INIS: THESAURUS

INTERNATIONAL ATOMIC ENERGY AGENCY, VIENNA, JANUARY 1992

Note

This replaces all previous revisions of this document and their supplements.

INIS: THESAURUS, IAEA, VIENNA, 1992
IAEA-INIS-13 (Rev. 31)
ISBN 92–0–100392–7
ISSN 1014-1561

Printed by the IAEA in Austria
December 1991

FOREWORD

This document, the Thesaurus, is one in a series of publications known as the **INIS Reference Series**. It contains the terminology to be used for subject description, as explained in the Manual for Indexing,[1] for the preparation of INIS input by national and regional centres.

The basis of the terminology in the original edition of the INIS Thesaurus was that in the December 1969 edition of the EURATOM Thesaurus [2]; the structure subsequently given to that terminology was the result of a systematic study performed by subject specialists.

The present revision of the Thesaurus is the result of continued editing carried out parallel to the processing of the INIS input, and of proposals for descriptors received from the contributors to the INIS Atomindex. Identification of errors as well as suggestions for improvements to the present document are welcome, particularly from parties that are contributing to or utilizing the INIS services. These should be addressed to:

>The Thesaurus Specialist, INIS Section
>Division of Scientific and Technical Information
>International Atomic Energy Agency
>P.O. Box 100
>A-1400 Vienna, Austria

---

[1] IAEA-INIS-12; INIS: Manual for Indexing.

[2] EUR 500e, Part 1; EURATOM-Thesaurus.

TABLE OF CONTENTS

Foreword iii

Introduction vii

List of the deleted and added terms since the last revision ix

Editor's Note xi

Dictionary 1

Appendix A-1

INTRODUCTION

"A thesaurus is a terminological control device used in translating from the natural language of documents, indexers or users into a more constrained 'system language' (document language, information language)." It is also "a controlled and dynamic vocabulary of semantically and generically related terms which covers a specific domain of knowledge". The INIS Thesaurus fits this definition adopted by UNESCO.[3]

The domain of knowledge covered by the INIS Thesaurus comprises general physics, high energy physics, nuclear physics, chemistry, materials, earth sciences, radiation biology, radioisotope effects and kinetics, applied life sciences, radiation protection and environment, radiology and nuclear medicine, isotopes, radiation sources, radiation applications, engineering, fission and fusion reactor technology, instrumentation, waste management, economics and sociology, nuclear law, safeguards and inspection, as well as the economic and environmental effects of non-nuclear energy sources. There are 17939 accepted terms (descriptors) and 6081 forbidden terms (non- descriptors) in this edition of the INIS Thesaurus.

The terms in the INIS Thesaurus are listed alphabetically, and with each alphabetic entry a "word block" containing all the terms associated with that particular entry is displayed. In the word block, terms which have a hierarchical relationship to the entry are identified by the symbols BT and NT, for *Broader Term* and *Narrower Term;* those with an affinitive relationship are identified by RT, for *Related Term;* and those with a preferential relationship are identified by USE or SEE and the reciprocals UF and SF, for *Used For* and *Seen For.* (If more than one descriptor should be used, the designation USE... AND... is given with the forbidden term and UF+... appears by each of the preferred descriptors. If more than one descriptor should be considered, the designation SEE... OR... is used.) A full description of the structure given to the terminology and detailed explanations of the various relationships existing between terms are given in the Manual for Indexing[4] and in the Guidelines[5]

To attract the indexer's attention to the narrower terms in the word block, the reference indicators "NT" are printed in bold face, upper case type. A non-descriptor sometimes refers to a descriptor which has Narrower Terms: users of the Thesaurus should always refer to the word block of that descriptor to ensure that the most specific appropriate term is chosen.

All descriptors deleted from or added to the previous revision are printed in a list preceding the main body of the Thesaurus. In addition, all new terms are indicated by an arrow to the left of the entry in the Thesaurus itself. These arrows are printed only in the front of the alphabetic entry of the descriptors concerned within the full alphabetic listing of all the terms in the Thesaurus. Other word blocks affected by the changes have been altered accordingly, but the changes are not indicated. With this presentation, users of INIS output tapes can easily identify these additions and corrections and adjust existing query profiles if necessary.

Some broad descriptors, such as "ISOTOPES" have very many narrower terms. Long lists of narrower terms in the word blocks of this type of cumulative term are not always of equal usefulness to indexers and retrievers. Hence the display of these word blocks has been truncated in the main body of the Thesaurus, and whenever this has been done it is indicated by an asterisk (*) at the level below which no narrower terms are listed. If the asterisk appears next to the alphabetic entry, i.e. when none of the narrower terms below the alphabetic entry is listed, the complete word block for the descriptor is given with full listings of narrower terms in the Appendix to the Thesaurus. Furthermore, the alphabetic entry is followed by the scope note: (For specific terms, consult the Appendix).

If the asterisk appears next to the reference indicator "NT" of a term within a word block, narrower terms more specific than that identified by the asterisk are not listed in that particular word block. They are listed, however, in the word block of the descriptor which is accompanied by the asterisk, where this descriptor is listed as the alphabetic entry, and no reference is made to the Appendix.

The symbols § and §§ next to some of the alphabetic entries indicate that the descriptor should rarely (§) or never (§§) be used as a main heading in the selection of M/Q pairs which form the subject headings in the printed subject index to Atomindex (see Manual for Indexing,[4] Chapter 11).

The numbers in square brackets listed to the right of each descriptor are the frequencies of use of that descriptor. The first figure is the number of times that the particular descriptor was actually assigned by indexers preparing INIS input

---

[3] SC/WS/555: Guidelines for the Establishment and Development of Monolingual Thesauri: United Nations Educations, Scientific and Cultural Organization, Paris, September 1973.

[4] IAEA-INIS-12; INIS: Manual for Indexing.

[5] IAEA-142; INIS: Guidelines for the Development and Maintenance of the INIS Thesaurus.

to pieces of literature reported to the system. The second is the sum of the first figure, i.e. the indexer assignment, and the number of times that the particular descriptor was added by the computer through the automatic hierarchical up-posting procedure. It follows that the two figures are always equal for those descriptors that have no narrower terms [6]. These figures refer to the documents published in INIS Atomindex Vol. 3, No. 5, through Vol. 22, No. 23 (Reference Numbers 019320-22:086041, i.e. 1534127 records altogether). The date printed after the frequency of use at each descriptor shows the month and the year when the term was introduced into the Thesaurus and hence its earliest possible appearance in the INIS data base, provided its introduction occurred after 30 June 1975. If the descriptor is not followed by a date, it already existed in the Thesaurus on 30 June 1975.

INIS descriptors are limited to a maximum length of 30 characters. In rare instances this limitation results in the truncation of the final word in multiword descriptors, e.g. KERNFORSCHUNGSZENTRUM KARLSRUH, REACTOR EXPERIMENTAL FACILITIE, THREE-NUCLEON TRANSFER REACTIO.

When searching for entries in the alphabetic listing, users should take note of the sort order, which is as follows:

space
asterisk *
dash (hyphen) -
Roman alphabet A-Z
Arabic numerals 0-9

This is particularly important with words that may or may not be hyphenated, since the space sorts before the hyphen. It should also be noted that if the mass numbers of the isotopes of the same element cover a range which includes a change from one digit to two, or from two to three, the descriptors are not filed in the normal manner; for example BORON 10 through BORON 19 file before BORON 7 through BORON 9, and RUTHENIUM 100 through RUTHENIUM 111 file before RUTHENIUM 92 through RUTHENIUM 99.

Each INIS inputting centre is supplied monthly with a cumulative list of terms deleted from or added to the Thesaurus since the most recent revision. These lists include the descriptors to be used for each new forbidden term and the first-level broader term, related terms and scope note, if any, for each new descriptor. Since these lists are cumulative, all changes made since the preceding list are marked with →. Revisions of the Thesaurus are published annually.

Detailed instructions for using the Thesaurus are given in the Manual for Indexing.[4]

Division of Scientific and Technical Information
International Atomic Energy Agency
January 1992

---

[6] In those few instances when this is not the case, the discrepancy is explained by a change in the hierarchical structure of such a descriptor which previously had a narrower term subsequently removed.

LIST OF THE DELETED AND ADDED TERMS SINCE THE LAST REVISION

DELETED TERMS

air flow
air pollution abatement
air pollution control
air quality
automobiles
benthos
biodegradation
brominated aliphatic hydrocarb
brominated aromatic hydrocarbo
certification
chars (coal)
chinsan-1 reactor
chinsan-2 reactor
chlorinated aliphatic hydrocar
chlorinated aromatic hydrocarb

combustion kinetics
design (computer-aided)
design (projective planning)
economic aspects
economic impact
energy demand
environmental effects
exhaust gases
fluorinated aliphatic hydrocar
gene repressors
GERMAN DEMOCRATIC REPUBLIC
GERMAN DR ORGANIZATIONS
halogenated aliphatic hydrocar
halogenated aromatic hydrocarb
hazardous materials spills

iodinated aliphatic hydrocarbo
mineral resources
offshore drilling
particulates
QINSHAN-1 REACTOR
QINSHAN-2 REACTOR
SAAS
social aspects
social impact
standards (specifications)
surface mining
underground mining
water pollution control
water quality
water removal

ADDED TERMS

ACID RAIN
ACOUSTIC MEASUREMENTS
ADITYA TOKAMAK
AHARONOV-BOHM EFFECT
AIR FLOW
AIR POLLUTION ABATEMENT
AIR POLLUTION CONTROL
AIR POLLUTION MONITORING
AIR POLLUTION MONITORS
AIR QUALITY
airborne particles
ALUMINIUM SELENIDES
ALUMINIUM TELLURIDES
AMERICIUM SILICIDES
AMERICIUM SULFATES
AMINE OXIDASES
AMMONIUM THIOCYANATES
ANADROMOUS FISHES
AQUACULTURE
aquiculture
ATMOSPHERIC CIRCULATION
AUTOMOBILES
AUTOMOTIVE FUELS
BAGHOUSES
BAY OF FUNDY
BEAUFORT SEA
BENTHOS
BERYLLIUM SELENIDES
BERYLLIUM TELLURIDES
bfs
BIOCONVERSION
BIODEGRADATION
BIOMASS CONVERSION PLANTS
BIOMASS PLANTATIONS
BIOTECHNOLOGY
BITUMINOUS COAL
BLACK COAL
BLOWOUTS
BONNEVILLE POWER ADMINISTRATIO
bpa
brazil lab for synchrotron rad
BRAZILIAN LNLS
brazilian lnls synchrotron
BRIDGES
BROMINATED ALIPHATIC HYDROCAR
BROMINATED AROMATIC HYDROCARBO
BUNDESAMT FUER STRAHLENSCHUTZ
CADMIUM TITANATES
CALCIUM PERCHLORATES
CALCIUM SILICIDES
CARBON 12 EMISSION DECAY
CERIUM TUNGSTATES
CERTIFICATION
CETACEANS
CHARS
CHEMICAL SPILLS

CHINSHAN-1 REACTOR
CHINSHAN-2 REACTOR
CHLORINATED ALIPHATIC HYDROCAR
CHLORINATED AROMATIC HYDROCARB
CHS TORSATRON
CHUKCHI SEA
CIVIL ENGINEERING
COAL DEPOSITS
COAL GAS
COAL GASIFICATION PLANTS
COAL INDUSTRY
COAL MINES
COAL MINING
COAL RANK
COAL RESERVES
COAL SEAMS
COASTAL REGIONS
COBALT ARSENIDES
COBALT PERCHLORATES
COBALT SELENIDES
COBALT TELLURIDES
COBALT TUNGSTATES
COCOMBUSTION
cofiring
coke-oven gas
COKING
COKING PLANTS
COLD FUSION
COLORADO RIVER BASIN
COLUMBIA HIGH-BETA TOKAMAK
COLUMBIA RIVER BASIN
COMBINED CYCLES
combined gas and steam cycle p
COMBINED-CYCLE POWER PLANTS
COMBUSTION CONTROL
COMBUSTION KINETICS
COMBUSTORS
compact helical system torsatr
COMPUTERIZED CONTROL SYSTEMS
CONTINENTAL MARGIN
CONTINENTAL SLOPE
CONTINUOUS CURRENT TOKAMAK
COPPER ARSENIDES
COPPER PHOSPHIDES
CREOSOTE
CURIUM SELENIDES
CURIUM TELLURIDES
DAMPIERRE-1 REACTOR
darmstadt synchrotron
DATA ANALYSIS
DAYA BAY REACTOR
DEFORESTATION
DESIGN
DIESEL FUELS
dolphins
DREDGE SPOIL

DREDGING
DRILLING
DRILLING FLUIDS
drilling mud
DYSPROSIUM PHOSPHIDES
DYSPROSIUM SILICATES
DYSPROSIUM TUNGSTATES
ECONOMIC IMPACT
elisa
ENDANGERED SPECIES
ENERGY DEMAND
ENERGY EFFICIENCY
ENERGY EFFICIENCY STANDARDS
energy performance standards
ENERGY SUPPLIES
energy technol data exchange
ENHANCED RECOVERY
enhanced recovery (biological)
ENVIRONMENTAL EFFECTS
ENVIRONMENTAL QUALITY
ERBIUM PERCHLORATES
ERBIUM TELLURIDES
ETDE
EUROPIUM PERCHLORATES
EXHAUST GASES
fish ladders
fish lifts
fish locks
FISH PASSAGE FACILITIES
fishways
FLUORINATED ALIPHATIC HYDROCAR
FLUORINATED AROMATIC HYDROCARB
FLUOROBORIC ACID
FOURIER TRANSFORM SPECTROMETER
frh reactor
FUZZY LOGIC
GALLIUM HALIDES
GAMBIA
GENERAL CIRCULATION MODELS
german democratic republic
german dr organizations
GERMANIUM BORIDES
GERMANIUM CARBIDES
GERMANIUM PHOSPHATES
GERMANIUM 85
GOLD TELLURIDES
HABITAT
HAFNIUM PERCHLORATES
HAFNIUM PHOSPHIDES
HALOGENATED ALIPHATIC HYDROCAR
HALOGENATED AROMATIC HYDROCARB
hannover-triga-mk-1 reactor
hard coal
HAZARDOUS MATERIALS SPILLS
HOLMIUM PERCHLORATES

Changes since the last revision

HUMAN CHROMOSOMES
HYBTOK TOKAMAKS
HYPERCUBE COMPUTERS
IMMUNE SYSTEM DISEASES
INDIUM TUNGSTATES
INJECTION WELLS
IODINATED ALIPHATIC HYDROCARBO
IODINATED AROMATIC HYDROCARBON
IODINE 108
IPEN-MB-1 REACTOR
IRIDIUM CARBIDES
JT-60U TOKAMAK
KANSAS CITY PLANT
KASHIWAZAKI-KARIWA-3 REACTOR
KEY LAKE MINE
KIRIBATI
KMR REACTOR
knu-10 reactor
knu-9 reactor
LABOR RELATIONS
LEADING ABSTRACT
LITHIUM ARSENIDES
LITHIUM PHOSPHIDES
LITHIUM SILICIDES
LITHIUM 8 TARGET
LITHIUM 9 REACTIONS
LNLS STORAGE RING
MAANSHAN-1 REACTOR
MAGNESIUM ARSENIDES
MAGNESIUM TELLURIDES
MANGANESE HALIDES
mariculture
microbial processes
MIDDLE EAST
MIGRATION
migration (kernel)
migration (radionuclide)
MINERAL RESOURCES
miniature neutron source react
MNS REACTOR
MODE CONVERSION
MODE RATIONAL SURFACES
MOLYBDENUM 84
monitors (air pollution)
NATURAL GAS DEPOSITS
NESTS
NICKEL ARSENIDES
NICKEL SELENIDES
NICKEL TUNGSTATES
NIOBIUM PHOSPHIDES
NITROGEN IODIDES
OIL SPILLS
OIL WELLS
OSMIUM CARBIDES
OSMIUM PHOSPHIDES
OSMIUM SULFIDES
OXYGEN 16 EMISSION DECAY
PALLADIUM ARSENIDES
PALLADIUM BORIDES
PALLADIUM PHOSPHIDES
PALLADIUM SELENIDES

PALLADIUM 119
PARTICULATES
pcb
pet scanning
petroleum coke
PETROLEUM DEPOSITS
PETROLEUM INDUSTRY
PLATINUM ARSENIDES
PLATINUM HYDROXIDES
PLATINUM PHOSPHIDES
polychlorinated biphenyl
porpoises
POST-TRANSLATION MODIFICATION
POTASSIUM PHOSPHIDES
POTASSIUM SELENIDES
POTASSIUM VANADATES
POTASSIUM 39 REACTIONS
PRASEODYMIUM TUNGSTATES
PROMETHIUM HYDROXIDES
PROTACTINIUM PHOSPHATES
QATAR
radio frequency quadrupoles
RADIUM OXIDES
rational surfaces
REMOVAL
RFLPS
rfq (accelerators)
RHENIUM CARBONATES
RHENIUM HALIDES
RHENIUM SELENIDES
RHENIUM TELLURIDES
RHODIUM SELENIDES
RHODIUM SULFIDES
RHODIUM TELLURIDES
rinderpest
rossendorf zfk
ROTATION-VIBRATION MODEL
RUBIDIUM PERCHLORATES
RUBIDIUM SELENIDES
RUBIDIUM SILICIDES
RUBIDIUM SULFIDES
RUTHENIUM ARSENIDES
RUTHENIUM NITRIDES
RUTHENIUM SELENIDES
RUTHENIUM TELLURIDES
RWANDA
saas
SAMARIUM ARSENIDES
SAMARIUM PERCHLORATES
SCANDIUM PERCHLORATES
SCANDIUM 53
SCANDIUM 54
SCANDIUM 55
secondary recovery
SELENIUM TELLURIDES
SILICON HALIDES
SILICON 29 BEAMS
SILVER ARSENIDES
SIS SYNCHROTRON
SODIUM SELENIDES

sonic measurements
STANDARDS
STRONTIUM URANATES
SULFATE-REDUCING BACTERIA
SULFUR CYCLE
SULFUR-OXIDIZING BACTERIA
SUPERCONDUCTING CYCLOTRONS
SUPPLY AND DEMAND
SURFACE MINING
TANTALUM PHOSPHIDES
TANTALUM SILICATES
TECHNOLOGY ASSESSMENT
TELLURIUM HALIDES
tertiary recovery
test heating reactor
THALLIUM TUNGSTATES
THR REACTOR
THULIUM HYDROXIDES
TIN ARSENIDES
TIN HALIDES
TIN TUNGSTATES
TIN 112 REACTIONS
TITANIUM PHOSPHIDES
TITANIUM TUNGSTATES
TITANIUM 55
TJ-1 TOKAMAK
TOKOLOSHE TOKAMAK
TORTUS TOKAMAK
TR-2 REACTOR
TRANSCRIPTION FACTORS
TRANSPOSONS
TRIGA-1-HANOVER REACTOR
TUNGSTEN TELLURIDES
turkish reactor-2
TUVALU
ULCHIN-1 REACTOR
ULCHIN-2 REACTOR
uljin-1 reactor
uljin-2 reactor
UNDERGROUND MINING
URANIUM 223
URANIUM 224
VANADIUM TELLURIDES
WATER POLLUTION CONTROL
WATER QUALITY
WATER REMOVAL
waterborne particles
waterborne particulates
WATERSHEDS
wecs
whales
wind energy conversion systems
WIND TURBINES
YEMEN
YTTERBIUM PERCHLORATES
YTTRIUM PERCHLORATES
YTTRIUM SELENIDES
zentralinst. f kernforschung
ZINC HALIDES
ZINC PERCHLORATES
ZINC SILICIDES

EDITOR'S NOTE

In 1991, a large number of forbidden terms were converted to valid descriptors as part of the expansion of INIS subject scope into the areas of Economic and Environmental aspects of all energy sources. The descriptors QINSHAN-1 REACTOR and QINSHAN-2 REACTOR were deleted and replaced by the correct spellings CHINSHAN-1 REACTOR and CHINSHAN-2 REACTOR. The reunification of Germany is reflected in the change of GERMAN DEMOCRATIC REPUBLIC and GERMAN DR ORGANIZATIONS and SAAS from descriptors to non-descriptors.

DICTIONARY

A CENTERS [114; 114] *Aug 82*
  BT1   color centers
    BT2   vacancies
      BT3   point defects
        BT4   crystal defects
          BT5   crystal structure

A CODES [2,212; 2,212]
  BT1   computer codes

a resonances
(Prior to December 1987 this was a valid descriptor.)
  USE   mesons

A-BOMB SURVIVORS [1,456; 1,456]
  RT   delayed radiation effects
  RT   epidemiology
  RT   hiroshima
  RT   nagasaki

a-1 reactor (bohunice)
  USE   bohunice a-1 reactor

a-1 reactor (calder hall)
  USE   calder hall a-1 reactor

a-2 reactor (bohunice)
  USE   bohunice a-2 reactor

a-2 reactor (calder hall)
  USE   calder hall a-2 reactor

AABO CYCLOTRON [9; 9]
  UF   *turku cyclotron*
  BT1   isochronous cyclotrons
    BT2   cyclotrons
      BT3   cyclic accelerators
        BT4   accelerators

AAEC [179; 179] *Feb 78*
(Australian Atomic Energy Commission, abolished on 27 April 1987 and replaced by ANSTO.)
  UF   *australian atom en commission*
  BT1   ansto
    BT2   australian organizations
      BT3   national organizations

ABANDONED SITES [488; 488] *Dec 80*
  RT   land reclamation
  RT   remedial action

abashian-booth-crowe effect
  USE   abc effect

ABC EFFECT [3; 3] *Sep 77*
  UF   *abashian-booth-crowe effect*
  RT   interactions
  RT   missing-mass spectra
  RT   pions

ABDOMEN [2,378; 2,378]
  BT1   body areas
    BT2   body
  RT   diaphragm
  RT   gastrointestinal tract
  RT   liver
  RT   peritoneum
  RT   spleen

aberdeen md. reactor
  USE   aprf reactor

aberration yield
  USE   mutation frequency

ABFST EQUATION [27; 27]
(Amati-Bertocchi-Fabini-Strangellini-Tonin Equation.)
  BT1   equations
  RT   multiperipheral model
  RT   regge poles
  RT   scattering amplitudes

ABLATION [1,209; 1,209]
(For the medical concept use SURGERY or RADIOTHERAPY.)
  RT   heat transfer
  RT   reentry
  RT   refractories
  RT   sublimation heat

abnormalities (chromosomal)
  USE   chromosomal aberrations

abnormalities (developmental)
  USE   malformations

ABORTION [93; 93]
  RT   pregnancy
  RT   reproductive disorders

abragam model
  USE   abragam-pound theory

ABRAGAM-POUND THEORY [25; 25]
  UF   *abragam model*
  RT   angular correlation
  RT   angular distribution

ABRASION [339; 339]
  RT   abrasives
  RT   erosion
  RT   wear

ABRASIVES [111; 111]
  RT   abrasion

ABRIKOSOV THEORY [167; 167]
  RT   magnetic properties
  RT   superconductivity
  RT   superconductors

ABS [17; 17]
  UF   *alkyl benzenesulfonates*
  BT1   sulfonic acid esters
    BT2   esters
      BT3   organic compounds
    BT2   organic sulfur compounds
      BT3   organic compounds

ABSCESSES [881; 881]
  BT1   pathological changes
    BT2   diseases

ABSCOPAL RADIATION EFFECTS [114; 114]
  BT1   biological radiation effects
    BT2   biological effects
    BT2   radiation effects
  RT   local irradiation
  RT   partial body irradiation
  RT   radiotoxins

ABSOLUTE COUNTING [354; 354]
  BT1   counting techniques
  RT   calibration

ABSOLUTE INSTABILITIES [103; 103]
(A class of plasma instabilities growing exponentially with time at any point in space; opposite to CONVECTIVE INSTABILITIES.)
  BT1   plasma instability
    BT2   instability
  RT   briggs criterion
  RT   convective instabilities

absolute liability
(Prior to December 1990, this was a valid descriptor.)
  USE   liabilities

ABSOLUTE ZERO TEMPERATURE [561; 561]
  UF   *temperature (0 k)*
  RT   cryogenics
  RT   temperature dependence
  RT   thermodynamics

absorbed doses
  USE   radiation doses

absorbed fraction (internal ir
  USE   internal irradiation
  AND   spatial dose distributions

§ **ABSORPTION** [10,587; 12,506]
(In quantum physics only. For reducing the intensity of waves and submolecular particles when passing through matter employing quantum physics use the above descriptor, when employing classical physics use ATTENUATION or CHEMISORPTION. For absorption cross sections, see also TOTAL CROSS SECTIONS.)
  UF   *stopping*
  NT1   k absorption
  NT1   polar-cap absorption
  NT1   resonance absorption
  NT1   self-absorption
  RT   absorption spectra
  RT   half-thickness
  RT   heterogeneous effects
  RT   point kernels
  RT   radiations
  RT   range
  RT   self-shielding
  RT   shielding
  RT   slowing-down
  RT   stopping power
  RT   transmission

absorption (intestinal)
  USE   intestinal absorption

absorption (leaves)
USE   foliar uptake

absorption (root)
USE   root absorption

absorption (skin)
USE   skin absorption

ABSORPTION HEAT [63; 63]
UF   *heat of absorption*
BT1   enthalpy
  BT2   thermodynamic properties
    BT3   physical properties

absorption models (linear)
USE   linear absorption models

ABSORPTION SPECTRA
[14,230; 14,230]
BT1   spectra
RT   absorption
RT   absorption spectroscopy
RT   optical depth curve
RT   spectroscopic curve of growth

ABSORPTION SPECTROSCOPY
[4,443; 4,443]
UF   *atomic absorption spectroscopy*
UF   *colorimetry*
SF   *spectrochemistry*
BT1   spectroscopy
RT   absorption spectra
RT   double resonance methods
RT   infrared spectra
RT   laser spectroscopy
RT   photoacoustic spectrometers
RT   structural chemical analysis
RT   ultraviolet spectra

absorptivity (optical)
USE   opacity

ABSTRACTS [117; 118]
(Use only for items about abstracts, not for items which are abstracts or collections of abstracts.)
NT1   leading abstract
RT   document types

abundance (chemical)
USE   chemical composition

abundance (element)
USE   element abundance

abundance (isotopic)
USE   isotope ratio

abundance (mineral)
USE   ore composition

AC AMPLIFIERS [36; 36]
BT1   amplifiers
  BT2   equipment
BT1   electronic equipment
  BT2   equipment

AC LOSSES [143; 143] Nov 82
BT1   energy losses
RT   electric impedance
RT   superconductivity

acceler pulsed fast cr assembl
USE   apfa-3 reactor

ACCELERATION [5,892; 7,024]
UF   *deceleration*
NT1   plasma acceleration
RT   accelerators
RT   gravimetry
RT   velocity
RT   wakefield accelerators

ACCELERATOR BREEDERS [176; 176]
Jul 78
(Accelerators used in the production of fissionable materials.)
RT   accelerators
RT   breeder reactors
RT   breeding
RT   fissionable materials
RT   nuclear fuels

ACCELERATOR FACILITIES
[2,238; 3,848]
UF   *exper. facilities (acceler.)*
NT1   target chambers
RT   accelerators
RT   beam dumps
RT   beam monitors
RT   laboratory equipment
RT   pigmi facilities

ACCELERATORS [6,276; 43,294]
NT1   bevalac
NT1   coherent accelerators
NT1   collective accelerators
  NT2   electron-ring accelerators
  NT2   plasma betatrons
NT1   cyclic accelerators
  NT2   betatrons
  NT2   cyclotrons
    NT3   calcutta cyclotron
    NT3   chandigarh cyclotron
    NT3   cracow u-120 cyclotron
    NT3   isochronous cyclotrons
      NT4   aabo cyclotron
      NT4   alice cyclotron
      NT4   apache
      NT4   brookhaven cyclotron
      NT4   chicago cyclotron
      NT4   cracow aic-144 cyclotron
      NT4   cracow c-48 cyclotron
      NT4   crnl superconducting cyclotron
      NT4   cyclone cyclotron
      NT4   debrecen cyclotron
      NT4   eindhoven cyclotron
      NT4   ganil cyclotron
      NT4   grenoble cyclotron
      NT4   haizy cyclotron
      NT4   hirfl cyclotron
      NT4   inr cyclotron
      NT4   ipcr cyclotron
      NT4   iu cyclotron
      NT4   jinr cyclotrons
        NT5   jinr u-400 cyclotron
      NT4   julic cyclotron
      NT4   karlsruhe cyclotron
      NT4   kazakhstan cyclotron
      NT4   kiev cyclotron
      NT4   kvi cyclotron
      NT4   milan superconducting cyclotro
      NT4   msu cyclotrons
      NT4   munich compact cyclotron
      NT4   munich suse cyclotron
      NT4   nac cyclotron
      NT4   nirs cyclotron
      NT4   nrl cyclotron
      NT4   ornl isochronous cyclotron
      NT4   orsay cyclotron
      NT4   oslo cyclotron
      NT4   princeton cyclotron
      NT4   rcnp cyclotron
      NT4   sara cyclotron
      NT4   sin cyclotron
      NT4   texas a and m cyclotron
      NT4   texas superconducting cyclotro
      NT4   tohoku cyclotron
      NT4   tokyo ins cyclotron
      NT4   triumf cyclotron
      NT4   uclrl cyclotrons
      NT5   lbl 88-inch cyclotron
      NT4   warsaw cyclotron
    NT3   microtrons
      NT4   racetrack microtrons
    NT3   nbi cyclotron
    NT3   separated orbit cyclotrons
      NT4   ornl separated orbit cyclotron
    NT3   superconducting cyclotrons
      NT4   milan superconducting cyclotro
      NT4   texas superconducting cyclotro
    NT3   variable energy cyclotrons
  NT2   synchrocyclotrons
    NT3   berkeley synchrocyclotron
    NT3   cern synchrocyclotron
    NT3   chicago synchrocyclotron
    NT3   dubna synchrocyclotron
    NT3   goettingen synchrocyclotron
    NT3   harvard synchrocyclotron
    NT3   harwell synchrocyclotron
    NT3   iko synchrocyclotron
    NT3   mcgill synchrocyclotron
    NT3   orsay synchrocyclotron
    NT3   uppsala synchrocyclotron
  NT2   synchrotrons
    NT3   bevatron
    NT3   birmingham synchrotron
    NT3   bonn synchrotron
    NT3   brookhaven ags
    NT3   caltech synchrotron
    NT3   cambridge electron accelerator
    NT3   cern ps synchrotron
    NT3   cern sps synchrotron
    NT3   cornell 10-gev synchrotron
    NT3   cornell 2-gev synchrotron
    NT3   cosmotron
    NT3   desy
    NT3   erevan synchrotron
    NT3   escar storage ring
    NT3   fermilab accelerator
    NT3   fermilab tevatron
    NT3   fian synchrotron
    NT3   frascati synchrotron
    NT3   glasgow synchrotron
    NT3   ipns-i synchrotron
    NT3   itep synchrotron
    NT3   jinr synchrotron
    NT3   kek synchrotron
    NT3   lampf ii synchrotron
    NT3   lusy
    NT3   mura synchrotron
    NT3   nimrod
    NT3   nina
    NT3   omnitron
    NT3   pakhra synchrotron
    NT3   princeton synchrotron
    NT3   saturne
    NT3   saturne ii
    NT3   serpukhov synchrotron
    NT3   serpukhov tevatron
    NT3   sis synchrotron
    NT3   superconducting super collider
    NT3   tokyo synchrotron
    NT3   tomsk synchrotron
    NT3   zgs
NT1   electron beam fusion accelerat
NT1   electrostatic accelerators
  NT2   cockcroft-walton accelerators
  NT2   dynamitrons
  NT2   pelletron accelerators
    NT3   5u pelletron accelerator
  NT2   tandem electrostatic accelerat
    NT3   crnl mp tandem accelerator
    NT3   jaeri tandem accelerator
    NT3   learn tandem accelerator
    NT3   orsay tandem accelerator
    NT3   vivitron tandem accelerator
  NT2   van de graaff accelerators
    NT3   crnl mp tandem accelerator
    NT3   jaeri tandem accelerator
    NT3   learn tandem accelerator
    NT3   orsay tandem accelerator
    NT3   vivitron tandem accelerator
NT1   heavy ion accelerators
  NT2   brookhaven rhic
  NT2   calcutta cyclotron

ACCELERATORS (continued)

- NT2 cracow u-120 cyclotron
- NT2 crnl superconducting cyclotron
- NT2 cyclone cyclotron
- NT2 ganil cyclotron
- NT2 hhirf accelerator
- NT2 hilacs
- NT3 atlas superconducting linac
- NT3 superhilac
- NT2 hirfl cyclotron
- NT2 ipcr cyclotron
- NT2 jinr u-400 cyclotron
- NT2 kvi cyclotron
- NT2 milan superconducting cyclotro
- NT2 munich suse cyclotron
- NT2 nac cyclotron
- NT2 numatron accelerator
- NT2 rcnp cyclotron
- NT2 rilac
- NT2 sis synchrotron
- NT2 texas superconducting cyclotro
- NT2 tohoku cyclotron
- NT2 tokyo ins cyclotron
- NT2 unilac
- NT2 vicksi accelerator
- NT2 warsaw cyclotron
- NT1 linear accelerators
- NT2 beat wave accelerators
- NT2 brookhaven 200-mev linac
- NT2 cebaf accelerator
- NT2 cern linac
- NT2 fmit linac
- NT2 frascati linac
- NT2 hilacs
- NT3 atlas superconducting linac
- NT3 superhilac
- NT2 ing linac
- NT2 jaeri linac
- NT2 kek linac
- NT2 kharkov linac
- NT2 lampf linac
- NT2 llnl advanced test accelerator
- NT2 mea linac
- NT2 minnesota univ linac
- NT2 mit bates linac
- NT2 nrl linac
- NT2 orela
- NT2 orsay linac
- NT2 quadrupole linacs
- NT2 rilac
- NT2 saclay linac
- NT2 stanford linear collider
- NT2 stanford 1200-mev linac
- NT2 stanford 20-gev linac
- NT2 swierk linac
- NT2 unilac
- NT2 wakefield accelerators
- NT2 zeran linac
- NT1 meson factories
- NT2 lampf ii synchrotron
- NT2 lampf linac
- NT1 particle beam fusion accelerat
- RT acceleration
- RT accelerator breeders
- RT accelerator facilities
- RT beam dumps
- RT beam dynamics
- RT beam separators
- RT impact fusion drivers
- RT isotope production
- RT particle boosters
- RT storage rings
- RT target chambers
- RT vacuum systems

ACCELEROMETERS [196; 196]
- BT1 measuring instruments
- RT velocimeters

acceptance (beam)
- USE beam acceptance

access denial systems
- USE entry control systems

ACCIDENT INSURANCE [17; 17]
Dec 76
- BT1 insurance
- RT accidents

accidental intake
- USE accidents
- AND single intake

accidental irradiation
- USE irradiation
- AND radiation accidents

ACCIDENTS [3,740; 38,414]
- UF *aircraft accidents*
- UF *disasters*
- UF *emergencies*
- UF *incidents*
- UF *marine vehicle accidents*
- UF *nuclear accidents*
- UF+ *accidental intake*
- NT1 blowouts
- NT1 chemical spills
- NT1 hazardous materials spills
- NT1 industrial accidents
- NT1 motor vehicle accidents
- NT1 oil spills
- NT1 radiation accidents
- NT1 reactor accidents
- NT2 design basis accidents
- NT3 atws
- NT3 maximum credible accident
- NT2 excursions
- NT2 fuel element failure
- NT2 loss of coolant
- NT2 loss of flow
- NT2 meltdown
- NT2 power-cooling-mismatch acciden
- NT2 reactor core disruption
- NT2 rod drop accidents
- NT2 rod ejection accidents
- NT2 transient overpower accidents
- RT accident insurance
- RT aerial monitoring
- RT environment
- RT evacuation
- RT explosions
- RT failures
- RT fallout
- RT fires
- RT first aid
- RT fission products
- RT hazards
- RT human factors
- RT industrial medicine
- RT injuries
- RT insurance
- RT liabilities
- RT nuclear damage
- RT on-site power generation
- RT outages
- RT population relocation
- RT preventive medicine
- RT radiation protection
- RT radioactive clouds
- RT reactor safety
- RT safety
- RT single intake
- RT site selection
- RT victims compensation
- RT workmens compensation

acclimation
(Prior to December 1990, this was a valid descriptor.)
- USE biological adaptation

ACCOUNTING [1,896; 2,046]
- UF *bookkeeping*
- BT1 management
- NT1 energy accounting
- RT audits
- RT inventories
- RT invoices
- RT losses
- RT material balance
- RT nuclear materials management
- RT safeguards

accretion (planet-system)
- USE planet-system accretion

accretion (stars)
- USE star accretion

ACCRETION DISKS [1,300; 1,300]
Apr 82
(Disks of matter which sometimes surround certain celestial objects, e.g. neutron stars.)
- UF *disks (accretion)*
- RT black holes
- RT cosmic x-ray sources
- RT eruptive variable stars
- RT neutron stars
- RT star accretion
- RT symbiotic stars

accumulation
- USE buildup

accumulation (radioecological)
- USE radioecological concentration

accumulators
- USE electric batteries

§§ ACCURACY [21,161; 21,161]
- UF *precision*
- RT calibration
- RT calibration standards
- RT data covariances
- RT errors
- RT inspection
- RT reliability
- RT resolution
- RT sensitivity
- RT signal-to-noise ratio
- RT specificity

ACENAPHTHENE [23; 23]
- BT1 condensed aromatics
- BT2 aromatics
- BT3 organic compounds
- BT1 hydrocarbons
- BT2 organic compounds
- RT naphthalene

aces
- USE quarks

ACETABULARIA [14; 14]
- BT1 algae
- BT2 plants

ACETAL [5; 5]
- UF *1,1-diethoxyethane*
- BT1 acetals
- BT2 ethers
- BT3 organic oxygen compounds
- BT4 organic compounds
- RT acetaldehyde

ACETALDEHYDE [147; 147]
- UF *acetic aldehyde*
- UF *ethanal*
- UF *ethylaldehyde*
- BT1 aldehydes
- BT2 organic compounds
- RT acetal
- RT chloral

ACETALS [43; 47]
BT1 ethers
BT2 organic oxygen compounds
BT3 organic compounds
NT1 acetal
RT polyacetals

ACETAMIDE [169; 183]
BT1 amides
BT2 organic nitrogen compounds
BT3 organic compounds
NT1 ioglycamic acid
RT acetic acid

ACETATES [1,722; 1,722]
BT1 carboxylic acid salts
RT acetic acid esters

ACETIC ACID [1,005; 1,005]
BT1 monocarboxylic acids
BT2 carboxylic acids
BT3 organic acids
BT4 organic compounds
RT acetamide
RT acetolysis
RT acetonitrile

ACETIC ACID ESTERS [329; 335]
UF *amyl acetate*
BT1 carboxylic acid esters
BT2 esters
BT3 organic compounds
NT1 isopentyl acetate
RT acetates

acetic aldehyde
USE acetaldehyde

ACETOACETATES [40; 40]
BT1 carboxylic acid salts

ACETOACETIC ACID [10; 10]
UF *ketobutyric acid-beta*
BT1 keto acids
BT2 carboxylic acids
BT3 organic acids
BT4 organic compounds

ACETOACETIC ACID ESTERS [35; 35]
BT1 carboxylic acid esters
BT2 esters
BT3 organic compounds

ACETOLYSIS [13; 13]
BT1 solvolysis
BT2 decomposition
BT3 chemical reactions
RT acetic acid

ACETONE [926; 926]
UF *dimethyl ketone*
UF *oxopropane*
UF *propanone*
BT1 ketones
BT2 organic compounds

ACETONITRILE [324; 324] *Jul 81*
BT1 nitriles
BT2 organic nitrogen compounds
BT3 organic compounds
RT acetic acid

ACETOPHENONE [121; 121]
UF *acetylbenzene*
UF *methyl phenyl ketone*
BT1 aromatics
BT2 organic compounds
BT1 ketones
BT2 organic compounds

acetyl propionyl
USE 2-3-pentanedione

ACETYL RADICALS [38; 38]
BT1 acyl radicals
BT2 radicals

ACETYLACETONE [445; 445]
UF *2,4-pentanedione*
BT1 chelating agents
BT1 ketones
BT2 organic compounds
BT1 reagents

ACETYLATION [149; 149]
BT1 acylation
BT2 chemical reactions

acetylbenzene
USE acetophenone

ACETYLCHOLINE [500; 500]
BT1 esters
BT2 organic compounds
BT1 neuroregulators
BT2 autonomic nervous system agent
BT3 drugs
BT1 parasympathomimetics
BT2 autonomic nervous system agent
BT3 drugs
BT1 quaternary compounds
BT2 amines
BT3 organic compounds
RT choline
RT cholinesterase

ACETYLENE [726; 726]
UF *ethine*
UF *ethyne*
BT1 alkynes
BT2 hydrocarbons
BT3 organic compounds

acetylenes
USE alkynes

acetylpropionic acid-beta
USE levulinic acid

ACETYLSALICYLIC ACID [72; 72] *Feb 76*
UF *aspirin*
BT1 analgesics
BT2 central nervous system depress
BT3 central nervous system agents
BT4 drugs
BT1 antipyretics
BT2 central nervous system depress
BT3 central nervous system agents
BT4 drugs
BT1 hydroxy acids
BT2 carboxylic acids
BT3 organic acids
BT4 organic compounds

ACHOLEPLASMA LAIDLAWII B [11; 11]
BT1 mycoplasma
BT2 microorganisms

ACHONDRITES [111; 111]
BT1 stone meteorites
BT2 meteorites

ACHROMATIC LESIONS [5; 5]
RT chromatin

ACID ANHYDRASES [4; 420] *Dec 86*
BT1 hydrolases
BT2 enzymes
BT3 organic compounds
NT1 phosphohydrolases
NT2 atp-ase

ACID CARBONATES [207; 207] *Aug 81*
(Prior to December 1985 BICARBONATES was used for this concept.)
UF *bicarbonates*
RT carbonates
RT inorganic acids

ACID CHROME DYES [7; 7]
BT1 azo dyes
BT2 azo compounds
BT3 organic nitrogen compounds
BT4 organic compounds
BT2 dyes
BT1 naphthols
BT2 phenols
BT3 aromatics
BT4 organic compounds
BT3 hydroxy compounds
BT4 organic compounds
BT1 sulfonic acids
BT2 organic acids
BT3 organic compounds
BT2 organic sulfur compounds
BT3 organic compounds

ACID PHOSPHATASE [291; 291]
BT1 phosphatases
BT2 esterases
BT3 hydrolases
BT4 enzymes
BT5 organic compounds

ACID PROTEINASES [1; 23] *Dec 86*
BT1 peptide hydrolases
BT2 hydrolases
BT3 enzymes
BT4 organic compounds
NT1 pepsin

→ **ACID RAIN** [0; 0] *Aug 91*
BT1 rain
BT2 atmospheric precipitations
RT air pollution

ACIDIFICATION [153; 153] *Mar 83*
(The act or process of acidifying.)
RT chemical reactions
RT inorganic acids
RT organic acids

acidity
USE ph value

acids (inorganic)
USE inorganic acids

acids (organic)
USE organic acids

ACO [65; 65]
BT1 storage rings

ACOUSTIC DETECTION [87; 87] *Jun 83*
(Charged particle detection technique based on sonic signal produced by charged particles traversing fluid media.)
BT1 acoustic measurements
BT1 charged particle detection
BT2 radiation detection
BT3 detection
RT acoustic monitoring
RT dumand project
RT sound waves

acoustic electron spin resonan
USE acoustic esr

ACOUSTIC EMISSION TESTING
[1,180; 1,180]
- BT1 acoustic testing
- BT2 nondestructive testing
-   BT3 materials testing
-    BT4 testing

ACOUSTIC ESR [47; 47]
- UF *acoustic electron spin resonan*
- UF *aepr*
- UF *aesr*
- UF *paramagn. res. (elec. acoust.)*
- BT1 electron spin resonance
- BT2 magnetic resonance
-   BT3 resonance
- RT attenuation
- RT phonons
- RT resonance scattering
- RT sound waves

ACOUSTIC HEATING [57; 57]
- BT1 magnetic-pumping heating
- BT2 high-frequency heating
-   BT3 plasma heating
-    BT4 heating

→ **ACOUSTIC MEASUREMENTS** [0; 2]
Sep 91
- UF *sonic measurements*
- NT1 acoustic detection
- RT acoustic monitoring
- RT acoustic testing
- RT seismic surveys
- RT seismographs
- RT sonic probes
- RT sound waves
- RT ultrasonic testing

ACOUSTIC MONITORING [867; 867]
- BT1 monitoring
- RT acoustic detection
- RT acoustic measurements
- RT in core instruments
- RT reactor instrumentation
- RT reactor monitoring systems
- RT sound waves

ACOUSTIC NMR [115; 115]
- UF *acoustic nucl. magn. resonance*
- UF *anmr*
- UF *nuclear acoustic resonance*
- UF *paramagn. res. (nucl. acoust.)*
- BT1 nuclear magnetic resonance
- BT2 magnetic resonance
-   BT3 resonance
- RT attenuation
- RT phonons
- RT resonance scattering
- RT sound waves

acoustic nucl. magn. resonance
- USE acoustic nmr

acoustic spark chambers
- USE sonic spark chambers

ACOUSTIC TESTING [289; 5,497]
- BT1 nondestructive testing
- BT2 materials testing
-   BT3 testing
- NT1 acoustic emission testing
- NT1 ultrasonic testing
- RT acoustic measurements

ACPR REACTOR [140; 140]
(Sandia Laboratories, Albuquerque, New Mexico, USA)
- UF *annular core pulse reactor*
- BT1 enriched uranium reactors
- BT2 reactors
- BT1 hydride moderated reactors
- BT2 reactors
- BT1 mixed spectrum reactors
- BT2 reactors
- BT1 pulsed reactors
- BT2 reactors
- BT1 research reactors
- BT2 research and test reactors
-   BT3 reactors
- BT1 solid homogeneous reactors
- BT2 homogeneous reactors
-   BT3 reactors
- BT1 water cooled reactors
- BT2 reactors
- BT1 water moderated reactors
- BT2 reactors

acquired immunodeficiency viru
- USE aids virus

acquisition (data)
- USE data acquisition

acraldehyde
- USE acrolein

ACRIDINE ORANGE [49; 49]
- BT1 acridines
- BT2 pyridines
-   BT3 azines
-    BT4 heterocyclic compounds
-     BT5 organic compounds
-    BT4 organic nitrogen compounds
-     BT5 organic compounds
- BT1 amines
- BT2 organic compounds
- BT1 dyes

ACRIDINES [106; 271]
- BT1 pyridines
- BT2 azines
-   BT3 heterocyclic compounds
-    BT4 organic compounds
-   BT3 organic nitrogen compounds
-    BT4 organic compounds
- NT1 acridine orange
- NT1 flavines
- NT2 acriflavine
- NT2 proflavine

ACRIFLAVINE [65; 65]
- UF *euflavine*
- UF *trypaflavine*
- BT1 flavines
- BT2 acridines
-   BT3 pyridines
-    BT4 azines
-     BT5 heterocyclic compounds
-      BT6 organic compounds
-     BT5 organic nitrogen compounds
-      BT6 organic compounds
- BT2 amines
-   BT3 organic compounds
- RT proflavine

ACROCENTRIC CHROMOSOMES [17; 17]
- BT1 chromosomes
- RT chromosomal aberrations
- RT karyotype

acroleic acid
- USE acrylic acid

ACROLEIN [61; 61]
- UF *acraldehyde*
- UF *acrylic aldehyde*
- UF *propenal*
- BT1 aldehydes
- BT2 organic compounds
- RT vinyl monomers

ACROMEGALY [70; 70]
- BT1 endocrine diseases
- BT2 diseases
- RT pituitary gland
- RT sth

ACRYLAMIDE [267; 267]
- BT1 amides
- BT2 organic nitrogen compounds
-   BT3 organic compounds
- RT acrylic acid
- RT vinyl monomers

ACRYLATES [288; 288]
- BT1 carboxylic acid salts
- RT acrylic acid esters
- RT vinyl monomers

ACRYLIC ACID [322; 322]
- UF *acroleic acid*
- UF *ethylenecarboxylic acid*
- BT1 monocarboxylic acids
- BT2 carboxylic acids
-   BT3 organic acids
-    BT4 organic compounds
- RT acrylamide
- RT acrylonitrile
- RT vinyl monomers

ACRYLIC ACID ESTERS [220; 220]
- BT1 carboxylic acid esters
- BT2 esters
-   BT3 organic compounds
- RT acrylates
- RT vinyl monomers

acrylic aldehyde
- USE acrolein

acrylic polymers
- USE polyacrylates

ACRYLONITRILE [284; 284]
- UF *vinyl cyanide*
- BT1 nitriles
- BT2 organic nitrogen compounds
-   BT3 organic compounds
- RT acrylic acid
- RT organic polymers
- RT vinyl monomers

ACT DEVICES [7; 7] *Dec 85*
(Advanced Concept Torus.)
- BT1 tokamak devices
- BT2 closed plasma devices
-   BT3 thermonuclear devices

ACTH [252; 252]
- UF *adrenocorticotropic hormone*
- BT1 pituitary hormones
- BT2 peptide hormones
-   BT3 hormones
- RT adrenal glands
- RT corticosteroids
- RT glucocorticoids

ACTIN [87; 87]
- BT1 proteins
- BT2 organic compounds
- RT muscles

ACTINIDE ALLOYS [86; 2,897]
- BT1 alloys
- NT1 americium alloys
- NT2 americium base alloys
- NT1 berkelium alloys
- NT1 californium alloys
- NT1 curium alloys
- NT2 curium base alloys
- NT1 neptunium alloys
- NT2 neptunium base alloys
- NT1 plutonium alloys
- NT2 plutonium base alloys
- NT1 protactinium alloys

ACTINIDE ALLOYS

    NT2   protactinium base alloys
    NT1   thorium alloys
    NT2   thorium base alloys
    NT1   uranium alloys
    NT2   uranium base alloys
    NT3   alloy-u90nb7zr3
    RT   rare earth alloys

ACTINIDE BURNER REACTORS [28; 28] *Jul 80*
(Reactors which convert radioactive waste actinides to useful or less harmful elements by fission reactions.)
    BT1   fast reactors
    BT2   epithermal reactors
    BT3   reactors
    RT   radioactive waste disposal

ACTINIDE COMPLEXES [335; 5,188]
    BT1   complexes
    NT1   actinium complexes
    NT1   americium complexes
    NT1   berkelium complexes
    NT1   californium complexes
    NT1   curium complexes
    NT1   einsteinium complexes
    NT1   fermium complexes
    NT1   lawrencium complexes
    NT1   mendelevium complexes
    NT1   neptunium complexes
    NT2   neptunyl complexes
    NT1   nobelium complexes
    NT1   plutonium complexes
    NT2   plutonyl complexes
    NT1   protactinium complexes
    NT1   thorium complexes
    NT1   uranium complexes
    NT2   uranyl complexes

ACTINIDE COMPOUNDS [593; 30,352]
    *NT1   actinium compounds
    *NT1   americium compounds
    *NT1   berkelium compounds
    *NT1   californium compounds
    *NT1   curium compounds
    *NT1   einsteinium compounds
    *NT1   fermium compounds
    *NT1   lawrencium compounds
    *NT1   mendelevium compounds
    *NT1   neptunium compounds
    *NT1   nobelium compounds
    *NT1   plutonium compounds
    *NT1   protactinium compounds
    *NT1   thorium compounds
    *NT1   uranium compounds

*ACTINIDE NUCLEI [647; 22,874]
(For specific terms, consult the Appendix.)
    BT1   heavy nuclei
    BT2   nuclei

ACTINIDES [2,396; 32,639]
    BT1   metals
    BT2   elements
    NT1   actinium
    NT1   americium
    NT1   berkelium
    NT1   californium
    NT1   curium
    NT1   einsteinium
    NT1   fermium
    NT1   lawrencium
    NT1   mendelevium
    NT1   neptunium
    NT2   neptunium-alpha
    NT2   neptunium-beta
    NT2   neptunium-gamma
    NT1   nobelium
    NT1   plutonium
    NT2   plutonium-alpha
    NT2   plutonium-beta
    NT2   plutonium-delta
    NT2   plutonium-epsilon
    NT2   plutonium-eta
    NT2   plutonium-gamma
    NT1   protactinium

    NT1   thorium
    NT2   thorium-alpha
    NT2   thorium-beta
    NT1   uranium
    NT2   depleted uranium
    NT2   enriched uranium
    NT3   highly enriched uranium
    NT3   moderately enriched uranium
    NT3   slightly enriched uranium
    NT2   natural uranium
    NT2   uranium-alpha
    NT2   uranium-beta
    NT2   uranium-gamma
    RT   transplutonium elements
    RT   transuranium elements

ACTINIUM [96; 96]
    BT1   actinides
    BT2   metals
    BT3   elements

actinium a
    USE   polonium 215

actinium b
    USE   lead 211

ACTINIUM BROMIDES [2; 2] *Jan 76*
    BT1   actinium compounds
    BT2   actinide compounds
    BT1   bromides
    BT2   bromine compounds
    BT3   halogen compounds
    BT2   halides
    BT3   halogen compounds

actinium c
    USE   bismuth 211

actinium c/
    USE   polonium 211

actinium c//
    USE   thallium 207

ACTINIUM CHLORIDES [4; 4] *Jan 76*
    BT1   actinium compounds
    BT2   actinide compounds
    BT1   chlorides
    BT2   chlorine compounds
    BT3   halogen compounds
    BT2   halides
    BT3   halogen compounds

ACTINIUM COMPLEXES [33; 33]
    BT1   actinide complexes
    BT2   complexes

ACTINIUM COMPOUNDS [40; 60]
    BT1   actinide compounds
    NT1   actinium bromides
    NT1   actinium chlorides
    NT1   actinium fluorides
    NT1   actinium hydrides
    NT1   actinium hydroxides
    NT1   actinium oxides
    NT1   actinium sulfates

actinium d
    USE   lead 207

ACTINIUM FLUORIDES [4; 4] *Jan 76*
    BT1   actinium compounds
    BT2   actinide compounds
    BT1   fluorides
    BT2   fluorine compounds
    BT3   halogen compounds
    BT2   halides
    BT3   halogen compounds

ACTINIUM HYDRIDES [3; 3] *Nov 84*
    BT1   actinium compounds
    BT2   actinide compounds
    BT1   hydrides
    BT2   hydrogen compounds

ACTINIUM HYDROXIDES [5; 5] *Oct 77*
    BT1   actinium compounds
    BT2   actinide compounds
    BT1   hydroxides
    BT2   hydrogen compounds
    BT2   oxygen compounds

ACTINIUM IONS [6; 6]
    BT1   ions
    BT2   charged particles

ACTINIUM ISOTOPES [58; 486]
    NT1   actinium 209
    NT1   actinium 210
    NT1   actinium 211
    NT1   actinium 212
    NT1   actinium 213
    NT1   actinium 214
    NT1   actinium 215
    NT1   actinium 216
    NT1   actinium 217
    NT1   actinium 218
    NT1   actinium 219
    NT1   actinium 220
    NT1   actinium 221
    NT1   actinium 222
    NT1   actinium 223
    NT1   actinium 224
    NT1   actinium 225
    NT1   actinium 226
    NT1   actinium 227
    NT1   actinium 228
    NT1   actinium 229
    NT1   actinium 230
    NT1   actinium 231
    NT1   actinium 232
    NT1   actinium 233
    NT1   actinium 234

actinium k
    USE   francium 223

ACTINIUM OXIDES [7; 7]
    BT1   actinium compounds
    BT2   actinide compounds
    BT1   oxides
    BT2   chalcogenides
    BT2   oxygen compounds

ACTINIUM SULFATES [4; 4] *Feb 79*
    BT1   actinium compounds
    BT2   actinide compounds
    BT1   sulfates
    BT2   oxygen compounds
    BT2   sulfur compounds

actinium x
    USE   radium 223

ACTINIUM 209 [0; 0] *May 86*
    BT1   actinide nuclei
    BT2   heavy nuclei
    BT3   nuclei
    BT1   actinium isotopes
    BT1   alpha decay radioisotopes
    BT2   radioisotopes
    BT3   isotopes
    BT1   millisec living radioisotopes
    BT2   radioisotopes
    BT3   isotopes
    BT1   odd-even nuclei
    BT2   nuclei

ACTINIUM 210 [2; 2] *May 86*
  BT1   actinide nuclei
    BT2   heavy nuclei
      BT3   nuclei
  BT1   actinium isotopes
  BT1   alpha decay radioisotopes
    BT2   radioisotopes
      BT3   isotopes
  BT1   millisec living radioisotopes
    BT2   radioisotopes
      BT3   isotopes
  BT1   odd-odd nuclei
    BT2   nuclei

ACTINIUM 211 [3; 3] *May 86*
  BT1   actinide nuclei
    BT2   heavy nuclei
      BT3   nuclei
  BT1   actinium isotopes
  BT1   alpha decay radioisotopes
    BT2   radioisotopes
      BT3   isotopes
  BT1   millisec living radioisotopes
    BT2   radioisotopes
      BT3   isotopes
  BT1   odd-even nuclei
    BT2   nuclei

ACTINIUM 212 [4; 4]
  BT1   actinide nuclei
    BT2   heavy nuclei
      BT3   nuclei
  BT1   actinium isotopes
  BT1   alpha decay radioisotopes
    BT2   radioisotopes
      BT3   isotopes
  BT1   millisec living radioisotopes
    BT2   radioisotopes
      BT3   isotopes
  BT1   odd-odd nuclei
    BT2   nuclei

ACTINIUM 213 [3; 3]
  BT1   actinide nuclei
    BT2   heavy nuclei
      BT3   nuclei
  BT1   actinium isotopes
  BT1   alpha decay radioisotopes
    BT2   radioisotopes
      BT3   isotopes
  BT1   millisec living radioisotopes
    BT2   radioisotopes
      BT3   isotopes
  BT1   odd-even nuclei
    BT2   nuclei

ACTINIUM 214 [6; 6] *May 86*
  BT1   actinide nuclei
    BT2   heavy nuclei
      BT3   nuclei
  BT1   actinium isotopes
  BT1   alpha decay radioisotopes
    BT2   radioisotopes
      BT3   isotopes
  BT1   electron capture radioisotopes
    BT2   beta decay radioisotopes
      BT3   radioisotopes
        BT4   isotopes
  BT1   odd-odd nuclei
    BT2   nuclei
  BT1   seconds living radioisotopes
    BT2   radioisotopes
      BT3   isotopes

ACTINIUM 215 [6; 6] *Jun 82*
  BT1   actinide nuclei
    BT2   heavy nuclei
      BT3   nuclei
  BT1   actinium isotopes
  BT1   alpha decay radioisotopes
    BT2   radioisotopes
      BT3   isotopes
  BT1   electron capture radioisotopes
    BT2   beta decay radioisotopes
      BT3   radioisotopes
        BT4   isotopes
  BT1   millisec living radioisotopes
    BT2   radioisotopes
      BT3   isotopes
  BT1   odd-even nuclei
    BT2   nuclei

ACTINIUM 216 [1; 1]
  BT1   actinide nuclei
    BT2   heavy nuclei
      BT3   nuclei
  BT1   actinium isotopes
  BT1   alpha decay radioisotopes
    BT2   radioisotopes
      BT3   isotopes
  BT1   microsec living radioisotopes
    BT2   radioisotopes
      BT3   isotopes
  BT1   odd-odd nuclei
    BT2   nuclei

ACTINIUM 217 [25; 25]
  BT1   actinide nuclei
    BT2   heavy nuclei
      BT3   nuclei
  BT1   actinium isotopes
  BT1   alpha decay radioisotopes
    BT2   radioisotopes
      BT3   isotopes
  BT1   nanosec living radioisotopes
    BT2   radioisotopes
      BT3   isotopes
  BT1   odd-even nuclei
    BT2   nuclei

ACTINIUM 218 [12; 12] *Mar 77*
  BT1   actinide nuclei
    BT2   heavy nuclei
      BT3   nuclei
  BT1   actinium isotopes
  BT1   alpha decay radioisotopes
    BT2   radioisotopes
      BT3   isotopes
  BT1   microsec living radioisotopes
    BT2   radioisotopes
      BT3   isotopes
  BT1   odd-odd nuclei
    BT2   nuclei

ACTINIUM 219 [10; 10] *Jun 85*
  BT1   actinide nuclei
    BT2   heavy nuclei
      BT3   nuclei
  BT1   actinium isotopes
  BT1   alpha decay radioisotopes
    BT2   radioisotopes
      BT3   isotopes
  BT1   microsec living radioisotopes
    BT2   radioisotopes
      BT3   isotopes
  BT1   odd-even nuclei
    BT2   nuclei

ACTINIUM 220 [6; 6] *Jul 76*
  BT1   actinide nuclei
    BT2   heavy nuclei
      BT3   nuclei
  BT1   actinium isotopes
  BT1   alpha decay radioisotopes
    BT2   radioisotopes
      BT3   isotopes
  BT1   millisec living radioisotopes
    BT2   radioisotopes
      BT3   isotopes
  BT1   odd-odd nuclei
    BT2   nuclei

ACTINIUM 221 [7; 7]
  BT1   actinide nuclei
    BT2   heavy nuclei
      BT3   nuclei
  BT1   actinium isotopes
  BT1   alpha decay radioisotopes
    BT2   radioisotopes
      BT3   isotopes
  BT1   millisec living radioisotopes
    BT2   radioisotopes
      BT3   isotopes
  BT1   odd-even nuclei
    BT2   nuclei

ACTINIUM 222 [9; 9]
  BT1   actinide nuclei
    BT2   heavy nuclei
      BT3   nuclei
  BT1   actinium isotopes
  BT1   alpha decay radioisotopes
    BT2   radioisotopes
      BT3   isotopes
  BT1   electron capture radioisotopes
    BT2   beta decay radioisotopes
      BT3   radioisotopes
        BT4   isotopes
  BT1   isomeric transition isotopes
    BT2   radioisotopes
      BT3   isotopes
  BT1   minutes living radioisotopes
    BT2   radioisotopes
      BT3   isotopes
  BT1   odd-odd nuclei
    BT2   nuclei
  BT1   seconds living radioisotopes
    BT2   radioisotopes
      BT3   isotopes

ACTINIUM 223 [11; 11]
  BT1   actinide nuclei
    BT2   heavy nuclei
      BT3   nuclei
  BT1   actinium isotopes
  BT1   alpha decay radioisotopes
    BT2   radioisotopes
      BT3   isotopes
  BT1   electron capture radioisotopes
    BT2   beta decay radioisotopes
      BT3   radioisotopes
        BT4   isotopes
  BT1   minutes living radioisotopes
    BT2   radioisotopes
      BT3   isotopes
  BT1   odd-even nuclei
    BT2   nuclei

ACTINIUM 224 [3; 3]
  BT1   actinide nuclei
    BT2   heavy nuclei
      BT3   nuclei
  BT1   actinium isotopes
  BT1   alpha decay radioisotopes
    BT2   radioisotopes
      BT3   isotopes
  BT1   electron capture radioisotopes
    BT2   beta decay radioisotopes
      BT3   radioisotopes
        BT4   isotopes
  BT1   hours living radioisotopes
    BT2   radioisotopes
      BT3   isotopes
  BT1   odd-odd nuclei
    BT2   nuclei

ACTINIUM 225 [49; 49]
  BT1   actinide nuclei
    BT2   heavy nuclei
      BT3   nuclei
  BT1   actinium isotopes
  BT1   alpha decay radioisotopes
    BT2   radioisotopes
      BT3   isotopes
  BT1   days living radioisotopes
    BT2   radioisotopes
      BT3   isotopes
  BT1   odd-even nuclei
    BT2   nuclei

ACTINIUM 226 [8; 8]
  BT1   actinide nuclei
    BT2   heavy nuclei
      BT3   nuclei
  BT1   actinium isotopes
  BT1   alpha decay radioisotopes
    BT2   radioisotopes
      BT3   isotopes
  BT1   beta-minus decay radioisotopes
    BT2   beta decay radioisotopes
      BT3   radioisotopes
        BT4   isotopes
  BT1   days living radioisotopes
    BT2   radioisotopes
      BT3   isotopes

ACTINIUM 226

BT1 electron capture radioisotopes
BT2 beta decay radioisotopes
BT3 radioisotopes
BT4 isotopes
BT1 odd-odd nuclei
BT2 nuclei

ACTINIUM 227 [182; 182]
BT1 actinide nuclei
BT2 heavy nuclei
BT3 nuclei
BT1 actinium isotopes
BT1 alpha decay radioisotopes
BT2 radioisotopes
BT3 isotopes
BT1 beta-minus decay radioisotopes
BT2 beta decay radioisotopes
BT3 radioisotopes
BT4 isotopes
BT1 internal conversion radioisoto
BT2 radioisotopes
BT3 isotopes
BT1 odd-even nuclei
BT2 nuclei
BT1 years living radioisotopes
BT2 radioisotopes
BT3 isotopes

ACTINIUM 227 TARGET [13; 13]
Oct 75
BT1 targets

ACTINIUM 228 [109; 109]
BT1 actinide nuclei
BT2 heavy nuclei
BT3 nuclei
BT1 actinium isotopes
BT1 beta-minus decay radioisotopes
BT2 beta decay radioisotopes
BT3 radioisotopes
BT4 isotopes
BT1 hours living radioisotopes
BT2 radioisotopes
BT3 isotopes
BT1 odd-odd nuclei
BT2 nuclei

ACTINIUM 229 [8; 8]
BT1 actinide nuclei
BT2 heavy nuclei
BT3 nuclei
BT1 actinium isotopes
BT1 beta-minus decay radioisotopes
BT2 beta decay radioisotopes
BT3 radioisotopes
BT4 isotopes
BT1 hours living radioisotopes
BT2 radioisotopes
BT3 isotopes
BT1 odd-even nuclei
BT2 nuclei

ACTINIUM 230 [7; 7]
BT1 actinide nuclei
BT2 heavy nuclei
BT3 nuclei
BT1 actinium isotopes
BT1 beta-minus decay radioisotopes
BT2 beta decay radioisotopes
BT3 radioisotopes
BT4 isotopes
BT1 minutes living radioisotopes
BT2 radioisotopes
BT3 isotopes
BT1 odd-odd nuclei
BT2 nuclei

ACTINIUM 231 [12; 12]
BT1 actinide nuclei
BT2 heavy nuclei
BT3 nuclei
BT1 actinium isotopes
BT1 beta-minus decay radioisotopes
BT2 beta decay radioisotopes
BT3 radioisotopes
BT4 isotopes
BT1 minutes living radioisotopes
BT2 radioisotopes
BT3 isotopes
BT1 odd-even nuclei
BT2 nuclei

ACTINIUM 232 [11; 11] Jan 78
BT1 actinide nuclei
BT2 heavy nuclei
BT3 nuclei
BT1 actinium isotopes
BT1 beta-minus decay radioisotopes
BT2 beta decay radioisotopes
BT3 radioisotopes
BT4 isotopes
BT1 minutes living radioisotopes
BT2 radioisotopes
BT3 isotopes
BT1 odd-odd nuclei
BT2 nuclei

ACTINIUM 233 [5; 5] Sep 83
BT1 actinide nuclei
BT2 heavy nuclei
BT3 nuclei
BT1 actinium isotopes
BT1 beta-minus decay radioisotopes
BT2 beta decay radioisotopes
BT3 radioisotopes
BT4 isotopes
BT1 minutes living radioisotopes
BT2 radioisotopes
BT3 isotopes
BT1 odd-even nuclei
BT2 nuclei

ACTINIUM 234 [5; 5] Jan 86
BT1 actinide nuclei
BT2 heavy nuclei
BT3 nuclei
BT1 actinium isotopes
BT1 beta-minus decay radioisotopes
BT2 beta decay radioisotopes
BT3 radioisotopes
BT4 isotopes
BT1 odd-odd nuclei
BT2 nuclei
BT1 seconds living radioisotopes
BT2 radioisotopes
BT3 isotopes

ACTINOMYCES [29; 29]
BT1 bacteria
BT2 microorganisms
RT nocardia

ACTINOMYCIN [286; 286]
BT1 antibiotics
BT2 drugs
BT2 organic compounds
BT1 antimitotic drugs
BT2 drugs
BT1 antineoplastic drugs
BT2 drugs

ACTION INTEGRAL [2,211; 2,211]
Jul 86
(An integral associated with the trajectory of a system in configuration space, equal to the sum of the integrals of the generalized momenta of the system over their canonically conjugate coordinates.)
BT1 integrals
RT field theories
RT mechanics

ACTIVATED CARBON [1,108; 1,108]
BT1 adsorbents
BT1 carbon
BT2 nonmetals
BT3 elements
RT adsorption
RT charcoal

activation (chemical)
USE chemical activation

activation (radio)
USE radioactivation

§ ### ACTIVATION ANALYSIS
[7,712; 13,699]
(Before the introduction of the specific narrower terms in November 1978, all types of activation analysis were indexed to the above descriptor.)
UF *analysis (activation)*
UF *radiochemical activation analy*
BT1 nondestructive analysis
BT2 chemical analysis
NT1 charged-particle activation an
NT1 neutron activation analysis
NT1 photon activation analysis
RT crime detection
RT impurities
RT nuclear reaction analysis
RT qualitative chemical analysis
RT quantitative chemical analysis
RT radioactivation
RT substoichiometry

ACTIVATION DETECTORS [995; 995]
BT1 neutron detectors
BT2 radiation detectors
BT3 measuring instruments
RT fission foil detectors
RT moderating detectors
RT radiator counters
RT threshold detectors

ACTIVATION ENERGY [7,897; 7,897]
UF *activation heat*
BT1 energy
RT arrhenius equation
RT chemical activation
RT chemical reaction kinetics
RT excitation
RT reaction kinetics

activation heat
USE activation energy

activity (optical)
USE optical activity

activity coefficient
USE thermodynamic activity

ACTIVITY LEVELS [766; 766] Oct 76
(May be used in any field. Prior to 1986 RADIOACTIVITY was used for this concept if appropriate.)
RT activity meters
RT enzyme activity
RT maximum permissible activity
RT radioactivity
RT solar activity

ACTIVITY METERS [133; 133]
RT activity levels
RT counting techniques

activity transport
(In reactor systems.)
USE radioactivity transport

ACTUATORS [192; 192] Aug 75
(Mechanism to activate process control equipment, e.g., valves.)
RT control equipment
RT servomechanisms
RT solenoids

ACUTE EXPOSURE [88; 513] Dec 85
(For acute exposure to radiation, use ACUTE IRRADIATION.)
NT1 acute irradiation
RT biological effects
RT dose-response relationships

RT   toxicity

ACUTE IRRADIATION [1,905; 1,905]
BT1   acute exposure
BT1   irradiation
RT   latency period
RT   radiation syndrome

ACYL RADICALS [37; 170]
BT1   radicals
NT1   acetyl radicals
NT1   butyryl radicals
NT1   formyl radicals

ACYLATION [127; 277]
BT1   chemical reactions
NT1   acetylation
NT1   benzoylation
RT   post-translation modification

adamantane
USE   cycloalkanes

adamellite
USE   quartz monzonite

adapted swim. pool r. austria
USE   astra reactor

added mass effect
USE   hydrodynamic mass effect

§ **ADDITIVES** [1,553; 1,988]
NT1   emulsifiers
NT2   detergents
NT3   pluronics
RT   catalysts
RT   solutes
RT   xenobiotics

ADDUCTS [1,026; 1,338]
(Chemical compounds with weak bonds, e.g. occlusive or Van der Waals bonds.)
NT1   dna adducts
RT   chemical bonds
RT   clathrates
RT   complexes

ADENINES [362; 411]
UF   *6-aminopurine*
BT1   amines
BT2   organic compounds
BT1   antimetabolites
BT2   drugs
BT1   purines
BT2   heterocyclic compounds
BT3   organic compounds
BT2   organic nitrogen compounds
BT3   organic compounds
NT1   kinetin
RT   adenosine
RT   adp
RT   amp
RT   atp
RT   vitamin b group

adenocarcinomas
USE   carcinomas

ADENOMAS [1,073; 1,073]
BT1   neoplasms
BT2   diseases
RT   glands

ADENOSINE [379; 379]
BT1   nucleosides
BT2   nucleotides
BT3   organic compounds
BT2   ribosides
RT   adenines
RT   atp

adenosine diphosphate
USE   adp

adenosine monophosphate
USE   amp

adenosine triphosphatase
USE   atp-ase

adenosine triphosphate
USE   atp

ADENOVIRUS [106; 106]
BT1   oncogenic viruses
BT2   viruses
BT3   microorganisms
BT3   parasites

adenylic acid
USE   amp

adgezator
USE   electron-ring accelerators

ADHESION [1,133; 1,133]
RT   adhesives
RT   agglomeration
RT   bonding
RT   coalescence
RT   surface properties

ADHESIVES [177; 177]
RT   adhesion
RT   binders

ADIABATIC APPROXIMATION [1,386; 1,386]
UF   *approximation (adiabatic)*
RT   born-oppenheimer approximation
RT   diabatic approximation
RT   quantum mechanics
RT   scattering

ADIABATIC COMPRESSION HEATING [332; 332]
BT1   plasma heating
BT2   heating

ADIABATIC DEMAGNETIZATION [133; 133]
BT1   demagnetization
RT   cryogenics
RT   magnetism

ADIABATIC INVARIANCE [219; 219]
RT   invariance principles
RT   quantum mechanics

ADIABATIC PROCESSES [1,270; 1,274]
UF   *processes (adiabatic)*
NT1   adiabatic surface ionization
RT   isentropic processes
RT   isothermal processes
RT   thermodynamics

ADIABATIC SURFACE IONIZATION [5; 5]
UF   *asi*
BT1   adiabatic processes
BT1   surface ionization
BT2   ionization

adiabatic toroidal compressors
USE   atc devices

ADIPIC ACID [38; 38]
BT1   dicarboxylic acids
BT2   carboxylic acids
BT3   organic acids
BT4   organic compounds

ADIPOSE TISSUE [631; 631]
BT1   connective tissue
BT2   tissues
BT3   body
RT   fat cells
RT   fats

→ **ADITYA TOKAMAK** [5; 5] *Feb 91*
BT1   tokamak devices
BT2   closed plasma devices
BT3   thermonuclear devices

ADJOINT DIFFERENCE METHOD [42; 42]
RT   neutron transport theory
RT   one-dimensional calculations
RT   three-dimensional calculations
RT   two-dimensional calculations

ADJOINT FLUX [190; 190]
BT1   neutron flux
BT2   radiation flux
RT   neutron importance function
RT   perturbation theory

administration
USE   management

ADMINISTRATIVE PROCEDURES [1,000; 1,895] *Dec 83*
UF   *permit applications*
NT1   licensing procedures
NT1   notification procedures
RT   agreements
RT   enforcement
RT   hearings
RT   implementation
RT   laws
RT   leasing
RT   legal aspects
RT   regulations
RT   reporting requirements

ADOLESCENTS [333; 333]
(Not limited to man, but referring to the stage between puberty and maturity.)
RT   adults
RT   age groups
RT   children
RT   education
RT   juveniles
RT   life cycle
RT   man

ADONE [82; 82]
BT1   storage rings

ADP [382; 382]
UF   *adenosine diphosphate*
BT1   nucleotides
BT2   organic compounds
RT   adenines

ADRENAL GLANDS [1,409; 1,409]
UF   *cortex (adrenal)*
BT1   endocrine glands
BT2   glands
BT3   organs
BT4   body
RT   acth
RT   adrenal hormones
RT   adrenalectomy
RT   androgens

ADRENAL HORMONES [76; 2,312]
- BT1 hormones
- NT1 adrenaline
- NT1 corticosteroids
  - NT2 glucocorticoids
    - NT3 corticosterone
    - NT3 cortisone
    - NT3 dexamethasone
    - NT3 hydrocortisone
    - NT3 prednisolone
    - NT3 prednisone
  - NT2 mineralocorticoids
    - NT3 aldosterone
    - NT3 doca
- NT1 noradrenaline
- RT adrenal glands
- RT adrenalectomy
- RT androgens

ADRENALECTOMY [111; 111]
- BT1 surgery
  - BT2 medicine
- RT adrenal glands
- RT adrenal hormones
- RT response modifying factors

ADRENALINE [343; 343]
- UF *epinephrine*
- BT1 adrenal hormones
  - BT2 hormones
- BT1 cardiotonics
  - BT2 cardiovascular agents
    - BT3 drugs
- BT1 neuroregulators
  - BT2 autonomic nervous system agent
    - BT3 drugs
- BT1 sympathomimetics
  - BT2 autonomic nervous system agent
    - BT3 drugs

adrenocorticotropic hormone
- USE acth

adriamycin
- USE doxorubicin

ADSORBENTS [1,462; 3,626]
- NT1 activated carbon
- NT1 bioadsorbents
- NT1 molecular sieves
- NT1 silica gel
- RT adsorption
- RT chemisorption

§ ## ADSORPTION [11,583; 11,583]
- SF *sorption*
- RT activated carbon
- RT adsorbents
- RT adsorption heat
- RT adsorption isotherms
- RT bioadsorbents
- RT chemisorption
- RT deposition
- RT desorption
- RT gettering
- RT hygroscopicity
- RT impregnation
- RT molecular sieves
- RT separation processes
- RT silica gel
- RT surface properties
- RT surfaces
- RT van der waals forces

ADSORPTION HEAT [294; 294]
- UF *heat of adsorption*
- BT1 enthalpy
  - BT2 thermodynamic properties
    - BT3 physical properties
- RT adsorption

ADSORPTION ISOTHERMS [401; 401]
- RT adsorption

ADU [180; 180]
- UF *ammonium diuranate*
- BT1 ammonium uranates
  - BT2 ammonium compounds
  - BT2 uranates
    - BT3 uranium compounds
      - BT4 actinide compounds

ADULTS [1,053; 1,267]
- NT1 aged adults
- NT2 elderly people
- RT adolescents
- RT age groups
- RT animal growth
- RT life cycle
- RT man
- RT men
- RT metamorphosis
- RT reference man
- RT reproduction
- RT women

adv. gas cooled graph. moderat
- USE agr type reactors

adv. reactivity meas. fac.-1
- USE armf-1 reactor

adv. test idaho reactor
- USE atr reactor

adv. test react. critical fac.
- USE atrc reactor

adv. thermal reactor fugen
- USE jatr reactor

advanced toroidal facil torsat
- USE atf torsatron

ADVECTION [185; 185] *Feb 76*
(The horizontal mass transport of a fluid as a result of current or pressure conditions.)
- BT1 mass transfer
- RT convection
- RT diffusion
- RT fluid flow
- RT osmosis
- RT water currents
- RT wind

ADVENTITIOUS BUD TECHNIQUE [20; 20]
- RT mutants
- RT mutations
- RT plant breeding
- RT vegetative propagation

adversaries
- USE interest groups

aec-nim
- USE nuclear instrument modules

aecb canada
- USE canadian aecb

aecl
- USE atomic energy of canada ltd

aecl radiochemical slowpoke re
- USE slowpoke-ottawa reactor

aedes
- USE mosquitoes

aeg pruefreaktor pr-10
- USE aeg-pr-10 reactor

AEG-PR-10 REACTOR [4; 4]
(KWU, Karlstein, Bayern, Federal Republic of Germany)
- UF *aeg pruefreaktor pr-10*
- UF *grosswelzheim pr-10 reactor*
- UF *pr-10 aeg pruefreaktor*
- BT1 argonaut type reactors
  - BT2 enriched uranium reactors
    - BT3 reactors
  - BT2 research and test reactors
    - BT3 reactors
  - BT2 water cooled reactors
    - BT3 reactors
  - BT2 water moderated reactors
    - BT3 reactors
- BT1 research reactors
  - BT2 research and test reactors
    - BT3 reactors
- BT1 thermal reactors
  - BT2 reactors

aepr
- USE acoustic esr

AERATION [101; 101] *Sep 80*
- RT air
- RT bubbles
- RT deaerators
- RT gases
- RT mixing

AERE [203; 203]
- UF *atomic energy research establi*
- BT1 ukaea
  - BT2 united kingdom organizations
    - BT3 national organizations

AERIAL MONITORING [1,764; 1,764]
(For monitoring FROM the air, e.g. by airplanes or balloons; not for monitoring OF the air.)
- UF *aerial surveying (radiat. mon)*
- BT1 radiation monitoring
  - BT2 monitoring
- RT accidents
- RT aerial prospecting
- RT aerial surveying
- RT aerosols
- RT air
- RT aircraft
- RT fallout
- RT magnetic surveys
- RT radioactive clouds

AERIAL PROSPECTING [952; 952]
- BT1 prospecting
- RT aerial monitoring
- RT aerial surveying
- RT exploration
- RT magnetic surveys
- RT radiometric surveys
- RT remote sensing

AERIAL SURVEYING [113; 113] *Dec 85*
(For surveying from the air, e.g. by aircraft.)
- RT aerial monitoring
- RT aerial prospecting
- RT aircraft
- RT landsat satellites
- RT magnetic surveys
- RT remote sensing

aerial surveying (radiat. mon)
  USE   aerial monitoring

AEROBACTER [16; 16]
  BT1   bacteria
  BT2   microorganisms
  RT   coliforms
  RT   intestines
  RT   soils

AEROBIC CONDITIONS [170; 170]
  Feb 83
  RT   biodegradation
  RT   biological radiation effects
  RT   decomposition
  RT   irradiation procedures
  RT   oxygen enhancement ratio

AERODYNAMICS [568; 568]
  BT1   fluid mechanics
  BT2   mechanics
  RT   aircraft
  RT   compressible flow
  RT   gas flow
  RT   mach number
  RT   particle resuspension
  RT   reentry
  RT   subsonic flow
  RT   supersonic flow
  RT   transonic flow
  RT   wind tunnels

AEROJET-GENERAL NUCLEONICS R
[3; 3]
  UF   *agn reactor series*
  BT1   enriched uranium reactors
  BT2   reactors
  BT1   research reactors
  BT2   research and test reactors
  BT3   reactors
  BT1   solid homogeneous reactors
  BT2   homogeneous reactors
  BT3   reactors
  BT1   thermal reactors
  BT2   reactors
  BT1   training reactors
  BT2   research and test reactors
  BT3   reactors

AEROSOL GENERATORS [219; 219]
  UF   *generators (aerosol)*
  RT   aerosols
  RT   nozzles

AEROSOL MONITORING [946; 946]
  BT1   monitoring
  RT   aerosols
  RT   air pollution monitors
  RT   air samplers
  RT   cascade impactors
  RT   radiation monitoring
  RT   radioactive aerosols
  RT   smoke detectors

AEROSOL WASTES [89; 670]
  BT1   wastes
  NT1   fly ash
  RT   aerosols
  RT   air pollution

AEROSOLS [4,233; 8,601]
  UF   *fumes*
  BT1   sols
  BT2   colloids
  BT3   dispersions
  NT1   radioactive aerosols
  NT1   smokes
  NT2   tobacco smokes
  RT   aerial monitoring
  RT   aerosol generators
  RT   aerosol monitoring
  RT   aerosol wastes
  RT   air
  RT   air pollution
  RT   air pollution monitoring
  RT   atomization
  RT   condensation nuclei
  RT   droplets
  RT   dusts
  RT   fallout
  RT   filters
  RT   flow visualization
  RT   inhalation
  RT   particle size
  RT   particles
  RT   radioactive clouds
  RT   respirators
  RT   sedimentation
  RT   smoke detectors
  RT   ventilation

AESCHYNITE [2; 2]
  BT1   oxide minerals
  BT2   minerals
  BT1   thorium minerals
  BT2   radioactive minerals
  BT3   minerals
  BT3   radioactive materials
  BT4   materials
  RT   niobium oxides
  RT   thorium oxides
  RT   titanium oxides

aesr
  USE   acoustic esr

AESTHETICS [24; 24] *Jun 83*
  UF   *esthetics*
  RT   environmental impacts
  RT   human factors
  RT   ornamental plants
  RT   pollution
  RT   public opinion
  RT   public relations
  RT   socio-economic factors
  RT   sociology

AET [316; 316]
  UF   *aminoethylisothiuronium bromid*
  UF   *aminoethylthiopseudourea*
  BT1   amines
  BT2   organic compounds
  BT1   radioprotective substances
  BT2   drugs
  BT2   response modifying factors
  BT1   thioureas
  BT2   carbonic acid derivatives
  BT3   organic compounds
  BT2   organic sulfur compounds
  BT3   organic compounds

AFFINITY [1,520; 1,520]
  RT   chemical properties
  RT   chemical reactions
  RT   electronegativity
  RT   free energy

AFGHANISTAN [4; 4]
  BT1   asia
  BT1   developing countries

AFLATOXINS [131; 131]
  BT1   toxins
  BT2   antigens
  RT   aspergillus
  RT   toxicity

afr storage
  USE   away-from-reactor storage

AFRICA [186; 2,634]
  NT1   algeria
  NT1   angola
  NT1   botswana
  NT1   cameroon
  NT1   central african republic
  NT1   chad
  NT1   congo peoples republic
  NT1   egyptian arab republic
  NT1   ethiopia
  NT1   gabon
  NT1   gambia
  NT1   ghana
  NT1   ivory coast
  NT1   kenya
  NT1   lesotho
  NT1   liberia
  NT1   libya
  NT1   madagascar
  NT1   malawi
  NT1   mali
  NT1   mauritania
  NT1   morocco
  NT1   mozambique
  NT1   niger
  NT1   nigeria
  NT1   rwanda
  NT1   senegal
  NT1   sierra leone
  NT1   somalia
  NT1   south africa
  NT2   transvaal
  NT1   south west africa
  NT1   sudan
  NT1   swaziland
  NT1   tanzania
  NT1   togo
  NT1   tunisia
  NT1   uganda
  NT1   upper volta
  NT1   zaire republic
  NT1   zambia
  NT1   zimbabwe
  NT2   southern rhodesia

AFRRI REACTOR [3; 3]
(Armed Forces Radiobiology Research Institute, Bethesda, Maryland, USA)
  UF   *def. at. supp. ag. triga-mk-f*
  UF   *triga-f-dasa reactor*
  BT1   isotope production reactors
  BT2   irradiation reactors
  BT3   reactors
  BT1   research reactors
  BT2   research and test reactors
  BT3   reactors
  BT1   thermal reactors
  BT2   reactors
  BT1   training reactors
  BT2   research and test reactors
  BT3   reactors
  BT1   triga type reactors
  BT2   enriched uranium reactors
  BT3   reactors
  BT2   hydride moderated reactors
  BT3   reactors
  BT2   research and test reactors
  BT3   reactors
  BT2   solid homogeneous reactors
  BT3   homogeneous reactors
  BT4   reactors
  BT2   water cooled reactors
  BT3   reactors
  BT2   water moderated reactors
  BT3   reactors

AFSR REACTOR [1; 1]
(ANL, Idaho Falls, Idaho, USA)
  UF   *argonne fast source reactor*
  UF   *fast source reactor aec*
  BT1   air cooled reactors
  BT2   gas cooled reactors
  BT3   reactors
  BT1   enriched uranium reactors
  BT2   reactors
  BT1   fast reactors
  BT2   epithermal reactors
  BT3   reactors
  BT1   research reactors
  BT2   research and test reactors
  BT3   reactors

AFTER-HEAT [1,154; 1,154]
(Heat derived from residual radioactivity after a reactor has been shut down.)
  SF   *decay heat*
  RT   after-heat removal
  RT   away-from-reactor storage
  RT   fuel cooling time
  RT   reactor shutdown
  RT   residual power

RT   spent fuel storage

AFTER-HEAT REMOVAL [2,072; 2,072]
UF   *pahr*
UF   *removal (after-heat)*
UF   *residual-heat removal*
UF   *rhr*
BT1   removal
RT   after-heat

AFTERGLOW [516; 516]
RT   electric discharges
RT   phosphorescence

AFTERLOADING [767; 767] *Aug 76*
(Method in radiotherapy whereby empty applicators are first positioned and the radiation source inserted automatically after the personnel has withdrawn.)
BT1   radiotherapy
  BT2   therapy
    BT3   medicine
RT   internal irradiation
RT   irradiation procedures
RT   radiation protection
RT   radiation source implants

AGAR [139; 139]
BT1   colloids
  BT2   dispersions
BT1   polysaccharides
  BT2   saccharides
    BT3   carbohydrates
      BT4   organic compounds

AGATA REACTOR [0; 0]
(Institute of Nuclear Research, Swierk, Poland)
UF   *swierk agata reactor*
BT1   beryllium moderated reactors
  BT2   metal moderated reactors
    BT3   reactors
BT1   pool type reactors
  BT2   water cooled reactors
    BT3   reactors
  BT2   water moderated reactors
    BT3   reactors
BT1   research reactors
  BT2   research and test reactors
    BT3   reactors
BT1   zero power reactors
  BT2   experimental reactors
    BT3   research and test reactors
      BT4   reactors

AGE DEPENDENCE [3,907; 3,907]
RT   growth
RT   life span
RT   menopause
RT   ripening

AGE ESTIMATION [3,047; 6,638]
UF   *dating*
UF   *geochronology*
NT1   isotope dating
RT   archaeology
RT   cultural objects
RT   fission tracks
RT   paleontology

AGE GROUPS [910; 910]
RT   adolescents
RT   adults
RT   aged adults
RT   children
RT   fetuses
RT   infants
RT   juveniles
RT   larvae
RT   life cycle
RT   neonates
RT   populations
RT   pupae

AGE HARDENING [313; 313]
BT1   hardening
RT   aging
RT   precipitation hardening

AGED ADULTS [128; 220] *Feb 83*
BT1   adults
NT1   elderly people
RT   age groups
RT   life cycle
RT   man

agedoite
USE   asparagine

AGESTA REACTOR [26; 26]
(Agesta, Stockholm, Sweden)
UF   *agesta-r3 reactor*
UF   *r-3/adam reactor*
BT1   natural uranium reactors
  BT2   reactors
BT1   phwr type reactors
  BT2   heavy water cooled reactors
    BT3   reactors
  BT2   heavy water moderated reactors
    BT3   reactors
BT1   process heat reactors
  BT2   power reactors
    BT3   reactors
BT1   thermal reactors
  BT2   reactors

agesta-r3 reactor
USE   agesta reactor

AGGLOMERATION [340; 340] *Dec 85*
UF   *aggregation*
RT   adhesion
RT   coalescence
RT   compacting
RT   precipitation
RT   sintering

agglutination
USE   antigen-antibody reactions

AGGLUTININS [69; 634]
NT1   hemagglutinins
  NT2   concanavalin a
  NT2   phytohemagglutinin
RT   antibodies

aggregation
USE   agglomeration

AGING [3,031; 3,397]
(For biological aging use LIFE CYCLE or LIFE SPAN.)
NT1   quench aging
NT1   strain aging
RT   age hardening
RT   heat treatments

AGIP NUCLEARE [4; 4]
BT1   italian organizations
  BT2   national organizations

agn reactor series
USE   aerojet-general nucleonics r

agr reactor (windscale)
USE   wagr reactor

AGR TYPE REACTORS [1,111; 1,673]
UF   *adv. gas cooled graph. moderat*
BT1   enriched uranium reactors
  BT2   reactors
BT1   gas cooled reactors
  BT2   reactors

BT1   graphite moderated reactors
  BT2   reactors
NT1   connah quay-b reactor
NT1   dungeness-b reactor
NT1   hartlepool reactor
NT1   heysham-a reactor
NT1   heysham-b reactor
NT1   hinkley point-b reactor
NT1   hunterston-b reactor
NT1   torness reactor
NT1   wagr reactor
RT   carbon dioxide cooled reactors
RT   power reactors

AGREEMENTS [141; 1,925]
UF   *conventions*
NT1   indemnification agreements
NT1   international agreements
  NT2   atomic energy agreements
  NT2   bcoclmcnm
  NT2   bcolons
  NT2   bcstpc
  NT2   bilateral agreements
  NT2   canare
  NT2   cenna
  NT2   cppnm
  NT2   iaea agreements
  NT2   lcpmpdpw
  NT2   multilateral agreements
  NT2   pcotpl
  NT2   solas convention
  NT2   vcoclnd
RT   administrative procedures
RT   contracts
RT   cooperation
RT   delivery
RT   implementation
RT   laws
RT   leasing
RT   recommendations
RT   regulations

agricultural information syste
USE   agris

agricultural wastes
USE   biological wastes

AGRICULTURE [1,163; 1,163]
RT   agris
RT   animal breeding
RT   biomass plantations
RT   crops
RT   cultivation techniques
RT   domestic animals
RT   ecosystems
RT   fao
RT   fertilizers
RT   food
RT   grain disinfestation
RT   irrigation
RT   pesticides
RT   plants
RT   soils
RT   sterile male technique

AGRIS [18; 18]
UF   *agricultural information syste*
BT1   information systems
RT   agriculture
RT   fao

aguirre-1 reactor
(Prior to December 1990, this was a valid descriptor.)
USE   north coast-1 reactor

→ **AHARONOV-BOHM EFFECT** [0; 0]
Sep 91
RT   electromagnetic fields
RT   gauge invariance
RT   magnetic flux
RT   phase shift
RT   quantum mechanics

AI-L-77 REACTOR [1; 1]
(Atomics International/Rockwell International, Canoga Park, California, USA)
- UF *atomics international l-77 r.*
- UF *l-77 atomics international r.*
- BT1 aqueous homogeneous reactors
  - BT2 liquid homogeneous reactors
    - BT3 fluid fueled reactors
      - BT4 reactors
    - BT3 homogeneous reactors
      - BT4 reactors
  - BT2 water cooled reactors
    - BT3 reactors
  - BT2 water moderated reactors
    - BT3 reactors
- BT1 enriched uranium reactors
  - BT2 reactors
- BT1 isotope production reactors
  - BT2 irradiation reactors
    - BT3 reactors
- BT1 research reactors
  - BT2 research and test reactors
    - BT3 reactors
- BT1 thermal reactors
  - BT2 reactors
- BT1 training reactors
  - BT2 research and test reactors
    - BT3 reactors

aic-144 cyclotron
- USE cracow aic-144 cyclotron

AIDS [205; 205] *Aug 86*
(Acquired Immuno-Deficiency Syndrome.)
- BT1 immune system diseases
  - BT2 diseases
- BT1 viral diseases
  - BT2 infectious diseases
    - BT3 diseases
- RT aids virus
- RT disease resistance
- RT immunity
- RT leukocytes

AIDS VIRUS [82; 82] *May 86*
(Virus responsible for Acquired Immuno-Deficiency Syndrome.)
- UF *acquired immunodeficiency viru*
- UF *htlv iii virus*
- UF *lav virus*
- BT1 viruses
  - BT2 microorganisms
  - BT2 parasites
- RT aids
- RT immune reactions
- RT immunity

AIPFR REACTOR [1; 1]
- UF *atomics int. prototype fast r.*
- BT1 fbr type reactors
  - BT2 breeder reactors
    - BT3 reactors
  - BT2 fast reactors
    - BT3 epithermal reactors
      - BT4 reactors
- BT1 power reactors
  - BT2 reactors
- BT1 test reactors
  - BT2 research and test reactors
    - BT3 reactors
  - BT2 test facilities

AIR [7,481; 8,731]
- UF+ *air heaters*
- BT1 gases
  - BT2 fluids
- NT1 surface air
- RT aeration
- RT aerial monitoring
- RT aerosols
- RT air conditioning
- RT air flow
- RT air infiltration
- RT aircraft
- RT breath
- RT carbon dioxide fixation
- RT earth atmosphere
- RT environmental materials
- RT fallout
- RT inhalation
- RT nitrogen fixation
- RT radioactive clouds
- RT respiration
- RT respirators
- RT respiratory system
- RT troposphere
- RT ventilation
- RT wind

AIR CLEANING [750; 750]
- UF *air purification*
- BT1 cleaning
- RT air conditioning
- RT air filters
- RT electrostatic precipitators
- RT pollution control equipment
- RT scrubbers
- RT ventilation

AIR CONDITIONING [244; 244]
- RT air
- RT air cleaning
- RT cooling
- RT environmental engineering
- RT heating
- RT humidity control
- RT radiative cooling
- RT temperature control
- RT thermal insulation
- RT ventilation
- RT working conditions

AIR COOLED REACTORS [12; 752]
- UF *air-cooled reactors*
- BT1 gas cooled reactors
  - BT2 reactors
- NT1 afsr reactor
- NT1 bepo reactor
- NT1 bgrr reactor
- NT1 br-1 reactor
- NT1 gleep reactor
- NT1 harmonie reactor
- NT1 hprr reactor
- NT1 kalpakkam pfr reactor
- NT1 sneak reactor
- NT1 stf reactor
- NT1 tory-2c reactor
- NT1 treat reactor
- NT1 windscale production reactors
- NT1 x-10 reactor
- NT1 zed-2 reactor

AIR FILTERS [1,758; 1,758]
- BT1 filters
- BT1 pollution control equipment
  - BT2 equipment
- RT air cleaning
- RT air pollution monitors
- RT scrubbers

→ **AIR FLOW** [9; 9] *Apr 84*
- BT1 gas flow
  - BT2 fluid flow
- RT air
- RT air infiltration
- RT ventilation

air heaters
- USE air
- AND heaters

AIR INFILTRATION [57; 57] *Dec 85*
(Air flow into an enclosed space, e.g. a building.)
- RT air
- RT air flow
- RT buildings
- RT containment
- RT gas flow
- RT leaks

AIR POLLUTION [4,562; 4,562]
(For nonradioactive pollution only; for radioactive pollution use CONTAMINATION.)
- UF *smog*
- UF+ *thermal pollution (air)*
- BT1 pollution
- RT acid rain
- RT aerosol wastes
- RT aerosols
- RT air pollution abatement
- RT air pollution monitoring
- RT air quality
- RT atmospheric chemistry
- RT fly ash
- RT particle resuspension
- RT plumes
- RT scrubbers
- RT temperature inversions

→ **AIR POLLUTION ABATEMENT** [2; 2]
Apr 84
(The prevention of formation of pollutants at the source.)
- BT1 pollution abatement
- RT air pollution
- RT desulfurization

→ **AIR POLLUTION CONTROL** [0; 0]
Apr 86
(The removal or management of pollutants after they are formed by a source.)
- BT1 pollution control
  - BT2 control
- RT baghouses

→ **AIR POLLUTION MONITORING** [2; 2]
Aug 91
- BT1 monitoring
- RT aerosols
- RT air pollution

→ **AIR POLLUTION MONITORS** [2; 2]
Sep 91
- UF *monitors (air pollution)*
- BT1 monitors
  - BT2 measuring instruments
- RT aerosol monitoring
- RT air filters
- RT air samplers
- RT cascade impactors
- RT electrostatic precipitators

air purification
- USE air cleaning

→ **AIR QUALITY** [2; 2] *Jan 77*
- BT1 environmental quality
- RT air pollution

AIR SAMPLERS [827; 827]
- BT1 samplers
  - BT2 laboratory equipment
    - BT3 equipment
- RT aerosol monitoring
- RT air pollution monitors
- RT cascade impactors

AIR TRANSPORT [201; 236] *Dec 76*
- BT1 transport
- NT1 supersonic transport
- RT aircraft

air wall ionization chambers
- USE bragg gray chambers

air-cooled reactors
- USE air cooled reactors

AIR-WATER INTERACTIONS [48; 48]
 Oct 83
 RT   carbon cycle
 RT   environmental transport
 RT   surface waters
 RT   troposphere

→ *airborne particles*
 USE   particulates

airborne particulates
 USE   particulates

AIRCRAFT [861; 861]
 RT   aerial monitoring
 RT   aerial surveying
 RT   aerodynamics
 RT   air
 RT   air transport
 RT   balloons
 RT   navigational instruments
 RT   propulsion systems
 RT   space shuttles
 RT   supersonic transport

aircraft accidents
 USE   accidents

AIRCRAFT PROPULSION REACTORS [19; 19]
 BT1   propulsion reactors
  BT2   power reactors
   BT3   reactors

AIRGLOW [374; 374]
 UF   *dayglow*
 UF   *nightglow*
 RT   aurorae
 RT   earth atmosphere

AIROX PROCESS [8; 8] *Jul 80*
 BT1   reprocessing
  BT2   separation processes

AIRY FUNCTIONS [108; 108]
 BT1   functions
 RT   differential equations

akm muehleberg reactor
 USE   muehleberg reactor

akm reactor
 USE   muehleberg reactor

akw1 rheinsberg reactor
 USE   rheinsberg akw1 reactor

ALABAMA [119; 119]
 BT1   usa
  BT2   developed countries
  BT2   north america

ALANINE-ALPHA [55; 136]
 UF   *aminopropionic acid-alpha*
 BT1   alanines
  BT2   amino acids
   BT3   carboxylic acids
    BT4   organic acids
     BT5   organic compounds
 NT1   alanine-l

ALANINE-BETA [44; 44]
 UF   *aminopropionic acid-beta*
 BT1   alanines
  BT2   amino acids
   BT3   carboxylic acids
    BT4   organic acids
     BT5   organic compounds
 RT   pantothenic acid

ALANINE-L [96; 96]
 UF   *l-alanine*
 UF   *l-alanine-alpha*
 BT1   alanine-alpha
  BT2   alanines
   BT3   amino acids
    BT4   carboxylic acids
     BT5   organic acids
      BT6   organic compounds

ALANINES [373; 534]
 BT1   amino acids
  BT2   carboxylic acids
   BT3   organic acids
    BT4   organic compounds
 NT1   alanine-alpha
  NT2   alanine-l
 NT1   alanine-beta

ALARA [839; 839] *Feb 81*
(All exposures shall be kept As Low As Reasonably Achievable, economic and social factors being taken into account.)
 UF   *as low as reasonably achievabl*
 RT   icrp
 RT   optimization
 RT   radiation doses
 RT   radiation hazards
 RT   radiation protection
 RT   risk assessment
 RT   safety
 RT   shielding
 RT   working conditions

alarm dosemeters
 USE   radiation monitors

ALARM SYSTEMS [1,182; 1,182]
 UF   *audible alarm*
 UF   *warning systems*
 RT   radiation monitoring
 RT   radiation monitors
 RT   reactor components
 RT   safety engineering
 RT   smoke detectors

ALASKA [495; 495]
 BT1   usa
  BT2   developed countries
  BT2   north america
 RT   aleutian islands
 RT   amchitka island area
 RT   chukchi sea

alaskites
 USE   aplites

ALBANIA [9; 9]
 BT1   developing countries
 BT1   europe
 RT   centrally planned economies

ALBEDO [980; 980]
 RT   illuminance
 RT   neutron transport theory
 RT   reflection

ALBEDO-NEUTRON DOSEMETERS [316; 316]
 BT1   dosemeters
  BT2   measuring instruments
 RT   backscattering
 RT   neutron dosimetry
 RT   personnel monitoring

ALBERTA [39; 40]
 BT1   canada
  BT2   developed countries
  BT2   north america

alberta univ. slowpoke reactor
 USE   slowpoke-alberta reactor

albite
 USE   feldspars

albumen
 USE   albumins

ALBUMINS [2,503; 2,516]
 UF   *albumen*
 UF+   *hsa*
 UF+   *human serum albumin*
 UF+   *risa*
 BT1   proteins
  BT2   organic compounds
 NT1   luciferin
 RT   albuminuria
 RT   polyamides

ALBUMINURIA [14; 14]
 RT   albumins

ALCATOR DEVICE [478; 478]
 UF   *massachus. inst. techn. alcato*
 BT1   tokamak devices
  BT2   closed plasma devices
   BT3   thermonuclear devices

alcoholates
 USE   alkoxides

ALCOHOLS [1,599; 8,867]
 UF   *alkylates*
 UF+   *amino alcohols*
 BT1   hydroxy compounds
  BT2   organic compounds
 NT1   batyl alcohol
 NT1   benzhydrol
 NT1   benzyl alcohol
 NT1   butanols
 NT1   choline
 NT1   decanols
 NT1   enols
 NT1   erythritol
 NT1   ethanol
 NT1   geraniol
 NT1   glycerol
 NT1   glycols
  NT2   benzopinacol
  NT2   carbitols
  NT2   cellosolves
  NT2   egta
  NT2   pinacol
 NT1   hexanols
 NT1   methanol
 NT1   metronidazole
 NT1   misonidazole
 NT1   octanols
 NT1   pentanols
 NT1   propanols
 NT1   pva
 NT1   2-methylpropanol
 RT   alkoxides

ALDEHYDES [548; 5,192]
 UF+   *aldehydo acids*
 BT1   organic compounds
 NT1   acetaldehyde
 NT1   acrolein
 NT1   aldosterone
 NT1   arabinose
 NT1   benzaldehyde
 NT1   chloral
 NT1   deoxyribose
 NT1   formaldehyde
 NT1   furfural
 NT1   galactose
 NT1   galacturonic acid
 NT1   glucose
 NT1   glucuronic acid
 NT1   glyoxal
 NT1   glyoxylic acid
 NT1   mannose
 NT1   pyridoxal
 NT1   ribose
 NT1   xylose
 RT   hydrazones
 RT   imines

```
    RT     oximes
    RT     semicarbazones


  aldehydo acids
    USE    aldehydes
    AND    carboxylic acids

ALDOLASES [43; 43]
    BT1    carbon-carbon lyases
    BT2      lyases
    BT3        enzymes
    BT4          organic compounds


ALDOSTERONE [248; 248]
    BT1    aldehydes
    BT2      organic compounds
    BT1    mineralocorticoids
    BT2      corticosteroids
    BT3        adrenal hormones
    BT4          hormones
    BT3        hydroxy compounds
    BT4          organic compounds
    BT3        ketones
    BT4          organic compounds
    BT3        pregnanes
    BT4          steroids
    BT5            organic compounds
    BT3        steroid hormones
    BT4          hormones
    RT     tubules

ALDRIN [17; 17] May 76
    BT1    chlorinated aromatic hydrocarb
    BT2      halogenated aromatic hydrocarb
    BT3        aromatics
    BT4          organic compounds
    BT3        organic halogen compounds
    BT4          organic compounds
    BT2      organic chlorine compounds
    BT3        organic halogen compounds
    BT4          organic compounds
    BT1    insecticides
    BT2      pesticides
    RT     dieldrin


ALEUTIAN ISLANDS [27; 101]
    BT1    islands
    NT1    amchitka island area
    RT     alaska
    RT     bering sea
    RT     nuclear explosions
    RT     pacific ocean


ALFALFA [121; 121]
    BT1    leguminosae
    BT2      plants


ALFVEN WAVES [2,550; 2,550]
    BT1    hydromagnetic waves
    RT     plasma waves


ALGAE [907; 1,631]
    UF+    diatoms
    BT1    plants
    NT1    acetabularia
    NT1    fucus
    NT1    laminaria
    NT1    lichens
    NT1    nitella
    NT1    porphyra
    NT1    ulva
    NT1    unicellular algae
    NT2      chlamydomonas
    NT2      chlorella
    NT2      euglena
    NT2      scenedesmus
    RT     aquatic organisms
    RT     biomass plantations
    RT     eutrophication


ALGEBRA [2,460; 2,460]
    BT1    mathematics
    RT     graded lie groups


ALGEBRAIC CURRENTS [866; 5,857]
    BT1    currents
    NT1    axial-vector currents
    NT1    charged currents
    NT2      weak charged currents
    NT1    neutral currents
    NT2      weak neutral currents
    NT1    second-class currents
    NT1    vector currents
    RT     current algebra
    RT     current commutators
    RT     current divergences


ALGEBRAIC FIELD THEORY
[504; 504] Nov 77
    UF     haag-araki field theory
    BT1    axiomatic field theory
    BT2      quantum field theory
    BT3        field theories


ALGERIA [49; 49]
    BT1    africa
    BT1    developing countries


ALGINATES [45; 45]
    RT     laminaria


ALGINIC ACID [18; 18]
    BT1    colloids
    BT2      dispersions
    BT1    polysaccharides
    BT2      saccharides
    BT3        carbohydrates
    BT4          organic compounds
    RT     carboxylic acids


ALGOL [246; 246]
    BT1    programming languages


ALGORITHMS [14,622; 14,622]
    RT     computer codes
    RT     mathematical logic
    RT     mathematics
    RT     parallel processing
    RT     vector processing


ali
    USE    annual limit of intake


ALICE [7; 7]
    BT1    magnetic mirrors
    BT2      open plasma devices
    BT3        thermonuclear devices


ALICE CYCLOTRON [22; 22]
    UF     orsay alice cyclotron
    BT1    isochronous cyclotrons
    BT2      cyclotrons
    BT3        cyclic accelerators
    BT4          accelerators


ALIGNED COUPLING SCHEME
[90; 90]
    UF     stretch model
    RT     coupling
    RT     deformed nuclei
    RT     particle-hole model
    RT     projection operators
    RT     shell models
    RT     slater method


ALIGNMENT [1,456; 1,456]
(Not for the concept covered by the descriptor NUCLEAR ALIGNMENT.)
    RT     beam optics
    RT     positioning


ALIZARIN [51; 51]
    UF     anthraquinonic acid
    UF     1,2-dihydroxyanthraquinone
    BT1    anthraquinones
    BT2      quinones
    BT3        aromatics
    BT4          organic compounds
    BT3        organic oxygen compounds
    BT4          organic compounds
    BT1    dyes
    BT1    hydroxy compounds
    BT2      organic compounds
    BT1    reagents


ALKALI METAL COMPLEXES
[80; 409]
    BT1    complexes
    NT1    cesium complexes
    NT1    francium complexes
    NT1    potassium complexes
    NT1    rubidium complexes
    NT1    sodium complexes


ALKALI METAL COMPOUNDS
[1,938; 35,346]
   *NT1    cesium compounds
   *NT1    francium compounds
   *NT1    lithium compounds
   *NT1    potassium compounds
   *NT1    rubidium compounds
   *NT1    sodium compounds


ALKALI METALS [955; 23,748]
    BT1    metals
    BT2      elements
    NT1    cesium
    NT1    francium
    NT1    lithium
    NT1    potassium
    NT1    rubidium
    NT1    sodium


ALKALINE EARTH METAL COMPLEXES [72; 833]
    BT1    complexes
    NT1    barium complexes
    NT1    beryllium complexes
    NT1    calcium complexes
    NT1    magnesium complexes
    NT1    radium complexes
    NT1    strontium complexes


ALKALINE EARTH METAL COMPOUNDS [710; 28,827]
   *NT1    barium compounds
   *NT1    beryllium compounds
   *NT1    calcium compounds
   *NT1    magnesium compounds
   *NT1    radium compounds
   *NT1    strontium compounds


ALKALINE EARTH METALS
[250; 15,247]
    BT1    metals
    BT2      elements
    NT1    barium
    NT1    beryllium
    NT2      beryllium-alpha
    NT2      beryllium-beta
    NT1    calcium
    NT1    magnesium
    NT1    radium
    NT1    strontium


ALKALINE PHOSPHATASE [382; 382]
    BT1    phosphatases
    BT2      esterases
    BT3        hydrolases
    BT4          enzymes
    BT5            organic compounds


ALKALOIDS [252; 1,125]
    UF     codeinone
    BT1    organic compounds
    NT1    atropine
    NT1    cinchonine
    NT1    cocaine
    NT1    codeine
    NT1    colchicine
    NT1    ephedrine
    NT1    ergotamine
    NT1    eserine
    NT1    heroin
    NT1    hyoscyamine
    NT1    lysergic acid
```

NT1 morphine
NT1 nicotine
NT1 oncovin
NT1 pilocarpine
NT1 quinine
NT1 reserpine
NT1 strychnine
NT1 thebaine
NT1 vinblastine
RT medicinal plants
RT plants

ALKANES [1,909; 9,479]
UF *paraffins*
BT1 hydrocarbons
BT2 organic compounds
NT1 butane
NT1 cycloalkanes
NT2 cyclohexane
NT2 decalin
NT1 decane
NT1 dodecane
NT1 ethane
NT1 heptane
NT1 hexadecane
NT1 hexane
NT1 methane
NT1 octane
NT1 paraffin
NT1 pentane
NT1 propane
NT1 squalane
NT1 2-methylbutane
NT1 2-methylpropane
NT1 2-2-dimethylpropane

alkanoic acids
USE carboxylic acids

ALKENES [939; 3,734]
UF *olefins*
BT1 hydrocarbons
BT2 organic compounds
NT1 butenes
NT1 cycloalkenes
NT2 camphene
NT2 cyclopentadiene
NT1 ethylene
NT1 heptenes
NT1 hexenes
NT1 pentenes
NT1 propylene
NT1 2-methylpropene
RT polyenes

alkenoic acids
USE carboxylic acids

alkines
USE alkynes

ALKOXIDES [189; 189] *Feb 82*
(A group of compounds in which a hydrogen atom of an alcohol or phenol hydroxide group is replaced by a metal.)
UF *alcoholates*
UF *phenolates*
RT alcohols
RT phenols

ALKOXY RADICALS [69; 152]
BT1 radicals
NT1 butoxy radicals
NT1 ethoxy radicals
NT1 methoxy radicals

alkyl benzenesulfonates
USE abs

ALKYL RADICALS [320; 1,232]
BT1 radicals
NT1 allyl radicals
NT1 butyl radicals
NT1 dodecyl radicals
NT1 ethyl radicals
NT1 heptyl radicals
NT1 hexyl radicals
NT1 isobutyl radicals
NT1 isopropyl radicals
NT1 methyl radicals
NT1 nonyl radicals
NT1 octyl radicals
NT1 pentyl radicals
NT1 propargyl radicals
NT1 propyl radicals
NT1 tridecyl radicals
NT1 vinyl radicals
RT alkylating agents
RT alkylation

alkylates
USE alcohols

ALKYLATING AGENTS [311; 823]
UF *chlorambucil*
UF *mannomustine*
UF *tem*
UF *tretamine*
UF *triethylenemelamine*
BT1 antimitotic drugs
BT2 drugs
NT1 endoxan
NT1 myleran
NT1 nitrogen mustard
RT alkyl radicals
RT alkylation
RT antimetabolites
RT chemosterilants
RT methyl methanesulfonate

ALKYLATION [319; 319]
BT1 chemical reactions
RT alkyl radicals
RT alkylating agents

alkylmagnesium compounds
USE grignard reagents

ALKYNES [246; 985]
UF *acetylenes*
UF *alkines*
BT1 hydrocarbons
BT2 organic compounds
NT1 acetylene
NT1 propyne

ALLANITE [18; 24]
BT1 silicate minerals
BT2 minerals
BT1 thorium minerals
BT2 radioactive minerals
BT3 minerals
BT3 radioactive materials
BT4 materials
NT1 orthite
RT thorium silicates

ALLANTOIN [10; 10]
BT1 imidazoles
BT2 azoles
BT3 heterocyclic compounds
BT4 organic compounds
BT3 organic nitrogen compounds
BT4 organic compounds
BT1 organic oxygen compounds
BT2 organic compounds
RT urea

ALLEGHENY RIVER [0; 0]
BT1 rivers
BT2 surface waters

ALLENE [42; 42]
UF *propadiene*
BT1 dienes
BT2 polyenes
BT3 hydrocarbons
BT4 organic compounds

ALLENS CREEK-1 REACTOR [21; 21]
(Wallis, Texas, USA)
BT1 bwr type reactors
BT2 enriched uranium reactors
BT3 reactors
BT2 power reactors
BT3 reactors
BT2 thermal reactors
BT3 reactors
BT2 water cooled reactors
BT3 reactors
BT2 water moderated reactors
BT3 reactors

ALLENS CREEK-2 REACTOR [20; 20]
(Wallis, Texas, USA)
BT1 bwr type reactors
BT2 enriched uranium reactors
BT3 reactors
BT2 power reactors
BT3 reactors
BT2 thermal reactors
BT3 reactors
BT2 water cooled reactors
BT3 reactors
BT2 water moderated reactors
BT3 reactors

ALLERGY [283; 283]
BT1 pathological changes
BT2 diseases
RT anaphylaxis
RT antihistaminics
RT eczema
RT histamine
RT immunity

ALLIUM CEPA [41; 41]
BT1 plants
RT onions

ALLOCATIONS [24; 24] *Dec 85*
UF *assignments*
UF *curtailments*
UF *rationing*
RT availability
RT budgets
RT distribution
RT economic policy
RT energy policy
RT management
RT planning

ALLOTROPY [704; 704]
(See also descriptors for specific allotropic forms, e.g., HELIUM I, IRON-ALPHA, and URANIUM-BETA.)
RT crystal structure
RT phase diagrams
RT phase transformations

ALLOXAN [22; 22]
BT1 organic oxygen compounds
BT2 organic compounds
BT1 pyrimidines
BT2 azines
BT3 heterocyclic compounds
BT4 organic compounds
BT3 organic nitrogen compounds
BT4 organic compounds

ALLOY NUCLEAR FUELS [152; 152]
BT1 solid fuels
BT2 nuclear fuels
BT3 energy sources
BT3 fuels
BT3 reactor materials
BT4 materials

ALLOY SYSTEMS [226; 8,263]
- NT1 binary alloy systems
- NT1 quaternary alloy systems
- NT1 ternary alloy systems
- RT alloys
- RT phase diagrams
- RT vegard law

alloy-a-286
USE steel-ni26cr15ti2movalb

ALLOY-AL95CU4 [23; 23]
- UF *duralumin*
- BT1 aluminium base alloys
- BT2 aluminium alloys
-   BT3 alloys
- BT1 copper alloys
- BT2 alloys
- BT1 iron additions
- BT1 magnesium additions
- BT1 manganese additions
- BT1 silicon additions

ALLOY-BI50PB25CD12SN12 [29; 29]
- UF *wood metal*
- BT1 bismuth base alloys
- BT2 bismuth alloys
-   BT3 alloys
- BT1 cadmium alloys
- BT2 alloys
- BT1 lead alloys
- BT2 alloys
- BT1 tin alloys
- BT2 alloys

alloy-ck-20
USE steel-cr25ni20

ALLOY-CO36CR22NI22W15FE3 [23; 23]
- UF *haynes 188 alloy*
- BT1 chromium alloys
- BT2 alloys
- BT1 corrosion resistant alloys
- BT2 alloys
- BT1 haynes alloys
- BT2 cobalt base alloys
-   BT3 cobalt alloys
-    BT4 alloys
- BT1 heat resisting alloys
- BT2 alloys
- BT1 iron alloys
- BT2 alloys
- BT1 lanthanum additions
- BT2 rare earth additions
- BT1 nickel alloys
- BT2 alloys
- BT1 tungsten alloys
- BT2 alloys

ALLOY-CO43CR20FE18NI13W3 [14; 14]
- UF *havar*
- BT1 carbon additions
- BT1 chromium alloys
- BT2 alloys
- BT1 cobalt base alloys
- BT2 cobalt alloys
-   BT3 alloys
- BT1 iron alloys
- BT2 alloys
- BT1 manganese alloys
- BT2 alloys
- BT1 molybdenum alloys
- BT2 alloys
- BT1 nickel alloys
- BT2 alloys
- BT1 tungsten alloys
- BT2 alloys

ALLOY-CO50FE50 [7; 7]
- UF *permendur*
- BT1 cobalt base alloys
- BT2 cobalt alloys
-   BT3 alloys
- BT1 iron base alloys
- BT2 iron alloys
-   BT3 alloys

ALLOY-CO52CR17FE15MO3SI3 [5; 5] *Dec 80*
- UF *tribaloy 800*
- BT1 chromium alloys
- BT2 alloys
- BT1 cobalt base alloys
- BT2 cobalt alloys
-   BT3 alloys
- BT1 corrosion resistant alloys
- BT2 alloys
- BT1 heat resisting alloys
- BT2 alloys
- BT1 iron alloys
- BT2 alloys
- BT1 molybdenum alloys
- BT2 alloys
- BT1 silicon alloys
- BT2 alloys

ALLOY-CO52FE35V10 [8; 8]
- UF *vikalloy 1*
- BT1 cobalt base alloys
- BT2 cobalt alloys
-   BT3 alloys
- BT1 iron alloys
- BT2 alloys
- BT1 vanadium alloys
- BT2 alloys

ALLOY-CO52FE35V13 [4; 4] *Nov 78*
- UF *vikalloy 2*
- BT1 cobalt base alloys
- BT2 cobalt alloys
-   BT3 alloys
- BT1 iron alloys
- BT2 alloys
- BT1 vanadium alloys
- BT2 alloys

ALLOY-CO54CR20W15NI10 [28; 28]
- UF *alloy-hs-25*
- UF *haynes 25 alloy*
- BT1 chromium alloys
- BT2 alloys
- BT1 corrosion resistant alloys
- BT2 alloys
- BT1 haynes alloys
- BT2 cobalt base alloys
-   BT3 cobalt alloys
-    BT4 alloys
- BT1 heat resisting alloys
- BT2 alloys
- BT1 iron alloys
- BT2 alloys
- BT1 nickel alloys
- BT2 alloys
- BT1 stellite
- BT2 cobalt base alloys
-   BT3 cobalt alloys
-    BT4 alloys
- BT1 tungsten alloys
- BT2 alloys

ALLOY-CO60CR30W4 [32; 32] *Apr 79*
- UF *haynes stellite 6b*
- UF *stellite 6*
- BT1 chromium alloys
- BT2 alloys
- BT1 corrosion resistant alloys
- BT2 alloys
- BT1 haynes alloys
- BT2 cobalt base alloys
-   BT3 cobalt alloys
-    BT4 alloys
- BT1 heat resisting alloys
- BT2 alloys
- BT1 iron alloys
- BT2 alloys
- BT1 nickel alloys
- BT2 alloys
- BT1 stellite
- BT2 cobalt base alloys
-   BT3 cobalt alloys
-    BT4 alloys
- BT1 tungsten alloys
- BT2 alloys

ALLOY-CO62CR28MO6NI3 [2; 2] *Dec 80*
- UF *alloy-hs-21*
- UF *haynes stellite no 21*
- BT1 boron additions
- BT1 chromium alloys
- BT2 alloys
- BT1 corrosion resistant alloys
- BT2 alloys
- BT1 haynes alloys
- BT2 cobalt base alloys
-   BT3 cobalt alloys
-    BT4 alloys
- BT1 heat resisting alloys
- BT2 alloys
- BT1 iron alloys
- BT2 alloys
- BT1 molybdenum alloys
- BT2 alloys
- BT1 nickel alloys
- BT2 alloys
- BT1 stellite
- BT2 cobalt base alloys
-   BT3 cobalt alloys
-    BT4 alloys

ALLOY-CO64CR29W4 [3; 3] *Apr 79*
- UF *stellite 156*
- BT1 chromium alloys
- BT2 alloys
- BT1 corrosion resistant alloys
- BT2 alloys
- BT1 heat resisting alloys
- BT2 alloys
- BT1 stellite
- BT2 cobalt base alloys
-   BT3 cobalt alloys
-    BT4 alloys
- BT1 tungsten alloys
- BT2 alloys

ALLOY-CO66CR26W6 [3; 3] *May 84*
- UF *deloro stellite 6*
- UF *stellite 6 (deloro)*
- BT1 carbon additions
- BT1 chromium alloys
- BT2 alloys
- BT1 corrosion resistant alloys
- BT2 alloys
- BT1 heat resisting alloys
- BT2 alloys
- BT1 stellite
- BT2 cobalt base alloys
-   BT3 cobalt alloys
-    BT4 alloys
- BT1 tungsten alloys
- BT2 alloys

ALLOY-CU52NI47 [17; 17]
- UF *constantan*
- BT1 copper base alloys
- BT2 copper alloys
-   BT3 alloys
- BT1 nickel alloys
- BT2 alloys

alloy-ehi 183
USE steel-cr17ni13mo3ti

alloy-ehi 397
USE steel-cr17ni13mo3ti

alloy-ehi 432
USE steel-cr17ni13mo3ti

alloy-ehi 437b
USE alloy-ni77cr20ti2

alloy-ehi 702
USE steel-ni36cr12ti3al-l

alloy-ehi 826
   USE   alloy-ni68cr15w6al3mo3fe2

alloy-ehi 868
   USE   alloy-ni60cr25w15

alloy-ehp 199
   USE   alloy-ni56cr21w10mo5fe4al2

alloy-ehp 567
   USE   alloy-ni65mo16cr15w4

ALLOY-FE31CR21CO20NI20MO3W2
[7; 7] *Feb 81*
   UF   *alloy-hd-556*
   UF   *alloy-n-155*
   BT1   carbon additions
   BT1   chromium alloys
     BT2   alloys
   BT1   cobalt alloys
     BT2   alloys
   BT1   corrosion resistant alloys
     BT2   alloys
   BT1   heat resisting alloys
     BT2   alloys
   BT1   iron base alloys
     BT2   iron alloys
       BT3   alloys
   BT1   molybdenum alloys
     BT2   alloys
   BT1   nickel alloys
     BT2   alloys
   BT1   niobium additions
   BT1   nitrogen additions
   BT1   tungsten alloys
     BT2   alloys

ALLOY-FE36NI33CR26 [10; 10] *Feb 81*
   UF   *manaurite 36x*
   BT1   chromium alloys
     BT2   alloys
   BT1   iron base alloys
     BT2   iron alloys
       BT3   alloys
   BT1   manganese alloys
     BT2   alloys
   BT1   nickel alloys
     BT2   alloys
   BT1   niobium additions
   BT1   silicon alloys
     BT2   alloys

ALLOY-FE40NI35CR22 [4; 4] *Feb 81*
   UF   *manaurite 900*
   BT1   chromium alloys
     BT2   alloys
   BT1   iron base alloys
     BT2   iron alloys
       BT3   alloys
   BT1   manganese additions
   BT1   nickel alloys
     BT2   alloys
   BT1   silicon additions

ALLOY-FE44NI33CR21 [143; 143]
Feb 82
   UF   *alloy-800h (incoloy)*
   UF   *incoloy 800h*
   BT1   aluminium additions
   BT1   chromium alloys
     BT2   alloys
   BT1   cobalt alloys
     BT2   alloys
   BT1   corrosion resistant alloys
     BT2   alloys
   BT1   heat resisting alloys
     BT2   alloys
   BT1   incoloy alloys
     BT2   alloys
   BT1   iron base alloys
     BT2   iron alloys
       BT3   alloys
   BT1   nickel alloys
     BT2   alloys
   BT1   titanium additions

ALLOY-FE46NI33CR21 [677; 677]
   UF   *alloy-800 (incoloy)*
   UF   *alloy-802 (incoloy)*
   UF   *incoloy 800*
   UF   *incoloy 802*
   UF   *sanicro 30*
   BT1   aluminium additions
   BT1   chromium alloys
     BT2   alloys
   BT1   corrosion resistant alloys
     BT2   alloys
   BT1   heat resisting alloys
     BT2   alloys
   BT1   incoloy alloys
     BT2   alloys
   BT1   iron base alloys
     BT2   iron alloys
       BT3   alloys
   BT1   nickel alloys
     BT2   alloys
   BT1   titanium additions

ALLOY-FE48CR24NI24 [7; 7] *Feb 83*
   UF   *alloy-in-519*
   BT1   aluminium additions
   BT1   chromium alloys
     BT2   alloys
   BT1   corrosion resistant alloys
     BT2   alloys
   BT1   heat resisting alloys
     BT2   alloys
   BT1   iron base alloys
     BT2   iron alloys
       BT3   alloys
   BT1   molybdenum additions
   BT1   nickel alloys
     BT2   alloys
   BT1   niobium alloys
     BT2   alloys

ALLOY-FE53NI29CO18 [22; 22]
   UF   *kovar*
   BT1   cobalt alloys
     BT2   alloys
   BT1   iron base alloys
     BT2   iron alloys
       BT3   alloys
   BT1   manganese additions
   BT1   nickel alloys
     BT2   alloys

alloy-hd-556
   USE   alloy-fe31cr21co20ni20mo3w2

alloy-hk-40
   USE   steel-cr25ni20

alloy-hs-21
   USE   alloy-co62cr28mo6ni3

alloy-hs-25
   USE   alloy-co54cr20w15ni10

alloy-ht-9
   USE   steel-cr12mov

alloy-in-100
   USE   alloy-ni60co15cr10al6ti5mo3

alloy-in-519
   USE   alloy-fe48cr24ni24

alloy-in-643
   USE   alloy-ni47cr25co12w9fe3

alloy-in-738
   USE   alloy-ni61cr16co9al3ti3w3

alloy-in-939
   USE   alloy-ni46cr23co19ti5al4

alloy-khn56vmtyu
   USE   alloy-ni56cr21w10mo5fe4al2

alloy-khn60mkbyut
   USE   alloy-ni60mo13co9cr8nb4al3

alloy-khn60v
   USE   alloy-ni60cr25w15

alloy-khn60vt
   USE   alloy-ni60cr25w15

alloy-khn67vmtyu
   USE   alloy-ni67cr19mo5w5ti3

alloy-khn77tyur
   USE   alloy-ni77cr20ti2

alloy-khn78t
   USE   alloy-ni78cr21

alloy-kh20n80
   USE   alloy-ni80cr20

alloy-m-813
   USE   steel-ni35cr18mo4ti2al

ALLOY-MO99 [165; 165]
   UF   *alloy-tzm*
   UF   *alloy-vm-1*
   UF   *alloy-zm-2a*
   BT1   corrosion resistant alloys
     BT2   alloys
   BT1   heat resisting alloys
     BT2   alloys
   BT1   molybdenum base alloys
     BT2   molybdenum alloys
       BT3   alloys
   BT1   titanium additions
   BT1   zirconium additions

ALLOY-MO99B [14; 14] *Sep 78*
   UF   *alloy-tsm6*
   BT1   boron additions
   BT1   molybdenum base alloys
     BT2   molybdenum alloys
       BT3   alloys
   BT1   zirconium additions

alloy-n-155
   USE   alloy-fe31cr21co20ni20mo3w2

ALLOY-NB94MO4 [5; 5]
   UF   *alloy-vn-2*
   BT1   heat resisting alloys
     BT2   alloys
   BT1   molybdenum alloys
     BT2   alloys
   BT1   niobium base alloys
     BT2   niobium alloys
       BT3   alloys
   BT1   tantalum additions
   BT1   titanium additions
   BT1   zirconium additions

alloy-ni-cr 50-50
   USE   alloy-ni51cr48

ALLOY-NI41FE40CR16NB3 [49; 49]
- UF *alloy-706 (inconel)*
- UF *inconel 706*
- BT1 chromium alloys
  - BT2 alloys
- BT1 corrosion resistant alloys
  - BT2 alloys
- BT1 heat resisting alloys
  - BT2 alloys
- BT1 inconel alloys
  - BT2 nickel base alloys
    - BT3 nickel alloys
      - BT4 alloys
- BT1 iron alloys
  - BT2 alloys
- BT1 niobium alloys
  - BT2 alloys
- BT1 titanium alloys
  - BT2 alloys

ALLOY-NI42FE36CR12MO6TI3 [7; 7]
- UF *alloy-901 (incoloy)*
- UF *incoloy 901*
- BT1 aluminium additions
- BT1 boron additions
- BT1 chromium alloys
  - BT2 alloys
- BT1 corrosion resistant alloys
  - BT2 alloys
- BT1 heat resisting alloys
  - BT2 alloys
- BT1 incoloy alloys
  - BT2 alloys
- BT1 iron alloys
  - BT2 alloys
- BT1 molybdenum alloys
  - BT2 alloys
- BT1 nickel base alloys
  - BT2 nickel alloys
    - BT3 alloys
- BT1 titanium alloys
  - BT2 alloys

ALLOY-NI43FE30CR22MO3 [17; 17]
Sep 83
- UF *alloy-825 (incoloy)*
- UF *incoloy 825*
- BT1 aluminium additions
- BT1 chromium alloys
  - BT2 alloys
- BT1 copper alloys
  - BT2 alloys
- BT1 corrosion resistant alloys
  - BT2 alloys
- BT1 heat resisting alloys
  - BT2 alloys
- BT1 incoloy alloys
  - BT2 alloys
- BT1 iron alloys
  - BT2 alloys
- BT1 molybdenum alloys
  - BT2 alloys
- BT1 nickel base alloys
  - BT2 nickel alloys
    - BT3 alloys
- BT1 titanium additions

ALLOY-NI43FE33CR16MO3 [177; 177]
- UF *nimonic pe16*
- UF *pe-16*
- BT1 aluminium alloys
  - BT2 alloys
- BT1 boron additions
- BT1 chromium alloys
  - BT2 alloys
- BT1 cobalt additions
- BT1 copper additions
- BT1 corrosion resistant alloys
  - BT2 alloys
- BT1 heat resisting alloys
  - BT2 alloys
- BT1 iron alloys
  - BT2 alloys
- BT1 molybdenum alloys
  - BT2 alloys
- BT1 nimonic
  - BT2 nickel base alloys
    - BT3 nickel alloys
      - BT4 alloys

- BT1 titanium alloys
  - BT2 alloys
- BT1 zirconium additions

ALLOY-NI45CR23FE19CO3MO3W3 [3; 3] *Feb 81*
- UF *alloy-ra-333*
- BT1 chromium alloys
  - BT2 alloys
- BT1 cobalt alloys
  - BT2 alloys
- BT1 corrosion resistant alloys
  - BT2 alloys
- BT1 heat resisting alloys
  - BT2 alloys
- BT1 iron alloys
  - BT2 alloys
- BT1 molybdenum alloys
  - BT2 alloys
- BT1 nickel base alloys
  - BT2 nickel alloys
    - BT3 alloys
- BT1 silicon alloys
  - BT2 alloys
- BT1 tungsten alloys
  - BT2 alloys

ALLOY-NI45FE34CR20 [13; 13]
- UF *steel-kh20n45b*
- BT1 chromium alloys
  - BT2 alloys
- BT1 corrosion resistant alloys
  - BT2 alloys
- BT1 iron alloys
  - BT2 alloys
- BT1 nickel base alloys
  - BT2 nickel alloys
    - BT3 alloys
- BT1 niobium additions

ALLOY-NI46CR23CO19TI5AL4 [6; 6] *Jan 82*
- UF *alloy-in-939*
- BT1 aluminium alloys
  - BT2 alloys
- BT1 boron additions
- BT1 chromium alloys
  - BT2 alloys
- BT1 cobalt alloys
  - BT2 alloys
- BT1 corrosion resistant alloys
  - BT2 alloys
- BT1 heat resisting alloys
  - BT2 alloys
- BT1 inconel alloys
  - BT2 nickel base alloys
    - BT3 nickel alloys
      - BT4 alloys
- BT1 iron additions
- BT1 niobium additions
- BT1 tantalum alloys
  - BT2 alloys
- BT1 titanium alloys
  - BT2 alloys
- BT1 zirconium additions

ALLOY-NI47CR25CO12W9FE3 [3; 3] *Apr 79*
- UF *alloy-in-643*
- UF *alloy 643 (inconel)*
- UF *inconel 643*
- BT1 chromium alloys
  - BT2 alloys
- BT1 cobalt alloys
  - BT2 alloys
- BT1 corrosion resistant alloys
  - BT2 alloys
- BT1 heat resisting alloys
  - BT2 alloys
- BT1 inconel alloys
  - BT2 nickel base alloys
    - BT3 nickel alloys
      - BT4 alloys
- BT1 iron alloys
  - BT2 alloys
- BT1 molybdenum additions
- BT1 niobium alloys
  - BT2 alloys
- BT1 titanium additions

- BT1 tungsten alloys
  - BT2 alloys
- BT1 zirconium additions

ALLOY-NI48CO28CR15AL3MO3TI2 [3; 3] *Apr 79*
- UF *alloy-700 (inconel)*
- UF *inconel 700*
- BT1 aluminium alloys
  - BT2 alloys
- BT1 chromium alloys
  - BT2 alloys
- BT1 cobalt alloys
  - BT2 alloys
- BT1 corrosion resistant alloys
  - BT2 alloys
- BT1 heat resisting alloys
  - BT2 alloys
- BT1 inconel alloys
  - BT2 nickel base alloys
    - BT3 nickel alloys
      - BT4 alloys
- BT1 iron additions
- BT1 molybdenum alloys
  - BT2 alloys
- BT1 titanium alloys
  - BT2 alloys

ALLOY-NI48CR22FE18MO9 [4; 4] *Sep 79*
- UF *nimonic pe13*
- UF *pe-13*
- BT1 chromium alloys
  - BT2 alloys
- BT1 cobalt alloys
  - BT2 alloys
- BT1 copper additions
- BT1 corrosion resistant alloys
  - BT2 alloys
- BT1 heat resisting alloys
  - BT2 alloys
- BT1 iron alloys
  - BT2 alloys
- BT1 molybdenum alloys
  - BT2 alloys
- BT1 nimonic
  - BT2 nickel base alloys
    - BT3 nickel alloys
      - BT4 alloys
- BT1 tungsten additions

ALLOY-NI49CR22FE18MO9 [412; 412]
- UF *hastelloy x*
- BT1 chromium alloys
  - BT2 alloys
- BT1 cobalt alloys
  - BT2 alloys
- BT1 corrosion resistant alloys
  - BT2 alloys
- BT1 hastelloys
  - BT2 nickel base alloys
    - BT3 nickel alloys
      - BT4 alloys
- BT1 heat resisting alloys
  - BT2 alloys
- BT1 iron alloys
  - BT2 alloys
- BT1 molybdenum alloys
  - BT2 alloys
- BT1 tungsten additions

ALLOY-NI50CO20CR15AL5MO5 [12; 12] *Mar 76*
- UF *nimonic 105*
- BT1 aluminium alloys
  - BT2 alloys
- BT1 chromium alloys
  - BT2 alloys
- BT1 cobalt alloys
  - BT2 alloys
- BT1 corrosion resistant alloys
  - BT2 alloys
- BT1 heat resisting alloys
  - BT2 alloys
- BT1 iron alloys
  - BT2 alloys
- BT1 molybdenum alloys
  - BT2 alloys
- BT1 nimonic

    BT2   nickel base alloys
      BT3   nickel alloys
        BT4   alloys
BT1   titanium alloys
  BT2   alloys

ALLOY-NI50CR22FE18MO9 [74; 74]
Feb 82
UF   *hastelloy xr*
BT1   chromium alloys
  BT2   alloys
BT1   corrosion resistant alloys
  BT2   alloys
BT1   hastelloys
  BT2   nickel base alloys
    BT3   nickel alloys
      BT4   alloys
BT1   heat resisting alloys
  BT2   alloys
BT1   iron alloys
  BT2   alloys
BT1   molybdenum alloys
  BT2   alloys
BT1   tungsten additions

ALLOY-NI50MO32CR15SI3 [14; 14]
Dec 80
UF   *tribaloy 700*
BT1   chromium alloys
  BT2   alloys
BT1   corrosion resistant alloys
  BT2   alloys
BT1   heat resisting alloys
  BT2   alloys
BT1   molybdenum alloys
  BT2   alloys
BT1   nickel base alloys
  BT2   nickel alloys
    BT3   alloys
BT1   silicon alloys
  BT2   alloys

ALLOY-NI51CR48 [4; 4] *Dec 80*
UF   *alloy-ni-cr 50-50*
UF   *alloy-671 (inconel)*
UF   *inconel 671*
BT1   chromium alloys
  BT2   alloys
BT1   corrosion resistant alloys
  BT2   alloys
BT1   heat resisting alloys
  BT2   alloys
BT1   inconel alloys
  BT2   nickel base alloys
    BT3   nickel alloys
      BT4   alloys
BT1   titanium additions

ALLOY-NI53CO19CR15MO5AL4TI3
[39; 39]
UF   *udimet 700*
BT1   aluminium alloys
  BT2   alloys
BT1   boron additions
BT1   chromium alloys
  BT2   alloys
BT1   cobalt alloys
  BT2   alloys
BT1   corrosion resistant alloys
  BT2   alloys
BT1   heat resisting alloys
  BT2   alloys
BT1   molybdenum alloys
  BT2   alloys
BT1   titanium alloys
  BT2   alloys
BT1   udimet alloys
  BT2   nickel base alloys
    BT3   nickel alloys
      BT4   alloys

ALLOY-NI53CR19FE19NB5MO3
[288; 288]
UF   *inconel 718*
BT1   aluminium additions
BT1   chromium alloys
  BT2   alloys
BT1   corrosion resistant alloys
  BT2   alloys
BT1   heat resisting alloys
  BT2   alloys
BT1   inconel alloys
  BT2   nickel base alloys
    BT3   nickel alloys
      BT4   alloys
BT1   iron alloys
  BT2   alloys
BT1   molybdenum alloys
  BT2   alloys
BT1   niobium alloys
  BT2   alloys
BT1   titanium additions

ALLOY-NI54CR22CO13MO9 [271; 271]
UF   *alloy-617 (inconel)*
UF   *inconel 617*
BT1   aluminium additions
BT1   chromium alloys
  BT2   alloys
BT1   cobalt alloys
  BT2   alloys
BT1   corrosion resistant alloys
  BT2   alloys
BT1   heat resisting alloys
  BT2   alloys
BT1   inconel alloys
  BT2   nickel base alloys
    BT3   nickel alloys
      BT4   alloys
BT1   molybdenum alloys
  BT2   alloys

ALLOY-NI54MO17CR16FE6W4 [55; 55]
UF   *hastelloy c*
BT1   chromium alloys
  BT2   alloys
BT1   cobalt alloys
  BT2   alloys
BT1   corrosion resistant alloys
  BT2   alloys
BT1   hastelloys
  BT2   nickel base alloys
    BT3   nickel alloys
      BT4   alloys
BT1   heat resisting alloys
  BT2   alloys
BT1   iron alloys
  BT2   alloys
BT1   molybdenum alloys
  BT2   alloys
BT1   tungsten alloys
  BT2   alloys
BT1   vanadium additions

ALLOY-NI55CO17CR15MO5AL4TI4
[24; 24]
UF   *astroloy*
BT1   aluminium alloys
  BT2   alloys
BT1   boron additions
BT1   chromium alloys
  BT2   alloys
BT1   cobalt alloys
  BT2   alloys
BT1   molybdenum alloys
  BT2   alloys
BT1   nickel base alloys
  BT2   nickel alloys
    BT3   alloys
BT1   titanium alloys
  BT2   alloys
BT1   zirconium additions

ALLOY-NI55CR19CO11MO10TI3
[20; 20]
UF   *rene 41*
BT1   aluminium alloys
  BT2   alloys
BT1   boron additions
BT1   chromium alloys
  BT2   alloys
BT1   cobalt alloys
  BT2   alloys
BT1   corrosion resistant alloys
  BT2   alloys
BT1   heat resisting alloys
  BT2   alloys
BT1   molybdenum alloys
  BT2   alloys
BT1   inconel alloys
  BT2   nickel base alloys
    BT3   nickel alloys
BT1   titanium alloys
  BT2   alloys

ALLOY-NI56CR21W10MO5FE4AL2
[6; 6] *Apr 78*
UF   *alloy-ehp 199*
UF   *alloy-khn56vmtyu*
BT1   aluminium alloys
  BT2   alloys
BT1   boron additions
BT1   chromium alloys
  BT2   alloys
BT1   corrosion resistant alloys
  BT2   alloys
BT1   heat resisting alloys
  BT2   alloys
BT1   iron alloys
  BT2   alloys
BT1   manganese additions
BT1   molybdenum alloys
  BT2   alloys
BT1   nickel base alloys
  BT2   nickel alloys
    BT3   alloys
BT1   silicon additions
BT1   titanium alloys
  BT2   alloys
BT1   tungsten alloys
  BT2   alloys

ALLOY-NI58CR14CO8AL4MO4NB4W4
[7; 7] *Jul 76*
UF   *rene 95*
BT1   aluminium alloys
  BT2   alloys
BT1   chromium alloys
  BT2   alloys
BT1   cobalt alloys
  BT2   alloys
BT1   corrosion resistant alloys
  BT2   alloys
BT1   heat resisting alloys
  BT2   alloys
BT1   iron additions
BT1   molybdenum alloys
  BT2   alloys
BT1   nickel base alloys
  BT2   nickel alloys
    BT3   alloys
BT1   niobium alloys
  BT2   alloys
BT1   titanium alloys
  BT2   alloys
BT1   tungsten alloys
  BT2   alloys

ALLOY-NI58CR20CO14MO4TI3 [20; 20]
UF   *waspaloy*
BT1   aluminium alloys
  BT2   alloys
BT1   boron additions
BT1   chromium alloys
  BT2   alloys
BT1   cobalt alloys
  BT2   alloys
BT1   corrosion resistant alloys
  BT2   alloys
BT1   heat resisting alloys
  BT2   alloys
BT1   iron alloys
  BT2   alloys
BT1   molybdenum alloys
  BT2   alloys
BT1   nickel base alloys
  BT2   nickel alloys
    BT3   alloys
BT1   titanium alloys
  BT2   alloys
BT1   zirconium additions

ALLOY-NI59CR20CO17TI2 [18; 18]
Apr 77
UF   *nimonic 90*
BT1   aluminium alloys
  BT2   alloys
BT1   boron additions
BT1   chromium alloys
  BT2   alloys
BT1   cobalt alloys
  BT2   alloys
BT1   corrosion resistant alloys
  BT2   alloys
BT1   heat resisting alloys
  BT2   alloys
BT1   iron alloys
  BT2   alloys
BT1   nimonic
  BT2   nickel base alloys
    BT3 nickel alloys
      BT4 alloys
BT1   titanium alloys
  BT2   alloys
BT1   zirconium additions

ALLOY-NI59CR30FE9 [88; 88] *Feb 81*
UF   *alloy-690 (inconel)*
UF   *inconel 690*
BT1   chromium alloys
  BT2   alloys
BT1   corrosion resistant alloys
  BT2   alloys
BT1   heat resisting alloys
  BT2   alloys
BT1   inconel alloys
  BT2   nickel base alloys
    BT3 nickel alloys
      BT4 alloys
BT1   iron alloys
  BT2   alloys
BT1   titanium additions

ALLOY-NI60CO15CR10AL6TI5MO3 [38; 38]
UF   *alloy-in-100*
BT1   aluminium alloys
  BT2   alloys
BT1   boron additions
BT1   carbon additions
BT1   chromium alloys
  BT2   alloys
BT1   cobalt alloys
  BT2   alloys
BT1   copper additions
BT1   corrosion resistant alloys
  BT2   alloys
BT1   heat resisting alloys
  BT2   alloys
BT1   inconel alloys
  BT2   nickel base alloys
    BT3 nickel alloys
      BT4 alloys
BT1   iron additions
BT1   molybdenum alloys
  BT2   alloys
BT1   titanium alloys
  BT2   alloys
BT1   vanadium additions
BT1   zirconium additions

ALLOY-NI60CR14CO10TI5MO4W4AL3 [7; 7] *Feb 80*
UF   *rene 80*
BT1   aluminium alloys
  BT2   alloys
BT1   boron additions
BT1   chromium alloys
  BT2   alloys
BT1   cobalt alloys
  BT2   alloys
BT1   corrosion resistant alloys
  BT2   alloys
BT1   heat resisting alloys
  BT2   alloys
BT1   molybdenum alloys
  BT2   alloys
BT1   nickel base alloys
  BT2   nickel alloys
    BT3 alloys

BT1   titanium alloys
  BT2   alloys
BT1   tungsten alloys
  BT2   alloys
BT1   zirconium additions

ALLOY-NI60CR25W15 [7; 7] *Dec 75*
UF   *alloy-ehi 868*
UF   *alloy-khn60v*
UF   *alloy-khn60vt*
UF   *alloy-vzh98*
BT1   aluminium additions
BT1   cerium additions
  BT2   rare earth additions
BT1   chromium alloys
  BT2   alloys
BT1   corrosion resistant alloys
  BT2   alloys
BT1   heat resisting alloys
  BT2   alloys
BT1   iron alloys
  BT2   alloys
BT1   nickel base alloys
  BT2   nickel alloys
    BT3 alloys
BT1   silicon additions
BT1   titanium additions
BT1   tungsten alloys
  BT2   alloys

ALLOY-NI60FE24CR16 [74; 74]
UF   *chromel c*
UF   *nichrome*
UF   *tophet c*
BT1   chromel
  BT2   nickel base alloys
    BT3 nickel alloys
      BT4 alloys
BT1   chromium alloys
  BT2   alloys
BT1   corrosion resistant alloys
  BT2   alloys
BT1   heat resisting alloys
  BT2   alloys
BT1   iron alloys
  BT2   alloys

ALLOY-NI60MO13CO9CR8NB4AL3 [2; 2] *Sep 77*
UF   *alloy-khn60mkbyut*
BT1   aluminium alloys
  BT2   alloys
BT1   boron additions
BT1   cerium additions
  BT2   rare earth additions
BT1   chromium alloys
  BT2   alloys
BT1   cobalt alloys
  BT2   alloys
BT1   corrosion resistant alloys
  BT2   alloys
BT1   heat resisting alloys
  BT2   alloys
BT1   molybdenum alloys
  BT2   alloys
BT1   nickel base alloys
  BT2   nickel alloys
    BT3 alloys
BT1   niobium alloys
  BT2   alloys
BT1   titanium alloys
  BT2   alloys

ALLOY-NI61CR16CO9AL3TI3W3 [17; 17] *Feb 80*
UF   *alloy-in-738*
BT1   aluminium alloys
  BT2   alloys
BT1   boron additions
BT1   chromium alloys
  BT2   alloys
BT1   cobalt alloys
  BT2   alloys
BT1   corrosion resistant alloys
  BT2   alloys
BT1   heat resisting alloys
  BT2   alloys

BT1   inconel alloys
  BT2   nickel base alloys
    BT3 nickel alloys
      BT4 alloys
BT1   molybdenum alloys
  BT2   alloys
BT1   niobium additions
BT1   tantalum alloys
  BT2   alloys
BT1   titanium alloys
  BT2   alloys
BT1   tungsten alloys
  BT2   alloys
BT1   zirconium additions

ALLOY-NI61CR22MO9NB4FE3 [250; 250]
UF   *alloy-625 (inconel)*
UF   *inconel 625*
BT1   aluminium additions
BT1   chromium alloys
  BT2   alloys
BT1   corrosion resistant alloys
  BT2   alloys
BT1   heat resisting alloys
  BT2   alloys
BT1   inconel alloys
  BT2   nickel base alloys
    BT3 nickel alloys
      BT4 alloys
BT1   iron alloys
  BT2   alloys
BT1   molybdenum alloys
  BT2   alloys
BT1   niobium alloys
  BT2   alloys
BT1   titanium additions

ALLOY-NI61CR23FE14 [5; 5] *Jan 85*
UF   *alloy-601 (inconel)*
UF   *inconel 601*
BT1   chromium alloys
  BT2   alloys
BT1   inconel alloys
  BT2   nickel base alloys
    BT3 nickel alloys
      BT4 alloys
BT1   iron alloys
  BT2   alloys

ALLOY-NI62CR16MO15FE3 [21; 21]
Dec 80
UF   *hastelloy s*
BT1   aluminium additions
BT1   boron additions
BT1   chromium alloys
  BT2   alloys
BT1   cobalt additions
BT1   corrosion resistant alloys
  BT2   alloys
BT1   hastelloys
  BT2   nickel base alloys
    BT3 nickel alloys
      BT4 alloys
BT1   heat resisting alloys
  BT2   alloys
BT1   iron alloys
  BT2   alloys
BT1   molybdenum alloys
  BT2   alloys
BT1   tungsten additions
BT1   vanadium additions

ALLOY-NI65CR25MO10 [38; 38] *Feb 82*
UF   *nimonic 86*
BT1   chromium alloys
  BT2   alloys
BT1   corrosion resistant alloys
  BT2   alloys
BT1   heat resisting alloys
  BT2   alloys
BT1   molybdenum alloys
  BT2   alloys
BT1   nimonic
  BT2   nickel base alloys
    BT3 nickel alloys
      BT4 alloys

ALLOY-NI65MO16CR15W4 [6; 6]
Nov 75
- UF   *alloy-ehp 567*
- UF   *alloy-0khn65mv*
- BT1   chromium alloys
  - BT2   alloys
- BT1   corrosion resistant alloys
  - BT2   alloys
- BT1   heat resisting alloys
  - BT2   alloys
- BT1   iron additions
- BT1   molybdenum alloys
  - BT2   alloys
- BT1   nickel base alloys
  - BT2   nickel alloys
    - BT3   alloys
- BT1   tungsten alloys
  - BT2   alloys

ALLOY-NI65MO28FE5 [21; 21]
- UF   *hastelloy b*
- BT1   chromium additions
- BT1   cobalt alloys
  - BT2   alloys
- BT1   corrosion resistant alloys
  - BT2   alloys
- BT1   hastelloys
  - BT2   nickel base alloys
    - BT3   nickel alloys
      - BT4   alloys
- BT1   vanadium additions

ALLOY-NI66CU32 [22; 22] *Apr 79*
- UF   *monel r-405*
- UF   *monel 400*
- BT1   copper alloys
  - BT2   alloys
- BT1   iron alloys
  - BT2   alloys
- BT1   manganese additions
- BT1   monel
  - BT2   nickel base alloys
    - BT3   nickel alloys
      - BT4   alloys

ALLOY-NI67CR19MO5W5TI3 [10; 10]
Oct 75
- UF   *alloy-khn67vmtyu*
- BT1   aluminium alloys
  - BT2   alloys
- BT1   boron additions
- BT1   cerium additions
  - BT2   rare earth additions
- BT1   chromium alloys
  - BT2   alloys
- BT1   corrosion resistant alloys
  - BT2   alloys
- BT1   heat resisting alloys
  - BT2   alloys
- BT1   molybdenum alloys
  - BT2   alloys
- BT1   nickel base alloys
  - BT2   nickel alloys
    - BT3   alloys
- BT1   silicon additions
- BT1   titanium alloys
  - BT2   alloys
- BT1   tungsten alloys
  - BT2   alloys

ALLOY-NI68CR15W6AL3MO3FE2 [7; 7]
- UF   *alloy-ehi 826*
- BT1   aluminium alloys
  - BT2   alloys
- BT1   boron additions
- BT1   chromium alloys
  - BT2   alloys
- BT1   corrosion resistant alloys
  - BT2   alloys
- BT1   heat resisting alloys
  - BT2   alloys
- BT1   iron alloys
  - BT2   alloys
- BT1   molybdenum alloys
  - BT2   alloys
- BT1   nickel base alloys
  - BT2   nickel alloys
    - BT3   alloys
- BT1   silicon additions
- BT1   titanium alloys
- BT2   alloys
- BT1   tungsten alloys
- BT2   alloys
- BT1   vanadium additions

ALLOY-NI70MO17CR7FE5 [52; 52]
- UF   *hastelloy n*
- UF   *inor-8*
- BT1   aluminium additions
- BT1   chromium alloys
  - BT2   alloys
- BT1   corrosion resistant alloys
  - BT2   alloys
- BT1   hastelloys
  - BT2   nickel base alloys
    - BT3   nickel alloys
      - BT4   alloys
- BT1   heat resisting alloys
  - BT2   alloys
- BT1   iron alloys
  - BT2   alloys
- BT1   molybdenum alloys
  - BT2   alloys
- BT1   titanium additions
- RT   inconel alloys

ALLOY-NI73CR15FE7TI3 [165; 165]
- UF   *alloy-x750 (inconel)*
- UF   *inconel x750*
- BT1   aluminium additions
- BT1   chromium alloys
  - BT2   alloys
- BT1   corrosion resistant alloys
  - BT2   alloys
- BT1   heat resisting alloys
  - BT2   alloys
- BT1   inconel alloys
  - BT2   nickel base alloys
    - BT3   nickel alloys
      - BT4   alloys
- BT1   iron alloys
  - BT2   alloys
- BT1   niobium additions
- BT1   titanium alloys
  - BT2   alloys

ALLOY-NI73CR20MN3NB3 [25; 25]
- UF   *alloy-82 (inconel)*
- UF   *inconel 82*
- BT1   chromium alloys
  - BT2   alloys
- BT1   corrosion resistant alloys
  - BT2   alloys
- BT1   heat resisting alloys
  - BT2   alloys
- BT1   inconel alloys
  - BT2   nickel base alloys
    - BT3   nickel alloys
      - BT4   alloys
- BT1   iron additions
- BT1   manganese alloys
  - BT2   alloys
- BT1   niobium alloys
  - BT2   alloys
- BT1   titanium additions

ALLOY-NI74CR13AL6MO4 [12; 12]
Feb 77
- UF   *alloy-713c (inconel)*
- UF   *inconel 713c*
- BT1   aluminium alloys
  - BT2   alloys
- BT1   boron additions
- BT1   chromium alloys
  - BT2   alloys
- BT1   corrosion resistant alloys
  - BT2   alloys
- BT1   heat resisting alloys
  - BT2   alloys
- BT1   inconel alloys
  - BT2   nickel base alloys
    - BT3   nickel alloys
      - BT4   alloys
- BT1   molybdenum alloys
  - BT2   alloys
- BT1   niobium alloys
  - BT2   alloys
- BT1   titanium additions
- BT1   tungsten alloys
  - BT2   alloys
- BT1   vanadium additions

ALLOY-NI75CR12AL6MO5 [15; 15]
Jul 81
- UF   *alloy-713-lc*
- UF   *alloy-713lc (inconel)*
- UF   *inconel 713lc*
- BT1   aluminium alloys
  - BT2   alloys
- BT1   boron additions
- BT1   chromium alloys
  - BT2   alloys
- BT1   corrosion resistant alloys
  - BT2   alloys
- BT1   heat resisting alloys
  - BT2   alloys
- BT1   inconel alloys
  - BT2   nickel base alloys
    - BT3   nickel alloys
      - BT4   alloys
- BT1   molybdenum alloys
  - BT2   alloys
- BT1   niobium alloys
  - BT2   alloys
- BT1   titanium additions
- BT1   zirconium additions

ALLOY-NI76CR15FE8 [758; 758]
- UF   *alloy-600 (inconel)*
- UF   *inconel 600*
- UF   *sanicro 70*
- BT1   aluminium additions
- BT1   chromium alloys
  - BT2   alloys
- BT1   corrosion resistant alloys
  - BT2   alloys
- BT1   heat resisting alloys
  - BT2   alloys
- BT1   inconel alloys
  - BT2   nickel base alloys
    - BT3   nickel alloys
      - BT4   alloys
- BT1   iron alloys
  - BT2   alloys
- BT1   nimonic
  - BT2   nickel base alloys
    - BT3   nickel alloys
      - BT4   alloys
- BT1   titanium additions

ALLOY-NI76CR20TI2 [27; 27] *Jan 77*
- UF   *nimonic 80a*
- BT1   aluminium alloys
  - BT2   alloys
- BT1   boron additions
- BT1   chromium alloys
  - BT2   alloys
- BT1   corrosion resistant alloys
  - BT2   alloys
- BT1   heat resisting alloys
  - BT2   alloys
- BT1   nimonic
  - BT2   nickel base alloys
    - BT3   nickel alloys
      - BT4   alloys
- BT1   titanium alloys
  - BT2   alloys
- BT1   zirconium additions

ALLOY-NI77CR17AL5 [0; 0] *Apr 85*
- BT1   aluminium alloys
  - BT2   alloys
- BT1   chromium alloys
  - BT2   alloys
- BT1   heat resisting alloys
  - BT2   alloys
- BT1   nickel base alloys
  - BT2   nickel alloys
    - BT3   alloys
- BT1   yttrium additions

ALLOY-NI77CR20TI2 [57; 57]
- UF   *alloy-ehi 437b*
- UF   *alloy-khn77tyur*
- BT1   aluminium additions
- BT1   boron additions
- BT1   chromium alloys
  - BT2   alloys

ALLOY-NI77CR20TI2 (continued)
- BT1   corrosion resistant alloys
- BT2   alloys
- BT1   heat resisting alloys
- BT2   alloys
- BT1   iron alloys
- BT2   alloys
- BT1   nickel base alloys
- BT2   nickel alloys
- BT3   alloys
- BT1   titanium alloys
- BT2   alloys

ALLOY-NI78CR16AL4 [7; 7]
- UF   alloy-702 (inconel)
- UF   inconel 702
- BT1   aluminium alloys
- BT2   alloys
- BT1   chromium alloys
- BT2   alloys
- BT1   corrosion resistant alloys
- BT2   alloys
- BT1   heat resisting alloys
- BT2   alloys
- BT1   inconel alloys
- BT2   nickel base alloys
- BT3   nickel alloys
- BT4   alloys
- BT1   iron additions
- BT1   titanium additions

ALLOY-NI78CR21 [16; 16]
- UF   alloy-khn78t
- BT1   aluminium additions
- BT1   chromium alloys
- BT2   alloys
- BT1   iron alloys
- BT2   alloys
- BT1   manganese additions
- BT1   nickel base alloys
- BT2   nickel alloys
- BT3   alloys
- BT1   silicon additions
- BT1   titanium additions

ALLOY-NI79FE16MO4 [10; 10] *Feb 76*
- UF   alloy-79nm
- BT1   iron alloys
- BT2   alloys
- BT1   molybdenum alloys
- BT2   alloys
- BT1   nickel base alloys
- BT2   nickel alloys
- BT3   alloys

ALLOY-NI80CR20 [24; 24]
- UF   alloy-kh20n80
- UF   chromel a
- UF   nichrome v
- UF   tophet a
- BT1   aluminium additions
- BT1   chromel
- BT2   nickel base alloys
- BT3   nickel alloys
- BT4   alloys
- BT1   chromium alloys
- BT2   alloys
- BT1   iron additions
- BT1   silicon additions

ALLOY-NI80FE16MO4 [6; 6] *Nov 83*
- UF   hymu-80
- UF   permalloy c
- BT1   iron alloys
- BT2   alloys
- BT1   molybdenum alloys
- BT2   alloys
- BT1   nickel base alloys
- BT2   nickel alloys
- BT3   alloys
- BT1   permalloy
- BT2   alloys

ALLOY-NI85CR15 [0; 0] *Nov 83*
- UF   chromel b
- BT1   chromel
- BT2   nickel base alloys
- BT3   nickel alloys
- BT4   alloys

- BT1   chromium alloys
- BT2   alloys

ALLOY-NI94MN3AL2 [44; 44]
- UF   alumel
- BT1   aluminium alloys
- BT2   alloys
- BT1   manganese alloys
- BT2   alloys
- BT1   nickel base alloys
- BT2   nickel alloys
- BT3   alloys
- BT1   silicon additions

alloy-ra-333
- USE   alloy-ni45cr23fe19co3mo3w3

ALLOY-TA90W8HF [87; 87]
- UF   tantalum alloy-t111
- BT1   hafnium alloys
- BT2   alloys
- BT1   tantalum base alloys
- BT2   tantalum alloys
- BT3   alloys
- BT1   tungsten alloys
- BT2   alloys

ALLOY-TI78CR11MO7AL3 [32; 32]
- UF   alloy-vt15
- BT1   aluminium alloys
- BT2   alloys
- BT1   chromium alloys
- BT2   alloys
- BT1   molybdenum alloys
- BT2   alloys
- BT1   titanium base alloys
- BT2   titanium alloys
- BT3   alloys

ALLOY-TI88MO8AL3 [87; 87]
- UF   alloy-vt22
- BT1   aluminium alloys
- BT2   alloys
- BT1   chromium alloys
- BT2   alloys
- BT1   iron additions
- BT1   molybdenum alloys
- BT2   alloys
- BT1   titanium base alloys
- BT2   titanium alloys
- BT3   alloys

ALLOY-TI89AL6MO3 [70; 70]
- UF   alloy-vt9
- BT1   aluminium alloys
- BT2   alloys
- BT1   molybdenum alloys
- BT2   alloys
- BT1   titanium base alloys
- BT2   titanium alloys
- BT3   alloys
- BT1   zirconium alloys
- BT2   alloys

ALLOY-TI90AL6 [34; 34] *Sep 78*
- UF   alloy-vt20
- BT1   aluminium alloys
- BT2   alloys
- BT1   molybdenum additions
- BT1   titanium base alloys
- BT2   titanium alloys
- BT3   alloys
- BT1   vanadium additions
- BT1   zirconium alloys
- BT2   alloys

ALLOY-TI90AL6MO3 [18; 18] *Jan 76*
- UF   alloy-vt8
- BT1   aluminium alloys
- BT2   alloys
- BT1   iron additions
- BT1   molybdenum alloys
- BT2   alloys
- BT1   titanium base alloys
- BT2   titanium alloys
- BT3   alloys

ALLOY-TI90AL6V4 [132; 132]
- UF   alloy-vt6
- BT1   aluminium alloys
- BT2   alloys
- BT1   iron additions
- BT1   titanium base alloys
- BT2   titanium alloys
- BT3   alloys
- BT1   vanadium alloys
- BT2   alloys

ALLOY-TI90MO7AL2 [40; 40]
- UF   alloy-vt16
- BT1   aluminium alloys
- BT2   alloys
- BT1   molybdenum alloys
- BT2   alloys
- BT1   titanium base alloys
- BT2   titanium alloys
- BT3   alloys

ALLOY-TI91AL4MO3 [73; 73]
- UF   alloy-vt14
- BT1   aluminium alloys
- BT2   alloys
- BT1   iron additions
- BT1   molybdenum alloys
- BT2   alloys
- BT1   titanium base alloys
- BT2   titanium alloys
- BT3   alloys
- BT1   vanadium alloys
- BT2   alloys

ALLOY-TI91AL5CR2 [103; 103] *Feb 77*
- UF   alloy-vtz-1
- UF   alloy-vt3-1
- BT1   aluminium alloys
- BT2   alloys
- BT1   chromium alloys
- BT2   alloys
- BT1   iron additions
- BT1   molybdenum alloys
- BT2   alloys
- BT1   titanium base alloys
- BT2   titanium alloys
- BT3   alloys

ALLOY-TI99 [114; 114]
- UF   alloy-vt1-0
- BT1   titanium base alloys
- BT2   titanium alloys
- BT3   alloys

alloy-tsm6
- USE   alloy-mo99b

alloy-tzm
- USE   alloy-mo99

ALLOY-U90NB7ZR3 [25; 25]
- UF   mulberry alloy
- BT1   niobium alloys
- BT2   alloys
- BT1   uranium base alloys
- BT2   uranium alloys
- BT3   actinide alloys
- BT4   alloys
- BT1   zirconium alloys
- BT2   alloys

alloy-vm-1
- USE   alloy-mo99

alloy-vn-2
- USE   alloy-nb94mo4

alloy-vtz-1
- USE   alloy-ti91al5cr2

alloy-vt1-0
   USE   alloy-ti99

alloy-vt14
   USE   alloy-ti91al4mo3

alloy-vt15
   USE   alloy-ti78cr11mo7al3

alloy-vt16
   USE   alloy-ti90mo7al2

alloy-vt20
   USE   alloy-ti90al6

alloy-vt22
   USE   alloy-ti88mo8al3

alloy-vt3-1
   USE   alloy-ti91al5cr2

alloy-vt6
   USE   alloy-ti90al6v4

alloy-vt8
   USE   alloy-ti90al6mo3

alloy-vt9
   USE   alloy-ti89al6mo3

alloy-vzh98
   USE   alloy-ni60cr25w15

ALLOY-V87CR9FE3 [17; 17]
   UF   *vanstar 7*
   BT1   chromium alloys
      BT2   alloys
   BT1   iron alloys
      BT2   alloys
   BT1   vanadium base alloys
      BT2   vanadium alloys
         BT3 alloys
   BT1   zirconium alloys
      BT2   alloys

alloy-x750 (inconel)
   USE   alloy-ni73cr15fe7ti3

alloy-zm-2a
   USE   alloy-mo99

ALLOY-ZR97NB3 [45; 45] *Jul 85*
   BT1   heat resisting alloys
      BT2   alloys
   BT1   niobium alloys
      BT2   alloys
   BT1   zirconium base alloys
      BT2   zirconium alloys
         BT3 alloys

ALLOY-ZR98SN-2 [874; 874]
   UF   *zircaloy 2*
   BT1   chromium additions
   BT1   corrosion resistant alloys
      BT2   alloys
   BT1   heat resisting alloys
      BT2   alloys
   BT1   iron additions
   BT1   nickel additions
   BT1   tin alloys
      BT2   alloys
   BT1   zircaloy
      BT2   zirconium base alloys
         BT3 zirconium alloys
            BT4 alloys

ALLOY-ZR98SN-4 [1,105; 1,105]
   UF   *zircaloy 4*
   BT1   chromium additions
   BT1   corrosion resistant alloys
      BT2   alloys
   BT1   heat resisting alloys
      BT2   alloys
   BT1   iron additions
   BT1   tin alloys
      BT2   alloys
   BT1   zircaloy
      BT2   zirconium base alloys
         BT3 zirconium alloys
            BT4 alloys

alloy-0khn65mv
   USE   alloy-ni65mo16cr15w4

alloy-600 (inconel)
   USE   alloy-ni76cr15fe8

alloy-601 (inconel)
   USE   alloy-ni61cr23fe14

alloy-617 (inconel)
   USE   alloy-ni54cr22co13mo9

alloy-625 (inconel)
   USE   alloy-ni61cr22mo9nb4fe3

alloy-643 (inconel)
   USE   alloy-ni47cr25co12w9fe3

alloy-671 (inconel)
   USE   alloy-ni51cr48

alloy-690 (inconel)
   USE   alloy-ni59cr30fe9

alloy-700 (inconel)
   USE   alloy-ni48co28cr15al3mo3ti2

alloy-702 (inconel)
   USE   alloy-ni78cr16al4

alloy-706 (inconel)
   USE   alloy-ni41fe40cr16nb3

alloy-713-lc
(Prior to July 1981 this was a valid term, and older information is so indexed.)
   USE   alloy-ni75cr12al6mo5

alloy-713c (inconel)
   USE   alloy-ni74cr13al6mo4

alloy-713lc (inconel)
   USE   alloy-ni75cr12al6mo5

alloy-79nm
   USE   alloy-ni79fe16mo4

alloy-800 (incoloy)
   USE   alloy-fe46ni33cr21

alloy-800h (incoloy)
   USE   alloy-fe44ni33cr21

alloy-802 (incoloy)
   USE   alloy-fe46ni33cr21

alloy-82 (inconel)
   USE   alloy-ni73cr20mn3nb3

alloy-825 (incoloy)
   USE   alloy-ni43fe30cr22mo3

alloy-901 (incoloy)
   USE   alloy-ni42fe36cr12mo6ti3

ALLOYS [2,578; 94,997]
 * NT1   actinide alloys
 * NT1   aluminium alloys
 * NT1   antimony alloys
    NT1   arsenic alloys
 * NT1   barium alloys
 * NT1   beryllium alloys
 * NT1   bismuth alloys
 * NT1   boron alloys
    NT1   brazing alloys
 * NT1   cadmium alloys
 * NT1   calcium alloys
 * NT1   cesium alloys
 * NT1   chromium alloys
 * NT1   cobalt alloys
 * NT1   copper alloys
 * NT1   corrosion resistant alloys
    NT1   dilute alloys
 * NT1   francium alloys
 * NT1   gallium alloys
 * NT1   germanium alloys
 * NT1   gold alloys
 * NT1   hafnium alloys
 * NT1   heat resisting alloys
 * NT1   incoloy alloys
 * NT1   indium alloys
 * NT1   intermetallic compounds
 * NT1   iron alloys
 * NT1   lead alloys
 * NT1   lithium alloys
 * NT1   magnesium alloys
 * NT1   manganese alloys
 * NT1   mercury alloys
 * NT1   molybdenum alloys
 * NT1   nickel alloys
 * NT1   niobium alloys
    NT1   permalloy
 * NT1   platinum metal alloys
 * NT1   polonium alloys
 * NT1   potassium alloys
 * NT1   rare earth alloys
 * NT1   rhenium alloys
 * NT1   rubidium alloys
 * NT1   scandium alloys
    NT1   selenium alloys
 * NT1   silicon alloys
 * NT1   silver alloys
 * NT1   sodium alloys
 * NT1   strontium alloys
 * NT1   tantalum alloys
 * NT1   technetium alloys
    NT1   tellurium alloys
 * NT1   thallium alloys
 * NT1   tin alloys
 * NT1   titanium alloys
 * NT1   tungsten alloys
 * NT1   vanadium alloys
 * NT1   yttrium alloys
 * NT1   zinc alloys
 * NT1   zirconium alloys
    RT   alloy systems
    RT   binary mixtures
    RT   metals
    RT   semimetals
    RT   solid solutions

ALLUVIAL DEPOSITS [184; 184]
- BT1 geologic deposits
- RT clays
- RT ground water
- RT placers
- RT sand
- RT sediments
- RT soils
- RT surface waters

ALLYL RADICALS [80; 80]
- BT1 alkyl radicals
- BT2 radicals

alma-ata wwr-k reactor
- USE wwr-k-alma-ata reactor

ALMARAZ-1 REACTOR [16; 16]
Apr 77
(Almaraz, Caceres, Spain)
- BT1 pwr type reactors
- BT2 enriched uranium reactors
- BT3 reactors
- BT2 power reactors
- BT3 reactors
- BT2 thermal reactors
- BT3 reactors
- BT2 water cooled reactors
- BT3 reactors
- BT2 water moderated reactors
- BT3 reactors

ALMARAZ-2 REACTOR [16; 16]
Apr 77
(Almaraz, Caceres, Spain)
- BT1 pwr type reactors
- BT2 enriched uranium reactors
- BT3 reactors
- BT2 power reactors
- BT3 reactors
- BT2 thermal reactors
- BT3 reactors
- BT2 water cooled reactors
- BT3 reactors
- BT2 water moderated reactors
- BT3 reactors

ALMENDRO EVENT [5; 5]
- BT1 contained explosions
- BT2 underground explosions
- BT3 explosions
- BT1 nuclear explosions
- BT2 explosions

ALNICO ALLOYS [52; 52]
- BT1 aluminium alloys
- BT2 alloys
- BT1 cobalt alloys
- BT2 alloys
- BT1 iron base alloys
- BT2 iron alloys
- BT3 alloys
- BT1 nickel alloys
- BT2 alloys

ALOE [8; 8]
- BT1 medicinal plants
- BT2 plants

ALOUETTE SATELLITES [21; 21]
- BT1 satellites

ALPHA BEAMS [1,929; 1,929]
- BT1 helium 4 beams
- BT2 ion beams
- BT3 beams
- RT alpha particles

ALPHA DECAY [2,690; 2,690]
- BT1 nuclear decay
- BT2 decay
- RT alpha decay radioisotopes
- RT alpha particles
- RT gamow barrier
- RT geiger-nuttall law

* ALPHA DECAY RADIOISOTOPES [324; 38,519]
(For specific terms, consult the Appendix.)
- UF *alpha-decay radioisotopes*
- BT1 radioisotopes
- BT2 isotopes
- RT alpha decay

ALPHA DETECTION [2,127; 2,127]
- BT1 charged particle detection
- BT2 radiation detection
- BT3 detection
- RT alpha dosimetry
- RT alpha spectrometers
- RT alpha spectroscopy

ALPHA DEVICE [2; 2]
- BT1 tlp devices
- BT2 toroidal pinch devices
- BT3 closed plasma devices
- BT4 thermonuclear devices
- BT3 pinch devices
- BT4 thermonuclear devices

ALPHA DOSIMETRY [359; 359]
- BT1 dosimetry
- RT alpha detection

alpha particle model
- USE cluster model

ALPHA PARTICLES [14,156; 14,325]
(Emitted by nuclei.)
- BT1 helium ions
- BT2 ions
- BT3 charged particles
- BT1 ionizing radiations
- BT2 radiations
- NT1 cosmic alpha particles
- NT1 delayed alpha particles
- NT1 solar alpha particles
- RT alpha beams
- RT alpha decay
- RT alpha sources
- RT alpha spectra
- RT geiger-nuttall law
- RT helium ash

ALPHA REACTIONS [8,020; 8,020]
- UF *helium 4 reactions*
- BT1 nuclear reactions

ALPHA SOURCES [826; 826]
- BT1 ion sources
- BT1 particle sources
- BT2 radiation sources
- RT alpha particles

ALPHA SPECTRA [2,426; 2,426]
- BT1 spectra
- RT alpha particles

ALPHA SPECTROMETERS [278; 278]
- BT1 spectrometers
- BT2 measuring instruments
- RT alpha detection

alpha spectrometry
- USE alpha spectroscopy

ALPHA SPECTROSCOPY [1,440; 1,440]
- UF *alpha spectrometry*
- BT1 spectroscopy
- RT alpha detection

ALPHA-BEARING WASTES [1,646; 1,646] *Apr 79*
- BT1 radioactive wastes
- BT2 radioactive materials
- BT3 materials
- BT2 wastes
- RT slagging pyrolysis process
- RT wipp

alpha-decay radioisotopes
- USE alpha decay radioisotopes

alpha-nitroso-beta-naphthol
- USE 1-nitroso-2-naphthol

ALPHA-TRANSFER REACTIONS [930; 930]
- BT1 four-nucleon transfer reaction
- BT2 multi-nucleon transfer reactio
- BT3 transfer reactions
- BT4 direct reactions
- BT5 nuclear reactions

ALPS [106; 106]
- BT1 mountains

ALRR REACTOR [23; 23]
(Ames Laboratory, Iowa State Univ., Ames, Iowa, USA)
- UF *ames laboratory research reac.*
- BT1 enriched uranium reactors
- BT2 reactors
- BT1 heavy water cooled reactors
- BT2 reactors
- BT1 heavy water moderated reactors
- BT2 reactors
- BT1 isotope production reactors
- BT2 irradiation reactors
- BT3 reactors
- BT1 research reactors
- BT2 research and test reactors
- BT3 reactors
- BT1 tank type reactors
- BT2 reactors
- BT1 thermal reactors
- BT2 reactors

ALTERNATING CURRENT [984; 984]
- UF *current (alternating)*
- BT1 electric currents
- BT2 currents
- RT alternators
- RT parametric instabilities

ALTERNATORS [101; 101]
- BT1 electric generators
- BT2 electrical equipment
- BT3 equipment
- RT alternating current

althein
- USE asparagine

ALTIMETERS [7; 7]
- BT1 measuring instruments

altitude
- USE levels

alto lazio-1 reactor
- USE montalto di castro-1 reactor

alto lazio-2 reactor
- USE montalto di castro-2 reactor

alumel
- USE alloy-ni94mn3al2

ALUMINATES [542; 542]
(Specific compounds should be indexed by coordination of a descriptor of the form (CATION) COMPOUNDS and the above anion descriptor.)
- BT1 aluminium compounds
- BT1 oxygen compounds
- RT aluminium oxides

aluminia
 USE aluminium oxides

ALUMINIUM [11,297; 11,297]
 BT1 metals
  BT2 elements
 RT sap

ALUMINIUM ADDITIONS [554; 1,895]
(Alloys containing not more than 1% Al are listed here.)
 NT1 alloy-fe44ni33cr21
 NT1 alloy-fe46ni33cr21
 NT1 alloy-fe48cr24ni24
 NT1 alloy-ni42fe36cr12mo6ti3
 NT1 alloy-ni43fe30cr22mo3
 NT1 alloy-ni53cr19fe19nb5mo3
 NT1 alloy-ni54cr22co13mo9
 NT1 alloy-ni60cr25w15
 NT1 alloy-ni61cr22mo9nb4fe3
 NT1 alloy-ni62cr16mo15fe3
 NT1 alloy-ni70mo17cr7fe5
 NT1 alloy-ni73cr15fe7ti3
 NT1 alloy-ni76cr15fe8
 NT1 alloy-ni77cr20ti2
 NT1 alloy-ni78cr21
 NT1 alloy-ni80cr20
 NT1 steel-cralnimo
 NT1 steel-cr13al
 NT1 steel-ni26cr15ti2movalb
 NT1 steel-ni36cr12ti3al-l
 RT aluminium alloys
 RT aluminium compounds

ALUMINIUM ALLOYS [5,495; 8,220]
(Alloys containing more than 1% Al.)
 BT1 alloys
 NT1 alloy-ni43fe33cr16mo3
 NT1 alloy-ni46cr23co19ti5al4
 NT1 alloy-ni48co28cr15al3mo3ti2
 NT1 alloy-ni50co20cr15al5mo5
 NT1 alloy-ni53co19cr15mo5al4ti3
 NT1 alloy-ni55co17cr15mo5al4ti4
 NT1 alloy-ni55cr19co11mo10ti3
 NT1 alloy-ni56cr21w10mo5fe4al2
 NT1 alloy-ni58cr14co8al4mo4nb4w4
 NT1 alloy-ni58cr20co14mo4ti3
 NT1 alloy-ni59cr20co17ti2
 NT1 alloy-ni60co15cr10al6ti5mo3
 NT1 alloy-ni60cr14co10ti5mo4w4al3
 NT1 alloy-ni60mo13co9cr8nb4al3
 NT1 alloy-ni61cr16co9al3ti3w3
 NT1 alloy-ni67cr19mo5w5ti3
 NT1 alloy-ni68cr15w6al3mo3fe2
 NT1 alloy-ni74cr13al6mo4
 NT1 alloy-ni75cr12al6mo5
 NT1 alloy-ni76cr20ti2
 NT1 alloy-ni77cr17al5
 NT1 alloy-ni78cr16al4
 NT1 alloy-ni94mn3al2
 NT1 alloy-ti78cr11mo7al3
 NT1 alloy-ti88mo8al3
 NT1 alloy-ti89al6mo3
 NT1 alloy-ti90al6
 NT1 alloy-ti90al6mo3
 NT1 alloy-ti90al6v4
 NT1 alloy-ti90mo7al2
 NT1 alloy-ti91al4mo3
 NT1 alloy-ti91al5cr2
 NT1 alnico alloys
 NT1 aluminium base alloys
  NT2 alloy-al95cu4
 NT1 heusler alloys
 NT1 steel-ni35cr18mo4ti2al
 NT1 tikonal
 RT aluminium additions

ALUMINIUM ARSENIDES [470; 470]
 BT1 aluminium compounds
 BT1 arsenides
  BT2 arsenic compounds
  BT2 pnictides

ALUMINIUM BASE ALLOYS
[1,319; 1,335]
 BT1 aluminium alloys
  BT2 alloys
 NT1 alloy-al95cu4

ALUMINIUM BORIDES [65; 65]
 BT1 aluminium compounds
 BT1 borides
  BT2 boron compounds

ALUMINIUM BROMIDES [30; 30]
 BT1 aluminium compounds
 BT1 bromides
  BT2 bromine compounds
   BT3 halogen compounds
  BT2 halides
   BT3 halogen compounds

ALUMINIUM CARBIDES [26; 26]
 BT1 aluminium compounds
 BT1 carbides
  BT2 carbon compounds

ALUMINIUM CHLORIDES [261; 261]
 BT1 aluminium compounds
 BT1 chlorides
  BT2 chlorine compounds
   BT3 halogen compounds
  BT2 halides
   BT3 halogen compounds

ALUMINIUM COMPLEXES [179; 179]
 BT1 complexes

ALUMINIUM COMPOUNDS
[1,074; 10,047]
 NT1 aluminates
 NT1 aluminium arsenides
 NT1 aluminium borides
 NT1 aluminium bromides
 NT1 aluminium carbides
 NT1 aluminium chlorides
 NT1 aluminium fluorides
 NT1 aluminium hydrides
 NT1 aluminium hydroxides
 NT1 aluminium iodides
 NT1 aluminium nitrates
 NT1 aluminium nitrides
 NT1 aluminium oxides
 NT1 aluminium perchlorates
 NT1 aluminium phosphates
 NT1 aluminium phosphides
 NT1 aluminium selenides
 NT1 aluminium silicates
 NT1 aluminium silicides
 NT1 aluminium sulfates
 NT1 aluminium sulfides
 NT1 aluminium tellurides
 NT1 aluminium tungstates
 RT aluminium additions

ALUMINIUM FLUORIDES [146; 146]
 BT1 aluminium compounds
 BT1 fluorides
  BT2 fluorine compounds
   BT3 halogen compounds
  BT2 halides
   BT3 halogen compounds

ALUMINIUM HYDRIDES [120; 120]
 BT1 aluminium compounds
 BT1 hydrides
  BT2 hydrogen compounds

ALUMINIUM HYDROXIDES [162; 162]
 BT1 aluminium compounds
 BT1 hydroxides
  BT2 hydrogen compounds
  BT2 oxygen compounds

ALUMINIUM IODIDES [23; 23]
 BT1 aluminium compounds
 BT1 iodides
  BT2 halides
   BT3 halogen compounds
  BT2 iodine compounds
   BT3 halogen compounds

ALUMINIUM IONS [686; 686]
 BT1 ions
  BT2 charged particles

ALUMINIUM ISOTOPES [133; 2,439]
 NT1 aluminium 22
 NT1 aluminium 23
 NT1 aluminium 24
 NT1 aluminium 25
 NT1 aluminium 26
 NT1 aluminium 27
 NT1 aluminium 28
 NT1 aluminium 29
 NT1 aluminium 30
 NT1 aluminium 31
 NT1 aluminium 32
 NT1 aluminium 33
 NT1 aluminium 34
 NT1 aluminium 35
 NT1 aluminium 36
 NT1 aluminium 37
 NT1 aluminium 38
 NT1 aluminium 39

ALUMINIUM NITRATES [140; 140]
 BT1 aluminium compounds
 BT1 nitrates
  BT2 nitrogen compounds
  BT2 oxygen compounds

ALUMINIUM NITRIDES [269; 269]
 BT1 aluminium compounds
 BT1 nitrides
  BT2 nitrogen compounds
  BT2 pnictides

ALUMINIUM ORES [11; 134]
 BT1 ores
 NT1 bauxite

ALUMINIUM OXIDES [5,639; 6,181]
 UF *aluminia*
 UF+ *sialon*
 UF+ *yttrium aluminium garnets*
 BT1 aluminium compounds
 BT1 oxides
  BT2 chalcogenides
  BT2 oxygen compounds
 RT aluminates
 RT corundum
 RT hollandite
 RT oxide minerals
 RT spinels

ALUMINIUM PERCHLORATES [0; 0]
Feb 89
 BT1 aluminium compounds
 BT1 perchlorates
  BT2 chlorine compounds
   BT3 halogen compounds
  BT2 oxygen compounds

ALUMINIUM PHOSPHATES [122; 123]
 BT1 aluminium compounds
 BT1 phosphates
  BT2 oxygen compounds
  BT2 phosphorus compounds
 RT florencite
 RT phosphate minerals

ALUMINIUM PHOSPHIDES [23; 23]
Feb 83
 BT1 aluminium compounds
 BT1 phosphides
  BT2 phosphorus compounds
  BT2 pnictides

→ **ALUMINIUM SELENIDES** [0; 0] *Sep 91*
 BT1 aluminium compounds
 BT1 selenides
  BT2 chalcogenides
  BT2 selenium compounds

ALUMINIUM SILICATES [463; 570]
BT1 aluminium compounds
BT1 silicates
  BT2 oxygen compounds
  BT2 silicon compounds
RT pollucite
RT silicate minerals
RT smectite
RT tourmaline
RT vermiculite

ALUMINIUM SILICIDES [10; 10]
Mar 77
BT1 aluminium compounds
BT1 silicides
  BT2 silicon compounds

ALUMINIUM SULFATES [84; 84]
BT1 aluminium compounds
BT1 sulfates
  BT2 oxygen compounds
  BT2 sulfur compounds
RT sulfate minerals

ALUMINIUM SULFIDES [22; 22]
BT1 aluminium compounds
BT1 sulfides
  BT2 chalcogenides
  BT2 sulfur compounds

→ **ALUMINIUM TELLURIDES** [0; 0]
Sep 91
BT1 aluminium compounds
BT1 tellurides
  BT2 chalcogenides
  BT2 tellurium compounds

ALUMINIUM TUNGSTATES [9; 9]
Sep 79
BT1 aluminium compounds
BT1 tungstates
  BT2 oxygen compounds
  BT2 tungsten compounds
    BT3 transition element compounds

ALUMINIUM 22 [22; 22] *Jun 77*
BT1 aluminium isotopes
BT1 beta-plus decay radioisotopes
  BT2 beta decay radioisotopes
    BT3 radioisotopes
      BT4 isotopes
BT1 light nuclei
  BT2 nuclei
BT1 millisec living radioisotopes
  BT2 radioisotopes
    BT3 isotopes
BT1 odd-odd nuclei
  BT2 nuclei

ALUMINIUM 23 [6; 6]
BT1 aluminium isotopes
BT1 beta-plus decay radioisotopes
  BT2 beta decay radioisotopes
    BT3 radioisotopes
      BT4 isotopes
BT1 light nuclei
  BT2 nuclei
BT1 millisec living radioisotopes
  BT2 radioisotopes
    BT3 isotopes
BT1 odd-even nuclei
  BT2 nuclei

ALUMINIUM 24 [59; 59]
BT1 aluminium isotopes
BT1 beta-plus decay radioisotopes
  BT2 beta decay radioisotopes
    BT3 radioisotopes
      BT4 isotopes
BT1 isomeric transition isotopes
  BT2 radioisotopes
    BT3 isotopes
BT1 light nuclei
  BT2 nuclei
BT1 millisec living radioisotopes
  BT2 radioisotopes
    BT3 isotopes
BT1 odd-odd nuclei
  BT2 nuclei
BT1 seconds living radioisotopes
  BT2 radioisotopes
    BT3 isotopes

ALUMINIUM 25 [95; 95]
BT1 aluminium isotopes
BT1 beta-plus decay radioisotopes
  BT2 beta decay radioisotopes
    BT3 radioisotopes
      BT4 isotopes
BT1 light nuclei
  BT2 nuclei
BT1 odd-even nuclei
  BT2 nuclei
BT1 seconds living radioisotopes
  BT2 radioisotopes
    BT3 isotopes

ALUMINIUM 25 TARGET [2; 2]
Apr 79
BT1 targets

ALUMINIUM 26 [694; 694]
BT1 aluminium isotopes
BT1 beta-plus decay radioisotopes
  BT2 beta decay radioisotopes
    BT3 radioisotopes
      BT4 isotopes
BT1 light nuclei
  BT2 nuclei
BT1 odd-odd nuclei
  BT2 nuclei
BT1 seconds living radioisotopes
  BT2 radioisotopes
    BT3 isotopes
BT1 years living radioisotopes
  BT2 radioisotopes
    BT3 isotopes

ALUMINIUM 26 TARGET [20; 20]
Jun 84
BT1 targets

ALUMINIUM 27 [1,167; 1,167]
BT1 aluminium isotopes
BT1 light nuclei
  BT2 nuclei
BT1 odd-even nuclei
  BT2 nuclei
BT1 stable isotopes
  BT2 isotopes

ALUMINIUM 27 BEAMS [34; 34]
Jan 77
BT1 ion beams
  BT2 beams

ALUMINIUM 27 REACTIONS [74; 74]
Aug 78
BT1 heavy ion reactions
  BT2 nuclear reactions

ALUMINIUM 27 TARGET [2,523; 2,523]
BT1 targets

ALUMINIUM 28 [307; 307]
BT1 aluminium isotopes
BT1 beta-minus decay radioisotopes
  BT2 beta decay radioisotopes
    BT3 radioisotopes
      BT4 isotopes
BT1 light nuclei
  BT2 nuclei
BT1 minutes living radioisotopes
  BT2 radioisotopes
    BT3 isotopes
BT1 odd-odd nuclei
  BT2 nuclei

ALUMINIUM 28 TARGET [7; 7]
Apr 79
BT1 targets

ALUMINIUM 29 [74; 74]
BT1 aluminium isotopes
BT1 beta-minus decay radioisotopes
  BT2 beta decay radioisotopes
    BT3 radioisotopes
      BT4 isotopes
BT1 light nuclei
  BT2 nuclei
BT1 minutes living radioisotopes
  BT2 radioisotopes
    BT3 isotopes
BT1 odd-even nuclei
  BT2 nuclei

ALUMINIUM 30 [10; 10]
BT1 aluminium isotopes
BT1 beta-minus decay radioisotopes
  BT2 beta decay radioisotopes
    BT3 radioisotopes
      BT4 isotopes
BT1 light nuclei
  BT2 nuclei
BT1 odd-odd nuclei
  BT2 nuclei
BT1 seconds living radioisotopes
  BT2 radioisotopes
    BT3 isotopes

ALUMINIUM 31 [13; 13]
BT1 aluminium isotopes
BT1 beta-minus decay radioisotopes
  BT2 beta decay radioisotopes
    BT3 radioisotopes
      BT4 isotopes
BT1 light nuclei
  BT2 nuclei
BT1 millisec living radioisotopes
  BT2 radioisotopes
    BT3 isotopes
BT1 odd-even nuclei
  BT2 nuclei

ALUMINIUM 32 [11; 11]
BT1 aluminium isotopes
BT1 beta-minus decay radioisotopes
  BT2 beta decay radioisotopes
    BT3 radioisotopes
      BT4 isotopes
BT1 light nuclei
  BT2 nuclei
BT1 millisec living radioisotopes
  BT2 radioisotopes
    BT3 isotopes
BT1 odd-odd nuclei
  BT2 nuclei

ALUMINIUM 33 [10; 10]
BT1 aluminium isotopes
BT1 light nuclei
  BT2 nuclei
BT1 odd-even nuclei
  BT2 nuclei

ALUMINIUM 34 [17; 17] *Oct 77*
BT1 aluminium isotopes
BT1 beta-minus decay radioisotopes
  BT2 beta decay radioisotopes
    BT3 radioisotopes
      BT4 isotopes
BT1 light nuclei
  BT2 nuclei
BT1 millisec living radioisotopes
  BT2 radioisotopes
    BT3 isotopes
BT1 odd-odd nuclei
  BT2 nuclei

ALUMINIUM 35 [9; 9] *Sep 79*
BT1 aluminium isotopes
BT1 light nuclei
  BT2 nuclei
BT1 odd-even nuclei
  BT2 nuclei

ALUMINIUM 36 [3; 3] *Jul 80*
  BT1   aluminium isotopes
  BT1   beta-minus decay radioisotopes
  BT2   beta decay radioisotopes
  BT3   radioisotopes
  BT4   isotopes
  BT1   light nuclei
  BT2   nuclei
  BT1   odd-odd nuclei
  BT2   nuclei

ALUMINIUM 37 [4; 4] *Jul 80*
  BT1   aluminium isotopes
  BT1   beta-minus decay radioisotopes
  BT2   beta decay radioisotopes
  BT3   radioisotopes
  BT4   isotopes
  BT1   light nuclei
  BT2   nuclei
  BT1   odd-even nuclei
  BT2   nuclei

ALUMINIUM 38 [2; 2] *Sep 89*
  BT1   aluminium isotopes
  BT1   light nuclei
  BT2   nuclei
  BT1   odd-odd nuclei
  BT2   nuclei

ALUMINIUM 39 [2; 2] *Sep 89*
  BT1   aluminium isotopes
  BT1   light nuclei
  BT2   nuclei
  BT1   odd-even nuclei
  BT2   nuclei

ALUMINON [3; 3]
  UF   *aurintricarboxylic acid*
  UF   *chrome violet*
  BT1   hydroxy acids
  BT2   carboxylic acids
  BT3   organic acids
  BT4   organic compounds
  BT1   reagents
  BT1   triphenylmethane dyes
  BT2   dyes

alveoli (dental)
  USE   jaw

alveoli (pulmonary)
  USE   lungs

ALVITE [1; 1]
  BT1   silicate minerals
  BT2   minerals
  RT   zirconium silicates

ALWAC COMPUTERS [0; 0]
  BT1   computers

am-1 reactor
  USE   aps reactor

amalgams
  USE   mercury alloys

AMAZON RIVER [32; 32] *Jun 82*
  BT1   rivers
  BT2   surface waters
  RT   brazil
  RT   peru

AMBER [6; 6]
  BT1   other organic compounds
  BT2   organic compounds

amberlite
  USE   organic ion exchangers

AMBIPLASMA [34; 34]
(Containing both matter and antimatter.)
  BT1   plasma
  RT   antimatter
  RT   matter

AMBIPOLAR DIFFUSION [390; 390]
  BT1   diffusion
  RT   electron drift
  RT   ion drift
  RT   plasma drift

ambr method
  USE   atomic beams
  AND   magnetic resonance

AMBROSIA LAKE [4; 4]
  BT1   lakes
  BT2   surface waters

AMCHITKA ISLAND AREA [81; 81]
  BT1   aleutian islands
  BT2   islands
  RT   alaska

ameba
  USE   amoeba

amenorrhea
  USE   menstruation disorders

AMERICIUM [1,503; 1,503]
  BT1   actinides
  BT2   metals
  BT3   elements
  BT1   transplutonium elements
  BT2   transuranium elements
  BT3   elements

AMERICIUM ADDITIONS [4; 4]
(Alloys containing not more than 1% Am are listed here.)
  RT   americium alloys
  RT   americium compounds

AMERICIUM ALLOYS [73; 75]
(Alloys containing more than 1% Am.)
  BT1   actinide alloys
  BT2   alloys
  NT1   americium base alloys
  RT   americium additions

AMERICIUM ARSENIDES [3; 3] *Oct 76*
  BT1   americium compounds
  BT2   actinide compounds
  BT2   transplutonium compounds
  BT3   transuranium compounds
  BT1   arsenides
  BT2   arsenic compounds
  BT2   pnictides

AMERICIUM BASE ALLOYS [1; 1]
  BT1   americium alloys
  BT2   actinide alloys
  BT3   alloys

AMERICIUM BROMIDES [6; 6]
  BT1   americium compounds
  BT2   actinide compounds
  BT2   transplutonium compounds
  BT3   transuranium compounds
  BT1   bromides
  BT2   bromine compounds
  BT3   halogen compounds
  BT2   halides
  BT3   halogen compounds

AMERICIUM CARBIDES [5; 5]
  BT1   americium compounds
  BT2   actinide compounds
  BT2   transplutonium compounds
  BT3   transuranium compounds
  BT1   carbides
  BT2   carbon compounds

AMERICIUM CARBONATES [28; 28]
  BT1   americium compounds
  BT2   actinide compounds
  BT2   transplutonium compounds
  BT3   transuranium compounds
  BT1   carbonates
  BT2   carbon compounds
  BT2   oxygen compounds

AMERICIUM CHLORIDES [42; 42]
  BT1   americium compounds
  BT2   actinide compounds
  BT2   transplutonium compounds
  BT3   transuranium compounds
  BT1   chlorides
  BT2   chlorine compounds
  BT3   halogen compounds
  BT2   halides
  BT3   halogen compounds

AMERICIUM COMPLEXES [465; 465]
  BT1   actinide complexes
  BT2   complexes
  BT1   transuranium complexes

AMERICIUM COMPOUNDS [525; 992]
  BT1   actinide compounds
  BT1   transplutonium compounds
  BT2   transuranium compounds
  NT1   americium arsenides
  NT1   americium bromides
  NT1   americium carbides
  NT1   americium carbonates
  NT1   americium chlorides
  NT1   americium fluorides
  NT1   americium hydrides
  NT1   americium hydroxides
  NT1   americium iodides
  NT1   americium nitrates
  NT1   americium nitrides
  NT1   americium oxides
  NT1   americium perchlorates
  NT1   americium phosphates
  NT1   americium selenides
  NT1   americium silicates
  NT1   americium silicides
  NT1   americium sulfates
  NT1   americium sulfides
  NT1   americium tellurides
  RT   americium additions

AMERICIUM FLUORIDES [44; 44]
  BT1   americium compounds
  BT2   actinide compounds
  BT2   transplutonium compounds
  BT3   transuranium compounds
  BT1   fluorides
  BT2   fluorine compounds
  BT3   halogen compounds
  BT2   halides
  BT3   halogen compounds

AMERICIUM HYDRIDES [4; 4] *Nov 84*
  BT1   americium compounds
  BT2   actinide compounds
  BT2   transplutonium compounds
  BT3   transuranium compounds
  BT1   hydrides
  BT2   hydrogen compounds

AMERICIUM HYDROXIDES [27; 27]
  BT1   americium compounds
  BT2   actinide compounds
  BT2   transplutonium compounds
  BT3   transuranium compounds
  BT1   hydroxides
  BT2   hydrogen compounds
  BT2   oxygen compounds

AMERICIUM IODIDES [10; 10]
  BT1   americium compounds
  BT2   actinide compounds
  BT2   transplutonium compounds
  BT3   transuranium compounds
  BT1   iodides

BT2　　halides
　　　BT3　　　halogen compounds
　　　BT2　　iodine compounds
　　　BT3　　　halogen compounds

AMERICIUM IONS [59; 59]
　　　BT1　ions
　　　BT2　　charged particles

AMERICIUM ISOTOPES [195; 4,311]
　　　NT1　americium 232
　　　NT1　americium 234
　　　NT1　americium 237
　　　NT1　americium 238
　　　NT1　americium 239
　　　NT1　americium 240
　　　NT1　americium 241
　　　NT1　americium 242
　　　NT1　americium 243
　　　NT1　americium 244
　　　NT1　americium 245
　　　NT1　americium 246
　　　NT1　americium 247

AMERICIUM NITRATES [79; 79]
　　　BT1　americium compounds
　　　BT2　　actinide compounds
　　　BT2　　transplutonium compounds
　　　BT3　　　transuranium compounds
　　　BT1　nitrates
　　　BT2　　nitrogen compounds
　　　BT2　　oxygen compounds

AMERICIUM NITRIDES [9; 9]
　　　BT1　americium compounds
　　　BT2　　actinide compounds
　　　BT2　　transplutonium compounds
　　　BT3　　　transuranium compounds
　　　BT1　nitrides
　　　BT2　　nitrogen compounds
　　　BT2　　pnictides

AMERICIUM OXIDES [246; 246]
　　　BT1　americium compounds
　　　BT2　　actinide compounds
　　　BT2　　transplutonium compounds
　　　BT3　　　transuranium compounds
　　　BT1　oxides
　　　BT2　　chalcogenides
　　　BT2　　oxygen compounds

AMERICIUM PERCHLORATES [5; 5]
Sep 78
　　　BT1　americium compounds
　　　BT2　　actinide compounds
　　　BT2　　transplutonium compounds
　　　BT3　　　transuranium compounds
　　　BT1　perchlorates
　　　BT2　　chlorine compounds
　　　BT3　　　halogen compounds
　　　BT2　　oxygen compounds

AMERICIUM PHOSPHATES [10; 10]
Jul 78
　　　BT1　americium compounds
　　　BT2　　actinide compounds
　　　BT2　　transplutonium compounds
　　　BT3　　　transuranium compounds
　　　BT1　phosphates
　　　BT2　　oxygen compounds
　　　BT2　　phosphorus compounds

AMERICIUM SELENIDES [4; 4] *Jul 78*
　　　BT1　americium compounds
　　　BT2　　actinide compounds
　　　BT2　　transplutonium compounds
　　　BT3　　　transuranium compounds
　　　BT1　selenides
　　　BT2　　chalcogenides
　　　BT2　　selenium compounds

AMERICIUM SILICATES [2; 2] *Jul 84*
　　　BT1　americium compounds
　　　BT2　　actinide compounds
　　　BT2　　transplutonium compounds
　　　BT3　　　transuranium compounds
　　　BT1　silicates
　　　BT2　　oxygen compounds
　　　BT2　　silicon compounds

→ **AMERICIUM SILICIDES** [0; 0] *Sep 91*
　　　BT1　americium compounds
　　　BT2　　actinide compounds
　　　BT2　　transplutonium compounds
　　　BT3　　　transuranium compounds
　　　BT1　silicides
　　　BT2　　silicon compounds

→ **AMERICIUM SULFATES** [0; 0] *Sep 91*
　　　BT1　americium compounds
　　　BT2　　actinide compounds
　　　BT2　　transplutonium compounds
　　　BT3　　　transuranium compounds
　　　BT1　sulfates
　　　BT2　　oxygen compounds
　　　BT2　　sulfur compounds

AMERICIUM SULFIDES [4; 4] *Oct 76*
　　　BT1　americium compounds
　　　BT2　　actinide compounds
　　　BT2　　transplutonium compounds
　　　BT3　　　transuranium compounds
　　　BT1　sulfides
　　　BT2　　chalcogenides
　　　BT2　　sulfur compounds

AMERICIUM TELLURIDES [6; 6]
Jul 78
　　　BT1　americium compounds
　　　BT2　　actinide compounds
　　　BT2　　transplutonium compounds
　　　BT3　　　transuranium compounds
　　　BT1　tellurides
　　　BT2　　chalcogenides
　　　BT2　　tellurium compounds

AMERICIUM 232 [4; 4]
　　　BT1　actinide nuclei
　　　BT2　　heavy nuclei
　　　BT3　　　nuclei
　　　BT1　alpha decay radioisotopes
　　　BT2　　radioisotopes
　　　BT3　　　isotopes
　　　BT1　americium isotopes
　　　BT1　electron capture radioisotopes
　　　BT2　　beta decay radioisotopes
　　　BT3　　　radioisotopes
　　　BT4　　　　isotopes
　　　BT1　odd-odd nuclei
　　　BT2　　nuclei
　　　BT1　seconds living radioisotopes
　　　BT2　　radioisotopes
　　　BT3　　　isotopes

AMERICIUM 234 [8; 8]
　　　BT1　actinide nuclei
　　　BT2　　heavy nuclei
　　　BT3　　　nuclei
　　　BT1　americium isotopes
　　　BT1　electron capture radioisotopes
　　　BT2　　beta decay radioisotopes
　　　BT3　　　radioisotopes
　　　BT4　　　　isotopes
　　　BT1　minutes living radioisotopes
　　　BT2　　radioisotopes
　　　BT3　　　isotopes
　　　BT1　odd-odd nuclei
　　　BT2　　nuclei

AMERICIUM 237 [13; 13]
　　　BT1　actinide nuclei
　　　BT2　　heavy nuclei
　　　BT3　　　nuclei
　　　BT1　alpha decay radioisotopes
　　　BT2　　radioisotopes
　　　BT3　　　isotopes
　　　BT1　americium isotopes
　　　BT1　electron capture radioisotopes
　　　BT2　　beta decay radioisotopes
　　　BT3　　　radioisotopes
　　　BT4　　　　isotopes
　　　BT1　hours living radioisotopes
　　　BT2　　radioisotopes
　　　BT3　　　isotopes
　　　BT1　odd-even nuclei
　　　BT2　　nuclei
　　　BT1　spontaneous fission radioisoto
　　　BT2　　radioisotopes
　　　BT3　　　isotopes

AMERICIUM 238 [9; 9]
　　　BT1　actinide nuclei
　　　BT2　　heavy nuclei
　　　BT3　　　nuclei
　　　BT1　alpha decay radioisotopes
　　　BT2　　radioisotopes
　　　BT3　　　isotopes
　　　BT1　americium isotopes
　　　BT1　electron capture radioisotopes
　　　BT2　　beta decay radioisotopes
　　　BT3　　　radioisotopes
　　　BT4　　　　isotopes
　　　BT1　hours living radioisotopes
　　　BT2　　radioisotopes
　　　BT3　　　isotopes
　　　BT1　odd-odd nuclei
　　　BT2　　nuclei
　　　BT1　spontaneous fission radioisoto
　　　BT2　　radioisotopes
　　　BT3　　　isotopes

AMERICIUM 239 [27; 27]
　　　BT1　actinide nuclei
　　　BT2　　heavy nuclei
　　　BT3　　　nuclei
　　　BT1　alpha decay radioisotopes
　　　BT2　　radioisotopes
　　　BT3　　　isotopes
　　　BT1　americium isotopes
　　　BT1　electron capture radioisotopes
　　　BT2　　beta decay radioisotopes
　　　BT3　　　radioisotopes
　　　BT4　　　　isotopes
　　　BT1　hours living radioisotopes
　　　BT2　　radioisotopes
　　　BT3　　　isotopes
　　　BT1　odd-even nuclei
　　　BT2　　nuclei
　　　BT1　spontaneous fission radioisoto
　　　BT2　　radioisotopes
　　　BT3　　　isotopes

AMERICIUM 240 [47; 47]
　　　BT1　actinide nuclei
　　　BT2　　heavy nuclei
　　　BT3　　　nuclei
　　　BT1　alpha decay radioisotopes
　　　BT2　　radioisotopes
　　　BT3　　　isotopes
　　　BT1　americium isotopes
　　　BT1　days living radioisotopes
　　　BT2　　radioisotopes
　　　BT3　　　isotopes
　　　BT1　electron capture radioisotopes
　　　BT2　　beta decay radioisotopes
　　　BT3　　　radioisotopes
　　　BT4　　　　isotopes
　　　BT1　odd-odd nuclei
　　　BT2　　nuclei
　　　BT1　spontaneous fission radioisoto
　　　BT2　　radioisotopes
　　　BT3　　　isotopes

AMERICIUM 241 [3,706; 3,706]
　　　BT1　actinide nuclei
　　　BT2　　heavy nuclei
　　　BT3　　　nuclei
　　　BT1　alpha decay radioisotopes
　　　BT2　　radioisotopes
　　　BT3　　　isotopes
　　　BT1　americium isotopes
　　　BT1　odd-even nuclei
　　　BT2　　nuclei
　　　BT1　spontaneous fission radioisoto
　　　BT2　　radioisotopes
　　　BT3　　　isotopes
　　　BT1　years living radioisotopes
　　　BT2　　radioisotopes
　　　BT3　　　isotopes

AMERICIUM 241 TARGET [177; 177]
BT1   targets

AMERICIUM 242 [168; 168]
BT1   actinide nuclei
BT2   heavy nuclei
BT3   nuclei
BT1   alpha decay radioisotopes
BT2   radioisotopes
BT3   isotopes
BT1   americium isotopes
BT1   beta-minus decay radioisotopes
BT2   beta decay radioisotopes
BT3   radioisotopes
BT4   isotopes
BT1   electron capture radioisotopes
BT2   beta decay radioisotopes
BT3   radioisotopes
BT4   isotopes
BT1   hours living radioisotopes
BT2   radioisotopes
BT3   isotopes
BT1   isomeric transition isotopes
BT2   radioisotopes
BT3   isotopes
BT1   odd-odd nuclei
BT2   nuclei
BT1   spontaneous fission radioisoto
BT2   radioisotopes
BT3   isotopes
BT1   years living radioisotopes
BT2   radioisotopes
BT3   isotopes

AMERICIUM 242 TARGET [40; 40]
BT1   targets

AMERICIUM 243 [394; 394]
BT1   actinide nuclei
BT2   heavy nuclei
BT3   nuclei
BT1   alpha decay radioisotopes
BT2   radioisotopes
BT3   isotopes
BT1   americium isotopes
BT1   odd-even nuclei
BT2   nuclei
BT1   spontaneous fission radioisoto
BT2   radioisotopes
BT3   isotopes
BT1   years living radioisotopes
BT2   radioisotopes
BT3   isotopes

AMERICIUM 243 TARGET [107; 107]
BT1   targets

AMERICIUM 244 [48; 48]
BT1   actinide nuclei
BT2   heavy nuclei
BT3   nuclei
BT1   americium isotopes
BT1   beta-minus decay radioisotopes
BT2   beta decay radioisotopes
BT3   radioisotopes
BT4   isotopes
BT1   electron capture radioisotopes
BT2   beta decay radioisotopes
BT3   radioisotopes
BT4   isotopes
BT1   hours living radioisotopes
BT2   radioisotopes
BT3   isotopes
BT1   minutes living radioisotopes
BT2   radioisotopes
BT3   isotopes
BT1   odd-odd nuclei
BT2   nuclei
BT1   spontaneous fission radioisoto
BT2   radioisotopes
BT3   isotopes

AMERICIUM 245 [13; 13]
BT1   actinide nuclei
BT2   heavy nuclei
BT3   nuclei
BT1   americium isotopes
BT1   beta-minus decay radioisotopes
BT2   beta decay radioisotopes
BT3   radioisotopes
BT4   isotopes
BT1   hours living radioisotopes
BT2   radioisotopes
BT3   isotopes
BT1   odd-even nuclei
BT2   nuclei
BT1   spontaneous fission radioisoto
BT2   radioisotopes
BT3   isotopes

AMERICIUM 246 [9; 9]
BT1   actinide nuclei
BT2   heavy nuclei
BT3   nuclei
BT1   americium isotopes
BT1   beta-minus decay radioisotopes
BT2   beta decay radioisotopes
BT3   radioisotopes
BT4   isotopes
BT1   minutes living radioisotopes
BT2   radioisotopes
BT3   isotopes
BT1   odd-odd nuclei
BT2   nuclei
BT1   spontaneous fission radioisoto
BT2   radioisotopes
BT3   isotopes

AMERICIUM 247 [6; 6]
BT1   actinide nuclei
BT2   heavy nuclei
BT3   nuclei
BT1   americium isotopes
BT1   beta-minus decay radioisotopes
BT2   beta decay radioisotopes
BT3   radioisotopes
BT4   isotopes
BT1   minutes living radioisotopes
BT2   radioisotopes
BT3   isotopes
BT1   odd-even nuclei
BT2   nuclei

AMES LABORATORY [43; 43]
BT1   us aec
BT2   us organizations
BT3   national organizations
BT1   us doe
BT2   us organizations
BT3   national organizations
BT1   us erda
BT2   us organizations
BT3   national organizations
RT   iowa

ames laboratory research reac.
USE   alrr reactor

ames, iowa state univ utr-10 r
USE   iowa utr-10 reactor

amethopterin
USE   methotrexate

AMEX PROCESS [9; 9]
BT1   reprocessing
BT2   separation processes
RT   amines
RT   solvent extraction

AMIDASES [19; 32] *Dec 86*
BT1   non-peptide c-n hydrolases
BT2   hydrolases
BT3   enzymes
BT4   organic compounds
NT1   urease

AMIDES [1,673; 3,159]
BT1   organic nitrogen compounds
BT2   organic compounds
NT1   acetamide
NT2   ioglycamic acid
NT1   acrylamide
NT1   asparagine
NT1   formamide
NT1   glutamine
NT1   hypaque
NT1   lactams
NT2   pyrrolidones
NT3   pvp
NT1   metrizamide
NT1   nicotinamide
NT1   phenatine
NT1   sulfonamides
NT2   sulfadiazine
NT1   thionalide
RT   bph
RT   cerebrosides
RT   chloramines
RT   guanidines
RT   polyamides
RT   thioureas
RT   urea

AMIDINASES [8; 12] *Dec 86*
BT1   non-peptide c-n hydrolases
BT2   hydrolases
BT3   enzymes
BT4   organic compounds
NT1   arginase

AMIDINES [66; 67]
UF   *iminoamides*
BT1   organic nitrogen compounds
BT2   organic compounds
NT1   stilbamidine

AMIDOL [4; 4]
BT1   amines
BT2   organic compounds
BT1   developers
BT1   phenols
BT2   aromatics
BT3   organic compounds
BT2   hydroxy compounds
BT3   organic compounds
BT1   reagents

AMINATION [42; 42]
BT1   chemical reactions
RT   deamination

→ **AMINE OXIDASES** [3; 3] *Dec 86*
(Code numbers 1.4 and 1.5)
BT1   oxidases
BT2   oxidoreductases
BT3   enzymes
BT4   organic compounds

AMINES [3,951; 15,561]
UF   *butylamine*
UF+   *amino alcohols*
UF+   *amino sugars*
UF+   *aminoglycides*
UF+   *bromamines*
UF+   *ndpp*
UF+   *p-nitrodimethylaminopropiophen*
UF+   *promethazine*
BT1   organic compounds
NT1   acridine orange
NT1   adenines
NT2   kinetin
NT1   aet
NT1   amidol
NT1   aminopterin
NT1   amphetamines
NT2   benzedrine
NT1   aniline
NT1   arsanilic acid
NT1   benzidine
NT1   bph
NT1   cadaverine
NT1   catecholamines
NT1   cephalins
NT1   chloramines
NT1   chlorpromazine
NT1   congo red
NT1   cupferron
NT1   cystamine
NT1   cystaphos

NT1 cytosine
NT1 deferoxamine
NT1 dopamine
NT1 ephedrine
NT1 flavines
NT2 acriflavine
NT2 proflavine
NT1 gammaphos
NT1 guanine
NT1 hexosamines
NT2 glucosamine
NT1 histamine
NT1 hydroxamic acids
NT2 benzohydroxamic acid
NT1 hydroxylamine
NT1 imipramine
NT1 mea
NT1 melamine
NT1 methyl orange
NT1 methyl violet
NT1 methylamine
NT1 methylene blue
NT1 morpholines
NT1 mucopolysaccharides
NT2 chitin
NT2 chondroitin
NT2 heparin
NT2 hyaluronic acid
NT1 neutral red
NT1 nitrogen mustard
NT1 oximes
NT2 benzoinoxime
NT2 dimethylglyoxime
NT2 furildioxime
NT1 papp
NT1 piperidines
NT2 pethidine
NT2 tmpn
NT2 triacetoneamine-n-oxyl
NT1 primene
NT1 putrescine
NT1 pyrrolidines
NT2 hydroxyproline
NT2 nicotine
NT2 proline
NT1 quaternary compounds
NT2 acetylcholine
NT2 betaine
NT2 choline
NT2 pyridinium compounds
NT2 teab
NT1 rhodamines
NT1 spermidine
NT1 spermine
NT1 sulfanilic acid
NT1 taurine
NT1 tda
NT1 teta
NT1 thiamine
NT1 thionine
NT1 tna
NT1 toa
NT1 toluidines
NT1 tridodecylamine
NT1 trypan blue
NT1 tryptamines
NT2 bufotenine
NT2 melatonin
NT2 serotonin
NT1 tyramine
NT1 urotropin
RT amex process
RT eurex process
RT piperazines
RT sialic acid
RT tramex process

amino acid sequence
  USE protein structure

AMINO ACIDS [2,562; 16,756]
  (For carboxylic acids only.)
  BT1 carboxylic acids
    BT2 organic acids
      BT3 organic compounds
  NT1 alanines
    NT2 alanine-alpha

NT3 alanine-l
NT2 alanine-beta
NT1 aminoadipic acid
NT1 aminobutyric acid
NT1 aminolevulinic acid
NT1 anthranilic acid
NT1 arginine
NT1 asparagine
NT1 aspartic acid
NT1 betaine
NT1 carnitine
NT1 cdta
NT1 citrulline
NT1 cpdta
NT1 creatine
NT1 cysteine
NT1 cystine
NT1 dcta
NT1 diiodotyrosine
NT1 dopa
NT1 dtpa
NT1 eddha
NT1 edta
NT1 ethionine
NT1 folic acid
NT1 glutamic acid
  NT2 pyridoxylideneglutamate
NT1 glutamine
NT1 glycine
NT1 glycylglycine
NT1 hedta
NT1 heida
NT1 hippuric acid
NT1 histidine
NT1 hmdta
NT1 homocysteine
NT1 homocystine
NT1 hydroxyproline
NT1 hydroxytryptophan
NT1 kynurenine
NT1 leucine
NT1 lysine
NT1 methionine
NT1 methyl red
NT1 methyl tyrosine
NT1 mimosine
NT1 mpg
NT1 nta
NT1 ornithine
NT1 paba
NT1 pantothenic acid
NT1 pas
NT1 penicillamine
NT1 phenylalanine
NT1 phosphocreatine
NT1 proline
NT1 sarcosine
NT1 serine
NT1 tetaha
NT1 threonine
NT1 thyronine
NT1 thyroxine
NT1 tryptophan
NT1 tyrosine
NT1 valine
RT lactams
RT protein structure
RT proteins

amino alcohols
  USE alcohols
  AND amines

amino sugars
  USE amines
  AND saccharides

aminoacetic acid
  USE glycine

AMINOADIPIC ACID [1; 1]
  BT1 amino acids
    BT2 carboxylic acids
      BT3 organic acids
        BT4 organic compounds

aminobenzene
  USE aniline

aminobenzenesulfonic acid-para
  USE sulfanilic acid

aminobenzoic acid-ortho
  USE anthranilic acid

aminobenzoic acid-para
  USE paba

AMINOBUTYRIC ACID [277; 277]
  BT1 amino acids
    BT2 carboxylic acids
      BT3 organic acids
        BT4 organic compounds
  BT1 neuroregulators
    BT2 autonomic nervous system agent
      BT3 drugs

aminoethanesulfonic acid
  USE taurine

aminoethanethiol
  USE mea

aminoethylisothiuronium bromid
  USE aet

aminoethylthiopseudourea
  USE aet

aminoglutaric acid-alpha
  USE glutamic acid

aminoglycides
  USE amines
  AND saccharides

aminohypoxanthine
  USE guanine

aminoisocaproic acid-alpha
  USE leucine

aminoisovaleric acid-alpha
  USE valine

AMINOLEVULINIC ACID [48; 48]
  BT1 amino acids
    BT2 carboxylic acids
      BT3 organic acids
        BT4 organic compounds

AMINOPEPTIDASES [19; 19] *Dec 86*
  BT1 peptide hydrolases
    BT2 hydrolases
      BT3 enzymes
        BT4 organic compounds

aminophenylacetic acid-alpha
  USE phenylalanine

aminopropionic acid-alpha
  USE alanine-alpha

aminopropionic acid-beta
USE alanine-beta

aminopropiophenone-para
USE papp

AMINOPTERIN [12; 12]
BT1 amines
BT2 organic compounds
BT1 antimetabolites
BT2 drugs
BT1 antimitotic drugs
BT2 drugs
BT1 antineoplastic drugs
BT2 drugs
BT1 pteridines
BT2 heterocyclic compounds
BT3 organic compounds
BT2 organic nitrogen compounds
BT3 organic compounds

aminopyrine
USE antipyretics
AND pyrazolines

aminosalicylic acid-para
USE pas

aminosuccinamic acid-alpha
USE asparagine

aminosuccinic acid
USE aspartic acid

aminotoluenes
USE toluidines

AMINOTRANSFERASES [237; 237]
UF *transaminases*
BT1 nitrogen transferases
BT2 transferases
BT3 enzymes
BT4 organic compounds

amipaque
USE metrizamide

AMMETERS [34; 34]
BT1 electric measuring instruments
BT2 electrical equipment
BT3 equipment
BT2 measuring instruments

ammines
(If possible, more specific complexes should be used.)
USE ammonia
AND complexes

AMMONIA [2,994; 2,994]
UF+ *ammines*
BT1 nitrogen hydrides
BT2 hydrides
BT3 hydrogen compounds
BT2 nitrogen compounds
RT ammonolysis
RT refrigerants

AMMONIUM CARBONATES [110; 170]
Nov 78
BT1 ammonium compounds
BT1 carbonates
BT2 carbon compounds
BT2 oxygen compounds
NT1 auc

AMMONIUM CHLORIDES [247; 247]
Apr 78
BT1 ammonium halides
BT2 ammonium compounds
BT2 halides
BT3 halogen compounds
BT1 chlorides
BT2 chlorine compounds
BT3 halogen compounds
BT2 halides
BT3 halogen compounds

AMMONIUM COMPLEXES [37; 37]
Dec 81
BT1 complexes

AMMONIUM COMPOUNDS
[2,362; 3,949]
NT1 ammonium carbonates
NT2 auc
NT1 ammonium halides
NT2 ammonium chlorides
NT2 ammonium fluorides
NT1 ammonium hydroxides
NT1 ammonium nitrates
NT1 ammonium perchlorates
NT1 ammonium phosphates
NT1 ammonium sulfates
NT1 ammonium thiocyanates
NT1 ammonium tungstates
NT1 ammonium uranates
NT2 adu

ammonium diuranate
USE adu

AMMONIUM FLUORIDES [110; 110]
Sep 79
BT1 ammonium halides
BT2 ammonium compounds
BT2 halides
BT3 halogen compounds
BT1 fluorides
BT2 fluorine compounds
BT3 halogen compounds
BT2 halides
BT3 halogen compounds

AMMONIUM HALIDES [29; 261]
Jan 84
BT1 ammonium compounds
BT1 halides
BT2 halogen compounds
NT1 ammonium chlorides
NT1 ammonium fluorides

AMMONIUM HYDROXIDES [222; 222]
BT1 ammonium compounds
BT1 hydroxides
BT2 hydrogen compounds
BT2 oxygen compounds

AMMONIUM NITRATES [264; 264]
Nov 75
BT1 ammonium compounds
BT1 nitrates
BT2 nitrogen compounds
BT2 oxygen compounds

AMMONIUM PERCHLORATES [3; 3]
Apr 89
BT1 ammonium compounds
BT1 perchlorates
BT2 chlorine compounds
BT3 halogen compounds
BT2 oxygen compounds

AMMONIUM PHOSPHATES [61; 61]
Feb 81
BT1 ammonium compounds
BT1 phosphates
BT2 oxygen compounds
BT2 phosphorus compounds

AMMONIUM SULFATES [325; 325]
Mar 77
BT1 ammonium compounds
BT1 sulfates
BT2 oxygen compounds
BT2 sulfur compounds

→ AMMONIUM THIOCYANATES [0; 0]
Sep 91
BT1 ammonium compounds
BT1 thiocyanates
BT2 antithyroid drugs
BT3 drugs
BT2 carbonic acid derivatives
BT3 organic compounds
BT2 organic sulfur compounds
BT3 organic compounds

AMMONIUM TUNGSTATES [31; 31]
Jul 78
BT1 ammonium compounds
BT1 tungstates
BT2 oxygen compounds
BT2 tungsten compounds
BT3 transition element compounds

AMMONIUM URANATES [106; 199]
BT1 ammonium compounds
BT1 uranates
BT2 uranium compounds
BT3 actinide compounds
NT1 adu

ammonium uranyl carbonate
USE auc

AMMONOLYSIS [31; 31]
BT1 solvolysis
BT2 decomposition
BT3 chemical reactions
RT ammonia

amnion
USE fetal membranes

amnion cells
USE embryonic cells

AMNIOTIC FLUID [88; 88] Oct 75
BT1 body fluids
BT2 biological materials
BT3 materials
RT embryos
RT fetuses

amobarbital
USE amytal

AMOEBA [76; 76]
UF *ameba*
BT1 protozoa
BT2 invertebrates
BT3 animals
BT2 microorganisms
RT phagocytosis

AMOEBA EFFECT [50; 50]
(Unidirectional migration and penetration of the fuel kernel through the particle coating, caused by thermal stresses occurring in the course of irradiation.)
UF *migration (kernel)*
RT coated fuel particles
RT failures
RT physical radiation effects
RT reliability

AMORPHOUS STATE [7,141; 7,141]
RT crystallization
RT metallic glasses

AMOUYAL-BENOIST-HOROWITZ METHO [0; 0]
   RT   neutron transport theory

AMP [833; 833]
   UF   *adenosine monophosphate*
   UF   *adenylic acid*
   UF   *camp*
   UF   *cyclic adenosine monophosphate*
   BT1 nucleotides
      BT2 organic compounds
   RT   adenines

AMP BEAM CURRENTS [781; 781]
   (From 1 to 1000 amp.)
   BT1 beam currents
      BT2 currents

AMPEROMETRY [242; 242]
   BT1 titration
   RT   quantitative chemical analysis

amphetamine
   USE benzedrine

AMPHETAMINES [323; 496] *Mar 85*
   BT1 amines
      BT2 organic compounds
   BT1 analeptics
      BT2 central nervous system agents
         BT3 drugs
   BT1 sympathomimetics
      BT2 autonomic nervous system agent
         BT3 drugs
   NT1 benzedrine

AMPHIBIANS [87; 504]
   UF+ *tadpoles*
   BT1 aquatic organisms
   BT1 vertebrates
      BT2 animals
   NT1 frogs
   NT1 salamanders
      NT2 axolotl
      NT2 triturus
   RT   larvae

AMPHIBOLE [65; 163]
   BT1 silicate minerals
      BT2 minerals
   NT1 hornblende

AMPLIFICATION [223; 1,191] *Dec 85*
   NT1 gain
   RT   amplifiers
   RT   amplitudes
   RT   fluidic devices

AMPLIFIERS [1,146; 17,692]
   BT1 equipment
   NT1 ac amplifiers
   NT1 dc amplifiers
   NT1 dielectric amplifiers
   NT1 gasers
   NT1 high frequency amplifiers
   NT1 lasers
      NT2 chemical lasers
      NT2 dye lasers
      NT2 free electron lasers
      NT2 gas lasers
         NT3 carbon dioxide lasers
         NT3 carbon monoxide lasers
         NT3 excimer lasers
            NT4 krypton fluoride lasers
         NT3 helium-neon lasers
      NT2 solid state lasers
         NT3 neodymium lasers
         NT3 ruby lasers
         NT3 semiconductor lasers
      NT2 x-ray lasers
   NT1 magnetic amplifiers
   NT1 microwave amplifiers
      NT2 masers
   NT1 operational amplifiers
   NT1 parametric amplifiers
   NT1 power amplifiers
   NT1 preamplifiers
   NT1 pulse amplifiers
   NT1 transistor amplifiers
   RT   amplification
   RT   electronic circuits
   RT   electronic equipment
   RT   gain

§§ **AMPLITUDES** [6,551; 23,431]
   NT1 scattering amplitudes
   NT1 transition amplitudes
   NT2 decay amplitudes
   RT   amplification
   RT   dimensions
   RT   mechanical vibrations
   RT   oscillations
   RT   wave propagation

AMSCO [10; 10]
   BT1 organic solvents
      BT2 nonaqueous solvents
         BT3 solvents
   RT   hydrocarbons

amygdalic acid
   USE mandelic acid

amyl acetate
   USE acetic acid esters

amyl alcohols
   USE pentanols

amyl radicals
   USE pentyl radicals

AMYLASE [209; 209]
   UF+ *isoamylase*
   BT1 o-glycosyl hydrolases
      BT2 glycosyl hydrolases
         BT3 hydrolases
            BT4 enzymes
               BT5 organic compounds
   RT   digestion
   RT   pancreas
   RT   saliva

amylum
   USE starch

AMYTAL [2; 2]
   UF   *amobarbital*
   BT1 barbiturates
      BT2 anesthetics
         BT3 central nervous system depress
            BT4 central nervous system agents
               BT5 drugs
      BT2 hypnotics and sedatives
         BT3 central nervous system depress
            BT4 central nervous system agents
               BT5 drugs
   BT2 organic oxygen compounds
      BT3 organic compounds
   BT2 pyrimidines
      BT3 azines
         BT4 heterocyclic compounds
            BT5 organic compounds
         BT4 organic nitrogen compounds
            BT5 organic compounds

ANABOLISM [45; 45]
   BT1 metabolism
   RT   androgens
   RT   biosynthesis
   RT   sth

ANACONDA URANIUM MILL [4; 4]
May 80
   BT1 feed materials plants
      BT2 industrial plants
      BT2 nuclear facilities
   RT   ore processing
   RT   uranium ores

→ **ANADROMOUS FISHES** [0; 2] *Aug 91*
   BT1 fishes
      BT2 aquatic organisms
      BT2 vertebrates
         BT3 animals
   NT1 salmon
   RT   fish passage facilities

ANAEROBIC CONDITIONS [171; 171]
Feb 83
   RT   anaerobic digestion
   RT   biodegradation
   RT   biological radiation effects
   RT   decomposition
   RT   irradiation procedures
   RT   oxygen enhancement ratio

ANAEROBIC DIGESTION [67; 67]
Sep 79
   SF   *microbial processes*
   BT1 bioconversion
   BT1 digestion
   RT   anaerobic conditions
   RT   fermentation
   RT   microorganisms
   RT   sewage sludge
   RT   waste processing

analcime
   USE zeolites

ANALEPTICS [8; 680] *May 84*
   UF   *central nervous system stimula*
   UF   *cns stimulants*
   UF   *stimulants (central nerv syst)*
   BT1 central nervous system agents
      BT2 drugs
   NT1 amphetamines
      NT2 benzedrine
   NT1 caffeine

ANALGESICS [144; 631]
   UF+ *phenacetin*
   BT1 central nervous system depress
      BT2 central nervous system agents
         BT3 drugs
   NT1 acetylsalicylic acid
   NT1 antipyrine
   NT1 codeine
   NT1 heroin
   NT1 morphine
   NT1 pethidine
   NT1 thebaine
   RT   anesthetics
   RT   antipyretics
   RT   hypnotics and sedatives
   RT   narcotics
   RT   pain

ANALOG COMPUTERS [128; 128]
   BT1 computers

analog resonances (isobaric)
   USE isobaric analogs
   AND resonance

analog resonances (strangeness
   USE strangeness analog resonances

analog states
   USE isobaric analogs

ANALOG SYSTEMS [617; 2,937]
- NT1 simulators
- NT2 reactor simulators
- RT analog-to-digital converters
- RT biological models
- RT computers
- RT digital-to-analog converters
- RT electronic circuits
- RT electronic equipment
- RT functional models
- RT real time systems

ANALOG-TO-DIGITAL CONVERTERS [1,569; 1,569]
- UF *converters (analog-digital)*
- BT1 electronic equipment
- BT2 equipment
- RT analog systems
- RT digital systems
- RT digitizers

analysis (activation)
- USE activation analysis

analysis (charged-particle act
- USE charged-particle activation an

analysis (fourier)
- USE fourier analysis

analysis (gas)
- USE gas analysis

analysis (neutron activation)
- USE neutron activation analysis

analysis (normal-mode)
- USE normal-mode analysis

analysis (nuclear reaction)
(Chemical analysis based on detection and analysis of prompt nuclear reaction products.)
- USE nuclear reaction analysis

analysis (photon activation)
- USE photon activation analysis

analysis (qualitative chemical
- USE qualitative chemical analysis

analysis (quantitative chemica
- USE quantitative chemical analysis

analysis (structural chemical)
- USE structural chemical analysis

analysis (thermal)
- USE thermal analysis

ANALYTIC FUNCTIONS [1,909; 1,909]
- BT1 functions
- RT continued fractions
- RT s matrix

§§ **ANALYTICAL SOLUTION** [20,674; 20,674]
(For the procedure only.)
- RT asymptotic solutions
- RT differential equations
- RT finite difference method
- RT galerkin-petrov method
- RT mathematics
- RT numerical solution

analyzers (pulse)
- USE pulse analyzers

analyzing power
- USE polarization-asymmetry ratio

anaphase
- USE mitosis

ANAPHYLAXIS [47; 47]
- RT allergy
- RT biological shock
- RT immunity

ANATOMY [1,943; 1,943]
- SF *morphology*
- BT1 biology
- RT body
- RT physiology

anbn
- USE 1-nitroso-2-naphthol

anchoring
- USE fastening

anchors
- USE fasteners

andco-torrax slagging pyrolysi
- USE slagging pyrolysis process

ANDERSONITE [5; 5]
- BT1 carbonate minerals
- BT2 minerals
- BT1 uranium minerals
- BT2 radioactive minerals
- BT3 minerals
- BT3 radioactive materials
- BT4 materials

ANDES [33; 33]
- UF *cordillera de los andes*
- BT1 mountains

ANDRADITE [3; 3]
- BT1 calcium silicates
- BT2 calcium compounds
- BT3 alkaline earth metal compounds
- BT2 silicates
- BT3 oxygen compounds
- BT3 silicon compounds
- BT1 garnets
- BT2 silicate minerals
- BT3 minerals
- BT1 iron silicates
- BT2 iron compounds
- BT3 transition element compounds
- BT2 silicates
- BT3 oxygen compounds
- BT3 silicon compounds

ANDROGENS [173; 777]
- BT1 androstanes
- BT2 steroids
- BT3 organic compounds
- BT1 steroid hormones
- BT2 hormones
- NT1 androstenedione
- NT1 androsterone
- NT1 dianabol
- NT1 hydroxyandrostenone
- NT1 testosterone
- RT adrenal glands
- RT adrenal hormones
- RT anabolism
- RT antiandrogens
- RT castration

- RT corticosteroids
- RT lh
- RT testes
- RT urinary ketosteroids

ANDROSTANES [26; 796]
- BT1 steroids
- BT2 organic compounds
- NT1 androgens
- NT2 androstenedione
- NT2 androsterone
- NT2 dianabol
- NT2 hydroxyandrostenone
- NT2 testosterone

ANDROSTENEDIONE [85; 85]
- BT1 androgens
- BT2 androstanes
- BT3 steroids
- BT4 organic compounds
- BT2 steroid hormones
- BT3 hormones
- BT1 ketones
- BT2 organic compounds

ANDROSTERONE [36; 36]
- BT1 androgens
- BT2 androstanes
- BT3 steroids
- BT4 organic compounds
- BT2 steroid hormones
- BT3 hormones
- BT1 hydroxy compounds
- BT2 organic compounds
- BT1 ketones
- BT2 organic compounds

ANEMIAS [612; 3,017]
- UF *aplastic anemia*
- UF *pernicious anemia*
- BT1 hemic diseases
- BT2 diseases
- BT1 symptoms
- NT1 ischemia
- NT1 megaloblastic anemia
- NT1 sickle cell anemia
- NT1 thalassemia
- RT erythrocytes
- RT folic acid
- RT hemoglobin
- RT hemolysis
- RT hemorrhage
- RT intrinsic factor
- RT vitamin b-12

ANEMOMETERS [154; 221]
- BT1 measuring instruments
- NT1 hot wire anemometers
- RT flowmeters

ANESTHESIA [177; 177]
- RT anesthetics
- RT medicine
- RT pain
- RT surgery

ANESTHETICS [176; 373]
- BT1 central nervous system depress
- BT2 central nervous system agents
- BT3 drugs
- NT1 barbiturates
- NT2 amytal
- NT2 nembutal
- NT2 phenobarbital
- NT2 thiopental
- NT1 cocaine
- NT1 procaine
- RT analgesics
- RT anesthesia
- RT hypnotics and sedatives
- RT narcotics

ANEUPLOIDY [83; 83]
- BT1 ploidy
- RT genome mutations
- RT non-disjunction

ANEX REACTOR [2; 2]
UF   *cfg reactor*
BT1   enriched uranium reactors
BT2   reactors
BT1   hydride moderated reactors
BT2   reactors
BT1   solid homogeneous reactors
BT2   homogeneous reactors
BT3   reactors
BT1   thermal reactors
BT2   reactors
BT1   zero power reactors
BT2   experimental reactors
BT3   research and test reactors
BT4   reactors

ANGARA-5 DEVICE [18; 18] *Aug 84*
BT1   icf devices
BT2   thermonuclear devices

angiography
USE   biomedical radiography
AND   blood vessels

ANGIOMAS [547; 547]
UF   *hemangiomas*
BT1   neoplasms
BT2   diseases
RT   blood vessels
RT   lymph vessels

ANGIOTENSIN [340; 340]
BT1   globulins
BT2   proteins
BT3   organic compounds
BT1   vasoconstrictors
BT2   cardiovascular agents
BT3   drugs

angle (incidence)
USE   incidence angle

angle of incidence
USE   incidence angle

ANGOLA [9; 9]
BT1   africa
BT1   developing countries

ANGRA-1 REACTOR [294; 294]
(Angra Dosreis, Rio de Janeiro, Brazil)
BT1   pwr type reactors
BT2   enriched uranium reactors
BT3   reactors
BT2   power reactors
BT3   reactors
BT2   thermal reactors
BT3   reactors
BT2   water cooled reactors
BT3   reactors
BT2   water moderated reactors
BT3   reactors

ANGRA-2 REACTOR [94; 94] *Jun 77*
(Angra Dosreis, Rio de Janeiro, Brazil)
BT1   pwr type reactors
BT2   enriched uranium reactors
BT3   reactors
BT2   power reactors
BT3   reactors
BT2   thermal reactors
BT3   reactors
BT2   water cooled reactors
BT3   reactors
BT2   water moderated reactors
BT3   reactors

ANGRA-3 REACTOR [42; 42] *Jun 77*
(Angra Dosreis, Rio de Janeiro, Brazil)
BT1   pwr type reactors
BT2   enriched uranium reactors
BT3   reactors
BT2   power reactors
BT3   reactors
BT2   thermal reactors
BT3   reactors
BT2   water cooled reactors
BT3   reactors
BT2   water moderated reactors
BT3   reactors

ANGULAR CORRELATION
[6,124; 8,076]
UF   *directional correlation*
BT1   correlations
NT1   perturbed angular correlation
NT2   differential pac
NT2   integral pac
RT   abragam-pound theory
RT   angular distribution
RT   biedenharn-rose theory
RT   decay
RT   particle kinematics

§§ **ANGULAR DISTRIBUTION**
[40,307; 40,307]
BT1   distribution
RT   abragam-pound theory
RT   angular correlation
RT   backscattering
RT   biedenharn-rose theory
RT   blatt-biedenharn formalism
RT   castagnoli formula
RT   differential cross sections
RT   emission
RT   halpern-strutinski theory
RT   incidence angle
RT   lambert law
RT   marshak boundary conditions
RT   milne problem
RT   minami ambiguity
RT   small angle scattering
RT   spatial distribution
RT   transverse energy
RT   yang theorem

ANGULAR MOMENTUM [7,428; 34,190]
UF   *momentum (angular)*
NT1   orbital angular momentum
NT1   spin
RT   angular momentum operators
RT   backbending
RT   chirality
RT   clebsch-gordan coefficients
RT   d waves
RT   f waves
RT   gyroelectric ratio
RT   gyromagnetic ratio
RT   helicity
RT   kinetic energy
RT   linear momentum
RT   motion
RT   p waves
RT   partial waves
RT   quantum mechanics
RT   racah coefficients
RT   s waves
RT   wigner coefficients
RT   yrast states

ANGULAR MOMENTUM OPERATORS
[368; 853]
BT1   quantum operators
BT2   mathematical operators
NT1   orbital momentum operators
NT1   pauli spin operators
RT   angular momentum

ANGULAR MOMENTUM TRANSFER
[537; 537] *Sep 78*
UF   *transfer (angular momentum)*
BT1   momentum transfer
RT   energy transfer

ANGULAR VELOCITY [727; 727]
BT1   velocity

ANHARMONIC CRYSTALS [254; 254]
BT1   crystals
RT   coherent scattering
RT   inelastic scattering
RT   lattice vibrations

ANHARMONIC OSCILLATORS
[376; 376] *Aug 81*
RT   equations of motion
RT   harmonic oscillators
RT   mathematics
RT   mechanics

ANHYDRIDES [234; 234]
RT   bases
RT   inorganic acids
RT   organic acids
RT   water

ANHYDRITE [71; 71] *Oct 82*
(Mineral consisting of an anhydrous calcium sulfate.)
BT1   sulfate minerals
BT2   minerals
RT   calcium sulfates
RT   gypsum

ANILINE [312; 312]
UF   *aminobenzene*
UF   *phenylamine*
BT1   amines
BT2   organic compounds
BT1   aromatics
BT2   organic compounds
RT   benzene

ANIMAL BREEDING [189; 264]
NT1   mass rearing
RT   agriculture
RT   domestic animals
RT   nests
RT   nutrition
RT   progeny

ANIMAL CELLS [5,460; 25,441]
(Includes human cells)
UF   *cells (animal)*
UF   *human cells*
UF+   *cell growth (animal)*
UF+   *melanocytes*
UF+   *pigment cells*
NT1   embryonic cells
NT1   hair follicles
NT1   hybridomas
NT1   somatic cells
NT2   cho cells
NT2   connective tissue cells
NT3   bone cells
NT3   bone marrow cells
NT3   fat cells
NT3   fibroblasts
NT3   lymphocytes
NT3   macrophages
NT3   mast cells
NT3   plasma cells
NT2   crypt cells
NT2   liver cells
NT2   nerve cells
NT2   phagocytes
NT3   macrophages
NT2   respiratory tract cells
NT2   spleen cells
NT2   stem cells
NT2   thymocytes
NT2   thymus cells
NT2   thyroid cells
NT1   tumor cells
NT2   ascites tumor cells
NT2   hela cells
NT1   xp cells
RT   cell constituents
RT   cell cultures
RT   cell flow systems
RT   clone cells
RT   colony formation
RT   cytology
RT   homogenates
RT   intracellular digestion

ANIMAL FEEDS [515; 754]
- UF *fodder*
- BT1 food
- NT1 forage
- RT diet
- RT nutrition

ANIMAL GROWTH [566; 566]
- BT1 growth
- RT adults
- RT animals
- RT molting
- RT rearing

animal tissues
- USE tissues

ANIMALS [1,226; 81,930]
- NT1 domestic animals
  - NT2 cattle
    - NT3 calves
    - NT3 cows
  - NT2 goats
  - NT2 sheep
  - NT2 swine
    - NT3 miniature swine
- NT1 germ-free animals
- NT1 invertebrates
  - NT2 annelids
  - NT2 arthropods
    - NT3 arachnids
      - NT4 mites
      - NT4 scorpions
      - NT4 spiders
      - NT4 ticks
    - NT3 crustaceans
      - NT4 artemia
      - NT4 daphnia
      - NT4 lobsters
      - NT4 prawns
      - NT4 shrimp
    - NT3 insects
      - NT4 beetles
        - NT5 boll weevil
        - NT5 tribolium
      - NT4 cockroaches
      - NT4 flies
        - NT5 fruit flies
          - NT6 ceratitis capitata
          - NT6 dacus
            - NT7 dacus oleae
          - NT6 drosophila
          - NT6 rhagoletis cerasi
        - NT5 glossina
        - NT5 hylemya antiqua
        - NT5 screwworm fly
      - NT4 grasshoppers
        - NT5 locusts
      - NT4 hemiptera
        - NT5 aphids
      - NT4 lepidoptera
        - NT5 moths
          - NT6 bollworm
          - NT6 codling moth
          - NT6 lymantria dispar
          - NT6 rice stem borers
          - NT6 silkworm
      - NT4 mosquitoes
      - NT4 wasps
        - NT5 habrobracon
  - NT2 coelenterata
    - NT3 cnidaria
      - NT4 corals
      - NT4 hydra
  - NT2 echinoderms
    - NT3 sea urchins
  - NT2 molluscs
    - NT3 clams
    - NT3 oysters
    - NT3 snails
  - NT2 nematodes
    - NT3 ascaridae
      - NT4 ascaris
    - NT3 dictyocaulus
    - NT3 hookworm
    - NT3 nippostrongylus
    - NT3 syngamus
    - NT3 trichinella
  - NT2 platyhelminths
    - NT3 cestodes
      - NT4 hymenolepis
    - NT3 trematodes
      - NT4 fasciola
      - NT4 schistosoma
    - NT3 turbellaria
      - NT4 planaria
  - NT2 protozoa
    - NT3 amoeba
    - NT3 babesidae
    - NT3 dinoflagellate
    - NT3 paramecium
    - NT3 plasmodium
    - NT3 tetrahymena
    - NT3 trypanosoma
- NT1 laboratory animals
- NT1 neonates
- NT1 vertebrates
  - NT2 amphibians
    - NT3 frogs
    - NT3 salamanders
      - NT4 axolotl
      - NT4 triturus
  - NT2 birds
    - NT3 fowl
      - NT4 chickens
      - NT4 ducks
    - NT3 pigeons
  - NT2 fishes
    - NT3 anadromous fishes
      - NT4 salmon
    - NT3 codfish
    - NT3 eel
    - NT3 goldfish
    - NT3 plaice
    - NT3 trout
    - NT3 tuna
  - NT2 mammals
    - NT3 burros
    - NT3 cats
    - NT3 cetaceans
    - NT3 dogs
      - NT4 beagles
    - NT3 horses
    - NT3 marsupials
    - NT3 pikas
    - NT3 primates
      - NT4 apes
      - NT4 man
        - NT5 children
          - NT6 infants
        - NT5 elderly people
        - NT5 men
        - NT5 patients
        - NT5 women
      - NT4 monkeys
        - NT5 baboons
        - NT5 macacus
    - NT3 rabbits
    - NT3 rodents
      - NT4 chipmunks
      - NT4 gerbils
      - NT4 guinea pigs
      - NT4 hamsters
      - NT4 mice
      - NT4 rats
      - NT4 squirrels
      - NT4 voles
    - NT3 ruminants
      - NT4 antelopes
      - NT4 buffalo
      - NT4 cattle
        - NT5 calves
        - NT5 cows
      - NT4 deer
      - NT4 goats
      - NT4 llamas
      - NT4 sheep
    - NT3 shrews
    - NT3 swine
      - NT4 miniature swine
  - NT2 reptiles
    - NT3 lizards
    - NT3 snakes
    - NT3 turtles
- NT1 wild animals
- RT animal growth
- RT aquatic organisms
- RT biological materials
- RT biology
- RT endangered species
- RT females
- RT males
- RT symbiosis
- RT translocation
- RT veterinary medicine

ANIONS [5,246; 7,143]
- UF *negative ions*
- UF+ *hydroxyl ions*
- BT1 ions
  - BT2 charged particles
- NT1 heteropolyanions
- NT1 hydrogen ions 1 minus
- RT chemical state
- RT electrolysis
- RT ion beams
- RT ion exchange materials

ANISOLE [81; 81]
- UF *methoxybenzene*
- UF *methyl phenyl ether*
- UF *phenyl methyl ether*
- BT1 ethers
  - BT2 organic oxygen compounds
  - BT3 organic compounds

ANISOTROPY [12,028; 12,028]
- RT asymmetry
- RT configuration
- RT distribution
- RT isotropy
- RT mass distribution
- RT orientation
- RT sherman tables
- RT transverse energy

ANISYL RADICALS [1; 1]
- BT1 aryl radicals
- BT2 radicals

ankylosing spondylitis
- USE spondylitis

ANL [795; 795]
- UF *argonne national laboratory*
- BT1 us aec
  - BT2 us organizations
  - BT3 national organizations
- BT1 us doe
  - BT2 us organizations
  - BT3 national organizations
- BT1 us erda
  - BT2 us organizations
  - BT3 national organizations
- RT illinois

anl zero power res. reactor-3
- USE zpr-3 reactor

anl zero power res. reactor-6
- USE zpr-6 reactor

anl zero power res. reactor-9
- USE zpr-9 reactor

anmr
- USE acoustic nmr

ANNA REACTOR [6; 6]
(Institute of Nuclear Research, Swierk, Poland)
- UF *swierk anna reactor*
- BT1 enriched uranium reactors
  - BT2 reactors
- BT1 graphite moderated reactors
  - BT2 reactors
- BT1 research reactors
  - BT2 research and test reactors
    - BT3 reactors
- BT1 thermal reactors

  BT2 reactors
  BT1 water cooled reactors
  BT2 reactors
  BT1 water moderated reactors
  BT2 reactors
  BT1 zero power reactors
  BT2 experimental reactors
   BT3 research and test reactors
    BT4 reactors

ANNEALING [16,714; 16,714]
  BT1 heat treatments
  RT recrystallization
  RT stress relaxation

ANNELIDS [108; 108]
  UF *worms (segmented)*
  BT1 invertebrates
  BT2 animals

ANNIE EVENT [3; 3] *Feb 82*
  BT1 atmospheric explosions
  BT2 explosions
  BT1 nuclear explosions
  BT2 explosions
  BT1 upshot project

ANNIHILATION [13,221; 13,221]
  SF *disintegration (nuclear part.)*
  BT1 particle interactions
  BT2 interactions
  RT electromagnetic interactions
  RT gribov-lipatov relation
  RT strong interactions

ANNIHILATION OPERATORS
[1,388; 1,388]
  UF+ *coherent states*
  BT1 quantum operators
  BT2 mathematical operators
  RT second quantization
  RT vacuum states

ANNUAL LIMIT OF INTAKE [91; 91]
Apr 85
(The greatest value of the annual intake of a given radionuclide which corresponds to a whole-body dose commitment of less than or equal to 5 rem and tissue dose commitment of less than or equal to 50 rem.)
  UF *ali*
  BT1 safety standards
  BT2 standards
  RT critical organs
  RT intake
  RT radioactivity

§§ **ANNUAL VARIATIONS** [485; 485]
  BT1 variations

annular core pulse reactor
  USE acpr reactor

ANNULAR FUEL ELEMENTS
[133; 133]
  BT1 fuel elements
  BT2 reactor components
  RT fuel washers

ANNULAR SPACE [939; 5,360]
  BT1 configuration
  NT1 toroidal configuration
  RT tori

ANODES [2,382; 2,382]
  BT1 electrodes
  RT thermionic collectors

ANODIZATION [377; 377]
  BT1 corrosion protection
  BT1 electrochemical coating
  BT2 chemical coating
   BT3 surface coating
    BT4 deposition
  BT1 electrolysis

ANOMALONS [164; 164] *Oct 84*
(Projectile fragments from relativistic heavy ion reactions with anomalously short mean free paths.)
  BT1 nuclear fragments
  RT heavy ion reactions
  RT mean free path

ANOMALOUS DIMENSION [545; 545]
  UF *non-canonical dimension*
  UF *noncanonical dimension*
  BT1 scale dimension

anopheles
  USE mosquitoes

ANOREXIA [34; 34]
  RT digestive system
  RT digestive system diseases

ANORTHOSITES [72; 72]
  BT1 plutonic rocks
  BT2 igneous rocks
   BT3 rocks
  RT feldspars
  RT lunar materials
  RT olivine

ANOXIA [1,991; 1,991]
  UF *hypoxia*
  RT biological stress
  RT ischemia
  RT oxidation
  RT respiration

ANSTO [103; 104] *Oct 88*
(Australian Nuclear Science and Technology Organization, created on 27 April 1987 and replacing the AAEC.)
  BT1 australian organizations
  BT2 national organizations
  NT1 aaec

ANTARCTIC REGIONS [174; 486]
  BT1 polar regions
  NT1 antarctica
  RT arctic regions
  RT auroral zones
  RT climates
  RT glaciers
  RT ice
  RT polar-cap aurorae
  RT snow

ANTARCTICA [313; 313]
  BT1 antarctic regions
  BT2 polar regions

ANTARES FACILITY [84; 84] *Sep 79*
(Large CO2 laser facility to be used at Los Alamos for laser fusion.)
  RT aurora facility
  RT carbon dioxide lasers
  RT helios facility
  RT lanl
  RT laser fusion reactors
  RT lasl

ANTELOPES [10; 10]
  BT1 ruminants
  BT2 mammals
   BT3 vertebrates
    BT4 animals

ANTENNAS [1,884; 2,129]
  BT1 electrical equipment
  BT2 equipment
  RT radio equipment

anthers
  USE stamen

anthonomus grandis
  USE boll weevil

ANTHRACENE [341; 341]
  BT1 condensed aromatics
  BT2 aromatics
   BT3 organic compounds
  BT1 hydrocarbons
  BT2 organic compounds
  RT anthraquinones
  RT organic crystal phosphors
  RT plastic scintillators

ANTHRACITE [34; 34]
  SF *hard coal*
  BT1 black coal
  BT2 coal
   BT3 carbonaceous materials
    BT4 materials
   BT3 fossil fuels
    BT4 energy sources
    BT4 fuels

ANTHRANILIC ACID [54; 54]
  UF *aminobenzoic acid-ortho*
  BT1 amino acids
  BT2 carboxylic acids
   BT3 organic acids
    BT4 organic compounds

ANTHRAQUINONES [125; 213]
  BT1 quinones
  BT2 aromatics
   BT3 organic compounds
  BT2 organic oxygen compounds
   BT3 organic compounds
  NT1 alizarin
  NT1 carminic acid
  NT1 quinizarin
  RT anthracene
  RT dyes

anthraquinonic acid
  USE alizarin

ANTI-B NEUTRAL MESONS [169; 169]
Dec 87
  BT1 antiparticles
  BT2 antimatter
   BT3 matter
  BT2 elementary particles
  BT1 b neutral mesons
  BT2 b mesons
   BT3 beauty particles
    BT4 elementary particles
   BT3 pseudoscalar mesons
    BT4 mesons
     BT5 bosons
     BT5 hadrons
      BT6 elementary particles

ANTI-D NEUTRAL MESONS [35; 35]
Dec 87
  BT1 antiparticles
  BT2 antimatter
   BT3 matter
  BT2 elementary particles
  BT1 d neutral mesons
  BT2 d mesons
   BT3 charmed mesons
    BT4 charm particles
     BT5 elementary particles
    BT4 mesons
     BT5 bosons
     BT5 hadrons
      BT6 elementary particles
   BT3 pseudoscalar mesons
    BT4 mesons
     BT5 bosons
     BT5 hadrons
      BT6 elementary particles

ANTIANDROGENS [7; 7] *Sep 79*
- BT1 drugs
- RT androgens
- RT biochemistry
- RT chemotherapy
- RT pharmacology
- RT physiology

ANTIBARYONS [187; 3,128]
- BT1 antiparticles
- BT2 antimatter
- BT3 matter
- BT2 elementary particles
- BT1 baryons
- BT2 fermions
- BT2 hadrons
- BT3 elementary particles
- NT1 antihyperons
- NT2 antilambda particles
- NT2 antiomega particles
- NT2 antisigma particles
- NT2 antixi particles
- NT1 antinucleons
- NT2 antineutrons
- NT2 antiprotons

ANTIBIOTICS [887; 3,247]
- UF *antimicrobial agents*
- UF *neomycin*
- BT1 drugs
- BT1 organic compounds
- NT1 actinomycin
- NT1 antimycin
- NT1 bleomycin
- NT1 chloramphenicol
- NT1 cinchonine
- NT1 cycloheximide
- NT1 doxorubicin
- NT1 erythromycin
- NT1 fudr
- NT1 isoniazid
- NT2 iproniazid
- NT1 methylene blue
- NT1 mitomycin
- NT1 neocarcinostatin
- NT1 pas
- NT1 penicillin
- NT1 puromycin
- NT1 quinine
- NT1 streptomycin
- NT1 sulfonamides
- NT2 sulfadiazine
- NT1 tetracyclines
- NT2 chlortetracycline
- NT2 oxytetracycline
- NT1 valinomycin
- RT antimitotic drugs
- RT bacterial diseases
- RT infectious diseases
- RT microorganisms
- RT mutagens

ANTIBODIES [2,818; 5,641]
- NT1 antitoxins
- NT1 monoclonal antibodies
- NT1 precipitins
- RT agglutinins
- RT antigen-antibody reactions
- RT complement
- RT enzyme immunoassay
- RT hemagglutinins
- RT hemolysins
- RT immune serums
- RT immunity
- RT lectins
- RT radioimmunoassay
- RT radioimmunodetection
- RT toxoids

ANTIBODY FORMATION [364; 364]
- RT antigen-antibody reactions
- RT germ-free animals
- RT immunity

ANTICOAGULANTS [109; 797]
- BT1 hematologic agents
- BT2 drugs
- NT1 coumarin
- NT1 dicumarol
- NT1 heparin
- NT1 psoralen
- NT1 tromexan
- RT blood coagulation
- RT vitamin k

ANTICOINCIDENCE [482; 482]
(Detector arrangement.)
- RT coincidence circuits
- RT counting techniques

ANTICONVULSANTS [47; 111] *May 84*
- BT1 central nervous system depress
- BT2 central nervous system agents
- BT3 drugs
- NT1 phenobarbital

anticorrosion
- USE corrosion protection

ANTIDEPRESSANTS [90; 180] *May 84*
- BT1 psychotropic drugs
- BT2 central nervous system agents
- BT3 drugs
- NT1 cocaine
- NT1 imipramine
- NT1 iproniazid

ANTIDEUTERON REACTIONS [5; 5]
Nov 88
- BT1 deuteron reactions
- BT2 nuclear reactions
- RT antideuterons

ANTIDEUTERONS [93; 93]
- BT1 antinuclei
- BT2 antimatter
- BT3 matter
- BT2 nuclei
- BT1 deuterons
- BT2 charged particles
- RT antideuteron reactions

antidiuretic hormone
- USE vasopressin

ANTIFERROELECTRIC MATERIALS
[109; 109]
- BT1 dielectric materials
- BT2 materials
- RT ferroelectric materials

ANTIFERROMAGNETIC MATERIALS
[1,295; 1,295]
- BT1 magnetic materials
- BT2 materials
- RT ferromagnetic materials
- RT kondo effect

ANTIFERROMAGNETISM [2,306; 2,306]
- BT1 magnetism
- RT ferrimagnetism
- RT ferromagnetism
- RT neel temperature

ANTIFOULANTS [6; 6] *Dec 85*
(Materials which prevent formation and/or deposition of foulants, e.g., on heat transfer surfaces or equipment.)
- RT corrosion
- RT deposits
- RT fouling

ANTIGEN-ANTIBODY REACTIONS
[1,578; 1,578]
- UF *agglutination*
- RT antibodies
- RT antibody formation
- RT antigens

- RT complement
- RT cpb
- RT enzyme immunoassay
- RT graft-host reaction
- RT immune reactions
- RT immunity
- RT lectins
- RT radioimmunoassay

ANTIGENS [2,370; 3,760]
- NT1 carcinoembryonic antigen
- NT1 toxins
- NT2 aflatoxins
- NT2 endotoxins
- NT1 tuberculin
- RT antigen-antibody reactions
- RT enzyme immunoassay
- RT freunds adjuvant
- RT immunity
- RT lectins
- RT radioimmunoassay
- RT vaccines

ANTIHISTAMINICS [65; 65]
- UF+ *promethazine*
- BT1 drugs
- RT allergy
- RT histamine

ANTIHYPERONS [45; 595]
- BT1 antibaryons
- BT2 antiparticles
- BT3 antimatter
- BT4 matter
- BT3 elementary particles
- BT2 baryons
- BT3 fermions
- BT3 hadrons
- BT4 elementary particles
- BT1 hyperons
- BT2 baryons
- BT3 fermions
- BT3 hadrons
- BT4 elementary particles
- BT2 strange particles
- BT3 elementary particles
- NT1 antilambda particles
- NT1 antiomega particles
- NT1 antisigma particles
- NT1 antixi particles

ANTIHYPERTENSIVE AGENTS
[105; 129] *May 84*
- BT1 cardiovascular agents
- BT2 drugs
- NT1 guanethidine
- NT1 reserpine

ANTIKAONS [256; 1,558]
- BT1 antiparticles
- BT2 antimatter
- BT3 matter
- BT2 elementary particles
- BT1 kaons
- BT2 pseudoscalar mesons
- BT3 mesons
- BT4 bosons
- BT4 hadrons
- BT5 elementary particles
- BT2 strange mesons
- BT3 mesons
- BT4 bosons
- BT4 hadrons
- BT5 elementary particles
- BT3 strange particles
- BT4 elementary particles
- NT1 antikaons neutral

ANTIKAONS NEUTRAL [701; 701]
- BT1 antikaons
- BT2 antiparticles
- BT3 antimatter
- BT4 matter
- BT3 elementary particles
- BT2 kaons
- BT3 pseudoscalar mesons
- BT4 mesons
- BT5 bosons

```
        BT5     hadrons
          BT6    elementary particles
      BT3   strange mesons
        BT4   mesons
          BT5    bosons
          BT5    hadrons
            BT6   elementary particles
        BT4   strange particles
          BT5    elementary particles
  BT1    kaons neutral
    BT2    kaons
      BT3    pseudoscalar mesons
        BT4    mesons
          BT5    bosons
          BT5    hadrons
            BT6   elementary particles
      BT3    strange mesons
        BT4    mesons
          BT5    bosons
          BT5    hadrons
            BT6   elementary particles
        BT4    strange particles
          BT5    elementary particles
```

ANTILAMBDA PARTICLES [507; 507]
```
  BT1    antihyperons
    BT2    antibaryons
      BT3    antiparticles
        BT4    antimatter
          BT5    matter
        BT4    elementary particles
      BT3    baryons
        BT4    fermions
        BT4    hadrons
          BT5    elementary particles
    BT2    hyperons
      BT3    baryons
        BT4    fermions
        BT4    hadrons
          BT5    elementary particles
      BT3    strange particles
        BT4    elementary particles
  BT1    lambda particles
    BT2    lambda baryons
      BT3    hyperons
        BT4    baryons
          BT5    fermions
          BT5    hadrons
            BT6    elementary particles
        BT4    strange particles
          BT5    elementary particles
```

ANTILEPTON-NEUTRON INTERACTION [1; 71] Jan 77
```
  BT1    lepton-neutron interactions
    BT2    lepton-nucleon interactions
      BT3    lepton-baryon interactions
        BT4    lepton-hadron interactions
          BT5    particle interactions
            BT6    interactions
  NT1    antineutrino-neutron interacti
```

ANTILEPTON-PROTON INTERACTIONS [5; 399]
```
  BT1    lepton-proton interactions
    BT2    lepton-nucleon interactions
      BT3    lepton-baryon interactions
        BT4    lepton-hadron interactions
          BT5    particle interactions
            BT6    interactions
  NT1    antineutrino-proton interactio
```

ANTILEPTONS [239; 12,167]
```
  BT1    antiparticles
    BT2    antimatter
      BT3    matter
    BT2    elementary particles
  BT1    leptons
    BT2    elementary particles
    BT2    fermions
  NT1    antineutrinos
    NT2    electron antineutrinos
    NT2    muon antineutrinos
  NT1    muons plus
  NT1    positrons
    NT2    cosmic positrons
```

ANTIMATTER [304; 22,689]
```
  BT1    matter
  NT1    antinuclei
    NT2    antideuterons
    NT2    antiprotons
    NT2    antitritons
  NT1    antiparticles
    NT2    anti-b neutral mesons
    NT2    anti-d neutral mesons
    NT2    antibaryons
      NT3    antihyperons
        NT4    antilambda particles
        NT4    antiomega particles
        NT4    antisigma particles
        NT4    antixi particles
      NT3    antinucleons
        NT4    antineutrons
        NT4    antiprotons
    NT2    antikaons
      NT3    antikaons neutral
    NT2    antileptons
      NT3    antineutrinos
        NT4    electron antineutrinos
        NT4    muon antineutrinos
      NT3    muons plus
      NT3    positrons
        NT4    cosmic positrons
  RT     ambiplasma
```

antimesons
(Prior to December 1987 this was a valid descriptor.)
```
  USE    antiparticles
  AND    mesons
```

ANTIMETABOLITES [134; 1,974]
```
  UF     azaguanine
  BT1    drugs
  NT1    adenines
    NT2    kinetin
  NT1    aminopterin
  NT1    bromouracils
    NT2    budr
  NT1    deoxyuridine
  NT1    ethionine
  NT1    fluorodeoxyglucose
  NT1    fluorouracils
    NT2    fudr
  NT1    iodouracils
    NT2    iododeoxyuridine
  NT1    mercaptopurine
  NT1    methotrexate
  NT1    thiouracil
  RT     alkylating agents
  RT     chemosterilants
  RT     synchronization
  RT     synchronous cultures
```

antimicrobial agents
```
  USE    antibiotics
```

ANTIMITOTIC DRUGS [417; 3,291]
```
  UF     cytostatics
  BT1    drugs
  NT1    actinomycin
  NT1    alkylating agents
    NT2    endoxan
    NT2    myleran
    NT2    nitrogen mustard
  NT1    aminopterin
  NT1    bleomycin
  NT1    colchicine
  NT1    mitomycin
  NT1    nem
  NT1    oncovin
  NT1    vinblastine
  RT     antibiotics
  RT     antineoplastic drugs
  RT     immunosuppression
  RT     mitosis
  RT     mutagens
  RT     neocarcinostatin
  RT     neoplasms
  RT     radiomimetic drugs
  RT     radiosensitizers
```

ANTIMONATES [47; 47] Sep 79
(Specific compounds should be indexed by coordination of a descriptor of the form (CATION) COMPOUNDS and the above anion descriptor.)
```
  BT1    antimony compounds
  BT1    oxygen compounds
  RT     antimony oxides
```

ANTIMONIDES [839; 879] Aug 78
(Specific compounds should be indexed by coordination of a descriptor of the form (CATION) COMPOUNDS and the above anion descriptor.)
```
  BT1    antimony compounds
  BT1    pnictides
  NT1    indium antimonides
  RT     antimony additions
  RT     antimony alloys
  RT     intermetallic compounds
```

ANTIMONY [1,561; 1,561]
```
  BT1    metals
    BT2    elements
```

ANTIMONY ADDITIONS [223; 223]
(Alloys containing not more than 1% Sb are listed here.)
```
  RT     antimonides
  RT     antimony alloys
  RT     antimony compounds
```

ANTIMONY ALLOYS [1,027; 1,063]
(Alloys containing more than 1% Sb.)
```
  BT1    alloys
  NT1    antimony base alloys
  RT     antimonides
  RT     antimony additions
```

ANTIMONY BASE ALLOYS [28; 28]
```
  BT1    antimony alloys
    BT2    alloys
```

ANTIMONY BORIDES [2; 2]
```
  BT1    antimony compounds
  BT1    borides
    BT2    boron compounds
```

ANTIMONY BROMIDES [12; 12]
```
  BT1    antimony compounds
  BT1    bromides
    BT2    bromine compounds
      BT3    halogen compounds
    BT2    halides
      BT3    halogen compounds
```

ANTIMONY CHLORIDES [71; 71]
```
  BT1    antimony compounds
  BT1    chlorides
    BT2    chlorine compounds
      BT3    halogen compounds
    BT2    halides
      BT3    halogen compounds
```

ANTIMONY COMPLEXES [78; 78]
```
  BT1    complexes
```

ANTIMONY COMPOUNDS [997; 2,708]
```
  NT1    antimonates
  NT1    antimonides
    NT2    indium antimonides
  NT1    antimony borides
  NT1    antimony bromides
  NT1    antimony chlorides
  NT1    antimony fluorides
  NT1    antimony hydrides
  NT1    antimony hydroxides
  NT1    antimony iodides
  NT1    antimony oxides
  NT1    antimony selenides
  NT1    antimony sulfides
  NT1    antimony tellurides
  RT     antimony additions
```

ANTIMONY FLUORIDES [84; 84]
- BT1 antimony compounds
- BT1 fluorides
  - BT2 fluorine compounds
    - BT3 halogen compounds
  - BT2 halides
    - BT3 halogen compounds

ANTIMONY HYDRIDES [15; 15]
- BT1 antimony compounds
- BT1 hydrides
  - BT2 hydrogen compounds

ANTIMONY HYDROXIDES [17; 17]
- BT1 antimony compounds
- BT1 hydroxides
  - BT2 hydrogen compounds
  - BT2 oxygen compounds

ANTIMONY IODIDES [97; 97]
- BT1 antimony compounds
- BT1 iodides
  - BT2 halides
    - BT3 halogen compounds
  - BT2 iodine compounds
    - BT3 halogen compounds

ANTIMONY IONS [238; 238]
- BT1 ions
  - BT2 charged particles

ANTIMONY ISOTOPES [158; 1,751]
- NT1 antimony 106
- NT1 antimony 108
- NT1 antimony 109
- NT1 antimony 110
- NT1 antimony 111
- NT1 antimony 112
- NT1 antimony 113
- NT1 antimony 114
- NT1 antimony 115
- NT1 antimony 116
- NT1 antimony 117
- NT1 antimony 118
- NT1 antimony 119
- NT1 antimony 120
- NT1 antimony 121
- NT1 antimony 122
- NT1 antimony 123
- NT1 antimony 124
- NT1 antimony 125
- NT1 antimony 126
- NT1 antimony 127
- NT1 antimony 128
- NT1 antimony 129
- NT1 antimony 130
- NT1 antimony 131
- NT1 antimony 132
- NT1 antimony 133
- NT1 antimony 134
- NT1 antimony 135
- NT1 antimony 136

ANTIMONY OXIDES [269; 269]
- BT1 antimony compounds
- BT1 oxides
  - BT2 chalcogenides
  - BT2 oxygen compounds
- RT antimonates

ANTIMONY SELENIDES [25; 25]
Nov 79
- BT1 antimony compounds
- BT1 selenides
  - BT2 chalcogenides
  - BT2 selenium compounds

ANTIMONY SULFIDES [151; 151]
- BT1 antimony compounds
- BT1 sulfides
  - BT2 chalcogenides
  - BT2 sulfur compounds

ANTIMONY TELLURIDES [151; 151]
Feb 79
- BT1 antimony compounds
- BT1 tellurides
  - BT2 chalcogenides
  - BT2 tellurium compounds

ANTIMONY 106 [4; 4] Jul 81
- BT1 antimony isotopes
- BT1 intermediate mass nuclei
  - BT2 nuclei
- BT1 odd-odd nuclei
  - BT2 nuclei
- BT1 seconds living radioisotopes
  - BT2 radioisotopes
    - BT3 isotopes

ANTIMONY 108 [3; 3] Jun 77
- BT1 antimony isotopes
- BT1 beta-plus decay radioisotopes
  - BT2 beta decay radioisotopes
    - BT3 radioisotopes
      - BT4 isotopes
- BT1 intermediate mass nuclei
  - BT2 nuclei
- BT1 odd-odd nuclei
  - BT2 nuclei
- BT1 seconds living radioisotopes
  - BT2 radioisotopes
    - BT3 isotopes

ANTIMONY 109 [13; 13]
- BT1 antimony isotopes
- BT1 electron capture radioisotopes
  - BT2 beta decay radioisotopes
    - BT3 radioisotopes
      - BT4 isotopes
- BT1 intermediate mass nuclei
  - BT2 nuclei
- BT1 odd-even nuclei
  - BT2 nuclei
- BT1 seconds living radioisotopes
  - BT2 radioisotopes
    - BT3 isotopes

ANTIMONY 110 [7; 7]
- BT1 antimony isotopes
- BT1 beta-plus decay radioisotopes
  - BT2 beta decay radioisotopes
    - BT3 radioisotopes
      - BT4 isotopes
- BT1 electron capture radioisotopes
  - BT2 beta decay radioisotopes
    - BT3 radioisotopes
      - BT4 isotopes
- BT1 intermediate mass nuclei
  - BT2 nuclei
- BT1 odd-odd nuclei
  - BT2 nuclei
- BT1 seconds living radioisotopes
  - BT2 radioisotopes
    - BT3 isotopes

ANTIMONY 111 [9; 9]
- BT1 antimony isotopes
- BT1 beta-plus decay radioisotopes
  - BT2 beta decay radioisotopes
    - BT3 radioisotopes
      - BT4 isotopes
- BT1 electron capture radioisotopes
  - BT2 beta decay radioisotopes
    - BT3 radioisotopes
      - BT4 isotopes
- BT1 intermediate mass nuclei
  - BT2 nuclei
- BT1 minutes living radioisotopes
  - BT2 radioisotopes
    - BT3 isotopes
- BT1 odd-even nuclei
  - BT2 nuclei

ANTIMONY 112 [32; 32]
- BT1 antimony isotopes
- BT1 beta-plus decay radioisotopes
  - BT2 beta decay radioisotopes
    - BT3 radioisotopes
      - BT4 isotopes
- BT1 electron capture radioisotopes

- BT2 beta decay radioisotopes
  - BT3 radioisotopes
    - BT4 isotopes
- BT1 intermediate mass nuclei
  - BT2 nuclei
- BT1 odd-odd nuclei
  - BT2 nuclei
- BT1 seconds living radioisotopes
  - BT2 radioisotopes
    - BT3 isotopes

ANTIMONY 113 [36; 36]
- BT1 antimony isotopes
- BT1 beta-plus decay radioisotopes
  - BT2 beta decay radioisotopes
    - BT3 radioisotopes
      - BT4 isotopes
- BT1 electron capture radioisotopes
  - BT2 beta decay radioisotopes
    - BT3 radioisotopes
      - BT4 isotopes
- BT1 intermediate mass nuclei
  - BT2 nuclei
- BT1 isomeric transition isotopes
  - BT2 radioisotopes
    - BT3 isotopes
- BT1 minutes living radioisotopes
  - BT2 radioisotopes
    - BT3 isotopes
- BT1 nanosec living radioisotopes
  - BT2 radioisotopes
    - BT3 isotopes
- BT1 odd-even nuclei
  - BT2 nuclei

ANTIMONY 114 [35; 35]
- BT1 antimony isotopes
- BT1 beta-plus decay radioisotopes
  - BT2 beta decay radioisotopes
    - BT3 radioisotopes
      - BT4 isotopes
- BT1 electron capture radioisotopes
  - BT2 beta decay radioisotopes
    - BT3 radioisotopes
      - BT4 isotopes
- BT1 intermediate mass nuclei
  - BT2 nuclei
- BT1 minutes living radioisotopes
  - BT2 radioisotopes
    - BT3 isotopes
- BT1 odd-odd nuclei
  - BT2 nuclei

ANTIMONY 115 [57; 57]
- BT1 antimony isotopes
- BT1 beta-plus decay radioisotopes
  - BT2 beta decay radioisotopes
    - BT3 radioisotopes
      - BT4 isotopes
- BT1 electron capture radioisotopes
  - BT2 beta decay radioisotopes
    - BT3 radioisotopes
      - BT4 isotopes
- BT1 intermediate mass nuclei
  - BT2 nuclei
- BT1 minutes living radioisotopes
  - BT2 radioisotopes
    - BT3 isotopes
- BT1 odd-even nuclei
  - BT2 nuclei

ANTIMONY 116 [67; 67]
- BT1 antimony isotopes
- BT1 beta-plus decay radioisotopes
  - BT2 beta decay radioisotopes
    - BT3 radioisotopes
      - BT4 isotopes
- BT1 electron capture radioisotopes
  - BT2 beta decay radioisotopes
    - BT3 radioisotopes
      - BT4 isotopes
- BT1 hours living radioisotopes
  - BT2 radioisotopes
    - BT3 isotopes
- BT1 intermediate mass nuclei
  - BT2 nuclei
- BT1 minutes living radioisotopes
  - BT2 radioisotopes
    - BT3 isotopes

ANTIMONY 117 [69; 69]
    BT1   antimony isotopes
    BT1   beta-plus decay radioisotopes
      BT2   beta decay radioisotopes
        BT3   radioisotopes
          BT4   isotopes
    BT1   electron capture radioisotopes
      BT2   beta decay radioisotopes
        BT3   radioisotopes
          BT4   isotopes
    BT1   hours living radioisotopes
      BT2   radioisotopes
        BT3   isotopes
    BT1   intermediate mass nuclei
      BT2   nuclei
    BT1   isomeric transition isotopes
      BT2   radioisotopes
        BT3   isotopes
    BT1   nanosec living radioisotopes
      BT2   radioisotopes
        BT3   isotopes
    BT1   odd-even nuclei
      BT2   nuclei

ANTIMONY 118 [45; 45]
    BT1   antimony isotopes
    BT1   beta-plus decay radioisotopes
      BT2   beta decay radioisotopes
        BT3   radioisotopes
          BT4   isotopes
    BT1   electron capture radioisotopes
      BT2   beta decay radioisotopes
        BT3   radioisotopes
          BT4   isotopes
    BT1   hours living radioisotopes
      BT2   radioisotopes
        BT3   isotopes
    BT1   intermediate mass nuclei
      BT2   nuclei
    BT1   minutes living radioisotopes
      BT2   radioisotopes
        BT3   isotopes
    BT1   odd-odd nuclei
      BT2   nuclei

ANTIMONY 119 [108; 108]
    BT1   antimony isotopes
    BT1   days living radioisotopes
      BT2   radioisotopes
        BT3   isotopes
    BT1   electron capture radioisotopes
      BT2   beta decay radioisotopes
        BT3   radioisotopes
          BT4   isotopes
    BT1   intermediate mass nuclei
      BT2   nuclei
    BT1   internal conversion radioisoto
      BT2   radioisotopes
        BT3   isotopes
    BT1   odd-even nuclei
      BT2   nuclei

ANTIMONY 120 [73; 73]
    BT1   antimony isotopes
    BT1   beta-plus decay radioisotopes
      BT2   beta decay radioisotopes
        BT3   radioisotopes
          BT4   isotopes
    BT1   days living radioisotopes
      BT2   radioisotopes
        BT3   isotopes
    BT1   electron capture radioisotopes
      BT2   beta decay radioisotopes
        BT3   radioisotopes
          BT4   isotopes
    BT1   intermediate mass nuclei
      BT2   nuclei
    BT1   minutes living radioisotopes
      BT2   radioisotopes
        BT3   isotopes
    BT1   odd-odd nuclei
      BT2   nuclei

ANTIMONY 120 TARGET [2; 2]
    BT1   targets

ANTIMONY 121 [205; 205]
    BT1   antimony isotopes
    BT1   intermediate mass nuclei
      BT2   nuclei
    BT1   odd-even nuclei
      BT2   nuclei
    BT1   stable isotopes
      BT2   isotopes

ANTIMONY 121 TARGET [97; 97]
    BT1   targets

ANTIMONY 122 [137; 137]
    BT1   antimony isotopes
    BT1   beta-minus decay radioisotopes
      BT2   beta decay radioisotopes
        BT3   radioisotopes
          BT4   isotopes
    BT1   beta-plus decay radioisotopes
      BT2   beta decay radioisotopes
        BT3   radioisotopes
          BT4   isotopes
    BT1   days living radioisotopes
      BT2   radioisotopes
        BT3   isotopes
    BT1   electron capture radioisotopes
      BT2   beta decay radioisotopes
        BT3   radioisotopes
          BT4   isotopes
    BT1   intermediate mass nuclei
      BT2   nuclei
    BT1   internal conversion radioisoto
      BT2   radioisotopes
        BT3   isotopes
    BT1   isomeric transition isotopes
      BT2   radioisotopes
        BT3   isotopes
    BT1   minutes living radioisotopes
      BT2   radioisotopes
        BT3   isotopes
    BT1   odd-odd nuclei
      BT2   nuclei

ANTIMONY 123 [69; 69]
    BT1   antimony isotopes
    BT1   intermediate mass nuclei
      BT2   nuclei
    BT1   odd-even nuclei
      BT2   nuclei
    BT1   stable isotopes
      BT2   isotopes

ANTIMONY 123 TARGET [87; 87]
    BT1   targets

ANTIMONY 124 [290; 290]
    BT1   antimony isotopes
    BT1   beta-minus decay radioisotopes
      BT2   beta decay radioisotopes
        BT3   radioisotopes
          BT4   isotopes
    BT1   days living radioisotopes
      BT2   radioisotopes
        BT3   isotopes
    BT1   intermediate mass nuclei
      BT2   nuclei
    BT1   internal conversion radioisoto
      BT2   radioisotopes
        BT3   isotopes
    BT1   isomeric transition isotopes
      BT2   radioisotopes
        BT3   isotopes
    BT1   minutes living radioisotopes
      BT2   radioisotopes
        BT3   isotopes
    BT1   odd-odd nuclei
      BT2   nuclei

ANTIMONY 125 [453; 453]
    BT1   antimony isotopes
    BT1   beta-minus decay radioisotopes
      BT2   beta decay radioisotopes
        BT3   radioisotopes
          BT4   isotopes
    BT1   intermediate mass nuclei
      BT2   nuclei
    BT1   odd-even nuclei
      BT2   nuclei
    BT1   years living radioisotopes
      BT2   radioisotopes
        BT3   isotopes

ANTIMONY 126 [26; 26]
    BT1   antimony isotopes
    BT1   beta-minus decay radioisotopes
      BT2   beta decay radioisotopes
        BT3   radioisotopes
          BT4   isotopes
    BT1   days living radioisotopes
      BT2   radioisotopes
        BT3   isotopes
    BT1   intermediate mass nuclei
      BT2   nuclei
    BT1   internal conversion radioisoto
      BT2   radioisotopes
        BT3   isotopes
    BT1   isomeric transition isotopes
      BT2   radioisotopes
        BT3   isotopes
    BT1   minutes living radioisotopes
      BT2   radioisotopes
        BT3   isotopes
    BT1   odd-odd nuclei
      BT2   nuclei
    BT1   seconds living radioisotopes
      BT2   radioisotopes
        BT3   isotopes

ANTIMONY 127 [25; 25]
    BT1   antimony isotopes
    BT1   beta-minus decay radioisotopes
      BT2   beta decay radioisotopes
        BT3   radioisotopes
          BT4   isotopes
    BT1   days living radioisotopes
      BT2   radioisotopes
        BT3   isotopes
    BT1   intermediate mass nuclei
      BT2   nuclei
    BT1   odd-even nuclei
      BT2   nuclei

ANTIMONY 127 TARGET [4; 4] *Jan 79*
    BT1   targets

ANTIMONY 128 [40; 40]
    BT1   antimony isotopes
    BT1   beta-minus decay radioisotopes
      BT2   beta decay radioisotopes
        BT3   radioisotopes
          BT4   isotopes
    BT1   hours living radioisotopes
      BT2   radioisotopes
        BT3   isotopes
    BT1   intermediate mass nuclei
      BT2   nuclei
    BT1   minutes living radioisotopes
      BT2   radioisotopes
        BT3   isotopes
    BT1   odd-odd nuclei
      BT2   nuclei

ANTIMONY 129 [28; 28]
    BT1   antimony isotopes
    BT1   beta-minus decay radioisotopes
      BT2   beta decay radioisotopes
        BT3   radioisotopes
          BT4   isotopes
    BT1   hours living radioisotopes
      BT2   radioisotopes
        BT3   isotopes
    BT1   intermediate mass nuclei
      BT2   nuclei
    BT1   minutes living radioisotopes
      BT2   radioisotopes
        BT3   isotopes
    BT1   odd-even nuclei
      BT2   nuclei

ANTIMONY 130 [44; 44]
BT1 antimony isotopes
BT1 beta-minus decay radioisotopes
  BT2 beta decay radioisotopes
    BT3 radioisotopes
      BT4 isotopes
BT1 intermediate mass nuclei
  BT2 nuclei
BT1 minutes living radioisotopes
  BT2 radioisotopes
    BT3 isotopes
BT1 odd-odd nuclei
  BT2 nuclei

ANTIMONY 131 [29; 29]
BT1 antimony isotopes
BT1 beta-minus decay radioisotopes
  BT2 beta decay radioisotopes
    BT3 radioisotopes
      BT4 isotopes
BT1 intermediate mass nuclei
  BT2 nuclei
BT1 isomeric transition isotopes
  BT2 radioisotopes
    BT3 isotopes
BT1 minutes living radioisotopes
  BT2 radioisotopes
    BT3 isotopes
BT1 odd-even nuclei
  BT2 nuclei

ANTIMONY 132 [43; 43]
BT1 antimony isotopes
BT1 beta-minus decay radioisotopes
  BT2 beta decay radioisotopes
    BT3 radioisotopes
      BT4 isotopes
BT1 intermediate mass nuclei
  BT2 nuclei
BT1 minutes living radioisotopes
  BT2 radioisotopes
    BT3 isotopes
BT1 odd-odd nuclei
  BT2 nuclei

ANTIMONY 133 [31; 31]
BT1 antimony isotopes
BT1 beta-minus decay radioisotopes
  BT2 beta decay radioisotopes
    BT3 radioisotopes
      BT4 isotopes
BT1 intermediate mass nuclei
  BT2 nuclei
BT1 minutes living radioisotopes
  BT2 radioisotopes
    BT3 isotopes
BT1 odd-even nuclei
  BT2 nuclei

ANTIMONY 134 [16; 16]
BT1 antimony isotopes
BT1 beta-minus decay radioisotopes
  BT2 beta decay radioisotopes
    BT3 radioisotopes
      BT4 isotopes
BT1 intermediate mass nuclei
  BT2 nuclei
BT1 millisec living radioisotopes
  BT2 radioisotopes
    BT3 isotopes
BT1 odd-odd nuclei
  BT2 nuclei
BT1 seconds living radioisotopes
  BT2 radioisotopes
    BT3 isotopes

ANTIMONY 135 [28; 28]
BT1 antimony isotopes
BT1 beta-minus decay radioisotopes
  BT2 beta decay radioisotopes
    BT3 radioisotopes
      BT4 isotopes
BT1 intermediate mass nuclei
  BT2 nuclei
BT1 odd-even nuclei
  BT2 nuclei
BT1 seconds living radioisotopes
  BT2 radioisotopes

    BT3 isotopes

ANTIMONY 136 [6; 6] *Jul 76*
BT1 antimony isotopes
BT1 beta-minus decay radioisotopes
  BT2 beta decay radioisotopes
    BT3 radioisotopes
      BT4 isotopes
BT1 intermediate mass nuclei
  BT2 nuclei
BT1 millisec living radioisotopes
  BT2 radioisotopes
    BT3 isotopes
BT1 odd-odd nuclei
  BT2 nuclei

antimuons
USE muons plus

ANTIMYCIN [7; 7] *May 84*
BT1 antibiotics
  BT2 drugs
  BT2 organic compounds

ANTINEOPLASTIC DRUGS [871; 2,245]
BT1 drugs
NT1 actinomycin
NT1 aminopterin
NT1 bleomycin
NT1 doxorubicin
NT1 metronidazole
NT1 misonidazole
NT1 mitomycin
NT1 neocarcinostatin
NT1 puromycin
RT antimitotic drugs

ANTINEUTRINO BEAMS [95; 95]
BT1 antiparticle beams
  BT2 beams
RT antineutrinos

ANTINEUTRINO REACTIONS [8; 8] *Nov 89*
BT1 nuclear reactions

ANTINEUTRINO-ELECTRON INTERACT [240; 240]
BT1 neutrino-electron interactions
  BT2 lepton-lepton interactions
    BT3 particle interactions
      BT4 interactions

ANTINEUTRINO-NEUTRON INTERACTI [70; 70] *Jan 77*
BT1 antilepton-neutron interaction
  BT2 lepton-neutron interactions
    BT3 lepton-nucleon interactions
      BT4 lepton-baryon interactions
        BT5 lepton-hadron interactions
          BT6 particle interactions
            BT7 interactions
BT1 antineutrino-nucleon interacti
  BT2 neutrino-nucleon interactions
    BT3 lepton-nucleon interactions
      BT4 lepton-baryon interactions
        BT5 lepton-hadron interactions
          BT6 particle interactions
            BT7 interactions
BT1 neutrino-neutron interactions
  BT2 neutrino-nucleon interactions
    BT3 lepton-nucleon interactions
      BT4 lepton-baryon interactions
        BT5 lepton-hadron interactions
          BT6 particle interactions
            BT7 interactions

ANTINEUTRINO-NUCLEON INTERACTI [628; 1,026]
BT1 neutrino-nucleon interactions
  BT2 lepton-nucleon interactions
    BT3 lepton-baryon interactions
      BT4 lepton-hadron interactions
        BT5 particle interactions
          BT6 interactions
NT1 antineutrino-neutron interacti
NT1 antineutrino-proton interactio

ANTINEUTRINO-PROTON INTERACTIO [395; 395] *Dec 75*
BT1 antilepton-proton interactions
  BT2 lepton-proton interactions
    BT3 lepton-nucleon interactions
      BT4 lepton-baryon interactions
        BT5 lepton-hadron interactions
          BT6 particle interactions
            BT7 interactions
BT1 antineutrino-nucleon interacti
  BT2 neutrino-nucleon interactions
    BT3 lepton-nucleon interactions
      BT4 lepton-baryon interactions
        BT5 lepton-hadron interactions
          BT6 particle interactions
            BT7 interactions
BT1 neutrino-proton interactions
  BT2 neutrino-nucleon interactions
    BT3 lepton-nucleon interactions
      BT4 lepton-baryon interactions
        BT5 lepton-hadron interactions
          BT6 particle interactions
            BT7 interactions

ANTINEUTRINOS [993; 1,840]
BT1 antileptons
  BT2 antiparticles
    BT3 antimatter
      BT4 matter
    BT3 elementary particles
  BT2 leptons
    BT3 elementary particles
    BT3 fermions
BT1 neutrinos
  BT2 leptons
    BT3 elementary particles
    BT3 fermions
  BT2 massless particles
    BT3 elementary particles
NT1 electron antineutrinos
NT1 muon antineutrinos
RT antineutrino beams

ANTINEUTRON REACTIONS [46; 46]
BT1 antinucleon reactions
  BT2 nucleon reactions
    BT3 baryon reactions
      BT4 hadron reactions
        BT5 nuclear reactions

ANTINEUTRONS [330; 330]
BT1 antinucleons
  BT2 antibaryons
    BT3 antiparticles
      BT4 antimatter
        BT5 matter
      BT4 elementary particles
    BT3 baryons
      BT4 fermions
      BT4 hadrons
        BT5 elementary particles
  BT2 nucleons
    BT3 baryons
      BT4 fermions
      BT4 hadrons
        BT5 elementary particles
BT1 neutrons
  BT2 nucleons
    BT3 baryons
      BT4 fermions
      BT4 hadrons
        BT5 elementary particles
RT neutron oscillation

antinuclear groups
USE interest groups

ANTINUCLEI [34; 1,966]
BT1 antimatter
  BT2 matter
BT1 nuclei
NT1 antideuterons
NT1 antiprotons
NT1 antitritons

ANTINUCLEON BEAMS [15; 947]
- BT1 antiparticle beams
- BT2 beams
- NT1 antiproton beams
- RT antinucleons

ANTINUCLEON REACTIONS [43; 962]
- BT1 nucleon reactions
- BT2 baryon reactions
- BT3 hadron reactions
- BT4 nuclear reactions
- NT1 antineutron reactions
- NT1 antiproton reactions

ANTINUCLEONS [197; 2,508]
- BT1 antibaryons
- BT2 antiparticles
- BT3 antimatter
- BT4 matter
- BT3 elementary particles
- BT2 baryons
- BT3 fermions
- BT3 hadrons
- BT4 elementary particles
- BT1 nucleons
- BT2 baryons
- BT3 fermions
- BT3 hadrons
- BT4 elementary particles
- NT1 antineutrons
- NT1 antiprotons
- RT antinucleon beams

ANTIOMEGA PARTICLES [22; 22]
- BT1 antihyperons
- BT2 antibaryons
- BT3 antiparticles
- BT4 antimatter
- BT5 matter
- BT4 elementary particles
- BT3 baryons
- BT4 fermions
- BT4 hadrons
- BT5 elementary particles
- BT2 hyperons
- BT3 baryons
- BT4 fermions
- BT4 hadrons
- BT5 elementary particles
- BT3 strange particles
- BT4 elementary particles
- BT1 omega particles
- BT2 omega baryons
- BT3 hyperons
- BT4 baryons
- BT5 fermions
- BT5 hadrons
- BT6 elementary particles
- BT4 strange particles
- BT5 elementary particles

ANTIOXIDANTS [263; 263]
- RT oxidation
- RT oxidizers

ANTIPARTICLE BEAMS [13; 1,097]
- BT1 beams
- NT1 antineutrino beams
- NT1 antinucleon beams
- NT2 antiproton beams
- RT pomeranchuk theorem

ANTIPARTICLES [387; 22,364]
- UF+ *antimesons*
- UF+ *pseudoscalar antimesons*
- BT1 antimatter
- BT2 matter
- BT1 elementary particles
- NT1 anti-b neutral mesons
- NT1 anti-d neutral mesons
- NT1 antibaryons
- NT2 antihyperons
- NT3 antilambda particles
- NT3 antiomega particles
- NT3 antisigma particles
- NT3 antixi particles
- NT2 antinucleons
- NT3 antineutrons
- NT3 antiprotons
- NT1 antikaons
- NT2 antikaons neutral
- NT1 antileptons
- NT2 antineutrinos
- NT3 electron antineutrinos
- NT3 muon antineutrinos
- NT2 muons plus
- NT2 positrons
- NT3 cosmic positrons

ANTIPROTON BEAMS [978; 978]
- BT1 antinucleon beams
- BT2 antiparticle beams
- BT3 beams

ANTIPROTON REACTIONS [896; 896]
- UF+ *antiproton-deuteron interactio*
- BT1 antinucleon reactions
- BT2 nucleon reactions
- BT3 baryon reactions
- BT4 hadron reactions
- BT5 nuclear reactions

ANTIPROTON SOURCES [61; 61]
Dec 85
- BT1 particle sources
- BT2 radiation sources
- RT antiprotons

antiproton-deuteron interactio
- USE antiproton reactions
- AND deuterium target

ANTIPROTON-NEUTRON INTERACTION [174; 174]
- BT1 nucleon-antinucleon interactio
- BT2 baryon-baryon interactions
- BT3 hadron-hadron interactions
- BT4 particle interactions
- BT5 interactions

antiproton-proton interactions
- USE proton-antiproton interactions

antiprotonic atoms
- USE hadronic atoms

ANTIPROTONS [2,077; 2,077]
- BT1 antinuclei
- BT2 antimatter
- BT3 matter
- BT2 nuclei
- BT1 antinucleons
- BT2 antibaryons
- BT3 antiparticles
- BT4 antimatter
- BT5 matter
- BT4 elementary particles
- BT3 baryons
- BT4 fermions
- BT4 hadrons
- BT5 elementary particles
- BT2 nucleons
- BT3 baryons
- BT4 fermions
- BT4 hadrons
- BT5 elementary particles
- BT1 protons
- BT2 hydrogen ions 1 plus
- BT3 cations
- BT4 ions
- BT5 charged particles
- BT3 hydrogen ions
- BT4 ions
- BT5 charged particles
- BT2 nucleons
- BT3 baryons
- BT4 fermions
- BT4 hadrons
- BT5 elementary particles
- RT antiproton sources
- RT protonium

ANTIPYRETICS [90; 448]
- UF+ *aminopyrine*
- UF+ *phenacetin*
- BT1 central nervous system depress
- BT2 central nervous system agents
- BT3 drugs
- NT1 acetylsalicylic acid
- NT1 antipyrine
- NT1 cinchonine
- NT1 colchicine
- NT1 quinine
- RT analgesics
- RT fever

ANTIPYRINE [236; 236]
- BT1 analgesics
- BT2 central nervous system depress
- BT3 central nervous system agents
- BT4 drugs
- BT1 antipyretics
- BT2 central nervous system depress
- BT3 central nervous system agents
- BT4 drugs
- BT1 pyrazolines
- BT2 pyrazoles
- BT3 azoles
- BT4 heterocyclic compounds
- BT5 organic compounds
- BT4 organic nitrogen compounds
- BT5 organic compounds

ANTIREFLECTION COATINGS [127; 127] *Oct 76*
- BT1 coatings
- RT dielectric materials
- RT optical properties
- RT optical systems
- RT reflective coatings

antiserum
- USE immune serums

ANTISIGMA PARTICLES [83; 83]
- BT1 antihyperons
- BT2 antibaryons
- BT3 antiparticles
- BT4 antimatter
- BT5 matter
- BT4 elementary particles
- BT3 baryons
- BT4 fermions
- BT4 hadrons
- BT5 elementary particles
- BT2 hyperons
- BT3 baryons
- BT4 fermions
- BT4 hadrons
- BT5 elementary particles
- BT3 strange particles
- BT4 elementary particles
- BT1 sigma particles
- BT2 sigma baryons
- BT3 hyperons
- BT4 baryons
- BT5 fermions
- BT5 hadrons
- BT6 elementary particles
- BT4 strange particles
- BT5 elementary particles

ANTITHYROID DRUGS [66; 716]
- UF *thyroid antagonists*
- BT1 drugs
- NT1 thiocyanates
- NT2 ammonium thiocyanates
- NT1 thiouracil
- NT1 thiourea
- RT hyperthyroidism
- RT hypothyroidism

ANTITOXINS [24; 24]
- BT1 antibodies
- RT toxins

ANTITRITONS [17; 17]
- BT1 antinuclei
- BT2 antimatter
- BT3 matter
- BT2 nuclei
- BT1 tritons
- BT2 charged particles

ANTITRUST REVIEW [9; 9] *Sep 79*
(A review to establish whether a situation would be created or maintained which would be inconsistent with antitrust laws.)
- RT legal aspects
- RT reactor licensing

ANTIXI PARTICLES [57; 57]
- BT1 antihyperons
- BT2 antibaryons
- BT3 antiparticles
- BT4 antimatter
- BT5 matter
- BT4 elementary particles
- BT3 baryons
- BT4 fermions
- BT4 hadrons
- BT5 elementary particles
- BT2 hyperons
- BT3 baryons
- BT4 fermions
- BT4 hadrons
- BT5 elementary particles
- BT3 strange particles
- BT4 elementary particles
- BT1 xi particles
- BT2 xi baryons
- BT3 hyperons
- BT4 baryons
- BT5 fermions
- BT5 hadrons
- BT6 elementary particles
- BT4 strange particles
- BT5 elementary particles

ANTLERS [1; 1]
- BT1 bone tissues
- BT2 connective tissue
- BT3 tissues
- BT4 body
- RT deer

ants
- USE insects

ANVIL PROJECT [3; 3] *Apr 78*
- UF *project anvil*
- RT contained explosions
- RT nuclear explosions
- RT underground explosions

AO-PHAI-1 REACTOR [2; 2] *Mar 85*
- UF *sriracha reactor*
- BT1 power reactors
- BT2 reactors

AORTA [1,259; 1,259]
- BT1 arteries
- BT2 blood vessels
- BT3 cardiovascular system
- BT3 organs
- BT4 body
- RT heart
- RT mediastinum

APACHE [1; 1]
(Accelerator for Physics And Chemistry of Heavy Elements)
- BT1 isochronous cyclotrons
- BT2 cyclotrons
- BT3 cyclic accelerators
- BT4 accelerators

APARTMENT BUILDINGS [20; 20] *Jul 85*
- UF *residential buildings (apartm)*
- BT1 buildings

APATITES [590; 590]
- UF+ *calcium hydroxyapatite*
- BT1 phosphate minerals
- BT2 minerals
- RT kimberlites

APERTURES [1,151; 1,151]
- BT1 openings
- RT orifices

APES [193; 193]
- BT1 primates
- BT2 mammals
- BT3 vertebrates
- BT4 animals

APFA-3 REACTOR [3; 3]
(Accelerator Pulsed Fast Critical Assembly)
- UF *acceler pulsed fast cr assembl*
- BT1 zero power reactors
- BT2 experimental reactors
- BT3 research and test reactors
- BT4 reactors

APHIDS [25; 25]
- BT1 hemiptera
- BT2 insects
- BT3 arthropods
- BT4 invertebrates
- BT5 animals

aplastic anemia
- USE anemias

APLITES [18; 18]
- UF *alaskites*
- BT1 granites
- BT2 plutonic rocks
- BT3 igneous rocks
- BT4 rocks
- RT feldspars
- RT quartz

apolipoproteins
- SEE lipoproteins

APOLLO PROJECT [398; 398]
- UF *project apollo*
- RT lunar materials
- RT moon
- RT space flight

APPALACHIAN MOUNTAINS [17; 17]
- BT1 mountains

apparatus
- USE equipment

appendix (vermiform)
- USE large intestine
- AND lymphatic system

APPENNINES [11; 11] *Oct 76*
- BT1 mountains

APPLES [140; 140]
- BT1 fruits
- BT2 food
- RT codling moth
- RT fruit trees

applications
- USE uses

applicators (radiotherapy)
- USE radiation sources

approximation (adiabatic)
- USE adiabatic approximation

approximation (bohr)
- USE nilsson-mottelson model

approximation (born)
- USE born approximation

approximation (born-oppenheim.
- USE born-oppenheimer approximation

approximation (brinkman-kram.)
- USE brinkman-kramers approximation

approximation (coupled-chann.)
- USE coupled channel born approxima

approximation (diabatic)
- USE diabatic approximation

approximation (distorted-wave)
- USE dwba

approximation (eikonal)
- USE eikonal approximation

approximation (equiv.-photon)
- USE equivalent-photon approximatio

approximation (fix scatt. cen)
- USE fsc approximation

approximation (p1)
- USE p1-approximation

approximation (p2)
- USE p2-approximation

approximation (p3)
- USE p3-approximation

approximation (semiclassical)
- USE semiclassical approximation

approximation (straight-line)
- USE straight-line path approximati

approximation (sudden)
- USE sudden approximation

approximation (tomonaga)
- USE tomonaga approximation

approximation (williams-weizs.
- USE equivalent-photon approximatio

apra reactor
- USE aprf reactor

APRF REACTOR [21; 21]
  UF   *aberdeen md. reactor*
  UF   *apra reactor*
  UF   *army pulsed reactor assembly*
  BT1   fast reactors
    BT2   epithermal reactors
      BT3   reactors
  BT1   research reactors
    BT2   research and test reactors
      BT3   reactors

APS REACTOR [16; 16]
(Obninsk, Kaluga, USSR)
  UF   *am-1 reactor*
  BT1   enriched uranium reactors
    BT2   reactors
  BT1   experimental reactors
    BT2   research and test reactors
      BT3   reactors
  BT1   lwgr type reactors
    BT2   graphite moderated reactors
      BT3   reactors
    BT2   water cooled reactors
      BT3   reactors
  BT1   power reactors
    BT2   reactors
  BT1   thermal reactors
    BT2   reactors

APSARA REACTOR [45; 45]
(Bhabha Atomic Research Center, Trombay, Maharashtra, India)
  BT1   enriched uranium reactors
    BT2   reactors
  BT1   isotope production reactors
    BT2   irradiation reactors
      BT3   reactors
  BT1   pool type reactors
    BT2   water cooled reactors
      BT3   reactors
    BT2   water moderated reactors
      BT3   reactors
  BT1   research reactors
    BT2   research and test reactors
      BT3   reactors
  BT1   thermal reactors
    BT2   reactors
  BT1   training reactors
    BT2   research and test reactors
      BT3   reactors

AQUA REGIA [28; 28]
  RT   hydrochloric acid
  RT   nitric acid

→ **AQUACULTURE** [0; 0] *Sep 91*
(Cultivation of natural faunal and/or floral resources of water.)
  UF   *aquiculture*
  UF   *mariculture*
  RT   fishes

AQUATIC ECOSYSTEMS [2,265; 2,265]
  UF   *brackish water ecosystems*
  UF   *estuarine ecosystems*
  UF   *fresh water ecosystems*
  UF   *marine ecosystems*
  BT1   ecosystems
  RT   aquatic organisms
  RT   benthos
  RT   eutrophication
  RT   hydrosphere
  RT   limnology
  RT   swamps

AQUATIC ORGANISMS [689; 4,159]
Oct 76
(Unspecified biota characteristic of aquatic ecosystems.)
  UF   *aufwuchs*
  NT1   amphibians
    NT2   frogs
    NT2   salamanders
      NT3   axolotl
      NT3   triturus
  NT1   benthos
  NT1   cetaceans
  NT1   crustaceans
    NT2   artemia
    NT2   daphnia
    NT2   lobsters
    NT2   prawns
    NT2   shrimp
  NT1   echinoderms
    NT2   sea urchins
  NT1   fishes
    NT2   anadromous fishes
      NT3   salmon
    NT2   codfish
    NT2   eel
    NT2   goldfish
    NT2   plaice
    NT2   trout
    NT2   tuna
  NT1   molluscs
    NT2   clams
    NT2   oysters
    NT2   snails
  NT1   plankton
  RT   algae
  RT   animals
  RT   aquatic ecosystems
  RT   plants

AQUEOUS HOMOGENEOUS REACTORS [18; 149]
  BT1   liquid homogeneous reactors
    BT2   fluid fueled reactors
      BT3   reactors
    BT2   homogeneous reactors
      BT3   reactors
  BT1   water cooled reactors
    BT2   reactors
  BT1   water moderated reactors
    BT2   reactors
  NT1   ai-l-77 reactor
  NT1   ber-2 reactor
  NT1   cesnef reactor
  NT1   dr-1 reactor
  NT1   frf reactor
  NT1   jrr-1 reactor
  NT1   kewb reactor
  NT1   kstr reactor
  NT1   ncscr-1 reactor
  NT1   prnc-l-77 reactor
  NT1   supo reactor
  NT1   wrrr reactor

aqueous humor
  USE   body fluids

AQUEOUS SOLUTIONS [16,952; 16,952]
  UF   *water solutions*
  BT1   solutions
    BT2   homogeneous mixtures
      BT3   mixtures
        BT4   dispersions
  RT   water
  RT   water influx

→ *aquiculture*
  USE   aquaculture

AQUIFERS [1,056; 1,056]
(A stratum of permeable rock, sand, or gravel that will yield a significant quantity of water.)
  RT   ground water
  RT   hydrology
  RT   reservoir pressure
  RT   rocks
  RT   sand
  RT   water influx
  RT   water tables

AQUILON REACTOR [2; 2]
  BT1   heavy water cooled reactors
    BT2   reactors
  BT1   heavy water moderated reactors
    BT2   reactors
  BT1   natural uranium reactors
    BT2   reactors
  BT1   tank type reactors
    BT2   reactors
  BT1   thermal reactors
    BT2   reactors
  BT1   zero power reactors
    BT2   experimental reactors
      BT3   research and test reactors
        BT4   reactors

arab republic of egypt
  USE   egyptian arab republic

ARABIAN SEA [37; 37]
  BT1   indian ocean
    BT2   seas
      BT3   surface waters

ARABIDOPSIS [45; 45]
  BT1   plants

ARABINOSE [66; 66]
  BT1   aldehydes
    BT2   organic compounds
  BT1   pentoses
    BT2   monosaccharides
      BT3   saccharides
        BT4   carbohydrates
          BT5   organic compounds
  RT   gum acacia

arachidic acid
  USE   eicosanoic acid

ARACHIDONIC ACID [367; 367]
  BT1   monocarboxylic acids
    BT2   carboxylic acids
      BT3   organic acids
        BT4   organic compounds

ARACHNIDS [20; 128]
  BT1   arthropods
    BT2   invertebrates
      BT3   animals
  NT1   mites
  NT1   scorpions
  NT1   spiders
  NT1   ticks

ARAGONITE [40; 40]
  BT1   carbonate minerals
    BT2   minerals
  RT   calcium carbonates

ARALDITE [38; 38]
  BT1   epoxides
    BT2   organic oxygen compounds
      BT3   organic compounds
  BT1   organic polymers
    BT2   organic compounds
    BT2   polymers
  RT   homalite
  RT   resins

aramids
  USE   polyamides

arbeitsgemeinsch. versuchs r.
  USE   avr reactor

ARBI REACTOR [1; 1]
(Bilbao, Vizcaya, Spain)
  UF   *argonaut bilbao reactor*
  UF   *bilbao argonaut reactor*
  BT1   argonaut type reactors
    BT2   enriched uranium reactors
      BT3   reactors
    BT2   research and test reactors
      BT3   reactors
    BT2   water cooled reactors
      BT3   reactors
    BT2   water moderated reactors
      BT3   reactors
  BT1   research reactors
    BT2   research and test reactors

BT3 reactors
BT1 thermal reactors
BT2 reactors
BT1 training reactors
BT2 research and test reactors
BT3 reactors

ARBITRATION [9; 9] *Dec 76*
RT dispute settlements
RT hearings
RT lawsuits

ARBOR PROJECT [2; 2]
RT contained explosions
RT nevada test site
RT nuclear explosions
RT underground explosions

ARBUS REACTOR [19; 19]
UF *ast-1 reactor*
UF *melekess-arbus reactor*
BT1 enriched uranium reactors
BT2 reactors
BT1 experimental reactors
BT2 research and test reactors
BT3 reactors
BT1 omr type reactors
BT2 organic cooled reactors
BT3 reactors
BT2 organic moderated reactors
BT3 reactors
BT1 power reactors
BT2 reactors
BT1 test reactors
BT2 research and test reactors
BT3 reactors
BT2 test facilities
BT1 thermal reactors
BT2 reactors

ARC FURNACES [172; 172]
BT1 electric furnaces
BT2 furnaces
RT plasma furnaces
RT vacuum furnaces

ARC WELDING [437; 1,416]
UF *flux cored arc welding*
BT1 welding
BT2 joining
BT3 fabrication
NT1 gas metal-arc welding
NT2 gas tungsten-arc welding
NT1 plasma arc welding
NT1 shielded metal-arc welding
NT1 submerged arc welding
RT electroslag welding
RT sputtering

ARCHAEOLOGICAL SITES [60; 60]
Dec 85
RT archaeological specimens
RT archaeology
RT cultural objects

ARCHAEOLOGICAL SPECIMENS
[657; 657]
RT archaeological sites
RT archaeology
RT cultural objects

ARCHAEOLOGY [502; 502]
RT age estimation
RT archaeological sites
RT archaeological specimens
RT historical aspects

arco process
USE reprocessing

ARCTIC OCEAN [35; 35] *Sep 77*
BT1 seas
BT2 surface waters

NT1 beaufort sea
NT1 chukchi sea
RT arctic regions
RT greenland

ARCTIC REGIONS [198; 198]
BT1 polar regions
RT antarctic regions
RT arctic ocean
RT auroral zones
RT chukchi sea
RT climates
RT eskimos
RT glaciers
RT greenland
RT ice
RT lapps
RT polar-cap aurorae
RT snow
RT tundra

ARDENNES B-1 REACTOR [18; 18]
Jul 84
UF *chooz b-1 reactor*
BT1 pwr type reactors
BT2 enriched uranium reactors
BT3 reactors
BT2 power reactors
BT3 reactors
BT2 thermal reactors
BT3 reactors
BT2 water cooled reactors
BT3 reactors
BT2 water moderated reactors
BT3 reactors

ARDENNES REACTOR [102; 102]
(Chooz, Ardennes, France)
UF *chooz reactor*
UF *sena reactor*
BT1 pwr type reactors
BT2 enriched uranium reactors
BT3 reactors
BT2 power reactors
BT3 reactors
BT2 thermal reactors
BT3 reactors
BT2 water cooled reactors
BT3 reactors
BT2 water moderated reactors
BT3 reactors

ARGAND DIAGRAMS [395; 395]
(The real part of a scattering amplitude plotted versus the imaginary one.)
BT1 diagrams
BT2 information
RT phase shift
RT scattering amplitudes

ARGENTINA [472; 476]
BT1 developing countries
BT1 south america
BT2 latin america
NT1 mendoza

ARGENTINE ORGANIZATIONS
[23; 23] *Jul 86*
BT1 national organizations

argentine reactor ra-0
USE ra-0 reactor

argentine reactor ra-1
USE ra-1 reactor

argentine reactor ra-2
USE ra-2 reactor

argentine reactor ra-3
USE ra-3 reactor

argentine reactor ra-5
USE ra-5 reactor

argillite
USE shales

ARGINASE [13; 13]
BT1 amidinases
BT2 non-peptide c-n hydrolases
BT3 hydrolases
BT4 enzymes
BT5 organic compounds
RT arginine

ARGININE [276; 276]
UF *guanidylaminovaleric acid*
BT1 amino acids
BT2 carboxylic acids
BT3 organic acids
BT4 organic compounds
RT arginase
RT guanidines

ARGON [10,194; 10,232]
BT1 rare gases
BT2 nonmetals
BT3 elements

ARGON BORIDES [0; 0]
BT1 argon compounds
BT2 rare gas compounds
BT1 borides
BT2 boron compounds

ARGON CHLORIDES [14; 14]
BT1 argon compounds
BT2 rare gas compounds
BT1 chlorides
BT2 chlorine compounds
BT3 halogen compounds
BT2 halides
BT3 halogen compounds

ARGON COMPLEXES [26; 26]
BT1 complexes

ARGON COMPOUNDS [40; 133]
BT1 rare gas compounds
NT1 argon borides
NT1 argon chlorides
NT1 argon fluorides
NT1 argon hydrides
NT1 argon iodides
NT1 argon nitrides
NT1 argon oxides

ARGON FLUORIDES [45; 45]
BT1 argon compounds
BT2 rare gas compounds
BT1 fluorides
BT2 fluorine compounds
BT3 halogen compounds
BT2 halides
BT3 halogen compounds

ARGON HYDRIDES [30; 30]
BT1 argon compounds
BT2 rare gas compounds
BT1 hydrides
BT2 hydrogen compounds

ARGON IODIDES [3; 3]
BT1 argon compounds
BT2 rare gas compounds
BT1 iodides
BT2 halides
BT3 halogen compounds
BT2 iodine compounds
BT3 halogen compounds

ARGON IONS [4,827; 4,827]
  BT1   ions
  BT2   charged particles

ARGON ISOTOPES [363; 2,562]
  NT1   argon 31
  NT1   argon 32
  NT1   argon 33
  NT1   argon 34
  NT1   argon 35
  NT1   argon 36
  NT1   argon 37
  NT1   argon 38
  NT1   argon 39
  NT1   argon 40
  NT1   argon 41
  NT1   argon 42
  NT1   argon 43
  NT1   argon 44
  NT1   argon 45
  NT1   argon 46
  NT1   argon 47
  NT1   argon 49
  NT1   argon 50
  NT1   argon 51

argon method
  USE   isotope dating

ARGON NITRIDES [3; 3]
  BT1   argon compounds
  BT2   rare gas compounds
  BT1   nitrides
  BT2   nitrogen compounds
  BT2   pnictides

ARGON OXIDES [5; 5] *Nov 81*
  BT1   argon compounds
  BT2   rare gas compounds
  BT1   oxides
  BT2   chalcogenides
  BT2   oxygen compounds

ARGON 31 [18; 18] *Aug 86*
  BT1   argon isotopes
  BT1   beta-plus decay radioisotopes
  BT2   beta decay radioisotopes
  BT3   radioisotopes
  BT4   isotopes
  BT1   even-odd nuclei
  BT2   nuclei
  BT1   light nuclei
  BT2   nuclei
  BT1   millisec living radioisotopes
  BT2   radioisotopes
  BT3   isotopes

ARGON 32 [21; 21]
  BT1   argon isotopes
  BT1   beta-plus decay radioisotopes
  BT2   beta decay radioisotopes
  BT3   radioisotopes
  BT4   isotopes
  BT1   even-even nuclei
  BT2   nuclei
  BT1   light nuclei
  BT2   nuclei
  BT1   millisec living radioisotopes
  BT2   radioisotopes
  BT3   isotopes

ARGON 33 [14; 14]
  BT1   argon isotopes
  BT1   beta-plus decay radioisotopes
  BT2   beta decay radioisotopes
  BT3   radioisotopes
  BT4   isotopes
  BT1   even-odd nuclei
  BT2   nuclei
  BT1   light nuclei
  BT2   nuclei
  BT1   millisec living radioisotopes
  BT2   radioisotopes
  BT3   isotopes

ARGON 34 [32; 32]
  BT1   argon isotopes
  BT1   beta-plus decay radioisotopes
  BT2   beta decay radioisotopes
  BT3   radioisotopes
  BT4   isotopes
  BT1   even-even nuclei
  BT2   nuclei
  BT1   light nuclei
  BT2   nuclei
  BT1   millisec living radioisotopes
  BT2   radioisotopes
  BT3   isotopes

ARGON 35 [32; 32]
  BT1   argon isotopes
  BT1   beta-plus decay radioisotopes
  BT2   beta decay radioisotopes
  BT3   radioisotopes
  BT4   isotopes
  BT1   even-odd nuclei
  BT2   nuclei
  BT1   light nuclei
  BT2   nuclei
  BT1   seconds living radioisotopes
  BT2   radioisotopes
  BT3   isotopes

ARGON 36 [477; 477]
  BT1   argon isotopes
  BT1   even-even nuclei
  BT2   nuclei
  BT1   light nuclei
  BT2   nuclei
  BT1   stable isotopes
  BT2   isotopes

ARGON 36 REACTIONS [110; 110] *Jul 80*
  BT1   heavy ion reactions
  BT2   nuclear reactions

ARGON 36 TARGET [87; 87]
  BT1   targets

ARGON 37 [300; 300]
  BT1   argon isotopes
  BT1   days living radioisotopes
  BT2   radioisotopes
  BT3   isotopes
  BT1   electron capture radioisotopes
  BT2   beta decay radioisotopes
  BT3   radioisotopes
  BT4   isotopes
  BT1   even-odd nuclei
  BT2   nuclei
  BT1   light nuclei
  BT2   nuclei

ARGON 37 TARGET [5; 5] *Feb 79*
  BT1   targets

ARGON 38 [245; 245]
  BT1   argon isotopes
  BT1   even-even nuclei
  BT2   nuclei
  BT1   light nuclei
  BT2   nuclei
  BT1   stable isotopes
  BT2   isotopes

ARGON 38 BEAMS [2; 2] *Dec 86*
  BT1   ion beams
  BT2   beams

ARGON 38 TARGET [50; 50]
  BT1   targets

ARGON 39 [396; 396]
  BT1   argon isotopes
  BT1   beta-minus decay radioisotopes
  BT2   beta decay radioisotopes
  BT3   radioisotopes
  BT4   isotopes
  BT1   even-odd nuclei
  BT2   nuclei
  BT1   light nuclei
  BT2   nuclei
  BT1   years living radioisotopes
  BT2   radioisotopes
  BT3   isotopes

ARGON 39 BEAMS [2; 2] *Dec 86*
  BT1   ion beams
  BT2   beams

ARGON 40 [943; 943]
  BT1   argon isotopes
  BT1   even-even nuclei
  BT2   nuclei
  BT1   light nuclei
  BT2   nuclei
  BT1   stable isotopes
  BT2   isotopes
  RT   argon 40 beams

ARGON 40 BEAMS [576; 576]
  BT1   ion beams
  BT2   beams
  RT   argon 40

ARGON 40 REACTIONS [1,809; 1,809]
  BT1   heavy ion reactions
  BT2   nuclear reactions

ARGON 40 TARGET [263; 263]
  BT1   targets

ARGON 41 [286; 286]
  BT1   argon isotopes
  BT1   beta-minus decay radioisotopes
  BT2   beta decay radioisotopes
  BT3   radioisotopes
  BT4   isotopes
  BT1   even-odd nuclei
  BT2   nuclei
  BT1   hours living radioisotopes
  BT2   radioisotopes
  BT3   isotopes
  BT1   intermediate mass nuclei
  BT2   nuclei

ARGON 42 [24; 24]
  BT1   argon isotopes
  BT1   beta-minus decay radioisotopes
  BT2   beta decay radioisotopes
  BT3   radioisotopes
  BT4   isotopes
  BT1   even-even nuclei
  BT2   nuclei
  BT1   intermediate mass nuclei
  BT2   nuclei
  BT1   years living radioisotopes
  BT2   radioisotopes
  BT3   isotopes

ARGON 43 [8; 8]
  BT1   argon isotopes
  BT1   beta-minus decay radioisotopes
  BT2   beta decay radioisotopes
  BT3   radioisotopes
  BT4   isotopes
  BT1   even-odd nuclei
  BT2   nuclei
  BT1   intermediate mass nuclei
  BT2   nuclei
  BT1   minutes living radioisotopes
  BT2   radioisotopes
  BT3   isotopes

ARGON 44 [11; 11]
  BT1   argon isotopes
  BT1   beta-minus decay radioisotopes
  BT2   beta decay radioisotopes
  BT3   radioisotopes
  BT4   isotopes
  BT1   even-even nuclei
  BT2   nuclei
  BT1   intermediate mass nuclei
  BT2   nuclei
  BT1   minutes living radioisotopes
  BT2   radioisotopes
  BT3   isotopes

ARGON 45 [11; 11]
- BT1 argon isotopes
- BT1 beta-minus decay radioisotopes
  - BT2 beta decay radioisotopes
    - BT3 radioisotopes
      - BT4 isotopes
- BT1 even-odd nuclei
  - BT2 nuclei
- BT1 intermediate mass nuclei
  - BT2 nuclei
- BT1 seconds living radioisotopes
  - BT2 radioisotopes
    - BT3 isotopes

ARGON 46 [17; 17]
- BT1 argon isotopes
- BT1 beta-minus decay radioisotopes
  - BT2 beta decay radioisotopes
    - BT3 radioisotopes
      - BT4 isotopes
- BT1 even-even nuclei
  - BT2 nuclei
- BT1 intermediate mass nuclei
  - BT2 nuclei
- BT1 seconds living radioisotopes
  - BT2 radioisotopes
    - BT3 isotopes

ARGON 47 [4; 4] *Aug 86*
- BT1 argon isotopes
- BT1 even-odd nuclei
  - BT2 nuclei
- BT1 intermediate mass nuclei
  - BT2 nuclei

ARGON 49 [2; 2] *Sep 89*
- BT1 argon isotopes
- BT1 even-odd nuclei
  - BT2 nuclei
- BT1 intermediate mass nuclei
  - BT2 nuclei

ARGON 50 [2; 2] *Sep 89*
- BT1 argon isotopes
- BT1 even-even nuclei
  - BT2 nuclei
- BT1 intermediate mass nuclei
  - BT2 nuclei

ARGON 51 [2; 2] *Sep 89*
- BT1 argon isotopes
- BT1 even-odd nuclei
  - BT2 nuclei
- BT1 intermediate mass nuclei
  - BT2 nuclei

argonaut barcelona reactor
- USE argos reactor

argonaut bilbao reactor
- USE arbi reactor

argonaut lemont reactor
- USE argonaut reactor

ARGONAUT REACTOR [11; 11]
(ANL, Argonne, Illinois, USA)
- UF *argonaut lemont reactor*
- UF *cp-11 reactor*
- BT1 argonaut type reactors
  - BT2 enriched uranium reactors
    - BT3 reactors
  - BT2 research and test reactors
    - BT3 reactors
  - BT2 water cooled reactors
    - BT3 reactors
  - BT2 water moderated reactors
    - BT3 reactors
- BT1 research reactors
  - BT2 research and test reactors
    - BT3 reactors
- BT1 thermal reactors
  - BT2 reactors

- BT1 training reactors
  - BT2 research and test reactors
    - BT3 reactors

ARGONAUT TYPE REACTORS
[40; 255]
- BT1 enriched uranium reactors
  - BT2 reactors
- BT1 research and test reactors
  - BT2 reactors
- BT1 water cooled reactors
  - BT2 reactors
- BT1 water moderated reactors
  - BT2 reactors
- NT1 aeg-pr-10 reactor
- NT1 arbi reactor
- NT1 argonaut reactor
- NT1 argos reactor
- NT1 jason reactor
- NT1 lfr reactor
- NT1 moata reactor
- NT1 nestor reactor
- NT1 queen mary college utr-b react
- NT1 ra-1 reactor
- NT1 rb-2 reactor
- NT1 rien-1 reactor
- NT1 srrc-utr-100 reactor
- NT1 stark reactor
- NT1 strasbourg-cronenbourg reactor
- NT1 uftr reactor
- NT1 ulysse reactor
- NT1 urr reactor
- NT1 utr-10-kinki reactor
- NT1 vpi-utr-10 reactor

argonauta rien-1 reactor
- USE rien-1 reactor

argonauta rio reactor
- USE rien-1 reactor

argonne fast source reactor
- USE afsr reactor

argonne heavy water reactor
- USE cp-3 reactor

argonne national laboratory
- USE anl

argonne research reactor
- USE cp-5 reactor

argonne superconducting linac
- USE atlas superconducting linac

argonne tandem/linear acceler.
- USE atlas superconducting linac

argonne zgs
- USE zgs

ARGOS REACTOR [1; 1]
(Barcelona, Spain)
- UF *argonaut barcelona reactor*
- UF *barcelona argonaut reactor*
- BT1 argonaut type reactors
  - BT2 enriched uranium reactors
    - BT3 reactors
  - BT2 research and test reactors
    - BT3 reactors
  - BT2 water cooled reactors
    - BT3 reactors
  - BT2 water moderated reactors
    - BT3 reactors
- BT1 research reactors
  - BT2 research and test reactors

  - BT3 reactors
- BT1 thermal reactors
  - BT2 reactors
- BT1 training reactors
  - BT2 research and test reactors
    - BT3 reactors

ARGUS EVENT [5; 5]
- BT1 atmospheric explosions
  - BT2 explosions
- BT1 nuclear explosions
  - BT2 explosions

arid lands
- USE deserts

ARIEL SATELLITES [73; 73]
- BT1 satellites

ARIZONA [353; 353]
- BT1 usa
  - BT2 developed countries
  - BT2 north america

ARKANSAS [147; 147]
- BT1 usa
  - BT2 developed countries
  - BT2 north america

arkansas power-light-1 reactor
- USE arkansas-1 reactor

arkansas power-light-2 reactor
- USE arkansas-2 reactor

ARKANSAS-1 REACTOR [161; 161]
(Pope, Arkansas, USA)
- UF *arkansas power-light-1 reactor*
- UF *russellville-1 arkansas react.*
- BT1 pwr type reactors
  - BT2 enriched uranium reactors
    - BT3 reactors
  - BT2 power reactors
    - BT3 reactors
  - BT2 thermal reactors
    - BT3 reactors
  - BT2 water cooled reactors
    - BT3 reactors
  - BT2 water moderated reactors
    - BT3 reactors

ARKANSAS-2 REACTOR [57; 57]
(Pope, Arkansas, USA)
- UF *arkansas power-light-2 reactor*
- UF *russellville-2 arkansas react.*
- BT1 pwr type reactors
  - BT2 enriched uranium reactors
    - BT3 reactors
  - BT2 power reactors
    - BT3 reactors
  - BT2 thermal reactors
    - BT3 reactors
  - BT2 water cooled reactors
    - BT3 reactors
  - BT2 water moderated reactors
    - BT3 reactors

arktika (nuclear ship)
- USE ns leonid brezhnev

arktika reactor
(Prior to the name change in November 1982 this was a valid descriptor, and older material is so indexed.)
- USE leonid brezhnev reactor

ARMATURES [50; 50] *Apr 84*
- BT1 electrical equipment
  - BT2 equipment
- RT rotors
- RT stators

ARMENIAN-1 REACTOR [13; 13]
Aug 84
UF   oktemberian-1 reactor
BT1   wwer type reactors
  BT2   pwr type reactors
    BT3   enriched uranium reactors
      BT4   reactors
    BT3   power reactors
      BT4   reactors
    BT3   thermal reactors
      BT4   reactors
    BT3   water cooled reactors
      BT4   reactors
    BT3   water moderated reactors
      BT4   reactors

ARMENIAN-2 REACTOR [7; 7] *Aug 84*
UF   oktemberian-2 reactor
BT1   wwer type reactors
  BT2   pwr type reactors
    BT3   enriched uranium reactors
      BT4   reactors
    BT3   power reactors
      BT4   reactors
    BT3   thermal reactors
      BT4   reactors
    BT3   water cooled reactors
      BT4   reactors
    BT3   water moderated reactors
      BT4   reactors

ARMF-1 REACTOR [12; 12]
(Idaho National Engineering Lab., Idaho Falls, Idaho, USA)
UF   adv. reactivity meas. fac.-1
BT1   enriched uranium reactors
  BT2   reactors
BT1   pool type reactors
  BT2   water cooled reactors
    BT3   reactors
  BT2   water moderated reactors
    BT3   reactors
BT1   research reactors
  BT2   research and test reactors
    BT3   reactors
BT1   thermal reactors
  BT2   reactors

ARMS [427; 1,130] *Feb 76*
BT1   limbs
  BT2   body areas
    BT3   body
NT1   hands
  NT2   fingers

ARMS CONTROL [35; 35] *May 88*
RT   nuclear weapons
RT   treaties
RT   verification

army personnel
USE   military personnel

army pulsed reactor assembly
USE   aprf reactor

aromatic acids
USE   carboxylic acids

aromatic compounds
USE   aromatics

aromatic hydrocarbons
USE   aromatics

AROMATICS [4,146; 15,465]
UF   aromatic compounds
UF   aromatic hydrocarbons
UF   polycyclic aromatic hydrocarbo
UF+   ndpp
UF+   p-nitrodimethylaminopropiophen
UF+   pcb (polychlorinated biphenyl)
BT1   organic compounds
NT1   acetophenone
NT1   aniline
NT1   benzene
NT1   benzidine
NT1   benzyl alcohol
NT1   bibenzyl
NT1   biphenyl
NT1   condensed aromatics
  NT2   acenaphthene
  NT2   anthracene
  NT2   benzanthracene
  NT2   benzopyrene
  NT2   cholanthrene
  NT2   chrysene
  NT2   dimethylbenzanthracene
  NT2   fluorene
  NT2   indene
  NT2   indocyanine green
  NT2   naphthalene
  NT2   perylene
  NT2   phenanthrene
  NT2   pyrene
  NT2   tetracene
  NT2   triphenylene
  NT2   violanthrone
  NT2   3-methylcholanthrene
NT1   cumene
NT1   cymene
NT1   ddt
NT1   divinylbenzene
NT1   durene
NT1   halogenated aromatic hydrocarb
  NT2   brominated aromatic hydrocarbo
  NT2   chlorinated aromatic hydrocarb
    NT3   aldrin
  NT2   fluorinated aromatic hydrocarb
  NT2   iodinated aromatic hydrocarbon
NT1   mesitylene
NT1   methyl tyrosine
NT1   oligophenylenes
NT1   pethidine
NT1   phenols
  NT2   amidol
  NT2   bamp
  NT2   cresols
  NT2   dinitrophenol
  NT2   eriochrome dyes
  NT2   naphthols
    NT3   acid chrome dyes
    NT3   beryllon
    NT3   nitroso-r salt
    NT3   pan
    NT3   thorin
    NT3   trypan blue
    NT3   1-nitroso-2-naphthol
  NT2   nitrophenol
  NT2   phenol
  NT2   phenolphthalein
  NT2   picric acid
  NT2   polyphenols
    NT3   arsenazo
    NT3   aurin
    NT3   bromosulfophthalein
    NT3   catecholamines
    NT3   curcumin
    NT3   dopamine
    NT3   fluorescein
    NT3   hematoxylin
    NT3   morin
    NT3   pyridylazoresorcinol
    NT3   pyrocatechol
    NT3   pyrogallol
    NT3   quercetin
    NT3   resorcinol
    NT3   stilbestrol
    NT3   tannic acid
    NT3   tiron
  NT2   pop
  NT2   thymol
  NT2   tyramine
NT1   phenylalanine
NT1   polyphenyls
  NT2   santowax
  NT2   terphenyls
    NT3   terphenyl-meta
    NT3   terphenyl-ortho
    NT3   terphenyl-para
NT1   quaterphenyls
NT1   quinones
  NT2   anthraquinones
    NT3   alizarin
    NT3   carminic acid
    NT3   quinizarin
  NT2   benzoquinones
    NT3   chloranil
    NT3   chloranilic acid
    NT3   quinhydrone
    NT3   ubiquinone
  NT2   rhodizonic acid
  NT2   vitamin k
NT1   stilbene
NT1   styrene
NT1   tetralin
NT1   thyronine
NT1   tolan
NT1   toluene
NT1   tyrosine
NT1   xylenes
  NT2   xylene-para
RT   aromatization
RT   cyanine dyes
RT   hydrocarbons
RT   ninhydrin
RT   organic coolants
RT   organic moderators
RT   solvesso

AROMATIZATION [11; 11] *May 86*
(Conversion of any nonaromatic hydrocarbon structure to aromatic hydrocarbon.)
BT1   chemical reactions
RT   aromatics

ARRAY PROCESSORS [393; 393]
Jul 85
(Multiprocessors composed of sets of identical CPUs, each set acting synchronously under the control of a common unit.)
BT1   digital computers
  BT2   computers
RT   data processing
RT   hypercube computers
RT   microprocessors

ARRHENIUS EQUATION [807; 807]
RT   activation energy
RT   chemical reaction kinetics
RT   partition
RT   reaction kinetics

ARSANILIC ACID [1; 1]
BT1   amines
  BT2   organic compounds
BT1   arsonic acids
  BT2   arsenic compounds
  BT2   organic acids
    BT3   organic compounds

ARSENATES [349; 349]
(Specific compounds should be indexed by coordination of a descriptor of the form (CATION) COMPOUNDS and the above anion descriptor.)
BT1   arsenic compounds
BT1   oxygen compounds
RT   arsenic oxides

ARSENAZO [351; 351]
BT1   arsonic acids
  BT2   arsenic compounds
  BT2   organic acids
    BT3   organic compounds
BT1   azo compounds
  BT2   organic nitrogen compounds
    BT3   organic compounds
BT1   polyphenols
  BT2   phenols
    BT3   aromatics
      BT4   organic compounds
    BT3   hydroxy compounds
      BT4   organic compounds
BT1   reagents
BT1   sulfonic acids
  BT2   organic acids

        BT3   organic compounds
        BT2   organic sulfur compounds
        BT3   organic compounds

ARSENIC [1,603; 1,603]
    BT1   semimetals
    BT2   elements

ARSENIC ADDITIONS [121; 121]
    RT   arsenic alloys
    RT   arsenides

ARSENIC ALLOYS [210; 212]
    (Alloys containing more than 1% As.)
    BT1   alloys
    RT   arsenic additions
    RT   arsenides

ARSENIC BROMIDES [8; 8]
    BT1   arsenic compounds
    BT1   bromides
    BT2   bromine compounds
        BT3   halogen compounds
    BT2   halides
        BT3   halogen compounds

ARSENIC CHLORIDES [36; 36]
    BT1   arsenic compounds
    BT1   chlorides
    BT2   chlorine compounds
        BT3   halogen compounds
    BT2   halides
        BT3   halogen compounds

ARSENIC COMPLEXES [44; 44]
    BT1   complexes

ARSENIC COMPOUNDS [514; 6,780]
    UF   arsonium compounds
    NT1   arsenates
    NT1   arsenic bromides
    NT1   arsenic chlorides
    NT1   arsenic fluorides
    NT1   arsenic hydrides
    NT1   arsenic iodides
    NT1   arsenic oxides
    NT1   arsenic selenides
    NT1   arsenic sulfides
    NT1   arsenic tellurides
    NT1   arsenides
        NT2   aluminium arsenides
        NT2   americium arsenides
        NT2   berkelium arsenides
        NT2   boron arsenides
        NT2   cadmium arsenides
        NT2   californium arsenides
        NT2   cerium arsenides
        NT2   cobalt arsenides
        NT2   copper arsenides
        NT2   curium arsenides
        NT2   europium arsenides
        NT2   gadolinium arsenides
        NT2   gallium arsenides
        NT2   germanium arsenides
        NT2   indium arsenides
        NT2   lithium arsenides
        NT2   magnesium arsenides
        NT2   manganese arsenides
        NT2   molybdenum arsenides
        NT2   neptunium arsenides
        NT2   nickel arsenides
        NT2   niobium arsenides
        NT2   palladium arsenides
        NT2   platinum arsenides
        NT2   plutonium arsenides
        NT2   praseodymium arsenides
        NT2   ruthenium arsenides
        NT2   samarium arsenides
        NT2   silicon arsenides
        NT2   silver arsenides
        NT2   terbium arsenides
        NT2   thorium arsenides
        NT2   thulium arsenides
        NT2   tin arsenides
        NT2   uranium arsenides
        NT2   vanadium arsenides
        NT2   yttrium arsenides

        NT2   zinc arsenides
        NT2   zirconium arsenides
    NT1   arsenic acids
        NT2   arsanilic acid
        NT2   arsenazo
        NT2   beryllon
    NT1   cacodylic acid
    NT1   thorin
    RT   organic arsenic compounds

ARSENIC FLUORIDES [76; 76]
    BT1   arsenic compounds
    BT1   fluorides
        BT2   fluorine compounds
            BT3   halogen compounds
        BT2   halides
            BT3   halogen compounds

ARSENIC HYDRIDES [40; 40]
    BT1   arsenic compounds
    BT1   hydrides
        BT2   hydrogen compounds

ARSENIC IODIDES [47; 47]
    BT1   arsenic compounds
    BT1   iodides
        BT2   halides
            BT3   halogen compounds
        BT2   iodine compounds
            BT3   halogen compounds

ARSENIC IONS [479; 479]
    BT1   ions
        BT2   charged particles

ARSENIC ISOTOPES [88; 885]
    NT1   arsenic 65
    NT1   arsenic 66
    NT1   arsenic 67
    NT1   arsenic 68
    NT1   arsenic 69
    NT1   arsenic 70
    NT1   arsenic 71
    NT1   arsenic 72
    NT1   arsenic 73
    NT1   arsenic 74
    NT1   arsenic 75
    NT1   arsenic 76
    NT1   arsenic 77
    NT1   arsenic 78
    NT1   arsenic 79
    NT1   arsenic 80
    NT1   arsenic 81
    NT1   arsenic 82
    NT1   arsenic 83
    NT1   arsenic 84
    NT1   arsenic 85
    NT1   arsenic 86
    NT1   arsenic 87

ARSENIC OXIDES [116; 117]
    BT1   arsenic compounds
    BT1   oxides
        BT2   chalcogenides
        BT2   oxygen compounds
    RT   arsenates
    RT   oxide minerals
    RT   zeunerite

ARSENIC SELENIDES [79; 79] Feb 78
    BT1   arsenic compounds
    BT1   selenides
        BT2   chalcogenides
        BT2   selenium compounds

ARSENIC SULFIDES [99; 99]
    BT1   arsenic compounds
    BT1   sulfides
        BT2   chalcogenides
        BT2   sulfur compounds

ARSENIC TELLURIDES [60; 60]
    Mar 77
    BT1   arsenic compounds
    BT1   tellurides
        BT2   chalcogenides
        BT2   tellurium compounds

ARSENIC 65 [4; 4] Dec 90
    BT1   arsenic isotopes
    BT1   intermediate mass nuclei
        BT2   nuclei
    BT1   odd-even nuclei
        BT2   nuclei

ARSENIC 66 [5; 5] Sep 79
    BT1   arsenic isotopes
    BT1   beta-plus decay radioisotopes
        BT2   beta decay radioisotopes
            BT3   radioisotopes
                BT4   isotopes
    BT1   intermediate mass nuclei
        BT2   nuclei
    BT1   millisec living radioisotopes
        BT2   radioisotopes
            BT3   isotopes
    BT1   odd-odd nuclei
        BT2   nuclei

ARSENIC 67 [6; 6] Jul 78
    BT1   arsenic isotopes
    BT1   beta-plus decay radioisotopes
        BT2   beta decay radioisotopes
            BT3   radioisotopes
                BT4   isotopes
    BT1   electron capture radioisotopes
        BT2   beta decay radioisotopes
            BT3   radioisotopes
                BT4   isotopes
    BT1   intermediate mass nuclei
        BT2   nuclei
    BT1   odd-even nuclei
        BT2   nuclei
    BT1   seconds living radioisotopes
        BT2   radioisotopes
            BT3   isotopes

ARSENIC 68 [16; 16]
    BT1   arsenic isotopes
    BT1   beta-plus decay radioisotopes
        BT2   beta decay radioisotopes
            BT3   radioisotopes
                BT4   isotopes
    BT1   intermediate mass nuclei
        BT2   nuclei
    BT1   minutes living radioisotopes
        BT2   radioisotopes
            BT3   isotopes
    BT1   odd-odd nuclei
        BT2   nuclei

ARSENIC 69 [38; 38]
    BT1   arsenic isotopes
    BT1   beta-plus decay radioisotopes
        BT2   beta decay radioisotopes
            BT3   radioisotopes
                BT4   isotopes
    BT1   intermediate mass nuclei
        BT2   nuclei
    BT1   minutes living radioisotopes
        BT2   radioisotopes
            BT3   isotopes
    BT1   odd-even nuclei
        BT2   nuclei

ARSENIC 70 [26; 26]
    BT1   arsenic isotopes
    BT1   beta-plus decay radioisotopes
        BT2   beta decay radioisotopes
            BT3   radioisotopes
                BT4   isotopes
    BT1   electron capture radioisotopes
        BT2   beta decay radioisotopes
            BT3   radioisotopes
                BT4   isotopes
    BT1   intermediate mass nuclei
        BT2   nuclei
    BT1   minutes living radioisotopes
        BT2   radioisotopes
            BT3   isotopes
    BT1   odd-odd nuclei
        BT2   nuclei

ARSENIC 71 [66; 66]
- BT1 arsenic isotopes
- BT1 beta-plus decay radioisotopes
  - BT2 beta decay radioisotopes
    - BT3 radioisotopes
      - BT4 isotopes
- BT1 days living radioisotopes
  - BT2 radioisotopes
    - BT3 isotopes
- BT1 electron capture radioisotopes
  - BT2 beta decay radioisotopes
    - BT3 radioisotopes
      - BT4 isotopes
- BT1 intermediate mass nuclei
  - BT2 nuclei
- BT1 odd-even nuclei
  - BT2 nuclei

ARSENIC 72 [39; 39]
- BT1 arsenic isotopes
- BT1 beta-plus decay radioisotopes
  - BT2 beta decay radioisotopes
    - BT3 radioisotopes
      - BT4 isotopes
- BT1 days living radioisotopes
  - BT2 radioisotopes
    - BT3 isotopes
- BT1 electron capture radioisotopes
  - BT2 beta decay radioisotopes
    - BT3 radioisotopes
      - BT4 isotopes
- BT1 intermediate mass nuclei
  - BT2 nuclei
- BT1 odd-odd nuclei
  - BT2 nuclei

ARSENIC 73 [77; 77]
- BT1 arsenic isotopes
- BT1 days living radioisotopes
  - BT2 radioisotopes
    - BT3 isotopes
- BT1 electron capture radioisotopes
  - BT2 beta decay radioisotopes
    - BT3 radioisotopes
      - BT4 isotopes
- BT1 intermediate mass nuclei
  - BT2 nuclei
- BT1 odd-even nuclei
  - BT2 nuclei

ARSENIC 74 [89; 89]
- BT1 arsenic isotopes
- BT1 beta-minus decay radioisotopes
  - BT2 beta decay radioisotopes
    - BT3 radioisotopes
      - BT4 isotopes
- BT1 beta-plus decay radioisotopes
  - BT2 beta decay radioisotopes
    - BT3 radioisotopes
      - BT4 isotopes
- BT1 days living radioisotopes
  - BT2 radioisotopes
    - BT3 isotopes
- BT1 electron capture radioisotopes
  - BT2 beta decay radioisotopes
    - BT3 radioisotopes
      - BT4 isotopes
- BT1 intermediate mass nuclei
  - BT2 nuclei
- BT1 odd-odd nuclei
  - BT2 nuclei

ARSENIC 75 [243; 243]
- BT1 arsenic isotopes
- BT1 intermediate mass nuclei
  - BT2 nuclei
- BT1 odd-even nuclei
  - BT2 nuclei
- BT1 stable isotopes
  - BT2 isotopes

ARSENIC 75 TARGET [98; 98]
- BT1 targets

ARSENIC 76 [175; 175]
- BT1 arsenic isotopes
- BT1 beta-minus decay radioisotopes
  - BT2 beta decay radioisotopes
    - BT3 radioisotopes
      - BT4 isotopes
- BT1 days living radioisotopes
  - BT2 radioisotopes
    - BT3 isotopes
- BT1 intermediate mass nuclei
  - BT2 nuclei
- BT1 odd-odd nuclei
  - BT2 nuclei

ARSENIC 77 [54; 54]
- BT1 arsenic isotopes
- BT1 beta-minus decay radioisotopes
  - BT2 beta decay radioisotopes
    - BT3 radioisotopes
      - BT4 isotopes
- BT1 days living radioisotopes
  - BT2 radioisotopes
    - BT3 isotopes
- BT1 intermediate mass nuclei
  - BT2 nuclei
- BT1 odd-even nuclei
  - BT2 nuclei

ARSENIC 78 [12; 12]
- BT1 arsenic isotopes
- BT1 beta-minus decay radioisotopes
  - BT2 beta decay radioisotopes
    - BT3 radioisotopes
      - BT4 isotopes
- BT1 hours living radioisotopes
  - BT2 radioisotopes
    - BT3 isotopes
- BT1 intermediate mass nuclei
  - BT2 nuclei
- BT1 odd-odd nuclei
  - BT2 nuclei

ARSENIC 79 [12; 12]
- BT1 arsenic isotopes
- BT1 beta-minus decay radioisotopes
  - BT2 beta decay radioisotopes
    - BT3 radioisotopes
      - BT4 isotopes
- BT1 intermediate mass nuclei
  - BT2 nuclei
- BT1 minutes living radioisotopes
  - BT2 radioisotopes
    - BT3 isotopes
- BT1 odd-even nuclei
  - BT2 nuclei

ARSENIC 80 [7; 7]
- BT1 arsenic isotopes
- BT1 beta-minus decay radioisotopes
  - BT2 beta decay radioisotopes
    - BT3 radioisotopes
      - BT4 isotopes
- BT1 intermediate mass nuclei
  - BT2 nuclei
- BT1 odd-odd nuclei
  - BT2 nuclei
- BT1 seconds living radioisotopes
  - BT2 radioisotopes
    - BT3 isotopes

ARSENIC 81 [15; 15]
- BT1 arsenic isotopes
- BT1 beta-minus decay radioisotopes
  - BT2 beta decay radioisotopes
    - BT3 radioisotopes
      - BT4 isotopes
- BT1 intermediate mass nuclei
  - BT2 nuclei
- BT1 odd-even nuclei
  - BT2 nuclei
- BT1 seconds living radioisotopes
  - BT2 radioisotopes
    - BT3 isotopes

ARSENIC 82 [5; 5]
- BT1 arsenic isotopes
- BT1 beta-minus decay radioisotopes
  - BT2 beta decay radioisotopes
    - BT3 radioisotopes
      - BT4 isotopes
- BT1 intermediate mass nuclei
  - BT2 nuclei
- BT1 odd-odd nuclei
  - BT2 nuclei
- BT1 seconds living radioisotopes
  - BT2 radioisotopes
    - BT3 isotopes

ARSENIC 83 [14; 14]
- BT1 arsenic isotopes
- BT1 beta-minus decay radioisotopes
  - BT2 beta decay radioisotopes
    - BT3 radioisotopes
      - BT4 isotopes
- BT1 intermediate mass nuclei
  - BT2 nuclei
- BT1 odd-even nuclei
  - BT2 nuclei
- BT1 seconds living radioisotopes
  - BT2 radioisotopes
    - BT3 isotopes

ARSENIC 84 [10; 10]
- BT1 arsenic isotopes
- BT1 beta-minus decay radioisotopes
  - BT2 beta decay radioisotopes
    - BT3 radioisotopes
      - BT4 isotopes
- BT1 intermediate mass nuclei
  - BT2 nuclei
- BT1 millisec living radioisotopes
  - BT2 radioisotopes
    - BT3 isotopes
- BT1 odd-odd nuclei
  - BT2 nuclei
- BT1 seconds living radioisotopes
  - BT2 radioisotopes
    - BT3 isotopes

ARSENIC 85 [27; 27]
- BT1 arsenic isotopes
- BT1 beta-minus decay radioisotopes
  - BT2 beta decay radioisotopes
    - BT3 radioisotopes
      - BT4 isotopes
- BT1 intermediate mass nuclei
  - BT2 nuclei
- BT1 odd-even nuclei
  - BT2 nuclei
- BT1 seconds living radioisotopes
  - BT2 radioisotopes
    - BT3 isotopes

ARSENIC 86 [7; 7]
- BT1 arsenic isotopes
- BT1 beta-minus decay radioisotopes
  - BT2 beta decay radioisotopes
    - BT3 radioisotopes
      - BT4 isotopes
- BT1 intermediate mass nuclei
  - BT2 nuclei
- BT1 millisec living radioisotopes
  - BT2 radioisotopes
    - BT3 isotopes
- BT1 odd-odd nuclei
  - BT2 nuclei

ARSENIC 87 [5; 5]
- BT1 arsenic isotopes
- BT1 beta-minus decay radioisotopes
  - BT2 beta decay radioisotopes
    - BT3 radioisotopes
      - BT4 isotopes
- BT1 intermediate mass nuclei
  - BT2 nuclei
- BT1 millisec living radioisotopes
  - BT2 radioisotopes
    - BT3 isotopes
- BT1 odd-even nuclei
  - BT2 nuclei

ARSENIDES [618; 5,246]
- BT1 arsenic compounds
- BT1 pnictides
- NT1 aluminium arsenides
- NT1 americium arsenides
- NT1 berkelium arsenides
- NT1 boron arsenides
- NT1 cadmium arsenides
- NT1 californium arsenides
- NT1 cerium arsenides
- NT1 cobalt arsenides
- NT1 copper arsenides
- NT1 curium arsenides
- NT1 europium arsenides
- NT1 gadolinium arsenides
- NT1 gallium arsenides
- NT1 germanium arsenides
- NT1 indium arsenides
- NT1 lithium arsenides
- NT1 magnesium arsenides
- NT1 manganese arsenides
- NT1 molybdenum arsenides
- NT1 neptunium arsenides
- NT1 nickel arsenides
- NT1 niobium arsenides
- NT1 palladium arsenides
- NT1 platinum arsenides
- NT1 plutonium arsenides
- NT1 praseodymium arsenides
- NT1 ruthenium arsenides
- NT1 samarium arsenides
- NT1 silicon arsenides
- NT1 silver arsenides
- NT1 terbium arsenides
- NT1 thorium arsenides
- NT1 thulium arsenides
- NT1 tin arsenides
- NT1 uranium arsenides
- NT1 vanadium arsenides
- NT1 yttrium arsenides
- NT1 zinc arsenides
- NT1 zirconium arsenides
- RT arsenic additions
- RT arsenic alloys
- RT intermetallic compounds

arsi reactor
- USE avogadro rs-1 reactor

arsonates
- USE organic arsenic compounds

ARSONIC ACIDS [20; 350]
- BT1 arsenic compounds
- BT1 organic acids
- BT2 organic compounds
- NT1 arsanilic acid
- NT1 arsenazo
- NT1 beryllon

arsonium compounds
- USE arsenic compounds

art objects
- USE cultural objects

ARTEMIA [39; 39]
- BT1 crustaceans
- BT2 aquatic organisms
- BT2 arthropods
- BT3 invertebrates
- BT4 animals

ARTERIES [3,028; 6,605]
- BT1 blood vessels
- BT2 cardiovascular system
- BT2 organs
- BT3 body
- NT1 aorta
- NT1 carotid arteries
- NT1 coronaries
- RT arteriosclerosis
- RT blood pressure

ARTERIOSCLEROSIS [507; 507]
- UF *atherosclerosis*
- BT1 cardiovascular diseases
- BT2 diseases
- RT arteries

arthritis
- USE rheumatic diseases

ARTHROPODS [62; 3,331]
- BT1 invertebrates
- BT2 animals
- NT1 arachnids
- NT2 mites
- NT2 scorpions
- NT2 spiders
- NT2 ticks
- NT1 crustaceans
- NT2 artemia
- NT2 daphnia
- NT2 lobsters
- NT2 prawns
- NT2 shrimp
- NT1 insects
- NT2 beetles
- NT3 boll weevil
- NT3 tribolium
- NT2 cockroaches
- NT2 flies
- NT3 fruit flies
- NT4 ceratitis capitata
- NT4 dacus
- NT5 dacus oleae
- NT4 drosophila
- NT4 rhagoletis cerasi
- NT3 glossina
- NT3 hylemya antiqua
- NT3 screwworm fly
- NT2 grasshoppers
- NT3 locusts
- NT2 hemiptera
- NT3 aphids
- NT2 lepidoptera
- NT3 moths
- NT4 bollworm
- NT4 codling moth
- NT4 lymantria dispar
- NT4 rice stem borers
- NT4 silkworm
- NT2 mosquitoes
- NT2 wasps
- NT3 habrobracon

ARTIFICIAL INTELLIGENCE [644; 644] *Dec 86*
- RT computers
- RT expert systems
- RT neural networks
- RT programming

ARTIFICIAL ORGANS [55; 61]
- NT1 mechanical heart
- RT organs

ARTIFICIAL RADIATION BELTS [5; 5]
- BT1 radiation belts
- RT nuclear explosions

ARYL RADICALS [81; 337]
- BT1 radicals
- NT1 anisyl radicals
- NT1 benzyl radicals
- NT1 mesityl radicals
- NT1 naphthyl radicals
- NT1 phenethyl radicals
- NT1 phenyl radicals
- NT1 tolyl radicals

arylmagnesium compounds
- USE grignard reagents

as low as reasonably achievabl
- USE alara

ASBESTOS [292; 292]
- RT refractories

ASCARIDAE [10; 26]
- BT1 nematodes
- BT2 invertebrates
- BT3 animals
- BT1 parasites
- NT1 ascaris
- RT chickens
- RT intestines
- RT man

ASCARIS [32; 32]
- BT1 ascaridae
- BT2 nematodes
- BT3 invertebrates
- BT4 animals
- BT2 parasites
- BT1 helminths
- BT2 parasites
- RT small intestine

ASCITES [111; 111]
- BT1 pathological changes
- BT2 diseases
- BT1 symptoms
- RT ascites tumor cells
- RT ehrlich ascites tumor
- RT peritoneum

ASCITES TUMOR CELLS [504; 504]
- BT1 tumor cells
- BT2 animal cells
- RT ascites
- RT ehrlich ascites tumor
- RT neoplasms

ASCO-1 REACTOR [12; 12] *Apr 77*
(Asco, Tarragona, Spain)
- BT1 pwr type reactors
- BT2 enriched uranium reactors
- BT3 reactors
- BT2 power reactors
- BT3 reactors
- BT2 thermal reactors
- BT3 reactors
- BT2 water cooled reactors
- BT3 reactors
- BT2 water moderated reactors
- BT3 reactors

ASCO-2 REACTOR [12; 12] *Apr 77*
(Asco, Tarragona, Spain)
- BT1 pwr type reactors
- BT2 enriched uranium reactors
- BT3 reactors
- BT2 power reactors
- BT3 reactors
- BT2 thermal reactors
- BT3 reactors
- BT2 water cooled reactors
- BT3 reactors
- BT2 water moderated reactors
- BT3 reactors

ASCORBIC ACID [525; 525]
- UF *vitamin c*
- BT1 vitamins
- RT redox process

ASDEX TOKAMAK [858; 858] *Mar 77*
- BT1 tokamak devices
- BT2 closed plasma devices
- BT3 thermonuclear devices

ASHES [871; 1,251] *Feb 76*
- BT1 combustion products
- BT1 solid wastes
- BT2 wastes
- NT1 fly ash
- RT residues

ashing (dry)
   USE   dry ashing

ashing (wet)
   USE   wet ashing

asi
   USE   adiabatic surface ionization

ASIA [208; 12,241]
- NT1   afghanistan
- NT1   bangladesh
- NT1   bhutan
- NT1   burma
- NT1   cambodia
- NT1   china
- NT1   hong kong
- NT1   india
- NT1   indonesia
- NT1   iran
- NT1   iraq
- NT1   israel
- NT1   japan
  - NT2   hiroshima
  - NT2   nagasaki
- NT1   jordan
- NT1   kuwait
- NT1   laos
- NT1   lebanon
- NT1   macao
- NT1   malaysia
- NT1   mongolian peoples republic
- NT1   nepal
- NT1   north korea
- NT1   oman
- NT1   pakistan
- NT1   philippines
- NT1   qatar
- NT1   republic of korea
- NT1   saudi arabia
- NT1   singapore
- NT1   sri lanka
- NT1   syria
- NT1   thailand
- NT1   turkey
- NT1   viet nam

ASPA DEVICE [0; 0]
- BT1   magnetic mirrors
  - BT2   open plasma devices
    - BT3   thermonuclear devices

asparagic acid
   USE   aspartic acid

ASPARAGINE [103; 103]
- UF   *agedoite*
- UF   *althein*
- UF   *aminosuccinamic acid-alpha*
- UF   *asparagine-beta*
- UF   *asparamide*
- BT1   amides
  - BT2   organic nitrogen compounds
    - BT3   organic compounds
- BT1   amino acids
  - BT2   carboxylic acids
    - BT3   organic acids
      - BT4   organic compounds
- RT   aspartic acid

asparagine-beta
   USE   asparagine

asparaginic acid
   USE   aspartic acid

asparamide
   USE   asparagine

ASPARTIC ACID [286; 286]
- UF   *aminosuccinic acid*
- UF   *asparagic acid*
- UF   *asparaginic acid*
- BT1   amino acids
  - BT2   carboxylic acids
    - BT3   organic acids
      - BT4   organic compounds
- RT   asparagine
- RT   succinic acid

ASPECT RATIO [994; 994]
- RT   closed plasma devices
- RT   plasma
- RT   tori

ASPERGILLUS [230; 230]
- BT1   fungi
  - BT2   plants
- RT   aflatoxins

asphaltenes
   USE   asphalts

ASPHALTITE [14; 14]
- BT1   other organic compounds
  - BT2   organic compounds
- RT   bitumens

ASPHALTS [245; 245]
- UF   *asphaltenes*
- BT1   bitumens
  - BT2   tar
    - BT3   other organic compounds
      - BT4   organic compounds

aspirin
   USE   acetylsalicylic acid

assaying (qualitative)
   USE   qualitative chemical analysis

assaying (quantitative)
   USE   quantitative chemical analysis

ASSE SALT MINE [105; 105] *May 88*
(Underground test facility in the Federal Republic of Germany for research and development in the field of radioactive waste storage and disposal.)
- BT1   mines
  - BT2   underground facilities
- BT1   radioactive waste facilities
  - BT2   nuclear facilities
- RT   federal republic of germany
- RT   radioactive waste disposal
- RT   salt deposits
- RT   underground disposal

assessments
   USE   charges

assignments
   USE   allocations

assistance nuc acc/rad emerg
   USE   canare

ast-1 reactor
   USE   arbus reactor

ASTATINATION [11; 11] *Sep 83*
- BT1   halogenation
  - BT2   chemical reactions

ASTATINE [75; 75]
- BT1   halogens
  - BT2   nonmetals
    - BT3   elements

ASTATINE BROMIDES [3; 3]
- BT1   astatine compounds
  - BT2   halogen compounds
- BT1   bromides
  - BT2   bromine compounds
    - BT3   halogen compounds
  - BT2   halides
    - BT3   halogen compounds

ASTATINE CHLORIDES [6; 6]
- BT1   astatine compounds
  - BT2   halogen compounds
- BT1   chlorides
  - BT2   chlorine compounds
    - BT3   halogen compounds
  - BT2   halides
    - BT3   halogen compounds

ASTATINE COMPLEXES [25; 25]
- BT1   complexes

ASTATINE COMPOUNDS [92; 99]
- BT1   halogen compounds
- NT1   astatine bromides
- NT1   astatine chlorides
- NT1   astatine iodides

ASTATINE IODIDES [3; 3]
- BT1   astatine compounds
  - BT2   halogen compounds
- BT1   iodides
  - BT2   halides
    - BT3   halogen compounds
  - BT2   iodine compounds
    - BT3   halogen compounds

ASTATINE IONS [16; 16]
- BT1   ions
  - BT2   charged particles

ASTATINE ISOTOPES [69; 599]
- NT1   astatine 194
- NT1   astatine 195
- NT1   astatine 196
- NT1   astatine 197
- NT1   astatine 198
- NT1   astatine 199
- NT1   astatine 200
- NT1   astatine 201
- NT1   astatine 202
- NT1   astatine 203
- NT1   astatine 204
- NT1   astatine 205
- NT1   astatine 206
- NT1   astatine 207
- NT1   astatine 208
- NT1   astatine 209
- NT1   astatine 210
- NT1   astatine 211
- NT1   astatine 212
- NT1   astatine 213
- NT1   astatine 214
- NT1   astatine 215
- NT1   astatine 216
- NT1   astatine 217
- NT1   astatine 218
- NT1   astatine 219
- NT1   astatine 220
- NT1   astatine 221
- NT1   astatine 222
- NT1   astatine 223

ASTATINE 194 [2; 2] *Nov 85*
- BT1   alpha decay radioisotopes
  - BT2   radioisotopes
    - BT3   isotopes
- BT1   astatine isotopes
- BT1   heavy nuclei
  - BT2   nuclei
- BT1   millisec living radioisotopes
  - BT2   radioisotopes
    - BT3   isotopes

ASTATINE 195 [3; 3]
BT1 astatine isotopes
BT1 electron capture radioisotopes
BT2 beta decay radioisotopes
BT3 radioisotopes
BT4 isotopes
BT1 heavy nuclei
BT2 nuclei
BT1 millisec living radioisotopes
BT2 radioisotopes
BT3 isotopes
BT1 odd-even nuclei
BT2 nuclei

ASTATINE 196 [1; 1]
BT1 alpha decay radioisotopes
BT2 radioisotopes
BT3 isotopes
BT1 astatine isotopes
BT1 heavy nuclei
BT2 nuclei
BT1 millisec living radioisotopes
BT2 radioisotopes
BT3 isotopes
BT1 odd-odd nuclei
BT2 nuclei

ASTATINE 197 [3; 3]
BT1 alpha decay radioisotopes
BT2 radioisotopes
BT3 isotopes
BT1 astatine isotopes
BT1 electron capture radioisotopes
BT2 beta decay radioisotopes
BT3 radioisotopes
BT4 isotopes
BT1 heavy nuclei
BT2 nuclei
BT1 millisec living radioisotopes
BT2 radioisotopes
BT3 isotopes
BT1 odd-even nuclei
BT2 nuclei

ASTATINE 198 [2; 2]
BT1 alpha decay radioisotopes
BT2 radioisotopes
BT3 isotopes
BT1 astatine isotopes
BT1 heavy nuclei
BT2 nuclei
BT1 odd-odd nuclei
BT2 nuclei
BT1 seconds living radioisotopes
BT2 radioisotopes
BT3 isotopes

ASTATINE 199 [6; 6]
BT1 alpha decay radioisotopes
BT2 radioisotopes
BT3 isotopes
BT1 astatine isotopes
BT1 electron capture radioisotopes
BT2 beta decay radioisotopes
BT3 radioisotopes
BT4 isotopes
BT1 heavy nuclei
BT2 nuclei
BT1 odd-even nuclei
BT2 nuclei
BT1 seconds living radioisotopes
BT2 radioisotopes
BT3 isotopes

ASTATINE 200 [2; 2]
BT1 alpha decay radioisotopes
BT2 radioisotopes
BT3 isotopes
BT1 astatine isotopes
BT1 electron capture radioisotopes
BT2 beta decay radioisotopes
BT3 radioisotopes
BT4 isotopes
BT1 heavy nuclei
BT2 nuclei
BT1 odd-odd nuclei
BT2 nuclei
BT1 seconds living radioisotopes
BT2 radioisotopes
BT3 isotopes

ASTATINE 201 [11; 11]
BT1 alpha decay radioisotopes
BT2 radioisotopes
BT3 isotopes
BT1 astatine isotopes
BT1 electron capture radioisotopes
BT2 beta decay radioisotopes
BT3 radioisotopes
BT4 isotopes
BT1 heavy nuclei
BT2 nuclei
BT1 minutes living radioisotopes
BT2 radioisotopes
BT3 isotopes
BT1 odd-even nuclei
BT2 nuclei

ASTATINE 202 [3; 3]
BT1 alpha decay radioisotopes
BT2 radioisotopes
BT3 isotopes
BT1 astatine isotopes
BT1 electron capture radioisotopes
BT2 beta decay radioisotopes
BT3 radioisotopes
BT4 isotopes
BT1 heavy nuclei
BT2 nuclei
BT1 isomeric transition isotopes
BT2 radioisotopes
BT3 isotopes
BT1 minutes living radioisotopes
BT2 radioisotopes
BT3 isotopes
BT1 odd-odd nuclei
BT2 nuclei
BT1 seconds living radioisotopes
BT2 radioisotopes
BT3 isotopes

ASTATINE 203 [16; 16]
BT1 alpha decay radioisotopes
BT2 radioisotopes
BT3 isotopes
BT1 astatine isotopes
BT1 electron capture radioisotopes
BT2 beta decay radioisotopes
BT3 radioisotopes
BT4 isotopes
BT1 heavy nuclei
BT2 nuclei
BT1 minutes living radioisotopes
BT2 radioisotopes
BT3 isotopes
BT1 odd-even nuclei
BT2 nuclei

ASTATINE 204 [12; 12]
BT1 alpha decay radioisotopes
BT2 radioisotopes
BT3 isotopes
BT1 astatine isotopes
BT1 electron capture radioisotopes
BT2 beta decay radioisotopes
BT3 radioisotopes
BT4 isotopes
BT1 heavy nuclei
BT2 nuclei
BT1 minutes living radioisotopes
BT2 radioisotopes
BT3 isotopes
BT1 odd-odd nuclei
BT2 nuclei

ASTATINE 205 [41; 41]
BT1 alpha decay radioisotopes
BT2 radioisotopes
BT3 isotopes
BT1 astatine isotopes
BT1 beta-plus decay radioisotopes
BT2 beta decay radioisotopes
BT3 radioisotopes
BT4 isotopes
BT1 electron capture radioisotopes
BT2 beta decay radioisotopes
BT3 radioisotopes
BT4 isotopes
BT1 heavy nuclei
BT2 nuclei
BT1 minutes living radioisotopes
BT2 radioisotopes
BT3 isotopes
BT1 odd-even nuclei
BT2 nuclei

ASTATINE 206 [19; 19]
BT1 alpha decay radioisotopes
BT2 radioisotopes
BT3 isotopes
BT1 astatine isotopes
BT1 beta-plus decay radioisotopes
BT2 beta decay radioisotopes
BT3 radioisotopes
BT4 isotopes
BT1 electron capture radioisotopes
BT2 beta decay radioisotopes
BT3 radioisotopes
BT4 isotopes
BT1 heavy nuclei
BT2 nuclei
BT1 minutes living radioisotopes
BT2 radioisotopes
BT3 isotopes
BT1 odd-odd nuclei
BT2 nuclei

ASTATINE 207 [21; 21]
BT1 alpha decay radioisotopes
BT2 radioisotopes
BT3 isotopes
BT1 astatine isotopes
BT1 electron capture radioisotopes
BT2 beta decay radioisotopes
BT3 radioisotopes
BT4 isotopes
BT1 heavy nuclei
BT2 nuclei
BT1 hours living radioisotopes
BT2 radioisotopes
BT3 isotopes
BT1 odd-even nuclei
BT2 nuclei

ASTATINE 208 [39; 39]
BT1 alpha decay radioisotopes
BT2 radioisotopes
BT3 isotopes
BT1 astatine isotopes
BT1 electron capture radioisotopes
BT2 beta decay radioisotopes
BT3 radioisotopes
BT4 isotopes
BT1 heavy nuclei
BT2 nuclei
BT1 hours living radioisotopes
BT2 radioisotopes
BT3 isotopes
BT1 odd-odd nuclei
BT2 nuclei

ASTATINE 209 [63; 63]
BT1 alpha decay radioisotopes
BT2 radioisotopes
BT3 isotopes
BT1 astatine isotopes
BT1 electron capture radioisotopes
BT2 beta decay radioisotopes
BT3 radioisotopes
BT4 isotopes
BT1 heavy nuclei
BT2 nuclei
BT1 hours living radioisotopes
BT2 radioisotopes
BT3 isotopes
BT1 odd-even nuclei
BT2 nuclei

ASTATINE 210 [64; 64]
BT1 alpha decay radioisotopes
BT2 radioisotopes
BT3 isotopes
BT1 astatine isotopes
BT1 electron capture radioisotopes
BT2 beta decay radioisotopes
BT3 radioisotopes
BT4 isotopes
BT1 heavy nuclei
BT2 nuclei
BT1 hours living radioisotopes
BT2 radioisotopes
BT3 isotopes
BT1 odd-odd nuclei
BT2 nuclei

ASTATINE 211 [238; 238]
BT1 alpha decay radioisotopes
BT2 radioisotopes
BT3 isotopes
BT1 astatine isotopes
BT1 electron capture radioisotopes
BT2 beta decay radioisotopes
BT3 radioisotopes
BT4 isotopes
BT1 heavy nuclei
BT2 nuclei
BT1 hours living radioisotopes
BT2 radioisotopes
BT3 isotopes
BT1 odd-even nuclei
BT2 nuclei

ASTATINE 212 [25; 25]
BT1 alpha decay radioisotopes
BT2 radioisotopes
BT3 isotopes
BT1 astatine isotopes
BT1 heavy nuclei
BT2 nuclei
BT1 internal conversion radioisoto
BT2 radioisotopes
BT3 isotopes
BT1 millisec living radioisotopes
BT2 radioisotopes
BT3 isotopes
BT1 odd-odd nuclei
BT2 nuclei

ASTATINE 213 [49; 49]
BT1 alpha decay radioisotopes
BT2 radioisotopes
BT3 isotopes
BT1 astatine isotopes
BT1 heavy nuclei
BT2 nuclei
BT1 nanosec living radioisotopes
BT2 radioisotopes
BT3 isotopes
BT1 odd-even nuclei
BT2 nuclei

ASTATINE 214 [5; 5]
BT1 alpha decay radioisotopes
BT2 radioisotopes
BT3 isotopes
BT1 astatine isotopes
BT1 heavy nuclei
BT2 nuclei
BT1 microsec living radioisotopes
BT2 radioisotopes
BT3 isotopes
BT1 odd-odd nuclei
BT2 nuclei

ASTATINE 215 [4; 4]
BT1 alpha decay radioisotopes
BT2 radioisotopes
BT3 isotopes
BT1 astatine isotopes
BT1 heavy nuclei
BT2 nuclei
BT1 microsec living radioisotopes
BT2 radioisotopes
BT3 isotopes
BT1 odd-even nuclei
BT2 nuclei

ASTATINE 216 [1; 1]
BT1 alpha decay radioisotopes
BT2 radioisotopes
BT3 isotopes
BT1 astatine isotopes
BT1 heavy nuclei
BT2 nuclei
BT1 microsec living radioisotopes
BT2 radioisotopes
BT3 isotopes
BT1 odd-odd nuclei
BT2 nuclei

ASTATINE 217 [6; 6]
BT1 alpha decay radioisotopes
BT2 radioisotopes
BT3 isotopes
BT1 astatine isotopes
BT1 beta-minus decay radioisotopes
BT2 beta decay radioisotopes
BT3 radioisotopes
BT4 isotopes
BT1 heavy nuclei
BT2 nuclei
BT1 millisec living radioisotopes
BT2 radioisotopes
BT3 isotopes
BT1 odd-even nuclei
BT2 nuclei

ASTATINE 218 [10; 10]
BT1 alpha decay radioisotopes
BT2 radioisotopes
BT3 isotopes
BT1 astatine isotopes
BT1 beta-minus decay radioisotopes
BT2 beta decay radioisotopes
BT3 radioisotopes
BT4 isotopes
BT1 heavy nuclei
BT2 nuclei
BT1 odd-odd nuclei
BT2 nuclei
BT1 seconds living radioisotopes
BT2 radioisotopes
BT3 isotopes

ASTATINE 219 [3; 3]
BT1 alpha decay radioisotopes
BT2 radioisotopes
BT3 isotopes
BT1 astatine isotopes
BT1 beta-minus decay radioisotopes
BT2 beta decay radioisotopes
BT3 radioisotopes
BT4 isotopes
BT1 heavy nuclei
BT2 nuclei
BT1 odd-even nuclei
BT2 nuclei
BT1 seconds living radioisotopes
BT2 radioisotopes
BT3 isotopes

ASTATINE 220 [3; 3] *Apr 89*
BT1 alpha decay radioisotopes
BT2 radioisotopes
BT3 isotopes
BT1 astatine isotopes
BT1 beta-minus decay radioisotopes
BT2 beta decay radioisotopes
BT3 radioisotopes
BT4 isotopes
BT1 heavy nuclei
BT2 nuclei
BT1 minutes living radioisotopes
BT2 radioisotopes
BT3 isotopes
BT1 odd-odd nuclei
BT2 nuclei

ASTATINE 221 [2; 2] *May 89*
BT1 astatine isotopes
BT1 beta-minus decay radioisotopes
BT2 beta decay radioisotopes
BT3 radioisotopes
BT4 isotopes
BT1 heavy nuclei
BT2 nuclei
BT1 minutes living radioisotopes
BT2 radioisotopes
BT3 isotopes
BT1 odd-even nuclei
BT2 nuclei

ASTATINE 222 [2; 2] *May 89*
BT1 astatine isotopes
BT1 beta-minus decay radioisotopes
BT2 beta decay radioisotopes
BT3 radioisotopes
BT4 isotopes
BT1 heavy nuclei
BT2 nuclei
BT1 odd-odd nuclei
BT2 nuclei
BT1 seconds living radioisotopes
BT2 radioisotopes
BT3 isotopes

ASTATINE 223 [2; 2] *May 89*
BT1 astatine isotopes
BT1 beta-minus decay radioisotopes
BT2 beta decay radioisotopes
BT3 radioisotopes
BT4 isotopes
BT1 heavy nuclei
BT2 nuclei
BT1 odd-even nuclei
BT2 nuclei
BT1 seconds living radioisotopes
BT2 radioisotopes
BT3 isotopes

ASTEROIDS [496; 496]
RT planets
RT solar system

ASTHMA [127; 127] *Feb 78*
BT1 respiratory system diseases
BT2 diseases

ASTRA REACTOR [38; 38]
(Oesterreichisches Forschungszentrum Seibersdorf GmbH.)
UF *adapted swim. pool r. austria*
UF *austrian research reactor*
UF *swimming pool tank r. austria*
BT1 enriched uranium reactors
BT2 reactors
BT1 isotope production reactors
BT2 irradiation reactors
BT3 reactors
BT1 pool type reactors
BT2 water cooled reactors
BT3 reactors
BT2 water moderated reactors
BT3 reactors
BT1 research reactors
BT2 research and test reactors
BT3 reactors
BT1 test reactors
BT2 research and test reactors
BT3 reactors
BT2 test facilities
BT1 thermal reactors
BT2 reactors
RT seibersdorf research centre

astrocytomas
USE neoplasms

astroloy
USE alloy-ni55co17cr15mo5al4ti4

ASTRON [116; 116]
BT1 closed plasma devices
BT2 thermonuclear devices

ASTRON SATELLITES [12; 12] *Jun 85*
- BT1 satellites

ASTRONAUTS [126; 126]
- BT1 personnel
- RT aviation personnel

ASTRONOMY [1,038; 2,334]
- NT1 gamma astronomy
- NT1 radioastronomy
- RT astrophysics
- RT eclipse
- RT stars

ASTROPHYSICS [2,869; 2,869]
- RT astronomy
- RT chandrasekhar theory
- RT cosmology
- RT force-free magnetic fields
- RT galactic evolution
- RT red shift

ASYMMETRY [6,259; 6,401]
- NT1 east-west asymmetry
- NT1 north-south asymmetry
- RT anisotropy
- RT asymmetry coefficients
- RT configuration
- RT distribution
- RT orientation
- RT symmetry

ASYMMETRY COEFFICIENTS [242; 242]
- RT asymmetry

asymptotic conditions
- USE boundary conditions

ASYMPTOTIC SOLUTIONS [5,146; 5,146]
- RT analytical solution
- RT boundary conditions
- RT limiting fragmentation
- RT mathematics
- RT numerical solution

ATC DEVICES [107; 107]
- UF *adiabatic toroidal compressors*
- BT1 tokamak devices
- BT2 closed plasma devices
- BT3 thermonuclear devices

ATF TORSATRON [309; 309] *Apr 84*
- UF *advanced toroidal facil torsat*
- UF *atf-1 torsatron*
- BT1 torsatron stellarators
- BT2 stellarators
- BT3 closed plasma devices
- BT4 thermonuclear devices

atf-1 torsatron
- USE atf torsatron

ATHABASCA LAKE [11; 11]
- BT1 lakes
- BT2 surface waters

atherosclerosis
- USE arteriosclerosis

ATLANTIC OCEAN [732; 1,203]
- BT1 seas
- BT2 surface waters
- NT1 bay of biscay
- NT1 bay of fundy
- NT1 biscayne bay
- NT1 caribbean sea
- NT2 gulf of mexico
- NT3 san antonio bay
- NT1 chesapeake bay
- NT1 gulf of maine
- NT1 irish sea
- NT1 north sea
- NT1 sargasso sea
- RT bahama islands
- RT bermuda
- RT faeroe islands
- RT iceland
- RT newfoundland
- RT prince edward island

ATLANTIC-1 REACTOR [10; 10]
- BT1 pwr type reactors
- BT2 enriched uranium reactors
- BT3 reactors
- BT2 power reactors
- BT3 reactors
- BT2 thermal reactors
- BT3 reactors
- BT2 water cooled reactors
- BT3 reactors
- BT2 water moderated reactors
- BT3 reactors
- RT offshore nuclear power plants

ATLANTIC-2 REACTOR [9; 9]
- BT1 pwr type reactors
- BT2 enriched uranium reactors
- BT3 reactors
- BT2 power reactors
- BT3 reactors
- BT2 thermal reactors
- BT3 reactors
- BT2 water cooled reactors
- BT3 reactors
- BT2 water moderated reactors
- BT3 reactors
- RT offshore nuclear power plants

ATLAS COMPUTERS [6; 6]
- BT1 computers

ATLAS ROCKETS [1; 1]
- BT1 rockets

ATLAS SUPERCONDUCTING LINAC [95; 95] *Nov 85*
(Argonne Tandem/Linear Accelerator.)
- UF *argonne superconducting linac*
- UF *argonne tandem/linear acceler.*
- BT1 hilacs
- BT2 heavy ion accelerators
- BT3 accelerators
- BT2 linear accelerators
- BT3 accelerators

ATMOSPHERES [427; 10,054]
(Not for concepts covered by EARTH ATMOSPHERE.)
- NT1 planetary atmospheres
- NT2 planetary ionospheres
- NT2 planetary magnetospheres
- NT1 satellite atmospheres
- NT2 lunar atmosphere
- NT1 stellar atmospheres
- NT2 solar atmosphere
- NT3 chromosphere
- NT3 heliosphere
- NT3 photosphere
- NT3 solar corona
- NT2 stellar chromospheres
- NT2 stellar coronae
- NT3 solar corona
- NT2 stellar magnetospheres

ATMOSPHERIC CHEMISTRY [461; 461] *May 81*
- BT1 chemistry
- RT air pollution
- RT ozone

→ **ATMOSPHERIC CIRCULATION** [0; 0] *Sep 91*
(Global or hemispheric air movements which can be treated by equations of motion, in contrast to atmospheric diffusion which is small random movement not amenable to treatment by these equations.)
- RT climates
- RT currents
- RT earth atmosphere
- RT general circulation models
- RT meteorology
- RT wind

ATMOSPHERIC EXPLOSIONS [284; 303]
- BT1 explosions
- NT1 annie event
- NT1 argus event
- NT1 harry event
- NT1 orange event
- NT1 romeo event
- NT1 smoky event
- NT1 starfish event
- NT1 swordfish event
- NT1 teak event
- NT1 tewa event
- NT1 yankee event
- RT buffalo project
- RT castle project
- RT crossroads project
- RT dominic project
- RT earth atmosphere
- RT nuclear explosion detection
- RT nuclear explosions
- RT redwing project

atmospheric exposure chambers
- USE exposure chambers

ATMOSPHERIC PRECIPITATIONS [1,088; 2,340]
- UF *fog (meteorological)*
- UF *precipitations (atmospheric)*
- NT1 hail
- NT1 rain
- NT2 acid rain
- NT1 snow
- RT climates
- RT clouds
- RT droplets
- RT earth atmosphere
- RT environmental materials
- RT fallout
- RT ground water
- RT hydrosphere
- RT meteorology
- RT seasons
- RT surface waters
- RT washout
- RT water
- RT weather

ATMOSPHERICS [70; 70]
- UF *sferics*
- BT1 radio noise
- BT2 noise
- BT2 radiowave radiation
- BT3 electromagnetic radiation
- BT4 radiations
- RT whistlers

ATOM COLLISIONS [1,510; 20,048]
- BT1 collisions
- NT1 atom-atom collisions
- NT1 atom-molecule collisions
- NT1 electron-atom collisions
- NT1 ion-atom collisions
- NT1 muon-atom collisions
- NT1 photon-atom collisions
- NT1 positron-atom collisions
- RT atomic physics

ATOM TRANSPORT [813; 813] *Sep 75*
- UF *transport (atom)*
- BT1 neutral-particle transport
- BT2 radiation transport
- RT diffusion
- RT mass transfer

ATOM-ATOM COLLISIONS
[2,510; 2,510]
- BT1 atom collisions
- BT2 collisions
- RT electron exchange

ATOM-MOLECULE COLLISIONS
[2,799; 2,799]
- BT1 atom collisions
- BT2 collisions
- BT1 molecule collisions
- BT2 collisions
- RT electron exchange

atomic absorption spectroscopy
- USE absorption spectroscopy

ATOMIC BEAM DIFFRACTION
[75; 75] Sep 75
- BT1 diffraction
- BT2 coherent scattering
- BT3 scattering
- RT crystallography

ATOMIC BEAM SOURCES [836; 836]
Sep 77
- BT1 neutral beam sources
- RT atomic beams
- RT beam injection heating
- RT ion sources
- RT neutral atom beam injection

ATOMIC BEAMS [2,426; 2,426]
- UF+ ambr method
- BT1 beams
- RT atomic beam sources
- RT beam strippers

atomic bombs
- USE nuclear weapons

ATOMIC CLOCKS [80; 80]
- RT electronic equipment
- RT time interval analyzers
- RT time measurement

atomic clouds
- USE radioactive clouds

ATOMIC DISPLACEMENTS [815; 815]
Nov 82
- UF displacements (atomic)
- UF dpa
- BT1 physical radiation effects
- BT2 radiation effects

atomic energy
- USE nuclear energy

ATOMIC ENERGY AGREEMENTS
[151; 151]
- BT1 international agreements
- BT2 agreements

atomic energy cont bd (canada)
(Atomic Energy Control Board of Canada.)
- USE canadian aecb

ATOMIC ENERGY CONTROL
[142; 473]
- NT1 international control
- NT1 national control
- RT legal aspects
- RT safeguards

atomic energy law
- USE atomic energy laws

ATOMIC ENERGY LAWS [1,554; 2,193]
(PRIOR TO December 1990, this was spelled ATOMIC ENERGY LAW.)
- UF atomic energy law
- BT1 laws
- NT1 nuclear waste policy acts
- RT secrecy protection

ATOMIC ENERGY OF CANADA LTD
[155; 407] Mar 77
- UF aecl
- BT1 canadian organizations
- BT2 national organizations
- NT1 chalk river nuclear labs
- NT1 wnre

atomic energy research establi
- USE aere

atomic explosions
- USE nuclear explosions

atomic fluoresc. spectroscopy
- USE fluorescence spectroscopy

atomic fluorescence spectro
- USE fluorescence spectroscopy

ATOMIC IONS [803; 17,905] Nov 75
- BT1 ions
- BT2 charged particles

ATOMIC MODELS [2,000; 2,604]
- UF models (atomic)
- UF+ molecular orbital model
- BT1 mathematical models
- RT atomic physics
- RT atomic radii
- RT bohr theory
- RT configuration interaction
- RT electron correlation
- RT electronic structure
- RT harmonic oscillator models
- RT hartree-fock method
- RT optical models
- RT self-consistent field
- RT single-particle model
- RT thomas-fermi model

ATOMIC NUMBER [3,641; 3,641]
- UF nuclear charge
- RT periodic system
- RT stopping power

ATOMIC PHYSICS [384; 384] Jun 83
(Use only for indexing articles of very broad coverage, such as annual reviews, text books, etc.)
- BT1 physics
- RT atom collisions
- RT atomic models

atomic power co. main yankee
- USE maine yankee reactor

ATOMIC RADII [466; 466]
- RT atomic models
- RT electronic structure

atomic shells
- USE electronic structure

atomic shells (k)
- USE k shell

atomic shells (l)
- USE l shell

atomic shells (m)
- USE m shell

atomic shells (n)
- USE n shell

atomic weapons
- USE nuclear weapons

atomics int. prototype fast r.
- USE aipfr reactor

ATOMICS INTERNATIONAL CANOGA P [4; 4] Sep 77
- BT1 us doe
- BT2 us organizations
- BT3 national organizations
- BT1 us erda
- BT2 us organizations
- BT3 national organizations
- RT california

atomics international l-77 r.
- USE ai-l-77 reactor

ATOMIZATION [476; 476]
- RT aerosols
- RT droplets
- RT sprays

ATOMKI [17; 17] Apr 86
- UF mta atommagkutato intezete
- BT1 hungarian organizations
- BT2 national organizations

atomki cyclotron
- USE debrecen cyclotron

atomkraftw. rheinsberg akw1 re
- USE rheinsberg akw1 reactor

atomkraftwerk muehleberg
- USE muehleberg reactor

ATOMS [9,970; 13,388]
- NT1 hadronic atoms
- NT2 mesic atoms
- NT3 kaonic atoms
- NT3 muonic atoms
- NT3 pionic atoms
- NT1 isoelectronic atoms
- RT aufbau principle
- RT fundamental constants
- RT kihara potential
- RT matrix isolation
- RT muonium
- RT positronium
- RT protonium

ATP [1,602; 1,602]
- UF adenosine triphosphate
- BT1 nucleotides
- BT2 organic compounds
- RT adenines
- RT adenosine
- RT atp-ase

ATP-ASE [660; 660]
- UF adenosine triphosphatase
- BT1 phosphohydrolases
- BT2 acid anhydrases
- BT3 hydrolases
- BT4 enzymes
- BT5 organic compounds
- RT atp

ATR REACTOR [131; 131]
(E.G. and G. Idaho, Inc., Idaho Falls, Idaho, USA)
UF   adv. test idaho reactor
UF   idaho advanced test reactor
BT1   enriched uranium reactors
  BT2   reactors
BT1   materials testing reactors
  BT2   irradiation reactors
    BT3   reactors
BT1   tank type reactors
  BT2   reactors
BT1   test reactors
  BT2   research and test reactors
    BT3   reactors
  BT2   test facilities
BT1   thermal reactors
  BT2   reactors
BT1   water cooled reactors
  BT2   reactors
BT1   water moderated reactors
  BT2   reactors

ATRC REACTOR [5; 5]
UF   adv. test react. critical fac.
BT1   enriched uranium reactors
  BT2   reactors
BT1   experimental reactors
  BT2   research and test reactors
    BT3   reactors
BT1   pool type reactors
  BT2   water cooled reactors
    BT3   reactors
  BT2   water moderated reactors
    BT3   reactors
BT1   thermal reactors
  BT2   reactors

ATROPA BELLADONNA [3; 3]
BT1   medicinal plants
  BT2   plants
RT   atropine

ATROPHY [640; 640]
BT1   pathological changes
  BT2   diseases

ATROPINE [95; 95]
BT1   alkaloids
  BT2   organic compounds
BT1   parasympatholytics
  BT2   autonomic nervous system agent
    BT3   drugs
RT   atropa belladonna

ATS SATELLITES [84; 84]
BT1   satellites

ATTAPULGITE [20; 20] May 80
BT1   clays
  BT2   silicate minerals
    BT3   minerals
RT   fullers earth

ATTENUATION [3,825; 3,825]
(In classical physics only. For reducing the intensity of waves and submolecular particles when passing through matter employing classical physics use the above descriptor, when employing quantum physics use ABSORPTION. For attenuation cross sections, see also TOTAL CROSS SECTIONS.)
RT   acoustic esr
RT   acoustic nmr
RT   damping
RT   energy losses
RT   opacity
RT   transmission

ATTITUDES [189; 189] Dec 85
RT   behavior
RT   human factors
RT   learning
RT   public opinion

ATTRACTORS [40; 40] Feb 87
RT   phase space
RT   randomness
RT   turbulence

ATUCHA REACTOR [112; 112]
(Lima, Buenos Aires, Argentina)
UF   atucha-1 reactor
UF   central nuclear en atucha rea.
UF   cna reactor
BT1   natural uranium reactors
  BT2   reactors
BT1   phwr type reactors
  BT2   heavy water cooled reactors
    BT3   reactors
  BT2   heavy water moderated reactors
    BT3   reactors
BT1   pressure tube reactors
  BT2   power reactors
    BT3   reactors
BT1   thermal reactors
  BT2   reactors

atucha-1 reactor
USE   atucha reactor

ATUCHA-2 REACTOR [33; 33] Feb 80
(Lima, Buenos Aires, Argentina)
BT1   natural uranium reactors
  BT2   reactors
BT1   phwr type reactors
  BT2   heavy water cooled reactors
    BT3   reactors
  BT2   heavy water moderated reactors
    BT3   reactors
BT1   pressure tube reactors
  BT2   power reactors
    BT3   reactors
BT1   thermal reactors
  BT2   reactors

ATWS [502; 502] Sep 75
(Anticipated Transients Without Scram)
BT1   design basis accidents
  BT2   reactor accidents
    BT3   accidents
RT   scram

AUC [64; 64] Nov 79
UF   ammonium uranyl carbonate
BT1   ammonium carbonates
  BT2   ammonium compounds
  BT2   carbonates
    BT3   carbon compounds
    BT3   oxygen compounds
BT1   uranyl compounds
  BT2   uranium compounds
    BT3   actinide compounds

audible alarm
USE   alarm systems

AUDITORY ORGANS [550; 550]
UF   ears
UF+   labyrinth
BT1   sense organs
  BT2   organs
    BT3   body
RT   vestibular apparatus

AUDITS [136; 136] Dec 85
(Documented activities undertaken to determine the adequacy of or the adherence to established procedures, instructions, specifications, codes, standards, etc., and the effectiveness of implementation.)
RT   accounting
RT   evaluation
RT   inspection
RT   licensing
RT   management
RT   quality assurance
RT   verification

AUFBAU PRINCIPLE [11; 11]
UF   aufbauprinzip
RT   atoms
RT   electronic structure

aufbauprinzip
USE   aufbau principle

aufwuchs
USE   aquatic organisms

AUGER EFFECT [2,285; 2,441]
(Includes all particles, processes, and spectra associated with the auger effect.)
NT1   coster-kronig transitions
RT   auger electron spectroscopy
RT   autoionization
RT   electron emission
RT   energy-level transitions
RT   inner-shell ionization

AUGER ELECTRON SPECTROSCOPY [2,578; 2,578]
BT1   electron spectroscopy
  BT2   spectroscopy
RT   auger effect

AUGMENTATION [180; 180] Dec 85
(Increasing or making more numerous, larger, or more intense, e.g., augmentation of heat transfer.)
RT   expansion
RT   minimization
RT   optimization
RT   shrinkage

AURATES [4; 4]
(Specific compounds should be indexed by coordination of a descriptor of the form (CATION) COMPOUNDS and the above anion descriptor.)
BT1   gold compounds
  BT2   transition element compounds
BT1   oxygen compounds
RT   gold oxides

AURIN [0; 0]
BT1   polyphenols
  BT2   phenols
    BT3   aromatics
      BT4   organic compounds
    BT3   hydroxy compounds
      BT4   organic compounds
BT1   triphenylmethane dyes
  BT2   dyes

aurintricarboxylic acid
USE   aluminon

AURORA FACILITY [47; 47] Jan 86
(Large KrF laser facility at Los Alamos.)
RT   antares facility
RT   icf devices
RT   krypton fluoride lasers
RT   lanl

AURORAE [1,671; 1,829]
NT1   midday aurorae
NT1   polar-cap aurorae
RT   airglow
RT   auroral oval
RT   auroral zones
RT   charged-particle precipitation
RT   electron precipitation
RT   harang discontinuity
RT   night sky
RT   proton precipitation
RT   trapped protons

auroral electrojets
USE   electrojets

AURORAL HISS [91; 91]
 BT1 electromagnetic radiation
  BT2 radiations
 RT ionosphere
 RT whistlers

AURORAL OVAL [334; 375]
 NT1 harang discontinuity
 RT aurorae
 RT auroral zones
 RT charged-particle precipitation
 RT electron precipitation
 RT ionosphere
 RT midday aurorae
 RT polar cusp
 RT polar-cap aurorae
 RT proton precipitation

auroral substorms
 USE magnetic bays

AURORAL ZONES [988; 988]
 UF *zones (auroral)*
 RT antarctic regions
 RT arctic regions
 RT aurorae
 RT auroral oval
 RT ionosphere
 RT midday aurorae
 RT polar-cap aurorae

AUSTENITE [1,337; 1,337]
 (A solid solution of carbon in gamma-iron)
 BT1 carbon additions
 BT1 iron alloys
  BT2 alloys
 RT austenitic steels
 RT decarburization
 RT iron-gamma
 RT martensite
 RT solid solutions

AUSTENITIC STEELS [2,386; 5,784]
 Aug 78
 BT1 steels
  BT2 carbon additions
  BT2 iron base alloys
   BT3 iron alloys
    BT4 alloys
 NT1 steel-cr13mn8ni8
 NT1 steel-cr13ni6mo-l
 NT1 steel-cr15ni15motib
 NT1 steel-cr16ni13monbv
 NT1 steel-cr16ni15mo3nb
 NT1 steel-cr16ni16monb
 NT1 steel-cr16ni8mo2
 NT1 steel-cr17mn15nni
 NT1 steel-cr17ni12monb
 NT1 steel-cr17ni12mo3
 NT1 steel-cr17ni12mo3-l
 NT1 steel-cr17ni13
 NT1 steel-cr17ni13mo2ti
 NT1 steel-cr17ni13mo3ti
 NT1 steel-cr17ni7
 NT1 steel-cr18ni10
 NT1 steel-cr18ni10-l
 NT1 steel-cr18ni10ti
 NT1 steel-cr18ni11
 NT1 steel-cr18ni11nb
 NT1 steel-cr18ni11nbco
 NT1 steel-cr18ni12
 NT1 steel-cr18ni12ti
 NT1 steel-cr18ni8
 NT1 steel-cr18ni9
 NT1 steel-cr18ni9ti
 NT1 steel-cr19ni10
 NT1 steel-cr19ni10-l
 NT1 steel-cr20ni11
 NT1 steel-cr20ni11-l
 NT1 steel-cr21mn9ni6
 NT1 steel-cr23ni14
 NT1 steel-cr23ni18
 NT1 steel-cr25ni20
 NT1 steel-ni17cr14moti-l
 NT1 steel-ni25cr20
 NT1 steel-ni26cr15ti2movalb
 NT1 steel-ni36cr18
 RT austenite
 RT corrosion resistant alloys
 RT heat resisting alloys

AUSTRALASIA [12; 2,534]
 NT1 australia
  NT2 new south wales
  NT2 northern territory
  NT2 queensland
  NT2 south australia
  NT2 tasmania
  NT2 victoria
  NT2 western australia
 NT1 micronesia
  NT2 kiribati
  NT2 marshall islands
   NT3 bikini
   NT3 eniwetok
  NT2 nauru
  NT2 tuvalu
 NT1 new guinea
 NT1 new zealand

AUSTRALIA [1,448; 2,262]
 BT1 australasia
 BT1 developed countries
 NT1 new south wales
 NT1 northern territory
 NT1 queensland
 NT1 south australia
 NT1 tasmania
 NT1 victoria
 NT1 western australia
 RT mary kathleen mines
 RT new guinea
 RT rum jungle

australian atom en commission
 USE aaec

australian moata reactor
 USE moata reactor

AUSTRALIAN ORGANIZATIONS
 [56; 322] *Feb 78*
 BT1 national organizations
 NT1 ansto
  NT2 aaec

australites
 USE tektites

AUSTRIA [737; 737]
 BT1 developed countries
 BT1 europe
 RT iaea
 RT unido

AUSTRIAN ORGANIZATIONS [15; 22]
 Dec 80
 BT1 national organizations
 NT1 seibersdorf research centre

austrian res cent seibersdorf
 USE seibersdorf research centre

austrian research reactor
 USE astra reactor

austrian triga-mk-2 reactor
 USE triga-2-vienna reactor

AUTOCLAVES [233; 233]
 RT laboratory equipment
 RT pressure vessels

AUTOIONIZATION [1,640; 1,640]
 BT1 ionization
 RT auger effect
 RT inner-shell ionization

AUTOLYSIS [27; 152]
 BT1 decomposition
  BT2 chemical reactions
 NT1 autoradiolysis
 RT enzymes

AUTOMATION [5,341; 5,341]
 RT computer-aided manufacturing
 RT distance
 RT man-machine systems
 RT reactor control systems
 RT remote handling
 RT work

→ **AUTOMOBILES** [0; 0]
 BT1 vehicles
 RT exhaust gases
 RT ignition systems

→ **AUTOMOTIVE FUELS** [0; 0] *Sep 91*
 BT1 fuels
 RT gasoline

AUTONOMIC NERVOUS SYSTEM
 [178; 221]
 UF *parasympathetic nervous system*
 UF *sympathetic nervous system*
 UF+ *sympathectomy*
 BT1 nervous system
 NT1 vagus
 RT ganglions
 RT hypothalamus
 RT parasympatholytics
 RT parasympathomimetics
 RT radiation syndrome
 RT sympatholytics
 RT sympathomimetics

**AUTONOMIC NERVOUS SYSTEM
AGENT** [38; 3,209] *May 84*
 BT1 drugs
 NT1 neuroregulators
  NT2 acetylcholine
  NT2 adrenaline
  NT2 aminobutyric acid
  NT2 dopa
  NT2 dopamine
  NT2 endorphins
   NT3 enkephalins
  NT2 noradrenaline
  NT2 serotonin
 NT1 parasympatholytics
  NT2 atropine
 NT1 parasympathomimetics
  NT2 acetylcholine
  NT2 eserine
  NT2 pilocarpine
 NT1 sympatholytics
  NT2 ergotamine
  NT2 reserpine
 NT1 sympathomimetics
  NT2 adrenaline
  NT2 amphetamines
   NT3 benzedrine
  NT2 dopamine
  NT2 ephedrine
  NT2 noradrenaline
  NT2 serotonin
  NT2 tyramine

AUTOPSY [828; 828]
 BT1 diagnostic techniques
 RT biopsy
 RT pathology

autoradiographs
 USE images

AUTORADIOGRAPHY [6,714; 6,714]
UF radioautography
UF radiography (auto)
RT ceramography
RT diagnostic techniques
RT industrial radiography
RT labelled compounds
RT nondestructive testing
RT nuclear emulsions
RT tracer techniques

AUTORADIOLYSIS [126; 126]
BT1 autolysis
BT2 decomposition
BT3 chemical reactions
BT1 radiolysis
BT2 chemical radiation effects
BT3 radiation effects
BT2 decomposition
BT3 chemical reactions
RT labelled compounds
RT self-irradiation

AUTUNITE [28; 28]
BT1 phosphate minerals
BT2 minerals
BT1 uranium minerals
BT2 radioactive minerals
BT3 minerals
BT3 radioactive materials
BT4 materials

AUXILIARY HEATING [112; 112]
Aug 84
BT1 heating
RT auxiliary systems
RT plasma heating

AUXILIARY SYSTEMS [186; 361]
Dec 85
(May be used in any field.)
NT1 auxiliary water systems
NT2 condenser cooling systems
RT auxiliary heating
RT electrical equipment
RT remote handling equipment

AUXILIARY WATER SYSTEMS [260; 331] Apr 76
(For service water systems or other water systems not intended to be part of the cooling or moderating water system of a reactor.)
UF service water systems
BT1 auxiliary systems
NT1 condenser cooling systems
RT reactor cooling systems

AUXINS [148; 148]
BT1 plant growth regulators
RT gibberellic acid

AVAILABILITY [2,920; 2,920]
UF supply
RT allocations
RT demand
RT domestic supplies
RT economics
RT geologic deposits
RT inventories
RT ore composition
RT outages

avalanche multiplication
USE townsend discharge

AVALANCHE QUENCHING [160; 160]
Jul 78
UF quenching (avalanche)
RT geiger-mueller counters
RT ionization chambers
RT proportional counters
RT townsend discharge

avena
USE oats

average magnetic well
USE minimum average-b configuratio

AVIATION PERSONNEL [44; 44]
BT1 personnel
RT astronauts
RT military personnel

AVOCADOS [17; 17] Jun 83
BT1 fruits
BT2 food

AVOGADRO RS-1 REACTOR [3; 3]
(Saluggia, Italy)
UF arsi reactor
UF rsi avogadro reactor
BT1 enriched uranium reactors
BT2 reactors
BT1 pool type reactors
BT2 water cooled reactors
BT3 reactors
BT2 water moderated reactors
BT3 reactors
BT1 research reactors
BT2 research and test reactors
BT3 reactors
BT1 thermal reactors
BT2 reactors

AVOIDANCE [60; 60]
(Limited to living systems.)
BT1 behavior
RT conditioned reflexes

AVR REACTOR [437; 437]
(Juelich, Federal Republic of Germany)
UF arbeitsgemeinsch. versuchs r.
BT1 enriched uranium reactors
BT2 reactors
BT1 helium cooled reactors
BT2 gas cooled reactors
BT3 reactors
BT1 htgr type reactors
BT2 gas cooled reactors
BT3 reactors
BT2 graphite moderated reactors
BT3 reactors
BT1 pebble bed reactors
BT2 solid homogeneous reactors
BT3 homogeneous reactors
BT4 reactors
BT1 power reactors
BT2 reactors
BT1 thermal reactors
BT2 reactors
BT1 thorium reactors
BT2 reactors

AWAY-FROM-REACTOR STORAGE [398; 398] Apr 80
UF afr storage
BT1 spent fuel storage
BT2 storage
RT after-heat
RT fuel storage pools
RT waste transportation

axerophtol
USE vitamin a

AXIAL RATIO [44; 44]
RT crystal structure

AXIAL SYMMETRY [1,816; 1,816]
BT1 symmetry
RT kerr field
RT rotational invariance

AXIAL VECTOR MESONS [68; 281]
Dec 87
(Mesons with spin and parity 1+.)
UF pseudovector mesons
BT1 mesons
BT2 bosons
BT2 hadrons
BT3 elementary particles
NT1 a1-1270 mesons
NT1 b1-1235 mesons
NT1 chi1-3510 mesons
NT1 f1-1285 mesons
NT1 f1-1420 mesons
NT1 f1-1530 mesons
NT1 h1-1190 mesons
NT1 k1-1280 mesons
NT1 k1-1400 mesons

AXIAL-VECTOR CURRENTS [1,632; 1,632]
BT1 algebraic currents
BT2 currents
RT pcac theory
RT v-a theory
RT vector currents

AXIOMATIC FIELD THEORY [151; 787] Nov 77
UF axiomatic s-matrix theory
UF general quantum field theory
UF non lagrangian quantum field t
UF non-lagrangian quantum field t
UF nonlagrangian quantum field th
BT1 quantum field theory
BT2 field theories
NT1 algebraic field theory
NT1 lsz theory
NT1 wightman field theory

axiomatic s-matrix theory
USE axiomatic field theory

AXIONS [866; 866] Aug 78
BT1 goldstone bosons
BT2 bosons
BT2 postulated particles
BT3 elementary particles

AXOLOTL [10; 10]
UF siredon
BT1 salamanders
BT2 amphibians
BT3 aquatic organisms
BT3 vertebrates
BT4 animals

axons
USE nerve cells

azaguanine
USE antimetabolites

AZBEL-KANER RESONANCE [11; 11]
(A type of cyclotron resonance in high-purity metals at liquid helium temperature.)
BT1 cyclotron resonance
BT2 resonance
RT metals

AZEOTROPE [45; 45]
RT boiling points
RT distillation

AZIDES [287; 287]
(For inorganic compounds only. For organic azides, use AZIDO COMPOUNDS.)
BT1 nitrogen compounds
RT azido compounds
RT hydrazoic acid

AZIDO COMPOUNDS [76; 76]
- BT1 organic nitrogen compounds
- BT2 organic compounds
- RT azides

azimuthal pinch devices (linea
- USE linear theta pinch devices

AZINES [111; 10,490]
(Compounds that contain a six-membered heterocyclic ring containing one or more nitrogen atoms.)
- BT1 heterocyclic compounds
- BT2 organic compounds
- BT1 organic nitrogen compounds
- BT2 organic compounds
- NT1 phenothiazines
- NT2 chlorpromazine
- NT2 methylene blue
- NT1 pyrazines
- NT2 neutral red
- NT2 phenazine
- NT2 piperazines
- NT1 pyridazines
- NT2 phthalazines
- NT1 pyridines
- NT2 acridines
- NT3 acridine orange
- NT3 flavines
- NT4 acriflavine
- NT4 proflavine
- NT2 bipyridines
- NT2 diodrast
- NT2 nicotinamide
- NT2 nicotine
- NT2 nicotinic acid
- NT2 pan
- NT2 phenatine
- NT2 picolines
- NT3 picolinic acid
- NT2 piperidines
- NT3 pethidine
- NT3 tmpn
- NT3 triacetoneamine-n-oxyl
- NT2 pyridinium compounds
- NT2 pyridoxal
- NT2 pyridoxine
- NT2 pyridoxylideneglutamate
- NT2 pyridylazoresorcinol
- NT2 quinolines
- NT3 ferron
- NT3 kynurenic acid
- NT3 oxine
- NT3 quinaldine
- NT1 pyrimidines
- NT2 alloxan
- NT2 barbiturates
- NT3 amytal
- NT3 nembutal
- NT3 phenobarbital
- NT3 thiopental
- NT2 cytidine
- NT2 cytosine
- NT2 deoxycytidine
- NT2 murexide
- NT2 sulfadiazine
- NT2 thiamine
- NT2 thymidine
- NT2 uracils
- NT3 bromouracils
- NT4 budr
- NT3 chlorouracils
- NT3 deoxyuridine
- NT3 fluorouracils
- NT4 fudr
- NT3 iodouracils
- NT4 iododeoxyuridine
- NT3 orotic acid
- NT3 thiouracil
- NT3 thymine
- NT3 uridine
- NT1 triazines
- NT2 cyanurates
- NT2 melamine

AZO COMPOUNDS [411; 983]
- BT1 organic nitrogen compounds
- BT2 organic compounds
- NT1 arsenazo
- NT1 azo dyes
- NT2 acid chrome dyes
- NT2 beryllon
- NT2 congo red
- NT2 eriochrome dyes
- NT2 erioglaucine
- NT2 evans blue
- NT2 methyl orange
- NT2 methyl red
- NT2 toluidine blue
- NT2 trypan blue

AZO DYES [147; 309]
- BT1 azo compounds
- BT2 organic nitrogen compounds
- BT3 organic compounds
- BT1 dyes
- NT1 acid chrome dyes
- NT1 beryllon
- NT1 congo red
- NT1 eriochrome dyes
- NT1 erioglaucine
- NT1 evans blue
- NT1 methyl orange
- NT1 methyl red
- NT1 toluidine blue
- NT1 trypan blue
- RT diazo compounds

AZOLES [92; 6,296]
(Compounds that contain a five-membered heterocyclic ring containing one or more nitrogen atoms.)
- BT1 heterocyclic compounds
- BT2 organic compounds
- BT1 organic nitrogen compounds
- BT2 organic compounds
- NT1 carbazoles
- NT1 imidazoles
- NT2 allantoin
- NT2 benzimidazoles
- NT2 biotin
- NT2 cmni
- NT2 creatinine
- NT2 histamine
- NT2 histidine
- NT2 metronidazole
- NT2 misonidazole
- NT2 urocanic acid
- NT1 oxadiazoles
- NT1 oxazoles
- NT2 benzoxazoles
- NT2 pemoline
- NT2 popop
- NT1 pyrazoles
- NT2 indazoles
- NT2 pyrazolines
- NT3 antipyrine
- NT1 pyrroles
- NT2 bilirubin
- NT2 biliverdin
- NT2 indoles
- NT3 indocyanine green
- NT3 lysergic acid
- NT3 reserpine
- NT3 strychnine
- NT3 tryptamines
- NT4 bufotenine
- NT4 melatonin
- NT4 serotonin
- NT3 tryptophan
- NT3 vinblastine
- NT2 pyrrolidines
- NT3 hydroxyproline
- NT3 nicotine
- NT3 proline
- NT2 pyrrolidones
- NT3 pvp
- NT2 stercobilin
- NT2 urobilinogen
- NT1 tetrazoles
- NT2 tetrazolium
- NT1 thiadiazoles
- NT1 thiazoles
- NT2 benzothiazoles
- NT2 saccharin
- NT2 thiamine
- NT1 triazoles

azomide
- USE hydrazoic acid

AZOTOBACTER [35; 35]
- BT1 bacteria
- BT2 microorganisms

AZULENE [30; 30]
- BT1 hydrocarbons
- BT2 organic compounds

A0-980 MESONS [215; 215]
(Prior to December 1987 this concept was indexed by DELTA-966 RESONANCES.)
- UF *delta-966 resonances*
- BT1 scalar mesons
- BT2 mesons
- BT3 bosons
- BT3 hadrons
- BT4 elementary particles

a1-1070 resonances
(Prior to December 1987 this was a valid descriptor.)
- USE a1-1270 mesons

A1-1270 MESONS [365; 365]
(Prior to December 1987 this concept was indexed by A1-1070 RESONANCES.)
- UF *a1-1070 resonances*
- BT1 axial vector mesons
- BT2 mesons
- BT3 bosons
- BT3 hadrons
- BT4 elementary particles

a2-1310 resonances
(Prior to December 1987 this was a valid descriptor.)
- USE a2-1320 mesons

A2-1320 MESONS [320; 320]
(Prior to December 1987 this concept was indexed by A2-1310 RESONANCES.)
- UF *a2-1310 resonances*
- BT1 tensor mesons
- BT2 mesons
- BT3 bosons
- BT3 hadrons
- BT4 elementary particles

a2h-1320 resonances
(Prior to December 1987 this was a valid descriptor.)
- USE mesons

a2l-1280 resonances
(Prior to December 1987 this was a valid descriptor.)
- USE mesons

A3-2050 MESONS [0; 0] *Dec 87*
- BT1 tensor mesons
- BT2 mesons
- BT3 bosons
- BT3 hadrons
- BT4 elementary particles

a4-1960 resonances
(Prior to December 1987 this was a valid descriptor.)
- USE a4-2040 mesons

A4-2040 MESONS [9; 9]
(Prior to December 1987 this concept was indexed by A4-1960 RESONANCES.)
UF   *a4-1960 resonances*
BT1   tensor mesons
  BT2   mesons
    BT3   bosons
    BT3   hadrons
      BT4   elementary particles

A6-2450 MESONS [2; 2] *Dec 87*
BT1   tensor mesons
  BT2   mesons
    BT3   bosons
    BT3   hadrons
      BT4   elementary particles

B CODES [1,013; 1,013]
BT1   computer codes

B MESONS [1,191; 1,406] *Jan 85*
(The 'Bottom' or 'Beauty' meson with mass approx. 5270 MeV.)
BT1   beauty particles
  BT2   elementary particles
BT1   pseudoscalar mesons
  BT2   mesons
    BT3   bosons
    BT3   hadrons
      BT4   elementary particles
NT1   b minus mesons
NT1   b neutral mesons
  NT2   anti-b neutral mesons
NT1   b plus mesons

B MINUS MESONS [53; 53] *Dec 87*
BT1   b mesons
  BT2   beauty particles
    BT3   elementary particles
  BT2   pseudoscalar mesons
    BT3   mesons
      BT4   bosons
      BT4   hadrons
        BT5   elementary particles

B NEUTRAL MESONS [194; 281] *Dec 87*
BT1   b mesons
  BT2   beauty particles
    BT3   elementary particles
  BT2   pseudoscalar mesons
    BT3   mesons
      BT4   bosons
      BT4   hadrons
        BT5   elementary particles
NT1   anti-b neutral mesons

B PLUS MESONS [43; 43] *Dec 87*
BT1   b mesons
  BT2   beauty particles
    BT3   elementary particles
  BT2   pseudoscalar mesons
    BT3   mesons
      BT4   bosons
      BT4   hadrons
        BT5   elementary particles

B*-5325 MESONS [7; 7] *Dec 87*
BT1   beauty mesons
  BT2   beauty particles
    BT3   elementary particles
  BT2   mesons
    BT3   bosons
    BT3   hadrons
      BT4   elementary particles

b-1235 resonances
(Prior to December 1987 this was a valid descriptor.)
USE   b1-1235 mesons

babcock and wilcox stand. reac
USE   bw standard reactor

babcock and wilcox test react.
USE   bawtr reactor

BABESIDAE [31; 31]
BT1   protozoa
  BT2   invertebrates
    BT3   animals
  BT2   microorganisms
RT   erythrocytes
RT   parasites

BABOONS [154; 154]
(Prior to 1986 APES was used for this concept.)
BT1   monkeys
  BT2   primates
    BT3   mammals
      BT4   vertebrates
        BT5   animals

BACH-TAMAID THEORY [1; 1]
RT   particle structure

BACILLUS [191; 738]
BT1   bacteria
  BT2   microorganisms
NT1   bacillus cereus
NT1   bacillus megaterium
NT1   bacillus subtilis
NT1   thiobacillus ferroxidans
NT1   thiobacillus oxidans

BACILLUS CEREUS [39; 39]
BT1   bacillus
  BT2   bacteria
    BT3   microorganisms

BACILLUS MEGATERIUM [80; 80]
BT1   bacillus
  BT2   bacteria
    BT3   microorganisms

BACILLUS SUBTILIS [361; 361]
BT1   bacillus
  BT2   bacteria
    BT3   microorganisms

BACKBENDING [584; 584] *Mar 77*
(The sudden increase of the moment of inertia of deformed nuclei at a critical angular momentum.)
RT   angular momentum
RT   coriolis force
RT   deformed nuclei
RT   high spin states
RT   moment of inertia
RT   nuclear structure
RT   rotation
RT   rotational states
RT   vmi model
RT   yrast states

BACKFILLING [480; 480] *Oct 83*
RT   coal mines
RT   land reclamation
RT   mines
RT   radioactive waste disposal
RT   radionuclide migration
RT   underground disposal
RT   waste-rock interactions

backfitting
USE   retrofitting

BACKGROUND NOISE [2,108; 2,108]
BT1   noise
RT   radio noise

BACKGROUND RADIATION [4,966; 4,966]
UF   *terrestrial background*
BT1   radiations
RT   cosmic radiation
RT   natural radioactivity
RT   relict radiation

backlund transformation
USE   baecklund transformation

BACKSCATTERING [5,774; 5,774]
BT1   scattering
RT   albedo-neutron dosemeters
RT   angular distribution
RT   reflection

BACKWARD WAVE TUBES [33; 33]
BT1   microwave tubes
  BT2   electron tubes
  BT2   microwave equipment
    BT3   electronic equipment
      BT4   equipment

bacon
USE   meat

BACTERIA [2,132; 7,879]
UF   *cells (bacterial)*
BT1   microorganisms
NT1   actinomyces
NT1   aerobacter
NT1   azotobacter
NT1   bacillus
  NT2   bacillus cereus
  NT2   bacillus megaterium
  NT2   bacillus subtilis
  NT2   thiobacillus ferroxidans
  NT2   thiobacillus oxidans
NT1   brucella
NT1   clostridium
  NT2   clostridium acetobutylicum
  NT2   clostridium botulinum
  NT2   clostridium butyricum
  NT2   clostridium perfringens
NT1   coliforms
NT1   corynebacterium parvum
NT1   escherichia coli
NT1   haemophilus
NT1   lactobacillus
NT1   meningococcus
NT1   methanogenic bacteria
NT1   micrococcus
  NT2   micrococcus luteus
  NT2   micrococcus lysodeicticus
  NT2   micrococcus radiodurans
NT1   mycobacterium
  NT2   mycobacterium tuberculosis
NT1   nocardia
NT1   pneumococcus
NT1   proteus
NT1   pseudomonas
NT1   rhodopseudomonas
NT1   rhodospirillum
NT1   salmonella
  NT2   salmonella typhimurium
NT1   serratia
NT1   shigella
NT1   spirochaetes
NT1   staphylococcus
NT1   streptococcus
NT1   streptomyces
NT1   sulfate-reducing bacteria
NT1   sulfur-oxidizing bacteria
  NT2   thiobacillus ferroxidans
  NT2   thiobacillus oxidans
RT   bacterial diseases
RT   bacterial spores
RT   bacteriophages
RT   disinfectants
RT   endotoxins
RT   germ-free animals
RT   host-cell reactivation
RT   infectivity
RT   mycoplasma
RT   nitrogen fixation
RT   plankton
RT   toxins
RT   vaccines

BACTERIAL DISEASES [260; 722] *Dec 82*
BT1   infectious diseases
  BT2   diseases
NT1   cholera

NT1 diphtheria
NT1 gonorrhea
NT1 leprosy
NT1 paratyphoid
NT1 syphilis
NT1 tetanus
NT1 tuberculosis
NT2 lupus
NT1 typhoid
RT antibiotics
RT bacteria
RT granulomas

BACTERIAL SPORES [289; 289]
BT1 spores
RT bacteria
RT preservation
RT sterilization

BACTERIOPHAGES [1,147; 1,147]
UF *phages*
BT1 viruses
BT2 microorganisms
BT2 parasites
RT bacteria
RT host-cell reactivation
RT plaque formation

BADDELEYITE [32; 32]
BT1 oxide minerals
BT2 minerals
BT1 radioactive minerals
BT2 minerals
BT2 radioactive materials
BT3 materials
RT caldasite
RT hafnium oxides
RT zirconium oxides

BAECKLUND TRANSFORMATION
[213; 213] *May 80*
UF *backlund transformation*
BT1 transformations
RT nonlinear problems
RT solitons

BAFFLED TUBES [45; 45]
BT1 tubes
RT baffles

BAFFLES [93; 93] *Apr 84*
(Plates that regulate the flow of a fluid, e.g. in heat exchangers.)
BT1 flow regulators
BT2 control equipment
BT3 equipment
RT baffled tubes
RT fluid flow

BAG MODEL [4,976; 4,976] *Mar 76*
UF *quark confinement*
BT1 extended particle model
BT2 particle models
BT3 mathematical models
RT quantum chromodynamics

baghdad wwr-s reactor
USE irt-baghdad reactor

→ **BAGHOUSES** [0; 0] *Sep 91*
(A structure for holding bag filters for removing suspended dusts and fumes from airstreams.)
BT1 pollution control equipment
BT2 equipment
RT air pollution control
RT filters

BAHAMA ISLANDS [4; 4]
BT1 developing countries
BT1 west indies
BT2 islands
RT atlantic ocean

BAHRAIN [4; 4] *Dec 82*
BT1 developing countries
BT1 islands
BT1 middle east

BAILLY-1 REACTOR [13; 13]
(Porter, Indiana, USA)
BT1 bwr type reactors
BT2 enriched uranium reactors
BT3 reactors
BT2 power reactors
BT3 reactors
BT2 thermal reactors
BT3 reactors
BT2 water cooled reactors
BT3 reactors
BT2 water moderated reactors
BT3 reactors

BAINITE [134; 134]
RT martensite
RT steels

BAKELITE [29; 29]
BT1 organic polymers
BT2 organic compounds
BT2 polymers
RT formaldehyde
RT phenols
RT resins

BAKING [184; 184]
BT1 heating

baking (food)
USE food processing

BAL [35; 35]
(British anti-Lewisite)
UF *dimercaprol*
UF *dimercaptopropanol*
BT1 chelating agents
BT1 dithiols
BT2 reagents
BT2 thiols
BT3 organic sulfur compounds
BT4 organic compounds
BT1 radioprotective substances
BT2 drugs
BT2 response modifying factors
RT unithiol

BALAKOVO-1 REACTOR [33; 33]
Aug 84
BT1 wwer type reactors
BT2 pwr type reactors
BT3 enriched uranium reactors
BT4 reactors
BT3 power reactors
BT4 reactors
BT3 thermal reactors
BT4 reactors
BT3 water cooled reactors
BT4 reactors
BT3 water moderated reactors
BT4 reactors

BALAKOVO-2 REACTOR [16; 16]
Dec 86
BT1 wwer type reactors
BT2 pwr type reactors
BT3 enriched uranium reactors
BT4 reactors
BT3 power reactors
BT4 reactors
BT3 thermal reactors
BT4 reactors
BT3 water cooled reactors
BT4 reactors
BT3 water moderated reactors
BT4 reactors

balance (energy)
USE energy balance

balance (mass)
USE mass balance

BALANCES [129; 186]
UF *weighing*
BT1 weight indicators
BT2 measuring instruments
NT1 microbalances

balances (magnetic)
USE magnetic balances

balescu theory
USE prigogine theorem

BALL BEARINGS [55; 55]
BT1 bearings

BALL LIGHTNING [19; 19]
BT1 lightning
BT2 electric discharges

BALLOONING INSTABILITY [900; 900]
May 79
BT1 plasma macroinstabilities
BT2 plasma instability
BT3 instability

BALLOONS [872; 872]
RT aircraft

BALMER LINES [3,076; 3,076]
(Includes all aspects of the transitions associated with balmer lines.)
UF *balmer spectra*
UF *h-alpha line*
UF *h-beta line*
UF *h-gamma line*
RT hydrogen
RT rydberg correction
RT spectra

balmer spectra
USE balmer lines

BALNEOLOGY [64; 64]
BT1 medicine
RT therapy
RT water

BALTIC SEA [226; 226]
BT1 seas
BT2 surface waters

BAMBP [1; 1]
UF *butyl-alpha-methylbenzylphenol*
BT1 phenols
BT2 aromatics
BT3 organic compounds
BT2 hydroxy compounds
BT3 organic compounds

BANACH SPACE [269; 3,680]
BT1 mathematical space
BT2 space
NT1 hilbert space
RT vectors

BANANA PLANTS [14; 14] *Dec 75*
BT1 plants
RT bananas

BANANA REGIME [324; 324]
(A specific mechanism of particle trapping in toroidal devices.)
BT1 trapping
RT neoclassical transport theory
RT stellarators
RT tokamak devices
RT toroidal pinch devices
RT trapped-particle instability

BANANAS [57; 57]
 BT1 fruits
 BT2 food
 RT banana plants

BAND THEORY [3,787; 3,787]
 RT brillouin zones
 RT electronic structure
 RT energy gap
 RT energy-level transitions
 RT fermi level
 RT wigner-seitz method

BANDING TECHNIQUES [40; 40]
 Apr 78
 (Techniques for making chromosomal aberrations visible.)
 RT biological localization
 RT chromosomal aberrations
 RT chromosomes
 RT human chromosomes
 RT stains

BANEBERRY EVENT [12; 12]
 BT1 contained explosions
 BT2 underground explosions
 BT3 explosions
 BT1 nuclear explosions
 BT2 explosions

BANGLADESH [87; 87]
 BT1 asia
 BT1 developing countries

BANGLADESH ORGANIZATIONS [5; 5] *Jul 83*
 BT1 national organizations

BARBITURATES [128; 284]
 UF *barbituric acid*
 BT1 anesthetics
 BT2 central nervous system depress
 BT3 central nervous system agents
 BT4 drugs
 BT1 hypnotics and sedatives
 BT2 central nervous system depress
 BT3 central nervous system agents
 BT4 drugs
 BT1 organic oxygen compounds
 BT2 organic compounds
 BT1 pyrimidines
 BT2 azines
 BT3 heterocyclic compounds
 BT4 organic compounds
 BT3 organic nitrogen compounds
 BT4 organic compounds
 NT1 amytal
 NT1 nembutal
 NT1 phenobarbital
 NT1 thiopental

barbituric acid
 USE barbiturates

BARC [204; 204]
 UF *bhabha atomic research center*
 BT1 indian organizations
 BT2 national organizations

barcelona argonaut reactor
 USE argos reactor

bardeen-cooper-schrieffer theo
 USE bcs theory

BARITE [100; 100]
 BT1 sulfate minerals
 BT2 minerals
 RT barium sulfates

BARIUM [2,209; 2,209]
 BT1 alkaline earth metals
 BT2 metals
 BT3 elements

BARIUM ADDITIONS [40; 40]
 (Alloys containing not more than 1% Ba are listed here.)
 RT barium alloys
 RT barium compounds

BARIUM ALLOYS [87; 101]
 (Alloys containing more than 1% Ba.)
 BT1 alloys
 NT1 barium base alloys
 RT barium additions

BARIUM BASE ALLOYS [11; 11]
 BT1 barium alloys
 BT2 alloys

BARIUM BORIDES [9; 9]
 BT1 barium compounds
 BT2 alkaline earth metal compounds
 BT1 borides
 BT2 boron compounds

BARIUM BROMIDES [33; 33]
 BT1 barium compounds
 BT2 alkaline earth metal compounds
 BT1 bromides
 BT2 bromine compounds
 BT3 halogen compounds
 BT2 halides
 BT3 halogen compounds

BARIUM CARBIDES [5; 5]
 BT1 barium compounds
 BT2 alkaline earth metal compounds
 BT1 carbides
 BT2 carbon compounds

BARIUM CARBONATES [142; 142]
 BT1 barium compounds
 BT2 alkaline earth metal compounds
 BT1 carbonates
 BT2 carbon compounds
 BT2 oxygen compounds

BARIUM CHLORIDES [216; 216]
 BT1 barium compounds
 BT2 alkaline earth metal compounds
 BT1 chlorides
 BT2 chlorine compounds
 BT3 halogen compounds
 BT2 halides
 BT3 halogen compounds

BARIUM COMPLEXES [46; 46]
 BT1 alkaline earth metal complexes
 BT2 complexes

BARIUM COMPOUNDS [2,147; 10,904]
 BT1 alkaline earth metal compounds
 NT1 barium borides
 NT1 barium bromides
 NT1 barium carbides
 NT1 barium carbonates
 NT1 barium chlorides
 NT1 barium fluorides
 NT1 barium hydrides
 NT1 barium hydroxides
 NT1 barium iodides
 NT1 barium nitrates
 NT1 barium nitrides
 NT1 barium oxides
 NT1 barium perchlorates
 NT1 barium phosphates
 NT1 barium silicates
 NT1 barium sulfates
 NT1 barium sulfides
 NT1 barium tungstates
 RT barium additions

BARIUM FLUORIDES [725; 725]
 BT1 barium compounds
 BT2 alkaline earth metal compounds
 BT1 fluorides
 BT2 fluorine compounds
 BT3 halogen compounds
 BT2 halides
 BT3 halogen compounds

BARIUM HYDRIDES [8; 8]
 BT1 barium compounds
 BT2 alkaline earth metal compounds
 BT1 hydrides
 BT2 hydrogen compounds

BARIUM HYDROXIDES [65; 65]
 BT1 barium compounds
 BT2 alkaline earth metal compounds
 BT1 hydroxides
 BT2 hydrogen compounds
 BT2 oxygen compounds

BARIUM IODIDES [44; 44]
 BT1 barium compounds
 BT2 alkaline earth metal compounds
 BT1 iodides
 BT2 halides
 BT3 halogen compounds
 BT2 iodine compounds
 BT3 halogen compounds

BARIUM IONS [318; 318]
 BT1 ions
 BT2 charged particles

BARIUM ISOTOPES [311; 2,276]
 NT1 barium 117
 NT1 barium 119
 NT1 barium 120
 NT1 barium 121
 NT1 barium 122
 NT1 barium 123
 NT1 barium 124
 NT1 barium 125
 NT1 barium 126
 NT1 barium 127
 NT1 barium 128
 NT1 barium 129
 NT1 barium 130
 NT1 barium 131
 NT1 barium 132
 NT1 barium 133
 NT1 barium 134
 NT1 barium 135
 NT1 barium 136
 NT1 barium 137
 NT1 barium 138
 NT1 barium 139
 NT1 barium 140
 NT1 barium 141
 NT1 barium 142
 NT1 barium 143
 NT1 barium 144
 NT1 barium 145
 NT1 barium 146
 NT1 barium 147
 NT1 barium 148
 NT1 barium 149

BARIUM NITRATES [73; 73]
 BT1 barium compounds
 BT2 alkaline earth metal compounds
 BT1 nitrates
 BT2 nitrogen compounds
 BT2 oxygen compounds

BARIUM NITRIDES [7; 7]
 BT1 barium compounds
 BT2 alkaline earth metal compounds
 BT1 nitrides
 BT2 nitrogen compounds
 BT2 pnictides

BARIUM OXIDES [6,995; 7,024]
  BT1 barium compounds
    BT2 alkaline earth metal compounds
  BT1 oxides
    BT2 chalcogenides
    BT2 oxygen compounds
  RT hollandite
  RT oxide minerals

BARIUM PERCHLORATES [4; 4]
  Oct 83
  BT1 barium compounds
    BT2 alkaline earth metal compounds
  BT1 perchlorates
    BT2 chlorine compounds
      BT3 halogen compounds
    BT2 oxygen compounds

BARIUM PHOSPHATES [57; 57]
  BT1 barium compounds
    BT2 alkaline earth metal compounds
  BT1 phosphates
    BT2 oxygen compounds
    BT2 phosphorus compounds
  RT phosphate minerals

BARIUM SILICATES [26; 26]
  BT1 barium compounds
    BT2 alkaline earth metal compounds
  BT1 silicates
    BT2 oxygen compounds
    BT2 silicon compounds

BARIUM SULFATES [417; 479]
  BT1 barium compounds
    BT2 alkaline earth metal compounds
  BT1 sulfates
    BT2 oxygen compounds
    BT2 sulfur compounds
  RT barite
  RT sulfate minerals
  RT uranocircite

BARIUM SULFIDES [42; 42]
  BT1 barium compounds
    BT2 alkaline earth metal compounds
  BT1 sulfides
    BT2 chalcogenides
    BT2 sulfur compounds

BARIUM TUNGSTATES [47; 47] Feb 78
  BT1 barium compounds
    BT2 alkaline earth metal compounds
  BT1 tungstates
    BT2 oxygen compounds
    BT2 tungsten compounds
      BT3 transition element compounds

BARIUM 117 [11; 11] Jun 77
  BT1 barium isotopes
  BT1 beta-plus decay radioisotopes
    BT2 beta decay radioisotopes
      BT3 radioisotopes
        BT4 isotopes
  BT1 electron capture radioisotopes
    BT2 beta decay radioisotopes
      BT3 radioisotopes
        BT4 isotopes
  BT1 even-odd nuclei
    BT2 nuclei
  BT1 intermediate mass nuclei
    BT2 nuclei
  BT1 seconds living radioisotopes
    BT2 radioisotopes
      BT3 isotopes

BARIUM 119 [16; 16]
  BT1 barium isotopes
  BT1 beta-plus decay radioisotopes
    BT2 beta decay radioisotopes
      BT3 radioisotopes
        BT4 isotopes
  BT1 electron capture radioisotopes
    BT2 beta decay radioisotopes
      BT3 radioisotopes
        BT4 isotopes
  BT1 even-odd nuclei
    BT2 nuclei
  BT1 intermediate mass nuclei
    BT2 nuclei
  BT1 seconds living radioisotopes
    BT2 radioisotopes
      BT3 isotopes

BARIUM 120 [9; 9]
  BT1 barium isotopes
  BT1 beta-plus decay radioisotopes
    BT2 beta decay radioisotopes
      BT3 radioisotopes
        BT4 isotopes
  BT1 electron capture radioisotopes
    BT2 beta decay radioisotopes
      BT3 radioisotopes
        BT4 isotopes
  BT1 even-even nuclei
    BT2 nuclei
  BT1 intermediate mass nuclei
    BT2 nuclei
  BT1 seconds living radioisotopes
    BT2 radioisotopes
      BT3 isotopes

BARIUM 121 [22; 22]
  BT1 barium isotopes
  BT1 beta-plus decay radioisotopes
    BT2 beta decay radioisotopes
      BT3 radioisotopes
        BT4 isotopes
  BT1 electron capture radioisotopes
    BT2 beta decay radioisotopes
      BT3 radioisotopes
        BT4 isotopes
  BT1 even-odd nuclei
    BT2 nuclei
  BT1 intermediate mass nuclei
    BT2 nuclei
  BT1 seconds living radioisotopes
    BT2 radioisotopes
      BT3 isotopes

BARIUM 122 [12; 12]
  BT1 barium isotopes
  BT1 beta-plus decay radioisotopes
    BT2 beta decay radioisotopes
      BT3 radioisotopes
        BT4 isotopes
  BT1 electron capture radioisotopes
    BT2 beta decay radioisotopes
      BT3 radioisotopes
        BT4 isotopes
  BT1 even-even nuclei
    BT2 nuclei
  BT1 intermediate mass nuclei
    BT2 nuclei
  BT1 minutes living radioisotopes
    BT2 radioisotopes
      BT3 isotopes

BARIUM 123 [20; 20]
  BT1 barium isotopes
  BT1 beta-plus decay radioisotopes
    BT2 beta decay radioisotopes
      BT3 radioisotopes
        BT4 isotopes
  BT1 electron capture radioisotopes
    BT2 beta decay radioisotopes
      BT3 radioisotopes
        BT4 isotopes
  BT1 even-odd nuclei
    BT2 nuclei
  BT1 intermediate mass nuclei
    BT2 nuclei
  BT1 minutes living radioisotopes
    BT2 radioisotopes
      BT3 isotopes

BARIUM 124 [30; 30]
  BT1 barium isotopes
  BT1 beta-plus decay radioisotopes
    BT2 beta decay radioisotopes
      BT3 radioisotopes
        BT4 isotopes
  BT1 electron capture radioisotopes
    BT2 beta decay radioisotopes
      BT3 radioisotopes
        BT4 isotopes
  BT1 even-even nuclei
    BT2 nuclei
  BT1 intermediate mass nuclei
    BT2 nuclei
  BT1 minutes living radioisotopes
    BT2 radioisotopes
      BT3 isotopes

BARIUM 125 [21; 21]
  BT1 barium isotopes
  BT1 beta-plus decay radioisotopes
    BT2 beta decay radioisotopes
      BT3 radioisotopes
        BT4 isotopes
  BT1 electron capture radioisotopes
    BT2 beta decay radioisotopes
      BT3 radioisotopes
        BT4 isotopes
  BT1 even-odd nuclei
    BT2 nuclei
  BT1 intermediate mass nuclei
    BT2 nuclei
  BT1 minutes living radioisotopes
    BT2 radioisotopes
      BT3 isotopes

BARIUM 126 [67; 67]
  BT1 barium isotopes
  BT1 beta-plus decay radioisotopes
    BT2 beta decay radioisotopes
      BT3 radioisotopes
        BT4 isotopes
  BT1 electron capture radioisotopes
    BT2 beta decay radioisotopes
      BT3 radioisotopes
        BT4 isotopes
  BT1 even-even nuclei
    BT2 nuclei
  BT1 hours living radioisotopes
    BT2 radioisotopes
      BT3 isotopes
  BT1 intermediate mass nuclei
    BT2 nuclei

BARIUM 127 [23; 23]
  BT1 barium isotopes
  BT1 beta-plus decay radioisotopes
    BT2 beta decay radioisotopes
      BT3 radioisotopes
        BT4 isotopes
  BT1 electron capture radioisotopes
    BT2 beta decay radioisotopes
      BT3 radioisotopes
        BT4 isotopes
  BT1 even-odd nuclei
    BT2 nuclei
  BT1 intermediate mass nuclei
    BT2 nuclei
  BT1 minutes living radioisotopes
    BT2 radioisotopes
      BT3 isotopes

BARIUM 128 [87; 87]
  BT1 barium isotopes
  BT1 days living radioisotopes
    BT2 radioisotopes
      BT3 isotopes
  BT1 electron capture radioisotopes
    BT2 beta decay radioisotopes
      BT3 radioisotopes
        BT4 isotopes
  BT1 even-even nuclei
    BT2 nuclei
  BT1 intermediate mass nuclei
    BT2 nuclei

BARIUM 129 [36; 36]
  BT1 barium isotopes
  BT1 beta-plus decay radioisotopes
    BT2 beta decay radioisotopes
      BT3 radioisotopes
        BT4 isotopes
  BT1 electron capture radioisotopes
    BT2 beta decay radioisotopes
      BT3 radioisotopes
        BT4 isotopes
  BT1 even-odd nuclei

BT2   nuclei
BT1   hours living radioisotopes
BT2   radioisotopes
BT3   isotopes
BT1   intermediate mass nuclei
BT2   nuclei

BARIUM 130 [64; 64]
BT1   barium isotopes
BT1   even-even nuclei
BT2   nuclei
BT1   intermediate mass nuclei
BT2   nuclei
BT1   stable isotopes
BT2   isotopes

BARIUM 130 TARGET [21; 21]
BT1   targets

BARIUM 131 [110; 110]
BT1   barium isotopes
BT1   days living radioisotopes
BT2   radioisotopes
BT3   isotopes
BT1   electron capture radioisotopes
BT2   beta decay radioisotopes
BT3   radioisotopes
BT4   isotopes
BT1   even-odd nuclei
BT2   nuclei
BT1   intermediate mass nuclei
BT2   nuclei
BT1   internal conversion radioisoto
BT2   radioisotopes
BT3   isotopes
BT1   isomeric transition isotopes
BT2   radioisotopes
BT3   isotopes
BT1   minutes living radioisotopes
BT2   radioisotopes
BT3   isotopes

BARIUM 132 [48; 48]
BT1   barium isotopes
BT1   even-even nuclei
BT2   nuclei
BT1   intermediate mass nuclei
BT2   nuclei
BT1   stable isotopes
BT2   isotopes

BARIUM 133 [376; 376]
BT1   barium isotopes
BT1   days living radioisotopes
BT2   radioisotopes
BT3   isotopes
BT1   electron capture radioisotopes
BT2   beta decay radioisotopes
BT3   radioisotopes
BT4   isotopes
BT1   even-odd nuclei
BT2   nuclei
BT1   intermediate mass nuclei
BT2   nuclei
BT1   internal conversion radioisoto
BT2   radioisotopes
BT3   isotopes
BT1   isomeric transition isotopes
BT2   radioisotopes
BT3   isotopes
BT1   years living radioisotopes
BT2   radioisotopes
BT3   isotopes

BARIUM 134 [93; 93]
BT1   barium isotopes
BT1   even-even nuclei
BT2   nuclei
BT1   intermediate mass nuclei
BT2   nuclei
BT1   stable isotopes
BT2   isotopes

BARIUM 134 TARGET [44; 44]
BT1   targets

BARIUM 135 [96; 96]
BT1   barium isotopes
BT1   days living radioisotopes
BT2   radioisotopes
BT3   isotopes
BT1   even-odd nuclei
BT2   nuclei
BT1   intermediate mass nuclei
BT2   nuclei
BT1   internal conversion radioisoto
BT2   radioisotopes
BT3   isotopes
BT1   isomeric transition isotopes
BT2   radioisotopes
BT3   isotopes
BT1   stable isotopes
BT2   isotopes

BARIUM 135 TARGET [19; 19] *Apr 77*
BT1   targets

BARIUM 136 [87; 87]
BT1   barium isotopes
BT1   even-even nuclei
BT2   nuclei
BT1   intermediate mass nuclei
BT2   nuclei
BT1   isomeric transition isotopes
BT2   radioisotopes
BT3   isotopes
BT1   millisec living radioisotopes
BT2   radioisotopes
BT3   isotopes
BT1   stable isotopes
BT2   isotopes

BARIUM 136 TARGET [48; 48] *Feb 76*
BT1   targets

BARIUM 137 [181; 181]
BT1   barium isotopes
BT1   even-odd nuclei
BT2   nuclei
BT1   intermediate mass nuclei
BT2   nuclei
BT1   isomeric transition isotopes
BT2   radioisotopes
BT3   isotopes
BT1   minutes living radioisotopes
BT2   radioisotopes
BT3   isotopes
BT1   stable isotopes
BT2   isotopes

BARIUM 137 TARGET [21; 21] *Apr 77*
BT1   targets

BARIUM 138 [177; 177]
BT1   barium isotopes
BT1   even-even nuclei
BT2   nuclei
BT1   intermediate mass nuclei
BT2   nuclei
BT1   isomeric transition isotopes
BT2   radioisotopes
BT3   isotopes
BT1   nanosec living radioisotopes
BT2   radioisotopes
BT3   isotopes
BT1   stable isotopes
BT2   isotopes

BARIUM 138 TARGET [156; 156]
BT1   targets

BARIUM 139 [86; 86]
BT1   barium isotopes
BT1   beta-minus decay radioisotopes
BT2   beta decay radioisotopes
BT3   radioisotopes
BT4   isotopes
BT1   even-odd nuclei
BT2   nuclei
BT1   hours living radioisotopes
BT2   radioisotopes
BT3   isotopes
BT1   intermediate mass nuclei
BT2   nuclei

BARIUM 139 TARGET [4; 4] *Oct 75*
BT1   targets

BARIUM 140 [620; 620]
BT1   barium isotopes
BT1   beta-minus decay radioisotopes
BT2   beta decay radioisotopes
BT3   radioisotopes
BT4   isotopes
BT1   days living radioisotopes
BT2   radioisotopes
BT3   isotopes
BT1   even-even nuclei
BT2   nuclei
BT1   intermediate mass nuclei
BT2   nuclei

BARIUM 141 [30; 30]
BT1   barium isotopes
BT1   beta-minus decay radioisotopes
BT2   beta decay radioisotopes
BT3   radioisotopes
BT4   isotopes
BT1   even-odd nuclei
BT2   nuclei
BT1   intermediate mass nuclei
BT2   nuclei
BT1   minutes living radioisotopes
BT2   radioisotopes
BT3   isotopes

BARIUM 142 [50; 50]
BT1   barium isotopes
BT1   beta-minus decay radioisotopes
BT2   beta decay radioisotopes
BT3   radioisotopes
BT4   isotopes
BT1   even-even nuclei
BT2   nuclei
BT1   intermediate mass nuclei
BT2   nuclei
BT1   minutes living radioisotopes
BT2   radioisotopes
BT3   isotopes

BARIUM 143 [31; 31]
BT1   barium isotopes
BT1   beta-minus decay radioisotopes
BT2   beta decay radioisotopes
BT3   radioisotopes
BT4   isotopes
BT1   even-odd nuclei
BT2   nuclei
BT1   intermediate mass nuclei
BT2   nuclei
BT1   seconds living radioisotopes
BT2   radioisotopes
BT3   isotopes

BARIUM 144 [50; 50]
BT1   barium isotopes
BT1   beta-minus decay radioisotopes
BT2   beta decay radioisotopes
BT3   radioisotopes
BT4   isotopes
BT1   even-even nuclei
BT2   nuclei
BT1   intermediate mass nuclei
BT2   nuclei
BT1   seconds living radioisotopes
BT2   radioisotopes
BT3   isotopes

BARIUM 145 [28; 28]
BT1   barium isotopes
BT1   beta-minus decay radioisotopes
BT2   beta decay radioisotopes
BT3   radioisotopes
BT4   isotopes
BT1   even-odd nuclei
BT2   nuclei
BT1   intermediate mass nuclei

BARIUM 146 [38; 38]
  BT2   nuclei
  BT1   seconds living radioisotopes
    BT2   radioisotopes
      BT3   isotopes

BARIUM 146 [38; 38]
  BT1   barium isotopes
  BT1   beta-minus decay radioisotopes
    BT2   beta decay radioisotopes
      BT3   radioisotopes
        BT4   isotopes
  BT1   even-even nuclei
    BT2   nuclei
  BT1   intermediate mass nuclei
    BT2   nuclei
  BT1   seconds living radioisotopes
    BT2   radioisotopes
      BT3   isotopes

BARIUM 147 [18; 18] *Jun 77*
  BT1   barium isotopes
  BT1   beta-minus decay radioisotopes
    BT2   beta decay radioisotopes
      BT3   radioisotopes
        BT4   isotopes
  BT1   even-odd nuclei
    BT2   nuclei
  BT1   intermediate mass nuclei
    BT2   nuclei
  BT1   millisec living radioisotopes
    BT2   radioisotopes
      BT3   isotopes

BARIUM 148 [24; 24] *Jun 77*
  BT1   barium isotopes
  BT1   beta-minus decay radioisotopes
    BT2   beta decay radioisotopes
      BT3   radioisotopes
        BT4   isotopes
  BT1   even-even nuclei
    BT2   nuclei
  BT1   intermediate mass nuclei
    BT2   nuclei
  BT1   millisec living radioisotopes
    BT2   radioisotopes
      BT3   isotopes

BARIUM 149 [3; 3] *Jan 86*
  BT1   barium isotopes
  BT1   beta-minus decay radioisotopes
    BT2   beta decay radioisotopes
      BT3   radioisotopes
        BT4   isotopes
  BT1   even-odd nuclei
    BT2   nuclei
  BT1   intermediate mass nuclei
    BT2   nuclei
  BT1   millisec living radioisotopes
    BT2   radioisotopes
      BT3   isotopes

BARK [11; 11] *Jul 86*
  BT1   plant tissues
  RT   cork
  RT   lignin
  RT   plant stems
  RT   trees

BARLEY [794; 794]
  UF   *hordeum*
  BT1   cereals
    BT2   gramineae
      BT3   plants

BARN REACTOR [2; 2]
(Institute for Atomic Sciences in Agriculture, Wageningen, Netherlands)
  UF   *wageningen barn reactor*
  BT1   pool type reactors
    BT2   water cooled reactors
      BT3   reactors
    BT2   water moderated reactors
      BT3   reactors
  BT1   research reactors
    BT2   research and test reactors
      BT3   reactors
  BT1   test reactors
    BT2   research and test reactors
      BT3   reactors
    BT2   test facilities

BARNWELL FUEL PROCESSING PLANT [191; 191]
  BT1   fuel reprocessing plants
    BT2   nuclear facilities

BAROMETERS [15; 15]
  BT1   pressure gages
    BT2   measuring instruments

BARSEBAECK-1 REACTOR [110; 110]
(Barsebaeck, Malmo, Sweden)
  UF   *sydsvenska kraft ab reactor 1*
  BT1   bwr type reactors
    BT2   enriched uranium reactors
      BT3   reactors
    BT2   power reactors
      BT3   reactors
    BT2   thermal reactors
      BT3   reactors
    BT2   water cooled reactors
      BT3   reactors
    BT2   water moderated reactors
      BT3   reactors

BARSEBAECK-2 REACTOR [89; 89] *Apr 78*
(Barsebaeck, Malmo, Sweden)
  UF   *sydsvenska kraft ab reactor 2*
  BT1   bwr type reactors
    BT2   enriched uranium reactors
      BT3   reactors
    BT2   power reactors
      BT3   reactors
    BT2   thermal reactors
      BT3   reactors
    BT2   water cooled reactors
      BT3   reactors
    BT2   water moderated reactors
      BT3   reactors

BARTON-1 REACTOR [6; 6]
  BT1   bwr type reactors
    BT2   enriched uranium reactors
      BT3   reactors
    BT2   power reactors
      BT3   reactors
    BT2   thermal reactors
      BT3   reactors
    BT2   water cooled reactors
      BT3   reactors
    BT2   water moderated reactors
      BT3   reactors

BARTON-2 REACTOR [6; 6]
  BT1   bwr type reactors
    BT2   enriched uranium reactors
      BT3   reactors
    BT2   power reactors
      BT3   reactors
    BT2   thermal reactors
      BT3   reactors
    BT2   water cooled reactors
      BT3   reactors
    BT2   water moderated reactors
      BT3   reactors

BARTON-3 REACTOR [6; 6]
  BT1   bwr type reactors
    BT2   enriched uranium reactors
      BT3   reactors
    BT2   power reactors
      BT3   reactors
    BT2   thermal reactors
      BT3   reactors
    BT2   water cooled reactors
      BT3   reactors
    BT2   water moderated reactors
      BT3   reactors

BARTON-4 REACTOR [6; 6]
  BT1   bwr type reactors
    BT2   enriched uranium reactors
      BT3   reactors
    BT2   power reactors
      BT3   reactors
    BT2   thermal reactors
      BT3   reactors
    BT2   water cooled reactors
      BT3   reactors
    BT2   water moderated reactors
      BT3   reactors

BARYON DECUPLETS [98; 98]
  BT1   particle multiplets
    BT2   multiplets

BARYON NUMBER [1,220; 1,220]
  RT   baryons
  RT   gauge invariance
  RT   neutron oscillation

BARYON OCTETS [257; 257]
  BT1   particle multiplets
    BT2   multiplets
  RT   octet model

BARYON REACTIONS [26; 38,304]
  BT1   hadron reactions
  BT2   nuclear reactions
  NT1   hyperon reactions
  NT1   nucleon reactions
    NT2   antinucleon reactions
      NT3   antineutron reactions
      NT3   antiproton reactions
    NT2   neutron reactions
      NT3   fast fission
      NT3   thermal fission
    NT2   proton reactions

baryon resonances
(Prior to December 1987 this was a valid descriptor.)
  USE   baryons

BARYON SPECTROSCOPY [98; 98] *Jan 79*
  BT1   spectroscopy

BARYON-BARYON INTERACTIONS [274; 20,258]
  BT1   hadron-hadron interactions
    BT2   particle interactions
      BT3   interactions
  NT1   hyperon-hyperon interactions
  NT1   nucleon-antinucleon interactio
    NT2   antiproton-antineutron interaction
    NT2   neutron-antineutron interactio
    NT2   proton-antineutron interaction
    NT2   proton-antiproton interactions
  NT1   nucleon-hyperon interactions
  NT1   nucleon-nucleon interactions
    NT2   neutron-neutron interactions
    NT2   proton-nucleon interactions
      NT3   proton-neutron interactions
      NT3   proton-proton interactions

BARYON-EXCHANGE MODELS [162; 162]
  BT1   peripheral models
    BT2   particle models
      BT3   mathematical models

BARYONIUM [446; 446] *Aug 78*
  BT1   mesons
    BT2   bosons
    BT2   hadrons
      BT3   elementary particles
  RT   baryons
  RT   quarkonium

BARYONS [3,260; 99,853]
- UF *baryon resonances*
- UF *d* plus resonances*
- UF *d* zero resonances*
- UF *d*resonances*
- UF *y*resonances*
- BT1 fermions
- BT1 hadrons
- BT2 elementary particles
- NT1 antibaryons
  - NT2 antihyperons
    - NT3 antilambda particles
    - NT3 antiomega particles
    - NT3 antisigma particles
    - NT3 antixi particles
  - NT2 antinucleons
    - NT3 antineutrons
    - NT3 antiprotons
- NT1 beauty baryons
  - NT2 lambda b neutral baryons
- NT1 charmed baryons
  - NT2 lambda c plus baryons
  - NT2 omega c neutral baryons
  - NT2 sigma c-2450 baryons
  - NT2 xi c plus baryons
- NT1 dibaryons
  - NT2 dineutrons
  - NT2 diprotons
  - NT2 lambda-n-2130 dibaryons
  - NT2 nn-2170 dibaryons
  - NT2 nn-2250 dibaryons
- NT1 hyperons
  - NT2 antihyperons
    - NT3 antilambda particles
    - NT3 antiomega particles
    - NT3 antisigma particles
    - NT3 antixi particles
  - NT2 lambda baryons
    - NT3 lambda particles
      - NT4 antilambda particles
    - NT3 lambda-1405 baryons
    - NT3 lambda-1520 baryons
    - NT3 lambda-1600 baryons
    - NT3 lambda-1670 baryons
    - NT3 lambda-1690 baryons
    - NT3 lambda-1800 baryons
    - NT3 lambda-1820 baryons
    - NT3 lambda-1830 baryons
    - NT3 lambda-1890 baryons
    - NT3 lambda-2000 baryons
    - NT3 lambda-2020 baryons
    - NT3 lambda-2100 baryons
    - NT3 lambda-2110 baryons
    - NT3 lambda-2325 baryons
    - NT3 lambda-2350 baryons
    - NT3 lambda-2585 baryons
  - NT2 lambda-n-2130 dibaryons
  - NT2 omega baryons
    - NT3 omega particles
      - NT4 antiomega particles
  - NT2 sigma baryons
    - NT3 sigma particles
      - NT4 antisigma particles
      - NT4 sigma minus particles
      - NT4 sigma neutral particles
      - NT4 sigma plus particles
    - NT3 sigma-1385 baryons
    - NT3 sigma-1480 baryons
    - NT3 sigma-1560 baryons
    - NT3 sigma-1580 baryons
    - NT3 sigma-1620 baryons
    - NT3 sigma-1660 baryons
    - NT3 sigma-1670 baryons
    - NT3 sigma-1690 baryons
    - NT3 sigma-1750 baryons
    - NT3 sigma-1770 baryons
    - NT3 sigma-1775 baryons
    - NT3 sigma-1840 baryons
    - NT3 sigma-1880 baryons
    - NT3 sigma-1915 baryons
    - NT3 sigma-1940 baryons
    - NT3 sigma-2000 baryons
    - NT3 sigma-2030 baryons
    - NT3 sigma-2070 baryons
    - NT3 sigma-2080 baryons
    - NT3 sigma-2100 baryons
    - NT3 sigma-2250 baryons
    - NT3 sigma-2455 baryons
    - NT3 sigma-2620 baryons
    - NT3 sigma-3000 baryons
    - NT3 sigma-3170 baryons
  - NT2 xi baryons
    - NT3 xi particles
      - NT4 antixi particles
      - NT4 xi minus particles
      - NT4 xi neutral particles
    - NT3 xi-1530 baryons
    - NT3 xi-1630 baryons
    - NT3 xi-1680 baryons
    - NT3 xi-1820 baryons
    - NT3 xi-1940 baryons
    - NT3 xi-2030 baryons
    - NT3 xi-2120 baryons
    - NT3 xi-2250 baryons
    - NT3 xi-2370 baryons
    - NT3 xi-2500 baryons
  - NT2 z*baryons
    - NT3 z0-1780 baryons
    - NT3 z0-1865 baryons
    - NT3 z1-1725 baryons
    - NT3 z1-1900 baryons
    - NT3 z1-2150 baryons
    - NT3 z1-2500 baryons
- NT1 n*baryons
  - NT2 delta baryons
    - NT3 delta-1232 baryons
    - NT3 delta-1550 baryons
    - NT3 delta-1600 baryons
    - NT3 delta-1620 baryons
    - NT3 delta-1700 baryons
    - NT3 delta-1900 baryons
    - NT3 delta-1905 baryons
    - NT3 delta-1910 baryons
    - NT3 delta-1920 baryons
    - NT3 delta-1930 baryons
    - NT3 delta-1940 baryons
    - NT3 delta-1950 baryons
    - NT3 delta-2000 baryons
    - NT3 delta-2150 baryons
    - NT3 delta-2200 baryons
    - NT3 delta-2300 baryons
    - NT3 delta-2350 baryons
    - NT3 delta-2390 baryons
    - NT3 delta-2400 baryons
    - NT3 delta-2420 baryons
    - NT3 delta-2750 baryons
    - NT3 delta-2950 baryons
    - NT3 delta-3000 baryons
  - NT2 n baryons
    - NT3 n-1440 baryons
    - NT3 n-1520 baryons
    - NT3 n-1535 baryons
    - NT3 n-1540 baryons
    - NT3 n-1650 baryons
    - NT3 n-1675 baryons
    - NT3 n-1680 baryons
    - NT3 n-1700 baryons
    - NT3 n-1710 baryons
    - NT3 n-1720 baryons
    - NT3 n-1960 baryons
    - NT3 n-1990 baryons
    - NT3 n-2000 baryons
    - NT3 n-2080 baryons
    - NT3 n-2090 baryons
    - NT3 n-2100 baryons
    - NT3 n-2190 baryons
    - NT3 n-2200 baryons
    - NT3 n-2220 baryons
    - NT3 n-2250 baryons
    - NT3 n-2600 baryons
    - NT3 n-2700 baryons
    - NT3 n-3000 baryons
- NT1 nucleons
  - NT2 antinucleons
    - NT3 antineutrons
    - NT3 antiprotons
  - NT2 neutrons
    - NT3 antineutrons
    - NT3 beta-delayed neutrons
    - NT3 cold neutrons
      - NT4 ultracold neutrons
    - NT3 cosmic neutrons
    - NT3 epithermal neutrons
    - NT3 fast neutrons
    - NT3 fission neutrons
      - NT4 delayed neutrons
      - NT4 prompt neutrons
    - NT3 intermediate neutrons
    - NT3 photoneutrons
    - NT3 pile neutrons
    - NT3 polyneutrons
      - NT4 dineutrons
      - NT4 tetraneutrons
      - NT4 trineutrons
    - NT3 resonance neutrons
    - NT3 slow neutrons
    - NT3 solar neutrons
    - NT3 thermal neutrons
  - NT2 photonucleons
    - NT3 photoneutrons
    - NT3 photoprotons
  - NT2 protons
    - NT3 antiprotons
    - NT3 cosmic protons
    - NT3 delayed protons
    - NT3 diprotons
    - NT3 photoprotons
    - NT3 prompt protons
    - NT3 solar protons
    - NT3 trapped protons
- RT baryon number
- RT baryonium

BASAL METABOLISM [41; 41]
- BT1 metabolism

BASALT [2,331; 2,331]
- BT1 igneous rocks
- BT2 rocks
- RT feldspars
- RT olivine

BASEBALL DEVICES [58; 58]
- BT1 open plasma devices
- BT2 thermonuclear devices

BASEBALL SEAM CONFIGURATIONS [19; 19]
- BT1 open configurations
- BT2 magnetic field configurations

basedow's disease
- USE hyperthyroidism

BASELINE ECOLOGY [66; 66] *Dec 82*
(The ecological situation or studies of that situation which exists at a site or geographical region before some development is made in the area; it provides a basis for evaluating impact of the development.)
- BT1 ecology
- RT site surveys

BASES [211; 211]
- RT anhydrides
- RT hydroxides
- RT ph value

basf-industriekernkraftw. r. 1
- USE basf-1 reactor

basf-industriekernkraftw. r. 2
- USE basf-2 reactor

BASF-1 REACTOR [16; 16]
- UF *basf-industriekernkraftw. r. 1*
- BT1 pwr type reactors
- BT2 enriched uranium reactors
- BT3 reactors
- BT2 power reactors
- BT3 reactors
- BT2 thermal reactors
- BT3 reactors
- BT2 water cooled reactors
- BT3 reactors
- BT2 water moderated reactors
- BT3 reactors

BASF-2 REACTOR [6; 6]
- UF *basf-industriekernkraftw. r. 2*
- BT1 pwr type reactors
- BT2 enriched uranium reactors
- BT3 reactors

```
    BT2     power reactors
      BT3     reactors
    BT2     thermal reactors
      BT3     reactors
    BT2     water cooled reactors
      BT3     reactors
    BT2     water moderated reactors
      BT3     reactors
```

BASIC [133; 133] *Jan 79*
- BT1   programming languages

BASIC INTERACTIONS [262; 31,323]
- NT1   electromagnetic interactions
  - NT2   compton effect
  - NT2   coulomb scattering
  - NT2   electroproduction
  - NT2   photon-hadron interactions
    - NT3   photon-baryon interactions
      - NT4   photon-hyperon interactions
      - NT4   photon-nucleon interactions
        - NT5   photon-neutron interactions
        - NT5   photon-proton interactions
    - NT3   photon-meson interactions
  - NT2   photon-photon interactions
  - NT2   photoproduction
    - NT3   primakoff effect
  - NT2   umklapp processes
- NT1   gravitational interactions
- NT1   strong interactions
  - NT2   charge-exchange interactions
  - NT2   peripheral collisions
- NT1   weak interactions
  - NT2   fermi interactions
  - NT2   leptonic decay
- RT   charged-current interactions
- RT   conservation laws
- RT   interactions
- RT   invariance principles
- RT   neutral-current interactions
- RT   potentials
- RT   unified-field theories

basins (sedimentary)
- USE   geologic structures

BASOPHILS [32; 32]
- BT1   leukocytes
  - BT2   blood cells
    - BT3   blood
      - BT4   body fluids
        - BT5   biological materials
          - BT6   materials

basophils (connective tissue)
- USE   mast cells

BASTNAESITE [50; 50]
- BT1   oxide minerals
  - BT2   minerals
- BT1   thorium minerals
  - BT2   radioactive minerals
    - BT3   minerals
    - BT3   radioactive materials
      - BT4   materials
- RT   thorium oxides

bataan philippine power plant
- USE   pnpp-1 reactor

BATCH LOADING [69; 69]
- BT1   reactor fueling

bates linac mit
- USE   mit bates linac

BATTELLE COLUMBUS LABORATORY [32; 32] *Sep 77*
- BT1   us erda
  - BT2   us organizations
    - BT3   national organizations

BATTELLE PACIFIC NORTHWEST LAB [390; 390] *Oct 76*
- BT1   us doe
  - BT2   us organizations
    - BT3   national organizations
- BT1   us erda
  - BT2   us organizations
    - BT3   national organizations
- RT   hanford reservation

battelle research reactor
- USE   brr reactor

batteries (electric)
- USE   electric batteries

batteries (isotopic)
- USE   radioisotope batteries

BATYL ALCOHOL [1; 1]
- UF   *octadecyl glyceryl ether-alpha*
- BT1   alcohols
  - BT2   hydroxy compounds
    - BT3   organic compounds
- BT1   ethers
  - BT2   organic oxygen compounds
    - BT3   organic compounds
- RT   glycerol

BAUXITE [123; 123]
- BT1   aluminium ores
  - BT2   ores

BAWTR REACTOR [8; 8]
(Babcock and Wilcox, Lynchburg Research Center, Lynchburg, Virginia, USA)
- UF   *babcock and wilcox test react.*
- BT1   enriched uranium reactors
  - BT2   reactors
- BT1   pool type reactors
  - BT2   water cooled reactors
    - BT3   reactors
  - BT2   water moderated reactors
    - BT3   reactors
- BT1   test reactors
  - BT2   research and test reactors
    - BT3   reactors
  - BT2   test facilities
- BT1   thermal reactors
  - BT2   reactors

BAY OF BISCAY [4; 4] *Jul 85*
- UF   *biscay bay (france, spain)*
- BT1   atlantic ocean
  - BT2   seas
    - BT3   surface waters
- RT   france
- RT   spain

→ **BAY OF FUNDY** [0; 0] *Sep 91*
- BT1   atlantic ocean
  - BT2   seas
    - BT3   surface waters
- RT   canada

BAYARD-ALPERT GAGES [32; 32]
- BT1   ionization gages
  - BT2   vacuum gages
    - BT3   pressure gages
      - BT4   measuring instruments

BAYLEYITE [3; 3]
- BT1   carbonate minerals
  - BT2   minerals
- BT1   uranium minerals
  - BT2   radioactive minerals
    - BT3   minerals
    - BT3   radioactive materials
      - BT4   materials
- RT   magnesium carbonates
- RT   uranium carbonates

bays (coastal waters)
- USE   coastal waters

bays (magnetic)
- USE   magnetic bays

BBGKY EQUATION [210; 210]
- UF   *bbgky hierarchy*
- UF   *bbgky theory*
- UF   *bogolyubov theory*
- UF   *born-bogol.-green-kirkw.-yvon*
- BT1   differential equations
  - BT2   equations
- RT   statistical mechanics

bbgky hierarchy
- USE   bbgky equation

bbgky theory
- USE   bbgky equation

BCC LATTICES [1,835; 1,835]
- UF   *body centered cubic*
- BT1   cubic lattices
  - BT2   crystal lattices
    - BT3   crystal structure

BCOCLMCNM [39; 39]
(Brussels Convention on Civil Liability for Maritime Carriage of Nuclear Materials)
- UF   *bruss conv maritime liab 1971*
- UF   *liabil conv marit car nucl mat*
- UF   *marit car liab conv bruss 1971*
- BT1   international agreements
  - BT2   agreements
- RT   civil liability

BCOLONS [38; 38]
(Brussels Convention on Liability for Operation of Nuclear Ships)
- UF   *bruss conv-liab opera nucl shi*
- UF   *liabil conv opera nucl ships*
- UF   *nucl. ship oper. lia. conv,bru*
- BT1   international agreements
  - BT2   agreements
- RT   civil liability
- RT   liabilities
- RT   nuclear ship visits
- RT   nuclear ships

BCS THEORY [1,423; 1,423]
- UF   *bardeen-cooper-schrieffer theo*
- RT   superconductivity

BCSTPC [99; 99]
(Brussels Convention - supplement to Paris Convention on Third Party Liability)
- UF   *bruss conv-suppl to paris conv*
- UF   *liabil conv on third party, br*
- UF   *third party liabil conv, bruss*
- BT1   international agreements
  - BT2   agreements
- RT   civil liability
- RT   pcotpl

BEAGLES [1,412; 1,412]
- BT1   dogs
  - BT2   mammals
    - BT3   vertebrates
      - BT4   animals

BEAM ACCEPTANCE [326; 326]
- UF   *acceptance (beam)*
- RT   beam optics

BEAM ANALYZERS [240; 1,091]
(For momentum analysis of charged particle beams.)
- NT1   electrostatic analyzers
- NT1   magnetic analyzers
- RT   beam monitors
- RT   monochromators

BEAM BENDING MAGNETS [1,558; 1,558]
- UF *beam-bending magnets*
- BT1 magnets
  - BT2 equipment
- RT beam optics
- RT magnetic analyzers

beam blowup
- USE beam dynamics

BEAM BUNCHERS [525; 525]
- RT beam bunching

BEAM BUNCHING [2,598; 2,598]
- UF *bunching (beam)*
- BT1 beam dynamics
  - BT2 dynamics
    - BT3 mechanics
- RT beam bunchers
- RT beam optics
- RT beam shaping

beam choppers
- USE beam pulsers

BEAM COOLING [212; 741] *Aug 75*
(For improving the quality of particle beams.)
- NT1 electron cooling
- NT1 stochastic cooling
  - NT2 momentum cooling
- RT beam dynamics

BEAM CURRENTS [2,949; 7,160]
- BT1 currents
- NT1 amp beam currents
- NT1 kilo amp beam currents
- NT1 mega amp beam currents
- NT1 micro amp beam currents
- NT1 milli amp beam currents
- NT1 nano amp beam currents
- NT1 pico amp beam currents
- RT beam monitoring
- RT beam monitors
- RT current density
- RT faraday cups

BEAM DUMPS [540; 540]
(Mass of shielding material to absorb an accelerator beam after experimental use.)
- RT accelerator facilities
- RT accelerators

BEAM DYNAMICS [4,486; 7,726]
(Particle beam motion inside an accelerator.)
- UF *beam blowup*
- UF *blowup (particle beams)*
- BT1 dynamics
  - BT2 mechanics
- NT1 beam bunching
- NT1 betatron oscillations
- NT1 phase oscillations
- NT1 synchrotron oscillations
- RT accelerators
- RT beam cooling
- RT beam optics
- RT beam stacking
- RT beam-beam interactions
- RT negative mass effect
- RT orbit stability
- RT orbits
- RT phase stability
- RT trajectories

BEAM EMITTANCE [2,876; 2,876]
- UF *emittance (beam)*
- RT beam optics
- RT brightness

BEAM EXTRACTION [2,573; 2,573]
- UF *extraction (beam)*
- RT beam optics
- RT kicker magnets
- RT septum magnets

BEAM FOCUSING MAGNETS [1,051; 1,051]
- UF *beam-focusing magnets*
- BT1 magnets
  - BT2 equipment
- RT beam optics

BEAM HOLES [128; 128]
(Hole through a reactor for the passage of a beam of radiation for experiments outside the reactor.)
- BT1 reactor channels
  - BT2 reactor components
- BT1 reactor experimental facilitie
  - BT2 reactor components

BEAM INJECTION [3,543; 9,506]
- UF *injection (beams)*
- NT1 cluster beam injection
- NT1 electron beam injection
- NT1 ion beam injection
  - NT2 molecular ion beam injection
- NT1 neutral atom beam injection
- NT1 plasma beam injection
- NT1 relativistic beam injection
- RT beam injection heating
- RT beam optics
- RT beam production
- RT particle boosters
- RT thermonuclear devices

BEAM INJECTION HEATING [1,904; 1,904]
- UF *beam-injection heating*
- BT1 plasma heating
  - BT2 heating
- RT atomic beam sources
- RT beam injection

BEAM LUMINOSITY [1,274; 1,274]
(Colliding beam interaction rate)
- RT colliding beams
- RT electron cooling
- RT interactions

BEAM MONITORING [2,074; 2,074]
- BT1 monitoring
- RT beam currents
- RT beam monitors
- RT beam position
- RT beam profiles
- RT magnetoinduction sensors

BEAM MONITORS [1,589; 2,291]
- BT1 monitors
  - BT2 measuring instruments
- NT1 beam scanners
- NT1 faraday cups
- NT1 magnetoinduction sensors
- RT accelerator facilities
- RT beam analyzers
- RT beam currents
- RT beam monitoring
- RT beam position
- RT beam profiles

BEAM NEUTRALIZATION [870; 870]
- UF *neutralization (beam)*
- RT charge exchange
- RT ionization
- RT particle beams

BEAM OPTICS [5,365; 5,365]
- RT alignment
- RT beam acceptance
- RT beam bending magnets
- RT beam bunching
- RT beam dynamics
- RT beam emittance
- RT beam extraction
- RT beam focusing magnets
- RT beam injection
- RT beam shaping
- RT beam splitting
- RT beam transport
- RT chromatic aberrations
- RT collimators
- RT electrostatic lenses
- RT electrostatic mirrors
- RT electrostatic septa
- RT focusing
- RT geometrical aberrations
- RT kicker magnets
- RT monochromators
- RT optical systems
- RT septum magnets

BEAM POSITION [737; 737]
- RT beam monitoring
- RT beam monitors
- RT beam scanners

BEAM PRODUCTION [1,794; 1,794]
- UF *production (beam)*
- RT beam injection

BEAM PROFILES [2,048; 2,048]
- UF *beam widths*
- RT beam monitoring
- RT beam monitors
- RT beam scanners
- RT beam shaping

BEAM PULSERS [400; 578]
- UF *beam choppers*
- UF *choppers (beams)*
- NT1 neutron choppers
- RT beams

BEAM SCANNERS [244; 244]
- UF *scanners (beam)*
- BT1 beam monitors
  - BT2 monitors
    - BT3 measuring instruments
- RT beam position
- RT beam profiles

BEAM SEPARATORS [256; 256]
(For velocity separation of secondary beams.)
- RT accelerators

BEAM SHAPING [721; 721] *Aug 75*
- RT beam bunching
- RT beam optics
- RT beam profiles
- RT focusing

BEAM SPLITTING [144; 144] *Oct 75*
- RT beam optics

BEAM STACKING [206; 206]
- RT beam dynamics
- RT beam-beam interactions

BEAM STRIPPERS [486; 486]
- UF *stripper foils*
- UF *strippers*
- RT atomic beams
- RT charge exchange
- RT charge states
- RT electron loss
- RT ion beams

BEAM TRANSPORT [5,421; 5,421]
- UF *transport (beam)*
- RT beam optics

beam widths
- USE beam profiles

BEAM-BEAM INTERACTIONS
[752; 752] *Sep 80*
- RT beam dynamics
- RT beam stacking
- RT colliding beams

beam-bending magnets
- USE beam bending magnets

beam-focusing magnets
- USE beam focusing magnets

beam-foil spectroscopy
- USE ion spectroscopy

beam-gas spectroscopy
- USE ion spectroscopy

beam-injection heating
- USE beam injection heating

BEAM-PLASMA SYSTEMS
[2,887; 2,887]
- RT beams
- RT pierce instability
- RT plasma
- RT whistler instability

BEAMS [883; 91,392]
- NT1 antiparticle beams
  - NT2 antineutrino beams
  - NT2 antinucleon beams
    - NT3 antiproton beams
- NT1 atomic beams
- NT1 cluster beams
- NT1 colliding beams
- NT1 ion beams
  - NT2 aluminium 27 beams
  - NT2 argon 38 beams
  - NT2 argon 39 beams
  - NT2 argon 40 beams
  - NT2 beryllium 7 beams
  - NT2 beryllium 9 beams
  - NT2 bismuth 209 beams
  - NT2 boron 10 beams
  - NT2 boron 11 beams
  - NT2 bromine 79 beams
  - NT2 calcium 40 beams
  - NT2 calcium 48 beams
  - NT2 carbon 10 beams
  - NT2 carbon 11 beams
  - NT2 carbon 12 beams
  - NT2 carbon 13 beams
  - NT2 carbon 14 beams
  - NT2 chlorine 35 beams
  - NT2 chlorine 39 beams
  - NT2 copper 63 beams
  - NT2 deuteron beams
  - NT2 fluorine 19 beams
  - NT2 gadolinium 155 beams
  - NT2 germanium 74 beams
  - NT2 germanium 76 beams
  - NT2 gold 197 beams
  - NT2 helium 3 beams
  - NT2 helium 4 beams
    - NT3 alpha beams
  - NT2 helium 8 beams
  - NT2 hydrogen 1 minus beams
  - NT2 iodine 127 beams
  - NT2 iron 56 beams
  - NT2 iron 58 beams
  - NT2 krypton 84 beams
  - NT2 krypton 86 beams
  - NT2 lanthanum 139 beams
  - NT2 lead 208 beams
  - NT2 lithium 6 beams
  - NT2 lithium 7 beams
  - NT2 magnesium 24 beams
  - NT2 neon 19 beams
  - NT2 neon 20 beams
  - NT2 neon 22 beams
  - NT2 nickel 58 beams
  - NT2 nickel 60 beams
  - NT2 nitrogen 13 beams
  - NT2 nitrogen 14 beams
  - NT2 nitrogen 15 beams
  - NT2 oxygen 16 beams
  - NT2 oxygen 18 beams
  - NT2 phosphorus 31 beams
  - NT2 potassium 39 beams
  - NT2 potassium 41 beams
  - NT2 silicon 28 beams
  - NT2 silicon 29 beams
  - NT2 silver 107 beams
  - NT2 sodium 23 beams
  - NT2 sulfur 32 beams
  - NT2 sulfur 38 beams
  - NT2 tin 120 beams
  - NT2 titanium 48 beams
  - NT2 titanium 50 beams
  - NT2 triton beams
  - NT2 tungsten 184 beams
  - NT2 uranium 238 beams
  - NT2 xenon 129 beams
  - NT2 xenon 131 beams
  - NT2 xenon 132 beams
  - NT2 xenon 136 beams
- NT1 molecular beams
- NT1 particle beams
  - NT2 hyperon beams
    - NT3 lambda particle beams
    - NT3 omega particle beams
    - NT3 sigma particle beams
    - NT3 xi particle beams
  - NT2 lepton beams
    - NT3 electron beams
    - NT3 muon beams
    - NT3 neutrino beams
    - NT3 positron beams
  - NT2 meson beams
    - NT3 eta meson beams
    - NT3 kaon beams
    - NT3 pion beams
  - NT2 nucleon beams
    - NT3 neutron beams
    - NT3 proton beams
- NT1 photon beams
- NT1 polarized beams
- NT1 secondary beams
- RT beam pulsers
- RT beam-plasma systems
- RT stern-gerlach experiment

beams (structural)
- USE supports

bean plant
- USE phaseolus

BEANS [290; 290]
- BT1 vegetables
- BT2 food
- RT phaseolus
- RT seeds

BEARINGS [396; 613]
- NT1 ball bearings
- NT1 gas bearings
- NT1 hydrostatic bearings
- NT1 journal bearings
- NT1 magnetic bearings
- NT1 roller bearings
- RT bushings
- RT lubrication
- RT wear

BEAT WAVE ACCELERATORS
[76; 76] *Feb 88*
- BT1 linear accelerators
- BT2 accelerators
- RT laser radiation
- RT plasma waves

→ **BEAUFORT SEA** [0; 0] *Sep 91*
- BT1 arctic ocean
- BT2 seas
- BT3 surface waters

BEAUTY BARYONS [13; 28] *Dec 87*
- UF bottom baryons
- BT1 baryons
- BT2 fermions
- BT2 hadrons
- BT3 elementary particles
- BT1 beauty particles
- BT2 elementary particles
- NT1 lambda b neutral baryons

BEAUTY MESONS [86; 91] *Dec 87*
- UF bottom mesons
- BT1 beauty particles
- BT2 elementary particles
- BT1 mesons
- BT2 bosons
- BT2 hadrons
- BT3 elementary particles
- NT1 b*-5325 mesons

beauty model
- USE flavor model

BEAUTY PARTICLES [878; 2,300]
Jan 82
- UF bottom particles
- BT1 elementary particles
- NT1 b mesons
  - NT2 b minus mesons
  - NT2 b neutral mesons
    - NT3 anti-b neutral mesons
  - NT2 b plus mesons
- NT1 beauty baryons
  - NT2 lambda b neutral baryons
- NT1 beauty mesons
  - NT2 b*-5325 mesons
- RT flavor model
- RT top particles

BEAVER VALLEY-1 REACTOR
[62; 62]
(Shippingport Pennsylvania, USA)
- BT1 pwr type reactors
- BT2 enriched uranium reactors
- BT3 reactors
- BT2 power reactors
- BT3 reactors
- BT2 thermal reactors
- BT3 reactors
- BT2 water cooled reactors
- BT3 reactors
- BT2 water moderated reactors
- BT3 reactors

BEAVER VALLEY-2 REACTOR
[64; 64]
(Shippingport Pennsylvania, USA)
- BT1 pwr type reactors
- BT2 enriched uranium reactors
- BT3 reactors
- BT2 power reactors
- BT3 reactors
- BT2 thermal reactors
- BT3 reactors
- BT2 water cooled reactors
- BT3 reactors
- BT2 water moderated reactors
- BT3 reactors

BEAVERLODGE [3; 3]
- BT1 saskatchewan
- BT2 canada
- BT3 developed countries
- BT3 north america

BEAVERLODGE MINE [17; 17] *Oct 75*
(Saskatchewan, Canada)
- BT1 uranium mines
- BT2 mines
- BT3 underground facilities
- RT saskatchewan

BECQUERELITE [4; 4]
- BT1 oxide minerals
- BT2 minerals
- BT1 uranium minerals
- BT2 radioactive minerals
- BT3 minerals
- BT3 radioactive materials
- BT4 materials
- RT calcium oxides
- RT uranium oxides

BEDROCK PROJECT [4; 4] *Nov 76*
- UF *project bedrock*
- RT nuclear explosions
- RT underground explosions

beef
- USE meat

bees
- USE insects

BEETLES [185; 258]
- UF *weevils*
- BT1 insects
- BT2 arthropods
- BT3 invertebrates
- BT4 animals
- NT1 boll weevil
- NT1 tribolium

BEETS [103; 103]
- BT1 vegetables
- BT2 food

BEHAVIOR [1,335; 1,373]
(Limited to living systems.)
- UF *psychology*
- NT1 avoidance
- RT attitudes
- RT central nervous system
- RT cerebral cortex
- RT competition
- RT human factors
- RT insect dispersal
- RT learning
- RT mating
- RT mental disorders
- RT physiology
- RT radiation syndrome
- RT reflexes

BELGIAN ORGANIZATIONS [39; 39]
Sep 80
- BT1 national organizations

belgian reactor 02
- USE br-02 reactor

belgian reactor 1
- USE br-1 reactor

belgian reactor 2
- USE br-2 reactor

belgian reactor 3
- USE br-3 reactor

belgian reactor-3/vulcain
- USE br-3-vn reactor

BELGIUM [817; 817]
- BT1 developed countries
- BT1 europe

bell inequality
- USE bell theorem

BELL REACTOR [1; 1]
- BT1 bwr type reactors
- BT2 enriched uranium reactors
- BT3 reactors
- BT2 power reactors
- BT3 reactors
- BT2 thermal reactors
- BT3 reactors
- BT2 water cooled reactors
- BT3 reactors
- BT2 water moderated reactors
- BT3 reactors

BELL THEOREM [190; 190] *Oct 77*
- UF *bell inequality*
- RT hidden variables
- RT quantum mechanics

BELLEFONTE-1 REACTOR [58; 58]
(Scottsboro, Alabama, USA)
- BT1 pwr type reactors
- BT2 enriched uranium reactors
- BT3 reactors
- BT2 power reactors
- BT3 reactors
- BT2 thermal reactors
- BT3 reactors
- BT2 water cooled reactors
- BT3 reactors
- BT2 water moderated reactors
- BT3 reactors

BELLEFONTE-2 REACTOR [52; 52]
(Scottsboro, Alabama, USA)
- BT1 pwr type reactors
- BT2 enriched uranium reactors
- BT3 reactors
- BT2 power reactors
- BT3 reactors
- BT2 thermal reactors
- BT3 reactors
- BT2 water cooled reactors
- BT3 reactors
- BT2 water moderated reactors
- BT3 reactors

BELLEVILLE SUR LOIRE-1 REACTOR
[3; 3] *Jul 84*
- BT1 pwr type reactors
- BT2 enriched uranium reactors
- BT3 reactors
- BT2 power reactors
- BT3 reactors
- BT2 thermal reactors
- BT3 reactors
- BT2 water cooled reactors
- BT3 reactors
- BT2 water moderated reactors
- BT3 reactors

BELLEVILLE SUR LOIRE-2 REACTOR
[3; 3] *Jul 84*
- BT1 pwr type reactors
- BT2 enriched uranium reactors
- BT3 reactors
- BT2 power reactors
- BT3 reactors
- BT2 thermal reactors
- BT3 reactors
- BT2 water cooled reactors
- BT3 reactors
- BT2 water moderated reactors
- BT3 reactors

BELLOWS [366; 366]
(Use only for the expandable structure. Coordinate with descriptors for the device of which the bellows is a component, e.g., VALVES or BLOWERS.)
- RT blowers
- RT expansion joints
- RT pressure gages
- RT pumps
- RT valves

BELOYARSK-1 REACTOR [57; 57]
(Zarechnyy, Sverdlovsk, USSR)
- UF *bnps-1 reactor*
- SF *urals atomic power station*
- BT1 enriched uranium reactors
- BT2 reactors
- BT1 lwgr type reactors
- BT2 graphite moderated reactors
- BT3 reactors
- BT2 water cooled reactors
- BT3 reactors
- BT1 power reactors
- BT2 reactors
- BT1 thermal reactors
- BT2 reactors

BELOYARSK-2 REACTOR [56; 56]
(Zarechnyy, Sverdlovsk, USSR)
- UF *bnps-2 reactor*
- SF *urals atomic power station*
- BT1 enriched uranium reactors
- BT2 reactors
- BT1 lwgr type reactors
- BT2 graphite moderated reactors
- BT3 reactors
- BT2 water cooled reactors
- BT3 reactors
- BT1 power reactors
- BT2 reactors
- BT1 thermal reactors
- BT2 reactors

BELOYARSK-3 REACTOR [239; 239]
(Zarechnyy, Sverdlovsk, USSR)
- UF *bn-600 reactor*
- SF *urals atomic power station*
- BT1 lmfbr type reactors
- BT2 fbr type reactors
- BT3 breeder reactors
- BT4 reactors
- BT3 fast reactors
- BT4 epithermal reactors
- BT5 reactors
- BT2 liquid metal cooled reactors
- BT3 reactors
- BT1 power reactors
- BT2 reactors
- BT1 sodium cooled reactors
- BT2 liquid metal cooled reactors
- BT3 reactors
- RT enriched uranium reactors
- RT plutonium reactors

BELOYARSK-4 REACTOR [2; 2]
Jan 90
(Zarechnyy, Sverdlovsk, USSR.)
- BT1 lmfbr type reactors
- BT2 fbr type reactors
- BT3 breeder reactors
- BT4 reactors
- BT3 fast reactors
- BT4 epithermal reactors
- BT5 reactors
- BT2 liquid metal cooled reactors
- BT3 reactors
- BT1 power reactors
- BT2 reactors
- BT1 sodium cooled reactors
- BT2 liquid metal cooled reactors
- BT3 reactors

BELT PINCH [111; 111]
- BT1 longitudinal pinch
- BT2 pinch effect

BELYAEV THEORY [8; 8]
- RT nuclear structure
- RT superconductivity

BENCH-SCALE EXPERIMENTS
[1,569; 1,569] *May 81*
- UF *laboratory scale experiments*
- RT feasibility studies
- RT field tests
- RT laboratory equipment
- RT testing

benchmark experiments
USE benchmarks

BENCHMARKS [1,746; 1,746] *May 79*
UF *benchmark experiments*
RT experimental data
RT standardization
RT standards

BENDING [1,860; 1,860]
BT1 deformation
RT flexural strength

BENHAM EVENT [3; 3]
BT1 contained explosions
BT2 underground explosions
BT3 explosions
BT1 nuclear explosions
BT2 explosions
RT seismic detection

beni oil
USE sesame oil

benne oil
USE sesame oil

→ BENTHOS [0; 0] *Apr 84*
(Aquatic bottom dwelling organisms.)
BT1 aquatic organisms
RT aquatic ecosystems

BENTONITE [629; 629]
BT1 clays
BT2 silicate minerals
BT3 minerals
BT1 inorganic ion exchangers
BT2 ion exchange materials
BT3 materials
RT montmorillonite

BENZALDEHYDE [113; 113]
UF *benzoic aldehyde*
BT1 aldehydes
BT2 organic compounds

BENZANTHRACENE [60; 68]
BT1 condensed aromatics
BT2 aromatics
BT3 organic compounds
BT1 hydrocarbons
BT2 organic compounds

BENZEDRINE [239; 239]
UF *amphetamine*
UF *phenylisopropylamine*
BT1 amphetamines
BT2 amines
BT3 organic compounds
BT2 analeptics
BT3 central nervous system agents
BT4 drugs
BT2 sympathomimetics
BT3 autonomic nervous system agent
BT4 drugs

BENZENE [2,218; 2,218]
BT1 aromatics
BT2 organic compounds
BT1 hydrocarbons
BT2 organic compounds
RT aniline
RT nitrobenzene

benzenedicarboxylic acid-ortho
USE phthalic acid

benzenedicarboxylic acid-para
USE terephthalic acid

BENZHYDROL [12; 12]
UF *benzohydrol*
UF *diphenylcarbinol*
UF *diphenylmethanol*
BT1 alcohols
BT2 hydroxy compounds
BT3 organic compounds

BENZIDINE [46; 46]
UF *biphenyldiamine*
UF *diaminobiphenyl*
BT1 amines
BT2 organic compounds
BT1 aromatics
BT2 organic compounds
RT biphenyl
RT congo red

BENZILIC ACID [54; 54]
UF *diphenylglycolic acid*
UF *hydroxydiphenylacetic acid*
BT1 hydroxy acids
BT2 carboxylic acids
BT3 organic acids
BT4 organic compounds

BENZIMIDAZOLES [95; 95]
BT1 imidazoles
BT2 azoles
BT3 heterocyclic compounds
BT4 organic compounds
BT3 organic nitrogen compounds
BT4 organic compounds

BENZOFURANS [60; 60]
BT1 furans
BT2 heterocyclic compounds
BT3 organic compounds
BT2 organic oxygen compounds
BT3 organic compounds
RT organic polymers
RT psoralen

benzohydrol
USE benzhydrol

BENZOHYDROXAMIC ACID [50; 50]
BT1 hydroxamic acids
BT2 amines
BT3 organic compounds
BT2 hydroxy compounds
BT3 organic compounds
RT benzoic acid

BENZOIC ACID [352; 366]
BT1 monocarboxylic acids
BT2 carboxylic acids
BT3 organic acids
BT4 organic compounds
NT1 ioglycamic acid
RT benzohydroxamic acid
RT benzoyl peroxide
RT hypaque

benzoic aldehyde
USE benzaldehyde

BENZOINOXIME [22; 22]
BT1 oximes
BT2 amines
BT3 organic compounds
BT2 hydroxy compounds
BT3 organic compounds
BT2 organic nitrogen compounds
BT3 organic compounds

BENZOPHENONE [116; 116]
UF *diphenyl ketone*
BT1 ketones
BT2 organic compounds

BENZOPINACOL [0; 0]
UF *tetraphenylethylene glycol*
BT1 glycols
BT2 alcohols
BT3 hydroxy compounds
BT4 organic compounds

BENZOPYRENE [317; 317]
BT1 condensed aromatics
BT2 aromatics
BT3 organic compounds
BT1 hydrocarbons
BT2 organic compounds

benzopyrroles
USE indoles

BENZOQUINONES [112; 174]
UF *chinone*
UF *quinone*
BT1 quinones
BT2 aromatics
BT3 organic compounds
BT2 organic oxygen compounds
BT3 organic compounds
NT1 chloranil
NT1 chloranilic acid
NT1 quinhydrone
NT1 ubiquinone

BENZOTHIAZOLES [63; 63]
BT1 thiazoles
BT2 azoles
BT3 heterocyclic compounds
BT4 organic compounds
BT3 organic nitrogen compounds
BT4 organic compounds
BT2 organic sulfur compounds
BT3 organic compounds

benzothiophenes
USE thionaphthenes

BENZOXAZOLES [17; 17]
BT1 oxazoles
BT2 azoles
BT3 heterocyclic compounds
BT4 organic compounds
BT3 organic nitrogen compounds
BT4 organic compounds
BT2 organic oxygen compounds
BT3 organic compounds

BENZOYL PEROXIDE [44; 44]
BT1 organic oxygen compounds
BT2 organic compounds
BT1 peroxides
BT2 oxygen compounds
RT benzoic acid

BENZOYL RADICALS [27; 27]
BT1 radicals

benzoylaminoacetic acid
USE hippuric acid

BENZOYLATION [11; 11]
BT1 acylation
BT2 chemical reactions

benzoylglycine
USE hippuric acid

benzoylglycocoll
USE hippuric acid

benzoylphenylhydroxylamine
USE bph

BENZYL ALCOHOL [36; 36] *Feb 82*
  UF   *phenylcarbinol*
  BT1   alcohols
    BT2   hydroxy compounds
      BT3   organic compounds
  BT1   aromatics
    BT2   organic compounds

BENZYL RADICALS [94; 94]
  BT1   aryl radicals
    BT2   radicals

BEPO REACTOR [3; 3]
  UF   *british exper. pile operation*
  BT1   air cooled reactors
    BT2   gas cooled reactors
      BT3   reactors
  BT1   graphite moderated reactors
    BT2   reactors
  BT1   isotope production reactors
    BT2   irradiation reactors
      BT3   reactors
  BT1   natural uranium reactors
    BT2   reactors
  BT1   research reactors
    BT2   research and test reactors
      BT3   reactors
  BT1   thermal reactors
    BT2   reactors

BER-2 REACTOR [76; 76]
(Hahn-Meitner-Institute fuer Kernforschung GmbH, Berlin, Federal Republic of Germany)
  UF   *berlin-2 research reactor*
  UF   *forschungsreaktor berlin-2*
  BT1   aqueous homogeneous reactors
    BT2   liquid homogeneous reactors
      BT3   fluid fueled reactors
        BT4   reactors
      BT3   homogeneous reactors
        BT4   reactors
    BT2   water cooled reactors
      BT3   reactors
    BT2   water moderated reactors
      BT3   reactors
  BT1   isotope production reactors
    BT2   irradiation reactors
      BT3   reactors
  BT1   pool type reactors
    BT2   water cooled reactors
      BT3   reactors
    BT2   water moderated reactors
      BT3   reactors
  BT1   research reactors
    BT2   research and test reactors
      BT3   reactors
  BT1   thermal reactors
    BT2   reactors

BERING SEA [12; 12]
  BT1   pacific ocean
    BT2   seas
      BT3   surface waters
  RT   aleutian islands

berkeley bevalac
  USE bevalac

berkeley escar storage ring
  USE escar storage ring

BERKELEY REACTOR [29; 29]
(River Severn, Gloucestershire, UK)
  BT1   magnox type reactors
    BT2   gcr type reactors
      BT3   gas cooled reactors
        BT4   reactors
      BT3   graphite moderated reactors
        BT4   reactors
    BT2   natural uranium reactors
      BT3   reactors
    BT2   power reactors
      BT3   reactors
  BT1   thermal reactors
    BT2   reactors

berkeley superhilac
  USE superhilac

BERKELEY SYNCHROCYCLOTRON [41; 41]
  BT1   synchrocyclotrons
    BT2   cyclic accelerators
      BT3   accelerators

berkeley triga reactor
  USE ucbrr reactor

BERKELIUM [163; 163]
  BT1   actinides
    BT2   metals
      BT3   elements
  BT1   transplutonium elements
    BT2   transuranium elements
      BT3   elements

BERKELIUM ALLOYS [10; 10] *Apr 79*
(Alloys containing more than 1% Bk.)
  BT1   actinide alloys
    BT2   alloys

BERKELIUM ARSENIDES [3; 3] *Apr 79*
  BT1   arsenides
    BT2   arsenic compounds
    BT2   pnictides
  BT1   berkelium compounds
    BT2   actinide compounds
    BT2   transplutonium compounds
      BT3   transuranium compounds

BERKELIUM BORIDES [0; 0]
  BT1   berkelium compounds
    BT2   actinide compounds
    BT2   transplutonium compounds
      BT3   transuranium compounds
  BT1   borides
    BT2   boron compounds

BERKELIUM BROMIDES [6; 6]
  BT1   berkelium compounds
    BT2   actinide compounds
    BT2   transplutonium compounds
      BT3   transuranium compounds
  BT1   bromides
    BT2   bromine compounds
      BT3   halogen compounds
    BT2   halides
      BT3   halogen compounds

BERKELIUM CARBIDES [0; 0]
  BT1   berkelium compounds
    BT2   actinide compounds
    BT2   transplutonium compounds
      BT3   transuranium compounds
  BT1   carbides
    BT2   carbon compounds

BERKELIUM CARBONATES [0; 0]
  BT1   berkelium compounds
    BT2   actinide compounds
    BT2   transplutonium compounds
      BT3   transuranium compounds
  BT1   carbonates
    BT2   carbon compounds
    BT2   oxygen compounds

BERKELIUM CHLORIDES [12; 12]
  BT1   berkelium compounds
    BT2   actinide compounds
    BT2   transplutonium compounds
      BT3   transuranium compounds
  BT1   chlorides
    BT2   chlorine compounds
      BT3   halogen compounds
    BT2   halides
      BT3   halogen compounds

BERKELIUM COMPLEXES [72; 72]
  BT1   actinide complexes
    BT2   complexes
  BT1   transuranium complexes

BERKELIUM COMPOUNDS [111; 189]
  BT1   actinide compounds
  BT1   transplutonium compounds
    BT2   transuranium compounds
  NT1   berkelium arsenides
  NT1   berkelium borides
  NT1   berkelium bromides
  NT1   berkelium carbides
  NT1   berkelium carbonates
  NT1   berkelium chlorides
  NT1   berkelium fluorides
  NT1   berkelium hydrides
  NT1   berkelium hydroxides
  NT1   berkelium iodides
  NT1   berkelium nitrates
  NT1   berkelium nitrides
  NT1   berkelium oxides
  NT1   berkelium phosphates
  NT1   berkelium phosphides
  NT1   berkelium selenides
  NT1   berkelium silicates
  NT1   berkelium sulfates
  NT1   berkelium sulfides
  NT1   berkelium tellurides

BERKELIUM FLUORIDES [14; 14]
  BT1   berkelium compounds
    BT2   actinide compounds
    BT2   transplutonium compounds
      BT3   transuranium compounds
  BT1   fluorides
    BT2   fluorine compounds
      BT3   halogen compounds
    BT2   halides
      BT3   halogen compounds

BERKELIUM HYDRIDES [6; 6]
  BT1   berkelium compounds
    BT2   actinide compounds
    BT2   transplutonium compounds
      BT3   transuranium compounds
  BT1   hydrides
    BT2   hydrogen compounds

BERKELIUM HYDROXIDES [0; 0]
  BT1   berkelium compounds
    BT2   actinide compounds
    BT2   transplutonium compounds
      BT3   transuranium compounds
  BT1   hydroxides
    BT2   hydrogen compounds
    BT2   oxygen compounds

BERKELIUM IODIDES [0; 0]
  BT1   berkelium compounds
    BT2   actinide compounds
    BT2   transplutonium compounds
      BT3   transuranium compounds
  BT1   iodides
    BT2   halides
      BT3   halogen compounds
    BT2   iodine compounds
      BT3   halogen compounds

BERKELIUM IONS [19; 19]
  BT1   ions
    BT2   charged particles

BERKELIUM ISOTOPES [51; 334]
  NT1   berkelium 240
  NT1   berkelium 241
  NT1   berkelium 242
  NT1   berkelium 243
  NT1   berkelium 244
  NT1   berkelium 245
  NT1   berkelium 246
  NT1   berkelium 247
  NT1   berkelium 248
  NT1   berkelium 249
  NT1   berkelium 250
  NT1   berkelium 251

BERKELIUM NITRATES [18; 18]
BT1　berkelium compounds
BT2　actinide compounds
BT2　transplutonium compounds
BT3　transuranium compounds
BT1　nitrates
BT2　nitrogen compounds
BT2　oxygen compounds

BERKELIUM NITRIDES [6; 6]
BT1　berkelium compounds
BT2　actinide compounds
BT2　transplutonium compounds
BT3　transuranium compounds
BT1　nitrides
BT2　nitrogen compounds
BT2　pnictides

BERKELIUM OXIDES [21; 21]
BT1　berkelium compounds
BT2　actinide compounds
BT2　transplutonium compounds
BT3　transuranium compounds
BT1　oxides
BT2　chalcogenides
BT2　oxygen compounds

BERKELIUM PHOSPHATES [4; 4]
BT1　berkelium compounds
BT2　actinide compounds
BT2　transplutonium compounds
BT3　transuranium compounds
BT1　phosphates
BT2　oxygen compounds
BT2　phosphorus compounds

BERKELIUM PHOSPHIDES [3; 3]
Apr 79
BT1　berkelium compounds
BT2　actinide compounds
BT2　transplutonium compounds
BT3　transuranium compounds
BT1　phosphides
BT2　phosphorus compounds
BT2　pnictides

BERKELIUM SELENIDES [2; 2] *Apr 79*
BT1　berkelium compounds
BT2　actinide compounds
BT2　transplutonium compounds
BT3　transuranium compounds
BT1　selenides
BT2　chalcogenides
BT2　selenium compounds

BERKELIUM SILICATES [0; 0]
BT1　berkelium compounds
BT2　actinide compounds
BT2　transplutonium compounds
BT3　transuranium compounds
BT1　silicates
BT2　oxygen compounds
BT2　silicon compounds

BERKELIUM SULFATES [2; 2]
BT1　berkelium compounds
BT2　actinide compounds
BT2　transplutonium compounds
BT3　transuranium compounds
BT1　sulfates
BT2　oxygen compounds
BT2　sulfur compounds

BERKELIUM SULFIDES [1; 1]
BT1　berkelium compounds
BT2　actinide compounds
BT2　transplutonium compounds
BT3　transuranium compounds
BT1　sulfides
BT2　chalcogenides
BT2　sulfur compounds

BERKELIUM TELLURIDES [2; 2]
Apr 79
BT1　berkelium compounds
BT2　actinide compounds
BT2　transplutonium compounds
BT3　transuranium compounds
BT1　tellurides
BT2　chalcogenides
BT2　tellurium compounds

BERKELIUM 240 [6; 6]
BT1　actinide nuclei
BT2　heavy nuclei
BT3　nuclei
BT1　berkelium isotopes
BT1　electron capture radioisotopes
BT2　beta decay radioisotopes
BT3　radioisotopes
BT4　isotopes
BT1　minutes living radioisotopes
BT2　radioisotopes
BT3　isotopes
BT1　odd-odd nuclei
BT2　nuclei

BERKELIUM 241 [4; 4]
BT1　actinide nuclei
BT2　heavy nuclei
BT3　nuclei
BT1　berkelium isotopes
BT1　odd-even nuclei
BT2　nuclei

BERKELIUM 242 [8; 8]
BT1　actinide nuclei
BT2　heavy nuclei
BT3　nuclei
BT1　berkelium isotopes
BT1　electron capture radioisotopes
BT2　beta decay radioisotopes
BT3　radioisotopes
BT4　isotopes
BT1　minutes living radioisotopes
BT2　radioisotopes
BT3　isotopes
BT1　odd-odd nuclei
BT2　nuclei
BT1　spontaneous fission radioisoto
BT2　radioisotopes
BT3　isotopes

BERKELIUM 243 [10; 10]
BT1　actinide nuclei
BT2　heavy nuclei
BT3　nuclei
BT1　alpha decay radioisotopes
BT2　radioisotopes
BT3　isotopes
BT1　berkelium isotopes
BT1　electron capture radioisotopes
BT2　beta decay radioisotopes
BT3　radioisotopes
BT4　isotopes
BT1　hours living radioisotopes
BT2　radioisotopes
BT3　isotopes
BT1　internal conversion radioisoto
BT2　radioisotopes
BT3　isotopes
BT1　odd-even nuclei
BT2　nuclei
BT1　spontaneous fission radioisoto
BT2　radioisotopes
BT3　isotopes

BERKELIUM 244 [3; 3]
BT1　actinide nuclei
BT2　heavy nuclei
BT3　nuclei
BT1　alpha decay radioisotopes
BT2　radioisotopes
BT3　isotopes
BT1　berkelium isotopes
BT1　electron capture radioisotopes
BT2　beta decay radioisotopes
BT3　radioisotopes
BT4　isotopes
BT1　hours living radioisotopes
BT2　radioisotopes
BT3　isotopes
BT1　odd-odd nuclei
BT2　nuclei
BT1　spontaneous fission radioisoto
BT2　radioisotopes
BT3　isotopes

BERKELIUM 245 [9; 9]
BT1　actinide nuclei
BT2　heavy nuclei
BT3　nuclei
BT1　alpha decay radioisotopes
BT2　radioisotopes
BT3　isotopes
BT1　berkelium isotopes
BT1　days living radioisotopes
BT2　radioisotopes
BT3　isotopes
BT1　electron capture radioisotopes
BT2　beta decay radioisotopes
BT3　radioisotopes
BT4　isotopes
BT1　odd-even nuclei
BT2　nuclei
BT1　spontaneous fission radioisoto
BT2　radioisotopes
BT3　isotopes

BERKELIUM 246 [2; 2]
BT1　actinide nuclei
BT2　heavy nuclei
BT3　nuclei
BT1　berkelium isotopes
BT1　days living radioisotopes
BT2　radioisotopes
BT3　isotopes
BT1　electron capture radioisotopes
BT2　beta decay radioisotopes
BT3　radioisotopes
BT4　isotopes
BT1　odd-odd nuclei
BT2　nuclei

BERKELIUM 247 [19; 19]
BT1　actinide nuclei
BT2　heavy nuclei
BT3　nuclei
BT1　alpha decay radioisotopes
BT2　radioisotopes
BT3　isotopes
BT1　berkelium isotopes
BT1　odd-even nuclei
BT2　nuclei
BT1　years living radioisotopes
BT2　radioisotopes
BT3　isotopes

BERKELIUM 248 [8; 8]
BT1　actinide nuclei
BT2　heavy nuclei
BT3　nuclei
BT1　berkelium isotopes
BT1　beta-minus decay radioisotopes
BT2　beta decay radioisotopes
BT3　radioisotopes
BT4　isotopes
BT1　electron capture radioisotopes
BT2　beta decay radioisotopes
BT3　radioisotopes
BT4　isotopes
BT1　hours living radioisotopes
BT2　radioisotopes
BT3　isotopes
BT1　odd-odd nuclei
BT2　nuclei

BERKELIUM 249 [189; 189]
BT1　actinide nuclei
BT2　heavy nuclei
BT3　nuclei
BT1　alpha decay radioisotopes
BT2　radioisotopes
BT3　isotopes
BT1　berkelium isotopes
BT1　beta-minus decay radioisotopes
BT2　beta decay radioisotopes
BT3　radioisotopes

```
        BT4      isotopes
    BT1     days living radioisotopes
    BT2     radioisotopes
        BT3      isotopes
    BT1     odd-even nuclei
    BT2     nuclei
    BT1     spontaneous fission radioisoto
    BT2     radioisotopes
        BT3      isotopes
```

BERKELIUM 249 TARGET [55; 55]
Oct 76
    BT1   targets

BERKELIUM 250 [42; 42]
    BT1   actinide nuclei
        BT2   heavy nuclei
            BT3   nuclei
    BT1   berkelium isotopes
    BT1   beta-minus decay radioisotopes
        BT2   beta decay radioisotopes
            BT3   radioisotopes
                BT4   isotopes
    BT1   hours living radioisotopes
        BT2   radioisotopes
            BT3   isotopes
    BT1   odd-odd nuclei
        BT2   nuclei

BERKELIUM 251 [8; 8]
    BT1   actinide nuclei
        BT2   heavy nuclei
            BT3   nuclei
    BT1   berkelium isotopes
    BT1   beta-minus decay radioisotopes
        BT2   beta decay radioisotopes
            BT3   radioisotopes
                BT4   isotopes
    BT1   minutes living radioisotopes
        BT2   radioisotopes
            BT3   isotopes
    BT1   odd-even nuclei
        BT2   nuclei

berl saddles
    USE   column packing

berlin-2 research reactor
    USE   ber-2 reactor

BERMUDA [2; 2] *Feb 84*
    BT1   islands
    RT   atlantic ocean

BERNOULLI LAW [55; 55]
    RT   fluid flow

BERNSTEIN MODE [566; 566]
    BT1   oscillation modes
    RT   cyclotron harmonics
    RT   ion wave instability
    RT   ion waves
    RT   plasma heating

BERRIES [36; 36]
    BT1   fruits
        BT2   food

BERYL [93; 93]
    BT1   silicate minerals
        BT2   minerals
    RT   beryllium silicates

beryllia
    USE   beryllium oxides

BERYLLIOSIS [16; 16]
    BT1   pneumoconioses
        BT2   respiratory system diseases
            BT3   diseases
    RT   beryllium compounds

BERYLLIUM [4,623; 4,628]
    UF   *beryllium moderators*
    BT1   alkaline earth metals
        BT2   metals
            BT3   elements
    NT1   beryllium-alpha
    NT1   beryllium-beta
    RT   moderators

BERYLLIUM ADDITIONS [116; 116]
(Alloys containing not more than 1% Be are listed here.)
    RT   beryllium alloys
    RT   beryllium compounds

BERYLLIUM ALLOYS [731; 864]
(Alloys containing more than 1% Be.)
    BT1   alloys
    NT1   beryllium base alloys
    RT   beryllium additions
    RT   moderators

BERYLLIUM BASE ALLOYS [117; 117]
    BT1   beryllium alloys
        BT2   alloys

BERYLLIUM BORIDES [21; 21]
    BT1   beryllium compounds
        BT2   alkaline earth metal compounds
    BT1   borides
        BT2   boron compounds

BERYLLIUM BROMIDES [3; 3]
    BT1   beryllium compounds
        BT2   alkaline earth metal compounds
    BT1   bromides
        BT2   bromine compounds
            BT3   halogen compounds
        BT2   halides
            BT3   halogen compounds

BERYLLIUM CARBIDES [21; 21]
    BT1   beryllium compounds
        BT2   alkaline earth metal compounds
    BT1   carbides
        BT2   carbon compounds

BERYLLIUM CARBONATES [12; 12]
    BT1   beryllium compounds
        BT2   alkaline earth metal compounds
    BT1   carbonates
        BT2   carbon compounds
        BT2   oxygen compounds

BERYLLIUM CHLORIDES [87; 87]
    BT1   beryllium compounds
        BT2   alkaline earth metal compounds
    BT1   chlorides
        BT2   chlorine compounds
            BT3   halogen compounds
        BT2   halides
            BT3   halogen compounds

BERYLLIUM COMPLEXES [364; 364]
    BT1   alkaline earth metal complexes
        BT2   complexes

BERYLLIUM COMPOUNDS [371; 2,126]
    BT1   alkaline earth metal compounds
    NT1   beryllium borides
    NT1   beryllium bromides
    NT1   beryllium carbides
    NT1   beryllium carbonates
    NT1   beryllium chlorides
    NT1   beryllium fluorides
    NT1   beryllium hydrides
    NT1   beryllium hydroxides
    NT1   beryllium iodides
    NT1   beryllium nitrates
    NT1   beryllium nitrides
    NT1   beryllium oxides
    NT1   beryllium phosphates
    NT1   beryllium phosphides
    NT1   beryllium selenides
    NT1   beryllium silicates
    NT1   beryllium sulfates
    NT1   beryllium sulfides
    NT1   beryllium tellurides
    RT   berylliosis
    RT   beryllium additions
    RT   moderators

BERYLLIUM FLUORIDES [384; 384]
    BT1   beryllium compounds
        BT2   alkaline earth metal compounds
    BT1   fluorides
        BT2   fluorine compounds
            BT3   halogen compounds
        BT2   halides
            BT3   halogen compounds
    RT   flibe

BERYLLIUM HYDRIDES [76; 76]
    BT1   beryllium compounds
        BT2   alkaline earth metal compounds
    BT1   hydrides
        BT2   hydrogen compounds

BERYLLIUM HYDROXIDES [63; 63]
    BT1   beryllium compounds
        BT2   alkaline earth metal compounds
    BT1   hydroxides
        BT2   hydrogen compounds
        BT2   oxygen compounds

BERYLLIUM IODIDES [3; 3]
    BT1   beryllium compounds
        BT2   alkaline earth metal compounds
    BT1   iodides
        BT2   halides
            BT3   halogen compounds
        BT2   iodine compounds
            BT3   halogen compounds

BERYLLIUM IONS [432; 432]
    BT1   ions
        BT2   charged particles

BERYLLIUM ISOTOPES [216; 4,296]
    NT1   beryllium 10
    NT1   beryllium 11
    NT1   beryllium 12
    NT1   beryllium 13
    NT1   beryllium 14
    NT1   beryllium 5
    NT1   beryllium 6
    NT1   beryllium 7
    NT1   beryllium 8
    NT1   beryllium 9

BERYLLIUM MODERATED REACTORS [6; 69]
    UF   *beryllium-moderated reactors*
    BT1   metal moderated reactors
        BT2   reactors
    NT1   agata reactor
    NT1   br-02 reactor
    NT1   ebor reactor
    NT1   maria reactor
    NT1   nuclear furnace reactor

beryllium moderators
    USE   beryllium

BERYLLIUM NITRATES [27; 27]
    BT1   beryllium compounds
        BT2   alkaline earth metal compounds
    BT1   nitrates
        BT2   nitrogen compounds
        BT2   oxygen compounds

BERYLLIUM NITRIDES [16; 16]
    BT1   beryllium compounds
        BT2   alkaline earth metal compounds
    BT1   nitrides
        BT2   nitrogen compounds
        BT2   pnictides

BERYLLIUM OXIDES [994; 994]
 UF beryllia
 BT1 beryllium compounds
  BT2 alkaline earth metal compounds
 BT1 oxides
  BT2 chalcogenides
  BT2 oxygen compounds
 RT moderators

BERYLLIUM PHOSPHATES [5; 5]
 BT1 beryllium compounds
  BT2 alkaline earth metal compounds
 BT1 phosphates
  BT2 oxygen compounds
  BT2 phosphorus compounds

BERYLLIUM PHOSPHIDES [2; 2]
Oct 77
 BT1 beryllium compounds
  BT2 alkaline earth metal compounds
 BT1 phosphides
  BT2 phosphorus compounds
  BT2 pnictides

→ **BERYLLIUM SELENIDES** [0; 0] Sep 91
 BT1 beryllium compounds
  BT2 alkaline earth metal compounds
 BT1 selenides
  BT2 chalcogenides
  BT2 selenium compounds

BERYLLIUM SILICATES [44; 94]
 BT1 beryllium compounds
  BT2 alkaline earth metal compounds
 BT1 silicates
  BT2 oxygen compounds
  BT2 silicon compounds
 RT beryl
 RT silicate minerals

BERYLLIUM SULFATES [41; 41]
 BT1 beryllium compounds
  BT2 alkaline earth metal compounds
 BT1 sulfates
  BT2 oxygen compounds
  BT2 sulfur compounds

BERYLLIUM SULFIDES [4; 4]
 BT1 beryllium compounds
  BT2 alkaline earth metal compounds
 BT1 sulfides
  BT2 chalcogenides
  BT2 sulfur compounds

→ **BERYLLIUM TELLURIDES** [0; 0]
Sep 91
 BT1 beryllium compounds
  BT2 alkaline earth metal compounds
 BT1 tellurides
  BT2 chalcogenides
  BT2 tellurium compounds

BERYLLIUM 10 [644; 644]
 BT1 beryllium isotopes
 BT1 beta-minus decay radioisotopes
  BT2 beta decay radioisotopes
   BT3 radioisotopes
    BT4 isotopes
 BT1 even-even nuclei
  BT2 nuclei
 BT1 light nuclei
  BT2 nuclei
 BT1 years living radioisotopes
  BT2 radioisotopes
   BT3 isotopes

BERYLLIUM 10 TARGET [28; 28]
 BT1 targets

BERYLLIUM 11 [91; 91]
 BT1 beryllium isotopes
 BT1 beta-minus decay radioisotopes
  BT2 beta decay radioisotopes
   BT3 radioisotopes
    BT4 isotopes
 BT1 even-odd nuclei
  BT2 nuclei
 BT1 light nuclei
  BT2 nuclei
 BT1 seconds living radioisotopes
  BT2 radioisotopes
   BT3 isotopes

BERYLLIUM 11 TARGET [6; 6] Sep 79
 BT1 targets

BERYLLIUM 12 [76; 76]
 BT1 beryllium isotopes
 BT1 beta-minus decay radioisotopes
  BT2 beta decay radioisotopes
   BT3 radioisotopes
    BT4 isotopes
 BT1 even-even nuclei
  BT2 nuclei
 BT1 light nuclei
  BT2 nuclei
 BT1 millisec living radioisotopes
  BT2 radioisotopes
   BT3 isotopes

BERYLLIUM 13 [10; 10]
 BT1 beryllium isotopes
 BT1 even-odd nuclei
  BT2 nuclei
 BT1 light nuclei
  BT2 nuclei

BERYLLIUM 14 [21; 21]
 BT1 beryllium isotopes
 BT1 beta-minus decay radioisotopes
  BT2 beta decay radioisotopes
   BT3 radioisotopes
    BT4 isotopes
 BT1 even-even nuclei
  BT2 nuclei
 BT1 light nuclei
  BT2 nuclei
 BT1 millisec living radioisotopes
  BT2 radioisotopes
   BT3 isotopes

BERYLLIUM 5 [4; 4]
 BT1 beryllium isotopes
 BT1 even-odd nuclei
  BT2 nuclei
 BT1 light nuclei
  BT2 nuclei

BERYLLIUM 6 [108; 108]
 BT1 beryllium isotopes
 BT1 even-even nuclei
  BT2 nuclei
 BT1 light nuclei
  BT2 nuclei

BERYLLIUM 7 [1,406; 1,406]
 BT1 beryllium isotopes
 BT1 days living radioisotopes
  BT2 radioisotopes
   BT3 isotopes
 BT1 electron capture radioisotopes
  BT2 beta decay radioisotopes
   BT3 radioisotopes
    BT4 isotopes
 BT1 even-odd nuclei
  BT2 nuclei
 BT1 light nuclei
  BT2 nuclei
 RT beryllium 7 beams

BERYLLIUM 7 BEAMS [11; 11]
 BT1 ion beams
  BT2 beams
 RT beryllium 7

BERYLLIUM 7 REACTIONS [19; 19]
Jan 84
 BT1 heavy ion reactions
  BT2 nuclear reactions

BERYLLIUM 7 TARGET [57; 57]
Nov 76
 BT1 targets

BERYLLIUM 8 [1,052; 1,052]
 BT1 alpha decay radioisotopes
  BT2 radioisotopes
   BT3 isotopes
 BT1 beryllium isotopes
 BT1 even-even nuclei
  BT2 nuclei
 BT1 light nuclei
  BT2 nuclei

BERYLLIUM 8 REACTIONS [7; 7]
Sep 83
 BT1 heavy ion reactions
  BT2 nuclear reactions

BERYLLIUM 8 TARGET [28; 28]
Feb 79
 BT1 targets

BERYLLIUM 9 [1,152; 1,152]
 BT1 beryllium isotopes
 BT1 even-odd nuclei
  BT2 nuclei
 BT1 light nuclei
  BT2 nuclei
 BT1 stable isotopes
  BT2 isotopes
 RT beryllium 9 beams

BERYLLIUM 9 BEAMS [43; 43]
 BT1 ion beams
  BT2 beams
 RT beryllium 9

BERYLLIUM 9 REACTIONS [253; 253]
 BT1 heavy ion reactions
  BT2 nuclear reactions

BERYLLIUM 9 TARGET [1,725; 1,725]
 BT1 targets

BERYLLIUM-ALPHA [3; 3]
 BT1 beryllium
  BT2 alkaline earth metals
   BT3 metals
    BT4 elements

BERYLLIUM-BETA [3; 3]
 BT1 beryllium
  BT2 alkaline earth metals
   BT3 metals
    BT4 elements

beryllium-moderated reactors
 USE beryllium moderated reactors

BERYLLON [1; 1]
 UF dsnadns
 BT1 arsonic acids
  BT2 arsenic compounds
  BT2 organic acids
   BT3 organic compounds
 BT1 azo dyes
  BT2 azo compounds
   BT3 organic nitrogen compounds
    BT4 organic compounds
  BT2 dyes
 BT1 dicarboxylic acids
  BT2 carboxylic acids
   BT3 organic acids
    BT4 organic compounds
 BT1 naphthols
  BT2 phenols
   BT3 aromatics
    BT4 organic compounds
   BT3 hydroxy compounds
    BT4 organic compounds
 BT1 sulfonic acids
  BT2 organic acids
   BT3 organic compounds
  BT2 organic sulfur compounds

BT3   organic compounds

BESM COMPUTERS [501; 501]
BT1   computers

bessel differential equation
USE   fokker-planck equation

BESSEL FUNCTIONS [1,121; 1,121]
UF   *hankel functions*
UF   *neumann functions*
BT1   functions
RT   neumann series

BESSY STORAGE RING [62; 62]
Apr 85
(Berliner Elektronenspeicherring-
Gesellschaft fuer Synchrotronstrahlung.)
BT1   storage rings

beta backscattering gages
USE   radiometric gages

beta beams (electrons)
USE   electron beams

beta beams (positrons)
USE   positron beams

BETA DECAY [4,159; 10,348]
(Neutron and nuclear beta decay.)
BT1   nuclear decay
BT2   decay
NT1   beta-minus decay
NT2   double beta decay
NT1   beta-plus decay
NT1   electron capture decay
NT2   k capture
NT2   l capture
NT2   m capture
RT   beta decay radioisotopes
RT   beta particles
RT   beta spectra
RT   fermi plot
RT   feynman-gell-mann theory
RT   fierz interference
RT   ft value
RT   gamow-teller rules
RT   internal ionization
RT   knipp-uhlenbeck theory
RT   lee-yang theory
RT   sargent diagrams
RT   two-component neutrino theory
RT   way-wigner formula

BETA DECAY RADIOISOTOPES
[256; 155,118]
UF   *beta-decay radioisotopes*
BT1   radioisotopes
BT2   isotopes
* NT1   beta-minus decay radioisotopes
* NT1   beta-plus decay radioisotopes
* NT1   electron capture radioisotopes
NT1   iron 45
NT1   niobium 85
NT1   vanadium 42
NT1   vanadium 45
RT   beta decay

BETA DETECTION [1,908; 1,908]
BT1   charged particle detection
BT2   radiation detection
BT3   detection
RT   beta dosimetry
RT   beta particles
RT   beta spectrometers
RT   beta spectroscopy
RT   positron detection

BETA DOSIMETRY [795; 795]
BT1   dosimetry
RT   beta detection

BETA II DEVICES [9; 9] *Oct 81*
BT1   magnetic mirrors
BT2   open plasma devices
BT3   thermonuclear devices

BETA PARTICLES [2,196; 2,196]
(Emitted by nuclei.)
BT1   charged particles
BT1   ionizing radiations
BT2   radiations
RT   beta decay
RT   beta detection
RT   beta sources
RT   electrons
RT   positrons

BETA RADIOGRAPHY [54; 54] *Oct 76*
RT   industrial radiography
RT   nondestructive testing

BETA RATIO [1,624; 1,624]
RT   high-beta plasma
RT   low-beta plasma
RT   magnetic fields
RT   medium-beta plasma
RT   plasma pressure

BETA SOURCES [1,027; 1,027]
BT1   particle sources
BT2   radiation sources
RT   beta particles

BETA SPECTRA [1,273; 1,273]
BT1   spectra
RT   beta decay
RT   beta spectrometers

BETA SPECTROMETERS [565; 565]
BT1   spectrometers
BT2   measuring instruments
RT   beta detection
RT   beta spectra
RT   electron detection

beta spectrometry
USE   beta spectroscopy

BETA SPECTROSCOPY [409; 409]
UF   *beta spectrometry*
BT1   spectroscopy
RT   beta detection

beta-decay radioisotopes
USE   beta decay radioisotopes

BETA-DELAYED NEUTRONS [27; 27]
Jan 85
BT1   neutrons
BT2   nucleons
BT3   baryons
BT4   fermions
BT4   hadrons
BT5   elementary particles
RT   beta-minus decay
RT   delayed neutron precursors
RT   neutron-rich isotopes

beta-delayed protons
USE   delayed protons

BETA-MINUS DECAY [2,582; 3,250]
BT1   beta decay
BT2   nuclear decay
BT3   decay
NT1   double beta decay
RT   beta-delayed neutrons
RT   beta-minus decay radioisotopes

* **BETA-MINUS DECAY
RADIOISOTOPES** [82; 109,388]
(For specific terms, consult the Appendix.)
BT1   beta decay radioisotopes
BT2   radioisotopes
BT3   isotopes
RT   beta-minus decay

BETA-PLUS DECAY [1,860; 1,860]
UF   *positron decay*
BT1   beta decay
BT2   nuclear decay
BT3   decay
RT   beta-plus decay radioisotopes
RT   delayed protons
RT   electron capture decay

* **BETA-PLUS DECAY RADIOISOTOPES**
[97; 26,160]
(For specific terms, consult the Appendix.)
BT1   beta decay radioisotopes
BT2   radioisotopes
BT3   isotopes
RT   beta-plus decay

BETA-W LATTICES [367; 367]
BT1   crystal lattices
BT2   crystal structure

BETAINE [25; 25]
BT1   amino acids
BT2   carboxylic acids
BT3   organic acids
BT4   organic compounds
BT1   lipotropic factors
BT2   drugs
BT1   quaternary compounds
BT2   amines
BT3   organic compounds
RT   carnitine

BETATRON OSCILLATIONS
[1,034; 1,034]
BT1   beam dynamics
BT2   dynamics
BT3   mechanics
BT1   oscillations
RT   q-shift

BETATRONS [1,025; 1,025]
BT1   cyclic accelerators
BT2   accelerators
RT   plasma betatrons

BETAVOLTAIC CELLS [31; 31]
BT1   direct collection converters
BT2   direct energy converters
RT   semiconductor diodes

bethe-goldstone approximation
USE   bethe-goldstone equation

BETHE-GOLDSTONE EQUATION
[245; 245]
UF   *bethe-goldstone approximation*
BT1   equations
RT   many-body problem

BETHE-HEITLER THEORY [111; 111]
UF   *bethe-heitler-schiff formula*
RT   branching ratio
RT   bremsstrahlung
RT   pair production

bethe-heitler-schiff formula
USE   bethe-heitler theory

bethe-hurwitz effect
USE   hurwitz effect

bethe-placzec model
   USE   placzec function

BETHE-SALPETER EQUATION
[1,191; 1,191]
   BT1   equations
   RT   blankenbecler-sugar equations
   RT   quantum field theory

BETHE-TAIT METHOD [51; 51]
   RT   mathematics
   RT   reactor safety

bethe-weizsaecker cycle
   USE   cno cycle

bethe-weizsaecker relation
   USE   weizsaecker formula

BETTIS [15; 15]
(Bettis Atomic Power Laboratory.)
   BT1   us aec
    BT2   us organizations
     BT3   national organizations
   BT1   us doe
    BT2   us organizations
     BT3   national organizations
   BT1   us erda
    BT2   us organizations
     BT3   national organizations
   RT   pennsylvania

betula
   USE   trees

BEVALAC [408; 408] *Jan 76*
(A linking of the Superhilac to the Bevatron.)
   UF   *berkeley bevalac*
   BT1   accelerators
   RT   bevatron
   RT   cyclic accelerators
   RT   superhilac

BEVATRON [113; 113]
   BT1   synchrotrons
    BT2   cyclic accelerators
     BT3   accelerators
   RT   bevalac

BEVERAGES [232; 232]
   UF   *coffee*
   UF   *juices*
   UF   *tea*
   UF   *wine*
   BT1   food
   RT   coffee beans
   RT   diet
   RT   drinking water
   RT   ingestion
   RT   milk
   RT   tea leaves
   RT   tea plants

BEZNAU-1 REACTOR [192; 192]
(Beznau, Doettingen, Switzerland)
   UF   *nok-1 reactor*
   UF   *nordost schweiz kraftw-1 react*
   BT1   pwr type reactors
    BT2   enriched uranium reactors
     BT3   reactors
    BT2   power reactors
     BT3   reactors
    BT2   thermal reactors
     BT3   reactors
    BT2   water cooled reactors
     BT3   reactors
    BT2   water moderated reactors
     BT3   reactors

BEZNAU-2 REACTOR [173; 173]
(Beznau, Doettingen, Switzerland)
   UF   *nok-2 reactor*
   UF   *nordost schweiz kraftw-2 react*
   BT1   pwr type reactors
    BT2   enriched uranium reactors
     BT3   reactors
    BT2   power reactors
     BT3   reactors
    BT2   thermal reactors
     BT3   reactors
    BT2   water cooled reactors
     BT3   reactors
    BT2   water moderated reactors
     BT3   reactors

bfs
   USE   bundesamt fuer strahlenschutz

BF3 COUNTERS [269; 269]
   BT1   neutron detectors
    BT2   radiation detectors
     BT3   measuring instruments
   BT1   proportional counters
    BT2   radiation detectors
     BT3   measuring instruments
   RT   moderating detectors

BGO DETECTORS [329; 329] *Aug 84*
   UF   *bismuth germanate detectors*
   BT1   solid scintillation detectors
    BT2   scintillation counters
     BT3   radiation detectors
      BT4   measuring instruments

BGRR REACTOR [2; 2]
(Brookhaven National Lab., Upton, New York, USA)
   UF   *brookhaven graph. res. reactor*
   BT1   air cooled reactors
    BT2   gas cooled reactors
     BT3   reactors
   BT1   enriched uranium reactors
    BT2   reactors
   BT1   graphite moderated reactors
    BT2   reactors
   BT1   isotope production reactors
    BT2   irradiation reactors
     BT3   reactors
   BT1   research reactors
    BT2   research and test reactors
     BT3   reactors
   BT1   test reactors
    BT2   research and test reactors
     BT3   reactors
    BT2   test facilities
   BT1   thermal reactors
    BT2   reactors
   BT1   training reactors
    BT2   research and test reactors
     BT3   reactors

bhabha atomic research center
   USE   barc

BHABHA SCATTERING [437; 437]
   BT1   elastic scattering
    BT2   scattering
   RT   moeller scattering
   RT   quantum electrodynamics

BHUTAN [2; 2] *Jan 90*
   BT1   asia
   BT1   developing countries

BHWR TYPE REACTORS [14; 221]
   UF   *boiling heavy water cool./mode*
   BT1   heavy water cooled reactors
    BT2   reactors
   BT1   heavy water moderated reactors
    BT2   reactors
   NT1   hbwr reactor
   NT1   marviken reactor
   RT   power reactors

BIBENZYL [11; 11]
   UF   *diphenylethane (1,2-)*
   UF   *1,2-diphenylethane*
   BT1   aromatics
    BT2   organic compounds

§ **BIBLIOGRAPHIES** [5,634; 5,634]
(Use only in conjunction with literary indicator Z for indexing true bibliographies.)
   BT1   document types

biblis reactor
(Prior to December 1990, this was a valid descriptor.)
   USE   biblis-1 reactor

biblis-b reactor
(Prior to December 1990, this was a valid descriptor.)
   USE   biblis-2 reactor

biblis-c reactor
   USE   biblis-3 reactor

biblis-d reactor
   USE   biblis-4 reactor

BIBLIS-1 REACTOR [296; 296] *Apr 84*
(Biblis, Hessen, Germany. Prior to December 1990, this was indexed by BIBLIS REACTOR.)
   UF   *biblis reactor*
   BT1   pwr type reactors
    BT2   enriched uranium reactors
     BT3   reactors
    BT2   power reactors
     BT3   reactors
    BT2   thermal reactors
     BT3   reactors
    BT2   water cooled reactors
     BT3   reactors
    BT2   water moderated reactors
     BT3   reactors

BIBLIS-2 REACTOR [158; 158] *Apr 84*
(Biblis, Hessen, Germany. Prior to December 1990, this was indexed by BIBLIS-B REACTOR.)
   UF   *biblis-b reactor*
   BT1   pwr type reactors
    BT2   enriched uranium reactors
     BT3   reactors
    BT2   power reactors
     BT3   reactors
    BT2   thermal reactors
     BT3   reactors
    BT2   water cooled reactors
     BT3   reactors
    BT2   water moderated reactors
     BT3   reactors

BIBLIS-3 REACTOR [31; 31] *Oct 76*
(Biblis, Hessen, Federal Republic of Germany)
   UF   *biblis-c reactor*
   UF   *kernkraftwerk biblis-3*
   BT1   pwr type reactors
    BT2   enriched uranium reactors
     BT3   reactors
    BT2   power reactors
     BT3   reactors
    BT2   thermal reactors
     BT3   reactors
    BT2   water cooled reactors
     BT3   reactors
    BT2   water moderated reactors
     BT3   reactors

BIBLIS-4 REACTOR [4; 4] *Oct 76*
(Biblis, Hessen, Federal Republic of Germany)
   UF   *biblis-d reactor*
   UF   *kernkraftwerk biblis-4*

```
         BT1     pwr type reactors
         BT2     enriched uranium reactors
           BT3     reactors
         BT2     power reactors
           BT3     reactors
         BT2     thermal reactors
           BT3     reactors
         BT2     water cooled reactors
           BT3     reactors
         BT2     water moderated reactors
           BT3     reactors
```

bicarbonates
(Prior to December 1985 this was a valid descriptor.)
   USE   acid carbonates

bicrystals
   USE   polycrystals

BIEDENHARN-ROSE THEORY [1; 1]
   RT   angular correlation
   RT   angular distribution

biexcitons
   USE   excitons

BIG ROCK POINT REACTOR [134; 134]
(Charlevoix, Michigan, USA)
```
         BT1     bwr type reactors
         BT2     enriched uranium reactors
           BT3     reactors
         BT2     power reactors
           BT3     reactors
         BT2     thermal reactors
           BT3     reactors
         BT2     water cooled reactors
           BT3     reactors
         BT2     water moderated reactors
           BT3     reactors
```

BIG TEN REACTOR [26; 26]
```
         BT1     zero power reactors
         BT2     experimental reactors
           BT3     research and test reactors
             BT4     reactors
```

BIGR REACTOR [2; 2] *Dec 86*
```
         BT1     enriched uranium reactors
         BT2     reactors
         BT1     fast reactors
         BT2     epithermal reactors
           BT3     reactors
         BT1     graphite moderated reactors
         BT2     reactors
         BT1     pulsed reactors
         BT2     reactors
         BT1     research reactors
         BT2     research and test reactors
           BT3     reactors
```

BIKINI [103; 103]
```
         BT1     marshall islands
         BT2     micronesia
           BT3     australasia
           BT3     islands
         RT      castle project
         RT      redwing project
```

BILATERAL AGREEMENTS [346; 346]
```
         BT1     international agreements
         BT2     agreements
         RT      transfrontier contamination
         RT      transfrontier pollution
```

bilbao argonaut reactor
   USE   arbi reactor

BILE [457; 457]
```
         BT1     body fluids
         BT2     biological materials
           BT3     materials
         RT      bile acids
         RT      biliary tract
         RT      bilirubin
         RT      biliverdin
         RT      stercobilin
         RT      urobilinogen
```

BILE ACIDS [201; 261]
```
         BT1     carboxylic acids
         BT2     organic acids
           BT3     organic compounds
         BT1     sterols
         BT2     hydroxy compounds
           BT3     organic compounds
         BT2     steroids
           BT3     organic compounds
         NT1     cholic acid
         RT      bile
```

bile ducts
   USE   biliary tract

BILIARY TRACT [2,228; 2,228]
```
         UF      bile ducts
         UF      gallbladder
         UF+     gallstones
         BT1     digestive system
         RT      bile
         RT      liver
```

BILIBIN REACTOR [44; 44]
(Chukotka region, USSR)
```
         UF      chukotka reactor
         BT1     lwgr type reactors
         BT2     graphite moderated reactors
           BT3     reactors
         BT2     water cooled reactors
           BT3     reactors
         BT1     power reactors
         BT2     reactors
         BT1     thermal reactors
         BT2     reactors
```

BILIRUBIN [127; 127]
```
         BT1     heterocyclic acids
         BT2     carboxylic acids
           BT3     organic acids
             BT4     organic compounds
         BT2     heterocyclic compounds
           BT3     organic compounds
         BT1     pigments
         BT1     pyrroles
         BT2     azoles
           BT3     heterocyclic compounds
             BT4     organic compounds
           BT3     organic nitrogen compounds
             BT4     organic compounds
         RT      bile
```

BILIVERDIN [3; 3]
```
         BT1     heterocyclic acids
         BT2     carboxylic acids
           BT3     organic acids
             BT4     organic compounds
         BT2     heterocyclic compounds
           BT3     organic compounds
         BT1     pigments
         BT1     pyrroles
         BT2     azoles
           BT3     heterocyclic compounds
             BT4     organic compounds
           BT3     organic nitrogen compounds
             BT4     organic compounds
         RT      bile
```

billitonites
   USE   tektites

bimetallic corrosion
   USE   electrochemical corrosion

BIMETALS [256; 256]
   RT   switches

BINARY ALLOY SYSTEMS [4,874; 4,874]
   BT1   alloy systems

BINARY ENCOUNTER METHOD [384; 384]
   RT   scattering

BINARY FISSION [175; 175]
```
         BT1     fission
         BT2     nuclear reactions
```

BINARY MIXTURES [3,098; 3,098]
```
         BT1     mixtures
         BT2     dispersions
         RT      alloys
```

BINARY STARS [5,840; 8,450]
```
         BT1     stars
         NT1     eruptive variable stars
           NT2     novae
           NT2     supernovae
           NT2     t tauri stars
         RT      roche equipotentials
         RT      symbiotic stars
```

BINDERS [584; 584]
```
         RT      adhesives
         RT      fillers
```

BINDING ENERGY [10,119; 10,978]
(For chemical and nuclear bonding. For bonding of materials, see also BONDING.)
```
         UF      separation energy
         UF+     electron acceptor
         UF+     electron donor
         BT1     energy
         NT1     neutron separation energy
         NT1     pairing energy
         RT      bond angle
         RT      bond lengths
         RT      chemical bonds
         RT      coulomb energy
         RT      covalence
         RT      double bonds
         RT      heitler-london theory
         RT      interatomic forces
         RT      intermolecular forces
         RT      ionization potential
         RT      majorana theory
         RT      mass defect
         RT      nuclear forces
         RT      work functions
```

BIOADSORBENTS [77; 77]
(Biological materials with adsorptive capacity.)
```
         BT1     adsorbents
         RT      adsorption
         RT      decontamination
         RT      fungi
         RT      liquid wastes
```

BIOASSAY [1,986; 1,986]
```
         UF      biological testing
         UF      testing (biological)
         BT1     performance testing
         BT2     testing
         RT      comparative evaluations
         RT      immunoassay
         RT      plaque formation
         RT      radioreceptor assay
```

biocenoses
   USE   ecosystems

biochemical activity
   USE   biochemistry

BIOCHEMICAL REACTION KINETICS
[7,732; 7,732]
- BT1 reaction kinetics
- BT2 kinetics
- RT biological markers
- RT detoxification
- RT enzyme activity
- RT metabolic diseases
- RT metabolism

BIOCHEMISTRY [3,408; 3,664]
- UF *biochemical activity*
- BT1 chemistry
- NT1 blood chemistry
- RT antiandrogens
- RT bioconversion
- RT biodegradation
- RT biological evolution
- RT biology
- RT bioluminescence
- RT biosynthesis
- RT carbon 14 compounds
- RT coenzymes
- RT cytochemistry
- RT enzymes
- RT fermentation
- RT hormones
- RT metabolism
- RT receptors
- RT synergism
- RT vitamins

→ **BIOCONVERSION** [0; 3] *Sep 91*
- SF *microbial processes*
- NT1 anaerobic digestion
- NT1 fermentation
- RT biochemistry
- RT biomass

→ **BIODEGRADATION** [9; 9] *Feb 76*
- SF *microbial processes*
- BT1 decomposition
- BT2 chemical reactions
- RT aerobic conditions
- RT anaerobic conditions
- RT biochemistry
- RT bioreactors

BIOELECTRICITY [134; 134] *Sep 83*
- BT1 electricity
- RT nerve cells
- RT receptors
- RT stimuli

BIOFLAVONOIDS [15; 15]
- UF *vitamin p*
- BT1 vitamins

biofouling
- USE fouling

biogeocenoses
- USE ecosystems

BIOGEOCHEMISTRY [170; 170]
- BT1 geochemistry
- RT biological evolution
- RT biology
- RT geobotany

BIOINTRUSION [24; 24] *Jul 85*
(Breaching by plants or animals of natural or man-made barriers, e.g. at waste disposal sites. Not for HUMAN INTRUSION.)
- UF *intrusion (animals)*
- UF *intrusion (plants)*
- RT environmental exposure pathway
- RT nuclear facilities
- RT physical protection
- RT radioactive waste disposal
- RT radioactive waste facilities
- RT security
- RT tailings

biologic. research reac. janus
- USE janus reactor

BIOLOGICAL ADAPTATION [134; 134]
May 76
(Prior to December 1990, this concept was indexed by ACCLIMATION.)
- UF *acclimation*
- RT biological recovery
- RT environment
- RT temperature dependence

BIOLOGICAL AVAILABILITY
[207; 207] *Dec 85*
(A measure of the ease with which a substance can be picked up by and incorporated into an organism.)
- RT environmental exposure pathway
- RT radionuclide migration
- RT retention
- RT uptake

BIOLOGICAL DOSEMETERS [390; 390]
- BT1 dosemeters
- BT2 measuring instruments
- RT biological indicators

§ **BIOLOGICAL EFFECTS** [7,813; 54,176]
- NT1 biological radiation effects
- NT2 abscopal radiation effects
- NT2 delayed radiation effects
- NT2 early radiation effects
- NT2 genetic radiation effects
- NT2 local radiation effects
- NT3 osteoradionecrosis
- NT3 radiation burns
- NT3 radiodermatitis
- NT2 radiation injuries
- NT3 osteoradionecrosis
- NT3 radiation burns
- NT3 radiodermatitis
- NT1 genetic effects
- NT2 genetic radiation effects
- RT acute exposure
- RT biology
- RT biophysics
- RT chronic exposure
- RT dose-response relationships
- RT molecular biology
- RT morphological changes
- RT prenatal exposure
- RT response modifying factors
- RT survival curves
- RT synergism
- RT toxicity

BIOLOGICAL EVOLUTION [146; 146]
Jun 83
- UF *speciation (biological)*
- RT biochemistry
- RT biogeochemistry
- RT biology
- RT biosynthesis
- RT fossils
- RT genetics
- RT geobotany
- RT molecular biology
- RT paleontology

BIOLOGICAL FATIGUE [57; 57]
- UF *fatigue (biological)*
- RT biological stress
- RT exercise

biological fouling
- USE fouling

BIOLOGICAL FUNCTIONS
[3,942; 3,942] *Oct 75*
(Coordinate with descriptors for the organs or functions involved.)
- UF *function (biological)*
- RT biological pathways
- RT dynamic function studies
- RT metabolism
- RT physiology

- RT structure-activity relationshi

BIOLOGICAL HALF-LIFE [1,719; 1,719]
- UF *effective half-life*
- UF *half-life (biological)*
- UF *half-life (effective)*
- RT body burden
- RT radionuclide kinetics

BIOLOGICAL HOT SPOTS [164; 164]
- UF *hot spots (biological)*
- RT biological localization
- RT bone seekers
- RT radionuclide kinetics
- RT retention

BIOLOGICAL INDICATORS [771; 771]
- RT biological dosemeters
- RT blood cells
- RT blood plasma
- RT bone marrow cells
- RT chromosomal aberrations
- RT dose-response relationships
- RT early radiation effects
- RT nucleosides
- RT radiation doses
- RT radiation injuries

BIOLOGICAL LOCALIZATION
[3,565; 3,565]
(The concentration of a specific material or a specific effect in a definite location of a biological system.)
- UF *localization (biological)*
- RT banding techniques
- RT biological hot spots
- RT bone seekers
- RT radiation effects
- RT radioecological concentration
- RT radioisotopes
- RT radionuclide kinetics
- RT radiopharmaceuticals
- RT retention
- RT tissue distribution

BIOLOGICAL MARKERS [380; 380]
Aug 84
- UF *reference materials (bio mark)*
- RT biochemical reaction kinetics
- RT biological pathways
- RT dynamic function studies
- RT metabolism
- RT tracer techniques

BIOLOGICAL MATERIALS
[2,070; 27,848]
- BT1 materials
- NT1 biological wastes
- NT2 feces
- NT2 sewage sludge
- NT2 sweat
- NT2 urine
- NT1 body fluids
- NT2 amniotic fluid
- NT2 bile
- NT2 blood
- NT3 blood cells
- NT4 blood platelets
- NT4 erythrocytes
- NT5 reticulocytes
- NT4 leukocytes
- NT5 basophils
- NT5 eosinophils
- NT5 lymphocytes
- NT5 monocytes
- NT5 neutrophils
- NT3 blood plasma
- NT4 blood serum
- NT2 cerebrospinal fluid
- NT2 gastric acid
- NT2 lymph
- NT2 milk
- NT2 saliva
- NT2 sweat
- NT2 urine
- NT1 forest litter
- NT1 tissue extracts
- RT animals

> RT biomass
> RT environmental materials
> RT food
> RT homogenates
> RT plankton
> RT plants
> RT tissues

BIOLOGICAL MODELS [2,737; 2,737]
> UF *models (biological)*
> RT analog systems
> RT environmental exposure pathway
> RT functional models
> RT mathematical models
> RT mockup
> RT phantoms

BIOLOGICAL PATHWAYS
[1,832; 1,832] *Nov 78*
> UF *metabolic pathways*
> UF *mutagenic pathways*
> UF *mutation induction pathways*
> UF *repair pathways*
> RT biological functions
> RT biological markers
> RT molecular biology

§ **BIOLOGICAL RADIATION EFFECTS**
[31,035; 47,014]
> UF *radiobiological effects*
> BT1 biological effects
> BT1 radiation effects
> NT1 abscopal radiation effects
> NT1 delayed radiation effects
> NT1 early radiation effects
> NT1 genetic radiation effects
> NT1 local radiation effects
>> NT2 osteoradionecrosis
>> NT2 radiation burns
>> NT2 radiodermatitis
> NT1 radiation injuries
>> NT2 osteoradionecrosis
>> NT2 radiation burns
>> NT2 radiodermatitis
> RT aerobic conditions
> RT anaerobic conditions
> RT biological stress
> RT oxygen enhancement ratio
> RT radiation chimeras
> RT radiation doses
> RT radiobiology
> RT radioimmunology
> RT radiosensitivity
> RT rbe
> RT strand breaks
> RT teratogenesis

biological reactors
> USE bioreactors

BIOLOGICAL RECOVERY
[1,743; 10,354]
> UF *enhanced recovery (biological)*
> UF *liquid holding recovery*
> UF *recovery (biological)*
> UF *restoration*
> NT1 biological regeneration
> NT1 biological repair
>> NT2 dna repair
>> NT2 host-cell reactivation
>> NT2 photoreactivation
> NT1 healing
> RT biological adaptation
> RT homeostasis
> RT post-irradiation therapy
> RT response modifying factors
> RT therapy

BIOLOGICAL REGENERATION
[802; 802]
> UF *regenerating liver*
> UF *regeneration (biological)*
> BT1 biological recovery
> RT growth
> RT organs
> RT tissues
> RT viability

BIOLOGICAL REPAIR [5,231; 7,484]
> UF *repair (biological)*
> BT1 biological recovery
> NT1 dna repair
> NT1 host-cell reactivation
> NT1 photoreactivation
> RT let
> RT molecular structure
> RT nucleic acids
> RT radiation injuries
> RT ultrastructural changes

BIOLOGICAL SHIELDING [759; 759]
> BT1 shielding
> RT radiation protection

BIOLOGICAL SHIELDS [617; 617]
> BT1 shields

BIOLOGICAL SHOCK [188; 188]
(For all types of shock in biology and medicine.)
> UF *shock (biological)*
> UF *shock (medical)*
> UF+ *electric shock*
> UF+ *traumatic shock*
> BT1 pathological changes
>> BT2 diseases
> RT anaphylaxis
> RT biological stress
> RT heart failure

BIOLOGICAL STRESS [763; 763]
> UF *stress (biological)*
> RT anoxia
> RT biological fatigue
> RT biological radiation effects
> RT biological shock
> RT chronic exposure
> RT exercise
> RT fasting
> RT heart failure
> RT hypertension
> RT hypotension
> RT physiology
> RT prenatal exposure

biological testing
> USE bioassay

BIOLOGICAL VARIABILITY [369; 988]
> UF *variability (biological)*
> NT1 genetic variability
>> NT2 rflps

BIOLOGICAL WASTES [170; 4,050]
> UF *agricultural wastes*
> UF *municipal wastes (biological)*
> UF+ *radioactive biological wastes*
> BT1 biological materials
>> BT2 materials
> BT1 wastes
> NT1 feces
> NT1 sewage sludge
> NT1 sweat
> NT1 urine
> RT excretion
> RT liquid wastes
> RT pollutants
> RT solid wastes

BIOLOGY [621; 5,481]
> NT1 anatomy
> NT1 botany
>> NT2 geobotany
> NT1 cytology
> NT1 genetics
> NT1 radiobiology
> NT1 zoology
> RT animals
> RT biochemistry
> RT biogeochemistry
> RT biological effects

> RT biological evolution
> RT biosphere
> RT ecosystems
> RT medicine
> RT microorganisms
> RT organs
> RT plants
> RT symbiosis
> RT taxonomy
> RT tissues

BIOLUMINESCENCE [21; 21] *Jul 86*
> BT1 chemiluminescence
>> BT2 luminescence
>>> BT3 photon emission
>>>> BT4 emission
> RT biochemistry

BIOMASS [355; 355] *Nov 75*
(Total weight of living organisms per unit area, or weight or volume of organisms per unit volume of habitat.)
> BT1 renewable energy sources
>> BT2 energy sources
> RT bioconversion
> RT biological materials
> RT biomass plantations
> RT deforestation
> RT plankton
> RT plants

→ **BIOMASS CONVERSION PLANTS**
[0; 0] *Sep 91*
(Plants converting biomass to fuel.)
> BT1 industrial plants

→ **BIOMASS PLANTATIONS** [0; 0] *Sep 91*
> BT1 energy sources
> RT agriculture
> RT algae
> RT biomass
> RT crops
> RT trees

BIOMATERIALS [0; 0]
(Materials foreign to the organism, inserted to remedy a physiological defect either temporarily or permanently. USE the name for the specific materials.)

BIOMEDICAL RADIOGRAPHY
[25,006; 25,908]
> UF *encephalography*
> UF *radiography (biomedical)*
> UF *x-ray radiography (biomedical)*
> UF+ *angiography*
> BT1 diagnostic techniques
> BT1 medicine
> NT1 fluoroscopy
> NT1 osteodensitometry
> RT cat scanning
> RT computerized tomography
> RT contrast media
> RT emission computed tomography
> RT ionographic imaging
> RT microradiography
> RT nuclear medicine
> RT proton computed tomography
> RT proton radiography
> RT radiological personnel
> RT radiology
> RT sequential scanning
> RT tomography
> RT x-ray radiography

BIOPHYSICS [531; 531]
> RT biological effects
> RT compartments
> RT molecular biology
> RT radiation doses
> RT radiation effects
> RT radiation protection
> RT radiations
> RT radiobiology
> RT radionuclide kinetics

BIOPSY [1,533; 1,533]
 BT1 diagnostic techniques
 RT autopsy
 RT tissues

BIOREACTORS [15; 15] *May 86*
 UF *biological reactors*
 RT biodegradation
 RT chemical reactors
 RT water treatment

BIOSATELLITES [43; 43]
 BT1 satellites

BIOSPHERE [560; 560]
 RT biology
 RT ecosystems
 RT environment
 RT populations

BIOSYNTHESIS [6,364; 6,368]
 UF *translation (macromolecules)*
 BT1 synthesis
 NT1 post-translation modification
 RT anabolism
 RT biochemistry
 RT biological evolution
 RT coenzymes
 RT enzymes
 RT gene regulation
 RT metabolism
 RT molecular biology
 RT photosynthesis
 RT precursor

BIOT-SAVART LAW [47; 47]
 RT magnetic fields

→ **BIOTECHNOLOGY** [2; 2] *Aug 91*
 (The application of the principles of technology or engineering to the life sciences.)
 NT1 genetic engineering
 RT commercialization

BIOTIN [82; 82]
 UF *vitamin h*
 BT1 heterocyclic acids
  BT2 carboxylic acids
   BT3 organic acids
    BT4 organic compounds
  BT2 heterocyclic compounds
   BT3 organic compounds
 BT1 imidazoles
  BT2 azoles
   BT3 heterocyclic compounds
    BT4 organic compounds
   BT3 organic nitrogen compounds
    BT4 organic compounds
 BT1 organic sulfur compounds
  BT2 organic compounds
 BT1 vitamin b group
  BT2 vitamins

BIOTITE [314; 314]
 BT1 mica
  BT2 silicate minerals
   BT3 minerals
 RT granites

BIPHENYL [225; 225]
 BT1 aromatics
  BT2 organic compounds
 BT1 hydrocarbons
  BT2 organic compounds
 RT benzidine

biphenyldiamine
 USE benzidine

BIPYRIDINES [316; 316]
 BT1 pyridines
  BT2 azines
   BT3 heterocyclic compounds

    BT4 organic compounds
   BT3 organic nitrogen compounds
    BT4 organic compounds

BIR REACTOR [2; 2] *Dec 86*
 BT1 enriched uranium reactors
  BT2 reactors
 BT1 fast reactors
  BT2 epithermal reactors
   BT3 reactors
 BT1 pulsed reactors
  BT2 reactors
 BT1 research reactors
  BT2 research and test reactors
   BT3 reactors

birches
 USE trees

BIRDS [322; 1,693]
 UF+ *bursa of fabricius*
 BT1 vertebrates
  BT2 animals
 NT1 fowl
  NT2 chickens
  NT2 ducks
 NT1 pigeons
 RT eggs
 RT feathers
 RT newcastle disease

birefringence
 USE refraction

BIRMINGHAM SYNCHROTRON [5; 5]
 BT1 synchrotrons
  BT2 cyclic accelerators
   BT3 accelerators

birth
 USE parturition

bis(2-ethylhexyl)phosphoric ac
 USE hdehp

bis-chloroethylamine
 USE nitrogen mustard

bis-phenyloxazolylbenzene
 USE popop

biscay bay (france, spain)
 USE bay of biscay

BISCAYNE BAY [10; 10]
 BT1 atlantic ocean
  BT2 seas
   BT3 surface waters
 RT florida

BISMUTH [1,558; 1,558]
 BT1 metals
  BT2 elements

BISMUTH ADDITIONS [106; 106]
 (Alloys containing not more than 1% Bi are listed here.)
 RT bismuth alloys
 RT bismuth compounds

BISMUTH ALLOYS [678; 770]
 (Alloys containing more than 1% Bi.)
 BT1 alloys
 NT1 bismuth base alloys
  NT2 alloy-bi50pb25cd12sn12
 RT bismuth additions

BISMUTH BASE ALLOYS [55; 86]
 BT1 bismuth alloys
  BT2 alloys
 NT1 alloy-bi50pb25cd12sn12

BISMUTH BORIDES [2; 2]
 BT1 bismuth compounds
 BT1 borides
  BT2 boron compounds

BISMUTH BROMIDES [16; 16]
 BT1 bismuth compounds
 BT1 bromides
  BT2 bromine compounds
   BT3 halogen compounds
  BT2 halides
   BT3 halogen compounds

BISMUTH CARBONATES [5; 5]
 BT1 bismuth compounds
 BT1 carbonates
  BT2 carbon compounds
  BT2 oxygen compounds

BISMUTH CHLORIDES [40; 40]
 BT1 bismuth compounds
 BT1 chlorides
  BT2 chlorine compounds
   BT3 halogen compounds
  BT2 halides
   BT3 halogen compounds

BISMUTH COMPLEXES [69; 69]
 BT1 complexes

BISMUTH COMPOUNDS [947; 3,393]
 NT1 bismuth borides
 NT1 bismuth bromides
 NT1 bismuth carbonates
 NT1 bismuth chlorides
 NT1 bismuth fluorides
 NT1 bismuth germanates
 NT1 bismuth hydrides
 NT1 bismuth hydroxides
 NT1 bismuth iodides
 NT1 bismuth nitrates
 NT1 bismuth oxides
 NT1 bismuth phosphates
 NT1 bismuth selenides
 NT1 bismuth sulfates
 NT1 bismuth sulfides
 NT1 bismuth tellurides
 NT1 bismuth tungstates
 RT bismuth additions

BISMUTH FLUORIDES [28; 28]
 BT1 bismuth compounds
 BT1 fluorides
  BT2 fluorine compounds
   BT3 halogen compounds
  BT2 halides
   BT3 halogen compounds

bismuth germanate detectors
 USE bgo detectors

BISMUTH GERMANATES [162; 162]
 Dec 83
 BT1 bismuth compounds
 BT1 germanates
  BT2 germanium compounds
  BT2 oxygen compounds

BISMUTH HYDRIDES [5; 5]
 BT1 bismuth compounds
 BT1 hydrides
  BT2 hydrogen compounds

BISMUTH HYDROXIDES [13; 13]
 BT1 bismuth compounds
 BT1 hydroxides
  BT2 hydrogen compounds
  BT2 oxygen compounds

BISMUTH IODIDES [90; 90]
BT1 bismuth compounds
BT1 iodides
BT2 halides
BT3 halogen compounds
BT2 iodine compounds
BT3 halogen compounds

BISMUTH IONS [219; 219]
BT1 ions
BT2 charged particles

BISMUTH ISOTOPES [116; 2,054]
NT1 bismuth 188
NT1 bismuth 189
NT1 bismuth 190
NT1 bismuth 191
NT1 bismuth 192
NT1 bismuth 193
NT1 bismuth 194
NT1 bismuth 195
NT1 bismuth 196
NT1 bismuth 197
NT1 bismuth 198
NT1 bismuth 199
NT1 bismuth 200
NT1 bismuth 201
NT1 bismuth 202
NT1 bismuth 203
NT1 bismuth 204
NT1 bismuth 205
NT1 bismuth 206
NT1 bismuth 207
NT1 bismuth 208
NT1 bismuth 209
NT1 bismuth 210
NT1 bismuth 211
NT1 bismuth 212
NT1 bismuth 213
NT1 bismuth 214
NT1 bismuth 215
NT1 bismuth 216

BISMUTH NITRATES [19; 19]
BT1 bismuth compounds
BT1 nitrates
BT2 nitrogen compounds
BT2 oxygen compounds

BISMUTH ORES [0; 0]
BT1 ores

BISMUTH OXIDES [1,770; 1,770]
BT1 bismuth compounds
BT1 oxides
BT2 chalcogenides
BT2 oxygen compounds

BISMUTH PHOSPHATES [31; 31]
BT1 bismuth compounds
BT1 phosphates
BT2 oxygen compounds
BT2 phosphorus compounds

BISMUTH SELENIDES [34; 34] *Sep 79*
BT1 bismuth compounds
BT1 selenides
BT2 chalcogenides
BT2 selenium compounds

BISMUTH SULFATES [6; 6]
BT1 bismuth compounds
BT1 sulfates
BT2 oxygen compounds
BT2 sulfur compounds

BISMUTH SULFIDES [52; 52]
BT1 bismuth compounds
BT1 sulfides
BT2 chalcogenides
BT2 sulfur compounds

BISMUTH TELLURIDES [248; 248]
BT1 bismuth compounds
BT1 tellurides
BT2 chalcogenides
BT2 tellurium compounds

BISMUTH TUNGSTATES [21; 21]
Nov 81
BT1 bismuth compounds
BT1 tungstates
BT2 oxygen compounds
BT2 tungsten compounds
BT3 transition element compounds

BISMUTH 188 [4; 4] *Nov 80*
BT1 alpha decay radioisotopes
BT2 radioisotopes
BT3 isotopes
BT1 bismuth isotopes
BT1 heavy nuclei
BT2 nuclei
BT1 odd-odd nuclei
BT2 nuclei

BISMUTH 189 [6; 6]
BT1 alpha decay radioisotopes
BT2 radioisotopes
BT3 isotopes
BT1 bismuth isotopes
BT1 heavy nuclei
BT2 nuclei
BT1 odd-even nuclei
BT2 nuclei
BT1 seconds living radioisotopes
BT2 radioisotopes
BT3 isotopes

BISMUTH 190 [5; 5]
BT1 alpha decay radioisotopes
BT2 radioisotopes
BT3 isotopes
BT1 bismuth isotopes
BT1 electron capture radioisotopes
BT2 beta decay radioisotopes
BT3 radioisotopes
BT4 isotopes
BT1 heavy nuclei
BT2 nuclei
BT1 odd-odd nuclei
BT2 nuclei
BT1 seconds living radioisotopes
BT2 radioisotopes
BT3 isotopes

BISMUTH 191 [7; 7]
BT1 alpha decay radioisotopes
BT2 radioisotopes
BT3 isotopes
BT1 bismuth isotopes
BT1 electron capture radioisotopes
BT2 beta decay radioisotopes
BT3 radioisotopes
BT4 isotopes
BT1 heavy nuclei
BT2 nuclei
BT1 odd-even nuclei
BT2 nuclei
BT1 seconds living radioisotopes
BT2 radioisotopes
BT3 isotopes

BISMUTH 192 [6; 6]
BT1 alpha decay radioisotopes
BT2 radioisotopes
BT3 isotopes
BT1 bismuth isotopes
BT1 electron capture radioisotopes
BT2 beta decay radioisotopes
BT3 radioisotopes
BT4 isotopes
BT1 heavy nuclei
BT2 nuclei
BT1 odd-odd nuclei
BT2 nuclei
BT1 seconds living radioisotopes
BT2 radioisotopes
BT3 isotopes

BISMUTH 193 [9; 9]
BT1 alpha decay radioisotopes
BT2 radioisotopes
BT3 isotopes
BT1 bismuth isotopes
BT1 electron capture radioisotopes
BT2 beta decay radioisotopes
BT3 radioisotopes
BT4 isotopes
BT1 heavy nuclei
BT2 nuclei
BT1 minutes living radioisotopes
BT2 radioisotopes
BT3 isotopes
BT1 odd-even nuclei
BT2 nuclei
BT1 seconds living radioisotopes
BT2 radioisotopes
BT3 isotopes

BISMUTH 194 [7; 7]
BT1 alpha decay radioisotopes
BT2 radioisotopes
BT3 isotopes
BT1 beta-plus decay radioisotopes
BT2 beta decay radioisotopes
BT3 radioisotopes
BT4 isotopes
BT1 bismuth isotopes
BT1 electron capture radioisotopes
BT2 beta decay radioisotopes
BT3 radioisotopes
BT4 isotopes
BT1 heavy nuclei
BT2 nuclei
BT1 minutes living radioisotopes
BT2 radioisotopes
BT3 isotopes
BT1 odd-odd nuclei
BT2 nuclei

BISMUTH 195 [12; 12]
BT1 alpha decay radioisotopes
BT2 radioisotopes
BT3 isotopes
BT1 bismuth isotopes
BT1 electron capture radioisotopes
BT2 beta decay radioisotopes
BT3 radioisotopes
BT4 isotopes
BT1 heavy nuclei
BT2 nuclei
BT1 minutes living radioisotopes
BT2 radioisotopes
BT3 isotopes
BT1 odd-even nuclei
BT2 nuclei

BISMUTH 196 [3; 3]
BT1 bismuth isotopes
BT1 electron capture radioisotopes
BT2 beta decay radioisotopes
BT3 radioisotopes
BT4 isotopes
BT1 heavy nuclei
BT2 nuclei
BT1 minutes living radioisotopes
BT2 radioisotopes
BT3 isotopes
BT1 odd-odd nuclei
BT2 nuclei

BISMUTH 197 [6; 6]
BT1 alpha decay radioisotopes
BT2 radioisotopes
BT3 isotopes
BT1 beta-plus decay radioisotopes
BT2 beta decay radioisotopes
BT3 radioisotopes
BT4 isotopes
BT1 bismuth isotopes
BT1 electron capture radioisotopes
BT2 beta decay radioisotopes
BT3 radioisotopes
BT4 isotopes
BT1 heavy nuclei
BT2 nuclei
BT1 minutes living radioisotopes
BT2 radioisotopes

BT3   isotopes
BT1   odd-even nuclei
BT2   nuclei

BISMUTH 198 [6; 6]
BT1   bismuth isotopes
BT1   electron capture radioisotopes
BT2   beta decay radioisotopes
BT3   radioisotopes
BT4   isotopes
BT1   heavy nuclei
BT2   nuclei
BT1   isomeric transition isotopes
BT2   radioisotopes
BT3   isotopes
BT1   minutes living radioisotopes
BT2   radioisotopes
BT3   isotopes
BT1   odd-odd nuclei
BT2   nuclei
BT1   seconds living radioisotopes
BT2   radioisotopes
BT3   isotopes

BISMUTH 199 [18; 18]
BT1   alpha decay radioisotopes
BT2   radioisotopes
BT3   isotopes
BT1   bismuth isotopes
BT1   electron capture radioisotopes
BT2   beta decay radioisotopes
BT3   radioisotopes
BT4   isotopes
BT1   heavy nuclei
BT2   nuclei
BT1   minutes living radioisotopes
BT2   radioisotopes
BT3   isotopes
BT1   odd-even nuclei
BT2   nuclei

BISMUTH 200 [10; 10]
BT1   beta-plus decay radioisotopes
BT2   beta decay radioisotopes
BT3   radioisotopes
BT4   isotopes
BT1   bismuth isotopes
BT1   electron capture radioisotopes
BT2   beta decay radioisotopes
BT3   radioisotopes
BT4   isotopes
BT1   heavy nuclei
BT2   nuclei
BT1   minutes living radioisotopes
BT2   radioisotopes
BT3   isotopes
BT1   odd-odd nuclei
BT2   nuclei

BISMUTH 201 [24; 24]
BT1   alpha decay radioisotopes
BT2   radioisotopes
BT3   isotopes
BT1   bismuth isotopes
BT1   electron capture radioisotopes
BT2   beta decay radioisotopes
BT3   radioisotopes
BT4   isotopes
BT1   heavy nuclei
BT2   nuclei
BT1   hours living radioisotopes
BT2   radioisotopes
BT3   isotopes
BT1   isomeric transition isotopes
BT2   radioisotopes
BT3   isotopes
BT1   minutes living radioisotopes
BT2   radioisotopes
BT3   isotopes
BT1   odd-even nuclei
BT2   nuclei

BISMUTH 202 [21; 21]
BT1   beta-plus decay radioisotopes
BT2   beta decay radioisotopes
BT3   radioisotopes
BT4   isotopes
BT1   bismuth isotopes

BT1   electron capture radioisotopes
BT2   beta decay radioisotopes
BT3   radioisotopes
BT4   isotopes
BT1   heavy nuclei
BT2   nuclei
BT1   hours living radioisotopes
BT2   radioisotopes
BT3   isotopes
BT1   odd-odd nuclei
BT2   nuclei

BISMUTH 203 [25; 25]
BT1   alpha decay radioisotopes
BT2   radioisotopes
BT3   isotopes
BT1   beta-plus decay radioisotopes
BT2   beta decay radioisotopes
BT3   radioisotopes
BT4   isotopes
BT1   bismuth isotopes
BT1   electron capture radioisotopes
BT2   beta decay radioisotopes
BT3   radioisotopes
BT4   isotopes
BT1   heavy nuclei
BT2   nuclei
BT1   hours living radioisotopes
BT2   radioisotopes
BT3   isotopes
BT1   odd-even nuclei
BT2   nuclei

BISMUTH 204 [45; 45]
BT1   bismuth isotopes
BT1   electron capture radioisotopes
BT2   beta decay radioisotopes
BT3   radioisotopes
BT4   isotopes
BT1   heavy nuclei
BT2   nuclei
BT1   hours living radioisotopes
BT2   radioisotopes
BT3   isotopes
BT1   odd-odd nuclei
BT2   nuclei

BISMUTH 205 [59; 59]
BT1   beta-plus decay radioisotopes
BT2   beta decay radioisotopes
BT3   radioisotopes
BT4   isotopes
BT1   bismuth isotopes
BT1   days living radioisotopes
BT2   radioisotopes
BT3   isotopes
BT1   electron capture radioisotopes
BT2   beta decay radioisotopes
BT3   radioisotopes
BT4   isotopes
BT1   heavy nuclei
BT2   nuclei
BT1   odd-even nuclei
BT2   nuclei

BISMUTH 206 [118; 118]
BT1   beta-plus decay radioisotopes
BT2   beta decay radioisotopes
BT3   radioisotopes
BT4   isotopes
BT1   bismuth isotopes
BT1   days living radioisotopes
BT2   radioisotopes
BT3   isotopes
BT1   electron capture radioisotopes
BT2   beta decay radioisotopes
BT3   radioisotopes
BT4   isotopes
BT1   heavy nuclei
BT2   nuclei
BT1   odd-odd nuclei
BT2   nuclei

BISMUTH 207 [205; 205]
BT1   beta-plus decay radioisotopes
BT2   beta decay radioisotopes
BT3   radioisotopes
BT4   isotopes

BT1   electron capture radioisotopes
BT2   beta decay radioisotopes
BT3   radioisotopes
BT4   isotopes
BT1   heavy nuclei
BT2   nuclei
BT1   odd-even nuclei
BT2   nuclei
BT1   years living radioisotopes
BT2   radioisotopes
BT3   isotopes

BISMUTH 207 TARGET [12; 12] *Jan 78*
BT1   targets

BISMUTH 208 [188; 188]
BT1   bismuth isotopes
BT1   electron capture radioisotopes
BT2   beta decay radioisotopes
BT3   radioisotopes
BT4   isotopes
BT1   heavy nuclei
BT2   nuclei
BT1   odd-odd nuclei
BT2   nuclei
BT1   years living radioisotopes
BT2   radioisotopes
BT3   isotopes

BISMUTH 208 TARGET [12; 12] *Sep 79*
BT1   targets

BISMUTH 209 [637; 637]
BT1   bismuth isotopes
BT1   heavy nuclei
BT2   nuclei
BT1   odd-even nuclei
BT2   nuclei
BT1   stable isotopes
BT2   isotopes

BISMUTH 209 BEAMS [28; 28] *Mar 83*
BT1   ion beams
BT2   beams

BISMUTH 209 REACTIONS [18; 18] *Nov 80*
BT1   heavy ion reactions
BT2   nuclear reactions

BISMUTH 209 TARGET [1,062; 1,062]
BT1   targets

BISMUTH 210 [231; 231]
UF   *radium e*
BT1   alpha decay radioisotopes
BT2   radioisotopes
BT3   isotopes
BT1   beta-minus decay radioisotopes
BT2   beta decay radioisotopes
BT3   radioisotopes
BT4   isotopes
BT1   bismuth isotopes
BT1   days living radioisotopes
BT2   radioisotopes
BT3   isotopes
BT1   heavy nuclei
BT2   nuclei
BT1   odd-odd nuclei
BT2   nuclei
BT1   years living radioisotopes
BT2   radioisotopes
BT3   isotopes

BISMUTH 210 TARGET [7; 7] *Oct 76*
BT1   targets

BISMUTH 211 [32; 32]
UF   *actinium c*
BT1   alpha decay radioisotopes
BT2   radioisotopes
BT3   isotopes
BT1   beta-minus decay radioisotopes
BT2   beta decay radioisotopes
BT3   radioisotopes

BT4   isotopes
BT1   bismuth isotopes
BT1   heavy nuclei
BT2   nuclei
BT1   isomeric transition isotopes
BT2   radioisotopes
BT3   isotopes
BT1   minutes living radioisotopes
BT2   radioisotopes
BT3   isotopes
BT1   nanosec living radioisotopes
BT2   radioisotopes
BT3   isotopes
BT1   odd-even nuclei
BT2   nuclei

BISMUTH 212 [146; 146]
UF   *thorium c*
BT1   alpha decay radioisotopes
BT2   radioisotopes
BT3   isotopes
BT1   beta-minus decay radioisotopes
BT2   beta decay radioisotopes
BT3   radioisotopes
BT4   isotopes
BT1   bismuth isotopes
BT1   heavy nuclei
BT2   nuclei
BT1   hours living radioisotopes
BT2   radioisotopes
BT3   isotopes
BT1   minutes living radioisotopes
BT2   radioisotopes
BT3   isotopes
BT1   odd-odd nuclei
BT2   nuclei

BISMUTH 213 [11; 11]
BT1   alpha decay radioisotopes
BT2   radioisotopes
BT3   isotopes
BT1   beta-minus decay radioisotopes
BT2   beta decay radioisotopes
BT3   radioisotopes
BT4   isotopes
BT1   bismuth isotopes
BT1   heavy nuclei
BT2   nuclei
BT1   minutes living radioisotopes
BT2   radioisotopes
BT3   isotopes
BT1   odd-even nuclei
BT2   nuclei

BISMUTH 214 [327; 327]
UF   *radium c*
BT1   alpha decay radioisotopes
BT2   radioisotopes
BT3   isotopes
BT1   beta-minus decay radioisotopes
BT2   beta decay radioisotopes
BT3   radioisotopes
BT4   isotopes
BT1   bismuth isotopes
BT1   heavy nuclei
BT2   nuclei
BT1   minutes living radioisotopes
BT2   radioisotopes
BT3   isotopes
BT1   odd-odd nuclei
BT2   nuclei

BISMUTH 215 [1; 1]
BT1   beta-minus decay radioisotopes
BT2   beta decay radioisotopes
BT3   radioisotopes
BT4   isotopes
BT1   bismuth isotopes
BT1   heavy nuclei
BT2   nuclei
BT1   minutes living radioisotopes
BT2   radioisotopes
BT3   isotopes
BT1   odd-even nuclei
BT2   nuclei

BISMUTH 216 [3; 3] *May 89*
BT1   beta-minus decay radioisotopes
BT2   beta decay radioisotopes
BT3   radioisotopes
BT4   isotopes
BT1   bismuth isotopes
BT1   heavy nuclei
BT2   nuclei
BT1   minutes living radioisotopes
BT2   radioisotopes
BT3   isotopes
BT1   odd-odd nuclei
BT2   nuclei

BITUMENS [775; 1,063]
BT1   tar
BT2   other organic compounds
BT3   organic compounds
NT1   asphalts
NT1   carburan
NT1   coal tar
NT1   thucholite
RT   asphaltite
RT   oil sands
RT   oil shales
RT   waste processing

→ **BITUMINOUS COAL** [0; 0] *Sep 91*
BT1   black coal
BT2   coal
BT3   carbonaceous materials
BT4   materials
BT3   fossil fuels
BT4   energy sources
BT4   fuels

BJORKLUND-FERNBACH MODEL [0; 0]
BT1   nuclear models
BT2   mathematical models
RT   optical models

BL LACERTAE OBJECTS [294; 294]
Oct 81
BT1   cosmic radio sources
BT1   cosmic x-ray sources
BT2   cosmic ray sources
RT   seyfert galaxies

→ **BLACK COAL** [0; 0] *Sep 91*
SF   *hard coal*
BT1   coal
BT2   carbonaceous materials
BT3   materials
BT2   fossil fuels
BT3   energy sources
BT3   fuels
NT1   anthracite
NT1   bituminous coal

BLACK DWARF STARS [13; 13]
BT1   dwarf stars
BT2   stars

BLACK FOX-1 REACTOR [4; 4] *Jul 76*
(Rogers, Oklahoma, USA)
BT1   bwr type reactors
BT2   enriched uranium reactors
BT3   reactors
BT2   power reactors
BT3   reactors
BT2   thermal reactors
BT3   reactors
BT2   water cooled reactors
BT3   reactors
BT2   water moderated reactors
BT3   reactors
RT   ge standard reactor

BLACK FOX-2 REACTOR [4; 4] *Jul 76*
(Rogers, Oklahoma, USA)
BT1   bwr type reactors
BT2   enriched uranium reactors
BT3   reactors
BT2   power reactors
BT3   reactors
BT2   thermal reactors
BT3   reactors
BT2   water cooled reactors
BT3   reactors
BT2   water moderated reactors
BT3   reactors
RT   ge standard reactor

BLACK HOLES [3,653; 3,653]
RT   accretion disks
RT   gravitational collapse
RT   kerr field
RT   schwarzschild radius
RT   stars
RT   white holes

BLACK NUCLEUS MODEL [17; 17]
UF   *black-nucleus model*
BT1   nuclear models
BT2   mathematical models

BLACK SANDS [9; 9]
BT1   minerals
BT1   sand
RT   magnetite
RT   thorianite
RT   thorite
RT   uraninites

BLACK SEA [86; 86]
BT1   seas
BT2   surface waters

black-nucleus model
USE   black nucleus model

BLACKBODY RADIATION [592; 592]
UF   *universal blackbody radiation*
BT1   electromagnetic radiation
BT2   radiations
RT   emissivity
RT   planck radiation formula
RT   thermal radiation

blackouts
USE   outages

BLADDER [1,374; 1,374]
BT1   urinary tract
BT2   organs
BT3   body
RT   pelvis

blades (turbines)
USE   turbine blades

BLAHUTOVICE-1 REACTOR [10; 10]
Apr 88
(North Moravia, Czechoslovakia.)
BT1   wwer type reactors
BT2   pwr type reactors
BT3   enriched uranium reactors
BT4   reactors
BT3   power reactors
BT4   reactors
BT3   thermal reactors
BT4   reactors
BT3   water cooled reactors
BT4   reactors
BT3   water moderated reactors
BT4   reactors

BLAIR MODEL [27; 27]
UF   *blair phase rule*
RT   elastic scattering

blair phase rule
USE   blair model

BLANKENBECLER-SUGAR
  EQUATIONS [66; 66]
  BT1   integral equations
  BT2   equations
  RT   bethe-salpeter equation
  RT   lippmann-schwinger equation
  RT   particle production
  RT   scattering

blankets (breeding)
  USE   breeding blankets

blankets (gas)
  USE   gas blankets

BLASCON DEVICES [7; 7]
(Spherical configuration using swirling lithium to create a vortex for injection of fusion fuel for laser ignition.)
  BT1   closed plasma devices
  BT2   thermonuclear devices

BLAST EFFECTS [240; 240]
  RT   explosions
  RT   landslides
  RT   seismic effects
  RT   shock waves

BLAST FURNACES [97; 97]
  BT1   furnaces

blasts
  USE   explosions

BLATT-BIEDENHARN FORMALISM
  [2; 2]
  RT   angular distribution

BLEACHING [439; 439]
  RT   coloration

blending
  USE   mixing

BLEOMYCIN [680; 680]
  BT1   antibiotics
  BT2   drugs
  BT2   organic compounds
  BT1   antimitotic drugs
  BT2   drugs
  BT1   antineoplastic drugs
  BT2   drugs
  RT   neoplasms
  RT   therapy

BLIND RIVER [6; 6]
  BT1   rivers
  BT2   surface waters

BLISTERS [538; 538] *Oct 76*
(Resulting near or on the surface of materials due to external physical or chemical effects.)
  RT   bubbles
  RT   heating
  RT   radiation effects
  RT   surfaces
  RT   swelling

BLIZZARD DEPOSIT [2; 2] *Feb 81*
  BT1   uranium deposits
  BT2   geologic deposits
  RT   british columbia
  RT   uranium ores

BLOCH EQUATIONS [210; 210]
  BT1   equations
  RT   magnetic resonance

BLOCH THEORY [232; 232]
  RT   quantum mechanics

BLOCH WALL [254; 254] *Feb 76*
(Transition layer with finite thickness of a few hundred lattice constants, between adjacent ferromagnetic domains.)
  BT1   domain structure

blocking
  USE   channeling

BLOCKING OSCILLATORS [11; 11]
  BT1   oscillators
  BT2   electronic equipment
  BT3   equipment
  RT   pulse generators

BLOOD [3,632; 20,073]
  BT1   body fluids
  BT2   biological materials
  BT3   materials
  NT1   blood cells
  NT2   blood platelets
  NT2   erythrocytes
  NT3   reticulocytes
  NT2   leukocytes
  NT3   basophils
  NT3   eosinophils
  NT3   lymphocytes
  NT3   monocytes
  NT3   neutrophils
  NT1   blood plasma
  NT2   blood serum
  RT   blood circulation
  RT   blood count
  RT   blood formation
  RT   blood groups
  RT   bone marrow
  RT   connective tissue
  RT   extracorporeal irradiation
  RT   hemic diseases
  RT   hemocyanin
  RT   hemorrhage
  RT   hemosiderin
  RT   homeostasis
  RT   respiration
  RT   septicemia
  RT   transfusions
  RT   uremia

BLOOD CELLS [670; 13,064]
  BT1   blood
  BT2   body fluids
  BT3   biological materials
  BT4   materials
  NT1   blood platelets
  NT1   erythrocytes
  NT2   reticulocytes
  NT1   leukocytes
  NT2   basophils
  NT2   eosinophils
  NT2   lymphocytes
  NT2   monocytes
  NT2   neutrophils
  RT   biological indicators
  RT   blood count
  RT   bone marrow

BLOOD CHEMISTRY [274; 274] *Jun 82*
  BT1   biochemistry
  BT2   chemistry
  RT   blood coagulation factors
  RT   blood plasma
  RT   blood serum
  RT   hemic diseases

BLOOD CIRCULATION [2,434; 2,434]
  UF   *cardiac output*
  UF   *circulation (blood)*
  RT   blood
  RT   blood flow
  RT   blood pressure
  RT   cardiography
  RT   cardiovascular system
  RT   emboli
  RT   heart
  RT   ischemia
  RT   kidneys
  RT   lungs
  RT   mechanical heart
  RT   myocardial infarction
  RT   parabiosis
  RT   physiology
  RT   spleen
  RT   vasoconstriction
  RT   vasodilation

blood clotting
  USE   blood coagulation

BLOOD COAGULATION [458; 458]
  UF   *blood clotting*
  UF   *coagulation (blood)*
  RT   anticoagulants
  RT   blood coagulation factors
  RT   blood platelets
  RT   blood serum
  RT   coalescence
  RT   fibrinolysin
  RT   hemophilia
  RT   hemorrhage
  RT   thrombosis

BLOOD COAGULATION FACTORS
  [218; 1,258]
  BT1   coagulants
  BT2   hematologic agents
  BT3   drugs
  NT1   fibrin
  NT1   fibrinogen
  NT1   fibrinolysin
  NT1   folic acid
  NT1   intrinsic factor
  NT1   kallikrein
  NT1   plasminogen
  NT1   protamines
  NT2   salmin
  NT1   prothrombin
  NT1   thrombin
  NT1   thromboplastin
  NT1   urokinase
  NT1   vitamin b-12
  NT1   vitamin k
  RT   blood chemistry
  RT   blood coagulation
  RT   blood platelets
  RT   calcium

BLOOD COUNT [499; 499]
  RT   blood
  RT   blood cells

blood diseases
  USE   hemic diseases

BLOOD FLOW [6,720; 6,720]
  RT   blood circulation
  RT   blood vessels
  RT   emboli
  RT   organs

BLOOD FORMATION [1,045; 1,441]
  UF   *hematopoiesis*
  UF   *hemopoiesis*
  NT1   erythropoiesis
  NT1   leukopoiesis
  NT1   thrombopoiesis
  RT   blood
  RT   bone marrow
  RT   bone marrow cells
  RT   cell differentiation
  RT   hematopoietic system
  RT   spleen
  RT   spleen colony formation
  RT   stem cells

BLOOD GROUPS [44; 44]
  RT   blood
  RT   erythrocytes
  RT   hemagglutinins
  RT   transfusions

BLOOD PLASMA [2,854; 4,484]
UF *plasma (blood)*
BT1 blood
  BT2 body fluids
    BT3 biological materials
      BT4 materials
NT1 blood serum
RT biological indicators
RT blood chemistry
RT blood substitutes
RT blood-plasma clearance
RT chylomicrons
RT complement
RT proteins

BLOOD PLATELETS [1,808; 1,808]
UF *thrombocytes*
BT1 blood cells
  BT2 blood
    BT3 body fluids
      BT4 biological materials
        BT5 materials
RT blood coagulation
RT blood coagulation factors
RT thrombopoiesis

BLOOD PRESSURE [931; 931]
RT arteries
RT blood circulation
RT cardiography
RT cardiovascular system
RT hypertension
RT hypotension
RT renin

BLOOD SERUM [3,947; 3,947]
UF *serum (blood)*
UF+ *hsa*
UF+ *human serum albumin*
BT1 blood plasma
  BT2 blood
    BT3 body fluids
      BT4 biological materials
        BT5 materials
RT blood chemistry
RT blood coagulation
RT immune serums

BLOOD SUBSTITUTES [19; 323]
NT1 dextran
NT1 pvp
RT blood plasma
RT hematologic agents
RT post-irradiation therapy
RT therapy
RT transfusions

BLOOD VESSELS [4,486; 12,695]
UF+ *angiography*
BT1 cardiovascular system
BT1 organs
  BT2 body
NT1 arteries
  NT2 aorta
  NT2 carotid arteries
  NT2 coronaries
NT1 capillaries
NT1 veins
  NT2 portal system
RT angiomas
RT blood flow
RT emboli
RT hemorrhage
RT ischemia
RT telangiectasis
RT thrombosis
RT vasoconstriction
RT vasodilation

BLOOD-BRAIN BARRIER [430; 430]
RT homeostasis
RT physiology

BLOOD-PLASMA CLEARANCE [931; 931]
UF *plasma clearance*
BT1 clearance
RT blood plasma
RT diagnostic techniques
RT pbi
RT radionuclide administration
RT radionuclide kinetics
RT thyroid
RT time dependence

BLOWDOWN [1,950; 1,950]
RT loss of coolant

BLOWERS [328; 328]
UF *fans*
RT bellows
RT compressors
RT pumps
RT reactor cooling systems

→ **BLOWOUTS** [0; 0] *Sep 91*
(The high-pressure, sometimes violent, uncontrolled ejection of water, gas, or oil from a borehole.)
BT1 accidents
RT oil wells
RT wells

blowup (particle beams)
USE beam dynamics

BLUE HILLS-1 REACTOR [5; 5]
(Newton, Texas, USA)
BT1 pwr type reactors
  BT2 enriched uranium reactors
    BT3 reactors
  BT2 power reactors
    BT3 reactors
  BT2 thermal reactors
    BT3 reactors
  BT2 water cooled reactors
    BT3 reactors
  BT2 water moderated reactors
    BT3 reactors

BLUE HILLS-2 REACTOR [5; 5]
(Newton, Texas, USA)
BT1 pwr type reactors
  BT2 enriched uranium reactors
    BT3 reactors
  BT2 power reactors
    BT3 reactors
  BT2 thermal reactors
    BT3 reactors
  BT2 water cooled reactors
    BT3 reactors
  BT2 water moderated reactors
    BT3 reactors

BLUE STELLAR OBJECTS [39; 39]
BT1 quasars
BT2 cosmic radio sources

blue-green algae
USE cyanobacteria

bmi reactor
USE brr reactor

BN-1600 REACTOR [52; 52] *Sep 79*
(USSR)
BT1 lmfbr type reactors
  BT2 fbr type reactors
    BT3 breeder reactors
      BT4 reactors
    BT3 fast reactors
      BT4 epithermal reactors
        BT5 reactors
  BT2 liquid metal cooled reactors
    BT3 reactors
BT1 power reactors
  BT2 reactors
BT1 sodium cooled reactors
  BT2 liquid metal cooled reactors
    BT3 reactors

BN-350 REACTOR [187; 187]
(Mangyshalk, Shevchenko, USSR)
UF *fort shevchenko reactor*
BT1 desalination reactors
  BT2 power reactors
    BT3 reactors
BT1 lmfbr type reactors
  BT2 fbr type reactors
    BT3 breeder reactors
      BT4 reactors
    BT3 fast reactors
      BT4 epithermal reactors
        BT5 reactors
  BT2 liquid metal cooled reactors
    BT3 reactors
BT1 sodium cooled reactors
  BT2 liquid metal cooled reactors
    BT3 reactors
RT enriched uranium reactors
RT plutonium reactors

bn-600 reactor
USE beloyarsk-3 reactor

BN-800 REACTOR [14; 14] *Feb 89*
BT1 lmfbr type reactors
  BT2 fbr type reactors
    BT3 breeder reactors
      BT4 reactors
    BT3 fast reactors
      BT4 epithermal reactors
        BT5 reactors
  BT2 liquid metal cooled reactors
    BT3 reactors
BT1 power reactors
  BT2 reactors
BT1 sodium cooled reactors
  BT2 liquid metal cooled reactors
    BT3 reactors

BNFL [375; 375] *Apr 80*
UF *british nuclear fuels limited*
BT1 united kingdom organizations
  BT2 national organizations

BNL [737; 737]
UF *brookhaven national laboratory*
BT1 us aec
  BT2 us organizations
    BT3 national organizations
BT1 us doe
  BT2 us organizations
    BT3 national organizations
BT1 us erda
  BT2 us organizations
    BT3 national organizations
RT new york

bnps-1 reactor
USE beloyarsk-1 reactor

bnps-2 reactor
USE beloyarsk-2 reactor

BODY [1,247; 116,622]
NT1 body areas
  NT2 abdomen
  NT2 chest
    NT3 mediastinum
  NT2 head
    NT3 face
      NT4 nose
  NT2 limbs
    NT3 arms
      NT4 hands
        NT5 fingers
    NT3 legs
      NT4 feet
  NT2 neck
  NT2 pelvis

NT1	hematopoietic system
NT2	bone marrow
NT1	organs
NT2	blood vessels
NT3	arteries
NT4	aorta
NT4	carotid arteries
NT4	coronaries
NT3	capillaries
NT3	veins
NT4	portal system
NT2	bone marrow
NT2	brain
NT3	cerebellum
NT3	cerebrum
NT4	cerebral cortex
NT3	hippocampus
NT3	hypothalamus
NT3	olfactory bulbs
NT3	thalamus
NT2	critical organs
NT2	diaphragm
NT2	esophagus
NT2	female genitals
NT3	ovaries
NT3	uterus
NT2	glands
NT3	endocrine glands
NT4	adrenal glands
NT4	pancreas
NT4	parathyroid glands
NT4	pituitary gland
NT4	thyroid
NT3	liver
NT3	mammary glands
NT3	pineal gland
NT3	prostate
NT3	salivary glands
NT2	heart
NT3	myocardium
NT3	pericardium
NT2	intestines
NT3	large intestine
NT4	rectum
NT3	small intestine
NT2	kidneys
NT3	glomeruli
NT3	tubules
NT2	lungs
NT2	male genitals
NT3	prostate
NT3	testes
NT2	perfused organs
NT2	pharynx
NT2	sense organs
NT3	auditory organs
NT3	eyes
NT4	conjunctiva
NT4	cornea
NT4	crystalline lens
NT4	lacrimal ducts
NT4	retina
NT4	uvea
NT3	taste buds
NT3	vestibular apparatus
NT2	skeleton
NT3	bone joints
NT3	exoskeleton
NT3	femur
NT3	skull
NT4	jaw
NT3	tibia
NT3	vertebrae
NT2	skin
NT3	epidermis
NT3	feathers
NT3	hair
NT3	nails
NT2	spleen
NT2	stomach
NT2	thymus
NT2	tongue
NT2	urinary tract
NT3	bladder
NT3	ureters
NT1	tissues
NT2	bone marrow

NT2	connective tissue
NT3	adipose tissue
NT3	bone tissues
NT4	antlers
NT4	trabecular bone
NT3	cartilage
NT3	fascia
NT3	ligaments
NT2	endothelium
NT2	epithelium
NT3	epidermis
NT2	nerve tissue
NT2	perfused tissues
NT2	reticuloendothelial system
RT	anatomy
RT	body composition
RT	retention
RT	whole-body counting
RT	whole-body irradiation

BODY AREAS [117; 14,063]
BT1	body
NT1	abdomen
NT1	chest
NT2	mediastinum
NT1	head
NT2	face
NT3	nose
NT1	limbs
NT2	arms
NT3	hands
NT4	fingers
NT2	legs
NT3	feet
NT1	neck
NT1	pelvis
RT	partial body irradiation

BODY BURDEN [1,194; 1,194]
RT	biological half-life
RT	contamination
RT	icrp critical group
RT	maximum permissible body burde
RT	pollution
RT	radioactivity
RT	radionuclide kinetics

body centered cubic
USE bcc lattices

BODY COMPOSITION [309; 309]
RT	body
RT	quantitative chemical analysis

BODY FLUIDS [620; 25,721]
UF	aqueous humor
BT1	biological materials
BT2	materials
NT1	amniotic fluid
NT1	bile
NT1	blood
NT2	blood cells
NT3	blood platelets
NT3	erythrocytes
NT4	reticulocytes
NT3	leukocytes
NT4	basophils
NT4	eosinophils
NT4	lymphocytes
NT4	monocytes
NT4	neutrophils
NT2	blood plasma
NT3	blood serum
NT1	cerebrospinal fluid
NT1	gastric acid
NT1	lymph
NT1	milk
NT1	saliva
NT1	sweat
NT1	urine
RT	edema
RT	excretion
RT	feces
RT	secretion

BODY TEMPERATURE [156; 1,553]
UF	temperature (body)
UF+	thermoregulation
NT1	hyperthermia
NT1	hypothermia
RT	fever
RT	physiology

body waves p (seismic)
USE seismic p waves

body waves s (seismic)
USE seismic s waves

BOGOLYUBOV METHOD [181; 181]
RT	superconductivity

bogolyubov theory
USE bbgky equation

BOGOLYUBOV TRANSFORMATION [424; 424]
UF	bogolyubov-valatin relation
BT1	canonical transformations
BT2	transformations
RT	hartree-fock-bogolyubov theory

bogolyubov-valatin relation
USE bogolyubov transformation

bogs
USE swamps

BOHM CRITERION [145; 145]
UF	bohm theory
UF	bohm-gross method
RT	plasma

bohm theory
USE bohm criterion

bohm-gross method
USE bohm criterion

bohm-pines theory
USE pines-bohm theory

bohr approximation
USE nilsson-mottelson model

BOHR THEORY [206; 206]
UF	bohr-sommerfeld quantum theory
RT	atomic models

bohr-mottelson model
USE nilsson-mottelson model

bohr-sommerfeld quantum theory
USE bohr theory

BOHR-WHEELER THEORY [63; 63]
RT	fission
RT	nuclear models

BOHUNICE A-1 REACTOR [340; 340]
(Trnava, West Slovakia, Czechoslovakia)
UF	a-1 reactor (bohunice)
UF	heavy water gcr of czechoslova
UF	hwgcr of czechoslovakia
UF	ks-150 reactor
BT1	hwgcr type reactors
BT2	gas cooled reactors
BT3	reactors
BT2	heavy water moderated reactors

```
          BT3      reactors
          BT1      natural uranium reactors
          BT2      reactors
          BT1      power reactors
          BT2      reactors
          BT1      thermal reactors
          BT2      reactors

BOHUNICE A-2 REACTOR [2; 2]
(Trnava, West Slovakia, Czechoslovakia)
     UF       a-2 reactor (bohunice)
     BT1      hwgcr type reactors
     BT2      gas cooled reactors
          BT3      reactors
     BT2      heavy water moderated reactors
          BT3      reactors
     BT1      natural uranium reactors
     BT2      reactors
     BT1      power reactors
     BT2      reactors
     BT1      thermal reactors
     BT2      reactors

BOHUNICE V-1 REACTOR [295; 295]
(Trnava, West Slovakia, Czechoslovakia)
     UF       v-1 reactor (bohunice)
     BT1      wwer type reactors
     BT2      pwr type reactors
          BT3      enriched uranium reactors
               BT4      reactors
          BT3      power reactors
               BT4      reactors
          BT3      thermal reactors
               BT4      reactors
          BT3      water cooled reactors
               BT4      reactors
          BT3      water moderated reactors
               BT4      reactors

BOHUNICE V-2 REACTOR [146; 146]
May 79
(Trnava, West Slovakia, Czecholslovakia)
     UF       v-2 reactor (bohunice)
     BT1      wwer type reactors
     BT2      pwr type reactors
          BT3      enriched uranium reactors
               BT4      reactors
          BT3      power reactors
               BT4      reactors
          BT3      thermal reactors
               BT4      reactors
          BT3      water cooled reactors
               BT4      reactors
          BT3      water moderated reactors
               BT4      reactors

BOILERS [673; 9,136]
     NT1      vapor generators
          NT2      steam generators
     RT       boiling
     RT       combustion control
     RT       deaerators
     RT       district heating
     RT       feedwater
     RT       heat transfer
     RT       reactor cooling systems

BOILING [1,697; 3,872]
     BT1      phase transformations
     NT1      film boiling
     NT1      nucleate boiling
          NT2      departure nucleate boiling
     NT1      pool boiling
     NT1      subcooled boiling
     NT1      transition boiling
     RT       boilers
     RT       boiling detection
     RT       bubble growth
     RT       evaporation
     RT       heat transfer
     RT       heating
     RT       steam generators
     RT       two-phase flow

BOILING DETECTION [324; 324]
     BT1      detection
     RT       boiling
     RT       bubble growth
     RT       bubbles
     RT       foams
     RT       reactor control systems
     RT       reactor safety
     RT       voids

*boiling heavy water cool./mode*
     USE      bhwr type reactors

*boiling nuclear superheater r.*
     USE      bonus reactor

BOILING POINTS [325; 325]
     BT1      transition temperature
          BT2      thermodynamic properties
               BT3      physical properties
     RT       azeotrope

*boiling reactor experiment 1*
     USE      borax-1 reactor

*boiling reactor experiment 2*
     USE      borax-2 reactor

*boiling reactor experiment 3*
     USE      borax-3 reactor

*boiling reactor experiment 4*
     USE      borax-4 reactor

*boiling water cooled and moder*
     USE      bwr type reactors

BOLIVIA [22; 82]
     BT1      developing countries
     BT1      south america
          BT2      latin america
     NT1      chacaltaya

BOLL WEEVIL [15; 15]
     UF       *anthonomus grandis*
     BT1      beetles
          BT2      insects
               BT3      arthropods
                    BT4      invertebrates
                         BT5      animals
     RT       cotton plants

BOLLWORM [16; 16]
     UF       *heliothis*
     BT1      moths
          BT2      lepidoptera
               BT3      insects
                    BT4      arthropods
                         BT5      invertebrates
                              BT6      animals
     RT       cotton plants

BOLOMETERS [407; 407]
     BT1      measuring instruments
     RT       temperature measurement
     RT       thermometers

BOLTED JOINTS [151; 151]
     BT1      joints

*bolting*
     USE      fastening

*bolts*
     USE      fasteners

BOLTWOODITE [7; 7]
     BT1      silicate minerals
          BT2      minerals
     BT1      uranium minerals
          BT2      radioactive minerals
               BT3      minerals
          BT3      radioactive materials
               BT4      materials
     RT       potassium silicates
     RT       uranium silicates

*boltzmann approximation*
     USE      boltzmann statistics

*boltzmann collision integral*
     USE      boltzmann equation

BOLTZMANN EQUATION [2,148; 2,148]
     UF       *boltzmann collision integral*
     UF       *boltzmann transport equation*
     UF       *born-green-yvon equation*
     UF       *maxwell-boltzmann equation*
     BT1      partial differential equations
          BT2      differential equations
               BT3      equations
     RT       collision integrals
     RT       gases
     RT       kinetic equations
     RT       p1-approximation
     RT       p3-approximation
     RT       statistical mechanics
     RT       transport theory

*boltzmann factor*
     USE      boltzmann statistics

BOLTZMANN STATISTICS
[1,435; 1,435]
     UF       *boltzmann approximation*
     UF       *boltzmann factor*
     UF       *maxwell distribution*
     UF       *maxwell statistics*
     UF       *maxwell velocity distribution*
     UF       *maxwell-boltzmann distribution*
     UF       *maxwell-boltzmann statistics*
     RT       distribution
     RT       h theorem
     RT       statistical mechanics

*boltzmann transport equation*
     USE      boltzmann equation

BOLTZMANN-VLASOV EQUATION
[2,317; 2,410]
     UF       *liouville equation*
     UF       *vlasov equation*
     UF       *vlasov instability*
     BT1      partial differential equations
          BT2      differential equations
               BT3      equations
     NT1      plasma fluid equations
     RT       plasma
     RT       quasilinear problems
     RT       transport theory

BOMB REDUCTION [19; 19]
     BT1      reduction
          BT2      chemical reactions

*bombyx*
     USE      silkworm

BOND ANGLE [2,024; 2,024]
     RT       binding energy
     RT       chemical bonds

BOND LENGTHS [2,139; 2,139]
     RT       binding energy
     RT       chemical bonds
     RT       molecular structure
```

BONDING [745; 745]
(For joining metals and other materials. For nuclear or chemical bonding, see also BINDING ENERGY.)
UF   fusion (bonding, nonmetallic)
BT1   joining
  BT2   fabrication
RT   adhesion
RT   coalescence
RT   grouting
RT   joints

BONE CELLS [178; 178]
UF   osteocytes
BT1   connective tissue cells
  BT2   somatic cells
    BT3   animal cells
RT   bone marrow
RT   bone marrow cells
RT   bone tissues

bone diseases
USE   skeletal diseases

BONE FRACTURES [1,146; 1,146]
UF   fractures (bone)
BT1   injuries
  BT2   diseases
BT1   skeletal diseases
  BT2   diseases

BONE JOINTS [2,361; 2,361]
UF   joints (anatomy)
UF   synovia
BT1   skeleton
  BT2   organs
    BT3   body
RT   cartilage
RT   rheumatic diseases

BONE MARROW [3,675; 3,675]
BT1   hematopoietic system
  BT2   body
BT1   organs
  BT2   body
BT1   tissues
  BT2   body
RT   blood
RT   blood cells
RT   blood formation
RT   bone cells
RT   bone marrow cells
RT   bone tissues
RT   leukemia
RT   plasma cells
RT   polycythemia
RT   radiation syndrome
RT   reticuloendothelial system
RT   stem cells
RT   trabecular bone

BONE MARROW CELLS [1,960; 1,960]
UF   erythroblasts
UF   megakaryocytes
BT1   connective tissue cells
  BT2   somatic cells
    BT3   animal cells
RT   biological indicators
RT   blood formation
RT   bone cells
RT   bone marrow

BONE SEEKERS [378; 378]
BT1   radioisotopes
  BT2   isotopes
RT   biological hot spots
RT   biological localization
RT   bone tissues
RT   calcium isotopes
RT   radionuclide kinetics
RT   radium isotopes
RT   strontium isotopes

BONE TISSUES [2,798; 2,870]
UF   endosteum
UF   epiphysis (bones)
UF   periosteum
BT1   connective tissue
  BT2   tissues
    BT3   body
NT1   antlers
NT1   trabecular bone
RT   bone cells
RT   bone marrow
RT   bone seekers
RT   calcium
RT   dentin
RT   hyperparathyroidism
RT   osteodensitometry
RT   osteomyelitis
RT   osteoporosis
RT   osteoradionecrosis
RT   osteosarcomas
RT   parathormone
RT   rheumatic diseases
RT   rickets
RT   skeleton
RT   teeth

bones
USE   skeleton

BONN SYNCHROTRON [61; 61]
BT1   synchrotrons
  BT2   cyclic accelerators
    BT3   accelerators

BONNER SPHERE DETECTORS [115; 115]
UF   multisphere neutron detectors
BT1   moderating detectors
  BT2   neutron detectors
    BT3   radiation detectors
      BT4   measuring instruments

BONNER SPHERE SPECTROMETERS [90; 90]
BT1   neutron spectrometers
  BT2   spectrometers
    BT3   measuring instruments

→ **BONNEVILLE POWER ADMINISTRATIO** [0; 0] *Aug 91*
UF   bpa
BT1   us doe
  BT2   us organizations
    BT3   national organizations
RT   electric power

BONUS REACTOR [6; 6]
UF   boiling nuclear superheater r.
UF   bwr superheater puerto rico r.
UF   puerto rico bonus reactor
BT1   bwr type reactors
  BT2   enriched uranium reactors
    BT3   reactors
  BT2   power reactors
    BT3   reactors
  BT2   thermal reactors
    BT3   reactors
  BT2   water cooled reactors
    BT3   reactors
  BT2   water moderated reactors
    BT3   reactors

bookkeeping
USE   accounting

boosters (particle)
USE   particle boosters

BOOTSTRAP CURRENT [96; 96]
Apr 89
BT1   electric currents
  BT2   currents
RT   neoclassical transport theory
RT   non-inductive current drive

RT   plasma

BOOTSTRAP MODEL [569; 569]
BT1   composite models
  BT2   particle models
    BT3   mathematical models
RT   coupling

BOPSSAR STANDARD PLANT [4; 4]
Oct 77
BT1   nuclear power plants
  BT2   nuclear facilities
  BT2   thermal power plants
    BT3   power plants
RT   westinghouse standard reactor

BOR-60 REACTOR [321; 321]
(Dimitrovgrad, USSR)
BT1   enriched uranium reactors
  BT2   reactors
BT1   experimental reactors
  BT2   research and test reactors
    BT3   reactors
BT1   lmfbr type reactors
  BT2   fbr type reactors
    BT3   breeder reactors
      BT4   reactors
    BT3   fast reactors
      BT4   epithermal reactors
        BT5   reactors
  BT2   liquid metal cooled reactors
    BT3   reactors
BT1   power reactors
  BT2   reactors
BT1   sodium cooled reactors
  BT2   liquid metal cooled reactors
    BT3   reactors

BORANES [516; 516]
UF   boron hydrides
UF   diborane
BT1   boron compounds
BT1   hydrides
  BT2   hydrogen compounds
RT   carboranes

BORATES [1,387; 1,458]
(Specific compounds should be indexed by coordination of a descriptor of the form (CATION) COMPOUNDS and the above anion descriptor with the exception of the one NT below.)
BT1   boron compounds
BT1   oxygen compounds
NT1   borax
RT   boric acid
RT   boron oxides

BORAX [77; 77]
BT1   borates
  BT2   boron compounds
  BT2   oxygen compounds
BT1   sodium compounds
  BT2   alkali metal compounds

BORAX-1 REACTOR [5; 5]
UF   boiling reactor experiment 1
BT1   enriched uranium reactors
  BT2   reactors
BT1   experimental reactors
  BT2   research and test reactors
    BT3   reactors
BT1   tank type reactors
  BT2   reactors
BT1   thermal reactors
  BT2   reactors
BT1   water cooled reactors
  BT2   reactors
BT1   water moderated reactors
  BT2   reactors

BORAX-2 REACTOR [3; 3]
UF   boiling reactor experiment 2
BT1   enriched uranium reactors
  BT2   reactors
BT1   experimental reactors
  BT2   research and test reactors

BT3   reactors
BT1   tank type reactors
BT2   reactors
BT1   thermal reactors
BT2   reactors
BT1   water cooled reactors
BT2   reactors
BT1   water moderated reactors
BT2   reactors

BORAX-3 REACTOR [3; 3]
UF   *boiling reactor experiment 3*
BT1   enriched uranium reactors
BT2   reactors
BT1   experimental reactors
BT2   research and test reactors
BT3   reactors
BT1   power reactors
BT2   reactors
BT1   tank type reactors
BT2   reactors
BT1   thermal reactors
BT2   reactors
BT1   water cooled reactors
BT2   reactors
BT1   water moderated reactors
BT2   reactors

BORAX-4 REACTOR [3; 3]
UF   *boiling reactor experiment 4*
BT1   enriched uranium reactors
BT2   reactors
BT1   experimental reactors
BT2   research and test reactors
BT3   reactors
BT1   power reactors
BT2   reactors
BT1   tank type reactors
BT2   reactors
BT1   thermal reactors
BT2   reactors
BT1   thorium reactors
BT2   reactors
BT1   water cooled reactors
BT2   reactors
BT1   water moderated reactors
BT2   reactors

bordentown nj newbold island-1
USE   newbold island-1 reactor

bordentown nj newbold island-2
USE   newbold island-2 reactor

BORDONI PEAK [39; 39]
RT   dislocations
RT   internal friction

BOREHOLES [3,475; 3,475]
BT1   cavities
RT   borescopes
RT   earthmoving equipment
RT   openings
RT   rock drilling
RT   subterrene penetrators
RT   well logging
RT   wells

BORESCOPES [16; 16] *Nov 75*
(A device, usually optical, for examining the inside surface of tubes, pipes, or bores.)
RT   boreholes
RT   pipes
RT   pressure tubes
RT   telescopes
RT   tubes

BORIC ACID [1,031; 1,031]
BT1   boron compounds
BT1   inorganic acids
BT2   hydrogen compounds
BT2   inorganic compounds
BT1   oxygen compounds
RT   borates

BORIDES [791; 3,251]
BT1   boron compounds
NT1   aluminium borides
NT1   antimony borides
NT1   argon borides
NT1   barium borides
NT1   berkelium borides
NT1   beryllium borides
NT1   bismuth borides
NT1   cadmium borides
NT1   calcium borides
NT1   cerium borides
NT1   chromium borides
NT1   cobalt borides
NT1   copper borides
NT1   dysprosium borides
NT1   erbium borides
NT1   europium borides
NT1   gadolinium borides
NT1   germanium borides
NT1   hafnium borides
NT1   holmium borides
NT1   indium borides
NT1   iridium borides
NT1   iron borides
NT1   lanthanum borides
NT1   lithium borides
NT1   lutetium borides
NT1   magnesium borides
NT1   manganese borides
NT1   molybdenum borides
NT1   neodymium borides
NT1   neptunium borides
NT1   nickel borides
NT1   niobium borides
NT1   osmium borides
NT1   palladium borides
NT1   plutonium borides
NT1   potassium borides
NT1   praseodymium borides
NT1   rhenium borides
NT1   rhodium borides
NT1   ruthenium borides
NT1   samarium borides
NT1   scandium borides
NT1   silicon borides
NT1   sodium borides
NT1   strontium borides
NT1   tantalum borides
NT1   terbium borides
NT1   thorium borides
NT1   thulium borides
NT1   tin borides
NT1   titanium borides
NT1   tungsten borides
NT1   uranium borides
NT1   vanadium borides
NT1   ytterbium borides
NT1   yttrium borides
NT1   zinc borides
NT1   zirconium borides
RT   boron additions
RT   ceramics
RT   intermetallic compounds

BORN APPROXIMATION [3,710; 11,169]
UF   *approximation (born)*
UF   *born cross sections*
UF   *plane-wave born approximation*
UF   *pwba*
NT1   coupled channel born approxima
NT1   dwba
RT   perturbation theory
RT   quantum mechanics
RT   scattering

born cross sections
USE   born approximation

born-bogol.-green-kirkw.-yvon
USE   bbgky equation

born-green-yvon equation
USE   boltzmann equation

BORN-INFELD THEORY [78; 78]
RT   electrodynamics
RT   maxwell equations

BORN-MAYER EQUATION [47; 47]
BT1   equations

BORN-OPPENHEIMER APPROXIMATION [440; 440]
UF   *approximation (born-oppenheim.*
RT   adiabatic approximation
RT   scattering

BORN-VON KARMAN THEORY [50; 50]
RT   specific heat

BOROHYDRIDES [480; 480]
(Specific compounds should be indexed by coordination of a descriptor of the form (CATION) COMPOUNDS and the above anion descriptor.)
BT1   boron compounds
BT1   hydrogen compounds

BORON [3,864; 3,864]
BT1   semimetals
BT2   elements

BORON ADDITIONS [908; 1,356]
(Alloys containing not more than 1% B are listed here.)
NT1   alloy-co62cr28mo6ni3
NT1   alloy-mo99b
NT1   alloy-ni42fe36cr12mo6ti3
NT1   alloy-ni43fe33cr16mo3
NT1   alloy-ni46cr23co19ti5al4
NT1   alloy-ni53co19cr15mo5al4ti3
NT1   alloy-ni55co17cr15mo5al4ti4
NT1   alloy-ni55cr19co11mo10ti3
NT1   alloy-ni56cr21w10mo5fe4al2
NT1   alloy-ni58cr20co14mo4ti3
NT1   alloy-ni59cr20co17ti2
NT1   alloy-ni60co15cr10al6ti5mo3
NT1   alloy-ni60cr14co10ti5mo4w4al3
NT1   alloy-ni60mo13co9cr8nb4al3
NT1   alloy-ni61cr16co9al3ti3w3
NT1   alloy-ni62cr16mo15fe3
NT1   alloy-ni67cr19mo5w5ti3
NT1   alloy-ni68cr15w6al3mo3fe2
NT1   alloy-ni74cr13al6mo4
NT1   alloy-ni75cr12al6mo5
NT1   alloy-ni76cr20ti2
NT1   alloy-ni77cr20ti2
NT1   steel-cr15ni15motib
NT1   steel-ni26cr15ti2movalb
RT   borides
RT   boron alloys

BORON ALLOYS [1,382; 1,446]
(Alloys containing more than 1% B.)
BT1   alloys
NT1   colmonoy
RT   boron additions

BORON ARSENIDES [8; 8] *Apr 89*
BT1   arsenides
BT2   arsenic compounds
BT2   pnictides
BT1   boron compounds

BORON BROMIDES [64; 64]
BT1   boron compounds
BT1   bromides
BT2   bromine compounds
BT3   halogen compounds
BT2   halides
BT3   halogen compounds

BORON CARBIDES [1,290; 1,290]
BT1   boron compounds
BT1   carbides
BT2   carbon compounds

BORON CHLORIDES [193; 193]
- BT1 boron compounds
- BT1 chlorides
  - BT2 chlorine compounds
    - BT3 halogen compounds
  - BT2 halides
    - BT3 halogen compounds

BORON COATED ION CHAMBERS [31; 31]
- UF *boron-coated ion chambers*
- BT1 ionization chambers
  - BT2 radiation detectors
    - BT3 measuring instruments
- BT1 neutron detectors
  - BT2 radiation detectors
    - BT3 measuring instruments

BORON COMPLEXES [397; 397]
- BT1 complexes

BORON COMPOUNDS [956; 10,439]
- NT1 boranes
- NT1 borates
  - NT2 borax
- NT1 boric acid
- *NT1 borides
- NT1 borohydrides
- NT1 boron arsenides
- NT1 boron bromides
- NT1 boron carbides
- NT1 boron chlorides
- NT1 boron fluorides
- NT1 boron hydroxides
- NT1 boron iodides
- NT1 boron nitrides
- NT1 boron oxides
- NT1 boron phosphates
- NT1 boron phosphides
- NT1 boron silicates
- NT1 boron silicides
- NT1 boron sulfides
- NT1 boronic acids
- NT1 fluoroboric acid
- RT organic boron compounds

BORON FLUORIDES [480; 480]
- BT1 boron compounds
- BT1 fluorides
  - BT2 fluorine compounds
    - BT3 halogen compounds
  - BT2 halides
    - BT3 halogen compounds

boron hydrides
- USE boranes

BORON HYDROXIDES [26; 26]
- BT1 boron compounds
- BT1 hydroxides
  - BT2 hydrogen compounds
  - BT2 oxygen compounds

BORON IODIDES [24; 24]
- BT1 boron compounds
- BT1 iodides
  - BT2 halides
    - BT3 halogen compounds
  - BT2 iodine compounds
    - BT3 halogen compounds

BORON IONS [1,118; 1,118]
- BT1 ions
  - BT2 charged particles

BORON ISOTOPES [359; 3,692]
- NT1 boron 10
- NT1 boron 11
- NT1 boron 12
- NT1 boron 13
- NT1 boron 14
- NT1 boron 15
- NT1 boron 17
- NT1 boron 18
- NT1 boron 19
- NT1 boron 7
- NT1 boron 8
- NT1 boron 9

BORON LINED COUNTERS [42; 42]
- UF *boron-lined counters*
- BT1 neutron detectors
  - BT2 radiation detectors
    - BT3 measuring instruments
- BT1 proportional counters
  - BT2 radiation detectors
    - BT3 measuring instruments

BORON NITRIDES [725; 725]
- BT1 boron compounds
- BT1 nitrides
  - BT2 nitrogen compounds
  - BT2 pnictides

BORON OXIDES [912; 912]
- BT1 boron compounds
- BT1 oxides
  - BT2 chalcogenides
  - BT2 oxygen compounds
- RT borates

BORON PHOSPHATES [24; 24]
- BT1 boron compounds
- BT1 phosphates
  - BT2 oxygen compounds
  - BT2 phosphorus compounds
- RT borophosphate glass

BORON PHOSPHIDES [40; 40] *Jul 78*
- BT1 boron compounds
- BT1 phosphides
  - BT2 phosphorus compounds
  - BT2 pnictides

BORON SILICATES [181; 208]
- BT1 boron compounds
- BT1 silicates
  - BT2 oxygen compounds
  - BT2 silicon compounds
- RT borosilicate glass
- RT silicate minerals
- RT tourmaline

BORON SILICIDES [11; 11] *Sep 85*
- BT1 boron compounds
- BT1 silicides
  - BT2 silicon compounds

BORON SULFIDES [10; 10]
- BT1 boron compounds
- BT1 sulfides
  - BT2 chalcogenides
  - BT2 sulfur compounds

BORON 10 [1,547; 1,547]
- BT1 boron isotopes
- BT1 light nuclei
  - BT2 nuclei
- BT1 odd-odd nuclei
  - BT2 nuclei
- BT1 stable isotopes
  - BT2 isotopes
- RT boron 10 beams

BORON 10 BEAMS [37; 37]
- BT1 ion beams
  - BT2 beams
- RT boron 10

BORON 10 REACTIONS [201; 201]
- BT1 heavy ion reactions
- BT2 nuclear reactions

BORON 10 TARGET [822; 822]
- BT1 targets

BORON 11 [1,280; 1,280]
- BT1 boron isotopes
- BT1 light nuclei
  - BT2 nuclei
- BT1 odd-even nuclei
  - BT2 nuclei
- BT1 stable isotopes
  - BT2 isotopes
- RT boron 11 beams

BORON 11 BEAMS [119; 119]
- BT1 ion beams
  - BT2 beams
- RT boron 11

BORON 11 REACTIONS [309; 309]
- BT1 heavy ion reactions
- BT2 nuclear reactions

BORON 11 TARGET [647; 647]
- BT1 targets

BORON 12 [519; 519]
- BT1 beta-minus decay radioisotopes
  - BT2 beta decay radioisotopes
    - BT3 radioisotopes
      - BT4 isotopes
- BT1 boron isotopes
- BT1 light nuclei
  - BT2 nuclei
- BT1 millisec living radioisotopes
  - BT2 radioisotopes
    - BT3 isotopes
- BT1 odd-odd nuclei
  - BT2 nuclei

BORON 12 TARGET [6; 6]
- BT1 targets

BORON 13 [58; 58]
- BT1 beta-minus decay radioisotopes
  - BT2 beta decay radioisotopes
    - BT3 radioisotopes
      - BT4 isotopes
- BT1 boron isotopes
- BT1 light nuclei
  - BT2 nuclei
- BT1 millisec living radioisotopes
  - BT2 radioisotopes
    - BT3 isotopes
- BT1 odd-even nuclei
  - BT2 nuclei

BORON 13 TARGET [3; 3] *Dec 75*
- BT1 targets

BORON 14 [36; 36]
- BT1 beta-minus decay radioisotopes
  - BT2 beta decay radioisotopes
    - BT3 radioisotopes
      - BT4 isotopes
- BT1 boron isotopes
- BT1 light nuclei
  - BT2 nuclei
- BT1 millisec living radioisotopes
  - BT2 radioisotopes
    - BT3 isotopes
- BT1 odd-odd nuclei
  - BT2 nuclei

BORON 15 [27; 27]
- BT1 beta-minus decay radioisotopes
  - BT2 beta decay radioisotopes
    - BT3 radioisotopes
      - BT4 isotopes
- BT1 boron isotopes
- BT1 light nuclei
  - BT2 nuclei
- BT1 millisec living radioisotopes
  - BT2 radioisotopes
    - BT3 isotopes
- BT1 odd-even nuclei
  - BT2 nuclei

BORON 17 [20; 20]
BT1 beta-minus decay radioisotopes
BT2 beta decay radioisotopes
BT3 radioisotopes
BT4 isotopes
BT1 boron isotopes
BT1 light nuclei
BT2 nuclei
BT1 millisec living radioisotopes
BT2 radioisotopes
BT3 isotopes
BT1 odd-even nuclei
BT2 nuclei

BORON 18 [5; 5] *Jul 85*
BT1 boron isotopes
BT1 light nuclei
BT2 nuclei
BT1 odd-odd nuclei
BT2 nuclei

BORON 19 [11; 11]
BT1 beta-minus decay radioisotopes
BT2 beta decay radioisotopes
BT3 radioisotopes
BT4 isotopes
BT1 boron isotopes
BT1 light nuclei
BT2 nuclei
BT1 odd-even nuclei
BT2 nuclei

BORON 7 [3; 3]
BT1 boron isotopes
BT1 light nuclei
BT2 nuclei
BT1 odd-even nuclei
BT2 nuclei

BORON 8 [197; 197]
BT1 beta-plus decay radioisotopes
BT2 beta decay radioisotopes
BT3 radioisotopes
BT4 isotopes
BT1 boron isotopes
BT1 light nuclei
BT2 nuclei
BT1 millisec living radioisotopes
BT2 radioisotopes
BT3 isotopes
BT1 odd-odd nuclei
BT2 nuclei

BORON 9 [134; 134]
BT1 alpha decay radioisotopes
BT2 radioisotopes
BT3 isotopes
BT1 boron isotopes
BT1 light nuclei
BT2 nuclei
BT1 odd-even nuclei
BT2 nuclei

boron-coated ion chambers
USE boron coated ion chambers

boron-lined counters
USE boron lined counters

BORONIC ACIDS [39; 39]
BT1 boron compounds
BT1 organic acids
BT2 organic compounds

BOROPHOSPHATE GLASS [31; 31]
Feb 81
(Low expansion heat resistant glass.)
UF *borophosphates*
BT1 phosphate glass
BT2 glass
RT boron phosphates

borophosphates
USE borophosphate glass

BOROSILICATE GLASS [1,440; 1,500]
Nov 80
(Low expansion heat resistant glass.)
UF *borosilicates*
BT1 glass
NT1 pyrex
RT boron silicates

borosilicates
USE borosilicate glass

BORSSELE REACTOR [72; 72]
(Borssele, Zeeland, Netherlands)
UF *kcb reactor*
UF *kernenergiecent borssele react*
BT1 pwr type reactors
BT2 enriched uranium reactors
BT3 reactors
BT2 power reactors
BT3 reactors
BT2 thermal reactors
BT3 reactors
BT2 water cooled reactors
BT3 reactors
BT2 water moderated reactors
BT3 reactors

BOSE-EINSTEIN CONDENSATION
[1,400; 1,400]
RT pion condensation
RT superfluidity

BOSE-EINSTEIN GAS [452; 452]
RT bose-einstein statistics
RT bosons
RT fermi gas

BOSE-EINSTEIN STATISTICS
[553; 553]
RT bose-einstein gas
RT bosons
RT cooper pairs
RT fermi statistics
RT parastatistics
RT statistical mechanics

BOSON EXPANSION [195; 195] *Jan 86*
RT boson-fermion symmetry
RT collective model
RT dyson representation
RT generator-coordinate method
RT hartree-fock-bogolyubov theory
RT interacting boson model
RT quantum operators
RT random phase approximation
RT series expansion
RT tamm-dancoff method

BOSON-EXCHANGE MODELS
[671; 5,413]
BT1 peripheral models
BT2 particle models
BT3 mathematical models
NT1 obe model
NT2 ope model
NT3 electric born model
NT1 sigma model
RT deep inelastic scattering

BOSON-FERMION SYMMETRY
[198; 198] *Dec 84*
(Symmetry of a system containing a conserved number of bosons as well as fermions in which bosons and fermions share a common symmetry.)
UF *dynamical boson-fermion symmet*
UF *fermion-boson symmetry*
UF *spinor symmetry*
BT1 symmetry
RT boson expansion
RT bosons
RT dynamical groups
RT fermions

RT interacting boson model

BOSONS [5,309; 64,316]
NT1 gluons
NT1 goldstone bosons
NT2 axions
NT1 intermediate bosons
NT2 intermediate vector bosons
NT3 w minus bosons
NT3 w plus bosons
NT3 z neutral bosons
NT1 mesons
NT2 axial vector mesons
NT3 a1-1270 mesons
NT3 b1-1235 mesons
NT3 chi1-3510 mesons
NT3 f1-1285 mesons
NT3 f1-1420 mesons
NT3 f1-1530 mesons
NT3 h1-1190 mesons
NT3 k1-1280 mesons
NT3 k1-1400 mesons
NT2 baryonium
NT2 beauty mesons
NT3 b*-5325 mesons
NT2 bottomonium
NT3 chi b0-10235 mesons
NT3 chi b0-9860 mesons
NT3 chi b1-10255 mesons
NT3 chi b1-9895 mesons
NT3 chi b2-10270 mesons
NT3 chi b2-9915 mesons
NT3 upsilon-10023 mesons
NT3 upsilon-10355 mesons
NT3 upsilon-10575 mesons
NT3 upsilon-10860 mesons
NT3 upsilon-11020 mesons
NT3 upsilon-9460 mesons
NT2 charmed mesons
NT3 d mesons
NT4 d minus mesons
NT4 d neutral mesons
NT5 anti-d neutral mesons
NT4 d plus mesons
NT3 d s mesons
NT3 d*-2010 mesons
NT3 d*-2420 mesons
NT3 d*s-2110 mesons
NT2 charmonium
NT3 chi0-3415 mesons
NT3 chi1-3510 mesons
NT3 chi2-3555 mesons
NT3 eta c-2980 mesons
NT3 eta c-3590 mesons
NT3 j psi-3097 mesons
NT3 psi-3685 mesons
NT3 psi-3770 mesons
NT3 psi-4030 mesons
NT3 psi-4160 mesons
NT3 psi-4415 mesons
NT2 pomeranchuk particles
NT2 pseudoscalar mesons
NT3 b mesons
NT4 b minus mesons
NT4 b neutral mesons
NT5 anti-b neutral mesons
NT4 b plus mesons
NT3 d mesons
NT4 d minus mesons
NT4 d neutral mesons
NT5 anti-d neutral mesons
NT4 d plus mesons
NT3 eta c-2980 mesons
NT3 eta c-3590 mesons
NT3 eta mesons
NT3 eta prime-958 mesons
NT3 eta-1275 mesons
NT3 eta-1440 mesons
NT3 k-1460 mesons
NT3 k-1830 mesons
NT3 kaons
NT4 antikaons
NT5 antikaons neutral
NT4 cosmic kaons
NT4 kaons minus
NT4 kaons neutral
NT5 antikaons neutral
NT5 kaons neutral long-lived
NT5 kaons neutral short-lived
NT4 kaons plus

NT3	pi-1300 mesons
NT3	pi-1770 mesons
NT3	pions
NT4	cosmic pions
NT4	pions minus
NT4	pions neutral
NT4	pions plus
NT2	scalar mesons
NT3	a0-980 mesons
NT3	chi0-3415 mesons
NT3	f0-1240 mesons
NT3	f0-1300 mesons
NT3	f0-1590 mesons
NT3	f0-1730 mesons
NT3	f0-975 mesons
NT3	k*0-1350 mesons
NT2	strange mesons
NT3	k*-1410 mesons
NT3	k*-1790 mesons
NT3	k*-892 mesons
NT3	k*0-1350 mesons
NT3	k*2-1430 mesons
NT3	k*3-1780 mesons
NT3	k*4-2060 mesons
NT3	k-1460 mesons
NT3	k-1830 mesons
NT3	kaons
NT4	antikaons
NT5	antikaons neutral
NT4	cosmic kaons
NT4	kaons minus
NT4	kaons neutral
NT5	antikaons neutral
NT5	kaons neutral long-lived
NT5	kaons neutral short-lived
NT4	kaons plus
NT3	k1-1280 mesons
NT3	k1-1400 mesons
NT3	k2-1580 mesons
NT3	k2-1770 mesons
NT3	k2-2250 mesons
NT3	k3-2320 mesons
NT3	k4-2500 mesons
NT2	strangeonium
NT3	f2-1525 mesons
NT3	phi j-1850 mesons
NT3	phi-1020 mesons
NT3	phi-1680 mesons
NT2	tensor mesons
NT3	a2-1320 mesons
NT3	a3-2050 mesons
NT3	a4-2040 mesons
NT3	a6-2450 mesons
NT3	chi2-3555 mesons
NT3	f2-1270 mesons
NT3	f2-1410 mesons
NT3	f2-1525 mesons
NT3	f2-1720 mesons
NT3	f2-1810 mesons
NT3	f2-2150 mesons
NT3	f2-2240 mesons
NT3	f4-2030 mesons
NT3	f4-2300 mesons
NT3	f6-2510 mesons
NT3	k*2-1430 mesons
NT3	k*3-1780 mesons
NT3	k*4-2060 mesons
NT3	k2-1580 mesons
NT3	k2-1770 mesons
NT3	k2-2250 mesons
NT3	k3-2320 mesons
NT3	k4-2500 mesons
NT3	omega3-1670 mesons
NT3	phi j-1850 mesons
NT3	pi2-1680 mesons
NT3	pi2-2100 mesons
NT3	rho3-1690 mesons
NT3	rho3-2250 mesons
NT3	rho5-2350 mesons
NT2	toponium
NT2	vector mesons
NT3	d*-2010 mesons
NT3	j psi-3097 mesons
NT3	k*-1410 mesons
NT3	k*-1790 mesons
NT3	k*-892 mesons
NT3	omega-783 mesons
NT3	phi-1020 mesons
NT3	phi-1680 mesons
NT3	psi-3685 mesons
NT3	psi-3770 mesons
NT3	psi-4030 mesons
NT3	psi-4160 mesons
NT3	psi-4415 mesons
NT3	rho-1250 mesons
NT3	rho-1600 mesons
NT3	rho-2150 mesons
NT3	rho-770 mesons
NT3	upsilon-10023 mesons
NT3	upsilon-10355 mesons
NT3	upsilon-10575 mesons
NT3	upsilon-10860 mesons
NT3	upsilon-11020 mesons
NT3	upsilon-9460 mesons
NT2	x-1700 mesons
NT2	x-1935 mesons
NT2	x-2220 mesons
NT2	x-3075 mesons
NT1	photons
NT2	cosmic photons
RT	bose-einstein gas
RT	bose-einstein statistics
RT	boson-fermion symmetry
RT	interacting boson model

BOTANY [33; 49]
- BT1 biology
- NT1 geobotany
- RT plants

BOTSWANA [20; 20]
- BT1 africa
- BT1 developing countries

bottom baryons
- USE beauty baryons

bottom mesons
- USE beauty mesons

bottom particles
- USE beauty particles

bottoming cycles
- USE thermodynamic cycles

BOTTOMONIUM [108; 298] *Dec 87*
(A bound state of bottom and antibottom quarks.)
- SF *upsilon resonances*
- BT1 mesons
- BT2 bosons
- BT2 hadrons
- BT3 elementary particles
- BT1 quarkonium
- NT1 chi b0-10235 mesons
- NT1 chi b0-9860 mesons
- NT1 chi b1-10255 mesons
- NT1 chi b1-9895 mesons
- NT1 chi b2-10270 mesons
- NT1 chi b2-9915 mesons
- NT1 upsilon-10023 mesons
- NT1 upsilon-10355 mesons
- NT1 upsilon-10575 mesons
- NT1 upsilon-10860 mesons
- NT1 upsilon-11020 mesons
- NT1 upsilon-9460 mesons

BOUND STATE [8,585; 8,585]
- RT coupling
- RT efimov effect
- RT energy levels
- RT impulse approximation
- RT kaonium
- RT pi-k atoms
- RT pi-mu atoms
- RT pionium
- RT quasibound state

boundaries (grain)
- USE grain boundaries

§§ **BOUNDARY CONDITIONS**
[12,923; 12,987]
- UF *asymptotic conditions*
- NT1 marshak boundary conditions
- NT1 moving-boundary conditions
- RT asymptotic solutions
- RT boundary-value problems
- RT cauchy problem
- RT differential equations
- RT phi4-field theory

BOUNDARY LAYERS [2,791; 3,748]
- BT1 layers
- NT1 plasma scrape-off layer
- NT1 plasmapause
- NT1 tropopause
- RT fluid flow
- RT plasma sheath
- RT rosseland approximation

boundary value problems
(Between April 1982 and July 1985 this was a valid descriptor.)
- USE boundary-value problems

BOUNDARY-VALUE PROBLEMS
[819; 1,353] *Jul 84*
(Prior to April 1982 this material was indexed to BOUNDARY CONDITIONS; from then till July 1985 the form BOUNDARY VALUE PROBLEMS was used.)
- UF *boundary value problems*
- NT1 cauchy problem
- NT1 dirichlet problem
- RT boundary conditions
- RT differential equations
- RT mathematics

bovine
- USE cattle

BOXCAR EVENT [8; 8]
- BT1 contained explosions
- BT2 underground explosions
- BT3 explosions
- BT1 nuclear explosions
- BT2 explosions
- RT seismic detection

→ *bpa*
- USE bonneville power administratio

BPH [86; 86]
- UF *benzoylphenylhydroxylamine*
- BT1 amines
- BT2 organic compounds
- BT1 hydroxy compounds
- BT2 organic compounds
- RT amides

BR-02 REACTOR [11; 11]
(C.E.N.-S.C.K. Mol, Belgium)
- UF *belgian reactor 02*
- UF *br-2 zero power mock-up react.*
- BT1 beryllium moderated reactors
- BT2 metal moderated reactors
- BT3 reactors
- BT1 enriched uranium reactors
- BT2 reactors
- BT1 research reactors
- BT2 research and test reactors
- BT3 reactors
- BT1 tank type reactors
- BT2 reactors
- BT1 test reactors
- BT2 research and test reactors
- BT3 reactors
- BT2 test facilities
- BT1 thermal reactors
- BT2 reactors
- BT1 water cooled reactors
- BT2 reactors
- BT1 water moderated reactors

```
             BT2    reactors
BR-1 REACTOR [18; 18]
(C.E.N.-S.C.K. Mol, Belgium)
      UF     belgian reactor 1
      BT1    air cooled reactors
         BT2    gas cooled reactors
            BT3    reactors
      BT1    graphite moderated reactors
         BT2    reactors
      BT1    natural uranium reactors
         BT2    reactors
      BT1    research reactors
         BT2    research and test reactors
            BT3    reactors
      BT1    tank type reactors
         BT2    reactors
      BT1    thermal reactors
         BT2    reactors


br-1 reactor (ussr)
      USE    sbr-1 reactor

BR-2 REACTOR [172; 172]
      UF     belgian reactor 2
      BT1    enriched uranium reactors
         BT2    reactors
      BT1    materials testing reactors
         BT2    irradiation reactors
            BT3    reactors
      BT1    tank type reactors
         BT2    reactors
      BT1    thermal reactors
         BT2    reactors
      BT1    water cooled reactors
         BT2    reactors
      BT1    water moderated reactors
         BT2    reactors


br-2 reactor (ussr)
      USE    sbr-2 reactor


br-2 zero power mock-up react.
      USE    br-02 reactor

BR-3 REACTOR [61; 61]
      UF     belgian reactor 3
      BT1    pwr type reactors
         BT2    enriched uranium reactors
            BT3    reactors
         BT2    power reactors
            BT3    reactors
         BT2    thermal reactors
            BT3    reactors
         BT2    water cooled reactors
            BT3    reactors
         BT2    water moderated reactors
            BT3    reactors

BR-3-VN REACTOR [1; 1]
      UF     belgian reactor-3/vulcain
      UF     br-3/vulcain reactor
      UF     vulcain/belgian-3 reactor
      BT1    enriched uranium reactors
         BT2    reactors
      BT1    experimental reactors
         BT2    research and test reactors
            BT3    reactors
      BT1    heavy water cooled reactors
         BT2    reactors
      BT1    heavy water moderated reactors
         BT2    reactors
      BT1    mixed spectrum reactors
         BT2    reactors
      BT1    tank type reactors
         BT2    reactors
      BT1    water cooled reactors
         BT2    reactors
      BT1    water moderated reactors
         BT2    reactors


br-3/vulcain reactor
      USE    br-3-vn reactor

br-5 reactor (ussr)
      USE    sbr-5 reactor


brackish water ecosystems
      USE    aquatic ecosystems

BRADWELL REACTOR [21; 21]
(Blackwater Estuary, Essex, UK)
      BT1    magnox type reactors
         BT2    gcr type reactors
            BT3    gas cooled reactors
               BT4    reactors
            BT3    graphite moderated reactors
               BT4    reactors
         BT2    natural uranium reactors
            BT3    reactors
         BT2    power reactors
            BT3    reactors
      BT1    thermal reactors
         BT2    reactors


bradykinin
      USE    kinins
      AND    peptide hormones


bragg angle
      USE    bragg reflection

BRAGG CURVE [328; 328]
      UF     bragg peak
      UF     bragg zone
      BT1    diagrams
         BT2    information
      RT     energy losses
      RT     ionization
      RT     let


bragg diffraction
      USE    bragg reflection

BRAGG GRAY CHAMBERS [246; 246]
      UF     air wall ionization chambers
      UF     bragg-gray chambers
      UF     cavity ionization chambers
      UF     tissue equivalent chambers
      BT1    dosemeters
         BT2    measuring instruments
      BT1    ionization chambers
         BT2    radiation detectors
            BT3    measuring instruments


bragg law
      USE    bragg reflection


bragg peak
      USE    bragg curve

BRAGG REFLECTION [1,730; 1,730]
      UF     bragg angle
      UF     bragg diffraction
      UF     bragg law
      UF     laue-bragg scattering
      BT1    reflection
      RT     x-ray diffraction


bragg zone
      USE    bragg curve


bragg-gray chambers
      USE    bragg gray chambers

BRAIDWOOD-1 REACTOR [27; 27]
(BRAIDWOOD, Illinois, USA)
      BT1    pwr type reactors
         BT2    enriched uranium reactors
            BT3    reactors
         BT2    power reactors
            BT3    reactors
         BT2    thermal reactors
            BT3    reactors
         BT2    water cooled reactors
            BT3    reactors
         BT2    water moderated reactors
            BT3    reactors

BRAIDWOOD-2 REACTOR [25; 25]
(BRAIDWOOD, Illinois, USA)
      BT1    pwr type reactors
         BT2    enriched uranium reactors
            BT3    reactors
         BT2    power reactors
            BT3    reactors
         BT2    thermal reactors
            BT3    reactors
         BT2    water cooled reactors
            BT3    reactors
         BT2    water moderated reactors
            BT3    reactors

BRAIN [12,010; 15,002]
      BT1    central nervous system
         BT2    nervous system
      BT1    organs
         BT2    body
      NT1    cerebellum
      NT1    cerebrum
         NT2    cerebral cortex
      NT1    hippocampus
      NT1    hypothalamus
      NT1    olfactory bulbs
      NT1    thalamus
      RT     electroencephalography
      RT     encephalitis
      RT     endorphins
      RT     head
      RT     mental disorders
      RT     pineal gland
      RT     skull

BRAKES [46; 46]
      BT1    machine parts


braking radiation
      USE    bremsstrahlung

BRANCHING RATIO [10,335; 10,335]
      RT     bethe-heitler theory
      RT     decay
      RT     ft value
      RT     mixing ratio

BRANNERITE [64; 64]
      BT1    oxide minerals
         BT2    minerals
      BT1    thorium minerals
         BT2    radioactive minerals
            BT3    minerals
            BT3    radioactive materials
               BT4    materials
      BT1    uranium minerals
         BT2    radioactive minerals
            BT3    minerals
            BT3    radioactive materials
               BT4    materials
      RT     thorium oxides
      RT     titanium oxides
      RT     uranium oxides


brasimone pec reactor
      USE    pec brasimone reactor

BRASS [237; 282]
      BT1    copper base alloys
         BT2    copper alloys
            BT3    alloys
      BT1    zinc alloys
         BT2    alloys
      NT1    brass-alpha
      NT1    brass-beta
      RT     heusler alloys
```

BRASS-ALPHA [32; 32]
BT1 brass
BT2 copper base alloys
BT3 copper alloys
BT4 alloys
BT2 zinc alloys
BT3 alloys

BRASS-BETA [18; 18]
BT1 brass
BT2 copper base alloys
BT3 copper alloys
BT4 alloys
BT2 zinc alloys
BT3 alloys

BRASSICA [188; 188]
UF cabbage
UF cauliflower
UF kale
UF mustard
UF sarson
UF turnips
BT1 plants
BT1 vegetables
BT2 food

braunschweig experimental r.
USE fmrb reactor

braunschweig research reactor
USE fmrb reactor

BRAVO EVENT [5; 5] *Jan 85*
BT1 castle project
BT1 surface explosions
BT2 explosions
BT1 thermonuclear explosions
BT2 nuclear explosions
BT3 explosions

BRAYTON CYCLE [283; 283]
UF+ *brayton cycle power systems*
BT1 thermodynamic cycles
RT thermodynamics

brayton cycle power systems
USE brayton cycle
AND power generation

BRAZED JOINTS [174; 174]
BT1 joints
RT brazing

BRAZIL [1,404; 1,404]
UF+ *goiania radiological emergency*
BT1 developing countries
BT1 south america
BT2 latin america
RT amazon river

→ *brazil lab for synchrotron rad*
USE brazilian lnls

brazil triga reactor
USE triga-brazil reactor

BRAZILIAN CNEN [186; 186] *Aug 82*
(Comissao Nacional de Energia Nuclear de Brasil.)
UF *cnen brazil*
UF *comissao nacional energia nucl*
BT1 brazilian organizations
BT2 national organizations

→ **BRAZILIAN LNLS** [2; 2] *Feb 91*
(Brazilian Laboratory for Synchrotron Radiation.)
UF *brazil lab for synchrotron rad*
BT1 brazilian organizations
BT2 national organizations

→ *brazilian lnls synchrotron*
USE lnls storage ring

BRAZILIAN ORGANIZATIONS [86; 364] *Mar 77*
BT1 national organizations
NT1 brazilian cnen
NT1 brazilian lnls
NT1 nuclebras

BRAZING [388; 388]
UF *hard soldering*
BT1 welding
BT2 joining
BT3 fabrication
RT brazed joints
RT brazing alloys
RT soldering

BRAZING ALLOYS [130; 130]
BT1 alloys
RT brazing
RT filler metals

BREAD [61; 61]
BT1 food
RT flour

BREAKDOWN [1,556; 1,556]
(Limited to electric discharge phenomena. See also CLEAVAGE or DECOMPOSITION.)
RT electric discharges
RT electric potential
RT electric sparks
RT electrical faults
RT flashover
RT lichtenberg figures
RT overvoltage
RT paschen law
RT spark gaps

breakers (circuit)
USE circuit breakers

BREAKEVEN [130; 130]
UF *zero energy balance*
BT1 energy balance
RT lawson criterion
RT plasma
RT thermonuclear reactors

breakup fusion
USE incomplete fusion reactions

BREAKUP REACTIONS [3,192; 3,192]
BT1 nuclear reactions

breasts
USE mammary glands

BREATH [350; 350]
UF *breathing*
RT air
RT exhalation
RT inhalation
RT respiration
RT respirators
RT respiratory system

breathing
USE breath

BREEDER REACTORS [1,046; 25,157]
BT1 reactors
NT1 fbr type reactors
NT2 aipfr reactor
NT2 gcfr type reactors
NT3 gcfr reactor
NT2 lmfbr type reactors
NT3 beloyarsk-3 reactor
NT3 beloyarsk-4 reactor
NT3 bn-1600 reactor
NT3 bn-350 reactor
NT3 bn-800 reactor
NT3 bor-60 reactor
NT3 cdfr reactor
NT3 clinch river breeder reactor
NT3 dfr reactor
NT3 ebr-1 reactor
NT3 ebr-2 reactor
NT3 enrico fermi-1 reactor
NT3 joyo reactor
NT3 kalpakkam lmfbr reactor
NT3 monju reactor
NT3 pfr reactor
NT3 phenix reactor
NT3 plbr reactor
NT3 rapsodie reactor
NT3 sbr-2 reactor
NT3 sbr-5 reactor
NT3 snr reactor
NT3 snr-2 reactor
NT3 super phenix reactor
NT2 pec brasimone reactor
NT2 sbr-1 reactor
NT2 zebra reactor
NT1 lwbr type reactors
RT accelerator breeders
RT breeding blankets
RT breeding pellets
RT zpr-9 reactor

BREEDING [1,053; 1,053]
(Fuel breeding only. See also ANIMAL BREEDING and PLANT BREEDING.)
BT1 nuclear fuel conversion
RT accelerator breeders
RT breeding blankets
RT breeding pellets
RT breeding ratio
RT transmutation

BREEDING BLANKETS [5,301; 5,301]
UF *blankets (breeding)*
RT breeder reactors
RT breeding
RT breeding pellets
RT fertile materials
RT flibe
RT lotus facility
RT reactor components
RT thermonuclear reactors
RT tritium recovery

BREEDING PELLETS [180; 180]
UF *pellets (breeding)*
RT breeder reactors
RT breeding
RT breeding blankets
RT pelletizing
RT thermonuclear reactors

BREEDING RATIO [1,107; 1,107]
BT1 conversion ratio
RT breeding

BREIT-WIGNER FORMULA [603; 603]
UF *single-level resonance formula*
RT cross sections
RT multilevel analysis

BREMSSTRAHLUNG [6,788; 13,423]
UF *braking radiation*
BT1 electromagnetic radiation
BT2 radiations
NT1 cyclotron radiation
NT1 internal bremsstrahlung
NT1 ondulator radiation
NT1 synchrotron radiation
RT bethe-heitler theory
RT migdal theory
RT peierls method
RT penfold-leiss method
RT radiation length
RT tagged photon method

bremsstrahlung (magnetic)
USE   synchrotron radiation

BRICKS [151; 151]
BT1   building materials
BT2   materials

→ **BRIDGES** [0; 0] *Sep 91*
BT1   mechanical structures

bridges (electric)
USE   electric bridges

BRIDGMAN METHOD [166; 166]
RT   crystal growth

BRIGGS CRITERION [2; 2]
(Allows distinguishing between absolute and convective plasma instabilities.)
RT   absolute instabilities
RT   convective instabilities

BRIGHTNESS [4,627; 4,627]
BT1   optical properties
BT2   physical properties
RT   beam emittance
RT   illuminance
RT   luminosity

BRILLOUIN EFFECT [674; 674]
UF   *brillouin scattering*
BT1   coherent scattering
BT2   scattering

brillouin scattering
USE   brillouin effect

BRILLOUIN ZONES [829; 829]
BT1   zones
RT   band theory

BRINELL HARDNESS [57; 57]
RT   hardness

BRINES [1,038; 1,038]
RT   salts
RT   solutions

BRINKMAN-KRAMERS APPROXIMATION [56; 56]
UF   *approximation (brinkman-kram.)*
RT   perturbation theory
RT   scattering

BRITISH COLUMBIA [55; 55]
BT1   canada
BT2   developed countries
BT2   north america
RT   blizzard deposit

british exper. pile operation
USE   bepo reactor

BRITISH GUIANA [1; 1]
BT1   guyana
BT2   developing countries
BT2   south america
BT3   latin america

british nuclear fuels limited
USE   bnfl

brittle-ductile transitions
USE   ductile-brittle transitions

BRITTLENESS [957; 957]
BT1   mechanical properties
RT   crack propagation
RT   ductile-brittle transitions
RT   embrittlement

broadening (line)
USE   line broadening

BROKDORF REACTOR [106; 106] *Sep 76*
(Wilstermarsch, Schleswig-Holstein, Federal Republic of Germany)
UF   *kernkraftwerk brokdorf*
BT1   pwr type reactors
BT2   enriched uranium reactors
BT3   reactors
BT2   power reactors
BT3   reactors
BT2   thermal reactors
BT3   reactors
BT2   water cooled reactors
BT3   reactors
BT2   water moderated reactors
BT3   reactors

BROKEN-PAIR APPROXIMATION [47; 47] *Aug 78*
RT   nuclear theory
RT   shell models

bromamines
USE   amines
AND   organic bromine compounds

BROMATES [241; 241]
(Specific compounds should be indexed by coordination of a descriptor of the form (CATION) COMPOUNDS and the above anion descriptor.)
BT1   bromine compounds
BT2   halogen compounds
BT1   oxygen compounds
RT   bromic acid

BROMIC ACID [28; 28]
BT1   bromine compounds
BT2   halogen compounds
BT1   inorganic acids
BT2   hydrogen compounds
BT2   inorganic compounds
BT1   oxygen compounds
RT   bromates

BROMIDES [747; 3,426]
BT1   bromine compounds
BT2   halogen compounds
BT1   halides
BT2   halogen compounds
NT1   actinium bromides
NT1   aluminium bromides
NT1   americium bromides
NT1   antimony bromides
NT1   arsenic bromides
NT1   astatine bromides
NT1   barium bromides
NT1   berkelium bromides
NT1   beryllium bromides
NT1   bismuth bromides
NT1   boron bromides
NT1   cadmium bromides
NT1   calcium bromides
NT1   californium bromides
NT1   cerium bromides
NT1   cesium bromides
NT1   chromium bromides
NT1   cobalt bromides
NT1   copper bromides
NT1   curium bromides
NT1   dysprosium bromides
NT1   einsteinium bromides
NT1   erbium bromides
NT1   europium bromides
NT1   fermium bromides
NT1   francium bromides
NT1   gadolinium bromides
NT1   gallium bromides
NT1   germanium bromides
NT1   gold bromides
NT1   hafnium bromides
NT1   holmium bromides
NT1   indium bromides
NT1   iodine bromides
NT1   iron bromides
NT1   lanthanum bromides
NT1   lead bromides
NT1   lithium bromides
NT1   lutetium bromides
NT1   magnesium bromides
NT1   manganese bromides
NT1   mercury bromides
NT1   molybdenum bromides
NT1   neodymium bromides
NT1   neptunium bromides
NT1   nickel bromides
NT1   niobium bromides
NT1   palladium bromides
NT1   phosphorus bromides
NT1   platinum bromides
NT1   plutonium bromides
NT1   polonium bromides
NT1   potassium bromides
NT1   praseodymium bromides
NT1   promethium bromides
NT1   protactinium bromides
NT1   radium bromides
NT1   rhenium bromides
NT1   rhodium bromides
NT1   rubidium bromides
NT1   ruthenium bromides
NT1   samarium bromides
NT1   scandium bromides
NT1   selenium bromides
NT1   silicon bromides
NT1   silver bromides
NT1   sodium bromides
NT1   strontium bromides
NT1   tantalum bromides
NT1   teab
NT1   technetium bromides
NT1   tellurium bromides
NT1   terbium bromides
NT1   thallium bromides
NT1   thorium bromides
NT1   thulium bromides
NT1   tin bromides
NT1   titanium bromides
NT1   tungsten bromides
NT1   uranium bromides
NT1   vanadium bromides
NT1   xenon bromides
NT1   ytterbium bromides
NT1   yttrium bromides
NT1   zinc bromides
NT1   zirconium bromides
RT   bromine additions
RT   hydrobromic acid
RT   oxybromides

→ **BROMINATED ALIPHATIC HYDROCARB** [0; 0]
(Prior to October 1991, this concept was indexed by ORGANIC BROMINE COMPOUNDS.)
BT1   halogenated aliphatic hydrocar
BT2   organic halogen compounds
BT3   organic compounds
BT1   organic bromine compounds
BT2   organic halogen compounds
BT3   organic compounds

→ **BROMINATED AROMATIC HYDROCARBO** [0; 0]
(Prior to October 1991, this concept was indexed by ORGANIC BROMINE COMPOUNDS and AROMATICS.)
BT1   halogenated aromatic hydrocarb
BT2   aromatics
BT3   organic compounds
BT2   organic halogen compounds
BT3   organic compounds
BT1   organic bromine compounds
BT2   organic halogen compounds
BT3   organic compounds

brominated hydrocarbons
  USE organic bromine compounds

BROMINATION [188; 188]
  BT1 halogenation
  BT2 chemical reactions

BROMINE [1,559; 1,559]
  UF *bromine bromides*
  BT1 halogens
  BT2 nonmetals
  BT3 elements

BROMINE ADDITIONS [34; 34]
  RT bromides
  RT crystal doping
  RT doped materials

bromine bromides
  USE bromine

BROMINE CHLORIDES [13; 13]
  UF *chlorine bromides*
  BT1 bromine compounds
  BT2 halogen compounds
  BT1 chlorides
  BT2 chlorine compounds
  BT3 halogen compounds
  BT2 halides
  BT3 halogen compounds

BROMINE COMPLEXES [31; 31]
  BT1 complexes

BROMINE COMPOUNDS [265; 4,014]
  BT1 halogen compounds
  NT1 bromates
  NT1 bromic acid
 *NT1 bromides
  NT1 bromine chlorides
  NT1 bromine fluorides
  NT1 bromine oxides
  NT1 hydrobromic acid
  NT1 oxybromides
  NT1 perbromates
  RT organic bromine compounds

BROMINE FLUORIDES [44; 44]
  UF *fluorine bromides*
  BT1 bromine compounds
  BT2 halogen compounds
  BT1 fluorides
  BT2 fluorine compounds
  BT3 halogen compounds
  BT2 halides
  BT3 halogen compounds

bromine iodides
  USE iodine bromides

BROMINE IONS [251; 251]
  BT1 ions
  BT2 charged particles

BROMINE ISOTOPES [141; 1,743]
  NT1 bromine 69
  NT1 bromine 70
  NT1 bromine 71
  NT1 bromine 72
  NT1 bromine 73
  NT1 bromine 74
  NT1 bromine 75
  NT1 bromine 76
  NT1 bromine 77
  NT1 bromine 78
  NT1 bromine 79
  NT1 bromine 80
  NT1 bromine 81
  NT1 bromine 82
  NT1 bromine 83
  NT1 bromine 84
  NT1 bromine 85
  NT1 bromine 86
  NT1 bromine 87
  NT1 bromine 88
  NT1 bromine 89
  NT1 bromine 90
  NT1 bromine 91
  NT1 bromine 92
  NT1 bromine 93

BROMINE OXIDES [10; 10]
  BT1 bromine compounds
  BT2 halogen compounds
  BT1 oxides
  BT2 chalcogenides
  BT2 oxygen compounds
  RT oxybromides

BROMINE 69 [10; 10]
  BT1 beta-plus decay radioisotopes
  BT2 beta decay radioisotopes
  BT3 radioisotopes
  BT4 isotopes
  BT1 bromine isotopes
  BT1 intermediate mass nuclei
  BT2 nuclei
  BT1 odd-even nuclei
  BT2 nuclei

BROMINE 70 [4; 4]
  BT1 beta-plus decay radioisotopes
  BT2 beta decay radioisotopes
  BT3 radioisotopes
  BT4 isotopes
  BT1 bromine isotopes
  BT1 intermediate mass nuclei
  BT2 nuclei
  BT1 millisec living radioisotopes
  BT2 radioisotopes
  BT3 isotopes
  BT1 odd-odd nuclei
  BT2 nuclei

BROMINE 71 [6; 6]
  BT1 beta-plus decay radioisotopes
  BT2 beta decay radioisotopes
  BT3 radioisotopes
  BT4 isotopes
  BT1 bromine isotopes
  BT1 electron capture radioisotopes
  BT2 beta decay radioisotopes
  BT3 radioisotopes
  BT4 isotopes
  BT1 intermediate mass nuclei
  BT2 nuclei
  BT1 odd-even nuclei
  BT2 nuclei
  BT1 seconds living radioisotopes
  BT2 radioisotopes
  BT3 isotopes

BROMINE 71 TARGET [3; 3] *May 80*
  BT1 targets

BROMINE 72 [21; 21]
  BT1 beta-plus decay radioisotopes
  BT2 beta decay radioisotopes
  BT3 radioisotopes
  BT4 isotopes
  BT1 bromine isotopes
  BT1 intermediate mass nuclei
  BT2 nuclei
  BT1 minutes living radioisotopes
  BT2 radioisotopes
  BT3 isotopes
  BT1 odd-odd nuclei
  BT2 nuclei

BROMINE 73 [30; 30]
  BT1 beta-plus decay radioisotopes
  BT2 beta decay radioisotopes
  BT3 radioisotopes
  BT4 isotopes
  BT1 bromine isotopes
  BT1 electron capture radioisotopes
  BT2 beta decay radioisotopes
  BT3 radioisotopes
  BT4 isotopes
  BT1 intermediate mass nuclei
  BT2 nuclei

BT1 minutes living radioisotopes
  BT2 radioisotopes
  BT3 isotopes
  BT1 odd-even nuclei
  BT2 nuclei

BROMINE 74 [39; 39]
  BT1 beta-plus decay radioisotopes
  BT2 beta decay radioisotopes
  BT3 radioisotopes
  BT4 isotopes
  BT1 bromine isotopes
  BT1 electron capture radioisotopes
  BT2 beta decay radioisotopes
  BT3 radioisotopes
  BT4 isotopes
  BT1 intermediate mass nuclei
  BT2 nuclei
  BT1 minutes living radioisotopes
  BT2 radioisotopes
  BT3 isotopes
  BT1 odd-odd nuclei
  BT2 nuclei

BROMINE 75 [140; 140]
  BT1 beta-plus decay radioisotopes
  BT2 beta decay radioisotopes
  BT3 radioisotopes
  BT4 isotopes
  BT1 bromine isotopes
  BT1 electron capture radioisotopes
  BT2 beta decay radioisotopes
  BT3 radioisotopes
  BT4 isotopes
  BT1 hours living radioisotopes
  BT2 radioisotopes
  BT3 isotopes
  BT1 intermediate mass nuclei
  BT2 nuclei
  BT1 odd-even nuclei
  BT2 nuclei

BROMINE 76 [118; 118]
  BT1 beta-plus decay radioisotopes
  BT2 beta decay radioisotopes
  BT3 radioisotopes
  BT4 isotopes
  BT1 bromine isotopes
  BT1 electron capture radioisotopes
  BT2 beta decay radioisotopes
  BT3 radioisotopes
  BT4 isotopes
  BT1 hours living radioisotopes
  BT2 radioisotopes
  BT3 isotopes
  BT1 intermediate mass nuclei
  BT2 nuclei
  BT1 isomeric transition isotopes
  BT2 radioisotopes
  BT3 isotopes
  BT1 odd-odd nuclei
  BT2 nuclei
  BT1 seconds living radioisotopes
  BT2 radioisotopes
  BT3 isotopes

BROMINE 76 TARGET [4; 4] *Feb 79*
  BT1 targets

BROMINE 77 [298; 298]
  BT1 beta-plus decay radioisotopes
  BT2 beta decay radioisotopes
  BT3 radioisotopes
  BT4 isotopes
  BT1 bromine isotopes
  BT1 days living radioisotopes
  BT2 radioisotopes
  BT3 isotopes
  BT1 electron capture radioisotopes
  BT2 beta decay radioisotopes
  BT3 radioisotopes
  BT4 isotopes
  BT1 intermediate mass nuclei
  BT2 nuclei
  BT1 internal conversion radioisoto
  BT2 radioisotopes
  BT3 isotopes
  BT1 isomeric transition isotopes

BT2   radioisotopes
BT3   isotopes
BT1   minutes living radioisotopes
BT2   radioisotopes
BT3   isotopes
BT1   odd-even nuclei
BT2   nuclei

BROMINE 78 [34; 34]
BT1   beta-plus decay radioisotopes
BT2   beta decay radioisotopes
BT3   radioisotopes
BT4   isotopes
BT1   bromine isotopes
BT1   electron capture radioisotopes
BT2   beta decay radioisotopes
BT3   radioisotopes
BT4   isotopes
BT1   intermediate mass nuclei
BT2   nuclei
BT1   minutes living radioisotopes
BT2   radioisotopes
BT3   isotopes
BT1   odd-odd nuclei
BT2   nuclei

BROMINE 79 [152; 152]
BT1   bromine isotopes
BT1   intermediate mass nuclei
BT2   nuclei
BT1   isomeric transition isotopes
BT2   radioisotopes
BT3   isotopes
BT1   odd-even nuclei
BT2   nuclei
BT1   seconds living radioisotopes
BT2   radioisotopes
BT3   isotopes
BT1   stable isotopes
BT2   isotopes
RT   bromine 79 beams

BROMINE 79 BEAMS [34; 34] *Jul 76*
BT1   ion beams
BT2   beams
RT   bromine 79

BROMINE 79 REACTIONS [4; 4]
May 87
BT1   heavy ion reactions
BT2   nuclear reactions

BROMINE 79 TARGET [132; 132]
BT1   targets

BROMINE 80 [220; 220]
BT1   beta-minus decay radioisotopes
BT2   beta decay radioisotopes
BT3   radioisotopes
BT4   isotopes
BT1   beta-plus decay radioisotopes
BT2   beta decay radioisotopes
BT3   radioisotopes
BT4   isotopes
BT1   bromine isotopes
BT1   electron capture radioisotopes
BT2   beta decay radioisotopes
BT3   radioisotopes
BT4   isotopes
BT1   hours living radioisotopes
BT2   radioisotopes
BT3   isotopes
BT1   intermediate mass nuclei
BT2   nuclei
BT1   internal conversion radioisoto
BT2   radioisotopes
BT3   isotopes
BT1   isomeric transition isotopes
BT2   radioisotopes
BT3   isotopes
BT1   minutes living radioisotopes
BT2   radioisotopes
BT3   isotopes
BT1   odd-odd nuclei
BT2   nuclei

BROMINE 81 [166; 166]
BT1   bromine isotopes
BT1   intermediate mass nuclei
BT2   nuclei
BT1   odd-even nuclei
BT2   nuclei
BT1   stable isotopes
BT2   isotopes

BROMINE 81 REACTIONS [12; 12]
Nov 79
BT1   heavy ion reactions
BT2   nuclear reactions

BROMINE 81 TARGET [133; 133]
BT1   targets

BROMINE 82 [584; 584]
BT1   beta-minus decay radioisotopes
BT2   beta decay radioisotopes
BT3   radioisotopes
BT4   isotopes
BT1   bromine isotopes
BT1   days living radioisotopes
BT2   radioisotopes
BT3   isotopes
BT1   intermediate mass nuclei
BT2   nuclei
BT1   internal conversion radioisoto
BT2   radioisotopes
BT3   isotopes
BT1   isomeric transition isotopes
BT2   radioisotopes
BT3   isotopes
BT1   minutes living radioisotopes
BT2   radioisotopes
BT3   isotopes
BT1   odd-odd nuclei
BT2   nuclei

BROMINE 83 [25; 25]
BT1   beta-minus decay radioisotopes
BT2   beta decay radioisotopes
BT3   radioisotopes
BT4   isotopes
BT1   bromine isotopes
BT1   hours living radioisotopes
BT2   radioisotopes
BT3   isotopes
BT1   intermediate mass nuclei
BT2   nuclei
BT1   isomeric transition isotopes
BT2   radioisotopes
BT3   isotopes
BT1   nanosec living radioisotopes
BT2   radioisotopes
BT3   isotopes
BT1   odd-even nuclei
BT2   nuclei

BROMINE 84 [12; 12]
BT1   beta-minus decay radioisotopes
BT2   beta decay radioisotopes
BT3   radioisotopes
BT4   isotopes
BT1   bromine isotopes
BT1   intermediate mass nuclei
BT2   nuclei
BT1   minutes living radioisotopes
BT2   radioisotopes
BT3   isotopes
BT1   odd-odd nuclei
BT2   nuclei

BROMINE 85 [18; 18]
BT1   beta-minus decay radioisotopes
BT2   beta decay radioisotopes
BT3   radioisotopes
BT4   isotopes
BT1   bromine isotopes
BT1   intermediate mass nuclei
BT2   nuclei
BT1   minutes living radioisotopes
BT2   radioisotopes
BT3   isotopes
BT1   odd-even nuclei
BT2   nuclei

BROMINE 86 [20; 20]
BT1   beta-minus decay radioisotopes
BT2   beta decay radioisotopes
BT3   radioisotopes
BT4   isotopes
BT1   bromine isotopes
BT1   intermediate mass nuclei
BT2   nuclei
BT1   odd-odd nuclei
BT2   nuclei
BT1   seconds living radioisotopes
BT2   radioisotopes
BT3   isotopes

BROMINE 87 [79; 79]
BT1   beta-minus decay radioisotopes
BT2   beta decay radioisotopes
BT3   radioisotopes
BT4   isotopes
BT1   bromine isotopes
BT1   intermediate mass nuclei
BT2   nuclei
BT1   odd-even nuclei
BT2   nuclei
BT1   seconds living radioisotopes
BT2   radioisotopes
BT3   isotopes

BROMINE 88 [45; 45]
BT1   beta-minus decay radioisotopes
BT2   beta decay radioisotopes
BT3   radioisotopes
BT4   isotopes
BT1   bromine isotopes
BT1   intermediate mass nuclei
BT2   nuclei
BT1   odd-odd nuclei
BT2   nuclei
BT1   seconds living radioisotopes
BT2   radioisotopes
BT3   isotopes

BROMINE 89 [32; 32]
BT1   beta-minus decay radioisotopes
BT2   beta decay radioisotopes
BT3   radioisotopes
BT4   isotopes
BT1   bromine isotopes
BT1   intermediate mass nuclei
BT2   nuclei
BT1   odd-even nuclei
BT2   nuclei
BT1   seconds living radioisotopes
BT2   radioisotopes
BT3   isotopes

BROMINE 90 [27; 27]
BT1   beta-minus decay radioisotopes
BT2   beta decay radioisotopes
BT3   radioisotopes
BT4   isotopes
BT1   bromine isotopes
BT1   intermediate mass nuclei
BT2   nuclei
BT1   odd-odd nuclei
BT2   nuclei
BT1   seconds living radioisotopes
BT2   radioisotopes
BT3   isotopes

BROMINE 91 [23; 23]
BT1   beta-minus decay radioisotopes
BT2   beta decay radioisotopes
BT3   radioisotopes
BT4   isotopes
BT1   bromine isotopes
BT1   intermediate mass nuclei
BT2   nuclei
BT1   millisec living radioisotopes
BT2   radioisotopes
BT3   isotopes
BT1   odd-even nuclei
BT2   nuclei

BROMINE 92 [17; 17]
  BT1   beta-minus decay radioisotopes
    BT2   beta decay radioisotopes
      BT3   radioisotopes
        BT4   isotopes
  BT1   bromine isotopes
  BT1   intermediate mass nuclei
    BT2   nuclei
  BT1   millisec living radioisotopes
    BT2   radioisotopes
      BT3   isotopes
  BT1   odd-odd nuclei
    BT2   nuclei

BROMINE 93 [2; 2] *Oct 88*
  BT1   beta-minus decay radioisotopes
    BT2   beta decay radioisotopes
      BT3   radioisotopes
        BT4   isotopes
  BT1   bromine isotopes
  BT1   intermediate mass nuclei
    BT2   nuclei
  BT1   millisec living radioisotopes
    BT2   radioisotopes
      BT3   isotopes
  BT1   odd-even nuclei
    BT2   nuclei

bromodeoxyuridine
  USE   budr

BROMOFORM [43; 43]
  BT1   organic bromine compounds
    BT2   organic halogen compounds
      BT3   organic compounds
  RT   hydrocarbons
  RT   methane

BROMOSULFOPHTHALEIN [65; 65]
  UF   *bromsulphalein*
  UF   *bsp*
  BT1   carboxylic acid esters
    BT2   esters
      BT3   organic compounds
  BT1   dyes
  BT1   indicators
  BT1   organic bromine compounds
    BT2   organic halogen compounds
      BT3   organic compounds
  BT1   polyphenols
    BT2   phenols
      BT3   aromatics
        BT4   organic compounds
      BT3   hydroxy compounds
        BT4   organic compounds
  BT1   reagents
  BT1   sulfonic acids
    BT2   organic acids
      BT3   organic compounds
    BT2   organic sulfur compounds
      BT3   organic compounds
  RT   phthalic acid
  RT   radiopharmaceuticals

BROMOURACILS [94; 417]
  BT1   antimetabolites
    BT2   drugs
  BT1   organic bromine compounds
    BT2   organic halogen compounds
      BT3   organic compounds
  BT1   uracils
    BT2   hydroxy compounds
      BT3   organic compounds
    BT2   pyrimidines
      BT3   azines
        BT4   heterocyclic compounds
          BT5   organic compounds
        BT4   organic nitrogen compounds
          BT5   organic compounds
  NT1   budr

bromsulphalein
  USE   bromosulfophthalein

BRONCHI [943; 943]
  BT1   respiratory system
  RT   bronchitis
  RT   lungs
  RT   respiratory tract cells

BRONCHITIS [139; 139]
  BT1   respiratory system diseases
    BT2   diseases
  RT   bronchi

bronchogenic carcinoma
  USE   carcinomas
  AND   respiratory system diseases

BRONCHOPNEUMONIA [17; 17]
  BT1   pneumonia
    BT2   respiratory system diseases
      BT3   diseases

BRONZE [321; 321]
  BT1   copper base alloys
    BT2   copper alloys
      BT3   alloys
  BT1   tin alloys
    BT2   alloys
  RT   heusler alloys

BROOKHAVEN AGS [846; 846]
  BT1   synchrotrons
    BT2   cyclic accelerators
      BT3   accelerators

BROOKHAVEN CYCLOTRON [21; 21]
  BT1   isochronous cyclotrons
    BT2   cyclotrons
      BT3   cyclic accelerators
        BT4   accelerators

brookhaven graph. res. reactor
  USE   bgrr reactor

brookhaven high flux beam r.
  USE   hfbr reactor

brookhaven inters. stor. accel
  USE   isabelle storage rings

brookhaven medical res. reacto
  USE   mrr reactor

brookhaven national laboratory
  USE   bnl

BROOKHAVEN RHIC [212; 212]
  May 86
  UF   *relat. heavy ion collid. (bnl)*
  UF   *rhic (brookhaven)*
  BT1   heavy ion accelerators
    BT2   accelerators
  BT1   storage rings

BROOKHAVEN 200-MEV LINAC
  [28; 28] *Sep 79*
  BT1   linear accelerators
    BT2   accelerators

BROWNIAN MOVEMENT [461; 461]
  RT   collisions
  RT   colloids

BROWNS FERRY-1 REACTOR
  [310; 310]
  (Decatur, Alabama, USA)
  BT1   bwr type reactors
    BT2   enriched uranium reactors
      BT3   reactors
    BT2   power reactors
      BT3   reactors
    BT2   thermal reactors
      BT3   reactors
    BT2   water cooled reactors
      BT3   reactors
    BT2   water moderated reactors
      BT3   reactors
  BT1   mixed spectrum reactors
    BT2   reactors

BROWNS FERRY-2 REACTOR
  [145; 145]
  (Decatur, Alabama, USA)
  BT1   bwr type reactors
    BT2   enriched uranium reactors
      BT3   reactors
    BT2   power reactors
      BT3   reactors
    BT2   thermal reactors
      BT3   reactors
    BT2   water cooled reactors
      BT3   reactors
    BT2   water moderated reactors
      BT3   reactors
  BT1   mixed spectrum reactors
    BT2   reactors

BROWNS FERRY-3 REACTOR
  [142; 142]
  (Decatur, Alabama, USA)
  BT1   bwr type reactors
    BT2   enriched uranium reactors
      BT3   reactors
    BT2   power reactors
      BT3   reactors
    BT2   thermal reactors
      BT3   reactors
    BT2   water cooled reactors
      BT3   reactors
    BT2   water moderated reactors
      BT3   reactors
  BT1   mixed spectrum reactors
    BT2   reactors

BRR REACTOR [10; 10]
  (Battelle Columbus Laboratories,
  Columbus, Ohio, USA)
  UF   *battelle research reactor*
  UF   *bmi reactor*
  BT1   enriched uranium reactors
    BT2   reactors
  BT1   isotope production reactors
    BT2   irradiation reactors
      BT3   reactors
  BT1   pool type reactors
    BT2   water cooled reactors
      BT3   reactors
    BT2   water moderated reactors
      BT3   reactors
  BT1   research reactors
    BT2   research and test reactors
      BT3   reactors
  BT1   test reactors
    BT2   research and test reactors
      BT3   reactors
    BT2   test facilities
  BT1   thermal reactors
    BT2   reactors

BRUCE-1 REACTOR [141; 141]
  (Tiverton, Ontario, Canada)
  BT1   candu type reactors
    BT2   heavy water moderated reactors
      BT3   reactors
    BT2   pressure tube reactors
      BT3   power reactors
        BT4   reactors
    BT2   thermal reactors
      BT3   reactors
  BT1   natural uranium reactors
    BT2   reactors
  BT1   phwr type reactors
    BT2   heavy water cooled reactors
      BT3   reactors
    BT2   heavy water moderated reactors
      BT3   reactors

BRUCE-2 REACTOR [72; 72]
(Tiverton, Ontario, Canada)
- BT1 candu type reactors
  - BT2 heavy water moderated reactors
    - BT3 reactors
  - BT2 pressure tube reactors
    - BT3 power reactors
      - BT4 reactors
  - BT2 thermal reactors
    - BT3 reactors
- BT1 natural uranium reactors
  - BT2 reactors
- BT1 phwr type reactors
  - BT2 heavy water cooled reactors
    - BT3 reactors
  - BT2 heavy water moderated reactors
    - BT3 reactors

BRUCE-3 REACTOR [60; 60]
(Tiverton, Ontario, Canada)
- BT1 candu type reactors
  - BT2 heavy water moderated reactors
    - BT3 reactors
  - BT2 pressure tube reactors
    - BT3 power reactors
      - BT4 reactors
  - BT2 thermal reactors
    - BT3 reactors
- BT1 natural uranium reactors
  - BT2 reactors
- BT1 phwr type reactors
  - BT2 heavy water cooled reactors
    - BT3 reactors
  - BT2 heavy water moderated reactors
    - BT3 reactors

BRUCE-4 REACTOR [54; 54]
(Tiverton, Ontario, Canada)
- BT1 candu type reactors
  - BT2 heavy water moderated reactors
    - BT3 reactors
  - BT2 pressure tube reactors
    - BT3 power reactors
      - BT4 reactors
  - BT2 thermal reactors
    - BT3 reactors
- BT1 natural uranium reactors
  - BT2 reactors
- BT1 phwr type reactors
  - BT2 heavy water cooled reactors
    - BT3 reactors
  - BT2 heavy water moderated reactors
    - BT3 reactors

BRUCE-5 REACTOR [32; 32] *Jul 78*
(Tiverton, Ontario, Canada)
- BT1 candu type reactors
  - BT2 heavy water moderated reactors
    - BT3 reactors
  - BT2 pressure tube reactors
    - BT3 power reactors
      - BT4 reactors
  - BT2 thermal reactors
    - BT3 reactors
- BT1 natural uranium reactors
  - BT2 reactors
- BT1 phwr type reactors
  - BT2 heavy water cooled reactors
    - BT3 reactors
  - BT2 heavy water moderated reactors
    - BT3 reactors

BRUCE-6 REACTOR [17; 17] *Jul 78*
(Tiverton, Ontario, Canada)
- BT1 candu type reactors
  - BT2 heavy water moderated reactors
    - BT3 reactors
  - BT2 pressure tube reactors
    - BT3 power reactors
      - BT4 reactors
  - BT2 thermal reactors
    - BT3 reactors
- BT1 natural uranium reactors
  - BT2 reactors
- BT1 phwr type reactors
  - BT2 heavy water cooled reactors
    - BT3 reactors
  - BT2 heavy water moderated reactors
    - BT3 reactors

BRUCE-7 REACTOR [13; 13] *Jul 78*
(Tiverton, Ontario, Canada)
- BT1 candu type reactors
  - BT2 heavy water moderated reactors
    - BT3 reactors
  - BT2 pressure tube reactors
    - BT3 power reactors
      - BT4 reactors
  - BT2 thermal reactors
    - BT3 reactors
- BT1 natural uranium reactors
  - BT2 reactors
- BT1 phwr type reactors
  - BT2 heavy water cooled reactors
    - BT3 reactors
  - BT2 heavy water moderated reactors
    - BT3 reactors

BRUCE-8 REACTOR [12; 12] *Jul 78*
(Tiverton, Ontario, Canada)
- BT1 candu type reactors
  - BT2 heavy water moderated reactors
    - BT3 reactors
  - BT2 pressure tube reactors
    - BT3 power reactors
      - BT4 reactors
  - BT2 thermal reactors
    - BT3 reactors
- BT1 natural uranium reactors
  - BT2 reactors
- BT1 phwr type reactors
  - BT2 heavy water cooled reactors
    - BT3 reactors
  - BT2 heavy water moderated reactors
    - BT3 reactors

BRUCELLA [36; 36]
- BT1 bacteria
  - BT2 microorganisms

brueckner approximation
- USE goldstone diagrams

BRUECKNER METHOD [294; 294]
- UF *brueckner-gammel potential*
- UF *brueckner-gammel-weitzner theo*
- RT brueckner model
- RT nuclear models
- RT nucleons

BRUECKNER MODEL [251; 251]
- UF *brueckner potential*
- UF *brueckner-watson theory*
- BT1 nuclear models
  - BT2 mathematical models
- RT brueckner method

brueckner potential
- USE brueckner model

brueckner-gammel potential
- USE brueckner method

brueckner-gammel-weitzner theo
- USE brueckner method

brueckner-goldstone theory
- USE goldstone diagrams

brueckner-sawada theory
- USE goldstone diagrams

brueckner-watson theory
- USE brueckner model

bruno leuschner-1 reactor
- USE greifswald-1 reactor

bruno leuschner-2 reactor
- USE greifswald-2 reactor

bruno leuschner-3 reactor
- USE greifswald-3 reactor

bruno leuschner-4 reactor
- USE greifswald-4 reactor

BRUNSBUETTEL REACTOR [150; 150]
- UF *kkb reactor*
- BT1 bwr type reactors
  - BT2 enriched uranium reactors
    - BT3 reactors
  - BT2 power reactors
    - BT3 reactors
  - BT2 thermal reactors
    - BT3 reactors
  - BT2 water cooled reactors
    - BT3 reactors
  - BT2 water moderated reactors
    - BT3 reactors

BRUNSWICK-1 REACTOR [100; 100]
(Southport, North Carolina, USA)
- BT1 bwr type reactors
  - BT2 enriched uranium reactors
    - BT3 reactors
  - BT2 power reactors
    - BT3 reactors
  - BT2 thermal reactors
    - BT3 reactors
  - BT2 water cooled reactors
    - BT3 reactors
  - BT2 water moderated reactors
    - BT3 reactors

BRUNSWICK-2 REACTOR [99; 99]
(Southport, North Carolina, USA)
- BT1 bwr type reactors
  - BT2 enriched uranium reactors
    - BT3 reactors
  - BT2 power reactors
    - BT3 reactors
  - BT2 thermal reactors
    - BT3 reactors
  - BT2 water cooled reactors
    - BT3 reactors
  - BT2 water moderated reactors
    - BT3 reactors

bruss conv maritime liab 1971
- USE bcoclmcnm

bruss conv-liab opera nucl shi
- USE bcolons

bruss conv-suppl to paris conv
- USE bcstpc

bsf reactor
- USE bsr-1 reactor

BSG DEVICES [5; 5]
- BT1 linear theta pinch devices
  - BT2 linear pinch devices
    - BT3 open plasma devices
      - BT4 thermonuclear devices
    - BT3 pinch devices
      - BT4 thermonuclear devices
- BT1 magnetic mirrors
  - BT2 open plasma devices
    - BT3 thermonuclear devices

bsp
- USE bromosulfophthalein

BSR-1 REACTOR [39; 39]
(Oak Ridge National Labs., Oak Ridge, Tennessee, USA)
  UF   *bsf reactor*
  UF   *bulk shielding reactor-1*
  BT1   enriched uranium reactors
    BT2   reactors
  BT1   pool type reactors
    BT2   water cooled reactors
      BT3   reactors
    BT2   water moderated reactors
      BT3   reactors
  BT1   research reactors
    BT2   research and test reactors
      BT3   reactors
  BT1   thermal reactors
    BT2   reactors

BSR-2 REACTOR [38; 38]
(Oak Ridge National Labs., Oak Ridge, Tennessee, USA)
  UF   *bulk shielding reactor-2*
  BT1   enriched uranium reactors
    BT2   reactors
  BT1   pool type reactors
    BT2   water cooled reactors
      BT3   reactors
    BT2   water moderated reactors
      BT3   reactors
  BT1   research reactors
    BT2   research and test reactors
      BT3   reactors
  BT1   thermal reactors
    BT2   reactors

BUBBLE CHAMBERS [1,637; 2,195]
  BT1   gas track detectors
    BT2   radiation detectors
      BT3   measuring instruments
  NT1   cryogenic bubble chambers
  NT1   heavy liquid bubble chambers
  NT1   ultrasonic bubble chambers
  RT   digitizers

BUBBLE GROWTH [654; 654]
  RT   boiling
  RT   boiling detection

BUBBLES [2,796; 2,796]
  RT   aeration
  RT   blisters
  RT   boiling detection
  RT   flow visualization
  RT   foams
  RT   voids

bucharest wwr-s reactor
  USE   wwr-s-bucharest reactor

BUCKINGHAM POTENTIAL [18, 18]
  BT1   potentials
  RT   interatomic forces

BUCKLING [255; 426]
(For neutron density distribution in reactors; for structural buckling see DEFORMATION or FAILURES.)
  NT1   geometric buckling
  NT1   material buckling
  RT   criticality

buckling (structural)
  USE   deformation

BUCKWHEAT [27; 27]
  BT1   plants
  RT   cereals

BUDAPEST TRAINING REACTOR [22; 22] *Sep 80*
(Technical Univ., Budapest, Hungary)
  BT1   thermal reactors
    BT2   reactors
  BT1   training reactors

    BT2   research and test reactors
      BT3   reactors
  BT1   wwr type reactors
    BT2   enriched uranium reactors
      BT3   reactors
    BT2   tank type reactors
      BT3   reactors
    BT2   water cooled reactors
      BT3   reactors
    BT2   water moderated reactors
      BT3   reactors

budapest wwr-s reactor
  USE   wwr-s-budapest reactor

BUDGETS [704; 704]
  RT   allocations
  RT   economics

budker accelerators
  USE   plasma betatrons

BUDR [329; 329]
  UF   *bromodeoxyuridine*
  BT1   bromouracils
    BT2   antimetabolites
      BT3   drugs
    BT2   organic bromine compounds
      BT3   organic halogen compounds
        BT4   organic compounds
    BT2   uracils
      BT3   hydroxy compounds
        BT4   organic compounds
      BT3   pyrimidines
        BT4   azines
          BT5   heterocyclic compounds
            BT6   organic compounds
          BT5   organic nitrogen compounds
            BT6   organic compounds
  BT1   nucleosides
    BT2   nucleotides
      BT3   organic compounds
    BT2   ribosides
  RT   deoxyuridine

BUDS [132; 132]
  RT   plants

BUFFALO [123; 123]
  BT1   ruminants
    BT2   mammals
      BT3   vertebrates
        BT4   animals
  RT   domestic animals

BUFFALO PROJECT [1; 1]
  UF   *project buffalo*
  RT   atmospheric explosions
  RT   nuclear explosions
  RT   surface explosions

buffalo pulstar reactor
  USE   pulstar-buffalo reactor

BUFFERS [621; 621]
  RT   gases
  RT   ph value
  RT   solutions

BUFOTENINE [1; 1]
  BT1   hallucinogens
    BT2   psychotropic drugs
      BT3   central nervous system agents
        BT4   drugs
  BT1   radioprotective substances
    BT2   drugs
    BT2   response modifying factors
  BT1   tryptamines
    BT2   amines
      BT3   organic compounds
    BT2   indoles
      BT3   pyrroles

        BT4   azoles
          BT5   heterocyclic compounds
            BT6   organic compounds
          BT5   organic nitrogen compounds
            BT6   organic compounds

BUGEY-1 REACTOR [69; 69]
(St-Vulbas, Ain, France)
  UF   *edf-5 reactor*
  BT1   gcr type reactors
    BT2   gas cooled reactors
      BT3   reactors
    BT2   graphite moderated reactors
      BT3   reactors
  BT1   power reactors
    BT2   reactors
  BT1   thermal reactors
    BT2   reactors

BUGEY-2 REACTOR [32; 32]
(St-Vulbas, Ain, France)
  BT1   pwr type reactors
    BT2   enriched uranium reactors
      BT3   reactors
    BT2   power reactors
      BT3   reactors
    BT2   thermal reactors
      BT3   reactors
    BT2   water cooled reactors
      BT3   reactors
    BT2   water moderated reactors
      BT3   reactors

BUGEY-3 REACTOR [12; 12] *Sep 83*
(St-Vulbas, Ain, France.)
  BT1   pwr type reactors
    BT2   enriched uranium reactors
      BT3   reactors
    BT2   power reactors
      BT3   reactors
    BT2   thermal reactors
      BT3   reactors
    BT2   water cooled reactors
      BT3   reactors
    BT2   water moderated reactors
      BT3   reactors

BUGEY-4 REACTOR [24; 24] *Jul 80*
(St-Vulbas, Ain, France)
  BT1   pwr type reactors
    BT2   enriched uranium reactors
      BT3   reactors
    BT2   power reactors
      BT3   reactors
    BT2   thermal reactors
      BT3   reactors
    BT2   water cooled reactors
      BT3   reactors
    BT2   water moderated reactors
      BT3   reactors

BUGEY-5 REACTOR [5; 5] *May 88*
(St-Vulbas, Ain, France.)
  BT1   pwr type reactors
    BT2   enriched uranium reactors
      BT3   reactors
    BT2   power reactors
      BT3   reactors
    BT2   thermal reactors
      BT3   reactors
    BT2   water cooled reactors
      BT3   reactors
    BT2   water moderated reactors
      BT3   reactors

building (constructing)
  USE   construction

building (manufacturing)
  USE   fabrication

building foundations
  USE   foundations

BUILDING MATERIALS [1,375; 9,659]
- UF structural materials
- BT1 materials
- NT1 bricks
- NT1 cements
  - NT2 gypsum cements
- NT1 concretes
  - NT2 prestressed concrete
  - NT2 reinforced concrete
- RT buildings
- RT composite materials
- RT mortars
- RT reinforced materials
- RT sand
- RT shielding materials

BUILDINGS [3,998; 6,770]
- UF greenhouses
- UF structures (buildings)
- NT1 apartment buildings
- NT1 containment buildings
- NT1 hospitals
- NT1 houses
- RT air infiltration
- RT building materials
- RT construction
- RT foundations
- RT laboratories
- RT mechanical structures
- RT roofs
- RT shelters
- RT soil-structure interactions
- RT stacks

BUILDUP [1,755; 1,755]
- UF accumulation
- UF radiation buildup
- RT depth dose distributions
- RT ionization
- RT ionizing radiations
- RT radiation doses
- RT radiations
- RT radioecological concentration
- RT scattering
- RT shielding
- RT spatial dose distributions

BULBS [33; 33]
- RT onions
- RT plants

BULGARIA [337; 337]
- BT1 developing countries
- BT1 europe
- RT centrally planned economies

bulgarian r. reactor irt-2000
- USE irt-sofia reactor

BULK SEMICONDUCTOR DETECTORS [20; 20]
- BT1 semiconductor detectors
  - BT2 radiation detectors
    - BT3 measuring instruments
- RT crystal counters

bulk shielding reactor-1
- USE bsr-1 reactor

bulk shielding reactor-2
- USE bsr-2 reactor

BUMP-IN-TAIL INSTABILITY [65; 65]
- BT1 plasma microinstabilities
  - BT2 plasma instability
    - BT3 instability
- RT resonance

BUMPY TORI [44; 317] *Feb 84*
- BT1 magnetic mirrors
  - BT2 open plasma devices
    - BT3 thermonuclear devices
- NT1 elmo bumpy torus
- RT tori

BUNA [8; 8]
- BT1 rubbers
  - BT2 elastomers
    - BT3 polymers
  - BT2 organic polymers
    - BT3 organic compounds
    - BT3 polymers
- RT butadiene

bunching (beam)
- USE beam bunching

→ **BUNDESAMT FUER STRAHLENSCHUTZ** [2; 2] *May 91*
(Federal Office for Radiation Protection, Federal Republic of Germany.)
- UF bfs
- UF saas
- UF staat amt atomsich strahlensch
- BT1 german fr organizations
  - BT2 national organizations

BUNDLE DIVERTORS [72; 72] *Jul 81*
(Divertors that extract a bundle of magnetic field lines.)
- BT1 divertors
- RT toroidal field divertors

bundles (fuel elements)
- USE fuel element clusters

bureau of mines (us)
- USE us bureau of mines

BURGERS VECTOR [396; 396]
- RT dislocations

BURMA [6; 6]
- BT1 asia
- BT1 developing countries

BURNABLE POISONS [936; 936]
- BT1 neutron absorbers
- BT1 nuclear poisons
  - BT2 reactor materials
    - BT3 materials
- RT burnup
- RT control elements
- RT fluid poison control
- RT poisoning
- RT reactor control systems
- RT reactor kinetics

BURNERS [35; 35] *Dec 85*
- RT combustion
- RT combustors
- RT furnaces
- RT incinerators

BURNOUT [445; 445]
- RT dryout
- RT fuel elements
- RT heat flux
- RT heat transfer
- RT hot spots
- RT reactor accidents

BURNOUT DEVICES [5; 5]
- BT1 magnetic mirrors
  - BT2 open plasma devices
    - BT3 thermonuclear devices

BURNS [189; 340]
- BT1 injuries
  - BT2 diseases
- NT1 flash burns
- NT1 radiation burns
- RT fires
- RT safety showers
- RT skin diseases

BURNUP [6,444; 6,444]
- UF depletion (nuclear fuels)
- RT burnable poisons
- RT fuel cooling time
- RT fuel scanning
- RT nuclear fuels
- RT spent fuel elements

BURROS [10; 10]
- BT1 mammals
  - BT2 vertebrates
    - BT3 animals

BURROUGHS COMPUTERS [6; 6] *Feb 80*
- BT1 computers

bursa of fabricius
- USE birds
- AND lymphatic system

burst can detection
- USE failed element detection

burst can monitors
- USE failed element monitors

burst reactors
- USE pulsed reactors

burst slug detection
- USE failed element detection

burst slug monitors
- USE failed element monitors

BUSHINGS [39; 39]
- RT bearings

buspr reactor
- USE pulstar-buffalo reactor

busulfan
- USE myleran

BUTADIENE [267; 267]
- BT1 dienes
  - BT2 polyenes
    - BT3 hydrocarbons
      - BT4 organic compounds
- RT buna
- RT neoprene
- RT organic polymers

BUTANE [297; 297]
- BT1 alkanes
  - BT2 hydrocarbons
    - BT3 organic compounds

butanoic acid
- USE butyric acid

BUTANOLS [543; 543]
- UF butyl alcohols
- UF butyric alcohols
- BT1 alcohols
  - BT2 hydroxy compounds
    - BT3 organic compounds

BUTENES [211; 211]
- UF butylenes
- BT1 alkenes
  - BT2 hydrocarbons
    - BT3 organic compounds

BUTEX PROCESS [2; 2]
BT1 reprocessing
BT2 separation processes
RT solvent extraction

BUTLER THEORY [18; 18]
UF *butler-born approximation*
RT stripping

butler-born approximation
USE butler theory

BUTOXY RADICALS [11; 11]
BT1 alkoxy radicals
BT2 radicals

butt welds
USE welded joints

BUTTER [9; 9]
BT1 milk products
BT2 food
RT butter fat

BUTTER FAT [6; 6]
BT1 fats
BT1 triglycerides
BT2 esters
BT3 organic compounds
BT2 lipids
BT3 organic compounds
RT butter

buttercups
USE ranunculaceae

butyl alcohols
USE butanols

BUTYL ETHER [28; 28]
UF *dibutyl ether*
BT1 ethers
BT2 organic oxygen compounds
BT3 organic compounds
RT organic solvents

BUTYL PHOSPHATES [65; 2,489]
BT1 phosphoric acid esters
BT2 esters
BT3 organic compounds
BT2 organic phosphorus compounds
BT3 organic compounds
NT1 dbp
NT1 mbp
NT1 tbp

BUTYL RADICALS [57; 57]
BT1 alkyl radicals
BT2 radicals

butyl-alpha-methylbenzylphenol
USE bambp

butylamine
USE amines

butylenes
USE butenes

BUTYRIC ACID [162; 162]
UF *butanoic acid*
BT1 monocarboxylic acids
BT2 carboxylic acids
BT3 organic acids
BT4 organic compounds

butyric alcohols
USE butanols

BUTYRYL RADICALS [2; 2]
BT1 acyl radicals
BT2 radicals

BW STANDARD REACTOR [82; 82]
Oct 75
UF *babcock and wilcox stand. reac*
UF *pwr/241 type reactor*
BT1 pwr type reactors
BT2 enriched uranium reactors
BT3 reactors
BT2 power reactors
BT3 reactors
BT2 thermal reactors
BT3 reactors
BT2 water cooled reactors
BT3 reactors
BT2 water moderated reactors
BT3 reactors

bwr superheater puerto rico r.
USE bonus reactor

BWR TYPE REACTORS
[19,449; 26,308]
UF *boiling water cooled and moder*
BT1 enriched uranium reactors
BT2 reactors
BT1 power reactors
BT2 reactors
BT1 thermal reactors
BT2 reactors
BT1 water cooled reactors
BT2 reactors
BT1 water moderated reactors
BT2 reactors
NT1 allens creek-1 reactor
NT1 allens creek-2 reactor
NT1 bailly-1 reactor
NT1 barsebaeck-1 reactor
NT1 barsebaeck-2 reactor
NT1 barton-1 reactor
NT1 barton-2 reactor
NT1 barton-3 reactor
NT1 barton-4 reactor
NT1 bell reactor
NT1 big rock point reactor
NT1 black fox-1 reactor
NT1 black fox-2 reactor
NT1 bonus reactor
NT1 browns ferry-1 reactor
NT1 browns ferry-2 reactor
NT1 browns ferry-3 reactor
NT1 brunsbuettel reactor
NT1 brunswick-1 reactor
NT1 brunswick-2 reactor
NT1 chinshan-1 reactor
NT1 chinshan-2 reactor
NT1 clinton-1 reactor
NT1 clinton-2 reactor
NT1 cofrentes reactor
NT1 cooper reactor
NT1 dodewaard reactor
NT1 douglas point-1 reactor
NT1 douglas point-2 reactor
NT1 dresden-1 reactor
NT1 dresden-2 reactor
NT1 dresden-3 reactor
NT1 duane arnold-1 reactor
NT1 ebwr reactor
NT1 enel-4 reactor
NT1 enrico fermi-2 reactor
NT1 err reactor
NT1 fitzpatrick reactor
NT1 forsmark-1 reactor
NT1 forsmark-2 reactor
NT1 forsmark-3 reactor
NT1 fukushima-ii-1 reactor
NT1 fukushima-ii-2 reactor
NT1 fukushima-ii-3 reactor
NT1 fukushima-ii-4 reactor
NT1 fukushima-1 reactor
NT1 fukushima-2 reactor
NT1 fukushima-3 reactor
NT1 fukushima-4 reactor
NT1 fukushima-5 reactor
NT1 fukushima-6 reactor
NT1 garigliano reactor
NT1 garona reactor
NT1 ge standard reactor
NT1 graben-1 reactor
NT1 grand gulf-1 reactor
NT1 grand gulf-2 reactor
NT1 gundremmingen-2 reactor
NT1 gundremmingen-3 reactor
NT1 hamaoka-1 reactor
NT1 hamaoka-2 reactor
NT1 hamaoka-3 reactor
NT1 hartsville-1 reactor
NT1 hartsville-2 reactor
NT1 hartsville-3 reactor
NT1 hartsville-4 reactor
NT1 hatch-1 reactor
NT1 hatch-2 reactor
NT1 hdr reactor
NT1 hope creek-1 reactor
NT2 newbold island-1 reactor
NT1 hope creek-2 reactor
NT2 newbold island-2 reactor
NT1 humboldt bay reactor
NT1 isar reactor
NT1 jpdr reactor
NT1 jpdr-2 reactor
NT1 kaiseraugst reactor
NT1 kashiwazaki-kariwa-1 reactor
NT1 kashiwazaki-kariwa-2 reactor
NT1 kashiwazaki-kariwa-3 reactor
NT1 kashiwazaki-kariwa-4 reactor
NT1 kashiwazaki-kariwa-5 reactor
NT1 kashiwazaki-kariwa-6 reactor
NT1 kashiwazaki-kariwa-7 reactor
NT1 kruemmel reactor
NT1 kuosheng-1 reactor
NT1 kuosheng-2 reactor
NT1 la salle county-1 reactor
NT1 la salle county-2 reactor
NT1 lacbwr reactor
NT1 laguna verde-1 reactor
NT1 laguna verde-2 reactor
NT1 leibstadt reactor
NT1 limerick-1 reactor
NT1 limerick-2 reactor
NT1 lingen reactor
NT1 mendocino-1 reactor
NT1 mendocino-2 reactor
NT1 millstone-1 reactor
NT1 montague-1 reactor
NT1 montague-2 reactor
NT1 montalto di castro-1 reactor
NT1 montalto di castro-2 reactor
NT1 monticello reactor
NT1 muehleberg reactor
NT1 nine mile point-1 reactor
NT1 nine mile point-2 reactor
NT1 okg-1 reactor
NT1 okg-2 reactor
NT1 onagawa-1 reactor
NT1 onagawa-2 reactor
NT1 oyster creek-1 reactor
NT1 pathfinder reactor
NT1 peach bottom-2 reactor
NT1 peach bottom-3 reactor
NT1 perry-1 reactor
NT1 perry-2 reactor
NT1 philippsburg-1 reactor
NT1 phipps bend-1 reactor
NT1 phipps bend-2 reactor
NT1 quad cities-1 reactor
NT1 quad cities-2 reactor
NT1 ringhals-1 reactor
NT1 river bend-1 reactor
NT1 river bend-2 reactor
NT1 rwe-bayernwerk reactor
NT1 shika-1 reactor
NT1 shimane-1 reactor
NT1 shimane-2 reactor
NT1 shoreham reactor
NT1 skagit-1 reactor
NT1 skagit-2 reactor
NT1 sl-1 reactor
NT1 susquehanna-1 reactor
NT1 susquehanna-2 reactor
NT1 tarapur-1 reactor
NT1 tarapur-2 reactor
NT1 tokai-2 reactor

NT1 tsuruga reactor
NT1 tullnerfeld reactor
NT1 tvo-1 reactor
NT1 tvo-2 reactor
NT1 vak reactor
NT1 vbwr reactor
NT1 vermont yankee reactor
NT1 verplanck-1 reactor
NT1 verplanck-2 reactor
NT1 vk-50 reactor
NT1 wnp-2 reactor
NT2 hanford-2 reactor
NT1 wuergassen reactor
NT1 zimmer-1 reactor
NT1 zimmer-2 reactor

bwr/6 type reactor
USE ge standard reactor

BY-PRODUCTS [94; 94] *Dec 85*
RT chars
RT industry
RT pyrolysis products
RT wastes

BYELORUSSIAN SSR [67; 67]
BT1 ussr
BT2 developed countries
BT2 europe

BYPASSES [658; 658]
UF *shunt (biomedical)*
UF *shunts*
RT coolant loops
RT reactor cooling systems

BYRON-1 REACTOR [40; 40]
(Byron, Illinois, USA)
BT1 pwr type reactors
BT2 enriched uranium reactors
BT3 reactors
BT2 power reactors
BT3 reactors
BT2 thermal reactors
BT3 reactors
BT2 water cooled reactors
BT3 reactors
BT2 water moderated reactors
BT3 reactors

BYRON-2 REACTOR [30; 30]
(Byron, Illinois, USA)
BT1 pwr type reactors
BT2 enriched uranium reactors
BT3 reactors
BT2 power reactors
BT3 reactors
BT2 thermal reactors
BT3 reactors
BT2 water cooled reactors
BT3 reactors
BT2 water moderated reactors
BT3 reactors

B1-1235 MESONS [209; 209]
(Prior to December 1987 this concept was indexed by B-1235 RESONANCES.)
UF *b-1235 resonances*
BT1 axial vector mesons
BT2 mesons
BT3 bosons
BT3 hadrons
BT4 elementary particles

C CODES [3,174; 3,174]
BT1 computer codes

C INVARIANCE [462; 462]
UF *charge conjugation invariance*
BT1 invariance principles
RT electric charges

C REACTOR [16; 16] *Nov 85*
UF *savannah riv. plant c reactor*
BT1 heavy water moderated reactors
BT2 reactors
BT1 special production reactors
BT2 production reactors
BT3 reactors

C REGION [2; 2] *Oct 82*
BT1 ionosphere
BT2 earth atmosphere

c-reactive protein
USE globulins

c-1430 resonances
(Prior to December 1987 this was a valid descriptor.)
USE mesons

cabbage
USE brassica

CABIBBO ANGLE [995; 995]
RT current algebra
RT kobayashi-maskawa matrix
RT weak interactions

CABLES [253; 1,508] *Jul 81*
(For both electric and structural cables.)
NT1 electric cables
NT2 coaxial cables
NT2 cryogenic cables
NT2 gas-insulated cables
NT2 superconducting cables

CABRI REACTOR [48; 48]
(Nuclear Protection and Safety Inst., CEA St. Paul Lez Durance, France)
UF *cadarache swimming pool react.*
BT1 enriched uranium reactors
BT2 reactors
BT1 pool type reactors
BT2 water cooled reactors
BT3 reactors
BT2 water moderated reactors
BT3 reactors
BT1 research reactors
BT2 research and test reactors
BT3 reactors
BT1 thermal reactors
BT2 reactors

CABRIOLET EVENT [5; 5]
BT1 cratering explosions
BT2 explosions
BT1 nuclear explosions
BT2 explosions
BT1 plowshare project
BT1 underground explosions
BT2 explosions

CACAO TREES [16; 16]
UF *theobroma*
BT1 trees
BT2 plants
RT cocoa products

CACODYLIC ACID [1; 1]
BT1 arsenic compounds
BT1 organic acids
BT2 organic compounds

cactaceae
USE cacti

CACTI [6; 6] *Sep 79*
UF *cactaceae*
BT1 plants

cadarache (cea)
USE cea cadarache

cadarache fuel el. testing r.
USE pegase reactor

cadarache maquette surgen. rea
USE masurca reactor

cadarache rapsodie reactor
USE rapsodie reactor

cadarache reactor marius
USE marius reactor

cadarache swimming pool react.
USE cabri reactor

CADAVERINE [16; 16]
UF *pentamethylenediamine*
UF *1,5-diaminopentane*
BT1 amines
BT2 organic compounds

CADMIUM [4,071; 4,071]
BT1 metals
BT2 elements

CADMIUM ADDITIONS [199; 203]
(Alloys containing not more than 1% Cd are listed here.)
RT cadmium alloys
RT cadmium compounds

CADMIUM ALLOYS [1,070; 1,220]
(Alloys containing more than 1% Cd.)
BT1 alloys
NT1 alloy-bi50pb25cd12sn12
NT1 cadmium base alloys
RT cadmium additions

CADMIUM ARSENIDES [114; 114] *Apr 78*
BT1 arsenides
BT2 arsenic compounds
BT2 pnictides
BT1 cadmium compounds

CADMIUM BASE ALLOYS [108; 108]
BT1 cadmium alloys
BT2 alloys

CADMIUM BORIDES [3; 3]
BT1 borides
BT2 boron compounds
BT1 cadmium compounds

CADMIUM BROMIDES [139; 139]
BT1 bromides
BT2 bromine compounds
BT3 halogen compounds
BT2 halides
BT3 halogen compounds
BT1 cadmium halides
BT2 cadmium compounds
BT2 halides
BT3 halogen compounds

CADMIUM CARBONATES [20; 20]
BT1 cadmium compounds
BT1 carbonates
BT2 carbon compounds
BT2 oxygen compounds

CADMIUM CHLORIDES [414; 414]
BT1 cadmium halides
BT2 cadmium compounds
BT2 halides
BT3 halogen compounds
BT1 chlorides

```
          BT2     chlorine compounds
          BT3       halogen compounds
          BT2     halides
          BT3       halogen compounds

CADMIUM COMPLEXES [1,423; 1,423]
     BT1   complexes

CADMIUM COMPOUNDS [1,857; 7,718]
     NT1   cadmium arsenides
     NT1   cadmium borides
     NT1   cadmium carbonates
     NT1   cadmium halides
      NT2     cadmium bromides
      NT2     cadmium chlorides
      NT2     cadmium fluorides
      NT2     cadmium iodides
     NT1   cadmium hydroxides
     NT1   cadmium nitrates
     NT1   cadmium oxides
     NT1   cadmium perchlorates
     NT1   cadmium phosphates
     NT1   cadmium phosphides
     NT1   cadmium selenides
     NT1   cadmium silicates
     NT1   cadmium sulfates
     NT1   cadmium sulfides
     NT1   cadmium tellurides
     NT1   cadmium titanates
     NT1   cadmium tungstates
     NT1   calcium perchlorates
     RT    cadmium additions

CADMIUM FLUORIDES [152; 152]
     BT1   cadmium halides
      BT2     cadmium compounds
      BT2     halides
       BT3      halogen compounds
     BT1   fluorides
      BT2     fluorine compounds
       BT3      halogen compounds
      BT2     halides
       BT3      halogen compounds

CADMIUM HALIDES [3; 342] Apr 84
     BT1   cadmium compounds
     BT1   halides
      BT2     halogen compounds
     NT1   cadmium bromides
     NT1   cadmium chlorides
     NT1   cadmium fluorides
     NT1   cadmium iodides

CADMIUM HYDROXIDES [77; 77]
     BT1   cadmium compounds
     BT1   hydroxides
      BT2     hydrogen compounds
      BT2     oxygen compounds

CADMIUM IODIDES [230; 230]
     BT1   cadmium halides
      BT2     cadmium compounds
      BT2     halides
       BT3      halogen compounds
     BT1   iodides
      BT2     halides
       BT3      halogen compounds
      BT2     iodine compounds
       BT3      halogen compounds

CADMIUM IONS [245; 245]
     BT1   ions
      BT2     charged particles

CADMIUM ISOTOPES [246; 2,489]
     NT1   cadmium 100
     NT1   cadmium 101
     NT1   cadmium 102
     NT1   cadmium 103
     NT1   cadmium 104
     NT1   cadmium 105
     NT1   cadmium 106
     NT1   cadmium 107
     NT1   cadmium 108
     NT1   cadmium 109
```

```
     NT1   cadmium 110
     NT1   cadmium 111
     NT1   cadmium 112
     NT1   cadmium 113
     NT1   cadmium 114
     NT1   cadmium 115
     NT1   cadmium 116
     NT1   cadmium 117
     NT1   cadmium 118
     NT1   cadmium 119
     NT1   cadmium 120
     NT1   cadmium 121
     NT1   cadmium 122
     NT1   cadmium 123
     NT1   cadmium 124
     NT1   cadmium 125
     NT1   cadmium 126
     NT1   cadmium 127
     NT1   cadmium 128
     NT1   cadmium 130
     NT1   cadmium 96
     NT1   cadmium 97
     NT1   cadmium 98
     NT1   cadmium 99

CADMIUM NITRATES [103; 103]
     BT1   cadmium compounds
     BT1   nitrates
      BT2     nitrogen compounds
      BT2     oxygen compounds

CADMIUM OXIDES [374; 374]
     BT1   cadmium compounds
     BT1   oxides
      BT2     chalcogenides
      BT2     oxygen compounds

CADMIUM PERCHLORATES [34; 34]
     BT1   cadmium compounds
     BT1   perchlorates
      BT2     chlorine compounds
       BT3      halogen compounds
      BT2     oxygen compounds

CADMIUM PHOSPHATES [42; 42]
     BT1   cadmium compounds
     BT1   phosphates
      BT2     oxygen compounds
      BT2     phosphorus compounds

CADMIUM PHOSPHIDES [149; 149]
     Jan 77
     BT1   cadmium compounds
     BT1   phosphides
      BT2     phosphorus compounds
      BT2     pnictides

CADMIUM SELENIDES [849; 849]
     BT1   cadmium compounds
     BT1   selenides
      BT2     chalcogenides
      BT2     selenium compounds

CADMIUM SILICATES [19; 19]
     BT1   cadmium compounds
     BT1   silicates
      BT2     oxygen compounds
      BT2     silicon compounds

CADMIUM SULFATES [176; 176]
     BT1   cadmium compounds
     BT1   sulfates
      BT2     oxygen compounds
      BT2     sulfur compounds

CADMIUM SULFIDES [1,794; 1,794]
     BT1   cadmium compounds
     BT1   sulfides
      BT2     chalcogenides
      BT2     sulfur compounds

*cadmium telluride detectors*
     USE    cdte semiconductor detectors
```

```
CADMIUM TELLURIDES [1,757; 1,757]
     BT1   cadmium compounds
     BT1   tellurides
      BT2     chalcogenides
      BT2     tellurium compounds

→ CADMIUM TITANATES [0; 0] Sep 91
     BT1   cadmium compounds
     BT1   titanates
      BT2     oxygen compounds
      BT2     titanium compounds
       BT3      transition element compounds

CADMIUM TUNGSTATES [66; 66]
     BT1   cadmium compounds
     BT1   tungstates
      BT2     oxygen compounds
      BT2     tungsten compounds
       BT3      transition element compounds

CADMIUM 100 [17; 17]
     BT1   beta-plus decay radioisotopes
      BT2     beta decay radioisotopes
       BT3      radioisotopes
        BT4       isotopes
     BT1   cadmium isotopes
     BT1   electron capture radioisotopes
      BT2     beta decay radioisotopes
       BT3      radioisotopes
        BT4       isotopes
     BT1   even-even nuclei
      BT2     nuclei
     BT1   intermediate mass nuclei
      BT2     nuclei
     BT1   isomeric transition isotopes
      BT2     radioisotopes
       BT3      isotopes
     BT1   minutes living radioisotopes
      BT2     radioisotopes
       BT3      isotopes

CADMIUM 101 [7; 7]
     BT1   beta-plus decay radioisotopes
      BT2     beta decay radioisotopes
       BT3      radioisotopes
        BT4       isotopes
     BT1   cadmium isotopes
     BT1   electron capture radioisotopes
      BT2     beta decay radioisotopes
       BT3      radioisotopes
        BT4       isotopes
     BT1   even-odd nuclei
      BT2     nuclei
     BT1   intermediate mass nuclei
      BT2     nuclei
     BT1   minutes living radioisotopes
      BT2     radioisotopes
       BT3      isotopes

CADMIUM 102 [23; 23]
     BT1   beta-plus decay radioisotopes
      BT2     beta decay radioisotopes
       BT3      radioisotopes
        BT4       isotopes
     BT1   cadmium isotopes
     BT1   electron capture radioisotopes
      BT2     beta decay radioisotopes
       BT3      radioisotopes
        BT4       isotopes
     BT1   even-even nuclei
      BT2     nuclei
     BT1   intermediate mass nuclei
      BT2     nuclei
     BT1   minutes living radioisotopes
      BT2     radioisotopes
       BT3      isotopes

CADMIUM 103 [24; 24]
     BT1   beta-plus decay radioisotopes
      BT2     beta decay radioisotopes
       BT3      radioisotopes
        BT4       isotopes
     BT1   cadmium isotopes
     BT1   electron capture radioisotopes
      BT2     beta decay radioisotopes
       BT3      radioisotopes
        BT4       isotopes
     BT1   even-odd nuclei
```

BT2   nuclei
BT1   intermediate mass nuclei
BT2   nuclei
BT1   minutes living radioisotopes
BT2   radioisotopes
BT3   isotopes

CADMIUM 104 [33; 33]
BT1   beta-plus decay radioisotopes
BT2   beta decay radioisotopes
BT3   radioisotopes
BT4   isotopes
BT1   cadmium isotopes
BT1   electron capture radioisotopes
BT2   beta decay radioisotopes
BT3   radioisotopes
BT4   isotopes
BT1   even-even nuclei
BT2   nuclei
BT1   intermediate mass nuclei
BT2   nuclei
BT1   minutes living radioisotopes
BT2   radioisotopes
BT3   isotopes

CADMIUM 105 [47; 47]
BT1   beta-plus decay radioisotopes
BT2   beta decay radioisotopes
BT3   radioisotopes
BT4   isotopes
BT1   cadmium isotopes
BT1   electron capture radioisotopes
BT2   beta decay radioisotopes
BT3   radioisotopes
BT4   isotopes
BT1   even-odd nuclei
BT2   nuclei
BT1   intermediate mass nuclei
BT2   nuclei
BT1   minutes living radioisotopes
BT2   radioisotopes
BT3   isotopes

CADMIUM 106 [101; 101]
BT1   cadmium isotopes
BT1   even-even nuclei
BT2   nuclei
BT1   intermediate mass nuclei
BT2   nuclei
BT1   stable isotopes
BT2   isotopes

CADMIUM 106 TARGET [104; 104]
BT1   targets

CADMIUM 107 [89; 89]
BT1   beta-plus decay radioisotopes
BT2   beta decay radioisotopes
BT3   radioisotopes
BT4   isotopes
BT1   cadmium isotopes
BT1   electron capture radioisotopes
BT2   beta decay radioisotopes
BT3   radioisotopes
BT4   isotopes
BT1   even-odd nuclei
BT2   nuclei
BT1   hours living radioisotopes
BT2   radioisotopes
BT3   isotopes
BT1   intermediate mass nuclei
BT2   nuclei

CADMIUM 108 [80; 80]
BT1   cadmium isotopes
BT1   even-even nuclei
BT2   nuclei
BT1   intermediate mass nuclei
BT2   nuclei
BT1   stable isotopes
BT2   isotopes

CADMIUM 108 TARGET [37; 37]
BT1   targets

CADMIUM 109 [692; 692]
BT1   cadmium isotopes
BT1   electron capture radioisotopes
BT2   beta decay radioisotopes
BT3   radioisotopes
BT4   isotopes
BT1   even-odd nuclei
BT2   nuclei
BT1   intermediate mass nuclei
BT2   nuclei
BT1   years living radioisotopes
BT2   radioisotopes
BT3   isotopes

CADMIUM 109 TARGET [5; 5] *Feb 79*
BT1   targets

CADMIUM 110 [150; 150]
BT1   cadmium isotopes
BT1   even-even nuclei
BT2   nuclei
BT1   intermediate mass nuclei
BT2   nuclei
BT1   stable isotopes
BT2   isotopes

CADMIUM 110 TARGET [140; 140]
BT1   targets

CADMIUM 111 [446; 446]
BT1   cadmium isotopes
BT1   even-odd nuclei
BT2   nuclei
BT1   intermediate mass nuclei
BT2   nuclei
BT1   internal conversion radioisoto
BT2   radioisotopes
BT3   isotopes
BT1   isomeric transition isotopes
BT2   radioisotopes
BT3   isotopes
BT1   minutes living radioisotopes
BT2   radioisotopes
BT3   isotopes
BT1   stable isotopes
BT2   isotopes

CADMIUM 111 TARGET [92; 92]
BT1   targets

CADMIUM 112 [144; 144]
BT1   cadmium isotopes
BT1   even-even nuclei
BT2   nuclei
BT1   intermediate mass nuclei
BT2   nuclei
BT1   stable isotopes
BT2   isotopes

CADMIUM 112 TARGET [118; 118]
BT1   targets

CADMIUM 113 [173; 173]
BT1   beta-minus decay radioisotopes
BT2   beta decay radioisotopes
BT3   radioisotopes
BT4   isotopes
BT1   cadmium isotopes
BT1   even-odd nuclei
BT2   nuclei
BT1   intermediate mass nuclei
BT2   nuclei
BT1   internal conversion radioisoto
BT2   radioisotopes
BT3   isotopes
BT1   isomeric transition isotopes
BT2   radioisotopes
BT3   isotopes
BT1   stable isotopes
BT2   isotopes
BT1   years living radioisotopes
BT2   radioisotopes
BT3   isotopes

CADMIUM 113 TARGET [84; 84]
BT1   targets

CADMIUM 114 [193; 193]
BT1   cadmium isotopes
BT1   even-even nuclei
BT2   nuclei
BT1   intermediate mass nuclei
BT2   nuclei
BT1   stable isotopes
BT2   isotopes

CADMIUM 114 TARGET [142; 142]
BT1   targets

CADMIUM 115 [277; 277]
BT1   beta-minus decay radioisotopes
BT2   beta decay radioisotopes
BT3   radioisotopes
BT4   isotopes
BT1   cadmium isotopes
BT1   days living radioisotopes
BT2   radioisotopes
BT3   isotopes
BT1   even-odd nuclei
BT2   nuclei
BT1   intermediate mass nuclei
BT2   nuclei

CADMIUM 116 [101; 101]
BT1   cadmium isotopes
BT1   even-even nuclei
BT2   nuclei
BT1   intermediate mass nuclei
BT2   nuclei
BT1   stable isotopes
BT2   isotopes

CADMIUM 116 TARGET [138; 138]
BT1   targets

CADMIUM 117 [44; 44]
BT1   beta-minus decay radioisotopes
BT2   beta decay radioisotopes
BT3   radioisotopes
BT4   isotopes
BT1   cadmium isotopes
BT1   even-odd nuclei
BT2   nuclei
BT1   hours living radioisotopes
BT2   radioisotopes
BT3   isotopes
BT1   intermediate mass nuclei
BT2   nuclei

CADMIUM 118 [20; 20]
BT1   beta-minus decay radioisotopes
BT2   beta decay radioisotopes
BT3   radioisotopes
BT4   isotopes
BT1   cadmium isotopes
BT1   even-even nuclei
BT2   nuclei
BT1   intermediate mass nuclei
BT2   nuclei
BT1   minutes living radioisotopes
BT2   radioisotopes
BT3   isotopes

CADMIUM 119 [18; 18]
BT1   beta-minus decay radioisotopes
BT2   beta decay radioisotopes
BT3   radioisotopes
BT4   isotopes
BT1   cadmium isotopes
BT1   even-odd nuclei
BT2   nuclei
BT1   intermediate mass nuclei
BT2   nuclei
BT1   minutes living radioisotopes
BT2   radioisotopes
BT3   isotopes

CADMIUM 120 [15; 15]
  BT1   beta-minus decay radioisotopes
    BT2   beta decay radioisotopes
      BT3   radioisotopes
        BT4   isotopes
  BT1   cadmium isotopes
  BT1   even-even nuclei
    BT2   nuclei
  BT1   intermediate mass nuclei
    BT2   nuclei
  BT1   seconds living radioisotopes
    BT2   radioisotopes
      BT3   isotopes

CADMIUM 121 [12; 12]
  BT1   beta-minus decay radioisotopes
    BT2   beta decay radioisotopes
      BT3   radioisotopes
        BT4   isotopes
  BT1   cadmium isotopes
  BT1   even-odd nuclei
    BT2   nuclei
  BT1   intermediate mass nuclei
    BT2   nuclei
  BT1   seconds living radioisotopes
    BT2   radioisotopes
      BT3   isotopes

CADMIUM 122 [14; 14]
  BT1   beta-minus decay radioisotopes
    BT2   beta decay radioisotopes
      BT3   radioisotopes
        BT4   isotopes
  BT1   cadmium isotopes
  BT1   even-even nuclei
    BT2   nuclei
  BT1   intermediate mass nuclei
    BT2   nuclei
  BT1   seconds living radioisotopes
    BT2   radioisotopes
      BT3   isotopes

CADMIUM 123 [12; 12]
  BT1   beta-minus decay radioisotopes
    BT2   beta decay radioisotopes
      BT3   radioisotopes
        BT4   isotopes
  BT1   cadmium isotopes
  BT1   even-odd nuclei
    BT2   nuclei
  BT1   intermediate mass nuclei
    BT2   nuclei
  BT1   seconds living radioisotopes
    BT2   radioisotopes
      BT3   isotopes

CADMIUM 124 [12; 12]
  BT1   beta-minus decay radioisotopes
    BT2   beta decay radioisotopes
      BT3   radioisotopes
        BT4   isotopes
  BT1   cadmium isotopes
  BT1   even-even nuclei
    BT2   nuclei
  BT1   intermediate mass nuclei
    BT2   nuclei
  BT1   millisec living radioisotopes
    BT2   radioisotopes
      BT3   isotopes

CADMIUM 125 [9; 9]
  BT1   beta-minus decay radioisotopes
    BT2   beta decay radioisotopes
      BT3   radioisotopes
        BT4   isotopes
  BT1   cadmium isotopes
  BT1   even-odd nuclei
    BT2   nuclei
  BT1   intermediate mass nuclei
    BT2   nuclei
  BT1   millisec living radioisotopes
    BT2   radioisotopes
      BT3   isotopes

CADMIUM 126 [12; 12]
  BT1   beta-minus decay radioisotopes
    BT2   beta decay radioisotopes
      BT3   radioisotopes
        BT4   isotopes
  BT1   cadmium isotopes
  BT1   even-even nuclei
    BT2   nuclei
  BT1   intermediate mass nuclei
    BT2   nuclei
  BT1   millisec living radioisotopes
    BT2   radioisotopes
      BT3   isotopes

CADMIUM 127 [7; 7]
  BT1   cadmium isotopes
  BT1   even-odd nuclei
    BT2   nuclei
  BT1   intermediate mass nuclei
    BT2   nuclei
  BT1   millisec living radioisotopes
    BT2   radioisotopes
      BT3   isotopes

CADMIUM 128 [8; 8]
  BT1   cadmium isotopes
  BT1   even-even nuclei
    BT2   nuclei
  BT1   intermediate mass nuclei
    BT2   nuclei
  BT1   millisec living radioisotopes
    BT2   radioisotopes
      BT3   isotopes

CADMIUM 130 [7; 7] *Feb 87*
  BT1   beta-minus decay radioisotopes
    BT2   beta decay radioisotopes
      BT3   radioisotopes
        BT4   isotopes
  BT1   cadmium isotopes
  BT1   even-even nuclei
    BT2   nuclei
  BT1   intermediate mass nuclei
    BT2   nuclei
  BT1   millisec living radioisotopes
    BT2   radioisotopes
      BT3   isotopes

CADMIUM 96 [3; 3] *Jun 84*
  BT1   cadmium isotopes
  BT1   electron capture radioisotopes
    BT2   beta decay radioisotopes
      BT3   radioisotopes
        BT4   isotopes
  BT1   even-even nuclei
    BT2   nuclei
  BT1   intermediate mass nuclei
    BT2   nuclei
  BT1   millisec living radioisotopes
    BT2   radioisotopes
      BT3   isotopes

CADMIUM 97 [7; 7] *Feb 80*
  BT1   beta-plus decay radioisotopes
    BT2   beta decay radioisotopes
      BT3   radioisotopes
        BT4   isotopes
  BT1   cadmium isotopes
  BT1   electron capture radioisotopes
    BT2   beta decay radioisotopes
      BT3   radioisotopes
        BT4   isotopes
  BT1   even-odd nuclei
    BT2   nuclei
  BT1   intermediate mass nuclei
    BT2   nuclei
  BT1   seconds living radioisotopes
    BT2   radioisotopes
      BT3   isotopes

CADMIUM 98 [15; 15] *Feb 77*
  BT1   beta-plus decay radioisotopes
    BT2   beta decay radioisotopes
      BT3   radioisotopes
        BT4   isotopes
  BT1   cadmium isotopes
  BT1   even-even nuclei
    BT2   nuclei
  BT1   intermediate mass nuclei
    BT2   nuclei
  BT1   seconds living radioisotopes
    BT2   radioisotopes
      BT3   isotopes

CADMIUM 99 [5; 5] *Feb 80*
  BT1   beta-plus decay radioisotopes
    BT2   beta decay radioisotopes
      BT3   radioisotopes
        BT4   isotopes
  BT1   cadmium isotopes
  BT1   even-odd nuclei
    BT2   nuclei
  BT1   intermediate mass nuclei
    BT2   nuclei
  BT1   seconds living radioisotopes
    BT2   radioisotopes
      BT3   isotopes

caesium
  USE   cesium

CAFFEINE [567; 567]
  UF   *1,3,7-trimethylxanthine*
  BT1   analeptics
    BT2   central nervous system agents
      BT3   drugs
  BT1   xanthines
    BT2   organic oxygen compounds
      BT3   organic compounds
    BT2   purines
      BT3   heterocyclic compounds
        BT4   organic compounds
      BT3   organic nitrogen compounds
        BT4   organic compounds

cairo wwr-s reactor
  USE   wwr-s-cairo reactor

CALABASH EVENT [0; 0]
  BT1   nuclear explosions
    BT2   explosions
  BT1   underground explosions
    BT2   explosions

CALANDRIAS [246; 246]
  BT1   containers
  RT   pressure tubes

CALCINATION [1,390; 1,390]
  BT1   pyrolysis
    BT2   decomposition
      BT3   chemical reactions
  RT   calcined wastes
  RT   pyrometallurgy
  RT   radioactive waste processing
  RT   waste processing

CALCINED WASTES [134; 134] *Mar 81*
(Waste forms resulting from the calcination of aqueous nuclear fuel reprocessing wastes and composed of granular solids of metallic oxides.)
  BT1   radioactive wastes
    BT2   radioactive materials
      BT3   materials
    BT2   wastes
  RT   calcination
  RT   radioactive waste processing
  RT   solid wastes

calcinosis
  USE   calcium compounds
  AND   metabolic diseases

CALCITE [383; 383]
  UF   *chalk*
  BT1   carbonate minerals
    BT2   minerals
  RT   calcium carbonates
  RT   dolomite
  RT   limestone

CALCITONIN [220; 220]
- BT1 peptide hormones
- BT2 hormones
- BT1 polypeptides
- BT2 peptides
- BT3 proteins
- BT4 organic compounds
- RT calcium
- RT parathyroid glands
- RT thymus
- RT thyroid

CALCIUM [4,472; 4,472]
- BT1 alkaline earth metals
- BT2 metals
- BT3 elements
- RT blood coagulation factors
- RT bone tissues
- RT calcitonin
- RT hyperparathyroidism
- RT parathormone
- RT teeth
- RT thyrocalcitonin

CALCIUM ADDITIONS [83; 83]
(Alloys containing not more than 1% Ca are listed here.)
- RT calcium alloys
- RT calcium compounds

CALCIUM ALLOYS [78; 95]
(Alloys containing more than 1% Ca.)
- BT1 alloys
- NT1 calcium base alloys
- RT calcium additions

CALCIUM BASE ALLOYS [9; 9]
- BT1 calcium alloys
- BT2 alloys

CALCIUM BORIDES [16; 16]
- BT1 borides
- BT2 boron compounds
- BT1 calcium compounds
- BT2 alkaline earth metal compounds

CALCIUM BROMIDES [41; 41]
- BT1 bromides
- BT2 bromine compounds
- BT3 halogen compounds
- BT2 halides
- BT3 halogen compounds
- BT1 calcium halides
- BT2 calcium compounds
- BT3 alkaline earth metal compounds
- BT2 halides
- BT3 halogen compounds

CALCIUM CARBIDES [16; 16]
- BT1 calcium compounds
- BT2 alkaline earth metal compounds
- BT1 carbides
- BT2 carbon compounds

CALCIUM CARBONATES [453; 695]
- UF+ *marble*
- BT1 calcium compounds
- BT2 alkaline earth metal compounds
- BT1 carbonates
- BT2 carbon compounds
- BT2 oxygen compounds
- RT aragonite
- RT calcite
- RT carbonate minerals
- RT dolomite
- RT liebigite
- RT limestone
- RT phosphate rocks
- RT schroeckingerite

CALCIUM CHLORIDES [481; 481]
- BT1 calcium halides
- BT2 calcium compounds
- BT3 alkaline earth metal compounds
- BT2 halides
- BT3 halogen compounds
- BT1 chlorides
- BT2 chlorine compounds
- BT3 halogen compounds
- BT2 halides
- BT3 halogen compounds

CALCIUM COMPLEXES [123; 123]
- BT1 alkaline earth metal complexes
- BT2 complexes

CALCIUM COMPOUNDS [2,414; 9,687]
- UF+ *calcinosis*
- BT1 alkaline earth metal compounds
- NT1 calcium borides
- NT1 calcium carbides
- NT1 calcium carbonates
- NT1 calcium halides
- NT2 calcium bromides
- NT2 calcium chlorides
- NT2 calcium fluorides
- NT2 calcium iodides
- NT1 calcium hydrides
- NT1 calcium hydroxides
- NT1 calcium nitrates
- NT1 calcium nitrides
- NT1 calcium oxides
- NT1 calcium phosphates
- NT1 calcium silicates
- NT2 andradite
- NT2 uranotile
- NT1 calcium silicides
- NT1 calcium sulfates
- NT1 calcium sulfides
- NT1 calcium tungstates
- RT calcium additions

CALCIUM FLUORIDES [1,413; 1,626]
- BT1 calcium halides
- BT2 calcium compounds
- BT3 alkaline earth metal compounds
- BT2 halides
- BT3 halogen compounds
- BT1 fluorides
- BT2 fluorine compounds
- BT3 halogen compounds
- BT2 halides
- BT3 halogen compounds
- RT fluorite
- RT halide minerals
- RT thermoluminescent dosemeters

CALCIUM HALIDES [1; 817] *Oct 83*
- BT1 calcium compounds
- BT2 alkaline earth metal compounds
- BT1 halides
- BT2 halogen compounds
- NT1 calcium bromides
- NT1 calcium chlorides
- NT1 calcium fluorides
- NT1 calcium iodides

CALCIUM HYDRIDES [46; 46]
- BT1 calcium compounds
- BT2 alkaline earth metal compounds
- BT1 hydrides
- BT2 hydrogen compounds

CALCIUM HYDROXIDES [173; 173]
- BT1 calcium compounds
- BT2 alkaline earth metal compounds
- BT1 hydroxides
- BT2 hydrogen compounds
- BT2 oxygen compounds

calcium hydroxyapatite
- USE apatites
- AND calcium phosphates

CALCIUM IODIDES [37; 37]
- BT1 calcium halides
- BT2 calcium compounds
- BT3 alkaline earth metal compounds
- BT2 halides
- BT3 halogen compounds
- BT1 iodides
- BT2 halides
- BT3 halogen compounds
- BT2 iodine compounds
- BT3 halogen compounds

CALCIUM IONS [873; 873]
- BT1 ions
- BT2 charged particles

CALCIUM ISOTOPES [376; 5,516]
- NT1 calcium 35
- NT1 calcium 36
- NT1 calcium 37
- NT1 calcium 38
- NT1 calcium 39
- NT1 calcium 40
- NT1 calcium 41
- NT1 calcium 42
- NT1 calcium 43
- NT1 calcium 44
- NT1 calcium 45
- NT1 calcium 46
- NT1 calcium 47
- NT1 calcium 48
- NT1 calcium 49
- NT1 calcium 50
- NT1 calcium 51
- NT1 calcium 52
- NT1 calcium 53
- RT bone seekers

CALCIUM NITRATES [107; 107]
- BT1 calcium compounds
- BT2 alkaline earth metal compounds
- BT1 nitrates
- BT2 nitrogen compounds
- BT2 oxygen compounds

CALCIUM NITRIDES [9; 9]
- BT1 calcium compounds
- BT2 alkaline earth metal compounds
- BT1 nitrides
- BT2 nitrogen compounds
- BT2 pnictides

CALCIUM OXIDES [2,693; 2,921]
- BT1 calcium compounds
- BT2 alkaline earth metal compounds
- BT1 oxides
- BT2 chalcogenides
- BT2 oxygen compounds
- RT becquerelite
- RT oxide minerals
- RT perovskite
- RT tyuyamunite
- RT zeunerite
- RT zirconolite

→ **CALCIUM PERCHLORATES** [0; 0]
Sep 91
- BT1 cadmium compounds
- BT1 perchlorates
- BT2 chlorine compounds
- BT3 halogen compounds
- BT2 oxygen compounds

CALCIUM PHOSPHATES [194; 194]
- UF+ *calcium hydroxyapatite*
- BT1 calcium compounds
- BT2 alkaline earth metal compounds
- BT1 phosphates
- BT2 oxygen compounds
- BT2 phosphorus compounds
- RT lermontovite
- RT phosphate rocks

CALCIUM SILICATES [122; 145]
- BT1 calcium compounds
- BT2 alkaline earth metal compounds
- BT1 silicates
- BT2 oxygen compounds
- BT2 silicon compounds
- NT1 andradite
- NT1 uranotile
- RT eudialyte

CALCIUM SILICATES
- RT garnets
- RT ilvaite
- RT silicate minerals
- RT uranophane

→ **CALCIUM SILICIDES** [0; 0] *Sep 91*
- BT1 calcium compounds
- BT2 alkaline earth metal compounds
- BT1 silicides
- BT2 silicon compounds

CALCIUM SULFATES [871; 981]
- BT1 calcium compounds
- BT2 alkaline earth metal compounds
- BT1 sulfates
- BT2 oxygen compounds
- BT2 sulfur compounds
- RT anhydrite
- RT gypsum
- RT polyhalite
- RT sulfate minerals
- RT thermoluminescent dosemeters

CALCIUM SULFIDES [89; 89]
- BT1 calcium compounds
- BT2 alkaline earth metal compounds
- BT1 sulfides
- BT2 chalcogenides
- BT2 sulfur compounds

CALCIUM TUNGSTATES [172; 172]
- BT1 calcium compounds
- BT2 alkaline earth metal compounds
- BT1 tungstates
- BT2 oxygen compounds
- BT2 tungsten compounds
- BT3 transition element compounds

CALCIUM 35 [11; 11]
- BT1 calcium isotopes
- BT1 even-odd nuclei
- BT2 nuclei
- BT1 light nuclei
- BT2 nuclei

CALCIUM 36 [7; 7]
- BT1 beta-plus decay radioisotopes
- BT2 beta decay radioisotopes
- BT3 radioisotopes
- BT4 isotopes
- BT1 calcium isotopes
- BT1 even-even nuclei
- BT2 nuclei
- BT1 light nuclei
- BT2 nuclei
- BT1 millisec living radioisotopes
- BT2 radioisotopes
- BT3 isotopes

CALCIUM 37 [12; 12]
- BT1 beta-plus decay radioisotopes
- BT2 beta decay radioisotopes
- BT3 radioisotopes
- BT4 isotopes
- BT1 calcium isotopes
- BT1 even-odd nuclei
- BT2 nuclei
- BT1 light nuclei
- BT2 nuclei
- BT1 millisec living radioisotopes
- BT2 radioisotopes
- BT3 isotopes

CALCIUM 38 [20; 20]
- BT1 beta-plus decay radioisotopes
- BT2 beta decay radioisotopes
- BT3 radioisotopes
- BT4 isotopes
- BT1 calcium isotopes
- BT1 even-even nuclei
- BT2 nuclei
- BT1 light nuclei
- BT2 nuclei
- BT1 millisec living radioisotopes
- BT2 radioisotopes
- BT3 isotopes

CALCIUM 39 [102; 102]
- BT1 beta-plus decay radioisotopes
- BT2 beta decay radioisotopes
- BT3 radioisotopes
- BT4 isotopes
- BT1 calcium isotopes
- BT1 even-odd nuclei
- BT2 nuclei
- BT1 light nuclei
- BT2 nuclei
- BT1 millisec living radioisotopes
- BT2 radioisotopes
- BT3 isotopes

CALCIUM 40 [2,294; 2,294]
- BT1 calcium isotopes
- BT1 even-even nuclei
- BT2 nuclei
- BT1 light nuclei
- BT2 nuclei
- BT1 stable isotopes
- BT2 isotopes

CALCIUM 40 BEAMS [52; 52] *Oct 76*
- BT1 ion beams
- BT2 beams

CALCIUM 40 REACTIONS [610; 610]
- BT1 heavy ion reactions
- BT2 nuclear reactions

CALCIUM 40 TARGET [3,162; 3,162]
- BT1 targets

CALCIUM 41 [444; 444]
- BT1 calcium isotopes
- BT1 electron capture radioisotopes
- BT2 beta decay radioisotopes
- BT3 radioisotopes
- BT4 isotopes
- BT1 even-odd nuclei
- BT2 nuclei
- BT1 intermediate mass nuclei
- BT2 nuclei
- BT1 years living radioisotopes
- BT2 radioisotopes
- BT3 isotopes

CALCIUM 41 TARGET [53; 53]
- BT1 targets

CALCIUM 42 [386; 386]
- BT1 calcium isotopes
- BT1 even-even nuclei
- BT2 nuclei
- BT1 intermediate mass nuclei
- BT2 nuclei
- BT1 stable isotopes
- BT2 isotopes

CALCIUM 42 REACTIONS [5; 5] *Nov 84*
- BT1 heavy ion reactions
- BT2 nuclear reactions

CALCIUM 42 TARGET [294; 294]
- BT1 targets

CALCIUM 43 [139; 139]
- BT1 calcium isotopes
- BT1 even-odd nuclei
- BT2 nuclei
- BT1 intermediate mass nuclei
- BT2 nuclei
- BT1 stable isotopes
- BT2 isotopes

CALCIUM 43 TARGET [27; 27]
- BT1 targets

CALCIUM 44 [330; 330]
- BT1 calcium isotopes
- BT1 even-even nuclei
- BT2 nuclei
- BT1 intermediate mass nuclei
- BT2 nuclei
- BT1 stable isotopes
- BT2 isotopes

CALCIUM 44 REACTIONS [15; 15] *Sep 77*
- BT1 heavy ion reactions
- BT2 nuclear reactions

CALCIUM 44 TARGET [321; 321]
- BT1 targets

CALCIUM 45 [1,302; 1,302]
- BT1 beta-minus decay radioisotopes
- BT2 beta decay radioisotopes
- BT3 radioisotopes
- BT4 isotopes
- BT1 calcium isotopes
- BT1 days living radioisotopes
- BT2 radioisotopes
- BT3 isotopes
- BT1 even-odd nuclei
- BT2 nuclei
- BT1 intermediate mass nuclei
- BT2 nuclei

CALCIUM 46 [96; 96]
- BT1 calcium isotopes
- BT1 even-even nuclei
- BT2 nuclei
- BT1 intermediate mass nuclei
- BT2 nuclei
- BT1 stable isotopes
- BT2 isotopes

CALCIUM 46 TARGET [19; 19]
- BT1 targets

CALCIUM 47 [264; 264]
- BT1 beta-minus decay radioisotopes
- BT2 beta decay radioisotopes
- BT3 radioisotopes
- BT4 isotopes
- BT1 calcium isotopes
- BT1 days living radioisotopes
- BT2 radioisotopes
- BT3 isotopes
- BT1 even-odd nuclei
- BT2 nuclei
- BT1 intermediate mass nuclei
- BT2 nuclei

CALCIUM 48 [676; 676]
- BT1 calcium isotopes
- BT1 even-even nuclei
- BT2 nuclei
- BT1 intermediate mass nuclei
- BT2 nuclei
- BT1 stable isotopes
- BT2 isotopes

CALCIUM 48 BEAMS [29; 29] *Apr 77*
- BT1 ion beams
- BT2 beams

CALCIUM 48 REACTIONS [219; 219] *Nov 76*
- BT1 heavy ion reactions
- BT2 nuclear reactions

CALCIUM 48 TARGET [828; 828]
- BT1 targets

CALCIUM 49 [99; 99]
- BT1 beta-minus decay radioisotopes
- BT2 beta decay radioisotopes
- BT3 radioisotopes
- BT4 isotopes
- BT1 calcium isotopes
- BT1 even-odd nuclei
- BT2 nuclei
- BT1 intermediate mass nuclei
- BT2 nuclei
- BT1 minutes living radioisotopes
- BT2 radioisotopes
- BT3 isotopes

CALCIUM 49 TARGET [4; 4] *Jun 84*
BT1 targets

CALCIUM 50 [25; 25]
BT1 beta-minus decay radioisotopes
BT2 beta decay radioisotopes
BT3 radioisotopes
BT4 isotopes
BT1 calcium isotopes
BT1 even-even nuclei
BT2 nuclei
BT1 intermediate mass nuclei
BT2 nuclei
BT1 seconds living radioisotopes
BT2 radioisotopes
BT3 isotopes

CALCIUM 51 [8; 8] *Jun 84*
BT1 beta-minus decay radioisotopes
BT2 beta decay radioisotopes
BT3 radioisotopes
BT4 isotopes
BT1 calcium isotopes
BT1 even-odd nuclei
BT2 nuclei
BT1 intermediate mass nuclei
BT2 nuclei
BT1 seconds living radioisotopes
BT2 radioisotopes
BT3 isotopes

CALCIUM 52 [3; 3] *Oct 84*
BT1 beta-minus decay radioisotopes
BT2 beta decay radioisotopes
BT3 radioisotopes
BT4 isotopes
BT1 calcium isotopes
BT1 even-even nuclei
BT2 nuclei
BT1 intermediate mass nuclei
BT2 nuclei
BT1 seconds living radioisotopes
BT2 radioisotopes
BT3 isotopes

CALCIUM 53 [3; 3] *Jun 84*
BT1 beta-minus decay radioisotopes
BT2 beta decay radioisotopes
BT3 radioisotopes
BT4 isotopes
BT1 calcium isotopes
BT1 even-odd nuclei
BT2 nuclei
BT1 intermediate mass nuclei
BT2 nuclei
BT1 millisec living radioisotopes
BT2 radioisotopes
BT3 isotopes

calcretes
USE limestone

calculations (computer)
USE computer calculations

calculations (many dimensions)
USE many-dimensional calculations

calculations (1-dimensional)
USE one-dimensional calculations

calculations (2-dimensional)
USE two-dimensional calculations

calculations (3-dimensional)
USE three-dimensional calculations

calculations (4-dimensional)
USE four-dimensional calculations

CALCULATORS [22; 22] *Dec 85*
(Small, often hand-held, devices capable of carrying out limited logic and arithmetic operations.)
UF *pocket calculators*
BT1 digital computers
BT2 computers
BT1 portable equipment
BT2 equipment
RT data processing

CALCULI [500; 500]
(In biology and medicine only; to be assigned in coordination with descriptors specifying their location such as URINARY TRACT, PANCREAS, etc.)
UF+ *gallstones*
UF+ *kidney stones*
RT kidneys
RT urinary tract

calculus (differential)
USE differential calculus

CALCUTTA CYCLOTRON [23; 23]
Jun 83
BT1 cyclotrons
BT2 cyclic accelerators
BT3 accelerators
BT1 heavy ion accelerators
BT2 accelerators

CALDASITE [12; 12]
BT1 rocks
RT baddeleyite
RT zircon

CALDER HALL A-1 REACTOR [21; 21]
(Seascale, Cumbria, UK)
UF *a-1 reactor (calder hall)*
BT1 carbon dioxide cooled reactors
BT2 gas cooled reactors
BT3 reactors
BT1 magnox type reactors
BT2 gcr type reactors
BT3 gas cooled reactors
BT4 reactors
BT3 graphite moderated reactors
BT4 reactors
BT2 natural uranium reactors
BT3 reactors
BT2 power reactors
BT3 reactors
BT1 plutonium production reactors
BT2 production reactors
BT3 reactors
BT1 thermal reactors
BT2 reactors

CALDER HALL A-2 REACTOR [15; 15]
(Seascale, Cumbria, UK)
UF *a-2 reactor (calder hall)*
BT1 carbon dioxide cooled reactors
BT2 gas cooled reactors
BT3 reactors
BT1 magnox type reactors
BT2 gcr type reactors
BT3 gas cooled reactors
BT4 reactors
BT3 graphite moderated reactors
BT4 reactors
BT2 natural uranium reactors
BT3 reactors
BT2 power reactors
BT3 reactors
BT1 plutonium production reactors
BT2 production reactors
BT3 reactors
BT1 thermal reactors
BT2 reactors

CALDER HALL B-3 REACTOR [14; 14]
(Seascale, Cumbria, UK)
BT1 carbon dioxide cooled reactors
BT2 gas cooled reactors
BT3 reactors
BT1 magnox type reactors
BT2 gcr type reactors
BT3 gas cooled reactors
BT4 reactors
BT3 graphite moderated reactors
BT4 reactors
BT2 natural uranium reactors
BT3 reactors
BT2 power reactors
BT3 reactors
BT1 plutonium production reactors
BT2 production reactors
BT3 reactors
BT1 thermal reactors
BT2 reactors

CALDER HALL B-4 REACTOR [15; 15]
(Seascale, Cumbria, UK)
BT1 carbon dioxide cooled reactors
BT2 gas cooled reactors
BT3 reactors
BT1 magnox type reactors
BT2 gcr type reactors
BT3 gas cooled reactors
BT4 reactors
BT3 graphite moderated reactors
BT4 reactors
BT2 natural uranium reactors
BT3 reactors
BT2 power reactors
BT3 reactors
BT1 plutonium production reactors
BT2 production reactors
BT3 reactors
BT1 thermal reactors
BT2 reactors

calderas
USE geologic structures
AND volcanoes

CALHOUN-1 REACTOR [100; 100]
UF *ft. calhoun-1 reactor*
BT1 pwr type reactors
BT2 enriched uranium reactors
BT3 reactors
BT2 power reactors
BT3 reactors
BT2 thermal reactors
BT3 reactors
BT2 water cooled reactors
BT3 reactors
BT2 water moderated reactors
BT3 reactors

CALHOUN-2 REACTOR [16; 16]
Feb 76
UF *ft. calhoun-2 reactor*
BT1 pwr type reactors
BT2 enriched uranium reactors
BT3 reactors
BT2 power reactors
BT3 reactors
BT2 thermal reactors
BT3 reactors
BT2 water cooled reactors
BT3 reactors
BT2 water moderated reactors
BT3 reactors

CALIBRATION [12,914; 12,914]
RT absolute counting
RT accuracy
RT calibration standards
RT inspection
RT scaling laws

CALIBRATION STANDARDS
[5,019; 5,019]
UF *reference materials (standard)*
UF *srm*
UF *standard reference materials*
UF *standards (calibration)*
BT1 standards
RT accuracy
RT calibration
RT interlaboratory comparisons
RT nisus facility

RT   ssdl
RT   standardization
RT   standards document

CALIFORNIA [728; 728]
- BT1   usa
  - BT2   developed countries
  - BT2   north america
- RT   atomics international canoga p
- RT   lawrence berkeley laboratory
- RT   lawrence livermore laboratory
- RT   lawrence livermore national la
- RT   sandia laboratories
- RT   sandia national laboratories
- RT   stanford linear accelerator ce
- RT   ucla

california berkeley triga reac
USE   ucbrr reactor

california irvine triga-mk-1 r
USE   triga-1-california reactor

CALIFORNIUM [274; 274]
- BT1   actinides
  - BT2   metals
    - BT3   elements
- BT1   transplutonium elements
  - BT2   transuranium elements
    - BT3   elements

CALIFORNIUM ALLOYS [8; 8] *Apr 79*
(Alloys containing more than 1% Cf.)
- BT1   actinide alloys
  - BT2   alloys

CALIFORNIUM ARSENIDES [4; 4] *Apr 79*
- BT1   arsenides
  - BT2   arsenic compounds
  - BT2   pnictides
- BT1   californium compounds
  - BT2   actinide compounds
  - BT2   transplutonium compounds
    - BT3   transuranium compounds

CALIFORNIUM BROMIDES [13; 13]
- BT1   bromides
  - BT2   bromine compounds
    - BT3   halogen compounds
  - BT2   halides
    - BT3   halogen compounds
- BT1   californium compounds
  - BT2   actinide compounds
  - BT2   transplutonium compounds
    - BT3   transuranium compounds

CALIFORNIUM CARBIDES [0; 0]
- BT1   californium compounds
  - BT2   actinide compounds
  - BT2   transplutonium compounds
    - BT3   transuranium compounds
- BT1   carbides
  - BT2   carbon compounds

CALIFORNIUM CHLORIDES [26; 26]
- BT1   californium compounds
  - BT2   actinide compounds
  - BT2   transplutonium compounds
    - BT3   transuranium compounds
- BT1   chlorides
  - BT2   chlorine compounds
    - BT3   halogen compounds
  - BT2   halides
    - BT3   halogen compounds

CALIFORNIUM COMPLEXES [103; 103]
- BT1   actinide complexes
  - BT2   complexes
- BT1   transuranium complexes

CALIFORNIUM COMPOUNDS [118; 232]
- BT1   actinide compounds
- BT1   transplutonium compounds
  - BT2   transuranium compounds
- NT1   californium arsenides
- NT1   californium bromides
- NT1   californium carbides
- NT1   californium chlorides
- NT1   californium fluorides
- NT1   californium iodides
- NT1   californium nitrates
- NT1   californium nitrides
- NT1   californium oxides
- NT1   californium selenides
- NT1   californium sulfates
- NT1   californium sulfides
- NT1   californium tellurides

CALIFORNIUM FLUORIDES [19; 19]
- BT1   californium compounds
  - BT2   actinide compounds
  - BT2   transplutonium compounds
    - BT3   transuranium compounds
- BT1   fluorides
  - BT2   fluorine compounds
    - BT3   halogen compounds
  - BT2   halides
    - BT3   halogen compounds

CALIFORNIUM IODIDES [7; 7]
- BT1   californium compounds
  - BT2   actinide compounds
  - BT2   transplutonium compounds
    - BT3   transuranium compounds
- BT1   iodides
  - BT2   halides
    - BT3   halogen compounds
  - BT2   iodine compounds
    - BT3   halogen compounds

CALIFORNIUM IONS [15; 15]
- BT1   ions
  - BT2   charged particles

CALIFORNIUM ISOTOPES [93; 3,843]
- NT1   californium 239
- NT1   californium 240
- NT1   californium 241
- NT1   californium 242
- NT1   californium 243
- NT1   californium 244
- NT1   californium 245
- NT1   californium 246
- NT1   californium 247
- NT1   californium 248
- NT1   californium 249
- NT1   californium 250
- NT1   californium 251
- NT1   californium 252
- NT1   californium 253
- NT1   californium 254
- NT1   californium 255
- NT1   californium 256

CALIFORNIUM NITRATES [9; 9]
- BT1   californium compounds
  - BT2   actinide compounds
  - BT2   transplutonium compounds
    - BT3   transuranium compounds
- BT1   nitrates
  - BT2   nitrogen compounds
  - BT2   oxygen compounds

CALIFORNIUM NITRIDES [1; 1]
- BT1   californium compounds
  - BT2   actinide compounds
  - BT2   transplutonium compounds
    - BT3   transuranium compounds
- BT1   nitrides
  - BT2   nitrogen compounds
  - BT2   pnictides

CALIFORNIUM OXIDES [47; 47]
- BT1   californium compounds
  - BT2   actinide compounds
  - BT2   transplutonium compounds
    - BT3   transuranium compounds
- BT1   oxides
  - BT2   chalcogenides
  - BT2   oxygen compounds

CALIFORNIUM SELENIDES [2; 2] *Apr 79*
- BT1   californium compounds
  - BT2   actinide compounds
  - BT2   transplutonium compounds
    - BT3   transuranium compounds
- BT1   selenides
  - BT2   chalcogenides
  - BT2   selenium compounds

CALIFORNIUM SULFATES [2; 2]
- BT1   californium compounds
  - BT2   actinide compounds
  - BT2   transplutonium compounds
    - BT3   transuranium compounds
- BT1   sulfates
  - BT2   oxygen compounds
  - BT2   sulfur compounds

CALIFORNIUM SULFIDES [2; 2]
- BT1   californium compounds
  - BT2   actinide compounds
  - BT2   transplutonium compounds
    - BT3   transuranium compounds
- BT1   sulfides
  - BT2   chalcogenides
  - BT2   sulfur compounds

CALIFORNIUM TELLURIDES [2; 2] *Apr 79*
- BT1   californium compounds
  - BT2   actinide compounds
  - BT2   transplutonium compounds
    - BT3   transuranium compounds
- BT1   tellurides
  - BT2   chalcogenides
  - BT2   tellurium compounds

CALIFORNIUM 239 [0; 0] *Jun 86*
- BT1   actinide nuclei
  - BT2   heavy nuclei
    - BT3   nuclei
- BT1   alpha decay radioisotopes
  - BT2   radioisotopes
    - BT3   isotopes
- BT1   californium isotopes
- BT1   even-odd nuclei
  - BT2   nuclei
- BT1   seconds living radioisotopes
  - BT2   radioisotopes
    - BT3   isotopes

CALIFORNIUM 240 [0; 0] *Jun 86*
- BT1   actinide nuclei
  - BT2   heavy nuclei
    - BT3   nuclei
- BT1   alpha decay radioisotopes
  - BT2   radioisotopes
    - BT3   isotopes
- BT1   californium isotopes
- BT1   even-even nuclei
  - BT2   nuclei
- BT1   minutes living radioisotopes
  - BT2   radioisotopes
    - BT3   isotopes

CALIFORNIUM 241 [0; 0] *Jun 86*
- BT1   actinide nuclei
  - BT2   heavy nuclei
    - BT3   nuclei
- BT1   alpha decay radioisotopes
  - BT2   radioisotopes
    - BT3   isotopes
- BT1   californium isotopes
- BT1   electron capture radioisotopes
  - BT2   beta decay radioisotopes
    - BT3   radioisotopes
      - BT4   isotopes

CALIFORNIUM 241
- BT1 even-odd nuclei
- BT2 nuclei
- BT1 minutes living radioisotopes
- BT2 radioisotopes
- BT3 isotopes

CALIFORNIUM 242 [15; 15]
- BT1 actinide nuclei
- BT2 heavy nuclei
- BT3 nuclei
- BT1 alpha decay radioisotopes
- BT2 radioisotopes
- BT3 isotopes
- BT1 californium isotopes
- BT1 even-even nuclei
- BT2 nuclei
- BT1 minutes living radioisotopes
- BT2 radioisotopes
- BT3 isotopes

CALIFORNIUM 243 [4; 4]
- BT1 actinide nuclei
- BT2 heavy nuclei
- BT3 nuclei
- BT1 alpha decay radioisotopes
- BT2 radioisotopes
- BT3 isotopes
- BT1 californium isotopes
- BT1 electron capture radioisotopes
- BT2 beta decay radioisotopes
- BT3 radioisotopes
- BT4 isotopes
- BT1 even-odd nuclei
- BT2 nuclei
- BT1 minutes living radioisotopes
- BT2 radioisotopes
- BT3 isotopes

CALIFORNIUM 244 [32; 32]
- BT1 actinide nuclei
- BT2 heavy nuclei
- BT3 nuclei
- BT1 alpha decay radioisotopes
- BT2 radioisotopes
- BT3 isotopes
- BT1 californium isotopes
- BT1 even-even nuclei
- BT2 nuclei
- BT1 minutes living radioisotopes
- BT2 radioisotopes
- BT3 isotopes

CALIFORNIUM 245 [15; 15]
- BT1 actinide nuclei
- BT2 heavy nuclei
- BT3 nuclei
- BT1 alpha decay radioisotopes
- BT2 radioisotopes
- BT3 isotopes
- BT1 californium isotopes
- BT1 electron capture radioisotopes
- BT2 beta decay radioisotopes
- BT3 radioisotopes
- BT4 isotopes
- BT1 even-odd nuclei
- BT2 nuclei
- BT1 minutes living radioisotopes
- BT2 radioisotopes
- BT3 isotopes

CALIFORNIUM 246 [35; 35]
- BT1 actinide nuclei
- BT2 heavy nuclei
- BT3 nuclei
- BT1 alpha decay radioisotopes
- BT2 radioisotopes
- BT3 isotopes
- BT1 californium isotopes
- BT1 days living radioisotopes
- BT2 radioisotopes
- BT3 isotopes
- BT1 even-even nuclei
- BT2 nuclei
- BT1 spontaneous fission radioisoto
- BT2 radioisotopes
- BT3 isotopes

CALIFORNIUM 247 [10; 10]
- BT1 actinide nuclei
- BT2 heavy nuclei
- BT3 nuclei
- BT1 alpha decay radioisotopes
- BT2 radioisotopes
- BT3 isotopes
- BT1 californium isotopes
- BT1 electron capture radioisotopes
- BT2 beta decay radioisotopes
- BT3 radioisotopes
- BT4 isotopes
- BT1 even-odd nuclei
- BT2 nuclei
- BT1 hours living radioisotopes
- BT2 radioisotopes
- BT3 isotopes
- BT1 internal conversion radioisoto
- BT2 radioisotopes
- BT3 isotopes

CALIFORNIUM 248 [37; 37]
- BT1 actinide nuclei
- BT2 heavy nuclei
- BT3 nuclei
- BT1 alpha decay radioisotopes
- BT2 radioisotopes
- BT3 isotopes
- BT1 californium isotopes
- BT1 days living radioisotopes
- BT2 radioisotopes
- BT3 isotopes
- BT1 even-even nuclei
- BT2 nuclei
- BT1 spontaneous fission radioisoto
- BT2 radioisotopes
- BT3 isotopes

CALIFORNIUM 249 [243; 243]
- BT1 actinide nuclei
- BT2 heavy nuclei
- BT3 nuclei
- BT1 alpha decay radioisotopes
- BT2 radioisotopes
- BT3 isotopes
- BT1 californium isotopes
- BT1 even-odd nuclei
- BT2 nuclei
- BT1 spontaneous fission radioisoto
- BT2 radioisotopes
- BT3 isotopes
- BT1 years living radioisotopes
- BT2 radioisotopes
- BT3 isotopes

CALIFORNIUM 249 TARGET [93; 93]
- BT1 targets

CALIFORNIUM 250 [69; 69]
- BT1 actinide nuclei
- BT2 heavy nuclei
- BT3 nuclei
- BT1 alpha decay radioisotopes
- BT2 radioisotopes
- BT3 isotopes
- BT1 californium isotopes
- BT1 even-even nuclei
- BT2 nuclei
- BT1 internal conversion radioisoto
- BT2 radioisotopes
- BT3 isotopes
- BT1 spontaneous fission radioisoto
- BT2 radioisotopes
- BT3 isotopes
- BT1 years living radioisotopes
- BT2 radioisotopes
- BT3 isotopes

CALIFORNIUM 250 TARGET [17; 17]
Jul 78
- BT1 targets

CALIFORNIUM 251 [33; 33]
- BT1 actinide nuclei
- BT2 heavy nuclei
- BT3 nuclei
- BT1 alpha decay radioisotopes
- BT2 radioisotopes
- BT3 isotopes
- BT1 californium isotopes
- BT1 even-odd nuclei
- BT2 nuclei
- BT1 years living radioisotopes
- BT2 radioisotopes
- BT3 isotopes

CALIFORNIUM 251 TARGET [6; 6]
- BT1 targets

CALIFORNIUM 252 [3,366; 3,366]
- BT1 actinide nuclei
- BT2 heavy nuclei
- BT3 nuclei
- BT1 alpha decay radioisotopes
- BT2 radioisotopes
- BT3 isotopes
- BT1 californium isotopes
- BT1 even-even nuclei
- BT2 nuclei
- BT1 spontaneous fission radioisoto
- BT2 radioisotopes
- BT3 isotopes
- BT1 years living radioisotopes
- BT2 radioisotopes
- BT3 isotopes

CALIFORNIUM 252 TARGET [64; 64]
- BT1 targets

CALIFORNIUM 253 [12; 12]
- BT1 actinide nuclei
- BT2 heavy nuclei
- BT3 nuclei
- BT1 alpha decay radioisotopes
- BT2 radioisotopes
- BT3 isotopes
- BT1 beta-minus decay radioisotopes
- BT2 beta decay radioisotopes
- BT3 radioisotopes
- BT4 isotopes
- BT1 californium isotopes
- BT1 days living radioisotopes
- BT2 radioisotopes
- BT3 isotopes
- BT1 even-odd nuclei
- BT2 nuclei

CALIFORNIUM 254 [31; 31]
- BT1 actinide nuclei
- BT2 heavy nuclei
- BT3 nuclei
- BT1 alpha decay radioisotopes
- BT2 radioisotopes
- BT3 isotopes
- BT1 californium isotopes
- BT1 days living radioisotopes
- BT2 radioisotopes
- BT3 isotopes
- BT1 even-even nuclei
- BT2 nuclei
- BT1 spontaneous fission radioisoto
- BT2 radioisotopes
- BT3 isotopes

CALIFORNIUM 254 TARGET [5; 5]
Sep 78
- BT1 targets

CALIFORNIUM 255 [5; 5] *Jan 77*
- BT1 actinide nuclei
- BT2 heavy nuclei
- BT3 nuclei
- BT1 beta-minus decay radioisotopes
- BT2 beta decay radioisotopes
- BT3 radioisotopes
- BT4 isotopes
- BT1 californium isotopes
- BT1 even-odd nuclei
- BT2 nuclei
- BT1 hours living radioisotopes
- BT2 radioisotopes
- BT3 isotopes

CALIFORNIUM 256 [8; 8] *Sep 78*
- BT1 actinide nuclei
- BT2 heavy nuclei
- BT3 nuclei
- BT1 californium isotopes
- BT1 even-even nuclei
- BT2 nuclei
- BT1 minutes living radioisotopes
- BT2 radioisotopes
- BT3 isotopes
- BT1 spontaneous fission radioisoto
- BT2 radioisotopes
- BT3 isotopes

CALLAWAY-1 REACTOR [27; 27]
(Fulton, Missouri, USA)
- BT1 pwr type reactors
- BT2 enriched uranium reactors
- BT3 reactors
- BT2 power reactors
- BT3 reactors
- BT2 thermal reactors
- BT3 reactors
- BT2 water cooled reactors
- BT3 reactors
- BT2 water moderated reactors
- BT3 reactors

CALLAWAY-2 REACTOR [14; 14]
(Fulton, Missouri, USA)
- BT1 pwr type reactors
- BT2 enriched uranium reactors
- BT3 reactors
- BT2 power reactors
- BT3 reactors
- BT2 thermal reactors
- BT3 reactors
- BT2 water cooled reactors
- BT3 reactors
- BT2 water moderated reactors
- BT3 reactors

calorimeter detectors
- USE shower counters

CALORIMETERS [2,304; 2,304]
- BT1 measuring instruments
- RT calorimetric dosemeters
- RT calorimetry
- RT temperature measurement

CALORIMETRIC DOSEMETERS [343; 343]
- BT1 dosemeters
- BT2 measuring instruments
- RT calorimeters
- RT thermocouples

CALORIMETRY [1,680; 1,680]
- RT calorimeters
- RT heat transfer
- RT temperature measurement

calorizing
- USE diffusion coating

CALTECH SYNCHROTRON [4; 4]
- UF *cit synchrotron*
- BT1 synchrotrons
- BT2 cyclic accelerators
- BT3 accelerators

CALVERT CLIFFS-1 REACTOR [176; 176]
(Lusby, Maryland, USA)
- BT1 pwr type reactors
- BT2 enriched uranium reactors
- BT3 reactors
- BT2 power reactors
- BT3 reactors
- BT2 thermal reactors
- BT3 reactors
- BT2 water cooled reactors
- BT3 reactors
- BT2 water moderated reactors
- BT3 reactors

CALVERT CLIFFS-2 REACTOR [121; 121]
(Lusby, Maryland, USA)
- BT1 pwr type reactors
- BT2 enriched uranium reactors
- BT3 reactors
- BT2 power reactors
- BT3 reactors
- BT2 thermal reactors
- BT3 reactors
- BT2 water cooled reactors
- BT3 reactors
- BT2 water moderated reactors
- BT3 reactors

CALVES [320; 320]
- BT1 cattle
- BT2 domestic animals
- BT3 animals
- BT2 ruminants
- BT3 mammals
- BT4 vertebrates
- BT5 animals

cam
- USE computer-aided manufacturing

CAMAC SYSTEM [3,722; 3,722]
(Computer Application to Measurement And Control.)
- RT computers
- RT data acquisition systems
- RT data transmission
- RT electronic equipment
- RT equipment interfaces
- RT fastbus system
- RT modular structures
- RT on-line control systems
- RT specifications

cambium
- USE meristems

CAMBODIA [0; 0]
- BT1 asia

CAMBRIDGE ELECTRON ACCELERATOR [14; 14]
- UF *cea (accelerator)*
- BT1 synchrotrons
- BT2 cyclic accelerators
- BT3 accelerators

camellia sinensis
- USE tea plants

CAMERA TUBES [102; 291]
- BT1 image tubes
- NT1 iconoscopes
- NT1 orthicons
- NT1 vidicons
- RT television

CAMERAS [1,423; 5,412]
- NT1 gamma cameras
- NT2 positron cameras
- NT1 neutron cameras
- NT1 streak cameras
- RT photography
- RT radioisotope scanning
- RT television

CAMEROON [16; 16]
- BT1 africa
- BT1 developing countries

camp
- USE amp

camp century medium p. p. 2a
- USE pm-2a reactor

CAMPBELLING CIRCUITS [9; 9] *Aug 76*
(Circuits based on Campbell's mean square theorem for evaluating the signal from an ionization chamber.)
- BT1 electronic circuits
- RT ionization chambers

CAMPHENE [7; 7]
- BT1 cycloalkenes
- BT2 alkenes
- BT3 hydrocarbons
- BT4 organic compounds
- BT1 terpenes
- BT2 organic compounds

CAMPHOR [34; 34]
- BT1 ketones
- BT2 organic compounds
- BT1 terpenes
- BT2 organic compounds
- RT celluloid

CANADA [2,278; 3,350]
- BT1 developed countries
- BT1 north america
- NT1 alberta
- NT1 british columbia
- NT1 manitoba
- NT1 new brunswick
- NT1 newfoundland
- NT1 northwest territories
- NT2 port radium
- NT1 nova scotia
- NT1 ontario
- NT2 chalk river
- NT2 deep river
- NT2 elliot lake
- NT1 prince edward island
- NT1 quebec
- NT1 saskatchewan
- NT2 beaverlodge
- NT1 yukon territory
- RT bay of fundy

canada nrx research reactor
- USE nrx reactor

canada-india reactor
- USE cirus reactor

CANADIAN AECB [145; 146] *Mar 77*
(Canadian Atomic Energy Control Board.)
- UF *aecb canada*
- UF *atomic energy cont bd (canada)*
- BT1 canadian organizations
- BT2 national organizations

canadian nru reactor
- USE nru reactor

CANADIAN ORGANIZATIONS [81; 655]
- BT1 national organizations
- NT1 atomic energy of canada ltd
- NT2 chalk river nuclear labs
- NT2 wnre
- NT1 canadian aecb

canals (waterways)
- USE inland waterways

CANARE [17; 17] *Feb 89*
(Convention on Assistance in the Case of a Nuclear Accident or Radiological Emergency.)
- UF *assistance nuc acc/rad emerg*
- UF *conv assist nuc acc/rad emerg*
- BT1 international agreements

BT2 agreements
RT iaea
RT radiation accidents
RT reactor accidents

canberra tokamak
   USE   lt-3 tokamak

CANCELLATION [47; 47] *Mar 85*
   RT   decommissioning
   RT   implementation
   RT   planning
   RT   shutdown

cancer
   USE   neoplasms

CANDIDA [138; 138]
   UF   *monilia*
   BT1   yeasts
     BT2   fungi
       BT3   plants
     BT2   microorganisms

candu reactor
   USE   douglas point ontario reactor

CANDU TYPE REACTORS
[2,325; 3,147] *Sep 75*
(Thermal power reactors of Canadian design characterized by heavy water moderator, pressure tube construction, and on-power refuelling.)
   BT1   heavy water moderated reactors
     BT2   reactors
   BT1   pressure tube reactors
     BT2   power reactors
       BT3   reactors
   BT1   thermal reactors
     BT2   reactors
   NT1   bruce-1 reactor
   NT1   bruce-2 reactor
   NT1   bruce-3 reactor
   NT1   bruce-4 reactor
   NT1   bruce-5 reactor
   NT1   bruce-6 reactor
   NT1   bruce-7 reactor
   NT1   bruce-8 reactor
   NT1   cernavoda-1 reactor
   NT1   cordoba reactor
   NT1   darlington-1 reactor
   NT1   darlington-2 reactor
   NT1   darlington-3 reactor
   NT1   darlington-4 reactor
   NT1   douglas point ontario reactor
   NT1   gentilly reactor
   NT1   gentilly-2 reactor
   NT1   kanupp reactor
   NT1   npd reactor
   NT1   pickering-1 reactor
   NT1   pickering-2 reactor
   NT1   pickering-3 reactor
   NT1   pickering-4 reactor
   NT1   pickering-5 reactor
   NT1   pickering-6 reactor
   NT1   pickering-7 reactor
   NT1   pickering-8 reactor
   NT1   point lepreau-1 reactor
   NT1   point lepreau-2 reactor
   NT1   rajasthan-1 reactor
   NT1   rajasthan-2 reactor
   NT1   wolsung-1 reactor

CANNIKIN EVENT [86; 86]
   BT1   contained explosions
     BT2   underground explosions
       BT3   explosions
   BT1   nuclear explosions
     BT2   explosions

CANNING [160; 160]
   UF   *sheathing*
   BT1   materials working
     BT2   fabrication
   RT   cladding
   RT   fuel cans

canning (food)
   USE   food processing

CANONICAL DIMENSION [217; 217]
(Scale dimension of quantum fields obeying canonical equal-time commutation relations.)
   BT1   scale dimension
   RT   commutation relations

canonical equations
   USE   differential equations

canonical quantum field theory
   USE   lagrangian field theory

CANONICAL TRANSFORMATIONS
[1,318; 1,841]
   BT1   transformations
   NT1   bogolyubov transformation
   NT1   foldy-wouthuysen transform
   RT   equations of motion
   RT   mathematics
   RT   mechanics
   RT   quantum mechanics

CAPACITANCE [482; 482] *Jan 84*
   BT1   electrical properties
   BT2   physical properties
   RT   electric impedance

CAPACITORS [1,651; 1,651]
   UF   *condensers (electric)*
   UF   *electric condensers*
   BT1   electrical equipment
     BT2   equipment
   BT1   energy storage systems
   RT   dielectric materials
   RT   electrostatics
   RT   energy storage
   RT   power supplies

CAPACITRONS [2; 2]
   BT1   rectifier tubes
     BT2   electron tubes
     BT2   rectifiers
       BT3   electrical equipment
         BT4   equipment

§§ **CAPACITY** [711; 711] *Dec 82*
(Coordinate with descriptor for appropriate other term. Not for electrical capacitance.)
   UF   *generating capacity*
   UF   *production capacity*
   UF   *reserve capacity*
   RT   load management
   RT   outages
   RT   power generation
   RT   production

CAPE FEAR RIVER [3; 3]
   BT1   rivers
     BT2   surface waters
   RT   north carolina

CAPE KENNEDY [3; 3]
   BT1   florida
     BT2   usa
       BT3   developed countries
       BT3   north america

CAPILLARIES [531; 531]
   BT1   blood vessels
     BT2   cardiovascular system
     BT2   organs
       BT3   body
   RT   glomeruli
   RT   histamine
   RT   respiration
   RT   tissues
   RT   vasoconstriction
   RT   vasodilation

CAPILLARY FLOW [296; 296]
   BT1   fluid flow
   RT   heat pipes

CAPITAL [391; 391]
   RT   economics
   RT   investment

CAPITALIZED COST [576; 576] *Dec 82*
(Prior to August 1985 CAPITAL COST was used.)
   BT1   cost
   RT   economic analysis

capric acid
   USE   decanoic acid

caproic acid
   USE   hexanoic acid

caprylic acid
   USE   octanoic acid

CAPSICUM [59; 59]
   BT1   plants
   RT   peppers

CAPSULES [687; 687]
   BT1   containers
   RT   encapsulation

capsules (irradiation)
   USE   irradiation capsules

CAPTURE [10,139; 13,325]
(For capture cross sections, see also INTEGRAL CROSS SECTIONS.)
   UF   *radiative capture*
   UF+   *neutron capture*
   NT1   electron capture
   RT   capture-to-fission ratio
   RT   electron capture decay
   RT   interactions
   RT   nuclear reactions
   RT   r process
   RT   stein theory

CAPTURE-TO-FISSION RATIO
[220; 220]
   UF   *neutron capture-to-fissi ratio*
   RT   capture
   RT   fission ratio
   RT   interactions
   RT   nuclear reactions

carassius
   USE   goldfish

caraway
   USE   ranunculaceae

CARBAMATES [310; 611]
   BT1   carbonic acid derivatives
     BT2   organic compounds
   BT1   carboxylic acid salts
   BT1   organic nitrogen compounds
     BT2   organic compounds
   NT1   dedtc

NT1 urethane
RT carbamic acid esters

CARBAMIC ACID ESTERS [25; 25]
BT1 carboxylic acid esters
BT2 esters
BT3 organic compounds
RT carbamates

carbamide
USE urea

CARBAZIDES [20; 20]
BT1 carbonic acid derivatives
BT2 organic compounds
BT1 organic nitrogen compounds
BT2 organic compounds

CARBAZOLES [63; 63]
UF *dibenzopyrroles*
BT1 azoles
BT2 heterocyclic compounds
BT3 organic compounds
BT2 organic nitrogen compounds
BT3 organic compounds
RT pyrroles

CARBAZONES [28; 163]
BT1 carbonic acid derivatives
BT2 organic compounds
BT1 organic nitrogen compounds
BT2 organic compounds
NT1 diphenylcarbazones
NT1 dithizone

CARBENES [51; 51] *Feb 83*
(Organic radicals containing divalent carbon as CH2, CHOH, CHF, etc.)
BT1 radicals

CARBIDES [1,593; 10,343]
BT1 carbon compounds
NT1 aluminium carbides
NT1 americium carbides
NT1 barium carbides
NT1 berkelium carbides
NT1 beryllium carbides
NT1 boron carbides
NT1 calcium carbides
NT1 californium carbides
NT1 cerium carbides
NT1 cesium carbides
NT1 chromium carbides
NT1 cobalt carbides
NT1 copper carbides
NT1 curium carbides
NT1 dysprosium carbides
NT1 einsteinium carbides
NT1 erbium carbides
NT1 europium carbides
NT1 fermium carbides
NT1 gadolinium carbides
NT1 gallium carbides
NT1 germanium carbides
NT1 hafnium carbides
NT1 helium carbides
NT1 holmium carbides
NT1 indium carbides
NT1 iridium carbides
NT1 iron carbides
NT2 cementite
NT1 lanthanum carbides
NT1 lithium carbides
NT1 lutetium carbides
NT1 magnesium carbides
NT1 manganese carbides
NT1 mendelevium carbides
NT1 molybdenum carbides
NT1 neodymium carbides
NT1 neptunium carbides
NT1 nickel carbides
NT1 niobium carbides
NT1 nitrogen carbides
NT1 nobelium carbides
NT1 osmium carbides
NT1 palladium carbides
NT1 platinum carbides
NT1 plutonium carbides
NT1 potassium carbides
NT1 praseodymium carbides
NT1 protactinium carbides
NT1 rhenium carbides
NT1 rhodium carbides
NT1 rubidium carbides
NT1 ruthenium carbides
NT1 samarium carbides
NT1 scandium carbides
NT1 selenium carbides
NT1 silicon carbides
NT1 sodium carbides
NT1 strontium carbides
NT1 tantalum carbides
NT1 technetium carbides
NT1 tellurium carbides
NT1 terbium carbides
NT1 thallium carbides
NT1 thorium carbides
NT1 thulium carbides
NT1 titanium carbides
NT1 tungsten carbides
NT1 uranium carbides
NT1 vanadium carbides
NT1 ytterbium carbides
NT1 yttrium carbides
NT1 zinc carbides
NT1 zirconium carbides
RT carbon additions
RT carbonitrides
RT ceramics
RT decarburization
RT oxycarbides

carbinol
USE methanol

CARBITOLS [3; 3]
UF *diglycol monoalkyl ethers*
BT1 ethers
BT2 organic oxygen compounds
BT3 organic compounds
BT1 glycols
BT2 alcohols
BT3 hydroxy compounds
BT4 organic compounds
BT1 organic solvents
BT2 nonaqueous solvents
BT3 solvents

CARBOHYDRATES [385; 10,838]
BT1 organic compounds
NT1 glycosides
NT2 digitalis glycosides
NT3 digitoxin
NT3 digoxin
NT2 hesperidin
NT2 ouabain
NT2 phlorizin
NT2 saponins
NT2 udpg
NT1 saccharides
NT2 gangliosides
NT2 glycolipids
NT3 cerebrosides
NT2 glycoproteins
NT3 lactoferrin
NT3 lh
NT3 ovalbumin
NT2 monosaccharides
NT3 erythritol
NT3 hexoses
NT4 fructose
NT4 galactose
NT4 glucose
NT4 hexosamines
NT5 glucosamine
NT4 mannose
NT4 sorbose
NT3 inositols
NT4 inositol
NT3 pentoses
NT4 arabinose
NT4 deoxyribose
NT4 ribose
NT4 ribulose
NT4 xylose
NT3 sedoheptulose
NT3 sorbitol
NT2 oligosaccharides
NT3 disaccharides
NT4 cellobiose
NT4 lactose
NT4 maltose
NT4 melibiose
NT4 saccharose
NT3 raffinose
NT2 polysaccharides
NT3 agar
NT3 alginic acid
NT3 cellophane
NT3 cellulose
NT3 dextran
NT3 dextrin
NT3 glycogen
NT3 gum acacia
NT3 inulin
NT3 lignin
NT3 lipopolysaccharides
NT3 mucopolysaccharides
NT4 chitin
NT4 chondroitin
NT4 heparin
NT4 hyaluronic acid
NT3 mucoproteins
NT4 haptoglobins
NT4 intrinsic factor
NT4 phytohemagglutinin
NT3 nitrocellulose
NT3 pectins
NT3 rayon
NT3 sialic acid
NT3 starch
NT3 viscose
RT food
RT glycolysis

CARBON [10,424; 20,278]
BT1 nonmetals
BT2 elements
NT1 activated carbon
NT1 carbon black
NT1 carbynes
NT1 diamonds
NT1 graphite
NT1 pyrolytic carbon
RT carbon fibers
RT decarburization

CARBON ADDITIONS [1,278; 33,582]
NT1 alloy-co43cr20fe18ni13w3
NT1 alloy-co66cr26w6
NT1 alloy-fe31cr21co20ni20mo3w2
NT1 alloy-ni60co15cr10al6ti5mo3
NT1 austenite
NT1 cast iron
NT1 ferrite
NT1 martensite
*NT1 steels
RT carbides

CARBON BLACK [87; 87]
BT1 carbon
BT2 nonmetals
BT3 elements

CARBON BURNING [98; 98] *Aug 78*
(Astrophysical processes only.)
BT1 star burning
RT nucleosynthesis
RT star evolution
RT star models
RT stars

CARBON COMPLEXES [21; 21]
BT1 complexes

CARBON COMPOUNDS [633; 30,884]
*NT1 carbides
NT1 carbon fluorides
NT1 carbon nitrides
NT1 carbon oxides
NT2 carbon dioxide
NT2 carbon monoxide
NT1 carbon sulfides

CARBON COMPOUNDS

   NT1   carbon 14 compounds
*NT1   carbonates
   NT1   carbonic acid
   NT1   carbonitrides
   NT1   oxycarbides

CARBON CYCLE [106; 106] *Jul 82*
   RT   air-water interactions
   RT   carbon dioxide fixation
   RT   deforestation
   RT   ecological concentration
   RT   ecosystems
   RT   metabolism
   RT   photosynthesis

CARBON DIOXIDE [6,388; 6,388]
   BT1   carbon oxides
    BT2   carbon compounds
    BT2   oxides
     BT3   chalcogenides
     BT3   oxygen compounds
   RT   carbon dioxide fixation
   RT   inert atmosphere

CARBON DIOXIDE COOLED REACTORS [96; 1,009]
   UF   *carbon dioxide-cooled reactors*
   BT1   gas cooled reactors
    BT2   reactors
   NT1   calder hall a-1 reactor
   NT1   calder hall a-2 reactor
   NT1   calder hall b-3 reactor
   NT1   calder hall b-4 reactor
   NT1   cesar reactor
   NT1   chapelcross-1 reactor
   NT1   chapelcross-2 reactor
   NT1   chapelcross-3 reactor
   NT1   chapelcross-4 reactor
   NT1   dungeness-a reactor
   NT1   dungeness-b reactor
   NT1   el-2 reactor
   NT1   hartlepool reactor
   NT1   hector reactor
   NT1   heysham-a reactor
   NT1   heysham-b reactor
   NT1   hinkley point-a reactor
   NT1   hinkley point-b reactor
   NT1   hunterston-a reactor
   NT1   hunterston-b reactor
   NT1   oldbury-a reactor
   NT1   oldbury-b reactor
   NT1   sizewell-a reactor
   NT1   tokai-mura reactor
   NT1   torness reactor
   NT1   trawsfynydd reactor
   NT1   vandellos reactor
   NT1   wagr reactor
   NT1   wylfa reactor
   RT   agr type reactors
   RT   gcr type reactors

CARBON DIOXIDE FIXATION [121; 121] *Feb 82*
   UF   *fixation (carbon.dioxide)*
   RT   air
   RT   carbon cycle
   RT   carbon dioxide
   RT   metabolism
   RT   photosynthesis
   RT   plant growth

CARBON DIOXIDE LASERS [2,279; 2,279]
   BT1   gas lasers
    BT2   lasers
     BT3   amplifiers
      BT4   equipment
   RT   antares facility
   RT   helios facility

carbon dioxide-cooled reactors
   USE   carbon dioxide cooled reactors

CARBON FIBERS [211; 211] *Mar 83*
   UF   *graphite fibers*
   BT1   fibers
   RT   carbon
   RT   graphite

CARBON FLUORIDES [256; 256]
   BT1   carbon compounds
   BT1   fluorides
    BT2   fluorine compounds
     BT3   halogen compounds
    BT2   halides
     BT3   halogen compounds

CARBON IONS [2,452; 2,452]
   BT1   ions
    BT2   charged particles

CARBON ISOTOPES [792; 18,262]
   NT1   carbon 10
   NT1   carbon 11
   NT1   carbon 12
   NT1   carbon 13
   NT1   carbon 14
   NT1   carbon 15
   NT1   carbon 16
   NT1   carbon 17
   NT1   carbon 18
   NT1   carbon 19
   NT1   carbon 20
   NT1   carbon 22
   NT1   carbon 8
   NT1   carbon 9

CARBON METERS [39; 39] *Jan 78*
   BT1   measuring instruments
   RT   chemical analysis

CARBON MONOXIDE [4,441; 4,441]
   BT1   carbon oxides
    BT2   carbon compounds
    BT2   oxides
     BT3   chalcogenides
     BT3   oxygen compounds
   RT   carbonyls

CARBON MONOXIDE LASERS [80; 80]
   BT1   gas lasers
    BT2   lasers
     BT3   amplifiers
      BT4   equipment

CARBON NITRIDES [101; 101]
   BT1   carbon compounds
   BT1   nitrides
    BT2   nitrogen compounds
    BT2   pnictides

CARBON OXIDES [302; 10,290]
   BT1   carbon compounds
   BT1   oxides
    BT2   chalcogenides
    BT2   oxygen compounds
   NT1   carbon dioxide
   NT1   carbon monoxide
   RT   oxycarbides

carbon oxychloride
   USE   phosgene

CARBON STARS [405; 405]
   BT1   main sequence stars
    BT2   stars

CARBON STEELS [2,226; 2,581]
(Steels with carbon as the only alloying element.)
   UF   *steel-astm-a105*
   UF   *steel-astm-a106*
   UF   *steel-astm-a212*
   UF   *steel-astm-a285*
   UF   *steel-astm-a350 (gr 1)*
   UF   *steel-astm-a350 (gr 2)*
   UF   *steel-astm-a416*
   UF   *steel-astm-a516*
   UF   *steel-sae-1006*
   UF   *steel-sae-1045*
   BT1   steels
    BT2   carbon additions
    BT2   iron base alloys
     BT3   iron alloys
      BT4   alloys

CARBON SULFIDES [345; 345]
   UF   *sulfur carbides*
   BT1   carbon compounds
   BT1   sulfides
    BT2   chalcogenides
    BT2   sulfur compounds

CARBON TETRACHLORIDE [1,047; 1,047]
(Prior to August 1985 TETRACHLOROMETHANE was used.)
   UF   *tetrachloromethane*
   BT1   chlorinated aliphatic hydrocar
    BT2   halogenated aliphatic hydrocar
     BT3   organic halogen compounds
      BT4   organic compounds
    BT2   organic chlorine compounds
     BT3   organic halogen compounds
      BT4   organic compounds
   RT   methane
   RT   organic solvents

CARBON TETRAFLUORIDE [177; 177]
(Prior to August 1985 TETRAFLUOROMETHANE was used.)
   UF   *tetrafluoromethane*
   BT1   organic fluorine compounds
    BT2   organic halogen compounds
     BT3   organic compounds
   RT   methane

CARBON 10 [116; 116]
   BT1   beta-plus decay radioisotopes
    BT2   beta decay radioisotopes
     BT3   radioisotopes
      BT4   isotopes
   BT1   carbon isotopes
   BT1   even-even nuclei
    BT2   nuclei
   BT1   light nuclei
    BT2   nuclei
   BT1   seconds living radioisotopes
    BT2   radioisotopes
     BT3   isotopes

CARBON 10 BEAMS [2; 2] *Nov 88*
   BT1   ion beams
    BT2   beams

CARBON 11 [2,071; 2,071]
   BT1   beta-plus decay radioisotopes
    BT2   beta decay radioisotopes
     BT3   radioisotopes
      BT4   isotopes
   BT1   carbon isotopes
   BT1   even-odd nuclei
    BT2   nuclei
   BT1   light nuclei
    BT2   nuclei
   BT1   minutes living radioisotopes
    BT2   radioisotopes
     BT3   isotopes

CARBON 11 BEAMS [2; 2] *May 85*
   BT1   ion beams
    BT2   beams

CARBON 11 TARGET [2; 2] *Apr 86*
   BT1   targets

CARBON 12 [5,540; 5,540]
   BT1   carbon isotopes
   BT1   even-even nuclei
    BT2   nuclei
   BT1   light nuclei
    BT2   nuclei
   BT1   stable isotopes
    BT2   isotopes
   RT   carbon 12 beams

CARBON 12 BEAMS [626; 626]
BT1 ion beams
BT2 beams
RT carbon 12

CARBON 12 EMISSION DECAY [2; 2]
May 91
BT1 heavy ion emission decay
BT2 nuclear decay
BT3 decay

CARBON 12 REACTIONS [3,606; 3,606]
BT1 heavy ion reactions
BT2 nuclear reactions

CARBON 12 TARGET [7,756; 7,756]
BT1 targets

CARBON 13 [5,180; 5,180]
BT1 carbon isotopes
BT1 even-odd nuclei
BT2 nuclei
BT1 light nuclei
BT2 nuclei
BT1 stable isotopes
BT2 isotopes
RT carbon 13 beams

CARBON 13 BEAMS [49; 49]
BT1 ion beams
BT2 beams
RT carbon 13

CARBON 13 REACTIONS [553; 553]
BT1 heavy ion reactions
BT2 nuclear reactions

CARBON 13 TARGET [1,099; 1,099]
BT1 targets

CARBON 14 [6,145; 6,145]
UF+ *radiocarbon dating*
BT1 beta-minus decay radioisotopes
BT2 beta decay radioisotopes
BT3 radioisotopes
BT4 isotopes
BT1 carbon isotopes
BT1 even-even nuclei
BT2 nuclei
BT1 light nuclei
BT2 nuclei
BT1 years living radioisotopes
BT2 radioisotopes
BT3 isotopes
RT carbon 14 beams
RT carbon 14 compounds
RT isotope dating

CARBON 14 BEAMS [40; 40]
BT1 ion beams
BT2 beams
RT carbon 14

CARBON 14 COMPOUNDS
[8,240; 8,240]
BT1 carbon compounds
RT biochemistry
RT carbon 14
RT labelled compounds
RT labelling

CARBON 14 DECAY RADIOISOTOPES
[6; 1,465] *Mar 86*
BT1 heavy ion decay radioisotopes
BT2 radioisotopes
BT3 isotopes
NT1 radium 222
NT1 radium 223
NT1 radium 224
NT1 radium 226
RT carbon 14 emission decay

CARBON 14 EMISSION DECAY
[63; 63] *Mar 86*
BT1 heavy ion emission decay
BT2 nuclear decay
BT3 decay
RT carbon 14 decay radioisotopes

CARBON 14 REACTIONS [140; 140]
BT1 heavy ion reactions
BT2 nuclear reactions

CARBON 14 TARGET [371; 371]
BT1 targets

CARBON 15 [91; 91]
BT1 beta-minus decay radioisotopes
BT2 beta decay radioisotopes
BT3 radioisotopes
BT4 isotopes
BT1 carbon isotopes
BT1 even-odd nuclei
BT2 nuclei
BT1 light nuclei
BT2 nuclei
BT1 seconds living radioisotopes
BT2 radioisotopes
BT3 isotopes

CARBON 16 [59; 59]
BT1 beta-minus decay radioisotopes
BT2 beta decay radioisotopes
BT3 radioisotopes
BT4 isotopes
BT1 carbon isotopes
BT1 even-even nuclei
BT2 nuclei
BT1 light nuclei
BT2 nuclei
BT1 millisec living radioisotopes
BT2 radioisotopes
BT3 isotopes

CARBON 17 [25; 25]
BT1 beta-minus decay radioisotopes
BT2 beta decay radioisotopes
BT3 radioisotopes
BT4 isotopes
BT1 carbon isotopes
BT1 even-odd nuclei
BT2 nuclei
BT1 light nuclei
BT2 nuclei
BT1 millisec living radioisotopes
BT2 radioisotopes
BT3 isotopes

CARBON 18 [40; 40]
BT1 beta-minus decay radioisotopes
BT2 beta decay radioisotopes
BT3 radioisotopes
BT4 isotopes
BT1 carbon isotopes
BT1 even-even nuclei
BT2 nuclei
BT1 light nuclei
BT2 nuclei
BT1 millisec living radioisotopes
BT2 radioisotopes
BT3 isotopes

CARBON 19 [10; 10]
BT1 carbon isotopes
BT1 even-odd nuclei
BT2 nuclei
BT1 light nuclei
BT2 nuclei

CARBON 20 [16; 16]
BT1 carbon isotopes
BT1 even-even nuclei
BT2 nuclei
BT1 light nuclei
BT2 nuclei

CARBON 22 [6; 6] *Feb 79*
BT1 carbon isotopes
BT1 even-even nuclei
BT2 nuclei
BT1 light nuclei
BT2 nuclei

CARBON 8 [6; 6]
BT1 carbon isotopes
BT1 even-even nuclei
BT2 nuclei
BT1 light nuclei
BT2 nuclei

CARBON 9 [15; 15]
BT1 beta-plus decay radioisotopes
BT2 beta decay radioisotopes
BT3 radioisotopes
BT4 isotopes
BT1 carbon isotopes
BT1 even-odd nuclei
BT2 nuclei
BT1 light nuclei
BT2 nuclei
BT1 millisec living radioisotopes
BT2 radioisotopes
BT3 isotopes

CARBON-CARBON LYASES [22; 112]
Dec 86
BT1 lyases
BT2 enzymes
BT3 organic compounds
NT1 aldolases
NT1 decarboxylases

CARBON-GROUP TRANSFERASES
[0; 51] *Dec 86*
BT1 transferases
BT2 enzymes
BT3 organic compounds
NT1 methyl transferases

carbon-nitrogen-oxygen cycle
USE cno cycle

CARBON-OXYGEN LYASES [8; 37]
Dec 86
UF *polysaccharide-lyases*
BT1 lyases
BT2 enzymes
BT3 organic compounds
NT1 hyaluronidase
NT1 hydro-lyases
NT2 carbonic anhydrase

CARBONACEOUS MATERIALS
[117; 2,248] *Jul 82*
(Materials rich in carbon.)
BT1 materials
NT1 coal
NT2 black coal
NT3 anthracite
NT3 bituminous coal
NT2 lignite
NT1 oil sands
NT1 oil shales
RT organic matter

CARBONATE MINERALS [58; 399]
Apr 84
BT1 minerals
NT1 andersonite
NT1 aragonite
NT1 bayleyite
NT1 calcite
NT1 cordylite
NT1 dolomite
NT1 liebigite
NT1 rutherfordite
NT1 schroeckingerite
RT calcium carbonates
RT cerium carbonates
RT iron carbonates
RT lanthanum carbonates
RT magnesium carbonates

RT	manganese carbonates	
RT	shales	
RT	sodium carbonates	
RT	uranium carbonates	

CARBONATE ROCKS [74; 262] *Dec 85*
(Rocks composed principally of carbonates, usually more than 50% by weight. See also CARBONATE MINERALS.)
- BT1 sedimentary rocks
- BT2 rocks
- NT1 limestone

CARBONATES [1,181; 4,155]
- BT1 carbon compounds
- BT1 oxygen compounds
- NT1 americium carbonates
- NT1 ammonium carbonates
- NT2 auc
- NT1 barium carbonates
- NT1 berkelium carbonates
- NT1 beryllium carbonates
- NT1 bismuth carbonates
- NT1 cadmium carbonates
- NT1 calcium carbonates
- NT1 cerium carbonates
- NT1 cesium carbonates
- NT1 cobalt carbonates
- NT1 copper carbonates
- NT1 curium carbonates
- NT1 erbium carbonates
- NT1 europium carbonates
- NT1 gadolinium carbonates
- NT1 holmium carbonates
- NT1 iron carbonates
- NT1 lanthanum carbonates
- NT1 lead carbonates
- NT1 lithium carbonates
- NT1 lutetium carbonates
- NT1 magnesium carbonates
- NT1 manganese carbonates
- NT1 molybdenum carbonates
- NT1 neodymium carbonates
- NT1 neptunium carbonates
- NT1 nickel carbonates
- NT1 plutonium carbonates
- NT1 polycarbonates
- NT1 potassium carbonates
- NT1 praseodymium carbonates
- NT1 radium carbonates
- NT1 rhenium carbonates
- NT1 rubidium carbonates
- NT1 samarium carbonates
- NT1 scandium carbonates
- NT1 silver carbonates
- NT1 sodium carbonates
- NT1 strontium carbonates
- NT1 terbium carbonates
- NT1 thallium carbonates
- NT1 thorium carbonates
- NT1 uranium carbonates
- NT1 uranyl carbonates
- NT1 ytterbium carbonates
- NT1 yttrium carbonates
- NT1 zinc carbonates
- NT1 zirconium carbonates
- RT acid carbonates

CARBONIC ACID [26; 26] *Apr 82*
- BT1 carbon compounds
- BT1 inorganic acids
- BT2 hydrogen compounds
- BT2 inorganic compounds
- BT1 oxygen compounds

CARBONIC ACID DERIVATIVES [222; 4,985]
- BT1 organic compounds
- NT1 carbamates
- NT2 dedtc
- NT2 urethane
- NT1 carbazides
- NT1 carbazones
- NT2 diphenylcarbazones
- NT2 dithizone
- NT1 cyanamides
- NT1 cyanates
- NT1 dpca
- NT1 guanethidine
- NT1 guanidines
- NT1 isonitriles
- NT1 meg
- NT1 phosgene
- NT1 semicarbazides
- NT1 semicarbazones
- NT1 thiocyanates
- NT2 ammonium thiocyanates
- NT1 thioureas
- NT2 aet
- NT2 thiourea
- NT1 urea

CARBONIC ANHYDRASE [48; 48]
- BT1 hydro-lyases
- BT2 carbon-oxygen lyases
-   BT3 lyases
-    BT4 enzymes
-     BT5 organic compounds

CARBONITRIDES [71; 71] *Jan 82*
(Specific compounds should be indexed by coordination of a descriptor of the form (CATION) COMPOUNDS and the above anion descriptor.)
- BT1 carbon compounds
- BT1 nitrogen compounds
- RT carbides
- RT nitrides

CARBONIZATION [262; 262]
- BT1 decomposition
- BT2 chemical reactions
- NT1 coking
- RT graphitization

carbonyl chloride
- USE phosgene

CARBONYL RADICALS [78; 78]
- BT1 radicals
- RT carbonyls

CARBONYLATION [36; 36] *Sep 81*
- BT1 chemical reactions

CARBONYLS [1,084; 1,084]
(Only for compounds of metals with carbonyl radicals.)
- RT carbon monoxide
- RT carbonyl radicals
- RT metals

CARBORANES [129; 129] *May 78*
- BT1 organic boron compounds
- BT2 organic compounds
- RT boranes

CARBOWAX [7; 7]
- BT1 polyethylene glycols
- BT2 organic polymers
-   BT3 organic compounds
-   BT3 polymers
- BT1 waxes
- BT2 other organic compounds
-   BT3 organic compounds

CARBOXYHEMOGLOBIN [10; 10] *Oct 84*
- BT1 hemoglobin
- BT2 globins
-   BT3 proteins
-    BT4 organic compounds
- BT2 pigments
- BT2 porphyrins
-   BT3 heterocyclic acids
-    BT4 carboxylic acids
-     BT5 organic acids
-      BT6 organic compounds
-    BT4 heterocyclic compounds
-     BT5 organic compounds
-   BT3 organic nitrogen compounds
-    BT4 organic compounds
- RT erythrocytes
- RT heme
- RT respiration

CARBOXYLASE [101; 101]
- BT1 ligases
- BT2 enzymes
-   BT3 organic compounds

CARBOXYLATION [96; 96]
- BT1 chemical reactions
- RT decarboxylation

CARBOXYLESTERASES [6; 312] *Dec 86*
- BT1 esterases
- BT2 hydrolases
-   BT3 enzymes
-    BT4 organic compounds
- NT1 cholinesterase
- NT1 lipases

CARBOXYLIC ACID ESTERS [488; 1,630]
- BT1 esters
- BT2 organic compounds
- NT1 acetic acid esters
- NT2 isopentyl acetate
- NT1 acetoacetic acid esters
- NT1 acrylic acid esters
- NT1 bromosulfophthalein
- NT1 carbamic acid esters
- NT1 citric acid esters
- NT1 malathion
- NT1 methacrylic acid esters
- NT1 oxalic acid esters
- NT1 phenolphthalein
- NT1 tartaric acid esters
- RT carboxylic acids

CARBOXYLIC ACID SALTS [661; 6,450]
- NT1 acetates
- NT1 acetoacetates
- NT1 acrylates
- NT1 carbamates
- NT2 dedtc
- NT2 urethane
- NT1 citrates
- NT1 formates
- NT1 lactates
- NT1 methacrylates
- NT1 oxalates
- NT1 phthalates
- NT1 tartrates
- NT2 rochelle salt
- RT carboxylic acids
- RT esters

CARBOXYLIC ACIDS [1,758; 28,826]
- UF *alkanoic acids*
- UF *alkenoic acids*
- UF *aromatic acids*
- UF *fatty acids*
- UF+ *aldehydo acids*
- BT1 organic acids
- BT2 organic compounds
- *NT1 amino acids
- NT1 bile acids
- NT2 cholic acid
- NT1 carminic acid
- *NT1 dicarboxylic acids
- NT1 egta
- NT1 glyoxylic acid
- *NT1 heterocyclic acids
- *NT1 hydroxy acids
- *NT1 keto acids
- NT1 mellitic acid
- *NT1 monocarboxylic acids
- NT1 tannic acid
- NT1 tricarballylic acid
- RT alginic acid
- RT carboxylic acid esters
- RT carboxylic acid salts
- RT ketenes
- RT nitriles

carboxypeptidase
(Prior to April 1985 this was a valid descriptor.)
USE   carboxypeptidases

CARBOXYPEPTIDASES [44; 44]
(Prior to April 1985 the singular form was used.)
UF   *carboxypeptidase*
BT1   peptide hydrolases
BT2   hydrolases
BT3   enzymes
BT4   organic compounds

CARBURAN [2; 2]
BT1   bitumens
BT2   tar
BT3   other organic compounds
BT4   organic compounds
BT1   uranium minerals
BT2   radioactive minerals
BT3   minerals
BT3   radioactive materials
BT4   materials
RT   thucholite

CARBURIZATION [569; 569]
BT1   surface hardening
BT2   hardening
BT2   surface treatments

CARBYNES [5; 5] *Mar 83*
(Triply bonded allotropes of carbon.)
BT1   carbon
BT2   nonmetals
BT3   elements

CARCINOEMBRYONIC ANTIGEN
[417; 417] *Sep 82*
UF   *cea (antigen)*
BT1   antigens
RT   embryos
RT   neoplasms

CARCINOGENESIS [3,550; 3,876]
BT1   pathogenesis
NT1   leukemogenesis
RT   carcinogens
RT   dna adducts
RT   neoplasms
RT   oncogenes
RT   oncogenic transformations
RT   oncogenic viruses

CARCINOGENS [829; 829]
RT   carcinogenesis
RT   dimethylbenzanthracene
RT   dna adducts
RT   mutagens
RT   neoplasms
RT   oncogenic transformations
RT   radiomimetic drugs
RT   teratogens
RT   tumor promoters

CARCINOMAS [14,355; 14,355]
UF   *adenocarcinomas*
UF   *pulmonary cancer*
UF+   *bronchogenic carcinoma*
UF+   *uterine cervix carcinoma*
BT1   neoplasms
BT2   diseases
RT   epithelium

cardiac output
USE   blood circulation

CARDIAC PACEMAKERS [352; 352]
UF   *pacemakers*
RT   electric batteries
RT   heart
RT   mechanical heart
RT   prostheses
RT   radioisotope batteries

CARDIOGRAPHY [382; 1,528]
BT1   diagnostic techniques
NT1   radiocardiography
RT   blood circulation
RT   blood pressure
RT   electrocardiograms
RT   heart

CARDIOLIPIN [9; 9]
BT1   phospholipids
BT2   esters
BT3   organic compounds
BT2   lipids
BT3   organic compounds
BT2   organic phosphorus compounds
BT3   organic compounds

cardiotonic glycosides
USE   cardiotonics

CARDIOTONICS [57; 1,546]
UF   *cardiotonic glycosides*
UF   *strophanthin*
BT1   cardiovascular agents
BT2   drugs
NT1   adrenaline
NT1   digitalis glycosides
NT2   digitoxin
NT2   digoxin
NT1   dopamine
NT1   noradrenaline
NT1   ouabain
RT   heart
RT   steroids

CARDIOVASCULAR AGENTS
[113; 2,181] *May 84*
BT1   drugs
NT1   antihypertensive agents
NT2   guanethidine
NT2   reserpine
NT1   cardiotonics
NT2   adrenaline
NT2   digitalis glycosides
NT3   digitoxin
NT3   digoxin
NT2   dopamine
NT2   noradrenaline
NT2   ouabain
NT1   vasoconstrictors
NT2   angiotensin
NT2   ephedrine
NT1   vasodilators
NT2   theobromine
NT2   theophylline

CARDIOVASCULAR DISEASES
[3,621; 10,280]
BT1   diseases
NT1   arteriosclerosis
NT1   hypertension
NT1   ischemia
NT1   myocardial infarction
NT1   nephrosclerosis
NT1   telangiectasis
NT1   thrombosis
RT   cardiovascular system
RT   heart failure

CARDIOVASCULAR SYSTEM
[407; 21,089]
NT1   blood vessels
NT2   arteries
NT3   aorta
NT3   carotid arteries
NT3   coronaries
NT2   capillaries
NT2   veins
NT3   portal system
NT1   heart
NT2   myocardium
NT2   pericardium
RT   blood circulation
RT   blood pressure
RT   cardiovascular diseases
RT   lymphatic system
RT   organs

CARIBBEAN SEA [31; 89]
BT1   atlantic ocean
BT2   seas
BT3   surface waters
NT1   gulf of mexico
NT2   san antonio bay
RT   west indies

caribou
USE   deer

CARIES [84; 84] *Sep 75*
BT1   pathological changes
BT2   diseases
RT   dentistry
RT   teeth

carlson method
USE   discrete ordinate method

carlton power reactor
USE   kewaunee reactor

CARMINIC ACID [15; 15]
BT1   anthraquinones
BT2   quinones
BT3   aromatics
BT4   organic compounds
BT3   organic oxygen compounds
BT4   organic compounds
BT1   carboxylic acids
BT2   organic acids
BT3   organic compounds
BT1   hydroxy compounds
BT2   organic compounds
RT   dyes

CARNALLITE [39; 39]
BT1   halide minerals
BT2   minerals
RT   magnesium chlorides
RT   potassium chlorides

CARNATIONS [16; 16]
BT1   plants

CARNITINE [47; 47]
UF   *novain*
UF   *vitamin b-t*
BT1   amino acids
BT2   carboxylic acids
BT3   organic acids
BT4   organic compounds
BT1   hydroxy acids
BT2   carboxylic acids
BT3   organic acids
BT4   organic compounds
BT1   vitamin b group
BT2   vitamins
RT   betaine

CARNOT CYCLE [52; 52]
BT1   thermodynamic cycles
RT   thermodynamics

CARNOTITE [69; 69]
BT1   uranium minerals
BT2   radioactive minerals
BT3   minerals
BT3   radioactive materials
BT4   materials

carol. pow. light robinson-2 r
USE   robinson-2 reactor

carolinas virginia tube react.
USE   cvtr reactor

CAROTENOIDS [139; 139]
- BT1 hydrocarbons
  - BT2 organic compounds
- BT1 pigments
- BT1 terpenes
  - BT2 organic compounds
- RT vitamin a
- RT vitamins

CAROTID ARTERIES [793; 793]
- BT1 arteries
  - BT2 blood vessels
    - BT3 cardiovascular system
    - BT3 organs
      - BT4 body
- RT head
- RT neck

CARPETBAG EVENT [6; 6]
- BT1 contained explosions
  - BT2 underground explosions
    - BT3 explosions
- BT1 nuclear explosions
  - BT2 explosions

carpocapsa pomonella
- USE codling moth

CARRIER DENSITY [2,067; 2,067]
- UF *density (carrier)*
- RT charge carriers
- RT current density

CARRIER LIFETIME [529; 529]
- BT1 lifetime
- RT charge carriers

CARRIER MOBILITY [1,384; 1,384]
- BT1 mobility
- RT charge carriers
- RT electric conductivity
- RT electron transfer

CARRIER-FREE ISOTOPES [782; 782]
- RT labelled compounds
- RT labelling
- RT radioisotopes
- RT trace amounts

CARRIERS [486; 486]
(For any substance accompanying, or carrying, an isotope of interest; see also CHARGE CARRIERS.)
- RT radioisotopes
- RT radionuclide kinetics
- RT stable isotopes

CARRIZO MOUNTAINS [3; 3]
- BT1 mountains

CARROTS [92; 92]
- BT1 vegetables
  - BT2 food

cars
- USE vehicles

cars (spectroscopy)
(Coherent Anti-stokes Raman Spectroscopy.)
- USE raman spectroscopy

CARTESIAN COORDINATES [203; 203]
- BT1 coordinates

CARTILAGE [776; 776]
- UF+ *disks (intervertebral)*
- UF+ *intervertebral disks*
- BT1 connective tissue
  - BT2 tissues
    - BT3 body
- RT bone joints

casaccia rana reactor
- USE rana reactor

casaccia rospo reactor
- USE rospo reactor

cascade (extraction)
- USE extraction columns

CASCADE IMPACTORS [111; 111]
- RT aerosol monitoring
- RT air pollution monitors
- RT air samplers

CASCADE REACTORS [33; 33] Oct 86
(A conceptual inertial confinement fusion reactor which uses a replenished layer of granules for wall protection, heat exchange, and fuel production.)
- RT icf devices
- RT laser fusion reactors

CASCADE SHOWERS [1,327; 1,327]
- BT1 showers
- RT cascade theory
- RT cosmic showers

CASCADE THEORY [785; 785]
- RT cascade showers
- RT gamma cascades

cascades (nuclear)
- USE nuclear cascades

CASE LAW [55; 55] Dec 76
- BT1 laws

CASE METHOD [38; 38]
- RT transport theory

CASEIN [119; 119]
- BT1 organic phosphorus compounds
  - BT2 organic compounds
- BT1 proteins
  - BT2 organic compounds

CASIMIR EFFECT [146; 146] May 86
(Attractive force between two uncharged, conducting, parallel plates due to vacuum fluctuations of the electromagnetic field, i.e. quantum electromagnetic zero-point energy.)
- UF *casimir force*
- RT electric fields
- RT vacuum polarization

casimir force
- USE casimir effect

CASIMIR OPERATORS [636; 636]
- BT1 mathematical operators
- RT symmetry groups

CASKS [3,495; 3,495]
- UF *flasks*
- UF *fuel casks*
- UF *spent fuel casks*
- BT1 containers

CASPIAN SEA [10; 10] Jan 76
- BT1 seas
  - BT2 surface waters

CASSAVA [46; 46]
- BT1 plants
- RT food

CAST IRON [474; 474]
- BT1 carbon additions
- BT1 iron base alloys
  - BT2 iron alloys
    - BT3 alloys
- BT1 silicon alloys
  - BT2 alloys
- RT iron carbides
- RT pearlite

CASTAGNOLI FORMULA [6; 6]
- RT angular distribution

caste (insects)
- USE insects
- AND occupations
- AND populations

castillejo-dalitz-dyson poles
- USE cdd poles

CASTING [730; 804]
- BT1 fabrication
- NT1 slip casting
- NT1 vacuum casting
- RT casting molds
- RT castings
- RT crucibles
- RT dies
- RT materials working
- RT melting
- RT molding

CASTING MOLDS [128; 128]
- UF *molds (casting)*
- RT casting
- RT castings
- RT dies
- RT molding

CASTINGS [658; 658] Jan 77
- RT casting
- RT casting molds
- RT degassing
- RT inclusions
- RT machine parts
- RT microstructure
- RT solidification

CASTLE PROJECT [2; 6]
- UF *project castle*
- NT1 bravo event
- NT1 romeo event
- NT1 yankee event
- RT atmospheric explosions
- RT bikini
- RT nuclear explosions
- RT nuclear weapons
- RT surface explosions
- RT thermonuclear explosions

CASTOR [31; 31]
- UF *ricinum communis*
- BT1 medicinal plants
  - BT2 plants
- RT castor oil

CASTOR OIL [15; 15]
- BT1 oils
  - BT2 other organic compounds
    - BT3 organic compounds
- RT castor
- RT plasticizers

CASTOR TOKAMAK [51; 51] May 87
(Institute of Plasma Physics, Czechoslovakian Academy of Sciences, Prague)
- BT1 tokamak devices
  - BT2 closed plasma devices
    - BT3 thermonuclear devices

CASTRATION [70; 70]
- BT1 surgery
- BT2 medicine
- RT androgens
- RT estrogens
- RT gonads
- RT reproductive disorders
- RT therapy

CAT SCANNING [7,012; 7,012] *Jan 78*
(Computerized Axial Tomography scanning.)
- UF *computer axial tomography scan*
- UF *ct scanning*
- UF+ *ecat scanning*
- BT1 computerized tomography
- BT2 tomography
- RT biomedical radiography

CATABOLISM [267; 267]
- BT1 metabolism
- RT decomposition
- RT glycolysis
- RT proteolysis

cataclysmic binary stars
- USE eruptive variable stars

cataclysmic variable stars
(Variable close binary systems, one star of which provides the other with accretion material.)
- USE eruptive variable stars

CATALASE [220; 220]
- BT1 peroxidases
- BT2 oxidoreductases
- BT3 enzymes
- BT4 organic compounds
- BT2 porphyrins
- BT3 heterocyclic acids
- BT4 carboxylic acids
- BT5 organic acids
- BT6 organic compounds
- BT4 heterocyclic compounds
- BT5 organic compounds
- BT3 organic nitrogen compounds
- BT4 organic compounds

catalogs
- USE indexes

§ **CATALYSIS** [4,988; 4,988]
- RT catalysts
- RT chemical reaction kinetics
- RT chemical reactions
- RT coenzymes
- RT enzyme activity
- RT enzymes
- RT ziegler catalyst

CATALYSTS [4,071; 4,076]
- SF *promoters*
- NT1 ziegler catalyst
- RT additives
- RT catalysis

cataphoresis
- USE electrophoresis

CATAPLEITE [1; 1]
- BT1 silicate minerals
- BT2 minerals
- RT sodium silicates
- RT zirconium silicates

CATARACTS [324; 324]
- UF *eye cataracts*
- BT1 sense organs diseases
- BT2 diseases
- RT crystalline lens

CATAWBA-1 REACTOR [94; 94]
(York County, South Carolina, USA)
- BT1 pwr type reactors
- BT2 enriched uranium reactors
- BT3 reactors
- BT2 power reactors
- BT3 reactors
- BT2 thermal reactors
- BT3 reactors
- BT2 water cooled reactors
- BT3 reactors
- BT2 water moderated reactors
- BT3 reactors

CATAWBA-2 REACTOR [85; 85]
(York County, South Carolina, USA)
- BT1 pwr type reactors
- BT2 enriched uranium reactors
- BT3 reactors
- BT2 power reactors
- BT3 reactors
- BT2 thermal reactors
- BT3 reactors
- BT2 water cooled reactors
- BT3 reactors
- BT2 water moderated reactors
- BT3 reactors

catechol
- USE pyrocatechol

CATECHOLAMINES [361; 361]
- BT1 amines
- BT2 organic compounds
- BT1 polyphenols
- BT2 phenols
- BT3 aromatics
- BT4 organic compounds
- BT3 hydroxy compounds
- BT4 organic compounds
- RT pyrocatechol

CATHEPSINS [51; 51]
- BT1 sh-proteinases
- BT2 peptide hydrolases
- BT3 hydrolases
- BT4 enzymes
- BT5 organic compounds

CATHODE FOLLOWERS [10; 10]
- BT1 electronic circuits
- RT pulse amplifiers

CATHODE RAY TUBE DIGITIZERS [55; 55]
- UF *pepr devices*
- BT1 digitizers

CATHODE RAY TUBES [361; 361]
- BT1 electron tubes
- RT display devices
- RT electron scanning
- RT image tubes
- RT oscillographs

CATHODE SPUTTERING [295; 295]
- BT1 sputtering
- RT vapor plating

CATHODES [2,902; 3,817]
- BT1 electrodes
- NT1 hollow cathodes
- NT1 photocathodes
- RT cathodoluminescence
- RT electron tubes
- RT thermionic emitters

cathodic protection
- USE corrosion protection

CATHODOLUMINESCENCE [460; 460]
(Cathode-ray-excited emission)
- BT1 luminescence
- BT2 photon emission
- BT3 emission
- RT cathodes
- RT emission spectroscopy

CATIONS [9,727; 41,581]
- UF *positive ions*
- BT1 ions
- BT2 charged particles
- NT1 hydrogen ions 1 plus
- NT2 protons
- NT3 antiprotons
- NT3 cosmic protons
- NT3 delayed protons
- NT3 diprotons
- NT3 photoprotons
- NT3 prompt protons
- NT3 solar protons
- NT3 trapped protons
- NT1 hydrogen ions 2 plus
- NT1 hydrogen ions 3 plus
- RT chemical state
- RT electrolysis
- RT ion beams
- RT ion exchange materials

CATS [372; 372]
- BT1 mammals
- BT2 vertebrates
- BT3 animals

CATTENOM-1 REACTOR [36; 36] *Jul 84*
- BT1 pwr type reactors
- BT2 enriched uranium reactors
- BT3 reactors
- BT2 power reactors
- BT3 reactors
- BT2 thermal reactors
- BT3 reactors
- BT2 water cooled reactors
- BT3 reactors
- BT2 water moderated reactors
- BT3 reactors

CATTENOM-2 REACTOR [10; 10] *Jul 84*
- BT1 pwr type reactors
- BT2 enriched uranium reactors
- BT3 reactors
- BT2 power reactors
- BT3 reactors
- BT2 thermal reactors
- BT3 reactors
- BT2 water cooled reactors
- BT3 reactors
- BT2 water moderated reactors
- BT3 reactors

CATTENOM-3 REACTOR [7; 7] *Jul 84*
- BT1 pwr type reactors
- BT2 enriched uranium reactors
- BT3 reactors
- BT2 power reactors
- BT3 reactors
- BT2 thermal reactors
- BT3 reactors
- BT2 water cooled reactors
- BT3 reactors
- BT2 water moderated reactors
- BT3 reactors

CATTENOM-4 REACTOR [6; 6] *Jul 84*
- BT1 pwr type reactors
- BT2 enriched uranium reactors
- BT3 reactors
- BT2 power reactors
- BT3 reactors
- BT2 thermal reactors
- BT3 reactors
- BT2 water cooled reactors
- BT3 reactors
- BT2 water moderated reactors
- BT3 reactors

CATTLE [1,658; 2,375]
UF bovine
BT1 domestic animals
BT2 animals
BT1 ruminants
BT2 mammals
BT3 vertebrates
BT4 animals
NT1 calves
NT1 cows
RT forage
RT gramineae
RT meat
RT pastures

CAUCHY PROBLEM [633; 633]
BT1 boundary-value problems
RT boundary conditions
RT partial differential equations

cauliflower
USE brassica

CAUSALITY [899; 899]
RT quantum mechanics
RT schwinger source theory

CAVES [228; 228]
BT1 cavities
RT geologic fissures
RT openings

CAVITATION [571; 571]
UF column separation (fluid mech)
RT fluid flow

CAVITIES [1,535; 6,104]
NT1 boreholes
NT1 caves
NT1 chimneys
NT1 craters
NT1 salt caverns
NT1 sinuses
RT crystal defects
RT excavation
RT nuclear explosions
RT openings
RT underground explosions
RT underground storage
RT voids
RT water influx

cavity ionization chambers
USE bragg gray chambers

CAVITY RESONATORS [3,167; 4,071]
UF resonance cavities
BT1 electronic equipment
BT2 equipment
BT1 resonators
BT2 equipment
NT1 superconducting cavity resonat
RT cyclic accelerators
RT microwave equipment
RT rf systems
RT tuning

ccba
USE coupled channel born approxima

ccd
USE charge-coupled devices

CDC COMPUTERS [521; 521]
BT1 computers

CDD POLES [29; 29]
UF castillejo-dalitz-dyson poles
RT dispersion relations
RT partial waves

CDFR REACTOR [101; 101] *Sep 79*
UF commercial demonstr fast react
BT1 lmfbr type reactors
BT2 fbr type reactors
BT3 breeder reactors
BT4 reactors
BT3 fast reactors
BT4 epithermal reactors
BT5 reactors
BT2 liquid metal cooled reactors
BT3 reactors
BT1 power reactors
BT2 reactors
BT1 sodium cooled reactors
BT2 liquid metal cooled reactors
BT3 reactors

CDTA [40; 40]
(Cyclohexylenedinitrilotetraacetic acid)
UF cyclohexylenedinitrilotetraace
BT1 amino acids
BT2 carboxylic acids
BT3 organic acids
BT4 organic compounds
BT1 chelating agents

CDTE SEMICONDUCTOR DETECTORS [320; 320]
UF cadmium telluride detectors
BT1 semiconductor detectors
BT2 radiation detectors
BT3 measuring instruments

CE STANDARD REACTOR [77; 77]
Oct 75
UF comb. eng. standard reactor
UF pwr/80 type reactor
BT1 pwr type reactors
BT2 enriched uranium reactors
BT3 reactors
BT2 power reactors
BT3 reactors
BT2 thermal reactors
BT3 reactors
BT2 water cooled reactors
BT3 reactors
BT2 water moderated reactors
BT3 reactors

CEA [425; 827]
UF commissariat a l'energie atomi
BT1 french organizations
BT2 national organizations
NT1 cea bruyeres-le-chatel
NT1 cea cadarache
NT1 cea fontenay-aux-roses
NT1 cea grenoble
NT1 cea la hague
NT1 cea marcoule
NT1 cea pierrelatte
NT1 cea saclay
RT france

cea (accelerator)
USE cambridge electron accelerator

cea (antigen)
USE carcinoembryonic antigen

CEA BRUYERES-LE-CHATEL [0; 0]
Dec 89
BT1 cea
BT2 french organizations
BT3 national organizations

CEA CADARACHE [95; 95]
UF cadarache (cea)
BT1 cea
BT2 french organizations
BT3 national organizations

CEA FONTENAY-AUX-ROSES [33; 33]
UF fontenay-aux-roses (cea)
BT1 cea
BT2 french organizations
BT3 national organizations

CEA GRENOBLE [46; 46]
BT1 cea
BT2 french organizations
BT3 national organizations

CEA LA HAGUE [75; 75]
BT1 cea
BT2 french organizations
BT3 national organizations
BT1 fuel reprocessing plants
BT2 nuclear facilities

CEA MARCOULE [65; 65]
UF marcoule (cea)
BT1 cea
BT2 french organizations
BT3 national organizations

CEA PIERRELATTE [11; 11]
UF pierrelatte (cea)
BT1 cea
BT2 french organizations
BT3 national organizations

CEA SACLAY [101; 101]
UF saclay (cea)
BT1 cea
BT2 french organizations
BT3 national organizations

CEBAF ACCELERATOR [113; 113]
May 87
(Continuous Electron Beam Accelerator Facility.)
BT1 linear accelerators
BT2 accelerators

cef-or reactor
USE or-cef reactor

CELESTIN REACTOR [3; 3]
BT1 heavy water cooled reactors
BT2 reactors
BT1 heavy water moderated reactors
BT2 reactors
BT1 isotope production reactors
BT2 irradiation reactors
BT3 reactors
BT1 tritium production reactors
BT2 irradiation reactors
BT3 reactors

CELL CONSTITUENTS [355; 8,886]
NT1 cell membranes
NT1 cell nuclei
NT2 nucleoli
NT1 cell wall
NT1 chloroplasts
NT1 cytoplasm
NT1 microtubules
NT1 mitochondria
NT1 organoids
NT2 endoplasmic reticulum
NT2 lysosomes
NT2 ribosomes
NT1 plasmids
RT animal cells
RT cytological techniques
RT cytology
RT genetics
RT liposomes
RT plant cells
RT tissue extracts
RT ultrastructural changes

INIS THESAURUS: CUMULATIVE UPDATE

This update to the INIS Thesaurus (IAEA-INIS-13/Rev. 31) covers the period from **January 1992** through **June 1992**. The June changes are marked with arrows (→).

DELETED TERMS

accumulators
agricultural wastes
antimicrobial agents
arid lands
bays (coastal waters)
birches
comminution
→ *cooling ponds*
corrosive effects
diatoms
engines
exports
geothermal resources
HIGH TEMPERATURE
imports
kale
land pollution abatement
land pollution control
liquefied natural gas
LOW TEMPERATURE
machinery
magma
manufacturing

MAPLE REACTOR
marshes
MEDIUM TEMPERATURE
mine shafts
morphology
mussels
NECKAR REACTOR
ORGANOPHOSPHINIC ACIDS
parametric analysis
→ *photovoltaic power plants*
polycyclic aromatic hydrocarbo
ponds
prices
PUBLIC LAW
public policy
pulverizing
residential buildings (apartm)
residential buildings (houses)
resource development
→ *rift zones*
rubber trees
→ *sedimentary basins*
service life
shafts (mines)
site characterization

sludges
sorption
sulfur dioxide
temperature (0000-0013 k)
temperature (0013-0065 k)
temperature (0065-0273 k)
temperature (0273-0400 k)
temperature (0400-1000 k)
temperature (1000-4000 k)
tendons
toxic materials
training
tribology
ULTRALOW TEMPERATURE
US WATER POLLUTION CONTROL ACT
VERY HIGH TEMPERATURE
VERY LOW TEMPERATURE
water pollution abatement
wetlands

ADDED TERMS

ABANDONED SHAFTS
BT1 mine shafts
RT mines
ABANDONED WELLS
(An oil or gas well that has been abandoned because its yield has fallen below that necessary for profitable production.)
BT1 wells
RT natural gas wells
RT oil wells
ABSORPTION REFRIGERATION CYCLE
BT1 thermodynamic cycles
RT cooling systems
RT refrigeration
RT refrigerators
abu dhabi
USE united arab emirates
ABUNDANCE
RT chemical composition
RT isotope ratio
RT ore composition
RT quantity ratio
AC SYSTEMS
UF *alternating current systems*
BT1 power systems
ACID ELECTROLYTE FUEL CELLS
BT1 fuel cells
ACID HYDROLYSIS
BT1 hydrolysis
RT enzymatic hydrolysis
ACID MINE DRAINAGE
RT coal mining
RT land pollution
RT liquid wastes
RT mine draining
RT mining
RT waste water

ACID NEUTRALIZING CAPACITY
(The total quantity of base in natural waters, usually in equilibrium with carbonate or bicarbonate, as determined by titration with strong acid.)
BT1 water chemistry
RT acid carbonates
RT acid rain
RT bases
RT buffers
RT carbonates
RT geochemistry
RT limnology
RT organic matter
RT ph value
RT soils
RT titration
ACIDIZATION
(Treatment of a reservoir formation with acid to assist the flow of crude oil or gas by improving the permeability of the reservoir rock.)
RT enhanced recovery
RT natural gas deposits
RT petroleum deposits
ACOUSTICS
RT photoacoustic effect
RT sound waves
ADRIATIC SEA
BT1 mediterranean sea
adsorptive properties
USE sorptive properties
AEROSPACE INDUSTRY
BT1 industry
RT aircraft
RT space vehicles

AGEAN SEA
BT1 mediterranean sea
agricultural residues
USE agricultural wastes
AGRICULTURAL WASTES
UF *agricultural residues*
UF *stover*
BT1 organic wastes
RT biological wastes
RT straw
→ **AHUACHAPAN GEOTHERMAL FIELD**
BT1 geothermal fields
RT el salvador
AIR CLEANING SYSTEMS
RT air cleaning
RT air conditioning
RT air filters
RT electrostatic precipitators
RT off-gas systems
RT pollution control equipment
RT scrubbers
RT ventilation
RT ventilation systems
AIR-BIOSPHERE INTERACTIONS
RT air-water interactions
RT environmental transport
RT mass transfer
RT mineral cycling
AIRPORTS
RT aircraft
ajman
USE united arab emirates
→ **ALASKA OIL PIPELINE**
UF *transalaska pipeline*
BT1 pipelines
RT alaskan north slope
RT petroleum

→ **ALASKAN NORTH SLOPE**
    BT1   alaska
    RT   alaska oil pipeline
ALCOHOL FUEL CELLS
    BT1   fuel cells
ALCOHOL FUELS
(For pure alcohols, alcohol-water mixtures, or alcohol with additives; for alcohol-gasoline mixtures use GASOHOL.)
    BT1   liquid fuels
    BT1   synthetic fuels
    RT   automotive fuels
    RT   diesel fuels
    RT   gasohol
ALKALINE ELECTROLYTE FUEL CELL
    BT1   fuel cells
ALLOY-CU70NI30
    BT1   copper base alloys
ALLOY-CU90NI10
    BT1   copper base alloys
→ **ALTAMAHA RIVER**
    BT1   rivers
    RT   georgia
    RT   hydroelectric power plants
alternating current systems
    USE   ac systems
→ **ALUMINIUM ARSENIDE SOLAR CELLS**
    BT1   solar cells
AMENDMENTS
    BT1   laws
AMMONIA FUEL CELLS
    BT1   fuel cells
ANTI-INFECTIVE AGENTS
    BT1   drugs
ANTIMICROBIAL AGENTS
(Prior to February 1992, this concept was indexed to ANTIBIOTICS.)
    BT1   anti-infective agents
ANYONS
    BT1   quasi particles
    RT   quantum field theory
    RT   statistical mechanics
    RT   superconductivity
→ **AQUICLUDES**
    RT   ground water
    RT   rocks
    RT   water reservoirs
ARAB ATOMIC ENERGY AGENCY
    BT1   international organizations
ARAB COUNTRIES
    RT   africa
    RT   asia
    RT   middle east
ARCHITECTURE
    RT   aesthetics
    RT   buildings
area pollution sources
    USE   pollution sources
ARID LANDS
→ **ARTIFICIAL LIFTS**
(Any method of lifting oil out of underground reservoirs, usually by injecting gas or foam into a rock or sand formation to force fluids from wells.)
    RT   oil wells
ASH CONTENT
    RT   ashes
    RT   chemical composition
    RT   coal
ASPENS
    BT1   poplars
    RT   cottonwoods
→ **ASPHALT RIDGE DEPOSIT**
    BT1   oil sand deposits
    RT   oil sands
    RT   utah
ASTRID STORAGE RING
(Aarhus University, Denmark.)
    BT1   storage rings
→ **ATHABASCA DEPOSIT**
    BT1   oil sand deposits
    RT   alberta
    RT   canada
    RT   oil sands

→ **ATLANTA**
    BT1   georgia
→ **AU SABLE RIVER**
    BT1   rivers
    RT   hydroelectric power plants
    RT   michigan
automobile industry
    USE   automotive industry
AUTOMOTIVE INDUSTRY
    UF   *automobile industry*
    BT1   industry
→ **BACK CONTACT SOLAR CELLS**
    BT1   solar cells
→ **BALTIMORE CANYON**
(Depression off the Middle Atlantic States.)
    BT1   atlantic ocean
BAMBOO
    BT1   gramineae
→ **BARBADOS**
    BT1   lesser antilles
BARGES
    RT   maritime transport
    RT   ships
BASEMENT ROCK
(Metamorphic or igneous rock underlying the sedimentary sequence.)
    BT1   geologic strata
    RT   igneous rocks
    RT   metamorphic rocks
    RT   rocks
BATCH CULTURE
    RT   anaerobic digestion
    RT   continuous culture
    RT   culture media
    RT   fermentation
    RT   semibatch culture
→ **BATHYMETRY**
(The measurement of ocean depths and the charting of the topography of the ocean floor.)
    RT   geophysics
    RT   oceanography
    RT   seas
BAYS
    BT1   coastal waters
BEECH TREES
    BT1   magnoliopsida
    BT1   trees
→ **BENIN**
    BT1   africa
→ **BEPPU GEOTHERMAL FIELD**
    BT1   geothermal fields
    RT   japan
BIOCHEMICAL FUEL CELLS
    BT1   fuel cells
BIOCHEMICAL OXYGEN DEMAND
(The amount of oxygen necessary for the oxidative decomposition of a material by microorganisms.)
    RT   aquatic ecosystems
    RT   biochemistry
    RT   dissolved gases
    RT   liquid wastes
biodiversity
    USE   species diversity
BIOLOGICAL WARFARE
    BT1   warfare
BIOPHOTOLYSIS
    BT1   bioconversion
    BT1   photolysis
    RT   photosynthesis
BIRCHES
    BT1   magnoliopsida
    BT1   trees
→ **BOREAL REGIONS**
(Those regions comprising the climate and biotic communities between the polar regions and the temperate zones.)
    RT   climates
    RT   polar regions
BOUNDARY ELEMENT METHOD
    BT1   finite element method
    RT   computer calculations
    RT   finite difference method
    RT   mathematics
    RT   mesh generation

BOX MODELS
    BT1   mathematical models
    RT   atmospheric circulation
    RT   climate models
    RT   oceanic circulation
    RT   simulation
→ **BRAWLEY GEOTHERMAL FIELD**
    BT1   california
    BT1   geothermal fields
→ **BRAZOS RIVER**
    BT1   rivers
    RT   texas
BROWN COAL
    BT1   coal
BRYOPHYTA
    BT1   plants
BUFFALO GOURD
    BT1   magnoliopsida
BULK DENSITY
    BT1   density
bunker oils
    USE   residual fuels
→ **BURUNDI**
    BT1   africa
    BT1   developing countries
BUSINESS
    RT   economy
    RT   industry
    RT   market
    RT   trade
buyers
    USE   marketers
→ **CADMIUM ARSENIDE SOLAR CELLS**
    BT1   solar cells
→ **CADMIUM SELENIDE SOLAR CELLS**
    BT1   solar cells
→ **CADMIUM SULFIDE SOLAR CELLS**
    BT1   solar cells
→ **CADMIUM TELLURIDE SOLAR CELLS**
    BT1   solar cells
CALCULATION METHODS
    RT   numerical solution
CALORIFIC VALUE
(Quantity of heat liberated on the complete combustion of a unit weight or unit volume of fuel.)
    RT   combustion
    RT   fuels
CALVIN CYCLE SPECIES
(Plants that fix carbon by the reductive pentose phosphate pathway only.)
    BT1   plants
    RT   carbon dioxide fixation
    RT   chloroplasts
    RT   c4 species
    RT   leaves
    RT   photosynthesis
CAMBRIAN PERIOD
    BT1   paleozoic era
CAMELS
    BT1   ruminants
CANOPIES
(Vegetative canopies only.)
    RT   forests
    RT   ground cover
    RT   leaves
    RT   trees
→ **CAPE VERDE ISLANDS**
    BT1   islands
    RT   atlantic ocean
CARBON DIOXIDE INJECTION
    UF   *co2 flooding*
    BT1   miscible-phase displacement
    RT   enhanced recovery
CARBONIFEROUS PERIOD
    UF   *mississippian period*
    UF   *pennsylvanian period*
    BT1   paleozoic era
→ **CASCADE MOUNTAINS**
    BT1   mountains
    RT   sierra nevada colorado
    RT   usa

→ **CASCADE SOLAR CELLS**
    UF   *graded band gap solar cells*
    BT1   solar cells
    RT   graded band gaps

casings (well)
    USE   well casings

CATALYST SUPPORTS
    UF   *supports (catalyst)*
    RT   catalysts
    RT   substrates
    RT   surfaces

CATALYTIC CONVERTERS
(Air pollution control devices using a catalytic reaction to change gaseous effluents to harmless gases.)
    BT1   pollution control equipment
    RT   air pollution control
    RT   catalysis
    RT   exhaust gases

CATALYTIC CRACKING
    BT1   pyrolysis
    RT   catalysis

CATALYTIC EFFECTS
    RT   catalysis
    RT   catalysts
    RT   electrocatalysts

CATTAILS
    BT1   liliopsida
    RT   aquatic ecosystems
    RT   biomass

cdf
    USE   fermilab collider detector

CEDAR COMPUTERS
    BT1   supercomputers
    RT   array processors
    RT   parallel processing
    RT   vector processing

CEDARS
    UF   *junipers*
    BT1   conifers
    BT1   trees

CENOZOIC ERA
    BT1   geologic ages

CERAMICS INDUSTRY
    BT1   industry
    RT   ceramics
    RT   metal industry

cercla
    USE   us superfund

→ **CERRO PRIETO GEOTHERMAL FIELD**
    BT1   geothermal fields
    RT   geothermal hot-water systems
    RT   mexico

→ *cfc*
    USE   chlorofluorocarbons

→ **CHATTAHOOCHEE RIVER**
    BT1   rivers
    RT   alabama
    RT   florida
    RT   georgia

CHEMICAL ATTRACTANTS
    RT   insects
    RT   odor
    RT   pest control

CHEMICAL ENGINEERING
    BT1   engineering
    RT   chemistry

CHEMICAL PLANTS
    BT1   industrial plants
    RT   biomass conversion plants
    RT   chemical industry

CHEMICAL WARFARE
    BT1   warfare

CHENOPODIACEAE
    BT1   magnoliopsida

CHESTNUT TREES
    BT1   magnoliopsida
    BT1   trees

CHINA SEA
    UF   *east china sea*
    UF   *south china sea*
    BT1   pacific ocean

CHINESE TALLOW TREE
    BT1   euphorbia

→ **CHLOROFLUOROCARBONS**
    UF   *cfc*
    BT1   organic chlorine compounds
    BT1   organic fluorine compounds
    RT   chlorinated aliphatic hydrocar
    RT   fluorinated aliphatic hydrocar
    RT   freons
    RT   greenhouse gases
    RT   refrigerants

CHLOROPHYCOTA
    BT1   algae

→ **CHLOROSIS**
    BT1   pathological changes
    RT   chlorophyll
    RT   leaves
    RT   plant diseases
    RT   plant tissues
    RT   symptoms

CHROMOPHYCOTA
    BT1   algae

→ **CIRCLE CLIFFS DEPOSIT**
    BT1   oil sand deposits
    RT   oil sands
    RT   utah

circular point collectors
    USE   parabolic dish collectors

CLASSIFIED INFORMATION
    BT1   information
    RT   secrecy protection
    RT   security

CLIMATE MODELS
    BT1   mathematical models
    RT   atmospheric circulation
    RT   box models
    RT   climates
    RT   general circulation models
    RT   meteorology
    RT   seasonal variations

CLIMATIC CHANGE
    UF   *global climate change*
    RT   acid rain
    RT   greenhouse effect
    RT   ozone layer

CLOUD COVER
    UF   *cloudiness (meteorology)*
    RT   clouds
    RT   meteorology
    RT   storms

cloudiness (meteorology)
    USE   cloud cover

→ **CNRS SOLAR FACILITY**
(The solar furnace facility at the National Center for Scientific Research, CNRS, at Odeillo, France.)
    BT1   test facilities
    RT   france
    RT   solar furnaces

COAL FINES
    BT1   coal
    RT   pulverized fuels

COAL FUEL CELLS
    BT1   fuel cells

COAL MINERS
    BT1   miners

COAL PREPARATION
    RT   cleaning
    RT   coal preparation plants
    RT   comminution
    RT   crushing
    RT   drying
    RT   flotation
    RT   us clean coal technology progr
    RT   washing
    RT   water removal

COAL PREPARATION PLANTS
    UF   *solvent-refining coal plants*
    BT1   industrial plants
    RT   coal preparation
    RT   solvent-refined coal

COAL PRODUCING DISTRICTS
    RT   coal deposits
    RT   coal mining

COAL-FIRED GAS TURBINES
    BT1   gas turbines
    RT   fossil-fuel power plants
    RT   gas turbine power plants

→ **COASTAL ZONE MANAGEMENT ACTS**
    BT1   laws
    RT   coastal regions
    RT   coastal waters
    RT   continental shelf

COLD FISSION
    BT1   fission
    RT   heavy ion emission decay
    RT   kinetic energy

COLD LAKE DEPOSIT
    BT1   oil sand deposits
    RT   alberta
    RT   canada
    RT   oil sands
    RT   saskatchewan

collider detector at fermilab
    USE   fermilab collider detector

→ **COMBINED COLLECTORS**
(Combined photovoltaic and thermal collectors.)
    RT   solar cells
    RT   solar collectors

COMBUSTION CHAMBERS
    RT   combustors
    RT   engines
    RT   furnaces
    RT   spark ignition engines

COMMINUTION
    UF   *pulverization*
    BT1   mechanical fragmentation
    RT   coal preparation
    RT   crushing
    RT   pulverizers

COMMUNITIES
    RT   human populations
    RT   socio-economic factors

→ **COMPLEX TERRAIN**
    RT   mountains
    RT   topography
    RT   valleys
    RT   watersheds

COMPOST
    BT1   organic wastes
    RT   composting

COMPOSTING
    BT1   waste processing
    RT   compost
    RT   decomposition

COMPRESSED AIR
    BT1   air
    BT1   compressed gases

COMPUTER-AIDED INSTRUCTION
    RT   education

CONCENTRATING COLLECTORS
    BT1   solar collectors
    RT   solar receivers

→ **CONCENTRATOR SOLAR CELLS**
    BT1   solar cells
    RT   solar concentrators
    RT   solar receivers

CONNECTICUT RIVER BASIN
    BT1   watersheds
    RT   connecticut
    RT   connecticut river
    RT   massachusetts
    RT   new hampshire
    RT   vermont

CONSTRUCTION INDUSTRY
    BT1   industry
    RT   buildings
    RT   construction
    RT   modular structures

CONSUMER PROTECTION
    RT   consumer products
    RT   interest groups
    RT   legal aspects
    RT   public relations
    RT   regulations
    RT   us natural gas policy act

CONTINUOUS CULTURE
    RT   anaerobic digestion
    RT   batch culture
    RT   culture media
    RT   fermentation
    RT   semibatch culture

→ *cook inlet*
    USE   gulf of alaska

→ **COOLING PONDS**
　UF　*ponds (cooling)*
　UF　*spray ponds*
　BT1　ponds
　BT1　water reservoirs
　RT　cooling
　RT　cooling systems
　RT　lakes

→ **COPPER OXIDE SOLAR CELLS**
　BT1　solar cells

→ **COPPER SELENIDE SOLAR CELLS**
　BT1　solar cells

→ **COPPER SULFIDE SOLAR CELLS**
　BT1　solar cells

COPPER 76
　BT1　beta-minus decay radioisotopes
　BT1　copper isotopes
　BT1　intermediate mass nuclei
　BT1　millisec living radioisotopes
　BT1　odd-odd nuclei

COPPER 77
　BT1　beta-minus decay radioisotopes
　BT1　copper isotopes
　BT1　intermediate mass nuclei
　BT1　millisec living radioisotopes
　BT1　odd-even nuclei

COPPER 78
　BT1　beta-minus decay radioisotopes
　BT1　copper isotopes
　BT1　intermediate mass nuclei
　BT1　millisec living radioisotopes
　BT1　odd-odd nuclei

COPPER 79
　BT1　beta-minus decay radioisotopes
　BT1　copper isotopes
　BT1　intermediate mass nuclei
　BT1　millisec living radioisotopes
　BT1　odd-even nuclei

CORROSIVE EFFECTS
　RT　corrosion

→ **COSO HOT SPRINGS**
　BT1　california

COST RECOVERY
　RT　charges
　RT　cost
　RT　financing

COSY STORAGE RING
(Cooled synchrotron storage ring at KFZ Juelich, Federal Republic of Germany.)
　UF　*juelich storage ring*
　BT1　storage rings

COTTONWOODS
　BT1　poplars
　RT　aspens

cowpea plants
　USE　vigna

co2 flooding
　USE　carbon dioxide injection

CRETACEOUS PERIOD
　BT1　mesozoic era

CROWN ETHERS
　BT1　ethers
　RT　chelating agents
　RT　complexes
　RT　ligands
　RT　solvent extraction

CRYSTAL GROWTH METHODS
　RT　crystal growth

cylindrical parabolic collecto
　USE　parabolic trough collectors

C4 SPECIES
(Plants having a preliminary step in their carbon fixation pathway whereby CO2 binds to phosphoenolpyruvate.)
　BT1　plants
　RT　calvin cycle species
　RT　carbon dioxide fixation
　RT　chloroplasts
　RT　leaves
　RT　photosynthesis

→ **DALHART BASIN**
　BT1　salt deposits
　RT　texas

darmstadt storage ring
　USE　esr storage ring

DC SYSTEMS
(Direct-current electric power systems.)
　BT1　power systems

dealers
　USE　marketers

DELAWARE BAY
　BT1　atlantic ocean
　BT1　bays
　RT　delaware

DENITRIFICATION
　BT1　chemical reactions
　RT　nitrogen
　RT　nitrogen compounds

→ **DEPLETION LAYER**
(An electric double layer formed at the surface of contact between a metal and a semiconductor having different work functions.)
　RT　semiconductor materials
　RT　solar cells
　RT　surface barrier detectors
　RT　surface barrier transistors

DERIVATIZATION
(Conversion of a chemical compound into a derivative, usually for the purpose of identification.)
　BT1　chemical reactions
　RT　chemical analysis
　RT　structural chemical analysis

DEVONIAN PERIOD
　BT1　paleozoic era

DIATOMS
(Algae of the class Bacillariophyceae. Prior to January 1992, this was indexed by ALGAE and PLANKTON.)
　BT1　chromophycota

→ **DIENG GEOTHERMAL FIELD**
　BT1　geothermal fields
　RT　indonesia

diesel oil (fraction)
　USE　diesel fuels

DIMETHYL SULFIDE
　UF　*dimethylsulfide*
　BT1　organic sulfur compounds
　BT1　sulfides

dimethylsulfide
　USE　dimethyl sulfide

→ **DIRECT DRIVE LASER IMPLOSION**
(Laser implosion where the driver energy is directly absorbed by the target capsule.)
　BT1　laser implosions
　RT　laser fusion reactors
　RT　laser targets
　RT　laser-produced plasma
　RT　laser-radiation heating
　RT　pulsed fusion reactors

disarmament
　SEE　arms control

DISPLACEMENT FLUIDS
　BT1　fluids
　RT　enhanced recovery
　RT　fluid injection

DISPOSAL WELLS
　BT1　wells
　RT　brines
　RT　radioactive waste disposal
　RT　underground disposal

DISTRIBUTED COLLECTOR POWER PL
　BT1　solar thermal power plants

DISTRIBUTED DATA PROCESSING
　BT1　data processing

DJIBOUTI
　BT1　africa
　BT1　arab countries

DNA CLONING
　BT1　dna hybridization

DNA HYBRIDIZATION
　BT1　nucleic acid hybridization
　RT　genetic mapping
　RT　recombinant dna

dnepr river
　USE　dnieper river

DNIEPER RIVER
　UF　*dnepr river*
　BT1　rivers
　RT　black sea
　RT　pripet river
　RT　ukrainian ssr

→ **DOUGLAS POINT SITE**
　BT1　reactor sites
　RT　maryland
　RT　nuclear power plants

DRAWDOWN
(Reduction of fluid level in reservoirs by intentional withdrawal.)
　RT　ground water
　RT　reservoir fluids

DRILL PIPES
　BT1　drilling equipment
　BT1　pipes
　RT　drills

DRILLING EQUIPMENT
　BT1　equipment
　RT　drilling fluids
　RT　well drilling

drilling platforms
　USE　offshore platforms

DRILLING RIGS
(A drill machine complete with all tools and accessory equipment needed to drill boreholes.)
　BT1　drilling equipment
　RT　well drilling

DRILLS
　BT1　drilling equipment
　RT　drill bits
　RT　drill pipes
　RT　rock drilling
　RT　well drilling

dubai
　USE　united arab emirates

east china sea
　USE　china sea

→ **EAST MESA GEOTHERMAL FIELD**
　BT1　geothermal fields
　RT　imperial valley

→ **EDNA DEPOSIT**
　BT1　oil sand deposits
　RT　california
　RT　oil sands

EDUCATIONAL TOOLS
(Activities or materials such as movies, slides, or computer media intended to assist in promoting learning or understanding.)
　RT　education
　RT　educational facilities
　RT　training

EHV DC SYSTEMS
(345-765 kV.)
　UF　*extrahigh voltage dc systems*
　BT1　dc systems

→ *el nino*
　USE　southern oscillation

→ **EL TATIO GEOTHERMAL FIELD**
　BT1　geothermal fields
　RT　chile

ELECTRIC POWER INDUSTRY
(Only for general papers when descriptors such as ELECTRIC POWER, ELECTRIC UTILITIES, or POWER SYSTEMS will not suffice.)
　BT1　industry
　RT　electric power
　RT　epri
　RT　nuclear power
　RT　power systems

ELECTRIC-POWERED VEHICLES
　BT1　vehicles
　RT　electric batteries
　RT　fuel cells
　RT　hybrid electric-powered vehicl

ELECTRICAL ENGINEERING
　BT1　engineering

ELECTROCATALYSTS
　UF　*fuel cell catalysts*
　BT1　catalysts
　RT　catalysis
　RT　catalytic effects

ELECTROCHEMICAL CELLS
　RT　electrochemistry

ELEMENT 105 263
　BT1　alpha decay radioisotopes
　BT1　element 105 isotopes
　BT1　odd-even nuclei
　BT1　seconds living radioisotopes
　BT1　spontaneous fission radioisoto

EMULSIFICATION
  RT   emulsifiers
  RT   emulsions
ENERGY AUDITS
(The analysis of a facility to determine the forms of energy used, the quantities and costs of various forms of energy used, the purposes for which the energy is used, and the identification of energy conservation opportunities.)
  BT1 audits
  RT   energy accounting
  RT   energy conservation
ENERGY EXPENSES
(Monetary outlays or charges for energy consumed; not for Energy Costs, for which see ENERGY ACCOUNTING.)
  RT   cost
  RT   energy consumption
  RT   prices
ENERGY MODELS
  RT   computerized simulation
  RT   energy analysis
  RT   mathematical models
ENERGY SOURCE DEVELOPMENT
  RT   energy sources
  RT   resource development
  RT   risk assessment
ENGINEERING DRAWINGS
  BT1 diagrams
  RT   design
  RT   specifications
ENGINES
  RT   combustion chambers
ENVIRONMENTAL EXPOSURE
  RT   acute exposure
  RT   air pollution
  RT   carcinogens
  RT   chronic exposure
  RT   hazardous materials
  RT   land pollution
  RT   mutagens
  RT   water pollution
environmental parks
  USE nature reserves
ENZYMATIC HYDROLYSIS
  BT1 hydrolysis
  RT   acid hydrolysis
  RT   biodegradation
  RT   cellulase
  RT   enzymes
  RT   hydrolases
  RT   pellicularia
  RT   thielavia
ENZYME INDUCTION
  BT1 gene regulation
  RT   biosynthesis
  RT   enzymes
  RT   gene repressors
EOCENE EPOCH
  BT1 tertiary period
ERZGEBIRGE DEPOSIT
  BT1 uranium deposits
  RT   federal republic of germany
  RT   uranium ores
ESR STORAGE RING
  UF   *darmstadt storage ring*
  BT1 storage rings
EUGLENOPHYCOTA
  BT1 plants
EUMYCOTA
  BT1 fungi
EUPHORBIA
(Latex bearing plants and possible source of hydrocarbons.)
  BT1 magnoliopsida
EVERGLADES NATIONAL PARK
  BT1 public lands
  RT   florida
  RT   swamps
EXPENDITURES
  UF   *spending*
  RT   budgets
  RT   capital
  RT   cost
  RT   economics
  RT   financing

EXPORTS
  BT1 trade
  RT   domestic supplies
  RT   tariffs
extrahigh voltage dc systems
  USE ehv dc systems
FABRIC FILTERS
  BT1 filters
  RT   baghouses
  RT   dust collectors
  RT   pollution control equipment
fed. energy reg. comm.
  USE us ferc
FEDERAL BUILDINGS
  BT1 public buildings
FELIX FACILITY
(Experimental test facility at Argonne National Laboratory, USA, for the study of electromagnetic effects in fusion reactor materials.)
  UF   *fusion e.m. induction exp*
  BT1 test facilities
  RT   thermonuclear reactors
FERMILAB COLLIDER DETECTOR
(Detector to study proton-antiproton collisions at 2 TeV center-of-mass energy.)
  UF   *cdf*
  UF   *collider detector at fermilab*
  BT1 radiation detectors
  RT   drift chambers
  RT   projection spark chambers
  RT   shower counters
FIORDS
  BT1 estuaries
  RT   salinity
  RT   seawater
FIRE DETECTORS
  BT1 measuring instruments
  RT   alarm systems
firewood
  USE wood fuels
FIRS
  BT1 conifers
  BT1 trees
fish culture
  USE fisheries
fish hatcheries
  USE fisheries
FISHERIES
  UF   *fish culture*
  UF   *fish hatcheries*
  RT   aquaculture
  RT   fishing industry
fixed beds
  USE packed beds
FLOOD CONTROL
  RT   coastal regions
  RT   dams
  RT   hydroelectric power plants
  RT   rivers
florida current
  USE gulf stream
FLUIDIZED BED BOILERS
  BT1 boilers
  RT   fluidized beds
  RT   fluidized-bed combustion
FOOD ADDITIVES
  BT1 additives
  RT   animal feeds
  RT   diet
  RT   drugs
  RT   food
  RT   vitamins
FOOD INDUSTRY
  BT1 industry
  RT   food processing
FORAMINIFERA
  BT1 sarcodina
FORESTRY
  RT   deforestation
  RT   forests
  RT   paper industry
  RT   wood products industry
FORMALDEHYDE FUEL CELLS
  BT1 fuel cells

FORMATE FUEL CELLS
  BT1 fuel cells
FORMIC ACID FUEL CELLS
  BT1 fuel cells
FRACTURED RESERVOIRS
  BT1 geologic structures
  RT   geologic fissures
  RT   reservoir rock
FUEL ADDITIVES
  BT1 additives
  RT   fuels
  RT   tel
fuel cell catalysts
  USE electrocatalysts
FUEL CELL POWER PLANTS
(For commercial, residential, or electric utility use.)
  BT1 power plants
  RT   fuel cells
FUEL CONSUMPTION
  BT1 energy consumption
  RT   automotive fuels
  RT   demand
  RT   fuels
FUEL OILS
  BT1 gas oils
  BT1 liquid fuels
FUEL SUBSTITUTION
  RT   energy shortages
  RT   energy supplies
  RT   fossil fuels
  RT   fuels
fuelwood
  USE wood fuels
fujaira
  USE united arab emirates
FULLERENES
(Carbon allotrope containing 60 carbon atoms in a hollow spherical configuration similar to a geodesic dome.)
  BT1 carbon
FUMAROLES
  RT   fumarolic fluids
  RT   hydrothermal systems
  RT   volcanoes
FUMAROLIC FLUIDS
  BT1 geothermal fluids
  RT   fumaroles
FURNITURE INDUSTRY
  BT1 industry
  RT   wood products industry
fusion e.m. induction exp
  USE felix facility
GALLIUM ARSENIDE SOLAR CELLS
  BT1 solar cells
GALLIUM PHOSPHIDE SOLAR CELLS
  BT1 solar cells
GALLIUM 84
  BT1 beta-minus decay radioisotopes
  BT1 gallium isotopes
  BT1 intermediate mass nuclei
  BT1 millisec living radioisotopes
  BT1 odd-odd nuclei
GALVESTON BAY
  BT1 bays
  BT1 gulf of mexico
  RT   texas
GAS BURNERS
  BT1 burners
  RT   combustion
gas fields
  USE natural gas fields
GAS METERS
  BT1 measuring instruments
  RT   energy consumption
  RT   natural gas
GAS OILS
(Petroleum distillates boiling within the general range 204 degrees to 593 degrees C)
  BT1 petroleum distillates
  BT1 petroleum products
GAS SPILLS
  UF   *lng spills*
  BT1 accidents
  RT   chemical spills
  RT   hazardous materials spills
  RT   natural gas
  RT   pollution

GAS TURBINE ENGINES
  BT1 engines
GAS UTILITIES
  BT1 public utilities
  RT   natural gas distribution syste
  RT   natural gas industry
GASOHOL
  (Blend of gasoline and an alchohol, usually methanol or ethanol.)
  BT1 liquid fuels
  RT   alcohol fuels
  RT   automotive fuels
  RT   diesel fuels
  RT   gasoline
  RT   methanol fuels
gasoline spills
  USE hazardous materials spills
GENE REPRESSORS
  RT   enzyme induction
GEOLOGIC AGES
  RT   age estimation
  RT   geologic history
→ **GEORGES BANK**
  (Submerged sandbank east of Massachusetts.)
  RT   atlantic ocean
  RT   mid-atlantic bight
GEOTHERMAL FLUIDS
  (Naturally occurring steam or hot water found in the earth's volcanic or young orogenic zones.)
  BT1 fluids
  RT   brines
  RT   hydrothermal systems
GEOTHERMAL HOT-WATER SYSTEMS
  (Hydrothermal convective systems characterized by liquid water as the continuous, pressure-controlling fluid phase.)
  BT1 hydrothermal systems
  RT   cerro prieto geothermal field
GEOTHERMAL INDUSTRY
  BT1 industry
  RT   geothermal energy
GEOTHERMAL RESOURCES
  (Until March 1992, this was indexed by GEOTHERMAL ENERGY and RESOURCES.)
  BT1 resources
  RT   geothermal systems
GEOTHERMAL SYSTEMS
  (Localized regions in which geothermal heat is carried close enough to the earth's surface by steam or hot water to be harnessed for use.)
  RT   geothermal fields
  RT   geothermal resources
GERMANIUM 70 REACTIONS
  BT1 heavy ion reactions
→ **GEYSERS GEOTHERMAL FIELD**
  UF   *the geysers*
  BT1 geothermal fields
  RT   california
  RT   vapor-dominated systems
→ **GLEN DAVIS FACILITY**
  BT1 oil shale processing plants
  RT   new south wales
global climate change
  USE climatic change
GLUCOSIDASE
  BT1 o-glycosyl hydrolases
→ *graded band gap solar cells*
  USE cascade solar cells
→ **GRADED BAND GAPS**
  RT   cascade solar cells
  RT   solar cells
→ **GRAND RIVER**
  BT1 rivers
  RT   hydroelectric power
  RT   michigan
→ **GREAT BASIN**
  (Area including Nevada, Western and Central Utah, Mohave county in Arizona, and the counties of Alpine, El Dorado, Inyo, Mono, and San Bernardino in California.)
  BT1 usa
  RT   arizona
  RT   california
  RT   nevada
  RT   utah

GREAT LAKES BASIN
  BT1 watersheds
  RT   great lakes
→ **GREAT SALT LAKE**
  BT1 lakes
  RT   utah
→ **GREATER ANTILLES**
  BT1 west indies
GREENHOUSE GASES
  RT   air pollution
  RT   atmospheric chemistry
  RT   carbon dioxide
  RT   chlorofluorocarbons
  RT   greenhouse effect
  RT   methane
  RT   nitrogen oxides
→ **GUAM**
  BT1 mariana islands
GUAYULE
  BT1 rubber trees
  RT   natural rubber
→ **GUINEA**
  BT1 africa
GULF OF ALASKA
  UF   *cook inlet*
  BT1 pacific ocean
GULF OF CALIFORNIA
  BT1 pacific ocean
→ **GULF OF SUEZ**
  BT1 red sea
GULF STREAM
  UF   *florida current*
  BT1 water currents
  RT   atlantic ocean
  RT   mid-atlantic bight
→ **HACHIMANTAI**
  BT1 japan
  RT   matsukawa geothermal field
  RT   onuma geothermal field
  RT   takinoue geothermal field
  RT   volcanic regions
HARVESTING
  RT   agriculture
  RT   biomass
  RT   crops
  RT   horticulture
  RT   silviculture
  RT   wood
→ **HATCHOBARU GEOTHERMAL FIELD**
  BT1 geothermal fields
  RT   japan
HEAT
  BT1 energy
  RT   energy recovery
  RT   heat recovery
  RT   heat transfer
  RT   heating
HEAT RECOVERY EQUIPMENT
  BT1 equipment
  RT   heat exchangers
  RT   heat recovery
  RT   waste heat boilers
HEATING OILS
  BT1 gas oils
  RT   liquefied petroleum gases
heavy fuels
  USE residual fuels
→ **HEBER GEOTHERMAL FIELD**
  BT1 geothermal fields
  RT   california
HELICOPTERS
  BT1 aircraft
HELIOSTATS
  BT1 solar equipment
  RT   control systems
→ **HELIUM EMBRITTLEMENT**
  (A decrease in the fracture strength of metals due to the incorporation of helium in the metal lattice.)
  BT1 embrittlement
  RT   brittleness
  RT   fracture properties
  RT   helium
  RT   interstitial helium generation

HEMLOCKS
  BT1 conifers
HETEROGENEOUS CATALYSIS
  (Catalysis occurring at a phase boundary, usually a solid-fluid interface.)
  BT1 catalysis
high temperature
  USE temperature range 0400-1000 k
high voltage dc systems
  USE hvdc systems
HIGH-TEMPERATURE FUEL CELLS
  BT1 fuel cells
highways
  USE roads
→ **HISPANIOLA**
  BT1 greater antilles
HOMOGENEOUS CATALYSIS
  (Catalysis occurring within a single phase, usually a gas or liquid.)
  BT1 catalysis
HONEYLOCUST TREES
  BT1 leguminosae
  BT1 trees
  RT   locust trees
HORTICULTURE
  (The science of growing fruits, vegetables, flowers and ornamental plants.)
  BT1 agriculture
  RT   harvesting
HUBBARD MODEL
  BT1 crystal models
  RT   antiferromagnetism
  RT   band theory
  RT   electronic structure
  RT   ferromagnetism
  RT   high-tc superconductors
  RT   superconductivity
HUMAN CHROMOSOME 16
  BT1 human chromosomes
HUMAN CHROMOSOME 17
  BT1 human chromosomes
HUMAN CHROMOSOME 18
  BT1 human chromosomes
HUMAN CHROMOSOME 19
  BT1 human chromosomes
HUMAN CHROMOSOME 21
  BT1 human chromosomes
HUMAN CHROMOSOME 5
  BT1 human chromosomes
HUMAN X CHROMOSOME
  BT1 human chromosomes
  BT1 x chromosome
HUMAN Y CHROMOSOME
  BT1 human chromosomes
  BT1 y chromosome
HVDC SYSTEMS
  (69-230 kV.)
  UF   *high voltage dc systems*
  BT1 dc systems
HYBRID ELECTRIC-POWERED VEHICL
  RT   electric batteries
  RT   electric-powered vehicles
  RT   hybrid systems
HYBRID SYSTEMS
  (Systems using two different types of components performing essentially the same function.)
  RT   hybrid electric-powered vehicl
  RT   hybrid reactors
HYDRAULIC FLUIDS
  BT1 working fluids
  RT   hydraulic equipment
HYDRAULIC FRACTURES
  BT1 fractures
  RT   cracks
  RT   hydraulic fracturing
HYDRAULIC TURBINES
  (Machines which convert the energy of an elevated water supply into mechanical energy of a rotating shaft.)
  BT1 turbines
HYDRAZINE FUEL CELLS
  BT1 fuel cells

HYDROCARBON FUEL CELLS
BT1 fuel cells

→ **HYDROGEN EMBRITTLEMENT**
(A decrease in fracture strength of metals due to the incorporation of hydrogen in the metal lattice.)
BT1 embrittlement
RT brittleness
RT fracture properties
RT hydridation
RT hydrogen
RT interstitial hydrogen generati

HYDROGEN STORAGE
BT1 storage
RT chemisorption
RT cryogenics
RT hydrides
RT hydrogen
RT tanks

HYDROTHERMAL SYSTEMS
(Geothermal system where most of the heat is transferred by the convective circulation of water or steam.)
BT1 geothermal systems
RT fumaroles
RT geothermal fluids
RT thermal springs

ICE CAPS
(Perennial cover of ice and snow on a land mass.)
BT1 ice
RT antarctic regions
RT arctic regions
RT glaciers
RT mountains

IFIEC
(International Federation of Industrial Energy Consumers)
UF *int. fed. ind. en. consumers*
BT1 international organizations
RT industry
RT international cooperation

→ **ILLINOIS BASIN**
(The geographic area that includes all of the coal reserves of Illinois, Indiana, and the western part of Kentucky.)
RT coal deposits
RT coal reserves
RT illinois
RT indiana
RT kentucky

→ **IMPERIAL VALLEY**
BT1 california
BT1 valleys
RT east mesa geothermal field
RT geothermal fields
RT salton sea
RT watersheds

IMPORTS
(Goods or services brought from another country. Until February 1992 this concept was indexed by TRADE.)
BT1 trade
RT tariffs

→ **INDIRECT DRIVE LASER IMPLOSION**
(Laser implosion where the driver energy is converted into x-rays before being absorbed by the target capsule.)
BT1 laser implosions
RT laser fusion reactors
RT laser targets
RT laser-produced plasma
RT laser-radiation heating
RT pulsed fusion reactors

→ **INDIUM PHOSPHIDE SOLAR CELLS**
BT1 solar cells

→ **INDIUM SELENIDE SOLAR CELLS**
BT1 solar cells

INDUCTANCE
BT1 electrical properties
RT capacitance
RT electric conductivity

INDUCTION GENERATORS
BT1 electric generators

→ **INFLATABLE COLLECTORS**
BT1 solar collectors
RT solar ponds

INFLATION
RT cost
RT economy
RT income

→ **INNER MONGOLIA**
UF *mongolia*
BT1 china

int. fed. ind. en. consumers
USE ifiec

INTERCONNECTED POWER SYSTEMS
(A system of two or more individual power systems normally operating with interconnecting tie lines enabling each system to draw on the other's reserves in time of need or for economic reasons.)
BT1 power systems
RT power generation
RT power transmission

INTERMEDIATE BTU GAS
BT1 fuel gas

IONIZATION FRONT ACCELERATORS
(Collective effect accelerator that produces controlled motion of a potential well at the head of an intense relativistic electron beam.)
BT1 collective accelerators

IVV-7 REACTOR
(Research Center in Tajura, Libya.)
BT1 pool type reactors
BT1 research reactors

JOINT VENTURES
(Commercial or maritime enterprises undertaken by several parties jointly.)
BT1 cooperation
RT industry
RT legal aspects
RT liabilities

JOJOBA
BT1 magnoliopsida
BT1 shrubs

JRR-3M REACTOR
(Tokai Research Establishment of JAERI, Ibaraki Prefecture, japan. This reactor replaces the JRR-3 Reactor which was shut down in 1983.)
BT1 enriched uranium reactors
BT1 isotope production reactors
BT1 materials testing reactors
BT1 pool type reactors
BT1 research reactors

juelich storage ring
USE cosy storage ring

junipers
USE cedars

JURASSIC PERIOD
BT1 mesozoic era

→ **KAKKONDA GEOTHERMAL FIELD**
BT1 geothermal fields
RT japan

KALE
BT1 brassica

→ **KAMCHATKA**
BT1 ussr

→ **KAMOJANG GEOTHERMAL FIELD**
BT1 geothermal fields
RT indonesia

kelp
USE seaweeds

→ **KENNEBEC RIVER**
BT1 rivers
RT maine

→ **KILAUEA VOLCANO**
BT1 volcanoes
RT hawaii

kiln incinerators
USE incinerators

KILNS
(Heated enclosures used for drying, burning, or firing materials.)
RT furnaces

KINGSTON STEAM PLANT
BT1 fossil-fuel power plants
RT tennessee
RT tennessee valley authority

→ **KIZILDERE GEOTHERMAL FIELD**
BT1 geothermal fields
RT turkey

KNOCK CONTROL
RT automotive fuels

KNOWLEDGE BASE
(Facts, assumptions, beliefs, and heuristics; used in dealing with a data base to achieve desired results such as a diagnosis, an interpretation or a solution to a problem.)
RT artificial intelligence
RT expert systems
RT programming

KOSTERLITZ-THOULESS THEORY
RT high-tc superconductors
RT phase transformations
RT superconductivity
RT superfluidity

→ **KRAFLA GEOTHERMAL FIELD**
BT1 geothermal fields
RT iceland

LAND LEASING
BT1 leasing
RT land resources
RT land use
RT leases
RT legal aspects

LAND OWNERSHIP
BT1 ownership
RT land resources
RT land use
RT legal aspects

LAND POLLUTION ABATEMENT
(The prevention of formation of pollutants at the source.)
BT1 pollution abatement
RT land pollution
RT land reclamation

LAND POLLUTION CONTROL
(The removal or management of pollutants after they are formed by a source.)
BT1 pollution control
RT land pollution
RT land reclamation
RT land use

LAND RESOURCES
BT1 resources
RT land leasing
RT land ownership
RT land reclamation
RT land use

→ **LARDERELLO GEOTHERMAL FIELD**
BT1 geothermal fields
RT italy

→ **LASER DOPPLER ANEMOMETERS**
BT1 anemometers
RT laser radiation

LASER-DOPPLER ANEMOMETERS
BT1 anemometers
RT lasers

LEAD-ACID BATTERIES
UF *storage batteries (lead-acid)*
BT1 electric batteries

LEASES
BT1 contracts
RT land leasing

→ **LESSER ANTILLES**
BT1 west indies

→ **LEWIS RIVER**
BT1 rivers
RT hydroelectric power plants
RT washington

LICADO PROCESS
BT1 coal preparation
BT1 separation processes

lidar
USE optical radar

LIFE-CYCLE COST
(The estimated total cost of a system during its entire service life.)
BT1 cost
RT cost benefit analysis
RT cost estimation
RT economics
RT payback period
RT service life

LIGHT TRANSMISSION
BT1 transmission
RT fiber optics
RT opacity
RT optical properties

LILIOPSIDA
  UF   *monocotyledons*
  BT1 magnoliophyta

LIMING
(The addition of limestone or its oxidized derivatives to soil or water as a means of modifying pH.)
  RT   calcium carbonates
  RT   calcium oxides
  RT   land reclamation
  RT   ph value
  RT   pollution control
  RT   soil chemistry
  RT   soils
  RT   water

limnanthes alba
  USE meadow foam

LIQUEFIED GASES
  BT1 liquids

LIQUEFIED NATURAL GAS
  BT1 liquefied gases
  BT1 natural gas
  RT   liquid fuels

LIQUEFIED PETROLEUM GASES
  BT1 liquefied gases
  BT1 natural gas liquids
  BT1 petroleum products
  RT   heating oils

liquid asphalt
  USE petroleum residues

→ **LITTLE TENNESSEE RIVER**
  BT1 rivers
  RT   hydroelectric power plants
  RT   tennessee
  RT   tennessee valley authority
  RT   tennessee valley region

lng spills
  USE gas spills

LOCUST TREES
  BT1 magnoliopsida
  BT1 trees
  RT   honeylocust trees

LONG ISLAND SOUND
  BT1 atlantic ocean
  BT1 estuaries
  RT   connecticut
  RT   mid-atlantic bight
  RT   new york

→ **LONG VALLEY**
  BT1 california

→ **LOS ALAMOS**
  BT1 new mexico

low temperature
  USE temperature range 0065-0273 k

LOW-HEAD HYDROELECTRIC POWER P
(Heads less than 15 meters.)
  BT1 hydroelectric power plants
  RT   small-scale hydroelectric powe

lumber industry
  USE wood products industry

MACHINERY
  BT1 equipment
  RT   manufacturing

MAGMA
  BT1 volcanoes
  RT   igneous rocks
  RT   lava
  RT   volcanism

MAGMA SYSTEMS
(A geothermal system in which the dominant heat source is a reservoir of magma.)
  BT1 geothermal systems

MAGNOLIOPHYTA
  BT1 plants

MAGNOLIOPSIDA
  BT1 magnoliophyta

→ **MAHOGANY ZONE**
  BT1 colorado
  BT1 green river formation
  RT   oil shales

→ **MALAGASY REPUBLIC**
  BT1 madagascar

→ **MANCHURIA**
  BT1 china

MANGROVES
  BT1 magnoliopsida
  BT1 trees

MANUFACTURERS
  RT   commercialization
  RT   industry

MANUFACTURING
(Large-scale commercial fabrication; for fabrication of single systems or components use FABRICATION.)
  RT   fabrication
  RT   industry
  RT   machinery

MANURES
  BT1 agricultural wastes

MAPLE TYPE REACTORS
(Multipurpose Applied Physics Lattice Experimental Reactor. Prior to January 1992, this information was indexed by MAPLE REACTOR.)
  UF   *multipurpose appl phys latt r.*
  BT1 enriched uranium reactors
  BT1 heavy water moderated reactors
  BT1 research and test reactors
  BT1 water cooled reactors
  BT1 water moderated reactors

MAPLES
  BT1 magnoliopsida
  BT1 trees

MAPPING
  RT   geometry
  RT   maps

→ **MARIANA ISLANDS**
  BT1 trust territory of the pacific

MARIHUANA
  UF   *marijuana*
  BT1 herbs
  BT1 magnoliopsida
  RT   hallucinogens

marijuana
  USE marihuana

→ **MARINAS**
  RT   harbors
  RT   inland waterways
  RT   seas

MARKETERS
  UF   *buyers*
  UF   *dealers*
  UF   *refiner-marketers*
  UF   *sellers*
  RT   commercial sector
  RT   competition
  RT   industry
  RT   market

MARKETING
(The aggregate of functions involved in moving goods from producer to customer.)
  BT1 business

MARSHES
  BT1 wetlands
  RT   surface waters

→ **MARTINIQUE**
  BT1 lesser antilles

MASKING
(Using a covering or coating on a semiconductor or other surface to provide a masked area for selective deposition or etching.)
  RT   coatings
  RT   deposition
  RT   etching

MASS DOUBLETS
  RT   mass spectroscopy

MATAGORDA BAY
  BT1 bays
  BT1 gulf of mexico
  RT   texas

MATERIALS RECOVERY
  BT1 waste processing
  RT   recycling

→ **MATSUKAWA GEOTHERMAL FIELD**
  BT1 geothermal fields
  RT   hachimantai
  RT   japan
  RT   vapor-dominated systems

→ **MAURITIUS**
  BT1 islands
  RT   indian ocean

MEADOW FOAM
  UF   *limnanthes alba*
  BT1 herbs
  BT1 magnoliopsida

MECHANICAL TRANSMISSIONS
  BT1 machine parts
  RT   automobiles
  RT   gears
  RT   vehicles

medium temperature
  USE temperature range 0273-0400 k

→ **MENOMINEE RIVER**
  BT1 rivers
  RT   hydroelectric power plants
  RT   michigan
  RT   wisconsin

MESOPHILIC CONDITIONS
(Temperature range centered at 40 degrees C favoring the growth of certain bacteria.)
  RT   anaerobic digestion
  RT   fermentation
  RT   thermophilic conditions

MESOZOIC ERA
  BT1 geologic ages

MESQUITE
  BT1 leguminosae
  BT1 trees

METABOLIC ACTIVATION
  BT1 chemical activation
  BT1 metabolism
  RT   enzyme activity
  RT   stimulation

METAL INDUSTRY
  UF   *steel industry*
  BT1 industry
  RT   ceramics industry
  RT   metals

→ *metal oxide-semiconductor sola*
  USE mos solar cells

METAL-GAS BATTERIES
  BT1 electric batteries
  RT   fuel cells

→ *metal-insulator solar cells*
  USE mi solar cells

→ *metal-insulator-semiconductor*
  USE mis solar cells

→ *metal-semiconductor solar cell*
  USE ms solar cells

METHANOL FUELS
(Pure methanol, methanol-water mixtures, or methanol with additives; for methanol-gasoline mixtures, use GASOHOL.)
  BT1 alcohol fuels
  RT   automotive fuels
  RT   diesel fuels
  RT   gasohol
  RT   methanol

MHD POWER PLANTS
  BT1 power plants
  RT   fossil-fuel power plants
  RT   magnetohydrodynamics
  RT   mhd channels
  RT   mhd generators

→ **MI SOLAR CELLS**
  UF   *metal-insulator solar cells*
  BT1 solar cells

micellar-polymer flooding
  USE microemulsion flooding

→ **MICROBIAL DRUG RESISTANCE**
(The resistance developed by microorganisms to a drug.)
  RT   drugs
  RT   microorganisms

microbial enhanced oil recover
  USE microbial eor

MICROBIAL EOR
  UF   *microbial enhanced oil recover*
  SF   *microbial processes*
  BT1 enhanced recovery
  RT   microbial leaching
  RT   microorganisms

MICROBIAL LEACHING
  BT1 leaching
  RT   microbial eor

MICROCLIMATES
(The local, rather uniform, climate of a specific place or habitat, compared with the climate of the entire area of which it is a part.)
- BT1 climates

MICROEMULSION FLOODING
- UF *micellar-polymer flooding*
- BT1 miscible-phase displacement
- RT enhanced recovery
- RT petroleum

MICROEMULSIONS
- BT1 emulsions

MID-ATLANTIC BIGHT
(The portion of the Atlantic Ocean overlying the continental shelf between Cape Hatteras and Georges Bank.)
- BT1 atlantic ocean
- RT chesapeake bay
- RT coastal waters
- RT continental shelf
- RT georges bank
- RT gulf stream
- RT long island sound
- RT south atlantic bight

MID-ATLANTIC RIDGE
- BT1 geologic structures
- RT atlantic ocean

middle distillates
- USE petroleum distillates

MILKWEED
- BT1 euphorbia

MINE DRAINING
- RT acid mine drainage
- RT coal mines
- RT drainage
- RT underground mining
- RT water influx

MINE SHAFTS
(Prior to January 1992, this concept was indexed to SHAFT EXCAVATIONS.)
- UF *shafts (mine)*
- BT1 shaft excavations

MINERAL CYCLING
(The cyclic movement of elemental mineral nutrients in ecosystems.)
- RT air-biosphere interactions
- RT biogeochemistry
- RT carbon cycle
- RT ecological concentration
- RT ecosystems
- RT sulfur cycle

MIOCENE EPOCH
- BT1 tertiary period

MIS SOLAR CELLS
- UF *metal-insulator-semiconductor*
- BT1 solar cells
- RT mis transistors
- RT schottky barrier solar cells

miscible flooding
- USE miscible-phase displacement

MISCIBLE-PHASE DISPLACEMENT
- UF *miscible flooding*
- BT1 fluid injection
- RT enhanced recovery

MISSISSIPPI RIVER BASIN
- BT1 watersheds
- RT mississippi river

mississippian period
- USE carboniferous period

MISSOURI RIVER BASIN
- BT1 watersheds
- RT missouri river

MOBILE POLLUTANT SOURCES
(Use for general articles when sources are not named. See also specific mobile sources e.g., AUTOMOBILES.)
- BT1 pollution sources
- RT air pollution
- RT point pollutant sources
- RT pollution
- RT stationary pollutant sources

MOLASSES
- BT1 food
- RT animal feeds
- RT saccharides
- RT sugar cane

MOLTEN CARBONATE FUEL CELLS
- BT1 high-temperature fuel cells

MOMOTOMBO GEOTHERMAL FIELD
- BT1 geothermal fields
- RT nicaragua

mongolia
- USE inner mongolia

monitors (water pollution)
- USE water pollution monitors

monochloroethylene
- USE vinyl chloride

monocotyledons
- USE liliopsida

MONONGAHELA RIVER BASIN
- BT1 watersheds
- RT pennsylvania
- RT west virginia

MONSOONS
- BT1 storms
- RT hurricanes
- RT rain

MONTE AMIATA GEOTHERMAL FIELD
- BT1 geothermal fields
- RT italy

MORPHOLOGY
(Study of structure or form.)
- RT crystal structure
- RT morphological changes
- RT shape
- RT structural models

MORSLEBEN SALT MINE
- BT1 radioactive waste facilities
- RT intermediate-level radioactive
- RT low-level radioactive wastes
- RT radioactive waste disposal
- RT salt caverns
- RT underground disposal

MOS SOLAR CELLS
- UF *metal oxide-semiconductor sola*
- BT1 solar cells

MS SOLAR CELLS
- UF *metal-semiconductor solar cell*
- BT1 solar cells

MT BAKER
- BT1 cascade mountains
- RT washington

MT HOOD
- BT1 cascade mountains
- RT oregon

MT ST HELENS
- BT1 cascade mountains
- RT volcanoes
- RT washington

MULTIVARIATE ANALYSIS
- BT1 statistics
- RT correlations

mungbean plants
- USE vigna

MUSSELS
- BT1 molluscs

MUTAGEN SCREENING
- RT biological indicators
- RT cell cultures
- RT mutagenesis
- RT mutants
- RT mutations

NAMAFJALL GEOTHERMAL FIELD
- BT1 geothermal fields
- RT iceland

NAMIBIA
- UF *southwest africa*
- BT1 africa
- RT south africa

nat inst petrol and ener res
- USE us niper

NATURAL GAS DISTRIBUTION SYSTE
- UF *natural gas gathering systems*
- RT gas utilities
- RT natural gas
- RT pipelines

NATURAL GAS FIELDS
- UF *gas fields*
- BT1 natural gas deposits
- RT natural gas wells
- RT reservoir fluids

NATURAL GAS FUEL CELLS
- BT1 fuel cells

natural gas gathering systems
- USE natural gas distribution syste

NATURAL GAS INDUSTRY
- BT1 industry
- RT gas utilities
- RT natural gas
- RT natural gas processing plants
- RT us natural gas policy act

NATURAL GAS LIQUIDS
(Liquid hydrocarbon mixtures that are gaseous at reservoir temperatures and pressures, but are recoverable by condensation or absorption.)
- UF *natural gasoline*
- BT1 liquids

NATURAL GAS PROCESSING PLANTS
- UF *natural gasoline plants*
- BT1 industrial plants
- RT natural gas industry

NATURAL GAS WELLS
- UF *gas wells*
- BT1 wells
- RT abandoned wells
- RT natural gas
- RT natural gas fields
- RT water influx
- RT well servicing
- RT wellhead prices
- RT wellheads

natural gasoline
- USE natural gas liquids

natural gasoline plants
- USE natural gas processing plants

NATURAL KILLER CELLS
- UF *nk cells*
- BT1 leukocytes
- RT immunity
- RT lymphocytes

NATURAL STEAM
(Geothermal steam containing incondensible gases such as carbon dioxide and hydrogen sulfide with minor amounts of other gases.)
- BT1 geothermal fluids
- BT1 steam

NATURE RESERVES
- UF *environmental parks*
- UF *wilderness areas*
- BT1 resources
- RT biosphere
- RT ecosystems
- RT environment
- RT land use
- RT wilderness protection acts

naval oil shale reserves
- SEE us naval oil shale reserves

NAVIGATION
(Steering a course.)
- RT aircraft
- RT ships
- RT transport

neckar reactor
- USE neckar-1 reactor

NECKAR-1 REACTOR
(Until March 1992, this information was indexed by NECKAR REACTOR.)
- UF *gemeinschaftskernkraftwerk nec*
- UF *gkn-1 reactor (neckar)*
- UF *neckar reactor*
- BT1 pwr type reactors

NELSON RIVER
- BT1 rivers
- RT canada

NEPTUNIUM 225
- BT1 actinide nuclei
- BT1 alpha decay radioisotopes
- BT1 neptunium isotopes
- BT1 odd-even nuclei

NETHERLANDS ANTILLES
- BT1 lesser antilles

NEW CALEDONIA
- BT1 oceania

NEW HEBRIDES ISLANDS
- BT1 islands
- RT pacific ocean

→ **NEW YORK BIGHT**
(The section of the continental margin and overlying water within the bend of the Atlantic coastline bounded by Long Island on the north and New Jersey on the west.)
   BT1   mid-atlantic bight
   RT   continental shelf
   RT   new jersey
   RT   new york

→ **NIAGARA RIVER**
   BT1   rivers
   RT   new york

NICKEL-HYDROGEN BATTERIES
   BT1   metal-gas batteries

NITROGEN 13 REACTIONS
   BT1   heavy ion reactions

nk cells
   USE natural killer cells

→ **NODULAR CORROSION**
   BT1   corrosion

NOISE DOSEMETERS
   BT1   measuring instruments
   RT   acoustic measurements
   RT   noise pollution

NOISE POLLUTION
(Objectionable or harmful levels of noise.)
   BT1   pollution
   RT   noise
   RT   noise dosemeters
   RT   noise pollution abatement
   RT   noise pollution control

NOISE POLLUTION ABATEMENT
(Reduction of noise at its source.)
   BT1   pollution abatement
   RT   noise
   RT   noise pollution
   RT   noise pollution control

NOISE POLLUTION CONTROL
(Reduction of noise after it has been produced by a source.)
   BT1   pollution control
   RT   noise
   RT   noise pollution
   RT   noise pollution abatement

NORTH PLATTE RIVER
   BT1   rivers
   RT   north platte river basin

NORTH PLATTE RIVER BASIN
   BT1   watersheds
   RT   colorado
   RT   nebraska
   RT   north platte river
   RT   wyoming

NUCLEIC ACID HYBRIDIZATION
   BT1   genetic engineering

NUMERICAL ANALYSIS
(Study of approximation methods using arithmetic techniques.)
   BT1   mathematics
   RT   computer calculations
   RT   computerized simulation
   RT   numerical solution

OCCUPANTS
   RT   automobiles
   RT   taxicabs
   RT   vehicles

OCEAN THERMAL ENERGY CONVERSIO
   UF   *otec*
   BT1 solar energy conversion
   RT   ocean thermal power plants

OCEAN THERMAL POWER PLANTS
   UF   *solar sea power plants*
   UF   *solar power plants*
   BT1 thermal power plants
   RT   ocean thermal energy conversio

→ **OCEANIA**
(Collective name for lands of the central and south Pacific Ocean, including Melanesia, Micronesia, and Polynesia; and sometimes including Australia, New Zealand, and the Malay Archipelago.)
   UF   *pacific islands*
   RT   australia
   RT   islands
   RT   new zealand

OCEANIC CIRCULATION
(Large-scale movement of discrete water masses which can be treated by equations of motion.)
   RT   box models
   RT   general circulation models
   RT   seas
   RT   water currents

OFFSHORE DRILLING
   BT1 drilling
   BT1 offshore operations
   RT   offshore platforms
   RT   offshore sites

OFFSHORE OPERATIONS
   RT   offshore platforms

OFFSHORE PLATFORMS
(Includes gravity or fixed, floating, and towed platforms.)
   UF   *drilling platforms*
   RT   offshore drilling
   RT   offshore operations
   RT   offshore sites
   RT   positioning

OIL FIELDS
(Surface boundary of an area from which petroleum is obtained; may correspond to an oil pool or may be circumscribed by political or legal limits.)
   BT1 petroleum deposits
   RT   oil wells
   RT   reservoir fluids
   RT   reservoir rock

OIL FURNACES
   BT1 furnaces
   RT   space heating

OIL POLLUTION CONTAINMENT
   BT1 pollution control
   RT   water pollution control

oil residues
   USE petroleum residues

OIL SAND DEPOSITS
   BT1 geologic deposits
   RT   oil sands
   RT   reserves

OIL SAND TAILINGS
   UF   *tar sand tailings*
   BT1 tailings

OIL SHALE DEPOSITS
   BT1 geologic deposits
   RT   piceance creek basin
   RT   rock springs sites
   RT   sand wash basin
   RT   washakie basin

OIL SHALE MINING
   BT1 mining
   RT   surface mining
   RT   underground mining

→ **OIL SHALE PROCESSING PLANTS**
   BT1 industrial plants

→ **OKINAWA**
   BT1 islands
   RT   japan

→ **ONIKOBE GEOTHERMAL FIELD**
   BT1 geothermal fields
   RT   japan

ONSLOW BAY
   BT1 atlantic ocean
   BT1 bays
   RT   north carolina
   RT   south atlantic bight

→ **ONUMA GEOTHERMAL FIELD**
   BT1 geothermal fields
   RT   hachimantai
   RT   japan

OPEC
(Organization of Oil Exporting Countries)
   BT1 international organizations
   RT   algeria
   RT   ecuador
   RT   gabon
   RT   indonesia
   RT   iran
   RT   iraq
   RT   kuwait
   RT   libya
   RT   middle east
   RT   nigeria
   RT   petroleum
   RT   qatar
   RT   saudi arabia
   RT   united arab emirates
   RT   venezuela

OPTICAL RADAR
   UF   *lidar*
   BT1 radar
   RT   laser radiation
   RT   lasers
   RT   optical systems
   RT   remote sensing

ORDOVICIAN PERIOD
   BT1 paleozoic era

→ **ORGANIC SEMICONDUCTORS**
   BT1 semiconductor materials
   RT   organic compounds
   RT   organic solar cells
   RT   organic superconductors

→ **ORGANIC SOLAR CELLS**
   BT1 solar cells
   RT   dyes
   RT   organic semiconductors
   RT   photovoltaic conversion
   RT   pis solar cells
   RT   ps solar cells

ORGANIC SUPERCONDUCTORS
   BT1 superconductors
   RT   organic compounds
   RT   organic semiconductors
   RT   tmtsf

ORGANIC WASTES
   BT1 wastes
   RT   biological wastes

organophosphinic acids
   USE phosphinic acids

→ **OTAKE GEOTHERMAL FIELD**
   BT1 geothermal fields
   BT1 geothermal hot-water systems
   RT   japan

otec
   USE ocean thermal energy conversio

→ **OVERHEAD POWER TRANSMISSION**
   BT1 power transmission

OXYGEN 14 REACTIONS
   BT1 heavy ion reactions

OZONIZATION
   BT1 chemical reactions
   RT   ozone
   RT   water treatment

→ *pacific islands*
   USE oceania

PACKED BEDS
   UF   *fixed beds*
   RT   fluidized beds

PALEOZOIC ERA
   BT1 geologic ages

→ **PALIMPINON GEOTHERMAL FIELD**
   UF   *southern negros geothermal fie*
   BT1 geothermal fields
   RT   philippines

PALLADIUM 110 REACTIONS
   BT1 heavy ion reactions

PANSTWOWA AGENCJA ATOMISTYKI
   BT1 polish organizations

PAPER INDUSTRY
   BT1 wood products industry
   RT   forestry
   RT   paper
   RT   wood

→ *papua*
   USE papua new guinea

→ **PAPUA NEW GUINEA**
(Prior to February 1992, this was indexed by NEW GUINEA.)
   UF   *papua*
   BT1 new guinea

PARABOLIC COLLECTORS
   BT1 concentrating collectors

PARABOLIC DISH COLLECTORS
   UF   *circular point collectors*
   UF   *parabolic point collectors*
   BT1 parabolic collectors

parabolic point collectors
   USE parabolic dish collectors

PARABOLIC TROUGH COLLECTORS
   UF   *cylindrical parabolic collecto*
   BT1 parabolic collectors

PARAMETRIC ANALYSIS
(Experimental or theoretical study of the changes in the characteristics of a system due to changes in design or operating parameters.)
  RT mathematical models
  RT multi-parameter analysis
  RT optimization
  RT response functions
  RT sensitivity analysis
  RT systems analysis

→ **PARATUNKA GEOTHERMAL FIELD**
  BT1 geothermal fields
  RT ussr

→ **PASCO BASIN**
  BT1 columbia river basin
  RT hanford reservation
  RT radioactive waste disposal
  RT washington

→ **PATHE GEOTHERMAL FIELD**
  BT1 geothermal fields
  BT1 geothermal hot-water systems
  RT mexico

→ **PAUZHETSK GEOTHERMAL FIELD**
  BT1 geothermal fields
  BT1 geothermal hot-water systems
  RT ussr

PAVEMENTS
  RT asphalts
  RT building materials
  RT concretes
  RT roads

→ **PEACE RIVER**
  BT1 rivers
  RT alberta
  RT british columbia

→ **PEACE RIVER DEPOSIT**
  BT1 oil sand deposits
  RT alberta
  RT canada
  RT oil sands

PECAN TREES
  BT1 magnoliopsida
  BT1 trees

PELLICULARIA
(Cellulase-producing fungus.)
  BT1 eumycota
  RT enzymatic hydrolysis

PENETROMETERS
  BT1 measuring instruments

pennsylvanian period
  USE carboniferous period

perfect flow
  SEE incompressible flow

PERMIAN PERIOD
  BT1 paleozoic era

→ **PERSIAN GULF**
  BT1 arabian sea

PETROCHEMICAL PLANTS
  BT1 chemical plants
  RT petroleum refineries

PETROLEUM DISTILLATES
(Boiling point range 0-600 degrees c.)
  UF *middle distillates*
  BT1 petroleum fractions
  RT petroleum products

PETROLEUM FRACTIONS
(Hydrocarbon mixtures occurring in petroleum that can be characterized by specific physical properties such as boiling range, density and viscosity.)
  BT1 petroleum
  RT petroleum products

PETROLEUM GEOLOGY
  BT1 geology
  RT exploration
  RT natural gas deposits
  RT petroleum deposits

PETROLEUM RESIDUES
(Boiling point over 593 degrees c; includes oil residues, residua.)
  UF *liquid asphalt*
  UF *oil residues*
  UF *resid*
  UF *residual oils*
  BT1 petroleum fractions
  RT residual fuels

PHANEROCHAETE
(Ligninolytic fungus.)
  BT1 eumycota

PHASE CHANGE MATERIALS
(Materials that undergo a phase change, e.g. from solid to liquid, at a temperature desired for heat storage.)
  BT1 materials
  RT eutectics
  RT fusion heat
  RT phase transformations
  RT transition heat

PHOSPHINE OXIDES
  BT1 organic phosphorus compounds

PHOSPHINIC ACIDS
(Before 1992, this information was indexed to ORGANOPHOSPHINIC ACIDS.)
  UF *organophosphinic acids*
  BT1 organic acids
  BT1 organic phosphorus compounds
  RT phosphinic acid esters

PHOTOANODES
  BT1 anodes
  RT photocathodes

PHOTOCHEMICAL REACTIONS
  BT1 chemical reactions
  RT atmospheric chemistry
  RT hydrogen transfer
  RT photochemistry
  RT photoelectrochemical cells

PHOTOELECTROCHEMICAL CELLS
  BT1 electrochemical cells
  RT electrochemistry
  RT photochemical reactions
  RT photochemistry
  RT photocurrents
  RT photovoltaic cells

→ **PHOTOVOLTAIC POWER PLANTS**
  BT1 solar power plants
  RT photovoltaic power supplies
  RT solar cell arrays

→ **PHOTOVOLTAIC POWER SUPPLIES**
(Solar cells or arrays with associated circuitry for small-scale or dispersed applications.)
  BT1 power supplies
  BT1 solar equipment
  RT photovoltaic power plants
  RT solar cell arrays
  RT solar cells

PHYSICAL VAPOR DEPOSITION
  BT1 surface coating
  RT cathode sputtering
  RT vacuum coating
  RT vacuum evaporation
  RT vapor deposited coatings
  RT vapor plating

PICEANCE CREEK
  BT1 rivers
  RT colorado

PICEANCE CREEK BASIN
  BT1 watersheds
  RT colorado
  RT green river formation
  RT oil shale deposits

PINOPHYTA
  BT1 plants

→ **PIS SOLAR CELLS**
  UF *polymer-insulator-semiconducto*
  BT1 solar cells
  RT organic solar cells

plating solutions
  USE process solutions

PLEISTOCENE EPOCH
  BT1 quaternary period

PLIOCENE EPOCH
  BT1 tertiary period

PLUGGING
  RT grouting
  RT oil wells
  RT permeability
  RT plugging agents
  RT reservoir rock

PLUGGING AGENTS
  RT cements
  RT gels
  RT oil wells
  RT plugging
  RT polymers
  RT reservoir rock

POINCARE-BERTRAND FORMULA
  RT integral calculus
  RT transport theory

POINT POLLUTANT SOURCES
(Use for general articles when sources are not named.)
  BT1 pollution sources
  RT air pollution
  RT mobile pollutant sources
  RT pollution
  RT water pollution

POLLUTION SOURCES
  UF *area pollution sources*
  RT pollutants

POLYCYCLIC AROMATIC HYDROCARBO
  BT1 aromatics
  BT1 hydrocarbons
  RT carcinogens
  RT mutagens

→ *polymer-insulator-semiconducto*
  USE pis solar cells

→ *polymer-semiconductor solar ce*
  USE ps solar cells

POLYPORUS VERSICOLOR
  BT1 fungi

PONDS
  UF *pools*
  BT1 surface waters
  RT lakes

→ *ponds (cooling)*
  USE cooling ponds

pools
  USE ponds

PORTLAND CEMENT
  BT1 cements
  RT spent shales

→ *portsmouth plant*
  SEE portsmouth centrifuge enrichme

POTOMAC RIVER BASIN
  BT1 watersheds

→ **POWDER RIVER BASIN**
  BT1 montana
  BT1 watersheds
  BT1 wyoming
  RT coal deposits
  RT natural gas deposits
  RT petroleum deposits
  RT sedimentary basins

POWER DISTRIBUTION SYSTEMS
(Systems for distributing electric power from convenient points on the transmission or bulk power system to the consumers.)
  RT power systems
  RT power transmission

→ **PR SPRINGS DEPOSIT**
  BT1 oil sand deposits
  RT oil sands
  RT utah

PRECAMBRIAN ERA
  BT1 geologic ages

PREDATOR-PREY INTERACTIONS
  RT behavior
  RT ecology
  RT ecosystems
  RT food chains
  RT population dynamics
  RT symbiosis

pressure effects
  USE pressure dependence

PRICES
  RT charges
  RT cost
  RT energy expenses
  RT pricing regulations
  RT spot market

PRICING REGULATIONS
  BT1 regulations
  RT deregulation
  RT economic policy
  RT prices

PRIPET RIVER
  UF *pripyat river*
  BT1 rivers
  RT chernobylsk-4 reactor
  RT dnieper river
  RT ukrainian ssr

pripyat river
  USE   pripet river

PROCESS CONTROL
  BT1   control
  RT   ore processing
  RT   waste processing

PROCESS SOLUTIONS
  UF   *plating solutions*
  BT1   solutions

PROCUREMENT
  BT1   business
  RT   accounting
  RT   cost
  RT   cost overruns

PROFITS
  RT   economics
  RT   income

→ **PROGRAM MANAGEMENT**
  UF+   *us doe program management*
  BT1   management
  RT   demonstration programs
  RT   research programs

PRUDHOE BAY
  BT1   bays
  BT1   beaufort sea
  RT   alaska

→ **PS SOLAR CELLS**
  UF   *polymer-semiconductor solar ce*
  BT1   solar cells
  RT   organic solar cells

PUBLIC ANXIETY
  RT   accidents
  RT   attitudes
  RT   behavior
  RT   nuclear facilities
  RT   sociology

PUBLIC BUILDINGS
(Government-owned buildings.)
  BT1   buildings

PUBLIC ENTERPRISES
(Government owned enterprises.)
  RT   government policies
  RT   ownership

PUBLIC POLICY
(Body of rules governing State action and relationship with citizens. Until March 1992, this concept was indexed by PUBLIC LAW.)
  RT   government policies
  RT   laws
  RT   legal aspects
  RT   legislation
  RT   regulations

→ **PUGET SOUND**
  BT1   pacific ocean
  RT   washington

pulverization
  USE   comminution

PULVERIZED FUELS
  RT   coal fines
  RT   powders
  RT   solid fuels

PULVERIZERS
  BT1   machinery
  RT   comminution
  RT   crushing
  RT   fuel feeding systems

PUMP TURBINES
(Reversible hydraulic turbines.)
  BT1   hydraulic turbines

QUATERNARY PERIOD
  BT1   cenozoic era

RABBIT BRUSH
  BT1   magnoliopsida
  BT1   shrubs

RADIOACTIVE ION BEAMS
  BT1   ion beams

RADIOLOGICAL WARFARE
  BT1   warfare

→ **RAFT RIVER VALLEY**
  BT1   idaho

RANKINE CYCLE POWER SYSTEMS
  BT1   power systems

RAROTONGA TREATY
  BT1   treaties
  RT   arms control
  RT   international agreements
  RT   nuclear weapons
  RT   tlatelolco treaty

ras al khaima
  USE   united arab emirates

RAW MATERIALS
  BT1   materials
  RT   resources

→ *receivers (solar)*
  USE   solar receivers

RECORDS MANAGEMENT
  BT1   management
  RT   information

REDOX FUEL CELLS
  BT1   regenerative fuel cells

REDOX REACTIONS
  BT1   chemical reactions
  RT   oxidation
  RT   reduction

REEDS
  BT1   gramineae

→ **REEFS**
(Chains of rocks or sand near the surface of water.)
  BT1   geologic structures
  RT   rocks
  RT   sand
  RT   seas

refiner-marketers
  USE   marketers

REFLECTIVITY
  BT1   optical properties
  BT1   surface properties

REFRIGERATING MACHINERY
(Machinery for cooling a volume to a temperature below that of the surrounding environment.)
  BT1   machinery
  RT   air conditioning
  RT   cooling systems
  RT   refrigeration
  RT   refrigerators

REFUSE DERIVED FUELS
(Fuels prepared from solid municipal or industrial wastes by removing all non-combustible materials, and put into burnable form.)
  BT1   fuels
  RT   industrial wastes
  RT   municipal wastes
  RT   refuse-fueled power plants
  RT   solid wastes
  RT   synthetic fuels

REFUSE-FUELED BOILERS
  UF   *waste-fueled boilers*
  BT1   boilers
  RT   refuse-fueled power plants

REFUSE-FUELED POWER PLANTS
  BT1   thermal power plants
  RT   cogeneration
  RT   dual-purpose power plants
  RT   power generation
  RT   refuse derived fuels
  RT   refuse-fueled boilers
  RT   steam generation

REGENERATIVE FUEL CELLS
  BT1   fuel cells

RESELLERS
  UF   *wholesale buyers*
  UF   *wholesale sellers*
  UF   *wholesalers*
  BT1   marketers
  RT   commercial sector
  RT   competition
  RT   economics
  RT   industry
  RT   market

RESERVOIR ENGINEERING
  BT1   engineering
  RT   civil engineering
  RT   reservoir rock
  RT   water reservoirs

RESERVOIR FLUIDS
  BT1   fluids
  RT   drawdown
  RT   natural gas fields
  RT   oil fields

RESERVOIR ROCK
(Porous and permeable rock containing producible oil, gas, or geothermal fluid in its pore spaces.)
  RT   carbonate rocks
  RT   fractured reservoirs
  RT   heterogeneous effects
  RT   oil fields
  RT   plugging

  RT   plugging agents
  RT   reservoir engineering
  RT   sand
  RT   water influx

resid
  USE   petroleum residues

RESIDENTIAL BUILDINGS
  BT1   buildings

residual fuel oil
  USE   residual fuels

RESIDUAL FUELS
  UF   *bunker oils*
  UF   *heavy fuels*
  UF   *residual fuel oil*
  UF   *residuums*
  BT1   fuel oils
  RT   petroleum residues

residual oils
  USE   petroleum residues

residuums
  USE   residual fuels

RESOURCE DEVELOPMENT
  RT   economic development
  RT   energy source development
  RT   resources

RESOURCE MANAGEMENT
  BT1   management
  RT   resources

→ **RESOURCE RECOVERY ACTS**
  UF   *us resource recovery acts*
  BT1   laws
  RT   energy conservation
  RT   regulations
  RT   resource conservation
  RT   waste disposal acts

RETAILERS
  BT1   marketers
  RT   commercial sector

retorted shales
  USE   spent shales

RHIZOBIUM
  BT1   bacteria
  RT   leguminosae
  RT   nitrogen fixation
  RT   symbiosis

RHODOPHYCOTA
  BT1   algae

→ **RIFT ZONES**
(Until June 1992, this concept was indexed by GEOLOGIC FAULTS.)
  BT1   geologic structures
  RT   geologic faults

→ **RIO GRANDE RIFT**
  BT1   rift zones
  RT   colorado
  RT   new mexico

→ **RIO GRANDE RIVER**
  BT1   rivers
  RT   colorado
  RT   mexico
  RT   new mexico
  RT   texas

→ **RIVER DELTAS**
  BT1   coastal regions
  RT   rivers
  RT   sediments
  RT   shores
  RT   wetlands

ROADS
  UF   *highways*
  UF   *streets*
  RT   bridges
  RT   pavements
  RT   road transport

ROCK BURSTS
(Explosive release of energy in rock strained beyond its elastic limit.)
  RT   hazards
  RT   mining
  RT   precursor
  RT   rock mechanics
  RT   seismic events

→ **ROCK SPRINGS SITES**
  BT1   wyoming
  RT   oil shale deposits

→ **ROOSEVELT HOT SPRINGS**
  BT1   utah
  RT   geothermal fields

ROSACEAE
- BT1 magnoliopsida
- RT apples
- RT cherries
- RT peaches
- RT pears
- RT plums
- RT raspberries

ROTARY DRILLS
- BT1 drills
- RT drill bits
- RT rock drilling
- RT well drilling

rotterdam spot market
- USE spot market

RUBBER TREES
- BT1 euphorbia

RUNOFF
- BT1 environmental transport
- RT atmospheric precipitations
- RT drainage
- RT floods
- RT rain water
- RT settling ponds
- RT storms
- RT watersheds

russian thistle
- USE tumbleweeds

→ **SAGINAW RIVER**
- BT1 rivers
- RT hydroelectric power plants
- RT michigan

SAINT VINCENT AND THE GRENADIN
- BT1 developing countries
- BT1 latin america
- BT1 west indies

salsola kali
- USE tumbleweeds

→ **SALTON SEA**
- BT1 lakes
- RT geothermal fields
- RT imperial valley
- RT salton sea geothermal field

→ **SALTON SEA GEOTHERMAL FIELD**
- BT1 geothermal fields
- RT california
- RT salton sea

→ **SAND WASH BASIN**
- BT1 colorado
- RT green river formation
- RT oil shale deposits

→ **SANTA BARBARA CHANNEL**
- BT1 pacific ocean
- RT california
- RT continental shelf

→ **SANTA ROSA DEPOSIT**
- BT1 oil sand deposits
- RT new mexico
- RT oil sands

→ **SANTEE RIVER**
- BT1 rivers
- RT south carolina

SARCODINA
- BT1 protozoa

SCALE CONTROL
- RT corrosion protection
- RT descaling
- RT scaling

→ **SCHOTTKY BARRIER SOLAR CELLS**
- BT1 solar cells
- RT mis solar cells
- RT schottky barrier diodes

→ **SEA-FLOOR SPREADING**
- RT geomorphology
- RT seas

→ **SEDIMENTARY BASINS**
- BT1 geologic structures
- RT limnology
- RT powder river basin

SEISMIC EVENTS
- RT explosions
- RT ground motion
- RT nuclear explosions
- RT rock bursts
- RT seismic effects
- RT seismic waves
- RT tsunamis

→ **SELENIUM SOLAR CELLS**
- BT1 solar cells

sellers
- USE marketers

SEMIBATCH CULTURE
- RT anaerobic digestion
- RT batch culture
- RT continuous culture
- RT culture media
- RT fermentation

seri
- USE solar energy research institut

SERVICE LIFE
- UF *useful life*
- BT1 lifetime
- RT life-cycle cost

SEVERN RIVER
- BT1 rivers

shafts (mine)
- USE mine shafts

sharja
- USE united arab emirates

→ **SHAWNEE STEAM PLANT**
- BT1 fossil-fuel power plants
- RT kentucky
- RT tennessee valley authority

SHORT ROTATION CULTIVATION
- BT1 cultivation techniques
- RT agriculture
- RT biomass plantations
- RT trees

→ **SICILY**
- BT1 italy

SILICON ARSENIDE SOLAR CELLS
- BT1 solar cells

→ *silicon on ceramic solar cells*
- USE soc solar cells

SILTSTONES
- BT1 sedimentary rocks
- RT sandstones
- RT shales

SILURIAN PERIOD
- BT1 paleozoic era

SILVICULTURE
- BT1 forestry
- RT biomass plantations
- RT harvesting
- RT plant breeding
- RT trees

→ **SKAGIT RIVER**
- BT1 rivers
- RT hydroelectric power plants
- RT washington

slc detectors
- USE stanford linear collider detec

sld
- SEE stanford linear collider detec

SLUDGES
- RT sediments
- RT slurries

SMALL BUSINESSES
(Businesses and commercial establishments employing fewer than 500 people.)
- BT1 business
- RT commercial sector
- RT economy
- RT industry
- RT market
- RT trade

SMALL-SCALE HYDROELECTRIC POWE
(Small-scale hydroelectric power plants generating from 100kW to 30MW.)
- BT1 hydroelectric power plants
- RT low-head hydroelectric power p

SNAKE RIVER PLAIN
- RT idaho
- RT nevada
- RT oregon
- RT wyoming
- RT yellowstone national park

→ **SOC SOLAR CELLS**
- UF *silicon on ceramic solar cells*
- BT1 silicon solar cells

SOCIAL IMPACT
- RT aesthetics
- RT socio-economic factors
- RT sociology
- RT technology impacts

sofc (solid oxide fuel cells)
- USE solid electrolyte fuel cells

SOIL CHEMISTRY
- BT1 chemistry
- RT agriculture
- RT biochemistry
- RT fertilizers
- RT liming
- RT soils

SOLAR ABSORBERS
- BT1 solar equipment
- RT antireflection coatings
- RT coatings
- RT solar collectors
- RT solar receivers

SOLAR ARCHITECTURE
(Building design that integrates the thermal, directional, and seasonal aspects of solar radiation.)
- BT1 architecture
- RT buildings
- RT solar energy

→ *solar batteries*
- USE solar cell arrays

→ **SOLAR CELL ARRAYS**
- UF *solar batteries*
- BT1 solar equipment
- RT photovoltaic cells
- RT photovoltaic power plants
- RT photovoltaic power supplies
- RT solar cells

→ *solar cell receivers*
- USE solar receivers

→ **SOLAR CONCENTRATORS**
- RT concentrator solar cells
- RT solar receivers

SOLAR ENERGY CONVERSION
- BT1 energy conversion

SOLAR ENERGY RESEARCH INSTITUT
- UF *seri*
- BT1 us doe
- RT solar energy

SOLAR EQUIPMENT
- BT1 equipment

SOLAR FLUX
- BT1 radiation flux
- RT solar radiation

SOLAR HEAT ENGINES
- BT1 engines
- RT stirling engines

SOLAR PONDS
- BT1 ponds
- BT1 solar collectors
- RT inflatable collectors
- RT solar water heaters

→ **SOLAR RECEIVERS**
(Systems designed to receive concentrated sunlight and convert it to some other energy form. They incorporate an absorber or a concentrator solar cell assembly.)
- UF *receivers (solar)*
- UF *solar cell receivers*
- UF *solar thermal receivers*
- RT concentrating collectors
- RT concentrator solar cells
- RT solar absorbers
- RT solar concentrators
- RT solar thermal conversion

solar sea power plants
- USE ocean thermal power plants

SOLAR THERMAL CONVERSION
- BT1 solar energy conversion
- RT solar receivers
- RT solar thermal power plants

SOLAR THERMAL POWER PLANTS
- BT1 solar power plants
- RT solar thermal conversion

→ *solar thermal receivers*
- USE solar receivers

SOLAR WATER HEATERS
- BT1 solar equipment
- BT1 water heaters
- RT solar ponds

SOLAR WATER PUMPS
 BT1 solar equipment

SOLID ELECTROLYTE FUEL CELLS
 UF *sofc (solid oxide fuel cells)*
 BT1 fuel cells

SOLVENT-REFINED COAL
 BT1 fuels
 RT coal
 RT coal preparation plants

solvent-refining coal plants
 USE coal preparation plants

SORBENT RECOVERY SYSTEMS
(Recovery using sorptive materials.)
 RT adsorbents
 RT oil spills
 RT water pollution control

SORPTION

SORPTIVE PROPERTIES
 UF *adsorptive properties*
 BT1 surface properties
 RT adsorbents
 RT adsorption

→ **SOUTH ATLANTIC BIGHT**
(The portion of the Atlantic Ocean overlying the continental shelf off North Carolina, South Carolina, Georgia, and Florida.)
 BT1 atlantic ocean
 RT coastal waters
 RT continental shelf
 RT mid-atlantic bight
 RT onslow bay

south china sea
 USE china sea

→ *southern negros geothermal fie*
 USE palimpinon geothermal field

→ **SOUTHERN OSCILLATION**
(A periodic barometric pressure fluctuation between the Indian Ocean region and the southeast Pacific Ocean.)
 UF *el nino*
 RT atmospheric circulation
 RT indian ocean
 RT pacific ocean

SPARK IGNITION ENGINES
 BT1 engines
 RT automobiles
 RT combustion
 RT combustion chambers
 RT gasoline

SPECIES DIVERSITY
 UF *biodiversity*
 RT animals
 RT baseline ecology
 RT ecological succession
 RT ecology
 RT ecosystems
 RT plants
 RT populations

spending
 USE expenditures

SPENT SHALES
 UF *retorted shales*
 RT oil shales
 RT portland cement
 RT shales
 RT solid wastes

SPOT MARKET
 UF *rotterdam spot market*
 BT1 market
 RT economics
 RT prices

→ *spray ponds*
 USE cooling ponds

SPRUCES
 BT1 conifers
 BT1 trees

stanford large detector
 USE stanford linear collider detec

STANFORD LINEAR COLLIDER DETEC
(A detector for the SLAC Linear Collider (SLC) designed to study electron-positron interactions up to 100 GeV.)
 UF *slc detectors*
 UF *stanford large detector*
 SF *sld*
 BT1 radiation detectors
 RT cherenkov counters
 RT drift chambers
 RT shower counters
 RT stanford linear collider

STATIONARY POLLUTANT SOURCES
(Use for general articles when sources are not named. See also specific stationary sources, e.g., FOSSIL-FUEL POWER PLANTS.)
 BT1 pollution sources
 RT air pollution
 RT emission
 RT mobile pollutant sources
 RT pollution
 RT water pollution

steel industry
 USE metal industry

STOKERS
 BT1 fuel feeding systems
 RT burners
 RT coal
 RT furnaces

storage batteries (lead-acid)
 USE lead-acid batteries

STORMS
 RT atmospheric precipitations
 RT cloud cover
 RT clouds
 RT lightning
 RT meteorology
 RT rain
 RT runoff
 RT snow
 RT weather

stover
 USE agricultural wastes

→ **STRAIT OF HORMUZ**
 BT1 persian gulf

STRATIFIED CHARGE ENGINES
 BT1 engines

STRAW
 RT agricultural wastes
 RT plant stems

streets
 USE roads

STRONTIUM 76
 BT1 beta-plus decay radioisotopes
 BT1 electron capture radioisotopes
 BT1 even-even nuclei
 BT1 intermediate mass nuclei
 BT1 seconds living radioisotopes
 BT1 strontium isotopes

SUBBITUMINOUS COAL
(Coal that is intermediate between bituminous coal and lignite.)
 BT1 coal
 RT bituminous coal
 RT lignite

→ **SUEZ CANAL**
 BT1 surface waters
 RT egyptian arab republic

SUGAR BEETS
 BT1 beets

SULFUR CONTENT
 RT chemical composition
 RT coal
 RT sulfur

SULFUR DIOXIDE
(Prior to January 1992, this was indexed by SULFUR OXIDES.)
 BT1 sulfur oxides

SULFUR TRIOXIDE
 BT1 sulfur oxides

→ **SUNNYSIDE DEPOSIT**
 BT1 oil sand deposits
 RT oil sands
 RT utah

SUPERCRITICAL STATE
(Homogeneous phase existing above critical temperature and above critical pressure.)
 RT critical pressure
 RT critical temperature
 RT phase transformations

SUPERSTRING MODELS
 BT1 string models
 RT particle structure
 RT supersymmetry

SUPPLY DISRUPTION
 RT energy supplies
 RT supply and demand

supports (catalyst)
 USE catalyst supports

SURFACE MINING ACTS
 BT1 mining laws

SWEET GUMS
 BT1 magnoliopsida

SYCAMORES
 BT1 magnoliopsida
 BT1 trees

→ **TAKENOYU GEOTHERMAL FIELD**
 BT1 geothermal fields
 RT japan

→ **TAKINOUE GEOTHERMAL FIELD**
 BT1 geothermal fields
 RT hachimantai
 RT japan

TANKER SHIPS
 BT1 ships
 RT maritime transport

tar sand tailings
 USE oil sand tailings

→ **TAR SAND TRIANGLE DEPOSIT**
 BT1 oil sand deposits
 RT oil sands
 RT utah

TARIFFS
 RT exports
 RT imports
 RT taxes

TASK SCHEDULING
(The routing of data within a computer.)
 BT1 data processing
 RT array processors
 RT executive codes
 RT parallel processing

→ **TASMAN SEA**
 BT1 seas
 RT australia
 RT new zealand

TAXICABS
 BT1 vehicles
 RT automobiles
 RT occupants

TELEVISION CAMERAS
 BT1 cameras
 RT television
 RT vidicons

TEMPERATURE RANGE
 RT temperature dependence
 RT thermophilic conditions

TEMPERATURE RANGE 0000-0013 K
 UF *milli k range*
 UF *ultralow temperature*
 BT1 temperature range
 RT cryogenics
 RT temperature dependence
 RT thermal boundary resistance

TEMPERATURE RANGE 0013-0065 K
 UF *very low temperature*
 BT1 temperature range
 RT cryogenics
 RT temperature dependence

TEMPERATURE RANGE 0065-0273 K
 UF *low temperature*
 BT1 temperature range
 RT cryogenics
 RT cryoscopy
 RT freezing out
 RT temperature dependence

TEMPERATURE RANGE 0273-0400 K
 UF *medium temperature*
 BT1 temperature range
 RT temperature dependence

TEMPERATURE RANGE 0400-1000 K
 UF *high temperature*
 BT1 temperature range
 RT critical heat flux
 RT scaling
 RT temperature dependence

TEMPERATURE RANGE 1000-4000 K
 UF *very high temperature*
 BT1 temperature range
 RT critical heat flux
 RT temperature dependence
 RT vhtr reactor

TENDONS
 BT1 connective tissue
 RT muscles

TENNESSEE VALLEY REGION
- BT1 watersheds
- RT alabama
- RT clinch river
- RT cumberland river
- RT kentucky
- RT little tennessee river
- RT tennessee
- RT tennessee river
- RT tennessee valley authority

TERTIARY PERIOD
- BT1 cenozoic era

the geysers
- USE geysers geothermal field

THERMAL RECOVERY
- BT1 enhanced recovery

THERMOCHEMICAL DIAGRAMS
- BT1 diagrams
- RT corrosion
- RT phase studies
- RT temperature dependence

THERMOMECHANICAL TREATMENTS
(Combination of material-forming processes with heat treatments in order to obtain specific material properties.)
- BT1 heat treatments
- BT1 materials working

THERMOPHILIC CONDITIONS
(Temperature range centered at 70 degrees C favoring the growth of certain bacteria.)
- RT anaerobic digestion
- RT fermentation
- RT mesophilic conditions
- RT temperature range

THIELAVIA
(Thermophilic fungus capable of degrading cellulose to glucose.)
- BT1 eumycota
- RT cellulase
- RT enzymatic hydrolysis

TIBET
- BT1 asia

TIME DELAY
- RT administrative procedures
- RT contracts
- RT legal aspects
- RT management
- RT schedules
- RT time measurement

TIRES
- RT vehicles

TIWI GEOTHERMAL FIELD
- BT1 geothermal fields
- RT philippines

TOLERANCE
- RT accuracy
- RT dimensions
- RT errors
- RT hysteresis
- RT quality control

TONGONAN GEOTHERMAL FIELD
- BT1 geothermal fields
- RT philippines

TOXIC MATERIALS
(Until March 1992, this concept was indexed by HAZARDOUS MATERIALS.)
- BT1 hazardous materials

TRAFFIC CONTROL
(Control of vehicular traffic.)
- BT1 control
- RT vehicles

TRAINING
- BT1 education
- RT educational tools

transalaska pipeline
- USE alaska oil pipeline

TRANSGENIC ANIMALS
- BT1 animals

TRANSGENIC MICE
- BT1 mice
- BT1 transgenic animals

TRANSITION ELEMENT ALLOYS
(From November 1983 until March 1992 this was indexed using the descriptors for the specific alloys or the broader term ALLOYS.)

TRAVALE GEOTHERMAL FIELD
- BT1 geothermal fields
- RT italy
- RT vapor-dominated systems

TRIASSIC PERIOD
- BT1 mesozoic era

TRIBOLOGY
- RT bearings
- RT friction
- RT lubricants
- RT lubricating oils
- RT lubrication
- RT surface properties
- RT wear

TRICHODERMA
- BT1 eumycota

trichoderma reesei
- USE trichoderma viride

TRICHODERMA VIRIDE
- UF trichoderma reesei
- BT1 trichoderma

TRINIDAD AND TOBAGO
- BT1 lesser antilles

TRUST TERRITORY OF THE PACIFIC
- BT1 islands
- RT pacific ocean

TUMBLEWEEDS
- UF russian thistle
- UF salsola kali
- BT1 magnoliopsida
- RT biomass

TURBODRILLS
- BT1 rotary drills
- BT1 turbomachinery

TURBOJET ENGINES
- BT1 engines

TURBOMACHINERY
- BT1 machinery
- RT compressors
- RT pumps

UHV DC SYSTEMS
(Over 765 kV.)
- UF ultrahigh voltage dc systems
- BT1 dc systems

ultrahigh voltage dc systems
- USE uhv dc systems

ultralow temperature
- USE temperature range 0000-0013 k

umm al qaiwan
- USE united arab emirates

UNITED ARAB EMIRATES
- UF abu dhabi
- UF ajman
- UF dubai
- UF fujaira
- UF ras al khaima
- UF sharja
- UF umm al qaiwan
- BT1 arab countries
- BT1 asia
- RT opec

URACH GEOTHERMAL FIELD
(Located in the Schwabian Alb, Federal Republic of Germany.)
- BT1 geothermal fields
- RT federal republic of germany

US CLEAN AIR ACT
- BT1 pollution laws
- RT air pollution
- RT air quality
- RT environment
- RT environmental policy
- RT pollution regulations

US CLEAN COAL TECHNOLOGY PROGR
- RT coal preparation
- RT desulfurization
- RT pollution control

US CLEAN WATER ACT
(US Federal Water Pollution Control Act.)
- UF federal water pollution contro
- UF fwpca
- BT1 pollution laws
- RT pollution regulations
- RT water pollution

US COAST GUARD
- BT1 us dot

US CORPS OF ENGINEERS
- BT1 us dod

us department of defense
- USE us dod

US DEPARTMENT OF TREASURY
- BT1 us organizations

US DEPLETION ALLOWANCES
(Deduction allowed to US income tax based on depletion of natural resources such as fossil fuels.)
- RT financial incentives
- RT taxes

US DOA
- BT1 us organizations

US DOD
- UF us department of defense
- BT1 us organizations

us doe program management
- USE program management

US DOI
- BT1 us organizations

US ECONOMIC RECOVERY TAX ACT
- BT1 laws
- RT economic development
- RT financial incentives
- RT legislation
- RT taxes

US EMERGENCY PREPAREDNESS ACT
- BT1 laws
- RT emergency plans
- RT energy supplies

US ENERGY EXTENSION SERVICE
- BT1 us doe

US ENERGY INFORMATION ADMINIST
- BT1 us doe

US ENERGY POLICY AND CONSERVAT
(US Energy Policy and Conservation Act.)
- BT1 laws
- RT energy conservation
- RT energy policy

US ENERGY SECURITY ACT
- BT1 laws

US ENERGY TAX ACT
- BT1 laws
- RT energy conservation
- RT energy consumption
- RT financial incentives

US FEDERAL POWER COMMISSION
- BT1 us organizations

US FERC
- UF fed. energy reg. comm.
- BT1 us doe

us geological survey
- USE us gs

US GS
- UF us geological survey
- BT1 us doi

US GULF COAST
- BT1 usa
- RT alabama
- RT florida
- RT gulf of mexico
- RT louisiana
- RT mississippi
- RT texas

US IRS
(U. S. Internal Revenue Service.)
- BT1 us department of treasury

US NAPAP
(United States National Acid Precipitation Assessment Program.)
- RT acid rain
- RT information needs
- RT research programs
- RT us organizations

US NATIONAL ENERGY ACT
- BT1 laws
- RT us national energy plan

US NATIONAL ENERGY PLAN
- BT1 energy policy
- RT energy conservation
- RT energy sources
- RT energy supplies
- RT us national energy act

US NATIONAL ENVIRONMENTAL POLI
(US National Environmental Policy Act.)
- BT1 laws
- RT environment
- RT environmental impact statement
- RT environmental policy

us national oceanic and atmosp
- USE us noaa

US NATURAL GAS POLICY ACT
- BT1 us national energy act
- RT consumer protection
- RT deregulation
- RT energy policy
- RT natural gas industry

→ **US NAVAL OIL SHALE RESERVES**
- SF *naval oil shale reserves*
- BT1 oil shale deposits
- BT1 reserves
- RT colorado
- RT utah

US NAVAL PETROLEUM RESERVES
- BT1 petroleum deposits
- BT1 reserves
- RT california
- RT energy supplies
- RT underground storage
- RT wyoming

US NIPER
(National Institute for Petroleum and Energy Research.)
- UF *nat inst petrol and ener res*
- BT1 us doe

US NOAA
- UF *us national oceanic and atmosp*
- BT1 us organizations

US OSM
(Office of Surface Mining, Reclamation and Enforcement, that regulates all coal mining activities in the USA.)
- BT1 us organizations
- RT coal mining

→ *us resource recovery acts*
- USE resource recovery acts

US SUPERFUND
- UF *cercla*
- BT1 pollution laws
- RT waste disposal acts

→ **US WEST COAST**
- UF *west coast*
- BT1 usa
- RT california
- RT oregon
- RT pacific ocean
- RT washington

useful life
- USE service life

→ **UVALDE DEPOSIT**
- BT1 oil sand deposits
- RT oil sands
- RT texas

VALLEYS
- RT complex terrain
- RT mountains
- RT watersheds

→ **VAPOR-DOMINATED SYSTEMS**
- BT1 hydrothermal systems
- RT geysers geothermal field
- RT matsukawa geothermal field
- RT travale geothermal field

VEGETABLE OILS
- BT1 oils

VENTILATION SYSTEMS
- RT air cleaning systems
- RT air conditioning
- RT air flow
- RT ventilation

very high temperature
- USE temperature range 1000-4000 k

very low temperature
- USE temperature range 0013-0065 k

VIGNA
- UF *cowpea plants*
- UF *mungbean plants*
- BT1 leguminosae
- RT mungbeans

VINYL CHLORIDE
- UF *monochloroethylene*
- BT1 chlorinated aliphatic hydrocar

→ **VIRGIN ISLANDS**
- BT1 lesser antilles

VOLCANISM
(The process by which magma and its associated gases rise into the earth's crust and are extruded onto the earth's surface and into the atmosphere.)
- RT lava
- RT magma
- RT volcanoes

VULNERABILITY
- RT sabotage
- RT safeguards
- RT warfare

→ **WABASCA DEPOSIT**
- BT1 oil sand deposits
- RT alberta
- RT canada
- RT oil sands

WALLS
- RT buildings

walls (cell)
- USE cell wall

walls (thermonuclear reactor)
- USE thermonuclear reactor walls

WANKEL ENGINES
- BT1 spark ignition engines
- RT automobiles

WARFARE
- RT national defense
- RT vulnerability

→ **WASHAKIE BASIN**
- BT1 wyoming
- RT green river formation
- RT oil shale deposits

WASHING
- BT1 cleaning
- RT coal preparation
- RT safety showers
- RT scrubbing

WASTE DISPOSAL ACTS
(For legislation of any country relating to the handling of nonradioactive wastes. For radioactive wastes, use NUCLEAR WASTE POLICY ACTS.)
- BT1 laws
- RT liquid wastes
- RT nonradioactive waste disposal
- RT nuclear waste policy acts
- RT resource recovery acts
- RT solid wastes
- RT us superfund
- RT waste disposal

WASTE HEAT BOILERS
- BT1 boilers
- RT cogeneration
- RT heat recovery equipment
- RT waste heat utilization

WASTE OILS
- BT1 oils
- RT lubricating oils
- RT recycling

→ **WASTE PROCESSING PLANTS**
- BT1 industrial plants
- RT waste processing

waste-fueled boilers
- USE refuse-fueled boilers

WATER HEATERS
- BT1 heaters

WATER HYACINTHS
- BT1 aquatic organisms
- BT1 liliopsida

WATER POLICY
- BT1 environmental policy

WATER POLLUTION ABATEMENT
(The prevention of formation of pollutants at the source.)
- BT1 pollution abatement
- RT ground cover
- RT water reclamation

WATER POLLUTION MONITORS
- UF *monitors (water pollution)*
- BT1 monitors
- RT chemical effluents
- RT liquid wastes
- RT monitoring
- RT water pollution

WATER RECLAMATION
- RT aesthetics
- RT public health
- RT water pollution abatement
- RT water quality

WATER TREATMENT PLANTS
- RT water pollution control
- RT water treatment

→ **WEDDELL SEA**
(An arm of the southern Atlantic Ocean in Antarctica.)
- BT1 atlantic ocean

WELL CASINGS
- UF *casings (well)*
- BT1 equipment
- RT pipes
- RT wells

WELL DRILLING
- BT1 drilling
- RT drilling equipment
- RT drilling rigs
- RT drills
- RT rotary drills
- RT wells

well maintenance
- USE well servicing

well reconditioning
- USE well servicing

WELL SERVICING
- UF *well maintenance*
- UF *well reconditioning*
- RT natural gas wells
- RT oil wells

WELLHEAD PRICES
(Prices paid at the wellhead for gas or oil produced.)
- BT1 prices
- RT natural gas wells
- RT oil wells

WELLHEADS
- RT natural gas wells
- RT oil wells

→ **WENDELL-AMEDEE HOT SPRINGS**
- RT california
- RT geothermal fields

→ *west coast*
- USE us west coast

WETLANDS
- BT1 aquatic ecosystems
- RT river deltas
- RT surface waters

wholesale buyers
- USE resellers

WHOLESALE PRICES
- BT1 prices

wholesale sellers
- USE resellers

wholesalers
- USE resellers

wilderness areas
- USE nature reserves

WILDERNESS PROTECTION ACTS
- BT1 laws
- RT environment
- RT land use
- RI nature reserves

→ **WILLISTON BASIN**
- BT1 sedimentary basins
- RT manitoba
- RT montana
- RT north dakota
- RT petroleum deposits
- RT saskatchewan
- RT south dakota

WILLOWS
- BT1 magnoliopsida
- BT1 trees

wind farms
- USE wind turbine arrays

WIND POWER INDUSTRY
- BT1 industry
- RT wind power

WIND POWER PLANTS
(Wind turbines supplying electric power to a grid.)
- BT1 power plants
- RT wind turbine arrays

WIND TURBINE ARRAYS
   UF   *wind farms*
   RT   wind power plants

WIND-POWERED PUMPS
(Wind-mechanical pumps only, for wind-electric pumps use WIND TURBINES and PUMPS.)
   BT1   pumps
   RT   wind turbines

WINDING MACHINES
(Equipment for winding coils.)
   BT1   machinery
   RT   electric coils

WOLSUNG-2 REACTOR
   BT1   candu type reactors
   BT1   natural uranium reactors
   BT1   phwr type reactors

WOOD FUELS
   UF   *firewood*
   UF   *fuelwood*
   BT1   energy sources
   BT1   fuels
   RT   biomass
   RT   charcoal
   RT   trees
   RT   wood

WOOD PRODUCTS INDUSTRY
(Industry producing products made from wood, including lumber.)
   UF   *lumber industry*
   BT1   industry
   RT   forestry
   RT   furniture industry
   RT   wood

WOOD WASTES
   BT1   organic wastes
   BT1   solid wastes

→ **YANGTZE RIVER**
   BT1   rivers
   RT   china

→ **YELLOW CREEK**
   BT1   rivers
   RT   colorado
   RT   yellow creek basin

→ **YELLOW CREEK BASIN**
   BT1   watersheds
   RT   colorado
   RT   yellow creek

→ **YELLOWSTONE NATIONAL PARK**
   BT1   public lands
   RT   idaho
   RT   montana
   RT   snake river plain
   RT   wyoming

YTTRIUM 79
   BT1   beta-plus decay radioisotopes
   BT1   electron capture radioisotopes
   BT1   intermediate mass nuclei
   BT1   odd-even nuclei
   BT1   seconds living radioisotopes
   BT1   yttrium isotopes

→ **YUKON RIVER**
   BT1   rivers
   RT   alaska

→ **ZINC PHOSPHIDE SOLAR CELLS**
   BT1   solar cells

→ **ZINC SULFIDE SOLAR CELLS**
   BT1   solar cells

ZINC 81
   BT1   beta-minus decay radioisotopes
   BT1   even-odd nuclei
   BT1   intermediate mass nuclei
   BT1   millisec living radioisotopes
   BT1   zinc isotopes

CELL CULTURES [6,168; 6,858]
- UF   cultures (cells)
- NT1 clone cells
- NT1 synchronous cultures
- RT   animal cells
- RT   cloning
- RT   colony formation
- RT   culture media
- RT   hybridomas
- RT   in vitro
- RT   microorganisms
- RT   plant cells
- RT   tissue cultures
- RT   tumor cells

CELL CYCLE [2,100; 2,100]
- RT   cell division
- RT   concanavalin a
- RT   dna replication
- RT   synchronization
- RT   synchronous cultures

CELL DIFFERENTIATION [891; 891]
- RT   blood formation
- RT   genetic engineering
- RT   growth factors
- RT   ontogenesis

CELL DIVISION [688; 2,313]
- NT1 meiosis
- NT1 mitosis
- RT   cell cycle
- RT   cell proliferation
- RT   gametogenesis
- RT   healing
- RT   in vivo
- RT   mitogens
- RT   non-disjunction

CELL FLOW SYSTEMS [403; 403]
Sep 77
(Fluid flow devices in which a stream of individual cells from biological cell samples flow through a chamber enabling the screening of cytological material.)
- RT   animal cells
- RT   chromosome sorting
- RT   cytological techniques
- RT   cytology
- RT   plant cells

cell growth (animal)
- USE animal cells
- AND growth

cell growth (plant)
- USE growth
- AND plant cells

CELL KILLING [2,396; 2,396]
- RT   death

CELL MEMBRANES [4,090; 4,090]
- BT1 cell constituents
- BT1 membranes
- RT   cell wall
- RT   radioreceptor assay
- RT   subcellular distribution

CELL NUCLEI [1,328; 1,336]
- UF   nuclei (cells)
- BT1 cell constituents
- NT1 nucleoli
- RT   chromatin
- RT   chromosomes
- RT   human chromosomes
- RT   nucleic acids
- RT   subcellular distribution

CELL PROLIFERATION [2,713; 2,713]
- UF   proliferation (cell)
- RT   cell division
- RT   cloning
- RT   concanavalin a

- RT   growth factors
- RT   in vivo
- RT   phytohemagglutinin

CELL TRANSFORMATIONS [112; 112]
Feb 87
- BT1 oncogenic transformations
- RT   viral diseases

CELL WALL [190; 190]
- BT1 cell constituents
- RT   cell membranes
- RT   plant cells

CELLOBIOSE [34; 34]
- BT1 disaccharides
- BT2 oligosaccharides
- BT3 saccharides
- BT4 carbohydrates
- BT5 organic compounds

CELLOPHANE [45; 45]
- BT1 polysaccharides
- BT2 saccharides
- BT3 carbohydrates
- BT4 organic compounds
- RT   cellulose

CELLOSOLVES [5; 5]
- UF   glycol monoalkyl ethers
- BT1 ethers
- BT2 organic oxygen compounds
- BT3 organic compounds
- BT1 glycols
- BT2 alcohols
- BT3 hydroxy compounds
- BT4 organic compounds
- BT1 organic solvents
- BT2 nonaqueous solvents
- BT3 solvents

cells (animal)
- USE animal cells

cells (bacterial)
- USE bacteria

cells (electrolytic)
- USE electrolytic cells

cells (plant)
- USE plant cells

cells (reactor)
- USE reactor cells

CELLULASE [40; 40] Feb 83
- UF+ cellulolytic activity

CELLULOID [20; 20]
- RT   camphor
- RT   cellulose esters
- RT   nitrocellulose

cellulolytic activity
- USE cellulase
- AND enzyme activity

CELLULOSE [1,100; 1,100]
- UF+ ethocel
- BT1 polysaccharides
- BT2 saccharides
- BT3 carbohydrates
- BT4 organic compounds
- RT   cellophane
- RT   cellulose esters
- RT   polyacetals
- RT   rayon

CELLULOSE ESTERS [240; 240]
- BT1 esters
- BT2 organic compounds
- RT   celluloid
- RT   cellulose

CELSIUS STORAGE RING [9; 9]
Jul 86
- BT1 storage rings
- RT   uppsala synchrocyclotron

cemented carbides
- USE cermets

CEMENTITE [69; 69]
(An intermetallic compound, Fe3C.)
- BT1 intermetallic compounds
- BT2 alloys
- BT1 iron carbides
- BT2 carbides
- BT3 carbon compounds
- BT2 iron compounds
- BT3 transition element compounds
- RT   martensite
- RT   pearlite
- RT   steels

CEMENTS [2,065; 2,089]
- BT1 building materials
- BT2 materials
- NT1 gypsum cements
- RT   concretes
- RT   grouting
- RT   mortars

CENNA [22; 22] Feb 89
(Convention on Early Notification of a Nuclear Accident.)
- UF   conv early notif nuc accident
- UF   early notification convention
- BT1 international agreements
- BT2 agreements
- RT   iaea
- RT   reactor accidents

CENTER-OF-MASS SYSTEM [1,259; 1,259]
- UF   centre-of-mass system
- RT   coordinates
- RT   laboratory system
- RT   longitudinal momentum
- RT   lorentz transformations
- RT   mechanics
- RT   scattering
- RT   transverse momentum

CENTRAL AFRICAN REPUBLIC [10; 10]
- BT1 africa
- BT1 developing countries

CENTRAL AMERICA [84; 133]
- BT1 latin america
- NT1 costa rica
- NT1 el salvador
- NT1 guatemala
- NT1 honduras
- NT1 nicaragua
- NT1 panama
- NT1 panama canal zone

CENTRAL NERVOUS SYSTEM [826; 17,163]
- BT1 nervous system
- NT1 brain
- NT2 cerebellum
- NT2 cerebrum
- NT3 cerebral cortex
- NT2 hippocampus
- NT2 hypothalamus
- NT2 olfactory bulbs
- NT2 thalamus
- NT1 spinal cord
- RT   behavior
- RT   cerebrospinal fluid
- RT   meninges

         RT   rabies
         RT   radiation syndrome
         RT   receptors

    **CENTRAL NERVOUS SYSTEM
    AGENTS** [94; 2,017] *May 84*
         BT1   drugs
         NT1   analeptics
            NT2   amphetamines
               NT3   benzedrine
            NT2   caffeine
         NT1   central nervous system depress
            NT2   analgesics
               NT3   acetylsalicylic acid
               NT3   antipyrine
               NT3   codeine
               NT3   heroin
               NT3   morphine
               NT3   pethidine
               NT3   thebaine
            NT2   anesthetics
               NT3   barbiturates
                  NT4   amytal
                  NT4   nembutal
                  NT4   phenobarbital
                  NT4   thiopental
               NT3   cocaine
               NT3   procaine
            NT2   anticonvulsants
               NT3   phenobarbital
            NT2   antipyretics
               NT3   acetylsalicylic acid
               NT3   antipyrine
               NT3   cinchonine
               NT3   colchicine
               NT3   quinine
            NT2   hypnotics and sedatives
               NT3   barbiturates
                  NT4   amytal
                  NT4   nembutal
                  NT4   phenobarbital
                  NT4   thiopental
               NT3   chlorpromazine
               NT3   codeine
               NT3   reserpine
            NT2   narcotics
               NT3   heroin
               NT3   methadone hydrochloride
               NT3   morphine
               NT3   pethidine
               NT3   thebaine
         NT1   psychotropic drugs
            NT2   antidepressants
               NT3   cocaine
               NT3   imipramine
               NT3   iproniazid
            NT2   hallucinogens
               NT3   bufotenine
            NT2   tranquilizers
               NT3   chlorpromazine
               NT3   reserpine

    **CENTRAL NERVOUS SYSTEM DE-
    PRESS** [15; 916] *May 84*
         UF   *cns depressants*
         UF   *depressants (central nerv sys)*
         BT1   central nervous system agents
            BT2   drugs
         NT1   analgesics
            NT2   acetylsalicylic acid
            NT2   antipyrine
            NT2   codeine
            NT2   heroin
            NT2   morphine
            NT2   pethidine
            NT2   thebaine
         NT1   anesthetics
            NT2   barbiturates
               NT3   amytal
               NT3   nembutal
               NT3   phenobarbital
               NT3   thiopental
            NT2   cocaine
            NT2   procaine
         NT1   anticonvulsants
            NT2   phenobarbital
         NT1   antipyretics
            NT2   acetylsalicylic acid

            NT2   antipyrine
            NT2   cinchonine
            NT2   colchicine
            NT2   quinine
         NT1   hypnotics and sedatives
            NT2   barbiturates
               NT3   amytal
               NT3   nembutal
               NT3   phenobarbital
               NT3   thiopental
            NT2   chlorpromazine
            NT2   codeine
            NT2   reserpine
         NT1   narcotics
            NT2   heroin
            NT2   methadone hydrochloride
            NT2   morphine
            NT2   pethidine
            NT2   thebaine

    central nervous system stimula
         USE   analeptics

    central nuclear de zorita-1
         USE   zorita-1 reactor

    central nuclear en atucha rea.
         USE   atucha reactor

    CENTRAL POTENTIAL [1,385; 1,385]
         BT1   potentials
         RT   coulomb field

    CENTRALLY PLANNED ECONOMIES
    [12; 12] *Dec 82*
    (Includes the economies of the countries
    in the list below.)
         RT   albania
         RT   bulgaria
         RT   china
         RT   czechoslovakia
         RT   economic development
         RT   economic policy
         RT   hungary
         RT   mongolian peoples republic
         RT   national government
         RT   nationalization
         RT   north korea
         RT   poland
         RT   romania
         RT   ussr
         RT   viet nam

    centre-of-mass system
         USE   center-of-mass system

    centrifugal separators
         USE   inertial separators

    CENTRIFUGATION [774; 1,299]
         BT1   separation processes
         NT1   gas centrifugation
         NT1   ultracentrifugation
         RT   centrifuge enrichment plants
         RT   isotope separation
         RT   podbielniak contactors
         RT   sedimentation
         RT   ultracentrifuges

    CENTRIFUGE ENRICHMENT PLANTS
    [293; 313] *Feb 78*
         UF   *enrichment plants (centrifuge)*
         UF   *enrichment plants (ultracentri*
         UF   *ultracentrifuge enrichment pla*
         BT1   isotope separation plants
            BT2   industrial plants
            BT2   nuclear facilities
         NT1   portsmouth centrifuge enrichme
         RT   centrifugation
         RT   ultracentrifugation

    CENTRIFUGES [256; 793]
         NT1   gas centrifuges
         NT1   plasma centrifuges
         NT1   ultracentrifuges

    centro informazioni studi espe
         USE   cise

    centro studi nucl. e. fermi r.
         USE   cesnef reactor

    CEPHALINS [8; 8]
         BT1   amines
            BT2   organic compounds
         BT1   phospholipids
            BT2   esters
               BT3   organic compounds
            BT2   lipids
               BT3   organic compounds
            BT2   organic phosphorus compounds
               BT3   organic compounds
         RT   glycerol

    CEPHEIDS [636; 636]
         BT1   pulsating variable stars
            BT2   variable stars
               BT3   stars

    CERAMIC MELTERS [304; 304] *Feb 81*
    (An electric furnace for vitrifying liquid
    or calcined high-level radioactive wastes.)
         BT1   electric furnaces
            BT2   furnaces
         RT   radioactive waste processing
         RT   vitrification

    CERAMICS [6,647; 6,647]
         RT   borides
         RT   carbides
         RT   ceramography
         RT   cermets
         RT   clays
         RT   dielectric track detectors
         RT   enamels
         RT   glass
         RT   glazes
         RT   mixed nitride fuels
         RT   mixed oxide fuels
         RT   nitrides
         RT   oxides
         RT   porcelain
         RT   refractories
         RT   slip casting

    CERAMOGRAPHY [119; 119] *Aug 78*
    (Methods for the characterization of
    microstructural features and stereometric
    and topologic parameters of ceramic ma-
    terials including sample preparation tech-
    niques.)
         RT   autoradiography
         RT   ceramics
         RT   cracks
         RT   electron microprobe analysis
         RT   etching
         RT   fractography
         RT   materials testing
         RT   microhardness
         RT   microradiography
         RT   microscopy
         RT   microstructure
         RT   particle size
         RT   photomicrography
         RT   porosity
         RT   post-irradiation examination
         RT   replica techniques
         RT   sample preparation
         RT   surface properties

    CERATITIS CAPITATA [115; 115]
         UF   *mediterranean fruit fly*
         BT1   fruit flies
            BT2   flies
               BT3   insects
                  BT4   arthropods

                BT5   invertebrates
                BT6   animals

cercaria
     USE   platyhelminths

CEREALS [432; 4,260]
     UF+   *grains (cereal)*
     BT1   gramineae
        BT2   plants
     NT1   barley
     NT1   maize
     NT1   millet
     NT1   oats
     NT1   rice
     NT1   rye
     NT1   sorghum
     NT1   wheat
     RT   buckwheat
     RT   crops
     RT   flour
     RT   food
     RT   grain disinfestation
     RT   ustilago
     RT   vernalization

CEREBELLUM [598; 598]
     BT1   brain
        BT2   central nervous system
           BT3   nervous system
        BT2   organs
           BT3   body

CEREBRAL CORTEX [718; 718]
     UF   *cortex (cerebral)*
     BT1   cerebrum
        BT2   brain
           BT3   central nervous system
              BT4   nervous system
           BT3   organs
              BT4   body
     RT   behavior
     RT   conditioned reflexes

CEREBROSIDES [22; 22]
     BT1   glycolipids
        BT2   lipids
           BT3   organic compounds
        BT2   saccharides
           BT3   carbohydrates
              BT4   organic compounds
     RT   amides
     RT   galactose

CEREBROSPINAL FLUID [714; 714]
     BT1   body fluids
        BT2   biological materials
           BT3   materials
     RT   central nervous system

CEREBRUM [1,620; 2,300]
     BT1   brain
        BT2   central nervous system
           BT3   nervous system
        BT2   organs
           BT3   body
     NT1   cerebral cortex

CERIANITE [1; 1]
     BT1   oxide minerals
        BT2   minerals
     BT1   thorium minerals
        BT2   radioactive minerals
           BT3   minerals
           BT3   radioactive materials
              BT4   materials
     RT   cerium oxides
     RT   thorium oxides

CERITE [1; 1]
     BT1   silicate minerals
        BT2   minerals
     RT   cerium silicates

CERIUM [1,955; 2,006]
     BT1   rare earths
        BT2   metals
           BT3   elements
     NT1   cerium-alpha
     NT1   cerium-beta
     NT1   cerium-gamma

CERIUM ADDITIONS [258; 270]
(Alloys containing not more than 1% Ce are listed here.)
     BT1   rare earth additions
     NT1   alloy-ni60cr25w15
     NT1   alloy-ni60mo13co9cr8nb4al3
     NT1   alloy-ni67cr19mo5w5ti3
     RT   cerium alloys
     RT   cerium compounds

CERIUM ALLOYS [1,177; 1,379]
(Alloys containing more than 1% Ce.)
     BT1   rare earth alloys
        BT2   alloys
     NT1   cerium base alloys
        NT2   misch metal
     RT   cerium additions

CERIUM ARSENIDES [10; 10] *Jul 78*
     BT1   arsenides
        BT2   arsenic compounds
        BT2   pnictides
     BT1   cerium compounds
        BT2   rare earth compounds

CERIUM BASE ALLOYS [94; 170]
     BT1   cerium alloys
        BT2   rare earth alloys
           BT3   alloys
     NT1   misch metal

CERIUM BORIDES [87; 87]
     BT1   borides
        BT2   boron compounds
     BT1   cerium compounds
        BT2   rare earth compounds

CERIUM BROMIDES [6; 6]
     BT1   bromides
        BT2   bromine compounds
           BT3   halogen compounds
        BT2   halides
           BT3   halogen compounds
     BT1   cerium compounds
        BT2   rare earth compounds

CERIUM CARBIDES [64; 64]
     BT1   carbides
        BT2   carbon compounds
     BT1   cerium compounds
        BT2   rare earth compounds

CERIUM CARBONATES [20; 22]
     BT1   carbonates
        BT2   carbon compounds
        BT2   oxygen compounds
     BT1   cerium compounds
        BT2   rare earth compounds
     RT   carbonate minerals
     RT   cordylite

CERIUM CHLORIDES [164; 164]
     BT1   cerium compounds
        BT2   rare earth compounds
     BT1   chlorides
        BT2   chlorine compounds
           BT3   halogen compounds
        BT2   halides
           BT3   halogen compounds

CERIUM COMPLEXES [655; 655]
     BT1   rare earth complexes
        BT2   complexes

CERIUM COMPOUNDS [1,084; 3,245]
     BT1   rare earth compounds
     NT1   cerium arsenides
     NT1   cerium borides
     NT1   cerium bromides
     NT1   cerium carbides
     NT1   cerium carbonates
     NT1   cerium chlorides
     NT1   cerium fluorides
     NT1   cerium hydrides
     NT1   cerium hydroxides
     NT1   cerium iodides
     NT1   cerium nitrates
     NT1   cerium nitrides
     NT1   cerium oxides
     NT1   cerium perchlorates
     NT1   cerium phosphates
     NT1   cerium phosphides
     NT1   cerium selenides
     NT1   cerium silicates
     NT1   cerium silicides
     NT1   cerium sulfates
     NT1   cerium sulfides
     NT1   cerium tellurides
     NT1   cerium tungstates
     RT   cerium additions

CERIUM FLUORIDES [133; 133]
     BT1   cerium compounds
        BT2   rare earth compounds
     BT1   fluorides
        BT2   fluorine compounds
           BT3   halogen compounds
        BT2   halides
           BT3   halogen compounds

CERIUM HYDRIDES [76; 76]
     BT1   cerium compounds
        BT2   rare earth compounds
     BT1   hydrides
        BT2   hydrogen compounds

CERIUM HYDROXIDES [28; 28]
     BT1   cerium compounds
        BT2   rare earth compounds
     BT1   hydroxides
        BT2   hydrogen compounds
        BT2   oxygen compounds

CERIUM IODIDES [31; 31]
     BT1   cerium compounds
        BT2   rare earth compounds
     BT1   iodides
        BT2   halides
           BT3   halogen compounds
        BT2   iodine compounds
           BT3   halogen compounds

CERIUM IONS [284; 284]
     BT1   ions
        BT2   charged particles

CERIUM ISOTOPES [191; 2,931]
     NT1   cerium 123
     NT1   cerium 124
     NT1   cerium 125
     NT1   cerium 126
     NT1   cerium 127
     NT1   cerium 128
     NT1   cerium 129
     NT1   cerium 130
     NT1   cerium 131
     NT1   cerium 132
     NT1   cerium 133
     NT1   cerium 134
     NT1   cerium 135
     NT1   cerium 136
     NT1   cerium 137
     NT1   cerium 138
     NT1   cerium 139
     NT1   cerium 140
     NT1   cerium 141
     NT1   cerium 142
     NT1   cerium 143
     NT1   cerium 144
     NT1   cerium 145
     NT1   cerium 146
     NT1   cerium 147

NT1 cerium 148
NT1 cerium 149
NT1 cerium 150
NT1 cerium 151
NT1 cerium 152

CERIUM NITRATES [155; 155]
BT1 cerium compounds
BT2 rare earth compounds
BT1 nitrates
BT2 nitrogen compounds
BT2 oxygen compounds

CERIUM NITRIDES [35; 35]
BT1 cerium compounds
BT2 rare earth compounds
BT1 nitrides
BT2 nitrogen compounds
BT2 pnictides

CERIUM OXIDES [951; 952]
BT1 cerium compounds
BT2 rare earth compounds
BT1 oxides
BT2 chalcogenides
BT2 oxygen compounds
RT cerianite
RT oxide minerals

CERIUM PERCHLORATES [12; 12]
BT1 cerium compounds
BT2 rare earth compounds
BT1 perchlorates
BT2 chlorine compounds
BT3 halogen compounds
BT2 oxygen compounds

CERIUM PHOSPHATES [90; 91]
BT1 cerium compounds
BT2 rare earth compounds
BT1 phosphates
BT2 oxygen compounds
BT2 phosphorus compounds
RT florencite
RT phosphate minerals

CERIUM PHOSPHIDES [18; 18] *Jul 78*
BT1 cerium compounds
BT2 rare earth compounds
BT1 phosphides
BT2 phosphorus compounds
BT2 pnictides

CERIUM SELENIDES [11; 11] *Oct 76*
BT1 cerium compounds
BT2 rare earth compounds
BT1 selenides
BT2 chalcogenides
BT2 selenium compounds

CERIUM SILICATES [11; 14]
BT1 cerium compounds
BT2 rare earth compounds
BT1 silicates
BT2 oxygen compounds
BT2 silicon compounds
RT cerite
RT silicate minerals
RT yttrialite

CERIUM SILICIDES [127; 127] *Oct 75*
BT1 cerium compounds
BT2 rare earth compounds
BT1 silicides
BT2 silicon compounds

CERIUM SULFATES [193; 193]
BT1 cerium compounds
BT2 rare earth compounds
BT1 sulfates
BT2 oxygen compounds
BT2 sulfur compounds

CERIUM SULFIDES [66; 66]
BT1 cerium compounds
BT2 rare earth compounds
BT1 sulfides
BT2 chalcogenides
BT2 sulfur compounds

CERIUM TELLURIDES [6; 6] *Mar 85*
BT1 cerium compounds
BT2 rare earth compounds
BT1 tellurides
BT2 chalcogenides
BT2 tellurium compounds

→ **CERIUM TUNGSTATES** [0; 0] *Sep 91*
BT1 cerium compounds
BT2 rare earth compounds
BT1 tungstates
BT2 oxygen compounds
BT2 tungsten compounds
BT3 transition element compounds

CERIUM 123 [5; 5] *Aug 84*
BT1 cerium isotopes
BT1 electron capture radioisotopes
BT2 beta decay radioisotopes
BT3 radioisotopes
BT4 isotopes
BT1 even-odd nuclei
BT2 nuclei
BT1 rare earth nuclei
BT2 intermediate mass nuclei
BT3 nuclei
BT1 seconds living radioisotopes
BT2 radioisotopes
BT3 isotopes

CERIUM 124 [11; 11] *Feb 79*
BT1 cerium isotopes
BT1 even-even nuclei
BT2 nuclei
BT1 rare earth nuclei
BT2 intermediate mass nuclei
BT3 nuclei
BT1 seconds living radioisotopes
BT2 radioisotopes
BT3 isotopes

CERIUM 125 [7; 7] *Feb 79*
BT1 beta-plus decay radioisotopes
BT2 beta decay radioisotopes
BT3 radioisotopes
BT4 isotopes
BT1 cerium isotopes
BT1 even-odd nuclei
BT2 nuclei
BT1 rare earth nuclei
BT2 intermediate mass nuclei
BT3 nuclei
BT1 seconds living radioisotopes
BT2 radioisotopes
BT3 isotopes

CERIUM 126 [11; 11]
BT1 cerium isotopes
BT1 electron capture radioisotopes
BT2 beta decay radioisotopes
BT3 radioisotopes
BT4 isotopes
BT1 even-even nuclei
BT2 nuclei
BT1 rare earth nuclei
BT2 intermediate mass nuclei
BT3 nuclei
BT1 seconds living radioisotopes
BT2 radioisotopes
BT3 isotopes

CERIUM 127 [7; 7] *Feb 78*
BT1 beta-plus decay radioisotopes
BT2 beta decay radioisotopes
BT3 radioisotopes
BT4 isotopes
BT1 cerium isotopes
BT1 electron capture radioisotopes
BT2 beta decay radioisotopes
BT3 radioisotopes
BT4 isotopes
BT1 even-odd nuclei
BT2 nuclei
BT1 rare earth nuclei
BT2 intermediate mass nuclei
BT3 nuclei
BT1 seconds living radioisotopes
BT2 radioisotopes
BT3 isotopes

CERIUM 128 [18; 18]
BT1 beta-plus decay radioisotopes
BT2 beta decay radioisotopes
BT3 radioisotopes
BT4 isotopes
BT1 cerium isotopes
BT1 electron capture radioisotopes
BT2 beta decay radioisotopes
BT3 radioisotopes
BT4 isotopes
BT1 even-even nuclei
BT2 nuclei
BT1 minutes living radioisotopes
BT2 radioisotopes
BT3 isotopes
BT1 rare earth nuclei
BT2 intermediate mass nuclei
BT3 nuclei

CERIUM 129 [12; 12]
BT1 beta-plus decay radioisotopes
BT2 beta decay radioisotopes
BT3 radioisotopes
BT4 isotopes
BT1 cerium isotopes
BT1 electron capture radioisotopes
BT2 beta decay radioisotopes
BT3 radioisotopes
BT4 isotopes
BT1 even-odd nuclei
BT2 nuclei
BT1 minutes living radioisotopes
BT2 radioisotopes
BT3 isotopes
BT1 rare earth nuclei
BT2 intermediate mass nuclei
BT3 nuclei

CERIUM 130 [56; 56]
BT1 beta-plus decay radioisotopes
BT2 beta decay radioisotopes
BT3 radioisotopes
BT4 isotopes
BT1 cerium isotopes
BT1 electron capture radioisotopes
BT2 beta decay radioisotopes
BT3 radioisotopes
BT4 isotopes
BT1 even-even nuclei
BT2 nuclei
BT1 minutes living radioisotopes
BT2 radioisotopes
BT3 isotopes
BT1 rare earth nuclei
BT2 intermediate mass nuclei
BT3 nuclei

CERIUM 131 [32; 32]
BT1 beta-plus decay radioisotopes
BT2 beta decay radioisotopes
BT3 radioisotopes
BT4 isotopes
BT1 cerium isotopes
BT1 electron capture radioisotopes
BT2 beta decay radioisotopes
BT3 radioisotopes
BT4 isotopes
BT1 even-odd nuclei
BT2 nuclei
BT1 minutes living radioisotopes
BT2 radioisotopes
BT3 isotopes
BT1 rare earth nuclei
BT2 intermediate mass nuclei
BT3 nuclei

CERIUM 132 [69; 69]
  BT1   cerium isotopes
  BT1   electron capture radioisotopes
    BT2   beta decay radioisotopes
      BT3   radioisotopes
        BT4   isotopes
  BT1   even-even nuclei
    BT2   nuclei
  BT1   hours living radioisotopes
    BT2   radioisotopes
      BT3   isotopes
  BT1   rare earth nuclei
    BT2   intermediate mass nuclei
      BT3   nuclei

CERIUM 133 [26; 26]
  BT1   beta-plus decay radioisotopes
    BT2   beta decay radioisotopes
      BT3   radioisotopes
        BT4   isotopes
  BT1   cerium isotopes
  BT1   electron capture radioisotopes
    BT2   beta decay radioisotopes
      BT3   radioisotopes
        BT4   isotopes
  BT1   even-odd nuclei
    BT2   nuclei
  BT1   hours living radioisotopes
    BT2   radioisotopes
      BT3   isotopes
  BT1   internal conversion radioisoto
    BT2   radioisotopes
      BT3   isotopes
  BT1   rare earth nuclei
    BT2   intermediate mass nuclei
      BT3   nuclei

CERIUM 134 [62; 62]
  BT1   cerium isotopes
  BT1   days living radioisotopes
    BT2   radioisotopes
      BT3   isotopes
  BT1   electron capture radioisotopes
    BT2   beta decay radioisotopes
      BT3   radioisotopes
        BT4   isotopes
  BT1   even-even nuclei
    BT2   nuclei
  BT1   rare earth nuclei
    BT2   intermediate mass nuclei
      BT3   nuclei

CERIUM 135 [27; 27]
  BT1   beta-plus decay radioisotopes
    BT2   beta decay radioisotopes
      BT3   radioisotopes
        BT4   isotopes
  BT1   cerium isotopes
  BT1   electron capture radioisotopes
    BT2   beta decay radioisotopes
      BT3   radioisotopes
        BT4   isotopes
  BT1   even-odd nuclei
    BT2   nuclei
  BT1   hours living radioisotopes
    BT2   radioisotopes
      BT3   isotopes
  BT1   isomeric transition isotopes
    BT2   radioisotopes
      BT3   isotopes
  BT1   rare earth nuclei
    BT2   intermediate mass nuclei
      BT3   nuclei
  BT1   seconds living radioisotopes
    BT2   radioisotopes
      BT3   isotopes

CERIUM 136 [39; 39]
  BT1   cerium isotopes
  BT1   even-even nuclei
    BT2   nuclei
  BT1   rare earth nuclei
    BT2   intermediate mass nuclei
      BT3   nuclei
  BT1   stable isotopes
    BT2   isotopes

CERIUM 136 TARGET [11; 11]
  BT1   targets

CERIUM 137 [51; 51]
  BT1   beta-plus decay radioisotopes
    BT2   beta decay radioisotopes
      BT3   radioisotopes
        BT4   isotopes
  BT1   cerium isotopes
  BT1   days living radioisotopes
    BT2   radioisotopes
      BT3   isotopes
  BT1   electron capture radioisotopes
    BT2   beta decay radioisotopes
      BT3   radioisotopes
        BT4   isotopes
  BT1   even-odd nuclei
    BT2   nuclei
  BT1   hours living radioisotopes
    BT2   radioisotopes
      BT3   isotopes
  BT1   internal conversion radioisoto
    BT2   radioisotopes
      BT3   isotopes
  BT1   isomeric transition isotopes
    BT2   radioisotopes
      BT3   isotopes
  BT1   rare earth nuclei
    BT2   intermediate mass nuclei
      BT3   nuclei

CERIUM 138 [61; 61]
  BT1   cerium isotopes
  BT1   even-even nuclei
    BT2   nuclei
  BT1   rare earth nuclei
    BT2   intermediate mass nuclei
      BT3   nuclei
  BT1   stable isotopes
    BT2   isotopes

CERIUM 138 TARGET [8; 8]
  BT1   targets

CERIUM 139 [141; 141]
  BT1   cerium isotopes
  BT1   days living radioisotopes
    BT2   radioisotopes
      BT3   isotopes
  BT1   electron capture radioisotopes
    BT2   beta decay radioisotopes
      BT3   radioisotopes
        BT4   isotopes
  BT1   even-odd nuclei
    BT2   nuclei
  BT1   isomeric transition isotopes
    BT2   radioisotopes
      BT3   isotopes
  BT1   rare earth nuclei
    BT2   intermediate mass nuclei
      BT3   nuclei
  BT1   seconds living radioisotopes
    BT2   radioisotopes
      BT3   isotopes

CERIUM 140 [296; 296]
  BT1   cerium isotopes
  BT1   even-even nuclei
    BT2   nuclei
  BT1   rare earth nuclei
    BT2   intermediate mass nuclei
      BT3   nuclei
  BT1   stable isotopes
    BT2   isotopes

CERIUM 140 TARGET [184; 184]
  BT1   targets

CERIUM 141 [585; 585]
  BT1   beta-minus decay radioisotopes
    BT2   beta decay radioisotopes
      BT3   radioisotopes
        BT4   isotopes
  BT1   cerium isotopes
  BT1   days living radioisotopes
    BT2   radioisotopes
      BT3   isotopes
  BT1   even-odd nuclei
    BT2   nuclei
  BT1   rare earth nuclei
    BT2   intermediate mass nuclei
      BT3   nuclei

CERIUM 141 TARGET [2; 2] *Oct 75*
  BT1   targets

CERIUM 142 [90; 90]
  BT1   cerium isotopes
  BT1   even-even nuclei
    BT2   nuclei
  BT1   rare earth nuclei
    BT2   intermediate mass nuclei
      BT3   nuclei
  BT1   stable isotopes
    BT2   isotopes

CERIUM 142 TARGET [63; 63] *Oct 75*
  BT1   targets

CERIUM 143 [79; 79]
  BT1   beta-minus decay radioisotopes
    BT2   beta decay radioisotopes
      BT3   radioisotopes
        BT4   isotopes
  BT1   cerium isotopes
  BT1   days living radioisotopes
    BT2   radioisotopes
      BT3   isotopes
  BT1   even-odd nuclei
    BT2   nuclei
  BT1   rare earth nuclei
    BT2   intermediate mass nuclei
      BT3   nuclei

CERIUM 144 [1,441; 1,441]
  BT1   beta-minus decay radioisotopes
    BT2   beta decay radioisotopes
      BT3   radioisotopes
        BT4   isotopes
  BT1   cerium isotopes
  BT1   days living radioisotopes
    BT2   radioisotopes
      BT3   isotopes
  BT1   even-even nuclei
    BT2   nuclei
  BT1   rare earth nuclei
    BT2   intermediate mass nuclei
      BT3   nuclei

CERIUM 145 [27; 27]
  BT1   beta-minus decay radioisotopes
    BT2   beta decay radioisotopes
      BT3   radioisotopes
        BT4   isotopes
  BT1   cerium isotopes
  BT1   even-odd nuclei
    BT2   nuclei
  BT1   minutes living radioisotopes
    BT2   radioisotopes
      BT3   isotopes
  BT1   rare earth nuclei
    BT2   intermediate mass nuclei
      BT3   nuclei

CERIUM 146 [34; 34]
  BT1   beta-minus decay radioisotopes
    BT2   beta decay radioisotopes
      BT3   radioisotopes
        BT4   isotopes
  BT1   cerium isotopes
  BT1   even-even nuclei
    BT2   nuclei
  BT1   minutes living radioisotopes
    BT2   radioisotopes
      BT3   isotopes
  BT1   rare earth nuclei
    BT2   intermediate mass nuclei
      BT3   nuclei

CERIUM 147 [24; 24]
 BT1 beta-minus decay radioisotopes
 BT2 beta decay radioisotopes
 BT3 radioisotopes
  BT4 isotopes
 BT1 cerium isotopes
 BT1 even-odd nuclei
 BT2 nuclei
 BT1 rare earth nuclei
 BT2 intermediate mass nuclei
 BT3 nuclei
 BT1 seconds living radioisotopes
 BT2 radioisotopes
 BT3 isotopes

CERIUM 148 [32; 32]
 BT1 beta-minus decay radioisotopes
 BT2 beta decay radioisotopes
 BT3 radioisotopes
  BT4 isotopes
 BT1 cerium isotopes
 BT1 even-even nuclei
 BT2 nuclei
 BT1 rare earth nuclei
 BT2 intermediate mass nuclei
 BT3 nuclei
 BT1 seconds living radioisotopes
 BT2 radioisotopes
 BT3 isotopes

CERIUM 149 [8; 8] *Jun 77*
 BT1 beta-minus decay radioisotopes
 BT2 beta decay radioisotopes
 BT3 radioisotopes
  BT4 isotopes
 BT1 cerium isotopes
 BT1 even-odd nuclei
 BT2 nuclei
 BT1 rare earth nuclei
 BT2 intermediate mass nuclei
 BT3 nuclei
 BT1 seconds living radioisotopes
 BT2 radioisotopes
 BT3 isotopes

CERIUM 150 [14; 14]
 BT1 beta-minus decay radioisotopes
 BT2 beta decay radioisotopes
 BT3 radioisotopes
  BT4 isotopes
 BT1 cerium isotopes
 BT1 even-even nuclei
 BT2 nuclei
 BT1 rare earth nuclei
 BT2 intermediate mass nuclei
 BT3 nuclei
 BT1 seconds living radioisotopes
 BT2 radioisotopes
 BT3 isotopes

CERIUM 151 [2; 2] *Jan 77*
 BT1 beta-minus decay radioisotopes
 BT2 beta decay radioisotopes
 BT3 radioisotopes
  BT4 isotopes
 BT1 cerium isotopes
 BT1 even-odd nuclei
 BT2 nuclei
 BT1 rare earth nuclei
 BT2 intermediate mass nuclei
 BT3 nuclei
 BT1 seconds living radioisotopes
 BT2 radioisotopes
 BT3 isotopes

CERIUM 152 [3; 3] *Jun 90*
 BT1 beta-minus decay radioisotopes
 BT2 beta decay radioisotopes
 BT3 radioisotopes
  BT4 isotopes
 BT1 cerium isotopes
 BT1 even-even nuclei
 BT2 nuclei
 BT1 rare earth nuclei
 BT2 intermediate mass nuclei

 BT3 nuclei
 BT1 seconds living radioisotopes
 BT2 radioisotopes
 BT3 isotopes

CERIUM-ALPHA [41; 41]
 BT1 cerium
 BT2 rare earths
 BT3 metals
  BT4 elements

CERIUM-BETA [6; 6] *Sep 77*
 BT1 cerium
 BT2 rare earths
 BT3 metals
  BT4 elements

CERIUM-GAMMA [40; 40]
 BT1 cerium
 BT2 rare earths
 BT3 metals
  BT4 elements

CERMETS [986; 1,034]
 UF *cemented carbides*
 UF *hard metals*
 BT1 composite materials
 BT2 materials
 NT1 td-nickel
 NT1 td-nickel chromium
 RT ceramics
 RT refractories

CERN [928; 928]
 UF *european organization for nucl*
 BT1 international organizations

cern ag synchrotron
 USE cern ps synchrotron

CERN CESAR [9; 9]
(CERN Electron Storage and Accumulation Ring)
 BT1 storage rings

cern ii synchrotron
 USE cern sps synchrotron

CERN ISR [662; 662]
(CERN Intersection Storage Rings)
 BT1 storage rings

CERN LEAR [355; 355] *Jun 84*
(Facility for antiproton physics at low energies with intense and cold beams of antiprotons. Located in the South Experimental Hall of CERN PS.)
 UF *cern low energy antiproton rin*
 UF *lear (cern)*
 RT cern ps synchrotron

cern lep
 USE lep storage rings

CERN LINAC [60; 60] *Aug 78*
 BT1 linear accelerators
 BT2 accelerators

cern low energy antiproton rin
 USE cern lear

CERN PS SYNCHROTRON [325; 325]
(CERN 28-GeV Proton Synchrotron)
 UF *cern ag synchrotron*
 BT1 synchrotrons
 BT2 cyclic accelerators
 BT3 accelerators
 RT cern lear

CERN SPS SYNCHROTRON [1,109; 1,109]
(CERN 400-GeV Proton Synchrotron)
 UF *cern ii synchrotron*
 BT1 synchrotrons
 BT2 cyclic accelerators
 BT3 accelerators

CERN SYNCHROCYCLOTRON [101; 101]
 BT1 synchrocyclotrons
 BT2 cyclic accelerators
 BT3 accelerators

CERNAVODA-1 REACTOR [3; 3] *Aug 82*
 BT1 candu type reactors
 BT2 heavy water moderated reactors
 BT3 reactors
 BT2 pressure tube reactors
 BT3 power reactors
  BT4 reactors
 BT2 thermal reactors
 BT3 reactors
 BT1 natural uranium reactors
 BT2 reactors
 BT1 phwr type reactors
 BT2 heavy water cooled reactors
 BT3 reactors
 BT2 heavy water moderated reactors
 BT3 reactors

CERTIFICATION [2; 2] *Apr 81*
(Prior to August 1991, this concept was indexed to LICENSING.)
 RT licensing
 RT performance testing
 RT quality assurance
 RT standards
 RT testing

CERULOPLASMIN [69; 69]
 BT1 copper complexes
 BT2 transition element complexes
 BT3 complexes
 BT1 globulins-alpha
 BT2 globulins
 BT3 proteins
  BT4 organic compounds

CESAR REACTOR [13; 13]
(CEA/CEN, Cadarache, St. Paul Lez Durance, France)
 BT1 carbon dioxide cooled reactors
 BT2 gas cooled reactors
 BT3 reactors
 BT1 experimental reactors
 BT2 research and test reactors
 BT3 reactors
 BT1 graphite moderated reactors
 BT2 reactors
 BT1 natural uranium reactors
 BT2 reactors
 BT1 research reactors
 BT2 research and test reactors
 BT3 reactors
 BT1 thermal reactors
 BT2 reactors
 RT enriched uranium reactors

CESIUM [4,163; 4,163]
 UF *caesium*
 BT1 alkali metals
 BT2 metals
 BT3 elements

CESIUM ADDITIONS [32; 32]
(Alloys containing not more than 1% Cs are listed here.)
 RT cesium alloys
 RT cesium compounds

CESIUM ALLOYS [174; 183]
(Alloys containing more than 1% Cs.)
- BT1 alloys
- NT1 cesium base alloys
- RT cesium additions

CESIUM BASE ALLOYS [8; 8]
- BT1 cesium alloys
- BT2 alloys

CESIUM BROMIDES [328; 328]
- BT1 bromides
- BT2 bromine compounds
- BT3 halogen compounds
- BT2 halides
- BT3 halogen compounds
- BT1 cesium compounds
- BT2 alkali metal compounds

CESIUM CARBIDES [7; 7]
- BT1 carbides
- BT2 carbon compounds
- BT1 cesium compounds
- BT2 alkali metal compounds

CESIUM CARBONATES [41; 41]
- BT1 carbonates
- BT2 carbon compounds
- BT2 oxygen compounds
- BT1 cesium compounds
- BT2 alkali metal compounds

CESIUM CHLORIDES [935; 935]
- BT1 cesium compounds
- BT2 alkali metal compounds
- BT1 chlorides
- BT2 chlorine compounds
- BT3 halogen compounds
- BT2 halides
- BT3 halogen compounds

CESIUM COMPLEXES [176; 176]
- BT1 alkali metal complexes
- BT2 complexes

CESIUM COMPOUNDS [1,641; 5,014]
- BT1 alkali metal compounds
- NT1 cesium bromides
- NT1 cesium carbides
- NT1 cesium carbonates
- NT1 cesium chlorides
- NT1 cesium fluorides
- NT1 cesium hydrides
- NT1 cesium hydroxides
- NT1 cesium iodides
- NT1 cesium nitrates
- NT1 cesium nitrides
- NT1 cesium oxides
- NT1 cesium perchlorates
- NT1 cesium phosphates
- NT1 cesium selenides
- NT1 cesium silicates
- NT1 cesium silicides
- NT1 cesium sulfates
- NT1 cesium sulfides
- NT1 cesium tellurides
- NT1 cesium tungstates
- NT1 cesium uranates
- RT cesium additions

CESIUM FLUORIDES [377; 377]
- BT1 cesium compounds
- BT2 alkali metal compounds
- BT1 fluorides
- BT2 fluorine compounds
- BT3 halogen compounds
- BT2 halides
- BT3 halogen compounds

CESIUM HYDRIDES [46; 46]
- BT1 cesium compounds
- BT2 alkali metal compounds
- BT1 hydrides
- BT2 hydrogen compounds

CESIUM HYDROXIDES [123; 123]
- BT1 cesium compounds
- BT2 alkali metal compounds
- BT1 hydroxides
- BT2 hydrogen compounds
- BT2 oxygen compounds

CESIUM IODIDES [1,095; 1,095]
- BT1 cesium compounds
- BT2 alkali metal compounds
- BT1 iodides
- BT2 halides
- BT3 halogen compounds
- BT2 iodine compounds
- BT3 halogen compounds

CESIUM IONS [658; 658]
- BT1 ions
- BT2 charged particles

CESIUM ISOTOPES [475; 12,449]
- NT1 cesium 113
- NT1 cesium 114
- NT1 cesium 115
- NT1 cesium 116
- NT1 cesium 117
- NT1 cesium 118
- NT1 cesium 119
- NT1 cesium 120
- NT1 cesium 121
- NT1 cesium 122
- NT1 cesium 123
- NT1 cesium 124
- NT1 cesium 125
- NT1 cesium 126
- NT1 cesium 127
- NT1 cesium 128
- NT1 cesium 129
- NT1 cesium 130
- NT1 cesium 131
- NT1 cesium 132
- NT1 cesium 133
- NT1 cesium 134
- NT1 cesium 135
- NT1 cesium 136
- NT1 cesium 137
- NT1 cesium 138
- NT1 cesium 139
- NT1 cesium 140
- NT1 cesium 141
- NT1 cesium 142
- NT1 cesium 143
- NT1 cesium 144
- NT1 cesium 145
- NT1 cesium 146
- NT1 cesium 147
- NT1 cesium 148

CESIUM NITRATES [188; 188]
- BT1 cesium compounds
- BT2 alkali metal compounds
- BT1 nitrates
- BT2 nitrogen compounds
- BT2 oxygen compounds

CESIUM NITRIDES [1; 1]
- BT1 cesium compounds
- BT2 alkali metal compounds
- BT1 nitrides
- BT2 nitrogen compounds
- BT2 pnictides

CESIUM OXIDES [200; 200]
- BT1 cesium compounds
- BT2 alkali metal compounds
- BT1 oxides
- BT2 chalcogenides
- BT2 oxygen compounds

CESIUM PERCHLORATES [18; 18]
Nov 78
- BT1 cesium compounds
- BT2 alkali metal compounds
- BT1 perchlorates
- BT2 chlorine compounds
- BT3 halogen compounds
- BT2 oxygen compounds

CESIUM PHOSPHATES [118; 118]
- BT1 cesium compounds
- BT2 alkali metal compounds
- BT1 phosphates
- BT2 oxygen compounds
- BT2 phosphorus compounds

CESIUM SELENIDES [10; 10] *Sep 79*
- BT1 cesium compounds
- BT2 alkali metal compounds
- BT1 selenides
- BT2 chalcogenides
- BT2 selenium compounds

CESIUM SILICATES [41; 41]
- BT1 cesium compounds
- BT2 alkali metal compounds
- BT1 silicates
- BT2 oxygen compounds
- BT2 silicon compounds
- RT pollucite

CESIUM SILICIDES [3; 3] *Feb 88*
- BT1 cesium compounds
- BT2 alkali metal compounds
- BT1 silicides
- BT2 silicon compounds

CESIUM SULFATES [223; 223]
- BT1 cesium compounds
- BT2 alkali metal compounds
- BT1 sulfates
- BT2 oxygen compounds
- BT2 sulfur compounds

CESIUM SULFIDES [29; 29]
- BT1 cesium compounds
- BT2 alkali metal compounds
- BT1 sulfides
- BT2 chalcogenides
- BT2 sulfur compounds

CESIUM TELLURIDES [17; 17] *Feb 83*
- BT1 cesium compounds
- BT2 alkali metal compounds
- BT1 tellurides
- BT2 chalcogenides
- BT2 tellurium compounds

CESIUM TUNGSTATES [22; 22]
May 78
- BT1 cesium compounds
- BT2 alkali metal compounds
- BT1 tungstates
- BT2 oxygen compounds
- BT2 tungsten compounds
- BT3 transition element compounds

CESIUM URANATES [30; 30] *Nov 75*
- BT1 cesium compounds
- BT2 alkali metal compounds
- BT1 uranates
- BT2 uranium compounds
- BT3 actinide compounds

CESIUM 113 [23; 23] *Jul 80*
- BT1 cesium isotopes
- BT1 intermediate mass nuclei
- BT2 nuclei
- BT1 nanosec living radioisotopes
- BT2 radioisotopes
- BT3 isotopes
- BT1 odd-even nuclei
- BT2 nuclei
- BT1 proton decay radioisotopes
- BT2 radioisotopes
- BT3 isotopes

CESIUM 114 [27; 27] *Jan 79*
- BT1 beta-plus decay radioisotopes
- BT2 beta decay radioisotopes
- BT3 radioisotopes
- BT4 isotopes
- BT1 cesium isotopes
- BT1 electron capture radioisotopes
- BT2 beta decay radioisotopes

CESIUM 115 [3; 3] Jan 79
- BT1 beta-plus decay radioisotopes
- BT2 beta decay radioisotopes
- BT3 radioisotopes
- BT4 isotopes
- BT1 cesium isotopes
- BT1 electron capture radioisotopes
- BT2 beta decay radioisotopes
- BT3 radioisotopes
- BT4 isotopes
- BT1 intermediate mass nuclei
- BT2 nuclei
- BT1 millisec living radioisotopes
- BT2 radioisotopes
- BT3 isotopes
- BT1 odd-odd nuclei
- BT2 nuclei

(continuing previous entry CESIUM 114)
- BT3 radioisotopes
- BT4 isotopes
- BT1 intermediate mass nuclei
- BT2 nuclei
- BT1 millisec living radioisotopes
- BT2 radioisotopes
- BT3 isotopes
- BT1 odd-odd nuclei
- BT2 nuclei

CESIUM 116 [22; 22]
- BT1 beta-plus decay radioisotopes
- BT2 beta decay radioisotopes
- BT3 radioisotopes
- BT4 isotopes
- BT1 cesium isotopes
- BT1 electron capture radioisotopes
- BT2 beta decay radioisotopes
- BT3 radioisotopes
- BT4 isotopes
- BT1 intermediate mass nuclei
- BT2 nuclei
- BT1 millisec living radioisotopes
- BT2 radioisotopes
- BT3 isotopes
- BT1 odd-odd nuclei
- BT2 nuclei
- BT1 seconds living radioisotopes
- BT2 radioisotopes
- BT3 isotopes

CESIUM 117 [8; 8]
- BT1 beta-plus decay radioisotopes
- BT2 beta decay radioisotopes
- BT3 radioisotopes
- BT4 isotopes
- BT1 cesium isotopes
- BT1 electron capture radioisotopes
- BT2 beta decay radioisotopes
- BT3 radioisotopes
- BT4 isotopes
- BT1 intermediate mass nuclei
- BT2 nuclei
- BT1 odd-even nuclei
- BT2 nuclei
- BT1 seconds living radioisotopes
- BT2 radioisotopes
- BT3 isotopes

CESIUM 118 [15; 15]
- BT1 beta-plus decay radioisotopes
- BT2 beta decay radioisotopes
- BT3 radioisotopes
- BT4 isotopes
- BT1 cesium isotopes
- BT1 electron capture radioisotopes
- BT2 beta decay radioisotopes
- BT3 radioisotopes
- BT4 isotopes
- BT1 intermediate mass nuclei
- BT2 nuclei
- BT1 odd-odd nuclei
- BT2 nuclei
- BT1 seconds living radioisotopes
- BT2 radioisotopes
- BT3 isotopes

CESIUM 119 [14; 14]
- BT1 beta-plus decay radioisotopes
- BT2 beta decay radioisotopes
- BT3 radioisotopes
- BT4 isotopes
- BT1 cesium isotopes
- BT1 electron capture radioisotopes
- BT2 beta decay radioisotopes
- BT3 radioisotopes
- BT4 isotopes
- BT1 intermediate mass nuclei
- BT2 nuclei
- BT1 odd-even nuclei
- BT2 nuclei
- BT1 seconds living radioisotopes
- BT2 radioisotopes
- BT3 isotopes

CESIUM 120 [15; 15]
- BT1 beta-plus decay radioisotopes
- BT2 beta decay radioisotopes
- BT3 radioisotopes
- BT4 isotopes
- BT1 cesium isotopes
- BT1 electron capture radioisotopes
- BT2 beta decay radioisotopes
- BT3 radioisotopes
- BT4 isotopes
- BT1 intermediate mass nuclei
- BT2 nuclei
- BT1 minutes living radioisotopes
- BT2 radioisotopes
- BT3 isotopes
- BT1 odd-odd nuclei
- BT2 nuclei

CESIUM 121 [26; 26]
- BT1 beta-plus decay radioisotopes
- BT2 beta decay radioisotopes
- BT3 radioisotopes
- BT4 isotopes
- BT1 cesium isotopes
- BT1 electron capture radioisotopes
- BT2 beta decay radioisotopes
- BT3 radioisotopes
- BT4 isotopes
- BT1 intermediate mass nuclei
- BT2 nuclei
- BT1 isomeric transition isotopes
- BT2 radioisotopes
- BT3 isotopes
- BT1 minutes living radioisotopes
- BT2 radioisotopes
- BT3 isotopes
- BT1 odd-even nuclei
- BT2 nuclei

CESIUM 122 [24; 24]
- BT1 beta-plus decay radioisotopes
- BT2 beta decay radioisotopes
- BT3 radioisotopes
- BT4 isotopes
- BT1 cesium isotopes
- BT1 electron capture radioisotopes
- BT2 beta decay radioisotopes
- BT3 radioisotopes
- BT4 isotopes
- BT1 intermediate mass nuclei
- BT2 nuclei
- BT1 minutes living radioisotopes
- BT2 radioisotopes
- BT3 isotopes
- BT1 odd-odd nuclei
- BT2 nuclei
- BT1 seconds living radioisotopes
- BT2 radioisotopes
- BT3 isotopes

CESIUM 123 [42; 42]
- BT1 beta-plus decay radioisotopes
- BT2 beta decay radioisotopes
- BT3 radioisotopes
- BT4 isotopes
- BT1 cesium isotopes
- BT1 electron capture radioisotopes
- BT2 beta decay radioisotopes
- BT3 radioisotopes
- BT4 isotopes
- BT1 intermediate mass nuclei
- BT2 nuclei
- BT1 internal conversion radioisoto
- BT2 radioisotopes
- BT3 isotopes
- BT1 isomeric transition isotopes
- BT2 radioisotopes
- BT3 isotopes
- BT1 minutes living radioisotopes
- BT2 radioisotopes
- BT3 isotopes
- BT1 odd-even nuclei
- BT2 nuclei
- BT1 seconds living radioisotopes
- BT2 radioisotopes
- BT3 isotopes

CESIUM 124 [36; 36]
- BT1 beta-plus decay radioisotopes
- BT2 beta decay radioisotopes
- BT3 radioisotopes
- BT4 isotopes
- BT1 cesium isotopes
- BT1 electron capture radioisotopes
- BT2 beta decay radioisotopes
- BT3 radioisotopes
- BT4 isotopes
- BT1 intermediate mass nuclei
- BT2 nuclei
- BT1 odd-odd nuclei
- BT2 nuclei
- BT1 seconds living radioisotopes
- BT2 radioisotopes
- BT3 isotopes

CESIUM 125 [30; 30]
- BT1 beta-plus decay radioisotopes
- BT2 beta decay radioisotopes
- BT3 radioisotopes
- BT4 isotopes
- BT1 cesium isotopes
- BT1 electron capture radioisotopes
- BT2 beta decay radioisotopes
- BT3 radioisotopes
- BT4 isotopes
- BT1 intermediate mass nuclei
- BT2 nuclei
- BT1 minutes living radioisotopes
- BT2 radioisotopes
- BT3 isotopes
- BT1 odd-even nuclei
- BT2 nuclei

CESIUM 126 [20; 20]
- BT1 beta-plus decay radioisotopes
- BT2 beta decay radioisotopes
- BT3 radioisotopes
- BT4 isotopes
- BT1 cesium isotopes
- BT1 electron capture radioisotopes
- BT2 beta decay radioisotopes
- BT3 radioisotopes
- BT4 isotopes
- BT1 intermediate mass nuclei
- BT2 nuclei
- BT1 minutes living radioisotopes
- BT2 radioisotopes
- BT3 isotopes
- BT1 odd-odd nuclei
- BT2 nuclei

CESIUM 127 [57; 57]
- BT1 beta-plus decay radioisotopes
- BT2 beta decay radioisotopes
- BT3 radioisotopes
- BT4 isotopes
- BT1 cesium isotopes
- BT1 electron capture radioisotopes
- BT2 beta decay radioisotopes
- BT3 radioisotopes
- BT4 isotopes
- BT1 hours living radioisotopes
- BT2 radioisotopes
- BT3 isotopes
- BT1 intermediate mass nuclei
- BT2 nuclei
- BT1 odd-even nuclei
- BT2 nuclei

CESIUM 128 [32; 32]
  BT1   beta-plus decay radioisotopes
    BT2   beta decay radioisotopes
      BT3   radioisotopes
        BT4   isotopes
  BT1   cesium isotopes
  BT1   electron capture radioisotopes
    BT2   beta decay radioisotopes
      BT3   radioisotopes
        BT4   isotopes
  BT1   intermediate mass nuclei
    BT2   nuclei
  BT1   minutes living radioisotopes
    BT2   radioisotopes
      BT3   isotopes
  BT1   odd-odd nuclei
    BT2   nuclei

CESIUM 129 [88; 88]
  BT1   beta-plus decay radioisotopes
    BT2   beta decay radioisotopes
      BT3   radioisotopes
        BT4   isotopes
  BT1   cesium isotopes
  BT1   days living radioisotopes
    BT2   radioisotopes
      BT3   isotopes
  BT1   electron capture radioisotopes
    BT2   beta decay radioisotopes
      BT3   radioisotopes
        BT4   isotopes
  BT1   intermediate mass nuclei
    BT2   nuclei
  BT1   odd-even nuclei
    BT2   nuclei

CESIUM 130 [29; 29]
  BT1   beta-minus decay radioisotopes
    BT2   beta decay radioisotopes
      BT3   radioisotopes
        BT4   isotopes
  BT1   beta-plus decay radioisotopes
    BT2   beta decay radioisotopes
      BT3   radioisotopes
        BT4   isotopes
  BT1   cesium isotopes
  BT1   electron capture radioisotopes
    BT2   beta decay radioisotopes
      BT3   radioisotopes
        BT4   isotopes
  BT1   intermediate mass nuclei
    BT2   nuclei
  BT1   minutes living radioisotopes
    BT2   radioisotopes
      BT3   isotopes
  BT1   odd-odd nuclei
    BT2   nuclei

CESIUM 131 [135; 135]
  BT1   cesium isotopes
  BT1   days living radioisotopes
    BT2   radioisotopes
      BT3   isotopes
  BT1   electron capture radioisotopes
    BT2   beta decay radioisotopes
      BT3   radioisotopes
        BT4   isotopes
  BT1   intermediate mass nuclei
    BT2   nuclei
  BT1   odd-even nuclei
    BT2   nuclei

CESIUM 131 TARGET [0; 0] *Feb 88*
  BT1   targets

CESIUM 132 [50; 50]
  BT1   beta-minus decay radioisotopes
    BT2   beta decay radioisotopes
      BT3   radioisotopes
        BT4   isotopes
  BT1   beta-plus decay radioisotopes
    BT2   beta decay radioisotopes
      BT3   radioisotopes
        BT4   isotopes
  BT1   cesium isotopes
  BT1   days living radioisotopes
    BT2   radioisotopes
      BT3   isotopes
  BT1   electron capture radioisotopes
    BT2   beta decay radioisotopes
      BT3   radioisotopes
        BT4   isotopes
  BT1   intermediate mass nuclei
    BT2   nuclei
  BT1   odd-odd nuclei
    BT2   nuclei

CESIUM 132 TARGET [3; 3] *Feb 79*
  BT1   targets

CESIUM 133 [268; 268]
  BT1   cesium isotopes
  BT1   intermediate mass nuclei
    BT2   nuclei
  BT1   odd-even nuclei
    BT2   nuclei
  BT1   stable isotopes
    BT2   isotopes

CESIUM 133 TARGET [99; 99]
  BT1   targets

CESIUM 134 [1,961; 1,961]
  BT1   beta-minus decay radioisotopes
    BT2   beta decay radioisotopes
      BT3   radioisotopes
        BT4   isotopes
  BT1   cesium isotopes
  BT1   electron capture radioisotopes
    BT2   beta decay radioisotopes
      BT3   radioisotopes
        BT4   isotopes
  BT1   hours living radioisotopes
    BT2   radioisotopes
      BT3   isotopes
  BT1   intermediate mass nuclei
    BT2   nuclei
  BT1   internal conversion radioisoto
    BT2   radioisotopes
      BT3   isotopes
  BT1   isomeric transition isotopes
    BT2   radioisotopes
      BT3   isotopes
  BT1   odd-odd nuclei
    BT2   nuclei
  BT1   years living radioisotopes
    BT2   radioisotopes
      BT3   isotopes

CESIUM 134 TARGET [0; 0] *Feb 88*
  BT1   targets

CESIUM 135 [100; 100]
  BT1   beta-minus decay radioisotopes
    BT2   beta decay radioisotopes
      BT3   radioisotopes
        BT4   isotopes
  BT1   cesium isotopes
  BT1   intermediate mass nuclei
    BT2   nuclei
  BT1   isomeric transition isotopes
    BT2   radioisotopes
      BT3   isotopes
  BT1   minutes living radioisotopes
    BT2   radioisotopes
      BT3   isotopes
  BT1   odd-even nuclei
    BT2   nuclei
  BT1   years living radioisotopes
    BT2   radioisotopes
      BT3   isotopes

CESIUM 135 TARGET [5; 5] *Feb 88*
  BT1   targets

CESIUM 136 [75; 75]
  BT1   beta-minus decay radioisotopes
    BT2   beta decay radioisotopes
      BT3   radioisotopes
        BT4   isotopes
  BT1   cesium isotopes
  BT1   days living radioisotopes
    BT2   radioisotopes
      BT3   isotopes
  BT1   intermediate mass nuclei
    BT2   nuclei
  BT1   isomeric transition isotopes
    BT2   radioisotopes
      BT3   isotopes
  BT1   odd-odd nuclei
    BT2   nuclei
  BT1   seconds living radioisotopes
    BT2   radioisotopes
      BT3   isotopes

CESIUM 137 [10,444; 10,444]
  BT1   beta-minus decay radioisotopes
    BT2   beta decay radioisotopes
      BT3   radioisotopes
        BT4   isotopes
  BT1   cesium isotopes
  BT1   intermediate mass nuclei
    BT2   nuclei
  BT1   odd-even nuclei
    BT2   nuclei
  BT1   years living radioisotopes
    BT2   radioisotopes
      BT3   isotopes
  RT   radioisotope generators

CESIUM 137 TARGET [4; 4] *Aug 88*
  BT1   targets

CESIUM 138 [72; 72]
  BT1   beta-minus decay radioisotopes
    BT2   beta decay radioisotopes
      BT3   radioisotopes
        BT4   isotopes
  BT1   cesium isotopes
  BT1   intermediate mass nuclei
    BT2   nuclei
  BT1   internal conversion radioisoto
    BT2   radioisotopes
      BT3   isotopes
  BT1   isomeric transition isotopes
    BT2   radioisotopes
      BT3   isotopes
  BT1   minutes living radioisotopes
    BT2   radioisotopes
      BT3   isotopes
  BT1   odd-odd nuclei
    BT2   nuclei

CESIUM 139 [39; 39]
  BT1   beta-minus decay radioisotopes
    BT2   beta decay radioisotopes
      BT3   radioisotopes
        BT4   isotopes
  BT1   cesium isotopes
  BT1   intermediate mass nuclei
    BT2   nuclei
  BT1   minutes living radioisotopes
    BT2   radioisotopes
      BT3   isotopes
  BT1   odd-even nuclei
    BT2   nuclei

CESIUM 140 [42; 42]
  BT1   beta-minus decay radioisotopes
    BT2   beta decay radioisotopes
      BT3   radioisotopes
        BT4   isotopes
  BT1   cesium isotopes
  BT1   intermediate mass nuclei
    BT2   nuclei
  BT1   minutes living radioisotopes
    BT2   radioisotopes
      BT3   isotopes
  BT1   odd-odd nuclei
    BT2   nuclei

CESIUM 141 [61; 61]
  BT1   beta-minus decay radioisotopes
    BT2   beta decay radioisotopes
      BT3   radioisotopes
        BT4   isotopes
  BT1   cesium isotopes
  BT1   intermediate mass nuclei
    BT2   nuclei
  BT1   odd-even nuclei
    BT2   nuclei
  BT1   seconds living radioisotopes
    BT2   radioisotopes

CESIUM 142 [35; 35]
BT3   isotopes
BT1   beta-minus decay radioisotopes
BT2   beta decay radioisotopes
BT3   radioisotopes
BT4   isotopes
BT1   cesium isotopes
BT1   intermediate mass nuclei
BT2   nuclei
BT1   odd-odd nuclei
BT2   nuclei
BT1   seconds living radioisotopes
BT2   radioisotopes
BT3   isotopes

CESIUM 143 [45; 45]
BT1   beta-minus decay radioisotopes
BT2   beta decay radioisotopes
BT3   radioisotopes
BT4   isotopes
BT1   cesium isotopes
BT1   intermediate mass nuclei
BT2   nuclei
BT1   odd-even nuclei
BT2   nuclei
BT1   seconds living radioisotopes
BT2   radioisotopes
BT3   isotopes

CESIUM 144 [89; 89]
BT1   beta-minus decay radioisotopes
BT2   beta decay radioisotopes
BT3   radioisotopes
BT4   isotopes
BT1   cesium isotopes
BT1   intermediate mass nuclei
BT2   nuclei
BT1   odd-odd nuclei
BT2   nuclei
BT1   seconds living radioisotopes
BT2   radioisotopes
BT3   isotopes

CESIUM 145 [40; 40]
BT1   beta-minus decay radioisotopes
BT2   beta decay radioisotopes
BT3   radioisotopes
BT4   isotopes
BT1   cesium isotopes
BT1   intermediate mass nuclei
BT2   nuclei
BT1   millisec living radioisotopes
BT2   radioisotopes
BT3   isotopes
BT1   odd-even nuclei
BT2   nuclei

CESIUM 146 [17; 17]
BT1   beta-minus decay radioisotopes
BT2   beta decay radioisotopes
BT3   radioisotopes
BT4   isotopes
BT1   cesium isotopes
BT1   intermediate mass nuclei
BT2   nuclei
BT1   millisec living radioisotopes
BT2   radioisotopes
BT3   isotopes
BT1   odd-odd nuclei
BT2   nuclei

CESIUM 147 [14; 14] *Apr 79*
BT1   beta-minus decay radioisotopes
BT2   beta decay radioisotopes
BT3   radioisotopes
BT4   isotopes
BT1   cesium isotopes
BT1   intermediate mass nuclei
BT2   nuclei
BT1   millisec living radioisotopes
BT2   radioisotopes
BT3   isotopes
BT1   odd-even nuclei
BT2   nuclei

CESIUM 148 [8; 8] *Apr 79*
BT1   beta-minus decay radioisotopes
BT2   beta decay radioisotopes
BT3   radioisotopes
BT4   isotopes
BT1   cesium isotopes
BT1   intermediate mass nuclei
BT2   nuclei
BT1   millisec living radioisotopes
BT2   radioisotopes
BT3   isotopes
BT1   odd-odd nuclei
BT2   nuclei

CESNEF REACTOR [4; 4]
(Centro Studi Nucleari E. Fermi, Milan, Italy)
UF   *centro studi nucl. e. fermi r.*
UF   *e. fermi nucl. res. center r.*
UF   *l-54 reactor*
BT1   aqueous homogeneous reactors
BT2   liquid homogeneous reactors
BT3   fluid fueled reactors
BT4   reactors
BT3   homogeneous reactors
BT4   reactors
BT2   water cooled reactors
BT3   reactors
BT2   water moderated reactors
BT3   reactors
BT1   enriched uranium reactors
BT2   reactors
BT1   isotope production reactors
BT2   irradiation reactors
BT3   reactors
BT1   research reactors
BT2   research and test reactors
BT3   reactors
BT1   test reactors
BT2   research and test reactors
BT3   reactors
BT2   test facilities
BT1   thermal reactors
BT2   reactors
BT1   training reactors
BT2   research and test reactors
BT3   reactors

CESR STORAGE RING [256; 256]
Jan 79
UF   *cornell electron-positron stor*
BT1   storage rings

CESTODES [62; 70]
UF   *tapeworms*
BT1   helminths
BT2   parasites
BT1   platyhelminths
BT2   invertebrates
BT3   animals
NT1   hymenolepis
RT   hydatidosis

→ **CETACEANS** [0; 0] *Sep 91*
(The order of aquatic mammals that includes whales, dolphins, and porpoises.)
UF   *dolphins*
UF   *porpoises*
UF   *whales*
BT1   aquatic organisms
BT1   mammals
BT2   vertebrates
BT3   animals

ceylon
USE   sri lanka

cfg reactor
USE   anex reactor

CFRMF REACTOR [68; 68]
UF   *coupled f.reactor meas.facili.*
BT1   fast reactors
BT2   epithermal reactors
BT3   reactors

BT1   zero power reactors
BT2   experimental reactors
BT3   research and test reactors
BT4   reactors

CFRP PROGRAM [131; 131] *Feb 81*
(Consolidated Fuel Reprocessing Program, a comprehensive program to develop and demonstrate breeder reprocessing and recycle.)
UF   *consol. fuel reproc. program*
BT1   coordinated research programs
BT2   research programs
RT   hef
RT   reprocessing

CFU [676; 676]
(Limited to colony formation on spleen.)
UF   *colony forming units*
RT   spleen colony formation
RT   stem cells

CHACALTAYA [60; 60]
BT1   bolivia
BT2   developing countries
BT2   south america
BT3   latin america

CHAD [9; 9]
BT1   africa
BT1   developing countries

CHAIN REACTIONS [234; 246]
RT   criticality
RT   fission
RT   fissioning plasma
RT   natural nuclear reactors
RT   nuclear reactions
RT   oklo phenomenon
RT   thermonuclear reactions

CHALCOGENIDES [493; 86,708]
*NT1   oxides
*NT1   selenides
*NT1   sulfides
*NT1   tellurides
RT   high-tc superconductors

CHALCOPYRITE [72; 72]
BT1   sulfide minerals
BT2   minerals
RT   copper sulfides
RT   iron sulfides

CHALICE DEVICES [1; 1]
BT1   linear theta pinch devices
BT2   linear pinch devices
BT3   open plasma devices
BT4   thermonuclear devices
BT3   pinch devices
BT4   thermonuclear devices

chalk
USE   calcite

CHALK RIVER [20; 20]
BT1   ontario
BT2   canada
BT3   developed countries
BT3   north america

CHALK RIVER NUCLEAR LABS [280; 280]
BT1   atomic energy of canada ltd
BT2   canadian organizations
BT3   national organizations

chalk river pool test reactor
USE   ptr reactor

chalk river supercond. cyclo.
USE   crnl superconducting cyclotron

chalk river zed-2 reactor
USE zed-2 reactor

CHANDIGARH CYCLOTRON [4; 4]
Jun 83
BT1 cyclotrons
BT2 cyclic accelerators
BT3 accelerators

CHANDRASEKHAR THEORY [71; 71]
UF *chandrasekhar-fermi theory*
RT astrophysics
RT stars

chandrasekhar-fermi theory
USE chandrasekhar theory

CHANNELING [1,445; 4,678]
UF *blocking*
UF *dechanneling*
NT1 electron channeling
NT1 ion channeling
NT1 positron channeling
NT1 proton channeling

channels (reactor)
USE reactor channels

CHAPELCROSS-1 REACTOR [18; 18]
(Annan, Scotland, UK)
BT1 carbon dioxide cooled reactors
  BT2 gas cooled reactors
    BT3 reactors
BT1 magnox type reactors
  BT2 gcr type reactors
    BT3 gas cooled reactors
      BT4 reactors
    BT3 graphite moderated reactors
      BT4 reactors
  BT2 natural uranium reactors
    BT3 reactors
  BT2 power reactors
    BT3 reactors
BT1 plutonium production reactors
  BT2 production reactors
    BT3 reactors
BT1 thermal reactors
  BT2 reactors

CHAPELCROSS-2 REACTOR [14; 14]
(Annan, Scotland, UK)
BT1 carbon dioxide cooled reactors
  BT2 gas cooled reactors
    BT3 reactors
BT1 magnox type reactors
  BT2 gcr type reactors
    BT3 gas cooled reactors
      BT4 reactors
    BT3 graphite moderated reactors
      BT4 reactors
  BT2 natural uranium reactors
    BT3 reactors
  BT2 power reactors
    BT3 reactors
BT1 plutonium production reactors
  BT2 production reactors
    BT3 reactors
BT1 thermal reactors
  BT2 reactors

CHAPELCROSS-3 REACTOR [12; 12]
(Annan, Scotland, UK)
BT1 carbon dioxide cooled reactors
  BT2 gas cooled reactors
    BT3 reactors
BT1 magnox type reactors
  BT2 gcr type reactors
    BT3 gas cooled reactors
      BT4 reactors
    BT3 graphite moderated reactors
      BT4 reactors
  BT2 natural uranium reactors
    BT3 reactors
  BT2 power reactors
    BT3 reactors
BT1 plutonium production reactors
  BT2 production reactors
    BT3 reactors
BT1 thermal reactors
  BT2 reactors

CHAPELCROSS-4 REACTOR [13; 13]
(Annan, Scotland, UK)
BT1 carbon dioxide cooled reactors
  BT2 gas cooled reactors
    BT3 reactors
BT1 magnox type reactors
  BT2 gcr type reactors
    BT3 gas cooled reactors
      BT4 reactors
    BT3 graphite moderated reactors
      BT4 reactors
  BT2 natural uranium reactors
    BT3 reactors
  BT2 power reactors
    BT3 reactors
BT1 plutonium production reactors
  BT2 production reactors
    BT3 reactors
BT1 thermal reactors
  BT2 reactors

CHAPMAN-ENSKOG THEORY
[147; 147]
RT transport theory

CHAPMAN-FERRARO PROBLEM
[11; 11]
RT solar wind
RT transport theory

CHAPMAN-KOLMOGOROV
EQUATION [133; 133]
(A set of equations used in the theory of stochastic processes, giving the state of a system as a probability distribution at a certain time in terms of the known states at previous times.)
UF *kolmogorov equation*
BT1 equations
RT markov process
RT stochastic processes

CHARCOAL [579; 579]
RT activated carbon

CHARGE CARRIERS [2,092; 2,092]
RT carrier density
RT carrier lifetime
RT carrier mobility
RT dember effect
RT electric charges
RT electron-hole droplets
RT electrons
RT holes

CHARGE COLLECTION [360; 360]
RT charge transport
RT charged particles
RT electric charges

charge conjugation invariance
USE c invariance

CHARGE CONSERVATION [169; 169]
UF *conservation (charge)*
RT electric charges
RT gauge invariance

CHARGE DENSITY [2,161; 2,161]
May 76
UF *density (charge)*
RT electric charges
RT energy density

CHARGE DISTRIBUTION [1,609; 1,609]
Dec 75
(Not for CHARGE STATES. Prior to January 1983 this concept was indexed by coordination of ELECTRIC CHARGES and SPATIAL DISTRIBUTION.)
RT electric charges
RT electrostatics
RT ion beams
RT multiple production
RT nuclear radii
RT space charge
RT spatial distribution

CHARGE EXCHANGE [4,931; 4,931]
UF *exchange (charge)*
RT beam neutralization
RT beam strippers
RT electron capture
RT electron loss
RT hydrogen transfer
RT ionization
RT plasma potential

CHARGE INDEPENDENCE [284; 284]
BT1 invariance principles
RT nucleons
RT strong interactions

CHARGE PLUNGER METHOD [74; 74]
Aug 78
(Method for the determination of lifetimes of nuclear levels.)
UF *plunger method*
UF *recoil distance method*
BT1 counting techniques
RT lifetime
RT time-of-flight method

charge radius (nuclear)
USE nuclear radii

charge radius (particle)
USE particle radii

CHARGE RENORMALIZATION
[144; 144]
BT1 renormalization
RT electrodynamics

charge state distributions
USE charge states

CHARGE STATES [834; 834] *Jun 84*
(NOT for electric batteries.)
UF *charge state distributions*
RT beam strippers
RT charged particles
RT electric charges
RT electron capture
RT electron loss
RT ionization
RT ions

CHARGE TRANSPORT [610; 610]
RT charge collection
RT electric charges

CHARGE-COUPLED DEVICES
[868; 868] *Sep 79*
(Semiconductor devices arrayed so that the electric charge at the output of one provides the input stimulus to the next.)
UF *ccd*
BT1 semiconductor devices

CHARGE-EXCHANGE INTERACTIONS
[1,345; 1,345]
BT1 strong interactions
  BT2 basic interactions
  BT2 interactions
RT cluster emission model

CHARGE-EXCHANGE REACTIONS
[3,252; 3,252]
- BT1 nuclear reactions

CHARGED CURRENTS [327; 807]
Aug 76
- BT1 algebraic currents
- BT2 currents
- NT1 weak charged currents
- RT charged-current interactions
- RT electromagnetic interactions
- RT neutral currents
- RT weak interactions

charged particle activation an
- USE charged-particle activation an

CHARGED PARTICLE DETECTION
[1,176; 8,316]
- UF *charged-particle detection*
- BT1 radiation detection
- BT2 detection
- NT1 acoustic detection
- NT1 alpha detection
- NT1 beta detection
- NT1 electron detection
- NT1 ion detection
- NT1 muon detection
- NT1 positron detection
- NT1 proton detection
- RT cosmic ray detection
- RT fission fragment detection
- RT radiation detectors
- RT radiation length
- RT superconducting colloid detect

charged particle precipitation
- USE charged-particle precipitation

charged particle transport
- USE charged-particle transport

charged particle transport the
- USE charged-particle transport the

CHARGED PARTICLES [6,939; 122,157]
(In addition to the specific charged particles listed below, see also the list under ELEMENTARY PARTICLES.)
- NT1 beta particles
- NT1 deuterons
- NT2 antideuterons
- NT1 ions
- NT2 actinium ions
- NT2 aluminium ions
- NT2 americium ions
- NT2 anions
-   NT3 heteropolyanions
-   NT3 hydrogen ions 1 minus
- NT2 antimony ions
- NT2 argon ions
- NT2 arsenic ions
- NT2 astatine ions
- NT2 atomic ions
- NT2 barium ions
- NT2 berkelium ions
- NT2 beryllium ions
- NT2 bismuth ions
- NT2 boron ions
- NT2 bromine ions
- NT2 cadmium ions
- NT2 calcium ions
- NT2 californium ions
- NT2 carbon ions
- NT2 cations
-   NT3 hydrogen ions 1 plus
-   *NT4 protons
-   NT3 hydrogen ions 2 plus
-   NT3 hydrogen ions 3 plus
- NT2 cerium ions
- NT2 cesium ions
- NT2 chlorine ions
- NT2 chromium ions
- NT2 cobalt ions
- NT2 copper ions
- NT2 curium ions
- NT2 deuterium ions
- NT2 dysprosium ions
- NT2 einsteinium ions
- NT2 erbium ions
- NT2 europium ions
- NT2 fermium ions
- NT2 fluorine ions
- NT2 francium ions
- NT2 gadolinium ions
- NT2 gallium ions
- NT2 germanium ions
- NT2 gold ions
- NT2 hafnium ions
- NT2 heavy ions
- NT2 helium ions
-   NT3 alpha particles
-    NT4 cosmic alpha particles
-    NT4 delayed alpha particles
-    NT4 solar alpha particles
-   NT3 helium ash
- NT2 holmium ions
- NT2 hydrogen ions
-   NT3 hydrogen ions 1 minus
-   NT3 hydrogen ions 1 plus
-   *NT4 protons
-   NT3 hydrogen ions 2 plus
-   NT3 hydrogen ions 3 plus
- NT2 indium ions
- NT2 iodine ions
- NT2 iridium ions
- NT2 iron ions
- NT2 krypton ions
- NT2 lanthanum ions
- NT2 lead ions
- NT2 light ions
- NT2 lithium ions
- NT2 lutetium ions
- NT2 magnesium ions
- NT2 manganese ions
- NT2 mendelevium ions
- NT2 mercury ions
- NT2 molecular ions
-   NT3 hydrogen ions 2 plus
-   NT3 hydrogen ions 3 plus
-   NT3 oxonium ions
- NT2 molybdenum ions
- NT2 multicharged ions
- NT2 muonic ions
- NT2 neodymium ions
- NT2 neon ions
- NT2 neptunium ions
- NT2 nickel ions
- NT2 niobium ions
- NT2 nitrogen ions
- NT2 nobelium ions
- NT2 osmium ions
- NT2 oxygen ions
- NT2 palladium ions
- NT2 phosphorus ions
- NT2 platinum ions
- NT2 plutonium ions
- NT2 polonium ions
- NT2 potassium ions
- NT2 praseodymium ions
- NT2 promethium ions
- NT2 protactinium ions
- NT2 radium ions
- NT2 radon ions
- NT2 rhenium ions
- NT2 rhodium ions
- NT2 rubidium ions
- NT2 ruthenium ions
- NT2 samarium ions
- NT2 scandium ions
- NT2 selenium ions
- NT2 silicon ions
- NT2 silver ions
- NT2 sodium ions
- NT2 strontium ions
- NT2 sulfur ions
- NT2 tantalum ions
- NT2 technetium ions
- NT2 tellurium ions
- NT2 terbium ions
- NT2 thallium ions
- NT2 thorium ions
- NT2 thulium ions
- NT2 tin ions
- NT2 titanium ions
- NT2 tritium ions
- NT2 tungsten ions
- NT2 uranium ions
- NT2 vanadium ions
- NT2 xenon ions
- NT2 ytterbium ions
- NT2 yttrium ions
- NT2 zinc ions
- NT2 zirconium ions
- NT1 tritons
- NT2 antitritons
- RT charge collection
- RT charge states
- RT charged-particle precipitation
- RT charged-particle transport
- RT charged-particle transport the
- RT guiding-center approximation
- RT ion beams
- RT lorentz force
- RT ponderomotive force
- RT stoermer theory
- RT test particles

CHARGED-CURRENT INTERACTION
[1,539; 1,539] *Aug 76*
- BT1 particle interactions
- BT2 interactions
- RT basic interactions
- RT charged currents

CHARGED-PARTICLE ACTIVATION AN [437; 437] *Feb 76*
(For the process.)
- UF *analysis (charged-particle act*
- UF *charged particle activation an*
- BT1 activation analysis
- BT2 nondestructive analysis
- BT3 chemical analysis

charged-particle detection
- USE charged particle detection

CHARGED-PARTICLE PRECIPITATION [338; 1,362]
- UF *charged particle precipitation*
- NT1 electron precipitation
- NT1 proton precipitation
- RT aurorae
- RT auroral oval
- RT charged particles
- RT midday aurorae
- RT radiation belts

CHARGED-PARTICLE TRANSPORT
[3,403; 3,567]
- UF *charged particle transport*
- UF *transport (charged-particle)*
- BT1 radiation transport
- NT1 proton transport
- RT charged particles
- RT charged-particle transport the
- RT energy deposition

CHARGED-PARTICLE TRANSPORT THE [570; 570]
- UF *charged particle transport the*
- BT1 transport theory
- RT charged particles
- RT charged-particle transport
- RT elementary particles

§§ CHARGES [1,001; 1,001]
- UF *assessments*
- UF *fees*
- UF *prices*
- UF+ *peak-load pricing*
- RT cost
- RT cost overruns
- RT income
- RT invoices

charging (fission reactor)
- USE reactor fueling

charging (fusion reactor)
  USE   thermonuclear reactor fueling

charging machines (fiss react)
  USE   reactor charging machines

CHARIOT EVENT [0; 0]
  BT1   plowshare project
  RT   harbors

CHARM PARTICLES [3,164; 4,367]
  BT1   elementary particles
  NT1   charmed baryons
    NT2   lambda c plus baryons
    NT2   omega c neutral baryons
    NT2   sigma c-2450 baryons
    NT2   xi c plus baryons
  NT1   charmed mesons
    NT2   d mesons
      NT3   d minus mesons
      NT3   d neutral mesons
        NT4   anti-d neutral mesons
      NT3   d plus mesons
    NT2   d s mesons
    NT2   d*-2010 mesons
    NT2   d*-2420 mesons
    NT2   d*s-2110 mesons
  RT   charmonium
  RT   hadrons
  RT   hypercharge
  RT   isospin
  RT   quark model
  RT   su-3 groups

charmed baryon resonances
(Prior to December 1987 this was a valid descriptor.)
  USE   charmed baryons

CHARMED BARYONS [279; 540]
Aug 78
(Prior to December 1987 this concept was indexed by CHARMED BARYON RESONANCES.)
  UF   *charmed baryon resonances*
  BT1   baryons
    BT2   fermions
    BT2   hadrons
      BT3   elementary particles
  BT1   charm particles
    BT2   elementary particles
  NT1   lambda c plus baryons
  NT1   omega c neutral baryons
  NT1   sigma c-2450 baryons
  NT1   xi c plus baryons

charmed meson resonances
(Prior to December 1987 this was a valid descriptor.)
  USE   charmed mesons

CHARMED MESONS [141; 753] *Dec 87*
  UF   *charmed meson resonances*
  UF   *d resonances*
  BT1   charm particles
    BT2   elementary particles
  BT1   mesons
    BT2   bosons
    BT2   hadrons
      BT3   elementary particles
  NT1   d mesons
    NT2   d minus mesons
    NT2   d neutral mesons
      NT3   anti-d neutral mesons
    NT2   d plus mesons
  NT1   d s mesons
  NT1   d*-2010 mesons
  NT1   d*-2420 mesons
  NT1   d*s-2110 mesons

CHARMONIUM [934; 1,483] *Aug 76*
(A bound state of charm and anticharm quarks.)
  BT1   mesons
    BT2   bosons
    BT2   hadrons
      BT3   elementary particles
  BT1   quarkonium
  NT1   chi0-3415 mesons
  NT1   chi1-3510 mesons
  NT1   chi2-3555 mesons
  NT1   eta c-2980 mesons
  NT1   eta c-3590 mesons
  NT1   j psi-3097 mesons
  NT1   psi-3685 mesons
  NT1   psi-3770 mesons
  NT1   psi-4030 mesons
  NT1   psi-4160 mesons
  NT1   psi-4415 mesons
  RT   charm particles
  RT   flavor model
  RT   muonium
  RT   positronium

charpak chambers
  USE   multiwire proportional chamber

CHARPY TEST [838; 838]
  BT1   destructive testing
    BT2   materials testing
      BT3   testing
  BT1   impact tests
    BT2   mechanical tests
      BT3   materials testing
        BT4   testing

→ CHARS [0; 0] *Sep 91*
  UF   *coal chars*
  BT1   pyrolysis products
  RT   by-products
  RT   coal

charts
  USE   diagrams

CHATTANOOGA FORMATION [10; 10]
Mar 77
  UF   *chattanooga shale*
  BT1   geologic formations
  RT   uranium deposits
  RT   uranium ores

chattanooga shale
  USE   chattanooga formation

CHEESE [30; 30]
  BT1   milk products
    BT2   food

CHELATES [1,851; 1,851]
  BT1   complexes
  RT   chelating agents

CHELATING AGENTS [1,549; 7,809]
  NT1   acetylacetone
  NT1   bal
  NT1   cdta
  NT1   cpdta
  NT1   dcta
  NT1   dedtc
  NT1   deferoxamine
  NT1   dithizone
  NT1   dtpa
  NT1   eddha
  NT1   edta
  NT1   egta
  NT1   hedta
  NT1   heida
  NT1   hmdta
  NT1   mdpa
  NT1   nta
  NT1   penicillamine
  NT1   tda
  NT1   tetaha
  NT1   tna
  NT1   toa
  NT1   tridodecylamine
  RT   chelates
  RT   decontamination
  RT   drugs

chem. eff. of nucl. transform.
  USE   hot atom chemistry

CHEMICAL ACTIVATION [903; 903]
  UF   *activation (chemical)*
  RT   activation energy
  RT   excitation

chemical activity
  USE   thermodynamic activity

CHEMICAL ANALYSIS [5,306; 50,355]
  UF   *content analysis*
  UF   *destructive chemical analysis*
  UF   *determination (chemical)*
  UF+   *esca*
  NT1   ion selective electrode analys
  NT1   multi-element analysis
  NT1   nondestructive analysis
    NT2   activation analysis
      NT3   charged-particle activation an
      NT3   neutron activation analysis
      NT3   photon activation analysis
    NT2   delayed neutron analysis
    NT2   deuteron microprobe analysis
    NT2   electron microprobe analysis
    NT2   ion microprobe analysis
    NT2   ion scattering analysis
    NT2   nuclear reaction analysis
    NT2   proton microprobe analysis
    NT2   radiation absorption analysis
    NT2   radiation scattering analysis
    NT2   x-ray emission analysis
      NT3   pixe analysis
      NT3   x-ray fluorescence analysis
  NT1   qualitative chemical analysis
  NT1   quantitative chemical analysis
    NT2   gravimetric analysis
      NT3   thermal gravimetric analysis
    NT2   radio-release analysis
    NT2   radiometric analysis
    NT2   volumetric analysis
  RT   carbon meters
  RT   crime detection
  RT   hydrogen meters
  RT   ion probes
  RT   oxygen meters
  RT   post-irradiation examination
  RT   sulfur meters
  RT   tritium meters
  RT   water chemistry

CHEMICAL BONDS [5,763; 5,859]
  NT1   double bonds
  RT   adducts
  RT   binding energy
  RT   bond angle
  RT   bond lengths
  RT   dna adducts

CHEMICAL COATING [104; 2,364]
  BT1   surface coating
    BT2   deposition
  NT1   chemical vapor deposition
  NT1   electrochemical coating
    NT2   anodization

§§ CHEMICAL COMPOSITION
[33,741; 33,741]
  UF   *abundance (chemical)*
  RT   cosmochemistry
  RT   element abundance
  RT   ionic composition
  RT   quantitative chemical analysis
  RT   stoichiometry
  RT   water chemistry

CHEMICAL DECLADDING [43; 43]
- BT1 decladding
- BT2 head end processes

CHEMICAL DOSEMETERS [655; 655]
- UF *fricke dosemeters*
- BT1 dosemeters
- BT2 measuring instruments
- RT chemical radiation detectors

CHEMICAL EFFLUENTS [727; 727]
Oct 75
- UF *effluents (chemical)*
- BT1 chemical wastes
- BT2 nonradioactive wastes
- BT3 nonradioactive waste managemen
- BT4 waste management
- BT5 management
- BT3 wastes
- RT gaseous wastes
- RT industrial wastes
- RT liquid wastes
- RT nonradioactive waste disposal
- RT particle resuspension
- RT pollutants
- RT pollution abatement
- RT stack disposal

CHEMICAL EXPLOSIONS [414; 416]
- UF *events (chemical explosions)*
- BT1 explosions
- NT1 cowboy event
- NT1 palanquin event
- NT1 pre-gondola i event
- NT1 pre-gondola ii event
- RT chemical explosives
- RT contained explosions
- RT cratering explosions
- RT essex i project
- RT explosive fracturing
- RT explosive stimulation

CHEMICAL EXPLOSIVES [231; 345]
- UF *high explosives*
- UF *shaped charges*
- BT1 explosives
- NT1 dynamite
- NT1 nitromethane
- NT1 petn
- NT1 tnt
- RT chemical explosions

CHEMICAL INDUSTRY [347; 347]
Oct 77
- BT1 industry

CHEMICAL LASERS [292; 301]
(The excitation process involves the making or breaking of a chemical bond.)
- BT1 lasers
- BT2 amplifiers
- BT3 equipment
- RT dye lasers

CHEMICAL MACHINING [13; 118]
- UF *chemical milling*
- BT1 machining
- NT1 electrochemical machining

chemical milling
- USE chemical machining

chemical mutagens
- USE mutagens

CHEMICAL POLISHING [125; 125]
- BT1 polishing
- BT2 surface finishing

CHEMICAL PREPARATION [22,290; 22,290]
- UF *preparation (chemical)*
- BT1 synthesis
- RT chemical reactions

CHEMICAL PROPERTIES [3,637; 3,637]
- RT affinity
- RT chemical reactions
- RT chemistry
- RT thermal degradation

CHEMICAL RADIATION DETECTORS [57; 57]
- BT1 radiation detectors
- BT2 measuring instruments
- RT chemical dosemeters

CHEMICAL RADIATION EFFECTS [9,116; 21,044]
- UF+ *radiation hardening (chemical)*
- UF+ *radiopolymerization*
- BT1 radiation effects
- NT1 lyoluminescence
- NT1 radiation curing
- NT1 radiolysis
- NT2 autoradiolysis
- RT host-cell reactivation
- RT radiation chemistry
- RT strand breaks

CHEMICAL REACTION KINETICS [23,363; 23,363]
- BT1 reaction kinetics
- BT2 kinetics
- NT1 combustion kinetics
- RT activation energy
- RT arrhenius equation
- RT catalysis
- RT enzyme activity
- RT reaction intermediates

CHEMICAL REACTION YIELD [5,457; 5,457]
- UF *yield (chemical reaction)*
- RT chemical reactions

CHEMICAL REACTIONS [13,512; 84,105]
- UF+ *ionic reactions*
- NT1 acylation
- NT2 acetylation
- NT2 benzoylation
- NT1 alkylation
- NT1 amination
- NT1 aromatization
- NT1 carbonylation
- NT1 carboxylation
- NT1 chemisorption
- NT1 claisen condensation
- NT1 corrosion
- NT2 crevice corrosion
- NT2 electrochemical corrosion
- NT2 fretting corrosion
- NT2 intergranular corrosion
- NT2 pitting corrosion
- NT2 scaling
- NT2 stress corrosion
- NT1 cyclization
- NT1 dealkylation
- NT1 deamination
- NT1 decarboxylation
- NT1 decarburization
- NT1 decomposition
- NT2 autolysis
- NT3 autoradiolysis
- NT2 biodegradation
- NT2 carbonization
- NT3 coking
- NT2 depolymerization
- NT2 glycolysis
- NT2 molysis
- NT2 photolysis
- NT2 proteolysis
- NT3 fibrinolysis
- NT2 pyrolysis
- NT3 calcination
- NT3 cracking
- NT2 radiolysis
- NT3 autoradiolysis
- NT2 solvolysis
- NT3 acetolysis
- NT3 ammonolysis
- NT3 hydrolysis
- NT4 saponification
- NT1 dehalogenation
- NT2 dechlorination
- NT2 deiodination
- NT1 dehydrogenation
- NT1 denitration
- NT1 desulfurization
- NT1 deuteration
- NT1 diazotization
- NT1 diels-alder reaction
- NT1 esterification
- NT1 fischer-tropsch synthesis
- NT1 friedel-crafts reaction
- NT1 halogenation
- NT2 astatination
- NT2 bromination
- NT2 chlorination
- NT3 sulfochlorination
- NT2 fluorination
- NT2 iodination
- NT1 hydration
- NT1 hydrogenation
- NT1 hydroxylation
- NT1 isomerization
- NT1 methylation
- NT1 nitration
- NT1 nitridation
- NT1 oxidation
- NT2 combustion
- NT3 cocombustion
- NT3 fluidized-bed combustion
- NT2 roasting
- NT1 phosphorylation
- NT1 photosynthesis
- NT1 polymerization
- NT2 copolymerization
- NT2 cross-linking
- NT2 dimerization
- NT2 telomerization
- NT1 reduction
- NT2 bomb reduction
- NT2 thermite process
- NT1 sulfidation
- NT1 sulfonation
- NT2 sulfochlorination
- RT acidification
- RT affinity
- RT catalysis
- RT chemical preparation
- RT chemical properties
- RT chemical reaction yield
- RT chemical reactors
- RT chemical state
- RT chemistry
- RT detonation waves
- RT detoxification
- RT equilibrium
- RT fermentation
- RT fluidized beds
- RT fuel-cladding interactions
- RT fuel-coolant interactions
- RT hydrogen transfer
- RT isotopic exchange
- RT molten metal-water reactions
- RT reaction intermediates
- RT rock-fluid interactions
- RT seed-slag interactions
- RT stoichiometry
- RT thermodynamic activity
- RT waste-rock interactions

CHEMICAL REACTORS [223; 223]
Dec 85
- UF *vessels (chemical reactions)*
- RT bioreactors
- RT chemical reactions
- RT containers
- RT fluidized beds

CHEMICAL SHIFT [2,741; 2,741]
   RT   nuclear magnetic resonance
   RT   spectral shift

chemical shimming
   USE fluid poison control

CHEMICAL SPILLS [0; 0] *Sep 91*
   BT1 accidents
   RT   chemical wastes
   RT   hazardous materials spills

CHEMICAL STATE [1,399; 1,399]
   UF   *speciation (chemical)*
   RT   anions
   RT   cations
   RT   chemical reactions
   RT   recoils

CHEMICAL VAPOR DEPOSITION [1,863; 1,863]
   BT1 chemical coating
     BT2 surface coating
       BT3 deposition
   RT   vapor deposited coatings
   RT   vapor plating

CHEMICAL WASTES [199; 445] *Jul 86*
(For wastes which are of concern because of their chemical properties. See also RADIOACTIVE WASTES.)
   UF   *waste chemicals*
   BT1 nonradioactive wastes
     BT2 nonradioactive waste managemen
       BT3 waste management
         BT4 management
     BT2 wastes
   NT1 chemical effluents
   RT   chemical spills
   RT   industrial wastes
   RT   municipal wastes

chemicals
(See specific compounds or classes of compounds, e.g., CARCINOGENS, DETERGENTS, PLASTICIZERS, and ORGANIC COMPOUNDS.)
   SEE pigments

CHEMILUMINESCENCE [536; 556]
   BT1 luminescence
     BT2 photon emission
       BT3 emission
   NT1 bioluminescence

CHEMISORPTION [2,384; 2,384]
(Dissolution or adsorption followed by chemical reaction.)
   SF   sorption
   BT1 chemical reactions
   BT1 separation processes
   RT   adsorbents
   RT   adsorption
   RT   scrubbing

CHEMISTRY [1,282; 17,483]
   NT1 atmospheric chemistry
   NT1 biochemistry
     NT2 blood chemistry
   NT1 cosmochemistry
   NT1 petrochemistry
   NT1 photochemistry
   NT1 physical chemistry
   NT1 radiation chemistry
   NT1 radiochemistry
     NT2 hot atom chemistry
       NT3 szilard-chalmers reaction
   RT   chemical properties
   RT   chemical reactions
   RT   nuclear chemistry
   RT   qualitative chemical analysis
   RT   quantitative chemical analysis
   RT   stoichiometry

CHEMONUCLEAR REACTORS [33; 33]
   BT1 irradiation reactors
     BT2 reactors

CHEMORECEPTORS [18; 18]
   RT   flavor
   RT   insects
   RT   odor
   RT   sense organs

CHEMOSTERILANTS [28; 28]
(A substance producing irreversible sterility in a reproductive system.)
   RT   alkylating agents
   RT   antimetabolites
   RT   sterilization

CHEMOTHERAPY [4,789; 4,789]
   UF   *pharmacotherapy*
   BT1 therapy
     BT2 medicine
   RT   antiandrogens
   RT   drugs
   RT   liposomes
   RT   misonidazole
   RT   neocarcinostatin

cheralite
   USE quartzites

CHERENKOV COUNTERS [2,109; 2,109]
   UF   *cherenkov detectors*
   BT1 radiation detectors
     BT2 measuring instruments

cherenkov detectors
   USE cherenkov counters

CHERENKOV RADIATION [1,424; 1,424]
   UF   *vavilov-cherenkov radiation*
   BT1 electromagnetic radiation
     BT2 radiations
   RT   light cone

CHERNOBYLSK-1 REACTOR [43; 43] *Aug 84*
   BT1 enriched uranium reactors
     BT2 reactors
   BT1 lwgr type reactors
     BT2 graphite moderated reactors
       BT3 reactors
     BT2 water cooled reactors
       BT3 reactors
   BT1 power reactors
     BT2 reactors
   BT1 thermal reactors
     BT2 reactors

CHERNOBYLSK-2 REACTOR [30; 30] *Aug 84*
   BT1 enriched uranium reactors
     BT2 reactors
   BT1 lwgr type reactors
     BT2 graphite moderated reactors
       BT3 reactors
     BT2 water cooled reactors
       BT3 reactors
   BT1 power reactors
     BT2 reactors
   BT1 thermal reactors
     BT2 reactors

CHERNOBYLSK-3 REACTOR [35; 35] *Aug 84*
   BT1 enriched uranium reactors
     BT2 reactors
   BT1 lwgr type reactors
     BT2 graphite moderated reactors
       BT3 reactors
     BT2 water cooled reactors
       BT3 reactors
   BT1 power reactors
     BT2 reactors
   BT1 thermal reactors
     BT2 reactors

CHERNOBYLSK-4 REACTOR [3,076; 3,076] *Aug 84*
   BT1 enriched uranium reactors
     BT2 reactors
   BT1 lwgr type reactors
     BT2 graphite moderated reactors
       BT3 reactors
     BT2 water cooled reactors
       BT3 reactors
   BT1 power reactors
     BT2 reactors
   BT1 thermal reactors
     BT2 reactors

CHEROKEE-1 REACTOR [12; 12]
(In Cherokee County, South Carolina, USA.)
   BT1 pwr type reactors
     BT2 enriched uranium reactors
       BT3 reactors
     BT2 power reactors
       BT3 reactors
     BT2 thermal reactors
       BT3 reactors
     BT2 water cooled reactors
       BT3 reactors
     BT2 water moderated reactors
       BT3 reactors

CHEROKEE-2 REACTOR [8; 8]
(In Cherokee County, South Carolina, USA.)
   BT1 pwr type reactors
     BT2 enriched uranium reactors
       BT3 reactors
     BT2 power reactors
       BT3 reactors
     BT2 thermal reactors
       BT3 reactors
     BT2 water cooled reactors
       BT3 reactors
     BT2 water moderated reactors
       BT3 reactors

CHEROKEE-3 REACTOR [8; 8]
(In Cherokee County, South Carolina, USA.)
   BT1 pwr type reactors
     BT2 enriched uranium reactors
       BT3 reactors
     BT2 power reactors
       BT3 reactors
     BT2 thermal reactors
       BT3 reactors
     BT2 water cooled reactors
       BT3 reactors
     BT2 water moderated reactors
       BT3 reactors

CHERRIES [34; 34]
   BT1 fruits
     BT2 food
   RT   fruit trees

cherry fruit fly
   USE rhagoletis cerasi

CHESAPEAKE BAY [78; 78]
   BT1 atlantic ocean
     BT2 seas
       BT3 surface waters

CHEST [2,985; 3,833]
   UF   *thorax*
   BT1 body areas
     BT2 body
   NT1 mediastinum
   RT   diaphragm
   RT   heart
   RT   lungs
   RT   mammary glands
   RT   pleura
   RT   respiratory system

RT　thymus

CHESTNUTS [6; 6] *Jan 82*
BT1　nuts
　BT2　fruits
　　BT3　food

CHEW-LOW METHOD [171; 171]
RT　strong interactions

CHI B0-10235 MESONS [6; 6] *Dec 87*
BT1　bottomonium
　BT2　mesons
　　BT3　bosons
　　BT3　hadrons
　　　BT4　elementary particles
　BT2　quarkonium

CHI B0-9860 MESONS [10; 10] *Dec 87*
BT1　bottomonium
　BT2　mesons
　　BT3　bosons
　　BT3　hadrons
　　　BT4　elementary particles
　BT2　quarkonium

CHI B1-10255 MESONS [10; 10] *Dec 87*
BT1　bottomonium
　BT2　mesons
　　BT3　bosons
　　BT3　hadrons
　　　BT4　elementary particles
　BT2　quarkonium

CHI B1-9895 MESONS [8; 8] *Dec 87*
BT1　bottomonium
　BT2　mesons
　　BT3　bosons
　　BT3　hadrons
　　　BT4　elementary particles
　BT2　quarkonium

CHI B2-10270 MESONS [7; 7] *Dec 87*
BT1　bottomonium
　BT2　mesons
　　BT3　bosons
　　BT3　hadrons
　　　BT4　elementary particles
　BT2　quarkonium

CHI B2-9915 MESONS [6; 6] *Dec 87*
BT1　bottomonium
　BT2　mesons
　　BT3　bosons
　　BT3　hadrons
　　　BT4　elementary particles
　BT2　quarkonium

chi resonances
(Prior to December 1987 this was a valid descriptor.)
USE　mesons

chi-2800 resonances
(Prior to December 1987 this was a valid descriptor.)
USE　mesons

chi-3410 resonances
(Prior to December 1987 this was a valid descriptor.)
USE　chi0-3415 mesons

chi-3455 resonances
(Prior to December 1987 this was a valid descriptor.)
USE　mesons

chi-3500 resonances
(Prior to December 1987 this was a valid descriptor.)
USE　chi1-3510 mesons

chi-3550 resonances
(Prior to December 1987 this was a valid descriptor.)
USE　chi2-3555 mesons

CHICAGO CYCLOTRON [5; 5]
BT1　isochronous cyclotrons
　BT2　cyclotrons
　　BT3　cyclic accelerators
　　　BT4　accelerators

chicago pile-2 reactor
USE　cp-2 reactor

CHICAGO SYNCHROCYCLOTRON [1; 1]
BT1　synchrocyclotrons
　BT2　cyclic accelerators
　　BT3　accelerators

CHICKENS [1,096; 1,096]
UF　hens
BT1　fowl
　BT2　birds
　　BT3　vertebrates
　　　BT4　animals
RT　ascaridae
RT　syngamus

CHILDREN [4,782; 6,269]
BT1　man
　BT2　primates
　　BT3　mammals
　　　BT4　vertebrates
　　　　BT5　animals
NT1　infants
RT　adolescents
RT　age groups
RT　education
RT　juveniles
RT　life cycle
RT　pediatrics
RT　progeny

CHILE [123; 123]
BT1　developing countries
BT1　south america
　BT2　latin america

CHIMERAS [87; 490]
BT1　mosaicism
NT1　radiation chimeras
RT　immunity
RT　spleen colony formation
RT　transplants

CHIMNEYS [42; 42] *Aug 75*
(Limited to pipelike vents in the earth. For gas disposal use STACKS.)
BT1　cavities
RT　explosive stimulation
RT　underground explosions

CHINA [1,466; 1,466]
BT1　asia
RT　centrally planned economies

china clay
USE　kaolin

chinese bean oil
USE　soybean oil

chinese hamster
USE　hamsters

chinese hamster ovary cells
USE　cho cells

CHINESE ORGANIZATIONS [8; 8] *May 87*
BT1　national organizations

CHINON-1 REACTOR [21; 21]
(Avoine, Chinon, France)
UF　*edf-1 reactor*
BT1　gcr type reactors
　BT2　gas cooled reactors
　　BT3　reactors
　BT2　graphite moderated reactors
　　BT3　reactors
BT1　power reactors
　BT2　reactors
BT1　thermal reactors
　BT2　reactors

CHINON-2 REACTOR [30; 30]
(Avoine, Chinon, France)
UF　*edf-2 reactor*
BT1　gcr type reactors
　BT2　gas cooled reactors
　　BT3　reactors
　BT2　graphite moderated reactors
　　BT3　reactors
BT1　power reactors
　BT2　reactors
BT1　thermal reactors
　BT2　reactors

CHINON-3 REACTOR [48; 48]
(Avoine, Chinon, France)
UF　*edf-3 reactor*
BT1　gcr type reactors
　BT2　gas cooled reactors
　　BT3　reactors
　BT2　graphite moderated reactors
　　BT3　reactors
BT1　power reactors
　BT2　reactors
BT1　thermal reactors
　BT2　reactors

chinone
USE　benzoquinones

→ **CHINSHAN-1 REACTOR** [23; 23]
(Taipei, Taiwan. This descriptor was spelled QINSHAN-1 REACTOR for items input in 1991, and prior to 1991 was spelled CHINSAN-1 REACTOR.)
BT1　bwr type reactors
　BT2　enriched uranium reactors
　　BT3　reactors
　BT2　power reactors
　　BT3　reactors
　BT2　thermal reactors
　　BT3　reactors
　BT2　water cooled reactors
　　BT3　reactors
　BT2　water moderated reactors
　　BT3　reactors

→ **CHINSHAN-2 REACTOR** [15; 15]
(Taipei, Taiwan. This descriptor was spelled QINSHAN-2 REACTOR for items input in 1991, and prior to 1991 was spelled CHINSAN-2 REACTOR.)
BT1　bwr type reactors
　BT2　enriched uranium reactors
　　BT3　reactors
　BT2　power reactors
　　BT3　reactors
　BT2　thermal reactors
　　BT3　reactors
　BT2　water cooled reactors
　　BT3　reactors
　BT2　water moderated reactors
　　BT3　reactors

CHIPMUNKS [10; 10]
  BT1   rodents
    BT2   mammals
      BT3   vertebrates
        BT4   animals
  RT   squirrels

CHIRAL SYMMETRY [4,805; 4,805]
  BT1   symmetry
  RT   chirality

CHIRALITY [3,095; 3,095]
  BT1   particle properties
  RT   angular momentum
  RT   chiral symmetry
  RT   helicity
  RT   quantum mechanics
  RT   spin

CHITIN [43; 43]
  BT1   mucopolysaccharides
    BT2   amines
      BT3   organic compounds
    BT2   polysaccharides
      BT3   saccharides
        BT4   carbohydrates
          BT5   organic compounds
  RT   glucosamine
  RT   polyacetals

CHI0-3415 MESONS [64; 64] *Nov 76*
(Prior to December 1987 this concept was indexed by CHI-3410 RESONANCES.)
  UF   *chi-3410 resonances*
  BT1   charmonium
    BT2   mesons
      BT3   bosons
      BT3   hadrons
        BT4   elementary particles
    BT2   quarkonium
  BT1   scalar mesons
    BT2   mesons
      BT3   bosons
      BT3   hadrons
        BT4   elementary particles

CHI1-3510 MESONS [73; 73] *Oct 77*
(Prior to December 1987 this concept was indexed by CHI-3500 RESONANCES.)
  UF   *chi-3500 resonances*
  BT1   axial vector mesons
    BT2   mesons
      BT3   bosons
      BT3   hadrons
        BT4   elementary particles
  BT1   charmonium
    BT2   mesons
      BT3   bosons
      BT3   hadrons
        BT4   elementary particles
    BT2   quarkonium

CHI2-3555 MESONS [80; 80] *Sep 77*
(Prior to December 1987 this concept was indexed by CHI-3550 RESONANCES.)
  UF   *chi-3550 resonances*
  BT1   charmonium
    BT2   mesons
      BT3   bosons
      BT3   hadrons
        BT4   elementary particles
    BT2   quarkonium
  BT1   tensor mesons
    BT2   mesons
      BT3   bosons
      BT3   hadrons
        BT4   elementary particles

CHLAMYDOMONAS [131; 131]
  BT1   unicellular algae
    BT2   algae
      BT3   plants
    BT2   microorganisms

CHLORAL [17; 17]
  UF   *trichloroacetaldehyde*
  BT1   aldehydes
    BT2   organic compounds
  BT1   organic chlorine compounds
    BT2   organic halogen compounds
      BT3   organic compounds
  RT   acetaldehyde

chlorambucil
  USE   alkylating agents

chloramine-b
  USE   chloramines

chloramine-t
  USE   chloramines

CHLORAMINES [251; 251]
  UF   *chloramine-b*
  UF   *chloramine-t*
  BT1   amines
    BT2   organic compounds
  BT1   organic chlorine compounds
    BT2   organic halogen compounds
      BT3   organic compounds
  RT   amides
  RT   sulfonic acids

CHLORAMPHENICOL [195; 195]
  BT1   antibiotics
    BT2   drugs
    BT2   organic compounds

CHLORANIL [15; 15]
  UF   *tetrachlorobenzoquinone*
  BT1   benzoquinones
    BT2   quinones
      BT3   aromatics
        BT4   organic compounds
      BT3   organic oxygen compounds
        BT4   organic compounds
  BT1   organic chlorine compounds
    BT2   organic halogen compounds
      BT3   organic compounds
  RT   chloranilic acid

CHLORANILIC ACID [3; 3]
  BT1   benzoquinones
    BT2   quinones
      BT3   aromatics
        BT4   organic compounds
      BT3   organic oxygen compounds
        BT4   organic compounds
  RT   chloranil
  RT   organic acids

CHLORATES [277; 277]
(Specific compounds should be indexed by coordination of a descriptor of the form (CATION) COMPOUNDS and the above anion descriptor.)
  BT1   chlorine compounds
    BT2   halogen compounds
  BT1   oxygen compounds
  RT   chloric acid

CHLORELLA [166; 166]
  BT1   unicellular algae
    BT2   algae
      BT3   plants
    BT2   microorganisms

CHLORIC ACID [82; 82]
  BT1   chlorine compounds
    BT2   halogen compounds
  BT1   inorganic acids
    BT2   hydrogen compounds
    BT2   inorganic compounds
  BT1   oxygen compounds
  RT   chlorates

CHLORIDE VOLATILITY PROCESS [31; 31]
  BT1   pyrometallurgy
    BT2   extractive metallurgy
      BT3   metallurgy
  BT1   reprocessing
    BT2   separation processes
  RT   distillation
  RT   refining
  RT   volatility

CHLORIDES [3,055; 16,811]
  BT1   chlorine compounds
    BT2   halogen compounds
  BT1   halides
    BT2   halogen compounds
  NT1   actinium chlorides
  NT1   aluminium chlorides
  NT1   americium chlorides
  NT1   ammonium chlorides
  NT1   antimony chlorides
  NT1   argon chlorides
  NT1   arsenic chlorides
  NT1   astatine chlorides
  NT1   barium chlorides
  NT1   berkelium chlorides
  NT1   beryllium chlorides
  NT1   bismuth chlorides
  NT1   boron chlorides
  NT1   bromine chlorides
  NT1   cadmium chlorides
  NT1   calcium chlorides
  NT1   californium chlorides
  NT1   cerium chlorides
  NT1   cesium chlorides
  NT1   chromium chlorides
  NT1   cobalt chlorides
  NT1   copper chlorides
  NT1   curium chlorides
  NT1   dysprosium chlorides
  NT1   einsteinium chlorides
  NT1   element 104 chlorides
  NT1   erbium chlorides
  NT1   europium chlorides
  NT1   fermium chlorides
  NT1   francium chlorides
  NT1   gadolinium chlorides
  NT1   gallium chlorides
  NT1   germanium chlorides
  NT1   gold chlorides
  NT1   hafnium chlorides
  NT1   helium chlorides
  NT1   holmium chlorides
  NT1   indium chlorides
  NT1   iodine chlorides
  NT1   iridium chlorides
  NT1   iron chlorides
  NT1   krypton chlorides
  NT1   lanthanum chlorides
  NT1   lawrencium chlorides
  NT1   lead chlorides
  NT1   lithium chlorides
  NT1   lutetium chlorides
  NT1   magnesium chlorides
  NT1   manganese chlorides
  NT1   mercury chlorides
  NT1   methylene blue
  NT1   molybdenum chlorides
  NT1   neodymium chlorides
  NT1   neon chlorides
  NT1   neptunium chlorides
  NT1   nickel chlorides
  NT1   niobium chlorides
  NT1   nitrogen chlorides
  NT1   nobelium chlorides
  NT1   osmium chlorides
  NT1   palladium chlorides
  NT1   phosphorus chlorides
  NT1   platinum chlorides
  NT1   plutonium chlorides
  NT1   polonium chlorides
  NT1   potassium chlorides
  NT1   praseodymium chlorides
  NT1   promethium chlorides
  NT1   protactinium chlorides
  NT1   radium chlorides
  NT1   radon chlorides
  NT1   rhenium chlorides
  NT1   rhodium chlorides
  NT1   rubidium chlorides

	NT1	ruthenium chlorides
	NT1	samarium chlorides
	NT1	scandium chlorides
	NT1	selenium chlorides
	NT1	silicon chlorides
	NT1	silver chlorides
	NT1	sodium chlorides
	NT1	strontium chlorides
	NT1	sulfur chlorides
	NT1	tantalum chlorides
	NT1	technetium chlorides
	NT1	tellurium chlorides
	NT1	terbium chlorides
	NT1	tetrazolium
	NT1	thallium chlorides
	NT1	thorium chlorides
	NT1	thulium chlorides
	NT1	tin chlorides
	NT1	titanium chlorides
	NT1	tungsten chlorides
	NT1	uranium chlorides
	NT1	uranyl chlorides
	NT1	vanadium chlorides
	NT1	xenon chlorides
	NT1	ytterbium chlorides
	NT1	yttrium chlorides
	NT1	zinc chlorides
	NT1	zirconium chlorides
	RT	chlorine additions
	RT	hydrochloric acid
	RT	oxychlorides

→ **CHLORINATED ALIPHATIC HYDROCAR** [0; 0]
(Prior to October 1991, this concept was indexed by ORGANIC CHLORINE COMPOUNDS.)
BT1　halogenated aliphatic hydrocar
　BT2　organic halogen compounds
　　BT3　organic compounds
BT1　organic chlorine compounds
　BT2　organic halogen compounds
　　BT3　organic compounds
NT1　carbon tetrachloride
NT1　chloroform
NT1　methyl chloride
NT1　pvc

→ **CHLORINATED AROMATIC HYDROCARB** [0; 0]
UF　pcb
UF　polychlorinated biphenyl
BT1　halogenated aromatic hydrocarb
　BT2　aromatics
　　BT3　organic compounds
　BT2　organic halogen compounds
　　BT3　organic compounds
BT1　organic chlorine compounds
　BT2　organic halogen compounds
　　BT3　organic compounds
NT1　aldrin

chlorinated hydrocarbons
USE　organic chlorine compounds

CHLORINATION [548; 563]
BT1　halogenation
　BT2　chemical reactions
NT1　sulfochlorination
RT　dechlorination

CHLORINE [2,231; 2,231]
UF　*chlorine chlorides*
BT1　halogens
　BT2　nonmetals
　　BT3　elements

CHLORINE ADDITIONS [104; 104]
RT　chlorides
RT　crystal doping
RT　doped materials

chlorine bromides
USE　bromine chlorides

chlorine chlorides
USE　chlorine

CHLORINE COMPLEXES [79; 79]
BT1　complexes

CHLORINE COMPOUNDS [607; 20,415]
UF+　*chlorites*
BT1　halogen compounds
NT1　chlorates
NT1　chloric acid
*NT1　chlorides
NT1　chlorine fluorides
NT1　chlorine oxides
NT1　chlorous acid
NT1　hydrochloric acid
NT1　hypochlorous acid
NT1　oxychlorides
*NT1　perchlorates
NT1　perchloric acid
RT　organic chlorine compounds

CHLORINE FLUORIDES [75; 75]
UF　*fluorine chlorides*
BT1　chlorine compounds
　BT2　halogen compounds
BT1　fluorides
　BT2　fluorine compounds
　　BT3　halogen compounds
　BT2　halides
　　BT3　halogen compounds

chlorine iodides
USE　iodine chlorides

CHLORINE IONS [741; 741]
BT1　ions
　BT2　charged particles

CHLORINE ISOTOPES [147; 2,036]
NT1　chlorine 31
NT1　chlorine 32
NT1　chlorine 33
NT1　chlorine 34
NT1　chlorine 35
NT1　chlorine 36
NT1　chlorine 37
NT1　chlorine 38
NT1　chlorine 39
NT1　chlorine 40
NT1　chlorine 41
NT1　chlorine 42
NT1　chlorine 43
NT1　chlorine 44
NT1　chlorine 45
NT1　chlorine 46
NT1　chlorine 47
NT1　chlorine 48
NT1　chlorine 49
NT1　chlorine 51

CHLORINE OXIDES [57; 57]
BT1　chlorine compounds
　BT2　halogen compounds
BT1　oxides
　BT2　chalcogenides
　BT2　oxygen compounds
RT　oxychlorides

CHLORINE 31 [9; 9]
BT1　beta-plus decay radioisotopes
　BT2　beta decay radioisotopes
　　BT3　radioisotopes
　　　BT4　isotopes
BT1　chlorine isotopes
BT1　light nuclei
　BT2　nuclei
BT1　millisec living radioisotopes
　BT2　radioisotopes
　　BT3　isotopes
BT1　odd-even nuclei
　BT2　nuclei

CHLORINE 32 [14; 14]
BT1　beta-plus decay radioisotopes
　BT2　beta decay radioisotopes
　　BT3　radioisotopes
　　　BT4　isotopes
BT1　chlorine isotopes
BT1　light nuclei
　BT2　nuclei
BT1　millisec living radioisotopes
　BT2　radioisotopes
　　BT3　isotopes
BT1　odd-odd nuclei
　BT2　nuclei

CHLORINE 33 [64; 64]
BT1　beta-plus decay radioisotopes
　BT2　beta decay radioisotopes
　　BT3　radioisotopes
　　　BT4　isotopes
BT1　chlorine isotopes
BT1　light nuclei
　BT2　nuclei
BT1　odd-even nuclei
　BT2　nuclei
BT1　seconds living radioisotopes
　BT2　radioisotopes
　　BT3　isotopes

CHLORINE 34 [176; 176]
BT1　beta-plus decay radioisotopes
　BT2　beta decay radioisotopes
　　BT3　radioisotopes
　　　BT4　isotopes
BT1　chlorine isotopes
BT1　isomeric transition isotopes
　BT2　radioisotopes
　　BT3　isotopes
BT1　light nuclei
　BT2　nuclei
BT1　minutes living radioisotopes
　BT2　radioisotopes
　　BT3　isotopes
BT1　odd-odd nuclei
　BT2　nuclei
BT1　seconds living radioisotopes
　BT2　radioisotopes
　　BT3　isotopes

CHLORINE 35 [557; 557]
BT1　chlorine isotopes
BT1　light nuclei
　BT2　nuclei
BT1　odd-even nuclei
　BT2　nuclei
BT1　stable isotopes
　BT2　isotopes
RT　chlorine 35 beams

CHLORINE 35 BEAMS [88; 88] *Nov 75*
BT1　ion beams
　BT2　beams
RT　chlorine 35

CHLORINE 35 REACTIONS [199; 199]
BT1　heavy ion reactions
BT2　nuclear reactions

CHLORINE 35 TARGET [193; 193]
BT1　targets

CHLORINE 36 [629; 629]
BT1　beta-minus decay radioisotopes
　BT2　beta decay radioisotopes
　　BT3　radioisotopes
　　　BT4　isotopes
BT1　beta-plus decay radioisotopes
　BT2　beta decay radioisotopes
　　BT3　radioisotopes
　　　BT4　isotopes
BT1　chlorine isotopes
BT1　electron capture radioisotopes
　BT2　beta decay radioisotopes
　　BT3　radioisotopes
　　　BT4　isotopes
BT1　light nuclei
　BT2　nuclei
BT1　odd-odd nuclei

```
BT2    nuclei
BT1    years living radioisotopes
BT2    radioisotopes
BT3    isotopes
```

CHLORINE 36 TARGET [16; 16] *Jul 85*
```
BT1    targets
```

CHLORINE 37 [385; 385]
```
BT1    chlorine isotopes
BT1    light nuclei
BT2    nuclei
BT1    odd-even nuclei
BT2    nuclei
BT1    stable isotopes
BT2    isotopes
```

CHLORINE 37 REACTIONS [102; 102]
```
BT1    heavy ion reactions
BT2    nuclear reactions
```

CHLORINE 37 TARGET [168; 168]
```
BT1    targets
```

CHLORINE 38 [299; 299]
```
BT1    beta-minus decay radioisotopes
BT2    beta decay radioisotopes
BT3    radioisotopes
BT4    isotopes
BT1    chlorine isotopes
BT1    isomeric transition isotopes
BT2    radioisotopes
BT3    isotopes
BT1    light nuclei
BT2    nuclei
BT1    minutes living radioisotopes
BT2    radioisotopes
BT3    isotopes
BT1    odd-odd nuclei
BT2    nuclei
BT1    seconds living radioisotopes
BT2    radioisotopes
BT3    isotopes
```

CHLORINE 39 [44; 44]
```
BT1    beta-minus decay radioisotopes
BT2    beta decay radioisotopes
BT3    radioisotopes
BT4    isotopes
BT1    chlorine isotopes
BT1    light nuclei
BT2    nuclei
BT1    minutes living radioisotopes
BT2    radioisotopes
BT3    isotopes
BT1    odd-even nuclei
BT2    nuclei
```

CHLORINE 39 BEAMS [2; 2] *Dec 86*
```
BT1    ion beams
BT2    beams
```

CHLORINE 40 [16; 16]
```
BT1    beta-minus decay radioisotopes
BT2    beta decay radioisotopes
BT3    radioisotopes
BT4    isotopes
BT1    chlorine isotopes
BT1    light nuclei
BT2    nuclei
BT1    minutes living radioisotopes
BT2    radioisotopes
BT3    isotopes
BT1    odd-odd nuclei
BT2    nuclei
```

CHLORINE 41 [11; 11]
```
BT1    beta-minus decay radioisotopes
BT2    beta decay radioisotopes
BT3    radioisotopes
BT4    isotopes
BT1    chlorine isotopes
BT1    intermediate mass nuclei
BT2    nuclei
BT1    odd-even nuclei
```

```
BT2    nuclei
BT1    seconds living radioisotopes
BT2    radioisotopes
BT3    isotopes
```

CHLORINE 42 [9; 9]
```
BT1    chlorine isotopes
BT1    intermediate mass nuclei
BT2    nuclei
BT1    odd-odd nuclei
BT2    nuclei
```

CHLORINE 43 [3; 3] *Mar 77*
```
BT1    chlorine isotopes
BT1    intermediate mass nuclei
BT2    nuclei
BT1    odd-even nuclei
BT2    nuclei
```

CHLORINE 44 [3; 3] *Mar 76*
```
BT1    chlorine isotopes
BT1    intermediate mass nuclei
BT2    nuclei
BT1    odd-odd nuclei
BT2    nuclei
```

CHLORINE 45 [0; 0] *Apr 86*
```
BT1    chlorine isotopes
BT1    intermediate mass nuclei
BT2    nuclei
BT1    odd-even nuclei
BT2    nuclei
```

CHLORINE 46 [2; 2] *Sep 89*
```
BT1    chlorine isotopes
BT1    intermediate mass nuclei
BT2    nuclei
BT1    odd-odd nuclei
BT2    nuclei
```

CHLORINE 47 [2; 2] *Sep 89*
```
BT1    chlorine isotopes
BT1    intermediate mass nuclei
BT2    nuclei
BT1    odd-even nuclei
BT2    nuclei
```

CHLORINE 48 [2; 2] *Sep 89*
```
BT1    chlorine isotopes
BT1    intermediate mass nuclei
BT2    nuclei
BT1    odd-odd nuclei
BT2    nuclei
```

CHLORINE 49 [2; 2] *Sep 89*
```
BT1    chlorine isotopes
BT1    intermediate mass nuclei
BT2    nuclei
BT1    odd-even nuclei
BT2    nuclei
```

CHLORINE 51 [0; 0] *Apr 90*
```
BT1    chlorine isotopes
BT1    intermediate mass nuclei
BT2    nuclei
BT1    odd-even nuclei
BT2    nuclei
```

CHLORITE MINERALS [68; 68]
(Greenish, platyhydrous monoclinic silicates of aluminium, ferrous iron, and magnesium.)
```
UF     chlorites (minerals)
BT1    silicate minerals
BT2    minerals
```

chlorites
(Salts of chlorous acid.)
```
USE    chlorine compounds
AND    oxygen compounds
```

chlorites (minerals)
```
USE    chlorite minerals
```

chlormerodrin
```
USE    neohydrin
```

chlorobutadiene
```
USE    neoprene
```

CHLOROFORM [1,194; 1,194]
```
UF     trichloromethane
BT1    chlorinated aliphatic hydrocar
BT2    halogenated aliphatic hydrocar
BT3    organic halogen compounds
BT4    organic compounds
BT2    organic chlorine compounds
BT3    organic halogen compounds
BT4    organic compounds
RT     methane
RT     organic solvents
```

chloromethane
```
USE    methyl chloride
```

CHLOROPHYLL [396; 396]
```
BT1    phytochromes
BT2    pigments
BT1    porphyrins
BT2    heterocyclic acids
BT3    carboxylic acids
BT4    organic acids
BT5    organic compounds
BT3    heterocyclic compounds
BT4    organic compounds
BT2    organic nitrogen compounds
BT3    organic compounds
RT     chloroplasts
RT     leaves
RT     photosynthesis
RT     plants
```

CHLOROPLASTS [252; 252]
```
BT1    cell constituents
RT     chlorophyll
RT     photosynthesis
RT     plant cells
```

chloroprene
```
USE    neoprene
```

CHLOROTHIAZIDE [4; 4]
```
BT1    diuretics
BT2    drugs
```

CHLOROURACILS [8; 8] *Jun 83*
```
BT1    organic chlorine compounds
BT2    organic halogen compounds
BT3    organic compounds
BT1    uracils
BT2    hydroxy compounds
BT3    organic compounds
BT2    pyrimidines
BT3    azines
BT4    heterocyclic compounds
BT5    organic compounds
BT4    organic nitrogen compounds
BT5    organic compounds
```

CHLOROUS ACID [?; ?]
```
BT1    chlorine compounds
BT2    halogen compounds
BT1    inorganic acids
BT2    hydrogen compounds
BT2    inorganic compounds
BT1    oxygen compounds
```

CHLORPROMAZINE [119; 119]
```
BT1    amines
BT2    organic compounds
BT1    hypnotics and sedatives
BT2    central nervous system depress
BT3    central nervous system agents
BT4    drugs
BT1    organic chlorine compounds
BT2    organic halogen compounds
BT3    organic compounds
BT1    phenothiazines
```

    BT2   azines
      BT3   heterocyclic compounds
        BT4   organic compounds
      BT3   organic nitrogen compounds
        BT4   organic compounds
    BT2   organic sulfur compounds
      BT3   organic compounds
  BT1   tranquilizers
    BT2   psychotropic drugs
      BT3   central nervous system agents
        BT4   drugs

CHLORTETRACYCLINE [11; 11]
  BT1   tetracyclines
    BT2   antibiotics
      BT3   drugs
      BT3   organic compounds

CHO CELLS [679; 679] *Jan 84*
  UF   *chinese hamster ovary cells*
  BT1   somatic cells
    BT2   animal cells

CHOLANTHRENE [18; 18]
  BT1   condensed aromatics
    BT2   aromatics
      BT3   organic compounds

CHOLECALCIFEROL [129; 129]
  UF   *vitamin d-3*
  BT1   vitamin d
    BT2   vitamins

CHOLERA [32; 32]
  BT1   bacterial diseases
    BT2   infectious diseases
      BT3   diseases

CHOLESTEROL [874; 874]
  BT1   sterols
    BT2   hydroxy compounds
      BT3   organic compounds
    BT2   steroids
      BT3   organic compounds
  RT   lanolin
  RT   lipids
  RT   myelin

CHOLIC ACID [86; 86]
  BT1   bile acids
    BT2   carboxylic acids
      BT3   organic acids
        BT4   organic compounds
    BT2   sterols
      BT3   hydroxy compounds
        BT4   organic compounds
      BT3   steroids
        BT4   organic compounds

CHOLINE [457; 457]
  BT1   alcohols
    BT2   hydroxy compounds
      BT3   organic compounds
  BT1   lipotropic factors
    BT2   drugs
  BT1   quaternary compounds
    BT2   amines
      BT3   organic compounds
  RT   acetylcholine
  RT   lecithins
  RT   lipids

CHOLINESTERASE [189; 189]
  BT1   carboxylesterases
    BT2   esterases
      BT3   hydrolases
        BT4   enzymes
          BT5   organic compounds
  RT   acetylcholine

CHONDRITES [852; 852]
  BT1   stone meteorites
    BT2   meteorites

CHONDROITIN [51; 51]
  BT1   mucopolysaccharides
    BT2   amines
      BT3   organic compounds
    BT2   polysaccharides
      BT3   saccharides
        BT4   carbohydrates
          BT5   organic compounds
  RT   mucoproteins

chondrosarcomas
  USE   sarcomas
  AND   skeletal diseases

chooz b-1 reactor
  USE   ardennes b-1 reactor

chooz reactor
  USE   ardennes reactor

choppers (beams)
  USE   beam pulsers

choppers (neutron)
  USE   neutron choppers

chorioallantoic membrane
  USE   fetal membranes

choroid
  USE   uvea

CHROMATES [624; 624]
(Specific compounds should be indexed by coordination of a descriptor of the form (CATION) COMPOUNDS and the above anion descriptor.)
  BT1   chromium compounds
    BT2   transition element compounds
  BT1   oxygen compounds
  RT   chromic acid
  RT   chromium oxides

CHROMATIC ABERRATIONS [293; 293]
  RT   beam optics

chromatid deletions
  USE   chromosomal aberrations

CHROMATIDS [151; 151]
  RT   chromatin
  RT   chromosomes
  RT   human chromosomes

CHROMATIN [594; 634]
  NT1   heterochromatin
  NT1   sex chromatin
  RT   achromatic lesions
  RT   cell nuclei
  RT   chromatids
  RT   chromosomes
  RT   human chromosomes
  RT   nucleosomes

chromatographic columns
  USE   extraction columns

CHROMATOGRAPHY [2,589; 11,719]
  UF   *paper chromatography*
  UF   *partition chromatography*
  BT1   separation processes
  NT1   extraction chromatography
  NT1   gas chromatography
  NT1   gel permeation chromatography
  NT1   ion exchange chromatography
  NT1   liquid column chromatography
  NT1   radiochromatography
  NT1   thermochromatography
  NT1   thin-layer chromatography
  RT   counter current

chrome violet
  USE   aluminon

CHROMEL [53; 70]
  BT1   nickel base alloys
    BT2   nickel alloys
      BT3   alloys
  NT1   alloy-ni60fe24cr16
  NT1   alloy-ni80cr20
  NT1   alloy-ni85cr15

chromel a
  USE   alloy-ni80cr20

chromel b
  USE   alloy-ni85cr15

chromel c
  USE   alloy-ni60fe24cr16

CHROMIC ACID [28; 28]
  BT1   chromium compounds
    BT2   transition element compounds
  BT1   inorganic acids
    BT2   hydrogen compounds
    BT2   inorganic compounds
  BT1   oxygen compounds
  RT   chromates
  RT   chromium oxides

CHROMIUM [3,909; 3,909]
  BT1   transition elements
    BT2   metals
      BT3   elements

CHROMIUM ADDITIONS [623; 2,281]
(Alloys containing not more than 1% Cr are listed here.)
  NT1   alloy-ni65mo28fe5
  NT1   alloy-zr98sn-2
  NT1   alloy-zr98sn-4
  NT1   steel-crmo
  NT1   steel-crni
  NT1   steel-mncumo
  NT1   steel-nicr
  NT1   steel-nicrmo
  NT1   steel-nimocr
  NT1   steel-ni3cr
  RT   chromium alloys
  RT   chromium compounds

CHROMIUM ALLOYS [3,912; 24,911]
(Alloys containing more than 1% Cr.)
  BT1   alloys
  NT1   alloy-co36cr22ni22w15fe3
  NT1   alloy-co43cr20fe18ni13w3
  NT1   alloy-co52cr17fe15mo3si3
  NT1   alloy-co54cr20w15ni10
  NT1   alloy-co60cr30w4
  NT1   alloy-co62cr28mo6ni3
  NT1   alloy-co64cr29w4
  NT1   alloy-co66cr26w6
  NT1   alloy-fe31cr21co20ni20mo3w2
  NT1   alloy-fe36ni33cr26
  NT1   alloy-fe40ni35cr22
  NT1   alloy-fe44ni33cr21
  NT1   alloy-fe46ni33cr21
  NT1   alloy-fe48cr24ni24
  NT1   alloy-ni41fe40cr16nb3
  NT1   alloy-ni42fe36cr12mo6ti3
  NT1   alloy-ni43fe30cr22mo3
  NT1   alloy-ni43fe33cr16mo3
  NT1   alloy-ni45cr23fe19co3mo3w3
  NT1   alloy-ni45fe34cr20
  NT1   alloy-ni46cr23co19ti5al4
  NT1   alloy-ni47cr25co12w9fe3
  NT1   alloy-ni48co28cr15al3mo3ti2
  NT1   alloy-ni48cr22fe18mo9

NT1	alloy-ni49cr22fe18mo9	NT1	steel-ni3crmov			

CHROMIUM ALLOYS (continued)

NT1 alloy-ni49cr22fe18mo9
NT1 alloy-ni50co20cr15al5mo5
NT1 alloy-ni50cr22fe18mo9
NT1 alloy-ni50mo32cr15si3
NT1 alloy-ni51cr48
NT1 alloy-ni53co19cr15mo5al4ti3
NT1 alloy-ni53cr19fe19nb5mo3
NT1 alloy-ni54cr22co13mo9
NT1 alloy-ni54mo17cr16fe6w4
NT1 alloy-ni55co17cr15mo5al4ti4
NT1 alloy-ni55cr19co11mo10ti3
NT1 alloy-ni56cr21w10mo5fe4al2
NT1 alloy-ni58cr14co8al4mo2nb4w4
NT1 alloy-ni58cr20co14mo4ti3
NT1 alloy-ni59cr20co17ti2
NT1 alloy-ni59cr30fe9
NT1 alloy-ni60co15cr10al6ti5mo3
NT1 alloy-ni60cr14co10ti5mo4w4al3
NT1 alloy-ni60cr25w15
NT1 alloy-ni60fe24cr16
NT1 alloy-ni60mo13co9cr8nb4al3
NT1 alloy-ni61cr16co9al3ti3w3
NT1 alloy-ni61cr22mo9nb4fe3
NT1 alloy-ni61cr23fe14
NT1 alloy-ni62cr16mo15fe3
NT1 alloy-ni65cr25mo10
NT1 alloy-ni65mo16cr15w4
NT1 alloy-ni67cr19mo5w5ti3
NT1 alloy-ni68cr15w6al3mo3fe2
NT1 alloy-ni70mo17cr7fe5
NT1 alloy-ni73cr15fe7ti3
NT1 alloy-ni73cr20mn3nb3
NT1 alloy-ni74cr13al6mo4
NT1 alloy-ni75cr12al6mo5
NT1 alloy-ni76cr15fe8
NT1 alloy-ni76cr20ti2
NT1 alloy-ni77cr17al5
NT1 alloy-ni77cr20ti2
NT1 alloy-ni78cr16al4
NT1 alloy-ni78cr21
NT1 alloy-ni80cr20
NT1 alloy-ni85cr15
NT1 alloy-ti78cr11mo7al3
NT1 alloy-ti88mo8al3
NT1 alloy-ti91al5cr2
NT1 alloy-v87cr9fe3
NT1 chromium base alloys
* NT1 chromium steels
NT1 chromium-nickel steels
* NT2 chromium-nickel-molybdenum ste
NT2 steel-cr13mn8ni8
NT2 steel-cr17ni13
NT2 steel-cr17ni7
NT2 steel-cr18ni10
NT2 steel-cr18ni10-l
NT2 steel-cr18ni10ti
NT2 steel-cr18ni11
NT2 steel-cr18ni11nb
NT2 steel-cr18ni11nbco
NT2 steel-cr18ni12
NT2 steel-cr18ni12ti
NT2 steel-cr18ni8
NT2 steel-cr18ni9
NT2 steel-cr18ni9ti
NT2 steel-cr19ni10
NT2 steel-cr19ni10-l
NT2 steel-cr20ni11
NT2 steel-cr20ni11-l
NT2 steel-cr23ni14
NT2 steel-cr23ni18
NT2 steel-cr25ni20
NT2 steel-ni25cr20
NT2 steel-ni36cr12ti3al-l
NT2 steel-ni36cr18
NT1 colmonoy
NT1 refractaloy
NT1 steel-cralnimo
NT1 steel-crmov
NT1 steel-cr17mn15nni
NT1 steel-cr2mo
NT1 steel-cr2moninb
NT1 steel-cr2mov
NT1 steel-cr2nimov
NT1 steel-cr21mn9ni6
NT1 steel-cr5mo
NT1 steel-ni3crmo

NT1 steel-ni3crmov
NT1 steel-ni4crw
NT1 td-nickel chromium
RT chromium additions

CHROMIUM BASE ALLOYS [291; 297]
BT1 chromium alloys
BT2 alloys

CHROMIUM BORIDES [67; 67]
BT1 borides
BT2 boron compounds
BT1 chromium compounds
BT2 transition element compounds

CHROMIUM BROMIDES [9; 9]
BT1 bromides
BT2 bromine compounds
BT3 halogen compounds
BT2 halides
BT3 halogen compounds
BT1 chromium compounds
BT2 transition element compounds

CHROMIUM CARBIDES [255; 255]
BT1 carbides
BT2 carbon compounds
BT1 chromium compounds
BT2 transition element compounds

CHROMIUM CHLORIDES [73; 73]
BT1 chlorides
BT2 chlorine compounds
BT3 halogen compounds
BT2 halides
BT3 halogen compounds
BT1 chromium compounds
BT2 transition element compounds

CHROMIUM COMPLEXES [410; 410]
BT1 transition element complexes
BT2 complexes

CHROMIUM COMPOUNDS [827; 3,353]
BT1 transition element compounds
NT1 chromates
NT1 chromic acid
NT1 chromium borides
NT1 chromium bromides
NT1 chromium carbides
NT1 chromium chlorides
NT1 chromium fluorides
NT1 chromium hydrides
NT1 chromium hydroxides
NT1 chromium iodides
NT1 chromium nitrates
NT1 chromium nitrides
NT1 chromium oxides
NT1 chromium perchlorates
NT1 chromium phosphates
NT1 chromium selenides
NT1 chromium silicates
NT1 chromium silicides
NT1 chromium sulfates
NT1 chromium sulfides
NT1 chromium tellurides
NT1 dichromates
RT chromium additions

CHROMIUM FLUORIDES [20; 20]
BT1 chromium compounds
BT2 transition element compounds
BT1 fluorides
BT2 fluorine compounds
BT3 halogen compounds
BT2 halides
BT3 halogen compounds

CHROMIUM HYDRIDES [30; 30]
Jul 78
BT1 chromium compounds
BT2 transition element compounds
BT1 hydrides
BT2 hydrogen compounds

CHROMIUM HYDROXIDES [14; 14]
BT1 chromium compounds
BT2 transition element compounds
BT1 hydroxides
BT2 hydrogen compounds
BT2 oxygen compounds

CHROMIUM IODIDES [18; 18]
BT1 chromium compounds
BT2 transition element compounds
BT1 iodides
BT2 halides
BT3 halogen compounds
BT2 iodine compounds
BT3 halogen compounds

CHROMIUM IONS [593; 593]
BT1 ions
BT2 charged particles

CHROMIUM ISOTOPES [223; 3,451]
NT1 chromium 42
NT1 chromium 43
NT1 chromium 44
NT1 chromium 45
NT1 chromium 46
NT1 chromium 47
NT1 chromium 48
NT1 chromium 49
NT1 chromium 50
NT1 chromium 51
NT1 chromium 52
NT1 chromium 53
NT1 chromium 54
NT1 chromium 55
NT1 chromium 56
NT1 chromium 57
NT1 chromium 58
NT1 chromium 59
NT1 chromium 60
NT1 chromium 61
NT1 chromium 62

CHROMIUM NITRATES [11; 11]
BT1 chromium compounds
BT2 transition element compounds
BT1 nitrates
BT2 nitrogen compounds
BT2 oxygen compounds

CHROMIUM NITRIDES [96; 96]
BT1 chromium compounds
BT2 transition element compounds
BT1 nitrides
BT2 nitrogen compounds
BT2 pnictides

CHROMIUM ORES [36; 36]
BT1 ores

CHROMIUM OXIDES [942; 942]
BT1 chromium compounds
BT2 transition element compounds
BT1 oxides
BT2 chalcogenides
BT2 oxygen compounds
RT chromates
RT chromic acid
RT dichromates

CHROMIUM PERCHLORATES [2; 2]
Jun 83
BT1 chromium compounds
BT2 transition element compounds
BT1 perchlorates
BT2 chlorine compounds
BT3 halogen compounds
BT2 oxygen compounds

CHROMIUM PHOSPHATES [39; 39]
BT1 chromium compounds
BT2 transition element compounds
BT1 phosphates
BT2 oxygen compounds
BT2 phosphorus compounds

CHROMIUM SELENIDES [171; 171]
Nov 76
- BT1 chromium compounds
- BT2 transition element compounds
- BT1 selenides
- BT2 chalcogenides
- BT2 selenium compounds

CHROMIUM SILICATES [3; 3]
- BT1 chromium compounds
- BT2 transition element compounds
- BT1 silicates
- BT2 oxygen compounds
- BT2 silicon compounds

CHROMIUM SILICIDES [45; 45]
Apr 82
- BT1 chromium compounds
- BT2 transition element compounds
- BT1 silicides
- BT2 silicon compounds

CHROMIUM STEELS [1,182; 9,090]
(High alloy steels containing Cr as main alloying element.)
- BT1 chromium alloys
- BT2 alloys
- BT1 stainless steels
- BT2 high alloy steels
- BT3 steels
- BT4 carbon additions
- BT4 iron base alloys
- BT5 iron alloys
- BT6 alloys
- NT1 steel-cr10mo2
- NT1 steel-cr12
- NT1 steel-cr12moniv
- NT1 steel-cr12mov
- NT1 steel-cr13
- NT1 steel-cr13al
- NT1 steel-cr16
- NT1 steel-cr16ni
- NT1 steel-cr17cu4ni4nb-l
- NT1 steel-cr17mo
- NT1 steel-cr17ni4mo3
- NT1 steel-cr18
- NT1 steel-cr21ni5ti
- NT1 steel-cr22ni5ti
- NT1 steel-cr25
- NT1 steel-cr26ni5mo-l
- NT1 steel-cr9mo
- NT1 steel-cr9monbv

CHROMIUM SULFATES [13; 13]
- BT1 chromium compounds
- BT2 transition element compounds
- BT1 sulfates
- BT2 oxygen compounds
- BT2 sulfur compounds

CHROMIUM SULFIDES [109; 109]
- BT1 chromium compounds
- BT2 transition element compounds
- BT1 sulfides
- BT2 chalcogenides
- BT2 sulfur compounds

CHROMIUM TELLURIDES [29; 29]
Nov 78
- BT1 chromium compounds
- BT2 transition element compounds
- BT1 tellurides
- BT2 chalcogenides
- BT2 tellurium compounds

CHROMIUM 42 [3; 3] *Nov 88*
- BT1 beta-plus decay radioisotopes
- BT2 beta decay radioisotopes
- BT3 radioisotopes
- BT4 isotopes
- BT1 chromium isotopes
- BT1 even-even nuclei
- BT2 nuclei
- BT1 intermediate mass nuclei
- BT2 nuclei

CHROMIUM 43 [1; 1]
- BT1 chromium isotopes
- BT1 even-odd nuclei
- BT2 nuclei
- BT1 intermediate mass nuclei
- BT2 nuclei

CHROMIUM 44 [2; 2]
- BT1 chromium isotopes
- BT1 even-even nuclei
- BT2 nuclei
- BT1 intermediate mass nuclei
- BT2 nuclei

CHROMIUM 45 [2; 2]
- BT1 beta-plus decay radioisotopes
- BT2 beta decay radioisotopes
- BT3 radioisotopes
- BT4 isotopes
- BT1 chromium isotopes
- BT1 even-odd nuclei
- BT2 nuclei
- BT1 intermediate mass nuclei
- BT2 nuclei
- BT1 millisec living radioisotopes
- BT2 radioisotopes
- BT3 isotopes

CHROMIUM 46 [4; 4]
- BT1 beta-plus decay radioisotopes
- BT2 beta decay radioisotopes
- BT3 radioisotopes
- BT4 isotopes
- BT1 chromium isotopes
- BT1 even-even nuclei
- BT2 nuclei
- BT1 intermediate mass nuclei
- BT2 nuclei
- BT1 millisec living radioisotopes
- BT2 radioisotopes
- BT3 isotopes

CHROMIUM 47 [14; 14]
- BT1 beta-plus decay radioisotopes
- BT2 beta decay radioisotopes
- BT3 radioisotopes
- BT4 isotopes
- BT1 chromium isotopes
- BT1 even-odd nuclei
- BT2 nuclei
- BT1 intermediate mass nuclei
- BT2 nuclei
- BT1 millisec living radioisotopes
- BT2 radioisotopes
- BT3 isotopes

CHROMIUM 48 [96; 96]
- BT1 chromium isotopes
- BT1 electron capture radioisotopes
- BT2 beta decay radioisotopes
- BT3 radioisotopes
- BT4 isotopes
- BT1 even-even nuclei
- BT2 nuclei
- BT1 hours living radioisotopes
- BT2 radioisotopes
- BT3 isotopes
- BT1 intermediate mass nuclei
- BT2 nuclei

CHROMIUM 49 [66; 66]
- BT1 beta-plus decay radioisotopes
- BT2 beta decay radioisotopes
- BT3 radioisotopes
- BT4 isotopes
- BT1 chromium isotopes
- BT1 electron capture radioisotopes
- BT2 beta decay radioisotopes
- BT3 radioisotopes
- BT4 isotopes
- BT1 even-odd nuclei
- BT2 nuclei
- BT1 intermediate mass nuclei
- BT2 nuclei
- BT1 minutes living radioisotopes
- BT2 radioisotopes
- BT3 isotopes

CHROMIUM 50 [229; 229]
- BT1 chromium isotopes
- BT1 even-even nuclei
- BT2 nuclei
- BT1 intermediate mass nuclei
- BT2 nuclei
- BT1 stable isotopes
- BT2 isotopes

CHROMIUM 50 TARGET [251; 251]
- BT1 targets

CHROMIUM 51 [2,314; 2,314]
- BT1 chromium isotopes
- BT1 days living radioisotopes
- BT2 radioisotopes
- BT3 isotopes
- BT1 electron capture radioisotopes
- BT2 beta decay radioisotopes
- BT3 radioisotopes
- BT4 isotopes
- BT1 even-odd nuclei
- BT2 nuclei
- BT1 intermediate mass nuclei
- BT2 nuclei

CHROMIUM 52 [406; 406]
- BT1 chromium isotopes
- BT1 even-even nuclei
- BT2 nuclei
- BT1 intermediate mass nuclei
- BT2 nuclei
- BT1 stable isotopes
- BT2 isotopes

CHROMIUM 52 REACTIONS [48; 48]
Apr 77
- BT1 heavy ion reactions
- BT2 nuclear reactions

CHROMIUM 52 TARGET [454; 454]
- BT1 targets

CHROMIUM 53 [186; 186]
- BT1 chromium isotopes
- BT1 even-odd nuclei
- BT2 nuclei
- BT1 intermediate mass nuclei
- BT2 nuclei
- BT1 stable isotopes
- BT2 isotopes

CHROMIUM 53 TARGET [105; 105]
- BT1 targets

CHROMIUM 54 [117; 117]
- BT1 chromium isotopes
- BT1 even-even nuclei
- BT2 nuclei
- BT1 intermediate mass nuclei
- BT2 nuclei
- BT1 stable isotopes
- BT2 isotopes

CHROMIUM 54 REACTIONS [36; 36]
Feb 78
- BT1 heavy ion reactions
- BT2 nuclear reactions

CHROMIUM 54 TARGET [122; 122]
- BT1 targets

CHROMIUM 55 [19; 19]
- BT1 beta-minus decay radioisotopes
- BT2 beta decay radioisotopes
- BT3 radioisotopes
- BT4 isotopes
- BT1 chromium isotopes
- BT1 even-odd nuclei
- BT2 nuclei
- BT1 intermediate mass nuclei
- BT2 nuclei
- BT1 minutes living radioisotopes
- BT2 radioisotopes
- BT3 isotopes

CHROMIUM 56 [12; 12]
- BT1 beta-minus decay radioisotopes
- BT2 beta decay radioisotopes
- BT3 radioisotopes
- BT4 isotopes
- BT1 chromium isotopes
- BT1 even-even nuclei
- BT2 nuclei
- BT1 intermediate mass nuclei
- BT2 nuclei
- BT1 minutes living radioisotopes
- BT2 radioisotopes
- BT3 isotopes

CHROMIUM 56 TARGET [2; 2] *Jul 81*
- BT1 targets

CHROMIUM 57 [10; 10]
- BT1 beta-minus decay radioisotopes
- BT2 beta decay radioisotopes
- BT3 radioisotopes
- BT4 isotopes
- BT1 chromium isotopes
- BT1 even-odd nuclei
- BT2 nuclei
- BT1 intermediate mass nuclei
- BT2 nuclei
- BT1 seconds living radioisotopes
- BT2 radioisotopes
- BT3 isotopes

CHROMIUM 58 [9; 9]
- BT1 beta-minus decay radioisotopes
- BT2 beta decay radioisotopes
- BT3 radioisotopes
- BT4 isotopes
- BT1 chromium isotopes
- BT1 even-even nuclei
- BT2 nuclei
- BT1 intermediate mass nuclei
- BT2 nuclei
- BT1 seconds living radioisotopes
- BT2 radioisotopes
- BT3 isotopes

CHROMIUM 59 [10; 10] *Nov 80*
- BT1 beta-minus decay radioisotopes
- BT2 beta decay radioisotopes
- BT3 radioisotopes
- BT4 isotopes
- BT1 chromium isotopes
- BT1 even-odd nuclei
- BT2 nuclei
- BT1 intermediate mass nuclei
- BT2 nuclei
- BT1 seconds living radioisotopes
- BT2 radioisotopes
- BT3 isotopes

CHROMIUM 60 [7; 7] *Aug 86*
- BT1 chromium isotopes
- BT1 even-even nuclei
- BT2 nuclei
- BT1 intermediate mass nuclei
- BT2 nuclei

CHROMIUM 61 [6; 6] *Aug 86*
- BT1 chromium isotopes
- BT1 even-odd nuclei
- BT2 nuclei
- BT1 intermediate mass nuclei
- BT2 nuclei

CHROMIUM 62 [3; 3] *Aug 86*
- BT1 chromium isotopes
- BT1 even-even nuclei
- BT2 nuclei
- BT1 intermediate mass nuclei
- BT2 nuclei

CHROMIUM-MOLYBDENUM STEELS [1,288; 1,652]
(Steels containing Cr and Mo as main alloying elements; Cr content is higher than Mo content. Prior to November 1983 this was a valid descriptor, and older material is so indexed. USE CHROMIUM-NICKEL-MOLYBDENUM STE if appropriate; if not, coordinate CHROMIUM ALLOYS and MOLYBDENUM ALLOYS with most specific appropriate term from STEELS hierarchy.)

CHROMIUM-NICKEL STEELS [2,963; 11,680]
(High alloy steels containing Cr and Ni as important alloying elements. Prior to November 1983 this descriptor included only steels in which the Cr content was higher than the Ni content.)
- UF nickel-chromium steels
- BT1 chromium alloys
- BT2 alloys
- BT1 nickel alloys
- BT2 alloys
- BT1 stainless steels
- BT2 high alloy steels
- BT3 steels
- BT4 carbon additions
- BT4 iron base alloys
- BT5 iron alloys
- BT6 alloys
- *NT1 chromium-nickel-molybdenum ste
- NT1 steel-cr13mn8ni8
- NT1 steel-cr17ni13
- NT1 steel-cr17ni7
- NT1 steel-cr18ni10
- NT1 steel-cr18ni10-l
- NT1 steel-cr18ni10ti
- NT1 steel-cr18ni11
- NT1 steel-cr18ni11nb
- NT1 steel-cr18ni11nbco
- NT1 steel-cr18ni12
- NT1 steel-cr18ni12ti
- NT1 steel-cr18ni8
- NT1 steel-cr18ni9
- NT1 steel-cr18ni9ti
- NT1 steel-cr19ni10
- NT1 steel-cr19ni10-l
- NT1 steel-cr20ni11
- NT1 steel-cr20ni11-l
- NT1 steel-cr23ni14
- NT1 steel-cr23ni18
- NT1 steel-cr25ni20
- NT1 steel-ni25cr20
- NT1 steel-ni36cr12ti3al-l
- NT1 steel-ni36cr18

CHROMIUM-NICKEL-MOLYBDENUM STE [205; 2,020] *Nov 83*
(Cr-Ni steels containing Mo.)
- BT1 chromium-nickel steels
- BT2 chromium alloys
- BT3 alloys
- BT2 nickel alloys
- BT3 alloys
- BT2 stainless steels
- BT3 high alloy steels
- BT4 steels
- BT5 carbon additions
- BT5 iron base alloys
- BT6 iron alloys
- BT7 alloys
- BT1 molybdenum alloys
- BT2 alloys
- NT1 steel-cr11ni10mo2ti-l
- NT1 steel-cr13ni6mo-l
- NT1 steel-cr15ni15motib
- NT1 steel-cr16ni13monbv
- NT1 steel-cr16ni15mo3nb
- NT1 steel-cr16ni16monb
- NT1 steel-cr16ni8mo2
- NT1 steel-cr17ni12monb
- NT1 steel-cr17ni12mo3
- NT1 steel-cr17ni12mo3-l
- NT1 steel-cr17ni13mo2ti
- NT1 steel-cr17ni13mo3ti
- NT1 steel-ni17cr14moti-l
- NT1 steel-ni26cr15ti2movalb
- NT1 steel-ni35cr18mo4ti2al

chromizing
USE diffusion coating

CHROMOSOMAL ABERRATIONS [4,018; 4,255]
- UF *abnormalities (chromosomal)*
- UF *chromatid deletions*
- UF *chromosome aberrations*
- UF *chromosome exchanges*
- UF *chromosome fragments*
- UF *deletions (chromosomal)*
- UF *reciprocal translocations*
- BT1 mutations
- NT1 chromosome breakage
- RT acrocentric chromosomes
- RT banding techniques
- RT biological indicators
- RT chromosomes
- RT dicentric chromosomes
- RT downs syndrome
- RT genetic control
- RT heterochromosomes
- RT human chromosomes
- RT karyotype

chromosome aberrations
USE chromosomal aberrations

CHROMOSOME BREAKAGE [284; 284]
- BT1 chromosomal aberrations
- BT2 mutations
- RT heterochromatin

chromosome exchanges
USE chromosomal aberrations

chromosome fragments
USE chromosomal aberrations

CHROMOSOME LOSSES [55; 55]
May 76
- RT genetic radiation effects

CHROMOSOME SORTING [3; 3]
Apr 88
(The physical separation of a karyotype to provide large quantities of an individual chromosome.)
- BT1 cytological techniques
- RT cell flow systems
- RT chromosomes
- RT human chromosomes

CHROMOSOMES [1,204; 1,717]
- NT1 acrocentric chromosomes
- NT1 dicentric chromosomes
- NT1 heterochromosomes
- NT2 x chromosome
- NT2 y chromosome
- NT1 human chromosomes
- NT2 philadelphia chromosome
- NT1 ring chromosomes
- RT banding techniques
- RT cell nuclei
- RT chromatids
- RT chromatin
- RT chromosomal aberrations
- RT chromosome sorting
- RT crossing-over
- RT dna
- RT dna repair
- RT gene operons
- RT gene regulation
- RT genes
- RT genetic effects
- RT genetic mapping
- RT karyotype
- RT mitosis
- RT nucleoli
- RT rflps

CHROMOSPHERE [1,396; 1,396]
- BT1 solar atmosphere
- BT2 stellar atmospheres
- BT3 atmospheres
- RT photosphere
- RT plages

RT solar flares
RT sun

CHROMOTROPIC ACID [31; 31]
BT1 hydroxy compounds
BT2 organic compounds
BT1 sulfonic acids
BT2 organic acids
BT3 organic compounds
BT2 organic sulfur compounds
BT3 organic compounds
RT dyes

chronic administration
USE chronic intake

CHRONIC EXPOSURE [167; 504]
Dec 85
(For chronic exposure to radiation use CHRONIC IRRADIATION.)
NT1 chronic irradiation
RT biological effects
RT biological stress
RT toxicity

CHRONIC INTAKE [405; 405]
UF *chronic administration*
UF *continuous intake*
UF *long term intake*
UF *long-term intake*
BT1 intake
RT chronic irradiation

CHRONIC IRRADIATION [1,880; 1,880]
UF *continuous irradiation*
UF *long term irradiation*
UF *long-term irradiation*
UF *protracted irradiation*
BT1 chronic exposure
BT1 irradiation
RT chronic intake
RT low dose irradiation
RT radiation doses
RT radiation syndrome
RT temporal dose distributions

chronic radiation effects
USE delayed radiation effects

CHRONOTRONS [7; 8]
BT1 time interval analyzers
BT2 measuring instruments
NT1 vernier chronotrons

CHRYSENE [21; 21]
BT1 condensed aromatics
BT2 aromatics
BT3 organic compounds
BT1 hydrocarbons
BT2 organic compounds

→ **CHS TORSATRON** [19; 19] Feb 91
(National Institute for Fusion Science, Nagoya, Japan.)
UF *compact helical system torsatr*
BT1 torsatron stellarators
BT2 stellarators
BT3 closed plasma devices
BT4 thermonuclear devices

chubu-1 reactor
USE hamaoka-1 reactor

chubu-2 reactor
USE hamaoka-2 reactor

chubu-3 reactor
USE hamaoka-3 reactor

chugoku el. power co. reactor
USE shimane-1 reactor

chugoku-1 reactor
USE shimane-1 reactor

chugoku-2 reactor
USE shimane-2 reactor

→ **CHUKCHI SEA** [0; 0] Oct 91
(Part of Arctic Ocean north of Bering Strait between Asia and North America.)
BT1 arctic ocean
BT2 seas
BT3 surface waters
RT alaska
RT arctic regions
RT ussr

chukotka reactor
USE bilibin reactor

CHYLOMICRONS [35; 35]
RT blood plasma
RT lipids

CHYMOTRYPSIN [88; 88]
BT1 serine proteinases
BT2 peptide hydrolases
BT3 hydrolases
BT4 enzymes
BT5 organic compounds
RT digestion
RT pancreas

CII COMPUTERS [6; 6]
BT1 digital computers
BT2 computers

CIM MODEL [55; 55] Aug 78
UF *constituent interchange model*
BT1 composite models
BT2 particle models
BT3 mathematical models
RT exchange interactions
RT hadrons
RT quantum chromodynamics
RT quark-hadron interactions
RT strong interactions

CIMARRON PLUTONIUM PLANT [3; 3] Sep 75
BT1 fuel fabrication plants
BT2 nuclear facilities
BT1 industrial plants
RT cimarron uranium plant

CIMARRON URANIUM PLANT [2; 2] Mar 76
BT1 fuel fabrication plants
BT2 nuclear facilities
BT1 industrial plants
RT cimarron plutonium plant

CINCHONINE [2; 2]
BT1 alkaloids
BT2 organic compounds
BT1 antibiotics
BT2 drugs
BT2 organic compounds
BT1 antipyretics
BT2 central nervous system depress
BT3 central nervous system agents
BT4 drugs
RT quinolines

CINDA [75; 75]
(Computer Index of Nuclear Data.)
BT1 information systems
RT cross sections
RT data
RT neutrons
RT nuclear data collections

RT nuclear reactions

CINEMATOGRAPHY [100; 100] Jan 86
(Motion picture photography.)
BT1 photography

CINNAMIC ACID [57; 57]
UF *phenylacrylic acid-beta*
BT1 monocarboxylic acids
BT2 carboxylic acids
BT3 organic acids
BT4 organic compounds

cir reactor
USE cirus reactor

circadian variations
USE daily variations

CIRCE DEVICES [10; 11]
BT1 magnetic mirrors
BT2 open plasma devices
BT3 thermonuclear devices
NT1 circe-25kw device

CIRCE-25KW DEVICE [2; 2]
BT1 circe devices
BT2 magnetic mirrors
BT3 open plasma devices
BT4 thermonuclear devices

CIRCUIT BREAKERS [342; 342]
UF *breakers (circuit)*
BT1 electrical equipment
BT2 equipment
BT1 equipment protection devices
RT current limiters
RT electric fuses
RT electronic circuits
RT lightning arresters
RT switches
RT switching circuits

CIRCUIT THEORY [85; 85]
RT electronic circuits
RT network analysis

circuits (electronic)
USE electronic circuits

circuits (magnetic)
USE magnetic circuits

CIRCULAR CONFIGURATION [629; 629]
BT1 configuration

circulation (blood)
USE blood circulation

CIRENE REACTOR [87; 87]
(Cirene, Latina, Italy)
BT1 hwlwr type reactors
BT2 heavy water moderated reactor
BT3 reactors
BT2 water cooled reactors
BT3 reactors
BT1 pressure tube reactors
BT2 power reactors
BT3 reactors
BT1 thermal reactors
BT2 reactors

CIRUS REACTOR [104; 104]
(Bhabha Atomic Research Centre, Trombay, Maharashtra, India)
UF *canada-india reactor*
UF *cir reactor*
BT1 heavy water moderated reactors
BT2 reactors

CIRUS REACTOR

```
BT1    isotope production reactors
BT2      irradiation reactors
BT3        reactors
BT1    natural uranium reactors
BT2      reactors
BT1    research reactors
BT2      research and test reactors
BT3        reactors
BT1    tank type reactors
BT2      reactors
BT1    test reactors
BT2      research and test reactors
BT3        reactors
BT2      test facilities
BT1    thermal reactors
BT2      reactors
BT1    training reactors
BT2      research and test reactors
BT3        reactors
BT1    water cooled reactors
BT2      reactors
```

CISE [6; 6]
```
UF     centro informazioni studi espe
BT1    italian organizations
BT2      national organizations
```

cistrons
```
USE    genes
```

cit synchrotron
```
USE    caltech synchrotron
```

cities
```
USE    urban areas
```

CITRATES [1,367; 1,367]
```
BT1    carboxylic acid salts
RT     citric acid esters
```

CITRIC ACID [347; 347]
```
BT1    hydroxy acids
BT2      carboxylic acids
BT3        organic acids
BT4          organic compounds
```

CITRIC ACID ESTERS [20; 20]
```
BT1    carboxylic acid esters
BT2      esters
BT3        organic compounds
RT     citrates
```

CITROVORUM FACTOR [13; 13]
```
UF     folinic acid
RT     folic acid
RT     vitamin b group
```

CITRULLINE [12; 12]
```
UF     ureidoaminovaleric acid
BT1    amino acids
BT2      carboxylic acids
BT3        organic acids
BT4          organic compounds
RT     urea
```

CITRUS [107; 107]
```
BT1    plants
RT     fruit trees
RT     grapefruits
RT     lemons
RT     oranges
```

CIVEX PROCESS [23; 23] *Nov 78*
```
BT1    reprocessing
BT2      separation processes
RT     solvent extraction
```

CIVIL DEFENSE [212; 212]
```
BT1    national defense
RT     evacuation
```
```
RT     human populations
RT     local fallout
RT     nuclear explosions
RT     nuclear weapons
RT     population relocation
RT     radiation protection
RT     safety
RT     shelters
RT     subsurface structures
```

→ **CIVIL ENGINEERING** [0; 0] *Oct 91*
```
BT1    engineering
```

CIVIL LIABILITY [222; 222]
```
BT1    liabilities
RT     bcoclmcnm
RT     bcolons
RT     bcstpc
RT     pcotpl
RT     solas convention
RT     vcoclnd
RT     workmens compensation
```

CLADDING [1,029; 1,029]
(For the process only.)
```
BT1    surface coating
BT2      deposition
RT     canning
RT     decladding
RT     fuel cans
RT     plating
RT     rolling
```

cladding-fuel interactions
```
USE    fuel-cladding interactions
```

CLAISEN CONDENSATION [13; 13]
```
BT1    chemical reactions
RT     esters
```

CLAMS [18; 18]
```
BT1    molluscs
BT2      aquatic organisms
BT2      invertebrates
BT3        animals
```

CLARKEITE [2; 2]
```
BT1    oxide minerals
BT2      minerals
BT1    uranium minerals
BT2      radioactive minerals
BT3        minerals
BT3        radioactive materials
BT4          materials
RT     potassium oxides
RT     sodium oxides
RT     uranium oxides
```

CLASP DEVICE [2; 2]
```
BT1    stellarators
BT2      closed plasma devices
BT3        thermonuclear devices
```

CLASSICAL MECHANICS [2,627; 2,627]
```
UF     newton mechanics
BT1    mechanics
RT     hamiltonian function
```

CLATHRATES [485; 485]
```
UF     inclusion complexes
UF     occlusion complexes
RT     adducts
RT     crystals
RT     matrix isolation
RT     organic compounds
RT     rare gases
```

CLAVICEPS [4; 4]
```
BT1    fungi
BT2      plants
BT1    parasites
RT     rye
```

CLAYS [1,810; 2,644]
```
UF     marlite
UF     marlstone
BT1    silicate minerals
BT2      minerals
NT1    attapulgite
NT1    bentonite
NT1    clinoptilolite
NT1    fullers earth
NT1    illite
NT1    kaolin
NT1    montmorillonite
NT1    smectite
RT     alluvial deposits
RT     ceramics
RT     decontamination
RT     ground water
RT     loam
RT     radionuclide migration
RT     sand
RT     shales
RT     soils
```

CLEAN ROOMS [16; 16] *Feb 83*
```
RT     contamination
RT     controlled atmospheres
RT     remote handling
```

§ **CLEANING** [1,155; 9,710]
```
NT1    air cleaning
NT1    decontamination
NT1    surface cleaning
RT     coolant cleanup systems
RT     decarbonization
RT     detergents
RT     electropolishing
RT     purification
RT     scrubbing
RT     stains
```

CLEARANCE [959; 6,801]
```
NT1    blood-plasma clearance
NT1    excretion
NT2      exhalation
NT2      lung clearance
NT2      renal clearance
RT     nuclear medicine
```

CLEAVAGE [365; 365]
```
BT1    microstructure
BT2      crystal structure
RT     crystal growth
RT     crystallization
```

CLEBSCH-GORDAN COEFFICIENTS
[600; 600]
```
UF     3j-symbols
RT     angular momentum
RT     group theory
RT     racah coefficients
RT     wigner coefficients
```

CLEMENTINE REACTOR [4; 4]
(Los Alamos Scientific Lab., Los Alamos, New Mexico, USA)
```
BT1    fast reactors
BT2      epithermal reactors
BT3        reactors
BT1    mercury cooled reactors
BT2      liquid metal cooled reactors
BT3        reactors
BT1    plutonium reactors
BT2      reactors
BT1    research reactors
BT2      research and test reactors
BT3        reactors
```

CLEO STELLARATOR [70; 70]
```
BT1    stellarators
BT2      closed plasma devices
BT3        thermonuclear devices
RT     proto-cleo stellarators
```

CLIFFORD ALGEBRA [304; 304]
RT group theory

CLIMATES [1,226; 1,226]
RT antarctic regions
RT arctic regions
RT atmospheric circulation
RT atmospheric precipitations
RT deserts
RT meteorology
RT nuclear winter
RT seasons
RT tropical regions
RT tundra
RT weather
RT wind

CLINCH RIVER [42; 42]
BT1 rivers
  BT2 surface waters
RT tennessee

CLINCH RIVER BREEDER REACTOR [691; 691]
UF crbr reactor
BT1 lmfbr type reactors
  BT2 fbr type reactors
    BT3 breeder reactors
      BT4 reactors
    BT3 fast reactors
      BT4 epithermal reactors
        BT5 reactors
  BT2 liquid metal cooled reactors
    BT3 reactors
BT1 power reactors
  BT2 reactors
BT1 sodium cooled reactors
  BT2 liquid metal cooled reactors
    BT3 reactors
RT enriched uranium reactors
RT plutonium reactors

CLINOPTILOLITE [114; 114]
BT1 clays
  BT2 silicate minerals
    BT3 minerals
BT1 inorganic ion exchangers
  BT2 ion exchange materials
    BT3 materials

CLINTON-1 REACTOR [43; 43]
(Dewitt, Illinois, USA)
BT1 bwr type reactors
  BT2 enriched uranium reactors
    BT3 reactors
  BT2 power reactors
    BT3 reactors
  BT2 thermal reactors
    BT3 reactors
  BT2 water cooled reactors
    BT3 reactors
  BT2 water moderated reactors
    BT3 reactors

CLINTON-2 REACTOR [26; 26]
(Dewitt, Illinois, USA)
BT1 bwr type reactors
  BT2 enriched uranium reactors
    BT3 reactors
  BT2 power reactors
    BT3 reactors
  BT2 thermal reactors
    BT3 reactors
  BT2 water cooled reactors
    BT3 reactors
  BT2 water moderated reactors
    BT3 reactors

clipping circuits
USE pulse shapers

CLONE CELLS [557; 601]
BT1 cell cultures
RT animal cells
RT cloning
RT hela cells

RT in vitro
RT l cells
RT monoclonal antibodies
RT plant cells
RT plaque formation

CLONING [281; 776] Oct 77
NT1 dna-cloning
RT cell cultures
RT cell proliferation
RT clone cells
RT colony formation

close-in fallout
USE local fallout

CLOSED CONFIGURATIONS [275; 1,757]
UF *magnetic traps (closed)*
BT1 magnetic field configurations
NT1 mayer-schmidt configurations
NT1 minimum average-b configuratio
NT1 multipolar configurations
  NT2 hexapolar configurations
  NT2 octupolar configurations
  NT2 quadrupolar configurations
NT1 toroidal configuration
RT closed plasma devices

closed cycle cooling systems
USE closed-cycle cooling systems

closed cycle mhd generators
USE closed-cycle mhd generators

closed cycle systems
USE closed-cycle systems

CLOSED PLASMA DEVICES [205; 30,605]
BT1 thermonuclear devices
NT1 astron
NT1 blascon devices
NT1 heliotron
NT1 internal ring devices
  NT2 fm devices
  NT2 levitron devices
  NT2 lm devices
  NT2 spherator
  NT2 stator-b device
  NT2 tokapole devices
  NT2 tornado devices
NT1 stellarators
  NT2 clasp device
  NT2 cleo stellarator
  NT2 h-1 heliac
  NT2 harmonica-2 device
  NT2 heliac stellarators
    NT3 sheila heliac
  NT2 ims stellarator
  NT2 jipp stellarator
  NT2 jippt-2 device
  NT2 l-2 stellarator
  NT2 proto-cleo stellarators
  NT2 pulsator stellarator
  NT2 sirius device
  NT2 stellarator model c
  NT2 torsatron stellarators
    NT3 atf torsatron
    NT3 chs torsatron
    NT3 vint torsatron
  NT2 uragan stellarator
  NT2 wega stellarator
  NT2 wendelstein-2b stellarator
  NT2 wendelstein-7 stellarator
NT1 tokamak devices
  NT2 act devices
  NT2 aditya tokamak
  NT2 alcator device
  NT2 asdex tokamak
  NT2 atc devices
  NT2 castor tokamak
  NT2 columbia high-beta tokamak

  NT2 compact ignition tokamak
  NT2 continuous current tokamak
  NT2 ct-6b tokamak
  NT2 dante tokamak
  NT2 dite tokamak
  NT2 doublet-1 device
  NT2 doublet-2 device
  NT2 doublet-3 device
  NT2 etf tokamak
  NT2 ft tokamak
  NT2 hl-1 tokamak
  NT2 ht-6b tokamak
  NT2 ht-6m tokamak
  NT2 hybtok tokamaks
  NT2 intor tokamak
  NT2 isx tokamak
  NT2 iter tokamak
  NT2 jet tokamak
  NT2 jft-2 tokamak
  NT2 jft-2a tokamak
  NT2 jft-2m tokamak
  NT2 jippt-2 device
  NT2 jt-60 tokamak
  NT2 jt-60u tokamak
  NT2 jxfr tokamak
  NT2 lt-3 tokamak
  NT2 lt-4 tokamak
  NT2 mt-1 tokamak
  NT2 net tokamak
  NT2 ormak devices
  NT2 pbx devices
  NT2 petula tokamak
  NT2 plt devices
  NT2 spheromak devices
    NT3 ctx spheromak
  NT2 st tokamak
  NT2 starfire tokamak
  NT2 surmac tokamak
  NT2 t-10 tokamak
  NT2 t-15 tokamak
  NT2 t-7 tokamak
  NT2 tbr tokamak
  NT2 tca tokamak
  NT2 text devices
  NT2 textor tokamak
  NT2 tfr tokamak
  NT2 tftr tokamak
  NT2 tiber-x tokamak
  NT2 tj-1 tokamak
  NT2 tnt-a tokamak
  NT2 tokapole devices
  NT2 tokoloshe tokamak
  NT2 tore supra tokamak
  NT2 tormac devices
  NT2 tortus tokamak
  NT2 torus-ii tokamak
  NT2 tosca tokamak
  NT2 triam-1 tokamak
  NT2 tuman devices
  NT2 two-component torus
  NT2 uwmak devices
  NT2 varennes tokamak
  NT2 versator tokamak
  NT2 wt-3 tokamak
NT1 toroidal pinch devices
  NT2 hbtx devices
  NT2 tlp devices
    NT3 alpha device
    NT3 zeta devices
  NT2 toroidal screw pinch devices
    NT3 tpe-2 device
  NT2 toroidal theta pinch devices
    NT3 scyllac devices
  NT2 tpe-1rm15 device
  NT2 zt-p devices
  NT2 zt-40 devices
RT aspect ratio
RT closed configurations
RT compact torus
RT trapped-particle instability

CLOSED-CYCLE COOLING SYSTEMS [225; 225]
UF *closed cycle cooling systems*
BT1 closed-cycle systems
BT1 cooling systems
RT coolant loops
RT cooling towers
RT reactor cooling systems

CLOSED-CYCLE MHD GENERATORS [98; 161]
- UF *closed cycle mhd generators*
- BT1 closed-cycle systems
- BT1 mhd generators
  - BT2 direct energy converters
- NT1 liquid-metal mhd generators
- RT open-cycle mhd generators

CLOSED-CYCLE SYSTEMS [197; 330]
Dec 82
- UF *closed cycle systems*
- NT1 closed-cycle cooling systems
- NT1 closed-cycle mhd generators
  - NT2 liquid-metal mhd generators
- RT thermodynamic cycles

CLOSED-LOOP CONTROL [148; 148]
Sep 76
(With feedback.)
- BT1 control
- RT feedback

CLOSTRIDIUM [93; 182]
- BT1 bacteria
  - BT2 microorganisms
- NT1 clostridium acetobutylicum
- NT1 clostridium botulinum
- NT1 clostridium butyricum
- NT1 clostridium perfringens
- RT proteolysis
- RT toxins

CLOSTRIDIUM ACETOBUTYLICUM [5; 5] *Sep 85*
- BT1 clostridium
  - BT2 bacteria
    - BT3 microorganisms

CLOSTRIDIUM BOTULINUM [61; 61]
- BT1 clostridium
  - BT2 bacteria
    - BT3 microorganisms

CLOSTRIDIUM BUTYRICUM [5; 5]
Sep 85
- BT1 clostridium
  - BT2 bacteria
    - BT3 microorganisms

CLOSTRIDIUM PERFRINGENS [24; 24]
- UF *clostridium welchii*
- BT1 clostridium
  - BT2 bacteria
    - BT3 microorganisms

clostridium welchii
- USE clostridium perfringens

CLOSURES [1,847; 1,847]
- UF *plugs*
- RT joints
- RT seals
- RT valves

CLOTHING [108; 540]
- UF *shoes*
- NT1 protective clothing
  - NT2 gloves
- RT consumer products
- RT textiles

CLOUD CHAMBERS [93; 208]
- BT1 gas track detectors
  - BT2 radiation detectors
    - BT3 measuring instruments
- NT1 diffusion chambers
- NT1 expansion chambers

CLOUDS [471; 919]
(Limited to clouds in the earth atmosphere; for interstellar clouds see COSMIC DUST or COSMIC GASES.)

- NT1 radioactive clouds
- RT atmospheric precipitations
- RT meteorology
- RT water
- RT weather

CLOUDY CRYSTAL BALL MODEL [10; 10]
- BT1 nuclear models
  - BT2 mathematical models
- RT optical models

CLOVER [59; 59]
- BT1 leguminosae
  - BT2 plants
- RT forage

CLUFF LAKE MINE [20; 20] *Feb 81*
- BT1 uranium mines
  - BT2 mines
    - BT3 underground facilities
- RT saskatchewan

CLUSTER BEAM INJECTION [55; 55]
- BT1 beam injection
- RT cluster beams

CLUSTER BEAMS [204; 204] *Mar 76*
- BT1 beams
- RT cluster beam injection

CLUSTER EMISSION MODEL [435; 523] *Feb 76*
(A particle interaction model describing the emission of clusters having the potential to transfer charge from one center of mass hemisphere to the other, depending upon the rapidities of the clusters.)
- UF *cluster model (particle)*
- BT1 multiperipheral model
  - BT2 peripheral models
    - BT3 particle models
      - BT4 mathematical models
- NT1 space-time model
- RT charge-exchange interactions

CLUSTER EXPANSION [282; 282]
- RT differential equations

CLUSTER MODEL [3,504; 3,504]
- UF *alpha particle model*
- UF *cluster model (nuclear)*
- BT1 nuclear models
  - BT2 mathematical models
- RT quartet model

cluster model (nuclear)
- USE cluster model

cluster model (particle)
- USE cluster emission model

clusters (fuel elements)
- USE fuel element clusters

clusters (galaxy)
- USE galaxy clusters

clusters (ion)
- USE ion pairs

clusters (solid)
- USE solid clusters

clusters (star)
- USE star clusters

cmea
- USE comecon

CML REACTOR [7; 7]
- UF *critical mass laboratory pnl*
- UF *pnl-cml reactor*
- BT1 zero power reactors
  - BT2 experimental reactors
    - BT3 research and test reactors
      - BT4 reactors

CMNI [4; 4] *Aug 81*
(5-chloro-1-methyl-4-nitroimidazole.)
- BT1 imidazoles
  - BT2 azoles
    - BT3 heterocyclic compounds
      - BT4 organic compounds
    - BT3 organic nitrogen compounds
      - BT4 organic compounds
- RT radiosensitizers

cn method
- USE placzec function
- AND spherical harmonics

cna reactor
- USE atucha reactor

CNEN [75; 75]
(Name changed to Comitato Nazionale per la Ricerca e lo Sviluppo dell'Energia Nucleare e delle Energie Alternative in April 1982, and more recent material should be indexed to ITALIAN ENEA.)
- UF *comitato nazionale energia nuc*
- BT1 italian enea
  - BT2 italian organizations
    - BT3 national organizations

cnen brazil
- USE brazilian cnen

CNIDARIA [13; 118]
- BT1 coelenterata
  - BT2 invertebrates
    - BT3 animals
- NT1 corals
- NT1 hydra

CNO CYCLE [143; 143] *Sep 78*
(Astrophysical processes only.)
- UF *bethe-weizsaecker cycle*
- UF *carbon-nitrogen-oxygen cycle*
- BT1 star burning
- RT main sequence stars
- RT nucleosynthesis
- RT star evolution
- RT star models

cns depressants
- USE central nervous system depress

cns stimulants
- USE analeptics

co-generation
- USE cogeneration

COAGULANTS [11; 916] *May 84*
- BT1 hematologic agents
  - BT2 drugs
- NT1 blood coagulation factors
  - NT2 fibrin
  - NT2 fibrinogen
  - NT2 fibrinolysin
  - NT2 folic acid
  - NT2 intrinsic factor
  - NT2 kallikrein
  - NT2 plasminogen
  - NT2 protamines

    NT3   salmin
    NT2   prothrombin
    NT2   thrombin
    NT2   thromboplastin
    NT2   urokinase
    NT2   vitamin b-12
    NT2   vitamin k

coagulation (blood)
    USE   blood coagulation

coagulation (colloid)
    USE   flocculation

COAL [3,539; 3,789]
    BT1   carbonaceous materials
      BT2   materials
    BT1   fossil fuels
      BT2   energy sources
      BT2   fuels
    NT1   black coal
      NT2   anthracite
      NT2   bituminous coal
    NT1   lignite
    RT   chars
    RT   coal deposits
    RT   coal gas
    RT   coal gasification
    RT   coal liquefaction
    RT   coal rank
    RT   coal reserves
    RT   coke
    RT   gasification
    RT   peat
    RT   wasatch formation

coal chars
    USE   chars

→ **COAL DEPOSITS** [0; 0] *Oct 91*
    BT1   geologic deposits
    NT1   coal seams
    RT   coal
    RT   coal reserves

→ **COAL GAS** [0; 0] *Oct 91*
    UF   *coke-oven gas*
    BT1   fuel gas
      BT2   energy sources
      BT2   fuels
      BT2   gases
        BT3 fluids
    RT   coal

COAL GASIFICATION [210; 210]
    BT1   gasification
    RT   coal
    RT   coal gasification plants
    RT   synthetic fuels
    RT   thunderbird project

→ **COAL GASIFICATION PLANTS** [0; 0] *Oct 91*
    BT1   industrial plants
    RT   coal gasification

→ **COAL INDUSTRY** [0; 0] *Oct 91*
    BT1   industry

COAL LIQUEFACTION [69; 69] *Dec 82*
    BT1   liquefaction
    RT   coal
    RT   synthetic fuels

coal liquids
    USE   hydrocarbons

→ **COAL MINES** [0; 0] *Aug 91*
    BT1   mines
      BT2   underground facilities
    RT   backfilling
    RT   coal mining

→ **COAL MINING** [0; 0] *Aug 91*
    BT1   mining
    RT   coal mines
    RT   surface mining
    RT   underground mining

→ **COAL RANK** [0; 0] *Oct 91*
(The degree of metamorphosis that the original plant debris has undergone during the geological ages since it was deposited.)
    RT   coal

→ **COAL RESERVES** [0; 0] *Oct 91*
    BT1   reserves
      BT2   resources
    RT   coal
    RT   coal deposits

→ **COAL SEAMS** [0; 0] *Oct 91*
    BT1   coal deposits
      BT2   geologic deposits
    RT   geologic strata
    RT   water influx

COAL TAR [31; 31]
    BT1   bitumens
      BT2   tar
        BT3 other organic compounds
          BT4 organic compounds
    RT   creosote

COALESCENCE [317; 317]
    RT   adhesion
    RT   agglomeration
    RT   blood coagulation
    RT   bonding
    RT   coprecipitation

coarse control rods
    USE   shim rods

coarse mesh method
    USE   finite difference method

coast
    USE   shores

→ **COASTAL REGIONS** [0; 0] *Oct 91*
(Land areas of unspecified dimensions near sea or lake coastlines.)
    NT1   shores
    RT   coastal waters

COASTAL WATERS [861; 1,017]
(For use only in its geographic connotation; for the legal connotation use TERRITORIAL WATERS.)
    UF   *bays (coastal waters)*
    BT1   surface waters
    NT1   estuaries
    RT   coastal regions
    RT   continental margin
    RT   continental shelf
    RT   continental slope
    RT   intake structures
    RT   offshore sites
    RT   seas
    RT   shores
    RT   territorial waters

COATED FUEL PARTICLES [1,771; 1,771]
    BT1   fuel particles
    RT   amoeba effect

coating (surface)
    USE   surface coating

coating processes
    USE   surface coating

COATINGS [3,825; 8,487]
    NT1   antireflection coatings
    NT1   diffusion coatings
    NT1   dipped coatings
    NT1   electrodeposited coatings
    NT1   enamels
    NT1   glazes
    NT1   lacquers
    NT1   paints
      NT2   luminous paints
    NT1   protective coatings
    NT1   reflective coatings
    NT1   sprayed coatings
    NT1   vapor deposited coatings
    NT1   varnishes
    RT   corrosion protection
    RT   deposits
    RT   films
    RT   latex
    RT   surface coating
    RT   surface finishing
    RT   thin films

COAXIAL CABLES [224; 224]
    BT1   electric cables
      BT2   cables
      BT2   conductor devices
        BT3 electrical equipment
          BT4 equipment

COAXIAL FLOW REACTORS [33; 33]
    BT1   gas fueled reactors
      BT2   fluid fueled reactors
        BT3 reactors
      BT2   homogeneous reactors
        BT3 reactors

COBALT [3,268; 3,268]
    BT1   transition elements
      BT2   metals
        BT3 elements

COBALT ADDITIONS [290; 363]
(Alloys containing not more than 1% Co are listed here.)
    NT1   alloy-ni43fe33cr16mo3
    NT1   alloy-ni62cr16mo15fe3
    NT1   steel-cr18ni11nbco
    RT   cobalt alloys
    RT   cobalt compounds

COBALT ALLOYS [3,475; 5,459]
(Alloys containing more than 1% Co.)
    BT1   alloys
    NT1   alloy-fe31cr21co20ni20mo3w2
    NT1   alloy-fe44ni33cr21
    NT1   alloy-fe53ni29co18
    NT1   alloy-ni45cr23fe19co3mo3w3
    NT1   alloy-ni46cr23co19ti5al4
    NT1   alloy-ni47cr25co12w9fe3
    NT1   alloy-ni48co28cr15al3mo3ti2
    NT1   alloy-ni48cr22fe18mo9
    NT1   alloy-ni49cr22fe18mo9
    NT1   alloy-ni50co20cr15al5mo5
    NT1   alloy-ni53co19cr15mo5al4ti3
    NT1   alloy-ni54cr22co13mo9
    NT1   alloy-ni54mo17cr16fe6w4
    NT1   alloy-ni55co17cr15mo5al4ti4
    NT1   alloy-ni55cr19co11mo10ti3
    NT1   alloy-ni58cr14co8al4mo4nb4w4
    NT1   alloy-ni58cr20co14mo4ti3
    NT1   alloy-ni59cr20co17ti2
    NT1   alloy-ni60co15cr10al6ti5mo3
    NT1   alloy-ni60cr14co10ti5mo4w4al3
    NT1   alloy-ni60mo13co9cr8nb4al3
    NT1   alloy-ni61cr16co9al3ti3w3
    NT1   alloy-ni65mo28fe5
    NT1   alnico alloys
    NT1   cobalt base alloys
      NT2   alloy-co43cr20fe18ni13w3
      NT2   alloy-co50fe50
      NT2   alloy-co52cr17fe15mo3si3
      NT2   alloy-co52fe35v10
      NT2   alloy-co52fe35v13
      NT2   haynes alloys
        NT3 alloy-co36cr22ni22w15fe3
        NT3 alloy-co54cr20w15ni10
        NT3 alloy-co60cr30w4

	NT3	alloy-co62cr28mo6ni3
	NT2	stellite
	NT3	alloy-co54cr20w15ni10
	NT3	alloy-co60cr30w4
	NT3	alloy-co62cr28mo6ni3
	NT3	alloy-co64cr29w4
	NT3	alloy-co66cr26w6
	NT1	tikonal
	RT	cobalt additions

COBALT ARSENIDES [0; 0] *Sep 91*
    BT1   arsenides
        BT2   arsenic compounds
        BT2   pnictides
    BT1   cobalt compounds
        BT2   transition element compounds

COBALT BASE ALLOYS [907; 1,092]
    BT1   cobalt alloys
        BT2   alloys
    NT1   alloy-co43cr20fe18ni13w3
    NT1   alloy-co50fe50
    NT1   alloy-co52cr17fe15mo3si3
    NT1   alloy-co52fe35v10
    NT1   alloy-co52fe35v13
    NT1   haynes alloys
        NT2   alloy-co36cr22ni22w15fe3
        NT2   alloy-co54cr20w15ni10
        NT2   alloy-co60cr30w4
        NT2   alloy-co62cr28mo6ni3
    NT1   stellite
        NT2   alloy-co54cr20w15ni10
        NT2   alloy-co60cr30w4
        NT2   alloy-co62cr28mo6ni3
        NT2   alloy-co64cr29w4
        NT2   alloy-co66cr26w6

COBALT BORIDES [121; 121]
    BT1   borides
        BT2   boron compounds
    BT1   cobalt compounds
        BT2   transition element compounds

COBALT BROMIDES [28; 28]
    BT1   bromides
        BT2   bromine compounds
            BT3   halogen compounds
        BT2   halides
            BT3   halogen compounds
    BT1   cobalt compounds
        BT2   transition element compounds

COBALT CARBIDES [28; 28]
    BT1   carbides
        BT2   carbon compounds
    BT1   cobalt compounds
        BT2   transition element compounds

COBALT CARBONATES [6; 6]
    BT1   carbonates
        BT2   carbon compounds
        BT2   oxygen compounds
    BT1   cobalt compounds
        BT2   transition element compounds

COBALT CHLORIDES [188; 188]
    BT1   chlorides
        BT2   chlorine compounds
            BT3   halogen compounds
        BT2   halides
            BT3   halogen compounds
    BT1   cobalt compounds
        BT2   transition element compounds

COBALT COMPLEXES [977; 977]
    BT1   transition element complexes
        BT2   complexes

COBALT COMPOUNDS [988; 2,222]
    BT1   transition element compounds
    NT1   cobalt arsenides
    NT1   cobalt borides
    NT1   cobalt bromides
    NT1   cobalt carbides
    NT1   cobalt carbonates
    NT1   cobalt chlorides
    NT1   cobalt fluorides
    NT1   cobalt hydrides
    NT1   cobalt hydroxides
    NT1   cobalt iodides
    NT1   cobalt nitrates
    NT1   cobalt oxides
    NT1   cobalt perchlorates
    NT1   cobalt phosphates
    NT1   cobalt phosphides
    NT1   cobalt selenides
    NT1   cobalt silicates
    NT1   cobalt silicides
    NT1   cobalt sulfates
    NT1   cobalt sulfides
    NT1   cobalt tellurides
    NT1   cobalt tungstates
    RT   cobalt additions

COBALT FLUORIDES [98; 98]
    BT1   cobalt compounds
        BT2   transition element compounds
    BT1   fluorides
        BT2   fluorine compounds
            BT3   halogen compounds
        BT2   halides
            BT3   halogen compounds

COBALT HYDRIDES [36; 36]
    BT1   cobalt compounds
        BT2   transition element compounds
    BT1   hydrides
        BT2   hydrogen compounds

COBALT HYDROXIDES [26; 26]
    BT1   cobalt compounds
        BT2   transition element compounds
    BT1   hydroxides
        BT2   hydrogen compounds
        BT2   oxygen compounds

COBALT IODIDES [22; 22]
    BT1   cobalt compounds
        BT2   transition element compounds
    BT1   iodides
        BT2   halides
            BT3   halogen compounds
        BT2   iodine compounds
            BT3   halogen compounds

COBALT IONS [229; 229]
    BT1   ions
        BT2   charged particles

COBALT ISOTOPES [212; 13,907]
    NT1   cobalt 53
    NT1   cobalt 54
    NT1   cobalt 55
    NT1   cobalt 56
    NT1   cobalt 57
    NT1   cobalt 58
    NT1   cobalt 59
    NT1   cobalt 60
    NT1   cobalt 61
    NT1   cobalt 62
    NT1   cobalt 63
    NT1   cobalt 64
    NT1   cobalt 65
    NT1   cobalt 66
    NT1   cobalt 67
    NT1   cobalt 68
    NT1   cobalt 69
    NT1   cobalt 70

COBALT NITRATES [42; 42]
    BT1   cobalt compounds
        BT2   transition element compounds
    BT1   nitrates
        BT2   nitrogen compounds
        BT2   oxygen compounds

COBALT ORES [4; 4]
    BT1   ores

COBALT OXIDES [460; 460]
    BT1   cobalt compounds
        BT2   transition element compounds
    BT1   oxides
        BT2   chalcogenides
        BT2   oxygen compounds
    RT   oxide minerals

→ **COBALT PERCHLORATES** [0; 0]
Sep 91
    BT1   cobalt compounds
        BT2   transition element compounds
    BT1   perchlorates
        BT2   chlorine compounds
            BT3   halogen compounds
        BT2   oxygen compounds

COBALT PHOSPHATES [19; 19]
    BT1   cobalt compounds
        BT2   transition element compounds
    BT1   phosphates
        BT2   oxygen compounds
        BT2   phosphorus compounds

COBALT PHOSPHIDES [23; 23] *Jul 77*
    BT1   cobalt compounds
        BT2   transition element compounds
    BT1   phosphides
        BT2   phosphorus compounds
        BT2   pnictides

→ **COBALT SELENIDES** [0; 0] *Sep 91*
    BT1   cobalt compounds
        BT2   transition element compounds
    BT1   selenides
        BT2   chalcogenides
        BT2   selenium compounds

COBALT SILICATES [14; 14]
    BT1   cobalt compounds
        BT2   transition element compounds
    BT1   silicates
        BT2   oxygen compounds
        BT2   silicon compounds

COBALT SILICIDES [104; 104] *Aug 78*
    BT1   cobalt compounds
        BT2   transition element compounds
    BT1   silicides
        BT2   silicon compounds

COBALT SULFATES [47; 47]
    BT1   cobalt compounds
        BT2   transition element compounds
    BT1   sulfates
        BT2   oxygen compounds
        BT2   sulfur compounds

COBALT SULFIDES [48; 48]
    BT1   cobalt compounds
        BT2   transition element compounds
    BT1   sulfides
        BT2   chalcogenides
        BT2   sulfur compounds

→ **COBALT TELLURIDES** [0; 0] *Sep 91*
    BT1   cobalt compounds
        BT2   transition element compounds
    BT1   tellurides
        BT2   chalcogenides
        BT2   tellurium compounds

→ **COBALT TUNGSTATES** [0; 0] *Sep 91*
    BT1   cobalt compounds
        BT2   transition element compounds
    BT1   tungstates
        BT2   oxygen compounds
        BT2   tungsten compounds
            BT3   transition element compounds

COBALT 53 [23; 23]
    BT1   beta-plus decay radioisotopes
        BT2   beta decay radioisotopes
            BT3   radioisotopes
                BT4   isotopes
    BT1   cobalt isotopes

BT1 intermediate mass nuclei
BT2 nuclei
BT1 millisec living radioisotopes
BT2 radioisotopes
BT3 isotopes
BT1 odd-even nuclei
BT2 nuclei
BT1 proton decay radioisotopes
BT2 radioisotopes
BT3 isotopes

COBALT 54 [65; 65]
BT1 beta-plus decay radioisotopes
BT2 beta decay radioisotopes
BT3 radioisotopes
BT4 isotopes
BT1 cobalt isotopes
BT1 intermediate mass nuclei
BT2 nuclei
BT1 millisec living radioisotopes
BT2 radioisotopes
BT3 isotopes
BT1 minutes living radioisotopes
BT2 radioisotopes
BT3 isotopes
BT1 odd-odd nuclei
BT2 nuclei

COBALT 55 [170; 170]
BT1 beta-plus decay radioisotopes
BT2 beta decay radioisotopes
BT3 radioisotopes
BT4 isotopes
BT1 cobalt isotopes
BT1 electron capture radioisotopes
BT2 beta decay radioisotopes
BT3 radioisotopes
BT4 isotopes
BT1 hours living radioisotopes
BT2 radioisotopes
BT3 isotopes
BT1 intermediate mass nuclei
BT2 nuclei
BT1 odd-even nuclei
BT2 nuclei

COBALT 56 [364; 364]
BT1 beta-plus decay radioisotopes
BT2 beta decay radioisotopes
BT3 radioisotopes
BT4 isotopes
BT1 cobalt isotopes
BT1 days living radioisotopes
BT2 radioisotopes
BT3 isotopes
BT1 electron capture radioisotopes
BT2 beta decay radioisotopes
BT3 radioisotopes
BT4 isotopes
BT1 intermediate mass nuclei
BT2 nuclei
BT1 odd-odd nuclei
BT2 nuclei

COBALT 56 TARGET [3; 3] *Oct 82*
BT1 targets

COBALT 57 [1,605; 1,605]
BT1 cobalt isotopes
BT1 days living radioisotopes
BT2 radioisotopes
BT3 isotopes
BT1 electron capture radioisotopes
BT2 beta decay radioisotopes
BT3 radioisotopes
BT4 isotopes
BT1 intermediate mass nuclei
BT2 nuclei
BT1 odd-even nuclei
BT2 nuclei

COBALT 57 TARGET [3; 3] *Jan 77*
BT1 targets

COBALT 58 [877; 877]
BT1 beta-plus decay radioisotopes
BT2 beta decay radioisotopes
BT3 radioisotopes
BT4 isotopes
BT1 cobalt isotopes
BT1 days living radioisotopes
BT2 radioisotopes
BT3 isotopes
BT1 electron capture radioisotopes
BT2 beta decay radioisotopes
BT3 radioisotopes
BT4 isotopes
BT1 hours living radioisotopes
BT2 radioisotopes
BT3 isotopes
BT1 intermediate mass nuclei
BT2 nuclei
BT1 internal conversion radioisoto
BT2 radioisotopes
BT3 isotopes
BT1 isomeric transition isotopes
BT2 radioisotopes
BT3 isotopes
BT1 odd-odd nuclei
BT2 nuclei

COBALT 58 TARGET [7; 7] *Jul 76*
BT1 targets

COBALT 59 [518; 518]
BT1 cobalt isotopes
BT1 intermediate mass nuclei
BT2 nuclei
BT1 odd-even nuclei
BT2 nuclei
BT1 stable isotopes
BT2 isotopes

COBALT 59 REACTIONS [8; 8] *Nov 84*
BT1 heavy ion reactions
BT2 nuclear reactions

COBALT 59 TARGET [606; 606]
BT1 targets

COBALT 60 [10,892; 10,892]
BT1 beta-minus decay radioisotopes
BT2 beta decay radioisotopes
BT3 radioisotopes
BT4 isotopes
BT1 cobalt isotopes
BT1 intermediate mass nuclei
BT2 nuclei
BT1 internal conversion radioisoto
BT2 radioisotopes
BT3 isotopes
BT1 isomeric transition isotopes
BT2 radioisotopes
BT3 isotopes
BT1 minutes living radioisotopes
BT2 radioisotopes
BT3 isotopes
BT1 odd-odd nuclei
BT2 nuclei
BT1 years living radioisotopes
BT2 radioisotopes
BT3 isotopes

COBALT 60 TARGET [13; 13] *Dec 75*
BT1 targets

COBALT 61 [39; 39]
BT1 beta-minus decay radioisotopes
BT2 beta decay radioisotopes
BT3 radioisotopes
BT4 isotopes
BT1 cobalt isotopes
BT1 hours living radioisotopes
BT2 radioisotopes
BT3 isotopes
BT1 intermediate mass nuclei
BT2 nuclei
BT1 odd-even nuclei
BT2 nuclei

COBALT 62 [20; 20]
BT1 beta-minus decay radioisotopes
BT2 beta decay radioisotopes
BT3 radioisotopes
BT4 isotopes
BT1 cobalt isotopes
BT1 intermediate mass nuclei
BT2 nuclei
BT1 minutes living radioisotopes
BT2 radioisotopes
BT3 isotopes
BT1 odd-odd nuclei
BT2 nuclei

COBALT 63 [17; 17]
BT1 beta-minus decay radioisotopes
BT2 beta decay radioisotopes
BT3 radioisotopes
BT4 isotopes
BT1 cobalt isotopes
BT1 intermediate mass nuclei
BT2 nuclei
BT1 odd-even nuclei
BT2 nuclei
BT1 seconds living radioisotopes
BT2 radioisotopes
BT3 isotopes

COBALT 64 [7; 7]
BT1 beta-minus decay radioisotopes
BT2 beta decay radioisotopes
BT3 radioisotopes
BT4 isotopes
BT1 cobalt isotopes
BT1 intermediate mass nuclei
BT2 nuclei
BT1 millisec living radioisotopes
BT2 radioisotopes
BT3 isotopes
BT1 odd-odd nuclei
BT2 nuclei

COBALT 65 [12; 12] *Sep 79*
BT1 beta-minus decay radioisotopes
BT2 beta decay radioisotopes
BT3 radioisotopes
BT4 isotopes
BT1 cobalt isotopes
BT1 intermediate mass nuclei
BT2 nuclei
BT1 odd-even nuclei
BT2 nuclei
BT1 seconds living radioisotopes
BT2 radioisotopes
BT3 isotopes

COBALT 66 [9; 9] *Jan 86*
BT1 beta-minus decay radioisotopes
BT2 beta decay radioisotopes
BT3 radioisotopes
BT4 isotopes
BT1 cobalt isotopes
BT1 intermediate mass nuclei
BT2 nuclei
BT1 millisec living radioisotopes
BT2 radioisotopes
BT3 isotopes
BT1 odd-odd nuclei
BT2 nuclei

COBALT 67 [8; 8] *Jan 86*
BT1 beta-minus decay radioisotopes
BT2 beta decay radioisotopes
BT3 radioisotopes
BT4 isotopes
BT1 cobalt isotopes
BT1 intermediate mass nuclei
BT2 nuclei
BT1 millisec living radioisotopes
BT2 radioisotopes
BT3 isotopes
BT1 odd-even nuclei
BT2 nuclei

COBALT 68 [2; 2] *Aug 86*
  BT1   cobalt isotopes
  BT1   intermediate mass nuclei
    BT2   nuclei
  BT1   odd-odd nuclei
    BT2   nuclei

COBALT 69 [3; 3] *Aug 86*
  BT1   cobalt isotopes
  BT1   intermediate mass nuclei
    BT2   nuclei
  BT1   odd-even nuclei
    BT2   nuclei

COBALT 70 [2; 2] *Aug 86*
  BT1   cobalt isotopes
  BT1   intermediate mass nuclei
    BT2   nuclei
  BT1   odd-odd nuclei
    BT2   nuclei

COBOL [8; 8]
  BT1   programming languages

COCAINE [39; 39]
  BT1   alkaloids
    BT2   organic compounds
  BT1   anesthetics
    BT2   central nervous system depress
      BT3   central nervous system agents
        BT4   drugs
  BT1   antidepressants
    BT2   psychotropic drugs
      BT3   central nervous system agents
        BT4   drugs

COCKCROFT-WALTON ACCELERATORS [169; 169]
  BT1   electrostatic accelerators
    BT2   accelerators

COCKROACHES [19; 19]
  BT1   insects
    BT2   arthropods
      BT3   invertebrates
        BT4   animals

cocoa beans
  USE   cocoa products

COCOA PRODUCTS [24; 24]
  UF   *cocoa beans*
  BT1   food
  RT   cacao trees

COCOMBUSTION [0; 0] *Oct 91*
(The simultaneous burning of two fuels in a boiler, e.g., coal and biomass.)
  UF   *cofiring*
  BT1   combustion
    BT2   oxidation
      BT3   chemical reactions

COCONUT PALMS [17; 17]
  BT1   trees
    BT2   plants
  RT   coconuts

COCONUTS [32; 32]
  BT1   fruits
    BT2   food
  RT   coconut palms

CODEINE [15; 15]
  BT1   alkaloids
    BT2   organic compounds
  BT1   analgesics
    BT2   central nervous system depress
      BT3   central nervous system agents
        BT4   drugs
  BT1   hypnotics and sedatives
    BT2   central nervous system depress
      BT3   central nervous system agents
        BT4   drugs
  RT   heroin
  RT   morphine
  RT   thebaine

codeinone
  USE   alkaloids

CODFISH [38; 38]
  BT1   fishes
    BT2   aquatic organisms
    BT2   vertebrates
      BT3   animals

coding circuits
  USE   digital circuits

CODLING MOTH [39; 39]
  UF   *carpocapsa pomonella*
  BT1   moths
    BT2   lepidoptera
      BT3   insects
        BT4   arthropods
          BT5   invertebrates
            BT6   animals
  RT   apples

CODONS [58; 58]
  RT   gene operons
  RT   gene regulation
  RT   genes
  RT   nucleotides
  RT   ribosomes

COELENTERATA [8; 92]
  UF   *coelenterates*
  BT1   invertebrates
    BT2   animals
  NT1   cnidaria
    NT2   corals
    NT2   hydra

coelenterates
  USE   coelenterata

coenzyme i
  USE   nad

coenzyme ii
  USE   nadp

COENZYMES [244; 640]
  NT1   nad
  NT1   nadh2
  NT1   nadp
  NT1   ubiquinone
  RT   biochemistry
  RT   biosynthesis
  RT   catalysis
  RT   cytochromes
  RT   enzymes
  RT   isoalloxazines
  RT   metabolism
  RT   pyridoxal
  RT   redox process
  RT   vitamin b group

COERCIVE FORCE [1,079; 1,079]
  RT   magnetic properties

COEXTRUSION [15; 15]
  BT1   extrusion
    BT2   materials working
      BT3   fabrication

coffee
  USE   beverages

COFFEE BEANS [19; 19] *Nov 78*
  BT1   seeds
  RT   beverages
  RT   coffee plants

COFFEE PLANTS [36; 36]
  BT1   plants
  RT   coffee beans

COFFINITE [81; 81]
  BT1   silicate minerals
    BT2   minerals
  BT1   uranium minerals
    BT2   radioactive minerals
      BT3   minerals
      BT3   radioactive materials
        BT4   materials

cofiring
  USE   cocombustion

COFRENTES REACTOR [8; 8] *Apr 77*
(Cofrents, Valencia, Spain)
  BT1   bwr type reactors
    BT2   enriched uranium reactors
      BT3   reactors
    BT2   power reactors
      BT3   reactors
    BT2   thermal reactors
      BT3   reactors
    BT2   water cooled reactors
      BT3   reactors
    BT2   water moderated reactors
      BT3   reactors

COGEMA [63; 236] *Mar 77*
  UF   *comp gener matieres nucleaires*
  BT1   french organizations
    BT2   national organizations
  NT1   cogema la hague
  NT1   cogema marcoule
  NT1   cogema pierrelatte

COGEMA LA HAGUE [157; 157]
Mar 77
  BT1   cogema
    BT2   french organizations
      BT3   national organizations
  BT1   fuel reprocessing plants
    BT2   nuclear facilities

COGEMA MARCOULE [19; 19] *Mar 77*
  BT1   cogema
    BT2   french organizations
      BT3   national organizations

COGEMA PIERRELATTE [10; 10]
Mar 77
  BT1   cogema
    BT2   french organizations
      BT3   national organizations
  BT1   gaseous diffusion plants
    BT2   isotope separation plants
      BT3   industrial plants
      BT3   nuclear facilities

COGENERATION [316; 316] *Dec 82*
  UF   *co-generation*
  UF   *combined heat-power generation*
  UF   *combined steam-power generatio*
  BT1   power generation
  BT1   steam generation
  RT   district heating
  RT   dual-purpose power plants
  RT   waste heat
  RT   waste product utilization

COHERENCE LENGTH [319; 319]
Nov 78
(The range of interaction between the electrons of a Cooper pair.)
  RT   cooper pairs
  RT   ginzburg-landau theory
  RT   superconductivity

COHERENT ACCELERATORS [9; 9]
(Prior to 1986 COLLECTIVE ACCELERATORS was used for this concept.)
BT1 accelerators
RT collective accelerators

coherent anti-stokes raman spe
USE raman spectroscopy

COHERENT PRODUCTION [794; 794]
BT1 particle interactions
BT2 interactions
BT1 particle production
RT coherent tube model

COHERENT RADIATION [1,024; 1,024]
BT1 electromagnetic radiation
BT2 radiations

COHERENT SCATTERING
[1,207; 31,480]
BT1 scattering
NT1 brillouin effect
NT1 diffraction
NT2 atomic beam diffraction
NT2 electron diffraction
NT2 neutron diffraction
NT2 x-ray diffraction
NT1 rayleigh scattering
RT anharmonic crystals
RT elastic scattering

coherent states
(Eigenstates of annihilation operators.)
USE annihilation operators
AND eigenstates

COHERENT TUBE MODEL [83; 83]
Jun 77
BT1 mathematical models
RT coherent production
RT incoherent production
RT multiple production
RT nuclear reactions
RT particle interactions

coils (electric)
USE electric coils

coils (magnetic)
USE magnet coils

COINCIDENCE CIRCUITS [641; 641]
BT1 electronic circuits
RT anticoincidence
RT coincidence methods
RT pulse circuits
RT telescope counters
RT time measurement

COINCIDENCE METHODS
[4,405; 7,405]
BT1 counting techniques
NT1 coincidence spectrometry
NT1 tagged photon method
RT coincidence circuits
RT positron cameras
RT synchronization

COINCIDENCE SPECTROMETRY
[3,148; 3,148]
BT1 coincidence methods
BT2 counting techniques
RT radiation detection
RT spectrometers

COKE [208; 208]
UF *petroleum coke*
RT coal
RT coking
RT fuels

→ *coke-oven gas*
USE coal gas

→ **COKING** [0; 0] *Oct 91*
(Destructive distillation of coal to make coke.)
BT1 carbonization
BT2 decomposition
BT3 chemical reactions
RT coke
RT coking plants
RT retorting

→ **COKING PLANTS** [0; 0] *Oct 91*
BT1 industrial plants
RT coking

COLCHICINE [134; 134]
BT1 alkaloids
BT2 organic compounds
BT1 antimitotic drugs
BT2 drugs
BT1 antipyretics
BT2 central nervous system depress
BT3 central nervous system agents
BT4 drugs
RT polyploidy

COLD CATHODE TUBES [55; 55]
BT1 electron tubes

→ **COLD FUSION** [37; 37] *Jul 91*
BT1 nuclear reactions
RT thermonuclear reactions

COLD NEUTRONS [720; 1,209]
(Neutrons of less velocity than thermal neutrons; at 15 c their energy is below 0.01 eV.)
BT1 neutrons
BT2 nucleons
BT3 baryons
BT4 fermions
BT4 hadrons
BT5 elementary particles
NT1 ultracold neutrons

COLD PLASMA [1,912; 1,912]
BT1 plasma

COLD PRESSING [183; 183]
BT1 pressing
BT2 materials working
BT3 fabrication
RT cold working

COLD TRAPS [317; 317]
BT1 traps
RT vapor condensers

COLD WORKING [1,351; 1,423]
BT1 materials working
BT2 fabrication
NT1 shot peening
RT cold pressing
RT dislocation pinning
RT drawing
RT extrusion
RT forging
RT hardening
RT rolling
RT strain aging
RT strain hardening
RT surface hardening

COLEOPTILE [26; 26]
RT germination
RT seedlings

COLEUS [7; 7]
BT1 herbs
BT2 plants

COLIFORMS [46; 46]
(Restricted to papers on water purity analysis.)
BT1 bacteria
BT2 microorganisms
RT aerobacter
RT escherichia coli

COLLAGEN [561; 561]
BT1 scleroproteins
BT2 proteins
BT3 organic compounds
RT connective tissue
RT fibroblasts
RT hydroxyproline
RT proline

collapse (gravitational)
USE gravitational collapse

COLLECTIVE ACCELERATORS
[464; 1,047]
BT1 accelerators
NT1 electron-ring accelerators
NT1 plasma betatrons
RT coherent accelerators

COLLECTIVE EXCITATIONS
[707; 707] *Dec 85*
(See also COLLECTIVE MODEL.)
BT1 excitation
BT2 energy-level transitions
RT superconductivity

COLLECTIVE MODEL [4,553; 4,554]
UF *collective motion (in nuclei)*
BT1 nuclear models
BT2 mathematical models
NT1 rotation-vibration model
RT boson expansion
RT davydov-filipov model
RT hill-wheeler theory
RT quasiparticle-phonon model

collective motion (in nuclei)
USE collective model

collective states (rotational)
USE rotational states

collective states (vibrational)
USE vibrational states

collectors (dust)
USE dust collectors

collectrons
USE self-powered neutron detectors

college station texas train. r
USE nscr reactor

colleges
USE educational facilities

COLLIDING BEAMS [3,768; 3,768]
UF *intersecting beams*
BT1 beams
RT beam luminosity
RT beam-beam interactions
RT interactions

COLLIMATORS [3,022; 3,022]
RT beam optics
RT radiotherapy
RT shielding
RT shutters

COLLISION INTEGRALS [499; 499]
BT1 integrals
RT boltzmann equation

collision matrix
USE s matrix

COLLISIONAL HEATING [61; 61]
BT1 magnetic-pumping heating
BT2 high-frequency heating
BT3 plasma heating
BT4 heating

COLLISIONAL PLASMA [1,944; 1,944]
BT1 plasma
RT pfirsch-schlueter regime

COLLISIONLESS PLASMA
[2,417; 2,417]
BT1 plasma

COLLISIONS [5,711; 38,253]
(For low-energy interactions involving photons, electrons, ions, atoms, and molecules; not for the concept covered by NUCLEAR REACTIONS. For collisions with elementary particles and radiations, see also INTERACTIONS.)
NT1 atom collisions
 NT2 atom-atom collisions
 NT2 atom-molecule collisions
 NT2 electron-atom collisions
 NT2 ion-atom collisions
 NT2 muon-atom collisions
 NT2 photon-atom collisions
 NT2 positron-atom collisions
NT1 electron collisions
 NT2 electron-atom collisions
 NT2 electron-electron collisions
 NT2 electron-ion collisions
 NT2 electron-molecule collisions
 NT2 electron-positron collisions
 NT2 photon-electron collisions
NT1 ion collisions
 NT2 electron-ion collisions
 NT2 ion-atom collisions
 NT2 ion-ion collisions
 NT2 ion-molecule collisions
 NT2 photon-ion collisions
 NT2 positron-ion collisions
NT1 molecule collisions
 NT2 atom-molecule collisions
 NT2 electron-molecule collisions
 NT2 ion-molecule collisions
 NT2 molecule-molecule collisions
 NT2 photon-molecule collisions
 NT2 positron-molecule collisions
NT1 photon collisions
 NT2 photon-atom collisions
 NT2 photon-electron collisions
 NT2 photon-ion collisions
 NT2 photon-molecule collisions
 NT2 photon-positron collisions
NT1 positron collisions
 NT2 electron-positron collisions
 NT2 photon-positron collisions
 NT2 positron-atom collisions
 NT2 positron-ion collisions
 NT2 positron-molecule collisions
 NT2 positron-positron collisions
RT brownian movement
RT colloids
RT coupled channel theory
RT dynamics
RT interactions
RT kinetic equations
RT kinetics
RT landau-zener formula
RT particle kinematics
RT pss method
RT scattering

collodion
USE nitrocellulose

colloid coagulation
USE flocculation

COLLOIDS [1,583; 14,181]
BT1 dispersions
NT1 agar
NT1 alginic acid
NT1 emulsions
NT1 foams
NT1 gelatin
NT1 gels
NT1 radiocolloids
 NT2 thorotrast
NT1 sols
 NT2 aerosols
  NT3 radioactive aerosols
  NT3 smokes
   NT4 tobacco smokes
RT brownian movement
RT collisions
RT dialysis
RT gelation
RT particle size
RT particles
RT sol-gel process
RT superconducting colloid detect

COLMONOY [21; 21]
BT1 boron alloys
 BT2 alloys
BT1 chromium alloys
 BT2 alloys
BT1 corrosion resistant alloys
 BT2 alloys
BT1 iron alloys
 BT2 alloys
BT1 nickel base alloys
 BT2 nickel alloys
  BT3 alloys
BT1 silicon alloys
 BT2 alloys

cologne spirits
USE ethanol

COLOMBIA [48; 48]
BT1 developing countries
BT1 south america
 BT2 latin america

COLOMBIAN ORGANIZATIONS [0; 20]
Apr 87
BT1 national organizations
NT1 ian

colon
USE large intestine

colonies
USE populations

COLONY FORMATION [679; 877]
Jul 76
NT1 spleen colony formation
RT animal cells
RT cell cultures
RT cloning

colony forming units
USE cfu

COLOR [3,214; 3,214]
BT1 optical properties
 BT2 physical properties
BT1 organoleptic properties
 BT2 dichroism

COLOR CENTERS [1,073; 3,269]
BT1 vacancies
 BT2 point defects
  BT3 crystal defects
   BT4 crystal structure

NT1 a centers
NT1 e centers
NT1 f centers
NT1 h centers
NT1 i centers
NT1 m centers
NT1 q centers
NT1 r centers
NT1 s centers
NT1 u centers
NT1 v centers
NT1 z centers

COLOR MODEL [3,923; 3,923] *Sep 75*
BT1 quark model
 BT2 composite models
  BT3 particle models
   BT4 mathematical models
RT glueballs
RT grace particles
RT preons
RT quantum chromodynamics
RT taste particles

COLORADO [690; 690]
BT1 usa
 BT2 developed countries
 BT2 north america
RT colorado river basin
RT green river formation
RT rocky flats plant
RT uinta formation
RT wasatch formation

COLORADO PLATEAU [35; 35]
UF *paradox basin*
BT1 mountains

COLORADO RIVER [15; 15]
BT1 rivers
 BT2 surface waters
RT colorado river basin

→ **COLORADO RIVER BASIN** [0; 0]
Oct 91
BT1 watersheds
RT colorado
RT colorado river

COLORATION [260; 260]
RT bleaching

COLORIMETRIC DOSEMETERS
[219; 219]
BT1 dosemeters
 BT2 measuring instruments
RT dyes
RT glass
RT polymers

colorimetry
USE absorption spectroscopy

columbia (missouri) res. reac
USE murr reactor

→ **COLUMBIA HIGH-BETA TOKAMAK**
[0; 0] *Aug 91*
BT1 tokamak devices
 BT2 closed plasma devices
  BT3 thermonuclear devices

COLUMBIA RIVER [281; 281]
BT1 rivers
 BT2 surface waters
RT columbia river basin
RT washington

→ **COLUMBIA RIVER BASIN** [0; 0]
Oct 91
BT1 watersheds
RT columbia river
RT idaho
RT oregon

RT washington

columbium
USE niobium

COLUMN PACKING [381; 381]
UF *berl saddles*
UF *packing (column)*
UF *raschig rings*
RT extraction columns

column separation (fluid mech)
(Prior to December 1990, this was a valid descriptor.)
USE cavitation

column separation (isotopes)
USE isotope separation

columns (extraction)
USE extraction columns

columns (structural)
(Prior to October 1983 MECHANICAL STRUCTURES was used for this concept.)
USE supports

columns (thermal)
USE thermal columns

COMANCHE PEAK-1 REACTOR [56; 56]
(Somervell, Texas, USA)
BT1 pwr type reactors
BT2 enriched uranium reactors
BT3 reactors
BT2 power reactors
BT3 reactors
BT2 thermal reactors
BT3 reactors
BT2 water cooled reactors
BT3 reactors
BT2 water moderated reactors
BT3 reactors

COMANCHE PEAK-2 REACTOR [48; 48]
(Somervell, Texas, USA)
BT1 pwr type reactors
BT2 enriched uranium reactors
BT3 reactors
BT2 power reactors
BT3 reactors
BT2 thermal reactors
BT3 reactors
BT2 water cooled reactors
BT3 reactors
BT2 water moderated reactors
BT3 reactors

comb. eng. standard reactor
USE ce standard reactor

→ COMBINED CYCLES [0; 0] *Oct 91*
BT1 thermodynamic cycles
RT combined-cycle power plants
RT electric power
RT power plants
RT total energy systems

→ *combined gas and steam cycle p*
(Combined gas and steam cycle power plants.)
USE combined-cycle power plants

combined heat-power generation
USE cogeneration

combined pinch devices (linear
USE linear screw pinch devices

combined steam-power generatio
USE cogeneration

→ COMBINED-CYCLE POWER PLANTS [0; 0] *Oct 91*
UF *combined gas and steam cycle p*
BT1 thermal power plants
BT2 power plants
RT combined cycles
RT gas turbine power plants

COMBUSTION [3,019; 3,180]
UF *spontaneous combustion*
BT1 oxidation
BT2 chemical reactions
NT1 cocombustion
NT1 fluidized-bed combustion
RT burners
RT combustion kinetics
RT combustion products
RT dry ashing
RT fire prevention
RT fires
RT flames
RT flammability
RT ignition systems
RT incinerators
RT wet ashing

→ COMBUSTION CONTROL [0; 0] *Oct 91*
(Control of factors (temperature, preheating, draft, excess or deficient air, etc.) which affect combustion efficiency.)
BT1 control
RT boilers
RT combustors

combustion gases
USE flue gas

COMBUSTION HEAT [88; 88]
UF *heat of combustion*
BT1 reaction heat
BT2 enthalpy
BT3 thermodynamic properties
BT4 physical properties

→ COMBUSTION KINETICS [0; 0] *Apr 84*
BT1 chemical reaction kinetics
BT2 reaction kinetics
BT3 kinetics
RT combustion

COMBUSTION PRODUCTS [240; 1,206]
Mar 83
UF *soot*
NT1 ashes
NT2 fly ash
RT combustion
RT exhaust gases
RT gaseous wastes
RT pyrolysis products
RT solid wastes

→ COMBUSTORS [0; 0] *Oct 91*
(Combustion chambers together with their associated burners, igniters, and fuel injection devices.)
RT burners
RT combustion control
RT ignition systems

COMECON [359; 359]
UF *cmea*
UF *council for mutual econ assist*
BT1 international organizations

COMETS [1,257; 1,619]
NT1 halley comet
RT planets
RT solar system

comissao nacional energia nucl
(Comissao Nacional de Energia Nuclear de Brasil.)
USE brazilian cnen

comitato nazionale en nuc e al
(Comitato Nazionale per la Ricerca e lo Sviluppo dell'Energia Nucleare e delle Energie Alternative.)
USE italian enea

comitato nazionale energia nuc
USE cnen

commensalism
USE symbiosis

commerce (nuclear)
USE nuclear trade

commercial demonstr fast react
USE cdfr reactor

COMMERCIAL LICENSES [36; 36]
Dec 76
BT1 licenses

commercial nuclear ships
USE nuclear merchant ships

COMMERCIAL SECTOR [66; 66]
Jul 86
RT commercialization
RT economic development
RT market
RT trade

COMMERCIALIZATION [647; 647]
Oct 84
(Establishment of a new technology for large-scale use after research, development, and demonstration.)
SF *technology development*
RT biotechnology
RT commercial sector
RT demonstration programs
RT economic development
RT feasibility studies
RT industry
RT market
RT technology impacts
RT technology transfer

comminution
USE mechanical fragmentation

commissariat a l'energie atomi
USE cea

commissioning (reactor)
USE reactor commissioning

COMMON MARKET [126; 126]
UF *european economic community*
BT1 european communities
BT2 international organizations

COMMUNICATIONS [822; 2,760]
    NT1   data transmission
        NT2   telemetry
    RT   data transmission systems
    RT   information theory
    RT   man-machine systems
    RT   radio equipment
    RT   signals

communities (ecological)
    USE   ecosystems

COMMUTATION RELATIONS
[3,319; 3,319]
    RT   canonical dimension
    RT   current algebra
    RT   mathematical operators
    RT   quantum mechanics

COMMUTATORS [860; 1,468]
    BT1   quantum operators
        BT2   mathematical operators
    NT1   current commutators
        NT2   sigma terms
    RT   current algebra

comp gener matieres nucleaires
    USE   cogema

compact helical system torsatr
    USE   chs torsatron

COMPACT IGNITION TOKAMAK
[363; 363] *Apr 87*
(A tokamak proposed as a next step after TFTR.)
    BT1   tokamak devices
        BT2   closed plasma devices
            BT3   thermonuclear devices
    RT   thermonuclear ignition

compact toroids
    USE   compact torus

COMPACT TORUS [394; 615] *Mar 83*
(Torus with aspect ratio nearly equal to one.)
    UF   *compact toroids*
    BT1   tori
    NT1   field-reversed theta pinch dev
    NT1   rotamak devices
    RT   closed plasma devices
    RT   plasma
    RT   plasma rings
    RT   toroidal configuration

COMPACTIFICATION [1,294; 1,294]
Oct 85
(Process by which the number of space-time dimensions may be reduced.)
    UF   *dimensional compactification*
    RT   dimensions
    RT   kaluza-klein theory
    RT   space-time
    RT   supergravity
    RT   symmetry breaking

COMPACTING [1,069; 1,069]
    BT1   fabrication
    RT   agglomeration
    RT   compacts
    RT   pelletizing
    RT   powder metallurgy
    RT   pressing
    RT   rolling

COMPACTS [476; 476]
    RT   compacting
    RT   powders

§§ **COMPARATIVE EVALUATIONS**
[54,710; 54,710]
(Use in coordination with the concepts being compared. In the case of numerical data see also EVALUATED DATA or COMPILED DATA.)
    BT1   evaluation
    RT   bioassay
    RT   correlations
    RT   cost benefit analysis
    RT   data
    RT   efficiency
    RT   errors
    RT   feasibility studies
    RT   functional models
    RT   hypothesis
    RT   interlaboratory comparisons
    RT   mathematical models
    RT   measuring methods
    RT   radiation effects
    RT   resolution
    RT   structural models

COMPARATOR CIRCUITS [320; 320]
(Provide indication of agreement or disagreement between signals.)
    BT1   electronic circuits

COMPARTMENTS [727; 727]
    RT   biophysics
    RT   extracellular space
    RT   radionuclide kinetics
    RT   retention
    RT   retention functions

§§ **COMPATIBILITY** [990; 990]
(Mutual behaviour of 2 or more materials joined or mixed together.)
    RT   joining
    RT   joints
    RT   mixtures

compatibility (immunological)
    USE   immunity

compensation (workmens)
    USE   workmens compensation

COMPETITION [111; 111] *Jul 86*
(Contest among individuals; may be used in any field.)
    RT   behavior
    RT   ecological succession
    RT   economics
    RT   population dynamics
    RT   trade

competitive protein binding
    USE   cpb

COMPILED DATA [7,759; 7,759]
(Use only in conjunction with literary indicator N for data flagging.)
    BT1   numerical data
        BT2   data
            BT3   information
    RT   data acquisition
    RT   data compilation
    RT   nuclear data collections

COMPLEMENT [231; 231]
    RT   antibodies
    RT   antigen-antibody reactions
    RT   blood plasma
    RT   hemolysins

COMPLEX MANIFOLDS [236; 236]
    BT1   mathematical manifolds

COMPLEXES [2,529; 29,817]
    UF+   *ammines*
    NT1   actinide complexes
        NT2   actinium complexes
        NT2   americium complexes
        NT2   berkelium complexes
        NT2   californium complexes
        NT2   curium complexes
        NT2   einsteinium complexes
        NT2   fermium complexes
        NT2   lawrencium complexes
        NT2   mendelevium complexes
        NT2   neptunium complexes
            NT3   neptunyl complexes
        NT2   nobelium complexes
        NT2   plutonium complexes
            NT3   plutonyl complexes
        NT2   protactinium complexes
        NT2   thorium complexes
        NT2   uranium complexes
            NT3   uranyl complexes
    NT1   alkali metal complexes
        NT2   cesium complexes
        NT2   francium complexes
        NT2   potassium complexes
        NT2   rubidium complexes
        NT2   sodium complexes
    NT1   alkaline earth metal complexes
        NT2   barium complexes
        NT2   beryllium complexes
        NT2   calcium complexes
        NT2   magnesium complexes
        NT2   radium complexes
        NT2   strontium complexes
    NT1   aluminium complexes
    NT1   ammonium complexes
    NT1   antimony complexes
    NT1   argon complexes
    NT1   arsenic complexes
    NT1   astatine complexes
    NT1   bismuth complexes
    NT1   boron complexes
    NT1   bromine complexes
    NT1   cadmium complexes
    NT1   carbon complexes
    NT1   chelates
    NT1   chlorine complexes
    NT1   element 104 complexes
    NT1   fluorine complexes
    NT1   gallium complexes
    NT1   germanium complexes
    NT1   helium complexes
    NT1   heteropolyanions
    NT1   hydrogen complexes
    NT1   indium complexes
    NT1   iodine complexes
    NT1   krypton complexes
    NT1   lead complexes
    NT1   lithium complexes
    NT1   mercury complexes
    NT1   neon complexes
    NT1   nitrogen complexes
    NT1   oxygen complexes
    NT1   phosphorus complexes
    NT1   polonium complexes
    NT1   radon complexes
    NT1   rare earth complexes
        NT2   cerium complexes
        NT2   dysprosium complexes
        NT2   erbium complexes
        NT2   europium complexes
        NT2   gadolinium complexes
        NT2   holmium complexes
        NT2   lanthanum complexes
        NT2   lutetium complexes
        NT2   neodymium complexes
        NT2   praseodymium complexes
        NT2   promethium complexes
        NT2   samarium complexes
        NT2   terbium complexes
        NT2   thulium complexes
        NT2   ytterbium complexes
    NT1   selenium complexes
    NT1   silicon complexes
    NT1   sulfur complexes
    NT1   tellurium complexes
    NT1   thallium complexes
    NT1   tin complexes
    NT1   transition element complexes
        NT2   chromium complexes

COMPLEXES

    NT2   cobalt complexes
    NT2   copper complexes
      NT3   ceruloplasmin
    NT2   gold complexes
    NT2   hafnium complexes
    NT2   iridium complexes
    NT2   iron complexes
      NT3   ferricyanides
      NT3   ferritin
      NT3   ferrocene
      NT3   ferrocyanides
    NT2   manganese complexes
    NT2   molybdenum complexes
    NT2   nickel complexes
    NT2   niobium complexes
    NT2   osmium complexes
    NT2   palladium complexes
    NT2   platinum complexes
    NT2   rhenium complexes
    NT2   rhodium complexes
    NT2   ruthenium complexes
    NT2   scandium complexes
    NT2   silver complexes
    NT2   tantalum complexes
    NT2   technetium complexes
    NT2   titanium complexes
    NT2   tungsten complexes
    NT2   vanadium complexes
    NT2   yttrium complexes
    NT2   zirconium complexes
    NT1   xenon complexes
    NT1   zinc complexes
    RT   adducts
    RT   complexometry
    RT   coordination number
    RT   coordination valences
    RT   ligands

COMPLEXOMETRY [950; 950]
    RT   complexes

COMPOSITE MATERIALS
[2,977; 7,188]
    BT1   materials
    NT1   cermets
    NT2   td-nickel
    NT2   td-nickel chromium
    NT1   concrete-plastic composites
    NT1   fiberglass
    NT1   prestressed concrete
    NT1   reinforced concrete
    NT1   superconducting composites
    NT1   wood-plastic composites
    RT   building materials
    RT   reinforced materials

COMPOSITE MODELS [1,737; 20,199]
    BT1   particle models
      BT2   mathematical models
    NT1   bootstrap model
    NT1   cim model
    NT1   parton model
    NT1   quark model
      NT2   color model
      NT2   flavor model
    RT   preons
    RT   quarks

COMPOUND NUCLEI [3,404; 3,404]
    RT   hauser-feshbach theory
    RT   jackson model
    RT   nuclear models
    RT   peierls method
    RT   porter-thomas distribution

COMPOUND-NUCLEUS REACTIONS
[4,508; 4,508]
    BT1   nuclear reactions
    RT   deep inelastic heavy ion react
    RT   incomplete fusion reactions
    RT   quasi-fission

compounds (inorganic)
    USE   inorganic compounds

compounds (organic)
    USE   organic compounds

COMPRESSED GASES [37; 37] *Jan 85*
    BT1   gases
      BT2   fluids
    RT   compressibility
    RT   compression
    RT   gas compressors

COMPRESSIBILITY [1,176; 1,176]
    BT1   mechanical properties
    RT   compressed gases
    RT   grueneisen constant

COMPRESSIBLE FLOW [454; 454]
    BT1   fluid flow
    RT   aerodynamics
    RT   gas flow
    RT   subsonic flow
    RT   supersonic flow
    RT   transonic flow

COMPRESSION [2,562; 3,234]
    NT1   magnetic compression
    RT   compressed gases
    RT   pressurization

COMPRESSION STRENGTH
[1,058; 1,058]
    UF   *strength (compression)*
    BT1   mechanical properties
    RT   tensile properties

compressor blades
    USE   compressors
    AND   turbine blades

COMPRESSORS [294; 428]
    UF+   *compressor blades*
    NT1   gas compressors
    NT1   magnetoplasma compressors
    RT   blowers
    RT   pressurizers
    RT   pumps
    RT   reactor cooling systems

COMPTON DIODE DETECTORS
[37; 37]
    BT1   radiation detectors
      BT2   measuring instruments
    RT   gamma detection
    RT   self-powered detectors

COMPTON EFFECT [3,445; 3,445]
    UF   *compton scattering*
    BT1   elastic scattering
      BT2   scattering
    BT1   electromagnetic interactions
      BT2   basic interactions
      BT2   interactions
    RT   compton scattering tomography
    RT   klein-nishina formula

compton scattering
    USE   compton effect

COMPTON SCATTERING TOMOGRAPHY [71; 71] *Apr 80*
(Based on the detection by a gamma camera of the 90 degree Compton scattering of a planar gamma beam produced by an external source.)
    BT1   tomography
    RT   compton effect
    RT   gamma cameras

COMPTON SPECTROMETERS
[240; 240]
    BT1   gamma spectrometers
      BT2   spectrometers
        BT3   measuring instruments

computed tomography
    USE   computerized tomography

COMPUTER ARCHITECTURE
[779; 779] *Feb 87*
(Assembly of logical elements to form a computing system.)
    RT   computers
    RT   digital systems
    RT   electronic equipment
    RT   equipment interfaces
    RT   neural networks

computer axial tomography scan
    USE   cat scanning

COMPUTER CALCULATIONS
[16,631; 16,631]
(Methods, not results.)
    UF   *calculations (computer)*
    RT   computer graphics
    RT   computer-graphics devices
    RT   computerized simulation
    RT   computers
    RT   data analysis
    RT   mathematical models
    RT   mesh generation
    RT   sensitivity analysis

§ **COMPUTER CODES** [16,006; 38,538]
(Computer codes are indexed by their initial letter and CODES, e.g., A CODES. If the code name begins with a number the code is indexed to NUMBER CODES.)
    UF   *computer programs*
    NT1   a codes
    NT1   b codes
    NT1   c codes
    NT1   d codes
    NT1   e codes
    NT1   executive codes
    NT1   f codes
    NT1   g codes
    NT1   h codes
    NT1   i codes
    NT1   j codes
    NT1   k codes
    NT1   l codes
    NT1   m codes
    NT1   n codes
    NT1   number codes
    NT1   o codes
    NT1   p codes
    NT1   q codes
    NT1   r codes
    NT1   s codes
    NT1   t codes
    NT1   translators
    NT1   u codes
    NT1   v codes
    NT1   w codes
    NT1   x codes
    NT1   y codes
    NT1   z codes
    RT   algorithms
    RT   computer program documentation
    RT   programming
    RT   programming languages

COMPUTER GRAPHICS [1,040; 1,040]
Dec 82
(The technique of combining computer calculations with various display devices, printers, plotters, etc., to render information in graphical or pictorial format.)
    RT   computer calculations
    RT   computer output devices
    RT   computer-aided design
    RT   computer-graphics devices
    RT   diagrams
    RT   display devices
    RT   plotters

computer graphics devices
    USE   computer-graphics devices

computer languages
  USE   programming languages

COMPUTER NETWORKS [1,265; 1,265]
Aug 76
(A complex consisting of two or more interconnected computing units.)
- UF   networks (computers)
- RT   computers
- RT   data transmission
- RT   information systems
- RT   on-line systems
- RT   real time systems

COMPUTER OUTPUT DEVICES
[3; 106] *Dec 90*
- NT1   computer-graphics devices
-   NT2   display devices
-     NT3   interactive display devices
-   NT2   plotters
- RT   computer graphics
- RT   computers

COMPUTER PROGRAM DOCUMENTATION [388; 388] *Sep 87*
(Use only in conjunction with literary indicator V for indexing the actual documentation which enables the installation and use of a computer code.)
- RT   computer codes
- RT   manuals
- RT   programming
- RT   programming languages

computer programming
  USE   programming

computer programs
  USE   computer codes

computer simulation
  USE   computerized simulation

COMPUTER-AIDED DESIGN
[1,249; 1,249] *Jul 77*
- BT1   design
- RT   computer graphics
- RT   computer-aided manufacturing
- RT   computer-graphics devices
- RT   computers
- RT   mathematical models
- RT   planning

COMPUTER-AIDED MANUFACTURING [77; 77] *Jan 84*
- UF   cam
- RT   automation
- RT   computer-aided design
- RT   fabrication
- RT   machine tools
- RT   on-line control systems
- RT   production

COMPUTER-GRAPHICS DEVICES
[275; 2,830]
- UF   computer graphics devices
- BT1   computer output devices
- NT1   display devices
-   NT2   interactive display devices
- NT1   plotters
- RT   computer calculations
- RT   computer graphics
- RT   computer-aided design
- RT   diagrams

→ ## COMPUTERIZED CONTROL SYSTEMS [0; 0] *Oct 91*
- BT1   on-line control systems
-   BT2   control systems
-   BT2   on-line systems
- RT   computers
- RT   control equipment

COMPUTERIZED SIMULATION
[17,003; 17,003] *Dec 79*
(Computer calculated representation of a process, device or concept in mathematical form.)
- UF   computer simulation
- BT1   simulation
- RT   computer calculations

COMPUTERIZED TOMOGRAPHY
[10,703; 23,488] *Apr 80*
(An imaging technique in which transmission measurements of a narrow beam of rays, photons or particles made at several different angles around an object may be used with a computer program to obtain a clear image of one plane of the object.)
- UF   computed tomography
- BT1   tomography
- NT1   cat scanning
- NT1   emission computed tomography
-   NT2   positron computed tomography
-   NT2   single photon ect
- NT1   proton computed tomography
- RT   biomedical radiography
- RT   image processing
- RT   image scanners
- RT   sequential scanning

COMPUTERS [5,403; 12,505]
- UF+   on-line computers
- NT1   alwac computers
- NT1   analog computers
- NT1   atlas computers
- NT1   besm computers
- NT1   burroughs computers
- NT1   cdc computers
- NT1   cray computers
- NT1   dec computers
-   NT2   pdp computers
- NT1   denelcor computers
- NT1   digital computers
-   NT2   array processors
-   NT2   calculators
-   NT2   cii computers
-   NT2   fault tolerant computers
-   NT2   microcomputers
-   NT2   parameter computers
-   NT2   supercomputers
- NT1   dpp computers
- NT1   es computers
- NT1   facom computers
- NT1   ferranti computers
- NT1   fluidic computers
- NT1   ge computers
- NT1   honeywell computers
- NT1   hp computers
- NT1   hybrid computers
- NT1   hypercube computers
- NT1   ibm computers
- NT1   icl computers
- NT1   illiac computers
- NT1   kdf computers
- NT1   maniac computers
- NT1   midas computer
- NT1   minsk computers
- NT1   nord computers
- NT1   orion computers
- NT1   philco computers
- NT1   process computers
- NT1   razdan computers
- NT1   sds computers
- NT1   serac computers
- NT1   siemens computers
- NT1   silliac computers
- NT1   univac computers
- NT1   ural computers
- NT1   xds computers
- RT   analog systems
- RT   artificial intelligence
- RT   camac system
- RT   computer architecture
- RT   computer calculations
- RT   computer networks
- RT   computer output devices
- RT   computer-aided design
- RT   computerized control systems
- RT   data processing
- RT   digital systems
- RT   electronic equipment
- RT   equipment interfaces
- RT   fastbus system
- RT   magnetic cores
- RT   parallel processing
- RT   programming
- RT   real time systems
- RT   vector processing

CONCANAVALIN A [190; 190] *Feb 81*
- BT1   hemagglutinins
-   BT2   agglutinins
- RT   cell cycle
- RT   cell proliferation
- RT   lymphocytes
- RT   mitosis

concentrates (ore)
  USE   ore concentrates

concentration (analytical)
  USE   quantity ratio

concentration dependence
  USE   quantity ratio

concentration processes (ecol)
  USE   ecological concentration

concentrations (radionuclides)
  USE   radioactivity

CONCRETE STRINGERS [28; 28]
- RT   reinforced concrete

CONCRETE-PLASTIC COMPOSITES
[47; 47] *Nov 75*
- BT1   composite materials
-   BT2   materials
- RT   concretes
- RT   organic polymers

CONCRETES [3,963; 6,488]
- BT1   building materials
-   BT2   materials
- NT1   prestressed concrete
- NT1   reinforced concrete
- RT   cements
- RT   concrete-plastic composites
- RT   mortars
- RT   sand
- RT   shielding materials

CONDENSATES [627; 627]
- RT   drainage
- RT   vapor condensation

condensation (vapor)
  USE   vapor condensation

CONDENSATION CHAMBERS
[366; 366]
- RT   control equipment
- RT   pressure suppression
- RT   reactor components
- RT   reactor cooling systems
- RT   reactor safety
- RT   vapor condensation

CONDENSATION NUCLEI [48; 48]
Sep 81
(Small particles upon which gases can condense, such as dust in the earth's atmosphere.)
- RT   aerosols
- RT   meteorology
- RT   particles
- RT   vapor condensation

CONDENSED AROMATICS [448; 1,901]
- UF polynuclear hydrocarbons
- BT1 aromatics
  - BT2 organic compounds
- NT1 acenaphthene
- NT1 anthracene
- NT1 benzanthracene
- NT1 benzopyrene
- NT1 cholanthrene
- NT1 chrysene
- NT1 dimethylbenzanthracene
- NT1 fluorene
- NT1 indene
- NT1 indocyanine green
- NT1 naphthalene
- NT1 perylene
- NT1 phenanthrene
- NT1 pyrene
- NT1 tetracene
- NT1 triphenylene
- NT1 violanthrone
- NT1 3-methylcholanthrene

CONDENSER COOLING SYSTEMS [73; 73] Jul 80
(For heat dissipation in either nuclear or fossil fueled power plants. May be of open circuit or closed cycle design.)
- BT1 auxiliary water systems
  - BT2 auxiliary systems
- BT1 cooling systems
- RT reactor cooling systems

CONDENSER IONIZATION CHAMBERS [151; 151]
- UF pocket chambers
- BT1 dosemeters
  - BT2 measuring instruments
- BT1 ionization chambers
  - BT2 radiation detectors
    - BT3 measuring instruments
- RT electrometers

condensers (electric)
- USE capacitors

condensers (steam)
- USE steam condensers

condensers (using ice)
(A steam condenser using ice as the heat sink.)
- USE ice condensers

condensers (vapor)
- USE vapor condensers

CONDITIONED REFLEXES [31; 31]
- BT1 reflexes
- RT avoidance
- RT cerebral cortex
- RT learning

conduction (thermal)
- USE thermal conduction

conductivity (electric)
- USE electric conductivity

conductivity (thermal)
- USE thermal conductivity

CONDUCTOR DEVICES [88; 2,520]
- BT1 electrical equipment
  - BT2 equipment
- NT1 connectors
- NT1 electric cables
  - NT2 coaxial cables
  - NT2 cryogenic cables
  - NT2 gas-insulated cables
  - NT2 superconducting cables
- NT1 electric fuses
- RT electric conductors
- RT resistors

conductors (electric)
- USE electric conductors

CONES [58; 58] Sep 83
- RT shape

conferences
- USE meetings

§§ CONFIGURATION [7,194; 25,293]
(For the relative arrangement of component parts; for electron configuration in atoms and molecules use ELECTRONIC STRUCTURE; for nuclear configuration use NUCLEAR STRUCTURE; for molecular configuration use MOLECULAR STRUCTURE.)
- NT1 annular space
  - NT2 toroidal configuration
- NT1 circular configuration
- NT1 conical configuration
- NT1 cylindrical configuration
- NT1 elliptical configuration
- NT1 helical configuration
- NT1 hexagonal configuration
- NT1 prismatic configuration
- NT1 rectangular configuration
  - NT2 square configuration
- NT1 spherical configuration
- NT1 spiral configuration
- NT1 triangular configuration
- RT anisotropy
- RT asymmetry
- RT crystal structure
- RT geometry
- RT isotropy
- RT mass distribution
- RT orientation
- RT reactor lattices
- RT rings
- RT shape
- RT symmetry

CONFIGURATION CONTROL [192; 289]
(Reactor control by varying the configuration of the fuel, reflector, coolant or moderator.)
- NT1 spectral shift control
- RT moderators
- RT neutron reflectors
- RT reactor control systems
- RT reactor lattices
- RT reflector savings

CONFIGURATION INTERACTION [2,442; 2,442]
(Not for interactions of elementary particles; for which see INTERACTIONS.)
- RT atomic models
- RT electronic structure
- RT molecular structure

CONFIGURATION MIXING [3,490; 3,490]
- BT1 interactions
- RT kobayashi-maskawa matrix

§ CONFINEMENT [3,646; 10,794]
- NT1 plasma confinement
  - NT2 h-mode plasma confinement
  - NT2 inertial confinement
  - NT2 magnetic confinement
- RT magnetic insulation
- RT mass balance

CONFINEMENT TIME [1,687; 1,687]
- RT h-mode plasma confinement
- RT lawson criterion
- RT plasma
- RT plasma confinement
- RT plasma disruption
- RT thermonuclear devices
- RT thermonuclear reactors
- RT time dependence

CONFORMAL GROUPS [1,314; 1,314]
- BT1 lie groups
  - BT2 symmetry groups
- RT conformal invariance
- RT conformal mapping

CONFORMAL INVARIANCE [3,209; 3,209]
- BT1 invariance principles
- RT conformal groups
- RT scale dimension
- RT scale invariance

CONFORMAL MAPPING [850; 850]
- BT1 topological mapping
  - BT2 transformations
- RT conformal groups
- RT mathematics
- RT smooth manifolds

CONGENITAL DISEASES [401; 486]
- BT1 diseases
- NT1 downs syndrome

CONGENITAL MALFORMATIONS [1,483; 1,561]
- BT1 malformations
  - BT2 pathological changes
    - BT3 diseases
- NT1 downs syndrome
- RT delayed radiation effects
- RT fetuses
- RT genetic effects
- RT mutations
- RT pediatrics
- RT teratogenesis
- RT teratogens

CONGLOMERATES [158; 158]
- BT1 rocks
- RT graywacke

congo democratic republic
- USE zaire republic

congo kinshasa triga reactor
- USE trico reactor

CONGO PEOPLES REPUBLIC [5; 5]
- BT1 africa
- BT1 developing countries

CONGO RED [6; 6]
- BT1 amines
  - BT2 organic compounds
- BT1 azo dyes
  - BT2 azo compounds
    - BT3 organic nitrogen compounds
      - BT4 organic compounds
  - BT2 dyes
- BT1 indicators
- BT1 sulfonic acids
  - BT2 organic acids
    - BT3 organic compounds
  - BT2 organic sulfur compounds
    - BT3 organic compounds
- RT benzidine

CONICAL CONFIGURATION [257; 257]
- BT1 configuration

CONIDIA [68; 68]
  BT1 spores
  RT   fungi

CONIFERS [67; 343]
  BT1 plants
  NT1 pines
  RT   shrubs
  RT   trees

conjugate points
  USE geomagnetic conjugacy

CONJUNCTIVA [43; 43]
  BT1 eyes
    BT2 sense organs
      BT3 organs
        BT4 body
  BT1 mucous membranes
  RT   conjunctivitis
  RT   epithelium

CONJUNCTIVITIS [12; 12]
  BT1 sense organs diseases
    BT2 diseases
  RT   conjunctiva

CONNAH QUAY-B REACTOR [1; 1]
  BT1 agr type reactors
    BT2 enriched uranium reactors
      BT3 reactors
    BT2 gas cooled reactors
      BT3 reactors
    BT2 graphite moderated reactors
      BT3 reactors
  BT1 power reactors
    BT2 reactors

CONNECTICUT [100; 100]
  BT1 usa
    BT2 developed countries
    BT2 north america

CONNECTICUT RIVER [9; 9]
  BT1 rivers
    BT2 surface waters

CONNECTICUT YANKEE REACTOR
[164; 164]
  UF   *haddam neck reactor*
  UF   *yankee connecticut reactor*
  BT1 pwr type reactors
    BT2 enriched uranium reactors
      BT3 reactors
    BT2 power reactors
      BT3 reactors
    BT2 thermal reactors
      BT3 reactors
    BT2 water cooled reactors
      BT3 reactors
    BT2 water moderated reactors
      BT3 reactors

connecting
  USE fastening

connections
  USE joints

CONNECTIVE TISSUE [388; 4,757]
  BT1 tissues
    BT2 body
  NT1 adipose tissue
  NT1 bone tissues
    NT2 antlers
    NT2 trabecular bone
  NT1 cartilage
  NT1 fascia
  NT1 ligaments
  RT   blood
  RT   collagen
  RT   connective tissue cells

  RT   fibrosis
  RT   reticuloendothelial system

CONNECTIVE TISSUE CELLS
[87; 10,798]
  UF   *osteoblasts*
  BT1 somatic cells
    BT2 animal cells
  NT1 bone cells
  NT1 bone marrow cells
  NT1 fat cells
  NT1 fibroblasts
  NT1 lymphocytes
  NT1 macrophages
  NT1 mast cells
  NT1 plasma cells
  RT   connective tissue

CONNECTORS [212; 212]
  BT1 conductor devices
    BT2 electrical equipment
      BT3 equipment
  RT   switches

conservation (charge)
  USE charge conservation

conservation (energy)
  USE energy conservation

conservation (resources)
  USE resource conservation

CONSERVATION LAWS [3,453; 3,453]
  RT   basic interactions
  RT   invariance principles
  RT   particle kinematics

consol. fuel reproc. program
  USE cfrp program

CONSOLES [297; 297]
  RT   control rooms
  RT   display devices
  RT   electronic equipment

consolidated edison thorium r.
  USE indian point-1 reactor

CONSORT-2 REACTOR [12; 12]
(Imperial College of Science and Technology for Univ. of London, Ascot, Berkshire, United Kingdom)
  BT1 enriched uranium reactors
    BT2 reactors
  BT1 isotope production reactors
    BT2 irradiation reactors
      BT3 reactors
  BT1 pool type reactors
    BT2 water cooled reactors
      BT3 reactors
    BT2 water moderated reactors
      BT3 reactors
  BT1 research reactors
    BT2 research and test reactors
      BT3 reactors
  BT1 thermal reactors
    BT2 reactors
  BT1 training reactors
    BT2 research and test reactors
      BT3 reactors

CONSPIRACY RELATIONS [13; 13]
  RT   regge poles
  RT   scattering

constantan
  USE alloy-cu52ni47

CONSTIPATION [18; 18]
  BT1 symptoms
  RT   diarrhea
  RT   digestive system diseases
  RT   intestines

constituent interchange model
  USE cim model

CONSTRUCTION [7,729; 7,729]
(For manufacturing see FABRICATION.)
  UF   *building (constructing)*
  UF+ *construction work in progress*
  UF+ *cwip*
  RT   buildings
  RT   contracts
  RT   excavation
  RT   foundations
  RT   mechanical structures
  RT   modifications
  RT   modular structures
  RT   nuclear industry
  RT   planning
  RT   retrofitting

CONSTRUCTION PERMITS [732; 732]
Dec 76
  BT1 licenses

construction work in progress
  USE construction
  AND financing

CONSTRUCTIVE FIELD THEORY
[233; 6,185] *Nov 77*
  UF+ *euclidean quantum field theory*
  BT1 quantum field theory
    BT2 field theories
  NT1 lattice field theory

consult mechan on sea dumping
(Multilateral Consultation and surveillance Mechanism for Sea Dumping of Radioactive Waste.)
  USE oecd mcmsdrw

CONSUMER PRODUCTS [107; 107]
Sep 80
(Articles of commerce available to the general public. When possible, use descriptors for the specific products, e.g., food, clothing, instruments and pharmaceuticals.)
  UF   *cosmetics*
  RT   clothing
  RT   drugs
  RT   food

consumers michigan palisades r
  USE palisades-1 reactor

consumers power co. midland-1
  USE midland-1 reactor

consumers power co. midland-2
  USE midland-2 reactor

CONTACT HANDLING [32; 32] *Dec 85*
(Handling by touch, perhaps made allowable because of low surface radiation dose rate.)
  RT   materials handling
  RT   materials handling equipment
  RT   remote handling

contact radiotherapy
  USE radiotherapy

contactors
  USE switches

contacts (electric)
  USE electric contacts

CONTAINED EXPLOSIONS [124; 491]
  BT1 underground explosions
   BT2 explosions
  NT1 almendro event
  NT1 baneberry event
  NT1 benham event
  NT1 boxcar event
  NT1 cannikin event
  NT1 carpetbag event
  NT1 dining car event
  NT1 gasbuggy event
  NT1 halfbeak event
  NT1 handley event
  NT1 marvel event
  NT1 monique event
  NT1 pokhran event
  NT1 rio blanco event
  NT1 rulison event
  NT1 scotch event
  NT1 wagon wheel event
  RT   anvil project
  RT   arbor project
  RT   chemical explosions
  RT   mining
  RT   nuclear explosions
  RT   plowshare project
  RT   thunderbird project

CONTAINERS [6,189; 25,232]
  UF   *vessels*
  NT1 calandrias
  NT1 capsules
  NT1 casks
  NT1 dewars
  NT1 gas cylinders
  NT1 pressure vessels
  NT1 reactor vessels
  NT1 tanks
  RT   chemical reactors
  RT   containment
  RT   liners
  RT   packaging
  RT   radiation sources
  RT   reactor components
  RT   shielding
  RT   transport

CONTAINMENT [4,466; 10,685]
(Means and methods for preventing the escape of radioactive materials to the biosphere, particularly in the case of reactor accidents and including entombment.)
  UF   *entombment (radioactive matls)*
  NT1 containment buildings
  NT1 containment shells
  NT1 containment systems
   NT2 containment spray systems
  RT   air infiltration
  RT   containers
  RT   containment mockup facility
  RT   containment research installat
  RT   fission product release
  RT   fission products
  RT   gloveboxes
  RT   leaks
  RT   radiation protection
  RT   reactor components
  RT   reactor safety
  RT   sealed sources
  RT   source terms

CONTAINMENT BUILDINGS
[2,599; 2,599]
  BT1 buildings
  BT1 containment

CONTAINMENT MOCKUP FACILITY
[33; 33]
  BT1 reactor safety experiments
  RT   containment

CONTAINMENT RESEARCH INSTALLAT [10; 10]
  BT1 reactor safety experiments
  RT   containment

CONTAINMENT SHELLS [1,321; 1,321]
  UF   *shells (containment)*
  BT1 containment

CONTAINMENT SPRAY SYSTEMS
[331; 331]
  UF   *spray systems (containment)*
  BT1 containment systems
   BT2 containment
  RT   pressure suppression
  RT   reactor safety

CONTAINMENT SYSTEMS
[2,497; 2,788]
  BT1 containment
  NT1 containment spray systems
  RT   containment systems experiment
  RT   fission products
  RT   ice condensers

CONTAINMENT SYSTEMS EXPERIMENT [76; 76]
  BT1 reactor safety experiments
  RT   containment systems

CONTAMINATION [9,099; 11,156]
(For radioactive contamination only; see also POLLUTION.)
  NT1 surface contamination
  NT1 transfrontier contamination
  RT   body burden
  RT   clean rooms
  RT   contamination regulations
  RT   environment
  RT   fallout
  RT   fission product release
  RT   global aspects
  RT   lcpmpdpw
  RT   liquid contamination monitors
  RT   maximum acceptable contaminati
  RT   medical surveillance
  RT   oecd mcmsdrw
  RT   radioactive wastes
  RT   radioactivity
  RT   radioactivity transport
  RT   radioecological concentration

contamination (internal)
  USE radionuclide kinetics

CONTAMINATION REGULATIONS
[244; 389]
(Regulations for radioactive contamination only; see also POLLUTION REGULATIONS.)
  BT1 regulations
   BT2 laws
  NT1 maximum acceptable contaminati
  RT   contamination
  RT   transfrontier contamination
  RT   us natl environment policy act

content analysis
  USE chemical analysis

CONTINENTAL CRUST [142; 142]
Sep 81
  BT1 earth crust
  RT   earth planet

→ **CONTINENTAL MARGIN** [0; 0] *Oct 91*
(The ocean floor that is between the shoreline and the abyssal ocean floor including the continental borderland, the continental shelf, the continental slope, and the continental rise.)
  NT1 continental shelf
  NT1 continental slope
  RT   coastal waters

CONTINENTAL SHELF [91; 91]
  BT1 continental margin
  RT   coastal waters
  RT   continental slope
  RT   territorial waters

→ **CONTINENTAL SLOPE** [0; 0] *Oct 91*
(That part of the continental margin that is between the continental shelf and the continental rise.)
  BT1 continental margin
  RT   coastal waters
  RT   continental shelf

CONTINUED FRACTIONS [81; 81]
(Finite or infinite.)
  RT   analytic functions
  RT   series expansion

CONTINUITY EQUATIONS [837; 837]
  BT1 partial differential equations
   BT2 differential equations
    BT3 equations
  RT   electromagnetism
  RT   fluid flow
  RT   heat transfer

→ **CONTINUOUS CURRENT TOKAMAK**
[3; 3] *Aug 91*
  BT1 tokamak devices
   BT2 closed plasma devices
    BT3 thermonuclear devices

continuous intake
  USE chronic intake

continuous irradiation
  USE chronic irradiation

continuous vacuum casting
  USE vacuum casting

continuum shell model
  USE shell models

CONTRACTION [543; 543]
  RT   expansion
  RT   expansion joints
  RT   shrinkage
  RT   thermal expansion

CONTRACTORS [98; 98] *Jul 86*
(Persons or companies which supply services under contract.)
  UF   *subcontractors*
  RT   contracts

§ **CONTRACTS** [624; 624]
  RT   agreements
  RT   construction
  RT   contractors
  RT   delivery

contractual liability
(Prior to December 1990, this was a valid descriptor.)
  USE liabilities

CONTRAST MEDIA [6,361; 7,918]
- NT1 diodrast
- NT1 hippuran
- NT1 hypaque
- NT1 ioglycamic acid
- NT1 iohexol
- NT1 iopamidol
- NT1 lipiodol
- NT1 metrizamide
- NT1 thorotrast
- RT biomedical radiography
- RT nuclear magnetic resonance

CONTROL [4,073; 14,533]
(Regulating a process, property or component in a qualitative or quantitative sense. Not to be confused with MONITORING which refers only to detection or measurement.)
- NT1 closed-loop control
- NT1 combustion control
- NT1 frequency control
- NT1 humidity control
- NT1 mode control
- NT1 open-loop control
- NT1 optimal control
- NT1 pollution control
  - NT2 air pollution control
  - NT2 water pollution control
- NT1 pressure control
- NT1 quality control
- NT1 remote control
- NT1 temperature control
- RT control systems
- RT control theory
- RT cybernetics
- RT decision tree analysis
- RT detection
- RT fault tree analysis
- RT feedback
- RT mitigation
- RT monitoring
- RT optimization

control (inspection)
USE inspection

control (radioactivity)
USE radiation monitoring

CONTROL ELEMENTS [3,579; 4,183]
- UF *control rods*
- UF *reactor control rods*
- UF *rods (control)*
- BT1 reactor components
- NT1 regulating rods
- NT1 scram rods
- NT1 shim rods
- RT burnable poisons
- RT control rod drives
- RT control rod worths
- RT guide tubes
- RT neutron absorbers
- RT reactor control systems
- RT reactor cores
- RT reactor kinetics
- RT rod drop accidents
- RT rod drop method
- RT rod ejection accidents

CONTROL EQUIPMENT [893; 8,294]
- BT1 equipment
- NT1 electric controllers
- NT1 flow regulators
  - NT2 baffles
  - NT2 valves
    - NT3 relief valves
- NT1 fluidic control devices
- NT1 humidistats
- NT1 hydraulic control devices
- NT1 pneumatic controllers
- NT1 pressure regulators
- NT1 servomechanisms
- NT1 speed regulators
- NT1 thermostats
  - NT2 cryostats
- RT actuators
- RT computerized control systems
- RT condensation chambers
- RT control rooms
- RT control systems
- RT reactor components
- RT robots

CONTROL ROD DRIVES [1,542; 1,542]
- BT1 reactor components
- RT control elements
- RT reactor control systems

control rod effectiveness
USE control rod worths

CONTROL ROD WORTHS [844; 844]
- UF *control rod effectiveness*
- RT control elements
- RT nordheim-scalettar method
- RT reactor kinetics

control rods
USE control elements

CONTROL ROOMS [1,159; 1,159]
Dec 79
(In the sense of the fully instrumented complex of control equipment, displays and instruments and their layout in a room at a particular facility and not in the limited sense of a part of a building.)
- RT consoles
- RT control equipment
- RT display devices
- RT man-machine systems
- RT reactor control systems
- RT reactor instrumentation
- RT reactor simulators

CONTROL SYSTEMS [5,432; 16,336]
(For automated processes including feedback.)
- NT1 electronic guidance
- NT1 on-line control systems
  - NT2 computerized control systems
- NT1 reactor control systems
- RT control
- RT control equipment
- RT identification systems
- RT interlocks
- RT man-machine systems
- RT optimization
- RT power conditioning circuits
- RT real time systems
- RT robots
- RT systems analysis

CONTROL THEORY [234; 234] Sep 76
- RT control
- RT differential equations
- RT feedback
- RT optimization

control theory (fiss reactor)
USE reactor kinetics

CONTROLLED AREAS [299; 299]
Dec 76
(Areas designated by radiation protection regulations for special monitoring.)
- RT nuclear facilities
- RT radiation monitoring
- RT radiation protection

CONTROLLED ATMOSPHERES [1,113; 2,089]
- NT1 inert atmosphere
  - NT2 cover gas
- RT clean rooms
- RT environment
- RT exhaust systems
- RT exposure chambers
- RT heat treatments

controlled terminology
USE standardized terminology

conv assist nuc acc/rad emerg
USE canare

conv early notif nuc accident
USE cenna

conv phys protec nucl material
USE cppnm

CONVECTION [3,007; 5,802]
(Heat transfer by convection.)
- BT1 heat transfer
  - BT2 energy transfer
- NT1 forced convection
- NT1 natural convection
- RT advection
- RT grashof number
- RT mass transfer

CONVECTIVE INSTABILITIES [357; 357]
- BT1 plasma instability
  - BT2 instability
- RT absolute instabilities
- RT briggs criterion

conventions
USE agreements

§ ## CONVERGENCE [620; 620]
(Approach to a limit, e.g. by an infinite sequence; prior to December 1982 this concept was indexed by SERIES EXPANSION.)
- RT mathematics
- RT series expansion
- RT superconvergence relations

CONVERSION [543; 6,158]
- NT1 energy conversion
  - NT2 direct energy conversion
    - NT3 photovoltaic conversion
    - NT3 thermionic conversion
    - NT3 thermoelectric conversion
    - NT3 thermomagnetic conversion
- NT1 external conversion
- NT1 internal conversion
  - NT2 internal pair production
  - NT2 k conversion
  - NT2 l conversion
  - NT2 m conversion

conversion (nuclear fuel)
USE nuclear fuel conversion

CONVERSION RATIO [317; 1,418]
- NT1 breeding ratio
- RT nuclear fuel conversion

converters (analog-digital)
USE analog-to-digital converters

converters (digital-analog)
USE digital-to-analog converters

converters (image)
USE image converters

converters (pulse)
USE pulse converters

CONVEX MANIFOLDS [36; 36] *Sep 76*
  BT1 mathematical manifolds

CONVEYORS [78; 78] *Dec 85*
  BT1 materials handling equipment
    BT2 equipment
  RT   transport

cony
  USE pikas

COOK-1 REACTOR [86; 86]
  UF   *donald c. cook-1 reactor*
  BT1 pwr type reactors
    BT2 enriched uranium reactors
      BT3 reactors
    BT2 power reactors
      BT3 reactors
    BT2 thermal reactors
      BT3 reactors
    BT2 water cooled reactors
      BT3 reactors
    BT2 water moderated reactors
      BT3 reactors

COOK-2 REACTOR [77; 77]
  UF   *donald c. cook-2 reactor*
  BT1 pwr type reactors
    BT2 enriched uranium reactors
      BT3 reactors
    BT2 power reactors
      BT3 reactors
    BT2 thermal reactors
      BT3 reactors
    BT2 water cooled reactors
      BT3 reactors
    BT2 water moderated reactors
      BT3 reactors

cooking (food)
  USE food processing

COOLANT CLEANUP SYSTEMS [598; 598] *Oct 77*
  RT   cleaning
  RT   decontamination
  RT   extraction apparatuses
  RT   filters
  RT   primary coolant circuits
  RT   purification

COOLANT LOOPS [1,164; 1,164]
(For reactors use REACTOR COOLING SYSTEMS or IN PILE LOOPS.)
  UF   *loops (coolant)*
  RT   bypasses
  RT   closed-cycle cooling systems
  RT   cooling
  RT   cooling systems
  RT   heat transfer

coolant-fuel interactions
  USE fuel-coolant interactions

COOLANTS [5,619; 5,728]
(See also specific coolant materials.)
  SF   *heat transfer fluids*
  NT1 organic coolants
  RT   cooling
  RT   fuel-coolant interactions
  RT   gases
  RT   heavy water
  RT   liquid metals
  RT   loss of coolant
  RT   molten salts
  RT   oils
  RT   reactor cooling systems
  RT   reactor materials
  RT   refrigerants
  RT   steam
  RT   thermonuclear reactor cooling
  RT   water
  RT   water chemistry

coolers
  USE heat exchangers

COOLING [5,226; 7,535]
  SF   *heat dissipation*
  NT1 evaporative cooling
  NT1 film cooling
  NT1 fog cooling
  NT1 gas cooling
  NT1 radiative cooling
  NT1 refrigeration
    NT2 helium dilution refrigeration
  NT1 splat cooling
  NT1 spray cooling
  NT1 subcooling
  NT1 sublimation cooling
  RT   air conditioning
  RT   coolant loops
  RT   coolants
  RT   cooling systems
  RT   cooling towers
  RT   fuel cooling time
  RT   heat exchangers
  RT   heat pumps
  RT   heat transfer
  RT   heating
  RT   ice condensers
  RT   reactor cooling systems
  RT   temperature control
  RT   temperature noise
  RT   thermonuclear reactor cooling
  RT   vapor condensation
  RT   water

cooling ponds
  USE water reservoirs

COOLING SYSTEMS [1,865; 17,384] *Feb 76*
  NT1 closed-cycle cooling systems
  NT1 condenser cooling systems
  NT1 open-cycle cooling systems
  NT1 reactor cooling systems
    NT2 direct cycle cooling systems
    NT2 dual cycle cooling systems
    NT2 integrated cooling systems
    NT2 primary coolant circuits
    NT2 secondary coolant circuits
    NT2 shrouds
  NT1 thermonuclear reactor cooling
  RT   coolant loops
  RT   cooling
  RT   cooling towers
  RT   intake structures
  RT   refrigerators

cooling systems (fiss reactor)
  USE reactor cooling systems

cooling systems (fus reactor)
  USE thermonuclear reactor cooling

cooling time
(The cooling time of spent fuel after its discharge from the reactor core.)
  USE fuel cooling time

COOLING TOWERS [1,001; 1,001]
  UF+ *counterflow cooling towers*
  UF+ *crossflow cooling towers*
  RT   closed-cycle cooling systems
  RT   cooling
  RT   cooling systems
  RT   counterflow systems
  RT   crossflow systems
  RT   evaporative cooling
  RT   heat exchangers
  RT   open-cycle cooling systems
  RT   reactor components
  RT   vapor condensers

cooling water chem. treatment
  USE water chemistry

COOPER PAIRS [654; 654]
  RT   bose-einstein statistics
  RT   coherence length
  RT   electrons
  RT   fermi level
  RT   superconductivity

COOPER REACTOR [75; 75]
(Brownsville, Nebraska, USA)
  BT1 bwr type reactors
    BT2 enriched uranium reactors
      BT3 reactors
    BT2 power reactors
      BT3 reactors
    BT2 thermal reactors
      BT3 reactors
    BT2 water cooled reactors
      BT3 reactors
    BT2 water moderated reactors
      BT3 reactors

COOPERATION [161; 2,218] *Jul 86*
  NT1 intergovernmental cooperation
  NT1 international cooperation
  NT1 regional cooperation
  RT   agreements
  RT   coordinated research programs
  RT   interlaboratory comparisons

cooperative spontaneous emissi
  USE superradiance

COORDINATED RESEARCH PROGRAMS [2,221; 2,367]
(Research based on a common plan but carried out in various locations. This descriptor to be used in coordination with descriptors for the institutions or countries involved.)
  UF   *large coil program*
  BT1 research programs
  NT1 cfrp program
  NT1 ifip
  RT   cooperation
  RT   dumand project
  RT   interlaboratory comparisons
  RT   international agreements
  RT   international cooperation
  RT   international organizations
  RT   planning

COORDINATES [3,765; 4,213]
  UF   *grids (coordinates)*
  UF   *position (optical)*
  UF   *position (radio)*
  NT1 cartesian coordinates
  NT1 curvilinear coordinates
    NT2 magnetic flux coordinates
  NT1 geomagnetic coordinates
  NT1 hylleraas coordinates
  RT   center-of-mass system
  RT   laboratory system
  RT   mathematics
  RT   mesh generation
  RT   position operators

COORDINATION NUMBER [1,900; 1,900]
  RT   complexes
  RT   coordination valences
  RT   ligands

COORDINATION VALENCES [753; 753]
  BT1 valence
  RT   complexes
  RT   coordination number
  RT   crystal lattices
  RT   structural chemical analysis

copepods
  USE   crustaceans

COPOLYMERIZATION [616; 616]
(Polymerization of molecules of different types.)
  BT1   polymerization
    BT2   chemical reactions

COPOLYMERS [489; 489] *Nov 75*
  BT1   organic polymers
    BT2   organic compounds
    BT2   polymers

COPPER [12,424; 12,424]
  BT1   transition elements
    BT2   metals
      BT3   elements

COPPER ADDITIONS [561; 1,303]
(Alloys containing not more than 1% Cu are listed here.)
  NT1   alloy-ni43fe33cr16mo3
  NT1   alloy-ni48cr22fe18mo9
  NT1   alloy-ni60co15cr10al6ti5mo3
  NT1   steel-crmov
  NT1   steel-crni
  NT1   steel-cr2mov
  NT1   steel-cr2nimov
  NT1   steel-mncumo
  NT1   steel-nicr
  NT1   steel-nicrmo
  NT1   steel-ni3cr
  NT1   steel-ni4crw
  RT   copper alloys
  RT   copper compounds

COPPER ALLOYS [3,027; 5,033]
(Alloys containing more than 1% Cu.)
  BT1   alloys
  NT1   alloy-al95cu4
  NT1   alloy-ni43fe30cr22mo3
  NT1   alloy-ni66cu32
  NT1   copper base alloys
    NT2   alloy-cu52ni47
    NT2   brass
      NT3   brass-alpha
      NT3   brass-beta
    NT2   bronze
    NT2   german silver
    NT2   heusler alloys
    NT2   tungsten bronze
  NT1   steel-cr17cu4ni4nb-l
  NT1   tikonal
  RT   copper additions

→ **COPPER ARSENIDES** [0; 0] *Sep 91*
  BT1   arsenides
    BT2   arsenic compounds
    BT2   pnictides
  BT1   copper compounds
    BT2   transition element compounds

COPPER BASE ALLOYS [1,092; 1,869]
  BT1   copper alloys
    BT2   alloys
  NT1   alloy-cu52ni47
  NT1   brass
    NT2   brass-alpha
    NT2   brass-beta
  NT1   bronze
  NT1   german silver
  NT1   heusler alloys
  NT1   tungsten bronze

COPPER BORIDES [10; 10]
  BT1   borides
    BT2   boron compounds
  BT1   copper compounds
    BT2   transition element compounds

COPPER BROMIDES [66; 66]
  BT1   bromides
    BT2   bromine compounds
      BT3   halogen compounds
    BT2   halides
      BT3   halogen compounds
  BT1   copper halides
    BT2   copper compounds
      BT3   transition element compounds
    BT2   halides
      BT3   halogen compounds

COPPER CARBIDES [5; 5]
  BT1   carbides
    BT2   carbon compounds
  BT1   copper compounds
    BT2   transition element compounds

COPPER CARBONATES [14; 14]
  BT1   carbonates
    BT2   carbon compounds
    BT2   oxygen compounds
  BT1   copper compounds
    BT2   transition element compounds

COPPER CHLORIDES [296; 296]
  BT1   chlorides
    BT2   chlorine compounds
      BT3   halogen compounds
    BT2   halides
      BT3   halogen compounds
  BT1   copper halides
    BT2   copper compounds
      BT3   transition element compounds
    BT2   halides
      BT3   halogen compounds

COPPER COMPLEXES [547; 616]
  BT1   transition element complexes
    BT2   complexes
  NT1   ceruloplasmin
  RT   phthalocyanines

COPPER COMPOUNDS [1,172; 12,789]
  BT1   transition element compounds
  NT1   copper arsenides
  NT1   copper borides
  NT1   copper carbides
  NT1   copper carbonates
  NT1   copper halides
    NT2   copper bromides
    NT2   copper chlorides
    NT2   copper fluorides
    NT2   copper iodides
  NT1   copper hydrides
  NT1   copper hydroxides
  NT1   copper nitrates
  NT1   copper nitrides
  NT1   copper oxides
  NT1   copper perchlorates
  NT1   copper phosphates
  NT1   copper phosphides
  NT1   copper selenides
  NT1   copper silicates
  NT1   copper silicides
  NT1   copper sulfates
  NT1   copper sulfides
  NT1   copper tellurides
  NT1   copper tungstates
  NT1   cuprates
  RT   copper additions

COPPER FLUORIDES [53; 53]
  BT1   copper halides
    BT2   copper compounds
      BT3   transition element compounds
    BT2   halides
      BT3   halogen compounds
  BT1   fluorides
    BT2   fluorine compounds
      BT3   halogen compounds
    BT2   halides
      BT3   halogen compounds

COPPER HALIDES [5; 136] *Apr 86*
  BT1   copper compounds
    BT2   transition element compounds
  BT1   halides
    BT2   halogen compounds
  NT1   copper bromides
  NT1   copper chlorides
  NT1   copper fluorides
  NT1   copper iodides

COPPER HYDRIDES [34; 34]
  BT1   copper compounds
    BT2   transition element compounds
  BT1   hydrides
    BT2   hydrogen compounds

COPPER HYDROXIDES [23; 23]
  BT1   copper compounds
    BT2   transition element compounds
  BT1   hydroxides
    BT2   hydrogen compounds
    BT2   oxygen compounds

COPPER IODIDES [89; 89]
  BT1   copper halides
    BT2   copper compounds
      BT3   transition element compounds
    BT2   halides
      BT3   halogen compounds
  BT1   iodides
    BT2   halides
      BT3   halogen compounds
    BT2   iodine compounds
      BT3   halogen compounds

COPPER IONS [837; 837]
  BT1   ions
    BT2   charged particles

COPPER ISOTOPES [181; 2,089]
  NT1   copper 57
  NT1   copper 58
  NT1   copper 59
  NT1   copper 60
  NT1   copper 61
  NT1   copper 62
  NT1   copper 63
  NT1   copper 64
  NT1   copper 65
  NT1   copper 66
  NT1   copper 67
  NT1   copper 68
  NT1   copper 69
  NT1   copper 70
  NT1   copper 71
  NT1   copper 72
  NT1   copper 73
  NT1   copper 74
  NT1   copper 75

COPPER NITRATES [46; 46]
  BT1   copper compounds
    BT2   transition element compounds
  BT1   nitrates
    BT2   nitrogen compounds
    BT2   oxygen compounds

COPPER NITRIDES [4; 4] *Dec 89*
  BT1   copper compounds
    BT2   transition element compounds
  BT1   nitrides
    BT2   nitrogen compounds
    BT2   pnictides

COPPER ORES [268; 268]
  BT1   ores

COPPER OXIDES [8,758; 8,758]
  BT1   copper compounds
    BT2   transition element compounds
  BT1   oxides
    BT2   chalcogenides
    BT2   oxygen compounds
  RT   cuprates
  RT   oxide minerals

COPPER PERCHLORATES [6; 6]
  BT1   copper compounds
    BT2   transition element compounds
  BT1   perchlorates
    BT2   chlorine compounds
      BT3   halogen compounds
    BT2   oxygen compounds

COPPER PHOSPHATES [16; 23]
- BT1 copper compounds
- BT2 transition element compounds
- BT1 phosphates
- BT2 oxygen compounds
- BT2 phosphorus compounds
- RT phosphate minerals
- RT torbernite

→ **COPPER PHOSPHIDES** [0; 0] *Sep 91*
- BT1 copper compounds
- BT2 transition element compounds
- BT1 phosphides
- BT2 phosphorus compounds
- BT2 pnictides

COPPER SELENIDES [218; 218] *Jul 76*
- BT1 copper compounds
- BT2 transition element compounds
- BT1 selenides
- BT2 chalcogenides
- BT2 selenium compounds

COPPER SILICATES [6; 7]
- BT1 copper compounds
- BT2 transition element compounds
- BT1 silicates
- BT2 oxygen compounds
- BT2 silicon compounds
- RT cuprosklodowskite

COPPER SILICIDES [108; 108] *Jan 77*
- BT1 copper compounds
- BT2 transition element compounds
- BT1 silicides
- BT2 silicon compounds

COPPER SULFATES [182; 183]
- BT1 copper compounds
- BT2 transition element compounds
- BT1 sulfates
- BT2 oxygen compounds
- BT2 sulfur compounds
- RT johannite
- RT sulfate minerals

COPPER SULFIDES [280; 312]
- BT1 copper compounds
- BT2 transition element compounds
- BT1 sulfides
- BT2 chalcogenides
- BT2 sulfur compounds
- RT chalcopyrite
- RT sulfide minerals

COPPER TELLURIDES [124; 124] *Feb 78*
- BT1 copper compounds
- BT2 transition element compounds
- BT1 tellurides
- BT2 chalcogenides
- BT2 tellurium compounds

COPPER TUNGSTATES [13; 13]
- BT1 copper compounds
- BT2 transition element compounds
- BT1 tungstates
- BT2 oxygen compounds
- BT2 tungsten compounds
- BT3 transition element compounds

copper vapor lasers
- USE gas lasers

COPPER 57 [17; 17] *May 80*
- BT1 beta-plus decay radioisotopes
- BT2 beta decay radioisotopes
- BT3 radioisotopes
- BT4 isotopes
- BT1 copper isotopes
- BT1 intermediate mass nuclei
- BT2 nuclei
- BT1 millisec living radioisotopes
- BT2 radioisotopes
- BT3 isotopes
- BT1 odd-even nuclei
- BT2 nuclei

COPPER 58 [29; 29]
- BT1 beta-plus decay radioisotopes
- BT2 beta decay radioisotopes
- BT3 radioisotopes
- BT4 isotopes
- BT1 copper isotopes
- BT1 electron capture radioisotopes
- BT2 beta decay radioisotopes
- BT3 radioisotopes
- BT4 isotopes
- BT1 intermediate mass nuclei
- BT2 nuclei
- BT1 odd-odd nuclei
- BT2 nuclei
- BT1 seconds living radioisotopes
- BT2 radioisotopes
- BT3 isotopes

COPPER 59 [127; 127]
- BT1 beta-plus decay radioisotopes
- BT2 beta decay radioisotopes
- BT3 radioisotopes
- BT4 isotopes
- BT1 copper isotopes
- BT1 intermediate mass nuclei
- BT2 nuclei
- BT1 minutes living radioisotopes
- BT2 radioisotopes
- BT3 isotopes
- BT1 odd-even nuclei
- BT2 nuclei

COPPER 60 [59; 59]
- BT1 beta-plus decay radioisotopes
- BT2 beta decay radioisotopes
- BT3 radioisotopes
- BT4 isotopes
- BT1 copper isotopes
- BT1 electron capture radioisotopes
- BT2 beta decay radioisotopes
- BT3 radioisotopes
- BT4 isotopes
- BT1 intermediate mass nuclei
- BT2 nuclei
- BT1 minutes living radioisotopes
- BT2 radioisotopes
- BT3 isotopes
- BT1 odd-odd nuclei
- BT2 nuclei

COPPER 61 [162; 162]
- BT1 beta-plus decay radioisotopes
- BT2 beta decay radioisotopes
- BT3 radioisotopes
- BT4 isotopes
- BT1 copper isotopes
- BT1 electron capture radioisotopes
- BT2 beta decay radioisotopes
- BT3 radioisotopes
- BT4 isotopes
- BT1 hours living radioisotopes
- BT2 radioisotopes
- BT3 isotopes
- BT1 intermediate mass nuclei
- BT2 nuclei
- BT1 odd-even nuclei
- BT2 nuclei

COPPER 61 TARGET [4; 4]
- BT1 targets

COPPER 62 [151; 151]
- BT1 beta-plus decay radioisotopes
- BT2 beta decay radioisotopes
- BT3 radioisotopes
- BT4 isotopes
- BT1 copper isotopes
- BT1 electron capture radioisotopes
- BT2 beta decay radioisotopes
- BT3 radioisotopes
- BT4 isotopes
- BT1 intermediate mass nuclei
- BT2 nuclei
- BT1 minutes living radioisotopes
- BT2 radioisotopes
- BT3 isotopes
- BT1 odd-odd nuclei
- BT2 nuclei

COPPER 63 [580; 580]
- BT1 copper isotopes
- BT1 intermediate mass nuclei
- BT2 nuclei
- BT1 odd-even nuclei
- BT2 nuclei
- BT1 stable isotopes
- BT2 isotopes

COPPER 63 BEAMS [48; 48] *Nov 78*
- BT1 ion beams
- BT2 beams

COPPER 63 REACTIONS [95; 95]
- BT1 heavy ion reactions
- BT2 nuclear reactions

COPPER 63 TARGET [849; 849]
- BT1 targets

COPPER 64 [616; 616]
- BT1 beta-minus decay radioisotopes
- BT2 beta decay radioisotopes
- BT3 radioisotopes
- BT4 isotopes
- BT1 beta-plus decay radioisotopes
- BT2 beta decay radioisotopes
- BT3 radioisotopes
- BT4 isotopes
- BT1 copper isotopes
- BT1 electron capture radioisotopes
- BT2 beta decay radioisotopes
- BT3 radioisotopes
- BT4 isotopes
- BT1 hours living radioisotopes
- BT2 radioisotopes
- BT3 isotopes
- BT1 intermediate mass nuclei
- BT2 nuclei
- BT1 odd-odd nuclei
- BT2 nuclei

COPPER 64 TARGET [152; 152] *Apr 78*
- BT1 targets

COPPER 65 [312; 312]
- BT1 copper isotopes
- BT1 intermediate mass nuclei
- BT2 nuclei
- BT1 odd-even nuclei
- BT2 nuclei
- BT1 stable isotopes
- BT2 isotopes

COPPER 65 REACTIONS [19; 19]
- BT1 heavy ion reactions
- BT2 nuclear reactions

COPPER 65 TARGET [345; 345]
- BT1 targets

COPPER 66 [54; 54]
- BT1 beta-minus decay radioisotopes
- BT2 beta decay radioisotopes
- BT3 radioisotopes
- BT4 isotopes
- BT1 copper isotopes
- BT1 intermediate mass nuclei
- BT2 nuclei
- BT1 minutes living radioisotopes
- BT2 radioisotopes
- BT3 isotopes
- BT1 odd-odd nuclei
- BT2 nuclei

COPPER 67 [139; 139]
- BT1 beta-minus decay radioisotopes
- BT2 beta decay radioisotopes
- BT3 radioisotopes
- BT4 isotopes
- BT1 copper isotopes
- BT1 days living radioisotopes

COPPER 68 [13; 13]
BT1 beta-minus decay radioisotopes
BT2 beta decay radioisotopes
BT3 radioisotopes
BT4 isotopes
BT1 copper isotopes
BT1 intermediate mass nuclei
BT2 nuclei
BT1 isomeric transition isotopes
BT2 radioisotopes
BT3 isotopes
BT1 minutes living radioisotopes
BT2 radioisotopes
BT3 isotopes
BT1 odd-odd nuclei
BT2 nuclei
BT1 seconds living radioisotopes
BT2 radioisotopes
BT3 isotopes

COPPER 69 [11; 11]
BT1 beta-minus decay radioisotopes
BT2 beta decay radioisotopes
BT3 radioisotopes
BT4 isotopes
BT1 copper isotopes
BT1 intermediate mass nuclei
BT2 nuclei
BT1 minutes living radioisotopes
BT2 radioisotopes
BT3 isotopes
BT1 odd-even nuclei
BT2 nuclei

COPPER 70 [5; 5]
BT1 beta-minus decay radioisotopes
BT2 beta decay radioisotopes
BT3 radioisotopes
BT4 isotopes
BT1 copper isotopes
BT1 intermediate mass nuclei
BT2 nuclei
BT1 odd-odd nuclei
BT2 nuclei
BT1 seconds living radioisotopes
BT2 radioisotopes
BT3 isotopes

COPPER 71 [7; 7] *Jul 82*
BT1 beta-minus decay radioisotopes
BT2 beta decay radioisotopes
BT3 radioisotopes
BT4 isotopes
BT1 copper isotopes
BT1 intermediate mass nuclei
BT2 nuclei
BT1 odd-even nuclei
BT2 nuclei
BT1 seconds living radioisotopes
BT2 radioisotopes
BT3 isotopes

COPPER 72 [6; 6] *Jul 82*
BT1 beta-minus decay radioisotopes
BT2 beta decay radioisotopes
BT3 radioisotopes
BT4 isotopes
BT1 copper isotopes
BT1 intermediate mass nuclei
BT2 nuclei
BT1 odd-odd nuclei
BT2 nuclei
BT1 seconds living radioisotopes
BT2 radioisotopes
BT3 isotopes

COPPER 73 [8; 8] *Jul 82*
BT1 beta-minus decay radioisotopes
BT2 beta decay radioisotopes
BT3 radioisotopes
BT4 isotopes
BT1 copper isotopes
BT1 intermediate mass nuclei
BT2 nuclei
BT1 odd-even nuclei
BT2 nuclei
BT1 seconds living radioisotopes
BT2 radioisotopes
BT3 isotopes

COPPER 74 [5; 5] *Jul 89*
BT1 beta-minus decay radioisotopes
BT2 beta decay radioisotopes
BT3 radioisotopes
BT4 isotopes
BT1 copper isotopes
BT1 intermediate mass nuclei
BT2 nuclei
BT1 odd-odd nuclei
BT2 nuclei
BT1 seconds living radioisotopes
BT2 radioisotopes
BT3 isotopes

COPPER 75 [2; 2] *May 90*
BT1 beta-minus decay radioisotopes
BT2 beta decay radioisotopes
BT3 radioisotopes
BT4 isotopes
BT1 copper isotopes
BT1 intermediate mass nuclei
BT2 nuclei
BT1 odd-even nuclei
BT2 nuclei
BT1 seconds living radioisotopes
BT2 radioisotopes
BT3 isotopes

COPRECIPITATION [1,230; 1,230]
BT1 precipitation
BT2 separation processes
RT coalescence
RT flocculation

CORAL-1 REACTOR [4; 4]
(Uncooled; Junta de Energia Nuclear, Madrid, Spain)
BT1 enriched uranium reactors
BT2 reactors
BT1 fast reactors
BT2 epithermal reactors
BT3 reactors
BT1 research reactors
BT2 research and test reactors
BT3 reactors
BT1 zero power reactors
BT2 experimental reactors
BT3 research and test reactors
BT4 reactors

CORALS [100; 100]
BT1 cnidaria
BT2 coelenterata
BT3 invertebrates
BT4 animals

CORCHORUS [4; 4]
BT1 plants

cordillera de los andes
USE andes

CORDOBA REACTOR [31; 31] *Feb 78*
BT1 candu type reactors
BT2 heavy water moderated reactors
BT3 reactors
BT2 pressure tube reactors
BT3 power reactors
BT4 reactors
BT2 thermal reactors
BT3 reactors
BT1 natural uranium reactors
BT2 reactors
BT1 phwr type reactors
BT2 heavy water cooled reactors
BT3 reactors
BT2 heavy water moderated reactors
BT3 reactors

cordova quad cities-1 reactor
USE quad cities-1 reactor

cordova quad cities-2 reactor
USE quad cities-2 reactor

CORDYLITE [2; 2]
BT1 carbonate minerals
BT2 minerals
BT1 radioactive minerals
BT2 minerals
BT2 radioactive materials
BT3 materials
RT cerium carbonates
RT lanthanum carbonates

core (earth)
USE earth core

CORE CATCHERS [276; 276]
BT1 reactor components
RT corium
RT meltdown
RT reactor cores

CORE FLOODING SYSTEMS [536; 536]
BT1 eccs
BT2 reactor protection systems
RT loss of coolant

core polarization (nuclei)
USE excitation
AND nuclear cores

CORE SPRAY SYSTEMS [306; 306]
BT1 eccs
BT2 reactor protection systems
RT fog cooled reactors
RT fog cooling
RT loss of coolant

cores (drill)
USE drill cores

cores (magnet)
USE magnet cores

cores (magnetic)
USE magnetic cores

cores (nuclear)
USE nuclear cores

cores (reactor)
USE reactor cores

CORIOLIS FORCE [994; 994]
RT backbending
RT rotation

CORIUM [1,258; 1,258] *Oct 77*
(Molten mixture of fuel, cladding and other core structural material resulting from a meltdown accident.)
RT core catchers
RT meltdown
RT reactor cores

CORK [7; 7]
RT bark
RT wood

corn (maize)
USE maize

CORN OIL [22; 22]
UF *maize oil*
BT1 oils
BT2 other organic compounds
BT3 organic compounds
BT1 triglycerides
BT2 esters
BT3 organic compounds
BT2 lipids
BT3 organic compounds

CORNEA [198; 198]
BT1 eyes
BT2 sense organs
BT3 organs
BT4 body

cornell electron-positron stor
USE cesr storage ring

CORNELL TRIGA-MK-2 REACTOR [10; 10]
(Cornell, Univ., Ithaca, New York, USA)
UF *triga-2-cornell reactor*
BT1 training reactors
BT2 research and test reactors
BT3 reactors
BT1 triga type reactors
BT2 enriched uranium reactors
BT3 reactors
BT2 hydride moderated reactors
BT3 reactors
BT2 research and test reactors
BT3 reactors
BT2 solid homogeneous reactors
BT3 homogeneous reactors
BT4 reactors
BT2 water cooled reactors
BT3 reactors
BT2 water moderated reactors
BT3 reactors

cornell univ. zero pow. react.
USE zpr reactor

CORNELL 10-GEV SYNCHROTRON [38; 38]
BT1 synchrotrons
BT2 cyclic accelerators
BT3 accelerators

CORNELL 2-GEV SYNCHROTRON [0; 0]
BT1 synchrotrons
BT2 cyclic accelerators
BT3 accelerators

corona (solar)
USE solar corona

CORONA COUNTERS [55; 55]
BT1 radiation detectors
BT2 measuring instruments
RT proportional counters
RT spark counters

CORONA DISCHARGES [202; 202]
BT1 electric discharges
RT lichtenberg figures

coronae (stellar)
USE stellar coronae

CORONARIES [1,775; 1,775]
BT1 arteries
BT2 blood vessels
BT3 cardiovascular system
BT3 organs
BT4 body
RT heart
RT myocardial infarction
RT myocardium

corporation law
(Prior to December 1990, this was a valid descriptor.)
USE laws

§§ **CORRECTIONS** [11,117; 14,623]
(See also REMEDIAL ACTION.)
NT1 coulomb correction
NT1 radiative corrections
NT1 rydberg correction
RT errors
RT mitigation
RT modifications

CORRELATED-PARTICLE MODELS [251; 251]
BT1 particle models
BT2 mathematical models
RT correlation functions
RT multiple production

correlation energy
USE electron correlation

CORRELATION FUNCTIONS [7,025; 7,025]
BT1 functions
RT correlated-particle models
RT reactor noise

§§ **CORRELATIONS** [15,193; 24,592]
NT1 angular correlation
NT2 perturbed angular correlation
NT3 differential pac
NT3 integral pac
NT1 electron correlation
NT1 kramers-kronig correlation
RT comparative evaluations
RT regression analysis

§ **CORROSION** [8,702; 13,787]
UF *corrosive effects*
BT1 chemical reactions
NT1 crevice corrosion
NT1 electrochemical corrosion
NT1 fretting corrosion
NT1 intergranular corrosion
NT1 pitting corrosion
NT1 scaling
NT1 stress corrosion
RT antifoulants
RT corrosion denting
RT corrosion fatigue
RT corrosion pickling
RT corrosion products
RT corrosion protection
RT corrosion resistance
RT erosion
RT failures
RT fouling
RT materials testing
RT oxidation
RT passivity
RT surface properties
RT weathering

CORROSION DENTING [154; 154]
May 79
UF *denting (corrosion)*
BT1 deformation
RT corrosion
RT tubes
RT water chemistry

CORROSION FATIGUE [283; 283]
Jul 81
BT1 fatigue
BT2 mechanical properties
RT corrosion

corrosion inhibition
USE corrosion protection

CORROSION INHIBITORS [490; 490]
UF *inhibitors (corrosion)*
RT corrosion protection

CORROSION PICKLING [38; 38]
BT1 pickling
BT2 surface treatments
RT corrosion

CORROSION PRODUCTS [2,155; 2,155]
RT corrosion
RT electromagnetic filters
RT oxidation
RT oxides
RT scaling

CORROSION PROTECTION [1,863; 2,232]
UF *anticorrosion*
UF *cathodic protection*
UF *corrosion inhibition*
UF *protection (corrosion)*
NT1 anodization
RT coatings
RT corrosion
RT corrosion inhibitors
RT corrosion resistance
RT paints
RT passivation
RT surface coating

CORROSION RESISTANCE [4,063; 4,063]
RT corrosion
RT corrosion protection
RT passivity

CORROSION RESISTANT ALLOYS [388; 13,833]
BT1 alloys
NT1 alloy-co36cr22ni22w15fe3
NT1 alloy-co52cr17fe15mo3si3
NT1 alloy-co54cr20w15ni10
NT1 alloy-co60cr30w4
NT1 alloy-co62cr28mo6ni3
NT1 alloy-co64cr29w4
NT1 alloy-co66cr26w6
NT1 alloy-fe31cr21co20ni20mo3w2
NT1 alloy-fe44ni33cr21
NT1 alloy-fe46ni33cr21
NT1 alloy-fe48cr24ni24
NT1 alloy-mo99
NT1 alloy-ni41fe40cr16nb3
NT1 alloy-ni42fe36cr12mo6ti3
NT1 alloy-ni43fe30cr22mo3
NT1 alloy-ni43fe33cr16mo3
NT1 alloy-ni45cr23fe19co3mo3w3
NT1 alloy-ni45fe34cr20
NT1 alloy-ni46cr23co19ti5al4
NT1 alloy-ni47cr25co12w9fe3
NT1 alloy-ni48co28cr15al3mo3ti2
NT1 alloy-ni48cr22fe18mo9
NT1 alloy-ni49cr22fe18mo9
NT1 alloy-ni50co20cr15al5mo5
NT1 alloy-ni50cr22fe18mo9
NT1 alloy-ni50mo32cr15si3
NT1 alloy-ni51cr48
NT1 alloy-ni53co19cr15mo5al4ti3
NT1 alloy-ni53cr19fe19nb5mo3
NT1 alloy-ni54cr22co13mo9
NT1 alloy-ni54mo17cr16fe6w4
NT1 alloy-ni55cr19co11mo10ti3
NT1 alloy-ni56cr21w10mo5fe4al2
NT1 alloy-ni58cr14co8al4mo4nb4w4
NT1 alloy-ni58cr20co14mo4ti3
NT1 alloy-ni59cr20co17ti2
NT1 alloy-ni59cr30fe9
NT1 alloy-ni60co15cr10al6ti5mo3

NT1	alloy-ni60cr14co10ti5mo4w4al3
NT1	alloy-ni60cr25w15
NT1	alloy-ni60fe24cr16
NT1	alloy-ni60mo13co9cr8nb4al3
NT1	alloy-ni61cr16co9al3ti3w3
NT1	alloy-ni61cr22mo9nb4fe3
NT1	alloy-ni62cr16mo15fe3
NT1	alloy-ni65cr25mo10
NT1	alloy-ni65mo16cr15w4
NT1	alloy-ni65mo28fe5
NT1	alloy-ni67cr19mo5w5ti3
NT1	alloy-ni68cr15w6al3mo3fe2
NT1	alloy-ni70mo17cr7fe5
NT1	alloy-ni73cr15fe7ti3
NT1	alloy-ni73cr20mn3nb3
NT1	alloy-ni74cr13al6mo4
NT1	alloy-ni75cr12al6mo5
NT1	alloy-ni76cr15fe8
NT1	alloy-ni76cr20ti2
NT1	alloy-ni77cr20ti2
NT1	alloy-ni78cr16al4
NT1	alloy-zr98sn-2
NT1	alloy-zr98sn-4
NT1	colmonoy
NT1	heusler alloys
NT1	refractaloy
NT1	steel-cr11ni10mo2ti-l
NT1	steel-cr12
NT1	steel-cr12moniv
NT1	steel-cr12mov
NT1	steel-cr13
NT1	steel-cr13al
NT1	steel-cr13mn8ni8
NT1	steel-cr13ni6mo-l
NT1	steel-cr15ni15motib
NT1	steel-cr16
NT1	steel-cr16ni
NT1	steel-cr16ni13monbv
NT1	steel-cr16ni15mo3nb
NT1	steel-cr16ni16monb
NT1	steel-cr16ni8mo2
NT1	steel-cr17cu4ni4nb-l
NT1	steel-cr17mn15nni
NT1	steel-cr17mo
NT1	steel-cr17ni12monb
NT1	steel-cr17ni12mo3
NT1	steel-cr17ni12mo3-l
NT1	steel-cr17ni13
NT1	steel-cr17ni13mo2ti
NT1	steel-cr17ni13mo3ti
NT1	steel-cr17ni4mo3
NT1	steel-cr17ni7
NT1	steel-cr18
NT1	steel-cr18ni10
NT1	steel-cr18ni10-l
NT1	steel-cr18ni10ti
NT1	steel-cr18ni11
NT1	steel-cr18ni11nb
NT1	steel-cr18ni11nbco
NT1	steel-cr18ni12
NT1	steel-cr18ni12ti
NT1	steel-cr18ni8
NT1	steel-cr18ni9
NT1	steel-cr18ni9ti
NT1	steel-cr19ni10
NT1	steel-cr19ni10-l
NT1	steel-cr20ni11
NT1	steel-cr20ni11-l
NT1	steel-cr21mn9ni6
NT1	steel-cr21ni5ti
NT1	steel-cr22ni5ti
NT1	steel-cr23ni14
NT1	steel-cr23ni18
NT1	steel-cr25
NT1	steel-cr25ni20
NT1	steel-cr26ni5mo-l
NT1	steel-ni17cr14moti-l
NT1	steel-ni25cr20
NT1	steel-ni26cr15ti2movalb
NT1	steel-ni35cr18mo4ti2al
NT1	steel-ni36cr12ti3al-l
NT1	steel-ni36cr18
RT	austenitic steels
RT	ferritic steels
RT	hastelloys
RT	stainless steels

corrosive effects
USE corrosion

cortex (adrenal)
USE adrenal glands

cortex (cerebral)
USE cerebral cortex

corticoids
USE corticosteroids

CORTICOSTEROIDS [221; 1,520]
UF   *corticoids*
BT1   adrenal hormones
  BT2   hormones
BT1   hydroxy compounds
  BT2   organic compounds
BT1   ketones
  BT2   organic compounds
BT1   pregnanes
  BT2   steroids
    BT3   organic compounds
BT1   steroid hormones
  BT2   hormones
NT1   glucocorticoids
  NT2   corticosterone
  NT2   cortisone
  NT2   dexamethasone
  NT2   hydrocortisone
  NT2   prednisolone
  NT2   prednisone
NT1   mineralocorticoids
  NT2   aldosterone
  NT2   doca
RT   acth
RT   androgens
RT   cushing syndrome

CORTICOSTERONE [157; 157]
BT1   glucocorticoids
  BT2   corticosteroids
    BT3   adrenal hormones
      BT4   hormones
    BT3   hydroxy compounds
      BT4   organic compounds
    BT3   ketones
      BT4   organic compounds
    BT3   pregnanes
      BT4   steroids
        BT5   organic compounds
    BT3   steroid hormones
      BT4   hormones

cortisol
USE hydrocortisone

CORTISONE [61; 61]
BT1   glucocorticoids
  BT2   corticosteroids
    BT3   adrenal hormones
      BT4   hormones
    BT3   hydroxy compounds
      BT4   organic compounds
    BT3   ketones
      BT4   organic compounds
    BT3   pregnanes
      BT4   steroids
        BT5   organic compounds
    BT3   steroid hormones
      BT4   hormones

CORUNDUM [157; 655]
BT1   oxide minerals
  BT2   minerals
NT1   ruby
NT1   sapphire
RT   aluminium oxides

CORYNEBACTERIUM PARVUM
[20; 20] *Sep 78*
BT1   bacteria
BT2   microorganisms

cosmetics
USE consumer products

COSMIC ALPHA PARTICLES [51; 51]
Nov 75
(Prior to March 1983 this concept was indexed by coordination of COSMIC RADIATION and ALPHA PARTICLES.)
BT1   alpha particles
  BT2   helium ions
    BT3   ions
      BT4   charged particles
  BT2   ionizing radiations
    BT3   radiations
BT1   primary cosmic radiation
  BT2   cosmic radiation
    BT3   ionizing radiations
      BT4   radiations

COSMIC DUST [4,051; 4,051]
BT1   dusts
RT   interstellar grains
RT   interstellar space
RT   nebulae
RT   star accretion

COSMIC ELECTRONS [384; 384]
Nov 75
(Prior to March 1983 this concept was indexed by coordination of COSMIC RADIATION and ELECTRONS.)
BT1   electrons
  BT2   leptons
    BT3   elementary particles
    BT3   fermions
BT1   secondary cosmic radiation
  BT2   cosmic radiation
    BT3   ionizing radiations
      BT4   radiations

COSMIC GAMMA BURSTS [946; 946]
BT1   primary cosmic radiation
  BT2   cosmic radiation
    BT3   ionizing radiations
      BT4   radiations
RT   cosmic gamma sources
RT   cosmic x-ray bursts

COSMIC GAMMA SOURCES
[1,312; 1,312]
BT1   cosmic ray sources
RT   cosmic gamma bursts
RT   gamma astronomy
RT   gamma radiation
RT   primary cosmic radiation

COSMIC GASES [5,991; 5,991]
BT1   gases
  BT2   fluids
RT   interstellar grains
RT   interstellar space
RT   nebulae
RT   optical depth curve
RT   spectroscopic curve of growth

COSMIC KAONS [55; 55] *Dec 85*
BT1   kaons
  BT2   pseudoscalar mesons
    BT3   mesons
      BT4   bosons
      BT4   hadrons
        BT5   elementary particles
  BT2   strange mesons
    BT3   mesons
      BT4   bosons
      BT4   hadrons
        BT5   elementary particles
    BT3   strange particles
      BT4   elementary particles
BT1   secondary cosmic radiation
  BT2   cosmic radiation

BT3   ionizing radiations
BT4   radiations

COSMIC MUONS [637; 637] *Feb 76*
(Prior to March 1983 this concept was indexed by coordination of COSMIC RADIATION and MUONS.)
BT1   muons
BT2   leptons
BT3   elementary particles
BT3   fermions
BT1   secondary cosmic radiation
BT2   cosmic radiation
BT3   ionizing radiations
BT4   radiations

COSMIC NEUTRINOS [761; 761] *Nov 75*
BT1   cosmic radiation
BT2   ionizing radiations
BT3   radiations
BT1   neutrinos
BT2   leptons
BT3   elementary particles
BT3   fermions
BT2   massless particles
BT3   elementary particles

COSMIC NEUTRONS [137; 137] *Nov 75*
(Prior to March 1983 this concept was indexed by coordination of COSMIC RADIATION and NEUTRONS.)
BT1   neutrons
BT2   nucleons
BT3   baryons
BT4   fermions
BT4   hadrons
BT5   elementary particles
BT1   secondary cosmic radiation
BT2   cosmic radiation
BT3   ionizing radiations
BT4   radiations

cosmic noise
USE   radio noise

COSMIC NUCLEI [455; 455] *Nov 75*
(Prior to March 1983 this concept was indexed by coordination of COSMIC RADIATION and NUCLEI.)
BT1   nuclei
BT1   primary cosmic radiation
BT2   cosmic radiation
BT3   ionizing radiations
BT4   radiations

cosmic particles
USE   cosmic radiation

COSMIC PHOTONS [607; 607] *Nov 75*
BT1   cosmic radiation
BT2   ionizing radiations
BT3   radiations
BT1   photons
BT2   bosons
BT2   massless particles
BT3   elementary particles

COSMIC PIONS [66; 66] *Mar 83*
BT1   pions
BT2   pseudoscalar mesons
BT3   mesons
BT4   bosons
BT4   hadrons
BT5   elementary particles
BT1   secondary cosmic radiation
BT2   cosmic radiation
BT3   ionizing radiations
BT4   radiations

COSMIC POSITRONS [64; 64] *Feb 76*
(Prior to March 1983 this concept was indexed by coordination of COSMIC RADIATION and POSITRONS.)
BT1   positrons
BT2   antileptons
BT3   antiparticles
BT4   antimatter
BT5   matter
BT4   elementary particles
BT3   leptons
BT4   elementary particles
BT4   fermions
BT1   secondary cosmic radiation
BT2   cosmic radiation
BT3   ionizing radiations
BT4   radiations

COSMIC PROTONS [410; 410] *Nov 75*
BT1   cosmic radiation
BT2   ionizing radiations
BT3   radiations
BT1   protons
BT2   hydrogen ions 1 plus
BT3   cations
BT4   ions
BT5   charged particles
BT3   hydrogen ions
BT4   ions
BT5   charged particles
BT2   nucleons
BT3   baryons
BT4   fermions
BT4   hadrons
BT5   elementary particles

COSMIC RADIATION [7,914; 15,647]
(Not for radiation from the sun for which see SOLAR RADIATION.)
UF   *cosmic particles*
BT1   ionizing radiations
BT2   radiations
NT1   cosmic neutrinos
NT1   cosmic photons
NT1   cosmic protons
NT1   hard component
NT1   primary cosmic radiation
NT2   cosmic alpha particles
NT2   cosmic gamma bursts
NT2   cosmic nuclei
NT2   cosmic x-ray bursts
NT1   secondary cosmic radiation
NT2   cosmic electrons
NT2   cosmic kaons
NT2   cosmic muons
NT2   cosmic neutrons
NT2   cosmic pions
NT2   cosmic positrons
NT2   cosmic showers
NT3   extensive air showers
NT1   soft component
RT   background radiation
RT   cosmic radio sources
RT   cosmic ray detection
RT   cosmic ray flux
RT   cosmic ray propagation
RT   cosmic x-ray sources
RT   east-west asymmetry
RT   forbush decrease
RT   gamma astronomy
RT   north-south asymmetry
RT   positive excess
RT   relict radiation
RT   solar radiation
RT   space flight
RT   stellar activity
RT   stellar radiation
RT   supersonic transport
RT   threshold rigidity
RT   x-ray galaxies

COSMIC RADIO SOURCES [3,565; 14,946]
NT1   bl lacertae objects
NT1   h1 regions
NT1   h2 regions
NT1   pulsars
NT1   quasars
NT2   blue stellar objects
NT1   radio galaxies
NT1   supernova remnants
NT2   crab nebula
RT   cosmic radiation
RT   cosmic ray sources
RT   markarian galaxies
RT   radioastronomy
RT   radiowave radiation

COSMIC RAY DETECTION [2,231; 2,231]
UF   *cosmic-ray detection*
BT1   radiation detection
BT2   detection
RT   charged particle detection
RT   cosmic radiation
RT   cosmic ray spectrometers
RT   muon detection
RT   radiation detectors
RT   shower counters
RT   telescope counters

COSMIC RAY FLUX [2,540; 2,540]
UF   *cosmic-ray flux*
UF   *flux (cosmic ray)*
BT1   radiation flux
RT   cosmic radiation
RT   cosmic ray propagation

COSMIC RAY PROPAGATION [985; 985]
UF   *cosmic-ray propagation*
RT   cosmic radiation
RT   cosmic ray flux

COSMIC RAY SOURCES [551; 6,576]
UF   *cosmic-ray sources*
NT1   cosmic gamma sources
NT1   cosmic x-ray sources
NT2   bl lacertae objects
NT2   x-ray galaxies
RT   cosmic radio sources
RT   primary cosmic radiation

COSMIC RAY SPECTROMETERS [330; 330]
UF   *cosmic-ray spectrometers*
BT1   spectrometers
BT2   measuring instruments
RT   cosmic ray detection

COSMIC SHOWERS [849; 2,653]
BT1   secondary cosmic radiation
BT2   cosmic radiation
BT3   ionizing radiations
BT4   radiations
BT1   showers
NT1   extensive air showers
RT   cascade showers

COSMIC X-RAY BURSTS [239; 239] *Feb 83*
BT1   primary cosmic radiation
BT2   cosmic radiation
BT3   ionizing radiations
BT4   radiations
RT   cosmic gamma bursts
RT   cosmic x-ray sources
RT   x radiation

COSMIC X-RAY SOURCES [5,075; 5,458]
BT1   cosmic ray sources
NT1   bl lacertae objects
NT1   x-ray galaxies
RT   accretion disks
RT   cosmic radiation
RT   cosmic x-ray bursts
RT   gamma astronomy
RT   x radiation

cosmic-ray detection
USE   cosmic ray detection

cosmic-ray flux
   USE   cosmic ray flux

cosmic-ray propagation
   USE   cosmic ray propagation

cosmic-ray sources
   USE   cosmic ray sources

cosmic-ray spectrometers
   USE   cosmic ray spectrometers

COSMOCHEMISTRY [2,011; 2,011]
   BT1   chemistry
   RT   chemical composition
   RT   element abundance
   RT   nucleosynthesis

cosmogony
   USE   cosmology

COSMOLOGICAL CONSTANT [660; 660] *Apr 84*
(Multiplicative constant for a term proportional to the metric in Einstein's equation relating the curvature of space to the energy-momentum tensor.)
   RT   einstein field equations
   RT   general relativity theory
   RT   space-time

COSMOLOGICAL MODELS [6,528; 6,878]
   UF   *einstein-de sitter model*
   UF   *models (cosmological)*
   BT1   mathematical models
   NT1   inflationary universe
   RT   expansion
   RT   galactic evolution
   RT   general relativity theory
   RT   planet-system accretion
   RT   protoplanets
   RT   protostars
   RT   solar nebula
   RT   star accretion
   RT   universe

COSMOLOGY [6,190; 6,291]
   UF   *cosmogony*
   NT1   dirac cosmology
   RT   astrophysics
   RT   fundamental constants
   RT   galactic evolution
   RT   hubble effect
   RT   matter
   RT   origin
   RT   red shift
   RT   relativity theory
   RT   schwarzschild metric
   RT   space-time
   RT   star evolution
   RT   universe
   RT   white holes

cosmos
   USE   universe

COSMOTRON [11; 11]
   BT1   synchrotrons
     BT2   cyclic accelerators
       BT3   accelerators

§ **COST** [13,638; 14,419]
   NT1   capitalized cost
   NT1   cost overruns
   NT1   operating cost
   RT   charges
   RT   cost benefit analysis
   RT   cost estimation
   RT   economics
   RT   fuel cycle
   RT   nuclear materials management
   RT   payback period
   RT   present worth method

COST BENEFIT ANALYSIS [3,260; 3,260]
   BT1   economic analysis
   RT   comparative evaluations
   RT   cost
   RT   cost estimation
   RT   cost overruns
   RT   economics
   RT   technology impacts

COST ESTIMATION [903; 903] *Dec 85*
   RT   cost
   RT   cost benefit analysis
   RT   forecasting

COST OVERRUNS [15; 15] *Dec 85*
   BT1   cost
   RT   charges
   RT   cost benefit analysis

COSTA RICA [18; 18]
   BT1   central america
     BT2   latin america
   BT1   developing countries

COSTER-KRONIG TRANSITIONS [218; 218]
   BT1   auger effect
   BT1   energy-level transitions

COTTON [163; 163]
   RT   cotton plants
   RT   fibers
   RT   textiles

COTTON PLANTS [173; 173]
   BT1   plants
   RT   boll weevil
   RT   bollworm
   RT   cotton
   RT   cottonseed oil

cotton-mouton effect
   USE   voigt effect

COTTONSEED OIL [9; 9] *Aug 81*
   BT1   oils
     BT2   other organic compounds
       BT3   organic compounds
   RT   cotton plants

COUETTE FLOW [79; 79]
   BT1   viscous flow
     BT2   fluid flow

coulomb attraction
   USE   coulomb field

coulomb barrier
   USE   coulomb field

COULOMB CORRECTION [528; 528]
   BT1   corrections
   RT   electromagnetic interactions

COULOMB ENERGY [663; 663]
   BT1   energy
   RT   binding energy
   RT   nolen-schiffer anomaly

COULOMB EXCITATION [2,182; 2,182]
   BT1   excitation
     BT2   energy-level transitions
   RT   coulomb scattering

COULOMB FIELD [6,757; 6,757]
   UF   *coulomb attraction*
   UF   *coulomb barrier*
   UF   *coulomb potential*
   UF   *coulomb repulsion*
   BT1   electric fields
   RT   central potential
   RT   coulomb ionization
   RT   nuclear screening
   RT   ponderomotive force

COULOMB IONIZATION [171; 171] *Sep 77*
(Ionization produced by Coulomb forces between a projectile and the target.)
   BT1   ionization
   RT   coulomb field
   RT   inner-shell ionization

coulomb potential
   USE   coulomb field

coulomb repulsion
   USE   coulomb field

COULOMB SCATTERING [1,611; 1,611]
   BT1   elastic scattering
     BT2   scattering
   BT1   electromagnetic interactions
     BT2   basic interactions
     BT2   interactions
   RT   coulomb excitation
   RT   electron cooling
   RT   potential scattering

coulometry
   USE   voltametry

COUMARIN [114; 114]
   BT1   anticoagulants
     BT2   hematologic agents
       BT3   drugs
   BT1   lactones
     BT2   esters
       BT3   organic compounds
     BT2   heterocyclic compounds
       BT3   organic compounds
   BT1   pyrans
     BT2   heterocyclic compounds
       BT3   organic compounds
     BT2   organic oxygen compounds
       BT3   organic compounds
   RT   psoralen

council for mutual econ assist
   USE   comecon

COUNTER CURRENT [429; 429]
   RT   chromatography
   RT   counterflow systems
   RT   solvent extraction

counterflow cooling towers
   USE   cooling towers
   AND   counterflow systems

COUNTERFLOW SYSTEMS [95; 95] *Apr 84*
   UF+   *counterflow cooling towers*
   RT   cooling towers
   RT   counter current
   RT   evaporation
   RT   hydrodynamics
   RT   vapor condensers

counters (radiation)
   USE   radiation detectors

COUNTING CIRCUITS [1,162; 1,162]
- BT1 electronic circuits
- RT counting ratemeters
- RT counting tubes
- RT pulse circuits
- RT pulse techniques
- RT radiation detection
- RT radiation detectors
- RT scalers
- RT switching circuits

COUNTING RATEMETERS [205; 252]
- UF *ratemeters (counting)*
- BT1 electronic equipment
- BT2 equipment
- NT1 linear ratemeters
- NT1 logarithmic ratemeters
- RT counting circuits
- RT counting rates
- RT exposure ratemeters
- RT pulse integrators
- RT pulse techniques

COUNTING RATES [2,946; 2,946]
- RT counting ratemeters
- RT time dependence

COUNTING TECHNIQUES [1,799; 38,600]
- NT1 absolute counting
- NT1 charge plunger method
- NT1 coincidence methods
  - NT2 coincidence spectrometry
  - NT2 tagged photon method
- NT1 dsa method
- NT1 four-pi counting
- NT1 low level counting
- NT1 photoelectron counting
- NT1 radioisotope scanning
  - NT2 scintiscanning
- NT1 scintillation counting
- NT1 sequential scanning
- NT1 whole-body counting
- RT activity meters
- RT anticoincidence
- RT electronic circuits
- RT electronic equipment
- RT hodoscopes
- RT position sensitive detectors
- RT pulse techniques
- RT radiation detectors
- RT radioassay
- RT recording systems
- RT telescope counters

COUNTING TUBES [32; 32]
- UF *dekatrons*
- UF *trochotrons*
- BT1 electron tubes
- RT counting circuits
- RT pulse techniques
- RT scalers

couple corrosion
- USE electrochemical corrosion

COUPLED CHANNEL BORN APPROXIMA [412; 412]
- UF *approximation (coupled-chann.)*
- UF *ccba*
- UF *coupled-channel born approxima*
- BT1 born approximation
- RT coupled channel theory
- RT nuclear reaction kinetics
- RT nuclear reactions
- RT scattering

COUPLED CHANNEL THEORY [3,343; 3,343]
- RT collisions
- RT coupled channel born approxima
- RT nuclear reactions

coupled f.reactor meas.facili.
- USE cfrmf reactor

COUPLED REACTOR CORES [164; 164]
- BT1 reactor cores
- BT2 reactor components

coupled-channel born approxima
- USE coupled channel born approxima

COUPLING [8,459; 14,517]
(Not for the concept covered by JOINING.)
- UF+ *electron-ion coupling*
- NT1 electron-hole coupling
- NT1 electron-phonon coupling
- NT1 intermediate coupling
  - NT2 j-j coupling
  - NT2 l-s coupling
- NT1 pseudovector coupling
- NT1 ruderman-kittel coupling
- RT aligned coupling scheme
- RT bootstrap model
- RT bound state
- RT coupling constants
- RT decoupling
- RT goldberger-treiman relation
- RT impulse approximation
- RT interactions
- RT particle-core coupling model
- RT quasibound state
- RT strong-coupling model
- RT weak-coupling model

COUPLING CONSTANTS [10,874; 10,874]
- RT coupling

couplings (machine parts)
- USE machine parts

COURTS [746; 746] *Dec 76*
- RT dispute settlements
- RT hearings
- RT lawsuits

COVALENCE [695; 695]
- UF *covalency*
- RT binding energy

covalency
- USE covalence

COVER GAS [469; 469]
(The inert gas blanket over the liquid metal in a liquid metal cooled reactor.)
- BT1 inert atmosphere
- BT2 controlled atmospheres

cow-milkers
- USE radioisotope generators

COWBOY EVENT [0; 0]
- BT1 chemical explosions
- BT2 explosions
- BT1 vela project

COWS [438; 438]
- BT1 cattle
- BT2 domestic animals
- BT3 animals
- BT2 ruminants
- BT3 mammals
- BT4 vertebrates
- BT5 animals
- RT milk

CP INVARIANCE [3,050; 3,050]
- BT1 invariance principles
- RT kobayashi-maskawa matrix

cp-11 reactor
- USE argonaut reactor

CP-2 REACTOR [1; 1]
(ANL, Argonne, Illinois, USA)
- UF *chicago pile-2 reactor*
- BT1 graphite moderated reactors
- BT2 reactors
- BT1 materials testing reactors
- BT2 irradiation reactors
- BT3 reactors
- BT1 natural uranium reactors
- BT2 reactors
- BT1 research reactors
- BT2 research and test reactors
- BT3 reactors
- BT1 thermal reactors
- BT2 reactors

CP-3 REACTOR [2; 2]
(ANL, Argonne, Illinois, USA)
- UF *argonne heavy water reactor*
- BT1 heavy water cooled reactors
- BT2 reactors
- BT1 heavy water moderated reactors
- BT2 reactors
- BT1 natural uranium reactors
- BT2 reactors
- BT1 research reactors
- BT2 research and test reactors
- BT3 reactors
- BT1 tank type reactors
- BT2 reactors
- BT1 thermal reactors
- BT2 reactors

CP-5 REACTOR [7; 7]
(ANL, Argonne, Illinois, USA)
- UF *argonne research reactor*
- BT1 enriched uranium reactors
- BT2 reactors
- BT1 heavy water cooled reactors
- BT2 reactors
- BT1 heavy water moderated reactors
- BT2 reactors
- BT1 isotope production reactors
- BT2 irradiation reactors
- BT3 reactors
- BT1 research reactors
- BT2 research and test reactors
- BT3 reactors
- BT1 tank type reactors
- BT2 reactors
- BT1 test reactors
- BT2 research and test reactors
- BT3 reactors
- BT2 test facilities
- BT1 thermal reactors
- BT2 reactors

CPB [219; 315]
- UF *competitive protein binding*
- NT1 pbi
- RT antigen-antibody reactions
- RT enzyme immunoassay
- RT proteins
- RT radioimmunoassay

CPDTA [1; 1]
(Cyclopentanediaminetetraacetic acid)
- UF *cyclopentanediaminetetraacetic*
- BT1 amino acids
- BT2 carboxylic acids
- BT3 organic acids
- BT4 organic compounds
- BT1 chelating agents

cpm
(Critical Path Method.)
- USE pert method

CPPNM [21; 21] *Jun 85*
(Convention on the Physical Protection of Nuclear Materials)
- UF *conv phys protec nucl material*
- UF *nucl mater, conv phys protec*
- UF *phys protec nucl mater, conv*
- UF *protec nucl mater, conv*
- BT1 international agreements
  - BT2 agreements
- RT nuclear materials diversion
- RT nuclear materials management
- RT physical protection

CPT THEOREM [273; 273]
- BT1 invariance principles

CRAB NEBULA [733; 733]
- BT1 nebulae
- BT1 supernova remnants
  - BT2 cosmic radio sources
- RT pulsars

crabs
- USE crustaceans

crack growth
- USE crack propagation

CRACK PROPAGATION [4,804; 4,804] *Sep 80*
- UF *crack growth*
- RT brittleness
- RT cracks
- RT fatigue
- RT fracture mechanics
- RT fractures
- RT stress intensity factors

CRACKING [521; 521]
- BT1 pyrolysis
  - BT2 decomposition
    - BT3 chemical reactions
- RT petrochemistry

CRACKS [9,519; 9,519]
- RT ceramography
- RT crack propagation
- RT defects
- RT fracture mechanics
- RT fracture properties
- RT fractures
- RT geologic fissures
- RT geologic fractures
- RT notches
- RT stress intensity factors

CRACOW AIC-144 CYCLOTRON [5; 5] *Jul 82*
- UF *aic-144 cyclotron*
- BT1 isochronous cyclotrons
  - BT2 cyclotrons
    - BT3 cyclic accelerators
      - BT4 accelerators

CRACOW C-48 CYCLOTRON [4; 4] *Jun 79*
- BT1 isochronous cyclotrons
  - BT2 cyclotrons
    - BT3 cyclic accelerators
      - BT4 accelerators

CRACOW U-120 CYCLOTRON [16; 16] *Apr 79*
- BT1 cyclotrons
  - BT2 cyclic accelerators
    - BT3 accelerators
- BT1 heavy ion accelerators
  - BT2 accelerators

CRANES [396; 396]
- UF *hoists*
- BT1 remote handling equipment
  - BT2 materials handling equipment
    - BT3 equipment

CRANKING MODEL [947; 947]
- BT1 nuclear models
  - BT2 mathematical models
- RT deformed nuclei
- RT governor model

CRATERING EXPLOSIONS [104; 126]
- BT1 explosions
- NT1 cabriolet event
- NT1 danny boy event
- NT1 palanquin event
- NT1 pre-gondola i event
- NT1 pre-gondola ii event
- NT1 schooner event
- NT1 sedan event
- RT chemical explosions
- RT craters
- RT essex i project
- RT mining
- RT nuclear excavation
- RT nuclear explosions
- RT plowshare project
- RT surface explosions
- RT underground explosions

CRATERS [290; 290]
- BT1 cavities
- RT cratering explosions
- RT excavation
- RT openings
- RT surface explosions
- RT underground explosions

CRAY COMPUTERS [267; 267] *Apr 80*
- BT1 computers

crbr reactor
- USE clinch river breeder reactor

cre
- USE cumulative radiation effects

CREATINE [91; 91]
- BT1 amino acids
  - BT2 carboxylic acids
    - BT3 organic acids
      - BT4 organic compounds
- RT creatinine
- RT guanidines
- RT phosphocreatine

CREATININE [207; 207]
- BT1 imidazoles
  - BT2 azoles
    - BT3 heterocyclic compounds
      - BT4 organic compounds
    - BT3 organic nitrogen compounds
      - BT4 organic compounds
- BT1 imines
  - BT2 organic nitrogen compounds
    - BT3 organic compounds
- RT creatine

CREATION OPERATORS [1,362; 1,362]
- BT1 quantum operators
  - BT2 mathematical operators
- RT second quantization
- RT vacuum states

creeks
- USE rivers

CREEP [7,898; 7,898]
- BT1 mechanical properties
- RT plasticity
- RT ratcheting
- RT stress relaxation

→ **CREOSOTE** [0; 0] *Oct 91*
(A yellowish oily liquid containing a mixture of phenolic compounds obtained by distillation of coal or wood tars.)
- RT coal tar
- RT cresols
- RT wood

CREPIS [98; 98]
- BT1 plants

CRESOLS [86; 86]
- UF *cresylic acid*
- UF *hydroxytoluenes*
- UF *methyl phenols*
- BT1 phenols
  - BT2 aromatics
    - BT3 organic compounds
  - BT2 hydroxy compounds
    - BT3 organic compounds
- RT creosote

cresylic acid
- USE cresols

CREVICE CORROSION [164; 164] *Nov 80*
- BT1 corrosion
  - BT2 chemical reactions

creys-malville reactor
- USE super phenix reactor

cricetulus
- USE hamsters

CRIME DETECTION [169; 169]
- BT1 detection
- RT activation analysis
- RT chemical analysis
- RT tracer techniques

CRISTOBALITE [33; 33]
- BT1 oxide minerals
  - BT2 minerals
- RT quartz
- RT silicate minerals
- RT silicon oxides

critical assemblies
- USE zero power reactors

CRITICAL CURRENT [4,147; 4,147]
- BT1 electric currents
  - BT2 currents
- RT superconductivity

critical exp. facility oak rid
- USE or-cef reactor

CRITICAL FIELD [2,748; 2,748]
- BT1 magnetic fields
- RT superconductivity

CRITICAL FLOW [386; 386]
- BT1 fluid flow
- RT critical velocity
- RT laminar flow
- RT turbulent flow

CRITICAL FREQUENCY [78; 78] *Oct 82*
- RT ionosphere
- RT radiowave radiation

critical group (icrp)
(Out of a general population, the group of persons most highly exposed to radiation by virtue of their occupations, diets, habits, etc.)
- USE icrp critical group

critical heat flow
USE   departure nucleate boiling

CRITICAL HEAT FLUX [1,242; 1,242]
BT1   heat flux
RT   heat transfer
RT   high temperature
RT   ultrahigh temperature
RT   very high temperature

CRITICAL MASS [430; 430]
RT   criticality
RT   reflector savings

critical mass laboratory pnl
USE   cml reactor

CRITICAL ORGANS [786; 786]
BT1   organs
 BT2   body
RT   annual limit of intake
RT   internal irradiation
RT   nonuniform irradiation
RT   radiation doses
RT   radionuclide kinetics
RT   retention

critical path method
USE   pert method

CRITICAL PRESSURE [247; 247]
UF   *pressure (critical)*
BT1   thermodynamic properties
BT2   physical properties

CRITICAL SIZE [237; 237]
BT1   size
RT   criticality
RT   reflector savings

CRITICAL TEMPERATURE
[2,803; 2,803]
(For superconducting transition use
TRANSITION TEMPERATURE.)
BT1   transition temperature
BT2   thermodynamic properties
 BT3   physical properties
RT   heat treatments
RT   phase diagrams
RT   phase transformations

CRITICAL VELOCITY [279; 279]
BT1   velocity
RT   critical flow

CRITICALITY [4,022; 4,022]
UF   *subcriticality*
UF+   *criticality accidents*
RT   buckling
RT   chain reactions
RT   critical mass
RT   critical size
RT   fission
RT   multiplication factors
RT   natural nuclear reactors
RT   oklo phenomenon
RT   reactor kinetics
RT   reactor safety
RT   reactors
RT   reflector savings
RT   response matrix method

criticality accidents
USE   criticality
AND   radiation accidents

CRNL MP TANDEM ACCELERATOR
[91; 91] *Jun 76*
UF   *mp tandem accelerator*
BT1   tandem electrostatic accelerat
 BT2   electrostatic accelerators
  BT3   accelerators

BT1   van de graaff accelerators
 BT2   electrostatic accelerators
  BT3   accelerators

**CRNL SUPERCONDUCTING
CYCLOTRON** [58; 58] *Sep 82*
UF   *chalk river supercond. cyclo.*
BT1   heavy ion accelerators
 BT2   accelerators
BT1   isochronous cyclotrons
 BT2   cyclotrons
  BT3   cyclic accelerators
   BT4   accelerators

CROCUS REACTOR [7; 7]
(Atomic Engineering Lab. of the Lausanne
Federal Polytechnic School, Lausanne,
Switzerland)
BT1   pool type reactors
 BT2   water cooled reactors
  BT3   reactors
 BT2   water moderated reactors
  BT3   reactors
BT1   research reactors
 BT2   research and test reactors
  BT3   reactors
BT1   zero power reactors
 BT2   experimental reactors
  BT3   research and test reactors
   BT4   reactors

CROLOY [22; 243]
(For unspecified Croloy alloys.)
BT1   steels
 BT2   carbon additions
 BT2   iron base alloys
  BT3   iron alloys
   BT4   alloys
NT1   steel-cr13
NT1   steel-cr16
NT1   steel-cr17mn15nni
NT1   steel-cr18ni10
NT1   steel-cr2mo
NT1   steel-cr5mo

croloy 12
USE   steel-cr13

croloy 18
USE   steel-cr16

croloy 2
USE   steel-cr2mo

croloy 299
USE   steel-cr17mn15nni

croloy 3035
USE   steel-cr18ni10

croloy 5
USE   steel-cr5mo

cropping systems
USE   cultivation techniques

CROPS [631; 631]
RT   agriculture
RT   biomass plantations
RT   cereals
RT   cultivation techniques
RT   food
RT   fruits
RT   ground cover
RT   sugar cane
RT   tobacco
RT   vegetables
RT   vernalization

§ **CROSS SECTIONS** [47,519; 97,681]
(Whenever appropriate see the more specific descriptors listed below.)
NT1   differential cross sections
NT1   group constants
NT1   integral cross sections
NT1   total cross sections
RT   breit-wigner formula
RT   cinda
RT   detailed balance principle
RT   four momentum transfer
RT   giant resonance
RT   giant resonance model
RT   intermediate resonance
RT   intermediate structure
RT   mean free path
RT   multilevel analysis
RT   nuclear reactions
RT   peierls method
RT   reciprocal v law
RT   rosenbluth formula
RT   shadow effect
RT   transfer matrix method

CROSS-LINKING [2,428; 2,428]
BT1   polymerization
 BT2   chemical reactions
RT   radiation curing

CROSSED FIELDS [719; 719]
UF   *fields (crossed)*
RT   electric fields
RT   magnetic fields

crossflow cooling towers
USE   cooling towers
AND   crossflow systems

CROSSFLOW SYSTEMS [93; 93]
Dec 85
UF+   *crossflow cooling towers*
RT   cooling towers
RT   evaporators
RT   hydrodynamics
RT   vapor condensers

CROSSING SYMMETRY [575; 575]
BT1   symmetry
RT   scattering amplitudes

CROSSING-OVER [98; 98]
RT   chromosomes
RT   gene recombination
RT   human chromosomes
RT   meiosis
RT   mitosis
RT   recombinant dna

CROSSROADS PROJECT [1; 1]
UF   *project crossroads*
RT   atmospheric explosions
RT   nuclear explosions
RT   underwater explosions

CROTON OIL [4; 4]
UF   *tiglium oil*
BT1   oils
 BT2   other organic compounds
  BT3   organic compounds
BT1   triglycerides
 BT2   esters
  BT3   organic compounds
 BT2   lipids
  BT3   organic compounds

CROTONIC ACID [22; 22]
BT1   monocarboxylic acids
 BT2   carboxylic acids
  BT3   organic acids
   BT4   organic compounds

CROWDIONS [86; 86]
  BT1 line defects
    BT2 crystal defects
      BT3 crystal structure
  RT   interstitials

crowfoot
  USE ranunculaceae

CRUAS-2 REACTOR [4; 4] *Nov 89*
(Cruas, France.)
  BT1 pwr type reactors
    BT2 enriched uranium reactors
      BT3 reactors
    BT2 power reactors
      BT3 reactors
    BT2 thermal reactors
      BT3 reactors
    BT2 water cooled reactors
      BT3 reactors
    BT2 water moderated reactors
      BT3 reactors

CRUAS-3 REACTOR [2; 2] *Nov 89*
(Cruas, France.)
  BT1 pwr type reactors
    BT2 enriched uranium reactors
      BT3 reactors
    BT2 power reactors
      BT3 reactors
    BT2 thermal reactors
      BT3 reactors
    BT2 water cooled reactors
      BT3 reactors
    BT2 water moderated reactors
      BT3 reactors

CRUCIBLES [208; 208]
  RT   casting
  RT   furnaces
  RT   melting

crude oil
  USE petroleum

CRUSHING [429; 429]
  UF   *pulverizing*
  BT1 mechanical fragmentation
  RT   explosive stimulation
  RT   ore processing

CRUSTACEANS [363; 556]
  UF   *copepods*
  UF   *crabs*
  BT1 aquatic organisms
  BT1 arthropods
    BT2 invertebrates
      BT3 animals
  NT1 artemia
  NT1 daphnia
  NT1 lobsters
  NT1 prawns
  NT1 shrimp
  RT   plankton

cryocables
  USE cryogenic cables

CRYOGENIC BUBBLE CHAMBERS
[348; 348]
  BT1 bubble chambers
    BT2 gas track detectors
      BT3 radiation detectors
        BT4 measuring instruments

CRYOGENIC CABLES [11; 11] *Aug 76*
(Prior to 1986 SUPERCONDUCTING
CABLES was used for this concept.)
  UF   *cryocables*
  BT1 electric cables
    BT2 cables
    BT2 conductor devices
      BT3 electrical equipment
        BT4 equipment

  RT   superconducting cables

CRYOGENIC FLUIDS [693; 693]
Mar 76
  UF   *cryogens*
  BT1 fluids
  RT   cryogenics
  RT   helium
  RT   hydrogen
  RT   methane
  RT   nitrogen
  RT   oxygen
  RT   refrigerants

CRYOGENIC STORAGE DEVICES
[30; 30]
  BT1 memory devices

CRYOGENICS [2,738; 2,738]
  RT   absolute zero temperature
  RT   adiabatic demagnetization
  RT   cryogenic fluids
  RT   cryopumps
  RT   cryostats
  RT   cryotrons
  RT   dewars
  RT   freons
  RT   helium dilution refrigeration
  RT   low temperature
  RT   magnetic refrigerators
  RT   superconductivity
  RT   superfluidity
  RT   ultralow temperature
  RT   very low temperature

cryogens
  USE cryogenic fluids

CRYOPUMPS [640; 640]
  BT1 vacuum pumps
    BT2 pumps
      BT3 equipment
  RT   cryogenics
  RT   high vacuum
  RT   medium vacuum
  RT   ultrahigh vacuum

CRYOSCOPY [53; 53]
(Measurement of freezing-point depression produced in a solvent by a solute to determine molecular weight of the solute or properties of solutions.)
  UF   *freezing point depression*
  RT   low temperature
  RT   molecular weight

CRYOSTATS [1,644; 1,644]
  BT1 thermostats
    BT2 control equipment
      BT3 equipment
  RT   cryogenics
  RT   equipment protection devices
  RT   magnetic refrigerators
  RT   refrigerators

CRYOTRONS [28; 28]
(Switching devices based on the magnetic control of superconductivity.)
  BT1 superconducting devices
  BT1 switches
    BT2 electrical equipment
      BT3 equipment
  RT   cryogenics

CRYPT CELLS [302; 302]
  BT1 somatic cells
    BT2 animal cells
  RT   epithelium
  RT   intestines

CRYSTAL COUNTERS [214; 216]
  UF   *diamond counters*
  BT1 radiation detectors
    BT2 measuring instruments
  NT1 filament crystal counters

  RT   bulk semiconductor detectors

CRYSTAL DEFECTS [7,651; 27,946]
  BT1 crystal structure
  NT1 line defects
    NT2 crowdions
    NT2 dislocations
      NT3 edge dislocations
      NT3 screw dislocations
  NT1 point defects
    NT2 interstitials
      NT3 i centers
    NT2 vacancies
      NT3 color centers
        NT4 a centers
        NT4 e centers
        NT4 f centers
        NT4 h centers
        NT4 i centers
        NT4 m centers
        NT4 q centers
        NT4 r centers
        NT4 s centers
        NT4 u centers
        NT4 v centers
        NT4 z centers
      NT3 frenkel defects
      NT3 schottky defects
  NT1 stacking faults
  RT   cavities
  RT   crystal lattices
  RT   inclusions
  RT   internal friction
  RT   microstructure
  RT   radiation effects
  RT   thermal spikes
  RT   varley mechanism

CRYSTAL DOPING [3,102; 3,102]
  UF   *doping (crystal)*
  RT   bromine additions
  RT   chlorine additions
  RT   doped materials
  RT   fluorine additions
  RT   iodine additions
  RT   ion implantation
  RT   trace amounts

CRYSTAL FIELD [3,916; 3,916]
  RT   crystal structure
  RT   electronic structure

CRYSTAL GROWTH [4,366; 4,366]
  UF   *growth (crystal)*
  RT   bridgman method
  RT   cleavage
  RT   crystallization
  RT   crystals
  RT   czochralski method
  RT   epitaxy
  RT   grain growth
  RT   nucleation
  RT   stockbarger method
  RT   zone melting

CRYSTAL LATTICES [9,585; 22,770]
  UF   *lattices (crystal)*
  UF   *space lattices*
  BT1 crystal structure
  NT1 beta-w lattices
  NT1 cubic lattices
    NT2 bcc lattices
    NT2 fcc lattices
  NT1 hexagonal lattices
    NT2 hcp lattices
  NT1 monoclinic lattices
  NT1 orthorhombic lattices
  NT1 tetragonal lattices
  NT1 triclinic lattices
  NT1 trigonal lattices
  RT   coordination valences
  RT   crystal defects
  RT   crystals
  RT   diffraction methods
  RT   electron channeling
  RT   electron-phonon coupling
  RT   habit planes
  RT   ion channeling

RT	lattice parameters	
RT	laue method	
RT	laves phases	
RT	microstructure	
RT	miller indices	
RT	muon spin relaxation	
RT	space groups	
RT	trapping	
RT	vegard law	

CRYSTAL MODELS [1,543; 3,914]
(For theories only.)
- UF   *models (crystal)*
- BT1   mathematical models
- NT1   heisenberg model
- NT1   ising model
- RT   crystal structure
- RT   replicas

crystal phase transitions
- USE   crystal-phase transformations

CRYSTAL RIVER-3 REACTOR [96; 96]
(Citrus, Florida, USA)
- UF   *red level-3 reactor*
- BT1   pwr type reactors
- BT2   enriched uranium reactors
-   BT3   reactors
- BT2   power reactors
-   BT3   reactors
- BT2   thermal reactors
-   BT3   reactors
- BT2   water cooled reactors
-   BT3   reactors
- BT2   water moderated reactors
-   BT3   reactors

CRYSTAL RIVER-4 REACTOR [8; 8]
(Citrus, Florida, USA)
- UF   *red level-4 reactor*
- BT1   pwr type reactors
- BT2   enriched uranium reactors
-   BT3   reactors
- BT2   power reactors
-   BT3   reactors
- BT2   thermal reactors
-   BT3   reactors
- BT2   water cooled reactors
-   BT3   reactors
- BT2   water moderated reactors
-   BT3   reactors

CRYSTAL STRUCTURE [13,971; 79,396]
- UF   *structure (crystal)*
- SF   *morphology*
- NT1   crystal defects
- NT2   line defects
-   NT3   crowdions
-   NT3   dislocations
-    NT4   edge dislocations
-    NT4   screw dislocations
- NT2   point defects
-   NT3   interstitials
-    NT4   i centers
-   NT3   vacancies
-    NT4   color centers
-     NT5   a centers
-     NT5   e centers
-     NT5   f centers
-     NT5   h centers
-     NT5   i centers
-     NT5   m centers
-     NT5   q centers
-     NT5   r centers
-     NT5   s centers
-     NT5   u centers
-     NT5   v centers
-     NT5   z centers
-    NT4   frenkel defects
-    NT4   schottky defects
- NT2   stacking faults
- NT1   crystal lattices
- NT2   beta-w lattices
- NT2   cubic lattices
-   NT3   bcc lattices
-   NT3   fcc lattices
- NT2   hexagonal lattices
-   NT3   hcp lattices
- NT2   monoclinic lattices
- NT2   orthorhombic lattices
- NT2   tetragonal lattices
- NT2   triclinic lattices
- NT2   trigonal lattices
- NT1   microstructure
- NT2   cleavage
- NT2   grain boundaries
- NT2   grain density
- NT2   grain orientation
- NT2   grain size
- NT2   widmanstaetten structure
- RT   allotropy
- RT   axial ratio
- RT   configuration
- RT   crystal field
- RT   crystal models
- RT   crystal-phase transformations
- RT   crystallography
- RT   guinier-preston zones
- RT   kikuchi lines
- RT   lattice vibrations
- RT   metamict state
- RT   optical activity
- RT   order parameters
- RT   peierls-nabarro force
- RT   physical metallurgy
- RT   solid state physics
- RT   structure factors
- RT   texture
- RT   twinning

CRYSTAL-PHASE TRANSFORMATIONS [5,994; 5,994]
- UF   *crystal phase transitions*
- BT1   phase transformations
- RT   crystal structure
- RT   graphitization
- RT   order-disorder transformations

CRYSTALLINE LENS [451; 451]
- UF   *lens (crystalline)*
- BT1   eyes
- BT2   sense organs
-   BT3   organs
-    BT4   body
- RT   cataracts

CRYSTALLIZATION [5,350; 5,350]
- BT1   phase transformations
- RT   amorphous state
- RT   cleavage
- RT   crystal growth
- RT   crystals
- RT   epitaxy
- RT   mineralization
- RT   nucleation
- RT   precipitation
- RT   purification
- RT   recrystallization
- RT   separation processes
- RT   solidification
- RT   solubility
- RT   zone refining

CRYSTALLOGRAPHY [1,970; 1,970]
- UF   *radiocrystallography*
- RT   atomic beam diffraction
- RT   crystal structure
- RT   crystals
- RT   diffraction methods
- RT   electron diffraction
- RT   gamma diffractometers
- RT   neutron diffraction
- RT   neutron diffractometers
- RT   patterson method
- RT   x-ray diffraction
- RT   x-ray diffractometers

CRYSTALS [10,269; 40,287]
- NT1   anharmonic crystals
- NT1   dendrites
- NT1   ionic crystals
- NT1   liquid crystals
- NT1   molecular crystals
- NT1   monocrystals
- NT2   whiskers
- NT1   polycrystals
- RT   clathrates
- RT   crystal growth
- RT   crystal lattices
- RT   crystallization
- RT   crystallography
- RT   ion implantation
- RT   solids
- RT   umklapp processes
- RT   varley mechanism

CSREX PROCESS [0; 0]
- BT1   reprocessing
- BT2   separation processes
- RT   solvent extraction

ct scanning
- USE   cat scanning

CT-6B TOKAMAK [5; 5] *Dec 89*
(Academia Sinica, Beijing, China.)
- BT1   tokamak devices
- BT2   closed plasma devices
-   BT3   thermonuclear devices

CTX SPHEROMAK [57; 57] *Nov 84*
(A LASL facility to investigate the production, equilibrium, stability and confinement properties of compact toroids of the spheromak type in the absence of externally supported toroidal fields.)
- BT1   spheromak devices
- BT2   tokamak devices
-   BT3   closed plasma devices
-    BT4   thermonuclear devices

CUBA [71; 71]
- BT1   developing countries
- BT1   latin america
- BT1   west indies
- BT2   islands

CUBIC LATTICES [2,666; 5,952]
- UF   *perovskite crystal structure*
- BT1   crystal lattices
- BT2   crystal structure
- NT1   bcc lattices
- NT1   fcc lattices

CUCUMBERS [77; 77]
- BT1   vegetables
- BT2   food

CUEX [9; 9] *Nov 75*
- UF   *cumulative exposure index*
- RT   human populations
- RT   icrp
- RT   integral doses

CULHAM LABORATORY [45; 45]
Feb 83
- BT1   ukaea
- BT2   united kingdom organizations
-   BT3   national organizations

CULTIVATION TECHNIQUES
[235; 235]
- UF   *cropping systems*
- UF   *plant cultivation*
- RT   agriculture
- RT   crops
- RT   irrigation

CULTURAL OBJECTS [258; 258]
Dec 81
(Objects of historical and/or artistic value.)
- UF   *art objects*
- UF   *museum objects*
- UF   *paintings*
- RT   age estimation
- RT   archaeological sites
- RT   archaeological specimens
- RT   historical aspects
- RT   preservation

CULTURE MEDIA [1,030; 1,030]
RT   cell cultures
RT   in vitro
RT   nutrients
RT   tissue cultures

cultures (cells)
USE   cell cultures

cultures (tissue)
USE   tissue cultures

CUMBERLAND RIVER [7; 7]
BT1   rivers
BT2   surface waters

CUMENE [61; 61]
UF   *isopropylbenzene*
BT1   aromatics
BT2   organic compounds
BT1   hydrocarbons
BT2   organic compounds

cumulative effect
(Production of particles in the region of limiting fragmentation of nuclei outside the limits allowed by one-nucleon collision kinematics.)
USE   limiting fragmentation
AND   particle production

cumulative exposure index
USE   cuex

cumulative liability
(Prior to December 1990, this was a valid descriptor.)
USE   liabilities

CUMULATIVE RADIATION EFFECTS [300; 300]
UF   *cre*
BT1   radiation effects
RT   fractionated irradiation
RT   radiation doses
RT   radiotherapy
RT   temporal dose distributions

CUPFERRON [69; 69]
UF   *phenylhydroxylamine*
BT1   amines
BT2   organic compounds
BT1   hydroxy compounds
BT2   organic compounds
BT1   reagents

CUPRATES [1,488; 1,488]
(Specific compounds should be indexed by coordination of a descriptor of the form (CATION) COMPOUNDS and the above anion descriptor.)
BT1   copper compounds
BT2   transition element compounds
BT1   oxygen compounds
RT   copper oxides

CUPROSKLODOWSKITE [2; 2]
BT1   silicate minerals
BT2   minerals
BT1   uranium minerals
BT2   radioactive minerals
BT3   minerals
BT3   radioactive materials
BT4   materials
RT   copper silicates
RT   uranium silicates

CURCUMIN [16; 16]
BT1   dyes
BT1   ethers
BT2   organic oxygen compounds
BT3   organic compounds
BT1   ketones
BT2   organic compounds
BT1   polyphenols
BT2   phenols
BT3   aromatics
BT4   organic compounds
BT3   hydroxy compounds
BT4   organic compounds

curie law
USE   curie-weiss law

CURIE POINT [2,665; 2,665]
UF   *curie temperature*
BT1   transition temperature
BT2   thermodynamic properties
BT3   physical properties
RT   ferromagnetism
RT   magnetic susceptibility

curie temperature
USE   curie point

CURIE-WEISS LAW [616; 616]
UF   *curie law*
RT   magnetic susceptibility

CURING [112; 616] Oct 82
NT1   radiation curing
RT   drying
RT   heat treatments
RT   polymerization
RT   vulcanization

CURITE [2; 2]
BT1   oxide minerals
BT2   minerals
BT1   uranium minerals
BT2   radioactive minerals
BT3   minerals
BT3   radioactive materials
BT4   materials
RT   lead oxides
RT   uranium oxides

CURIUM [649; 649]
BT1   actinides
BT2   metals
BT3   elements
BT1   transplutonium elements
BT2   transuranium elements
BT3   elements

CURIUM ADDITIONS [1; 1]
(Alloys containing not more than 1% Cm are listed here.)
RT   curium alloys
RT   curium compounds

CURIUM ALLOYS [32; 33]
(Alloys containing more than 1% Cm.)
BT1   actinide alloys
BT2   alloys
NT1   curium base alloys
RT   curium additions

CURIUM ARSENIDES [3; 3] Oct 76
BT1   arsenides
BT2   arsenic compounds
BT2   pnictides
BT1   curium compounds
BT2   actinide compounds
BT2   transplutonium compounds
BT3   transuranium compounds

CURIUM BASE ALLOYS [1; 1]
BT1   curium alloys
BT2   actinide alloys
BT3   alloys

CURIUM BROMIDES [3; 3]
BT1   bromides
BT2   bromine compounds
BT3   halogen compounds
BT2   halides
BT3   halogen compounds
BT1   curium compounds
BT2   actinide compounds
BT2   transplutonium compounds
BT3   transuranium compounds

CURIUM CARBIDES [0; 0]
BT1   carbides
BT2   carbon compounds
BT1   curium compounds
BT2   actinide compounds
BT2   transplutonium compounds
BT3   transuranium compounds

CURIUM CARBONATES [1; 1]
BT1   carbonates
BT2   carbon compounds
BT2   oxygen compounds
BT1   curium compounds
BT2   actinide compounds
BT2   transplutonium compounds
BT3   transuranium compounds

CURIUM CHLORIDES [14; 14]
BT1   chlorides
BT2   chlorine compounds
BT3   halogen compounds
BT2   halides
BT3   halogen compounds
BT1   curium compounds
BT2   actinide compounds
BT2   transplutonium compounds
BT3   transuranium compounds

CURIUM COMPLEXES [183; 183]
BT1   actinide complexes
BT2   complexes
BT1   transuranium complexes

CURIUM COMPOUNDS [215; 494]
BT1   actinide compounds
BT1   transplutonium compounds
BT2   transuranium compounds
NT1   curium arsenides
NT1   curium bromides
NT1   curium carbides
NT1   curium carbonates
NT1   curium chlorides
NT1   curium fluorides
NT1   curium hydrides
NT1   curium hydroxides
NT1   curium iodides
NT1   curium nitrates
NT1   curium nitrides
NT1   curium oxides
NT1   curium phosphides
NT1   curium selenides
NT1   curium silicates
NT1   curium silicides
NT1   curium sulfates
NT1   curium sulfides
NT1   curium tellurides
RT   curium additions

CURIUM FLUORIDES [27; 27]
BT1   curium compounds
BT2   actinide compounds
BT2   transplutonium compounds
BT3   transuranium compounds
BT1   fluorides
BT2   fluorine compounds
BT3   halogen compounds
BT2   halides
BT3   halogen compounds

CURIUM HYDRIDES [4; 4] *Nov 84*
 BT1 curium compounds
  BT2 actinide compounds
  BT2 transplutonium compounds
   BT3 transuranium compounds
 BT1 hydrides
  BT2 hydrogen compounds

CURIUM HYDROXIDES [2; 2]
 BT1 curium compounds
  BT2 actinide compounds
  BT2 transplutonium compounds
   BT3 transuranium compounds
 BT1 hydroxides
  BT2 hydrogen compounds
  BT2 oxygen compounds

CURIUM IODIDES [2; 2] *Aug 87*
 BT1 curium compounds
  BT2 actinide compounds
  BT2 transplutonium compounds
   BT3 transuranium compounds
 BT1 iodides
  BT2 halides
   BT3 halogen compounds
  BT2 iodine compounds
   BT3 halogen compounds

CURIUM IONS [31; 31]
 BT1 ions
  BT2 charged particles

CURIUM ISOTOPES [187; 1,643]
 NT1 curium 236
 NT1 curium 238
 NT1 curium 239
 NT1 curium 240
 NT1 curium 241
 NT1 curium 242
 NT1 curium 243
 NT1 curium 244
 NT1 curium 245
 NT1 curium 246
 NT1 curium 247
 NT1 curium 248
 NT1 curium 249
 NT1 curium 250
 NT1 curium 251
 NT1 curium 252

CURIUM NITRATES [24; 24]
 BT1 curium compounds
  BT2 actinide compounds
  BT2 transplutonium compounds
   BT3 transuranium compounds
 BT1 nitrates
  BT2 nitrogen compounds
  BT2 oxygen compounds

CURIUM NITRIDES [9; 9]
 BT1 curium compounds
  BT2 actinide compounds
  BT2 transplutonium compounds
   BT3 transuranium compounds
 BT1 nitrides
  BT2 nitrogen compounds
  BT2 pnictides

CURIUM OXIDES [209; 209]
 BT1 curium compounds
  BT2 actinide compounds
  BT2 transplutonium compounds
   BT3 transuranium compounds
 BT1 oxides
  BT2 chalcogenides
  BT2 oxygen compounds

CURIUM PHOSPHIDES [5; 5] *Jul 78*
 BT1 curium compounds
  BT2 actinide compounds
  BT2 transplutonium compounds
   BT3 transuranium compounds
 BT1 phosphides
  BT2 phosphorus compounds
  BT2 pnictides

→ **CURIUM SELENIDES** [0; 0] *Sep 91*
 BT1 curium compounds
  BT2 actinide compounds
  BT2 transplutonium compounds
   BT3 transuranium compounds
 BT1 selenides
  BT2 chalcogenides
  BT2 selenium compounds

CURIUM SILICATES [2; 2] *Jul 84*
 BT1 curium compounds
  BT2 actinide compounds
  BT2 transplutonium compounds
   BT3 transuranium compounds
 BT1 silicates
  BT2 oxygen compounds
  BT2 silicon compounds

CURIUM SILICIDES [0; 0] *Oct 83*
 BT1 curium compounds
  BT2 actinide compounds
  BT2 transplutonium compounds
   BT3 transuranium compounds
 BT1 silicides
  BT2 silicon compounds

CURIUM SULFATES [4; 4]
 BT1 curium compounds
  BT2 actinide compounds
  BT2 transplutonium compounds
   BT3 transuranium compounds
 BT1 sulfates
  BT2 oxygen compounds
  BT2 sulfur compounds

CURIUM SULFIDES [4; 4]
 BT1 curium compounds
  BT2 actinide compounds
  BT2 transplutonium compounds
   BT3 transuranium compounds
 BT1 sulfides
  BT2 chalcogenides
  BT2 sulfur compounds

→ **CURIUM TELLURIDES** [0; 0] *Sep 91*
 BT1 curium compounds
  BT2 actinide compounds
  BT2 transplutonium compounds
   BT3 transuranium compounds
 BT1 tellurides
  BT2 chalcogenides
  BT2 tellurium compounds

CURIUM 236 [4; 4] *Mar 86*
 BT1 actinide nuclei
  BT2 heavy nuclei
   BT3 nuclei
 BT1 alpha decay radioisotopes
  BT2 radioisotopes
   BT3 isotopes
 BT1 curium isotopes
 BT1 even-even nuclei
  BT2 nuclei
 BT1 minutes living radioisotopes
  BT2 radioisotopes
   BT3 isotopes

CURIUM 238 [4; 4]
 BT1 actinide nuclei
  BT2 heavy nuclei
   BT3 nuclei
 BT1 alpha decay radioisotopes
  BT2 radioisotopes
   BT3 isotopes
 BT1 curium isotopes
 BT1 electron capture radioisotopes
  BT2 beta decay radioisotopes
   BT3 radioisotopes
    BT4 isotopes
 BT1 even-even nuclei
  BT2 nuclei
 BT1 hours living radioisotopes
  BT2 radioisotopes
   BT3 isotopes

CURIUM 239 [1; 1]
 BT1 actinide nuclei
  BT2 heavy nuclei
   BT3 nuclei
 BT1 curium isotopes
 BT1 electron capture radioisotopes
  BT2 beta decay radioisotopes
   BT3 radioisotopes
    BT4 isotopes
 BT1 even-odd nuclei
  BT2 nuclei
 BT1 hours living radioisotopes
  BT2 radioisotopes
   BT3 isotopes

CURIUM 240 [25; 25]
 BT1 actinide nuclei
  BT2 heavy nuclei
   BT3 nuclei
 BT1 alpha decay radioisotopes
  BT2 radioisotopes
   BT3 isotopes
 BT1 curium isotopes
 BT1 days living radioisotopes
  BT2 radioisotopes
   BT3 isotopes
 BT1 even-even nuclei
  BT2 nuclei
 BT1 spontaneous fission radioisoto
  BT2 radioisotopes
   BT3 isotopes

CURIUM 241 [16; 16]
 BT1 actinide nuclei
  BT2 heavy nuclei
   BT3 nuclei
 BT1 alpha decay radioisotopes
  BT2 radioisotopes
   BT3 isotopes
 BT1 curium isotopes
 BT1 days living radioisotopes
  BT2 radioisotopes
   BT3 isotopes
 BT1 electron capture radioisotopes
  BT2 beta decay radioisotopes
   BT3 radioisotopes
    BT4 isotopes
 BT1 even-odd nuclei
  BT2 nuclei
 BT1 spontaneous fission radioisoto
  BT2 radioisotopes
   BT3 isotopes

CURIUM 242 [310; 310]
 BT1 actinide nuclei
  BT2 heavy nuclei
   BT3 nuclei
 BT1 alpha decay radioisotopes
  BT2 radioisotopes
   BT3 isotopes
 BT1 curium isotopes
 BT1 days living radioisotopes
  BT2 radioisotopes
   BT3 isotopes
 BT1 even-even nuclei
  BT2 nuclei
 BT1 spontaneous fission radioisoto
  BT2 radioisotopes
   BT3 isotopes

CURIUM 242 TARGET [22; 22]
 BT1 targets

CURIUM 243 [138; 138]
 BT1 actinide nuclei
  BT2 heavy nuclei
   BT3 nuclei
 BT1 alpha decay radioisotopes
  BT2 radioisotopes
   BT3 isotopes
 BT1 curium isotopes
 BT1 even-odd nuclei
  BT2 nuclei
 BT1 spontaneous fission radioisoto
  BT2 radioisotopes
   BT3 isotopes
 BT1 years living radioisotopes
  BT2 radioisotopes

    BT3   isotopes

CURIUM 243 TARGET [20; 20] *Oct 76*
    BT1   targets

CURIUM 244 [967; 967]
    BT1   actinide nuclei
    BT2   heavy nuclei
    BT3   nuclei
    BT1   alpha decay radioisotopes
    BT2   radioisotopes
    BT3   isotopes
    BT1   curium isotopes
    BT1   even-even nuclei
    BT2   nuclei
    BT1   spontaneous fission radioisoto
    BT2   radioisotopes
    BT3   isotopes
    BT1   years living radioisotopes
    BT2   radioisotopes
    BT3   isotopes

CURIUM 244 TARGET [37; 37]
    BT1   targets

CURIUM 245 [119; 119]
    BT1   actinide nuclei
    BT2   heavy nuclei
    BT3   nuclei
    BT1   alpha decay radioisotopes
    BT2   radioisotopes
    BT3   isotopes
    BT1   curium isotopes
    BT1   even-odd nuclei
    BT2   nuclei
    BT1   spontaneous fission radioisoto
    BT2   radioisotopes
    BT3   isotopes
    BT1   years living radioisotopes
    BT2   radioisotopes
    BT3   isotopes

CURIUM 245 TARGET [49; 49]
    BT1   targets

CURIUM 246 [85; 85]
    BT1   actinide nuclei
    BT2   heavy nuclei
    BT3   nuclei
    BT1   alpha decay radioisotopes
    BT2   radioisotopes
    BT3   isotopes
    BT1   curium isotopes
    BT1   even-even nuclei
    BT2   nuclei
    BT1   spontaneous fission radioisoto
    BT2   radioisotopes
    BT3   isotopes
    BT1   years living radioisotopes
    BT2   radioisotopes
    BT3   isotopes

CURIUM 246 TARGET [37; 37] *Oct 76*
    BT1   targets

CURIUM 247 [46; 46]
    BT1   actinide nuclei
    BT2   heavy nuclei
    BT3   nuclei
    BT1   alpha decay radioisotopes
    BT2   radioisotopes
    BT3   isotopes
    BT1   curium isotopes
    BT1   even-odd nuclei
    BT2   nuclei
    BT1   years living radioisotopes
    BT2   radioisotopes
    BT3   isotopes

CURIUM 247 TARGET [19; 19] *Jul 78*
    BT1   targets

CURIUM 248 [163; 163]
    BT1   actinide nuclei
    BT2   heavy nuclei
    BT3   nuclei
    BT1   alpha decay radioisotopes
    BT2   radioisotopes
    BT3   isotopes
    BT1   curium isotopes
    BT1   even-even nuclei
    BT2   nuclei
    BT1   spontaneous fission radioisoto
    BT2   radioisotopes
    BT3   isotopes
    BT1   years living radioisotopes
    BT2   radioisotopes
    BT3   isotopes

CURIUM 248 TARGET [182; 182]
    BT1   targets

CURIUM 249 [15; 15]
    BT1   actinide nuclei
    BT2   heavy nuclei
    BT3   nuclei
    BT1   beta-minus decay radioisotopes
    BT2   beta decay radioisotopes
    BT3   radioisotopes
    BT4   isotopes
    BT1   curium isotopes
    BT1   even-odd nuclei
    BT2   nuclei
    BT1   hours living radioisotopes
    BT2   radioisotopes
    BT3   isotopes

CURIUM 250 [19; 19]
    BT1   actinide nuclei
    BT2   heavy nuclei
    BT3   nuclei
    BT1   alpha decay radioisotopes
    BT2   radioisotopes
    BT3   isotopes
    BT1   beta-minus decay radioisotopes
    BT2   beta decay radioisotopes
    BT3   radioisotopes
    BT4   isotopes
    BT1   curium isotopes
    BT1   even-even nuclei
    BT2   nuclei
    BT1   spontaneous fission radioisoto
    BT2   radioisotopes
    BT3   isotopes
    BT1   years living radioisotopes
    BT2   radioisotopes
    BT3   isotopes

CURIUM 250 TARGET [5; 5]
    BT1   targets

CURIUM 251 [3; 3] *Feb 78*
    BT1   actinide nuclei
    BT2   heavy nuclei
    BT3   nuclei
    BT1   beta-minus decay radioisotopes
    BT2   beta decay radioisotopes
    BT3   radioisotopes
    BT4   isotopes
    BT1   curium isotopes
    BT1   even-odd nuclei
    BT2   nuclei
    BT1   minutes living radioisotopes
    BT2   radioisotopes
    BT3   isotopes

CURIUM 252 [2; 2]
    BT1   actinide nuclei
    BT2   heavy nuclei
    BT3   nuclei
    BT1   curium isotopes
    BT1   even-even nuclei
    BT2   nuclei

current (alternating)
    USE   alternating current

current (direct)
    USE   direct current

current (leakage)
    USE   leakage current

CURRENT ALGEBRA [2,012; 2,012]
    RT   algebraic currents
    RT   cabibbo angle
    RT   commutation relations
    RT   commutators
    RT   current commutators
    RT   current divergences
    RT   cvc theory
    RT   field algebra
    RT   low-energy theorem
    RT   pcac theory
    RT   pcvc theory
    RT   quantum field theory
    RT   symmetry groups
    RT   v-a theory

CURRENT COMMUTATORS [433; 616]
(For operators in current algebra; in electric circuitry use SWITCHES.)
    BT1   commutators
    BT2   quantum operators
    BT3   mathematical operators
    NT1   sigma terms
    RT   algebraic currents
    RT   current algebra
    RT   schwinger terms

CURRENT DENSITY [5,393; 5,393]
    UF   *density (current)*
    RT   beam currents
    RT   carrier density
    RT   electric currents
    RT   electron density

CURRENT DIVERGENCES [60; 60]
    RT   algebraic currents
    RT   current algebra

CURRENT LIMITERS [54; 54] *Aug 78*
    UF   *demand limiters*
    BT1   electrical equipment
    BT2   equipment
    RT   circuit breakers
    RT   electric currents
    RT   power transmission lines

CURRENT-DRIVE HEATING
[1,038; 1,038] *Mar 83*
    BT1   plasma heating
    BT2   heating
    RT   non-inductive current drive

CURRENTS [752; 32,639]
    NT1   algebraic currents
    NT2   axial-vector currents
    NT2   charged currents
    NT3   weak charged currents
    NT2   neutral currents
    NT3   weak neutral currents
    NT2   second-class currents
    NT2   vector currents
    NT1   beam currents
    NT2   amp beam currents
    NT2   kilo amp beam currents
    NT2   mega amp beam currents
    NT2   micro amp beam currents
    NT2   milli amp beam currents
    NT2   nano amp beam currents
    NT2   pico amp beam currents
    NT1   electric currents
    NT2   alternating current
    NT2   bootstrap current
    NT2   critical current
    NT2   direct current
    NT2   eddy currents
    NT2   electric arcs
    NT2   electrojets
    NT2   faraday current
    NT2   leakage current
    NT2   overcurrent

```
        NT2    photocurrents
        NT2    ring currents
     NT1    water currents
     RT     atmospheric circulation
     RT     voltametry

  curtailments
     USE    allocations

  curve of growth (spectroscopic
     USE    spectroscopic curve of growth

  curve of growth(spectroscopic)
     USE    spectroscopic curve of growth

  curves
     USE    diagrams

  CURVILINEAR COORDINATES
     [104; 145] Jul 85
     BT1    coordinates
     NT1    magnetic flux coordinates
     RT     metrics
     RT     riemann space

  CUSHING SYNDROME [170; 170]
     BT1    endocrine diseases
        BT2    diseases
     RT     corticosteroids
     RT     pituitary gland

  cusp
     USE    cusped geometries

  CUSPED GEOMETRIES [588; 588]
     UF     cusp
     UF     picket fence
     BT1    open configurations
        BT2    magnetic field configurations
     RT     geometry

  CUTTING [569; 569]
     BT1    machining
     RT     cutting tools
     RT     mechanical decladding

  CUTTING TOOLS [454; 454]
     BT1    tools
        BT2    equipment
     RT     cutting
     RT     shredders

  CVC THEORY [425; 425]
     RT     current algebra
     RT     vector currents

  CVTR REACTOR [8; 8]
     UF     carolinas virginia tube react.
     UF     parr carolinas cvtr reactor
     BT1    enriched uranium reactors
        BT2    reactors
     BT1    phwr type reactors
        BT2    heavy water cooled reactors
           BT3    reactors
        BT2    heavy water moderated reactors
           BT3    reactors
     BT1    pressure tube reactors
        BT2    power reactors
           BT3    reactors
     BT1    thermal reactors
        BT2    reactors

  cwip
     (Construction work in progress.)
     USE    construction
     AND    financing
```

```
  CYANAMIDES [37; 37]
     BT1    carbonic acid derivatives
        BT2    organic compounds
     BT1    organic nitrogen compounds
        BT2    organic compounds

  CYANATES [237; 237]
  (Specific compounds should be indexed
  by coordination of a descriptor of the form
  (CATION) COMPOUNDS and the above
  anion descriptor.)
     UF     isocyanates
     BT1    carbonic acid derivatives
        BT2    organic compounds
     BT1    nitrogen compounds
     RT     cyanides
     RT     oxygen compounds

  CYANIDES [1,073; 1,073]
  (Specific compounds should be indexed
  by coordination of a descriptor of the form
  (CATION) COMPOUNDS and the above
  anion descriptor.)
     RT     cyanates
     RT     cyanogen
     RT     hydrocyanic acid

  CYANINE DYES [27; 27] Jun 83
     BT1    dyes
     RT     aromatics
     RT     heterocyclic compounds

  CYANOBACTERIA [80; 80] Feb 83
     UF     blue-green algae
     BT1    microorganisms

  cyanocobalamin
     USE    vitamin b-12

  cyanoferrates
     USE    ferricyanides

  CYANOGEN [223; 223]
     RT     cyanides

  CYANURATES [30; 30]
     BT1    organic oxygen compounds
        BT2    organic compounds
     BT1    triazines
        BT2    azines
           BT3    heterocyclic compounds
              BT4    organic compounds
           BT3    organic nitrogen compounds
              BT4    organic compounds

  CYBERNETICS [44; 44]
     RT     control
     RT     information theory
     RT     man-machine systems

  CYCLASES [258; 258] Feb 83
     BT1    lyases
        BT2    enzymes
           BT3    organic compounds

  cycles (thermodynamic)
     USE    thermodynamic cycles

  CYCLIC ACCELERATORS [380; 21,431]
     BT1    accelerators
     NT1    betatrons
     NT1    cyclotrons
        NT2    calcutta cyclotron
        NT2    chandigarh cyclotron
        NT2    cracow u-120 cyclotron
        NT2    isochronous cyclotrons
           NT3    aabo cyclotron
           NT3    alice cyclotron
           NT3    apache
           NT3    brookhaven cyclotron
           NT3    chicago cyclotron
           NT3    cracow aic-144 cyclotron
           NT3    cracow c-48 cyclotron
```

```
           NT3    crnl superconducting
                     cyclotron
           NT3    cyclone cyclotron
           NT3    debrecen cyclotron
           NT3    eindhoven cyclotron
           NT3    ganil cyclotron
           NT3    grenoble cyclotron
           NT3    haizy cyclotron
           NT3    hirfl cyclotron
           NT3    inr cyclotron
           NT3    ipcr cyclotron
           NT3    iu cyclotron
           NT3    jinr cyclotrons
              NT4    jinr u-400 cyclotron
           NT3    julic cyclotron
           NT3    karlsruhe cyclotron
           NT3    kazakhstan cyclotron
           NT3    kiev cyclotron
           NT3    kvi cyclotron
           NT3    milan superconducting
                     cyclotro
           NT3    msu cyclotrons
           NT3    munich compact cyclotron
           NT3    munich suse cyclotron
           NT3    nac cyclotron
           NT3    nirs cyclotron
           NT3    nrl cyclotron
           NT3    ornl isochronous cyclotron
           NT3    orsay cyclotron
           NT3    oslo cyclotron
           NT3    princeton cyclotron
           NT3    rcnp cyclotron
           NT3    sara cyclotron
           NT3    sin cyclotron
           NT3    texas a and m cyclotron
           NT3    texas superconducting
                     cyclotro
           NT3    tohoku cyclotron
           NT3    tokyo ins cyclotron
           NT3    triumf cyclotron
           NT3    uclrl cyclotrons
              NT4    lbl 88-inch cyclotron
           NT3    warsaw cyclotron
        NT2    microtrons
           NT3    racetrack microtrons
        NT2    nbi cyclotron
        NT2    separated orbit cyclotrons
           NT3    ornl separated orbit cyclotron
        NT2    superconducting cyclotrons
           NT3    milan superconducting
                     cyclotro
           NT3    texas superconducting
                     cyclotro
        NT2    variable energy cyclotrons
     NT1    synchrocyclotrons
        NT2    berkeley synchrocyclotron
        NT2    cern synchrocyclotron
        NT2    chicago synchrocyclotron
        NT2    dubna synchrocyclotron
        NT2    goettingen synchrocyclotron
        NT2    harvard synchrocyclotron
        NT2    harwell synchrocyclotron
        NT2    iko synchrocyclotron
        NT2    mcgill synchrocyclotron
        NT2    orsay synchrocyclotron
        NT2    uppsala synchrocyclotron
     NT1    synchrotrons
        NT2    bevatron
        NT2    birmingham synchrotron
        NT2    bonn synchrotron
        NT2    brookhaven ags
        NT2    caltech synchrotron
        NT2    cambridge electron accelerator
        NT2    cern ps synchrotron
        NT2    cern sps synchrotron
        NT2    cornell 10-gev synchrotron
        NT2    cornell 2-gev synchrotron
        NT2    cosmotron
        NT2    desy
        NT2    erevan synchrotron
        NT2    escar storage ring
        NT2    fermilab accelerator
        NT2    fermilab tevatron
        NT2    fian synchrotron
        NT2    frascati synchrotron
        NT2    glasgow synchrotron
        NT2    ipns-i synchrotron
        NT2    itep synchrotron
        NT2    jinr synchrotron
        NT2    kek synchrotron
```

NT2	lampf ii synchrotron
NT2	lusy
NT2	mura synchrotron
NT2	nimrod
NT2	nina
NT2	omnitron
NT2	pakhra synchrotron
NT2	princeton synchrotron
NT2	saturne
NT2	saturne ii
NT2	serpukhov synchrotron
NT2	serpukhov tevatron
NT2	sis synchrotron
NT2	superconducting super collider
NT2	tokyo synchrotron
NT2	tomsk synchrotron
NT2	zgs
RT	bevalac
RT	cavity resonators
RT	rf systems
RT	superconducting cavity resonat
RT	waveguides

cyclic adenosine monophosphate
   USE   amp

cyclic amides
   USE   lactams

cyclic esters
   USE   lactones

CYCLIZATION [37; 37] *Jun 85*
| UF+ | *dehydrocyclization* |
| BT1 | chemical reactions |

CYCLOALKANES [735; 1,465]
UF	*adamantane*
BT1	alkanes
BT2	hydrocarbons
BT3	organic compounds
NT1	cyclohexane
NT1	decalin

CYCLOALKENES [703; 952]
UF+	*ttf-tcnq*
BT1	alkenes
BT2	hydrocarbons
BT3	organic compounds
NT1	camphene
NT1	cyclopentadiene

cycloheptatrienones
   USE   tropones

CYCLOHEXANE [734; 734]
BT1	cycloalkanes
BT2	alkanes
BT3	hydrocarbons
BT4	organic compounds
RT	hexane

cyclohexanol
   USE   hexanols

cyclohexanone
   USE   ketones

CYCLOHEXIMIDE [246; 246]
BT1	antibiotics
BT2	drugs
BT2	organic compounds
BT1	fungicides
BT2	pesticides

cyclohexylenedinitrilotetraace
(Cyclohexylenedinitrilotetraacetic acid)
   USE   cdta

CYCLONE CYCLOTRON [18; 18]
Jan 84
UF	*louvain isochronous cyclotron*
UF	*univ. catholique louvain cycl.*
BT1	heavy ion accelerators
BT2	accelerators
BT1	isochronous cyclotrons
BT2	cyclotrons
BT3	cyclic accelerators
BT4	accelerators

CYCLONE SEPARATORS [88; 88]
BT1	inertial separators
BT2	separation equipment
BT3	equipment
RT	scrubbers
RT	separation processes

CYCLOPENTADIENE [275; 275]
BT1	cycloalkenes
BT2	alkenes
BT3	hydrocarbons
BT4	organic compounds
BT1	dienes
BT2	polyenes
BT3	hydrocarbons
BT4	organic compounds

cyclopentanediaminetetraacetic
(Cyclopentanediaminetetraacetic acid)
   USE   cpdta

cyclophosphamide
   USE   endoxan

CYCLOTRON FREQUENCY
[1,203; 1,203]
UF	*frequency (cyclotron)*
RT	cyclotron harmonics
RT	cyclotron instability
RT	cyclotron radiation
RT	gyrofrequency

CYCLOTRON HARMONICS [403; 403]
BT1	harmonics
BT2	oscillations
RT	bernstein mode
RT	cyclotron frequency

CYCLOTRON INSTABILITY [631; 631]
BT1	plasma microinstabilities
BT2	plasma instability
BT3	instability
RT	cyclotron frequency

CYCLOTRON RADIATION [844; 844]
BT1	bremsstrahlung
BT2	electromagnetic radiation
BT3	radiations
RT	cyclotron frequency
RT	cyclotron resonance
RT	synchrotron radiation

CYCLOTRON RESONANCE [964; 2,331]
BT1	resonance
NT1	azbel-kaner resonance
NT1	electron cyclotron-resonance
NT1	ion cyclotron-resonance
RT	cyclotron radiation

CYCLOTRONS [2,526; 6,843]
BT1	cyclic accelerators
BT2	accelerators
NT1	calcutta cyclotron
NT1	chandigarh cyclotron
NT1	cracow u-120 cyclotron
NT1	isochronous cyclotrons
NT2	aabo cyclotron
NT2	alice cyclotron
NT2	apache
NT2	brookhaven cyclotron
NT2	chicago cyclotron
NT2	cracow aic-144 cyclotron
NT2	cracow c-48 cyclotron
NT2	crnl superconducting cyclotron
NT2	cyclone cyclotron
NT2	debrecen cyclotron
NT2	eindhoven cyclotron
NT2	ganil cyclotron
NT2	grenoble cyclotron
NT2	haizy cyclotron
NT2	hirfl cyclotron
NT2	inr cyclotron
NT2	ipcr cyclotron
NT2	iu cyclotron
NT2	jinr cyclotrons
NT3	jinr u-400 cyclotron
NT2	julic cyclotron
NT2	karlsruhe cyclotron
NT2	kazakhstan cyclotron
NT2	kiev cyclotron
NT2	kvi cyclotron
NT2	milan superconducting cyclotro
NT2	msu cyclotrons
NT2	munich compact cyclotron
NT2	munich suse cyclotron
NT2	nac cyclotron
NT2	nirs cyclotron
NT2	nrl cyclotron
NT2	ornl isochronous cyclotron
NT2	orsay cyclotron
NT2	oslo cyclotron
NT2	princeton cyclotron
NT2	rcnp cyclotron
NT2	sara cyclotron
NT2	sin cyclotron
NT2	texas a and m cyclotron
NT2	texas superconducting cyclotro
NT2	tohoku cyclotron
NT2	tokyo ins cyclotron
NT2	triumf cyclotron
NT2	uclrl cyclotrons
NT3	lbl 88-inch cyclotron
NT2	warsaw cyclotron
NT1	microtrons
NT2	racetrack microtrons
NT1	nbi cyclotron
NT1	separated orbit cyclotrons
NT2	ornl separated orbit cyclotron
NT1	superconducting cyclotrons
NT2	milan superconducting cyclotro
NT2	texas superconducting cyclotro
NT1	variable energy cyclotrons
RT	dees
RT	synchrocyclotrons

CYLINDERS [2,044; 2,044]
(Objects of cylindrical shape. For containers see headings such as GAS CYLINDERS.)
RT	pipes
RT	rods
RT	shape
RT	tubes

CYLINDRICAL CONFIGURATION
[4,066; 4,066]
| BT1 | configuration |

CYMENE [6; 6]
UF	*isopropyltoluene-para*
BT1	aromatics
BT2	organic compounds
BT1	hydrocarbons
BT2	organic compounds
RT	thymol

CYPRUS [18; 18]
BT1	islands
BT1	middle east
RT	mediterranean sea

cyric cyclotron
(At CYclotron and RadioIsotope Center, Tohoku University, Sendai, Japan.)
   USE   tohoku cyclotron

CYRTOLITE [2; 2]
BT1 silicate minerals
BT2 minerals
BT1 uranium minerals
BT2 radioactive minerals
BT3 minerals
BT3 radioactive materials
BT4 materials
RT zirconium silicates

cystamin
USE urotropin

CYSTAMINE [293; 293]
UF *2,2-dithiobisethylamine*
BT1 amines
BT2 organic compounds
BT1 organic sulfur compounds
BT2 organic compounds
BT1 radioprotective substances
BT2 drugs
BT2 response modifying factors
RT mea

CYSTAPHOS [26; 26] *Nov 75*
UF *sodium aminoethylthiophosphate*
BT1 amines
BT2 organic compounds
BT1 radioprotective substances
BT2 drugs
BT2 response modifying factors
BT1 thiophosphoric acid esters
BT2 esters
BT3 organic compounds

cysteamine
USE mea

CYSTEINE [585; 585]
UF *mercaptoalanine-beta*
BT1 amino acids
BT2 carboxylic acids
BT3 organic acids
BT4 organic compounds
BT1 thiols
BT2 organic sulfur compounds
BT3 organic compounds
RT cystine
RT homocysteine

CYSTINE [123; 123]
BT1 amino acids
BT2 carboxylic acids
BT3 organic acids
BT4 organic compounds
BT1 disulfides
BT2 organic sulfur compounds
BT3 organic compounds
RT cysteine
RT homocystine

CYSTS [65; 65] *Nov 88*
BT1 pathological changes
BT2 diseases

CYTIDINE [105; 105]
BT1 nucleosides
BT2 nucleotides
BT3 organic compounds
BT2 ribosides
BT1 pyrimidines
BT2 azines
BT3 heterocyclic compounds
BT4 organic compounds
BT3 organic nitrogen compounds
BT4 organic compounds
RT cytidylic acid
RT cytosine
RT deoxycytidine

CYTIDYLIC ACID [20; 20]
BT1 nucleotides
BT2 organic compounds
RT cytidine
RT cytosine
RT deoxycytidylic acid

CYTOCHEMISTRY [300; 300]
RT biochemistry
RT cytology
RT feulgen method

CYTOCHROME OXIDASE [90; 90]
BT1 oxidases
BT2 oxidoreductases
BT3 enzymes
BT4 organic compounds
RT cytochromes

CYTOCHROMES [357; 357]
BT1 pigments
RT coenzymes
RT cytochrome oxidase
RT diaphorases
RT redox process

CYTOLOGICAL TECHNIQUES
[439; 441] *Oct 75*
NT1 chromosome sorting
RT cell constituents
RT cell flow systems
RT cytology
RT electron microscopy

CYTOLOGY [681; 681]
BT1 biology
RT animal cells
RT cell constituents
RT cell flow systems
RT cytochemistry
RT cytological techniques
RT genetics
RT microorganisms
RT plant cells
RT ultrastructural changes

CYTOPLASM [544; 544]
BT1 cell constituents
RT liposomes
RT mitochondria
RT plasmids

CYTOSINE [276; 276]
BT1 amines
BT2 organic compounds
BT1 organic oxygen compounds
BT2 organic compounds
BT1 pyrimidines
BT2 azines
BT3 heterocyclic compounds
BT4 organic compounds
BT3 organic nitrogen compounds
BT4 organic compounds
RT cytidine
RT cytidylic acid

cytostatics
USE antimitotic drugs

czech wwr-s reactor
USE wwr-s-prague reactor

czechoslovak lr-0 reactor
USE lr-0 reactor

CZECHOSLOVAK ORGANIZATIONS
[239; 443]
BT1 national organizations
NT1 ujv
NT1 uvvvr

czechoslovak tr-0 reactor
USE tr-0 reactor

CZECHOSLOVAKIA [1,054; 1,054]
BT1 developing countries
BT1 europe
RT centrally planned economies

CZOCHRALSKI METHOD [364; 364]
RT crystal growth

D CODES [1,564; 1,564]
BT1 computer codes

D MESONS [921; 1,131] *Mar 77*
UF *d-1865 resonances*
BT1 charmed mesons
BT2 charm particles
BT3 elementary particles
BT2 mesons
BT3 bosons
BT3 hadrons
BT4 elementary particles
BT1 pseudoscalar mesons
BT2 mesons
BT3 bosons
BT3 hadrons
BT4 elementary particles
NT1 d minus mesons
NT1 d neutral mesons
NT2 anti-d neutral mesons
NT1 d plus mesons

D MINUS MESONS [36; 36] *Dec 87*
BT1 d mesons
BT2 charmed mesons
BT3 charm particles
BT4 elementary particles
BT3 mesons
BT4 bosons
BT4 hadrons
BT5 elementary particles
BT2 pseudoscalar mesons
BT3 mesons
BT4 bosons
BT4 hadrons
BT5 elementary particles

D NEUTRAL MESONS [443; 463]
Nov 78
(Prior to December 1987 this concept was indexed by D ZERO RESONANCES.)
UF *d zero resonances*
UF *d-zero resonances*
BT1 d mesons
BT2 charmed mesons
BT3 charm particles
BT4 elementary particles
BT3 mesons
BT4 bosons
BT4 hadrons
BT5 elementary particles
BT2 pseudoscalar mesons
BT3 mesons
BT4 bosons
BT4 hadrons
BT5 elementary particles
NT1 anti-d neutral mesons

D PLUS MESONS [287; 287] *Nov 78*
(Prior to December 1987 this concept was indexed by D PLUS RESONANCES.)
UF *d plus resonances*
UF *d-plus resonances*
BT1 d mesons
BT2 charmed mesons
BT3 charm particles
BT4 elementary particles
BT3 mesons
BT4 bosons
BT4 hadrons
BT5 elementary particles
BT2 pseudoscalar mesons
BT3 mesons
BT4 bosons
BT4 hadrons
BT5 elementary particles

d plus resonances
(Prior to December 1987 this was a valid descriptor.)
    USE   d plus mesons

D REGION [362; 362]
    BT1   ionosphere
    BT2   earth atmosphere

d resonances
(Prior to December 1987 this was a valid descriptor.)
    USE   charmed mesons

D S MESONS [399; 399] *Jul 78*
(Prior to December 1987 this concept was indexed by F MESONS.)
    UF   *d strange mesons*
    UF   *f mesons*
    UF   *f-2030 resonances*
    BT1   charmed mesons
      BT2   charm particles
        BT3   elementary particles
      BT2   mesons
        BT3   bosons
        BT3   hadrons
          BT4   elementary particles

D STATES [2,621; 2,621]
    BT1   energy levels

d strange mesons
    USE   d s mesons

D WAVES [851; 851]
    BT1   partial waves
    RT   angular momentum
    RT   quantum mechanics

d zero resonances
(Prior to December 1987 this was a valid descriptor.)
    USE   d neutral mesons

d* plus resonances
(Prior to December 1987 this was a valid descriptor.)
    USE   baryons

d* zero resonances
(Prior to December 1987 this was a valid descriptor.)
    USE   baryons

D*-2010 MESONS [199; 199] *Aug 78*
(Prior to December 1987 this concept was indexed by D-2007 RESONANCES.)
    UF   *d-2007 resonances*
    BT1   charmed mesons
      BT2   charm particles
        BT3   elementary particles
      BT2   mesons
        BT3   bosons
        BT3   hadrons
          BT4   elementary particles
    BT1   vector mesons
      BT2   mesons
        BT3   bosons
        BT3   hadrons
          BT4   elementary particles

D*-2420 MESONS [11; 11] *Dec 87*
    BT1   charmed mesons
      BT2   charm particles
        BT3   elementary particles
      BT2   mesons
        BT3   bosons
        BT3   hadrons
          BT4   elementary particles

d*resonances
(Prior to December 1987 this was a valid descriptor.)
    USE   baryons

D*S-2110 MESONS [99; 99] *Jul 78*
(Prior to December 1987 this concept was indexed by F* RESONANCES.)
    UF   *f*resonances*
    BT1   charmed mesons
      BT2   charm particles
        BT3   elementary particles
      BT2   mesons
        BT3   bosons
        BT3   hadrons
          BT4   elementary particles
    BT1   strange particles
      BT2   elementary particles

D-D REACTORS [79; 79] *Oct 83*
    BT1   thermonuclear reactors

d-plus resonances
    USE   d plus mesons

D-T REACTORS [729; 952]
    BT1   thermonuclear reactors
    NT1   pulsed d-t reactors
    NT2   reference theta pinch reactor
    NT1   steady-state d-t reactors

d-zero resonances
    USE   d neutral mesons

d-1285 resonances
(Prior to December 1987 this was a valid descriptor.)
    USE   f1-1285 mesons

d-1865 resonances
    USE   d mesons

d-2007 resonances
(Prior to December 1987 this was a valid descriptor.)
    USE   d*-2010 mesons

DACRON [53; 53]
    UF   *terylene*
    BT1   polyesters
      BT2   esters
        BT3   organic compounds
      BT2   organic polymers
        BT3   organic compounds
        BT3   polymers
    RT   fibers
    RT   glycols
    RT   terephthalic acid
    RT   textiles

DACUS [34; 48]
    BT1   fruit flies
      BT2   flies
        BT3   insects
          BT4   arthropods
            BT5   invertebrates
              BT6   animals
    NT1   dacus oleae

DACUS OLEAE [15; 15]
    BT1   dacus
      BT2   fruit flies
        BT3   flies
          BT4   insects
            BT5   arthropods
              BT6   invertebrates
                BT7   animals
    RT   olives

§§ **DAILY VARIATIONS** [1,968; 1,968]
(Includes day-to-day, diurnal, and semidiurnal variations.)
    UF   *circadian variations*
    UF   *diurnal variation*
    UF   *semidiurnal variation*
    BT1   variations
    RT   night sky

dalat triga-mk-2 reactor
    USE   triga-2-dalat reactor

dalhousie univ. slowpoke react
    USE   slowpoke-dalhousie reactor

DALITZ PLOT [697; 697]
(Phase-space plot of momentum or mass distribution of final-state particles.)
    BT1   scatterplots
      BT2   diagrams
        BT3   information
    RT   linear momentum
    RT   mass
    RT   phase space
    RT   resonance particles

dam
(Diantipyrylmethane.)
    USE   pyrazolines

damage (nuclear)
    USE   nuclear damage

damage (radiation, biological)
    USE   radiation injuries

damage (radiation, chemical)
    USE   radiolysis

damage (radiation, physical)
    USE   physical radiation effects

damage, vienna conv liability
    USE   vcoclnd

DAMAGING NEUTRON FLUENCE [800; 802] *May 76*
    BT1   neutron fluence
    NT1   equivalent fission fluence
    RT   interstitial helium generation
    RT   interstitial hydrogen generati
    RT   irradiation
    RT   neutron flux
    RT   neutronic damage functions
    RT   physical radiation effects

DAMPA [12; 12]
    UF   *diisoamyl methylphosphonate*
    UF   *diisopentyl methylphosphonate*
    BT1   phosphonic acid esters
      BT2   esters
        BT3   organic compounds
      BT2   organic phosphorus compounds
        BT3   organic compounds

→ **DAMPIERRE-1 REACTOR** [3; 3]
    Mar 91
(Ouzouer-sur-Loire, France.)
    BT1   pwr type reactors
      BT2   enriched uranium reactors
        BT3   reactors
      BT2   power reactors
        BT3   reactors
      BT2   thermal reactors
        BT3   reactors
      BT2   water cooled reactors
        BT3   reactors
      BT2   water moderated reactors
        BT3   reactors

DAMPING [4,175; 5,667]
- NT1 landau damping
- RT attenuation
- RT energy losses
- RT hydrodynamic mass effect
- RT hysteresis
- RT internal friction
- RT mechanical vibrations
- RT restraints
- RT shock absorbers

DAMS [200; 200]
- RT fish passage facilities
- RT hydroelectric power plants
- RT water reservoirs

DANCOFF CORRECTION [46; 46]
- RT resonance escape probability

DANGER COEFFICIENT [9; 9]
- BT1 reactivity coefficients

DANISH ATOMIC ENERGY COMMISSIO [11; 11]
- BT1 danish organizations
- BT2 national organizations

DANISH ORGANIZATIONS [22; 191]
- BT1 national organizations
- NT1 danish atomic energy commissio
- NT1 risoe national laboratory
- NT2 risoe research establishment

danish reactor-1
- USE dr-1 reactor

danish reactor-2
- USE dr-2 reactor

danish reactor-3
- USE dr-3 reactor

DANNY BOY EVENT [2; 2]
- BT1 cratering explosions
- BT2 explosions
- BT1 nuclear explosions
- BT2 explosions
- BT1 plowshare project
- BT1 underground explosions
- BT2 explosions

DANTE TOKAMAK [5; 5] *Aug 84*
(DANish Tokamak Experiment.)
- BT1 tokamak devices
- BT2 closed plasma devices
- BT3 thermonuclear devices

DANUBE RIVER [183; 183]
- BT1 rivers
- BT2 surface waters

DAPEX PROCESS [6; 6]
- BT1 reprocessing
- BT2 separation processes
- RT solvent extraction

DAPHNIA [30; 30]
- BT1 crustaceans
- BT2 aquatic organisms
- BT2 arthropods
- BT3 invertebrates
- BT4 animals
- RT plankton

DARCY LAW [94; 94]
- RT fluid flow

daresbury synchrotron
- USE nina

DAREX PROCESS [2; 2]
- BT1 reprocessing
- BT2 separation processes
- RT solvent extraction

dark matter
(In outer space.)
- USE nonluminous matter

dark repair
- USE dna repair

DARLINGTON-1 REACTOR [73; 73]
Nov 76
(Darlington, Ontario, Canada)
- BT1 candu type reactors
- BT2 heavy water moderated reactors
- BT3 reactors
- BT2 pressure tube reactors
- BT3 power reactors
- BT4 reactors
- BT2 thermal reactors
- BT3 reactors
- BT1 natural uranium reactors
- BT2 reactors
- BT1 phwr type reactors
- BT2 heavy water cooled reactors
- BT3 reactors
- BT2 heavy water moderated reactors
- BT3 reactors

DARLINGTON-2 REACTOR [35; 35]
Nov 76
(Darlington, Ontario, Canada)
- BT1 candu type reactors
- BT2 heavy water moderated reactors
- BT3 reactors
- BT2 pressure tube reactors
- BT3 power reactors
- BT4 reactors
- BT2 thermal reactors
- BT3 reactors
- BT1 natural uranium reactors
- BT2 reactors
- BT1 phwr type reactors
- BT2 heavy water cooled reactors
- BT3 reactors
- BT2 heavy water moderated reactors
- BT3 reactors

DARLINGTON-3 REACTOR [31; 31]
Nov 76
(Darlington, Ontario, Canada)
- BT1 candu type reactors
- BT2 heavy water moderated reactors
- BT3 reactors
- BT2 pressure tube reactors
- BT3 power reactors
- BT4 reactors
- BT2 thermal reactors
- BT3 reactors
- BT1 natural uranium reactors
- BT2 reactors
- BT1 phwr type reactors
- BT2 heavy water cooled reactors
- BT3 reactors
- BT2 heavy water moderated reactors
- BT3 reactors

DARLINGTON-4 REACTOR [34; 34]
Nov 76
(Darlington, Ontario, Canada)
- BT1 candu type reactors
- BT2 heavy water moderated reactors
- BT3 reactors
- BT2 pressure tube reactors
- BT3 power reactors
- BT4 reactors
- BT2 thermal reactors
- BT3 reactors
- BT1 natural uranium reactors
- BT2 reactors
- BT1 phwr type reactors
- BT2 heavy water cooled reactors
- BT3 reactors
- BT2 heavy water moderated reactors
- BT3 reactors

→ *darmstadt synchrotron*
- USE sis synchrotron

DATA [12,463; 134,419]
(For data flagging always use a more specific term.)
- BT1 information
- NT1 numerical data
- NT2 compiled data
- NT2 evaluated data
- NT2 experimental data
- NT2 statistical data
- NT2 theoretical data
- RT cinda
- RT comparative evaluations
- RT data covariances
- RT data processing
- RT information needs

DATA ACQUISITION [4,557; 4,557]
- UF *acquisition (data)*
- RT compiled data
- RT data compilation
- RT data processing
- RT recording systems
- RT reporting requirements

DATA ACQUISITION SYSTEMS [6,296; 6,296]
(Systems for converting data to machine readable form and gathering it into a computer store.)
- RT camac system
- RT electronic equipment
- RT fastbus system
- RT identification systems
- RT readout systems
- RT recording systems

→ **DATA ANALYSIS** [0; 0] *Oct 91*
- RT computer calculations
- RT data processing

DATA BASE MANAGEMENT [1,620; 1,620] *Jul 86*
- BT1 management
- RT data compilation
- RT data processing
- RT information systems
- RT nuclear data collections

DATA COMPILATION [700; 700]
Oct 78
(The process of compiling large volumes of data. For data flagging use COMPILED DATA.)
- RT compiled data
- RT data acquisition
- RT data base management
- RT documentation
- RT information systems
- RT nuclear data collections

data compilation (evaluated)
- USE evaluated data

DATA COVARIANCES [1,043; 1,043]
Dec 85
(Relates to statistical uncertainties in measured quantities.)
- UF *uncertainty in measured values*
- RT accuracy
- RT data
- RT statistics

data display devices
- USE display devices

data display systems
   USE   display devices

DATA PROCESSING [18,685; 20,196]
(Manipulation of unit facts.)
   UF   *electronic data processing*
   UF   *handling (data)*
   UF   *processing (data)*
   NT1   spectra unfolding
   RT   array processors
   RT   calculators
   RT   computers
   RT   data
   RT   data acquisition
   RT   data analysis
   RT   data base management
   RT   data transmission
   RT   data transmission systems
   RT   digital filters
   RT   digitizers
   RT   expert systems
   RT   frequency analysis
   RT   image processing
   RT   image scanners
   RT   information theory
   RT   multi-parameter analysis
   RT   pattern recognition
   RT   recording systems

data processors
   USE   digital computers

data storage devices
   USE   memory devices

DATA TRANSMISSION [1,769; 2,002]
   UF   *transmission (data)*
   BT1   communications
   NT1   telemetry
   RT   camac system
   RT   computer networks
   RT   data processing
   RT   data transmission systems
   RT   equipment interfaces
   RT   multiplexers
   RT   signal conditioning
   RT   signal distortion
   RT   signals

DATA TRANSMISSION SYSTEMS
[325; 325] *Mar 85*
   RT   communications
   RT   data processing
   RT   data transmission

DATES [36; 36]
   BT1   fruits
   BT2   food

dating
   USE   age estimation

datum pressure
   USE   reservoir pressure

DAUGHTER PRODUCTS [3,557; 3,557]
   UF   *decay products*
   BT1   isotopes
   RT   natural radioactivity
   RT   radioisotope generators

DAVIDITE [9; 9]
   BT1   oxide minerals
     BT2   minerals
   BT1   uranium minerals
     BT2   radioactive minerals
       BT3   minerals
       BT3   radioactive materials
         BT4   materials

davis besse reactor
(Prior to December 1990, this was a valid descriptor.)
   USE   davis besse-1 reactor

DAVIS BESSE-1 REACTOR [72; 72]
Oct 75
(Ottawa, Ohio, USA)
   UF   *davis besse reactor*
   UF   *oak harbor ohio reactor*
   BT1   pwr type reactors
     BT2   enriched uranium reactors
       BT3   reactors
     BT2   power reactors
       BT3   reactors
     BT2   thermal reactors
       BT3   reactors
     BT2   water cooled reactors
       BT3   reactors
     BT2   water moderated reactors
       BT3   reactors

DAVIS BESSE-2 REACTOR [19; 19]
Oct 77
   BT1   pwr type reactors
     BT2   enriched uranium reactors
       BT3   reactors
     BT2   power reactors
       BT3   reactors
     BT2   thermal reactors
       BT3   reactors
     BT2   water cooled reactors
       BT3   reactors
     BT2   water moderated reactors
       BT3   reactors

DAVIS BESSE-3 REACTOR [17; 17]
Oct 77
   BT1   pwr type reactors
     BT2   enriched uranium reactors
       BT3   reactors
     BT2   power reactors
       BT3   reactors
     BT2   thermal reactors
       BT3   reactors
     BT2   water cooled reactors
       BT3   reactors
     BT2   water moderated reactors
       BT3   reactors

davydov model
   USE   davydov-filipov model

DAVYDOV-FILIPOV MODEL [76; 76]
   UF   *davydov model*
   BT1   nuclear models
     BT2   mathematical models
   RT   collective model

→ **DAYA BAY REACTOR** [2; 2] *Sep 91*
(Shenzhen, Guangdong, China)
   BT1   pwr type reactors
     BT2   enriched uranium reactors
       BT3   reactors
     BT2   power reactors
       BT3   reactors
     BT2   thermal reactors
       BT3   reactors
     BT2   water cooled reactors
       BT3   reactors
     BT2   water moderated reactors
       BT3   reactors

dayglow
   USE   airglow

* **DAYS LIVING RADIOISOTOPES**
[46; 72,030]
(For specific terms, consult the Appendix.)
   BT1   radioisotopes
     BT2   isotopes
   RT   half-life

DBP [180; 180]
   UF   *dibutyl phosphate*
   BT1   butyl phosphates
     BT2   phosphoric acid esters
       BT3   esters
         BT4   organic compounds
       BT3   organic phosphorus compounds
         BT4   organic compounds

DC AMPLIFIERS [94; 94]
   BT1   amplifiers
     BT2   equipment
   BT1   electronic equipment
     BT2   equipment

DC RESINS [1; 1]
   BT1   silicones
     BT2   polymers
     BT2   siloxanes

dc to ac inverters
   USE   inverters

DC TO DC CONVERTERS [33; 33]
Jun 83
   BT1   electrical equipment
     BT2   equipment
   RT   inverters
   RT   rectifiers
   RT   transformers

DCA REACTOR [13; 13]
   BT1   heavy water cooled reactors
     BT2   reactors
   BT1   heavy water moderated reactors
     BT2   reactors
   BT1   tank type reactors
     BT2   reactors
   BT1   zero power reactors
     BT2   experimental reactors
       BT3   research and test reactors
         BT4   reactors

DCI ORSAY STORAGE RING [77; 77]
   BT1   storage rings

DCTA [71; 71]
(Diaminocyclohexanetetraacetic acid)
   UF   *diaminocyclohexanetetraacetic*
   BT1   amino acids
     BT2   carboxylic acids
       BT3   organic acids
         BT4   organic compounds
   BT1   chelating agents

DCX DEVICES [1; 1]
   BT1   magnetic mirrors
     BT2   open plasma devices
       BT3   thermonuclear devices

DDT [105; 105]
   UF   *dichlorodiphenyltrichloroethan*
   BT1   aromatics
     BT2   organic compounds
   BT1   insecticides
     BT2   pesticides
   BT1   organic chlorine compounds
     BT2   organic halogen compounds
       BT3   organic compounds
   RT   ethane

DE BROGLIE WAVELENGTH
[153; 153]
   RT   quantum mechanics

DE HAAS-VAN ALPHEN EFFECT
[255; 255]
   RT   diamagnetism

DE SITTER GROUP [464; 464]
- BT1 lie groups
- BT2 symmetry groups

DE-EXCITATION [4,270; 4,539]
- BT1 energy-level transitions
- NT1 radiationless decay
- RT excitation
- RT relaxation

deactivation
- USE inactivation

DEAD SEA [18; 18] *Apr 78*
- BT1 lakes
- BT2 surface waters

§ **DEAD TIME** [820; 820]
- UF *live time*
- BT1 timing properties
- RT sensitivity
- RT time measurement
- RT timing circuits

DEAERATORS [32; 32] *Apr 84*
(Devices that remove dissolved gases from liquids.)
- RT aeration
- RT boilers
- RT dissolved gases
- RT feedwater
- RT water treatment

DEALKYLATION [32; 32]
- BT1 chemical reactions

DEAMINATION [85; 85]
- BT1 chemical reactions
- RT amination

DEATH [655; 655]
- RT cell killing
- RT lethal irradiation
- RT life span
- RT mortality
- RT supralethal irradiation

DEBRECEN CYCLOTRON [37; 37] *May 85*
(At ATOMKI, Debrecen, Hungary.)
- UF *atomki cyclotron*
- BT1 isochronous cyclotrons
- BT2 cyclotrons
- BT3 cyclic accelerators
- BT4 accelerators

debris (nuclear)
- USE fission products

debye cutoff
- USE debye length

DEBYE LENGTH [483; 483]
- UF *debye cutoff*
- UF *debye shield*
- UF *debye shielding length*
- RT plasma density

debye shield
- USE debye length

debye shielding length
- USE debye length

DEBYE TEMPERATURE [1,095; 1,095]
- UF *temperature (debye)*
- RT specific heat

DEBYE-SCHERRER METHOD [259; 259]
- BT1 diffraction methods
- RT powders
- RT structural chemical analysis
- RT x-ray diffraction

DEBYE-WALLER FACTOR [543; 543]
- RT diffraction
- RT lattice vibrations

DEC COMPUTERS [561; 886] *Sep 80*
- UF *vax computers*
- BT1 computers
- NT1 pdp computers

DECA DEVICES [7; 7]
- BT1 magnetic mirrors
- BT2 open plasma devices
- BT3 thermonuclear devices

decahydronaphthalene
- USE decalin

DECALIN [51; 51]
- UF *decahydronaphthalene*
- BT1 cycloalkanes
- BT2 alkanes
- BT3 hydrocarbons
- BT4 organic compounds
- RT naphthalene

decalso
- USE ion exchange materials

DECANE [45; 45] *Apr 84*
- BT1 alkanes
- BT2 hydrocarbons
- BT3 organic compounds

DECANOIC ACID [96; 96]
- UF *capric acid*
- BT1 monocarboxylic acids
- BT2 carboxylic acids
- BT3 organic acids
- BT4 organic compounds

DECANOLS [40; 40]
- UF *decyl alcohols*
- BT1 alcohols
- BT2 hydroxy compounds
- BT3 organic compounds

DECANTATION [62; 62]
- BT1 separation processes
- RT sedimentation

DECARBONIZATION [85; 85]
- RT cleaning
- RT decontamination

decarboxylase
(Prior to June 1982 this was a valid term, and older material is so indexed.)
- USE decarboxylases

DECARBOXYLASES [107; 107] *Jun 82*
- UF *decarboxylase*
- BT1 carbon-carbon lyases
- BT2 lyases
- BT3 enzymes
- BT4 organic compounds

DECARBOXYLATION [147; 147]
- BT1 chemical reactions
- RT carboxylation

DECARBURIZATION [184; 184] *Jun 76*
- BT1 chemical reactions
- RT austenite
- RT carbides
- RT carbon
- RT heat treatments
- RT steels

DECAY [9,166; 44,953]
(For nuclear or particle decay only. For chemical or biological decay, see DECOMPOSITION.)
- UF *degradation (nuclear)*
- UF *disintegration (nuclear)*
- UF *fragments (decay)*
- NT1 nuclear decay
- NT2 alpha decay
- NT2 beta decay
- NT3 beta-minus decay
- NT4 double beta decay
- NT3 beta-plus decay
- NT3 electron capture decay
- NT4 k capture
- NT4 l capture
- NT4 m capture
- NT2 gamma decay
- NT2 heavy ion emission decay
- NT3 carbon 12 emission decay
- NT3 carbon 14 emission decay
- NT3 magnesium 28 emission decay
- NT3 magnesium 30 emission decay
- NT3 neon 24 emission decay
- NT3 oxygen 16 emission decay
- NT3 silicon 32 emission decay
- NT3 silicon 34 emission decay
- NT2 internal conversion
- NT3 internal pair production
- NT3 k conversion
- NT3 l conversion
- NT3 m conversion
- NT2 proton-emission decay
- NT2 spontaneous fission
- NT1 particle decay
- NT2 electromagnetic particle decay
- NT2 hadronic particle decay
- NT2 radiative decay
- NT2 weak particle decay
- NT3 leptonic decay
- NT3 semileptonic decay
- NT3 weak hadronic decay
- RT angular correlation
- RT branching ratio
- RT energy-level transitions
- RT forbidden transitions
- RT ft value
- RT half-life
- RT interactions
- RT isomeric transitions
- RT lifetime
- RT mixing ratio
- RT particle kinematics
- RT radioisotope generators
- RT selection rules

decay (biological)
- USE decomposition

DECAY AMPLITUDES [1,834; 1,834]
- BT1 transition amplitudes
- BT2 amplitudes

decay heat
- SEE after-heat

DECAY INSTABILITY [343; 343]
- BT1 plasma instability
- BT2 instability
- RT plasma macroinstabilities
- RT plasma microinstabilities
- RT plasma waves

decay products
   USE   daughter products

deceleration
   USE   acceleration

dechanneling
   USE   channeling

DECHLORINATION [58; 58]
   BT1   dehalogenation
      BT2   chemical reactions
   RT   chlorination

deciduous trees
   USE   trees

decimeter wave radiat (1-3 dm)
   USE   ghz range 01-100
   AND   radiowave radiation

decimeter wave radiat (3-10dm)
   USE   mhz range 100-1000
   AND   radiowave radiation

DECISION TREE ANALYSIS [214; 214]
   RT   control
   RT   planning

DECK EFFECT [153; 153]
(Kinematic peak in the mass spectrum of resonance particles.)
   RT   kinetics
   RT   resonance particles

DECLADDING [136; 320]
   BT1   head end processes
   NT1   chemical decladding
   NT1   mechanical decladding
   RT   cladding
   RT   fuel cans
   RT   fuel elements
   RT   reprocessing

DECOMMISSIONING [1,342; 2,884]
   NT1   reactor decommissioning
   RT   cancellation
   RT   shutdown

DECOMPOSITION [4,234; 25,953]
   UF   *decay (biological)*
   UF   *degradation (chemical)*
   UF   *disintegration (biological)*
   UF   *disintegration (chemical)*
   UF   *lysis*
   BT1   chemical reactions
   NT1   autolysis
      NT2   autoradiolysis
   NT1   biodegradation
   NT1   carbonization
      NT2   coking
   NT1   depolymerization
   NT1   glycolysis
   NT1   hemolysis
   NT1   photolysis
   NT1   proteolysis
      NT2   fibrinolysis
   NT1   pyrolysis
      NT2   calcination
      NT2   cracking
   NT1   radiolysis
      NT2   autoradiolysis
   NT1   solvolysis
      NT2   acetolysis
      NT2   ammonolysis
      NT2   hydrolysis
         NT3   saponification
   RT   aerobic conditions
   RT   anaerobic conditions
   RT   catabolism
   RT   dissociation
   RT   nucleic acid denaturation
   RT   strand breaks
   RT   thermal gravimetric analysis
   RT   weathering

DECONTAMINATION [7,234; 7,234]
   UF   *radioactive decontamination*
   UF+   *decontamination factor*
   BT1   cleaning
   RT   bioadsorbents
   RT   chelating agents
   RT   clays
   RT   coolant cleanup systems
   RT   decarbonization
   RT   detergents
   RT   lavage
   RT   protective coatings
   RT   purification
   RT   radiation protection
   RT   remedial action
   RT   safety showers
   RT   scrubbing
   RT   surface cleaning
   RT   surface contamination
   RT   washout

decontamination factor
   USE   decontamination
   AND   efficiency

DECOUPLING [648; 648]
   RT   coupling
   RT   ft value

decyl alcohols
   USE   decanols

decylamine-tris
   USE   tda

DEDTC [218; 218]
   UF   *diethyldithiocarbamates*
   BT1   carbamates
      BT2   carbonic acid derivatives
         BT3   organic compounds
      BT2   carboxylic acid salts
      BT2   organic nitrogen compounds
         BT3   organic compounds
   BT1   chelating agents
   BT1   organic sulfur compounds
      BT2   organic compounds

deep inelastic heavy ion colli
   USE   quasi-fission

DEEP INELASTIC HEAVY ION REACT [2,280; 2,280] Aug 78
   UF   *deep inelastic transfer reacti*
   UF   *strongly damped heavy ion reac*
   BT1   heavy ion reactions
      BT2   nuclear reactions
   RT   compound-nucleus reactions
   RT   heavy ion fusion reactions
   RT   incomplete fusion reactions
   RT   nuclear fragmentation
   RT   precompound-nucleus emission
   RT   quasi-fission

DEEP INELASTIC SCATTERING [4,381; 4,381] Sep 75
(Lepton-nucleon inelastic scattering involving an exchange of a virtual photon.)
   BT1   inelastic scattering
      BT2   scattering
   BT1   lepton-nucleon interactions
      BT2   lepton-baryon interactions
         BT3   lepton-hadron interactions
            BT4   particle interactions
               BT5   interactions
   RT   boson-exchange models
   RT   emc effect
   RT   parton model
   RT   resonance scattering
   RT   virtual particles

deep inelastic transfer reacti
   USE   deep inelastic heavy ion react

DEEP RIVER [9; 9]
   BT1   ontario
      BT2   canada
         BT3   developed countries
         BT3   north america

DEER [292; 292]
   UF   *caribou*
   UF   *mule deer*
   UF   *odocoileus*
   UF   *reindeer*
   BT1   ruminants
      BT2   mammals
         BT3   vertebrates
            BT4   animals
   RT   antlers

DEES [169; 169]
   BT1   electrodes
   RT   cyclotrons
   RT   mass spectrometers

def. at. supp. ag. triga-mk-f
   USE   afrri reactor

DEFECTS [4,688; 4,688]
(Not for the concept covered by CRYSTAL DEFECTS.)
   UF   *flaws*
   UF   *imperfections*
   RT   cracks
   RT   fracture mechanics
   RT   fractures
   RT   porosity
   RT   stress intensity factors
   RT   voids

DEFEROXAMINE [90; 90]
   UF   *dfa*
   BT1   amines
      BT2   organic compounds
   BT1   chelating agents

deficiency (nutritional)
   USE   nutritional deficiency

→ **DEFORESTATION** [0; 0] Oct 91
   RT   biomass
   RT   carbon cycle
   RT   forests
   RT   revegetation

DEFORMATION [11,473; 22,505]
   UF   *buckling (structural)*
   UF   *structural buckling*
   NT1   bending
   NT1   corrosion denting
   NT1   elongation
   NT1   nuclear deformation
   NT1   ratcheting
   NT1   swelling
   RT   dynamic loads
   RT   fractures
   RT   magnetostriction
   RT   materials working
   RT   mechanical properties
   RT   plasticity
   RT   rheology
   RT   slip
   RT   static loads
   RT   strains
   RT   torsion

DEFORMED NUCLEI [4,386; 4,386]
(Nuclei which are deformed even in the ground state.)
   UF   *nonaxial nuclei*
   BT1   nuclei
   RT   aligned coupling scheme
   RT   backbending
   RT   cranking model
   RT   governor model

RT   nuclear deformation
RT   nuclear models
RT   rotation-vibration model

DEGASSING [1,241; 1,241]
UF   *outgassing*
RT   castings
RT   desorption

degradation (chemical)
USE   decomposition

degradation (energy)
USE   energy losses

degradation (nuclear)
USE   decay

degradation (radioinduced)
USE   radiolysis

DEGREES OF FREEDOM [745; 745]
Jul 85
RT   mechanics
RT   statistics
RT   thermodynamics
RT   variations

DEHALOGENATION [60; 106] *Oct 82*
BT1   chemical reactions
NT1   dechlorination
NT1   deiodination

dehpa
SEE   hdehp
OR   phosphonic acid esters

dehumidifiers
USE   dryers

DEHYDRATION [1,129; 1,129]
RT   desiccants
RT   drying
RT   evaporation
RT   water removal

dehydrocyclization
USE   cyclization
AND   dehydrogenation

dehydroepiandrosterone
USE   hydroxyandrostenone

DEHYDROGENASES [322; 558]
BT1   oxidoreductases
BT2   enzymes
BT3   organic compounds
NT1   diaphorases
NT1   lactate dehydrogenase
NT1   nitrogenase

DEHYDROGENATION [274; 274]
UF+   *dehydrocyclization*
BT1   chemical reactions
RT   deuteration
RT   hydrogenation

DEIODINATION [46; 46]
BT1   dehalogenation
BT2   chemical reactions
RT   iodination

dekatrons
USE   counting tubes

DELAWARE [53; 53]
BT1   usa
BT2   developed countries
BT2   north america

DELAWARE RIVER [8; 8]
BT1   rivers
BT2   surface waters

DELAY CIRCUITS [613; 613]
BT1   electronic circuits
RT   pulse techniques

DELAYED ALPHA PARTICLES
[80; 80]
BT1   alpha particles
BT2   helium ions
BT3   ions
BT4   charged particles
BT2   ionizing radiations
BT3   radiations

DELAYED GAMMA RADIATION
[241; 241]
BT1   gamma radiation
BT2   electromagnetic radiation
BT3   radiations
BT2   ionizing radiations
BT3   radiations
RT   nuclear reactions
RT   photons

DELAYED NEUTRON ANALYSIS
[296; 296] *Jan 77*
BT1   nondestructive analysis
BT2   chemical analysis
RT   delayed neutrons

DELAYED NEUTRON FRACTION
[84; 84]
RT   delayed neutrons

DELAYED NEUTRON PRECURSORS
[254; 254]
UF   *precursors (delayed neutrons)*
RT   beta-delayed neutrons

DELAYED NEUTRONS [1,347; 1,347]
(For fission neutrons only. For delayed neutrons not resulting from fission, see BETA-DELAYED NEUTRONS. (Scope note added in 1985.))
BT1   fission neutrons
BT2   neutrons
BT3   nucleons
BT4   baryons
BT5   fermions
BT5   hadrons
BT6   elementary particles
RT   delayed neutron analysis
RT   delayed neutron fraction
RT   reactor kinetics

DELAYED PROTON PRECURSORS
[50; 50] *Oct 76*
UF   *precursors (delayed protons)*
RT   delayed protons

DELAYED PROTONS [310; 310]
UF   *beta-delayed protons*
BT1   protons
BT2   hydrogen ions 1 plus
BT3   cations
BT4   ions
BT5   charged particles
BT3   hydrogen ions
BT4   ions
BT5   charged particles
BT2   nucleons
BT3   baryons
BT4   fermions
BT4   hadrons
BT5   elementary particles
RT   beta-plus decay

RT   delayed proton precursors
RT   electron capture decay
RT   neutron-deficient isotopes

DELAYED RADIATION EFFECTS
[6,276; 6,276]
UF   *chronic radiation effects*
UF   *late radiation effects*
UF+   *delayed radiation injuries*
BT1   biological radiation effects
BT2   biological effects
BT2   radiation effects
RT   a-bomb survivors
RT   congenital malformations
RT   dose commitments
RT   early radiation effects
RT   genetic radiation effects
RT   latency period
RT   medical surveillance
RT   neoplasms
RT   radiation syndrome
RT   time dependence

delayed radiation injuries
USE   delayed radiation effects
AND   radiation injuries

DELBRUECK SCATTERING [112; 112]
BT1   inelastic scattering
BT2   scattering

deletions (chromosomal)
USE   chromosomal aberrations

delft hoger onderwijs reactor
USE   hor reactor

DELIVERY [11; 11] *Dec 85*
RT   agreements
RT   contracts
RT   materials handling
RT   transport

deloro stellite 6
USE   alloy-co66cr26w6

delphinium
USE   ranunculaceae

DELTA BARYONS [99; 667] *Dec 87*
UF   *delta-1960 resonances*
UF   *delta-2850 resonances*
BT1   n*baryons
BT2   baryons
BT3   fermions
BT3   hadrons
BT4   elementary particles
NT1   delta-1232 baryons
NT1   delta-1550 baryons
NT1   delta-1600 baryons
NT1   delta-1620 baryons
NT1   delta-1700 baryons
NT1   delta-1900 baryons
NT1   delta-1905 baryons
NT1   delta-1910 baryons
NT1   delta-1920 baryons
NT1   delta-1930 baryons
NT1   delta-1940 baryons
NT1   delta-1950 baryons
NT1   delta-2000 baryons
NT1   delta-2150 baryons
NT1   delta-2200 baryons
NT1   delta-2300 baryons
NT1   delta-2350 baryons
NT1   delta-2390 baryons
NT1   delta-2400 baryons
NT1   delta-2420 baryons
NT1   delta-2750 baryons
NT1   delta-2950 baryons
NT1   delta-3000 baryons

DELTA FUNCTION [559; 559]
- UF   *dirac delta function*
- BT1   functions
- RT   schwinger terms

DELTA RAYS [333; 333]
- BT1   radiations
- RT   electrons
- RT   ionizing radiations
- RT   recoils

delta resonances (baryon)
- USE   n*baryons

DELTA-1232 BARYONS [2,692; 2,692]
(Prior to December 1987 this concept was indexed by DELTA-1236 RESONANCES.)
- UF   *delta-1236 resonances*
- BT1   delta baryons
- BT2   n*baryons
- BT3   baryons
- BT4   fermions
- BT4   hadrons
- BT5   elementary particles

delta-1236 resonances
(Prior to December 1987 this was a valid descriptor.)
- USE   delta-1232 baryons

DELTA-1550 BARYONS [2; 2] *Dec 87*
- BT1   delta baryons
- BT2   n*baryons
- BT3   baryons
- BT4   fermions
- BT4   hadrons
- BT5   elementary particles

DELTA-1600 BARYONS [27; 27]
(Prior to December 1987 this concept was indexed by DELTA-1650 RESONANCES.)
- UF   *delta-1650 resonances*
- BT1   delta baryons
- BT2   n*baryons
- BT3   baryons
- BT4   fermions
- BT4   hadrons
- BT5   elementary particles

DELTA-1620 BARYONS [8; 8] *Dec 87*
- BT1   delta baryons
- BT2   n*baryons
- BT3   baryons
- BT4   fermions
- BT4   hadrons
- BT5   elementary particles

delta-1650 resonances
(Prior to December 1987 this was a valid descriptor.)
- USE   delta-1600 baryons

delta-1670 resonances
(Prior to December 1987 this was a valid descriptor.)
- USE   delta-1700 baryons

DELTA-1700 BARYONS [31; 31]
(Prior to December 1987 this concept was indexed by DELTA-1670 RESONANCES.)
- UF   *delta-1670 resonances*
- BT1   delta baryons
- BT2   n*baryons
- BT3   baryons
- BT4   fermions
- BT4   hadrons
- BT5   elementary particles

delta-1890 resonances
(Prior to December 1987 this was a valid descriptor.)
- USE   delta-1900 baryons

DELTA-1900 BARYONS [18; 18]
(Prior to December 1987 this concept was indexed by DELTA-1890 RESONANCES.)
- UF   *delta-1890 resonances*
- BT1   delta baryons
- BT2   n*baryons
- BT3   baryons
- BT4   fermions
- BT4   hadrons
- BT5   elementary particles

DELTA-1905 BARYONS [2; 2] *Dec 87*
- BT1   delta baryons
- BT2   n*baryons
- BT3   baryons
- BT4   fermions
- BT4   hadrons
- BT5   elementary particles

DELTA-1910 BARYONS [20; 20]
(Prior to December 1987 this concept was indexed by DELTA-1910 RESONANCES.)
- UF   *delta-1910 resonances*
- BT1   delta baryons
- BT2   n*baryons
- BT3   baryons
- BT4   fermions
- BT4   hadrons
- BT5   elementary particles

delta-1910 resonances
(Prior to December 1987 this was a valid descriptor.)
- USE   delta-1910 baryons

DELTA-1920 BARYONS [3; 3] *Dec 87*
- BT1   delta baryons
- BT2   n*baryons
- BT3   baryons
- BT4   fermions
- BT4   hadrons
- BT5   elementary particles

DELTA-1930 BARYONS [2; 2] *Dec 87*
- BT1   delta baryons
- BT2   n*baryons
- BT3   baryons
- BT4   fermions
- BT4   hadrons
- BT5   elementary particles

DELTA-1940 BARYONS [0; 0] *Dec 87*
- BT1   delta baryons
- BT2   n*baryons
- BT3   baryons
- BT4   fermions
- BT4   hadrons
- BT5   elementary particles

DELTA-1950 BARYONS [45; 45]
(Prior to December 1987 this concept was indexed by DELTA-1950 RESONANCES.)
- UF   *delta-1950 resonances*
- BT1   delta baryons
- BT2   n*baryons
- BT3   baryons
- BT4   fermions
- BT4   hadrons
- BT5   elementary particles

delta-1950 resonances
(Prior to December 1987 this was a valid descriptor.)
- USE   delta-1950 baryons

delta-1960 resonances
(Prior to December 1987 this was a valid descriptor.)
- USE   delta baryons

DELTA-2000 BARYONS [2; 2] *Dec 87*
- BT1   delta baryons
- BT2   n*baryons
- BT3   baryons
- BT4   fermions
- BT4   hadrons
- BT5   elementary particles

DELTA-2150 BARYONS [2; 2] *Dec 87*
- BT1   delta baryons
- BT2   n*baryons
- BT3   baryons
- BT4   fermions
- BT4   hadrons
- BT5   elementary particles

DELTA-2200 BARYONS [13; 13]
(Prior to December 1987 this concept was indexed by DELTA-2200 RESONANCES.)
- UF   *delta-2200 resonances*
- BT1   delta baryons
- BT2   n*baryons
- BT3   baryons
- BT4   fermions
- BT4   hadrons
- BT5   elementary particles

delta-2200 resonances
(Prior to December 1987 this was a valid descriptor.)
- USE   delta-2200 baryons

DELTA-2300 BARYONS [0; 0] *Dec 87*
- BT1   delta baryons
- BT2   n*baryons
- BT3   baryons
- BT4   fermions
- BT4   hadrons
- BT5   elementary particles

DELTA-2350 BARYONS [0; 0] *Dec 87*
- BT1   delta baryons
- BT2   n*baryons
- BT3   baryons
- BT4   fermions
- BT4   hadrons
- BT5   elementary particles

DELTA-2390 BARYONS [0; 0] *Dec 87*
- BT1   delta baryons
- BT2   n*baryons
- BT3   baryons
- BT4   fermions
- BT4   hadrons
- BT5   elementary particles

DELTA-2400 BARYONS [0; 0] *Dec 87*
- BT1   delta baryons
- BT2   n*baryons
- BT3   baryons
- BT4   fermions
- BT4   hadrons
- BT5   elementary particles

DELTA-2420 BARYONS [11; 11]
(Prior to December 1987 this concept was indexed by DELTA-2420 RESONANCES.)
- UF   *delta-2420 resonances*
- BT1   delta baryons
- BT2   n*baryons
- BT3   baryons
- BT4   fermions
- BT4   hadrons
- BT5   elementary particles

delta-2420 resonances
(Prior to December 1987 this was a valid descriptor.)
- USE   delta-2420 baryons

DELTA-2750 BARYONS [0; 0] *Dec 87*
- BT1 delta baryons
- BT2 n*baryons
- BT3 baryons
- BT4 fermions
- BT4 hadrons
- BT5 elementary particles

delta-2850 resonances
(Prior to December 1987 this was a valid descriptor.)
- USE delta baryons

DELTA-2950 BARYONS [0; 0] *Dec 87*
- BT1 delta baryons
- BT2 n*baryons
- BT3 baryons
- BT4 fermions
- BT4 hadrons
- BT5 elementary particles

DELTA-3000 BARYONS [24; 24]
(Prior to December 1987 this concept was indexed by DELTA-3230 RESONANCES.)
- UF *delta-3230 resonances*
- BT1 delta baryons
- BT2 n*baryons
- BT3 baryons
- BT4 fermions
- BT4 hadrons
- BT5 elementary particles

delta-3230 resonances
(Prior to December 1987 this was a valid descriptor.)
- USE delta-3000 baryons

delta-966 resonances
(Prior to December 1987 this was a valid descriptor.)
- USE a0-980 mesons

DEMAGNETIZATION [156; 245] *Sep 77*
- NT1 adiabatic demagnetization
- RT magnetic fields
- RT magnetism
- RT magnets

DEMAND [47; 764] *Dec 85*
- NT1 energy demand
- NT1 power demand
- NT1 uranium requirements
- NT1 water requirements
- RT availability
- RT energy consumption
- RT supply and demand

DEMAND FACTORS [17; 17] *Dec 85*
(Ratios of the maximum demand to the total connected load.)
- RT electric power
- RT energy consumption
- RT energy demand
- RT power demand

demand limiters
- USE current limiters

DEMBER EFFECT [14; 14]
- RT charge carriers

demerol
- USE pethidine

DEMESMAEKERITE [2; 2]
- BT1 oxide minerals
- BT2 minerals
- BT1 uranium minerals
- BT2 radioactive minerals
- BT3 minerals

- BT3 radioactive materials
- BT4 materials
- RT lead oxides
- RT uranium oxides

DEMINERALIZATION [186; 611]
- BT1 separation processes
- NT1 desalination
- RT demineralizers
- RT distillation
- RT feedwater
- RT ion exchange
- RT water chemistry

DEMINERALIZERS [169; 169]
- RT demineralization
- RT reactor cooling systems
- RT water

DEMOCRITUS REACTOR [28; 28]
(Greek Atomic Energy Commission, Demokritos, Greece)
- UF *greek research reactor*
- UF *grr reactor*
- BT1 enriched uranium reactors
- BT2 reactors
- BT1 pool type reactors
- BT2 water cooled reactors
- BT3 reactors
- BT2 water moderated reactors
- BT3 reactors
- BT1 research reactors
- BT2 research and test reactors
- BT3 reactors
- BT1 thermal reactors
- BT2 reactors

demography
(The statistical study of human populations with reference to natality, mortality, migratory movements, age, and sex, among other social, ethnic, and economic factors.)
- USE human populations
- AND statistics

DEMOLITION [137; 1,075]
- NT1 reactor dismantling

demonstration plants
- USE pilot plants

DEMONSTRATION PROGRAMS [658; 658] *Dec 85*
- RT commercialization
- RT experiment planning
- RT planning
- RT research programs

denaturation (nucleic acid)
- USE nucleic acid denaturation

denaturation (protein)
- USE protein denaturation

DENATURED FUEL [95; 95] *May 78*
(Fuel which has been diluted or spiked so that it is not suitable for weapons use.)
- BT1 nuclear fuels
- BT2 energy sources
- BT2 fuels
- BT2 reactor materials
- BT3 materials
- RT proliferation
- RT safeguards

DENDRITES [262; 262]
- BT1 crystals

DENELCOR COMPUTERS [5; 5] *Sep 86*
- BT1 computers

DENITRATION [349; 349]
- BT1 chemical reactions
- RT nitric acid
- RT reprocessing

DENMARK [549; 549]
- BT1 developed countries
- BT1 scandinavia
- BT2 europe
- RT faeroe islands
- RT greenland

DENSIMETERS [724; 745]
- BT1 measuring instruments
- NT1 pycnometers
- RT density
- RT radiometric gages
- RT weight indicators

DENSITOMETERS [562; 562]
- BT1 photometers
- BT2 measuring instruments
- RT photometry

DENSITY [12,667; 12,667]
(For specific weight only; see also descriptors such as CARRIER DENSITY, CURRENT DENSITY, and FLUX DENSITY.)
- UF *specific gravity*
- UF *specific volume*
- UF *specific weight*
- BT1 physical properties
- RT densimeters
- RT fuel densification
- RT mass distribution
- RT stopping power
- RT weight

density (carrier)
- USE carrier density

density (charge)
- USE charge density

density (current)
- USE current density

density (electron)
- USE electron density

density (energy)
- USE energy density

density (energy-level)
- USE energy-level density

density (flux)
- USE flux density

density (grain)
- USE grain density

density (ion)
- USE ion density

density (neutron)
- USE neutron density

density (plasma)
- USE plasma density

density (population)
   USE   population density

density (power)
   USE   power density

density (proton)
   USE   proton density

density (spectral)
   USE   spectral density

DENSITY MATRIX [2,957; 2,957]
   BT1   matrices
   RT   mathematical operators
   RT   quantum mechanics

DENTIN [102; 102]
   RT   bone tissues
   RT   teeth

denting (corrosion)
   USE   corrosion denting

DENTISTRY [697; 697]
   BT1   medicine
   RT   caries
   RT   teeth

deoxidation
   USE   reduction

DEOXYCYTIDINE [91; 91]
   UF+   *deoxycytidinuria*
   BT1   nucleosides
     BT2   nucleotides
       BT3   organic compounds
     BT2   ribosides
   BT1   pyrimidines
     BT2   azines
       BT3   heterocyclic compounds
         BT4   organic compounds
       BT3   organic nitrogen compounds
         BT4   organic compounds
   RT   cytidine

deoxycytidinuria
   USE   deoxycytidine
   AND   urine

DEOXYCYTIDYLIC ACID [4; 4]
   BT1   nucleotides
     BT2   organic compounds
   RT   cytidylic acid

deoxypentose nucleic acid
   USE   dna

deoxyribonuclease
   USE   dna-ase

deoxyribonucleic acid
   USE   dna

DEOXYRIBOSE [48; 48]
   BT1   aldehydes
     BT2   organic compounds
   BT1   pentoses
     BT2   monosaccharides
       BT3   saccharides
         BT4   carbohydrates
           BT5   organic compounds
   RT   ribosides

DEOXYURIDINE [165; 165]
   BT1   antimetabolites
     BT2   drugs
   BT1   nucleosides
     BT2   nucleotides
       BT3   organic compounds
     BT2   ribosides
   BT1   uracils
     BT2   hydroxy compounds
       BT3   organic compounds
     BT2   pyrimidines
       BT3   azines
         BT4   heterocyclic compounds
           BT5   organic compounds
         BT4   organic nitrogen compounds
           BT5   organic compounds
   RT   budr
   RT   fudr
   RT   iododeoxyuridine

DEPARTURE NUCLEATE BOILING [474; 474]
   UF   *critical heat flow*
   UF   *dnb*
   BT1   nucleate boiling
     BT2   boiling
       BT3   phase transformations

DEPLETED URANIUM [392; 392]
   BT1   uranium
     BT2   actinides
       BT3   metals
         BT4   elements
   RT   fuel cycle

depletion (isotopic)
   USE   isotope separation

depletion (nuclear fuels)
   USE   burnup

DEPOLARIZATION [1,159; 1,159]
   RT   polarization

DEPOLYMERIZATION [121; 121]
   BT1   decomposition
     BT2   chemical reactions
   RT   molecular weight
   RT   polymerization

DEPOSITION [3,967; 12,419]
(For the laying down of a substance on a surface; for deposition of elements and nuclides in tissues of living organisms use RETENTION.)
   NT1   surface coating
     NT2   chemical coating
       NT3   chemical vapor deposition
       NT3   electrochemical coating
         NT4   anodization
     NT2   cladding
     NT2   diffusion coating
     NT2   dip coating
       NT3   hot dipping
     NT2   electrodeposition
       NT3   electroplating
     NT2   plating
       NT3   electroplating
       NT3   vapor plating
     NT2   spray coating
       NT3   flame spraying
       NT3   plasma arc spraying
     NT2   vacuum coating
   RT   adsorption
   RT   deposits
   RT   fouling
   RT   precipitation
   RT   sputtering
   RT   thin films

deposition (gravitational)
   USE   sedimentation

DEPOSITS [932; 932]
   RT   antifoulants
   RT   coatings
   RT   deposition

deposits (geological)
   USE   geologic deposits

depressants (central nerv sys)
   USE   central nervous system depress

DEPRESSURIZATION [655; 655]
   RT   depressurization systems
   RT   pressure vessels
   RT   pressurization
   RT   reactor safety

DEPRESSURIZATION SYSTEMS [61; 61] *Dec 85*
   RT   depressurization
   RT   eccs
   RT   pressure vessels
   RT   reactor protection systems

§§ **DEPTH** [4,392; 4,392]
(For elevation use LEVELS.)
   UF+   *depth distribution*
   BT1   dimensions

depth distribution
   USE   depth
   AND   spatial distribution

DEPTH DOSE DISTRIBUTIONS [3,144; 3,144]
   UF   *depth doses*
   BT1   spatial dose distributions
     BT2   radiation dose distributions
     BT2   spatial distribution
       BT3   distribution
   RT   buildup
   RT   isodose curves
   RT   phantoms
   RT   radiotherapy
   RT   range

depth doses
   USE   depth dose distributions

derby zpr neptune
   USE   neptune reactor

DEREGULATION [8; 8] *Dec 85*
   RT   economic policy
   RT   economics
   RT   government policies
   RT   regulations

DERMATITIS [54; 334]
   BT1   skin diseases
     BT2   diseases
   NT1   radiodermatitis

DESALINATION [427; 427]
   BT1   demineralization
     BT2   separation processes
   RT   desalination plants
   RT   desalination reactors
   RT   distillation
   RT   dual-purpose power plants
   RT   evaporators
   RT   freezing out
   RT   ion exchange
   RT   salinity
   RT   salts
   RT   seawater

DESALINATION PLANTS [15; 15]
Apr 86
- BT1 industrial plants
- RT desalination
- RT desalination reactors
- RT dual-purpose power plants
- RT seawater

DESALINATION REACTORS [77; 263]
- BT1 power reactors
- BT2 reactors
- NT1 bn-350 reactor
- RT desalination
- RT desalination plants

DESCALING [99; 99]
- BT1 surface finishing
- RT scaling
- RT scrubbing
- RT shot peening
- RT surface cleaning

desertron
- USE superconducting super collider

DESERTS [336; 336]
- UF *arid lands*
- RT climates
- RT sand
- RT terrestrial ecosystems

DESICCANTS [3; 3] *Dec 85*
- RT dehydration
- RT dryers
- RT drying
- RT resins
- RT zeolites

→ ## DESIGN [0; 0] *Oct 91*
(For conceptual design only; use of a more specific descriptor is recommended.)
- NT1 computer-aided design
- RT diagrams
- RT feasibility studies
- RT planning
- RT specifications

design (technical drawings)
- USE diagrams

design (technical specificat.)
- USE specifications

DESIGN BASIS ACCIDENTS
[1,000; 1,751]
- BT1 reactor accidents
- BT2 accidents
- NT1 atws
- NT1 maximum credible accident

desiodothyroxine
- USE thyronine

DESORPTION [3,234; 3,234]
- RT adsorption
- RT degassing

desoxycorticosterone acetate
- USE doca

desoxyribonucleic acid
- USE dna

destructive chemical analysis
(Prior to December 1990, this concept was indexed by DESTRUCTIVE ANALYSIS which is no longer a valid descriptor.)
- USE chemical analysis

DESTRUCTIVE TESTING [1,106; 1,887]
- BT1 materials testing
- BT2 testing
- NT1 charpy test
- RT impact tests
- RT mechanical properties
- RT post-irradiation examination

DESULFURIZATION [235; 235]
- BT1 chemical reactions
- RT air pollution abatement
- RT sulfate-reducing bacteria
- RT thiobacillus oxidans

DESY [329; 329]
(Deutsches Elektronen Synchrotron)
- UF *hamburg synchrotron*
- BT1 synchrotrons
- BT2 cyclic accelerators
- BT3 accelerators

DETAILED BALANCE PRINCIPLE
[157; 157]
- BT1 t invariance
- BT2 invariance principles
- RT cross sections
- RT hamiltonians
- RT nuclear reactions
- RT s matrix
- RT scattering

DETECTION [1,985; 14,558] *Sep 83*
- NT1 boiling detection
- NT1 crime detection
- NT1 failed element detection
- NT1 fuel motion detection
- NT1 nuclear explosion detection
- NT1 radiation detection
- NT2 charged particle detection
- NT3 acoustic detection
- NT3 alpha detection
- NT3 beta detection
- NT3 electron detection
- NT3 ion detection
- NT3 muon detection
- NT3 positron detection
- NT3 proton detection
- NT2 cosmic ray detection
- NT2 fission fragment detection
- NT2 gamma detection
- NT2 kaon detection
- NT2 neutrino detection
- NT2 neutron detection
- NT2 pion detection
- NT2 x-ray detection
- NT1 seismic detection
- RT control
- RT monitoring
- RT motion detection systems
- RT nuclear materials diversion
- RT nuclear materials management
- RT safeguards

detection limits
- USE sensitivity

detectors (radiation)
- USE radiation detectors

DETERGENTS [370; 374]
- BT1 emulsifiers
- BT2 additives
- BT1 wetting agents
- BT2 surfactants
- NT1 pluronics
- RT cleaning
- RT decontamination
- RT soaps
- RT xenobiotics

determination (chemical)
- USE chemical analysis

DETONATION WAVES [57; 57]
(Shock waves caused by release of chemical energy through chemical reactions.)
- BT1 shock waves
- RT chemical reactions

detonations
- USE explosions

DETONATORS [50; 50]
- RT exploding wires
- RT explosions

DETOXIFICATION [90; 90] *Apr 84*
- RT biochemical reaction kinetics
- RT chemical reactions
- RT hazardous materials
- RT toxicity
- RT toxins

DEUTERATION [717; 717]
- BT1 chemical reactions
- RT dehydrogenation
- RT hydrogenation

DEUTERIDES [112; 327] *Feb 76*
- BT1 deuterium compounds
- BT2 hydrogen compounds
- NT1 hydrogen deuteride
- NT1 lithium deuterides

DEUTERIUM [14,110; 14,110]
- UF *hydrogen 2*
- BT1 hydrogen isotopes
- BT1 light nuclei
- BT2 nuclei
- BT1 odd-odd nuclei
- BT2 nuclei
- BT1 stable isotopes
- BT2 isotopes
- RT deuterons
- RT hydrogen deuteride
- RT thermonuclear fuels

DEUTERIUM COMPOUNDS
[4,239; 5,551]
- UF+ *dto*
- UF+ *hdo*
- BT1 hydrogen compounds
- NT1 deuterides
- NT2 hydrogen deuteride
- NT2 lithium deuterides
- NT1 deuterium tritide
- RT heavy water

deuterium hydride
- USE hydrogen deuteride

DEUTERIUM IONS [1,296; 1,296]
- BT1 ions
- BT2 charged particles

deuterium mod. pile low energy
- USE dimple reactor

deuterium oxide
- USE heavy water

DEUTERIUM TARGET [6,702; 6,702]
- UF *deuteron target*
- UF+ *antiproton-deuteron interactio*
- UF+ *electron-deuteron interactions*
- UF+ *kaon-deuteron interactions*
- UF+ *lepton-deuteron interactions*
- UF+ *meson-deuteron interactions*
- UF+ *muon-deuteron interactions*
- UF+ *neutrino-deuteron interactions*
- UF+ *neutron-deuteron interactions*
- UF+ *nucleon-deuteron interactions*
- UF+ *photon-deuteron interactions*
- UF+ *pion-deuteron interactions*
- UF+ *proton-deuteron interactions*

```
       BT1     targets

DEUTERIUM TRITIDE [421; 421]
    Feb 76
       BT1     deuterium compounds
          BT2     hydrogen compounds
       BT1     tritides
          BT2     tritium compounds
             BT3     hydrogen compounds
       RT      muon-catalyzed fusion


DEUTERON BEAMS [2,426; 2,426]
       BT1     ion beams
          BT2     beams
       RT      deuterons

DEUTERON MICROPROBE ANALYSIS
    [23; 23] Jul 81
       BT1     microanalysis
       BT1     nondestructive analysis
          BT2     chemical analysis
       RT      deuteron probes


DEUTERON PROBES [6; 6] Jul 81
       BT1     probes
       RT      deuteron microprobe analysis
       RT      deuteron sources
       RT      ion probes


DEUTERON REACTIONS [6,908; 6,911]
       BT1     nuclear reactions
       NT1     antideuteron reactions


DEUTERON SOURCES [49; 49]
       BT1     particle sources
          BT2     radiation sources
       RT      deuteron probes
       RT      deuterons


DEUTERON SPECTRA [489; 489]
       BT1     spectra
       RT      deuterons


deuteron target
    USE      deuterium target


DEUTERONS [8,011; 8,083]
       BT1     charged particles
       NT1     antideuterons
       RT      deuterium
       RT      deuteron beams
       RT      deuteron sources
       RT      deuteron spectra


DEVELOPED COUNTRIES [113; 32,147]
    Dec 82
       UF      industrialized countries
     * NT1     australia
       NT1     austria
       NT1     belgium
     * NT1     canada
       NT1     denmark
       NT1     federal republic of germany
       NT1     finland
       NT1     france
       NT1     ireland
       NT1     italy
     * NT1     japan
       NT1     luxembourg
       NT1     monaco
       NT1     netherlands
       NT1     new zealand
       NT1     norway
     * NT1     south africa
       NT1     sweden
       NT1     switzerland
       NT1     united kingdom
     * NT1     usa
     * NT1     ussr
       RT      developing countries
       RT      economic development
```

```
DEVELOPERS [90; 381]
       NT1     amidol
       NT1     pyrocatechol
       NT1     pyrogallol
       NT1     resorcinol
       RT      photography


DEVELOPING COUNTRIES
    [988; 11,504]
       NT1     afghanistan
       NT1     albania
       NT1     algeria
       NT1     angola
     * NT1     argentina
       NT1     bahama islands
       NT1     bahrain
       NT1     bangladesh
       NT1     bhutan
     * NT1     bolivia
       NT1     botswana
       NT1     brazil
       NT1     bulgaria
       NT1     burma
       NT1     cameroon
       NT1     central african republic
       NT1     chad
       NT1     chile
       NT1     colombia
       NT1     congo peoples republic
       NT1     costa rica
       NT1     cuba
       NT1     czechoslovakia
       NT1     dominican republic
       NT1     ecuador
       NT1     egyptian arab republic
       NT1     el salvador
       NT1     ethiopia
       NT1     gabon
       NT1     gambia
       NT1     ghana
       NT1     greece
       NT1     guatemala
     * NT1     guyana
       NT1     haiti
       NT1     honduras
       NT1     hungary
       NT1     iceland
       NT1     india
       NT1     indonesia
       NT1     iran
       NT1     iraq
       NT1     israel
       NT1     ivory coast
       NT1     jamaica
       NT1     jordan
       NT1     kenya
       NT1     kuwait
       NT1     laos
       NT1     lebanon
       NT1     lesotho
       NT1     liberia
       NT1     libya
       NT1     madagascar
       NT1     malawi
       NT1     malaysia
       NT1     mali
       NT1     mauritania
       NT1     mexico
       NT1     morocco
       NT1     mozambique
       NT1     nepal
       NT1     nicaragua
       NT1     niger
       NT1     nigeria
       NT1     north korea
       NT1     oman
       NT1     pakistan
       NT1     panama
       NT1     paraguay
       NT1     peru
       NT1     philippines
       NT1     poland
       NT1     portugal
       NT1     qatar
       NT1     republic of korea
       NT1     romania
       NT1     rwanda
       NT1     saint lucia
       NT1     saudi arabia
```

```
       NT1     senegal
       NT1     sierra leone
       NT1     singapore
       NT1     somalia
       NT1     spain
       NT1     sri lanka
       NT1     sudan
       NT1     surinam
       NT1     swaziland
       NT1     syria
       NT1     tanzania
       NT1     thailand
       NT1     togo
       NT1     tunisia
       NT1     turkey
       NT1     uganda
       NT1     upper volta
       NT1     uruguay
       NT1     venezuela
       NT1     viet nam
       NT1     yemen
       NT1     yugoslavia
       NT1     zaire republic
       NT1     zambia
     * NT1     zimbabwe
       RT      developed countries
       RT      industry
       RT      technology transfer


devices
    USE      equipment


DEW POINT [44; 44] Oct 76
       BT1     transition temperature
          BT2     thermodynamic properties
             BT3     physical properties
       RT      humidity
       RT      phase transformations
       RT      vapor condensation


dewar flasks
    (Prior to August 1985 this was a valid
    descriptor.)
    USE      dewars


DEWARS [181; 181] Jul 76
    (Prior to August 1985 DEWAR FLASKS
    was used.)
       UF      dewar flasks
       BT1     containers
       RT      cryogenics


DEXAMETHASONE [217; 217]
       BT1     glucocorticoids
          BT2     corticosteroids
             BT3     adrenal hormones
                BT4     hormones
             BT3     hydroxy compounds
                BT4     organic compounds
             BT3     ketones
                BT4     organic compounds
             BT3     pregnanes
                BT4     steroids
                   BT5     organic compounds
             BT3     steroid hormones
                BT4     hormones


DEXTRAN [228; 228]
       BT1     blood substitutes
       BT1     polysaccharides
          BT2     saccharides
             BT3     carbohydrates
                BT4     organic compounds


DEXTRIN [39; 39]
       UF      starch gum
       BT1     polysaccharides
          BT2     saccharides
             BT3     carbohydrates
                BT4     organic compounds


dextronic acid
    USE      gluconic acid
```

dfa
   USE   deferoxamine

DFR REACTOR [181; 181]
  UF   *dfr-350 reactor*
  UF   *dounreay fast reactor*
  BT1   enriched uranium reactors
    BT2   reactors
  BT1   experimental reactors
    BT2   research and test reactors
      BT3   reactors
  BT1   lmfbr type reactors
    BT2   fbr type reactors
      BT3   breeder reactors
        BT4   reactors
      BT3   fast reactors
        BT4   epithermal reactors
          BT5   reactors
    BT2   liquid metal cooled reactors
      BT3   reactors
  BT1   power reactors
    BT2   reactors

dfr-350 reactor
   USE   dfr reactor

DHDECMP [41; 41] *Jul 81*
(Dihexyl-n,n-diethylcarbamyl methylenephosphonate.)
  BT1   phosphonic acid esters
    BT2   esters
      BT3   organic compounds
    BT2   organic phosphorus compounds
      BT3   organic compounds
  RT   organic solvents

DHRUVA REACTOR [119; 119]
(Bhabha Atomic Research Centre, Trombay, Maharashtra, India. Prior to March 1986 known as TROMBAY R-5 REACTOR.)
  UF   *trombay r-5 reactor*
  BT1   heavy water cooled reactors
    BT2   reactors
  BT1   heavy water moderated reactors
    BT2   reactors
  BT1   isotope production reactors
    BT2   irradiation reactors
      BT3   reactors
  BT1   natural uranium reactors
    BT2   reactors
  BT1   research reactors
    BT2   research and test reactors
      BT3   reactors
  BT1   test reactors
    BT2   research and test reactors
      BT3   reactors
    BT2   test facilities
  BT1   thermal reactors
    BT2   reactors

di-(2-propyl) ether
   USE   isopropyl ether

di-2-ethylhexylphosphoric acid
   USE   hdehp

DIABATIC APPROXIMATION [98; 98]
  UF   *approximation (diabatic)*
  RT   adiabatic approximation
  RT   electron-promotion model
  RT   quantum mechanics
  RT   scattering

DIABETES MELLITUS [627; 627]
  BT1   endocrine diseases
    BT2   diseases
  RT   insulin
  RT   metabolic diseases
  RT   metabolism

DIABLO CANYON-1 REACTOR [123; 123]
(Avila Beach, California, USA)
  UF   *pacific gas diablo canyon-1 r.*
  BT1   pwr type reactors
    BT2   enriched uranium reactors
      BT3   reactors
    BT2   power reactors
      BT3   reactors
    BT2   thermal reactors
      BT3   reactors
    BT2   water cooled reactors
      BT3   reactors
    BT2   water moderated reactors
      BT3   reactors

DIABLO CANYON-2 REACTOR [101; 101]
(Avila Beach, California, USA)
  UF   *pacific gas diablo canyon-2 r.*
  BT1   pwr type reactors
    BT2   enriched uranium reactors
      BT3   reactors
    BT2   power reactors
      BT3   reactors
    BT2   thermal reactors
      BT3   reactors
    BT2   water cooled reactors
      BT3   reactors
    BT2   water moderated reactors
      BT3   reactors

diacetylmorphine
   USE   heroin

DIAGENESIS [227; 227]
  RT   sediments

DIAGNOSIS [37,308; 37,308]
  UF+   *radiodiagnosis (radionuclides)*
  RT   diagnostic techniques
  RT   labelled compounds
  RT   medical examinations
  RT   medicine
  RT   nuclear medicine
  RT   radiology
  RT   radiopharmaceuticals
  RT   scintiscanning
  RT   symptoms
  RT   tracer techniques

DIAGNOSTIC TECHNIQUES
[5,476; 64,794]
  NT1   autopsy
  NT1   biomedical radiography
    NT2   fluoroscopy
    NT2   osteodensitometry
  NT1   biopsy
  NT1   cardiography
    NT2   radiocardiography
  NT1   electroencephalography
  NT1   nmr imaging
  NT1   photon emission scanning
  NT1   photon transmission scanning
  NT1   radioimmunodetection
  NT1   renography
  NT1   scintiscanning
  NT1   ultrasonography
  RT   autoradiography
  RT   blood-plasma clearance
  RT   diagnosis
  RT   electrocardiograms
  RT   medicine
  RT   nuclear medicine
  RT   radioisotope generators
  RT   radiology
  RT   tomography
  RT   tracer techniques
  RT   x-ray equipment

DIAGRAMS [15,709; 46,483]
(FOR SIGNIFICANT DIAGRAMS, CHARTS, GRAPHS, AND DRAWINGS ONLY.)
  UF   *charts*
  UF   *curves*

  UF   *design (technical drawings)*
  BT1   information
  NT1   argand diagrams
  NT1   bragg curve
  NT1   electrocardiograms
  NT1   fermi plot
  NT1   feynman diagram
  NT1   flowsheets
  NT1   goldstone diagrams
  NT1   hertzsprung-russell diagram
  NT1   nomograms
  NT1   nyquist diagrams
  NT1   optical depth curve
    NT2   spectroscopic curve of growth
  NT1   phase diagrams
  NT1   s-n diagram
  NT1   sargent diagrams
  NT1   scatterplots
    NT2   dalitz plot
    NT2   prism plot
  NT1   young diagram
  RT   computer graphics
  RT   computer-graphics devices
  RT   design
  RT   maps
  RT   pattern recognition

DIAL PAINTERS [180; 180]
  BT1   personnel
  RT   luminous paints

DIALYSIS [515; 515]
  BT1   separation processes
  RT   colloids
  RT   diffusion
  RT   mass transfer
  RT   membranes
  RT   permeability
  RT   proteins

DIAMAGNETISM [653; 861]
  BT1   magnetism
  NT1   plasma diamagnetism
  RT   de haas-van alphen effect

diaminobiphenyl
   USE   benzidine

diaminocaproic acid
   USE   lysine

diaminocyclohexanetetraacetic
(Diaminocyclohexanetetraacetic acid)
   USE   dcta

diamond counters
   USE   crystal counters

DIAMONDS [1,162; 1,162]
  BT1   carbon
    BT2   nonmetals
      BT3   elements
  BT1   minerals

diamyl sulfoxide
   USE   dpso

DIANABOL [11; 11]
  BT1   androgens
    BT2   androstanes
      BT3   steroids
        BT4   organic compounds
    BT2   steroid hormones
      BT3   hormones
  BT1   hydroxy compounds
    BT2   organic compounds
  BT1   ketones
    BT2   organic compounds
  BT1   radioprotective substances
    BT2   drugs
    BT2   response modifying factors

diantipyrylmethane
USE pyrazolines

DIAPHORASES [5; 5]
UF *flavoprotein enzymes*
BT1 dehydrogenases
  BT2 oxidoreductases
    BT3 enzymes
      BT4 organic compounds
BT1 isoalloxazines
  BT2 heterocyclic compounds
    BT3 organic compounds
  BT2 organic nitrogen compounds
    BT3 organic compounds
  BT2 organic oxygen compounds
    BT3 organic compounds
RT cytochromes

DIAPHRAGM [132; 132] *Sep 80*
(Partition separating the chest and abdominal cavities.)
BT1 muscles
BT1 organs
  BT2 body
RT abdomen
RT chest
RT lungs
RT respiration

diaphragms (thermonucl. device
USE limiters

DIARRHEA [184; 184]
BT1 symptoms
RT constipation
RT digestive system diseases
RT enteritis
RT intestines

diatoms
(Algae of the class Bacillariophyceae.)
USE algae
AND plankton

DIAZO COMPOUNDS [242; 467]
BT1 organic nitrogen compounds
  BT2 organic compounds
NT1 pan
NT1 pyridylazoresorcinol
NT1 thorin
RT azo dyes
RT dyes

DIAZOTIZATION [15; 15]
BT1 chemical reactions
RT organic nitrogen compounds

dibaryon resonances
(Prior to December 1987 this was a valid descriptor.)
USE dibaryons

DIBARYONS [861; 924] *Feb 81*
(Prior to December 1987 this concept was indexed by DIBARYON RESONANCES.)
UF *dibaryon resonances*
BT1 baryons
  BT2 fermions
  BT2 hadrons
    BT3 elementary particles
NT1 dineutrons
NT1 diprotons
NT1 lambda-n-2130 dibaryons
NT1 nn-2170 dibaryons
NT1 nn-2250 dibaryons

dibenzopyrroles
USE carbazoles

diborane
USE boranes

dibutyl ether
USE butyl ether

dibutyl phosphate
USE dbp

DICARBOXYLIC ACIDS [301; 1,687]
BT1 carboxylic acids
  BT2 organic acids
    BT3 organic compounds
NT1 adipic acid
NT1 beryllon
NT1 fumaric acid
NT1 glutaric acid
NT1 itaconic acid
NT1 maleic acid
NT1 malonic acid
NT1 oxalic acid
NT1 phthalic acid
NT1 sebacic acid
NT1 succinic acid
NT1 terephthalic acid
RT imides
RT imidines

DICENTRIC CHROMOSOMES [250; 250]
UF *dicentrics*
BT1 chromosomes
RT chromosomal aberrations

dicentrics
USE dicentric chromosomes

dichlorodiethylamine
USE nitrogen mustard

dichlorodiphenyltrichloroethan
USE ddt

dichloromethane
USE methylene chloride

DICHROISM [446; 446]
RT color
RT optical properties

DICHROMATES [46; 46] *Oct 83*
(Specific compounds should be indexed by coordination of a descriptor of the form (CATION) COMPOUNDS and the above anion descriptor.)
BT1 chromium compounds
  BT2 transition element compounds
BT1 oxygen compounds
RT chromium oxides

DICTYOCAULUS [18; 18]
BT1 nematodes
  BT2 invertebrates
    BT3 animals
RT parasitic diseases
RT sheep

DICUMAROL [3; 3]
BT1 anticoagulants
  BT2 hematologic agents
    BT3 drugs

DIDO REACTOR [81; 81]
(UKAEA Atomic Energy Research Establishment, Harwell)
UF *ukaea-dido reactor*
BT1 enriched uranium reactors
  BT2 reactors
BT1 heavy water cooled reactors
  BT2 reactors
BT1 heavy water moderated reactors
  BT2 reactors
BT1 isotope production reactors
  BT2 irradiation reactors
    BT3 reactors
BT1 materials testing reactors
  BT2 irradiation reactors
    BT3 reactors
BT1 research reactors
  BT2 research and test reactors
    BT3 reactors
BT1 tank type reactors
  BT2 reactors
BT1 thermal reactors
  BT2 reactors

dido-juelich reactor
USE frj-2 reactor

DIELDRIN [29; 29]
BT1 insecticides
  BT2 pesticides
RT aldrin

DIELECTRIC AMPLIFIERS [3; 3]
BT1 amplifiers
  BT2 equipment
BT1 electronic equipment
  BT2 equipment

dielectric constant
USE permittivity

DIELECTRIC MATERIALS [2,605; 4,221]
UF *dielectrics*
BT1 materials
NT1 antiferroelectric materials
NT1 electrets
NT1 ferroelectric materials
RT antireflection coatings
RT capacitors
RT dielectric properties
RT dielectric tensor
RT dielectric track detectors
RT electrical insulation
RT electrical insulators
RT lichtenberg figures
RT mica
RT natural rubber
RT organic insulators
RT paper
RT potting
RT potting materials
RT ritad dosemeters
RT rubbers
RT varnishes

DIELECTRIC PROPERTIES [2,186; 3,812]
BT1 electrical properties
  BT2 physical properties
NT1 kerr effect
NT1 permittivity
RT dielectric materials
RT dielectric tensor
RT relaxation losses

DIELECTRIC TENSOR [105; 105] *Aug 81*
BT1 tensors
RT dielectric materials
RT dielectric properties

DIELECTRIC TRACK DETECTORS [3,291; 3,291]
UF *track detectors (dielectric)*
BT1 radiation detectors
  BT2 measuring instruments
RT ceramics
RT dielectric materials
RT electron microscopy
RT etching
RT fission foil detectors
RT glass
RT latent images
RT lithium fluorides
RT luminescent dosemeters
RT mica

RT   olivine
RT   particle tracks
RT   polymers
RT   tourmaline

dielectrics
USE   dielectric materials

DIELS-ALDER REACTION [9; 9]
BT1   chemical reactions

DIENES [539; 1,275]
BT1   polyenes
BT2   hydrocarbons
BT3   organic compounds
NT1   allene
NT1   butadiene
NT1   cyclopentadiene
NT1   ferrocene
NT1   isoprene

DIES [124; 124]
RT   casting
RT   casting molds
RT   extrusion
RT   forging
RT   pressing

DIESEL ENGINES [452; 452]
(Prior to December 1990, this concept was indexed by DIESEL MOTORS.)
UF   *diesel motors*
BT1   motors

→ **DIESEL FUELS** [0; 0] *Oct 91*
BT1   liquid fuels
BT2   fuels
BT1   petroleum products

diesel motors
(Prior to December 1990, this was a valid descriptor.)
USE   diesel engines

DIET [2,006; 2,006]
RT   animal feeds
RT   beverages
RT   drinking water
RT   fasting
RT   feeding
RT   food
RT   food chains
RT   icrp critical group
RT   ingestion
RT   mass rearing
RT   nutrients
RT   nutrition
RT   nutritional deficiency
RT   rearing
RT   therapy
RT   vitamins

diethyl ether
USE   ethyl ether

diethyldithiocarbamates
USE   dedtc

diethylenetriaminepentaacetic
(Diethylenetriaminepentaacetic acid)
USE   dtpa

DIFFERENTIAL CALCULUS [501; 501]
UF   *calculus (differential)*
BT1   mathematics
RT   differential geometry

§ **DIFFERENTIAL CROSS SECTIONS**
[34,147; 34,147]
BT1   cross sections
RT   angular distribution
RT   excitation functions

DIFFERENTIAL EQUATIONS
[5,570; 40,938]
UF   *canonical equations*
BT1   equations
NT1   bbgky equation
NT1   dirac-hestenes equation
NT1   hill equation
NT1   joos-weinberg equation
NT1   mathieu equation
NT1   partial differential equations
NT2   boltzmann equation
NT2   boltzmann-vlasov equation
NT3   plasma fluid equations
NT2   continuity equations
NT2   equations of motion
NT2   fokker-planck equation
NT2   fourier heat equation
NT2   grad-shafranov equation
NT2   hamilton-jacobi equations
NT2   korteweg-de vries equation
NT2   lagrange equations
NT2   laplace equation
NT2   maxwell equations
NT2   navier-stokes equations
NT2   poisson equation
NT2   proca equations
NT2   wave equations
NT3   dirac equation
NT3   klein-gordon equation
NT3   schroedinger equation
NT1   riccati equation
NT1   schwinger functional equations
NT1   sturm-liouville equation
RT   airy functions
RT   analytical solution
RT   boundary conditions
RT   boundary-value problems
RT   cluster expansion
RT   control theory
RT   finite difference method
RT   finite element method
RT   floquet function
RT   green function
RT   integral equations
RT   lyapunov method
RT   mathematics
RT   recursion relations
RT   riemann function

DIFFERENTIAL GEOMETRY [795; 795]
Mar 83
BT1   geometry
BT2   mathematics
RT   differential calculus
RT   mathematical space

DIFFERENTIAL PAC [858; 858]
UF   *perturbed ang. corr. (differ.)*
BT1   perturbed angular correlation
BT2   angular correlation
BT3   correlations
RT   time dependence

DIFFERENTIAL THERMAL ANALYSIS
[2,338; 2,338]
UF   *dta*
BT1   thermal analysis
RT   transition heat

DIFFERENTIAL TOPOLOGY [129; 129]
BT1   topology
BT2   mathematics
RT   mapping fibration
RT   smooth manifolds
RT   topological foliation

DIFFRACTION [1,575; 29,347]
BT1   coherent scattering
BT2   scattering
NT1   atomic beam diffraction
NT1   electron diffraction
NT1   neutron diffraction
NT1   x-ray diffraction
RT   debye-waller factor
RT   diffraction gratings
RT   diffractometers
RT   gamma diffractometers
RT   optical dispersion

diffraction dissociation
USE   diffraction models

DIFFRACTION GRATINGS [299; 299]
Jan 84
UF   *echelle gratings*
UF   *echelon gratings*
SF   *gratings*
RT   diffraction
RT   diffractometers
RT   optical systems
RT   spectrometers
RT   x-ray equipment

DIFFRACTION METHODS [309; 990]
NT1   debye-scherrer method
NT1   laue method
NT1   rotating crystal method
RT   crystal lattices
RT   crystallography
RT   patterson method
RT   schulz method
RT   x-ray diffractometers

DIFFRACTION MODELS [2,103; 2,103]
UF   *diffraction dissociation*
UF   *diffraction production*
BT1   particle models
BT2   mathematical models

diffraction production
USE   diffraction models

diffractive dissociation
(In high-energy hadron collisions)
USE   multiperipheral model
AND   particle production

DIFFRACTOMETERS [123; 1,081]
BT1   measuring instruments
NT1   gamma diffractometers
NT1   neutron diffractometers
NT1   x-ray diffractometers
RT   diffraction
RT   diffraction gratings

DIFFUSION [21,666; 24,165]
NT1   ambipolar diffusion
NT1   gaseous diffusion
NT1   self-diffusion
NT1   thermal diffusion
RT   advection
RT   atom transport
RT   dialysis
RT   donnan theory
RT   fick laws
RT   kirkendall effect
RT   leaching
RT   mass transfer
RT   mean free path
RT   membrane transport
RT   mixing
RT   osmosis
RT   particle resuspension
RT   radionuclide migration
RT   turbulence

diffusion area
USE   diffusion length

DIFFUSION BARRIERS [252; 252]
Nov 75
RT   gaseous diffusion plants
RT   gaseous diffusion process

DIFFUSION CHAMBERS [93; 93]
- BT1 cloud chambers
- BT2 gas track detectors
- BT3 radiation detectors
- BT4 measuring instruments

DIFFUSION COATING [273; 273]
(The process)
- UF *calorizing*
- UF *chromizing*
- UF *sherardizing*
- UF *siliconizing*
- BT1 surface coating
- BT2 deposition
- RT diffusion coatings

DIFFUSION COATINGS [322; 322]
- BT1 coatings
- RT diffusion coating

DIFFUSION LENGTH [552; 552]
- UF *diffusion area*
- RT migration length

DIFFUSION WELDING [212; 212]
- BT1 welding
- BT2 joining
- BT3 fabrication

digallic acid
- USE tannic acid

DIGESTION [381; 461]
- NT1 anaerobic digestion
- NT1 intracellular digestion
- RT amylase
- RT chymotrypsin
- RT digestive system
- RT enzymes
- RT gastric acid
- RT ingestion
- RT intestinal absorption
- RT pepsin
- RT physiology
- RT trypsin

DIGESTIVE SYSTEM [201; 26,589]
- NT1 biliary tract
- NT1 esophagus
- NT1 gastrointestinal tract
  - NT2 intestines
    - NT3 large intestine
      - NT4 rectum
    - NT3 small intestine
  - NT2 stomach
- NT1 liver
- NT1 oral cavity
  - NT2 teeth
  - NT2 tongue
- NT1 pancreas
- NT1 pharynx
- RT anorexia
- RT digestion
- RT digestive system diseases
- RT organs

DIGESTIVE SYSTEM DISEASES [2,469; 3,826]
- BT1 diseases
- NT1 enteritis
- NT1 hepatitis
- NT1 liver cirrhosis
- NT1 peritonitis
- NT1 proctitis
- RT anorexia
- RT constipation
- RT diarrhea
- RT digestive system
- RT gastrectomy
- RT nausea
- RT vomiting

DIGITAL CIRCUITS [468; 468]
- UF *coding circuits*
- BT1 electronic circuits
- RT sequential circuits

DIGITAL COMPUTERS [822; 2,180]
- UF *data processors*
- BT1 computers
- NT1 array processors
- NT1 calculators
- NT1 cii computers
- NT1 fault tolerant computers
- NT1 microcomputers
- NT1 parameter computers
- NT1 supercomputers

DIGITAL FILTERS [143; 143] *Mar 86*
(Computational means of attenuating undesired frequencies in a set of time-dependent data.)
- RT data processing
- RT frequency analysis
- RT image processing
- RT mathematical models

DIGITAL SYSTEMS [2,754; 2,754]
- RT analog-to-digital converters
- RT computer architecture
- RT computers
- RT digital-to-analog converters
- RT electronic circuits
- RT electronic equipment

DIGITAL-TO-ANALOG CONVERTERS [239; 239]
- UF *converters (digital-analog)*
- BT1 electronic equipment
- BT2 equipment
- RT analog systems
- RT digital systems

DIGITALIS [30; 30]
- BT1 medicinal plants
- BT2 plants

DIGITALIS GLYCOSIDES [17; 216]
- BT1 cardiotonics
- BT2 cardiovascular agents
- BT3 drugs
- BT1 glycosides
- BT2 carbohydrates
- BT3 organic compounds
- NT1 digitoxin
- NT1 digoxin

DIGITIZERS [526; 931]
(Devices for converting non-digital information into digits.)
- NT1 cathode ray tube digitizers
- NT1 flying spot digitizers
- NT1 scanning measuring projectors
- NT1 spiral reader digitizers
- RT analog-to-digital converters
- RT bubble chambers
- RT data processing
- RT electronic equipment
- RT image scanners
- RT on-line measurement systems
- RT signal conditioning
- RT spark chambers
- RT video tapes

DIGITOXIN [37; 37]
- BT1 digitalis glycosides
- BT2 cardiotonics
- BT3 cardiovascular agents
- BT4 drugs
- BT2 glycosides
- BT3 carbohydrates
- BT4 organic compounds
- RT digoxin

diglycol monoalkyl ethers
- USE carbitols

DIGOXIN [187; 187]
- UF *lanoxin*
- BT1 digitalis glycosides
- BT2 cardiotonics
- BT3 cardiovascular agents
- BT4 drugs
- BT2 glycosides
- BT3 carbohydrates
- BT4 organic compounds
- RT digitoxin

dihydroxyaromatics
- USE polyphenols

dihydroxybenzene-meta
- USE resorcinol

dihydroxybenzene-ortho
- USE pyrocatechol

dihydroxypropionic acid
- USE glyceric acid

dihydroxysuccinic acid
- USE tartaric acid

DIIODOTHYRONINE [10; 10] *Sep 83*
- BT1 thyroid hormones
- BT2 peptide hormones
- BT3 hormones
- RT thyronine
- RT triiodothyronine

DIIODOTYROSINE [31; 31]
- BT1 amino acids
- BT2 carboxylic acids
- BT3 organic acids
- BT4 organic compounds
- BT1 hydroxy acids
- BT2 carboxylic acids
- BT3 organic acids
- BT4 organic compounds
- BT1 organic iodine compounds
- BT2 organic halogen compounds
- BT3 organic compounds
- RT tyrosine

diisoamyl methylphosphonate
- USE dampa

diisopentyl methylphosphonate
- USE dampa

diisopropyl ether
- USE isopropyl ether

DILATOMETRY [361; 361]
- BT1 thermal analysis
- RT extensometers
- RT shrinkage
- RT thermal expansion

diluents
- USE solvents

DILUTE ALLOYS [877; 877]
- BT1 alloys

DILUTION [725; 725]
- RT isotope dilution
- RT solutions

dimensional compactification
- USE compactification

DIMENSIONS [3,681; 18,843]
- NT1 depth
- NT1 height
- NT1 length
- NT1 thickness
- NT1 width
- RT amplitudes
- RT compactification
- RT distance
- RT shape
- RT size
- RT topology
- RT volume

dimercaprol
- USE bal

dimercaptoethane
- USE dithiols

dimercaptopropanol
- USE bal

DIMERIZATION [259; 259]
- BT1 polymerization
- BT2 chemical reactions

DIMERS [1,602; 1,812]
- NT1 pyrimidine dimers
- RT monomers
- RT polymers

dimethyl ether
- USE methyl ether

dimethyl ketone
- USE acetone

dimethyl sulfoxide
- USE dmso

DIMETHYLBENZANTHRACENE [54; 54] *May 80*
- UF dmba
- BT1 condensed aromatics
- BT2 aromatics
- BT3 organic compounds
- RT carcinogens
- RT neoplasms

dimethylbenzenes
- USE xylenes

DIMETHYLGLYOXIME [41; 41]
- BT1 oximes
- BT2 amines
- BT3 organic compounds
- BT2 hydroxy compounds
- BT3 organic compounds
- BT2 organic nitrogen compounds
- BT3 organic compounds
- BT1 reagents

dimethylpropane (2,2-)
- USE 2-2-dimethylpropane

dimethylpropionic acid
- USE pivalic acid

DIMPLE REACTOR [16; 16]
(Uncooled, variably fueled reactor at UKAEA Atomic Energy Establishment, Winfrith, UK.)
- UF *deuterium mod. pile low energy*
- BT1 heavy water moderated reactors
- BT2 reactors
- BT1 test reactors
- BT2 research and test reactors
- BT3 reactors
- BT2 test facilities
- BT1 thermal reactors
- BT2 reactors
- BT1 zero power reactors
- BT2 experimental reactors
- BT3 research and test reactors
- BT4 reactors

DINEUTRONS [69; 69] *Jan 78*
- BT1 dibaryons
- BT2 baryons
- BT3 fermions
- BT3 hadrons
- BT4 elementary particles
- BT1 polyneutrons
- BT2 neutrons
- BT3 nucleons
- BT4 baryons
- BT5 fermions
- BT5 hadrons
- BT6 elementary particles

DINING CAR EVENT [3; 3] *Apr 79*
- BT1 contained explosions
- BT2 underground explosions
- BT3 explosions
- BT1 nuclear explosions
- BT2 explosions

DINITROPHENOL [114; 114]
- UF *dnp*
- BT1 nitro compounds
- BT2 organic nitrogen compounds
- BT3 organic compounds
- BT1 phenols
- BT2 aromatics
- BT3 organic compounds
- BT2 hydroxy compounds
- BT3 organic compounds
- RT nitrophenol

DINOFLAGELLATE [13; 13] *Sep 80*
- BT1 protozoa
- BT2 invertebrates
- BT3 animals
- BT2 microorganisms

diode transistors
- USE transistors

DIODE TUBES [423; 779]
- BT1 electron tubes
- NT1 thermionic diodes

diodes (semiconductor)
- USE semiconductor diodes

DIODRAST [3; 3]
- UF *iodopyracet*
- BT1 contrast media
- BT1 heterocyclic acids
- BT2 carboxylic acids
- BT3 organic acids
- BT4 organic compounds
- BT2 heterocyclic compounds
- BT3 organic compounds
- BT1 organic iodine compounds
- BT2 organic halogen compounds
- BT3 organic compounds
- BT1 pyridines
- BT2 azines
- BT3 heterocyclic compounds
- BT4 organic compounds
- BT3 organic nitrogen compounds
- BT4 organic compounds

diols
- USE glycols

DIORIT REACTOR [28; 28]
(Eidgenoessiches Institute fuer Reaktorforschung, Wuerlingen, Switzerland)
- BT1 heavy water cooled reactors
- BT2 reactors
- BT1 heavy water moderated reactors
- BT2 reactors
- BT1 mixed spectrum reactors
- BT2 reactors
- BT1 natural uranium reactors
- BT2 reactors
- BT1 research reactors
- BT2 research and test reactors
- BT3 reactors
- BT1 tank type reactors
- BT2 reactors
- BT1 test reactors
- BT2 research and test reactors
- BT3 reactors
- BT2 test facilities

DIOXANE [331; 331]
- UF *dioxyethylene ether*
- UF *1,4-dioxane*
- BT1 heterocyclic compounds
- BT2 organic compounds
- BT1 organic oxygen compounds
- BT2 organic compounds

DIOXIN [81; 81] *Feb 87*
- BT1 heterocyclic compounds
- BT2 organic compounds
- BT1 organic oxygen compounds
- BT2 organic compounds

dioxyethylene ether
- USE dioxane

DIP COATING [20; 29]
- BT1 surface coating
- BT2 deposition
- NT1 hot dipping
- RT dipped coatings

dipentyl sulfoxide
- USE dpso

diphenyl ketone
- USE benzophenone

diphenylcarbazides
- USE dpca

DIPHENYLCARBAZONES [13; 13]
- BT1 carbazones
- BT2 carbonic acid derivatives
- BT3 organic compounds
- BT2 organic nitrogen compounds
- BT3 organic compounds

diphenylcarbinol
- USE benzhydrol

diphenylethane (1,2-)
- USE bibenzyl

diphenylglycolic acid
- USE benzilic acid

diphenylmethanol
- USE benzhydrol

diphenylphosphine oxide
- USE organic phosphorus compounds

diphenylpicrylhydrazyl
USE   dpph

diphenylthiocarbazone
USE   dithizone

diphosphodihydropyridine nucle
(Diphosphodihydropyridine nucleotide)
USE   nadh2

DIPHTHERIA [13; 13]
BT1   bacterial diseases
BT2   infectious diseases
BT3   diseases

diplococcus pneumoniae
USE   pneumococcus

DIPLOIDY [152; 152]
BT1   ploidy

DIPOLE MOMENTS [1,031; 3,903]
NT1   electric dipole moments
NT1   magnetic dipole moments
RT   dipoles

DIPOLES [1,808; 3,588]
BT1   multipoles
NT1   electric dipoles
NT1   magnetic dipoles
RT   dipole moments
RT   relaxation losses

DIPPED COATINGS [28; 28]
BT1   coatings
RT   dip coating

DIPROTONS [172; 172]
BT1   dibaryons
BT2   baryons
BT3   fermions
BT3   hadrons
BT4   elementary particles
BT1   protons
BT2   hydrogen ions 1 plus
BT3   cations
BT4   ions
BT5   charged particles
BT3   hydrogen ions
BT4   ions
BT5   charged particles
BT2   nucleons
BT3   baryons
BT4   fermions
BT4   hadrons
BT5   elementary particles

DIRAC APPROXIMATION [112; 112]
RT   quantum mechanics

DIRAC COSMOLOGY [111; 111]
BT1   cosmology

dirac delta function
USE   delta function

DIRAC EQUATION [3,841; 3,841]
BT1   field equations
BT2   equations
BT1   wave equations
BT2   partial differential equations
BT3   differential equations
BT4   equations
RT   dirac operators
RT   electrons
RT   foldy-wouthuysen transform
RT   joos-weinberg equation
RT   quantum electrodynamics
RT   relativity theory
RT   schroedinger equation

DIRAC FORM FACTORS [63; 63]
BT1   form factors
BT2   particle properties

dirac matrices
USE   dirac operators

dirac monopoles
USE   magnetic monopoles

DIRAC OPERATORS [944; 944]
UF   *dirac matrices*
BT1   quantum operators
BT2   mathematical operators
RT   dirac equation
RT   quantum electrodynamics

DIRAC-HESTENES EQUATION [4; 4]
BT1   differential equations
BT2   equations

DIRECT COLLECTION CONVERTERS [16; 36]
UF   *radioelectric cells*
BT1   direct energy converters
NT1   betavoltaic cells
RT   radioisotope batteries

DIRECT CURRENT [1,122; 1,122]
UF   *current (direct)*
BT1   electric currents
BT2   currents

DIRECT CYCLE COOLING SYSTEMS [170; 170]
UF   *direct-cycle cooling systems*
BT1   reactor cooling systems
BT2   cooling systems
BT2   reactor components

DIRECT ENERGY CONVERSION [308; 643]
BT1   energy conversion
BT2   conversion
NT1   photovoltaic conversion
NT1   thermionic conversion
NT1   thermoelectric conversion
NT1   thermomagnetic conversion
RT   direct energy converters
RT   electrohydrodynamics
RT   magnetohydrodynamics

DIRECT ENERGY CONVERTERS [170; 4,832]
NT1   direct collection converters
NT2   betavoltaic cells
NT1   ehd generators
NT1   fuel cells
NT1   mhd generators
NT2   closed-cycle mhd generators
NT3   liquid-metal mhd generators
NT2   open-cycle mhd generators
NT1   photoelectric cells
NT2   photoconductive cells
NT2   photovoltaic cells
NT1   radioisotope batteries
NT2   snap batteries
NT3   snap 1 battery
NT3   snap 11 battery
NT3   snap 13 battery
NT3   snap 15 battery
NT3   snap 17 battery
NT3   snap 19 battery
NT3   snap 21 battery
NT3   snap 23 battery
NT3   snap 25 battery
NT3   snap 27 battery
NT3   snap 29 battery
NT3   snap 3 battery
NT3   snap 5 battery
NT3   snap 7 battery
NT3   snap 9 battery
NT1   solar cells
NT2   silicon solar cells
NT1   thermionic converters
NT1   thermoelectric generators
NT1   thermoelectric refrigerators
RT   direct energy conversion
RT   power supplies

DIRECT REACTIONS [1,218; 16,271]
BT1   nuclear reactions
NT1   knock-on reactions
NT1   knock-out reactions
NT1   quasi-free reactions
NT1   transfer reactions
NT2   multi-nucleon transfer reactio
NT3   four-nucleon transfer reaction
NT4   alpha-transfer reactions
NT3   many-nucleon transfer reaction
NT3   three-nucleon transfer reactio
NT3   two-nucleon transfer reactions
NT2   one-nucleon transfer reactions
NT2   pickup reactions
NT2   stripping
RT   oppenheimer-phillips process

direct-cycle cooling systems
USE   direct cycle cooling systems

directional correlation
USE   angular correlation

DIRECTIONAL RADIATION DETECTOR [95; 95]
BT1   radiation detectors
BT2   measuring instruments

directories
USE   indexes

DIRICHLET PROBLEM [251; 251]
BT1   boundary-value problems
RT   partial differential equations

DISACCHARIDES [46; 749]
BT1   oligosaccharides
BT2   saccharides
BT3   carbohydrates
BT4   organic compounds
NT1   cellobiose
NT1   lactose
NT1   maltose
NT1   melibiose
NT1   saccharose

DISADVANTAGE FACTOR [24; 24]
RT   multiplication factors
RT   neutron flux

disaster (exceptional natural)
USE   exceptional natural disaster

disasters
USE   accidents

discharges (electric)
USE   electric discharges

discharges (ionization)
USE   ionization

discharges (wastes)
USE   waste disposal

discharging (fission reactor)
USE   reactor fueling

DISCRETE ORDINATE METHOD
[769; 769]
UF   *carlson method*
UF   *discrete ordinates*
UF   *sn method*
RT   transport theory

discrete ordinates
USE   discrete ordinate method

DISCRIMINATORS [258; 1,072]
BT1   electronic circuits
NT1   pulse discriminators
RT   timing circuits

disease free period
(The time between disease treatment and recurrence of symptoms.)
USE   latency period

DISEASE INCIDENCE [449; 449] *Jan 85*
RT   disease resistance
RT   diseases
RT   epidemiology
RT   plant diseases

DISEASE RESISTANCE [425; 425]
RT   aids
RT   disease incidence
RT   diseases
RT   epidemiology
RT   immunity
RT   mutants
RT   plant breeding
RT   plant diseases

DISEASE VECTORS [58; 58]
RT   diseases
RT   glossina
RT   insects
RT   mites
RT   parasites
RT   rodents
RT   snails

DISEASES [1,061; 92,826]
(Limited to diseases of man and animals; see also PLANT DISEASES.)
NT1   cardiovascular diseases
  NT2   arteriosclerosis
  NT2   hypertension
  NT2   ischemia
  NT2   myocardial infarction
  NT2   nephrosclerosis
  NT2   telangiectasis
  NT2   thrombosis
NT1   congenital diseases
  NT2   downs syndrome
NT1   digestive system diseases
  NT2   enteritis
  NT2   hepatitis
  NT2   liver cirrhosis
  NT2   peritonitis
  NT2   proctitis
NT1   endocrine diseases
  NT2   acromegaly
  NT2   cushing syndrome
  NT2   diabetes mellitus
  NT2   goiter
  NT2   hyperparathyroidism
  NT2   hyperthyroidism
  NT2   hypothyroidism
  NT2   thyroiditis
NT1   hemic diseases
  NT2   anemias
    NT3   ischemia
    NT3   megaloblastic anemia
    NT3   sickle cell anemia
    NT3   thalassemia
  NT2   hemophilia
  NT2   leukopenia
    NT3   lymphopenia
  NT2   malaria
  NT2   polycythemia
  NT2   purpura

NT1   hereditary diseases
  NT2   hemophilia
NT1   immune system diseases
  NT2   aids
  NT2   leukemia
    NT3   myeloid leukemia
  NT2   leukopenia
    NT3   lymphopenia
  NT2   lupus
  NT2   lymphomas
    NT3   hodgkins disease
    NT3   lymphosarcomas
NT1   infectious diseases
  NT2   bacterial diseases
    NT3   cholera
    NT3   diphtheria
    NT3   gonorrhea
    NT3   leprosy
    NT3   paratyphoid
    NT3   syphilis
    NT3   tetanus
    NT3   tuberculosis
      NT4   lupus
    NT3   typhoid
  NT2   fungal diseases
    NT3   mycoses
  NT2   parasitic diseases
    NT3   fascioliasis
    NT3   filariasis
    NT3   hydatidosis
    NT3   malaria
    NT3   schistosomiasis
    NT3   trichinosis
    NT3   trypanosomiasis
  NT2   rickettsial diseases
    NT3   typhus
  NT2   viral diseases
    NT3   aids
    NT3   herpes simplex
    NT3   herpes zoster
    NT3   influenza
    NT3   measles
    NT3   newcastle disease
    NT3   poliomyelitis
    NT3   rabies
NT1   injuries
  NT2   bone fractures
  NT2   burns
    NT3   flash burns
    NT3   radiation burns
  NT2   radiation injuries
    NT3   osteoradionecrosis
    NT3   radiation burns
    NT3   radiodermatitis
  NT2   wounds
NT1   metabolic diseases
NT1   neoplasms
  NT2   adenomas
  NT2   angiomas
  NT2   carcinomas
  NT2   epitheliomas
  NT2   experimental neoplasms
    NT3   ehrlich ascites tumor
  NT2   gliomas
  NT2   hepatomas
  NT2   leukemia
    NT3   myeloid leukemia
  NT2   lymphomas
    NT3   hodgkins disease
    NT3   lymphosarcomas
  NT2   melanomas
  NT2   sarcomas
    NT3   fibrosarcomas
    NT3   lymphosarcomas
    NT3   myosarcomas
      NT4   rhabdomyosarcomas
    NT3   osteosarcomas
NT1   nervous system diseases
  NT2   encephalitis
  NT2   epilepsy
  NT2   gliomas
  NT2   mental disorders
  NT2   myelitis
  NT2   poliomyelitis
  NT2   rabies
NT1   occupational diseases
NT1   pathological changes
  NT2   abscesses
  NT2   allergy
  NT2   ascites

  NT2   atrophy
  NT2   biological shock
  NT2   caries
  NT2   cysts
  NT2   edema
  NT2   emphysema
  NT2   fibrosis
  NT2   fistulae
  NT2   granulomas
  NT2   hemorrhage
  NT2   hypertrophy
  NT2   inflammation
  NT2   jaundice
  NT2   leukopenia
    NT3   lymphopenia
  NT2   malformations
    NT3   congenital malformations
      NT4   downs syndrome
  NT2   necrosis
    NT3   gangrene
    NT3   osteoradionecrosis
  NT2   splenomegaly
  NT2   ulcers
NT1   respiratory system diseases
  NT2   asthma
  NT2   bronchitis
  NT2   pneumoconioses
    NT3   berylliosis
  NT2   pneumonia
    NT3   bronchopneumonia
NT1   sense organs diseases
  NT2   cataracts
  NT2   conjunctivitis
NT1   skeletal diseases
  NT2   bone fractures
  NT2   osteomyelitis
  NT2   osteoporosis
  NT2   osteoradionecrosis
  NT2   osteosarcomas
  NT2   rheumatic diseases
  NT2   rickets
  NT2   spondylitis
NT1   skin diseases
  NT2   dermatitis
    NT3   radiodermatitis
  NT2   eczema
  NT2   herpes simplex
  NT2   psoriasis
NT1   urogenital system diseases
  NT2   menstruation disorders
  NT2   nephritis
  NT2   nephrosclerosis
  NT2   reproductive disorders
  NT2   uremia
NT1   vascular diseases
  NT2   hypertension
RT   disease incidence
RT   disease resistance
RT   disease vectors
RT   etiology
RT   pathogens
RT   pathology
RT   quarantine
RT   symptoms

DISINFECTANTS [20; 20] *Jul 86*
RT   bacteria
RT   infectivity
RT   pesticides

disinfection
USE   sterilization

DISINFESTATION [178; 504]
NT1   grain disinfestation
NT1   radiodisinfestation
RT   pesticides
RT   preservation
RT   sterilization

disintegration (biological)
USE   decomposition

disintegration (chemical)
USE   decomposition

disintegration (fission)
  USE   fission

disintegration (nuclear part.)
  SEE   annihilation
  OR   particle decay

disintegration (nuclear)
  USE   decay

disks (accretion)
  USE   accretion disks

disks (intervertebral)
  USE   cartilage
  AND   vertebrae

disks (magnetic)
  USE   magnetic disks

DISLOCATION PINNING [227; 227]
  RT   cold working
  RT   dislocations
  RT   grain boundaries

DISLOCATIONS [6,387; 6,928]
  BT1   line defects
    BT2   crystal defects
      BT3   crystal structure
  NT1   edge dislocations
  NT1   screw dislocations
  RT   bordoni peak
  RT   burgers vector
  RT   dislocation pinning
  RT   kikuchi lines
  RT   peierls-nabarro force
  RT   slip
  RT   stacking faults
  RT   superdislocations

dismantling (fission reactor)
  USE   reactor dismantling

dismantling (fuel assembly)
  USE   fuel assembly dismantling

dispersal (insect)
  USE   insect dispersal

disperse systems
  USE   dispersions

DISPERSION HARDENING [442; 442]
  BT1   hardening

DISPERSION NUCLEAR FUELS [174; 174]
(A dispersion of nuclear fuel particles in a solid.)
  BT1   solid fuels
    BT2   nuclear fuels
      BT3   energy sources
      BT3   fuels
      BT3   reactor materials
        BT4   materials
  RT   fuel dispersion reactors
  RT   fuel particles

DISPERSION RELATIONS [9,704; 9,704]
(For dispersion of light use OPTICAL DISPERSION.)
  UF   dispersion theory
  UF   fracer-fulco method
  RT   cdd poles
  RT   mandelstam representation
  RT   n-d method
  RT   partial waves
  RT   plasma instability
  RT   plasma waves
  RT   quantum field theory
  RT   scattering
  RT   scattering amplitudes
  RT   spectral functions

dispersion theory
  USE   dispersion relations

DISPERSIONS [1,433; 58,511]
(For the state of aggregation in materials; if related to wave phenomena see DISPERSION RELATIONS or OPTICAL DISPERSION.)
  UF   disperse systems
  NT1   colloids
  NT2   agar
  NT2   alginic acid
  NT2   emulsions
  NT2   foams
  NT2   gelatin
  NT2   gels
  NT2   radiocolloids
    NT3   thorotrast
  NT2   sols
    NT3   aerosols
      NT4   radioactive aerosols
      NT4   smokes
        NT5   tobacco smokes
  NT1   mixtures
  NT2   binary mixtures
  NT2   homogeneous mixtures
    NT3   solutions
      NT4   aqueous solutions
      NT4   hypertonic solutions
      NT4   isotonic solutions
      NT4   leachates
      NT4   solid solutions
  NT2   mixed solvents
  NT2   slurries
  NT1   suspensions
  NT2   slurries
  NT1   td-nickel
  NT1   td-nickel chromium
  RT   dusts
  RT   elutriation
  RT   gases
  RT   liquids
  RT   microspheres
  RT   particle resuspension
  RT   particle size
  RT   particles
  RT   solids
  RT   sprays

dispersive ion waves
  USE   ion plasma waves

DISPLACEMENT GAGES [302; 302]
  UF   position indicators
  BT1   measuring instruments

displacements (atomic)
  USE   atomic displacements

displacements (seismic)
  USE   ground motion

DISPLAY DEVICES [2,295; 2,794]
  UF   data display devices
  UF   data display systems
  BT1   computer-graphics devices
    BT2   computer output devices
  NT1   interactive display devices
  RT   cathode ray tubes
  RT   computer graphics
  RT   consoles
  RT   control rooms
  RT   electronic equipment
  RT   image tubes
  RT   images
  RT   man-machine systems
  RT   pattern recognition
  RT   plotters
  RT   semiconductor devices

disposal (wastes)
  USE   waste disposal

disproportionation
  USE   oxidation
  AND   reduction

DISPUTE SETTLEMENTS [105; 105] Dec 76
  UF   settlements (disputes)
  RT   arbitration
  RT   courts
  RT   hearings
  RT   lawsuits

DISSIPATION FACTOR [1,070; 1,070]
  RT   energy losses

DISSOCIATING GASES [61; 61] Dec 85
  BT1   gases
    BT2   fluids
  RT   dissociation

DISSOCIATION [4,670; 4,866]
  NT1   predissociation
  RT   decomposition
  RT   dissociating gases
  RT   dissociation energy
  RT   dissociation heat
  RT   electrolysis
  RT   electrolytes
  RT   ionization
  RT   photolysis
  RT   pyrolysis
  RT   radiolysis
  RT   reaction kinetics

DISSOCIATION ENERGY [539; 539]
(For the bond property only; for the reaction property see DISSOCIATION HEAT.)
  UF   energy of dissociation
  BT1   energy
  RT   dissociation
  RT   formation heat
  RT   molecular structure

DISSOCIATION HEAT [196; 196]
  UF   heat of dissociation
  BT1   reaction heat
    BT2   enthalpy
      BT3   thermodynamic properties
        BT4   physical properties
  RT   dissociation
  RT   formation heat

DISSOLUTION [3,217; 9,811]
  NT1   leaching
  RT   fractionation
  RT   solubility
  RT   solutes
  RT   solutions
  RT   solvent extraction
  RT   solvents

DISSOLVED GASES [122; 122] Oct 83
  BT1   gases
    BT2   fluids
  BT1   solutes
  RT   deaerators
  RT   reactor cooling systems
  RT   water pollution
  RT   water treatment

dissolved liquids
  USE   solutes

dissolved solids
   USE   solutes

DISTANCE [2,790; 9,726]
- NT1   interaction range
- NT1   interatomic distances
- RT   automation
- RT   dimensions
- RT   manipulators
- RT   radiation protection
- RT   range
- RT   remote handling
- RT   shielding
- RT   thickness

DISTILLATION [1,219; 1,219]
- UF+   *solar distillation*
- BT1   separation processes
- RT   azeotrope
- RT   chloride volatility process
- RT   demineralization
- RT   desalination
- RT   distillation equipment
- RT   evaporation
- RT   evaporators
- RT   flash heating
- RT   fluoride volatility process
- RT   fractionation
- RT   petroleum
- RT   petroleum refineries
- RT   volatility

DISTILLATION EQUIPMENT [50; 50]
Dec 85
- BT1   equipment
- RT   distillation
- RT   petroleum refineries

distorted wave born approximat
   USE   dwba

DISTORTED WAVE THEORY
[1,778; 1,778]
- RT   dwba
- RT   nuclear reaction kinetics

§§ **DISTRIBUTION** [13,717; 85,101]
(For energy distribution use ENERGY SPECTRA.)
- UF+   *inclusive distribution*
- NT1   angular distribution
- NT1   spatial distribution
- NT2   mass distribution
- NT2   power distribution
- NT2   spatial dose distributions
- NT3   depth dose distributions
- NT1   subcellular distribution
- NT1   tissue distribution
- RT   allocations
- RT   anisotropy
- RT   asymmetry
- RT   boltzmann statistics
- RT   gauss function
- RT   gaussian processes
- RT   isotropy
- RT   particle kinematics
- RT   symmetry

distribution constants
   USE   distribution functions

distribution factor (rad doses
   USE   spatial dose distributions

DISTRIBUTION FUNCTIONS
[11,654; 11,654]
- UF   *distribution constants*
- RT   ion exchange
- RT   ion exchange chromatography
- RT   plasma
- RT   solvent extraction

DISTRICT HEATING [1,196; 1,196]
- BT1   heating
- RT   boilers
- RT   cogeneration
- RT   dual-purpose power plants
- RT   heat transfer
- RT   power transmission
- RT   process heat
- RT   slowpoke-wnre reactor
- RT   space heating
- RT   steam
- RT   thermal power plants
- RT   waste heat

district of columbia
   USE   washington dc

DISTURBANCES [5,002; 5,457]
- UF   *perturbations*
- NT1   ionospheric storms
- NT2   sudden ionospheric disturbance
- NT2   travelling ionospheric disturb
- RT   magnetic storms
- RT   modifications
- RT   oscillations
- RT   pulsations
- RT   variations

DISULFIDES [146; 275]
- BT1   organic sulfur compounds
- BT2   organic compounds
- NT1   cystine
- NT1   thioctic acid

disulfodiphenylpicrylhydrazyl
   USE   sdpph

DITE TOKAMAK [152; 152] *Jul 81*
- BT1   tokamak devices
- BT2   closed plasma devices
- BT3   thermonuclear devices

DITHIOLS [123; 180]
- UF   *dimercaptoethane*
- UF   *1,2-ethanedithiol*
- BT1   reagents
- BT1   thiols
- BT2   organic sulfur compounds
- BT3   organic compounds
- NT1   bal
- NT1   unithiol

DITHIZONE [122; 122]
- UF   *diphenylthiocarbazone*
- BT1   carbazones
- BT2   carbonic acid derivatives
- BT3   organic compounds
- BT2   organic nitrogen compounds
- BT3   organic compounds
- BT1   chelating agents
- BT1   organic sulfur compounds
- BT2   organic compounds
- BT1   reagents

DIURETICS [156; 369]
- BT1   drugs
- NT1   chlorothiazide
- NT1   neohydrin
- NT1   theobromine
- NT1   theophylline
- RT   edema
- RT   urine

diurnal variation
   USE   daily variations

diva tokamak
   USE   jft-2a tokamak

divergences (infrared)
   USE   infrared divergences

divergences (ultraviolet)
   USE   ultraviolet divergences

DIVERTORS [1,970; 2,629]
- NT1   bundle divertors
- NT1   poloidal field divertors
- NT1   toroidal field divertors
- RT   exhaust systems
- RT   h-mode plasma confinement
- RT   magnetic field configurations
- RT   magnetic surfaces
- RT   plasma impurities
- RT   stellarators
- RT   tokamak devices

DIVINYLBENZENE [19; 19] *Jun 82*
- BT1   aromatics
- BT2   organic compounds
- BT1   hydrocarbons
- BT2   organic compounds

djakarta irt-2000 reactor
   USE   irt-2000 djakarta reactor

dmba
   USE   dimethylbenzanthracene

DME [25; 25]
- UF   *1,2-dimethoxyethane*
- BT1   ethers
- BT2   organic oxygen compounds
- BT3   organic compounds
- RT   organic solvents

DMSO [780; 780]
- UF   *dimethyl sulfoxide*
- BT1   sulfoxides
- BT2   organic sulfur compounds
- BT3   organic compounds

DMTR REACTOR [13; 13]
- UF   *dounreay mater. testing react.*
- BT1   enriched uranium reactors
- BT2   reactors
- BT1   heavy water cooled reactors
- BT2   reactors
- BT1   heavy water moderated reactors
- BT2   reactors
- BT1   isotope production reactors
- BT2   irradiation reactors
- BT3   reactors
- BT1   materials testing reactors
- BT2   irradiation reactors
- BT3   reactors
- BT1   research reactors
- BT2   research and test reactors
- BT3   reactors
- BT1   tank type reactors
- BT2   reactors
- BT1   thermal reactors
- BT2   reactors

DNA [10,386; 10,997]
- UF   *deoxypentose nucleic acid*
- UF   *deoxyribonucleic acid*
- UF   *desoxyribonucleic acid*
- BT1   nucleic acids
- BT2   organic compounds
- NT1   recombinant dna
- RT   chromosomes
- RT   dna adducts
- RT   dna polymerases
- RT   dna repair
- RT   dna replication
- RT   dna sequencing
- RT   dna-ase
- RT   dna-cloning
- RT   feulgen method
- RT   gene operons
- RT   genetic engineering
- RT   helical configuration
- RT   host-cell reactivation
- RT   human chromosomes
- RT   nucleosomes
- RT   strand breaks

DNA ADDUCTS [313; 313] *Apr 84*
- BT1 adducts
- RT carcinogenesis
- RT carcinogens
- RT chemical bonds
- RT dna
- RT metabolism
- RT metabolites
- RT mutagenesis
- RT mutagens
- RT radiomimetic drugs

DNA POLYMERASES [280; 280] *Jun 84*
- BT1 polymerases
- BT2 nucleotidyltransferases
- BT3 phosphorus-group transferases
- BT4 transferases
- BT5 enzymes
- BT6 organic compounds
- RT dna
- RT dna repair
- RT genes
- RT rna polymerases
- RT transcription

DNA REPAIR [1,734; 1,734] *Apr 84*
- UF *dark repair*
- UF *excision repair*
- BT1 biological repair
- BT2 biological recovery
- RT chromosomes
- RT dna
- RT dna polymerases
- RT human chromosomes
- RT pyrimidine dimers
- RT strand breaks

DNA REPLICATION [1,477; 1,477]
- BT1 nucleic acid replication
- RT cell cycle
- RT dna
- RT dna-cloning
- RT transcription

DNA SEQUENCING [972; 972] *Dec 84*
- BT1 structural chemical analysis
- RT dna
- RT molecular structure
- RT nucleic acid denaturation
- RT nucleotides
- RT strand breaks

DNA-ASE [254; 284]
- UF *deoxyribonuclease*
- UF *nuclease (deoxyribonuclease)*
- BT1 nucleases
- BT2 phosphodiesterases
- BT3 esterases
- BT4 hydrolases
- BT5 enzymes
- BT6 organic compounds
- RT dna

DNA-CLONING [496; 496] *Oct 77*
- BT1 cloning
- RT dna
- RT dna replication
- RT transposons

dnb
- USE departure nucleate boiling

dnp
- USE dinitrophenol

DOCA [9; 9]
- UF *desoxycorticosterone acetate*
- BT1 mineralocorticoids
- BT2 corticosteroids
- BT3 adrenal hormones
- BT4 hormones
- BT3 hydroxy compounds
- BT4 organic compounds
- BT3 ketones

- BT4 organic compounds
- BT3 pregnanes
- BT4 steroids
- BT5 organic compounds
- BT3 steroid hormones
- BT4 hormones

document retrieval
- USE information retrieval

DOCUMENT TYPES [396; 46,102]
(See scope note for each of the descriptors below for its proper usage.)
- NT1 bibliographies
- NT1 indexes
- NT1 lectures
- NT1 manuals
- NT1 regulatory guides
- NT1 reviews
- RT abstracts
- RT environmental impact statement
- RT patents
- RT proceedings
- RT safety reports

DOCUMENTATION [1,819; 1,819]
(The assembling, coding, and disseminating of recorded knowledge.)
- RT data compilation
- RT information retrieval
- RT information systems
- RT reporting requirements

DODECANE [329; 329]
- BT1 alkanes
- BT2 hydrocarbons
- BT3 organic compounds

DODECANOIC ACID [49; 49]
- UF *lauric acid*
- BT1 monocarboxylic acids
- BT2 carboxylic acids
- BT3 organic acids
- BT4 organic compounds

DODECYL RADICALS [38; 38]
- UF *lauryl radicals*
- BT1 alkyl radicals
- BT2 radicals

DODEWAARD REACTOR [114; 114]
(Dodewaard, Gelderland, Netherlands)
- UF *gkn reactor (dodewaard)*
- BT1 bwr type reactors
- BT2 enriched uranium reactors
- BT3 reactors
- BT2 power reactors
- BT3 reactors
- BT2 thermal reactors
- BT3 reactors
- BT2 water cooled reactors
- BT3 reactors
- BT2 water moderated reactors
- BT3 reactors

DOEL-1 REACTOR [43; 43]
(Doel-Beveren, Flandre, Belgium)
- BT1 pwr type reactors
- BT2 enriched uranium reactors
- BT3 reactors
- BT2 power reactors
- BT3 reactors
- BT2 thermal reactors
- BT3 reactors
- BT2 water cooled reactors
- BT3 reactors
- BT2 water moderated reactors
- BT3 reactors

DOEL-2 REACTOR [50; 50]
(Doel-Beveren, Flandre, Belgium)
- BT1 pwr type reactors
- BT2 enriched uranium reactors
- BT3 reactors
- BT2 power reactors

- BT3 reactors
- BT2 thermal reactors
- BT3 reactors
- BT2 water cooled reactors
- BT3 reactors
- BT2 water moderated reactors
- BT3 reactors

DOEL-3 REACTOR [41; 41] *Sep 77*
(Doel-Beveren, Flandre, Belgium)
- BT1 pwr type reactors
- BT2 enriched uranium reactors
- BT3 reactors
- BT2 power reactors
- BT3 reactors
- BT2 thermal reactors
- BT3 reactors
- BT2 water cooled reactors
- BT3 reactors
- BT2 water moderated reactors
- BT3 reactors

DOEL-4 REACTOR [21; 21] *May 81*
(Doel-Beveren, Flandre, belgium)
- BT1 pwr type reactors
- BT2 enriched uranium reactors
- BT3 reactors
- BT2 power reactors
- BT3 reactors
- BT2 thermal reactors
- BT3 reactors
- BT2 water cooled reactors
- BT3 reactors
- BT2 water moderated reactors
- BT3 reactors

DOGS [3,648; 4,992]
- BT1 mammals
- BT2 vertebrates
- BT3 animals
- NT1 beagles

dolantal
- USE pethidine

DOLLARS [7; 7]
- BT1 reactivity units

DOLOMITE [257; 257]
- BT1 carbonate minerals
- BT2 minerals
- RT calcite
- RT calcium carbonates
- RT limestone
- RT magnesium carbonates

dolomite rock
- USE limestone

→ *dolphins*
- USE cetaceans

DOMAIN STRUCTURE [2,144; 2,364]
- UF *landau domain structure*
- NT1 bloch wall
- RT magnetic properties

DOMESTIC ANIMALS [225; 4,893]
- UF *farm animals*
- UF *livestock*
- BT1 animals
- NT1 cattle
- NT2 calves
- NT2 cows
- NT1 goats
- NT1 sheep
- NT1 swine
- NT2 miniature swine
- RT agriculture
- RT animal breeding
- RT buffalo
- RT rearing
- RT screwworm fly

DOMESTIC SAFEGUARDS [226; 226]
BT1 safeguards

DOMESTIC SUPPLIES [28; 28] *Jul 86*
(Goods whose source country is the same as the place of use, i.e. native goods not requiring import from another country.)
RT availability
RT gross national product
RT market
RT trade

domestic wastes
(Prior to August 1985 this was a valid descriptor.)
USE municipal wastes

DOMINANT MUTATIONS [188; 188]
BT1 mutations

DOMINIC PROJECT [2; 12]
UF *project dominic*
NT1 starfish event
NT1 swordfish event
RT atmospheric explosions
RT nuclear explosions
RT underwater explosions

DOMINICAN REPUBLIC [5; 5]
BT1 developing countries
BT1 latin america
BT1 west indies
BT2 islands

donald c. cook-1 reactor
USE cook-1 reactor

donald c. cook-2 reactor
USE cook-2 reactor

DONNAN THEORY [6; 6]
RT diffusion
RT electrolytes
RT osmosis

DOORS [159; 159]
BT1 openings

DOPA [162; 162]
UF *3,4-dihydroxyphenylalanine*
BT1 amino acids
BT2 carboxylic acids
BT3 organic acids
BT4 organic compounds
BT1 hydroxy acids
BT2 carboxylic acids
BT3 organic acids
BT4 organic compounds
BT1 neuroregulators
BT2 autonomic nervous system agent
BT3 drugs
RT dopamine
RT phenylalanine

DOPAMINE [849; 849]
BT1 amines
BT2 organic compounds
BT1 cardiotonics
BT2 cardiovascular agents
BT3 drugs
BT1 neuroregulators
BT2 autonomic nervous system agent
BT3 drugs
BT1 polyphenols
BT2 phenols
BT3 aromatics
BT4 organic compounds
BT3 hydroxy compounds
BT4 organic compounds
BT1 sympathomimetics

BT2 autonomic nervous system agent
BT3 drugs
RT dopa
RT pyrocatechol

DOPED MATERIALS [7,043; 7,043]
BT1 materials
RT bromine additions
RT chlorine additions
RT crystal doping
RT fluorine additions
RT iodine additions
RT ion implantation
RT trace amounts

doping (crystal)
USE crystal doping

DOPPLER BROADENING [1,220; 1,220]
BT1 line broadening
RT doppler coefficient
RT doppler effect

DOPPLER COEFFICIENT [285; 285]
BT1 reactivity coefficients
RT doppler broadening
RT temperature coefficient

DOPPLER EFFECT [3,389; 3,389]
RT doppler broadening
RT dsa method
RT red shift
RT spectral shift

doppler shift attenuation meth
USE dsa method

DORIS STORAGE RING [318; 318]
BT1 storage rings

DOSE COMMITMENTS [962; 962]
RT delayed radiation effects
RT internal irradiation
RT life span
RT medical surveillance
RT radiation doses
RT radionuclide kinetics

dose distributions
USE radiation dose distributions

DOSE EQUIVALENTS [3,608; 3,608]
UF+ *rem*
UF+ *roentgen equivalent man*
RT let
RT quality factor
RT radiation doses
RT tissue-equivalent detectors

dose fractionation
USE fractionated irradiation

DOSE LIMITS [1,784; 1,784]
BT1 safety standards
BT2 standards
RT maximum permissible dose
RT radiation doses
RT unscear

DOSE RATEMETERS [337; 337]
UF *ratemeters (dose)*
RT dosimetry

DOSE RATES [10,029; 10,029]
RT low dose irradiation
RT pulsed irradiation
RT radiation doses
RT radiation effects
RT temporal dose distributions
RT time dependence

dose reduction factor
USE efficiency
AND radioprotective substances

dose relative factor
USE efficiency
AND radioprotective substances

DOSE-RESPONSE RELATIONSHIPS
[17,248; 17,248]
RT acute exposure
RT biological effects
RT biological indicators
RT fractionated irradiation
RT lethal irradiation
RT low dose irradiation
RT radiation dose distributions
RT radiation doses
RT radiation effects
RT radiosensitivity
RT sublethal irradiation
RT supralethal irradiation
RT survival curves
RT toxicity

DOSEMETERS [2,408; 9,213]
UF *dosimeters*
UF *radiation dosemeters*
BT1 measuring instruments
NT1 albedo-neutron dosemeters
NT1 biological dosemeters
NT1 bragg gray chambers
NT1 calorimetric dosemeters
NT1 chemical dosemeters
NT1 colorimetric dosemeters
NT1 condenser ionization chambers
NT1 exoelectron dosemeters
NT1 extrapolation chambers
NT1 luminescent dosemeters
NT2 rpl dosemeters
NT2 thermoluminescent dosemeters
NT1 photographic film dosemeters
NT1 ritac dosemeters
NT1 ritad dosemeters
RT dosimetry
RT radiation detection
RT radiation detectors
RT radiation doses
RT radiation monitoring
RT radiation monitors
RT scintillation counters
RT semiconductor detectors

doses (lethal)
USE lethal doses

doses (radiation)
USE radiation doses

dosimeters
USE dosemeters

DOSIMETRY [6,157; 18,749]
UF *radiation dosimetry*
NT1 alpha dosimetry
NT1 beta dosimetry
NT1 electron dosimetry
NT1 film dosimetry
NT1 gamma dosimetry
NT1 ion dosimetry
NT1 microdosimetry
NT1 neutron dosimetry
NT1 personnel dosimetry
NT1 pion dosimetry
NT1 proton dosimetry
NT1 thermoluminescent dosimetry
NT1 x-ray dosimetry
RT dose ratemeters
RT dosemeters
RT icru
RT lyoluminescence
RT measuring methods
RT radiation detection
RT radiation dose units

RT radiation doses
RT radiation monitoring
RT radiation protection
RT radiations
RT ssdl

DOUBLE BETA DECAY [679; 679]
Jun 83
(Decay (A,Z) yields (A,Z+2), and related reactions.)
BT1 beta-minus decay
BT2 beta decay
BT3 nuclear decay
BT4 decay

DOUBLE BONDS [105; 105]
BT1 chemical bonds
RT binding energy

double focusing spectrometers
USE flat magnetic spectrometers

DOUBLE LABELLING [474; 474]
BT1 labelling
RT labelled compounds

DOUBLE RESONANCE METHODS [320; 320] *Mar 77*
(Simultaneous excitation of two resonance transitions of different frequencies increasing the sensitivity of high frequency spectroscopy.)
RT absorption spectroscopy
RT eldor
RT electron spin resonance
RT endor
RT nuclear magnetic resonance
RT optical pumping
RT zeeman effect

DOUBLET-1 DEVICE [4; 4]
(Quadrupolar configuration)
BT1 tokamak devices
BT2 closed plasma devices
BT3 thermonuclear devices

DOUBLET-2 DEVICE [47; 47]
(Octupolar configuration)
BT1 tokamak devices
BT2 closed plasma devices
BT3 thermonuclear devices

DOUBLET-3 DEVICE [819; 819] *May 76*
BT1 tokamak devices
BT2 closed plasma devices
BT3 thermonuclear devices

DOUGLAS POINT ONTARIO REACTOR [178; 178]
UF *candu reactor*
UF *douglas point power station*
BT1 candu type reactors
BT2 heavy water moderated reactors
BT3 reactors
BT2 pressure tube reactors
BT3 power reactors
BT4 reactors
BT2 thermal reactors
BT3 reactors
BT1 natural uranium reactors
BT2 reactors
BT1 phwr type reactors
BT2 heavy water cooled reactors
BT3 reactors
BT2 heavy water moderated reactors
BT3 reactors

douglas point power station
USE douglas point ontario reactor

DOUGLAS POINT-1 REACTOR [27; 27]
(Nanjamoy, Maryland, USA)
BT1 bwr type reactors
BT2 enriched uranium reactors
BT3 reactors
BT2 power reactors
BT3 reactors
BT2 thermal reactors
BT3 reactors
BT2 water cooled reactors
BT3 reactors
BT2 water moderated reactors
BT3 reactors

DOUGLAS POINT-2 REACTOR [26; 26]
(Nanjamoy, Maryland, USA)
BT1 bwr type reactors
BT2 enriched uranium reactors
BT3 reactors
BT2 power reactors
BT3 reactors
BT2 thermal reactors
BT3 reactors
BT2 water cooled reactors
BT3 reactors
BT2 water moderated reactors
BT3 reactors

dounreay fast reactor
USE dfr reactor

dounreay mater. testing react.
USE dmtr reactor

dounreay prototype fast r.
USE pfr reactor

dow chemical triga-mk-1 react.
USE dow triga-mk-1 reactor

DOW TRIGA-MK-1 REACTOR [2; 2]
(Midland, Michigan, USA)
UF *dow chemical triga-mk-1 react.*
BT1 isotope production reactors
BT2 irradiation reactors
BT3 reactors
BT1 research reactors
BT2 research and test reactors
BT3 reactors
BT1 thermal reactors
BT2 reactors
BT1 training reactors
BT2 research and test reactors
BT3 reactors
BT1 triga type reactors
BT2 enriched uranium reactors
BT3 reactors
BT2 hydride moderated reactors
BT3 reactors
BT2 research and test reactors
BT3 reactors
BT2 solid homogeneous reactors
BT3 homogeneous reactors
BT4 reactors
BT2 water cooled reactors
BT3 reactors
BT2 water moderated reactors
BT3 reactors

dowex
USE organic ion exchangers

DOWNS SYNDROME [86; 86]
UF *mongolism*
BT1 congenital diseases
BT2 diseases
BT1 congenital malformations
BT2 malformations
BT3 pathological changes
BT4 diseases
RT chromosomal aberrations

DOXORUBICIN [310; 310] *Nov 80*
UF *adriamycin*
BT1 antibiotics
BT2 drugs
BT2 organic compounds
BT1 antineoplastic drugs
BT2 drugs
RT mutagenesis

dpa
(Displacements per atom.)
USE atomic displacements

DPCA [14; 14]
UF *diphenylcarbazides*
BT1 carbonic acid derivatives
BT2 organic compounds
BT1 organic nitrogen compounds
BT2 organic compounds

dpo
(Diphenylphosphine oxide)
USE organic phosphorus compounds

DPP COMPUTERS [0; 0]
BT1 computers

DPPH [41; 41]
UF *diphenylpicrylhydrazyl*
BT1 nitro compounds
BT2 organic nitrogen compounds
BT3 organic compounds
BT1 radicals
RT hydrazine

DPSO [33; 33]
UF *diamyl sulfoxide*
UF *dipentyl sulfoxide*
BT1 sulfoxides
BT2 organic sulfur compounds
BT3 organic compounds

DR-1 REACTOR [3; 3]
(Risoe National Lab., Roskilde, Denmark)
UF *danish reactor-1*
BT1 aqueous homogeneous reactors
BT2 liquid homogeneous reactors
BT3 fluid fueled reactors
BT4 reactors
BT3 homogeneous reactors
BT4 reactors
BT2 water cooled reactors
BT3 reactors
BT2 water moderated reactors
BT3 reactors
BT1 enriched uranium reactors
BT2 reactors
BT1 research reactors
BT2 research and test reactors
BT3 reactors
BT1 thermal reactors
BT2 reactors
BT1 training reactors
BT2 research and test reactors
BT3 reactors

DR-2 REACTOR [4; 4]
(Risoe National Lab., Roskilde, Denmark)
UF *danish reactor-2*
BT1 enriched uranium reactors
BT2 reactors
BT1 isotope production reactors
BT2 irradiation reactors
BT3 reactors
BT1 pool type reactors
BT2 water cooled reactors
BT3 reactors
BT2 water moderated reactors
BT3 reactors
BT1 research reactors
BT2 research and test reactors
BT3 reactors
BT1 thermal reactors
BT2 reactors

DR-3 REACTOR [31; 31]
(Risoe National Lab., Roskilde, Denmark)
- UF   *danish reactor-3*
- BT1 enriched uranium reactors
  - BT2 reactors
- BT1 heavy water cooled reactors
  - BT2 reactors
- BT1 heavy water moderated reactors
  - BT2 reactors
- BT1 isotope production reactors
  - BT2 irradiation reactors
    - BT3 reactors
- BT1 materials testing reactors
  - BT2 irradiation reactors
    - BT3 reactors
- BT1 research reactors
  - BT2 research and test reactors
    - BT3 reactors
- BT1 tank type reactors
  - BT2 reactors
- BT1 thermal reactors
  - BT2 reactors

DRAG [439; 439]
- UF   *drag coefficient*
- RT   fluid mechanics

drag coefficient
- USE   drag

drag effect
- USE   electrophoresis

DRAGON REACTOR [124; 124]
- BT1 enriched uranium reactors
  - BT2 reactors
- BT1 experimental reactors
  - BT2 research and test reactors
    - BT3 reactors
- BT1 helium cooled reactors
  - BT2 gas cooled reactors
    - BT3 reactors
- BT1 htgr type reactors
  - BT2 gas cooled reactors
    - BT3 reactors
  - BT2 graphite moderated reactors
    - BT3 reactors
- BT1 power reactors
  - BT2 reactors
- BT1 thermal reactors
  - BT2 reactors
- BT1 thorium reactors
  - BT2 reactors

DRAINAGE [350; 350] *Aug 84*
- RT   condensates
- RT   floods
- RT   fluid flow
- RT   hydrology
- RT   rivers
- RT   settling ponds
- RT   waste water

DRAWING [318; 318]
- BT1 materials working
  - BT2 fabrication
- RT   cold working

→ **DREDGE SPOIL** [0; 0] *Oct 91*
- RT   dredging
- RT   sediments
- RT   solid wastes

→ **DREDGING** [0; 0] *Oct 91*
- RT   dredge spoil
- RT   excavation

DRELL MODEL [735; 735]
- RT   photoproduction

DRESDEN-1 REACTOR [174; 174]
(Morris, Illinois, USA)
- BT1 bwr type reactors
  - BT2 enriched uranium reactors
    - BT3 reactors
  - BT2 power reactors
    - BT3 reactors
  - BT2 thermal reactors
    - BT3 reactors
  - BT2 water cooled reactors
    - BT3 reactors
  - BT2 water moderated reactors
    - BT3 reactors

DRESDEN-2 REACTOR [190; 190]
(Morris, Illinois, USA)
- BT1 bwr type reactors
  - BT2 enriched uranium reactors
    - BT3 reactors
  - BT2 power reactors
    - BT3 reactors
  - BT2 thermal reactors
    - BT3 reactors
  - BT2 water cooled reactors
    - BT3 reactors
  - BT2 water moderated reactors
    - BT3 reactors

DRESDEN-3 REACTOR [149; 149]
(Morris, Illinois, USA)
- BT1 bwr type reactors
  - BT2 enriched uranium reactors
    - BT3 reactors
  - BT2 power reactors
    - BT3 reactors
  - BT2 thermal reactors
    - BT3 reactors
  - BT2 water cooled reactors
    - BT3 reactors
  - BT2 water moderated reactors
    - BT3 reactors

drf
(Dose Reduction Factor.)
- USE   efficiency
- AND   radioprotective substances

drift (electron)
- USE   electron drift

drift (ion)
- USE   ion drift

drift (plasma)
- USE   plasma drift

DRIFT CHAMBERS [2,320; 2,372]
- UF   *multiwire drift chambers*
- BT1 multiwire proportional chamber
  - BT2 proportional counters
    - BT3 radiation detectors
      - BT4 measuring instruments
- NT1 time projection chambers

DRIFT INSTABILITY [1,658; 1,658]
- BT1 plasma instability
  - BT2 instability
- RT   plasma drift

DRIFT TUBES [805; 805]
- RT   linear accelerators

DRILL BITS [39; 39] *Mar 76*
- BT1 tools
  - BT2 equipment
- RT   machine tools
- RT   materials drilling

DRILL CORES [770; 770]
- UF   *cores (drill)*
- RT   well logging

→ **DRILLING** [0; 10] *Aug 91*
- NT1 rock drilling
- RT   drilling fluids

drilling (materials)
- USE   materials drilling

drilling (rock)
- USE   rock drilling

→ **DRILLING FLUIDS** [0; 0] *Oct 91*
(Limited to materials used in well drilling.)
- UF   *drilling mud*
- BT1 fluids
- RT   drilling
- RT   suspensions

→ *drilling mud*
- USE   drilling fluids

DRINKING WATER [1,585; 1,585]
- BT1 water
  - BT2 hydrogen compounds
  - BT2 oxygen compounds
- RT   beverages
- RT   diet
- RT   food
- RT   fresh water
- RT   ingestion

DROPLET MODEL [243; 243]
- BT1 nuclear models
  - BT2 mathematical models

DROPLETS [1,333; 1,333]
- BT1 particles
- RT   aerosols
- RT   atmospheric precipitations
- RT   atomization
- RT   liquids
- RT   particle size
- RT   rain
- RT   spray cooling
- RT   sprays
- RT   washout

DROPWISE CONDENSATION [37; 37]
- BT1 vapor condensation

DROSOPHILA [649; 649]
- BT1 fruit flies
  - BT2 flies
    - BT3 insects
      - BT4 arthropods
        - BT5 invertebrates
          - BT6 animals

DRUG ABUSE [17; 17] *May 88*
- RT   drugs
- RT   health hazards
- RT   human factors
- RT   man-machine systems
- RT   occupational safety

DRUGS [2,281; 40,605]
- UF   *medicines*
- UF   *pharmaceuticals*
- UF   *therapeutic agents*
- NT1 antiandrogens
- NT1 antibiotics
  - NT2 actinomycin
  - NT2 antimycin
  - NT2 bleomycin
  - NT2 chloramphenicol
  - NT2 cinchonine
  - NT2 cycloheximide
  - NT2 doxorubicin
  - NT2 erythromycin

NT2	fudr		NT3	tyramine		NT4	fibrinolysin
NT2	isoniazid		NT1	cardiovascular agents		NT4	folic acid
NT3	iproniazid		NT2	antihypertensive agents		NT4	intrinsic factor
NT2	methylene blue		NT3	guanethidine		NT4	kallikrein
NT2	mitomycin		NT3	reserpine		NT4	plasminogen
NT2	neocarcinostatin		NT2	cardiotonics		NT4	protamines
NT2	pas		NT3	adrenaline		NT5	salmin
NT2	penicillin		NT3	digitalis glycosides		NT4	prothrombin
NT2	puromycin		NT4	digitoxin		NT4	thrombin
NT2	quinine		NT4	digoxin		NT4	thromboplastin
NT2	streptomycin		NT3	dopamine		NT4	urokinase
NT2	sulfonamides		NT3	noradrenaline		NT4	vitamin b-12
NT3	sulfadiazine		NT3	ouabain		NT4	vitamin k
NT2	tetracyclines		NT2	vasoconstrictors		NT1	lipotropic factors
NT3	chlortetracycline		NT3	angiotensin		NT2	betaine
NT3	oxytetracycline		NT3	ephedrine		NT2	choline
NT2	valinomycin		NT2	vasodilators		NT2	ethionine
NT1	antihistaminics		NT3	theobromine		NT2	inositol
NT1	antimetabolites		NT3	theophylline		NT2	methionine
NT2	adenines		NT1	central nervous system agents		NT2	phytic acid
NT3	kinetin		NT2	analeptics		NT2	thioctic acid
NT2	aminopterin		NT3	amphetamines		NT1	radiomimetic drugs
NT2	bromouracils		NT4	benzedrine		NT2	neocarcinostatin
NT3	budr		NT3	caffeine		NT1	radiopharmaceuticals
NT2	deoxyuridine		NT2	central nervous system depress		NT1	radioprotective substances
NT2	ethionine		NT3	analgesics		NT2	aet
NT2	fluorodeoxyglucose		NT4	acetylsalicylic acid		NT2	bal
NT2	fluorouracils		NT4	antipyrine		NT2	bufotenine
NT3	fudr		NT4	codeine		NT2	cystamine
NT2	iodouracils		NT4	heroin		NT2	cystaphos
NT3	iododeoxyuridine		NT4	morphine		NT2	dianabol
NT2	mercaptopurine		NT4	pethidine		NT2	dtpa
NT2	methotrexate		NT4	thebaine		NT2	gammaphos
NT2	thiouracil		NT3	anesthetics		NT2	glutathione
NT1	antimitotic drugs		NT4	barbiturates		NT2	hydroxytryptophan
NT2	actinomycin		NT5	amytal		NT2	kallikrein
NT2	alkylating agents		NT5	nembutal		NT2	mea
NT3	endoxan		NT5	phenobarbital		NT2	meg
NT3	myleran		NT5	thiopental		NT2	mercaptopropylamine
NT3	nitrogen mustard		NT4	cocaine		NT2	mexamine
NT2	aminopterin		NT4	procaine		NT2	mpg
NT2	bleomycin		NT3	anticonvulsants		NT2	penicillamine
NT2	colchicine		NT4	phenobarbital		NT2	royal jelly
NT2	mitomycin		NT3	antipyretics		NT2	serotonin
NT2	nem		NT4	acetylsalicylic acid		NT1	radiosensitizers
NT2	oncovin		NT4	antipyrine		NT2	fudr
NT2	vinblastine		NT4	cinchonine		NT2	metronidazole
NT1	antineoplastic drugs		NT4	colchicine		NT2	misonidazole
NT2	actinomycin		NT4	quinine		NT2	nem
NT2	aminopterin		NT3	hypnotics and sedatives		NT2	triacetoneamine-n-oxyl
NT2	bleomycin		NT4	barbiturates		RT	chelating agents
NT2	doxorubicin		NT5	amytal		RT	chemotherapy
NT2	metronidazole		NT5	nembutal		RT	consumer products
NT2	misonidazole		NT5	phenobarbital		RT	drug abuse
NT2	mitomycin		NT5	thiopental		RT	medical supplies
NT2	neocarcinostatin		NT4	chlorpromazine		RT	medicinal plants
NT2	puromycin		NT4	codeine		RT	mutagens
NT1	antithyroid drugs		NT4	reserpine		RT	ointments
NT2	thiocyanates		NT3	narcotics		RT	pharmacology
NT3	ammonium thiocyanates		NT4	heroin		RT	teratogens
NT2	thiouracil		NT4	methadone hydrochloride		RT	therapy
NT2	thiourea		NT4	morphine		RT	toxicity
NT1	autonomic nervous system agent		NT4	pethidine		RT	vitamins
NT2	neuroregulators		NT4	thebaine		RT	xenobiotics
NT3	acetylcholine		NT2	psychotropic drugs			
NT3	adrenaline		NT3	antidepressants			
NT3	aminobutyric acid		NT4	cocaine			
NT3	dopa		NT4	imipramine			
NT3	dopamine		NT4	iproniazid			
NT3	endorphins		NT3	hallucinogens			
NT4	enkephalins		NT4	bufotenine			
NT3	noradrenaline		NT3	tranquilizers			
NT3	serotonin		NT4	chlorpromazine			
NT2	parasympatholytics		NT4	reserpine			
NT3	atropine		NT1	diuretics			
NT2	parasympathomimetics		NT2	chlorothiazide			
NT3	acetylcholine		NT2	neohydrin			
NT3	eserine		NT2	theobromine			
NT3	pilocarpine		NT2	theophylline			
NT2	sympatholytics		NT1	hematologic agents			
NT3	ergotamine		NT2	anticoagulants			
NT3	reserpine		NT3	coumarin			
NT2	sympathomimetics		NT3	dicumarol			
NT3	adrenaline		NT3	heparin			
NT3	amphetamines		NT3	psoralen			
NT4	benzedrine		NT3	tromexan			
NT3	dopamine		NT2	coagulants			
NT3	ephedrine		NT3	blood coagulation factors			
NT3	noradrenaline		NT4	fibrin			
NT3	serotonin		NT4	fibrinogen			

DRY ASHING [130; 130]
UF *ashing (dry)*
RT combustion
RT sample preparation

DRY STORAGE [693; 693] *Feb 82*
BT1 storage
RT radioactive waste storage
RT spent fuel storage

DRYERS [156; 156] *Oct 76*
UF *dehumidifiers*
RT desiccants
RT drying
RT evaporators

DRYING [777; 828]
UF *solar drying*
NT1 spray drying
RT curing
RT dehydration
RT desiccants
RT dryers
RT evaporation

RT   lyophilization

DRYOUT [804; 804]
- RT   burnout
- RT   heat flux
- RT   hot spots
- RT   rewetting

DSA METHOD [265; 265] *Dec 79*
(Used for the determination of lifetimes of nuclear levels.)
- UF   *doppler shift attenuation meth*
- BT1   counting techniques
- RT   doppler effect
- RT   lifetime

dsnadns
- USE   beryllon

dta
- USE   differential thermal analysis

dto
- USE   deuterium compounds
- AND   heavy water
- AND   tritium compounds

DTPA [3,070; 3,070]
(Diethylenetriaminepentaacetic acid)
- UF   *diethylenetriaminepentaacetic*
- BT1   amino acids
  - BT2   carboxylic acids
    - BT3   organic acids
      - BT4   organic compounds
- BT1   chelating agents
- BT1   radioprotective substances
  - BT2   drugs
  - BT2   response modifying factors

DUAL ABSORPTION MODEL [108; 108]
- BT1   particle models
  - BT2   mathematical models

DUAL CYCLE COOLING SYSTEMS [52; 52]
- UF   *dual-cycle cooling systems*
- BT1   reactor cooling systems
  - BT2   cooling systems
  - BT2   reactor components

DUAL RESONANCE MODEL [823; 823]
- BT1   veneziano model
  - BT2   particle models
    - BT3   mathematical models
- RT   duality

DUAL TEMPERATURE PROCESS [113; 113]
- UF   *gs process*
- BT1   isotope separation
  - BT2   separation processes
- BT1   isotopic exchange
- RT   heavy water
- RT   hydrogen sulfides

dual-cycle cooling systems
- USE   dual cycle cooling systems

DUAL-ISOTOPE SUBTRACTION TEC [454; 454]
- BT1   tracer techniques
  - BT2   isotope applications
- RT   radiopharmaceuticals
- RT   scintiscanning

DUAL-PURPOSE POWER PLANTS [588; 588] *Jan 77*
- BT1   power plants
- RT   cogeneration
- RT   desalination
- RT   desalination plants

- RT   district heating
- RT   power generation
- RT   process heat

DUALITY [2,228; 2,228]
(Correlation between resonance poles and scattering amplitudes.)
- RT   dual resonance model
- RT   scattering amplitudes

DUANE ARNOLD-1 REACTOR [82; 82]
(Palo, Iowa, USA)
- BT1   bwr type reactors
  - BT2   enriched uranium reactors
    - BT3   reactors
  - BT2   power reactors
    - BT3   reactors
  - BT2   thermal reactors
    - BT3   reactors
  - BT2   water cooled reactors
    - BT3   reactors
  - BT2   water moderated reactors
    - BT3   reactors

DUBNA [16; 16]
- BT1   ussr
  - BT2   developed countries
  - BT2   europe

dubna ibr-2 reactor
- USE   ibr-2 reactor

DUBNA SYNCHROCYCLOTRON [225; 225]
- BT1   synchrocyclotrons
  - BT2   cyclic accelerators
    - BT3   accelerators

dubna, jinr
- USE   jinr

DUCKS [68; 68]
- BT1   fowl
  - BT2   birds
    - BT3   vertebrates
      - BT4   animals

DUCTILE-BRITTLE TRANSITIONS [912; 912]
- UF   *brittle-ductile transitions*
- UF   *transitions (ductile-brittle)*
- RT   brittleness
- RT   ductility
- RT   embrittlement
- RT   transition temperature

DUCTILITY [2,647; 2,647]
- BT1   tensile properties
  - BT2   mechanical properties
- RT   ductile-brittle transitions
- RT   plasticity

DUCTS [1,092; 1,092]
- RT   openings
- RT   pipes
- RT   tubes

ducts (tear)
- USE   lacrimal ducts

DUKOVANY V-2 REACTOR [216; 216]
(Dukovany, South Moravia, Czechoslovakia)
- UF   *v-2 reactor (dukovany)*
- BT1   wwer type reactors
  - BT2   pwr type reactors
    - BT3   enriched uranium reactors
      - BT4   reactors
    - BT3   power reactors
      - BT4   reactors
    - BT3   thermal reactors
      - BT4   reactors
    - BT3   water cooled reactors

- BT4   reactors
- BT3   water moderated reactors
  - BT4   reactors

DUMAND PROJECT [85; 85] *Apr 80*
(Deep Underwater Muon And Neutrino Detection Project.)
- RT   acoustic detection
- RT   coordinated research programs
- RT   international cooperation
- RT   muon detection
- RT   neutrino detection
- RT   underwater

DUMONTITE [2; 2]
- BT1   phosphate minerals
  - BT2   minerals
- BT1   uranium minerals
  - BT2   radioactive minerals
    - BT3   minerals
    - BT3   radioactive materials
      - BT4   materials
- RT   lead phosphates
- RT   uranium phosphates

DUNGENESS-A REACTOR [22; 22]
(Dungeness Point, Kent, UK)
- BT1   carbon dioxide cooled reactors
  - BT2   gas cooled reactors
    - BT3   reactors
- BT1   magnox type reactors
  - BT2   gcr type reactors
    - BT3   gas cooled reactors
      - BT4   reactors
    - BT3   graphite moderated reactors
      - BT4   reactors
  - BT2   natural uranium reactors
    - BT3   reactors
  - BT2   power reactors
    - BT3   reactors
- BT1   thermal reactors
  - BT2   reactors

DUNGENESS-B REACTOR [56; 56]
(Romney Marsh, Kent, UK)
- BT1   agr type reactors
  - BT2   enriched uranium reactors
    - BT3   reactors
  - BT2   gas cooled reactors
    - BT3   reactors
  - BT2   graphite moderated reactors
    - BT3   reactors
- BT1   carbon dioxide cooled reactors
  - BT2   gas cooled reactors
    - BT3   reactors
- BT1   power reactors
  - BT2   reactors
- BT1   thermal reactors
  - BT2   reactors

duodenum
- USE   small intestine

DUOPLASMATRONS [449; 449]
- BT1   ion sources
- BT1   plasmatrons
  - BT2   electron tubes

duralumin
- USE   alloy-al95cu4

DURENE [26; 26]
- UF   *1,2,4,5-tetramethylbenzene*
- BT1   aromatics
  - BT2   organic compounds
- BT1   hydrocarbons
  - BT2   organic compounds

DUST COLLECTORS [79; 79] *Oct 76*
- UF   *collectors (dust)*
- RT   dusts
- RT   electrostatic precipitators
- RT   filters
- RT   inertial separators
- RT   scrubbers

RT   separation processes

DUST COOLED REACTORS [1; 1]
BT1   reactors

dust fueled reactors
USE   fluid fueled reactors

DUSTS [1,761; 5,810]
NT1   cosmic dust
RT   aerosols
RT   dispersions
RT   dust collectors
RT   elutriation
RT   filters
RT   inhalation
RT   lunar materials
RT   overburden
RT   particle resuspension
RT   particle size
RT   particles
RT   pneumoconioses
RT   powders
RT   respirators
RT   sedimentation

DWARF STARS [931; 2,880]
BT1   stars
NT1   black dwarf stars
NT1   red dwarf stars
NT1   white dwarf stars
RT   helium burning

DWBA [7,312; 7,312]
UF   *approximation (distorted-wave)*
UF   *distorted wave born approximat*
BT1   born approximation
RT   distorted wave theory
RT   nuclear reaction kinetics
RT   scattering

DYE LASERS [1,117; 1,117]
(Based on transitions between vibrationally broadened electronic states of polyatomic molecules.)
BT1   lasers
BT2   amplifiers
BT3   equipment
RT   chemical lasers

DYES [734; 2,454]
NT1   acridine orange
NT1   alizarin
NT1   azo dyes
NT2   acid chrome dyes
NT2   beryllon
NT2   congo red
NT2   eriochrome dyes
NT2   erioglaucine
NT2   evans blue
NT2   methyl orange
NT2   methyl red
NT2   toluidine blue
NT2   trypan blue
NT1   bromosulfophthalein
NT1   curcumin
NT1   cyanine dyes
NT1   eosin
NT1   fluorescein
NT1   hematoxylin
NT1   indocyanine green
NT1   morin
NT1   murexide
NT1   phthalocyanines
NT1   pyrocatechol violet
NT1   quinizarin
NT1   rhodamines
NT1   rose bengal
NT1   triphenylmethane dyes
NT2   aluminon
NT2   aurin
NT2   methyl violet
NT2   methylthymol blue
NT1   xylenol orange

RT   anthraquinones
RT   carminic acid
RT   chromotropic acid
RT   colorimetric dosemeters
RT   diazo compounds
RT   inks
RT   stains
RT   violanthrone

DYNAMIC FUNCTION STUDIES
[5,129; 5,129] Oct 75
UF   *dynamic studies (biological)*
RT   biological functions
RT   biological markers
RT   equilibrium
RT   flow rate
RT   radionuclide kinetics
RT   sequential scanning
RT   structure-activity relationshi
RT   tracer techniques

DYNAMIC LOADS [3,273; 3,273] Feb 81
UF   *loads (dynamic)*
RT   deformation
RT   mechanical tests
RT   mechanical vibrations
RT   pipe whip
RT   ratcheting
RT   soil-structure interactions
RT   static loads
RT   stresses

DYNAMIC MASS SPECTROMETERS
[39; 338]
UF   *r-f mass spectrometers*
BT1   mass spectrometers
BT2   spectrometers
BT3   measuring instruments
NT1   energy balance mass spectromet
NT1   time-of-flight mass spectromet

DYNAMIC PROGRAMMING [81; 81]
RT   econometrics
RT   linear programming
RT   mathematical models
RT   nonlinear programming
RT   optimization

dynamic studies (biological)
USE   dynamic function studies

dynamical boson-fermion symmet
USE   boson-fermion symmetry

DYNAMICAL GROUPS [197; 2,153]
BT1   symmetry groups
NT1   o groups
RT   boson-fermion symmetry

DYNAMICS [2,775; 7,889]
(Study of the motion of a system of particles under the influence of forces.)
BT1   mechanics
NT1   beam dynamics
NT2   beam bunching
NT2   betatron oscillations
NT2   phase oscillations
NT2   synchrotron oscillations
RT   collisions
RT   kinetics

DYNAMITE [5; 5]
BT1   chemical explosives
BT2   explosives

DYNAMITRONS [94; 94]
BT1   electrostatic accelerators
BT2   accelerators

DYNAMOMETERS [11; 11]
BT1   measuring instruments

DYNODES [125; 125]
RT   electron multipliers

DYONS [337; 337]
(Hypothetical particles endowed with both electric and magnetic charges.)
BT1   postulated particles
BT2   elementary particles

DYSON REPRESENTATION [637; 637]
RT   boson expansion
RT   quantum field theory

DYSPROSIUM [1,302; 1,302]
BT1   rare earths
BT2   metals
BT3   elements

DYSPROSIUM ADDITIONS [166; 166]
(Alloys containing not more than 1% Dy are listed here.)
BT1   rare earth additions
RT   dysprosium alloys
RT   dysprosium compounds

DYSPROSIUM ALLOYS [703; 742]
(Alloys containing more than 1% Dy.)
BT1   rare earth alloys
BT2   alloys
NT1   dysprosium base alloys
RT   dysprosium additions

DYSPROSIUM BASE ALLOYS [36; 36]
BT1   dysprosium alloys
BT2   rare earth alloys
BT3   alloys

DYSPROSIUM BORIDES [40; 40]
BT1   borides
BT2   boron compounds
BT1   dysprosium compounds
BT2   rare earth compounds

DYSPROSIUM BROMIDES [11; 11]
BT1   bromides
BT2   bromine compounds
BT3   halogen compounds
BT2   halides
BT3   halogen compounds
BT1   dysprosium compounds
BT2   rare earth compounds

DYSPROSIUM CARBIDES [21; 21]
BT1   carbides
BT2   carbon compounds
BT1   dysprosium compounds
BT2   rare earth compounds

DYSPROSIUM CHLORIDES [80; 80]
BT1   chlorides
BT2   chlorine compounds
BT3   halogen compounds
BT2   halides
BT3   halogen compounds
BT1   dysprosium compounds
BT2   rare earth compounds

DYSPROSIUM COMPLEXES [363; 363]
BT1   rare earth complexes
BT2   complexes

DYSPROSIUM COMPOUNDS
[534; 1,287]
BT1   rare earth compounds
NT1   dysprosium borides
NT1   dysprosium bromides
NT1   dysprosium carbides
NT1   dysprosium chlorides
NT1   dysprosium fluorides
NT1   dysprosium hydrides
NT1   dysprosium hydroxides
NT1   dysprosium iodides
NT1   dysprosium nitrates
NT1   dysprosium nitrides
NT1   dysprosium oxides

DYSPROSIUM COMPOUNDS

    NT1   dysprosium perchlorates
    NT1   dysprosium phosphates
    NT1   dysprosium phosphides
    NT1   dysprosium selenides
    NT1   dysprosium silicates
    NT1   dysprosium silicides
    NT1   dysprosium sulfates
    NT1   dysprosium sulfides
    NT1   dysprosium tellurides
    NT1   dysprosium tungstates
    RT   dysprosium additions

DYSPROSIUM FLUORIDES [54; 54]
    BT1   dysprosium compounds
    BT2   rare earth compounds
    BT1   fluorides
    BT2   fluorine compounds
    BT3   halogen compounds
    BT2   halides
    BT3   halogen compounds

DYSPROSIUM HYDRIDES [27; 27]
    BT1   dysprosium compounds
    BT2   rare earth compounds
    BT1   hydrides
    BT2   hydrogen compounds

DYSPROSIUM HYDROXIDES [12; 12]
    BT1   dysprosium compounds
    BT2   rare earth compounds
    BT1   hydroxides
    BT2   hydrogen compounds
    BT2   oxygen compounds

DYSPROSIUM IODIDES [16; 16]
    BT1   dysprosium compounds
    BT2   rare earth compounds
    BT1   iodides
    BT2   halides
    BT3   halogen compounds
    BT2   iodine compounds
    BT3   halogen compounds

DYSPROSIUM IONS [165; 165]
    BT1   ions
    BT2   charged particles

DYSPROSIUM ISOTOPES [249; 2,014]
    NT1   dysprosium 141
    NT1   dysprosium 142
    NT1   dysprosium 143
    NT1   dysprosium 144
    NT1   dysprosium 145
    NT1   dysprosium 146
    NT1   dysprosium 147
    NT1   dysprosium 148
    NT1   dysprosium 149
    NT1   dysprosium 150
    NT1   dysprosium 151
    NT1   dysprosium 152
    NT1   dysprosium 153
    NT1   dysprosium 154
    NT1   dysprosium 155
    NT1   dysprosium 156
    NT1   dysprosium 157
    NT1   dysprosium 158
    NT1   dysprosium 159
    NT1   dysprosium 160
    NT1   dysprosium 161
    NT1   dysprosium 162
    NT1   dysprosium 163
    NT1   dysprosium 164
    NT1   dysprosium 165
    NT1   dysprosium 166
    NT1   dysprosium 167
    NT1   dysprosium 168
    NT1   dysprosium 169

DYSPROSIUM NITRATES [21; 21]
    BT1   dysprosium compounds
    BT2   rare earth compounds
    BT1   nitrates
    BT2   nitrogen compounds
    BT2   oxygen compounds

DYSPROSIUM NITRIDES [1; 1]
    BT1   dysprosium compounds
    BT2   rare earth compounds
    BT1   nitrides
    BT2   nitrogen compounds
    BT2   pnictides

DYSPROSIUM OXIDES [373; 373]
    BT1   dysprosium compounds
    BT2   rare earth compounds
    BT1   oxides
    BT2   chalcogenides
    BT2   oxygen compounds

DYSPROSIUM PERCHLORATES [4; 4]
    BT1   dysprosium compounds
    BT2   rare earth compounds
    BT1   perchlorates
    BT2   chlorine compounds
    BT3   halogen compounds
    BT2   oxygen compounds

DYSPROSIUM PHOSPHATES [20; 20]
Oct 75
    BT1   dysprosium compounds
    BT2   rare earth compounds
    BT1   phosphates
    BT2   oxygen compounds
    BT2   phosphorus compounds

→ ### DYSPROSIUM PHOSPHIDES [0; 0]
Sep 91
    BT1   dysprosium compounds
    BT2   rare earth compounds
    BT1   phosphides
    BT2   phosphorus compounds
    BT2   pnictides

DYSPROSIUM SELENIDES [9; 9]
Feb 82
    BT1   dysprosium compounds
    BT2   rare earth compounds
    BT1   selenides
    BT2   chalcogenides
    BT2   selenium compounds

→ ### DYSPROSIUM SILICATES [0; 0]
Sep 91
    BT1   dysprosium compounds
    BT2   rare earth compounds
    BT1   silicates
    BT2   oxygen compounds
    BT2   silicon compounds

DYSPROSIUM SILICIDES [28; 28]
    BT1   dysprosium compounds
    BT2   rare earth compounds
    BT1   silicides
    BT2   silicon compounds

DYSPROSIUM SULFATES [15; 15]
    BT1   dysprosium compounds
    BT2   rare earth compounds
    BT1   sulfates
    BT2   oxygen compounds
    BT2   sulfur compounds

DYSPROSIUM SULFIDES [60; 60]
    BT1   dysprosium compounds
    BT2   rare earth compounds
    BT1   sulfides
    BT2   chalcogenides
    BT2   sulfur compounds

DYSPROSIUM TELLURIDES [6; 6]
Feb 78
    BT1   dysprosium compounds
    BT2   rare earth compounds
    BT1   tellurides
    BT2   chalcogenides
    BT2   tellurium compounds

→ ### DYSPROSIUM TUNGSTATES [0; 0]
Sep 91
    BT1   dysprosium compounds
    BT2   rare earth compounds
    BT1   tungstates
    BT2   oxygen compounds
    BT2   tungsten compounds
    BT3   transition element compounds

DYSPROSIUM 141 [5; 5] *Aug 84*
    BT1   dysprosium isotopes
    BT1   electron capture radioisotopes
    BT2   beta decay radioisotopes
    BT3   radioisotopes
    BT4   isotopes
    BT1   even-odd nuclei
    BT2   nuclei
    BT1   rare earth nuclei
    BT2   intermediate mass nuclei
    BT3   nuclei
    BT1   seconds living radioisotopes
    BT2   radioisotopes
    BT3   isotopes

DYSPROSIUM 142 [4; 4] *Feb 87*
    BT1   dysprosium isotopes
    BT1   even-even nuclei
    BT2   nuclei
    BT1   rare earth nuclei
    BT2   intermediate mass nuclei
    BT3   nuclei
    BT1   seconds living radioisotopes
    BT2   radioisotopes
    BT3   isotopes

DYSPROSIUM 143 [5; 5] *Aug 84*
    BT1   dysprosium isotopes
    BT1   electron capture radioisotopes
    BT2   beta decay radioisotopes
    BT3   radioisotopes
    BT4   isotopes
    BT1   even-odd nuclei
    BT2   nuclei
    BT1   rare earth nuclei
    BT2   intermediate mass nuclei
    BT3   nuclei
    BT1   seconds living radioisotopes
    BT2   radioisotopes
    BT3   isotopes

DYSPROSIUM 144 [7; 7] *Oct 86*
    BT1   dysprosium isotopes
    BT1   electron capture radioisotopes
    BT2   beta decay radioisotopes
    BT3   radioisotopes
    BT4   isotopes
    BT1   even-even nuclei
    BT2   nuclei
    BT1   rare earth nuclei
    BT2   intermediate mass nuclei
    BT3   nuclei
    BT1   seconds living radioisotopes
    BT2   radioisotopes
    BT3   isotopes

DYSPROSIUM 145 [10; 10] *Aug 82*
    BT1   beta-plus decay radioisotopes
    BT2   beta decay radioisotopes
    BT3   radioisotopes
    BT4   isotopes
    BT1   dysprosium isotopes
    BT1   electron capture radioisotopes
    BT2   beta decay radioisotopes
    BT3   radioisotopes
    BT4   isotopes
    BT1   even-odd nuclei
    BT2   nuclei
    BT1   rare earth nuclei
    BT2   intermediate mass nuclei
    BT3   nuclei
    BT1   seconds living radioisotopes
    BT2   radioisotopes
    BT3   isotopes

DYSPROSIUM 146 [21; 21] *Sep 81*
BT1   beta-plus decay radioisotopes
BT2   beta decay radioisotopes
BT3   radioisotopes
BT4   isotopes
BT1   dysprosium isotopes
BT1   even-even nuclei
BT2   nuclei
BT1   rare earth nuclei
BT2   intermediate mass nuclei
BT3   nuclei
BT1   seconds living radioisotopes
BT2   radioisotopes
BT3   isotopes

DYSPROSIUM 147 [52; 52]
BT1   beta-plus decay radioisotopes
BT2   beta decay radioisotopes
BT3   radioisotopes
BT4   isotopes
BT1   dysprosium isotopes
BT1   electron capture radioisotopes
BT2   beta decay radioisotopes
BT3   radioisotopes
BT4   isotopes
BT1   even-odd nuclei
BT2   nuclei
BT1   isomeric transition isotopes
BT2   radioisotopes
BT3   isotopes
BT1   minutes living radioisotopes
BT2   radioisotopes
BT3   isotopes
BT1   rare earth nuclei
BT2   intermediate mass nuclei
BT3   nuclei
BT1   seconds living radioisotopes
BT2   radioisotopes
BT3   isotopes

DYSPROSIUM 148 [87; 87]
BT1   beta-plus decay radioisotopes
BT2   beta decay radioisotopes
BT3   radioisotopes
BT4   isotopes
BT1   dysprosium isotopes
BT1   electron capture radioisotopes
BT2   beta decay radioisotopes
BT3   radioisotopes
BT4   isotopes
BT1   even-even nuclei
BT2   nuclei
BT1   minutes living radioisotopes
BT2   radioisotopes
BT3   isotopes
BT1   rare earth nuclei
BT2   intermediate mass nuclei
BT3   nuclei

DYSPROSIUM 149 [57; 57]
BT1   beta-plus decay radioisotopes
BT2   beta decay radioisotopes
BT3   radioisotopes
BT4   isotopes
BT1   dysprosium isotopes
BT1   electron capture radioisotopes
BT2   beta decay radioisotopes
BT3   radioisotopes
BT4   isotopes
BT1   even-odd nuclei
BT2   nuclei
BT1   isomeric transition isotopes
BT2   radioisotopes
BT3   isotopes
BT1   millisec living radioisotopes
BT2   radioisotopes
BT3   isotopes
BT1   minutes living radioisotopes
BT2   radioisotopes
BT3   isotopes
BT1   rare earth nuclei
BT2   intermediate mass nuclei
BT3   nuclei

DYSPROSIUM 150 [72; 72]
BT1   alpha decay radioisotopes
BT2   radioisotopes
BT3   isotopes
BT1   beta-plus decay radioisotopes
BT2   beta decay radioisotopes
BT3   radioisotopes
BT4   isotopes
BT1   dysprosium isotopes
BT1   electron capture radioisotopes
BT2   beta decay radioisotopes
BT3   radioisotopes
BT4   isotopes
BT1   even-even nuclei
BT2   nuclei
BT1   minutes living radioisotopes
BT2   radioisotopes
BT3   isotopes
BT1   rare earth nuclei
BT2   intermediate mass nuclei
BT3   nuclei

DYSPROSIUM 151 [91; 91]
BT1   alpha decay radioisotopes
BT2   radioisotopes
BT3   isotopes
BT1   beta-plus decay radioisotopes
BT2   beta decay radioisotopes
BT3   radioisotopes
BT4   isotopes
BT1   dysprosium isotopes
BT1   electron capture radioisotopes
BT2   beta decay radioisotopes
BT3   radioisotopes
BT4   isotopes
BT1   even-odd nuclei
BT2   nuclei
BT1   minutes living radioisotopes
BT2   radioisotopes
BT3   isotopes
BT1   rare earth nuclei
BT2   intermediate mass nuclei
BT3   nuclei

DYSPROSIUM 152 [244; 244]
BT1   alpha decay radioisotopes
BT2   radioisotopes
BT3   isotopes
BT1   dysprosium isotopes
BT1   electron capture radioisotopes
BT2   beta decay radioisotopes
BT3   radioisotopes
BT4   isotopes
BT1   even-even nuclei
BT2   nuclei
BT1   hours living radioisotopes
BT2   radioisotopes
BT3   isotopes
BT1   rare earth nuclei
BT2   intermediate mass nuclei
BT3   nuclei

DYSPROSIUM 153 [59; 59]
BT1   alpha decay radioisotopes
BT2   radioisotopes
BT3   isotopes
BT1   beta-plus decay radioisotopes
BT2   beta decay radioisotopes
BT3   radioisotopes
BT4   isotopes
BT1   dysprosium isotopes
BT1   electron capture radioisotopes
BT2   beta decay radioisotopes
BT3   radioisotopes
BT4   isotopes
BT1   even-odd nuclei
BT2   nuclei
BT1   hours living radioisotopes
BT2   radioisotopes
BT3   isotopes
BT1   rare earth nuclei
BT2   intermediate mass nuclei
BT3   nuclei

DYSPROSIUM 154 [82; 82]
BT1   alpha decay radioisotopes
BT2   radioisotopes
BT3   isotopes
BT1   dysprosium isotopes
BT1   even-even nuclei
BT2   nuclei
BT1   rare earth nuclei
BT2   intermediate mass nuclei
BT3   nuclei
BT1   years living radioisotopes
BT2   radioisotopes
BT3   isotopes

DYSPROSIUM 154 TARGET [5; 5]
Sep 77
BT1   targets

DYSPROSIUM 155 [75; 75]
BT1   beta-plus decay radioisotopes
BT2   beta decay radioisotopes
BT3   radioisotopes
BT4   isotopes
BT1   dysprosium isotopes
BT1   electron capture radioisotopes
BT2   beta decay radioisotopes
BT3   radioisotopes
BT4   isotopes
BT1   even-odd nuclei
BT2   nuclei
BT1   hours living radioisotopes
BT2   radioisotopes
BT3   isotopes
BT1   rare earth nuclei
BT2   intermediate mass nuclei
BT3   nuclei

DYSPROSIUM 156 [173; 173]
BT1   dysprosium isotopes
BT1   even-even nuclei
BT2   nuclei
BT1   rare earth nuclei
BT2   intermediate mass nuclei
BT3   nuclei
BT1   stable isotopes
BT2   isotopes

DYSPROSIUM 156 TARGET [24; 24]
Feb 76
BT1   targets

DYSPROSIUM 157 [83; 83]
BT1   dysprosium isotopes
BT1   electron capture radioisotopes
BT2   beta decay radioisotopes
BT3   radioisotopes
BT4   isotopes
BT1   even-odd nuclei
BT2   nuclei
BT1   hours living radioisotopes
BT2   radioisotopes
BT3   isotopes
BT1   rare earth nuclei
BT2   intermediate mass nuclei
BT3   nuclei

DYSPROSIUM 158 [179; 179]
BT1   dysprosium isotopes
BT1   even-even nuclei
BT2   nuclei
BT1   rare earth nuclei
BT2   intermediate mass nuclei
BT3   nuclei
BT1   stable isotopes
BT2   isotopes

DYSPROSIUM 158 TARGET [23; 23]
Sep 75
BT1   targets

DYSPROSIUM 159 [92; 92]
BT1   days living radioisotopes
BT2   radioisotopes
BT3   isotopes
BT1   dysprosium isotopes
BT1   electron capture radioisotopes
BT2   beta decay radioisotopes

BT3 radioisotopes
    BT4 isotopes
BT1 even-odd nuclei
BT2 nuclei
BT1 internal conversion radioisoto
  BT2 radioisotopes
    BT3 isotopes
BT1 rare earth nuclei
  BT2 intermediate mass nuclei
    BT3 nuclei

DYSPROSIUM 160 [237; 237]
BT1 dysprosium isotopes
BT1 even-even nuclei
  BT2 nuclei
BT1 rare earth nuclei
  BT2 intermediate mass nuclei
    BT3 nuclei
BT1 stable isotopes
  BT2 isotopes

DYSPROSIUM 160 TARGET [62; 62]
BT1 targets

DYSPROSIUM 161 [252; 252]
BT1 dysprosium isotopes
BT1 even-odd nuclei
  BT2 nuclei
BT1 rare earth nuclei
  BT2 intermediate mass nuclei
    BT3 nuclei
BT1 stable isotopes
  BT2 isotopes

DYSPROSIUM 161 REACTIONS [3; 3]
Nov 84
BT1 heavy ion reactions
  BT2 nuclear reactions

DYSPROSIUM 161 TARGET [68; 68]
BT1 targets

DYSPROSIUM 162 [194; 194]
BT1 dysprosium isotopes
BT1 even-even nuclei
  BT2 nuclei
BT1 rare earth nuclei
  BT2 intermediate mass nuclei
    BT3 nuclei
BT1 stable isotopes
  BT2 isotopes

DYSPROSIUM 162 TARGET [129; 129]
BT1 targets

DYSPROSIUM 163 [129; 129]
BT1 dysprosium isotopes
BT1 even-odd nuclei
  BT2 nuclei
BT1 rare earth nuclei
  BT2 intermediate mass nuclei
    BT3 nuclei
BT1 stable isotopes
  BT2 isotopes

DYSPROSIUM 163 TARGET [73; 73]
BT1 targets

DYSPROSIUM 164 [190; 190]
BT1 dysprosium isotopes
BT1 even-even nuclei
  BT2 nuclei
BT1 rare earth nuclei
  BT2 intermediate mass nuclei
    BT3 nuclei
BT1 stable isotopes
  BT2 isotopes

DYSPROSIUM 164 TARGET [168; 168]
BT1 targets

DYSPROSIUM 165 [97; 97]
BT1 beta-minus decay radioisotopes
  BT2 beta decay radioisotopes
    BT3 radioisotopes
      BT4 isotopes
BT1 dysprosium isotopes
BT1 even-odd nuclei
  BT2 nuclei
BT1 hours living radioisotopes
  BT2 radioisotopes
    BT3 isotopes
BT1 isomeric transition isotopes
  BT2 radioisotopes
    BT3 isotopes
BT1 minutes living radioisotopes
  BT2 radioisotopes
    BT3 isotopes
BT1 rare earth nuclei
  BT2 intermediate mass nuclei
    BT3 nuclei

DYSPROSIUM 165 TARGET [7; 7]
Aug 81
BT1 targets

DYSPROSIUM 166 [16; 16]
BT1 beta-minus decay radioisotopes
  BT2 beta decay radioisotopes
    BT3 radioisotopes
      BT4 isotopes
BT1 days living radioisotopes
  BT2 radioisotopes
    BT3 isotopes
BT1 dysprosium isotopes
BT1 even-even nuclei
  BT2 nuclei
BT1 rare earth nuclei
  BT2 intermediate mass nuclei
    BT3 nuclei

DYSPROSIUM 167 [4; 4]
BT1 beta-minus decay radioisotopes
  BT2 beta decay radioisotopes
    BT3 radioisotopes
      BT4 isotopes
BT1 dysprosium isotopes
BT1 even-odd nuclei
  BT2 nuclei
BT1 minutes living radioisotopes
  BT2 radioisotopes
    BT3 isotopes
BT1 rare earth nuclei
  BT2 intermediate mass nuclei
    BT3 nuclei

DYSPROSIUM 168 [3; 3] *Aug 82*
BT1 beta-minus decay radioisotopes
  BT2 beta decay radioisotopes
    BT3 radioisotopes
      BT4 isotopes
BT1 dysprosium isotopes
BT1 even-even nuclei
  BT2 nuclei
BT1 minutes living radioisotopes
  BT2 radioisotopes
    BT3 isotopes
BT1 rare earth nuclei
  BT2 intermediate mass nuclei
    BT3 nuclei

DYSPROSIUM 169 [0; 0] *Dec 90*
BT1 beta-minus decay radioisotopes
  BT2 beta decay radioisotopes
    BT3 radioisotopes
      BT4 isotopes
BT1 dysprosium isotopes
BT1 even-odd nuclei
  BT2 nuclei
BT1 rare earth nuclei
  BT2 intermediate mass nuclei
    BT3 nuclei
BT1 seconds living radioisotopes
  BT2 radioisotopes
    BT3 isotopes

E CENTERS [211; 211]
BT1 color centers
  BT2 vacancies
    BT3 point defects
      BT4 crystal defects
        BT5 crystal structure

E CODES [1,280; 1,280]
BT1 computer codes

e layer
USE e region

E REGION [558; 657]
UF *e layer*
BT1 ionosphere
  BT2 earth atmosphere
NT1 sporadic e

E STATES [51; 51]
BT1 energy levels

e. fermi nucl. res. center r.
USE cesnef reactor

e-beam type reactors
USE electron beam fusion reactors

e-1422 resonances
(Prior to December 1987 this was a valid descriptor.)
USE f1-1420 mesons

EARLY BIRD SATELLITES [0; 0]
BT1 satellites

early notification convention
USE cenna

EARLY RADIATION EFFECTS
[1,605; 1,605]
UF *immediate radiation effects*
UF+ *early radiation injuries*
BT1 biological radiation effects
  BT2 biological effects
  BT2 radiation effects
RT biological indicators
RT delayed radiation effects
RT time dependence

early radiation injuries
USE early radiation effects
AND radiation injuries

ears
USE auditory organs

earth (electric grounds)
USE electric grounds

EARTH ATMOSPHERE [4,566; 14,849]
NT1 earth magnetosphere
NT1 exosphere
NT1 ionosphere
  NT2 c region
  NT2 d region
  NT2 e region
    NT3 sporadic e
  NT2 f region
    NT3 f1 layer
    NT3 f2 layer
    NT3 spread f
NT1 mesosphere
NT1 stratosphere
NT1 thermosphere
NT1 troposphere
RT air
RT airglow

EARTH ATMOSPHERE

RT	atmospheric circulation
RT	atmospheric explosions
RT	atmospheric precipitations
RT	earth planet
RT	environment
RT	fallout
RT	geocorona
RT	global aspects
RT	greenhouse effect
RT	meteorology
RT	radioactive clouds
RT	residence half-time
RT	surface air
RT	temperature inversions
RT	tropopause

EARTH CORE [17; 17] Feb 88
UF	core (earth)
RT	earth crust
RT	earth mantle
RT	earth planet

EARTH CRUST [867; 1,019]
NT1	continental crust
NT1	oceanic crust
RT	earth core
RT	earth mantle
RT	earth planet
RT	geology
RT	geomorphology
RT	geothermal energy
RT	natural occurrence
RT	particle resuspension
RT	sea bed
RT	soil mechanics
RT	volcanoes

EARTH MAGNETOSPHERE [4,640; 4,640]
UF	magnetosphere (earth)
BT1	earth atmosphere
RT	geomagnetic field
RT	international magnetospheric s
RT	loss cone
RT	magnetic storms
RT	magnetopause
RT	magnetosheath
RT	magnetotail
RT	planetary magnetospheres
RT	plasma sheet
RT	plasmapause
RT	plasmasphere
RT	polar cusp
RT	radiation belts

EARTH MANTLE [245; 245] Dec 85
(Intermediate shell zone of the earth below the crust and above the core.)
RT	earth core
RT	earth crust
RT	earth planet

EARTH PLANET [1,189; 1,189]
BT1	planets
RT	continental crust
RT	earth atmosphere
RT	earth core
RT	earth crust
RT	earth mantle
RT	geography
RT	geology
RT	geophysics
RT	northern hemisphere
RT	oceanic crust
RT	oceanography
RT	southern hemisphere
RT	topography

earthing (electric grounds)
USE	electric grounds

EARTHMOVING EQUIPMENT [32; 32]
Jun 83
UF	excavators
SF	mining equipment
BT1	materials handling equipment
BT2	equipment
RT	boreholes
RT	excavation
RT	mining
RT	shaft excavations
RT	slope stability
RT	tunnels
RT	vehicles

EARTHQUAKES [4,262; 4,262]
UF	seismicity
RT	epicenters
RT	exceptional natural disaster
RT	geologic faults
RT	ground motion
RT	landslides
RT	rayleigh waves
RT	seismic effects
RT	seismic isolation
RT	seismic p waves
RT	seismic s waves
RT	seismic waves
RT	seismographs
RT	seismology
RT	shock waves
RT	soil-structure interactions
RT	tsunamis

EAST-WEST ASYMMETRY [34; 34]
(For cosmic radiation only.)
BT1	asymmetry
RT	cosmic radiation

easton power reactor
USE	fitzpatrick reactor

EBASCO STANDARD PLANT [3; 3]
Nov 78
(Ebasco Services reference PWR nuclear power plant.)
BT1	nuclear power plants
BT2	nuclear facilities
BT2	thermal power plants
BT3	power plants

ebfa
USE	electron beam fusion accelerat

EBONITE [5; 5]
BT1	vulcanized elastomers
BT2	elastomers
BT3	polymers

EBOR REACTOR [2; 2]
UF	exp. beryllium oxide reactor
BT1	beryllium moderated reactors
BT2	metal moderated reactors
BT3	reactors
BT1	enriched uranium reactors
BT2	reactors
BT1	helium cooled reactors
BT2	gas cooled reactors
BT3	reactors
BT1	power reactors
BT2	reactors
BT1	research reactors
BT2	research and test reactors
BT3	reactors
BT1	solid homogeneous reactors
BT2	homogeneous reactors
BT3	reactors
BT1	test reactors
BT2	research and test reactors
BT3	reactors
BT2	test facilities
BT1	thermal reactors
BT2	reactors

EBR-1 REACTOR [31; 31]
(ANL, Argonne, Illinois, USA)
UF	exp. breeder reactor-1
BT1	experimental reactors
BT2	research and test reactors
BT3	reactors
BT1	lmfbr type reactors
BT2	fbr type reactors
BT3	breeder reactors
BT4	reactors
BT3	fast reactors
BT4	epithermal reactors
BT5	reactors
BT2	liquid metal cooled reactors
BT3	reactors
BT1	nak cooled reactors
BT2	liquid metal cooled reactors
BT3	reactors
BT1	plutonium reactors
BT2	reactors
BT1	potassium cooled reactors
BT2	liquid metal cooled reactors
BT3	reactors
BT1	power reactors
BT2	reactors
BT1	research reactors
BT2	research and test reactors
BT3	reactors
BT1	sodium cooled reactors
BT2	liquid metal cooled reactors
BT3	reactors
BT1	test reactors
BT2	research and test reactors
BT3	reactors
BT2	test facilities
RT	natural uranium reactors

EBR-2 REACTOR [1,212; 1,212]
UF	exp. breeder reactor-2
BT1	experimental reactors
BT2	research and test reactors
BT3	reactors
BT1	lmfbr type reactors
BT2	fbr type reactors
BT3	breeder reactors
BT4	reactors
BT3	fast reactors
BT4	epithermal reactors
BT5	reactors
BT2	liquid metal cooled reactors
BT3	reactors
BT1	power reactors
BT2	reactors
BT1	sodium cooled reactors
BT2	liquid metal cooled reactors
BT3	reactors
RT	enriched uranium reactors
RT	plutonium reactors

EBWR REACTOR [11; 11]
UF	exp. boiling water reactor
BT1	bwr type reactors
BT2	enriched uranium reactors
BT3	reactors
BT2	power reactors
BT3	reactors
BT2	thermal reactors
BT3	reactors
BT2	water cooled reactors
BT3	reactors
BT2	water moderated reactors
BT3	reactors
BT1	experimental reactors
BT2	research and test reactors
BT3	reactors

ecat scanning
USE	cat scanning
AND	emission computed tomography

eccles-jordan circuits
USE	flip-flop circuits

ECCS [3,131; 4,054]
UF	emergency core cooling system
BT1	reactor protection systems
NT1	core flooding systems
NT1	core spray systems
NT1	high pressure coolant injectio
NT1	low pressure coolant injection
RT	depressurization systems
RT	reactor safety experiments

ECEL REACTOR [3; 3]
BT1 fast reactors
BT2 epithermal reactors
BT3 reactors
BT1 zero power reactors
BT2 experimental reactors
BT3 research and test reactors
BT4 reactors

echelle gratings
USE diffraction gratings

echelon gratings
USE diffraction gratings

ECHINODERMS [36; 97]
BT1 aquatic organisms
BT1 invertebrates
BT2 animals
NT1 sea urchins
RT exoskeleton

echography
(Method to detect inhomogenities in the human body by means of reflected ultrasonic waves.)
USE images
AND ultrasonic waves

ECLIPSE [1,369; 1,369]
UF *lunar occultation*
UF *occultation*
UF *solar occultation*
RT astronomy

ECN [72; 75] *Feb 77*
(Energieonderzoek Centrum Nederland; prior to 1 August 1976 known as Reactor Centrum Nederland, and documents written before that date should be indexed to RCN.)
UF *energieonderzoek centrum neder*
BT1 netherlands organizations
BT2 national organizations
NT1 rcn

ECO REACTOR [14; 14]
UF *experience critique orgel*
BT1 heavy water moderated reactors
BT2 reactors
BT1 natural uranium reactors
BT2 reactors
BT1 organic cooled reactors
BT2 reactors
BT1 research reactors
BT2 research and test reactors
BT3 reactors
BT1 tank type reactors
BT2 reactors
BT1 test reactors
BT2 research and test reactors
BT3 reactors
BT2 test facilities

ecological communities
USE ecosystems

ECOLOGICAL CONCENTRATION [596; 4,686] *Jul 76*
UF *concentration processes (ecol)*
UF *transfer factors (biological)*
NT1 radioecological concentration
RT carbon cycle
RT environmental transport

ECOLOGICAL SUCCESSION [5; 5]
Jul 86
(Orderly and progressive change in animal and/or plant communities.)
RT competition
RT ecology
RT population dynamics

ECOLOGY [897; 1,971]
NT1 baseline ecology
NT1 radioecology
RT ecological succession
RT ecosystems
RT regional analysis
RT regional cooperation

ECONOMETRICS [98; 131]
(The application of mathematical methods to the study of economic data and problems.)
BT1 economic analysis
BT1 economics
RT dynamic programming
RT linear programming
RT nonlinear programming
RT optimization

ECONOMIC ANALYSIS [1,127; 3,140]
Dec 82
UF *input-output analysis*
NT1 cost benefit analysis
NT1 econometrics
RT capitalized cost
RT economics
RT economy
RT energy analysis
RT operating cost
RT regional analysis
RT regression analysis

ECONOMIC DEVELOPMENT [650; 650]
UF+ *resource development*
RT centrally planned economies
RT commercial sector
RT commercialization
RT developed countries
RT economic policy
RT energy analysis
RT gross national product
RT industry
RT nuclear trade

→ **ECONOMIC IMPACT** [0; 0] *Apr 84*
RT economics
RT socio-economic factors
RT technology impacts

ECONOMIC POLICY [467; 467]
RT allocations
RT centrally planned economies
RT deregulation
RT economic development
RT economics
RT forecasting
RT nationalization
RT nuclear trade
RT taxes

ECONOMICS [10,023; 10,136]
NT1 econometrics
RT availability
RT budgets
RT capital
RT competition
RT cost
RT cost benefit analysis
RT deregulation
RT economic analysis
RT economic impact
RT economic policy
RT economy
RT energy consumption
RT energy policy
RT environmental policy
RT feasibility studies
RT financial incentives
RT gross national product
RT income
RT investment
RT market
RT payback period
RT regional analysis
RT socio-economic factors
RT trade

ECONOMIZERS [55; 55]
RT reactor cooling systems
RT steam generators

ECONOMY [588; 588]
(The structure of economic life in a country or area.)
RT economic analysis
RT economics
RT financing
RT forecasting
RT gross national product
RT technology impacts

ECOSYSTEMS [746; 3,766]
UF *biocenoses*
UF *biogeocenoses*
UF *communities (ecological)*
UF *ecological communities*
NT1 aquatic ecosystems
NT1 terrestrial ecosystems
RT agriculture
RT biology
RT biosphere
RT carbon cycle
RT ecology
RT environment
RT forest litter
RT pesticides
RT population dynamics
RT populations
RT radioecological concentration
RT radionuclide migration
RT recreational areas
RT soils
RT sulfur cycle

ecr
USE electron cyclotron-resonance

ECR HEATING [2,264; 2,264]
UF *electron cyclotron-resonance h*
BT1 high-frequency heating
BT2 plasma heating
BT3 heating
RT electron cyclotron-resonance

ECSC [1; 1]
UF *european coal and steel commun*
BT1 european communities
BT2 international organizations

ECUADOR [27; 27]
BT1 developing countries
BT1 south america
BT2 latin america

ECZEMA [18; 18]
BT1 skin diseases
BT2 diseases
RT allergy

EDDHA [7; 7]
BT1 amino acids
BT2 carboxylic acids
BT3 organic acids
BT4 organic compounds
BT1 chelating agents
BT1 hydroxy acids
BT2 carboxylic acids
BT3 organic acids
BT4 organic compounds

EDDINGTON THEORY [107; 107]
RT spectra

EDDY CURRENT TESTING [1,059; 1,059]
BT1 electromagnetic testing
BT2 nondestructive testing
BT3 materials testing
BT4 testing
RT eddy currents

EDDY CURRENTS [819; 819]
(Limited to electric currents.)
BT1 electric currents
BT2 currents
RT eddy current testing

EDEMA [878; 878]
BT1 pathological changes
BT2 diseases
BT1 symptoms
RT body fluids
RT diuretics
RT extracellular space
RT retention

edf-1 reactor
USE chinon-1 reactor

edf-2 reactor
USE chinon-2 reactor

edf-3 reactor
USE chinon-3 reactor

edf-4 reactor
USE saint laurent-1 reactor

edf-5 reactor
USE bugey-1 reactor

EDGE DISLOCATIONS [330; 330]
BT1 dislocations
BT2 line defects
BT3 crystal defects
BT4 crystal structure

EDGE LOCALIZED MODES [68; 68] Dec 89
UF *elm (plasma physics)*
BT1 plasma macroinstabilities
BT2 plasma instability
BT3 instability
RT h-mode plasma confinement

EDTA [2,018; 2,018]
UF *ethylenediaminetetraacetic aci*
UF *sequestrene*
UF *versene*
BT1 amino acids
BT2 carboxylic acids
BT3 organic acids
BT4 organic compounds
BT1 chelating agents

EDUCATION [6,358; 6,358]
UF *teaching*
UF *training*
RT adolescents
RT children
RT educational facilities
RT learning
RT manuals
RT technology transfer

EDUCATIONAL FACILITIES [678; 678] Jun 83
UF *colleges*
UF *museums*
UF *schools*
UF *teaching facilities*
UF *training facilities*
UF *universities*
RT education

edwin i. hatch-1 reactor
USE hatch-1 reactor

edwin i. hatch-2 reactor
USE hatch-2 reactor

EEL [40; 40]
BT1 fishes
BT2 aquatic organisms
BT2 vertebrates
BT3 animals

EEV RANGE [116; 116] Jan 77
(From 10 exp 18 to 10 exp 21 ev.)
BT1 energy range

EFDR-50 REACTOR [3; 3] Apr 77
(Entwickelter Fortschrittlicher Druckwasser Reactor for ship propulsion with 50000 SHP.)
UF *entwick. fortschr. druckw reac*
BT1 pwr type reactors
BT2 enriched uranium reactors
BT3 reactors
BT2 power reactors
BT3 reactors
BT2 thermal reactors
BT3 reactors
BT2 water cooled reactors
BT3 reactors
BT2 water moderated reactors
BT3 reactors
BT1 ship propulsion reactors
BT2 propulsion reactors
BT3 power reactors
BT4 reactors

EFFECTIVE CHARGE [683; 683]
(Observed charge of nucleus or atom, less than Ze because of screening effects.)
RT nuclear screening

effective energy (internal irr
USE internal irradiation
AND spatial dose distributions

effective half-life
USE biological half-life

EFFECTIVE MASS [4,351; 4,351]
BT1 mass

EFFECTIVE RANGE THEORY [498; 498]
RT efimov effect
RT interactions
RT nucleons
RT scattering

§§ **EFFICIENCY** [21,805; 22,936]
UF+ *decontamination factor*
UF+ *dose reduction factor*
UF+ *dose relative factor*
UF+ *drf*
SF *promoters*
NT1 energy efficiency
NT1 mechanical efficiency
NT1 quantum efficiency
NT1 thermal efficiency
RT comparative evaluations
RT energy conservation
RT energy yield
RT feasibility studies
RT performance
RT productivity
RT uses

effluents (chemical)
USE chemical effluents

effluents (gaseous)
USE gaseous wastes

effluents (liquid)
USE liquid wastes

effluents (radioactive)
USE radioactive effluents

effluents (thermal)
USE thermal effluents

EFIMOV EFFECT [13; 13] Nov 85
(The conjectured possibility of an anomalous behaviour of a resonant interacting three-body system near the three-body breakup threshold.)
RT bound state
RT effective range theory
RT three-body problem

efr reactor
USE joyo reactor

EGCR REACTOR [10; 10]
UF *exp. gas cooled reactor*
BT1 enriched uranium reactors
BT2 reactors
BT1 experimental reactors
BT2 research and test reactors
BT3 reactors
BT1 graphite moderated reactors
BT2 reactors
BT1 helium cooled reactors
BT2 gas cooled reactors
BT3 reactors
BT1 power reactors
BT2 reactors
BT1 thermal reactors
BT2 reactors

EGGS [724; 724]
UF *yolk*
RT birds
RT food
RT ova

EGTA [65; 65] Sep 77
(Ethyleneglycol-bis(2-aminoethylether) tetraacetic acid)
BT1 carboxylic acids
BT2 organic acids
BT3 organic compounds
BT1 chelating agents
BT1 glycols
BT2 alcohols
BT3 hydroxy compounds
BT4 organic compounds

EGYPTIAN ARAB REPUBLIC [334; 334]
UF *arab republic of egypt*
UF *uar*
UF *united arab republic*
BT1 africa
BT1 developing countries
BT1 middle east

EHD GENERATORS [15; 15]
UF *electrohydrodynamic generators*
BT1 direct energy converters
RT electrohydrodynamics

ehf radiation
USE microwave radiation

EHRLICH ASCITES TUMOR [418; 418]
BT1 experimental neoplasms
BT2 neoplasms
BT3 diseases
RT ascites
RT ascites tumor cells

EICOSANOIC ACID [89; 89]
  UF   *arachidic acid*
  BT1   monocarboxylic acids
    BT2   carboxylic acids
      BT3   organic acids
        BT4   organic compounds

EIGENFREQUENCY [874; 874]
  UF   *frequency (eigen)*
  RT   eigenvalues
  RT   hydrodynamic mass effect

EIGENFUNCTIONS [2,886; 2,886]
  BT1   functions
  RT   expectation value
  RT   quantum mechanics
  RT   sturm-liouville equation
  RT   wave functions

EIGENSTATES [3,006; 3,006]
  UF+ *coherent states*
  RT   energy levels
  RT   quantum mechanics

EIGENVALUES [7,228; 7,228]
  RT   eigenfrequency
  RT   expectation value
  RT   mathematical operators
  RT   multiplicity
  RT   quantum mechanics
  RT   secular equation

EIGENVECTORS [936; 936]
  RT   mathematical operators
  RT   mathematics
  RT   vectors

eightfold way
  USE   octet model

EIKONAL APPROXIMATION
[1,657; 1,657]
  UF   *approximation (eikonal)*
  RT   scattering amplitudes
  RT   straight-line path approximati

EINDHOVEN CYCLOTRON [7; 7]
Jun 83
(Eindhoven AVF cyclotron.)
  BT1   isochronous cyclotrons
    BT2   cyclotrons
      BT3   cyclic accelerators
        BT4   accelerators

EINSTEIN COEFFICIENTS [127; 127]
  RT   energy-level transitions
  RT   oscillator strengths
  RT   stimulated emission

EINSTEIN EFFECT [40; 40] *Oct 75*
(A shift towards longer wavelengths of spectral lines emitted by atoms in strong gravitational fields.)
  UF   *einstein shift*
  RT   general relativity theory
  RT   gravitational fields
  RT   red shift

EINSTEIN FIELD EQUATIONS
[4,174; 4,174]
  BT1   field equations
    BT2   equations
  RT   cosmological constant
  RT   general relativity theory
  RT   gravitational fields
  RT   kerr field

einstein gravitation theory
  USE   general relativity theory

einstein shift
  USE   einstein effect

einstein-de sitter model
  USE   cosmological models

EINSTEIN-MAXWELL EQUATIONS
[750; 750]
  UF   *electrovac equations*
  BT1   field equations
    BT2   equations
  RT   electromagnetic fields
  RT   general relativity theory
  RT   gravitational fields
  RT   gravitational waves

EINSTEIN-SCHROEDINGER THEORY
[234; 234]
  BT1   unified-field theories
    BT2   field theories

EINSTEINIUM [107; 107]
  BT1   actinides
    BT2   metals
      BT3   elements
  BT1   transplutonium elements
    BT2   transuranium elements
      BT3   elements

EINSTEINIUM BROMIDES [11; 11]
Jan 76
  BT1   bromides
    BT2   bromine compounds
      BT3   halogen compounds
    BT2   halides
      BT3   halogen compounds
  BT1   einsteinium compounds
    BT2   actinide compounds
    BT2   transplutonium compounds
      BT3   transuranium compounds

EINSTEINIUM CARBIDES [0; 0]
  BT1   carbides
    BT2   carbon compounds
  BT1   einsteinium compounds
    BT2   actinide compounds
    BT2   transplutonium compounds
      BT3   transuranium compounds

EINSTEINIUM CHLORIDES [19; 19]
  BT1   chlorides
    BT2   chlorine compounds
      BT3   halogen compounds
    BT2   halides
      BT3   halogen compounds
  BT1   einsteinium compounds
    BT2   actinide compounds
    BT2   transplutonium compounds
      BT3   transuranium compounds

EINSTEINIUM COMPLEXES [27; 27]
  BT1   actinide complexes
    BT2   complexes
  BT1   transuranium complexes

EINSTEINIUM COMPOUNDS [62; 107]
  BT1   actinide compounds
  BT1   transplutonium compounds
    BT2   transuranium compounds
  NT1   einsteinium bromides
  NT1   einsteinium carbides
  NT1   einsteinium chlorides
  NT1   einsteinium fluorides
  NT1   einsteinium hydroxides
  NT1   einsteinium iodides
  NT1   einsteinium nitrates
  NT1   einsteinium nitrides
  NT1   einsteinium oxides
  NT1   einsteinium sulfides

EINSTEINIUM FLUORIDES [6; 6]
Dec 80
  BT1   einsteinium compounds
    BT2   actinide compounds
    BT2   transplutonium compounds
      BT3   transuranium compounds
  BT1   fluorides
    BT2   fluorine compounds
      BT3   halogen compounds
    BT2   halides
      BT3   halogen compounds

EINSTEINIUM HYDROXIDES [2; 2]
  BT1   einsteinium compounds
    BT2   actinide compounds
    BT2   transplutonium compounds
      BT3   transuranium compounds
  BT1   hydroxides
    BT2   hydrogen compounds
    BT2   oxygen compounds

EINSTEINIUM IODIDES [7; 7]
  BT1   einsteinium compounds
    BT2   actinide compounds
    BT2   transplutonium compounds
      BT3   transuranium compounds
  BT1   iodides
    BT2   halides
      BT3   halogen compounds
    BT2   iodine compounds
      BT3   halogen compounds

EINSTEINIUM IONS [11; 11]
  BT1   ions
    BT2   charged particles

EINSTEINIUM ISOTOPES [42; 306]
  NT1   einsteinium 243
  NT1   einsteinium 244
  NT1   einsteinium 245
  NT1   einsteinium 246
  NT1   einsteinium 247
  NT1   einsteinium 248
  NT1   einsteinium 249
  NT1   einsteinium 250
  NT1   einsteinium 251
  NT1   einsteinium 252
  NT1   einsteinium 253
  NT1   einsteinium 254
  NT1   einsteinium 255
  NT1   einsteinium 256

EINSTEINIUM NITRATES [13; 13]
  BT1   einsteinium compounds
    BT2   actinide compounds
    BT2   transplutonium compounds
      BT3   transuranium compounds
  BT1   nitrates
    BT2   nitrogen compounds
    BT2   oxygen compounds

EINSTEINIUM NITRIDES [0; 0]
  BT1   einsteinium compounds
    BT2   actinide compounds
    BT2   transplutonium compounds
      BT3   transuranium compounds
  BT1   nitrides
    BT2   nitrogen compounds
    BT2   pnictides

EINSTEINIUM OXIDES [9; 9]
  BT1   einsteinium compounds
    BT2   actinide compounds
    BT2   transplutonium compounds
      BT3   transuranium compounds
  BT1   oxides
    BT2   chalcogenides
    BT2   oxygen compounds

EINSTEINIUM SULFIDES [0; 0]
  BT1   einsteinium compounds
    BT2   actinide compounds
    BT2   transplutonium compounds
      BT3   transuranium compounds
  BT1   sulfides
    BT2   chalcogenides
    BT2   sulfur compounds

EINSTEINIUM 243 [5; 5]
  BT1   actinide nuclei
    BT2   heavy nuclei
      BT3   nuclei
  BT1   alpha decay radioisotopes
    BT2   radioisotopes
      BT3   isotopes
  BT1   einsteinium isotopes
  BT1   odd-even nuclei

EINSTEINIUM 243
- BT2 nuclei
- BT1 seconds living radioisotopes
- BT2 radioisotopes
- BT3 isotopes

EINSTEINIUM 244 [6; 6]
- BT1 actinide nuclei
- BT2 heavy nuclei
- BT3 nuclei
- BT1 alpha decay radioisotopes
- BT2 radioisotopes
- BT3 isotopes
- BT1 einsteinium isotopes
- BT1 electron capture radioisotopes
- BT2 beta decay radioisotopes
- BT3 radioisotopes
- BT4 isotopes
- BT1 odd-odd nuclei
- BT2 nuclei
- BT1 seconds living radioisotopes
- BT2 radioisotopes
- BT3 isotopes

EINSTEINIUM 245 [7; 7]
- BT1 actinide nuclei
- BT2 heavy nuclei
- BT3 nuclei
- BT1 alpha decay radioisotopes
- BT2 radioisotopes
- BT3 isotopes
- BT1 einsteinium isotopes
- BT1 electron capture radioisotopes
- BT2 beta decay radioisotopes
- BT3 radioisotopes
- BT4 isotopes
- BT1 minutes living radioisotopes
- BT2 radioisotopes
- BT3 isotopes
- BT1 odd-even nuclei
- BT2 nuclei

EINSTEINIUM 246 [6; 6]
- BT1 actinide nuclei
- BT2 heavy nuclei
- BT3 nuclei
- BT1 alpha decay radioisotopes
- BT2 radioisotopes
- BT3 isotopes
- BT1 einsteinium isotopes
- BT1 electron capture radioisotopes
- BT2 beta decay radioisotopes
- BT3 radioisotopes
- BT4 isotopes
- BT1 minutes living radioisotopes
- BT2 radioisotopes
- BT3 isotopes
- BT1 odd-odd nuclei
- BT2 nuclei

EINSTEINIUM 247 [4; 4]
- BT1 actinide nuclei
- BT2 heavy nuclei
- BT3 nuclei
- BT1 alpha decay radioisotopes
- BT2 radioisotopes
- BT3 isotopes
- BT1 einsteinium isotopes
- BT1 electron capture radioisotopes
- BT2 beta decay radioisotopes
- BT3 radioisotopes
- BT4 isotopes
- BT1 minutes living radioisotopes
- BT2 radioisotopes
- BT3 isotopes
- BT1 odd-even nuclei
- BT2 nuclei

EINSTEINIUM 248 [6; 6]
- BT1 actinide nuclei
- BT2 heavy nuclei
- BT3 nuclei
- BT1 alpha decay radioisotopes
- BT2 radioisotopes
- BT3 isotopes
- BT1 einsteinium isotopes
- BT1 electron capture radioisotopes
- BT2 beta decay radioisotopes
- BT3 radioisotopes
- BT4 isotopes
- BT1 minutes living radioisotopes
- BT2 radioisotopes
- BT3 isotopes
- BT1 odd-odd nuclei
- BT2 nuclei

EINSTEINIUM 249 [8; 8]
- BT1 actinide nuclei
- BT2 heavy nuclei
- BT3 nuclei
- BT1 alpha decay radioisotopes
- BT2 radioisotopes
- BT3 isotopes
- BT1 einsteinium isotopes
- BT1 electron capture radioisotopes
- BT2 beta decay radioisotopes
- BT3 radioisotopes
- BT4 isotopes
- BT1 hours living radioisotopes
- BT2 radioisotopes
- BT3 isotopes
- BT1 odd-even nuclei
- BT2 nuclei

EINSTEINIUM 250 [6; 6]
- BT1 actinide nuclei
- BT2 heavy nuclei
- BT3 nuclei
- BT1 einsteinium isotopes
- BT1 electron capture radioisotopes
- BT2 beta decay radioisotopes
- BT3 radioisotopes
- BT4 isotopes
- BT1 hours living radioisotopes
- BT2 radioisotopes
- BT3 isotopes
- BT1 odd-odd nuclei
- BT2 nuclei

EINSTEINIUM 251 [20; 20]
- BT1 actinide nuclei
- BT2 heavy nuclei
- BT3 nuclei
- BT1 alpha decay radioisotopes
- BT2 radioisotopes
- BT3 isotopes
- BT1 days living radioisotopes
- BT2 radioisotopes
- BT3 isotopes
- BT1 einsteinium isotopes
- BT1 electron capture radioisotopes
- BT2 beta decay radioisotopes
- BT3 radioisotopes
- BT4 isotopes
- BT1 odd-even nuclei
- BT2 nuclei

EINSTEINIUM 252 [15; 15]
- BT1 actinide nuclei
- BT2 heavy nuclei
- BT3 nuclei
- BT1 alpha decay radioisotopes
- BT2 radioisotopes
- BT3 isotopes
- BT1 einsteinium isotopes
- BT1 electron capture radioisotopes
- BT2 beta decay radioisotopes
- BT3 radioisotopes
- BT4 isotopes
- BT1 odd-odd nuclei
- BT2 nuclei
- BT1 years living radioisotopes
- BT2 radioisotopes
- BT3 isotopes

EINSTEINIUM 253 [155; 155]
- BT1 actinide nuclei
- BT2 heavy nuclei
- BT3 nuclei
- BT1 alpha decay radioisotopes
- BT2 radioisotopes
- BT3 isotopes
- BT1 days living radioisotopes
- BT2 radioisotopes
- BT3 isotopes
- BT1 einsteinium isotopes
- BT1 odd-even nuclei
- BT2 nuclei
- BT1 spontaneous fission radioisoto
- BT2 radioisotopes
- BT3 isotopes

EINSTEINIUM 253 TARGET [8; 8]
Jan 78
- BT1 targets

EINSTEINIUM 254 [72; 72]
- BT1 actinide nuclei
- BT2 heavy nuclei
- BT3 nuclei
- BT1 alpha decay radioisotopes
- BT2 radioisotopes
- BT3 isotopes
- BT1 beta-minus decay radioisotopes
- BT2 beta decay radioisotopes
- BT3 radioisotopes
- BT4 isotopes
- BT1 days living radioisotopes
- BT2 radioisotopes
- BT3 isotopes
- BT1 einsteinium isotopes
- BT1 electron capture radioisotopes
- BT2 beta decay radioisotopes
- BT3 radioisotopes
- BT4 isotopes
- BT1 internal conversion radioisoto
- BT2 radioisotopes
- BT3 isotopes
- BT1 odd-odd nuclei
- BT2 nuclei
- BT1 spontaneous fission radioisoto
- BT2 radioisotopes
- BT3 isotopes

EINSTEINIUM 254 TARGET [44; 44]
- BT1 targets

EINSTEINIUM 255 [13; 13]
- BT1 actinide nuclei
- BT2 heavy nuclei
- BT3 nuclei
- BT1 alpha decay radioisotopes
- BT2 radioisotopes
- BT3 isotopes
- BT1 beta-minus decay radioisotopes
- BT2 beta decay radioisotopes
- BT3 radioisotopes
- BT4 isotopes
- BT1 days living radioisotopes
- BT2 radioisotopes
- BT3 isotopes
- BT1 einsteinium isotopes
- BT1 odd-even nuclei
- BT2 nuclei
- BT1 spontaneous fission radioisoto
- BT2 radioisotopes
- BT3 isotopes

EINSTEINIUM 255 TARGET [5; 5]
Sep 78
- BT1 targets

EINSTEINIUM 256 [7; 7] *Jan 77*
- BT1 actinide nuclei
- BT2 heavy nuclei
- BT3 nuclei
- BT1 beta-minus decay radioisotopes
- BT2 beta decay radioisotopes
- BT3 radioisotopes
- BT4 isotopes
- BT1 einsteinium isotopes
- BT1 hours living radioisotopes
- BT2 radioisotopes
- BT3 isotopes
- BT1 minutes living radioisotopes
- BT2 radioisotopes
- BT3 isotopes
- BT1 odd-odd nuclei
- BT2 nuclei

eku
USE erevan synchrotron

EL SALVADOR [6; 6]
BT1 central america
BT2 latin america
BT1 developing countries

EL-1 REACTOR [2; 2]
UF *zoe reactor*
BT1 experimental reactors
BT2 research and test reactors
BT3 reactors
BT1 heavy water cooled reactors
BT2 reactors
BT1 heavy water moderated reactors
BT2 reactors
BT1 isotope production reactors
BT2 irradiation reactors
BT3 reactors
BT1 natural uranium reactors
BT2 reactors
BT1 research reactors
BT2 research and test reactors
BT3 reactors
BT1 tank type reactors
BT2 reactors
BT1 thermal reactors
BT2 reactors

EL-2 REACTOR [2; 2]
BT1 carbon dioxide cooled reactors
BT2 gas cooled reactors
BT3 reactors
BT1 heavy water moderated reactors
BT2 reactors
BT1 isotope production reactors
BT2 irradiation reactors
BT3 reactors
BT1 natural uranium reactors
BT2 reactors
BT1 research reactors
BT2 research and test reactors
BT3 reactors
BT1 tank type reactors
BT2 reactors
BT1 thermal reactors
BT2 reactors

EL-3 REACTOR [21; 21]
(Saclay, France)
BT1 enriched uranium reactors
BT2 reactors
BT1 heavy water cooled reactors
BT2 reactors
BT1 heavy water moderated reactors
BT2 reactors
BT1 isotope production reactors
BT2 irradiation reactors
BT3 reactors
BT1 materials testing reactors
BT2 irradiation reactors
BT3 reactors
BT1 research reactors
BT2 research and test reactors
BT3 reactors
BT1 tank type reactors
BT2 reactors

EL-4 REACTOR [22; 22]
(Brennilis, Monts Arrel, France)
BT1 enriched uranium reactors
BT2 reactors
BT1 hwgcr type reactors
BT2 gas cooled reactors
BT3 reactors
BT2 heavy water moderated reactors
BT3 reactors
BT1 pressure tube reactors
BT2 power reactors
BT3 reactors
BT1 thermal reactors
BT2 reactors

elastic properties
USE elasticity

ELASTIC SCATTERING [23,849; 33,030]
BT1 scattering
NT1 bhabha scattering
NT1 compton effect
NT1 coulomb scattering
NT1 moeller scattering
NT1 mott scattering
NT1 potential scattering
NT1 rutherford scattering
NT1 wigner scattering
RT blair model
RT coherent scattering
RT quasi-elastic scattering
RT ramsauer effect
RT rosenbluth formula
RT skyrme potential
RT zero-range approximation

ELASTICITY [4,836; 5,753]
UF *elastic properties*
BT1 mechanical properties
NT1 photoelasticity
NT1 thermoelasticity
RT hooke law
RT poisson ratio
RT strains
RT young modulus

ELASTOMERS [254; 1,093]
BT1 polymers
NT1 neoprene
NT1 polyisoprene
NT1 rubbers
NT2 buna
NT2 latex
NT2 natural rubber
NT2 silastic
NT2 viton
NT1 vulcanized elastomers
NT2 ebonite
RT gutta percha

ELDERLY PEOPLE [93; 93] *Jul 85*
BT1 aged adults
BT2 adults
BT1 man
BT2 primates
BT3 mammals
BT4 vertebrates
BT5 animals

ELDOR [31; 31]
UF *electron-electron double res.*
BT1 magnetic resonance
BT2 resonance
RT double resonance methods

ELECTRETS [211; 211]
BT1 dielectric materials
BT2 materials
RT polarization

ELECTRIC ARCS [1,541; 1,541]
BT1 electric currents
BT2 currents
BT1 electric discharges
RT electrical faults
RT flashover
RT plasma

ELECTRIC BATTERIES [507; 507]
(Devices for production and/or storage of electrical energy from chemical reactions; excludes FUEL CELLS and RADIOISOTOPE BATTERIES.)
UF *accumulators*
UF *batteries (electric)*
UF *voltaic cells*
BT1 energy storage systems
RT cardiac pacemakers
RT electrical equipment
RT electrolytic cells
RT electromotive force
RT energy storage
RT spacecraft power supplies

ELECTRIC BORN MODEL [12; 12]
BT1 ope model
BT2 obe model
BT3 boson-exchange models
BT4 peripheral models
BT5 particle models
BT6 mathematical models
RT electroproduction
RT photoproduction

ELECTRIC BRIDGES [227; 227]
UF *bridges (electric)*
BT1 electrical equipment
BT2 equipment
RT electric measuring instruments

ELECTRIC CABLES [1,135; 2,228]
BT1 cables
BT1 conductor devices
BT2 electrical equipment
BT3 equipment
NT1 coaxial cables
NT1 cryogenic cables
NT1 gas-insulated cables
NT1 superconducting cables
RT power transmission lines

ELECTRIC CHARGES [4,091; 4,378]
UF *electric monopoles*
UF+ *pyroelectricity*
NT1 point charge
RT c invariance
RT charge carriers
RT charge collection
RT charge conservation
RT charge density
RT charge distribution
RT charge states
RT charge transport
RT electrostatic charge eliminato
RT electrostatics
RT minus-plus ratio
RT positive excess
RT space charge

ELECTRIC COILS [733; 8,328]
UF *coils (electric)*
BT1 electrical equipment
BT2 equipment
NT1 magnet coils
NT2 pulsed magnet coils
NT1 rogowski coil
NT1 solenoids
NT1 superconducting coils
RT electromagnets
RT magnetic circuits
RT transformers

electric condensers
USE capacitors

ELECTRIC CONDUCTIVITY
[22,488; 39,606]
UF *conductivity (electric)*
UF *electric resistivity*
UF *electrical conductivity*
UF *electrical resistance*
UF *electrical resistivity*
UF *i-v characteristic*
UF *ohmic resistance*
UF *resistivity (electric)*
UF *va characteristic*
UF *volt-ampere characteristic*
BT1 electrical properties
BT2 physical properties
NT1 ionic conductivity
NT1 magnetoresistance
NT1 photoconductivity
NT1 superconductivity
RT carrier mobility
RT electric conductors
RT electric impedance
RT electrical testing
RT grueneisen formula
RT matthiessen rule
RT ohm law
RT umklapp processes

RT wiedemann-franz law

ELECTRIC CONDUCTORS [778; 778]
UF conductors (electric)
RT conductor devices
RT electric conductivity
RT electric grounds
RT electron mobility
RT hall effect
RT penetration depth
RT photoconductors
RT semiconductor materials
RT skin effect
RT superconductors

electric contactors
USE switches

ELECTRIC CONTACTS [877; 877]
UF contacts (electric)
UF point contacts
BT1 electrical equipment
BT2 equipment
RT switches

ELECTRIC CONTROLLERS [200; 200]
BT1 control equipment
BT2 equipment
RT surges
RT voltage regulators

ELECTRIC CURRENTS [9,439; 19,061]
UF plasma currents
BT1 currents
NT1 alternating current
NT1 bootstrap current
NT1 critical current
NT1 direct current
NT1 eddy currents
NT1 electric arcs
NT1 electrojets
NT1 faraday current
NT1 leakage current
NT1 overcurrent
NT1 photocurrents
NT1 ring currents
RT current density
RT current limiters
RT electrical transients
RT electricity
RT electrocardiograms
RT flashover
RT joule heating
RT kruskal limit
RT non-inductive current drive
RT skin effect
RT surges

ELECTRIC DIPOLE MOMENTS
[1,088; 1,088]
BT1 dipole moments
BT1 electric moments
RT nuclear electric moments
RT polarizability

electric dipole transitions
USE e1-transitions

ELECTRIC DIPOLES [453; 453]
BT1 dipoles
BT2 multipoles
RT electric fields

electric discharge pumping
USE electrical pumping

ELECTRIC DISCHARGES [4,199; 8,821]
UF discharges (electric)
NT1 corona discharges
NT1 electric arcs
NT1 electric sparks
NT1 flashover
NT1 glow discharges

NT1 high-frequency discharges
NT1 lightning
NT2 ball lightning
NT1 penning discharges
NT1 townsend discharge
RT afterglow
RT breakdown
RT electric grounds
RT electrical faults
RT paschen law
RT positive column
RT saha equation
RT spark gaps
RT striations
RT switches

ELECTRIC FIELDS [15,904; 22,573]
UF fields (electric)
NT1 coulomb field
RT casimir effect
RT crossed fields
RT electric dipoles
RT electromagnetic fields
RT inhomogeneous fields
RT nuclear quadrupole resonance
RT parametric instabilities
RT stark effect

ELECTRIC FILTERS [294; 294]
BT1 filters

ELECTRIC FURNACES [168; 594]
BT1 furnaces
NT1 arc furnaces
NT1 ceramic melters
NT1 induction furnaces

ELECTRIC FUSES [48; 48]
UF fuses (electric)
BT1 conductor devices
BT2 electrical equipment
BT3 equipment
BT1 equipment protection devices
RT circuit breakers
RT switches

ELECTRIC GENERATORS [758; 1,643]
(Excludes the concept DIRECT ENERGY CONVERTERS.)
UF generators (electric)
BT1 electrical equipment
BT2 equipment
NT1 alternators
NT1 flux pumps
NT1 rotating generators
NT2 superconducting generators
NT1 turbogenerators

ELECTRIC GROUNDS [42; 42] *Jun 82*
UF earth (electric grounds)
UF earthing (electric grounds)
UF grounds (electric)
RT electric conductors
RT electric discharges
RT electrical faults
RT electrical insulators
RT electronic circuits

electric heating
USE joule heating

electric hexadecapole transiti
USE e4-transitions

ELECTRIC IMPEDANCE [1,048; 1,048]
Nov 75
BT1 impedance
RT ac losses
RT capacitance
RT electric conductivity

electric logging
USE well logging

ELECTRIC MEASURING INSTRUMENTS [194; 582]
BT1 electrical equipment
BT2 equipment
BT1 measuring instruments
NT1 ammeters
NT1 electrometers
NT1 electroscopes
NT1 galvanometers
NT1 potentiometers
NT1 voltmeters
RT electric bridges
RT electronic equipment
RT faraday cups

ELECTRIC MOMENTS [335; 2,734]
NT1 electric dipole moments
NT1 nuclear electric moments
RT gyroelectric ratio
RT quadrupole moments

electric monopole transitions
USE e0-transitions

electric monopoles
USE electric charges

ELECTRIC MOTORS [368; 388]
BT1 electrical equipment
BT2 equipment
BT1 motors
NT1 superconducting motors

electric octupole transitions
USE e3-transitions

ELECTRIC POTENTIAL [8,028; 9,202]
UF potential (electric)
UF voltage
NT1 electromotive force
NT1 overvoltage
NT1 plasma potential
RT breakdown
RT electrical transients
RT paschen law
RT potentiometers
RT surges

ELECTRIC POWER [4,394; 4,628]
BT1 power
NT1 hydroelectric power
RT bonneville power administratio
RT combined cycles
RT demand factors
RT electric utilities
RT electricity
RT epri
RT load management
RT nuclear power
RT power demand
RT power generation
RT power losses
RT power plants
RT power supplies
RT power transmission
RT power transmission lines
RT public utilities

electric power research inst.
USE epri

electric power systems
USE power systems

ELECTRIC PROBES [585; 1,685]
BT1 probes
NT1 langmuir probe
NT1 plasma eaters

electric properties
   USE   electrical properties

electric pulses
   USE   pulses

electric quadrupole transition
   USE   e2-transitions

electric resistivity
   USE   electric conductivity

ELECTRIC RESONANCE [51; 62]
BT1   resonance
NT1   paraelectric resonance

electric shock
(Coordinate the descriptors below with THERAPY if appropriate.)
   USE   biological shock
   AND   electricity

ELECTRIC SPARKS [520; 520]
UF   *sparks (electric)*
BT1   electric discharges
RT   breakdown
RT   electrical faults
RT   electrostatics
RT   flashover
RT   spark gaps

electric switches
   USE   switches

ELECTRIC UTILITIES [1,392; 1,392]
Feb 79
BT1   public utilities
RT   electric power
RT   epri
RT   peak load

electrical conductivity
   USE   electric conductivity

ELECTRICAL EQUIPMENT
[1,422; 27,305]
BT1   equipment
NT1   antennas
NT1   armatures
NT1   capacitors
NT1   circuit breakers
NT1   conductor devices
  NT2   connectors
  NT2   electric cables
    NT3   coaxial cables
    NT3   cryogenic cables
    NT3   gas-insulated cables
    NT3   superconducting cables
  NT2   electric fuses
NT1   current limiters
NT1   dc to dc converters
NT1   electric bridges
NT1   electric coils
  NT2   magnet coils
    NT3   pulsed magnet coils
  NT2   rogowski coil
  NT2   solenoids
  NT2   superconducting coils
NT1   electric contacts
NT1   electric generators
  NT2   alternators
  NT2   flux pumps
  NT2   rotating generators
    NT3   superconducting generators
  NT2   turbogenerators
NT1   electric measuring instruments
  NT2   ammeters
  NT2   electrometers
  NT2   electroscopes
  NT2   galvanometers
  NT2   potentiometers
  NT2   voltmeters
NT1   electric motors
  NT2   superconducting motors
NT1   electrical insulators
NT1   electromagnets
  NT2   superconducting magnets
NT1   inverters
NT1   lightning arresters
NT1   rectifiers
  NT2   rectifier tubes
    NT3   capacitrons
    NT3   ignitrons
  NT2   semiconductor rectifiers
NT1   relays
NT1   resistors
  NT2   photoresistors
  NT2   rheostats
  NT2   semiconductor resistors
NT1   switches
  NT2   cryotrons
  NT2   plasma switches
  NT2   semiconductor switches
NT1   transformers
RT   auxiliary systems
RT   electric batteries
RT   electron tubes
RT   electronic circuits
RT   electronic equipment
RT   lighting systems
RT   miniaturization
RT   potting
RT   potting materials
RT   radar
RT   reactor components
RT   semiconductor devices
RT   transducers
RT   waveguides

ELECTRICAL FAULTS [149; 149]
Oct 83
UF   *short circuits*
UF   *shorts (electrical)*
RT   breakdown
RT   electric arcs
RT   electric discharges
RT   electric grounds
RT   electric sparks
RT   failures
RT   flashover

ELECTRICAL INSULATION [527; 527]
(Prior to January 1983 this concept was indexed by DIELECTRIC MATERIALS.)
UF   *insulation (electr.,by diel.m)*
RT   dielectric materials
RT   electrical insulators
RT   organic insulators

ELECTRICAL INSULATORS
[1,202; 1,202] *May 76*
UF   *insulators (electrical)*
BT1   electrical equipment
  BT2   equipment
RT   dielectric materials
RT   electric grounds
RT   electrical insulation

ELECTRICAL PROPERTIES
[2,915; 47,115]
UF   *electric properties*
UF+   *magnetoelectricity*
BT1   physical properties
NT1   capacitance
NT1   dielectric properties
  NT2   kerr effect
  NT2   permittivity
NT1   electric conductivity
  NT2   ionic conductivity
  NT2   magnetoresistance
  NT2   photoconductivity
  NT2   superconductivity
NT1   polarizability
NT1   thermoelectric properties
RT   electricity
RT   electro-optical effects
RT   magnetic properties

ELECTRICAL PUMPING [146; 146]
Jul 82
(Pumping achieved by allowing a suitable electric current to pass through the lasing medium.)
UF   *electric discharge pumping*
RT   excitation
RT   lasers
RT   nuclear pumping
RT   optical pumping
RT   stimulated emission

electrical resistance
   USE   electric conductivity

electrical resistivity
   USE   electric conductivity

ELECTRICAL SURVEYS [74; 142]
UF   *resistivity surveys*
BT1   geophysical surveys
  BT2   geologic surveys
NT1   electromagnetic surveys
  NT2   magnetotelluric surveys
RT   exploration
RT   prospecting

ELECTRICAL TESTING [211; 211]
BT1   nondestructive testing
  BT2   materials testing
    BT3   testing
RT   electric conductivity

ELECTRICAL TRANSIENTS [190; 190]
Jun 83
BT1   transients
RT   electric currents
RT   electric potential
RT   overcurrent
RT   overvoltage
RT   power systems
RT   pulses
RT   surges

ELECTRICITY [698; 2,015]
UF+   *electric shock*
NT1   bioelectricity
NT1   piezoelectricity
NT1   thermoelectricity
RT   electric currents
RT   electric power
RT   electrical properties

electricity supply com. reacto
   USE   escom reactor

ELECTRO-OPTICAL EFFECTS
[323; 323] *Nov 78*
RT   electrical properties
RT   magneto-optical effects
RT   optical properties

ELECTROCARDIOGRAMS
[1,085; 1,085]
BT1   diagrams
  BT2   information
RT   cardiography
RT   diagnostic techniques
RT   electric currents
RT   heart
RT   pulses
RT   recording systems

ELECTROCHEMICAL COATING
[74; 451]
BT1   chemical coating
  BT2   surface coating
    BT3   deposition
NT1   anodization

ELECTROCHEMICAL CORROSION
[616; 616]
- UF   *bimetallic corrosion*
- UF   *couple corrosion*
- UF   *electrolytic corrosion*
- UF   *galvanic corrosion*
- BT1 corrosion
-   BT2 chemical reactions
- RT   electrochemistry
- RT   electrolysis

ELECTROCHEMICAL MACHINING
[140; 140]
- BT1 chemical machining
-   BT2 machining

ELECTROCHEMISTRY [2,351; 2,351]
- RT   electrochemical corrosion
- RT   electrometallurgy
- RT   electromotive force
- RT   fuel cells

ELECTRODEPOSITED COATINGS
[346; 346]
- BT1 coatings
- RT   electroplating

ELECTRODEPOSITION [1,222; 1,552]
- BT1 electrolysis
- BT1 surface coating
-   BT2 deposition
- NT1 electroplating
- RT   electrometallurgy

ELECTRODES [6,228; 12,305]
- NT1 anodes
- NT1 cathodes
-   NT2 hollow cathodes
-   NT2 photocathodes
- NT1 dees
- NT1 grids
- RT   electron tubes
- RT   ion selective electrode analys
- RT   welding rods

ELECTRODYNAMICS [1,454; 7,247]
- UF   *electrokinetics*
- NT1 quantum electrodynamics
-   NT2 schwinger-tomonaga formalism
- RT   born-infeld theory
- RT   charge renormalization
- RT   electromagnetic fields
- RT   electromagnetic interactions
- RT   electromagnetism
- RT   field theories
- RT   maxwell equations

ELECTROENCEPHALOGRAPHY
[183; 183] *Jul 80*
- BT1 diagnostic techniques
- RT   brain

ELECTROFISSION [190; 190] *Mar 77*
(Fission of heavy nuclei by MeV range electrons.)
- BT1 electron reactions
-   BT2 lepton reactions
-     BT3 nuclear reactions
- BT1 fission
-   BT2 nuclear reactions

ELECTROGASDYNAMICS [33; 33]
- BT1 fluid mechanics
-   BT2 mechanics
- RT   gas flow

electrohydrodynamic generators
- USE ehd generators

ELECTROHYDRODYNAMICS
[163; 163]
- BT1 hydrodynamics
-   BT2 fluid mechanics
-     BT3 mechanics
- RT   direct energy conversion
- RT   ehd generators

ELECTROJETS [575; 575]
- UF   *auroral electrojets*
- UF   *equatorial electrojets*
- BT1 electric currents
-   BT2 currents
- RT   ring currents

electrokinetics
- USE electrodynamics

ELECTROLUMINESCENCE [301; 301]
- BT1 luminescence
-   BT2 photon emission
-     BT3 emission

ELECTROLYSIS [2,632; 5,054]
- NT1 anodization
- NT1 electrodeposition
-   NT2 electroplating
- NT1 electropolishing
- NT1 electrorefining
- RT   anions
- RT   cations
- RT   dissociation
- RT   electrochemical corrosion
- RT   electrolytic cells
- RT   electrometallurgy
- RT   electromotive force
- RT   faraday laws
- RT   polarography
- RT   voltametry

ELECTROLYTES [2,592; 2,940]
- NT1 solid electrolytes
- RT   dissociation
- RT   donnan theory

ELECTROLYTIC CELLS [808; 808]
- UF   *cells (electrolytic)*
- RT   electric batteries
- RT   electrolysis
- RT   electromotive force
- RT   voltametry

electrolytic corrosion
- USE electrochemical corrosion

ELECTROMAG ISOTOPE SEPARATORS [339; 360]
- NT1 tristan separator
- RT   electromagnetic isotope separa
- RT   isotope separation
- RT   mass spectrometers

ELECTROMAGNETIC FIELDS
[6,857; 6,857]
- UF   *fields (electromagnetic)*
- RT   aharonov-bohm effect
- RT   einstein-maxwell equations
- RT   electric fields
- RT   electrodynamics
- RT   inhomogeneous fields
- RT   magnetic fields
- RT   maxwell equations
- RT   ponderomotive force
- RT   potentials
- RT   weyl unified theory

ELECTROMAGNETIC FILTERS
[140; 140] *May 80*
- BT1 filters
- RT   corrosion products
- RT   primary coolant circuits
- RT   water

ELECTROMAGNETIC FORM FACTORS [2,456; 2,456]
- BT1 form factors
-   BT2 particle properties
- RT   four momentum transfer

ELECTROMAGNETIC INTERACTIONS
[4,706; 17,702]
- BT1 basic interactions
- BT1 interactions
- NT1 compton effect
- NT1 coulomb scattering
- NT1 electroproduction
- NT1 photon-hadron interactions
-   NT2 photon-baryon interactions
-     NT3 photon-hyperon interactions
-     NT3 photon-nucleon interactions
-       NT4 photon-neutron interactions
-       NT4 photon-proton interactions
-   NT2 photon-meson interactions
- NT1 photon-photon interactions
- NT1 photoproduction
-   NT2 primakoff effect
- NT1 umklapp processes
- RT   annihilation
- RT   charged currents
- RT   coulomb correction
- RT   electrodynamics
- RT   electron-quark interactions
- RT   grand unified theory
- RT   hadron-hadron interactions
- RT   internal pair production
- RT   lepton-hadron interactions
- RT   lepton-lepton interactions
- RT   neutral currents
- RT   photon-lepton interactions
- RT   radiative corrections
- RT   standard model
- RT   weinberg lepton model

ELECTROMAGNETIC ISOTOPE SEPARA [486; 486]
(The process)
- BT1 isotope separation
-   BT2 separation processes
- RT   electromag isotope separators

ELECTROMAGNETIC LENSES
[747; 747]
- UF   *plasma lens*
- BT1 lenses
- RT   end effects
- RT   magnetic analyzers
- RT   magnets

ELECTROMAGNETIC PARTICLE DECAY [316; 517] *Feb 78*
- BT1 particle decay
-   BT2 decay
- RT   radiative decay

ELECTROMAGNETIC PULSES
[514; 545]
- UF   *emp*
- BT1 electromagnetic radiation
-   BT2 radiations
- NT1 internal electromagnetic pulse
- RT   nuclear explosions

ELECTROMAGNETIC PUMPS
[303; 303]
- BT1 pumps
-   BT2 equipment

ELECTROMAGNETIC RADIATION
[5,336; 161,222]
- UF   *electromagnetic waves*
- BT1 radiations
- NT1 auroral hiss
- NT1 blackbody radiation
- NT1 bremsstrahlung
-   NT2 cyclotron radiation
-   NT2 internal bremsstrahlung
-   NT2 ondulator radiation
-   NT2 synchrotron radiation
- NT1 cherenkov radiation
- NT1 coherent radiation
- NT1 electromagnetic pulses
-   NT2 internal electromagnetic pulse
- NT1 gamma radiation
-   NT2 delayed gamma radiation
-   NT2 prompt gamma radiation
- NT1 helicon waves
- NT1 infrared radiation

NT2	far infrared radiation
NT2	intermediate infrared radiatio
NT2	near infrared radiation
NT1	laser radiation
NT1	microwave radiation
NT2	relict radiation
NT1	monochromatic radiation
NT1	multipole radiation
NT1	radiowave radiation
NT2	long wave radiation
NT2	luxemburg effect
NT2	medium wave radiation
NT2	radio noise
NT3	atmospherics
NT3	whistlers
NT2	radioecho
NT2	short wave radiation
NT2	solar radio bursts
NT1	thermal radiation
NT1	transition radiation
NT1	ultralow frequency radiation
NT1	ultraviolet radiation
NT2	extreme ultraviolet radiation
NT2	far ultraviolet radiation
NT2	near ultraviolet radiation
NT1	visible radiation
NT1	x radiation
NT2	hard x radiation
NT2	soft x radiation
NT1	zodiacal light
RT	faraday effect
RT	frequency mixing
RT	harmonic generation
RT	photons
RT	radiation pressure
RT	signal distortion
RT	standing waves
RT	travelling waves
RT	wave forms

ELECTROMAGNETIC SURVEYS
[59; 76] *Feb 81*
(A subgroup of methods of electrical exploration based on the measurement of alternating magnetic fields associated with currents artificially or naturally maintained in the subsurface.)
BT1	electrical surveys
BT2	geophysical surveys
BT3	geologic surveys
NT1	magnetotelluric surveys

ELECTROMAGNETIC TESTING
[106; 1,160]
BT1	nondestructive testing
BT2	materials testing
BT3	testing
NT1	eddy current testing

electromagnetic transitions
USE   energy-level transitions

electromagnetic waves
USE   electromagnetic radiation

ELECTROMAGNETISM [549; 549]
BT1	magnetism
RT	continuity equations
RT	electrodynamics
RT	kaluza-klein theory

electromagnetostriction
USE   magnetostriction

ELECTROMAGNETS [1,265; 7,957]
BT1	electrical equipment
BT2	equipment
BT1	magnets
BT2	equipment
NT1	superconducting magnets
RT	electric coils
RT	magnetic properties

ELECTROMECHANICS [73; 73]
BT1	mechanics

ELECTROMETALLURGY [136; 136]
UF	*electrowinning*
BT1	metallurgy
RT	electrochemistry
RT	electrodeposition
RT	electrolysis
RT	electrorefining
RT	extractive metallurgy

ELECTROMETERS [191; 191]
BT1	electric measuring instruments
BT2	electrical equipment
BT3	equipment
BT2	measuring instruments
RT	condenser ionization chambers
RT	electromotive force

electromigration
USE   electrophoresis

ELECTROMOTIVE FORCE
[1,049; 1,049]
UF	*emf*
BT1	electric potential
RT	electric batteries
RT	electrochemistry
RT	electrolysis
RT	electrolytic cells
RT	electrometers
RT	potentiometry
RT	voltametry

electron acceptor
USE	binding energy
AND	electrons
AND	valence

electron acoustic waves
USE   electron plasma waves

ELECTRON ANTINEUTRINOS
[586; 586]
BT1	antineutrinos
BT2	antileptons
BT3	antiparticles
BT4	antimatter
BT5	matter
BT4	elementary particles
BT3	leptons
BT4	elementary particles
BT4	fermions
BT2	neutrinos
BT3	leptons
BT4	elementary particles
BT4	fermions
BT3	massless particles
BT4	elementary particles
BT1	electron neutrinos
BT2	neutrinos
BT3	leptons
BT4	elementary particles
BT4	fermions
BT3	massless particles
BT4	elementary particles

ELECTRON ATTACHMENT [645; 645]
(A(neutral) + e yields A(1 minus).)
RT	electron capture
RT	ionization

ELECTRON BEAM FURNACES [35; 35]
BT1	furnaces
RT	vacuum furnaces

ELECTRON BEAM FUSION ACCELERAT [43; 43] *Feb 81*
(Electron beam accelerator at Sandia Laboratories to be used for inertial confinement fusion experiments.)
UF	*ebfa*
BT1	accelerators
RT	electron beam fusion reactors
RT	energy deposition
RT	inertial confinement

ELECTRON BEAM FUSION REACTORS [34; 34] *Nov 82*
UF	*e-beam type reactors*
UF	*electron beam type reactors*
BT1	thermonuclear reactors
RT	electron beam fusion accelerat
RT	energy deposition
RT	icf devices
RT	inertial confinement

ELECTRON BEAM INJECTION
[1,169; 1,169]
BT1	beam injection

ELECTRON BEAM ION SOURCES
[377; 377] *Aug 76*
(Ion source creating high charge states by sequential electron impact ionization.)
BT1	ion sources
RT	electron beams

ELECTRON BEAM MACHINING
[60; 60]
BT1	machining

ELECTRON BEAM MELTING
[307; 307]
BT1	melting
BT2	phase transformations

ELECTRON BEAM TARGETS
[130; 130] *Nov 82*
BT1	targets
RT	energy deposition
RT	inertial confinement
RT	ion beam targets
RT	laser targets
RT	thermonuclear fuels

electron beam type reactors
USE   electron beam fusion reactors

ELECTRON BEAM WELDING
[704; 704]
BT1	welding
BT2	joining
BT3	fabrication
RT	vacuum welding

ELECTRON BEAMS [26,511; 26,511]
UF	*beta beams (electrons)*
BT1	lepton beams
BT2	particle beams
BT3	beams
RT	electron beam ion sources
RT	electron cooling
RT	electrons
RT	llnl advanced test accelerator
RT	pierce instability
RT	wiggler magnets

ELECTRON CAPTURE [3,195; 3,195]
(By projectiles in collisions; not for ELECTRON CAPTURE DECAY.)
BT1	capture
RT	charge exchange
RT	charge states
RT	electron attachment
RT	recombination

ELECTRON CAPTURE DECAY
[1,640; 2,001]
BT1	beta decay
BT2	nuclear decay
BT3	decay
NT1	k capture
NT1	l capture
NT1	m capture
RT	beta-plus decay
RT	capture
RT	delayed protons

RT   electron capture radioisotopes

* **ELECTRON CAPTURE**
RADIOISOTOPES [64; 56,254]
(For specific terms, consult the Appendix.)
UF   *electron-capture radioisotopes*
BT1   beta decay radioisotopes
BT2   radioisotopes
BT3   isotopes
RT   electron capture decay

ELECTRON CHANNELING
[1,055; 1,055]
BT1   channeling
RT   crystal lattices

ELECTRON COLLISIONS
[1,820; 11,238]
BT1   collisions
NT1   electron-atom collisions
NT1   electron-electron collisions
NT1   electron-ion collisions
NT1   electron-molecule collisions
NT1   electron-positron collisions
NT1   photon-electron collisions

electron configuration (atoms)
USE   electronic structure

ELECTRON COOLING [501; 501]
Aug 75
(Reduction of particle beam oscillations by collisions with a low energy electron beam.)
BT1   beam cooling
RT   beam luminosity
RT   coulomb scattering
RT   electron beams
RT   proton beams

ELECTRON CORRELATION
[1,182; 1,182]
(In atomic models.)
UF   *correlation energy*
BT1   correlations
RT   atomic models

ELECTRON
CYCLOTRON-RESONANCE
[1,082; 1,082]
UF   *ecr*
BT1   cyclotron resonance
BT2   resonance
RT   ecr heating

electron cyclotron-resonance h
USE   ecr heating

ELECTRON DENSITY [11,768; 11,768]
UF   *density (electron)*
RT   current density
RT   electrons
RT   plasma eaters

ELECTRON DETACHMENT [542; 542]
(A(1 minus) yields A(neutral) + e.)
RT   electron loss
RT   ionization

ELECTRON DETECTION [1,505; 1,505]
BT1   charged particle detection
BT2   radiation detection
BT3   detection
RT   beta spectrometers
RT   electron dosimetry
RT   electron spectrometers
RT   positron detection

ELECTRON DIFFRACTION
[3,058; 3,058]
UF   *leed*

UF   *low energy electron diffractio*
BT1   diffraction
BT2   coherent scattering
BT3   scattering
RT   crystallography
RT   kikuchi lines

electron donor
USE   binding energy
AND   electrons
AND   valence

ELECTRON DOSIMETRY [594; 594]
BT1   dosimetry
RT   electron detection

ELECTRON DRIFT [1,542; 1,542]
UF   *drift (electron)*
RT   ambipolar diffusion
RT   electrons

ELECTRON EMISSION [2,723; 3,257]
BT1   emission
NT1   photoelectric emission
RT   auger effect
RT   electron sources
RT   field emission
RT   internal electromagnetic pulse
RT   thermionic emission
RT   work functions

ELECTRON EXCHANGE [345; 345]
UF   *exchange (electron)*
BT1   electron transfer
RT   atom-atom collisions
RT   atom-molecule collisions

ELECTRON GAS [1,232; 1,232]
RT   fermi gas
RT   pines-bohm theory
RT   solid-state plasma

ELECTRON GUNS [1,250; 1,250]
UF   *guns (electron)*
RT   electron tubes

electron holes
USE   holes

ELECTRON LOSS [786; 786]
RT   beam strippers
RT   charge exchange
RT   charge states
RT   electron detachment
RT   ionization

ELECTRON MICROPROBE ANALYSIS
[1,194; 1,194]
BT1   microanalysis
BT1   nondestructive analysis
BT2   chemical analysis
RT   ceramography
RT   electron probes
RT   post-irradiation examination

ELECTRON MICROSCOPES [573; 573]
BT1   microscopes

ELECTRON MICROSCOPY
[7,099; 11,741]
BT1   microscopy
NT1   scanning electron microscopy
NT1   transmission electron microsco
RT   cytological techniques
RT   dielectric track detectors
RT   electron scanning
RT   labelled compounds
RT   replicas
RT   resolution
RT   sample preparation
RT   ultrastructural changes

ELECTRON MOBILITY [974; 974]
BT1   particle mobility
BT2   mobility
RT   electric conductors
RT   semiconductor materials

ELECTRON MULTIPLIER DETEC-
TORS [177; 177]
BT1   radiation detectors
BT2   measuring instruments
RT   electron multipliers

ELECTRON MULTIPLIERS [263; 728]
UF   *multiplier tubes*
BT1   electron tubes
NT1   microchannel electron multipli
RT   dynodes
RT   electron multiplier detectors
RT   photomultipliers

ELECTRON NEUTRINOS [1,219; 1,756]
BT1   neutrinos
BT2   leptons
BT3   elementary particles
BT3   fermions
BT2   massless particles
BT3   elementary particles
NT1   electron antineutrinos

electron nuclear double resona
USE   endor

electron paramagnetic resonanc
USE   electron spin resonance

ELECTRON PAIRS [1,108; 1,108]
RT   electrons
RT   pair production
RT   positrons

electron paramagnetic resonanc
USE   electron spin resonance

ELECTRON PLASMA WAVES
[1,027; 1,027]
UF   *electron acoustic waves*
BT1   plasma waves

ELECTRON PRECIPITATION
[1,155; 1,155]
BT1   charged-particle precipitation
RT   aurorae
RT   auroral oval
RT   midday aurorae
RT   polar cusp
RT   radiation belts
RT   trapped electrons

ELECTRON PROBES [365; 365]
BT1   probes
RT   electron microprobe analysis
RT   x-ray emission analysis

electron promotion model
USE   electron-promotion model

ELECTRON REACTIONS [5,053; 5,227]
UF+   *electron-deuteron interactions*
BT1   lepton reactions
BT2   nuclear reactions
NT1   electrofission

ELECTRON RINGS [619; 619] *May 76*
RT   electron-ring accelerators
RT   magnetic confinement

ELECTRON SCANNING [477; 477]
UF   *scanning (electron)*
RT   cathode ray tubes
RT   electron microscopy

ELECTRON SOURCES [906; 969]
- BT1 particle sources
  - BT2 radiation sources
- NT1 pierce electron guns
- RT electron emission
- RT thermionic emitters

ELECTRON SPECTRA [4,314; 4,314]
Nov 75
- BT1 spectra
- RT electron spectrometers
- RT electron spectroscopy
- RT electrons

ELECTRON SPECTROMETERS
[699; 699]
- BT1 spectrometers
  - BT2 measuring instruments
- RT electron detection
- RT electron spectra

ELECTRON SPECTROSCOPY
[1,459; 6,493]
- UF+ *esca*
- BT1 spectroscopy
- NT1 auger electron spectroscopy
- NT1 photoelectron spectroscopy
- RT electron spectra
- RT electrons

ELECTRON SPIN RESONANCE
[8,876; 8,917]
- UF *electron paramagnetic resonanc*
- UF *epr*
- UF *esr*
- UF *paramagnetic resonance (electr*
- BT1 magnetic resonance
  - BT2 resonance
- NT1 acoustic esr
- RT double resonance methods
- RT overhauser effect
- RT structural chemical analysis

ELECTRON TEMPERATURE
[9,182; 9,182]
- UF *temperature (electron)*
- UF+ *plasma temperature*
- RT electrons
- RT energy

ELECTRON TRANSFER [1,832; 2,170]
(Not for the concept covered by CHARGE EXCHANGE.)
- UF *transfer (electron)*
- NT1 electron exchange
- RT carrier mobility
- RT point defects
- RT valence

ELECTRON TUBES [170; 6,355]
- UF+ *storage tubes*
- NT1 cathode ray tubes
- NT1 cold cathode tubes
- NT1 counting tubes
- NT1 diode tubes
  - NT2 thermionic diodes
- NT1 electron multipliers
  - NT2 microchannel electron multipli
- NT1 gas discharge tubes
  - NT2 flash tubes
  - NT2 geissler tubes
  - NT2 ignitrons
  - NT2 thyratrons
- NT1 gyrocons
- NT1 microwave tubes
  - NT2 backward wave tubes
  - NT2 klystrons
  - NT2 lasertrons
  - NT2 magnetrons
  - NT2 travelling wave tubes
- NT1 plasmatrons
  - NT2 duoplasmatrons
  - NT2 triplasmatrons
- NT1 rectifier tubes
  - NT2 capacitrons
  - NT2 ignitrons
- NT1 thermionic tubes

  - NT2 thermionic diodes
- NT1 triode tubes
- NT1 x-ray tubes
- RT cathodes
- RT electrical equipment
- RT electrodes
- RT electron guns
- RT electronic equipment
- RT gettering
- RT getters
- RT image tubes
- RT phototubes
- RT space charge
- RT thermionic emission
- RT work functions

ELECTRON-ATOM COLLISIONS
[4,475; 4,475]
- BT1 atom collisions
  - BT2 collisions
- BT1 electron collisions
  - BT2 collisions

ELECTRON-CAPTURE DETECTORS
[91; 91]
(Instrument for gas analysis which incorporates an ionization chamber and internal beta source.)
- BT1 radiometric gages
  - BT2 measuring instruments
- RT gas analysis
- RT ionization chambers

electron-capture radioisotopes
- USE electron capture radioisotopes

electron-deuteron interactions
- USE deuterium target
- AND electron reactions

ELECTRON-ELECTRON COLLISIONS
[308; 308]
- BT1 electron collisions
  - BT2 collisions

electron-electron double res.
- USE eldor

ELECTRON-ELECTRON INTERACTIONS [576; 576]
- BT1 lepton-lepton interactions
  - BT2 particle interactions
    - BT3 interactions

ELECTRON-HOLE COUPLING
[124; 124] *Sep 89*
- BT1 coupling
- RT electrons
- RT holes
- RT superconductivity

ELECTRON-HOLE DROPLETS
[100; 100] *Jun 83*
- RT charge carriers
- RT excitons
- RT solid-state plasma

electron-hole plasma
- USE solid-state plasma

ELECTRON-ION COLLISIONS
[1,998; 1,998]
- BT1 electron collisions
  - BT2 collisions
- BT1 ion collisions
  - BT2 collisions

electron-ion coupling
- USE coupling
- AND electrons
- AND ions

ELECTRON-MESON INTERACTIONS
[29; 51]
- BT1 lepton-meson interactions
  - BT2 lepton-hadron interactions
    - BT3 particle interactions
      - BT4 interactions
- NT1 electron-pion interactions

ELECTRON-MOLECULE COLLISIONS
[2,618; 2,618]
- BT1 electron collisions
  - BT2 collisions
- BT1 molecule collisions
  - BT2 collisions

ELECTRON-MUON INTERACTIONS
[73; 73]
- BT1 lepton-lepton interactions
  - BT2 particle interactions
    - BT3 interactions

ELECTRON-MUON UNIVERSALITY
[120; 120]
(Identity of all properties but mass.)
- BT1 electron-muon-tau universality
- RT electrons
- RT muons

ELECTRON-MUON-TAU UNIVERSALITY [0; 20] *Sep 89*
(Identity of all properties but mass.)
- NT1 electron-muon universality
- RT electrons
- RT muons
- RT tau particles

ELECTRON-NEUTRON INTERACTIONS [125; 125]
- BT1 electron-nucleon interactions
  - BT2 lepton-nucleon interactions
    - BT3 lepton-baryon interactions
      - BT4 lepton-hadron interactions
        - BT5 particle interactions
          - BT6 interactions

ELECTRON-NUCLEON INTERACTIONS [630; 2,035]
- BT1 lepton-nucleon interactions
  - BT2 lepton-baryon interactions
    - BT3 lepton-hadron interactions
      - BT4 particle interactions
        - BT5 interactions
- NT1 electron-neutron interactions
- NT1 electron-proton interactions

ELECTRON-PHONON COUPLING
[1,129; 1,129] *Mar 83*
- BT1 coupling
- RT crystal lattices
- RT electrons
- RT phonons
- RT superconductivity

ELECTRON-PION INTERACTIONS
[23; 23] *Aug 82*
- BT1 electron-meson interactions
  - BT2 lepton-meson interactions
    - BT3 lepton-hadron interactions
      - BT4 particle interactions
        - BT5 interactions

ELECTRON-POSITRON COLLISIONS
[649; 649]
- BT1 electron collisions
  - BT2 collisions
- BT1 positron collisions
  - BT2 collisions

ELECTRON-POSITRON INTERACTIONS [9,497; 9,497]
- BT1 lepton-lepton interactions
  - BT2 particle interactions
    - BT3 interactions

ELECTRON-PROMOTION MODEL
[42; 42]
- UF *electron promotion model*
- UF *fano-lichten model*
- BT1 mathematical models
- RT diabatic approximation
- RT ion-atom collisions

ELECTRON-PROTON INTERACTIONS
[1,364; 1,364]
- BT1 electron-nucleon interactions
- BT2 lepton-nucleon interactions
- BT3 lepton-baryon interactions
- BT4 lepton-hadron interactions
- BT5 particle interactions
- BT6 interactions

ELECTRON-QUARK INTERACTIONS
[45; 45] *Jul 85*
- BT1 particle interactions
- BT2 interactions
- RT electromagnetic interactions
- RT intermediate vector bosons
- RT weak interactions
- RT weinberg lepton model

ELECTRON-RING ACCELERATORS
[578; 578]
- UF *adgezator*
- UF *ion-drag accelerators*
- UF *ringotron*
- UF *smokatron*
- BT1 collective accelerators
- BT2 accelerators
- RT electron rings

ELECTRONEGATIVITY [310; 310]
- RT affinity
- RT ionization potential

ELECTRONIC CIRCUITS
[3,507; 15,826]
- UF *circuits (electronic)*
- NT1 campbelling circuits
- NT1 cathode followers
- NT1 coincidence circuits
- NT1 comparator circuits
- NT1 counting circuits
- NT1 delay circuits
- NT1 digital circuits
- NT1 discriminators
- NT2 pulse discriminators
- NT1 equivalent circuits
- NT1 gating circuits
- NT1 integrated circuits
- NT1 limiter circuits
- NT1 logic circuits
- NT1 microelectronic circuits
- NT2 microprocessors
- NT1 printed circuits
- NT1 pulse circuits
- NT2 multivibrators
- NT3 flip-flop circuits
- NT2 pulse discriminators
- NT2 pulse shapers
- NT2 trigger circuits
- NT3 transistor trigger circuits
- NT1 sequential circuits
- NT1 sweep circuits
- NT1 switching circuits
- NT2 transistor switching circuits
- NT1 tank circuits
- NT1 timing circuits
- RT amplifiers
- RT analog systems
- RT circuit breakers
- RT circuit theory
- RT counting techniques
- RT digital systems
- RT electric grounds
- RT electrical equipment
- RT electronic equipment
- RT microelectronics
- RT network analysis
- RT nuclear instrument modules
- RT oscillators
- RT response functions
- RT transistors

electronic data processing
- USE data processing

ELECTRONIC EQUIPMENT
[2,507; 24,764]
- BT1 equipment
- NT1 ac amplifiers
- NT1 analog-to-digital converters
- NT1 cavity resonators
- NT2 superconducting cavity resonat
- NT1 counting ratemeters
- NT2 linear ratemeters
- NT2 logarithmic ratemeters
- NT1 dc amplifiers
- NT1 dielectric amplifiers
- NT1 digital-to-analog converters
- NT1 function generators
- NT2 pulse generators
- NT3 high-voltage pulse generators
- NT4 marx generators
- NT1 high frequency amplifiers
- NT1 magnetic amplifiers
- NT1 microwave equipment
- NT2 heterodyne receivers
- NT2 microwave amplifiers
- NT3 masers
- NT2 microwave tubes
- NT3 backward wave tubes
- NT3 klystrons
- NT3 lasertrons
- NT3 magnetrons
- NT3 travelling wave tubes
- NT2 squid devices
- NT1 multiplexers
- NT1 operational amplifiers
- NT1 oscillators
- NT2 blocking oscillators
- NT2 transistor oscillators
- NT1 oscillographs
- NT1 parametric amplifiers
- NT1 power amplifiers
- NT1 power supplies
- NT2 spacecraft power supplies
- NT1 preamplifiers
- NT1 pulse amplifiers
- NT1 pulse analyzers
- NT2 multi-channel analyzers
- NT1 pulse converters
- NT2 time-to-amplitude converters
- NT1 pulse integrators
- NT1 radio equipment
- NT2 heterodyne receivers
- NT2 ionosondes
- NT2 radio telescopes
- NT1 scalers
- NT1 solar cells
- NT2 silicon solar cells
- NT1 transistor amplifiers
- RT amplifiers
- RT analog systems
- RT atomic clocks
- RT camac system
- RT computer architecture
- RT computers
- RT consoles
- RT counting techniques
- RT data acquisition systems
- RT digital systems
- RT digitizers
- RT display devices
- RT electric measuring instruments
- RT electrical equipment
- RT electron tubes
- RT electronic circuits
- RT electronic guidance
- RT equipment interfaces
- RT image scanners
- RT miniaturization
- RT nuclear instrument modules
- RT potting
- RT potting materials
- RT pulse techniques
- RT radar
- RT reactor components
- RT recording systems
- RT resonators
- RT semiconductor devices
- RT x-ray equipment

ELECTRONIC GUIDANCE [157; 157]
- UF *guidance (electronic)*
- BT1 control systems
- RT electronic equipment
- RT navigational instruments
- RT rockets
- RT space vehicles

ELECTRONIC SPECIFIC HEAT
[501; 501]
(Electron contribution to the specific heat of electronic conductors.)
- BT1 specific heat
- BT2 thermodynamic properties
- BT3 physical properties
- RT nuclear specific heat

ELECTRONIC STRUCTURE
[17,938; 20,833]
(For electron configuration in atoms and molecules, and electron band structure in solids.)
- UF *atomic shells*
- UF *electron configuration (atoms)*
- NT1 k shell
- NT1 l shell
- NT1 m shell
- NT1 n shell
- RT atomic models
- RT atomic radii
- RT aufbau principle
- RT band theory
- RT configuration interaction
- RT crystal field
- RT energy levels
- RT hartree-fock method
- RT heisenberg model
- RT hsk procedure
- RT hybridization
- RT isoelectronic atoms
- RT molecular orbital method
- RT muffin-tin potential
- RT photoelectron spectroscopy
- RT rydberg states
- RT rydberg-klein-rees method
- RT slater method
- RT ultraviolet spectra

electronics (quantum)
- USE quantum electronics

ELECTRONS [33,251; 36,919]
- UF *knock-on electrons*
- UF *negatons*
- UF *negatrons*
- UF+ *electron acceptor*
- UF+ *electron donor*
- UF+ *electron-ion coupling*
- UF+ *valence electrons*
- BT1 leptons
- BT2 elementary particles
- BT2 fermions
- NT1 cosmic electrons
- NT1 exoelectrons
- NT1 prompt electrons
- NT1 runaway electrons
- NT1 solar electrons
- NT1 solvated electrons
- NT1 trapped electrons
- RT beta particles
- RT charge carriers
- RT cooper pairs
- RT delta rays
- RT dirac equation
- RT electron beams
- RT electron density
- RT electron drift
- RT electron pairs
- RT electron spectra
- RT electron spectroscopy
- RT electron temperature
- RT electron-hole coupling
- RT electron-muon universality
- RT electron-muon-tau universality
- RT electron-phonon coupling
- RT muonium
- RT positronium
- RT positrons

RT traps
RT umklapp processes

ELECTROPHORESIS [3,718; 3,718]
UF *cataphoresis*
UF *drag effect*
UF *electromigration*
UF *ionophoresis*
RT thermophoresis
RT transfer numbers

ELECTROPLATING [350; 350]
BT1 electrodeposition
BT2 electrolysis
BT2 surface coating
BT3 deposition
BT1 plating
BT2 surface coating
BT3 deposition
RT electrodeposited coatings

ELECTROPOLISHING [348; 348]
BT1 electrolysis
BT1 polishing
BT2 surface finishing
RT cleaning

ELECTROPRODUCTION [2,010; 2,010]
BT1 electromagnetic interactions
BT2 basic interactions
BT2 interactions
BT1 particle interactions
BT2 interactions
BT1 particle production
RT electric born model

ELECTROREFINING [227; 227]
BT1 electrolysis
BT1 refining
RT electrometallurgy

ELECTROSCOPES [14; 14]
BT1 electric measuring instruments
BT2 electrical equipment
BT3 equipment
BT2 measuring instruments

ELECTROSLAG WELDING [153; 153]
BT1 welding
BT2 joining
BT3 fabrication
RT arc welding

ELECTROSTATIC ACCELERATORS
[1,035; 4,202]
BT1 accelerators
NT1 cockcroft-walton accelerators
NT1 dynamitrons
NT1 pelletron accelerators
NT2 5u pelletron accelerator
NT1 tandem electrostatic accelerat
NT2 crnl mp tandem accelerator
NT2 jaeri tandem accelerator
NT2 learn tandem accelerator
NT2 orsay tandem accelerator
NT2 vivitron tandem accelerator
NT1 van de graaff accelerators
NT2 crnl mp tandem accelerator
NT2 jaeri tandem accelerator
NT2 learn tandem accelerator
NT2 orsay tandem accelerator
NT2 vivitron tandem accelerator

ELECTROSTATIC ANALYZERS
[583; 583]
BT1 beam analyzers
RT electrostatic lenses

ELECTROSTATIC CHARGE ELIMINATO [46; 46]
UF *static electricity eliminators*
RT electric charges
RT electrostatics

ELECTROSTATIC LENSES [481; 481]
BT1 lenses
RT beam optics
RT electrostatic analyzers
RT electrostatic mirrors
RT electrostatic septa

ELECTROSTATIC MIRRORS [18; 18]
Mar 86
BT1 mirrors
RT beam optics
RT electrostatic lenses
RT electrostatics
RT reflection

ELECTROSTATIC PRECIPITATORS
[115; 115]
BT1 pollution control equipment
BT2 equipment
RT air cleaning
RT air pollution monitors
RT dust collectors
RT electrostatics
RT gaseous wastes
RT separation processes
RT stack disposal

ELECTROSTATIC PROBES [243; 243]
BT1 probes

ELECTROSTATIC SEPTA [39; 39]
RT beam optics
RT electrostatic lenses
RT magnetic analyzers
RT septum magnets

ELECTROSTATIC SPECTROMETERS
[161; 161]
BT1 spectrometers
BT2 measuring instruments

electrostatic waves
USE plasma waves

ELECTROSTATICS [1,315; 1,315]
RT capacitors
RT charge distribution
RT electric charges
RT electric sparks
RT electrostatic charge eliminato
RT electrostatic mirrors
RT electrostatic precipitators
RT xerography

electrovac equations
USE einstein-maxwell equations

electroweak interaction model
USE weinberg lepton model

electrowinning
USE electrometallurgy

ELEMENT ABUNDANCE [3,389; 3,389]
(Always coordinate with descriptor(s) for element(s) involved.)
UF *abundance (element)*
BT1 quantity ratio
RT chemical composition
RT cosmochemistry
RT isotope ratio
RT optical depth curve
RT quantitative chemical analysis
RT spectroscopic curve of growth

ELEMENT 104 [102; 102]
UF *kurchatovium*
UF *rutherfordium*
UF *unnilquadium*
BT1 transplutonium elements
BT2 transuranium elements
BT3 elements

ELEMENT 104 CHLORIDES [5; 5]
BT1 chlorides
BT2 chlorine compounds
BT3 halogen compounds
BT2 halides
BT3 halogen compounds
BT1 element 104 compounds
BT2 transplutonium compounds
BT3 transuranium compounds

ELEMENT 104 COMPLEXES [2; 2]
BT1 complexes

ELEMENT 104 COMPOUNDS [15; 20]
BT1 transplutonium compounds
BT2 transuranium compounds
NT1 element 104 chlorides

ELEMENT 104 ISOTOPES [67; 94]
NT1 element 104 253
NT1 element 104 254
NT1 element 104 255
NT1 element 104 256
NT1 element 104 257
NT1 element 104 258
NT1 element 104 259
NT1 element 104 260
NT1 element 104 261
NT1 element 104 262

ELEMENT 104 253 [0; 0] *Jun 86*
BT1 element 104 isotopes
BT1 even-odd nuclei
BT2 nuclei
BT1 seconds living radioisotopes
BT2 radioisotopes
BT3 isotopes
BT1 spontaneous fission radioisoto
BT2 radioisotopes
BT3 isotopes

ELEMENT 104 254 [5; 5] *Jun 86*
BT1 element 104 isotopes
BT1 even-even nuclei
BT2 nuclei
BT1 microsec living radioisotopes
BT2 radioisotopes
BT3 isotopes
BT1 spontaneous fission radioisoto
BT2 radioisotopes
BT3 isotopes

ELEMENT 104 255 [5; 5] *Jun 86*
BT1 alpha decay radioisotopes
BT2 radioisotopes
BT3 isotopes
BT1 element 104 isotopes
BT1 even-odd nuclei
BT2 nuclei
BT1 seconds living radioisotopes
BT2 radioisotopes
BT3 isotopes
BT1 spontaneous fission radioisoto
BT2 radioisotopes
BT3 isotopes

ELEMENT 104 256 [10; 10] *Jun 86*
BT1 element 104 isotopes
BT1 even-even nuclei
BT2 nuclei
BT1 millisec living radioisotopes
BT2 radioisotopes
BT3 isotopes
BT1 spontaneous fission radioisoto
BT2 radioisotopes
BT3 isotopes

ELEMENT 104 257 [2; 2] *Jun 86*
BT1 alpha decay radioisotopes
BT2 radioisotopes
BT3 isotopes
BT1 element 104 isotopes
BT1 even-odd nuclei
BT2 nuclei
BT1 seconds living radioisotopes
BT2 radioisotopes
BT3 isotopes

ELEMENT 104 258 [6; 6] *Jun 86*
   BT1   element 104 isotopes
   BT1   even-even nuclei
      BT2   nuclei
   BT1   millisec living radioisotopes
      BT2   radioisotopes
         BT3   isotopes
   BT1   spontaneous fission radioisoto
      BT2   radioisotopes
         BT3   isotopes

ELEMENT 104 259 [5; 5] *Jun 86*
   BT1   alpha decay radioisotopes
      BT2   radioisotopes
         BT3   isotopes
   BT1   element 104 isotopes
   BT1   even-odd nuclei
      BT2   nuclei
   BT1   seconds living radioisotopes
      BT2   radioisotopes
         BT3   isotopes
   BT1   spontaneous fission radioisoto
      BT2   radioisotopes
         BT3   isotopes

ELEMENT 104 260 [14; 14] *Jun 86*
   BT1   element 104 isotopes
   BT1   even-even nuclei
      BT2   nuclei
   BT1   millisec living radioisotopes
      BT2   radioisotopes
         BT3   isotopes
   BT1   spontaneous fission radioisoto
      BT2   radioisotopes
         BT3   isotopes

ELEMENT 104 261 [4; 4] *Jun 86*
   BT1   alpha decay radioisotopes
      BT2   radioisotopes
         BT3   isotopes
   BT1   element 104 isotopes
   BT1   even-odd nuclei
      BT2   nuclei
   BT1   minutes living radioisotopes
      BT2   radioisotopes
         BT3   isotopes
   BT1   spontaneous fission radioisoto
      BT2   radioisotopes
         BT3   isotopes

ELEMENT 104 262 [8; 8] *Jun 86*
   BT1   element 104 isotopes
   BT1   even-even nuclei
      BT2   nuclei
   BT1   millisec living radioisotopes
      BT2   radioisotopes
         BT3   isotopes
   BT1   spontaneous fission radioisoto
      BT2   radioisotopes
         BT3   isotopes

ELEMENT 105 [85; 85]
   UF   *hahnium*
   UF   *unnilpentium*
   BT1   trans 104 elements
      RT2   transplutonium elements
         BT3   transuranium elements
            BT4   elements

ELEMENT 105 COMPOUNDS [17; 17]
   BT1   trans 104 element compounds
      BT2   transplutonium compounds
         BT3   transuranium compounds

ELEMENT 105 ISOTOPES [11; 25]
Jun 86
   NT1   element 105 255
   NT1   element 105 257
   NT1   element 105 258
   NT1   element 105 259
   NT1   element 105 260
   NT1   element 105 261
   NT1   element 105 262

ELEMENT 105 255 [0; 0] *Jun 86*
   BT1   element 105 isotopes
   BT1   odd-even nuclei
      BT2   nuclei
   BT1   seconds living radioisotopes
      BT2   radioisotopes
         BT3   isotopes
   BT1   spontaneous fission radioisoto
      BT2   radioisotopes
         BT3   isotopes

ELEMENT 105 257 [3; 3] *Jun 86*
   BT1   alpha decay radioisotopes
      BT2   radioisotopes
         BT3   isotopes
   BT1   element 105 isotopes
   BT1   odd-even nuclei
      BT2   nuclei
   BT1   seconds living radioisotopes
      BT2   radioisotopes
         BT3   isotopes
   BT1   spontaneous fission radioisoto
      BT2   radioisotopes
         BT3   isotopes

ELEMENT 105 258 [5; 5] *Jun 86*
   BT1   alpha decay radioisotopes
      BT2   radioisotopes
         BT3   isotopes
   BT1   electron capture radioisotopes
      BT2   beta decay radioisotopes
         BT3   radioisotopes
            BT4   isotopes
   BT1   element 105 isotopes
   BT1   odd-odd nuclei
      BT2   nuclei
   BT1   seconds living radioisotopes
      BT2   radioisotopes
         BT3   isotopes

ELEMENT 105 259 [0; 0] *Jun 86*
   BT1   element 105 isotopes
   BT1   odd-even nuclei
      BT2   nuclei
   BT1   seconds living radioisotopes
      BT2   radioisotopes
         BT3   isotopes
   BT1   spontaneous fission radioisoto
      BT2   radioisotopes
         BT3   isotopes

ELEMENT 105 260 [2; 2] *Jun 86*
   BT1   alpha decay radioisotopes
      BT2   radioisotopes
         BT3   isotopes
   BT1   element 105 isotopes
   BT1   odd-odd nuclei
      BT2   nuclei
   BT1   seconds living radioisotopes
      BT2   radioisotopes
         BT3   isotopes
   BT1   spontaneous fission radioisoto
      BT2   radioisotopes
         BT3   isotopes

ELEMENT 105 261 [0; 0] *Jun 86*
   BT1   alpha decay radioisotopes
      BT2   radioisotopes
         BT3   isotopes
   BT1   element 105 isotopes
   BT1   odd-even nuclei
      BT2   nuclei
   BT1   seconds living radioisotopes
      BT2   radioisotopes
         BT3   isotopes
   BT1   spontaneous fission radioisoto
      BT2   radioisotopes
         BT3   isotopes

ELEMENT 105 262 [11; 11] *Jun 86*
   BT1   alpha decay radioisotopes
      BT2   radioisotopes
         BT3   isotopes
   BT1   element 105 isotopes
   BT1   odd-odd nuclei
      BT2   nuclei
   BT1   seconds living radioisotopes

   BT2   radioisotopes
   BT3   isotopes
   BT1   spontaneous fission radioisoto
      BT2   radioisotopes
      BT3   isotopes

ELEMENT 106 [53; 53]
   UF   *unnilhexium*
   BT1   trans 104 elements
      BT2   transplutonium elements
         BT3   transuranium elements
            BT4   elements

ELEMENT 106 COMPOUNDS [3; 3]
   BT1   trans 104 element compounds
      BT2   transplutonium compounds
         BT3   transuranium compounds

ELEMENT 106 ISOTOPES [36; 45]
Mar 76
   NT1   element 106 259
   NT1   element 106 260
   NT1   element 106 261
   NT1   element 106 263

ELEMENT 106 259 [2; 2] *Jun 86*
   BT1   element 106 isotopes
   BT1   even-odd nuclei
      BT2   nuclei
   BT1   millisec living radioisotopes
      BT2   radioisotopes
         BT3   isotopes
   BT1   spontaneous fission radioisoto
      BT2   radioisotopes
         BT3   isotopes

ELEMENT 106 260 [8; 8] *Jun 86*
   BT1   alpha decay radioisotopes
      BT2   radioisotopes
         BT3   isotopes
   BT1   element 106 isotopes
   BT1   even-even nuclei
      BT2   nuclei
   BT1   millisec living radioisotopes
      BT2   radioisotopes
         BT3   isotopes
   BT1   spontaneous fission radioisoto
      BT2   radioisotopes
         BT3   isotopes

ELEMENT 106 261 [2; 2] *Jun 86*
   BT1   alpha decay radioisotopes
      BT2   radioisotopes
         BT3   isotopes
   BT1   element 106 isotopes
   BT1   even-odd nuclei
      BT2   nuclei
   BT1   millisec living radioisotopes
      BT2   radioisotopes
         BT3   isotopes

ELEMENT 106 263 [3; 3] *Jun 86*
   BT1   alpha decay radioisotopes
      BT2   radioisotopes
         BT3   isotopes
   BT1   element 106 isotopes
   BT1   even-odd nuclei
      RT2   nuclei
   BT1   millisec living radioisotopes
      BT2   radioisotopes
         BT3   isotopes
   BT1   spontaneous fission radioisoto
      BT2   radioisotopes
         BT3   isotopes

ELEMENT 107 [53; 53]
   UF   *unnilseptium*
   BT1   trans 104 elements
      BT2   transplutonium elements
         BT3   transuranium elements
            BT4   elements

ELEMENT 107 COMPOUNDS [3; 3]
   BT1   trans 104 element compounds
      BT2   transplutonium compounds
         BT3   transuranium compounds

ELEMENT 107 ISOTOPES [14; 27]
Jun 86
NT1 element 107 261
NT1 element 107 262

ELEMENT 107 261 [11; 11] *Jun 86*
BT1 alpha decay radioisotopes
BT2 radioisotopes
BT3 isotopes
BT1 element 107 isotopes
BT1 millisec living radioisotopes
BT2 radioisotopes
BT3 isotopes
BT1 odd-even nuclei
BT2 nuclei
BT1 spontaneous fission radioisoto
BT2 radioisotopes
BT3 isotopes

ELEMENT 107 262 [12; 12] *Jun 86*
BT1 alpha decay radioisotopes
BT2 radioisotopes
BT3 isotopes
BT1 element 107 isotopes
BT1 millisec living radioisotopes
BT2 radioisotopes
BT3 isotopes
BT1 odd-odd nuclei
BT2 nuclei

ELEMENT 108 [46; 46]
UF *unniloctium*
BT1 trans 104 elements
BT2 transplutonium elements
BT3 transuranium elements
BT4 elements

ELEMENT 108 COMPOUNDS [0; 0]
BT1 trans 104 element compounds
BT2 transplutonium compounds
BT3 transuranium compounds

ELEMENT 108 ISOTOPES [23; 37]
Jun 86
NT1 element 108 264
NT1 element 108 265

ELEMENT 108 264 [15; 15] *Oct 86*
BT1 alpha decay radioisotopes
BT2 radioisotopes
BT3 isotopes
BT1 element 108 isotopes
BT1 even-even nuclei
BT2 nuclei
BT1 microsec living radioisotopes
BT2 radioisotopes
BT3 isotopes

ELEMENT 108 265 [6; 6] *Jun 86*
BT1 alpha decay radioisotopes
BT2 radioisotopes
BT3 isotopes
BT1 element 108 isotopes
BT1 even-even nuclei
BT2 nuclei
BT1 millisec living radioisotopes
BT2 radioisotopes
BT3 isotopes

ELEMENT 109 [31; 31]
UF *unnilennium*
BT1 trans 104 elements
BT2 transplutonium elements
BT3 transuranium elements
BT4 elements

ELEMENT 109 COMPOUNDS [0; 0]
BT1 trans 104 element compounds
BT2 transplutonium compounds
BT3 transuranium compounds

ELEMENT 109 ISOTOPES [11; 25]
Jun 86
NT1 element 109 266

ELEMENT 109 266 [14; 14] *Jun 86*
BT1 alpha decay radioisotopes
BT2 radioisotopes
BT3 isotopes
BT1 element 109 isotopes
BT1 odd-odd nuclei
BT2 nuclei
BT1 seconds living radioisotopes
BT2 radioisotopes
BT3 isotopes

ELEMENT 110 [35; 35]
UF *unnnilium*
BT1 trans 104 elements
BT2 transplutonium elements
BT3 transuranium elements
BT4 elements

ELEMENT 110 COMPOUNDS [5; 5]
BT1 trans 104 element compounds
BT2 transplutonium compounds
BT3 transuranium compounds

ELEMENT 111 [14; 14]
UF *unununium*
BT1 trans 104 elements
BT2 transplutonium elements
BT3 transuranium elements
BT4 elements

ELEMENT 111 COMPOUNDS [2; 2]
BT1 trans 104 element compounds
BT2 transplutonium compounds
BT3 transuranium compounds

ELEMENT 112 [26; 26]
UF *ununbium*
BT1 trans 104 elements
BT2 transplutonium elements
BT3 transuranium elements
BT4 elements

ELEMENT 112 COMPOUNDS [2; 2]
BT1 trans 104 element compounds
BT2 transplutonium compounds
BT3 transuranium compounds

ELEMENT 113 [10; 10]
UF *ununtrium*
BT1 trans 104 elements
BT2 transplutonium elements
BT3 transuranium elements
BT4 elements

ELEMENT 113 COMPOUNDS [4; 4]
BT1 trans 104 element compounds
BT2 transplutonium compounds
BT3 transuranium compounds

ELEMENT 114 [79; 79]
UF *ununquadium*
BT1 trans 104 elements
BT2 transplutonium elements
BT3 transuranium elements
BT4 elements

ELEMENT 114 COMPOUNDS [10; 10]
BT1 trans 104 element compounds
BT2 transplutonium compounds
BT3 transuranium compounds

ELEMENT 115 [11; 11]
UF *ununpentium*
BT1 trans 104 elements
BT2 transplutonium elements
BT3 transuranium elements
BT4 elements

ELEMENT 116 [11; 11] *Mar 77*
UF *ununhexium*
BT1 trans 104 elements
BT2 transplutonium elements
BT3 transuranium elements
BT4 elements

ELEMENT 117 [4; 4]
UF *unurseptium*
BT1 trans 104 elements
BT2 transplutonium elements
BT3 transuranium elements
BT4 elements

ELEMENT 118 [5; 5] *Oct 75*
UF *ununoctium*
BT1 trans 104 elements
BT2 transplutonium elements
BT3 transuranium elements
BT4 elements

ELEMENT 119 [3; 3] *Nov 81*
UF *ununennium*
BT1 trans 104 elements
BT2 transplutonium elements
BT3 transuranium elements
BT4 elements

ELEMENT 120 [2; 2] *Nov 81*
UF *unbinilium*
BT1 trans 104 elements
BT2 transplutonium elements
BT3 transuranium elements
BT4 elements

ELEMENT 126 [20; 20]
UF *unbihexium*
BT1 trans 104 elements
BT2 transplutonium elements
BT3 transuranium elements
BT4 elements

ELEMENT 126 COMPOUNDS [0; 0]
BT1 trans 104 element compounds
BT2 transplutonium compounds
BT3 transuranium compounds

ELEMENT 128 [4; 4] *Sep 77*
UF *unbioctium*
BT1 trans 104 elements
BT2 transplutonium elements
BT3 transuranium elements
BT4 elements

ELEMENT 134 [2; 2] *Sep 77*
UF *untriquadium*
BT1 trans 104 elements
BT2 transplutonium elements
BT3 transuranium elements
BT4 elements

ELEMENT 145 [2; 2] *Sep 77*
UF *unquadpentium*
BT1 trans 104 elements
BT2 transplutonium elements
BT3 transuranium elements
BT4 elements

ELEMENT 164 [4; 4] *Sep 77*
UF *unhexquadium*
BT1 trans 104 elements
BT2 transplutonium elements
BT3 transuranium elements
BT4 elements

ELEMENT 173 [3; 3] *Sep 77*
UF *unsepttrium*
BT1 trans 104 elements
BT2 transplutonium elements
BT3 transuranium elements
BT4 elements

elementary length
USE fundamental constants
AND length

ELEMENTARY PARTICLES
[2,248; 214,203]
UF *fundamental particles*
NT1 antiparticles
NT2 anti-b neutral mesons
NT2 anti-d neutral mesons

NT2	antibaryons
NT3	antihyperons
NT4	antilambda particles
NT4	antiomega particles
NT4	antisigma particles
NT4	antixi particles
NT3	antinucleons
NT4	antineutrons
NT4	antiprotons
NT2	antikaons
NT3	antikaons neutral
NT2	antileptons
NT3	antineutrinos
NT4	electron antineutrinos
NT4	muon antineutrinos
NT3	muons plus
NT3	positrons
NT4	cosmic positrons
NT1	beauty particles
NT2	b mesons
NT3	b minus mesons
NT3	b neutral mesons
NT4	anti-b neutral mesons
NT3	b plus mesons
NT2	beauty baryons
NT3	lambda b neutral baryons
NT2	beauty mesons
NT3	b*-5325 mesons
NT1	charm particles
NT2	charmed baryons
NT3	lambda c plus baryons
NT3	omega c neutral baryons
NT3	sigma c-2450 baryons
NT3	xi c plus baryons
NT2	charmed mesons
NT3	d mesons
NT4	d minus mesons
NT4	d neutral mesons
NT5	anti-d neutral mesons
NT4	d plus mesons
NT3	d s mesons
NT3	d*-2010 mesons
NT3	d*-2420 mesons
NT3	d*s-2110 mesons
NT1	hadrons
*NT2	baryons
*NT2	mesons
*NT2	resonance particles
NT1	intermediate bosons
NT2	intermediate vector bosons
NT3	w minus bosons
NT3	w plus bosons
NT3	z neutral bosons
NT1	leading particles
NT1	leptons
NT2	antileptons
NT3	antineutrinos
NT4	electron antineutrinos
NT4	muon antineutrinos
NT3	muons plus
NT3	positrons
NT4	cosmic positrons
*NT2	electrons
NT2	heavy leptons
NT3	tau neutrinos
NT3	tau particles
NT2	muons
NT3	cosmic muons
NT3	muons minus
NT3	muons plus
NT2	neutrinos
NT3	antineutrinos
NT4	electron antineutrinos
NT4	muon antineutrinos
NT3	cosmic neutrinos
NT3	electron neutrinos
NT4	electron antineutrinos
NT3	muon neutrinos
NT4	muon antineutrinos
NT3	solar neutrinos
NT3	tau neutrinos
NT1	massless particles
NT2	gravitons
NT2	neutrinos
NT3	antineutrinos
NT4	electron antineutrinos
NT4	muon antineutrinos
NT3	cosmic neutrinos
NT3	electron neutrinos
NT4	electron antineutrinos

NT3	muon neutrinos
NT4	muon antineutrinos
NT3	solar neutrinos
NT3	tau neutrinos
NT2	photons
NT3	cosmic photons
NT1	postulated particles
NT2	dyons
NT2	gluons
NT2	goldstone bosons
NT3	axions
NT2	grace particles
NT2	gravitons
NT2	higgs bosons
NT2	magnetic monopoles
NT2	partons
NT2	pomeranchuk particles
NT2	preons
NT2	quarks
NT2	sparticles
NT2	spurions
NT2	tachyons
NT2	taste particles
NT2	top particles
NT1	strange particles
NT2	d*s-2110 mesons
*NT2	hyperons
NT2	spurions
NT2	strange mesons
NT3	k*-1410 mesons
NT3	k*-1790 mesons
NT3	k*-892 mesons
NT3	k*0-1350 mesons
NT3	k*2-1430 mesons
NT3	k*3-1780 mesons
NT3	k*4-2060 mesons
NT3	k-1460 mesons
NT3	k-1830 mesons
NT3	kaons
NT4	antikaons
NT5	antikaons neutral
NT4	cosmic kaons
NT4	kaons minus
NT4	kaons neutral
NT5	antikaons neutral
NT5	kaons neutral long-lived
NT5	kaons neutral short-lived
NT4	kaons plus
NT3	k1-1280 mesons
NT3	k1-1400 mesons
NT3	k2-1580 mesons
NT3	k2-1770 mesons
NT3	k2-2250 mesons
NT3	k3-2320 mesons
NT3	k4-2500 mesons
NT1	virtual particles
RT	charged-particle transport the
RT	fundamental constants
RT	schwinger source theory

ELEMENTS [1,781; 263,482]
(For chemical elements only.)
UF	trace elements
*NT1	metals
*NT1	nonmetals
*NT1	semimetals
*NT1	transuranium elements
RT	periodic system

eliashberg equations
USE gorkov-eliashberg theory

→ *elisa*
(Enzyme-Linked Immunosorbent Assay.)
USE enzyme immunoassay

elk river reactor
USE err reactor

ELLIOT LAKE [69; 69]
BT1	ontario
BT2	canada
BT3	developed countries
BT3	north america
RT	stanleigh mine

ELLIOT MODEL [43; 43]
BT1	nuclear models
BT2	mathematical models
RT	shell models

ELLIPTICAL CONFIGURATION
[1,152; 1,152]
BT1	configuration

elm (plasma physics)
USE edge localized modes

ELMO BUMPY TORUS [801; 801]
BT1	bumpy tori
BT2	magnetic mirrors
BT3	open plasma devices
BT4	thermonuclear devices
BT1	elmo devices
BT2	magnetic mirrors
BT3	open plasma devices
BT4	thermonuclear devices

ELMO DEVICES [26; 824]
BT1	magnetic mirrors
BT2	open plasma devices
BT3	thermonuclear devices
NT1	elmo bumpy torus

ELONGATION [1,415; 1,415]
BT1	deformation
RT	expansion
RT	thermal expansion

ELPIDITE [1; 1]
BT1	silicate minerals
BT2	minerals
RT	sodium silicates
RT	zirconium silicates

elution (insoluble particles)
USE elutriation

elution (soluble constituents)
USE leaching

ELUTRIATION [301; 301]
UF	elution (insoluble particles)
BT1	separation processes
RT	dispersions
RT	dusts
RT	particle size
RT	particles
RT	powders
RT	sampling

EMANATION METHOD [149; 215]
NT1	emanation thermal analysis
RT	materials testing
RT	radiochemistry
RT	rare gases

EMANATION THERMAL ANALYSIS
[69; 69]
BT1	emanation method
BT1	thermal analysis
RT	rare gases

EMANOMETERS [198; 198]
UF	radon monitors
BT1	radiation detectors
BT2	measuring instruments

EMBOLI [1,051; 1,051]
UF	gas bubble disease
RT	blood circulation
RT	blood flow
RT	blood vessels

EMBRITTLEMENT [3,121; 3,121]
- RT brittleness
- RT ductile-brittle transitions

EMBRYONIC CELLS [406; 406]
- UF *amnion cells*
- BT1 animal cells
- RT embryos

EMBRYOS [1,449; 1,449]
- UF *zygotes*
- RT amniotic fluid
- RT carcinoembryonic antigen
- RT embryonic cells
- RT fetal membranes
- RT fetuses
- RT ontogenesis
- RT pregnancy
- RT prenatal irradiation
- RT reproduction
- RT uterus

EMC EFFECT [503; 503] *Nov 85*
(The unexpected variation of the structure functions of nucleons bound in nuclei as compared with the structure functions of nucleons bound in the deuteron.)
- UF *european muon collab. effect*
- RT deep inelastic scattering
- RT lepton reactions
- RT particle structure
- RT structure functions

emergencies
- USE accidents

emergency core cooling system
- USE eccs

EMERGENCY PLANS [3,206; 3,206] *Aug 76*
(Prior to August 1985 EMERGENCY PROVISIONS was used.)
- UF *emergency provisions*
- RT evacuation
- RT external zones
- RT on-site power generation
- RT planning
- RT radiation accidents
- RT reactor accidents

emergency provisions
(Prior to August 1985 this was a valid descriptor.)
- USE emergency plans

emergency rods
- USE scram rods

emergency showers
- USE safety showers

emergency shutdown
- USE scram

emf
- USE electromotive force

§ **EMISSION** [4,386; 22,854]
- NT1 electron emission
- NT2 photoelectric emission
- NT1 field emission
- NT1 ion emission
- NT1 neutron emission
- NT1 photon emission
- NT2 luminescence
-   NT3 cathodoluminescence
-   NT3 chemiluminescence
-    NT4 bioluminescence
-   NT3 electroluminescence
-   NT3 fluorescence
-    NT4 resonance fluorescence
-   NT3 lyoluminescence
-   NT3 phosphorescence
-   NT3 photoluminescence
-   NT3 radioluminescence
-    NT4 radiothermoluminescence
-   NT3 thermoluminescence
-    NT4 radiothermoluminescence
- NT2 superradiance
- NT1 secondary emission
- NT2 photoemission
- NT1 stimulated emission
- NT1 thermionic emission
- RT angular distribution
- RT emission spectra

emission (cooperative spontane
- USE superradiance

EMISSION COMPUTED TOMOGRAPHY [714; 6,533] *Apr 80*
- UF+ *ecat scanning*
- BT1 computerized tomography
- BT2 tomography
- NT1 positron computed tomography
- NT1 single photon ect
- RT biomedical radiography
- RT gamma cameras
- RT photon emission scanning
- RT positron cameras
- RT radioisotope scanning

EMISSION SPECTRA [13,871; 13,871]
- BT1 spectra
- RT emission

EMISSION SPECTROSCOPY [2,907; 4,761]
- SF *spectrochemistry*
- BT1 spectroscopy
- NT1 fluorescence spectroscopy
- RT cathodoluminescence
- RT fourier transform spectrometer
- RT qualitative chemical analysis
- RT quantitative chemical analysis

EMISSIVITY [637; 637]
- BT1 optical properties
- BT2 physical properties
- BT1 surface properties
- RT blackbody radiation
- RT radiant heat transfer

emittance (beam)
- USE beam emittance

emp
- USE electromagnetic pulses

EMPHYSEMA [137; 137] *Jan 79*
- BT1 pathological changes
- BT2 diseases
- RT lungs
- RT respiratory system diseases

emplacement
- USE positioning

employees
- USE personnel

employment
- USE occupations

EMS [458; 458]
- UF *ethyl methanesulfonate*
- BT1 mutagens
- BT1 sulfonic acid esters
- BT2 esters
-   BT3 organic compounds
- BT2 organic sulfur compounds
-   BT3 organic compounds
- RT methane

EMSLAND REACTOR [62; 62] *Feb 80*
(Lingen, Niedersachsen, Federal Republic of Germany)
- UF *kernkraftwerk emsland*
- BT1 pwr type reactors
- BT2 enriched uranium reactors
-   BT3 reactors
- BT2 power reactors
-   BT3 reactors
- BT2 thermal reactors
-   BT3 reactors
- BT2 water cooled reactors
-   BT3 reactors
- BT2 water moderated reactors
-   BT3 reactors

EMULSIFIERS [69; 440]
- BT1 additives
- NT1 detergents
- NT2 pluronics
- RT emulsions
- RT soaps

EMULSIONS [645; 645]
- BT1 colloids
- BT2 dispersions
- RT emulsifiers
- RT latex

ENAMELS [156; 156]
- BT1 coatings
- RT ceramics

enanthic acid
- USE heptanoic acid

enantiomorphs
- USE isomers

ENCAPSULATION [826; 826] *Nov 78*
(May be used for biological systems, radioactive waste processing, etc.)
- RT capsules
- RT potting
- RT potting materials
- RT radioactive waste processing

ENCEPHALITIS [144; 144]
- BT1 nervous system diseases
- BT2 diseases
- RT brain

encephalography
- USE biomedical radiography

END EFFECTS [206; 206] *Nov 82*
- UF *end losses*
- RT electromagnetic lenses
- RT magnetic fields
- RT mhd generators
- RT pinch devices
- RT wall effects

end losses
- USE end effects

→ **ENDANGERED SPECIES** [0; 0] *Oct 91*
(A species in danger of extinction in all or a significant part of its range.)
- RT animals
- RT plants

ENDOCRINE DISEASES [809; 3,401]
- BT1 diseases
- NT1 acromegaly
- NT1 cushing syndrome
- NT1 diabetes mellitus
- NT1 goiter
- NT1 hyperparathyroidism
- NT1 hyperthyroidism
- NT1 hypothyroidism
- NT1 thyroiditis
- RT endocrine glands
- RT hormones

ENDOCRINE GLANDS [171; 10,022]
- BT1 glands
- BT2 organs
- BT3 body
- NT1 adrenal glands
- NT1 pancreas
- NT1 parathyroid glands
- NT1 pituitary gland
- NT1 thyroid
- RT endocrine diseases
- RT gonads
- RT homeostasis
- RT hormones
- RT hypothalamus
- RT pineal gland
- RT receptors

endometrium
- USE uterus

ENDONUCLEASES [186; 186] *Jan 85*
- BT1 nucleases
- BT2 phosphodiesterases
- BT3 esterases
- BT4 hydrolases
- BT5 enzymes
- BT6 organic compounds
- RT rflps

ENDOPLASMIC RETICULUM [182; 182]
- BT1 organoids
- BT2 cell constituents

ENDOR [499; 499]
- UF *electron nuclear double resona*
- BT1 magnetic resonance
- BT2 resonance
- RT double resonance methods

ENDORPHINS [153; 247] *Sep 82*
- BT1 neuroregulators
- BT2 autonomic nervous system agent
- BT3 drugs
- BT1 polypeptides
- BT2 peptides
- BT3 proteins
- BT4 organic compounds
- NT1 enkephalins
- RT brain

ENDOSPERM [67; 67]
- BT1 plant tissues
- RT seeds

endosteum
- USE bone tissues

ENDOTHELIUM [531; 531]
- BT1 tissues
- BT2 body
- RT epithelium

ENDOTOXINS [196; 196]
- BT1 toxins
- BT2 antigens
- RT bacteria
- RT infectivity
- RT polysaccharides

ENDOXAN [439; 439]
- UF *cyclophosphamide*
- BT1 alkylating agents
- BT2 antimitotic drugs
- BT3 drugs

ENEA [46; 46]
(Name changed to OECD Nuclear Energy Agency in April 1972, and the more recent material should be indexed to NEA.)
- UF *european nuclear energy agency*
- BT1 nea
- BT2 oecd
- BT3 international organizations

enea italy
(Comitato Nazionale per la Ricerca e lo Sviluppo dell'Energia Nucleare e delle Energie Alternative.)
- USE italian enea

ENEL-4 REACTOR [42; 42]
(Caorso, Italy)
- BT1 bwr type reactors
- BT2 enriched uranium reactors
- BT3 reactors
- BT2 power reactors
- BT3 reactors
- BT2 thermal reactors
- BT3 reactors
- BT2 water cooled reactors
- BT3 reactors
- BT2 water moderated reactors
- BT3 reactors

enel-6 reactor
- USE montalto di castro-1 reactor

enel-8 reactor
- USE montalto di castro-2 reactor

energetic solar particles
(Prior to December 1985 this was a valid descriptor.)
- USE solar particles

energia nucl e altern, com naz
(Comitato Nazionale per la Ricerca e lo Sviluppo dell'Energia Nucleare e delle Energie Alternative.)
- USE italian enea

energieonderzoek centrum neder
- USE ecn

ENERGY [4,956; 49,666]
- NT1 activation energy
- NT1 binding energy
- NT2 neutron separation energy
- NT2 pairing energy
- NT1 coulomb energy
- NT1 dissociation energy
- NT1 exergy
- NT1 free energy
- NT2 formation free energy
- NT1 free enthalpy
- NT2 formation free enthalpy
- NT2 oxygen potential
- NT1 geothermal energy
- NT1 kinetic energy
- NT2 transverse energy
- NT1 nuclear energy
- NT1 potential energy
- NT2 fission barrier
- NT1 q-value
- NT1 self-energy
- NT1 solar energy
- NT1 stored energy
- NT1 threshold energy
- RT electron temperature
- RT energy dependence
- RT energy policy
- RT energy range
- RT energy recovery
- RT energy sources
- RT energy-momentum tensor
- RT ion temperature
- RT neutron temperature
- RT nuclear temperature
- RT photon temperature
- RT proton temperature
- RT radioisotope heat sources
- RT sargent diagrams
- RT thermodynamics
- RT work functions

energy absorption
(Prior to January 1983 ENERGY TRANSFER was used for this concept.)
- USE energy deposition

ENERGY ACCOUNTING [150; 150] *Dec 82*
(Procedure of preparing an 'energy balance sheet' of all energy inputs, outputs, and losses of a process or facility; energy forms, quantities, costs, and flows through the system are considered.)
- UF *energy costs*
- BT1 accounting
- BT2 management
- RT energy analysis
- RT energy conservation
- RT energy consumption
- RT energy conversion
- RT energy losses
- RT energy transfer
- RT energy yield
- RT systems analysis

ENERGY ANALYSIS [223; 223] *Sep 79*
(Any analysis or methodology to discover how energy is used by economies.)
- RT economic analysis
- RT economic development
- RT energy accounting
- RT systems analysis

ENERGY BALANCE [1,999; 2,122]
(For energy economics studies use ENERGY ACCOUNTING.)
- UF *balance (energy)*
- NT1 breakeven
- RT energy recovery
- RT energy transfer

ENERGY BALANCE MASS SPECTROMET [12; 12]
- BT1 dynamic mass spectrometers
- BT2 mass spectrometers
- BT3 spectrometers
- BT4 measuring instruments

ENERGY CONSERVATION [929; 929] *Oct 77*
(Conservation of energy resources.)
- UF *conservation (energy)*
- RT efficiency
- RT energy accounting
- RT energy consumption
- RT energy efficiency
- RT energy losses
- RT energy recovery
- RT recycling
- RT resource conservation
- RT thermal insulation
- RT total energy systems

ENERGY CONSUMPTION [1,470; 1,470]
- RT demand
- RT demand factors
- RT economics
- RT energy accounting
- RT energy conservation
- RT energy efficiency
- RT energy shortages
- RT fuels
- RT power
- RT total energy systems

ENERGY CONVERSION [1,459; 2,074]
- BT1 conversion
- NT1 direct energy conversion
  - NT2 photovoltaic conversion
  - NT2 thermionic conversion
  - NT2 thermoelectric conversion
  - NT2 thermomagnetic conversion
- RT energy accounting
- RT energy transfer
- RT energy yield
- RT photovoltaic effect
- RT working fluids

energy costs
- USE energy accounting

→ **ENERGY DEMAND** [11; 11]
(For general reference to all forms of energy; for electric-power demand use POWER DEMAND.)
- BT1 demand
- RT demand factors
- RT energy efficiency
- RT energy shortages
- RT energy supplies
- RT power demand
- RT supply and demand

ENERGY DENSITY [2,104; 2,104]
Sep 80
- UF *density (energy)*
- RT charge density
- RT quantum mechanics

ENERGY DEPENDENCE [23,496; 23,496]
(For explicit dependence of a certain quantity or phenomenon on the energy.)
- RT energy
- RT energy range
- RT excitation functions

ENERGY DEPOSITION [2,051; 2,051]
Nov 82
- UF *energy absorption*
- RT charged-particle transport
- RT electron beam fusion accelerat
- RT electron beam fusion reactors
- RT electron beam targets
- RT energy losses
- RT energy transfer
- RT excitation
- RT impact fusion
- RT inertial confinement
- RT ion beam fusion reactors
- RT ion beam targets
- RT ionization
- RT kerma
- RT laser targets
- RT let
- RT particle beam fusion accelerat
- RT plasma heating
- RT radiation doses

energy dissipation
- USE energy losses

energy distribution
- USE energy spectra

→ **ENERGY EFFICIENCY** [3; 3] *Aug 91*
- BT1 efficiency
- RT energy conservation
- RT energy consumption
- RT energy demand
- RT energy efficiency standards

→ **ENERGY EFFICIENCY STANDARDS** [0; 0] *Aug 91*
- UF *energy performance standards*
- BT1 standards
- RT energy efficiency

energy exchange
- USE energy transfer

ENERGY GAP [3,548; 3,548]
- RT band theory
- RT superconductivity

ENERGY LEVELS [23,398; 84,595]
- UF *energy-level schemes*
- UF *level schemes*
- UF *resonance states*
- UF *states (energy)*
- NT1 d states
- NT1 e states
- NT1 excited states
  - NT2 metastable states
  - NT2 rotational states
  - NT2 rydberg states
  - NT2 vibrational states
- NT1 f states
- NT1 fermi level
- NT1 g states
- NT1 ground states
- NT1 high spin states
- NT1 isobaric analogs
- NT1 negative energy states
- NT1 p states
- NT1 s states
- NT1 virtual states
- NT1 yrast states
- RT bound state
- RT eigenstates
- RT electronic structure
- RT energy-level density
- RT energy-level transitions
- RT external conversion
- RT fine structure
- RT internal conversion
- RT jahn-teller effect
- RT lamb shift
- RT lande factor
- RT level widths
- RT nuclear cascades
- RT nuclear structure
- RT population inversion
- RT quasibound state
- RT rydberg correction
- RT strangeness analog resonances
- RT strength functions

ENERGY LOSSES [13,283; 13,542]
- UF *degradation (energy)*
- UF *energy dissipation*
- UF *ionization loss*
- UF *losses (energy)*
- UF *ohmic plasma losses*
- UF+ *heat losses*
- SF *heat dissipation*
- NT1 ac losses
- NT1 relaxation losses
- RT attenuation
- RT bragg curve
- RT damping
- RT dissipation factor
- RT energy accounting
- RT energy conservation
- RT energy deposition
- RT energy recovery
- RT hysteresis
- RT ionization
- RT ionizing radiations
- RT landau fluctuations
- RT let
- RT microdosimetry
- RT particle losses
- RT power losses
- RT radiation effects
- RT radiation length
- RT radiation quality
- RT range
- RT shock absorbers
- RT slowing-down
- RT stopping power

energy management
- USE energy policy

energy of dissociation
- USE dissociation energy

energy operators
- USE hamiltonians

→ *energy performance standards*
- USE energy efficiency standards

ENERGY POLICY [4,143; 4,143]
(Overall policy concerning development, production, use, and conservation of energy and its sources.)
- UF *energy management*
- RT allocations
- RT economics
- RT energy
- RT government policies
- RT international energy agency
- RT nuclear power phaseout
- RT planning
- RT wends

ENERGY RANGE [795; 153,732]
- NT1 eev range
- NT1 ev range
  - NT2 ev range 01-10
  - NT2 ev range 10-100
  - NT2 ev range 100-1000
- NT1 gev range
  - NT2 gev range 01-10
  - NT2 gev range 10-100
  - NT2 gev range 100-1000
- NT1 kev range
  - NT2 kev range 01-10
  - NT2 kev range 10-100
  - NT2 kev range 100-1000
- NT1 mev range
  - NT2 mev range 01-10
  - NT2 mev range 10-100
  - NT2 mev range 100-1000
- NT1 milli ev range
- NT1 pev range
- NT1 relativistic range
- NT1 tev range
  - NT2 tev range 01-10
  - NT2 tev range 10-100
  - NT2 tev range 100-1000
- RT energy
- RT energy dependence
- RT group constants

ENERGY RECOVERY [54; 130] *Dec 85*
- NT1 heat recovery
- RT energy
- RT energy balance
- RT energy conservation
- RT energy losses
- RT recycling
- RT waste heat
- RT waste product utilization

ENERGY RESOLUTION [6,102; 6,102]
(Full Width at Half-Maximum of energy spectra.)
- BT1 resolution
- RT energy spectra
- RT energy-level density

ENERGY SHORTAGES [191; 191]
- RT energy consumption
- RT energy demand
- RT energy supplies
- RT international energy agency

ENERGY SOURCES [2,334; 26,284]
- NT1 biomass plantations
- NT1 fossil fuels
  - NT2 coal
    - NT3 black coal
      - NT4 anthracite
      - NT4 bituminous coal
    - NT3 lignite
  - NT2 gasoline
  - NT2 kerosene

```
         NT2     natural gas
         NT2     peat
         NT2     petroleum
            NT3     shale oil
         NT1     fuel gas
         NT2     coal gas
         NT2     natural gas
         NT1     nuclear fuels
         NT2     denatured fuel
         NT2     fuel slurries
         NT2     gas fuels
         NT2     solid fuels
            NT3     alloy nuclear fuels
            NT3     dispersion nuclear fuels
            NT3     mixed carbide fuels
            NT3     mixed nitride fuels
            NT3     mixed oxide fuels
         NT2     spent fuels
         NT1     radioisotope heat sources
         NT1     renewable energy sources
         NT2     biomass
         NT2     geothermal energy
         NT2     hydroelectric power
         NT2     solar energy
         NT2     tidal power
         NT2     wave power
         NT2     wind power
         NT1     waste heat
         RT      energy
         RT      energy supplies
         RT      energy yield
         RT      power generation
         RT      spacecraft power supplies
         RT      sun

ENERGY SPECTRA [30,659; 30,659]
         UF      energy distribution
         BT1     spectra
         RT      energy resolution
         RT      energy yield
         RT      group constants
         RT      rydberg correction
         RT      spectral density
         RT      transverse energy

ENERGY STORAGE [1,151; 1,402]
         UF      off-peak energy storage
         BT1     storage
         NT1     heat storage
         NT1     pumped storage
         NT1     superconductive energy storage
         RT      capacitors
         RT      electric batteries
         RT      energy storage systems
         RT      flywheels
         RT      water reservoirs

ENERGY STORAGE SYSTEMS
         [176; 1,552] Nov 80
         NT1     capacitors
         NT1     electric batteries
         NT1     flywheels
         RT      energy storage
         RT      plasma switches
         RT      water reservoirs

→  ENERGY SUPPLIES [0; 0] Oct 91
         RT      energy demand
         RT      energy shortages
         RT      energy sources
         RT      supply and demand

→  energy technol data exchange
         USE     etde


ENERGY TRANSFER [6,608; 32,972]
         UF      energy exchange
         UF      transfer (energy)
         NT1     heat transfer
         NT2     convection
            NT3     forced convection
            NT3     natural convection
         NT2     radiant heat transfer
         NT2     thermal conduction
         NT1     let
         NT1     radiationless decay
         RT      angular momentum transfer
         RT      energy accounting
         RT      energy balance
         RT      energy conversion
         RT      energy deposition
         RT      linear momentum transfer
         RT      mass transfer


energy transmission
         USE     power transmission

ENERGY YIELD [272; 272] Nov 75
         RT      efficiency
         RT      energy accounting
         RT      energy conversion
         RT      energy sources
         RT      energy spectra

ENERGY-LEVEL DENSITY
         [4,231; 4,231]
         UF      density (energy-level)
         UF      level density
         RT      energy levels
         RT      energy resolution
         RT      level widths


energy-level schemes
         USE     energy levels

ENERGY-LEVEL TRANSITIONS
         [18,529; 55,638]
         UF      electromagnetic transitions
         UF      transitions (energy level)
         NT1     coster-kronig transitions
         NT1     de-excitation
            NT2     radiationless decay
         NT1     excitation
            NT2     collective excitations
            NT2     coulomb excitation
            NT2     inner-shell excitation
         NT1     forbidden transitions
         NT1     isomeric transitions
         NT1     multipole transitions
            NT2     e0-transitions
            NT2     e1-transitions
            NT2     e2-transitions
            NT2     e3-transitions
            NT2     e4-transitions
            NT2     m1-transitions
            NT2     m2-transitions
            NT2     m3-transitions
            NT2     m4-transitions
         NT1     nuclear cascades
            NT2     gamma cascades
         NT1     stimulated emission
         RT      auger effect
         RT      band theory
         RT      decay
         RT      einstein coefficients
         RT      energy levels
         RT      franck-condon principle
         RT      mixing ratio
         RT      multi-photon processes
         RT      oscillator strengths
         RT      selection rules

ENERGY-LOSS SPECTROSCOPY
         [210; 210] Jan 86
         BT1     spectroscopy

ENERGY-MOMENTUM TENSOR
         [1,432; 1,432] Mar 83
         BT1     tensors
         RT      energy
         RT      general relativity theory
         RT      linear momentum
         RT      space-time


enewetak
         USE     eniwetok

ENFORCEMENT [161; 161] Nov 78
         RT      administrative procedures
         RT      implementation
         RT      laws
         RT      legal aspects
         RT      regulations


ENGINEERING [2,317; 4,172]
         NT1     civil engineering
         NT1     nuclear engineering


engineering test facil tokamak
         USE     etf tokamak


engineering test reactor
         USE     etr reactor


engines
         USE     motors


england
         USE     united kingdom

→  ENHANCED RECOVERY [0; 0] Oct 91
         UF      secondary recovery
         UF      tertiary recovery


→  enhanced recovery (biological)
         USE     biological recovery

ENIWETOK [74; 74]
         UF      enewetak
         BT1     marshall islands
            BT2     micronesia
               BT3     australasia
               BT3     islands
         RT      greenhouse project
         RT      hardtack project
         RT      holly event
         RT      ivy project

ENKEPHALINS [151; 151] Nov 78
         BT1     endorphins
            BT2     neuroregulators
               BT3     autonomic nervous system
                          agent
                  BT4     drugs
            BT2     polypeptides
               BT3     peptides
                  BT4     proteins
                     BT5     organic compounds
         RT      narcotics

ENOLS [60; 60]
         BT1     alcohols
            BT2     hydroxy compounds
               BT3     organic compounds
         RT      ketones


enriched materials (isotopes)
         USE     isotope enriched materials


enriched materials (ores)
         USE     ore concentrates

ENRICHED URANIUM [1,399; 2,612]
         BT1     isotope enriched materials
            BT2     materials
         BT1     uranium
            BT2     actinides
               BT3     metals
                  BT4     elements
         NT1     highly enriched uranium
         NT1     moderately enriched uranium
         NT1     slightly enriched uranium
         RT      enriched uranium reactors
```

ENRICHED URANIUM REACTORS
[138; 58,189]
(Reactors fuelled primarily with enriched uranium.)

- BT1 reactors
- NT1 acpr reactor
- NT1 aerojet-general nucleonics r
- NT1 afsr reactor
- NT1 agr type reactors
  - NT2 connah quay-b reactor
  - NT2 dungeness-b reactor
  - NT2 hartlepool reactor
  - NT2 heysham-a reactor
  - NT2 heysham-b reactor
  - NT2 hinkley point-b reactor
  - NT2 hunterston-b reactor
  - NT2 torness reactor
  - NT2 wagr reactor
- NT1 ai-l-77 reactor
- NT1 alrr reactor
- NT1 anex reactor
- NT1 anna reactor
- NT1 aps reactor
- NT1 apsara reactor
- NT1 arbus reactor
- NT1 argonaut type reactors
  - NT2 aeg-pr-10 reactor
  - NT2 arbi reactor
  - NT2 argonaut reactor
  - NT2 argos reactor
  - NT2 jason reactor
  - NT2 lfr reactor
  - NT2 moata reactor
  - NT2 nestor reactor
  - NT2 queen mary college utr-b react
  - NT2 ra-1 reactor
  - NT2 rb-2 reactor
  - NT2 rien-1 reactor
  - NT2 srrc-utr-100 reactor
  - NT2 stark reactor
  - NT2 strasbourg-cronenbourg reactor
  - NT2 uftr reactor
  - NT2 ulysse reactor
  - NT2 urr reactor
  - NT2 utr-10-kinki reactor
  - NT2 vpi-utr-10 reactor
- NT1 armf-1 reactor
- NT1 astra reactor
- NT1 atr reactor
- NT1 atrc reactor
- NT1 avogadro rs-1 reactor
- NT1 avr reactor
- NT1 bawtr reactor
- NT1 beloyarsk-1 reactor
- NT1 beloyarsk-2 reactor
- NT1 bgrr reactor
- NT1 bigr reactor
- NT1 bir reactor
- NT1 bor-60 reactor
- NT1 borax-1 reactor
- NT1 borax-2 reactor
- NT1 borax-3 reactor
- NT1 borax-4 reactor
- NT1 br-02 reactor
- NT1 br-2 reactor
- NT1 br-3-vn reactor
- NT1 brr reactor
- NT1 bsr-1 reactor
- NT1 bsr-2 reactor
- NT1 bwr type reactors
  - NT2 allens creek-1 reactor
  - NT2 allens creek-2 reactor
  - NT2 bailly-1 reactor
  - NT2 barsebaeck-1 reactor
  - NT2 barsebaeck-2 reactor
  - NT2 barton-1 reactor
  - NT2 barton-2 reactor
  - NT2 barton-3 reactor
  - NT2 barton-4 reactor
  - NT2 bell reactor
  - NT2 big rock point reactor
  - NT2 black fox-1 reactor
  - NT2 black fox-2 reactor
  - NT2 bonus reactor
  - NT2 browns ferry-1 reactor
  - NT2 browns ferry-2 reactor
  - NT2 browns ferry-3 reactor
  - NT2 brunsbuettel reactor
  - BT2 brunswick-1 reactor
  - NT2 brunswick-2 reactor
  - NT2 chinshan-1 reactor
  - NT2 chinshan-2 reactor
  - NT2 clinton-1 reactor
  - NT2 clinton-2 reactor
  - NT2 cofrentes reactor
  - NT2 cooper reactor
  - NT2 dodewaard reactor
  - NT2 douglas point-1 reactor
  - NT2 douglas point-2 reactor
  - NT2 dresden-1 reactor
  - NT2 dresden-2 reactor
  - NT2 dresden-3 reactor
  - NT2 duane arnold-1 reactor
  - NT2 ebwr reactor
  - NT2 enel-4 reactor
  - NT2 enrico fermi-2 reactor
  - NT2 err reactor
  - NT2 fitzpatrick reactor
  - NT2 forsmark-1 reactor
  - NT2 forsmark-2 reactor
  - NT2 forsmark-3 reactor
  - NT2 fukushima-ii-1 reactor
  - NT2 fukushima-ii-2 reactor
  - NT2 fukushima-ii-3 reactor
  - NT2 fukushima-ii-4 reactor
  - NT2 fukushima-1 reactor
  - NT2 fukushima-2 reactor
  - NT2 fukushima-3 reactor
  - NT2 fukushima-4 reactor
  - NT2 fukushima-5 reactor
  - NT2 fukushima-6 reactor
  - NT2 garigliano reactor
  - NT2 garona reactor
  - NT2 ge standard reactor
  - NT2 graben-1 reactor
  - NT2 grand gulf-1 reactor
  - NT2 grand gulf-2 reactor
  - NT2 gundremmingen-2 reactor
  - NT2 gundremmingen-3 reactor
  - NT2 hamaoka-1 reactor
  - NT2 hamaoka-2 reactor
  - NT2 hamaoka-3 reactor
  - NT2 hartsville-1 reactor
  - NT2 hartsville-2 reactor
  - NT2 hartsville-3 reactor
  - NT2 hartsville-4 reactor
  - NT2 hatch-1 reactor
  - NT2 hatch-2 reactor
  - NT2 hdr reactor
  - NT2 hope creek-1 reactor
  - NT3 newbold island-1 reactor
  - NT2 hope creek-2 reactor
  - NT3 newbold island-2 reactor
  - NT2 humboldt bay reactor
  - NT2 isar reactor
  - NT2 jpdr reactor
  - NT2 jpdr-2 reactor
  - NT2 kaiseraugst reactor
  - NT2 kashiwazaki-kariwa-1 reactor
  - NT2 kashiwazaki-kariwa-2 reactor
  - NT2 kashiwazaki-kariwa-3 reactor
  - NT2 kashiwazaki-kariwa-4 reactor
  - NT2 kashiwazaki-kariwa-5 reactor
  - NT2 kashiwazaki-kariwa-6 reactor
  - NT2 kashiwazaki-kariwa-7 reactor
  - NT2 kruemmel reactor
  - NT2 kuosheng-1 reactor
  - NT2 kuosheng-2 reactor
  - NT2 la salle county-1 reactor
  - NT2 la salle county-2 reactor
  - NT2 lacbwr reactor
  - NT2 laguna verde-1 reactor
  - NT2 laguna verde-2 reactor
  - NT2 leibstadt reactor
  - NT2 limerick-1 reactor
  - NT2 limerick-2 reactor
  - NT2 lingen reactor
  - NT2 mendocino-1 reactor
  - NT2 mendocino-2 reactor
  - NT2 millstone-1 reactor
  - NT2 montague-1 reactor
  - NT2 montague-2 reactor
  - NT2 montalto di castro-1 reactor
  - NT2 montalto di castro-2 reactor
  - NT2 monticello reactor
  - NT2 muehleberg reactor
  - NT2 nine mile point-1 reactor
  - NT2 nine mile point-2 reactor
  - NT2 okg-1 reactor
  - NT2 okg-2 reactor
  - NT2 onagawa-1 reactor
  - NT2 onagawa-2 reactor
  - NT2 oyster creek-1 reactor
  - NT2 pathfinder reactor
  - NT2 peach bottom-2 reactor
  - NT2 peach bottom-3 reactor
  - NT2 perry-1 reactor
  - NT2 perry-2 reactor
  - NT2 philippsburg-1 reactor
  - NT2 phipps bend-1 reactor
  - NT2 phipps bend-2 reactor
  - NT2 quad cities-1 reactor
  - NT2 quad cities-2 reactor
  - NT2 ringhals-1 reactor
  - NT2 river bend-1 reactor
  - NT2 river bend-2 reactor
  - NT2 rwe-bayernwerk reactor
  - NT2 shika-1 reactor
  - NT2 shimane-1 reactor
  - NT2 shimane-2 reactor
  - NT2 shoreham reactor
  - NT2 skagit-1 reactor
  - NT2 skagit-2 reactor
  - NT2 sl-1 reactor
  - NT2 susquehanna-1 reactor
  - NT2 susquehanna-2 reactor
  - NT2 tarapur-1 reactor
  - NT2 tarapur-2 reactor
  - NT2 tokai-2 reactor
  - NT2 tsuruga reactor
  - NT2 tullnerfeld reactor
  - NT2 tvo-1 reactor
  - NT2 tvo-2 reactor
  - NT2 vak reactor
  - NT2 vbwr reactor
  - NT2 vermont yankee reactor
  - NT2 verplanck-1 reactor
  - NT2 verplanck-2 reactor
  - NT2 vk-50 reactor
  - NT2 wnp-2 reactor
  - NT3 hanford-2 reactor
  - NT2 wuergassen reactor
  - NT2 zimmer-1 reactor
  - NT2 zimmer-2 reactor
- NT1 cabri reactor
- NT1 cesnef reactor
- NT1 chernobylsk-1 reactor
- NT1 chernobylsk-2 reactor
- NT1 chernobylsk-3 reactor
- NT1 chernobylsk-4 reactor
- NT1 consort-2 reactor
- NT1 coral-1 reactor
- NT1 cp-5 reactor
- NT1 cvtr reactor
- NT1 democritus reactor
- NT1 dfr reactor
- NT1 dido reactor
- NT1 dmtr reactor
- NT1 dr-1 reactor
- NT1 dr-2 reactor
- NT1 dr-3 reactor
- NT1 dragon reactor
- NT1 ebor reactor
- NT1 egcr reactor
- NT1 el-3 reactor
- NT1 el-4 reactor
- NT1 enrico fermi-1 reactor
- NT1 eocr reactor
- NT1 esada-vesr reactor
- NT1 essor reactor
- NT1 etr reactor
- NT1 fmrb reactor
- NT1 fnr reactor
- NT1 fr-0 reactor
- NT1 frf reactor
- NT1 frg-1 reactor
- NT1 frg-2 reactor
- NT1 frj-1 reactor
- NT1 frj-2 reactor
- NT1 frm reactor
- NT1 fulton-1 reactor
- NT1 fulton-2 reactor
- NT1 ga standard reactor
- NT1 getr reactor
- NT1 gtrr reactor
- NT1 harmonie reactor
- NT1 hbwr reactor
- NT1 hector reactor
- NT1 herald reactor
- NT1 hero reactor

NT1	hfbr reactor	NT1	prr reactor	NT2	flamanville-2 reactor
NT1	hfetr reactor	NT1	prr-1 reactor	NT2	forked river-1 reactor
NT1	hfir reactor	NT1	ptr reactor	NT2	genkai-1 reactor
NT1	hfr reactor	NT1	pulstar-buffalo reactor	NT2	genkai-2 reactor
NT1	hifar reactor	NT1	pwr type reactors	NT2	genkai-3 reactor
NT1	hnpf reactor	NT2	almaraz-1 reactor	NT2	genkai-4 reactor
NT1	hor reactor	NT2	almaraz-2 reactor	NT2	ginna-1 reactor
NT1	horace reactor	NT2	angra-1 reactor	NT2	goesgen reactor
NT1	hprr reactor	NT2	angra-2 reactor	NT2	golfech-1 reactor
NT1	htltr reactor	NT2	angra-3 reactor	NT2	grafenrheinfeld reactor
NT1	htr reactor	NT2	ardennes b-1 reactor	NT2	gravelines-b1 reactor
NT1	httr reactor	NT2	ardennes reactor	NT2	gravelines-c6 reactor
NT1	hwctr reactor	NT2	arkansas-1 reactor	NT2	greene county reactor
NT1	ian-r1 reactor	NT2	arkansas-2 reactor	NT2	greenwood-2 reactor
NT1	iear-1 reactor	NT2	asco-1 reactor	NT2	greenwood-3 reactor
NT1	ignalinsk-1 reactor	NT2	asco-2 reactor	NT2	grohnde reactor
NT1	ignalinsk-2 reactor	NT2	atlantic-1 reactor	NT2	hamm-uentrop reactor
NT1	irl reactor	NT2	atlantic-2 reactor	NT2	harris-1 reactor
NT1	irr-1 reactor	NT2	basf-1 reactor	NT2	harris-2 reactor
NT1	irt reactor	NT2	basf-2 reactor	NT2	harris-3 reactor
NT1	irt-sofia reactor	NT2	beaver valley-1 reactor	NT2	harris-4 reactor
NT1	irt-2000 djakarta reactor	NT2	beaver valley-2 reactor	NT2	haven-1 reactor
NT1	irt-2000 moscow reactor	NT2	bellefonte-1 reactor	NT3	koshkonong-1 reactor
NT1	isis reactor	NT2	bellefonte-2 reactor	NT2	haven-2 reactor
NT1	ispra-1 reactor	NT2	belleville sur loire-1 reactor	NT3	koshkonong-2 reactor
NT1	janus reactor	NT2	belleville sur loire-2 reactor	NT2	ikata reactor
NT1	jeep-2 reactor	NT2	beznau-1 reactor	NT2	ikata-2 reactor
NT1	jen reactor	NT2	beznau-2 reactor	NT2	ikata-3 reactor
NT1	jen-1 reactor	NT2	biblis-1 reactor	NT2	indian point-1 reactor
NT1	jmtr reactor	NT2	biblis-2 reactor	NT2	indian point-2 reactor
NT1	jrr-1 reactor	NT2	biblis-3 reactor	NT2	indian point-3 reactor
NT1	jrr-2 reactor	NT2	biblis-4 reactor	NT2	iran-1 reactor
NT1	jrr-4 reactor	NT2	blue hills-1 reactor	NT2	iran-2 reactor
NT1	kmr reactor	NT2	blue hills-2 reactor	NT2	isar-2 reactor
NT1	knk reactor	NT2	borssele reactor	NT2	jamesport-1 reactor
NT1	knk-2 reactor	NT2	br-3 reactor	NT2	jamesport-2 reactor
NT1	kuca reactor	NT2	braidwood-1 reactor	NT2	kewaunee reactor
NT1	kuhfr reactor	NT2	braidwood-2 reactor	NT2	kori-1 reactor
NT1	kur reactor	NT2	brokdorf reactor	NT2	kori-2 reactor
NT1	kursk-1 reactor	NT2	bugey-2 reactor	NT2	krsko reactor
NT1	kursk-2 reactor	NT2	bugey-3 reactor	NT2	lemoniz-1 reactor
NT1	kursk-3 reactor	NT2	bugey-4 reactor	NT2	lemoniz-2 reactor
NT1	kursk-4 reactor	NT2	bugey-5 reactor	NT2	lenin reactor
NT1	leningrad-1 reactor	NT2	bw standard reactor	NT2	leonid brezhnev reactor
NT1	leningrad-2 reactor	NT2	byron-1 reactor	NT2	loft reactor
NT1	leningrad-3 reactor	NT2	byron-2 reactor	NT2	lucie-1 reactor
NT1	leningrad-4 reactor	NT2	calhoun-1 reactor	NT2	lucie-2 reactor
NT1	lido reactor	NT2	calhoun-2 reactor	NT2	maanshan-1 reactor
NT1	litr reactor	NT2	callaway-1 reactor	NT2	maine yankee reactor
NT1	lptr reactor	NT2	callaway-2 reactor	NT2	marble hill-1 reactor
NT1	lucens reactor	NT2	calvert cliffs-1 reactor	NT2	marble hill-2 reactor
NT1	maple reactor	NT2	calvert cliffs-2 reactor	NT2	mc guire-1 reactor
NT1	maria reactor	NT2	catawba-1 reactor	NT2	mc guire-2 reactor
NT1	marviken reactor	NT2	catawba-2 reactor	NT2	mh-1a reactor
NT1	maryla reactor	NT2	cattenom-1 reactor	NT2	midland-1 reactor
NT1	masurca reactor	NT2	cattenom-2 reactor	NT2	midland-2 reactor
NT1	melusine-1 reactor	NT2	cattenom-3 reactor	NT2	mihama-1 reactor
NT1	minerve reactor	NT2	cattenom-4 reactor	NT2	mihama-2 reactor
NT1	mitr reactor	NT2	ce standard reactor	NT2	mihama-3 reactor
NT1	mnr reactor	NT2	cherokee-1 reactor	NT2	millstone-2 reactor
NT1	mrr reactor	NT2	cherokee-2 reactor	NT2	millstone-3 reactor
NT1	msre reactor	NT2	cherokee-3 reactor	NT2	muelheim-kaerlich reactor
NT1	mtr reactor	NT2	comanche peak-1 reactor	NT2	mutsu reactor
NT1	murr reactor	NT2	comanche peak-2 reactor	NT2	neckar reactor
NT1	n-reactor	NT2	connecticut yankee reactor	NT2	neckar-2 reactor
NT1	ncscr-1 reactor	NT2	cook-1 reactor	NT2	nep-1 reactor
NT1	niederaichbach reactor	NT2	cook-2 reactor	NT2	nep-2 reactor
NT1	nsrr reactor	NT2	cruas-2 reactor	NT2	neupotz-1 reactor
NT1	ntr reactor	NT2	cruas-3 reactor	NT2	neupotz-2 reactor
NT1	nuclear furnace reactor	NT2	crystal river-3 reactor	NT2	nogent sur seine-1 reactor
NT1	oldbury-b reactor	NT2	crystal river-4 reactor	NT2	nogent sur seine-2 reactor
NT1	omro reactor	NT2	dampierre-1 reactor	NT2	north anna-1 reactor
NT1	orr reactor	NT2	davis besse-1 reactor	NT2	north anna-2 reactor
NT1	osiris reactor	NT2	davis besse-2 reactor	NT2	north anna-3 reactor
NT1	owr reactor	NT2	davis besse-3 reactor	NT2	north anna-4 reactor
NT1	parr reactor	NT2	daya bay reactor	NT2	north coast-1 reactor
NT1	pbr reactor	NT2	diablo canyon-1 reactor	NT2	obrigheim reactor
NT1	pctr reactor	NT2	diablo canyon-2 reactor	NT2	oconee-1 reactor
NT1	peach bottom-1 reactor	NT2	doel-1 reactor	NT2	oconee-2 reactor
NT1	pegase reactor	NT2	doel-2 reactor	NT2	oconee-3 reactor
NT1	peggy reactor	NT2	doel-3 reactor	NT2	oi-1 reactor
NT1	pelinduna reactor	NT2	doel-4 reactor	NT2	oi-2 reactor
NT1	perryman-1 reactor	NT2	efdr-50 reactor	NT2	oi-3 reactor
NT1	perryman-2 reactor	NT2	emsland reactor	NT2	oi-4 reactor
NT1	phebus reactor	NT2	erie-1 reactor	NT2	otto hahn reactor
NT1	phenix reactor	NT2	erie-2 reactor	NT2	palisades-1 reactor
NT1	pluto reactor	NT2	farley-1 reactor	NT2	palo verde-1 reactor
NT1	pnpf reactor	NT2	farley-2 reactor	NT2	palo verde-2 reactor
NT1	prnc-l-77 reactor	NT2	fessenheim-1 reactor	NT2	palo verde-3 reactor
NT1	proteus reactor	NT2	flamanville-1 reactor	NT2	palo verde-4 reactor

NT2	palo verde-5 reactor	NT2	ulchin-2 reactor	NT1	rospo reactor
NT2	paluel-1 reactor	NT2	unterweser reactor	NT1	rpt reactor
NT2	paluel-2 reactor	NT2	vahnum-1 reactor	NT1	rts-1 reactor
NT2	paluel-3 reactor	NT2	vahnum-2 reactor	NT1	rv-1 reactor
NT2	paluel-4 reactor	NT2	vogtle-1 reactor	NT1	r2-0 reactor
NT2	pebble springs-1 reactor	NT2	vogtle-2 reactor	NT1	safari-1 reactor
NT2	pebble springs-2 reactor	NT2	vogtle-3 reactor	NT1	saphir reactor
NT2	penly-1 reactor	NT2	vogtle-4 reactor	NT1	sbr-1 reactor
NT2	perkins-1 reactor	NT2	waterford-3 reactor	NT1	schmehausen reactor
NT2	perkins-2 reactor	NT2	waterford-4 reactor	NT1	ser reactor
NT2	perkins-3 reactor	NT2	watts bar-1 reactor	NT1	sghwr reactor
NT2	philippsburg-2 reactor	NT2	watts bar-2 reactor	NT1	shca reactor
NT2	pilgrim-1 reactor	NT2	westinghouse standard reactor	NT1	silene reactor
NT2	pilgrim-2 reactor	NT2	wnp-1 reactor	NT1	siloe reactor
NT2	pilgrim-3 reactor	NT2	wnp-3 reactor	NT1	siloette reactor
NT2	pm-2a reactor	NT2	wnp-4 reactor	NT1	slowpoke type reactors
NT2	pm-3a reactor	NT2	wnp-5 reactor	NT2	slowpoke-alberta reactor
NT2	pnpp-1 reactor	NT2	wolf creek-1 reactor	NT2	slowpoke-dalhousie reactor
NT2	point beach-1 reactor	NT2	wup-3 reactor	NT2	slowpoke-montreal reactor
NT2	point beach-2 reactor	NT2	wup-4 reactor	NT2	slowpoke-ottawa reactor
NT2	prairie island-1 reactor	NT2	wup-5 reactor	NT2	slowpoke-toronto reactor
NT2	prairie island-2 reactor	NT2	wup-6 reactor	NT2	slowpoke-wnre reactor
NT2	qinshan reactor	NT2	wwer type reactors	NT1	smolensk-1 reactor
NT2	quanicassee-1 reactor	NT3	armenian-1 reactor	NT1	smolensk-2 reactor
NT2	quanicassee-2 reactor	NT3	armenian-2 reactor	NT1	snap 10 reactor
NT2	rancho seco-1 reactor	NT3	balakovo-1 reactor	NT2	s10fs-1 reactor
NT2	remerschen reactor	NT3	balakovo-2 reactor	NT2	s10fs-3 reactor
NT2	rheinsberg akw1 reactor	NT3	blahutovice-1 reactor	NT2	s10fs-4 reactor
NT2	ringhals-2 reactor	NT3	bohunice v-1 reactor	NT1	snap 2 reactor
NT2	ringhals-3 reactor	NT3	bohunice v-2 reactor	NT2	s2ds reactor
NT2	ringhals-4 reactor	NT3	dukovany v-2 reactor	NT1	snap 8 reactor
NT2	robinson-2 reactor	NT3	greifswald-1 reactor	NT2	s8dr reactor
NT2	rooppur reactor	NT3	greifswald-2 reactor	NT2	s8er reactor
NT2	rowe yankee reactor	NT3	greifswald-3 reactor	NT1	snaptran reactors
NT2	saint alban-1 reactor	NT3	greifswald-4 reactor	NT1	spert-1 reactor
NT2	saint alban-2 reactor	NT3	greifswald-5 reactor	NT1	spert-2 reactor
NT2	salem-1 reactor	NT3	greifswald-6 reactor	NT1	spert-3 reactor
NT2	salem-2 reactor	NT3	kalinin-1 reactor	NT1	spert-4 reactor
NT2	san onofre-1 reactor	NT3	kalinin-3 reactor	NT1	sr-oa reactor
NT2	san onofre-2 reactor	NT3	kecerovce-1 reactor	NT1	sr-1 reactor
NT2	san onofre-3 reactor	NT3	khmelnitskij-1 reactor	NT1	sre reactor
NT2	savannah reactor	NT3	kola-1 reactor	NT1	stek reactor
NT2	saxton reactor	NT3	kola-2 reactor	NT1	stir reactor
NT2	seabrook-1 reactor	NT3	kola-3 reactor	NT1	summit-1 reactor
NT2	seabrook-2 reactor	NT3	kola-4 reactor	NT1	summit-2 reactor
NT2	selni reactor	NT3	kozloduy-1 reactor	NT1	super phenix reactor
NT2	sendai-1 reactor	NT3	kozloduy-2 reactor	NT1	supo reactor
NT2	sendai-2 reactor	NT3	kozloduy-3 reactor	NT1	sur-100 series reactor
NT2	sequoyah-1 reactor	NT3	loviisa-1 reactor	NT1	tca reactor
NT2	sequoyah-2 reactor	NT3	loviisa-2 reactor	NT1	thetis reactor
NT2	shippingport reactor	NT3	mochovce-1 reactor	NT1	thor reactor
NT2	sizewell-b reactor	NT3	paks-1 reactor	NT1	thtr-300 reactor
NT2	sm-1 reactor	NT3	paks-2 reactor	NT1	tibr reactor
NT2	sm-1a reactor	NT3	paks-3 reactor	NT1	toshiba reactor
NT2	south texas project-1 reactor	NT3	paks-4 reactor	NT1	tr-1 reactor
NT2	south texas project-2 reactor	NT3	rovno-1 reactor	NT1	treat reactor
NT2	stade reactor	NT3	rovno-2 reactor	NT1	triga type reactors
NT2	sterling-1 reactor	NT3	rovno-3 reactor	NT2	afrri reactor
NT2	summer-1 reactor	NT3	rovno-4 reactor	NT2	cornell triga-mk-2 reactor
NT2	sundesert-1 reactor	NT3	rovno-5 reactor	NT2	dow triga-mk-1 reactor
NT2	sundesert-2 reactor	NT3	south ukrainian-1 reactor	NT2	fir-1 reactor
NT2	surry-1 reactor	NT3	south ukrainian-2 reactor	NT2	frf-2 reactor
NT2	surry-2 reactor	NT3	south ukrainian-3 reactor	NT2	frn reactor
NT2	surry-3 reactor	NT3	stendal-1 reactor	NT2	gulf triga-mk-3 reactor
NT2	surry-4 reactor	NT3	tatarian reactor	NT2	lopra reactor
NT2	slc prototype reactor	NT3	temelin-1 reactor	NT2	nscr reactor
NT2	takahama-1 reactor	NT3	wwer-1 reactor	NT2	ostr reactor
NT2	takahama-2 reactor	NT3	wwer-2 reactor	NT2	prpr reactor
NT2	takahama-3 reactor	NT3	wwer-3 reactor	NT2	pstr reactor
NT2	takahama-4 reactor	NT3	wwer-4 reactor	NT2	rtp reactor
NT2	thr reactor	NT3	wwer-5 reactor	NT2	trico reactor
NT2	three mile island-1 reactor	NT3	zaporozhe-1 reactor	NT2	triga-brazil reactor
NT2	three mile island-2 reactor	NT3	zaporozhe-2 reactor	NT2	triga-texas reactor
NT2	tihange reactor	NT3	zaporozhe-3 reactor	NT2	triga-veterans reactor
NT2	tihange-2 reactor	NT3	zaporozhe-4 reactor	NT2	triga-1-arizona reactor
NT2	tihange-3 reactor	NT2	wyhl-1 reactor	NT2	triga-1-california reactor
NT2	tomari-1 reactor	NT2	wyhl-2 reactor	NT2	triga-1-hanford reactor
NT2	tomari-2 reactor	NT2	yellow creek-1 reactor	NT2	triga-1-hanover reactor
NT2	tricastin-1 reactor	NT2	yellow creek-2 reactor	NT2	triga-1-heidelberg reactor
NT2	tricastin-4 reactor	NT2	zion-1 reactor	NT2	triga-1-michigan reactor
NT2	trillo-1 reactor	NT2	zion-2 reactor	NT2	triga-2 reactor
NT2	trojan reactor	NT2	zorita-1 reactor	NT2	triga-2-dalat reactor
NT2	tsuruga-2 reactor	NT1	r-a reactor	NT2	triga-2-illinois reactor
NT2	turkey point-3 reactor	NT1	r-2 reactor	NT2	triga-2-kansas reactor
NT2	turkey point-4 reactor	NT1	ra-5 reactor	NT2	triga-2-ljubljana reactor
NT2	tva-1 reactor	NT1	rana reactor	NT2	triga-2-mainz reactor
NT2	tva-2 reactor	NT1	rapsodie reactor	NT2	triga-2-musashi reactor
NT2	tyrone-1 reactor	NT1	rb-1 reactor	NT2	triga-2-pavia reactor
NT2	tyrone-2 reactor	NT1	rg-1m reactor	NT2	triga-2-rikkyo reactor
NT2	ulchin-1 reactor	NT1	ritmo reactor	NT2	triga-2-rome reactor

NT2	triga-2-seoul reactor		*enrichment plants (ultracentri*			RT	thermodynamics
NT2	triga-2-vienna reactor		USE	centrifuge enrichment plants			

NT2 triga-2-seoul reactor
NT2 triga-2-vienna reactor
NT2 triga-3-la jolla reactor
NT2 triga-3-salazar reactor
NT2 triga-3-seoul reactor
NT2 ucbrr reactor
NT2 wsur reactor
NT1 triton reactor
NT1 trr-1 reactor
NT1 tsr-1 reactor
NT1 tz1 reactor
NT1 tz2 reactor
NT1 uhtrex reactor
NT1 umne-1 reactor
NT1 umrr reactor
NT1 utrr reactor
NT1 uvar reactor
NT1 uwnr reactor
NT1 uwtr reactor
NT1 venus reactor
NT1 vg-400 reactor
NT1 vgr-50 reactor
NT1 vhtr reactor
NT1 vidal-1 reactor
NT1 vidal-2 reactor
NT1 viper reactor
NT1 vr-1 reactor
NT1 vrain reactor
NT1 wntr reactor
NT1 wpir reactor
NT1 wr-1·reactor
NT1 wrrr reactor
NT1 wtr reactor
NT1 wwr type reactors
  NT2 budapest training reactor
  NT2 irt-baghdad reactor
  NT2 wwr-k-alma-ata reactor
  NT2 wwr-m-kiev reactor
  NT2 wwr-m-leningrad reactor
  NT2 wwr-s-bucharest reactor
  NT2 wwr-s-budapest reactor
  NT2 wwr-s-cairo reactor
  NT2 wwr-s-moscow reactor
  NT2 wwr-s-prague reactor
  NT2 wwr-s-tashkent reactor
  NT2 wwr-sm rossendorf reactor
  NT2 wwr-2 reactor
NT1 zlfr reactor
NT1 zpr reactor
RT beloyarsk-3 reactor
RT bn-350 reactor
RT cesar reactor
RT clinch river breeder reactor
RT ebr-2 reactor
RT enriched uranium
RT eole reactor
RT iea-zpr reactor
RT lwgr type reactors
RT nora reactor
RT pdp reactor
RT pfr reactor
RT sneak reactor
RT vera reactor
RT zebra reactor
RT zenith reactor

enrichment (isotopic)
  USE isotope separation

enrichment (ores)
  USE ore enrichment

enrichment (uranium)
  USE isotope separation

enrichment plants (centrifuge)
  USE centrifuge enrichment plants

enrichment plants (gas diffusi
  USE gaseous diffusion plants

enrichment plants (ultracentri
  USE centrifuge enrichment plants

ENRICO FERMI-1 REACTOR [78; 78]
(Lagoona Beach, Michigan, USA)
BT1 enriched uranium reactors
  BT2 reactors
BT1 lmfbr type reactors
  BT2 fbr type reactors
    BT3 breeder reactors
      BT4 reactors
    BT3 fast reactors
      BT4 epithermal reactors
        BT5 reactors
  BT2 liquid metal cooled reactors
    BT3 reactors
BT1 power reactors
  BT2 reactors
BT1 sodium cooled reactors
  BT2 liquid metal cooled reactors
    BT3 reactors

ENRICO FERMI-2 REACTOR [59; 59]
(New Port, Michigan, USA)
BT1 bwr type reactors
  BT2 enriched uranium reactors
    BT3 reactors
  BT2 power reactors
    BT3 reactors
  BT2 thermal reactors
    BT3 reactors
  BT2 water cooled reactors
    BT3 reactors
  BT2 water moderated reactors
    BT3 reactors

enstatite
  USE magnesium silicates

ENTERITIS [118; 118]
BT1 digestive system diseases
  BT2 diseases
RT diarrhea
RT intestines

ENTHALPY [2,993; 7,395]
BT1 thermodynamic properties
  BT2 physical properties
NT1 absorption heat
NT1 adsorption heat
NT1 mixing heat
NT1 reaction heat
  NT2 combustion heat
  NT2 dissociation heat
  NT2 formation heat
NT1 solution heat
NT1 transition heat
  NT2 fusion heat
  NT2 sublimation heat
  NT2 vaporization heat
RT entropy
RT thermodynamics

enthalpy of formation
  USE formation heat

entombment (radioactive matls)
  USE containment

entomology
  USE insects

ENTRAINMENT [449; 449]
RT extraction apparatuses
RT solvent extraction

ENTROPY [5,202; 5,202]
BT1 thermodynamic properties
  BT2 physical properties
RT enthalpy
RT formation free enthalpy
RT h theorem
RT isentropic processes

RT thermodynamics

ENTRY CONTROL SYSTEMS [67; 67]
Jul 86
(Systems for controlling access to areas of a facility.)
UF *access denial systems*
RT human intrusion
RT identification systems
RT physical protection
RT physical protection devices
RT security

entwick. fortschr. druckw reac
  USE efdr-50 reactor

ENVIRONMENT [14,427; 14,499]
RT accidents
RT biological adaptation
RT biosphere
RT contamination
RT controlled atmospheres
RT earth atmosphere
RT ecosystems
RT environmental effects
RT environmental impact statement
RT environmental impacts
RT environmental policy
RT environmental transport
RT fallout deposits
RT habitat
RT hydrosphere
RT land use
RT pollution
RT populations
RT preventive medicine
RT radiation protection
RT radionuclide migration
RT reactor sites
RT recreational areas
RT regional analysis
RT regional cooperation
RT site selection
RT source terms
RT us natl environment policy act
RT water use

→ **ENVIRONMENTAL EFFECTS** [0; 0]
Dec 82
RT environment
RT environmental impact statement
RT environmental impacts
RT environmental policy
RT land pollution
RT thermal pollution
RT water pollution

ENVIRONMENTAL ENGINEERING [108; 108]
RT air conditioning
RT pollution control equipment
RT remedial action

environmental exposure chamber
  USE exposure chambers

ENVIRONMENTAL EXPOSURE PATHWAY [2,354; 2,354]
RT biointrusion
RT biological availability
RT biological models
RT food chains
RT radioactive waste disposal
RT radionuclide migration

ENVIRONMENTAL IMPACT STATEMENT [574; 574]
(Use only for items about Environmental Impact Statements, not for documents which are such statements.)
RT document types
RT environment
RT environmental effects
RT environmental impacts
RT us natl environment policy act

ENVIRONMENTAL IMPACTS
[6,376; 6,376] *Jul 77*
- RT aesthetics
- RT environment
- RT environmental effects
- RT environmental impact statement
- RT environmental policy
- RT nuclear winter
- RT site surveys

ENVIRONMENTAL MATERIALS
[630; 630] *Dec 80*
(Use only for unspecified samples from the environment.)
- BT1 materials
- RT air
- RT atmospheric precipitations
- RT biological materials
- RT minerals
- RT ores
- RT rocks
- RT sediments
- RT soils
- RT water

ENVIRONMENTAL POLICY [625; 625]
Feb 81
- RT economics
- RT environment
- RT environmental effects
- RT environmental impacts
- RT government policies
- RT planning

environmental protection agenc
- USE us epa

→ ### ENVIRONMENTAL QUALITY [0; 2]
Aug 91
- NT1 air quality
- NT1 water quality

ENVIRONMENTAL TRANSPORT
[1,405; 10,151] *Dec 82*
(For movement of chemicals, nuclides, etc., in the environment; not for goods and persons.)
- BT1 mass transfer
- NT1 radionuclide migration
- RT air-water interactions
- RT ecological concentration
- RT environment
- RT leachates
- RT transfrontier contamination
- RT transfrontier pollution

ENZYME ACTIVITY [3,098; 3,098]
- UF+ *cellulolytic activity*
- RT activity levels
- RT biochemical reaction kinetics
- RT catalysis
- RT chemical reaction kinetics
- RT enzymes
- RT metabolism
- RT structure-activity relationshi

ENZYME IMMUNOASSAY [243; 243]
Jan 85
- UF *elisa*
- BT1 immunoassay
- RT antibodies
- RT antigen-antibody reactions
- RT antigens
- RT cpb
- RT enzymes
- RT tracer techniques

ENZYME INHIBITORS [1,308; 1,308]
Aug 78
- UF *inhibitors (enzyme)*
- RT enzymes
- RT inhibition

ENZYMES [2,472; 13,404]
- UF+ *pre*
- BT1 organic compounds
- NT1 hydrolases
- NT2 acid anhydrases
- NT3 phosphohydrolases
- NT4 atp-ase
- NT2 esterases
- NT3 carboxylesterases
- NT4 cholinesterase
- NT4 lipases
- NT3 phosphatases
- NT4 acid phosphatase
- NT4 alkaline phosphatase
- NT4 nucleotidases
- NT3 phosphodiesterases
- NT4 nucleases
- NT5 dna-ase
- NT5 endonucleases
- NT5 rna-ase
- NT2 glycosyl hydrolases
- NT3 o-glycosyl hydrolases
- NT4 amylase
- NT4 galactosidase
- NT4 glucuronidase
- NT4 lysozyme
- NT2 non-peptide c-n hydrolases
- NT3 amidases
- NT4 urease
- NT3 amidinases
- NT4 arginase
- NT2 peptide hydrolases
- NT3 acid proteinases
- NT4 pepsin
- NT3 aminopeptidases
- NT3 carboxypeptidases
- NT3 nonspecific peptidases
- NT4 renin
- NT4 urokinase
- NT3 serine proteinases
- NT4 chymotrypsin
- NT4 fibrinolysin
- NT4 kallikrein
- NT4 thrombin
- NT4 trypsin
- NT3 sh-proteinases
- NT4 cathepsins
- NT4 papain
- NT4 streptococcal proteinase
- NT1 isomerases
- NT1 ligases
- NT2 carboxylase
- NT1 lyases
- NT2 carbon-carbon lyases
- NT3 aldolases
- NT3 decarboxylases
- NT2 carbon-oxygen lyases
- NT3 hyaluronidase
- NT3 hydro-lyases
- NT4 carbonic anhydrase
- NT2 cyclases
- NT1 oxidoreductases
- NT2 dehydrogenases
- NT3 diaphorases
- NT3 lactate dehydrogenase
- NT3 nitrogenase
- NT2 hydrogenases
- NT2 hydroxylases
- NT3 tyrosinase
- NT2 oxidases
- NT3 amine oxidases
- NT3 cytochrome oxidase
- NT3 histaminase
- NT3 luciferase
- NT3 uricase
- NT2 oxygenases
- NT3 tryptophan oxygenase
- NT2 peroxidases
- NT3 catalase
- NT2 superoxide dismutase
- NT1 transferases
- NT2 carbon-group transferases
- NT3 methyl transferases
- NT2 glycosyl transferases
- NT2 nitrogen transferases
- NT3 aminotransferases
- NT2 phosphorus-group transferases
- NT3 nucleotidyltransferases
- NT4 polymerases
- NT5 dna polymerases
- NT5 rna polymerases
- NT3 phosphotransferases
- NT4 hexokinase
- RT autolysis
- RT biochemistry
- RT biosynthesis
- RT catalysis
- RT coenzymes
- RT digestion
- RT enzyme activity
- RT enzyme immunoassay
- RT enzyme inhibitors
- RT glycolysis
- RT isoenzymes
- RT metabolism
- RT mitochondria
- RT precursor
- RT protein denaturation
- RT radioenzymatic assay
- RT substrates

EOCR REACTOR [2; 2]
(Idaho National Engineering Lab., Idaho Falls, Idaho, USA)
- UF *exp. organic cooled reactor*
- BT1 enriched uranium reactors
- BT2 reactors
- BT1 experimental reactors
- BT2 research and test reactors
- BT3 reactors
- BT1 organic cooled reactors
- BT2 reactors
- BT1 organic moderated reactors
- BT2 reactors
- BT1 research reactors
- BT2 research and test reactors
- BT3 reactors
- BT1 tank type reactors
- BT2 reactors
- BT1 test reactors
- BT2 research and test reactors
- BT3 reactors
- BT2 test facilities
- BT1 thermal reactors
- BT2 reactors

EOLE REACTOR [13; 13]
(CEA/CEN, Cadarache, St. Paul Lez Durance, France)
- BT1 heavy water cooled reactors
- BT2 reactors
- BT1 heavy water moderated reactors
- BT2 reactors
- BT1 research reactors
- BT2 research and test reactors
- BT3 reactors
- BT1 tank type reactors
- BT2 reactors
- RT enriched uranium reactors
- RT natural uranium reactors

EOSIN [43; 43]
- BT1 dyes
- BT1 hydroxy acids
- BT2 carboxylic acids
- BT3 organic acids
- BT4 organic compounds
- BT1 indicators
- BT1 organic bromine compounds
- BT2 organic halogen compounds
- BT3 organic compounds
- RT phthalic acid

EOSINOPHILS [96; 96]
- BT1 leukocytes
- BT2 blood cells
- BT3 blood
- BT4 body fluids
- BT5 biological materials
- BT6 materials

epa
- USE us epa

EPEC REACTOR [5; 5]
BT1 power reactors
BT2 reactors

EPHEDRINE [13; 13]
BT1 alkaloids
BT2 organic compounds
BT1 amines
BT2 organic compounds
BT1 hydroxy compounds
BT2 organic compounds
BT1 sympathomimetics
BT2 autonomic nervous system agent
BT3 drugs
BT1 vasoconstrictors
BT2 cardiovascular agents
BT3 drugs

EPIC STORAGE RING [19; 19]
BT1 storage rings

EPICENTERS [22; 22] Jan 85
(The parts of the earth's surface directly above the foci of earthquakes.)
RT earthquakes
RT ground motion
RT seismic waves

EPIDEMIOLOGY [1,415; 1,415]
RT a-bomb survivors
RT disease incidence
RT disease resistance
RT human populations
RT infectious diseases
RT preventive medicine

EPIDERMIS [560; 560]
BT1 epithelium
BT2 tissues
BT3 body
BT1 skin
BT2 organs
BT3 body

EPILATION [63; 63]
RT hair
RT skin

EPILEPSY [268; 268] Jul 80
BT1 nervous system diseases
BT2 diseases

epinephrine
USE adrenaline

epiphysis (bones)
USE bone tissues

epiphysis (pineal gland)
USE pineal gland

EPITAXY [2,962; 2,962]
RT crystal growth
RT crystallization

EPITHELIOMAS [82; 82]
BT1 neoplasms
BT2 diseases
RT epithelium

EPITHELIUM [1,334; 1,881]
BT1 tissues
BT2 body
NT1 epidermis
RT carcinomas
RT conjunctiva
RT crypt cells
RT endothelium
RT epitheliomas
RT hair follicles
RT mucous membranes

EPITHERMAL NEUTRONS [1,037; 1,037]
BT1 neutrons
BT2 nucleons
BT3 baryons
BT4 fermions
BT4 hadrons
BT5 elementary particles
RT epithermal reactors

EPITHERMAL REACTORS [42; 29,442]
BT1 reactors
NT1 fast reactors
NT2 actinide burner reactors
NT2 afsr reactor
NT2 aprf reactor
NT2 bigr reactor
NT2 bir reactor
NT2 cfrmf reactor
NT2 clementine reactor
NT2 coral-1 reactor
NT2 ecel reactor
NT2 fbr type reactors
NT3 aipfr reactor
NT3 gcfr type reactors
NT4 gcfr reactor
NT3 lmfbr type reactors
NT4 beloyarsk-3 reactor
NT4 beloyarsk-4 reactor
NT4 bn-1600 reactor
NT4 bn-350 reactor
NT4 bn-800 reactor
NT4 bor-60 reactor
NT4 cdfr reactor
NT4 clinch river breeder reactor
NT4 dfr reactor
NT4 ebr-1 reactor
NT4 ebr-2 reactor
NT4 enrico fermi-1 reactor
NT4 joyo reactor
NT4 kalpakkam lmfbr reactor
NT4 monju reactor
NT4 pfr reactor
NT4 phenix reactor
NT4 plbr reactor
NT4 rapsodie reactor
NT4 sbr-2 reactor
NT4 sbr-5 reactor
NT4 snr reactor
NT4 snr-2 reactor
NT4 super phenix reactor
NT3 pec brasimone reactor
NT3 sbr-1 reactor
NT3 zebra reactor
NT2 fbrf reactor
NT2 fca reactor
NT2 fftf reactor
NT2 fr-0 reactor
NT2 harmonie reactor
NT2 hprr reactor
NT2 ibr-2 reactor
NT2 ibr-30 reactor
NT2 ifr reactor
NT2 kalpakkam pfr reactor
NT2 knk-2 reactor
NT2 lampre-1 reactor
NT2 masurca reactor
NT2 purnima reactor
NT2 purnima-2 reactor
NT2 saref reactor
NT2 sefor reactor
NT2 sneak reactor
NT2 sora reactor
NT2 stf reactor
NT2 tapiro reactor
NT2 tibr reactor
NT2 vera reactor
NT2 viper reactor
NT2 wntr reactor
NT2 yayoi reactor
NT2 zephyr reactor
NT2 zppr reactor
NT2 zpr-3 reactor
NT2 zpr-6 reactor
NT2 zpr-9 reactor
NT2 zrr reactor
NT1 intermediate reactors
NT2 thor reactor
RT epithermal neutrons

EPOXIDES [1,218; 1,254]
UF *epoxy compounds*
UF *oxirans*
BT1 organic oxygen compounds
BT2 organic compounds
NT1 araldite
RT heterocyclic compounds
RT potting materials

epoxy compounds
USE epoxides

epr
USE electron spin resonance

EPR SPECTROMETERS [139; 139]
BT1 spectrometers
BT2 measuring instruments

EPRI [860; 860] Dec 82
(Organization founded by US utilities to develop and carry out broad, coordinated technology program for improving electric power.)
UF *electric power research inst.*
RT electric power
RT electric utilities

epstein-barr virus
USE oncogenic viruses

EQUATIONS [6,767; 73,908]
NT1 abfst equation
NT1 bethe-goldstone equation
NT1 bethe-salpeter equation
NT1 bloch equations
NT1 born-mayer equation
NT1 chapman-kolmogorov equation
NT1 differential equations
NT2 bbgky equation
NT2 dirac-hestenes equation
NT2 hill equation
NT2 joos-weinberg equation
NT2 mathieu equation
NT2 partial differential equations
NT3 boltzmann equation
NT3 boltzmann-vlasov equation
NT4 plasma fluid equations
NT3 continuity equations
NT3 equations of motion
NT3 fokker-planck equation
NT3 fourier heat equation
NT3 grad-shafranov equation
NT3 hamilton-jacobi equations
NT3 korteweg-de vries equation
NT3 lagrange equations
NT3 laplace equation
NT3 maxwell equations
NT3 navier-stokes equations
NT3 poisson equation
NT3 proca equations
NT3 wave equations
NT4 dirac equation
NT4 klein-gordon equation
NT4 schroedinger equation
NT2 riccati equation
NT2 schwinger functional equations
NT2 sturm-liouville equation
NT1 equations of state
NT1 faddeev equations
NT1 field equations
NT2 dirac equation
NT2 einstein field equations
NT2 einstein-maxwell equations
NT2 klein-gordon equation
NT2 sine-gordon equation
NT1 gribov-lipatov relation
NT1 integral equations
NT2 blankenbecler-sugar equations
NT2 fredholm equation
NT2 lippmann-schwinger equation
NT2 quasipotential equation
NT2 volterra integral equations
NT1 kinetic equations
NT1 langevin equation

NT1 london equation
NT1 low equation
NT1 massey-mohr equation
NT1 percus-yevick equation
NT1 prediction equations
NT1 reactor kinetics equations
  NT2 response matrix method
NT1 richardson equation
NT1 rydberg equation
NT1 saha equation
NT1 secular equation
NT1 selengut-goertzel equation
NT1 sum rules
NT1 weil equation
NT1 wilkins equation
RT functions
RT galerkin-petrov method
RT mathematics
RT series expansion

§ **EQUATIONS OF MOTION**
[9,017; 9,017]
BT1 partial differential equations
  BT2 differential equations
    BT3 equations
RT anharmonic oscillators
RT canonical transformations
RT hamilton-jacobi equations
RT hamiltonian function
RT harmonic oscillators
RT lagrangian function
RT mechanics
RT particle kinematics

EQUATIONS OF STATE [3,563; 3,563]
BT1 equations
RT thermodynamics
RT virial equation

EQUATOR [379; 379]
RT geomagnetic equator
RT latitude effect

equatorial electrojets
USE electrojets

EQUILIBRIUM [8,378; 11,264]
NT1 lte
NT1 mhd equilibrium
NT1 thermal equilibrium
RT chemical reactions
RT dynamic function studies
RT partition
RT population dynamics
RT reaction kinetics
RT stability
RT steady-state conditions
RT thermodynamic activity

EQUILIBRIUM PLASMA [1,343; 1,343]
BT1 plasma
RT magnetic surfaces

§ **EQUIPMENT** [1,440; 57,012] *Dec 82*
(Use of a more specific term is strongly recommended.)
UF *apparatus*
UF *devices*
UF *machinery*
NT1 amplifiers
  NT2 ac amplifiers
  NT2 dc amplifiers
  NT2 dielectric amplifiers
  NT2 gasers
  NT2 high frequency amplifiers
  NT2 lasers
    NT3 chemical lasers
    NT3 dye lasers
    NT3 free electron lasers
    NT3 gas lasers
      NT4 carbon dioxide lasers
      NT4 carbon monoxide lasers
      NT4 excimer lasers
        NT5 krypton fluoride lasers
      NT4 helium-neon lasers
    NT3 solid state lasers
      NT4 neodymium lasers
      NT4 ruby lasers
      NT4 semiconductor lasers
    NT3 x-ray lasers
  NT2 magnetic amplifiers
  NT2 microwave amplifiers
    NT3 masers
  NT2 operational amplifiers
  NT2 parametric amplifiers
  NT2 power amplifiers
  NT2 preamplifiers
  NT2 pulse amplifiers
  NT2 transistor amplifiers
NT1 control equipment
  NT2 electric controllers
  NT2 flow regulators
    NT3 baffles
    NT3 valves
      NT4 relief valves
  NT2 fluidic control devices
  NT2 humidistats
  NT2 hydraulic control devices
  NT2 pneumatic controllers
  NT2 pressure regulators
  NT2 servomechanisms
  NT2 speed regulators
  NT2 thermostats
    NT3 cryostats
NT1 distillation equipment
NT1 electrical equipment
  NT2 antennas
  NT2 armatures
  NT2 capacitors
  NT2 circuit breakers
  NT2 conductor devices
    NT3 connectors
    NT3 electric cables
      NT4 coaxial cables
      NT4 cryogenic cables
      NT4 gas-insulated cables
      NT4 superconducting cables
    NT3 electric fuses
  NT2 current limiters
  NT2 dc to dc converters
  NT2 electric bridges
  NT2 electric coils
    NT3 magnet coils
      NT4 pulsed magnet coils
    NT3 rogowski coil
    NT3 solenoids
    NT3 superconducting coils
  NT2 electric contacts
  NT2 electric generators
    NT3 alternators
    NT3 flux pumps
    NT3 rotating generators
      NT4 superconducting generators
    NT3 turbogenerators
  NT2 electric measuring instruments
    NT3 ammeters
    NT3 electrometers
    NT3 electroscopes
    NT3 galvanometers
    NT3 potentiometers
    NT3 voltmeters
  NT2 electric motors
    NT3 superconducting motors
  NT2 electrical insulators
  NT2 electromagnets
    NT3 superconducting magnets
  NT2 inverters
  NT2 lightning arresters
  NT2 rectifiers
    NT3 rectifier tubes
      NT4 capacitrons
      NT4 ignitrons
    NT3 semiconductor rectifiers
  NT2 relays
  NT2 resistors
    NT3 photoresistors
    NT3 rheostats
    NT3 semiconductor resistors
  NT2 switches
    NT3 cryotrons
    NT3 plasma switches
    NT3 semiconductor switches
  NT2 transformers
NT1 electronic equipment
  NT2 ac amplifiers
  NT2 analog-to-digital converters
  NT2 cavity resonators
    NT3 superconducting cavity resonat
  NT2 counting ratemeters
    NT3 linear ratemeters
    NT3 logarithmic ratemeters
  NT2 dc amplifiers
  NT2 dielectric amplifiers
  NT2 digital-to-analog converters
  NT2 function generators
    NT3 pulse generators
      NT4 high-voltage pulse generators
        NT5 marx generators
  NT2 high frequency amplifiers
  NT2 magnetic amplifiers
  NT2 microwave equipment
    NT3 heterodyne receivers
    NT3 microwave amplifiers
      NT4 masers
    NT3 microwave tubes
      NT4 backward wave tubes
      NT4 klystrons
      NT4 lasertrons
      NT4 magnetrons
      NT4 travelling wave tubes
    NT3 squid devices
  NT2 multiplexers
  NT2 operational amplifiers
  NT2 oscillators
    NT3 blocking oscillators
    NT3 transistor oscillators
  NT2 oscillographs
  NT2 parametric amplifiers
  NT2 power amplifiers
  NT2 power supplies
    NT3 spacecraft power supplies
  NT2 preamplifiers
  NT2 pulse amplifiers
  NT2 pulse analyzers
    NT3 multi-channel analyzers
  NT2 pulse converters
    NT3 time-to-amplitude converters
  NT2 pulse integrators
  NT2 radio equipment
    NT3 heterodyne receivers
    NT3 ionosondes
    NT3 radio telescopes
  NT2 scalers
  NT2 solar cells
    NT3 silicon solar cells
  NT2 transistor amplifiers
NT1 hydraulic equipment
  NT2 hydraulic control devices
NT1 laboratory equipment
  NT2 fume hoods
  NT2 gloveboxes
  NT2 hot cells
  NT2 manipulators
  NT2 samplers
    NT3 air samplers
NT1 magnets
  NT2 beam bending magnets
  NT2 beam focusing magnets
  NT2 electromagnets
    NT3 superconducting magnets
  NT2 kicker magnets
  NT2 permanent magnets
  NT2 septum magnets
  NT2 wiggler magnets
NT1 materials handling equipment
  NT2 conveyors
  NT2 earthmoving equipment
  NT2 grabs
  NT2 remote handling equipment
    NT3 cranes
    NT3 manipulators
  NT2 shredders
NT1 pollution control equipment
  NT2 air filters
  NT2 baghouses
  NT2 electrostatic precipitators
  NT2 scrubbers
NT1 portable equipment
  NT2 calculators
NT1 pumps
  NT2 electromagnetic pumps
  NT2 heat pumps
  NT2 vacuum pumps
    NT3 cryopumps
    NT3 sputter-ion pumps

```
            NT3     turbomolecular pumps
        NT1     remote viewing equipment
        NT1     resonators
            NT2     cavity resonators
                NT3     superconducting cavity
                            resonat
        NT1     robots
        NT1     separation equipment
            NT2     extraction apparatuses
                NT3     extraction columns
                NT3     mixer-settlers
                NT3     podbielniak contactors
            NT2     inertial separators
                NT3     cyclone separators
            NT2     vapor separators
                NT3     steam separators
        NT1     solar collectors
        NT1     solar furnaces
        NT1     subterrene penetrators
        NT1     tools
            NT2     cutting tools
            NT2     drill bits
        NT1     well logging equipment
        NT1     winches
        NT1     x-ray equipment
            NT2     x-ray tubes
        RT      equipment interfaces
        RT      equipment protection devices

EQUIPMENT INTERFACES
[1,922; 1,922]
        UF      interfaces (equipment)
        RT      camac system
        RT      computer architecture
        RT      computers
        RT      data transmission
        RT      electronic equipment
        RT      equipment
        RT      fastbus system

EQUIPMENT PROTECTION DEVICES
[578; 924]
        NT1     circuit breakers
        NT1     electric fuses
        RT      cryostats
        RT      equipment
        RT      reactor protection systems
        RT      relays
        RT      switches


EQUIVALENCE PRINCIPLE [498; 498]
        RT      general relativity theory
        RT      gravitational fields
        RT      mass

EQUIVALENT CIRCUITS [414; 414]
        BT1     electronic circuits


EQUIVALENT FISSION FLUENCE
[15; 15] May 76
        BT1     damaging neutron fluence
            BT2     neutron fluence
        RT      irradiation
        RT      neutronic damage functions
        RT      physical radiation effects

EQUIVALENT-PHOTON
APPROXIMATIO [83; 83]
        UF      approximation (equiv.-photon)
        UF      approximation (williams-weizs.
        UF      williams-weizsaecker approxima
        RT      photon-photon interactions
        RT      quantum electrodynamics


ERBIUM [712; 712]
        BT1     rare earths
            BT2     metals
                BT3     elements

ERBIUM ADDITIONS [157; 157]
(Alloys containing not more than 1% Er
are listed here.)
        BT1     rare earth additions
        RT      erbium alloys
        RT      erbium compounds
```

```
ERBIUM ALLOYS [555; 581]
(Alloys containing more than 1% Er.)
        BT1     rare earth alloys
            BT2     alloys
        NT1     erbium base alloys
        RT      erbium additions

ERBIUM BASE ALLOYS [25; 25]
        BT1     erbium alloys
            BT2     rare earth alloys
                BT3     alloys


ERBIUM BORIDES [193; 193]
        BT1     borides
            BT2     boron compounds
        BT1     erbium compounds
            BT2     rare earth compounds

ERBIUM BROMIDES [12; 12]
        BT1     bromides
            BT2     bromine compounds
                BT3     halogen compounds
            BT2     halides
                BT3     halogen compounds
        BT1     erbium compounds
            BT2     rare earth compounds

ERBIUM CARBIDES [17; 17]
        BT1     carbides
            BT2     carbon compounds
        BT1     erbium compounds
            BT2     rare earth compounds

ERBIUM CARBONATES [6; 6]
        BT1     carbonates
            BT2     carbon compounds
            BT2     oxygen compounds
        BT1     erbium compounds
            BT2     rare earth compounds

ERBIUM CHLORIDES [69; 69]
        BT1     chlorides
            BT2     chlorine compounds
                BT3     halogen compounds
            BT2     halides
                BT3     halogen compounds
        BT1     erbium compounds
            BT2     rare earth compounds

ERBIUM COMPLEXES [328; 328]
        BT1     rare earth complexes
            BT2     complexes

ERBIUM COMPOUNDS [542; 1,504]
        BT1     rare earth compounds
        NT1     erbium borides
        NT1     erbium bromides
        NT1     erbium carbides
        NT1     erbium carbonates
        NT1     erbium chlorides
        NT1     erbium fluorides
        NT1     erbium hydrides
        NT1     erbium hydroxides
        NT1     erbium iodides
        NT1     erbium nitrates
        NT1     erbium nitrides
        NT1     erbium oxides
        NT1     erbium perchlorates
        NT1     erbium phosphates
        NT1     erbium phosphides
        NT1     erbium selenides
        NT1     erbium silicides
        NT1     erbium sulfates
        NT1     erbium sulfides
        NT1     erbium tellurides
        NT1     erbium tungstates
        RT      erbium additions

ERBIUM FLUORIDES [56; 56]
        BT1     erbium compounds
            BT2     rare earth compounds
        BT1     fluorides
            BT2     fluorine compounds
                BT3     halogen compounds
            BT2     halides
                BT3     halogen compounds
```

```
ERBIUM HYDRIDES [72; 72]
        BT1     erbium compounds
            BT2     rare earth compounds
        BT1     hydrides
            BT2     hydrogen compounds

ERBIUM HYDROXIDES [10; 10]
        BT1     erbium compounds
            BT2     rare earth compounds
        BT1     hydroxides
            BT2     hydrogen compounds
            BT2     oxygen compounds

ERBIUM IODIDES [9; 9]
        BT1     erbium compounds
            BT2     rare earth compounds
        BT1     iodides
            BT2     halides
                BT3     halogen compounds
            BT2     iodine compounds
                BT3     halogen compounds

ERBIUM IONS [286; 286]
        BT1     ions
            BT2     charged particles

ERBIUM ISOTOPES [244; 2,037]
        NT1     erbium 145
        NT1     erbium 147
        NT1     erbium 148
        NT1     erbium 149
        NT1     erbium 150
        NT1     erbium 151
        NT1     erbium 152
        NT1     erbium 153
        NT1     erbium 154
        NT1     erbium 155
        NT1     erbium 156
        NT1     erbium 157
        NT1     erbium 158
        NT1     erbium 159
        NT1     erbium 160
        NT1     erbium 161
        NT1     erbium 162
        NT1     erbium 163
        NT1     erbium 164
        NT1     erbium 165
        NT1     erbium 166
        NT1     erbium 167
        NT1     erbium 168
        NT1     erbium 169
        NT1     erbium 170
        NT1     erbium 171
        NT1     erbium 172
        NT1     erbium 173
        NT1     erbium 174

ERBIUM NITRATES [28; 28]
        BT1     erbium compounds
            BT2     rare earth compounds
        BT1     nitrates
            BT2     nitrogen compounds
            BT2     oxygen compounds

ERBIUM NITRIDES [4; 4]
        BT1     erbium compounds
            BT2     rare earth compounds
        BT1     nitrides
            BT2     nitrogen compounds
            BT2     pnictides

ERBIUM OXIDES [428; 428]
        BT1     erbium compounds
            BT2     rare earth compounds
        BT1     oxides
            BT2     chalcogenides
            BT2     oxygen compounds

→ ERBIUM PERCHLORATES [0; 0]
Sep 91
        BT1     erbium compounds
            BT2     rare earth compounds
        BT1     perchlorates
            BT2     chlorine compounds
                BT3     halogen compounds
            BT2     oxygen compounds
```

ERBIUM PHOSPHATES [13; 13] *Jan 86*
- BT1 erbium compounds
- BT2 rare earth compounds
- BT1 phosphates
- BT2 oxygen compounds
- BT2 phosphorus compounds

ERBIUM PHOSPHIDES [4; 4] *Aug 81*
- BT1 erbium compounds
- BT2 rare earth compounds
- BT1 phosphides
- BT2 phosphorus compounds
- BT2 pnictides

ERBIUM SELENIDES [10; 10] *Aug 78*
- BT1 erbium compounds
- BT2 rare earth compounds
- BT1 selenides
- BT2 chalcogenides
- BT2 selenium compounds

ERBIUM SILICIDES [27; 27] *Oct 75*
- BT1 erbium compounds
- BT2 rare earth compounds
- BT1 silicides
- BT2 silicon compounds

ERBIUM SULFATES [8; 8]
- BT1 erbium compounds
- BT2 rare earth compounds
- BT1 sulfates
- BT2 oxygen compounds
- BT2 sulfur compounds

ERBIUM SULFIDES [26; 26]
- BT1 erbium compounds
- BT2 rare earth compounds
- BT1 sulfides
- BT2 chalcogenides
- BT2 sulfur compounds

→ **ERBIUM TELLURIDES** [0; 0] *Sep 91*
- BT1 erbium compounds
- BT2 rare earth compounds
- BT1 tellurides
- BT2 chalcogenides
- BT2 tellurium compounds

ERBIUM TUNGSTATES [3; 3] *Feb 88*
- BT1 erbium compounds
- BT2 rare earth compounds
- BT1 tungstates
- BT2 oxygen compounds
- BT2 tungsten compounds
- BT3 transition element compounds

ERBIUM 145 [2; 2] *Jul 89*
- BT1 beta-plus decay radioisotopes
- BT2 beta decay radioisotopes
- BT3 radioisotopes
- BT4 isotopes
- BT1 erbium isotopes
- BT1 even-odd nuclei
- BT2 nuclei
- BT1 rare earth nuclei
- BT2 intermediate mass nuclei
- BT3 nuclei

ERBIUM 147 [6; 6] *Sep 83*
- BT1 beta-plus decay radioisotopes
- BT2 beta decay radioisotopes
- BT3 radioisotopes
- BT4 isotopes
- BT1 electron capture radioisotopes
- BT2 beta decay radioisotopes
- BT3 radioisotopes
- BT4 isotopes
- BT1 erbium isotopes
- BT1 even-odd nuclei
- BT2 nuclei
- BT1 rare earth nuclei
- BT2 intermediate mass nuclei
- BT3 nuclei
- BT1 seconds living radioisotopes
- BT2 radioisotopes
- BT3 isotopes

ERBIUM 148 [9; 9] *Sep 81*
- BT1 beta-plus decay radioisotopes
- BT2 beta decay radioisotopes
- BT3 radioisotopes
- BT4 isotopes
- BT1 erbium isotopes
- BT1 even-even nuclei
- BT2 nuclei
- BT1 rare earth nuclei
- BT2 intermediate mass nuclei
- BT3 nuclei
- BT1 seconds living radioisotopes
- BT2 radioisotopes
- BT3 isotopes

ERBIUM 149 [21; 21] *Oct 84*
- BT1 beta-plus decay radioisotopes
- BT2 beta decay radioisotopes
- BT3 radioisotopes
- BT4 isotopes
- BT1 electron capture radioisotopes
- BT2 beta decay radioisotopes
- BT3 radioisotopes
- BT4 isotopes
- BT1 erbium isotopes
- BT1 even-odd nuclei
- BT2 nuclei
- BT1 rare earth nuclei
- BT2 intermediate mass nuclei
- BT3 nuclei
- BT1 seconds living radioisotopes
- BT2 radioisotopes
- BT3 isotopes

ERBIUM 150 [58; 58] *Jan 77*
- BT1 beta-plus decay radioisotopes
- BT2 beta decay radioisotopes
- BT3 radioisotopes
- BT4 isotopes
- BT1 electron capture radioisotopes
- BT2 beta decay radioisotopes
- BT3 radioisotopes
- BT4 isotopes
- BT1 erbium isotopes
- BT1 even-even nuclei
- BT2 nuclei
- BT1 rare earth nuclei
- BT2 intermediate mass nuclei
- BT3 nuclei
- BT1 seconds living radioisotopes
- BT2 radioisotopes
- BT3 isotopes

ERBIUM 151 [25; 25] *Jan 77*
- BT1 beta-plus decay radioisotopes
- BT2 beta decay radioisotopes
- BT3 radioisotopes
- BT4 isotopes
- BT1 electron capture radioisotopes
- BT2 beta decay radioisotopes
- BT3 radioisotopes
- BT4 isotopes
- BT1 erbium isotopes
- BT1 even-odd nuclei
- BT2 nuclei
- BT1 isomeric transition isotopes
- BT2 radioisotopes
- BT3 isotopes
- BT1 millisec living radioisotopes
- BT2 radioisotopes
- BT3 isotopes
- BT1 rare earth nuclei
- BT2 intermediate mass nuclei
- BT3 nuclei
- BT1 seconds living radioisotopes
- BT2 radioisotopes
- BT3 isotopes

ERBIUM 152 [61; 61]
- BT1 alpha decay radioisotopes
- BT2 radioisotopes
- BT3 isotopes
- BT1 beta-plus decay radioisotopes
- BT2 beta decay radioisotopes
- BT3 radioisotopes
- BT4 isotopes
- BT1 electron capture radioisotopes
- BT2 beta decay radioisotopes
- BT3 radioisotopes
- BT4 isotopes
- BT1 erbium isotopes
- BT1 even-even nuclei
- BT2 nuclei
- BT1 rare earth nuclei
- BT2 intermediate mass nuclei
- BT3 nuclei
- BT1 seconds living radioisotopes
- BT2 radioisotopes
- BT3 isotopes

ERBIUM 153 [42; 42]
- BT1 alpha decay radioisotopes
- BT2 radioisotopes
- BT3 isotopes
- BT1 beta-plus decay radioisotopes
- BT2 beta decay radioisotopes
- BT3 radioisotopes
- BT4 isotopes
- BT1 electron capture radioisotopes
- BT2 beta decay radioisotopes
- BT3 radioisotopes
- BT4 isotopes
- BT1 erbium isotopes
- BT1 even-odd nuclei
- BT2 nuclei
- BT1 rare earth nuclei
- BT2 intermediate mass nuclei
- BT3 nuclei
- BT1 seconds living radioisotopes
- BT2 radioisotopes
- BT3 isotopes

ERBIUM 154 [56; 56]
- BT1 alpha decay radioisotopes
- BT2 radioisotopes
- BT3 isotopes
- BT1 beta-plus decay radioisotopes
- BT2 beta decay radioisotopes
- BT3 radioisotopes
- BT4 isotopes
- BT1 electron capture radioisotopes
- BT2 beta decay radioisotopes
- BT3 radioisotopes
- BT4 isotopes
- BT1 erbium isotopes
- BT1 even-even nuclei
- BT2 nuclei
- BT1 minutes living radioisotopes
- BT2 radioisotopes
- BT3 isotopes
- BT1 rare earth nuclei
- BT2 intermediate mass nuclei
- BT3 nuclei

ERBIUM 155 [27; 27]
- BT1 alpha decay radioisotopes
- BT2 radioisotopes
- BT3 isotopes
- BT1 beta-plus decay radioisotopes
- BT2 beta decay radioisotopes
- BT3 radioisotopes
- BT4 isotopes
- BT1 electron capture radioisotopes
- BT2 beta decay radioisotopes
- BT3 radioisotopes
- BT4 isotopes
- BT1 erbium isotopes
- BT1 even-odd nuclei
- BT2 nuclei
- BT1 minutes living radioisotopes
- BT2 radioisotopes
- BT3 isotopes
- BT1 rare earth nuclei
- BT2 intermediate mass nuclei
- BT3 nuclei

ERBIUM 156 [128; 128]
- BT1 beta-plus decay radioisotopes
- BT2 beta decay radioisotopes
- BT3 radioisotopes
- BT4 isotopes
- BT1 electron capture radioisotopes
- BT2 beta decay radioisotopes
- BT3 radioisotopes
- BT4 isotopes
- BT1 erbium isotopes
- BT1 even-even nuclei
- BT2 nuclei

```
BT1    internal conversion radioisoto
BT2    radioisotopes
  BT3    isotopes
BT1    minutes living radioisotopes
BT2    radioisotopes
  BT3    isotopes
BT1    rare earth nuclei
BT2    intermediate mass nuclei
  BT3    nuclei
```

ERBIUM 157 [46; 46]
```
BT1    beta-plus decay radioisotopes
BT2    beta decay radioisotopes
  BT3    radioisotopes
    BT4    isotopes
BT1    electron capture radioisotopes
BT2    beta decay radioisotopes
  BT3    radioisotopes
    BT4    isotopes
BT1    erbium isotopes
BT1    even-odd nuclei
BT2    nuclei
BT1    minutes living radioisotopes
BT2    radioisotopes
  BT3    isotopes
BT1    rare earth nuclei
BT2    intermediate mass nuclei
  BT3    nuclei
```

ERBIUM 158 [205; 205]
```
BT1    beta-plus decay radioisotopes
BT2    beta decay radioisotopes
  BT3    radioisotopes
    BT4    isotopes
BT1    electron capture radioisotopes
BT2    beta decay radioisotopes
  BT3    radioisotopes
    BT4    isotopes
BT1    erbium isotopes
BT1    even-even nuclei
BT2    nuclei
BT1    hours living radioisotopes
BT2    radioisotopes
  BT3    isotopes
BT1    rare earth nuclei
BT2    intermediate mass nuclei
  BT3    nuclei
```

ERBIUM 159 [62; 62]
```
BT1    beta-plus decay radioisotopes
BT2    beta decay radioisotopes
  BT3    radioisotopes
    BT4    isotopes
BT1    electron capture radioisotopes
BT2    beta decay radioisotopes
  BT3    radioisotopes
    BT4    isotopes
BT1    erbium isotopes
BT1    even-odd nuclei
BT2    nuclei
BT1    minutes living radioisotopes
BT2    radioisotopes
  BT3    isotopes
BT1    rare earth nuclei
BT2    intermediate mass nuclei
  BT3    nuclei
```

ERBIUM 160 [121; 121]
```
BT1    days living radioisotopes
BT2    radioisotopes
  BT3    isotopes
BT1    electron capture radioisotopes
BT2    beta decay radioisotopes
  BT3    radioisotopes
    BT4    isotopes
BT1    erbium isotopes
BT1    even-even nuclei
BT2    nuclei
BT1    rare earth nuclei
BT2    intermediate mass nuclei
  BT3    nuclei
```

ERBIUM 161 [63; 63]
```
BT1    beta-plus decay radioisotopes
BT2    beta decay radioisotopes
  BT3    radioisotopes
    BT4    isotopes
BT1    electron capture radioisotopes
BT2    beta decay radioisotopes
  BT3    radioisotopes
    BT4    isotopes
BT1    erbium isotopes
BT1    even-odd nuclei
BT2    nuclei
BT1    hours living radioisotopes
BT2    radioisotopes
  BT3    isotopes
BT1    rare earth nuclei
BT2    intermediate mass nuclei
  BT3    nuclei
```

ERBIUM 162 [129; 129]
```
BT1    erbium isotopes
BT1    even-even nuclei
BT2    nuclei
BT1    rare earth nuclei
BT2    intermediate mass nuclei
  BT3    nuclei
BT1    stable isotopes
BT2    isotopes
```

ERBIUM 162 TARGET [12; 12]
```
BT1    targets
```

ERBIUM 163 [54; 54]
```
BT1    beta-plus decay radioisotopes
BT2    beta decay radioisotopes
  BT3    radioisotopes
    BT4    isotopes
BT1    electron capture radioisotopes
BT2    beta decay radioisotopes
  BT3    radioisotopes
    BT4    isotopes
BT1    erbium isotopes
BT1    even-odd nuclei
BT2    nuclei
BT1    hours living radioisotopes
BT2    radioisotopes
  BT3    isotopes
BT1    rare earth nuclei
BT2    intermediate mass nuclei
  BT3    nuclei
```

ERBIUM 163 TARGET [2; 2] *Feb 79*
```
BT1    targets
```

ERBIUM 164 [234; 234]
```
BT1    erbium isotopes
BT1    even-even nuclei
BT2    nuclei
BT1    rare earth nuclei
BT2    intermediate mass nuclei
  BT3    nuclei
BT1    stable isotopes
BT2    isotopes
```

ERBIUM 164 TARGET [39; 39]
```
BT1    targets
```

ERBIUM 165 [83; 83]
```
BT1    electron capture radioisotopes
BT2    beta decay radioisotopes
  BT3    radioisotopes
    BT4    isotopes
BT1    erbium isotopes
BT1    even-odd nuclei
BT2    nuclei
BT1    hours living radioisotopes
BT2    radioisotopes
  BT3    isotopes
BT1    rare earth nuclei
BT2    intermediate mass nuclei
  BT3    nuclei
```

ERBIUM 165 TARGET [3; 3] *Feb 79*
```
BT1    targets
```

ERBIUM 166 [338; 338]
```
BT1    erbium isotopes
BT1    even-even nuclei
BT2    nuclei
BT1    rare earth nuclei
BT2    intermediate mass nuclei
  BT3    nuclei
BT1    stable isotopes
BT2    isotopes
```

ERBIUM 166 REACTIONS [3; 3]
Nov 85
```
BT1    heavy ion reactions
BT2    nuclear reactions
```

ERBIUM 166 TARGET [220; 220]
```
BT1    targets
```

ERBIUM 167 [133; 133]
```
BT1    erbium isotopes
BT1    even-odd nuclei
BT2    nuclei
BT1    isomeric transition isotopes
BT2    radioisotopes
  BT3    isotopes
BT1    rare earth nuclei
BT2    intermediate mass nuclei
  BT3    nuclei
BT1    seconds living radioisotopes
BT2    radioisotopes
  BT3    isotopes
BT1    stable isotopes
BT2    isotopes
```

ERBIUM 167 TARGET [78; 78]
```
BT1    targets
```

ERBIUM 168 [340; 340]
```
BT1    erbium isotopes
BT1    even-even nuclei
BT2    nuclei
BT1    rare earth nuclei
BT2    intermediate mass nuclei
  BT3    nuclei
BT1    stable isotopes
BT2    isotopes
```

ERBIUM 168 TARGET [120; 120]
```
BT1    targets
```

ERBIUM 169 [74; 74]
```
BT1    beta-minus decay radioisotopes
BT2    beta decay radioisotopes
  BT3    radioisotopes
    BT4    isotopes
BT1    days living radioisotopes
BT2    radioisotopes
  BT3    isotopes
BT1    erbium isotopes
BT1    even-odd nuclei
BT2    nuclei
BT1    internal conversion radioisoto
BT2    radioisotopes
  BT3    isotopes
BT1    rare earth nuclei
BT2    intermediate mass nuclei
  BT3    nuclei
```

ERBIUM 170 [85; 85]
```
BT1    erbium isotopes
BT1    even-even nuclei
BT2    nuclei
BT1    rare earth nuclei
BT2    intermediate mass nuclei
  BT3    nuclei
BT1    stable isotopes
BT2    isotopes
```

ERBIUM 170 TARGET [105; 105]
```
BT1    targets
```

ERBIUM 171 [33; 33]
```
BT1    beta-minus decay radioisotopes
BT2    beta decay radioisotopes
  BT3    radioisotopes
    BT4    isotopes
BT1    erbium isotopes
BT1    even-odd nuclei
BT2    nuclei
BT1    hours living radioisotopes
BT2    radioisotopes
  BT3    isotopes
BT1    rare earth nuclei
BT2    intermediate mass nuclei
```

BT3 nuclei

ERBIUM 172 [9; 9]
BT1 beta-minus decay radioisotopes
BT2 beta decay radioisotopes
BT3 radioisotopes
BT4 isotopes
BT1 days living radioisotopes
BT2 radioisotopes
BT3 isotopes
BT1 erbium isotopes
BT1 even-even nuclei
BT2 nuclei
BT1 rare earth nuclei
BT2 intermediate mass nuclei
BT3 nuclei

ERBIUM 173 [5; 5]
BT1 beta-minus decay radioisotopes
BT2 beta decay radioisotopes
BT3 radioisotopes
BT4 isotopes
BT1 erbium isotopes
BT1 even-odd nuclei
BT2 nuclei
BT1 minutes living radioisotopes
BT2 radioisotopes
BT3 isotopes
BT1 rare earth nuclei
BT2 intermediate mass nuclei
BT3 nuclei

ERBIUM 174 [5; 5] *Apr 89*
BT1 beta-minus decay radioisotopes
BT2 beta decay radioisotopes
BT3 radioisotopes
BT4 isotopes
BT1 erbium isotopes
BT1 even-even nuclei
BT2 nuclei
BT1 minutes living radioisotopes
BT2 radioisotopes
BT3 isotopes
BT1 rare earth nuclei
BT2 intermediate mass nuclei
BT3 nuclei

EREVAN SYNCHROTRON [129; 129]
UF *eku*
UF *yerevan synchrotron*
BT1 synchrotrons
BT2 cyclic accelerators
BT3 accelerators

ERGOCALCIFEROL [11; 11]
UF *vitamin d-2*
BT1 vitamin d
BT2 vitamins

ERGODIC HYPOTHESIS [262; 262]
BT1 hypothesis
RT phase space
RT probability
RT statistical mechanics

ERGOSTEROL [17; 17]
BT1 sterols
BT2 hydroxy compounds
BT3 organic compounds
BT2 steroids
BT3 organic compounds

ERGOTAMINE [29; 29]
BT1 alkaloids
BT2 organic compounds
BT1 sympatholytics
BT2 autonomic nervous system agent
BT3 drugs
RT indoles

ericson fluctuations
USE ericson theory

ERICSON THEORY [182; 182]
UF *ericson fluctuations*
RT random phase approximation

ERIE-1 REACTOR [3; 3] *Sep 77*
BT1 pwr type reactors
BT2 enriched uranium reactors
BT3 reactors
BT2 power reactors
BT3 reactors
BT2 thermal reactors
BT3 reactors
BT2 water cooled reactors
BT3 reactors
BT2 water moderated reactors
BT3 reactors

ERIE-2 REACTOR [3; 3] *Sep 77*
BT1 pwr type reactors
BT2 enriched uranium reactors
BT3 reactors
BT2 power reactors
BT3 reactors
BT2 thermal reactors
BT3 reactors
BT2 water cooled reactors
BT3 reactors
BT2 water moderated reactors
BT3 reactors

ERIOCHROME DYES [53; 53]
BT1 azo dyes
BT2 azo compounds
BT3 organic nitrogen compounds
BT4 organic compounds
BT2 dyes
BT1 phenols
BT2 aromatics
BT3 organic compounds
BT2 hydroxy compounds
BT3 organic compounds
BT1 sulfonic acids
BT2 organic acids
BT3 organic compounds
BT2 organic sulfur compounds
BT3 organic compounds

ERIOGLAUCINE [0; 0]
BT1 azo dyes
BT2 azo compounds
BT3 organic nitrogen compounds
BT4 organic compounds
BT2 dyes
BT1 indicators
BT1 sulfonic acids
BT2 organic acids
BT3 organic compounds
BT2 organic sulfur compounds
BT3 organic compounds

ERMINE REACTOR [14; 14]
BT1 zero power reactors
BT2 experimental reactors
BT3 research and test reactors
BT4 reactors

EROSION [2,682; 2,682]
RT abrasion
RT corrosion
RT ground cover
RT particle resuspension
RT wear

ERR REACTOR [36; 36]
UF *elk river reactor*
BT1 bwr type reactors
BT2 enriched uranium reactors
BT3 reactors
BT2 power reactors
BT3 reactors
BT2 thermal reactors
BT3 reactors
BT2 water cooled reactors
BT3 reactors
BT2 water moderated reactors

BT3 reactors
BT1 thorium reactors
BT2 reactors

§§ **ERRORS** [12,934; 12,934]
(For considerations of causes of errors. For data uncertainties use DATA COVARIANCES.)
RT accuracy
RT comparative evaluations
RT corrections
RT performance
RT quality control
RT reliability
RT resolution
RT sensitivity analysis

eruptive binary stars
USE eruptive variable stars

ERUPTIVE VARIABLE STARS [462; 4,045] *Nov 78*
(Variable close binary systems, one star of which provides the other with accretion material.)
UF *cataclysmic binary stars*
UF *cataclysmic variable stars*
UF *eruptive binary stars*
BT1 binary stars
BT2 stars
BT1 variable stars
BT2 stars
NT1 novae
NT1 supernovae
NT1 t tauri stars
RT accretion disks
RT star accretion

ERYTHEMA [244; 244]
BT1 symptoms
RT skin
RT skin diseases

ERYTHRITOL [13; 13]
UF *tetrahydroxybutane*
BT1 alcohols
BT2 hydroxy compounds
BT3 organic compounds
BT1 monosaccharides
BT2 saccharides
BT3 carbohydrates
BT4 organic compounds

erythroblasts
USE bone marrow cells

ERYTHROCYTES [3,303; 3,434]
BT1 blood cells
BT2 blood
BT3 body fluids
BT4 biological materials
BT5 materials
NT1 reticulocytes
RT anemias
RT babesidae
RT blood groups
RT carboxyhemoglobin
RT hemagglutinins
RT hemoglobin
RT hemolysis
RT megaloblastic anemia
RT methemoglobin
RT sickle cell anemia

ERYTHROMYCIN [28; 28]
BT1 antibiotics
BT2 drugs
BT2 organic compounds

ERYTHROPOIESIS [300; 300]
BT1 blood formation
RT erythropoietin
RT hematopoietic system

ERYTHROPOIETIN [150; 150]
  RT   erythropoiesis
  RT   growth factors
  RT   hormones

ERYTHROSINE [9; 9]
  BT1   organic iodine compounds
    BT2   organic halogen compounds
      BT3   organic compounds
  RT   fluorescein

ES COMPUTERS [242; 242] *Feb 82*
  BT1   computers

ESA [17; 20] *Nov 80*
(Prior to 1975 known as ESRO, and documents written before the name change should be indexed to ESRO.)
  UF   *european space agency*
  BT1   international organizations
  NT1   esro

ESADA-VESR REACTOR [1; 1]
  BT1   enriched uranium reactors
    BT2   reactors
  BT1   experimental reactors
    BT2   research and test reactors
      BT3   reactors
  BT1   tank type reactors
    BT2   reactors
  BT1   test reactors
    BT2   research and test reactors
      BT3   reactors
    BT2   test facilities
  BT1   thermal reactors
    BT2   reactors
  BT1   water cooled reactors
    BT2   reactors
  BT1   water moderated reactors
    BT2   reactors

ESARDA [27; 27] *Sep 76*
(European Safeguards Research and Development Association.)
  UF   *europ safeg res develop assoc*
  BT1   international organizations
  RT   european communities

esca
(Electron-Spectroscopy Chemical Analysis)
  USE   chemical analysis
  AND   electron spectroscopy

ESCAPE PEAKS [81; 81]
  BT1   peaks
  RT   gamma spectra

ESCAR STORAGE RING [21; 21] *Feb 76*
(Experimental SuperConducting Accelerating Ring at Berkeley)
  UF   *berkeley escar storage ring*
  BT1   storage rings
  BT1   synchrotrons
    BT2   cyclic accelerators
      BT3   accelerators

ESCHERICHIA COLI [3,267; 3,267]
  BT1   bacteria
    BT2   microorganisms
  RT   coliforms
  RT   intestines

ESCOM REACTOR [7; 7]
  UF   *electricity supply com. reacto*
  BT1   power reactors
    BT2   reactors

escom-1 reactor
  USE   koeberg-1 reactor

ESERINE [6; 6]
  UF   *physostigmine*
  BT1   alkaloids
    BT2   organic compounds
  BT1   parasympathomimetics
    BT2   autonomic nervous system agent
      BT3   drugs

ESKIMOS [19; 19]
  BT1   human populations
    BT2   populations
  RT   arctic regions
  RT   lapps

ESOPHAGUS [1,701; 1,701]
  BT1   digestive system
  BT1   organs
    BT2   body
  RT   mediastinum

esr
  USE   electron spin resonance

ESRO [28; 28]
(Name changed in 1975 to ESA, and documents written after the change should be indexed to ESA.)
  UF   *european space research organi*
  BT1   esa
    BT2   international organizations

ESSENTIAL OILS [82; 82]
  BT1   oils
    BT2   other organic compounds
      BT3   organic compounds
  RT   plants

ESSEX I PROJECT [4; 4] *Apr 78*
  RT   chemical explosions
  RT   cratering explosions
  RT   simulation

ESSOR REACTOR [24; 24]
(Joint Research Centre, Ispra, Italy)
  UF   *orgel reactor*
  BT1   enriched uranium reactors
    BT2   reactors
  BT1   heavy water cooled reactors
    BT2   reactors
  BT1   heavy water moderated reactors
    BT2   reactors
  BT1   natural uranium reactors
    BT2   reactors
  BT1   organic cooled reactors
    BT2   reactors
  BT1   tank type reactors
    BT2   reactors
  BT1   test reactors
    BT2   research and test reactors
      BT3   reactors
    BT2   test facilities
  BT1   thermal reactors
    BT2   reactors

ESTERASES [143; 2,448]
  BT1   hydrolases
    BT2   enzymes
      BT3   organic compounds
  NT1   carboxylesterases
    NT2   cholinesterase
    NT2   lipases
  NT1   phosphatases
    NT2   acid phosphatase
    NT2   alkaline phosphatase
    NT2   nucleotidases
  NT1   phosphodiesterases
    NT2   nucleases
      NT3   dna-ase
      NT3   endonucleases
      NT3   rna-ase
  RT   esters

ESTERIFICATION [109; 109]
  BT1   chemical reactions
  RT   esters

ESTERS [647; 13,176]
(Includes esters of organic and inorganic acids.)
  BT1   organic compounds
  NT1   acetylcholine
  NT1   carboxylic acid esters
    NT2   acetic acid esters
      NT3   isopentyl acetate
    NT2   acetoacetic acid esters
    NT2   acrylic acid esters
    NT2   bromosulfophthalein
    NT2   carbamic acid esters
    NT2   citric acid esters
    NT2   malathion
    NT2   methacrylic acid esters
    NT2   oxalic acid esters
    NT2   phenolphthalein
    NT2   tartaric acid esters
  NT1   cellulose esters
  NT1   lactones
    NT2   coumarin
    NT2   gibberellic acid
  NT1   lanolin
  NT1   nitric acid esters
    NT2   nitrocellulose
    NT2   petn
  NT1   phorbol esters
  NT1   phosphinic acid esters
  NT1   phospholipids
    NT2   cardiolipin
    NT2   cephalins
    NT2   lecithins
    NT2   sphingomyelins
  NT1   phosphonic acid esters
    NT2   dampa
    NT2   dhdecmp
  NT1   phosphoric acid esters
    NT2   butyl phosphates
      NT3   dbp
      NT3   mbp
      NT3   tbp
    NT2   hdehp
    NT2   mdpa
    NT2   phytic acid
    NT2   tcp
  NT1   phthalic acid esters
  NT1   polyacrylates
    NT2   lucite
    NT2   perspex
    NT2   plexiglas
    NT2   pmma
  NT1   polyesters
    NT2   dacron
    NT2   homalite
    NT2   laminac
    NT2   mylar
  NT1   sulfonic acid esters
    NT2   abs
    NT2   ems
    NT2   methyl methanesulfonate
  NT1   sulfuric acid esters
  NT1   thiophosphoric acid esters
    NT2   cystaphos
    NT2   gammaphos
    NT2   parathion
  NT1   triglycerides
    NT2   butter fat
    NT2   corn oil
    NT2   croton oil
    NT2   linseed oil
    NT2   olive oil
    NT2   peanut oil
    NT2   soybean oil
    NT2   triolein
  RT   carboxylic acid salts
  RT   claisen condensation
  RT   esterases
  RT   esterification
  RT   hydrolysis
  RT   lipids

esthetics
  USE   aesthetics

ESTRADIOL [612; 612]
BT1 estranes
BT2 steroids
BT3 organic compounds
BT1 estrogens
BT2 steroid hormones
BT3 hormones
BT1 hydroxy compounds
BT2 organic compounds

ESTRANES [15; 728]
BT1 steroids
BT2 organic compounds
NT1 estradiol
NT1 estriol
NT1 estrone
RT estrogens

ESTRIOL [84; 84]
BT1 estranes
BT2 steroids
BT3 organic compounds
BT1 estrogens
BT2 steroid hormones
BT3 hormones
BT1 hydroxy compounds
BT2 organic compounds

ESTROGENS [455; 1,099]
BT1 steroid hormones
BT2 hormones
NT1 estradiol
NT1 estriol
NT1 estrone
RT castration
RT estranes
RT estrous cycle
RT fsh
RT ovaries
RT stilbestrol
RT tamoxifen

ESTRONE [102; 102]
BT1 estranes
BT2 steroids
BT3 organic compounds
BT1 estrogens
BT2 steroid hormones
BT3 hormones
BT1 hydroxy compounds
BT2 organic compounds
BT1 ketones
BT2 organic compounds

ESTROUS CYCLE [261; 261]
RT estrogens
RT female genitals
RT lh
RT menopause
RT menstrual cycle
RT menstruation disorders
RT ovulation
RT rhythmicity

ESTUARIES [547; 547]
BT1 coastal waters
BT2 surface waters
RT eutrophication
RT fresh water
RT offshore nuclear power plants
RT offshore sites
RT rivers
RT salinity
RT seas
RT seawater

estuarine ecosystems
USE aquatic ecosystems

ETA C-2980 MESONS [84; 84] *Jul 85*
(Prior to December 1987 this concept was indexed by ETA-2980 RESONANCES.)
UF *eta-2980 resonances*
BT1 charmonium
BT2 mesons
BT3 bosons
BT3 hadrons
BT4 elementary particles
BT2 quarkonium
BT1 pseudoscalar mesons
BT2 mesons
BT3 bosons
BT3 hadrons
BT4 elementary particles

ETA C-3590 MESONS [2; 2] *Dec 87*
BT1 charmonium
BT2 mesons
BT3 bosons
BT3 hadrons
BT4 elementary particles
BT2 quarkonium
BT1 pseudoscalar mesons
BT2 mesons
BT3 bosons
BT3 hadrons
BT4 elementary particles

ETA MESON BEAMS [5; 5]
BT1 meson beams
BT2 particle beams
BT3 beams

ETA MESONS [1,877; 1,877]
UF *eta-549*
BT1 pseudoscalar mesons
BT2 mesons
BT3 bosons
BT3 hadrons
BT4 elementary particles

ETA PRIME-958 MESONS [612; 612]
(Prior to December 1987 this concept was indexed by ETA-958 RESONANCES.)
UF *eta-958 resonances*
UF *x-zero resonances*
BT1 pseudoscalar mesons
BT2 mesons
BT3 bosons
BT3 hadrons
BT4 elementary particles

eta-1060 resonances
(Prior to December 1987 this was a valid descriptor.)
USE eta-1275 mesons

ETA-1275 MESONS [11; 11]
(Prior to December 1987 this concept was indexed by ETA-1060 RESONANCES.)
UF *eta-1060 resonances*
BT1 pseudoscalar mesons
BT2 mesons
BT3 bosons
BT3 hadrons
BT4 elementary particles

ETA-1440 MESONS [129; 129] *Jul 85*
(Prior to December 1987 this concept was indexed by IOTA-1440 RESONANCES.)
UF *iota-1440 resonances*
BT1 pseudoscalar mesons
BT2 mesons
BT3 bosons
BT3 hadrons
BT4 elementary particles

eta-2980 resonances
(Prior to December 1987 this was a valid descriptor.)
USE eta c-2980 mesons

eta-549
USE eta mesons

eta-700 resonances
(Prior to December 1987 this was a valid descriptor.)
USE mesons

eta-958 resonances
(Prior to December 1987 this was a valid descriptor.)
USE eta prime-958 mesons

ETCHING [3,850; 3,850]
RT ceramography
RT dielectric track detectors
RT metallography
RT particle tracks
RT surface finishing

ETDE [0; 0] *Feb 91*
UF *energy technol data exchange*
BT1 information systems
RT international energy agency

ETF TOKAMAK [40; 40] *Jul 81*
UF *engineering test facil tokamak*
BT1 tokamak devices
BT2 closed plasma devices
BT3 thermonuclear devices

ethanal
USE acetaldehyde

ETHANE [751; 751]
BT1 alkanes
BT2 hydrocarbons
BT3 organic compounds
RT ddt

ETHANOL [2,001; 2,001]
UF *cologne spirits*
UF *ethyl alcohol*
UF *fermentation alcohol*
UF *grain alcohol*
BT1 alcohols
BT2 hydroxy compounds
BT3 organic compounds

ether
USE ethyl ether

ETHERS [764; 1,498]
UF+ *ethocel*
BT1 organic oxygen compounds
BT2 organic compounds
NT1 acetals
NT2 acetal
NT1 anisole
NT1 batyl alcohol
NT1 butyl ether
NT1 carbitols
NT1 cellosolves
NT1 curcumin
NT1 dme
NT1 ethyl ether
NT1 ioglycamic acid
NT1 isopropyl ether
NT1 methyl ether
NT1 methylal
NT1 mexamine
NT1 morpholines
RT polyethylene glycols
RT tetrahydropyran
RT thyronine
RT thyroxine

ETHICAL ASPECTS [210; 210] *Feb 82*
RT hazards
RT political aspects
RT public opinion
RT radiation protection
RT safety
RT sociology

ethine
USE acetylene

ETHIONINE [20; 20]
  UF   *ethylmercaptoaminobutyric acid*
  UF   *ethylthioaminobutyric acid*
  BT1 amino acids
    BT2 carboxylic acids
      BT3 organic acids
        BT4 organic compounds
  BT1 antimetabolites
    BT2 drugs
  BT1 lipotropic factors
    BT2 drugs
  BT1 organic sulfur compounds
    BT2 organic compounds

ETHIOPIA [19; 19]
  BT1 africa
  BT1 developing countries

ethocel
  USE cellulose
  AND ethers

ETHOXY RADICALS [16; 16]
  BT1 alkoxy radicals
    BT2 radicals

ethyl alcohol
  USE ethanol

ETHYL ETHER [188; 188]
  UF   *diethyl ether*
  UF   *ether*
  BT1 ethers
    BT2 organic oxygen compounds
      BT3 organic compounds
  RT   organic solvents

ethyl methanesulfonate
  USE ems

ETHYL RADICALS [128; 128]
  BT1 alkyl radicals
    BT2 radicals

ethylaldehyde
  USE acetaldehyde

ETHYLENE [1,261; 1,261]
  BT1 alkenes
    BT2 hydrocarbons
      BT3 organic compounds

ethylene glycol
  USE glycols

ethylene polymers
  USE polyethylenes

ethylenecarboxylic acid
  USE acrylic acid

ethylenediaminetetraacetic aci
  USE edta

ethylmercaptoaminobutyric acid
  USE ethionine

ethylthioaminobutyric acid
  USE ethionine

ethyne
  USE acetylene

ETIOLOGY [546; 546]
(Dealing with all causes of a disease or abnormal condition of an organism.)
  RT   diseases

ETR REACTOR [111; 111]
(E.G. and G. Idaho, Inc., Idaho Falls, Idaho, USA)
  UF   *engineering test reactor*
  UF   *nrts-etr reactor*
  BT1 enriched uranium reactors
    BT2 reactors
  BT1 isotope production reactors
    BT2 irradiation reactors
      BT3 reactors
  BT1 research reactors
    BT2 research and test reactors
      BT3 reactors
  BT1 tank type reactors
    BT2 reactors
  BT1 test reactors
    BT2 research and test reactors
      BT3 reactors
    BT2 test facilities
  BT1 thermal reactors
    BT2 reactors
  BT1 water cooled reactors
    BT2 reactors
  BT1 water moderated reactors
    BT2 reactors

ETRR-1 REACTOR [0; 0] *Aug 90*
(Egypt Thermal Research Reactor, Cairo, Egypt.)
  BT1 research reactors
    BT2 research and test reactors
      BT3 reactors
  BT1 tank type reactors
    BT2 reactors

ETTINGHAUSEN EFFECT [27; 27]
  RT   hall effect

EUCALYPTUSES [14; 14] *Jan 78*
  BT1 trees
    BT2 plants

euclidean quantum field theory
  USE constructive field theory
  AND euclidean space

EUCLIDEAN SPACE [2,398; 2,398]
  UF+ *euclidean quantum field theory*
  BT1 riemann space
    BT2 mathematical space
      BT3 space

EUDIALYTE [7; 7] *Aug 75*
  BT1 silicate minerals
    BT2 minerals
  RT   calcium silicates
  RT   iron silicates
  RT   zirconium silicates

euflavine
  USE acriflavine

EUGLENA [39; 39]
  BT1 unicellular algae
    BT2 algae
      BT3 plants
    BT2 microorganisms

EURATOM [543; 543]
  UF   *european atomic energy comm*
  BT1 european communities
    BT2 international organizations

EUREX PROCESS [28; 28]
  BT1 reprocessing
    BT2 separation processes
  RT   amines
  RT   solvent extraction

EUROCHEMIC [111; 111]
  RT   reprocessing

EURODIF [69; 69] *Nov 75*
(International association founded in march 1972 to promote the construction of a European gaseous diffusion plant.)
  BT1 international organizations
  RT   gaseous diffusion plants

europ safeg res develop assoc
  USE esarda

EUROPE [1,207; 32,523]
  NT1 albania
  NT1 austria
  NT1 belgium
  NT1 bulgaria
  NT1 czechoslovakia
  NT1 federal republic of germany
  NT1 france
  NT1 greece
  NT1 hungary
  NT1 iceland
  NT1 ireland
  NT1 italy
  NT1 luxembourg
  NT1 malta
  NT1 monaco
  NT1 netherlands
  NT1 poland
  NT1 portugal
  NT1 romania
  NT1 scandinavia
    NT2 denmark
    NT2 finland
    NT2 norway
    NT2 sweden
  NT1 spain
  NT1 switzerland
  NT1 united kingdom
  NT1 ussr
    NT2 byelorussian ssr
    NT2 dubna
    NT2 ukrainian ssr
  NT1 yugoslavia
  RT   european communities

european atomic energy comm
  USE euratom

european coal and steel commun
  USE ecsc

EUROPEAN COMMUNITIES [1,065; 1,686]
  BT1 international organizations
  NT1 common market
  NT1 ecsc
  NT1 euratom
  RT   esarda
  RT   europe

european economic community
  USE common market

european muon collab. effect
  USE emc effect

european nuclear energy agency
  USE enea

european organization for nucl
  USE cern

european space agency
  USE esa

european space research organi
　USE　esro

EUROPIUM [1,611; 1,611]
　BT1　rare earths
　　BT2　metals
　　　BT3　elements

EUROPIUM ADDITIONS [205; 205]
(Alloys containing not more than 1% Eu are listed here.)
　BT1　rare earth additions
　RT　europium alloys
　RT　europium compounds

EUROPIUM ALLOYS [253; 265]
(Alloys containing more than 1% Eu.)
　BT1　rare earth alloys
　　BT2　alloys
　NT1　europium base alloys
　RT　europium additions

EUROPIUM ARSENIDES [2; 2] *Sep 89*
　BT1　arsenides
　　BT2　arsenic compounds
　　BT2　pnictides
　BT1　europium compounds
　　BT2　rare earth compounds

EUROPIUM BASE ALLOYS [8; 8]
　BT1　europium alloys
　　BT2　rare earth alloys
　　　BT3　alloys

EUROPIUM BORIDES [90; 90]
　BT1　borides
　　BT2　boron compounds
　BT1　europium compounds
　　BT2　rare earth compounds

EUROPIUM BROMIDES [16; 16]
　BT1　bromides
　　BT2　bromine compounds
　　　BT3　halogen compounds
　　BT2　halides
　　　BT3　halogen compounds
　BT1　europium compounds
　　BT2　rare earth compounds

EUROPIUM CARBIDES [11; 11]
　BT1　carbides
　　BT2　carbon compounds
　BT1　europium compounds
　　BT2　rare earth compounds

EUROPIUM CARBONATES [12; 12]
　BT1　carbonates
　　BT2　carbon compounds
　　BT2　oxygen compounds
　BT1　europium compounds
　　BT2　rare earth compounds

EUROPIUM CHLORIDES [141; 141]
　BT1　chlorides
　　BT2　chlorine compounds
　　　BT3　halogen compounds
　　BT2　halides
　　　BT3　halogen compounds
　BT1　europium compounds
　　BT2　rare earth compounds

EUROPIUM COMPLEXES [860; 860]
　BT1　rare earth complexes
　　BT2　complexes

EUROPIUM COMPOUNDS
[1,134; 2,809]
　BT1　rare earth compounds
　NT1　europium arsenides
　NT1　europium borides
　NT1　europium bromides
　NT1　europium carbides
　NT1　europium carbonates
　NT1　europium chlorides
　NT1　europium fluorides
　NT1　europium hydrides
　NT1　europium hydroxides
　NT1　europium iodides
　NT1　europium nitrates
　NT1　europium nitrides
　NT1　europium oxides
　NT1　europium perchlorates
　NT1　europium phosphates
　NT1　europium phosphides
　NT1　europium selenides
　NT1　europium silicates
　NT1　europium silicides
　NT1　europium sulfates
　NT1　europium sulfides
　NT1　europium tellurides
　RT　europium additions

EUROPIUM FLUORIDES [62; 62]
　BT1　europium compounds
　　BT2　rare earth compounds
　BT1　fluorides
　　BT2　fluorine compounds
　　　BT3　halogen compounds
　　BT2　halides
　　　BT3　halogen compounds

EUROPIUM HYDRIDES [19; 19]
　BT1　europium compounds
　　BT2　rare earth compounds
　BT1　hydrides
　　BT2　hydrogen compounds

EUROPIUM HYDROXIDES [15; 15]
　BT1　europium compounds
　　BT2　rare earth compounds
　BT1　hydroxides
　　BT2　hydrogen compounds
　　BT2　oxygen compounds

EUROPIUM IODIDES [22; 22]
　BT1　europium compounds
　　BT2　rare earth compounds
　BT1　iodides
　　BT2　halides
　　　BT3　halogen compounds
　　BT2　iodine compounds
　　　BT3　halogen compounds

EUROPIUM IONS [511; 511]
　BT1　ions
　　BT2　charged particles

EUROPIUM ISOTOPES [145; 1,882]
　NT1　europium 134
　NT1　europium 135
　NT1　europium 136
　NT1　europium 137
　NT1　europium 138
　NT1　europium 139
　NT1　europium 140
　NT1　europium 141
　NT1　europium 142
　NT1　europium 143
　NT1　europium 144
　NT1　europium 145
　NT1　europium 146
　NT1　europium 147
　NT1　europium 148
　NT1　europium 149
　NT1　europium 150
　NT1　europium 151
　NT1　europium 152
　NT1　europium 153
　NT1　europium 154
　NT1　europium 155
　NT1　europium 156
　NT1　europium 157
　NT1　europium 158
　NT1　europium 159
　NT1　europium 160
　NT1　europium 161
　NT1　europium 162

EUROPIUM NITRATES [78; 78]
　BT1　europium compounds
　　BT2　rare earth compounds
　BT1　nitrates
　　BT2　nitrogen compounds
　　BT2　oxygen compounds

EUROPIUM NITRIDES [10; 10]
　BT1　europium compounds
　　BT2　rare earth compounds
　BT1　nitrides
　　BT2　nitrogen compounds
　　BT2　pnictides

EUROPIUM OXIDES [860; 860]
　BT1　europium compounds
　　BT2　rare earth compounds
　BT1　oxides
　　BT2　chalcogenides
　　BT2　oxygen compounds

→ **EUROPIUM PERCHLORATES** [0; 0]
Sep 91
　BT1　europium compounds
　　BT2　rare earth compounds
　BT1　perchlorates
　　BT2　chlorine compounds
　　　BT3　halogen compounds
　　BT2　oxygen compounds

EUROPIUM PHOSPHATES [52; 52]
Oct 75
　BT1　europium compounds
　　BT2　rare earth compounds
　BT1　phosphates
　　BT2　oxygen compounds
　　BT2　phosphorus compounds

EUROPIUM PHOSPHIDES [7; 7]
Oct 83
　BT1　europium compounds
　　BT2　rare earth compounds
　BT1　phosphides
　　BT2　phosphorus compounds
　　BT2　pnictides

EUROPIUM SELENIDES [67; 67]
Oct 76
　BT1　europium compounds
　　BT2　rare earth compounds
　BT1　selenides
　　BT2　chalcogenides
　　BT2　selenium compounds

EUROPIUM SILICATES [6; 6]
　BT1　europium compounds
　　BT2　rare earth compounds
　BT1　silicates
　　BT2　oxygen compounds
　　BT2　silicon compounds

EUROPIUM SILICIDES [22; 22] *Oct 75*
　BT1　europium compounds
　　BT2　rare earth compounds
　BT1　silicides
　　BT2　silicon compounds

EUROPIUM SULFATES [39; 39]
　BT1　europium compounds
　　BT2　rare earth compounds
　BT1　sulfates
　　BT2　oxygen compounds
　　BT2　sulfur compounds

EUROPIUM SULFIDES [295; 295]
　BT1　europium compounds
　　BT2　rare earth compounds
　BT1　sulfides
　　BT2　chalcogenides
　　BT2　sulfur compounds

EUROPIUM TELLURIDES [54; 54]
May 76
BT1   europium compounds
BT2   rare earth compounds
BT1   tellurides
BT2   chalcogenides
BT2   tellurium compounds

EUROPIUM 134 [2; 2] *Oct 89*
BT1   beta-plus decay radioisotopes
BT2   beta decay radioisotopes
BT3   radioisotopes
BT4   isotopes
BT1   europium isotopes
BT1   millisec living radioisotopes
BT2   radioisotopes
BT3   isotopes
BT1   odd-odd nuclei
BT2   nuclei
BT1   rare earth nuclei
BT2   intermediate mass nuclei
BT3   nuclei

EUROPIUM 135 [2; 2] *Oct 89*
BT1   beta-plus decay radioisotopes
BT2   beta decay radioisotopes
BT3   radioisotopes
BT4   isotopes
BT1   europium isotopes
BT1   odd-even nuclei
BT2   nuclei
BT1   rare earth nuclei
BT2   intermediate mass nuclei
BT3   nuclei
BT1   seconds living radioisotopes
BT2   radioisotopes
BT3   isotopes

EUROPIUM 136 [9; 9] *Apr 86*
BT1   beta-plus decay radioisotopes
BT2   beta decay radioisotopes
BT3   radioisotopes
BT4   isotopes
BT1   europium isotopes
BT1   odd-odd nuclei
BT2   nuclei
BT1   rare earth nuclei
BT2   intermediate mass nuclei
BT3   nuclei
BT1   seconds living radioisotopes
BT2   radioisotopes
BT3   isotopes

EUROPIUM 137 [2; 2] *Apr 88*
BT1   europium isotopes
BT1   odd-even nuclei
BT2   nuclei
BT1   rare earth nuclei
BT2   intermediate mass nuclei
BT3   nuclei

EUROPIUM 138 [14; 14] *Jun 77*
BT1   beta-plus decay radioisotopes
BT2   beta decay radioisotopes
BT3   radioisotopes
BT4   isotopes
BT1   europium isotopes
BT1   odd-odd nuclei
BT2   nuclei
BT1   rare earth nuclei
BT2   intermediate mass nuclei
BT3   nuclei
BT1   seconds living radioisotopes
BT2   radioisotopes
BT3   isotopes

EUROPIUM 139 [11; 11]
BT1   beta-plus decay radioisotopes
BT2   beta decay radioisotopes
BT3   radioisotopes
BT4   isotopes
BT1   electron capture radioisotopes
BT2   beta decay radioisotopes
BT3   radioisotopes
BT4   isotopes
BT1   europium isotopes
BT1   odd-even nuclei
BT2   nuclei

BT1   rare earth nuclei
BT2   intermediate mass nuclei
BT3   nuclei
BT1   seconds living radioisotopes
BT2   radioisotopes
BT3   isotopes

EUROPIUM 140 [10; 10]
BT1   beta-plus decay radioisotopes
BT2   beta decay radioisotopes
BT3   radioisotopes
BT4   isotopes
BT1   electron capture radioisotopes
BT2   beta decay radioisotopes
BT3   radioisotopes
BT4   isotopes
BT1   europium isotopes
BT1   odd-odd nuclei
BT2   nuclei
BT1   rare earth nuclei
BT2   intermediate mass nuclei
BT3   nuclei
BT1   seconds living radioisotopes
BT2   radioisotopes
BT3   isotopes

EUROPIUM 141 [22; 22]
BT1   beta-plus decay radioisotopes
BT2   beta decay radioisotopes
BT3   radioisotopes
BT4   isotopes
BT1   electron capture radioisotopes
BT2   beta decay radioisotopes
BT3   radioisotopes
BT4   isotopes
BT1   europium isotopes
BT1   isomeric transition isotopes
BT2   radioisotopes
BT3   isotopes
BT1   odd-even nuclei
BT2   nuclei
BT1   rare earth nuclei
BT2   intermediate mass nuclei
BT3   nuclei
BT1   seconds living radioisotopes
BT2   radioisotopes
BT3   isotopes

EUROPIUM 142 [19; 19]
BT1   beta-plus decay radioisotopes
BT2   beta decay radioisotopes
BT3   radioisotopes
BT4   isotopes
BT1   electron capture radioisotopes
BT2   beta decay radioisotopes
BT3   radioisotopes
BT4   isotopes
BT1   europium isotopes
BT1   minutes living radioisotopes
BT2   radioisotopes
BT3   isotopes
BT1   odd-odd nuclei
BT2   nuclei
BT1   rare earth nuclei
BT2   intermediate mass nuclei
BT3   nuclei
BT1   seconds living radioisotopes
BT2   radioisotopes
BT3   isotopes

EUROPIUM 143 [40; 40]
BT1   beta-plus decay radioisotopes
BT2   beta decay radioisotopes
BT3   radioisotopes
BT4   isotopes
BT1   electron capture radioisotopes
BT2   beta decay radioisotopes
BT3   radioisotopes
BT4   isotopes
BT1   europium isotopes
BT1   minutes living radioisotopes
BT2   radioisotopes
BT3   isotopes
BT1   odd-even nuclei
BT2   nuclei
BT1   rare earth nuclei
BT2   intermediate mass nuclei
BT3   nuclei

EUROPIUM 144 [31; 31]
BT1   beta-plus decay radioisotopes
BT2   beta decay radioisotopes
BT3   radioisotopes
BT4   isotopes
BT1   electron capture radioisotopes
BT2   beta decay radioisotopes
BT3   radioisotopes
BT4   isotopes
BT1   europium isotopes
BT1   odd-odd nuclei
BT2   nuclei
BT1   rare earth nuclei
BT2   intermediate mass nuclei
BT3   nuclei
BT1   seconds living radioisotopes
BT2   radioisotopes
BT3   isotopes

EUROPIUM 145 [105; 105]
BT1   beta-plus decay radioisotopes
BT2   beta decay radioisotopes
BT3   radioisotopes
BT4   isotopes
BT1   days living radioisotopes
BT2   radioisotopes
BT3   isotopes
BT1   electron capture radioisotopes
BT2   beta decay radioisotopes
BT3   radioisotopes
BT4   isotopes
BT1   europium isotopes
BT1   odd-even nuclei
BT2   nuclei
BT1   rare earth nuclei
BT2   intermediate mass nuclei
BT3   nuclei

EUROPIUM 146 [54; 54]
BT1   beta-plus decay radioisotopes
BT2   beta decay radioisotopes
BT3   radioisotopes
BT4   isotopes
BT1   days living radioisotopes
BT2   radioisotopes
BT3   isotopes
BT1   electron capture radioisotopes
BT2   beta decay radioisotopes
BT3   radioisotopes
BT4   isotopes
BT1   europium isotopes
BT1   odd-odd nuclei
BT2   nuclei
BT1   rare earth nuclei
BT2   intermediate mass nuclei
BT3   nuclei

EUROPIUM 147 [77; 77]
BT1   alpha decay radioisotopes
BT2   radioisotopes
BT3   isotopes
BT1   beta-plus decay radioisotopes
BT2   beta decay radioisotopes
BT3   radioisotopes
BT4   isotopes
BT1   days living radioisotopes
BT2   radioisotopes
BT3   isotopes
BT1   electron capture radioisotopes
BT2   beta decay radioisotopes
BT3   radioisotopes
BT4   isotopes
BT1   europium isotopes
BT1   odd-even nuclei
BT2   nuclei
BT1   rare earth nuclei
BT2   intermediate mass nuclei
BT3   nuclei

EUROPIUM 148 [33; 33]
BT1   alpha decay radioisotopes
BT2   radioisotopes
BT3   isotopes
BT1   beta-plus decay radioisotopes
BT2   beta decay radioisotopes
BT3   radioisotopes
BT4   isotopes
BT1   days living radioisotopes
BT2   radioisotopes

BT3   isotopes
BT1   electron capture radioisotopes
BT2   beta decay radioisotopes
BT3   radioisotopes
BT4   isotopes
BT1   europium isotopes
BT1   odd-odd nuclei
BT2   nuclei
BT1   rare earth nuclei
BT2   intermediate mass nuclei
BT3   nuclei

EUROPIUM 149 [74; 74]
BT1   days living radioisotopes
BT2   radioisotopes
BT3   isotopes
BT1   electron capture radioisotopes
BT2   beta decay radioisotopes
BT3   radioisotopes
BT4   isotopes
BT1   europium isotopes
BT1   odd-even nuclei
BT2   nuclei
BT1   rare earth nuclei
BT2   intermediate mass nuclei
BT3   nuclei

EUROPIUM 150 [29; 29]
BT1   beta-minus decay radioisotopes
BT2   beta decay radioisotopes
BT3   radioisotopes
BT4   isotopes
BT1   beta-plus decay radioisotopes
BT2   beta decay radioisotopes
BT3   radioisotopes
BT4   isotopes
BT1   electron capture radioisotopes
BT2   beta decay radioisotopes
BT3   radioisotopes
BT4   isotopes
BT1   europium isotopes
BT1   hours living radioisotopes
BT2   radioisotopes
BT3   isotopes
BT1   odd-odd nuclei
BT2   nuclei
BT1   rare earth nuclei
BT2   intermediate mass nuclei
BT3   nuclei
BT1   years living radioisotopes
BT2   radioisotopes
BT3   isotopes

EUROPIUM 151 [409; 409]
BT1   europium isotopes
BT1   odd-even nuclei
BT2   nuclei
BT1   rare earth nuclei
BT2   intermediate mass nuclei
BT3   nuclei
BT1   stable isotopes
BT2   isotopes

EUROPIUM 151 TARGET [85; 85]
BT1   targets

EUROPIUM 152 [569; 569]
BT1   beta-minus decay radioisotopes
BT2   beta decay radioisotopes
BT3   radioisotopes
BT4   isotopes
BT1   beta-plus decay radioisotopes
BT2   beta decay radioisotopes
BT3   radioisotopes
BT4   isotopes
BT1   electron capture radioisotopes
BT2   beta decay radioisotopes
BT3   radioisotopes
BT4   isotopes
BT1   europium isotopes
BT1   hours living radioisotopes
BT2   radioisotopes
BT3   isotopes
BT1   isomeric transition isotopes
BT2   radioisotopes
BT3   isotopes
BT1   odd-odd nuclei
BT2   nuclei
BT1   rare earth nuclei
BT2   intermediate mass nuclei
BT3   nuclei
BT1   years living radioisotopes
BT2   radioisotopes
BT3   isotopes

EUROPIUM 152 TARGET [14; 14]
Nov 77
BT1   targets

EUROPIUM 153 [209; 209]
BT1   europium isotopes
BT1   odd-even nuclei
BT2   nuclei
BT1   rare earth nuclei
BT2   intermediate mass nuclei
BT3   nuclei
BT1   stable isotopes
BT2   isotopes

EUROPIUM 153 TARGET [77; 77]
BT1   targets

EUROPIUM 154 [329; 329]
BT1   beta-minus decay radioisotopes
BT2   beta decay radioisotopes
BT3   radioisotopes
BT4   isotopes
BT1   electron capture radioisotopes
BT2   beta decay radioisotopes
BT3   radioisotopes
BT4   isotopes
BT1   europium isotopes
BT1   isomeric transition isotopes
BT2   radioisotopes
BT3   isotopes
BT1   minutes living radioisotopes
BT2   radioisotopes
BT3   isotopes
BT1   odd-odd nuclei
BT2   nuclei
BT1   rare earth nuclei
BT2   intermediate mass nuclei
BT3   nuclei
BT1   years living radioisotopes
BT2   radioisotopes
BT3   isotopes

EUROPIUM 154 TARGET [13; 13]
Nov 77
BT1   targets

EUROPIUM 155 [189; 189]
BT1   beta-minus decay radioisotopes
BT2   beta decay radioisotopes
BT3   radioisotopes
BT4   isotopes
BT1   europium isotopes
BT1   odd-even nuclei
BT2   nuclei
BT1   rare earth nuclei
BT2   intermediate mass nuclei
BT3   nuclei
BT1   years living radioisotopes
BT2   radioisotopes
BT3   isotopes

EUROPIUM 155 TARGET [4; 4] Dec 79
BT1   targets

EUROPIUM 156 [43; 43]
BT1   beta-minus decay radioisotopes
BT2   beta decay radioisotopes
BT3   radioisotopes
BT4   isotopes
BT1   days living radioisotopes
BT2   radioisotopes
BT3   isotopes
BT1   europium isotopes
BT1   odd-odd nuclei
BT2   nuclei
BT1   rare earth nuclei
BT2   intermediate mass nuclei
BT3   nuclei

EUROPIUM 157 [14; 14]
BT1   beta-minus decay radioisotopes
BT2   beta decay radioisotopes
BT3   radioisotopes
BT4   isotopes
BT1   europium isotopes
BT1   hours living radioisotopes
BT2   radioisotopes
BT3   isotopes
BT1   odd-even nuclei
BT2   nuclei
BT1   rare earth nuclei
BT2   intermediate mass nuclei
BT3   nuclei

EUROPIUM 158 [11; 11]
BT1   beta-minus decay radioisotopes
BT2   beta decay radioisotopes
BT3   radioisotopes
BT4   isotopes
BT1   europium isotopes
BT1   minutes living radioisotopes
BT2   radioisotopes
BT3   isotopes
BT1   odd-odd nuclei
BT2   nuclei
BT1   rare earth nuclei
BT2   intermediate mass nuclei
BT3   nuclei

EUROPIUM 159 [10; 10]
BT1   beta-minus decay radioisotopes
BT2   beta decay radioisotopes
BT3   radioisotopes
BT4   isotopes
BT1   europium isotopes
BT1   minutes living radioisotopes
BT2   radioisotopes
BT3   isotopes
BT1   odd-even nuclei
BT2   nuclei
BT1   rare earth nuclei
BT2   intermediate mass nuclei
BT3   nuclei

EUROPIUM 160 [6; 6]
BT1   beta-minus decay radioisotopes
BT2   beta decay radioisotopes
BT3   radioisotopes
BT4   isotopes
BT1   europium isotopes
BT1   odd-odd nuclei
BT2   nuclei
BT1   rare earth nuclei
BT2   intermediate mass nuclei
BT3   nuclei
BT1   seconds living radioisotopes
BT2   radioisotopes
BT3   isotopes

EUROPIUM 161 [0; 0] Oct 86
BT1   beta-minus decay radioisotopes
BT2   beta decay radioisotopes
BT3   radioisotopes
BT4   isotopes
BT1   europium isotopes
BT1   odd-even nuclei
BT2   nuclei
BT1   rare earth nuclei
BT2   intermediate mass nuclei
BT3   nuclei
BT1   seconds living radioisotopes
BT2   radioisotopes
BT3   isotopes

EUROPIUM 162 [0; 0] Aug 87
BT1   beta-minus decay radioisotopes
BT2   beta decay radioisotopes
BT3   radioisotopes
BT4   isotopes
BT1   europium isotopes
BT1   odd-odd nuclei
BT2   nuclei
BT1   rare earth nuclei
BT2   intermediate mass nuclei
BT3   nuclei
BT1   seconds living radioisotopes
BT2   radioisotopes

BT3 isotopes

EUTECTICS [2,655; 2,655]
RT monotectics
RT phase diagrams
RT phase transformations

EUTECTOIDS [90; 90]
RT monotectoids
RT phase diagrams
RT phase transformations

EUTROPHICATION [47; 47]
RT algae
RT aquatic ecosystems
RT estuaries
RT fertilizers
RT lakes
RT limnology
RT nutrients
RT water pollution

EV RANGE [1,612; 10,338]
BT1 energy range
NT1 ev range 01-10
NT1 ev range 10-100
NT1 ev range 100-1000

EV RANGE 01-10 [2,828; 2,828]
BT1 ev range
BT2 energy range

EV RANGE 10-100 [4,101; 4,101]
BT1 ev range
BT2 energy range

EV RANGE 100-1000 [4,433; 4,433]
BT1 ev range
BT2 energy range

EVACUATION [208; 208] *Feb 84*
(An organized withdrawal of people from a place or area as a protective measure.)
RT accidents
RT civil defense
RT emergency plans
RT external zones
RT population relocation
RT routing

EVALUATED DATA [3,595; 3,595]
Oct 78
(Use only in conjunction with literary indicator N for data flagging; refers to data gathered from other sources and may consist of a compilation of data which, however, has been evaluated and some judgement as to its accuracy or value is expressed or implied.)
UF *data compilation (evaluated)*
BT1 numerical data
BT2 data
BT3 information
RT nuclear data collections

EVALUATION [4,732; 22,504] *Dec 85*
(Process of subjecting to critical judgement or interpretation.)
NT1 comparative evaluations
RT audits
RT feasibility studies
RT forecasting
RT inspection
RT management
RT performance
RT quality assurance
RT testing
RT verification

EVANS BLUE [15; 15]
BT1 azo dyes
BT2 azo compounds
BT3 organic nitrogen compounds
BT4 organic compounds
BT2 dyes
BT1 reagents

BT1 sulfonic acids
BT2 organic acids
BT3 organic compounds
BT2 organic sulfur compounds
BT3 organic compounds

EVAPORATION [4,919; 5,731]
UF *flashing*
UF *vaporization*
UF *volatilization*
BT1 phase transformations
NT1 sublimation
NT1 vacuum evaporation
RT boiling
RT counterflow systems
RT dehydration
RT distillation
RT drying
RT evaporative cooling
RT evaporators
RT flash heating
RT spray drying
RT transpiration
RT vaporization heat
RT vapors
RT waste processing

EVAPORATION MODEL [2,007; 2,111]
UF *nuclear evaporation*
BT1 nuclear models
BT2 mathematical models
NT1 weisskopf model
RT nuclear fireball model
RT nuclear temperature

EVAPORATIVE COOLING [58; 58]
Sep 76
(Cooling of a liquid by using the vaporization heat of part of the liquid or cooling air by evaporating water into it.)
BT1 cooling
RT cooling towers
RT evaporation
RT vaporization heat

EVAPORATORS [608; 608]
RT crossflow systems
RT desalination
RT distillation
RT dryers
RT evaporation
RT heat exchangers
RT vapor condensers

evaporites
USE sedimentary rocks

* **EVEN-EVEN NUCLEI** [1,805; 84,557]
(Even protons, even neutrons. For specific terms, consult the Appendix.)
BT1 nuclei
RT nuclear structure

* **EVEN-ODD NUCLEI** [567; 73,852]
(Even protons, odd neutrons. For specific terms, consult the Appendix.)
BT1 nuclei
RT nuclear structure

event tree analysis
(For specific terms, consult the Appendix.)
USE failure mode analysis

events (chemical explosions)
(See also under CHEMICAL EXPLOSIONS the list of specific chemical explosion events.)
USE chemical explosions

events (nuclear explosions)
(See also under NUCLEAR EXPLOSIONS the list of specific named nuclear events.)
USE nuclear explosions

EWA REACTOR [36; 36]
(Inst. of Nuclear Research, Swierk, Poland)
UF *swierk ewa reactor*
BT1 isotope production reactors
BT2 irradiation reactors
BT3 reactors
BT1 research reactors
BT2 research and test reactors
BT3 reactors
BT1 tank type reactors
BT2 reactors
BT1 water cooled reactors
BT2 reactors
BT1 water moderated reactors
BT2 reactors

EXCAVATION [336; 415]
NT1 nuclear excavation
RT cavities
RT construction
RT craters
RT dredging
RT earthmoving equipment
RT explosions
RT mining
RT nuclear explosions
RT schooner event
RT shaft excavations
RT slope stability
RT subterrene penetrators
RT surface mining
RT tunnels

excavators
USE earthmoving equipment

EXCEPTIONAL NATURAL DISASTER [13; 13] *Dec 76*
(In the legal sense when so declared by the competent authority in relation to compensation for damages.)
UF *disaster (exceptional natural)*
UF *natural disaster (exceptional)*
RT earthquakes
RT floods
RT liabilities
RT tsunamis
RT victims compensation

EXCER PROCESS [1; 1]
BT1 reprocessing
BT2 separation processes
RT solvent extraction

exchange (charge)
USE charge exchange

exchange (electron)
USE electron exchange

exchange (heat)
USE heat transfer

exchange (ion)
USE ion exchange

exchange (isotopic)
USE isotopic exchange

EXCHANGE DEGENERACY [413; 413]
RT regge poles

EXCHANGE INTERACTIONS [3,972; 3,972]
(Not for chemical reactions.)
BT1 interactions
RT cim model
RT morrison rule
RT quark-hadron interactions
RT spin exchange

exchange models
   USE   peripheral models

EXCIMER LASERS [358; 520] *Jul 85*
(Lasers whose lasing medium is a dimer that exists in the excited state and dissociates in the ground state.)
   BT1   gas lasers
     BT2   lasers
       BT3   amplifiers
         BT4   equipment
   NT1   krypton fluoride lasers

excision repair
   USE   dna repair

EXCITATION [20,519; 23,416]
(Addition of energy to a nuclear, atomic or molecular system transferring it to another energy state.)
   UF+   *core polarization (nuclei)*
   BT1   energy-level transitions
   NT1   collective excitations
   NT1   coulomb excitation
   NT1   inner-shell excitation
   RT   activation energy
   RT   chemical activation
   RT   de-excitation
   RT   electrical pumping
   RT   energy deposition
   RT   excited states
   RT   fission barrier
   RT   optical pumping

EXCITATION FUNCTIONS [9,650; 9,650]
   RT   differential cross sections
   RT   energy dependence
   RT   gerjuoy-stein theory
   RT   integral cross sections
   RT   nuclear reactions
   RT   total cross sections

EXCITED STATES [23,414; 42,152]
   BT1   energy levels
   NT1   metastable states
   NT1   rotational states
   NT1   rydberg states
   NT1   vibrational states
   RT   excitation

EXCITON MODEL [301; 301] *Jan 82*
   BT1   nuclear models
     BT2   mathematical models

EXCITONS [2,191; 2,191]
   UF   *biexcitons*
   BT1   quasi particles
   RT   electron-hole droplets

exclusion principle
   USE   pauli principle

exclusions (liability)
   USE   liability exclusions

EXCLUSIVE INTERACTIONS [1,477; 1,490]
(The group of all interactions of two particles producing a specific final state but excluding the final-state particle itself.)
   BT1   particle interactions
     BT2   interactions
   NT1   semi-exclusive interactions
   RT   inclusive interactions

exclusive liability
(Prior to December 1990, this was a valid descriptor.)
   USE   liabilities

EXCRETION [3,432; 5,378]
   UF+   *excretion analysis*
   BT1   clearance
   NT1   exhalation
   NT1   lung clearance
   NT1   renal clearance
   RT   biological wastes
   RT   body fluids
   RT   feces
   RT   glands
   RT   kidneys
   RT   large intestine
   RT   lavage
   RT   phagocytosis
   RT   physiology
   RT   radionuclide kinetics
   RT   retention
   RT   secretion
   RT   sweat
   RT   urinary tract
   RT   urine

excretion analysis
   USE   excretion
   AND   personnel monitoring

excretion functions
   USE   retention functions

EXCURSIONS [580; 580]
   UF   *power excursions*
   UF   *runaway (reactor accident)*
   BT1   reactor accidents
     BT2   accidents
   RT   hazards
   RT   reactors

EXECUTIVE CODES [24; 24] *Nov 88*
(A digital computer code that controls other codes, allocates storage to these codes and controls the servicing of peripheral devices.)
   UF   *monitor codes*
   UF   *operating systems (computer)*
   UF   *supervisor codes*
   BT1   computer codes
   RT   programming

EXERCISE [1,630; 1,630]
   UF   *physical effort*
   UF   *swimming*
   RT   biological fatigue
   RT   biological stress
   RT   muscles

EXERGY [29; 29] *Feb 80*
(That portion of energy which is converted into the desired, economically utilizable form.)
   BT1   energy
   RT   thermodynamics

EXHALATION [274; 274]
   BT1   excretion
     BT2   clearance
   RT   breath
   RT   lung clearance

→ **EXHAUST GASES** [0; 0] *Apr 84*
   BT1   gaseous wastes
     BT2   wastes
   BT1   gases
     BT2   fluids
   RT   automobiles
   RT   combustion products
   RT   exhaust systems

EXHAUST SYSTEMS [180; 180] *Mar 83*
   RT   controlled atmospheres
   RT   divertors
   RT   exhaust gases
   RT   gloveboxes
   RT   reactor components
   RT   tokamak devices
   RT   ventilation

EXOELECTRON DOSEMETERS [268; 268]
   BT1   dosemeters
     BT2   measuring instruments

EXOELECTRONS [305; 305]
   BT1   electrons
     BT2   leptons
       BT3   elementary particles
       BT3   fermions

EXOSKELETON [14; 14]
   BT1   skeleton
     BT2   organs
       BT3   body
   RT   echinoderms

EXOSPHERE [109; 109]
   BT1   earth atmosphere

exotic atoms
   USE   hadronic atoms

EXOTIC RESONANCES [680; 680]
   BT1   resonance particles
     BT2   hadrons
       BT3   elementary particles

exp multipurp high temp gas cr
   USE   vhtr reactor

exp. beryllium oxide reactor
   USE   ebor reactor

exp. boiling water reactor
   USE   ebwr reactor

exp. breeder reactor-1
   USE   ebr-1 reactor

exp. breeder reactor-2
   USE   ebr-2 reactor

exp. gas cooled reactor
   USE   egcr reactor

exp. organic cooled reactor
   USE   eocr reactor

exp. propulsion test reactor
   USE   tory-2c reactor

EXPANSION [2,925; 7,235]
(Increase in size or volume, not for the concept covered by SERIES EXPANSION.)
   NT1   plasma expansion
   NT1   thermal expansion
   RT   augmentation
   RT   contraction
   RT   cosmological models
   RT   elongation
   RT   hubble effect
   RT   solar wind
   RT   swelling

EXPANSION CHAMBERS [28; 28]
   BT1   cloud chambers
     BT2   gas track detectors
       BT3   radiation detectors
         BT4   measuring instruments

EXPANSION JOINTS [93; 93] *Oct 75*
  BT1 joints
  RT   bellows
  RT   contraction
  RT   pipe fittings
  RT   pipe joints
  RT   thermal expansion

EXPECTATION VALUE [2,636; 2,636]
  RT   eigenfunctions
  RT   eigenvalues
  RT   probability
  RT   quantum mechanics
  RT   statistics

exper. facilities (acceler.)
  USE accelerator facilities

experience critique orgel
  USE eco reactor

EXPERIMENT PLANNING
[1,713; 1,713] *Feb 83*
  BT1 planning
  RT   demonstration programs
  RT   research programs

EXPERIMENTAL CHANNELS
[387; 387]
  UF   *irradiation channels*
  BT1 reactor channels
    BT2 reactor components
  BT1 reactor experimental facilitie
    BT2 reactor components
  RT   in pile loops
  RT   irradiation capsules

EXPERIMENTAL DATA [89,101; 89,101]
Oct 78
(Use only in conjunction with literary indicator N for data flagging.)
  UF   *measured values*
  BT1 numerical data
    BT2 data
      BT3 information
  RT   benchmarks

EXPERIMENTAL NEOPLASMS
[1,577; 1,992]
  UF   *jensen sarcoma*
  UF   *walker carcinoma*
  UF   *yoshida sarcoma*
  BT1 neoplasms
    BT2 diseases
  NT1 ehrlich ascites tumor
  RT   leukemia viruses

EXPERIMENTAL REACTORS
[195; 7,301]
(For engineering testing of reactor components such as fuel elements, cooling systems, etc.)
  BT1 research and test reactors
    BT2 reactors
  NT1 aps reactor
  NT1 arbus reactor
  NT1 auc reactor
  NT1 bor-60 reactor
  NT1 borax-1 reactor
  NT1 borax-2 reactor
  NT1 borax-3 reactor
  NT1 borax-4 reactor
  NT1 br-3-vn reactor
  NT1 cesar reactor
  NT1 dfr reactor
  NT1 dragon reactor
  NT1 ebr-1 reactor
  NT1 ebr-2 reactor
  NT1 ebwr reactor
  NT1 egcr reactor
  NT1 el-1 reactor
  NT1 eocr reactor
  NT1 esada-vesr reactor
  NT1 hbwr reactor
  NT1 hdr reactor
  NT1 httr reactor
  NT1 joyo reactor
  NT1 jpdr reactor
  NT1 kiwi reactors
  NT1 knk reactor
  NT1 knk-2 reactor
  NT1 lampre-1 reactor
  NT1 mh-1a reactor
  NT1 mir reactor
  NT1 msre reactor
  NT1 nrx-a2 reactor
  NT1 nrx-a3 reactor
  NT1 nrx-a4-est reactor
  NT1 nrx-a5 reactor
  NT1 nrx-a6 reactor
  NT1 omre reactor
  NT1 rover reactors
  NT1 sefor reactor
  NT1 spert-1 reactor
  NT1 spert-2 reactor
  NT1 spert-3 reactor
  NT1 spert-4 reactor
  NT1 sre reactor
  NT1 subcritical assemblies
    NT2 pse reactor
    NT2 stsf assembly
  NT1 topaz reactor
  NT1 tory-2c reactor
  NT1 treat reactor
  NT1 tz1 reactor
  NT1 tz2 reactor
  NT1 uhtrex reactor
  NT1 venus reactor
  NT1 vhtr reactor
  NT1 zero power reactors
    NT2 agata reactor
    NT2 anex reactor
    NT2 anna reactor
    NT2 apfa-3 reactor
    NT2 aquilon reactor
    NT2 big ten reactor
    NT2 cfrmf reactor
    NT2 cml reactor
    NT2 coral-1 reactor
    NT2 crocus reactor
    NT2 dca reactor
    NT2 dimple reactor
    NT2 ecel reactor
    NT2 ermine reactor
    NT2 fca reactor
    NT2 flattop reactor
    NT2 fr-0 reactor
    NT2 godiva reactor
    NT2 hero reactor
    NT2 hitrex-1 reactor
    NT2 horace reactor
    NT2 iea-zpr reactor
    NT2 ifr reactor
    NT2 ipen-mb-1 reactor
    NT2 jezebel reactor
    NT2 juno reactor
    NT2 kahter reactor
    NT2 kuca reactor
    NT2 lptf reactor
    NT2 lr-0 reactor
    NT2 marius reactor
    NT2 maryla reactor
    NT2 masurca reactor
    NT2 minerve reactor
    NT2 neptune reactor
    NT2 nsf-rfp reactor
    NT2 or-cef reactor
    NT2 ornl-pca reactor
    NT2 parka reactor
    NT2 pdp reactor
    NT2 peggy reactor
    NT2 pelinduna reactor
    NT2 plasma core assembly
    NT2 prcf reactor
    NT2 ptf-unc reactor
    NT2 purnima reactor
    NT2 purnima-2 reactor
    NT2 r-b reactor
    NT2 ra-0 reactor
    NT2 ra-2 reactor
    NT2 rake-2 reactor
    NT2 rb-1 reactor
    NT2 rb-3 reactor
    NT2 rensselaer critical facility
    NT2 ritmo reactor
    NT2 rospo reactor
    NT2 saref reactor
    NT2 shca reactor
    NT2 silene reactor
    NT2 siloette reactor
    NT2 sneak reactor
    NT2 split table reactor
    NT2 sr-oa reactor
    NT2 tca reactor
    NT2 tr-0 reactor
    NT2 vera reactor
    NT2 zebra reactor
    NT2 zeep reactor
    NT2 zenith reactor
    NT2 zephyr reactor
    NT2 zerlina reactor
    NT2 zlfr reactor
    NT2 zppr reactor
    NT2 zpr reactor
    NT2 zpr-3 reactor
    NT2 zpr-6 reactor
    NT2 zpr-9 reactor
    NT2 zr-6 reactor
  NT1 zrr reactor

EXPERT SYSTEMS [955; 955] *Sep 86*
(Computer programs comprising a knowledge-based component, constructed from an expert skill, operating in such a way that the system can offer intelligent advice or take an intelligent decision about a processing function.)
  RT   artificial intelligence
  RT   data processing
  RT   information systems
  RT   neural networks

EXPLODING WIRES [147; 147]
  BT1 wires
  RT   detonators

EXPLORATION [2,580; 2,580]
  RT   aerial prospecting
  RT   electrical surveys
  RT   geochemical surveys
  RT   geologic surveys
  RT   geophysical surveys
  RT   magnetic surveys
  RT   prospecting
  RT   radiometric surveys
  RT   remote sensing

EXPLORER SATELLITES [420; 420]
  BT1 satellites

EXPLOSION WELDING [144; 144]
  BT1 welding
    BT2 joining
      BT3 fabrication

EXPLOSIONS [1,935; 6,282]
  UF   *blasts*
  UF   *detonations*
  NT1 atmospheric explosions
    NT2 annie event
    NT2 argus event
    NT2 harry event
    NT2 orange event
    NT2 romeo event
    NT2 smoky event
    NT2 starfish event
    NT2 swordfish event
    NT2 teak event
    NT2 tewa event
    NT2 yankee event
  NT1 chemical explosions
    NT2 cowboy event
    NT2 palanquin event
    NT2 pre-gondola i event
    NT2 pre-gondola ii event
  NT1 cratering explosions
    NT2 cabriolet event
    NT2 danny boy event
    NT2 palanquin event
    NT2 pre-gondola i event
    NT2 pre-gondola ii event
    NT2 schooner event
    NT2 sedan event

NT1	nuclear explosions	RT	implosions	

NT1 nuclear explosions
  NT2 almendro event
  NT2 annie event
  NT2 argus event
  NT2 baneberry event
  NT2 benham event
  NT2 boxcar event
  NT2 cabriolet event
  NT2 calabash event
  NT2 cannikin event
  NT2 carpetbag event
  NT2 danny boy event
  NT2 dining car event
  NT2 faultless event
  NT2 gasbuggy event
  NT2 greeley event
  NT2 halfbeak event
  NT2 handcar event
  NT2 handley event
  NT2 harry event
  NT2 holly event
  NT2 hutch event
  NT2 jorum event
  NT2 marvel event
  NT2 milrow event
  NT2 monique event
  NT2 orange event
  NT2 pokhran event
  NT2 rio blanco event
  NT2 romeo event
  NT2 rulison event
  NT2 scotch event
  NT2 smoky event
  NT2 starfish event
  NT2 swordfish event
  NT2 teak event
  NT2 tewa event
  NT2 thermonuclear explosions
    NT3 bravo event
    NT3 mike event
    NT3 schooner event
  NT2 trinity event
  NT2 wagon wheel event
  NT2 yankee event
  NT2 zuni event
NT1 surface explosions
  NT2 bravo event
  NT2 holly event
  NT2 mike event
  NT2 zuni event
NT1 underground explosions
  NT2 cabriolet event
  NT2 calabash event
  NT2 contained explosions
    NT3 almendro event
    NT3 baneberry event
    NT3 benham event
    NT3 boxcar event
    NT3 cannikin event
    NT3 carpetbag event
    NT3 dining car event
    NT3 gasbuggy event
    NT3 halfbeak event
    NT3 handley event
    NT3 marvel event
    NT3 monique event
    NT3 pokhran event
    NT3 rio blanco event
    NT3 rulison event
    NT3 scotch event
    NT3 wagon wheel event
  NT2 danny boy event
  NT2 faultless event
  NT2 greeley event
  NT2 handcar event
  NT2 hutch event
  NT2 jorum event
  NT2 milrow event
  NT2 palanquin event
  NT2 pre-gondola i event
  NT2 pre-gondola ii event
  NT2 schooner event
NT1 underwater explosions
  NT2 swordfish event
RT accidents
RT blast effects
RT detonators
RT excavation
RT fires
RT implosions
RT molten metal-water reactions
RT projectiles
RT shock waves

EXPLOSIVE FORMING [54; 54]
BT1 materials working
  BT2 fabrication

EXPLOSIVE FRACTURING [74; 74]
Jan 77
BT1 fracturing
RT chemical explosions
RT fractures
RT nuclear explosions
RT underground explosions

EXPLOSIVE INSTABILITY [105; 105]
BT1 plasma instability
  BT2 instability

EXPLOSIVE STIMULATION [88; 88]
UF *stimulation (explosive)*
RT chemical explosions
RT chimneys
RT crushing
RT natural gas
RT nuclear explosions
RT oil shales
RT underground explosions

EXPLOSIVES [195; 711]
NT1 chemical explosives
  NT2 dynamite
  NT2 nitromethane
  NT2 petn
  NT2 tnt
NT1 nuclear explosives
NT1 picric acid
RT guns
RT nitrocellulose

exponential piles
  USE subcritical assemblies

exports
  USE trade

exposure (radiation doses)
  USE radiation doses

EXPOSURE CHAMBERS [79; 79]
Sep 78
UF *atmospheric exposure chambers*
UF *environmental exposure chamber*
UF *inhalation exposure chambers*
RT controlled atmospheres

EXPOSURE RATEMETERS [182; 182]
UF *ratemeters (exposure)*
BT1 radiation monitors
  BT2 monitors
    BT3 measuring instruments
RT counting ratemeters
RT radiation monitoring

EXTENDED PARTICLE MODEL [284; 12,866]
BT1 particle models
  BT2 mathematical models
NT1 bag model
NT1 string models

EXTENSIVE AIR SHOWERS [1,827; 1,827]
BT1 cosmic showers
  BT2 secondary cosmic radiation
    BT3 cosmic radiation
      BT4 ionizing radiations
        BT5 radiations
  BT2 showers

EXTENSOMETERS [94; 94]
RT dilatometry
RT strain gages

EXTERNAL CONVERSION [13; 13]
BT1 conversion
RT energy levels

EXTERNAL IRRADIATION [3,915; 10,491]
BT1 irradiation
NT1 extracorporeal irradiation
NT1 partial body irradiation
NT1 whole-body irradiation
RT irradiation devices
RT irradiation plants
RT irradiation procedures
RT local fallout
RT local irradiation
RT personnel dosimetry
RT radiation protection
RT radioactive clouds
RT shielding

external magnetic fields
  USE magnetic fields

EXTERNAL ZONES [66; 66] *May 84*
(Areas immediately surrounding nuclear facility sites in which population distribution and density, and land and water uses, are considered with respect to the possibility of implementing emergency measures.)
RT emergency plans
RT evacuation
RT land use
RT nuclear facilities
RT population relocation
RT reactor sites
RT routing
RT site selection
RT water use

EXTRACELLULAR SPACE [127; 127]
RT compartments
RT edema

EXTRACORPOREAL IRRADIATION [141; 141]
(In vivo irradiation of organ, tissue or body fluid while outside the body.)
BT1 external irradiation
  BT2 irradiation
RT blood

extraction (beam)
  USE beam extraction

extraction (solvent)
  USE solvent extraction

EXTRACTION APPARATUSES [282; 1,419]
BT1 separation equipment
  BT2 equipment
NT1 extraction columns
NT1 mixer-settlers
NT1 podbielniak contactors
RT coolant cleanup systems
RT entrainment
RT laboratory equipment
RT solvent extraction

EXTRACTION CHROMATOGRAPHY [815; 815]
BT1 chromatography
  BT2 separation processes

EXTRACTION COLUMNS [925; 925]
  UF   *cascade (extraction)*
  UF   *chromatographic columns*
  UF   *columns (extraction)*
  UF   *pulse columns*
  UF   *towers (extraction)*
  BT1   extraction apparatuses
    BT2   separation equipment
      BT3   equipment
  RT   column packing

EXTRACTIVE METALLURGY
[315; 953]
  BT1   metallurgy
  NT1   hydrometallurgy
  NT1   pyrometallurgy
    NT2   chloride volatility process
    NT2   fluoride volatility process
  RT   electrometallurgy
  RT   refining

EXTRAPOLATION [1,037; 1,037]
  BT1   numerical solution
  RT   extrapolation length
  RT   interpolation
  RT   mathematics

EXTRAPOLATION CHAMBERS
[115; 115]
  BT1   dosemeters
    BT2   measuring instruments
  BT1   ionization chambers
    BT2   radiation detectors
      BT3   measuring instruments

EXTRAPOLATION LENGTH [61; 61]
  RT   extrapolation
  RT   neutron transport theory

EXTREME ULTRAVIOLET RADIATION [1,120; 1,120]
(Wavelength range 400-100 A.)
  UF   *xuv*
  BT1   ultraviolet radiation
    BT2   electromagnetic radiation
      BT3   radiations
  RT   extreme ultraviolet spectra

EXTREME ULTRAVIOLET SPECTRA
[28; 28] *Sep 89*
  BT1   spectra
  RT   extreme ultraviolet radiation

EXTREME-VALUE PROBLEMS [34; 34]
Oct 76
  RT   mathematics

extremely high freq radiation
  USE   microwave radiation

EXTRUSION [547; 562]
  BT1   materials working
    BT2   fabrication
  NT1   coextrusion
  RT   cold working
  RT   dies
  RT   hot working
  RT   presses
  RT   pressing

EXXON FUEL FABRICATION FACILIT [22; 22]
  BT1   fuel fabrication plants
    BT2   nuclear facilities

exxon recovery and recycle pla
(Prior to December 1990, this was a valid descriptor.)
  USE   nuclear fuel recovery and recy

eye cataracts
  USE   cataracts

EYES [1,485; 2,625]
  UF   *sclera*
  BT1   sense organs
    BT2   organs
      BT3   body
  NT1   conjunctiva
  NT1   cornea
  NT1   crystalline lens
  NT1   lacrimal ducts
  NT1   retina
  NT1   uvea
  RT   face
  RT   ophthalmology
  RT   vision

ezeiza argentine ra-3 reactor
  USE   ra-3 reactor

E0-TRANSITIONS [687; 687] *Feb 78*
(Electric monopole transitions.)
  UF   *electric monopole transitions*
  BT1   multipole transitions
    BT2   energy-level transitions

E1-TRANSITIONS [2,622; 2,622] *Feb 78*
(Electric dipole transitions.)
  UF   *electric dipole transitions*
  BT1   multipole transitions
    BT2   energy-level transitions

E2-TRANSITIONS [4,570; 4,570] *Feb 78*
(Electric quadrupole transitions.)
  UF   *electric quadrupole transition*
  BT1   multipole transitions
    BT2   energy-level transitions

E3-TRANSITIONS [677; 677] *Feb 78*
(Electric octupole transitions.)
  UF   *electric octupole transitions*
  BT1   multipole transitions
    BT2   energy-level transitions

E4-TRANSITIONS [268; 268] *Feb 78*
(Electric hexadecapole transitions.)
  UF   *electric hexadecapole transiti*
  BT1   multipole transitions
    BT2   energy-level transitions

F CENTERS [1,419; 1,419]
  BT1   color centers
    BT2   vacancies
      BT3   point defects
        BT4   crystal defects
          BT5   crystal structure

F CODES [1,818; 1,818]
  BT1   computer codes

f mesons
(Prior to December 1987 this was a valid descriptor.)
  USE   d s mesons

F REGION [838; 1,126]
  BT1   ionosphere
    BT2   earth atmosphere
  NT1   f1 layer
  NT1   f2 layer
  NT1   spread f

F STATES [1,227; 1,227]
  BT1   energy levels

F WAVES [194; 194]
  BT1   partial waves
  RT   angular momentum
  RT   quantum mechanics

f*resonances
(Prior to December 1987 this was a valid descriptor.)
  USE   d*s-2110 mesons

F-1 REACTOR [5; 5] *Sep 79*
  BT1   graphite moderated reactors
    BT2   reactors
  BT1   natural uranium reactors
    BT2   reactors
  BT1   research reactors
    BT2   research and test reactors
      BT3   reactors

f-1260 resonances
(Prior to December 1987 this was a valid descriptor.)
  USE   f2-1270 mesons

f-1514 resonances
(Prior to December 1987 this was a valid descriptor.)
  USE   f2-1525 mesons

f-1540 resonances
(Prior to December 1987 this was a valid descriptor.)
  USE   mesons

f-2030 resonances
  USE   d s mesons

§ **FABRICATION** [16,385; 32,617]
(Limited to the concepts of shaping and manufacturing, use of a more specific term is recommended; for large scale building see CONSTRUCTION.)
  UF   *building (manufacturing)*
  UF   *manufacturing*
  SF   *processing*
  NT1   casting
    NT2   slip casting
    NT2   vacuum casting
  NT1   compacting
  NT1   joining
    NT2   bonding
    NT2   fastening
    NT2   welding
      NT3   arc welding
        NT4   gas metal-arc welding
          NT5   gas tungsten-arc welding
        NT4   plasma arc welding
        NT4   shielded metal-arc welding
        NT4   submerged arc welding
      NT3   brazing
      NT3   diffusion welding
      NT3   electron beam welding
      NT3   electroslag welding
      NT3   explosion welding
      NT3   forge welding
      NT3   friction welding
      NT3   gas welding
      NT3   induction welding
      NT3   laser welding
      NT3   magnetic force welding
      NT3   resistance welding
        NT4   flash welding
        NT4   projection welding
      NT3   soldering
      NT3   ultrasonic welding
      NT3   vacuum welding
  NT1   materials working
    NT2   canning
    NT2   cold working
      NT3   shot peening
    NT2   drawing
    NT2   explosive forming
    NT2   extrusion
      NT3   coextrusion
    NT2   forging
    NT2   hot working
    NT2   magnetic forming
    NT2   pressing
      NT3   cold pressing
      NT3   hot pressing
    NT2   rolling
    NT2   swaging
  NT1   molding
    NT2   pelletizing
  NT1   sintering

```
RT    computer-aided manufacturing
RT    fuel fabrication plants
RT    modular structures
RT    production
```

FABRY-PEROT INTERFEROMETER
[338; 338]
```
BT1   interferometers
BT2   measuring instruments
```

FACE [379; 845]
```
BT1   head
BT2   body areas
BT3   body
NT1   nose
RT    eyes
RT    respirators
RT    sinuses
```

face centered cubic
```
USE   fcc lattices
```

facilities (test)
```
USE   test facilities
```

facilities (underground)
```
USE   underground facilities
```

FACOM COMPUTERS [25; 25] *Nov 85*
```
BT1   computers
```

FACTORIZATION [1,651; 1,651]
```
RT    mathematics
```

FACULAE [203; 203]
```
BT1   solar activity
RT    photosphere
RT    plages
```

FADDEEV EQUATIONS [1,848; 1,848]
```
BT1   equations
RT    lippmann-schwinger equation
RT    multiple scattering
RT    three-body problem
```

FAEROE ISLANDS [38; 38]
```
UF    faroe islands
BT1   islands
RT    atlantic ocean
RT    denmark
```

FAILED ELEMENT DETECTION
[1,019; 1,019]
```
UF    burst can detection
UF    burst slug detection
UF    fedal
BT1   detection
RT    failed element monitors
RT    fuel cans
RT    fuel element failure
RT    fuel elements
RT    fuel motion detection
```

FAILED ELEMENT MONITORS
[379; 379]
```
UF    burst can monitors
UF    burst slug monitors
BT1   monitors
BT2   measuring instruments
RT    failed element detection
RT    fuel cans
RT    fuel element failure
RT    fuel elements
RT    reactor monitoring systems
```

FAILURE MODE ANALYSIS
[2,119; 2,119]
```
UF    event tree analysis
BT1   system failure analysis
BT2   systems analysis
RT    markov process
RT    reliability
```

FAILURES [9,157; 15,963]
```
NT1   fractures
NT2   thermal fractures
NT1   ruptures
RT    accidents
RT    amoeba effect
RT    corrosion
RT    electrical faults
RT    fatigue
RT    fracture properties
RT    hazards
RT    human factors
RT    impact shock
RT    leaks
RT    outages
RT    reliability
RT    safety
RT    systems analysis
```

FALLOUT [3,443; 5,449]
(For radioactive fallout only.)
```
UF    fragments (fallout)
UF+   fallout particulates
NT1   fallout deposits
NT1   global fallout
NT1   local fallout
NT1   washout
RT    accidents
RT    aerial monitoring
RT    aerosols
RT    air
RT    atmospheric precipitations
RT    contamination
RT    earth atmosphere
RT    fission products
RT    global aspects
RT    nuclear explosions
RT    nuclear weapons
RT    particle resuspension
RT    radiation hazards
RT    radiation protection
RT    radioactive aerosols
RT    radioactive clouds
RT    regional analysis
RT    residence half-time
RT    sedimentation
RT    sunshine project
RT    wind
```

FALLOUT DEPOSITS [1,120; 1,120]
```
BT1   fallout
RT    environment
RT    food chains
RT    radionuclide migration
RT    sedimentation
RT    soils
```

fallout particulates
```
USE   fallout
AND   particles
```

FALLOUT SHELTERS [60; 60]
```
BT1   shelters
RT    local fallout
RT    radiation protection
RT    subsurface structures
```

FANO FACTOR [139; 139]
```
RT    ionization
RT    semiconductor materials
```

fano-lichten model
```
USE   electron-promotion model
```

fans
```
USE   blowers
```

FAO [97; 97]
```
UF    food and agriculture org
BT1   international organizations
RT    agriculture
RT    agris
RT    food
RT    united nations
```

FAR INFRARED RADIATION
[1,501; 1,501]
(Wavelength range 50-1000 microns)
```
BT1   infrared radiation
BT2   electromagnetic radiation
BT3   radiations
```

FAR ULTRAVIOLET RADIATION
[1,491; 1,491]
(Wavelength range 2000-400 A.)
```
UF    vacuum ultraviolet radiation
BT1   ultraviolet radiation
BT2   electromagnetic radiation
BT3   radiations
```

faraday cages
```
USE   faraday cups
```

FARADAY CUPS [473; 473]
```
UF    faraday cages
BT1   beam monitors
BT2   monitors
BT3   measuring instruments
RT    beam currents
RT    electric measuring instruments
```

FARADAY CURRENT [24; 24]
```
BT1   electric currents
BT2   currents
```

FARADAY EFFECT [822; 822]
```
UF    faraday rotation
RT    electromagnetic radiation
RT    magneto-optical effects
RT    polarization
```

faraday generators
```
USE   mhd generators
```

FARADAY INDUCTION [106; 106]
```
BT1   induction
```

FARADAY LAWS [25; 25]
```
RT    electrolysis
```

FARADAY METHOD [48; 48]
```
RT    magnetic fields
```

faraday rotation
```
USE   faraday effect
```

FARLEY-1 REACTOR [63; 63]
(Dothan, Alabama, USA)
```
UF    joseph m. farley-1 reactor
BT1   pwr type reactors
BT2   enriched uranium reactors
BT3   reactors
BT2   power reactors
BT3   reactors
BT2   thermal reactors
BT3   reactors
BT2   water cooled reactors
BT3   reactors
BT2   water moderated reactors
BT3   reactors
```

FARLEY-2 REACTOR [47; 47]
(Dothan, Alabama, USA)
```
UF    joseph m. farley-2 reactor
BT1   pwr type reactors
BT2   enriched uranium reactors
BT3   reactors
BT2   power reactors
BT3   reactors
BT2   thermal reactors
BT3   reactors
BT2   water cooled reactors
BT3   reactors
BT2   water moderated reactors
BT3   reactors
```

farm animals
  USE   domestic animals

faroe islands
  USE   faeroe islands

FASCIA [20; 20]
  BT1   connective tissue
    BT2   tissues
      BT3   body

FASCIOLA [29; 29]
  BT1   trematodes
    BT2   helminths
      BT3   parasites
    BT2   platyhelminths
      BT3   invertebrates
        BT4   animals
  RT   fascioliasis

FASCIOLIASIS [16; 16]
  BT1   parasitic diseases
    BT2   infectious diseases
      BT3   diseases
  RT   fasciola

fast breeder test r. (kalpakka
  USE   kalpakkam lmfbr reactor

fast breeder type reactors
  USE   fbr type reactors

fast burst reactor facility
  USE   fbrf reactor

fast experim. breed. rea. japa
  USE   joyo reactor

FAST FISSION [817; 817]
  BT1   fission
    BT2   nuclear reactions
  BT1   neutron reactions
    BT2   nucleon reactions
      BT3   baryon reactions
        BT4   hadron reactions
          BT5   nuclear reactions
  RT   fast fission factor
  RT   fast neutrons

FAST FISSION FACTOR [20; 20]
  RT   fast fission
  RT   fast reactors
  RT   fission
  RT   multiplication factors

fast flux test facility
  USE   fftf reactor

FAST MAGNETOACOUSTIC WAVES [118; 118]
  BT1   magnetoacoustic waves
    BT2   hydromagnetic waves
  RT   transit-time magnetic pumping

FAST NEUTRONS [11,062; 11,062]
  BT1   neutrons
    BT2   nucleons
      BT3   baryons
        BT4   fermions
        BT4   hadrons
          BT5   elementary particles
  RT   fast fission
  RT   fast reactors
  RT   nisus facility

fast prototype reactor japan
  USE   monju reactor

fast reactor core test facilit
  USE   frctf reactor

FAST REACTORS [3,189; 29,387]
  BT1   epithermal reactors
    BT2   reactors
  NT1   actinide burner reactors
  NT1   afsr reactor
  NT1   aprf reactor
  NT1   bigr reactor
  NT1   bir reactor
  NT1   cfrmf reactor
  NT1   clementine reactor
  NT1   coral-1 reactor
  NT1   ecel reactor
  NT1   fbr type reactors
    NT2   aipfr reactor
    NT2   gcfr type reactors
      NT3   gcfr reactor
    NT2   lmfbr type reactors
      NT3   beloyarsk-3 reactor
      NT3   beloyarsk-4 reactor
      NT3   bn-1600 reactor
      NT3   bn-350 reactor
      NT3   bn-800 reactor
      NT3   bor-60 reactor
      NT3   cdfr reactor
      NT3   clinch river breeder reactor
      NT3   dfr reactor
      NT3   ebr-1 reactor
      NT3   ebr-2 reactor
      NT3   enrico fermi-1 reactor
      NT3   joyo reactor
      NT3   kalpakkam lmfbr reactor
      NT3   monju reactor
      NT3   pfr reactor
      NT3   phenix reactor
      NT3   plbr reactor
      NT3   rapsodie reactor
      NT3   sbr-2 reactor
      NT3   sbr-5 reactor
      NT3   snr reactor
      NT3   snr-2 reactor
      NT3   super phenix reactor
    NT2   pec brasimone reactor
    NT2   sbr-1 reactor
    NT2   zebra reactor
  NT1   fbrf reactor
  NT1   fca reactor
  NT1   fftf reactor
  NT1   fr-0 reactor
  NT1   harmonie reactor
  NT1   hprr reactor
  NT1   ibr-2 reactor
  NT1   ibr-30 reactor
  NT1   ifr reactor
  NT1   kalpakkam pfr reactor
  NT1   knk-2 reactor
  NT1   lampre-1 reactor
  NT1   masurca reactor
  NT1   purnima reactor
  NT1   purnima-2 reactor
  NT1   saref reactor
  NT1   sefor reactor
  NT1   sneak reactor
  NT1   sora reactor
  NT1   stf reactor
  NT1   tapiro reactor
  NT1   tibr reactor
  NT1   vera reactor
  NT1   viper reactor
  NT1   wntr reactor
  NT1   yayoi reactor
  NT1   zephyr reactor
  NT1   zppr reactor
  NT1   zpr-3 reactor
  NT1   zpr-6 reactor
  NT1   zpr-9 reactor
  NT1   zrr reactor
  RT   fast fission factor
  RT   fast neutrons

fast source reactor aec
  USE   afsr reactor

FASTBUS SYSTEM [381; 381] Sep 83
  RT   camac system
  RT   computers
  RT   data acquisition systems
  RT   equipment interfaces
  RT   nuclear instrument modules
  RT   on-line control systems
  RT   on-line measurement systems

FASTENERS [1,235; 1,235]
  UF   anchors
  UF   bolts
  UF   nuts (mechanical)
  UF   rivets
  UF   screws
  UF   studs
  RT   fastening
  RT   joining
  RT   restraints

FASTENING [406; 406]
  UF   anchoring
  UF   bolting
  UF   connecting
  UF   riveting
  UF   screwing
  BT1   joining
    BT2   fabrication
  RT   fasteners
  RT   joints

FASTING [296; 296]
  UF   starvation
  RT   biological stress
  RT   diet
  RT   metabolism

FAT CELLS [166; 166]
  BT1   connective tissue cells
    BT2   somatic cells
      BT3   animal cells
  RT   adipose tissue

FATIGUE [5,036; 6,019]
  BT1   mechanical properties
  NT1   corrosion fatigue
  NT1   thermal fatigue
  RT   crack propagation
  RT   failures
  RT   s-n diagram

fatigue (biological)
  USE   biological fatigue

FATS [343; 348]
  NT1   butter fat
  RT   adipose tissue
  RT   food
  RT   lipids

fatty acids
  USE   carboxylic acids

fault liability
(Prior to December 1990, this was a valid descriptor.)
  USE   liabilities

FAULT TOLERANT COMPUTERS [18; 18] Nov 88
(Systems which have the ability to produce correct results even in the presence of a fault.)
  BT1   digital computers
    BT2   computers
  RT   reliability

FAULT TREE ANALYSIS [1,481; 1,481]
  UF   fault tree systems
  BT1   system failure analysis
    BT2   systems analysis
  RT   control
  RT   monte carlo method

    RT   planning
    RT   probabilistic estimation
    RT   statistics

fault tree systems
    USE   fault tree analysis

FAULTLESS EVENT [4; 4]
    BT1   nuclear explosions
      BT2   explosions
    BT1   underground explosions
      BT2   explosions
    RT   seismology

faults (geologic)
    USE   geologic faults

faure cyclotron
    USE   nac cyclotron

FBR TYPE REACTORS [4,839; 23,790]
    UF   *fast breeder type reactors*
    BT1   breeder reactors
      BT2   reactors
    BT1   fast reactors
      BT2   epithermal reactors
        BT3   reactors
    NT1   aipfr reactor
    NT1   gcfr type reactors
      NT2   gcfr reactor
    NT1   lmfbr type reactors
      NT2   beloyarsk-3 reactor
      NT2   beloyarsk-4 reactor
      NT2   bn-1600 reactor
      NT2   bn-350 reactor
      NT2   bn-800 reactor
      NT2   bor-60 reactor
      NT2   cdfr reactor
      NT2   clinch river breeder reactor
      NT2   dfr reactor
      NT2   ebr-1 reactor
      NT2   ebr-2 reactor
      NT2   enrico fermi-1 reactor
      NT2   joyo reactor
      NT2   kalpakkam lmfbr reactor
      NT2   monju reactor
      NT2   pfr reactor
      NT2   phenix reactor
      NT2   plbr reactor
      NT2   rapsodie reactor
      NT2   sbr-2 reactor
      NT2   sbr-5 reactor
      NT2   snr reactor
      NT2   snr-2 reactor
      NT2   super phenix reactor
    NT1   pec brasimone reactor
    NT1   sbr-1 reactor
    NT1   zebra reactor
    RT   heterogeneous reactor cores
    RT   power reactors

FBRF REACTOR [24; 24]
(Fast Burst Reactor Facility, White Sands Missile Range, New Mexico, USA)
    UF   *fast burst reactor facility*
    BT1   fast reactors
      BT2   epithermal reactors
        BT3   reactors
    BT1   pulsed reactors
      BT2   reactors
    BT1   research reactors
      BT2   research and test reactors
        BT3   reactors

fbtr reactor (kalpakkam)
    USE   kalpakkam lmfbr reactor

FCA REACTOR [123; 123]
    UF   *tokai-mura fast critical assem*
    BT1   fast reactors
      BT2   epithermal reactors

        BT3   reactors
    BT1   zero power reactors
      BT2   experimental reactors
        BT3   research and test reactors
          BT4   reactors

FCC LATTICES [1,910; 1,910]
    UF   *face centered cubic*
    BT1   cubic lattices
      BT2   crystal lattices
        BT3   crystal structure

§ **FEASIBILITY STUDIES** [11,109; 11,109]
    RT   bench-scale experiments
    RT   commercialization
    RT   comparative evaluations
    RT   design
    RT   economics
    RT   efficiency
    RT   evaluation
    RT   field tests
    RT   implementation
    RT   performance
    RT   planning
    RT   productivity
    RT   technology assessment
    RT   testing

FEATHERS [22; 22]
    BT1   skin
      BT2   organs
        BT3   body
    RT   birds

FECES [1,225; 1,225]
    BT1   biological wastes
      BT2   biological materials
        BT3   materials
      BT2   wastes
    RT   body fluids
    RT   excretion
    RT   large intestine
    RT   proteus
    RT   rectum

fedal
    USE   failed element detection

federal energy administration
    USE   us fea

federal government
    USE   national government

FEDERAL RADIATION COUNCIL [11; 11]
    UF   *frc*
    BT1   us organizations
      BT2   national organizations
    RT   radiation protection
    RT   radiation protection laws
    RT   safety standards

FEDERAL REPUBLIC OF GERMANY [9,367; 9,367]
    UF   *german democratic republic*
    UF   *german federal republic*
    UF   *germany (democratic republic)*
    UF   *germany, federal republic of*
    BT1   developed countries
    BT1   europe
    RT   asse salt mine
    RT   german fr organizations

federal water pollution contro
    USE   us water pollution control act

federation of malaya
    USE   malaysia

FEED MATERIALS PLANTS [782; 863]
Jun 76
(Plants for the production of refined uranium or plutonium metal or their pure compounds in a form suitable for use in nuclear reactor fuel elements or as feed for uranium enrichment processes.)
    BT1   industrial plants
    BT1   nuclear facilities
    NT1   anaconda uranium mill
    NT1   feed materials production cent
    NT1   highland uranium mill
    NT1   shirley basin uranium mill
    NT1   west valley uf6 facility
    RT   fuel cycle centers

FEED MATERIALS PRODUCTION CENT [85; 85]
    BT1   feed materials plants
      BT2   industrial plants
      BT2   nuclear facilities
    BT1   us aec
      BT2   us organizations
        BT3   national organizations
    BT1   us doe
      BT2   us organizations
        BT3   national organizations
    BT1   us erda
      BT2   us organizations
        BT3   national organizations
    RT   ohio

FEEDBACK [2,261; 2,261]
    RT   closed-loop control
    RT   control
    RT   control theory
    RT   nyquist diagrams
    RT   servomechanisms

FEEDING [266; 266]
    RT   diet
    RT   food
    RT   nutrients

FEEDWATER [2,132; 2,132]
    BT1   water
      BT2   hydrogen compounds
      BT2   oxygen compounds
    RT   boilers
    RT   deaerators
    RT   demineralization
    RT   feedwater heaters
    RT   reactor cooling systems
    RT   steam generators
    RT   water chemistry

FEEDWATER HEATERS [274; 274]
    BT1   heaters
    RT   feedwater
    RT   reactor cooling systems

fees
    USE   charges

FEET [424; 424]
    BT1   legs
      BT2   limbs
        BT3   body areas
          BT4   body

FEINBERG-PAIS THEORY [3; 3]
    UF   *peratization procedure*
    RT   leptons
    RT   weak interactions

FELDSPARS [416; 416]
    UF   *albite*
    BT1   silicate minerals
      BT2   minerals
    RT   anorthosites
    RT   aplites
    RT   basalt
    RT   gabbros
    RT   granites
    RT   granodiorites
    RT   pegmatites

```
    RT    quartz monzonite
    RT    rhyolites
    RT    shales
    RT    syenites
```

FEMALE GENITALS [657; 4,023]
```
    UF    genitals (female)
    UF    vagina
    BT1   organs
     BT2    body
    NT1   ovaries
    NT1   uterus
    RT    estrous cycle
    RT    fertility
    RT    gonads
    RT    gynecology
    RT    menstrual cycle
    RT    menstruation disorders
    RT    pelvis
    RT    reproduction
    RT    sex
    RT    urogenital system diseases
```

FEMALES [1,085; 2,866]
```
    NT1   women
    RT    animals
    RT    sex
    RT    sex dependence
```

FEMUR [1,094; 1,094]
```
    BT1   skeleton
     BT2    organs
      BT3     body
    RT    legs
```

FERMAT PRINCIPLE [23; 23]
```
    RT    wave propagation
```

FERMENTATION [184; 184]
```
    SF    microbial processes
    BT1   bioconversion
    RT    anaerobic digestion
    RT    biochemistry
    RT    chemical reactions
```

fermentation alcohol
```
    USE   ethanol
```

fermi age
```
    USE   fermi age theory
    AND   neutron age
```

FERMI AGE THEORY [38; 38]
```
    UF+   fermi age
    BT1   neutron slowing-down theory
    RT    neutron age
    RT    slowing-down
```

fermi beta theory
```
    USE   fermi interactions
```

fermi constants
```
    USE   fermi interactions
```

fermi diagram
```
    USE   fermi plot
```

fermi fluid
```
    USE   fermi gas
```

FERMI GAS [1,145; 1,145]
```
    UF    fermi fluid
    UF    fermi liquid
    UF    fermi-dirac gas
    RT    bose-einstein gas
    RT    electron gas
    RT    fermi statistics
```

FERMI GAS MODEL [1,090; 1,090]
```
    BT1   nuclear models
     BT2    mathematical models
```

FERMI INTERACTIONS [1,042; 1,042]
```
    UF    fermi beta theory
    UF    fermi constants
    UF    fermi pseudopotential
    UF    fermi-weizsaecker formula
    UF    four-fermion interaction
    BT1   weak interactions
     BT2    basic interactions
     BT2    interactions
    RT    primakoff theory
    RT    v-a theory
```

FERMI LEVEL [4,424; 4,424]
```
    UF    fermi surface
    BT1   energy levels
    RT    band theory
    RT    cooper pairs
```

fermi liquid
```
    USE   fermi gas
```

FERMI PLOT [168; 168]
```
    UF    fermi diagram
    UF    fermi-kurie plot
    UF    kurie plot
    BT1   diagrams
     BT2    information
    RT    beta decay
```

fermi pseudopotential
```
    USE   fermi interactions
```

FERMI RESONANCE [55; 55]
```
    BT1   resonance
```

FERMI STATISTICS [508; 508] *Sep 75*
```
    UF    fermi-dirac statistics
    RT    bose-einstein statistics
    RT    fermi gas
    RT    fermions
    RT    parastatistics
    RT    statistical mechanics
```

fermi surface
```
    USE   fermi level
```

fermi-dirac gas
```
    USE   fermi gas
```

fermi-dirac statistics
```
    USE   fermi statistics
```

fermi-kurie plot
```
    USE   fermi plot
```

FERMI-SEGRE FORMULA [6; 6]
```
    RT    magnetic moments
```

fermi-thomas model
```
    USE   thomas-fermi model
```

fermi-weizsaecker formula
```
    USE   fermi interactions
```

FERMILAB ACCELERATOR [1,154; 1,177] *Feb 76*
(Facility at Fermi National Accelerator Laboratory, Batavia, Illinois, includes main synchrotron, booster synchrotron, and linac.)
```
    UF    nal synchrotron
    BT1   synchrotrons
     BT2    cyclic accelerators
      BT3     accelerators
    RT    fermilab tevatron
```

FERMILAB TEVATRON [785; 785] *Feb 84*
```
    UF    tevatron (fermilab)
    BT1   synchrotrons
     BT2    cyclic accelerators
      BT3     accelerators
    RT    fermilab accelerator
```

fermion-boson symmetry
```
    USE   boson-fermion symmetry
```

FERMIONS [8,908; 166,118]
```
    NT1   baryons
     NT2    antibaryons
      NT3     antihyperons
       NT4      antilambda particles
       NT4      antiomega particles
       NT4      antisigma particles
       NT4      antixi particles
      NT3     antinucleons
       NT4      antineutrons
       NT4      antiprotons
     NT2    beauty baryons
      NT3     lambda b neutral baryons
     NT2    charmed baryons
      NT3     lambda c plus baryons
      NT3     omega c neutral baryons
      NT3     sigma c-2450 baryons
      NT3     xi c plus baryons
     NT2    dibaryons
      NT3     dineutrons
      NT3     diprotons
      NT3     lambda-n-2130 dibaryons
      NT3     nn-2170 dibaryons
      NT3     nn-2250 dibaryons
    *NT2    hyperons
     NT2    n*baryons
      NT3     delta baryons
       NT4      delta-1232 baryons
       NT4      delta-1550 baryons
       NT4      delta-1600 baryons
       NT4      delta-1620 baryons
       NT4      delta-1700 baryons
       NT4      delta-1900 baryons
       NT4      delta-1905 baryons
       NT4      delta-1910 baryons
       NT4      delta-1920 baryons
       NT4      delta-1930 baryons
       NT4      delta-1940 baryons
       NT4      delta-1950 baryons
       NT4      delta-2000 baryons
       NT4      delta-2150 baryons
       NT4      delta-2200 baryons
       NT4      delta-2300 baryons
       NT4      delta-2350 baryons
       NT4      delta-2390 baryons
       NT4      delta-2400 baryons
       NT4      delta-2420 baryons
       NT4      delta-2750 baryons
       NT4      delta-2950 baryons
       NT4      delta-3000 baryons
      NT3     n baryons
       NT4      n-1440 baryons
       NT4      n-1520 baryons
       NT4      n-1535 baryons
       NT4      n-1540 baryons
       NT4      n-1650 baryons
       NT4      n-1675 baryons
       NT4      n-1680 baryons
       NT4      n-1700 baryons
       NT4      n-1710 baryons
       NT4      n-1720 baryons
       NT4      n-1960 baryons
       NT4      n-1990 baryons
       NT4      n-2000 baryons
       NT4      n-2080 baryons
       NT4      n-2090 baryons
       NT4      n-2100 baryons
       NT4      n-2190 baryons
       NT4      n-2200 baryons
       NT4      n-2220 baryons
       NT4      n-2250 baryons
       NT4      n-2600 baryons
       NT4      n-2700 baryons
       NT4      n-3000 baryons
     NT2    nucleons
```

FERMIONS 262 FERMIUM 247

    NT3   antinucleons
      NT4   antineutrons
      NT4   antiprotons
*NT3   neutrons
    NT3   photonucleons
      NT4   photoneutrons
      NT4   photoprotons
    NT3   protons
      NT4   antiprotons
      NT4   cosmic protons
      NT4   delayed protons
      NT4   diprotons
      NT4   photoprotons
      NT4   prompt protons
      NT4   solar protons
      NT4   trapped protons
NT1   leptons
  NT2   antileptons
    NT3   antineutrinos
      NT4   electron antineutrinos
      NT4   muon antineutrinos
    NT3   muons plus
    NT3   positrons
      NT4   cosmic positrons
  NT2   electrons
    NT3   cosmic electrons
    NT3   exoelectrons
    NT3   prompt electrons
    NT3   runaway electrons
    NT3   solar electrons
    NT3   solvated electrons
    NT3   trapped electrons
  NT2   heavy leptons
    NT3   tau neutrinos
    NT3   tau particles
  NT2   muons
    NT3   cosmic muons
    NT3   muons minus
    NT3   muons plus
  NT2   neutrinos
    NT3   antineutrinos
      NT4   electron antineutrinos
      NT4   muon antineutrinos
    NT3   cosmic neutrinos
    NT3   electron neutrinos
      NT4   electron antineutrinos
    NT3   muon neutrinos
      NT4   muon antineutrinos
    NT3   solar neutrinos
    NT3   tau neutrinos
NT1   quarks
RT   boson-fermion symmetry
RT   fermi statistics

FERMIUM [104; 104]
  BT1   actinides
    BT2   metals
      BT3   elements
  BT1   transplutonium elements
    BT2   transuranium elements
      BT3   elements

FERMIUM BROMIDES [0; 0] *Aug 87*
  BT1   bromides
    BT2   bromine compounds
      BT3   halogen compounds
    BT2   halides
      BT3   halogen compounds
  BT1   fermium compounds
    BT2   actinide compounds
    BT2   transplutonium compounds
      BT3   transuranium compounds

FERMIUM CARBIDES [0; 0]
  BT1   carbides
    BT2   carbon compounds
  BT1   fermium compounds
    BT2   actinide compounds
    BT2   transplutonium compounds
      BT3   transuranium compounds

FERMIUM CHLORIDES [4; 4]
  BT1   chlorides
    BT2   chlorine compounds
      BT3   halogen compounds
    BT2   halides

      BT3   halogen compounds
  BT1   fermium compounds
    BT2   actinide compounds
    BT2   transplutonium compounds
      BT3   transuranium compounds

FERMIUM COMPLEXES [15; 15]
  BT1   actinide complexes
    BT2   complexes
  BT1   transuranium complexes

FERMIUM COMPOUNDS [23; 30]
  BT1   actinide compounds
  BT1   transplutonium compounds
    BT2   transuranium compounds
  NT1   fermium bromides
  NT1   fermium carbides
  NT1   fermium chlorides
  NT1   fermium iodides
  NT1   fermium nitrides
  NT1   fermium oxides
  NT1   fermium sulfides

FERMIUM IODIDES [2; 2] *Aug 87*
  BT1   fermium compounds
    BT2   actinide compounds
    BT2   transplutonium compounds
      BT3   transuranium compounds
  BT1   iodides
    BT2   halides
      BT3   halogen compounds
    BT2   iodine compounds
      BT3   halogen compounds

FERMIUM IONS [8; 8]
  BT1   ions
    BT2   charged particles

FERMIUM ISOTOPES [89; 393]
  NT1   fermium 242
  NT1   fermium 243
  NT1   fermium 244
  NT1   fermium 245
  NT1   fermium 246
  NT1   fermium 247
  NT1   fermium 248
  NT1   fermium 249
  NT1   fermium 250
  NT1   fermium 251
  NT1   fermium 252
  NT1   fermium 253
  NT1   fermium 254
  NT1   fermium 255
  NT1   fermium 256
  NT1   fermium 257
  NT1   fermium 258
  NT1   fermium 259

FERMIUM NITRIDES [0; 0]
  BT1   fermium compounds
    BT2   actinide compounds
    BT2   transplutonium compounds
      BT3   transuranium compounds
  BT1   nitrides
    BT2   nitrogen compounds
    BT2   pnictides

FERMIUM OXIDES [2; 2]
  BT1   fermium compounds
    BT2   actinide compounds
    BT2   transplutonium compounds
      BT3   transuranium compounds
  BT1   oxides
    BT2   chalcogenides
    BT2   oxygen compounds

FERMIUM SULFIDES [0; 0]
  BT1   fermium compounds
    BT2   actinide compounds
    BT2   transplutonium compounds
      BT3   transuranium compounds
  BT1   sulfides
    BT2   chalcogenides
    BT2   sulfur compounds

FERMIUM 242 [13; 13] *Mar 76*
  BT1   actinide nuclei
    BT2   heavy nuclei
      BT3   nuclei
  BT1   even-even nuclei
    BT2   nuclei
  BT1   fermium isotopes
  BT1   microsec living radioisotopes
    BT2   radioisotopes
      BT3   isotopes
  BT1   spontaneous fission radioisoto
    BT2   radioisotopes
      BT3   isotopes

FERMIUM 243 [0; 0] *Jun 86*
  BT1   actinide nuclei
    BT2   heavy nuclei
      BT3   nuclei
  BT1   alpha decay radioisotopes
    BT2   radioisotopes
      BT3   isotopes
  BT1   even-odd nuclei
    BT2   nuclei
  BT1   fermium isotopes
  BT1   millisec living radioisotopes
    BT2   radioisotopes
      BT3   isotopes

FERMIUM 244 [29; 29]
  BT1   actinide nuclei
    BT2   heavy nuclei
      BT3   nuclei
  BT1   even-even nuclei
    BT2   nuclei
  BT1   fermium isotopes
  BT1   millisec living radioisotopes
    BT2   radioisotopes
      BT3   isotopes
  BT1   spontaneous fission radioisoto
    BT2   radioisotopes
      BT3   isotopes

FERMIUM 245 [3; 3]
  BT1   actinide nuclei
    BT2   heavy nuclei
      BT3   nuclei
  BT1   alpha decay radioisotopes
    BT2   radioisotopes
      BT3   isotopes
  BT1   even-odd nuclei
    BT2   nuclei
  BT1   fermium isotopes
  BT1   seconds living radioisotopes
    BT2   radioisotopes
      BT3   isotopes

FERMIUM 246 [35; 35]
  BT1   actinide nuclei
    BT2   heavy nuclei
      BT3   nuclei
  BT1   alpha decay radioisotopes
    BT2   radioisotopes
      BT3   isotopes
  BT1   even-even nuclei
    BT2   nuclei
  BT1   fermium isotopes
  BT1   seconds living radioisotopes
    BT2   radioisotopes
      BT3   isotopes
  BT1   spontaneous fission radioisoto
    BT2   radioisotopes
      BT3   isotopes

FERMIUM 247 [3; 3]
  BT1   actinide nuclei
    BT2   heavy nuclei
      BT3   nuclei
  BT1   alpha decay radioisotopes
    BT2   radioisotopes
      BT3   isotopes
  BT1   electron capture radioisotopes
    BT2   beta decay radioisotopes
      BT3   radioisotopes
        BT4   isotopes
  BT1   even-odd nuclei
    BT2   nuclei
  BT1   fermium isotopes
  BT1   seconds living radioisotopes

FERMIUM 248 [19; 19]
BT2 radioisotopes
BT3 isotopes

FERMIUM 248 [19; 19]
BT1 actinide nuclei
BT2 heavy nuclei
BT3 nuclei
BT1 alpha decay radioisotopes
BT2 radioisotopes
BT3 isotopes
BT1 even-even nuclei
BT2 nuclei
BT1 fermium isotopes
BT1 seconds living radioisotopes
BT2 radioisotopes
BT3 isotopes
BT1 spontaneous fission radioisoto
BT2 radioisotopes
BT3 isotopes

FERMIUM 249 [2; 2]
BT1 actinide nuclei
BT2 heavy nuclei
BT3 nuclei
BT1 alpha decay radioisotopes
BT2 radioisotopes
BT3 isotopes
BT1 electron capture radioisotopes
BT2 beta decay radioisotopes
BT3 radioisotopes
BT4 isotopes
BT1 even-odd nuclei
BT2 nuclei
BT1 fermium isotopes
BT1 minutes living radioisotopes
BT2 radioisotopes
BT3 isotopes

FERMIUM 250 [26; 26]
BT1 actinide nuclei
BT2 heavy nuclei
BT3 nuclei
BT1 alpha decay radioisotopes
BT2 radioisotopes
BT3 isotopes
BT1 even-even nuclei
BT2 nuclei
BT1 fermium isotopes
BT1 isomeric transition isotopes
BT2 radioisotopes
BT3 isotopes
BT1 minutes living radioisotopes
BT2 radioisotopes
BT3 isotopes
BT1 seconds living radioisotopes
BT2 radioisotopes
BT3 isotopes
BT1 spontaneous fission radioisoto
BT2 radioisotopes
BT3 isotopes

FERMIUM 251 [7; 7]
BT1 actinide nuclei
BT2 heavy nuclei
BT3 nuclei
BT1 alpha decay radioisotopes
BT2 radioisotopes
BT3 isotopes
BT1 electron capture radioisotopes
BT2 beta decay radioisotopes
BT3 radioisotopes
BT4 isotopes
BT1 even-odd nuclei
BT2 nuclei
BT1 fermium isotopes
BT1 hours living radioisotopes
BT2 radioisotopes
BT3 isotopes

FERMIUM 252 [40; 40]
BT1 actinide nuclei
BT2 heavy nuclei
BT3 nuclei
BT1 alpha decay radioisotopes
BT2 radioisotopes
BT3 isotopes
BT1 days living radioisotopes
BT2 radioisotopes
BT3 isotopes
BT1 even-even nuclei
BT2 nuclei
BT1 fermium isotopes
BT1 spontaneous fission radioisoto
BT2 radioisotopes
BT3 isotopes

FERMIUM 253 [11; 11]
BT1 actinide nuclei
BT2 heavy nuclei
BT3 nuclei
BT1 alpha decay radioisotopes
BT2 radioisotopes
BT3 isotopes
BT1 days living radioisotopes
BT2 radioisotopes
BT3 isotopes
BT1 electron capture radioisotopes
BT2 beta decay radioisotopes
BT3 radioisotopes
BT4 isotopes
BT1 even-odd nuclei
BT2 nuclei
BT1 fermium isotopes

FERMIUM 253 TARGET [2; 2] *May 80*
BT1 targets

FERMIUM 254 [49; 49]
BT1 actinide nuclei
BT2 heavy nuclei
BT3 nuclei
BT1 alpha decay radioisotopes
BT2 radioisotopes
BT3 isotopes
BT1 even-even nuclei
BT2 nuclei
BT1 fermium isotopes
BT1 hours living radioisotopes
BT2 radioisotopes
BT3 isotopes
BT1 spontaneous fission radioisoto
BT2 radioisotopes
BT3 isotopes

FERMIUM 254 TARGET [4; 4]
BT1 targets

FERMIUM 255 [41; 41]
BT1 actinide nuclei
BT2 heavy nuclei
BT3 nuclei
BT1 alpha decay radioisotopes
BT2 radioisotopes
BT3 isotopes
BT1 even-odd nuclei
BT2 nuclei
BT1 fermium isotopes
BT1 hours living radioisotopes
BT2 radioisotopes
BT3 isotopes
BT1 spontaneous fission radioisoto
BT2 radioisotopes
BT3 isotopes

FERMIUM 255 TARGET [3; 3]
BT1 targets

FERMIUM 256 [57; 57]
BT1 actinide nuclei
BT2 heavy nuclei
BT3 nuclei
BT1 alpha decay radioisotopes
BT2 radioisotopes
BT3 isotopes
BT1 even-even nuclei
BT2 nuclei
BT1 fermium isotopes
BT1 hours living radioisotopes
BT2 radioisotopes
BT3 isotopes
BT1 isomeric transition isotopes
BT2 radioisotopes
BT3 isotopes
BT1 nanosec living radioisotopes
BT2 radioisotopes
BT3 isotopes
BT1 spontaneous fission radioisoto
BT2 radioisotopes
BT3 isotopes

FERMIUM 256 TARGET [2; 2] *May 80*
BT1 targets

FERMIUM 257 [52; 52]
BT1 actinide nuclei
BT2 heavy nuclei
BT3 nuclei
BT1 alpha decay radioisotopes
BT2 radioisotopes
BT3 isotopes
BT1 days living radioisotopes
BT2 radioisotopes
BT3 isotopes
BT1 even-odd nuclei
BT2 nuclei
BT1 fermium isotopes
BT1 spontaneous fission radioisoto
BT2 radioisotopes
BT3 isotopes

FERMIUM 257 TARGET [9; 9] *Mar 76*
BT1 targets

FERMIUM 258 [62; 62]
BT1 actinide nuclei
BT2 heavy nuclei
BT3 nuclei
BT1 even-even nuclei
BT2 nuclei
BT1 fermium isotopes
BT1 microsec living radioisotopes
BT2 radioisotopes
BT3 isotopes
BT1 spontaneous fission radioisoto
BT2 radioisotopes
BT3 isotopes

FERMIUM 258 TARGET [2; 2] *May 80*
BT1 targets

FERMIUM 259 [18; 18]
BT1 actinide nuclei
BT2 heavy nuclei
BT3 nuclei
BT1 even-odd nuclei
BT2 nuclei
BT1 fermium isotopes
BT1 seconds living radioisotopes
BT2 radioisotopes
BT3 isotopes
BT1 spontaneous fission radioisoto
BT2 radioisotopes
BT3 isotopes

FERMIUM 259 TARGET [2; 2] *May 80*
BT1 targets

FERMIUM 260 TARGET [2; 2] *May 80*
BT1 targets

FERNS [41; 41]
BT1 plants

FERRANTI COMPUTERS [3; 3]
BT1 computers

FERRATES [96; 96]
(Specific compounds should be indexed by coordination of a descriptor of the form (CATION) COMPOUNDS and the above anion descriptor.)
BT1 iron compounds
BT2 transition element compounds
BT1 oxygen compounds
RT iron oxides

ferric compounds
USE iron compounds

FERRICYANIDES [194; 194]
  UF   *cyanoferrates*
  BT1   iron complexes
    BT2   transition element complexes
      BT3   complexes

FERRIMAGNETIC MATERIALS
[206; 995]
  BT1   magnetic materials
    BT2   materials
  NT1   ferrites
  RT   ferrimagnetic resonance
  RT   ferrimagnetism
  RT   ferrite garnets

FERRIMAGNETIC RESONANCE [8; 8]
Sep 77
  BT1   magnetic resonance
    BT2   resonance
  RT   ferrimagnetic materials
  RT   ferrimagnetism

FERRIMAGNETISM [183; 183]
  BT1   magnetism
  RT   antiferromagnetism
  RT   ferrimagnetic materials
  RT   ferrimagnetic resonance
  RT   ferromagnetism

FERRITE [793; 793]
(A solid solution of carbon in alpha-iron.)
  BT1   carbon additions
  BT1   iron alloys
    BT2   alloys
  RT   ferritic steels
  RT   iron-alpha
  RT   magnetite
  RT   martensite
  RT   pearlite
  RT   solid solutions
  RT   steel-cr2moninb
  RT   steels

FERRITE GARNETS [1,422; 1,422]
(Minerals with the general formula $Y_3M_5O_{12}$, where Y is yttrium or other rare earth, and M is usually iron, but may be another metal. For silicate garnets use GARNETS.)
  UF+ *yttrium aluminium garnets*
  BT1   oxide minerals
    BT2   minerals
  RT   ferrimagnetic materials
  RT   garnets

FERRITES [796; 796]
  BT1   ferrimagnetic materials
    BT2   magnetic materials
      BT3   materials

FERRITIC STEELS [1,107; 1,279]
May 79
  BT1   steels
    BT2   carbon additions
    BT2   iron base alloys
      BT3   iron alloys
        BT4   alloys
  NT1   steel-cr12moniv
  NT1   steel-cr13al
  NT1   steel-cr16
  NT1   steel-cr25
  NT1   steel-cr9mo
  NT1   steel-cr9monbv
  RT   corrosion resistant alloys
  RT   ferrite

FERRITIN [276; 276]
  BT1   iron complexes
    BT2   transition element complexes
      BT3   complexes
  BT1   proteins
    BT2   organic compounds
  RT   hemosiderin
  RT   iron

FERROCENE [144; 144]
  BT1   dienes
    BT2   polyenes
      BT3   hydrocarbons
        BT4   organic compounds
  BT1   iron complexes
    BT2   transition element complexes
      BT3   complexes

FERROCYANIDES [349; 349]
  UF+ *prussian blue*
  BT1   iron complexes
    BT2   transition element complexes
      BT3   complexes

FERROELECTRIC MATERIALS
[1,371; 1,371]
  BT1   dielectric materials
    BT2   materials
  RT   antiferroelectric materials

FERROIN [19; 19]
  BT1   phenanthrolines
    BT2   heterocyclic compounds
      BT3   organic compounds
    BT2   organic nitrogen compounds
      BT3   organic compounds
  BT1   reagents
  RT   iron complexes
  RT   phenanthroline-ortho

FERROMAGNETIC MATERIALS
[2,810; 2,810]
  BT1   magnetic materials
    BT2   materials
  RT   antiferromagnetic materials
  RT   ferromagnetic resonance
  RT   magnetic semiconductors
  RT   spin glass state

FERROMAGNETIC RESONANCE
[227; 227] *May 76*
  BT1   magnetic resonance
    BT2   resonance
  RT   ferromagnetic materials
  RT   ferromagnetism

FERROMAGNETISM [2,171; 2,171]
  UF+ *nuclear ferromagnetism*
  BT1   magnetism
  RT   antiferromagnetism
  RT   curie point
  RT   ferrimagnetism
  RT   ferromagnetic resonance
  RT   heisenberg model

FERRON [10; 10]
  BT1   hydroxy compounds
    BT2   organic compounds
  BT1   organic iodine compounds
    BT2   organic halogen compounds
      BT3   organic compounds
  BT1   quinolines
    BT2   pyridines
      BT3   azines
        BT4   heterocyclic compounds
          BT5   organic compounds
        BT4   organic nitrogen compounds
          BT5   organic compounds
  BT1   reagents
  BT1   sulfonic acids
    BT2   organic acids
      BT3   organic compounds
    BT2   organic sulfur compounds
      BT3   organic compounds

ferrous compounds
  USE   iron compounds

FERTILE MATERIALS [259; 259]
(Materials containing nuclides capable of being transformed into fissile nuclides by neutron capture.)
  BT1   materials
  RT   breeding blankets
  RT   nuclear fuel conversion
  RT   nuclear fuels

FERTILITY [640; 640]
  RT   female genitals
  RT   fertilization
  RT   gonads
  RT   male genitals
  RT   menopause
  RT   menstrual cycle
  RT   progeny
  RT   reproduction
  RT   reproductive disorders
  RT   sterility

FERTILIZATION [43; 43] *Dec 86*
  RT   fertility
  RT   gametes
  RT   ovulation
  RT   reproduction

FERTILIZERS [1,055; 1,196]
  NT1   superphosphates
  RT   agriculture
  RT   eutrophication
  RT   nitrogen cycle
  RT   nutrients
  RT   plants

feshbach-porter-weisskopf mode
  USE   optical models

FESHBACH-WEISSKOPF MODEL
[40; 40]
  RT   nuclear reactions

FESSENHEIM-1 REACTOR [80; 80]
(Fessenheim, Haut-Rhine, France)
  BT1   pwr type reactors
    BT2   enriched uranium reactors
      BT3   reactors
    BT2   power reactors
      BT3   reactors
    BT2   thermal reactors
      BT3   reactors
    BT2   water cooled reactors
      BT3   reactors
    BT2   water moderated reactors
      BT3   reactors

FESSENHEIM-2 REACTOR [36; 36]
(Fessenheim, Haut-Rhine, France)
  BT1   power reactors
    BT2   reactors

FETAL MEMBRANES [61; 635]
  UF   *amnion*
  UF   *chorioallantoic membrane*
  BT1   membranes
  NT1   placenta
  RT   embryos
  RT   fetuses

FETUSES [1,462; 1,462]
  RT   age groups
  RT   amniotic fluid
  RT   congenital malformations
  RT   embryos
  RT   fetal membranes
  RT   ontogenesis
  RT   pregnancy
  RT   prenatal exposure
  RT   prenatal irradiation
  RT   teratogens
  RT   uterus

FEULGEN METHOD [11; 11]
  RT   cytochemistry
  RT   dna

FEVER [74; 74]
  BT1   symptoms
  RT   antipyretics
  RT   body temperature
  RT   hyperthermia
  RT   pyrogens

FEYNMAN DIAGRAM [7,627; 7,627]
BT1 diagrams
BT2 information
RT quantum field theory

FEYNMAN GAS MODEL [44; 44]
BT1 particle models
BT2 mathematical models
BT1 statistical models
BT2 mathematical models

FEYNMAN METHOD [75; 75]
UF *welton method*
RT neutron transport theory
RT transport theory

FEYNMAN PATH INTEGRAL
[2,572; 2,572]
BT1 integrals
RT propagator
RT quantum mechanics
RT wilson loop

FEYNMAN-GELL-MANN THEORY
[28; 28]
RT beta decay
RT neutrinos

FFTF REACTOR [1,773; 1,773]
(Westinghouse Hanford Company, Richland, Washington, USA)
UF *fast flux test facility*
UF *richland fftf reactor*
BT1 fast reactors
BT2 epithermal reactors
BT3 reactors
BT1 research reactors
BT2 research and test reactors
BT3 reactors
BT1 sodium cooled reactors
BT2 liquid metal cooled reactors
BT3 reactors
BT1 test reactors
BT2 research and test reactors
BT3 reactors
BT2 test facilities

FIAN SYNCHROTRON [16; 16]
UF *lebedev synchrotron*
BT1 synchrotrons
BT2 cyclic accelerators
BT3 accelerators

FIBER OPTICS [958; 958] *Apr 79*
(The technique of transmitting light through long, thin, flexible fibers of glass, plastic or other transparent materials.)
BT1 optics
RT optical fibers
RT optical properties
RT optical systems

FIBERGLASS [243; 243] *Aug 78*
BT1 composite materials
BT2 materials
RT fibers
RT glass
RT organic polymers

FIBERS [1,349; 2,374]
NT1 carbon fibers
NT1 optical fibers
RT cotton
RT dacron
RT fiberglass
RT jute
RT rayon
RT textiles
RT wool

fibration (topological maps)
USE mapping fibration

FIBRIN [172; 172]
BT1 blood coagulation factors
BT2 coagulants
BT3 hematologic agents
BT4 drugs
BT1 scleroproteins
BT2 proteins
BT3 organic compounds

FIBRINOGEN [492; 492]
BT1 blood coagulation factors
BT2 coagulants
BT3 hematologic agents
BT4 drugs
BT1 globulins
BT2 proteins
BT3 organic compounds

FIBRINOLYSIN [45; 45]
BT1 blood coagulation factors
BT2 coagulants
BT3 hematologic agents
BT4 drugs
BT1 serine proteinases
BT2 peptide hydrolases
BT3 hydrolases
BT4 enzymes
BT5 organic compounds
RT blood coagulation
RT fibrinolysis
RT thrombosis

FIBRINOLYSIS [109; 109]
BT1 proteolysis
BT2 decomposition
BT3 chemical reactions
RT fibrinolysin
RT streptococcal proteinase
RT urokinase

FIBROBLASTS [2,411; 2,411]
BT1 connective tissue cells
BT2 somatic cells
BT3 animal cells
RT collagen
RT fibrosis
RT l cells

FIBROSARCOMAS [271; 271]
BT1 sarcomas
BT2 neoplasms
BT3 diseases

FIBROSIS [1,163; 1,163]
BT1 pathological changes
BT2 diseases
RT connective tissue
RT fibroblasts

FICK LAWS [169; 169]
RT diffusion
RT neutron diffusion equation
RT neutron transport theory

FIELD ALGEBRA [613; 613]
RT current algebra
RT parastatistics
RT quantum field theory

FIELD EFFECT TRANSISTORS
[555; 801]
UF *unipolar transistors*
BT1 transistors
BT2 semiconductor devices
NT1 mosfet

FIELD EMISSION [679; 679]
BT1 emission
RT electron emission
RT ion emission
RT ion microscopy

field emission microscopy
USE ion microscopy

FIELD EQUATIONS [4,484; 14,134]
BT1 equations
NT1 dirac equation
NT1 einstein field equations
NT1 einstein-maxwell equations
NT1 klein-gordon equation
NT1 sine-gordon equation
RT field theories
RT general relativity theory
RT instantons
RT maxwell equations
RT merons

field ion microscopy
USE ion microscopy

FIELD OPERATORS [1,285; 1,285]
BT1 quantum operators
BT2 mathematical operators
RT quantum field theory
RT vacuum states

FIELD TESTS [1,075; 1,075] *May 81*
RT bench-scale experiments
RT feasibility studies
RT testing

FIELD THEORIES [3,518; 65,934]
NT1 general relativity theory
NT1 quantum field theory
NT2 axiomatic field theory
NT3 algebraic field theory
NT3 lsz theory
NT3 wightman field theory
NT2 constructive field theory
NT3 lattice field theory
NT2 lagrangian field theory
NT2 phi4-field theory
NT2 quantum chromodynamics
NT2 quantum electrodynamics
NT3 schwinger-tomonaga formalism
NT2 quantum flavordynamics
NT2 quantum gravity
NT2 unified gauge models
NT3 grand unified theory
NT4 standard model
NT3 weinberg lepton model
NT2 yukawa nonlocal theory
NT1 relativity theory
NT1 unified-field theories
NT2 einstein-schroedinger theory
NT2 kaluza-klein theory
NT2 supergravity
NT2 weyl unified theory
RT action integral
RT electrodynamics
RT field equations
RT instantons

field-reversed configurations
USE field-reversed theta pinch dev

field-reversed mirrors
USE reversed-field mirrors

FIELD-REVERSED THETA PINCH DEV [179; 179] *Aug 86*
(A type of compact torus with poloidal magnetic field only.)
UF *field-reversed configurations*
BT1 compact torus
BT2 tori
BT1 pinch devices
BT2 thermonuclear devices

fields (crossed)
USE crossed fields

fields (electric)
USE electric fields

fields (electromagnetic)
  USE   electromagnetic fields

fields (gravitational)
  USE   gravitational fields

fields (magnetic)
  USE   magnetic fields

FIERZ INTERFERENCE [11; 11]
  RT   beta decay

FIERZ-PAULI THEORY [28; 28]
  RT   quantum mechanics

FIFTH SOUND [12; 12] *Sep 77*
  RT   superfluidity

FIGS [13; 13]
  BT1   fruits
    BT2   food

figure of merit
  USE   performance

FIJI [8; 8]
  BT1   islands
  RT   pacific ocean

filament (plasma)
  USE   plasma filament

FILAMENT CRYSTAL COUNTERS [3; 3]
(Gamma counter filled with crystalline argon, xenon, methane, etc. at cryogenic temperatures.)
  BT1   crystal counters
    BT2   radiation detectors
      BT3   measuring instruments
  RT   gamma detection

FILAMENTS [1,538; 1,538]
  RT   wires

FILARIASIS [25; 25] *Sep 75*
  BT1   parasitic diseases
    BT2   infectious diseases
      BT3   diseases
  RT   nematodes
  RT   parasites

FILLER METALS [462; 462]
  RT   brazing alloys
  RT   welding

FILLERS [306; 306]
  RT   binders
  RT   grouting

film badges
  USE   photographic film dosemeters

FILM BOILING [684; 684]
  BT1   boiling
    BT2   phase transformations

FILM CONDENSATION [90; 90]
  BT1   vapor condensation
  RT   steam condensers

FILM COOLING [39; 39]
  BT1   cooling

film dosemeters
  USE   photographic film dosemeters

FILM DOSIMETRY [251; 251]
  BT1   dosimetry
  RT   photographic film dosemeters

FILM FLOW [244; 244] *Aug 75*
  BT1   fluid flow
  RT   helium ii
  RT   superfluidity

FILMLESS SPARK CHAMBERS [22; 417]
  BT1   spark chambers
    BT2   gas track detectors
      BT3   radiation detectors
        BT4   measuring instruments
  NT1   sonic spark chambers
  NT1   wire spark chambers

FILMS [12,062; 18,555]
(Not for the concepts covered by PHOTOGRAPHIC FILMS or NUCLEAR EMULSIONS.)
  NT1   superconducting films
  NT1   thin films
  RT   coatings
  RT   foils
  RT   layers

FILTERS [3,222; 6,091]
(See also DIGITAL FILTERS.)
  NT1   air filters
  NT1   electric filters
  NT1   electromagnetic filters
  NT1   magnetic filters
  NT1   mechanical filters
  NT1   optical filters
  RT   aerosols
  RT   baghouses
  RT   coolant cleanup systems
  RT   dust collectors
  RT   dusts
  RT   filtration
  RT   fouling
  RT   respirators
  RT   samplers
  RT   screens
  RT   scrubbing
  RT   sorting
  RT   suspensions
  RT   ultrafiltration
  RT   ventilation

§ **FILTRATION** [1,826; 2,057]
  BT1   separation processes
  NT1   ultrafiltration
  RT   filters
  RT   scrubbing

FINAL-STATE INTERACTIONS [2,055; 2,055]
  BT1   interactions
  RT   proximity scattering

financial assistance
  USE   financing

FINANCIAL INCENTIVES [115; 115] *Dec 82*
  UF   property tax exemption
  UF   subsidies
  UF   tax credits
  RT   economics
  RT   financing
  RT   legal aspects
  RT   payback period
  RT   socio-economic factors
  RT   taxes

FINANCIAL SECURITY [57; 57] *Dec 76*
(Insurance or other financial security a nuclear operator must have to cover his civil liability.)
  UF   security (financial)
  RT   insurance
  RT   liabilities
  RT   victims compensation

  RT   workmens compensation

FINANCING [1,348; 1,348]
  UF   financial assistance
  UF   grants
  UF   loan guarantees
  UF+   construction work in progress
  UF+   cwip
  RT   economy
  RT   financial incentives

fine control rods
  USE   regulating rods

FINE STRUCTURE [3,110; 3,110]
  RT   energy levels
  RT   paschen-back effect
  RT   sommerfeld constant
  RT   spectra

FINGERS [266; 266]
  BT1   hands
    BT2   arms
      BT3   limbs
        BT4   body areas
          BT5   body
  RT   nails

finishing (surface)
  USE   surface finishing

FINITE DIFFERENCE METHOD [2,381; 2,381]
  UF   coarse mesh method
  BT1   iterative methods
  BT1   numerical solution
  RT   analytical solution
  RT   differential equations
  RT   finite element method
  RT   mathematics
  RT   mesh generation
  RT   nodal expansion method

FINITE ELEMENT METHOD [5,975; 5,975]
  BT1   numerical solution
  RT   differential equations
  RT   finite difference method
  RT   mathematics
  RT   mesh generation
  RT   nodal expansion method

FINITE-RANGE INTERACTIONS [581; 581]
  BT1   interactions
  RT   nuclear reaction kinetics
  RT   zero-range approximation

FINLAND [872; 872]
  BT1   developed countries
  BT1   scandinavia
    BT2   europe

FINNISH ORGANIZATIONS [22; 22] *Aug 76*
  BT1   national organizations

finnish reactor-1
  USE   fir-1 reactor

FINS [365; 365]
  RT   reactor components
  RT   spacers
  RT   vanes

FIR-1 REACTOR [13; 13]
(Technical Research Centre of Finland Reactor Lab., Espoo, Finland)
  UF   finnish reactor-1
  BT1   isotope production reactors
    BT2   irradiation reactors
      BT3   reactors
  BT1   pulsed reactors

```
    BT2      reactors
  BT1      research reactors
    BT2      research and test reactors
      BT3      reactors
  BT1      tank type reactors
    BT2      reactors
  BT1      test reactors
    BT2      research and test reactors
      BT3      reactors
    BT2      test facilities
  BT1      thermal reactors
    BT2      reactors
  BT1      training reactors
    BT2      research and test reactors
      BT3      reactors
  BT1      triga type reactors
    BT2      enriched uranium reactors
      BT3      reactors
    BT2      hydride moderated reactors
      BT3      reactors
    BT2      research and test reactors
      BT3      reactors
    BT2      solid homogeneous reactors
      BT3      homogeneous reactors
        BT4      reactors
    BT2      water cooled reactors
      BT3      reactors
    BT2      water moderated reactors
      BT3      reactors
```

FIRE EXTINGUISHERS [156; 156]
RT   fire fighting
RT   fires
RT   safety

FIRE FIGHTING [105; 105] Dec 85
RT   fire extinguishers
RT   fire hazards
RT   fires

FIRE HAZARDS [585; 585]
BT1   hazards
RT   fire fighting
RT   fire prevention
RT   fires

FIRE PREVENTION [230; 230] Dec 85
RT   combustion
RT   fire hazards
RT   fire resistance
RT   fires
RT   safety

FIRE RESISTANCE [350; 350]
RT   fire prevention
RT   fires
RT   thermal insulation

FIREBALL MODEL [706; 706]
UF   *two-fireball model*
BT1   particle models
BT2   mathematical models

fireballs (nuclear)
USE   nuclear fireballs

firehose instability
USE   hose instability

FIRES [1,571; 1,571]
RT   accidents
RT   burns
RT   combustion
RT   explosions
RT   fire extinguishers
RT   fire fighting
RT   fire hazards
RT   fire prevention
RT   fire resistance
RT   flammability
RT   hazards
RT   safety engineering
RT   smoke detectors

firestreak model
USE   nuclear fireball model

FIRST AID [170; 170]
BT1   therapy
BT2   medicine
RT   accidents
RT   health hazards
RT   injuries
RT   safety showers
RT   single intake

FIRST WALL [4,245; 4,245] Aug 75
BT1   thermonuclear reactor walls
RT   steel-cr10mo2
RT   wall loading

FISCHER-TROPSCH SYNTHESIS [44; 44]
BT1   chemical reactions
RT   hydrocarbons

→ *fish ladders*
USE   fish passage facilities

→ *fish lifts*
USE   fish passage facilities

→ *fish locks*
USE   fish passage facilities

fish meal
USE   fish products

FISH OIL [11; 11] Oct 76
BT1   oils
BT2   other organic compounds
BT3   organic compounds
RT   fishes
RT   hydrocarbons

→ ## FISH PASSAGE FACILITIES [0; 0] Aug 91
(Structures that carry water around dams thus facilitating the migration of fish.)
UF   *fish ladders*
UF   *fish lifts*
UF   *fish locks*
UF   *fishways*
RT   anadromous fishes
RT   dams
RT   hydroelectric power plants
RT   migration

FISH PRODUCTS [47; 450]
UF   *fish meal*
NT1   seafood

FISHBONE INSTABILITY [58; 58] Jun 84
BT1   plasma macroinstabilities
BT2   plasma instability
BT3   instability

FISHERY LAWS [2; 2]
(Prior to December 1990, this descriptor was spelled FISHERY LAW.)
BT1   laws
RT   high seas
RT   territorial waters

FISHES [2,695; 3,061]
(Not for the concept of the edible flesh of a fish for which use SEAFOOD.)
UF   *flukes (fishes)*
UF   *misgurnus*
BT1   aquatic organisms
BT1   vertebrates
BT2   animals
NT1   anadromous fishes
NT2   salmon
NT1   codfish
NT1   eel
NT1   goldfish
NT1   plaice
NT1   trout
NT1   tuna
RT   aquaculture
RT   fish oil
RT   food
RT   gills
RT   seafood
RT   surface waters

FISHING INDUSTRY [57; 57] Dec 75
BT1   industry

→ *fishways*
USE   fish passage facilities

FISSILE MATERIALS [1,505; 1,505]
(Materials containing nuclides capable of undergoing fission by interaction with slow neutrons.)
BT1   fissionable materials
BT2   materials
RT   fission
RT   nuclear fuels
RT   nuclear materials management

FISSION [7,008; 11,968]
UF   *disintegration (fission)*
BT1   nuclear reactions
NT1   binary fission
NT1   electrofission
NT1   fast fission
NT1   photofission
NT1   quaternary fission
NT1   spontaneous fission
NT1   ternary fission
NT1   thermal fission
RT   bohr-wheeler theory
RT   chain reactions
RT   criticality
RT   fast fission factor
RT   fissile materials
RT   fission barrier
RT   fission fragments
RT   fission products
RT   fission spectra
RT   fission yield
RT   fissionable materials
RT   fissioning plasma
RT   governor model
RT   nuclear explosions
RT   nuclear fragmentation
RT   nuclear fragments
RT   order-disorder model
RT   quasi-fission
RT   reactors
RT   recoils
RT   scission-point model
RT   snell experiment
RT   spallation
RT   strutinsky theory
RT   thermal fission factor
RT   watt fission spectrum

FISSION BARRIER [1,271; 1,271]
BT1   potential energy
BT2   energy
RT   excitation
RT   fission

FISSION CHAMBERS [581; 581]
BT1   ionization chambers
BT2   radiation detectors
BT3   measuring instruments
BT1   neutron detectors
BT2   radiation detectors
BT3   measuring instruments
RT   threshold detectors

FISSION FOIL DETECTORS [362; 362]
BT1   neutron detectors
BT2   radiation detectors
BT3   measuring instruments
RT   activation detectors
RT   dielectric track detectors

RT threshold detectors

FISSION FRAGMENT DETECTION [796; 796]
- BT1 radiation detection
- BT2 detection
- RT charged particle detection
- RT radiation detectors

FISSION FRAGMENT SPECTROMETERS [84; 84]
- BT1 spectrometers
- BT2 measuring instruments

FISSION FRAGMENTS [5,053; 5,053]
- UF *fragments (fission)*
- BT1 nuclear fragments
- RT fission
- RT fission tracks

FISSION ISOMERS [423; 423]
- RT isomeric nuclei
- RT spontaneous fission

FISSION NEUTRONS [1,585; 3,810]
- BT1 neutrons
- BT2 nucleons
- BT3 baryons
- BT4 fermions
- BT4 hadrons
- BT5 elementary particles
- NT1 delayed neutrons
- NT1 prompt neutrons
- RT multiplication factors

FISSION POISONS [31; 31]
- BT1 nuclear poisons
- BT2 reactor materials
- BT3 materials

FISSION PRODUCT RELEASE [5,411; 5,411]
(Coordinate with descriptors for the area of release, such as BIOSPHERE or COOLANTS, and for the specific fission products, if known.)
- UF *release (fission product)*
- RT containment
- RT contamination
- RT leaks
- RT radiation hazards
- RT radioactive waste disposal
- RT source terms

FISSION PRODUCTS [10,310; 10,310]
- UF *debris (nuclear)*
- BT1 isotopes
- BT1 radioactive materials
- BT2 materials
- RT accidents
- RT containment
- RT containment systems
- RT fallout
- RT fission
- RT fission yield
- RT fissium
- RT fong theory
- RT fuel cooling time
- RT fuel reprocessing plants
- RT nuclear explosions
- RT radioactive wastes
- RT reactors
- RT source terms
- RT spent fuels

FISSION RATIO [254; 254]
- RT capture-to-fission ratio
- RT resonance neutrons

fission reactor control theory
- USE reactor kinetics

FISSION SPECTRA [455; 455]
- BT1 spectra
- RT fission
- RT prompt neutrons

FISSION TRACKS [1,331; 1,331]
- BT1 particle tracks
- RT age estimation
- RT fission fragments

FISSION YIELD [2,021; 2,021]
- UF *yield (fission)*
- BT1 nuclear reaction yield
- RT fission
- RT fission products

fission-like reactions
- USE quasi-fission

FISSIONABLE MATERIALS [667; 2,153]
(Materials containing nuclides capable of undergoing fission by any process.)
- BT1 materials
- NT1 fissile materials
- RT accelerator breeders
- RT fission
- RT fuel cycle
- RT nuclear materials management
- RT radioactive wastes

fissionable materials manageme
- USE nuclear materials management

FISSIONING PLASMA [54; 54]
- BT1 plasma
- RT chain reactions
- RT fission
- RT gas fuels
- RT space propulsion reactors

FISSIUM [18; 18]
- RT fission products
- RT nuclear fuels

FISTULAE [510; 510]
- BT1 pathological changes
- BT2 diseases
- RT necrosis
- RT ulcers

FITZPATRICK REACTOR [71; 71]
(Oswego, New York, USA)
- UF *easton power reactor*
- UF *james a. fitzpatrick reactor*
- BT1 bwr type reactors
- BT2 enriched uranium reactors
- BT3 reactors
- BT2 power reactors
- BT3 reactors
- BT2 thermal reactors
- BT3 reactors
- BT2 water cooled reactors
- BT3 reactors
- BT2 water moderated reactors
- BT3 reactors

five-dimensional calculations
- USE many-dimensional calculations

fixation (carbon dioxide)
- USE carbon dioxide fixation

fixation (nitrogen)
- USE nitrogen fixation

fixation (waste treatment)
- USE solidification

fixed scatt. cent. approx.
- USE fsc approximation

flagyl
- USE metronidazole

FLAMANVILLE-1 REACTOR [4; 4] *Jul 84*
- BT1 pwr type reactors
- BT2 enriched uranium reactors
- BT3 reactors
- BT2 power reactors
- BT3 reactors
- BT2 thermal reactors
- BT3 reactors
- BT2 water cooled reactors
- BT3 reactors
- BT2 water moderated reactors
- BT3 reactors

FLAMANVILLE-2 REACTOR [2; 2] *Jul 84*
- BT1 pwr type reactors
- BT2 enriched uranium reactors
- BT3 reactors
- BT2 power reactors
- BT3 reactors
- BT2 thermal reactors
- BT3 reactors
- BT2 water cooled reactors
- BT3 reactors
- BT2 water moderated reactors
- BT3 reactors

FLAME SPRAYING [29; 29]
- BT1 spray coating
- BT2 surface coating
- BT3 deposition

FLAMES [569; 569]
- RT combustion

FLAMMABILITY [234; 234] *Nov 77*
- RT combustion
- RT fires

FLANGES [416; 416]
- RT joints

FLASH BURNS [42; 42]
- BT1 burns
- BT2 injuries
- BT3 diseases

FLASH HEATING [162; 162]
- BT1 heating
- RT distillation
- RT evaporation
- RT steam

FLASH TUBES [179; 179]
- BT1 gas discharge tubes
- BT2 electron tubes

FLASH WELDING [14; 14]
- BT1 resistance welding
- BT2 welding
- BT3 joining
- BT4 fabrication

flashing
(The evaporation of a heated liquid as a consequence of rapid pressure reduction.)
- USE evaporation

FLASHOVER [44; 44] *Dec 85*
- BT1 electric discharges
- RT breakdown
- RT electric arcs
- RT electric currents
- RT electric sparks
- RT electrical faults

flasks
  USE   casks

FLAT MAGNETIC SPECTROMETERS [250; 250]
  UF   *double focusing spectrometers*
  UF   *iron-free spectrometers*
  UF   *orange-type spectrometers*
  UF   *semicircular spectrometers*
  UF   *siegbahn spectrometers*
  UF   *spiral orbit spectrometers*
  BT1   magnetic spectrometers
    BT2   spectrometers
      BT3   measuring instruments

flattening (neutron flux)
  USE   neutron flux flattening

FLATTOP REACTOR [15; 15]
  BT1   zero power reactors
    BT2   experimental reactors
      BT3   research and test reactors
        BT4   reactors

FLAVENOIDS [49; 157]
  BT1   organic oxygen compounds
    BT2   organic compounds
  NT1   flavones
  NT2   hesperidin
  NT2   morin
  NT2   quercetin

FLAVINES [21; 122]
  BT1   acridines
    BT2   pyridines
      BT3   azines
        BT4   heterocyclic compounds
          BT5   organic compounds
        BT4   organic nitrogen compounds
          BT5   organic compounds
  BT1   amines
    BT2   organic compounds
  NT1   acriflavine
  NT1   proflavine

flavins
  USE   isoalloxazines

FLAVONES [68; 132]
  BT1   flavenoids
    BT2   organic oxygen compounds
      BT3   organic compounds
  NT1   hesperidin
  NT1   morin
  NT1   quercetin

flavoprotein enzymes
  USE   diaphorases

FLAVOR [154; 154]
(Not for elementary particles.)
  BT1   organoleptic properties
  RT   chemoreceptors
  RT   spices
  RT   taste buds

FLAVOR MODEL [3,629; 3,629] *Jul 77*
  UF   *beauty model*
  UF   *top quark model*
  UF   *truth model*
  BT1   quark model
    BT2   composite models
      BT3   particle models
        BT4   mathematical models
  RT   beauty particles
  RT   charmonium
  RT   kobayashi-maskawa matrix
  RT   quantum chromodynamics
  RT   quantum flavordynamics
  RT   quantum numbers
  RT   top particles
  RT   toponium

flaws
  USE   defects

FLAX PLANTS [25; 25]
  UF   *linseed plants*
  BT1   plants
  RT   linseed oil

flaxseed oil
  USE   linseed oil

FLEXIBILITY [383; 383]
  UF   *stiffness*
  BT1   tensile properties
    BT2   mechanical properties
  RT   flexural strength

FLEXURAL STRENGTH [689; 689]
  UF   *strength (flexural)*
  BT1   mechanical properties
  RT   bending
  RT   flexibility

FLIBE [104; 104] *Aug 75*
(Molten salt of fluorine, lithium and beryllium.)
  BT1   molten salts
    BT2   salts
  RT   beryllium fluorides
  RT   breeding blankets
  RT   lithium fluorides
  RT   thermonuclear reactor walls

FLIES [146; 1,149]
  BT1   insects
    BT2   arthropods
      BT3   invertebrates
        BT4   animals
  NT1   fruit flies
  NT2   ceratitis capitata
  NT2   dacus
  NT3   dacus oleae
  NT2   drosophila
  NT2   rhagoletis cerasi
  NT1   glossina
  NT1   hylemya antiqua
  NT1   screwworm fly

FLIP-FLOP CIRCUITS [111; 111]
  UF   *eccles-jordan circuits*
  BT1   multivibrators
    BT2   pulse circuits
      BT3   electronic circuits

float. nuc. pow. plant-sturgis
  USE   mh-1a reactor

floating nuclear power plants
  USE   offshore nuclear power plants

floating zone techniques
  USE   zone melting

FLOCCULATION [310; 310]
  UF   *coagulation (colloid)*
  UF   *colloid coagulation*
  BT1   precipitation
    BT2   separation processes
  RT   coprecipitation

FLOODS [319; 319]
  RT   drainage
  RT   exceptional natural disaster
  RT   hydrology
  RT   surface waters

FLOQUET FUNCTION [67; 67]
  BT1   functions
  RT   differential equations

florence oil
  USE   olive oil

FLORENCITE [2; 2]
  BT1   phosphate minerals
    BT2   minerals
  BT1   radioactive minerals
    BT2   minerals
    BT2   radioactive materials
      BT3   materials
  RT   aluminium phosphates
  RT   cerium phosphates

FLORIDA [229; 231]
  BT1   usa
    BT2   developed countries
    BT2   north america
  NT1   cape kennedy
  RT   biscayne bay
  RT   pinellas plant

florida university reactor
  USE   uftr reactor

FLOTATION [516; 516]
  BT1   separation processes
  RT   foam separation
  RT   ore enrichment
  RT   ore processing
  RT   waste processing

FLOUR [127; 127]
  BT1   food
  RT   bread
  RT   cereals

flow (fluid)
  USE   fluid flow

FLOW BLOCKAGE [1,067; 1,067]
  RT   fluid flow

FLOW COUNTERS [284; 284]
  UF   *fluid flow counters*
  BT1   radiation detectors
    BT2   measuring instruments
  RT   geiger-mueller counters
  RT   proportional counters

FLOW MODELS [3,924; 3,924]
  UF   *models (flow)*
  BT1   mathematical models
  RT   fluid flow

FLOW RATE [7,635; 7,635]
  RT   dynamic function studies
  RT   flow regulators
  RT   flowmeters
  RT   fluid flow
  RT   hydraulics
  RT   mach number
  RT   plasma eaters
  RT   pressure drop
  RT   time dependence
  RT   velocity

FLOW REGULATORS [481; 4,793]
  BT1   control equipment
    BT2   equipment
  NT1   baffles
  NT1   valves
  NT2   relief valves
  RT   flow rate

flow sheets
  USE   flowsheets

FLOW STRESS [526; 526]
  BT1   stresses
  RT   plasticity

FLOW VISUALIZATION [268; 268]
Oct 86
- RT aerosols
- RT bubbles
- RT fluid flow

FLOWERS [215; 275]
(For reproductive organs of plants.)
- NT1 stamen
- RT plants
- RT pollen
- RT reproduction

FLOWMETERS [947; 989]
- BT1 measuring instruments
- NT1 plasma eaters
- RT anemometers
- RT flow rate
- RT nozzles
- RT orifices
- RT pitot tubes
- RT venturi tubes

FLOWSHEETS [6,300; 6,300]
- UF *flow sheets*
- BT1 diagrams
- BT2 information

§§ FLUCTUATIONS [8,768; 8,768]
(Stochastic variations)
- BT1 variations
- RT noise

FLUE GAS [304; 304] *Jul 76*
- UF *combustion gases*
- BT1 gaseous wastes
- BT2 wastes
- RT scrubbing

fluence (neutron)
USE neutron fluence

fluid equations (plasma)
USE plasma fluid equations

FLUID FLOW [7,629; 25,980]
- UF *flow (fluid)*
- NT1 capillary flow
- NT1 compressible flow
- NT1 critical flow
- NT1 film flow
- NT1 gas flow
- NT2 air flow
- NT2 knudsen flow
- NT2 slip flow
- NT1 hypersonic flow
- NT1 incompressible flow
- NT2 ideal flow
- NT1 laminar flow
- NT1 liquid flow
- NT1 multiphase flow
- NT1 potential flow
- NT1 steady flow
- NT2 ideal flow
- NT1 subsonic flow
- NT1 supersonic flow
- NT1 transition flow
- NT1 transonic flow
- NT1 turbulent flow
- NT1 two-phase flow
- NT1 unsteady flow
- NT1 viscous flow
- NT2 couette flow
- NT1 vortex flow
- RT advection
- RT baffles
- RT bernoulli law
- RT boundary layers
- RT cavitation
- RT continuity equations
- RT darcy law
- RT drainage
- RT flow blockage
- RT flow models
- RT flow rate
- RT flow visualization
- RT fluid mechanics
- RT fluid-structure interactions
- RT fluids
- RT friction factor
- RT froude number
- RT hartmann number
- RT heat transfer
- RT helmholtz instability
- RT hydraulics
- RT hydrodynamics
- RT jets
- RT magnetohydrodynamics
- RT mass transfer
- RT oseen method
- RT pressure drop
- RT rayleigh-taylor instability
- RT reactor cooling systems
- RT reynolds number
- RT rheology
- RT shear
- RT stagnation
- RT superfluidity
- RT surges
- RT turbulence
- RT two-stream instability
- RT viscosity

fluid flow counters
USE flow counters

FLUID FUELED REACTORS [13; 430]
- UF *dust fueled reactors*
- UF *fluid-fueled reactors*
- BT1 reactors
- NT1 gas fueled reactors
- NT2 coaxial flow reactors
- NT2 light bulb reactors
- NT2 plasma core assembly
- NT1 liquid homogeneous reactors
- NT2 aqueous homogeneous reactors
- NT3 ai-l-77 reactor
- NT3 ber-2 reactor
- NT3 cesnef reactor
- NT3 dr-1 reactor
- NT3 frf reactor
- NT3 jrr-1 reactor
- NT3 kewb reactor
- NT3 kstr reactor
- NT3 ncscr-1 reactor
- NT3 prnc-l-77 reactor
- NT3 supo reactor
- NT3 wrrr reactor
- NT1 molten salt fueled reactors
- RT fluidized bed reactors
- RT liquid metal fuels

FLUID INJECTION [88; 306] *Aug 82*
- NT1 gas injection
- RT hydraulic fracturing
- RT hydrology
- RT pressurization
- RT underground disposal

FLUID MECHANICS [1,483; 15,775]
- BT1 mechanics
- NT1 aerodynamics
- NT1 electrogasdynamics
- NT1 hydrodynamics
- NT2 electrohydrodynamics
- NT2 magnetohydrodynamics
- NT1 magnetogasdynamics
- RT drag
- RT fluid flow
- RT fluid-structure interactions
- RT fluids
- RT friction factor
- RT general circulation models
- RT gravity waves
- RT hydraulic conductivity
- RT hydraulics
- RT hydrostatics

FLUID POISON CONTROL [232; 232]
- UF *chemical shimming*
- RT burnable poisons
- RT poisoning
- RT reactor control systems
- RT scram
- RT soluble poisons

fluid-fueled reactors
USE fluid fueled reactors

FLUID-STRUCTURE INTERACTIONS [904; 904] *Nov 80*
(Interactions between fluids, usually coolants, and structural components involving distortion of components such as shields, spacers, supports etc. in reactors.)
- RT fluid flow
- RT fluid mechanics
- RT fuel-coolant interactions
- RT reactor components
- RT reactor cooling systems
- RT reactor cores

FLUIDIC COMPUTERS [0; 0]
- BT1 computers

FLUIDIC CONTROL DEVICES [61; 61]
- BT1 control equipment
- BT2 equipment
- BT1 fluidic devices

FLUIDIC DEVICES [22; 81]
- NT1 fluidic control devices
- RT amplification

FLUIDIZATION [93; 93] *Dec 75*
- RT fluidized beds
- RT suspensions

FLUIDIZED BED REACTORS [117; 117]
- UF *fluidized-bed reactors*
- BT1 fuel dispersion reactors
- BT2 homogeneous reactors
- BT3 reactors
- RT fluid fueled reactors

FLUIDIZED BEDS [743; 743]
- RT chemical reactions
- RT chemical reactors
- RT fluidization
- RT suspensions

FLUIDIZED-BED COMBUSTION [189; 189] *Feb 76*
- BT1 combustion
- BT2 oxidation
- BT3 chemical reactions

fluidized-bed reactors
USE fluidized bed reactors

FLUIDS [1,796; 47,917]
(Not for the concepts covered by BODY FLUIDS.)
- NT1 cryogenic fluids
- NT1 drilling fluids
- NT1 gases
- NT2 air
- NT3 surface air
- NT2 compressed gases
- NT2 cosmic gases
- NT2 dissociating gases
- NT2 dissolved gases
- NT2 exhaust gases
- NT2 fuel gas
- NT3 coal gas
- NT3 natural gas
- NT2 ionized gases
- NT3 fully ionized gases
- NT4 lorentz gas
- NT3 strongly ionized gases
- NT3 weakly ionized gases

NT2	rarefied gases
NT2	vapors
NT3	water vapor
NT1	liquids
NT2	liquid crystals
NT2	liquid metals
NT1	quantum fluids
NT2	helium ii
NT1	working fluids
RT	fluid flow
RT	fluid mechanics

flukes (fishes)
   USE   fishes

flukes (trematodes)
   USE   trematodes

FLUORATES [21; 21]
(Specific compounds should be indexed by coordination of a descriptor of the form (CATION) COMPOUNDS and the above anion descriptor.)
   BT1   fluorine compounds
      BT2   halogen compounds
   BT1   oxygen compounds

FLUORENE [68; 68]
   BT1   condensed aromatics
      BT2   aromatics
         BT3   organic compounds
   BT1   hydrocarbons
      BT2   organic compounds

FLUORESCEIN [162; 164]
   BT1   dyes
   BT1   hydroxy acids
      BT2   carboxylic acids
         BT3   organic acids
            BT4   organic compounds
   BT1   polyphenols
      BT2   phenols
         BT3   aromatics
            BT4   organic compounds
         BT3   hydroxy compounds
            BT4   organic compounds
   RT   erythrosine
   RT   fluorescence
   RT   phthalic acid

FLUORESCENCE [4,700; 4,971]
   UF   *quenching (fluorescence)*
   BT1   luminescence
      BT2   photon emission
         BT3   emission
   NT1   resonance fluorescence
   RT   fluorescein
   RT   fluorescence spectroscopy
   RT   radiationless decay
   RT   superradiance
   RT   x-ray fluorescence analysis

FLUORESCENCE SPECTROSCOPY [2,062; 2,062]
   UF   *atomic fluoresc. spectroscopy*
   UF   *atomic fluorescence spectro*
   UF   *fluorimetry*
   UF   *molecular fluorescence spec*
   BT1   emission spectroscopy
      BT2   spectroscopy
   RT   fluorescence
   RT   fluorimeters
   RT   laser spectroscopy
   RT   quantitative chemical analysis
   RT   x-ray fluorescence analysis

fluorescent penetrant tests
   USE   liquid penetrant inspection

FLUORIDE VOLATILITY PROCESS [147; 147]
   BT1   pyrometallurgy
      BT2   extractive metallurgy
         BT3   metallurgy

   BT1   reprocessing
      BT2   separation processes
   RT   distillation
   RT   refining
   RT   volatility

FLUORIDES [1,815; 15,881]
   BT1   fluorine compounds
      BT2   halogen compounds
   BT1   halides
      BT2   halogen compounds
   NT1   actinium fluorides
   NT1   aluminium fluorides
   NT1   americium fluorides
   NT1   ammonium fluorides
   NT1   antimony fluorides
   NT1   argon fluorides
   NT1   arsenic fluorides
   NT1   barium fluorides
   NT1   berkelium fluorides
   NT1   beryllium fluorides
   NT1   bismuth fluorides
   NT1   boron fluorides
   NT1   bromine fluorides
   NT1   cadmium fluorides
   NT1   calcium fluorides
   NT1   californium fluorides
   NT1   carbon fluorides
   NT1   cerium fluorides
   NT1   cesium fluorides
   NT1   chlorine fluorides
   NT1   chromium fluorides
   NT1   cobalt fluorides
   NT1   copper fluorides
   NT1   curium fluorides
   NT1   dysprosium fluorides
   NT1   einsteinium fluorides
   NT1   erbium fluorides
   NT1   europium fluorides
   NT1   francium fluorides
   NT1   gadolinium fluorides
   NT1   gallium fluorides
   NT1   germanium fluorides
   NT1   gold fluorides
   NT1   hafnium fluorides
   NT1   helium fluorides
   NT1   holmium fluorides
   NT1   indium fluorides
   NT1   iodine fluorides
   NT1   iridium fluorides
   NT1   iron fluorides
   NT1   krypton fluorides
   NT1   lanthanum fluorides
   NT1   lead fluorides
   NT1   lithium fluorides
   NT1   lutetium fluorides
   NT1   magnesium fluorides
   NT1   manganese fluorides
   NT1   mercury fluorides
   NT1   molybdenum fluorides
   NT1   neodymium fluorides
   NT1   neon fluorides
   NT1   neptunium fluorides
   NT1   nickel fluorides
   NT1   niobium fluorides
   NT1   nitrogen fluorides
   NT1   osmium fluorides
   NT1   palladium fluorides
   NT1   phosphorus fluorides
   NT1   platinum fluorides
   NT1   plutonium fluorides
   NT1   polonium fluorides
   NT1   potassium fluorides
   NT1   praseodymium fluorides
   NT1   promethium fluorides
   NT1   protactinium fluorides
   NT1   radium fluorides
   NT1   radon fluorides
   NT1   rhenium fluorides
   NT1   rhodium fluorides
   NT1   rubidium fluorides
   NT1   ruthenium fluorides
   NT1   samarium fluorides
   NT1   scandium fluorides
   NT1   selenium fluorides
   NT1   silicon fluorides
   NT1   silver fluorides
   NT1   sodium fluorides
   NT1   strontium fluorides

   NT1   sulfur fluorides
   NT1   tantalum fluorides
   NT1   technetium fluorides
   NT1   tellurium fluorides
   NT1   terbium fluorides
   NT1   thallium fluorides
   NT1   thorium fluorides
   NT1   thulium fluorides
   NT1   tin fluorides
   NT1   titanium fluorides
   NT1   tungsten fluorides
   NT1   uranium fluorides
      NT2   uranium hexafluoride
      NT2   uranium pentafluoride
      NT2   uranium tetrafluoride
   NT1   uranyl fluorides
   NT1   vanadium fluorides
   NT1   xenon fluorides
   NT1   ytterbium fluorides
   NT1   yttrium fluorides
   NT1   zinc fluorides
   NT1   zirconium fluorides
   RT   fluorine additions
   RT   hydrofluoric acid
   RT   oxyfluorides

FLUORIMETERS [60; 60]
(Instrument for measuring fluorescent radiation emitted by a sample exposed to monochromatic radiation, used in chemical analysis or to determine the intensity of the radiation producing fluorescence.)
   UF   *fluorometers*
   BT1   measuring instruments
   RT   fluorescence spectroscopy

fluorimetry
   USE   fluorescence spectroscopy

→ **FLUORINATED ALIPHATIC HYDROCAR** [0; 0]
(Prior to October 1991, this concept was indexed by ORGANIC FLUORINE COMPOUNDS.)
   BT1   halogenated aliphatic hydrocar
      BT2   organic halogen compounds
         BT3   organic compounds
   BT1   organic fluorine compounds
      BT2   organic halogen compounds
         BT3   organic compounds

→ **FLUORINATED AROMATIC HYDROCARB** [0; 0] Oct 91
   BT1   halogenated aromatic hydrocarb
      BT2   aromatics
         BT3   organic compounds
      BT2   organic halogen compounds
         BT3   organic compounds
   BT1   organic fluorine compounds
      BT2   organic halogen compounds
         BT3   organic compounds

fluorinated hydrocarbons
   USE   organic fluorine compounds

FLUORINATION [504; 504]
   BT1   halogenation
      BT2   chemical reactions

FLUORINE [1,748; 1,748]
   UF   *fluorine fluorides*
   BT1   halogens
      BT2   nonmetals
         BT3   elements

FLUORINE ADDITIONS [19; 19]
Feb 89
   RT   crystal doping
   RT   doped materials
   RT   fluorides

fluorine bromides
   USE   bromine fluorides

fluorine chlorides
USE chlorine fluorides

FLUORINE COMPLEXES [59; 59]
BT1 complexes

FLUORINE COMPOUNDS [672; 16,147]
BT1 halogen compounds
NT1 fluorates
*NT1 fluorides
NT1 fluorine oxides
NT1 fluoroboric acid
NT1 hydrofluoric acid
NT1 oxyfluorides
RT   organic fluorine compounds

fluorine fluorides
USE fluorine

fluorine iodides
USE iodine fluorides

FLUORINE IONS [637; 637]
BT1 ions
BT2 charged particles

FLUORINE ISOTOPES [109; 3,974]
NT1 fluorine 14
NT1 fluorine 15
NT1 fluorine 16
NT1 fluorine 17
NT1 fluorine 18
NT1 fluorine 19
NT1 fluorine 20
NT1 fluorine 21
NT1 fluorine 22
NT1 fluorine 23
NT1 fluorine 24
NT1 fluorine 25
NT1 fluorine 26
NT1 fluorine 27
NT1 fluorine 29

FLUORINE OXIDES [35; 35]
UF   *oxygen fluorides*
BT1 fluorine compounds
BT2 halogen compounds
BT1 oxides
BT2 chalcogenides
BT2 oxygen compounds
RT   oxyfluorides

FLUORINE 14 [2; 2]
BT1 fluorine isotopes
BT1 light nuclei
BT2 nuclei
BT1 odd-odd nuclei
BT2 nuclei

FLUORINE 15 [7; 7] *Nov 78*
BT1 fluorine isotopes
BT1 light nuclei
BT2 nuclei
BT1 odd-even nuclei
BT2 nuclei

FLUORINE 16 [65; 65]
BT1 fluorine isotopes
BT1 light nuclei
BT2 nuclei
BT1 odd-odd nuclei
BT2 nuclei

FLUORINE 17 [193; 193]
BT1 beta-plus decay radioisotopes
BT2 beta decay radioisotopes
BT3 radioisotopes
BT4 isotopes
BT1 fluorine isotopes
BT1 light nuclei
BT2 nuclei
BT1 minutes living radioisotopes
BT2 radioisotopes

BT3 isotopes
BT1 odd-even nuclei
BT2 nuclei

FLUORINE 18 [2,271; 2,271]
BT1 beta-plus decay radioisotopes
BT2 beta decay radioisotopes
BT3 radioisotopes
BT4 isotopes
BT1 fluorine isotopes
BT1 hours living radioisotopes
BT2 radioisotopes
BT3 isotopes
BT1 isomeric transition isotopes
BT2 radioisotopes
BT3 isotopes
BT1 light nuclei
BT2 nuclei
BT1 nanosec living radioisotopes
BT2 radioisotopes
BT3 isotopes
BT1 odd-odd nuclei
BT2 nuclei

FLUORINE 18 TARGET [11; 11]
Apr 80
BT1 targets

FLUORINE 19 [1,230; 1,230]
BT1 fluorine isotopes
BT1 light nuclei
BT2 nuclei
BT1 odd-even nuclei
BT2 nuclei
BT1 stable isotopes
BT2 isotopes

FLUORINE 19 BEAMS [79; 79] *Oct 76*
BT1 ion beams
BT2 beams

FLUORINE 19 REACTIONS [382; 382]
BT1 heavy ion reactions
BT2 nuclear reactions

FLUORINE 19 TARGET [532; 532]
BT1 targets

FLUORINE 20 [194; 194]
BT1 beta-minus decay radioisotopes
BT2 beta decay radioisotopes
BT3 radioisotopes
BT4 isotopes
BT1 fluorine isotopes
BT1 light nuclei
BT2 nuclei
BT1 odd-odd nuclei
BT2 nuclei
BT1 seconds living radioisotopes
BT2 radioisotopes
BT3 isotopes

FLUORINE 21 [27; 27]
BT1 beta-minus decay radioisotopes
BT2 beta decay radioisotopes
BT3 radioisotopes
BT4 isotopes
BT1 fluorine isotopes
BT1 light nuclei
BT2 nuclei
BT1 odd-even nuclei
BT2 nuclei
BT1 seconds living radioisotopes
BT2 radioisotopes
BT3 isotopes

FLUORINE 22 [8; 8]
BT1 beta-minus decay radioisotopes
BT2 beta decay radioisotopes
BT3 radioisotopes
BT4 isotopes
BT1 fluorine isotopes
BT1 light nuclei
BT2 nuclei
BT1 odd-odd nuclei
BT2 nuclei

BT1 seconds living radioisotopes
BT2 radioisotopes
BT3 isotopes

FLUORINE 23 [17; 17]
BT1 beta-minus decay radioisotopes
BT2 beta decay radioisotopes
BT3 radioisotopes
BT4 isotopes
BT1 fluorine isotopes
BT1 light nuclei
BT2 nuclei
BT1 odd-even nuclei
BT2 nuclei
BT1 seconds living radioisotopes
BT2 radioisotopes
BT3 isotopes

FLUORINE 24 [22; 22]
BT1 beta-minus decay radioisotopes
BT2 beta decay radioisotopes
BT3 radioisotopes
BT4 isotopes
BT1 fluorine isotopes
BT1 light nuclei
BT2 nuclei
BT1 millisec living radioisotopes
BT2 radioisotopes
BT3 isotopes
BT1 odd-odd nuclei
BT2 nuclei

FLUORINE 25 [11; 11]
BT1 fluorine isotopes
BT1 light nuclei
BT2 nuclei
BT1 odd-even nuclei
BT2 nuclei

FLUORINE 26 [9; 9] *Jul 80*
BT1 beta-minus decay radioisotopes
BT2 beta decay radioisotopes
BT3 radioisotopes
BT4 isotopes
BT1 fluorine isotopes
BT1 light nuclei
BT2 nuclei
BT1 odd-odd nuclei
BT2 nuclei

FLUORINE 27 [4; 4] *Apr 86*
BT1 fluorine isotopes
BT1 light nuclei
BT2 nuclei
BT1 odd-even nuclei
BT2 nuclei

FLUORINE 29 [2; 2] *Sep 89*
BT1 fluorine isotopes
BT1 light nuclei
BT2 nuclei
BT1 odd-even nuclei
BT2 nuclei

FLUORITE [340; 340]
BT1 halide minerals
BT2 minerals
RT   calcium fluorides

→ **FLUOROBORIC ACID** [0; 0] *Sep 91*
BT1 boron compounds
BT1 fluorine compounds
BT2 halogen compounds
BT1 inorganic acids
BT2 hydrogen compounds
BT2 inorganic compounds

fluorod
USE rpl dosemeters

FLUORODEOXYGLUCOSE [161; 161]
May 86
BT1 antimetabolites
BT2 drugs
RT   glucose

fluorodeoxyuridine
USE   fudr

FLUOROFORM [66; 66]
BT1   organic fluorine compounds
BT2   organic halogen compounds
BT3   organic compounds
RT   hydrocarbons
RT   methane

fluorometers
USE   fluorimeters

FLUOROSCOPY [880; 880]
BT1   biomedical radiography
BT2   diagnostic techniques
BT2   medicine
RT   image intensifiers
RT   x radiation

FLUOROURACILS [396; 475]
BT1   antimetabolites
BT2   drugs
BT1   organic fluorine compounds
BT2   organic halogen compounds
BT3   organic compounds
BT1   uracils
BT2   hydroxy compounds
BT3   organic compounds
BT2   pyrimidines
BT3   azines
BT4   heterocyclic compounds
BT5   organic compounds
BT4   organic nitrogen compounds
BT5   organic compounds
NT1   fudr

FLUOROX PROCESS [1; 1]
BT1   reprocessing
BT2   separation processes
RT   solvent extraction

fluors
USE   phosphors

FLUREX PROCESS [0; 0]
BT1   reprocessing
BT2   separation processes
RT   solvent extraction

FLUTE INSTABILITY [669; 669]
UF   *interchange instability*
BT1   plasma macroinstabilities
BT2   plasma instability
BT3   instability
RT   hydrodynamics
RT   mercier criterion

flux (cosmic ray)
USE   cosmic ray flux

flux (magnetic)
USE   magnetic flux

flux (metallurgy)
USE   metallurgical flux

flux (neutron)
USE   neutron flux

flux (radiation)
USE   radiation flux

flux cored arc welding
USE   arc welding

FLUX DENSITY [4,652; 4,652]
(Coordinate with descriptors for the flux considered, e.g., MAGNETIC FLUX, NEUTRON FLUX, etc.)
UF   *density (flux)*
UF+   *neutron flux density*
RT   magnetic flux
RT   poynting theorem
RT   radiation flux

flux jumps
USE   magnetic flux

flux pinning
USE   magnetic flux

FLUX PUMPS [16; 16] *Aug 75*
(A cryogenic dc generator.)
BT1   electric generators
BT2   electrical equipment
BT3   equipment
RT   superconducting devices

FLUX QUANTIZATION [152; 152] *Oct 75*
RT   magnetic flux
RT   superconductivity

flux surfaces
USE   magnetic surfaces

FLUX SYNTHESIS [78; 78]
RT   neutron diffusion equation
RT   neutron flux

FLUXGATE MAGNETOMETERS [24; 24]
UF   *saturable core magnetometers*
BT1   magnetometers
BT2   measuring instruments

FLUXMETERS [59; 1,026]
BT1   measuring instruments
NT1   squid devices
RT   magnetometers

fluxoids
USE   magnetic flux

FLY ASH [587; 587]
BT1   aerosol wastes
BT2   wastes
BT1   ashes
BT2   combustion products
BT2   solid wastes
BT3   wastes
RT   air pollution

FLYING SPOT DIGITIZERS [99; 99]
(Mechanical flying spot digitizers; see also CATHODE RAY TUBE DIGITIZERS.)
UF   *fsd devices*
UF   *hough-powell devices*
UF   *hpd devices*
BT1   digitizers

FLYWHEELS [134; 134]
BT1   energy storage systems
BT1   rotors
RT   energy storage

fm cyclotrons
(Frequency-modulated cyclotrons.)
USE   synchrocyclotrons

FM DEVICES [39; 39]
(Floating multipoles.)
BT1   internal ring devices
BT2   closed plasma devices
BT3   thermonuclear devices
RT   multipolar configurations

FMIT LINAC [219; 219] *Dec 79*
(Linear accelerator at the Hanford Fusion Materials Irradiation Test facility.)
BT1   linear accelerators
BT2   accelerators
RT   materials testing
RT   quadrupole linacs
RT   thermonuclear reactor material

FMRB REACTOR [59; 59]
(Physikalisch-Technische Bundesanstalt, Braunschweig, Niedersachsen, Federal Republic of Germany)
UF   *braunschweig experimental r.*
UF   *braunschweig research reactor*
UF   *forschungs und messreaktor bra*
BT1   enriched uranium reactors
BT2   reactors
BT1   pool type reactors
BT2   water cooled reactors
BT3   reactors
BT2   water moderated reactors
BT3   reactors
BT1   research reactors
BT2   research and test reactors
BT3   reactors
BT1   test reactors
BT2   research and test reactors
BT3   reactors
BT2   test facilities

FNR REACTOR [44; 44]
(University of Michigan, Ann Arbor, Michigan, USA)
UF   *ford nuclear reactor*
BT1   enriched uranium reactors
BT2   reactors
BT1   isotope production reactors
BT2   irradiation reactors
BT3   reactors
BT1   pool type reactors
BT2   water cooled reactors
BT3   reactors
BT2   water moderated reactors
BT3   reactors
BT1   research reactors
BT2   research and test reactors
BT3   reactors
BT1   test reactors
BT2   research and test reactors
BT3   reactors
BT2   test facilities
BT1   thermal reactors
BT2   reactors
BT1   training reactors
BT2   research and test reactors
BT3   reactors

FOAM SEPARATION [83; 83]
BT1   separation processes
RT   flotation
RT   foams

FOAMS [357; 357]
BT1   colloids
BT2   dispersions
RT   boiling detection
RT   bubbles
RT   foam separation

foce verde reactor
USE   latina reactor

fock method
USE   hartree-fock method

FOCK REPRESENTATION [378; 378]
RT   mathematical space
RT   quantum field theory

fock self-consistent field
    USE   hartree-fock method

FOCUSING [4,742; 4,742]
    RT   beam optics
    RT   beam shaping

FOCUSONS [17; 17] *Mar 76*
(Focussed collision sequences behaving like particles in solids.)
    BT1   quasi particles

fodder
    USE   animal feeds

fog (meteorological)
    USE   atmospheric precipitations

fog (sprays)
    USE   sprays

FOG COOLED REACTORS [2; 2]
    BT1   reactors
    RT   core·spray systems
    RT   fog cooling

FOG COOLING [11; 11]
    BT1   cooling
    RT   core spray systems
    RT   fog cooled reactors
    RT   spray cooling

FOILS [4,780; 4,780]
(Thinner than plates or sheets.)
    RT   films
    RT   plates
    RT   sheets

fokker-planck coefficients
    USE   fokker-planck equation

FOKKER-PLANCK EQUATION [2,391; 2,391]
    UF   *bessel differential equation*
    UF   *fokker-planck coefficients*
    BT1   partial differential equations
       BT2   differential equations
          BT3   equations
    RT   ionized gases
    RT   transport theory

FOLDING MODEL [10; 10] *Nov 89*
    BT1   nuclear models
       BT2   mathematical models

FOLDY-WOUTHUYSEN TRANSFORM [103; 103]
    BT1   canonical transformations
       BT2   transformations
    RT   dirac equation

foliage
    USE   leaves

FOLIAR UPTAKE [248; 248]
    UF   *absorption (leaves)*
    BT1   uptake
    RT   leaves

FOLIC ACID [164; 164]
    UF   *formylpteroic acid*
    UF   *pteroylglutamic acid*
    UF   *rhizopterin*
    BT1   amino acids
       BT2   carboxylic acids
          BT3   organic acids
             BT4   organic compounds
    BT1   blood coagulation factors
       BT2   coagulants
          BT3   hematologic agents
             BT4   drugs
    BT1   hydroxy compounds
       BT2   organic compounds
    BT1   pteridines
       BT2   heterocyclic compounds
          BT3   organic compounds
       BT2   organic nitrogen compounds
          BT3   organic compounds
    BT1   vitamin b group
       BT2   vitamins
    RT   anemias
    RT   citrovorum factor
    RT   paba

folinic acid
    USE   citrovorum factor

follicle stimulating hormone
    USE   fsh

FONG THEORY [4; 4]
    UF   *fong-newton theory*
    RT   fission products

fong-newton theory
    USE   fong theory

fontenay-aux-roses (cea)
    USE   cea fontenay-aux-roses

FOOD [3,171; 10,498]
    UF   *foodstuffs*
    NT1   animal feeds
       NT2   forage
    NT1   beverages
    NT1   bread
    NT1   cocoa products
    NT1   flour
    NT1   fruits
       NT2   apples
       NT2   avocados
       NT2   bananas
       NT2   berries
       NT2   cherries
       NT2   coconuts
       NT2   dates
       NT2   figs
       NT2   grapefruits
       NT2   grapes
       NT2   lemons
       NT2   mangoes
       NT2   nuts
          NT3   chestnuts
          NT3   peanuts
       NT2   olives
       NT2   oranges
       NT2   papayas
       NT2   peaches
       NT2   pears
       NT2   plums
       NT2   raspberries
       NT2   strawberries
    NT1   honey
    NT1   meat
    NT1   milk
    NT1   milk products
       NT2   butter
       NT2   cheese
    NT1   seafood
    NT1   vegetables
       NT2   beans
       NT2   beets
       NT2   brassica
       NT2   carrots
       NT2   cucumbers
       NT2   lettuce
       NT2   mungbeans
       NT2   onions
       NT2   peas
       NT2   peppers
       NT2   potatoes
       NT2   radishes
       NT2   soybeans
       NT2   spinach
       NT2   tomatoes
       NT2   yams
    RT   agriculture
    RT   biological materials
    RT   carbohydrates
    RT   cassava
    RT   cereals
    RT   consumer products
    RT   crops
    RT   diet
    RT   drinking water
    RT   eggs
    RT   fao
    RT   fats
    RT   feeding
    RT   fishes
    RT   food chains
    RT   food processing
    RT   fowl
    RT   ifip
    RT   ingestion
    RT   nutrients
    RT   nutrition
    RT   organoleptic properties
    RT   preservation
    RT   proteins
    RT   radappertization
    RT   radicidation
    RT   radurization
    RT   seeds
    RT   spices
    RT   sterilization
    RT   vitamins
    RT   wholesomeness

food and agriculture org
    USE   fao

food and drug administration
    USE   us fda

FOOD CHAINS [2,639; 2,639]
    RT   diet
    RT   environmental exposure pathway
    RT   fallout deposits
    RT   food
    RT   radioecological concentration
    RT   radionuclide migration

food irradiation (radiopasteur
    USE   radicidation

food irradiation (radiopreserv
    USE   radurization

food irradiation (radiosterili
    USE   radappertization

FOOD PROCESSING [438; 1,333]
Apr 84
(Processing of food by individuals or large-scale commercial establishments.)
    UF   *baking (food)*
    UF   *canning (food)*
    UF   *cooking (food)*
    UF   *freezing (food)*
    NT1   pasteurization
       NT2   radicidation
    NT1   radappertization
    NT1   radurization
    RT   food
    RT   heat treatments
    RT   preservation

foodstuffs
    USE   food

FORAGE [301; 301]
- BT1 animal feeds
- BT2 food
- BT1 plants
- RT cattle
- RT clover
- RT glycine hispida
- RT gramineae
- RT pastures

FORATOM [4; 4] *Feb 78*
(Forum Atomique Europeen)
- BT1 international organizations

FORBIDDEN TRANSITIONS
[1,402; 1,402]
- UF *transitions (forbidden)*
- BT1 energy-level transitions
- RT decay
- RT selection rules

FORBUSH DECREASE [376; 376]
- UF *forbush depression*
- UF *forbush event*
- RT cosmic radiation
- RT magnetic storms
- RT solar flares
- RT solar wind

forbush depression
USE forbush decrease

forbush event
USE forbush decrease

FORCE-FREE MAGNETIC FIELDS
[227; 227]
- BT1 magnetic fields
- RT astrophysics

FORCED CONVECTION [869; 869]
(Heat transfer by forced convection.)
- BT1 convection
- BT2 heat transfer
- BT3 energy transfer

ford nuclear reactor
USE fnr reactor

FORECASTING [7,457; 7,457]
- UF *prediction*
- RT cost estimation
- RT economic policy
- RT economy
- RT evaluation
- RT management
- RT market
- RT planning
- RT probabilistic estimation
- RT regression analysis
- RT schedules
- RT time-series analysis
- RT weather

foreign policy
USE government policies

FOREST LITTER [76; 76]
(Natural organic debris on the forest floor.)
- BT1 biological materials
- BT2 materials
- RT ecosystems
- RT forests
- RT humus
- RT leaves

FORESTS [463; 463]
- RT deforestation
- RT forest litter
- RT ground cover
- RT terrestrial ecosystems
- RT trees

FORGE WELDING [8; 8]
- UF *roll welding*
- BT1 welding
- BT2 joining
- BT3 fabrication

FORGING [521; 521]
- BT1 materials working
- BT2 fabrication
- RT cold working
- RT dies
- RT hot working
- RT presses
- RT pressing
- RT swaging

FORKED RIVER-1 REACTOR [31; 31]
- UF *oyster creek-2 reactor*
- BT1 pwr type reactors
- BT2 enriched uranium reactors
- BT3 reactors
- BT2 power reactors
- BT3 reactors
- BT2 thermal reactors
- BT3 reactors
- BT2 water cooled reactors
- BT3 reactors
- BT2 water moderated reactors
- BT3 reactors

FORM FACTORS [7,609; 10,090]
- BT1 particle properties
- NT1 dirac form factors
- NT1 electromagnetic form factors
- NT1 pauli form factors
- RT nuclear reactions
- RT vertex functions

formal
USE methylal

FORMALDEHYDE [856; 856]
- UF *formalin*
- UF *formalith*
- UF *formic aldehyde*
- UF *formol*
- UF *oxymethylene*
- BT1 aldehydes
- BT2 organic compounds
- RT bakelite
- RT formyl radicals
- RT methylal
- RT polyoxymethylenes

formaldehydedimethylacetal
USE methylal

formalin
USE formaldehyde

formalith
USE formaldehyde

FORMAMIDE [172; 172]
- BT1 amides
- BT2 organic nitrogen compounds
- BT3 organic compounds
- RT formic acid

FORMATES [367; 367] *Feb 76*
- BT1 carboxylic acid salts
- RT formic acid

formation
USE synthesis

formation enthalpy
USE formation heat

FORMATION FREE ENERGY
[463; 463]
- BT1 free energy
- BT2 energy
- BT2 thermodynamic properties
- BT3 physical properties
- RT formation heat

FORMATION FREE ENTHALPY
[361; 361] *Mar 76*
- UF *gibbs formation free energy*
- BT1 free enthalpy
- BT2 energy
- BT2 thermodynamic properties
- BT3 physical properties
- RT entropy
- RT formation heat

FORMATION HEAT [1,976; 1,976]
- UF *enthalpy of formation*
- UF *formation enthalpy*
- UF *heat of formation*
- BT1 reaction heat
- BT2 enthalpy
- BT3 thermodynamic properties
- BT4 physical properties
- RT dissociation energy
- RT dissociation heat
- RT formation free energy
- RT formation free enthalpy

formation pressure
USE reservoir pressure

FORMIC ACID [470; 470]
- BT1 monocarboxylic acids
- BT2 carboxylic acids
- BT3 organic acids
- BT4 organic compounds
- RT formamide
- RT formates

formic aldehyde
USE formaldehyde

forming (materials)
USE materials working

formol
USE formaldehyde

FORMVAR [30; 30]
- BT1 polyacetals
- BT2 organic polymers
- BT3 organic compounds
- BT3 polymers

FORMYL RADICALS [95; 95]
- BT1 acyl radicals
- BT2 radicals
- RT formaldehyde

formylpteroic acid
USE folic acid

forschungs und messreaktor bra
USE fmrb reactor

forschungsreaktor berlin-2
USE ber-2 reactor

forschungsreaktor frankfurt
USE frf reactor

forschungsreaktor geesthacht-1
USE frg-1 reactor

forschungsreaktor geesthacht-2
USE   frg-2 reactor

forschungsreaktor muenchen
USE   frm reactor

forschungsreaktor neuherberg
USE   frn reactor

forschungsreaktor-2 frankfurt
USE   frf-2 reactor

FORSMARK-1 REACTOR [51; 51]
(Oesthammar, Uppsala, Sweden)
- BT1   bwr type reactors
- BT2   enriched uranium reactors
- BT3   reactors
- BT2   power reactors
- BT3   reactors
- BT2   thermal reactors
- BT3   reactors
- BT2   water cooled reactors
- BT3   reactors
- BT2   water moderated reactors
- BT3   reactors

FORSMARK-2 REACTOR [30; 30]
Feb 77
(Oesthammar, Uppsala, Sweden)
- BT1   bwr type reactors
- BT2   enriched uranium reactors
- BT3   reactors
- BT2   power reactors
- BT3   reactors
- BT2   thermal reactors
- BT3   reactors
- BT2   water cooled reactors
- BT3   reactors
- BT2   water moderated reactors
- BT3   reactors

FORSMARK-3 REACTOR [48; 48]
Sep 76
(Oesthammar, Uppsala, Sweden)
- BT1   bwr type reactors
- BT2   enriched uranium reactors
- BT3   reactors
- BT2   power reactors
- BT3   reactors
- BT2   thermal reactors
- BT3   reactors
- BT2   water cooled reactors
- BT3   reactors
- BT2   water moderated reactors
- BT3   reactors

fort shevchenko reactor
USE   bn-350 reactor

fort st. vrain reactor
USE   vrain reactor

fort worth gtr reactor
USE   gtr reactor

FORTRAN [2,767; 2,767]
- BT1   programming languages

fossil fuel power plants
USE   fossil-fuel power plants

fossil fuel reserves
USE   fossil fuels
AND   reserves

FOSSIL FUELS [771; 7,186]
- UF+   *fossil fuel reserves*
- BT1   energy sources
- BT1   fuels
- NT1   coal
- NT2   black coal
- NT3   anthracite
- NT3   bituminous coal
- NT2   lignite
- NT1   gasoline
- NT1   kerosene
- NT1   natural gas
- NT1   peat
- NT1   petroleum
- NT2   shale oil
- RT   fuel feeding systems

FOSSIL-FUEL POWER PLANTS [2,005; 2,005]
- UF   *fossil fuel power plants*
- BT1   thermal power plants
- BT2   power plants

FOSSILS [181; 181] Jul 80
- UF   *plant fossils*
- UF   *skeletal fossils*
- RT   biological evolution
- RT   paleontology

FOULING [190; 190] Apr 79
(Deposition of unwanted materials on equipment, e.g., heat exchangers, usually in a water environment.)
- UF   *biofouling*
- UF   *biological fouling*
- UF+   *impingement*
- RT   antifoulants
- RT   corrosion
- RT   deposition
- RT   filters
- RT   screens
- RT   water pollution

FOUNDATIONS [768; 768] Dec 75
- UF   *building foundations*
- BT1   supports
- BT2   mechanical structures
- RT   buildings
- RT   construction
- RT   soil-structure interactions

FOUR MOMENTUM TRANSFER [575; 575] Feb 78
- UF   *four-momentum transfer*
- UF   *transfer (four momentum)*
- UF   *transfer (q-squared)*
- BT1   momentum transfer
- RT   cross sections
- RT   electromagnetic form factors
- RT   particle interactions
- RT   rosenbluth formula
- RT   scattering

FOUR-BODY PROBLEM [864; 864]
- BT1   many-body problem

FOUR-DIMENSIONAL CALCULATIONS [2,944; 2,944]
- UF   *calculations (4-dimensional)*
- UF   *4-dimensional calculations*
- RT   many-dimensional calculations
- RT   mathematics

four-fermion interaction
USE   fermi interactions

four-momentum transfer
USE   four momentum transfer

four-nucleon structure
USE   quartet model

FOUR-NUCLEON TRANSFER REACTION [174; 1,097]
- BT1   multi-nucleon transfer reactio
- BT2   transfer reactions
- BT3   direct reactions
- BT4   nuclear reactions
- NT1   alpha-transfer reactions

FOUR-PI COUNTING [571; 571]
- BT1   counting techniques

FOURIER ANALYSIS [1,779; 1,779]
- UF   *analysis (fourier)*
- RT   frequency analysis
- RT   mathematics
- RT   normal-mode analysis

FOURIER HEAT EQUATION [129; 129]
- BT1   partial differential equations
- BT2   differential equations
- BT3   equations
- RT   heat transfer

→ **FOURIER TRANSFORM SPECTROMETER** [0; 0] Oct 91
- BT1   spectrometers
- BT2   measuring instruments
- RT   emission spectroscopy

FOURIER TRANSFORMATION [3,285; 3,285]
- BT1   integral transformations
- BT2   transformations

FOURTH SOUND [94; 94]
- RT   superfluidity

FOWL [196; 1,341]
- UF   *poultry*
- BT1   birds
- BT2   vertebrates
- BT3   animals
- NT1   chickens
- NT1   ducks
- RT   food

fowler equation
USE   fowler-nordheim theory

FOWLER-NORDHEIM THEORY [60; 60]
- UF   *fowler equation*
- RT   photoelectric effect

FR-0 REACTOR [5; 5]
- UF   *studsvik fr-0 reactor*
- BT1   enriched uranium reactors
- BT2   reactors
- BT1   fast reactors
- BT2   epithermal reactors
- BT3   reactors
- BT1   research reactors
- BT2   research and test reactors
- BT3   reactors
- BT1   training reactors
- BT2   research and test reactors
- BT3   reactors
- BT1   zero power reactors
- BT2   experimental reactors
- BT3   research and test reactors
- BT4   reactors

FR-2 REACTOR [111; 111]
(Gesellschaft fuer Kernforschung mbH, Karlsruhe, Baden-Wuerttemberg, Federal Republic of Germany)
- UF   *karlsruhe research r. fr-2*
- BT1   heavy water cooled reactors
- BT2   reactors
- BT1   heavy water moderated reactor
- BT2   reactors
- BT1   isotope production reactors
- BT2   irradiation reactors
- BT3   reactors
- BT1   natural uranium reactors

```
    BT2    reactors
    BT1    research reactors
      BT2    research and test reactors
        BT3    reactors
    BT1    tank type reactors
      BT2    reactors
    BT1    test reactors
      BT2    research and test reactors
        BT3    reactors
      BT2    test facilities
    BT1    thermal reactors
      BT2    reactors
```

fracer-fulco method
   USE   dispersion relations

FRACTALS [345; 345] *May 87*
(Fractals have structure which looks the same for any level of magnification.)
   RT   metrics
   RT   topology

FRACTIONAL-PARENTAGE COEFFICIE [101; 101]
(Numerical coefficients for proper antisymmetric combinations of wave functions for (n-1) and 1 particles to form wave functions for n-particle states.)
   RT   n*baryons
   RT   orbital angular momentum
   RT   wave functions

FRACTIONATED IRRADIATION [5,690; 5,690]
```
    UF     dose fractionation
    UF     split dose irradiation
    BT1    irradiation
    RT     cumulative radiation effects
    RT     dose-response relationships
    RT     radiation doses
    RT     radiotherapy
    RT     temporal dose distributions
```

FRACTIONATION [573; 573] *Dec 85*
```
    BT1    separation processes
    RT     dissolution
    RT     distillation
```

FRACTOGRAPHY [594; 594]
```
    RT     ceramography
    RT     fractures
    RT     metallography
    RT     photomicrography
```

FRACTURE MECHANICS [2,592; 2,592] *Sep 80*
```
    BT1    mechanics
    RT     crack propagation
    RT     cracks
    RT     defects
    RT     fracture properties
    RT     fractures
    RT     stress intensity factors
```

FRACTURE PROPERTIES [5,832; 5,832]
```
    UF     fracture strength
    UF     fracture toughness
    UF     strength (fracture)
    UF     toughness (fracture)
    BT1    mechanical properties
    RT     cracks
    RT     failures
    RT     fracture mechanics
    RT     fractures
    RT     ruptures
    RT     stress intensity factors
```

fracture strength
   USE   fracture properties

fracture toughness
   USE   fracture properties

FRACTURES [3,826; 3,861]
```
    BT1    failures
    NT1    thermal fractures
    RT     crack propagation
    RT     cracks
    RT     defects
    RT     deformation
    RT     explosive fracturing
    RT     fractography
    RT     fracture mechanics
    RT     fracture properties
    RT     fracturing
    RT     geologic fractures
    RT     hydraulic fracturing
    RT     mechanical fragmentation
    RT     ruptures
    RT     stress intensity factors
```

fractures (bone)
   USE   bone fractures

FRACTURING [89; 270] *Feb 81*
```
    NT1    explosive fracturing
    NT1    hydraulic fracturing
    RT     fractures
    RT     mechanical fragmentation
    RT     surface mining
```

fragmentation (limiting)
   USE   limiting fragmentation

fragmentation (mechanical)
   USE   mechanical fragmentation

fragmentation (nuclear)
   USE   nuclear fragmentation

fragments (decay)
   USE   decay

fragments (fallout)
   USE   fallout

fragments (fission)
   USE   fission fragments

fragments (nuclear)
   USE   nuclear fragments

fragments (particles)
   USE   particles

fragments (spallation)
   USE   spallation fragments

FRANCE [4,420; 4,420]
```
    BT1    developed countries
    BT1    europe
    RT     bay of biscay
    RT     cea
```

FRANCEVILLITE [5; 5]
```
    BT1    oxide minerals
      BT2    minerals
    BT1    uranium minerals
      BT2    radioactive minerals
        BT3    minerals
        BT3    radioactive materials
          BT4    materials
    RT     uranium oxides
    RT     vanadium oxides
```

FRANCIUM [57; 57]
```
    BT1    alkali metals
      BT2    metals
        BT3    elements
```

FRANCIUM ADDITIONS [1; 1]
(Alloys containing not more than 1% Fr are listed here.)
```
    RT     francium alloys
    RT     francium compounds
```

FRANCIUM ALLOYS [0; 0]
(Alloys containing more than 1% Fr.)
```
    BT1    alloys
    NT1    francium base alloys
    RT     francium additions
```

FRANCIUM BASE ALLOYS [0; 0]
```
    BT1    francium alloys
      BT2    alloys
```

FRANCIUM BROMIDES [0; 0]
```
    BT1    bromides
      BT2    bromine compounds
        BT3    halogen compounds
      BT2    halides
        BT3    halogen compounds
    BT1    francium compounds
      BT2    alkali metal compounds
```

FRANCIUM CHLORIDES [1; 1]
```
    BT1    chlorides
      BT2    chlorine compounds
        BT3    halogen compounds
      BT2    halides
        BT3    halogen compounds
    BT1    francium compounds
      BT2    alkali metal compounds
```

FRANCIUM COMPLEXES [1; 1]
```
    BT1    alkali metal complexes
      BT2    complexes
```

FRANCIUM COMPOUNDS [9; 10]
```
    BT1    alkali metal compounds
    NT1    francium bromides
    NT1    francium chlorides
    NT1    francium fluorides
    NT1    francium iodides
    NT1    francium oxides
    RT     francium additions
```

FRANCIUM FLUORIDES [0; 0]
```
    BT1    fluorides
      BT2    fluorine compounds
        BT3    halogen compounds
      BT2    halides
        BT3    halogen compounds
    BT1    francium compounds
      BT2    alkali metal compounds
```

FRANCIUM IODIDES [0; 0]
```
    BT1    francium compounds
      BT2    alkali metal compounds
    BT1    iodides
      BT2    halides
        BT3    halogen compounds
      BT2    iodine compounds
        BT3    halogen compounds
```

FRANCIUM IONS [10; 10]
```
    BT1    ions
      BT2    charged particles
```

FRANCIUM ISOTOPES [86; 288]
```
    NT1    francium 201
    NT1    francium 202
    NT1    francium 203
    NT1    francium 204
    NT1    francium 205
    NT1    francium 206
    NT1    francium 207
    NT1    francium 208
    NT1    francium 209
    NT1    francium 210
    NT1    francium 211
```

NT1	francium 212
NT1	francium 213
NT1	francium 214
NT1	francium 215
NT1	francium 216
NT1	francium 217
NT1	francium 218
NT1	francium 219
NT1	francium 220
NT1	francium 221
NT1	francium 222
NT1	francium 223
NT1	francium 224
NT1	francium 225
NT1	francium 226
NT1	francium 227
NT1	francium 228
NT1	francium 229
NT1	francium 230
NT1	francium 231
NT1	francium 232

FRANCIUM OXIDES [0; 0]
BT1 francium compounds
BT2 alkali metal compounds
BT1 oxides
BT2 chalcogenides
BT2 oxygen compounds

FRANCIUM 201 [3; 3] May 79
BT1 alpha decay radioisotopes
BT2 radioisotopes
BT3 isotopes
BT1 francium isotopes
BT1 heavy nuclei
BT2 nuclei
BT1 millisec living radioisotopes
BT2 radioisotopes
BT3 isotopes
BT1 odd-even nuclei
BT2 nuclei

FRANCIUM 202 [3; 3] May 79
BT1 alpha decay radioisotopes
BT2 radioisotopes
BT3 isotopes
BT1 francium isotopes
BT1 heavy nuclei
BT2 nuclei
BT1 millisec living radioisotopes
BT2 radioisotopes
BT3 isotopes
BT1 odd-odd nuclei
BT2 nuclei

FRANCIUM 203 [2; 2]
BT1 alpha decay radioisotopes
BT2 radioisotopes
BT3 isotopes
BT1 francium isotopes
BT1 heavy nuclei
BT2 nuclei
BT1 millisec living radioisotopes
BT2 radioisotopes
BT3 isotopes
BT1 odd-even nuclei
BT2 nuclei

FRANCIUM 204 [4; 4]
BT1 alpha decay radioisotopes
BT2 radioisotopes
BT3 isotopes
BT1 electron capture radioisotopes
BT2 beta decay radioisotopes
BT3 radioisotopes
BT4 isotopes
BT1 francium isotopes
BT1 heavy nuclei
BT2 nuclei
BT1 odd-odd nuclei
BT2 nuclei
BT1 seconds living radioisotopes
BT2 radioisotopes
BT3 isotopes

FRANCIUM 205 [7; 7]
BT1 alpha decay radioisotopes
BT2 radioisotopes
BT3 isotopes
BT1 francium isotopes
BT1 heavy nuclei
BT2 nuclei
BT1 odd-even nuclei
BT2 nuclei
BT1 seconds living radioisotopes
BT2 radioisotopes
BT3 isotopes

FRANCIUM 206 [9; 9]
BT1 alpha decay radioisotopes
BT2 radioisotopes
BT3 isotopes
BT1 electron capture radioisotopes
BT2 beta decay radioisotopes
BT3 radioisotopes
BT4 isotopes
BT1 francium isotopes
BT1 heavy nuclei
BT2 nuclei
BT1 isomeric transition isotopes
BT2 radioisotopes
BT3 isotopes
BT1 millisec living radioisotopes
BT2 radioisotopes
BT3 isotopes
BT1 odd-odd nuclei
BT2 nuclei
BT1 seconds living radioisotopes
BT2 radioisotopes
BT3 isotopes

FRANCIUM 207 [6; 6]
BT1 alpha decay radioisotopes
BT2 radioisotopes
BT3 isotopes
BT1 electron capture radioisotopes
BT2 beta decay radioisotopes
BT3 radioisotopes
BT4 isotopes
BT1 francium isotopes
BT1 heavy nuclei
BT2 nuclei
BT1 odd-even nuclei
BT2 nuclei
BT1 seconds living radioisotopes
BT2 radioisotopes
BT3 isotopes

FRANCIUM 208 [11; 11]
BT1 alpha decay radioisotopes
BT2 radioisotopes
BT3 isotopes
BT1 electron capture radioisotopes
BT2 beta decay radioisotopes
BT3 radioisotopes
BT4 isotopes
BT1 francium isotopes
BT1 heavy nuclei
BT2 nuclei
BT1 odd-odd nuclei
BT2 nuclei
BT1 seconds living radioisotopes
BT2 radioisotopes
BT3 isotopes

FRANCIUM 209 [8; 8]
BT1 alpha decay radioisotopes
BT2 radioisotopes
BT3 isotopes
BT1 electron capture radioisotopes
BT2 beta decay radioisotopes
BT3 radioisotopes
BT4 isotopes
BT1 francium isotopes
BT1 heavy nuclei
BT2 nuclei
BT1 odd-even nuclei
BT2 nuclei
BT1 seconds living radioisotopes
BT2 radioisotopes
BT3 isotopes

FRANCIUM 210 [5; 5]
BT1 alpha decay radioisotopes
BT2 radioisotopes
BT3 isotopes
BT1 electron capture radioisotopes
BT2 beta decay radioisotopes
BT3 radioisotopes
BT4 isotopes
BT1 francium isotopes
BT1 heavy nuclei
BT2 nuclei
BT1 minutes living radioisotopes
BT2 radioisotopes
BT3 isotopes
BT1 odd-odd nuclei
BT2 nuclei

FRANCIUM 211 [12; 12]
BT1 alpha decay radioisotopes
BT2 radioisotopes
BT3 isotopes
BT1 electron capture radioisotopes
BT2 beta decay radioisotopes
BT3 radioisotopes
BT4 isotopes
BT1 francium isotopes
BT1 heavy nuclei
BT2 nuclei
BT1 isomeric transition isotopes
BT2 radioisotopes
BT3 isotopes
BT1 minutes living radioisotopes
BT2 radioisotopes
BT3 isotopes
BT1 nanosec living radioisotopes
BT2 radioisotopes
BT3 isotopes
BT1 odd-even nuclei
BT2 nuclei

FRANCIUM 212 [33; 33]
BT1 alpha decay radioisotopes
BT2 radioisotopes
BT3 isotopes
BT1 electron capture radioisotopes
BT2 beta decay radioisotopes
BT3 radioisotopes
BT4 isotopes
BT1 francium isotopes
BT1 heavy nuclei
BT2 nuclei
BT1 isomeric transition isotopes
BT2 radioisotopes
BT3 isotopes
BT1 microsec living radioisotopes
BT2 radioisotopes
BT3 isotopes
BT1 minutes living radioisotopes
BT2 radioisotopes
BT3 isotopes
BT1 nanosec living radioisotopes
BT2 radioisotopes
BT3 isotopes
BT1 odd-odd nuclei
BT2 nuclei

FRANCIUM 213 [39; 39]
BT1 alpha decay radioisotopes
BT2 radioisotopes
BT3 isotopes
BT1 electron capture radioisotopes
BT2 beta decay radioisotopes
BT3 radioisotopes
BT4 isotopes
BT1 francium isotopes
BT1 heavy nuclei
BT2 nuclei
BT1 isomeric transition isotopes
BT2 radioisotopes
BT3 isotopes
BT1 microsec living radioisotopes
BT2 radioisotopes
BT3 isotopes
BT1 nanosec living radioisotopes
BT2 radioisotopes
BT3 isotopes
BT1 odd-even nuclei
BT2 nuclei
BT1 seconds living radioisotopes

BT2 radioisotopes
BT3 isotopes

FRANCIUM 214 [9; 9]
BT1 alpha decay radioisotopes
BT2 radioisotopes
BT3 isotopes
BT1 francium isotopes
BT1 heavy nuclei
BT2 nuclei
BT1 millisec living radioisotopes
BT2 radioisotopes
BT3 isotopes
BT1 odd-odd nuclei
BT2 nuclei

FRANCIUM 215 [17; 17]
BT1 alpha decay radioisotopes
BT2 radioisotopes
BT3 isotopes
BT1 francium isotopes
BT1 heavy nuclei
BT2 nuclei
BT1 nanosec living radioisotopes
BT2 radioisotopes
BT3 isotopes
BT1 odd-even nuclei
BT2 nuclei

FRANCIUM 216 [2; 2]
BT1 alpha decay radioisotopes
BT2 radioisotopes
BT3 isotopes
BT1 francium isotopes
BT1 heavy nuclei
BT2 nuclei
BT1 nanosec living radioisotopes
BT2 radioisotopes
BT3 isotopes
BT1 odd-odd nuclei
BT2 nuclei

FRANCIUM 217 [9; 9]
BT1 alpha decay radioisotopes
BT2 radioisotopes
BT3 isotopes
BT1 francium isotopes
BT1 heavy nuclei
BT2 nuclei
BT1 microsec living radioisotopes
BT2 radioisotopes
BT3 isotopes
BT1 odd-even nuclei
BT2 nuclei

FRANCIUM 218 [4; 4]
BT1 alpha decay radioisotopes
BT2 radioisotopes
BT3 isotopes
BT1 francium isotopes
BT1 heavy nuclei
BT2 nuclei
BT1 microsec living radioisotopes
BT2 radioisotopes
BT3 isotopes
BT1 odd-odd nuclei
BT2 nuclei

FRANCIUM 219 [2; 2]
BT1 alpha decay radioisotopes
BT2 radioisotopes
BT3 isotopes
BT1 francium isotopes
BT1 heavy nuclei
BT2 nuclei
BT1 millisec living radioisotopes
BT2 radioisotopes
BT3 isotopes
BT1 odd-even nuclei
BT2 nuclei

FRANCIUM 220 [7; 7]
BT1 alpha decay radioisotopes
BT2 radioisotopes
BT3 isotopes
BT1 beta-minus decay radioisotopes
BT2 beta decay radioisotopes
BT3 radioisotopes
BT4 isotopes
BT1 francium isotopes
BT1 heavy nuclei
BT2 nuclei
BT1 odd-odd nuclei
BT2 nuclei
BT1 seconds living radioisotopes
BT2 radioisotopes
BT3 isotopes

FRANCIUM 221 [42; 42]
BT1 alpha decay radioisotopes
BT2 radioisotopes
BT3 isotopes
BT1 francium isotopes
BT1 heavy nuclei
BT2 nuclei
BT1 minutes living radioisotopes
BT2 radioisotopes
BT3 isotopes
BT1 odd-even nuclei
BT2 nuclei

FRANCIUM 222 [10; 10]
BT1 alpha decay radioisotopes
BT2 radioisotopes
BT3 isotopes
BT1 beta-minus decay radioisotopes
BT2 beta decay radioisotopes
BT3 radioisotopes
BT4 isotopes
BT1 francium isotopes
BT1 heavy nuclei
BT2 nuclei
BT1 minutes living radioisotopes
BT2 radioisotopes
BT3 isotopes
BT1 odd-odd nuclei
BT2 nuclei

FRANCIUM 223 [13; 13]
UF *actinium k*
BT1 alpha decay radioisotopes
BT2 radioisotopes
BT3 isotopes
BT1 beta-minus decay radioisotopes
BT2 beta decay radioisotopes
BT3 radioisotopes
BT4 isotopes
BT1 francium isotopes
BT1 heavy nuclei
BT2 nuclei
BT1 minutes living radioisotopes
BT2 radioisotopes
BT3 isotopes
BT1 odd-even nuclei
BT2 nuclei

FRANCIUM 224 [10; 10]
BT1 beta-minus decay radioisotopes
BT2 beta decay radioisotopes
BT3 radioisotopes
BT4 isotopes
BT1 francium isotopes
BT1 heavy nuclei
BT2 nuclei
BT1 minutes living radioisotopes
BT2 radioisotopes
BT3 isotopes
BT1 odd-odd nuclei
BT2 nuclei

FRANCIUM 225 [9; 9]
BT1 beta-minus decay radioisotopes
BT2 beta decay radioisotopes
BT3 radioisotopes
BT4 isotopes
BT1 francium isotopes
BT1 heavy nuclei
BT2 nuclei
BT1 minutes living radioisotopes
BT2 radioisotopes
BT3 isotopes
BT1 odd-even nuclei
BT2 nuclei

FRANCIUM 226 [7; 7] *Jul 76*
BT1 beta-minus decay radioisotopes
BT2 beta decay radioisotopes
BT3 radioisotopes
BT4 isotopes
BT1 francium isotopes
BT1 heavy nuclei
BT2 nuclei
BT1 odd-odd nuclei
BT2 nuclei
BT1 seconds living radioisotopes
BT2 radioisotopes
BT3 isotopes

FRANCIUM 227 [10; 10] *Jul 76*
BT1 beta-minus decay radioisotopes
BT2 beta decay radioisotopes
BT3 radioisotopes
BT4 isotopes
BT1 francium isotopes
BT1 heavy nuclei
BT2 nuclei
BT1 minutes living radioisotopes
BT2 radioisotopes
BT3 isotopes
BT1 odd-even nuclei
BT2 nuclei

FRANCIUM 228 [8; 8] *Jul 76*
BT1 beta-minus decay radioisotopes
BT2 beta decay radioisotopes
BT3 radioisotopes
BT4 isotopes
BT1 francium isotopes
BT1 heavy nuclei
BT2 nuclei
BT1 odd-odd nuclei
BT2 nuclei
BT1 seconds living radioisotopes
BT2 radioisotopes
BT3 isotopes

FRANCIUM 229 [2; 2] *Jan 79*
BT1 beta-minus decay radioisotopes
BT2 beta decay radioisotopes
BT3 radioisotopes
BT4 isotopes
BT1 francium isotopes
BT1 heavy nuclei
BT2 nuclei
BT1 odd-even nuclei
BT2 nuclei
BT1 seconds living radioisotopes
BT2 radioisotopes
BT3 isotopes

FRANCIUM 230 [5; 5] *May 79*
BT1 beta-minus decay radioisotopes
BT2 beta decay radioisotopes
BT3 radioisotopes
BT4 isotopes
BT1 francium isotopes
BT1 heavy nuclei
BT2 nuclei
BT1 odd-odd nuclei
BT2 nuclei
BT1 seconds living radioisotopes
BT2 radioisotopes
BT3 isotopes

FRANCIUM 231 [2; 2] *May 85*
BT1 beta-minus decay radioisotopes
BT2 beta decay radioisotopes
BT3 radioisotopes
BT4 isotopes
BT1 francium isotopes
BT1 heavy nuclei
BT2 nuclei
BT1 odd-even nuclei
BT2 nuclei
BT1 seconds living radioisotopes
BT2 radioisotopes
BT3 isotopes

FRANCIUM 232 [2; 2] *Dec 90*
  BT1   francium isotopes
  BT1   heavy nuclei
    BT2   nuclei
  BT1   odd-odd nuclei
    BT2   nuclei
  BT1   seconds living radioisotopes
    BT2   radioisotopes
      BT3   isotopes

FRANCK-CONDON PRINCIPLE
[349; 349]
  RT   energy-level transitions

franckenstein
  USE   scanning measuring projectors

franco-german high flux reacto
  USE   grenoble reactor

frank dislocations
  USE   screw dislocations

frank loops
  USE   screw dislocations

frankfurt research reactor
  USE   frf reactor

frankfurt research reactor-2
  USE   frf-2 reactor

FRASCATI LINAC [21; 21]
  BT1   linear accelerators
    BT2   accelerators

FRASCATI SYNCHROTRON [17; 17]
  BT1   synchrotrons
    BT2   cyclic accelerators
      BT3   accelerators

frascati tokamak
  USE   ft tokamak

FRAUNHOFER LINES [179; 179]
  UF   *fraunhofer spectrum*
  RT   spectra

fraunhofer spectrum
  USE   fraunhofer lines

frc
  USE   federal radiation council

FRCTF REACTOR [6; 6]
  UF   *fast reactor core test facilit*
  UF   *lampre-2 reactor*
  BT1   test reactors
    BT2   research and test reactors
      BT3   reactors
    BT2   test facilities

FREDHOLM EQUATION [356; 356]
  BT1   integral equations
    BT2   equations

free convection
  USE   natural convection

FREE ELECTRON LASERS
[1,314; 1,314] *Apr 81*
  UF   *free-electron lasers*
  BT1   lasers
    BT2   amplifiers
      BT3   equipment

FREE ENERGY [2,522; 2,977]
  UF   *free energy (helmholtz)*
  UF   *helmholtz free energy*
  BT1   energy
  BT1   thermodynamic properties
    BT2   physical properties
  NT1   formation free energy
  RT   affinity

free energy (gibbs)
  USE   free enthalpy

free energy (helmholtz)
  USE   free energy

FREE ENTHALPY [881; 1,326]
  UF   *free energy (gibbs)*
  UF   *gibbs free energy*
  BT1   energy
  BT1   thermodynamic properties
    BT2   physical properties
  NT1   formation free enthalpy
  NT1   oxygen potential

free radicals
  USE   radicals

free-electron lasers
  USE   free electron lasers

freeze-drying
  USE   lyophilization

FREEZING [665; 665]
  RT   lyophilization
  RT   melting
  RT   phase transformations
  RT   solidification

freezing (food)
  USE   food processing

FREEZING OUT [66; 66]
  BT1   separation processes
  RT   desalination
  RT   low temperature
  RT   waste processing

freezing point depression
  USE   cryoscopy

freezing points
  USE   melting points

FRENCH GUIANA [3; 3]
  BT1   south america
    BT2   latin america

french minerve reactor
  USE   minerve reactor

FRENCH ORGANIZATIONS
[225; 1,255]
  BT1   national organizations
  NT1   cea
    NT2   cea bruyeres-le-chatel
    NT2   cea cadarache
    NT2   cea fontenay-aux-roses
    NT2   cea grenoble
    NT2   cea la hague
    NT2   cea marcoule
    NT2   cea pierrelatte
    NT2   cea saclay
  NT1   cogema
    NT2   cogema la hague
    NT2   cogema marcoule
    NT2   cogema pierrelatte

FRENKEL DEFECTS [904; 904]
  BT1   vacancies
    BT2   point defects
      BT3   crystal defects
        BT4   crystal structure

FREONS [821; 821]
  BT1   organic halogen compounds
    BT2   organic compounds
  RT   cryogenics
  RT   hydrocarbons
  RT   refrigerants

frequency (cyclotron)
  USE   cyclotron frequency

frequency (eigen)
  USE   eigenfrequency

frequency (gyro)
  USE   gyrofrequency

frequency (langmuir)
  USE   langmuir frequency

FREQUENCY ANALYSIS [632; 632]
May 79
  RT   data processing
  RT   digital filters
  RT   fourier analysis
  RT   frequency measurement

FREQUENCY CONTROL [273; 273]
Feb 76
  BT1   control
  RT   frequency dependence
  RT   frequency measurement
  RT   frequency modulation
  RT   tuning

FREQUENCY CONVERTERS [204; 204]
  RT   frequency range
  RT   heterodyne receivers
  RT   parametric amplifiers
  RT   pulse generators

FREQUENCY DEPENDENCE
[5,150; 5,150]
  UF   *wavelength dependence*
  RT   frequency control
  RT   frequency measurement
  RT   frequency range

FREQUENCY MEASUREMENT
[491; 491]
  RT   frequency analysis
  RT   frequency control
  RT   frequency dependence
  RT   measuring methods

FREQUENCY MIXING [110; 110]
Sep 86
  RT   electromagnetic radiation
  RT   frequency modulation
  RT   harmonic generation
  RT   nonlinear optics
  RT   nonlinear problems
  RT   plasma waves
  RT   sound waves

frequency modulated cyclotrons
  USE   synchrocyclotrons

FREQUENCY MODULATION [224; 224]
Oct 85
  BT1   modulation
  RT   frequency control
  RT   frequency mixing

FREQUENCY RANGE [1,509; 10,179]
NT1 ghz range
NT2 ghz range 01-100
NT2 ghz range 100-1000
NT1 hz range
NT1 khz range
NT2 khz range 01-100
NT2 khz range 100-1000
NT1 mhz range
NT2 mhz range 01-100
NT2 mhz range 100-1000
NT1 milli hz range
RT frequency converters
RT frequency dependence
RT radar
RT wavelengths

FREQUENCY RESPONSE TESTING [185; 185] *Jul 76*
BT1 testing
RT reactor stability

frequency selection
USE tuning

FRESH WATER [699; 699]
BT1 water
BT2 hydrogen compounds
BT2 oxygen compounds
RT drinking water
RT estuaries
RT irrigation
RT lakes
RT limnology
RT rivers
RT water reservoirs

fresh water ecosystems
USE aquatic ecosystems

FRESNEL COEFFICIENT [57; 57]
(One minus the reciprocal of the square of the refractive index.)
RT refraction
RT refractive index
RT visible radiation

FRESNEL LENS [51; 51] *Jun 76*
(A lens with a surface consisting of a concentric series of simple lens sections.)
BT1 lenses

FRETTING CORROSION [161; 161]
BT1 corrosion
BT2 chemical reactions

FREUNDS ADJUVANT [14; 14]
RT antigens

FRF REACTOR [4; 4]
(Johann Wolfgang Goethe-Univ., Frankfurt am Main, Essen, Federal Republic of Germany)
UF *forschungsreaktor frankfurt*
UF *frankfurt research reactor*
BT1 aqueous homogeneous reactors
BT2 liquid homogeneous reactors
BT3 fluid fueled reactors
BT4 reactors
BT3 homogeneous reactors
BT4 reactors
BT2 water cooled reactors
BT3 reactors
BT2 water moderated reactors
BT3 reactors
BT1 enriched uranium reactors
BT2 reactors
BT1 isotope production reactors
BT2 irradiation reactors
BT3 reactors
BT1 research reactors
BT2 research and test reactors
BT3 reactors
BT1 training reactors
BT2 research and test reactors
BT3 reactors

FRF-2 REACTOR [9; 9]
UF *forschungsreaktor-2 frankfurt*
UF *frankfurt research reactor-2*
BT1 triga type reactors
BT2 enriched uranium reactors
BT3 reactors
BT2 hydride moderated reactors
BT3 reactors
BT2 research and test reactors
BT3 reactors
BT2 solid homogeneous reactors
BT3 homogeneous reactors
BT4 reactors
BT2 water cooled reactors
BT3 reactors
BT2 water moderated reactors
BT3 reactors

FRG-1 REACTOR [58; 58]
(Gesellschaft fuer Kernenergieverwertung in Schiffbau und Schiffarht mbH, Geesthacht, Schleswig-Holstein, Federal Republic of Germany)
UF *forschungsreaktor geesthacht-1*
UF *geesthacht-1 research reactor*
BT1 enriched uranium reactors
BT2 reactors
BT1 pool type reactors
BT2 water cooled reactors
BT3 reactors
BT2 water moderated reactors
BT3 reactors
BT1 research reactors
BT2 research and test reactors
BT3 reactors
BT1 test reactors
BT2 research and test reactors
BT3 reactors
BT2 test facilities
BT1 thermal reactors
BT2 reactors
BT1 training reactors
BT2 research and test reactors
BT3 reactors

FRG-2 REACTOR [72; 72]
(Gesellschaft fuer Kernenergieverwertung in Schiffbau and Schiffahrt mbH, Geesthacht, Schleswig-Holstein, Federal Republic of Germany)
UF *forschungsreaktor geesthacht-2*
UF *geesthacht-2 research reactor*
BT1 enriched uranium reactors
BT2 reactors
BT1 isotope production reactors
BT2 irradiation reactors
BT3 reactors
BT1 materials testing reactors
BT2 irradiation reactors
BT3 reactors
BT1 pool type reactors
BT2 water cooled reactors
BT3 reactors
BT2 water moderated reactors
BT3 reactors
BT1 research reactors
BT2 research and test reactors
BT3 reactors

→ *frh reactor*
USE triga-1-hanover reactor

fricke dosemeters
USE chemical dosemeters

FRICTION [1,871; 3,293]
NT1 internal friction
NT1 rolling friction
NT1 sliding friction
RT friction factor
RT wear

FRICTION FACTOR [249; 249] *Mar 83*
(Dimensionless number used in study of fluid friction in conduits; not for coefficient of friction.)
RT fluid flow
RT fluid mechanics
RT friction
RT hydraulics
RT reynolds number

FRICTION WELDING [60; 60]
BT1 welding
BT2 joining
BT3 fabrication

frictionless flow
USE ideal flow

FRIEDEL-CRAFTS REACTION [14; 14]
BT1 chemical reactions

FRJ-1 REACTOR [30; 30]
(Kernforschungsanlage Juelich GmbH, Juelich, Nordrhein-Westfalen, Federal Republic of Germany)
UF *juelich-merlin reactor*
UF *merlin-juelich reactor*
BT1 enriched uranium reactors
BT2 reactors
BT1 pool type reactors
BT2 water cooled reactors
BT3 reactors
BT2 water moderated reactors
BT3 reactors
BT1 research reactors
BT2 research and test reactors
BT3 reactors

FRJ-2 REACTOR [95; 95]
(Kernforschungsanlage Juelich GmbH, Juelich, Nordrhein-Westfalen, Federal Republic of Germany)
UF *dido-juelich reactor*
UF *juelich-dido reactor*
BT1 enriched uranium reactors
BT2 reactors
BT1 heavy water cooled reactors
BT2 reactors
BT1 heavy water moderated reactors
BT2 reactors
BT1 isotope production reactors
BT2 irradiation reactors
BT3 reactors
BT1 materials testing reactors
BT2 irradiation reactors
BT3 reactors
BT1 research reactors
BT2 research and test reactors
BT3 reactors
BT1 tank type reactors
BT2 reactors

FRM REACTOR [42; 42]
(Technische Universitaet Muenchen, Ministry for Education and Culture, Garching, Bayern, Federal Republic of Germany)
UF *forschungsreaktor muenchen*
UF *munich research reactor*
BT1 enriched uranium reactors
BT2 reactors
BT1 pool type reactors
BT2 water cooled reactors
BT3 reactors
BT2 water moderated reactors
BT3 reactors
BT1 research reactors
BT2 research and test reactors
BT3 reactors

frm reactors (thermonuclear)
(Field-reversed mirror reactors.)
USE reversed-field mirrors

FRN REACTOR [30; 30]
(Gesellschaft fuer Strahlen und Umweltforschung mbH, Neuherberg, Bayern, Federal Republic of Germany)
UF   *forschungsreaktor neuherberg*
UF   *neuherberg research reactor*
BT1   pool type reactors
  BT2   water cooled reactors
    BT3   reactors
  BT2   water moderated reactors
    BT3   reactors
BT1   research reactors
  BT2   research and test reactors
    BT3   reactors
BT1   test reactors
  BT2   research and test reactors
    BT3   reactors
  BT2   test facilities
BT1   triga type reactors
  BT2   enriched uranium reactors
    BT3   reactors
  BT2   hydride moderated reactors
    BT3   reactors
  BT2   research and test reactors
    BT3   reactors
  BT2   solid homogeneous reactors
    BT3   homogeneous reactors
      BT4   reactors
  BT2   water cooled reactors
    BT3   reactors
  BT2   water moderated reactors
    BT3   reactors

FROGS [358; 358]
UF   *rana*
UF   *toads*
BT1   amphibians
  BT2   aquatic organisms
  BT2   vertebrates
    BT3   animals

frost
USE   ice

FROST TESTS [4; 4]
BT1   thermal testing
  BT2   nondestructive testing
    BT3   materials testing
      BT4   testing

FROUDE NUMBER [100; 100]
RT   fluid flow

FRUCTOSE [129; 129]
UF   *levulose*
BT1   hexoses
  BT2   monosaccharides
    BT3   saccharides
      BT4   carbohydrates
        BT5   organic compounds
BT1   ketones
  BT2   organic compounds

fruit (seeds)
USE   seeds

FRUIT FLIES [106; 906]
BT1   flies
  BT2   insects
    BT3   arthropods
      BT4   invertebrates
        BT5   animals
NT1   ceratitis capitata
NT1   dacus
  NT2   dacus oleae
NT1   drosophila
NT1   rhagoletis cerasi

FRUIT TREES [135; 135]
BT1   trees
  BT2   plants
RT   apples
RT   cherries
RT   citrus
RT   fruits

FRUITS [464; 1,291]
(Edible parts of plants only.)
BT1   food
NT1   apples
NT1   avocados
NT1   bananas
NT1   berries
NT1   cherries
NT1   coconuts
NT1   dates
NT1   figs
NT1   grapefruits
NT1   grapes
NT1   lemons
NT1   mangoes
NT1   nuts
  NT2   chestnuts
  NT2   peanuts
NT1   olives
NT1   oranges
NT1   papayas
NT1   peaches
NT1   pears
NT1   plums
NT1   raspberries
NT1   strawberries
RT   crops
RT   fruit trees

fsa
(Fixed scatterer approximation.)
USE   fsc approximation

FSC APPROXIMATION [28; 28]
(Fixed Scattering Centres approximation.)
UF   *approximation (fix scatt. cen)*
UF   *fixed scatt. cent. approx.*
UF   *fsa*
RT   glauber theory
RT   many-body problem
RT   optical models
RT   scattering

fsd devices
USE   flying spot digitizers

FSH [390; 390]
UF   *follicle stimulating hormone*
BT1   gonadotropins
  BT2   pituitary hormones
    BT3   peptide hormones
      BT4   hormones
RT   estrogens

FT TOKAMAK [195; 195] *Oct 83*
UF   *frascati tokamak*
BT1   tokamak devices
  BT2   closed plasma devices
  BT3   thermonuclear devices

FT VALUE [1,425; 1,425]
RT   beta decay
RT   branching ratio
RT   decay
RT   decoupling
RT   half-life

ft. calhoun-1 reactor
USE   calhoun-1 reactor

ft. calhoun-2 reactor
USE   calhoun-2 reactor

fucose
USE   hexoses

FUCUS [76; 76]
BT1   algae
  BT2   plants
BT1   seaweeds

FUDR [85; 85]
UF   *fluorodeoxyuridine*
BT1   antibiotics
  BT2   drugs
  BT2   organic compounds
BT1   fluorouracils
  BT2   antimetabolites
    BT3   drugs
  BT2   organic fluorine compounds
    BT3   organic halogen compounds
      BT4   organic compounds
  BT2   uracils
    BT3   hydroxy compounds
      BT4   organic compounds
    BT3   pyrimidines
      BT4   azines
        BT5   heterocyclic compounds
          BT6   organic compounds
        BT5   organic nitrogen compounds
          BT6   organic compounds
BT1   nucleosides
  BT2   nucleotides
    BT3   organic compounds
  BT2   ribosides
BT1   radiosensitizers
  BT2   drugs
  BT2   response modifying factors
RT   deoxyuridine

FUEL ASSEMBLIES [7,060; 10,213]
NT1   fuel element clusters
RT   fuel assembly dismantling
RT   fuel elements
RT   guide tubes
RT   reactor cores
RT   shrouds

FUEL ASSEMBLY DISMANTLING [267; 267]
UF   *dismantling (fuel assembly)*
RT   fuel assemblies
RT   reactor dismantling

fuel bundles
USE   fuel element clusters

FUEL CANS [6,663; 6,663]
UF   *fuel sheaths*
UF   *sheaths (fuel)*
RT   canning
RT   cladding
RT   decladding
RT   failed element detection
RT   failed element monitors
RT   fuel elements
RT   fuel-cladding interactions
RT   hot spots
RT   jackets

fuel casks
USE   casks

FUEL CELLS [393; 393]
UF   *hydrogen fuel cells*
BT1   direct energy converters
RT   electrochemistry

FUEL CHANNELS [1,081; 1,081]
BT1   reactor channels
  BT2   reactor components
RT   fuel elements
RT   hot channel
RT   shrouds

fuel cooling installations
USE   spent fuel storage

FUEL COOLING TIME [97; 97] *Jul 80*
(The cooling time of spent fuel after its discharge from the reactor core.)
UF   *cooling time*
RT   after-heat
RT   burnup

FUEL COOLING TIME

- RT cooling
- RT fission products
- RT fuel storage pools
- RT gamma spectroscopy
- RT spent fuel storage
- RT spent fuels

FUEL CYCLE [7,679; 8,782]
- UF *recycle (fuel)*
- NT1 plutonium recycle
- NT1 thorium cycle
- NT1 uranium recycle
- RT cost
- RT depleted uranium
- RT fissionable materials
- RT fuel cycle centers
- RT fuel management
- RT nuclear fuels
- RT nuclear materials management
- RT present worth method
- RT proliferation
- RT reprocessing
- RT sol-gel process
- RT westinghouse recycle fuels pla

FUEL CYCLE CENTERS [263; 263]
Jul 78
- UF *nuclear fuel centers*
- BT1 nuclear facilities
- RT feed materials plants
- RT fuel cycle
- RT fuel fabrication plants
- RT fuel reprocessing plants
- RT fuel storage pools
- RT plutonium recycle
- RT radioactive waste disposal
- RT radioactive waste facilities
- RT radioactive waste processing
- RT radioactive waste storage
- RT spent fuel storage
- RT uranium recycle

FUEL DENSIFICATION [356; 356]
(The increase in density of nuclear fuel resulting from thermal and/or radiation effects.)
- RT density
- RT fuel elements
- RT nuclear fuels
- RT physical radiation effects
- RT reactor safety

FUEL DISPERSION REACTORS [2; 124]
- BT1 homogeneous reactors
- BT2 reactors
- NT1 fluidized bed reactors
- NT1 slurry reactors
- RT dispersion nuclear fuels

FUEL ELEMENT CLUSTERS [3,279; 3,279]
- UF *bundles (fuel elements)*
- UF *clusters (fuel elements)*
- UF *fuel bundles*
- UF *rod bundles*
- BT1 fuel assemblies
- RT spacers

FUEL ELEMENT FAILURE [2,418; 2,418]
- BT1 reactor accidents
- BT2 accidents
- RT failed element detection
- RT failed element monitors
- RT fuel motion detection
- RT radiation hazards
- RT reactor operation
- RT reactor safety

FUEL ELEMENTS [8,608; 21,451]
- UF *nuclear fuel elements*
- UF *reactor fuel elements*
- BT1 reactor components
- NT1 annular fuel elements
- NT1 fuel pins
- NT1 fuel plates
- NT1 fuel rods
- NT2 hollow fuel rods
- NT1 fuel wires
- NT1 spent fuel elements
- NT1 thermionic fuel elements
- RT burnout
- RT decladding
- RT failed element detection
- RT failed element monitors
- RT fuel assemblies
- RT fuel cans
- RT fuel channels
- RT fuel densification
- RT fuel fabrication plants
- RT fuel integrity
- RT fuel storage pools
- RT matrix materials
- RT nuclear fuels
- RT positioning
- RT post-irradiation examination
- RT reactor cores
- RT reactor lattices
- RT reactors

FUEL FABRICATION PLANTS [1,484; 1,738]
- BT1 nuclear facilities
- NT1 cimarron plutonium plant
- NT1 cimarron uranium plant
- NT1 exxon fuel fabrication facilit
- NT1 general atomic fuel fabricatio
- NT1 mixed oxide fuel plant
- NT1 westinghouse recycle fuels pla
- RT fabrication
- RT fuel cycle centers
- RT fuel elements
- RT industrial plants
- RT nuclear industry
- RT nuclear parks

FUEL FEEDING SYSTEMS [174; 174]
Mar 83
- RT fossil fuels
- RT fuel gas
- RT materials handling
- RT pellet injection
- RT thermonuclear fuels
- RT thermonuclear reactor fueling

FUEL GAS [110; 1,301]
- BT1 energy sources
- BT1 fuels
- BT1 gases
- BT2 fluids
- NT1 coal gas
- NT1 natural gas
- RT fuel feeding systems
- RT public utilities

FUEL INTEGRITY [181; 181] *Mar 86*
- UF *integrity (fuel)*
- RT fuel elements
- RT nuclear fuels

fuel kernels
  USE fuel pellets

fuel loading (fission reactor)
  USE reactor fueling

FUEL MANAGEMENT [1,979; 1,979]
- UF *in-core fuel management*
- BT1 nuclear materials management
- BT2 management
- RT fuel cycle
- RT reactor cores
- RT reactor fueling

FUEL MOTION DETECTION [170; 170]
Sep 79
(Determination of in-core nuclear fuel behavior.)
- BT1 detection
- RT failed element detection
- RT fuel element failure

FUEL PARTICLES [450; 2,211]
- UF *particles (fuel)*
- NT1 coated fuel particles
- RT dispersion nuclear fuels
- RT nuclear fuels

FUEL PELLETS [4,429; 4,429]
- UF *fuel kernels*
- UF *kernels (fuel)*
- UF *pellets (fuel)*
- RT fuel rods
- RT nuclear fuels
- RT pellet injection
- RT pelletizing

fuel pencils
  USE fuel pins

FUEL PINS [3,958; 3,958]
- UF *fuel pencils*
- UF *pins (fuel)*
- BT1 fuel elements
- BT2 reactor components

FUEL PLATES [500; 500]
- UF *plates (fuel)*
- BT1 fuel elements
- BT2 reactor components

fuel pools
  USE fuel storage pools

FUEL RACKS [381; 381] *Apr 80*
- UF *racks (fuel)*
- BT1 supports
- BT2 mechanical structures
- RT fuel storage pools
- RT spent fuel storage

fuel reprocessing
  USE reprocessing

FUEL REPROCESSING PLANTS [4,734; 6,564]
- BT1 nuclear facilities
- NT1 barnwell fuel processing plant
- NT1 cea la hague
- NT1 cogema la hague
- NT1 hef
- NT1 idaho chemical processing plan
- NT1 midwest fuel recovery plant
- NT1 nuclear fuel recovery and recy
- NT1 sellafield reprocessing plant
- NT1 wackersdorf reprocessing plant
- NT1 wak
- NT1 west valley processing plant
- NT1 westinghouse recycle fuels pla
- RT fission products
- RT fuel cycle centers
- RT industry
- RT nuclear industry
- RT nuclear parks
- RT radioactive waste facilities
- RT reprocessing
- RT spent fuels

FUEL RODS [5,905; 5,995]
- UF *fuel slugs*
- UF *rods (fuel)*
- UF *slugs (fuel)*
- BT1 fuel elements
- BT2 reactor components
- NT1 hollow fuel rods
- RT fuel pellets

FUEL SCANNING [134; 559]
- UF *scanning (fuel)*
- NT1 gamma fuel scanning
- RT burnup
- RT nondestructive testing

fuel sheaths
   USE   fuel cans

fuel slugs
   USE   fuel rods

FUEL SLURRIES [34; 34]
- UF   *fuel suspensions*
- UF   *slurries (fuel)*
- UF   *suspensions (fuel)*
- BT1   nuclear fuels
- BT2   energy sources
- BT2   fuels
- BT2   reactor materials
- BT3   materials
- RT   slurry reactors

FUEL SOLUTIONS [93; 93]
- BT1   liquid fuels
- BT2   fuels
- RT   liquid homogeneous reactors

FUEL STORAGE POOLS [1,154; 1,154]
Feb 76
- UF   *fuel pools*
- UF   *pools (fuel storage)*
- UF   *storage pools (fuel)*
- RT   away-from-reactor storage
- RT   fuel cooling time
- RT   fuel cycle centers
- RT   fuel elements
- RT   fuel racks
- RT   spent fuel storage

fuel suspensions
   USE   fuel slurries

FUEL WASHERS [17; 17]
- UF   *washers (fuel)*
- RT   annular fuel elements
- RT   nuclear fuels

FUEL WIRES [20; 20]
- UF   *wires (fuel)*
- BT1   fuel elements
- BT2   reactor components

FUEL-CLADDING INTERACTIONS [2,224; 2,224]
- UF   *cladding-fuel interactions*
- RT   chemical reactions
- RT   fuel cans
- RT   nuclear fuels

FUEL-COOLANT INTERACTIONS [1,086; 1,086]
- UF   *coolant-fuel interactions*
- RT   chemical reactions
- RT   coolants
- RT   fluid-structure interactions
- RT   molten metal-water reactions
- RT   nuclear fuels
- RT   reactor accidents

fueling machines (fiss react)
   USE   reactor charging machines

FUELS [635; 26,128]
- NT1   automotive fuels
- NT1   fossil fuels
- NT2   coal
- NT3   black coal
- NT4   anthracite
- NT4   bituminous coal
- NT3   lignite
- NT2   gasoline
- NT2   kerosene
- NT2   natural gas
- NT2   peat
- NT2   petroleum
- NT3   shale oil
- NT1   fuel gas
- NT2   coal gas
- NT2   natural gas
- NT1   liquid fuels
- NT2   diesel fuels
- NT2   fuel solutions
- NT2   gasoline
- NT2   liquid metal fuels
- NT2   molten salt fuels
- NT1   nuclear fuels
- NT2   denatured fuel
- NT2   fuel slurries
- NT2   gas fuels
- NT2   solid fuels
- NT3   alloy nuclear fuels
- NT3   dispersion nuclear fuels
- NT3   mixed carbide fuels
- NT3   mixed nitride fuels
- NT3   mixed oxide fuels
- NT2   spent fuels
- NT1   synthetic fuels
- NT1   thermonuclear fuels
- RT   coke
- RT   energy consumption
- RT   wood

fugen atr
   USE   jatr reactor

FUKUSHIMA-II-1 REACTOR [25; 25]
Sep 79
(Naraha, Fukushima, Japan)
- BT1   bwr type reactors
- BT2   enriched uranium reactors
- BT3   reactors
- BT2   power reactors
- BT3   reactors
- BT2   thermal reactors
- BT3   reactors
- BT2   water cooled reactors
- BT3   reactors
- BT2   water moderated reactors
- BT3   reactors

FUKUSHIMA-II-2 REACTOR [44; 44]
Sep 79
(Naraha, Fukushima, Japan)
- BT1   bwr type reactors
- BT2   enriched uranium reactors
- BT3   reactors
- BT2   power reactors
- BT3   reactors
- BT2   thermal reactors
- BT3   reactors
- BT2   water cooled reactors
- BT3   reactors
- BT2   water moderated reactors
- BT3   reactors

FUKUSHIMA-II-3 REACTOR [27; 27]
Jul 81
- BT1   bwr type reactors
- BT2   enriched uranium reactors
- BT3   reactors
- BT2   power reactors
- BT3   reactors
- BT2   thermal reactors
- BT3   reactors
- BT2   water cooled reactors
- BT3   reactors
- BT2   water moderated reactors
- BT3   reactors

FUKUSHIMA-II-4 REACTOR [17; 17]
Jul 81
- BT1   bwr type reactors
- BT2   enriched uranium reactors
- BT3   reactors
- BT2   power reactors
- BT3   reactors
- BT2   thermal reactors
- BT3   reactors
- BT2   water cooled reactors
- BT3   reactors
- BT2   water moderated reactors
- BT3   reactors

FUKUSHIMA-1 REACTOR [50; 50]
(Okuma, Fukushima, Japan)
- UF   *tokyo-1 reactor*
- BT1   bwr type reactors
- BT2   enriched uranium reactors
- BT3   reactors
- BT2   power reactors
- BT3   reactors
- BT2   thermal reactors
- BT3   reactors
- BT2   water cooled reactors
- BT3   reactors
- BT2   water moderated reactors
- BT3   reactors

FUKUSHIMA-2 REACTOR [28; 28]
(Okuma, Fukushima, Japan)
- UF   *tokyo-2 reactor*
- BT1   bwr type reactors
- BT2   enriched uranium reactors
- BT3   reactors
- BT2   power reactors
- BT3   reactors
- BT2   thermal reactors
- BT3   reactors
- BT2   water cooled reactors
- BT3   reactors
- BT2   water moderated reactors
- BT3   reactors

FUKUSHIMA-3 REACTOR [28; 28]
(Okuma, Fukushima, Japan)
- UF   *tokyo-3 reactor*
- BT1   bwr type reactors
- BT2   enriched uranium reactors
- BT3   reactors
- BT2   power reactors
- BT3   reactors
- BT2   thermal reactors
- BT3   reactors
- BT2   water cooled reactors
- BT3   reactors
- BT2   water moderated reactors
- BT3   reactors

FUKUSHIMA-4 REACTOR [20; 20]
(Okuma, Fukushima, Japan)
- UF   *tokyo-4 reactor*
- BT1   bwr type reactors
- BT2   enriched uranium reactors
- BT3   reactors
- BT2   power reactors
- BT3   reactors
- BT2   thermal reactors
- BT3   reactors
- BT2   water cooled reactors
- BT3   reactors
- BT2   water moderated reactors
- BT3   reactors

FUKUSHIMA-5 REACTOR [22; 22]
(Futaba, Fukushima, Japan)
- BT1   bwr type reactors
- BT2   enriched uranium reactors
- BT3   reactors
- BT2   power reactors
- BT3   reactors
- BT2   thermal reactors
- BT3   reactors
- BT2   water cooled reactors
- BT3   reactors
- BT2   water moderated reactors
- BT3   reactors

FUKUSHIMA-6 REACTOR [28; 28]
(Futaba, Fukushima, Japan)
- BT1   bwr type reactors
- BT2   enriched uranium reactors
- BT3   reactors
- BT2   power reactors
- BT3   reactors
- BT2   thermal reactors
- BT3   reactors
- BT2   water cooled reactors
- BT3   reactors
- BT2   water moderated reactors
- BT3   reactors

FULLERS EARTH [6; 6]
- BT1 clays
  - BT2 silicate minerals
    - BT3 minerals
- RT attapulgite

FULLY IONIZED GASES [62; 154]
(Use only when the gas is not macroscopically electrically neutral; otherwise use PLASMA.)
- BT1 ionized gases
  - BT2 gases
    - BT3 fluids
- NT1 lorentz gas

FULTON-1 REACTOR [31; 31]
- BT1 enriched uranium reactors
  - BT2 reactors
- BT1 helium cooled reactors
  - BT2 gas cooled reactors
    - BT3 reactors
- BT1 htgr type reactors
  - BT2 gas cooled reactors
    - BT3 reactors
  - BT2 graphite moderated reactors
    - BT3 reactors
- BT1 power reactors
  - BT2 reactors
- BT1 thermal reactors
  - BT2 reactors

FULTON-2 REACTOR [30; 30]
- BT1 enriched uranium reactors
  - BT2 reactors
- BT1 helium cooled reactors
  - BT2 gas cooled reactors
    - BT3 reactors
- BT1 htgr type reactors
  - BT2 gas cooled reactors
    - BT3 reactors
  - BT2 graphite moderated reactors
    - BT3 reactors
- BT1 power reactors
  - BT2 reactors
- BT1 thermal reactors
  - BT2 reactors

FULVIC ACIDS [130; 130]
- BT1 organic acids
  - BT2 organic compounds
- RT humic acids
- RT humus
- RT soils

FUMARIC ACID [47; 47]
- BT1 dicarboxylic acids
  - BT2 carboxylic acids
    - BT3 organic acids
      - BT4 organic compounds

FUME HOODS [15; 15] Sep 80
- BT1 laboratory equipment
  - BT2 equipment
- RT gaseous wastes
- RT ventilation

fumes
- USE aerosols

FUMIGANTS [53; 53]
- BT1 pesticides
- RT grain disinfestation
- RT methyl bromide
- RT preservation

function (biological)
- USE biological functions

FUNCTION GENERATORS [90; 2,206]
- UF *sine generators*
- UF *square-wave generators*
- BT1 electronic equipment
  - BT2 equipment
- NT1 pulse generators
  - NT2 high-voltage pulse generators
    - NT3 marx generators

FUNCTIONAL ANALYSIS [959; 959] Sep 76
- BT1 mathematics
- RT mathematical space

FUNCTIONAL MODELS [1,817; 6,784]
- UF *models (functional)*
- NT1 pilot plants
  - NT2 wipp
- NT1 simulators
  - NT2 reactor simulators
- RT analog systems
- RT biological models
- RT comparative evaluations
- RT hypothesis
- RT mathematical models
- RT mockup
- RT phantoms
- RT plasma simulation
- RT scale models
- RT simulation
- RT structural models

FUNCTIONALS [2,425; 2,425]
- RT functions
- RT variational methods

FUNCTIONS [1,454; 78,579]
- NT1 airy functions
- NT1 analytic functions
- NT1 bessel functions
- NT1 correlation functions
- NT1 delta function
- NT1 eigenfunctions
- NT1 floquet function
- NT1 gamma function
- NT1 gauss function
- NT1 green function
- NT1 hamiltonian function
- NT1 hypergeometric functions
- NT1 jacobian function
- NT1 jost function
- NT1 lagrangian function
- NT1 partition functions
- NT1 placzec function
- NT1 polynomials
  - NT2 hermite polynomials
  - NT2 laguerre polynomials
  - NT2 legendre polynomials
- NT1 response functions
- NT1 riemann function
- NT1 spectral functions
  - NT2 spectral density
- NT1 spherical harmonics
- NT1 spline functions
- NT1 strength functions
- NT1 structure functions
- NT1 transfer functions
- NT1 vertex functions
- NT1 wave functions
- NT1 weighting functions
- RT equations
- RT functionals
- RT mathematics
- RT recursion relations
- RT series expansion
- RT singularity

FUNDAMENTAL CONSTANTS [760; 760]
- UF+ *elementary length*
- UF+ *gravitational charges*
- RT atoms
- RT cosmology
- RT elementary particles
- RT natural units
- RT nuclei

fundamental particles
- USE elementary particles

FUNGAL DISEASES [113; 165] Dec 82
- BT1 infectious diseases
  - BT2 diseases
- NT1 mycoses
- RT fungi

FUNGI [656; 3,192]
- UF *molds*
- BT1 plants
- NT1 aspergillus
- NT1 claviceps
- NT1 fusarium
- NT1 lichens
- NT1 mildew
- NT1 mushrooms
- NT1 myxomycetes
- NT1 neurospora
- NT1 penicillium
- NT1 phycomyces
- NT1 physarum
- NT1 rhizopus
- NT1 ustilago
- NT1 yeasts
  - NT2 candida
  - NT2 saccharomyces
    - NT3 saccharomyces cerevisiae
  - NT2 torula
- RT bioadsorbents
- RT conidia
- RT fungal diseases
- RT mycelium
- RT mycoses
- RT parasites
- RT pathogens
- RT spores
- RT vaccines

FUNGICIDES [173; 419]
- BT1 pesticides
- NT1 cycloheximide

FURANS [490; 875]
- UF *methyltetrahydrofuran*
- UF *mthf*
- BT1 heterocyclic compounds
  - BT2 organic compounds
- BT1 organic oxygen compounds
  - BT2 organic compounds
- NT1 benzofurans
- NT1 furfural
- NT1 furildioxime
- NT1 tetrahydrofuran
- RT kinetin

FURFURAL [29; 29]
- UF *2-furalaldehyde*
- BT1 aldehydes
  - BT2 organic compounds
- BT1 furans
  - BT2 heterocyclic compounds
    - BT3 organic compounds
  - BT2 organic oxygen compounds
    - BT3 organic compounds

FURILDIOXIME [10; 10]
- BT1 furans
  - BT2 heterocyclic compounds
    - BT3 organic compounds
  - BT2 organic oxygen compounds
    - BT3 organic compounds
- BT1 oximes
  - BT2 amines
    - BT3 organic compounds
  - BT2 hydroxy compounds
    - BT3 organic compounds
  - BT2 organic nitrogen compounds
    - BT3 organic compounds
- BT1 reagents

FURNACES [732; 1,775]
- NT1 blast furnaces
- NT1 electric furnaces
  - NT2 arc furnaces
  - NT2 ceramic melters
  - NT2 induction furnaces
- NT1 electron beam furnaces
- NT1 plasma furnaces
- NT1 solar furnaces

NT1   vacuum furnaces
RT   burners
RT   crucibles
RT   incinerators
RT   melting
RT   sintering

FURSOV PILE [0; 0]
BT1   graphite moderated reactors
BT2   reactors
BT1   research reactors
BT2   research and test reactors
BT3   reactors

FUSARIUM [44; 44]
BT1   fungi
BT2   plants
BT1   parasites

fused salt fuels
USE   molten salt fuels

fused salts
USE   molten salts

fuses (electric)
USE   electric fuses

fuses (reactor safety)
USE   reactor safety fuses

fusion (bonding, nonmetallic)
USE   bonding

fusion (melting)
USE   melting

fusion (welding)
USE   welding

FUSION HEAT [326; 326]
UF   *heat of fusion*
UF   *latent heat of fusion*
BT1   transition heat
BT2   enthalpy
BT3   thermodynamic properties
BT4   physical properties

fusion reactions (endoenergeti
USE   heavy ion fusion reactions

fusion reactions (exoenergetic
USE   thermonuclear reactions

fusion reactions (heavy ion)
USE   heavy ion fusion reactions

fusion reactions (thermonuclea
USE   thermonuclear reactions

fusion reactors
USE   thermonuclear reactors

FUSION YIELD [620; 620] *Sep 75*
UF   *yield (fusion)*
BT1   nuclear reaction yield
RT   laser implosions
RT   thermonuclear fuels
RT   thermonuclear reactions
RT   thermonuclear reactors

fusion-reactor materials
USE   thermonuclear reactor material

→ **FUZZY LOGIC** [2; 2] *Jul 91*
BT1   mathematical logic
RT   mathematical models
RT   probability
RT   set theory

fwpca
(Federal Water Pollution Control Act.)
USE   us water pollution control act

F0-1240 MESONS [6; 6] *Dec 87*
BT1   scalar mesons
BT2   mesons
BT3   bosons
BT3   hadrons
BT4   elementary particles

F0-1300 MESONS [9; 9] *Dec 87*
BT1   scalar mesons
BT2   mesons
BT3   bosons
BT3   hadrons
BT4   elementary particles

F0-1590 MESONS [15; 15] *Dec 87*
BT1   scalar mesons
BT2   mesons
BT3   bosons
BT3   hadrons
BT4   elementary particles

F0-1730 MESONS [4; 4] *Dec 87*
BT1   scalar mesons
BT2   mesons
BT3   bosons
BT3   hadrons
BT4   elementary particles

F0-975 MESONS [107; 107] *Sep 75*
(Prior to December 1987 this concept was indexed by S-993 RESONANCES.)
UF   *s-993 resonances*
BT1   scalar mesons
BT2   mesons
BT3   bosons
BT3   hadrons
BT4   elementary particles

F1 LAYER [23; 23]
BT1   f region
BT2   ionosphere
BT3   earth atmosphere

F1-1285 MESONS [151; 151]
(Prior to December 1987 this concept was indexed by D-1285 RESONANCES.)
UF   *d-1285 resonances*
BT1   axial vector mesons
BT2   mesons
BT3   bosons
BT3   hadrons
BT4   elementary particles

F1-1420 MESONS [172; 172]
(Prior to December 1987 this concept was indexed by E-1422 RESONANCES.)
UF   *e-1422 resonances*
BT1   axial vector mesons
BT2   mesons
BT3   bosons
BT3   hadrons
BT4   elementary particles

F1-1530 MESONS [5; 5] *Dec 87*
BT1   axial vector mesons
BT2   mesons
BT3   bosons
BT3   hadrons
BT4   elementary particles

F2 LAYER [164; 164]
BT1   f region
BT2   ionosphere
BT3   earth atmosphere

F2-1270 MESONS [472; 472]
(Prior to December 1987 this concept was indexed by F-1260 RESONANCES.)
UF   *f-1260 resonances*
BT1   tensor mesons
BT2   mesons
BT3   bosons
BT3   hadrons
BT4   elementary particles

F2-1410 MESONS [2; 2] *Dec 87*
BT1   tensor mesons
BT2   mesons
BT3   bosons
BT3   hadrons
BT4   elementary particles

F2-1525 MESONS [138; 138]
(Prior to December 1987 this concept was indexed by F-1514 RESONANCES.)
UF   *f-1514 resonances*
BT1   strangeonium
BT2   mesons
BT3   bosons
BT3   hadrons
BT4   elementary particles
BT2   quarkonium
BT1   tensor mesons
BT2   mesons
BT3   bosons
BT3   hadrons
BT4   elementary particles

F2-1720 MESONS [74; 74] *Dec 85*
(Prior to December 1987 this concept was indexed by THETA-1690 RESONANCES.)
UF   *theta-1690 resonances*
BT1   tensor mesons
BT2   mesons
BT3   bosons
BT3   hadrons
BT4   elementary particles

F2-1810 MESONS [6; 6] *Dec 87*
BT1   tensor mesons
BT2   mesons
BT3   bosons
BT3   hadrons
BT4   elementary particles

F2-2150 MESONS [0; 0] *Dec 87*
BT1   tensor mesons
BT2   mesons
BT3   bosons
BT3   hadrons
BT4   elementary particles

F2-2240 MESONS [0; 0] *Dec 87*
BT1   tensor mesons
BT2   mesons
BT3   bosons
BT3   hadrons
BT4   elementary particles

F4-2030 MESONS [38; 38] *Aug 76*
(Prior to December 1987 this concept was indexed by H-2050 RESONANCES.)
UF   *h-2050 resonances*
BT1   tensor mesons
BT2   mesons
BT3   bosons
BT3   hadrons
BT4   elementary particles

F4-2300 MESONS [21; 21]
(Prior to December 1987 this concept was indexed by U-2375 RESONANCES.)
UF   *u-2375 resonances*
BT1   tensor mesons
BT2   mesons
BT3   bosons
BT3   hadrons

BT4   elementary particles

F6-2510 MESONS [5; 5] *Jun 84*
(Prior to December 1987 this concept was indexed by R-2510 RESONANCES.)
UF   r-2510 resonances
BT1   tensor mesons
  BT2   mesons
    BT3   bosons
    BT3   hadrons
      BT4   elementary particles

G CODES [1,003; 1,003]
BT1   computer codes

g factor (gyromagnetic ratio)
USE   gyromagnetic ratio

g factor (lande)
USE   lande factor

G MATRIX [488; 488]
(Limited to the theory of nuclear reactions.)
BT1   matrices
RT   nuclear reactions

G PARITY [183; 183]
(Property peculiar to mesons, not related to the concept covered by PARITY.)
BT1   particle properties
RT   g-parity invariance

g resonances
USE   rho3-1690 mesons

G STATES [146; 146] *Sep 79*
BT1   energy levels

G VALUE [2,764; 2,764]
(Limited to use in radiation chemistry; see also GYROMAGNETIC RATIO.)
RT   radiation chemistry
RT   radiolysis

G-PARITY INVARIANCE [48; 48]
BT1   invariance principles
RT   g parity

G-1 REACTOR [2; 2]
UF   marcoule g-1 reactor
BT1   gcr type reactors
  BT2   gas cooled reactors
    BT3   reactors
  BT2   graphite moderated reactors
    BT3   reactors
BT1   plutonium production reactors
  BT2   production reactors
    BT3   reactors
BT1   thermal reactors
  BT2   reactors

G-2 REACTOR [13; 13]
UF   marcoule g-2 reactor
BT1   gcr type reactors
  BT2   gas cooled reactors
    BT3   reactors
  BT2   graphite moderated reactors
    BT3   reactors
BT1   plutonium production reactors
  BT2   production reactors
    BT3   reactors
BT1   thermal reactors
  BT2   reactors

G-3 REACTOR [9; 9]
(Marcoule, France)
UF   marcoule g-3 reactor
BT1   gcr type reactors
  BT2   gas cooled reactors
    BT3   reactors
  BT2   graphite moderated reactors

BT3   reactors
BT1   plutonium production reactors
  BT2   production reactors
    BT3   reactors
BT1   thermal reactors
  BT2   reactors

GA STANDARD REACTOR [12; 12]
Oct 75
UF   gen. atomic standard reactor
BT1   enriched uranium reactors
  BT2   reactors
BT1   htgr type reactors
  BT2   gas cooled reactors
    BT3   reactors
  BT2   graphite moderated reactors
    BT3   reactors
BT1   power reactors
  BT2   reactors
BT1   thermal reactors
  BT2   reactors

GABBROS [35; 35] *Aug 84*
BT1   plutonic rocks
  BT2   igneous rocks
    BT3   rocks
RT   feldspars
RT   silicate minerals

GABON [117; 117]
BT1   africa
BT1   developing countries

GADOLINIUM [2,122; 2,122]
BT1   rare earths
  BT2   metals
    BT3   elements

GADOLINIUM ADDITIONS [226; 226]
(Alloys containing not more than 1% Gd are listed here.)
BT1   rare earth additions
RT   gadolinium alloys
RT   gadolinium compounds

GADOLINIUM ALLOYS [1,167; 1,280]
(Alloys containing more than 1% Gd.)
BT1   rare earth alloys
  BT2   alloys
NT1   gadolinium base alloys
RT   gadolinium additions

GADOLINIUM ARSENIDES [15; 15]
Oct 77
BT1   arsenides
  BT2   arsenic compounds
  BT2   pnictides
BT1   gadolinium compounds
  BT2   rare earth compounds

GADOLINIUM BASE ALLOYS [98; 98]
BT1   gadolinium alloys
  BT2   rare earth alloys
    BT3   alloys

GADOLINIUM BORIDES [68; 68]
BT1   borides
  BT2   boron compounds
BT1   gadolinium compounds
  BT2   rare earth compounds

GADOLINIUM BROMIDES [21; 21]
BT1   bromides
  BT2   bromine compounds
    BT3   halogen compounds
  BT2   halides
    BT3   halogen compounds
BT1   gadolinium compounds
  BT2   rare earth compounds

GADOLINIUM CARBIDES [24; 24]
BT1   carbides
  BT2   carbon compounds
BT1   gadolinium compounds
  BT2   rare earth compounds

GADOLINIUM CARBONATES [12; 12]
BT1   carbonates
  BT2   carbon compounds
  BT2   oxygen compounds
BT1   gadolinium compounds
  BT2   rare earth compounds

GADOLINIUM CHLORIDES [126; 126]
BT1   chlorides
  BT2   chlorine compounds
    BT3   halogen compounds
  BT2   halides
    BT3   halogen compounds
BT1   gadolinium compounds
  BT2   rare earth compounds

GADOLINIUM COMPLEXES [647; 647]
BT1   rare earth complexes
  BT2   complexes

GADOLINIUM COMPOUNDS
[1,108; 2,966]
BT1   rare earth compounds
NT1   gadolinium arsenides
NT1   gadolinium borides
NT1   gadolinium bromides
NT1   gadolinium carbides
NT1   gadolinium carbonates
NT1   gadolinium chlorides
NT1   gadolinium fluorides
NT1   gadolinium hydrides
NT1   gadolinium hydroxides
NT1   gadolinium iodides
NT1   gadolinium nitrates
NT1   gadolinium nitrides
NT1   gadolinium oxides
NT1   gadolinium perchlorates
NT1   gadolinium phosphates
NT1   gadolinium phosphides
NT1   gadolinium selenides
NT1   gadolinium silicides
NT1   gadolinium sulfates
NT1   gadolinium sulfides
NT1   gadolinium tellurides
NT1   gadolinium tungstates
RT   gadolinium additions

GADOLINIUM FLUORIDES [81; 81]
BT1   fluorides
  BT2   fluorine compounds
    BT3   halogen compounds
  BT2   halides
    BT3   halogen compounds
BT1   gadolinium compounds
  BT2   rare earth compounds

GADOLINIUM HYDRIDES [37; 37]
BT1   gadolinium compounds
  BT2   rare earth compounds
BT1   hydrides
  BT2   hydrogen compounds

GADOLINIUM HYDROXIDES [22; 22]
BT1   gadolinium compounds
  BT2   rare earth compounds
BT1   hydroxides
  BT2   hydrogen compounds
  BT2   oxygen compounds

GADOLINIUM IODIDES [22; 22]
BT1   gadolinium compounds
  BT2   rare earth compounds
BT1   iodides
  BT2   halides
    BT3   halogen compounds
  BT2   iodine compounds
    BT3   halogen compounds

GADOLINIUM IONS [374; 374]
BT1   ions
  BT2   charged particles

GADOLINIUM ISOTOPES [246; 2,229]
- NT1 gadolinium 137
- NT1 gadolinium 138
- NT1 gadolinium 139
- NT1 gadolinium 140
- NT1 gadolinium 141
- NT1 gadolinium 142
- NT1 gadolinium 143
- NT1 gadolinium 144
- NT1 gadolinium 145
- NT1 gadolinium 146
- NT1 gadolinium 147
- NT1 gadolinium 148
- NT1 gadolinium 149
- NT1 gadolinium 150
- NT1 gadolinium 151
- NT1 gadolinium 152
- NT1 gadolinium 153
- NT1 gadolinium 154
- NT1 gadolinium 155
- NT1 gadolinium 156
- NT1 gadolinium 157
- NT1 gadolinium 158
- NT1 gadolinium 159
- NT1 gadolinium 160
- NT1 gadolinium 161
- NT1 gadolinium 162
- NT1 gadolinium 163
- NT1 gadolinium 164

GADOLINIUM NITRATES [76; 76]
- BT1 gadolinium compounds
- BT2 rare earth compounds
- BT1 nitrates
- BT2 nitrogen compounds
- BT2 oxygen compounds

GADOLINIUM NITRIDES [14; 14]
- BT1 gadolinium compounds
- BT2 rare earth compounds
- BT1 nitrides
- BT2 nitrogen compounds
- BT2 pnictides

GADOLINIUM OXIDES [1,164; 1,164]
- BT1 gadolinium compounds
- BT2 rare earth compounds
- BT1 oxides
- BT2 chalcogenides
- BT2 oxygen compounds

GADOLINIUM PERCHLORATES [6; 6]
- BT1 gadolinium compounds
- BT2 rare earth compounds
- BT1 perchlorates
- BT2 chlorine compounds
- BT3 halogen compounds
- BT2 oxygen compounds

GADOLINIUM PHOSPHATES [32; 32]
- BT1 gadolinium compounds
- BT2 rare earth compounds
- BT1 phosphates
- BT2 oxygen compounds
- BT2 phosphorus compounds

GADOLINIUM PHOSPHIDES [7; 7]
Feb 79
- BT1 gadolinium compounds
- BT2 rare earth compounds
- BT1 phosphides
- BT2 phosphorus compounds
- BT2 pnictides

GADOLINIUM SELENIDES [35; 35]
Jan 77
- BT1 gadolinium compounds
- BT2 rare earth compounds
- BT1 selenides
- BT2 chalcogenides
- BT2 selenium compounds

GADOLINIUM SILICIDES [37; 37]
- BT1 gadolinium compounds
- BT2 rare earth compounds
- BT1 silicides
- BT2 silicon compounds

GADOLINIUM SULFATES [30; 30]
- BT1 gadolinium compounds
- BT2 rare earth compounds
- BT1 sulfates
- BT2 oxygen compounds
- BT2 sulfur compounds

GADOLINIUM SULFIDES [121; 121]
- BT1 gadolinium compounds
- BT2 rare earth compounds
- BT1 sulfides
- BT2 chalcogenides
- BT2 sulfur compounds

GADOLINIUM TELLURIDES [19; 19]
Jan 77
- BT1 gadolinium compounds
- BT2 rare earth compounds
- BT1 tellurides
- BT2 chalcogenides
- BT2 tellurium compounds

GADOLINIUM TUNGSTATES [4; 4]
Feb 88
- BT1 gadolinium compounds
- BT2 rare earth compounds
- BT1 tungstates
- BT2 oxygen compounds
- BT2 tungsten compounds
- BT3 transition element compounds

GADOLINIUM 137 [2; 2] *Oct 84*
- BT1 beta-plus decay radioisotopes
- BT2 beta decay radioisotopes
- BT3 radioisotopes
- BT4 isotopes
- BT1 even-odd nuclei
- BT2 nuclei
- BT1 gadolinium isotopes
- BT1 rare earth nuclei
- BT2 intermediate mass nuclei
- BT3 nuclei

GADOLINIUM 138 [3; 3] *Mar 86*
- BT1 even-even nuclei
- BT2 nuclei
- BT1 gadolinium isotopes
- BT1 rare earth nuclei
- BT2 intermediate mass nuclei
- BT3 nuclei

GADOLINIUM 139 [8; 8] *Oct 84*
- BT1 beta-plus decay radioisotopes
- BT2 beta decay radioisotopes
- BT3 radioisotopes
- BT4 isotopes
- BT1 even-odd nuclei
- BT2 nuclei
- BT1 gadolinium isotopes
- BT1 rare earth nuclei
- BT2 intermediate mass nuclei
- BT3 nuclei

GADOLINIUM 140 [9; 9] *Mar 86*
- BT1 even-even nuclei
- BT2 nuclei
- BT1 gadolinium isotopes
- BT1 rare earth nuclei
- BT2 intermediate mass nuclei
- BT3 nuclei
- BT1 seconds living radioisotopes
- BT2 radioisotopes
- BT3 isotopes

GADOLINIUM 141 [10; 10] *Aug 84*
- BT1 electron capture radioisotopes
- BT2 beta decay radioisotopes
- BT3 radioisotopes
- BT4 isotopes
- BT1 even-odd nuclei
- BT2 nuclei
- BT1 gadolinium isotopes
- BT1 isomeric transition isotopes
- BT2 radioisotopes
- BT3 isotopes
- BT1 rare earth nuclei
- BT2 intermediate mass nuclei
- BT3 nuclei
- BT1 seconds living radioisotopes
- BT2 radioisotopes
- BT3 isotopes

GADOLINIUM 142 [19; 19]
- BT1 beta-plus decay radioisotopes
- BT2 beta decay radioisotopes
- BT3 radioisotopes
- BT4 isotopes
- BT1 even-even nuclei
- BT2 nuclei
- BT1 gadolinium isotopes
- BT1 minutes living radioisotopes
- BT2 radioisotopes
- BT3 isotopes
- BT1 rare earth nuclei
- BT2 intermediate mass nuclei
- BT3 nuclei

GADOLINIUM 143 [20; 20]
- BT1 beta-plus decay radioisotopes
- BT2 beta decay radioisotopes
- BT3 radioisotopes
- BT4 isotopes
- BT1 electron capture radioisotopes
- BT2 beta decay radioisotopes
- BT3 radioisotopes
- BT4 isotopes
- BT1 even-odd nuclei
- BT2 nuclei
- BT1 gadolinium isotopes
- BT1 minutes living radioisotopes
- BT2 radioisotopes
- BT3 isotopes
- BT1 rare earth nuclei
- BT2 intermediate mass nuclei
- BT3 nuclei
- BT1 seconds living radioisotopes
- BT2 radioisotopes
- BT3 isotopes

GADOLINIUM 144 [50; 50]
- BT1 beta-plus decay radioisotopes
- BT2 beta decay radioisotopes
- BT3 radioisotopes
- BT4 isotopes
- BT1 electron capture radioisotopes
- BT2 beta decay radioisotopes
- BT3 radioisotopes
- BT4 isotopes
- BT1 even-even nuclei
- BT2 nuclei
- BT1 gadolinium isotopes
- BT1 minutes living radioisotopes
- BT2 radioisotopes
- BT3 isotopes
- BT1 rare earth nuclei
- BT2 intermediate mass nuclei
- BT3 nuclei

GADOLINIUM 145 [61; 61]
- BT1 beta-plus decay radioisotopes
- BT2 beta decay radioisotopes
- BT3 radioisotopes
- BT4 isotopes
- BT1 electron capture radioisotopes
- BT2 beta decay radioisotopes
- BT3 radioisotopes
- BT4 isotopes
- BT1 even-odd nuclei
- BT2 nuclei
- BT1 gadolinium isotopes
- BT1 isomeric transition isotopes
- BT2 radioisotopes
- BT3 isotopes
- BT1 minutes living radioisotopes
- BT2 radioisotopes
- BT3 isotopes
- BT1 rare earth nuclei
- BT2 intermediate mass nuclei
- BT3 nuclei

GADOLINIUM 146 [211; 211]
  BT1   beta-plus decay radioisotopes
  BT2   beta decay radioisotopes
  BT3   radioisotopes
  BT4   isotopes
  BT1   days living radioisotopes
  BT2   radioisotopes
  BT3   isotopes
  BT1   electron capture radioisotopes
  BT2   beta decay radioisotopes
  BT3   radioisotopes
  BT4   isotopes
  BT1   even-even nuclei
  BT2   nuclei
  BT1   gadolinium isotopes
  BT1   rare earth nuclei
  BT2   intermediate mass nuclei
  BT3   nuclei

GADOLINIUM 147 [152; 152]
  BT1   beta-plus decay radioisotopes
  BT2   beta decay radioisotopes
  BT3   radioisotopes
  BT4   isotopes
  BT1   days living radioisotopes
  BT2   radioisotopes
  BT3   isotopes
  BT1   electron capture radioisotopes
  BT2   beta decay radioisotopes
  BT3   radioisotopes
  BT4   isotopes
  BT1   even-odd nuclei
  BT2   nuclei
  BT1   gadolinium isotopes
  BT1   isomeric transition isotopes
  BT2   radioisotopes
  BT3   isotopes
  BT1   nanosec living radioisotopes
  BT2   radioisotopes
  BT3   isotopes
  BT1   rare earth nuclei
  BT2   intermediate mass nuclei
  BT3   nuclei

GADOLINIUM 148 [98; 98]
  BT1   alpha decay radioisotopes
  BT2   radioisotopes
  BT3   isotopes
  BT1   even-even nuclei
  BT2   nuclei
  BT1   gadolinium isotopes
  BT1   isomeric transition isotopes
  BT2   radioisotopes
  BT3   isotopes
  BT1   nanosec living radioisotopes
  BT2   radioisotopes
  BT3   isotopes
  BT1   rare earth nuclei
  BT2   intermediate mass nuclei
  BT3   nuclei
  BT1   years living radioisotopes
  BT2   radioisotopes
  BT3   isotopes

GADOLINIUM 148 TARGET [19; 19]
Jan 82
  BT1   targets

GADOLINIUM 149 [76; 76]
  BT1   alpha decay radioisotopes
  BT2   radioisotopes
  BT3   isotopes
  BT1   days living radioisotopes
  BT2   radioisotopes
  BT3   isotopes
  BT1   electron capture radioisotopes
  BT2   beta decay radioisotopes
  BT3   radioisotopes
  BT4   isotopes
  BT1   even-odd nuclei
  BT2   nuclei
  BT1   gadolinium isotopes
  BT1   rare earth nuclei
  BT2   intermediate mass nuclei
  BT3   nuclei

GADOLINIUM 150 [90; 90]
  BT1   alpha decay radioisotopes
  BT2   radioisotopes
  BT3   isotopes
  BT1   even-even nuclei
  BT2   nuclei
  BT1   gadolinium isotopes
  BT1   rare earth nuclei
  BT2   intermediate mass nuclei
  BT3   nuclei
  BT1   years living radioisotopes
  BT2   radioisotopes
  BT3   isotopes

GADOLINIUM 151 [68; 68]
  BT1   alpha decay radioisotopes
  BT2   radioisotopes
  BT3   isotopes
  BT1   days living radioisotopes
  BT2   radioisotopes
  BT3   isotopes
  BT1   electron capture radioisotopes
  BT2   beta decay radioisotopes
  BT3   radioisotopes
  BT4   isotopes
  BT1   even-odd nuclei
  BT2   nuclei
  BT1   gadolinium isotopes
  BT1   rare earth nuclei
  BT2   intermediate mass nuclei
  BT3   nuclei

GADOLINIUM 152 [146; 146]
  BT1   alpha decay radioisotopes
  BT2   radioisotopes
  BT3   isotopes
  BT1   even-even nuclei
  BT2   nuclei
  BT1   gadolinium isotopes
  BT1   rare earth nuclei
  BT2   intermediate mass nuclei
  BT3   nuclei
  BT1   years living radioisotopes
  BT2   radioisotopes
  BT3   isotopes

GADOLINIUM 152 TARGET [37; 37]
Oct 75
  BT1   targets

GADOLINIUM 153 [318; 318]
  BT1   days living radioisotopes
  BT2   radioisotopes
  BT3   isotopes
  BT1   electron capture radioisotopes
  BT2   beta decay radioisotopes
  BT3   radioisotopes
  BT4   isotopes
  BT1   even-odd nuclei
  BT2   nuclei
  BT1   gadolinium isotopes
  BT1   rare earth nuclei
  BT2   intermediate mass nuclei
  BT3   nuclei

GADOLINIUM 154 [236; 236]
  BT1   even-even nuclei
  BT2   nuclei
  BT1   gadolinium isotopes
  BT1   rare earth nuclei
  BT2   intermediate mass nuclei
  BT3   nuclei
  BT1   stable isotopes
  BT2   isotopes

GADOLINIUM 154 TARGET [94; 94]
  BT1   targets

GADOLINIUM 155 [272; 272]
  BT1   even-odd nuclei
  BT2   nuclei
  BT1   gadolinium isotopes
  BT1   rare earth nuclei
  BT2   intermediate mass nuclei
  BT3   nuclei
  BT1   stable isotopes
  BT2   isotopes

GADOLINIUM 155 BEAMS [2; 2]
Dec 86
  BT1   ion beams
  BT2   beams

GADOLINIUM 155 REACTIONS [3; 3]
Nov 84
  BT1   heavy ion reactions
  BT2   nuclear reactions

GADOLINIUM 155 TARGET [58; 58]
  BT1   targets

GADOLINIUM 156 [305; 305]
  BT1   even-even nuclei
  BT2   nuclei
  BT1   gadolinium isotopes
  BT1   rare earth nuclei
  BT2   intermediate mass nuclei
  BT3   nuclei
  BT1   stable isotopes
  BT2   isotopes

GADOLINIUM 156 TARGET [128; 128]
  BT1   targets

GADOLINIUM 157 [154; 154]
  BT1   even-odd nuclei
  BT2   nuclei
  BT1   gadolinium isotopes
  BT1   rare earth nuclei
  BT2   intermediate mass nuclei
  BT3   nuclei
  BT1   stable isotopes
  BT2   isotopes

GADOLINIUM 157 TARGET [51; 51]
  BT1   targets

GADOLINIUM 158 [204; 204]
  BT1   even-even nuclei
  BT2   nuclei
  BT1   gadolinium isotopes
  BT1   rare earth nuclei
  BT2   intermediate mass nuclei
  BT3   nuclei
  BT1   stable isotopes
  BT2   isotopes

GADOLINIUM 158 TARGET [119; 119]
  BT1   targets

GADOLINIUM 159 [44; 44]
  BT1   beta-minus decay radioisotopes
  BT2   beta decay radioisotopes
  BT3   radioisotopes
  BT4   isotopes
  BT1   even-odd nuclei
  BT2   nuclei
  BT1   gadolinium isotopes
  BT1   hours living radioisotopes
  BT2   radioisotopes
  BT3   isotopes
  BT1   rare earth nuclei
  BT2   intermediate mass nuclei
  BT3   nuclei

GADOLINIUM 159 TARGET [3; 3]
Apr 76
  BT1   targets

GADOLINIUM 160 [113; 113]
  BT1   even-even nuclei
  BT2   nuclei
  BT1   gadolinium isotopes
  BT1   rare earth nuclei
  BT2   intermediate mass nuclei
  BT3   nuclei
  BT1   stable isotopes
  BT2   isotopes

GADOLINIUM 160 TARGET [155; 155]
   BT1   targets

GADOLINIUM 161 [23; 23]
   BT1   beta-minus decay radioisotopes
     BT2   beta decay radioisotopes
       BT3   radioisotopes
         BT4   isotopes
   BT1   even-odd nuclei
     BT2   nuclei
   BT1   gadolinium isotopes
   BT1   minutes living radioisotopes
     BT2   radioisotopes
       BT3   isotopes
   BT1   rare earth nuclei
     BT2   intermediate mass nuclei
       BT3   nuclei

GADOLINIUM 162 [6; 6]
   BT1   beta-minus decay radioisotopes
     BT2   beta decay radioisotopes
       BT3   radioisotopes
         BT4   isotopes
   BT1   even-even nuclei
     BT2   nuclei
   BT1   gadolinium isotopes
   BT1   minutes living radioisotopes
     BT2   radioisotopes
       BT3   isotopes
   BT1   rare earth nuclei
     BT2   intermediate mass nuclei
       BT3   nuclei

GADOLINIUM 163 [5; 5] *Apr 82*
   BT1   beta-minus decay radioisotopes
     BT2   beta decay radioisotopes
       BT3   radioisotopes
         BT4   isotopes
   BT1   even-odd nuclei
     BT2   nuclei
   BT1   gadolinium isotopes
   BT1   minutes living radioisotopes
     BT2   radioisotopes
       BT3   isotopes
   BT1   rare earth nuclei
     BT2   intermediate mass nuclei
       BT3   nuclei

GADOLINIUM 164 [2; 2] *Oct 88*
   BT1   beta-minus decay radioisotopes
     BT2   beta decay radioisotopes
       BT3   radioisotopes
         BT4   isotopes
   BT1   even-even nuclei
     BT2   nuclei
   BT1   gadolinium isotopes
   BT1   rare earth nuclei
     BT2   intermediate mass nuclei
       BT3   nuclei
   BT1   seconds living radioisotopes
     BT2   radioisotopes
       BT3   isotopes

gages (pressure)
   USE   pressure gages

gages (strain)
   USE   strain gages

GAIN [1,993; 1,993]
   BT1   amplification
   RT   amplifiers

GALACTIC EVOLUTION [3,720; 3,720]
   RT   astrophysics
   RT   cosmological models
   RT   cosmology
   RT   galaxies
   RT   planet-system accretion
   RT   star evolution
   RT   universe

GALACTOSE [167; 167]
   BT1   aldehydes
     BT2   organic compounds
   BT1   hexoses
     BT2   monosaccharides
       BT3   saccharides
         BT4   carbohydrates
           BT5   organic compounds
   RT   cerebrosides

GALACTOSIDASE [62; 62]
   BT1   o-glycosyl hydrolases
     BT2   glycosyl hydrolases
       BT3   hydrolases
         BT4   enzymes
           BT5   organic compounds

GALACTURONIC ACID [3; 3]
   BT1   aldehydes
     BT2   organic compounds
   BT1   hydroxy acids
     BT2   carboxylic acids
       BT3   organic acids
         BT4   organic compounds
   RT   pectins

GALAXIES [7,676; 14,875]
   UF   *local group*
   NT1   magellanic clouds
   NT1   markarian galaxies
   NT1   milky way
   NT1   radio galaxies
   NT1   seyfert galaxies
   NT1   x-ray galaxies
   RT   galactic evolution
   RT   galaxy clusters
   RT   galaxy nuclei
   RT   nebulae
   RT   nonluminous matter

GALAXY CLUSTERS [3,118; 3,118]
   UF   *clusters (galaxy)*
   RT   galaxies

GALAXY NUCLEI [2,691; 2,691] *Nov 78*
(Central part of galaxies.)
   RT   galaxies

GALENA [106; 106]
   BT1   sulfide minerals
     BT2   minerals
   RT   lead sulfides

GALERKIN-PETROV METHOD [231; 231]
   UF   *petrov-galerkin method*
   BT1   iterative methods
   RT   analytical solution
   RT   equations
   RT   mathematics
   RT   numerical solution

GALILEI TRANSFORMATIONS [218; 218]
   BT1   lorentz transformations
   RT   group theory
   RT   mechanics
   RT   relativity theory
   RT   space-time

galileo galilei italy
   USE   rts-1 reactor

gallbladder
   USE   biliary tract

GALLIC ACID [44; 44]
   UF   *trihydroxybenzoic acid*
   BT1   hydroxy acids
     BT2   carboxylic acids
       BT3   organic acids
         BT4   organic compounds

GALLIUM [1,068; 1,068]
   BT1   metals
     BT2   elements

GALLIUM ADDITIONS [238; 238]
(Alloys containing not more than 1% Ga are listed here.)
   RT   gallium alloys
   RT   gallium compounds

GALLIUM ALLOYS [1,272; 1,343]
(Alloys containing more than 1% Ga.)
   BT1   alloys
   NT1   gallium base alloys
   RT   gallium additions

GALLIUM ARSENIDES [3,919; 3,919]
   BT1   arsenides
     BT2   arsenic compounds
     BT2   pnictides
   BT1   gallium compounds

GALLIUM BASE ALLOYS [63; 63]
   BT1   gallium alloys
     BT2   alloys

GALLIUM BROMIDES [13; 13]
   BT1   bromides
     BT2   bromine compounds
       BT3   halogen compounds
     BT2   halides
       BT3   halogen compounds
   BT1   gallium halides
     BT2   gallium compounds
     BT2   halides
       BT3   halogen compounds

GALLIUM CARBIDES [1; 1]
   BT1   carbides
     BT2   carbon compounds
   BT1   gallium compounds

GALLIUM CHLORIDES [56; 56]
   BT1   chlorides
     BT2   chlorine compounds
       BT3   halogen compounds
     BT2   halides
       BT3   halogen compounds
   BT1   gallium halides
     BT2   gallium compounds
     BT2   halides
       BT3   halogen compounds

GALLIUM COMPLEXES [150; 150]
   BT1   complexes

GALLIUM COMPOUNDS [1,063; 6,386]
   NT1   gallium arsenides
   NT1   gallium carbides
   NT1   gallium halides
     NT2   gallium bromides
     NT2   gallium chlorides
     NT2   gallium fluorides
     NT2   gallium iodides
   NT1   gallium hydroxides
   NT1   gallium nitrates
   NT1   gallium nitrides
   NT1   gallium oxides
   NT1   gallium phosphates
   NT1   gallium phosphides
   NT1   gallium selenides
   NT1   gallium sulfates
   NT1   gallium sulfides
   NT1   gallium tellurides
   RT   gallium additions

GALLIUM FLUORIDES [13; 13]
   BT1   fluorides
     BT2   fluorine compounds
       BT3   halogen compounds
     BT2   halides
       BT3   halogen compounds
   BT1   gallium halides
     BT2   gallium compounds
     BT2   halides
       BT3   halogen compounds

GALLIUM HALIDES [0; 4] *Sep 91*
- BT1   gallium compounds
- BT1   halides
-     BT2   halogen compounds
- NT1   gallium bromides
- NT1   gallium chlorides
- NT1   gallium fluorides
- NT1   gallium iodides

GALLIUM HYDROXIDES [12; 12]
- BT1   gallium compounds
- BT1   hydroxides
-     BT2   hydrogen compounds
-     BT2   oxygen compounds

GALLIUM IODIDES [15; 15]
- BT1   gallium halides
-     BT2   gallium compounds
-     BT2   halides
-        BT3   halogen compounds
- BT1   iodides
-     BT2   halides
-        BT3   halogen compounds
-     BT2   iodine compounds
-        BT3   halogen compounds

GALLIUM IONS [236; 236]
- BT1   ions
-     BT2   charged particles

GALLIUM ISOTOPES [151; 3,559]
- NT1   gallium 61
- NT1   gallium 62
- NT1   gallium 63
- NT1   gallium 64
- NT1   gallium 65
- NT1   gallium 66
- NT1   gallium 67
- NT1   gallium 68
- NT1   gallium 69
- NT1   gallium 70
- NT1   gallium 71
- NT1   gallium 72
- NT1   gallium 73
- NT1   gallium 74
- NT1   gallium 75
- NT1   gallium 76
- NT1   gallium 77
- NT1   gallium 78
- NT1   gallium 79
- NT1   gallium 80
- NT1   gallium 81
- NT1   gallium 82
- NT1   gallium 83

GALLIUM NITRATES [12; 12] *Jun 77*
- BT1   gallium compounds
- BT1   nitrates
-     BT2   nitrogen compounds
-     BT2   oxygen compounds

GALLIUM NITRIDES [30; 30]
- BT1   gallium compounds
- BT1   nitrides
-     BT2   nitrogen compounds
-     BT2   pnictides

GALLIUM OXIDES [509; 509]
- BT1   gallium compounds
- BT1   oxides
-     BT2   chalcogenides
-     BT2   oxygen compounds

GALLIUM PHOSPHATES [20; 20]
Sep 77
- BT1   gallium compounds
- BT1   phosphates
-     BT2   oxygen compounds
-     BT2   phosphorus compounds

GALLIUM PHOSPHIDES [727; 727]
- BT1   gallium compounds
- BT1   phosphides
-     BT2   phosphorus compounds
-     BT2   pnictides

GALLIUM SELENIDES [171; 171]
Jul 76
- BT1   gallium compounds
- BT1   selenides
-     BT2   chalcogenides
-     BT2   selenium compounds

GALLIUM SULFATES [11; 11]
- BT1   gallium compounds
- BT1   sulfates
-     BT2   oxygen compounds
-     BT2   sulfur compounds

GALLIUM SULFIDES [179; 179]
- BT1   gallium compounds
- BT1   sulfides
-     BT2   chalcogenides
-     BT2   sulfur compounds

GALLIUM TELLURIDES [135; 135]
Sep 77
- BT1   gallium compounds
- BT1   tellurides
-     BT2   chalcogenides
-     BT2   tellurium compounds

GALLIUM 61 [4; 4] *May 80*
- BT1   gallium isotopes
- BT1   intermediate mass nuclei
-     BT2   nuclei
- BT1   odd-even nuclei
-     BT2   nuclei

GALLIUM 62 [10; 10]
- BT1   beta-plus decay radioisotopes
-     BT2   beta decay radioisotopes
-        BT3   radioisotopes
-           BT4   isotopes
- BT1   electron capture radioisotopes
-     BT2   beta decay radioisotopes
-        BT3   radioisotopes
-           BT4   isotopes
- BT1   gallium isotopes
- BT1   intermediate mass nuclei
-     BT2   nuclei
- BT1   millisec living radioisotopes
-     BT2   radioisotopes
-        BT3   isotopes
- BT1   odd-odd nuclei
-     BT2   nuclei

GALLIUM 63 [9; 9]
- BT1   beta-plus decay radioisotopes
-     BT2   beta decay radioisotopes
-        BT3   radioisotopes
-           BT4   isotopes
- BT1   electron capture radioisotopes
-     BT2   beta decay radioisotopes
-        BT3   radioisotopes
-           BT4   isotopes
- BT1   gallium isotopes
- BT1   intermediate mass nuclei
-     BT2   nuclei
- BT1   odd-even nuclei
-     BT2   nuclei
- BT1   seconds living radioisotopes
-     BT2   radioisotopes
-        BT3   isotopes

GALLIUM 64 [32; 32]
- BT1   beta-plus decay radioisotopes
-     BT2   beta decay radioisotopes
-        BT3   radioisotopes
-           BT4   isotopes
- BT1   electron capture radioisotopes
-     BT2   beta decay radioisotopes
-        BT3   radioisotopes
-           BT4   isotopes
- BT1   gallium isotopes
- BT1   intermediate mass nuclei
-     BT2   nuclei
- BT1   minutes living radioisotopes
-     BT2   radioisotopes
-        BT3   isotopes
- BT1   odd-odd nuclei
-     BT2   nuclei

GALLIUM 65 [62; 62]
- BT1   beta-plus decay radioisotopes
-     BT2   beta decay radioisotopes
-        BT3   radioisotopes
-           BT4   isotopes
- BT1   electron capture radioisotopes
-     BT2   beta decay radioisotopes
-        BT3   radioisotopes
-           BT4   isotopes
- BT1   gallium isotopes
- BT1   intermediate mass nuclei
-     BT2   nuclei
- BT1   minutes living radioisotopes
-     BT2   radioisotopes
-        BT3   isotopes
- BT1   odd-even nuclei
-     BT2   nuclei

GALLIUM 65 TARGET [2; 2]
- BT1   targets

GALLIUM 66 [73; 73]
- BT1   beta-plus decay radioisotopes
-     BT2   beta decay radioisotopes
-        BT3   radioisotopes
-           BT4   isotopes
- BT1   electron capture radioisotopes
-     BT2   beta decay radioisotopes
-        BT3   radioisotopes
-           BT4   isotopes
- BT1   gallium isotopes
- BT1   hours living radioisotopes
-     BT2   radioisotopes
-        BT3   isotopes
- BT1   intermediate mass nuclei
-     BT2   nuclei
- BT1   odd-odd nuclei
-     BT2   nuclei

GALLIUM 67 [2,632; 2,632]
- BT1   days living radioisotopes
-     BT2   radioisotopes
-        BT3   isotopes
- BT1   electron capture radioisotopes
-     BT2   beta decay radioisotopes
-        BT3   radioisotopes
-           BT4   isotopes
- BT1   gallium isotopes
- BT1   intermediate mass nuclei
-     BT2   nuclei
- BT1   odd-even nuclei
-     BT2   nuclei

GALLIUM 67 TARGET [4; 4]
- BT1   targets

GALLIUM 68 [310; 310]
- BT1   beta-plus decay radioisotopes
-     BT2   beta decay radioisotopes
-        BT3   radioisotopes
-           BT4   isotopes
- BT1   electron capture radioisotopes
-     BT2   beta decay radioisotopes
-        BT3   radioisotopes
-           BT4   isotopes
- BT1   gallium isotopes
- BT1   hours living radioisotopes
-     BT2   radioisotopes
-        BT3   isotopes
- BT1   intermediate mass nuclei
-     BT2   nuclei
- BT1   odd-odd nuclei
-     BT2   nuclei

GALLIUM 69 [141; 141]
- BT1   gallium isotopes
- BT1   intermediate mass nuclei
-     BT2   nuclei
- BT1   odd-even nuclei
-     BT2   nuclei
- BT1   stable isotopes
-     BT2   isotopes

GALLIUM 69 TARGET [56; 56]
  BT1   targets

GALLIUM 70 [43; 43]
  BT1   beta-minus decay radioisotopes
    BT2   beta decay radioisotopes
      BT3   radioisotopes
        BT4   isotopes
  BT1   electron capture radioisotopes
    BT2   beta decay radioisotopes
      BT3   radioisotopes
        BT4   isotopes
  BT1   gallium isotopes
  BT1   intermediate mass nuclei
    BT2   nuclei
  BT1   minutes living radioisotopes
    BT2   radioisotopes
      BT3   isotopes
  BT1   odd-odd nuclei
    BT2   nuclei

GALLIUM 71 [144; 144]
  BT1   gallium isotopes
  BT1   intermediate mass nuclei
    BT2   nuclei
  BT1   odd-even nuclei
    BT2   nuclei
  BT1   stable isotopes
    BT2   isotopes

GALLIUM 71 TARGET [126; 126]
  BT1   targets

GALLIUM 72 [56; 56]
  BT1   beta-minus decay radioisotopes
    BT2   beta decay radioisotopes
      BT3   radioisotopes
        BT4   isotopes
  BT1   gallium isotopes
  BT1   hours living radioisotopes
    BT2   radioisotopes
      BT3   isotopes
  BT1   intermediate mass nuclei
    BT2   nuclei
  BT1   odd-odd nuclei
    BT2   nuclei

GALLIUM 73 [26; 26]
  BT1   beta-minus decay radioisotopes
    BT2   beta decay radioisotopes
      BT3   radioisotopes
        BT4   isotopes
  BT1   gallium isotopes
  BT1   hours living radioisotopes
    BT2   radioisotopes
      BT3   isotopes
  BT1   intermediate mass nuclei
    BT2   nuclei
  BT1   odd-even nuclei
    BT2   nuclei

GALLIUM 74 [20; 20]
  BT1   beta-minus decay radioisotopes
    BT2   beta decay radioisotopes
      BT3   radioisotopes
        BT4   isotopes
  BT1   gallium isotopes
  BT1   intermediate mass nuclei
    BT2   nuclei
  BT1   isomeric transition isotopes
    BT2   radioisotopes
      BT3   isotopes
  BT1   minutes living radioisotopes
    BT2   radioisotopes
      BT3   isotopes
  BT1   odd-odd nuclei
    BT2   nuclei
  BT1   seconds living radioisotopes
    BT2   radioisotopes
      BT3   isotopes

GALLIUM 75 [10; 10]
  BT1   beta-minus decay radioisotopes
    BT2   beta decay radioisotopes
      BT3   radioisotopes
        BT4   isotopes
  BT1   gallium isotopes
  BT1   intermediate mass nuclei
    BT2   nuclei
  BT1   minutes living radioisotopes
    BT2   radioisotopes
      BT3   isotopes
  BT1   odd-even nuclei
    BT2   nuclei

GALLIUM 76 [5; 5]
  BT1   beta-minus decay radioisotopes
    BT2   beta decay radioisotopes
      BT3   radioisotopes
        BT4   isotopes
  BT1   gallium isotopes
  BT1   intermediate mass nuclei
    BT2   nuclei
  BT1   odd-odd nuclei
    BT2   nuclei
  BT1   seconds living radioisotopes
    BT2   radioisotopes
      BT3   isotopes

GALLIUM 77 [6; 6]
  BT1   beta-minus decay radioisotopes
    BT2   beta decay radioisotopes
      BT3   radioisotopes
        BT4   isotopes
  BT1   gallium isotopes
  BT1   intermediate mass nuclei
    BT2   nuclei
  BT1   odd-even nuclei
    BT2   nuclei
  BT1   seconds living radioisotopes
    BT2   radioisotopes
      BT3   isotopes

GALLIUM 78 [5; 5]
  BT1   beta-minus decay radioisotopes
    BT2   beta decay radioisotopes
      BT3   radioisotopes
        BT4   isotopes
  BT1   gallium isotopes
  BT1   intermediate mass nuclei
    BT2   nuclei
  BT1   odd-odd nuclei
    BT2   nuclei
  BT1   seconds living radioisotopes
    BT2   radioisotopes
      BT3   isotopes

GALLIUM 79 [11; 11] *Jan 76*
  BT1   beta-minus decay radioisotopes
    BT2   beta decay radioisotopes
      BT3   radioisotopes
        BT4   isotopes
  BT1   gallium isotopes
  BT1   intermediate mass nuclei
    BT2   nuclei
  BT1   odd-even nuclei
    BT2   nuclei
  BT1   seconds living radioisotopes
    BT2   radioisotopes
      BT3   isotopes

GALLIUM 80 [14; 14] *Jan 76*
  BT1   beta-minus decay radioisotopes
    BT2   beta decay radioisotopes
      BT3   radioisotopes
        BT4   isotopes
  BT1   gallium isotopes
  BT1   intermediate mass nuclei
    BT2   nuclei
  BT1   odd-odd nuclei
    BT2   nuclei
  BT1   seconds living radioisotopes
    BT2   radioisotopes
      BT3   isotopes

GALLIUM 81 [12; 12] *Jun 77*
  BT1   beta-minus decay radioisotopes
    BT2   beta decay radioisotopes
      BT3   radioisotopes
        BT4   isotopes
  BT1   gallium isotopes
  BT1   intermediate mass nuclei
    BT2   nuclei
  BT1   odd-even nuclei
    BT2   nuclei
  BT1   seconds living radioisotopes
    BT2   radioisotopes
      BT3   isotopes

GALLIUM 82 [7; 7] *Jul 80*
  BT1   beta-minus decay radioisotopes
    BT2   beta decay radioisotopes
      BT3   radioisotopes
        BT4   isotopes
  BT1   gallium isotopes
  BT1   intermediate mass nuclei
    BT2   nuclei
  BT1   millisec living radioisotopes
    BT2   radioisotopes
      BT3   isotopes
  BT1   odd-odd nuclei
    BT2   nuclei

GALLIUM 83 [3; 3] *Jul 80*
  BT1   beta-minus decay radioisotopes
    BT2   beta decay radioisotopes
      BT3   radioisotopes
        BT4   isotopes
  BT1   gallium isotopes
  BT1   intermediate mass nuclei
    BT2   nuclei
  BT1   millisec living radioisotopes
    BT2   radioisotopes
      BT3   isotopes
  BT1   odd-even nuclei
    BT2   nuclei

gallotannic acid
  USE   tannic acid

gallstones
  USE   biliary tract
  AND   calculi

galvanic corrosion
  USE   electrochemical corrosion

GALVANOMAGNETIC EFFECT [158; 158]
  RT   magnetic fields

GALVANOMETERS [24; 24]
  BT1   electric measuring instruments
    BT2   electrical equipment
      BT3   equipment
    BT2   measuring instruments

→ **GAMBIA** [0; 0] *Oct 91*
  BT1   africa
  BT1   developing countries

GAMETES [41; 1,134]
  BT1   germ cells
  NT1   ova
  NT1   pollen
  NT1   spermatozoa
  RT   fertilization
  RT   gametogenesis
  RT   haploidy

GAMETOGENESIS [32; 380]
  NT1   oogenesis
  NT1   spermatogenesis
  RT   cell division
  RT   gametes
  RT   germ cells
  RT   gonads
  RT   meiosis

GAMMA ASTRONOMY [641; 641]
Jul 78
(For photon energies above 100 kev.)
  BT1   astronomy
  RT   cosmic gamma sources
  RT   cosmic radiation
  RT   cosmic x-ray sources

gamma benzene hexachloride
  USE lindane

GAMMA CAMERAS [3,380; 3,777]
  UF   *scintillation cameras*
  BT1 cameras
  NT1 positron cameras
  RT   compton scattering tomography
  RT   emission computed tomography
  RT   nuclear medicine
  RT   radioisotope scanners
  RT   single photon ect

GAMMA CASCADES [2,235; 2,235]
  BT1 nuclear cascades
  BT2   energy-level transitions
  RT   cascade theory

GAMMA DECAY [1,954; 3,172] *Feb 78*
  BT1 nuclear decay
  BT2   decay
  RT   internal conversion
  RT   internal pair production

GAMMA DETECTION [5,477; 5,477]
  BT1 radiation detection
  BT2   detection
  RT   compton diode detectors
  RT   filament crystal counters
  RT   gamma dosimetry
  RT   gamma spectrometers
  RT   gamma spectroscopy
  RT   radiation detectors
  RT   radioisotope scanning

GAMMA DIFFRACTOMETERS [49; 49]
  BT1 diffractometers
  BT2   measuring instruments
  RT   crystallography
  RT   diffraction

GAMMA DOSIMETRY [2,564; 2,564]
  BT1 dosimetry
  RT   gamma detection

GAMMA FUEL SCANNING [430; 430]
  BT1 fuel scanning

GAMMA FUNCTION [76; 76]
  BT1 functions
  RT   mathematics

gamma heating
  USE radiation heating

gamma hexachlorohexane
  USE lindane

GAMMA LOGGING [577; 577] *Oct 76*
(Logging the natural gamma activity of a well.)
  BT1 radioactivity logging
  DT2   well logging
  RT   natural radioactivity

GAMMA RADIATION [59,270; 60,298]
  BT1 electromagnetic radiation
  BT2   radiations
  BT1 ionizing radiations
  BT2   radiations
  NT1 delayed gamma radiation
  NT1 prompt gamma radiation
  RT   cosmic gamma sources
  RT   gamma sources
  RT   gamma spectra
  RT   photons
  RT   x radiation

GAMMA RADIOGRAPHY [804; 997]
  RT   industrial radiography
  RT   nondestructive testing

GAMMA SOURCES [3,155; 3,155]
(For cosmic sources of gamma radiation use COSMIC GAMMA SOURCES.)
  BT1 radiation sources
  RT   gamma radiation
  RT   gasers

GAMMA SPECTRA [16,430; 16,430]
  BT1 spectra
  RT   escape peaks
  RT   gamma radiation

GAMMA SPECTROMETERS [2,920; 3,830]
  BT1 spectrometers
  BT2   measuring instruments
  NT1 compton spectrometers
  NT1 moessbauer spectrometers
  NT1 pair spectrometers
  RT   gamma detection
  RT   whole-body counters

gamma spectrometry
  USE gamma spectroscopy

GAMMA SPECTROSCOPY [7,601; 7,601]
  UF   *gamma spectrometry*
  BT1 spectroscopy
  RT   fuel cooling time
  RT   gamma detection

gamma transmission scanning
  USE photon transmission scanning

GAMMA TRANSPORT THEORY [289; 289]
  BT1 transport theory
  RT   photon transport

GAMMA 10 DEVICES [16; 16] *Feb 89*
(Tsukuba University, Japan.)
  BT1 tandem mirrors
  BT2   magnetic mirrors
  BT3   open plasma devices
  BT4   thermonuclear devices

GAMMA-GAMMA LOGGING [274; 274] *Oct 76*
(Gamma source and gamma detector.)
  BT1 radioactivity logging
  BT2   well logging

gamma-ray lasers
  USE gasers

GAMMAPHOS [27; 27] *May 84*
(S-2-(Omega-aminopropylaminoethyl) phosphorothioate.)
  BT1 amines
  BT2   organic compounds
  BT1 radioprotective substances
  BT2   drugs
  BT2   response modifying factors
  BT1 thiophosphoric acid esters
  BT2   esters
  BT3   organic compounds

gammel-christian-thaler theory
  USE gammel-thaler potential

GAMMEL-THALER POTENTIAL [7; 7]
  UF   *gammel-christian-thaler theory*
  BT1 ope potential
  BT2   potentials

GAMOW BARRIER [40; 40]
  UF   *gamow factor*
  RT   alpha decay

gamow factor
  USE gamow barrier

gamow-teller decay
  USE gamow-teller rules

GAMOW-TELLER RULES [1,117; 1,117]
  UF   *gamow-teller decay*
  UF   *gamow-teller theory*
  RT   beta decay

gamow-teller theory
  USE gamow-teller rules

GANGA RIVER [5; 5]
  BT1 rivers
  BT2   surface waters

GANGLIONS [163; 163]
  BT1 nervous system
  RT   autonomic nervous system
  RT   spinal cord
  RT   thalamus

GANGLIOSIDES [77; 77]
  BT1 lipids
  BT2   organic compounds
  BT1 organic nitrogen compounds
  BT2   organic compounds
  BT1 saccharides
  BT2   carbohydrates
  BT3   organic compounds

GANGRENE [17; 17]
  BT1 necrosis
  BT2   pathological changes
  BT3   diseases
  RT   ulcers

GANGUE [30; 30]
  BT1 residues
  RT   slags

GANIL CYCLOTRON [322; 322] *Jul 76*
(Grand Accelerateur National a Ions Lourds; a heavy ion accelerator consisting of two identical isochronous cyclotrons and a particle booster for injection, located in Caen, France.)
  UF   *grand acc. nat. ions lourds*
  BT1 heavy ion accelerators
  BT2   accelerators
  BT1 isochronous cyclotrons
  BT2   cyclotrons
  BT3   cyclic accelerators
  BT4   accelerators

garching, ipp
(Max-Planck-Institut fuer Plasmaphysik)
  USE ipp garching

gardenhose instability
  USE hose instability

GARIGLIANO REACTOR [54; 54]
(Sessa Aurunea, Caserta, Italy)
  UF   *senn reactor*
  BT1 bwr type reactors
  BT2   enriched uranium reactors
  BT3   reactors
  BT2   power reactors
  BT3   reactors
  BT2   thermal reactors
  BT3   reactors
  BT2   water cooled reactors
  BT3   reactors
  BT2   water moderated reactors
  BT3   reactors

GARNETS [364; 366]
(For silicate garnets only.)
- BT1 silicate minerals
- BT2 minerals
- NT1 andradite
- RT calcium silicates
- RT ferrite garnets
- RT iron silicates

GARONA REACTOR [24; 24]
- UF santa maria de garona pow. rea
- UF sta maria garona nuc. pow. pla
- BT1 bwr type reactors
- BT2 enriched uranium reactors
- BT3 reactors
- BT2 power reactors
- BT3 reactors
- BT2 thermal reactors
- BT3 reactors
- BT2 water cooled reactors
- BT3 reactors
- BT2 water moderated reactors
- BT3 reactors

GARTENHAUS POTENTIAL [1; 1]
- BT1 potentials
- RT nucleon-nucleon potential

GAS ANALYSIS [778; 778]
- UF analysis (gas)
- RT electron-capture detectors
- RT gas chromatography
- RT gases
- RT orsat apparatus
- RT photoacoustic spectrometers
- RT quantitative chemical analysis
- RT radio-release analysis

GAS BEARINGS [37; 37]
- BT1 bearings

GAS BLANKETS [165; 165] Aug 75
(For plasma confinement. For other gas blankets see COVER GAS or INERT ATMOSPHERE.)
- UF blankets (gas)
- RT plasma
- RT plasma confinement

gas bubble disease
- USE emboli

GAS CENTRIFUGATION [276; 276]
Jan 76
- BT1 centrifugation
- BT2 separation processes
- RT gas centrifuges
- RT isotope enriched materials
- RT isotope separation

GAS CENTRIFUGES [417; 417]
- BT1 centrifuges
- RT gas centrifugation
- RT isotope separation

GAS CHROMATOGRAPHY [2,364; 2,364]
- BT1 chromatography
- BT2 separation processes
- RT gas analysis
- RT partition

GAS COMPRESSORS [110; 110]
- BT1 compressors
- RT compressed gases

gas coolants
- USE gases

gas cooled f. breeder reactor
- USE gcfr reactor

gas cooled fast breed reactors
- USE gcfr type reactors

gas cooled graphite moder. rea
- USE gcr type reactors

GAS COOLED REACTORS [1,074; 15,138]
- UF gas-cooled reactors
- BT1 reactors
- NT1 agr type reactors
- NT2 connah quay-b reactor
- NT2 dungeness-b reactor
- NT2 hartlepool reactor
- NT2 heysham-a reactor
- NT2 heysham-b reactor
- NT2 hinkley point-b reactor
- NT2 hunterston-b reactor
- NT2 torness reactor
- NT2 wagr reactor
- NT1 air cooled reactors
- NT2 afsr reactor
- NT2 bepo reactor
- NT2 bgrr reactor
- NT2 br-1 reactor
- NT2 gleep reactor
- NT2 harmonie reactor
- NT2 hprr reactor
- NT2 kalpakkam pfr reactor
- NT2 sneak reactor
- NT2 stf reactor
- NT2 tory-2c reactor
- NT2 treat reactor
- NT2 windscale production reactors
- NT2 x-10 reactor
- NT2 zed-2 reactor
- NT1 carbon dioxide cooled reactors
- NT2 calder hall a-1 reactor
- NT2 calder hall a-2 reactor
- NT2 calder hall b-3 reactor
- NT2 calder hall b-4 reactor
- NT2 cesar reactor
- NT2 chapelcross-1 reactor
- NT2 chapelcross-2 reactor
- NT2 chapelcross-3 reactor
- NT2 chapelcross-4 reactor
- NT2 dungeness-a reactor
- NT2 dungeness-b reactor
- NT2 el-2 reactor
- NT2 hartlepool reactor
- NT2 hector reactor
- NT2 heysham-a reactor
- NT2 heysham-b reactor
- NT2 hinkley point-a reactor
- NT2 hinkley point-b reactor
- NT2 hunterston-a reactor
- NT2 hunterston-b reactor
- NT2 oldbury-a reactor
- NT2 oldbury-b reactor
- NT2 sizewell-a reactor
- NT2 tokai-mura reactor
- NT2 torness reactor
- NT2 trawsfynydd reactor
- NT2 vandellos reactor
- NT2 wagr reactor
- NT2 wylfa reactor
- NT1 gcfr type reactors
- NT2 gcfr reactor
- NT1 gcr type reactors
- NT2 bugey-1 reactor
- NT2 chinon-1 reactor
- NT2 chinon-2 reactor
- NT2 chinon-3 reactor
- NT2 g-1 reactor
- NT2 g-2 reactor
- NT2 g-3 reactor
- NT2 magnox type reactors
- NT3 berkeley reactor
- NT3 bradwell reactor
- NT3 calder hall a-1 reactor
- NT3 calder hall a-2 reactor
- NT3 calder hall b-3 reactor
- NT3 calder hall b-4 reactor
- NT3 chapelcross-1 reactor
- NT3 chapelcross-2 reactor
- NT3 chapelcross-3 reactor
- NT3 chapelcross-4 reactor
- NT3 dungeness-a reactor
- NT3 hinkley point-a reactor
- NT3 hunterston-a reactor
- NT3 latina reactor
- NT3 oldbury-a reactor
- NT3 sizewell-a reactor
- NT3 tokai-mura reactor
- NT3 trawsfynydd reactor
- NT3 wylfa reactor
- NT2 saint laurent-1 reactor
- NT2 saint laurent-2 reactor
- NT2 vandellos reactor
- NT1 helium cooled reactors
- NT2 avr reactor
- NT2 dragon reactor
- NT2 ebor reactor
- NT2 egcr reactor
- NT2 fulton-1 reactor
- NT2 fulton-2 reactor
- NT2 httr reactor
- NT2 iea-zpr reactor
- NT2 peach bottom-1 reactor
- NT2 schmehausen reactor
- NT2 thtr-300 reactor
- NT2 uhtrex reactor
- NT2 vg-400 reactor
- NT2 vgr-50 reactor
- NT2 vhtr reactor
- NT2 vidal-1 reactor
- NT2 vidal-2 reactor
- NT1 htgr type reactors
- NT2 avr reactor
- NT2 dragon reactor
- NT2 fulton-1 reactor
- NT2 fulton-2 reactor
- NT2 ga standard reactor
- NT2 httr reactor
- NT2 kahter reactor
- NT2 peach bottom-1 reactor
- NT2 schmehausen reactor
- NT2 summit-1 reactor
- NT2 summit-2 reactor
- NT2 thtr-300 reactor
- NT2 vg-400 reactor
- NT2 vgr-50 reactor
- NT2 vhtr reactor
- NT2 vidal-1 reactor
- NT2 vidal-2 reactor
- NT2 vrain reactor
- NT1 hwgcr type reactors
- NT2 bohunice a-1 reactor
- NT2 bohunice a-2 reactor
- NT2 el-4 reactor
- NT2 lucens reactor
- NT2 niederaichbach reactor
- NT1 hydrogen cooled reactors
- NT2 kiwi reactors
- NT2 nrx-a2 reactor
- NT2 nrx-a3 reactor
- NT2 nrx-a4-est reactor
- NT2 nrx-a5 reactor
- NT2 nrx-a6 reactor
- NT2 rover reactors
- NT1 nitrogen cooled reactors
- NT2 htltr reactor
- NT1 phoebus-1a reactor
- NT1 phoebus-1b reactor
- NT1 phoebus-2a reactor
- NT1 steam cooled reactors

GAS COOLING [225; 225]
- BT1 cooling

GAS CYLINDERS [59; 59]
- BT1 containers

GAS DISCHARGE TUBES [223; 610]
- BT1 electron tubes
- NT1 flash tubes
- NT1 geissler tubes
- NT1 ignitrons
- NT1 thyratrons

GAS FLOW [4,405; 4,763]
- BT1 fluid flow
- NT1 air flow
- NT1 knudsen flow
- NT1 slip flow
- RT aerodynamics
- RT air infiltration
- RT compressible flow

RT electrogasdynamics
RT magnetogasdynamics
RT two-phase flow

GAS FUELED REACTORS [191; 261]
UF *gas-fueled reactors*
BT1 fluid fueled reactors
BT2 reactors
BT1 homogeneous reactors
BT2 reactors
NT1 coaxial flow reactors
NT1 light bulb reactors
NT1 plasma core assembly
RT gas fuels

GAS FUELS [52; 52]
(Limited to nuclear fuels.)
BT1 nuclear fuels
BT2 energy sources
BT2 fuels
BT2 reactor materials
BT3 materials
RT fissioning plasma
RT gas fueled reactors

GAS INJECTION [232; 232] *Jul 81*
BT1 fluid injection
RT thermonuclear reactor fueling

GAS LASERS [1,313; 4,265]
UF *copper vapor lasers*
UF *metal vapor lasers*
BT1 lasers
BT2 amplifiers
BT3 equipment
NT1 carbon dioxide lasers
NT1 carbon monoxide lasers
NT1 excimer lasers
NT2 krypton fluoride lasers
NT1 helium-neon lasers

GAS LUBRICANTS [4; 4]
BT1 lubricants

GAS METAL-ARC WELDING
[183; 319]
BT1 arc welding
BT2 welding
BT3 joining
BT4 fabrication
NT1 gas tungsten-arc welding

GAS SCINTILLATION DETECTORS
[409; 409]
BT1 scintillation counters
BT2 radiation detectors
BT3 measuring instruments
RT proportional counters
RT rare gases

GAS TRACK DETECTORS [165; 4,864]
UF *track detectors (gas)*
BT1 radiation detectors
BT2 measuring instruments
NT1 bubble chambers
NT2 cryogenic bubble chambers
NT2 heavy liquid bubble chambers
NT2 ultrasonic bubble chambers
NT1 cloud chambers
NT2 diffusion chambers
NT2 expansion chambers
NT1 spark chambers
NT2 filmless spark chambers
NT3 sonic spark chambers
NT3 wire spark chambers
NT2 projection spark chambers
NT2 streamer spark chambers
NT2 wide gap spark chambers

GAS TUNGSTEN-ARC WELDING
[410; 410]
BT1 gas metal-arc welding
BT2 arc welding
BT3 welding
BT4 joining
BT5 fabrication

GAS TURBINE POWER PLANTS
[21; 21] *Dec 82*
BT1 power plants
RT combined-cycle power plants
RT gas turbines

GAS TURBINES [826; 826]
BT1 turbines
RT gas turbine power plants

GAS WELDING [27; 27]
BT1 welding
BT2 joining
BT3 fabrication

gas wells
USE wells

gas-cooled reactors
USE gas cooled reactors

gas-fueled reactors
USE gas fueled reactors

GAS-INSULATED CABLES [13; 13]
Aug 76
BT1 electric cables
BT2 cables
BT2 conductor devices
BT3 electrical equipment
BT4 equipment
RT power transmission lines
RT superconducting cables

GASBUGGY EVENT [59; 59]
BT1 contained explosions
BT2 underground explosions
BT3 explosions
BT1 nuclear explosions
BT2 explosions
BT1 plowshare project
RT natural gas
RT oil shales

GASEOUS DIFFUSION [543; 543]
BT1 diffusion

GASEOUS DIFFUSION PLANTS
[293; 509]
UF *enrichment plants (gas diffusi*
BT1 isotope separation plants
BT2 industrial plants
BT2 nuclear facilities
NT1 cogema pierrelatte
NT1 orgdp
NT1 paducah plant
NT1 portsmouth gaseous diffusion p
RT diffusion barriers
RT eurodif
RT gaseous diffusion process
RT nuclear industry

GASEOUS DIFFUSION PROCESS
[467; 467]
BT1 isotope separation
BT2 separation processes
RT diffusion barriers
RT gaseous diffusion plants

gaseous effluents
USE gaseous wastes

GASEOUS WASTES [3,946; 4,231]
UF *effluents (gaseous)*
UF *gaseous effluents*
UF+ *radioactive gaseous wastes*
BT1 wastes
NT1 exhaust gases
NT1 flue gas
RT chemical effluents
RT combustion products
RT electrostatic precipitators
RT fume hoods
RT gases
RT ground release
RT off-gas systems
RT plumes
RT radioactive effluents
RT stack disposal
RT stacks
RT ventilation

GASERS [52; 52] *Mar 76*
(Gamma-ray Amplification by Stimulated Emission of Radiation)
UF *gamma-ray lasers*
UF *grasers*
BT1 amplifiers
BT2 equipment
RT gamma sources
RT lasers
RT masers
RT nuclear pumping
RT stimulated emission

GASES [10,017; 32,558]
(See also ELECTRON GAS and FERMI GAS)
UF *gas coolants*
BT1 fluids
NT1 air
NT2 surface air
NT1 compressed gases
NT1 cosmic gases
NT1 dissociating gases
NT1 dissolved gases
NT1 exhaust gases
NT1 fuel gas
NT2 coal gas
NT2 natural gas
NT1 ionized gases
NT2 fully ionized gases
NT3 lorentz gas
NT2 strongly ionized gases
NT2 weakly ionized gases
NT1 rarefied gases
NT1 vapors
NT2 water vapor
RT aeration
RT boltzmann equation
RT buffers
RT coolants
RT dispersions
RT gas analysis
RT gaseous wastes
RT hard-sphere model
RT jesse effect
RT kinetic equations
RT kinetics
RT paschen law
RT phase diagrams
RT underground disposal
RT virial equation

GASIFICATION [475; 681]
(Any technique for converting coal or other products into gaseous fuel. For other types of gasification, see EVAPORATION, BOILING, or DISTILLATION.)
NT1 coal gasification
RT coal

GASKETS [176; 176]
BT1 seals

GASOLINE [84; 84]
BT1 fossil fuels
BT2 energy sources
BT2 fuels
BT1 liquid fuels
BT2 fuels
BT1 petroleum products
RT automotive fuels

gasteropods
USE molluscs

GASTRECTOMY [94; 94]
  BT1   surgery
  BT2   medicine
  RT   digestive system diseases
  RT   stomach

GASTRIC ACID [91; 91]
  BT1   body fluids
  BT2   biological materials
  BT3   materials
  RT   digestion
  RT   gastrin
  RT   secretion
  RT   stomach

gastric administration
  USE   oral administration

GASTRIN [171; 171]
  BT1   peptide hormones
  BT2   hormones
  BT1   polypeptides
  BT2   peptides
  BT3   proteins
  BT4   organic compounds
  RT   gastric acid
  RT   secretion
  RT   stomach

GASTROINTESTINAL TRACT
[1,971; 9,195]
  BT1   digestive system
  NT1   intestines
  NT2   large intestine
  NT3   rectum
  NT2   small intestine
  NT1   stomach
  RT   abdomen
  RT   nippostrongylus
  RT   peritoneum
  RT   radiation syndrome
  RT   trichinosis

GATING CIRCUITS [574; 574]
  BT1   electronic circuits
  RT   logic circuits
  RT   switching circuits

GAUGE INVARIANCE [15,224; 15,224]
  UF   *gauge transformations*
  BT1   invariance principles
  RT   aharonov-bohm effect
  RT   baryon number
  RT   charge conservation
  RT   hypercharge
  RT   instantons
  RT   lattice field theory
  RT   lepton number
  RT   operator product expansion
  RT   quantum chromodynamics
  RT   quantum field theory
  RT   strangeness
  RT   supergravity
  RT   unified gauge models
  RT   ward identity

gauge transformations
  USE   gauge invariance

gauss distribution
  USE   gauss function

GAUSS FUNCTION [1,625; 1,625]
  UF   *gauss distribution*
  BT1   functions
  RT   distribution
  RT   gaussian processes
  RT   statistics

gauss nuclear model
  USE   gauss potential

GAUSS POTENTIAL [239; 239]
  UF   *gauss nuclear model*
  BT1   nucleon-nucleon potential
  BT2   potentials

gauss quadratures
  USE   quadratures

GAUSSIAN PROCESSES [728; 728]
  RT   distribution
  RT   gauss function
  RT   stochastic processes

gcep
  USE   portsmouth centrifuge enrichme

GCFR REACTOR [394; 394]
  UF   *gas cooled f. breeder reactor*
  UF   *gulf general atom. fast breed.*
  BT1   gcfr type reactors
  BT2   fbr type reactors
  BT3   breeder reactors
  BT4   reactors
  BT3   fast reactors
  BT4   epithermal reactors
  BT5   reactors
  BT2   gas cooled reactors
  BT3   reactors

GCFR TYPE REACTORS [455; 688]
Nov 75
  UF   *gas cooled fast breed reactors*
  BT1   fbr type reactors
  BT2   breeder reactors
  BT3   reactors
  BT2   fast reactors
  BT3   epithermal reactors
  BT4   reactors
  BT1   gas cooled reactors
  BT2   reactors
  NT1   gcfr reactor

GCR TYPE REACTORS [158; 641]
  UF   *gas cooled graphite moder. rea*
  BT1   gas cooled reactors
  BT2   reactors
  BT1   graphite moderated reactors
  BT2   reactors
  NT1   bugey-1 reactor
  NT1   chinon-1 reactor
  NT1   chinon-2 reactor
  NT1   chinon-3 reactor
  NT1   g-1 reactor
  NT1   g-2 reactor
  NT1   g-3 reactor
  NT1   magnox type reactors
  NT2   berkeley reactor
  NT2   bradwell reactor
  NT2   calder hall a-1 reactor
  NT2   calder hall a-2 reactor
  NT2   calder hall b-3 reactor
  NT2   calder hall b-4 reactor
  NT2   chapelcross-1 reactor
  NT2   chapelcross-2 reactor
  NT2   chapelcross-3 reactor
  NT2   chapelcross-4 reactor
  NT2   dungeness-a reactor
  NT2   hinkley point-a reactor
  NT2   hunterston-a reactor
  NT2   latina reactor
  NT2   oldbury-a reactor
  NT2   sizewell-a reactor
  NT2   tokai-mura reactor
  NT2   trawsfynydd reactor
  NT2   wylfa reactor
  NT1   saint laurent-1 reactor
  NT1   saint laurent-2 reactor
  NT1   vandellos reactor
  RT   carbon dioxide cooled reactors
  RT   power reactors

GDL FACILITY [8; 8] *May 86*
(Nd glass laser facility at University of Rochester.)
  UF   *glass development laser facil.*
  RT   laser fusion reactors
  RT   neodymium lasers

GE COMPUTERS [5; 5]
  BT1   computers

ge detectors (high-purity)
  USE   high-purity ge detectors

GE SEMICONDUCTOR DETECTORS
[1,057; 4,297]
  BT1   semiconductor detectors
  BT2   radiation detectors
  BT3   measuring instruments
  NT1   high-purity ge detectors
  NT1   li-drifted ge detectors

GE STANDARD REACTOR [97; 97]
Sep 75
  UF   *bwr/6 type reactor*
  BT1   bwr type reactors
  BT2   enriched uranium reactors
  BT3   reactors
  BT2   power reactors
  BT3   reactors
  BT2   thermal reactors
  BT3   reactors
  BT2   water cooled reactors
  BT3   reactors
  BT2   water moderated reactors
  BT3   reactors
  RT   black fox-1 reactor
  RT   black fox-2 reactor
  RT   phipps bend-1 reactor
  RT   phipps bend-2 reactor

ge(li) detectors
  USE   li-drifted ge detectors

GEARS [59; 59] *Nov 80*
  BT1   machine parts
  RT   lubrication
  RT   power transmission
  RT   rolling friction
  RT   wear
  RT   wear resistance

geesthacht-1 research reactor
  USE   frg-1 reactor

geesthacht-2 research reactor
  USE   frg-2 reactor

gegenschein
  USE   zodiacal light

GEIGER-MUELLER COUNTERS
[1,002; 1,002]
  BT1   radiation detectors
  BT2   measuring instruments
  RT   avalanche quenching
  RT   flow counters

GEIGER-NUTTALL LAW [13; 13]
Aug 86
  RT   alpha decay
  RT   alpha particles
  RT   half-life
  RT   mean free path

GEISSLER TUBES [0; 0]
  BT1   gas discharge tubes
  BT2   electron tubes

GEKKO FACILITY [54; 54] *Sep 85*
(Nd glass laser facility at Osaka University for laser fusion experiments.)
RT   neodymium lasers

GEL PERMEATION CHROMATOGRAPHY [176; 176]
Apr 84
BT1   chromatography
BT2   separation processes

GELATIN [142; 142]
BT1   colloids
BT2   dispersions
BT1   proteins
BT2   organic compounds

GELATION [222; 222]
RT   colloids
RT   sol-gel process

GELL-MANN THEORY [164; 164]
RT   quantum numbers
RT   strangeness

GELS [1,090; 1,090]
BT1   colloids
BT2   dispersions

gemeinschaftskernkraftwerk nec
USE   neckar reactor

gen. atomic standard reactor
USE   ga standard reactor

gen. electric nuclear test rea
USE   ntr reactor

gen. electric test reactor
USE   getr reactor

gene activators
USE   gene regulation

gene loci
USE   genes

GENE MUTATIONS [681; 681]
UF   *point mutations*
BT1   mutations
RT   gene recombination
RT   genes
RT   genetic engineering
RT   recombinant dna

GENE OPERONS [54; 54] *Nov 85*
RT   chromosomes
RT   codons
RT   dna
RT   genes
RT   rna

gene promotors
USE   gene regulation

GENE RECOMBINATION [519; 519]
UF   *recombination (genetic)*
RT   crossing-over
RT   gene mutations
RT   genes
RT   genetic variability
RT   recombinant dna

GENE REGULATION [880; 880] *Nov 85*
UF   *gene activators*
UF   *gene promotors*
RT   biosynthesis
RT   chromosomes
RT   codons
RT   genes
RT   genetic engineering
RT   human chromosomes
RT   transcription
RT   transcription factors

GENERAL ATOMIC FUEL FABRICATIO [5; 5]
BT1   fuel fabrication plants
BT2   nuclear facilities

→ **GENERAL CIRCULATION MODELS** [2; 2] *Jul 91*
BT1   mathematical models
RT   atmospheric circulation
RT   fluid mechanics
RT   meteorology
RT   three-dimensional calculations

general law
(Prior to December 1990, this was a valid descriptor.)
USE   laws

general quantum field theory
USE   axiomatic field theory

GENERAL RELATIVITY THEORY [6,883; 7,352]
UF   *einstein gravitation theory*
BT1   field theories
RT   cosmological constant
RT   cosmological models
RT   einstein effect
RT   einstein field equations
RT   einstein-maxwell equations
RT   energy-momentum tensor
RT   equivalence principle
RT   field equations
RT   gravitation
RT   gravitational fields
RT   gravitational lenses
RT   gravitational radiation
RT   kaluza-klein theory
RT   mach principle
RT   quantum gravity
RT   regge calculus
RT   schwarzschild metric

generating capacity
USE   capacity

GENERATOR-COORDINATE METHOD [741; 741]
RT   boson expansion
RT   nuclear structure
RT   pairing interactions
RT   quantum mechanics

generators (aerosol)
USE   aerosol generators

generators (electric)
USE   electric generators

generators (pulse)
USE   pulse generators

generators (radioisotope)
USE   radioisotope generators

generators (steam)
USE   steam generators

generators (vapor)
USE   vapor generators

GENES [1,700; 2,019]
UF   *cistrons*
UF   *gene loci*
NT1   lethal genes
NT1   oncogenes
RT   chromosomes
RT   codons
RT   dna polymerases
RT   gene mutations
RT   gene operons
RT   gene recombination
RT   gene regulation
RT   genetic effects
RT   genetic engineering
RT   genetic mapping
RT   genotype
RT   human chromosomes
RT   plasmids
RT   rflps
RT   transcription
RT   transposons

GENETIC CONTROL [163; 163]
BT1   pest control
RT   chromosomal aberrations
RT   insects
RT   mutagenesis
RT   mutations
RT   sterility

GENETIC EFFECTS [631; 5,534]
BT1   biological effects
NT1   genetic radiation effects
RT   chromosomes
RT   congenital malformations
RT   genes
RT   genetics
RT   gonads
RT   human chromosomes
RT   mosaicism
RT   mutations
RT   sister chromatid exchanges
RT   teratogens

GENETIC ENGINEERING [119; 119] *Dec 84*
BT1   biotechnology
RT   cell differentiation
RT   dna
RT   gene mutations
RT   gene regulation
RT   genes
RT   genetic radiation effects
RT   molecular biology
RT   transposons

GENETIC MAPPING [428; 428] *Dec 79*
(The graphical representation of the linear arrangement of genes on a chromosome.)
RT   chromosomes
RT   genes
RT   human chromosomes
RT   rflps

GENETIC RADIATION EFFECTS [5,033; 5,033]
BT1   biological radiation effects
BT2   biological effects
BT2   radiation effects
BT1   genetic effects
BT2   biological effects
RT   chromosome losses
RT   delayed radiation effects
RT   genetic engineering
RT   genetically significant dose
RT   sister chromatid exchanges

GENETIC VARIABILITY [627; 630]
- UF variability (genetic)
- BT1 biological variability
- NT1 rflps
- RT gene recombination
- RT transposons

GENETICALLY SIGNIFICANT DOSE [311; 311]
- UF gsd
- BT1 radiation doses
- RT genetic radiation effects
- RT populations
- RT radiation hazards

GENETICS [951; 1,064]
- UF heredity
- BT1 biology
- RT biological evolution
- RT cell constituents
- RT cytology
- RT genetic effects
- RT hereditary diseases
- RT hybridization
- RT nucleic acids
- RT plasmids

genitals (female)
- USE female genitals

genitals (male)
- USE male genitals

GENKAI-1 REACTOR [42; 42]
(Genkai, Saga, Japan)
- UF kyushu-1 reactor
- BT1 pwr type reactors
- BT2 enriched uranium reactors
- BT3 reactors
- BT2 power reactors
- BT3 reactors
- BT2 thermal reactors
- BT3 reactors
- BT2 water cooled reactors
- BT3 reactors
- BT2 water moderated reactors
- BT3 reactors

GENKAI-2 REACTOR [21; 21] Sep 79
(Genkai, Saga, Japan)
- UF kyushu-2 reactor
- BT1 pwr type reactors
- BT2 enriched uranium reactors
- BT3 reactors
- BT2 power reactors
- BT3 reactors
- BT2 thermal reactors
- BT3 reactors
- BT2 water cooled reactors
- BT3 reactors
- BT2 water moderated reactors
- BT3 reactors

GENKAI-3 REACTOR [9; 9] Jun 85
- UF+ kyushu-3 reactor
- BT1 pwr type reactors
- BT2 enriched uranium reactors
- BT3 reactors
- BT2 power reactors
- BT3 reactors
- BT2 thermal reactors
- BT3 reactors
- BT2 water cooled reactors
- BT3 reactors
- BT2 water moderated reactors
- BT3 reactors

GENKAI-4 REACTOR [9; 9] Jun 85
- UF kyushu-4 reactor
- BT1 pwr type reactors
- BT2 enriched uranium reactors
- BT3 reactors
- BT2 power reactors
- BT3 reactors

- BT2 thermal reactors
- BT3 reactors
- BT2 water cooled reactors
- BT3 reactors
- BT2 water moderated reactors
- BT3 reactors

GENOME MUTATIONS [154; 154]
- BT1 mutations
- RT aneuploidy
- RT karyotype
- RT non-disjunction
- RT ploidy
- RT polyploidy

GENOTYPE [415; 415]
- RT genes
- RT mutagenesis
- RT ontogenesis
- RT phenotype

GENTILLY REACTOR [99; 99]
(Nicolet, Quebec, Canada)
- UF gentilly-1 reactor
- BT1 candu type reactors
- BT2 heavy water moderated reactors
- BT3 reactors
- BT2 pressure tube reactors
- BT3 power reactors
- BT4 reactors
- BT2 thermal reactors
- BT3 reactors
- BT1 hwlwr type reactors
- BT2 heavy water moderated reactors
- BT3 reactors
- BT2 water cooled reactors
- BT3 reactors
- BT1 natural uranium reactors
- BT2 reactors

gentilly-1 reactor
- USE gentilly reactor

GENTILLY-2 REACTOR [60; 60]
(Nicolet, Quebec, Canada)
- BT1 candu type reactors
- BT2 heavy water moderated reactors
- BT3 reactors
- BT2 pressure tube reactors
- BT3 power reactors
- BT4 reactors
- BT2 thermal reactors
- BT3 reactors
- BT1 natural uranium reactors
- BT2 reactors
- BT1 phwr type reactors
- BT2 heavy water cooled reactors
- BT3 reactors
- BT2 heavy water moderated reactors
- BT3 reactors

GEOBOTANY [17; 17]
- BT1 botany
- BT2 biology
- RT biogeochemistry
- RT biological evolution

GEOCHEMICAL SURVEYS [1,564; 1,564]
- BT1 geologic surveys
- RT exploration
- RT geochemistry
- RT geology
- RT prospecting

GEOCHEMISTRY [4,048; 4,209]
- NT1 biogeochemistry
- RT geochemical surveys
- RT geology
- RT natural occurrence
- RT organic matter

geochronology
- USE age estimation

GEOCORONA [29; 29]
- RT earth atmosphere
- RT interplanetary space
- RT solar wind

GEODESICS [1,056; 1,056]
(Lines along which the distance between two points reaches an extremum.)
- RT mathematical space

GEODESY [219; 219]
- RT mathematics

§§ ## GEOGRAPHICAL VARIATIONS [330; 330] Jul 77
- BT1 variations

GEOGRAPHY [186; 186]
- RT earth planet
- RT oceanography

geoisotherms
- USE isotherms

GEOLOGIC DEPOSITS [7,313; 11,387]
- UF deposits (geological)
- NT1 alluvial deposits
- NT1 coal deposits
- NT2 coal seams
- NT1 moraines
- NT1 natural gas deposits
- NT1 petroleum deposits
- NT1 placers
- NT1 salt deposits
- NT1 thorium deposits
- NT1 uranium deposits
- NT2 blizzard deposit
- NT2 jabiluka deposit
- NT2 koongarra deposit
- NT2 nabarlek deposit
- NT2 ranger deposit
- NT2 ranstad deposit
- NT2 roxby downs deposit
- NT2 south alligator deposit
- NT2 yeelirrie deposit
- RT availability
- RT ores
- RT sediments
- RT underground storage

GEOLOGIC FAULTS [591; 591]
(Fractures in rock along which the adjacent rock surfaces are differentially displaced.)
- UF faults (geologic)
- UF rift zones
- BT1 geologic fractures
- BT2 geologic structures
- RT earthquakes
- RT geologic fissures
- RT geology
- RT geomorphology
- RT seismology

GEOLOGIC FISSURES [57; 57] Feb 76
- BT1 geologic structures
- RT caves
- RT cracks
- RT geologic faults
- RT geologic fractures

GEOLOGIC FORMATIONS [715; 725] Feb 81
- NT1 chattanooga formation
- NT1 green river formation
- NT1 uinta formation
- NT1 wasatch formation
- RT geologic structures
- RT reservoir pressure

GEOLOGIC FRACTURES [558; 846] Dec 85
(Breaks in rock, whether or not there is displacement, due to mechanical failure by stress.)
- BT1 geologic structures

```
NT1     geologic faults
RT      cracks
RT      fractures
RT      geologic fissures
```

GEOLOGIC HISTORY [367; 367]
Dec 85
```
RT      geologic models
RT      geologic structures
RT      geology
```

GEOLOGIC MODELS [260; 260]
Dec 85
```
RT      geologic history
RT      geologic structures
```

GEOLOGIC STRATA [400; 400] Dec 75
```
BT1     geologic structures
RT      coal seams
RT      stratification
RT      stratigraphy
```

GEOLOGIC STRUCTURES
[1,294; 2,720] Nov 75
```
UF        basins (sedimentary)
UF        sedimentary basins
UF+       calderas
NT1     geologic fissures
NT1     geologic fractures
  NT2     geologic faults
NT1     geologic strata
RT      geologic formations
RT      geologic history
RT      geologic models
RT      seismic surveys
RT      seismology
RT      water influx
```

GEOLOGIC SURVEYS [942; 4,427]
Nov 75
```
NT1     geochemical surveys
NT1     geophysical surveys
  NT2     electrical surveys
  NT3       electromagnetic surveys
    NT4       magnetotelluric surveys
  NT2     magnetic surveys
NT1     radiometric surveys
NT1     seismic surveys
RT      exploration
RT      prospecting
RT      site surveys
```

GEOLOGY [4,630; 4,826]
```
NT1     geomorphology
RT      earth crust
RT      earth planet
RT      geochemical surveys
RT      geochemistry
RT      geologic faults
RT      geologic history
RT      geophysical surveys
RT      geophysics
RT      geothermal energy
RT      metamorphism
RT      mohole project
RT      regional analysis
RT      rock mechanics
RT      stratigraphy
RT      volcanoes
```

GEOMAGNETIC CONJUGACY
[111; 111]
```
UF        conjugate points
RT      geomagnetic field
```

GEOMAGNETIC COORDINATES
[58; 58]
```
BT1     coordinates
RT      geomagnetic field
```

geomagnetic cut-off rigidity
```
  USE     threshold rigidity
```

GEOMAGNETIC EQUATOR [293; 293]
```
RT      equator
RT      geomagnetic field
```

GEOMAGNETIC FIELD [2,817; 2,817]
```
BT1     magnetic fields
RT      earth magnetosphere
RT      geomagnetic conjugacy
RT      geomagnetic coordinates
RT      geomagnetic equator
RT      geophysics
RT      inclination
RT      international magnetospheric s
RT      magnetosheath
RT      magnetotail
RT      threshold rigidity
```

geomagnetic storms
```
  USE     magnetic storms
```

GEOMETRIC BUCKLING [42; 42]
(A form of neutron density distribution in reactors. For buckling of materials, see DEFORMATION or FAILURES.)
```
BT1     buckling
```

GEOMETRICAL ABERRATIONS
[225; 225]
```
RT      beam optics
```

GEOMETRY [4,925; 5,704]
```
BT1     mathematics
NT1     differential geometry
RT      configuration
RT      cusped geometries
RT      invariant imbedding
RT      spheres
RT      spheroids
```

GEOMORPHOLOGY [232; 232] Sep 80
```
BT1     geology
RT      earth crust
RT      geologic faults
RT      geophysics
RT      regional analysis
RT      sea bed
RT      stratigraphy
```

GEOPHYSICAL SURVEYS [683; 1,503]
Mar 77
```
UF+       gravity surveys
BT1     geologic surveys
NT1     electrical surveys
  NT2     electromagnetic surveys
    NT3       magnetotelluric surveys
NT1     magnetic surveys
RT      exploration
RT      geology
RT      geophysics
RT      prospecting
```

GEOPHYSICS [811; 811]
```
RT      earth planet
RT      geology
RT      geomagnetic field
RT      geomorphology
RT      geophysical surveys
RT      international geophysical year
```

GEORGIA [177; 177]
```
BT1     usa
  BT2     developed countries
  BT2     north america
```

georgia tech. research reactor
```
  USE     gtrr reactor
```

GEOS SATELLITES [135; 135]
```
BT1     satellites
```

geothermal areas
```
  USE     geothermal fields
```

GEOTHERMAL ENERGY [442; 442]
```
UF+       geothermal resources
BT1     energy
BT1     renewable energy sources
  BT2     energy sources
RT      earth crust
RT      geology
RT      geothermal fields
RT      geothermal power plants
RT      thermal springs
RT      volcanoes
```

GEOTHERMAL FIELDS [2; 2] Dec 90
```
UF        geothermal areas
UF        geothermal regions
RT      geothermal energy
RT      thermal springs
```

GEOTHERMAL POWER PLANTS
[60; 60]
```
BT1     thermal power plants
  BT2     power plants
RT      geothermal energy
```

geothermal regions
```
  USE     geothermal fields
```

geothermal resources
```
  USE     geothermal energy
  AND     resources
```

geothermal springs
```
  USE     thermal springs
```

GERANIOL [4; 4]
```
BT1     alcohols
  BT2     hydroxy compounds
    BT3       organic compounds
BT1     terpenes
  BT2     organic compounds
```

GERBILS [52; 52]
```
BT1     rodents
  BT2     mammals
    BT3       vertebrates
      BT4       animals
```

GERJUOY-STEIN THEORY [1; 1]
```
RT      excitation functions
```

GERM CELLS [318; 2,167]
```
NT1     gametes
  NT2     ova
  NT2     pollen
  NT2     spermatozoa
NT1     oocytes
NT1     oogonia
NT1     spermatocytes
NT1     spermatogonia
RT      gametogenesis
RT      gonads
```

GERM-FREE ANIMALS [57; 57]
```
UF        gnothobionts
BT1     animals
RT      antibody formation
RT      bacteria
```

german (mainz) triga-mk-2 reac
```
  USE     triga-2-mainz reactor
```

german democratic republic
(Prior to May 1991, this was a valid descriptor.)
```
  USE     federal republic of germany
```

german dr organizations
(Prior to May 1991, this was a valid descriptor.)
```
  USE     german fr organizations
```

german federal republic
  USE   federal republic of germany

GERMAN FR ORGANIZATIONS
[695; 2,213]
  UF   *german dr organizations*
  BT1 national organizations
  NT1 bundesamt fuer strahlenschutz
  NT1 ges fuer reaktorsicherheit
  NT1 ipp garching
  NT1 kernforschungsanlage juelich
  NT1 kernforschungszentrum karlsruh
  NT1 reaktorsicherheitskommission
  NT1 strahlenschutzkommission
  NT1 wak
  NT1 zfi leipzig
  NT1 zfk rossendorf
  RT   federal republic of germany

german measles
  USE   measles

GERMAN SILVER [5; 5]
  UF   *nickel silver*
  UF   *white copper*
  BT1 copper base alloys
  BT2 copper alloys
  BT3 alloys
  BT1 nickel alloys
  BT2 alloys
  BT1 zinc alloys
  BT2 alloys

GERMANATES [318; 479]
(Specific compounds should be indexed by coordination of a descriptor of the form (CATION) COMPOUNDS and the above anion descriptor with the exception of the one NT below.)
  BT1 germanium compounds
  BT1 oxygen compounds
  NT1 bismuth germanates
  RT   germanium oxides

germanes
  USE   germanium hydrides

GERMANIDES [10; 10] *Jul 89*
  BT1 germanium compounds

GERMANIUM [3,160; 3,160]
  BT1 metals
  BT2 elements

GERMANIUM ADDITIONS [211; 211]
(Alloys containing not more than 1% Ge are listed here.)
  RT   germanium alloys
  RT   germanium compounds

GERMANIUM ALLOYS [1,627; 1,681]
(Alloys containing more than 1% Ge.)
  BT1 alloys
  NT1 germanium base alloys
  RT   germanium additions

GERMANIUM ARSENIDES [40; 40]
Feb 78
  BT1 arsenides
  BT2 arsenic compounds
  BT2 pnictides
  BT1 germanium compounds

GERMANIUM BASE ALLOYS [48; 48]
  BT1 germanium alloys
  BT2 alloys

→ **GERMANIUM BORIDES** [0; 0] *Sep 91*
  BT1 borides
  BT2 boron compounds
  BT1 germanium compounds

GERMANIUM BROMIDES [9; 9]
  BT1 bromides
  BT2 bromine compounds
  BT3 halogen compounds
  BT2 halides
  BT3 halogen compounds
  BT1 germanium compounds

→ **GERMANIUM CARBIDES** [0; 0] *Sep 91*
  BT1 carbides
  BT2 carbon compounds
  BT1 germanium compounds

GERMANIUM CHLORIDES [46; 46]
  BT1 chlorides
  BT2 chlorine compounds
  BT3 halogen compounds
  BT2 halides
  BT3 halogen compounds
  BT1 germanium compounds

GERMANIUM COMPLEXES [53; 53]
  BT1 complexes

GERMANIUM COMPOUNDS
[528; 1,964]
  NT1 germanates
    NT2 bismuth germanates
  NT1 germanides
  NT1 germanium arsenides
  NT1 germanium borides
  NT1 germanium bromides
  NT1 germanium carbides
  NT1 germanium chlorides
  NT1 germanium fluorides
  NT1 germanium hydrides
  NT1 germanium hydroxides
  NT1 germanium iodides
  NT1 germanium nitrides
  NT1 germanium oxides
  NT1 germanium phosphates
  NT1 germanium phosphides
  NT1 germanium selenides
  NT1 germanium silicates
  NT1 germanium silicides
  NT1 germanium sulfides
  NT1 germanium tellurides
  RT   germanium additions

GERMANIUM DIODES [60; 60]
  BT1 semiconductor diodes
  BT2 semiconductor devices

GERMANIUM FLUORIDES [19; 19]
  BT1 fluorides
  BT2 fluorine compounds
  BT3 halogen compounds
  BT2 halides
  BT3 halogen compounds
  BT1 germanium compounds

GERMANIUM HYDRIDES [75; 75]
  UF   *germanes*
  BT1 germanium compounds
  BT1 hydrides
  BT2 hydrogen compounds

GERMANIUM HYDROXIDES [3; 3]
Jul 78
  BT1 germanium compounds
  BT1 hydroxides
  BT2 hydrogen compounds
  BT2 oxygen compounds

GERMANIUM IODIDES [34; 34]
  BT1 germanium compounds
  BT1 iodides
  BT2 halides
  BT3 halogen compounds
  BT2 iodine compounds
  BT3 halogen compounds

GERMANIUM IONS [179; 179]
  BT1 ions
  BT2 charged particles

GERMANIUM ISOTOPES [165; 1,443]
  NT1 germanium 61
  NT1 germanium 64
  NT1 germanium 65
  NT1 germanium 66
  NT1 germanium 67
  NT1 germanium 68
  NT1 germanium 69
  NT1 germanium 70
  NT1 germanium 71
  NT1 germanium 72
  NT1 germanium 73
  NT1 germanium 74
  NT1 germanium 75
  NT1 germanium 76
  NT1 germanium 77
  NT1 germanium 78
  NT1 germanium 79
  NT1 germanium 80
  NT1 germanium 81
  NT1 germanium 82
  NT1 germanium 83
  NT1 germanium 84
  NT1 germanium 85

GERMANIUM NITRIDES [5; 5] *Apr 79*
  BT1 germanium compounds
  BT1 nitrides
  BT2 nitrogen compounds
  BT2 pnictides

GERMANIUM OXIDES [368; 368]
  BT1 germanium compounds
  BT1 oxides
  BT2 chalcogenides
  BT2 oxygen compounds
  RT   germanates

→ **GERMANIUM PHOSPHATES** [0; 0]
Sep 91
  BT1 germanium compounds
  BT1 phosphates
  BT2 oxygen compounds
  BT2 phosphorus compounds

GERMANIUM PHOSPHIDES [32; 32]
Jul 78
  BT1 germanium compounds
  BT1 phosphides
  BT2 phosphorus compounds
  BT2 pnictides

GERMANIUM SELENIDES [87; 87]
Oct 77
  BT1 germanium compounds
  BT1 selenides
  BT2 chalcogenides
  BT2 selenium compounds

GERMANIUM SILICATES [7; 7]
  BT1 germanium compounds
  BT1 silicates
  BT2 oxygen compounds
  BT2 silicon compounds

GERMANIUM SILICIDES [4; 4] *Sep 90*
  BT1 germanium compounds
  BT1 silicides
  BT2 silicon compounds

GERMANIUM SULFIDES [76; 76]
  BT1 germanium compounds
  BT1 sulfides
  BT2 chalcogenides
  BT2 sulfur compounds

GERMANIUM TELLURIDES [225; 225]
Oct 77
  BT1 germanium compounds
  BT1 tellurides
  BT2 chalcogenides
  BT2 tellurium compounds

GERMANIUM 61 [8; 8] *Jan 78*
- BT1 beta-plus decay radioisotopes
- BT2 beta decay radioisotopes
- BT3 radioisotopes
- BT4 isotopes
- BT1 even-odd nuclei
- BT2 nuclei
- BT1 germanium isotopes
- BT1 intermediate mass nuclei
- BT2 nuclei
- BT1 millisec living radioisotopes
- BT2 radioisotopes
- BT3 isotopes

GERMANIUM 64 [15; 15]
- BT1 beta-plus decay radioisotopes
- BT2 beta decay radioisotopes
- BT3 radioisotopes
- BT4 isotopes
- BT1 electron capture radioisotopes
- BT2 beta decay radioisotopes
- BT3 radioisotopes
- BT4 isotopes
- BT1 even-even nuclei
- BT2 nuclei
- BT1 germanium isotopes
- BT1 intermediate mass nuclei
- BT2 nuclei
- BT1 minutes living radioisotopes
- BT2 radioisotopes
- BT3 isotopes

GERMANIUM 65 [11; 11]
- BT1 beta-plus decay radioisotopes
- BT2 beta decay radioisotopes
- BT3 radioisotopes
- BT4 isotopes
- BT1 electron capture radioisotopes
- BT2 beta decay radioisotopes
- BT3 radioisotopes
- BT4 isotopes
- BT1 even-odd nuclei
- BT2 nuclei
- BT1 germanium isotopes
- BT1 intermediate mass nuclei
- BT2 nuclei
- BT1 seconds living radioisotopes
- BT2 radioisotopes
- BT3 isotopes

GERMANIUM 66 [29; 29]
- BT1 beta-plus decay radioisotopes
- BT2 beta decay radioisotopes
- BT3 radioisotopes
- BT4 isotopes
- BT1 electron capture radioisotopes
- BT2 beta decay radioisotopes
- BT3 radioisotopes
- BT4 isotopes
- BT1 even-even nuclei
- BT2 nuclei
- BT1 germanium isotopes
- BT1 hours living radioisotopes
- BT2 radioisotopes
- BT3 isotopes
- BT1 intermediate mass nuclei
- BT2 nuclei

GERMANIUM 67 [39; 39]
- BT1 beta-plus decay radioisotopes
- BT2 beta decay radioisotopes
- BT3 radioisotopes
- BT4 isotopes
- BT1 electron capture radioisotopes
- BT2 beta decay radioisotopes
- BT3 radioisotopes
- BT4 isotopes
- BT1 even-odd nuclei
- BT2 nuclei
- BT1 germanium isotopes
- BT1 intermediate mass nuclei
- BT2 nuclei
- BT1 minutes living radioisotopes
- BT2 radioisotopes
- BT3 isotopes

GERMANIUM 68 [185; 185]
- BT1 days living radioisotopes
- BT2 radioisotopes
- BT3 isotopes
- BT1 electron capture radioisotopes
- BT2 beta decay radioisotopes
- BT3 radioisotopes
- BT4 isotopes
- BT1 even-even nuclei
- BT2 nuclei
- BT1 germanium isotopes
- BT1 intermediate mass nuclei
- BT2 nuclei
- RT radioisotope generators

GERMANIUM 69 [101; 101]
- BT1 beta-plus decay radioisotopes
- BT2 beta decay radioisotopes
- BT3 radioisotopes
- BT4 isotopes
- BT1 days living radioisotopes
- BT2 radioisotopes
- BT3 isotopes
- BT1 electron capture radioisotopes
- BT2 beta decay radioisotopes
- BT3 radioisotopes
- BT4 isotopes
- BT1 even-odd nuclei
- BT2 nuclei
- BT1 germanium isotopes
- BT1 intermediate mass nuclei
- BT2 nuclei

GERMANIUM 70 [175; 175]
- BT1 even-even nuclei
- BT2 nuclei
- BT1 germanium isotopes
- BT1 intermediate mass nuclei
- BT2 nuclei
- BT1 stable isotopes
- BT2 isotopes

GERMANIUM 70 TARGET [161; 161]
- BT1 targets

GERMANIUM 71 [179; 179]
- BT1 days living radioisotopes
- BT2 radioisotopes
- BT3 isotopes
- BT1 electron capture radioisotopes
- BT2 beta decay radioisotopes
- BT3 radioisotopes
- BT4 isotopes
- BT1 even-odd nuclei
- BT2 nuclei
- BT1 germanium isotopes
- BT1 intermediate mass nuclei
- BT2 nuclei

GERMANIUM 71 TARGET [7; 7]
- BT1 targets

GERMANIUM 72 [193; 193]
- BT1 even-even nuclei
- BT2 nuclei
- BT1 germanium isotopes
- BT1 intermediate mass nuclei
- BT2 nuclei
- BT1 stable isotopes
- BT2 isotopes

GERMANIUM 72 TARGET [160; 160]
- BT1 targets

GERMANIUM 73 [100; 100]
- BT1 even-odd nuclei
- BT2 nuclei
- BT1 germanium isotopes
- BT1 intermediate mass nuclei
- BT2 nuclei
- BT1 internal conversion radioisoto
- BT2 radioisotopes
- BT3 isotopes
- BT1 isomeric transition isotopes
- BT2 radioisotopes
- BT3 isotopes
- BT1 millisec living radioisotopes
- BT2 radioisotopes
- BT3 isotopes
- BT1 stable isotopes
- BT2 isotopes

GERMANIUM 73 TARGET [46; 46]
- BT1 targets

GERMANIUM 74 [194; 194]
- BT1 even-even nuclei
- BT2 nuclei
- BT1 germanium isotopes
- BT1 intermediate mass nuclei
- BT2 nuclei
- BT1 stable isotopes
- BT2 isotopes
- RT germanium 74 beams

GERMANIUM 74 BEAMS [18; 18]
- BT1 ion beams
- BT2 beams
- RT germanium 74

GERMANIUM 74 REACTIONS [37; 37]
Nov 78
- BT1 heavy ion reactions
- BT2 nuclear reactions

GERMANIUM 74 TARGET [215; 215]
- BT1 targets

GERMANIUM 75 [65; 65]
- BT1 beta-minus decay radioisotopes
- BT2 beta decay radioisotopes
- BT3 radioisotopes
- BT4 isotopes
- BT1 even-odd nuclei
- BT2 nuclei
- BT1 germanium isotopes
- BT1 hours living radioisotopes
- BT2 radioisotopes
- BT3 isotopes
- BT1 intermediate mass nuclei
- BT2 nuclei
- BT1 internal conversion radioisoto
- BT2 radioisotopes
- BT3 isotopes
- BT1 isomeric transition isotopes
- BT2 radioisotopes
- BT3 isotopes
- BT1 seconds living radioisotopes
- BT2 radioisotopes
- BT3 isotopes

GERMANIUM 75 TARGET [4; 4]
- BT1 targets

GERMANIUM 76 [307; 307]
- BT1 even-even nuclei
- BT2 nuclei
- BT1 germanium isotopes
- BT1 intermediate mass nuclei
- BT2 nuclei
- BT1 stable isotopes
- BT2 isotopes
- RT germanium 76 beams

GERMANIUM 76 BEAMS [7; 7]
- BT1 ion beams
- BT2 beams
- RT germanium 76

GERMANIUM 76 REACTIONS [20; 20]
Mar 76
- BT1 heavy ion reactions
- BT2 nuclear reactions

GERMANIUM 76 TARGET [188; 188]
- BT1 targets

GERMANIUM 77 [46; 46]
- BT1 beta-minus decay radioisotopes
- BT2 beta decay radioisotopes
- BT3 radioisotopes
- BT4 isotopes

BT1 even-odd nuclei
BT2 nuclei
BT1 germanium isotopes
BT1 hours living radioisotopes
BT2 radioisotopes
BT3 isotopes
BT1 intermediate mass nuclei
BT2 nuclei
BT1 isomeric transition isotopes
BT2 radioisotopes
BT3 isotopes
BT1 seconds living radioisotopes
BT2 radioisotopes
BT3 isotopes

GERMANIUM 78 [18; 18]
BT1 beta-minus decay radioisotopes
BT2 beta decay radioisotopes
BT3 radioisotopes
BT4 isotopes
BT1 even-even nuclei
BT2 nuclei
BT1 germanium isotopes
BT1 hours living radioisotopes
BT2 radioisotopes
BT3 isotopes
BT1 intermediate mass nuclei
BT2 nuclei

GERMANIUM 79 [8; 8]
BT1 beta-minus decay radioisotopes
BT2 beta decay radioisotopes
BT3 radioisotopes
BT4 isotopes
BT1 even-odd nuclei
BT2 nuclei
BT1 germanium isotopes
BT1 intermediate mass nuclei
BT2 nuclei
BT1 seconds living radioisotopes
BT2 radioisotopes
BT3 isotopes

GERMANIUM 80 [13; 13]
BT1 beta-minus decay radioisotopes
BT2 beta decay radioisotopes
BT3 radioisotopes
BT4 isotopes
BT1 even-even nuclei
BT2 nuclei
BT1 germanium isotopes
BT1 intermediate mass nuclei
BT2 nuclei
BT1 seconds living radioisotopes
BT2 radioisotopes
BT3 isotopes

GERMANIUM 81 [10; 10]
BT1 beta-minus decay radioisotopes
BT2 beta decay radioisotopes
BT3 radioisotopes
BT4 isotopes
BT1 even-odd nuclei
BT2 nuclei
BT1 germanium isotopes
BT1 intermediate mass nuclei
BT2 nuclei
BT1 seconds living radioisotopes
BT2 radioisotopes
BT3 isotopes

GERMANIUM 82 [13; 13]
BT1 beta-minus decay radioisotopes
BT2 beta decay radioisotopes
BT3 radioisotopes
BT4 isotopes
BT1 even-even nuclei
BT2 nuclei
BT1 germanium isotopes
BT1 intermediate mass nuclei
BT2 nuclei
BT1 seconds living radioisotopes
BT2 radioisotopes
BT3 isotopes

GERMANIUM 83 [10; 10]
BT1 beta-minus decay radioisotopes
BT2 beta decay radioisotopes
BT3 radioisotopes
BT4 isotopes
BT1 even-odd nuclei
BT2 nuclei
BT1 germanium isotopes
BT1 intermediate mass nuclei
BT2 nuclei
BT1 seconds living radioisotopes
BT2 radioisotopes
BT3 isotopes

GERMANIUM 84 [4; 4]
BT1 beta-minus decay radioisotopes
BT2 beta decay radioisotopes
BT3 radioisotopes
BT4 isotopes
BT1 even-even nuclei
BT2 nuclei
BT1 germanium isotopes
BT1 intermediate mass nuclei
BT2 nuclei
BT1 seconds living radioisotopes
BT2 radioisotopes
BT3 isotopes

→ **GERMANIUM 85** [2; 2] *May 91*
BT1 beta-minus decay radioisotopes
BT2 beta decay radioisotopes
BT3 radioisotopes
BT4 isotopes
BT1 even-odd nuclei
BT2 nuclei
BT1 germanium isotopes
BT1 intermediate mass nuclei
BT2 nuclei
BT1 millisec living radioisotopes
BT2 radioisotopes
BT3 isotopes

GERMANIUM 86 TARGET [3; 3]
Jul 80
BT1 targets

germany (democratic republic)
USE federal republic of germany

germany, federal republic of
USE federal republic of germany

GERMINATION [636; 636]
RT coleoptile
RT seedlings
RT seeds

germs (microorganisms)
USE microorganisms

gerontine
USE spermine

GES FUER REAKTORSICHERHEIT
[60; 60] *Dec 75*
(A section of the Technical Inspection Associations of the German Federal Republic)
UF *grs*
UF *institute for reactor safety*
BT1 german fr organizations
BT2 national organizations
RT inspection
RT reactor licensing
RT reactor safety
RT safety standards

GETR REACTOR [17; 17]
(General Electric Company, Vallecitos Nuclear Center, Pleasanton, California, USA)
UF *gen. electric test reactor*
BT1 enriched uranium reactors
BT2 reactors
BT1 isotope production reactors
BT2 irradiation reactors
BT3 reactors
BT1 tank type reactors
BT2 reactors
BT1 test reactors
BT2 research and test reactors
BT3 reactors
BT2 test facilities
BT1 thermal reactors
BT2 reactors
BT1 water cooled reactors
BT2 reactors
BT1 water moderated reactors
BT2 reactors

GETTERING [491; 491]
RT adsorption
RT electron tubes
RT getters
RT high vacuum

GETTERS [514; 514]
(Materials used for the purification of vacuum atmosphers; see also the specific materials.)
RT electron tubes
RT gettering
RT high vacuum
RT sputter-ion pumps
RT vacuum pumps

GEV RANGE [2,106; 34,573]
(From 10 exp 9 to 10 exp 12 ev.)
BT1 energy range
NT1 gev range 01-10
NT1 gev range 10-100
NT1 gev range 100-1000
RT shower counters

GEV RANGE 01-10 [14,877; 14,877]
BT1 gev range
BT2 energy range

GEV RANGE 10-100 [14,412; 14,412]
BT1 gev range
BT2 energy range

GEV RANGE 100-1000 [8,215; 8,215]
BT1 gev range
BT2 energy range

geysers
USE thermal springs

GHANA [29; 29]
BT1 africa
BT1 developing countries

GHZ RANGE [224; 3,230]
BT1 frequency range
NT1 ghz range 01-100
NT1 ghz range 100-1000
RT radioastronomy

GHZ RANGE 01-100 [2,791; 2,791]
UF *uhf (lower range)*
UF *ultrahigh frequency (low. r.)*
UF+ *decimeter wave radiat (1-3 dm)*
UF+ *shf radiation*
UF+ *super high freq radiation*
UF+ *uhf radiation (upper range)*
UF+ *uhf radiation (01-100 ghz)*
UF+ *ultrahigh fr rad (01-100 ghz)*
UF+ *ultrahigh freq rad (upper r.)*
BT1 ghz range
BT2 frequency range

GHZ RANGE 100-1000 [273; 273]
UF *uhf (upper range)*
UF *ultrahigh frequency (upp. r.)*
BT1 ghz range
BT2 frequency range

giant cells
  USE tumor cells

GIANT RESONANCE [5,136; 5,136]
  BT1 resonance
  RT   cross sections
  RT   giant resonance model
  RT   nuclear reactions
  RT   photonuclear reactions

GIANT RESONANCE MODEL
[191; 191]
  UF   *goldhaber-teller model*
  RT   cross sections
  RT   giant resonance
  RT   photonuclear reactions
  RT   resonance

GIANT STARS [947; 2,596]
  BT1 stars
  NT1 red giant stars
  NT1 supergiant stars

GIBBERELLIC ACID [144; 144]
  UF   *gibberellin a3*
  BT1 hydroxy acids
    BT2 carboxylic acids
      BT3 organic acids
        BT4 organic compounds
  BT1 lactones
    BT2 esters
      BT3 organic compounds
    BT2 heterocyclic compounds
      BT3 organic compounds
  RT   auxins

gibberellin a3
  USE gibberellic acid

gibbs formation free energy
  USE formation free enthalpy

gibbs free energy
  USE free enthalpy

GIBBSSAR STANDARD PLANT [4; 4]
  Oct 77
  (Gibbs and Hill reference PWR nuclear power plant.)
  BT1 nuclear power plants
    BT2 nuclear facilities
    BT2 thermal power plants
      BT3 power plants
  RT   westinghouse standard reactor

GIGAWATT POWER RANGE [0; 14]
  Apr 88
  BT1 power range
  NT1 power range 01-10 gw
  NT1 power range 10-100 gw
  NT1 power range 100-1000 gw

gigily oil
  USE sesame oil

GILLS [77; 77]
  BT1 respiratory system
  RT   fishes

gingelly oil
  USE sesame oil

gingily oil
  USE sesame oil

GINNA-1 REACTOR [170; 170]
  UF   *robert e. ginna-1 reactor*
  BT1 pwr type reactors
    BT2 enriched uranium reactors
      BT3 reactors
    BT2 power reactors
      BT3 reactors
    BT2 thermal reactors
      BT3 reactors
    BT2 water cooled reactors
      BT3 reactors
    BT2 water moderated reactors
      BT3 reactors

GINNA-2 REACTOR [24; 24]
  UF   *robert e. ginna-2 reactor*
  BT1 power reactors
  BT2 reactors

GINZBURG-LANDAU THEORY
[1,247; 1,247]
  UF   *maki parameter*
  RT   coherence length
  RT   penetration depth
  RT   superconductivity

GINZBURG-PITAEVSKII THEORY
[45; 45]
  UF   *landau-ginzburg-pitaevskii the*
  RT   superfluidity

gkn reactor (dodewaard)
  USE dodewaard reactor

gkn-1 reactor (neckar)
  USE neckar reactor

gkn-2 reaktor (neckar)
  USE neckar-2 reactor

GLACIERS [183; 183]
  RT   antarctic regions
  RT   arctic regions
  RT   hydrosphere
  RT   ice
  RT   snow
  RT   water

GLANDS [131; 26,957]
  UF+ *sebaceous glands*
  UF+ *sweat glands*
  BT1 organs
  BT2 body
  NT1 endocrine glands
    NT2 adrenal glands
    NT2 pancreas
    NT2 parathyroid glands
    NT2 pituitary gland
    NT2 thyroid
  NT1 liver
  NT1 mammary glands
  NT1 pineal gland
  NT1 prostate
  NT1 salivary glands
  RT   adenomas
  RT   excretion
  RT   secretion

GLASGOW SYNCHROTRON [0; 0]
  BT1 synchrotrons
    BT2 cyclic accelerators
      BT3 accelerators

glasgow utr-100 reactor
  USE srrc-utr-100 reactor

GLASS [8,083; 9,758]
  (A hard, amorphous, brittle substance made by fusing silicates, sometimes borates and phosphates, with basic oxides and then rapidly cooling.)
  NT1 borosilicate glass
    NT2 pyrex
  NT1 phosphate glass
    NT2 borophosphate glass
  RT   ceramics
  RT   colorimetric dosemeters
  RT   dielectric track detectors
  RT   fiberglass
  RT   metallic glasses
  RT   phase diagrams
  RT   phase transformations
  RT   silicon oxides
  RT   solids
  RT   vitrification
  RT   vycor

glass development laser facil.
(At University of Rochester.)
  USE gdl facility

glass dosemeters
  USE rpl dosemeters

GLASS SCINTILLATORS [141; 141]
  BT1 phosphors
  RT   luminescent dosemeters
  RT   solid scintillation detectors

glassy alloys
  USE metallic glasses

glassy metals
  USE metallic glasses

GLAUBER THEORY [1,902; 1,902]
  RT   fsc approximation
  RT   multiple scattering
  RT   scattering

GLAZES [44; 44]
  BT1 coatings
  RT   ceramics

GLEEP REACTOR [10; 10]
(UKAEA Atomic Energy Research Establishment, Harwell, United Kingdom)
  UF   *graphite low-energy expe. pile*
  BT1 air cooled reactors
    BT2 gas cooled reactors
      BT3 reactors
  BT1 graphite moderated reactors
    BT2 reactors
  BT1 materials testing reactors
    BT2 irradiation reactors
      BT3 reactors
  BT1 natural uranium reactors
    BT2 reactors
  BT1 research reactors
    BT2 research and test reactors
      BT3 reactors
  BT1 thermal reactors
    BT2 reactors
  BT1 training reactors
    BT2 research and test reactors
      BT3 reactors

glioblastomas
  USE gliomas

GLIOMAS [500; 500]
  UF   *glioblastomas*
  BT1 neoplasms
    BT2 diseases
  BT1 nervous system diseases
    BT2 diseases

GLOBAL ANALYSIS [642; 642]
(Studies mathematical manifolds with topology which is locally Euclidean but globally non-Euclidean.)
  BT1 mathematics
  RT   topology

GLOBAL ASPECTS [1,142; 1,142]
- UF+ *global risk*
- RT contamination
- RT earth atmosphere
- RT fallout
- RT pollution
- RT waste disposal

GLOBAL FALLOUT [473; 473]
- UF *world-wide fallout*
- BT1 fallout
- RT nuclear explosions
- RT stratosphere
- RT tropopause

global risk
- USE global aspects
- AND hazards

GLOBINS [66; 969]
(Prior to January 1983 the form GLOBIN was used.)
- BT1 proteins
- BT2 organic compounds
- NT1 hemoglobin
- NT2 carboxyhemoglobin
- NT2 methemoglobin
- NT1 myoglobin

GLOBULINS [330; 3,937]
- UF *c-reactive protein*
- BT1 proteins
- BT2 organic compounds
- NT1 angiotensin
- NT1 fibrinogen
- NT1 globulins-alpha
- NT2 ceruloplasmin
- NT2 haptoglobins
- NT1 globulins-beta
- NT2 transferrin
- NT1 globulins-gamma
- NT1 immunoglobulins
- NT1 lactoferrin
- NT1 myosin
- NT1 thyroglobulin

GLOBULINS-ALPHA [99; 187]
- BT1 globulins
- BT2 proteins
- BT3 organic compounds
- NT1 ceruloplasmin
- NT1 haptoglobins

GLOBULINS-BETA [109; 551]
- BT1 globulins
- BT2 proteins
- BT3 organic compounds
- NT1 transferrin

GLOBULINS-GAMMA [164; 164]
- BT1 globulins
- BT2 proteins
- BT3 organic compounds

GLOMERULI [281; 281]
- BT1 kidneys
- BT2 organs
- BT3 body
- RT capillaries
- RT renal clearance
- RT ultrafiltration

GLOSSINA [99; 99]
- UF *tsetse fly*
- BT1 flies
- BT2 insects
- BT3 arthropods
- BT4 invertebrates
- BT5 animals
- RT disease vectors
- RT trypanosoma

GLOVEBOXES [702; 702]
- BT1 laboratory equipment
- BT2 equipment
- RT containment
- RT exhaust systems
- RT gloves
- RT hot cells
- RT leaks
- RT radiation protection
- RT remote handling
- RT shielding

GLOVES [78; 78]
- BT1 protective clothing
- BT2 clothing
- RT gloveboxes
- RT radiation protection
- RT shielding
- RT skin
- RT skin absorption

GLOW CURVE [1,549; 1,549]
- RT luminescence

GLOW DISCHARGES [1,384; 1,384]
- BT1 electric discharges

GLUCAGON [216; 216]
- BT1 peptide hormones
- BT2 hormones
- BT1 polypeptides
- BT2 peptides
- BT3 proteins
- BT4 organic compounds
- RT glucose
- RT metabolism
- RT pancreas

GLUCOCORTICOIDS [196; 1,125]
- BT1 corticosteroids
- BT2 adrenal hormones
- BT3 hormones
- BT2 hydroxy compounds
- BT3 organic compounds
- BT2 ketones
- BT3 organic compounds
- BT2 pregnanes
- BT3 steroids
- BT4 organic compounds
- BT2 steroid hormones
- BT3 hormones
- NT1 corticosterone
- NT1 cortisone
- NT1 dexamethasone
- NT1 hydrocortisone
- NT1 prednisolone
- NT1 prednisone
- RT acth
- RT immunosuppression

GLUCONIC ACID [103; 103]
- UF *dextronic acid*
- UF *glyconic acid*
- UF *glykogenic acid*
- BT1 hydroxy acids
- BT2 carboxylic acids
- BT3 organic acids
- BT4 organic compounds
- RT monosaccharides

glucoproteins
- USE glycoproteins

GLUCOSAMINE [243; 243]
- BT1 hexosamines
- BT2 amines
- BT3 organic compounds
- BT2 hexoses
- BT3 monosaccharides
- BT4 saccharides
- BT5 carbohydrates
- BT6 organic compounds
- RT chitin

GLUCOSE [2,605; 2,605]
- BT1 aldehydes
- BT2 organic compounds
- BT1 hexoses
- BT2 monosaccharides
- BT3 saccharides
- BT4 carbohydrates
- BT5 organic compounds
- RT fluorodeoxyglucose
- RT glucagon
- RT insulin
- RT udpg

GLUCURONIC ACID [51; 51]
- BT1 aldehydes
- BT2 organic compounds
- BT1 hydroxy acids
- BT2 carboxylic acids
- BT3 organic acids
- BT4 organic compounds
- RT glucuronidase
- RT hyaluronic acid
- RT pectins

GLUCURONIDASE [60; 60]
- BT1 o-glycosyl hydrolases
- BT2 glycosyl hydrolases
- BT3 hydrolases
- BT4 enzymes
- BT5 organic compounds
- RT glucuronic acid

GLUEBALLS [1,017; 1,017] *Oct 83*
(Bound states of gluons.)
- UF *gluonium*
- RT color model
- RT gluon model
- RT gluons

GLUON CONDENSATION [18; 18] *Apr 89*
- RT gluons
- RT quantum operators
- RT vacuum states

GLUON MODEL [2,778; 2,778]
- UF *massive vector-meson model*
- BT1 particle models
- BT2 mathematical models
- RT glueballs
- RT gluons
- RT quantum chromodynamics
- RT vector mesons

GLUON-GLUON INTERACTIONS [109; 109] *Nov 88*
- BT1 particle interactions
- BT2 interactions
- RT gluons
- RT quantum chromodynamics

gluonium
- USE glueballs

GLUONS [5,455; 5,455] *Jan 79*
- BT1 bosons
- BT1 postulated particles
- BT2 elementary particles
- RT glueballs
- RT gluon condensation
- RT gluon model
- RT gluon-gluon interactions
- RT quantum chromodynamics
- RT quark matter
- RT quark-gluon interactions
- RT vector mesons

GLUTAMIC ACID [473; 513]
- UF *aminoglutaric acid-alpha*
- BT1 amino acids
- BT2 carboxylic acids
- BT3 organic acids
- BT4 organic compounds
- NT1 pyridoxylideneglutamate
- RT glutamine
- RT glutaric acid

GLUTAMINE [189; 189]
  BT1   amides
    BT2   organic nitrogen compounds
      BT3   organic compounds
  BT1   amino acids
    BT2   carboxylic acids
      BT3   organic acids
        BT4   organic compounds
  RT   glutamic acid

GLUTARIC ACID [70; 70]
  BT1   dicarboxylic acids
    BT2   carboxylic acids
      BT3   organic acids
        BT4   organic compounds
  RT   glutamic acid

GLUTATHIONE [554; 554]
  BT1   polypeptides
    BT2   peptides
      BT3   proteins
        BT4   organic compounds
  BT1   radioprotective substances
    BT2   drugs
    BT2   response modifying factors

GLUTIN [13; 13]
  BT1   scleroproteins
    BT2   proteins
      BT3   organic compounds

GLYCERIC ACID [17; 17]
  UF   dihydroxypropionic acid
  BT1   hydroxy acids
    BT2   carboxylic acids
      BT3   organic acids
        BT4   organic compounds

glycerin
  USE   glycerol

GLYCEROL [496; 496]
  UF   glycerin
  UF   1,2,3-propanetriol
  BT1   alcohols
    BT2   hydroxy compounds
      BT3   organic compounds
  RT   batyl alcohol
  RT   cephalins
  RT   lecithins
  RT   lugol
  RT   triglycerides

glyceryl trioleate
  USE   triolein

glycides
  USE   saccharides

GLYCINE [859; 859]
  UF   aminoacetic acid
  UF   glycocoll
  BT1   amino acids
    BT2   carboxylic acids
      BT3   organic acids
        BT4   organic compounds
  RT   glycylglycine
  RT   hippuric acid
  RT   sarcosine

GLYCINE HISPIDA [221; 221]
  UF   soybean plant
  BT1   leguminosae
    BT2   plants
  RT   forage
  RT   soybeans

glycocoll
  USE   glycine

GLYCOGEN [238; 238]
  BT1   polysaccharides
    BT2   saccharides
      BT3   carbohydrates
        BT4   organic compounds
  RT   liver

glycol monoalkyl ethers
  USE   cellosolves

GLYCOLIC ACID [131; 131]
  UF   hydroxyacetic acid
  BT1   hydroxy acids
    BT2   carboxylic acids
      BT3   organic acids
        BT4   organic compounds
  BT1   monocarboxylic acids
    BT2   carboxylic acids
      BT3   organic acids
        BT4   organic compounds
  RT   thionalide

GLYCOLIPIDS [64; 85]
  BT1   lipids
    BT2   organic compounds
  BT1   saccharides
    BT2   carbohydrates
      BT3   organic compounds
  NT1   cerebrosides

GLYCOLS [706; 782]
  UF   diols
  UF   ethylene glycol
  UF   1,2-ethanediol
  BT1   alcohols
    BT2   hydroxy compounds
      BT3   organic compounds
  NT1   benzopinacol
  NT1   carbitols
  NT1   cellosolves
  NT1   egta
  NT1   pinacol
  RT   dacron
  RT   mylar
  RT   polyethylene glycols

GLYCOLYSIS [130; 130]
  BT1   decomposition
    BT2   chemical reactions
  RT   carbohydrates
  RT   catabolism
  RT   enzymes
  RT   saccharides

glyconic acid
  USE   gluconic acid

GLYCOPROTEINS [1,055; 1,530]
  UF   glucoproteins
  BT1   proteins
    BT2   organic compounds
  BT1   saccharides
    BT2   carbohydrates
      BT3   organic compounds
  NT1   lactoferrin
  NT1   lh
  NT1   ovalbumin
  RT   post-translation modification

GLYCOSIDES [145; 641]
  BT1   carbohydrates
    BT2   organic compounds
  NT1   digitalis glycosides
    NT2   digitoxin
    NT2   digoxin
  NT1   hesperidin
  NT1   ouabain
  NT1   phlorizin
  NT1   saponins
  NT1   udpg
  RT   lignin
  RT   quercetin

GLYCOSURIA [5; 5]
  RT   saccharides

GLYCOSYL HYDROLASES [113; 648]
  BT1   hydrolases
    BT2   enzymes
      BT3   organic compounds
  NT1   o-glycosyl hydrolases
  NT2   amylase
  NT2   galactosidase
  NT2   glucuronidase
  NT2   lysozyme

GLYCOSYL TRANSFERASES [71; 71] *Jun 82*
  BT1   transferases
    BT2   enzymes
      BT3   organic compounds

GLYCYLGLYCINE [50; 50]
  BT1   amino acids
    BT2   carboxylic acids
      BT3   organic acids
        BT4   organic compounds
  RT   glycine
  RT   peptides

glykogenic acid
  USE   gluconic acid

GLYOXAL [51; 51]
  UF   oxalaldehyde
  UF   1,2-ethanedial
  BT1   aldehydes
    BT2   organic compounds

GLYOXYLIC ACID [27; 27]
  UF   oxoacetic acid
  BT1   aldehydes
    BT2   organic compounds
  BT1   carboxylic acids
    BT2   organic acids
      BT3   organic compounds

GNEISSES [183; 183] *Feb 84*
  BT1   metamorphic rocks
    BT2   rocks

GNOME EVENT [14; 14]
  BT1   plowshare project
  BT1   vela project

gnothobionts
  USE   germ-free animals

GOATS [289; 289]
  BT1   domestic animals
    BT2   animals
  BT1   ruminants
    BT2   mammals
      BT3   vertebrates
        BT4   animals

GODIVA REACTOR [40; 40]
  BT1   zero power reactors
    BT2   experimental reactors
      BT3   research and test reactors
        BT4   reactors

GOES SATELLITES [53; 53] *Mar 83*
  BT1   satellites

GOESGEN REACTOR [138; 138]
  (Daeniken, Soleure, Switzerland)
  UF   kernkraftwerk goesgen-daeniken
  BT1   pwr type reactors
    BT2   enriched uranium reactors
      BT3   reactors
    BT2   power reactors
      BT3   reactors
    BT2   thermal reactors
      BT3   reactors
    BT2   water cooled reactors

```
        BT3    reactors
        BT2    water moderated reactors
        BT3    reactors

GOETTINGEN SYNCHROCYCLOTRON
[0; 0]
        BT1    synchrocyclotrons
        BT2    cyclic accelerators
        BT3    accelerators


goiania radiological emergency
(Goiania, Goias, Brazil.)
        USE    brazil
        AND    radiation accidents


GOITER [424; 424]
        BT1    endocrine diseases
        BT2    diseases
        RT     hyperthyroidism
        RT     hypothyroidism
        RT     thyroid

GOLD [5,566; 5,566]
        BT1    transition elements
        BT2    metals
        BT3    elements

GOLD ADDITIONS [157; 157]
(Alloys containing not more than 1% Au
are listed here.)
        RT     gold alloys
        RT     gold compounds

GOLD ALLOYS [897; 1,077]
(Alloys containing more than 1% Au.)
        BT1    alloys
        NT1    gold base alloys
        RT     gold additions

GOLD BASE ALLOYS [183; 183]
        BT1    gold alloys
        BT2    alloys

GOLD BROMIDES [7; 7]
        BT1    bromides
        BT2    bromine compounds
        BT3    halogen compounds
        BT2    halides
        BT3    halogen compounds
        BT1    gold compounds
        BT2    transition element compounds

GOLD CHLORIDES [34; 34]
        BT1    chlorides
        BT2    chlorine compounds
        BT3    halogen compounds
        BT2    halides
        BT3    halogen compounds
        BT1    gold compounds
        BT2    transition element compounds

GOLD COMPLEXES [107; 107]
        BT1    transition element complexes
        BT2    complexes

GOLD COMPOUNDS [161; 234]
        BT1    transition element compounds
        NT1    aurates
        NT1    gold bromides
        NT1    gold chlorides
        NT1    gold fluorides
        NT1    gold hydrides
        NT1    gold iodides
        NT1    gold oxides
        NT1    gold silicides
        NT1    gold tellurides
        RT     gold additions

GOLD FLUORIDES [5; 5]
        BT1    fluorides
        BT2    fluorine compounds
        BT3    halogen compounds
        BT2    halides
```
```
        BT3    halogen compounds
        BT1    gold compounds
        BT2    transition element compounds

GOLD HYDRIDES [9; 9] Nov 78
        BT1    gold compounds
        BT2    transition element compounds
        BT1    hydrides
        BT2    hydrogen compounds

GOLD IODIDES [13; 13]
        BT1    gold compounds
        BT2    transition element compounds
        BT1    iodides
        BT2    halides
        BT3    halogen compounds
        BT2    iodine compounds
        BT3    halogen compounds

GOLD IONS [328; 328]
        BT1    ions
        BT2    charged particles

GOLD ISOTOPES [216; 2,547]
        NT1    gold 173
        NT1    gold 174
        NT1    gold 175
        NT1    gold 176
        NT1    gold 177
        NT1    gold 178
        NT1    gold 179
        NT1    gold 180
        NT1    gold 181
        NT1    gold 182
        NT1    gold 183
        NT1    gold 184
        NT1    gold 185
        NT1    gold 186
        NT1    gold 187
        NT1    gold 188
        NT1    gold 189
        NT1    gold 190
        NT1    gold 191
        NT1    gold 192
        NT1    gold 193
        NT1    gold 194
        NT1    gold 195
        NT1    gold 196
        NT1    gold 197
        NT1    gold 198
        NT1    gold 199
        NT1    gold 200
        NT1    gold 201
        NT1    gold 202
        NT1    gold 203
        NT1    gold 204

GOLD ORES [244; 244]
        BT1    ores

GOLD OXIDES [6; 6]
        BT1    gold compounds
        BT2    transition element compounds
        BT1    oxides
        BT2    chalcogenides
        BT2    oxygen compounds
        RT     aurates

GOLD SILICIDES [11; 11] Jan 85
        BT1    gold compounds
        BT2    transition element compounds
        BT1    silicides
        BT2    silicon compounds

→ GOLD TELLURIDES [0; 0] Sep 91
        BT1    gold compounds
        BT2    transition element compounds
        BT1    tellurides
        BT2    chalcogenides
        BT2    tellurium compounds

GOLD 173 [3; 3] Sep 83
        BT1    alpha decay radioisotopes
        BT2    radioisotopes
        BT3    isotopes
```
```
        BT1    gold isotopes
        BT1    intermediate mass nuclei
        BT2    nuclei
        BT1    millisec living radioisotopes
        BT2    radioisotopes
        BT3    isotopes
        BT1    odd-even nuclei
        BT2    nuclei

GOLD 174 [2; 2] Sep 83
        BT1    alpha decay radioisotopes
        BT2    radioisotopes
        BT3    isotopes
        BT1    gold isotopes
        BT1    intermediate mass nuclei
        BT2    nuclei
        BT1    millisec living radioisotopes
        BT2    radioisotopes
        BT3    isotopes
        BT1    odd-odd nuclei
        BT2    nuclei

GOLD 175 [4; 4]
        BT1    alpha decay radioisotopes
        BT2    radioisotopes
        BT3    isotopes
        BT1    gold isotopes
        BT1    intermediate mass nuclei
        BT2    nuclei
        BT1    millisec living radioisotopes
        BT2    radioisotopes
        BT3    isotopes
        BT1    odd-even nuclei
        BT2    nuclei

GOLD 176 [5; 5]
        BT1    alpha decay radioisotopes
        BT2    radioisotopes
        BT3    isotopes
        BT1    gold isotopes
        BT1    intermediate mass nuclei
        BT2    nuclei
        BT1    odd-odd nuclei
        BT2    nuclei
        BT1    seconds living radioisotopes
        BT2    radioisotopes
        BT3    isotopes

GOLD 177 [7; 7]
        BT1    alpha decay radioisotopes
        BT2    radioisotopes
        BT3    isotopes
        BT1    gold isotopes
        BT1    intermediate mass nuclei
        BT2    nuclei
        BT1    odd-even nuclei
        BT2    nuclei
        BT1    seconds living radioisotopes
        BT2    radioisotopes
        BT3    isotopes

GOLD 178 [6; 6]
        BT1    alpha decay radioisotopes
        BT2    radioisotopes
        BT3    isotopes
        BT1    gold isotopes
        BT1    intermediate mass nuclei
        BT2    nuclei
        BT1    odd-odd nuclei
        BT2    nuclei
        BT1    seconds living radioisotopes
        BT2    radioisotopes
        BT3    isotopes

GOLD 179 [11; 11]
        BT1    alpha decay radioisotopes
        BT2    radioisotopes
        BT3    isotopes
        BT1    gold isotopes
        BT1    intermediate mass nuclei
        BT2    nuclei
        BT1    odd-even nuclei
        BT2    nuclei
        BT1    seconds living radioisotopes
        BT2    radioisotopes
        BT3    isotopes
```

GOLD 180 [2; 2]
  BT1   electron capture radioisotopes
    BT2   beta decay radioisotopes
      BT3   radioisotopes
        BT4   isotopes
  BT1   gold isotopes
  BT1   intermediate mass nuclei
    BT2   nuclei
  BT1   odd-odd nuclei
    BT2   nuclei
  BT1   seconds living radioisotopes
    BT2   radioisotopes
      BT3   isotopes

GOLD 181 [8; 8]
  BT1   alpha decay radioisotopes
    BT2   radioisotopes
      BT3   isotopes
  BT1   electron capture radioisotopes
    BT2   beta decay radioisotopes
      BT3   radioisotopes
        BT4   isotopes
  BT1   gold isotopes
  BT1   heavy nuclei
    BT2   nuclei
  BT1   odd-even nuclei
    BT2   nuclei
  BT1   seconds living radioisotopes
    BT2   radioisotopes
      BT3   isotopes

GOLD 182 [4; 4]
  BT1   beta-plus decay radioisotopes
    BT2   beta decay radioisotopes
      BT3   radioisotopes
        BT4   isotopes
  BT1   electron capture radioisotopes
    BT2   beta decay radioisotopes
      BT3   radioisotopes
        BT4   isotopes
  BT1   gold isotopes
  BT1   heavy nuclei
    BT2   nuclei
  BT1   odd-odd nuclei
    BT2   nuclei
  BT1   seconds living radioisotopes
    BT2   radioisotopes
      BT3   isotopes

GOLD 183 [11; 11]
  BT1   alpha decay radioisotopes
    BT2   radioisotopes
      BT3   isotopes
  BT1   electron capture radioisotopes
    BT2   beta decay radioisotopes
      BT3   radioisotopes
        BT4   isotopes
  BT1   gold isotopes
  BT1   heavy nuclei
    BT2   nuclei
  BT1   odd-even nuclei
    BT2   nuclei
  BT1   seconds living radioisotopes
    BT2   radioisotopes
      BT3   isotopes

GOLD 184 [11; 11]
  BT1   alpha decay radioisotopes
    BT2   radioisotopes
      BT3   isotopes
  BT1   beta-plus decay radioisotopes
    BT2   beta decay radioisotopes
      BT3   radioisotopes
        BT4   isotopes
  BT1   electron capture radioisotopes
    BT2   beta decay radioisotopes
      BT3   radioisotopes
        BT4   isotopes
  BT1   gold isotopes
  BT1   heavy nuclei
    BT2   nuclei
  BT1   odd-odd nuclei
    BT2   nuclei
  BT1   seconds living radioisotopes
    BT2   radioisotopes
      BT3   isotopes

GOLD 185 [49; 49]
  BT1   alpha decay radioisotopes
    BT2   radioisotopes
      BT3   isotopes
  BT1   beta-plus decay radioisotopes
    BT2   beta decay radioisotopes
      BT3   radioisotopes
        BT4   isotopes
  BT1   electron capture radioisotopes
    BT2   beta decay radioisotopes
      BT3   radioisotopes
        BT4   isotopes
  BT1   gold isotopes
  BT1   heavy nuclei
    BT2   nuclei
  BT1   minutes living radioisotopes
    BT2   radioisotopes
      BT3   isotopes
  BT1   odd-even nuclei
    BT2   nuclei

GOLD 186 [19; 19]
  BT1   beta-plus decay radioisotopes
    BT2   beta decay radioisotopes
      BT3   radioisotopes
        BT4   isotopes
  BT1   electron capture radioisotopes
    BT2   beta decay radioisotopes
      BT3   radioisotopes
        BT4   isotopes
  BT1   gold isotopes
  BT1   heavy nuclei
    BT2   nuclei
  BT1   minutes living radioisotopes
    BT2   radioisotopes
      BT3   isotopes
  BT1   odd-odd nuclei
    BT2   nuclei

GOLD 187 [59; 59]
  BT1   beta-plus decay radioisotopes
    BT2   beta decay radioisotopes
      BT3   radioisotopes
        BT4   isotopes
  BT1   electron capture radioisotopes
    BT2   beta decay radioisotopes
      BT3   radioisotopes
        BT4   isotopes
  BT1   gold isotopes
  BT1   heavy nuclei
    BT2   nuclei
  BT1   minutes living radioisotopes
    BT2   radioisotopes
      BT3   isotopes
  BT1   odd-even nuclei
    BT2   nuclei

GOLD 187 TARGET [5; 5] *Nov 78*
  BT1   targets

GOLD 188 [11; 11]
  BT1   beta-plus decay radioisotopes
    BT2   beta decay radioisotopes
      BT3   radioisotopes
        BT4   isotopes
  BT1   electron capture radioisotopes
    BT2   beta decay radioisotopes
      BT3   radioisotopes
        BT4   isotopes
  BT1   gold isotopes
  BT1   heavy nuclei
    BT2   nuclei
  BT1   minutes living radioisotopes
    BT2   radioisotopes
      BT3   isotopes
  BT1   odd-odd nuclei
    BT2   nuclei

GOLD 189 [40; 40]
  BT1   beta-plus decay radioisotopes
    BT2   beta decay radioisotopes
      BT3   radioisotopes
        BT4   isotopes
  BT1   electron capture radioisotopes
    BT2   beta decay radioisotopes
      BT3   radioisotopes
        BT4   isotopes
  BT1   gold isotopes
  BT1   heavy nuclei
    BT2   nuclei
  BT1   minutes living radioisotopes
    BT2   radioisotopes
      BT3   isotopes
  BT1   odd-even nuclei
    BT2   nuclei

GOLD 190 [20; 20]
  BT1   beta-plus decay radioisotopes
    BT2   beta decay radioisotopes
      BT3   radioisotopes
        BT4   isotopes
  BT1   electron capture radioisotopes
    BT2   beta decay radioisotopes
      BT3   radioisotopes
        BT4   isotopes
  BT1   gold isotopes
  BT1   heavy nuclei
    BT2   nuclei
  BT1   minutes living radioisotopes
    BT2   radioisotopes
      BT3   isotopes
  BT1   odd-odd nuclei
    BT2   nuclei

GOLD 191 [48; 48]
  BT1   electron capture radioisotopes
    BT2   beta decay radioisotopes
      BT3   radioisotopes
        BT4   isotopes
  BT1   gold isotopes
  BT1   heavy nuclei
    BT2   nuclei
  BT1   hours living radioisotopes
    BT2   radioisotopes
      BT3   isotopes
  BT1   internal conversion radioisoto
    BT2   radioisotopes
      BT3   isotopes
  BT1   isomeric transition isotopes
    BT2   radioisotopes
      BT3   isotopes
  BT1   millisec living radioisotopes
    BT2   radioisotopes
      BT3   isotopes
  BT1   odd-even nuclei
    BT2   nuclei

GOLD 192 [26; 26]
  BT1   beta-plus decay radioisotopes
    BT2   beta decay radioisotopes
      BT3   radioisotopes
        BT4   isotopes
  BT1   electron capture radioisotopes
    BT2   beta decay radioisotopes
      BT3   radioisotopes
        BT4   isotopes
  BT1   gold isotopes
  BT1   heavy nuclei
    BT2   nuclei
  BT1   hours living radioisotopes
    BT2   radioisotopes
      BT3   isotopes
  BT1   odd-odd nuclei
    BT2   nuclei

GOLD 193 [55; 55]
  BT1   electron capture radioisotopes
    BT2   beta decay radioisotopes
      BT3   radioisotopes
        BT4   isotopes
  BT1   gold isotopes
  BT1   heavy nuclei
    BT2   nuclei
  BT1   hours living radioisotopes
    BT2   radioisotopes
      BT3   isotopes
  BT1   internal conversion radioisoto
    BT2   radioisotopes
      BT3   isotopes
  BT1   isomeric transition isotopes
    BT2   radioisotopes
      BT3   isotopes
  BT1   odd-even nuclei
    BT2   nuclei
  BT1   seconds living radioisotopes
    BT2   radioisotopes
      BT3   isotopes

GOLD 193 TARGET [2; 2] *Nov 77*
  BT1   targets

GOLD 194 [50; 50]
  BT1   beta-plus decay radioisotopes
    BT2   beta decay radioisotopes
      BT3   radioisotopes
        BT4   isotopes
  BT1   days living radioisotopes
    BT2   radioisotopes
      BT3   isotopes
  BT1   electron capture radioisotopes
    BT2   beta decay radioisotopes
      BT3   radioisotopes
        BT4   isotopes
  BT1   gold isotopes
  BT1   heavy nuclei
    BT2   nuclei
  BT1   odd-odd nuclei
    BT2   nuclei

GOLD 194 TARGET [4; 4] *Nov 77*
  BT1   targets

GOLD 195 [246; 246]
  BT1   days living radioisotopes
    BT2   radioisotopes
      BT3   isotopes
  BT1   electron capture radioisotopes
    BT2   beta decay radioisotopes
      BT3   radioisotopes
        BT4   isotopes
  BT1   gold isotopes
  BT1   heavy nuclei
    BT2   nuclei
  BT1   internal conversion radioisoto
    BT2   radioisotopes
      BT3   isotopes
  BT1   isomeric transition isotopes
    BT2   radioisotopes
      BT3   isotopes
  BT1   odd-even nuclei
    BT2   nuclei
  BT1   seconds living radioisotopes
    BT2   radioisotopes
      BT3   isotopes

GOLD 195 TARGET [2; 2] *Nov 77*
  BT1   targets

GOLD 196 [108; 108]
  BT1   beta-minus decay radioisotopes
    BT2   beta decay radioisotopes
      BT3   radioisotopes
        BT4   isotopes
  BT1   beta-plus decay radioisotopes
    BT2   beta decay radioisotopes
      BT3   radioisotopes
        BT4   isotopes
  BT1   days living radioisotopes
    BT2   radioisotopes
      BT3   isotopes
  BT1   electron capture radioisotopes
    BT2   beta decay radioisotopes
      BT3   radioisotopes
        BT4   isotopes
  BT1   gold isotopes
  BT1   heavy nuclei
    BT2   nuclei
  BT1   hours living radioisotopes
    BT2   radioisotopes
      BT3   isotopes
  BT1   internal conversion radioisoto
    BT2   radioisotopes
      BT3   isotopes
  BT1   isomeric transition isotopes
    BT2   radioisotopes
      BT3   isotopes
  BT1   odd-odd nuclei
    BT2   nuclei
  BT1   seconds living radioisotopes
    BT2   radioisotopes
      BT3   isotopes

GOLD 196 TARGET [23; 23] *Nov 77*
  BT1   targets

GOLD 197 [681; 681]
  BT1   gold isotopes
  BT1   heavy nuclei
    BT2   nuclei
  BT1   internal conversion radioisoto
    BT2   radioisotopes
      BT3   isotopes
  BT1   isomeric transition isotopes
    BT2   radioisotopes
      BT3   isotopes
  BT1   odd-even nuclei
    BT2   nuclei
  BT1   seconds living radioisotopes
    BT2   radioisotopes
      BT3   isotopes
  BT1   stable isotopes
    BT2   isotopes

GOLD 197 BEAMS [67; 67] *Apr 79*
  BT1   ion beams
    BT2   beams

GOLD 197 REACTIONS [121; 121]
Jun 84
  BT1   heavy ion reactions
  BT2   nuclear reactions

GOLD 197 TARGET [2,245; 2,245]
  BT1   targets

GOLD 198 [1,088; 1,088]
  BT1   beta-minus decay radioisotopes
    BT2   beta decay radioisotopes
      BT3   radioisotopes
        BT4   isotopes
  BT1   days living radioisotopes
    BT2   radioisotopes
      BT3   isotopes
  BT1   gold isotopes
  BT1   heavy nuclei
    BT2   nuclei
  BT1   isomeric transition isotopes
    BT2   radioisotopes
      BT3   isotopes
  BT1   odd-odd nuclei
    BT2   nuclei
  RT   radiocolloids

GOLD 198 TARGET [12; 12] *Nov 77*
  BT1   targets

GOLD 199 [72; 72]
  BT1   beta-minus decay radioisotopes
    BT2   beta decay radioisotopes
      BT3   radioisotopes
        BT4   isotopes
  BT1   days living radioisotopes
    BT2   radioisotopes
      BT3   isotopes
  BT1   gold isotopes
  BT1   heavy nuclei
    BT2   nuclei
  BT1   odd-even nuclei
    BT2   nuclei

GOLD 199 TARGET [8; 8] *Nov 77*
  BT1   targets

GOLD 200 [20; 20]
  BT1   beta-minus decay radioisotopes
    BT2   beta decay radioisotopes
      BT3   radioisotopes
        BT4   isotopes
  BT1   gold isotopes
  BT1   heavy nuclei
    BT2   nuclei
  BT1   hours living radioisotopes
    BT2   radioisotopes
      BT3   isotopes
  BT1   isomeric transition isotopes
    BT2   radioisotopes
      BT3   isotopes
  BT1   minutes living radioisotopes
    BT2   radioisotopes
      BT3   isotopes
  BT1   odd-odd nuclei
    BT2   nuclei

GOLD 201 [5; 5]
  BT1   beta-minus decay radioisotopes
    BT2   beta decay radioisotopes
      BT3   radioisotopes
        BT4   isotopes
  BT1   gold isotopes
  BT1   heavy nuclei
    BT2   nuclei
  BT1   minutes living radioisotopes
    BT2   radioisotopes
      BT3   isotopes
  BT1   odd-even nuclei
    BT2   nuclei

GOLD 202 [2; 2]
  BT1   beta-minus decay radioisotopes
    BT2   beta decay radioisotopes
      BT3   radioisotopes
        BT4   isotopes
  BT1   gold isotopes
  BT1   heavy nuclei
    BT2   nuclei
  BT1   odd-odd nuclei
    BT2   nuclei
  BT1   seconds living radioisotopes
    BT2   radioisotopes
      BT3   isotopes

GOLD 203 [8; 8]
  BT1   beta-minus decay radioisotopes
    BT2   beta decay radioisotopes
      BT3   radioisotopes
        BT4   isotopes
  BT1   gold isotopes
  BT1   heavy nuclei
    BT2   nuclei
  BT1   odd-even nuclei
    BT2   nuclei
  BT1   seconds living radioisotopes
    BT2   radioisotopes
      BT3   isotopes

GOLD 204 [3; 3]
  BT1   beta-minus decay radioisotopes
    BT2   beta decay radioisotopes
      BT3   radioisotopes
        BT4   isotopes
  BT1   gold isotopes
  BT1   heavy nuclei
    BT2   nuclei
  BT1   odd-odd nuclei
    BT2   nuclei
  BT1   seconds living radioisotopes
    BT2   radioisotopes
      BT3   isotopes

GOLDBERGER MODEL [7; 7]
  UF   *serber-goldberger model*
  BT1   nuclear models
    BT2   mathematical models

GOLDBERGER-TREIMAN RELATION
[150; 150]
  RT   coupling
  RT   pions
  RT   quantum field theory
  RT   weak interactions

GOLDFISH [51; 51]
  UF   *carassius*
  BT1   fishes
    BT2   aquatic organisms
    BT2   vertebrates
      BT3   animals

goldhaber-teller model
  USE   giant resonance model

GOLDSTONE BOSONS [1,312; 2,130]
(Massless particles occurring in certain broken-symmetry theories.)
- BT1 bosons
- BT1 postulated particles
- BT2 elementary particles
- NT1 axions
- RT invariance principles
- RT su groups

GOLDSTONE DIAGRAMS [159; 159]
- UF *brueckner approximation*
- UF *brueckner-goldstone theory*
- UF *brueckner-sawada theory*
- UF *sawada method*
- BT1 diagrams
- BT2 information
- RT many-body problem

GOLFECH-1 REACTOR [6; 6] Jul 84
- BT1 pwr type reactors
- BT2 enriched uranium reactors
- BT3 reactors
- BT2 power reactors
- BT3 reactors
- BT2 thermal reactors
- BT3 reactors
- BT2 water cooled reactors
- BT3 reactors
- BT2 water moderated reactors
- BT3 reactors

golgi apparatus
- USE organoids

GONADOTROPINS [259; 1,266]
- BT1 pituitary hormones
- BT2 peptide hormones
- BT3 hormones
- NT1 fsh
- NT1 hcg
- NT1 lh
- NT1 lth
- RT gonads

GONADS [727; 3,628]
- NT1 ovaries
- NT1 testes
- RT castration
- RT endocrine glands
- RT female genitals
- RT fertility
- RT gametogenesis
- RT genetic effects
- RT germ cells
- RT gonadotropins
- RT hcg
- RT male genitals
- RT pelvis
- RT reproduction
- RT sex

GONIOMETERS [273; 273]
- BT1 measuring instruments

GONORRHEA [12; 12] Jun 76
- BT1 bacterial diseases
- BT2 infectious diseases
- BT3 diseases
- RT urogenital system diseases

GORKOV-ELIASHBERG THEORY
[294; 294] Jul 77
(Theory of gapless superconductivity arising from magnetic impurities.)
- UF *eliashberg equations*
- RT superconductivity

GORLEBEN SALT DOME [64; 64]
Nov 89
- BT1 radioactive waste facilities
- BT2 nuclear facilities
- RT high-level radioactive wastes
- RT radioactive waste disposal
- RT salt caverns
- RT salt deposits
- RT underground disposal

GOSATOMNADZOR [10; 10] Mar 77
- BT1 ussr organizations
- BT2 national organizations

GOVERNMENT POLICIES
[4,109; 4,109] Jul 76
- UF *foreign policy*
- SF *public policy*
- RT deregulation
- RT energy policy
- RT environmental policy
- RT implementation
- RT local government
- RT national government
- RT nationalization
- RT non-proliferation policy
- RT nuclear power phaseout
- RT planning
- RT political aspects
- RT public officials
- RT regional cooperation
- RT regulations
- RT state government

GOVERNOR MODEL [11; 11]
- BT1 shell models
- BT2 nuclear models
- BT3 mathematical models
- RT cranking model
- RT deformed nuclei
- RT fission

GRABEN-1 REACTOR [9; 9]
- BT1 bwr type reactors
- BT2 enriched uranium reactors
- BT3 reactors
- BT2 power reactors
- BT3 reactors
- BT2 thermal reactors
- BT3 reactors
- BT2 water cooled reactors
- BT3 reactors
- BT2 water moderated reactors
- BT3 reactors

GRABS [129; 129]
- BT1 materials handling equipment
- BT2 equipment

GRACE PARTICLES [5; 5] Aug 78
- BT1 postulated particles
- BT2 elementary particles
- RT color model
- RT hadrons
- RT hypercharge
- RT quarks
- RT su-3 groups

GRAD-SHAFRANOV EQUATION
[149; 149] Oct 83
- BT1 partial differential equations
- BT2 differential equations
- BT3 equations
- RT mercier criterion
- RT plasma
- RT transport theory

GRADED LIE GROUPS [1,320; 1,320]
Nov 78
(Lie groups defined by an algebraic structure which contains commutation and anticommutation relations.)
- UF *lie superalgebra*
- BT1 lie groups
- BT2 symmetry groups
- RT algebra
- RT supergravity
- RT supersymmetry

GRAFENRHEINFELD REACTOR
[97; 97]
- BT1 pwr type reactors
- BT2 enriched uranium reactors
- BT3 reactors
- BT2 power reactors
- BT3 reactors
- BT2 thermal reactors
- BT3 reactors
- BT2 water cooled reactors
- BT3 reactors
- BT2 water moderated reactors
- BT3 reactors

GRAFT POLYMERS [1,037; 1,037]
- BT1 organic polymers
- BT2 organic compounds
- BT2 polymers
- RT ion exchange materials

GRAFT-HOST REACTION [865; 865]
- RT antigen-antibody reactions
- RT grafts
- RT host
- RT immunity
- RT transplants

GRAFTS [1,077; 1,077]
- BT1 transplants
- RT graft-host reaction
- RT radioimmunology

grain alcohol
- USE ethanol

GRAIN BOUNDARIES [4,214; 4,214]
- UF *boundaries (grain)*
- BT1 microstructure
- BT2 crystal structure
- RT dislocation pinning
- RT grain growth
- RT intergranular corrosion

GRAIN DENSITY [204; 204]
- UF *density (grain)*
- BT1 microstructure
- BT2 crystal structure
- RT granular materials

GRAIN DISINFESTATION [111; 111]
- BT1 disinfestation
- RT agriculture
- RT cereals
- RT fumigants
- RT insects
- RT pesticides
- RT preservation
- RT radiodisinfestation
- RT sterilization

GRAIN GROWTH [824; 824]
- UF *growth (grain)*
- RT crystal growth
- RT grain boundaries
- RT grain refinement
- RT grain size
- RT recrystallization

GRAIN ORIENTATION [1,073; 1,073]
- UF *preferred orientation*
- BT1 microstructure
- BT2 crystal structure
- BT1 orientation
- RT texture

GRAIN REFINEMENT [166; 166]
- UF *refinement (grain)*
- RT grain growth
- RT grain size
- RT heat treatments

GRAIN SIZE [4,196; 4,196]
(See also PARTICLE SIZE.)
- BT1 microstructure
- BT2 crystal structure
- BT1 size
- RT grain growth
- RT grain refinement
- RT granular materials

grains (cereal)
   USE   cereals
   AND   seeds

GRAMINEAE [640; 4,678]
   UF   *grass*
   BT1   plants
   NT1   cereals
      NT2   barley
      NT2   maize
      NT2   millet
      NT2   oats
      NT2   rice
      NT2   rye
      NT2   sorghum
      NT2   wheat
   NT1   sugar cane
   RT   cattle
   RT   forage
   RT   ground cover
   RT   pastures
   RT   preferred species

grand acc. nat. ions lourds
   USE   ganil cyclotron

GRAND GULF-1 REACTOR [152; 152]
(Port Gibson, Mississipi, USA)
   BT1   bwr type reactors
      BT2   enriched uranium reactors
         BT3   reactors
      BT2   power reactors
         BT3   reactors
      BT2   thermal reactors
         BT3   reactors
      BT2   water cooled reactors
         BT3   reactors
      BT2   water moderated reactors
         BT3   reactors

GRAND GULF-2 REACTOR [109; 109]
(Port Gibson, Mississipi, USA)
   BT1   bwr type reactors
      BT2   enriched uranium reactors
         BT3   reactors
      BT2   power reactors
         BT3   reactors
      BT2   thermal reactors
         BT3   reactors
      BT2   water cooled reactors
         BT3   reactors
      BT2   water moderated reactors
         BT3   reactors

grand unification
   USE   grand unified theory

GRAND UNIFIED THEORY
[2,651; 5,227] Dec 83
(Gauge field theory to unify electromagnetic, weak and strong interactions. For unified theories involving gravitation see UNIFIED-FIELD THEORIES.)
   UF   *grand unification*
   BT1   unified gauge models
      BT2   particle models
         BT3   mathematical models
      BT2   quantum field theory
         BT3   field theories
   NT1   standard model
   RT   electromagnetic interactions
   RT   quantum chromodynamics
   RT   strong interactions
   RT   su-5 groups
   RT   unified-field theories
   RT   weak interactions
   RT   weinberg lepton model

GRANITES [2,705; 2,752]
   BT1   plutonic rocks
      BT2   igneous rocks
         BT3   rocks
   NT1   aplites
   NT1   granodiorites
   NT1   quartz monzonite
   RT   biotite
   RT   feldspars
   RT   hornblende
   RT   monique event
   RT   pegmatites
   RT   quartz
   RT   rhyolites
   RT   xenotime

GRANODIORITES [110; 110]
   BT1   granites
      BT2   plutonic rocks
         BT3   igneous rocks
            BT4   rocks
   RT   feldspars
   RT   quartz

grants
   USE   financing

granular bed filters
   USE   mechanical filters

GRANULAR MATERIALS [543; 543]
Sep 82
(For unspecified materials having a granular texture.)
   BT1   materials
   RT   grain density
   RT   grain size
   RT   particles
   RT   powders

granulation (solar)
   USE   solar granulation

granulocytes
   USE   leukocytes

GRANULOMAS [243; 243]
   BT1   pathological changes
      BT2   diseases
   RT   bacterial diseases
   RT   infectious diseases
   RT   inflammation
   RT   neoplasms

GRAPEFRUITS [21; 21]
   BT1   fruits
      BT2   food
   RT   citrus

GRAPES [88; 88]
   BT1   fruits
      BT2   food

GRAPHITE [7,260; 7,260]
   UF   *graphite moderator*
   BT1   carbon
      BT2   nonmetals
         BT3   elements
   RT   carbon fibers
   RT   graphitization
   RT   matrix materials
   RT   moderators
   RT   refractories
   RT   solid lubricants
   RT   wigner effect

graphite fibers
   USE   carbon fibers

graphite low-energy expe. pile
   USE   gleep reactor

GRAPHITE MODERATED REACTORS
[214; 17,084]
   BT1   reactors
   NT1   agr type reactors
      NT2   connah quay-b reactor
      NT2   dungeness-b reactor
      NT2   hartlepool reactor
      NT2   heysham-a reactor
      NT2   heysham-b reactor
      NT2   hinkley point-b reactor
      NT2   hunterston-b reactor
      NT2   torness reactor
      NT2   wagr reactor
   NT1   anna reactor
   NT1   bepo reactor
   NT1   bgrr reactor
   NT1   bigr reactor
   NT1   br-1 reactor
   NT1   cesar reactor
   NT1   cp-2 reactor
   NT1   egcr reactor
   NT1   f-1 reactor
   NT1   fursov pile
   NT1   gcr type reactors
      NT2   bugey-1 reactor
      NT2   chinon-1 reactor
      NT2   chinon-2 reactor
      NT2   chinon-3 reactor
      NT2   g-1 reactor
      NT2   g-2 reactor
      NT2   g-3 reactor
      NT2   magnox type reactors
         NT3   berkeley reactor
         NT3   bradwell reactor
         NT3   calder hall a-1 reactor
         NT3   calder hall a-2 reactor
         NT3   calder hall b-3 reactor
         NT3   calder hall b-4 reactor
         NT3   chapelcross-1 reactor
         NT3   chapelcross-2 reactor
         NT3   chapelcross-3 reactor
         NT3   chapelcross-4 reactor
         NT3   dungeness-a reactor
         NT3   hinkley point-a reactor
         NT3   hunterston-a reactor
         NT3   latina reactor
         NT3   oldbury-a reactor
         NT3   sizewell-a reactor
         NT3   tokai-mura reactor
         NT3   trawsfynydd reactor
         NT3   wylfa reactor
      NT2   saint laurent-1 reactor
      NT2   saint laurent-2 reactor
      NT2   vandellos reactor
   NT1   gleep reactor
   NT1   hector reactor
   NT1   hero reactor
   NT1   hitrex-1 reactor
   NT1   hnpf reactor
   NT1   htgr type reactors
      NT2   avr reactor
      NT2   dragon reactor
      NT2   fulton-1 reactor
      NT2   fulton-2 reactor
      NT2   ga standard reactor
      NT2   httr reactor
      NT2   kahter reactor
      NT2   peach bottom-1 reactor
      NT2   schmehausen reactor
      NT2   summit-1 reactor
      NT2   summit-2 reactor
      NT2   thtr-300 reactor
      NT2   vg-400 reactor
      NT2   vgr-50 reactor
      NT2   vhtr reactor
      NT2   vidal-1 reactor
      NT2   vidal-2 reactor
      NT2   vrain reactor
   NT1   htltr reactor
   NT1   iea-zpr reactor
   NT1   iowa utr-10 reactor
   NT1   kuca reactor
   NT1   lwgr type reactors
      NT2   aps reactor
      NT2   beloyarsk-1 reactor
      NT2   beloyarsk-2 reactor
      NT2   bilibin reactor
      NT2   chernobylsk-1 reactor
      NT2   chernobylsk-2 reactor
      NT2   chernobylsk-3 reactor

NT2 chernobylsk-4 reactor
NT2 ignalinsk-1 reactor
NT2 ignalinsk-2 reactor
NT2 kursk-1 reactor
NT2 kursk-2 reactor
NT2 kursk-3 reactor
NT2 kursk-4 reactor
NT2 leningrad-1 reactor
NT2 leningrad-2 reactor
NT2 leningrad-3 reactor
NT2 leningrad-4 reactor
NT2 n-reactor
NT2 rpt reactor
NT2 smolensk-1 reactor
NT2 smolensk-2 reactor
NT2 uwtr reactor
NT1 marius reactor
NT1 msre reactor
NT1 ntr reactor
NT1 pctr reactor
NT1 proteus reactor
NT1 rb-1 reactor
NT1 sgr type reactors
NT2 sre reactor
NT1 shca reactor
NT1 sr-305 reactor
NT1 treat reactor
NT1 uhtrex reactor
NT1 windscale production reactors
NT1 x-10 reactor
NT1 zenith reactor

graphite moderator
USE graphite

GRAPHITIZATION [33; 33] *Jul 84*
RT carbonization
RT crystal-phase transformations
RT graphite

grasers
USE gasers

GRASHOF NUMBER [113; 113]
RT convection
RT reynolds number

grass
USE gramineae

GRASSHOPPERS [31; 36]
BT1 insects
BT2 arthropods
BT3 invertebrates
BT4 animals
NT1 locusts

gratings
SEE diffraction gratings
OR intake structures
OR screens

GRAVELINES-B1 REACTOR [6; 6]
Feb 80
(Gravelines, Nord, France)
BT1 pwr type reactors
BT2 enriched uranium reactors
BT3 reactors
BT2 power reactors
BT3 reactors
BT2 thermal reactors
BT3 reactors
BT2 water cooled reactors
BT3 reactors
BT2 water moderated reactors
BT3 reactors

GRAVELINES-C6 REACTOR [2; 2]
Sep 90
(Gravelines, Nord, France.)
BT1 pwr type reactors

BT2 enriched uranium reactors
BT3 reactors
BT2 power reactors
BT3 reactors
BT2 thermal reactors
BT3 reactors
BT2 water cooled reactors
BT3 reactors
BT2 water moderated reactors
BT3 reactors

GRAVIMETRIC ANALYSIS [401; 2,213]
BT1 quantitative chemical analysis
BT2 chemical analysis
NT1 thermal gravimetric analysis

GRAVIMETRY [183; 183]
(For gravitation measurement only; see also GRAVIMETRIC ANALYSIS.)
UF+ *gravity surveys*
RT acceleration
RT gravitation

GRAVITATION [5,311; 5,311]
RT general relativity theory
RT gravimetry
RT gravitational fields
RT gravitational interactions
RT gravitational lenses
RT gravity waves
RT kaluza-klein theory
RT quantum gravity
RT schwarzschild metric
RT supergravity
RT twistor theory
RT unified-field theories

gravitational charges
USE fundamental constants
AND gravitons

GRAVITATIONAL COLLAPSE
[2,216; 2,216]
UF *collapse (gravitational)*
RT black holes
RT neutron stars
RT schwarzschild radius
RT star evolution

GRAVITATIONAL FIELDS
[6,408; 6,626]
UF *fields (gravitational)*
NT1 kerr field
RT einstein effect
RT einstein field equations
RT einstein-maxwell equations
RT equivalence principle
RT general relativity theory
RT gravitation
RT gravitational interactions
RT gravitational lenses
RT gravitational radiation
RT mass
RT metrics
RT potentials
RT quantum gravity
RT roche equipotentials
RT uniton
RT weyl unified theory

GRAVITATIONAL INTERACTIONS
[1,952; 1,952]
BT1 basic interactions
RT gravitation
RT gravitational fields
RT gravitational radiation
RT gravitational waves

GRAVITATIONAL LENSES [345; 345]
Feb 83
BT1 lenses
RT general relativity theory
RT gravitation
RT gravitational fields

GRAVITATIONAL RADIATION
[1,142; 1,988]
BT1 radiations
NT1 gravitons
RT general relativity theory
RT gravitational fields
RT gravitational interactions
RT gravitational wave detectors
RT gravitational waves

GRAVITATIONAL WAVE DETECTORS [482; 482] *Mar 76*
BT1 radiation detectors
BT2 measuring instruments
RT gravitational radiation
RT gravitational waves

GRAVITATIONAL WAVES
[1,352; 1,352]
RT einstein-maxwell equations
RT gravitational interactions
RT gravitational radiation
RT gravitational wave detectors

GRAVITONS [878; 878]
UF+ *gravitational charges*
BT1 gravitational radiation
BT2 radiations
BT1 massless particles
BT2 elementary particles
BT1 postulated particles
BT2 elementary particles
RT quantum gravity
RT supergravity
RT uniton

gravity logging
(Well logging by detection of gravitational anomalies.)
USE well logging

gravity surveys
USE geophysical surveys
AND gravimetry

GRAVITY WAVES [307; 307]
RT fluid mechanics
RT gravitation

gray
USE radiation dose units

GRAYWACKE [7; 7]
BT1 sandstones
BT2 sedimentary rocks
BT3 rocks
RT conglomerates

GRAZING INCIDENCE TOMOGRAPHY [7; 7] *May 81*
BT1 tomography

GREASES [56; 56]
BT1 lubricants
RT lubrication
RT oils

great britain
USE united kingdom

GREAT LAKES [58; 273]
BT1 lakes
BT2 surface waters
NT1 lake erie
NT1 lake huron
NT1 lake michigan
NT1 lake ontario
NT1 lake superior

GREECE [244; 244]
BT1 developing countries
BT1 europe

GREEK ORGANIZATIONS [2; 2]
Nov 84
BT1 national organizations

greek research reactor
USE democritus reactor

GREELEY EVENT [1; 1]
BT1 nuclear explosions
BT2 explosions
BT1 underground explosions
BT2 explosions

GREEN FUNCTION [8,239; 8,239]
BT1 functions
RT differential equations
RT sturm-liouville equation

GREEN RIVER FORMATION [5; 5]
Apr 84
BT1 geologic formations
RT colorado
RT oil shales
RT uranium deposits
RT uranium ores
RT utah
RT wyoming

GREENE COUNTY REACTOR [5; 5]
Feb 76
BT1 pwr type reactors
BT2 enriched uranium reactors
BT3 reactors
BT2 power reactors
BT3 reactors
BT2 thermal reactors
BT3 reactors
BT2 water cooled reactors
BT3 reactors
BT2 water moderated reactors
BT3 reactors

GREENHOUSE EFFECT [220; 220]
Dec 82
RT earth atmosphere
RT heat transfer
RT reflection
RT trapping

GREENHOUSE PROJECT [5; 5]
UF *project greenhouse*
RT eniwetok
RT nuclear explosions

greenhouses
USE buildings

GREENLAND [305; 305]
BT1 islands
RT arctic ocean
RT arctic regions
RT denmark

GREENWOOD-2 REACTOR [14; 14]
BT1 pwr type reactors
BT2 enriched uranium reactors
BT3 reactors
BT2 power reactors
BT3 reactors
BT2 thermal reactors
BT3 reactors
BT2 water cooled reactors
BT3 reactors
BT2 water moderated reactors
BT3 reactors

GREENWOOD-3 REACTOR [14; 14]
BT1 pwr type reactors
BT2 enriched uranium reactors
BT3 reactors
BT2 power reactors
BT3 reactors
BT2 thermal reactors
BT3 reactors
BT2 water cooled reactors
BT3 reactors
BT2 water moderated reactors
BT3 reactors

GREIFSWALD-1 REACTOR [70; 70]
(Greifswald, Federal Republic of Germany.)
UF *bruno leuschner-1 reactor*
UF *kkw greifswald-1 reactor*
BT1 wwer type reactors
BT2 pwr type reactors
BT3 enriched uranium reactors
BT4 reactors
BT3 power reactors
BT4 reactors
BT3 thermal reactors
BT4 reactors
BT3 water cooled reactors
BT4 reactors
BT3 water moderated reactors
BT4 reactors

GREIFSWALD-2 REACTOR [48; 48]
(Greifswald, Federal Republic of Germany.)
UF *bruno leuschner-2 reactor*
UF *kkw greifswald-2 reactor*
BT1 wwer type reactors
BT2 pwr type reactors
BT3 enriched uranium reactors
BT4 reactors
BT3 power reactors
BT4 reactors
BT3 thermal reactors
BT4 reactors
BT3 water cooled reactors
BT4 reactors
BT3 water moderated reactors
BT4 reactors

GREIFSWALD-3 REACTOR [43; 43]
Jul 78
(Greifswald, Federal Republic of Germany.)
UF *bruno leuschner-3 reactor*
UF *kkw greifswald-3 reactor*
BT1 wwer type reactors
BT2 pwr type reactors
BT3 enriched uranium reactors
BT4 reactors
BT3 power reactors
BT4 reactors
BT3 thermal reactors
BT4 reactors
BT3 water cooled reactors
BT4 reactors
BT3 water moderated reactors
BT4 reactors

GREIFSWALD-4 REACTOR [46; 46]
Jul 78
(Greifswald, Federal Republic of Germany.)
UF *bruno leuschner-4 reactor*
UF *kkw greifswald-4 reactor*
BT1 wwer type reactors
BT2 pwr type reactors
BT3 enriched uranium reactors
BT4 reactors
BT3 power reactors
BT4 reactors
BT3 thermal reactors
BT4 reactors
BT3 water cooled reactors
BT4 reactors
BT3 water moderated reactors
BT4 reactors

GREIFSWALD-5 REACTOR [4; 4]
Jul 90
(Greifswald, German Democratic Republic)
BT1 wwer type reactors
BT2 pwr type reactors
BT3 enriched uranium reactors
BT4 reactors
BT3 power reactors
BT4 reactors
BT3 thermal reactors
BT4 reactors
BT3 water cooled reactors
BT4 reactors
BT3 water moderated reactors
BT4 reactors

GREIFSWALD-6 REACTOR [3; 3]
Jul 90
(Greifswald, German Democratic Republic)
BT1 wwer type reactors
BT2 pwr type reactors
BT3 enriched uranium reactors
BT4 reactors
BT3 power reactors
BT4 reactors
BT3 thermal reactors
BT4 reactors
BT3 water cooled reactors
BT4 reactors
BT3 water moderated reactors
BT4 reactors

GRENOBLE CYCLOTRON [40; 40]
BT1 isochronous cyclotrons
BT2 cyclotrons
BT3 cyclic accelerators
BT4 accelerators
RT sara cyclotron

GRENOBLE REACTOR [143; 143]
UF *franco-german high flux reacto*
BT1 heavy water cooled reactors
BT2 reactors
BT1 heavy water moderated reactors
BT2 reactors
BT1 research reactors
BT2 research and test reactors
BT3 reactors
BT1 tank type reactors
BT2 reactors
BT1 test reactors
BT2 research and test reactors
BT3 reactors
BT2 test facilities

grenoble reactor melusine-1
USE melusine-1 reactor

grenoble reactor melusine-2
USE siloette reactor

GRIBOV-LIPATOV RELATION [38; 38]
BT1 equations
RT annihilation
RT scattering
RT structure functions

GRIDS [562; 562]
BT1 electrodes

grids (coordinates)
USE coordinates

GRIGNARD REAGENTS [45; 45]
UF *alkylmagnesium compounds*
UF *arylmagnesium compounds*
BT1 magnesium compounds
BT2 alkaline earth metal compound
BT1 organometallic compounds
BT2 organic compounds

GRINDING [399; 399]
(For grinding in the sense of pulverizing, use CRUSHING.)
BT1 machining
RT grinding machines
RT honing
RT wear

GRINDING MACHINES [46; 46]
BT1 machine tools
RT grinding

GROHNDE REACTOR [93; 93] *Jul 76*
(Grohnde, Niedersachsen, Federal Republic of Germany)
BT1 pwr type reactors
BT2 enriched uranium reactors
BT3 reactors
BT2 power reactors
BT3 reactors
BT2 thermal reactors
BT3 reactors
BT2 water cooled reactors
BT3 reactors
BT2 water moderated reactors
BT3 reactors

groningen (kvi) cyclotron
USE kvi cyclotron

groningen versneller instituut
USE kvi

gross domestic product
USE gross national product

GROSS NATIONAL PRODUCT [12; 12] *Dec 86*
(Sum of a nation's economic output measured in terms of expenditures for goods and services by consumers, government, business, and foreign countries and the earnings from foreign investments.)
UF *gross domestic product*
RT domestic supplies
RT economic development
RT economics
RT economy
RT market

gross-neveu model
USE lagrangian field theory

grosswelzheim hdr reactor
USE hdr reactor

grosswelzheim pr-10 reactor
USE aeg-pr-10 reactor

GROUND COVER [92; 92] *Nov 81*
(Vegetation or other means for ensuring soil stability, usually in connection with buried wastes.)
RT crops
RT erosion
RT forests
RT gramineae
RT plants
RT revegetation
RT underground disposal

GROUND DISPOSAL [1,080; 1,080]
(For disposal of wastes near the earth's surface, e.g. in trenches.)
SF *waste burial*
BT1 waste disposal
BT2 waste management
BT3 management
RT liquid wastes
RT radioactive wastes
RT sanitary landfills
RT sewage sludge
RT solid wastes
RT underground disposal

GROUND LEVEL [297; 297]
BT1 levels

GROUND MOTION [1,316; 1,316]
UF *displacements (seismic)*
BT1 motion
BT1 seismic effects
RT earthquakes
RT epicenters
RT ground subsidence
RT landslides
RT nuclear explosions
RT seismic waves
RT seismographs
RT seismology
RT shock waves
RT slope stability
RT soil-structure interactions
RT underground explosions

GROUND RELEASE [180; 180]
(Release of gaseous effluents at ground level.)
BT1 waste disposal
BT2 waste management
BT3 management
RT gaseous wastes
RT radioactive waste disposal
RT stack disposal

GROUND STATES [12,612; 12,612]
BT1 energy levels

GROUND SUBSIDENCE [80; 80] *Jul 82*
(Gradual sinking of the ground surface, e.g. due to collapse of an underground cavity.)
UF *subsidence (ground)*
RT ground motion

GROUND WATER [9,487; 9,487]
UF *water springs*
BT1 water
BT2 hydrogen compounds
BT2 oxygen compounds
RT alluvial deposits
RT aquifers
RT atmospheric precipitations
RT clays
RT hydraulic conductivity
RT hydrology
RT leachates
RT liquid wastes
RT radionuclide migration
RT reservoir pressure
RT rock-fluid interactions
RT soil mechanics
RT soils
RT surface waters
RT water influx
RT water tables

groundnuts
(Arachis hypogaea)
USE peanuts

grounds (electric)
USE electric grounds

GROUP CONSTANTS [1,016; 1,016]
BT1 cross sections
RT energy range
RT energy spectra
RT multigroup theory

group iva metal compounds
USE transition element compounds

GROUP THEORY [2,634; 2,634]
(For mathematical groups only; for neutron-energy groups use MULTIGROUP THEORY.)
BT1 mathematics
RT clebsch-gordan coefficients
RT clifford algebra
RT galilei transformations
RT irreducible representations
RT nonunitary representations
RT r matrix
RT racah coefficients
RT space groups
RT supersymmetry
RT symmetry groups
RT wigner coefficients
RT young diagram

group va metal compounds
USE transition element compounds

group via metal compounds
USE transition element compounds

groups (space)
USE space groups

GROUTING [358; 358] *Feb 81*
UF *grouts*
RT bonding
RT cements
RT fillers
RT mortars
RT sealing materials
RT seals

grouts
USE grouting

GROWTH [3,327; 5,735]
UF+ *cell growth (animal)*
UF+ *cell growth (plant)*
UF+ *growth inhibition*
UF+ *growth stimulation*
NT1 animal growth
NT1 plant growth
RT age dependence
RT biological regeneration
RT life cycle
RT metabolism
RT physiology
RT population dynamics
RT ripening
RT sth
RT teratogenesis
RT viability

growth (crystal)
USE crystal growth

growth (grain)
USE grain growth

GROWTH FACTORS [206; 206] *Apr 90*
(Tissue specific proteins released by a cell which act on neighboring cells to stimulate their replication.)
BT1 mitogens
BT1 proteins
BT2 organic compounds
RT cell differentiation
RT cell proliferation
RT erythropoietin
RT oncogenes

growth hormone
USE sth

growth inhibition
(If possible, use a more specific term for growth.)
USE growth
AND inhibition

growth stimulation
USE growth
AND stimulation

grr reactor
USE democritus reactor

grs
USE ges fuer reaktorsicherheit

GRUENEISEN CONSTANT [309; 309]
RT compressibility
RT specific heat
RT thermal expansion

GRUENEISEN FORMULA [21; 21]
RT electric conductivity
RT metals

gs process
USE dual temperature process

gsd
USE genetically significant dose

GTR REACTOR [1; 1]
(General Dynamics--Convair/U.S. Air Force, Fort Worth, Texas, USA)
UF *fort worth gtr reactor*
BT1 pool type reactors
BT2 water cooled reactors
BT3 reactors
BT2 water moderated reactors
BT3 reactors
BT1 test reactors
BT2 research and test reactors
BT3 reactors
BT2 test facilities

GTRR REACTOR [14; 14]
(Georgia Institute of Technology, Atlanta, Georgia, USA)
UF *georgia tech. research reactor*
BT1 enriched uranium reactors
BT2 reactors
BT1 heavy water cooled reactors
BT2 reactors
BT1 heavy water moderated reactors
BT2 reactors
BT1 isotope production reactors
BT2 irradiation reactors
BT3 reactors
BT1 research reactors
BT2 research and test reactors
BT3 reactors
BT1 tank type reactors
BT2 reactors
BT1 test reactors
BT2 research and test reactors
BT3 reactors
BT2 test facilities
BT1 training reactors
BT2 research and test reactors
BT3 reactors

GUANETHIDINE [6; 6]
BT1 antihypertensive agents
BT2 cardiovascular agents
BT3 drugs
BT1 carbonic acid derivatives
BT2 organic compounds
BT1 heterocyclic compounds
BT2 organic compounds
BT1 organic nitrogen compounds
BT2 organic compounds
RT guanidines

GUANIDINES [526; 526]
UF *iminourea*
BT1 carbonic acid derivatives
BT2 organic compounds
BT1 organic nitrogen compounds
BT2 organic compounds
RT amides
RT arginine
RT creatine
RT guanethidine
RT imines
RT meg

guanidylaminovaleric acid
USE arginine

GUANINE [292; 292]
UF *aminohypoxanthine*
BT1 amines
BT2 organic compounds
BT1 hydroxy compounds
BT2 organic compounds
BT1 purines
BT2 heterocyclic compounds
BT3 organic compounds
BT2 organic nitrogen compounds
BT3 organic compounds
RT guanosine
RT guanylic acid

GUANOSINE [180; 180]
BT1 nucleosides
BT2 nucleotides
BT3 organic compounds
BT2 ribosides
BT1 purines
BT2 heterocyclic compounds
BT3 organic compounds
BT2 organic nitrogen compounds
BT3 organic compounds
RT guanine
RT guanylic acid

GUANYLIC ACID [53; 53]
BT1 nucleotides
BT2 organic compounds
RT guanine
RT guanosine

guards
USE security personnel

GUATEMALA [12; 12]
BT1 central america
BT2 latin america
BT1 developing countries

guidance (electronic)
USE electronic guidance

GUIDE TUBES [109; 109] *Feb 86*
(Tubes which are a part of a reactor core and serve as guides for control rods or monitoring instruments.)
BT1 tubes
RT control elements
RT fuel assemblies

guidelines
USE recommendations

GUIDING-CENTER APPROXIMATION [385; 385]
RT charged particles
RT magnetic fields
RT motion
RT plasma
RT rotation

GUINEA PIGS [1,013; 1,013]
BT1 rodents
BT2 mammals
BT3 vertebrates
BT4 animals

GUINIER-PRESTON ZONES [112; 112]
BT1 zones
RT crystal structure
RT phase transformations
RT segregation

gulf general atom. fast breed.
USE gcfr reactor

gulf general atomic triga-mk-3
USE gulf triga-mk-3 reactor

GULF OF MAINE [3; 3] *Dec 75*
BT1 atlantic ocean
BT2 seas
BT3 surface waters

GULF OF MEXICO [60; 60]
BT1 caribbean sea
BT2 atlantic ocean
BT3 seas
BT4 surface waters
NT1 san antonio bay

GULF TRIGA-MK-3 REACTOR [1; 1]
UF *gulf general atomic triga-mk-3*
UF *triga-3-gulf reactor*
BT1 isotope production reactors
BT2 irradiation reactors
BT3 reactors
BT1 pool type reactors
BT2 water cooled reactors
BT3 reactors
BT2 water moderated reactors
BT3 reactors
BT1 research reactors
BT2 research and test reactors
BT3 reactors
BT1 training reactors
BT2 research and test reactors
BT3 reactors
BT1 triga type reactors
BT2 enriched uranium reactors
BT3 reactors
BT2 hydride moderated reactors
BT3 reactors
BT2 research and test reactors
BT3 reactors
BT2 solid homogeneous reactors
BT3 homogeneous reactors
BT4 reactors
BT2 water cooled reactors
BT3 reactors
BT2 water moderated reactors
BT3 reactors

GUM ACACIA [3; 3]
UF *gum arabic*
BT1 polysaccharides
BT2 saccharides
BT3 carbohydrates
BT4 organic compounds
RT arabinose

gum arabic
USE gum acacia

GUMMITE [6; 6]
BT1 oxide minerals
BT2 minerals
BT1 uranium minerals
BT2 radioactive minerals
BT3 minerals
BT3 radioactive materials
BT4 materials
RT uranium oxides

gun cotton
   USE   nitrocellulose

gundremmingen-1 reactor
   USE   rwe-bayernwerk reactor

GUNDREMMINGEN-2 REACTOR
[105; 105] *Aug 75*
   UF   *krb ii-b reactor*
   UF   *rwe-bayernwerk-b reactor*
   BT1   bwr type reactors
     BT2   enriched uranium reactors
       BT3   reactors
     BT2   power reactors
       BT3   reactors
     BT2   thermal reactors
       BT3   reactors
     BT2   water cooled reactors
       BT3   reactors
     BT2   water moderated reactors
       BT3   reactors

GUNDREMMINGEN-3 REACTOR
[62; 62] *Aug 75*
   UF   *krb ii-c reactor*
   UF   *rwe-bayernwerk-c reactor*
   BT1   bwr type reactors
     BT2   enriched uranium reactors
       BT3   reactors
     BT2   power reactors
       BT3   reactors
     BT2   thermal reactors
       BT3   reactors
     BT2   water cooled reactors
       BT3   reactors
     BT2   water moderated reactors
       BT3   reactors

GUNNISON RIVER [1; 1]
   BT1   rivers
     BT2   surface waters

GUNS [83; 83] *May 76*
   RT   explosives
   RT   projectiles

guns (electron)
   USE   electron guns

guns (plasma)
   USE   plasma guns

GUTTA PERCHA [0; 0]
   RT   elastomers

GUYANA [3; 3] *Dec 82*
   BT1   developing countries
   BT1   south america
     BT2   latin america
   NT1   british guiana

GYNECOLOGY [323; 323]
(Including obstetrics)
   UF   *obstetrics*
   BT1   medicine
   RT   female genitals
   RT   pregnancy
   RT   urogenital system diseases
   RT   women

GYPSUM [229; 229]
   BT1   sulfate minerals
     BT2   minerals
   RT   anhydrite
   RT   calcium sulfates

GYPSUM CEMENTS [29; 29]
   UF   *plaster of paris*
   BT1   cements
     BT2   building materials
       BT3   materials

gypsy moth
   USE   lymantria dispar

GYROCONS [46; 46] *Mar 81*
   BT1   electron tubes
   RT   klystrons
   RT   power supplies
   RT   rf systems

GYROELECTRIC RATIO [4; 4]
   RT   angular momentum
   RT   electric moments

GYROFREQUENCY [394; 394]
   UF   *frequency (gyro)*
   RT   cyclotron frequency

gyromagnetic radius
   USE   larmor radius

GYROMAGNETIC RATIO [1,960; 1,960]
   UF   *g factor (gyromagnetic ratio)*
   RT   angular momentum
   RT   magnetic moments

GYROSCOPES [122; 122]
   RT   measuring instruments
   RT   precession
   RT   rotation

H CENTERS [202; 202]
   BT1   color centers
     BT2   vacancies
       BT3   point defects
         BT4   crystal defects
           BT5   crystal structure

H CODES [919; 919]
   BT1   computer codes

H THEOREM [38; 38]
   RT   boltzmann statistics
   RT   entropy

h-alpha line
   USE   balmer lines

h-beta line
   USE   balmer lines

h-gamma line
   USE   balmer lines

H-MODE PLASMA CONFINEMENT
[335; 335] *Nov 88*
(An operational regime in neutral-beam-injection-heated divertor tokamaks.)
   BT1   plasma confinement
     BT2   confinement
   RT   confinement time
   RT   divertors
   RT   edge localized modes
   RT   tokamak devices

H-1 HELIAC [9; 9] *Apr 90*
   BT1   stellarators
     BT2   closed plasma devices
       BT3   thermonuclear devices
   RT   sheila heliac

h-2050 resonances
(Prior to December 1987 this was a valid descriptor.)
   USE   f4-2030 mesons

HAAG THEOREM [36; 36]
   RT   phi4-field theory
   RT   quantum field theory

haag-araki field theory
   USE   algebraic field theory

HABIT PLANES [61; 61]
   RT   crystal lattices
   RT   phase transformations

→ **HABITAT** [0; 0] *Aug 91*
(The area or type of environment in which a plant or animal normally occurs or lives.)
   RT   environment
   RT   nests

HABROBRACON [7; 7]
   BT1   wasps
     BT2   insects
       BT3   arthropods
         BT4   invertebrates
           BT5   animals

haddam neck reactor
   USE   connecticut yankee reactor

HADRON REACTIONS [1,374; 45,967]
   BT1   nuclear reactions
   NT1   baryon reactions
     NT2   hyperon reactions
     NT2   nucleon reactions
       NT3   antinucleon reactions
         NT4   antineutron reactions
         NT4   antiproton reactions
       NT3   neutron reactions
         NT4   fast fission
         NT4   thermal fission
       NT3   proton reactions
   NT1   meson reactions
     NT2   kaon reactions
       NT3   kaon minus reactions
       NT3   kaon neutral reactions
       NT3   kaon plus reactions
     NT2   pion reactions
       NT3   pion minus reactions
       NT3   pion plus reactions
   RT   space-time model

HADRON-HADRON INTERACTIONS
[3,386; 32,426]
   BT1   particle interactions
     BT2   interactions
   NT1   baryon-baryon interactions
     NT2   hyperon-hyperon interactions
     NT2   nucleon-antinucleon interactio
       NT3   antiproton-neutron interaction
       NT3   neutron-antineutron interactio
       NT3   proton-antineutron interaction
       NT3   proton-antiproton interactions
     NT2   nucleon-hyperon interactions
     NT2   nucleon-nucleon interactions
       NT3   neutron-neutron interactions
       NT3   proton-nucleon interactions
         NT4   proton-neutron interactions
         NT4   proton-proton interactions
   NT1   meson-baryon interactions
     NT2   meson-hyperon interactions
       NT3   kaon-hyperon interactions
       NT3   pion-hyperon interactions
     NT2   meson-nucleon interactions
       NT3   kaon-nucleon interactions
         NT4   kaon-neutron interactions
           NT5   kaon minus-neutron interaction
           NT5   kaon neutral-neutron interacti
           NT5   kaon plus-neutron interactions
         NT4   kaon-proton interactions
           NT5   kaon minus-proton interactions
           NT5   kaon neutral-proton interactio

	NT5	kaon plus-proton interactions
	NT3	pion-nucleon interactions
	NT4	pion-neutron interactions
	NT5	pion minus-neutron interaction
	NT5	pion plus-neutron interactions
	NT4	pion-proton interactions
	NT5	pion minus-proton interactions
	NT5	pion plus-proton interactions
NT1		meson-meson interactions
NT2		kaon-kaon interactions
NT2		pion-kaon interactions
NT2		pion-pion interactions
RT		electromagnetic interactions
RT		strong interactions

HADRONIC ATOMS [455; 2,276]
(Atoms with a hadron such as an antiproton or a sigma-minus particle bound in atomic orbits.)
 UF *antiprotonic atoms*
 UF *exotic atoms*
 UF *sigma-minus atoms*
 BT1 atoms
 NT1 mesic atoms
 NT2 kaonic atoms
 NT2 muonic atoms
 NT2 pionic atoms

HADRONIC PARTICLE DECAY [2,397; 2,397] *Feb 78*
(Particle decay due to hadronic interaction.)
 BT1 particle decay
 BT2 decay

HADRONS [9,387; 139,113]
 BT1 elementary particles
 *NT1 baryons
 *NT1 mesons
 *NT1 resonance particles
 RT charm particles
 RT cim model
 RT grace particles
 RT melosh transformation
 RT taste particles

HAEMOPHILUS [89; 89]
 UF *hemophilus*
 BT1 bacteria
 BT2 microorganisms

HAFNATES [54; 54]
(Specific compounds should be indexed by coordination of a descriptor of the form (CATION) COMPOUNDS and the above anion descriptor.)
 BT1 hafnium compounds
 BT2 transition element compounds
 BT1 oxygen compounds
 RT hafnium oxides

HAFNIUM [1,455; 1,468]
 BT1 transition elements
 BT2 metals
 BT3 elements
 NT1 hafnium-alpha
 NT1 hafnium-beta

HAFNIUM ADDITIONS [151; 155]
(Alloys containing not more than 1% Hf are listed here.)
 RT hafnium alloys
 RT hafnium compounds

HAFNIUM ALLOYS [680; 789]
(Alloys containing more than 1% Hf.)
 BT1 alloys
 NT1 alloy-ta90w8hf
 NT1 hafnium base alloys
 RT hafnium additions

HAFNIUM BASE ALLOYS [77; 77]
 BT1 hafnium alloys
 BT2 alloys

HAFNIUM BORIDES [63; 63]
 BT1 borides
 BT2 boron compounds
 BT1 hafnium compounds
 BT2 transition element compounds

HAFNIUM BROMIDES [18; 18]
 BT1 bromides
 BT2 bromine compounds
 BT3 halogen compounds
 BT2 halides
 BT3 halogen compounds
 BT1 hafnium compounds
 BT2 transition element compounds

HAFNIUM CARBIDES [276; 276]
 BT1 carbides
 BT2 carbon compounds
 BT1 hafnium compounds
 BT2 transition element compounds

HAFNIUM CHLORIDES [116; 116]
 BT1 chlorides
 BT2 chlorine compounds
 BT3 halogen compounds
 BT2 halides
 BT3 halogen compounds
 BT1 hafnium compounds
 BT2 transition element compounds

HAFNIUM COMPLEXES [470; 470]
 BT1 transition element complexes
 BT2 complexes

HAFNIUM COMPOUNDS [348; 1,881]
 BT1 transition element compounds
 NT1 hafnates
 NT1 hafnium borides
 NT1 hafnium bromides
 NT1 hafnium carbides
 NT1 hafnium chlorides
 NT1 hafnium fluorides
 NT1 hafnium hydrides
 NT1 hafnium hydroxides
 NT1 hafnium iodides
 NT1 hafnium nitrates
 NT1 hafnium nitrides
 NT1 hafnium oxides
 NT1 hafnium perchlorates
 NT1 hafnium phosphates
 NT1 hafnium phosphides
 NT1 hafnium selenides
 NT1 hafnium silicates
 NT1 hafnium silicides
 NT1 hafnium sulfates
 NT1 hafnium sulfides
 NT1 hafnium tellurides
 NT1 hafnium tungstates
 RT hafnium additions

HAFNIUM FLUORIDES [89; 89]
 BT1 fluorides
 BT2 fluorine compounds
 BT3 halogen compounds
 BT2 halides
 BT3 halogen compounds
 BT1 hafnium compounds
 BT2 transition element compounds

HAFNIUM HYDRIDES [65; 65]
 BT1 hafnium compounds
 BT2 transition element compounds
 BT1 hydrides
 BT2 hydrogen compounds

HAFNIUM HYDROXIDES [14; 14]
 BT1 hafnium compounds
 BT2 transition element compounds
 BT1 hydroxides
 BT2 hydrogen compounds
 BT2 oxygen compounds

HAFNIUM IODIDES [19; 19]
 BT1 hafnium compounds
 BT2 transition element compounds
 BT1 iodides
 BT2 halides
 BT3 halogen compounds
 BT2 iodine compounds
 BT3 halogen compounds

HAFNIUM IONS [41; 41]
 BT1 ions
 BT2 charged particles

HAFNIUM ISOTOPES [159; 1,271]
 NT1 hafnium 154
 NT1 hafnium 155
 NT1 hafnium 156
 NT1 hafnium 157
 NT1 hafnium 158
 NT1 hafnium 159
 NT1 hafnium 160
 NT1 hafnium 161
 NT1 hafnium 162
 NT1 hafnium 163
 NT1 hafnium 164
 NT1 hafnium 165
 NT1 hafnium 166
 NT1 hafnium 167
 NT1 hafnium 168
 NT1 hafnium 169
 NT1 hafnium 170
 NT1 hafnium 171
 NT1 hafnium 172
 NT1 hafnium 173
 NT1 hafnium 174
 NT1 hafnium 175
 NT1 hafnium 176
 NT1 hafnium 177
 NT1 hafnium 178
 NT1 hafnium 179
 NT1 hafnium 180
 NT1 hafnium 181
 NT1 hafnium 182
 NT1 hafnium 183
 NT1 hafnium 184
 NT1 hafnium 185
 NT1 hafnium 186

HAFNIUM NITRATES [16; 16]
 BT1 hafnium compounds
 BT2 transition element compounds
 BT1 nitrates
 BT2 nitrogen compounds
 BT2 oxygen compounds

HAFNIUM NITRIDES [153; 153]
 BT1 hafnium compounds
 BT2 transition element compounds
 BT1 nitrides
 BT2 nitrogen compounds
 BT2 pnictides

HAFNIUM OXIDES [589; 611]
 BT1 hafnium compounds
 BT2 transition element compounds
 BT1 oxides
 BT2 chalcogenides
 BT2 oxygen compounds
 RT baddeleyite
 RT hafnates
 RT oxide minerals

→ **HAFNIUM PERCHLORATES** [0; 0] *Sep 91*
 BT1 hafnium compounds
 BT2 transition element compounds
 BT1 perchlorates
 BT2 chlorine compounds
 BT3 halogen compounds
 BT2 oxygen compounds

HAFNIUM PHOSPHATES [32; 32]
 BT1 hafnium compounds
 BT2 transition element compounds
 BT1 phosphates
 BT2 oxygen compounds
 BT2 phosphorus compounds

HAFNIUM PHOSPHIDES [0; 0] *Sep 91*
BT1 hafnium compounds
BT2 transition element compounds
BT1 phosphides
BT2 phosphorus compounds
BT2 pnictides

HAFNIUM SELENIDES [13; 13]
BT1 hafnium compounds
BT2 transition element compounds
BT1 selenides
BT2 chalcogenides
BT2 selenium compounds

HAFNIUM SILICATES [14; 14]
BT1 hafnium compounds
BT2 transition element compounds
BT1 silicates
BT2 oxygen compounds
BT2 silicon compounds

HAFNIUM SILICIDES [20; 20] *Apr 79*
BT1 hafnium compounds
BT2 transition element compounds
BT1 silicides
BT2 silicon compounds

HAFNIUM SULFATES [63; 63]
BT1 hafnium compounds
BT2 transition element compounds
BT1 sulfates
BT2 oxygen compounds
BT2 sulfur compounds

HAFNIUM SULFIDES [39; 39]
BT1 hafnium compounds
BT2 transition element compounds
BT1 sulfides
BT2 chalcogenides
BT2 sulfur compounds

HAFNIUM TELLURIDES [5; 5] *Sep 85*
BT1 hafnium compounds
BT2 transition element compounds
BT1 tellurides
BT2 chalcogenides
BT2 tellurium compounds

HAFNIUM TUNGSTATES [2; 2] *Sep 78*
BT1 hafnium compounds
BT2 transition element compounds
BT1 tungstates
BT2 oxygen compounds
BT2 tungsten compounds
BT3 transition element compounds

HAFNIUM 154 [4; 4] *May 86*
BT1 beta-plus decay radioisotopes
BT2 beta decay radioisotopes
BT3 radioisotopes
BT4 isotopes
BT1 electron capture radioisotopes
BT2 beta decay radioisotopes
BT3 radioisotopes
BT4 isotopes
BT1 even-even nuclei
BT2 nuclei
BT1 hafnium isotopes
BT1 intermediate mass nuclei
BT2 nuclei
BT1 seconds living radioisotopes
BT2 radioisotopes
BT3 isotopes

HAFNIUM 155 [0; 0] *May 86*
BT1 beta-plus decay radioisotopes
BT2 beta decay radioisotopes
BT3 radioisotopes
BT4 isotopes
BT1 electron capture radioisotopes
BT2 beta decay radioisotopes
BT3 radioisotopes
BT4 isotopes
BT1 even-odd nuclei
BT2 nuclei
BT1 hafnium isotopes
BT1 intermediate mass nuclei
BT2 nuclei
BT1 millisec living radioisotopes
BT2 radioisotopes
BT3 isotopes

HAFNIUM 156 [5; 5] *Sep 79*
BT1 alpha decay radioisotopes
BT2 radioisotopes
BT3 isotopes
BT1 even-even nuclei
BT2 nuclei
BT1 hafnium isotopes
BT1 intermediate mass nuclei
BT2 nuclei
BT1 millisec living radioisotopes
BT2 radioisotopes
BT3 isotopes

HAFNIUM 157 [4; 4]
BT1 alpha decay radioisotopes
BT2 radioisotopes
BT3 isotopes
BT1 electron capture radioisotopes
BT2 beta decay radioisotopes
BT3 radioisotopes
BT4 isotopes
BT1 even-odd nuclei
BT2 nuclei
BT1 hafnium isotopes
BT1 intermediate mass nuclei
BT2 nuclei
BT1 millisec living radioisotopes
BT2 radioisotopes
BT3 isotopes

HAFNIUM 158 [4; 4]
BT1 alpha decay radioisotopes
BT2 radioisotopes
BT3 isotopes
BT1 electron capture radioisotopes
BT2 beta decay radioisotopes
BT3 radioisotopes
BT4 isotopes
BT1 even-even nuclei
BT2 nuclei
BT1 hafnium isotopes
BT1 intermediate mass nuclei
BT2 nuclei
BT1 seconds living radioisotopes
BT2 radioisotopes
BT3 isotopes

HAFNIUM 159 [4; 4]
BT1 alpha decay radioisotopes
BT2 radioisotopes
BT3 isotopes
BT1 electron capture radioisotopes
BT2 beta decay radioisotopes
BT3 radioisotopes
BT4 isotopes
BT1 even-odd nuclei
BT2 nuclei
BT1 hafnium isotopes
BT1 intermediate mass nuclei
BT2 nuclei
BT1 seconds living radioisotopes
BT2 radioisotopes
BT3 isotopes

HAFNIUM 160 [12; 12]
BT1 alpha decay radioisotopes
BT2 radioisotopes
BT3 isotopes
BT1 electron capture radioisotopes
BT2 beta decay radioisotopes
BT3 radioisotopes
BT4 isotopes
BT1 even-even nuclei
BT2 nuclei
BT1 hafnium isotopes
BT1 intermediate mass nuclei
BT2 nuclei
BT1 seconds living radioisotopes
BT2 radioisotopes
BT3 isotopes

HAFNIUM 161 [9; 9]
BT1 alpha decay radioisotopes
BT2 radioisotopes
BT3 isotopes
BT1 even-odd nuclei
BT2 nuclei
BT1 hafnium isotopes
BT1 intermediate mass nuclei
BT2 nuclei
BT1 seconds living radioisotopes
BT2 radioisotopes
BT3 isotopes

HAFNIUM 162 [18; 18] *Jun 82*
BT1 alpha decay radioisotopes
BT2 radioisotopes
BT3 isotopes
BT1 beta-plus decay radioisotopes
BT2 beta decay radioisotopes
BT3 radioisotopes
BT4 isotopes
BT1 electron capture radioisotopes
BT2 beta decay radioisotopes
BT3 radioisotopes
BT4 isotopes
BT1 even-even nuclei
BT2 nuclei
BT1 hafnium isotopes
BT1 intermediate mass nuclei
BT2 nuclei
BT1 seconds living radioisotopes
BT2 radioisotopes
BT3 isotopes

HAFNIUM 163 [15; 15] *Dec 80*
BT1 beta-plus decay radioisotopes
BT2 beta decay radioisotopes
BT3 radioisotopes
BT4 isotopes
BT1 electron capture radioisotopes
BT2 beta decay radioisotopes
BT3 radioisotopes
BT4 isotopes
BT1 even-odd nuclei
BT2 nuclei
BT1 hafnium isotopes
BT1 intermediate mass nuclei
BT2 nuclei
BT1 seconds living radioisotopes
BT2 radioisotopes
BT3 isotopes

HAFNIUM 164 [27; 27] *Apr 82*
BT1 even-even nuclei
BT2 nuclei
BT1 hafnium isotopes
BT1 intermediate mass nuclei
BT2 nuclei
BT1 minutes living radioisotopes
BT2 radioisotopes
BT3 isotopes

HAFNIUM 165 [12; 12] *Jun 82*
BT1 even-odd nuclei
BT2 nuclei
BT1 hafnium isotopes
BT1 intermediate mass nuclei
BT2 nuclei
BT1 minutes living radioisotopes
BT2 radioisotopes
BT3 isotopes

HAFNIUM 166 [28; 28]
BT1 beta-plus decay radioisotopes
BT2 beta decay radioisotopes
BT3 radioisotopes
BT4 isotopes
BT1 electron capture radioisotopes
BT2 beta decay radioisotopes
BT3 radioisotopes
BT4 isotopes
BT1 even-even nuclei
BT2 nuclei
BT1 hafnium isotopes
BT1 intermediate mass nuclei
BT2 nuclei
BT1 minutes living radioisotopes
BT2 radioisotopes

BT3 isotopes

HAFNIUM 167 [16; 16]
BT1 beta-plus decay radioisotopes
BT2 beta decay radioisotopes
BT3 radioisotopes
BT4 isotopes
BT1 electron capture radioisotopes
BT2 beta decay radioisotopes
BT3 radioisotopes
BT4 isotopes
BT1 even-odd nuclei
BT2 nuclei
BT1 hafnium isotopes
BT1 intermediate mass nuclei
BT2 nuclei
BT1 minutes living radioisotopes
BT2 radioisotopes
BT3 isotopes

HAFNIUM 168 [67; 67]
BT1 beta-plus decay radioisotopes
BT2 beta decay radioisotopes
BT3 radioisotopes
BT4 isotopes
BT1 electron capture radioisotopes
BT2 beta decay radioisotopes
BT3 radioisotopes
BT4 isotopes
BT1 even-even nuclei
BT2 nuclei
BT1 hafnium isotopes
BT1 intermediate mass nuclei
BT2 nuclei
BT1 minutes living radioisotopes
BT2 radioisotopes
BT3 isotopes

HAFNIUM 169 [14; 14]
BT1 beta-plus decay radioisotopes
BT2 beta decay radioisotopes
BT3 radioisotopes
BT4 isotopes
BT1 electron capture radioisotopes
BT2 beta decay radioisotopes
BT3 radioisotopes
BT4 isotopes
BT1 even-odd nuclei
BT2 nuclei
BT1 hafnium isotopes
BT1 intermediate mass nuclei
BT2 nuclei
BT1 minutes living radioisotopes
BT2 radioisotopes
BT3 isotopes

HAFNIUM 170 [44; 44]
BT1 electron capture radioisotopes
BT2 beta decay radioisotopes
BT3 radioisotopes
BT4 isotopes
BT1 even-even nuclei
BT2 nuclei
BT1 hafnium isotopes
BT1 hours living radioisotopes
BT2 radioisotopes
BT3 isotopes
BT1 intermediate mass nuclei
BT2 nuclei

HAFNIUM 171 [24; 24]
BT1 electron capture radioisotopes
BT2 beta decay radioisotopes
BT3 radioisotopes
BT4 isotopes
BT1 even-odd nuclei
BT2 nuclei
BT1 hafnium isotopes
BT1 hours living radioisotopes
BT2 radioisotopes
BT3 isotopes
BT1 intermediate mass nuclei
BT2 nuclei

HAFNIUM 172 [70; 70]
BT1 electron capture radioisotopes
BT2 beta decay radioisotopes
BT3 radioisotopes
BT4 isotopes
BT1 even-even nuclei
BT2 nuclei
BT1 hafnium isotopes
BT1 intermediate mass nuclei
BT2 nuclei
BT1 years living radioisotopes
BT2 radioisotopes
BT3 isotopes

HAFNIUM 173 [41; 41]
BT1 electron capture radioisotopes
BT2 beta decay radioisotopes
BT3 radioisotopes
BT4 isotopes
BT1 even-odd nuclei
BT2 nuclei
BT1 hafnium isotopes
BT1 hours living radioisotopes
BT2 radioisotopes
BT3 isotopes
BT1 intermediate mass nuclei
BT2 nuclei

HAFNIUM 174 [71; 71]
BT1 alpha decay radioisotopes
BT2 radioisotopes
BT3 isotopes
BT1 even-even nuclei
BT2 nuclei
BT1 hafnium isotopes
BT1 intermediate mass nuclei
BT2 nuclei
BT1 years living radioisotopes
BT2 radioisotopes
BT3 isotopes

HAFNIUM 174 TARGET [8; 8] *Sep 77*
BT1 targets

HAFNIUM 175 [96; 96]
BT1 days living radioisotopes
BT2 radioisotopes
BT3 isotopes
BT1 electron capture radioisotopes
BT2 beta decay radioisotopes
BT3 radioisotopes
BT4 isotopes
BT1 even-odd nuclei
BT2 nuclei
BT1 hafnium isotopes
BT1 intermediate mass nuclei
BT2 nuclei

HAFNIUM 176 [107; 107]
BT1 even-even nuclei
BT2 nuclei
BT1 hafnium isotopes
BT1 intermediate mass nuclei
BT2 nuclei
BT1 stable isotopes
BT2 isotopes

HAFNIUM 176 TARGET [32; 32]
Apr 76
BT1 targets

HAFNIUM 177 [126; 126]
BT1 even-odd nuclei
BT2 nuclei
BT1 hafnium isotopes
BT1 intermediate mass nuclei
BT2 nuclei
BT1 isomeric transition isotopes
BT2 radioisotopes
BT3 isotopes
BT1 minutes living radioisotopes
BT2 radioisotopes
BT3 isotopes
BT1 seconds living radioisotopes
BT2 radioisotopes
BT3 isotopes
BT1 stable isotopes
BT2 isotopes

HAFNIUM 177 TARGET [46; 46]
BT1 targets

HAFNIUM 178 [167; 167]
BT1 even-even nuclei
BT2 nuclei
BT1 hafnium isotopes
BT1 intermediate mass nuclei
BT2 nuclei
BT1 internal conversion radioisoto
BT2 radioisotopes
BT3 isotopes
BT1 isomeric transition isotopes
BT2 radioisotopes
BT3 isotopes
BT1 seconds living radioisotopes
BT2 radioisotopes
BT3 isotopes
BT1 stable isotopes
BT2 isotopes
BT1 years living radioisotopes
BT2 radioisotopes
BT3 isotopes

HAFNIUM 178 TARGET [68; 68]
BT1 targets

HAFNIUM 179 [132; 132]
BT1 days living radioisotopes
BT2 radioisotopes
BT3 isotopes
BT1 even-odd nuclei
BT2 nuclei
BT1 hafnium isotopes
BT1 intermediate mass nuclei
BT2 nuclei
BT1 internal conversion radioisoto
BT2 radioisotopes
BT3 isotopes
BT1 isomeric transition isotopes
BT2 radioisotopes
BT3 isotopes
BT1 seconds living radioisotopes
BT2 radioisotopes
BT3 isotopes
BT1 stable isotopes
BT2 isotopes

HAFNIUM 179 TARGET [55; 55]
BT1 targets

HAFNIUM 180 [182; 182]
BT1 even-even nuclei
BT2 nuclei
BT1 hafnium isotopes
BT1 hours living radioisotopes
BT2 radioisotopes
BT3 isotopes
BT1 intermediate mass nuclei
BT2 nuclei
BT1 internal conversion radioisoto
BT2 radioisotopes
BT3 isotopes
BT1 isomeric transition isotopes
BT2 radioisotopes
BT3 isotopes
BT1 stable isotopes
BT2 isotopes

HAFNIUM 180 TARGET [95; 95]
BT1 targets

HAFNIUM 181 [223; 223]
BT1 beta-minus decay radioisotopes
BT2 beta decay radioisotopes
BT3 radioisotopes
BT4 isotopes
BT1 days living radioisotopes
BT2 radioisotopes
BT3 isotopes
BT1 even-odd nuclei
BT2 nuclei
BT1 hafnium isotopes
BT1 heavy nuclei
BT2 nuclei

HAFNIUM 182 [10; 10]
  BT1 beta-minus decay radioisotopes
    BT2 beta decay radioisotopes
      BT3 radioisotopes
        BT4 isotopes
  BT1 even-even nuclei
    BT2 nuclei
  BT1 hafnium isotopes
  BT1 heavy nuclei
    BT2 nuclei
  BT1 hours living radioisotopes
    BT2 radioisotopes
      BT3 isotopes
  BT1 isomeric transition isotopes
    BT2 radioisotopes
      BT3 isotopes
  BT1 years living radioisotopes
    BT2 radioisotopes
      BT3 isotopes

HAFNIUM 183 [4; 4]
  BT1 beta-minus decay radioisotopes
    BT2 beta decay radioisotopes
      BT3 radioisotopes
        BT4 isotopes
  BT1 even-odd nuclei
    BT2 nuclei
  BT1 hafnium isotopes
  BT1 heavy nuclei
    BT2 nuclei
  BT1 hours living radioisotopes
    BT2 radioisotopes
      BT3 isotopes

HAFNIUM 184 [5; 5]
  BT1 beta-minus decay radioisotopes
    BT2 beta decay radioisotopes
      BT3 radioisotopes
        BT4 isotopes
  BT1 even-even nuclei
    BT2 nuclei
  BT1 hafnium isotopes
  BT1 heavy nuclei
    BT2 nuclei
  BT1 hours living radioisotopes
    BT2 radioisotopes
      BT3 isotopes

HAFNIUM 185 [1; 1]
  BT1 even-odd nuclei
    BT2 nuclei
  BT1 hafnium isotopes
  BT1 heavy nuclei
    BT2 nuclei

HAFNIUM 186 [0; 0]
  BT1 even-even nuclei
    BT2 nuclei
  BT1 hafnium isotopes
  BT1 heavy nuclei
    BT2 nuclei

HAFNIUM-ALPHA [14; 14]
  BT1 hafnium
    BT2 transition elements
      BT3 metals
        BT4 elements

HAFNIUM-BETA [6; 6]
  BT1 hafnium
    BT2 transition elements
      BT3 metals
        BT4 elements

hahn-meitner vicksi accelerato
  USE vicksi accelerator

hahnium
  USE element 105

HAIL [18; 18]
  BT1 atmospheric precipitations
  RT ice

HAIR [609; 609]
  BT1 skin
    BT2 organs
      BT3 body
  RT epilation
  RT hair follicles
  RT melanin

HAIR FOLLICLES [42; 42] *Sep 75*
  BT1 animal cells
  RT epithelium
  RT hair
  RT skin

HAITI [4; 4] *Apr 88*
  BT1 developing countries
  BT1 latin america
  BT1 west indies
    BT2 islands

HAIWEEITE [1; 1]
  BT1 silicate minerals
    BT2 minerals
  BT1 uranium minerals
    BT2 radioactive minerals
      BT3 minerals
      BT3 radioactive materials
        BT4 materials

HAIZY CYCLOTRON [8; 8] *Jun 83*
(Hamburg isochronous cyclotron.)
  BT1 isochronous cyclotrons
    BT2 cyclotrons
      BT3 cyclic accelerators
        BT4 accelerators

halden heavy boil. wa. reactor
  USE hbwr reactor

HALEX PROCESS [0; 0]
  BT1 purex process
    BT2 reprocessing
      BT3 separation processes

HALF-LIFE [6,601; 6,601]
  UF *halftime*
  RT days living radioisotopes
  RT decay
  RT ft value
  RT geiger-nuttall law
  RT hours living radioisotopes
  RT lifetime
  RT microsec living radioisotopes
  RT millisec living radioisotopes
  RT minutes living radioisotopes
  RT nanosec living radioisotopes
  RT radioisotope generators
  RT residence half-time
  RT seconds living radioisotopes
  RT years living radioisotopes

half-life (biological)
  USE biological half-life

half-life (effective)
  USE biological half-life

§§ **HALF-THICKNESS** [108; 108]
(Thickness of material which reduces the intensity of a beam of radiation passing through it to one-half its initial value.)
  BT1 physical properties
  RT absorption
  RT radiation length
  RT radiation protection
  RT radiation quality
  RT shielding
  RT thickness

HALFBEAK EVENT [2; 2] *Jun 77*
  BT1 contained explosions
    BT2 underground explosions
      BT3 explosions
  BT1 nuclear explosions
    BT2 explosions

halftime
  USE half-life

HALIDE MINERALS [17; 155] *Apr 84*
  BT1 minerals
  NT1 carnallite
  NT1 fluorite
  NT1 schroeckingerite
  RT calcium fluorides
  RT magnesium chlorides
  RT potassium chlorides

HALIDES [1,433; 38,703]
  BT1 halogen compounds
  *NT1 ammonium halides
  *NT1 bromides
  *NT1 cadmium halides
  *NT1 calcium halides
  *NT1 chlorides
  *NT1 copper halides
  *NT1 fluorides
  *NT1 gallium halides
  *NT1 iodides
  *NT1 lead halides
  *NT1 lithium halides
  *NT1 manganese halides
  *NT1 mercury halides
  *NT1 rhenium halides
  *NT1 silicon halides
  *NT1 tellurium halides
  *NT1 thallium halides
  *NT1 tin halides
  *NT1 zinc halides

HALL EFFECT [3,572; 3,572]
  RT electric conductors
  RT ettinghausen effect
  RT nernst effect
  RT righi-leduc effect
  RT shubnikov-de haas effect

hall generators
  USE mhd generators

hallam nuclear power facility
  USE hnpf reactor

HALLEY COMET [440; 440] *Aug 86*
  BT1 comets
  RT solar system

HALLUCINOGENS [50; 51]
  BT1 psychotropic drugs
    BT2 central nervous system agents
      BT3 drugs
  NT1 bufotenine

HALOGEN COMPOUNDS [239; 45,010]
(For inorganic compounds only; see also ORGANIC HALOGEN COMPOUNDS.)
  *NT1 astatine compounds
  *NT1 bromine compounds
  *NT1 chlorine compounds
  *NT1 fluorine compounds
  *NT1 halides
  *NT1 iodine compounds
  *NT1 oxyhalides
  RT organic halogen compounds

→ **HALOGENATED ALIPHATIC HYDROCAR** [0; 0]
(Prior to October 1991, this concept was indexed by ORGANIC HALOGEN COMPOUNDS.)
  BT1 organic halogen compounds
    BT2 organic compounds
  NT1 brominated aliphatic hydrocarb

    NT1   chlorinated aliphatic hydrocar
    NT2   carbon tetrachloride
    NT2   chloroform
    NT2   methyl chloride
    NT2   pvc
    NT1   fluorinated aliphatic hydrocar
    NT1   iodinated aliphatic hydrocarbo

→ **HALOGENATED AROMATIC HYDROCARB** [0; 0]
(Prior to October 1991, this concept was indexed by AROMATICS and ORGANIC HALOGEN COMPOUNDS.)
    BT1   aromatics
    BT2   organic compounds
    BT1   organic halogen compounds
    BT2   organic compounds
    NT1   brominated aromatic hydrocarbo
    NT1   chlorinated aromatic hydrocarb
    NT2   aldrin
    NT1   fluorinated aromatic hydrocarb
    NT1   iodinated aromatic hydrocarbon

halogenated hydrocarbons
    USE   organic halogen compounds

HALOGENATION [85; 2,094]
    BT1   chemical reactions
    NT1   astatination
    NT1   bromination
    NT1   chlorination
    NT2   sulfochlorination
    NT1   fluorination
    NT1   iodination

HALOGENS [316; 8,835]
    BT1   nonmetals
    BT2   elements
    NT1   astatine
    NT1   bromine
    NT1   chlorine
    NT1   fluorine
    NT1   iodine

HALPERN-STRUTINSKI THEORY [3; 3]
    RT   angular distribution

ham
    USE   meat

HAMADA-JOHNSTON POTENTIAL [244; 244]
    BT1   nucleon-nucleon potential
    BT2   potentials
    RT   nuclear models
    RT   nuclear potential

HAMAOKA-1 REACTOR [49; 49]
(Hamaoka, Shizuoka, Japan)
    UF   *chubu-1 reactor*
    BT1   bwr type reactors
    BT2   enriched uranium reactors
    BT3   reactors
    BT2   power reactors
    BT3   reactors
    BT2   thermal reactors
    BT3   reactors
    BT2   water cooled reactors
    BT3   reactors
    BT2   water moderated reactors
    BT3   reactors

HAMAOKA-2 REACTOR [40; 40]
(Hamaoka, Shizuoka, Japan)
    UF   *chubu-2 reactor*
    BT1   bwr type reactors
    BT2   enriched uranium reactors
    BT3   reactors
    BT2   power reactors
    BT3   reactors
    BT2   thermal reactors
    BT3   reactors
    BT2   water cooled reactors
    BT3   reactors
    BT2   water moderated reactors
    BT3   reactors

HAMAOKA-3 REACTOR [38; 38]
(Hamaoka, Shizuoka, Japan)
    UF   *chubu-3 reactor*
    BT1   bwr type reactors
    BT2   enriched uranium reactors
    BT3   reactors
    BT2   power reactors
    BT3   reactors
    BT2   thermal reactors
    BT3   reactors
    BT2   water cooled reactors
    BT3   reactors
    BT2   water moderated reactors
    BT3   reactors

hamburg synchrotron
    USE   desy

hamilton operators
    USE   hamiltonians

HAMILTON-JACOBI EQUATIONS [400; 400]
    BT1   partial differential equations
    BT2   differential equations
    BT3   equations
    RT   equations of motion
    RT   hamiltonian function
    RT   mechanics

HAMILTONIAN FUNCTION [1,431; 1,431]
    BT1   functions
    RT   classical mechanics
    RT   equations of motion
    RT   hamilton-jacobi equations
    RT   hamiltonians

HAMILTONIANS [20,145; 20,145]
    UF   *energy operators*
    UF   *hamilton operators*
    BT1   quantum operators
    BT2   mathematical operators
    RT   detailed balance principle
    RT   hamiltonian function
    RT   sudden approximation

HAMM-UENTROP REACTOR [11; 11] *Feb 76*
    BT1   pwr type reactors
    BT2   enriched uranium reactors
    BT3   reactors
    BT2   power reactors
    BT3   reactors
    BT2   thermal reactors
    BT3   reactors
    BT2   water cooled reactors
    BT3   reactors
    BT2   water moderated reactors
    BT3   reactors

HAMSTERS [2,490; 2,498]
    UF   *chinese hamster*
    UF   *cricetulus*
    UF   *mesocricetus*
    UF   *syrian hamster*
    BT1   rodents
    BT2   mammals
    BT3   vertebrates
    BT4   animals

HANDCAR EVENT [0; 0]
    BT1   nuclear explosions
    BT2   explosions
    BT1   underground explosions
    BT2   explosions

HANDLEY EVENT [3; 3]
    BT1   contained explosions
    BT2   underground explosions
    BT3   explosions
    BT1   nuclear explosions
    BT2   explosions

handling (data)
    USE   data processing

handling (materials)
    USE   materials handling

handling (wastes)
    USE   waste management

handling licenses
(If appropriate use the descriptor MATERIALS HANDLING together with the one below.)
    USE   licenses

HANDS [590; 830]
    BT1   arms
    BT2   limbs
    BT3   body areas
    BT4   body
    NT1   fingers

hanford atomic products operat
    USE   hapo

HANFORD ENGINEERING DEVELOPMEN [83; 83] *Dec 85*
(Hanford Engineering Development Laboratory)
    UF   *hedl*
    BT1   us doe
    BT2   us organizations
    BT3   national organizations
    RT   hanford reservation
    RT   hapo
    RT   washington

hanford neutron radiography fa
    USE   triga-1-hanford reactor

HANFORD PRODUCTION REACTORS [96; 96]
    BT1   plutonium production reactors
    BT2   production reactors
    BT3   reactors

HANFORD RESERVATION [1,782; 1,782] *Oct 76*
    BT1   us doe
    BT2   us organizations
    BT3   national organizations
    RT   battelle pacific northwest lab
    RT   hanford engineering developmen
    RT   hapo
    RT   us erda
    RT   washington

HANFORD-2 REACTOR [39; 39]
(Name changed to Washington Public Power Supply System Nuclear Project Number 2, and current items are indexed to the abbreviated form WNP-2 REACTOR.)
    BT1   wnp-2 reactor
    BT2   bwr type reactors
    BT3   enriched uranium reactors
    BT4   reactors
    BT3   power reactors
    BT4   reactors
    BT3   thermal reactors
    BT4   reactors
    BT3   water cooled reactors
    BT4   reactors
    BT3   water moderated reactors

    BT4   reactors

hankel functions
    USE   bessel functions

HANKEL TRANSFORM [41; 41]
    BT1   integral transformations
    BT2   transformations

hannover-triga-mk-1 reactor
    USE   triga-1-hanover reactor

HAPLOIDY [94; 94]
    BT1   ploidy
    RT   gametes

HAPO [452; 452]
    UF   *hanford atomic products operat*
    BT1   us aec
    BT2   us organizations
    BT3   national organizations
    BT1   us doe
    BT2   us organizations
    BT3   national organizations
    BT1   us erda
    BT2   us organizations
    BT3   national organizations
    RT   hanford engineering developmen
    RT   hanford reservation
    RT   sequim bay

HAPTOGLOBINS [27; 27]
    BT1   globulins-alpha
    BT2   globulins
    BT3   proteins
    BT4   organic compounds
    BT1   mucoproteins
    BT2   polysaccharides
    BT3   saccharides
    BT4   carbohydrates
    BT5   organic compounds
    BT2   proteins
    BT3   organic compounds

HARANG DISCONTINUITY [51; 51]
    UF   *midnight discontinuity*
    BT1   auroral oval
    RT   aurorae
    RT   ionosphere

HARBORS [117; 117]
    RT   chariot event
    RT   inland waterways
    RT   seas

hard coal
    SEE   anthracite
    OR   black coal

HARD COLLISION MODELS [145; 145]
Jul 78
(Models which reduce the origin of high systems to a binary collision of the projectiles or some subunits thereof.)
    UF   *hard-collision models*
    BT1   particle models
    BT2   mathematical models

HARD COMPONENT [116; 116]
    BT1   cosmic radiation
    BT2   ionizing radiations
    BT3   radiations

HARD CORE PINCH [12; 12]
    BT1   pinch effect
    RT   linear hard core pinch devices

hard metals
    USE   cermets

hard soldering
    USE   brazing

HARD X RADIATION [1,468; 1,468]
    BT1   x radiation
    BT2   electromagnetic radiation
    BT3   radiations
    BT2   ionizing radiations
    BT3   radiations

hard-collision models
    USE   hard collision models

HARD-CORE POTENTIAL [331; 331]
    BT1   nuclear potential
    BT2   potentials
    RT   jastrow theory
    RT   massey-mohr equation
    RT   nucleons

HARD-SPHERE MODEL [276; 276]
    RT   gases

HARDENING [928; 5,756]
    NT1   age hardening
    NT1   dispersion hardening
    NT1   precipitation hardening
    NT1   quench hardening
    NT1   radiation hardening
    NT1   strain hardening
    NT1   surface hardening
    NT2   carburization
    RT   cold working
    RT   hardness
    RT   heat treatments

hardening (spectral)
    USE   spectral hardening

HARDHAT EVENT [3; 3]
    BT1   plowshare project

HARDNESS [2,184; 5,099]
    BT1   mechanical properties
    NT1   microhardness
    RT   brinell hardness
    RT   hardening
    RT   knoop hardness
    RT   rockwell hardness
    RT   vickers hardness

HARDTACK PROJECT [0; 0]
    UF   *project hardtack*
    RT   eniwetok
    RT   holly event
    RT   nuclear explosions
    RT   orange event

HARMONIC GENERATION [243; 243]
Sep 86
    RT   electromagnetic radiation
    RT   frequency mixing
    RT   nonlinear optics
    RT   nonlinear problems
    RT   sound waves

HARMONIC OSCILLATOR MODELS [1,439; 1,439]
    BT1   mathematical models
    RT   atomic models
    RT   harmonic oscillators
    RT   nuclear models
    RT   particle models

HARMONIC OSCILLATORS [2,006; 2,006]
    RT   anharmonic oscillators
    RT   equations of motion
    RT   harmonic oscillator models
    RT   mathematics
    RT   mechanics

HARMONIC POTENTIAL [357; 357]
    BT1   nuclear potential
    BT2   potentials

HARMONICA-2 DEVICE [2; 2]
    BT1   stellarators
    BT2   closed plasma devices
    BT3   thermonuclear devices

HARMONICS [1,862; 2,262]
(Eigenfrequency oscillations excited in a vibrating system.)
    BT1   oscillations
    NT1   cyclotron harmonics
    RT   lattice vibrations
    RT   mechanical vibrations
    RT   nonlinear problems
    RT   oscillation modes
    RT   plasma waves
    RT   resonance

HARMONIE REACTOR [19; 19]
(CEA/CEN, Cadarache, St. Paul Lez Durance, France)
    BT1   air cooled reactors
    BT2   gas cooled reactors
    BT3   reactors
    BT1   enriched uranium reactors
    BT2   reactors
    BT1   fast reactors
    BT2   epithermal reactors
    BT3   reactors
    BT1   research reactors
    BT2   research and test reactors
    BT3   reactors
    BT1   test reactors
    BT2   research and test reactors
    BT3   reactors
    BT2   test facilities

HARRIS-1 REACTOR [60; 60]
    UF   *shearon harris-1 reactor*
    BT1   pwr type reactors
    BT2   enriched uranium reactors
    BT3   reactors
    BT2   power reactors
    BT3   reactors
    BT2   thermal reactors
    BT3   reactors
    BT2   water cooled reactors
    BT3   reactors
    BT2   water moderated reactors
    BT3   reactors

HARRIS-2 REACTOR [48; 48]
    UF   *shearon harris-2 reactor*
    BT1   pwr type reactors
    BT2   enriched uranium reactors
    BT3   reactors
    BT2   power reactors
    BT3   reactors
    BT2   thermal reactors
    BT3   reactors
    BT2   water cooled reactors
    BT3   reactors
    BT2   water moderated reactors
    BT3   reactors

HARRIS-3 REACTOR [43; 43]
    UF   *shearon harris-3 reactor*
    BT1   pwr type reactors
    BT2   enriched uranium reactors
    BT3   reactors
    BT2   power reactors
    BT3   reactors
    BT2   thermal reactors
    BT3   reactors
    BT2   water cooled reactors
    BT3   reactors
    BT2   water moderated reactors
    BT3   reactors

HARRIS-4 REACTOR [43; 43]
    UF   *shearon harris-4 reactor*
    BT1   pwr type reactors
    BT2   enriched uranium reactors
    BT3   reactors

BT2   power reactors
  BT3   reactors
  BT2   thermal reactors
  BT3   reactors
  BT2   water cooled reactors
  BT3   reactors
  BT2   water moderated reactors
  BT3   reactors

HARRY EVENT [4; 4] *Feb 82*
  BT1   atmospheric explosions
  BT2   explosions
  BT1   nuclear explosions
  BT2   explosions
  BT1   upshot project

HARTLEPOOL REACTOR [91; 91]
(Hartlepool, Durham, UK)
  BT1   agr type reactors
  BT2   enriched uranium reactors
  BT3   reactors
  BT2   gas cooled reactors
  BT3   reactors
  BT2   graphite moderated reactors
  BT3   reactors
  BT1   carbon dioxide cooled reactors
  BT2   gas cooled reactors
  BT3   reactors
  BT1   power reactors
  BT2   reactors
  BT1   thermal reactors
  BT2   reactors

HARTMANN NUMBER [216; 216]
  RT   fluid flow
  RT   magnetohydrodynamics

hartree approximation
  USE   hartree-fock method

HARTREE-FOCK METHOD
[6,359; 6,359]
  UF   *fock method*
  UF   *fock self-consistent field*
  UF   *hartree approximation*
  RT   atomic models
  RT   electronic structure
  RT   hartree-fock-bogolyubov theory
  RT   nuclear models
  RT   nuclear structure
  RT   self-consistent field

HARTREE-FOCK-BOGOLYUBOV THEORY [688; 688] *Feb 76*
(The Hartree-Fock approach as applied to self-consistent fields in nuclei.)
  RT   bogolyubov transformation
  RT   boson expansion
  RT   hartree-fock method
  RT   nuclear models
  RT   nuclear structure
  RT   self-consistent field

HARTSVILLE-1 REACTOR [11; 11]
(Hartsville, Tennessee, USA)
  BT1   bwr type reactors
  BT2   enriched uranium reactors
  BT3   reactors
  BT2   power reactors
  BT3   reactors
  BT2   thermal reactors
  BT3   reactors
  BT2   water cooled reactors
  BT3   reactors
  BT2   water moderated reactors
  BT3   reactors

HARTSVILLE-2 REACTOR [10; 10]
(Hartsville, Tennessee, USA)
  BT1   bwr type reactors
  BT2   enriched uranium reactors
  BT3   reactors
  BT2   power reactors
  BT3   reactors
  BT2   thermal reactors
  BT3   reactors

  BT2   water cooled reactors
  BT3   reactors
  BT2   water moderated reactors
  BT3   reactors

HARTSVILLE-3 REACTOR [10; 10]
(Hartsville, Tennessee, USA)
  BT1   bwr type reactors
  BT2   enriched uranium reactors
  BT3   reactors
  BT2   power reactors
  BT3   reactors
  BT2   thermal reactors
  BT3   reactors
  BT2   water cooled reactors
  BT3   reactors
  BT2   water moderated reactors
  BT3   reactors

HARTSVILLE-4 REACTOR [10; 10]
(Hartsville, Tennessee, USA)
  BT1   bwr type reactors
  BT2   enriched uranium reactors
  BT3   reactors
  BT2   power reactors
  BT3   reactors
  BT2   thermal reactors
  BT3   reactors
  BT2   water cooled reactors
  BT3   reactors
  BT2   water moderated reactors
  BT3   reactors

HARVARD SYNCHROCYCLOTRON
[9; 9]
  BT1   synchrocyclotrons
  BT2   cyclic accelerators
  BT3   accelerators

harwell pluto reactor
  USE   pluto reactor

HARWELL SYNCHROCYCLOTRON
[11; 11]
  BT1   synchrocyclotrons
  BT2   cyclic accelerators
  BT3   accelerators

harwell synchrotron
  USE   nimrod

hastelloy b
  USE   alloy-ni65mo28fe5

hastelloy c
  USE   alloy-ni54mo17cr16fe6w4

hastelloy n
  USE   alloy-ni70mo17cr7fe5

hastelloy s
  USE   alloy-ni62cr16mo15fe3

hastelloy x
  USE   alloy-ni49cr22fe18mo9

hastelloy xr
  USE   alloy-ni50cr22fe18mo9

HASTELLOYS [159; 694]
  BT1   nickel base alloys
  BT2   nickel alloys
  BT3   alloys
  NT1   alloy-ni49cr22fe18mo9
  NT1   alloy-ni50cr22fe18mo9
  NT1   alloy-ni54mo17cr16fe6w4
  NT1   alloy-ni62cr16mo15fe3
  NT1   alloy-ni65mo28fe5

  NT1   alloy-ni70mo17cr7fe5
  RT   corrosion resistant alloys

HATCH-1 REACTOR [95; 95]
(Baxley, Georgia, USA)
  UF   *edwin i. hatch-1 reactor*
  BT1   bwr type reactors
  BT2   enriched uranium reactors
  BT3   reactors
  BT2   power reactors
  BT3   reactors
  BT2   thermal reactors
  BT3   reactors
  BT2   water cooled reactors
  BT3   reactors
  BT2   water moderated reactors
  BT3   reactors

HATCH-2 REACTOR [47; 47]
  UF   *edwin i. hatch-2 reactor*
  BT1   bwr type reactors
  BT2   enriched uranium reactors
  BT3   reactors
  BT2   power reactors
  BT3   reactors
  BT2   thermal reactors
  BT3   reactors
  BT2   water cooled reactors
  BT3   reactors
  BT2   water moderated reactors
  BT3   reactors

HATCHETTOLITE [1; 1]
  BT1   oxide minerals
  BT2   minerals
  BT1   uranium minerals
  BT2   radioactive minerals
  BT3   minerals
  BT3   radioactive materials
  BT4   materials
  RT   niobium oxides
  RT   tantalum oxides
  RT   uranium oxides

HAUSDORFF SPACE [74; 74]
  BT1   mathematical space
  BT2   space

HAUSER-FESHBACH THEORY
[1,303; 1,303]
  BT1   nuclear theory
  RT   compound nuclei
  RT   inelastic scattering
  RT   nuclear reactions

havar
  USE   alloy-co43cr20fe18ni13w3

HAVEN-1 REACTOR [0; 0] *Aug 78*
(Standardized plant of the Wisconsin Utilities Project. Prior to July 1978 known as KOSHKONONG-1 REACTOR, and older material is so indexed.)
  UF   *wup-1 reactor*
  BT1   pwr type reactors
  BT2   enriched uranium reactors
  BT3   reactors
  BT2   power reactors
  BT3   reactors
  BT2   thermal reactors
  BT3   reactors
  BT2   water cooled reactors
  BT3   reactors
  BT2   water moderated reactors
  BT3   reactors
  NT1   koshkonong-1 reactor

HAVEN-2 REACTOR [0; 0] *Aug 78*
(Standardized plant of the Wisconsin Utilities Project. Prior to July 1978 known as KOSHKONONG-2 REACTOR, and older material is so indexed.)
  UF   *wup-2 reactor*
  BT1   pwr type reactors
  BT2   enriched uranium reactors
  BT3   reactors

BT2   power reactors
　BT3   reactors
BT2   thermal reactors
　BT3   reactors
BT2   water cooled reactors
　BT3   reactors
BT2   water moderated reactors
　BT3   reactors
NT1   koshkonong-2 reactor

HAWAII [125; 125]
BT1   islands
BT1   usa
　BT2   developed countries
　BT2   north america
RT   pacific ocean

HAYNES ALLOYS [20; 42]
BT1   cobalt base alloys
　BT2   cobalt alloys
　　BT3   alloys
NT1   alloy-co36cr22ni22w15fe3
NT1   alloy-co54cr20w15ni10
NT1   alloy-co60cr30w4
NT1   alloy-co62cr28mo6ni3

haynes stellite no 21
USE   alloy-co62cr28mo6ni3

haynes stellite 6b
USE   alloy-co60cr30w4

haynes 188 alloy
USE   alloy-co36cr22ni22w15fe3

haynes 25 alloy
USE   alloy-co54cr20w15ni10

HAYWOOD MODEL [4; 4]
RT   neutrons
RT   scattering
RT   transport theory

haz
USE   heat affected zone

HAZARDOUS MATERIALS
[1,506; 1,506] *Aug 81*
(Not for RADIOACTIVE MATERIALS.)
UF   *poisons (chemical)*
UF   *toxic materials*
BT1   materials
RT   detoxification
RT   lethal doses
RT   nonradioactive wastes
RT   toxicity
RT   waste management
RT   wastes

HAZARDOUS MATERIALS SPILLS
[0; 0] *Apr 84*
(Prior to October 1991, this concept was indexed by HAZARDOUS MATERIALS and ACCIDENTS.)
BT1   accidents
RT   chemical spills

HAZARDS [2,191; 15,100]
UF   *risks*
UF+   *global risk*
NT1   fire hazards
NT1   health hazards
　NT2   radiation hazards
RT   accidents
RT   ethical aspects
RT   excursions
RT   failures
RT   fires
RT   insurance
RT   liabilities

RT   pressure release
RT   public relations
RT   reliability
RT   risk assessment
RT   sabotage
RT   safety
RT   safety engineering
RT   workmens compensation

hb robinson-2
USE   robinson-2 reactor

HBTX DEVICES [44; 44] *Nov 85*
BT1   toroidal pinch devices
　BT2   closed plasma devices
　　BT3   thermonuclear devices
　BT2   pinch devices
　　BT3   thermonuclear devices
RT   reverse-field pinch

HBWR REACTOR [166; 166]
UF   *halden heavy boil. wa. reactor*
BT1   bhwr type reactors
　BT2   heavy water cooled reactors
　　BT3   reactors
　BT2   heavy water moderated reactors
　　BT3   reactors
BT1   enriched uranium reactors
　BT2   reactors
BT1   experimental reactors
　BT2   research and test reactors
　　BT3   reactors
BT1   power reactors
　BT2   reactors
BT1   tank type reactors
　BT2   reactors
BT1   thermal reactors
　BT2   reactors

HCG [185; 185]
UF   *human chorionic gonadotropin*
BT1   gonadotropins
　BT2   pituitary hormones
　　BT3   peptide hormones
　　　BT4   hormones
RT   gonads

HCLWR TYPE REACTORS [78; 78]
Feb 88
(High conversion light water reactors.)
BT1   plutonium reactors
　BT2   reactors
BT1   water cooled reactors
　BT2   reactors
BT1   water moderated reactors
　BT2   reactors

HCP LATTICES [965; 965]
UF   *hexagonal close packed*
BT1   hexagonal lattices
　BT2   crystal lattices
　　BT3   crystal structure

HDEHP [757; 757]
UF   *bis(2-ethylhexyl)phosphoric ac*
UF   *di-2-ethylhexylphosphoric acid*
SF   *dehpa*
BT1   phosphoric acid esters
　BT2   esters
　　BT3   organic compounds
　BT2   organic phosphorus compounds
　　BT3   organic compounds

hdo
USE   deuterium compounds
AND   heavy water

HDR REACTOR [392; 392]
UF   *grosswelzheim hdr reactor*
UF   *heissdampfreaktoranlage*
UF   *kahl-main reactor*
BT1   bwr type reactors
　BT2   enriched uranium reactors

　　BT3   reactors
　BT2   power reactors
　　BT3   reactors
　BT2   thermal reactors
　　BT3   reactors
　BT2   water cooled reactors
　　BT3   reactors
　BT2   water moderated reactors
　　BT3   reactors
BT1   experimental reactors
　BT2   research and test reactors
　　BT3   reactors

HE-3 COUNTERS [444; 444]
BT1   neutron detectors
　BT2   radiation detectors
　　BT3   measuring instruments
BT1   proportional counters
　BT2   radiation detectors
　　BT3   measuring instruments

HEAD [2,339; 3,115]
BT1   body areas
　BT2   body
NT1   face
　NT2   nose
RT   brain
RT   carotid arteries
RT   oral cavity
RT   sense organs
RT   skull

HEAD END PROCESSES [349; 655]
NT1   decladding
　NT2   chemical decladding
　NT2   mechanical decladding
NT1   voloxidation process
RT   reprocessing

HEALING [498; 498]
BT1   biological recovery
RT   cell division
RT   wounds

health (public)
USE   public health

HEALTH HAZARDS [3,592; 12,468]
BT1   hazards
NT1   radiation hazards
RT   drug abuse
RT   first aid
RT   injuries
RT   maximum credible accident
RT   occupational safety
RT   preventive medicine
RT   public health
RT   quarantine
RT   radiation protection
RT   radicidation
RT   safety

health insurance
(Prior to December 1990, this was a valid descriptor.)
USE   insurance

health physics
USE   radiation protection

health physics research r.
USE   hprr reactor

HEARINGS [857; 857]
RT   administrative procedures
RT   arbitration
RT   courts
RT   dispute settlements
RT   laws
RT   lawsuits
RT   legislation
RT   licensing procedures

HEART [6,315; 10,497]
  BT1 cardiovascular system
  BT1 organs
    BT2 body
  NT1 myocardium
  NT1 pericardium
  RT aorta
  RT blood circulation
  RT cardiac pacemakers
  RT cardiography
  RT cardiotonics
  RT chest
  RT coronaries
  RT electrocardiograms
  RT mechanical heart
  RT mediastinum

HEART FAILURE [100; 100] *Aug 81*
  BT1 symptoms
  RT biological shock
  RT biological stress
  RT cardiovascular diseases

heat (process)
  USE process heat

HEAT AFFECTED ZONE [933; 933]
  UF *haz*
  UF *heat-affected zone*
  RT welding

heat capacity
  USE specific heat

heat dissipation
(Prior to 1985 THERMAL DIFFUSION was used for this concept.)
  SEE cooling
  OR energy losses
  OR heat transfer
  OR thermal diffusivity

HEAT EXCHANGERS [4,340; 4,576]
  UF *coolers*
  NT1 in-vessel heat exchangers
  NT1 radiators
  RT cooling
  RT cooling towers
  RT evaporators
  RT heat pumps
  RT heat transfer
  RT heating
  RT reactor components
  RT reactor cooling systems
  RT regenerators
  RT steam condensers
  RT steam generators
  RT working fluids

heat extraction
  USE heat recovery

heat flow
(Prior to January 1983 HEAT TRANSFER was used for this concept.)
  USE heat flux

HEAT FLUX [2,944; 3,970] *Mar 77*
  UF *heat flow*
  NT1 critical heat flux
  RT burnout
  RT dryout
  RT heat transfer

heat losses
  USE energy losses
  AND heat transfer

heat of absorption
  USE absorption heat

heat of adsorption
  USE adsorption heat

heat of combustion
  USE combustion heat

heat of dissociation
  USE dissociation heat

heat of formation
  USE formation heat

heat of fusion
  USE fusion heat

heat of mixing
  USE mixing heat

heat of reaction
  USE reaction heat

heat of solution
  USE solution heat

heat of sublimation
  USE sublimation heat

heat of transition
  USE transition heat

heat of vaporization
  USE vaporization heat

HEAT PIPES [608; 608]
(Heat-transfer devices, frequently associated with thermionic converters. Not pipes for transporting hot fluids from place to place.)
  RT capillary flow
  RT heat transfer

HEAT PUMPS [72; 72] *Sep 79*
  BT1 pumps
    BT2 equipment
  RT cooling
  RT heat exchangers
  RT heating
  RT working fluids

HEAT RECOVERY [77; 77] *Dec 85*
  UF *heat extraction*
  BT1 energy recovery
  RT heat transfer
  RT waste heat
  RT waste heat utilization
  RT waste product utilization

HEAT RESISTING ALLOYS
[1,552; 11,835]
  UF *heat-resisting alloys*
  BT1 alloys
  NT1 alloy-co36cr22ni22w15fe3
  NT1 alloy-co52cr17fe15mo3si3
  NT1 alloy-co54cr20w15ni10
  NT1 alloy-co60cr30w4
  NT1 alloy-co62cr28mo6ni3
  NT1 alloy-co64cr29w4
  NT1 alloy-co66cr26w6
  NT1 alloy-fe31cr21co20ni20mo3w2
  NT1 alloy-fe44ni33cr21
  NT1 alloy-fe46ni33cr21
  NT1 alloy-fe48cr24ni24
  NT1 alloy-mo99
  NT1 alloy-nb94mo4
  NT1 alloy-ni41fe40cr16nb3
  NT1 alloy-ni42fe36cr12mo6ti3
  NT1 alloy-ni43fe30cr22mo3
  NT1 alloy-ni43fe33cr16mo3
  NT1 alloy-ni45cr23fe19co3mo3w3
  NT1 alloy-ni46cr23co19ti5al4
  NT1 alloy-ni47cr25co12w9fe3
  NT1 alloy-ni48co28cr15al3mo3ti2
  NT1 alloy-ni48cr22fe18mo9
  NT1 alloy-ni49cr22fe18mo9
  NT1 alloy-ni50co20cr15al5mo5
  NT1 alloy-ni50cr22fe18mo9
  NT1 alloy-ni50mo32cr15si3
  NT1 alloy-ni51cr48
  NT1 alloy-ni53co19cr15mo5al4ti3
  NT1 alloy-ni53cr19fe19nb5mo3
  NT1 alloy-ni54cr22co13mo9
  NT1 alloy-ni54mo17cr16fe6w4
  NT1 alloy-ni55cr19co11mo10ti3
  NT1 alloy-ni56cr21w10mo5fe4al2
  NT1 alloy-ni58cr14co8al4mo4nb4w4
  NT1 alloy-ni58cr20co14mo4ti3
  NT1 alloy-ni59cr20co17ti2
  NT1 alloy-ni59cr30fe9
  NT1 alloy-ni60co15cr10al6ti5mo3
  NT1 alloy-ni60cr14co10ti5mo4w4al3
  NT1 alloy-ni60cr25w15
  NT1 alloy-ni60fe24cr16
  NT1 alloy-ni60mo13co9cr8nb4al3
  NT1 alloy-ni61cr16co9al3ti3w3
  NT1 alloy-ni61cr22mo9nb4fe3
  NT1 alloy-ni62cr16mo15fe3
  NT1 alloy-ni65cr25mo10
  NT1 alloy-ni65mo16cr15w4
  NT1 alloy-ni67cr19mo5w5ti3
  NT1 alloy-ni68cr15w6al3mo3fe2
  NT1 alloy-ni70mo17cr7fe5
  NT1 alloy-ni73cr15fe7ti3
  NT1 alloy-ni73cr20mn3nb3
  NT1 alloy-ni74cr13al6mo4
  NT1 alloy-ni75cr12al6mo5
  NT1 alloy-ni76cr15fe8
  NT1 alloy-ni76cr20ti2
  NT1 alloy-ni77cr17al5
  NT1 alloy-ni77cr20ti2
  NT1 alloy-ni78cr16al4
  NT1 alloy-zr97nb3
  NT1 alloy-zr98sn-2
  NT1 alloy-zr98sn-4
  NT1 refractaloy
  NT1 steel-cr12
  NT1 steel-cr12moniv
  NT1 steel-cr12mov
  NT1 steel-cr13
  NT1 steel-cr13al
  NT1 steel-cr13ni6mo-l
  NT1 steel-cr15ni15motib
  NT1 steel-cr16
  NT1 steel-cr16ni
  NT1 steel-cr16ni13monbv
  NT1 steel-cr16ni15mo3nb
  NT1 steel-cr16ni16monb
  NT1 steel-cr16ni8mo2
  NT1 steel-cr17cu4ni4nb-l
  NT1 steel-cr17mo
  NT1 steel-cr17ni12monb
  NT1 steel-cr17ni12mo3
  NT1 steel-cr17ni12mo3-l
  NT1 steel-cr17ni13
  NT1 steel-cr17ni13mo2ti
  NT1 steel-cr17ni13mo3ti
  NT1 steel-cr17ni4mo3
  NT1 steel-cr17ni7
  NT1 steel-cr18ni10
  NT1 steel-cr18ni10-l
  NT1 steel-cr18ni10ti
  NT1 steel-cr18ni11
  NT1 steel-cr18ni11nb
  NT1 steel-cr18ni11nbco
  NT1 steel-cr18ni12
  NT1 steel-cr18ni12ti
  NT1 steel-cr18ni8
  NT1 steel-cr18ni9
  NT1 steel-cr18ni9ti
  NT1 steel-cr19ni10
  NT1 steel-cr19ni10-l
  NT1 steel-cr2moninb
  NT1 steel-cr20ni11

NT1	steel-cr20ni11-l
NT1	steel-cr21mn9ni6
NT1	steel-cr23ni14
NT1	steel-cr23ni18
NT1	steel-cr25
NT1	steel-cr25ni20
NT1	steel-cr26ni5mo-l
NT1	steel-nimocr
NT1	steel-ni17cr14moti-l
NT1	steel-ni25cr20
NT1	steel-ni26cr15ti2movalb
NT1	steel-ni36cr18
RT	austenitic steels
RT	refractories
RT	stainless steels

HEAT SINKS [288; 288]
RT	heat transfer
RT	thermal effluents
RT	thermodynamics
RT	vapor condensers
RT	waste heat

heat sources (radioisotope)
USE   radioisotope heat sources

heat stability
USE   sensitivity
AND   thermal degradation

HEAT STORAGE [131; 131] *Jan 79*
UF	*thermal storage*
BT1	energy storage
BT2	storage
RT	regenerators

HEAT TRANSFER [18,593; 24,989]
UF	*exchange (heat)*
UF	*heat transmission*
UF	*transfer (heat)*
UF	*transmission (heat)*
UF+	*heat losses*
SF	*heat dissipation*
BT1	energy transfer
NT1	convection
NT2	forced convection
NT2	natural convection
NT1	radiant heat transfer
NT1	thermal conduction
RT	ablation
RT	boilers
RT	boiling
RT	burnout
RT	calorimetry
RT	continuity equations
RT	coolant loops
RT	cooling
RT	critical heat flux
RT	district heating
RT	fluid flow
RT	fourier heat equation
RT	greenhouse effect
RT	heat exchangers
RT	heat flux
RT	heat pipes
RT	heat recovery
RT	heat sinks
RT	heaters
RT	heating
RT	hot spots
RT	nucleate boiling
RT	nusselt number
RT	reactor cooling systems
RT	rewetting
RT	righi-leduc effect
RT	rosseland approximation
RT	steam condensers
RT	steam generators
RT	thermal boundary resistance
RT	thermal conductivity
RT	thermal diffusion
RT	thermal insulation
RT	thermal radiation
RT	thermodynamics
RT	thermonuclear reactor cooling
RT	thermosyphons
RT	two-phase flow

RT	vapor condensation
RT	working fluids

heat transfer fluids
(Use descriptor for particular coolant or working fluid if appropriate.)
SEE   coolants
OR   working fluids

heat transmission
USE   heat transfer

HEAT TREATMENTS [7,387; 27,814]
(In metallurgy as well as for the biological effects of heat.)
NT1	annealing
NT1	quench hardening
NT1	quenching
NT1	tempering
RT	aging
RT	controlled atmospheres
RT	critical temperature
RT	curing
RT	decarburization
RT	food processing
RT	grain refinement
RT	hardening
RT	heating
RT	nucleic acid denaturation
RT	protein denaturation
RT	recrystallization
RT	stress relaxation
RT	thermal shock

heat-affected zone
USE   heat affected zone

heat-resisting alloys
USE   heat resisting alloys

heated effluents
USE   thermal effluents

HEATERS [799; 1,068]
UF+	*air heaters*
NT1	feedwater heaters
RT	heat transfer

HEATING [6,938; 25,730]
UF+	*solar heating*
NT1	auxiliary heating
NT1	baking
NT1	district heating
NT1	flash heating
NT1	joule heating
NT1	plasma heating
NT2	adiabatic compression heating
NT2	beam injection heating
NT2	current-drive heating
NT2	high-frequency heating
NT3	ecr heating
NT3	icr heating
NT3	lower hybrid heating
NT3	magnetic-pumping heating
NT4	acoustic heating
NT4	collisional heating
NT4	transit-time magnetic pumping
NT2	laser-radiation heating
NT2	shock heating
NT2	turbulent heating
NT1	radiation heating
NT1	space heating
NT1	superheating
NT2	nuclear superheating
RT	air conditioning
RT	blisters
RT	boiling
RT	cooling
RT	heat exchangers
RT	heat pumps
RT	heat transfer
RT	heat treatments

RT	heating rate
RT	incubation
RT	melting
RT	retorting
RT	subterrene penetrators
RT	temperature control
RT	thermal degradation

HEATING RATE [66; 66] *Mar 86*
RT	heating
RT	time dependence

HEAVY ION ACCELERATORS
[1,906; 4,078] *Feb 76*
UF	*heavy-ion accelerators*
BT1	accelerators
NT1	brookhaven rhic
NT1	calcutta cyclotron
NT1	cracow u-120 cyclotron
NT1	crnl superconducting cyclotron
NT1	cyclone cyclotron
NT1	ganil cyclotron
NT1	hhirf accelerator
NT1	hilacs
NT2	atlas superconducting linac
NT2	superhilac
NT1	hirfl cyclotron
NT1	ipcr cyclotron
NT1	jinr u-400 cyclotron
NT1	kvi cyclotron
NT1	milan superconducting cyclotro
NT1	munich suse cyclotron
NT1	nac cyclotron
NT1	numatron accelerator
NT1	rcnp cyclotron
NT1	rilac
NT1	sis synchrotron
NT1	texas superconducting cyclotro
NT1	tohoku cyclotron
NT1	tokyo ins cyclotron
NT1	unilac
NT1	vicksi accelerator
NT1	warsaw cyclotron

HEAVY ION DECAY RADIOISOTOPES
[5; 2,283] *Mar 86*
BT1	radioisotopes
BT2	isotopes
NT1	carbon 14 decay radioisotopes
NT2	radium 222
NT2	radium 223
NT2	radium 224
NT2	radium 226
NT1	magnesium 28 decay radioisotop
NT2	plutonium 236
NT2	uranium 234
NT1	neon 24 decay radioisotopes
NT2	protactinium 231
NT2	thorium 230
NT2	uranium 232
NT2	uranium 233
NT2	uranium 234
NT1	silicon 32 decay radioisotopes
NT2	plutonium 238
RT	heavy ion emission decay

HEAVY ION EMISSION DECAY
[101; 148] *Mar 86*
BT1	nuclear decay
BT2	decay
NT1	carbon 12 emission decay
NT1	carbon 14 emission decay
NT1	magnesium 28 emission decay
NT1	magnesium 30 emission decay
NT1	neon 24 emission decay
NT1	oxygen 16 emission decay
NT1	silicon 32 emission decay
NT1	silicon 34 emission decay
RT	heavy ion decay radioisotopes

HEAVY ION FUSION REACTIONS
[5,138; 5,138]
(Endoenergetic fusion reactions)
UF	*fusion reactions (endoenergeti*
UF	*fusion reactions (heavy ion)*
UF	*heavy-ion fusion reactions*
BT1	heavy ion reactions
BT2	nuclear reactions

BT1 nucleosynthesis
BT2 synthesis
RT deep inelastic heavy ion react
RT incomplete fusion reactions
RT quasi-fission
RT thermonuclear reactions

heavy ion linear accelerators
USE hilacs

HEAVY ION REACTIONS
[8,057; 27,746]
UF *heavy-ion reactions*
BT1 nuclear reactions
NT1 aluminium 27 reactions
NT1 argon 36 reactions
NT1 argon 40 reactions
NT1 beryllium 7 reactions
NT1 beryllium 8 reactions
NT1 beryllium 9 reactions
NT1 bismuth 209 reactions
NT1 boron 10 reactions
NT1 boron 11 reactions
NT1 bromine 79 reactions
NT1 bromine 81 reactions
NT1 calcium 40 reactions
NT1 calcium 42 reactions
NT1 calcium 44 reactions
NT1 calcium 48 reactions
NT1 carbon 12 reactions
NT1 carbon 13 reactions
NT1 carbon 14 reactions
NT1 chlorine 35 reactions
NT1 chlorine 37 reactions
NT1 chromium 52 reactions
NT1 chromium 54 reactions
NT1 cobalt 59 reactions
NT1 copper 63 reactions
NT1 copper 65 reactions
NT1 deep inelastic heavy ion react
NT1 dysprosium 161 reactions
NT1 erbium 166 reactions
NT1 fluorine 19 reactions
NT1 gadolinium 155 reactions
NT1 germanium 74 reactions
NT1 germanium 76 reactions
NT1 gold 197 reactions
NT1 heavy ion fusion reactions
NT1 helium 6 reactions
NT1 helium 8 reactions
NT1 holmium 165 reactions
NT1 incomplete fusion reactions
NT1 iodine 127 reactions
NT1 iron 54 reactions
NT1 iron 56 reactions
NT1 iron 58 reactions
NT1 krypton 80 reactions
NT1 krypton 82 reactions
NT1 krypton 83 reactions
NT1 krypton 84 reactions
NT1 krypton 86 reactions
NT1 lanthanum 139 reactions
NT1 lead 206 reactions
NT1 lead 208 reactions
NT1 lithium 11 reactions
NT1 lithium 6 reactions
NT1 lithium 7 reactions
NT1 lithium 8 reactions
NT1 lithium 9 reactions
NT1 magnesium 24 reactions
NT1 magnesium 25 reactions
NT1 magnesium 26 reactions
NT1 manganese 55 reactions
NT1 molybdenum 100 reactions
NT1 molybdenum 92 reactions
NT1 molybdenum 96 reactions
NT1 molybdenum 98 reactions
NT1 neodymium 142 reactions
NT1 neodymium 150 reactions
NT1 neon 20 reactions
NT1 neon 22 reactions
NT1 nickel 58 reactions
NT1 nickel 59 reactions
NT1 nickel 60 reactions
NT1 nickel 61 reactions
NT1 nickel 64 reactions
NT1 niobium 93 reactions
NT1 nitrogen 14 reactions
NT1 nitrogen 15 reactions
NT1 oxygen 16 reactions
NT1 oxygen 17 reactions
NT1 oxygen 18 reactions
NT1 palladium 118 reactions
NT1 phosphorus 31 reactions
NT1 potassium 39 reactions
NT1 quasi-fission
NT1 ruthenium 104 reactions
NT1 samarium 144 reactions
NT1 samarium 154 reactions
NT1 scandium 45 reactions
NT1 selenium 76 reactions
NT1 selenium 80 reactions
NT1 selenium 82 reactions
NT1 silicon 28 reactions
NT1 silicon 29 reactions
NT1 silicon 30 reactions
NT1 silver 109 reactions
NT1 sodium 23 reactions
NT1 sulfur 32 reactions
NT1 sulfur 33 reactions
NT1 sulfur 34 reactions
NT1 sulfur 36 reactions
NT1 tellurium 130 reactions
NT1 thallium 205 reactions
NT1 thorium 232 reactions
NT1 tin 112 reactions
NT1 tin 116 reactions
NT1 tin 118 reactions
NT1 tin 120 reactions
NT1 tin 122 reactions
NT1 tin 124 reactions
NT1 titanium 46 reactions
NT1 titanium 48 reactions
NT1 titanium 50 reactions
NT1 tungsten 183 reactions
NT1 tungsten 184 reactions
NT1 uranium 235 reactions
NT1 uranium 238 reactions
NT1 vanadium 51 reactions
NT1 xenon 129 reactions
NT1 xenon 132 reactions
NT1 xenon 134 reactions
NT1 xenon 136 reactions
NT1 zinc 64 reactions
NT1 zinc 68 reactions
NT1 zinc 70 reactions
NT1 zirconium 90 reactions
NT1 zirconium 92 reactions
NT1 zirconium 96 reactions
RT anomalons
RT hilacs
RT nuclear fireball model
RT peripheral collisions

heavy ion res fac lanzhou cycl
USE hirfl cyclotron

HEAVY ION SPECTROMETERS
[254; 254]
UF *heavy-ion spectrometers*
BT1 spectrometers
BT2 measuring instruments

HEAVY IONS [5,436; 5,436]
(Whenever appropriate use one of the specific terms listed under ION BEAMS.)
BT1 ions
BT2 charged particles
RT hilacs
RT ion beams
RT ion detection
RT multicharged ions

HEAVY LEPTONS [1,068; 2,574]
BT1 leptons
BT2 elementary particles
BT2 fermions
NT1 tau neutrinos
NT1 tau particles

HEAVY LIQUID BUBBLE CHAMBERS
[214; 214]
BT1 bubble chambers
BT2 gas track detectors
BT3 radiation detectors
BT4 measuring instruments

* HEAVY NUCLEI [2,632; 54,405]
(For nuclei from mass 181 upwards. For specific terms, consult the Appendix.)
BT1 nuclei
RT nuclear structure

HEAVY WATER [4,092; 4,092]
UF *deuterium oxide*
UF *heavy water coolant*
UF *heavy water moderator*
UF+ *dto*
UF+ *hdo*
UF+ *hto*
UF+ *tritiated water*
BT1 water
BT2 hydrogen compounds
BT2 oxygen compounds
RT coolants
RT deuterium compounds
RT dual temperature process
RT heavy water plants
RT moderators
RT tritium compounds
RT tritium extraction plants

heavy water components test re
USE hwctr reactor

heavy water coolant
USE heavy water

HEAVY WATER COOLED REACTORS
[218; 3,966]
UF *heavy water-cooled reactors*
BT1 reactors
NT1 alrr reactor
NT1 aquilon reactor
NT1 bhwr type reactors
NT2 hbwr reactor
NT2 marviken reactor
NT1 br-3-vn reactor
NT1 celestin reactor
NT1 cp-3 reactor
NT1 cp-5 reactor
NT1 dca reactor
NT1 dhruva reactor
NT1 dido reactor
NT1 diorit reactor
NT1 dmtr reactor
NT1 dr-3 reactor
NT1 el-1 reactor
NT1 el-3 reactor
NT1 eole reactor
NT1 essor reactor
NT1 fr-2 reactor
NT1 frj-2 reactor
NT1 grenoble reactor
NT1 gtrr reactor
NT1 hfbr reactor
NT1 hifar reactor
NT1 hwctr reactor
NT1 irr-2 reactor
NT1 ispra-1 reactor
NT1 jeep-2 reactor
NT1 jrr-2 reactor
NT1 jrr-3 reactor
NT1 mitr reactor
NT1 nbsr reactor
NT1 nora reactor
NT1 nru reactor
NT1 nrx reactor
NT1 pdp reactor
NT1 pelinduna reactor
NT1 phwr type reactors
NT2 agesta reactor
NT2 atucha reactor
NT2 atucha-2 reactor
NT2 bruce-1 reactor
NT2 bruce-2 reactor
NT2 bruce-3 reactor
NT2 bruce-4 reactor
NT2 bruce-5 reactor
NT2 bruce-6 reactor
NT2 bruce-7 reactor
NT2 bruce-8 reactor
NT2 cernavoda-1 reactor
NT2 cordoba reactor

NT2	cvtr reactor	NT2	point lepreau-1 reactor	NT2	pickering-7 reactor
NT2	darlington-1 reactor	NT2	point lepreau-2 reactor	NT2	pickering-8 reactor
NT2	darlington-2 reactor	NT2	rajasthan-1 reactor	NT2	point lepreau-1 reactor
NT2	darlington-3 reactor	NT2	rajasthan-2 reactor	NT2	point lepreau-2 reactor
NT2	darlington-4 reactor	NT2	wolsung-1 reactor	NT2	rajasthan-1 reactor
NT2	douglas point ontario reactor	NT1	celestin reactor	NT2	rajasthan-2 reactor
NT2	gentilly-2 reactor	NT1	cirus reactor	NT2	wolsung-1 reactor
NT2	kalpakkam-1 reactor	NT1	cp-3 reactor	NT1	pluto reactor
NT2	kalpakkam-2 reactor	NT1	cp-5 reactor	NT1	prr reactor
NT2	kanupp reactor	NT1	dca reactor	NT1	prtr reactor
NT2	mzfr reactor	NT1	dhruva reactor	NT1	pse reactor
NT2	narora-1 reactor	NT1	dido reactor	NT1	r reactor
NT2	narora-2 reactor	NT1	dimple reactor	NT1	r-a reactor
NT2	npd reactor	NT1	diorit reactor	NT1	r-b reactor
NT2	pickering-1 reactor	NT1	dmtr reactor	NT1	r-1 reactor
NT2	pickering-2 reactor	NT1	dr-3 reactor	NT1	rb-3 reactor
NT2	pickering-3 reactor	NT1	eco reactor	NT1	rtr reactor
NT2	pickering-4 reactor	NT1	el-1 reactor	NT1	sghwr reactor
NT2	pickering-5 reactor	NT1	el-2 reactor	NT1	spert-2 reactor
NT2	pickering-6 reactor	NT1	el-3 reactor	NT1	taiwan research reactor
NT2	pickering-7 reactor	NT1	eole reactor	NT1	tr-0 reactor
NT2	pickering-8 reactor	NT1	essor reactor	NT1	venus reactor
NT2	point lepreau-1 reactor	NT1	fr-2 reactor	NT1	wr-1 reactor
NT2	point lepreau-2 reactor	NT1	frj-2 reactor	NT1	zed-2 reactor
NT2	rajasthan-1 reactor	NT1	grenoble reactor	NT1	zeep reactor
NT2	rajasthan-2 reactor	NT1	gtrr reactor	NT1	zerlina reactor
NT2	wolsung-1 reactor	NT1	hfbr reactor		
NT1	pluto reactor	NT1	hifar reactor		
NT1	prr reactor	NT1	hwctr reactor		
NT1	prtr reactor	NT1	hwgcr type reactors	*heavy water moderator*	
NT1	pse reactor	NT2	bohunice a-1 reactor	USE	heavy water
NT1	r-a reactor	NT2	bohunice a-2 reactor		
NT1	r-1 reactor	NT2	el-4 reactor	**HEAVY WATER PLANTS** [191; 191]	
NT1	spert-2 reactor	NT2	lucens reactor	*Nov 78*	
NT1	taiwan research reactor	NT2	niederaichbach reactor	BT1	isotope separation plants
NT1	venus reactor	NT1	hwlwr type reactors	BT2	industrial plants
NT1	zed-2 reactor	NT2	cirene reactor	BT2	nuclear facilities
		NT2	gentilly reactor	RT	heavy water
		NT2	jatr reactor	RT	isotope separation
heavy water gcr of czechoslova		NT1	irr-2 reactor		
USE	bohunice a-1 reactor	NT1	ispra-1 reactor		
		NT1	jeep-2 reactor		
		NT1	jrr-2 reactor	*heavy water-cooled reactors*	
heavy water mod./gas cool. rea		NT1	jrr-3 reactor	USE	heavy water cooled reactors
USE	hwgcr type reactors	NT1	juno reactor		
		NT1	k reactor		
		NT1	l reactor	*heavy water-moderated reactors*	
heavy water mod./water cool. r		NT1	maple reactor	USE	heavy water moderated reactors
USE	hwlwr type reactors	NT1	mitr reactor		
		NT1	nbsr reactor		
HEAVY WATER MODERATED REACTORS [497; 8,145]		NT1	nora reactor	*heavy-ion accelerators*	
		NT1	nru reactor	USE	heavy ion accelerators
UF	*heavy water-moderated reactors*	NT1	nrx reactor		
BT1	reactors	NT1	p reactor		
NT1	alrr reactor	NT1	pdp reactor	*heavy-ion fusion reactions*	
NT1	aquilon reactor	NT1	pelinduna reactor	USE	heavy ion fusion reactions
NT1	bhwr type reactors	NT1	phwr type reactors		
NT2	hbwr reactor	NT2	agesta reactor		
NT2	marviken reactor	NT2	atucha reactor	*heavy-ion reactions*	
NT1	br-3-vn reactor	NT2	atucha-2 reactor	USE	heavy ion reactions
NT1	c reactor	NT2	bruce-1 reactor		
NT1	candu type reactors	NT2	bruce-2 reactor		
NT2	bruce-1 reactor	NT2	bruce-3 reactor	*heavy-ion spectrometers*	
NT2	bruce-2 reactor	NT2	bruce-4 reactor	USE	heavy ion spectrometers
NT2	bruce-3 reactor	NT2	bruce-5 reactor		
NT2	bruce-4 reactor	NT2	bruce-6 reactor	**HECTOR REACTOR** [8; 8]	
NT2	bruce-5 reactor	NT2	bruce-7 reactor	(UKAEA, Winfrith, United Kingdom)	
NT2	bruce-6 reactor	NT2	bruce-8 reactor	UF	*hot enr. carbon mod. th. osc.*
NT2	bruce-7 reactor	NT2	cernavoda-1 reactor	BT1	carbon dioxide cooled reactors
NT2	bruce-8 reactor	NT2	cordoba reactor	BT2	gas cooled reactors
NT2	cernavoda-1 reactor	NT2	cvtr reactor	BT3	reactors
NT2	cordoba reactor	NT2	darlington-1 reactor	BT1	enriched uranium reactors
NT2	darlington-1 reactor	NT2	darlington-2 reactor	BT2	reactors
NT2	darlington-2 reactor	NT2	darlington-3 reactor	BT1	graphite moderated reactors
NT2	darlington-3 reactor	NT2	darlington-4 reactor	BT2	reactors
NT2	darlington-4 reactor	NT2	douglas point ontario reactor	BT1	materials testing reactors
NT2	douglas point ontario reactor	NT2	gentilly-2 reactor	BT2	irradiation reactors
NT2	gentilly reactor	NT2	kalpakkam-1 reactor	BT3	reactors
NT2	gentilly-2 reactor	NT2	kalpakkam-2 reactor	BT1	pulsed reactors
NT2	kanupp reactor	NT2	kanupp reactor	BT2	reactors
NT2	mzfr reactor	NT2	mzfr reactor	BT1	research reactors
NT2	npd reactor	NT2	narora-1 reactor	BT2	research and test reactors
NT2	pickering-1 reactor	NT2	narora-2 reactor	BT3	reactors
NT2	pickering-2 reactor	NT2	npd reactor	BT1	thermal reactors
NT2	pickering-3 reactor	NT2	pickering-1 reactor	BT2	reactors
NT2	pickering-4 reactor	NT2	pickering-2 reactor		
NT2	pickering-5 reactor	NT2	pickering-3 reactor		
NT2	pickering-6 reactor	NT2	pickering-4 reactor	*hectorite*	
NT2	pickering-7 reactor	NT2	pickering-5 reactor	USE	montmorillonite
NT2	pickering-8 reactor	NT2	pickering-6 reactor		

hedl
    USE   hanford engineering developmen

HEDTA [106; 106]
(Hydroxyethylethylenediaminetriacetic acid)
    UF   *hydroxyethylethylenediaminetri*
    BT1   amino acids
       BT2   carboxylic acids
         BT3   organic acids
            BT4   organic compounds
    BT1   chelating agents
    BT1   hydroxy acids
       BT2   carboxylic acids
         BT3   organic acids
            BT4   organic compounds

HEF [10; 10] *Jun 82*
(To demonstrate breeder reactor fuel reprocessing. prior to December 1990, this concept was indexed by HOT EXPERIMENTAL FACILITY.)
    UF   *hot experimental facility*
    BT1   fuel reprocessing plants
       BT2   nuclear facilities
    RT   cfrp program

HEIDA [22; 22]
    UF   *hydroxyethyliminodiacetic acid*
    BT1   amino acids
       BT2   carboxylic acids
         BT3   organic acids
            BT4   organic compounds
    BT1   chelating agents
    BT1   hydroxy acids
       BT2   carboxylic acids
         BT3   organic acids
            BT4   organic compounds

heidelberg triga-mk-1-dkfz re.
    USE   triga-1-heidelberg reactor

§§ **HEIGHT** [544; 544]
(For elevation use LEVELS.)
    BT1   dimensions
    RT   levels
    RT   scale height

HEISENBERG MODEL [753; 753]
    BT1   crystal models
       BT2   mathematical models
    RT   electronic structure
    RT   ferromagnetism
    RT   phi4-field theory
    RT   spin

HEISENBERG PICTURE [528; 528]
    UF   *heisenberg representation*
    RT   quantum field theory
    RT   quantum mechanics
    RT   schroedinger picture

heisenberg principle
    USE   uncertainty principle

heisenberg representation
    USE   heisenberg picture

heissdampfreaktoranlage
    USE   hdr reactor

HEITLER-LONDON THEORY [36; 36]
    RT   binding energy
    RT   heitler-london waves

HEITLER-LONDON WAVES [4; 4]
    RT   heitler-london theory

HELA CELLS [780; 780]
    BT1   tumor cells
       BT2   animal cells
    RT   clone cells
    RT   in vitro

HELIAC STELLARATORS [71; 93] *May 87*
(Helical magnetic axis stellarators.)
    BT1   stellarators
       BT2   closed plasma devices
         BT3   thermonuclear devices
    NT1   sheila heliac

helianthus annuus
    USE   sunflowers

HELICAL CONFIGURATION [1,166; 1,166]
    BT1   configuration
    RT   dna
    RT   magnetic field configurations
    RT   molecular structure

HELICAL INSTABILITY [249; 249]
    UF   *screw instability*
    BT1   plasma macroinstabilities
       BT2   plasma instability
         BT3   instability

HELICAL WAVEGUIDES [39; 39]
    BT1   waveguides

HELICITY [3,051; 3,051]
    BT1   particle properties
    RT   angular momentum
    RT   chirality
    RT   spin

HELICON RESONANCE [13; 13]
    BT1   resonance
    RT   superconductivity

HELICON WAVES [99; 99]
    BT1   electromagnetic radiation
       BT2   radiations

HELIOS DEVICES [11; 11]
    BT1   q devices
       BT2   open plasma devices
         BT3   thermonuclear devices

HELIOS FACILITY [40; 40] *Jul 81*
(Large CO2 laser facility at Los Alamos for laser fusion experiments.)
    RT   antares facility
    RT   carbon dioxide lasers
    RT   lanl
    RT   laser fusion reactors
    RT   lasl

HELIOSPHERE [125; 125] *Feb 87*
(Influence zone of the sun in interstellar space, delimited by the ejected solar plasma.)
    BT1   solar atmosphere
       BT2   stellar atmospheres
         BT3   atmospheres

heliothis
    USE   bollworm

HELIOTRON [418; 418]
    BT1   closed plasma devices
       BT2   thermonuclear devices

HELIUM [18,671; 19,061]
    BT1   rare gases
       BT2   nonmetals
         BT3   elements
    RT   cryogenic fluids

HELIUM ASH [18; 18] *Feb 90*
(A thermonuclear reaction product.)
    BT1   helium ions
       BT2   ions
         BT3   charged particles
    RT   alpha particles
    RT   pumped limiters
    RT   thermonuclear reactions

HELIUM BURNING [336; 336] *Sep 78*
(Astrophysical processes only.)
    BT1   star burning
    RT   dwarf stars
    RT   nucleosynthesis
    RT   red giant stars
    RT   star evolution

HELIUM CARBIDES [1; 1]
    BT1   carbides
       BT2   carbon compounds
    BT1   helium compounds
       BT2   rare gas compounds

HELIUM CHLORIDES [2; 2]
    BT1   chlorides
       BT2   chlorine compounds
         BT3   halogen compounds
       BT2   halides
         BT3   halogen compounds
    BT1   helium compounds
       BT2   rare gas compounds

HELIUM COMPLEXES [10; 10]
    BT1   complexes

HELIUM COMPOUNDS [35; 250]
    BT1   rare gas compounds
    NT1   helium carbides
    NT1   helium chlorides
    NT1   helium fluorides
    NT1   helium hydrides
    NT1   helium hydroxides
    NT1   helium nitrides
    NT1   helium oxides
    NT1   helium tritides

HELIUM COOLED REACTORS [483; 2,232]
    UF   *helium-cooled reactors*
    BT1   gas cooled reactors
       BT2   reactors
    NT1   avr reactor
    NT1   dragon reactor
    NT1   ebor reactor
    NT1   egcr reactor
    NT1   fulton-1 reactor
    NT1   fulton-2 reactor
    NT1   httr reactor
    NT1   iea-zpr reactor
    NT1   peach bottom-1 reactor
    NT1   schmehausen reactor
    NT1   thtr-300 reactor
    NT1   uhtrex reactor
    NT1   vg-400 reactor
    NT1   vgr-50 reactor
    NT1   vhtr reactor
    NT1   vidal-1 reactor
    NT1   vidal-2 reactor

HELIUM DILUTION REFRIGERATION [357; 357]
    BT1   refrigeration
       BT2   cooling
    RT   cryogenics
    RT   helium dilution refrigerators

HELIUM DILUTION REFRIGERATORS [231; 231] *Jun 82*
    BT1   refrigerators
    RT   helium dilution refrigeration

HELIUM FLUORIDES [0; 0]
    BT1   fluorides
       BT2   fluorine compounds
         BT3   halogen compounds
       BT2   halides
         BT3   halogen compounds

```
BT1    helium compounds
BT2    rare gas compounds
```

helium generation
(Prior to December 1990, this was a valid descriptor.)
```
USE    interstitial helium generation
```

HELIUM HYDRIDES [196; 196]
```
BT1    helium compounds
BT2    rare gas compounds
BT1    hydrides
BT2    hydrogen compounds
```

HELIUM HYDROXIDES [1; 1]
```
BT1    helium compounds
BT2    rare gas compounds
BT1    hydroxides
BT2    hydrogen compounds
BT2    oxygen compounds
```

HELIUM I [282; 282]
```
BT1    helium 4
BT2    even-even nuclei
BT3    nuclei
BT2    helium isotopes
BT2    light nuclei
BT3    nuclei
BT2    stable isotopes
BT3    isotopes
```

HELIUM II [1,929; 1,929]
```
BT1    helium 4
BT2    even-even nuclei
BT3    nuclei
BT2    helium isotopes
BT2    light nuclei
BT3    nuclei
BT2    stable isotopes
BT3    isotopes
BT1    quantum fluids
BT2    fluids
RT     film flow
RT     landau liquid helium theory
RT     superfluidity
```

HELIUM IONS [6,504; 18,679]
```
BT1    ions
BT2    charged particles
NT1    alpha particles
NT2    cosmic alpha particles
NT2    delayed alpha particles
NT2    solar alpha particles
NT1    helium ash
```

HELIUM ISOTOPES [412; 14,720]
```
NT1    helium 10
NT1    helium 2
NT1    helium 3
NT2    helium 3 a
NT2    helium 3 a1
NT2    helium 3 b
NT1    helium 4
NT2    helium i
NT2    helium ii
NT1    helium 5
NT1    helium 6
NT1    helium 7
NT1    helium 8
NT1    helium 9
```

helium jet method
```
USE    reaction product transport
```

helium method
```
USE    isotope dating
```

HELIUM NITRIDES [0; 0]
```
BT1    helium compounds
BT2    rare gas compounds
BT1    nitrides
BT2    nitrogen compounds
BT2    pnictides
```

HELIUM OXIDES [1; 1]
```
BT1    helium compounds
BT2    rare gas compounds
BT1    oxides
BT2    chalcogenides
BT2    oxygen compounds
```

HELIUM TRITIDES [20; 20] *Sep 77*
```
BT1    helium compounds
BT2    rare gas compounds
BT1    tritides
BT2    tritium compounds
BT3    hydrogen compounds
```

HELIUM 10 [26; 26]
```
BT1    even-even nuclei
BT2    nuclei
BT1    helium isotopes
BT1    light nuclei
BT2    nuclei
```

HELIUM 2 [104; 104] *Feb 80*
```
BT1    helium isotopes
BT1    light nuclei
BT2    nuclei
```

HELIUM 3 [6,737; 7,712]
```
BT1    even-odd nuclei
BT2    nuclei
BT1    helium isotopes
BT1    light nuclei
BT2    nuclei
BT1    stable isotopes
BT2    isotopes
NT1    helium 3 a
NT1    helium 3 a1
NT1    helium 3 b
RT     helium 3 beams
RT     quantum fluids
```

HELIUM 3 A [642; 642] *Oct 75*
(A phase of superfluid helium 3.)
```
BT1    helium 3
BT2    even-odd nuclei
BT3    nuclei
BT2    helium isotopes
BT2    light nuclei
BT3    nuclei
BT2    stable isotopes
BT3    isotopes
RT     superfluidity
```

HELIUM 3 A1 [35; 35] *Aug 81*
(A phase of superfluid helium 3.)
```
BT1    helium 3
BT2    even-odd nuclei
BT3    nuclei
BT2    helium isotopes
BT2    light nuclei
BT3    nuclei
BT2    stable isotopes
BT3    isotopes
RT     superfluidity
```

HELIUM 3 B [601; 601] *Oct 75*
(A phase of superfluid helium 3.)
```
BT1    helium 3
BT2    even-odd nuclei
BT3    nuclei
BT2    helium isotopes
BT2    light nuclei
BT3    nuclei
BT2    stable isotopes
BT3    isotopes
RT     superfluidity
```

HELIUM 3 BEAMS [804; 804]
```
BT1    ion beams
BT2    beams
RT     helium 3
```

HELIUM 3 REACTIONS [3,295; 3,295]
```
BT1    nuclear reactions
```

HELIUM 3 TARGET [1,879; 1,879]
```
BT1    targets
```

HELIUM 4 [5,261; 7,225]
```
BT1    even-even nuclei
BT2    nuclei
BT1    helium isotopes
BT1    light nuclei
BT2    nuclei
BT1    stable isotopes
BT2    isotopes
NT1    helium i
NT1    helium ii
RT     helium 4 beams
RT     lambda point
RT     quantum fluids
```

HELIUM 4 BEAMS [661; 1,835]
```
BT1    ion beams
BT2    beams
NT1    alpha beams
RT     helium 4
```

helium 4 reactions
```
USE    alpha reactions
```

HELIUM 4 TARGET [2,354; 2,354]
```
BT1    targets
```

HELIUM 5 [445; 445]
```
BT1    alpha decay radioisotopes
BT2    radioisotopes
BT3    isotopes
BT1    even-odd nuclei
BT2    nuclei
BT1    helium isotopes
BT1    light nuclei
BT2    nuclei
```

HELIUM 6 [636; 636]
```
BT1    beta-minus decay radioisotopes
BT2    beta decay radioisotopes
BT3    radioisotopes
BT4    isotopes
BT1    even-even nuclei
BT2    nuclei
BT1    helium isotopes
BT1    light nuclei
BT2    nuclei
BT1    millisec living radioisotopes
BT2    radioisotopes
BT3    isotopes
```

HELIUM 6 REACTIONS [20; 20] *Jul 85*
```
BT1    heavy ion reactions
BT2    nuclear reactions
```

HELIUM 6 TARGET [5; 5] *Jan 86*
```
BT1    targets
```

HELIUM 7 [45; 45]
```
BT1    beta-minus decay radioisotopes
BT2    beta decay radioisotopes
BT3    radioisotopes
BT4    isotopes
BT1    even-odd nuclei
BT2    nuclei
BT1    helium isotopes
BT1    light nuclei
BT2    nuclei
```

HELIUM 8 [108; 108]
```
BT1    beta-minus decay radioisotopes
BT2    beta decay radioisotopes
BT3    radioisotopes
BT4    isotopes
BT1    even-even nuclei
BT2    nuclei
BT1    helium isotopes
BT1    light nuclei
BT2    nuclei
BT1    millisec living radioisotopes
BT2    radioisotopes
BT3    isotopes
```

HELIUM 8 BEAMS [3; 3] *May 85*
- BT1 ion beams
- BT2 beams

HELIUM 8 REACTIONS [12; 12] *Jul 85*
- BT1 heavy ion reactions
- BT2 nuclear reactions

HELIUM 9 [23; 23]
- BT1 even-odd nuclei
- BT2 nuclei
- BT1 helium isotopes
- BT1 light nuclei
- BT2 nuclei

helium-cooled reactors
- USE helium cooled reactors

HELIUM-NEON LASERS [250; 250] *May 76*
- BT1 gas lasers
- BT2 lasers
- BT3 amplifiers
- BT4 equipment

helmholtz free energy
- USE free energy

HELMHOLTZ INSTABILITY [359; 359]
- UF *kelvin-helmholtz instability*
- BT1 plasma macroinstabilities
- BT2 plasma instability
- BT3 instability
- RT fluid flow

HELMHOLTZ THEOREM [64; 64]
- RT vectors

HELMINTHS [48; 355]
- BT1 parasites
- NT1 ascaris
- NT1 cestodes
- NT2 hymenolepis
- NT1 trematodes
- NT2 fasciola
- NT2 schistosoma
- NT1 trichinella
- RT nematodes

hemagglutination
- USE hemagglutinins

HEMAGGLUTININS [95; 571]
- UF *hemagglutination*
- BT1 agglutinins
- NT1 concanavalin a
- NT1 phytohemagglutinin
- RT antibodies
- RT blood groups
- RT erythrocytes

hemangiomas
- USE angiomas

hematin
- USE heme

HEMATITE [300; 300]
- BT1 iron ores
- BT2 ores
- BT1 oxide minerals
- BT2 minerals
- RT iron oxides
- RT limonite

HEMATOLOGIC AGENTS [35; 1,357] *May 84*
- BT1 drugs
- NT1 anticoagulants
- NT2 coumarin
- NT2 dicumarol
- NT2 heparin
- NT2 psoralen
- NT2 tromexan
- NT1 coagulants
- NT2 blood coagulation factors
- NT3 fibrin
- NT3 fibrinogen
- NT3 fibrinolysin
- NT3 folic acid
- NT3 intrinsic factor
- NT3 kallikrein
- NT3 plasminogen
- NT3 protamines
- NT4 salmin
- NT3 prothrombin
- NT3 thrombin
- NT3 thromboplastin
- NT3 urokinase
- NT3 vitamin b-12
- NT3 vitamin k
- RT blood substitutes

HEMATOLOGY [243; 243]
- BT1 medicine
- RT hemic diseases

hematopoiesis
- USE blood formation

HEMATOPOIETIC SYSTEM [503; 4,045]
- BT1 body
- NT1 bone marrow
- RT blood formation
- RT erythropoiesis

hematoporphyrin (heme)
- USE heme

HEMATOPORPHYRINS [89; 89]
- BT1 pigments
- BT1 porphyrins
- BT2 heterocyclic acids
- BT3 carboxylic acids
- BT4 organic acids
- BT5 organic compounds
- BT3 heterocyclic compounds
- BT4 organic compounds
- BT2 organic nitrogen compounds
- BT3 organic compounds
- RT hemoglobin

HEMATOXYLIN [3; 3]
- BT1 dyes
- BT1 polyphenols
- BT2 phenols
- BT3 aromatics
- BT4 organic compounds
- BT3 hydroxy compounds
- BT4 organic compounds
- BT1 pyrans
- BT2 heterocyclic compounds
- BT3 organic compounds
- BT2 organic oxygen compounds
- BT3 organic compounds

HEME [171; 171]
- UF *hematin*
- UF *hematoporphyrin (heme)*
- UF *hemin*
- BT1 pigments
- BT1 porphyrins
- BT2 heterocyclic acids
- BT3 carboxylic acids
- BT4 organic acids
- BT5 organic compounds
- BT3 heterocyclic compounds
- BT4 organic compounds
- BT2 organic nitrogen compounds
- BT3 organic compounds
- RT carboxyhemoglobin
- RT hemoglobin
- RT iron
- RT methemoglobin

HEMIC DISEASES [410; 6,678]
- UF *blood diseases*
- BT1 diseases
- NT1 anemias
- NT2 ischemia
- NT2 megaloblastic anemia
- NT2 sickle cell anemia
- NT2 thalassemia
- NT1 hemophilia
- NT1 leukopenia
- NT2 lymphopenia
- NT1 malaria
- NT1 polycythemia
- NT1 purpura
- RT blood
- RT blood chemistry
- RT hematology
- RT hemolysis
- RT hemorrhage
- RT splenomegaly

hemin
- USE heme

HEMIPTERA [26; 51]
- BT1 insects
- BT2 arthropods
- BT3 invertebrates
- BT4 animals
- NT1 aphids

HEMOCYANIN [30; 30]
- BT1 proteins
- BT2 organic compounds
- RT blood

HEMOGLOBIN [662; 722]
- BT1 globins
- BT2 proteins
- BT3 organic compounds
- BT1 pigments
- BT1 porphyrins
- BT2 heterocyclic acids
- BT3 carboxylic acids
- BT4 organic acids
- BT5 organic compounds
- BT3 heterocyclic compounds
- BT4 organic compounds
- BT2 organic nitrogen compounds
- BT3 organic compounds
- NT1 carboxyhemoglobin
- NT1 methemoglobin
- RT anemias
- RT erythrocytes
- RT hematoporphyrins
- RT heme
- RT hemosiderin
- RT iron
- RT protoporphyrins
- RT respiration

HEMOLYSINS [16; 16]
- RT antibodies
- RT complement
- RT hemolysis

HEMOLYSIS [206; 206]
(The alteration, dissolution, or destruction of red blood cells in such a manner that hemoglobin is liberated into the medium in which the cells are suspended.)
- BT1 decomposition
- BT2 chemical reactions
- RT anemias
- RT erythrocytes
- RT hemic diseases
- RT hemolysins
- RT immunity
- RT pathological changes

HEMOPHILIA [17; 17] *Mar 87*
- BT1 hemic diseases
- BT2 diseases
- BT1 hereditary diseases
- BT2 diseases
- RT blood coagulation
- RT hemorrhage

hemophilus
  USE   haemophilus

hemopoiesis
  USE   blood formation

HEMORRHAGE [2,022; 2,022]
  BT1   pathological changes
    BT2   diseases
  BT1   symptoms
  RT   anemias
  RT   blood
  RT   blood coagulation
  RT   blood vessels
  RT   hemic diseases
  RT   hemophilia

HEMOSIDERIN [26; 26]
  BT1   pigments
  BT1   porphyrins
    BT2   heterocyclic acids
      BT3   carboxylic acids
        BT4   organic acids
          BT5   organic compounds
      BT3   heterocyclic compounds
        BT4   organic compounds
    BT2   organic nitrogen compounds
      BT3   organic compounds
  RT   blood
  RT   ferritin
  RT   hemoglobin
  RT   iron

hens
  USE   chickens

HEPARIN [292; 292]
  BT1   anticoagulants
    BT2   hematologic agents
      BT3   drugs
  BT1   mucopolysaccharides
    BT2   amines
      BT3   organic compounds
    BT2   polysaccharides
      BT3   saccharides
        BT4   carbohydrates
          BT5   organic compounds
  BT1   organic sulfur compounds
    BT2   organic compounds
  RT   mast cells

HEPATECTOMY [138; 138]
  BT1   surgery
    BT2   medicine
  RT   liver

HEPATITIS [660; 660]
  UF+   *hepatitis (infectious)*
  BT1   digestive system diseases
    BT2   diseases
  RT   jaundice
  RT   liver

hepatitis (infectious)
  USE   hepatitis
  AND   viral diseases

hepatocytes
  USE   liver cells

HEPATOMAS [851; 851]
  BT1   neoplasms
    BT2   diseases
  RT   liver

HEPTANE [199; 199]
  BT1   alkanes
    BT2   hydrocarbons
      BT3   organic compounds

HEPTANOIC ACID [25; 25]
  UF   *enanthic acid*
  UF   *heptylic acid*
  BT1   monocarboxylic acids
    BT2   carboxylic acids
      BT3   organic acids
        BT4   organic compounds

HEPTENES [15; 15]
  BT1   alkenes
    BT2   hydrocarbons
      BT3   organic compounds

HEPTYL RADICALS [5; 5]
  BT1   alkyl radicals
    BT2   radicals

heptylic acid
  USE   heptanoic acid

HERA STORAGE RING [544; 544]
May 84
(Hadron-Elektron-Ring Anlage.)
  BT1   storage rings

HERALD REACTOR [13; 13]
(UK Ministry of Defence, Aldermaston, Reading, Berkshire, United Kingdom)
  BT1   enriched uranium reactors
    BT2   reactors
  BT1   pool type reactors
    BT2   water cooled reactors
      BT3   reactors
    BT2   water moderated reactors
      BT3   reactors
  BT1   research reactors
    BT2   research and test reactors
      BT3   reactors
  BT1   test reactors
    BT2   research and test reactors
      BT3   reactors
    BT2   test facilities
  BT1   thermal reactors
    BT2   reactors

HERBICIDES [322; 322]
  BT1   pesticides

HERBS [135; 141]
  BT1   plants
  NT1   coleus

HEREDITARY DISEASES [708; 723]
  BT1   diseases
  NT1   hemophilia
  RT   genetics
  RT   mutants
  RT   mutations
  RT   sister chromatid exchanges

heredity
  USE   genetics

HERMEX PROCESS [1; 1]
  BT1   reprocessing
    BT2   separation processes
  RT   solvent extraction

HERMITE POLYNOMIALS [155; 155]
  BT1   polynomials
    BT2   functions

HERMITIAN MATRIX [264; 264]
  BT1   matrices

HERMITIAN OPERATORS [557; 557]
  BT1   mathematical operators

HERO REACTOR [2; 2]
  UF   *hot experi. reactor zero energ*
  BT1   enriched uranium reactors
    BT2   reactors
  BT1   graphite moderated reactors
    BT2   reactors
  BT1   research reactors
    BT2   research and test reactors
      BT3   reactors
  BT1   test reactors
    BT2   research and test reactors
      BT3   reactors
    BT2   test facilities
  BT1   zero power reactors
    BT2   experimental reactors
      BT3   research and test reactors
        BT4   reactors

HEROIN [13; 13]
  UF   *diacetylmorphine*
  BT1   alkaloids
    BT2   organic compounds
  BT1   analgesics
    BT2   central nervous system depress
      BT3   central nervous system agents
        BT4   drugs
  BT1   narcotics
    BT2   central nervous system depress
      BT3   central nervous system agents
        BT4   drugs
  RT   codeine
  RT   morphine
  RT   thebaine

HERPES SIMPLEX [285; 285]
  BT1   skin diseases
    BT2   diseases
  BT1   viral diseases
    BT2   infectious diseases
      BT3   diseases
  RT   viruses

HERPES ZOSTER [20; 20]
  BT1   viral diseases
    BT2   infectious diseases
      BT3   diseases
  RT   nerves
  RT   viruses

HERTZSPRUNG-RUSSELL DIAGRAM [715; 715]
  BT1   diagrams
    BT2   information
  RT   star evolution

HESPERIDIN [1; 1]
  BT1   flavones
    BT2   flavenoids
      BT3   organic oxygen compounds
        BT4   organic compounds
  BT1   glycosides
    BT2   carbohydrates
      BT3   organic compounds

HETEROCHROMATIN [35; 35]
  BT1   chromatin
  RT   chromosome breakage

HETEROCHROMOSOMES [139; 243]
  UF   *sex chromosomes*
  BT1   chromosomes
  NT1   x chromosome
  NT1   y chromosome
  RT   chromosomal aberrations
  RT   sex

HETEROCYCLIC ACIDS [33; 4,291]
  BT1   carboxylic acids
    BT2   organic acids
      BT3   organic compounds
  BT1   heterocyclic compounds
    BT2   organic compounds
  NT1   bilirubin
  NT1   biliverdin
  NT1   biotin
  NT1   diodrast
  NT1   histidine

NT1 hydroxyproline
NT1 kynurenic acid
NT1 lysergic acid
NT1 orotic acid
NT1 picolinic acid
NT1 porphyrins
  NT2 chlorophyll
  NT2 hematoporphyrins
  NT2 heme
  NT2 hemoglobin
    NT3 carboxyhemoglobin
    NT3 methemoglobin
  NT2 hemosiderin
  NT2 myoglobin
  NT2 peroxidases
    NT3 catalase
  NT2 protoporphyrins
NT1 proline
NT1 rhodamines
NT1 stercobilin
NT1 thioctic acid
NT1 tryptophan
NT1 urobilinogen
NT1 urocanic acid
RT nicotinamide

HETEROCYCLIC COMPOUNDS
[1,067; 25,850]
UF+ *heterocyclic oxygen compounds*
UF+ *tetrathiafulvalene*
UF+ *ttf*
UF+ *ttf-tcnq*
BT1 organic compounds
NT1 azines
  NT2 phenothiazines
    NT3 chlorpromazine
    NT3 methylene blue
  NT2 pyrazines
    NT3 neutral red
    NT3 phenazine
    NT3 piperazines
  NT2 pyridazines
    NT3 phthalazines
  NT2 pyridines
    NT3 acridines
      NT4 acridine orange
      NT4 flavines
        NT5 acriflavine
        NT5 proflavine
    NT3 bipyridines
    NT3 diodrast
    NT3 nicotinamide
    NT3 nicotine
    NT3 nicotinic acid
    NT3 pan
    NT3 phenatine
    NT3 picolines
      NT4 picolinic acid
    NT3 piperidines
      NT4 pethidine
      NT4 tmpn
      NT4 triacetoneamine-n-oxyl
    NT3 pyridinium compounds
    NT3 pyridoxal
    NT3 pyridoxine
    NT3 pyridoxylideneglutamate
    NT3 pyridylazoresorcinol
    NT3 quinolines
      NT4 ferron
      NT4 kynurenic acid
      NT4 oxine
      NT4 quinaldine
  NT2 pyrimidines
    NT3 alloxan
    NT3 barbiturates
      NT4 amytal
      NT4 nembutal
      NT4 phenobarbital
      NT4 thiopental
    NT3 cytidine
    NT3 cytosine
    NT3 deoxycytidine
    NT3 murexide
    NT3 sulfadiazine
    NT3 thiamine
    NT3 thymidine
    NT3 uracils
      NT4 bromouracils
        NT5 budr
      NT4 chlorouracils
      NT4 deoxyuridine
      NT4 fluorouracils
        NT5 fudr
      NT4 iodouracils
        NT5 iododeoxyuridine
      NT4 orotic acid
      NT4 thiouracil
      NT4 thymine
      NT4 uridine
  NT2 triazines
    NT3 cyanurates
    NT3 melamine
NT1 azoles
  NT2 carbazoles
  NT2 imidazoles
    NT3 allantoin
    NT3 benzimidazoles
    NT3 biotin
    NT3 cmni
    NT3 creatinine
    NT3 histamine
    NT3 histidine
    NT3 metronidazole
    NT3 misonidazole
    NT3 urocanic acid
  NT2 oxadiazoles
  NT2 oxazoles
    NT3 benzoxazoles
    NT3 pemoline
    NT3 popop
  NT2 pyrazoles
    NT3 indazoles
    NT3 pyrazolines
      NT4 antipyrine
  NT2 pyrroles
    NT3 bilirubin
    NT3 biliverdin
    NT3 indoles
      NT4 indocyanine green
      NT4 lysergic acid
      NT4 reserpine
      NT4 strychnine
      NT4 tryptamines
        NT5 bufotenine
        NT5 melatonin
        NT5 serotonin
      NT4 tryptophan
      NT4 vinblastine
    NT3 pyrrolidines
      NT4 hydroxyproline
      NT4 nicotine
      NT4 proline
    NT3 pyrrolidones
      NT4 pvp
    NT3 stercobilin
    NT3 urobilinogen
  NT2 tetrazoles
    NT3 tetrazolium
  NT2 thiadiazoles
  NT2 thiazoles
    NT3 benzothiazoles
    NT3 saccharin
    NT3 thiamine
  NT2 triazoles
NT1 dioxane
NT1 dioxin
NT1 furans
  NT2 benzofurans
  NT2 furfural
  NT2 furildioxime
  NT2 tetrahydrofuran
NT1 guanethidine
NT1 heterocyclic acids
  NT2 bilirubin
  NT2 biliverdin
  NT2 biotin
  NT2 diodrast
  NT2 histidine
  NT2 hydroxyproline
  NT2 kynurenic acid
  NT2 lysergic acid
  NT2 orotic acid
  NT2 picolinic acid
  NT2 porphyrins
    NT3 chlorophyll
    NT3 hematoporphyrins
    NT3 heme
    NT3 hemoglobin
      NT4 carboxyhemoglobin
      NT4 methemoglobin
    NT3 hemosiderin
    NT3 myoglobin
    NT3 peroxidases
      NT4 catalase
    NT3 protoporphyrins
  NT2 proline
  NT2 rhodamines
  NT2 stercobilin
  NT2 thioctic acid
  NT2 tryptophan
  NT2 urobilinogen
  NT2 urocanic acid
NT1 imipramine
NT1 isoalloxazines
  NT2 diaphorases
NT1 lactones
  NT2 coumarin
  NT2 gibberellic acid
NT1 morpholines
NT1 phenanthrolines
  NT2 ferroin
  NT2 phenanthroline-ortho
NT1 phthalocyanines
NT1 psoralen
NT1 pteridines
  NT2 aminopterin
  NT2 folic acid
NT1 purines
  NT2 adenines
    NT3 kinetin
  NT2 guanine
  NT2 guanosine
  NT2 hypoxanthine
  NT2 inosine
  NT2 mercaptopurine
  NT2 xanthines
    NT3 caffeine
    NT3 theobromine
    NT3 theophylline
    NT3 uric acid
NT1 pyrans
  NT2 coumarin
  NT2 hematoxylin
  NT2 quercetin
  NT2 tetrahydropyran
NT1 thionaphthenes
NT1 thionine
NT1 thiophene
NT1 tmtsf
NT1 trioxanes
NT1 tta
RT cyanine dyes
RT epoxides
RT lactams

heterocyclic oxygen compounds
USE heterocyclic compounds
AND organic oxygen compounds

HETERODYNE RECEIVERS [153; 153]
Feb 76
UF *superheterodyne receivers*
BT1 microwave equipment
  BT2 electronic equipment
    BT3 equipment
BT1 radio equipment
  BT2 electronic equipment
    BT3 equipment
RT frequency converters
RT radiometers

HETEROGENEOUS EFFECTS
[624; 624]
(Effects of dissimilar constituents on neutron diffusion in shielding or reactor cores.)
RT absorption
RT homogenization methods
RT neutron flux
RT reactor kinetics
RT shielding

HETEROGENEOUS REACTOR CORES
[220; 220] *May 81*
(Reactor cores using various types of fuel simultaneously.)
BT1 reactor cores
  BT2 reactor components

RT   fbr type reactors

HETEROJUNCTIONS [528; 528] *Aug 82*
BT1   semiconductor junctions

HETEROPOLYANIONS [550; 550]
BT1   anions
    BT2   ions
       BT3   charged particles
BT1   complexes
RT   molybdophosphoric acid
RT   tungstophosphoric acid

heterozygotes
USE   hybridization

HEUSLER ALLOYS [145; 145]
BT1   aluminium alloys
    BT2   alloys
BT1   copper base alloys
    BT2   copper alloys
       BT3   alloys
BT1   corrosion resistant alloys
    BT2   alloys
BT1   manganese alloys
    BT2   alloys
RT   brass
RT   bronze

HEVEA [11; 11]
UF   *rubber trees*
BT1   trees
    BT2   plants

hewlett-packard computers
USE   hp computers

HEXADECANE [42; 42]
BT1   alkanes
    BT2   hydrocarbons
       BT3   organic compounds

HEXADECANOIC ACID [301; 301]
UF   *palmitic acid*
BT1   monocarboxylic acids
    BT2   carboxylic acids
       BT3   organic acids
          BT4   organic compounds

HEXADECAPOLES [82; 82] *Nov 77*
BT1   multipoles

hexagonal close packed
USE   hcp lattices

HEXAGONAL CONFIGURATION [403; 403]
BT1   configuration

HEXAGONAL LATTICES [1,588; 2,546]
BT1   crystal lattices
    BT2   crystal structure
NT1   hcp lattices

hexahydropyridines
USE   piperidines

hexamethylenediaminetetraaceti (Hexamethylenediaminetetraacetic acid)
USE   hmdta

hexamethylenetetramine
USE   urotropin

HEXANE [500; 500]
BT1   alkanes
    BT2   hydrocarbons
       BT3   organic compounds
RT   cyclohexane

HEXANOIC ACID [53; 53]
UF   *caproic acid*
BT1   monocarboxylic acids
    BT2   carboxylic acids
       BT3   organic acids
          BT4   organic compounds

HEXANOLS [94; 94]
UF   *cyclohexanol*
UF   *hexyl alcohols*
BT1   alcohols
    BT2   hydroxy compounds
       BT3   organic compounds

HEXAPOLAR CONFIGURATIONS [18; 18]
BT1   multipolar configurations
    BT2   closed configurations
       BT3   magnetic field configurations

HEXAPOLES [144; 144]
BT1   multipoles

HEXENES [96; 96]
BT1   alkenes
    BT2   hydrocarbons
       BT3   organic compounds

HEXOKINASE [46; 46]
BT1   phosphotransferases
    BT2   phosphorus-group transferases
       BT3   transferases
          BT4   enzymes
             BT5   organic compounds

HEXOSAMINES [46; 282]
BT1   amines
    BT2   organic compounds
BT1   hexoses
    BT2   monosaccharides
       BT3   saccharides
          BT4   carbohydrates
             BT5   organic compounds
NT1   glucosamine

HEXOSES [155; 3,290]
UF   *fucose*
BT1   monosaccharides
    BT2   saccharides
       BT3   carbohydrates
          BT4   organic compounds
NT1   fructose
NT1   galactose
NT1   glucose
NT1   hexosamines
    NT2   glucosamine
NT1   mannose
NT1   sorbose

hexyl alcohols
USE   hexanols

HEXYL RADICALS [23; 23]
BT1   alkyl radicals
    BT2   radicals

HEYSHAM-A REACTOR [84; 84]
(Heysham, Lanchashire, UK)
BT1   agr type reactors
    BT2   enriched uranium reactors
       BT3   reactors
    BT2   gas cooled reactors
       BT3   reactors
    BT2   graphite moderated reactors
       BT3   reactors
BT1   carbon dioxide cooled reactors
    BT2   gas cooled reactors
       BT3   reactors
BT1   power reactors
    BT2   reactors
BT1   thermal reactors
    BT2   reactors

HEYSHAM-B REACTOR [169; 169]
(Heysham, Lanchashire, UK)
BT1   agr type reactors
    BT2   enriched uranium reactors
       BT3   reactors
    BT2   gas cooled reactors
       BT3   reactors
    BT2   graphite moderated reactors
       BT3   reactors
BT1   carbon dioxide cooled reactors
    BT2   gas cooled reactors
       BT3   reactors
BT1   power reactors
    BT2   reactors
BT1   thermal reactors
    BT2   reactors

hf radiation
USE   short wave radiation

HFBR REACTOR [85; 85]
(Association of Universities Inc., Upton, New York, USA)
UF   *brookhaven high flux beam r.*
BT1   enriched uranium reactors
    BT2   reactors
BT1   heavy water cooled reactors
    BT2   reactors
BT1   heavy water moderated reactors
    BT2   reactors
BT1   research reactors
    BT2   research and test reactors
       BT3   reactors
BT1   tank type reactors
    BT2   reactors
BT1   thermal reactors
    BT2   reactors
RT   tristan separator

HFETR REACTOR [55; 55] *Apr 86*
UF   *high flux engineering test r.*
BT1   enriched uranium reactors
    BT2   reactors
BT1   materials testing reactors
    BT2   irradiation reactors
       BT3   reactors
BT1   thermal reactors
    BT2   reactors
BT1   water cooled reactors
    BT2   reactors
BT1   water moderated reactors
    BT2   reactors

HFIR REACTOR [469; 469]
(Oak Ridge National Lab., Oak Ridge, Tennessee, USA)
UF   *high flux isotope reactor*
UF   *high-flux isotope reactor*
BT1   enriched uranium reactors
    BT2   reactors
BT1   isotope production reactors
    BT2   irradiation reactors
       BT3   reactors
BT1   research reactors
    BT2   research and test reactors
       BT3   reactors
BT1   tank type reactors
    BT2   reactors
BT1   test reactors
    BT2   research and test reactors
       BT3   reactors
    BT2   test facilities
BT1   thermal reactors
    BT2   reactors
BT1   water cooled reactors
    BT2   reactors
BT1   water moderated reactors
    BT2   reactors

HFR REACTOR [251; 251]
(Commission of the European Communities, Joint Research Centre, Petten, Netherlands)
UF   *high flux reactor petten*
UF   *high-flux reactor petten*
UF   *petten high flux reactor*
BT1   enriched uranium reactors
BT2   reactors
BT1   materials testing reactors
BT2   irradiation reactors
BT3   reactors
BT1   research reactors
BT2   research and test reactors
BT3   reactors
BT1   tank type reactors
BT2   reactors
BT1   thermal reactors
BT2   reactors
BT1   water cooled reactors
BT2   reactors
BT1   water moderated reactors
BT2   reactors

hfs
USE   hyperfine structure

HGI2 SEMICONDUCTOR DETECTORS [234; 234] *Dec 75*
(Mercury iodide semiconductor detectors)
UF   *mercuric iodide detectors*
BT1   semiconductor detectors
BT2   radiation detectors
BT3   measuring instruments

HHIRF ACCELERATOR [116; 116] *Aug 78*
UF   *holifield heavy ion research f*
BT1   heavy ion accelerators
BT2   accelerators
RT   ornl isochronous cyclotron

HIBERNATION [21; 21]
RT   hypothermia
RT   sleep

HIDDEN VARIABLES [312; 312]
(Prior to December 1985 NONMEASURABLE VARIABLES was used for this concept.)
UF   *non-measurable variables*
UF   *nonmeasurable variables*
RT   bell theorem
RT   quantum mechanics
RT   wave functions

HIFAR REACTOR [130; 130]
(Australian Atomic Energy Commission, Nuclear Science and Technology Branch, Lucas Heights, Australia)
UF   *high flux australian reactor*
UF   *high-flux australian reactor*
BT1   enriched uranium reactors
BT2   reactors
BT1   heavy water cooled reactors
BT2   reactors
BT1   heavy water moderated reactors
BT2   reactors
BT1   isotope production reactors
BT2   irradiation reactors
BT3   reactors
BT1   materials testing reactors
BT2   irradiation reactors
BT3   reactors
BT1   research reactors
BT2   research and test reactors
BT3   reactors
BT1   tank type reactors
BT2   reactors
BT1   test reactors
BT2   research and test reactors
BT3   reactors
BT2   test facilities
BT1   thermal reactors
BT2   reactors

HIGGS BOSONS [3,576; 3,576] *Jul 76*
BT1   postulated particles
BT2   elementary particles
RT   symmetry breaking

HIGGS MODEL [3,137; 3,137] *Jan 77*
(A gauge invariant model describing massive vector bosons, in which the scalar fields form an octet under su-3.)
BT1   particle models
BT2   mathematical models
RT   instantons
RT   quantum field theory
RT   su-3 groups
RT   vector mesons

HIGH ALLOY STEELS [45; 8,262] *Nov 83*
UF   *high-alloy steels*
BT1   steels
BT2   carbon additions
BT2   iron base alloys
BT3   iron alloys
BT4   alloys
NT1   stainless steels
* NT2   chromium steels
* NT2   chromium-nickel steels
* NT2   low carbon-high alloy steels
NT2   steel-cr17mn15nni
NT2   steel-cr21mn9ni6

high altitude (stratosphere)
USE   stratosphere

high beta plasma
USE   high-beta plasma

HIGH ENERGY PHYSICS [2,926; 2,926]
(Use only for articles of a very broad nature such as an annual research program, etc.)
UF   *high-energy physics*
BT1   physics
RT   nuclear physics

high energy radiotherapy
USE   radiotherapy

high explosives
USE   chemical explosives

high flux australian reactor
USE   hifar reactor

high flux engineering test r.
USE   hfetr reactor

high flux isotope reactor
USE   hfir reactor

high flux reactor petten
USE   hfr reactor

HIGH FREQUENCY AMPLIFIERS [65; 65]
UF   *high-frequency amplifiers*
BT1   amplifiers
BT2   equipment
BT1   electronic equipment
BT2   equipment

high frequency discharges
USE   high-frequency discharges

high frequency heating
USE   high-frequency heating

high frequency radiation
USE   short wave radiation

high level radioactive wastes
USE   high-level radioactive wastes

HIGH PRESSURE [2,745; 2,745]
UF   *pressure (0100-1000 atm)*
UF   *pressure (10-100 mpa)*
RT   pressure dependence

HIGH PRESSURE COOLANT INJECTIO [252; 252] *Jan 79*
UF   *high-pressure coolant injectio*
UF   *hpci*
BT1   eccs
BT2   reactor protection systems
RT   reactor safety

high purity ge detectors
USE   high-purity ge detectors

HIGH SEAS [9; 9] *Dec 76*
RT   fishery laws
RT   maritime laws
RT   seas
RT   territorial waters

HIGH SPIN STATES [4,834; 4,834]
UF   *high-spin states*
BT1   energy levels
RT   backbending
RT   spin

high tem. lattice test reactor
USE   htltr reactor

high temper. gas cool./grap. m
USE   htgr type reactors

HIGH TEMPERATURE [34,085; 34,085]
UF   *temperature (0400-1000 k)*
RT   critical heat flux
RT   scaling
RT   temperature dependence

high temperature test reactor
USE   httr reactor

HIGH VACUUM [2,644; 2,644]
UF   *vacuum (0.13-0.13x10(-5) pa)*
UF   *vacuum (10(-3)-10(-8) torr)*
RT   cryopumps
RT   gettering
RT   getters
RT   pressure dependence
RT   turbomolecular pumps
RT   vacuum pumps

high voltage pulse generators
USE   high-voltage pulse generators

high-alloy steels
USE   high alloy steels

HIGH-BETA PLASMA [1,624; 1,624]
(Plasma with Beta ratio of from 0.1 to 1.0.)
UF   *high beta plasma*
BT1   plasma
RT   beta ratio

high-energy physics
   USE   high energy physics

high-flux australian reactor
   USE   hifar reactor

high-flux isotope reactor
   USE   hfir reactor

high-flux reactor petten
   USE   hfr reactor

high-frequency amplifiers
   USE   high frequency amplifiers

HIGH-FREQUENCY DISCHARGES [480; 480]
   UF   *high frequency discharges*
   UF   *microwave discharges*
   BT1   electric discharges
   RT   high-frequency heating
   RT   plasma production

HIGH-FREQUENCY HEATING [1,380; 6,330]
   UF   *high frequency heating*
   BT1   plasma heating
     BT2   heating
   NT1   ecr heating
   NT1   icr heating
   NT1   lower hybrid heating
   NT1   magnetic-pumping heating
     NT2   acoustic heating
     NT2   collisional heating
     NT2   transit-time magnetic pumping
   RT   high-frequency discharges

high-frequency radiation
   USE   short wave radiation

HIGH-LEVEL RADIOACTIVE WASTES [10,486; 10,486] *May 78*
(Wastes containing more than 100 microcuries/milliliter of radioactivity.)
   UF   *high level radioactive wastes*
   BT1   radioactive wastes
     BT2   radioactive materials
       BT3   materials
     BT2   wastes
   RT   gorleben salt dome
   RT   pamela plant
   RT   us mrs project
   RT   wipp

high-pressure coolant injectio
   USE   high pressure coolant injectio

HIGH-PURITY GE DETECTORS [616; 616] *Dec 75*
   UF   *ge detectors (high-purity)*
   UF   *high purity ge detectors*
   BT1   ge semiconductor detectors
     BT2   semiconductor detectors
       BT3   radiation detectors
         BT4   measuring instruments

high-spin states
   USE   high spin states

HIGH-TC SUPERCONDUCTORS [2,010; 2,010] *Aug 90*
(Superconductors having critical temperature greater than 30 degrees Kelvin.)
   BT1   superconductors
   RT   chalcogenides
   RT   superconductivity

HIGH-VOLTAGE PULSE GENERATORS [766; 901]
   UF   *high voltage pulse generators*
   BT1   pulse generators
     BT2   function generators
       BT3   electronic equipment
         BT4   equipment
   NT1   marx generators

HIGHLAND URANIUM MILL [3; 3] *Nov 78*
   BT1   feed materials plants
     BT2   industrial plants
     BT2   nuclear facilities
   RT   ore processing
   RT   uranium ores

HIGHLY ENRICHED URANIUM [471; 471]
(80 - 100 per cent.)
   BT1   enriched uranium
     BT2   isotope enriched materials
       BT3   materials
     BT2   uranium
       BT3   actinides
         BT4   metals
           BT5   elements

HILACS [317; 593]
   UF   *heavy ion linear accelerators*
   BT1   heavy ion accelerators
     BT2   accelerators
   BT1   linear accelerators
     BT2   accelerators
   NT1   atlas superconducting linac
   NT1   superhilac
   RT   heavy ion reactions
   RT   heavy ions

HILBERT SPACE [3,428; 3,428]
   BT1   banach space
     BT2   mathematical space
       BT3   space

HILBERT TRANSFORMATION [68; 68]
   BT1   integral transformations
     BT2   transformations

HILL EQUATION [63; 63]
   BT1   differential equations
     BT2   equations

HILL-WHEELER THEORY [124; 124]
   RT   collective model
   RT   nuclear models

HIMALAYAS [41; 41] *Nov 77*
   BT1   mountains

HINKLEY POINT-A REACTOR [32; 32]
(Hinkley Point, Somerset, UK)
   BT1   carbon dioxide cooled reactors
     BT2   gas cooled reactors
       BT3   reactors
   BT1   magnox type reactors
     BT2   gcr type reactors
       BT3   gas cooled reactors
         BT4   reactors
     BT2   graphite moderated reactors
       BT4   reactors
     BT2   natural uranium reactors
       BT3   reactors
     BT2   power reactors
       BT3   reactors
   BT1   thermal reactors
     BT2   reactors

HINKLEY POINT-B REACTOR [137; 137]
(Hinkley Point, Somerset, UK)
   BT1   agr type reactors
     BT2   enriched uranium reactors
       BT3   reactors
     BT2   gas cooled reactors
       BT3   reactors
     BT2   graphite moderated reactors
       BT3   reactors
   BT1   carbon dioxide cooled reactors
     BT2   gas cooled reactors
       BT3   reactors
   BT1   power reactors
     BT2   reactors
   BT1   thermal reactors
     BT2   reactors

HIPPOCAMPUS [146; 146] *Feb 82*
   BT1   brain
     BT2   central nervous system
       BT3   nervous system
     BT2   organs
       BT3   body
   RT   receptors

HIPPURAN [823; 823]
   UF   *iodohippurate*
   UF   *n-o-iodobenzoylaminoacetate*
   UF   *orthoiodohippurate*
   UF   *sodium iodohippurate*
   UF   *sodium n-o-iodobenzoylaminoace*
   UF   *sodium orthoiodohippurate*
   BT1   contrast media
   RT   hippuric acid

HIPPURIC ACID [133; 133]
   UF   *benzoylaminoacetic acid*
   UF   *benzoylglycine*
   UF   *benzoylglycocoll*
   BT1   amino acids
     BT2   carboxylic acids
       BT3   organic acids
         BT4   organic compounds
   RT   glycine
   RT   hippuran

HIRFL CYCLOTRON [37; 37] *Jun 83*
(Heavy Ion Research Facility, Lanzhou, China.)
   UF   *heavy ion res fac lanzhou cycl*
   UF   *lanzhou cyclotron*
   BT1   heavy ion accelerators
     BT2   accelerators
   BT1   isochronous cyclotrons
     BT2   cyclotrons
       BT3   cyclic accelerators
         BT4   accelerators

HIROSHIMA [842; 842]
   BT1   japan
     BT2   asia
     BT2   developed countries
   RT   a-bomb survivors
   RT   nuclear explosions
   RT   nuclear weapons

HISTAMINASE [10; 10]
   BT1   oxidases
     BT2   oxidoreductases
       BT3   enzymes
         BT4   organic compounds

HISTAMINE [320; 320]
   BT1   amines
     BT2   organic compounds
   BT1   imidazoles
     BT2   azoles
       BT3   heterocyclic compounds
         BT4   organic compounds
       BT3   organic nitrogen compounds
         BT4   organic compounds
   RT   allergy
   RT   antihistaminics
   RT   capillaries

HISTIDINE [331; 331]
   BT1   amino acids
     BT2   carboxylic acids
       BT3   organic acids
         BT4   organic compounds
   BT1   heterocyclic acids
     BT2   carboxylic acids
       BT3   organic acids
         BT4   organic compounds
     BT2   heterocyclic compounds

```
        BT3     organic compounds
    BT1     imidazoles
      BT2     azoles
        BT3     heterocyclic compounds
          BT4     organic compounds
        BT3     organic nitrogen compounds
          BT4     organic compounds
```

HISTOLOGICAL TECHNIQUES
[310; 310] Oct 75
- RT   histology
- RT   microscopy
- RT   stains
- RT   tissues

HISTOLOGY [2,617; 2,617]
- RT   histological techniques
- RT   microscopy
- RT   tissues

HISTONES [307; 307]
- BT1   proteins
  - BT2   organic compounds
- RT   nucleosomes

HISTORICAL ASPECTS [2,389; 2,389]
Jun 83
(For documents concerning the history of scientific and technical activities.)
- RT   archaeology
- RT   cultural objects
- RT   research programs
- RT   sociology

hitachi training reactor
- USE   htr reactor

HITREX-1 REACTOR [3; 3] Feb 77
- BT1   graphite moderated reactors
  - BT2   reactors
- BT1   thermal reactors
  - BT2   reactors
- BT1   zero power reactors
  - BT2   experimental reactors
    - BT3   research and test reactors
      - BT4   reactors

HL-1 TOKAMAK [20; 20] Dec 89
(Southwestern Institute of Physics, Leshan, Sichuan, China.)
- BT1   tokamak devices
  - BT2   closed plasma devices
    - BT3   thermonuclear devices

HMDTA [12; 12]
(Hexamethylenediaminetetraacetic acid)
- UF   *hexamethylenediaminetetraaceti*
- BT1   amino acids
  - BT2   carboxylic acids
    - BT3   organic acids
      - BT4   organic compounds
- BT1   chelating agents

HNPF REACTOR [18; 18]
- UF   *hallam nuclear power facility*
- BT1   enriched uranium reactors
  - BT2   reactors
- BT1   graphite moderated reactors
  - BT2   reactors
- BT1   power reactors
  - BT2   reactors
- BT1   sodium cooled reactors
  - BT2   liquid metal cooled reactors
    - BT3   reactors
- BT1   thermal reactors
  - BT2   reactors

HODGKINS DISEASE [1,064; 1,064]
- UF   *lymphogranuloma malignum*
- UF   *lymphogranulomatosis*
- BT1   lymphomas
  - BT2   immune system diseases
    - BT3   diseases
  - BT2   neoplasms
    - BT3   diseases

HODOSCOPES [978; 978]
- RT   counting techniques
- RT   telescope counters

hoger onderwijs reactor
- USE   hor reactor

hoists
- USE   cranes

HOLE MOBILITY [405; 405]
- BT1   mobility

HOLES [2,574; 2,574]
(Absence of electrons from otherwise filled electron bands; see also BLACK HOLES, CAVITIES, OPENINGS, BOREHOLES, and VOIDS.)
- UF   *electron holes*
- RT   charge carriers
- RT   electron-hole coupling
- RT   point defects
- RT   quasi particles
- RT   trapping
- RT   traps

holifield heavy ion research f
- USE   hhirf accelerator

HOLLANDITE [79; 79] Sep 81
- BT1   oxide minerals
  - BT2   minerals
- RT   aluminium oxides
- RT   barium oxides
- RT   synroc process
- RT   titanium oxides

HOLLOW CATHODES [510; 510]
- BT1   cathodes
  - BT2   electrodes

HOLLOW FUEL RODS [93; 93]
- BT1   fuel rods
  - BT2   fuel elements
    - BT3   reactor components

HOLLY EVENT [2; 2] Jan 76
- BT1   nuclear explosions
  - BT2   explosions
- BT1   surface explosions
  - BT2   explosions
- RT   eniwetok
- RT   hardtack project

HOLMIUM [666; 666]
- BT1   rare earths
  - BT2   metals
    - BT3   elements

HOLMIUM ADDITIONS [57; 57]
(Alloys containing not more than 1% Ho are listed here.)
- BT1   rare earth additions
- RT   holmium alloys
- RT   holmium compounds

HOLMIUM ALLOYS [493; 524]
(Alloys containing more than 1% Ho.)
- BT1   rare earth alloys
  - BT2   alloys
- NT1   holmium base alloys
- RT   holmium additions

HOLMIUM BASE ALLOYS [31; 31]
- BT1   holmium alloys
  - BT2   rare earth alloys
    - BT3   alloys

HOLMIUM BORIDES [65; 65]
- BT1   borides
  - BT2   boron compounds
- BT1   holmium compounds
  - BT2   rare earth compounds

HOLMIUM BROMIDES [14; 14]
- BT1   bromides
  - BT2   bromine compounds
    - BT3   halogen compounds
  - BT2   halides
    - BT3   halogen compounds
- BT1   holmium compounds
  - BT2   rare earth compounds

HOLMIUM CARBIDES [15; 15]
- BT1   carbides
  - BT2   carbon compounds
- BT1   holmium compounds
  - BT2   rare earth compounds

HOLMIUM CARBONATES [0; 0]
Apr 89
- BT1   carbonates
  - BT2   carbon compounds
  - BT2   oxygen compounds
- BT1   holmium compounds
  - BT2   rare earth compounds

HOLMIUM CHLORIDES [55; 55]
- BT1   chlorides
  - BT2   chlorine compounds
    - BT3   halogen compounds
  - BT2   halides
    - BT3   halogen compounds
- BT1   holmium compounds
  - BT2   rare earth compounds

HOLMIUM COMPLEXES [285; 285]
- BT1   rare earth complexes
  - BT2   complexes

HOLMIUM COMPOUNDS [394; 1,016]
- BT1   rare earth compounds
- NT1   holmium borides
- NT1   holmium bromides
- NT1   holmium carbides
- NT1   holmium carbonates
- NT1   holmium chlorides
- NT1   holmium fluorides
- NT1   holmium hydrides
- NT1   holmium hydroxides
- NT1   holmium iodides
- NT1   holmium nitrates
- NT1   holmium nitrides
- NT1   holmium oxides
- NT1   holmium perchlorates
- NT1   holmium phosphates
- NT1   holmium phosphides
- NT1   holmium selenides
- NT1   holmium silicates
- NT1   holmium silicides
- NT1   holmium sulfates
- NT1   holmium sulfides
- NT1   holmium tellurides
- RT   holmium additions

HOLMIUM FLUORIDES [60; 60]
- BT1   fluorides
  - BT2   fluorine compounds
    - BT3   halogen compounds
  - BT2   halides
    - BT3   halogen compounds
- BT1   holmium compounds
  - BT2   rare earth compounds

HOLMIUM HYDRIDES [17; 17]
- BT1   holmium compounds
  - BT2   rare earth compounds
- BT1   hydrides
  - BT2   hydrogen compounds

HOLMIUM HYDROXIDES [13; 13]
- BT1 holmium compounds
- BT2 rare earth compounds
- BT1 hydroxides
- BT2 hydrogen compounds
- BT2 oxygen compounds

HOLMIUM IODIDES [12; 12]
- BT1 holmium compounds
- BT2 rare earth compounds
- BT1 iodides
- BT2 halides
- BT3 halogen compounds
- BT2 iodine compounds
- BT3 halogen compounds

HOLMIUM IONS [143; 143]
- BT1 ions
- BT2 charged particles

HOLMIUM ISOTOPES [74; 923]
- NT1 holmium 144
- NT1 holmium 145
- NT1 holmium 146
- NT1 holmium 147
- NT1 holmium 148
- NT1 holmium 149
- NT1 holmium 150
- NT1 holmium 151
- NT1 holmium 152
- NT1 holmium 153
- NT1 holmium 154
- NT1 holmium 155
- NT1 holmium 156
- NT1 holmium 157
- NT1 holmium 158
- NT1 holmium 159
- NT1 holmium 160
- NT1 holmium 161
- NT1 holmium 162
- NT1 holmium 163
- NT1 holmium 164
- NT1 holmium 165
- NT1 holmium 166
- NT1 holmium 167
- NT1 holmium 168
- NT1 holmium 169
- NT1 holmium 170
- NT1 holmium 171
- NT1 holmium 172

HOLMIUM NITRATES [17; 17]
- BT1 holmium compounds
- BT2 rare earth compounds
- BT1 nitrates
- BT2 nitrogen compounds
- BT2 oxygen compounds

HOLMIUM NITRIDES [4; 4]
- BT1 holmium compounds
- BT2 rare earth compounds
- BT1 nitrides
- BT2 nitrogen compounds
- BT2 pnictides

HOLMIUM OXIDES [261; 261]
- BT1 holmium compounds
- BT2 rare earth compounds
- BT1 oxides
- BT2 chalcogenides
- BT2 oxygen compounds

→ ## HOLMIUM PERCHLORATES [0; 0]
Sep 91
- BT1 holmium compounds
- BT2 rare earth compounds
- BT1 perchlorates
- BT2 chlorine compounds
- BT3 halogen compounds
- BT2 oxygen compounds

HOLMIUM PHOSPHATES [12; 12]
Oct 75
- BT1 holmium compounds
- BT2 rare earth compounds
- BT1 phosphates
- BT2 oxygen compounds

- BT2 phosphorus compounds

HOLMIUM PHOSPHIDES [10; 10]
Jul 78
- BT1 holmium compounds
- BT2 rare earth compounds
- BT1 phosphides
- BT2 phosphorus compounds
- BT2 pnictides

HOLMIUM SELENIDES [6; 6] *Aug 84*
- BT1 holmium compounds
- BT2 rare earth compounds
- BT1 selenides
- BT2 chalcogenides
- BT2 selenium compounds

HOLMIUM SILICATES [0; 0] *Jul 90*
- BT1 holmium compounds
- BT2 rare earth compounds
- BT1 silicates
- BT2 oxygen compounds
- BT2 silicon compounds

HOLMIUM SILICIDES [18; 18] *Oct 75*
- BT1 holmium compounds
- BT2 rare earth compounds
- BT1 silicides
- BT2 silicon compounds

HOLMIUM SULFATES [13; 13]
- BT1 holmium compounds
- BT2 rare earth compounds
- BT1 sulfates
- BT2 oxygen compounds
- BT2 sulfur compounds

HOLMIUM SULFIDES [64; 64]
- BT1 holmium compounds
- BT2 rare earth compounds
- BT1 sulfides
- BT2 chalcogenides
- BT2 sulfur compounds

HOLMIUM TELLURIDES [2; 2] *Feb 88*
- BT1 holmium compounds
- BT2 rare earth compounds
- BT1 tellurides
- BT2 chalcogenides
- BT2 tellurium compounds

HOLMIUM 144 [3; 3] *Feb 87*
- BT1 holmium isotopes
- BT1 millisec living radioisotopes
- BT2 radioisotopes
- BT3 isotopes
- BT1 odd-odd nuclei
- BT2 nuclei
- BT1 rare earth nuclei
- BT2 intermediate mass nuclei
- BT3 nuclei

HOLMIUM 145 [3; 3] *Apr 88*
- BT1 beta-plus decay radioisotopes
- BT2 beta decay radioisotopes
- BT3 radioisotopes
- BT4 isotopes
- BT1 electron capture radioisotopes
- BT2 beta decay radioisotopes
- BT3 radioisotopes
- BT4 isotopes
- BT1 holmium isotopes
- BT1 odd-even nuclei
- BT2 nuclei
- BT1 rare earth nuclei
- BT2 intermediate mass nuclei
- BT3 nuclei
- BT1 seconds living radioisotopes
- BT2 radioisotopes
- BT3 isotopes

HOLMIUM 146 [6; 6] *Sep 81*
- BT1 beta-plus decay radioisotopes
- BT2 beta decay radioisotopes
- BT3 radioisotopes

- BT4 isotopes
- BT1 holmium isotopes
- BT1 odd-odd nuclei
- BT2 nuclei
- BT1 rare earth nuclei
- BT2 intermediate mass nuclei
- BT3 nuclei
- BT1 seconds living radioisotopes
- BT2 radioisotopes
- BT3 isotopes

HOLMIUM 147 [4; 4] *Jun 82*
- BT1 beta-plus decay radioisotopes
- BT2 beta decay radioisotopes
- BT3 radioisotopes
- BT4 isotopes
- BT1 electron capture radioisotopes
- BT2 beta decay radioisotopes
- BT3 radioisotopes
- BT4 isotopes
- BT1 holmium isotopes
- BT1 odd-even nuclei
- BT2 nuclei
- BT1 rare earth nuclei
- BT2 intermediate mass nuclei
- BT3 nuclei

HOLMIUM 148 [18; 18] *Sep 79*
- BT1 beta-plus decay radioisotopes
- BT2 beta decay radioisotopes
- BT3 radioisotopes
- BT4 isotopes
- BT1 holmium isotopes
- BT1 isomeric transition isotopes
- BT2 radioisotopes
- BT3 isotopes
- BT1 millisec living radioisotopes
- BT2 radioisotopes
- BT3 isotopes
- BT1 odd-odd nuclei
- BT2 nuclei
- BT1 rare earth nuclei
- BT2 intermediate mass nuclei
- BT3 nuclei
- BT1 seconds living radioisotopes
- BT2 radioisotopes
- BT3 isotopes

HOLMIUM 149 [34; 34]
- BT1 beta-plus decay radioisotopes
- BT2 beta decay radioisotopes
- BT3 radioisotopes
- BT4 isotopes
- BT1 electron capture radioisotopes
- BT2 beta decay radioisotopes
- BT3 radioisotopes
- BT4 isotopes
- BT1 holmium isotopes
- BT1 odd-even nuclei
- BT2 nuclei
- BT1 rare earth nuclei
- BT2 intermediate mass nuclei
- BT3 nuclei
- BT1 seconds living radioisotopes
- BT2 radioisotopes
- BT3 isotopes

HOLMIUM 150 [41; 41]
- BT1 beta-plus decay radioisotopes
- BT2 beta decay radioisotopes
- BT3 radioisotopes
- BT4 isotopes
- BT1 electron capture radioisotopes
- BT2 beta decay radioisotopes
- BT3 radioisotopes
- BT4 isotopes
- BT1 holmium isotopes
- BT1 minutes living radioisotopes
- BT2 radioisotopes
- BT3 isotopes
- BT1 odd-odd nuclei
- BT2 nuclei
- BT1 rare earth nuclei
- BT2 intermediate mass nuclei
- BT3 nuclei
- BT1 seconds living radioisotopes
- BT2 radioisotopes
- BT3 isotopes

HOLMIUM 151 [42; 42]
BT1 alpha decay radioisotopes
BT2 radioisotopes
BT3 isotopes
BT1 beta-plus decay radioisotopes
BT2 beta decay radioisotopes
BT3 radioisotopes
BT4 isotopes
BT1 electron capture radioisotopes
BT2 beta decay radioisotopes
BT3 radioisotopes
BT4 isotopes
BT1 holmium isotopes
BT1 odd-even nuclei
BT2 nuclei
BT1 rare earth nuclei
BT2 intermediate mass nuclei
BT3 nuclei
BT1 seconds living radioisotopes
BT2 radioisotopes
BT3 isotopes

HOLMIUM 152 [49; 49]
BT1 alpha decay radioisotopes
BT2 radioisotopes
BT3 isotopes
BT1 beta-plus decay radioisotopes
BT2 beta decay radioisotopes
BT3 radioisotopes
BT4 isotopes
BT1 electron capture radioisotopes
BT2 beta decay radioisotopes
BT3 radioisotopes
BT4 isotopes
BT1 holmium isotopes
BT1 minutes living radioisotopes
BT2 radioisotopes
BT3 isotopes
BT1 odd-odd nuclei
BT2 nuclei
BT1 rare earth nuclei
BT2 intermediate mass nuclei
BT3 nuclei
BT1 seconds living radioisotopes
BT2 radioisotopes
BT3 isotopes

HOLMIUM 153 [39; 39]
BT1 alpha decay radioisotopes
BT2 radioisotopes
BT3 isotopes
BT1 beta-plus decay radioisotopes
BT2 beta decay radioisotopes
BT3 radioisotopes
BT4 isotopes
BT1 electron capture radioisotopes
BT2 beta decay radioisotopes
BT3 radioisotopes
BT4 isotopes
BT1 holmium isotopes
BT1 minutes living radioisotopes
BT2 radioisotopes
BT3 isotopes
BT1 odd-even nuclei
BT2 nuclei
BT1 rare earth nuclei
BT2 intermediate mass nuclei
BT3 nuclei

HOLMIUM 154 [18; 18]
BT1 alpha decay radioisotopes
BT2 radioisotopes
BT3 isotopes
BT1 beta-plus decay radioisotopes
BT2 beta decay radioisotopes
BT3 radioisotopes
BT4 isotopes
BT1 electron capture radioisotopes
BT2 beta decay radioisotopes
BT3 radioisotopes
BT4 isotopes
BT1 holmium isotopes
BT1 minutes living radioisotopes
BT2 radioisotopes
BT3 isotopes
BT1 odd-odd nuclei
BT2 nuclei
BT1 rare earth nuclei
BT2 intermediate mass nuclei
BT3 nuclei

HOLMIUM 155 [32; 32]
BT1 alpha decay radioisotopes
BT2 radioisotopes
BT3 isotopes
BT1 beta-plus decay radioisotopes
BT2 beta decay radioisotopes
BT3 radioisotopes
BT4 isotopes
BT1 electron capture radioisotopes
BT2 beta decay radioisotopes
BT3 radioisotopes
BT4 isotopes
BT1 holmium isotopes
BT1 minutes living radioisotopes
BT2 radioisotopes
BT3 isotopes
BT1 odd-even nuclei
BT2 nuclei
BT1 rare earth nuclei
BT2 intermediate mass nuclei
BT3 nuclei

HOLMIUM 156 [17; 17]
BT1 beta-plus decay radioisotopes
BT2 beta decay radioisotopes
BT3 radioisotopes
BT4 isotopes
BT1 electron capture radioisotopes
BT2 beta decay radioisotopes
BT3 radioisotopes
BT4 isotopes
BT1 holmium isotopes
BT1 isomeric transition isotopes
BT2 radioisotopes
BT3 isotopes
BT1 minutes living radioisotopes
BT2 radioisotopes
BT3 isotopes
BT1 odd-odd nuclei
BT2 nuclei
BT1 rare earth nuclei
BT2 intermediate mass nuclei
BT3 nuclei

HOLMIUM 157 [58; 58]
BT1 beta-plus decay radioisotopes
BT2 beta decay radioisotopes
BT3 radioisotopes
BT4 isotopes
BT1 electron capture radioisotopes
BT2 beta decay radioisotopes
BT3 radioisotopes
BT4 isotopes
BT1 holmium isotopes
BT1 minutes living radioisotopes
BT2 radioisotopes
BT3 isotopes
BT1 odd-even nuclei
BT2 nuclei
BT1 rare earth nuclei
BT2 intermediate mass nuclei
BT3 nuclei

HOLMIUM 158 [31; 31]
BT1 beta-plus decay radioisotopes
BT2 beta decay radioisotopes
BT3 radioisotopes
BT4 isotopes
BT1 electron capture radioisotopes
BT2 beta decay radioisotopes
BT3 radioisotopes
BT4 isotopes
BT1 holmium isotopes
BT1 internal conversion radioisoto
BT2 radioisotopes
BT3 isotopes
BT1 isomeric transition isotopes
BT2 radioisotopes
BT3 isotopes
BT1 minutes living radioisotopes
BT2 radioisotopes
BT3 isotopes
BT1 odd-odd nuclei
BT2 nuclei
BT1 rare earth nuclei
BT2 intermediate mass nuclei
BT3 nuclei

HOLMIUM 159 [37; 37]
BT1 electron capture radioisotopes
BT2 beta decay radioisotopes
BT3 radioisotopes
BT4 isotopes
BT1 holmium isotopes
BT1 isomeric transition isotopes
BT2 radioisotopes
BT3 isotopes
BT1 minutes living radioisotopes
BT2 radioisotopes
BT3 isotopes
BT1 odd-even nuclei
BT2 nuclei
BT1 rare earth nuclei
BT2 intermediate mass nuclei
BT3 nuclei
BT1 seconds living radioisotopes
BT2 radioisotopes
BT3 isotopes

HOLMIUM 160 [36; 36]
BT1 beta-plus decay radioisotopes
BT2 beta decay radioisotopes
BT3 radioisotopes
BT4 isotopes
BT1 electron capture radioisotopes
BT2 beta decay radioisotopes
BT3 radioisotopes
BT4 isotopes
BT1 holmium isotopes
BT1 hours living radioisotopes
BT2 radioisotopes
BT3 isotopes
BT1 internal conversion radioisoto
BT2 radioisotopes
BT3 isotopes
BT1 isomeric transition isotopes
BT2 radioisotopes
BT3 isotopes
BT1 minutes living radioisotopes
BT2 radioisotopes
BT3 isotopes
BT1 odd-odd nuclei
BT2 nuclei
BT1 rare earth nuclei
BT2 intermediate mass nuclei
BT3 nuclei

HOLMIUM 161 [52; 52]
BT1 electron capture radioisotopes
BT2 beta decay radioisotopes
BT3 radioisotopes
BT4 isotopes
BT1 holmium isotopes
BT1 hours living radioisotopes
BT2 radioisotopes
BT3 isotopes
BT1 isomeric transition isotopes
BT2 radioisotopes
BT3 isotopes
BT1 odd-even nuclei
BT2 nuclei
BT1 rare earth nuclei
BT2 intermediate mass nuclei
BT3 nuclei
BT1 seconds living radioisotopes
BT2 radioisotopes
BT3 isotopes

HOLMIUM 162 [20; 20]
BT1 beta-plus decay radioisotopes
BT2 beta decay radioisotopes
BT3 radioisotopes
BT4 isotopes
BT1 electron capture radioisotopes
BT2 beta decay radioisotopes
BT3 radioisotopes
BT4 isotopes
BT1 holmium isotopes
BT1 hours living radioisotopes
BT2 radioisotopes
BT3 isotopes
BT1 isomeric transition isotopes
BT2 radioisotopes
BT3 isotopes
BT1 minutes living radioisotopes
BT2 radioisotopes
BT3 isotopes

BT1 odd-odd nuclei
BT2 nuclei
BT1 rare earth nuclei
BT2 intermediate mass nuclei
BT3 nuclei

HOLMIUM 163 [104; 104]
BT1 electron capture radioisotopes
BT2 beta decay radioisotopes
BT3 radioisotopes
BT4 isotopes
BT1 holmium isotopes
BT1 isomeric transition isotopes
BT2 radioisotopes
BT3 isotopes
BT1 odd-even nuclei
BT2 nuclei
BT1 rare earth nuclei
BT2 intermediate mass nuclei
BT3 nuclei
BT1 seconds living radioisotopes
BT2 radioisotopes
BT3 isotopes
BT1 years living radioisotopes
BT2 radioisotopes
BT3 isotopes

HOLMIUM 164 [24; 24]
BT1 beta-minus decay radioisotopes
BT2 beta decay radioisotopes
BT3 radioisotopes
BT4 isotopes
BT1 electron capture radioisotopes
BT2 beta decay radioisotopes
BT3 radioisotopes
BT4 isotopes
BT1 holmium isotopes
BT1 internal conversion radioisoto
BT2 radioisotopes
BT3 isotopes
BT1 isomeric transition isotopes
BT2 radioisotopes
BT3 isotopes
BT1 minutes living radioisotopes
BT2 radioisotopes
BT3 isotopes
BT1 odd-odd nuclei
BT2 nuclei
BT1 rare earth nuclei
BT2 intermediate mass nuclei
BT3 nuclei

HOLMIUM 165 [207; 207]
BT1 holmium isotopes
BT1 odd-even nuclei
BT2 nuclei
BT1 rare earth nuclei
BT2 intermediate mass nuclei
BT3 nuclei
BT1 stable isotopes
BT2 isotopes

HOLMIUM 165 REACTIONS [39; 39]
Sep 83
BT1 heavy ion reactions
BT2 nuclear reactions

HOLMIUM 165 TARGET [552; 552]
BT1 targets

HOLMIUM 166 [123; 123]
BT1 beta-minus decay radioisotopes
BT2 beta decay radioisotopes
BT3 radioisotopes
BT4 isotopes
BT1 days living radioisotopes
BT2 radioisotopes
BT3 isotopes
BT1 holmium isotopes
BT1 odd-odd nuclei
BT2 nuclei
BT1 rare earth nuclei
BT2 intermediate mass nuclei
BT3 nuclei
BT1 years living radioisotopes
BT2 radioisotopes
BT3 isotopes

HOLMIUM 167 [10; 10]
BT1 beta-minus decay radioisotopes
BT2 beta decay radioisotopes
BT3 radioisotopes
BT4 isotopes
BT1 holmium isotopes
BT1 hours living radioisotopes
BT2 radioisotopes
BT3 isotopes
BT1 odd-even nuclei
BT2 nuclei
BT1 rare earth nuclei
BT2 intermediate mass nuclei
BT3 nuclei

HOLMIUM 168 [8; 8]
BT1 beta-minus decay radioisotopes
BT2 beta decay radioisotopes
BT3 radioisotopes
BT4 isotopes
BT1 holmium isotopes
BT1 isomeric transition isotopes
BT2 radioisotopes
BT3 isotopes
BT1 minutes living radioisotopes
BT2 radioisotopes
BT3 isotopes
BT1 odd-odd nuclei
BT2 nuclei
BT1 rare earth nuclei
BT2 intermediate mass nuclei
BT3 nuclei

HOLMIUM 169 [5; 5]
BT1 beta-minus decay radioisotopes
BT2 beta decay radioisotopes
BT3 radioisotopes
BT4 isotopes
BT1 holmium isotopes
BT1 minutes living radioisotopes
BT2 radioisotopes
BT3 isotopes
BT1 odd-even nuclei
BT2 nuclei
BT1 rare earth nuclei
BT2 intermediate mass nuclei
BT3 nuclei

HOLMIUM 170 [6; 6]
BT1 beta-minus decay radioisotopes
BT2 beta decay radioisotopes
BT3 radioisotopes
BT4 isotopes
BT1 holmium isotopes
BT1 minutes living radioisotopes
BT2 radioisotopes
BT3 isotopes
BT1 odd-odd nuclei
BT2 nuclei
BT1 rare earth nuclei
BT2 intermediate mass nuclei
BT3 nuclei
BT1 seconds living radioisotopes
BT2 radioisotopes
BT3 isotopes

HOLMIUM 171 [4; 4] *Mar 88*
BT1 beta-minus decay radioisotopes
BT2 beta decay radioisotopes
BT3 radioisotopes
BT4 isotopes
BT1 holmium isotopes
BT1 odd-even nuclei
BT2 nuclei
BT1 rare earth nuclei
BT2 intermediate mass nuclei
BT3 nuclei
BT1 seconds living radioisotopes
BT2 radioisotopes
BT3 isotopes

HOLMIUM 172 [3; 3] *Dec 90*
BT1 beta-minus decay radioisotopes
BT2 beta decay radioisotopes
BT3 radioisotopes
BT4 isotopes
BT1 holmium isotopes
BT1 odd-odd nuclei
BT2 nuclei
BT1 rare earth nuclei
BT2 intermediate mass nuclei
BT3 nuclei
BT1 seconds living radioisotopes
BT2 radioisotopes
BT3 isotopes

HOLOGRAPHY [925; 925]
RT photography

HOLTSMARK THEORY [9; 9]
RT plasma

HOMALITE [4; 4] *Sep 79*
BT1 polyesters
BT2 esters
BT3 organic compounds
BT2 organic polymers
BT3 organic compounds
BT3 polymers
RT araldite
RT photoelasticity
RT stress analysis

HOMEOSTASIS [235; 235]
RT biological recovery
RT blood
RT blood-brain barrier
RT endocrine glands
RT hormones
RT hypothalamus
RT physiology
RT pituitary gland

HOMOCYSTEINE [25; 25]
BT1 amino acids
BT2 carboxylic acids
BT3 organic acids
BT4 organic compounds
RT cysteine

HOMOCYSTINE [4; 4]
BT1 amino acids
BT2 carboxylic acids
BT3 organic acids
BT4 organic compounds
RT cystine

HOMOGENATES [221; 221]
RT animal cells
RT biological materials
RT in vitro
RT organs
RT tissues

HOMOGENEOUS MIXTURES
[326; 26,843]
BT1 mixtures
BT2 dispersions
NT1 solutions
NT2 aqueous solutions
NT2 hypertonic solutions
NT2 isotonic solutions
NT2 leachates
NT2 solid solutions

HOMOGENEOUS PLASMA
[1,023; 1,023]
BT1 plasma

HOMOGENEOUS REACTORS
[83; 4,063]
BT1 reactors
NT1 fuel dispersion reactors
NT2 fluidized bed reactors
NT2 slurry reactors
NT1 gas fueled reactors
NT2 coaxial flow reactors
NT2 light bulb reactors
NT2 plasma core assembly
NT1 liquid homogeneous reactors
NT2 aqueous homogeneous reactors
NT3 ai-l-77 reactor
NT3 ber-2 reactor
NT3 cesnef reactor

```
NT3    dr-1 reactor
NT3    frf reactor
NT3    jrr-1 reactor
NT3    kewb reactor
NT3    kstr reactor
NT3    ncscr-1 reactor
NT3    prnc-l-77 reactor
NT3    supo reactor
NT3    wrrr reactor
NT1  solid homogeneous reactors
NT2    acpr reactor
NT2    aerojet-general nucleonics r
NT2    anex reactor
NT2    ebor reactor
NT2    nsrr reactor
NT2    pebble bed reactors
NT3      avr reactor
NT3      thtr-300 reactor
NT3      vg-400 reactor
NT3      vgr-50 reactor
NT2    romashka reactor
NT2    shca reactor
NT2    sur-100 series reactor
NT2    treat reactor
NT2    triga type reactors
NT3      afrri reactor
NT3      cornell triga-mk-2 reactor
NT3      dow triga-mk-1 reactor
NT3      fir-1 reactor
NT3      frf-2 reactor
NT3      frn reactor
NT3      gulf triga-mk-3 reactor
NT3      lopra reactor
NT3      nscr reactor
NT3      ostr reactor
NT3      prpr reactor
NT3      pstr reactor
NT3      rtp reactor
NT3      trico reactor
NT3      triga-brazil reactor
NT3      triga-texas reactor
NT3      triga-veterans reactor
NT3      triga-1-arizona reactor
NT3      triga-1-california reactor
NT3      triga-1-hanford reactor
NT3      triga-1-hanover reactor
NT3      triga-1-heidelberg reactor
NT3      triga-1-michigan reactor
NT3      triga-2 reactor
NT3      triga-2-dalat reactor
NT3      triga-2-illinois reactor
NT3      triga-2-kansas reactor
NT3      triga-2-ljubljana reactor
NT3      triga-2-mainz reactor
NT3      triga-2-musashi reactor
NT3      triga-2-pavia reactor
NT3      triga-2-rikkyo reactor
NT3      triga-2-rome reactor
NT3      triga-2-seoul reactor
NT3      triga-2-vienna reactor
NT3      triga-3-la jolla reactor
NT3      triga-3-salazar reactor
NT3      triga-3-seoul reactor
NT3      ucbrr reactor
NT3      wsur reactor
```

HOMOGENIZATION METHODS [196; 196] *Jun 81*
(Methods in which the heterogeneities of the reactor core must be considered in separate calculations in which the equivalent homogenized parameters are produced for use in subsequent calculations of the overall flux distribution in the reactor.)
```
RT     heterogeneous effects
RT     neutron diffusion equation
RT     neutron flux
RT     neutron transport theory
RT     reactor lattice parameters
```

homopolar generators
USE   rotating generators

homozygotes
USE   hybridization

HONDURAS [4; 4]
```
BT1    central america
BT2    latin america
BT1    developing countries
```

HONEY [28; 28]
```
BT1    food
```

HONEYWELL COMPUTERS [24; 24]
```
BT1    computers
```

HONG KONG [23; 23]
```
BT1    asia
```

HONING [10; 10]
```
BT1    machining
RT     grinding
```

HOOKE LAW [50; 50]
```
RT     elasticity
RT     poisson ratio
RT     young modulus
```

HOOKWORM [11; 11]
```
BT1    nematodes
BT2      invertebrates
BT3        animals
RT     parasites
RT     parasitic diseases
```

HOPE CREEK-1 REACTOR [33; 33]
(Salem, New Jersey, USA. Prior to November 1973 known as NEWBOLD ISLAND- 1 REACTOR for the initially planned site, and older material is so indexed.)
```
BT1    bwr type reactors
BT2      enriched uranium reactors
BT3        reactors
BT2      power reactors
BT3        reactors
BT2      thermal reactors
BT3        reactors
BT2      water cooled reactors
BT3        reactors
BT2      water moderated reactors
BT3        reactors
NT1    newbold island-1 reactor
```

HOPE CREEK-2 REACTOR [29; 29]
(Salem, New Jersey, USA. Prior to November 1973 known as NEWBOLD ISLAND- 2 REACTOR for the initially planned site, and older material is so indexed.)
```
BT1    bwr type reactors
BT2      enriched uranium reactors
BT3        reactors
BT2      power reactors
BT3        reactors
BT2      thermal reactors
BT3        reactors
BT2      water cooled reactors
BT3        reactors
BT2      water moderated reactors
BT3        reactors
NT1    newbold island-2 reactor
```

HOR REACTOR [18; 18]
(Interuniversitair Reactor Instituut/ Technische Hogeschool Delft, Delft, Netherlands)
```
UF     delft hoger onderwijs reactor
UF     hoger onderwijs reactor
BT1    enriched uranium reactors
BT2      reactors
BT1    pool type reactors
BT2      water cooled reactors
BT3        reactors
BT2      water moderated reactors
BT3        reactors
BT1    research reactors
BT2      research and test reactors
BT3        reactors
BT1    thermal reactors
BT2      reactors
BT1    training reactors
BT2      research and test reactors
BT3        reactors
```

HORACE REACTOR [1; 1]
```
BT1    enriched uranium reactors
BT2      reactors
BT1    pool type reactors
BT2      water cooled reactors
BT3        reactors
BT2      water moderated reactors
BT3        reactors
BT1    research reactors
BT2      research and test reactors
BT3        reactors
BT1    zero power reactors
BT2      experimental reactors
BT3        research and test reactors
BT4          reactors
```

hordeum
USE   barley

HORMONES [955; 11,149]
```
NT1    adrenal hormones
NT2      adrenaline
NT2      corticosteroids
NT3        glucocorticoids
NT4          corticosterone
NT4          cortisone
NT4          dexamethasone
NT4          hydrocortisone
NT4          prednisolone
NT4          prednisone
NT3        mineralocorticoids
NT4          aldosterone
NT4          doca
NT2      noradrenaline
NT1    peptide hormones
NT2      calcitonin
NT2      gastrin
NT2      glucagon
NT2      insulin
NT2      lactogens
NT3        hpl
NT2      parathormone
NT2      pituitary hormones
NT3        acth
NT3        gonadotropins
NT4          fsh
NT4          hcg
NT4          lh
NT4          lth
NT3        liberins
NT4          lh-rh
NT3        oxytocin
NT3        sth
NT3        tsh
NT3        vasopressin
NT2      thyroid hormones
NT3        diiodothyronine
NT3        thyrocalcitonin
NT3        thyroxine
NT3        triiodothyronine
NT2      thyronine
NT2      trh
NT1    secretin
NT1    steroid hormones
NT2      androgens
NT3        androstenedione
NT3        androsterone
NT3        dianabol
NT3        hydroxyandrostenone
NT3        testosterone
NT2      corticosteroids
NT3        glucocorticoids
NT4          corticosterone
NT4          cortisone
NT4          dexamethasone
NT4          hydrocortisone
NT4          prednisolone
NT4          prednisone
NT3        mineralocorticoids
NT4          aldosterone
NT4          doca
NT2      estrogens
NT3        estradiol
NT3        estriol
NT3        estrone
```

NT2 progesterone
RT biochemistry
RT endocrine diseases
RT endocrine glands
RT erythropoietin
RT homeostasis
RT intrinsic factor
RT physiology
RT prostaglandins
RT somatostatin
RT steroids
RT stimulation

HORNBLENDE [98; 98]
BT1 amphibole
BT2 silicate minerals
BT3 minerals
RT granites
RT peridotites

HORSES [165; 165]
BT1 mammals
BT2 vertebrates
BT3 animals

HOSE INSTABILITY [93; 93]
UF *firehose instability*
UF *gardenhose instability*
BT1 plasma microinstabilities
BT2 plasma instability
BT3 instability

HOSPITALS [834; 834]
BT1 buildings
BT1 medical establishments
RT medicine

HOST [122; 122]
RT graft-host reaction
RT transplants

HOST-CELL REACTIVATION [257; 257]
BT1 biological repair
BT2 biological recovery
RT bacteria
RT bacteriophages
RT chemical radiation effects
RT dna
RT radiation injuries

HOT ATOM CHEMISTRY [1,612; 1,718]
(Chemical reactions of atoms or ions of high kinetic energies (more than 1 ev) resulting from nuclear transformations.)
UF *chem. eff. of nucl. transform.*
UF *hot-atom chemistry*
UF *recoil chemistry*
BT1 radiochemistry
BT2 chemistry
NT1 szilard-chalmers reaction
RT nuclear reactions
RT recoils
RT scavenging
RT valence

HOT CELLS [1,400; 1,400]
(Shielded chambers for remote handling of radioactive materials.)
BT1 laboratory equipment
BT2 equipment
RT gloveboxes
RT hot labs
RT manipulators
RT periscopes
RT radiation protection
RT remote handling
RT remote handling equipment
RT remote viewing equipment
RT shielding

HOT CHANNEL [82; 82]
RT fuel channels
RT hot channel factor
RT reactor cooling systems

HOT CHANNEL FACTOR [71; 71]
RT hot channel
RT reactor safety

HOT DIPPING [9; 9]
BT1 dip coating
BT2 surface coating
BT3 deposition

hot enr. carbon mod. th. osc.
USE hector reactor

hot experi. reactor zero energ
USE hero reactor

hot experimental facility
(Prior to December 1990, this was a valid descriptor.)
USE hef

HOT LABS [651; 651]
UF *radiochemical laboratories*
BT1 laboratories
BT1 nuclear facilities
RT hot cells
RT laboratory equipment
RT manipulators
RT periscopes
RT radiation hazards
RT radiation protection
RT radioactivity
RT remote handling

HOT PLASMA [3,037; 3,037]
BT1 plasma

HOT PRESSING [1,137; 1,137]
BT1 pressing
BT2 materials working
BT3 fabrication
RT hot working

HOT SPOT FACTOR [49; 49]
RT hot spots
RT reactor safety

HOT SPOTS [353; 353]
RT burnout
RT dryout
RT fuel cans
RT heat transfer
RT hot spot factor
RT reactor cooling systems
RT rewetting

hot spots (biological)
USE biological hot spots

hot springs
USE thermal springs

HOT WIRE ANEMOMETERS [67; 67]
UF *hot-wire anemometers*
BT1 anemometers
BT2 measuring instruments

hot wire gages
USE hot-wire gages

HOT WORKING [488; 488]
BT1 materials working
BT2 fabrication
RT extrusion
RT forging
RT hot pressing
RT rolling

hot-atom chemistry
USE hot atom chemistry

hot-wire anemometers
USE hot wire anemometers

HOT-WIRE GAGES [16; 33]
UF *hot wire gages*
BT1 pressure gages
BT2 measuring instruments
NT1 pirani gages

hough-powell devices
USE flying spot digitizers

§ **HOURLY VARIATIONS** [87; 87] *Jul 81*
(Variations from hour to hour.)
BT1 variations

* **HOURS LIVING RADIOISOTOPES** [99; 44,413]
(For specific terms, consult the Appendix.)
BT1 radioisotopes
BT2 isotopes
RT half-life

HOUSES [632; 632] *Jul 85*
UF *residential buildings (houses)*
BT1 buildings

ho2
USE hydroperoxy radicals

HP COMPUTERS [188; 188]
UF *hewlett-packard computers*
BT1 computers

hpci
USE high pressure coolant injectio

hpd devices
USE flying spot digitizers

HPL [62; 62]
UF *human placental lactogen*
BT1 lactogens
BT2 peptide hormones
BT3 hormones
RT placenta
RT pregnancy
RT sth

HPRR REACTOR [76; 76]
(Oak Ridge National Lab., Oak Ridge, Tennessee, USA)
UF *health physics research r.*
BT1 air cooled reactors
BT2 gas cooled reactors
BT3 reactors
BT1 enriched uranium reactors
BT2 reactors
BT1 fast reactors
BT2 epithermal reactors
BT3 reactors
BT1 pulsed reactors
BT2 reactors
BT1 research reactors
BT2 research and test reactors
BT3 reactors

hsa
(Human serum albumin.)
USE albumins
AND blood serum

HSK PROCEDURE [11; 11]
- UF hylleraas-scherr-knight proc.
- BT1 perturbation theory
- BT1 variational methods
- RT electronic structure
- RT quantum mechanics

HT-6B TOKAMAK [6; 6] *Dec 89*
(Academia Sinica, Hefei, Anhui, China.)
- BT1 tokamak devices
- BT2 closed plasma devices
-   BT3 thermonuclear devices

HT-6M TOKAMAK [5; 5] *Dec 89*
(Academia Sinica, Hefei, Anhui, China.)
- BT1 tokamak devices
- BT2 closed plasma devices
-   BT3 thermonuclear devices

htgr peach bottom reactor
- USE peach bottom-1 reactor

HTGR TYPE REACTORS [7,843; 9,721]
- UF *high temper. gas cool./grap. m*
- BT1 gas cooled reactors
- BT2 reactors
- BT1 graphite moderated reactors
- BT2 reactors
- NT1 avr reactor
- NT1 dragon reactor
- NT1 fulton-1 reactor
- NT1 fulton-2 reactor
- NT1 ga standard reactor
- NT1 httr reactor
- NT1 kahter reactor
- NT1 peach bottom-1 reactor
- NT1 schmehausen reactor
- NT1 summit-1 reactor
- NT1 summit-2 reactor
- NT1 thtr-300 reactor
- NT1 vg-400 reactor
- NT1 vgr-50 reactor
- NT1 vhtr reactor
- NT1 vidal-1 reactor
- NT1 vidal-2 reactor
- NT1 vrain reactor
- RT   power reactors

HTLTR REACTOR [21; 21]
(Pacific Northwest Laboratory, Battelle Memorial Institute, Richland, Washington, USA)
- UF *high tem. lattice test reactor*
- BT1 enriched uranium reactors
- BT2 reactors
- BT1 graphite moderated reactors
- BT2 reactors
- BT1 nitrogen cooled reactors
- BT2 gas cooled reactors
-   BT3 reactors
- BT1 research reactors
- BT2 research and test reactors
-   BT3 reactors
- BT1 test reactors
- BT2 research and test reactors
-   BT3 reactors
- BT2 test facilities

htlv iii virus
- USE aids virus

hto
- USE heavy water
- AND tritium compounds

HTR REACTOR [88; 88]
(Tokyo Atomic Industrial Research Lab., Ltd, Kanagawa Prefecture, Japan)
- UF *hitachi training reactor*
- UF *japan htr*
- UF *kawasaki-hitachi training reac*
- BT1 enriched uranium reactors
- BT2 reactors
- BT1 isotope production reactors
- BT2 irradiation reactors
-   BT3 reactors
- BT1 pool type reactors
- BT2 water cooled reactors
-   BT3 reactors
- BT2 water moderated reactors
-   BT3 reactors
- BT1 research reactors
- BT2 research and test reactors
-   BT3 reactors
- BT1 thermal reactors
- BT2 reactors
- BT1 training reactors
- BT2 research and test reactors
-   BT3 reactors

HTTR REACTOR [125; 125] *Oct 88*
(Oarai Research Establishment of JAERI, Ibaraki Prefecture, Japan.)
- UF *high temperature test reactor*
- BT1 enriched uranium reactors
- BT2 reactors
- BT1 experimental reactors
- BT2 research and test reactors
-   BT3 reactors
- BT1 helium cooled reactors
- BT2 gas cooled reactors
-   BT3 reactors
- BT1 htgr type reactors
- BT2 gas cooled reactors
-   BT3 reactors
- BT2 graphite moderated reactors
-   BT3 reactors

HUBBLE EFFECT [823; 823]
- UF *hubble-humason shift*
- RT cosmology
- RT expansion
- RT red shift
- RT universe

hubble-humason shift
- USE hubble effect

HUDSON RIVER [85; 85]
- BT1 rivers
- BT2 surface waters

hugenholtz-pines theory
- USE van hove-hugenholtz theory

HULTHEN POTENTIAL [73; 73] *Jul 76*
- BT1 nuclear potential
- BT2 potentials

human cells
- USE animal cells

human chorionic gonadotropin
- USE hcg

→ **HUMAN CHROMOSOMES** [0; 0] *Sep 91*
(Prior to October 1991, this was indexed with CHROMOSOMES.)
- BT1 chromosomes
- NT1 philadelphia chromosome
- RT banding techniques
- RT cell nuclei
- RT chromatids
- RT chromatin
- RT chromosomal aberrations
- RT chromosome sorting
- RT crossing-over
- RT dna
- RT dna repair
- RT gene regulation
- RT genes
- RT genetic effects
- RT genetic mapping
- RT karyotype
- RT mitosis
- RT nucleoli
- RT rflps

HUMAN FACTORS [2,394; 2,394] *Feb 82*
(Aspects of human behavior which influence events or situations, e.g. actions of operators at nuclear power plants.)
- RT accidents
- RT aesthetics
- RT attitudes
- RT behavior
- RT drug abuse
- RT failures
- RT man-machine systems
- RT personnel
- RT safety
- RT safety engineering
- RT sociology

HUMAN INTRUSION [60; 60] *Jul 85*
(Unauthorized entering of people into restricted areas, facilities, etc. See also BIOINTRUSION.)
- UF *infiltration (by people)*
- UF *intrusion (human)*
- RT entry control systems
- RT interest groups
- RT nuclear facilities
- RT physical protection
- RT sabotage
- RT security

human placental lactogen
- USE hpl

HUMAN POPULATIONS [6,823; 7,076]
- UF+ *demography*
- BT1 populations
- NT1 eskimos
- NT1 lapps
- NT1 rural populations
- NT1 urban populations
- RT civil defense
- RT cuex
- RT epidemiology
- RT icrp critical group
- RT interest groups
- RT man
- RT patients
- RT personnel
- RT population relocation
- RT public health
- RT regional analysis
- RT sociology

human serum albumin
- USE albumins
- AND blood serum

HUMBOLDT BAY [3; 3]
- BT1 pacific ocean
- BT2 seas
-   BT3 surface waters

HUMBOLDT BAY REACTOR [75; 75]
(Eureka, California, USA)
- BT1 bwr type reactors
- BT2 enriched uranium reactors
-   BT3 reactors
- BT2 power reactors
-   BT3 reactors
- BT2 thermal reactors
-   BT3 reactors
- BT2 water cooled reactors
-   BT3 reactors
- BT2 water moderated reactors
-   BT3 reactors

HUMECA URANIUM MILL [2; 2] *Oct 76*
- BT1 industrial plants
- BT1 nuclear facilities
- RT ore processing
- RT uranium ores

HUMIC ACIDS [330; 330]
BT1 organic acids
BT2 organic compounds
RT fulvic acids
RT humus
RT soils

HUMIDISTATS [5; 5]
BT1 control equipment
BT2 equipment
RT humidity control

HUMIDITY [2,822; 2,822]
UF *moisture*
UF *water content*
RT dew point
RT hygrometry
RT moisture gages
RT water vapor

HUMIDITY CONTROL [105; 105]
BT1 control
RT air conditioning
RT humidistats

HUMUS [170; 170]
(Material resulting from partial decomposition of plant or animal matter and forming the organic portion of soil.)
RT forest litter
RT fulvic acids
RT humic acids
RT soils

HUNGARIAN ORGANIZATIONS
[17; 33] *Apr 86*
BT1 national organizations
NT1 atomki

hungarian paks-1 reactor
USE paks-1 reactor

hungarian paks-2 reactor
USE paks-2 reactor

hungarian paks-3 reactor
USE paks-3 reactor

hungarian paks-4 reactor
USE paks-4 reactor

hungarian wwr-c reactor
USE wwr-s-budapest reactor

HUNGARY [577; 577]
BT1 developing countries
BT1 europe
RT centrally planned economies

HUNTERSTON-A REACTOR [28; 28]
(Hunterston, Ayrshire, UK)
BT1 carbon dioxide cooled reactors
BT2 gas cooled reactors
BT3 reactors
BT1 magnox type reactors
BT2 gcr type reactors
BT3 gas cooled reactors
BT4 reactors
BT3 graphite moderated reactors
BT4 reactors
BT2 natural uranium reactors
BT3 reactors
BT2 power reactors
BT3 reactors
BT1 thermal reactors
BT2 reactors

HUNTERSTON-B REACTOR [95; 95]
(Hunterston, Ayrshire, UK)
BT1 agr type reactors
BT2 enriched uranium reactors
BT3 reactors
BT2 gas cooled reactors
BT3 reactors
BT2 graphite moderated reactors
BT3 reactors
BT1 carbon dioxide cooled reactors
BT2 gas cooled reactors
BT3 reactors
BT1 power reactors
BT2 reactors
BT1 thermal reactors
BT2 reactors

HURRICANES [49; 49]
RT turbulence
RT weather
RT wind

HURWITZ EFFECT [10; 10]
UF *bethe-hurwitz effect*
RT nuclear models

HUTCH EVENT [1; 1]
BT1 nuclear explosions
BT2 explosions
BT1 underground explosions
BT2 explosions
RT radioisotopes

hutchinson island-1 reactor
USE lucie-1 reactor

hutchinson island-2 reactor
USE lucie-2 reactor

HUTTONITE [7; 7]
BT1 silicate minerals
BT2 minerals
BT1 thorium minerals
BT2 radioactive minerals
BT3 minerals
BT3 radioactive materials
BT4 materials
RT thorium silicates

HUYGENS PRINCIPLE [45; 45]
RT wave propagation

HWCTR REACTOR [7; 7]
UF *heavy water components test re*
BT1 enriched uranium reactors
BT2 reactors
BT1 heavy water cooled reactors
BT2 reactors
BT1 heavy water moderated reactors
BT2 reactors
BT1 materials testing reactors
BT2 irradiation reactors
BT3 reactors
BT1 tank type reactors
BT2 reactors
BT1 thermal reactors
BT2 reactors

hwgcr of czechoslovakia
USE bohunice a-1 reactor

HWGCR TYPE REACTORS [24; 477]
UF *heavy water mod./gas cool. rea*
BT1 gas cooled reactors
BT2 reactors
BT1 heavy water moderated reactors
BT2 reactors
NT1 bohunice a-1 reactor
NT1 bohunice a-2 reactor
NT1 el-4 reactor
NT1 lucens reactor
NT1 niederaichbach reactor
RT power reactors

HWLWR TYPE REACTORS [107; 654]
UF *heavy water mod./water cool. r*
BT1 heavy water moderated reactors
BT2 reactors
BT1 water cooled reactors
BT2 reactors
NT1 cirene reactor
NT1 gentilly reactor
NT1 jatr reactor
RT power reactors

HYALURONIC ACID [44; 44]
BT1 mucopolysaccharides
BT2 amines
BT3 organic compounds
BT2 polysaccharides
BT3 saccharides
BT4 carbohydrates
BT5 organic compounds
RT glucuronic acid
RT hyaluronidase

HYALURONIDASE [20; 20]
BT1 carbon-oxygen lyases
BT2 lyases
BT3 enzymes
BT4 organic compounds
RT hyaluronic acid

HYBRID COMPUTERS [115; 115]
BT1 computers

HYBRID REACTORS [1,174; 1,174]
(Devices in which controlled self-sustaining fission-fusion processes take place.)
RT lotus facility
RT reactors
RT thermonuclear reactors

HYBRID RESONANCE [1,139; 1,139]
BT1 resonance

HYBRIDIZATION [2,121; 2,121]
UF *heterozygotes*
UF *homozygotes*
UF *hybrids*
UF *mixing (genetic)*
RT electronic structure
RT genetics
RT wave functions

HYBRIDOMAS [95; 95] *May 86*
(Hybrid cells resulting from the fusion of myeloma cells with lymphocytes; often used in the production of monoclonal antibodies.)
BT1 animal cells
RT cell cultures
RT lymphocytes
RT monoclonal antibodies

hybrids
USE hybridization

→ **HYBTOK TOKAMAKS** [2; 2] *Aug 91*
BT1 tokamak devices
BT2 closed plasma devices
BT3 thermonuclear devices

HYDATIDOSIS [36; 36]
BT1 parasitic diseases
BT2 infectious diseases
BT3 diseases
RT cestodes
RT parasites

HYDRA [11; 11]
BT1 cnidaria
BT2 coelenterata
BT3 invertebrates
BT4 animals

hydratation
  USE   hydration

hydrated electrons
  USE   hydration
  AND   solvated electrons

HYDRATES [4,119; 4,186]
(For chemical compounds or minerals.)
  NT1   unh

HYDRATION [1,447; 1,447]
(Addition of water; for addition of hydrogen use HYDROGENATION.)
  UF   *hydratation*
  UF+   *hydrated electrons*
  BT1   solvation

HYDRAULIC CONDUCTIVITY [765; 765] *Jun 83*
(Rate of water flow through porous rock, soil, etc.)
  UF   *meinzer unit*
  UF   *permeability coef (fluid mech)*
  RT   fluid mechanics
  RT   ground water
  RT   hydrology
  RT   liquid flow
  RT   underground disposal

HYDRAULIC CONTROL DEVICES [202; 202]
  BT1   control equipment
  BT2   equipment
  BT1   hydraulic equipment
  BT2   equipment
  RT   hydraulics
  RT   remote control

HYDRAULIC EQUIPMENT [54; 108]
Jul 86
  BT1   equipment
  NT1   hydraulic control devices
  RT   hydraulics

HYDRAULIC FRACTURING [156; 156]
Dec 75
(Fracturing of deep rock strata by hydraulic pressure, frequently for the deposition of radioactive wastes.)
  BT1   fracturing
  RT   fluid injection
  RT   fractures
  RT   waste disposal

HYDRAULIC TRANSPORT [73; 73]
Feb 84
  BT1   transport
  RT   hydraulics
  RT   materials handling
  RT   pipelines
  RT   slurries

HYDRAULICS [8,836; 8,836]
  RT   flow rate
  RT   fluid flow
  RT   fluid mechanics
  RT   friction factor
  RT   hydraulic control devices
  RT   hydraulic equipment
  RT   hydraulic transport
  RT   hydrodynamics
  RT   pneumatics
  RT   surges
  RT   water hammer

HYDRAZIDES [154; 179]
  BT1   organic nitrogen compounds
  BT2   organic compounds
  NT1   isoniazid
    NT2   iproniazid
  RT   hydrazine
  RT   organic acids

HYDRAZINE [640; 640]
  RT   dpph
  RT   hydrazides
  RT   hydrazones
  RT   sdpph

HYDRAZOIC ACID [10; 10] *Jun 88*
  UF   *azomide*
  BT1   inorganic acids
  BT2   hydrogen compounds
  BT2   inorganic compounds
  RT   azides

HYDRAZONES [131; 131]
  BT1   organic nitrogen compounds
  BT2   organic compounds
  RT   aldehydes
  RT   hydrazine
  RT   ketones

HYDRIDATION [762; 762]
  BT1   chemical reactions
  RT   hydrides
  RT   hydrogen

HYDRIDE MODERATED REACTORS [32; 1,467]
  BT1   reactors
  NT1   acpr reactor
  NT1   anex reactor
  NT1   nsrr reactor
  NT1   stir reactor
  NT1   szr type reactors
    NT2   knk reactor
    NT2   knk-2 reactor
  NT1   topaz reactor
  NT1   triga type reactors
    NT2   afrri reactor
    NT2   cornell triga-mk-2 reactor
    NT2   dow triga-mk-1 reactor
    NT2   fir-1 reactor
    NT2   frf-2 reactor
    NT2   frn reactor
    NT2   gulf triga-mk-3 reactor
    NT2   lopra reactor
    NT2   nscr reactor
    NT2   ostr reactor
    NT2   prpr reactor
    NT2   pstr reactor
    NT2   rtp reactor
    NT2   trico reactor
    NT2   triga-brazil reactor
    NT2   triga-texas reactor
    NT2   triga-veterans reactor
    NT2   triga-1-arizona reactor
    NT2   triga-1-california reactor
    NT2   triga-1-hanford reactor
    NT2   triga-1-hanover reactor
    NT2   triga-1-heidelberg reactor
    NT2   triga-1-michigan reactor
    NT2   triga-2 reactor
    NT2   triga-2-dalat reactor
    NT2   triga-2-illinois reactor
    NT2   triga-2-kansas reactor
    NT2   triga-2-ljubljana reactor
    NT2   triga-2-mainz reactor
    NT2   triga-2-musashi reactor
    NT2   triga-2-pavia reactor
    NT2   triga-2-rikkyo reactor
    NT2   triga-2-rome reactor
    NT2   triga-2-seoul reactor
    NT2   triga-2-vienna reactor
    NT2   triga-3-la jolla reactor
    NT2   triga-3-salazar reactor
    NT2   triga-3-seoul reactor
    NT2   ucbrr reactor
    NT2   wsur reactor
  RT   hydride moderators

HYDRIDE MODERATORS [44; 44]
  BT1   moderators
  RT   hydride moderated reactors
  RT   hydrides
  RT   szr type reactors
  RT   topaz reactor
  RT   zirconium hydrides

HYDRIDES [1,285; 8,801]
  BT1   hydrogen compounds
  NT1   actinium hydrides
  NT1   aluminium hydrides
  NT1   americium hydrides
  NT1   antimony hydrides
  NT1   argon hydrides
  NT1   arsenic hydrides
  NT1   barium hydrides
  NT1   berkelium hydrides
  NT1   beryllium hydrides
  NT1   bismuth hydrides
  NT1   boranes
  NT1   calcium hydrides
  NT1   cerium hydrides
  NT1   cesium hydrides
  NT1   chromium hydrides
  NT1   cobalt hydrides
  NT1   copper hydrides
  NT1   curium hydrides
  NT1   dysprosium hydrides
  NT1   erbium hydrides
  NT1   europium hydrides
  NT1   gadolinium hydrides
  NT1   germanium hydrides
  NT1   gold hydrides
  NT1   hafnium hydrides
  NT1   helium hydrides
  NT1   holmium hydrides
  NT1   indium hydrides
  NT1   iridium hydrides
  NT1   iron hydrides
  NT1   krypton hydrides
  NT1   lanthanum hydrides
  NT1   lithium hydrides
    NT2   lithium deuterides
    NT2   lithium tritides
  NT1   lutetium hydrides
  NT1   magnesium hydrides
  NT1   manganese hydrides
  NT1   mercury hydrides
  NT1   molybdenum hydrides
  NT1   neodymium hydrides
  NT1   neon hydrides
  NT1   neptunium hydrides
  NT1   nickel hydrides
  NT1   niobium hydrides
  NT1   nitrogen hydrides
    NT2   ammonia
  NT1   palladium hydrides
  NT1   phosphorus hydrides
  NT1   platinum hydrides
  NT1   plutonium hydrides
  NT1   potassium hydrides
  NT1   praseodymium hydrides
  NT1   protactinium hydrides
  NT1   rhenium hydrides
  NT1   rhodium hydrides
  NT1   rubidium hydrides
  NT1   ruthenium hydrides
  NT1   samarium hydrides
  NT1   scandium hydrides
  NT1   selenium hydrides
  NT1   silanes
  NT1   silver hydrides
  NT1   sodium hydrides
  NT1   strontium hydrides
  NT1   tantalum hydrides
  NT1   technetium hydrides
  NT1   tellurium hydrides
  NT1   terbium hydrides
  NT1   thallium hydrides
  NT1   thorium hydrides
  NT1   thulium hydrides
  NT1   tin hydrides
  NT1   titanium hydrides
  NT1   tungsten hydrides
  NT1   uranium hydrides
  NT1   vanadium hydrides
  NT1   xenon hydrides
  NT1   ytterbium hydrides
  NT1   yttrium hydrides
  NT1   zinc hydrides
  NT1   zirconium hydrides
  RT   hydridation
  RT   hydride moderators
  RT   hydrogen additions

HYDRIODIC ACID [227; 227]
- BT1 inorganic acids
- BT2 hydrogen compounds
- BT2 inorganic compounds
- BT1 iodine compounds
- BT2 halogen compounds
- RT iodides

HYDRO-LYASES [6; 23] *Dec 86*
- BT1 carbon-oxygen lyases
- BT2 lyases
- BT3 enzymes
- BT4 organic compounds
- NT1 carbonic anhydrase

HYDROBROMIC ACID [364; 364]
- UF *hydrogen bromides*
- BT1 bromine compounds
- BT2 halogen compounds
- BT1 inorganic acids
- BT2 hydrogen compounds
- BT2 inorganic compounds
- RT bromides

HYDROCARBONS [2,606; 21,614]
- UF *coal liquids*
- BT1 organic compounds
- NT1 acenaphthene
- NT1 alkanes
- NT2 butane
- NT2 cycloalkanes
- NT3 cyclohexane
- NT3 decalin
- NT2 decane
- NT2 dodecane
- NT2 ethane
- NT2 heptane
- NT2 hexadecane
- NT2 hexane
- NT2 methane
- NT2 octane
- NT2 paraffin
- NT2 pentane
- NT2 propane
- NT2 squalane
- NT2 2-methylbutane
- NT2 2-methylpropane
- NT2 2-2-dimethylpropane
- NT1 alkenes
- NT2 butenes
- NT2 cycloalkenes
- NT3 camphene
- NT3 cyclopentadiene
- NT2 ethylene
- NT2 heptenes
- NT2 hexenes
- NT2 pentenes
- NT2 propylene
- NT2 2-methylpropene
- NT1 alkynes
- NT2 acetylene
- NT2 propyne
- NT1 anthracene
- NT1 azulene
- NT1 benzanthracene
- NT1 benzene
- NT1 benzopyrene
- NT1 biphenyl
- NT1 carotenoids
- NT1 chrysene
- NT1 cumene
- NT1 cymene
- NT1 divinylbenzene
- NT1 durene
- NT1 fluorene
- NT1 indene
- NT1 mesitylene
- NT1 naphthalene
- NT1 oligophenylenes
- NT1 phenanthrene
- NT1 polyenes
- NT2 dienes
- NT3 allene
- NT3 butadiene
- NT3 cyclopentadiene
- NT3 ferrocene
- NT3 isoprene
- NT2 squalene
- NT1 polyphenyls
- NT2 santowax
- NT2 terphenyls
- NT3 terphenyl-meta
- NT3 terphenyl-ortho
- NT3 terphenyl-para
- NT1 pyrene
- NT1 quaterphenyls
- NT1 stilbene
- NT1 styrene
- NT1 tetracene
- NT1 tetralin
- NT1 tolan
- NT1 toluene
- NT1 triphenylene
- NT1 violanthrone
- NT1 xylenes
- NT2 xylene-para
- RT amsco
- RT aromatics
- RT bromoform
- RT fischer-tropsch synthesis
- RT fish oil
- RT fluoroform
- RT freons
- RT iodoform
- RT oils
- RT petroleum
- RT turpentine

hydrocephalus
- USE malformations

HYDROCHLORIC ACID [3,552; 3,552]
- UF *hydrogen chlorides*
- BT1 chlorine compounds
- BT2 halogen compounds
- BT1 inorganic acids
- BT2 hydrogen compounds
- BT2 inorganic compounds
- RT aqua regia
- RT chlorides

HYDROCORTISONE [415; 415]
- UF *cortisol*
- BT1 glucocorticoids
- BT2 corticosteroids
- BT3 adrenal hormones
- BT4 hormones
- BT3 hydroxy compounds
- BT4 organic compounds
- BT3 ketones
- BT4 organic compounds
- BT3 pregnanes
- BT4 steroids
- BT5 organic compounds
- BT3 steroid hormones
- BT4 hormones

HYDROCYANIC ACID [335; 335]
- BT1 inorganic acids
- BT2 hydrogen compounds
- BT2 inorganic compounds
- RT cyanides

HYDRODYNAMIC MASS EFFECT
[84; 84] *Mar 76*
(A virtual increase of the mass of solids when vibrating in fluids.)
- UF *added mass effect*
- UF *virtual mass effect*
- RT damping
- RT eigenfrequency
- RT hydrodynamics
- RT mechanical vibrations

HYDRODYNAMIC MODEL
[1,174; 1,174]
- BT1 thermodynamic model
- BT2 particle models
- BT3 mathematical models
- BT2 statistical models
- BT3 mathematical models
- RT nuclear models
- RT particle production

HYDRODYNAMICS [6,040; 13,727]
- BT1 fluid mechanics
- BT2 mechanics
- NT1 electrohydrodynamics
- NT1 magnetohydrodynamics
- RT counterflow systems
- RT crossflow systems
- RT fluid flow
- RT flute instability
- RT hydraulics
- RT hydrodynamic mass effect
- RT liquid flow
- RT rayleigh-taylor instability
- RT working fluids

HYDROELECTRIC POWER [294; 294]
- UF *hydroelectricity*
- BT1 electric power
- BT2 power
- BT1 renewable energy sources
- BT2 energy sources
- RT hydroelectric power plants

HYDROELECTRIC POWER PLANTS
[261; 261]
- BT1 power plants
- RT dams
- RT fish passage facilities
- RT hydroelectric power
- RT pumped storage
- RT turbines

hydroelectricity
- USE hydroelectric power

HYDROFLUORIC ACID [1,416; 1,416]
- UF *hydrogen fluorides*
- BT1 fluorine compounds
- BT2 halogen compounds
- BT1 inorganic acids
- BT2 hydrogen compounds
- BT2 inorganic compounds
- RT fluorides

HYDROGEN [31,817; 31,817]
- UF+ *hydrogen production*
- BT1 nonmetals
- BT2 elements
- RT balmer lines
- RT cryogenic fluids
- RT hydridation
- RT h1 regions
- RT lyman lines

HYDROGEN ADDITIONS [1,020; 1,020]
- RT hydrides

hydrogen bromides
- USE hydrobromic acid

HYDROGEN BURNING [260; 260]
Nov 78
(Astrophysical processes only.)
- UF *pp chain*
- UF *proton-proton cycle*
- BT1 star burning
- RT main sequence stars
- RT nucleosynthesis
- RT star evolution
- RT star models

hydrogen chlorides
- USE hydrochloric acid

HYDROGEN COMPLEXES [39; 39]
- BT1 complexes

HYDROGEN COMPOUNDS
[904; 79,779]
- NT1 borohydrides
- NT1 deuterium compounds
- NT2 deuterides
- NT3 hydrogen deuteride

HYDROGEN COMPOUNDS

    NT3   lithium deuterides
    NT2   deuterium tritide
* NT1   hydrides
    NT1   hydrogen peroxide
    NT1   hydrogen sulfides
* NT1   hydroxides
* NT1   inorganic acids
    NT1   tritium compounds
    NT2   tritides
    NT3   deuterium tritide
    NT3   helium tritides
    NT3   hydrogen tritide
    NT3   lithium tritides
    NT2   tritium oxides
* NT1   water

HYDROGEN COOLED REACTORS
[5; 61]
  UF   *hydrogen-cooled reactors*
  BT1   gas cooled reactors
    BT2 reactors
  NT1   kiwi reactors
  NT1   nrx-a2 reactor
  NT1   nrx-a3 reactor
  NT1   nrx-a4-est reactor
  NT1   nrx-a5 reactor
  NT1   nrx-a6 reactor
  NT1   rover reactors

HYDROGEN DEUTERIDE [546; 546]
  UF   *deuterium hydride*
  BT1   deuterides
    BT2 deuterium compounds
      BT3 hydrogen compounds
  RT   deuterium
  RT   hydrogen 1

hydrogen donor reactions
  USE   hydrogen transfer

hydrogen fluorides
  USE   hydrofluoric acid

hydrogen fuel cells
  USE   fuel cells

hydrogen generation
(Prior to December 1990, this was a valid descriptor.)
  USE   interstitial hydrogen generati

hydrogen hydroxides
  USE   water

HYDROGEN IONS [2,562; 35,697]
  BT1   ions
    BT2 charged particles
  NT1   hydrogen ions 1 minus
  NT1   hydrogen ions 1 plus
    NT2 protons
      NT3 antiprotons
      NT3 cosmic protons
      NT3 delayed protons
      NT3 diprotons
      NT3 photoprotons
      NT3 prompt protons
      NT3 solar protons
      NT3 trapped protons
  NT1   hydrogen ions 2 plus
  NT1   hydrogen ions 3 plus

HYDROGEN IONS 1 MINUS
[1,470; 1,470]
  BT1   anions
    BT2 ions
      BT3 charged particles
  BT1   hydrogen ions
    BT2 ions
      BT3 charged particles

HYDROGEN IONS 1 PLUS
[2,775; 31,483]
  UF+   *proton-atom collisions*
  UF+   *proton-molecule collisions*
  BT1   cations
    BT2 ions
      BT3 charged particles
  BT1   hydrogen ions
    BT2 ions
      BT3 charged particles
  NT1   protons
    NT2 antiprotons
    NT2 cosmic protons
    NT2 delayed protons
    NT2 diprotons
    NT2 photoprotons
    NT2 prompt protons
    NT2 solar protons
    NT2 trapped protons
  RT   h2 regions
  RT   oxonium ions

HYDROGEN IONS 2 PLUS [684; 684]
  BT1   cations
    BT2 ions
      BT3 charged particles
  BT1   hydrogen ions
    BT2 ions
      BT3 charged particles
  BT1   molecular ions
    BT2 ions
      BT3 charged particles

HYDROGEN IONS 3 PLUS [236; 236]
  BT1   cations
    BT2 ions
      BT3 charged particles
  BT1   hydrogen ions
    BT2 ions
      BT3 charged particles
  BT1   molecular ions
    BT2 ions
      BT3 charged particles

HYDROGEN ISOTOPES [877; 29,775]
  NT1   deuterium
  NT1   hydrogen 1
  NT1   hydrogen 4
  NT1   hydrogen 5
  NT1   hydrogen 6
  NT1   hydrogen 7
  NT1   tritium

HYDROGEN METERS [104; 104]
Oct 77
  BT1   measuring instruments
  RT   chemical analysis

hydrogen nitrates
  USE   nitric acid

HYDROGEN PEROXIDE [1,391; 1,391]
  BT1   hydrogen compounds
  BT1   peroxides
    BT2 oxygen compounds

hydrogen phosphates
  USE   phosphoric acid

hydrogen production
(Industrial production of hydrogen.)
  USE   hydrogen
  AND   production

hydrogen silicates
  USE   silicic acid

hydrogen sulfates
  USE   sulfuric acid

HYDROGEN SULFIDES [735; 735]
  UF   *sulfur hydrides*
  BT1   hydrogen compounds
  BT1   sulfides
    BT2 chalcogenides
    BT2 sulfur compounds
  RT   dual temperature process

HYDROGEN TRANSFER [235; 235]
Feb 81
  UF   *hydrogen donor reactions*
  RT   charge exchange
  RT   chemical reactions
  RT   isotopic exchange

HYDROGEN TRITIDE [133; 133] *Jul 76*
  UF   *tritium hydride*
  BT1   tritides
    BT2 tritium compounds
      BT3 hydrogen compounds

HYDROGEN 1 [1,419; 1,419]
  UF   *protium*
  BT1   hydrogen isotopes
  BT1   light nuclei
    BT2 nuclei
  BT1   odd-even nuclei
    BT2 nuclei
  BT1   stable isotopes
    BT2 isotopes
  RT   hydrogen deuteride

HYDROGEN 1 MINUS BEAMS
[520; 520] *Aug 78*
  BT1   ion beams
    BT2 beams

HYDROGEN 1 TARGET [2,049; 2,049]
  BT1   targets

hydrogen 2
  USE   deuterium

hydrogen 3
  USE   tritium

HYDROGEN 4 [149; 149]
  BT1   hydrogen isotopes
  BT1   light nuclei
    BT2 nuclei
  BT1   odd-odd nuclei
    BT2 nuclei

HYDROGEN 5 [29; 29]
  BT1   hydrogen isotopes
  BT1   light nuclei
    BT2 nuclei
  BT1   odd-even nuclei
    BT2 nuclei

HYDROGEN 6 [34; 34]
  BT1   hydrogen isotopes
  BT1   light nuclei
    BT2 nuclei
  BT1   odd-odd nuclei
    BT2 nuclei

HYDROGEN 7 [22; 22]
  BT1   hydrogen isotopes
  BT1   light nuclei
    BT2 nuclei
  BT1   odd-even nuclei
    BT2 nuclei

hydrogen-cooled reactors
  USE   hydrogen cooled reactors

hydrogenase
(Prior to July 1984 this was a valid descriptor, and older material is so indexed
  USE   hydrogenases

HYDROGENASES [37; 37]
UF *hydrogenase*
BT1 oxidoreductases
BT2   enzymes
BT3   organic compounds

HYDROGENATION [1,305; 1,305]
BT1 chemical reactions
RT dehydrogenation
RT deuteration

HYDROLASES [224; 5,143]
BT1 enzymes
BT2   organic compounds
NT1 acid anhydrases
NT2   phosphohydrolases
NT3   atp-ase
NT1 esterases
NT2   carboxylesterases
NT3   cholinesterase
NT3   lipases
NT2   phosphatases
NT3   acid phosphatase
NT3   alkaline phosphatase
NT3   nucleotidases
NT2   phosphodiesterases
NT3   nucleases
NT4   dna-ase
NT4   endonucleases
NT4   rna-ase
NT1 glycosyl hydrolases
NT2   o-glycosyl hydrolases
NT3   amylase
NT3   galactosidase
NT3   glucuronidase
NT3   lysozyme
NT1 non-peptide c-n hydrolases
NT2   amidases
NT3   urease
NT2   amidinases
NT3   arginase
NT1 peptide hydrolases
NT2   acid proteinases
NT3   pepsin
NT2   aminopeptidases
NT2   carboxypeptidases
NT2   nonspecific peptidases
NT3   renin
NT3   urokinase
NT2   serine proteinases
NT3   chymotrypsin
NT3   fibrinolysin
NT3   kallikrein
NT3   thrombin
NT3   trypsin
NT2   sh-proteinases
NT3   cathepsins
NT3   papain
NT3   streptococcal proteinase

HYDROLOGY [4,200; 4,200]
RT aquifers
RT drainage
RT floods
RT fluid injection
RT ground water
RT hydraulic conductivity
RT lakes
RT rivers
RT rock-fluid interactions
RT site surveys
RT surface waters
RT water influx
RT water tables
RT water use

HYDROLYSIS [2,532; 2,553]
BT1 solvolysis
BT2   decomposition
BT3   chemical reactions
NT1 saponification
RT esters

HYDROMAGNETIC WAVES [1,014; 4,087]
UF *magnetohydrodynamic waves*
NT1 alfven waves
NT1 magnetoacoustic waves
NT2   fast magnetoacoustic waves
RT magnetoacoustics
RT plasma waves
RT shock waves

HYDROMETALLURGY [331; 331]
BT1 extractive metallurgy
BT2   metallurgy
RT leaching
RT precipitation
RT solvent extraction

HYDRONIUM RADICALS [55; 55]
BT1 radicals
RT water

HYDROPEROXY RADICALS [93; 93]
(HO2)
UF *ho2*
BT1 radicals

HYDROSPHERE [143; 143]
RT aquatic ecosystems
RT atmospheric precipitations
RT environment
RT glaciers
RT limnology
RT surface waters
RT water

HYDROSTATIC BEARINGS [35; 35]
Aug 78
BT1 bearings
RT liquids
RT lubrication

HYDROSTATICS [393; 393]
RT fluid mechanics

hydrothermal alteration
USE metamorphism

HYDROTHERMAL STAGE [338; 338]
RT metamorphism

HYDROXAMIC ACIDS [197; 247]
BT1 amines
BT2   organic compounds
BT1 hydroxy compounds
BT2   organic compounds
NT1 benzohydroxamic acid
RT organic acids

HYDROXIDE MODERATORS [4; 4]
BT1 moderators
RT hydroxides

HYDROXIDES [1,200; 5,094]
UF+ *hydroxyl ions*
BT1 hydrogen compounds
BT1 oxygen compounds
NT1 actinium hydroxides
NT1 aluminium hydroxides
NT1 americium hydroxides
NT1 ammonium hydroxides
NT1 antimony hydroxides
NT1 barium hydroxides
NT1 berkelium hydroxides
NT1 beryllium hydroxides
NT1 bismuth hydroxides
NT1 boron hydroxides
NT1 cadmium hydroxides
NT1 calcium hydroxides
NT1 cerium hydroxides
NT1 cesium hydroxides
NT1 chromium hydroxides
NT1 cobalt hydroxides
NT1 copper hydroxides
NT1 curium hydroxides
NT1 dysprosium hydroxides
NT1 einsteinium hydroxides
NT1 erbium hydroxides
NT1 europium hydroxides
NT1 gadolinium hydroxides
NT1 gallium hydroxides
NT1 germanium hydroxides
NT1 hafnium hydroxides
NT1 helium hydroxides
NT1 holmium hydroxides
NT1 indium hydroxides
NT1 iron hydroxides
NT1 lanthanum hydroxides
NT1 lead hydroxides
NT1 lithium hydroxides
NT1 lutetium hydroxides
NT1 magnesium hydroxides
NT1 manganese hydroxides
NT1 molybdenum hydroxides
NT1 neodymium hydroxides
NT1 neptunium hydroxides
NT1 nickel hydroxides
NT1 niobium hydroxides
NT1 palladium hydroxides
NT1 platinum hydroxides
NT1 plutonium hydroxides
NT1 polonium hydroxides
NT1 potassium hydroxides
NT1 praseodymium hydroxides
NT1 promethium hydroxides
NT1 protactinium hydroxides
NT1 rhenium hydroxides
NT1 rhodium hydroxides
NT1 rubidium hydroxides
NT1 ruthenium hydroxides
NT1 samarium hydroxides
NT1 scandium hydroxides
NT1 selenium hydroxides
NT1 silicon hydroxides
NT1 sodium hydroxides
NT1 strontium hydroxides
NT1 tantalum hydroxides
NT1 tellurium hydroxides
NT1 terbium hydroxides
NT1 thallium hydroxides
NT1 thorium hydroxides
NT1 thulium hydroxides
NT1 tin hydroxides
NT1 titanium hydroxides
NT1 tungsten hydroxides
NT1 uranium hydroxides
NT1 vanadium hydroxides
NT1 xenon hydroxides
NT1 ytterbium hydroxides
NT1 yttrium hydroxides
NT1 zinc hydroxides
NT1 zirconium hydroxides
RT bases
RT hydroxide moderators
RT hydroxyl radicals

HYDROXY ACIDS [361; 4,007]
(For carboxylic acids only; for other acids see HYDROXY COMPOUNDS coordinated with the descriptor for the particular acid group, e.g., SULFONIC ACIDS.)
BT1 carboxylic acids
BT2   organic acids
BT3   organic compounds
NT1 acetylsalicylic acid
NT1 aluminon
NT1 benzilic acid
NT1 carnitine
NT1 citric acid
NT1 diiodotyrosine
NT1 dopa
NT1 eddha
NT1 eosin
NT1 fluorescein
NT1 galacturonic acid
NT1 gallic acid
NT1 gibberellic acid
NT1 gluconic acid
NT1 glucuronic acid
NT1 glyceric acid
NT1 glycolic acid
NT1 hedta
NT1 heida
NT1 hydroxyproline
NT1 hydroxytryptophan
NT1 lactic acid
NT1 malic acid
NT1 mandelic acid
NT1 melilotic acid
NT1 methyl tyrosine
NT1 mevalonic acid

NT1 pantothenic acid
NT1 podophyllic acid
NT1 rose bengal
NT1 salicylic acid
NT1 serine
NT1 shikimic acid
NT1 tartaric acid
NT1 threonine
NT1 thyronine
NT1 trihydroxyglutaric acid
NT1 tyrosine
RT hydroxy compounds
RT lactones

HYDROXY COMPOUNDS
[1,077; 23,170]
BT1 organic compounds
NT1 alcohols
  NT2 batyl alcohol
  NT2 benzhydrol
  NT2 benzyl alcohol
  NT2 butanols
  NT2 choline
  NT2 decanols
  NT2 enols
  NT2 erythritol
  NT2 ethanol
  NT2 geraniol
  NT2 glycerol
  NT2 glycols
    NT3 benzopinacol
    NT3 carbitols
    NT3 cellosolves
    NT3 egta
    NT3 pinacol
  NT2 hexanols
  NT2 methanol
  NT2 metronidazole
  NT2 misonidazole
  NT2 octanols
  NT2 pentanols
  NT2 propanols
  NT2 pva
  NT2 2-methylpropanol
NT1 alizarin
NT1 androsterone
NT1 bph
NT1 carminic acid
NT1 chromotropic acid
NT1 corticosteroids
  NT2 glucocorticoids
    NT3 corticosterone
    NT3 cortisone
    NT3 dexamethasone
    NT3 hydrocortisone
    NT3 prednisolone
    NT3 prednisone
  NT2 mineralocorticoids
    NT3 aldosterone
    NT3 doca
NT1 cupferron
NT1 dianabol
NT1 ephedrine
NT1 estradiol
NT1 estriol
NT1 estrone
NT1 ferron
NT1 folic acid
NT1 guanine
NT1 hydroxamic acids
  NT2 benzohydroxamic acid
NT1 hydroxyandrostenone
NT1 hydroxypregnenone
NT1 hypoxanthine
NT1 kynurenic acid
NT1 melanin
NT1 oximes
  NT2 benzoinoxime
  NT2 dimethylglyoxime
  NT2 furildioxime
NT1 oxine
NT1 phenols
  NT2 amidol
  NT2 bambp
  NT2 cresols
  NT2 dinitrophenol
  NT2 eriochrome dyes
  NT2 naphthols
    NT3 acid chrome dyes
    NT3 beryllon
    NT3 nitroso-r salt
    NT3 pan
    NT3 thorin
    NT3 trypan blue
    NT3 1-nitroso-2-naphthol
  NT2 nitrophenol
  NT2 phenol
  NT2 phenolphthalein
  NT2 picric acid
  NT2 polyphenols
    NT3 arsenazo
    NT3 aurin
    NT3 bromosulfophthalein
    NT3 catecholamines
    NT3 curcumin
    NT3 dopamine
    NT3 fluorescein
    NT3 hematoxylin
    NT3 morin
    NT3 pyridylazoresorcinol
    NT3 pyrocatechol
    NT3 pyrogallol
    NT3 quercetin
    NT3 resorcinol
    NT3 stilbestrol
    NT3 tannic acid
    NT3 tiron
  NT2 pop
  NT2 thymol
  NT2 tyramine
NT1 pregnanediol
NT1 pregnanetriol
NT1 pyridoxine
NT1 quinizarin
NT1 rhodizonic acid
NT1 serotonin
NT1 sterols
  NT2 bile acids
    NT3 cholic acid
  NT2 cholesterol
  NT2 ergosterol
  NT2 lanolin
  NT2 sitosterol
NT1 testosterone
NT1 thiamine
NT1 tmpn
NT1 uracils
  NT2 bromouracils
    NT3 budr
  NT2 chlorouracils
  NT2 deoxyuridine
  NT2 fluorouracils
    NT3 fudr
  NT2 iodouracils
    NT3 iododeoxyuridine
  NT2 orotic acid
  NT2 thiouracil
  NT2 thymine
  NT2 uridine
RT hydroxy acids
RT hydroxylation
RT inositols

hydroxy-alpha-alanine-beta
USE serine

hydroxy-para-cymene
USE thymol

hydroxyacetic acid
USE glycolic acid

HYDROXYANDROSTENONE [30; 30]
UF *dehydroepiandrosterone*
BT1 androgens
  BT2 androstanes
    BT3 steroids
      BT4 organic compounds
  BT2 steroid hormones
    BT3 hormones
BT1 hydroxy compounds
  BT2 organic compounds
BT1 ketones
  BT2 organic compounds

hydroxybenzene
USE phenol

hydroxybenzoic acid-ortho
USE salicylic acid

hydroxydiphenylacetic acid
USE benzilic acid

hydroxyethylethylenediaminetri
(Hydroxyethylethylenediaminetriacetic acid)
USE hedta

hydroxyethyliminodiacetic acid
USE heida

hydroxyl ions
USE anions
AND hydroxides

HYDROXYL RADICALS [2,187; 2,187]
BT1 radicals
RT hydroxides
RT oxygen compounds

HYDROXYLAMINE [194; 194]
BT1 amines
  BT2 organic compounds
RT oximes

HYDROXYLASES [170; 203]
(Prior to February 1982 HYDROXYLASE was a valid term, and older information is so indexed.)
BT1 oxidoreductases
  BT2 enzymes
    BT3 organic compounds
NT1 tyrosinase

HYDROXYLATION [111; 111] *Jul 77*
BT1 chemical reactions
RT hydroxy compounds

hydroxynaphthalenes
USE naphthols

HYDROXYPREGNENONE [40; 40]
UF *pregnenolone*
BT1 hydroxy compounds
  BT2 organic compounds
BT1 ketones
  BT2 organic compounds
BT1 pregnanes
  BT2 steroids
    BT3 organic compounds
RT progesterone

HYDROXYPROLINE [113; 113]
BT1 amino acids
  BT2 carboxylic acids
    BT3 organic acids
      BT4 organic compounds
BT1 heterocyclic acids
  BT2 carboxylic acids
    BT3 organic acids
      BT4 organic compounds
  BT2 heterocyclic compounds
    BT3 organic compounds
BT1 hydroxy acids
  BT2 carboxylic acids
    BT3 organic acids
      BT4 organic compounds
BT1 pyrrolidines
  BT2 amines
    BT3 organic compounds
  BT2 pyrroles
    BT3 azoles
      BT4 heterocyclic compounds
        BT5 organic compounds
      BT4 organic nitrogen compounds

```
            BT5   organic compounds
     RT     collagen
     RT     proline

hydroxypropionic acid-alpha
     USE    lactic acid

hydroxypropiophenone
     USE    pop

hydroxysuccinic acid
     USE    malic acid

hydroxytoluenes
     USE    cresols

HYDROXYTRYPTOPHAN [37; 37]
     BT1    amino acids
        BT2    carboxylic acids
           BT3    organic acids
              BT4    organic compounds
     BT1    hydroxy acids
        BT2    carboxylic acids
           BT3    organic acids
              BT4    organic compounds
     BT1    radioprotective substances
        BT2    drugs
        BT2    response modifying factors
     RT     tryptophan

HYGROMETRY [63; 63]
     RT     humidity
     RT     moisture gages

HYGROSCOPICITY [63; 63]
     RT     adsorption

HYLEMYA ANTIQUA [13; 13]
     BT1    flies
        BT2    insects
           BT3    arthropods
              BT4    invertebrates
                 BT5    animals
     RT     onions

HYLIFE CONVERTER [66; 66] Sep 79
(High Yield Lithium Injection Fusion Energy Converter.)
     BT1    thermonuclear devices

HYLLERAAS COORDINATES [50; 50]
     BT1    coordinates
     RT     quantum mechanics

hylleraas-scherr-knight proc.
     USE    hsk procedure

HYMENOLEPIS [8; 8]
     BT1    cestodes
        BT2    helminths
           BT3    parasites
        BT2    platyhelminths
           BT3    invertebrates
              BT4    animals

hymu-80
     USE    alloy-ni80fe16mo4

HYOSCYAMINE [4; 4]
     BT1    alkaloids
        BT2    organic compounds

HYPAQUE [16; 16]
     BT1    amides
        BT2    organic nitrogen compounds
           BT3    organic compounds
     BT1    contrast media
     BT1    organic iodine compounds
        BT2    organic halogen compounds
```

```
        BT3    organic compounds
     BT1    sodium compounds
        BT2    alkali metal compounds
     RT     benzoic acid

HYPERCHARGE [305; 305]
     BT1    particle properties
     RT     charm particles
     RT     gauge invariance
     RT     grace particles
     RT     taste particles

→ HYPERCUBE COMPUTERS [0; 0]
     Oct 91
     (Computer architecture in which each processor has its own memory and is connected to a number of other processors.)
     BT1    computers
     RT     array processors
     RT     supercomputers

HYPERFINE STRUCTURE
[8,415; 8,415]
     UF     hfs
     RT     spectra

hyperfragments
     USE    hypernuclei

HYPERGEOMETRIC FUNCTIONS
[449; 449]
     BT1    functions

HYPERGLYCEMIA [142; 142]
     RT     saccharides

HYPERNUCLEI [1,588; 1,588]
     UF     hyperfragments
     BT1    nuclei
     RT     hyperons

HYPERON BEAMS [68; 111]
     BT1    particle beams
        BT2    beams
     NT1    lambda particle beams
     NT1    omega particle beams
     NT1    sigma particle beams
     NT1    xi particle beams

HYPERON REACTIONS [144; 144]
     BT1    baryon reactions
        BT2    hadron reactions
           BT3    nuclear reactions

HYPERON-HYPERON INTERACTIONS
[67; 67]
     RT     baryon-baryon interactions
        BT2    hadron-hadron interactions
           BT3    particle interactions
              BT4    interactions

HYPERONS [818; 5,530]
     UF     strange baryons
     BT1    baryons
        BT2    fermions
        BT2    hadrons
           BT3    elementary particles
     BT1    strange particles
        BT2    elementary particles
     NT1    antihyperons
     NT2    antilambda particles
     NT2    antiomega particles
     NT2    antisigma particles
     NT2    antixi particles
     NT1    lambda baryons
        NT2    lambda particles
           NT3    antilambda particles
        NT2    lambda-1405 baryons
        NT2    lambda-1520 baryons
        NT2    lambda-1600 baryons
        NT2    lambda-1670 baryons
        NT2    lambda-1690 baryons
        NT2    lambda-1800 baryons
```

```
     NT2    lambda-1820 baryons
     NT2    lambda-1830 baryons
     NT2    lambda-1890 baryons
     NT2    lambda-2000 baryons
     NT2    lambda-2020 baryons
     NT2    lambda-2100 baryons
     NT2    lambda-2110 baryons
     NT2    lambda-2325 baryons
     NT2    lambda-2350 baryons
     NT2    lambda-2585 baryons
     NT1    lambda-n-2130 dibaryons
     NT1    omega baryons
        NT2    omega particles
           NT3    antiomega particles
     NT1    sigma baryons
        NT2    sigma particles
           NT3    antisigma particles
           NT3    sigma minus particles
           NT3    sigma neutral particles
           NT3    sigma plus particles
        NT2    sigma-1385 baryons
        NT2    sigma-1480 baryons
        NT2    sigma-1560 baryons
        NT2    sigma-1580 baryons
        NT2    sigma-1620 baryons
        NT2    sigma-1660 baryons
        NT2    sigma-1670 baryons
        NT2    sigma-1690 baryons
        NT2    sigma-1750 baryons
        NT2    sigma-1770 baryons
        NT2    sigma-1775 baryons
        NT2    sigma-1840 baryons
        NT2    sigma-1880 baryons
        NT2    sigma-1915 baryons
        NT2    sigma-1940 baryons
        NT2    sigma-2000 baryons
        NT2    sigma-2030 baryons
        NT2    sigma-2070 baryons
        NT2    sigma-2080 baryons
        NT2    sigma-2100 baryons
        NT2    sigma-2250 baryons
        NT2    sigma-2455 baryons
        NT2    sigma-2620 baryons
        NT2    sigma-3000 baryons
        NT2    sigma-3170 baryons
     NT1    xi baryons
        NT2    xi particles
           NT3    antixi particles
           NT3    xi minus particles
           NT3    xi neutral particles
        NT2    xi-1530 baryons
        NT2    xi-1630 baryons
        NT2    xi-1680 baryons
        NT2    xi-1820 baryons
        NT2    xi-1940 baryons
        NT2    xi-2030 baryons
        NT2    xi-2120 baryons
        NT2    xi-2250 baryons
        NT2    xi-2370 baryons
        NT2    xi-2500 baryons
     NT1    z*baryons
        NT2    z0-1780 baryons
        NT2    z0-1865 baryons
        NT2    z1-1725 baryons
        NT2    z1-1900 baryons
        NT2    z1-2150 baryons
        NT2    z1-2500 baryons
     RT     hypernuclei

HYPERPARATHYROIDISM [149; 149]
Dec 84
     BT1    endocrine diseases
        BT2    diseases
     RT     bone tissues
     RT     calcium
     RT     parathyroid glands

HYPERSONIC FLOW [68; 68]
     BT1    fluid flow

HYPERTENSION [1,179; 1,179]
     BT1    cardiovascular diseases
        BT2    diseases
     BT1    symptoms
     BT1    vascular diseases
        BT2    diseases
     RT     biological stress
     RT     blood pressure
```

HYPERTHERMIA [1,340; 1,340] *Feb 81*
BT1 body temperature
RT fever
RT hypothermia

HYPERTHYROIDISM [994; 994]
UF *basedow's disease*
UF *thyrotoxicosis*
BT1 endocrine diseases
BT2 diseases
RT antithyroid drugs
RT goiter
RT thyroid hormones

HYPERTONIC SOLUTIONS [70; 70]
BT1 solutions
BT2 homogeneous mixtures
BT3 mixtures
BT4 dispersions
RT isotonic solutions
RT osmosis

HYPERTROPHY [332; 332]
BT1 pathological changes
BT2 diseases

HYPNOTICS AND SEDATIVES [60; 407]
UF *sedatives*
UF+ *promethazine*
BT1 central nervous system depress
BT2 central nervous system agents
BT3 drugs
NT1 barbiturates
NT2 amytal
NT2 nembutal
NT2 phenobarbital
NT2 thiopental
NT1 chlorpromazine
NT1 codeine
NT1 reserpine
RT analgesics
RT anesthetics
RT narcotics
RT sleep

HYPOCHLOROUS ACID [39; 39]
BT1 chlorine compounds
BT2 halogen compounds
BT1 inorganic acids
BT2 hydrogen compounds
BT2 inorganic compounds
BT1 oxygen compounds

HYPOIODOUS ACID [33; 33] *Dec 80*
BT1 inorganic acids
BT2 hydrogen compounds
BT2 inorganic compounds
BT1 iodine compounds
BT2 halogen compounds
BT1 oxygen compounds

hypophosphites
(Specific hypophosphites should be indexed by coordination of a descriptor of the form (CATION) COMPOUNDS and HYPOPHOSPHOROUS ACID.)
USE hypophosphorous acid

HYPOPHOSPHOROUS ACID [50; 50]
UF *hypophosphites*
BT1 inorganic acids
BT2 hydrogen compounds
BT2 inorganic compounds
BT1 oxygen compounds
BT1 phosphorus compounds

HYPOPHYSECTOMY [62; 62]
BT1 surgery
BT2 medicine
RT hypothalamus
RT pituitary gland
RT pituitary hormones

hypophysis
USE pituitary gland

HYPOTENSION [84; 84]
RT biological stress
RT blood pressure

HYPOTHALAMUS [388; 388]
BT1 brain
BT2 central nervous system
BT3 nervous system
BT2 organs
BT3 body
RT autonomic nervous system
RT endocrine glands
RT homeostasis
RT hypophysectomy
RT metabolism
RT pituitary gland
RT trh

HYPOTHERMIA [88; 88]
BT1 body temperature
RT hibernation
RT hyperthermia

HYPOTHESIS [591; 2,565]
NT1 ergodic hypothesis
NT1 limiting fragmentation
NT1 mach principle
NT1 negative mass
RT comparative evaluations
RT functional models
RT mathematical models
RT structural models

HYPOTHYROIDISM [693; 693]
UF *myxedema*
BT1 endocrine diseases
BT2 diseases
RT antithyroid drugs
RT goiter
RT thyroid hormones

HYPOXANTHINE [96; 96]
BT1 hydroxy compounds
BT2 organic compounds
BT1 purines
BT2 heterocyclic compounds
BT3 organic compounds
BT2 organic nitrogen compounds
BT3 organic compounds
RT inosine
RT nucleotides
RT xanthines

hypoxia
USE anoxia

HYSTERESIS [1,814; 1,814]
RT damping
RT energy losses
RT internal friction

HZ RANGE [1,078; 1,125]
BT1 frequency range

H1 REGIONS [1,107; 1,107]
BT1 cosmic radio sources
RT hydrogen

H1-1190 MESONS [3; 3] *Dec 87*
BT1 axial vector mesons
BT2 mesons
BT3 bosons
BT3 hadrons
BT4 elementary particles

H2 REGIONS [2,351; 2,351]
BT1 cosmic radio sources
RT hydrogen ions 1 plus
RT nebulae

I CENTERS [32; 32]
(Interstitial halogen-ion centers)
BT1 color centers
BT2 vacancies
BT3 point defects
BT4 crystal defects
BT5 crystal structure
BT1 interstitials
BT2 point defects
BT3 crystal defects
BT4 crystal structure

I CODES [736; 736]
BT1 computer codes

i-beam type reactors
USE ion beam fusion reactors

i-inositol
USE inositol

i-v characteristic
USE electric conductivity

IAEA [2,748; 2,788]
UF *internat atomic energy agency*
BT1 international organizations
NT1 ictp
NT1 ilmr
NT1 seibersdorf iaea laboratory
RT austria
RT canare
RT cenna
RT iaea agreements
RT iaea safeguards
RT inis
RT recommendations
RT united nations

IAEA AGREEMENTS [223; 223]
BT1 international agreements
BT2 agreements
RT iaea

IAEA SAFEGUARDS [1,167; 1,167]
BT1 safeguards
RT iaea

iaea seibersdorf laboratory
USE seibersdorf iaea laboratory

IAN [20; 20] *May 87*
(Instituto de Asuntos Nucleares, Bogota.)
BT1 colombian organizations
BT2 national organizations

IAN-R1 REACTOR [7; 7]
(Institute of Nuclear Affairs, Bogota, Colombia.)
UF *instituto de asuntos nucle. r1*
BT1 enriched uranium reactors
BT2 reactors
BT1 isotope production reactors
BT2 irradiation reactors
BT3 reactors
BT1 pool type reactors
BT2 water cooled reactors
BT3 reactors
BT2 water moderated reactors
BT3 reactors
BT1 research reactors
BT2 research and test reactors
BT3 reactors
BT1 thermal reactors
BT2 reactors
BT1 training reactors
BT2 research and test reactors
BT3 reactors

IBM COMPUTERS [739; 739]
BT1 computers

ibr-1 reactor
USE ifr reactor

IBR-2 REACTOR [148; 148] *Jan 78*
UF *dubna ibr-2 reactor*
BT1 fast reactors
BT2 epithermal reactors
BT3 reactors
BT1 pulsed reactors
BT2 reactors
BT1 research reactors
BT2 research and test reactors
BT3 reactors

IBR-30 REACTOR [101; 101]
(Dubna, USSR)
BT1 fast reactors
BT2 epithermal reactors
BT3 reactors
BT1 pulsed reactors
BT2 reactors
BT1 research reactors
BT2 research and test reactors
BT3 reactors

ICE [1,118; 1,118]
UF *frost*
RT antarctic regions
RT arctic regions
RT glaciers
RT hail
RT snow
RT water

ICE CONDENSERS [111; 111] *Jan 77*
(A steam condenser using ice as the heat sink. Incorporated for example in the containment systems of McGuire, Watts Bar and other reactors.)
UF *condensers (using ice)*
BT1 steam condensers
BT2 vapor condensers
RT containment systems
RT cooling
RT reactor cooling systems

icebreaker arktika reactor
USE leonid brezhnev reactor

icebreaker lenin reactor
USE lenin reactor

icebreaker leonid brezhnev rea
USE leonid brezhnev reactor

icebreaker sibir reactor
USE sibir reactor

ICELAND [79; 79]
BT1 developing countries
BT1 europe
BT1 islands
RT atlantic ocean

ICF DEVICES [460; 478] *Aug 84*
UF *inertial confinement fusion de*
BT1 thermonuclear devices
NT1 angara-5 device
RT aurora facility
RT cascade reactors
RT electron beam fusion reactors
RT inertial confinement
RT ion beam fusion reactors
RT laser fusion reactors

ICL COMPUTERS [56; 56]
BT1 computers

ICONOSCOPES [1; 1]
BT1 camera tubes
BT2 image tubes

icr
USE ion cyclotron-resonance

ICR HEATING [2,161; 2,161]
UF *ion cyclotron-resonance heatin*
BT1 high-frequency heating
BT2 plasma heating
BT3 heating
RT ion cyclotron-resonance

ICRP [1,374; 1,374]
UF *internat comm radiol protect*
BT1 international organizations
RT alara
RT cuex
RT icru
RT radiation protection
RT recommendations
RT reference man

ICRP CRITICAL GROUP [193; 193]
(Out of a general population, the group of persons most highly exposed to radiation by virtue of their occupations, diets, habits, etc.)
UF *critical group (icrp)*
RT body burden
RT diet
RT human populations
RT occupational exposure
RT occupations
RT radiation doses
RT radiation hazards
RT working conditions

ICRU [304; 304]
UF *internat comm rad units measur*
UF *internat comm radiat units*
BT1 international organizations
RT dosimetry
RT icrp
RT radiation dose units
RT recommendations

icsd
(Ionization chamber smoke detectors.)
USE smoke detectors

ICTP [24; 24] *Nov 79*
(International Centre for Theoretical Physics, Trieste.)
UF *internat center theoret phys*
BT1 iaea
BT2 international organizations

IDAHO [248; 248]
BT1 usa
BT2 developed countries
BT2 north america
RT columbia river basin
RT idaho chemical processing plan
RT idaho national engineering lab

idaho advanced test reactor
USE atr reactor

IDAHO CHEMICAL PROCESSING PLAN [310; 310]
BT1 fuel reprocessing plants
BT2 nuclear facilities
BT1 us aec
BT2 us organizations
BT3 national organizations
BT1 us doe
BT2 us organizations
BT3 national organizations
BT1 us erda
BT2 us organizations
BT3 national organizations
RT idaho

idaho materials testing reacto
USE mtr reactor

IDAHO NATIONAL ENGINEERING LAB [733; 734] *May 76*
(Name changed in 1976 from NRTS and older material should be so indexed.)
UF *inel*
BT1 us doe
BT2 us organizations
BT3 national organizations
BT1 us erda
BT2 us organizations
BT3 national organizations
NT1 nrts
RT idaho

IDEAL FLOW [101; 101] *Mar 86*
UF *frictionless flow*
UF *inviscid flow*
UF *nonviscous flow*
BT1 incompressible flow
BT2 fluid flow
BT1 steady flow
BT2 fluid flow
RT laminar flow

IDENTIFICATION SYSTEMS [160; 160] *Dec 85*
(For persons or objects. Not for systems for PARTICLE IDENTIFICATION.)
RT control systems
RT data acquisition systems
RT entry control systems
RT nuclear materials management
RT pattern recognition
RT physical protection devices
RT safeguards
RT secrecy protection
RT security

iea
USE international energy agency

IEA-ZPR REACTOR [7; 7]
(Zero power reactor at Instituto de Energia Atomica, Sao Paulo, Brazil.)
UF *instituto de energia atom. zpr*
UF *sao paulo iea zero power reac.*
BT1 graphite moderated reactors
BT2 reactors
BT1 helium cooled reactors
BT2 gas cooled reactors
BT3 reactors
BT1 research reactors
BT2 research and test reactors
BT3 reactors
BT1 zero power reactors
BT2 experimental reactors
BT3 research and test reactors
BT4 reactors
RT enriched uranium reactors
RT thorium reactors

IEAR-1 REACTOR [106; 106]
(Research reactor at Instituto de Energia Atomica, Sao Paulo, Brazil.)
UF *instituto de energia atom. r1*
UF *sao paulo iear-1 reactor*
BT1 enriched uranium reactors
BT2 reactors
BT1 pool type reactors
BT2 water cooled reactors
BT3 reactors
BT2 water moderated reactors
BT3 reactors
BT1 research reactors
BT2 research and test reactors
BT3 reactors
BT1 thermal reactors
BT2 reactors

IFIP [19; 19]
UF   internat food irradiation proj
BT1   coordinated research programs
BT2   research programs
RT   food
RT   irradiation procedures
RT   radappertization
RT   radicidation
RT   radurization

IFR REACTOR [95; 95]
UF   ibr-1 reactor
BT1   fast reactors
BT2   epithermal reactors
BT3   reactors
BT1   zero power reactors
BT2   experimental reactors
BT3   research and test reactors
BT4   reactors

ifve
(Inst. Fiziki Vysokikh Ehnergij.)
USE   ihep

IGCAR [33; 33] *Mar 77*
(Indira Gandhi Centre for Atomic Research, Kalpakkam, Tamilnadu, India.)
UF   kalpakkam reactor research cen
UF   rrc, kalpakkam
BT1   indian organizations
BT2   national organizations

IGNALINSK-1 REACTOR [24; 24] *Aug 84*
UF   rbmk-1500 reactor
BT1   enriched uranium reactors
BT2   reactors
BT1   lwgr type reactors
BT2   graphite moderated reactors
BT3   reactors
BT2   water cooled reactors
BT3   reactors
BT1   power reactors
BT2   reactors
BT1   thermal reactors
BT2   reactors

IGNALINSK-2 REACTOR [10; 10] *Aug 84*
BT1   enriched uranium reactors
BT2   reactors
BT1   lwgr type reactors
BT2   graphite moderated reactors
BT3   reactors
BT2   water cooled reactors
BT3   reactors
BT1   power reactors
BT2   reactors
BT1   thermal reactors
BT2   reactors

IGNEOUS ROCKS [1,725; 8,103]
UF   magma
UF   volcanic rocks
BT1   rocks
NT1   basalt
NT1   lava
NT1   plutonic rocks
NT2   anorthosites
NT2   gabbros
NT2   granites
NT3   aplites
NT3   granodiorites
NT3   quartz monzonite
NT2   pegmatites
NT2   peridotites
NT3   kimberlites
NT2   syenites
NT1   rhyolites
NT1   tuff

igniters
USE   ignition systems

ignition (thermonuclear)
USE   thermonuclear ignition

IGNITION SYSTEMS [76; 76] *Jul 84*
(Not for THERMONUCLEAR IGNITION.)
UF   igniters
RT   automobiles
RT   combustion
RT   combustors
RT   vehicles

IGNITRONS [45; 45]
BT1   gas discharge tubes
BT2   electron tubes
BT1   rectifier tubes
BT2   electron tubes
BT2   rectifiers
BT3   electrical equipment
BT4   equipment

igy
USE   international geophysical year

IHEP [27; 27] *Oct 75*
(Institute for High Energy Physics, Serpukhov, USSR)
UF   ifve
UF   inst fiziki vysokikh ehnergij
UF   institute for high energy phys
BT1   ussr organizations
BT2   national organizations
RT   serpukhov synchrotron

iisnr reactor
USE   thetis reactor

IKATA REACTOR [50; 50]
(Ikata, Ehime, Japan)
BT1   pwr type reactors
BT2   enriched uranium reactors
BT3   reactors
BT2   power reactors
BT3   reactors
BT2   thermal reactors
BT3   reactors
BT2   water cooled reactors
BT3   reactors
BT2   water moderated reactors
BT3   reactors

IKATA-2 REACTOR [8; 8] *Nov 85*
(Ikata, Ehime, Japan)
BT1   pwr type reactors
BT2   enriched uranium reactors
BT3   reactors
BT2   power reactors
BT3   reactors
BT2   thermal reactors
BT3   reactors
BT2   water cooled reactors
BT3   reactors
BT2   water moderated reactors
BT3   reactors

IKATA-3 REACTOR [5; 5] *Oct 89*
(Ikata, Ehime, Japan.)
BT1   pwr type reactors
BT2   enriched uranium reactors
BT3   reactors
BT2   power reactors
BT3   reactors
BT2   thermal reactors
BT3   reactors
BT2   water cooled reactors
BT3   reactors
BT2   water moderated reactors
BT3   reactors

IKO [17; 17] *Jul 78*
UF   inst v. kernph onder amsterdam
UF   nucl. phys. res. in. amsterdam
BT1   netherlands organizations
BT2   national organizations

IKO SYNCHROCYCLOTRON [12; 12]
(IKO - Nuclear Physics Research Institute, Amsterdam)
UF   inst v. kernph onder synchrocy
BT1   synchrocyclotrons
BT2   cyclic accelerators
BT3   accelerators

ileum
USE   small intestine

ILLIAC COMPUTERS [5; 5]
BT1   computers

illinium
USE   promethium

ILLINOIS [341; 341]
BT1   usa
BT2   developed countries
BT2   north america
RT   anl

illinois univ. triga-mk-2 reac
USE   triga-2-illinois reactor

ILLITE [138; 138]
BT1   clays
BT2   silicate minerals
BT3   minerals

ILLUMINANCE [72; 72] *Jul 86*
(Density of luminous flux on a surface.)
UF   illumination
UF   luminous flux density
RT   albedo
RT   brightness
RT   lighting systems

illumination
USE   illuminance

ILMENITE [130; 130]
BT1   oxide minerals
BT2   minerals
RT   iron oxides
RT   titanium oxides

ILMR [7; 7] *Mar 87*
(IAEA Marine Environment Laboratory)
BT1   iaea
BT2   international organizations

ILO [24; 24]
UF   internat labour organisation
BT1   international organizations
RT   united nations
RT   work

ILVAITE [5; 5] *Feb 78*
BT1   silicate minerals
BT2   minerals
RT   calcium silicates
RT   iron silicates

IMAGE CONVERTERS [384; 384]
UF   converters (image)
BT1   image tubes
RT   image intensifiers
RT   image processing

IMAGE INTENSIFIERS [1,420; 1,420]
UF   intensifiers (image)
RT   fluoroscopy
RT   image converters
RT   image processing
RT   radiation protection

IMAGE PROCESSING [11,480; 11,480]
Nov 77
(Procedure for restoring or enhancing images, often by computer.)
- RT   computerized tomography
- RT   data processing
- RT   digital filters
- RT   image converters
- RT   image intensifiers
- RT   image scanners
- RT   images
- RT   photography
- RT   radioisotope scanners
- RT   video tapes

IMAGE SCANNERS [1,796; 1,796]
- UF   *scanners (image)*
- RT   computerized tomography
- RT   data processing
- RT   digitizers
- RT   electronic equipment
- RT   image processing
- RT   particle tracks
- RT   pattern recognition
- RT   photographic films
- RT   proton computed tomography
- RT   radioisotope scanners
- RT   sequential scanning

IMAGE STORAGE TUBES [40; 40]
- UF+   *storage tubes*
- BT1   image tubes

IMAGE TUBES [194; 877]
- NT1   camera tubes
  - NT2   iconoscopes
  - NT2   orthicons
  - NT2   vidicons
- NT1   image converters
- NT1   image storage tubes
- RT   cathode ray tubes
- RT   display devices
- RT   electron tubes
- RT   images
- RT   pattern recognition
- RT   photoelectric cells

IMAGES [27,365; 27,365]
- UF   *autoradiographs*
- UF   *photographs*
- UF   *radiographs*
- UF+   *echography*
- RT   display devices
- RT   image processing
- RT   image tubes
- RT   nuclear emulsions
- RT   pattern recognition
- RT   photographic films
- RT   radioisotope scanners
- RT   scintiscanning
- RT   video tapes
- RT   visibility

imatran voima-1 reactor
- USE   loviisa-1 reactor

imatran voima-2 reactor
- USE   loviisa-2 reactor

IMCO [10; 10]
- UF   *int. maritime consultative org*
- UF   *inter-gov marit consult organ*
- BT1   international organizations

IMIDAZOLES [594; 2,360]
(Compounds that contain a five-membered heterocyclic ring containing nitrogen atoms in the 1 and 3 positions.)
- UF+   *parabanic acid*
- BT1   azoles
  - BT2   heterocyclic compounds
    - BT3   organic compounds
  - BT2   organic nitrogen compounds
    - BT3   organic compounds
- NT1   allantoin
- NT1   benzimidazoles
- NT1   biotin
- NT1   cmni
- NT1   creatinine
- NT1   histamine
- NT1   histidine
- NT1   metronidazole
- NT1   misonidazole
- NT1   urocanic acid

IMIDES [401; 435]
- BT1   organic nitrogen compounds
  - BT2   organic compounds
- NT1   nem
- RT   dicarboxylic acids

IMIDINES [4; 4]
- BT1   organic nitrogen compounds
  - BT2   organic compounds
- RT   dicarboxylic acids

IMINES [335; 924]
(For aldehyde and ketone derivatives only, i.e., for compounds containing the =N- group; for those containing the -NH- group, see ORGANIC NITROGEN COMPOUNDS or appropriate specific descriptors listed thereunder.)
- BT1   organic nitrogen compounds
  - BT2   organic compounds
- NT1   creatinine
- NT1   pemoline
- NT1   schiff bases
- RT   aldehydes
- RT   guanidines
- RT   ketones

iminoamides
- USE   amidines

iminourea
- USE   guanidines

IMIPRAMINE [93; 93]
- BT1   amines
  - BT2   organic compounds
- BT1   antidepressants
  - BT2   psychotropic drugs
    - BT3   central nervous system agents
      - BT4   drugs
- BT1   heterocyclic compounds
  - BT2   organic compounds
- BT1   organic nitrogen compounds
  - BT2   organic compounds

immediate radiation effects
- USE   early radiation effects

immobilization (wastes)
(Prior to December 1990, this was a valid descriptor.)
- SEE   solidification
- OR   vitrification

IMMUNE REACTIONS [2,086; 2,086]
(Limited to immune reactions to foreign antigens in vivo.)
- RT   aids virus
- RT   antigen-antibody reactions
- RT   immunity
- RT   phagocytosis
- RT   toxoids

immune sera
- USE   immune serums

IMMUNE SERUMS [1,504; 1,504]
- UF   *antiserum*
- UF   *immune sera*
- UF   *serum (immune)*
- RT   antibodies
- RT   blood serum
- RT   inoculation

→ **IMMUNE SYSTEM DISEASES** [6; 154]
Jul 91
- BT1   diseases
- NT1   aids
- NT1   leukemia
  - NT2   myeloid leukemia
- NT1   leukopenia
  - NT2   lymphopenia
- NT1   lupus
- NT1   lymphomas
  - NT2   hodgkins disease
  - NT2   lymphosarcomas

immune tolerance
- USE   immunity

IMMUNITY [1,932; 1,932]
- UF   *compatibility (immunological)*
- UF   *immune tolerance*
- RT   aids
- RT   aids virus
- RT   allergy
- RT   anaphylaxis
- RT   antibodies
- RT   antibody formation
- RT   antigen-antibody reactions
- RT   antigens
- RT   chimeras
- RT   disease resistance
- RT   graft-host reaction
- RT   hemolysis
- RT   immune reactions
- RT   immunoglobulins
- RT   immunology
- RT   immunosuppression
- RT   inoculation
- RT   interferon
- RT   lymphocytes
- RT   lymphokines
- RT   preventive medicine
- RT   properdin
- RT   radioimmunology
- RT   receptors
- RT   thymectomy
- RT   toxoids
- RT   transplants
- RT   vaccines

IMMUNOASSAY [137; 2,002] *Feb 88*
- NT1   enzyme immunoassay
- NT1   radioimmunoassay
- RT   bioassay

IMMUNOGLOBULINS [1,465; 1,465]
- BT1   globulins
  - BT2   proteins
    - BT3   organic compounds
- RT   immunity

IMMUNOLOGY [653; 1,003]
- NT1   radioimmunology
- RT   immunity
- RT   mitogens

IMMUNOSUPPRESSION [1,088; 1,088]
- RT   antimitotic drugs
- RT   glucocorticoids
- RT   immunity
- RT   transplants

IMMUNOTHERAPY [463; 463] *May 81*
- UF+   *radioimmunotherapy*
- BT1   therapy
  - BT2   medicine

IMP DEVICE [6; 6]
- BT1   magnetic mirrors
  - BT2   open plasma devices
    - BT3   thermonuclear devices

IMP SATELLITES [193; 193]
  BT1 satellites

IMPACT FUSION [112; 112] *Jun 81*
  BT1 thermonuclear reactions
    BT2 nuclear reactions
    BT2 nucleosynthesis
      BT3 synthesis
  RT energy deposition
  RT inertial confinement
  RT magnetic gradient accelerators
  RT railgun accelerators

IMPACT FUSION DRIVERS [137; 330] *Oct 82*
(Macroparticle accelerators to be used in inertial confinement fusion.)
  NT1 magnetic gradient accelerators
  NT1 railgun accelerators
  RT accelerators
  RT plasma guns

IMPACT PARAMETER [2,544; 2,544]
  RT nuclear reactions
  RT peripheral collisions
  RT scattering

IMPACT SHOCK [1,353; 1,353]
  UF *shock (impact)*
  RT failures
  RT impact strength
  RT missile protection
  RT potting
  RT shock absorbers
  RT shock waves
  RT water hammer

IMPACT STRENGTH [1,668; 1,668]
  UF *strength (impact)*
  BT1 mechanical properties
  RT impact shock
  RT impact tests

IMPACT TESTS [1,247; 1,996]
  BT1 mechanical tests
    BT2 materials testing
      BT3 testing
  NT1 charpy test
  RT destructive testing
  RT impact strength
  RT notches

IMPEDANCE [785; 1,862]
  NT1 electric impedance
  NT1 mechanical impedance

imperfections
  USE defects

impingement
  USE fouling
  AND screens

IMPLANTS [195; 1,317] *Nov 81*
(For emplacement of materials into organisms; not for ION IMPLANTATION, CRYSTAL DOPING, etc.)
  NT1 radiation source implants

IMPLEMENTATION [934; 934] *Mar 85*
  RT administrative procedures
  RT agreements
  RT cancellation
  RT enforcement
  RT feasibility studies
  RT government policies
  RT legislation
  RT planning
  RT recommendations
  RT regulations

IMPLOSIONS [884; 2,824]
  NT1 laser implosions
  RT explosions
  RT linus reactors
  RT shock waves

importance function (neutron)
  USE neutron importance function

imports
(Goods or services brought from a foreign country.)
  USE trade

IMPREGNATION [586; 586]
(The infusion or permeation of one substance into another.)
  RT adsorption

impulse (linear momentum)
  USE linear momentum

impulse (pulses)
  USE pulses

IMPULSE APPROXIMATION [2,621; 2,621]
  RT bound state
  RT coupling
  RT scattering

§ **IMPURITIES** [19,680; 19,856]
(Unwanted constituents only, not for metal and nonmetal additions, or for the concepts covered by TRACE AMOUNTS and INTERFERING ELEMENTS.)
  UF *purity*
  NT1 plasma impurities
  RT activation analysis
  RT inclusions
  RT interfering elements
  RT jesse effect
  RT microanalysis
  RT plasma
  RT purification
  RT segregation
  RT substoichiometry
  RT trace amounts

impurity study experiment toka
  USE isx tokamak

ims
  USE international magnetospheric s

IMS STELLARATOR [5; 5] *Dec 90*
(Interchangeable Module Stellarator at University of Wisconsin, Madison, Wisconsin, USA.)
  BT1 stellarators
    BT2 closed plasma devices
      BT3 thermonuclear devices

IN CORE INSTRUMENTS [1,854; 1,854]
(See also specific instruments plus FUEL ASSEMBLIES or REACTOR CORES.)
  UF *in-core instruments*
  RT acoustic monitoring
  RT in-service inspection
  RT noise thermometers
  RT positioning
  RT reactor cores
  RT reactor instrumentation
  RT temperature monitoring

IN PILE LOOPS [844; 844]
  UF *in-pile loops*
  UF *loops (in pile)*
  BT1 reactor experimental facilitie
  BT2 reactor components
  RT experimental channels
  RT irradiation capsules

in situ processing
  USE in-situ processing

in utero irradiation
  USE prenatal irradiation

in vessel heat exchangers
  USE in-vessel heat exchangers

IN VITRO [7,725; 7,732]
(As opposite to in vivo.)
  RT cell cultures
  RT clone cells
  RT culture media
  RT hela cells
  RT homogenates
  RT l cells
  RT tissue cultures

IN VIVO [4,795; 4,795]
(To be used only to differentiate from in vitro studies at the cellular or tissue level.)
  RT cell division
  RT cell proliferation
  RT neoplasms
  RT organs
  RT plant cells
  RT tissues
  RT tumor cells

IN-BEAM SPECTROSCOPY [467; 467] *Jun 77*
  BT1 spectroscopy

in-core fuel management
  USE fuel management

in-core instruments
  USE in core instruments

in-pile loops
  USE in pile loops

IN-SERVICE INSPECTION [2,354; 2,354] *Jun 77*
  BT1 inspection
  RT in core instruments
  RT nondestructive testing
  RT reactor maintenance

IN-SITU PROCESSING [461; 764]
  UF *in situ processing*
  BT1 ore processing
  NT1 solution mining
  RT leachates
  RT leaching
  RT oil shales
  RT retorting
  RT separation processes
  RT underground explosions

IN-VESSEL HEAT EXCHANGERS [101; 101]
  UF *in vessel heat exchangers*
  BT1 heat exchangers

INACTIVATION [1,105; 1,105]
  UF *deactivation*
  RT inhibition
  RT preservation
  RT sterilization

INCIDENCE ANGLE [1,176; 1,176]
Apr 84
(Use only when the incidence angle is a significant parameter.)
- UF   *angle (incidence)*
- UF   *angle of incidence*
- RT   angular distribution
- RT   inclination
- RT   optics
- RT   orientation
- RT   reflection
- RT   refraction
- RT   scattering

incidents
USE   accidents

INCINERATORS [765; 765]
- RT   burners
- RT   combustion
- RT   furnaces

INCLINATION [718; 718]
(Angle between velocity vector of a charged particle and the magnetic field in which particle moves.)
- UF   *pitch angle*
- RT   geomagnetic field
- RT   incidence angle

inclusion complexes
USE   clathrates

INCLUSIONS [1,247; 1,247]
- RT   castings
- RT   crystal defects
- RT   impurities
- RT   ion implantation
- RT   microstructure
- RT   trace amounts

inclusive distribution
- USE   distribution
- AND   inclusive interactions

INCLUSIVE INTERACTIONS [11,590; 11,659]
(The group of all interactions of two particles producing a specific final state.)
- UF+   *inclusive distribution*
- BT1   particle interactions
- BT2   interactions
- NT1   semi-inclusive interactions
- RT   exclusive interactions
- RT   limiting fragmentation
- RT   nuclear fireball model

INCOHERENT PRODUCTION [76; 76]
- BT1   particle interactions
- BT2   interactions
- BT1   particle production
- RT   coherent tube model

INCOHERENT SCATTERING [913; 913]
- BT1   scattering
- RT   inelastic scattering

INCOLOY ALLOYS [107; 935]
- BT1   alloys
- NT1   alloy-fe44ni33cr21
- NT1   alloy-fe46ni33cr21
- NT1   alloy-ni42fe36cr12mo6ti3
- NT1   alloy-ni43fe30cr22mo3

incoloy 800
USE   alloy-fe46ni33cr21

incoloy 800h
USE   alloy-fe44ni33cr21

incoloy 802
USE   alloy-fe46ni33cr21

incoloy 825
USE   alloy-ni43fe30cr22mo3

incoloy 901
USE   alloy-ni42fe36cr12mo6ti3

INCOME [65; 65]
- RT   charges
- RT   economics

INCOMPLETE FUSION REACTIONS [209; 209] *Jan 85*
- UF   *breakup fusion*
- UF   *massive transfer reactions*
- BT1   heavy ion reactions
- BT2   nuclear reactions
- RT   compound-nucleus reactions
- RT   deep inelastic heavy ion react
- RT   heavy ion fusion reactions
- RT   nuclear fragmentation
- RT   precompound-nucleus emission
- RT   transfer reactions

INCOMPRESSIBLE FLOW [750; 839]
- BT1   fluid flow
- NT1   ideal flow
- RT   navier-stokes equations

INCONEL ALLOYS [489; 2,166]
- BT1   nickel base alloys
- BT2   nickel alloys
- BT3   alloys
- NT1   alloy-ni41fe40cr16nb3
- NT1   alloy-ni46cr23co19ti5al4
- NT1   alloy-ni47cr25co12w9fe3
- NT1   alloy-ni48co28cr15al3mo3ti2
- NT1   alloy-ni51cr48
- NT1   alloy-ni53cr19fe19nb5mo3
- NT1   alloy-ni54cr22co13mo9
- NT1   alloy-ni59cr30fe9
- NT1   alloy-ni60co15cr10al6ti5mo3
- NT1   alloy-ni61cr16co9al3ti3w3
- NT1   alloy-ni61cr22mo9nb4fe3
- NT1   alloy-ni61cr23fe14
- NT1   alloy-ni73cr15fe7ti3
- NT1   alloy-ni73cr20mn3nb3
- NT1   alloy-ni74cr13al6mo4
- NT1   alloy-ni75cr12al6mo5
- NT1   alloy-ni76cr15fe8
- NT1   alloy-ni78cr16al4
- RT   alloy-ni70mo17cr7fe5
- RT   nimonic

inconel x750
USE   alloy-ni73cr15fe7ti3

inconel 600
USE   alloy-ni76cr15fe8

inconel 601
USE   alloy-ni61cr23fe14

inconel 617
USE   alloy-ni54cr22co13mo9

inconel 625
USE   alloy-ni61cr22mo9nb4fe3

inconel 643
USE   alloy-ni47cr25co12w9fe3

inconel 671
USE   alloy-ni51cr48

inconel 690
USE   alloy-ni59cr30fe9

inconel 700
USE   alloy-ni48co28cr15al3mo3ti2

inconel 702
USE   alloy-ni78cr16al4

inconel 706
USE   alloy-ni41fe40cr16nb3

inconel 713c
USE   alloy-ni74cr13al6mo4

inconel 713lc
USE   alloy-ni75cr12al6mo5

inconel 718
USE   alloy-ni53cr19fe19nb5mo3

inconel 82
USE   alloy-ni73cr20mn3nb3

incorporation (biological)
USE   uptake

INCUBATION [660; 660]
- RT   heating
- RT   infectious diseases
- RT   latency period
- RT   quarantine
- RT   time dependence

INDAZOLES [10; 10]
- BT1   pyrazoles
- BT2   azoles
- BT3   heterocyclic compounds
- BT4   organic compounds
- BT3   organic nitrogen compounds
- BT4   organic compounds

indc
USE   international nuclear data com

INDEMNIFICATION AGREEMENTS [23; 23] *Dec 76*
(Agreements whereby the State undertakes to compensate for nuclear damage involving the civil liability of the nuclear operator.)
- BT1   agreements
- RT   liabilities
- RT   workmens compensation

INDENE [25; 25]
- BT1   condensed aromatics
- BT2   aromatics
- BT3   organic compounds
- BT1   hydrocarbons
- BT2   organic compounds

independent-particle model
USE   single-particle model

index of refraction
USE   refractive index

INDEXES [1,187; 1,187]
(Should be used to index all pieces of literature which are indexes.)
- UF   *catalogs*
- UF   *directories*
- BT1   document types
- RT   information retrieval

INDIA [1,780; 1,780]
  BT1 asia
  BT1 developing countries

INDIA INK [3; 3]
  BT1 inks
  BT1 pigments

INDIAN OCEAN [119; 153]
  BT1 seas
    BT2 surface waters
  NT1 arabian sea
  RT madagascar
  RT sri lanka
  RT tasmania

INDIAN ORGANIZATIONS [132; 361]
  BT1 national organizations
  NT1 barc
  NT1 igcar

INDIAN POINT-1 REACTOR [139; 139]
(Buchanan, New York, USA)
  UF consolidated edison thorium r.
  BT1 pwr type reactors
    BT2 enriched uranium reactors
      BT3 reactors
    BT2 power reactors
      BT3 reactors
    BT2 thermal reactors
      BT3 reactors
    BT2 water cooled reactors
      BT3 reactors
    BT2 water moderated reactors
      BT3 reactors

INDIAN POINT-2 REACTOR [171; 171]
(Buchanan, New York, USA)
  BT1 pwr type reactors
    BT2 enriched uranium reactors
      BT3 reactors
    BT2 power reactors
      BT3 reactors
    BT2 thermal reactors
      BT3 reactors
    BT2 water cooled reactors
      BT3 reactors
    BT2 water moderated reactors
      BT3 reactors

INDIAN POINT-3 REACTOR [135; 135]
(Buchanan, New York, USA)
  BT1 pwr type reactors
    BT2 enriched uranium reactors
      BT3 reactors
    BT2 power reactors
      BT3 reactors
    BT2 thermal reactors
      BT3 reactors
    BT2 water cooled reactors
      BT3 reactors
    BT2 water moderated reactors
      BT3 reactors

INDIANA [113; 113]
  BT1 usa
    BT2 developed countries
    BT2 north america

indiana university cyclotron
  USE iu cyclotron

INDICATORS [246; 816]
  NT1 bromosulfophthalein
  NT1 congo red
  NT1 eosin
  NT1 erioglaucine
  NT1 indocyanine green
  NT1 methyl orange
  NT1 methyl red
  NT1 methylthymol blue
  NT1 neutral red
  NT1 phenolphthalein
  NT1 pyrocatechol violet
  NT1 rose bengal
  NT1 xylenol orange

INDIUM [2,461; 2,461]
  BT1 metals
    BT2 elements

INDIUM ADDITIONS [407; 407]
(Alloys containing not more than 1% In are listed here.)
  RT indium alloys
  RT indium compounds

INDIUM ALLOYS [1,884; 2,096]
(Alloys containing more than 1% In.)
  BT1 alloys
  NT1 indium base alloys
  RT indium additions

indium antimonide detectors
  USE insb semiconductor detectors

INDIUM ANTIMONIDES [48; 48]
May 89
  BT1 antimonides
    BT2 antimony compounds
    BT2 pnictides
  BT1 indium compounds

INDIUM ARSENIDES [850; 850]
  BT1 arsenides
    BT2 arsenic compounds
    BT2 pnictides
  BT1 indium compounds

INDIUM BASE ALLOYS [202; 202]
  BT1 indium alloys
    BT2 alloys

INDIUM BORIDES [6; 6]
  BT1 borides
    BT2 boron compounds
  BT1 indium compounds

INDIUM BROMIDES [84; 84]
  BT1 bromides
    BT2 bromine compounds
      BT3 halogen compounds
    BT2 halides
      BT3 halogen compounds
  BT1 indium compounds

INDIUM CARBIDES [4; 4]
  BT1 carbides
    BT2 carbon compounds
  BT1 indium compounds

INDIUM CHLORIDES [266; 266]
  BT1 chlorides
    BT2 chlorine compounds
      BT3 halogen compounds
    BT2 halides
      BT3 halogen compounds
  BT1 indium compounds

INDIUM COMPLEXES [738; 738]
  BT1 complexes

INDIUM COMPOUNDS [1,865; 5,624]
  NT1 indium antimonides
  NT1 indium arsenides
  NT1 indium borides
  NT1 indium bromides
  NT1 indium carbides
  NT1 indium chlorides
  NT1 indium fluorides
  NT1 indium hydrides
  NT1 indium hydroxides
  NT1 indium iodides
  NT1 indium nitrates
  NT1 indium nitrides
  NT1 indium oxides
  NT1 indium perchlorates
  NT1 indium phosphates
  NT1 indium phosphides
  NT1 indium selenides
  NT1 indium silicates
  NT1 indium sulfates
  NT1 indium sulfides
  NT1 indium tellurides
  NT1 indium tungstates
  RT indium additions

INDIUM FLUORIDES [43; 43]
  BT1 fluorides
    BT2 fluorine compounds
      BT3 halogen compounds
    BT2 halides
      BT3 halogen compounds
  BT1 indium compounds

INDIUM HYDRIDES [6; 6]
  BT1 hydrides
    BT2 hydrogen compounds
  BT1 indium compounds

INDIUM HYDROXIDES [29; 29]
  BT1 hydroxides
    BT2 hydrogen compounds
    BT2 oxygen compounds
  BT1 indium compounds

INDIUM IODIDES [76; 76]
  BT1 indium compounds
  BT1 iodides
    BT2 halides
      BT3 halogen compounds
    BT2 iodine compounds
      BT3 halogen compounds

INDIUM IONS [243; 243]
  BT1 ions
    BT2 charged particles

INDIUM ISOTOPES [204; 5,413]
  NT1 indium 100
  NT1 indium 101
  NT1 indium 102
  NT1 indium 103
  NT1 indium 104
  NT1 indium 105
  NT1 indium 106
  NT1 indium 107
  NT1 indium 108
  NT1 indium 109
  NT1 indium 110
  NT1 indium 111
  NT1 indium 112
  NT1 indium 113
  NT1 indium 114
  NT1 indium 115
  NT1 indium 116
  NT1 indium 117
  NT1 indium 118
  NT1 indium 119
  NT1 indium 120
  NT1 indium 121
  NT1 indium 122
  NT1 indium 123
  NT1 indium 124
  NT1 indium 125
  NT1 indium 126
  NT1 indium 127
  NT1 indium 128
  NT1 indium 129
  NT1 indium 130
  NT1 indium 131
  NT1 indium 132

INDIUM NITRATES [25; 25]
  BT1 indium compounds
  BT1 nitrates
    BT2 nitrogen compounds
    BT2 oxygen compounds

INDIUM NITRIDES [23; 23]
  BT1 indium compounds
  BT1 nitrides
    BT2 nitrogen compounds
    BT2 pnictides

INDIUM OXIDES [455; 455]
BT1 indium compounds
BT1 oxides
BT2 chalcogenides
BT2 oxygen compounds

INDIUM PERCHLORATES [9; 9]
Sep 78
BT1 indium compounds
BT1 perchlorates
BT2 chlorine compounds
BT3 halogen compounds
BT2 oxygen compounds

INDIUM PHOSPHATES [20; 20] *Sep 78*
BT1 indium compounds
BT1 phosphates
BT2 oxygen compounds
BT2 phosphorus compounds

INDIUM PHOSPHIDES [1,237; 1,237]
BT1 indium compounds
BT1 phosphides
BT2 phosphorus compounds
BT2 pnictides

INDIUM SELENIDES [496; 496] *Mar 76*
BT1 indium compounds
BT1 selenides
BT2 chalcogenides
BT2 selenium compounds

INDIUM SILICATES [3; 3]
BT1 indium compounds
BT1 silicates
BT2 oxygen compounds
BT2 silicon compounds

INDIUM SULFATES [41; 41]
BT1 indium compounds
BT1 sulfates
BT2 oxygen compounds
BT2 sulfur compounds

INDIUM SULFIDES [367; 367]
BT1 indium compounds
BT1 sulfides
BT2 chalcogenides
BT2 sulfur compounds

INDIUM TELLURIDES [265; 265]
BT1 indium compounds
BT1 tellurides
BT2 chalcogenides
BT2 tellurium compounds

→ **INDIUM TUNGSTATES** [0; 0] *Sep 91*
BT1 indium compounds
BT1 tungstates
BT2 oxygen compounds
BT2 tungsten compounds
BT3 transition element compounds

INDIUM 100 [4; 4] *Jun 82*
BT1 beta-plus decay radioisotopes
BT2 beta decay radioisotopes
BT3 radioisotopes
BT4 isotopes
BT1 indium isotopes
BT1 intermediate mass nuclei
BT2 nuclei
BT1 odd-odd nuclei
BT2 nuclei

INDIUM 101 [2; 2] *Jun 88*
BT1 indium isotopes
BT1 intermediate mass nuclei
BT2 nuclei
BT1 odd-even nuclei
BT2 nuclei
BT1 seconds living radioisotopes
BT2 radioisotopes
BT3 isotopes

INDIUM 102 [9; 9] *Feb 81*
BT1 electron capture radioisotopes
BT2 beta decay radioisotopes
BT3 radioisotopes
BT4 isotopes
BT1 indium isotopes
BT1 intermediate mass nuclei
BT2 nuclei
BT1 odd-odd nuclei
BT2 nuclei
BT1 seconds living radioisotopes
BT2 radioisotopes
BT3 isotopes

INDIUM 103 [20; 20] *Nov 78*
BT1 beta-plus decay radioisotopes
BT2 beta decay radioisotopes
BT3 radioisotopes
BT4 isotopes
BT1 electron capture radioisotopes
BT2 beta decay radioisotopes
BT3 radioisotopes
BT4 isotopes
BT1 indium isotopes
BT1 intermediate mass nuclei
BT2 nuclei
BT1 minutes living radioisotopes
BT2 radioisotopes
BT3 isotopes
BT1 odd-even nuclei
BT2 nuclei

INDIUM 104 [35; 35]
BT1 beta-plus decay radioisotopes
BT2 beta decay radioisotopes
BT3 radioisotopes
BT4 isotopes
BT1 electron capture radioisotopes
BT2 beta decay radioisotopes
BT3 radioisotopes
BT4 isotopes
BT1 indium isotopes
BT1 intermediate mass nuclei
BT2 nuclei
BT1 isomeric transition isotopes
BT2 radioisotopes
BT3 isotopes
BT1 minutes living radioisotopes
BT2 radioisotopes
BT3 isotopes
BT1 odd-odd nuclei
BT2 nuclei
BT1 seconds living radioisotopes
BT2 radioisotopes
BT3 isotopes

INDIUM 105 [28; 28]
BT1 beta-plus decay radioisotopes
BT2 beta decay radioisotopes
BT3 radioisotopes
BT4 isotopes
BT1 electron capture radioisotopes
BT2 beta decay radioisotopes
BT3 radioisotopes
BT4 isotopes
BT1 indium isotopes
BT1 intermediate mass nuclei
BT2 nuclei
BT1 minutes living radioisotopes
BT2 radioisotopes
BT3 isotopes
BT1 odd-even nuclei
BT2 nuclei
BT1 seconds living radioisotopes
BT2 radioisotopes
BT3 isotopes

INDIUM 106 [41; 41]
BT1 beta-plus decay radioisotopes
BT2 beta decay radioisotopes
BT3 radioisotopes
BT4 isotopes
BT1 electron capture radioisotopes
BT2 beta decay radioisotopes
BT3 radioisotopes
BT4 isotopes
BT1 indium isotopes
BT1 intermediate mass nuclei
BT2 nuclei
BT1 minutes living radioisotopes
BT2 radioisotopes
BT3 isotopes
BT1 odd-odd nuclei
BT2 nuclei

INDIUM 107 [49; 49]
BT1 beta-plus decay radioisotopes
BT2 beta decay radioisotopes
BT3 radioisotopes
BT4 isotopes
BT1 electron capture radioisotopes
BT2 beta decay radioisotopes
BT3 radioisotopes
BT4 isotopes
BT1 indium isotopes
BT1 intermediate mass nuclei
BT2 nuclei
BT1 isomeric transition isotopes
BT2 radioisotopes
BT3 isotopes
BT1 minutes living radioisotopes
BT2 radioisotopes
BT3 isotopes
BT1 odd-even nuclei
BT2 nuclei
BT1 seconds living radioisotopes
BT2 radioisotopes
BT3 isotopes

INDIUM 108 [72; 72]
BT1 beta-plus decay radioisotopes
BT2 beta decay radioisotopes
BT3 radioisotopes
BT4 isotopes
BT1 electron capture radioisotopes
BT2 beta decay radioisotopes
BT3 radioisotopes
BT4 isotopes
BT1 indium isotopes
BT1 intermediate mass nuclei
BT2 nuclei
BT1 minutes living radioisotopes
BT2 radioisotopes
BT3 isotopes
BT1 odd-odd nuclei
BT2 nuclei

INDIUM 109 [64; 64]
BT1 beta-plus decay radioisotopes
BT2 beta decay radioisotopes
BT3 radioisotopes
BT4 isotopes
BT1 electron capture radioisotopes
BT2 beta decay radioisotopes
BT3 radioisotopes
BT4 isotopes
BT1 hours living radioisotopes
BT2 radioisotopes
BT3 isotopes
BT1 indium isotopes
BT1 intermediate mass nuclei
BT2 nuclei
BT1 isomeric transition isotopes
BT2 radioisotopes
BT3 isotopes
BT1 minutes living radioisotopes
BT2 radioisotopes
BT3 isotopes
BT1 odd-even nuclei
BT2 nuclei

INDIUM 110 [70; 70]
BT1 beta-plus decay radioisotopes
BT2 beta decay radioisotopes
BT3 radioisotopes
BT4 isotopes
BT1 electron capture radioisotopes
BT2 beta decay radioisotopes
BT3 radioisotopes
BT4 isotopes
BT1 hours living radioisotopes
BT2 radioisotopes
BT3 isotopes
BT1 indium isotopes
BT1 intermediate mass nuclei
BT2 nuclei
BT1 odd-odd nuclei
BT2 nuclei

INDIUM 110 TARGET [2; 2]
BT1 targets

INDIUM 111 [3,256; 3,256]
BT1 days living radioisotopes
  BT2 radioisotopes
    BT3 isotopes
BT1 electron capture radioisotopes
  BT2 beta decay radioisotopes
    BT3 radioisotopes
      BT4 isotopes
BT1 indium isotopes
BT1 intermediate mass nuclei
  BT2 nuclei
BT1 isomeric transition isotopes
  BT2 radioisotopes
    BT3 isotopes
BT1 minutes living radioisotopes
  BT2 radioisotopes
    BT3 isotopes
BT1 odd-even nuclei
  BT2 nuclei

INDIUM 112 [68; 68]
BT1 beta-minus decay radioisotopes
  BT2 beta decay radioisotopes
    BT3 radioisotopes
      BT4 isotopes
BT1 beta-plus decay radioisotopes
  BT2 beta decay radioisotopes
    BT3 radioisotopes
      BT4 isotopes
BT1 electron capture radioisotopes
  BT2 beta decay radioisotopes
    BT3 radioisotopes
      BT4 isotopes
BT1 indium isotopes
BT1 intermediate mass nuclei
  BT2 nuclei
BT1 internal conversion radioisoto
  BT2 radioisotopes
    BT3 isotopes
BT1 isomeric transition isotopes
  BT2 radioisotopes
    BT3 isotopes
BT1 minutes living radioisotopes
  BT2 radioisotopes
    BT3 isotopes
BT1 odd-odd nuclei
  BT2 nuclei

INDIUM 113 [922; 922]
BT1 hours living radioisotopes
  BT2 radioisotopes
    BT3 isotopes
BT1 indium isotopes
BT1 intermediate mass nuclei
  BT2 nuclei
BT1 isomeric transition isotopes
  BT2 radioisotopes
    BT3 isotopes
BT1 odd-even nuclei
  BT2 nuclei
BT1 stable isotopes
  BT2 isotopes

INDIUM 113 TARGET [94; 94]
BT1 targets

INDIUM 114 [209; 209]
BT1 beta-minus decay radioisotopes
  BT2 beta decay radioisotopes
    BT3 radioisotopes
      BT4 isotopes
BT1 beta-plus decay radioisotopes
  BT2 beta decay radioisotopes
    BT3 radioisotopes
      BT4 isotopes
BT1 days living radioisotopes
  BT2 radioisotopes
    BT3 isotopes
BT1 electron capture radioisotopes
  BT2 beta decay radioisotopes
    BT3 radioisotopes
      BT4 isotopes
BT1 indium isotopes
BT1 intermediate mass nuclei
  BT2 nuclei
BT1 internal conversion radioisoto
  BT2 radioisotopes
    BT3 isotopes
BT1 isomeric transition isotopes
  BT2 radioisotopes
    BT3 isotopes
BT1 millisec living radioisotopes
  BT2 radioisotopes
    BT3 isotopes
BT1 minutes living radioisotopes
  BT2 radioisotopes
    BT3 isotopes
BT1 odd-odd nuclei
  BT2 nuclei

INDIUM 115 [392; 392]
BT1 beta-minus decay radioisotopes
  BT2 beta decay radioisotopes
    BT3 radioisotopes
      BT4 isotopes
BT1 hours living radioisotopes
  BT2 radioisotopes
    BT3 isotopes
BT1 indium isotopes
BT1 intermediate mass nuclei
  BT2 nuclei
BT1 internal conversion radioisoto
  BT2 radioisotopes
    BT3 isotopes
BT1 isomeric transition isotopes
  BT2 radioisotopes
    BT3 isotopes
BT1 odd-even nuclei
  BT2 nuclei
BT1 years living radioisotopes
  BT2 radioisotopes
    BT3 isotopes

INDIUM 115 TARGET [349; 349]
BT1 targets

INDIUM 116 [138; 138]
BT1 beta-minus decay radioisotopes
  BT2 beta decay radioisotopes
    BT3 radioisotopes
      BT4 isotopes
BT1 indium isotopes
BT1 intermediate mass nuclei
  BT2 nuclei
BT1 internal conversion radioisoto
  BT2 radioisotopes
    BT3 isotopes
BT1 isomeric transition isotopes
  BT2 radioisotopes
    BT3 isotopes
BT1 minutes living radioisotopes
  BT2 radioisotopes
    BT3 isotopes
BT1 odd-odd nuclei
  BT2 nuclei
BT1 seconds living radioisotopes
  BT2 radioisotopes
    BT3 isotopes

INDIUM 117 [69; 69]
BT1 beta-minus decay radioisotopes
  BT2 beta decay radioisotopes
    BT3 radioisotopes
      BT4 isotopes
BT1 hours living radioisotopes
  BT2 radioisotopes
    BT3 isotopes
BT1 indium isotopes
BT1 intermediate mass nuclei
  BT2 nuclei
BT1 isomeric transition isotopes
  BT2 radioisotopes
    BT3 isotopes
BT1 minutes living radioisotopes
  BT2 radioisotopes
    BT3 isotopes
BT1 odd-even nuclei
  BT2 nuclei

INDIUM 118 [14; 14]
BT1 beta-minus decay radioisotopes
  BT2 beta decay radioisotopes
    BT3 radioisotopes
      BT4 isotopes
BT1 indium isotopes
BT1 intermediate mass nuclei
  BT2 nuclei
BT1 isomeric transition isotopes
  BT2 radioisotopes
    BT3 isotopes
BT1 minutes living radioisotopes
  BT2 radioisotopes
    BT3 isotopes
BT1 odd-odd nuclei
  BT2 nuclei
BT1 seconds living radioisotopes
  BT2 radioisotopes
    BT3 isotopes

INDIUM 119 [41; 41]
BT1 beta-minus decay radioisotopes
  BT2 beta decay radioisotopes
    BT3 radioisotopes
      BT4 isotopes
BT1 indium isotopes
BT1 intermediate mass nuclei
  BT2 nuclei
BT1 isomeric transition isotopes
  BT2 radioisotopes
    BT3 isotopes
BT1 minutes living radioisotopes
  BT2 radioisotopes
    BT3 isotopes
BT1 odd-even nuclei
  BT2 nuclei

INDIUM 120 [26; 26]
BT1 beta-minus decay radioisotopes
  BT2 beta decay radioisotopes
    BT3 radioisotopes
      BT4 isotopes
BT1 indium isotopes
BT1 intermediate mass nuclei
  BT2 nuclei
BT1 odd-odd nuclei
  BT2 nuclei
BT1 seconds living radioisotopes
  BT2 radioisotopes
    BT3 isotopes

INDIUM 121 [25; 25]
BT1 beta-minus decay radioisotopes
  BT2 beta decay radioisotopes
    BT3 radioisotopes
      BT4 isotopes
BT1 indium isotopes
BT1 intermediate mass nuclei
  BT2 nuclei
BT1 internal conversion radioisoto
  BT2 radioisotopes
    BT3 isotopes
BT1 isomeric transition isotopes
  BT2 radioisotopes
    BT3 isotopes
BT1 minutes living radioisotopes
  BT2 radioisotopes
    BT3 isotopes
BT1 odd-even nuclei
  BT2 nuclei
BT1 seconds living radioisotopes
  BT2 radioisotopes
    BT3 isotopes

INDIUM 122 [13; 13]
BT1 beta-minus decay radioisotopes
  BT2 beta decay radioisotopes
    BT3 radioisotopes
      BT4 isotopes
BT1 indium isotopes
BT1 intermediate mass nuclei
  BT2 nuclei
BT1 odd-odd nuclei
  BT2 nuclei
BT1 seconds living radioisotopes
  BT2 radioisotopes
    BT3 isotopes

INDIUM 123 [27; 27]
- BT1 beta-minus decay radioisotopes
  - BT2 beta decay radioisotopes
    - BT3 radioisotopes
      - BT4 isotopes
- BT1 indium isotopes
- BT1 intermediate mass nuclei
  - BT2 nuclei
- BT1 odd-even nuclei
  - BT2 nuclei
- BT1 seconds living radioisotopes
  - BT2 radioisotopes
    - BT3 isotopes

INDIUM 124 [17; 17]
- BT1 beta-minus decay radioisotopes
  - BT2 beta decay radioisotopes
    - BT3 radioisotopes
      - BT4 isotopes
- BT1 indium isotopes
- BT1 intermediate mass nuclei
  - BT2 nuclei
- BT1 odd-odd nuclei
  - BT2 nuclei
- BT1 seconds living radioisotopes
  - BT2 radioisotopes
    - BT3 isotopes

INDIUM 125 [12; 12]
- BT1 beta-minus decay radioisotopes
  - BT2 beta decay radioisotopes
    - BT3 radioisotopes
      - BT4 isotopes
- BT1 indium isotopes
- BT1 intermediate mass nuclei
  - BT2 nuclei
- BT1 odd-even nuclei
  - BT2 nuclei
- BT1 seconds living radioisotopes
  - BT2 radioisotopes
    - BT3 isotopes

INDIUM 126 [16; 16]
- BT1 beta-minus decay radioisotopes
  - BT2 beta decay radioisotopes
    - BT3 radioisotopes
      - BT4 isotopes
- BT1 indium isotopes
- BT1 intermediate mass nuclei
  - BT2 nuclei
- BT1 odd-odd nuclei
  - BT2 nuclei
- BT1 seconds living radioisotopes
  - BT2 radioisotopes
    - BT3 isotopes

INDIUM 127 [18; 18]
- BT1 beta-minus decay radioisotopes
  - BT2 beta decay radioisotopes
    - BT3 radioisotopes
      - BT4 isotopes
- BT1 indium isotopes
- BT1 intermediate mass nuclei
  - BT2 nuclei
- BT1 odd-even nuclei
  - BT2 nuclei
- BT1 seconds living radioisotopes
  - BT2 radioisotopes
    - BT3 isotopes

INDIUM 127 TARGET [2; 2] *Sep 79*
- BT1 targets

INDIUM 128 [16; 16]
- BT1 beta-minus decay radioisotopes
  - BT2 beta decay radioisotopes
    - BT3 radioisotopes
      - BT4 isotopes
- BT1 indium isotopes
- BT1 intermediate mass nuclei
  - BT2 nuclei
- BT1 millisec living radioisotopes
  - BT2 radioisotopes
    - BT3 isotopes
- BT1 odd-odd nuclei
  - BT2 nuclei

INDIUM 129 [16; 16]
- BT1 beta-minus decay radioisotopes
  - BT2 beta decay radioisotopes
    - BT3 radioisotopes
      - BT4 isotopes
- BT1 indium isotopes
- BT1 intermediate mass nuclei
  - BT2 nuclei
- BT1 millisec living radioisotopes
  - BT2 radioisotopes
    - BT3 isotopes
- BT1 odd-even nuclei
  - BT2 nuclei
- BT1 seconds living radioisotopes
  - BT2 radioisotopes
    - BT3 isotopes

INDIUM 130 [18; 18]
- BT1 beta-minus decay radioisotopes
  - BT2 beta decay radioisotopes
    - BT3 radioisotopes
      - BT4 isotopes
- BT1 indium isotopes
- BT1 intermediate mass nuclei
  - BT2 nuclei
- BT1 millisec living radioisotopes
  - BT2 radioisotopes
    - BT3 isotopes
- BT1 odd-odd nuclei
  - BT2 nuclei

INDIUM 131 [26; 26] *Jul 76*
- BT1 beta-minus decay radioisotopes
  - BT2 beta decay radioisotopes
    - BT3 radioisotopes
      - BT4 isotopes
- BT1 indium isotopes
- BT1 intermediate mass nuclei
  - BT2 nuclei
- BT1 millisec living radioisotopes
  - BT2 radioisotopes
    - BT3 isotopes
- BT1 odd-even nuclei
  - BT2 nuclei

INDIUM 132 [12; 12]
- BT1 beta-minus decay radioisotopes
  - BT2 beta decay radioisotopes
    - BT3 radioisotopes
      - BT4 isotopes
- BT1 indium isotopes
- BT1 intermediate mass nuclei
  - BT2 nuclei
- BT1 millisec living radioisotopes
  - BT2 radioisotopes
    - BT3 isotopes
- BT1 odd-odd nuclei
  - BT2 nuclei

INDOCYANINE GREEN [17; 17] *Oct 75*
- BT1 condensed aromatics
  - BT2 aromatics
    - BT3 organic compounds
- BT1 dyes
- BT1 indicators
- BT1 indoles
  - BT2 pyrroles
    - BT3 azoles
      - BT4 heterocyclic compounds
        - BT5 organic compounds
      - BT4 organic nitrogen compounds
        - BT5 organic compounds
- BT1 sulfonates
  - BT2 organic sulfur compounds
    - BT3 organic compounds

INDOLES [249; 1,751]
- UF *benzopyrroles*
- BT1 pyrroles
  - BT2 azoles
    - BT3 heterocyclic compounds
      - BT4 organic compounds
    - BT3 organic nitrogen compounds
      - BT4 organic compounds
- NT1 indocyanine green
- NT1 lysergic acid
- NT1 reserpine
- NT1 strychnine
- NT1 tryptamines
  - NT2 bufotenine
  - NT2 melatonin
  - NT2 serotonin
- NT1 tryptophan
- NT1 vinblastine
- RT ergotamine

INDONESIA [225; 225]
- BT1 asia
- BT1 developing countries
- BT1 islands
- RT pacific ocean

induced radioactivity
- USE radioactivity

INDUCTION [1,342; 1,448]
- NT1 faraday induction
- RT llnl advanced test accelerator

INDUCTION FURNACES [105; 105]
- BT1 electric furnaces
  - BT2 furnaces

induction logging
- USE well logging

INDUCTION WELDING [14; 14]
- BT1 welding
  - BT2 joining
    - BT3 fabrication

inductors
- USE solenoids

INDUSTRIAL ACCIDENTS [113; 113]
- BT1 accidents

INDUSTRIAL MEDICINE [195; 195]
- BT1 medicine
- RT accidents
- RT occupational diseases
- RT occupational safety
- RT radiation protection
- RT working conditions

INDUSTRIAL PLANTS [1,385; 3,809]
- UF *plants (industrial)*
- NT1 biomass conversion plants
- NT1 cimarron plutonium plant
- NT1 cimarron uranium plant
- NT1 coal gasification plants
- NT1 coking plants
- NT1 desalination plants
- NT1 feed materials plants
  - NT2 anaconda uranium mill
  - NT2 feed materials production cent
  - NT2 highland uranium mill
  - NT2 shirley basin uranium mill
  - NT2 west valley uf6 facility
- NT1 humeca uranium mill
- NT1 isotope separation plants
  - NT2 centrifuge enrichment plants
    - NT3 portsmouth centrifuge enrichme
  - NT2 gaseous diffusion plants
    - NT3 cogema pierrelatte
    - NT3 orgdp
    - NT3 paducah plant
    - NT3 portsmouth gaseous diffusion p
  - NT2 heavy water plants
  - NT2 tritium extraction plants
- NT1 sequoyah uf6 production plant
- RT fuel fabrication plants
- RT industry
- RT modular structures
- RT petroleum refineries
- RT pilot plants

INDUSTRIAL RADIOGRAPHY
[2,293; 3,256]
- UF *radiography (industrial)*
- BT1 nondestructive testing
  - BT2 materials testing
    - BT3 testing
- RT autoradiography
- RT beta radiography
- RT gamma radiography
- RT microradiography
- RT neutron radiography
- RT proton radiography
- RT radiation attenuation testing
- RT radiological personnel
- RT tomography
- RT x-ray radiography

INDUSTRIAL WASTES [447; 447]
Nov 75
- UF *municipal wastes (industrial)*
- BT1 wastes
- RT chemical effluents
- RT chemical wastes
- RT pollutants
- RT scrap

industrialized countries
- USE developed countries

INDUSTRY [2,745; 7,578]
- NT1 chemical industry
- NT1 coal industry
- NT1 fishing industry
- NT1 nuclear industry
- NT1 petroleum industry
- RT by-products
- RT commercialization
- RT developing countries
- RT economic development
- RT fuel reprocessing plants
- RT industrial plants
- RT labor relations
- RT mining
- RT technology assessment
- RT technology impacts
- RT technology transfer

inel
- USE idaho national engineering lab

inel safety res exper fac reac
- USE saref reactor

INELASTIC SCATTERING
[21,326; 28,649]
- BT1 scattering
- NT1 deep inelastic scattering
- NT1 delbrueck scattering
- NT1 resonance scattering
- NT1 thomson scattering
- RT anharmonic crystals
- RT hauser-feshbach theory
- RT incoherent scattering
- RT levinson-banerjee theory
- RT skyrme potential
- RT spin flip

INERT ATMOSPHERE [631; 1,096]
- BT1 controlled atmospheres
- NT1 cover gas
- RT carbon dioxide
- RT nitrogen
- RT rare gases

inertia
- USE moment of inertia

INERTIAL CONFINEMENT
[2,912; 2,912] *Feb 78*
(A dynamic plasma confinement by inertial forces.)
- BT1 plasma confinement
  - BT2 confinement
- RT electron beam fusion accelerat
- RT electron beam fusion reactors
- RT electron beam targets
- RT energy deposition
- RT icf devices
- RT impact fusion
- RT ion beam fusion reactors
- RT ion beam targets
- RT laser fusion reactors
- RT laser implosions
- RT laser targets
- RT particle beam fusion accelerat

inertial confinement fusion de
- USE icf devices

INERTIAL SEPARATORS [64; 127]
Oct 76
- UF *centrifugal separators*
- UF *separators (inertial)*
- BT1 separation equipment
  - BT2 equipment
- NT1 cyclone separators
- RT dust collectors
- RT pollution control equipment

INFANTS [1,768; 1,768]
- BT1 children
  - BT2 man
    - BT3 primates
      - BT4 mammals
        - BT5 vertebrates
          - BT6 animals
- RT age groups
- RT life cycle
- RT neonates

INFECTIOUS DISEASES [860; 3,201]
- BT1 diseases
- NT1 bacterial diseases
  - NT2 cholera
  - NT2 diphtheria
  - NT2 gonorrhea
  - NT2 leprosy
  - NT2 paratyphoid
  - NT2 syphilis
  - NT2 tetanus
  - NT2 tuberculosis
    - NT3 lupus
  - NT2 typhoid
- NT1 fungal diseases
  - NT2 mycoses
- NT1 parasitic diseases
  - NT2 fascioliasis
  - NT2 filariasis
  - NT2 hydatidosis
  - NT2 malaria
  - NT2 schistosomiasis
  - NT2 trichinosis
  - NT2 trypanosomiasis
- NT1 rickettsial diseases
  - NT2 typhus
- NT1 viral diseases
  - NT2 aids
  - NT2 herpes simplex
  - NT2 herpes zoster
  - NT2 influenza
  - NT2 measles
  - NT2 newcastle disease
  - NT2 poliomyelitis
  - NT2 rabies
- RT antibiotics
- RT epidemiology
- RT granulomas
- RT incubation
- RT inflammation
- RT microorganisms
- RT septicemia
- RT virulence

INFECTIVITY [381; 381]
- RT bacteria
- RT disinfectants
- RT endotoxins

infiltration (by people)
- USE human intrusion

infiltration (rock)
(Deposition in rocks of mineral matter by permeation of water carrying the matter in solution. Coordinate the descriptor below with an appropriate descriptor from the work block of ROCKS.)
- USE water influx

infiltration (water)
- USE water influx

INFLAMMATION [2,100; 2,871]
- BT1 pathological changes
  - BT2 diseases
- RT granulomas
- RT infectious diseases
- RT pneumonitis
- RT trichinosis

INFLATABLE SEALS [31; 31]
- BT1 seals

INFLATIONARY UNIVERSE [456; 456]
Jul 85
- BT1 cosmological models
  - BT2 mathematical models
- RT unified gauge models

INFLUENZA [19; 19]
- BT1 viral diseases
  - BT2 infectious diseases
    - BT3 diseases
- RT influenza viruses

INFLUENZA VIRUSES [104; 104]
- BT1 viruses
  - BT2 microorganisms
  - BT2 parasites
- RT influenza

influx (water)
- USE water influx

INFORMATION [1,350; 167,981]
- UF *recorded information*
- UF+ *information validation*
- NT1 data
  - NT2 numerical data
    - NT3 compiled data
    - NT3 evaluated data
    - NT3 experimental data
    - NT3 statistical data
    - NT3 theoretical data
- NT1 diagrams
  - NT2 argand diagrams
  - NT2 bragg curve
  - NT2 electrocardiograms
  - NT2 fermi plot
  - NT2 feynman diagram
  - NT2 flowsheets
  - NT2 goldstone diagrams
  - NT2 hertzsprung-russell diagram
  - NT2 nomograms
  - NT2 nyquist diagrams
  - NT2 optical depth curve
    - NT3 spectroscopic curve of grow
  - NT2 phase diagrams
  - NT2 s-n diagram
  - NT2 sargent diagrams
  - NT2 scatterplots
    - NT3 dalitz plot
    - NT3 prism plot
  - NT2 young diagram
- RT information theory
- RT manuals
- RT technology transfer

INFORMATION DISSEMINATION
[547; 547] *Jun 81*
- RT information needs
- RT information systems
- RT technology transfer

INFORMATION NEEDS [1,013; 1,013]
Mar 76
(Identification of subject areas or types of data on which information is needed in order to further specific areas of research. Coordinate with descriptors for the specific areas of research.)
- RT data
- RT information dissemination
- RT reporting requirements
- RT research programs

INFORMATION RETRIEVAL [945; 945]
- UF *document retrieval*
- UF *records retrieval*
- RT documentation
- RT indexes
- RT information systems
- RT standardized terminology
- RT unisist

INFORMATION SYSTEMS
[2,445; 2,756]
- NT1 agris
- NT1 cinda
- NT1 etde
- NT1 inis
- NT1 wends
- RT computer networks
- RT data base management
- RT data compilation
- RT documentation
- RT expert systems
- RT information dissemination
- RT information retrieval
- RT information theory
- RT nuclear data collections
- RT standardized terminology
- RT unisist

INFORMATION THEORY [299; 299]
- RT communications
- RT cybernetics
- RT data processing
- RT information
- RT information systems

information validation
- USE information
- AND verification

INFRARED DIVERGENCES
[1,441; 1,441]
- UF *divergences (infrared)*
- RT quantum electrodynamics

INFRARED RADIATION [4,736; 7,807]
- BT1 electromagnetic radiation
- BT2 radiations
- NT1 far infrared radiation
- NT1 intermediate infrared radiatio
- NT1 near infrared radiation
- RT infrared spectra
- RT infrared thermography
- RT thermal radiation
- RT thermography

INFRARED SPECTRA [14,053; 14,053]
- BT1 spectra
- RT absorption spectroscopy
- RT infrared radiation
- RT structural chemical analysis
- RT vibrational states

INFRARED SPECTROMETERS
[218; 282] *Feb 76*
- BT1 spectrometers
- BT2 measuring instruments
- NT1 photoacoustic spectrometers

INFRARED THERMOGRAPHY [95; 95]
Jul 78
- UF *thermal photography*
- RT infrared radiation
- RT surfaces
- RT temperature monitoring

INFUSION [347; 347]
- BT1 intake

ING LINAC [2; 2]
- UF *intense neutron generator lina*
- BT1 linear accelerators
- BT2 accelerators

INGESTION [1,408; 1,408]
- BT1 intake
- RT beverages
- RT diet
- RT digestion
- RT drinking water
- RT food
- RT intestinal absorption
- RT oral administration
- RT oral cavity

INHALATION [4,485; 4,485]
- BT1 intake
- RT aerosols
- RT air
- RT breath
- RT dusts
- RT intratracheal administration
- RT maximum inhalation quantity
- RT radionuclide administration
- RT respiration
- RT respirators
- RT respiratory system

inhalation exposure chambers
- USE exposure chambers

§ ## INHIBITION [4,296; 4,296]
- UF+ *growth inhibition*
- RT enzyme inhibitors
- RT inactivation

inhibitors (corrosion)
- USE corrosion inhibitors

inhibitors (enzyme)
- USE enzyme inhibitors

INHOMOGENEOUS FIELDS [641; 641]
- RT electric fields
- RT electromagnetic fields
- RT magnetic fields

INHOMOGENEOUS PLASMA
[2,486; 2,486]
- BT1 plasma

INHOUR EQUATION [21; 21]
- UF *nordheim equation*
- RT reactivity
- RT reactor kinetics

INHOURS [3; 3]
- BT1 reactivity units

INIS [301; 301]
- UF *internat nucl information syst*
- BT1 information systems
- RT iaea

initial reservoir pressure
- USE reservoir pressure

INJECTION [1,767; 6,799]
- BT1 intake
- NT1 intramuscular injection
- NT1 intraperitoneal injection
- NT1 intravenous injection
- NT1 subcutaneous injection
- RT radionuclide administration
- RT therapy

injection (beams)
- USE beam injection

injection (pellets)
- USE pellet injection

→ ## INJECTION WELLS [0; 0] *Oct 91*
(A well used for injecting fluids into underground strata.)
- BT1 wells

INJURIES [2,251; 11,209]
- UF *trauma*
- UF+ *traumatic shock*
- BT1 diseases
- NT1 bone fractures
- NT1 burns
- NT2 flash burns
- NT2 radiation burns
- NT1 radiation injuries
- NT2 osteoradionecrosis
- NT2 radiation burns
- NT2 radiodermatitis
- NT1 wounds
- RT accidents
- RT first aid
- RT health hazards
- RT safety
- RT single intake

INKS [39; 42]
- NT1 india ink
- RT dyes

INLAND WATERWAYS [70; 70]
- UF *canals (waterways)*
- RT harbors
- RT lakes
- RT rivers
- RT territorial waters

inner bremsstrahlung
- USE internal bremsstrahlung

INNER-SHELL EXCITATION [70; 70]
Nov 87
- BT1 excitation
- BT2 energy-level transitions
- RT inner-shell ionization

INNER-SHELL IONIZATION
[1,792; 1,792] *Jul 76*
- BT1 ionization
- RT auger effect
- RT autoionization
- RT coulomb ionization
- RT inner-shell excitation

INOCULATION [217; 217]
- RT immune serums
- RT immunity
- RT vaccines
- RT viruses

inor-8
- USE alloy-ni70mo17cr7fe5

INORGANIC ACIDS [1,006; 16,040]
- UF *acids (inorganic)*
- UF *mineral acids*
- UF+ *polythionic acids*
- BT1 hydrogen compounds
- BT1 inorganic compounds

NT1 boric acid
NT1 bromic acid
NT1 carbonic acid
NT1 chloric acid
NT1 chlorous acid
NT1 chromic acid
NT1 fluoroboric acid
NT1 hydrazoic acid
NT1 hydriodic acid
NT1 hydrobromic acid
NT1 hydrochloric acid
NT1 hydrocyanic acid
NT1 hydrofluoric acid
NT1 hypochlorous acid
NT1 hypoiodous acid
NT1 hypophosphorous acid
NT1 iodic acid
NT1 molybdophosphoric acid
NT1 nitric acid
NT1 nitrous acid
NT1 perchloric acid
NT1 periodic acid
NT1 phosphoric acid
NT1 phosphorous acid
NT1 silicic acid
NT1 sulfuric acid
NT1 sulfurous acid
NT1 telluric acid
NT1 tungstophosphoric acid
RT acid carbonates
RT acidification
RT anhydrides
RT ph value

INORGANIC COMPOUNDS [95; 4,616]
Jul 86
(For very general papers only. Use of a more specific term is recommended.)
UF compounds (inorganic)
NT1 inorganic acids
NT2 boric acid
NT2 bromic acid
NT2 carbonic acid
NT2 chloric acid
NT2 chlorous acid
NT2 chromic acid
NT2 fluoroboric acid
NT2 hydrazoic acid
NT2 hydriodic acid
NT2 hydrobromic acid
NT2 hydrochloric acid
NT2 hydrocyanic acid
NT2 hydrofluoric acid
NT2 hypochlorous acid
NT2 hypoiodous acid
NT2 hypophosphorous acid
NT2 iodic acid
NT2 molybdophosphoric acid
NT2 nitric acid
NT2 nitrous acid
NT2 perchloric acid
NT2 periodic acid
NT2 phosphoric acid
NT2 phosphorous acid
NT2 silicic acid
NT2 sulfuric acid
NT2 sulfurous acid
NT2 telluric acid
NT2 tungstophosphoric acid
NT1 inorganic phosphors

INORGANIC ION EXCHANGERS
[792; 3,164]
UF permutit (inorganic)
BT1 ion exchange materials
BT2 materials
NT1 bentonite
NT1 clinoptilolite
NT1 montmorillonite
NT1 mullite
NT1 vermiculite
NT1 zeolites

INORGANIC PHOSPHORS [477; 3,795]
BT1 inorganic compounds
BT1 phosphors
RT solid scintillation detectors

INORGANIC POLYMERS [191; 191]
BT1 polymers

INOSINE [54; 54]
BT1 nucleosides
BT2 nucleotides
BT3 organic compounds
BT2 ribosides
BT1 purines
BT2 heterocyclic compounds
BT3 organic compounds
BT2 organic nitrogen compounds
BT3 organic compounds
RT hypoxanthine

INOSITOL [183; 185]
UF i-inositol
BT1 inositols
BT2 monosaccharides
BT3 saccharides
BT4 carbohydrates
BT5 organic compounds
BT1 lipotropic factors
BT2 drugs
RT phytic acid

INOSITOLS [87; 272]
BT1 monosaccharides
BT2 saccharides
BT3 carbohydrates
BT4 organic compounds
NT1 inositol
RT hydroxy compounds

input-output analysis
(A type of economic analysis.)
USE economic analysis

INR CYCLOTRON [11; 11] *Jun 83*
(Institute of Nuclear Research, Academia Sinica, Shanghai.)
UF ins nuc res (shanghai) cyclotr
UF shanghai inr cyclotron
BT1 isochronous cyclotrons
BT2 cyclotrons
BT3 cyclic accelerators
BT4 accelerators

ins cyclotron (tokyo)
USE tokyo ins cyclotron

ins nuc res (shanghai) cyclotr
USE inr cyclotron

INSB SEMICONDUCTOR DETECTORS
[2; 2] *Apr 88*
UF indium antimonide detectors
BT1 semiconductor detectors
BT2 radiation detectors
BT3 measuring instruments

INSECT DISPERSAL [44; 44]
UF dispersal (insect)
RT behavior
RT insects
RT sterile insect release
RT sterile male technique

INSECTICIDES [380; 607]
BT1 pesticides
NT1 aldrin
NT1 ddt
NT1 dieldrin
NT1 lindane
NT1 malathion
NT1 parathion
RT insects

INSECTS [774; 2,623]
UF ants
UF bees
UF entomology
UF+ caste (insects)
BT1 arthropods
BT2 invertebrates
BT3 animals
NT1 beetles
NT2 boll weevil
NT2 tribolium
NT1 cockroaches
NT1 flies
NT2 fruit flies
NT3 ceratitis capitata
NT3 dacus
NT4 dacus oleae
NT3 drosophila
NT3 rhagoletis cerasi
NT2 glossina
NT2 hylemya antiqua
NT2 screwworm fly
NT1 grasshoppers
NT2 locusts
NT1 hemiptera
NT2 aphids
NT1 lepidoptera
NT2 moths
NT3 bollworm
NT3 codling moth
NT3 lymantria dispar
NT3 rice stem borers
NT3 silkworm
NT1 mosquitoes
NT1 wasps
NT2 habrobracon
RT chemoreceptors
RT disease vectors
RT genetic control
RT grain disinfestation
RT insect dispersal
RT insecticides
RT larvae
RT mass rearing
RT parasites
RT pest control
RT pest eradication
RT pheromone
RT pupae
RT radiodisinfestation
RT rearing
RT rickettsiae
RT royal jelly
RT sterile male technique

insolation
USE solar radiation

§ **INSPECTION** [7,231; 9,542]
UF control (inspection)
UF surveillance
NT1 in-service inspection
RT accuracy
RT audits
RT calibration
RT evaluation
RT ges fuer reaktorsicherheit
RT legal aspects
RT licensing
RT materials testing
RT nondestructive testing
RT performance testing
RT post-irradiation examination
RT preventive medicine
RT quality control
RT radiation monitoring
RT radiation protection
RT reactor maintenance
RT recommendations
RT safeguards
RT sampling
RT specifications
RT testing

inst fiziki vysokikh ehnergij
USE ihep

inst phys chem res cyclotron
USE ipcr cyclotron

inst phys chem res rilac
   USE   rilac

inst v. kernph onder amsterdam
   USE   iko

inst v. kernph onder synchrocy
   USE   iko synchrocyclotron

inst. nucl. studies cyclotron
   USE   tokyo ins cyclotron

INSTABILITY [4,291; 20,837]
   NT1   pierce instability
   NT1   plasma instability
     NT2   absolute instabilities
     NT2   convective instabilities
     NT2   decay instability
     NT2   drift instability
     NT2   explosive instability
     NT2   plasma macroinstabilities
       NT3   ballooning instability
       NT3   edge localized modes
       NT3   fishbone instability
       NT3   flute instability
       NT3   helical instability
       NT3   helmholtz instability
       NT3   kink instability
       NT3   parametric instabilities
       NT3   sausage instability
       NT3   tearing instability
       NT3   tilting instability
     NT2   plasma microinstabilities
       NT3   bump-in-tail instability
       NT3   cyclotron instability
       NT3   hose instability
       NT3   ion wave instability
       NT3   loss cone instability
       NT3   negative mass instability
       NT3   two-stream instability
       NT3   whistler instability
     NT2   trapped-particle instability
   NT1   rayleigh-taylor instability
   RT   stability

INSTABILITY GROWTH RATES
[2,090; 2,090]
   RT   plasma instability
   RT   time dependence

installation sites
(If appropriate use one of the specific types of facilities.)
   USE   nuclear facilities

INSTANTONS [1,676; 1,676] *Jan 78*
(Finite action solutions to Euclidean field equations, localized in time and space.)
   BT1   quasi particles
   RT   field equations
   RT   field theories
   RT   gauge invariance
   RT   higgs model
   RT   lattice field theory
   RT   merons
   RT   quantum chromodynamics
   RT   su groups
   RT   symmetry breaking
   RT   vacuum states
   RT   yang-mills theory

institut isotop. stral leipzig
   USE   zfi leipzig

institute for high energy phys
   USE   ihep

institute for reactor safety
   USE   ges fuer reaktorsicherheit

instituto de asuntos nucle. rl
   USE   ian-r1 reactor

instituto de energia atom. rl
   USE   iear-1 reactor

instituto de energia atom. zpr
   USE   iea-zpr reactor

instituto engen. nucl. rio r.
   USE   rien-1 reactor

instruments (measuring)
   USE   measuring instruments

insulating limiters
   USE   limiters

insulation (electr., by diel.m)
   USE   electrical insulation

insulation (electr., by mag.f.)
   USE   magnetic insulation

insulation (thermal)
   USE   thermal insulation

insulators (electrical)
   USE   electrical insulators

INSULIN [1,297; 1,297]
   BT1   peptide hormones
    BT2   hormones
   RT   diabetes mellitus
   RT   glucose
   RT   metabolism
   RT   pancreas

INSURANCE [155; 565]
   UF   health insurance
   UF   marine insurance
   UF   property insurance
   UF   transport insurance
   UF+   insurance law
   NT1   accident insurance
   NT1   nuclear insurance
   RT   accidents
   RT   financial security
   RT   hazards
   RT   legal aspects
   RT   liabilities
   RT   victims compensation

insurance law
(Prior to December 1990, this was a valid descriptor.)
   USE   insurance
   AND   legal aspects

int. maritime consultative org
   USE   imco

INTAKE [854; 13,957]
   NT1   chronic intake
   NT1   infusion
   NT1   ingestion
   NT1   inhalation
   NT1   injection
     NT2   intramuscular injection
     NT2   intraperitoneal injection
     NT2   intravenous injection
     NT2   subcutaneous injection
   NT1   oral administration
   NT1   rectal administration
   NT1   single intake
   RT   annual limit of intake
   RT   maximum permissible intake
   RT   radionuclide administration
   RT   radionuclide kinetics
   RT   uptake

INTAKE STRUCTURES [91; 91] *Jul 80*
   SF   gratings
   BT1   mechanical structures
   RT   coastal waters
   RT   cooling systems
   RT   rivers
   RT   screens
   RT   water

INTEGRAL CALCULUS [575; 575]
   UF+   residues (mathematical)
   BT1   mathematics

INTEGRAL CROSS SECTIONS
[5,939; 5,939] *May 76*
(Cross sections integrated over all angles; a measure of the reaction probability, not of the angular distribution.)
   BT1   cross sections
   RT   excitation functions
   RT   nuclear reactions

INTEGRAL DOSES [1,397; 1,397]
   BT1   radiation doses
   RT   cuex
   RT   maximum permissible exposure
   RT   spatial dose distributions
   RT   temporal dose distributions

INTEGRAL EQUATIONS [3,127; 4,699]
   BT1   equations
   NT1   blankenbecler-sugar equations
   NT1   fredholm equation
   NT1   lippmann-schwinger equation
   NT1   quasipotential equation
   NT1   volterra integral equations
   RT   differential equations
   RT   integrals
   RT   kernels
   RT   mathematics
   RT   point kernels

INTEGRAL PAC [185; 185]
   UF   perturbed ang. corr. (integr.)
   BT1   perturbed angular correlation
    BT2   angular correlation
     BT3   correlations

INTEGRAL TRANSFORMATIONS
[374; 4,650]
   BT1   transformations
   NT1   fourier transformation
   NT1   hankel transform
   NT1   hilbert transformation
   NT1   laplace transformation
   NT1   mellin transform
   RT   integrals
   RT   mathematics

INTEGRALS [2,546; 8,078]
   NT1   action integral
   NT1   collision integrals
   NT1   feynman path integral
   NT1   resonance integrals
   NT1   talmi integrals
   RT   integral equations
   RT   integral transformations
   RT   mathematics
   RT   quadratures

INTEGRATED CIRCUITS [1,928; 1,928]
   BT1   electronic circuits

INTEGRATED COOLING SYSTEMS
[128; 128]
   BT1   reactor cooling systems
    BT2   cooling systems
    BT2   reactor components

integrated utility systems
　USE　total energy systems

integrators (pulse)
　USE　pulse integrators

integrity (fuel)
　USE　fuel integrity

intense neutron generator lina
　USE　ing linac

intensifiers (image)
　USE　image intensifiers

inter-gov marit consult organ
　USE　imco

INTERACTING BOSON MODEL
[2,022; 2,022]
　BT1　shell models
　　BT2　nuclear models
　　　BT3　mathematical models
　RT　boson expansion
　RT　boson-fermion symmetry
　RT　bosons
　RT　nuclear structure

INTERACTION RANGE [3,405; 3,405]
　UF　*long range interactions*
　UF　*long-range interactions*
　UF　*short range interactions*
　UF　*short-range interactions*
　BT1　distance
　RT　interactions

INTERACTIONS [6,645; 110,531]
(For elementary particles and radiations only. See also CONFIGURATION INTERACTION.)
　NT1　configuration mixing
　NT1　electromagnetic interactions
　　NT2　compton effect
　　NT2　coulomb scattering
　　NT2　electroproduction
　*NT2　photon-hadron interactions
　　NT2　photon-photon interactions
　　NT2　photoproduction
　　　NT3　primakoff effect
　　NT2　umklapp processes
　NT1　exchange interactions
　NT1　final-state interactions
　NT1　finite-range interactions
　NT1　pairing interactions
　NT1　particle interactions
　　NT2　annihilation
　　NT2　charged-current interactions
　　NT2　coherent production
　　NT2　electron-quark interactions
　　NT2　electroproduction
　　NT2　exclusive interactions
　　　NT3　semi-exclusive interactions
　　NT2　gluon-gluon interactions
　*NT2　hadron-hadron interactions
　　NT2　inclusive interactions
　　　NT3　semi-inclusive interactions
　　NT2　incoherent production
　*NT2　lepton-hadron interactions
　*NT2　lepton-lepton interactions
　　NT2　neutral-current interactions
　*NT2　photon-hadron interactions
　*NT2　photon-lepton interactions
　　NT2　photon-photon interactions
　　NT2　photoproduction
　　　NT3　primakoff effect
　　NT2　quark-antiquark interactions
　　NT2　quark-gluon interactions
　　NT2　quark-hadron interactions
　　NT2　quark-quark interactions
　NT1　residual interactions

　NT1　strong interactions
　　NT2　charge-exchange interactions
　　NT2　peripheral collisions
　NT1　weak interactions
　　NT2　fermi interactions
　　NT2　leptonic decay
　RT　abc effect
　RT　basic interactions
　RT　beam luminosity
　RT　capture
　RT　capture-to-fission ratio
　RT　colliding beams
　RT　collisions
　RT　coupling
　RT　decay
　RT　effective range theory
　RT　interaction range
　RT　lorentz force
　RT　nuclear molecules
　RT　nucleon-nucleon potential
　RT　pomeranchuk theorem
　RT　scattering
　RT　selection rules
　RT　threshold energy
　RT　transverse momentum
　RT　wolfenstein parameters

INTERACTIVE DISPLAY DEVICES
[506; 506]
　UF　*interactive graphics*
　BT1　display devices
　　BT2　computer-graphics devices
　　BT3　computer output devices

interactive graphics
　USE　interactive display devices

INTERATOMIC DISTANCES
[3,567; 3,567]
　BT1　distance
　RT　molecular structure

INTERATOMIC FORCES [1,436; 1,436]
　RT　binding energy
　RT　buckingham potential
　RT　lennard-jones potential
　RT　morse potential
　RT　potentials

interchange instability
　USE　flute instability

intercrystalline corrosion
　USE　intergranular corrosion

INTEREM DEVICE [2; 2]
　BT1　magnetic mirrors
　　BT2　open plasma devices
　　　BT3　thermonuclear devices

INTEREST GROUPS [324; 324] *Dec 82*
(For groups formed to further a particular interest, e.g. antinuclear groups, industry groups.)
　UF　*adversaries*
　UF　*antinuclear groups*
　UF　*intervenors*
　UF　*lobbies*
　UF　*pressure groups*
　RT　human intrusion
　RT　human populations

INTERFACES [4,616; 4,728]
(Not in the sense of EQUIPMENT INTERFACES.)
　NT1　sediment-water interfaces
　RT　surfaces

interfaces (equipment)
　USE　equipment interfaces

INTERFERENCE [2,346; 2,346]
　RT　radio noise
　RT　wave propagation

INTERFERING ELEMENTS
[2,728; 2,728]
　RT　impurities

INTERFEROMETERS [1,222; 1,793]
　UF　*vlb systems*
　BT1　measuring instruments
　NT1　fabry-perot interferometer
　NT1　mach-zehnder interferometer
　NT1　michelson interferometer
　RT　interferometry
　RT　radio telescopes
　RT　spectrometers
　RT　squid devices

INTERFEROMETRY [2,443; 2,443]
　RT　interferometers

INTERFERON [335; 335]
　RT　immunity
　RT　viruses

INTERGALACTIC SPACE [862; 862]
　BT1　space
　RT　nonluminous matter
　RT　universe

INTERGOVERNMENTAL COOPERATION [50; 50] *Apr 85*
(Limited to cooperation between the national government and the government of one or more of the country's administrative subdivisions, or between the governments of some of the subdivisions. Not for INTERNATIONAL COOPERATION.)
　BT1　cooperation

INTERGRANULAR CORROSION
[1,296; 1,296]
　UF　*intercrystalline corrosion*
　BT1　corrosion
　　BT2　chemical reactions
　RT　grain boundaries

interim storage
　USE　waste storage

INTERKOSMOS SATELLITES
[179; 179]
　BT1　satellites
　RT　kosmos satellites
　RT　proton satellites

INTERLABORATORY COMPARISONS
[895; 895] *Aug 82*
　RT　calibration standards
　RT　comparative evaluations
　RT　cooperation
　RT　coordinated research programs

INTERLOCKS [57; 57] *May 86*
　RT　control systems
　RT　switches

INTERMEDIATE BOSONS [872; 6,466]
　UF　*w boson*
　UF　*weak boson*
　BT1　bosons
　BT1　elementary particles
　NT1　intermediate vector bosons
　　NT2　w minus bosons
　　NT2　w plus bosons
　　NT2　z neutral bosons

INTERMEDIATE COUPLING
[296; 4,766]
　BT1　coupling
　NT1　j-j coupling
　NT1　l-s coupling
　RT　tomonaga approximation

intermediate coupling approxim
   USE   tomonaga approximation

intermediate image spectromete
   USE   magnetic lens spectrometers

INTERMEDIATE INFRARED RADIATIO [285; 285] *May 76*
(Wave length range 2.5-50 microns)
- BT1   infrared radiation
- BT2   electromagnetic radiation
- BT3   radiations

intermediate level radioactive
(Radioactive wastes containing from 5 x 10 exp(-5) to 100 microcuries/ milliliter of radioactivity.)
   USE   intermediate-level radioactive

* INTERMEDIATE MASS NUCLEI [2,661; 126,476]
(For nuclei with mass 41-180. For specific terms, consult the Appendix.)
- BT1   nuclei
- RT   nuclear structure

INTERMEDIATE NEUTRONS [565; 565]
- BT1   neutrons
- BT2   nucleons
- BT3   baryons
- BT4   fermions
- BT4   hadrons
- BT5   elementary particles
- RT   resonance neutrons

INTERMEDIATE REACTORS [8; 29]
- BT1   epithermal reactors
- BT2   reactors
- NT1   thor reactor
- RT   resonance neutrons

INTERMEDIATE RESONANCE [334; 334]
- BT1   resonance
- RT   cross sections
- RT   intermediate structure
- RT   nuclear reactions

intermediate storage
   USE   waste storage

INTERMEDIATE STRUCTURE [562; 562]
- RT   cross sections
- RT   intermediate resonance
- RT   nuclear reactions

INTERMEDIATE VECTOR BOSONS [2,929; 4,799]
- BT1   intermediate bosons
- BT2   bosons
- BT2   elementary particles
- NT1   w minus bosons
- NT1   w plus bosons
- NT1   z neutral bosons
- RT   electron-quark interactions
- RT   weinberg angle

INTERMEDIATE-LEVEL RADIOAC-TIVE [1,921; 1,921] *May 78*
(Wastes containing from 5 x 10 exp(-5) to 100 microcuries/milliliter of radioactivity.)
- UF   *intermediate level radioactive*
- UF   *medium level wastes*
- UF   *medium-level wastes*
- BT1   radioactive wastes
- BT2   radioactive materials
- BT3   materials
- BT2   wastes
- RT   konrad ore mine

INTERMETALLIC COMPOUNDS [11,546; 11,612]
- BT1   alloys
- NT1   cementite
- RT   antimonides
- RT   arsenides
- RT   borides
- RT   laves phases
- RT   selenides
- RT   semimetals
- RT   silicides
- RT   tellurides

INTERMOLECULAR FORCES [760; 760]
- RT   binding energy
- RT   potentials
- RT   van der waals forces

INTERNAL BREMSSTRAHLUNG [247; 247]
- UF   *inner bremsstrahlung*
- BT1   bremsstrahlung
- BT2   electromagnetic radiation
- BT3   radiations

internal contamination
   USE   radionuclide kinetics

INTERNAL CONVERSION [2,558; 3,540]
- BT1   conversion
- BT1   nuclear decay
- BT2   decay
- NT1   internal pair production
- NT1   k conversion
- NT1   l conversion
- NT1   m conversion
- RT   energy levels
- RT   gamma decay
- RT   internal conversion radioisoto

* INTERNAL CONVERSION RADIOISOTO [12; 38,764]
(For specific terms, consult the Appendix.)
- BT1   radioisotopes
- BT2   isotopes
- RT   internal conversion

INTERNAL ELECTROMAGNETIC PULSE [37; 37]
- BT1   electromagnetic pulses
- BT2   electromagnetic radiation
- BT3   radiations
- RT   electron emission

INTERNAL FRICTION [1,191; 1,191]
- BT1   friction
- RT   bordoni peak
- RT   crystal defects
- RT   damping
- RT   hysteresis
- RT   viscosity

INTERNAL IONIZATION [48; 48]
- BT1   ionization
- RT   beta decay

INTERNAL IRRADIATION [3,324; 3,324]
- UF+   *absorbed fraction (internal ir*
- UF+   *effective energy (internal irr*
- BT1   irradiation
- RT   afterloading
- RT   critical organs
- RT   dose commitments
- RT   radiation source implants
- RT   radionuclide kinetics
- RT   unsealed sources

internal medicine
   USE   medicine

INTERNAL PAIR PRODUCTION [149; 149]
(Creation of an electron-positron pair by internal conversion of a nucleus with excitation of more than 1.022 MeV.)
- UF   *pair conversion*
- BT1   internal conversion
- BT2   conversion
- BT2   nuclear decay
- BT3   decay
- BT1   pair production
- BT2   particle production
- RT   electromagnetic interactions
- RT   gamma decay

INTERNAL RING DEVICES [22; 243]
- BT1   closed plasma devices
- BT2   thermonuclear devices
- NT1   fm devices
- NT1   levitron devices
- NT1   lm devices
- NT1   spherator
- NT1   stator-b device
- NT1   tokapole devices
- NT1   tornado devices
- RT   minimum average-b configuratio
- RT   multipolar configurations

internat
(See also INTERNATL.)

internat atomic energy agency
   USE   iaea

internat center theoret phys
   USE   ictp

internat comm rad units measur
   USE   icru

internat comm radiat units
   USE   icru

internat comm radiol protect
   USE   icrp

internat food irradiation proj
   USE   ifip

internat labour organisation
   USE   ilo

internat nucl information syst
   USE   inis

internat rad protection assoc
   USE   irpa

internat standard organization
   USE   iso

INTERNATIONAL AGREEMENTS [757; 1,768]
(Including agreements involving international organizations. The countries or organizations parties to the agreement are also indexed if appropriate.)
- BT1   agreements
- NT1   atomic energy agreements
- NT1   bcoclmcnm
- NT1   bcolons
- NT1   bcstpc
- NT1   bilateral agreements
- NT1   canare
- NT1   cenna
- NT1   cppnm

- NT1 iaea agreements
- NT1 lcpmpdpw
- NT1 multilateral agreements
- NT1 pcotpl
- NT1 solas convention
- NT1 vcoclnd
- RT coordinated research programs
- RT international cooperation
- RT treaties

INTERNATIONAL CONTROL
[173; 173]
- BT1 atomic energy control
- RT international cooperation

INTERNATIONAL COOPERATION
[4,242; 4,242]
(The cooperating countries or organizations are also indexed if appropriate.)
- BT1 cooperation
- RT coordinated research programs
- RT dumand project
- RT international agreements
- RT international control
- RT international organizations
- RT technology transfer

INTERNATIONAL ENERGY AGENCY
[45; 45] *Apr 77*
- UF iea
- BT1 international organizations
- RT energy policy
- RT energy shortages
- RT etde

INTERNATIONAL GEOPHYSICAL YEAR [19; 19]
- UF igy
- RT geophysics
- RT sun

INTERNATIONAL LAWS [177; 177]
(Prior to December 1990, this descriptor was spelled INTERNATIONAL LAW.)
- BT1 laws
- RT treaties

INTERNATIONAL MAGNETOSPHERIC S [55; 55] *Apr 77*
(The study covers the years 1976-1978. Prior to December 1990, this descriptor was spelled INTERNATL MAGNETOSPHERIC STUDY, and documents were indexed with this spelling.)
- UF ims
- UF internatl magnetospheric study
- RT earth magnetosphere
- RT geomagnetic field
- RT magnetopause
- RT magnetosheath
- RT magnetotail
- RT plasmapause
- RT plasmasphere

INTERNATIONAL NUCLEAR DATA COM [122; 122] *Jul 76*
- UF indc
- BT1 international organizations
- RT nuclear data collections

INTERNATIONAL ORGANIZATIONS
[438; 8,873]
- NT1 cern
- NT1 comecon
- NT1 esa
  - NT2 esro
- NT1 esarda
- NT1 eurodif
- NT1 european communities
  - NT2 common market
  - NT2 ecsc
  - NT2 euratom
- NT1 fao
- NT1 foratom
- NT1 iaea
  - NT2 ictp
  - NT2 ilmr
  - NT2 seibersdorf iaea laboratory
- NT1 icrp
- NT1 icru
- NT1 ilo
- NT1 imco
- NT1 international energy agency
- NT1 international nuclear data com
- NT1 irpa
- NT1 iso
- NT1 jinr
- NT1 nato
- NT1 oecd
  - NT2 nea
    - NT3 enea
- NT1 unido
- NT1 united nations
  - NT2 unscear
- NT1 uranium institute
- NT1 wano
- NT1 who
- RT coordinated research programs
- RT international cooperation
- RT member states
- RT national organizations

INTERNATIONAL QUIET SUN YEAR
[6; 6]
- UF iqsy
- RT sun

INTERNATIONAL REGULATIONS
[175; 188] *Jul 76*
- BT1 regulations
- BT2 laws
- NT1 oecd mcmsdrw

INTERNATIONAL SOLAR MAXIMUM YE [5; 5] *Apr 84*
(Began in October 1979. Prior to December 1990, this descriptor was spelled INTERNATL SOLAR MAXIMUM YEAR, and documents were indexed with this spelling.)
- UF internatl solar maximum year
- RT solar cycle
- RT sun

international tokamak reactor
- USE intor tokamak

internatl
(See also INTERNAT.)

internatl magnetospheric study
(Prior to December 1990, this was a valid descriptor.)
- USE international magnetospheric s

internatl solar maximum year
(Prior to December 1990, this was a valid descriptor.)
- USE international solar maximum ye

INTERPLANETARY MAGNETIC FIELDS [2,304; 2,304]
- BT1 magnetic fields
- RT interplanetary space

INTERPLANETARY SPACE
[2,490; 2,490]
- BT1 space
- RT geocorona
- RT interplanetary magnetic fields
- RT solar system
- RT zodiacal light

INTERPOLATION [672; 817]
- BT1 numerical solution
- NT1 runge-kutta method
- RT extrapolation
- RT mathematics
- RT spline functions

intersect. storage accelerator
- USE isabelle storage rings

intersecting beams
- USE colliding beams

INTERSTELLAR GRAINS [1,742; 1,742]
- BT1 particles
- RT cosmic dust
- RT cosmic gases
- RT star accretion

INTERSTELLAR MAGNETIC FIELDS
[564; 564]
- BT1 magnetic fields

INTERSTELLAR SPACE [5,548; 5,548]
- BT1 space
- RT cosmic dust
- RT cosmic gases
- RT milky way
- RT star accretion

interstitial cell stim hormone
- USE lh

INTERSTITIAL HELIUM GENERATION [244; 244] *Nov 82*
(Generation of helium in the lattice structure of structural materials due to neutron irradiation. Prior to December 1990, this concept was indexed by HELIUM GENERATION.)
- UF helium generation
- BT1 physical radiation effects
- BT2 radiation effects
- RT damaging neutron fluence

INTERSTITIAL HYDROGEN GENERATI [224; 224] *Nov 82*
(Generation of hydrogen in the lattice structure of structural materials due to neutron irradiation. Prior to December 1990, this concept was indexed by HYDROGEN GENERATION.)
- UF hydrogen generation
- BT1 physical radiation effects
- BT2 radiation effects
- RT damaging neutron fluence

INTERSTITIALS [5,062; 5,091]
- BT1 point defects
- BT2 crystal defects
- BT3 crystal structure
- NT1 i centers
- RT crowdions
- RT varley mechanism

interuniversitair reactor inst
(Delft, the Netherlands)
- USE iri

intervenors
- USE interest groups

intervertebral disks
- USE cartilage
- AND vertebrae

INTESTINAL ABSORPTION
[1,255; 1,255]
- UF absorption (intestinal)
- BT1 uptake
- RT digestion
- RT ingestion
- RT oral administration
- RT portal system
- RT rectal administration
- RT small intestine

INTESTINES [1,373; 5,743]
- BT1 gastrointestinal tract
- BT2 digestive system
- BT1 organs
- BT2 body
- NT1 large intestine
- NT2 rectum
- NT1 small intestine
- RT aerobacter
- RT ascaridae
- RT constipation
- RT crypt cells
- RT diarrhea
- RT enteritis
- RT escherichia coli
- RT paratyphoid
- RT portal system

INTOR TOKAMAK [725; 725] *Sep 80*
- UF *international tokamak reactor*
- BT1 tokamak devices
- BT2 closed plasma devices
- BT3 thermonuclear devices

INTRACELLULAR DIGESTION [15; 15]
- BT1 digestion
- RT animal cells
- RT phagocytosis

INTRAMUSCULAR INJECTION [227; 227]
- BT1 injection
- BT2 intake

intranuclear cascades
- USE nuclear cascades

INTRAPERITONEAL INJECTION [1,220; 1,220]
- BT1 injection
- BT2 intake
- RT peritoneum

INTRATRACHEAL ADMINISTRATION [206; 206]
- RT inhalation
- RT radionuclide administration
- RT trachea

INTRAVENOUS INJECTION [3,498; 3,498]
- BT1 injection
- BT2 intake
- RT veins

INTRINSIC FACTOR [36; 36]
- BT1 blood coagulation factors
- BT2 coagulants
- BT3 hematologic agents
- BT4 drugs
- BT1 mucoproteins
- BT2 polysaccharides
- BT3 saccharides
- BT4 carbohydrates
- BT5 organic compounds
- BT2 proteins
- BT3 organic compounds
- RT anemias
- RT hormones
- RT stomach
- RT vitamin b-12

intrusion (animals)
- USE biointrusion

intrusion (human)
- USE human intrusion

intrusion (plants)
- USE biointrusion

intrusion (rock)
(Process of emplacement of fluid material into pre-existing rock. Coordinate the descriptor below with other appropriate descriptor(s), e.g. POSITIONING, PETROGENESIS.)
- USE plutonic rocks

intrusion (water)
- USE water influx

intrusive rocks
(Rocks formed from emplacement of fluid material into pre-existing rock.)
- USE plutonic rocks

INULIN [157; 157]
- BT1 polysaccharides
- BT2 saccharides
- BT3 carbohydrates
- BT4 organic compounds
- RT polyacetals

INVAR [229; 229]
- BT1 iron base alloys
- BT2 iron alloys
- BT3 alloys
- BT1 nickel alloys
- BT2 alloys

INVARIANCE PRINCIPLES [2,424; 30,547]
- NT1 c invariance
- NT1 charge independence
- NT1 conformal invariance
- NT1 cp invariance
- NT1 cpt theorem
- NT1 g-parity invariance
- NT1 gauge invariance
- NT1 lorentz invariance
- NT1 p invariance
- NT1 rotational invariance
- NT1 scale invariance
- NT1 t invariance
- NT2 detailed balance principle
- RT adiabatic invariance
- RT basic interactions
- RT conservation laws
- RT goldstone bosons
- RT symmetry

INVARIANT IMBEDDING [180; 180]
- RT geometry
- RT topology
- RT transport theory

INVENTORIES [1,928; 1,928]
- UF *stockpiles*
- RT accounting
- RT availability
- RT material balance
- RT safeguards
- RT storage
- RT storage facilities

inverse pinch devices (linear)
- USE linear hard core pinch devices

INVERSE SCATTERING PROBLEM [1,137; 1,137]
(Problem of determining scattering potential from phase shifts.)
- RT scattering

inversions (temperature)
- USE temperature inversions

INVERTEBRATES [172; 5,524]
- BT1 animals
- NT1 annelids
- NT1 arthropods
- NT2 arachnids
- NT3 mites
- NT3 scorpions
- NT3 spiders
- NT3 ticks
- NT2 crustaceans
- NT3 artemia
- NT3 daphnia
- NT3 lobsters
- NT3 prawns
- NT3 shrimp
- NT2 insects
- NT3 beetles
- NT4 boll weevil
- NT4 tribolium
- NT3 cockroaches
- NT3 flies
- NT4 fruit flies
- NT5 ceratitis capitata
- NT5 dacus
- NT6 dacus oleae
- NT5 drosophila
- NT5 rhagoletis cerasi
- NT4 glossina
- NT4 hylemya antiqua
- NT4 screwworm fly
- NT3 grasshoppers
- NT4 locusts
- NT3 hemiptera
- NT4 aphids
- NT3 lepidoptera
- NT4 moths
- NT5 bollworm
- NT5 codling moth
- NT5 lymantria dispar
- NT5 rice stem borers
- NT5 silkworm
- NT3 mosquitoes
- NT3 wasps
- NT4 habrobracon
- NT1 coelenterata
- NT2 cnidaria
- NT3 corals
- NT3 hydra
- NT1 echinoderms
- NT2 sea urchins
- NT1 molluscs
- NT2 clams
- NT2 oysters
- NT2 snails
- NT1 nematodes
- NT2 ascaridae
- NT3 ascaris
- NT2 dictyocaulus
- NT2 hookworm
- NT2 nippostrongylus
- NT2 syngamus
- NT2 trichinella
- NT1 platyhelminths
- NT2 cestodes
- NT3 hymenolepis
- NT2 trematodes
- NT3 fasciola
- NT3 schistosoma
- NT2 turbellaria
- NT3 planaria
- NT1 protozoa
- NT2 amoeba
- NT2 babesidae
- NT2 dinoflagellate
- NT2 paramecium
- NT2 plasmodium
- NT2 tetrahymena
- NT2 trypanosoma

INVERTERS [98; 98] *Sep 76*
(Excludes AC to DC converters for which use RECTIFIERS.)
- UF *dc to ac inverters*
- BT1 electrical equipment
- BT2 equipment
- RT dc to dc converters
- RT power conditioning circuits
- RT power supplies

INVESTMENT [1,056; 1,056]
- RT capital
- RT economics
- RT payback period

inviscid flow
  USE   ideal flow

INVOICES [0; 0]
  RT   accounting
  RT   charges

IODATES [518; 518]
(Specific compounds should be indexed by coordination of a descriptor of the form (CATION) COMPOUNDS and the above anion descriptor.)
  BT1   iodine compounds
    BT2   halogen compounds
  BT1   oxygen compounds
  RT   iodic acid

IODIC ACID [120; 120]
  BT1   inorganic acids
    BT2   hydrogen compounds
    BT2   inorganic compounds
  BT1   iodine compounds
    BT2   halogen compounds
  BT1   oxygen compounds
  RT   iodates

IODIDES [1,213; 6,283]
  BT1   halides
    BT2   halogen compounds
  BT1   iodine compounds
    BT2   halogen compounds
  NT1   aluminium iodides
  NT1   americium iodides
  NT1   antimony iodides
  NT1   argon iodides
  NT1   arsenic iodides
  NT1   astatine iodides
  NT1   barium iodides
  NT1   berkelium iodides
  NT1   beryllium iodides
  NT1   bismuth iodides
  NT1   boron iodides
  NT1   cadmium iodides
  NT1   calcium iodides
  NT1   californium iodides
  NT1   cerium iodides
  NT1   cesium iodides
  NT1   chromium iodides
  NT1   cobalt iodides
  NT1   copper iodides
  NT1   curium iodides
  NT1   dysprosium iodides
  NT1   einsteinium iodides
  NT1   erbium iodides
  NT1   europium iodides
  NT1   fermium iodides
  NT1   francium iodides
  NT1   gadolinium iodides
  NT1   gallium iodides
  NT1   germanium iodides
  NT1   gold iodides
  NT1   hafnium iodides
  NT1   holmium iodides
  NT1   indium iodides
  NT1   iron iodides
  NT1   lanthanum iodides
  NT1   lead iodides
  NT1   lithium iodides
  NT1   lutetium iodides
  NT1   magnesium iodides
  NT1   manganese iodides
  NT1   mercury iodides
  NT1   molybdenum iodides
  NT1   neodymium iodides
  NT1   neon iodides
  NT1   neptunium iodides
  NT1   nickel iodides
  NT1   niobium iodides
  NT1   nitrogen iodides
  NT1   palladium iodides
  NT1   phosphorus iodides
  NT1   platinum iodides
  NT1   plutonium iodides
  NT1   polonium iodides
  NT1   potassium iodides
  NT1   praseodymium iodides
  NT1   promethium iodides
  NT1   protactinium iodides
  NT1   rhenium iodides
  NT1   rubidium iodides
  NT1   samarium iodides
  NT1   scandium iodides
  NT1   selenium iodides
  NT1   silicon iodides
  NT1   silver iodides
  NT1   sodium iodides
  NT1   strontium iodides
  NT1   tantalum iodides
  NT1   technetium iodides
  NT1   tellurium iodides
  NT1   terbium iodides
  NT1   thallium iodides
  NT1   thorium iodides
  NT1   thulium iodides
  NT1   tin iodides
  NT1   titanium iodides
  NT1   tungsten iodides
  NT1   uranium iodides
  NT1   vanadium iodides
  NT1   xenon iodides
  NT1   ytterbium iodides
  NT1   yttrium iodides
  NT1   zinc iodides
  NT1   zirconium iodides
  RT   hydriodic acid
  RT   iodine additions
  RT   oxyiodides

→ **IODINATED ALIPHATIC HYDROCARBO** [0; 0]
(Prior to October 1991, this concept was indexed by ORGANIC IODINE COMPOUNDS.)
  BT1   halogenated aliphatic hydrocar
    BT2   organic halogen compounds
      BT3   organic compounds
  BT1   organic iodine compounds
    BT2   organic halogen compounds
      BT3   organic compounds

→ **IODINATED AROMATIC HYDROCARBON** [0; 0] *Oct 91*
  BT1   halogenated aromatic hydrocarb
    BT2   aromatics
      BT3   organic compounds
    BT2   organic halogen compounds
      BT3   organic compounds
  BT1   organic iodine compounds
    BT2   organic halogen compounds
      BT3   . organic compounds

iodinated hydrocarbons
  USE   organic iodine compounds

IODINATION [810; 810]
  BT1   halogenation
    BT2   chemical reactions
  RT   deiodination

IODINE [4,115; 4,115]
  UF   *iodine iodides*
  BT1   halogens
    BT2   nonmetals
      BT3   elements
  RT   iodox process
  RT   lugol
  RT   thyroglobulin
  RT   thyroid
  RT   thyroid hormones

IODINE ADDITIONS [54; 54] *Jul 76*
  RT   crystal doping
  RT   doped materials
  RT   iodides

IODINE BROMIDES [45; 45]
  UF   *bromine iodides*
  BT1   bromides
    BT2   bromine compounds
      BT3   halogen compounds
    BT2   halides
      BT3   halogen compounds
  BT1   iodine compounds
    BT2   halogen compounds

IODINE CHLORIDES [119; 119]
  UF   *chlorine iodides*
  BT1   chlorides
    BT2   chlorine compounds
      BT3   halogen compounds
    BT2   halides
      BT3   halogen compounds
  BT1   iodine compounds
    BT2   halogen compounds

IODINE COMPLEXES [193; 193]
  BT1   complexes

IODINE COMPOUNDS [807; 7,600]
  BT1   halogen compounds
  NT1   hydriodic acid
  NT1   hypoiodous acid
  NT1   iodates
  NT1   iodic acid
*NT1   iodides
  NT1   iodine bromides
  NT1   iodine chlorides
  NT1   iodine fluorides
  NT1   iodine oxides
  NT1   oxyiodides
  NT1   periodates
  NT1   periodic acid
  RT   organic iodine compounds

IODINE FLUORIDES [44; 44]
  UF   *fluorine iodides*
  BT1   fluorides
    BT2   fluorine compounds
      BT3   halogen compounds
    BT2   halides
      BT3   halogen compounds
  BT1   iodine compounds
    BT2   halogen compounds

iodine iodides
  USE   iodine

IODINE IONS [358; 358]
  BT1   ions
    BT2   charged particles

IODINE ISOTOPES [1,201; 24,234]
  NT1   iodine 108
  NT1   iodine 109
  NT1   iodine 110
  NT1   iodine 111
  NT1   iodine 112
  NT1   iodine 113
  NT1   iodine 114
  NT1   iodine 115
  NT1   iodine 116
  NT1   iodine 117
  NT1   iodine 118
  NT1   iodine 119
  NT1   iodine 120
  NT1   iodine 121
  NT1   iodine 122
  NT1   iodine 123
  NT1   iodine 124
  NT1   iodine 125
  NT1   iodine 126
  NT1   iodine 127
  NT1   iodine 128
  NT1   iodine 129
  NT1   iodine 130
  NT1   iodine 131
  NT1   iodine 132
  NT1   iodine 133
  NT1   iodine 134
  NT1   iodine 135
  NT1   iodine 136
  NT1   iodine 137
  NT1   iodine 138
  NT1   iodine 139
  NT1   iodine 140
  NT1   iodine 141
  NT1   iodine 142

IODINE OXIDES [44; 44]
  BT1 iodine compounds
    BT2 halogen compounds
  BT1 oxides
    BT2 chalcogenides
    BT2 oxygen compounds
  RT   oxyiodides

IODINE 108 [2; 2] *Mar 91*
  BT1 intermediate mass nuclei
    BT2 nuclei
  BT1 iodine isotopes
  BT1 odd-odd nuclei
    BT2 nuclei

IODINE 109 [20; 20] *Jun 84*
  BT1 intermediate mass nuclei
    BT2 nuclei
  BT1 iodine isotopes
  BT1 odd-even nuclei
    BT2 nuclei
  BT1 proton decay radioisotopes
    BT2 radioisotopes
      BT3 isotopes

IODINE 110 [18; 18] *Feb 78*
  BT1 beta-plus decay radioisotopes
    BT2 beta decay radioisotopes
      BT3 radioisotopes
        BT4 isotopes
  BT1 electron capture radioisotopes
    BT2 beta decay radioisotopes
      BT3 radioisotopes
        BT4 isotopes
  BT1 intermediate mass nuclei
    BT2 nuclei
  BT1 iodine isotopes
  BT1 millisec living radioisotopes
    BT2 radioisotopes
      BT3 isotopes
  BT1 odd-odd nuclei
    BT2 nuclei

IODINE 111 [12; 12] *Feb 78*
  BT1 alpha decay radioisotopes
    BT2 radioisotopes
      BT3 isotopes
  BT1 beta-plus decay radioisotopes
    BT2 beta decay radioisotopes
      BT3 radioisotopes
        BT4 isotopes
  BT1 electron capture radioisotopes
    BT2 beta decay radioisotopes
      BT3 radioisotopes
        BT4 isotopes
  BT1 intermediate mass nuclei
    BT2 nuclei
  BT1 iodine isotopes
  BT1 odd-even nuclei
    BT2 nuclei
  BT1 seconds living radioisotopes
    BT2 radioisotopes
      BT3 isotopes

IODINE 112 [15; 15] *Feb 78*
  BT1 beta-plus decay radioisotopes
    BT2 beta decay radioisotopes
      BT3 radioisotopes
        BT4 isotopes
  BT1 electron capture radioisotopes
    BT2 beta decay radioisotopes
      BT3 radioisotopes
        BT4 isotopes
  BT1 intermediate mass nuclei
    BT2 nuclei
  BT1 iodine isotopes
  BT1 odd-odd nuclei
    BT2 nuclei
  BT1 seconds living radioisotopes
    BT2 radioisotopes
      BT3 isotopes

IODINE 113 [14; 14] *Feb 78*
  BT1 beta-plus decay radioisotopes
    BT2 beta decay radioisotopes
      BT3 radioisotopes
        BT4 isotopes
  BT1 electron capture radioisotopes
    BT2 beta decay radioisotopes
      BT3 radioisotopes
        BT4 isotopes
  BT1 intermediate mass nuclei
    BT2 nuclei
  BT1 iodine isotopes
  BT1 odd-even nuclei
    BT2 nuclei
  BT1 seconds living radioisotopes
    BT2 radioisotopes
      BT3 isotopes

IODINE 114 [4; 4] *Feb 78*
  BT1 beta-plus decay radioisotopes
    BT2 beta decay radioisotopes
      BT3 radioisotopes
        BT4 isotopes
  BT1 electron capture radioisotopes
    BT2 beta decay radioisotopes
      BT3 radioisotopes
        BT4 isotopes
  BT1 intermediate mass nuclei
    BT2 nuclei
  BT1 iodine isotopes
  BT1 odd-odd nuclei
    BT2 nuclei
  BT1 seconds living radioisotopes
    BT2 radioisotopes
      BT3 isotopes

IODINE 115 [10; 10] *Jul 78*
  BT1 beta-plus decay radioisotopes
    BT2 beta decay radioisotopes
      BT3 radioisotopes
        BT4 isotopes
  BT1 electron capture radioisotopes
    BT2 beta decay radioisotopes
      BT3 radioisotopes
        BT4 isotopes
  BT1 intermediate mass nuclei
    BT2 nuclei
  BT1 iodine isotopes
  BT1 minutes living radioisotopes
    BT2 radioisotopes
      BT3 isotopes
  BT1 odd-even nuclei
    BT2 nuclei

IODINE 116 [7; 7]
  BT1 beta-plus decay radioisotopes
    BT2 beta decay radioisotopes
      BT3 radioisotopes
        BT4 isotopes
  BT1 electron capture radioisotopes
    BT2 beta decay radioisotopes
      BT3 radioisotopes
        BT4 isotopes
  BT1 intermediate mass nuclei
    BT2 nuclei
  BT1 iodine isotopes
  BT1 isomeric transition isotopes
    BT2 radioisotopes
      BT3 isotopes
  BT1 microsec living radioisotopes
    BT2 radioisotopes
      BT3 isotopes
  BT1 odd-odd nuclei
    BT2 nuclei
  BT1 seconds living radioisotopes
    BT2 radioisotopes
      BT3 isotopes

IODINE 117 [18; 18]
  BT1 beta-plus decay radioisotopes
    BT2 beta decay radioisotopes
      BT3 radioisotopes
        BT4 isotopes
  BT1 electron capture radioisotopes
    BT2 beta decay radioisotopes
      BT3 radioisotopes
        BT4 isotopes
  BT1 intermediate mass nuclei
    BT2 nuclei
  BT1 iodine isotopes
  BT1 minutes living radioisotopes
    BT2 radioisotopes
      BT3 isotopes
  BT1 odd-even nuclei
    BT2 nuclei

IODINE 118 [11; 11]
  BT1 beta-plus decay radioisotopes
    BT2 beta decay radioisotopes
      BT3 radioisotopes
        BT4 isotopes
  BT1 electron capture radioisotopes
    BT2 beta decay radioisotopes
      BT3 radioisotopes
        BT4 isotopes
  BT1 intermediate mass nuclei
    BT2 nuclei
  BT1 iodine isotopes
  BT1 minutes living radioisotopes
    BT2 radioisotopes
      BT3 isotopes
  BT1 odd-odd nuclei
    BT2 nuclei

IODINE 119 [19; 19]
  BT1 beta-plus decay radioisotopes
    BT2 beta decay radioisotopes
      BT3 radioisotopes
        BT4 isotopes
  BT1 electron capture radioisotopes
    BT2 beta decay radioisotopes
      BT3 radioisotopes
        BT4 isotopes
  BT1 intermediate mass nuclei
    BT2 nuclei
  BT1 iodine isotopes
  BT1 minutes living radioisotopes
    BT2 radioisotopes
      BT3 isotopes
  BT1 odd-even nuclei
    BT2 nuclei

IODINE 120 [16; 16]
  BT1 beta-plus decay radioisotopes
    BT2 beta decay radioisotopes
      BT3 radioisotopes
        BT4 isotopes
  BT1 electron capture radioisotopes
    BT2 beta decay radioisotopes
      BT3 radioisotopes
        BT4 isotopes
  BT1 hours living radioisotopes
    BT2 radioisotopes
      BT3 isotopes
  BT1 intermediate mass nuclei
    BT2 nuclei
  BT1 iodine isotopes
  BT1 minutes living radioisotopes
    BT2 radioisotopes
      BT3 isotopes
  BT1 odd-odd nuclei
    BT2 nuclei

IODINE 121 [62; 62]
  BT1 beta-plus decay radioisotopes
    BT2 beta decay radioisotopes
      BT3 radioisotopes
        BT4 isotopes
  BT1 electron capture radioisotopes
    BT2 beta decay radioisotopes
      BT3 radioisotopes
        BT4 isotopes
  BT1 hours living radioisotopes
    BT2 radioisotopes
      BT3 isotopes
  BT1 intermediate mass nuclei
    BT2 nuclei
  BT1 iodine isotopes
  BT1 isomeric transition isotopes
    BT2 radioisotopes
      BT3 isotopes
  BT1 microsec living radioisotopes
    BT2 radioisotopes
      BT3 isotopes
  BT1 odd-even nuclei
    BT2 nuclei

IODINE 122 [58; 58]
  BT1 beta-plus decay radioisotopes
    BT2 beta decay radioisotopes
      BT3 radioisotopes
        BT4 isotopes
  BT1 electron capture radioisotopes
    BT2 beta decay radioisotopes
      BT3 radioisotopes

IODINE 122
- BT4 isotopes
- BT1 intermediate mass nuclei
- BT2 nuclei
- BT1 iodine isotopes
- BT1 isomeric transition isotopes
- BT2 radioisotopes
- BT3 isotopes
- BT1 microsec living radioisotopes
- BT2 radioisotopes
- BT3 isotopes
- BT1 minutes living radioisotopes
- BT2 radioisotopes
- BT3 isotopes
- BT1 odd-odd nuclei
- BT2 nuclei

IODINE 123 [2,575; 2,575]
- BT1 electron capture radioisotopes
- BT2 beta decay radioisotopes
- BT3 radioisotopes
- BT4 isotopes
- BT1 hours living radioisotopes
- BT2 radioisotopes
- BT3 isotopes
- BT1 intermediate mass nuclei
- BT2 nuclei
- BT1 iodine isotopes
- BT1 odd-even nuclei
- BT2 nuclei

IODINE 124 [104; 104]
- BT1 beta-plus decay radioisotopes
- BT2 beta decay radioisotopes
- BT3 radioisotopes
- BT4 isotopes
- BT1 days living radioisotopes
- BT2 radioisotopes
- BT3 isotopes
- BT1 electron capture radioisotopes
- BT2 beta decay radioisotopes
- BT3 radioisotopes
- BT4 isotopes
- BT1 intermediate mass nuclei
- BT2 nuclei
- BT1 iodine isotopes
- BT1 odd-odd nuclei
- BT2 nuclei

IODINE 125 [9,922; 9,922]
- BT1 days living radioisotopes
- BT2 radioisotopes
- BT3 isotopes
- BT1 electron capture radioisotopes
- BT2 beta decay radioisotopes
- BT3 radioisotopes
- BT4 isotopes
- BT1 intermediate mass nuclei
- BT2 nuclei
- BT1 internal conversion radioisoto
- BT2 radioisotopes
- BT3 isotopes
- BT1 iodine isotopes
- BT1 odd-even nuclei
- BT2 nuclei

IODINE 126 [74; 74]
- BT1 beta-minus decay radioisotopes
- BT2 beta decay radioisotopes
- BT3 radioisotopes
- BT4 isotopes
- BT1 beta-plus decay radioisotopes
- BT2 beta decay radioisotopes
- BT3 radioisotopes
- BT4 isotopes
- BT1 days living radioisotopes
- BT2 radioisotopes
- BT3 isotopes
- BT1 electron capture radioisotopes
- BT2 beta decay radioisotopes
- BT3 radioisotopes
- BT4 isotopes
- BT1 intermediate mass nuclei
- BT2 nuclei
- BT1 iodine isotopes
- BT1 odd-odd nuclei
- BT2 nuclei

IODINE 127 [525; 525]
- BT1 intermediate mass nuclei
- BT2 nuclei
- BT1 iodine isotopes
- BT1 odd-even nuclei
- BT2 nuclei
- BT1 stable isotopes
- BT2 isotopes

IODINE 127 BEAMS [49; 49] *Apr 79*
- BT1 ion beams
- BT2 beams

IODINE 127 REACTIONS [12; 12] *May 84*
- BT1 heavy ion reactions
- BT2 nuclear reactions

IODINE 127 TARGET [170; 170]
- BT1 targets

IODINE 128 [210; 210]
- BT1 beta-minus decay radioisotopes
- BT2 beta decay radioisotopes
- BT3 radioisotopes
- BT4 isotopes
- BT1 beta-plus decay radioisotopes
- BT2 beta decay radioisotopes
- BT3 radioisotopes
- BT4 isotopes
- BT1 electron capture radioisotopes
- BT2 beta decay radioisotopes
- BT3 radioisotopes
- BT4 isotopes
- BT1 intermediate mass nuclei
- BT2 nuclei
- BT1 iodine isotopes
- BT1 minutes living radioisotopes
- BT2 radioisotopes
- BT3 isotopes
- BT1 odd-odd nuclei
- BT2 nuclei

IODINE 128 TARGET [2; 2] *Jul 84*
- BT1 targets

IODINE 129 [1,270; 1,270]
- BT1 beta-minus decay radioisotopes
- BT2 beta decay radioisotopes
- BT3 radioisotopes
- BT4 isotopes
- BT1 intermediate mass nuclei
- BT2 nuclei
- BT1 internal conversion radioisoto
- BT2 radioisotopes
- BT3 isotopes
- BT1 iodine isotopes
- BT1 odd-even nuclei
- BT2 nuclei
- BT1 years living radioisotopes
- BT2 radioisotopes
- BT3 isotopes

IODINE 129 TARGET [22; 22]
- BT1 targets

IODINE 130 [85; 85]
- BT1 beta-minus decay radioisotopes
- BT2 beta decay radioisotopes
- BT3 radioisotopes
- BT4 isotopes
- BT1 hours living radioisotopes
- BT2 radioisotopes
- BT3 isotopes
- BT1 intermediate mass nuclei
- BT2 nuclei
- BT1 internal conversion radioisoto
- BT2 radioisotopes
- BT3 isotopes
- BT1 iodine isotopes
- BT1 isomeric transition isotopes
- BT2 radioisotopes
- BT3 isotopes
- BT1 minutes living radioisotopes
- BT2 radioisotopes
- BT3 isotopes
- BT1 odd-odd nuclei
- BT2 nuclei

IODINE 131 [9,832; 9,832]
- BT1 beta-minus decay radioisotopes
- BT2 beta decay radioisotopes
- BT3 radioisotopes
- BT4 isotopes
- BT1 days living radioisotopes
- BT2 radioisotopes
- BT3 isotopes
- BT1 intermediate mass nuclei
- BT2 nuclei
- BT1 iodine isotopes
- BT1 odd-even nuclei
- BT2 nuclei

IODINE 132 [219; 219]
- BT1 beta-minus decay radioisotopes
- BT2 beta decay radioisotopes
- BT3 radioisotopes
- BT4 isotopes
- BT1 hours living radioisotopes
- BT2 radioisotopes
- BT3 isotopes
- BT1 intermediate mass nuclei
- BT2 nuclei
- BT1 internal conversion radioisoto
- BT2 radioisotopes
- BT3 isotopes
- BT1 iodine isotopes
- BT1 isomeric transition isotopes
- BT2 radioisotopes
- BT3 isotopes
- BT1 odd-odd nuclei
- BT2 nuclei

IODINE 133 [190; 190]
- BT1 beta-minus decay radioisotopes
- BT2 beta decay radioisotopes
- BT3 radioisotopes
- BT4 isotopes
- BT1 hours living radioisotopes
- BT2 radioisotopes
- BT3 isotopes
- BT1 intermediate mass nuclei
- BT2 nuclei
- BT1 internal conversion radioisoto
- BT2 radioisotopes
- BT3 isotopes
- BT1 iodine isotopes
- BT1 isomeric transition isotopes
- BT2 radioisotopes
- BT3 isotopes
- BT1 odd-even nuclei
- BT2 nuclei
- BT1 seconds living radioisotopes
- BT2 radioisotopes
- BT3 isotopes

IODINE 134 [89; 89]
- BT1 beta-minus decay radioisotopes
- BT2 beta decay radioisotopes
- BT3 radioisotopes
- BT4 isotopes
- BT1 intermediate mass nuclei
- BT2 nuclei
- BT1 iodine isotopes
- BT1 isomeric transition isotopes
- BT2 radioisotopes
- BT3 isotopes
- BT1 minutes living radioisotopes
- BT2 radioisotopes
- BT3 isotopes
- BT1 odd-odd nuclei
- BT2 nuclei

IODINE 135 [185; 185]
- BT1 beta-minus decay radioisotopes
- BT2 beta decay radioisotopes
- BT3 radioisotopes
- BT4 isotopes
- BT1 hours living radioisotopes
- BT2 radioisotopes
- BT3 isotopes
- BT1 intermediate mass nuclei
- BT2 nuclei
- BT1 iodine isotopes
- BT1 odd-even nuclei

IODINE 136 [34; 34]
BT1 beta-minus decay radioisotopes
BT2 beta decay radioisotopes
BT3 radioisotopes
BT4 isotopes
BT1 intermediate mass nuclei
BT2 nuclei
BT1 iodine isotopes
BT1 minutes living radioisotopes
BT2 radioisotopes
BT3 isotopes
BT1 odd-odd nuclei
BT2 nuclei
BT1 seconds living radioisotopes
BT2 radioisotopes
BT3 isotopes

IODINE 137 [74; 74]
BT1 beta-minus decay radioisotopes
BT2 beta decay radioisotopes
BT3 radioisotopes
BT4 isotopes
BT1 intermediate mass nuclei
BT2 nuclei
BT1 iodine isotopes
BT1 odd-even nuclei
BT2 nuclei
BT1 seconds living radioisotopes
BT2 radioisotopes
BT3 isotopes

IODINE 138 [31; 31]
BT1 beta-minus decay radioisotopes
BT2 beta decay radioisotopes
BT3 radioisotopes
BT4 isotopes
BT1 intermediate mass nuclei
BT2 nuclei
BT1 iodine isotopes
BT1 odd-odd nuclei
BT2 nuclei
BT1 seconds living radioisotopes
BT2 radioisotopes
BT3 isotopes

IODINE 139 [25; 25]
BT1 beta-minus decay radioisotopes
BT2 beta decay radioisotopes
BT3 radioisotopes
BT4 isotopes
BT1 intermediate mass nuclei
BT2 nuclei
BT1 iodine isotopes
BT1 odd-even nuclei
BT2 nuclei
BT1 seconds living radioisotopes
BT2 radioisotopes
BT3 isotopes

IODINE 140 [19; 19]
BT1 beta-minus decay radioisotopes
BT2 beta decay radioisotopes
BT3 radioisotopes
BT4 isotopes
BT1 intermediate mass nuclei
BT2 nuclei
BT1 iodine isotopes
BT1 millisec living radioisotopes
BT2 radioisotopes
BT3 isotopes
BT1 odd-odd nuclei
BT2 nuclei

IODINE 141 [15; 15]
BT1 beta-minus decay radioisotopes
BT2 beta decay radioisotopes
BT3 radioisotopes
BT4 isotopes
BT1 intermediate mass nuclei
BT2 nuclei
BT1 iodine isotopes
BT1 millisec living radioisotopes
BT2 radioisotopes
BT3 isotopes
BT1 odd-even nuclei
BT2 nuclei

IODINE 142 [0; 0] Apr 86
BT1 beta-minus decay radioisotopes
BT2 beta decay radioisotopes
BT3 radioisotopes
BT4 isotopes
BT1 intermediate mass nuclei
BT2 nuclei
BT1 iodine isotopes
BT1 millisec living radioisotopes
BT2 radioisotopes
BT3 isotopes
BT1 odd-odd nuclei
BT2 nuclei

IODOCHLOROQUINE [4; 4] Aug 81
BT1 organic chlorine compounds
BT2 organic halogen compounds
BT3 organic compounds
BT1 organic iodine compounds
BT2 organic halogen compounds
BT3 organic compounds
RT radiopharmaceuticals

IODODEOXYURIDINE [236; 236]
UF iudr
BT1 iodouracils
BT2 antimetabolites
BT3 drugs
BT2 organic iodine compounds
BT3 organic halogen compounds
BT4 organic compounds
BT2 uracils
BT3 hydroxy compounds
BT4 organic compounds
BT3 pyrimidines
BT4 azines
BT5 heterocyclic compounds
BT6 organic compounds
BT5 organic nitrogen compounds
BT6 organic compounds
BT1 nucleosides
BT2 nucleotides
BT3 organic compounds
BT2 ribosides
RT deoxyuridine

IODOFORM [20; 20]
BT1 organic iodine compounds
BT2 organic halogen compounds
BT3 organic compounds
RT hydrocarbons
RT methane

iodohippurate
USE hippuran

IODOMETRY [64; 64]
BT1 titration
RT quantitative chemical analysis

iodopyracet
USE diodrast

IODOURACILS [59; 293]
BT1 antimetabolites
BT2 drugs
BT1 organic iodine compounds
BT2 organic halogen compounds
BT3 organic compounds
BT1 uracils
BT2 hydroxy compounds
BT3 organic compounds
BT2 pyrimidines
BT3 azines
BT4 heterocyclic compounds
BT5 organic compounds
BT4 organic nitrogen compounds
BT5 organic compounds
NT1 iododeoxyuridine

IODOX PROCESS [36; 36]
BT1 reprocessing
BT2 separation processes
RT iodine
RT methyl iodide

IOGLYCAMIC ACID [16; 16] Oct 75
BT1 acetamide
BT2 amides
BT3 organic nitrogen compounds
BT4 organic compounds
BT1 benzoic acid
BT2 monocarboxylic acids
BT3 carboxylic acids
BT4 organic acids
BT5 organic compounds
BT1 contrast media
BT1 ethers
BT2 organic oxygen compounds
BT3 organic compounds
BT1 organic iodine compounds
BT2 organic halogen compounds
BT3 organic compounds

IOHEXOL [124; 124] Jun 83
BT1 contrast media

ION ACOUSTIC WAVES [2,239; 2,239]
(Non-dispersive ion waves)
UF *non-dispersive ion waves*
UF *nondispersive ion waves*
BT1 ion waves
BT2 plasma waves
RT sonic probes

ION BEAM FUSION REACTORS [466; 466] Nov 82
UF *i-beam type reactors*
UF *ion beam type reactors*
BT1 thermonuclear reactors
RT energy deposition
RT icf devices
RT inertial confinement
RT particle beam fusion accelerat

ION BEAM INJECTION [838; 859]
BT1 beam injection
NT1 molecular ion beam injection

ION BEAM TARGETS [490; 490] Nov 82
BT1 targets
RT electron beam targets
RT energy deposition
RT inertial confinement
RT laser targets
RT thermonuclear fuels

ion beam type reactors
USE ion beam fusion reactors

ION BEAMS [15,775; 24,410]
BT1 beams
NT1 aluminium 27 beams
NT1 argon 38 beams
NT1 argon 39 beams
NT1 argon 40 beams
NT1 beryllium 7 beams
NT1 beryllium 9 beams
NT1 bismuth 209 beams
NT1 boron 10 beams
NT1 boron 11 beams
NT1 bromine 79 beams
NT1 calcium 40 beams
NT1 calcium 48 beams
NT1 carbon 10 beams
NT1 carbon 11 beams
NT1 carbon 12 beams
NT1 carbon 13 beams
NT1 carbon 14 beams
NT1 chlorine 35 beams
NT1 chlorine 39 beams
NT1 copper 63 beams
NT1 deuteron beams
NT1 fluorine 19 beams
NT1 gadolinium 155 beams

ION BEAMS

NT1 germanium 74 beams
NT1 germanium 76 beams
NT1 gold 197 beams
NT1 helium 3 beams
NT1 helium 4 beams
NT2 alpha beams
NT1 helium 8 beams
NT1 hydrogen 1 minus beams
NT1 iodine 127 beams
NT1 iron 56 beams
NT1 iron 58 beams
NT1 krypton 84 beams
NT1 krypton 86 beams
NT1 lanthanum 139 beams
NT1 lead 208 beams
NT1 lithium 6 beams
NT1 lithium 7 beams
NT1 magnesium 24 beams
NT1 neon 19 beams
NT1 neon 20 beams
NT1 neon 22 beams
NT1 nickel 58 beams
NT1 nickel 60 beams
NT1 nitrogen 13 beams
NT1 nitrogen 14 beams
NT1 nitrogen 15 beams
NT1 oxygen 16 beams
NT1 oxygen 18 beams
NT1 phosphorus 31 beams
NT1 potassium 39 beams
NT1 potassium 41 beams
NT1 silicon 28 beams
NT1 silicon 29 beams
NT1 silver 107 beams
NT1 sodium 23 beams
NT1 sulfur 32 beams
NT1 sulfur 38 beams
NT1 tin 120 beams
NT1 titanium 48 beams
NT1 titanium 50 beams
NT1 triton beams
NT1 tungsten 184 beams
NT1 uranium 238 beams
NT1 xenon 129 beams
NT1 xenon 131 beams
NT1 xenon 132 beams
NT1 xenon 136 beams
RT anions
RT beam strippers
RT cations
RT charge distribution
RT charged particles
RT heavy ions
RT ion implantation
RT ion probes
RT ion scattering analysis
RT ion spectroscopy
RT ions
RT learn tandem accelerator
RT light ions
RT migma devices
RT particle beams
RT sputtering

ion blocking
USE ion channeling

ION CHANNELING [1,724; 1,724]
UF *ion blocking*
BT1 channeling
RT crystal lattices
RT ions

ion clusters
USE ion pairs

ION COLLISIONS [2,738; 15,659]
BT1 collisions
NT1 electron-ion collisions
NT1 ion-atom collisions
NT1 ion-ion collisions
NT1 ion-molecule collisions
NT1 photon-ion collisions
NT1 positron-ion collisions

ION CYCLOTRON-RESONANCE
[298; 298] *Dec 83*
UF *icr*
BT1 cyclotron resonance
BT2 resonance
RT icr heating

ion cyclotron-resonance heatin
USE icr heating

ION DENSITY [2,050; 2,050]
UF *density (ion)*
RT ions

ION DETECTION [965; 965]
BT1 charged particle detection
BT2 radiation detection
BT3 detection
RT heavy ions
RT ion dosimetry
RT ions
RT light ions

ION DOSIMETRY [91; 91]
BT1 dosimetry
RT ion detection

ION DRIFT [932; 932]
UF *drift (ion)*
RT ambipolar diffusion
RT ions

ION EMISSION [811; 811]
BT1 emission
RT field emission

ION EXCHANGE [5,299; 5,299]
UF *exchange (ion)*
UF+ *ligand exchange*
SF *sorption*
RT demineralization
RT desalination
RT distribution functions
RT ion exchange chromatography
RT separation processes

ION EXCHANGE CHROMATOGRAPHY [2,200; 2,200]
BT1 chromatography
BT2 separation processes
RT distribution functions
RT ion exchange
RT ion exchange materials
RT leaching
RT resins

ION EXCHANGE MATERIALS
[1,933; 6,692]
UF *decalso*
UF+ *ion exchange membranes*
BT1 materials
NT1 inorganic ion exchangers
NT2 bentonite
NT2 clinoptilolite
NT2 montmorillonite
NT2 mullite
NT2 vermiculite
NT2 zeolites
NT1 liquid ion exchangers
NT1 mixed bed ion exchangers
NT1 organic ion exchangers
NT2 polystyrene-dvb
RT anions
RT cations
RT graft polymers
RT ion exchange chromatography
RT leaching
RT resins
RT silica gel

ion exchange membranes
USE ion exchange materials
AND membranes

ION SOURCES

ION IMPLANTATION [11,035; 11,035]
RT crystal doping
RT crystals
RT doped materials
RT inclusions
RT ion beams
RT ions
RT trace amounts

ION MICROPROBE ANALYSIS
[692; 692]
BT1 microanalysis
BT1 nondestructive analysis
BT2 chemical analysis
RT ion probes

ION MICROSCOPES [85; 85]
BT1 microscopes

ION MICROSCOPY [603; 603]
UF *field emission microscopy*
UF *field ion microscopy*
BT1 microscopy
RT field emission

ION MOBILITY [657; 657]
BT1 particle mobility
BT2 mobility

ION PAIRS [1,094; 1,094]
UF *clusters (ion)*
UF *ion clusters*
RT ions

ION PLASMA WAVES [541; 557]
(Dispersive ion waves)
UF *dispersive ion waves*
BT1 ion waves
BT2 plasma waves

ION PROBES [419; 419]
BT1 probes
RT chemical analysis
RT deuteron probes
RT ion beams
RT ion microprobe analysis
RT ion sources
RT proton probes
RT secondary beams
RT secondary emission

ION PROPULSION [29; 29] *Feb 76*
(Vehicular motion caused by reaction from the high-speed discharge of a beam of electrically equally charged minute particles.)
BT1 propulsion
RT ion thrusters

ION RINGS [208; 208]
RT magnetic confinement
RT minimum-b configurations

ION SCATTERING ANALYSIS
[790; 790]
BT1 nondestructive analysis
BT2 chemical analysis
RT ion beams
RT radiation scattering analysis
RT scattering

ION SELECTIVE ELECTRODE ANALYS [229; 229]
BT1 chemical analysis
RT electrodes

ION SOURCES [6,732; 8,655]
NT1 alpha sources
NT1 duoplasmatrons
NT1 electron beam ion sources
NT1 penning ion sources
NT1 triplasmatrons
RT atomic beam sources
RT ion probes
RT ions

RT	neutral beam sources						
RT	particle sources						

ION SPECTROSCOPY [1,492; 1,492]
- UF *beam-foil spectroscopy*
- UF *beam-gas spectroscopy*
- UF *ion-neutralization spectroscop*
- BT1 spectroscopy
- RT ion beams

ION TEMPERATURE [4,352; 4,352]
- UF *temperature (ion)*
- UF+ *plasma temperature*
- RT energy
- RT ions

ION THRUSTERS [38; 38] Oct 75
- RT ion propulsion
- RT propulsion systems
- RT surface ionization

ION WAVE INSTABILITY [309; 309]
- BT1 plasma microinstabilities
- BT2 plasma instability
- BT3 instability
- RT bernstein mode

ION WAVES [356; 2,895]
- BT1 plasma waves
- NT1 ion acoustic waves
- NT1 ion plasma waves
- RT bernstein mode

ION-ATOM COLLISIONS [8,459; 8,459]
- UF+ *proton-atom collisions*
- BT1 atom collisions
- BT2 collisions
- BT1 ion collisions
- BT2 collisions
- RT electron-promotion model

ion-drag accelerators
- USE electron-ring accelerators

ION-ION COLLISIONS [878; 878]
- BT1 ion collisions
- BT2 collisions

ION-MOLECULE COLLISIONS [2,423; 2,423]
- UF+ *proton-molecule collisions*
- BT1 ion collisions
- BT2 collisions
- BT1 molecule collisions
- BT2 collisions

ion-neutralization spectroscop
- USE ion spectroscopy

IONIC COMPOSITION [565; 565]
- RT chemical composition
- RT ionosphere
- RT ions
- RT plasma

IONIC CONDUCTIVITY [911; 911]
- BT1 electric conductivity
- BT2 electrical properties
- BT3 physical properties

IONIC CRYSTALS [1,029; 1,029]
- BT1 crystals

ionic reactions
- USE chemical reactions
- AND ions

IONIZATION [15,017; 22,089]
- UF *discharges (ionization)*
- NT1 autoionization
- NT1 coulomb ionization
- NT1 inner-shell ionization
- NT1 internal ionization
- NT1 photoionization
- NT1 surface ionization
- NT2 adiabatic surface ionization
- RT beam neutralization
- RT bragg curve
- RT buildup
- RT charge exchange
- RT charge states
- RT dissociation
- RT electron attachment
- RT electron detachment
- RT electron loss
- RT energy deposition
- RT energy losses
- RT fano factor
- RT ionization potential
- RT ionizing radiations
- RT jesse effect
- RT kerma
- RT let
- RT penning effect
- RT plasma production
- RT plasma seeding
- RT radiation quality
- RT wall effects

ionization chamber smoke detec
- USE smoke detectors

IONIZATION CHAMBERS [3,957; 5,363]
- BT1 radiation detectors
- BT2 measuring instruments
- NT1 boron coated ion chambers
- NT1 bragg gray chambers
- NT1 condenser ionization chambers
- NT1 extrapolation chambers
- NT1 fission chambers
- NT1 liquid ionization chambers
- NT1 multiwire ionization chambers
- RT avalanche quenching
- RT campbelling circuits
- RT electron-capture detectors
- RT multiwire proportional chamber
- RT wall effects
- RT wall-less counters

IONIZATION GAGES [89; 159]
- BT1 vacuum gages
- BT2 pressure gages
- BT3 measuring instruments
- NT1 bayard-alpert gages
- NT1 philips gages
- NT1 radioactive ionization gages

ionization loss
- USE energy losses

IONIZATION POTENTIAL [1,475; 1,475]
- RT binding energy
- RT electronegativity
- RT ionization
- RT plasma seeding

IONIZED GASES [1,155; 1,590]
- BT1 gases
- BT2 fluids
- NT1 fully ionized gases
- NT2 lorentz gas
- NT1 strongly ionized gases
- NT1 weakly ionized gases
- RT fokker-planck equation
- RT plasma

IONIZING RADIATIONS [6,095; 107,197]
- BT1 radiations

- NT1 alpha particles
- NT2 cosmic alpha particles
- NT2 delayed alpha particles
- NT2 solar alpha particles
- NT1 beta particles
- NT1 cosmic radiation
- NT2 cosmic neutrinos
- NT2 cosmic photons
- NT2 cosmic protons
- NT2 hard component
- NT2 primary cosmic radiation
- NT3 cosmic alpha particles
- NT3 cosmic gamma bursts
- NT3 cosmic nuclei
- NT3 cosmic x-ray bursts
- NT2 secondary cosmic radiation
- NT3 cosmic electrons
- NT3 cosmic kaons
- NT3 cosmic muons
- NT3 cosmic neutrons
- NT3 cosmic pions
- NT3 cosmic positrons
- NT3 cosmic showers
- NT4 extensive air showers
- NT2 soft component
- NT1 gamma radiation
- NT2 delayed gamma radiation
- NT2 prompt gamma radiation
- NT1 x radiation
- NT2 hard x radiation
- NT2 soft x radiation
- RT buildup
- RT delta rays
- RT energy losses
- RT ionization
- RT mutagens
- RT teratogens

IONOGRAPHIC IMAGING [44; 44]
Feb 76
(A process whereby a pattern of electrical charges is formed on a foil by the accumulation of ions from a gas of high atomic number ionized by the incident radiation.)
- RT biomedical radiography

ionophoresis
- USE electrophoresis

IONOSONDES [92; 92]
- BT1 radio equipment
- BT2 electronic equipment
- BT3 equipment
- RT measuring instruments
- RT space vehicles

IONOSPHERE [4,037; 5,575]
- BT1 earth atmosphere
- NT1 c region
- NT1 d region
- NT1 e region
- NT2 sporadic e
- NT1 f region
- NT2 f1 layer
- NT2 f2 layer
- NT2 spread f
- RT auroral hiss
- RT auroral oval
- RT auroral zones
- RT critical frequency
- RT harang discontinuity
- RT ionic composition
- RT midday aurorae
- RT polar cusp
- RT polar-cap aurorae
- RT scale height
- RT sudden ionospheric disturbance
- RT travelling ionospheric disturb

IONOSPHERIC STORMS [141; 403]
Nov 75
- BT1 disturbances
- NT1 sudden ionospheric disturbance
- NT1 travelling ionospheric disturb

IONS [8,598; 104,205]
(Ions in liquid and solid solutions are indexed as compounds; ions in gases by the precoordinated descriptor consisting of the element name and the word IONS; ions in beams by assigning either the specific descriptor if available, e.g. ARGON 40 BEAMS or the isotope name together with ION BEAMS.)
- UF+   *electron-ion coupling*
- UF+   *ionic reactions*
- BT1   charged particles
- NT1   actinium ions
- NT1   aluminium ions
- NT1   americium ions
- NT1   anions
  - NT2   heteropolyanions
  - NT2   hydrogen ions 1 minus
- NT1   antimony ions
- NT1   argon ions
- NT1   arsenic ions
- NT1   astatine ions
- NT1   atomic ions
- NT1   barium ions
- NT1   berkelium ions
- NT1   beryllium ions
- NT1   bismuth ions
- NT1   boron ions
- NT1   bromine ions
- NT1   cadmium ions
- NT1   calcium ions
- NT1   californium ions
- NT1   carbon ions
- NT1   cations
  - NT2   hydrogen ions 1 plus
    - NT3   protons
      - NT4   antiprotons
      - NT4   cosmic protons
      - NT4   delayed protons
      - NT4   diprotons
      - NT4   photoprotons
      - NT4   prompt protons
      - NT4   solar protons
      - NT4   trapped protons
  - NT2   hydrogen ions 2 plus
  - NT2   hydrogen ions 3 plus
- NT1   cerium ions
- NT1   cesium ions
- NT1   chlorine ions
- NT1   chromium ions
- NT1   cobalt ions
- NT1   copper ions
- NT1   curium ions
- NT1   deuterium ions
- NT1   dysprosium ions
- NT1   einsteinium ions
- NT1   erbium ions
- NT1   europium ions
- NT1   fermium ions
- NT1   fluorine ions
- NT1   francium ions
- NT1   gadolinium ions
- NT1   gallium ions
- NT1   germanium ions
- NT1   gold ions
- NT1   hafnium ions
- NT1   heavy ions
- NT1   helium ions
  - NT2   alpha particles
    - NT3   cosmic alpha particles
    - NT3   delayed alpha particles
    - NT3   solar alpha particles
  - NT2   helium ash
- NT1   holmium ions
- NT1   hydrogen ions
  - NT2   hydrogen ions 1 minus
  - NT2   hydrogen ions 1 plus
    - NT3   protons
      - NT4   antiprotons
      - NT4   cosmic protons
      - NT4   delayed protons
      - NT4   diprotons
      - NT4   photoprotons
      - NT4   prompt protons
      - NT4   solar protons
      - NT4   trapped protons
  - NT2   hydrogen ions 2 plus
  - NT2   hydrogen ions 3 plus
- NT1   indium ions
- NT1   iodine ions
- NT1   iridium ions
- NT1   iron ions
- NT1   krypton ions
- NT1   lanthanum ions
- NT1   lead ions
- NT1   light ions
- NT1   lithium ions
- NT1   lutetium ions
- NT1   magnesium ions
- NT1   manganese ions
- NT1   mendelevium ions
- NT1   mercury ions
- NT1   molecular ions
  - NT2   hydrogen ions 2 plus
  - NT2   hydrogen ions 3 plus
  - NT2   oxonium ions
- NT1   molybdenum ions
- NT1   multicharged ions
- NT1   muonic ions
- NT1   neodymium ions
- NT1   neon ions
- NT1   neptunium ions
- NT1   nickel ions
- NT1   niobium ions
- NT1   nitrogen ions
- NT1   nobelium ions
- NT1   osmium ions
- NT1   oxygen ions
- NT1   palladium ions
- NT1   phosphorus ions
- NT1   platinum ions
- NT1   plutonium ions
- NT1   polonium ions
- NT1   potassium ions
- NT1   praseodymium ions
- NT1   promethium ions
- NT1   protactinium ions
- NT1   radium ions
- NT1   radon ions
- NT1   rhenium ions
- NT1   rhodium ions
- NT1   rubidium ions
- NT1   ruthenium ions
- NT1   samarium ions
- NT1   scandium ions
- NT1   selenium ions
- NT1   silicon ions
- NT1   silver ions
- NT1   sodium ions
- NT1   strontium ions
- NT1   sulfur ions
- NT1   tantalum ions
- NT1   technetium ions
- NT1   tellurium ions
- NT1   terbium ions
- NT1   thallium ions
- NT1   thorium ions
- NT1   thulium ions
- NT1   tin ions
- NT1   titanium ions
- NT1   tritium ions
- NT1   tungsten ions
- NT1   uranium ions
- NT1   vanadium ions
- NT1   xenon ions
- NT1   ytterbium ions
- NT1   yttrium ions
- NT1   zinc ions
- NT1   zirconium ions
- RT   charge states
- RT   ion beams
- RT   ion channeling
- RT   ion density
- RT   ion detection
- RT   ion drift
- RT   ion implantation
- RT   ion pairs
- RT   ion sources
- RT   ion temperature
- RT   ionic composition
- RT   translocation

IOPAMIDOL [96; 96] *Feb 84*
- BT1   contrast media

iota-1440 resonances
(Prior to December 1987 this was a valid descriptor.)
- USE   eta-1440 mesons

IOWA [96; 96]
- BT1   usa
- BT2   developed countries
- BT2   north america
- RT   ames laboratory

IOWA UTR-10 REACTOR [5; 5]
(University Test Reactor, Iowa State Univ., Ames, Iowa, USA)
- UF   *ames, iowa state univ utr-10 r*
- UF   *utr-10 iowa state university r*
- BT1   graphite moderated reactors
- BT2   reactors
- BT1   training reactors
- BT2   research and test reactors
- BT3   reactors
- BT1   water cooled reactors
- BT2   reactors

IPCR CYCLOTRON [109; 109] *Jun 83*
(Separated-sector cyclotron of the Institute of Physical and Chemical Research, Saitama, Japan.)
- UF   *inst phys chem res cyclotron*
- UF   *riken ssc*
- UF   *saitama cyclotron*
- BT1   heavy ion accelerators
- BT2   accelerators
- BT1   isochronous cyclotrons
- BT2   cyclotrons
- BT3   cyclic accelerators
- BT4   accelerators

ipcr linac
- USE   rilac

→ **IPEN-MB-1 REACTOR** [0; 0] *Aug 91*
(Instituto de Pesquisas Energeticas e Nucleares, Sao Paulo, Brazil.)
- BT1   zero power reactors
- BT2   experimental reactors
- BT3   research and test reactors
- BT4   reactors

IPNS-I SYNCHROTRON [73; 73] *Nov 80*
(Intense Pulsed Neutron Source; 500-MeV rapid cycling synchroton at ANL.)
- BT1   synchrotrons
- BT2   cyclic accelerators
- BT3   accelerators

IPP GARCHING [100; 100]
(Max-Planck-Institut fuer Plasmaphysik)
- UF   *garching, ipp*
- UF   *max-planck-inst f plasmaphysik*
- BT1   german fr organizations
- BT2   national organizations

IPRONIAZID [2; 2]
- BT1   antidepressants
- BT2   psychotropic drugs
- BT3   central nervous system agent
- BT4   drugs
- BT1   isoniazid
- BT2   antibiotics
- BT3   drugs
- BT3   organic compounds
- BT2   hydrazides
- BT3   organic nitrogen compounds
- BT4   organic compounds

iqsy
- USE   international quiet sun year

IRAN [184; 184]
- BT1   asia
- BT1   developing countries
- BT1   middle east

IRAN-1 REACTOR [10; 10] *Jun 77*
  BT1   pwr type reactors
    BT2   enriched uranium reactors
      BT3   reactors
    BT2   power reactors
      BT3   reactors
    BT2   thermal reactors
      BT3   reactors
    BT2   water cooled reactors
      BT3   reactors
    BT2   water moderated reactors
      BT3   reactors

IRAN-2 REACTOR [10; 10] *Jun 77*
  BT1   pwr type reactors
    BT2   enriched uranium reactors
      BT3   reactors
    BT2   power reactors
      BT3   reactors
    BT2   thermal reactors
      BT3   reactors
    BT2   water cooled reactors
      BT3   reactors
    BT2   water moderated reactors
      BT3   reactors

IRANIAN ATOMIC ENERGY ORGANIZA [23; 23] *Oct 76*
  BT1   iranian organizations
    BT2   national organizations

IRANIAN ORGANIZATIONS [0; 34] *Oct 76*
  BT1   national organizations
  NT1   iranian atomic energy organiza
  NT1   tehran nuclear research centre

IRAQ [78; 78]
  BT1   asia
  BT1   developing countries
  BT1   middle east
  RT   tigris river

IRAQI ATOMIC ENERGY COMMISSION [2; 5] *Jun 85*
  BT1   iraqi organizations
    BT2   national organizations
  NT1   iraqi nuclear research centre

IRAQI NUCLEAR RESEARCH CENTRE [3; 3] *Jun 85*
  BT1   iraqi atomic energy commission
    BT2   iraqi organizations
      BT3   national organizations

IRAQI ORGANIZATIONS [0; 5] *Jun 85*
  BT1   national organizations
  NT1   iraqi atomic energy commission
  NT2   iraqi nuclear research centre

IRELAND [107; 107]
  BT1   developed countries
  BT1   europe

IRI [24; 24]
  (Interuniversitair Reactor Instituut, Delft, the Netherlands)
  UF   interuniversitair reactor inst
  BT1   netherlands organizations
    BT2   national organizations

IRIDIUM [685; 685]
  BT1   platinum metals
    BT2   transition elements
      BT3   metals
        BT4   elements

IRIDIUM ADDITIONS [26; 26]
  (Alloys containing not more than 1% Ir are listed here.)
  RT   iridium alloys
  RT   iridium compounds

IRIDIUM ALLOYS [322; 377]
  (Alloys containing more than 1% Ir.)
  BT1   platinum metal alloys
    BT2   alloys
  NT1   iridium base alloys
  RT   iridium additions

IRIDIUM BASE ALLOYS [51; 51]
  BT1   iridium alloys
    BT2   platinum metal alloys
      BT3   alloys

IRIDIUM BORIDES [29; 29]
  BT1   borides
    BT2   boron compounds
  BT1   iridium compounds
    BT2   transition element compounds

→ **IRIDIUM CARBIDES** [0; 0] *Sep 91*
  BT1   carbides
    BT2   carbon compounds
  BT1   iridium compounds
    BT2   transition element compounds

IRIDIUM CHLORIDES [35; 35]
  BT1   chlorides
    BT2   chlorine compounds
      BT3   halogen compounds
    BT2   halides
      BT3   halogen compounds
  BT1   iridium compounds
    BT2   transition element compounds

IRIDIUM COMPLEXES [122; 122]
  BT1   transition element complexes
    BT2   complexes

IRIDIUM COMPOUNDS [116; 257]
  BT1   transition element compounds
  NT1   iridium borides
  NT1   iridium carbides
  NT1   iridium chlorides
  NT1   iridium fluorides
  NT1   iridium hydrides
  NT1   iridium oxides
  NT1   iridium silicides
  RT   iridium additions

IRIDIUM FLUORIDES [12; 12]
  BT1   fluorides
    BT2   fluorine compounds
      BT3   halogen compounds
    BT2   halides
      BT3   halogen compounds
  BT1   iridium compounds
    BT2   transition element compounds

IRIDIUM HYDRIDES [8; 8] *Nov 79*
  BT1   hydrides
    BT2   hydrogen compounds
  BT1   iridium compounds
    BT2   transition element compounds

IRIDIUM IONS [17; 17]
  BT1   ions
    BT2   charged particles

IRIDIUM ISOTOPES [127; 1,761]
  NT1   iridium 166
  NT1   iridium 167
  NT1   iridium 168
  NT1   iridium 169
  NT1   iridium 170
  NT1   iridium 171
  NT1   iridium 172
  NT1   iridium 173
  NT1   iridium 174
  NT1   iridium 175
  NT1   iridium 176
  NT1   iridium 177
  NT1   iridium 178
  NT1   iridium 179
  NT1   iridium 180
  NT1   iridium 181
  NT1   iridium 182
  NT1   iridium 183
  NT1   iridium 184
  NT1   iridium 185
  NT1   iridium 186
  NT1   iridium 187
  NT1   iridium 188
  NT1   iridium 189
  NT1   iridium 190
  NT1   iridium 191
  NT1   iridium 192
  NT1   iridium 193
  NT1   iridium 194
  NT1   iridium 195
  NT1   iridium 196
  NT1   iridium 197
  NT1   iridium 198

IRIDIUM OXIDES [48; 48]
  BT1   iridium compounds
    BT2   transition element compounds
  BT1   oxides
    BT2   chalcogenides
    BT2   oxygen compounds

IRIDIUM SILICIDES [15; 15] *Apr 84*
  BT1   iridium compounds
    BT2   transition element compounds
  BT1   silicides
    BT2   silicon compounds

IRIDIUM 166 [0; 0] *May 86*
  BT1   alpha decay radioisotopes
    BT2   radioisotopes
      BT3   isotopes
  BT1   intermediate mass nuclei
    BT2   nuclei
  BT1   iridium isotopes
  BT1   millisec living radioisotopes
    BT2   radioisotopes
      BT3   isotopes
  BT1   odd-odd nuclei
    BT2   nuclei

IRIDIUM 167 [0; 0] *May 86*
  BT1   alpha decay radioisotopes
    BT2   radioisotopes
      BT3   isotopes
  BT1   intermediate mass nuclei
    BT2   nuclei
  BT1   iridium isotopes
  BT1   millisec living radioisotopes
    BT2   radioisotopes
      BT3   isotopes
  BT1   odd-even nuclei
    BT2   nuclei

IRIDIUM 168 [4; 4] *Nov 78*
  BT1   alpha decay radioisotopes
    BT2   radioisotopes
      BT3   isotopes
  BT1   intermediate mass nuclei
    BT2   nuclei
  BT1   iridium isotopes
  BT1   odd-odd nuclei
    BT2   nuclei

IRIDIUM 169 [10; 10] *Nov 78*
  BT1   alpha decay radioisotopes
    BT2   radioisotopes
      BT3   isotopes
  BT1   intermediate mass nuclei
    BT2   nuclei
  BT1   iridium isotopes
  BT1   millisec living radioisotopes
    BT2   radioisotopes
      BT3   isotopes
  BT1   odd-even nuclei
    BT2   nuclei

IRIDIUM 170 [8; 8] *Feb 78*
  BT1   alpha decay radioisotopes
    BT2   radioisotopes
      BT3   isotopes
  BT1   intermediate mass nuclei
    BT2   nuclei
  BT1   iridium isotopes
  BT1   odd-odd nuclei
    BT2   nuclei

BT1 seconds living radioisotopes
BT2 radioisotopes
BT3 isotopes

IRIDIUM 171 [6; 6]
BT1 alpha decay radioisotopes
BT2 radioisotopes
BT3 isotopes
BT1 intermediate mass nuclei
BT2 nuclei
BT1 iridium isotopes
BT1 odd-even nuclei
BT2 nuclei
BT1 seconds living radioisotopes
BT2 radioisotopes
BT3 isotopes

IRIDIUM 172 [4; 4]
BT1 alpha decay radioisotopes
BT2 radioisotopes
BT3 isotopes
BT1 intermediate mass nuclei
BT2 nuclei
BT1 iridium isotopes
BT1 odd-odd nuclei
BT2 nuclei
BT1 seconds living radioisotopes
BT2 radioisotopes
BT3 isotopes

IRIDIUM 173 [6; 6]
BT1 alpha decay radioisotopes
BT2 radioisotopes
BT3 isotopes
BT1 intermediate mass nuclei
BT2 nuclei
BT1 iridium isotopes
BT1 odd-even nuclei
BT2 nuclei
BT1 seconds living radioisotopes
BT2 radioisotopes
BT3 isotopes

IRIDIUM 174 [2; 2]
BT1 alpha decay radioisotopes
BT2 radioisotopes
BT3 isotopes
BT1 intermediate mass nuclei
BT2 nuclei
BT1 iridium isotopes
BT1 odd-odd nuclei
BT2 nuclei
BT1 seconds living radioisotopes
BT2 radioisotopes
BT3 isotopes

IRIDIUM 175 [11; 11]
BT1 alpha decay radioisotopes
BT2 radioisotopes
BT3 isotopes
BT1 intermediate mass nuclei
BT2 nuclei
BT1 iridium isotopes
BT1 odd-even nuclei
BT2 nuclei
BT1 seconds living radioisotopes
BT2 radioisotopes
BT3 isotopes

IRIDIUM 176 [2; 2]
BT1 alpha decay radioisotopes
BT2 radioisotopes
BT3 isotopes
BT1 intermediate mass nuclei
BT2 nuclei
BT1 iridium isotopes
BT1 odd-odd nuclei
BT2 nuclei
BT1 seconds living radioisotopes
BT2 radioisotopes
BT3 isotopes

IRIDIUM 177 [7; 7]
BT1 alpha decay radioisotopes
BT2 radioisotopes
BT3 isotopes
BT1 intermediate mass nuclei
BT2 nuclei
BT1 iridium isotopes
BT1 odd-even nuclei
BT2 nuclei
BT1 seconds living radioisotopes
BT2 radioisotopes
BT3 isotopes

IRIDIUM 178 [4; 4]
BT1 beta-plus decay radioisotopes
BT2 beta decay radioisotopes
BT3 radioisotopes
BT4 isotopes
BT1 electron capture radioisotopes
BT2 beta decay radioisotopes
BT3 radioisotopes
BT4 isotopes
BT1 intermediate mass nuclei
BT2 nuclei
BT1 iridium isotopes
BT1 odd-odd nuclei
BT2 nuclei
BT1 seconds living radioisotopes
BT2 radioisotopes
BT3 isotopes

IRIDIUM 179 [7; 7]
BT1 beta-plus decay radioisotopes
BT2 beta decay radioisotopes
BT3 radioisotopes
BT4 isotopes
BT1 electron capture radioisotopes
BT2 beta decay radioisotopes
BT3 radioisotopes
BT4 isotopes
BT1 intermediate mass nuclei
BT2 nuclei
BT1 iridium isotopes
BT1 minutes living radioisotopes
BT2 radioisotopes
BT3 isotopes
BT1 odd-even nuclei
BT2 nuclei

IRIDIUM 180 [6; 6]
BT1 beta-plus decay radioisotopes
BT2 beta decay radioisotopes
BT3 radioisotopes
BT4 isotopes
BT1 electron capture radioisotopes
BT2 beta decay radioisotopes
BT3 radioisotopes
BT4 isotopes
BT1 intermediate mass nuclei
BT2 nuclei
BT1 iridium isotopes
BT1 minutes living radioisotopes
BT2 radioisotopes
BT3 isotopes
BT1 odd-odd nuclei
BT2 nuclei

IRIDIUM 181 [20; 20]
BT1 beta-plus decay radioisotopes
BT2 beta decay radioisotopes
BT3 radioisotopes
BT4 isotopes
BT1 electron capture radioisotopes
BT2 beta decay radioisotopes
BT3 radioisotopes
BT4 isotopes
BT1 heavy nuclei
BT2 nuclei
BT1 iridium isotopes
BT1 minutes living radioisotopes
BT2 radioisotopes
BT3 isotopes
BT1 odd-even nuclei
BT2 nuclei

IRIDIUM 182 [11; 11]
BT1 beta-plus decay radioisotopes
BT2 beta decay radioisotopes
BT3 radioisotopes
BT4 isotopes
BT1 electron capture radioisotopes
BT2 beta decay radioisotopes
BT3 radioisotopes
BT4 isotopes
BT1 heavy nuclei
BT2 nuclei
BT1 iridium isotopes
BT1 minutes living radioisotopes
BT2 radioisotopes
BT3 isotopes
BT1 odd-odd nuclei
BT2 nuclei

IRIDIUM 183 [18; 18]
BT1 beta-plus decay radioisotopes
BT2 beta decay radioisotopes
BT3 radioisotopes
BT4 isotopes
BT1 electron capture radioisotopes
BT2 beta decay radioisotopes
BT3 radioisotopes
BT4 isotopes
BT1 heavy nuclei
BT2 nuclei
BT1 iridium isotopes
BT1 minutes living radioisotopes
BT2 radioisotopes
BT3 isotopes
BT1 odd-even nuclei
BT2 nuclei

IRIDIUM 184 [23; 23]
BT1 beta-plus decay radioisotopes
BT2 beta decay radioisotopes
BT3 radioisotopes
BT4 isotopes
BT1 electron capture radioisotopes
BT2 beta decay radioisotopes
BT3 radioisotopes
BT4 isotopes
BT1 heavy nuclei
BT2 nuclei
BT1 hours living radioisotopes
BT2 radioisotopes
BT3 isotopes
BT1 iridium isotopes
BT1 odd-odd nuclei
BT2 nuclei

IRIDIUM 185 [38; 38]
BT1 beta-plus decay radioisotopes
BT2 beta decay radioisotopes
BT3 radioisotopes
BT4 isotopes
BT1 electron capture radioisotopes
BT2 beta decay radioisotopes
BT3 radioisotopes
BT4 isotopes
BT1 heavy nuclei
BT2 nuclei
BT1 hours living radioisotopes
BT2 radioisotopes
BT3 isotopes
BT1 iridium isotopes
BT1 odd-even nuclei
BT2 nuclei

IRIDIUM 186 [37; 37]
BT1 beta-plus decay radioisotopes
BT2 beta decay radioisotopes
BT3 radioisotopes
BT4 isotopes
BT1 electron capture radioisotopes
BT2 beta decay radioisotopes
BT3 radioisotopes
BT4 isotopes
BT1 heavy nuclei
BT2 nuclei
BT1 hours living radioisotopes
BT2 radioisotopes
BT3 isotopes
BT1 iridium isotopes
BT1 odd-odd nuclei
BT2 nuclei

IRIDIUM 187 [47; 47]
BT1 electron capture radioisotopes
BT2 beta decay radioisotopes
BT3 radioisotopes
BT4 isotopes
BT1 heavy nuclei

BT2   nuclei
BT1   hours living radioisotopes
BT2   radioisotopes
BT3   isotopes
BT1   iridium isotopes
BT1   odd-even nuclei
BT2   nuclei

IRIDIUM 188 [25; 25]
BT1   beta-plus decay radioisotopes
BT2   beta decay radioisotopes
BT3   radioisotopes
BT4   isotopes
BT1   days living radioisotopes
BT2   radioisotopes
BT3   isotopes
BT1   electron capture radioisotopes
BT2   beta decay radioisotopes
BT3   radioisotopes
BT4   isotopes
BT1   heavy nuclei
BT2   nuclei
BT1   iridium isotopes
BT1   odd-odd nuclei
BT2   nuclei

IRIDIUM 189 [49; 49]
BT1   days living radioisotopes
BT2   radioisotopes
BT3   isotopes
BT1   electron capture radioisotopes
BT2   beta decay radioisotopes
BT3   radioisotopes
BT4   isotopes
BT1   heavy nuclei
BT2   nuclei
BT1   iridium isotopes
BT1   odd-even nuclei
BT2   nuclei

IRIDIUM 189 TARGET [2; 2] *Jan 78*
BT1   targets

IRIDIUM 190 [15; 15]
BT1   beta-plus decay radioisotopes
BT2   beta decay radioisotopes
BT3   radioisotopes
BT4   isotopes
BT1   days living radioisotopes
BT2   radioisotopes
BT3   isotopes
BT1   electron capture radioisotopes
BT2   beta decay radioisotopes
BT3   radioisotopes
BT4   isotopes
BT1   heavy nuclei
BT2   nuclei
BT1   hours living radioisotopes
BT2   radioisotopes
BT3   isotopes
BT1   internal conversion radioisoto
BT2   radioisotopes
BT3   isotopes
BT1   iridium isotopes
BT1   isomeric transition isotopes
BT2   radioisotopes
BT3   isotopes
BT1   odd-odd nuclei
BT2   nuclei

IRIDIUM 191 [207; 207]
BT1   heavy nuclei
BT2   nuclei
BT1   internal conversion radioisoto
BT2   radioisotopes
BT3   isotopes
BT1   iridium isotopes
BT1   isomeric transition isotopes
BT2   radioisotopes
BT3   isotopes
BT1   odd-even nuclei
BT2   nuclei
BT1   seconds living radioisotopes
BT2   radioisotopes
BT3   isotopes
BT1   stable isotopes
BT2   isotopes

IRIDIUM 191 TARGET [68; 68]
BT1   targets

IRIDIUM 192 [1,082; 1,082]
BT1   beta-minus decay radioisotopes
BT2   beta decay radioisotopes
BT3   radioisotopes
BT4   isotopes
BT1   days living radioisotopes
BT2   radioisotopes
BT3   isotopes
BT1   electron capture radioisotopes
BT2   beta decay radioisotopes
BT3   radioisotopes
BT4   isotopes
BT1   heavy nuclei
BT2   nuclei
BT1   internal conversion radioisoto
BT2   radioisotopes
BT3   isotopes
BT1   iridium isotopes
BT1   isomeric transition isotopes
BT2   radioisotopes
BT3   isotopes
BT1   minutes living radioisotopes
BT2   radioisotopes
BT3   isotopes
BT1   odd-odd nuclei
BT2   nuclei
BT1   years living radioisotopes
BT2   radioisotopes
BT3   isotopes

IRIDIUM 193 [138; 138]
BT1   days living radioisotopes
BT2   radioisotopes
BT3   isotopes
BT1   heavy nuclei
BT2   nuclei
BT1   internal conversion radioisoto
BT2   radioisotopes
BT3   isotopes
BT1   iridium isotopes
BT1   isomeric transition isotopes
BT2   radioisotopes
BT3   isotopes
BT1   odd-even nuclei
BT2   nuclei
BT1   stable isotopes
BT2   isotopes

IRIDIUM 193 TARGET [73; 73]
BT1   targets

IRIDIUM 194 [35; 35]
BT1   beta-minus decay radioisotopes
BT2   beta decay radioisotopes
BT3   radioisotopes
BT4   isotopes
BT1   days living radioisotopes
BT2   radioisotopes
BT3   isotopes
BT1   heavy nuclei
BT2   nuclei
BT1   hours living radioisotopes
BT2   radioisotopes
BT3   isotopes
BT1   iridium isotopes
BT1   odd-odd nuclei
BT2   nuclei

IRIDIUM 194 TARGET [2; 2] *Jun 87*
BT1   targets

IRIDIUM 195 [18; 18]
BT1   beta-minus decay radioisotopes
BT2   beta decay radioisotopes
BT3   radioisotopes
BT4   isotopes
BT1   heavy nuclei
BT2   nuclei
BT1   hours living radioisotopes
BT2   radioisotopes
BT3   isotopes
BT1   iridium isotopes
BT1   odd-even nuclei
BT2   nuclei

IRIDIUM 196 [5; 5]
BT1   beta-minus decay radioisotopes
BT2   beta decay radioisotopes
BT3   radioisotopes
BT4   isotopes
BT1   heavy nuclei
BT2   nuclei
BT1   hours living radioisotopes
BT2   radioisotopes
BT3   isotopes
BT1   iridium isotopes
BT1   odd-odd nuclei
BT2   nuclei
BT1   seconds living radioisotopes
BT2   radioisotopes
BT3   isotopes

IRIDIUM 197 [10; 10]
BT1   beta-minus decay radioisotopes
BT2   beta decay radioisotopes
BT3   radioisotopes
BT4   isotopes
BT1   heavy nuclei
BT2   nuclei
BT1   iridium isotopes
BT1   minutes living radioisotopes
BT2   radioisotopes
BT3   isotopes
BT1   odd-even nuclei
BT2   nuclei

IRIDIUM 198 [3; 3]
BT1   beta-minus decay radioisotopes
BT2   beta decay radioisotopes
BT3   radioisotopes
BT4   isotopes
BT1   heavy nuclei
BT2   nuclei
BT1   iridium isotopes
BT1   odd-odd nuclei
BT2   nuclei
BT1   seconds living radioisotopes
BT2   radioisotopes
BT3   isotopes

IRIGINITE [3; 3]
BT1   oxide minerals
BT2   minerals
BT1   uranium minerals
BT2   radioactive minerals
BT3   minerals
BT3   radioactive materials
BT4   materials
RT   molybdenum oxides
RT   uranium oxides

IRISH SEA [147; 147] *May 80*
BT1   atlantic ocean
BT2   seas
BT3   surface waters

IRL REACTOR [2; 2]
(Columbia University/Industrial Research Labs., Inc., USA)
UF   *plainsboro irl pool type react*
BT1   enriched uranium reactors
BT2   reactors
BT1   pool type reactors
BT2   water cooled reactors
BT3   reactors
BT2   water moderated reactors
BT3   reactors
BT1   research reactors
BT2   research and test reactors
BT3   reactors
BT1   test reactors
BT2   research and test reactors
BT3   reactors
BT2   test facilities
BT1   thermal reactors
BT2   reactors

IRON [12,229; 12,704]
BT1   transition elements
BT2   metals
BT3   elements
NT1   iron-alpha
NT1   iron-beta

IRON

NT1 iron-delta
NT1 iron-gamma
RT ferritin
RT heme
RT hemoglobin
RT hemosiderin

IRON ADDITIONS [813; 2,702]
(Alloys containing not more than 1% Fe are listed here.)
NT1 alloy-al95cu4
NT1 alloy-ni46cr23co19ti5al4
NT1 alloy-ni48co28cr15al3mo3ti2
NT1 alloy-ni58cr14co8al4mo4nb4w4
NT1 alloy-ni60co15cr10al6ti5mo3
NT1 alloy-ni65mo16cr15w4
NT1 alloy-ni73cr20mn3nb3
NT1 alloy-ni78cr16al4
NT1 alloy-ni80cr20
NT1 alloy-ti88mo8al3
NT1 alloy-ti90al6mo3
NT1 alloy-ti90al6v4
NT1 alloy-ti91al4mo3
NT1 alloy-ti91al5cr2
NT1 alloy-zr98sn-2
NT1 alloy-zr98sn-4
RT iron alloys
RT iron compounds

IRON ALLOYS [5,526; 45,526]
(Alloys containing more than 1% Fe.)
BT1 alloys
NT1 alloy-co36cr22ni22w15fe3
NT1 alloy-co43cr20fe18ni13w3
NT1 alloy-co52cr17fe15mo3si3
NT1 alloy-co52fe35v10
NT1 alloy-co52fe35v13
NT1 alloy-co54cr20w15ni10
NT1 alloy-co60cr30w4
NT1 alloy-co62cr28mo6ni3
NT1 alloy-ni41fe40cr16nb3
NT1 alloy-ni42fe36cr12mo6ti3
NT1 alloy-ni43fe30cr22mo3
NT1 alloy-ni43fe33cr16mo3
NT1 alloy-ni45cr23fe19co3mo3w3
NT1 alloy-ni45fe34cr20
NT1 alloy-ni47cr25co12w9fe3
NT1 alloy-ni48cr22fe18mo9
NT1 alloy-ni49cr22fe18mo9
NT1 alloy-ni50co20cr15al5mo5
NT1 alloy-ni50cr22fe18mo9
NT1 alloy-ni53cr19fe19nb5mo3
NT1 alloy-ni54mo17cr16fe6w4
NT1 alloy-ni56cr21w10mo5fe4al2
NT1 alloy-ni58cr20co14mo4ti3
NT1 alloy-ni59cr20co17ti2
NT1 alloy-ni59cr30fe9
NT1 alloy-ni60cr25w15
NT1 alloy-ni60fe24cr16
NT1 alloy-ni61cr22mo9nb4fe3
NT1 alloy-ni61cr23fe14
NT1 alloy-ni62cr16mo15fe3
NT1 alloy-ni66cu32
NT1 alloy-ni68cr15w6al3mo3fe2
NT1 alloy-ni70mo17cr7fe5
NT1 alloy-ni73cr15fe7ti3
NT1 alloy-ni76cr15fe8
NT1 alloy-ni77cr20ti2
NT1 alloy-ni78cr21
NT1 alloy-ni79fe16mo4
NT1 alloy-ni80fe16mo4
NT1 alloy-v87cr9fe3
NT1 austenite
NT1 colmonoy
NT1 ferrite
*NT1 iron base alloys
NT1 martensite
NT1 refractaloy
RT iron additions
RT shape memory effect

IRON BASE ALLOYS [2,894; 36,225]
BT1 iron alloys
BT2 alloys
NT1 alloy-co50fe50
NT1 alloy-fe31cr21co20ni20mo3w2
NT1 alloy-fe36ni33cr26
NT1 alloy-fe40ni35cr22
NT1 alloy-fe44ni33cr21

NT1 alloy-fe46ni33cr21
NT1 alloy-fe48cr24ni24
NT1 alloy-fe53ni29co18
NT1 alnico alloys
NT1 cast iron
NT1 invar
*NT1 steels
NT1 tikonal

IRON BORIDES [501; 501]
BT1 borides
BT2 boron compounds
BT1 iron compounds
BT2 transition element compounds

IRON BROMIDES [15; 15]
BT1 bromides
BT2 bromine compounds
BT3 halogen compounds
BT2 halides
BT3 halogen compounds
BT1 iron compounds
BT2 transition element compounds

IRON CARBIDES [136; 258]
BT1 carbides
BT2 carbon compounds
BT1 iron compounds
BT2 transition element compounds
NT1 cementite
RT cast iron

IRON CARBONATES [25; 25]
BT1 carbonates
BT2 carbon compounds
BT2 oxygen compounds
BT1 iron compounds
BT2 transition element compounds
RT carbonate minerals

IRON CHLORIDES [418; 418]
BT1 chlorides
BT2 chlorine compounds
BT3 halogen compounds
BT2 halides
BT3 halogen compounds
BT1 iron compounds
BT2 transition element compounds

IRON COMPLEXES [986; 1,885]
BT1 transition element complexes
BT2 complexes
NT1 ferricyanides
NT1 ferritin
NT1 ferrocene
NT1 ferrocyanides
RT ferroin
RT lactoferrin

IRON COMPOUNDS [2,422; 8,636]
UF ferric compounds
UF ferrous compounds
BT1 transition element compounds
NT1 ferrates
NT1 iron borides
NT1 iron bromides
NT1 iron carbides
NT2 cementite
NT1 iron carbonates
NT1 iron chlorides
NT1 iron fluorides
NT1 iron hydrides
NT1 iron hydroxides
NT1 iron iodides
NT1 iron nitrates
NT1 iron nitrides
NT1 iron oxides
NT1 iron perchlorates
NT1 iron phosphates
NT1 iron phosphides
NT1 iron selenides
NT1 iron silicates
NT2 andradite
NT1 iron silicides
NT1 iron sulfates
NT1 iron sulfides
NT1 iron tellurides

NT1 iron tungstates
RT iron additions

IRON FLUORIDES [149; 149]
BT1 fluorides
BT2 fluorine compounds
BT3 halogen compounds
BT2 halides
BT3 halogen compounds
BT1 iron compounds
BT2 transition element compounds

IRON HYDRIDES [95; 95]
BT1 hydrides
BT2 hydrogen compounds
BT1 iron compounds
BT2 transition element compounds

IRON HYDROXIDES [467; 467]
BT1 hydroxides
BT2 hydrogen compounds
BT2 oxygen compounds
BT1 iron compounds
BT2 transition element compounds

IRON IODIDES [30; 30]
BT1 iodides
BT2 halides
BT3 halogen compounds
BT2 iodine compounds
BT3 halogen compounds
BT1 iron compounds
BT2 transition element compounds

IRON IONS [2,149; 2,149]
BT1 ions
BT2 charged particles

IRON ISOTOPES [331; 6,898]
NT1 iron 45
NT1 iron 47
NT1 iron 48
NT1 iron 49
NT1 iron 50
NT1 iron 51
NT1 iron 52
NT1 iron 53
NT1 iron 54
NT1 iron 55
NT1 iron 56
NT1 iron 57
NT1 iron 58
NT1 iron 59
NT1 iron 60
NT1 iron 61
NT1 iron 62
NT1 iron 63
NT1 iron 64
NT1 iron 65
NT1 iron 66
NT1 iron 67
NT1 iron 68

IRON METEORITES [162; 162]
BT1 meteorites

IRON NITRATES [72; 72]
BT1 iron compounds
BT2 transition element compounds
BT1 nitrates
BT2 nitrogen compounds
BT2 oxygen compounds

IRON NITRIDES [90; 90]
BT1 iron compounds
BT2 transition element compounds
BT1 nitrides
BT2 nitrogen compounds
BT2 pnictides

IRON ORES [377; 1,128]
BT1 ores
NT1 hematite
NT1 limonite
NT1 magnetite
RT pyrite

IRON OXIDES [2,706; 3,143]
BT1 iron compounds
BT2 transition element compounds
BT1 oxides
BT2 chalcogenides
BT2 oxygen compounds
RT ferrates
RT hematite
RT ilmenite
RT limonite
RT magnetite
RT oxide minerals
RT shales
RT tantalite
RT wolframite

IRON PERCHLORATES [4; 4] *Oct 83*
BT1 iron compounds
BT2 transition element compounds
BT1 perchlorates
BT2 chlorine compounds
BT3 halogen compounds
BT2 oxygen compounds

IRON PHOSPHATES [83; 83]
BT1 iron compounds
BT2 transition element compounds
BT1 phosphates
BT2 oxygen compounds
BT2 phosphorus compounds

IRON PHOSPHIDES [73; 73] *Nov 76*
BT1 iron compounds
BT2 transition element compounds
BT1 phosphides
BT2 phosphorus compounds
BT2 pnictides

IRON SELENIDES [18; 18] *Nov 76*
BT1 iron compounds
BT2 transition element compounds
BT1 selenides
BT2 chalcogenides
BT2 selenium compounds

IRON SILICATES [69; 200]
BT1 iron compounds
BT2 transition element compounds
BT1 silicates
BT2 oxygen compounds
BT2 silicon compounds
NT1 andradite
RT eudialyte
RT garnets
RT ilvaite
RT olivine
RT silicate minerals
RT vermiculite

IRON SILICIDES [124; 124] *Jan 77*
BT1 iron compounds
BT2 transition element compounds
BT1 silicides
BT2 silicon compounds

IRON SULFATES [377; 377]
BT1 iron compounds
BT2 transition element compounds
BT1 sulfates
BT2 oxygen compounds
BT2 sulfur compounds

IRON SULFIDES [249; 401]
BT1 iron compounds
BT2 transition element compounds
BT1 sulfides
BT2 chalcogenides
BT2 sulfur compounds
RT chalcopyrite
RT marcasite
RT pyrite
RT sulfide minerals

IRON TELLURIDES [17; 17] *Jul 84*
BT1 iron compounds
BT2 transition element compounds
BT1 tellurides
BT2 chalcogenides
BT2 tellurium compounds

IRON TUNGSTATES [12; 12] *Sep 77*
BT1 iron compounds
BT2 transition element compounds
BT1 tungstates
BT2 oxygen compounds
BT2 tungsten compounds
BT3 transition element compounds

IRON 45 [4; 4] *Sep 78*
BT1 beta decay radioisotopes
BT2 radioisotopes
BT3 isotopes
BT1 even-odd nuclei
BT2 nuclei
BT1 intermediate mass nuclei
BT2 nuclei
BT1 iron isotopes

IRON 47 [0; 0]
BT1 even-odd nuclei
BT2 nuclei
BT1 intermediate mass nuclei
BT2 nuclei
BT1 iron isotopes

IRON 48 [2; 2]
BT1 even-even nuclei
BT2 nuclei
BT1 intermediate mass nuclei
BT2 nuclei
BT1 iron isotopes

IRON 49 [4; 4]
BT1 beta-plus decay radioisotopes
BT2 beta decay radioisotopes
BT3 radioisotopes
BT4 isotopes
BT1 even-odd nuclei
BT2 nuclei
BT1 intermediate mass nuclei
BT2 nuclei
BT1 iron isotopes
BT1 millisec living radioisotopes
BT2 radioisotopes
BT3 isotopes

IRON 50 [11; 11]
BT1 even-even nuclei
BT2 nuclei
BT1 intermediate mass nuclei
BT2 nuclei
BT1 iron isotopes

IRON 51 [15; 15]
BT1 beta-plus decay radioisotopes
BT2 beta decay radioisotopes
BT3 radioisotopes
BT4 isotopes
BT1 even-odd nuclei
BT2 nuclei
BT1 intermediate mass nuclei
BT2 nuclei
BT1 iron isotopes
BT1 millisec living radioisotopes
BT2 radioisotopes
BT3 isotopes

IRON 52 [184; 184]
BT1 beta-plus decay radioisotopes
BT2 beta decay radioisotopes
BT3 radioisotopes
BT4 isotopes
BT1 electron capture radioisotopes
BT2 beta decay radioisotopes
BT3 radioisotopes
BT4 isotopes
BT1 even-even nuclei
BT2 nuclei
BT1 hours living radioisotopes
BT2 radioisotopes
BT3 isotopes
BT1 intermediate mass nuclei
BT2 nuclei
BT1 iron isotopes
BT1 seconds living radioisotopes
BT2 radioisotopes
BT3 isotopes

IRON 53 [93; 93]
BT1 beta-plus decay radioisotopes
BT2 beta decay radioisotopes
BT3 radioisotopes
BT4 isotopes
BT1 electron capture radioisotopes
BT2 beta decay radioisotopes
BT3 radioisotopes
BT4 isotopes
BT1 even-odd nuclei
BT2 nuclei
BT1 intermediate mass nuclei
BT2 nuclei
BT1 iron isotopes
BT1 isomeric transition isotopes
BT2 radioisotopes
BT3 isotopes
BT1 minutes living radioisotopes
BT2 radioisotopes
BT3 isotopes

IRON 54 [441; 441]
BT1 even-even nuclei
BT2 nuclei
BT1 intermediate mass nuclei
BT2 nuclei
BT1 iron isotopes
BT1 stable isotopes
BT2 isotopes

IRON 54 REACTIONS [15; 15] *Aug 84*
BT1 heavy ion reactions
BT2 nuclear reactions

IRON 54 TARGET [720; 720]
BT1 targets

IRON 55 [777; 777]
BT1 electron capture radioisotopes
BT2 beta decay radioisotopes
BT3 radioisotopes
BT4 isotopes
BT1 even-odd nuclei
BT2 nuclei
BT1 intermediate mass nuclei
BT2 nuclei
BT1 iron isotopes
BT1 years living radioisotopes
BT2 radioisotopes
BT3 isotopes

IRON 55 TARGET [11; 11]
BT1 targets

IRON 56 [881; 881]
BT1 even-even nuclei
BT2 nuclei
BT1 intermediate mass nuclei
BT2 nuclei
BT1 iron isotopes
BT1 stable isotopes
BT2 isotopes

IRON 56 BEAMS [71; 71]
BT1 ion beams
BT2 beams

IRON 56 REACTIONS [355; 355]
BT1 heavy ion reactions
BT2 nuclear reactions

IRON 56 TARGET [1,315; 1,315]
BT1 targets

IRON 57 [3,002; 3,002]
- BT1 even-odd nuclei
- BT2 nuclei
- BT1 intermediate mass nuclei
- BT2 nuclei
- BT1 iron isotopes
- BT1 stable isotopes
- BT2 isotopes

IRON 57 TARGET [116; 116]
- BT1 targets

IRON 58 [170; 170]
- BT1 even-even nuclei
- BT2 nuclei
- BT1 intermediate mass nuclei
- BT2 nuclei
- BT1 iron isotopes
- BT1 stable isotopes
- BT2 isotopes

IRON 58 BEAMS [6; 6] *Aug 76*
- BT1 ion beams
- BT2 beams

IRON 58 REACTIONS [49; 49] *Aug 76*
- BT1 heavy ion reactions
- BT2 nuclear reactions

IRON 58 TARGET [148; 148]
- BT1 targets

IRON 59 [1,439; 1,439]
- BT1 beta-minus decay radioisotopes
- BT2 beta decay radioisotopes
- BT3 radioisotopes
- BT4 isotopes
- BT1 days living radioisotopes
- BT2 radioisotopes
- BT3 isotopes
- BT1 even-odd nuclei
- BT2 nuclei
- BT1 intermediate mass nuclei
- BT2 nuclei
- BT1 iron isotopes

IRON 60 [43; 43]
- BT1 beta-minus decay radioisotopes
- BT2 beta decay radioisotopes
- BT3 radioisotopes
- BT4 isotopes
- BT1 even-even nuclei
- BT2 nuclei
- BT1 intermediate mass nuclei
- BT2 nuclei
- BT1 iron isotopes
- BT1 years living radioisotopes
- BT2 radioisotopes
- BT3 isotopes

IRON 61 [9; 9]
- BT1 beta-minus decay radioisotopes
- BT2 beta decay radioisotopes
- BT3 radioisotopes
- BT4 isotopes
- BT1 even-odd nuclei
- BT2 nuclei
- BT1 intermediate mass nuclei
- BT2 nuclei
- BT1 iron isotopes
- BT1 minutes living radioisotopes
- BT2 radioisotopes
- BT3 isotopes

IRON 62 [20; 20] *Feb 76*
- BT1 beta-minus decay radioisotopes
- BT2 beta decay radioisotopes
- BT3 radioisotopes
- BT4 isotopes
- BT1 even-even nuclei
- BT2 nuclei
- BT1 intermediate mass nuclei
- BT2 nuclei
- BT1 iron isotopes
- BT1 minutes living radioisotopes
- BT2 radioisotopes
- BT3 isotopes

IRON 63 [13; 13] *Nov 80*
- BT1 beta-minus decay radioisotopes
- BT2 beta decay radioisotopes
- BT3 radioisotopes
- BT4 isotopes
- BT1 even-odd nuclei
- BT2 nuclei
- BT1 intermediate mass nuclei
- BT2 nuclei
- BT1 iron isotopes
- BT1 seconds living radioisotopes
- BT2 radioisotopes
- BT3 isotopes

IRON 64 [9; 9] *Nov 80*
- BT1 beta-minus decay radioisotopes
- BT2 beta decay radioisotopes
- BT3 radioisotopes
- BT4 isotopes
- BT1 even-even nuclei
- BT2 nuclei
- BT1 intermediate mass nuclei
- BT2 nuclei
- BT1 iron isotopes
- BT1 seconds living radioisotopes
- BT2 radioisotopes
- BT3 isotopes

IRON 65 [2; 2] *Aug 86*
- BT1 even-odd nuclei
- BT2 nuclei
- BT1 intermediate mass nuclei
- BT2 nuclei
- BT1 iron isotopes

IRON 66 [3; 3] *Aug 86*
- BT1 even-even nuclei
- BT2 nuclei
- BT1 intermediate mass nuclei
- BT2 nuclei
- BT1 iron isotopes

IRON 67 [3; 3] *Aug 86*
- BT1 even-odd nuclei
- BT2 nuclei
- BT1 intermediate mass nuclei
- BT2 nuclei
- BT1 iron isotopes

IRON 68 [3; 3] *Aug 86*
- BT1 even-even nuclei
- BT2 nuclei
- BT1 intermediate mass nuclei
- BT2 nuclei
- BT1 iron isotopes

IRON-ALPHA [322; 322]
- BT1 iron
- BT2 transition elements
- BT3 metals
- BT4 elements
- RT ferrite
- RT martensite

IRON-BETA [4; 4]
- BT1 iron
- BT2 transition elements
- BT3 metals
- BT4 elements
- RT martensite

IRON-DELTA [9; 9]
- BT1 iron
- BT2 transition elements
- BT3 metals
- BT4 elements

iron-free spectrometers
- USE flat magnetic spectrometers

IRON-GAMMA [59; 59]
- BT1 iron
- BT2 transition elements
- BT3 metals
- BT4 elements

- RT austenite

IRPA [65; 65]
(International Radiation Protection Association)
- UF *internat rad protection assoc*
- BT1 international organizations

IRR-1 REACTOR [16; 16]
(Nahal Sorero, Israel)
- UF *israel. research reactor-1*
- BT1 enriched uranium reactors
- BT2 reactors
- BT1 pool type reactors
- BT2 water cooled reactors
- BT3 reactors
- BT2 water moderated reactors
- BT3 reactors
- BT1 research reactors
- BT2 research and test reactors
- BT3 reactors
- BT1 test reactors
- BT2 research and test reactors
- BT3 reactors
- BT2 test facilities
- BT1 thermal reactors
- BT2 reactors

IRR-2 REACTOR [8; 8]
(Dimona, Israel)
- UF *israel. research reactor-2*
- BT1 heavy water cooled reactors
- BT2 reactors
- BT1 heavy water moderated reactors
- BT2 reactors
- BT1 research reactors
- BT2 research and test reactors
- BT3 reactors
- BT1 tank type reactors
- BT2 reactors

irradiated fuel elements
- USE spent fuel elements

irradiated fuels
- USE spent fuels

§ **IRRADIATION** [24,218; 54,689]
- UF+ *accidental irradiation*
- NT1 acute irradiation
- NT1 chronic irradiation
- NT1 external irradiation
- NT2 extracorporeal irradiation
- NT2 partial body irradiation
- NT2 whole-body irradiation
- NT1 fractionated irradiation
- NT1 internal irradiation
- NT1 lethal irradiation
- NT1 local irradiation
- NT1 low dose irradiation
- NT1 nonuniform irradiation
- NT1 perinatal irradiation
- NT1 prenatal irradiation
- NT1 pulsed irradiation
- NT1 radicidation
- NT1 radiodisinfestation
- NT1 radiopreservation
- NT2 radurization
- NT1 radiosterilization
- NT2 radappertization
- NT1 self-irradiation
- NT1 sublethal irradiation
- NT1 supralethal irradiation
- RT damaging neutron fluence
- RT equivalent fission fluence
- RT irradiation devices
- RT irradiation procedures
- RT neutronic damage functions
- RT plant breeding
- RT radiation dose distributions
- RT radiation doses
- RT radiation effects
- RT radiation hazards
- RT radiation sources
- RT radiations
- RT radioimmunology

RT   radiotherapy

IRRADIATION CAPSULES [878; 878]
UF   *capsules (irradiation)*
UF   *irradiation rigs*
RT   experimental channels
RT   in pile loops
RT   radiation source implants

irradiation channels
USE   experimental channels

IRRADIATION DEVICES [2,246; 2,246]
RT   external irradiation
RT   irradiation
RT   irradiation plants
RT   irradiation procedures
RT   pigmi facilities
RT   radiation sources

IRRADIATION PLANTS [1,031; 1,045]
BT1   nuclear facilities
NT1   isomed
RT   external irradiation
RT   irradiation devices
RT   irradiation procedures
RT   radiation sources

IRRADIATION PROCEDURES
[2,634; 2,634]
RT   aerobic conditions
RT   afterloading
RT   anaerobic conditions
RT   external irradiation
RT   ifip
RT   irradiation
RT   irradiation devices
RT   irradiation plants
RT   spatial dose distributions
RT   temporal dose distributions

IRRADIATION REACTORS [117; 4,927]
(For isotope production and irradiation
purposes; for producing fissile materials
see PRODUCTION REACTORS.)
BT1   reactors
NT1   chemonuclear reactors
NT1   isotope production reactors
NT2   afrri reactor
NT2   ai-1-77 reactor
NT2   alrr reactor
NT2   apsara reactor
NT2   astra reactor
NT2   bepo reactor
NT2   ber-2 reactor
NT2   bgrr reactor
NT2   brr reactor
NT2   celestin reactor
NT2   cesnef reactor
NT2   cirus reactor
NT2   consort-2 reactor
NT2   cp-5 reactor
NT2   dhruva reactor
NT2   dido reactor
NT2   dmtr reactor
NT2   dow triga-mk-1 reactor
NT2   dr-2 reactor
NT2   dr-3 reactor
NT2   el-1 reactor
NT2   el-2 reactor
NT2   el-3 reactor
NT2   etr reactor
NT2   ewa reactor
NT2   fir-1 reactor
NT2   fnr reactor
NT2   fr-2 reactor
NT2   frf reactor
NT2   frg-2 reactor
NT2   frj-2 reactor
NT2   getr reactor
NT2   gtrr reactor
NT2   gulf triga-mk-3 reactor
NT2   hfir reactor
NT2   hifar reactor
NT2   htr reactor
NT2   ian-r1 reactor

NT2   irt reactor
NT2   irt-sofia reactor
NT2   ispra-1 reactor
NT2   jeep-2 reactor
NT2   jrr-1 reactor
NT2   jrr-3 reactor
NT2   kmr reactor
NT2   kuhfr reactor
NT2   lptr reactor
NT2   maria reactor
NT2   melusine-1 reactor
NT2   mnr reactor
NT2   mrr reactor
NT2   nru reactor
NT2   nrx reactor
NT2   ostr reactor
NT2   pulstar-buffalo reactor
NT2   r-a reactor
NT2   r-1 reactor
NT2   rtp reactor
NT2   rts-1 reactor
NT2   r2-0 reactor
NT2   siloe reactor
NT2   slowpoke type reactors
NT3   slowpoke-alberta reactor
NT3   slowpoke-dalhousie reactor
NT3   slowpoke-montreal reactor
NT3   slowpoke-ottawa reactor
NT3   slowpoke-toronto reactor
NT3   slowpoke-wnre reactor
NT2   taiwan research reactor
NT2   thetis reactor
NT2   thor reactor
NT2   tr-1 reactor
NT2   trico reactor
NT2   triga-brazil reactor
NT2   triga-texas reactor
NT2   triga-veterans reactor
NT2   triga-1-california reactor
NT2   triga-1-hanover reactor
NT2   triga-1-michigan reactor
NT2   triga-2 reactor
NT2   triga-2-dalat reactor
NT2   triga-2-illinois reactor
NT2   triga-2-kansas reactor
NT2   triga-2-ljubljana reactor
NT2   triga-2-mainz reactor
NT2   triga-2-musashi reactor
NT2   triga-2-pavia reactor
NT2   triga-2-rikkyo reactor
NT2   triga-2-rome reactor
NT2   triga-2-seoul reactor
NT2   triga-2-vienna reactor
NT2   triga-3-salazar reactor
NT2   triga-3-seoul reactor
NT2   tz1 reactor
NT2   ucbrr reactor
NT2   uftr reactor
NT2   uvar reactor
NT2   uwnr reactor
NT2   wtr reactor
NT2   wwr-m-kiev reactor
NT2   wwr-m-leningrad reactor
NT2   wwr-s-budapest reactor
NT2   wwr-s-moscow reactor
NT2   wwr-sm rossendorf reactor
NT2   wwr-2 reactor
NT2   x-10 reactor
NT1   materials processing reactors
NT1   materials testing reactors
NT2   atr reactor
NT2   br-2 reactor
NT2   cp-2 reactor
NT2   dido reactor
NT2   dmtr reactor
NT2   dr-3 reactor
NT2   el-3 reactor
NT2   frg-2 reactor
NT2   frj-2 reactor
NT2   gleep reactor
NT2   hector reactor
NT2   hfetr reactor
NT2   hfr reactor
NT2   hifar reactor
NT2   hwctr reactor
NT2   jmtr reactor
NT2   jrr-3 reactor
NT2   kmr reactor
NT2   kstr reactor

NT2   mtr reactor
NT2   nbsr reactor
NT2   nrx reactor
NT2   osiris reactor
NT2   pbr reactor
NT2   pluto reactor
NT2   r-2 reactor
NT2   rv-1 reactor
NT2   sm-2 reactor
NT2   taiwan research reactor
NT2   triga-1-hanford reactor
NT2   wr-1 reactor
NT2   wwr-m-kiev reactor
NT2   wwr-m-leningrad reactor
NT2   zephyr reactor
NT1   tritium production reactors
NT2   celestin reactor

irradiation rigs
USE   irradiation capsules

IRREDUCIBLE REPRESENTATIONS
[4,048; 4,048]
UF   *representations (irreducible)*
RT   group theory
RT   nonunitary representations
RT   symmetry groups

IRREVERSIBLE PROCESSES [742; 742]
RT   onsager relations
RT   prigogine theorem
RT   thermodynamics

IRRIGATION [308; 308]
RT   agriculture
RT   cultivation techniques
RT   fresh water
RT   radionuclide migration
RT   soils
RT   surface waters

IRT REACTOR [59; 59]
(Moscow, USSR)
UF   *soviet research reactor irt*
BT1   enriched uranium reactors
BT2   reactors
BT1   isotope production reactors
BT2   irradiation reactors
BT3   reactors
BT1   pool type reactors
BT2   water cooled reactors
BT3   reactors
BT2   water moderated reactors
BT3   reactors
BT1   research reactors
BT2   research and test reactors
BT3   reactors
BT1   thermal reactors
BT2   reactors

IRT-BAGHDAD REACTOR [3; 3]
(Prior to June 1985 WWR-S-BAGHDAD
REACTOR was used.)
UF   *baghdad wwr-s reactor*
UF   *irt-5000 baghdad reactor*
UF   *wwr-c-baghdad reactor*
UF   *wwr-s-baghdad reactor*
BT1   research reactors
BT2   research and test reactors
BT3   reactors
BT1   test reactors
BT2   research and test reactors
BT3   reactors
BT2   test facilities
BT1   thermal reactors
BT2   reactors
BT1   wwr type reactors
BT2   enriched uranium reactors
BT3   reactors
BT2   tank type reactors
BT3   reactors
BT2   water cooled reactors
BT3   reactors
BT2   water moderated reactors
BT3   reactors

IRT-SOFIA REACTOR [37; 37]
(Institute for Nuclear Research and Nuclear Power, Sofia, Bulgaria)
- UF *bulgarian r. reactor irt-2000*
- UF *irt-2000 sofia reactor*
- UF *sofia irt-2000 reactor*
- BT1 enriched uranium reactors
- BT2 reactors
- BT1 isotope production reactors
- BT2 irradiation reactors
- BT3 reactors
- BT1 pool type reactors
- BT2 water cooled reactors
- BT3 reactors
- BT2 water moderated reactors
- BT3 reactors
- BT1 research reactors
- BT2 research and test reactors
- BT3 reactors
- BT1 thermal reactors
- BT2 reactors

IRT-2000 DJAKARTA REACTOR [0; 0]
- UF *djakarta irt-2000 reactor*
- BT1 enriched uranium reactors
- BT2 reactors
- BT1 pool type reactors
- BT2 water cooled reactors
- BT3 reactors
- BT2 water moderated reactors
- BT3 reactors
- BT1 research reactors
- BT2 research and test reactors
- BT3 reactors
- BT1 test reactors
- BT2 research and test reactors
- BT3 reactors
- BT2 test facilities
- BT1 thermal reactors
- BT2 reactors

IRT-2000 MOSCOW REACTOR [24; 24]
- UF *mifi irt-2000 reactor*
- UF *moscow irt-2000 reactor*
- BT1 enriched uranium reactors
- BT2 reactors
- BT1 pool type reactors
- BT2 water cooled reactors
- BT3 reactors
- BT2 water moderated reactors
- BT3 reactors
- BT1 research reactors
- BT2 research and test reactors
- BT3 reactors
- BT1 test reactors
- BT2 research and test reactors
- BT3 reactors
- BT2 test facilities
- BT1 thermal reactors
- BT2 reactors

irt-2000 sofia reactor
- USE irt-sofia reactor

irt-5000 baghdad reactor
(IRT-Baghdad reactor after upgrading from 2 MW(th) to 5 MW(th).)
- USE irt-baghdad reactor

irvine triga-mk-1 reactor
- USE triga-1-california reactor

isabelle
- USE isabelle storage rings

ISABELLE STORAGE RINGS [804; 804]
- UF *brookhaven inters. stor. accel*
- UF *intersect. storage accelerator*
- UF *isabelle*
- BT1 storage rings

ISAR DEVICES [28; 28]
- BT1 linear theta pinch devices
- BT2 linear pinch devices
- BT3 open plasma devices
- BT4 thermonuclear devices
- BT3 pinch devices
- BT4 thermonuclear devices

ISAR REACTOR [103; 103]
- UF *kernkraftwerk isar*
- UF *kki isar*
- BT1 bwr type reactors
- BT2 enriched uranium reactors
- BT3 reactors
- BT2 power reactors
- BT3 reactors
- BT2 thermal reactors
- BT3 reactors
- BT2 water cooled reactors
- BT3 reactors
- BT2 water moderated reactors
- BT3 reactors

ISAR-2 REACTOR [48; 48] *Oct 82*
- BT1 pwr type reactors
- BT2 enriched uranium reactors
- BT3 reactors
- BT2 power reactors
- BT3 reactors
- BT2 thermal reactors
- BT3 reactors
- BT2 water cooled reactors
- BT3 reactors
- BT2 water moderated reactors
- BT3 reactors

ISCHEMIA [2,279; 2,279]
- BT1 anemias
- BT2 hemic diseases
- BT3 diseases
- BT2 symptoms
- BT1 cardiovascular diseases
- BT2 diseases
- RT anoxia
- RT blood circulation
- RT blood vessels
- RT myocardial infarction
- RT necrosis

ISENTROPIC PROCESSES [87; 87]
(Accomplished at constant value of the entropy.)
- UF *processes (isentropic)*
- RT adiabatic processes
- RT entropy
- RT isothermal processes
- RT thermodynamics

ISHIKAWAITE [1; 1]
- BT1 oxide minerals
- BT2 minerals
- BT1 uranium minerals
- BT2 radioactive minerals
- BT3 minerals
- BT3 radioactive materials
- BT4 materials

ISING MODEL [1,775; 1,775]
- BT1 crystal models
- BT2 mathematical models
- RT order-disorder transformations
- RT phi4-field theory
- RT two-dimensional calculations

ISIS REACTOR [21; 21]
(CEA/CEN de Saclay, Gif-sur-Yvette, France)
- BT1 enriched uranium reactors
- BT2 reactors
- BT1 pool type reactors
- BT2 water cooled reactors
- BT3 reactors
- BT2 water moderated reactors
- BT3 reactors
- BT1 research reactors
- BT2 research and test reactors

- BT3 reactors
- BT1 thermal reactors
- BT2 reactors

islamabad reactor pakistan
- USE parr reactor

ISLANDS [156; 1,212]
- NT1 aleutian islands
- NT2 amchitka island area
- NT1 bahrain
- NT1 bermuda
- NT1 cyprus
- NT1 faeroe islands
- NT1 fiji
- NT1 greenland
- NT1 hawaii
- NT1 iceland
- NT1 indonesia
- NT1 madagascar
- NT1 malta
- NT1 micronesia
- NT2 kiribati
- NT2 marshall islands
- NT3 bikini
- NT3 eniwetok
- NT2 nauru
- NT2 tuvalu
- NT1 new guinea
- NT1 new zealand
- NT1 philippines
- NT1 prince edward island
- NT1 singapore
- NT1 sri lanka
- NT1 tasmania
- NT1 west indies
- NT2 bahama islands
- NT2 cuba
- NT2 dominican republic
- NT2 haiti
- NT2 jamaica
- NT2 puerto rico
- NT2 saint lucia
- RT newfoundland
- RT seas
- RT terrestrial ecosystems

ISO [92; 92]
- UF *internat standard organization*
- BT1 international organizations
- RT recommendations
- RT standardized terminology
- RT standards document

ISOALLOXAZINES [22; 27]
- UF *flavins*
- BT1 heterocyclic compounds
- BT2 organic compounds
- BT1 organic nitrogen compounds
- BT2 organic compounds
- BT1 organic oxygen compounds
- BT2 organic compounds
- NT1 diaphorases
- RT coenzymes

isoamyl acetate
- USE isopentyl acetate

isoamylase
- USE amylase
- AND isoenzymes

ISOBAR MODEL [384; 384]
- UF *isobaric model*
- BT1 particle models
- BT2 mathematical models

ISOBARIC ANALOGS [1,878; 1,878]
- UF *analog states*
- UF+ *analog resonances (isobaric)*
- BT1 energy levels
- RT isobaric nuclei
- RT nolen-schiffer anomaly

isobaric model
USE   isobar model

ISOBARIC NUCLEI [377; 377]
(Nuclei having identical mass number.)
BT1   nuclei
RT   isobaric analogs
RT   mirror nuclei

isobaric spin
USE   isospin

isobars (nucleon)
USE   n*baryons

isobutane
USE   2-methylpropane

isobutyl alcohol
USE   2-methylpropanol

ISOBUTYL RADICALS [6; 6]
BT1   alkyl radicals
BT2   radicals

isobutylene
USE   2-methylpropene

ISOBUTYRIC ACID [45; 45]
BT1   monocarboxylic acids
BT2   carboxylic acids
BT3   organic acids
BT4   organic compounds

ISOCHRONOUS CYCLOTRONS
[771; 3,553]
BT1   cyclotrons
BT2   cyclic accelerators
BT3   accelerators
NT1   aabo cyclotron
NT1   alice cyclotron
NT1   apache
NT1   brookhaven cyclotron
NT1   chicago cyclotron
NT1   cracow aic-144 cyclotron
NT1   cracow c-48 cyclotron
NT1   crnl superconducting cyclotron
NT1   cyclone cyclotron
NT1   debrecen cyclotron
NT1   eindhoven cyclotron
NT1   ganil cyclotron
NT1   grenoble cyclotron
NT1   haizy cyclotron
NT1   hirfl cyclotron
NT1   inr cyclotron
NT1   ipcr cyclotron
NT1   iu cyclotron
NT1   jinr cyclotrons
NT2   jinr u-400 cyclotron
NT1   julic cyclotron
NT1   karlsruhe cyclotron
NT1   kazakhstan cyclotron
NT1   kiev cyclotron
NT1   kvi cyclotron
NT1   milan superconducting cyclotro
NT1   msu cyclotrons
NT1   munich compact cyclotron
NT1   munich suse cyclotron
NT1   nac cyclotron
NT1   nirs cyclotron
NT1   nrl cyclotron
NT1   ornl isochronous cyclotron
NT1   orsay cyclotron
NT1   oslo cyclotron
NT1   princeton cyclotron
NT1   rcnp cyclotron
NT1   sara cyclotron
NT1   sin cyclotron
NT1   texas a and m cyclotron
NT1   texas superconducting cyclotro
NT1   tohoku cyclotron
NT1   tokyo ins cyclotron

NT1   triumf cyclotron
NT1   uclrl cyclotrons
NT2   lbl 88-inch cyclotron
NT1   warsaw cyclotron
RT   vicksi accelerator

isocyanates
USE   cyanates

ISODOSE CURVES [1,615; 1,615]
RT   depth dose distributions
RT   nonuniform irradiation
RT   phantoms
RT   radiation dose distributions
RT   radiotherapy
RT   spatial dose distributions

ISOELECTRONIC ATOMS [812; 812]
BT1   atoms
RT   electronic structure

ISOENZYMES [185; 185]
UF+   isoamylase
BT1   organic compounds
RT   enzymes

ISOMED [17; 17] Nov 75
(Radiation Plant for Sterilization of Medical Products)
BT1   irradiation plants
BT2   nuclear facilities
RT   medical supplies
RT   radiosterilization
RT   surgical materials

ISOMER RATIO [141; 141] May 86
(Ratio of cross sections for populating excited and ground states of the same nuclide in a nuclear reaction.)
RT   isomeric nuclei

ISOMER SHIFT [1,896; 1,896]
(Property shift between the isomeric and the ground states of a nucleus.)
RT   isomeric nuclei

ISOMERASES [153; 153]
BT1   enzymes
BT2   organic compounds
RT   isomers

ISOMERIC NUCLEI [11,879; 11,879]
BT1   nuclei
RT   fission isomers
RT   isomer ratio
RT   isomer shift
RT   isomeric transition isotopes
RT   isomeric transitions

* ISOMERIC TRANSITION ISOTOPES
[102; 67,851]
(For specific terms, consult the Appendix.)
BT1   radioisotopes
BT2   isotopes
RT   isomeric nuclei
RT   isomeric transitions

ISOMERIC TRANSITIONS
[1,175; 1,175]
BT1   energy-level transitions
RT   decay
RT   isomeric nuclei
RT   isomeric transition isotopes

ISOMERIZATION [616; 616]
BT1   chemical reactions

ISOMERS [1,384; 1,384]
(Only for geometrical isomers and stereoisomers in chemistry; see also ISOMERIC NUCLEI.)
UF   enantiomorphs
RT   isomerases
RT   stereochemistry

ISONIAZID [23; 24]
BT1   antibiotics
BT2   drugs
BT2   organic compounds
BT1   hydrazides
BT2   organic nitrogen compounds
BT3   organic compounds
NT1   iproniazid
RT   pyridines

ISONITRILES [111; 111]
BT1   carbonic acid derivatives
BT2   organic compounds
RT   nitriles

isopentane
USE   2-methylbutane

ISOPENTYL ACETATE [6; 6]
UF   isoamyl acetate
BT1   acetic acid esters
BT2   carboxylic acid esters
BT3   esters
BT4   organic compounds

ISOPRENE [42; 42]
UF   2-methylbutadiene
BT1   dienes
BT2   polyenes
BT3   hydrocarbons
BT4   organic compounds
RT   polyisoprene

isopropyl cresol
USE   thymol

ISOPROPYL ETHER [35; 35]
UF   di-(2-propyl) ether
UF   diisopropyl ether
BT1   ethers
BT2   organic oxygen compounds
BT3   organic compounds
RT   organic solvents

ISOPROPYL RADICALS [36; 36]
BT1   alkyl radicals
BT2   radicals

isopropylbenzene
USE   cumene

isopropyltoluene-para
USE   cymene

ISOSPIN [6,250; 6,250]
UF   isobaric spin
UF   isotopic spin
BT1   particle properties
RT   charm particles
RT   salam-polkinghorne theory
RT   yang-mills theory

ISOTHERMAL PROCESSES
[1,472; 1,472]
UF   processes (isothermal)
RT   adiabatic processes
RT   isentropic processes
RT   thermodynamics

ISOTHERMS [432; 432] Feb 83
(Lines connecting points of equal temperature.)
UF   geoisotherms
RT   temperature measurement

isothiocyanates
USE   thiocyanates

isotones
　USE　isotonic nuclei

ISOTONIC NUCLEI [296; 296]
(Nuclei having identical number of neutrons.)
　UF　　*isotones*
　BT1　nuclei

ISOTONIC SOLUTIONS [18; 18] *Feb 81*
(Solutions having the same osmotic pressure.)
　BT1　solutions
　　BT2　homogeneous mixtures
　　　BT3　mixtures
　　　　BT4　dispersions
　RT　hypertonic solutions
　RT　osmosis

isotope analysis (quantitative
　USE　isotope ratio

ISOTOPE APPLICATIONS
[1,269; 42,030]
　NT1　tracer techniques
　　NT2　dual-isotope subtraction tec
　　NT2　isotope dilution
　　NT2　labelled pool techniques
　　NT2　radioactive tracer logging
　　NT2　radioimmunoassay
　　NT2　radioimmunodetection
　　NT2　radioreceptor assay
　RT　radiocolloids

isotope composition
　USE　isotope ratio

isotope composition (quantitat
　USE　isotope ratio

ISOTOPE DATING [3,864; 3,864]
　UF　　*argon method*
　UF　　*helium method*
　UF　　*lead method*
　UF+　*radiocarbon dating*
　BT1　age estimation
　RT　carbon 14

ISOTOPE DILUTION [2,060; 2,060]
　BT1　tracer techniques
　　BT2　isotope applications
　RT　dilution
　RT　quantitative chemical analysis
　RT　substoichiometry

ISOTOPE EFFECTS [6,002; 6,002]
　UF　　*isotopic effects*
　RT　isotopes
　RT　isotopic exchange

ISOTOPE ENRICHED MATERIALS
[531; 3,139]
　UF　　*enriched materials (isotopes)*
　UF　　*isotope-enriched materials*
　BT1　materials
　NT1　enriched uranium
　　NT2　highly enriched uranium
　　NT2　moderately enriched uranium
　　NT2　slightly enriched uranium
　RT　gas centrifugation
　RT　isotope separation
　RT　isotopic exchange

isotope enrichment
　USE　isotope separation

isotope exchange
　USE　isotopic exchange

ISOTOPE PRODUCTION [3,983; 3,983]
　RT　accelerators
　RT　isotope production reactors
　RT　isotopes
　RT　production
　RT　radioisotope generators
　RT　transmutation

ISOTOPE PRODUCTION REACTORS
[123; 3,311]
(For the production of radioisotopes to be used in medicine, agriculture, industry, etc.; for the production of fissile materials, see also PRODUCTION REACTORS, and for the production of tritium, see also TRITIUM PRODUCTION REACTORS.)
　BT1　irradiation reactors
　　BT2　reactors
　NT1　afrri reactor
　NT1　ai-l-77 reactor
　NT1　alrr reactor
　NT1　apsara reactor
　NT1　astra reactor
　NT1　bepo reactor
　NT1　ber-2 reactor
　NT1　bgrr reactor
　NT1　brr reactor
　NT1　celestin reactor
　NT1　cesnef reactor
　NT1　cirus reactor
　NT1　consort-2 reactor
　NT1　cp-5 reactor
　NT1　dhruva reactor
　NT1　dido reactor
　NT1　dmtr reactor
　NT1　dow triga-mk-1 reactor
　NT1　dr-2 reactor
　NT1　dr-3 reactor
　NT1　el-1 reactor
　NT1　el-2 reactor
　NT1　el-3 reactor
　NT1　etr reactor
　NT1　ewa reactor
　NT1　fir-1 reactor
　NT1　fnr reactor
　NT1　fr-2 reactor
　NT1　frf reactor
　NT1　frg-2 reactor
　NT1　frj-2 reactor
　NT1　getr reactor
　NT1　gtrr reactor
　NT1　gulf triga-mk-3 reactor
　NT1　hfir reactor
　NT1　hifar reactor
　NT1　htr reactor
　NT1　ian-r1 reactor
　NT1　irt reactor
　NT1　irt-sofia reactor
　NT1　ispra-1 reactor
　NT1　jeep-2 reactor
　NT1　jrr-1 reactor
　NT1　jrr-3 reactor
　NT1　kmr reactor
　NT1　kuhfr reactor
　NT1　lptr reactor
　NT1　maria reactor
　NT1　melusine-1 reactor
　NT1　mnr reactor
　NT1　mrr reactor
　NT1　nru reactor
　NT1　nrx reactor
　NT1　ostr reactor
　NT1　pulstar-buffalo reactor
　NT1　r-a reactor
　NT1　r-1 reactor
　NT1　rtp reactor
　NT1　rts-1 reactor
　NT1　r2-0 reactor
　NT1　siloe reactor
　NT1　slowpoke type reactors
　　NT2　slowpoke-alberta reactor
　　NT2　slowpoke-dalhousie reactor
　　NT2　slowpoke-montreal reactor
　　NT2　slowpoke-ottawa reactor
　　NT2　slowpoke-toronto reactor
　　NT2　slowpoke-wnre reactor
　NT1　taiwan research reactor
　NT1　thetis reactor
　NT1　thor reactor
　NT1　tr-1 reactor

　NT1　trico reactor
　NT1　triga-brazil reactor
　NT1　triga-texas reactor
　NT1　triga-veterans reactor
　NT1　triga-1-california reactor
　NT1　triga-1-hanover reactor
　NT1　triga-1-michigan reactor
　NT1　triga-2 reactor
　NT1　triga-2-dalat reactor
　NT1　triga-2-illinois reactor
　NT1　triga-2-kansas reactor
　NT1　triga-2-ljubljana reactor
　NT1　triga-2-mainz reactor
　NT1　triga-2-musashi reactor
　NT1　triga-2-pavia reactor
　NT1　triga-2-rikkyo reactor
　NT1　triga-2-rome reactor
　NT1　triga-2-seoul reactor
　NT1　triga-2-vienna reactor
　NT1　triga-3-salazar reactor
　NT1　triga-3-seoul reactor
　NT1　tz1 reactor
　NT1　ucbrr reactor
　NT1　uftr reactor
　NT1　uvar reactor
　NT1　uwnr reactor
　NT1　wtr reactor
　NT1　wwr-m-kiev reactor
　NT1　wwr-m-leningrad reactor
　NT1　wwr-s-budapest reactor
　NT1　wwr-s-moscow reactor
　NT1　wwr-sm rossendorf reactor
　NT1　wwr-2 reactor
　NT1　x-10 reactor
　RT　isotope production

ISOTOPE RATIO [11,454; 11,454]
　UF　　*abundance (isotopic)*
　UF　　*isotope analysis (quantitative*
　UF　　*isotope composition*
　UF　　*isotope composition (quantitat*
　UF　　*isotopic analysis (quantitativ*
　UF　　*isotopic composition (quantita*
　RT　element abundance
　RT　isotopes
　RT　natural occurrence
　RT　x-ray fluorescence analysis

ISOTOPE SEPARATION [4,568; 6,953]
(For separation of isotopes of the same element only.)
　UF　　*column separation (isotopes)*
　UF　　*depletion (isotopic)*
　UF　　*enrichment (isotopic)*
　UF　　*enrichment (uranium)*
　UF　　*isotope enrichment*
　UF　　*isotopic separation*
　UF　　*uranium enrichment*
　BT1　separation processes
　NT1　dual temperature process
　NT1　electromagnetic isotope separa
　NT1　gaseous diffusion process
　NT1　laser isotope separation
　NT1　separation nozzle method
　RT　centrifugation
　RT　electromag isotope separators
　RT　gas centrifugation
　RT　gas centrifuges
　RT　heavy water plants
　RT　isotope enriched materials
　RT　isotopes
　RT　plasma centrifuges
　RT　radioisotope generators
　RT　ultracentrifuges

ISOTOPE SEPARATION PLANTS
[508; 1,535] *Apr 76*
　UF　　*uranium enrichment plants*
　BT1　industrial plants
　BT1　nuclear facilities
　NT1　centrifuge enrichment plants
　　NT2　portsmouth centrifuge enrichm
　NT1　gaseous diffusion plants
　　NT2　cogema pierrelatte
　　NT2　orgdp
　　NT2　paducah plant
　　NT2　portsmouth gaseous diffusion p
　NT1　heavy water plants

    NT1   tritium extraction plants

isotope shift
    USE   spectral shift

isotope-enriched materials
    USE   isotope enriched materials

ISOTOPES [1,065; 271,817]
- UF   *nuclides*
- NT1   daughter products
- NT1   fission products
- NT1   radioisotopes
- *NT2 alpha decay radioisotopes
- NT2   beta decay radioisotopes
- *NT3 beta-minus decay radioisotopes
- *NT3 beta-plus decay radioisotopes
- *NT3 electron capture radioisotopes
- NT3   iron 45
- NT3   niobium 85
- NT3   vanadium 42
- NT3   vanadium 45
- NT2   bone seekers
- *NT2 days living radioisotopes
- NT2   heavy ion decay radioisotopes
- NT3   carbon 14 decay radioisotopes
- NT4   radium 222
- NT4   radium 223
- NT4   radium 224
- NT4   radium 226
- NT3   magnesium 28 decay radioisotop
- NT4   plutonium 236
- NT4   uranium 234
- NT3   neon 24 decay radioisotopes
- NT4   protactinium 231
- NT4   thorium 230
- NT4   uranium 232
- NT4   uranium 233
- NT4   uranium 234
- NT3   silicon 32 decay radioisotopes
- NT4   plutonium 238
- *NT2 hours living radioisotopes
- *NT2 internal conversion radioisoto
- *NT2 isomeric transition isotopes
- *NT2 microsec living radioisotopes
- *NT2 millisec living radioisotopes
- *NT2 minutes living radioisotopes
- *NT2 nanosec living radioisotopes
- NT2   neutron-deficient isotopes
- NT2   proton decay radioisotopes
- NT3   cesium 113
- NT3   cobalt 53
- NT3   iodine 109
- NT3   lutetium 151
- NT3   scandium 39
- NT3   thulium 147
- *NT2 seconds living radioisotopes
- *NT2 spontaneous fission radioisoto
- *NT2 years living radioisotopes
- *NT1 stable isotopes
- RT   isotope effects
- RT   isotope production
- RT   isotope ratio
- RT   isotope separation
- RT   nuclei

isotopic analysis (quantitativ
    USE   isotope ratio

isotopic composition (quantita
    USE   isotope ratio

isotopic effects
    USE   isotope effects

ISOTOPIC EXCHANGE [3,818; 3,922]
- UF   *exchange (isotopic)*
- UF   *isotope exchange*
- UF   *isotopic substitution*
- NT1   dual temperature process
- RT   chemical reactions
- RT   hydrogen transfer
- RT   isotope effects
- RT   isotope enriched materials
- RT   labelling

isotopic separation
    USE   isotope separation

isotopic shift
    USE   spectral shift

isotopic spin
    USE   isospin

isotopic substitution
    USE   isotopic exchange

ISOTROPY [1,602; 1,602]
- RT   anisotropy
- RT   configuration
- RT   distribution
- RT   orientation

ISOVALERIC ACID [12; 12]
- BT1   monocarboxylic acids
- BT2   carboxylic acids
- BT3   organic acids
- BT4   organic compounds

ISOVECTORS [429; 429]
- BT1   vectors
- BT2   tensors

ISPRA-1 REACTOR [14; 14]
- BT1   enriched uranium reactors
- BT2   reactors
- BT1   heavy water cooled reactors
- BT2   reactors
- BT1   heavy water moderated reactors
- BT2   reactors
- BT1   isotope production reactors
- BT2   irradiation reactors
- BT3   reactors
- BT1   research reactors
- BT2   research and test reactors
- BT3   reactors
- BT1   tank type reactors
- BT2   reactors
- BT1   test reactors
- BT2   research and test reactors
- BT3   reactors
- BT2   test facilities

ispra-2 rana reactor
    USE   rana reactor

ISRAEL [357; 357]
- BT1   asia
- BT1   developing countries
- BT1   middle east

ISRAEL ATOMIC ENERGY COMMISSIO [3; 13] *Nov 79*
- BT1   israeli organizations
- BT2   national organizations
- NT1   negev nuclear research center
- NT1   soreq nuclear research center

israel research reactor-1
    USE   irr-1 reactor

israel research reactor-2
    USE   irr-2 reactor

ISRAELI ORGANIZATIONS [4; 17] *Nov 79*
- BT1   national organizations
- NT1   israel atomic energy commissio
- NT2   negev nuclear research center
- NT2   soreq nuclear research center

ISX TOKAMAK [420; 420] *Sep 77*
- UF   *impurity study experiment toka*
- BT1   tokamak devices
- BT2   closed plasma devices
- BT3   thermonuclear devices

ITACONIC ACID [30; 30]
- BT1   dicarboxylic acids
- BT2   carboxylic acids
- BT3   organic acids
- BT4   organic compounds

ITALIAN ENEA [41; 44] *Mar 85*
(Comitato Nazionale per la Ricerca e lo Sviluppo dell'Energia Nucleare e delle Energie Alternative; prior to April 1982 known as Comitato Nazionale per Energia Nucleare, and documents written before that date should be indexed to CNEN.)
- UF   *comitato nazionale en nuc e al*
- UF   *enea italy*
- UF   *energia nucl e altern, com naz*
- BT1   italian organizations
- BT2   national organizations
- NT1   cnen

ITALIAN ORGANIZATIONS [66; 187]
- BT1   national organizations
- NT1   agip nucleare
- NT1   cise
- NT1   italian enea
- NT2   cnen

italian triga-mk-2 reactor
    USE   triga-2-rome reactor

ITALY [1,249; 1,249]
- BT1   developed countries
- BT1   europe

ITEP SYNCHROTRON [130; 130]
(Institute of Theoretical and Experimental Physics Synchrotron)
- BT1   synchrotrons
- BT2   cyclic accelerators
- BT3   accelerators

ITER TOKAMAK [349; 349] *Apr 89*
(International Thermonuclear Experimental Reactor.)
- BT1   tokamak devices
- BT2   closed plasma devices
- BT3   thermonuclear devices

ITERATIVE METHODS [2,894; 5,596]
- NT1   finite difference method
- NT1   galerkin-petrov method
- NT1   newton method
- RT   mathematics
- RT   numerical solution

IU CYCLOTRON [113; 113] *Apr 79*
- UF   *indiana university cyclotron*
- BT1   isochronous cyclotrons
- BT2   cyclotrons
- BT3   cyclic accelerators
- BT4   accelerators

iudr
    USE   iododeoxyuridine

ius
(Integrated utility systems.)
    USE   total energy systems

IVORY COAST [9; 9] *Dec 75*
BT1   africa
BT1   developing countries

IVY PROJECT [0; 1]
UF   *project ivy*
NT1   mike event
RT   eniwetok
RT   nuclear explosions
RT   surface explosions

J CODES [210; 210]
BT1   computer codes

J PSI-3097 MESONS [1,751; 1,751]
(Prior to December 1987 this concept was indexed by PSI-3105 RESONANCES.)
UF   *j-3105 resonances*
UF   *psi-3105 resonances*
BT1   charmonium
  BT2   mesons
    BT3   bosons
    BT3   hadrons
      BT4   elementary particles
  BT2   quarkonium
BT1   vector mesons
  BT2   mesons
    BT3   bosons
    BT3   hadrons
      BT4   elementary particles

J-J COUPLING [1,411; 1,411]
UF   *spin-spin interaction*
BT1   intermediate coupling
  BT2   coupling
RT   orbital angular momentum

j-3105 resonances
  USE   j psi-3097 mesons

JABILUKA DEPOSIT [68; 68] *Jul 78*
BT1   uranium deposits
  BT2   geologic deposits
RT   northern territory
RT   uranium ores

JACKETS [154; 154]
(Device surrounding an object to be heated or cooled, e.g., water jackets.)
RT   fuel cans
RT   reactor components
RT   shrouds
RT   sleeves

JACKSON MODEL [8; 8]
RT   compound nuclei
RT   nuclear reactions

JACOBIAN FUNCTION [344; 344]
BT1   functions

JAERI [812; 812]
(Japan Atomic Energy Research Institute)
UF   *japan atom. en. res. institute*
BT1   japanese organizations
  BT2   national organizations

jaeri exper. fusion reactor
  USE   jxfr tokamak

jaeri fusion torus-2a
  USE   jft-2a tokamak

JAERI LINAC [29; 29]
BT1   linear accelerators
  BT2   accelerators

JAERI TANDEM ACCELERATOR [52; 52] *Apr 82*
BT1   tandem electrostatic accelerat
  BT2   electrostatic accelerators
    BT3   accelerators
BT1   van de graaff accelerators
  BT2   electrostatic accelerators
    BT3   accelerators

JAHN-TELLER EFFECT [502; 502]
RT   energy levels
RT   molecules

JAMAICA [12; 12]
BT1   developing countries
BT1   west indies
  BT2   islands

james a. fitzpatrick reactor
  USE   fitzpatrick reactor

JAMES RIVER [15; 15]
BT1   rivers
  BT2   surface waters
RT   virginia

JAMESPORT-1 REACTOR [6; 6]
BT1   pwr type reactors
  BT2   enriched uranium reactors
    BT3   reactors
  BT2   power reactors
    BT3   reactors
  BT2   thermal reactors
    BT3   reactors
  BT2   water cooled reactors
    BT3   reactors
  BT2   water moderated reactors
    BT3   reactors

JAMESPORT-2 REACTOR [6; 6]
BT1   pwr type reactors
  BT2   enriched uranium reactors
    BT3   reactors
  BT2   power reactors
    BT3   reactors
  BT2   thermal reactors
    BT3   reactors
  BT2   water cooled reactors
    BT3   reactors
  BT2   water moderated reactors
    BT3   reactors

JANGLE PROJECT [0; 0]
UF   *project jangle*
RT   nuclear explosions
RT   surface explosions
RT   underground explosions

JANUS REACTOR [27; 27]
(ANL, Argonne, Illinois, USA)
UF   *biologic. research reac. janus*
BT1   enriched uranium reactors
  BT2   reactors
BT1   research reactors
  BT2   research and test reactors
    BT3   reactors
BT1   tank type reactors
  BT2   reactors
BT1   thermal reactors
  BT2   reactors
BT1   water cooled reactors
  BT2   reactors
BT1   water moderated reactors
  BT2   reactors

JAPAN [6,003; 6,992]
BT1   asia
BT1   developed countries
NT1   hiroshima
NT1   nagasaki

japan atom. en. res. institute
  USE   jaeri

japan atr fugen
  USE   jatr reactor

japan fast experim. breed. rea
  USE   joyo reactor

japan htr
  USE   htr reactor

japan inst plasma phys stellar
  USE   jipp stellarator

japan materials testing reacto
  USE   jmtr reactor

japan nucl. ship dev. agency
  USE   jnsda

japan oceanog. ship rea. mutsu
  USE   mutsu reactor

japan power demonstr reactor-2
  USE   jpdr-2 reactor

japan power demonstration reac
  USE   jpdr reactor

japan prototype fast reactor
  USE   monju reactor

japan research reactor-1
  USE   jrr-1 reactor

japan research reactor-2
  USE   jrr-2 reactor

japan research reactor-3
  USE   jrr-3 reactor

japan research reactor-4
  USE   jrr-4 reactor

JAPANESE ORGANIZATIONS [597; 1,781]
BT1   national organizations
NT1   jaeri
NT1   jnsda
NT1   pnc

japco-1 reactor
  USE   tokai-mura reactor

japco-2 reactor
  USE   tsuruga reactor

japco-3 reactor
  USE   tokai-2 reactor

japco-4 reactor
  USE   tsuruga-2 reactor

JASON REACTOR [6; 6]
(UK Ministry of Defence, Dept. of Nuclear Science and Technology, Royal Naval College, London, United Kingdom)
UF   *uk royal nav. coll.-jason reac*
BT1   argonaut type reactors
  BT2   enriched uranium reactors
    BT3   reactors
  BT2   research and test reactors
    BT3   reactors
  BT2   water cooled reactors
    BT3   reactors

```
    BT2    water moderated reactors
    BT3    reactors
  BT1    research reactors
    BT2    research and test reactors
    BT3    reactors
  BT1    training reactors
    BT2    research and test reactors
    BT3    reactors
```

JASTROW THEORY [243; 243]
  RT   hard-core potential
  RT   nucleon-nucleon potential

JATR REACTOR [365; 365]
  UF   adv. thermal reactor fugen
  UF   fugen atr
  UF   japan atr fugen
  BT1   hwlwr type reactors
    BT2   heavy water moderated reactors
    BT3   reactors
    BT2   water cooled reactors
    BT3   reactors
  BT1   natural uranium reactors
    BT2   reactors
  BT1   plutonium reactors
    BT2   reactors
  BT1   pressure tube reactors
    BT2   power reactors
    BT3   reactors
  BT1   thermal reactors
    BT2   reactors

JAUNDICE [257; 257]
  BT1   pathological changes
    BT2   diseases
  BT1   symptoms
  RT   hepatitis
  RT   liver

JAW [826; 826]
  UF   alveoli (dental)
  UF   mandible
  BT1   skull
    BT2   skeleton
    BT3   organs
    BT4   body
  RT   teeth

JEEP-2 REACTOR [12; 12]
(Institut for Atomenergi, Kjeller, Norway)
  UF   joint establ. exp. pile-2
  BT1   enriched uranium reactors
    BT2   reactors
  BT1   heavy water cooled reactors
    BT2   reactors
  BT1   heavy water moderated reactors
    BT2   reactors
  BT1   isotope production reactors
    BT2   irradiation reactors
    BT3   reactors
  BT1   research reactors
    BT2   research and test reactors
    BT3   reactors
  BT1   tank type reactors
    BT2   reactors

jejunum
  USE   small intestine

JEN [0; 0]
(Junta de Energia Nuclear)

JEN REACTOR [8; 8]
  UF   junta en nucl (portugal) reac
  UF   portuguese jen research reacto
  BT1   enriched uranium reactors
    BT2   reactors
  BT1   pool type reactors
    BT2   water cooled reactors
    BT3   reactors
    BT2   water moderated reactors
    BT3   reactors
  BT1   research reactors

```
    BT2    research and test reactors
    BT3    reactors
  BT1    thermal reactors
    BT2    reactors
```

JEN-1 REACTOR [8; 8]
(Nuclear Energy Board, Juan Vigon National Nuclear Energy Centre, Madrid, Spain)
  UF   junta en nucl (spain)-1 reac
  UF   spanish jen-1 research reactor
  BT1   enriched uranium reactors
    BT2   reactors
  BT1   pool type reactors
    BT2   water cooled reactors
    BT3   reactors
    BT2   water moderated reactors
    BT3   reactors
  BT1   research reactors
    BT2   research and test reactors
    BT3   reactors
  BT1   thermal reactors
    BT2   reactors

JEN-2 REACTOR [4; 4]
  UF   junta en nucl (spain)-2 reac
  UF   spanish jen-2 research reactor
  BT1   pool type reactors
    BT2   water cooled reactors
    BT3   reactors
    BT2   water moderated reactors
    BT3   reactors
  BT1   research reactors
    BT2   research and test reactors
    BT3   reactors

jensen sarcoma
  USE   experimental neoplasms

JERVIS BAY REACTOR [17; 17]
  BT1   power reactors
    BT2   reactors

JESSE EFFECT [12; 12]
(Change of ionization characteristics when impurities are added to certain gases.)
  RT   gases
  RT   impurities
  RT   ionization

JET MODEL [3,979; 3,979] *Aug 76*
  UF   ujm
  UF   uncorrelated-jet model
  BT1   particle models
    BT2   mathematical models
  RT   uncorrelated-particle model

JET TOKAMAK [1,648; 1,648] *Nov 75*
  BT1   tokamak devices
    BT2   closed plasma devices
    BT3   thermonuclear devices

JETS [2,240; 2,240]
  RT   fluid flow
  RT   nozzles

JEZEBEL REACTOR [23; 23]
  BT1   zero power reactors
    BT2   experimental reactors
    BT3   research and test reactors
    BT4   reactors

jfer reactor
  USE   joyo reactor

JFT-2 TOKAMAK [221; 221]
(Tokamak device with circular cross section and no divertor.)
  BT1   tokamak devices
    BT2   closed plasma devices
    BT3   thermonuclear devices

JFT-2A TOKAMAK [61; 61] *Jul 76*
(Tokamak device with teardrop-like cross section and with an axisymmetric divertor.)
  UF   diva tokamak
  UF   jaeri fusion torus-2a
  BT1   tokamak devices
    BT2   closed plasma devices
    BT3   thermonuclear devices

JFT-2M TOKAMAK [139; 139] *Dec 85*
(Tokamak device with a D-shaped cross section and a divertor.)
  BT1   tokamak devices
    BT2   closed plasma devices
    BT3   thermonuclear devices

JINR [164; 164]
  UF   dubna, jinr
  UF   joint inst for nuclear researc
  UF   ob. inst. yadern. issled.
  UF   oiyai
  BT1   international organizations

JINR CYCLOTRONS [148; 211]
  BT1   isochronous cyclotrons
    BT2   cyclotrons
    BT3   cyclic accelerators
    BT4   accelerators
  NT1   jinr u-400 cyclotron

JINR SYNCHROTRON [313; 313]
  BT1   synchrotrons
    BT2   cyclic accelerators
    BT3   accelerators

JINR U-400 CYCLOTRON [65; 65] *Jul 82*
  BT1   heavy ion accelerators
    BT2   accelerators
  BT1   jinr cyclotrons
    BT2   isochronous cyclotrons
    BT3   cyclotrons
    BT4   cyclic accelerators
    BT5   accelerators

JIPP STELLARATOR [79; 79]
  UF   japan inst plasma phys stellar
  BT1   stellarators
    BT2   closed plasma devices
    BT3   thermonuclear devices

JIPPT-2 DEVICE [186; 186] *Aug 82*
  BT1   stellarators
    BT2   closed plasma devices
    BT3   thermonuclear devices
  BT1   tokamak devices
    BT2   closed plasma devices
    BT3   thermonuclear devices

JMTR REACTOR [223; 223]
(Oari Research Establishment of JAERI, Ibaraki Prefecture, Japan)
  UF   japan materials testing reacto
  UF   materials testing react japan
  BT1   enriched uranium reactors
    BT2   reactors
  BT1   materials testing reactors
    BT2   irradiation reactors
    BT3   reactors
  BT1   research reactors
    BT2   research and test reactors
    BT3   reactors
  BT1   tank type reactors
    BT2   reactors
  BT1   test reactors
    BT2   research and test reactors
    BT3   reactors
    BT2   test facilities
  BT1   water cooled reactors
    BT2   reactors
  BT1   water moderated reactors
    BT2   reactors

JNSDA [23; 23]
(Japan Nuclear Ship Development Agency)
UF *japan nucl. ship dev. agency*
BT1 japanese organizations
BT2 national organizations

JOHANNITE [3; 3]
BT1 sulfate minerals
BT2 minerals
BT1 uranium minerals
BT2 radioactive minerals
BT3 minerals
BT3 radioactive materials
BT4 materials
RT copper sulfates
RT uranium sulfates

JOINING [219; 6,759]
BT1 fabrication
NT1 bonding
NT1 fastening
NT1 welding
NT2 arc welding
NT3 gas metal-arc welding
NT4 gas tungsten-arc welding
NT3 plasma arc welding
NT3 shielded metal-arc welding
NT3 submerged arc welding
NT2 brazing
NT2 diffusion welding
NT2 electron beam welding
NT2 electroslag welding
NT2 explosion welding
NT2 forge welding
NT2 friction welding
NT2 gas welding
NT2 induction welding
NT2 laser welding
NT2 magnetic force welding
NT2 resistance welding
NT3 flash welding
NT3 projection welding
NT2 soldering
NT2 ultrasonic welding
NT2 vacuum welding
RT compatibility
RT fasteners

joint committee on atomic ener
USE us jcae

joint establ. exp. pile-2
USE jeep-2 reactor

joint inst for nuclear researc
USE jinr

joint liability
(Prior to December 1990, this was a valid descriptor.)
USE liabilities

JOINTS [841; 8,705]
(Mechanical joints only; see also BONE JOINTS.)
UF *connections*
UF *junctions*
NT1 bolted joints
NT1 brazed joints
NT1 expansion joints
NT1 pipe joints
NT1 soldered joints
NT1 threaded joints
NT1 welded joints
RT bonding
RT closures
RT compatibility
RT fastening
RT flanges

joints (anatomy)
USE bone joints

JOMINY END-QUENCH TECHNIQUE [1; 1]
RT quench hardening

JOOS-WEINBERG EQUATION [7; 7]
BT1 differential equations
BT2 equations
RT dirac equation
RT quantum electrodynamics
RT relativity theory
RT spin

JORDAN [29; 29] *Dec 79*
BT1 asia
BT1 developing countries
BT1 middle east

JORUM EVENT [4; 4]
BT1 nuclear explosions
BT2 explosions
BT1 underground explosions
BT2 explosions

jose cabrera reactor
USE zorita-1 reactor

joseph m. farley-1 reactor
USE farley-1 reactor

joseph m. farley-2 reactor
USE farley-2 reactor

JOSEPHSON EFFECT [899; 899]
RT josephson junctions
RT superconductivity

JOSEPHSON JUNCTIONS [2,179; 2,179]
BT1 semiconductor junctions
RT josephson effect
RT superconducting junctions

JOST FUNCTION [312; 312]
BT1 functions
RT scattering
RT schroedinger equation

JOULE HEATING [2,125; 2,125]
UF *electric heating*
UF *ohmic plasma heating*
BT1 heating
RT electric currents
RT plasma heating

JOURNAL BEARINGS [31; 31]
BT1 bearings

JOYO REACTOR [414; 414]
UF *efr reactor*
UF *fast experim. breed. rea. japa*
UF *japan fast experim. breed. rea*
UF *jfer reactor*
BT1 experimental reactors
BT2 research and test reactors
BT3 reactors
BT1 lmfbr type reactors
BT2 fbr type reactors
BT3 breeder reactors
BT4 reactors
BT3 fast reactors
BT4 epithermal reactors
BT5 reactors
BT2 liquid metal cooled reactors
BT3 reactors
BT1 power reactors
BT2 reactors

JPDR REACTOR [140; 140]
(Tokaimura, Ibaraki, Japan)
UF *japan power demonstration reac*
BT1 bwr type reactors
BT2 enriched uranium reactors
BT3 reactors
BT2 power reactors
BT3 reactors
BT2 thermal reactors
BT3 reactors
BT2 water cooled reactors
BT3 reactors
BT2 water moderated reactors
BT3 reactors
BT1 experimental reactors
BT2 research and test reactors
BT3 reactors

JPDR-2 REACTOR [17; 17] *Sep 79*
(Tokaimura, Ibaraki, Japan)
UF *japan power demonstr reactor-2*
BT1 bwr type reactors
BT2 enriched uranium reactors
BT3 reactors
BT2 power reactors
BT3 reactors
BT2 thermal reactors
BT3 reactors
BT2 water cooled reactors
BT3 reactors
BT2 water moderated reactors
BT3 reactors

jpfr reactor
USE monju reactor

JRR-1 REACTOR [10; 10]
UF *japan research reactor-1*
BT1 aqueous homogeneous reactors
BT2 liquid homogeneous reactors
BT3 fluid fueled reactors
BT4 reactors
BT3 homogeneous reactors
BT4 reactors
BT2 water cooled reactors
BT3 reactors
BT2 water moderated reactors
BT3 reactors
BT1 enriched uranium reactors
BT2 reactors
BT1 isotope production reactors
BT2 irradiation reactors
BT3 reactors
BT1 research reactors
BT2 research and test reactors
BT3 reactors
BT1 training reactors
BT2 research and test reactors
BT3 reactors

JRR-2 REACTOR [95; 95]
(Tokai Research Establishment of JAERI, Ibaraki Prefecture, Japan)
UF *japan research reactor-2*
BT1 enriched uranium reactors
BT2 reactors
BT1 heavy water cooled reactors
BT2 reactors
BT1 heavy water moderated reactors
BT2 reactors
BT1 research reactors
BT2 research and test reactors
BT3 reactors
BT1 tank type reactors
BT2 reactors

JRR-3 REACTOR [147; 147]
(Tokai Research Establishment of JAERI, Ibaraki Prefecture, Japan)
UF *japan research reactor-3*
BT1 heavy water cooled reactors
BT2 reactors
BT1 heavy water moderated reactors
BT2 reactors
BT1 isotope production reactors
BT2 irradiation reactors
BT3 reactors
BT1 materials testing reactors
BT2 irradiation reactors
BT3 reactors
BT1 natural uranium reactors
BT2 reactors
BT1 research reactors
BT2 research and test reactors

BT3   reactors
BT1   tank type reactors
BT2   reactors

JRR-4 REACTOR [88; 88]
(Tokai Research Establishment of JAERI, Ibaraki Prefecture, Japan)
UF   *japan research reactor-4*
BT1   enriched uranium reactors
BT2   reactors
BT1   pool type reactors
BT2   water cooled reactors
BT3   reactors
BT2   water moderated reactors
BT3   reactors
BT1   research reactors
BT2   research and test reactors
BT3   reactors

JT-60 TOKAMAK [819; 819] *Jan 77*
BT1   tokamak devices
BT2   closed plasma devices
BT3   thermonuclear devices
RT   jt-60u tokamak

→ **JT-60U TOKAMAK** [4; 4] *Mar 91*
BT1   tokamak devices
BT2   closed plasma devices
BT3   thermonuclear devices
RT   jt-60 tokamak

juelich (kernforschungsanlage)
USE   kernforschungsanlage juelich

juelich-dido reactor
USE   frj-2 reactor

juelich-merlin reactor
USE   frj-1 reactor

juices
USE   beverages

JULIC CYCLOTRON [54; 54] *Jun 83*
BT1   isochronous cyclotrons
BT2   cyclotrons
BT3   cyclic accelerators
BT4   accelerators

JUNCTION DETECTORS [162; 177]
UF   *p-n counters*
BT1   semiconductor detectors
BT2   radiation detectors
BT3   measuring instruments
NT1   li-drifted junction detectors
RT   semiconductor junctions

JUNCTION DIODES [160; 160]
UF   *zener diodes*
BT1   semiconductor diodes
BT2   semiconductor devices

JUNCTION TRANSISTORS [109; 109]
BT1   transistors
BT2   semiconductor devices
RT   semiconductor junctions

junctions
USE   joints

junctions (semiconductor)
USE   semiconductor junctions

JUNO REACTOR [1; 1]
UF   *ukaea-juno reactor*
BT1   heavy water moderated reactors
BT2   reactors
BT1   research reactors
BT2   research and test reactors

BT3   reactors
BT1   tank type reactors
BT2   reactors
BT1   thermal reactors
BT2   reactors
BT1   water moderated reactors
BT2   reactors
BT1   zero power reactors
BT2   experimental reactors
BT3   research and test reactors
BT4   reactors

junta en nucl (portugal) reac
USE   jen reactor

junta en nucl (spain)-1 reac
USE   jen-1 reactor

junta en nucl (spain)-2 reac
USE   jen-2 reactor

JUPITER PLANET [1,551; 1,551]
BT1   planets

JUTE [42; 42]
BT1   plants
RT   fibers
RT   textiles

JUVENILES [36; 36] *Mar 86*
RT   adolescents
RT   age groups
RT   children

jxfr reactor
USE   jxfr tokamak

JXFR TOKAMAK [78; 78] *Jun 81*
UF   *jaeri exper. fusion reactor*
UF   *jxfr reactor*
BT1   tokamak devices
BT2   closed plasma devices
BT3   thermonuclear devices

K ABSORPTION [238; 238]
BT1   absorption

K CAPTURE [375; 375]
BT1   electron capture decay
BT2   beta decay
BT3   nuclear decay
BT4   decay

K CODES [617; 617]
BT1   computer codes

K CONVERSION [843; 843]
UF   *k-conversion coefficient*
BT1   internal conversion
BT2   conversion
BT2   nuclear decay
BT3   decay

K MATRIX [504; 504]
BT1   matrices
RT   nuclear reactions
RT   unitary pole approximation

K REACTOR [76; 76]
UF   *savannah riv. plant k reactor*
BT1   heavy water moderated reactors
BT2   reactors
BT1   special production reactors
BT2   production reactors
BT3   reactors

K SHELL [2,231; 2,231] *Jul 76*
(Atomic electron shells)
UF   *atomic shells (k)*
BT1   electronic structure

K*-1410 MESONS [5; 5] *Dec 87*
BT1   strange mesons
BT2   mesons
BT3   bosons
BT3   hadrons
BT4   elementary particles
BT2   strange particles
BT3   elementary particles
BT1   vector mesons
BT2   mesons
BT3   bosons
BT3   hadrons
BT4   elementary particles

K*-1790 MESONS [0; 0] *Dec 87*
BT1   strange mesons
BT2   mesons
BT3   bosons
BT3   hadrons
BT4   elementary particles
BT2   strange particles
BT3   elementary particles
BT1   vector mesons
BT2   mesons
BT3   bosons
BT3   hadrons
BT4   elementary particles

K*-892 MESONS [721; 721]
(Prior to December 1987 this concept was indexed by K-892 RESONANCES.)
UF   *k-892 resonances*
BT1   strange mesons
BT2   mesons
BT3   bosons
BT3   hadrons
BT4   elementary particles
BT2   strange particles
BT3   elementary particles
BT1   vector mesons
BT2   mesons
BT3   bosons
BT3   hadrons
BT4   elementary particles

*k*resonances*
(Prior to December 1987 this was a valid descriptor.)
USE   strange mesons

K*0-1350 MESONS [16; 16]
(Prior to December 1987 this concept was indexed by K-1320 RESONANCES.)
UF   *k-1320 resonances*
BT1   scalar mesons
BT2   mesons
BT3   bosons
BT3   hadrons
BT4   elementary particles
BT1   strange mesons
BT2   mesons
BT3   bosons
BT3   hadrons
BT4   elementary particles
BT2   strange particles
BT3   elementary particles

K*2-1430 MESONS [215; 215]
(Prior to December 1987 this concept was indexed by K-1420 RESONANCES.)
UF   *k-1420 resonances*
BT1   strange mesons
BT2   mesons
BT3   bosons
BT3   hadrons
BT4   elementary particles
BT2   strange particles
BT3   elementary particles
BT1   tensor mesons
BT2   mesons
BT3   bosons
BT3   hadrons
BT4   elementary particles

K*3-1780 MESONS [8; 8] *Dec 87*
 BT1 strange mesons
  BT2 mesons
   BT3 bosons
   BT3 hadrons
    BT4 elementary particles
  BT2 strange particles
   BT3 elementary particles
 BT1 tensor mesons
  BT2 mesons
   BT3 bosons
   BT3 hadrons
    BT4 elementary particles

K*4-2060 MESONS [8; 8] *Sep 79*
(Prior to December 1987 this concept was indexed by K-2130 RESONANCES.)
 UF k-2130 resonances
 BT1 strange mesons
  BT2 mesons
   BT3 bosons
   BT3 hadrons
    BT4 elementary particles
  BT2 strange particles
   BT3 elementary particles
 BT1 tensor mesons
  BT2 mesons
   BT3 bosons
   BT3 hadrons
    BT4 elementary particles

k-conversion coefficient
 USE k conversion

K-HARMONICS METHOD [94; 94]
Nov 78
 RT nuclear structure

k-1240 resonances
(Prior to December 1987 this was a valid descriptor.)
 USE strange mesons

k-1320 resonances
(Prior to December 1987 this was a valid descriptor.)
 USE k*0-1350 mesons

k-1420 resonances
(Prior to December 1987 this was a valid descriptor.)
 USE k*2-1430 mesons

K-1460 MESONS [2; 2] *Dec 87*
 BT1 pseudoscalar mesons
  BT2 mesons
   BT3 bosons
   BT3 hadrons
    BT4 elementary particles
 BT1 strange mesons
  BT2 mesons
   BT3 bosons
   BT3 hadrons
    BT4 elementary particles
  BT2 strange particles
   BT3 elementary particles

k-1775 resonances
(Prior to December 1987 this was a valid descriptor.)
 USE k2-1770 mesons

K-1830 MESONS [2; 2] *Dec 87*
 BT1 pseudoscalar mesons
  BT2 mesons
   BT3 bosons
   BT3 hadrons
    BT4 elementary particles
 BT1 strange mesons
  BT2 mesons
   BT3 bosons

   BT3 hadrons
    BT4 elementary particles
  BT2 strange particles
   BT3 elementary particles

k-1871 resonances
(Prior to December 1987 this was a valid descriptor.)
 USE strange mesons

k-2130 resonances
(Prior to December 1987 this was a valid descriptor.)
 USE k*4-2060 mesons

k-25 plant
 USE orgdp

k-892 resonances
(Prior to December 1987 this was a valid descriptor.)
 USE k*-892 mesons

KAERI [38; 38] *Dec 81*
(Korea Atomic Energy Research Institute. Prior to December 1989 this descriptor was used to index Korea Advanced Energy Research Institute.)
 UF korea adv. en. res. institute
 UF korea atom. en. res. institute
 BT1 korean organizations
 BT2 national organizations

kahl-main reactor
 USE hdr reactor

kahl-vak reactor
 USE vak reactor

KAHTER REACTOR [5; 5] *May 80*
 BT1 htgr type reactors
  BT2 gas cooled reactors
   BT3 reactors
  BT2 graphite moderated reactors
   BT3 reactors
 BT1 zero power reactors
  BT2 experimental reactors
   BT3 research and test reactors
    BT4 reactors

KAISERAUGST REACTOR [41; 41]
 BT1 bwr type reactors
  BT2 enriched uranium reactors
   BT3 reactors
  BT2 power reactors
   BT3 reactors
  BT2 thermal reactors
   BT3 reactors
  BT2 water cooled reactors
   BT3 reactors
  BT2 water moderated reactors
   BT3 reactors

kale
 USE brassica

KALININ-1 REACTOR [15; 15] *Aug 84*
 BT1 wwer type reactors
  BT2 pwr type reactors
   BT3 enriched uranium reactors
    BT4 reactors
   BT3 power reactors
    BT4 reactors
   BT3 thermal reactors
    BT4 reactors
   BT3 water cooled reactors
    BT4 reactors
   BT3 water moderated reactors
    BT4 reactors

KALININ-3 REACTOR [2; 2] *Jan 90*
(Kalinin NPP, Kalinin, USSR.)
 BT1 wwer type reactors
  BT2 pwr type reactors
   BT3 enriched uranium reactors
    BT4 reactors
   BT3 power reactors
    BT4 reactors
   BT3 thermal reactors
    BT4 reactors
   BT3 water cooled reactors
    BT4 reactors
   BT3 water moderated reactors
    BT4 reactors

KALLIKREIN [38; 38]
 BT1 blood coagulation factors
  BT2 coagulants
   BT3 hematologic agents
    BT4 drugs
 BT1 radioprotective substances
  BT2 drugs
  BT2 response modifying factors
 BT1 serine proteinases
  BT2 peptide hydrolases
   BT3 hydrolases
    BT4 enzymes
     BT5 organic compounds

KALPAKKAM LMFBR REACTOR
[126; 126]
(Kalpakkam, Tamilnadu, India.)
 UF fast breeder test r. (kalpakka
 UF fbtr reactor (kalpakkam)
 UF test fast breeder r. kalpakkam
 BT1 lmfbr type reactors
  BT2 fbr type reactors
   BT3 breeder reactors
    BT4 reactors
   BT3 fast reactors
    BT4 epithermal reactors
     BT5 reactors
  BT2 liquid metal cooled reactors
   BT3 reactors
 BT1 test reactors
  BT2 research and test reactors
   BT3 reactors
  BT2 test facilities

KALPAKKAM PFR REACTOR [10; 10]
Oct 75
(Kalpakkam, Tamilnadu, India.)
 UF kalpakkam pulsed fast reactor
 BT1 air cooled reactors
  BT2 gas cooled reactors
   BT3 reactors
 BT1 fast reactors
  BT2 epithermal reactors
   BT3 reactors
 BT1 pulsed reactors
  BT2 reactors
 BT1 research and test reactors
  BT2 reactors

kalpakkam pulsed fast reactor
 USE kalpakkam pfr reactor

kalpakkam reactor research cen
 USE igcar

KALPAKKAM-1 REACTOR [73; 73]
(Kalpakkam, Tamilnadu, India)
 BT1 phwr type reactors
  BT2 heavy water cooled reactors
   BT3 reactors
  BT2 heavy water moderated reactors
   BT3 reactors
 BT1 pressure tube reactors
  BT2 power reactors
   BT3 reactors

KALPAKKAM-2 REACTOR [64; 64]
(Kalpakkam, Tamilnadu, India)
- BT1 phwr type reactors
- BT2 heavy water cooled reactors
- BT3 reactors
- BT2 heavy water moderated reactors
- BT3 reactors
- BT1 pressure tube reactors
- BT2 power reactors
- BT3 reactors

KALUZA-KLEIN THEORY [952; 952] *Jan 84*
(Approach to unify electromagnetism and gravitation in the framework of general relativity theory by introducing a fifth space-time coordinate, the generator of which is the electric charge.)
- BT1 unified-field theories
- BT2 field theories
- RT compactification
- RT electromagnetism
- RT general relativity theory
- RT gravitation
- RT supergravity
- RT unified gauge models

KAMINI REACTOR [10; 10] *Dec 89*
(IGCAR, Kalpakkam, Tamilnadu, India.)
- BT1 research and test reactors
- BT2 reactors
- BT1 tank type reactors
- BT2 reactors
- BT1 thermal reactors
- BT2 reactors
- BT1 water cooled reactors
- BT2 reactors
- BT1 water moderated reactors
- BT2 reactors

kangaroo rat
(Long-tailed jumping rat of western U.S.A.)
- USE rodents

kansai-1 reactor
- USE mihama-1 reactor

kansai-2 reactor
- USE mihama-2 reactor

kansai-3 reactor
- USE takahama-1 reactor

kansai-4 reactor
- USE takahama-2 reactor

KANSAS [135; 135]
- BT1 usa
- BT2 developed countries
- BT2 north america

→ **KANSAS CITY PLANT** [2; 2] *Feb 91*
(US DOE Facility in Kansas City, Missouri.)
- BT1 us doe
- BT2 us organizations
- BT3 national organizations
- BT1 us erda
- BT2 us organizations
- BT3 national organizations
- RT missouri

kansas state univ. triga-mk-2
- USE triga-2-kansas reactor

KANUPP REACTOR [47; 47]
(Paradise Point, Sind, Pakistan)
- UF *karachi nuclear power plant*
- BT1 candu type reactors
- BT2 heavy water moderated reactors
- BT3 reactors
- BT2 pressure tube reactors
- BT3 power reactors
- BT4 reactors
- BT2 thermal reactors
- BT3 reactors
- BT1 natural uranium reactors
- BT2 reactors
- BT1 phwr type reactors
- BT2 heavy water cooled reactors
- BT3 reactors
- BT2 heavy water moderated reactors
- BT3 reactors

KAOLIN [164; 164]
- UF *china clay*
- BT1 clays
- BT2 silicate minerals
- BT3 minerals
- BT1 oxide minerals
- BT2 minerals

KAON BEAMS [766; 766]
- BT1 meson beams
- BT2 particle beams
- BT3 beams

KAON DETECTION [129; 129] *Feb 76*
- BT1 radiation detection
- BT2 detection

KAON MINUS REACTIONS [556; 556] *Mar 77*
- BT1 kaon reactions
- BT2 meson reactions
- BT3 hadron reactions
- BT4 nuclear reactions

KAON MINUS-NEUTRON INTERACTION [65; 65] *Jan 77*
- BT1 kaon-neutron interactions
- BT2 kaon-nucleon interactions
- BT3 meson-nucleon interactions
- BT4 meson-baryon interactions
- BT5 hadron-hadron interactions
- BT6 particle interactions
- BT7 interactions

KAON MINUS-PROTON INTERACTIONS [912; 912] *Jan 77*
- BT1 kaon-proton interactions
- BT2 kaon-nucleon interactions
- BT3 meson-nucleon interactions
- BT4 meson-baryon interactions
- BT5 hadron hadron interactions
- BT6 particle interactions
- BT7 interactions

KAON NEUTRAL REACTIONS [44; 44] *Sep 79*
- BT1 kaon reactions
- BT2 meson reactions
- BT3 hadron reactions
- BT4 nuclear reactions

KAON NEUTRAL-NEUTRON INTERACTI [4; 4] *Sep 79*
- BT1 kaon-neutron interactions
- BT2 kaon-nucleon interactions
- BT3 meson-nucleon interactions
- BT4 meson-baryon interactions
- BT5 hadron-hadron interactions
- BT6 particle interactions
- BT7 interactions

KAON NEUTRAL-PROTON INTERACTIO [40; 40] *Jun 77*
- BT1 kaon-proton interactions
- BT2 kaon-nucleon interactions
- BT3 meson-nucleon interactions
- BT4 meson-baryon interactions
- BT5 hadron-hadron interactions
- BT6 particle interactions
- BT7 interactions

KAON PLUS REACTIONS [240; 240] *Sep 77*
- BT1 kaon reactions
- BT2 meson reactions
- BT3 hadron reactions
- BT4 nuclear reactions

KAON PLUS-NEUTRON INTERACTIONS [74; 74] *Jan 77*
- BT1 kaon-neutron interactions
- BT2 kaon-nucleon interactions
- BT3 meson-nucleon interactions
- BT4 meson-baryon interactions
- BT5 hadron-hadron interactions
- BT6 particle interactions
- BT7 interactions

KAON PLUS-PROTON INTERACTIONS [530; 530] *Jan 77*
- BT1 kaon-proton interactions
- BT2 kaon-nucleon interactions
- BT3 meson-nucleon interactions
- BT4 meson-baryon interactions
- BT5 hadron-hadron interactions
- BT6 particle interactions
- BT7 interactions

KAON REACTIONS [450; 1,205]
- UF+ *kaon-deuteron interactions*
- BT1 meson reactions
- BT2 hadron reactions
- BT3 nuclear reactions
- NT1 kaon minus reactions
- NT1 kaon neutral reactions
- NT1 kaon plus reactions

kaon-deuteron interactions
- USE deuterium target
- AND kaon reactions

KAON-HYPERON INTERACTIONS [12; 12]
- BT1 meson-hyperon interactions
- BT2 meson-baryon interactions
- BT3 hadron-hadron interactions
- BT4 particle interactions
- BT5 interactions

KAON-KAON INTERACTIONS [83; 83]
- BT1 meson-meson interactions
- BT2 hadron-hadron interactions
- BT3 particle interactions
- BT4 interactions

KAON-NEUTRON INTERACTIONS [96; 222]
- BT1 kaon-nucleon interactions
- BT2 meson-nucleon interactions
- BT3 meson-baryon interactions
- BT4 hadron-hadron interactions
- BT5 particle interactions
- BT6 interactions
- NT1 kaon minus neutron interaction
- NT1 kaon neutral-neutron interacti
- NT1 kaon plus-neutron interactions

KAON-NUCLEON INTERACTIONS [540; 2,941]
- BT1 meson-nucleon interactions
- BT2 meson-baryon interactions
- BT3 hadron-hadron interactions
- BT4 particle interactions
- BT5 interactions
- NT1 kaon-neutron interactions
- NT2 kaon minus-neutron interaction
- NT2 kaon neutral-neutron interacti
- NT2 kaon plus-neutron interactions
- NT1 kaon-proton interactions
- NT2 kaon minus-proton interactions
- NT2 kaon neutral-proton interactio
- NT2 kaon plus-proton interactions

KAON-PROTON INTERACTIONS
[987; 2,300]
  BT1   kaon-nucleon interactions
  BT2   meson-nucleon interactions
  BT3   meson-baryon interactions
  BT4   hadron-hadron interactions
  BT5   particle interactions
  BT6   interactions
  NT1   kaon minus-proton interactions
  NT1   kaon neutral-proton interactio
  NT1   kaon plus-proton interactions

KAONIC ATOMS [229; 229]
  BT1   mesic atoms
  BT2   hadronic atoms
  BT3   atoms
  RT   kaonium

KAONIUM [9; 9] *Nov 85*
  RT   bound state
  RT   kaonic atoms
  RT   kaons minus
  RT   kaons plus
  RT   muonium
  RT   pionium

KAONS [2,688; 9,547]
  BT1   pseudoscalar mesons
  BT2   mesons
  BT3   bosons
  BT3   hadrons
  BT4   elementary particles
  BT1   strange mesons
  BT2   mesons
  BT3   bosons
  BT3   hadrons
  BT4   elementary particles
  BT2   strange particles
  BT3   elementary particles
  NT1   antikaons
  NT2   antikaons neutral
  NT1   cosmic kaons
  NT1   kaons minus
  NT1   kaons neutral
  NT2   antikaons neutral
  NT2   kaons neutral long-lived
  NT2   kaons neutral short-lived
  NT1   kaons plus
  RT   pi-k atoms

KAONS MINUS [2,543; 2,543]
  BT1   kaons
  BT2   pseudoscalar mesons
  BT3   mesons
  BT4   bosons
  BT4   hadrons
  BT5   elementary particles
  BT2   strange mesons
  BT3   mesons
  BT4   bosons
  BT4   hadrons
  BT5   elementary particles
  BT3   strange particles
  BT4   elementary particles
  RT   kaonium

KAONS NEUTRAL [1,562; 3,384]
  BT1   kaons
  BT2   pseudoscalar mesons
  BT3   mesons
  BT4   bosons
  BT4   hadrons
  BT5   elementary particles
  BT2   strange mesons
  BT3   mesons
  BT4   bosons
  BT4   hadrons
  BT5   elementary particles
  BT3   strange particles
  BT4   elementary particles
  NT1   antikaons neutral
  NT1   kaons neutral long-lived
  NT1   kaons neutral short-lived

KAONS NEUTRAL LONG-LIVED
[923; 923]
  UF   *kaons 2*
  UF   *k02*
  BT1   kaons neutral
  BT2   kaons
  BT3   pseudoscalar mesons
  BT4   mesons
  BT5   bosons
  BT5   hadrons
  BT6   elementary particles
  BT3   strange mesons
  BT4   mesons
  BT5   bosons
  BT5   hadrons
  BT6   elementary particles
  BT4   strange particles
  BT5   elementary particles

KAONS NEUTRAL SHORT-LIVED
[1,111; 1,111]
  UF   *kaons 1*
  UF   *k01*
  BT1   kaons neutral
  BT2   kaons
  BT3   pseudoscalar mesons
  BT4   mesons
  BT5   bosons
  BT5   hadrons
  BT6   elementary particles
  BT3   strange mesons
  BT4   mesons
  BT5   bosons
  BT5   hadrons
  BT6   elementary particles
  BT4   strange particles
  BT5   elementary particles

KAONS PLUS [2,968; 2,968]
  BT1   kaons
  BT2   pseudoscalar mesons
  BT3   mesons
  BT4   bosons
  BT4   hadrons
  BT5   elementary particles
  BT2   strange mesons
  BT3   mesons
  BT4   bosons
  BT4   hadrons
  BT5   elementary particles
  BT3   strange particles
  BT4   elementary particles
  RT   kaonium

kaons 1
  USE   kaons neutral short-lived

kaons 2
  USE   kaons neutral long-lived

KAPITZA RESISTANCE [153; 153]
  BT1   thermal boundary resistance

KAPL [18; 18]
  UF   *knolls atomic power laboratory*
  BT1   us aec
  BT2   us organizations
  BT3   national organizations
  BT1   us doe
  BT2   us organizations
  BT3   national organizations
  BT1   us erda
  BT2   us organizations
  BT3   national organizations
  RT   new york

kappa-725 resonances
(Prior to December 1987 this was a valid descriptor.)
  USE   mesons

kapur-peierls method
  USE   peierls method

karachi nuclear power plant
  USE   kanupp reactor

karlsruhe (kernforschungszentr
  USE   kernforschungszentrum karlsruh

KARLSRUHE CYCLOTRON [92; 92]
  BT1   isochronous cyclotrons
  BT2   cyclotrons
  BT3   cyclic accelerators
  BT4   accelerators

karlsruhe reprocessing plant
(Wiederaufarbeitungsanlage Karlsruhe)
  USE   wak

karlsruhe research r. fr-2
  USE   fr-2 reactor

KARYOTYPE [203; 203]
  RT   acrocentric chromosomes
  RT   chromosomal aberrations
  RT   chromosomes
  RT   genome mutations
  RT   human chromosomes

kashima-1 reactor
  USE   shimane-1 reactor

kashima-2 reactor
  USE   shimane-2 reactor

KASHIWAZAKI-KARIWA-1 REACTOR
[14; 14] *Jan 87*
(Niigata, Japan.)
  UF   *tokyo-denrioku k-1 reactor*
  BT1   bwr type reactors
  BT2   enriched uranium reactors
  BT3   reactors
  BT2   power reactors
  BT3   reactors
  BT2   thermal reactors
  BT3   reactors
  BT2   water cooled reactors
  BT3   reactors
  BT2   water moderated reactors
  BT3   reactors

KASHIWAZAKI-KARIWA-2 REACTOR
[14; 14] *Apr 85*
(Niigata, Japan.)
  UF   *tokyo-denryoku k-2 reactor*
  BT1   bwr type reactors
  BT2   enriched uranium reactors
  BT3   reactors
  BT2   power reactors
  BT3   reactors
  BT2   thermal reactors
  BT3   reactors
  BT2   water cooled reactors
  BT3   reactors
  BT2   water moderated reactors
  BT3   reactors

→ **KASHIWAZAKI-KARIWA-3 REACTOR**
[0; 0] *Oct 91*
(Niigata, Japan)
  BT1   bwr type reactors
  BT2   enriched uranium reactors
  BT3   reactors
  BT2   power reactors
  BT3   reactors
  BT2   thermal reactors
  BT3   reactors
  BT2   water cooled reactors
  BT3   reactors
  BT2   water moderated reactors
  BT3   reactors

KASHIWAZAKI-KARIWA-4 REACTOR
[2; 2] *Dec 90*
(Niigata, Japan.)
BT1   bwr type reactors
BT2   enriched uranium reactors
BT3   reactors
BT2   power reactors
BT3   reactors
BT2   thermal reactors
BT3   reactors
BT2   water cooled reactors
BT3   reactors
BT2   water moderated reactors
BT3   reactors

KASHIWAZAKI-KARIWA-5 REACTOR
[11; 11] *Nov 88*
(Niigata, Japan.)
BT1   bwr type reactors
BT2   enriched uranium reactors
BT3   reactors
BT2   power reactors
BT3   reactors
BT2   thermal reactors
BT3   reactors
BT2   water cooled reactors
BT3   reactors
BT2   water moderated reactors
BT3   reactors

KASHIWAZAKI-KARIWA-6 REACTOR
[2; 2] *Sep 89*
(Niigata, Japan.)
BT1   bwr type reactors
BT2   enriched uranium reactors
BT3   reactors
BT2   power reactors
BT3   reactors
BT2   thermal reactors
BT3   reactors
BT2   water cooled reactors
BT3   reactors
BT2   water moderated reactors
BT3   reactors

KASHIWAZAKI-KARIWA-7 REACTOR
[2; 2] *Sep 89*
(Niigata, Japan.)
BT1   bwr type reactors
BT2   enriched uranium reactors
BT3   reactors
BT2   power reactors
BT3   reactors
BT2   thermal reactors
BT3   reactors
BT2   water cooled reactors
BT3   reactors
BT2   water moderated reactors
BT3   reactors

kawasaki-hitachi training reac
USE   htr reactor

KAZAKHSTAN CYCLOTRON [16; 16]
BT1   isochronous cyclotrons
BT2   cyclotrons
BT3   cyclic accelerators
BT4   accelerators

kcb reactor
(Kernenergiecentrale borssele)
USE   borssele reactor

KDF COMPUTERS [4; 4]
BT1   computers

KECEROVCE-1 REACTOR [9; 9]
Jan 90
(East Slovakia, Czechoslovakia.)
BT1   wwer type reactors
BT2   pwr type reactors
BT3   enriched uranium reactors
BT4   reactors
BT3   power reactors

BT4   reactors
BT3   thermal reactors
BT4   reactors
BT3   water cooled reactors
BT4   reactors
BT3   water moderated reactors
BT4   reactors

kek inters. stor. accel.
USE   tristan storage rings

KEK LINAC [120; 120]
BT1   linear accelerators
BT2   accelerators

KEK PHOTON FACTORY [153; 153]
Jul 84
BT1   synchrotron radiation sources
BT2   radiation sources
RT   linear accelerators
RT   storage rings
RT   synchrotron radiation

KEK SYNCHROTRON [422; 422]
(Japan National Laboratory for High Energy Physics Synchrotron)
UF   tsukuba kek synchrotron
BT1   synchrotrons
BT2   cyclic accelerators
BT3   accelerators

KEL-F [11; 11]
BT1   organic chlorine compounds
BT2   organic halogen compounds
BT3   organic compounds
BT1   organic fluorine compounds
BT2   organic halogen compounds
BT3   organic compounds
BT1   polyethylenes
BT2   polyolefins
BT3   organic polymers
BT4   organic compounds
BT4   polymers

kelvin-helmholtz instability
USE   helmholtz instability

kema suspension test reactor
USE   kstr reactor

KENTUCKY [197; 197]
BT1   usa
BT2   developed countries
BT2   north america
RT   paducah plant

KENYA [37; 37]
BT1   africa
BT1   developing countries

kepco oshima oi-1 reactor
USE   oi-1 reactor

kepco oshima oi-2 reactor
USE   oi-2 reactor

KERATIN [97; 97]
BT1   scleroproteins
BT2   proteins
BT3   organic compounds

KERMA [847; 847]
(Total kinetic energy of charged particles produced by ionizing radiation per unit mass of irradiated material in ergs per gram.)
RT   energy deposition
RT   ionization
RT   kinetic energy
RT   radiation doses

KERNELS [1,535; 1,629]
NT1   point kernels
RT   integral equations

kernels (fuel)
USE   fuel pellets

kernels (slowing-down)
USE   slowing-down kernels

kernenergiecent borssele react
USE   borssele reactor

KERNFORSCHUNGSANLAGE JUELICH [253; 253]
UF   juelich (kernforschungsanlage)
BT1   german fr organizations
BT2   national organizations

KERNFORSCHUNGSZENTRUM KARLSRUH [786; 786]
UF   karlsruhe (kernforschungszentr
BT1   german fr organizations
BT2   national organizations

kernfys. vers. inst. cyclotron
USE   kvi cyclotron

kernfysisch versneller institu
USE   kvi

kernkraftwerk biblis-3
USE   biblis-3 reactor

kernkraftwerk biblis-4
USE   biblis-4 reactor

kernkraftwerk brokdorf
USE   brokdorf reactor

kernkraftwerk emsland
USE   emsland reactor

kernkraftwerk goesgen-daeniken
USE   goesgen reactor

kernkraftwerk isar
USE   isar reactor

kernkraftwerk lingen
USE   lingen reactor

kernkraftwerk niederaichbach
USE   niederaichbach reactor

kernkraftwerk obrigheim
USE   obrigheim reactor

kernkraftwerk philippsburg-1
USE   philippsburg-1 reactor

kernkraftwerk philippsburg-2
USE   philippsburg-2 reactor

kernkraftwerk rwe-bayernwerk
USE   rwe-bayernwerk reactor

kernkraftwerk stade
  USE   stade reactor

kernkraftwerk vahnum-1
  USE   vahnum-1 reactor

kernkraftwerk vahnum-2
  USE   vahnum-2 reactor

kernkraftwerk wuergassen
  USE   wuergassen reactor

KEROSENE [313; 313]
  BT1   fossil fuels
  BT2   energy sources
  BT2   fuels
  BT1   petroleum products

KERR EFFECT [276; 276]
  BT1   dielectric properties
  BT2   electrical properties
  BT3   physical properties
  RT   magneto-optical effects
  RT   polarization
  RT   visible radiation

KERR FIELD [293; 293]
  BT1   gravitational fields
  RT   axial symmetry
  RT   black holes
  RT   einstein field equations
  RT   kerr metric

KERR METRIC [539; 539]
  BT1   metrics
  RT   kerr field

KETENES [39; 39]
  BT1   organic oxygen compounds
  BT2   organic compounds
  RT   carboxylic acids

KETO ACIDS [68; 290]
  (For carboxyl acids only.)
  UF   *oxocarboxylic acids*
  BT1   carboxylic acids
  BT2   organic acids
  BT3   organic compounds
  NT1   acetoacetic acid
  NT1   kynurenine
  NT1   levulinic acid
  NT1   pyruvic acid

ketobutyric acid-beta
  USE   acetoacetic acid

KETONES [1,899; 6,877]
  UF   *cyclohexanone*
  UF+   *ndpp*
  UF+   *p-nitrodimethylaminopropiophen*
  BT1   organic compounds
  NT1   acetone
  NT1   acetophenone
  NT1   acetylacetone
  NT1   androstenedione
  NT1   androsterone
  NT1   benzophenone
  NT1   camphor
  NT1   corticosteroids
    NT2   glucocorticoids
      NT3   corticosterone
      NT3   cortisone
      NT3   dexamethasone
      NT3   hydrocortisone
      NT3   prednisolone
      NT3   prednisone
    NT2   mineralocorticoids
      NT3   aldosterone
      NT3   doca
  NT1   curcumin

  NT1   dianabol
  NT1   estrone
  NT1   fructose
  NT1   hydroxyandrostenone
  NT1   hydroxypregnenone
  NT1   methyl isobutyl ketone
  NT1   ninhydrin
  NT1   papp
  NT1   phlorizin
  NT1   pop
  NT1   progesterone
  NT1   ribulose
  NT1   sedoheptulose
  NT1   sorbose
  NT1   testosterone
  NT1   triacetoneamine-n-oxyl
  NT1   tropones
  NT1   tta
  NT1   violanthrone
  NT1   2-3-pentanedione
  RT   enols
  RT   hydrazones
  RT   imines
  RT   oximes
  RT   quinones
  RT   semicarbazones

ketopropionic acid-alpha
  USE   pyruvic acid

ketosteroids (urinary)
  USE   urinary ketosteroids

ketovaleric acid-gamma
  USE   levulinic acid

KEV RANGE [2,685; 27,288]
  BT1   energy range
  NT1   kev range 01-10
  NT1   kev range 10-100
  NT1   kev range 100-1000

KEV RANGE 01-10 [6,695; 6,695]
  BT1   kev range
  BT2   energy range

KEV RANGE 10-100 [10,919; 10,919]
  BT1   kev range
  BT2   energy range

KEV RANGE 100-1000 [12,919; 12,919]
  BT1   kev range
  BT2   energy range

KEWAUNEE REACTOR [85; 85]
  (Carlton, Wisconsin, USA)
  UF   *carlton power reactor*
  UF   *wisconsin publ. serv. pow. rea*
  BT1   pwr type reactors
  BT2   enriched uranium reactors
  BT3   reactors
  BT2   power reactors
  BT3   reactors
  BT2   thermal reactors
  BT3   reactors
  BT2   water cooled reactors
  BT3   reactors
  BT2   water moderated reactors
  BT3   reactors

KEWB REACTOR [2; 2]
  UF   *kinetic exper. on water boiler*
  BT1   aqueous homogeneous reactors
  BT2   liquid homogeneous reactors
  BT3   fluid fueled reactors
  BT4   reactors
  BT3   homogeneous reactors
  BT4   reactors
  BT2   water cooled reactors
  BT3   reactors
  BT2   water moderated reactors
  BT3   reactors

→ **KEY LAKE MINE** [2; 2] *Jul 91*
  BT1   uranium mines
  BT2   mines
  BT3   underground facilities
  RT   saskatchewan

KHALATNIKOV THEORY [30; 30]
  RT   superfluidity
  RT   thermodynamics

KHARKOV LINAC [178; 178]
  BT1   linear accelerators
  BT2   accelerators

KHMELNITSKIJ-1 REACTOR [13; 13]
  Sep 89
  (Ukrainian SSR, USSR.)
  BT1   wwer type reactors
  BT2   pwr type reactors
  BT3   enriched uranium reactors
  BT4   reactors
  BT3   power reactors
  BT4   reactors
  BT3   thermal reactors
  BT4   reactors
  BT3   water cooled reactors
  BT4   reactors
  BT3   water moderated reactors
  BT4   reactors

KHURI REPRESENTATION [5; 5]
  RT   mandelstam representation

KHZ RANGE [276; 1,346]
  BT1   frequency range
  NT1   khz range 01-100
  NT1   khz range 100-1000

KHZ RANGE 01-100 [790; 790]
  BT1   khz range
  BT2   frequency range

KHZ RANGE 100-1000 [378; 378]
  BT1   khz range
  BT2   frequency range

KICKER MAGNETS [211; 211] *Oct 81*
  BT1   magnets
  BT2   equipment
  RT   beam extraction
  RT   beam optics

kicksorters
  USE   pulse analyzers

kidney stones
  USE   calculi
  AND   kidneys

KIDNEYS [7,912; 8,216]
  UF+   *kidney stones*
  BT1   organs
  BT2   body
  NT1   glomeruli
  NT1   tubules
  RT   blood circulation
  RT   calculi
  RT   excretion
  RT   nephrectomy
  RT   nephritis
  RT   nephrosclerosis
  RT   renal clearance
  RT   renin
  RT   renography
  RT   uremia
  RT   urinary tract
  RT   urine
  RT   urogenital system diseases

KIEV CYCLOTRON [33; 33] *Dec 81*
BT1 isochronous cyclotrons
BT2 cyclotrons
BT3 cyclic accelerators
BT4 accelerators

kiev wwr-m reactor
USE wwr-m-kiev reactor

kihara core
USE kihara potential

KIHARA POTENTIAL [11; 11]
UF *kihara core*
UF *kihara theory*
BT1 potentials
RT atoms
RT molecules

kihara theory
USE kihara potential

KIKUCHI LINES [70; 70]
RT crystal structure
RT dislocations
RT electron diffraction

KILO AMP BEAM CURRENTS
[1,048; 1,048]
(From 1000 to 10 exp 6 amp.)
BT1 beam currents
BT2 currents

KILOWATT POWER RANGE [3; 29]
Apr 88
BT1 power range
NT1 power range 01-10 kw
NT1 power range 10-100 kw
NT1 power range 100-1000 kw

KIMBERLITES [81; 81]
BT1 peridotites
BT2 plutonic rocks
BT3 igneous rocks
BT4 rocks
RT apatites
RT mica
RT olivine
RT oxide minerals
RT perovskite
RT silicate minerals

kinases (phosphotransferases)
USE phosphotransferases

kinematics (particle)
USE particle kinematics

KINETIC ENERGY [4,540; 4,657]
BT1 energy
NT1 transverse energy
RT angular momentum
RT kerma
RT lagrangian function
RT linear momentum
RT moment of inertia
RT motion
RT particle rapidity
RT potential energy
RT velocity
RT virial theorem

KINETIC EQUATIONS [4,335; 4,335]
(For reactor kinetics see REACTOR KINETICS EQUATIONS.)
BT1 equations
RT boltzmann equation
RT collisions
RT gases
RT plasma
RT statistical mechanics

kinetic exper. on water boiler
USE kewb reactor

kinetic intense neutron genera
USE king reactor

§§ **KINETICS** [5,579; 63,442]
NT1 radionuclide kinetics
NT1 reaction kinetics
NT2 biochemical reaction kinetics
NT2 chemical reaction kinetics
NT3 combustion kinetics
NT2 nuclear reaction kinetics
NT1 reactor kinetics
RT collisions
RT deck effect
RT dynamics
RT gases
RT mechanics
RT statistical mechanics
RT translocation

kinetics equations (reactor)
USE reactor kinetics equations

KINETIN [51; 51]
UF *6-furfurylaminopurine*
BT1 adenines
BT2 amines
BT3 organic compounds
BT2 antimetabolites
BT3 drugs
BT2 purines
BT3 heterocyclic compounds
BT4 organic compounds
BT3 organic nitrogen compounds
BT4 organic compounds
RT furans
RT plant growth
RT plant growth regulators

KING REACTOR [2; 2]
UF *kinetic intense neutron genera*
BT1 research reactors
BT2 research and test reactors
BT3 reactors

KININS [206; 206]
UF+ *bradykinin*
BT1 polypeptides
BT2 peptides
BT3 proteins
BT4 organic compounds

KINK INSTABILITY [771; 771]
BT1 plasma macroinstabilities
BT2 plasma instability
BT3 instability
RT sawtooth oscillations

kinki univ. utr-10 reactor
USE utr-10-kinki reactor

→ **KIRIBATI** [2; 2] *Mar 91*
BT1 micronesia
BT2 australasia
BT2 islands
RT pacific ocean

KIRKENDALL EFFECT [45; 45]
RT diffusion

kisslinger model
USE optical models

KISSLINGER-SORENSEN THEORY
[23; 23]
RT nuclear models
RT superconductivity

KIWI REACTORS [5; 5] *May 80*
(Prior to August 1985 KIWI TYPE REACTORS was used.)
UF *kiwi type reactors*
BT1 experimental reactors
BT2 research and test reactors
BT3 reactors
BT1 hydrogen cooled reactors
BT2 gas cooled reactors
BT3 reactors
BT1 space propulsion reactors
BT2 propulsion reactors
BT3 power reactors
BT4 reactors
BT2 space power reactors
BT3 mobile reactors
BT4 reactors
BT3 power reactors
BT4 reactors

kiwi type reactors
(Prior to August 1985 this was a valid descriptor.)
USE kiwi reactors

KJELDAHL METHOD [58; 58]
RT nitrogen
RT quantitative chemical analysis

kkb reactor
USE brunsbuettel reactor

kki isar
USE isar reactor

kkk reactor
USE kruemmel reactor

kkn reactor
USE niederaichbach reactor

kkp-1 philippsburg reactor
USE philippsburg-1 reactor

kkp-2 philippsburg reactor
USE philippsburg-2 reactor

kks reactor
USE stade reactor

kku reactor
USE unterweser reactor

kkw greifswald-1 reactor
USE greifswald-1 reactor

kkw greifswald-2 reactor
USE greifswald-2 reactor

kkw greifswald-3 reactor
USE greifswald-3 reactor

kkw greifswald-4 reactor
USE greifswald-4 reactor

KLEIN-GORDON EQUATION
[1,324; 1,324]
BT1 field equations
BT2 equations
BT1 wave equations
BT2 partial differential equations
BT3 differential equations
BT4 equations

  RT quantum mechanics

KLEIN-NISHINA FORMULA [101; 101]
  RT compton effect

KLYSTRONS [825; 825]
  BT1 microwave tubes
   BT2 electron tubes
  BT2 microwave equipment
   BT3 electronic equipment
    BT4 equipment
  RT gyrocons
  RT magnetrons
  RT power supplies
  RT rf systems

→ **KMR REACTOR** [9; 9] *Jul 91*
  BT1 enriched uranium reactors
   BT2 reactors
  BT1 isotope production reactors
   BT2 irradiation reactors
    BT3 reactors
  BT1 materials testing reactors
   BT2 irradiation reactors
    BT3 reactors
  BT1 pool type reactors
   BT2 water cooled reactors
    BT3 reactors
   BT2 water moderated reactors
    BT3 reactors
  BT1 research reactors
   BT2 research and test reactors
    BT3 reactors
  BT1 test reactors
   BT2 research and test reactors
    BT3 reactors
   BT2 test facilities

KNIGHT EFFECT [11; 11]
  RT spectral shift

KNIGHT SHIFT [733; 733]
  RT nuclear magnetic resonance
  RT spectral shift

knipp-bloch theory
  USE knipp-uhlenbeck theory

KNIPP-UHLENBECK THEORY [5; 5]
  UF knipp-bloch theory
  RT beta decay

KNK REACTOR [110; 110]
(Leopoldshafen, Karlsruhe, Federal Republic of Germany)
  UF kompakte natriumgekuehlte reak
  BT1 enriched uranium reactors
   BT2 reactors
  BT1 experimental reactors
   BT2 research and test reactors
    BT3 reactors
  BT1 power reactors
   BT2 reactors
  BT1 sodium cooled reactors
   BT2 liquid metal cooled reactors
    BT3 reactors
  BT1 szr type reactors
   BT2 hydride moderated reactors
    BT3 reactors
   BT2 liquid metal cooled reactors
    BT3 reactors
  BT1 thermal reactors
   BT2 reactors

KNK-2 REACTOR [278; 278]
(Leopoldshafen, Karlsruhe, Federal Republic of Germany)
  BT1 enriched uranium reactors
   BT2 reactors
  BT1 experimental reactors
   BT2 research and test reactors
    BT3 reactors
  BT1 fast reactors
   BT2 epithermal reactors
    BT3 reactors
  BT1 power reactors
   BT2 reactors
  BT1 sodium cooled reactors
   BT2 liquid metal cooled reactors
    BT3 reactors
  BT1 szr type reactors
   BT2 hydride moderated reactors
    BT3 reactors
   BT2 liquid metal cooled reactors
    BT3 reactors

KNOCK-ON [197; 197]
  RT recoils

knock-on electrons
  USE electrons

KNOCK-ON REACTIONS [178; 178]
  BT1 direct reactions
   BT2 nuclear reactions
  RT knock-out reactions

KNOCK-OUT REACTIONS
[2,363; 2,363]
  BT1 direct reactions
   BT2 nuclear reactions
  RT knock-on reactions
  RT recoils

knolls atomic power laboratory
  USE kapl

KNOOP HARDNESS [65; 65]
  RT hardness

→ *knu-10 reactor*
  USE ulchin-2 reactor

→ *knu-9 reactor*
  USE ulchin-1 reactor

knudsen effusion
  USE knudsen flow

KNUDSEN FLOW [328; 328]
  UF knudsen effusion
  UF knudsen number
  BT1 gas flow
  BT2 fluid flow
  RT vapor pressure

KNUDSEN GAGES [22; 22]
  BT1 vacuum gages
  BT2 pressure gages
  BT3 measuring instruments

knudsen number
  USE knudsen flow

KOBAYASHI-MASKAWA MATRIX
[1,044; 1,044] *Jan 84*
(Matrix describing the mixing between the three quark-lepton generations (u,d,e), (c,s,mu) and (t,b,tau) as a generalization of Cabibbo mixing with allowance of CP violation in the charged-current transition amplitude.)
  UF mixing matrix (kobayashi-mask)
  BT1 matrices
  RT cabibbo angle
  RT configuration mixing
  RT cp invariance
  RT flavor model
  RT standard model

KOEBERG-1 REACTOR [228; 228]
Nov 75
(Duynefontein, Cape, South Africa)
  UF escom-1 reactor
  BT1 power reactors
   BT2 reactors
  BT1 water cooled reactors
   BT2 reactors
  BT1 water moderated reactors
   BT2 reactors

KOEBERG-2 REACTOR [25; 25] *Jan 82*
  BT1 power reactors
   BT2 reactors
  BT1 water cooled reactors
   BT2 reactors
  BT1 water moderated reactors
   BT2 reactors

KOLA-1 REACTOR [20; 20] *Oct 81*
  BT1 wwer type reactors
   BT2 pwr type reactors
    BT3 enriched uranium reactors
     BT4 reactors
    BT3 power reactors
     BT4 reactors
    BT3 thermal reactors
     BT4 reactors
    BT3 water cooled reactors
     BT4 reactors
    BT3 water moderated reactors
     BT4 reactors

KOLA-2 REACTOR [10; 10] *Oct 81*
  BT1 wwer type reactors
   BT2 pwr type reactors
    BT3 enriched uranium reactors
     BT4 reactors
    BT3 power reactors
     BT4 reactors
    BT3 thermal reactors
     BT4 reactors
    BT3 water cooled reactors
     BT4 reactors
    BT3 water moderated reactors
     BT4 reactors

KOLA-3 REACTOR [5; 5] *Oct 81*
  BT1 wwer type reactors
   BT2 pwr type reactors
    BT3 enriched uranium reactors
     BT4 reactors
    BT3 power reactors
     BT4 reactors
    BT3 thermal reactors
     BT4 reactors
    BT3 water cooled reactors
     BT4 reactors
    BT3 water moderated reactors
     BT4 reactors

KOLA-4 REACTOR [5; 5] *Oct 81*
  BT1 wwer type reactors
   BT2 pwr type reactors
    BT3 enriched uranium reactors
     BT4 reactors
    BT3 power reactors
     BT4 reactors
    BT3 thermal reactors
     BT4 reactors
    BT3 water cooled reactors
     BT4 reactors
    BT3 water moderated reactors
     BT4 reactors

kolmogorov equation
  USE chapman-kolmogorov equation

kompakte natriumgekuehlte reak
  USE knk reactor

KONDO EFFECT [756; 756]
  RT antiferromagnetic materials

KONRAD ORE MINE [46; 46] *Nov 89*
  BT1 mines
   BT2 underground facilities
  BT1 radioactive waste facilities
   BT2 nuclear facilities
  RT intermediate-level radioactive
  RT low-level radioactive wastes

RT radioactive waste disposal
RT shaft excavations
RT underground disposal

KOONGARRA DEPOSIT [75; 75] *Jul 78*
BT1 uranium deposits
BT2 geologic deposits
RT northern territory
RT uranium ores

korea (north)
USE north korea

korea (south)
USE republic of korea

korea adv. en. res. institute
USE kaeri

korea atom. en. res. institute
USE kaeri

korean (seoul) triga-mk-2 reac
USE triga-2-seoul reactor

korean (seoul) triga-mk-3 reac
USE triga-3-seoul reactor

KOREAN ORGANIZATIONS [1; 39]
Dec 81
BT1 national organizations
NT1 kaeri

KORI-1 REACTOR [96; 96]
UF pusan kori-1 reactor
BT1 pwr type reactors
BT2 enriched uranium reactors
BT3 reactors
BT2 power reactors
BT3 reactors
BT2 thermal reactors
BT3 reactors
BT2 water cooled reactors
BT3 reactors
BT2 water moderated reactors
BT3 reactors

KORI-2 REACTOR [7; 7] *Sep 86*
UF pusan kori-2 reactor
BT1 pwr type reactors
BT2 enriched uranium reactors
BT3 reactors
BT2 power reactors
BT3 reactors
BT2 thermal reactors
BT3 reactors
BT2 water cooled reactors
BT3 reactors
BT2 water moderated reactors
BT3 reactors

KORTEWEG-DE VRIES EQUATION [677; 677]
BT1 partial differential equations
BT2 differential equations
BT3 equations

KOSHKONONG-1 REACTOR [3; 3]
(As of July 1978 known as HAVEN-1 REACTOR, and from that date material is so indexed.)
BT1 haven-1 reactor
BT2 pwr type reactors
BT3 enriched uranium reactors
BT4 reactors
BT3 power reactors
BT4 reactors
BT3 thermal reactors
BT4 reactors
BT3 water cooled reactors
BT4 reactors
BT3 water moderated reactors
BT4 reactors

KOSHKONONG-2 REACTOR [3; 3]
(As of July 1978 known as HAVEN-2 REACTOR, and from that date material is so indexed.)
BT1 haven-2 reactor
BT2 pwr type reactors
BT3 enriched uranium reactors
BT4 reactors
BT3 power reactors
BT4 reactors
BT3 thermal reactors
BT4 reactors
BT3 water cooled reactors
BT4 reactors
BT3 water moderated reactors
BT4 reactors

KOSMOS SATELLITES [244; 244]
BT1 satellites
RT interkosmos satellites
RT proton satellites

KOSSEL METHOD [44; 44]
RT laue method

kovar
USE alloy-fe53ni29co18

KOZLODUY-1 REACTOR [65; 65]
Mar 77
(Kozloduy, Bulgaria. Prior to December 1990, this descriptor was spelled KOZLODUJ-1 REACTOR.)
BT1 wwer type reactors
BT2 pwr type reactors
BT3 enriched uranium reactors
BT4 reactors
BT3 power reactors
BT4 reactors
BT3 thermal reactors
BT4 reactors
BT3 water cooled reactors
BT4 reactors
BT3 water moderated reactors
BT4 reactors

KOZLODUY-2 REACTOR [60; 60]
Mar 77
(Kozloduy, Bulgaria. Prior to December 1990, this descriptor was spelled KOZLODUJ-2 REACTOR.)
BT1 wwer type reactors
BT2 pwr type reactors
BT3 enriched uranium reactors
BT4 reactors
BT3 power reactors
BT4 reactors
BT3 thermal reactors
BT4 reactors
BT3 water cooled reactors
BT4 reactors
BT3 water moderated reactors
BT4 reactors

KOZLODUY-3 REACTOR [19; 19]
Oct 85
(Kozloduy, Bulgaria. Prior to December 1990, this descriptor was spelled KOZLODUJ-3 REACTOR.)
BT1 wwer type reactors
BT2 pwr type reactors
BT3 enriched uranium reactors
BT4 reactors
BT3 power reactors
BT4 reactors
BT3 thermal reactors
BT4 reactors
BT3 water cooled reactors
BT4 reactors
BT3 water moderated reactors
BT4 reactors

KRAMERS THEOREM [58; 58]
RT quantum mechanics

KRAMERS-KRONIG CORRELATION [235; 235]
BT1 correlations

krb ii-b reactor
USE gundremmingen-2 reactor

krb ii-c reactor
USE gundremmingen-3 reactor

krb reactor
USE rwe-bayernwerk reactor

KREBS CYCLE [36; 36]
RT metabolism
RT metabolites
RT mitochondria
RT respiration

krito critical assembly
USE stek reactor

KROLL PROCESS [8; 8]
RT reduction
RT titanium

KROLL-RUDERMAN THEOREM [9; 9]
(Prior to March, 1989, this descriptor was spelled KROLL-RUDERMANN THEOREM.)
RT photoproduction

KRSKO REACTOR [58; 58] *Jan 78*
(Krsko, Yugoslavia)
BT1 pwr type reactors
BT2 enriched uranium reactors
BT3 reactors
BT2 power reactors
BT3 reactors
BT2 thermal reactors
BT3 reactors
BT2 water cooled reactors
BT3 reactors
BT2 water moderated reactors
BT3 reactors

KRUEMMEL REACTOR [124; 124]
UF kkk reactor
BT1 bwr type reactors
BT2 enriched uranium reactors
BT3 reactors
BT2 power reactors
BT3 reactors
BT2 thermal reactors
BT3 reactors
BT2 water cooled reactors
BT3 reactors
BT2 water moderated reactors
BT3 reactors

KRUSKAL LIMIT [51; 51]
RT electric currents
RT stellarators

KRYPTON [2,899; 2,899]
BT1 rare gases
BT2 nonmetals
BT3 elements

KRYPTON CHLORIDES [5; 5]
BT1 chlorides
BT2 chlorine compounds
BT3 halogen compounds
BT2 halides
BT3 halogen compounds
BT1 krypton compounds
BT2 rare gas compounds

KRYPTON COMPLEXES [8; 8]
BT1   complexes

KRYPTON COMPOUNDS [94; 310]
UF   *kryptonates*
BT1   rare gas compounds
NT1   krypton chlorides
NT1   krypton fluorides
NT1   krypton hydrides
NT1   krypton oxides

KRYPTON FLUORIDE LASERS
[169; 169] *Jan 86*
BT1   excimer lasers
 BT2   gas lasers
  BT3   lasers
   BT4   amplifiers
    BT5   equipment
RT   aurora facility

KRYPTON FLUORIDES [199; 199]
BT1   fluorides
 BT2   fluorine compounds
  BT3   halogen compounds
 BT2   halides
  BT3   halogen compounds
BT1   krypton compounds
 BT2   rare gas compounds

KRYPTON HYDRIDES [7; 7]
BT1   hydrides
 BT2   hydrogen compounds
BT1   krypton compounds
 BT2   rare gas compounds

KRYPTON IONS [1,170; 1,170]
BT1   ions
 BT2   charged particles

KRYPTON ISOTOPES [364; 3,901]
NT1   krypton 70
NT1   krypton 71
NT1   krypton 72
NT1   krypton 73
NT1   krypton 74
NT1   krypton 75
NT1   krypton 76
NT1   krypton 77
NT1   krypton 78
NT1   krypton 79
NT1   krypton 80
NT1   krypton 81
NT1   krypton 82
NT1   krypton 83
NT1   krypton 84
NT1   krypton 85
NT1   krypton 86
NT1   krypton 87
NT1   krypton 88
NT1   krypton 89
NT1   krypton 90
NT1   krypton 91
NT1   krypton 92
NT1   krypton 93
NT1   krypton 94
NT1   krypton 95
NT1   krypton 96
NT1   krypton 97
NT1   krypton 98

KRYPTON OXIDES [7; 7]
BT1   krypton compounds
 BT2   rare gas compounds
BT1   oxides
 BT2   chalcogenides
 BT2   oxygen compounds

KRYPTON 70 [0; 0]
BT1   even-even nuclei
 BT2   nuclei
BT1   intermediate mass nuclei
 BT2   nuclei
BT1   krypton isotopes

KRYPTON 71 [2; 2]
BT1   beta-plus decay radioisotopes
 BT2   beta decay radioisotopes
  BT3   radioisotopes
   BT4   isotopes
BT1   electron capture radioisotopes
 BT2   beta decay radioisotopes
  BT3   radioisotopes
   BT4   isotopes
BT1   even-odd nuclei
 BT2   nuclei
BT1   intermediate mass nuclei
 BT2   nuclei
BT1   krypton isotopes
BT1   millisec living radioisotopes
 BT2   radioisotopes
  BT3   isotopes

KRYPTON 72 [12; 12]
BT1   beta-plus decay radioisotopes
 BT2   beta decay radioisotopes
  BT3   radioisotopes
   BT4   isotopes
BT1   electron capture radioisotopes
 BT2   beta decay radioisotopes
  BT3   radioisotopes
   BT4   isotopes
BT1   even-even nuclei
 BT2   nuclei
BT1   intermediate mass nuclei
 BT2   nuclei
BT1   krypton isotopes
BT1   seconds living radioisotopes
 BT2   radioisotopes
  BT3   isotopes

KRYPTON 73 [17; 17]
BT1   beta-plus decay radioisotopes
 BT2   beta decay radioisotopes
  BT3   radioisotopes
   BT4   isotopes
BT1   electron capture radioisotopes
 BT2   beta decay radioisotopes
  BT3   radioisotopes
   BT4   isotopes
BT1   even-odd nuclei
 BT2   nuclei
BT1   intermediate mass nuclei
 BT2   nuclei
BT1   krypton isotopes
BT1   seconds living radioisotopes
 BT2   radioisotopes
  BT3   isotopes

KRYPTON 74 [49; 49]
BT1   beta-plus decay radioisotopes
 BT2   beta decay radioisotopes
  BT3   radioisotopes
   BT4   isotopes
BT1   electron capture radioisotopes
 BT2   beta decay radioisotopes
  BT3   radioisotopes
   BT4   isotopes
BT1   even-even nuclei
 BT2   nuclei
BT1   intermediate mass nuclei
 BT2   nuclei
BT1   krypton isotopes
BT1   minutes living radioisotopes
 BT2   radioisotopes
  BT3   isotopes

KRYPTON 75 [34; 34]
BT1   beta-plus decay radioisotopes
 BT2   beta decay radioisotopes
  BT3   radioisotopes
   BT4   isotopes
BT1   electron capture radioisotopes
 BT2   beta decay radioisotopes
  BT3   radioisotopes
   BT4   isotopes
BT1   even-odd nuclei
 BT2   nuclei
BT1   intermediate mass nuclei
 BT2   nuclei
BT1   krypton isotopes
BT1   minutes living radioisotopes
 BT2   radioisotopes
  BT3   isotopes

KRYPTON 76 [84; 84]
BT1   electron capture radioisotopes
 BT2   beta decay radioisotopes
  BT3   radioisotopes
   BT4   isotopes
BT1   even-even nuclei
 BT2   nuclei
BT1   hours living radioisotopes
 BT2   radioisotopes
  BT3   isotopes
BT1   intermediate mass nuclei
 BT2   nuclei
BT1   krypton isotopes

KRYPTON 77 [85; 85]
BT1   beta-plus decay radioisotopes
 BT2   beta decay radioisotopes
  BT3   radioisotopes
   BT4   isotopes
BT1   electron capture radioisotopes
 BT2   beta decay radioisotopes
  BT3   radioisotopes
   BT4   isotopes
BT1   even-odd nuclei
 BT2   nuclei
BT1   hours living radioisotopes
 BT2   radioisotopes
  BT3   isotopes
BT1   intermediate mass nuclei
 BT2   nuclei
BT1   krypton isotopes

KRYPTON 78 [125; 125]
BT1   even-even nuclei
 BT2   nuclei
BT1   intermediate mass nuclei
 BT2   nuclei
BT1   krypton isotopes
BT1   stable isotopes
 BT2   isotopes

KRYPTON 78 TARGET [28; 28] *Jan 77*
BT1   targets

KRYPTON 79 [72; 72]
BT1   beta-plus decay radioisotopes
 BT2   beta decay radioisotopes
  BT3   radioisotopes
   BT4   isotopes
BT1   days living radioisotopes
 BT2   radioisotopes
  BT3   isotopes
BT1   electron capture radioisotopes
 BT2   beta decay radioisotopes
  BT3   radioisotopes
   BT4   isotopes
BT1   even-odd nuclei
 BT2   nuclei
BT1   intermediate mass nuclei
 BT2   nuclei
BT1   internal conversion radioisoto
 BT2   radioisotopes
  BT3   isotopes
BT1   isomeric transition isotopes
 BT2   radioisotopes
  BT3   isotopes
BT1   krypton isotopes
BT1   seconds living radioisotopes
 BT2   radioisotopes
  BT3   isotopes

KRYPTON 80 [102; 102]
BT1   even-even nuclei
 BT2   nuclei
BT1   intermediate mass nuclei
 BT2   nuclei
BT1   krypton isotopes
BT1   stable isotopes
 BT2   isotopes

KRYPTON 80 REACTIONS [3; 3]
Oct 86
BT1   heavy ion reactions
 BT2   nuclear reactions

KRYPTON 80 TARGET [35; 35] *Oct 75*
BT1   targets

KRYPTON 81 [679; 679]
BT1   electron capture radioisotopes
 BT2   beta decay radioisotopes
  BT3   radioisotopes
   BT4   isotopes
BT1   even-odd nuclei
 BT2   nuclei
BT1   intermediate mass nuclei
 BT2   nuclei
BT1   isomeric transition isotopes
 BT2   radioisotopes
  BT3   isotopes
BT1   krypton isotopes
BT1   seconds living radioisotopes
 BT2   radioisotopes
  BT3   isotopes
BT1   years living radioisotopes
 BT2   radioisotopes
  BT3   isotopes

KRYPTON 82 [101; 101]
BT1   even-even nuclei
 BT2   nuclei
BT1   intermediate mass nuclei
 BT2   nuclei
BT1   krypton isotopes
BT1   stable isotopes
 BT2   isotopes

KRYPTON 82 REACTIONS [4; 4]
May 87
BT1   heavy ion reactions
 BT2   nuclear reactions

KRYPTON 82 TARGET [41; 41] *Jan 77*
BT1   targets

KRYPTON 83 [119; 119]
BT1   even-odd nuclei
 BT2   nuclei
BT1   hours living radioisotopes
 BT2   radioisotopes
  BT3   isotopes
BT1   intermediate mass nuclei
 BT2   nuclei
BT1   internal conversion radioisoto
 BT2   radioisotopes
  BT3   isotopes
BT1   isomeric transition isotopes
 BT2   radioisotopes
  BT3   isotopes
BT1   krypton isotopes
BT1   stable isotopes
 BT2   isotopes

KRYPTON 83 REACTIONS [5; 5]
BT1   heavy ion reactions
BT2   nuclear reactions

KRYPTON 83 TARGET [18; 18] *Jan 77*
BT1   targets

KRYPTON 84 [189; 189]
BT1   even-even nuclei
 BT2   nuclei
BT1   intermediate mass nuclei
 BT2   nuclei
BT1   isomeric transition isotopes
 BT2   radioisotopes
  BT3   isotopes
BT1   krypton isotopes
BT1   microsec living radioisotopes
 BT2   radioisotopes
  BT3   isotopes
BT1   stable isotopes
 BT2   isotopes
RT   krypton 84 beams

KRYPTON 84 BEAMS [127; 127]
BT1   ion beams
 BT2   beams
RT   krypton 84

KRYPTON 84 REACTIONS [339; 339]
BT1   heavy ion reactions
 BT2   nuclear reactions

KRYPTON 84 TARGET [59; 59]
BT1   targets

KRYPTON 85 [1,992; 1,992]
BT1   beta-minus decay radioisotopes
 BT2   beta decay radioisotopes
  BT3   radioisotopes
   BT4   isotopes
BT1   even-odd nuclei
 BT2   nuclei
BT1   hours living radioisotopes
 BT2   radioisotopes
  BT3   isotopes
BT1   intermediate mass nuclei
 BT2   nuclei
BT1   isomeric transition isotopes
 BT2   radioisotopes
  BT3   isotopes
BT1   krypton isotopes
BT1   microsec living radioisotopes
 BT2   radioisotopes
  BT3   isotopes
BT1   years living radioisotopes
 BT2   radioisotopes
  BT3   isotopes

KRYPTON 85 TARGET [3; 3] *Nov 85*
BT1   targets

KRYPTON 86 [134; 134]
BT1   even-even nuclei
 BT2   nuclei
BT1   intermediate mass nuclei
 BT2   nuclei
BT1   isomeric transition isotopes
 BT2   radioisotopes
  BT3   isotopes
BT1   krypton isotopes
BT1   nanosec living radioisotopes
 BT2   radioisotopes
  BT3   isotopes
BT1   stable isotopes
 BT2   isotopes

KRYPTON 86 BEAMS [36; 36] *Sep 79*
BT1   ion beams
 BT2   beams

KRYPTON 86 REACTIONS [412; 412]
Oct 76
BT1   heavy ion reactions
 BT2   nuclear reactions

KRYPTON 86 TARGET [60; 60]
BT1   targets

KRYPTON 87 [118; 118]
BT1   beta-minus decay radioisotopes
 BT2   beta decay radioisotopes
  BT3   radioisotopes
   BT4   isotopes
BT1   even-odd nuclei
 BT2   nuclei
BT1   hours living radioisotopes
 BT2   radioisotopes
  BT3   isotopes
BT1   intermediate mass nuclei
 BT2   nuclei
BT1   krypton isotopes

KRYPTON 88 [133; 133]
BT1   beta-minus decay radioisotopes
 BT2   beta decay radioisotopes
  BT3   radioisotopes
   BT4   isotopes
BT1   even-even nuclei
 BT2   nuclei
BT1   hours living radioisotopes
 BT2   radioisotopes
  BT3   isotopes
BT1   intermediate mass nuclei
 BT2   nuclei
BT1   krypton isotopes

KRYPTON 89 [50; 50]
BT1   beta-minus decay radioisotopes
 BT2   beta decay radioisotopes
  BT3   radioisotopes
   BT4   isotopes
BT1   even-odd nuclei
 BT2   nuclei
BT1   intermediate mass nuclei
 BT2   nuclei
BT1   krypton isotopes
BT1   minutes living radioisotopes
 BT2   radioisotopes
  BT3   isotopes

KRYPTON 90 [32; 32]
BT1   beta-minus decay radioisotopes
 BT2   beta decay radioisotopes
  BT3   radioisotopes
   BT4   isotopes
BT1   even-even nuclei
 BT2   nuclei
BT1   intermediate mass nuclei
 BT2   nuclei
BT1   krypton isotopes
BT1   seconds living radioisotopes
 BT2   radioisotopes
  BT3   isotopes

KRYPTON 91 [20; 20]
BT1   beta-minus decay radioisotopes
 BT2   beta decay radioisotopes
  BT3   radioisotopes
   BT4   isotopes
BT1   even-odd nuclei
 BT2   nuclei
BT1   intermediate mass nuclei
 BT2   nuclei
BT1   krypton isotopes
BT1   seconds living radioisotopes
 BT2   radioisotopes
  BT3   isotopes

KRYPTON 92 [17; 17]
BT1   beta-minus decay radioisotopes
 BT2   beta decay radioisotopes
  BT3   radioisotopes
   BT4   isotopes
BT1   even-even nuclei
 BT2   nuclei
BT1   intermediate mass nuclei
 BT2   nuclei
BT1   krypton isotopes
BT1   seconds living radioisotopes
 BT2   radioisotopes
  BT3   isotopes

KRYPTON 93 [18; 18]
BT1   beta-minus decay radioisotopes
 BT2   beta decay radioisotopes
  BT3   radioisotopes
   BT4   isotopes
BT1   even-odd nuclei
 BT2   nuclei
BT1   intermediate mass nuclei
 BT2   nuclei
BT1   krypton isotopes
BT1   seconds living radioisotopes
 BT2   radioisotopes
  BT3   isotopes

KRYPTON 94 [6; 6]
BT1   beta-minus decay radioisotopes
 BT2   beta decay radioisotopes
  BT3   radioisotopes
   BT4   isotopes
BT1   even-even nuclei
 BT2   nuclei
BT1   intermediate mass nuclei
 BT2   nuclei
BT1   krypton isotopes
BT1   millisec living radioisotopes
 BT2   radioisotopes
  BT3   isotopes

KRYPTON 95 [3; 3]
  BT1   beta-minus decay radioisotopes
  BT2   beta decay radioisotopes
  BT3   radioisotopes
  BT4   isotopes
  BT1   even-odd nuclei
  BT2   nuclei
  BT1   intermediate mass nuclei
  BT2   nuclei
  BT1   krypton isotopes
  BT1   millisec living radioisotopes
  BT2   radioisotopes
  BT3   isotopes

KRYPTON 96 [1; 1]
  BT1   even-even nuclei
  BT2   nuclei
  BT1   intermediate mass nuclei
  BT2   nuclei
  BT1   krypton isotopes

KRYPTON 97 [1; 1]
  BT1   beta-minus decay radioisotopes
  BT2   beta decay radioisotopes
  BT3   radioisotopes
  BT4   isotopes
  BT1   even-odd nuclei
  BT2   nuclei
  BT1   intermediate mass nuclei
  BT2   nuclei
  BT1   krypton isotopes
  BT1   millisec living radioisotopes
  BT2   radioisotopes
  BT3   isotopes

KRYPTON 98 [0; 0]
  BT1   even-even nuclei
  BT2   nuclei
  BT1   intermediate mass nuclei
  BT2   nuclei
  BT1   krypton isotopes

kryptonates
  USE   krypton compounds

ks-150 reactor
  USE   bohunice a-1 reactor

KSTR REACTOR [21; 21]
(Keuring van Electrotechnische Materialen N.V., Arnhem, Netherlands)
  UF   *kema suspension test reactor*
  BT1   aqueous homogeneous reactors
  BT2   liquid homogeneous reactors
  BT3   fluid fueled reactors
  BT4   reactors
  BT3   homogeneous reactors
  BT4   reactors
  BT2   water cooled reactors
  BT3   reactors
  BT2   water moderated reactors
  BT3   reactors
  BT1   materials testing reactors
  BT2   irradiation reactors
  BT3   reactors
  BT1   research reactors
  BT2   research and test reactors
  BT3   reactors

KUBO FORMULA [125; 125]
  UF   *kubo method*
  UF   *kubo theory*
  RT   statistical mechanics

kubo method
  USE   kubo formula

kubo theory
  USE   kubo formula

KUCA REACTOR [55; 55] *Oct 83*
  UF   *kyoto univ. critical assembly*
  BT1   enriched uranium reactors
  BT2   reactors
  BT1   graphite moderated reactors
  BT2   reactors
  BT1   water moderated reactors
  BT2   reactors
  BT1   zero power reactors
  BT2   experimental reactors
  BT3   research and test reactors
  BT4   reactors

KUHFR REACTOR [28; 28] *Nov 79*
  UF   *kyoto university high flux rea*
  BT1   enriched uranium reactors
  BT2   reactors
  BT1   isotope production reactors
  BT2   irradiation reactors
  BT3   reactors
  BT1   research reactors
  BT2   research and test reactors
  BT3   reactors
  BT1   thermal reactors
  BT2   reactors
  BT1   water cooled reactors
  BT2   reactors
  BT1   water moderated reactors
  BT2   reactors

KUOSHENG-1 REACTOR [35; 35] *Feb 78*
  BT1   bwr type reactors
  BT2   enriched uranium reactors
  BT3   reactors
  BT2   power reactors
  BT3   reactors
  BT2   thermal reactors
  BT3   reactors
  BT2   water cooled reactors
  BT3   reactors
  BT2   water moderated reactors
  BT3   reactors

KUOSHENG-2 REACTOR [27; 27] *Feb 78*
  BT1   bwr type reactors
  BT2   enriched uranium reactors
  BT3   reactors
  BT2   power reactors
  BT3   reactors
  BT2   thermal reactors
  BT3   reactors
  BT2   water cooled reactors
  BT3   reactors
  BT2   water moderated reactors
  BT3   reactors

kupffer cells
  USE   reticuloendothelial system

KUR REACTOR [261; 261]
(Research Reactor Institute, Kyoto Univ., Osaka Prefecture, Japan)
  UF   *kyoto university reactor*
  UF   *training-research react. kyoto*
  BT1   enriched uranium reactors
  BT2   reactors
  BT1   pool type reactors
  BT2   water cooled reactors
  BT3   reactors
  BT2   water moderated reactors
  BT3   reactors
  BT1   research reactors
  BT2   research and test reactors
  BT3   reactors
  BT1   training reactors
  BT2   research and test reactors
  BT3   reactors

kurchatov institute romashka r
  USE   romashka reactor

kurchatovium
  USE   element 104

kurie plot
  USE   fermi plot

KURSK-1 REACTOR [11; 11] *Jun 83*
  BT1   enriched uranium reactors
  BT2   reactors
  BT1   lwgr type reactors
  BT2   graphite moderated reactors
  BT3   reactors
  BT2   water cooled reactors
  BT3   reactors
  BT1   power reactors
  BT2   reactors
  BT1   thermal reactors
  BT2   reactors

KURSK-2 REACTOR [8; 8] *Aug 84*
  BT1   enriched uranium reactors
  BT2   reactors
  BT1   lwgr type reactors
  BT2   graphite moderated reactors
  BT3   reactors
  BT2   water cooled reactors
  BT3   reactors
  BT1   power reactors
  BT2   reactors
  BT1   thermal reactors
  BT2   reactors

KURSK-3 REACTOR [6; 6] *Aug 84*
  BT1   enriched uranium reactors
  BT2   reactors
  BT1   lwgr type reactors
  BT2   graphite moderated reactors
  BT3   reactors
  BT2   water cooled reactors
  BT3   reactors
  BT1   power reactors
  BT2   reactors
  BT1   thermal reactors
  BT2   reactors

KURSK-4 REACTOR [12; 12] *Aug 84*
  BT1   enriched uranium reactors
  BT2   reactors
  BT1   lwgr type reactors
  BT2   graphite moderated reactors
  BT3   reactors
  BT2   water cooled reactors
  BT3   reactors
  BT1   power reactors
  BT2   reactors
  BT1   thermal reactors
  BT2   reactors

KUWAIT [24; 24] *Nov 76*
  BT1   asia
  BT1   developing countries
  BT1   middle east

KVI [33; 33] *Sep 77*
  UF   *groningen versneller instituut*
  UF   *kernfysisch versneller institu*
  BT1   netherlands organizations
  BT2   national organizations

KVI CYCLOTRON [19; 19] *Jun 83*
(Kernfysisch Versneller Instituut, Groningen.)
  UF   *groningen (kvi) cyclotron*
  UF   *kernfys. vers. inst. cyclotron*
  BT1   heavy ion accelerators
  BT2   accelerators
  BT1   isochronous cyclotrons
  BT2   cyclotrons
  BT3   cyclic accelerators
  BT4   accelerators

kwl reactor
  USE   lingen reactor

kwo reactor
   USE   obrigheim reactor

kws-1 wyhl reactor
   USE   wyhl-1 reactor

kws-2 wyhl reactor
   USE   wyhl-2 reactor

KYNURENIC ACID [4; 4]
   BT1   heterocyclic acids
     BT2   carboxylic acids
       BT3   organic acids
         BT4   organic compounds
     BT2   heterocyclic compounds
       BT3   organic compounds
   BT1   hydroxy compounds
     BT2   organic compounds
   BT1   quinolines
     BT2   pyridines
       BT3   azines
         BT4   heterocyclic compounds
           BT5   organic compounds
         BT4   organic nitrogen compounds
           BT5   organic compounds
   RT   kynurenine
   RT   quinaldine

KYNURENINE [16; 16]
   BT1   amino acids
     BT2   carboxylic acids
       BT3   organic acids
         BT4   organic compounds
   BT1   keto acids
     BT2   carboxylic acids
       BT3   organic acids
         BT4   organic compounds
   RT   kynurenic acid

kyoto univ. critical assembly
   USE   kuca reactor

kyoto university high flux rea
   USE   kuhfr reactor

kyoto university reactor
   USE   kur reactor

kyushu-1 reactor
   USE   genkai-1 reactor

kyushu-2 reactor
   USE   genkai-2 reactor

kyushu-3 reactor
   USE   genkai-3 reactor
   AND   sendai-1 reactor

kyushu-4 reactor
   USE   genkai-4 reactor

k01
   USE   kaons neutral short-lived

k02
   USE   kaons neutral long-lived

K1-1280 MESONS [12; 12] *Dec 87*
   SF   *q resonances*
   BT1   axial vector mesons
     BT2   mesons
       BT3   bosons
       BT3   hadrons
         BT4   elementary particles
   BT1   strange mesons
     BT2   mesons
       BT3   bosons
       BT3   hadrons
         BT4   elementary particles
     BT2   strange particles
       BT3   elementary particles

K1-1400 MESONS [10; 10] *Dec 87*
   SF   *q resonances*
   BT1   axial vector mesons
     BT2   mesons
       BT3   bosons
       BT3   hadrons
         BT4   elementary particles
   BT1   strange mesons
     BT2   mesons
       BT3   bosons
       BT3   hadrons
         BT4   elementary particles
     BT2   strange particles
       BT3   elementary particles

K2-1580 MESONS [0; 0] *Dec 87*
   SF   *l resonances*
   BT1   strange mesons
     BT2   mesons
       BT3   bosons
       BT3   hadrons
         BT4   elementary particles
     BT2   strange particles
       BT3   elementary particles
   BT1   tensor mesons
     BT2   mesons
       BT3   bosons
       BT3   hadrons
         BT4   elementary particles

K2-1770 MESONS [44; 44]
(Prior to December 1987 this concept was indexed by K-1775 RESONANCES.)
   UF   *k-1775 resonances*
   SF   *l resonances*
   BT1   strange mesons
     BT2   mesons
       BT3   bosons
       BT3   hadrons
         BT4   elementary particles
     BT2   strange particles
       BT3   elementary particles
   BT1   tensor mesons
     BT2   mesons
       BT3   bosons
       BT3   hadrons
         BT4   elementary particles

K2-2250 MESONS [0; 0] *Dec 87*
   BT1   strange mesons
     BT2   mesons
       BT3   bosons
       BT3   hadrons
         BT4   elementary particles
     BT2   strange particles
       BT3   elementary particles
   BT1   tensor mesons
     BT2   mesons
       BT3   bosons
       BT3   hadrons
         BT4   elementary particles

K3-2320 MESONS [0; 0] *Dec 87*
   BT1   strange mesons
     BT2   mesons
       BT3   bosons
       BT3   hadrons
         BT4   elementary particles
     BT2   strange particles
       BT3   elementary particles
   BT1   tensor mesons
     BT2   mesons
       BT3   bosons
       BT3   hadrons
         BT4   elementary particles

K4-2500 MESONS [0; 0] *Dec 87*
   BT1   strange mesons
     BT2   mesons
       BT3   bosons
       BT3   hadrons
         BT4   elementary particles
     BT2   strange particles
       BT3   elementary particles
   BT1   tensor mesons
     BT2   mesons
       BT3   bosons
       BT3   hadrons
         BT4   elementary particles

L CAPTURE [84; 84]
   BT1   electron capture decay
     BT2   beta decay
       BT3   nuclear decay
         BT4   decay

L CELLS [140; 140]
   RT   clone cells
   RT   fibroblasts
   RT   in vitro

L CODES [876; 876]
   BT1   computer codes

L CONVERSION [397; 397]
   UF   *l-conversion coefficient*
   BT1   internal conversion
     BT2   conversion
     BT2   nuclear decay
       BT3   decay

L REACTOR [51; 51] *Mar 83*
   UF   *savannah riv. plant l reactor*
   BT1   heavy water moderated reactors
     BT2   reactors
   BT1   special production reactors
     BT2   production reactors
       BT3   reactors

l resonances
   SEE   k2-1580 mesons
   OR   k2-1770 mesons

L SHELL [1,164; 1,164] *Jul 76*
(Atomic electron shells)
   UF   *atomic shells (l)*
   BT1   electronic structure

l-alanine
   USE   alanine-l

l-alanine-alpha
   USE   alanine-l

l-conversion coefficient
   USE   l conversion

L-S COUPLING [3,304; 3,304]
   UF   *russell-saunders coupling*
   UF   *spin-orbit interaction*
   BT1   intermediate coupling
     BT2   coupling
   RT   orbital angular momentum

L-2 STELLARATOR [102; 102] *Nov 77*
   BT1   stellarators
     BT2   closed plasma devices
       BT3   thermonuclear devices

l-54 reactor
   USE   cesnef reactor

l-77 atomics international r.
   USE   ai-l-77 reactor

l-77 puerto rico reactor
  USE   prnc-l-77 reactor

la crosse boiling water reacto
  USE   lacbwr reactor

la jolla triga-mk-3 reactor
  USE   triga-3-la jolla reactor

LA REINA RECH-1 REACTOR [2; 2]
Feb 89
(La Reina, Santiago, Chile.)
  BT1   pool type reactors
   BT2   water cooled reactors
    BT3   reactors
   BT2   water moderated reactors
    BT3   reactors
  BT1   research reactors
   BT2   research and test reactors
    BT3   reactors

LA SALLE COUNTY-1 REACTOR [65; 65]
  BT1   bwr type reactors
   BT2   enriched uranium reactors
    BT3   reactors
   BT2   power reactors
    BT3   reactors
   BT2   thermal reactors
    BT3   reactors
   BT2   water cooled reactors
    BT3   reactors
   BT2   water moderated reactors
    BT3   reactors

LA SALLE COUNTY-2 REACTOR [87; 87]
  BT1   bwr type reactors
   BT2   enriched uranium reactors
    BT3   reactors
   BT2   power reactors
    BT3   reactors
   BT2   thermal reactors
    BT3   reactors
   BT2   water cooled reactors
    BT3   reactors
   BT2   water moderated reactors
    BT3   reactors

LABELLED COMPOUNDS [15,513; 31,735]
(Compounds labelled with either stable or radioactive isotopes.)
  NT1   radiopharmaceuticals
  RT   autoradiography
  RT   autoradiolysis
  RT   carbon 14 compounds
  RT   carrier-free isotopes
  RT   diagnosis
  RT   double labelling
  RT   electron microscopy
  RT   labelling
  RT   nuclear medicine
  RT   radioenzymatic assay
  RT   radioimmunoassay
  RT   radioimmunodetection
  RT   scintiscanning
  RT   tracer techniques
  RT   tritium compounds
  RT   wilzbach method

labelled pool technique
(Prior to August 1985 this was a valid descriptor.)
  USE   labelled pool techniques

LABELLED POOL TECHNIQUES [234; 234] *Sep 75*
(Prior to August 1985 the singular form was used.)
  UF   *labelled pool technique*
  BT1   tracer techniques
   BT2   isotope applications
  RT   labelling

  RT   metabolism

LABELLING [9,954; 10,428]
(For labelling of packages use PACKAGING RULES.)
  NT1   double labelling
  NT1   wilzbach method
  RT   carbon 14 compounds
  RT   carrier-free isotopes
  RT   isotopic exchange
  RT   labelled compounds
  RT   labelled pool techniques
  RT   radioactivation

labelling (packages)
  USE   packaging rules

labor
  USE   work

→ **LABOR RELATIONS** [0; 0] *Oct 91*
  RT   industry
  RT   management
  RT   personnel
  RT   working conditions

LABORATORIES [251; 517] *Mar 86*
  NT1   hot labs
  RT   buildings
  RT   laboratory animals
  RT   laboratory equipment
  RT   nuclear facilities
  RT   research programs
  RT   test facilities

LABORATORY ANIMALS [660; 660]
  BT1   animals
  RT   laboratories

LABORATORY EQUIPMENT [1,654; 6,009]
  BT1   equipment
  NT1   fume hoods
  NT1   gloveboxes
  NT1   hot cells
  NT1   manipulators
  NT1   samplers
   NT2   air samplers
  RT   accelerator facilities
  RT   autoclaves
  RT   bench-scale experiments
  RT   extraction apparatuses
  RT   hot labs
  RT   laboratories
  RT   mixer-settlers
  RT   portable equipment
  RT   remote handling equipment
  RT   remote viewing equipment
  RT   sample changers
  RT   test facilities
  RT   vacuum pumps

laboratory scale experiments
  USE   bench-scale experiments

LABORATORY SYSTEM [323; 323]
  RT   center-of-mass system
  RT   coordinates
  RT   limiting fragmentation
  RT   lorentz transformations
  RT   mechanics
  RT   scattering

labyrinth
  USE   auditory organs
  AND   vestibular apparatus

LACBWR REACTOR [121; 121]
  UF   *la crosse boiling water reacto*
  BT1   bwr type reactors
   BT2   enriched uranium reactors
    BT3   reactors

   BT2   power reactors
    BT3   reactors
   BT2   thermal reactors
    BT3   reactors
   BT2   water cooled reactors
    BT3   reactors
   BT2   water moderated reactors
    BT3   reactors

LACQUERS [91; 91]
  BT1   coatings

LACRIMAL DUCTS [78; 78] *Jul 77*
  UF   *ducts (tear)*
  UF   *tear canals*
  BT1   eyes
   BT2   sense organs
    BT3   organs
     BT4   body

LACTAMS [53; 216]
  UF   *cyclic amides*
  BT1   amides
   BT2   organic nitrogen compounds
    BT3   organic compounds
  NT1   pyrrolidones
   NT2   pvp
  RT   amino acids
  RT   heterocyclic compounds

LACTATE DEHYDROGENASE [222; 222]
  BT1   dehydrogenases
   BT2   oxidoreductases
    BT3   enzymes
     BT4   organic compounds

LACTATES [154; 154] *Sep 81*
  BT1   carboxylic acid salts
  RT   lactic acid

LACTATION [289; 289]
  RT   mammary glands
  RT   milk

LACTIC ACID [235; 235]
  UF   *hydroxypropionic acid-alpha*
  BT1   hydroxy acids
   BT2   carboxylic acids
    BT3   organic acids
     BT4   organic compounds
  RT   lactates

LACTOBACILLUS [65; 65]
  BT1   bacteria
   BT2   microorganisms

LACTOFERRIN [30; 30] *Aug 81*
  BT1   globulins
   BT2   proteins
    BT3   organic compounds
  BT1   glycoproteins
   BT2   proteins
    BT3   organic compounds
   BT2   saccharides
    BT3   carbohydrates
     BT4   organic compounds
  BT1   organometallic compounds
   BT2   organic compounds
  RT   iron complexes

LACTOGENS [12; 32] *Dec 82*
  BT1   peptide hormones
   BT2   hormones
  NT1   hpl
  RT   pituitary gland
  RT   placenta

LACTONES [171; 428]
  UF   *cyclic esters*
  BT1   esters
   BT2   organic compounds
  BT1   heterocyclic compounds
   BT2   organic compounds
  NT1   coumarin
  NT1   gibberellic acid

RT   hydroxy acids

LACTOSE [76; 76]
UF   *milk sugar*
BT1   disaccharides
  BT2   oligosaccharides
    BT3   saccharides
      BT4   carbohydrates
        BT5   organic compounds

LADDER APPROXIMATION [509; 509]
RT   quantum field theory

lage flux reaktor petten
USE   lfr reactor

LAGO MAGGIORE [5; 5]
BT1   lakes
  BT2   surface waters

LAGRANGE EQUATIONS [1,509; 1,509]
BT1   partial differential equations
  BT2   differential equations
    BT3   equations
RT   lagrangian function
RT   mechanics

lagrange field equations
USE   lagrangian field theory

lagrangian
USE   lagrangian function

LAGRANGIAN FIELD THEORY [7,255; 7,255]
UF   *canonical quantum field theory*
UF   *gross-neveu model*
UF   *lagrange field equations*
BT1   quantum field theory
  BT2   field theories

LAGRANGIAN FUNCTION [8,508; 8,508]
UF   *lagrangian*
BT1   functions
RT   equations of motion
RT   kinetic energy
RT   lagrange equations
RT   mechanics
RT   potential energy

LAGUERRE POLYNOMIALS [174; 174]
BT1   polynomials
  BT2   functions

LAGUNA VERDE-1 REACTOR [27; 27]
Feb 78
(Alto Lucero, Veracruz, Mexico)
BT1   bwr type reactors
  BT2   enriched uranium reactors
    BT3   reactors
  BT2   power reactors
    BT3   reactors
  BT2   thermal reactors
    BT3   reactors
  BT2   water cooled reactors
    BT3   reactors
  BT2   water moderated reactors
    BT3   reactors

LAGUNA VERDE-2 REACTOR [11; 11]
Feb 87
(Alto Lucero, Veracruz, Mexico.)
BT1   bwr type reactors
  BT2   enriched uranium reactors
    BT3   reactors
  BT2   power reactors
    BT3   reactors
  BT2   thermal reactors
    BT3   reactors
  BT2   water cooled reactors
    BT3   reactors
  BT2   water moderated reactors

    BT3   reactors

LAKE BAIKAL [11; 11] *Oct 84*
BT1   lakes
  BT2   surface waters

LAKE BALATON [5; 5] *Sep 83*
BT1   lakes
  BT2   surface waters

LAKE ERIE [30; 30]
BT1   great lakes
  BT2   lakes
    BT3   surface waters

LAKE HURON [20; 20]
BT1   great lakes
  BT2   lakes
    BT3   surface waters

LAKE MICHIGAN [154; 154]
BT1   great lakes
  BT2   lakes
    BT3   surface waters

LAKE ONTARIO [57; 57]
BT1   great lakes
  BT2   lakes
    BT3   surface waters

LAKE SUPERIOR [9; 9] *Jul 80*
BT1   great lakes
  BT2   lakes
    BT3   surface waters

LAKES [1,192; 1,529]
UF   *ponds*
BT1   surface waters
NT1   ambrosia lake
NT1   athabasca lake
NT1   dead sea
NT1   great lakes
  NT2   lake erie
  NT2   lake huron
  NT2   lake michigan
  NT2   lake ontario
  NT2   lake superior
NT1   lago maggiore
NT1   lake baikal
NT1   lake balaton
RT   eutrophication
RT   fresh water
RT   hydrology
RT   inland waterways
RT   shores
RT   water reservoirs

LAMB SHIFT [641; 641]
UF   *lamb-retherford shift*
BT1   spectral shift
RT   energy levels

lamb-retherford shift
USE   lamb shift

LAMBDA B NEUTRAL BARYONS [19; 19] *Dec 87*
BT1   beauty baryons
  BT2   baryons
    BT3   fermions
    BT3   hadrons
      BT4   elementary particles
  BT2   beauty particles
    BT3   elementary particles

LAMBDA BARYONS [55; 870] *Dec 87*
BT1   hyperons
  BT2   baryons
    BT3   fermions
    BT3   hadrons
      BT4   elementary particles
  BT2   strange particles
    BT3   elementary particles
NT1   lambda particles

  NT2   antilambda particles
NT1   lambda-1405 baryons
NT1   lambda-1520 baryons
NT1   lambda-1600 baryons
NT1   lambda-1670 baryons
NT1   lambda-1690 baryons
NT1   lambda-1800 baryons
NT1   lambda-1820 baryons
NT1   lambda-1830 baryons
NT1   lambda-1890 baryons
NT1   lambda-2000 baryons
NT1   lambda-2020 baryons
NT1   lambda-2100 baryons
NT1   lambda-2110 baryons
NT1   lambda-2325 baryons
NT1   lambda-2350 baryons
NT1   lambda-2585 baryons

lambda c plus
(Prior to December 1987 this was a valid descriptor.)
USE   lambda c plus baryons

LAMBDA C PLUS BARYONS [342; 342]
Feb 79
(Prior to December 1987 this concept was indexed by LAMBDA C PLUS.)
UF   *lambda c plus*
UF   *lambda-2250 resonances*
BT1   charmed baryons
  BT2   baryons
    BT3   fermions
    BT3   hadrons
      BT4   elementary particles
  BT2   charm particles
    BT3   elementary particles

lambda neutral
USE   lambda particles

LAMBDA PARTICLE BEAMS [20; 20]
BT1   hyperon beams
  BT2   particle beams
    BT3   beams

LAMBDA PARTICLES [3,322; 3,371]
UF   *lambda neutral*
UF   *lambda-1115 resonances*
BT1   lambda baryons
  BT2   hyperons
    BT3   baryons
      BT4   fermions
      BT4   hadrons
        BT5   elementary particles
    BT3   strange particles
      BT4   elementary particles
NT1   antilambda particles

LAMBDA POINT [323; 323]
BT1   transition temperature
  BT2   thermodynamic properties
    BT3   physical properties
RT   helium 4
RT   superfluidity

LAMBDA-N-2130 DIBARYONS [7; 7]
Dec 87
BT1   dibaryons
  BT2   baryons
    BT3   fermions
    BT3   hadrons
      BT4   elementary particles
BT1   hyperons
  BT2   baryons
    BT3   fermions
    BT3   hadrons
      BT4   elementary particles
  BT2   strange particles
    BT3   elementary particles

lambda-1115 resonances
(Prior to December 1987 this was a valid descriptor.)
USE   lambda particles

LAMBDA-1405 BARYONS [139; 139]
(Prior to December 1987 this concept was indexed by LAMBDA-1405 RESONANCES.)
UF   *lambda-1405 resonances*
BT1   lambda baryons
  BT2   hyperons
    BT3   baryons
      BT4   fermions
      BT4   hadrons
        BT5   elementary particles
    BT3   strange particles
      BT4   elementary particles

lambda-1405 resonances
(Prior to December 1987 this was a valid descriptor.)
  USE   lambda-1405 baryons

LAMBDA-1520 BARYONS [97; 97]
(Prior to December 1987 this concept was indexed by LAMBDA-1520 RESONANCES.)
UF   *lambda-1520 resonances*
BT1   lambda baryons
  BT2   hyperons
    BT3   baryons
      BT4   fermions
      BT4   hadrons
        BT5   elementary particles
    BT3   strange particles
      BT4   elementary particles

lambda-1520 resonances
(Prior to December 1987 this was a valid descriptor.)
  USE   lambda-1520 baryons

LAMBDA-1600 BARYONS [2; 2] *Dec 87*
BT1   lambda baryons
  BT2   hyperons
    BT3   baryons
      BT4   fermions
      BT4   hadrons
        BT5   elementary particles
    BT3   strange particles
      BT4   elementary particles

LAMBDA-1670 BARYONS [17; 17]
(Prior to December 1987 this concept was indexed by LAMBDA-1670 RESONANCES.)
UF   *lambda-1670 resonances*
BT1   lambda baryons
  BT2   hyperons
    BT3   baryons
      BT4   fermions
      BT4   hadrons
        BT5   elementary particles
    BT3   strange particles
      BT4   elementary particles

lambda-1670 resonances
(Prior to December 1987 this was a valid descriptor.)
  USE   lambda-1670 baryons

LAMBDA-1690 BARYONS [15; 15]
(Prior to December 1987 this concept was indexed by LAMBDA-1690 RESONANCES.)
UF   *lambda-1690 resonances*
BT1   lambda baryons
  BT2   hyperons
    BT3   baryons
      BT4   fermions
      BT4   hadrons
        BT5   elementary particles
    BT3   strange particles
      BT4   elementary particles

lambda-1690 resonances
(Prior to December 1987 this was a valid descriptor.)
  USE   lambda-1690 baryons

LAMBDA-1800 BARYONS [0; 0] *Dec 87*
BT1   lambda baryons
  BT2   hyperons
    BT3   baryons
      BT4   fermions
      BT4   hadrons
        BT5   elementary particles
    BT3   strange particles
      BT4   elementary particles

lambda-1815 resonances
(Prior to December 1987 this was a valid descriptor.)
  USE   lambda-1820 baryons

LAMBDA-1820 BARYONS [9; 9]
(Prior to December 1987 this concept was indexed by LAMBDA-1815 RESONANCES.)
UF   *lambda-1815 resonances*
BT1   lambda baryons
  BT2   hyperons
    BT3   baryons
      BT4   fermions
      BT4   hadrons
        BT5   elementary particles
    BT3   strange particles
      BT4   elementary particles

LAMBDA-1830 BARYONS [7; 7]
(Prior to December 1987 this concept was indexed by LAMBDA-1830 RESONANCES.)
UF   *lambda-1830 resonances*
BT1   lambda baryons
  BT2   hyperons
    BT3   baryons
      BT4   fermions
      BT4   hadrons
        BT5   elementary particles
    BT3   strange particles
      BT4   elementary particles

lambda-1830 resonances
(Prior to December 1987 this was a valid descriptor.)
  USE   lambda-1830 baryons

LAMBDA-1890 BARYONS [0; 0] *Dec 87*
BT1   lambda baryons
  BT2   hyperons
    BT3   baryons
      BT4   fermions
      BT4   hadrons
        BT5   elementary particles
    BT3   strange particles
      BT4   elementary particles

LAMBDA-2000 BARYONS [0; 0] *Dec 87*
BT1   lambda baryons
  BT2   hyperons
    BT3   baryons
      BT4   fermions
      BT4   hadrons
        BT5   elementary particles
    BT3   strange particles
      BT4   elementary particles

LAMBDA-2020 BARYONS [0; 0] *Dec 87*
BT1   lambda baryons
  BT2   hyperons
    BT3   baryons
      BT4   fermions
      BT4   hadrons
        BT5   elementary particles
    BT3   strange particles
      BT4   elementary particles

LAMBDA-2100 BARYONS [4; 4]
(Prior to December 1987 this concept was indexed by LAMBDA-2100 RESONANCES.)
UF   *lambda-2100 resonances*
BT1   lambda baryons
  BT2   hyperons
    BT3   baryons
      BT4   fermions
      BT4   hadrons
        BT5   elementary particles
    BT3   strange particles
      BT4   elementary particles

lambda-2100 resonances
(Prior to December 1987 this was a valid descriptor.)
  USE   lambda-2100 baryons

LAMBDA-2110 BARYONS [2; 2] *Dec 87*
BT1   lambda baryons
  BT2   hyperons
    BT3   baryons
      BT4   fermions
      BT4   hadrons
        BT5   elementary particles
    BT3   strange particles
      BT4   elementary particles

lambda-2250 resonances
  USE   lambda c plus baryons

LAMBDA-2325 BARYONS [0; 0] *Dec 87*
BT1   lambda baryons
  BT2   hyperons
    BT3   baryons
      BT4   fermions
      BT4   hadrons
        BT5   elementary particles
    BT3   strange particles
      BT4   elementary particles

LAMBDA-2350 BARYONS [1; 1]
(Prior to december 1987 this concept was indexed by LAMBDA-2350 RESONANCES.)
UF   *lambda-2350 resonances*
BT1   lambda baryons
  BT2   hyperons
    BT3   baryons
      BT4   fermions
      BT4   hadrons
        BT5   elementary particles
    BT3   strange particles
      BT4   elementary particles

lambda-2350 resonances
(Prior to December 1987 this was a valid descriptor.)
  USE   lambda-2350 baryons

LAMBDA-2585 BARYONS [0; 0] *Dec 8*
BT1   lambda baryons
  BT2   hyperons
    BT3   baryons
      BT4   fermions
      BT4   hadrons
        BT5   elementary particles
    BT3   strange particles
      BT4   elementary particles

LAMBERT LAW [11; 11]
  RT   angular distribution

lambs
  USE   sheep

LAMELLAE [234; 234]
  RT   layers

LAMINAC [2; 2]
  BT1   polyesters
    BT2   esters
      BT3   organic compounds
    BT2   organic polymers
      BT3   organic compounds
      BT3   polymers

LAMINAR FLOW [1,192; 1,192]
  UF   *poiseuille flow*
  UF   *subcritical flow*
  BT1   fluid flow
  RT   critical flow
  RT   ideal flow
  RT   turbulent flow
  RT   viscous flow

LAMINARIA [18; 18]
  BT1   algae
    BT2   plants
  BT1   seaweeds
  RT   alginates

laminography
  USE   tomography

LAMPF II SYNCHROTRON [258; 258]
Jun 83
(6 to 32 GeV proton synchrotron addition to Los Alamos Meson Physics Facility.)
  BT1   meson factories
    BT2   accelerators
  BT1   synchrotrons
    BT2   cyclic accelerators
      BT3   accelerators

LAMPF LINAC [1,166; 1,166]
  UF   *los alamos meson physics facil*
  BT1   linear accelerators
    BT2   accelerators
  BT1   meson factories
    BT2   accelerators

LAMPRE-1 REACTOR [3; 3]
  UF   *los alam. molt. plut. rea. exp*
  BT1   experimental reactors
    BT2   research and test reactors
      BT3   reactors
  BT1   fast reactors
    BT2   epithermal reactors
      BT3   reactors
  BT1   plutonium reactors
    BT2   reactors
  BT1   power reactors
    BT2   reactors
  BT1   sodium cooled reactors
    BT2   liquid metal cooled reactors
      BT3   reactors

lampre-2 reactor
  USE   frctf reactor

land fills
  USE   sanitary landfills

LAND POLLUTION [424; 424]
(For nonradioactive pollution only; for radioactive pollution use CONTAMINATION.)
  UF+   *land pollution abatement*
  UF+   *land pollution control*
  BT1   pollution
  RT   environmental effects
  RT   land use

land pollution abatement
  USE   land pollution
  AND   pollution abatement

land pollution control
  USE   land pollution
  AND   pollution control

LAND RECLAMATION [335; 335]
Jul 76
  RT   abandoned sites
  RT   backfilling
  RT   land use
  RT   preferred species
  RT   remedial action
  RT   revegetation

LAND TRANSPORT [471; 1,067] *Jan 76*
  BT1   transport
  NT1   rail transport
  NT1   road transport

LAND USE [478; 478] *Jul 76*
  RT   environment
  RT   external zones
  RT   land pollution
  RT   land reclamation
  RT   recreational areas
  RT   regional analysis
  RT   regional cooperation
  RT   site selection
  RT   water use

landau absorption
  USE   landau damping

LANDAU CURVES [33; 33]
  RT   s matrix
  RT   scattering
  RT   singularity

LANDAU DAMPING [1,524; 1,524]
  UF   *landau absorption*
  BT1   damping
  RT   plasma waves
  RT   transit-time magnetic pumping

landau distribution
  USE   landau fluctuations

landau domain structure
  USE   domain structure

LANDAU FLUCTUATIONS [149; 149]
  UF   *landau distribution*
  RT   energy losses
  RT   variations

LANDAU LIQUID HELIUM THEORY [354; 354]
  UF   *two-fluid theory*
  RT   helium ii
  RT   phonons
  RT   rotons
  RT   superfluidity

LANDAU QUASI PARTICLES [49; 49]
  BT1   quasi particles
  RT   particle structure
  RT   quark model

landau-ginzburg-pitaevskii the
  USE   ginzburg-pitaevskii theory

LANDAU-ZENER FORMULA [205; 205]
  RT   collisions
  RT   potential energy

LANDE FACTOR [751; 751]
  UF   *g factor (lande)*
  UF   *lande g factor*
  UF   *lande interval factor*
  UF   *lande splitting factor*
  RT   energy levels

lande g factor
  USE   lande factor

lande interval factor
  USE   lande factor

lande splitting factor
  USE   lande factor

landfills
  USE   sanitary landfills

LANDSAT SATELLITES [36; 36] *Jun 83*
  BT1   satellites
  RT   aerial surveying

LANDSLIDES [28; 28] *Sep 80*
  RT   blast effects
  RT   earthquakes
  RT   ground motion
  RT   rain
  RT   seismic effects
  RT   slope stability
  RT   underground explosions

LANE-ROBSON THEORY [10; 10]
  RT   nuclear reactions
  RT   scattering

LANE-THOMAS-WIGNER MODEL [17; 17]
  BT1   nuclear models
    BT2   mathematical models

LANGEVIN EQUATION [714; 714]
  BT1   equations
  RT   magnetic fields

LANGMUIR FREQUENCY [1,497; 1,497]
  UF   *frequency (langmuir)*
  UF   *plasma frequency*
  RT   plasma

langmuir oscillations
  USE   plasma waves

LANGMUIR PROBE [1,080; 1,080]
  BT1   electric probes
    BT2   probes

languages (programming)
  USE   programming languages

LANL [169; 784] *Apr 84*
(Formerly known as Los Alamos Scientific Laboratory, and older material is indexed to LASL.)
  UF   *los alamos national laboratory*
  BT1   us doe
    BT2   us organizations
      BT3   national organizations
  NT1   lasl
  RT   antares facility
  RT   aurora facility
  RT   helios facility
  RT   new mexico

LANOLIN [8; 8]
  UF   *wool fat*
  BT1   esters
    BT2   organic compounds
  BT1   lipids
    BT2   organic compounds
  BT1   sterols
    BT2   hydroxy compounds
      BT3   organic compounds
    BT2   steroids
      BT3   organic compounds
  RT   cholesterol

lanoxin
  USE   digoxin

lanthanides
  USE rare earths

LANTHANUM [1,714; 1,714]
  BT1 rare earths
    BT2 metals
      BT3 elements

LANTHANUM ADDITIONS [153; 154]
(Alloys containing not more than 1% La are listed here.)
  BT1 rare earth additions
  NT1 alloy-co36cr22ni22w15fe3
  RT   lanthanum alloys
  RT   lanthanum compounds

LANTHANUM ALLOYS [1,086; 1,311]
(Alloys containing more than 1% La.)
  BT1 rare earth alloys
    BT2 alloys
  NT1 lanthanum base alloys
  NT1 misch metal
  RT   lanthanum additions

LANTHANUM BASE ALLOYS [129; 129]
  BT1 lanthanum alloys
    BT2 rare earth alloys
      BT3 alloys

LANTHANUM BORIDES [345; 345]
  BT1 borides
    BT2 boron compounds
  BT1 lanthanum compounds
    BT2 rare earth compounds

LANTHANUM BROMIDES [53; 53]
  BT1 bromides
    BT2 bromine compounds
      BT3 halogen compounds
    BT2 halides
      BT3 halogen compounds
  BT1 lanthanum compounds
    BT2 rare earth compounds

LANTHANUM CARBIDES [42; 42]
  BT1 carbides
    BT2 carbon compounds
  BT1 lanthanum compounds
    BT2 rare earth compounds

LANTHANUM CARBONATES [23; 25]
  BT1 carbonates
    BT2 carbon compounds
    BT2 oxygen compounds
  BT1 lanthanum compounds
    BT2 rare earth compounds
  RT   carbonate minerals
  RT   cordylite

LANTHANUM CHLORIDES [229; 229]
  BT1 chlorides
    BT2 chlorine compounds
      BT3 halogen compounds
    BT2 halides
      BT3 halogen compounds
  BT1 lanthanum compounds
    BT2 rare earth compounds

LANTHANUM COMPLEXES [754; 754]
  BT1 rare earth complexes
    BT2 complexes

LANTHANUM COMPOUNDS [1,572; 5,616]
  BT1 rare earth compounds
  NT1 lanthanum borides
  NT1 lanthanum bromides
  NT1 lanthanum carbides
  NT1 lanthanum carbonates
  NT1 lanthanum chlorides
  NT1 lanthanum fluorides
  NT1 lanthanum hydrides
  NT1 lanthanum hydroxides
  NT1 lanthanum iodides
  NT1 lanthanum nitrates
  NT1 lanthanum nitrides
  NT1 lanthanum oxides
  NT1 lanthanum perchlorates
  NT1 lanthanum phosphates
  NT1 lanthanum phosphides
  NT1 lanthanum selenides
  NT1 lanthanum silicates
  NT1 lanthanum silicides
  NT1 lanthanum sulfates
  NT1 lanthanum sulfides
  NT1 lanthanum tellurides
  NT1 lanthanum tungstates
  NT1 plzt
  RT   lanthanum additions

LANTHANUM FLUORIDES [308; 308]
  BT1 fluorides
    BT2 fluorine compounds
      BT3 halogen compounds
    BT2 halides
      BT3 halogen compounds
  BT1 lanthanum compounds
    BT2 rare earth compounds

LANTHANUM HYDRIDES [146; 146]
  BT1 hydrides
    BT2 hydrogen compounds
  BT1 lanthanum compounds
    BT2 rare earth compounds

LANTHANUM HYDROXIDES [57; 57]
  BT1 hydroxides
    BT2 hydrogen compounds
    BT2 oxygen compounds
  BT1 lanthanum compounds
    BT2 rare earth compounds

LANTHANUM IODIDES [25; 25]
  BT1 iodides
    BT2 halides
      BT3 halogen compounds
    BT2 iodine compounds
      BT3 halogen compounds
  BT1 lanthanum compounds
    BT2 rare earth compounds

LANTHANUM IONS [145; 145]
  BT1 ions
    BT2 charged particles

LANTHANUM ISOTOPES [104; 1,304]
  NT1 lanthanum 120
  NT1 lanthanum 121
  NT1 lanthanum 122
  NT1 lanthanum 123
  NT1 lanthanum 124
  NT1 lanthanum 125
  NT1 lanthanum 126
  NT1 lanthanum 127
  NT1 lanthanum 128
  NT1 lanthanum 129
  NT1 lanthanum 130
  NT1 lanthanum 131
  NT1 lanthanum 132
  NT1 lanthanum 133
  NT1 lanthanum 134
  NT1 lanthanum 135
  NT1 lanthanum 136
  NT1 lanthanum 137
  NT1 lanthanum 138
  NT1 lanthanum 139
  NT1 lanthanum 140
  NT1 lanthanum 141
  NT1 lanthanum 142
  NT1 lanthanum 143
  NT1 lanthanum 144
  NT1 lanthanum 145
  NT1 lanthanum 146
  NT1 lanthanum 147
  NT1 lanthanum 148
  NT1 lanthanum 149

LANTHANUM NITRATES [137; 137]
  BT1 lanthanum compounds
    BT2 rare earth compounds
  BT1 nitrates
    BT2 nitrogen compounds
    BT2 oxygen compounds

LANTHANUM NITRIDES [27; 27]
  BT1 lanthanum compounds
    BT2 rare earth compounds
  BT1 nitrides
    BT2 nitrogen compounds
    BT2 pnictides

LANTHANUM OXIDES [2,353; 2,353]
  BT1 lanthanum compounds
    BT2 rare earth compounds
  BT1 oxides
    BT2 chalcogenides
    BT2 oxygen compounds

LANTHANUM PERCHLORATES [15; 15]
  BT1 lanthanum compounds
    BT2 rare earth compounds
  BT1 perchlorates
    BT2 chlorine compounds
      BT3 halogen compounds
    BT2 oxygen compounds

LANTHANUM PHOSPHATES [100; 100]
  BT1 lanthanum compounds
    BT2 rare earth compounds
  BT1 phosphates
    BT2 oxygen compounds
    BT2 phosphorus compounds

LANTHANUM PHOSPHIDES [14; 14]
Sep 79
  BT1 lanthanum compounds
    BT2 rare earth compounds
  BT1 phosphides
    BT2 phosphorus compounds
    BT2 pnictides

LANTHANUM SELENIDES [28; 28]
  BT1 lanthanum compounds
    BT2 rare earth compounds
  BT1 selenides
    BT2 chalcogenides
    BT2 selenium compounds

LANTHANUM SILICATES [19; 19]
  BT1 lanthanum compounds
    BT2 rare earth compounds
  BT1 silicates
    BT2 oxygen compounds
    BT2 silicon compounds
  RT   orthite

LANTHANUM SILICIDES [16; 16]
Apr 84
  BT1 lanthanum compounds
    BT2 rare earth compounds
  BT1 silicides
    BT2 silicon compounds

LANTHANUM SULFATES [37; 37]
  BT1 lanthanum compounds
    BT2 rare earth compounds
  BT1 sulfates
    BT2 oxygen compounds
    BT2 sulfur compounds

LANTHANUM SULFIDES [214; 214]
  BT1 lanthanum compounds
    BT2 rare earth compounds
  BT1 sulfides
    BT2 chalcogenides
    BT2 sulfur compounds

LANTHANUM TELLURIDES [26; 26]
  BT1 lanthanum compounds
    BT2 rare earth compounds
  BT1 tellurides
    BT2 chalcogenides
    BT2 tellurium compounds

LANTHANUM TUNGSTATES [16; 16]
Jun 83
  BT1   lanthanum compounds
    BT2   rare earth compounds
  BT1   tungstates
    BT2   oxygen compounds
    BT2   tungsten compounds
      BT3   transition element compounds

LANTHANUM 120 [3; 3] *Aug 84*
  BT1   electron capture radioisotopes
    BT2   beta decay radioisotopes
      BT3   radioisotopes
        BT4   isotopes
  BT1   lanthanum isotopes
  BT1   odd-odd nuclei
    BT2   nuclei
  BT1   rare earth nuclei
    BT2   intermediate mass nuclei
      BT3   nuclei
  BT1   seconds living radioisotopes
    BT2   radioisotopes
      BT3   isotopes

LANTHANUM 121 [3; 3] *Feb 89*
  BT1   beta-plus decay radioisotopes
    BT2   beta decay radioisotopes
      BT3   radioisotopes
        BT4   isotopes
  BT1   electron capture radioisotopes
    BT2   beta decay radioisotopes
      BT3   radioisotopes
        BT4   isotopes
  BT1   lanthanum isotopes
  BT1   odd-even nuclei
    BT2   nuclei
  BT1   rare earth nuclei
    BT2   intermediate mass nuclei
      BT3   nuclei
  BT1   seconds living radioisotopes
    BT2   radioisotopes
      BT3   isotopes

LANTHANUM 122 [4; 4] *Aug 84*
  BT1   electron capture radioisotopes
    BT2   beta decay radioisotopes
      BT3   radioisotopes
        BT4   isotopes
  BT1   lanthanum isotopes
  BT1   odd-odd nuclei
    BT2   nuclei
  BT1   rare earth nuclei
    BT2   intermediate mass nuclei
      BT3   nuclei
  BT1   seconds living radioisotopes
    BT2   radioisotopes
      BT3   isotopes

LANTHANUM 123 [5; 5] *Feb 79*
  BT1   electron capture radioisotopes
    BT2   beta decay radioisotopes
      BT3   radioisotopes
        BT4   isotopes
  BT1   lanthanum isotopes
  BT1   odd-even nuclei
    BT2   nuclei
  BT1   rare earth nuclei
    BT2   intermediate mass nuclei
      BT3   nuclei
  BT1   seconds living radioisotopes
    BT2   radioisotopes
      BT3   isotopes

LANTHANUM 124 [10; 10]
  BT1   electron capture radioisotopes
    BT2   beta decay radioisotopes
      BT3   radioisotopes
        BT4   isotopes
  BT1   lanthanum isotopes
  BT1   odd-odd nuclei
    BT2   nuclei
  BT1   rare earth nuclei
    BT2   intermediate mass nuclei
      BT3   nuclei
  BT1   seconds living radioisotopes
    BT2   radioisotopes
      BT3   isotopes

LANTHANUM 125 [9; 9]
  BT1   beta-plus decay radioisotopes
    BT2   beta decay radioisotopes
      BT3   radioisotopes
        BT4   isotopes
  BT1   electron capture radioisotopes
    BT2   beta decay radioisotopes
      BT3   radioisotopes
        BT4   isotopes
  BT1   lanthanum isotopes
  BT1   minutes living radioisotopes
    BT2   radioisotopes
      BT3   isotopes
  BT1   odd-even nuclei
    BT2   nuclei
  BT1   rare earth nuclei
    BT2   intermediate mass nuclei
      BT3   nuclei

LANTHANUM 126 [9; 9]
  BT1   beta-plus decay radioisotopes
    BT2   beta decay radioisotopes
      BT3   radioisotopes
        BT4   isotopes
  BT1   electron capture radioisotopes
    BT2   beta decay radioisotopes
      BT3   radioisotopes
        BT4   isotopes
  BT1   lanthanum isotopes
  BT1   minutes living radioisotopes
    BT2   radioisotopes
      BT3   isotopes
  BT1   odd-odd nuclei
    BT2   nuclei
  BT1   rare earth nuclei
    BT2   intermediate mass nuclei
      BT3   nuclei

LANTHANUM 127 [13; 13]
  BT1   beta-plus decay radioisotopes
    BT2   beta decay radioisotopes
      BT3   radioisotopes
        BT4   isotopes
  BT1   electron capture radioisotopes
    BT2   beta decay radioisotopes
      BT3   radioisotopes
        BT4   isotopes
  BT1   lanthanum isotopes
  BT1   minutes living radioisotopes
    BT2   radioisotopes
      BT3   isotopes
  BT1   odd-even nuclei
    BT2   nuclei
  BT1   rare earth nuclei
    BT2   intermediate mass nuclei
      BT3   nuclei

LANTHANUM 128 [9; 9]
  BT1   beta-plus decay radioisotopes
    BT2   beta decay radioisotopes
      BT3   radioisotopes
        BT4   isotopes
  BT1   electron capture radioisotopes
    BT2   beta decay radioisotopes
      BT3   radioisotopes
        BT4   isotopes
  BT1   lanthanum isotopes
  BT1   minutes living radioisotopes
    BT2   radioisotopes
      BT3   isotopes
  BT1   odd-odd nuclei
    BT2   nuclei
  BT1   rare earth nuclei
    BT2   intermediate mass nuclei
      BT3   nuclei

LANTHANUM 129 [20; 20]
  BT1   beta-plus decay radioisotopes
    BT2   beta decay radioisotopes
      BT3   radioisotopes
        BT4   isotopes
  BT1   electron capture radioisotopes
    BT2   beta decay radioisotopes
      BT3   radioisotopes
        BT4   isotopes
  BT1   lanthanum isotopes
  BT1   minutes living radioisotopes
    BT2   radioisotopes
      BT3   isotopes
  BT1   odd-even nuclei
    BT2   nuclei
  BT1   rare earth nuclei
    BT2   intermediate mass nuclei
      BT3   nuclei

LANTHANUM 130 [16; 16]
  BT1   beta-plus decay radioisotopes
    BT2   beta decay radioisotopes
      BT3   radioisotopes
        BT4   isotopes
  BT1   electron capture radioisotopes
    BT2   beta decay radioisotopes
      BT3   radioisotopes
        BT4   isotopes
  BT1   lanthanum isotopes
  BT1   minutes living radioisotopes
    BT2   radioisotopes
      BT3   isotopes
  BT1   odd-odd nuclei
    BT2   nuclei
  BT1   rare earth nuclei
    BT2   intermediate mass nuclei
      BT3   nuclei

LANTHANUM 131 [34; 34]
  BT1   beta-plus decay radioisotopes
    BT2   beta decay radioisotopes
      BT3   radioisotopes
        BT4   isotopes
  BT1   electron capture radioisotopes
    BT2   beta decay radioisotopes
      BT3   radioisotopes
        BT4   isotopes
  BT1   lanthanum isotopes
  BT1   minutes living radioisotopes
    BT2   radioisotopes
      BT3   isotopes
  BT1   odd-even nuclei
    BT2   nuclei
  BT1   rare earth nuclei
    BT2   intermediate mass nuclei
      BT3   nuclei

LANTHANUM 132 [21; 21]
  BT1   beta-plus decay radioisotopes
    BT2   beta decay radioisotopes
      BT3   radioisotopes
        BT4   isotopes
  BT1   electron capture radioisotopes
    BT2   beta decay radioisotopes
      BT3   radioisotopes
        BT4   isotopes
  BT1   hours living radioisotopes
    BT2   radioisotopes
      BT3   isotopes
  BT1   isomeric transition isotopes
    BT2   radioisotopes
      BT3   isotopes
  BT1   lanthanum isotopes
  BT1   minutes living radioisotopes
    BT2   radioisotopes
      BT3   isotopes
  BT1   odd-odd nuclei
    BT2   nuclei
  BT1   rare earth nuclei
    BT2   intermediate mass nuclei
      BT3   nuclei

LANTHANUM 133 [44; 44]
  BT1   beta-plus decay radioisotopes
    BT2   beta decay radioisotopes
      BT3   radioisotopes
        BT4   isotopes
  BT1   electron capture radioisotopes
    BT2   beta decay radioisotopes
      BT3   radioisotopes
        BT4   isotopes
  BT1   hours living radioisotopes
    BT2   radioisotopes
      BT3   isotopes
  BT1   lanthanum isotopes
  BT1   odd-even nuclei
    BT2   nuclei
  BT1   rare earth nuclei
    BT2   intermediate mass nuclei
      BT3   nuclei

LANTHANUM 134 [27; 27]
   BT1   beta-plus decay radioisotopes
     BT2   beta decay radioisotopes
       BT3   radioisotopes
         BT4   isotopes
   BT1   electron capture radioisotopes
     BT2   beta decay radioisotopes
       BT3   radioisotopes
         BT4   isotopes
   BT1   lanthanum isotopes
   BT1   minutes living radioisotopes
     BT2   radioisotopes
       BT3   isotopes
   BT1   odd-odd nuclei
     BT2   nuclei
   BT1   rare earth nuclei
     BT2   intermediate mass nuclei
       BT3   nuclei

LANTHANUM 135 [42; 42]
   BT1   beta-plus decay radioisotopes
     BT2   beta decay radioisotopes
       BT3   radioisotopes
         BT4   isotopes
   BT1   electron capture radioisotopes
     BT2   beta decay radioisotopes
       BT3   radioisotopes
         BT4   isotopes
   BT1   hours living radioisotopes
     BT2   radioisotopes
       BT3   isotopes
   BT1   lanthanum isotopes
   BT1   odd-even nuclei
     BT2   nuclei
   BT1   rare earth nuclei
     BT2   intermediate mass nuclei
       BT3   nuclei

LANTHANUM 136 [9; 9]
   BT1   beta-plus decay radioisotopes
     BT2   beta decay radioisotopes
       BT3   radioisotopes
         BT4   isotopes
   BT1   electron capture radioisotopes
     BT2   beta decay radioisotopes
       BT3   radioisotopes
         BT4   isotopes
   BT1   lanthanum isotopes
   BT1   minutes living radioisotopes
     BT2   radioisotopes
       BT3   isotopes
   BT1   odd-odd nuclei
     BT2   nuclei
   BT1   rare earth nuclei
     BT2   intermediate mass nuclei
       BT3   nuclei

LANTHANUM 137 [20; 20]
   BT1   electron capture radioisotopes
     BT2   beta decay radioisotopes
       BT3   radioisotopes
         BT4   isotopes
   BT1   lanthanum isotopes
   BT1   odd-even nuclei
     BT2   nuclei
   BT1   rare earth nuclei
     BT2   intermediate mass nuclei
       BT3   nuclei
   BT1   years living radioisotopes
     BT2   radioisotopes
       BT3   isotopes

LANTHANUM 138 [63; 63]
   BT1   beta-minus decay radioisotopes
     BT2   beta decay radioisotopes
       BT3   radioisotopes
         BT4   isotopes
   BT1   electron capture radioisotopes
     BT2   beta decay radioisotopes
       BT3   radioisotopes
         BT4   isotopes
   BT1   lanthanum isotopes
   BT1   odd-odd nuclei
     BT2   nuclei
   BT1   rare earth nuclei
     BT2   intermediate mass nuclei
       BT3   nuclei
   BT1   years living radioisotopes
     BT2   radioisotopes
       BT3   isotopes

LANTHANUM 139 [240; 240]
   BT1   lanthanum isotopes
   BT1   odd-even nuclei
     BT2   nuclei
   BT1   rare earth nuclei
     BT2   intermediate mass nuclei
       BT3   nuclei
   BT1   stable isotopes
     BT2   isotopes

LANTHANUM 139 BEAMS [4; 4]
Jan 79
   BT1   ion beams
     BT2   beams

LANTHANUM 139 REACTIONS
[112; 112] *Jan 76*
   BT1   heavy ion reactions
     BT2   nuclear reactions

LANTHANUM 139 TARGET [286; 286]
   BT1   targets

LANTHANUM 140 [568; 568]
   BT1   beta-minus decay radioisotopes
     BT2   beta decay radioisotopes
       BT3   radioisotopes
         BT4   isotopes
   BT1   days living radioisotopes
     BT2   radioisotopes
       BT3   isotopes
   BT1   lanthanum isotopes
   BT1   odd-odd nuclei
     BT2   nuclei
   BT1   rare earth nuclei
     BT2   intermediate mass nuclei
       BT3   nuclei

LANTHANUM 141 [22; 22]
   BT1   beta-minus decay radioisotopes
     BT2   beta decay radioisotopes
       BT3   radioisotopes
         BT4   isotopes
   BT1   hours living radioisotopes
     BT2   radioisotopes
       BT3   isotopes
   BT1   lanthanum isotopes
   BT1   odd-even nuclei
     BT2   nuclei
   BT1   rare earth nuclei
     BT2   intermediate mass nuclei
       BT3   nuclei

LANTHANUM 142 [34; 34]
   BT1   beta-minus decay radioisotopes
     BT2   beta decay radioisotopes
       BT3   radioisotopes
         BT4   isotopes
   BT1   hours living radioisotopes
     BT2   radioisotopes
       BT3   isotopes
   BT1   lanthanum isotopes
   BT1   odd-odd nuclei
     BT2   nuclei
   BT1   rare earth nuclei
     BT2   intermediate mass nuclei
       BT3   nuclei

LANTHANUM 143 [23; 23]
   BT1   beta-minus decay radioisotopes
     BT2   beta decay radioisotopes
       BT3   radioisotopes
         BT4   isotopes
   BT1   lanthanum isotopes
   BT1   minutes living radioisotopes
     BT2   radioisotopes
       BT3   isotopes
   BT1   odd-even nuclei
     BT2   nuclei
   BT1   rare earth nuclei
     BT2   intermediate mass nuclei
       BT3   nuclei

LANTHANUM 144 [34; 34]
   BT1   beta-minus decay radioisotopes
     BT2   beta decay radioisotopes
       BT3   radioisotopes
         BT4   isotopes
   BT1   lanthanum isotopes
   BT1   odd-odd nuclei
     BT2   nuclei
   BT1   rare earth nuclei
     BT2   intermediate mass nuclei
       BT3   nuclei
   BT1   seconds living radioisotopes
     BT2   radioisotopes
       BT3   isotopes

LANTHANUM 145 [15; 15]
   BT1   beta-minus decay radioisotopes
     BT2   beta decay radioisotopes
       BT3   radioisotopes
         BT4   isotopes
   BT1   lanthanum isotopes
   BT1   odd-even nuclei
     BT2   nuclei
   BT1   rare earth nuclei
     BT2   intermediate mass nuclei
       BT3   nuclei
   BT1   seconds living radioisotopes
     BT2   radioisotopes
       BT3   isotopes

LANTHANUM 146 [23; 23]
   BT1   beta-minus decay radioisotopes
     BT2   beta decay radioisotopes
       BT3   radioisotopes
         BT4   isotopes
   BT1   lanthanum isotopes
   BT1   odd-odd nuclei
     BT2   nuclei
   BT1   rare earth nuclei
     BT2   intermediate mass nuclei
       BT3   nuclei
   BT1   seconds living radioisotopes
     BT2   radioisotopes
       BT3   isotopes

LANTHANUM 147 [25; 25] *Jun 77*
   BT1   beta-minus decay radioisotopes
     BT2   beta decay radioisotopes
       BT3   radioisotopes
         BT4   isotopes
   BT1   lanthanum isotopes
   BT1   odd-even nuclei
     BT2   nuclei
   BT1   rare earth nuclei
     BT2   intermediate mass nuclei
       BT3   nuclei
   BT1   seconds living radioisotopes
     BT2   radioisotopes
       BT3   isotopes

LANTHANUM 148 [17; 17] *Jun 77*
   BT1   beta-minus decay radioisotopes
     BT2   beta decay radioisotopes
       BT3   radioisotopes
         BT4   isotopes
   BT1   lanthanum isotopes
   BT1   odd-odd nuclei
     BT2   nuclei
   BT1   rare earth nuclei
     BT2   intermediate mass nuclei
       BT3   nuclei
   BT1   seconds living radioisotopes
     BT2   radioisotopes
       BT3   isotopes

LANTHANUM 149 [2; 2] *Mar 86*
   BT1   beta-minus decay radioisotopes
     BT2   beta decay radioisotopes
       BT3   radioisotopes
         BT4   isotopes
   BT1   lanthanum isotopes
   BT1   odd-even nuclei
     BT2   nuclei
   BT1   rare earth nuclei
     BT2   intermediate mass nuclei
       BT3   nuclei
   BT1   seconds living radioisotopes
     BT2   radioisotopes

BT3 isotopes

lanzhou cyclotron
USE hirfl cyclotron

LAOS [1; 1]
BT1 asia
BT1 developing countries

lap welds
USE welded joints

LAPLACE EQUATION [411; 411]
BT1 partial differential equations
BT2 differential equations
BT3 equations
RT poisson equation
RT spherical harmonics

laplace operator
USE laplacian

LAPLACE TRANSFORMATION [819; 819] .
BT1 integral transformations
BT2 transformations

LAPLACIAN [362; 362]
UF *laplace operator*
BT1 mathematical operators
RT vectors

LAPPS [36; 36]
BT1 human populations
BT2 populations
RT arctic regions
RT eskimos

large coil program
(Coordinate descriptor below with descriptor for aspect of program discussed, e.g. SUPERCONDUCTING MAGNETS.)
USE coordinated research programs

LARGE INTESTINE [1,490; 2,692]
UF colon
UF+ appendix (vermiform)
BT1 intestines
BT2 gastrointestinal tract
BT3 digestive system
BT2 organs
BT3 body
NT1 rectum
RT excretion
RT feces

larmor electrons
USE larmor radius

larmor nuclear precession
USE larmor precession

LARMOR PRECESSION [388; 388]
UF *larmor nuclear precession*
BT1 precession

LARMOR RADIUS [868; 868]
UF *gyromagnetic radius*
UF *larmor electrons*
RT magnetic fields

LARVAE [688; 688]
UF *larval stage*
UF *metacercariae*
UF *nymphs*
UF+ *tadpoles*
RT age groups

RT amphibians
RT insects
RT metamorphosis

larval stage
USE larvae

LARYNGECTOMY [35; 35] Aug 81
BT1 surgery
BT2 medicine
RT larynx

LARYNX [793; 793]
BT1 respiratory system
RT laryngectomy
RT neck

LASER BEAM MACHINING [85; 85] Sep 82
UF *laser-beam machining*
BT1 machining

LASER CAVITIES [344; 344] Aug 75
RT lasers

LASER DRILLING [51; 51] Jul 76
BT1 materials drilling
BT2 machining
RT laser radiation

LASER FUSION REACTORS [705; 705] Jul 81
BT1 thermonuclear reactors
RT antares facility
RT cascade reactors
RT gdl facility
RT helios facility
RT icf devices
RT inertial confinement
RT laser implosions
RT omega facility

LASER IMPLOSIONS [1,963; 1,963]
UF *thermonuclear implosions(laser*
BT1 implosions
RT fusion yield
RT inertial confinement
RT laser fusion reactors
RT laser targets
RT laser-produced plasma
RT laser-radiation heating
RT pulsed fusion reactors

LASER ISOTOPE SEPARATION [1,433; 1,433]
(A laser photon beam selectively excites or ionizes one of the isotopes which can then be isolated by electromagnetic, chemical, or other methods.)
BT1 isotope separation
BT2 separation processes
RT lasers

LASER MIRRORS [273; 273]
RT lasers

laser pumping
USE optical pumping

LASER RADIATION [11,311; 11,311]
BT1 electromagnetic radiation
BT2 radiations
RT beat wave accelerators
RT laser drilling
RT laser targets
RT laser welding
RT laser-radiation heating
RT lasers
RT monochromatic radiation
RT superradiance
RT visible radiation

LASER SPECTROSCOPY [2,016; 2,330] Sep 79
BT1 spectroscopy
NT1 raman spectroscopy
RT absorption spectroscopy
RT fluorescence spectroscopy
RT raman spectra

LASER TARGETS [1,697; 1,697] Aug 81
BT1 targets
RT electron beam targets
RT energy deposition
RT inertial confinement
RT ion beam targets
RT laser implosions
RT laser radiation
RT thermonuclear fuels

LASER WELDING [221; 221]
BT1 welding
BT2 joining
BT3 fabrication
RT laser radiation

laser-beam machining
USE laser beam machining

LASER-PRODUCED PLASMA [5,159; 5,159]
BT1 plasma
RT laser implosions
RT laser-radiation heating
RT plasma production

LASER-RADIATION HEATING [1,769; 1,769]
BT1 plasma heating
BT2 heating
RT laser implosions
RT laser radiation
RT laser-produced plasma

LASERS [4,973; 14,559]
(Light Amplification by Stimulated Emission of Radiation)
BT1 amplifiers
BT2 equipment
NT1 chemical lasers
NT1 dye lasers
NT1 free electron lasers
NT1 gas lasers
NT2 carbon dioxide lasers
NT2 carbon monoxide lasers
NT2 excimer lasers
NT3 krypton fluoride lasers
NT2 helium-neon lasers
NT1 solid state lasers
NT2 neodymium lasers
NT2 ruby lasers
NT2 semiconductor lasers
NT1 x-ray lasers
RT electrical pumping
RT gasers
RT laser cavities
RT laser isotope separation
RT laser mirrors
RT laser radiation
RT light sources
RT masers
RT mode control
RT mode locking
RT multi-photon processes
RT optical pumping
RT q-switching
RT quantum electronics
RT stimulated emission

LASERTRONS [52; 52] May 86
BT1 microwave tubes
BT2 electron tubes
BT2 microwave equipment
BT3 electronic equipment
BT4 equipment
RT power supplies
RT rf systems

LASL [1,064; 1,064]
(Name changed to Los Alamos National Laboratory, and more recent material should be indexed to LANL.)
- UF   los alamos scientific lab
- BT1   lanl
- BT2   us doe
- BT3   us organizations
- BT4   national organizations
- BT1   us aec
- BT2   us organizations
- BT3   national organizations
- BT1   us erda
- BT2   us organizations
- BT3   national organizations
- RT   antares facility
- RT   helios facility
- RT   new mexico

lasl cold critical assembly
- USE   plasma core assembly

lasl critical assembly
- USE   parka reactor

late radiation effects
- USE   delayed radiation effects

LATENCY PERIOD [454; 454]
- UF   disease free period
- RT   acute irradiation
- RT   delayed radiation effects
- RT   incubation
- RT   quarantine
- RT   radiation syndrome

latent heat of fusion
- USE   fusion heat

latent heat of sublimation
- USE   sublimation heat

latent heat of transition
- USE   transition heat

latent heat of vaporization
- USE   vaporization heat

LATENT IMAGES [91; 91]
- RT   dielectric track detectors
- RT   nuclear emulsions
- RT   photographic emulsions
- RT   photographic films

LATEX [173; 173]
- BT1   rubbers
- BT2   elastomers
- BT3   polymers
- BT2   organic polymers
- BT3   organic compounds
- BT3   polymers
- RT   coatings
- RT   emulsions
- RT   natural rubber
- RT   protective coatings

LATHES [12; 12] *May 80*
- BT1   machine tools
- RT   machining

latin am nucl weap prohib trea
- USE   tlatelolco treaty

LATIN AMERICA [29; 1,235] *Mar 86*
- NT1   central america
- NT2   costa rica
- NT2   el salvador
- NT2   guatemala
- NT2   honduras
- NT2   nicaragua
- NT2   panama
- NT2   panama canal zone
- NT1   cuba
- NT1   dominican republic
- NT1   haiti
- NT1   mexico
- NT1   puerto rico
- NT1   saint lucia
- NT1   south america
- NT2   argentina
- NT3   mendoza
- NT2   bolivia
- NT3   chacaltaya
- NT2   brazil
- NT2   chile
- NT2   colombia
- NT2   ecuador
- NT2   french guiana
- NT2   guyana
- NT3   british guiana
- NT2   paraguay
- NT2   peru
- NT2   surinam
- NT2   uruguay
- NT2   venezuela
- RT   west indies

LATINA REACTOR [26; 26]
(Borgo Sabotino, Latina, Italy)
- UF   foce verde reactor
- BT1   magnox type reactors
- BT2   gcr type reactors
- BT3   gas cooled reactors
- BT4   reactors
- BT3   graphite moderated reactors
- BT4   reactors
- BT2   natural uranium reactors
- BT3   reactors
- BT2   power reactors
- BT3   reactors
- BT1   thermal reactors
- BT2   reactors

LATITUDE EFFECT [954; 954]
- RT   equator

LATTICE FIELD THEORY
[5,965; 5,965] *Nov 78*
- BT1   constructive field theory
- BT2   quantum field theory
- BT3   field theories
- RT   gauge invariance
- RT   instantons
- RT   lie groups
- RT   wilson loop

LATTICE PARAMETERS
[15,547; 15,547]
- RT   crystal lattices

LATTICE VIBRATIONS [2,625; 2,625]
- UF   vibrations (lattice)
- RT   anharmonic crystals
- RT   crystal structure
- RT   debye-waller factor
- RT   harmonics
- RT   nuclear specific heat
- RT   oscillation modes
- RT   rayleigh waves
- RT   vibrational states

lattices (crystal)
- USE   crystal lattices

lattices (reactor)
- USE   reactor lattices

LAUE METHOD [353; 353]
- BT1   diffraction methods
- RT   crystal lattices
- RT   kossel method
- RT   structural chemical analysis

laue-bragg scattering
- USE   bragg reflection

LAUNCHING [94; 94]
- RT   missiles
- RT   rockets
- RT   space vehicles

lauric acid
- USE   dodecanoic acid

lauryl radicals
- USE   dodecyl radicals

lausanne tokamak
- USE   tca tokamak

lav virus
- USE   aids virus

LAVA [281; 281]
- BT1   igneous rocks
- BT2   rocks
- RT   magnesium silicates
- RT   silicate minerals
- RT   volcanoes

LAVAGE [233; 233]
(Washing out of hollow organ by copious injections and rejections of water.)
- UF+   pulmonary lavage
- RT   decontamination
- RT   excretion
- RT   lungs
- RT   respiratory system

LAVES PHASES [1,058; 1,058]
- RT   crystal lattices
- RT   intermetallic compounds

LAWRENCE BERKELEY LABORATORY [428; 428]
- UF   lbl
- UF   uclbl
- UF   univ. of calif. lawr. rad. lab
- BT1   us aec
- BT2   us organizations
- BT3   national organizations
- BT1   us doe
- BT2   us organizations
- BT3   national organizations
- BT1   us erda
- BT2   us organizations
- BT3   national organizations
- RT   california

LAWRENCE LIVERMORE LABORATORY [822; 822]
(Name changed to Lawrence Livermore National Laboratory, and more recent material should be indexed to LAWRENCE LIVERMORE NATIONAL LA.)
- UF   uclll
- BT1   lawrence livermore national la
- BT2   us doe
- BT3   us organizations
- BT4   national organizations
- BT1   us aec
- BT2   us organizations
- BT3   national organizations
- BT1   us erda
- BT2   us organizations
- BT3   national organizations
- RT   california
- RT   nova facility
- RT   shiva facility
- RT   tmx devices

LAWRENCE LIVERMORE NATIONAL LA [16; 510] *Apr 84*
(Formerly known as Lawrence Livermore Laboratory, and older material is so indexed.)
  UF   llnl
  BT1   us doe
    BT2   us organizations
      BT3   national organizations
  NT1   lawrence livermore laboratory
  RT   california
  RT   nova facility
  RT   novette facility
  RT   shiva facility

LAWRENCIUM [63; 63]
  BT1   actinides
    BT2   metals
      BT3   elements
  BT1   transplutonium elements
    BT2   transuranium elements
      BT3   elements

LAWRENCIUM CHLORIDES [0; 0]
  BT1   chlorides
    BT2   chlorine compounds
      BT3   halogen compounds
    BT2   halides
      BT3   halogen compounds
  BT1   lawrencium compounds
    BT2   actinide compounds
    BT2   transplutonium compounds
      BT3   transuranium compounds

LAWRENCIUM COMPLEXES [4; 4]
  BT1   actinide complexes
    BT2   complexes
  BT1   transuranium complexes

LAWRENCIUM COMPOUNDS [8; 9]
  BT1   actinide compounds
  BT1   transplutonium compounds
    BT2   transuranium compounds
  NT1   lawrencium chlorides
  NT1   lawrencium oxides

LAWRENCIUM ISOTOPES [35; 60]
  NT1   lawrencium 253
  NT1   lawrencium 254
  NT1   lawrencium 255
  NT1   lawrencium 256
  NT1   lawrencium 257
  NT1   lawrencium 258
  NT1   lawrencium 259
  NT1   lawrencium 260
  NT1   lawrencium 261
  NT1   lawrencium 262
  NT1   lawrencium 263

LAWRENCIUM OXIDES [1; 1]
  BT1   lawrencium compounds
    BT2   actinide compounds
    BT2   transplutonium compounds
      BT3   transuranium compounds
  BT1   oxides
    BT2   chalcogenides
    BT2   oxygen compounds

LAWRENCIUM 253 [2; 2] *Jun 86*
  BT1   actinide nuclei
    BT2   heavy nuclei
      BT3   nuclei
  BT1   alpha decay radioisotopes
    BT2   radioisotopes
      BT3   isotopes
  BT1   lawrencium isotopes
  BT1   odd-even nuclei
    BT2   nuclei
  BT1   seconds living radioisotopes
    BT2   radioisotopes
      BT3   isotopes

LAWRENCIUM 254 [4; 4] *Jun 86*
  BT1   actinide nuclei
    BT2   heavy nuclei
      BT3   nuclei
  BT1   alpha decay radioisotopes
    BT2   radioisotopes
      BT3   isotopes
  BT1   electron capture radioisotopes
    BT2   beta decay radioisotopes
      BT3   radioisotopes
        BT4   isotopes
  BT1   lawrencium isotopes
  BT1   odd-odd nuclei
    BT2   nuclei
  BT1   seconds living radioisotopes
    BT2   radioisotopes
      BT3   isotopes

LAWRENCIUM 255 [3; 3] *Jan 77*
  BT1   actinide nuclei
    BT2   heavy nuclei
      BT3   nuclei
  BT1   alpha decay radioisotopes
    BT2   radioisotopes
      BT3   isotopes
  BT1   electron capture radioisotopes
    BT2   beta decay radioisotopes
      BT3   radioisotopes
        BT4   isotopes
  BT1   lawrencium isotopes
  BT1   odd-even nuclei
    BT2   nuclei
  BT1   seconds living radioisotopes
    BT2   radioisotopes
      BT3   isotopes

LAWRENCIUM 256 [2; 2]
  BT1   actinide nuclei
    BT2   heavy nuclei
      BT3   nuclei
  BT1   alpha decay radioisotopes
    BT2   radioisotopes
      BT3   isotopes
  BT1   electron capture radioisotopes
    BT2   beta decay radioisotopes
      BT3   radioisotopes
        BT4   isotopes
  BT1   lawrencium isotopes
  BT1   odd-odd nuclei
    BT2   nuclei
  BT1   seconds living radioisotopes
    BT2   radioisotopes
      BT3   isotopes

LAWRENCIUM 257 [4; 4]
  BT1   actinide nuclei
    BT2   heavy nuclei
      BT3   nuclei
  BT1   alpha decay radioisotopes
    BT2   radioisotopes
      BT3   isotopes
  BT1   lawrencium isotopes
  BT1   millisec living radioisotopes
    BT2   radioisotopes
      BT3   isotopes
  BT1   odd-even nuclei
    BT2   nuclei

LAWRENCIUM 258 [3; 3] *Jun 86*
  BT1   actinide nuclei
    BT2   heavy nuclei
      BT3   nuclei
  BT1   alpha decay radioisotopes
    BT2   radioisotopes
      BT3   isotopes
  BT1   lawrencium isotopes
  BT1   odd-odd nuclei
    BT2   nuclei
  BT1   seconds living radioisotopes
    BT2   radioisotopes
      BT3   isotopes

LAWRENCIUM 259 [4; 4] *Jan 77*
  BT1   actinide nuclei
    BT2   heavy nuclei
      BT3   nuclei
  BT1   alpha decay radioisotopes
    BT2   radioisotopes
      BT3   isotopes
  BT1   lawrencium isotopes
  BT1   odd-even nuclei
    BT2   nuclei
  BT1   seconds living radioisotopes
    BT2   radioisotopes
      BT3   isotopes

LAWRENCIUM 260 [10; 10] *Mar 86*
  BT1   actinide nuclei
    BT2   heavy nuclei
      BT3   nuclei
  BT1   alpha decay radioisotopes
    BT2   radioisotopes
      BT3   isotopes
  BT1   lawrencium isotopes
  BT1   minutes living radioisotopes
    BT2   radioisotopes
      BT3   isotopes
  BT1   odd-odd nuclei
    BT2   nuclei

LAWRENCIUM 261 [7; 7] *Feb 87*
  BT1   actinide nuclei
    BT2   heavy nuclei
      BT3   nuclei
  BT1   lawrencium isotopes
  BT1   odd-even nuclei
    BT2   nuclei

LAWRENCIUM 262 [6; 6] *Feb 87*
  BT1   actinide nuclei
    BT2   heavy nuclei
      BT3   nuclei
  BT1   lawrencium isotopes
  BT1   odd-odd nuclei
    BT2   nuclei

LAWRENCIUM 263 [2; 2] *Feb 87*
  BT1   actinide nuclei
    BT2   heavy nuclei
      BT3   nuclei
  BT1   lawrencium isotopes
  BT1   odd-even nuclei
    BT2   nuclei

LAWS [623; 12,383]
(The whole body of laws, regulations, agreements, judicial or administrative decisions or practices which are binding or accepted as a rule of conduct. prior to December 1990, this descriptor was spelled LAW.)
  UF   *corporation law*
  UF   *general law*
  UF   *municipal law*
  UF   *private law*
  NT1   atomic energy laws
    NT2   nuclear waste policy acts
  NT1   case law
  NT1   fishery laws
  NT1   international laws
  NT1   maritime laws
  NT1   mining laws
  NT1   patent laws
  NT1   pollution laws
    NT2   us water pollution control act
  NT1   price-anderson act
  NT1   public law
  NT1   radiation protection laws
  NT1   regulations
    NT2   contamination regulations
      NT3   maximum acceptable contaminati
    NT2   international regulations
      NT3   oecd mcmsdrw
    NT2   licensing regulations
    NT2   packaging rules
    NT2   pollution regulations
    NT2   safeguard regulations
    NT2   transport regulations
  NT1   tax laws
  NT1   us natl environment policy act
  RT   administrative procedures
  RT   agreements
  RT   enforcement
  RT   hearings
  RT   legislation

RT   legislative text

LAWSON CRITERION [127; 127]
May 78
(The energy output from a thermonuclear reactor can only exceed the plasma energy input if the product of plasma density and confinement time is higher than 10 exp 14 s/cm exp 3.)
RT   breakeven
RT   confinement time
RT   plasma density
RT   thermonuclear devices

LAWSUITS [448; 448] *Dec 76*
RT   arbitration
RT   courts
RT   dispute settlements
RT   hearings

LAX THEOREM [126; 126]
RT   shock waves

LAYERS [8,070; 11,861]
NT1   boundary layers
  NT2   plasma scrape-off layer
  NT2   plasmapause
  NT2   tropopause
NT1   ozone layer
RT   films
RT   lamellae
RT   stratification
RT   stratigraphy
RT   substrates

lbl
USE   lawrence berkeley laboratory

LBL 88-INCH CYCLOTRON [12; 12]
Aug 88
(Lawrence Berkeley Laboratory, Berkeley, California, USA.)
BT1   uclrl cyclotrons
  BT2   isochronous cyclotrons
    BT3   cyclotrons
      BT4   cyclic accelerators
        BT5   accelerators

lcao calculations
USE   lcao method

LCAO METHOD [661; 661]
UF   *lcao calculations*
UF   *lcao mo calculations*
UF   *lcao scf treatment*
UF   *lcao theory*
UF   *linear comb of atomic orbitals*
RT   molecular orbital method
RT   molecular structure
RT   self-consistent field

lcao mo calculations
USE   lcao method

lcao scf treatment
USE   lcao method

lcao theory
USE   lcao method

LCPMPDPW [42; 42] *Mar 76*
(1972 London Convention on Prevention of Marine Pollution by Dumping of Waste and other Matter)
UF   *london conv preven marine poll*
UF   *marine poll preven, london con*
UF   *pollution prev mar, london con*
UF   *preven marine poll, london con*

BT1   international agreements
  BT2   agreements
RT   contamination
RT   marine disposal
RT   oecd mcmsdrw
RT   pollution

ld 50
USE   lethal radiation dose

LEACHATES [523; 523] *Feb 81*
(The liquid that has percolated through soil or other media; a solution obtained by leaching.)
BT1   solutions
  BT2   homogeneous mixtures
    BT3   mixtures
      BT4   dispersions
RT   environmental transport
RT   ground water
RT   in-situ processing
RT   leaching
RT   liquid wastes
RT   solvent extraction

LEACHING [6,525; 6,525]
UF   *elution (soluble constituents)*
UF   *lixiviation*
BT1   dissolution
BT1   separation processes
RT   diffusion
RT   hydrometallurgy
RT   in-situ processing
RT   ion exchange chromatography
RT   ion exchange materials
RT   leachates
RT   ore enrichment
RT   ore processing
RT   slurex process
RT   solubility
RT   solution mining
RT   solvent extraction
RT   thiobacillus ferroxidans
RT   thiobacillus oxidans

LEAD [7,919; 7,919]
BT1   metals
  BT2   elements
RT   shielding materials

LEAD ADDITIONS [173; 173]
(Alloys containing not more than 1% Pb are listed here.)
RT   lead alloys
RT   lead compounds

LEAD ALLOYS [1,377; 1,757]
(Alloys containing more than 1% Pb.)
BT1   alloys
NT1   alloy-bi50pb25cd12sn12
NT1   lead base alloys
RT   lead additions

LEAD BASE ALLOYS [341; 341]
BT1   lead alloys
  BT2   alloys

LEAD BROMIDES [24; 24]
BT1   bromides
  BT2   bromine compounds
    BT3   halogen compounds
  BT2   halides
    BT3   halogen compounds
BT1   lead halides
  BT2   halides
    BT3   halogen compounds
  BT2   lead compounds

LEAD CARBONATES [18; 18]
BT1   carbonates
  BT2   carbon compounds
  BT2   oxygen compounds
BT1   lead compounds

LEAD CHLORIDES [115; 115]
BT1   chlorides
  BT2   chlorine compounds
    BT3   halogen compounds
  BT2   halides
    BT3   halogen compounds
BT1   lead halides
  BT2   halides
    BT3   halogen compounds
  BT2   lead compounds

LEAD COMPLEXES [83; 83]
BT1   complexes

LEAD COMPOUNDS [1,268; 4,206]
NT1   lead carbonates
NT1   lead halides
  NT2   lead bromides
  NT2   lead chlorides
  NT2   lead fluorides
  NT2   lead iodides
NT1   lead hydroxides
NT1   lead nitrates
NT1   lead nitrides
NT1   lead oxides
NT1   lead phosphates
NT1   lead selenides
NT1   lead silicates
NT1   lead sulfates
NT1   lead sulfides
NT1   lead tellurides
NT1   lead tungstates
NT1   plumbates
NT1   plzt
NT1   pzt
NT1   tel
RT   lead additions

LEAD FLUORIDES [149; 149]
BT1   fluorides
  BT2   fluorine compounds
    BT3   halogen compounds
  BT2   halides
    BT3   halogen compounds
BT1   lead halides
  BT2   halides
    BT3   halogen compounds
  BT2   lead compounds

LEAD HALIDES [1; 161] *Apr 84*
BT1   halides
  BT2   halogen compounds
BT1   lead compounds
NT1   lead bromides
NT1   lead chlorides
NT1   lead fluorides
NT1   lead iodides

LEAD HYDROXIDES [14; 14]
BT1   hydroxides
  BT2   hydrogen compounds
  BT2   oxygen compounds
BT1   lead compounds

LEAD IODIDES [134; 134]
BT1   iodides
  BT2   halides
    BT3   halogen compounds
  BT2   iodine compounds
    BT3   halogen compounds
BT1   lead halides
  BT2   halides
    BT3   halogen compounds
  BT2   lead compounds

LEAD IONS [465; 465]
BT1   ions
  BT2   charged particles

LEAD ISOTOPES [884; 6,997]
NT1   lead 182
NT1   lead 183
NT1   lead 184
NT1   lead 185
NT1   lead 186
NT1   lead 187
NT1   lead 188

NT1 lead 189
NT1 lead 190
NT1 lead 191
NT1 lead 192
NT1 lead 193
NT1 lead 194
NT1 lead 195
NT1 lead 196
NT1 lead 197
NT1 lead 198
NT1 lead 199
NT1 lead 200
NT1 lead 201
NT1 lead 202
NT1 lead 203
NT1 lead 204
NT1 lead 205
NT1 lead 206
NT1 lead 207
NT1 lead 208
NT1 lead 209
NT1 lead 210
NT1 lead 211
NT1 lead 212
NT1 lead 213
NT1 lead 214
NT1 lead 215
NT1 lead 216

lead method
USE isotope dating

LEAD NITRATES [67; 67]
BT1 lead compounds
BT1 nitrates
BT2 nitrogen compounds
BT2 oxygen compounds

LEAD NITRIDES [2; 2]
BT1 lead compounds
BT1 nitrides
BT2 nitrogen compounds
BT2 pnictides

LEAD ORES [95; 95]
BT1 ores

LEAD OXIDES [1,045; 1,051]
BT1 lead compounds
BT1 oxides
BT2 chalcogenides
BT2 oxygen compounds
RT curite
RT demesmaekerite
RT oxide minerals
RT plumbates
RT wulfenite

LEAD PHOSPHATES [32; 35]
BT1 lead compounds
BT1 phosphates
BT2 oxygen compounds
BT2 phosphorus compounds
RT dumontite
RT parsonsite
RT phosphate minerals

LEAD SELENIDES [142; 142] *Jan 77*
BT1 lead compounds
BT1 selenides
BT2 chalcogenides
BT2 selenium compounds

LEAD SILICATES [22; 22]
BT1 lead compounds
BT1 silicates
BT2 oxygen compounds
BT2 silicon compounds

LEAD SULFATES [53; 53]
BT1 lead compounds
BT1 sulfates
BT2 oxygen compounds
BT2 sulfur compounds

LEAD SULFIDES [288; 353]
BT1 lead compounds
BT1 sulfides
BT2 chalcogenides
BT2 sulfur compounds
RT galena
RT sulfide minerals

LEAD TELLURIDES [874; 874]
BT1 lead compounds
BT1 tellurides
BT2 chalcogenides
BT2 tellurium compounds

LEAD TUNGSTATES [24; 24] *Apr 79*
BT1 lead compounds
BT1 tungstates
BT2 oxygen compounds
BT2 tungsten compounds
BT3 transition element compounds

LEAD 182 [2; 2] *Feb 88*
BT1 alpha decay radioisotopes
BT2 radioisotopes
BT3 isotopes
BT1 even-even nuclei
BT2 nuclei
BT1 heavy nuclei
BT2 nuclei
BT1 lead isotopes
BT1 millisec living radioisotopes
BT2 radioisotopes
BT3 isotopes

LEAD 183 [3; 3] *Feb 81*
BT1 alpha decay radioisotopes
BT2 radioisotopes
BT3 isotopes
BT1 even-odd nuclei
BT2 nuclei
BT1 heavy nuclei
BT2 nuclei
BT1 lead isotopes

LEAD 184 [7; 7] *Jul 80*
BT1 alpha decay radioisotopes
BT2 radioisotopes
BT3 isotopes
BT1 even-even nuclei
BT2 nuclei
BT1 heavy nuclei
BT2 nuclei
BT1 lead isotopes
BT1 millisec living radioisotopes
BT2 radioisotopes
BT3 isotopes

LEAD 185 [4; 4]
BT1 alpha decay radioisotopes
BT2 radioisotopes
BT3 isotopes
BT1 even-odd nuclei
BT2 nuclei
BT1 heavy nuclei
BT2 nuclei
BT1 lead isotopes
BT1 seconds living radioisotopes
BT2 radioisotopes
BT3 isotopes

LEAD 186 [19; 19]
BT1 alpha decay radioisotopes
BT2 radioisotopes
BT3 isotopes
BT1 electron capture radioisotopes
BT2 beta decay radioisotopes
BT3 radioisotopes
BT4 isotopes
BT1 even-even nuclei
BT2 nuclei
BT1 heavy nuclei
BT2 nuclei
BT1 lead isotopes
BT1 seconds living radioisotopes
BT2 radioisotopes
BT3 isotopes

LEAD 187 [11; 11]
BT1 alpha decay radioisotopes
BT2 radioisotopes
BT3 isotopes
BT1 beta-plus decay radioisotopes
BT2 beta decay radioisotopes
BT3 radioisotopes
BT4 isotopes
BT1 electron capture radioisotopes
BT2 beta decay radioisotopes
BT3 radioisotopes
BT4 isotopes
BT1 even-odd nuclei
BT2 nuclei
BT1 heavy nuclei
BT2 nuclei
BT1 lead isotopes
BT1 seconds living radioisotopes
BT2 radioisotopes
BT3 isotopes

LEAD 188 [21; 21]
BT1 alpha decay radioisotopes
BT2 radioisotopes
BT3 isotopes
BT1 beta-plus decay radioisotopes
BT2 beta decay radioisotopes
BT3 radioisotopes
BT4 isotopes
BT1 electron capture radioisotopes
BT2 beta decay radioisotopes
BT3 radioisotopes
BT4 isotopes
BT1 even-even nuclei
BT2 nuclei
BT1 heavy nuclei
BT2 nuclei
BT1 lead isotopes
BT1 seconds living radioisotopes
BT2 radioisotopes
BT3 isotopes

LEAD 189 [8; 8]
BT1 alpha decay radioisotopes
BT2 radioisotopes
BT3 isotopes
BT1 beta-plus decay radioisotopes
BT2 beta decay radioisotopes
BT3 radioisotopes
BT4 isotopes
BT1 electron capture radioisotopes
BT2 beta decay radioisotopes
BT3 radioisotopes
BT4 isotopes
BT1 even-odd nuclei
BT2 nuclei
BT1 heavy nuclei
BT2 nuclei
BT1 lead isotopes
BT1 seconds living radioisotopes
BT2 radioisotopes
BT3 isotopes

LEAD 190 [40; 40]
BT1 alpha decay radioisotopes
BT2 radioisotopes
BT3 isotopes
BT1 beta-plus decay radioisotopes
BT2 beta decay radioisotopes
BT3 radioisotopes
BT4 isotopes
BT1 electron capture radioisotopes
BT2 beta decay radioisotopes
BT3 radioisotopes
BT4 isotopes
BT1 even-even nuclei
BT2 nuclei
BT1 heavy nuclei
BT2 nuclei
BT1 lead isotopes
BT1 minutes living radioisotopes
BT2 radioisotopes
BT3 isotopes

LEAD 191 [9; 9]
  BT1   alpha decay radioisotopes
    BT2   radioisotopes
      BT3   isotopes
  BT1   beta-plus decay radioisotopes
    BT2   beta decay radioisotopes
      BT3   radioisotopes
        BT4   isotopes
  BT1   electron capture radioisotopes
    BT2   beta decay radioisotopes
      BT3   radioisotopes
        BT4   isotopes
  BT1   even-odd nuclei
    BT2   nuclei
  BT1   heavy nuclei
    BT2   nuclei
  BT1   lead isotopes
  BT1   minutes living radioisotopes
    BT2   radioisotopes
      BT3   isotopes

LEAD 192 [63; 63]
  BT1   alpha decay radioisotopes
    BT2   radioisotopes
      BT3   isotopes
  BT1   beta-plus decay radioisotopes
    BT2   beta decay radioisotopes
      BT3   radioisotopes
        BT4   isotopes
  BT1   electron capture radioisotopes
    BT2   beta decay radioisotopes
      BT3   radioisotopes
        BT4   isotopes
  BT1   even-even nuclei
    BT2   nuclei
  BT1   heavy nuclei
    BT2   nuclei
  BT1   lead isotopes
  BT1   minutes living radioisotopes
    BT2   radioisotopes
      BT3   isotopes

LEAD 193 [10; 10] *Oct 75*
  BT1   beta-plus decay radioisotopes
    BT2   beta decay radioisotopes
      BT3   radioisotopes
        BT4   isotopes
  BT1   electron capture radioisotopes
    BT2   beta decay radioisotopes
      BT3   radioisotopes
        BT4   isotopes
  BT1   even-odd nuclei
    BT2   nuclei
  BT1   heavy nuclei
    BT2   nuclei
  BT1   lead isotopes
  BT1   minutes living radioisotopes
    BT2   radioisotopes
      BT3   isotopes

LEAD 194 [67; 67]
  BT1   beta-plus decay radioisotopes
    BT2   beta decay radioisotopes
      BT3   radioisotopes
        BT4   isotopes
  BT1   electron capture radioisotopes
    BT2   beta decay radioisotopes
      BT3   radioisotopes
        BT4   isotopes
  BT1   even-even nuclei
    BT2   nuclei
  BT1   heavy nuclei
    BT2   nuclei
  BT1   isomeric transition isotopes
    BT2   radioisotopes
      BT3   isotopes
  BT1   lead isotopes
  BT1   minutes living radioisotopes
    BT2   radioisotopes
      BT3   isotopes
  BT1   nanosec living radioisotopes
    BT2   radioisotopes
      BT3   isotopes

LEAD 195 [34; 34]
  BT1   beta-plus decay radioisotopes
    BT2   beta decay radioisotopes
      BT3   radioisotopes
        BT4   isotopes
  BT1   electron capture radioisotopes
    BT2   beta decay radioisotopes
      BT3   radioisotopes
        BT4   isotopes
  BT1   even-odd nuclei
    BT2   nuclei
  BT1   heavy nuclei
    BT2   nuclei
  BT1   lead isotopes
  BT1   minutes living radioisotopes
    BT2   radioisotopes
      BT3   isotopes

LEAD 196 [68; 68]
  BT1   electron capture radioisotopes
    BT2   beta decay radioisotopes
      BT3   radioisotopes
        BT4   isotopes
  BT1   even-even nuclei
    BT2   nuclei
  BT1   heavy nuclei
    BT2   nuclei
  BT1   lead isotopes
  BT1   minutes living radioisotopes
    BT2   radioisotopes
      BT3   isotopes

LEAD 197 [34; 34]
  BT1   electron capture radioisotopes
    BT2   beta decay radioisotopes
      BT3   radioisotopes
        BT4   isotopes
  BT1   even-odd nuclei
    BT2   nuclei
  BT1   heavy nuclei
    BT2   nuclei
  BT1   isomeric transition isotopes
    BT2   radioisotopes
      BT3   isotopes
  BT1   lead isotopes
  BT1   minutes living radioisotopes
    BT2   radioisotopes
      BT3   isotopes

LEAD 198 [64; 64]
  BT1   electron capture radioisotopes
    BT2   beta decay radioisotopes
      BT3   radioisotopes
        BT4   isotopes
  BT1   even-even nuclei
    BT2   nuclei
  BT1   heavy nuclei
    BT2   nuclei
  BT1   hours living radioisotopes
    BT2   radioisotopes
      BT3   isotopes
  BT1   lead isotopes

LEAD 199 [37; 37]
  BT1   beta-plus decay radioisotopes
    BT2   beta decay radioisotopes
      BT3   radioisotopes
        BT4   isotopes
  BT1   electron capture radioisotopes
    BT2   beta decay radioisotopes
      BT3   radioisotopes
        BT4   isotopes
  BT1   even-odd nuclei
    BT2   nuclei
  BT1   heavy nuclei
    BT2   nuclei
  BT1   hours living radioisotopes
    BT2   radioisotopes
      BT3   isotopes
  BT1   internal conversion radioisoto
    BT2   radioisotopes
      BT3   isotopes
  BT1   isomeric transition isotopes
    BT2   radioisotopes
      BT3   isotopes
  BT1   lead isotopes
  BT1   minutes living radioisotopes
    BT2   radioisotopes
      BT3   isotopes

LEAD 200 [94; 94]
  BT1   electron capture radioisotopes
    BT2   beta decay radioisotopes
      BT3   radioisotopes
        BT4   isotopes
  BT1   even-even nuclei
    BT2   nuclei
  BT1   heavy nuclei
    BT2   nuclei
  BT1   hours living radioisotopes
    BT2   radioisotopes
      BT3   isotopes
  BT1   isomeric transition isotopes
    BT2   radioisotopes
      BT3   isotopes
  BT1   lead isotopes
  BT1   nanosec living radioisotopes
    BT2   radioisotopes
      BT3   isotopes

LEAD 200 TARGET [6; 6] *Dec 79*
  BT1   targets

LEAD 201 [72; 72]
  BT1   beta-plus decay radioisotopes
    BT2   beta decay radioisotopes
      BT3   radioisotopes
        BT4   isotopes
  BT1   electron capture radioisotopes
    BT2   beta decay radioisotopes
      BT3   radioisotopes
        BT4   isotopes
  BT1   even-odd nuclei
    BT2   nuclei
  BT1   heavy nuclei
    BT2   nuclei
  BT1   hours living radioisotopes
    BT2   radioisotopes
      BT3   isotopes
  BT1   isomeric transition isotopes
    BT2   radioisotopes
      BT3   isotopes
  BT1   lead isotopes
  BT1   minutes living radioisotopes
    BT2   radioisotopes
      BT3   isotopes

LEAD 202 [83; 83]
  BT1   electron capture radioisotopes
    BT2   beta decay radioisotopes
      BT3   radioisotopes
        BT4   isotopes
  BT1   even-even nuclei
    BT2   nuclei
  BT1   heavy nuclei
    BT2   nuclei
  BT1   hours living radioisotopes
    BT2   radioisotopes
      BT3   isotopes
  BT1   internal conversion radioisoto
    BT2   radioisotopes
      BT3   isotopes
  BT1   isomeric transition isotopes
    BT2   radioisotopes
      BT3   isotopes
  BT1   lead isotopes
  BT1   years living radioisotopes
    BT2   radioisotopes
      BT3   isotopes

LEAD 202 TARGET [4; 4] *Jul 78*
  BT1   targets

LEAD 203 [170; 170]
  BT1   days living radioisotopes
    BT2   radioisotopes
      BT3   isotopes
  BT1   electron capture radioisotopes
    BT2   beta decay radioisotopes
      BT3   radioisotopes
        BT4   isotopes
  BT1   even-odd nuclei
    BT2   nuclei
  BT1   heavy nuclei
    BT2   nuclei
  BT1   isomeric transition isotopes
    BT2   radioisotopes
      BT3   isotopes

BT1 lead isotopes
BT1 seconds living radioisotopes
BT2 radioisotopes
BT3 isotopes

LEAD 204 [539; 539]
BT1 even-even nuclei
BT2 nuclei
BT1 heavy nuclei
BT2 nuclei
BT1 hours living radioisotopes
BT2 radioisotopes
BT3 isotopes
BT1 isomeric transition isotopes
BT2 radioisotopes
BT3 isotopes
BT1 lead isotopes
BT1 stable isotopes
BT2 isotopes

LEAD 204 TARGET [129; 129]
BT1 targets

LEAD 205 [138; 138]
BT1 electron capture radioisotopes
BT2 beta decay radioisotopes
BT3 radioisotopes
BT4 isotopes
BT1 even-odd nuclei
BT2 nuclei
BT1 heavy nuclei
BT2 nuclei
BT1 lead isotopes
BT1 years living radioisotopes
BT2 radioisotopes
BT3 isotopes

LEAD 205 TARGET [10; 10] *Nov 78*
BT1 targets

LEAD 206 [876; 876]
UF *radium g*
BT1 even-even nuclei
BT2 nuclei
BT1 heavy nuclei
BT2 nuclei
BT1 lead isotopes
BT1 stable isotopes
BT2 isotopes

LEAD 206 REACTIONS [12; 12] *Aug 86*
BT1 heavy ion reactions
BT2 nuclear reactions

LEAD 206 TARGET [312; 312]
BT1 targets

LEAD 207 [928; 928]
UF *actinium d*
BT1 even-odd nuclei
BT2 nuclei
BT1 heavy nuclei
BT2 nuclei
BT1 isomeric transition isotopes
BT2 radioisotopes
BT3 isotopes
BT1 lead isotopes
BT1 millisec living radioisotopes
BT2 radioisotopes
BT3 isotopes
BT1 stable isotopes
BT2 isotopes

LEAD 207 TARGET [375; 375]
BT1 targets

LEAD 208 [2,709; 2,709]
UF *thorium d*
BT1 even-even nuclei
BT2 nuclei
BT1 heavy nuclei
BT2 nuclei
BT1 lead isotopes
BT1 stable isotopes
BT2 isotopes

LEAD 208 BEAMS [84; 84] *May 78*
BT1 ion beams
BT2 beams

LEAD 208 REACTIONS [346; 346] *Apr 78*
BT1 heavy ion reactions
BT2 nuclear reactions

LEAD 208 TARGET [3,456; 3,456]
BT1 targets

LEAD 209 [231; 231]
BT1 beta-minus decay radioisotopes
BT2 beta decay radioisotopes
BT3 radioisotopes
BT4 isotopes
BT1 even-odd nuclei
BT2 nuclei
BT1 heavy nuclei
BT2 nuclei
BT1 hours living radioisotopes
BT2 radioisotopes
BT3 isotopes
BT1 lead isotopes

LEAD 209 TARGET [19; 19] *Jul 76*
BT1 targets

LEAD 210 [1,444; 1,444]
UF *radium d*
BT1 alpha decay radioisotopes
BT2 radioisotopes
BT3 isotopes
BT1 beta-minus decay radioisotopes
BT2 beta decay radioisotopes
BT3 radioisotopes
BT4 isotopes
BT1 even-even nuclei
BT2 nuclei
BT1 heavy nuclei
BT2 nuclei
BT1 lead isotopes
BT1 years living radioisotopes
BT2 radioisotopes
BT3 isotopes

LEAD 210 TARGET [19; 19] *Jul 76*
BT1 targets

LEAD 211 [18; 18]
UF *actinium b*
BT1 beta-minus decay radioisotopes
BT2 beta decay radioisotopes
BT3 radioisotopes
BT4 isotopes
BT1 even-odd nuclei
BT2 nuclei
BT1 heavy nuclei
BT2 nuclei
BT1 lead isotopes
BT1 minutes living radioisotopes
BT2 radioisotopes
BT3 isotopes

LEAD 212 [258; 258]
UF *thorium b*
BT1 beta-minus decay radioisotopes
BT2 beta decay radioisotopes
BT3 radioisotopes
BT4 isotopes
BT1 even-even nuclei
BT2 nuclei
BT1 heavy nuclei
BT2 nuclei
BT1 hours living radioisotopes
BT2 radioisotopes
BT3 isotopes
BT1 lead isotopes

LEAD 213 [4; 4]
BT1 beta-minus decay radioisotopes
BT2 beta decay radioisotopes
BT3 radioisotopes
BT4 isotopes

BT1 even-odd nuclei
BT2 nuclei
BT1 heavy nuclei
BT2 nuclei
BT1 lead isotopes
BT1 minutes living radioisotopes
BT2 radioisotopes
BT3 isotopes

LEAD 214 [265; 265]
UF *radium b*
BT1 beta-minus decay radioisotopes
BT2 beta decay radioisotopes
BT3 radioisotopes
BT4 isotopes
BT1 even-even nuclei
BT2 nuclei
BT1 heavy nuclei
BT2 nuclei
BT1 lead isotopes
BT1 minutes living radioisotopes
BT2 radioisotopes
BT3 isotopes

LEAD 215 [0; 0]
BT1 even-odd nuclei
BT2 nuclei
BT1 heavy nuclei
BT2 nuclei
BT1 lead isotopes

LEAD 216 [1; 1]
BT1 even-even nuclei
BT2 nuclei
BT1 heavy nuclei
BT2 nuclei
BT1 lead isotopes

→ **LEADING ABSTRACT** [2; 2] *Aug 91*
BT1 abstracts

LEADING PARTICLES [149; 149]
Nov 81
(Charged interaction products with large longitudinal momentum.)
BT1 elementary particles
RT particle models
RT particle production

LEAK DETECTORS [813; 813]
RT leak testing
RT leaks
RT reactor components

LEAK TESTING [1,513; 1,513]
BT1 testing
RT leak detectors
RT leaks
RT sealed sources

leakage
USE leaks

leakage (neutron)
USE neutron leakage

LEAKAGE CURRENT [432; 432]
UF *current (leakage)*
BT1 electric currents
BT2 currents

LEAKS [4,044; 4,044]
UF *leakage*
RT air infiltration
RT containment
RT failures
RT fission product release
RT gloveboxes
RT leak detectors
RT leak testing
RT porosity
RT sealed sources

lear (cern)
(Low Energy Antiproton Ring)
USE   cern lear

LEARN TANDEM ACCELERATOR
[3; 3]
BT1   tandem electrostatic accelerat
BT2   electrostatic accelerators
BT3   accelerators
BT1   van de graaff accelerators
BT2   electrostatic accelerators
BT3   accelerators
RT   ion beams

LEARNING [242; 242]
RT   attitudes
RT   behavior
RT   conditioned reflexes
RT   education

LEASING [5; 5] *Jul 86*
RT   administrative procedures
RT   agreements

LEAST SQUARE FIT [2,516; 2,516]
BT1   maximum-likelihood fit
BT2   numerical solution

LEATHER [32; 32]
RT   skin

LEAVES [1,452; 1,514]
UF   *foliage*
NT1   tea leaves
RT   chlorophyll
RT   foliar uptake
RT   forest litter
RT   photosynthesis
RT   plants
RT   transpiration

LEBANON [5; 5]
BT1   asia
BT1   developing countries
BT1   middle east

lebedev synchrotron
USE   fian synchrotron

LECITHINS [150; 150]
BT1   phospholipids
BT2   esters
BT3   organic compounds
BT2   lipids
BT3   organic compounds
BT2   organic phosphorus compounds
BT3   organic compounds
RT   choline
RT   glycerol

LECTINS [110; 110] *Dec 82*
RT   antibodies
RT   antigen-antibody reactions
RT   antigens

§   **LECTURES** [2,935; 2,935]
(Should be used to index all pieces of literature which are a lecture or a collection of lectures.)
BT1   document types

led
USE   light emitting diodes

LEE MODEL [125; 125]
BT1   particle models
BT2   mathematical models

LEE-YANG THEORY [35; 35]
UF   *salam hypothesis*
UF   *yang-lee distribution*
RT   beta decay
RT   p invariance

leed
USE   electron diffraction

LEGAL ASPECTS [7,578; 7,578]
UF+   *insurance law*
RT   administrative procedures
RT   antitrust review
RT   atomic energy control
RT   enforcement
RT   financial incentives
RT   inspection
RT   insurance
RT   liabilities
RT   licenses
RT   licensing
RT   ownership
RT   patents
RT   political aspects
RT   property rights
RT   radiation protection
RT   regulatory guides
RT   safeguards
RT   safety standards
RT   workmens compensation

LEGENDRE POLYNOMIALS
[1,169; 1,169]
BT1   polynomials
BT2   functions
RT   spherical harmonics method

LEGISLATION [1,330; 1,330]
RT   hearings
RT   implementation
RT   laws
RT   legislative text
RT   local government
RT   national government
RT   regulations
RT   state government

LEGISLATIVE TEXT [507; 507] *Sep 87*
(Use only in conjunction with literary indicator Q for indexing the text of a piece of legislation.)
RT   laws
RT   legislation
RT   regulations

LEGS [1,288; 1,695]
BT1   limbs
BT2   body areas
BT3   body
NT1   feet
RT   femur
RT   sciatic nerve
RT   tibia

LEGUMINOSAE [356; 1,640]
BT1   plants
NT1   alfalfa
NT1   clover
NT1   glycine hispida
NT1   mungbeans
NT1   phaseolus
NT1   pisum
NT1   vicia
RT   mimosine
RT   peanuts

LEHMANN-KAELLEN REPRESENTATION [42; 42]
RT   quantum field theory

lehmann-symanzik-zimmermann me
USE   lsz theory

LEIBSTADT REACTOR [132; 132]
BT1   bwr type reactors
BT2   enriched uranium reactors
BT3   reactors
BT2   power reactors
BT3   reactors
BT2   thermal reactors
BT3   reactors
BT2   water cooled reactors
BT3   reactors
BT2   water moderated reactors
BT3   reactors

leipzig zfi
USE   zfi leipzig

LEMONIZ-1 REACTOR [9; 9] *Apr 77*
(Lemoniz, Vizcaya, Spain)
BT1   pwr type reactors
BT2   enriched uranium reactors
BT3   reactors
BT2   power reactors
BT3   reactors
BT2   thermal reactors
BT3   reactors
BT2   water cooled reactors
BT3   reactors
BT2   water moderated reactors
BT3   reactors

LEMONIZ-2 REACTOR [6; 6] *Apr 77*
(Lemoniz, Vizcaya, Spain)
BT1   pwr type reactors
BT2   enriched uranium reactors
BT3   reactors
BT2   power reactors
BT3   reactors
BT2   thermal reactors
BT3   reactors
BT2   water cooled reactors
BT3   reactors
BT2   water moderated reactors
BT3   reactors

LEMONS [9; 9]
BT1   fruits
BT2   food
RT   citrus

lena triga-mk-2 pulsed reactor
USE   triga-2-pavia reactor

§§ **LENGTH** [939; 939]
UF+   *elementary length*
BT1   dimensions

lenin (nuclear ship)
USE   ns lenin

LENIN REACTOR [8; 8]
UF   *icebreaker lenin reactor*
UF   *nucl. ship lenin reactor*
BT1   pwr type reactors
BT2   enriched uranium reactors
BT3   reactors
BT2   power reactors
BT3   reactors
BT2   thermal reactors
BT3   reactors
BT2   water cooled reactors
BT3   reactors
BT2   water moderated reactors
BT3   reactors
BT1   ship propulsion reactors
BT2   propulsion reactors
BT3   power reactors
BT4   reactors
RT   ns lenin

leningrad inst nuclear physics
(Prior to December 1990, this was a valid descriptor.)
USE   leningrad institute of nuclear

**LENINGRAD INSTITUTE OF NU-
CLEAR** [9; 9] *Mar 77*
(Leningrad Institute of Nuclear Physics
(LIYaF).)
 UF *leningrad inst nuclear physics*
 BT1 ussr organizations
 BT2 national organizations

leningrad wwr-m reactor
 USE wwr-m-leningrad reactor

LENINGRAD-1 REACTOR [153; 153]
(Sosnovyy bor, Leningrad, USSR)
 UF *rbmk-1000 reactor*
 BT1 enriched uranium reactors
 BT2 reactors
 BT1 lwgr type reactors
 BT2 graphite moderated reactors
 BT3 reactors
 BT2 water cooled reactors
 BT3 reactors
 BT1 power reactors
 BT2 reactors
 BT1 thermal reactors
 BT2 reactors

LENINGRAD-2 REACTOR [25; 25]
(Sosnovyy bor, Leningrad, USSR)
 BT1 enriched uranium reactors
 BT2 reactors
 BT1 lwgr type reactors
 BT2 graphite moderated reactors
 BT3 reactors
 BT2 water cooled reactors
 BT3 reactors
 BT1 power reactors
 BT2 reactors
 BT1 thermal reactors
 BT2 reactors

LENINGRAD-3 REACTOR [11; 11]
Aug 84
 BT1 enriched uranium reactors
 BT2 reactors
 BT1 lwgr type reactors
 BT2 graphite moderated reactors
 BT3 reactors
 BT2 water cooled reactors
 BT3 reactors
 BT1 power reactors
 BT2 reactors
 BT1 thermal reactors
 BT2 reactors

LENINGRAD-4 REACTOR [10; 10]
Aug 84
 BT1 enriched uranium reactors
 BT2 reactors
 BT1 lwgr type reactors
 BT2 graphite moderated reactors
 BT3 reactors
 BT2 water cooled reactors
 BT3 reactors
 BT1 power reactors
 BT2 reactors
 BT1 thermal reactors
 BT2 reactors

LENNARD-JONES POTENTIAL
[513; 513]
 BT1 potentials
 RT interatomic forces

lens (crystalline)
 USE crystalline lens

LENSES [468; 2,047]
 NT1 electromagnetic lenses
 NT1 electrostatic lenses
 NT1 fresnel lens
 NT1 gravitational lenses
 RT optical systems

leonid brezhnev (nuclear ship)
 USE ns leonid brezhnev

LEONID BREZHNEV REACTOR [2; 2]
Nov 76
(Prior to November 1982 known as
ARKTIKA REACTOR.)
 UF *arktika reactor*
 UF *icebreaker arktika reactor*
 UF *icebreaker leonid brezhnev rea*
 UF *nucl. ship arktika reactor*
 UF *nucl. ship leonid brezhnev rea*
 BT1 pwr type reactors
 BT2 enriched uranium reactors
 BT3 reactors
 BT2 power reactors
 BT3 reactors
 BT2 thermal reactors
 BT3 reactors
 BT2 water cooled reactors
 BT3 reactors
 BT2 water moderated reactors
 BT3 reactors
 BT1 ship propulsion reactors
 BT2 propulsion reactors
 BT3 power reactors
 BT4 reactors
 RT ns leonid brezhnev

LEP STORAGE RINGS [1,086; 1,086]
Sep 77
(European Large Electron-Positron storage rings.)
 UF *cern lep*
 BT1 storage rings

LEPIDOPTERA [25; 102] *Mar 85*
 BT1 insects
 BT2 arthropods
 BT3 invertebrates
 BT4 animals
 NT1 moths
 NT2 bollworm
 NT2 codling moth
 NT2 lymantria dispar
 NT2 rice stem borers
 NT2 silkworm

LEPROSY [22; 22]
 BT1 bacterial diseases
 BT2 infectious diseases
 BT3 diseases
 RT mycobacterium

LEPTON BEAMS [61; 28,436]
 BT1 particle beams
 BT2 beams
 NT1 electron beams
 NT1 muon beams
 NT1 neutrino beams
 NT1 positron beams

LEPTON NUMBER [750; 912]
 NT1 muon number
 RT gauge invariance
 RT leptons

LEPTON REACTIONS [379; 8,104]
 UF+ *lepton-deuteron interactions*
 BT1 nuclear reactions
 NT1 electron reactions
 NT2 electrofission
 NT1 muon reactions
 NT1 neutrino reactions
 NT1 positron reactions
 RT emc effect

LEPTON-BARYON INTERACTIONS
[10; 8,637]
 BT1 lepton-hadron interactions
 BT2 particle interactions
 BT3 interactions
 NT1 lepton-hyperon interactions
 NT1 lepton-nucleon interactions
 NT2 deep inelastic scattering
 NT2 electron-nucleon interactions
 NT3 electron-neutron interactions

 NT3 electron-proton interactions
 NT2 lepton-neutron interactions
 NT3 antilepton-neutron interaction
 NT4 antineutrino-neutron interacti
 NT2 lepton-proton interactions
 NT3 antilepton-proton interactions
 NT4 antineutrino-proton
    interactio
 NT2 muon-nucleon interactions
 NT3 muon-neutron interactions
 NT3 muon-proton interactions
 NT2 neutrino-nucleon interactions
 NT3 antineutrino-nucleon interacti
 NT4 antineutrino-neutron interacti
 NT4 antineutrino-proton
    interactio
 NT3 neutrino-neutron interactions
 NT4 antineutrino-neutron interacti
 NT3 neutrino-proton interactions
 NT4 antineutrino-proton
    interactio

lepton-deuteron interactions
 USE deuterium target
 AND lepton reactions

LEPTON-HADRON INTERACTIONS
[327; 8,933]
 BT1 particle interactions
 BT2 interactions
 NT1 lepton-baryon interactions
 NT2 lepton-hyperon interactions
 NT2 lepton-nucleon interactions
 NT3 deep inelastic scattering
 NT3 electron-nucleon interactions
 NT4 electron-neutron interactions
 NT4 electron-proton interactions
 NT3 lepton-neutron interactions
 NT4 antilepton-neutron inter-
    action
 NT5 antineutrino-neutron
    interacti
 NT3 lepton-proton interactions
 NT4 antilepton-proton inter-
    actions
 NT5 antineutrino-proton
    interactio
 NT3 muon-nucleon interactions
 NT4 muon-neutron interactions
 NT4 muon-proton interactions
 NT3 neutrino-nucleon interactions
 NT4 antineutrino-nucleon
    interacti
 NT5 antineutrino-neutron
    interacti
 NT5 antineutrino-proton
    interactio
 NT4 neutrino-neutron interactions
 NT5 antineutrino-neutron
    interacti
 NT4 neutrino-proton interactions
 NT5 antineutrino-proton
    interactio
 NT1 lepton-meson interactions
 NT2 electron-meson interactions
 NT3 electron-pion interactions
 NT2 muon-meson interactions
 NT2 neutrino-meson interactions
 RT electromagnetic interactions
 RT weak interactions

LEPTON-HYPERON INTERACTIONS
[3; 3]
 BT1 lepton-baryon interactions
 BT2 lepton-hadron interactions
 BT3 particle interactions
 BT4 interactions

LEPTON-LEPTON INTERACTIONS
[97; 11,069]
 BT1 particle interactions
 BT2 interactions
 NT1 electron-electron interactions
 NT1 electron-muon interactions
 NT1 electron-positron interactions
 NT1 muon-muon interactions
 NT1 neutrino-electron interactions
 NT2 antineutrino-electron interact

NT1 neutrino-muon interactions
NT1 neutrino-neutrino interactions
NT1 positron-positron interactions
RT electromagnetic interactions
RT weak interactions

LEPTON-MESON INTERACTIONS
[16; 84]
BT1 lepton-hadron interactions
BT2 particle interactions
BT3 interactions
NT1 electron-meson interactions
NT2 electron-pion interactions
NT1 muon-meson interactions
NT1 neutrino-meson interactions

LEPTON-NEUTRON INTERACTIONS
[0; 71] Jan 77
BT1 lepton-nucleon interactions
BT2 lepton-baryon interactions
BT3 lepton-hadron interactions
BT4 particle interactions
BT5 interactions
NT1 antilepton-neutron interaction
NT2 antineutrino-neutron interacti

LEPTON-NUCLEON INTERACTIONS
[254; 8,626]
BT1 lepton-baryon interactions
BT2 lepton-hadron interactions
BT3 particle interactions
BT4 interactions
NT1 deep inelastic scattering
NT1 electron-nucleon interactions
NT2 electron-neutron interactions
NT2 electron-proton interactions
NT1 lepton-neutron interactions
NT2 antilepton-neutron interaction
NT3 antineutrino-neutron interacti
NT1 lepton-proton interactions
NT2 antilepton-proton interactions
NT3 antineutrino-proton interactio
NT1 muon-nucleon interactions
NT2 muon-neutron interactions
NT2 muon-proton interactions
NT1 neutrino-nucleon interactions
NT2 antineutrino-nucleon interacti
NT3 antineutrino-neutron interacti
NT3 antineutrino-proton interactio
NT2 neutrino-neutron interactions
NT3 antineutrino-neutron interacti
NT2 neutrino-proton interactions
NT3 antineutrino-proton interactio

LEPTON-PROTON INTERACTIONS
[74; 470]
BT1 lepton-nucleon interactions
BT2 lepton-baryon interactions
BT3 lepton-hadron interactions
BT4 particle interactions
BT5 interactions
NT1 antilepton-proton interactions
NT2 antineutrino-proton interactio

LEPTONIC DECAY [3,122; 6,140]
BT1 weak interactions
BT2 basic interactions
BT2 interactions
BT1 weak particle decay
BT2 particle decay
BT3 decay

LEPTONS [4,153; 61,926]
BT1 elementary particles
BT1 fermions
NT1 antileptons
NT2 antineutrinos
NT3 electron antineutrinos
NT3 muon antineutrinos
NT2 muons plus
NT2 positrons
NT3 cosmic positrons
NT1 electrons
NT2 cosmic electrons
NT2 exoelectrons
NT2 prompt electrons
NT2 runaway electrons
NT2 solar electrons
NT2 solvated electrons
NT2 trapped electrons
NT1 heavy leptons
NT2 tau neutrinos
NT2 tau particles
NT1 muons
NT2 cosmic muons
NT2 muons minus
NT2 muons plus
NT1 neutrinos
NT2 antineutrinos
NT3 electron antineutrinos
NT3 muon antineutrinos
NT2 cosmic neutrinos
NT2 electron neutrinos
NT3 electron antineutrinos
NT2 muon neutrinos
NT3 muon antineutrinos
NT2 solar neutrinos
NT2 tau neutrinos
RT feinberg-pais theory
RT lepton number
RT preons

LERMONTOVITE [1; 1]
BT1 phosphate minerals
BT2 minerals
BT1 uranium minerals
BT2 radioactive minerals
BT3 minerals
BT3 radioactive materials
BT4 materials
RT calcium phosphates
RT uranium phosphates

LESOTHO [5; 5]
BT1 africa
BT1 developing countries

LET [2,728; 2,728]
UF *linear energy transfer*
BT1 energy transfer
RT biological repair
RT bragg curve
RT dose equivalents
RT energy deposition
RT energy losses
RT ionization
RT microdosimetry
RT oxygen enhancement ratio
RT quality factor
RT radiation quality
RT rbe

LETHAL DOSES [31; 307] Mar 86
UF *doses (lethal)*
NT1 lethal radiation dose
RT hazardous materials
RT toxicity

LETHAL GENES [22; 22]
BT1 genes
RT lethal mutations

LETHAL IRRADIATION [1,552; 1,552]
BT1 irradiation
RT death
RT dose-response relationships
RT lethal radiation dose
RT mortality
RT radiation doses
RT sublethal irradiation
RT supralethal irradiation
RT survival curves
RT survival time

LETHAL MUTATIONS [442; 442]
UF *lethals*
BT1 mutations
RT lethal genes

LETHAL RADIATION DOSE
[1,075; 1,075]
(Referring to a percentage kill, frequently with a time indication.)
UF *ld 50*
BT1 lethal doses
BT1 radiation doses
RT lethal irradiation
RT sublethal irradiation
RT supralethal irradiation

lethals
USE lethal mutations

LETTUCE [76; 76]
BT1 vegetables
BT2 food

LEUCINE [1,035; 1,035]
UF *aminoisocaproic acid-alpha*
BT1 amino acids
BT2 carboxylic acids
BT3 organic acids
BT4 organic compounds

leucocytes
USE leukocytes

LEUKEMIA [2,582; 2,826]
BT1 immune system diseases
BT2 diseases
BT1 neoplasms
BT2 diseases
NT1 myeloid leukemia
RT bone marrow
RT leukemia viruses
RT leukemogenesis
RT leukocytes
RT lymphatic system
RT oncogenic viruses
RT splenomegaly
RT vinblastine

LEUKEMIA VIRUSES [136; 136] Sep 77
BT1 oncogenic viruses
BT2 viruses
BT3 microorganisms
BT3 parasites
RT experimental neoplasms
RT leukemia

LEUKEMOGENESIS [391; 391]
BT1 carcinogenesis
BT2 pathogenesis
RT leukemia

LEUKOCYTES [2,244; 8,082]
UF *granulocytes*
UF *leucocytes*
BT1 blood cells
BT2 blood
BT3 body fluids
BT4 biological materials
BT5 materials
NT1 basophils
NT1 eosinophils
NT1 lymphocytes
NT1 monocytes
NT1 neutrophils
RT aids
RT leukemia
RT leukopenia
RT leukopoiesis
RT phagocytes

LEUKOPENIA [252; 360]
BT1 hemic diseases
BT2 diseases
BT1 immune system diseases
BT2 diseases
BT1 pathological changes
BT2 diseases
BT1 symptoms
NT1 lymphopenia
RT leukocytes

LEUKOPOIESIS [82; 82]
- UF   *lymphopoiesis*
- BT1 blood formation
- RT   leukocytes

level density
- USE   energy-level density

LEVEL INDICATORS [679; 679]
- BT1 measuring instruments
- RT   radiometric gages

LEVEL MIXING RESONANCE [25; 25]
Aug 86
(A resonant method which measures nuclear electric quadrupole and magnetic dipole interactions.)
- BT1 resonance
- RT   nuclear magnetic resonance
- RT   nuclear quadrupole resonance

level schemes
- USE   energy levels

LEVEL WIDTHS [4,650; 4,650]
- RT   energy levels
- RT   energy-level density
- RT   lifetime
- RT   line widths
- RT   porter-thomas distribution

LEVELS [1,924; 4,039]
(Limited to vertical distance; see also ENERGY LEVELS.)
- UF   *altitude*
- NT1 ground level
- NT1 sea level
- NT1 underground
- NT1 underwater
- RT   height

levinger method
- USE   levinger-bethe theory

LEVINGER-BETHE THEORY [20; 20]
- UF   *levinger method*
- RT   nucleons
- RT   photoproduction

LEVINSON THEOREM [81; 81]
- RT   quantum mechanics
- RT   scattering

LEVINSON-BANERJEE THEORY [0; 0]
- RT   inelastic scattering

LEVITATION [258; 258]
- RT   magnetic fields

LEVITRON DEVICES [80; 80]
- BT1 internal ring devices
- BT2 closed plasma devices
- BT3 thermonuclear devices

LEVULINIC ACID [9; 9]
- UF   *acetylpropionic acid-beta*
- UF   *ketovaleric acid-gamma*
- BT1 keto acids
- BT2 carboxylic acids
- BT3 organic acids
- BT4 organic compounds

levulose
- USE   fructose

levy potential
- USE   levy-klein potential

LEVY-KLEIN POTENTIAL [1; 1]
- UF   *levy potential*
- BT1 potentials
- RT   nucleon-nucleon potential

lewis effect
- USE   lewis peak

LEWIS PEAK [1; 1]
- UF   *lewis effect*
- RT   nuclear reactions

LFR REACTOR [23; 23]
(Stichting Energieonderzoek Centrum Nederland, Petten, Netherlands)
- UF   *lage flux reaktor petten*
- UF   *low flux reactor petten*
- UF   *low-flux reactor petten*
- UF   *petten low flux reactor*
- BT1 argonaut type reactors
- BT2   enriched uranium reactors
- BT3   reactors
- BT2   research and test reactors
- BT3   reactors
- BT2   water cooled reactors
- BT3   reactors
- BT2   water moderated reactors
- BT3   reactors
- BT1 research reactors
- BT2   research and test reactors
- BT3   reactors
- BT1 thermal reactors
- BT2   reactors
- BT1 training reactors
- BT2   research and test reactors
- BT3   reactors

LH [474; 474]
- UF   *interstitial cell stim hormone*
- UF   *luteinizing hormone*
- BT1 glycoproteins
- BT2   proteins
- BT3   organic compounds
- BT2   saccharides
- BT3   carbohydrates
- BT4   organic compounds
- BT1 gonadotropins
- BT2   pituitary hormones
- BT3   peptide hormones
- BT4   hormones
- RT   androgens
- RT   estrous cycle
- RT   lh-rh

LH-RH [72; 72]
(LH-Releasing Hormone)
- BT1 liberins
- BT2   pituitary hormones
- BT3   peptide hormones
- BT4   hormones
- RT   lh

lhr heating
(Lower hybrid resonance heating.)
- USE   lower hybrid heating

LI-DRIFTED DETECTORS [67; 3,345]
- BT1 semiconductor detectors
- BT2   radiation detectors
- BT3   measuring instruments
- NT1 li-drifted ge detectors
- NT1 li-drifted junction detectors
- NT1 li-drifted si detectors

LI-DRIFTED GE DETECTORS [2,741; 2,741]
- UF   *ge(li) detectors*
- BT1 ge semiconductor detectors
- BT2   semiconductor detectors
- BT3   radiation detectors
- BT4   measuring instruments
- BT1 li-drifted detectors
- BT2   semiconductor detectors
- BT3   radiation detectors
- BT4   measuring instruments

LI-DRIFTED JUNCTION DETECTORS [16; 16]
- BT1 junction detectors
- BT2   semiconductor detectors
- BT3   radiation detectors
- BT4   measuring instruments
- BT1 li-drifted detectors
- BT2   semiconductor detectors
- BT3   radiation detectors
- BT4   measuring instruments

LI-DRIFTED SI DETECTORS [1,070; 1,070]
- UF   *si(li) detectors*
- BT1 li-drifted detectors
- BT2   semiconductor detectors
- BT3   radiation detectors
- BT4   measuring instruments
- BT1 si semiconductor detectors
- BT2   semiconductor detectors
- BT3   radiation detectors
- BT4   measuring instruments

liabil conv marit car nucl mat
- USE   bcoclmcnm

liabil conv nucl damage, vienn
- USE   vcoclnd

liabil conv on third party, br
- USE   bcstpc

liabil conv on third party, pa
- USE   pcotpl

liabil conv opera nucl ships
- USE   bcolons

LIABILITIES [510; 1,040]
- UF   *absolute liability*
- UF   *contractual liability*
- UF   *cumulative liability*
- UF   *exclusive liability*
- UF   *fault liability*
- UF   *joint liability*
- UF   *state liability*
- NT1 civil liability
- NT1 nuclear liability
- RT   accidents
- RT   bcolons
- RT   exceptional natural disaster
- RT   financial security
- RT   hazards
- RT   indemnification agreements
- RT   insurance
- RT   legal aspects
- RT   liability exclusions
- RT   liability limitations
- RT   pcotpl
- RT   time limitations
- RT   victims compensation

LIABILITY EXCLUSIONS [16; 16]
Dec 76
(When under an international convention or national law the nuclear operator is not liable for the damage caused.)
- UF   *exclusions (liability)*
- RT   liabilities
- RT   nuclear liability

LIABILITY LIMITATIONS [43; 43]
Dec 76
(When under an international convention or national law the liability of the nuclear operator for the damage caused is limited.)
- UF   *limitations (liability)*
- RT   liabilities
- RT   nuclear liability
- RT   time limitations

liapunov method
  USE   lyapunov method

LIBERIA [5; 5]
  BT1   africa
  BT1   developing countries

LIBERINS [20; 60] *Feb 83*
  UF   *releasing factors*
  UF   *releasing hormones*
  BT1   pituitary hormones
    BT2   peptide hormones
      BT3   hormones
  NT1   lh-rh

LIBYA [39; 39]
  BT1   africa
  BT1   developing countries

LICENSES [288; 1,344]
  UF   *handling licenses*
  UF   *permits*
  UF   *research licenses*
  NT1   commercial licenses
  NT1   construction permits
  NT1   operating licenses
  RT   legal aspects
  RT   licensing procedures
  RT   licensing regulations
  RT   property rights
  RT   site approvals

LICENSING [3,171; 9,591]
  NT1   reactor licensing
  RT   audits
  RT   certification
  RT   inspection
  RT   legal aspects
  RT   patents
  RT   quality assurance
  RT   radiation protection
  RT   recommendations
  RT   regulations
  RT   safety standards
  RT   site selection

LICENSING PROCEDURES
  [1,789; 1,789] *Dec 76*
  BT1   administrative procedures
  RT   hearings
  RT   licenses
  RT   operating licenses

LICENSING REGULATIONS [788; 788]
  Dec 76
  BT1   regulations
    BT2   laws
  RT   licenses
  RT   operating licenses
  RT   retrofitting
  RT   risk assessment
  RT   safety analysis
  RT   safety reports

LICHENS [218; 218]
  BT1   algae
    BT2   plants
  BT1   fungi
    BT2   plants

LICHTENBERG FIGURES [13; 13]
  RT   breakdown
  RT   corona discharges
  RT   dielectric materials

LIDO REACTOR [2; 2]
  UF   *ukaea-lido reactor*
  BT1   enriched uranium reactors
    BT2   reactors
  BT1   pool type reactors
    BT2   water cooled reactors
      BT3   reactors
    BT2   water moderated reactors
      BT3   reactors
  BT1   research reactors

  BT2   research and test reactors
    BT3   reactors
  BT1   thermal reactors
    BT2   reactors

LIE GROUPS [2,091; 28,444]
  BT1   symmetry groups
  NT1   conformal groups
  NT1   de sitter group
  NT1   graded lie groups
  NT1   o groups
  NT1   poincare groups
    NT2   lorentz groups
  NT1   sl groups
  NT1   so groups
    NT2   so-10 groups
    NT2   so-12 groups
    NT2   so-2 groups
    NT2   so-3 groups
    NT2   so-4 groups
    NT2   so-6 groups
    NT2   so-8 groups
  NT1   sp groups
  NT1   su groups
    NT2   su-2 groups
    NT2   su-3 groups
    NT2   su-4 groups
    NT2   su-5 groups
    NT2   su-6 groups
    NT2   su-7 groups
    NT2   su-8 groups
    NT2   su-9 groups
  NT1   sw groups
    NT2   sw-3 groups
  NT1   u groups
    NT2   u-1 groups
    NT2   u-12 groups
    NT2   u-2 groups
    NT2   u-3 groups
    NT2   u-4 groups
    NT2   u-5 groups
    NT2   u-6 groups
  RT   lattice field theory

lie superalgebra
  USE   graded lie groups

LIEBIGITE [3; 3]
  BT1   carbonate minerals
    BT2   minerals
  BT1   uranium minerals
    BT2   radioactive minerals
      BT3   minerals
    BT3   radioactive materials
      BT4   materials
  RT   calcium carbonates
  RT   uranium carbonates

LIFE CYCLE [258; 258]
  RT   adolescents
  RT   adults
  RT   age groups
  RT   aged adults
  RT   children
  RT   growth
  RT   infants
  RT   life span
  RT   ova
  RT   pregnancy
  RT   pupae
  RT   reproduction
  RT   ripening
  RT   viability

life shortening
  USE   life span

LIFE SPAN [1,628; 1,628]
  UF   *life shortening*
  RT   age dependence
  RT   death
  RT   dose commitments
  RT   life cycle
  RT   mortality

LIFETIME [14,810; 15,337]
  UF   *mean life*
  UF   *service life*
  NT1   carrier lifetime
  RT   charge plunger method
  RT   decay
  RT   dsa method
  RT   half-life
  RT   level widths
  RT   particle properties
  RT   particle widths

LIGAMENTS [251; 251]
  BT1   connective tissue
    BT2   tissues
      BT3   body

ligand exchange
  USE   ion exchange
  AND   ligands

LIGANDS [5,384; 5,384]
  UF+   *ligand exchange*
  RT   complexes
  RT   coordination number
  RT   stereochemistry

LIGASES [390; 434]
  UF   *synthetases*
  BT1   enzymes
    BT2   organic compounds
  NT1   carboxylase

light
  USE   visible radiation

light (zodiacal)
  USE   zodiacal light

LIGHT BULB REACTORS [36; 36]
  BT1   gas fueled reactors
    BT2   fluid fueled reactors
      BT3   reactors
    BT2   homogeneous reactors
      BT3   reactors

LIGHT CONE [1,736; 1,736]
  BT1   space-time
  RT   cherenkov radiation
  RT   minkowski space
  RT   relativity theory

LIGHT EMITTING DIODES [282; 282]
  UF   *led*
  UF   *light-emitting diodes*
  BT1   semiconductor diodes
    BT2   semiconductor devices

LIGHT IONS [515; 515] *Sep 77*
  (Whenever appropriate use one of the specific terms listed under ION BEAMS.
  BT1   ions
    BT2   charged particles
  RT   ion beams
  RT   ion detection
  RT   multicharged ions

* **LIGHT NUCLEI** [3,151; 99,052]
  (For nuclei with mass 1-40. For specific terms, consult the Appendix.)
  BT1   nuclei
  RT   nuclear structure

LIGHT PIPES [317; 317]
  RT   scintillation counters

LIGHT SOURCES [605; 605]
  BT1   radiation sources
  RT   lasers
  RT   nsls
  RT   photon beams
  RT   visible radiation

light-emitting diodes
  USE   light emitting diodes

LIGHTING SYSTEMS [30; 30] *Mar 86*
  RT   electrical equipment
  RT   illuminance
  RT   optical systems
  RT   remote viewing equipment
  RT   visible radiation

LIGHTNING [165; 183]
  BT1   electric discharges
  NT1   ball lightning
  RT   whistlers

LIGHTNING ARRESTERS [34; 34]
  BT1   electrical equipment
  BT2   equipment
  RT   circuit breakers

LIGNIN [180; 180]
  BT1   polysaccharides
  BT2   saccharides
  BT3   carbohydrates
  BT4   organic compounds
  RT   bark
  RT   glycosides
  RT   polyacetals
  RT   wood

LIGNITE [267; 267]
  BT1   coal
  BT2   carbonaceous materials
  BT3   materials
  BT2   fossil fuels
  BT3   energy sources
  BT3   fuels

LILIUM [15; 15]
  BT1   plants

LIMBS [527; 3,316]
  BT1   body areas
  BT2   body
  NT1   arms
  NT2   hands
  NT3   fingers
  NT1   legs
  NT2   feet
  RT   muscles
  RT   skeleton

LIMERICK-1 REACTOR [85; 85]
(Limerick, Pennsylvania, USA)
  UF   *philadelp. elect.-pow. reac.-1*
  BT1   bwr type reactors
  BT2   enriched uranium reactors
  BT3   reactors
  BT2   power reactors
  BT3   reactors
  BT2   thermal reactors
  BT3   reactors
  BT2   water cooled reactors
  BT3   reactors
  BT2   water moderated reactors
  BT3   reactors

LIMERICK-2 REACTOR [76; 76]
(Limerick, Pennsylvania, USA)
  UF   *philadelp. elect.-pow. reac.-2*
  BT1   bwr type reactors
  BT2   enriched uranium reactors
  BT3   reactors
  BT2   power reactors
  BT3   reactors
  BT2   thermal reactors
  BT3   reactors
  BT2   water cooled reactors
  BT3   reactors
  BT2   water moderated reactors
  BT3   reactors

LIMESTONE [563; 563]
  UF   *calcretes*
  UF   *dolomite rock*
  BT1   carbonate rocks
  BT2   sedimentary rocks
  BT3   rocks
  RT   calcite
  RT   calcium carbonates
  RT   dolomite
  RT   magnesium carbonates

limitations (liability)
  USE   liability limitations

LIMITER CIRCUITS [20; 20]
  BT1   electronic circuits

LIMITERS [2,436; 2,587]
  UF   *diaphragms (thermonucl. device*
  UF   *insulating limiters*
  NT1   pumped limiters
  RT   pinch devices
  RT   pinch effect
  RT   plasma confinement
  RT   plasma impurities

LIMITING FRAGMENTATION [1,532; 1,532]
  UF   *fragmentation (limiting)*
  UF+ *cumulative effect*
  BT1   hypothesis
  RT   asymptotic solutions
  RT   inclusive interactions
  RT   laboratory system
  RT   lorentz transformations
  RT   multiple production
  RT   particle models

LIMITING VALUES [5,984; 5,984]
(Upper and/or lower bounds on a physical property determined theoretically or experimentally.)
  RT   nuclear properties
  RT   particle properties
  RT   thermodynamic properties

LIMNOLOGY [81; 81]
  RT   aquatic ecosystems
  RT   eutrophication
  RT   fresh water
  RT   hydrosphere
  RT   oceanography
  RT   sediment-water interfaces

LIMONITE [23; 23]
  BT1   iron ores
  BT2   ores
  BT1   oxide minerals
  BT2   minerals
  RT   hematite
  RT   iron oxides

linacs
  USE   linear accelerators

LINDANE [54; 54] *May 76*
  UF   *gamma benzene hexachloride*
  UF   *gamma hexachlorohexane*
  BT1   insecticides
  BT2   pesticides
  BT1   organic chlorine compounds
  BT2   organic halogen compounds
  BT3   organic compounds

LINE BROADENING [2,753; 3,917]
  UF   *broadening (line)*
  UF   *spectral broadening*
  NT1   doppler broadening
  RT   line narrowing
  RT   line widths
  RT   optical depth curve
  RT   spectra
  RT   spectroscopic curve of growth
  RT   stark effect

LINE DEFECTS [41; 7,033]
  BT1   crystal defects
  BT2   crystal structure
  NT1   crowdions
  NT1   dislocations
  NT2   edge dislocations
  NT2   screw dislocations

LINE NARROWING [148; 148] *Jul 76*
  UF   *spectral narrowing*
  RT   line broadening
  RT   line widths
  RT   spectra

LINE WIDTHS [6,451; 6,451]
  RT   level widths
  RT   line broadening
  RT   line narrowing
  RT   spectra

LINEAR ABSORPTION MODELS [51; 51] *Feb 76*
  UF   *absorption models (linear)*
  UF   *models (linear absorption)*
  BT1   particle models
  BT2   mathematical models
  RT   partial waves
  RT   regge poles
  RT   scattering amplitudes

LINEAR ACCELERATORS [8,312; 12,870]
  UF   *linacs*
  BT1   accelerators
  NT1   beat wave accelerators
  NT1   brookhaven 200-mev linac
  NT1   cebaf accelerator
  NT1   cern linac
  NT1   fmit linac
  NT1   frascati linac
  NT1   hilacs
  NT2   atlas superconducting linac
  NT2   superhilac
  NT1   ing linac
  NT1   jaeri linac
  NT1   kek linac
  NT1   kharkov linac
  NT1   lampf linac
  NT1   llnl advanced test accelerator
  NT1   mea linac
  NT1   minnesota univ linac
  NT1   mit bates linac
  NT1   nrl linac
  NT1   orela
  NT1   orsay linac
  NT1   quadrupole linacs
  NT1   rilac
  NT1   saclay linac
  NT1   stanford linear collider
  NT1   stanford 1200-mev linac
  NT1   stanford 20-gev linac
  NT1   swierk linac
  NT1   unilac
  NT1   wakefield accelerators
  NT1   zeran linac
  RT   drift tubes
  RT   kek photon factory
  RT   pigmi facilities

linear comb of atomic orbitals
  USE   lcao method

linear energy transfer
  USE   let

LINEAR HARD CORE PINCH DEVICES [6; 6]
  UF   *inverse pinch devices (linear)*
  UF   *tubular pinch devices (linear)*
  UF   *unpinch devices*
  BT1   linear pinch devices
  BT2   open plasma devices
  BT3   thermonuclear devices
  BT2   pinch devices
  BT3   thermonuclear devices
  RT   hard core pinch

LINEAR MOMENTUM [3,152; 11,404]
- UF *impulse (linear momentum)*
- UF *momentum (linear)*
- NT1 longitudinal momentum
- NT1 transverse momentum
- RT angular momentum
- RT dalitz plot
- RT energy-momentum tensor
- RT kinetic energy
- RT linear momentum operators
- RT linear momentum resolution
- RT mass
- RT motion
- RT prism plot
- RT velocity

LINEAR MOMENTUM OPERATORS [184; 184]
- BT1 quantum operators
- BT2 mathematical operators
- RT linear momentum

LINEAR MOMENTUM RESOLUTION [67; 67]
- BT1 resolution
- RT linear momentum

LINEAR MOMENTUM TRANSFER [1,236; 1,236]
- UF *transfer (linear momentum)*
- BT1 momentum transfer
- RT energy transfer
- RT straight-line path approximati

LINEAR PINCH DEVICES [78; 1,086]
- BT1 open plasma devices
- BT2 thermonuclear devices
- BT1 pinch devices
- BT2 thermonuclear devices
- NT1 linear hard core pinch devices
- NT1 linear screw pinch devices
- NT1 linear theta pinch devices
- NT2 bsg devices
- NT2 chalice devices
- NT2 isar devices
- NT2 pharos devices
- NT2 scylla devices
- NT1 linear z pinch devices
- NT1 megatron

LINEAR PROGRAMMING [193; 193]
(Optimization of operations or procedures in terms of maximized, or minimized, functions of many variables subject to constraints.)
- RT dynamic programming
- RT econometrics
- RT mathematical models
- RT nonlinear programming
- RT optimization

LINEAR RATEMETERS [26; 26]
- BT1 counting ratemeters
- BT2 electronic equipment
- BT3 equipment

LINEAR SCREW PINCH DEVICES [20; 20]
- UF *combined pinch devices (linear*
- BT1 linear pinch devices
- BT2 open plasma devices
- BT3 thermonuclear devices
- BT2 pinch devices
- BT3 thermonuclear devices
- RT screw pinch

LINEAR THETA PINCH DEVICES [294; 361]
- UF *azimuthal pinch devices (linea*
- UF *orthogonal pinch devices (line*
- BT1 linear pinch devices
- BT2 open plasma devices
- BT3 thermonuclear devices
- BT2 pinch devices
- BT3 thermonuclear devices
- NT1 bsg devices
- NT1 chalice devices
- NT1 isar devices
- NT1 pharos devices
- NT1 scylla devices
- RT theta pinch

LINEAR Z PINCH DEVICES [635; 635]
- UF *longitudinal pinch devices (ln*
- UF *z pinch devices (linear)*
- BT1 linear pinch devices
- BT2 open plasma devices
- BT3 thermonuclear devices
- BT2 pinch devices
- BT3 thermonuclear devices
- RT longitudinal pinch

LINERS [1,226; 1,226] *Nov 77*
- UF *linings*
- RT containers
- RT lining processes
- RT linus reactors
- RT seals
- RT shells
- RT surface coating

LINGEN REACTOR [127; 127]
- UF *kernkraftwerk lingen*
- UF *kwl reactor*
- BT1 bwr type reactors
- BT2 enriched uranium reactors
- BT3 reactors
- BT2 power reactors
- BT3 reactors
- BT2 thermal reactors
- BT3 reactors
- BT2 water cooled reactors
- BT3 reactors
- BT2 water moderated reactors
- BT3 reactors

LINING PROCESSES [64; 64]
- RT liners
- RT surface coating

linings
- USE liners

LINOLEIC ACID [124; 124]
- BT1 monocarboxylic acids
- BT2 carboxylic acids
- BT3 organic acids
- BT4 organic compounds

LINOLENIC ACID [43; 43]
- BT1 monocarboxylic acids
- BT2 carboxylic acids
- BT3 organic acids
- BT4 organic compounds

LINSEED OIL [6; 6]
- UF *flaxseed oil*
- BT1 oils
- BT2 other organic compounds
- BT3 organic compounds
- BT1 triglycerides
- BT2 esters
- BT3 organic compounds
- BT2 lipids
- BT3 organic compounds
- RT flax plants
- RT plasticizers

linseed plants
- USE flax plants

LINUS REACTORS [14; 14] *Aug 81*
- BT1 thermonuclear reactors
- RT implosions
- RT liners
- RT magnetic compression

liouville equation
- USE boltzmann-vlasov equation

LIOUVILLE THEOREM [267; 267]
- RT phase space
- RT statistical mechanics

LIPASES [306; 306]
- BT1 carboxylesterases
- BT2 esterases
- BT3 hydrolases
- BT4 enzymes
- BT5 organic compounds

LIPIDS [1,406; 3,959]
- BT1 organic compounds
- NT1 gangliosides
- NT1 glycolipids
- NT2 cerebrosides
- NT1 lanolin
- NT1 lipopolysaccharides
- NT1 lipoproteins
- NT2 myelin
- NT1 phospholipids
- NT2 cardiolipin
- NT2 cephalins
- NT2 lecithins
- NT2 sphingomyelins
- NT1 triglycerides
- NT2 butter fat
- NT2 corn oil
- NT2 croton oil
- NT2 linseed oil
- NT2 olive oil
- NT2 peanut oil
- NT2 soybean oil
- NT2 triolein
- RT cholesterol
- RT choline
- RT chylomicrons
- RT esters
- RT fats
- RT liposomes
- RT lipotropic factors
- RT valinomycin

LIPIODOL [92; 92]
- BT1 contrast media
- BT1 oils
- BT2 other organic compounds
- BT3 organic compounds
- BT1 organic iodine compounds
- BT2 organic halogen compounds
- BT3 organic compounds

lipoic acid (alpha)
- USE thioctic acid

LIPOPOLYSACCHARIDES [154; 154]
- BT1 lipids
- BT2 organic compounds
- BT1 polysaccharides
- BT2 saccharides
- BT3 carbohydrates
- BT4 organic compounds

LIPOPROTEINS [551; 715]
- UF *proteolipids*
- SF *apolipoproteins*
- BT1 lipids
- BT2 organic compounds
- BT1 proteins
- BT2 organic compounds
- NT1 myelin

LIPOSOMES [364; 364] *Feb 80*
- RT cell constituents
- RT chemotherapy
- RT cytoplasm
- RT lipids

LIPOTROPIC FACTORS [24; 2,248]
- BT1 drugs
- NT1 betaine
- NT1 choline
- NT1 ethionine
- NT1 inositol
- NT1 methionine
- NT1 phytic acid

NT1 thioctic acid
RT lipids
RT vitamin b group

LIPPMANN-SCHWINGER EQUATION
[819; 819]
BT1 integral equations
BT2 equations
RT blankenbecler-sugar equations
RT faddeev equations
RT quantum mechanics
RT quasipotential equation
RT schwinger variational method

lips
USE oral cavity

LIQUEFACTION [331; 397]
UF *liquefying*
NT1 coal liquefaction
RT melting
RT vapor condensation

liquefied natural gas
USE natural gas

liquefying
USE liquefaction

LIQUID COLUMN CHROMATOGRAPHY [2,344; 2,344]
Apr 77
BT1 chromatography
BT2 separation processes

LIQUID CONTAMINATION MONITORS [60; 60]
BT1 radiation monitors
BT2 monitors
BT3 measuring instruments
RT contamination

LIQUID CRYSTALS [735; 735]
BT1 crystals
BT1 liquids
BT2 fluids

LIQUID DROP MODEL [1,077; 1,077]
UF *liquid-drop model*
BT1 nuclear models
BT2 mathematical models
RT neutron emission
RT weizsaecker formula

liquid effluents
USE liquid wastes

LIQUID FLOW [3,175; 3,175]
BT1 fluid flow
RT hydraulic conductivity
RT hydrodynamics
RT liquids
RT two-phase flow

LIQUID FUELS [54; 378]
BT1 fuels
NT1 diesel fuels
NT1 fuel solutions
NT1 gasoline
NT1 liquid metal fuels
NT1 molten salt fuels

liquid holding recovery
USE biological recovery

LIQUID HOMOGENEOUS REACTORS
[2; 151]
BT1 fluid fueled reactors
BT2 reactors
BT1 homogeneous reactors

BT2 reactors
NT1 aqueous homogeneous reactors
NT2 ai-l-77 reactor
NT2 ber-2 reactor
NT2 cesnef reactor
NT2 dr-1 reactor
NT2 frf reactor
NT2 jrr-1 reactor
NT2 kewb reactor
NT2 kstr reactor
NT2 ncscr-1 reactor
NT2 prnc-l-77 reactor
NT2 supo reactor
NT2 wrrr reactor
RT fuel solutions

LIQUID ION EXCHANGERS [109; 109]
BT1 ion exchange materials
BT2 materials

LIQUID IONIZATION CHAMBERS
[249; 249]
BT1 ionization chambers
BT2 radiation detectors
BT3 measuring instruments

liquid metal coolant
USE liquid metals

LIQUID METAL COOLED REACTORS
[1,090; 22,628]
UF *liquid metal-cooled reactors*
UF *liquid-metal-cooled reactors*
BT1 reactors
NT1 lithium cooled reactors
NT1 lmfbr type reactors
NT2 beloyarsk-3 reactor
NT2 beloyarsk-4 reactor
NT2 bn-1600 reactor
NT2 bn-350 reactor
NT2 bn-800 reactor
NT2 bor-60 reactor
NT2 cdfr reactor
NT2 clinch river breeder reactor
NT2 dfr reactor
NT2 ebr-1 reactor
NT2 ebr-2 reactor
NT2 enrico fermi-1 reactor
NT2 joyo reactor
NT2 kalpakkam lmfbr reactor
NT2 monju reactor
NT2 pfr reactor
NT2 phenix reactor
NT2 plbr reactor
NT2 rapsodie reactor
NT2 sbr-2 reactor
NT2 sbr-5 reactor
NT2 snr reactor
NT2 snr-2 reactor
NT2 super phenix reactor
NT1 mercury cooled reactors
NT2 clementine reactor
NT2 sbr-2 reactor
NT1 nak cooled reactors
NT2 ebr-1 reactor
NT2 ser reactor
NT2 snaptran reactors
NT2 s10fs-1 reactor
NT2 s10fs-3 reactor
NT2 s10fs-4 reactor
NT2 s2ds reactor
NT2 s8dr reactor
NT2 s8er reactor
NT1 potassium cooled reactors
NT2 ebr-1 reactor
NT2 ser reactor
NT2 snap 10 reactor
NT3 s10fs-1 reactor
NT3 s10fs-3 reactor
NT3 s10fs-4 reactor
NT2 snaptran reactors
NT1 sodium cooled reactors
NT2 beloyarsk-3 reactor
NT2 beloyarsk-4 reactor
NT2 bn-1600 reactor
NT2 bn-350 reactor
NT2 bn-800 reactor
NT2 bor-60 reactor

NT2 cdfr reactor
NT2 clinch river breeder reactor
NT2 ebr-1 reactor
NT2 ebr-2 reactor
NT2 enrico fermi-1 reactor
NT2 fftf reactor
NT2 hnpf reactor
NT2 knk reactor
NT2 knk-2 reactor
NT2 lampre-1 reactor
NT2 monju reactor
NT2 pfr reactor
NT2 phenix reactor
NT2 rapsodie reactor
NT2 sbr-5 reactor
NT2 sefor reactor
NT2 ser reactor
NT2 sgr type reactors
NT3 sre reactor
NT2 snap 10 reactor
NT3 s10fs-1 reactor
NT3 s10fs-3 reactor
NT3 s10fs-4 reactor
NT2 snaptran reactors
NT2 snr reactor
NT2 snr-2 reactor
NT2 super phenix reactor
NT2 zrr reactor
NT1 szr type reactors
NT2 knk reactor
NT2 knk-2 reactor

LIQUID METAL FUELS [42; 42]
BT1 liquid fuels
BT2 fuels
RT fluid fueled reactors

liquid metal-cooled reactors
USE liquid metal cooled reactors

LIQUID METALS [6,583; 6,583]
UF *liquid metal coolant*
BT1 liquids
BT2 fluids
BT1 metals
BT2 elements
RT coolants

LIQUID PENETRANT INSPECTION
[144; 144]
UF *fluorescent penetrant tests*
UF *penetrant inspection (liquid)*
BT1 nondestructive testing
BT2 materials testing
BT3 testing

LIQUID PROPORTIONAL COUNTERS
[32; 32]
BT1 proportional counters
BT2 radiation detectors
BT3 measuring instruments

LIQUID SCINTILLATION DETECTORS
[2,294; 2,294]
BT1 scintillation counters
BT2 radiation detectors
BT3 measuring instruments
RT liquid scintillators
RT scintillation quenching

LIQUID SCINTILLATORS [821; 821]
BT1 phosphors
RT liquid scintillation detectors
RT terphenyls

liquid sodium-water reactions
USE molten metal-water reactions

LIQUID WASTES [6,275; 6,953]
UF *effluents (liquid)*
UF *liquid effluents*
UF *sewage*
UF *waste solutions*
UF+ *sewage disposal*
UF+ *sewage treatment*

LIQUID WASTES
BT1 wastes
NT1 waste water
RT bioadsorbents
RT biological wastes
RT chemical effluents
RT ground disposal
RT ground water
RT leachates
RT plumes
RT radioactive effluents
RT surface waters
RT waste disposal
RT waste processing
RT water

liquid-drop model
USE liquid drop model

liquid-liquid extraction
USE solvent extraction

LIQUID-METAL MHD GENERATORS
[68; 68] *Dec 75*
BT1 closed-cycle mhd generators
BT2 closed-cycle systems
BT2 mhd generators
BT3 direct energy converters

liquid-metal-cooled reactors
USE liquid metal cooled reactors

liquid-phase sintering
USE sintering

LIQUIDS [5,995; 13,250]
BT1 fluids
NT1 liquid crystals
NT1 liquid metals
RT dispersions
RT droplets
RT hydrostatic bearings
RT liquid flow
RT phase diagrams
RT structure factors
RT vapors
RT void fraction

LITHIUM [4,852; 4,989]
BT1 alkali metals
BT2 metals
BT3 elements

LITHIUM ADDITIONS [196; 196]
(Alloys containing not more than 1% Li are listed here.)
RT lithium alloys
RT lithium compounds

LITHIUM ALLOYS [756; 803]
(Alloys containing more than 1% Li.)
BT1 alloys
NT1 lithium base alloys
RT lithium additions

→ ## LITHIUM ARSENIDES [0; 0] *Sep 91*
BT1 arsenides
BT2 arsenic compounds
BT2 pnictides
BT1 lithium compounds
BT2 alkali metal compounds

LITHIUM BASE ALLOYS [36; 36]
BT1 lithium alloys
BT2 alloys

LITHIUM BORIDES [17; 17]
BT1 borides
BT2 boron compounds
BT1 lithium compounds
BT2 alkali metal compounds

LITHIUM BROMIDES [92; 92]
BT1 bromides
BT2 bromine compounds
BT3 halogen compounds
BT2 halides
BT3 halogen compounds
BT1 lithium halides
BT2 halides
BT3 halogen compounds
BT2 lithium compounds
BT3 alkali metal compounds

LITHIUM CARBIDES [24; 24]
BT1 carbides
BT2 carbon compounds
BT1 lithium compounds
BT2 alkali metal compounds

LITHIUM CARBONATES [148; 148]
BT1 carbonates
BT2 carbon compounds
BT2 oxygen compounds
BT1 lithium compounds
BT2 alkali metal compounds

LITHIUM CHLORIDES [657; 657]
BT1 chlorides
BT2 chlorine compounds
BT3 halogen compounds
BT2 halides
BT3 halogen compounds
BT1 lithium halides
BT2 halides
BT3 halogen compounds
BT2 lithium compounds
BT3 alkali metal compounds

LITHIUM COMPLEXES [96; 96]
BT1 complexes

LITHIUM COMPOUNDS [2,393; 9,151]
BT1 alkali metal compounds
NT1 lithium arsenides
NT1 lithium borides
NT1 lithium carbides
NT1 lithium carbonates
NT1 lithium halides
NT2 lithium bromides
NT2 lithium chlorides
NT2 lithium fluorides
NT2 lithium iodides
NT1 lithium hydrides
NT2 lithium deuterides
NT2 lithium tritides
NT1 lithium hydroxides
NT1 lithium nitrates
NT1 lithium nitrides
NT1 lithium oxides
NT1 lithium perchlorates
NT1 lithium phosphates
NT1 lithium phosphides
NT1 lithium selenides
NT1 lithium silicates
NT1 lithium silicides
NT1 lithium sulfates
NT1 lithium sulfides
NT1 lithium tellurides
NT1 lithium tungstates
NT1 lithium uranates
RT lithium additions

LITHIUM COOLED REACTORS
[61; 61] *May 76*
UF *lithium-cooled reactors*
BT1 liquid metal cooled reactors
BT2 reactors

LITHIUM DEUTERIDES [166; 166]
BT1 deuterides
BT2 deuterium compounds
BT3 hydrogen compounds
BT1 lithium hydrides
BT2 hydrides
BT3 hydrogen compounds
BT2 lithium compounds
BT3 alkali metal compounds

LITHIUM FLUORIDES [3,155; 3,155]
BT1 fluorides
BT2 fluorine compounds
BT3 halogen compounds
BT2 halides
BT3 halogen compounds
BT1 lithium halides
BT2 halides
BT3 halogen compounds
BT2 lithium compounds
BT3 alkali metal compounds
RT dielectric track detectors
RT flibe
RT thermoluminescent dosemeters

LITHIUM HALIDES [4; 1,991] *Aug 81*
BT1 halides
BT2 halogen compounds
BT1 lithium compounds
BT2 alkali metal compounds
NT1 lithium bromides
NT1 lithium chlorides
NT1 lithium fluorides
NT1 lithium iodides

LITHIUM HYDRIDES [515; 651]
BT1 hydrides
BT2 hydrogen compounds
BT1 lithium compounds
BT2 alkali metal compounds
NT1 lithium deuterides
NT1 lithium tritides

LITHIUM HYDROXIDES [239; 239]
BT1 hydroxides
BT2 hydrogen compounds
BT2 oxygen compounds
BT1 lithium compounds
BT2 alkali metal compounds

LITHIUM IODIDES [154; 154]
BT1 iodides
BT2 halides
BT3 halogen compounds
BT2 iodine compounds
BT3 halogen compounds
BT1 lithium halides
BT2 halides
BT3 halogen compounds
BT2 lithium compounds
BT3 alkali metal compounds

LITHIUM IONS [1,407; 1,407]
BT1 ions
BT2 charged particles

LITHIUM ISOTOPES [287; 4,614]
NT1 lithium 10
NT1 lithium 11
NT1 lithium 13
NT1 lithium 3
NT1 lithium 4
NT1 lithium 5
NT1 lithium 6
NT1 lithium 7
NT1 lithium 8
NT1 lithium 9

LITHIUM NITRATES [249; 249]
BT1 lithium compounds
BT2 alkali metal compounds
BT1 nitrates
BT2 nitrogen compounds
BT2 oxygen compounds

LITHIUM NITRIDES [49; 49]
BT1 lithium compounds
BT2 alkali metal compounds
BT1 nitrides
BT2 nitrogen compounds
BT2 pnictides

LITHIUM OXIDES [1,350; 1,350]
  BT1   lithium compounds
    BT2   alkali metal compounds
  BT1   oxides
    BT2   chalcogenides
    BT2   oxygen compounds

LITHIUM PERCHLORATES [48; 48]
Oct 77
  BT1   lithium compounds
    BT2   alkali metal compounds
  BT1   perchlorates
    BT2   chlorine compounds
      BT3   halogen compounds
    BT2   oxygen compounds

LITHIUM PHOSPHATES [65; 65]
  BT1   lithium compounds
    BT2   alkali metal compounds
  BT1   phosphates
    BT2   oxygen compounds
    BT2   phosphorus compounds

→ **LITHIUM PHOSPHIDES** [0; 0] *Sep 91*
  BT1   lithium compounds
    BT2   alkali metal compounds
  BT1   phosphides
    BT2   phosphorus compounds
    BT2   pnictides

LITHIUM SELENIDES [16; 16]
  BT1   lithium compounds
    BT2   alkali metal compounds
  BT1   selenides
    BT2   chalcogenides
    BT2   selenium compounds

LITHIUM SILICATES [183; 183]
  BT1   lithium compounds
    BT2   alkali metal compounds
  BT1   silicates
    BT2   oxygen compounds
    BT2   silicon compounds

→ **LITHIUM SILICIDES** [0; 0] *Sep 91*
  BT1   lithium compounds
    BT2   alkali metal compounds
  BT1   silicides
    BT2   silicon compounds

LITHIUM SULFATES [153; 153]
  BT1   lithium compounds
    BT2   alkali metal compounds
  BT1   sulfates
    BT2   oxygen compounds
    BT2   sulfur compounds

LITHIUM SULFIDES [23; 23]
  BT1   lithium compounds
    BT2   alkali metal compounds
  BT1   sulfides
    BT2   chalcogenides
    BT2   sulfur compounds

LITHIUM TELLURIDES [15; 15] *Jun 77*
  BT1   lithium compounds
    BT2   alkali metal compounds
  BT1   tellurides
    BT2   chalcogenides
    BT2   tellurium compounds

LITHIUM TRITIDES [53; 53] *Feb 76*
  BT1   lithium hydrides
    BT2   hydrides
      BT3   hydrogen compounds
    BT2   lithium compounds
      BT3   alkali metal compounds
  BT1   tritides
    BT2   tritium compounds
    BT3   hydrogen compounds

LITHIUM TUNGSTATES [39; 39]
May 78
  BT1   lithium compounds
    BT2   alkali metal compounds
  BT1   tungstates
    BT2   oxygen compounds
    BT2   tungsten compounds
      BT3   transition element compounds

LITHIUM URANATES [14; 14] *Nov 75*
  BT1   lithium compounds
    BT2   alkali metal compounds
  BT1   uranates
    BT2   uranium compounds
      BT3   actinide compounds

LITHIUM 10 [17; 17]
  BT1   light nuclei
    BT2   nuclei
  BT1   lithium isotopes
  BT1   millisec living radioisotopes
    BT2   radioisotopes
      BT3   isotopes
  BT1   odd-odd nuclei
    BT2   nuclei

LITHIUM 11 [107; 107]
  BT1   beta-minus decay radioisotopes
    BT2   beta decay radioisotopes
      BT3   radioisotopes
        BT4   isotopes
  BT1   light nuclei
    BT2   nuclei
  BT1   lithium isotopes
  BT1   millisec living radioisotopes
    BT2   radioisotopes
      BT3   isotopes
  BT1   odd-even nuclei
    BT2   nuclei

LITHIUM 11 REACTIONS [19; 19]
Jan 90
  BT1   heavy ion reactions
    BT2   nuclear reactions

LITHIUM 13 [4; 4]
  BT1   beta-minus decay radioisotopes
    BT2   beta decay radioisotopes
      BT3   radioisotopes
        BT4   isotopes
  BT1   light nuclei
    BT2   nuclei
  BT1   lithium isotopes
  BT1   odd-even nuclei
    BT2   nuclei

LITHIUM 3 [9; 9]
  BT1   light nuclei
    BT2   nuclei
  BT1   lithium isotopes
  BT1   odd-even nuclei
    BT2   nuclei

LITHIUM 4 [23; 23]
  BT1   light nuclei
    BT2   nuclei
  BT1   lithium isotopes
  RT1   odd-odd nuclei
    BT2   nuclei

LITHIUM 5 [210; 210]
  BT1   alpha decay radioisotopes
    BT2   radioisotopes
      BT3   isotopes
  BT1   light nuclei
    BT2   nuclei
  BT1   lithium isotopes
  BT1   odd-even nuclei
    BT2   nuclei

LITHIUM 6 [2,399; 2,399]
  BT1   light nuclei
    BT2   nuclei
  BT1   lithium isotopes
  BT1   odd-odd nuclei
    BT2   nuclei

  BT1   stable isotopes
    BT2   isotopes
  RT   lithium 6 beams

LITHIUM 6 BEAMS [221; 221]
  BT1   ion beams
    BT2   beams
  RT   lithium 6

LITHIUM 6 REACTIONS [1,170; 1,170]
  BT1   heavy ion reactions
    BT2   nuclear reactions

LITHIUM 6 TARGET [1,795; 1,795]
  BT1   targets

LITHIUM 7 [1,903; 1,903]
  BT1   light nuclei
    BT2   nuclei
  BT1   lithium isotopes
  BT1   odd-even nuclei
    BT2   nuclei
  BT1   stable isotopes
    BT2   isotopes
  RT   lithium 7 beams

LITHIUM 7 BEAMS [213; 213]
  BT1   ion beams
    BT2   beams
  RT   lithium 7

LITHIUM 7 REACTIONS [725; 725]
  BT1   heavy ion reactions
    BT2   nuclear reactions

LITHIUM 7 TARGET [1,249; 1,249]
  BT1   targets

LITHIUM 8 [302; 302]
  BT1   beta-minus decay radioisotopes
    BT2   beta decay radioisotopes
      BT3   radioisotopes
        BT4   isotopes
  BT1   light nuclei
    BT2   nuclei
  BT1   lithium isotopes
  BT1   millisec living radioisotopes
    BT2   radioisotopes
      BT3   isotopes
  BT1   odd-odd nuclei
    BT2   nuclei

LITHIUM 8 REACTIONS [15; 15]
Sep 79
  BT1   heavy ion reactions
    BT2   nuclear reactions

→ **LITHIUM 8 TARGET** [0; 0] *Oct 91*
  BT1   targets

LITHIUM 9 [142; 142]
  BT1   beta-minus decay radioisotopes
    BT2   beta decay radioisotopes
      BT3   radioisotopes
        BT4   isotopes
  BT1   light nuclei
    BT2   nuclei
  BT1   lithium isotopes
  BT1   millisec living radioisotopes
    BT2   radioisotopes
      BT3   isotopes
  BT1   odd-even nuclei
    BT2   nuclei

→ **LITHIUM 9 REACTIONS** [4; 4] *Mar 91*
  BT1   heavy ion reactions
    BT2   nuclear reactions

LITHIUM 9 TARGET [3; 3] *Mar 76*
  BT1   targets

lithium-cooled reactors
  USE   lithium cooled reactors

lithology
   USE   petrology

LITR REACTOR [1; 1]
   UF   *low intensity test reactor*
   UF   *low-intensity test reactor*
   UF   *us aec low inten. test reactor*
   BT1   enriched uranium reactors
     BT2   reactors
   BT1   tank type reactors
     BT2   reactors
   BT1   thermal reactors
     BT2   reactors
   BT1   water cooled reactors
     BT2   reactors
   BT1   water moderated reactors
     BT2   reactors

LITTER SIZE [65; 65]
   RT   progeny

live time
(Time during which equipment is actually sensitive to incoming signals.)
   USE   dead time

LIVER [11,947; 11,947]
   BT1   digestive system
   BT1   glands
     BT2   organs
       BT3   body
   RT   abdomen
   RT   biliary tract
   RT   glycogen
   RT   hepatectomy
   RT   hepatitis
   RT   hepatomas
   RT   jaundice
   RT   liver cells
   RT   liver cirrhosis
   RT   metabolism
   RT   peritoneum
   RT   portal system
   RT   reticuloendothelial system

LIVER CELLS [582; 582] *Jun 83*
   UF   *hepatocytes*
   BT1   somatic cells
     BT2   animal cells
   RT   liver

LIVER CIRRHOSIS [718; 718]
   BT1   digestive system diseases
     BT2   diseases
   RT   liver

livermore pool type reactor
   USE   lptr reactor

livestock
   USE   domestic animals

lixiviation
   USE   leaching

LIZARDS [41; 41]
   BT1   reptiles
     BT2   vertebrates
       BT3   animals

ljubljana triga-mk-2 reactor
   USE   triga-2-ljubljana reactor

LLAMAS [10; 10]
   BT1   ruminants
     BT2   mammals
       BT3   vertebrates
         BT4   animals

llnl
   USE   lawrence livermore national la

LLNL ADVANCED TEST ACCELERATOR [14; 14] *May 88*
(Linear induction accelerator at Lawrence Livermore Laboratory, Livermore, California, USA.)
   BT1   linear accelerators
     BT2   accelerators
   RT   electron beams
   RT   induction

LM DEVICES [0; 0]
(Linear multipoles.)
   BT1   internal ring devices
     BT2   closed plasma devices
       BT3   thermonuclear devices
   RT   multipolar configurations

LMFBR TYPE REACTORS [12,490; 14,465]
   BT1   fbr type reactors
     BT2   breeder reactors
       BT3   reactors
     BT2   fast reactors
       BT3   epithermal reactors
         BT4   reactors
   BT1   liquid metal cooled reactors
     BT2   reactors
   NT1   beloyarsk-3 reactor
   NT1   beloyarsk-4 reactor
   NT1   bn-1600 reactor
   NT1   bn-350 reactor
   NT1   bn-800 reactor
   NT1   bor-60 reactor
   NT1   cdfr reactor
   NT1   clinch river breeder reactor
   NT1   dfr reactor
   NT1   ebr-1 reactor
   NT1   ebr-2 reactor
   NT1   enrico fermi-1 reactor
   NT1   joyo reactor
   NT1   kalpakkam lmfbr reactor
   NT1   monju reactor
   NT1   pfr reactor
   NT1   phenix reactor
   NT1   plbr reactor
   NT1   rapsodie reactor
   NT1   sbr-2 reactor
   NT1   sbr-5 reactor
   NT1   snr reactor
   NT1   snr-2 reactor
   NT1   super phenix reactor

→ **LNLS STORAGE RING** [0; 0] *Feb 91*
(Brazilian Synchrotron Radiation Source.)
   UF   *brazilian lnls synchrotron*
   BT1   storage rings
   BT1   synchrotron radiation sources
     BT2   radiation sources

LO AGUIRRE RECH-2 REACTOR [5; 5] *Feb 89*
(Lo Aguirre, Santiago, Chile.)
   BT1   pool type reactors
     BT2   water cooled reactors
       BT3   reactors
     BT2   water moderated reactors
       BT3   reactors
   BT1   research reactors
     BT2   research and test reactors
       BT3   reactors

LOAD MANAGEMENT [619; 619]
Nov 77
(Management of electric power demands on a distribution grid to achieve maximum power-production efficiency.)
   BT1   management
   RT   capacity
   RT   electric power
   RT   peak load

loading (fission reactor)
   USE   reactor fueling

loading (materials handling)
   USE   materials handling

loading machines (fiss react)
   USE   reactor charging machines

loads (dynamic)
   USE   dynamic loads

loads (power demand)
   USE   power demand

loads (static)
   USE   static loads

loads (stresses)
   USE   stresses

LOAM [111; 111]
   BT1   soils
   RT   clays

loan guarantees
   USE   financing

LOBACHEVSKY GEOMETRY [70; 70]
   UF   *lobachevsky space*
   UF   *lobachevsky-bolyai geometry*
   RT   mathematical space

lobachevsky space
   USE   lobachevsky geometry

lobachevsky-bolyai geometry
   USE   lobachevsky geometry

lobbies
   USE   interest groups

LOBSTERS [20; 20] *Apr 77*
   BT1   crustaceans
     BT2   aquatic organisms
     BT2   arthropods
       BT3   invertebrates
         BT4   animals
   RT   seafood

local boiling
   USE   subcooled boiling

LOCAL FALLOUT [255; 255]
   UF   *close-in fallout*
   BT1   fallout
   RT   civil defense
   RT   external irradiation
   RT   fallout shelters
   RT   nuclear weapons
   RT   shelters

local galaxy
   USE   milky way

LOCAL GOVERNMENT [248; 248]
Feb 81
   RT   government policies
   RT   legislation
   RT   national government
   RT   public officials
   RT   regional cooperation
   RT   regulations
   RT   state government

local group
　USE　galaxies

LOCAL IRRADIATION [1,827; 1,827]
　BT1　irradiation
　RT　abscopal radiation effects
　RT　external irradiation
　RT　local radiation effects
　RT　partial body irradiation
　RT　spatial dose distributions

LOCAL RADIATION EFFECTS
[350; 1,012]
　BT1　biological radiation effects
　BT2　biological effects
　BT2　radiation effects
　NT1　osteoradionecrosis
　NT1　radiation burns
　NT1　radiodermatitis
　RT　local irradiation

local thermodynamic equilibriu
　USE　lte

LOCALITY [1,772; 1,772]
　RT　nonlocal potential
　RT　phi4-field theory
　RT　quantum field theory

localization (biological)
　USE　biological localization

locks (security)
　USE　physical protection devices

LOCUSTS [22; 22]
　BT1　grasshoppers
　BT2　insects
　BT3　arthropods
　BT4　invertebrates
　BT5　animals

LOFT REACTOR [866; 866]
(E.G. and G. Idaho, Inc., Idaho Falls, Idaho, USA)
　UF　loss of fluid test reactor
　BT1　pwr type reactors
　BT2　enriched uranium reactors
　BT3　reactors
　BT2　power reactors
　BT3　reactors
　BT2　thermal reactors
　BT3　reactors
　BT2　water cooled reactors
　BT3　reactors
　BT2　water moderated reactors
　BT3　reactors
　BT1　tank type reactors
　BT2　reactors
　BT1　test reactors
　BT2　research and test reactors
　BT3　reactors
　BT2　test facilities

LOGARITHMIC RATEMETERS
[24; 24]
　BT1　counting ratemeters
　BT2　electronic equipment
　BT3　equipment

logic (mathematical)
　USE　mathematical logic

LOGIC CIRCUITS [1,290; 1,290]
　BT1　electronic circuits
　RT　gating circuits

LOLLIPOP EVENT [0; 0]
　BT1　vela project

london conv preven marine poll
(1972 London Convention on Prevention of Marine Pollution by Dumping of Waste and other Matter)
　USE　lcpmpdpw

LONDON EQUATION [146; 146]
　BT1　equations
　RT　superconductivity

london safety of life at sea c
　USE　solas convention

LONG COUNTERS [60; 60]
　BT1　moderating detectors
　BT2　neutron detectors
　BT3　radiation detectors
　BT4　measuring instruments

long range interactions
　USE　interaction range

LONG SHOT EVENT [18; 18]
　BT1　vela project

long term intake
　USE　chronic intake

long term irradiation
　USE　chronic irradiation

LONG WAVE RADIATION [269; 269]
　UF　long-wave radiation
　UF　low frequency radiation
　UF　low-frequency radiation
　BT1　radiowave radiation
　BT2　electromagnetic radiation
　BT3　radiations

long-lens spectrometers
　USE　magnetic lens spectrometers

long-range interactions
　USE　interaction range

long-term intake
　USE　chronic intake

long-term irradiation
　USE　chronic irradiation

long-wave radiation
　USE　long wave radiation

LONGITUDINAL MOMENTUM
[973; 973]
　UF　momentum (longitudinal)
　BT1　linear momentum
　RT　center-of-mass system
　RT　nuclear reactions
　RT　particle interactions
　RT　particle rapidity
　RT　transverse momentum

LONGITUDINAL PINCH [224; 334]
　UF　zet pinch
　BT1　pinch effect
　NT1　belt pinch
　RT　linear z pinch devices
　RT　tlp devices

longitudinal pinch devices (ln
　USE　linear z pinch devices

longitudinal pinch devices (tr
　USE　tlp devices

loops (coolant)
　USE　coolant loops

loops (in pile)
　USE　in pile loops

LOOSE PARTS MONITORING
[163; 163] *Aug 81*
(Monitoring foreign, misplaced, or loose objects in reactor cores and cooling systems.)
　BT1　monitoring
　RT　reactor instrumentation
　RT　reactor monitoring systems

LOPRA REACTOR [2; 2]
　BT1　triga type reactors
　BT2　enriched uranium reactors
　BT3　reactors
　BT2　hydride moderated reactors
　BT3　reactors
　BT2　research and test reactors
　BT3　reactors
　BT2　solid homogeneous reactors
　BT3　homogeneous reactors
　BT4　reactors
　BT2　water cooled reactors
　BT3　reactors
　BT2　water moderated reactors
　BT3　reactors

LORENTZ FORCE [582; 582]
　RT　charged particles
　RT　interactions
　RT　ponderomotive force

LORENTZ GAS [106; 106]
　UF　lorentz plasma
　BT1　fully ionized gases
　BT2　ionized gases
　BT3　gases
　BT4　fluids

LORENTZ GROUPS [803; 803]
　BT1　poincare groups
　BT2　lie groups
　BT3　symmetry groups

LORENTZ INVARIANCE [1,990; 1,990]
　BT1　invariance principles

lorentz plasma
　USE　lorentz gas

LORENTZ POLES [11; 11]
　UF　toller poles
　RT　regge poles

LORENTZ TRANSFORMATIONS
[1,420; 1,620]
　NT1　galilei transformations
　RT　center-of-mass system
　RT　laboratory system
　RT　limiting fragmentation
　RT　minkowski space
　RT　poincare groups
　RT　relativity theory
　RT　space-time

los alam. molt. plut. rea. exp
　USE　lampre-1 reactor

los alam. omega west reactor
　USE　owr reactor

los alamos meson physics facil
  USE   lampf linac

los alamos national laboratory
  USE   lanl

los alamos scientific lab
  USE   lasl

LOSS CONE [295; 295]
  RT   earth magnetosphere
  RT   loss cone instability
  RT   plasma
  RT   plasmapause
  RT   solar wind

LOSS CONE INSTABILITY [271; 271]
  BT1   plasma microinstabilities
    BT2   plasma instability
      BT3   instability
  RT   loss cone

LOSS OF COOLANT [9,394; 9,394]
  BT1   reactor accidents
    BT2   accidents
  RT   blowdown
  RT   coolants
  RT   core flooding systems
  RT   core spray systems
  RT   loss of flow
  RT   reactor cooling systems

LOSS OF FLOW [1,415; 1,415]
  BT1   reactor accidents
    BT2   accidents
  RT   loss of coolant

loss of fluid test reactor
  USE   loft reactor

LOSSES [1,603; 1,603]
  RT   accounting
  RT   safeguards

losses (energy)
  USE   energy losses

losses (particles)
  USE   particle losses

losses (power)
  USE   power losses

LOTUS FACILITY [27; 27] Dec 85
  RT   breeding blankets
  RT   hybrid reactors

LOUISIANA [212; 212]
  BT1   usa
    BT2   developed countries
    BT2   north america

louvain isochronous cyclotron
  USE   cyclone cyclotron

LOVIISA-1 REACTOR [220; 220]
(Loviisa, Finland)
  UF   *imatran voima-1 reactor*
  BT1   wwer type reactors
    BT2   pwr type reactors
      BT3   enriched uranium reactors
        BT4   reactors
      BT3   power reactors
        BT4   reactors
      BT3   thermal reactors
        BT4   reactors
      BT3   water cooled reactors
        BT4   reactors
      BT3   water moderated reactors
        BT4   reactors

LOVIISA-2 REACTOR [168; 168]
Aug 76
(Loviisa, Finland)
  UF   *imatran voima-2 reactor*
  BT1   wwer type reactors
    BT2   pwr type reactors
      BT3   enriched uranium reactors
        BT4   reactors
      BT3   power reactors
        BT4   reactors
      BT3   thermal reactors
        BT4   reactors
      BT3   water cooled reactors
        BT4   reactors
      BT3   water moderated reactors
        BT4   reactors

LOW ALLOY STEELS [784; 1,936]
Nov 83
  UF   *low-alloy steels*
  BT1   steels
    BT2   carbon additions
    BT2   iron base alloys
      BT3   iron alloys
        BT4   alloys
  NT1   steel-cralnimo
  NT1   steel-crmo
  NT1   steel-crmov
  NT1   steel-crni
  NT1   steel-cr2mo
  NT1   steel-cr2moninb
  NT1   steel-cr2mov
  NT1   steel-cr2nimov
  NT1   steel-cr5mo
  NT1   steel-mncumo
  NT1   steel-mnmo
  NT1   steel-mnnimo
  NT1   steel-mnnimov
  NT1   steel-nicr
  NT1   steel-nicrmo
  NT1   steel-nimocr
  NT1   steel-ni3cr
  NT1   steel-ni3crmo
  NT1   steel-ni3crmov
  NT1   steel-ni3mov
  NT1   steel-ni4
  NT1   steel-ni4crw

low beta plasma
  USE   low-beta plasma

LOW CARBON-HIGH ALLOY STEELS
[35; 550] Nov 83
(High alloy steels with not more than 0.05% C.)
  UF   *low-carbon-high-alloy steels*
  BT1   stainless steels
    BT2   high alloy steels
      BT3   steels
        BT4   carbon additions
        BT4   iron base alloys
          BT5   iron alloys
            BT6   alloys
  NT1   steel-cr11ni10mo2ti-l
  NT1   steel-cr13ni6mo-l
  NT1   steel-cr17cu4ni4nb-l
  NT1   steel-cr17ni12mo3-l
  NT1   steel-cr18ni10-l
  NT1   steel-cr19ni10-l
  NT1   steel-cr20ni11-l
  NT1   steel-cr26ni5mo-l
  NT1   steel-ni17cr14moti-l
  NT1   steel-ni36cr12ti3al-l

LOW DOSE IRRADIATION
[3,503; 3,503]
  UF   *low-dose irradiation*
  BT1   irradiation
  RT   chronic irradiation
  RT   dose rates
  RT   dose-response relationships
  RT   radiation doses

low energy electron diffractio
  USE   electron diffraction

low energy theorem
  USE   low-energy theorem

LOW EQUATION [78; 78]
  BT1   equations

low flux reactor petten
  USE   lfr reactor

low frequency radiation
  USE   long wave radiation

low intensity test reactor
  USE   litr reactor

LOW LEVEL COUNTERS [487; 487]
  UF   *low-level counters*
  BT1   radiation detectors
    BT2   measuring instruments
  RT   low level counting

LOW LEVEL COUNTING [798; 798]
Aug 76
  UF   *low-level counting*
  BT1   counting techniques
  RT   low level counters

low level radioactive wastes
  USE   low-level radioactive wastes

low power test facility-nrts
  USE   lptf reactor

LOW PRESSURE [2,673; 2,673]
  UF   *pressure (1-760 torr)*
  UF   *pressure (133 pa-0.1 mpa)*
  UF   *rough vacuum*
  UF   *vacuum (rough)*
  UF   *vacuum (1-760 torr)*
  UF   *vacuum (133 pa-0.1 mpa)*
  RT   pressure dependence

LOW PRESSURE COOLANT INJECTION [130; 130] Sep 77
  UF   *low-pressure coolant injection*
  UF   *lpci*
  BT1   eccs
    BT2   reactor protection systems
  RT   reactor safety

LOW TEMPERATURE [23,564; 23,564]
  UF   *temperature (0065-0273 k)*
  RT   cryogenics
  RT   cryoscopy
  RT   freezing out
  RT   temperature dependence

low-alloy steels
  USE   low alloy steels

LOW-BETA PLASMA [496; 496]
(Beta from 0 to 0.01.)
  UF   *low beta plasma*
  BT1   plasma
  RT   beta ratio

low-carbon-high-alloy steels
  USE   low carbon-high alloy steels

low-dose irradiation
  USE   low dose irradiation

LOW-ENERGY THEOREM [225; 225]
UF low energy theorem
RT current algebra

low-flux reactor petten
USE lfr reactor

low-frequency radiation
USE long wave radiation

low-intensity test reactor
USE litr reactor

low-level counters
USE low level counters

low-level counting
USE low level counting

LOW-LEVEL RADIOACTIVE WASTES
[6,982; 6,982] *May 78*
(Wastes containing less than 5 x 10 exp(-5) microcuries/milliliter of radioactivity.)
UF low level radioactive wastes
BT1 radioactive wastes
BT2 radioactive materials
BT3 materials
BT2 wastes
RT konrad ore mine

low-power test facility-nrts
USE lptf reactor

low-pressure coolant injection
USE low pressure coolant injection

lowell techn. instit. reactor
USE ltir reactor

LOWER HYBRID CURRENT DRIVE
[127; 127] *Jul 89*
BT1 non-inductive current drive
RT lower hybrid heating

LOWER HYBRID HEATING [922; 922]
Mar 83
UF lhr heating
UF lower hybrid resonance heating
BT1 high-frequency heating
BT2 plasma heating
BT3 heating
RT lower hybrid current drive

lower hybrid resonance heating
USE lower hybrid heating

lpci
USE low pressure coolant injection

LPTF REACTOR [2; 2]
UF low power test facility-nrts
UF low-power test facility-nrts
UF nrts-lptf reactor
BT1 zero power reactors
BT2 experimental reactors
BT3 research and test reactors
BT4 reactors

LPTR REACTOR [18; 18]
(University of California, Lawrence Livermore Lab., Livermore, California, USA)
UF livermore pool type reactor
UF us aec lptr reactor
BT1 enriched uranium reactors
BT2 reactors
BT1 isotope production reactors
BT2 irradiation reactors
BT3 reactors
BT1 pool type reactors
BT2 water cooled reactors
BT3 reactors
BT2 water moderated reactors
BT3 reactors
BT1 research reactors
BT2 research and test reactors
BT3 reactors
BT1 tank type reactors
BT2 reactors
BT1 thermal reactors
BT2 reactors

LR-0 REACTOR [57; 57] *Nov 81*
(Lehkovodni Reaktor nuloveho vykonu.)
UF czechoslovak lr-0 reactor
UF rez lr-0 reactor
BT1 water cooled reactors
BT2 reactors
BT1 water moderated reactors
BT2 reactors
BT1 zero power reactors
BT2 experimental reactors
BT3 research and test reactors
BT4 reactors

LSZ THEORY [66; 66]
UF lehmann-symanzik-zimmermann me
BT1 axiomatic field theory
BT2 quantum field theory
BT3 field theories

LT-3 TOKAMAK [24; 24]
UF canberra tokamak
BT1 tokamak devices
BT2 closed plasma devices
BT3 thermonuclear devices

LT-4 TOKAMAK [19; 19] *Jun 84*
BT1 tokamak devices
BT2 closed plasma devices
BT3 thermonuclear devices

LTE [625; 625]
UF local thermodynamic equilibriu
BT1 equilibrium
RT thermodynamics

LTH [411; 411]
UF luteotropic hormone
UF prolactin
BT1 gonadotropins
BT2 pituitary hormones
BT3 peptide hormones
BT4 hormones
RT mammary glands
RT progesterone

LTIR REACTOR [6; 6]
(Univ. of Lowell, Lowell, Massachusetts, USA)
UF lowell techn. instit. reactor
BT1 pool type reactors
BT2 water cooled reactors
BT3 reactors
BT2 water moderated reactors
BT3 reactors
BT1 research reactors
BT2 research and test reactors
BT3 reactors

LUBRICANTS [193; 511]
UF mineral oil
NT1 gas lubricants
NT1 greases
NT1 lubricating oils
NT1 solid lubricants
RT lubrication

LUBRICATING OILS [199; 199]
BT1 lubricants
BT1 petroleum products

LUBRICATION [203; 203]
RT bearings
RT gears
RT greases
RT hydrostatic bearings
RT lubricants

luccu oil
USE olive oil

LUCENS REACTOR [18; 18]
BT1 enriched uranium reactors
BT2 reactors
BT1 hwgcr type reactors
BT2 gas cooled reactors
BT3 reactors
BT2 heavy water moderated reactors
BT3 reactors
BT1 pressure tube reactors
BT2 power reactors
BT3 reactors
BT1 thermal reactors
BT2 reactors

LUCIE-1 REACTOR [64; 64]
UF hutchinson island-1 reactor
UF st lucie-1 reactor
BT1 pwr type reactors
BT2 enriched uranium reactors
BT3 reactors
BT2 power reactors
BT3 reactors
BT2 thermal reactors
BT3 reactors
BT2 water cooled reactors
BT3 reactors
BT2 water moderated reactors
BT3 reactors

LUCIE-2 REACTOR [45; 45]
UF hutchinson island-2 reactor
UF st lucie-2 reactor
BT1 pwr type reactors
BT2 enriched uranium reactors
BT3 reactors
BT2 power reactors
BT3 reactors
BT2 thermal reactors
BT3 reactors
BT2 water cooled reactors
BT3 reactors
BT2 water moderated reactors
BT3 reactors

LUCIFERASE [14; 14]
BT1 oxidases
BT2 oxidoreductases
BT3 enzymes
BT4 organic compounds

LUCIFERIN [13; 13]
BT1 albumins
BT2 proteins
BT3 organic compounds

LUCITE [128; 128]
BT1 polyacrylates
BT2 esters
BT3 organic compounds
BT2 polyvinyls
BT3 organic polymers
BT4 organic compounds
BT4 polymers
RT pmma

LUGOL [8; 8]
UF lugol solution
RT glycerol
RT iodine
RT potassium iodides

lugol solution
   USE   lugol

luminal
   USE   phenobarbital

LUMINESCENCE [3,744; 15,103]
   BT1   photon emission
      BT2   emission
   NT1   cathodoluminescence
   NT1   chemiluminescence
      NT2   bioluminescence
   NT1   electroluminescence
   NT1   fluorescence
      NT2   resonance fluorescence
   NT1   lyoluminescence
   NT1   phosphorescence
   NT1   photoluminescence
   NT1   radioluminescence
      NT2   radiothermoluminescence
   NT1   thermoluminescence
      NT2   radiothermoluminescence
   RT   glow curve
   RT   traps

LUMINESCENT CHAMBERS [19; 19]
   RT   phosphors
   RT   scintillation counters

LUMINESCENT DOSEMETERS
[103; 4,268]
   BT1   dosemeters
      BT2   measuring instruments
   NT1   rpl dosemeters
   NT1   thermoluminescent dosemeters
   RT   dielectric track detectors
   RT   glass scintillators
   RT   phosphors

LUMINOSITY [7,234; 7,234]
   BT1   optical properties
      BT2   physical properties
   RT   brightness
   RT   visibility

luminous flux density
   USE   illuminance

LUMINOUS PAINTS [98; 98]
   BT1   paints
      BT2   coatings
   RT   dial painters

LUNA SPACE PROBES [25; 25] *Feb 79*
   BT1   space vehicles

LUNAR ATMOSPHERE [24; 24]
   BT1   satellite atmospheres
      BT2   atmospheres
   RT   lunar materials
   RT   moon

LUNAR MATERIALS [1,012; 1,012]
   BT1   materials
   RT   anorthosites
   RT   apollo project
   RT   dusts
   RT   lunar atmosphere
   RT   moon
   RT   rocks

lunar occultation
   USE   eclipse

lund synchrotron
   USE   lusy

lung cells
   USE   respiratory tract cells

LUNG CLEARANCE [754; 754]
   BT1   excretion
      BT2   clearance
   RT   exhalation
   RT   lungs
   RT   respiratory system

LUNGS [12,663; 12,663]
   UF   *alveoli (pulmonary)*
   UF+   *pulmonary lavage*
   BT1   organs
      BT2   body
   BT1   respiratory system
   RT   blood circulation
   RT   bronchi
   RT   chest
   RT   diaphragm
   RT   emphysema
   RT   lavage
   RT   lung clearance
   RT   lymphatic system
   RT   pleura
   RT   pneumoconioses
   RT   pneumonia
   RT   pneumonitis
   RT   respiration
   RT   respiratory tract cells

LUPUS [113; 113]
   BT1   immune system diseases
      BT2   diseases
   BT1   tuberculosis
      BT2   bacterial diseases
         BT3   infectious diseases
            BT4   diseases
   RT   skin

LUSY [8; 8]
   UF   *lund synchrotron*
   BT1   synchrotrons
      BT2   cyclic accelerators
         BT3   accelerators

luteinizing hormone
   USE   lh

luteotropic hormone
   USE   lth

LUTETIUM [628; 628]
   BT1   rare earths
      BT2   metals
         BT3   elements

LUTETIUM ADDITIONS [14; 14]
(Alloys containing not more than 1% Lu are listed here.)
   BT1   rare earth additions
   RT   lutetium alloys
   RT   lutetium compounds

LUTETIUM ALLOYS [194; 220]
(Alloys containing more than 1% Lu.)
   BT1   rare earth alloys
      BT2   alloys
   NT1   lutetium base alloys
   RT   lutetium additions

LUTETIUM BASE ALLOYS [26; 26]
   BT1   lutetium alloys
      BT2   rare earth alloys
         BT3   alloys

LUTETIUM BORIDES [29; 29]
   BT1   borides
      BT2   boron compounds
   BT1   lutetium compounds
      BT2   rare earth compounds

LUTETIUM BROMIDES [7; 7]
   BT1   bromides
      BT2   bromine compounds
         BT3   halogen compounds
      BT2   halides
         BT3   halogen compounds
   BT1   lutetium compounds
      BT2   rare earth compounds

LUTETIUM CARBIDES [10; 10]
   BT1   carbides
      BT2   carbon compounds
   BT1   lutetium compounds
      BT2   rare earth compounds

LUTETIUM CARBONATES [0; 0]
Apr 89
   BT1   carbonates
      BT2   carbon compounds
      BT2   oxygen compounds
   BT1   lutetium compounds
      BT2   rare earth compounds

LUTETIUM CHLORIDES [39; 39]
   BT1   chlorides
      BT2   chlorine compounds
         BT3   halogen compounds
      BT2   halides
         BT3   halogen compounds
   BT1   lutetium compounds
      BT2   rare earth compounds

LUTETIUM COMPLEXES [167; 167]
   BT1   rare earth complexes
      BT2   complexes

LUTETIUM COMPOUNDS [280; 755]
   BT1   rare earth compounds
   NT1   lutetium borides
   NT1   lutetium bromides
   NT1   lutetium carbides
   NT1   lutetium carbonates
   NT1   lutetium chlorides
   NT1   lutetium fluorides
   NT1   lutetium hydrides
   NT1   lutetium hydroxides
   NT1   lutetium iodides
   NT1   lutetium nitrates
   NT1   lutetium oxides
   NT1   lutetium perchlorates
   NT1   lutetium phosphates
   NT1   lutetium selenides
   NT1   lutetium silicates
   NT1   lutetium silicides
   NT1   lutetium sulfates
   NT1   lutetium sulfides
   NT1   lutetium tungstates
   RT   lutetium additions

LUTETIUM FLUORIDES [56; 56]
   BT1   fluorides
      BT2   fluorine compounds
         BT3   halogen compounds
      BT2   halides
         BT3   halogen compounds
   BT1   lutetium compounds
      BT2   rare earth compounds

LUTETIUM HYDRIDES [37; 37]
   BT1   hydrides
      BT2   hydrogen compounds
   BT1   lutetium compounds
      BT2   rare earth compounds

LUTETIUM HYDROXIDES [6; 6]
   BT1   hydroxides
      BT2   hydrogen compounds
      BT2   oxygen compounds
   BT1   lutetium compounds
      BT2   rare earth compounds

LUTETIUM IODIDES [11; 11]
   BT1   iodides
      BT2   halides
         BT3   halogen compounds
      BT2   iodine compounds
         BT3   halogen compounds
   BT1   lutetium compounds
      BT2   rare earth compounds

LUTETIUM IONS [29; 29]
BT1 ions
BT2 charged particles

LUTETIUM ISOTOPES [88; 951]
NT1 lutetium 151
NT1 lutetium 152
NT1 lutetium 153
NT1 lutetium 154
NT1 lutetium 155
NT1 lutetium 156
NT1 lutetium 157
NT1 lutetium 158
NT1 lutetium 159
NT1 lutetium 160
NT1 lutetium 161
NT1 lutetium 162
NT1 lutetium 163
NT1 lutetium 164
NT1 lutetium 165
NT1 lutetium 166
NT1 lutetium 167
NT1 lutetium 168
NT1 lutetium 169
NT1 lutetium 170
NT1 lutetium 171
NT1 lutetium 172
NT1 lutetium 173
NT1 lutetium 174
NT1 lutetium 175
NT1 lutetium 176
NT1 lutetium 177
NT1 lutetium 178
NT1 lutetium 179
NT1 lutetium 180
NT1 lutetium 181
NT1 lutetium 182
NT1 lutetium 183
NT1 lutetium 184

LUTETIUM NITRATES [23; 23]
BT1 lutetium compounds
BT2 rare earth compounds
BT1 nitrates
BT2 nitrogen compounds
BT2 oxygen compounds

LUTETIUM OXIDES [185; 185]
BT1 lutetium compounds
BT2 rare earth compounds
BT1 oxides
BT2 chalcogenides
BT2 oxygen compounds

LUTETIUM PERCHLORATES [4; 4]
BT1 lutetium compounds
BT2 rare earth compounds
BT1 perchlorates
BT2 chlorine compounds
BT3 halogen compounds
BT2 oxygen compounds

LUTETIUM PHOSPHATES [44; 44]
Oct 75
BT1 lutetium compounds
BT2 rare earth compounds
BT1 phosphates
BT2 oxygen compounds
BT2 phosphorus compounds

LUTETIUM SELENIDES [3; 3] *Sep 79*
BT1 lutetium compounds
BT2 rare earth compounds
BT1 selenides
BT2 chalcogenides
BT2 selenium compounds

LUTETIUM SILICATES [7; 7] *Feb 79*
BT1 lutetium compounds
BT2 rare earth compounds
BT1 silicates
BT2 oxygen compounds
BT2 silicon compounds

LUTETIUM SILICIDES [21; 21] *Jul 78*
BT1 lutetium compounds
BT2 rare earth compounds
BT1 silicides
BT2 silicon compounds

LUTETIUM SULFATES [8; 8]
BT1 lutetium compounds
BT2 rare earth compounds
BT1 sulfates
BT2 oxygen compounds
BT2 sulfur compounds

LUTETIUM SULFIDES [14; 14]
BT1 lutetium compounds
BT2 rare earth compounds
BT1 sulfides
BT2 chalcogenides
BT2 sulfur compounds

LUTETIUM TUNGSTATES [0; 0]
Apr 90
BT1 lutetium compounds
BT2 rare earth compounds
BT1 tungstates
BT2 oxygen compounds
BT2 tungsten compounds
BT3 transition element compounds

LUTETIUM 151 [14; 14] *Sep 83*
BT1 lutetium isotopes
BT1 millisec living radioisotopes
BT2 radioisotopes
BT3 isotopes
BT1 odd-even nuclei
BT2 nuclei
BT1 proton decay radioisotopes
BT2 radioisotopes
BT3 isotopes
BT1 rare earth nuclei
BT2 intermediate mass nuclei
BT3 nuclei

LUTETIUM 152 [2; 2] *Oct 88*
BT1 lutetium isotopes
BT1 millisec living radioisotopes
BT2 radioisotopes
BT3 isotopes
BT1 odd-odd nuclei
BT2 nuclei
BT1 rare earth nuclei
BT2 intermediate mass nuclei
BT3 nuclei

LUTETIUM 153 [5; 5] *May 86*
BT1 beta-plus decay radioisotopes
BT2 beta decay radioisotopes
BT3 radioisotopes
BT4 isotopes
BT1 electron capture radioisotopes
BT2 beta decay radioisotopes
BT3 radioisotopes
BT4 isotopes
BT1 isomeric transition isotopes
BT2 radioisotopes
BT3 isotopes
BT1 lutetium isotopes
BT1 millisec living radioisotopes
BT2 radioisotopes
BT3 isotopes
BT1 odd-even nuclei
BT2 nuclei
BT1 rare earth nuclei
BT2 intermediate mass nuclei
BT3 nuclei

LUTETIUM 154 [7; 7] *Nov 84*
BT1 electron capture radioisotopes
BT2 beta decay radioisotopes
BT3 radioisotopes
BT4 isotopes
BT1 isomeric transition isotopes
BT2 radioisotopes
BT3 isotopes
BT1 lutetium isotopes
BT1 microsec living radioisotopes
BT2 radioisotopes

BT3 isotopes
BT1 odd-odd nuclei
BT2 nuclei
BT1 rare earth nuclei
BT2 intermediate mass nuclei
BT3 nuclei
BT1 seconds living radioisotopes
BT2 radioisotopes
BT3 isotopes

LUTETIUM 155 [5; 5] *Jan 76*
BT1 alpha decay radioisotopes
BT2 radioisotopes
BT3 isotopes
BT1 electron capture radioisotopes
BT2 beta decay radioisotopes
BT3 radioisotopes
BT4 isotopes
BT1 lutetium isotopes
BT1 millisec living radioisotopes
BT2 radioisotopes
BT3 isotopes
BT1 odd-even nuclei
BT2 nuclei
BT1 rare earth nuclei
BT2 intermediate mass nuclei
BT3 nuclei

LUTETIUM 156 [3; 3] *Nov 76*
BT1 alpha decay radioisotopes
BT2 radioisotopes
BT3 isotopes
BT1 electron capture radioisotopes
BT2 beta decay radioisotopes
BT3 radioisotopes
BT4 isotopes
BT1 lutetium isotopes
BT1 millisec living radioisotopes
BT2 radioisotopes
BT3 isotopes
BT1 odd-odd nuclei
BT2 nuclei
BT1 rare earth nuclei
BT2 intermediate mass nuclei
BT3 nuclei

LUTETIUM 157 [6; 6] *Apr 78*
BT1 alpha decay radioisotopes
BT2 radioisotopes
BT3 isotopes
BT1 electron capture radioisotopes
BT2 beta decay radioisotopes
BT3 radioisotopes
BT4 isotopes
BT1 lutetium isotopes
BT1 odd-even nuclei
BT2 nuclei
BT1 rare earth nuclei
BT2 intermediate mass nuclei
BT3 nuclei
BT1 seconds living radioisotopes
BT2 radioisotopes
BT3 isotopes

LUTETIUM 158 [11; 11] *Dec 79*
BT1 alpha decay radioisotopes
BT2 radioisotopes
BT3 isotopes
BT1 electron capture radioisotopes
BT2 beta decay radioisotopes
BT3 radioisotopes
BT4 isotopes
BT1 lutetium isotopes
BT1 odd-odd nuclei
BT2 nuclei
BT1 rare earth nuclei
BT2 intermediate mass nuclei
BT3 nuclei
BT1 seconds living radioisotopes
BT2 radioisotopes
BT3 isotopes

LUTETIUM 159 [5; 5] *Dec 80*
BT1 alpha decay radioisotopes
BT2 radioisotopes
BT3 isotopes
BT1 electron capture radioisotopes
BT2 beta decay radioisotopes

```
      BT3     radioisotopes
         BT4     isotopes
      BT1     lutetium isotopes
      BT1     odd-even nuclei
         BT2     nuclei
      BT1     rare earth nuclei
         BT2     intermediate mass nuclei
            BT3     nuclei
      BT1     seconds living radioisotopes
         BT2     radioisotopes
            BT3     isotopes
```

LUTETIUM 160 [10; 10] *Dec 79*
```
      BT1     electron capture radioisotopes
         BT2     beta decay radioisotopes
            BT3     radioisotopes
               BT4     isotopes
      BT1     lutetium isotopes
      BT1     odd-odd nuclei
         BT2     nuclei
      BT1     rare earth nuclei
         BT2     intermediate mass nuclei
            BT3     nuclei
      BT1     seconds living radioisotopes
         BT2     radioisotopes
            BT3     isotopes
```

LUTETIUM 161 [20; 20]
```
      BT1     electron capture radioisotopes
         BT2     beta decay radioisotopes
            BT3     radioisotopes
               BT4     isotopes
      BT1     lutetium isotopes
      BT1     minutes living radioisotopes
         BT2     radioisotopes
            BT3     isotopes
      BT1     odd-even nuclei
         BT2     nuclei
      BT1     rare earth nuclei
         BT2     intermediate mass nuclei
            BT3     nuclei
```

LUTETIUM 162 [15; 15] *Jul 76*
```
      BT1     beta-plus decay radioisotopes
         BT2     beta decay radioisotopes
            BT3     radioisotopes
               BT4     isotopes
      BT1     electron capture radioisotopes
         BT2     beta decay radioisotopes
            BT3     radioisotopes
               BT4     isotopes
      BT1     lutetium isotopes
      BT1     minutes living radioisotopes
         BT2     radioisotopes
            BT3     isotopes
      BT1     odd-odd nuclei
         BT2     nuclei
      BT1     rare earth nuclei
         BT2     intermediate mass nuclei
            BT3     nuclei
```

LUTETIUM 163 [25; 25] *Dec 79*
```
      BT1     beta-plus decay radioisotopes
         BT2     beta decay radioisotopes
            BT3     radioisotopes
               BT4     isotopes
      BT1     electron capture radioisotopes
         BT2     beta decay radioisotopes
            BT3     radioisotopes
               BT4     isotopes
      BT1     lutetium isotopes
      BT1     minutes living radioisotopes
         BT2     radioisotopes
            BT3     isotopes
      BT1     odd-even nuclei
         BT2     nuclei
      BT1     rare earth nuclei
         BT2     intermediate mass nuclei
            BT3     nuclei
```

LUTETIUM 164 [15; 15]
```
      BT1     beta-plus decay radioisotopes
         BT2     beta decay radioisotopes
            BT3     radioisotopes
               BT4     isotopes
      BT1     electron capture radioisotopes
         BT2     beta decay radioisotopes
```

```
            BT3     radioisotopes
               BT4     isotopes
      BT1     lutetium isotopes
      BT1     minutes living radioisotopes
         BT2     radioisotopes
            BT3     isotopes
      BT1     odd-odd nuclei
         BT2     nuclei
      BT1     rare earth nuclei
         BT2     intermediate mass nuclei
            BT3     nuclei
```

LUTETIUM 165 [37; 37]
```
      BT1     beta-plus decay radioisotopes
         BT2     beta decay radioisotopes
            BT3     radioisotopes
               BT4     isotopes
      BT1     electron capture radioisotopes
         BT2     beta decay radioisotopes
            BT3     radioisotopes
               BT4     isotopes
      BT1     lutetium isotopes
      BT1     minutes living radioisotopes
         BT2     radioisotopes
            BT3     isotopes
      BT1     odd-even nuclei
         BT2     nuclei
      BT1     rare earth nuclei
         BT2     intermediate mass nuclei
            BT3     nuclei
```

LUTETIUM 166 [7; 7]
```
      BT1     beta-plus decay radioisotopes
         BT2     beta decay radioisotopes
            BT3     radioisotopes
               BT4     isotopes
      BT1     electron capture radioisotopes
         BT2     beta decay radioisotopes
            BT3     radioisotopes
               BT4     isotopes
      BT1     lutetium isotopes
      BT1     minutes living radioisotopes
         BT2     radioisotopes
            BT3     isotopes
      BT1     odd-odd nuclei
         BT2     nuclei
      BT1     rare earth nuclei
         BT2     intermediate mass nuclei
            BT3     nuclei
```

LUTETIUM 167 [31; 31]
```
      BT1     beta-plus decay radioisotopes
         BT2     beta decay radioisotopes
            BT3     radioisotopes
               BT4     isotopes
      BT1     electron capture radioisotopes
         BT2     beta decay radioisotopes
            BT3     radioisotopes
               BT4     isotopes
      BT1     lutetium isotopes
      BT1     minutes living radioisotopes
         BT2     radioisotopes
            BT3     isotopes
      BT1     odd-even nuclei
         BT2     nuclei
      BT1     rare earth nuclei
         BT2     intermediate mass nuclei
            BT3     nuclei
```

LUTETIUM 168 [11; 11]
```
      BT1     beta-plus decay radioisotopes
         BT2     beta decay radioisotopes
            BT3     radioisotopes
               BT4     isotopes
      BT1     electron capture radioisotopes
         BT2     beta decay radioisotopes
            BT3     radioisotopes
               BT4     isotopes
      BT1     lutetium isotopes
      BT1     minutes living radioisotopes
         BT2     radioisotopes
            BT3     isotopes
      BT1     odd-odd nuclei
         BT2     nuclei
      BT1     rare earth nuclei
         BT2     intermediate mass nuclei
            BT3     nuclei
```

LUTETIUM 169 [42; 42]
```
      BT1     beta-plus decay radioisotopes
         BT2     beta decay radioisotopes
            BT3     radioisotopes
               BT4     isotopes
      BT1     days living radioisotopes
         BT2     radioisotopes
            BT3     isotopes
      BT1     electron capture radioisotopes
         BT2     beta decay radioisotopes
            BT3     radioisotopes
               BT4     isotopes
      BT1     internal conversion radioisoto
         BT2     radioisotopes
            BT3     isotopes
      BT1     isomeric transition isotopes
         BT2     radioisotopes
            BT3     isotopes
      BT1     lutetium isotopes
      BT1     minutes living radioisotopes
         BT2     radioisotopes
            BT3     isotopes
      BT1     odd-even nuclei
         BT2     nuclei
      BT1     rare earth nuclei
         BT2     intermediate mass nuclei
            BT3     nuclei
```

LUTETIUM 170 [17; 17]
```
      BT1     beta-plus decay radioisotopes
         BT2     beta decay radioisotopes
            BT3     radioisotopes
               BT4     isotopes
      BT1     days living radioisotopes
         BT2     radioisotopes
            BT3     isotopes
      BT1     electron capture radioisotopes
         BT2     beta decay radioisotopes
            BT3     radioisotopes
               BT4     isotopes
      BT1     internal conversion radioisoto
         BT2     radioisotopes
            BT3     isotopes
      BT1     isomeric transition isotopes
         BT2     radioisotopes
            BT3     isotopes
      BT1     lutetium isotopes
      BT1     millisec living radioisotopes
         BT2     radioisotopes
            BT3     isotopes
      BT1     odd-odd nuclei
         BT2     nuclei
      BT1     rare earth nuclei
         BT2     intermediate mass nuclei
            BT3     nuclei
```

LUTETIUM 171 [97; 97]
```
      BT1     beta-plus decay radioisotopes
         BT2     beta decay radioisotopes
            BT3     radioisotopes
               BT4     isotopes
      BT1     days living radioisotopes
         BT2     radioisotopes
            BT3     isotopes
      BT1     electron capture radioisotopes
         BT2     beta decay radioisotopes
            BT3     radioisotopes
               BT4     isotopes
      BT1     internal conversion radioisoto
         BT2     radioisotopes
            BT3     isotopes
      BT1     isomeric transition isotopes
         BT2     radioisotopes
            BT3     isotopes
      BT1     lutetium isotopes
      BT1     minutes living radioisotopes
         BT2     radioisotopes
            BT3     isotopes
      BT1     odd-even nuclei
         BT2     nuclei
      BT1     rare earth nuclei
         BT2     intermediate mass nuclei
            BT3     nuclei
```

LUTETIUM 172 [69; 69]
 BT1　days living radioisotopes
 　BT2　radioisotopes
 　　BT3　isotopes
 BT1　electron capture radioisotopes
 　BT2　beta decay radioisotopes
 　　BT3　radioisotopes
 　　　BT4　isotopes
 BT1　internal conversion radioisoto
 　BT2　radioisotopes
 　　BT3　isotopes
 BT1　isomeric transition isotopes
 　BT2　radioisotopes
 　　BT3　isotopes
 BT1　lutetium isotopes
 BT1　minutes living radioisotopes
 　BT2　radioisotopes
 　　BT3　isotopes
 BT1　odd-odd nuclei
 　BT2　nuclei
 BT1　rare earth nuclei
 　BT2　intermediate mass nuclei
 　　BT3　nuclei

LUTETIUM 173 [65; 65]
 BT1　electron capture radioisotopes
 　BT2　beta decay radioisotopes
 　　BT3　radioisotopes
 　　　BT4　isotopes
 BT1　lutetium isotopes
 BT1　odd-even nuclei
 　BT2　nuclei
 BT1　rare earth nuclei
 　BT2　intermediate mass nuclei
 　　BT3　nuclei
 BT1　years living radioisotopes
 　BT2　radioisotopes
 　　BT3　isotopes

LUTETIUM 174 [52; 52]
 BT1　beta-plus decay radioisotopes
 　BT2　beta decay radioisotopes
 　　BT3　radioisotopes
 　　　BT4　isotopes
 BT1　days living radioisotopes
 　BT2　radioisotopes
 　　BT3　isotopes
 BT1　electron capture radioisotopes
 　BT2　beta decay radioisotopes
 　　BT3　radioisotopes
 　　　BT4　isotopes
 BT1　isomeric transition isotopes
 　BT2　radioisotopes
 　　BT3　isotopes
 BT1　lutetium isotopes
 BT1　odd-odd nuclei
 　BT2　nuclei
 BT1　rare earth nuclei
 　BT2　intermediate mass nuclei
 　　BT3　nuclei
 BT1　years living radioisotopes
 　BT2　radioisotopes
 　　BT3　isotopes

LUTETIUM 174 TARGET [3; 3]
 BT1　targets

LUTETIUM 175 [158; 158]
 BT1　lutetium isotopes
 BT1　odd-even nuclei
 　BT2　nuclei
 BT1　rare earth nuclei
 　BT2　intermediate mass nuclei
 　　BT3　nuclei
 BT1　stable isotopes
 　BT2　isotopes

LUTETIUM 175 TARGET [122; 122]
 BT1　targets

LUTETIUM 176 [169; 169]
 BT1　beta-minus decay radioisotopes
 　BT2　beta decay radioisotopes
 　　BT3　radioisotopes
 　　　BT4　isotopes
 BT1　hours living radioisotopes
 　BT2　radioisotopes
 　　BT3　isotopes
 BT1　internal conversion radioisoto
 　BT2　radioisotopes
 　　BT3　isotopes
 BT1　lutetium isotopes
 BT1　odd-odd nuclei
 　BT2　nuclei
 BT1　rare earth nuclei
 　BT2　intermediate mass nuclei
 　　BT3　nuclei
 BT1　years living radioisotopes
 　BT2　radioisotopes
 　　BT3　isotopes

LUTETIUM 176 TARGET [70; 70]
 BT1　targets

LUTETIUM 177 [126; 126]
 BT1　beta-minus decay radioisotopes
 　BT2　beta decay radioisotopes
 　　BT3　radioisotopes
 　　　BT4　isotopes
 BT1　days living radioisotopes
 　BT2　radioisotopes
 　　BT3　isotopes
 BT1　isomeric transition isotopes
 　BT2　radioisotopes
 　　BT3　isotopes
 BT1　lutetium isotopes
 BT1　odd-even nuclei
 　BT2　nuclei
 BT1　rare earth nuclei
 　BT2　intermediate mass nuclei
 　　BT3　nuclei

LUTETIUM 178 [18; 18]
 BT1　beta-minus decay radioisotopes
 　BT2　beta decay radioisotopes
 　　BT3　radioisotopes
 　　　BT4　isotopes
 BT1　lutetium isotopes
 BT1　minutes living radioisotopes
 　BT2　radioisotopes
 　　BT3　isotopes
 BT1　odd-odd nuclei
 　BT2　nuclei
 BT1　rare earth nuclei
 　BT2　intermediate mass nuclei
 　　BT3　nuclei

LUTETIUM 179 [6; 6]
 BT1　beta-minus decay radioisotopes
 　BT2　beta decay radioisotopes
 　　BT3　radioisotopes
 　　　BT4　isotopes
 BT1　hours living radioisotopes
 　BT2　radioisotopes
 　　BT3　isotopes
 BT1　lutetium isotopes
 BT1　odd-even nuclei
 　BT2　nuclei
 BT1　rare earth nuclei
 　BT2　intermediate mass nuclei
 　　BT3　nuclei

LUTETIUM 180 [16; 16]
 BT1　beta-minus decay radioisotopes
 　BT2　beta decay radioisotopes
 　　BT3　radioisotopes
 　　　BT4　isotopes
 BT1　lutetium isotopes
 BT1　minutes living radioisotopes
 　BT2　radioisotopes
 　　BT3　isotopes
 BT1　odd-odd nuclei
 　BT2　nuclei
 BT1　rare earth nuclei
 　BT2　intermediate mass nuclei
 　　BT3　nuclei

LUTETIUM 181 [10; 10] *Jun 82*
 BT1　beta-minus decay radioisotopes
 　BT2　beta decay radioisotopes
 　　BT3　radioisotopes
 　　　BT4　isotopes
 BT1　heavy nuclei
 　BT2　nuclei
 BT1　lutetium isotopes
 BT1　minutes living radioisotopes
 　BT2　radioisotopes
 　　BT3　isotopes
 BT1　odd-even nuclei
 　BT2　nuclei
 BT1　rare earth nuclei
 　BT2　intermediate mass nuclei
 　　BT3　nuclei

LUTETIUM 182 [8; 8] *Jun 82*
 BT1　beta-minus decay radioisotopes
 　BT2　beta decay radioisotopes
 　　BT3　radioisotopes
 　　　BT4　isotopes
 BT1　heavy nuclei
 　BT2　nuclei
 BT1　lutetium isotopes
 BT1　minutes living radioisotopes
 　BT2　radioisotopes
 　　BT3　isotopes
 BT1　odd-odd nuclei
 　BT2　nuclei
 BT1　rare earth nuclei
 　BT2　intermediate mass nuclei
 　　BT3　nuclei

LUTETIUM 183 [6; 6] *Mar 83*
 BT1　beta-minus decay radioisotopes
 　BT2　beta decay radioisotopes
 　　BT3　radioisotopes
 　　　BT4　isotopes
 BT1　heavy nuclei
 　BT2　nuclei
 BT1　lutetium isotopes
 BT1　odd-even nuclei
 　BT2　nuclei
 BT1　rare earth nuclei
 　BT2　intermediate mass nuclei
 　　BT3　nuclei
 BT1　seconds living radioisotopes
 　BT2　radioisotopes
 　　BT3　isotopes

LUTETIUM 184 [4; 4] *Mar 88*
 BT1　beta-minus decay radioisotopes
 　BT2　beta decay radioisotopes
 　　BT3　radioisotopes
 　　　BT4　isotopes
 BT1　heavy nuclei
 　BT2　nuclei
 BT1　lutetium isotopes
 BT1　odd-odd nuclei
 　BT2　nuclei
 BT1　rare earth nuclei
 　BT2　intermediate mass nuclei
 　　BT3　nuclei
 BT1　seconds living radioisotopes
 　BT2　radioisotopes
 　　BT3　isotopes

LUXEMBOURG [67; 67]
 BT1　developed countries
 BT1　europe

LUXEMBURG EFFECT [2; 2]
 BT1　radiowave radiation
 　BT2　electromagnetic radiation
 　　BT3　radiations

LWBR TYPE REACTORS [480; 480]
 BT1　breeder reactors
 　BT2　reactors
 BT1　thermal reactors
 　BT2　reactors
 BT1　water cooled reactors
 　BT2　reactors
 BT1　water moderated reactors
 　BT2　reactors

LWGR TYPE REACTORS [550; 4,324]
 UF　*rbmk type reactors*
 UF　*water cooled graphite mod. rea*
 BT1　graphite moderated reactors
 　BT2　reactors
 BT1　water cooled reactors
 　BT2　reactors
 NT1　aps reactor
 NT1　beloyarsk-1 reactor

NT1 beloyarsk-2 reactor
NT1 bilibin reactor
NT1 chernobylsk-1 reactor
NT1 chernobylsk-2 reactor
NT1 chernobylsk-3 reactor
NT1 chernobylsk-4 reactor
NT1 ignalinsk-1 reactor
NT1 ignalinsk-2 reactor
NT1 kursk-1 reactor
NT1 kursk-2 reactor
NT1 kursk-3 reactor
NT1 kursk-4 reactor
NT1 leningrad-1 reactor
NT1 leningrad-2 reactor
NT1 leningrad-3 reactor
NT1 leningrad-4 reactor
NT1 n-reactor
NT1 rpt reactor
NT1 smolensk-1 reactor
NT1 smolensk-2 reactor
NT1 uwtr reactor
RT enriched uranium reactors
RT power reactors
RT thermal reactors

LWOR TYPE REACTORS [9; 9]
UF *water moderated organic cooled*
BT1 organic cooled reactors
BT2 reactors
BT1 water moderated reactors
BT2 reactors
RT power reactors

LYAPUNOV METHOD [254; 254]
UF *liapunov method*
RT differential equations
RT stability

LYASES [156; 759]
BT1 enzymes
BT2 organic compounds
NT1 carbon-carbon lyases
NT2 aldolases
NT2 decarboxylases
NT1 carbon-oxygen lyases
NT2 hyaluronidase
NT2 hydro-lyases
NT3 carbonic anhydrase
NT1 cyclases

lyman alpha emission
USE lyman lines

lyman alpha radiation
USE lyman lines

lyman continuum
USE lyman lines

LYMAN LINES [1,484; 1,484]
(Includes all aspects of the transitions associated with Lyman lines.)
UF *lyman alpha emission*
UF *lyman alpha radiation*
UF *lyman continuum*
UF *lyman series*
RT hydrogen
RT spectra

lyman series
USE lyman lines

LYMANTRIA DISPAR [7; 7]
UF *gypsy moth*
BT1 moths
BT2 lepidoptera
BT3 insects
BT4 arthropods
BT5 invertebrates
BT6 animals

LYMPH [127; 127]
BT1 body fluids
BT2 biological materials
BT3 materials
RT lymphatic system

LYMPH NODES [2,873; 2,873]
BT1 lymphatic system
RT lymph vessels
RT reticuloendothelial system

LYMPH VESSELS [327; 327]
UF *thoracic duct*
BT1 lymphatic system
RT angiomas
RT lymph nodes
RT veins

LYMPHATIC SYSTEM [844; 5,030]
UF+ *appendix (vermiform)*
UF+ *bursa of fabricius*
UF+ *tonsils*
NT1 lymph nodes
NT1 lymph vessels
NT1 thymus
RT cardiovascular system
RT leukemia
RT lungs
RT lymph
RT lymphocytes
RT lymphomas
RT organs
RT radiation syndrome
RT reticuloendothelial system
RT spleen
RT splenectomy

lymphoblastomas
USE lymphomas

LYMPHOCYTES [5,459; 5,459]
UF *lymphoid cells*
BT1 connective tissue cells
BT2 somatic cells
BT3 animal cells
BT1 leukocytes
BT2 blood cells
BT3 blood
BT4 body fluids
BT5 biological materials
BT6 materials
RT concanavalin a
RT hybridomas
RT immunity
RT lymphatic system
RT lymphokines
RT lymphomas
RT lymphopenia
RT phytohemagglutinin
RT plasma cells
RT radiation syndrome
RT thymus

lymphogranuloma malignum
USE hodgkins disease

lymphogranulomas
USE lymphomas

lymphogranulomatosis
USE hodgkins disease

lymphoid cells
USE lymphocytes

LYMPHOKINES [364; 364] *Dec 80*
(Biologically active molecules released from lymphocytes stimulated by antigens of mitogens.)
RT immunity
RT lymphocytes

LYMPHOMAS [1,861; 2,984]
UF *lymphoblastomas*
UF *lymphogranulomas*
BT1 immune system diseases
BT2 diseases
BT1 neoplasms
BT2 diseases
NT1 hodgkins disease
NT1 lymphosarcomas
RT lymphatic system
RT lymphocytes

LYMPHOPENIA [120; 120]
BT1 leukopenia
BT2 hemic diseases
BT3 diseases
BT2 immune system diseases
BT3 diseases
BT2 pathological changes
BT3 diseases
BT2 symptoms
RT lymphocytes

lymphopoiesis
USE leukopoiesis

LYMPHOSARCOMAS [195; 195]
BT1 lymphomas
BT2 immune system diseases
BT3 diseases
BT2 neoplasms
BT3 diseases
BT1 sarcomas
BT2 neoplasms
BT3 diseases

LYOLUMINESCENCE [177; 177] *Sep 77*
BT1 chemical radiation effects
BT2 radiation effects
BT1 luminescence
BT2 photon emission
BT3 emission
RT dosimetry

LYOPHILIZATION [217; 217]
UF *freeze-drying*
RT drying
RT freezing

LYSERGIC ACID [28; 28]
BT1 alkaloids
BT2 organic compounds
BT1 heterocyclic acids
BT2 carboxylic acids
BT3 organic acids
BT4 organic compounds
BT2 heterocyclic compounds
BT3 organic compounds
BT1 indoles
BT2 pyrroles
BT3 azoles
BT4 heterocyclic compounds
BT5 organic compounds
BT4 organic nitrogen compounds
BT5 organic compounds

LYSIMETERS [82; 82] *Jul 86*
(Devices for measuring the percolation of water through soils and for determining the soluble constituents removed in the drainage.)
BT1 measuring instruments

LYSINE [506; 506]
UF *diaminocaproic acid*
BT1 amino acids
BT2 carboxylic acids
BT3 organic acids
BT4 organic compounds

lysis
(The destruction of antigens by a specific lysin.)
USE decomposition

LYSOSOMES [380; 380]
  BT1   organoids
  BT2   cell constituents

LYSOZYME [170; 170]
  BT1   o-glycosyl hydrolases
  BT2   glycosyl hydrolases
  BT3   hydrolases
  BT4   enzymes
  BT5   organic compounds
  RT   mucoproteins
  RT   polysaccharides

M CAPTURE [22; 22] *Sep 79*
  BT1   electron capture decay
  BT2   beta decay
  BT3   nuclear decay
  BT4   decay

M CENTERS [102; 102]
  BT1   color centers
  BT2   vacancies
  BT3   point defects
  BT4   crystal defects
  BT5   crystal structure

M CODES [2,735; 2,735]
  BT1   computer codes

M CONVERSION [138; 138]
  UF   *m-conversion coefficient*
  BT1   internal conversion
  BT2   conversion
  BT2   nuclear decay
  BT3   decay

M SHELL [277; 277] *Jul 76*
(Atomic electron shells)
  UF   *atomic shells (m)*
  BT1   electronic structure

m+s configuration
  USE   mayer-schmidt configurations

m-conversion coefficient
  USE   m conversion

→ **MAANSHAN-1 REACTOR** [0; 0] *Oct 91*
(Taiwan, China)
  BT1   pwr type reactors
  BT2   enriched uranium reactors
  BT3   reactors
  BT2   power reactors
  BT3   reactors
  BT2   thermal reactors
  BT3   reactors
  BT2   water cooled reactors
  BT3   reactors
  BT2   water moderated reactors
  BT3   reactors

mac
  USE   maximum acceptable contaminati

macaca
  USE   macacus

MACACUS [210; 210]
  UF   *macaca*
  UF   *rhesus monkeys*
  BT1   monkeys
  BT2   primates
  BT3   mammals
  BT4   vertebrates
  BT5   animals

MACAO [0; 0]
  BT1   asia

MACH NUMBER [688; 688]
  BT1   velocity
  RT   aerodynamics
  RT   flow rate
  RT   shock waves

MACH PRINCIPLE [150; 150]
  BT1   hypothesis
  RT   general relativity theory
  RT   space-time

MACH-ZEHNDER INTERFEROMETER [110; 110]
  BT1   interferometers
  BT2   measuring instruments

MACHINE PARTS [531; 1,323]
  UF   *couplings (machine parts)*
  NT1   brakes
  NT1   gears
  NT1   mechanical shafts
  NT1   springs
  RT   castings
  RT   rotors
  RT   stators

MACHINE TOOLS [144; 243]
  NT1   grinding machines
  NT1   lathes
  NT1   milling machines
  RT   computer-aided manufacturing
  RT   drill bits
  RT   machining
  RT   presses
  RT   tools

machinery
  USE   equipment

MACHINING [398; 2,823]
  NT1   chemical machining
  NT2   electrochemical machining
  NT1   cutting
  NT1   electron beam machining
  NT1   grinding
  NT1   honing
  NT1   laser beam machining
  NT1   materials drilling
  NT2   laser drilling
  NT2   rock drilling
  NT1   milling
  NT1   spark machining
  NT1   ultrasonic machining
  RT   lathes
  RT   machine tools
  RT   materials working
  RT   surface finishing
  RT   tools

MACROPHAGES [871; 871]
  BT1   connective tissue cells
  BT2   somatic cells
  BT3   animal cells
  BT1   phagocytes
  BT2   somatic cells
  BT3   animal cells
  RT   phagocytosis
  RT   reticuloendothelial system
  RT   spleen

MADAGASCAR [17; 17]
  BT1   africa
  BT1   developing countries
  BT1   islands
  RT   indian ocean

MAGELLANIC CLOUDS [1,261; 1,261]
  BT1   galaxies

MAGIC NUCLEI [670; 670]
  UF   *magic numbers*
  BT1   nuclei
  RT   nuclear structure
  RT   stable isotopes

magic numbers
  USE   magic nuclei

magma
  USE   igneous rocks

MAGNESIUM [2,865; 2,865]
  BT1   alkaline earth metals
  BT2   metals
  BT3   elements

MAGNESIUM ADDITIONS [242; 255]
(Alloys containing not more than 1% Mg are listed here.)
  NT1   alloy-al95cu4
  RT   magnesium alloys
  RT   magnesium compounds

MAGNESIUM ALLOYS [686; 1,061]
(Alloys containing more than 1% Mg.)
  BT1   alloys
  NT1   magnesium base alloys
  NT2   magnox
  RT   magnesium additions

→ **MAGNESIUM ARSENIDES** [0; 0] *Sep 91*
  BT1   arsenides
  BT2   arsenic compounds
  BT2   pnictides
  BT1   magnesium compounds
  BT2   alkaline earth metal compounds

MAGNESIUM BASE ALLOYS [258; 352]
  BT1   magnesium alloys
  BT2   alloys
  NT1   magnox

MAGNESIUM BORIDES [19; 19]
  BT1   borides
  BT2   boron compounds
  BT1   magnesium compounds
  BT2   alkaline earth metal compounds

MAGNESIUM BROMIDES [19; 19]
  BT1   bromides
  BT2   bromine compounds
  BT3   halogen compounds
  BT2   halides
  BT3   halogen compounds
  BT1   magnesium compounds
  BT2   alkaline earth metal compounds

MAGNESIUM CARBIDES [2; 2]
  BT1   carbides
  BT2   carbon compounds
  BT1   magnesium compounds
  BT2   alkaline earth metal compounds

MAGNESIUM CARBONATES [42; 175]
  BT1   carbonates
  BT2   carbon compounds
  BT2   oxygen compounds
  BT1   magnesium compounds
  BT2   alkaline earth metal compounds
  RT   bayleyite
  RT   carbonate minerals
  RT   dolomite
  RT   limestone

MAGNESIUM CHLORIDES [361; 379]
  BT1   chlorides
  BT2   chlorine compounds
  BT3   halogen compounds
  BT2   halides
  BT3   halogen compounds
  BT1   magnesium compounds
  BT2   alkaline earth metal compounds
  RT   carnallite
  RT   halide minerals

MAGNESIUM COMPLEXES [68; 68]
BT1 alkaline earth metal complexes
BT2 complexes

MAGNESIUM COMPOUNDS
[921; 4,852]
BT1 alkaline earth metal compounds
NT1 grignard reagents
NT1 magnesium arsenides
NT1 magnesium borides
NT1 magnesium bromides
NT1 magnesium carbides
NT1 magnesium carbonates
NT1 magnesium chlorides
NT1 magnesium fluorides
NT1 magnesium hydrides
NT1 magnesium hydroxides
NT1 magnesium iodides
NT1 magnesium nitrates
NT1 magnesium nitrides
NT1 magnesium oxides
NT1 magnesium perchlorates
NT1 magnesium phosphates
NT1 magnesium silicates
NT1 magnesium silicides
NT1 magnesium sulfates
NT1 magnesium sulfides
NT1 magnesium tellurides
RT magnesium additions

MAGNESIUM FLUORIDES [288; 288]
BT1 fluorides
BT2 fluorine compounds
BT3 halogen compounds
BT2 halides
BT3 halogen compounds
BT1 magnesium compounds
BT2 alkaline earth metal compounds

MAGNESIUM HYDRIDES [60; 60]
BT1 hydrides
BT2 hydrogen compounds
BT1 magnesium compounds
BT2 alkaline earth metal compounds

MAGNESIUM HYDROXIDES [100; 100]
BT1 hydroxides
BT2 hydrogen compounds
BT2 oxygen compounds
BT1 magnesium compounds
BT2 alkaline earth metal compounds

MAGNESIUM IODIDES [26; 26]
BT1 iodides
BT2 halides
BT3 halogen compounds
BT2 iodine compounds
BT3 halogen compounds
BT1 magnesium compounds
BT2 alkaline earth metal compounds

MAGNESIUM IONS [716; 716]
BT1 ions
BT2 charged particles

MAGNESIUM ISOTOPES [183; 2,900]
NT1 magnesium 20
NT1 magnesium 21
NT1 magnesium 22
NT1 magnesium 23
NT1 magnesium 24
NT1 magnesium 25
NT1 magnesium 26
NT1 magnesium 27
NT1 magnesium 28
NT1 magnesium 29
NT1 magnesium 30
NT1 magnesium 31
NT1 magnesium 32
NT1 magnesium 33
NT1 magnesium 34
NT1 magnesium 35
NT1 magnesium 36

MAGNESIUM NITRATES [125; 125]
BT1 magnesium compounds
BT2 alkaline earth metal compounds
BT1 nitrates
BT2 nitrogen compounds
BT2 oxygen compounds

MAGNESIUM NITRIDES [12; 12]
BT1 magnesium compounds
BT2 alkaline earth metal compounds
BT1 nitrides
BT2 nitrogen compounds
BT2 pnictides

MAGNESIUM OXIDES [2,100; 2,329]
BT1 magnesium compounds
BT2 alkaline earth metal compounds
BT1 oxides
BT2 chalcogenides
BT2 oxygen compounds
RT oxide minerals
RT spinels

MAGNESIUM PERCHLORATES
[20; 20]
BT1 magnesium compounds
BT2 alkaline earth metal compounds
BT1 perchlorates
BT2 chlorine compounds
BT3 halogen compounds
BT2 oxygen compounds

MAGNESIUM PHOSPHATES [26; 30]
BT1 magnesium compounds
BT2 alkaline earth metal compounds
BT1 phosphates
BT2 oxygen compounds
BT2 phosphorus compounds
RT phosphate minerals
RT saleeite

MAGNESIUM SILICATES [165; 309]
UF *enstatite*
BT1 magnesium compounds
BT2 alkaline earth metal compounds
BT1 silicates
BT2 oxygen compounds
BT2 silicon compounds
RT lava
RT olivine
RT silicate minerals
RT talc
RT vermiculite

MAGNESIUM SILICIDES [14; 14]
Oct 76
BT1 magnesium compounds
BT2 alkaline earth metal compounds
BT1 silicides
BT2 silicon compounds

MAGNESIUM SULFATES [91; 93]
BT1 magnesium compounds
BT2 alkaline earth metal compounds
BT1 sulfates
BT2 oxygen compounds
BT2 sulfur compounds
RT polyhalite
RT sulfate minerals

MAGNESIUM SULFIDES [18; 18]
BT1 magnesium compounds
BT2 alkaline earth metal compounds
BT1 sulfides
BT2 chalcogenides
BT2 sulfur compounds

→ **MAGNESIUM TELLURIDES** [0; 0]
Sep 91
BT1 magnesium compounds
BT2 alkaline earth metal compounds
BT1 tellurides
BT2 chalcogenides
BT2 tellurium compounds

MAGNESIUM 20 [13; 13]
BT1 beta-plus decay radioisotopes
BT2 beta decay radioisotopes
BT3 radioisotopes
BT4 isotopes
BT1 even-even nuclei
BT2 nuclei
BT1 light nuclei
BT2 nuclei
BT1 magnesium isotopes
BT1 millisec living radioisotopes
BT2 radioisotopes
BT3 isotopes

MAGNESIUM 21 [14; 14]
BT1 beta-plus decay radioisotopes
BT2 beta decay radioisotopes
BT3 radioisotopes
BT4 isotopes
BT1 even-odd nuclei
BT2 nuclei
BT1 light nuclei
BT2 nuclei
BT1 magnesium isotopes
BT1 millisec living radioisotopes
BT2 radioisotopes
BT3 isotopes

MAGNESIUM 22 [34; 34]
BT1 beta-plus decay radioisotopes
BT2 beta decay radioisotopes
BT3 radioisotopes
BT4 isotopes
BT1 even-even nuclei
BT2 nuclei
BT1 light nuclei
BT2 nuclei
BT1 magnesium isotopes
BT1 seconds living radioisotopes
BT2 radioisotopes
BT3 isotopes

MAGNESIUM 23 [105; 105]
BT1 beta-plus decay radioisotopes
BT2 beta decay radioisotopes
BT3 radioisotopes
BT4 isotopes
BT1 even-odd nuclei
BT2 nuclei
BT1 light nuclei
BT2 nuclei
BT1 magnesium isotopes
BT1 seconds living radioisotopes
BT2 radioisotopes
BT3 isotopes

MAGNESIUM 23 TARGET [9; 9]
Apr 76
BT1 targets

MAGNESIUM 24 [1,633; 1,633]
BT1 even-even nuclei
BT2 nuclei
BT1 light nuclei
BT2 nuclei
BT1 magnesium isotopes
BT1 stable isotopes
BT2 isotopes
RT magnesium 24 beams

MAGNESIUM 24 BEAMS [35; 35]
Jan 76
BT1 ion beams
BT2 beams
RT magnesium 24

MAGNESIUM 24 REACTIONS
[213; 213]
BT1 heavy ion reactions
BT2 nuclear reactions

MAGNESIUM 24 TARGET
[1,250; 1,250]
BT1 targets

MAGNESIUM 25 [366; 366]
 BT1 even-odd nuclei
 BT2 nuclei
 BT1 light nuclei
 BT2 nuclei
 BT1 magnesium isotopes
 BT1 stable isotopes
 BT2 isotopes

MAGNESIUM 25 REACTIONS [7; 7]
 Apr 82
 BT1 heavy ion reactions
 BT2 nuclear reactions

MAGNESIUM 25 TARGET [239; 239]
 BT1 targets

MAGNESIUM 26 [558; 558]
 BT1 even-even nuclei
 BT2 nuclei
 BT1 light nuclei
 BT2 nuclei
 BT1 magnesium isotopes
 BT1 stable isotopes
 BT2 isotopes

MAGNESIUM 26 REACTIONS [29; 29]
 Jun 82
 BT1 heavy ion reactions
 BT2 nuclear reactions

MAGNESIUM 26 TARGET [684; 684]
 BT1 targets

MAGNESIUM 27 [166; 166]
 BT1 beta-minus decay radioisotopes
 BT2 beta decay radioisotopes
 BT3 radioisotopes
 BT4 isotopes
 BT1 even-odd nuclei
 BT2 nuclei
 BT1 light nuclei
 BT2 nuclei
 BT1 magnesium isotopes
 BT1 minutes living radioisotopes
 BT2 radioisotopes
 BT3 isotopes

MAGNESIUM 27 TARGET [2; 2]
 Apr 79
 BT1 targets

MAGNESIUM 28 [162; 162]
 BT1 beta-minus decay radioisotopes
 BT2 beta decay radioisotopes
 BT3 radioisotopes
 BT4 isotopes
 BT1 even-even nuclei
 BT2 nuclei
 BT1 hours living radioisotopes
 BT2 radioisotopes
 BT3 isotopes
 BT1 light nuclei
 BT2 nuclei
 BT1 magnesium isotopes
 RT radioisotope generators

MAGNESIUM 28 DECAY RADIOISOTOP [0; 138] *Jan 90*
 BT1 heavy ion decay radioisotopes
 BT2 radioisotopes
 BT3 isotopes
 NT1 plutonium 236
 NT1 uranium 234
 RT magnesium 28 emission decay

MAGNESIUM 28 EMISSION DECAY
 [2; 2] *Jan 90*
 BT1 heavy ion emission decay
 BT2 nuclear decay
 BT3 decay
 RT magnesium 28 decay radioisotop

MAGNESIUM 29 [32; 32]
 BT1 beta-minus decay radioisotopes
 BT2 beta decay radioisotopes
 BT3 radioisotopes
 BT4 isotopes
 BT1 even-odd nuclei
 BT2 nuclei
 BT1 light nuclei
 BT2 nuclei
 BT1 magnesium isotopes
 BT1 seconds living radioisotopes
 BT2 radioisotopes
 BT3 isotopes

MAGNESIUM 30 [27; 27]
 BT1 beta-minus decay radioisotopes
 BT2 beta decay radioisotopes
 BT3 radioisotopes
 BT4 isotopes
 BT1 even-even nuclei
 BT2 nuclei
 BT1 light nuclei
 BT2 nuclei
 BT1 magnesium isotopes
 BT1 millisec living radioisotopes
 BT2 radioisotopes
 BT3 isotopes

MAGNESIUM 30 EMISSION DECAY
 [0; 0] *Oct 89*
 BT1 heavy ion emission decay
 BT2 nuclear decay
 BT3 decay

MAGNESIUM 31 [20; 20]
 BT1 beta-minus decay radioisotopes
 BT2 beta decay radioisotopes
 BT3 radioisotopes
 BT4 isotopes
 BT1 even-odd nuclei
 BT2 nuclei
 BT1 light nuclei
 BT2 nuclei
 BT1 magnesium isotopes
 BT1 millisec living radioisotopes
 BT2 radioisotopes
 BT3 isotopes

MAGNESIUM 32 [23; 23] *Oct 77*
 BT1 beta-minus decay radioisotopes
 BT2 beta decay radioisotopes
 BT3 radioisotopes
 BT4 isotopes
 BT1 even-even nuclei
 BT2 nuclei
 BT1 light nuclei
 BT2 nuclei
 BT1 magnesium isotopes

MAGNESIUM 33 [7; 7] *Jul 80*
 BT1 beta-minus decay radioisotopes
 BT2 beta decay radioisotopes
 BT3 radioisotopes
 BT4 isotopes
 BT1 even-odd nuclei
 BT2 nuclei
 BT1 light nuclei
 BT2 nuclei
 BT1 magnesium isotopes

MAGNESIUM 34 [5; 5] *Jul 80*
 BT1 beta-minus decay radioisotopes
 BT2 beta decay radioisotopes
 BT3 radioisotopes
 BT4 isotopes
 BT1 even-even nuclei
 BT2 nuclei
 BT1 light nuclei
 BT2 nuclei
 BT1 magnesium isotopes

MAGNESIUM 35 [2; 2] *Sep 89*
 BT1 even-odd nuclei
 BT2 nuclei
 BT1 light nuclei
 BT2 nuclei
 BT1 magnesium isotopes

MAGNESIUM 36 [2; 2] *Sep 89*
 BT1 even-even nuclei
 BT2 nuclei
 BT1 light nuclei
 BT2 nuclei
 BT1 magnesium isotopes

MAGNET COILS [4,977; 5,201]
 UF *coils (magnetic)*
 UF *magnetic coils*
 BT1 electric coils
 BT2 electrical equipment
 BT3 equipment
 NT1 pulsed magnet coils
 RT magnets
 RT septum magnets
 RT solenoids
 RT superconducting coils
 RT superconducting magnets

MAGNET CORES [169; 169]
 UF *cores (magnet)*
 RT magnet pole pieces
 RT magnets

MAGNET POLE PIECES [230; 230]
 RT magnet cores
 RT magnets

MAGNETIC AMPLIFIERS [11; 11]
 BT1 amplifiers
 BT2 equipment
 BT1 electronic equipment
 BT2 equipment

MAGNETIC ANALYZERS [328; 328]
 BT1 beam analyzers
 RT beam bending magnets
 RT electromagnetic lenses
 RT electrostatic septa
 RT septum magnets

MAGNETIC BALANCES [11; 11]
 UF *balances (magnetic)*
 BT1 measuring instruments
 RT magnetic susceptibility

MAGNETIC BAYS [821; 821]
 UF *auroral substorms*
 UF *bays (magnetic)*
 UF *polar substorms*
 RT magnetic storms

MAGNETIC BEARINGS [41; 41]
 BT1 bearings

magnetic bremsstrahlung
 USE synchrotron radiation

MAGNETIC CIRCUITS [126; 126]
 UF *circuits (magnetic)*
 RT electric coils

magnetic coils
 USE magnet coils

MAGNETIC COMPRESSION [683; 683]
 BT1 compression
 RT linus reactors
 RT magnetic fields
 RT pinch effect

MAGNETIC CONFINEMENT [856; 856]
 Nov 82
 BT1 plasma confinement
 BT2 confinement
 RT electron rings
 RT ion rings
 RT magnetic field configurations
 RT rotational transform

MAGNETIC CORES [84; 84]
(For the storage of information in machine-readable form only.)
UF   *cores (magnetic)*
BT1   magnetic storage devices
BT2   memory devices
RT   computers

MAGNETIC DIPOLE MOMENTS
[1,879; 1,879]
BT1   dipole moments
BT1   magnetic moments
RT   nuclear magnetic moments

magnetic dipole transitions
USE m1-transitions

MAGNETIC DIPOLES [1,386; 1,386]
BT1   dipoles
BT2   multipoles
RT   magnetic fields

MAGNETIC DISKS [172; 172]
UF   *disks (magnetic)*
BT1   magnetic storage devices
BT2   memory devices

MAGNETIC DRUMS [13; 13]
BT1   magnetic storage devices
BT2   memory devices

MAGNETIC FIELD CONFIGURATIONS [3,975; 8,660]
(For pinch configurations, use the narrower terms of PINCH EFFECT.)
NT1   closed configurations
NT2   mayer-schmidt configurations
NT2   minimum average-b configuratio
NT2   multipolar configurations
NT3   hexapolar configurations
NT3   octupolar configurations
NT3   quadrupolar configurations
NT2   toroidal configuration
NT1   magnetic field reversal
NT1   magnetic field ripples
NT1   magnetic islands
NT1   magnetic surfaces
NT2   mode rational surfaces
NT1   open configurations
NT2   baseball seam configurations
NT2   cusped geometries
NT2   magnetic mirror configurations
NT3   tlm configurations
NT2   minimum-b configurations
RT   divertors
RT   helical configuration
RT   magnetic confinement
RT   magnetic fields
RT   magnetic reconnection
RT   pinch effect
RT   plasma
RT   rotational transform
RT   thermonuclear devices

MAGNETIC FIELD REVERSAL
[467; 467] *Aug 81*
BT1   magnetic field configurations
RT   magnetic fields
RT   magnetic reconnection
RT   reverse-field pinch
RT   reversed-field mirrors

MAGNETIC FIELD RIPPLES [236; 236]
Jul 81
BT1   magnetic field configurations
RT   magnetic fields
RT   plasma

MAGNETIC FIELDS [45,991; 53,617]
UF   *external magnetic fields*
UF   *fields (magnetic)*
UF+ *magnetic shielding*
UF+ *magnetoelectricity*
UF+ *photoelectromagnetic effect*
UF+ *photomagnetoelectric effect*
NT1   critical field
NT1   force-free magnetic fields
NT1   geomagnetic field
NT1   interplanetary magnetic fields
NT1   interstellar magnetic fields
RT   beta ratio
RT   biot-savart law
RT   crossed fields
RT   demagnetization
RT   electromagnetic fields
RT   end effects
RT   faraday method
RT   galvanomagnetic effect
RT   guiding-center approximation
RT   inhomogeneous fields
RT   langevin equation
RT   larmor radius
RT   levitation
RT   magnetic compression
RT   magnetic dipoles
RT   magnetic field configurations
RT   magnetic field reversal
RT   magnetic field ripples
RT   magnetic flux
RT   magnetic islands
RT   magnetic mirror configurations
RT   magnetic mirrors
RT   magnetic properties
RT   magnetic rigidity
RT   magnetism
RT   magnetization
RT   magneto-thermal effects
RT   mirror ratio
RT   righi-leduc effect
RT   rotational transform
RT   shear
RT   shubnikov-de haas effect
RT   stoermer theory
RT   tlm configurations
RT   trapping
RT   zeeman effect

MAGNETIC FILTERS [89; 89] *Mar 83*
UF   *magnetic separators*
BT1   filters

MAGNETIC FLUX [5,498; 5,498]
UF   *flux (magnetic)*
UF   *flux jumps*
UF   *flux pinning*
UF   *fluxoids*
UF   *magnetic vortices*
UF   *pinning force*
UF   *vortices (magnetic)*
RT   aharonov-bohm effect
RT   flux density
RT   flux quantization
RT   magnetic fields
RT   skin effect

MAGNETIC FLUX COORDINATES
[42; 42] *Nov 88*
(A coordinate system for a toroidally confined plasma in which the radial coordinate is defined by the magnetic flux contained within a given magnetic flux surface.)
BT1   curvilinear coordinates
BT2   coordinates
RT   magnetic surfaces
RT   plasma radial profiles
RT   rotational transform

MAGNETIC FORCE WELDING [11; 11]
BT1   welding
BT2   joining
BT3   fabrication
RT   magnetic forming

MAGNETIC FORMING [5; 5]
BT1   materials working
BT2   fabrication
RT   magnetic force welding

MAGNETIC GRADIENT ACCELERATORS [24; 24] *Oct 82*
(Type of macroparticle accelerator which uses a high-gradient magnetic field to accelerate a projectile. The magnetic field motion of the accelerator is synchronized with the projectile.)
BT1   impact fusion drivers
RT   impact fusion

magnetic hexadecapole transiti
USE m4-transitions

MAGNETIC INSULATION [337; 337]
(Insulation of electric fields by means of magnetic fields; not for insulation of the magnetic fields themselves.)
UF   *insulation (electr.,by mag.f.)*
RT   confinement
RT   thermionic diodes

MAGNETIC ISLANDS [512; 512] *Jul 81*
BT1   magnetic field configurations
RT   magnetic fields
RT   plasma

MAGNETIC LENS SPECTROMETERS
[211; 211]
UF   *intermediate image spectrome*
UF   *long-lens spectrometers*
UF   *short-lens spectrometers*
UF   *slatis-siegbahn spectrometers*
BT1   magnetic spectrometers
BT2   spectrometers
BT3   measuring instruments

MAGNETIC MATERIALS [869; 5,718]
BT1   materials
NT1   antiferromagnetic materials
NT1   ferrimagnetic materials
NT2   ferrites
NT1   ferromagnetic materials
RT   magnetism

MAGNETIC MIRROR CONFIGURATIONS [546; 555]
BT1   open configurations
BT2   magnetic field configurations
NT1   tlm configurations
RT   magnetic fields
RT   magnetic mirrors
RT   mirror ratio
RT   plasma potential

MAGNETIC MIRRORS [2,330; 5,147]
(Including systems with minimum-B configuration.)
UF   *mirrors (magnetic)*
BT1   open plasma devices
BT2   thermonuclear devices
NT1   alice
NT1   aspa device
NT1   beta ii devices
NT1   bsg devices
NT1   bumpy tori
NT2   elmo bumpy torus
NT1   burnout devices
NT1   circe devices
NT2   circe-25kw device
NT1   dcx devices
NT1   deca devices
NT1   elmo devices
NT2   elmo bumpy torus
NT1   imp device
NT1   interem device
NT1   mftf devices
NT1   ogra
NT1   phoenix devices
NT1   pleiade device
NT1   pr devices
NT2   pr-6 device
NT2   pr-7 device
NT2   pr-8 device
NT1   reversed-field mirrors
NT1   tandem mirrors
NT2   gamma 10 devices
NT2   phaedrus mirror devices

MAGNETIC MIRRORS

NT2   tara devices
NT2   tmx devices
NT1   vgl devices
NT1   2x devices
RT   magnetic fields
RT   magnetic mirror configurations
RT   mirror ratio
RT   plasma potential
RT   q devices
RT   tlm configurations
RT   tmr reactors

MAGNETIC MOMENTS [6,422; 15,013]
NT1   magnetic dipole moments
NT1   magnetization
NT1   nuclear magnetic moments
RT   fermi-segre formula
RT   gyromagnetic ratio
RT   magnetism
RT   quadrupole moments

MAGNETIC MONOPOLES
[2,085; 2,085]
UF   *dirac monopoles*
BT1   monopoles
BT1   postulated particles
  BT2   elementary particles

magnetic octupole transitions
USE   m3-transitions

magnetic permeability
USE   magnetic susceptibility

MAGNETIC PROBES [594; 594]
BT1   probes
RT   magnetometers

MAGNETIC PROPERTIES
[6,800; 19,206]
BT1   physical properties
NT1   magnetic susceptibility
NT1   magnetization
NT1   magnetostriction
RT   abrikosov theory
RT   coercive force
RT   domain structure
RT   electrical properties
RT   electromagnets
RT   magnetic fields
RT   magnetism
RT   magneto-optical effects
RT   muon spin relaxation
RT   permanent magnets

magnetic quadrupole transition
USE   m2-transitions

MAGNETIC RECONNECTION
[342; 342] *Mar 87*
(A topological rearrangement of the magnetic field lines surrounding a plasma.)
RT   magnetic field configurations
RT   magnetic field reversal
RT   sawtooth oscillations

MAGNETIC REFRIGERATORS [94; 94]
Aug 78
BT1   refrigerators
RT   cryogenics
RT   cryostats
RT   refrigeration

MAGNETIC RESONANCE [890; 21,623]
UF+   *ambr method*
BT1   resonance
NT1   eldor
NT1   electron spin resonance
  NT2   acoustic esr
NT1   endor
NT1   ferrimagnetic resonance
NT1   ferromagnetic resonance
NT1   nuclear magnetic resonance
  NT2   acoustic nmr

RT   bloch equations
RT   muon spin relaxation

MAGNETIC REYNOLDS NUMBER
[227; 227]
BT1   reynolds number
RT   magnetohydrodynamics

MAGNETIC RIGIDITY [156; 156]
RT   magnetic fields
RT   stratosphere

MAGNETIC SEMICONDUCTORS
[228; 228] *Jan 76*
BT1   semiconductor materials
  BT2   materials
RT   ferromagnetic materials

magnetic separators
USE   magnetic filters

magnetic shielding
USE   magnetic fields
AND   shielding

MAGNETIC SPECTROMETERS
[2,022; 2,476]
BT1   spectrometers
  BT2   measuring instruments
NT1   flat magnetic spectrometers
NT1   magnetic lens spectrometers

MAGNETIC STARS [672; 672]
UF   *peculiar a-stars*
BT1   stars
RT   stellar magnetospheres
RT   variable stars

MAGNETIC STORAGE DEVICES
[108; 784]
BT1   memory devices
NT1   magnetic cores
NT1   magnetic disks
NT1   magnetic drums
NT1   magnetic tapes
  NT2   video tapes

MAGNETIC STORMS [1,752; 1,752]
UF   *geomagnetic storms*
RT   disturbances
RT   earth magnetosphere
RT   forbush decrease
RT   magnetic bays
RT   sudden commencements

MAGNETIC SURFACES [1,013; 1,018]
UF   *flux surfaces*
BT1   magnetic field configurations
NT1   mode rational surfaces
RT   divertors
RT   equilibrium plasma
RT   magnetic flux coordinates
RT   plasma confinement
RT   plasma radial profiles
RT   rotational transform
RT   stellarators
RT   tokamak devices

MAGNETIC SURVEYS [780; 782]
Jan 79
BT1   geophysical surveys
  BT2   geologic surveys
RT   aerial monitoring
RT   aerial prospecting
RT   aerial surveying
RT   exploration

§ MAGNETIC SUSCEPTIBILITY
[7,939; 7,939]
UF   *magnetic permeability*
UF   *permeability (magnetic)*
UF   *susceptibility (magnetic)*
UF+   *photomagnetic effect*
BT1   magnetic properties

  BT2   physical properties
RT   curie point
RT   curie-weiss law
RT   magnetic balances
RT   neel temperature

MAGNETIC TAPES [321; 462]
BT1   magnetic storage devices
  BT2   memory devices
NT1   video tapes

MAGNETIC TESTING [204; 204]
BT1   nondestructive testing
  BT2   materials testing
    BT3   testing

magnetic traps (closed)
USE   closed configurations

magnetic traps (open)
USE   open configurations

magnetic vortices
USE   magnetic flux

magnetic well
USE   minimum-b configurations

MAGNETIC-PUMPING HEATING
[67; 249]
BT1   high-frequency heating
  BT2   plasma heating
    BT3   heating
NT1   acoustic heating
NT1   collisional heating
NT1   transit-time magnetic pumping

MAGNETISM [1,105; 8,462]
NT1   antiferromagnetism
NT1   diamagnetism
  NT2   plasma diamagnetism
NT1   electromagnetism
NT1   ferrimagnetism
NT1   ferromagnetism
NT1   nuclear magnetism
NT1   paramagnetism
NT1   superparamagnetism
NT1   thermomagnetism
RT   adiabatic demagnetization
RT   demagnetization
RT   magnetic fields
RT   magnetic materials
RT   magnetic moments
RT   magnetic properties
RT   magnetization
RT   magnets
RT   spin glass state

MAGNETITE [504; 504]
BT1   iron ores
  BT2   ores
BT1   oxide minerals
  BT2   minerals
RT   black sands
RT   ferrite
RT   iron oxides
RT   spinels

§ MAGNETIZATION [5,922; 5,922] *Feb 76*
(Magnetic moment of unit volume of a material.)
BT1   magnetic moments
BT1   magnetic properties
  BT2   physical properties
RT   magnetic fields
RT   magnetism

MAGNETO-OPTICAL EFFECTS
[555; 607]
NT1   voigt effect
RT   electro-optical effects
RT   faraday effect

RT kerr effect
RT magnetic properties
RT optical properties
RT stark effect
RT zeeman effect

MAGNETO-THERMAL EFFECTS
[68; 68] Oct 75
RT magnetic fields

MAGNETOACOUSTIC WAVES
[746; 859]
UF *magnetosonic waves*
BT1 hydromagnetic waves
NT1 fast magnetoacoustic waves
RT magnetoacoustics

MAGNETOACOUSTICS [109; 109]
RT hydromagnetic waves
RT magnetoacoustic waves
RT sound waves

magnetoelectricity
(Appearance of an electric field in certain substances when they are subjected to a static magnetic field.)
USE electrical properties
AND magnetic fields

MAGNETOGASDYNAMICS [153; 153]
BT1 fluid mechanics
BT2 mechanics
RT gas flow
RT magnetohydrodynamics

magnetohydrodynamic channels
USE mhd channels

magnetohydrodynamic generators
USE mhd generators

magnetohydrodynamic waves
USE hydromagnetic waves

MAGNETOHYDRODYNAMICS
[7,606; 7,606]
BT1 hydrodynamics
BT2 fluid mechanics
BT3 mechanics
RT direct energy conversion
RT fluid flow
RT hartmann number
RT magnetic reynolds number
RT magnetogasdynamics
RT mercier criterion
RT mhd equilibrium
RT mhd generators
RT plasma
RT plasma fluid equations

MAGNETOINDUCTION SENSORS
[72; 72]
BT1 beam monitors
BT2 monitors
BT3 measuring instruments
RT beam monitoring

MAGNETOMETERS [689; 798]
BT1 measuring instruments
NT1 fluxgate magnetometers
NT1 moving coil magnetometers
NT1 proton precession magnetometer
NT1 vibrating sample magnetometers
RT fluxmeters
RT magnetic probes

MAGNETOPAUSE [769; 769]
RT earth magnetosphere
RT international magnetospheric s
RT magnetosheath

MAGNETOPLASMA COMPRESSORS
[26; 26]
BT1 compressors

MAGNETORESISTANCE [1,101; 1,101]
BT1 electric conductivity
BT2 electrical properties
BT3 physical properties
RT shubnikov-de haas effect

MAGNETOSHEATH [465; 465]
RT earth magnetosphere
RT geomagnetic field
RT international magnetospheric s
RT magnetopause
RT solar wind

magnetosonic waves
USE magnetoacoustic waves

magnetosphere (earth)
USE earth magnetosphere

magnetospheres (planetary)
USE planetary magnetospheres

magnetospheres (stellar)
USE stellar magnetospheres

MAGNETOSTRICTION [891; 891]
UF *electromagnetostriction*
BT1 magnetic properties
BT2 physical properties
RT deformation

MAGNETOTAIL [976; 976]
RT earth magnetosphere
RT geomagnetic field
RT international magnetospheric s
RT plasma sheet
RT plasmapause
RT plasmasphere

MAGNETOTELLURIC SURVEYS
[20; 20] Feb 79
(The measurement of natural electrical and magnetic fields of the earth.)
BT1 electromagnetic surveys
BT2 electrical surveys
BT3 geophysical surveys
BT4 geologic surveys

MAGNETRONS [757; 757]
BT1 microwave tubes
BT2 electron tubes
BT2 microwave equipment
BT3 electronic equipment
BT4 equipment
RT klystrons
RT rf systems

MAGNETS [1,824; 13,719]
BT1 equipment
NT1 beam bending magnets
NT1 beam focusing magnets
NT1 electromagnets
NT2 superconducting magnets
NT1 kicker magnets
NT1 permanent magnets
NT1 septum magnets
NT1 wiggler magnets
RT demagnetization
RT electromagnetic lenses
RT magnet coils
RT magnet cores
RT magnet pole pieces
RT magnetism

MAGNONS [612; 612]
BT1 quasi particles
RT spin waves

MAGNOX [94; 94]
BT1 magnesium base alloys
BT2 magnesium alloys
BT3 alloys
RT magnox type reactors

MAGNOX TYPE REACTORS [537; 846]
BT1 gcr type reactors
BT2 gas cooled reactors
BT3 reactors
BT2 graphite moderated reactors
BT3 reactors
BT1 natural uranium reactors
BT2 reactors
BT1 power reactors
BT2 reactors
NT1 berkeley reactor
NT1 bradwell reactor
NT1 calder hall a-1 reactor
NT1 calder hall a-2 reactor
NT1 calder hall b-3 reactor
NT1 calder hall b-4 reactor
NT1 chapelcross-1 reactor
NT1 chapelcross-2 reactor
NT1 chapelcross-3 reactor
NT1 chapelcross-4 reactor
NT1 dungeness-a reactor
NT1 hinkley point-a reactor
NT1 hunterston-a reactor
NT1 latina reactor
NT1 oldbury-a reactor
NT1 sizewell-a reactor
NT1 tokai-mura reactor
NT1 trawsfynydd reactor
NT1 wylfa reactor
RT magnox

mahogany trees
USE trees

MAIN SEQUENCE STARS [1,595; 5,010]
BT1 stars
NT1 carbon stars
NT1 sun
NT1 wolf-rayet stars
RT cno cycle
RT hydrogen burning

MAINE [131; 131]
BT1 usa
BT2 developed countries
BT2 north america

MAINE YANKEE REACTOR [162; 162]
(Wiscasset, Maine, USA)
UF *atomic power co. main yankee*
UF *yankee maine reactor*
BT1 pwr type reactors
BT2 enriched uranium reactors
BT3 reactors
BT2 power reactors
BT3 reactors
BT2 thermal reactors
BT3 reactors
BT2 water cooled reactors
BT3 reactors
BT2 water moderated reactors
BT3 reactors

MAINTENANCE [3,340; 7,269]
NT1 reactor maintenance
RT modifications
RT operation
RT outages
RT repair

mainz triga-mk-2 reactor
USE triga-2-mainz reactor

MAIZE [928; 928]
  UF   corn (maize)
  UF   zea mays
  BT1   cereals
    BT2   gramineae
      BT3   plants

maize oil
  USE corn oil

MAJORANA THEORY [830; 830]
  RT   binding energy

maki parameter
  USE ginzburg-landau theory

MALARIA [75; 75]
  BT1   hemic diseases
    BT2   diseases
  BT1   parasitic diseases
    BT2   infectious diseases
      BT3   diseases
  RT   mosquitoes
  RT   plasmodium

MALATHION [55; 55]
  BT1   carboxylic acid esters
    BT2   esters
      BT3   organic compounds
  BT1   insecticides
    BT2   pesticides
  BT1   organic oxygen compounds
    BT2   organic compounds
  BT1   organic phosphorus compounds
    BT2   organic compounds
  BT1   thiols
    BT2   organic sulfur compounds
      BT3   organic compounds

MALAWI [3; 3]
  BT1   africa
  BT1   developing countries

malaya
  USE malaysia

MALAYSIA [118; 118]
  UF   federation of malaya
  UF   malaya
  BT1   asia
  BT1   developing countries

MALAYSIAN ORGANIZATIONS [2; 57] Dec 84
  BT1   national organizations
  NT1   puspati

MALE GENITALS [308; 2,854]
  UF   genitals (male)
  UF   seminal vesicles
  BT1   organs
    BT2   body
  NT1   prostate
  NT1   testes
  RT   fertility
  RT   gonads
  RT   reproduction
  RT   sex
  RT   urogenital system diseases

MALEIC ACID [194; 194]
  UF   maleinic acid
  BT1   dicarboxylic acids
    BT2   carboxylic acids
      BT3   organic acids
        BT4   organic compounds

maleinic acid
  USE maleic acid

MALES [1,546; 2,246]
  NT1   men
  RT   animals
  RT   sex
  RT   sex dependence

MALFORMATIONS [1,457; 3,012]
  UF   abnormalities (developmental)
  UF   hydrocephalus
  UF   microcephaly
  BT1   pathological changes
    BT2   diseases
  NT1   congenital malformations
    NT2   downs syndrome

MALI [11; 11] *Jul 76*
  BT1   africa
  BT1   developing countries

MALIC ACID [108; 108]
  UF   hydroxysuccinic acid
  BT1   hydroxy acids
    BT2   carboxylic acids
      BT3   organic acids
        BT4   organic compounds

malnutrition
  USE nutritional deficiency

MALONIC ACID [220; 220]
  BT1   dicarboxylic acids
    BT2   carboxylic acids
      BT3   organic acids
        BT4   organic compounds

MALTA [2; 2] *Dec 90*
  BT1   europe
  BT1   islands
  RT   mediterranean sea

MALTOSE [37; 37]
  BT1   disaccharides
    BT2   oligosaccharides
      BT3   saccharides
        BT4   carbohydrates
          BT5   organic compounds

MAMMALS [852; 71,043]
  BT1   vertebrates
    BT2   animals
  NT1   burros
  NT1   cats
  NT1   cetaceans
  NT1   dogs
    NT2   beagles
  NT1   horses
  NT1   marsupials
  NT1   pikas
  NT1   primates
    NT2   apes
    NT2   man
      NT3   children
        NT4   infants
      NT3   elderly people
      NT3   men
      NT3   patients
      NT3   women
    NT2   monkeys
      NT3   baboons
      NT3   macacus
  NT1   rabbits
  NT1   rodents
    NT2   chipmunks
    NT2   gerbils
    NT2   guinea pigs
    NT2   hamsters
    NT2   mice
    NT2   rats
    NT2   squirrels
    NT2   voles
  NT1   ruminants
    NT2   antelopes
    NT2   buffalo
    NT2   cattle
      NT3   calves
      NT3   cows
    NT2   deer
    NT2   goats
    NT2   llamas
    NT2   sheep
  NT1   shrews
  NT1   swine
    NT2   miniature swine
  RT   syngamus

MAMMARY GLANDS [4,516; 4,516]
  UF   breasts
  BT1   glands
    BT2   organs
      BT3   body
  RT   chest
  RT   lactation
  RT   lth
  RT   milk

MAN [13,377; 22,171]
(All of mankind, of any age or of either sex.)
  BT1   primates
    BT2   mammals
      BT3   vertebrates
        BT4   animals
  NT1   children
    NT2   infants
  NT1   elderly people
  NT1   men
  NT1   patients
  NT1   women
  RT   adolescents
  RT   adults
  RT   aged adults
  RT   ascaridae
  RT   human populations
  RT   personnel
  RT   reference man
  RT   sociology

MAN-MACHINE SYSTEMS [1,192; 1,192] *Feb 83*
(People, machines and the processes by which they interact.)
  RT   automation
  RT   communications
  RT   control rooms
  RT   control systems
  RT   cybernetics
  RT   display devices
  RT   drug abuse
  RT   human factors
  RT   personnel
  RT   remote handling
  RT   systems analysis

§ **MANAGEMENT** [5,575; 55,428]
  UF   administration
  SF   operations research
  NT1   accounting
    NT2   energy accounting
  NT1   data base management
  NT1   load management
  NT1   nuclear materials management
    NT2   fuel management
  NT1   waste management
    NT2   nonradioactive waste managemen
      NT3   nonradioactive waste disposal
      NT3   nonradioactive wastes
        NT4   chemical wastes
          NT5   chemical effluents
    NT2   radioactive waste management
    NT2   waste disposal
      NT3   ground disposal
      NT3   ground release
      NT3   marine disposal
      NT3   nonradioactive waste disposal
      NT3   radioactive waste disposal
      NT3   stack disposal
      NT3   underground disposal
    NT2   waste processing
      NT3   radioactive waste processing
    NT2   waste retrieval
    NT2   waste storage
      NT3   radioactive waste storage
    NT2   waste transportation
  RT   allocations

RT	audits
RT	evaluation
RT	forecasting
RT	labor relations
RT	organizational models
RT	personnel
RT	public relations
RT	regional cooperation
RT	schedules

manaurite 36x
USE   alloy-fe36ni33cr26

manaurite 900
USE   alloy-fe40ni35cr22

manch. liverp. univ. res. re.
USE   urr reactor

MANDELIC ACID [75; 75]
UF	*amygdalic acid*
BT1	hydroxy acids
BT2	carboxylic acids
BT3	organic acids
BT4	organic compounds

MANDELSTAM REPRESENTATION
[265; 265]
RT	dispersion relations
RT	khuri representation
RT	s channel
RT	t channel
RT	u channel

mandible
USE   jaw

MANGANATES [61; 61]
(Specific compounds should be indexed by coordination of a descriptor of the form (CATION) COMPOUNDS and the above anion descriptor.)
BT1	manganese compounds
BT2	transition element compounds
BT1	oxygen compounds
RT	manganese oxides

MANGANESE [2,940; 2,954]
BT1	transition elements
BT2	metals
BT3	elements
NT1	manganese-alpha
NT1	manganese-beta
NT1	manganese-gamma
NT1	manganese-sigma

MANGANESE ADDITIONS [686; 1,681]
(Alloys containing not more than 1% Mn are listed here.)
NT1	alloy-al95cu4
NT1	alloy-fe40ni35cr22
NT1	alloy-fe53ni29co18
NT1	alloy-ni56cr21w10mo5fe4al2
NT1	alloy-ni66cu32
NT1	alloy-ni78cr21
RT	manganese alloys
RT	manganese compounds

MANGANESE ALLOYS [1,856; 3,687]
(Alloys containing more than 1% Mn.)
BT1	alloys
NT1	alloy-co43cr20fe18ni13w3
NT1	alloy-fe36ni33cr26
NT1	alloy-ni73cr20mn3nb3
NT1	alloy-ni94mn3al2
NT1	heusler alloys
NT1	manganese base alloys
NT1	steel-cr13mn8ni8
NT1	steel-cr17mn15nni
NT1	steel-cr21mn9ni6
NT1	steel-mncumo
NT1	steel-mnmo
NT1	steel-mnnimo
NT1	steel-mnnimov
RT	manganese additions

MANGANESE ARSENIDES [10; 10]
Nov 76
BT1	arsenides
BT2	arsenic compounds
BT2	pnictides
BT1	manganese compounds
BT2	transition element compounds

MANGANESE BASE ALLOYS [94; 94]
BT1	manganese alloys
BT2	alloys

MANGANESE BORIDES [27; 27]
BT1	borides
BT2	boron compounds
BT1	manganese compounds
BT2	transition element compounds

MANGANESE BROMIDES [24; 24]
BT1	bromides
BT2	bromine compounds
BT3	halogen compounds
BT2	halides
BT3	halogen compounds
BT1	manganese halides
BT2	halides
BT3	halogen compounds
BT2	manganese compounds
BT3	transition element compounds

MANGANESE CARBIDES [13; 13]
BT1	carbides
BT2	carbon compounds
BT1	manganese compounds
BT2	transition element compounds

MANGANESE CARBONATES [32; 32]
BT1	carbonates
BT2	carbon compounds
BT2	oxygen compounds
BT1	manganese compounds
BT2	transition element compounds
RT	carbonate minerals

MANGANESE CHLORIDES [178; 178]
BT1	chlorides
BT2	chlorine compounds
BT3	halogen compounds
BT2	halides
BT3	halogen compounds
BT1	manganese halides
BT2	halides
BT3	halogen compounds
BT2	manganese compounds
BT3	transition element compounds

MANGANESE COMPLEXES [242; 242]
BT1	transition element complexes
BT2	complexes

MANGANESE COMPOUNDS
[818; 2,721]
BT1	transition element compounds
NT1	manganates
NT1	manganese arsenides
NT1	manganese borides
NT1	manganese carbides
NT1	manganese carbonates
NT1	manganese halides
NT2	manganese bromides
NT2	manganese chlorides
NT2	manganese fluorides
NT2	manganese iodides
NT1	manganese hydrides
NT1	manganese hydroxides
NT1	manganese nitrates
NT1	manganese nitrides
NT1	manganese oxides
NT1	manganese perchlorates
NT1	manganese phosphates
NT1	manganese phosphides
NT1	manganese selenides
NT1	manganese silicates
NT1	manganese silicides
NT1	manganese sulfates
NT1	manganese sulfides
NT1	manganese tellurides
NT1	manganese tungstates
NT1	permanganates
RT	manganese additions

MANGANESE FLUORIDES [212; 212]
BT1	fluorides
BT2	fluorine compounds
BT3	halogen compounds
BT2	halides
BT3	halogen compounds
BT1	manganese halides
BT2	halides
BT3	halogen compounds
BT2	manganese compounds
BT3	transition element compounds

MANGANESE HALIDES [0; 0] *Sep 91*
BT1	halides
BT2	halogen compounds
BT1	manganese compounds
BT2	transition element compounds
NT1	manganese bromides
NT1	manganese chlorides
NT1	manganese fluorides
NT1	manganese iodides

MANGANESE HYDRIDES [31; 31]
Oct 77
BT1	hydrides
BT2	hydrogen compounds
BT1	manganese compounds
BT2	transition element compounds

MANGANESE HYDROXIDES [27; 27]
BT1	hydroxides
BT2	hydrogen compounds
BT2	oxygen compounds
BT1	manganese compounds
BT2	transition element compounds

MANGANESE IODIDES [15; 15]
BT1	iodides
BT2	halides
BT3	halogen compounds
BT2	iodine compounds
BT3	halogen compounds
BT1	manganese halides
BT2	halides
BT3	halogen compounds
BT2	manganese compounds
BT3	transition element compounds

MANGANESE IONS [402; 402]
BT1	ions
BT2	charged particles

MANGANESE ISOTOPES [97; 2,674]
NT1	manganese 44
NT1	manganese 46
NT1	manganese 47
NT1	manganese 48
NT1	manganese 49
NT1	manganese 50
NT1	manganese 51
NT1	manganese 52
NT1	manganese 53
NT1	manganese 54
NT1	manganese 55
NT1	manganese 56
NT1	manganese 57
NT1	manganese 58
NT1	manganese 59
NT1	manganese 60
NT1	manganese 61
NT1	manganese 62
NT1	manganese 63
NT1	manganese 64
NT1	manganese 65

MANGANESE NITRATES [11; 11]
- BT1 manganese compounds
- BT2 transition element compounds
- BT1 nitrates
- BT2 nitrogen compounds
- BT2 oxygen compounds

MANGANESE NITRIDES [12; 12]
- BT1 manganese compounds
- BT2 transition element compounds
- BT1 nitrides
- BT2 nitrogen compounds
- BT2 pnictides

manganese nodules
- USE manganese ores

MANGANESE ORES [132; 132]
- UF *manganese nodules*
- BT1 ores

MANGANESE OXIDES [677; 685]
- BT1 manganese compounds
- BT2 transition element compounds
- BT1 oxides
- BT2 chalcogenides
- BT2 oxygen compounds
- RT manganates
- RT oxide minerals
- RT permanganates
- RT tantalite

MANGANESE PERCHLORATES [5; 5]
Jan 77
- BT1 manganese compounds
- BT2 transition element compounds
- BT1 perchlorates
- BT2 chlorine compounds
- BT3 halogen compounds
- BT2 oxygen compounds

MANGANESE PHOSPHATES [25; 25]
- BT1 manganese compounds
- BT2 transition element compounds
- BT1 phosphates
- BT2 oxygen compounds
- BT2 phosphorus compounds

MANGANESE PHOSPHIDES [17; 17]
Nov 80
- BT1 manganese compounds
- BT2 transition element compounds
- BT1 phosphides
- BT2 phosphorus compounds
- BT2 pnictides

MANGANESE SELENIDES [25; 25]
Apr 79
- BT1 manganese compounds
- BT2 transition element compounds
- BT1 selenides
- BT2 chalcogenides
- BT2 selenium compounds

MANGANESE SILICATES [24; 24]
- BT1 manganese compounds
- BT2 transition element compounds
- BT1 silicates
- BT2 oxygen compounds
- BT2 silicon compounds
- RT silicate minerals

MANGANESE SILICIDES [42; 42]
Jan 77
- BT1 manganese compounds
- BT2 transition element compounds
- BT1 silicides
- BT2 silicon compounds

MANGANESE SULFATES [89; 89]
- BT1 manganese compounds
- BT2 transition element compounds
- BT1 sulfates
- BT2 oxygen compounds
- BT2 sulfur compounds

MANGANESE SULFIDES [77; 77]
- BT1 manganese compounds
- BT2 transition element compounds
- BT1 sulfides
- BT2 chalcogenides
- BT2 sulfur compounds

MANGANESE TELLURIDES [167; 167]
Nov 78
- BT1 manganese compounds
- BT2 transition element compounds
- BT1 tellurides
- BT2 chalcogenides
- BT2 tellurium compounds

MANGANESE TUNGSTATES [4; 4]
Sep 79
- BT1 manganese compounds
- BT2 transition element compounds
- BT1 tungstates
- BT2 oxygen compounds
- BT2 tungsten compounds
- BT3 transition element compounds

MANGANESE 44 [1; 1]
- BT1 intermediate mass nuclei
- BT2 nuclei
- BT1 manganese isotopes
- BT1 odd-odd nuclei
- BT2 nuclei

MANGANESE 46 [5; 5]
- BT1 intermediate mass nuclei
- BT2 nuclei
- BT1 manganese isotopes
- BT1 odd-odd nuclei
- BT2 nuclei

MANGANESE 47 [2; 2]
- BT1 intermediate mass nuclei
- BT2 nuclei
- BT1 manganese isotopes
- BT1 odd-even nuclei
- BT2 nuclei

MANGANESE 48 [9; 9]
- BT1 intermediate mass nuclei
- BT2 nuclei
- BT1 manganese isotopes
- BT1 odd-odd nuclei
- BT2 nuclei

MANGANESE 49 [14; 14]
- BT1 beta-plus decay radioisotopes
- BT2 beta decay radioisotopes
- BT3 radioisotopes
- BT4 isotopes
- BT1 intermediate mass nuclei
- BT2 nuclei
- BT1 manganese isotopes
- BT1 millisec living radioisotopes
- BT2 radioisotopes
- BT3 isotopes
- BT1 odd-even nuclei
- BT2 nuclei

MANGANESE 50 [38; 38]
- BT1 beta-plus decay radioisotopes
- BT2 beta decay radioisotopes
- BT3 radioisotopes
- BT4 isotopes
- BT1 intermediate mass nuclei
- BT2 nuclei
- BT1 manganese isotopes
- BT1 millisec living radioisotopes
- BT2 radioisotopes
- BT3 isotopes
- BT1 minutes living radioisotopes
- BT2 radioisotopes
- BT3 isotopes
- BT1 odd-odd nuclei
- BT2 nuclei

MANGANESE 51 [64; 64]
- BT1 beta-plus decay radioisotopes
- BT2 beta decay radioisotopes
- BT3 radioisotopes
- BT4 isotopes
- BT1 electron capture radioisotopes
- BT2 beta decay radioisotopes
- BT3 radioisotopes
- BT4 isotopes
- BT1 intermediate mass nuclei
- BT2 nuclei
- BT1 manganese isotopes
- BT1 minutes living radioisotopes
- BT2 radioisotopes
- BT3 isotopes
- BT1 odd-even nuclei
- BT2 nuclei

MANGANESE 51 TARGET [2; 2]
- BT1 targets

MANGANESE 52 [167; 167]
- BT1 beta-plus decay radioisotopes
- BT2 beta decay radioisotopes
- BT3 radioisotopes
- BT4 isotopes
- BT1 days living radioisotopes
- BT2 radioisotopes
- BT3 isotopes
- BT1 electron capture radioisotopes
- BT2 beta decay radioisotopes
- BT3 radioisotopes
- BT4 isotopes
- BT1 intermediate mass nuclei
- BT2 nuclei
- BT1 manganese isotopes
- BT1 minutes living radioisotopes
- BT2 radioisotopes
- BT3 isotopes
- BT1 odd-odd nuclei
- BT2 nuclei

MANGANESE 53 [271; 271]
- BT1 electron capture radioisotopes
- BT2 beta decay radioisotopes
- BT3 radioisotopes
- BT4 isotopes
- BT1 intermediate mass nuclei
- BT2 nuclei
- BT1 manganese isotopes
- BT1 odd-even nuclei
- BT2 nuclei
- BT1 years living radioisotopes
- BT2 radioisotopes
- BT3 isotopes

MANGANESE 53 TARGET [7; 7]
- BT1 targets

MANGANESE 54 [1,440; 1,440]
- BT1 days living radioisotopes
- BT2 radioisotopes
- BT3 isotopes
- BT1 electron capture radioisotopes
- BT2 beta decay radioisotopes
- BT3 radioisotopes
- BT4 isotopes
- BT1 intermediate mass nuclei
- BT2 nuclei
- BT1 manganese isotopes
- BT1 odd-odd nuclei
- BT2 nuclei

MANGANESE 54 TARGET [9; 9]
Sep 79
- BT1 targets

MANGANESE 55 [336; 336]
- BT1 intermediate mass nuclei
- BT2 nuclei
- BT1 manganese isotopes
- BT1 odd-even nuclei
- BT2 nuclei
- BT1 stable isotopes
- BT2 isotopes

MANGANESE 55 REACTIONS [6; 6]
Nov 84
  BT1   heavy ion reactions
    BT2   nuclear reactions

MANGANESE 55 TARGET [270; 270]
  BT1   targets

MANGANESE 56 [355; 355]
  BT1   beta-minus decay radioisotopes
    BT2   beta decay radioisotopes
        BT3   radioisotopes
            BT4   isotopes
  BT1   hours living radioisotopes
    BT2   radioisotopes
        BT3   isotopes
  BT1   intermediate mass nuclei
    BT2   nuclei
  BT1   manganese isotopes
  BT1   odd-odd nuclei
    BT2   nuclei

MANGANESE 57 [24; 24]
  BT1   beta-minus decay radioisotopes
    BT2   beta decay radioisotopes
        BT3   radioisotopes
            BT4   isotopes
  BT1   intermediate mass nuclei
    BT2   nuclei
  BT1   manganese isotopes
  BT1   minutes living radioisotopes
    BT2   radioisotopes
        BT3   isotopes
  BT1   odd-even nuclei
    BT2   nuclei

MANGANESE 58 [11; 11]
  BT1   beta-minus decay radioisotopes
    BT2   beta decay radioisotopes
        BT3   radioisotopes
            BT4   isotopes
  BT1   intermediate mass nuclei
    BT2   nuclei
  BT1   manganese isotopes
  BT1   minutes living radioisotopes
    BT2   radioisotopes
        BT3   isotopes
  BT1   odd-odd nuclei
    BT2   nuclei
  BT1   seconds living radioisotopes
    BT2   radioisotopes
        BT3   isotopes

MANGANESE 59 [9; 9] *Nov 76*
  BT1   beta-minus decay radioisotopes
    BT2   beta decay radioisotopes
        BT3   radioisotopes
            BT4   isotopes
  BT1   intermediate mass nuclei
    BT2   nuclei
  BT1   manganese isotopes
  BT1   odd-even nuclei
    BT2   nuclei
  BT1   seconds living radioisotopes
    BT2   radioisotopes
        BT3   isotopes

MANGANESE 60 [12; 12] *Jul 78*
  BT1   beta-minus decay radioisotopes
    BT2   beta decay radioisotopes
        BT3   radioisotopes
            BT4   isotopes
  BT1   intermediate mass nuclei
    BT2   nuclei
  BT1   manganese isotopes
  BT1   odd-odd nuclei
    BT2   nuclei
  BT1   seconds living radioisotopes
    BT2   radioisotopes
        BT3   isotopes

MANGANESE 61 [7; 7] *Nov 80*
  BT1   beta-minus decay radioisotopes
    BT2   beta decay radioisotopes
        BT3   radioisotopes
            BT4   isotopes
  BT1   intermediate mass nuclei
    BT2   nuclei
  BT1   manganese isotopes
  BT1   millisec living radioisotopes
    BT2   radioisotopes
        BT3   isotopes
  BT1   odd-even nuclei
    BT2   nuclei

MANGANESE 62 [9; 9] *Jun 82*
  BT1   beta-minus decay radioisotopes
    BT2   beta decay radioisotopes
        BT3   radioisotopes
            BT4   isotopes
  BT1   intermediate mass nuclei
    BT2   nuclei
  BT1   manganese isotopes
  BT1   millisec living radioisotopes
    BT2   radioisotopes
        BT3   isotopes
  BT1   odd-odd nuclei
    BT2   nuclei

MANGANESE 63 [6; 6] *Jan 86*
  BT1   beta-minus decay radioisotopes
    BT2   beta decay radioisotopes
        BT3   radioisotopes
            BT4   isotopes
  BT1   intermediate mass nuclei
    BT2   nuclei
  BT1   manganese isotopes
  BT1   millisec living radioisotopes
    BT2   radioisotopes
        BT3   isotopes
  BT1   odd-even nuclei
    BT2   nuclei

MANGANESE 64 [3; 3] *Aug 86*
  BT1   intermediate mass nuclei
    BT2   nuclei
  BT1   manganese isotopes
  BT1   odd-odd nuclei
    BT2   nuclei

MANGANESE 65 [4; 4] *Aug 86*
  BT1   intermediate mass nuclei
    BT2   nuclei
  BT1   manganese isotopes
  BT1   odd-even nuclei
    BT2   nuclei

MANGANESE-ALPHA [12; 12]
  BT1   manganese
    BT2   transition elements
        BT3   metals
            BT4   elements

MANGANESE-BETA [3; 3]
  BT1   manganese
    BT2   transition elements
        BT3   metals
            BT4   elements

MANGANESE-GAMMA [1; 1]
  BT1   manganese
    BT2   transition elements
        BT3   metals
            BT4   elements

MANGANESE-SIGMA [0; 0]
  BT1   manganese
    BT2   transition elements
        BT3   metals
            BT4   elements

MANGOES [109; 109]
  BT1   fruits
    BT2   food

MANHATTAN PROJECT [51; 51]
  RT   nuclear weapons

MANIAC COMPUTERS [2; 2]
  BT1   computers

MANIPULATORS [1,216; 1,216]
  BT1   laboratory equipment
    BT2   equipment
  BT1   remote handling equipment
    BT2   materials handling equipment
        BT3   equipment
  RT   distance
  RT   hot cells
  RT   hot labs
  RT   remote handling
  RT   shielding

MANITOBA [63; 63]
  BT1   canada
    BT2   developed countries
    BT2   north america

mannomustine
  USE   alkylating agents

MANNOSE [214; 214]
  BT1   aldehydes
    BT2   organic compounds
  BT1   hexoses
    BT2   monosaccharides
        BT3   saccharides
            BT4   carbohydrates
                BT5   organic compounds

manometers
  USE   pressure gages

manpower
  USE   personnel

MANUALS [2,172; 2,172]
(Should be used to index all pieces of literature which are manuals.)
  BT1   document types
  RT   computer program documentation
  RT   education
  RT   information
  RT   recommendations

manufacturing
  USE   fabrication

MANY-BODY PROBLEM [5,263; 13,652]
  NT1   four-body problem
  NT1   three-body problem
  NT1   two-body problem
  RT   bethe-goldstone equation
  RT   fsc approximation
  RT   goldstone diagrams
  RT   martin-schwinger theory
  RT   mean-field theory
  RT   multiple scattering
  RT   percus-yevick equation
  RT   quasi particles
  RT   unitary pole approximation
  RT   van hove-hugenholtz theory
  RT   wick theorem

MANY-DIMENSIONAL CALCULATIONS [3,312; 3,312]
(More than four dimensions.)
  UF   *calculations (many dimensions)*
  UF   *five-dimensional calculations*
  RT   four-dimensional calculations
  RT   mathematics
  RT   three-dimensional calculations
  RT   two-dimensional calculations

MANY-NUCLEON TRANSFER REACTION [341; 341]
(More than four nucleons transfered.)
  BT1   multi-nucleon transfer reactio
    BT2   transfer reactions
        BT3   direct reactions

BT4 nuclear reactions

MAPLE REACTOR [42; 42] *Dec 85*
(Multipurpose Applied Physics lattice Experimental reactor)
UF   *multipurpose appl phys latt r.*
BT1   enriched uranium reactors
BT2   reactors
BT1   heavy water moderated reactors
BT2   reactors
BT1   research and test reactors
BT2   reactors
BT1   water cooled reactors
BT2   reactors
BT1   water moderated reactors
BT2   reactors

mapping (topological)
USE   topological mapping

MAPPING FIBRATION [102; 102]
UF   *fibration (topological maps)*
RT   differential topology
RT   topological mapping

MAPS [3,794; 3,794]
RT   diagrams
RT   topography

mar-m509 alloy
USE   maraging steels

mar-250 alloy
USE   maraging steels

MARAGING STEELS [142; 142] *May 79*
(Strong tough low-carbon martensitic steels which contain up to 25% nickel and in which hardening precipitates are formed by aging.)
UF   *mar-m509 alloy*
UF   *mar-250 alloy*
BT1   martensitic steels
BT2   steels
BT3   carbon additions
BT3   iron base alloys
BT4   iron alloys
BT5   alloys

marble
USE   calcium carbonates
AND   metamorphic rocks

MARBLE HILL-1 REACTOR [9; 9]
May 76
(Jefferson, Indiana, USA)
BT1   pwr type reactors
BT2   enriched uranium reactors
BT3   reactors
BT2   power reactors
BT3   reactors
BT2   thermal reactors
BT3   reactors
BT2   water cooled reactors
BT3   reactors
BT2   water moderated reactors
BT3   reactors

MARBLE HILL-2 REACTOR [10; 10]
May 76
(Jefferson, Indiana, USA)
BT1   pwr type reactors
BT2   enriched uranium reactors
BT3   reactors
BT2   power reactors
BT3   reactors
BT2   thermal reactors
BT3   reactors
BT2   water cooled reactors
BT3   reactors
BT2   water moderated reactors
BT3   reactors

MARCASITE [9; 9] *Sep 83*
BT1   sulfide minerals
BT2   minerals
RT   iron sulfides
RT   pyrite

marcoule (cea)
USE   cea marcoule

marcoule g-1 reactor
USE   g-1 reactor

marcoule g-2 reactor
USE   g-2 reactor

marcoule g-3 reactor
USE   g-3 reactor

marcoule phenix reactor
USE   phenix reactor

MARFE [13; 13] *May 90*
(Multifaceted Asymmetric Radiation From the Edge is the result of a radiative thermal instability caused by light impurities in a peripheral plasma.)
RT   plasma confinement
RT   plasma instability
RT   plasma sheath
RT   stellarators
RT   tokamak devices

MARIA REACTOR [45; 45]
(Institute of Nuclear Research, Swierk, Poland)
UF   *swierk maria reactor*
BT1   beryllium moderated reactors
BT2   metal moderated reactors
BT3   reactors
BT1   enriched uranium reactors
BT2   reactors
BT1   isotope production reactors
BT2   irradiation reactors
BT3   reactors
BT1   pool type reactors
BT2   water cooled reactors
BT3   reactors
BT2   water moderated reactors
BT3   reactors
BT1   research and test reactors
BT2   reactors
BT1   thermal reactors
BT2   reactors

→ *mariculture*
USE   aquaculture

MARINE DISPOSAL [1,664; 1,664]
UF   *sea disposal*
BT1   waste disposal
BT2   waste management
BT3   management
RT   lcpmpdpw
RT   oecd mcmsdrw
RT   radioactive waste disposal

marine ecosystems
USE   aquatic ecosystems

marine insurance
USE   insurance

marine poll preven, london con
USE   lcpmpdpw

marine vehicle accidents
USE   accidents

MARINER SPACE PROBES [97; 97]
BT1   space vehicles

marit car liab conv bruss 1971
USE   bcoclmcnm

MARITIME LAWS [71; 71]
(Prior to December 1990, this descriptor was spelled MARITIME LAW.)
BT1   laws
RT   high seas
RT   maritime transport
RT   nuclear ship visits
RT   territorial waters
RT   transport regulations

MARITIME TRANSPORT [282; 282]
Dec 76
BT1   transport
RT   maritime laws

MARIUS REACTOR [8; 8]
(CEA/CEN, Cadarache, St. Paul Lez Durance, France)
UF   *cadarache reactor marius*
BT1   graphite moderated reactors
BT2   reactors
BT1   natural uranium reactors
BT2   reactors
BT1   research reactors
BT2   research and test reactors
BT3   reactors
BT1   thermal reactors
BT2   reactors
BT1   zero power reactors
BT2   experimental reactors
BT3   research and test reactors
BT4   reactors

mark v synchrotron
USE   mura synchrotron

MARKARIAN GALAXIES [202; 202]
(With abnormally strong continuum in the ultraviolet spectral region.)
BT1   galaxies
RT   cosmic radio sources

MARKET [1,964; 1,964]
(The chance to buy or sell.)
RT   commercial sector
RT   commercialization
RT   domestic supplies
RT   economics
RT   forecasting
RT   gross national product
RT   trade

market life
USE   storage life

MARKOV PROCESS [721; 721]
BT1   stochastic processes
RT   chapman-kolmogorov equation
RT   failure mode analysis

MARLEX [0; 0]
BT1   polyethylenes
BT2   polyolefins
BT3   organic polymers
BT4   organic compounds
BT4   polymers

marlite
USE   clays

marlstone
USE clays

MARMARA SEA [2; 2]
BT1 seas
BT2 surface waters

marmen effect
USE shape memory effect

MARS PLANET [768; 768]
BT1 planets

mars reactor
USE tmr reactors

MARS SPACE PROBES [86; 86] *Feb 78*
BT1 space vehicles

MARSHAK BOUNDARY CONDITIONS
[17; 17]
UF+ *marshak conditions*
BT1 boundary conditions
RT angular distribution
RT milne problem
RT spherical harmonics method

marshak conditions
USE marshak boundary conditions
AND martin-schwinger theory

MARSHALL ISLANDS [72; 216]
BT1 micronesia
BT2 australasia
BT2 islands
NT1 bikini
NT1 eniwetok
RT nuclear explosions
RT pacific ocean

marshes
USE swamps

MARSUPIALS [55; 55]
UF *opossum*
UF *potorous*
BT1 mammals
BT2 vertebrates
BT3 animals

MARTENSITE [1,016; 1,016]
BT1 carbon additions
BT1 iron alloys
BT2 alloys
RT austenite
RT bainite
RT cementite
RT ferrite
RT iron-alpha
RT iron-beta
RT martensitic steels
RT steels

MARTENSITIC STEELS [205; 618]
Nov 83
BT1 steels
BT2 carbon additions
BT2 iron base alloys
BT3 iron alloys
BT4 alloys
NT1 maraging steels
NT1 steel-cr10mo2
NT1 steel-cr12
NT1 steel-cr12mov
NT1 steel-cr13
NT1 steel-cr16ni
NT1 steel-cr17cu4ni4nb-l
NT1 steel-cr17mo
NT1 steel-cr18
RT martensite

martin-puff-schwinger theory
USE martin-schwinger theory

MARTIN-SCHWINGER THEORY
[10; 10]
UF *martin-puff-schwinger theory*
UF+ *marshak conditions*
RT many-body problem

MARVEL EVENT [2; 2]
BT1 contained explosions
BT2 underground explosions
BT3 explosions
BT1 nuclear explosions
BT2 explosions
BT1 plowshare project

MARVIKEN REACTOR [41; 41]
BT1 bhwr type reactors
BT2 heavy water cooled reactors
BT3 reactors
BT2 heavy water moderated reactors
BT3 reactors
BT1 enriched uranium reactors
BT2 reactors
BT1 power reactors
BT2 reactors

MARX GENERATORS [147; 147]
Apr 84
BT1 high-voltage pulse generators
BT2 pulse generators
BT3 function generators
BT4 electronic equipment
BT5 equipment

MARY KATHLEEN MINES [35; 35]
BT1 uranium mines
BT2 mines
BT3 underground facilities
RT australia

MARYLA REACTOR [2; 2]
(Institute of Nuclear Research, Academy of Mining and Metallurgy, Cracow, Poland)
UF *polish government maryla reac*
UF *swierk research reactor maryla*
BT1 enriched uranium reactors
BT2 reactors
BT1 pool type reactors
BT2 water cooled reactors
BT3 reactors
BT2 water moderated reactors
BT3 reactors
BT1 research reactors
BT2 research and test reactors
BT3 reactors
BT1 zero power reactors
BT2 experimental reactors
BT3 research and test reactors
BT4 reactors

MARYLAND [154; 154]
BT1 usa
BT2 developed countries
BT2 north america

maryland univ. reactor
USE umne-1 reactor

MASERS [853; 853]
(Microwave Amplification by Stimulated Emission of Radiation)
BT1 microwave amplifiers
BT2 amplifiers
BT3 equipment
BT2 microwave equipment
BT3 electronic equipment
BT4 equipment
RT gasers
RT lasers
RT microwave radiation
RT quantum electronics
RT radiation sources
RT stimulated emission

masks
USE respirators

MASS [17,107; 29,065]
NT1 effective mass
NT1 missing mass
NT1 negative mass
NT1 rest mass
RT dalitz plot
RT equivalence principle
RT gravitational fields
RT linear momentum
RT mass difference
RT mass distribution
RT mass formulae
RT moment of inertia
RT weight

MASS BALANCE [189; 189]
UF *balance (mass)*
RT confinement
RT plasma
RT thermonuclear devices
RT thermonuclear reactors

MASS DEFECT [458; 458]
(Mass lost to binding energy.)
RT binding energy
RT nuclear forces

MASS DIFFERENCE [1,762; 1,762]
(Unexpected difference between particles of the same family, e.g., between pi plus and pi minus.)
BT1 particle properties
RT mass

MASS DISTRIBUTION [1,322; 1,322]
Aug 84
(The way matter is distributed in space or throughout a body.)
BT1 spatial distribution
BT2 distribution
RT anisotropy
RT configuration
RT density
RT mass
RT shape

MASS FORMULAE [1,804; 1,896]
NT1 okubo mass formula
RT mass
RT quantum field theory

mass loss
SEE mass transfer
OR stellar winds

MASS NUMBER [2,605; 2,605]
RT mass spectroscopy
RT weizsaecker formula

mass radius (nuclear)
USE nuclear radii

mass radius (particle)
USE particle radii

MASS REARING [75; 75]
BT1 animal breeding
RT diet
RT insects
RT nutrition
RT sterile male technique

MASS RENORMALIZATION [394; 394]
BT1 renormalization

MASS RESOLUTION [636; 636]
BT1 resolution

MASS SPECTRA [10,561; 10,561]
BT1 spectra

MASS SPECTROMETERS [2,780; 3,299]
BT1 spectrometers
BT2 measuring instruments
NT1 dynamic mass spectrometers
NT2 energy balance mass spectromet
NT2 time-of-flight mass spectromet
NT1 spark mass spectrometers
NT1 static mass spectrometers
RT dees
RT electromag isotope separators
RT mass spectroscopy

mass spectrometry
USE mass spectroscopy

MASS SPECTROSCOPY [7,879; 8,040]
UF *mass spectrometry*
BT1 spectroscopy
NT1 resonance ionization mass spec
RT mass number
RT mass spectrometers

MASS TRANSFER [5,813; 15,912]
UF *transfer (mass)*
SF *mass loss*
NT1 advection
NT1 environmental transport
NT2 radionuclide migration
RT atom transport
RT convection
RT dialysis
RT diffusion
RT energy transfer
RT fluid flow
RT membrane transport
RT osmosis

massachus. inst. techn. alcato
USE alcator device

massachus. inst. techn. reacto
USE mitr reactor

MASSACHUSETTS [131; 131]
BT1 usa
BT2 developed countries
BT2 north america

MASSEY-MOHR EQUATION [2; 2]
BT1 equations
RT hard-core potential
RT nucleons

massive transfer reactions
USE incomplete fusion reactions

massive vector-meson model
USE gluon model

MASSLESS PARTICLES [1,970; 25,699]
BT1 elementary particles
NT1 gravitons
NT1 neutrinos
NT2 antineutrinos
NT3 electron antineutrinos
NT3 muon antineutrinos
NT2 cosmic neutrinos
NT2 electron neutrinos
NT3 electron antineutrinos
NT2 muon neutrinos
NT3 muon antineutrinos
NT2 solar neutrinos
NT2 tau neutrinos
NT1 photons

NT2 cosmic photons
RT quantum field theory
RT relativity theory

MAST CELLS [126; 126]
UF *basophils (connective tissue)*
BT1 connective tissue cells
BT2 somatic cells
BT3 animal cells
RT heparin

MASURCA REACTOR [52; 52]
UF *cadarache maquette surgen. rea*
BT1 enriched uranium reactors
BT2 reactors
BT1 fast reactors
BT2 epithermal reactors
BT3 reactors
BT1 plutonium reactors
BT2 reactors
BT1 zero power reactors
BT2 experimental reactors
BT3 research and test reactors
BT4 reactors

masurium
USE technetium

MASUYITE [2; 2]
BT1 oxide minerals
BT2 minerals
BT1 uranium minerals
BT2 radioactive minerals
BT3 minerals
BT3 radioactive materials
BT4 materials
RT uranium oxides

MATERIAL BALANCE [593; 593]
RT accounting
RT inventories
RT material unaccounted for
RT materials
RT shipper-receiver differences

MATERIAL BALANCE AREA [179; 179]
RT safeguards
RT strategic points

MATERIAL BUCKLING [135; 135]
(A form of neutron density distribution in reactors. For buckling of materials, see DEFORMATION or FAILURES.)
BT1 buckling

MATERIAL UNACCOUNTED FOR [309; 309]
UF *muf*
RT material balance
RT safeguards
RT shipper-receiver differences

MATERIALS [1,906; 103,857] Dec 82
(Use of a more specific term is strongly recommended.)
NT1 biological materials
NT2 biological wastes
NT3 feces
NT3 sewage sludge
NT3 sweat
NT3 urine
NT2 body fluids
NT3 amniotic fluid
NT3 bile
NT3 blood
NT4 blood cells
NT5 blood platelets
NT5 erythrocytes
NT6 reticulocytes
NT5 leukocytes
NT6 basophils
NT6 eosinophils
NT6 lymphocytes
NT6 monocytes
NT6 neutrophils

NT4 blood plasma
NT5 blood serum
NT3 cerebrospinal fluid
NT3 gastric acid
NT3 lymph
NT3 milk
NT3 saliva
NT3 sweat
NT3 urine
NT2 forest litter
NT2 tissue extracts
NT1 building materials
NT2 bricks
NT2 cements
NT3 gypsum cements
NT2 concretes
NT3 prestressed concrete
NT3 reinforced concrete
NT1 carbonaceous materials
NT2 coal
NT3 black coal
NT4 anthracite
NT4 bituminous coal
NT3 lignite
NT2 oil sands
NT2 oil shales
NT1 composite materials
NT2 cermets
NT3 td-nickel
NT3 td-nickel chromium
NT2 concrete-plastic composites
NT2 fiberglass
NT2 prestressed concrete
NT2 reinforced concrete
NT2 superconducting composites
NT2 wood-plastic composites
NT1 dielectric materials
NT2 antiferroelectric materials
NT2 electrets
NT2 ferroelectric materials
NT1 doped materials
NT1 environmental materials
NT1 fertile materials
NT1 fissionable materials
NT2 fissile materials
NT1 granular materials
NT1 hazardous materials
NT1 ion exchange materials
NT2 inorganic ion exchangers
NT3 bentonite
NT3 clinoptilolite
NT3 montmorillonite
NT3 mullite
NT3 vermiculite
NT3 zeolites
NT2 liquid ion exchangers
NT2 mixed bed ion exchangers
NT2 organic ion exchangers
NT3 polystyrene-dvb
NT1 isotope enriched materials
NT2 enriched uranium
NT3 highly enriched uranium
NT3 moderately enriched uranium
NT3 slightly enriched uranium
NT1 lunar materials
NT1 magnetic materials
NT2 antiferromagnetic materials
NT2 ferrimagnetic materials
NT3 ferrites
NT2 ferromagnetic materials
NT1 matrix materials
NT1 porous materials
NT1 potting materials
NT1 radioactive materials
NT2 fission products
*NT2 radioactive minerals
NT2 radioactive wastes
NT3 alpha-bearing wastes
NT3 calcined wastes
NT3 high-level radioactive wastes
NT3 intermediate-level radioactive
NT3 low-level radioactive wastes
NT3 radioactive effluents
NT2 radiopharmaceuticals
NT1 reactor materials
NT2 nuclear fuels
NT3 denatured fuel
NT3 fuel slurries
NT3 gas fuels
NT3 solid fuels

MATERIALS

- NT4 alloy nuclear fuels
- NT4 dispersion nuclear fuels
- NT4 mixed carbide fuels
- NT4 mixed nitride fuels
- NT4 mixed oxide fuels
- NT3 spent fuels
- NT2 nuclear poisons
- NT3 burnable poisons
- NT3 fission poisons
- NT3 soluble poisons
- NT1 reinforced materials
- NT2 reinforced concrete
- NT2 reinforced plastics
- NT1 sealing materials
- NT1 semiconductor materials
- NT2 magnetic semiconductors
- NT2 n-type conductors
- NT2 p-type conductors
- NT1 shielding materials
- NT1 sintered materials
- NT2 sap
- NT1 surgical materials
- NT1 thermonuclear reactor material
- NT1 tissue-equivalent materials
- RT material balance
- RT materials drilling
- RT materials handling
- RT materials testing
- RT materials working

MATERIALS DRILLING [65; 670]
- UF *drilling (materials)*
- BT1 machining
- NT1 laser drilling
- NT1 rock drilling
- RT drill bits
- RT materials
- RT subterrene penetrators

MATERIALS HANDLING [2,076; 2,076]
- UF *handling (materials)*
- UF *loading (materials handling)*
- UF *unloading*
- RT contact handling
- RT delivery
- RT fuel feeding systems
- RT hydraulic transport
- RT materials
- RT materials handling equipment
- RT recycling
- RT remote handling
- RT sample changers
- RT transport
- RT waste retrieval

MATERIALS HANDLING EQUIPMENT
[385; 2,625] *Sep 83*
- BT1 equipment
- NT1 conveyors
- NT1 earthmoving equipment
- NT1 grabs
- NT1 remote handling equipment
- NT2 cranes
- NT2 manipulators
- NT1 shredders
- RT contact handling
- RT materials handling
- RT transport
- RT winches

MATERIALS PROCESSING REACTORS [11; 11]
(For routine irradiation of production items to obtain desirable changes in properties.)
- BT1 irradiation reactors
- BT2 reactors

MATERIALS TESTING [8,250; 27,369]
- BT1 testing
- NT1 destructive testing
- NT2 charpy test
- NT1 mechanical tests
- NT2 impact tests
- NT3 charpy test
- NT1 nondestructive testing
- NT2 acoustic testing
- NT3 acoustic emission testing
- NT3 ultrasonic testing
- NT2 electrical testing
- NT2 electromagnetic testing
- NT3 eddy current testing
- NT2 industrial radiography
- NT2 liquid penetrant inspection
- NT2 magnetic testing
- NT2 radiation attenuation testing
- NT2 thermal testing
- NT3 frost tests
- NT3 thermography
- RT ceramography
- RT corrosion
- RT emanation method
- RT fmit linac
- RT inspection
- RT materials
- RT metallography
- RT photoelasticity
- RT quality control
- RT s-n diagram
- RT stresses

materials testing react. idaho
- USE mtr reactor

materials testing react. japan
- USE jmtr reactor

MATERIALS TESTING REACTORS [167; 2,164]
(For testing properties of materials or equipment in a radioactive environment.)
- BT1 irradiation reactors
- BT2 reactors
- NT1 atr reactor
- NT1 br-2 reactor
- NT1 cp-2 reactor
- NT1 dido reactor
- NT1 dmtr reactor
- NT1 dr-3 reactor
- NT1 el-3 reactor
- NT1 frg-2 reactor
- NT1 frj-2 reactor
- NT1 gleep reactor
- NT1 hector reactor
- NT1 hfetr reactor
- NT1 hfr reactor
- NT1 hifar reactor
- NT1 hwctr reactor
- NT1 jmtr reactor
- NT1 jrr-3 reactor
- NT1 kmr reactor
- NT1 kstr reactor
- NT1 mtr reactor
- NT1 nbsr reactor
- NT1 nrx reactor
- NT1 osiris reactor
- NT1 pbr reactor
- NT1 pluto reactor
- NT1 r-2 reactor
- NT1 rv-1 reactor
- NT1 sm-2 reactor
- NT1 taiwan research reactor
- NT1 triga-1-hanford reactor
- NT1 wr-1 reactor
- NT1 wwr-m-kiev reactor
- NT1 wwr-m-leningrad reactor
- NT1 zephyr reactor

MATERIALS WORKING [508; 6,629]
(Covers metal and non-metal working.)
- UF *forming (materials)*
- UF *working (materials)*
- BT1 fabrication
- NT1 canning
- NT1 cold working
- NT2 shot peening
- NT1 drawing
- NT1 explosive forming
- NT1 extrusion
- NT2 coextrusion
- NT1 forging
- NT1 hot working
- NT1 magnetic forming
- NT1 pressing
- NT2 cold pressing
- NT2 hot pressing
- NT1 rolling
- NT1 swaging
- RT casting
- RT deformation
- RT machining
- RT materials
- RT molding

MATHEMATICAL LOGIC [96; 97]
Jul 86
- UF *logic (mathematical)*
- UF *symbolic logic*
- NT1 fuzzy logic
- RT algorithms
- RT mathematical models
- RT mathematics
- RT system failure analysis

MATHEMATICAL MANIFOLDS
[1,686; 3,012]
- NT1 complex manifolds
- NT1 convex manifolds
- NT1 smooth manifolds
- RT mathematical space
- RT mathematics
- RT measure theory
- RT topological mapping
- RT topology

MATHEMATICAL MODELS
[43,892; 166,321]
- UF *models (mathematical)*
- NT1 atomic models
- NT1 coherent tube model
- NT1 cosmological models
- NT2 inflationary universe
- NT1 crystal models
- NT2 heisenberg model
- NT2 ising model
- NT1 electron-promotion model
- NT1 flow models
- NT1 general circulation models
- NT1 harmonic oscillator models
- NT1 molecular models
- NT2 thermodynamic molecular model
- NT1 nuclear models
- NT2 bjorklund-fernbach model
- NT2 black nucleus model
- NT2 brueckner model
- NT2 cloudy crystal ball model
- NT2 cluster model
- NT2 collective model
- NT3 rotation-vibration model
- NT2 cranking model
- NT2 davydov-filipov model
- NT2 droplet model
- NT2 elliot model
- NT2 evaporation model
- NT3 weisskopf model
- NT2 exciton model
- NT2 fermi gas model
- NT2 folding model
- NT2 goldberger model
- NT2 lane-thomas-wigner model
- NT2 liquid drop model
- NT2 nilsson-mottelson model
- NT2 nuclear fireball model
- NT2 order-disorder model
- NT2 particle-core coupling model
- NT2 particle-hole model
- NT2 perey-buck model
- NT2 quartet model
- NT2 quasiparticle-phonon model
- NT2 scission-point model
- NT2 shell models
- NT3 governor model
- NT3 interacting boson model
- NT3 multi-center shell model
- NT2 spherical model
- NT2 strong-absorption model
- NT2 superfluid model
- NT2 unified model
- NT2 vmi model
- NT2 walecka model
- NT2 weak-coupling model
- NT1 optical models
- NT1 particle models
- NT2 composite models

MATHEMATICAL MODELS

- NT3 bootstrap model
- NT3 cim model
- NT3 parton model
- NT3 quark model
  - NT4 color model
  - NT4 flavor model
- NT2 correlated-particle models
- NT2 diffraction models
- NT2 dual absorption model
- NT2 extended particle model
  - NT3 bag model
  - NT3 string models
- NT2 feynman gas model
- NT2 fireball model
- NT2 gluon model
- NT2 hard collision models
- NT2 higgs model
- NT2 isobar model
- NT2 jet model
- NT2 lee model
- NT2 linear absorption models
- NT2 nova model
- NT2 octet model
- NT2 peripheral models
  - NT3 baryon-exchange models
  - NT3 boson-exchange models
    - NT4 obe model
      - NT5 ope model
        - NT6 electric born model
    - NT4 sigma model
  - NT3 multiperipheral model
    - NT4 cluster emission model
      - NT5 space-time model
- NT2 strong-coupling model
- NT2 tensor dominance model
- NT2 thermodynamic model
  - NT3 hydrodynamic model
- NT2 uncorrelated-particle model
- NT2 unified gauge models
  - NT3 grand unified theory
    - NT4 standard model
- NT3 weinberg lepton model
- NT2 van hove model
- NT2 vector dominance model
- NT2 veneziano model
  - NT3 dual resonance model
- NT1 star models
- NT1 statistical models
  - NT2 feynman gas model
  - NT2 thermodynamic model
    - NT3 hydrodynamic model
- NT1 thermal-nelson model
- NT1 thomas-fermi model
- RT biological models
- RT comparative evaluations
- RT computer calculations
- RT computer-aided design
- RT digital filters
- RT dynamic programming
- RT functional models
- RT fuzzy logic
- RT hypothesis
- RT linear programming
- RT mathematical logic
- RT mockup
- RT nonlinear programming
- RT response functions
- RT scaling laws
- RT sensitivity analysis
- RT structural models

MATHEMATICAL OPERATORS
[1,997; 31,597]
- UF operators (mathematical)
- NT1 casimir operators
- NT1 hermitian operators
- NT1 laplacian
- NT1 projection operators
- NT1 quantum operators
  - NT2 angular momentum operators
    - NT3 orbital momentum operators
    - NT3 pauli spin operators
  - NT2 annihilation operators
  - NT2 commutators
    - NT3 current commutators
      - NT4 sigma terms
  - NT2 creation operators
  - NT2 dirac operators
  - NT2 field operators
  - NT2 hamiltonians
  - NT2 linear momentum operators
  - NT2 position operators
- NT1 superoperators
- RT commutation relations
- RT density matrix
- RT eigenvalues
- RT eigenvectors
- RT mathematics
- RT quantum mechanics
- RT transfer matrix method

MATHEMATICAL SPACE
[1,530; 17,021]
- BT1 space
- NT1 banach space
  - NT2 hilbert space
- NT1 hausdorff space
- NT1 minkowski space
- NT1 phase space
- NT1 riemann space
  - NT2 euclidean space
- RT differential geometry
- RT fock representation
- RT functional analysis
- RT geodesics
- RT lobachevsky geometry
- RT mathematical manifolds
- RT mathematics
- RT measure theory
- RT metrics
- RT space dependence
- RT space-time

MATHEMATICS [2,144; 25,884]
- NT1 algebra
- NT1 differential calculus
- NT1 functional analysis
- NT1 geometry
  - NT2 differential geometry
- NT1 global analysis
- NT1 group theory
- NT1 integral calculus
- NT1 measure theory
- NT1 set theory
- NT1 statistics
  - NT2 regression analysis
  - NT2 time-series analysis
- NT1 topology
  - NT2 differential topology
- RT algorithms
- RT analytical solution
- RT anharmonic oscillators
- RT asymptotic solutions
- RT bethe-tait method
- RT boundary-value problems
- RT canonical transformations
- RT conformal mapping
- RT convergence
- RT coordinates
- RT differential equations
- RT eigenvectors
- RT equations
- RT extrapolation
- RT extreme-value problems
- RT factorization
- RT finite difference method
- RT finite element method
- RT four-dimensional calculations
- RT fourier analysis
- RT functions
- RT galerkin-petrov method
- RT gamma function
- RT geodesy
- RT harmonic oscillators
- RT integral equations
- RT integral transformations
- RT integrals
- RT interpolation
- RT iterative methods
- RT many-dimensional calculations
- RT mathematical logic
- RT mathematical manifolds
- RT mathematical operators
- RT mathematical space
- RT matrices
- RT mesh generation
- RT metrics
- RT newton method
- RT nodal expansion method
- RT nonlinear problems
- RT numerical solution
- RT one-dimensional calculations
- RT perturbation theory
- RT phase space
- RT polynomials
- RT power series
- RT quasilinear problems
- RT regge calculus
- RT saddle-point method
- RT scalars
- RT series expansion
- RT spherical harmonics
- RT spline functions
- RT superconvergence relations
- RT tensors
- RT three-dimensional calculations
- RT two-dimensional calculations
- RT variational methods
- RT vectors

MATHIEU EQUATION [118; 118]
- BT1 differential equations
  - BT2 equations

MATING [196; 196]
- RT behavior
- RT reproduction
- RT sex

MATRICES [5,597; 19,301]
- NT1 density matrix
- NT1 g matrix
- NT1 hermitian matrix
- NT1 k matrix
- NT1 kobayashi-maskawa matrix
- NT1 nuclear matrix
- NT1 r matrix
- NT1 s matrix
- RT mathematics
- RT matrix elements
- RT metrics
- RT secular equation

MATRIX ELEMENTS [14,144; 14,144]
- RT matrices

MATRIX ISOLATION [429; 429] *Aug 78*
(Method for investigating chemical, physical, spectroscopic and other properties of reactive species of atoms or molecules while trapped in matrices at low temperatures.)
- RT atoms
- RT clathrates
- RT molecular structure
- RT molecules
- RT spectroscopy

MATRIX MATERIALS [1,143; 1,143]
- BT1 materials
- RT fuel elements
- RT graphite
- RT reactor materials
- RT resins

MATTER [1,611; 31,095]
- NT1 antimatter
  - NT2 antinuclei
    - NT3 antideuterons
    - NT3 antiprotons
    - NT3 antitritons
  - NT2 antiparticles
    - NT3 anti-b neutral mesons
    - NT3 anti-d neutral mesons
    - NT3 antibaryons
      - NT4 antihyperons
        - NT5 antilambda particles
        - NT5 antiomega particles
        - NT5 antisigma particles
        - NT5 antixi particles
      - NT4 antinucleons
        - NT5 antineutrons
        - NT5 antiprotons
    - NT3 antikaons
      - NT4 antikaons neutral
    - NT3 antileptons

MATTER (cont.)

- NT4 antineutrinos
  - NT5 electron antineutrinos
  - NT5 muon antineutrinos
- NT4 muons plus
- NT4 positrons
  - NT5 cosmic positrons
- NT1 nonluminous matter
- NT1 nuclear matter
- NT1 organic matter
- NT1 quark matter
- NT1 volatile matter
- RT ambiplasma
- RT cosmology
- RT rheology

MATTERHORN PROJECT [0; 0]
- RT thermonuclear reactions

MATTHIESSEN RULE [75; 75]
- RT electric conductivity
- RT thermal conductivity

MAURITANIA [7; 7]
- BT1 africa
- BT1 developing countries

max-planck-inst f plasmaphysik
- USE ipp garching

MAXIMUM ACCEPTABLE CONTAMINATI [152; 152]
- UF mac
- BT1 contamination regulations
  - BT2 regulations
    - BT3 laws
- BT1 safety standards
  - BT2 standards
- RT contamination

MAXIMUM CREDIBLE ACCIDENT [302; 302]
- UF mca
- BT1 design basis accidents
  - BT2 reactor accidents
    - BT3 accidents
- RT health hazards
- RT reactor safety

MAXIMUM INHALATION QUANTITY [37; 37]
- UF miq
- BT1 safety standards
  - BT2 standards
- RT inhalation
- RT radioactivity

maximum likelihood fit
- USE maximum-likelihood fit

MAXIMUM PERMISSIBLE ACTIVITY [173; 173]
- UF mpa
- BT1 safety standards
  - BT2 standards
- RT activity levels
- RT radioactivity

MAXIMUM PERMISSIBLE BODY BURDE [108; 108]
- UF mpbb
- BT1 safety standards
  - BT2 standards
- RT body burden
- RT radioactivity
- RT retention

MAXIMUM PERMISSIBLE CONCENTRAT [430; 430]
- UF mpc
- BT1 safety standards
  - BT2 standards

MAXIMUM PERMISSIBLE DOSE [672; 672]
- UF mpd
- BT1 safety standards
  - BT2 standards
- RT dose limits
- RT maximum permissible exposure
- RT radiation doses

MAXIMUM PERMISSIBLE EXPOSURE [315; 315]
- UF mpe
- BT1 safety standards
  - BT2 standards
- RT integral doses
- RT maximum permissible dose
- RT radiation doses

MAXIMUM PERMISSIBLE INTAKE [148; 148]
- UF mpi
- BT1 safety standards
  - BT2 standards
- RT intake
- RT radioactivity

MAXIMUM PERMISSIBLE LEVEL [170; 170]
- UF mpl
- BT1 safety standards
  - BT2 standards
- RT radioactivity

MAXIMUM-LIKELIHOOD FIT [479; 2,749]
- UF *maximum likelihood fit*
- BT1 numerical solution
- NT1 least square fit
- RT probability
- RT statistics

maxwell distribution
- USE boltzmann statistics

MAXWELL EQUATIONS [2,526; 2,526]
- BT1 partial differential equations
  - BT2 differential equations
    - BT3 equations
- RT born-infeld theory
- RT electrodynamics
- RT electromagnetic fields
- RT field equations
- RT poynting theorem
- RT quasilinear problems

maxwell statistics
- USE boltzmann statistics

maxwell velocity distribution
- USE boltzmann statistics

maxwell-boltzmann distribution
- USE boltzmann statistics

maxwell-boltzmann equation
- USE boltzmann equation

maxwell-boltzmann statistics
- USE boltzmann statistics

mayaguez p. r. pool reactor
- USE prpr reactor

mayaguez puerto rico l-77 r.
- USE prnc-l-77 reactor

MAYER-SCHMIDT CONFIGURATIONS [0; 0]
- UF *m+s configuration*
- BT1 closed configurations
  - BT2 magnetic field configurations

MBP [13; 13] *Aug 88*
- UF *monobutyl phosphate*
- BT1 butyl phosphates
  - BT2 phosphoric acid esters
    - BT3 esters
      - BT4 organic compounds
    - BT3 organic phosphorus compounds
      - BT4 organic compounds

MC GUIRE-1 REACTOR [60; 60]
(Cornelius, North Carolina, USA)
- UF *w. b. mc guire-1 reactor*
- BT1 pwr type reactors
  - BT2 enriched uranium reactors
    - BT3 reactors
  - BT2 power reactors
    - BT3 reactors
  - BT2 thermal reactors
    - BT3 reactors
  - BT2 water cooled reactors
    - BT3 reactors
  - BT2 water moderated reactors
    - BT3 reactors

MC GUIRE-2 REACTOR [52; 52]
(Cornelius, North Carolina, USA)
- UF *w. b. mc guire-2 reactor*
- BT1 pwr type reactors
  - BT2 enriched uranium reactors
    - BT3 reactors
  - BT2 power reactors
    - BT3 reactors
  - BT2 thermal reactors
    - BT3 reactors
  - BT2 water cooled reactors
    - BT3 reactors
  - BT2 water moderated reactors
    - BT3 reactors

MC LEOD GAGES [2; 2]
- BT1 vacuum gages
  - BT2 pressure gages
    - BT3 measuring instruments

mc master univ. nuclear reacto
- USE mnr reactor

mca
- USE maximum credible accident

MCGILL SYNCHROCYCLOTRON [7; 7]
- BT1 synchrocyclotrons
  - BT2 cyclic accelerators
    - BT3 accelerators

mcmurdo sound medium p. p. 3a
- USE pm-3a reactor

MDPA [15; 15]
- UF *monododecylphosphoric acid*
- BT1 chelating agents
- BT1 organic acids
  - BT2 organic compounds
- BT1 phosphoric acid esters
  - BT2 esters
    - BT3 organic compounds
  - BT2 organic phosphorus compounds
    - BT3 organic compounds

MEA [501; 501]
- UF *aminoethanethiol*
- UF *cysteamine*
- UF *mercamine*
- UF *mercaptoethylamine*
- BT1 amines
  - BT2 organic compounds

```
BT1    radioprotective substances
  BT2    drugs
  BT2    response modifying factors
BT1    thiols
  BT2    organic sulfur compounds
    BT3    organic compounds
RT     cystamine
```

MEA LINAC [75; 75] Oct 76
(500 MeV linac at NIKHEF, Amsterdam.)
```
BT1    linear accelerators
  BT2    accelerators
```

MEAN FREE PATH [1,518; 1,518]
```
RT     anomalons
RT     cross sections
RT     diffusion
RT     geiger-nuttall law
```

mean life
  USE   lifetime

MEAN-FIELD THEORY [1,541; 1,541]
Aug 84
(An approach for quantum-mechanical many-body problems by definition of a mean field which is derived from the interactions of single bodies.)
```
RT     many-body problem
RT     self-consistent field
RT     statistical mechanics
```

MEASLES [7; 7] Jun 76
```
UF     german measles
UF     rubeola
BT1    viral diseases
  BT2    infectious diseases
    BT3    diseases
RT     measles virus
```

MEASLES VIRUS [34; 34] Jun 76
```
UF     rubella virus
UF     rubeola virus
BT1    viruses
  BT2    microorganisms
  BT2    parasites
RT     measles
```

MEASURE THEORY [726; 726]
(Relates to the property of sigma algebras or Borel fields referred to as measure.)
```
BT1    mathematics
RT     mathematical manifolds
RT     mathematical space
RT     metrics
```

measured values
  USE   experimental data

MEASURING INSTRUMENTS [5,303; 101,253]
(Use of a more specific term is recommended.)
```
UF     instruments (measuring)
NT1    accelerometers
NT1    altimeters
NT1    anemometers
  NT2    hot wire anemometers
NT1    bolometers
NT1    calorimeters
NT1    carbon meters
NT1    densimeters
  NT2    pycnometers
NT1    diffractometers
  NT2    gamma diffractometers
  NT2    neutron diffractometers
  NT2    x-ray diffractometers
NT1    displacement gages
NT1    dosemeters
  NT2    albedo-neutron dosemeters
  NT2    biological dosemeters
  NT2    bragg gray chambers
  NT2    calorimetric dosemeters
  NT2    chemical dosemeters
  NT2    colorimetric dosemeters
  NT2    condenser ionization chambers
  NT2    exoelectron dosemeters
  NT2    extrapolation chambers
  NT2    luminescent dosemeters
    NT3    rpl dosemeters
    NT3    thermoluminescent dosemeters
  NT2    photographic film dosemeters
  NT2    ritac dosemeters
  NT2    ritad dosemeters
NT1    dynamometers
NT1    electric measuring instruments
  NT2    ammeters
  NT2    electrometers
  NT2    electroscopes
  NT2    galvanometers
  NT2    potentiometers
  NT2    voltmeters
NT1    flowmeters
  NT2    plasma eaters
NT1    fluorimeters
NT1    fluxmeters
  NT2    squid devices
NT1    goniometers
NT1    hydrogen meters
NT1    interferometers
  NT2    fabry-perot interferometer
  NT2    mach-zehnder interferometer
  NT2    michelson interferometer
NT1    level indicators
NT1    lysimeters
NT1    magnetic balances
NT1    magnetometers
  NT2    fluxgate magnetometers
  NT2    moving coil magnetometers
  NT2    proton precession magnetometer
  NT2    vibrating sample magnetometers
NT1    moisture gages
NT1    monitors
  NT2    air pollution monitors
  NT2    beam monitors
    NT3    beam scanners
    NT3    faraday cups
    NT3    magnetoinduction sensors
  NT2    failed element monitors
  NT2    radiation monitors
    NT3    exposure ratemeters
    NT3    liquid contamination monitors
    NT3    neutron monitors
    NT3    surface contamination monitors
    NT3    survey monitors
NT1    neutron activation analyzers
NT1    nuclear reaction analyzers
NT1    oxygen meters
NT1    photometers
  NT2    densitometers
NT1    porosimeters
NT1    pressure gages
  NT2    barometers
  NT2    hot-wire gages
    NT3    pirani gages
  NT2    vacuum gages
    NT3    ionization gages
      NT4    bayard-alpert gages
      NT4    philips gages
      NT4    radioactive ionization gages
    NT3    knudsen gages
    NT3    mc leod gages
    NT3    pirani gages
NT1    pyrometers
  NT2    optical pyrometers
*NT1    radiation detectors
NT1    radiometric gages
  NT2    electron-capture detectors
NT1    range finders
  NT2    radar
NT1    riometers
NT1    seismographs
NT1    smoke detectors
*NT1    spectrometers
NT1    spectrophotometers
NT1    strain gages
NT1    sulfur meters
NT1    thermocouples
NT1    thermometers
  NT2    noise thermometers
NT1    thickness gages
NT1    time interval analyzers
  NT2    chronotrons
    NT3    vernier chronotrons
NT1    tritium meters
NT1    velocimeters
NT1    viscosimeters
NT1    weight indicators
  NT2    balances
    NT3    microbalances
RT     gyroscopes
RT     ionosondes
RT     miniaturization
RT     nisus facility
RT     on-line measurement systems
RT     probes
RT     reactor instrumentation
RT     recording systems
RT     response functions
RT     temperature measurement
RT     time measurement
RT     transducers
```

§§ MEASURING METHODS [14,686; 14,686]
(Important new measuring techniques only.)
```
RT     comparative evaluations
RT     dosimetry
RT     frequency measurement
RT     particle discrimination
RT     stern-gerlach experiment
```

MEAT [817; 817]
```
UF     bacon
UF     beef
UF     ham
UF     pork
BT1    food
RT     cattle
RT     sheep
RT     swine
RT     trichinella
```

MECHANICAL DECLADDING [132; 147]
```
BT1    decladding
  BT2    head end processes
RT     cutting
RT     milling
```

MECHANICAL EFFICIENCY [54; 54]
```
BT1    efficiency
```

MECHANICAL FILTERS [232; 232]
```
UF     granular bed filters
BT1    filters
```

MECHANICAL FRAGMENTATION [1,520; 1,900] Nov 75
```
UF     comminution
UF     fragmentation (mechanical)
UF     shattering
NT1    crushing
RT     fractures
RT     fracturing
```

MECHANICAL HEART [128; 128]
```
BT1    artificial organs
BT1    prostheses
  BT2    medical supplies
RT     blood circulation
RT     cardiac pacemakers
RT     heart
RT     radioisotope batteries
```

MECHANICAL IMPEDANCE [34; 34] Nov 75
```
BT1    impedance
```

MECHANICAL POLISHING [134; 134]
```
BT1    polishing
  BT2    surface finishing
```

MECHANICAL PROPERTIES
[8,314; 46,847]
- NT1 brittleness
- NT1 compressibility
- NT1 compression strength
- NT1 creep
- NT1 elasticity
  - NT2 photoelasticity
  - NT2 thermoelasticity
- NT1 fatigue
  - NT2 corrosion fatigue
  - NT2 thermal fatigue
- NT1 flexural strength
- NT1 fracture properties
- NT1 hardness
  - NT2 microhardness
- NT1 impact strength
- NT1 plasticity
- NT1 poisson ratio
- NT1 shear properties
- NT1 tensile properties
  - NT2 ductility
  - NT2 flexibility
- NT1 ultimate strength
- NT1 wear resistance
- NT1 yield strength
- NT1 young modulus
- RT deformation
- RT destructive testing
- RT physical metallurgy
- RT rheology
- RT rock mechanics
- RT stresses
- RT thermal degradation

MECHANICAL SHAFTS [190; 190]
Sep 76
- UF shafts (mechanical)
- BT1 machine parts

MECHANICAL STRUCTURES
[4,963; 9,585]
- UF structures (mechanics)
- UF towers (structures)
- NT1 bridges
- NT1 intake structures
- NT1 roofs
- NT1 supports
  - NT2 foundations
  - NT2 fuel racks
- RT buildings
- RT construction
- RT modular structures
- RT ratcheting
- RT response functions
- RT shells
- RT soil-structure interactions

MECHANICAL TESTS [3,341; 5,303]
(See also descriptors for the properties tested.)
- BT1 materials testing
  - BT2 testing
- NT1 impact tests
  - NT2 charpy test
- RT dynamic loads
- RT static loads
- RT strain gages
- RT stress intensity factors
- RT stresses
- RT thermal cycling
- RT wear

MECHANICAL VIBRATIONS
[4,923; 4,923]
- UF vibrations (mechanical)
- RT amplitudes
- RT damping
- RT dynamic loads
- RT harmonics
- RT hydrodynamic mass effect
- RT oscillations
- RT springs
- RT standing waves
- RT travelling waves

MECHANICS [1,107; 44,708]
- UF translation (mechanical)
- NT1 classical mechanics
- NT1 dynamics
  - NT2 beam dynamics
    - NT3 beam bunching
    - NT3 betatron oscillations
    - NT3 phase oscillations
    - NT3 synchrotron oscillations
- NT1 electromechanics
- NT1 fluid mechanics
  - NT2 aerodynamics
  - NT2 electrogasdynamics
  - NT2 hydrodynamics
    - NT3 electrohydrodynamics
    - NT3 magnetohydrodynamics
  - NT2 magnetogasdynamics
- NT1 fracture mechanics
- NT1 quantum mechanics
- NT1 rock mechanics
- NT1 soil mechanics
- NT1 statistical mechanics
- RT action integral
- RT anharmonic oscillators
- RT canonical transformations
- RT center-of-mass system
- RT degrees of freedom
- RT equations of motion
- RT galilei transformations
- RT hamilton-jacobi equations
- RT harmonic oscillators
- RT kinetics
- RT laboratory system
- RT lagrange equations
- RT lagrangian function
- RT moment of inertia
- RT physical metallurgy
- RT virial theorem

MEDIASTINUM [1,022; 1,022]
- BT1 chest
  - BT2 body areas
    - BT3 body
- RT aorta
- RT esophagus
- RT heart
- RT pleura
- RT thymus
- RT trachea

medical centres
- USE medical establishments

MEDICAL ESTABLISHMENTS
[270; 985] Dec 76
- UF medical centres
- NT1 hospitals
- RT public health

MEDICAL EXAMINATIONS [696; 696]
Dec 76
- BT1 medical surveillance
- RT diagnosis
- RT preventive medicine

MEDICAL PERSONNEL [1,393; 1,393]
- BT1 personnel
- RT medicine
- RT radiological personnel

MEDICAL RECORDS [139; 139] Dec 76
- RT medical surveillance

medical res. reactor, bnl
- USE mrr reactor

MEDICAL SUPPLIES [653; 1,571]
- NT1 prostheses
  - NT2 mechanical heart
- NT1 surgical materials
- RT drugs
- RT isomed
- RT medicine

MEDICAL SURVEILLANCE [982; 1,658]
- UF surveillance (medical)
- NT1 medical examinations
- RT contamination
- RT delayed radiation effects
- RT dose commitments
- RT medical records
- RT personnel
- RT personnel monitoring
- RT preventive medicine
- RT radiation doses

MEDICINAL PLANTS [142; 228]
- BT1 plants
- NT1 aloe
- NT1 atropa belladonna
- NT1 castor
- NT1 digitalis
- NT1 papaver somniferum
- RT alkaloids
- RT drugs

MEDICINE [1,102; 73,920]
- UF internal medicine
- NT1 balneology
- NT1 biomedical radiography
  - NT2 fluoroscopy
  - NT2 osteodensitometry
- NT1 dentistry
- NT1 gynecology
- NT1 hematology
- NT1 industrial medicine
- NT1 neurology
- NT1 nuclear medicine
- NT1 ophthalmology
- NT1 pediatrics
- NT1 preventive medicine
  - NT2 public health
- NT1 radiology
- NT1 surgery
  - NT2 adrenalectomy
  - NT2 castration
  - NT2 gastrectomy
  - NT2 hepatectomy
  - NT2 hypophysectomy
  - NT2 laryngectomy
  - NT2 nephrectomy
  - NT2 plastic surgery
  - NT2 splenectomy
  - NT2 thymectomy
  - NT2 thyroidectomy
- NT1 therapy
  - NT2 chemotherapy
  - NT2 first aid
  - NT2 immunotherapy
  - NT2 post-irradiation therapy
  - NT2 radiotherapy
    - NT3 afterloading
    - NT3 neutron therapy
      - NT4 neutron capture therapy
  - NT2 transfusions
- NT1 tropical medicine
- NT1 veterinary medicine
- RT anesthesia
- RT biology
- RT diagnosis
- RT diagnostic techniques
- RT hospitals
- RT medical personnel
- RT medical supplies
- RT pathology
- RT patients
- RT who

medicines
- USE drugs

mediterranean fruit fly
- USE ceratitis capitata

MEDITERRANEAN SEA [166; 166]
- BT1 seas
  - BT2 surface waters
- RT cyprus
- RT malta

medium beta plasma
   USE   medium-beta plasma

medium level wastes
   USE   intermediate-level radioactive

MEDIUM PRESSURE [3,681; 3,681]
   UF   *pressure (0.1-10 mpa)*
   UF   *pressure (0001-0100 atm)*
   RT   pressure dependence

MEDIUM TEMPERATURE [30,725; 30,725]
   UF   *temperature (0273-0400 k)*
   RT   temperature dependence

MEDIUM VACUUM [1,379; 1,379]
   UF   *pressure (1-10(-3) torr)*
   UF   *pressure (133-0.13 pa)*
   UF   *vacuum (1-10(-3) torr)*
   UF   *vacuum (133-0.13 pa)*
   UF   *very low pressure*
   RT   cryopumps
   RT   pressure dependence
   RT   turbomolecular pumps
   RT   vacuum pumps

MEDIUM WAVE RADIATION [13; 13]
   UF   *medium-wave radiation*
   BT1   radiowave radiation
   BT2   electromagnetic radiation
   BT3   radiations

MEDIUM-BETA PLASMA [42; 42]
(Beta from 0.01 to 0.1.)
   UF   *medium beta plasma*
   BT1   plasma
   RT   beta ratio

medium-level wastes
   USE   intermediate-level radioactive

medium-wave radiation
   USE   medium wave radiation

MEETINGS [6,904; 6,904]
   UF   *conferences*
   UF   *symposia*

MEG [21; 21]
   UF   *mercaptoethylguanidine*
   BT1   carbonic acid derivatives
   BT2   organic compounds
   BT1   radioprotective substances
   BT2   drugs
   BT2   response modifying factors
   BT1   thiols
   BT2   organic sulfur compounds
   BT3   organic compounds
   RT   guanidines

MEGA AMP BEAM CURRENTS [52; 52] *Oct 76*
(From 10 exp 6 to 10 exp 9 amp.)
   BT1   beam currents
   BT2   currents

megakaryocytes
   USE   bone marrow cells

MEGALOBLASTIC ANEMIA [10; 10]
   BT1   anemias
   BT2   hemic diseases
   BT3   diseases
   BT2   symptoms
   RT   erythrocytes

MEGATRON [1; 1]
   BT1   linear pinch devices
   BT2   open plasma devices
   BT3   thermonuclear devices
   BT2   pinch devices
   BT3   thermonuclear devices

MEGAWATT POWER RANGE [4; 117]
Apr 88
   BT1   power range
   NT1   power range 01-10 mw
   NT1   power range 10-100 mw
   NT1   power range 100-1000 mw

mehrzweck-forschungsreaktor
   USE   mzfr reactor

meinzer unit
   USE   hydraulic conductivity

MEIOSIS [259; 259]
   BT1   cell division
   RT   crossing-over
   RT   gametogenesis
   RT   mutations

MEISSNER-OCHSENFELD EFFECT [428; 428]
   RT   superconductivity

MELAMINE [25; 25]
   BT1   amines
   BT2   organic compounds
   BT1   triazines
   BT2   azines
   BT3   heterocyclic compounds
   BT4   organic compounds
   BT3   organic nitrogen compounds
   BT4   organic compounds
   RT   organic polymers

MELANIN [191; 191]
   UF+   *melanocytes*
   BT1   hydroxy compounds
   BT2   organic compounds
   BT1   organic nitrogen compounds
   BT2   organic compounds
   BT1   pigments
   RT   hair
   RT   methyl tyrosine
   RT   skin
   RT   tyrosine

melanocytes
   USE   animal cells
   AND   melanin

MELANOMAS [1,335; 1,335]
   BT1   neoplasms
   BT2   diseases

MELATONIN [71; 71]
   BT1   tryptamines
   BT2   amines
   BT3   organic compounds
   BT2   indoles
   BT3   pyrroles
   BT4   azoles
   BT5   heterocyclic compounds
   BT6   organic compounds
   BT5   organic nitrogen compounds
   BT6   organic compounds
   RT   pineal gland

melekess-arbus reactor
   USE   arbus reactor

melekess-mir reactor
   USE   mir reactor

melekess-sm-2 reactor
   USE   sm-2 reactor

MELIBIOSE [4; 4]
   BT1   disaccharides
   BT2   oligosaccharides
   BT3   saccharides
   BT4   carbohydrates
   BT5   organic compounds

MELILOTIC ACID [1; 1]
   BT1   hydroxy acids
   BT2   carboxylic acids
   BT3   organic acids
   BT4   organic compounds

MELLIN TRANSFORM [189; 189]
   BT1   integral transformations
   BT2   transformations

MELLITIC ACID [21; 21]
   BT1   carboxylic acids
   BT2   organic acids
   BT3   organic compounds

MELOSH TRANSFORMATION [95; 95]
   RT   hadrons
   RT   quantum field theory
   RT   quarks

melt refining process
   USE   pyrochemical reprocessing

MELTDOWN [3,566; 3,566]
   BT1   reactor accidents
   BT2   accidents
   RT   core catchers
   RT   corium
   RT   source terms

MELTING [4,361; 5,295]
   UF   *fusion (melting)*
   BT1   phase transformations
   NT1   electron beam melting
   NT1   vacuum melting
   NT1   zone melting
   RT   casting
   RT   crucibles
   RT   freezing
   RT   furnaces
   RT   heating
   RT   liquefaction
   RT   melting points
   RT   metallurgical flux
   RT   smelting
   RT   solidification
   RT   subterrene penetrators
   RT   welding

MELTING POINTS [3,157; 3,157]
   UF   *freezing points*
   BT1   transition temperature
   BT2   thermodynamic properties
   BT3   physical properties
   RT   melting
   RT   phase diagrams

MELUSINE-1 REACTOR [41; 41]
(CEA-Grenoble Nuclear Studies Centre, Grenoble Cedex, France)
   UF   *grenoble reactor melusine-1*
   BT1   enriched uranium reactors
   BT2   reactors
   BT1   isotope production reactors
   BT2   irradiation reactors
   BT3   reactors
   BT1   pool type reactors
   BT2   water cooled reactors
   BT3   reactors
   BT2   water moderated reactors
   BT3   reactors
   BT1   research reactors
   BT2   research and test reactors
   BT3   reactors
   BT1   thermal reactors

BT2 reactors
BT1 training reactors
BT2 research and test reactors
BT3 reactors

melusine-2 reactor
USE siloette reactor

MEMBER STATES [313; 313]
(Countries participating in an international organization.)
RT international organizations

MEMBRANE TRANSPORT
[1,468; 1,468] *Jul 86*
RT diffusion
RT mass transfer
RT membranes
RT osmosis

MEMBRANES [2,214; 8,207]
UF+ *ion exchange membranes*
NT1 cell membranes
NT1 fetal membranes
NT2 placenta
NT1 meninges
NT1 serous membranes
NT2 mesentery
NT2 pericardium
NT2 peritoneum
NT2 pleura
RT dialysis
RT membrane transport
RT osmosis
RT permeability

MEMORY DEVICES [1,350; 2,345]
UF *data storage devices*
UF *storage devices (data)*
NT1 cryogenic storage devices
NT1 magnetic storage devices
NT2 magnetic cores
NT2 magnetic disks
NT2 magnetic drums
NT2 magnetic tapes
NT3 video tapes
NT1 semiconductor storage devices
NT1 thin film storage devices
RT punched cards
RT punched tapes

MEN [753; 753]
BT1 males
BT1 man
BT2 primates
BT3 mammals
BT4 vertebrates
BT5 animals
RT adults

mendeleev periodic system
USE periodic system

MENDELEVIUM [56; 56]
BT1 actinides
BT2 metals
BT3 elements
BT1 transplutonium elements
BT2 transuranium elements
BT3 elements

MENDELEVIUM CARBIDES [0; 0]
BT1 carbides
BT2 carbon compounds
BT1 mendelevium compounds
BT2 actinide compounds
BT2 transplutonium compounds
BT3 transuranium compounds

MENDELEVIUM COMPLEXES [13; 13]
BT1 actinide complexes
BT2 complexes
BT1 transuranium complexes

MENDELEVIUM COMPOUNDS [26; 28]
BT1 actinide compounds
BT1 transplutonium compounds
BT2 transuranium compounds
NT1 mendelevium carbides
NT1 mendelevium nitrides
NT1 mendelevium oxides
NT1 mendelevium sulfides

MENDELEVIUM IONS [3; 3]
BT1 ions
BT2 charged particles

MENDELEVIUM ISOTOPES [34; 106]
NT1 mendelevium 247
NT1 mendelevium 248
NT1 mendelevium 249
NT1 mendelevium 250
NT1 mendelevium 251
NT1 mendelevium 252
NT1 mendelevium 253
NT1 mendelevium 254
NT1 mendelevium 255
NT1 mendelevium 256
NT1 mendelevium 257
NT1 mendelevium 258
NT1 mendelevium 259
NT1 mendelevium 260
NT1 mendelevium 261

MENDELEVIUM NITRIDES [0; 0]
BT1 mendelevium compounds
BT2 actinide compounds
BT2 transplutonium compounds
BT3 transuranium compounds
BT1 nitrides
BT2 nitrogen compounds
BT2 pnictides

MENDELEVIUM OXIDES [2; 2]
BT1 mendelevium compounds
BT2 actinide compounds
BT2 transplutonium compounds
BT3 transuranium compounds
BT1 oxides
BT2 chalcogenides
BT2 oxygen compounds

MENDELEVIUM SULFIDES [0; 0]
BT1 mendelevium compounds
BT2 actinide compounds
BT2 transplutonium compounds
BT3 transuranium compounds
BT1 sulfides
BT2 chalcogenides
BT2 sulfur compounds

MENDELEVIUM 247 [0; 0] *Jun 86*
BT1 actinide nuclei
BT2 heavy nuclei
BT3 nuclei
BT1 alpha decay radioisotopes
BT2 radioisotopes
BT3 isotopes
BT1 mendelevium isotopes
BT1 odd-even nuclei
BT2 nuclei
BT1 seconds living radioisotopes
BT2 radioisotopes
BT3 isotopes

MENDELEVIUM 248 [4; 4] *Jul 80*
BT1 actinide nuclei
BT2 heavy nuclei
BT3 nuclei
BT1 alpha decay radioisotopes
BT2 radioisotopes
BT3 isotopes
BT1 electron capture radioisotopes
BT2 beta decay radioisotopes
BT3 radioisotopes
BT4 isotopes
BT1 mendelevium isotopes
BT1 odd-odd nuclei
BT2 nuclei
BT1 seconds living radioisotopes
BT2 radioisotopes
BT3 isotopes

MENDELEVIUM 249 [4; 4] *Jan 77*
BT1 actinide nuclei
BT2 heavy nuclei
BT3 nuclei
BT1 alpha decay radioisotopes
BT2 radioisotopes
BT3 isotopes
BT1 electron capture radioisotopes
BT2 beta decay radioisotopes
BT3 radioisotopes
BT4 isotopes
BT1 mendelevium isotopes
BT1 odd-even nuclei
BT2 nuclei
BT1 seconds living radioisotopes
BT2 radioisotopes
BT3 isotopes

MENDELEVIUM 250 [3; 3]
BT1 actinide nuclei
BT2 heavy nuclei
BT3 nuclei
BT1 alpha decay radioisotopes
BT2 radioisotopes
BT3 isotopes
BT1 electron capture radioisotopes
BT2 beta decay radioisotopes
BT3 radioisotopes
BT4 isotopes
BT1 mendelevium isotopes
BT1 odd-odd nuclei
BT2 nuclei
BT1 seconds living radioisotopes
BT2 radioisotopes
BT3 isotopes

MENDELEVIUM 251 [2; 2] *Jan 77*
BT1 actinide nuclei
BT2 heavy nuclei
BT3 nuclei
BT1 alpha decay radioisotopes
BT2 radioisotopes
BT3 isotopes
BT1 electron capture radioisotopes
BT2 beta decay radioisotopes
BT3 radioisotopes
BT4 isotopes
BT1 mendelevium isotopes
BT1 minutes living radioisotopes
BT2 radioisotopes
BT3 isotopes
BT1 odd-even nuclei
BT2 nuclei

MENDELEVIUM 252 [1; 1]
BT1 actinide nuclei
BT2 heavy nuclei
BT3 nuclei
BT1 electron capture radioisotopes
BT2 beta decay radioisotopes
BT3 radioisotopes
BT4 isotopes
BT1 mendelevium isotopes
BT1 minutes living radioisotopes
BT2 radioisotopes
BT3 isotopes
BT1 odd-odd nuclei
BT2 nuclei

MENDELEVIUM 253 [2; 2] *Jan 77*
BT1 actinide nuclei
BT2 heavy nuclei
BT3 nuclei
BT1 mendelevium isotopes
BT1 odd-even nuclei
BT2 nuclei

MENDELEVIUM 254 [0; 0]
BT1 actinide nuclei
BT2 heavy nuclei
BT3 nuclei
BT1 electron capture radioisotopes
BT2 beta decay radioisotopes
BT3 radioisotopes
BT4 isotopes
BT1 mendelevium isotopes

BT1 minutes living radioisotopes
BT2 radioisotopes
BT3 isotopes
BT1 odd-odd nuclei
BT2 nuclei

MENDELEVIUM 255 [2; 2]
BT1 actinide nuclei
BT2 heavy nuclei
BT3 nuclei
BT1 alpha decay radioisotopes
BT2 radioisotopes
BT3 isotopes
BT1 electron capture radioisotopes
BT2 beta decay radioisotopes
BT3 radioisotopes
BT4 isotopes
BT1 mendelevium isotopes
BT1 minutes living radioisotopes
BT2 radioisotopes
BT3 isotopes
BT1 odd-even nuclei
BT2 nuclei

MENDELEVIUM 256 [29; 29]
BT1 actinide nuclei
BT2 heavy nuclei
BT3 nuclei
BT1 alpha decay radioisotopes
BT2 radioisotopes
BT3 isotopes
BT1 electron capture radioisotopes
BT2 beta decay radioisotopes
BT3 radioisotopes
BT4 isotopes
BT1 hours living radioisotopes
BT2 radioisotopes
BT3 isotopes
BT1 mendelevium isotopes
BT1 odd-odd nuclei
BT2 nuclei

MENDELEVIUM 257 [3; 3]
BT1 actinide nuclei
BT2 heavy nuclei
BT3 nuclei
BT1 alpha decay radioisotopes
BT2 radioisotopes
BT3 isotopes
BT1 electron capture radioisotopes
BT2 beta decay radioisotopes
BT3 radioisotopes
BT4 isotopes
BT1 hours living radioisotopes
BT2 radioisotopes
BT3 isotopes
BT1 mendelevium isotopes
BT1 odd-even nuclei
BT2 nuclei

MENDELEVIUM 258 [11; 11]
BT1 actinide nuclei
BT2 heavy nuclei
BT3 nuclei
BT1 alpha decay radioisotopes
BT2 radioisotopes
BT3 isotopes
BT1 days living radioisotopes
BT2 radioisotopes
BT3 isotopes
BT1 electron capture radioisotopes
BT2 beta decay radioisotopes
BT3 radioisotopes
BT4 isotopes
BT1 mendelevium isotopes
BT1 minutes living radioisotopes
BT2 radioisotopes
BT3 isotopes
BT1 odd-odd nuclei
BT2 nuclei

MENDELEVIUM 259 [22; 22]
BT1 actinide nuclei
BT2 heavy nuclei
BT3 nuclei
BT1 alpha decay radioisotopes
BT2 radioisotopes
BT3 isotopes
BT1 hours living radioisotopes
BT2 radioisotopes
BT3 isotopes
BT1 mendelevium isotopes
BT1 odd-even nuclei
BT2 nuclei
BT1 spontaneous fission radioisoto
BT2 radioisotopes
BT3 isotopes

MENDELEVIUM 260 [21; 21] *Mar 86*
BT1 actinide nuclei
BT2 heavy nuclei
BT3 nuclei
BT1 mendelevium isotopes
BT1 odd-odd nuclei
BT2 nuclei

MENDELEVIUM 261 [2; 2] *Feb 87*
BT1 actinide nuclei
BT2 heavy nuclei
BT3 nuclei
BT1 mendelevium isotopes
BT1 odd-even nuclei
BT2 nuclei

MENDELSSOHN MODEL [0; 0]
RT superconductivity

MENDOCINO-1 REACTOR [13; 13]
BT1 bwr type reactors
BT2 enriched uranium reactors
BT3 reactors
BT2 power reactors
BT3 reactors
BT2 thermal reactors
BT3 reactors
BT2 water cooled reactors
BT3 reactors
BT2 water moderated reactors
BT3 reactors

MENDOCINO-2 REACTOR [13; 13]
BT1 bwr type reactors
BT2 enriched uranium reactors
BT3 reactors
BT2 power reactors
BT3 reactors
BT2 thermal reactors
BT3 reactors
BT2 water cooled reactors
BT3 reactors
BT2 water moderated reactors
BT3 reactors

MENDOZA [6; 6]
BT1 argentina
BT2 developing countries
BT2 south america
BT3 latin america

MENINGES [432; 432]
BT1 membranes
RT central nervous system
RT meningococcus

MENINGOCOCCUS [16; 16]
BT1 bacteria
BT2 microorganisms
RT meninges
RT nervous system diseases

MENOPAUSE [101; 101]
RT age dependence
RT estrous cycle
RT fertility
RT menstrual cycle
RT menstruation disorders

menorrhagia
USE menstruation disorders

MENSTRUAL CYCLE [44; 44] *Oct 84*
RT estrous cycle
RT female genitals
RT fertility
RT menopause
RT menstruation disorders
RT ovulation
RT rhythmicity

MENSTRUATION DISORDERS [68; 68]
UF *amenorrhea*
UF *menorrhagia*
BT1 urogenital system diseases
BT2 diseases
RT estrous cycle
RT female genitals
RT menopause
RT menstrual cycle
RT reproductive disorders

MENTAL DISORDERS [614; 614]
UF *psychoses*
BT1 nervous system diseases
BT2 diseases
RT behavior
RT brain
RT psychotropic drugs

mercamine
USE mea

mercaptans
USE thiols

mercaptoalanine-beta
USE cysteine

mercaptoaminoisovaleric acid
USE penicillamine

mercaptoethylamine
USE mea

mercaptoethylguanidine
USE meg

MERCAPTOPROPYLAMINE [6; 6]
BT1 radioprotective substances
BT2 drugs
BT2 response modifying factors

MERCAPTOPURINE [29; 29]
BT1 antimetabolites
BT2 drugs
BT1 purines
BT2 heterocyclic compounds
BT3 organic compounds
BT2 organic nitrogen compounds
BT3 organic compounds
BT1 thiols
BT2 organic sulfur compounds
BT3 organic compounds

mercaptovaline
USE penicillamine

MERCIER CRITERION [87; 87] *Oct 85*
RT flute instability
RT grad-shafranov equation
RT magnetohydrodynamics
RT plasma instability
RT suydam criterion

mercuric iodide detectors
USE hgi2 semiconductor detectors

MERCURY [2,667; 2,667]
BT1 metals
BT2 elements

MERCURY ADDITIONS [30; 30]
(Alloys containing not more than 1% Hg are listed here.)
RT mercury alloys
RT mercury compounds

MERCURY ALLOYS [551; 567]
(Alloys containing more than 1% Hg.)
UF *amalgams*
BT1 alloys
NT1 mercury base alloys
RT mercury additions

MERCURY BASE ALLOYS [14; 14]
BT1 mercury alloys
BT2 alloys

MERCURY BROMIDES [68; 68]
BT1 bromides
BT2 bromine compounds
BT3 halogen compounds
BT2 halides
BT3 halogen compounds
BT1 mercury halides
BT2 halides
BT3 halogen compounds
BT2 mercury compounds

MERCURY CHLORIDES [262; 262]
BT1 chlorides
BT2 chlorine compounds
BT3 halogen compounds
BT2 halides
BT3 halogen compounds
BT1 mercury halides
BT2 halides
BT3 halogen compounds
BT2 mercury compounds

MERCURY COMPLEXES [142; 142]
BT1 complexes

MERCURY COMPOUNDS [466; 1,891]
NT1 mercury halides
NT2 mercury bromides
NT2 mercury chlorides
NT2 mercury fluorides
NT2 mercury iodides
NT1 mercury hydrides
NT1 mercury nitrates
NT1 mercury oxides
NT1 mercury selenides
NT1 mercury sulfates
NT1 mercury sulfides
NT1 mercury tellurides
RT mercury additions

MERCURY COOLED REACTORS [1; 6]
UF *mercury-cooled reactors*
BT1 liquid metal cooled reactors
BT2 reactors
NT1 clementine reactor
NT1 sbr-2 reactor

MERCURY FLUORIDES [28; 28]
BT1 fluorides
BT2 fluorine compounds
BT3 halogen compounds
BT2 halides
BT3 halogen compounds
BT1 mercury halides
BT2 halides
BT3 halogen compounds
BT2 mercury compounds

MERCURY HALIDES [3; 87] Nov 88
BT1 halides
BT2 halogen compounds
BT1 mercury compounds
NT1 mercury bromides

NT1 mercury chlorides
NT1 mercury fluorides
NT1 mercury iodides

MERCURY HYDRIDES [2; 2] Mar 87
BT1 hydrides
BT2 hydrogen compounds
BT1 mercury compounds

MERCURY IODIDES [299; 299]
BT1 iodides
BT2 halides
BT3 halogen compounds
BT2 iodine compounds
BT3 halogen compounds
BT1 mercury halides
BT2 halides
BT3 halogen compounds
BT2 mercury compounds

MERCURY IONS [161; 161]
BT1 ions
BT2 charged particles

MERCURY ISOTOPES [334; 2,129]
NT1 mercury 175
NT1 mercury 176
NT1 mercury 177
NT1 mercury 178
NT1 mercury 179
NT1 mercury 180
NT1 mercury 181
NT1 mercury 182
NT1 mercury 183
NT1 mercury 184
NT1 mercury 185
NT1 mercury 186
NT1 mercury 187
NT1 mercury 188
NT1 mercury 189
NT1 mercury 190
NT1 mercury 191
NT1 mercury 192
NT1 mercury 193
NT1 mercury 194
NT1 mercury 195
NT1 mercury 196
NT1 mercury 197
NT1 mercury 198
NT1 mercury 199
NT1 mercury 200
NT1 mercury 201
NT1 mercury 202
NT1 mercury 203
NT1 mercury 204
NT1 mercury 205
NT1 mercury 206
NT1 mercury 207
NT1 mercury 208
NT1 mercury 209
NT1 mercury 210
NT1 mercury 211
NT1 mercury 212

MERCURY NITRATES [49; 49]
BT1 mercury compounds
BT1 nitrates
BT2 nitrogen compounds
BT2 oxygen compounds

MERCURY OXIDES [32; 32]
BT1 mercury compounds
BT1 oxides
BT2 chalcogenides
BT2 oxygen compounds

MERCURY PLANET [220; 220]
BT1 planets

MERCURY SELENIDES [45; 45] Mar 76
BT1 mercury compounds
BT1 selenides
BT2 chalcogenides
BT2 selenium compounds

MERCURY SULFATES [6; 6]
BT1 mercury compounds
BT1 sulfates
BT2 oxygen compounds
BT2 sulfur compounds

MERCURY SULFIDES [50; 50]
BT1 mercury compounds
BT1 sulfides
BT2 chalcogenides
BT2 sulfur compounds
RT sulfide minerals

MERCURY TELLURIDES [677; 677]
BT1 mercury compounds
BT1 tellurides
BT2 chalcogenides
BT2 tellurium compounds

MERCURY 175 [0; 0] Sep 83
BT1 alpha decay radioisotopes
BT2 radioisotopes
BT3 isotopes
BT1 even-odd nuclei
BT2 nuclei
BT1 intermediate mass nuclei
BT2 nuclei
BT1 mercury isotopes
BT1 millisec living radioisotopes
BT2 radioisotopes
BT3 isotopes

MERCURY 176 [3; 3] Sep 83
BT1 alpha decay radioisotopes
BT2 radioisotopes
BT3 isotopes
BT1 even-even nuclei
BT2 nuclei
BT1 intermediate mass nuclei
BT2 nuclei
BT1 mercury isotopes
BT1 millisec living radioisotopes
BT2 radioisotopes
BT3 isotopes

MERCURY 177 [5; 5] May 76
BT1 alpha decay radioisotopes
BT2 radioisotopes
BT3 isotopes
BT1 electron capture radioisotopes
BT2 beta decay radioisotopes
BT3 radioisotopes
BT4 isotopes
BT1 even-odd nuclei
BT2 nuclei
BT1 intermediate mass nuclei
BT2 nuclei
BT1 mercury isotopes
BT1 millisec living radioisotopes
BT2 radioisotopes
BT3 isotopes

MERCURY 178 [11; 11]
BT1 alpha decay radioisotopes
BT2 radioisotopes
BT3 isotopes
BT1 electron capture radioisotopes
BT2 beta decay radioisotopes
BT3 radioisotopes
BT4 isotopes
BT1 even-even nuclei
BT2 nuclei
BT1 intermediate mass nuclei
BT2 nuclei
BT1 mercury isotopes
BT1 millisec living radioisotopes
BT2 radioisotopes
BT3 isotopes

MERCURY 179 [8; 8]
BT1 alpha decay radioisotopes
BT2 radioisotopes
BT3 isotopes
BT1 beta-plus decay radioisotopes
BT2 beta decay radioisotopes
BT3 radioisotopes
BT4 isotopes

        BT1   electron capture radioisotopes
        BT2   beta decay radioisotopes
        BT3   radioisotopes
        BT4   isotopes
        BT1   even-odd nuclei
        BT2   nuclei
        BT1   intermediate mass nuclei
        BT2   nuclei
        BT1   mercury isotopes
        BT1   seconds living radioisotopes
        BT2   radioisotopes
        BT3   isotopes

MERCURY 180 [29; 29]
        BT1   alpha decay radioisotopes
        BT2   radioisotopes
        BT3   isotopes
        BT1   electron capture radioisotopes
        BT2   beta decay radioisotopes
        BT3   radioisotopes
        BT4   isotopes
        BT1   even-even nuclei
        BT2   nuclei
        BT1   intermediate mass nuclei
        BT2   nuclei
        BT1   mercury isotopes
        BT1   seconds living radioisotopes
        BT2   radioisotopes
        BT3   isotopes

MERCURY 181 [11; 11]
        BT1   alpha decay radioisotopes
        BT2   radioisotopes
        BT3   isotopes
        BT1   beta-plus decay radioisotopes
        BT2   beta decay radioisotopes
        BT3   radioisotopes
        BT4   isotopes
        BT1   electron capture radioisotopes
        BT2   beta decay radioisotopes
        BT3   radioisotopes
        BT4   isotopes
        BT1   even-odd nuclei
        BT2   nuclei
        BT1   heavy nuclei
        BT2   nuclei
        BT1   mercury isotopes
        BT1   seconds living radioisotopes
        BT2   radioisotopes
        BT3   isotopes

MERCURY 182 [23; 23]
        BT1   alpha decay radioisotopes
        BT2   radioisotopes
        BT3   isotopes
        BT1   beta-plus decay radioisotopes
        BT2   beta decay radioisotopes
        BT3   radioisotopes
        BT4   isotopes
        BT1   electron capture radioisotopes
        BT2   beta decay radioisotopes
        BT3   radioisotopes
        BT4   isotopes
        BT1   even-even nuclei
        BT2   nuclei
        BT1   heavy nuclei
        BT2   nuclei
        BT1   mercury isotopes
        BT1   seconds living radioisotopes
        BT2   radioisotopes
        BT3   isotopes

MERCURY 183 [14; 14]
        BT1   alpha decay radioisotopes
        BT2   radioisotopes
        BT3   isotopes
        BT1   beta-plus decay radioisotopes
        BT2   beta decay radioisotopes
        BT3   radioisotopes
        BT4   isotopes
        BT1   electron capture radioisotopes
        BT2   beta decay radioisotopes
        BT3   radioisotopes
        BT4   isotopes
        BT1   even-odd nuclei
        BT2   nuclei
        BT1   heavy nuclei
        BT2   nuclei
        BT1   mercury isotopes
        BT1   seconds living radioisotopes
        BT2   radioisotopes
        BT3   isotopes

MERCURY 184 [43; 43]
        BT1   alpha decay radioisotopes
        BT2   radioisotopes
        BT3   isotopes
        BT1   beta-plus decay radioisotopes
        BT2   beta decay radioisotopes
        BT3   radioisotopes
        BT4   isotopes
        BT1   electron capture radioisotopes
        BT2   beta decay radioisotopes
        BT3   radioisotopes
        BT4   isotopes
        BT1   even-even nuclei
        BT2   nuclei
        BT1   heavy nuclei
        BT2   nuclei
        BT1   mercury isotopes
        BT1   seconds living radioisotopes
        BT2   radioisotopes
        BT3   isotopes

MERCURY 185 [40; 40]
        BT1   alpha decay radioisotopes
        BT2   radioisotopes
        BT3   isotopes
        BT1   beta-plus decay radioisotopes
        BT2   beta decay radioisotopes
        BT3   radioisotopes
        BT4   isotopes
        BT1   electron capture radioisotopes
        BT2   beta decay radioisotopes
        BT3   radioisotopes
        BT4   isotopes
        BT1   even-odd nuclei
        BT2   nuclei
        BT1   heavy nuclei
        BT2   nuclei
        BT1   mercury isotopes
        BT1   seconds living radioisotopes
        BT2   radioisotopes
        BT3   isotopes

MERCURY 186 [54; 54]
        BT1   alpha decay radioisotopes
        BT2   radioisotopes
        BT3   isotopes
        BT1   beta-plus decay radioisotopes
        BT2   beta decay radioisotopes
        BT3   radioisotopes
        BT4   isotopes
        BT1   electron capture radioisotopes
        BT2   beta decay radioisotopes
        BT3   radioisotopes
        BT4   isotopes
        BT1   even-even nuclei
        BT2   nuclei
        BT1   heavy nuclei
        BT2   nuclei
        BT1   mercury isotopes
        BT1   minutes living radioisotopes
        BT2   radioisotopes
        BT3   isotopes

MERCURY 187 [35; 35]
        BT1   alpha decay radioisotopes
        BT2   radioisotopes
        BT3   isotopes
        BT1   beta-plus decay radioisotopes
        BT2   beta decay radioisotopes
        BT3   radioisotopes
        BT4   isotopes
        BT1   electron capture radioisotopes
        BT2   beta decay radioisotopes
        BT3   radioisotopes
        BT4   isotopes
        BT1   even-odd nuclei
        BT2   nuclei
        BT1   heavy nuclei
        BT2   nuclei
        BT1   mercury isotopes
        BT1   minutes living radioisotopes
        BT2   radioisotopes
        BT3   isotopes

MERCURY 188 [67; 67]
        BT1   alpha decay radioisotopes
        BT2   radioisotopes
        BT3   isotopes
        BT1   beta-plus decay radioisotopes
        BT2   beta decay radioisotopes
        BT3   radioisotopes
        BT4   isotopes
        BT1   electron capture radioisotopes
        BT2   beta decay radioisotopes
        BT3   radioisotopes
        BT4   isotopes
        BT1   even-even nuclei
        BT2   nuclei
        BT1   heavy nuclei
        BT2   nuclei
        BT1   mercury isotopes
        BT1   minutes living radioisotopes
        BT2   radioisotopes
        BT3   isotopes

MERCURY 189 [28; 28]
        BT1   electron capture radioisotopes
        BT2   beta decay radioisotopes
        BT3   radioisotopes
        BT4   isotopes
        BT1   even-odd nuclei
        BT2   nuclei
        BT1   heavy nuclei
        BT2   nuclei
        BT1   mercury isotopes
        BT1   minutes living radioisotopes
        BT2   radioisotopes
        BT3   isotopes

MERCURY 190 [62; 62]
        BT1   electron capture radioisotopes
        BT2   beta decay radioisotopes
        BT3   radioisotopes
        BT4   isotopes
        BT1   even-even nuclei
        BT2   nuclei
        BT1   heavy nuclei
        BT2   nuclei
        BT1   mercury isotopes
        BT1   minutes living radioisotopes
        BT2   radioisotopes
        BT3   isotopes

MERCURY 191 [49; 49]
        BT1   beta-plus decay radioisotopes
        BT2   beta decay radioisotopes
        BT3   radioisotopes
        BT4   isotopes
        BT1   electron capture radioisotopes
        BT2   beta decay radioisotopes
        BT3   radioisotopes
        BT4   isotopes
        BT1   even-odd nuclei
        BT2   nuclei
        BT1   heavy nuclei
        BT2   nuclei
        BT1   mercury isotopes
        BT1   minutes living radioisotopes
        BT2   radioisotopes
        BT3   isotopes

MERCURY 192 [56; 56]
        BT1   electron capture radioisotopes
        BT2   beta decay radioisotopes
        BT3   radioisotopes
        BT4   isotopes
        BT1   even-even nuclei
        BT2   nuclei
        BT1   heavy nuclei
        BT2   nuclei
        BT1   hours living radioisotopes
        BT2   radioisotopes
        BT3   isotopes
        BT1   mercury isotopes

MERCURY 193 [42; 42]
        BT1   beta-plus decay radioisotopes
        BT2   beta decay radioisotopes
        BT3   radioisotopes
        BT4   isotopes
        BT1   electron capture radioisotopes
        BT2   beta decay radioisotopes

        BT3   radioisotopes
          BT4   isotopes
  BT1   even-odd nuclei
    BT2   nuclei
  BT1   heavy nuclei
    BT2   nuclei
  BT1   hours living radioisotopes
    BT2   radioisotopes
      BT3   isotopes
  BT1   internal conversion radioisoto
    BT2   radioisotopes
      BT3   isotopes
  BT1   isomeric transition isotopes
    BT2   radioisotopes
      BT3   isotopes
  BT1   mercury isotopes

MERCURY 194 [98; 98]
  BT1   electron capture radioisotopes
    BT2   beta decay radioisotopes
      BT3   radioisotopes
        BT4   isotopes
  BT1   even-even nuclei
    BT2   nuclei
  BT1   heavy nuclei
    BT2   nuclei
  BT1   mercury isotopes
  BT1   years living radioisotopes
    BT2   radioisotopes
      BT3   isotopes

MERCURY 195 [77; 77]
  BT1   days living radioisotopes
    BT2   radioisotopes
      BT3   isotopes
  BT1   electron capture radioisotopes
    BT2   beta decay radioisotopes
      BT3   radioisotopes
        BT4   isotopes
  BT1   even-odd nuclei
    BT2   nuclei
  BT1   heavy nuclei
    BT2   nuclei
  BT1   hours living radioisotopes
    BT2   radioisotopes
      BT3   isotopes
  BT1   internal conversion radioisoto
    BT2   radioisotopes
      BT3   isotopes
  BT1   isomeric transition isotopes
    BT2   radioisotopes
      BT3   isotopes
  BT1   mercury isotopes

MERCURY 196 [80; 80]
  BT1   even-even nuclei
    BT2   nuclei
  BT1   heavy nuclei
    BT2   nuclei
  BT1   mercury isotopes
  BT1   stable isotopes
    BT2   isotopes

MERCURY 196 TARGET [9; 9] *Jun 84*
  BT1   targets

MERCURY 197 [432; 432]
  BT1   days living radioisotopes
    BT2   radioisotopes
      BT3   isotopes
  BT1   electron capture radioisotopes
    BT2   beta decay radioisotopes
      BT3   radioisotopes
        BT4   isotopes
  BT1   even-odd nuclei
    BT2   nuclei
  BT1   heavy nuclei
    BT2   nuclei
  BT1   hours living radioisotopes
    BT2   radioisotopes
      BT3   isotopes
  BT1   internal conversion radioisoto
    BT2   radioisotopes
      BT3   isotopes
  BT1   isomeric transition isotopes
    BT2   radioisotopes
      BT3   isotopes
  BT1   mercury isotopes

MERCURY 198 [141; 141]
  BT1   even-even nuclei
    BT2   nuclei
  BT1   heavy nuclei
    BT2   nuclei
  BT1   mercury isotopes
  BT1   stable isotopes
    BT2   isotopes

MERCURY 198 TARGET [45; 45]
  BT1   targets

MERCURY 199 [148; 148]
  BT1   even-odd nuclei
    BT2   nuclei
  BT1   heavy nuclei
    BT2   nuclei
  BT1   internal conversion radioisoto
    BT2   radioisotopes
      BT3   isotopes
  BT1   isomeric transition isotopes
    BT2   radioisotopes
      BT3   isotopes
  BT1   mercury isotopes
  BT1   minutes living radioisotopes
    BT2   radioisotopes
      BT3   isotopes
  BT1   stable isotopes
    BT2   isotopes

MERCURY 199 TARGET [31; 31]
  BT1   targets

MERCURY 200 [121; 121]
  BT1   even-even nuclei
    BT2   nuclei
  BT1   heavy nuclei
    BT2   nuclei
  BT1   mercury isotopes
  BT1   stable isotopes
    BT2   isotopes

MERCURY 200 TARGET [39; 39]
  BT1   targets

MERCURY 201 [62; 62]
  BT1   even-odd nuclei
    BT2   nuclei
  BT1   heavy nuclei
    BT2   nuclei
  BT1   isomeric transition isotopes
    BT2   radioisotopes
      BT3   isotopes
  BT1   mercury isotopes
  BT1   microsec living radioisotopes
    BT2   radioisotopes
      BT3   isotopes
  BT1   stable isotopes
    BT2   isotopes

MERCURY 201 TARGET [12; 12]
  BT1   targets

MERCURY 202 [91; 91]
  BT1   even-even nuclei
    BT2   nuclei
  BT1   heavy nuclei
    BT2   nuclei
  BT1   mercury isotopes
  BT1   stable isotopes
    BT2   isotopes

MERCURY 202 TARGET [56; 56]
  BT1   targets

MERCURY 203 [619; 619]
  BT1   beta-minus decay radioisotopes
    BT2   beta decay radioisotopes
      BT3   radioisotopes
        BT4   isotopes
  BT1   days living radioisotopes
    BT2   radioisotopes
      BT3   isotopes
  BT1   even-odd nuclei
    BT2   nuclei
  BT1   heavy nuclei
    BT2   nuclei
  BT1   mercury isotopes

MERCURY 204 [74; 74]
  BT1   even-even nuclei
    BT2   nuclei
  BT1   heavy nuclei
    BT2   nuclei
  BT1   mercury isotopes
  BT1   stable isotopes
    BT2   isotopes

MERCURY 204 TARGET [90; 90]
  BT1   targets

MERCURY 205 [20; 20]
  BT1   beta-minus decay radioisotopes
    BT2   beta decay radioisotopes
      BT3   radioisotopes
        BT4   isotopes
  BT1   even-odd nuclei
    BT2   nuclei
  BT1   heavy nuclei
    BT2   nuclei
  BT1   mercury isotopes
  BT1   minutes living radioisotopes
    BT2   radioisotopes
      BT3   isotopes

MERCURY 206 [36; 36]
  BT1   beta-minus decay radioisotopes
    BT2   beta decay radioisotopes
      BT3   radioisotopes
        BT4   isotopes
  BT1   even-even nuclei
    BT2   nuclei
  BT1   heavy nuclei
    BT2   nuclei
  BT1   mercury isotopes
  BT1   minutes living radioisotopes
    BT2   radioisotopes
      BT3   isotopes

MERCURY 206 TARGET [2; 2] *May 86*
  BT1   targets

MERCURY 207 [3; 3]
  BT1   even-odd nuclei
    BT2   nuclei
  BT1   heavy nuclei
    BT2   nuclei
  BT1   mercury isotopes

MERCURY 208 [6; 6]
  BT1   even-even nuclei
    BT2   nuclei
  BT1   heavy nuclei
    BT2   nuclei
  BT1   mercury isotopes

MERCURY 209 [0; 0]
  BT1   even-odd nuclei
    BT2   nuclei
  BT1   heavy nuclei
    BT2   nuclei
  BT1   mercury isotopes

MERCURY 210 [1; 1]
  BT1   even-even nuclei
    BT2   nuclei
  BT1   heavy nuclei
    BT2   nuclei
  BT1   mercury isotopes

MERCURY 211 [0; 0]
  BT1   even-odd nuclei
    BT2   nuclei
  BT1   heavy nuclei
    BT2   nuclei
  BT1   mercury isotopes

MERCURY 212 [0; 0]
  BT1   even-even nuclei
   BT2   nuclei
  BT1   heavy nuclei
   BT2   nuclei
  BT1   mercury isotopes

mercury-cooled reactors
  USE   mercury cooled reactors

MERISTEMS [209; 209]
  UF   *cambium*
  BT1   plant tissues

merlin-juelich reactor
  USE   frj-1 reactor

MERONS [36; 36] *Feb 83*
(Class of solutions of certain field equations; merons appear as particles with one-half unit of topological charge.)
  BT1   quasi particles
  RT   field equations
  RT   instantons
  RT   quark model
  RT   thirring model

MESENTERY [116; 116]
  UF   *omentum*
  BT1   serous membranes
   BT2   membranes
  RT   peritoneum
  RT   small intestine

MESH GENERATION [575; 575] *Oct 82*
(Procedure of preparing coordinate grid for complex calculations, e.g. neutron transport calculations.)
  RT   computer calculations
  RT   coordinates
  RT   finite difference method
  RT   finite element method
  RT   mathematics
  RT   nodal expansion method

MESIC ATOMS [244; 1,882]
  UF   *mesoatoms*
  BT1   hadronic atoms
   BT2   atoms
  NT1   kaonic atoms
  NT1   muonic atoms
  NT1   pionic atoms
  RT   mesic molecules
  RT   mesons
  RT   pi-k atoms
  RT   pi mu atoms

MESIC MOLECULES [137; 685]
  BT1   molecules
  NT1   muonic molecules
  RT   mesic atoms
  RT   mesons

MESITYL RADICALS [2; 2]
  BT1   aryl radicals
   BT2   radicals

MESITYLENE [53; 53]
  UF   *trimethylbenzene-sym*
  UF   *1,3,5-trimethylbenzene*
  BT1   aromatics
   BT2   organic compounds
  BT1   hydrocarbons
   BT2   organic compounds

mesoatoms
  USE   mesic atoms

mesocricetus
  USE   hamsters

MESON BEAMS [125; 2,768]
  BT1   particle beams
   BT2   beams
  NT1   eta meson beams
  NT1   kaon beams
  NT1   pion beams

MESON FACTORIES [398; 1,637]
  BT1   accelerators
  NT1   lampf ii synchrotron
  NT1   lampf linac
  RT   pigmi facilities

MESON NONETS [235; 235]
  BT1   particle multiplets
   BT2   multiplets

MESON OCTETS [96; 96]
  BT1   particle multiplets
   BT2   multiplets

MESON REACTIONS [106; 7,739]
  UF+   *meson-deuteron interactions*
  BT1   hadron reactions
   BT2   nuclear reactions
  NT1   kaon reactions
   NT2   kaon minus reactions
   NT2   kaon neutral reactions
   NT2   kaon plus reactions
  NT1   pion reactions
   NT2   pion minus reactions
   NT2   pion plus reactions

meson resonances
(Prior to December 1987 this was a valid descriptor.)
  USE   mesons

MESON SPECTROSCOPY [365; 365]
  BT1   spectroscopy
  RT   mesons

MESON-BARYON INTERACTIONS [220; 10,292]
  BT1   hadron-hadron interactions
   BT2   particle interactions
    BT3   interactions
  NT1   meson-hyperon interactions
   NT2   kaon-hyperon interactions
   NT2   pion-hyperon interactions
  NT1   meson-nucleon interactions
   NT2   kaon-nucleon interactions
    NT3   kaon-neutron interactions
     NT4   kaon minus-neutron interaction
     NT4   kaon neutral-neutron interacti
     NT4   kaon plus-neutron interactions
    NT3   kaon-proton interactions
     NT4   kaon minus-proton interactions
     NT4   kaon neutral-proton interactio
     NT4   kaon plus-proton interactions
   NT2   pion-nucleon interactions
    NT3   pion-neutron interactions
     NT4   pion minus-neutron interaction
     NT4   pion plus-neutron interactions
    NT3   pion-proton interactions
     NT4   pion minus-proton interactions
     NT4   pion plus-proton interactions

meson-deuteron interactions
  USE   deuterium target
  AND   meson reactions

MESON-HYPERON INTERACTIONS [6; 38]
  BT1   meson-baryon interactions
   BT2   hadron-hadron interactions
    BT3   particle interactions
     BT4   interactions
  NT1   kaon-hyperon interactions
  NT1   pion-hyperon interactions

MESON-MESON INTERACTIONS [249; 1,285]
  BT1   hadron-hadron interactions
   BT2   particle interactions
    BT3   interactions
  NT1   kaon-kaon interactions
  NT1   pion-kaon interactions
  NT1   pion-pion interactions

MESON-NUCLEON INTERACTIONS [445; 10,081]
  BT1   meson-baryon interactions
   BT2   hadron-hadron interactions
    BT3   particle interactions
     BT4   interactions
  NT1   kaon-nucleon interactions
   NT2   kaon-neutron interactions
    NT3   kaon minus-neutron interaction
    NT3   kaon neutral-neutron interacti
    NT3   kaon plus-neutron interactions
   NT2   kaon-proton interactions
    NT3   kaon minus-proton interactions
    NT3   kaon neutral-proton interactio
    NT3   kaon plus-proton interactions
  NT1   pion-nucleon interactions
   NT2   pion-neutron interactions
    NT3   pion minus-neutron interaction
    NT3   pion plus-neutron interactions
   NT2   pion-proton interactions
    NT3   pion minus-proton interactions
    NT3   pion plus-proton interactions

MESONS [3,503; 46,383]
  UF   *a resonances*
  UF   *a2h-1320 resonances*
  UF   *a2l-1280 resonances*
  UF   *c-1430 resonances*
  UF   *chi resonances*
  UF   *chi-2800 resonances*
  UF   *chi-3455 resonances*
  UF   *eta-700 resonances*
  UF   *f-1540 resonances*
  UF   *kappa-725 resonances*
  UF   *meson resonances*
  UF   *omega-1778 resonances*
  UF   *psi resonances*
  UF   *psi-4300 resonances*
  UF   *r-1650 resonances*
  UF   *rho-1500 resonances*
  UF   *rho-1700 resonances*
  UF   *s-1000 resonances*
  UF   *x-2830 resonances*
  UF+   *antimesons*
  BT1   bosons
  BT1   hadrons
   BT2   elementary particles
  NT1   axial vector mesons
   NT2   a1-1270 mesons
   NT2   b1-1235 mesons
   NT2   chi1-3510 mesons
   NT2   f1-1285 mesons
   NT2   f1-1420 mesons
   NT2   f1-1530 mesons
   NT2   h1-1190 mesons
   NT2   k1-1280 mesons
   NT2   k1-1400 mesons
  NT1   baryonium
  NT1   beauty mesons
   NT2   b*-5325 mesons
  NT1   bottomonium
   NT2   chi b0-10235 mesons
   NT2   chi b0-9860 mesons
   NT2   chi b1-10255 mesons
   NT2   chi b1-9895 mesons
   NT2   chi b2-10270 mesons
   NT2   chi b2-9915 mesons

NT2	upsilon-10023 mesons	NT3	kaons neutral	**METABOLIC DISEASES** [884; 884]	
NT2	upsilon-10355 mesons	NT4	antikaons neutral	UF	obesity
NT2	upsilon-10575 mesons	NT4	kaons neutral long-lived	UF+	calcinosis
NT2	upsilon-10860 mesons	NT4	kaons neutral short-lived	BT1	diseases
NT2	upsilon-11020 mesons	NT3	kaons plus	RT	biochemical reaction kinetics
NT2	upsilon-9460 mesons	NT2	k1-1280 mesons	RT	diabetes mellitus
NT1	charmed mesons	NT2	k1-1400 mesons	RT	metabolism
NT2	d mesons	NT2	k2-1580 mesons		
NT3	d minus mesons	NT2	k2-1770 mesons		
NT3	d neutral mesons	NT2	k2-2250 mesons		
NT4	anti-d neutral mesons	NT2	k3-2320 mesons	*metabolic pathways*	
NT3	d plus mesons	NT2	k4-2500 mesons	USE	biological pathways
NT2	d s mesons	NT1	strangeonium		
NT2	d*-2010 mesons	NT2	f2-1525 mesons	**METABOLISM** [13,029; 13,329]	
NT2	d*-2420 mesons	NT2	phi j-1850 mesons	NT1	anabolism
NT2	d*s-2110 mesons	NT2	phi-1020 mesons	NT1	basal metabolism
NT1	charmonium	NT2	phi-1680 mesons	NT1	catabolism
NT2	chi0-3415 mesons	NT1	tensor mesons	RT	biochemical reaction kinetics
NT2	chi1-3510 mesons	NT2	a2-1320 mesons	RT	biochemistry
NT2	chi2-3555 mesons	NT2	a3-2050 mesons	RT	biological functions
NT2	eta c-2980 mesons	NT2	a4-2040 mesons	RT	biological markers
NT2	eta c-3590 mesons	NT2	a6-2450 mesons	RT	biosynthesis
NT2	j psi-3097 mesons	NT2	chi2-3555 mesons	RT	carbon cycle
NT2	psi-3685 mesons	NT2	f2-1270 mesons	RT	carbon dioxide fixation
NT2	psi-3770 mesons	NT2	f2-1410 mesons	RT	coenzymes
NT2	psi-4030 mesons	NT2	f2-1525 mesons	RT	diabetes mellitus
NT2	psi-4160 mesons	NT2	f2-1720 mesons	RT	dna adducts
NT2	psi-4415 mesons	NT2	f2-1810 mesons	RT	enzyme activity
NT1	pomeranchuk particles	NT2	f2-2150 mesons	RT	enzymes
NT1	pseudoscalar mesons	NT2	f2-2240 mesons	RT	fasting
NT2	b mesons	NT2	f4-2030 mesons	RT	glucagon
NT3	b minus mesons	NT2	f4-2300 mesons	RT	growth
NT3	b neutral mesons	NT2	f6-2510 mesons	RT	hypothalamus
NT4	anti-b neutral mesons	NT2	k*2-1430 mesons	RT	insulin
NT3	b plus mesons	NT2	k*3-1780 mesons	RT	krebs cycle
NT2	d mesons	NT2	k*4-2060 mesons	RT	labelled pool techniques
NT3	d minus mesons	NT2	k2-1580 mesons	RT	liver
NT3	d neutral mesons	NT2	k2-1770 mesons	RT	metabolic diseases
NT4	anti-d neutral mesons	NT2	k2-2250 mesons	RT	metabolites
NT3	d plus mesons	NT2	k3-2320 mesons	RT	molecular biology
NT2	eta c-2980 mesons	NT2	k4-2500 mesons	RT	nitrogen cycle
NT2	eta c-3590 mesons	NT2	omega3-1670 mesons	RT	nitrogen fixation
NT2	eta mesons	NT2	phi j-1850 mesons	RT	physiology
NT2	eta prime-958 mesons	NT2	pi2-1680 mesons	RT	precursor
NT2	eta-1275 mesons	NT2	pi2-2100 mesons	RT	radionuclide kinetics
NT2	eta-1440 mesons	NT2	rho3-1690 mesons	RT	renal clearance
NT2	k-1460 mesons	NT2	rho3-2250 mesons	RT	respiration
NT2	k-1830 mesons	NT2	rho5-2350 mesons	RT	sulfur cycle
NT2	kaons	NT1	toponium	RT	symbiosis
NT3	antikaons	NT1	vector mesons	RT	thyroid hormones
NT4	antikaons neutral	NT2	d*-2010 mesons	RT	vitamins
NT3	cosmic kaons	NT2	j psi-3097 mesons		
NT3	kaons minus	NT2	k*-1410 mesons	**METABOLITES** [1,346; 1,346] Jan 78	
NT3	kaons neutral	NT2	k*-1790 mesons	RT	dna adducts
NT4	antikaons neutral	NT2	k*-892 mesons	RT	krebs cycle
NT4	kaons neutral long-lived	NT2	omega-783 mesons	RT	metabolism
NT4	kaons neutral short-lived	NT2	phi-1020 mesons	RT	pregnanediol
NT3	kaons plus	NT2	phi-1680 mesons	RT	pregnanetriol
NT2	pi-1300 mesons	NT2	psi-3685 mesons		
NT2	pi-1770 mesons	NT2	psi-3770 mesons		
NT2	pions	NT2	psi-4030 mesons		
NT3	cosmic pions	NT2	psi-4160 mesons	*metacercariae*	
NT3	pions minus	NT2	psi-4415 mesons	USE	larvae
NT3	pions neutral	NT2	rho-1250 mesons		
NT3	pions plus	NT2	rho-1600 mesons		
NT1	scalar mesons	NT2	rho-2150 mesons	*metagalaxy*	
NT2	a0-980 mesons	NT2	rho-770 mesons	USE	universe
NT2	chi0-3415 mesons	NT2	upsilon-10023 mesons		
NT2	f0-1240 mesons	NT2	upsilon-10355 mesons	**METAL MODERATED REACTORS** [3; 140]	
NT2	f0-1300 mesons	NT2	upsilon-10575 mesons	UF	metal-moderated reactors
NT2	f0-1590 mesons	NT2	upsilon-10860 mesons	BT1	reactors
NT2	f0-1730 mesons	NT2	upsilon-11020 mesons	NT1	beryllium moderated reactors
NT2	f0-975 mesons	NT2	upsilon-9460 mesons	NT2	agata reactor
NT2	k*0-1350 mesons	NT1	x-1700 mesons	NT2	br-02 reactor
NT1	strange mesons	NT1	x-1935 mesons	NT2	ebor reactor
NT2	k*-1410 mesons	NT1	x-2220 mesons	NT2	maria reactor
NT2	k*-1790 mesons	NT1	x-3075 mesons	NT2	nuclear furnace reactor
NT2	k*-892 mesons	RT	mesic atoms		
NT2	k*0-1350 mesons	RT	mesic molecules		
NT2	k*2-1430 mesons	RT	meson spectroscopy	*metal spraying*	
NT2	k*3-1780 mesons			USE	spray coating
NT2	k*4-2060 mesons	**MESOSPHERE** [171; 171]			
NT2	k-1460 mesons	BT1	earth atmosphere	**METAL TRANSFER PROCESS** [12; 12	
NT2	k-1830 mesons			BT1	separation processes
NT2	kaons	**MESSENGER-RNA** [833; 833]		RT	molten salt reactors
NT3	antikaons	BT1	rna		
NT4	antikaons neutral	BT2	nucleic acids		
NT3	cosmic kaons	BT3	organic compounds		
NT3	kaons minus	RT	transcription		

metal vapor lasers
  USE   gas lasers

metal-moderated reactors
  USE   metal moderated reactors

metal-water reactions
  USE   molten metal-water reactions

METALLIC GLASSES [868; 868] *Jan 84*
(Amorphous alloys produced by extremely rapid quenching of molten material.)
  UF   *glassy alloys*
  UF   *glassy metals*
  UF   *metglass*
  RT   amorphous state
  RT   glass
  RT   vitrification

METALLOGRAPHY [2,348; 2,348]
(Limited to the branch of metallurgy concerned with the preparation and examination of the surface of metals.)
  RT   etching
  RT   fractography
  RT   materials testing
  RT   microscopy
  RT   microstructure
  RT   photomicrography
  RT   polishing
  RT   surface finishing

metalloids
  USE   semimetals

METALLOTHIONEIN [144; 144] *May 76*
(Low molecular weight metal-binding proteins controlling heavy metal detoxification.)
  BT1   proteins
    BT2   organic compounds
  RT   metals

METALLURGICAL FLUX [225; 225]
  UF   *flux (metallurgy)*
  UF   *soldering fluxes*
  UF   *welding fluxes*
  RT   melting
  RT   welding

METALLURGY [1,743; 4,028]
(Use of a more specific descriptor is recommended; see also FABRICATION.)
  NT1   electrometallurgy
  NT1   extractive metallurgy
    NT2   hydrometallurgy
    NT2   pyrometallurgy
      NT3   chloride volatility process
      NT3   fluoride volatility process
  NT1   physical metallurgy
  NT1   powder metallurgy
  RT   zone refining

METALS [8,756; 162,305]
  BT1   elements
  *NT1   actinides
  *NT1   alkali metals
  *NT1   alkaline earth metals
  NT1   aluminium
  NT1   antimony
  NT1   bismuth
  NT1   cadmium
  NT1   gallium
  NT1   germanium
  NT1   indium
  NT1   lead
  NT1   liquid metals
  NT1   mercury
  NT1   polonium
  *NT1   rare earths
  NT1   thallium
  NT1   tin
  *NT1   transition elements
  NT1   zinc

  RT   alloys
  RT   azbel-kaner resonance
  RT   carbonyls
  RT   grueneisen formula
  RT   metallothionein
  RT   semimetals
  RT   work functions

METAMICT STATE [25; 25] *Jun 85*
(State of a radioactive mineral, exhibiting lattice disruption due to radiation damage while the original external morphology is retained.)
  RT   crystal structure
  RT   minerals
  RT   physical radiation effects

METAMORPHIC ROCKS [742; 1,477]
  UF+   *marble*
  BT1   rocks
  NT1   gneisses
  NT1   quartzites
  NT1   schists

METAMORPHISM [780; 780]
  UF   *hydrothermal alteration*
  RT   geology
  RT   hydrothermal stage
  RT   tectonics

METAMORPHOSIS [66; 66]
  RT   adults
  RT   larvae
  RT   ontogenesis
  RT   pupae

metaphase
  USE   mitosis

METASTABLE STATES [3,025; 3,025]
(For atomic and molecular states only; for nuclear states use ISOMERIC NUCLEI.)
  BT1   excited states
    BT2   energy levels

METASTASES [6,245; 6,245]
  RT   neoplasms

METEORITES [1,213; 2,217]
  NT1   iron meteorites
  NT1   stone meteorites
    NT2   achondrites
    NT2   chondrites
  RT   meteoroids
  RT   tektites

METEOROIDS [258; 258]
  UF   *meteors*
  RT   meteorites
  RT   solar system

METEOROLOGY [2,415; 2,415]
  RT   atmospheric circulation
  RT   atmospheric precipitations
  RT   climates
  RT   clouds
  RT   condensation nuclei
  RT   earth atmosphere
  RT   general circulation models
  RT   seasons
  RT   site selection
  RT   site surveys
  RT   temperature inversions
  RT   weather
  RT   wind

meteors
  USE   meteoroids

meter wave radiation
  USE   mhz range
  AND   radiowave radiation

metglass
  USE   metallic glasses

METHACRYLATES [246; 246]
  BT1   carboxylic acid salts
  RT   vinyl monomers

METHACRYLIC ACID [127; 127]
  UF   *methacrylic acid-alpha*
  BT1   monocarboxylic acids
    BT2   carboxylic acids
      BT3   organic acids
        BT4   organic compounds
  RT   polyacrylates
  RT   vinyl monomers

METHACRYLIC ACID ESTERS [444; 444]
  UF   *methyl methacrylate*
  BT1   carboxylic acid esters
    BT2   esters
      BT3   organic compounds
  RT   pmma
  RT   vinyl monomers

methacrylic acid-alpha
  USE   methacrylic acid

METHADONE HYDROCHLORIDE [12; 12] *May 84*
  BT1   narcotics
    BT2   central nervous system depress
      BT3   central nervous system agents
        BT4   drugs

METHANE [3,758; 3,758]
  BT1   alkanes
    BT2   hydrocarbons
      BT3   organic compounds
  RT   bromoform
  RT   carbon tetrachloride
  RT   carbon tetrafluoride
  RT   chloroform
  RT   cryogenic fluids
  RT   ems
  RT   fluoroform
  RT   iodoform
  RT   methyl chloride
  RT   methylene chloride
  RT   nitromethane

METHANOGENIC BACTERIA [61; 61] *May 81*
(Bacteria which ferment various organic materials with the production of methane.)
  BT1   bacteria
    BT2   microorganisms

METHANOL [1,995; 1,995]
  UF   *carbinol*
  UF   *methyl alcohol*
  UF   *wood alcohol*
  BT1   alcohols
    BT2   hydroxy compounds
      BT3   organic compounds

METHEMOGLOBIN [66; 66]
  BT1   hemoglobin
    BT2   globins
      BT3   proteins
        BT4   organic compounds
    BT2   pigments
    BT2   porphyrins
      BT3   heterocyclic acids
        BT4   carboxylic acids
          BT5   organic acids
            BT6   organic compounds
        BT4   heterocyclic compounds
          BT5   organic compounds
      BT3   organic nitrogen compounds
        BT4   organic compounds
  RT   erythrocytes
  RT   heme
  RT   respiration

methenamine
USE urotropin

METHIONINE [1,476; 1,476]
UF *methylmercaptoaminobutyric aci*
UF *methylthioaminobutyric acid*
BT1 amino acids
BT2 carboxylic acids
BT3 organic acids
BT4 organic compounds
BT1 lipotropic factors
BT2 drugs
BT1 organic sulfur compounds
BT2 organic compounds

METHOTREXATE [343; 343]
UF *amethopterin*
BT1 antimetabolites
BT2 drugs

METHOXY RADICALS [63; 63]
BT1 alkoxy radicals
BT2 radicals

methoxybenzene
USE anisole

methyl alcohol
USE methanol

METHYL BROMIDE [81; 81] *Aug 76*
BT1 organic bromine compounds
BT2 organic halogen compounds
BT3 organic compounds
RT fumigants

METHYL CHLORIDE [77; 77] *Jul 78*
UF *chloromethane*
BT1 chlorinated aliphatic hydrocar
BT2 halogenated aliphatic hydrocar
BT3 organic halogen compounds
BT4 organic compounds
BT2 organic chlorine compounds
BT3 organic halogen compounds
BT4 organic compounds
RT methane

METHYL ETHER [53; 53] *Jul 76*
UF *dimethyl ether*
BT1 ethers
BT2 organic oxygen compounds
BT3 organic compounds
RT organic solvents

methyl ethyl diketone
USE 2-3-pentanedione

METHYL FLUORIDE [64; 64] *Jul 78*
BT1 organic fluorine compounds
BT2 organic halogen compounds
BT3 organic compounds

methyl glycocoll
USE sarcosine

METHYL IODIDE [623; 623]
BT1 organic iodine compounds
BT2 organic halogen compounds
BT3 organic compounds
RT iodox process

METHYL ISOBUTYL KETONE [127; 127]
UF *mibk*
BT1 ketones
BT2 organic compounds

methyl methacrylate
USE methacrylic acid esters

METHYL METHANESULFONATE [159; 159] *Apr 76*
(Prior to August 1985 MMS was used.)
UF *mms*
BT1 mutagens
BT1 sulfonic acid esters
BT2 esters
BT3 organic compounds
BT2 organic sulfur compounds
BT3 organic compounds
RT alkylating agents

METHYL ORANGE [17; 17]
BT1 amines
BT2 organic compounds
BT1 azo dyes
BT2 azo compounds
BT3 organic nitrogen compounds
BT4 organic compounds
BT2 dyes
BT1 indicators
BT1 sulfonic acids
BT2 organic acids
BT3 organic compounds
BT2 organic sulfur compounds
BT3 organic compounds

methyl phenols
USE cresols

methyl phenyl ether
USE anisole

methyl phenyl ketone
USE acetophenone

methyl pyridines
USE picolines

METHYL RADICALS [507; 507]
BT1 alkyl radicals
BT2 radicals

METHYL RED [10; 10]
BT1 amino acids
BT2 carboxylic acids
BT3 organic acids
BT4 organic compounds
BT1 azo dyes
BT2 azo compounds
BT3 organic nitrogen compounds
BT4 organic compounds
BT2 dyes
BT1 indicators

METHYL TRANSFERASES [51; 51] *Dec 85*
BT1 carbon-group transferases
BT2 transferases
BT3 enzymes
BT4 organic compounds
RT methylation

METHYL TYROSINE [8; 8] *Aug 81*
UF *methyltyrosine*
BT1 amino acids
BT2 carboxylic acids
BT3 organic acids
BT4 organic compounds
BT1 aromatics
BT2 organic compounds
BT1 hydroxy acids
BT2 carboxylic acids
BT3 organic acids
BT4 organic compounds
RT melanin
RT radiopharmaceuticals
RT tyrosine

METHYL VIOLET [16; 16]
BT1 amines
BT2 organic compounds
BT1 triphenylmethane dyes
BT2 dyes

methylacetylene
USE propyne

METHYLAL [63; 63]
UF *formal*
UF *formaldehydedimethylacetal*
UF *1,2-dimethoxymethane*
BT1 ethers
BT2 organic oxygen compounds
BT3 organic compounds
RT formaldehyde

METHYLAMINE [114; 114] *Sep 75*
BT1 amines
BT2 organic compounds

methylaminoacetic acid
USE sarcosine

METHYLATION [395; 395]
BT1 chemical reactions
RT methyl transferases
RT post-translation modification

methylbenzene
USE toluene

methylbutane (2-)
USE 2-methylbutane

METHYLENE BLUE [128; 128]
BT1 amines
BT2 organic compounds
BT1 antibiotics
BT2 drugs
BT2 organic compounds
BT1 chlorides
BT2 chlorine compounds
BT3 halogen compounds
BT2 halides
BT3 halogen compounds
BT1 phenothiazines
BT2 azines
BT3 heterocyclic compounds
BT4 organic compounds
BT3 organic nitrogen compounds
BT4 organic compounds
BT2 organic sulfur compounds
BT3 organic compounds

METHYLENE CHLORIDE [73; 73] *Feb 82*
UF *dichloromethane*
BT1 organic chlorine compounds
BT2 organic halogen compounds
BT3 organic compounds
RT methane

METHYLENE RADICALS [139; 139]
UF *methylidene radicals*
BT1 radicals

methylidene radicals
USE methylene radicals

methylmercaptoaminobutyric aci
USE methionine

methylmercury
USE organic mercury compounds

methylpropane (2-)
 USE 2-methylpropane

methylpropanol (2-)
 USE 2-methylpropanol

methylpropene (2-)
 USE 2-methylpropene

methyltetrahydrofuran
 USE furans

methylthioaminobutyric acid
 USE methionine

METHYLTHYMOL BLUE [33; 33]
 BT1 indicators
 BT1 triphenylmethane dyes
 BT2 dyes

methyltyrosine
 USE methyl tyrosine

METRICS [6,489; 8,006]
 NT1 kerr metric
 NT1 schwarzschild metric
 RT curvilinear coordinates
 RT fractals
 RT gravitational fields
 RT mathematical space
 RT mathematics
 RT matrices
 RT measure theory
 RT relativity theory
 RT space-time
 RT tensors

METRIZAMIDE [231; 231] *Aug 81*
 UF *amipaque*
 BT1 amides
  BT2 organic nitrogen compounds
   BT3 organic compounds
 BT1 contrast media

METRONIDAZOLE [299; 299]
 UF *flagyl*
 BT1 alcohols
  BT2 hydroxy compounds
   BT3 organic compounds
 BT1 antineoplastic drugs
  BT2 drugs
 BT1 imidazoles
  BT2 azoles
   BT3 heterocyclic compounds
    BT4 organic compounds
   BT3 organic nitrogen compounds
    BT4 organic compounds
 BT1 nitro compounds
  BT2 organic nitrogen compounds
   BT3 organic compounds
 BT1 radiosensitizers
  BT2 drugs
  BT2 response modifying factors

metropolitan areas
 USE urban areas

MEV RANGE [2,550; 79,045]
 (From 10 exp 6 to 10 exp 9 ev.)
 BT1 energy range
 NT1 mev range 01-10
 NT1 mev range 10-100
 NT1 mev range 100-1000

MEV RANGE 01-10 [25,514; 25,514]
 BT1 mev range
  BT2 energy range

MEV RANGE 10-100 [38,034; 38,034]
 BT1 mev range
  BT2 energy range

MEV RANGE 100-1000 [22,585; 22,585]
 BT1 mev range
  BT2 energy range

MEVALONIC ACID [55; 55]
 BT1 hydroxy acids
  BT2 carboxylic acids
   BT3 organic acids
    BT4 organic compounds

MEXAMINE [139; 139]
 BT1 ethers
  BT2 organic oxygen compounds
   BT3 organic compounds
 BT1 radioprotective substances
  BT2 drugs
  BT2 response modifying factors
 RT serotonin

MEXICAN ORGANIZATIONS [12; 12]
 Dec 75
 BT1 national organizations

mexican triga-mk-3 reactor
 USE triga-3-salazar reactor

MEXICO [405; 405]
 BT1 developing countries
 BT1 latin america
 BT1 north america

MFTF DEVICES [585; 585] *Apr 78*
 (Mirror Fusion Test Facility.)
 BT1 magnetic mirrors
  BT2 open plasma devices
   BT3 thermonuclear devices

MH-1A REACTOR [2; 2]
 UF *float. nuc. pow. plant-sturgis*
 UF *sturgis-float. nuc. pow. plant*
 BT1 experimental reactors
  BT2 research and test reactors
   BT3 reactors
 BT1 mobile reactors
  BT2 reactors
 BT1 pwr type reactors
  BT2 enriched uranium reactors
   BT3 reactors
  BT2 power reactors
   BT3 reactors
  BT2 thermal reactors
   BT3 reactors
  BT2 water cooled reactors
   BT3 reactors
  BT2 water moderated reactors
   BT3 reactors

MHD CHANNELS [514; 514]
 UF *magnetohydrodynamic channels*
 RT mhd generators
 RT plasma seeding

MHD EQUILIBRIUM [971; 971] *May 84*
 BT1 equilibrium
 RT magnetohydrodynamics
 RT plasma instability

MHD GENERATORS [1,218; 1,477]
 UF *faraday generators*
 UF *hall generators*
 UF *magnetohydrodynamic generators*
 BT1 direct energy converters
 NT1 closed-cycle mhd generators
  NT2 liquid-metal mhd generators
 NT1 open-cycle mhd generators
 RT end effects
 RT magnetohydrodynamics
 RT mhd channels
 RT plasma seeding
 RT seed-slag interactions
 RT vapor jet ejectors

 RT vapor separators

mhd instabilities (plasma)
 USE plasma macroinstabilities

MHZ RANGE [462; 3,845]
 UF *very high frequency*
 UF *vhf*
 UF+ *meter wave radiation*
 UF+ *very high frequency radiation*
 UF+ *vhf radiation*
 BT1 frequency range
 NT1 mhz range 01-100
 NT1 mhz range 100-1000
 RT radioastronomy

MHZ RANGE 01-100 [2,054; 2,054]
 BT1 mhz range
  BT2 frequency range

MHZ RANGE 100-1000 [1,538; 1,538]
 UF+ *decimeter wave radiat (3-10dm)*
 UF+ *uhf radiation (lower range)*
 UF+ *uhf radiation (100-1000 mhz)*
 UF+ *ultrahi. fr rad (100-1000 mhz)*
 UF+ *ultrahigh freq rad (lower r.)*
 BT1 mhz range
  BT2 frequency range

MI VIDA MINE [0; 0]
 BT1 uranium mines
  BT2 mines
   BT3 underground facilities
 RT utah

mibk
 USE methyl isobutyl ketone

MICA [491; 971]
 BT1 silicate minerals
  BT2 minerals
 NT1 biotite
 NT1 muscovite
 RT dielectric materials
 RT dielectric track detectors
 RT kimberlites
 RT pegmatites

MICE [15,673; 15,673]
 BT1 rodents
  BT2 mammals
   BT3 vertebrates
    BT4 animals

MICHELSON INTERFEROMETER
 [157; 157] *Mar 77*
 BT1 interferometers
  BT2 measuring instruments

MICHIGAN [222; 222]
 BT1 usa
  BT2 developed countries
  BT2 north america

michigan state triga-mk 1 reac
 USE triga-1-michigan reactor

michigan state univ cyclotrons
 USE msu cyclotrons

MICRO AMP BEAM CURRENTS
 [964; 964]
 (From 10 exp -6 to .001 amp.)
 BT1 beam currents
  BT2 currents

MICROANALYSIS [1,698; 3,124]
 NT1 deuteron microprobe analysis
 NT1 electron microprobe analysis
 NT1 ion microprobe analysis
 NT1 proton microprobe analysis

```
    RT      impurities
    RT      qualitative chemical analysis
    RT      quantitative chemical analysis
    RT      trace amounts

MICROBALANCES [57; 57]
    BT1     balances
    BT2     weight indicators
        BT3     measuring instruments


microbial flora
    USE     microorganisms


→ microbial processes
    SEE     anaerobic digestion
    OR      bioconversion
    OR      biodegradation
    OR      fermentation



microcephaly
    USE     malformations


MICROCHANNEL ELECTRON
    MULTIPLI [468; 468] Feb 76
    BT1     electron multipliers
    BT2     electron tubes


MICROCOCCUS [86; 249]
    BT1     bacteria
    BT2     microorganisms
    NT1     micrococcus luteus
    NT1     micrococcus lysodeicticus
    NT1     micrococcus radiodurans


MICROCOCCUS LUTEUS [54; 54]
    Oct 77
    BT1     micrococcus
    BT2     bacteria
        BT3     microorganisms
    RT      nucleases


MICROCOCCUS LYSODEICTICUS
    [10; 10]
    BT1     micrococcus
    BT2     bacteria
        BT3     microorganisms


MICROCOCCUS RADIODURANS
    [106; 106]
    BT1     micrococcus
    BT2     bacteria
        BT3     microorganisms


MICROCOMPUTERS [623; 623] Mar 77
    UF      personal computers
    BT1     digital computers
    BT2     computers


MICRODOSIMETRY [1,203; 1,203]
    BT1     dosimetry
    RT      energy losses
    RT      let
    RT      spatial dose distributions
    RT      wall effects


MICROELECTRONIC CIRCUITS
    [306; 2,943] Mar 76
    BT1     electronic circuits
    NT1     microprocessors
    RT      microelectronics
    RT      printed circuits


MICROELECTRONICS [399; 399]
    RT      electronic circuits
    RT      microelectronic circuits


microflora
    USE     microorganisms

MICROHARDNESS [2,927; 2,927]
    BT1     hardness
    BT2     mechanical properties
    RT      ceramography


MICRONESIA [3; 52] Jun 85
    BT1     australasia
    BT1     islands
    NT1     kiribati
    NT1     marshall islands
    NT2     bikini
    NT2     eniwetok
    NT1     nauru
    NT1     tuvalu
    RT      pacific ocean


MICROORGANISMS [1,208; 13,964]
    UF      germs (microorganisms)
    UF      microbial flora
    UF      microflora
    NT1     bacteria
    NT2     actinomyces
    NT2     aerobacter
    NT2     azotobacter
    NT2     bacillus
    NT3     bacillus cereus
    NT3     bacillus megaterium
    NT3     bacillus subtilis
    NT3     thiobacillus ferroxidans
    NT3     thiobacillus oxidans
    NT2     brucella
    NT2     clostridium
    NT3     clostridium acetobutylicum
    NT3     clostridium botulinum
    NT3     clostridium butyricum
    NT3     clostridium perfringens
    NT2     coliforms
    NT2     corynebacterium parvum
    NT2     escherichia coli
    NT2     haemophilus
    NT2     lactobacillus
    NT2     meningococcus
    NT2     methanogenic bacteria
    NT2     micrococcus
    NT3     micrococcus luteus
    NT3     micrococcus lysodeicticus
    NT3     micrococcus radiodurans
    NT2     mycobacterium
    NT3     mycobacterium tuberculosis
    NT2     nocardia
    NT2     pneumococcus
    NT2     proteus
    NT2     pseudomonas
    NT2     rhodopseudomonas
    NT2     rhodospirillum
    NT2     salmonella
    NT3     salmonella typhimurium
    NT2     serratia
    NT2     shigella
    NT2     spirochaetes
    NT2     staphylococcus
    NT2     streptococcus
    NT2     streptomyces
    NT2     sulfate-reducing bacteria
    NT2     sulfur-oxidizing bacteria
    NT3     thiobacillus ferroxidans
    NT3     thiobacillus oxidans
    NT1     cyanobacteria
    NT1     mycoplasma
    NT2     acholeplasma laidlawii b
    NT1     protozoa
    NT2     amoeba
    NT2     babesidae
    NT2     dinoflagellate
    NT2     paramecium
    NT2     plasmodium
    NT2     tetrahymena
    NT2     trypanosoma
    NT1     rickettsiae
    NT1     unicellular algae
    NT2     chlamydomonas
    NT2     chlorella
    NT2     euglena
    NT2     scenedesmus
    NT1     viruses
    NT2     aids virus

    NT2     bacteriophages
    NT2     influenza viruses
    NT2     measles virus
    NT2     oncogenic viruses
    NT3     adenovirus
    NT3     leukemia viruses
    NT3     polyoma virus
    NT2     polio virus
    NT2     simian virus
    NT2     tobacco mosaic virus
    NT2     vaccinia virus
    NT1     yeasts
    NT2     candida
    NT2     saccharomyces
    NT3     saccharomyces cerevisiae
    NT2     torula
    RT      anaerobic digestion
    RT      antibiotics
    RT      biology
    RT      cell cultures
    RT      cytology
    RT      infectious diseases
    RT      parasites
    RT      pathogens
    RT      photoreactivation
    RT      virulence


MICROPROCESSORS [3,138; 3,138]
    Mar 77
    BT1     microelectronic circuits
    BT2     electronic circuits
    RT      array processors


micropulsations
    USE     pulsations


MICRORADIOGRAPHY [104; 104]
    Mar 83
    UF      radiography (micro)
    RT      biomedical radiography
    RT      ceramography
    RT      industrial radiography


MICROSCOPES [185; 971]
    NT1     electron microscopes
    NT1     ion microscopes
    NT1     optical microscopes
    RT      microscopy


MICROSCOPY [757; 13,486]
    NT1     electron microscopy
    NT2     scanning electron microscopy
    NT2     transmission electron microsco
    NT1     ion microscopy
    NT1     optical microscopy
    RT      ceramography
    RT      histological techniques
    RT      histology
    RT      metallography
    RT      microscopes
    RT      morphological changes
    RT      photomicrography


*MICROSEC LIVING RADIOISOTOPES
    [2; 379] Mar 84
    (From 10 exp -6 to 0.001 sec. For specific
    terms, consult the Appendix.)
    BT1     radioisotopes
    BT2     isotopes
    RT      half-life


MICROSOMES [590; 590]
    RT      ribosomes
    RT      rna


MICROSPHERES [1,697; 1,697]
    RT      dispersions
    RT      particle size
    RT      radiopharmaceuticals


MICROSPORES [27; 27]
    BT1     spores
    RT      pollen
```

MICROSTRUCTURE [15,910; 24,091]
- BT1 crystal structure
- NT1 cleavage
- NT1 grain boundaries
- NT1 grain density
- NT1 grain orientation
- NT1 grain size
- NT1 widmanstaetten structure
- RT castings
- RT ceramography
- RT crystal defects
- RT crystal lattices
- RT inclusions
- RT metallography
- RT phase diagrams
- RT phase transformations
- RT solids
- RT twinning

MICROTRONS [548; 621]
- BT1 cyclotrons
- BT2 cyclic accelerators
- BT3 accelerators
- NT1 racetrack microtrons

MICROTUBULES [71; 71] *Feb 82*
- BT1 cell constituents
- RT proteins

MICROWAVE AMPLIFIERS [451; 1,284]
- BT1 amplifiers
- BT2 equipment
- BT1 microwave equipment
- BT2 electronic equipment
- BT3 equipment
- NT1 masers

microwave discharges
- USE high-frequency discharges

MICROWAVE EQUIPMENT [791; 4,842]
- BT1 electronic equipment
- BT2 equipment
- NT1 heterodyne receivers
- NT1 microwave amplifiers
- NT2 masers
- NT1 microwave tubes
- NT2 backward wave tubes
- NT2 klystrons
- NT2 lasertrons
- NT2 magnetrons
- NT2 travelling wave tubes
- NT1 squid devices
- RT cavity resonators
- RT microwave radiation
- RT radio equipment
- RT resonators
- RT superconducting cavity resonat
- RT waveguides

MICROWAVE RADIATION [5,441; 5,934]
- UF *ehf radiation*
- UF *extremely high freq radiation*
- BT1 electromagnetic radiation
- BT2 radiations
- NT1 relict radiation
- RT masers
- RT microwave equipment
- RT microwave spectra

MICROWAVE SPECTRA [703; 703]
- BT1 spectra
- RT microwave radiation

MICROWAVE TUBES [203; 1,853]
- BT1 electron tubes
- BT1 microwave equipment
- BT2 electronic equipment
- BT3 equipment
- NT1 backward wave tubes
- NT1 klystrons
- NT1 lasertrons
- NT1 magnetrons
- NT1 travelling wave tubes
- RT thermionic tubes

MIDAS COMPUTER [5; 5]
- BT1 computers

MIDDAY AURORAE [34; 34]
- BT1 aurorae
- RT auroral oval
- RT auroral zones
- RT charged-particle precipitation
- RT electron precipitation
- RT ionosphere
- RT proton precipitation

→ **MIDDLE EAST** [0; 0] *Nov 91*
- NT1 bahrain
- NT1 cyprus
- NT1 egyptian arab republic
- NT1 iran
- NT1 iraq
- NT1 israel
- NT1 jordan
- NT1 kuwait
- NT1 lebanon
- NT1 oman
- NT1 qatar
- NT1 saudi arabia
- NT1 syria
- NT1 turkey
- NT1 yemen

MIDLAND-1 REACTOR [47; 47]
(Midland, Michigan, USA)
- UF *consumers power co. midland-1*
- BT1 process heat reactors
- BT2 power reactors
- BT3 reactors
- BT1 pwr type reactors
- BT2 enriched uranium reactors
- BT3 reactors
- BT2 power reactors
- BT3 reactors
- BT2 thermal reactors
- BT3 reactors
- BT2 water cooled reactors
- BT3 reactors
- BT2 water moderated reactors
- BT3 reactors

MIDLAND-2 REACTOR [47; 47]
(Midland, Michigan, USA)
- UF *consumers power co. midland-2*
- BT1 process heat reactors
- BT2 power reactors
- BT3 reactors
- BT1 pwr type reactors
- BT2 enriched uranium reactors
- BT3 reactors
- BT2 power reactors
- BT3 reactors
- BT2 thermal reactors
- BT3 reactors
- BT2 water cooled reactors
- DT3 reactors
- BT2 water moderated reactors
- BT3 reactors

midnight discontinuity
- USE harang discontinuity

MIDWEST FUEL RECOVERY PLANT [32; 32]
- BT1 fuel reprocessing plants
- BT2 nuclear facilities

mifi irt-2000 reactor
(Moskovskij Inzhenerno-Fizicheskij Inst.)
- USE irt-2000 moscow reactor

MIGDAL THEORY [91; 91]
- RT bremsstrahlung

MIGMA DEVICES [72; 72]
(Nonplasma, nonthermal, nonpulsed devices, in which fusion occurs among the ions of a self-colliding beam.)
- BT1 thermonuclear devices
- RT ion beams
- RT precession

→ **MIGRATION** [0; 0] *Aug 91*
- RT fish passage facilities
- RT population dynamics

→ *migration (kernel)*
- USE amoeba effect

→ *migration (radionuclide)*
- USE radionuclide migration

migration area
- USE migration length

MIGRATION LENGTH [304; 304]
- UF *migration area*
- RT diffusion length
- RT slowing-down length

MIHAMA-1 REACTOR [51; 51]
(Mihama, Fukui, Japan)
- UF *kansai-1 reactor*
- BT1 pwr type reactors
- BT2 enriched uranium reactors
- BT3 reactors
- BT2 power reactors
- BT3 reactors
- BT2 thermal reactors
- BT3 reactors
- BT2 water cooled reactors
- BT3 reactors
- BT2 water moderated reactors
- BT3 reactors

MIHAMA-2 REACTOR [35; 35]
(Mihama, Fukui, Japan)
- UF *kansai-2 reactor*
- BT1 pwr type reactors
- BT2 enriched uranium reactors
- BT3 reactors
- BT2 power reactors
- BT3 reactors
- BT2 thermal reactors
- BT3 reactors
- BT2 water cooled reactors
- BT3 reactors
- BT2 water moderated reactors
- BT3 reactors

MIHAMA-3 REACTOR [20; 20]
(Mihama, Fukui, Japan)
- BT1 pwr type reactors
- BT2 enriched uranium reactors
- BT3 reactors
- BT2 power reactors
- BT3 reactors
- BT2 thermal reactors
- BT3 reactors
- BT2 water cooled reactors
- BT3 reactors
- BT2 water moderated reactors
- BT3 reactors

MIKE EVENT [2; 2] *Jan 85*
- BT1 ivy project
- BT1 surface explosions
- BT2 explosions
- BT1 thermonuclear explosions
- BT2 nuclear explosions
- BT3 explosions

milan supercond cyclotron
(Prior to December 1990, this was a valid descriptor.)
USE   milan superconducting cyclotro

MILAN SUPERCONDUCTING CYCLOTRO [44; 44] *Jun 83*
(Prior to December 1990, this descriptor was spelled MILAN SUPERCOND CYCLOTRON.)
UF   *milan supercond cyclotron*
BT1   heavy ion accelerators
BT2   accelerators
BT1   isochronous cyclotrons
BT2   cyclotrons
BT3   cyclic accelerators
BT4   accelerators
BT1   superconducting cyclotrons
BT2   cyclotrons
BT3   cyclic accelerators
BT4   accelerators

MILDEW [56; 56]
BT1   fungi
BT2   plants
BT1   parasites
RT   plant diseases

MILITARY PERSONNEL [81; 81]
UF   *army personnel*
BT1   personnel
RT   aviation personnel

MILK [2,291; 2,291]
BT1   body fluids
BT2   biological materials
BT3   materials
BT1   food
RT   beverages
RT   cows
RT   lactation
RT   mammary glands
RT   milk products

MILK PRODUCTS [140; 174]
BT1   food
NT1   butter
NT1   cheese
RT   milk

milk sugar
USE   lactose

MILKY WAY [3,913; 3,913]
UF   *local galaxy*
BT1   galaxies
RT   interstellar space

MILL TAILINGS [494; 494] *Jan 78*
BT1   tailings
BT2   solid wastes
BT3   wastes
RT   radioactive wastes

MILLER INDICES [280; 280]
RT   crystal lattices

MILLET [50; 50]
BT1   cereals
BT2   gramineae
BT3   plants

MILLI AMP BEAM CURRENTS [1,320; 1,320]
(From .001 to 1 amp.)
BT1   beam currents
BT2   currents

MILLI EV RANGE [1,672; 1,672]
BT1   energy range

MILLI HZ RANGE [109; 109]
BT1   frequency range

milli k range
USE   ultralow temperature

MILLING [532; 532]
(For milling in the sense of pulverizing, use CRUSHING.)
BT1   machining
RT   mechanical decladding
RT   milling machines

MILLING MACHINES [49; 49]
BT1   machine tools
RT   milling

* **MILLISEC LIVING RADIOISOTOPES** [57; 2,728]
(From 0.001 to 1 sec. For specific terms, consult the Appendix.)
BT1   radioisotopes
BT2   isotopes
RT   half-life

MILLIWATT POWER RANGE [0; 0]
Apr 88
BT1   power range

MILLSTONE-1 REACTOR [226; 226]
(Waterford, Connecticut, USA)
BT1   bwr type reactors
BT2   enriched uranium reactors
BT3   reactors
BT2   power reactors
BT3   reactors
BT2   thermal reactors
BT3   reactors
BT2   water cooled reactors
BT3   reactors
BT2   water moderated reactors
BT3   reactors

MILLSTONE-2 REACTOR [106; 106]
(Waterford, Connecticut, USA)
BT1   pwr type reactors
BT2   enriched uranium reactors
BT3   reactors
BT2   power reactors
BT3   reactors
BT2   thermal reactors
BT3   reactors
BT2   water cooled reactors
BT3   reactors
BT2   water moderated reactors
BT3   reactors

MILLSTONE-3 REACTOR [93; 93]
(Waterford, Connecticut, USA)
BT1   pwr type reactors
BT2   enriched uranium reactors
BT3   reactors
BT2   power reactors
BT3   reactors
BT2   thermal reactors
BT3   reactors
BT2   water cooled reactors
BT3   reactors
BT2   water moderated reactors
BT3   reactors

MILNE PROBLEM [93; 93]
RT   angular distribution
RT   marshak boundary conditions
RT   neutron transport theory

MILROW EVENT [47; 47]
BT1   nuclear explosions
BT2   explosions
BT1   underground explosions
BT2   explosions
RT   seismic waves

MIM JUNCTIONS [61; 61]
(Metal-Insulator-Metal junctions.)
BT1   semiconductor junctions

MIMOSINE [4; 4]
BT1   amino acids
BT2   carboxylic acids
BT3   organic acids
BT4   organic compounds
RT   leguminosae
RT   toxicity

MINAMI AMBIGUITY [3; 3]
RT   angular distribution
RT   parity

minas gerais univ. triga react
USE   triga-brazil reactor

mine shafts
USE   shaft excavations

mine site rehabilitation
USE   remedial action

mine tailings
USE   tailings

mineral acids
USE   inorganic acids

mineral oil
USE   lubricants

→ **MINERAL RESOURCES** [4; 4] *Aug 76*
BT1   resources
NT1   natural gas deposits
NT1   petroleum deposits

mineral va. north anna-1 react
USE   north anna-1 reactor

mineral va. north anna-2 react
USE   north anna-2 reactor

mineral va. north anna-3 react
USE   north anna-3 reactor

§ **MINERALIZATION** [1,805; 1,805]
RT   crystallization
RT   mineralogy
RT   plutonic rocks

MINERALOCORTICOIDS [10; 263]
BT1   corticosteroids
BT2   adrenal hormones
BT3   hormones
BT2   hydroxy compounds
BT3   organic compounds
BT2   ketones
BT3   organic compounds
BT2   pregnanes
BT3   steroids
BT4   organic compounds
BT2   steroid hormones
BT3   hormones
NT1   aldosterone
NT1   doca

MINERALOGY [1,148; 1,148]
RT   mineralization
RT   minerals

MINERALS [3,180; 19,683]
- NT1 black sands
- NT1 carbonate minerals
  - NT2 andersonite
  - NT2 aragonite
  - NT2 bayleyite
  - NT2 calcite
  - NT2 cordylite
  - NT2 dolomite
  - NT2 liebigite
  - NT2 rutherfordite
  - NT2 schroeckingerite
- NT1 diamonds
- NT1 halide minerals
  - NT2 carnallite
  - NT2 fluorite
  - NT2 schroeckingerite
- NT1 oxide minerals
  - NT2 aeschynite
  - NT2 baddeleyite
  - NT2 bastnaesite
  - NT2 becquerelite
  - NT2 brannerite
  - NT2 cerianite
  - NT2 clarkeite
  - NT2 corundum
    - NT3 ruby
    - NT3 sapphire
  - NT2 cristobalite
  - NT2 curite
  - NT2 davidite
  - NT2 demesmaekerite
  - NT2 ferrite garnets
  - NT2 francevillite
  - NT2 gummite
  - NT2 hatchettolite
  - NT2 hematite
  - NT2 hollandite
  - NT2 ilmenite
  - NT2 iriginite
  - NT2 ishikawaite
  - NT2 kaolin
  - NT2 limonite
  - NT2 magnetite
  - NT2 masuyite
  - NT2 moluranite
  - NT2 mullite
  - NT2 perovskite
  - NT2 quartz
  - NT2 rutile
  - NT2 schoepite
  - NT2 spinels
  - NT2 strelkinite
  - NT2 tantalite
  - NT2 thorianite
  - NT2 tyuyamunite
  - NT2 umohoite
  - NT2 uraninites
    - NT3 pitchblende
  - NT2 uranium black
  - NT2 uranothorianite
  - NT2 wolframite
  - NT2 wulfenite
  - NT2 zeunerite
  - NT2 zirconolite
- NT1 phosphate minerals
  - NT2 apatites
  - NT2 autunite
  - NT2 dumontite
  - NT2 florencite
  - NT2 lermontovite
  - NT2 monazites
  - NT2 ningyoite
  - NT2 parsonsite
  - NT2 phosphuranylite
  - NT2 saleeite
  - NT2 steenstrupine
  - NT2 torbernite
  - NT2 uranocircite
  - NT2 xenotime
- *NT1 radioactive minerals
- NT1 silicate minerals
  - NT2 allanite
    - NT3 orthite
  - NT2 alvite
  - NT2 amphibole
    - NT3 hornblende
  - NT2 beryl
  - NT2 boltwoodite
  - NT2 catapleite
  - NT2 cerite
  - NT2 chlorite minerals
  - NT2 clays
    - NT3 attapulgite
    - NT3 bentonite
    - NT3 clinoptilolite
    - NT3 fullers earth
    - NT3 illite
    - NT3 kaolin
    - NT3 montmorillonite
    - NT3 smectite
  - NT2 coffinite
  - NT2 cuprosklodowskite
  - NT2 cyrtolite
  - NT2 elpidite
  - NT2 eudialyte
  - NT2 feldspars
  - NT2 garnets
    - NT3 andradite
  - NT2 haiweeite
  - NT2 huttonite
  - NT2 ilvaite
  - NT2 mica
    - NT3 biotite
    - NT3 muscovite
  - NT2 olivine
  - NT2 pollucite
  - NT2 soddyite
  - NT2 steenstrupine
  - NT2 talc
  - NT2 thorite
  - NT2 thorogummite
  - NT2 titanite
  - NT2 tourmaline
  - NT2 uranophane
  - NT2 uranothorite
  - NT2 vermiculite
  - NT2 yttrialite
  - NT2 zeolites
  - NT2 zircon
- NT1 sulfate minerals
  - NT2 anhydrite
  - NT2 barite
  - NT2 gypsum
  - NT2 johannite
  - NT2 polyhalite
  - NT2 schroeckingerite
  - NT2 zippeite
- NT1 sulfide minerals
  - NT2 chalcopyrite
  - NT2 galena
  - NT2 marcasite
  - NT2 pyrite
- NT1 tektites
- RT environmental materials
- RT metamict state
- RT mineralogy
- RT ores
- RT rocks
- RT translocation

MINERS [777; 777]
- BT1 personnel

MINERVE REACTOR [12; 12]
(CEA/CEN Cadarache, St. Paul Lez Durance, France)
- UF *french minerve reactor*
- UF *zero power crit. expe. minerve*
- BT1 enriched uranium reactors
  - BT2 reactors
- BT1 pool type reactors
  - BT2 water cooled reactors
    - BT3 reactors
  - BT2 water moderated reactors
    - BT3 reactors
- BT1 research reactors
  - BT2 research and test reactors
    - BT3 reactors
- BT1 thermal reactors
  - BT2 reactors
- BT1 zero power reactors
  - BT2 experimental reactors
    - BT3 research and test reactors
      - BT4 reactors

MINES [1,134; 3,708]
- BT1 underground facilities
- NT1 asse salt mine
- NT1 coal mines
- NT1 konrad ore mine
- NT1 uranium mines
  - NT2 beaverlodge mine
  - NT2 cluff lake mine
  - NT2 key lake mine
  - NT2 mary kathleen mines
  - NT2 mi vida mine
  - NT2 olympic dam mine
  - NT2 rum jungle
  - NT2 stanleigh mine
- RT backfilling
- RT mining
- RT shaft excavations
- RT surface mining
- RT tunnels
- RT water influx

→ *miniature neutron source react*
- USE mns reactor

MINIATURE SWINE [115; 115]
- BT1 swine
  - BT2 domestic animals
    - BT3 animals
  - BT2 mammals
    - BT3 vertebrates
      - BT4 animals

MINIATURIZATION [242; 242]
- RT electrical equipment
- RT electronic equipment
- RT measuring instruments
- RT semiconductor devices

MINIMIZATION [641; 641] *Jun 83*
- BT1 optimization
- RT augmentation

MINIMUM AVERAGE-B CONFIGURATIO [35; 35]
- UF *average magnetic well*
- BT1 closed configurations
  - BT2 magnetic field configurations
- RT internal ring devices

MINIMUM-B CONFIGURATIONS [190; 190]
- UF *magnetic well*
- BT1 open configurations
  - BT2 magnetic field configurations
- RT ion rings
- RT tlm configurations

MINING [2,291; 2,641]
- UF *open pit mining*
- UF *quarrying*
- UF *strip mining*
- NT1 coal mining
- NT1 solution mining
- NT1 surface mining
- NT1 underground mining
- RT contained explosions
- RT cratering explosions
- RT earthmoving equipment
- RT excavation
- RT industry
- RT mines
- RT ore composition
- RT sloop event
- RT underground explosions
- RT uranium ores

mining equipment
- SEE earthmoving equipment

MINING LAWS [67; 67]
(Prior to December 1990, this descriptor was spelled MINING LAW.)
- BT1 laws

MINKOWSKI SPACE [2,500; 2,500]
BT1 mathematical space
BT2 space
RT light cone
RT lorentz transformations

MINNESOTA [189; 189]
BT1 usa
BT2 developed countries
BT2 north america

MINNESOTA UNIV LINAC [0; 0]
BT1 linear accelerators
BT2 accelerators

MINSK COMPUTERS [188; 188]
BT1 computers

MINUS-PLUS RATIO [101; 101]
RT electric charges

*****MINUTES LIVING RADIOISOTOPES**
[150; 40,822]
(For specific terms, consult the Appendix.)
BT1 radioisotopes
BT2 isotopes
RT half-life

miq
(For specific terms, consult the Appendix.)
USE maximum inhalation quantity

MIR ORBITAL STATION [7; 7] *Oct 89*
BT1 satellites
BT1 space vehicles

MIR REACTOR [16; 16]
UF *melekess-mir reactor*
BT1 experimental reactors
BT2 research and test reactors
BT3 reactors
BT1 tank type reactors
BT2 reactors
BT1 thermal reactors
BT2 reactors
BT1 water cooled reactors
BT2 reactors
BT1 water moderated reactors
BT2 reactors

MIRROR NUCLEI [329; 329]
BT1 nuclei
RT isobaric nuclei

MIRROR RATIO [93; 93] *Aug 75*
RT magnetic fields
RT magnetic mirror configurations
RT magnetic mirrors

MIRRORS [1,022; 1,039] *Oct 75*
NT1 electrostatic mirrors
RT optical properties
RT optical systems
RT telescopes

mirrors (magnetic)
USE magnetic mirrors

MIS TRANSISTORS [125; 125]
(Metal Insulator Silicon transistors)
BT1 transistors
BT2 semiconductor devices

MISCH METAL [76; 76]
BT1 cerium base alloys
BT2 cerium alloys
BT3 rare earth alloys
BT4 alloys
BT1 lanthanum alloys
BT2 rare earth alloys
BT3 alloys

misgurnus
USE fishes

MISONIDAZOLE [570; 570] *Aug 81*
UF *ro-07-0582*
BT1 alcohols
BT2 hydroxy compounds
BT3 organic compounds
BT1 antineoplastic drugs
BT2 drugs
BT1 imidazoles
BT2 azoles
BT3 heterocyclic compounds
BT4 organic compounds
BT3 organic nitrogen compounds
BT4 organic compounds
BT1 nitro compounds
BT2 organic nitrogen compounds
BT3 organic compounds
BT1 radiosensitizers
BT2 drugs
BT2 response modifying factors
RT chemotherapy

MISSILE PROTECTION [246; 246] *Oct 75*
RT impact shock
RT reactor accidents
RT reactor protection systems
RT reactor safety

MISSILES [238; 238]
RT launching
RT propulsion systems
RT reentry
RT rockets

MISSING MASS [979; 981]
(The unobserved mass resulting from neutral particles in a particle- particle interaction.)
BT1 mass
RT missing-mass spectra
RT missing-mass spectrometers
RT neutral particles

MISSING-MASS SPECTRA [255; 255]
BT1 spectra
RT abc effect
RT missing mass
RT missing-mass spectrometers

MISSING-MASS SPECTROMETERS
[43; 43]
BT1 spectrometers
BT2 measuring instruments
RT missing mass
RT missing-mass spectra
RT neutral particles

MISSISSIPPI [203; 203]
BT1 usa
BT2 developed countries
BT2 north america

MISSISSIPPI RIVER [40; 40]
BT1 rivers
BT2 surface waters

MISSOURI [256; 256]
BT1 usa
BT2 developed countries
BT2 north america
RT kansas city plant

MISSOURI RIVER [6; 6]
BT1 rivers
BT2 surface waters

missouri school of mines react
USE umrr reactor

missouri univ./columbia res. r
USE murr reactor

missouri univ./rolla res. reac
USE umrr reactor

MIT BATES LINAC [47; 47] *Nov 77*
(Bates Electron Linear Accelerator Facility at MIT.)
UF *bates linac mit*
BT1 linear accelerators
BT2 accelerators

MITES [43; 43]
BT1 arachnids
BT2 arthropods
BT3 invertebrates
BT4 animals
RT disease vectors
RT parasites
RT pest control

MITIGATION [494; 494] *Sep 85*
(Abatement or diminution of something painful, injurious, severe, or calamitous.)
RT control
RT corrections
RT modifications
RT optimization
RT pollution abatement

MITOCHONDRIA [1,061; 1,061]
BT1 cell constituents
RT cytoplasm
RT enzymes
RT krebs cycle

MITOGENS [190; 550] *Oct 81*
(Substances that induce cell division or stimulate cells to undergo blastogenic activity.)
NT1 growth factors
NT1 phytohemagglutinin
RT cell division
RT immunology
RT response modifying factors
RT stimulation
RT tissue extracts

MITOMYCIN [318; 318]
BT1 antibiotics
BT2 drugs
BT2 organic compounds
BT1 antimitotic drugs
BT2 drugs
BT1 antineoplastic drugs
BT2 drugs

MITOSIS [1,460; 1,460]
UF *anaphase*
UF *metaphase*
UF *prophase*
UF *telophase*
BT1 cell division
RT antimitotic drugs
RT chromosomes
RT concanavalin a
RT crossing-over
RT human chromosomes
RT mitotic delay
RT mitotic index
RT phytohemagglutinin

MITOTIC DELAY [226; 226]
RT mitosis

MITOTIC INDEX [392; 392]
RT mitosis

MITR REACTOR [57; 57]
(Massachusetts Institute of Technology, Nuclear Research Lab., Cambridge Massachusetts, USA)
UF *massachus. inst. techn. reacto*
BT1 enriched uranium reactors

```
     BT2     reactors
   BT1    heavy water cooled reactors
     BT2     reactors
   BT1    heavy water moderated reactors
     BT2     reactors
   BT1    research reactors
     BT2     research and test reactors
       BT3     reactors
   BT1    tank type reactors
     BT2     reactors
   BT1    thermal reactors
     BT2     reactors
   BT1    training reactors
     BT2     research and test reactors
       BT3     reactors
```

MIXED BED ION EXCHANGERS
[52; 52]
```
   UF     mixed-bed ion exchangers
   BT1    ion exchange materials
     BT2     materials
```

MIXED CARBIDE FUELS [134; 134]
Sep 82
(Index also the specific carbides if important.)
```
   BT1    solid fuels
     BT2     nuclear fuels
       BT3     energy sources
       BT3     fuels
       BT3     reactor materials
         BT4     materials
```

mixed media
USE   mixed solvents

MIXED NITRIDE FUELS [31; 31]
Oct 88
(Uranium nitride mixed with plutonium nitride or other nitrides. Index other nitrides if important.)
```
   BT1    solid fuels
     BT2     nuclear fuels
       BT3     energy sources
       BT3     fuels
       BT3     reactor materials
         BT4     materials
   RT     ceramics
   RT     plutonium nitrides
   RT     uranium nitrides
```

mixed oxide fuel fabrication p
USE   mixed oxide fuel plant

MIXED OXIDE FUEL PLANT
[241; 241]
```
   UF     mixed oxide fuel fabrication p
   UF     uranium oxide fuel plant
   BT1    fuel fabrication plants
     BT2     nuclear facilities
```

MIXED OXIDE FUELS [1,670; 1,670]
Apr 80
(Uranium dioxide mixed with other oxide(s); index also the other oxide(s) if important.)
```
   BT1    solid fuels
     BT2     nuclear fuels
       BT3     energy sources
       BT3     fuels
       BT3     reactor materials
         BT4     materials
   RT     ceramics
```

MIXED SOLVENTS [481; 481]
```
   UF     mixed media
   BT1    mixtures
     BT2     dispersions
   BT1    solvents
```

MIXED SPECTRUM REACTORS
[20; 738]
```
   UF     mixed-spectrum reactors
   BT1    reactors
   NT1    acpr reactor
   NT1    br-3-vn reactor
   NT1    browns ferry-1 reactor
   NT1    browns ferry-2 reactor
   NT1    browns ferry-3 reactor
   NT1    diorit reactor
   NT1    nsrr reactor
   NT1    omre reactor
   NT1    rpt reactor
```

mixed-bed ion exchangers
USE   mixed bed ion exchangers

mixed-spectrum reactors
USE   mixed spectrum reactors

MIXER-SETTLERS [297; 297]
```
   BT1    extraction apparatuses
     BT2     separation equipment
       BT3     equipment
   RT     laboratory equipment
   RT     mixing
```

§ **MIXING** [2,748; 2,748]
(Not for the concept covered by CONFIGURATION MIXING.)
```
   UF     blending
   RT     aeration
   RT     diffusion
   RT     mixer-settlers
   RT     mixtures
   RT     solubility
   RT     stirring
   RT     turbulence
```

mixing (genetic)
USE   hybridization

MIXING HEAT [303; 303]
```
   UF     heat of mixing
   BT1    enthalpy
     BT2     thermodynamic properties
       BT3     physical properties
   RT     solution heat
```

mixing matrix (kobayashi-mask)
USE   kobayashi-maskawa matrix

MIXING RATIO [3,295; 3,295]
```
   RT     branching ratio
   RT     decay
   RT     energy-level transitions
   RT     multipolarity
   RT     multipoles
   RT     neutrino oscillation
   RT     particle production
   RT     weinberg angle
```

MIXTURES [4,710; 12,964]
```
   BT1    dispersions
   NT1    binary mixtures
   NT1    homogeneous mixtures
     NT2     solutions
       NT3     aqueous solutions
       NT3     hypertonic solutions
       NT3     isotonic solutions
       NT3     leachates
       NT3     solid solutions
   NT1    mixed solvents
   NT1    slurries
   RT     compatibility
   RT     mixing
```

mms
(Prior to August 1985 this was a valid descriptor.)
USE   methyl methanesulfonate

MNR REACTOR [11; 11]
(McMaster University, Ontario, Canada)
```
   UF     mc master univ. nuclear reacto
   BT1    enriched uranium reactors
     BT2     reactors
   BT1    isotope production reactors
     BT2     irradiation reactors
       BT3     reactors
   BT1    pool type reactors
     BT2     water cooled reactors
       BT3     reactors
     BT2     water moderated reactors
       BT3     reactors
   BT1    research reactors
     BT2     research and test reactors
       BT3     reactors
```

→ **MNS REACTOR** [0; 0] *Feb 91*
(Iae, China.)
```
   UF     miniature neutron source react
   BT1    research reactors
     BT2     research and test reactors
       BT3     reactors
   RT     tank type reactors
```

MOATA REACTOR [25; 25]
(Australian Atomic Energy Commission Research Establishment, Lucas Heights, Australia)
```
   UF     australian moata reactor
   BT1    argonaut type reactors
     BT2     enriched uranium reactors
       BT3     reactors
     BT2     research and test reactors
       BT3     reactors
     BT2     water cooled reactors
       BT3     reactors
     BT2     water moderated reactors
       BT3     reactors
   BT1    research reactors
     BT2     research and test reactors
       BT3     reactors
   BT1    training reactors
     BT2     research and test reactors
       BT3     reactors
```

MOBILE REACTORS [48; 1,526]
(Designed to be movable while in operation.)
```
   BT1    reactors
   NT1    mh-1a reactor
   NT1    space power reactors
     NT2     snap reactors
       NT3     snap 10 reactor
         NT4     s10fs-1 reactor
         NT4     s10fs-3 reactor
         NT4     s10fs-4 reactor
       NT3     snap 2 reactor
         NT4     s2ds reactor
       NT3     snap 8 reactor
         NT4     s8dr reactor
         NT4     s8er reactor
     NT2     space propulsion reactors
       NT3     kiwi reactors
       NT3     nerva reactor
       NT3     nrx-a2 reactor
       NT3     nrx-a3 reactor
       NT3     nrx-a4-est reactor
       NT3     nrx-a5 reactor
       NT3     nrx-a6 reactor
       NT3     pewee-1 reactor
       NT3     pewee-2 reactor
       NT3     pewee-3 reactor
       NT3     pewee-4 reactor
       NT3     phoebus-1a reactor
       NT3     phoebus-1b reactor
       NT3     phoebus-2a reactor
       NT3     rover reactors
   NT1    s1c prototype reactor
   RT     thermionic reactors
```

MOBILITY [840; 4,281]
(For material movement use TRANSPORT.)
```
   NT1    carrier mobility
   NT1    hole mobility
   NT1    particle mobility
     NT2     electron mobility
     NT2     ion mobility
```

MOCHOVCE-1 REACTOR [65; 65]
Oct 84
- BT1 wwer type reactors
  - BT2 pwr type reactors
    - BT3 enriched uranium reactors
      - BT4 reactors
    - BT3 power reactors
      - BT4 reactors
    - BT3 thermal reactors
      - BT4 reactors
    - BT3 water cooled reactors
      - BT4 reactors
    - BT3 water moderated reactors
      - BT4 reactors

MOCKUP [2,693; 9,005]
- BT1 structural models
- NT1 phantoms
- RT biological models
- RT functional models
- RT mathematical models
- RT pilot plants
- RT simulators
- RT test facilities

MODE CONTROL [100; 100] *May 84*
- UF *mode selection*
- BT1 control
- RT lasers
- RT oscillation modes
- RT wave propagation

→ **MODE CONVERSION** [8; 8] *Mar 91*
(Transformation of an electromagnetic wave from one mode of propagation to another.)
- RT oscillation modes
- RT plasma heating
- RT resonance
- RT wave propagation

MODE LOCKING [320; 320]
- RT lasers

→ **MODE RATIONAL SURFACES** [6; 6] *Mar 91*
- UF *rational surfaces*
- BT1 magnetic surfaces
  - BT2 magnetic field configurations
- RT stellarators
- RT tokamak devices

mode selection
  USE mode control

modeling
  USE simulation

models (atomic)
  USE atomic models

models (biological)
  USE biological models

models (cosmological)
  USE cosmological models

models (crystal)
  USE crystal models

models (flow)
  USE flow models

models (functional)
  USE functional models

models (linear absorption)
  USE linear absorption models

models (mathematical)
  USE mathematical models

models (nuclear)
  USE nuclear models

models (optical)
  USE optical models

models (organizational)
  USE organizational models

models (particle)
  USE particle models

models (plasma)
  USE plasma simulation

models (scale)
  USE scale models

models (shell)
  USE shell models

models (star)
  USE star models

models (statistical)
  USE statistical models

models (structural)
  USE structural models

MODERATELY ENRICHED URANIUM [447; 447]
(5 - 80 per cent.)
- BT1 enriched uranium
  - BT2 isotope enriched materials
    - BT3 materials
  - BT2 uranium
    - BT3 actinides
      - BT4 metals
        - BT5 elements

MODERATING DETECTORS [110; 278]
- BT1 neutron detectors
  - BT2 radiation detectors
    - BT3 measuring instruments
- NT1 bonner sphere detectors
- NT1 long counters
- RT activation detectors
- RT bf3 counters

MODERATING RATIO [53; 53]
- RT moderators

MODERATOR PELLETS [18; 18]
Sep 75
- UF *pellets (moderator)*
- RT moderators
- RT pelletizing

MODERATOR-FUEL RATIO [131; 131]
- RT moderators

MODERATORS [1,536; 1,747]
(See also descriptors for specific moderator materials.)
- NT1 hydride moderators
- NT1 hydroxide moderators
- NT1 organic moderators
- RT beryllium
- RT beryllium alloys
- RT beryllium compounds
- RT beryllium oxides
- RT configuration control
- RT graphite
- RT heavy water
- RT moderating ratio
- RT moderator pellets
- RT moderator-fuel ratio
- RT neutron slowing-down theory
- RT reactor cores
- RT reactor materials
- RT sigma piles
- RT thermal columns
- RT water

modes (optical)
  USE optical modes

modes (oscillation)
  USE oscillation modes

modes (single-particle)
  USE single-particle modes

§ **MODIFICATIONS** [3,125; 3,125] *Jan 85*
- RT construction
- RT corrections
- RT disturbances
- RT maintenance
- RT mitigation
- RT modulation
- RT operation
- RT optimization
- RT planning
- RT retrofitting
- RT shutdown
- RT specifications
- RT variations

modified surface delta potenti
  USE surface delta potential

modular construction
  USE modular structures

MODULAR STRUCTURES [1,017; 1,017]
Sep 83
- UF *modular construction*
- RT camac system
- RT construction
- RT fabrication
- RT industrial plants
- RT mechanical structures
- RT nuclear instrument modules

MODULATION [3,132; 3,350]
- NT1 frequency modulation
- RT modifications
- RT variations

MOELLER SCATTERING [78; 78]
- BT1 elastic scattering
  - BT2 scattering
- RT bhabha scattering
- RT quantum electrodynamics

MOESSBAUER EFFECT [9,526; 9,526]
- UF *moessbauer spectroscopy*
- RT recoils
- RT resonance fluorescence
- RT structural chemical analysis

MOESSBAUER SPECTROMETERS [562; 562]
- BT1 gamma spectrometers
  - BT2 spectrometers
    - BT3 measuring instruments

moessbauer spectroscopy
  USE   moessbauer effect

MOHAWK RIVER [1; 1]
  BT1   rivers
    BT2   surface waters

MOHOLE PROJECT [2; 2]
  RT   geology

moisture
  USE   humidity

MOISTURE GAGES [768; 768]
  UF   *neutron moisture meters*
  BT1   measuring instruments
  RT   humidity
  RT   hygrometry
  RT   neutron probes
  RT   radiometric gages

moldavites
  USE   tektites

MOLDING [163; 350]
  BT1   fabrication
  NT1   pelletizing
  RT   casting
  RT   casting molds
  RT   materials working

molds
  USE   fungi

molds (casting)
  USE   casting molds

MOLECULAR BEAMS [2,214; 2,214]
  BT1   beams
  RT   molecules

MOLECULAR BIOLOGY [1,101; 1,101]
  RT   biological effects
  RT   biological evolution
  RT   biological pathways
  RT   biophysics
  RT   biosynthesis
  RT   genetic engineering
  RT   metabolism
  RT   molecules
  RT   physiology
  RT   radiobiology
  RT   strand breaks

MOLECULAR CRYSTALS [374; 374]
  BT1   crystals

molecular fluorescence spec
  USE   fluorescence spectroscopy

MOLECULAR ION BEAM INJECTION [22; 22]
  BT1   ion beam injection
    BT2   beam injection

MOLECULAR IONS [2,567; 3,183]
  Nov 75
  BT1   ions
    BT2   charged particles
  NT1   hydrogen ions 2 plus
  NT1   hydrogen ions 3 plus
  NT1   oxonium ions

MOLECULAR MODELS [694; 725]
  BT1   mathematical models
  NT1   thermodynamic molecular model

MOLECULAR ORBITAL METHOD [1,309; 1,309]
  RT   electronic structure
  RT   lcao method
  RT   molecular structure

molecular orbital model
  USE   atomic models
  AND   molecules

MOLECULAR SIEVES [315; 315]
  BT1   adsorbents
  RT   adsorption

MOLECULAR STRUCTURE [11,582; 11,582]
  RT   biological repair
  RT   bond lengths
  RT   configuration interaction
  RT   dissociation energy
  RT   dna sequencing
  RT   helical configuration
  RT   interatomic distances
  RT   lcao method
  RT   matrix isolation
  RT   molecular orbital method
  RT   molecules
  RT   nucleic acid denaturation
  RT   optical activity
  RT   photoelectron spectroscopy
  RT   photoreactivation
  RT   protein denaturation
  RT   protein structure
  RT   stereochemistry
  RT   structural chemical analysis

MOLECULAR WEIGHT [2,290; 2,290]
  RT   cryoscopy
  RT   depolymerization
  RT   molecules
  RT   osmosis
  RT   polymerization
  RT   weight

MOLECULE COLLISIONS [785; 9,639]
  BT1   collisions
  NT1   atom-molecule collisions
  NT1   electron-molecule collisions
  NT1   ion-molecule collisions
  NT1   molecule-molecule collisions
  NT1   photon-molecule collisions
  NT1   positron-molecule collisions

MOLECULE-MOLECULE COLLISIONS [894; 894]
  BT1   molecule collisions
    BT2   collisions

MOLECULES [9,152; 9,862]
  UF+   *molecular orbital model*
  NT1   mesic molecules
    NT2   muonic molecules
  RT   jahn-teller effect
  RT   kihara potential
  RT   matrix isolation
  RT   molecular beams
  RT   molecular biology
  RT   molecular structure
  RT   molecular weight
  RT   van der waals forces

MOLIERE THEORY [94; 94]
  RT   multiple scattering

MOLLIER DIAGRAMS [23; 23]
  RT   steam
  RT   thermodynamics

MOLLUSCS [665; 925]
  UF   *gasteropods*
  UF   *mussels*
  BT1   aquatic organisms
  BT1   invertebrates
    BT2   animals
  NT1   clams

  NT1   oysters
  NT1   snails

MOLNIYA SATELLITES [35; 35]
  BT1   satellites

MOLTEN METAL-WATER REACTIONS [611; 611] *Sep 77*
  UF   *liquid sodium-water reactions*
  UF   *metal-water reactions*
  UF   *sodium(liquid)-water reactions*
  RT   chemical reactions
  RT   explosions
  RT   fuel-coolant interactions
  RT   reactor accidents
  RT   reactor safety

molten salt coolants
  USE   molten salts

MOLTEN SALT COOLED REACTORS [32; 88]
  UF   *molten salt-cooled reactors*
  BT1   molten salt reactors
    BT2   reactors
  NT1   msre reactor

MOLTEN SALT FUELED REACTORS [96; 96]
  UF   *molten salt-fueled reactors*
  BT1   fluid fueled reactors
    BT2   reactors
  BT1   molten salt reactors
    BT2   reactors

MOLTEN SALT FUELS [189; 189]
  UF   *fused salt fuels*
  BT1   liquid fuels
    BT2   fuels
  RT   molten salt reactors

molten salt reactor experiment
  USE   msre reactor

MOLTEN SALT REACTORS [322; 479]
  BT1   reactors
  NT1   molten salt cooled reactors
    NT2   msre reactor
  NT1   molten salt fueled reactors
  RT   metal transfer process
  RT   molten salt fuels
  RT   reductive extraction

molten salt-cooled reactors
  USE   molten salt cooled reactors

molten salt-fueled reactors
  USE   molten salt fueled reactors

MOLTEN SALTS [2,867; 2,964]
  UF   *fused salts*
  UF   *molten salt coolants*
  BT1   salts
  NT1   flibe
  RT   coolants

MOLTING [13; 13] *Jul 81*
(The shedding of an outer covering as a part of a periodic process of growth.)
  UF   *moulting*
  RT   animal growth

MOLURANITE [1; 1]
  BT1   oxide minerals
    BT2   minerals
  BT1   uranium minerals
    BT2   radioactive minerals
      BT3   minerals
      BT3   radioactive materials
        BT4   materials
  RT   molybdenum oxides
  RT   uranium oxides

MOLYBDATES [1,750; 1,750]
(Specific compounds should be indexed by coordination of a descriptor of the form (CATION) COMPOUNDS and the above anion descriptor.)
- BT1 molybdenum compounds
- BT2 transition element compounds
- BT1 oxygen compounds
- RT molybdenum oxides

MOLYBDENUM [7,874; 7,874]
- BT1 transition elements
- BT2 metals
- BT3 elements

MOLYBDENUM ADDITIONS
[757; 2,486]
(Alloys containing not more than 1% Mo are listed here.)
- NT1 alloy-fe48cr24ni24
- NT1 alloy-ni47cr25co12w9fe3
- NT1 alloy-ti90al6
- NT1 steel-cralnimo
- NT1 steel-crmo
- NT1 steel-crmov
- NT1 steel-cr12moniv
- NT1 steel-cr12mov
- NT1 steel-cr17mo
- NT1 steel-cr2mo
- NT1 steel-cr2moninb
- NT1 steel-cr2mov
- NT1 steel-cr2nimov
- NT1 steel-cr5mo
- NT1 steel-cr9mo
- NT1 steel-mncumo
- NT1 steel-mnmo
- NT1 steel-mnnimo
- NT1 steel-mnnimov
- NT1 steel-nicrmo
- NT1 steel-nimocr
- NT1 steel-ni3crmo
- NT1 steel-ni3crmov
- NT1 steel-ni3mov
- RT molybdenum alloys
- RT molybdenum compounds

MOLYBDENUM ALLOYS
[3,849; 12,330]
(Alloys containing more than 1% Mo.)
- BT1 alloys
- NT1 alloy-co43cr20fe18ni13w3
- NT1 alloy-co52cr17fe15mo3si3
- NT1 alloy-co62cr28mo6ni3
- NT1 alloy-fe31cr21co20ni20mo3w2
- NT1 alloy-nb94mo4
- NT1 alloy-ni42fe36cr12mo6ti3
- NT1 alloy-ni43fe30cr22mo3
- NT1 alloy-ni43fe33cr16mo3
- NT1 alloy-ni45cr23fe19co3mo3w3
- NT1 alloy-ni48co28cr15al3mo3ti2
- NT1 alloy-ni48cr22fe18mo9
- NT1 alloy-ni49cr22fe18mo9
- NT1 alloy-ni50co20cr15al5mo5
- NT1 alloy-ni50cr22fe18mo9
- NT1 alloy-ni50mo32cr15si3
- NT1 alloy-ni53co19cr15mo5al4ti3
- NT1 alloy-ni53cr19fe19nb5mo3
- NT1 alloy-ni54cr22co13mo9
- NT1 alloy-ni54mo17cr16fe6w4
- NT1 alloy-ni55co17cr15mo5al4ti4
- NT1 alloy-ni55cr19co11mo10ti3
- NT1 alloy-ni56cr21w10mo5fe4al2
- NT1 alloy-ni58cr14co8al4mo4nb4w4
- NT1 alloy-ni58cr20co14mo4ti3
- NT1 alloy-ni60co15cr10al6ti5mo3
- NT1 alloy-ni60cr14co10ti5mo4w4al3
- NT1 alloy-ni60mo13co9cr8nb4al3
- NT1 alloy-ni61cr16co9al3ti3w3
- NT1 alloy-ni61cr22mo9nb4fe3
- NT1 alloy-ni62cr16mo15fe3
- NT1 alloy-ni65cr25mo10
- NT1 alloy-ni65mo16cr15w4
- NT1 alloy-ni67cr19mo5w5ti3
- NT1 alloy-ni68cr15w6al3mo3fe2
- NT1 alloy-ni70mo17cr7fe5
- NT1 alloy-ni74cr13al6mo4
- NT1 alloy-ni75cr12al6mo5
- NT1 alloy-ni79fe16mo4
- NT1 alloy-ni80fe16mo4
- NT1 alloy-ti78cr11mo7al3
- NT1 alloy-ti88mo8al3
- NT1 alloy-ti89al6mo3
- NT1 alloy-ti90al6mo3
- NT1 alloy-ti90mo7al2
- NT1 alloy-ti91al4mo3
- NT1 alloy-ti91al5cr2
- NT1 chromium-nickel-molybdenum ste
- NT2 steel-cr11ni10mo2ti-1
- NT2 steel-cr13ni6mo-1
- NT2 steel-cr15ni15motib
- NT2 steel-cr16ni13monbv
- NT2 steel-cr16ni15mo3nb
- NT2 steel-cr16ni16monb
- NT2 steel-cr16ni8mo2
- NT2 steel-cr17ni12monb
- NT2 steel-cr17ni12mo3
- NT2 steel-cr17ni12mo3-1
- NT2 steel-cr17ni13mo2ti
- NT2 steel-cr17ni13mo3ti
- NT2 steel-ni17cr14moti-1
- NT2 steel-ni26cr15ti2movalb
- NT2 steel-ni35cr18mo4ti2al
- NT1 molybdenum base alloys
- NT2 alloy-mo99
- NT2 alloy-mo99b
- NT1 refractaloy
- NT1 steel-cr10mo2
- NT1 steel-cr17ni4mo3
- NT1 steel-cr26ni5mo-1
- NT1 steel-cr9monbv
- RT molybdenum additions

MOLYBDENUM ARSENIDES [0; 0]
Feb 89
- BT1 arsenides
- BT2 arsenic compounds
- BT2 pnictides
- BT1 molybdenum compounds
- BT2 transition element compounds

MOLYBDENUM BASE ALLOYS
[718; 899]
- BT1 molybdenum alloys
- BT2 alloys
- NT1 alloy-mo99
- NT1 alloy-mo99b

MOLYBDENUM BLUE [23; 23]
- BT1 molybdenum oxides
- BT2 molybdenum compounds
- BT3 transition element compounds
- BT2 oxides
- BT3 chalcogenides
- BT3 oxygen compounds
- BT1 pigments

MOLYBDENUM BORIDES [101; 101]
- BT1 borides
- BT2 boron compounds
- BT1 molybdenum compounds
- BT2 transition element compounds

MOLYBDENUM BROMIDES [26; 26]
- BT1 bromides
- BT2 bromine compounds
- BT3 halogen compounds
- BT2 halides
- BT3 halogen compounds
- BT1 molybdenum compounds
- BT2 transition element compounds

MOLYBDENUM CARBIDES [327; 327]
- BT1 carbides
- BT2 carbon compounds
- BT1 molybdenum compounds
- BT2 transition element compounds

MOLYBDENUM CARBONATES [6; 6]
Jan 79
- BT1 carbonates
- BT2 carbon compounds
- BT2 oxygen compounds
- BT1 molybdenum compounds
- BT2 transition element compounds

MOLYBDENUM CHLORIDES
[189; 189]
- BT1 chlorides
- BT2 chlorine compounds
- BT3 halogen compounds
- BT2 halides
- BT3 halogen compounds
- BT1 molybdenum compounds
- BT2 transition element compounds

MOLYBDENUM COMPLEXES
[1,536; 1,536]
- BT1 transition element complexes
- BT2 complexes

MOLYBDENUM COMPOUNDS
[1,389; 6,404]
- BT1 transition element compounds
- NT1 molybdates
- NT1 molybdenum arsenides
- NT1 molybdenum borides
- NT1 molybdenum bromides
- NT1 molybdenum carbides
- NT1 molybdenum carbonates
- NT1 molybdenum chlorides
- NT1 molybdenum fluorides
- NT1 molybdenum hydrides
- NT1 molybdenum hydroxides
- NT1 molybdenum iodides
- NT1 molybdenum nitrates
- NT1 molybdenum nitrides
- NT1 molybdenum oxides
- NT2 molybdenum blue
- NT1 molybdenum phosphates
- NT1 molybdenum phosphides
- NT1 molybdenum selenides
- NT1 molybdenum silicates
- NT1 molybdenum silicides
- NT1 molybdenum sulfates
- NT1 molybdenum sulfides
- NT1 molybdenum tellurides
- NT1 molybdophosphates
- NT1 molybdophosphoric acid
- RT molybdenum additions

MOLYBDENUM FLUORIDES [148; 148]
- BT1 fluorides
- BT2 fluorine compounds
- BT3 halogen compounds
- BT2 halides
- BT3 halogen compounds
- BT1 molybdenum compounds
- BT2 transition element compounds

MOLYBDENUM HYDRIDES [24; 24]
- BT1 hydrides
- BT2 hydrogen compounds
- BT1 molybdenum compounds
- BT2 transition element compounds

MOLYBDENUM HYDROXIDES [12; 12]
- BT1 hydroxides
- BT2 hydrogen compounds
- BT2 oxygen compounds
- BT1 molybdenum compounds
- BT2 transition element compounds

MOLYBDENUM IODIDES [34; 34]
- BT1 iodides
- BT2 halides
- BT3 halogen compounds
- BT2 iodine compounds
- BT3 halogen compounds
- BT1 molybdenum compounds
- BT2 transition element compounds

MOLYBDENUM IONS [377; 377]
- BT1 ions
- BT2 charged particles

MOLYBDENUM ISOTOPES [274; 2,271]
- NT1 molybdenum 100
- NT1 molybdenum 101
- NT1 molybdenum 102
- NT1 molybdenum 103
- NT1 molybdenum 104
- NT1 molybdenum 105

NT1 molybdenum 106
NT1 molybdenum 107
NT1 molybdenum 108
NT1 molybdenum 84
NT1 molybdenum 85
NT1 molybdenum 87
NT1 molybdenum 88
NT1 molybdenum 89
NT1 molybdenum 90
NT1 molybdenum 91
NT1 molybdenum 92
NT1 molybdenum 93
NT1 molybdenum 94
NT1 molybdenum 95
NT1 molybdenum 96
NT1 molybdenum 97
NT1 molybdenum 98
NT1 molybdenum 99

MOLYBDENUM NITRATES [3; 3]
Oct 76
BT1 molybdenum compounds
BT2 transition element compounds
BT1 nitrates
BT2 nitrogen compounds
BT2 oxygen compounds

MOLYBDENUM NITRIDES [101; 101]
BT1 molybdenum compounds
BT2 transition element compounds
BT1 nitrides
BT2 nitrogen compounds
BT2 pnictides

MOLYBDENUM ORES [132; 132]
BT1 ores

MOLYBDENUM OXIDES [1,297; 1,325]
BT1 molybdenum compounds
BT2 transition element compounds
BT1 oxides
BT2 chalcogenides
BT2 oxygen compounds
NT1 molybdenum blue
RT iriginite
RT moluranite
RT molybdates
RT molybdophosphoric acid
RT oxide minerals
RT umohoite
RT wulfenite

MOLYBDENUM PHOSPHATES [37; 37]
BT1 molybdenum compounds
BT2 transition element compounds
BT1 phosphates
BT2 oxygen compounds
BT2 phosphorus compounds

MOLYBDENUM PHOSPHIDES [17; 17]
Jul 78
BT1 molybdenum compounds
BT2 transition element compounds
BT1 phosphides
BT2 phosphorus compounds
BT2 pnictides

MOLYBDENUM SELENIDES [166; 166]
BT1 molybdenum compounds
BT2 transition element compounds
BT1 selenides
BT2 chalcogenides
BT2 selenium compounds

MOLYBDENUM SILICATES [10; 10]
BT1 molybdenum compounds
BT2 transition element compounds
BT1 silicates
BT2 oxygen compounds
BT2 silicon compounds

MOLYBDENUM SILICIDES [197; 197]
Oct 75
BT1 molybdenum compounds
BT2 transition element compounds
BT1 silicides
BT2 silicon compounds

MOLYBDENUM SULFATES [9; 9]
BT1 molybdenum compounds
BT2 transition element compounds
BT1 sulfates
BT2 oxygen compounds
BT2 sulfur compounds

MOLYBDENUM SULFIDES [830; 830]
BT1 molybdenum compounds
BT2 transition element compounds
BT1 sulfides
BT2 chalcogenides
BT2 sulfur compounds

MOLYBDENUM TELLURIDES [39; 39]
BT1 molybdenum compounds
BT2 transition element compounds
BT1 tellurides
BT2 chalcogenides
BT2 tellurium compounds

MOLYBDENUM 100 [239; 239]
BT1 even-even nuclei
BT2 nuclei
BT1 intermediate mass nuclei
BT2 nuclei
BT1 molybdenum isotopes
BT1 stable isotopes
BT2 isotopes

MOLYBDENUM 100 REACTIONS
[36; 36] *Jun 84*
BT1 heavy ion reactions
BT2 nuclear reactions

MOLYBDENUM 100 TARGET
[338; 338]
BT1 targets

MOLYBDENUM 101 [44; 44]
BT1 beta-minus decay radioisotopes
BT2 beta decay radioisotopes
BT3 radioisotopes
BT4 isotopes
BT1 even-odd nuclei
BT2 nuclei
BT1 intermediate mass nuclei
BT2 nuclei
BT1 minutes living radioisotopes
BT2 radioisotopes
BT3 isotopes
BT1 molybdenum isotopes

MOLYBDENUM 102 [43; 43]
BT1 beta-minus decay radioisotopes
BT2 beta decay radioisotopes
BT3 radioisotopes
BT4 isotopes
BT1 even-even nuclei
BT2 nuclei
BT1 intermediate mass nuclei
BT2 nuclei
BT1 minutes living radioisotopes
BT2 radioisotopes
BT3 isotopes
BT1 molybdenum isotopes

MOLYBDENUM 103 [21; 21]
BT1 beta-minus decay radioisotopes
BT2 beta decay radioisotopes
BT3 radioisotopes
BT4 isotopes
BT1 even-odd nuclei
BT2 nuclei
BT1 intermediate mass nuclei
BT2 nuclei
BT1 minutes living radioisotopes
BT2 radioisotopes
BT3 isotopes
BT1 molybdenum isotopes

MOLYBDENUM 104 [40; 40]
BT1 beta-minus decay radioisotopes
BT2 beta decay radioisotopes
BT3 radioisotopes
BT4 isotopes
BT1 even-even nuclei
BT2 nuclei
BT1 intermediate mass nuclei
BT2 nuclei
BT1 minutes living radioisotopes
BT2 radioisotopes
BT3 isotopes
BT1 molybdenum isotopes

MOLYBDENUM 105 [22; 22]
BT1 beta-minus decay radioisotopes
BT2 beta decay radioisotopes
BT3 radioisotopes
BT4 isotopes
BT1 even-odd nuclei
BT2 nuclei
BT1 intermediate mass nuclei
BT2 nuclei
BT1 molybdenum isotopes
BT1 seconds living radioisotopes
BT2 radioisotopes
BT3 isotopes

MOLYBDENUM 106 [23; 23]
BT1 beta-minus decay radioisotopes
BT2 beta decay radioisotopes
BT3 radioisotopes
BT4 isotopes
BT1 even-even nuclei
BT2 nuclei
BT1 intermediate mass nuclei
BT2 nuclei
BT1 molybdenum isotopes
BT1 seconds living radioisotopes
BT2 radioisotopes
BT3 isotopes

MOLYBDENUM 107 [10; 10]
BT1 beta-minus decay radioisotopes
BT2 beta decay radioisotopes
BT3 radioisotopes
BT4 isotopes
BT1 even-odd nuclei
BT2 nuclei
BT1 intermediate mass nuclei
BT2 nuclei
BT1 molybdenum isotopes
BT1 seconds living radioisotopes
BT2 radioisotopes
BT3 isotopes

MOLYBDENUM 108 [8; 8]
BT1 beta-minus decay radioisotopes
BT2 beta decay radioisotopes
BT3 radioisotopes
BT4 isotopes
BT1 even-even nuclei
BT2 nuclei
BT1 intermediate mass nuclei
BT2 nuclei
BT1 molybdenum isotopes
BT1 seconds living radioisotopes
BT2 radioisotopes
BT3 isotopes

→ **MOLYBDENUM 84** [0; 0] *Mar 91*
BT1 even-even nuclei
BT2 nuclei
BT1 intermediate mass nuclei
BT2 nuclei
BT1 molybdenum isotopes

MOLYBDENUM 85 [3; 3] *Apr 78*
BT1 even-odd nuclei
BT2 nuclei
BT1 intermediate mass nuclei
BT2 nuclei
BT1 molybdenum isotopes

MOLYBDENUM 87 [9; 9] *Nov 77*
BT1 beta-plus decay radioisotopes
BT2 beta decay radioisotopes
BT3 radioisotopes
BT4 isotopes
BT1 electron capture radioisotopes
BT2 beta decay radioisotopes
BT3 radioisotopes
BT4 isotopes

MOLYBDENUM 87
- BT1 even-odd nuclei
- BT2 nuclei
- BT1 intermediate mass nuclei
- BT2 nuclei
- BT1 molybdenum isotopes
- BT1 seconds living radioisotopes
- BT2 radioisotopes
- BT3 isotopes

MOLYBDENUM 88 [8; 8] *Nov 76*
- BT1 beta-plus decay radioisotopes
- BT2 beta decay radioisotopes
- BT3 radioisotopes
- BT4 isotopes
- BT1 electron capture radioisotopes
- BT2 beta decay radioisotopes
- BT3 radioisotopes
- BT4 isotopes
- BT1 even-even nuclei
- BT2 nuclei
- BT1 intermediate mass nuclei
- BT2 nuclei
- BT1 minutes living radioisotopes
- BT2 radioisotopes
- BT3 isotopes
- BT1 molybdenum isotopes

MOLYBDENUM 89 [15; 15]
- BT1 beta-plus decay radioisotopes
- BT2 beta decay radioisotopes
- BT3 radioisotopes
- BT4 isotopes
- BT1 electron capture radioisotopes
- BT2 beta decay radioisotopes
- BT3 radioisotopes
- BT4 isotopes
- BT1 even-odd nuclei
- BT2 nuclei
- BT1 intermediate mass nuclei
- BT2 nuclei
- BT1 isomeric transition isotopes
- BT2 radioisotopes
- BT3 isotopes
- BT1 millisec living radioisotopes
- BT2 radioisotopes
- BT3 isotopes
- BT1 minutes living radioisotopes
- BT2 radioisotopes
- BT3 isotopes
- BT1 molybdenum isotopes

MOLYBDENUM 90 [31; 31]
- BT1 beta-plus decay radioisotopes
- BT2 beta decay radioisotopes
- BT3 radioisotopes
- BT4 isotopes
- BT1 electron capture radioisotopes
- BT2 beta decay radioisotopes
- BT3 radioisotopes
- BT4 isotopes
- BT1 even-even nuclei
- BT2 nuclei
- BT1 hours living radioisotopes
- BT2 radioisotopes
- BT3 isotopes
- BT1 intermediate mass nuclei
- BT2 nuclei
- BT1 molybdenum isotopes

MOLYBDENUM 91 [55; 55]
- BT1 beta-plus decay radioisotopes
- BT2 beta decay radioisotopes
- BT3 radioisotopes
- BT4 isotopes
- BT1 electron capture radioisotopes
- BT2 beta decay radioisotopes
- BT3 radioisotopes
- BT4 isotopes
- BT1 even-odd nuclei
- BT2 nuclei
- BT1 intermediate mass nuclei
- BT2 nuclei
- BT1 isomeric transition isotopes
- BT2 radioisotopes
- BT3 isotopes
- BT1 minutes living radioisotopes
- BT2 radioisotopes
- BT3 isotopes
- BT1 molybdenum isotopes

MOLYBDENUM 92 [262; 262]
- BT1 even-even nuclei
- BT2 nuclei
- BT1 intermediate mass nuclei
- BT2 nuclei
- BT1 isomeric transition isotopes
- BT2 radioisotopes
- BT3 isotopes
- BT1 molybdenum isotopes
- BT1 nanosec living radioisotopes
- BT2 radioisotopes
- BT3 isotopes
- BT1 stable isotopes
- BT2 isotopes

MOLYBDENUM 92 REACTIONS [50; 50] *Oct 83*
- BT1 heavy ion reactions
- BT2 nuclear reactions

MOLYBDENUM 92 TARGET [505; 505]
- BT1 targets

MOLYBDENUM 93 [136; 136]
- BT1 electron capture radioisotopes
- BT2 beta decay radioisotopes
- BT3 radioisotopes
- BT4 isotopes
- BT1 even-odd nuclei
- BT2 nuclei
- BT1 hours living radioisotopes
- BT2 radioisotopes
- BT3 isotopes
- BT1 intermediate mass nuclei
- BT2 nuclei
- BT1 internal conversion radioisoto
- BT2 radioisotopes
- BT3 isotopes
- BT1 isomeric transition isotopes
- BT2 radioisotopes
- BT3 isotopes
- BT1 molybdenum isotopes
- BT1 years living radioisotopes
- BT2 radioisotopes
- BT3 isotopes

MOLYBDENUM 94 [147; 147]
- BT1 even-even nuclei
- BT2 nuclei
- BT1 intermediate mass nuclei
- BT2 nuclei
- BT1 isomeric transition isotopes
- BT2 radioisotopes
- BT3 isotopes
- BT1 molybdenum isotopes
- BT1 nanosec living radioisotopes
- BT2 radioisotopes
- BT3 isotopes
- BT1 stable isotopes
- BT2 isotopes

MOLYBDENUM 94 TARGET [198; 198]
- BT1 targets

MOLYBDENUM 95 [163; 163]
- BT1 even-odd nuclei
- BT2 nuclei
- BT1 intermediate mass nuclei
- BT2 nuclei
- BT1 molybdenum isotopes
- BT1 stable isotopes
- BT2 isotopes

MOLYBDENUM 95 TARGET [84; 84]
- BT1 targets

MOLYBDENUM 96 [145; 145]
- BT1 even-even nuclei
- BT2 nuclei
- BT1 intermediate mass nuclei
- BT2 nuclei
- BT1 molybdenum isotopes
- BT1 stable isotopes
- BT2 isotopes

MOLYBDENUM 96 REACTIONS [5; 5] *Dec 89*
- BT1 heavy ion reactions
- BT2 nuclear reactions

MOLYBDENUM 96 TARGET [189; 189]
- BT1 targets

MOLYBDENUM 97 [94; 94]
- BT1 even-odd nuclei
- BT2 nuclei
- BT1 intermediate mass nuclei
- BT2 nuclei
- BT1 molybdenum isotopes
- BT1 stable isotopes
- BT2 isotopes

MOLYBDENUM 97 TARGET [45; 45]
- BT1 targets

MOLYBDENUM 98 [169; 169]
- BT1 even-even nuclei
- BT2 nuclei
- BT1 intermediate mass nuclei
- BT2 nuclei
- BT1 molybdenum isotopes
- BT1 stable isotopes
- BT2 isotopes

MOLYBDENUM 98 REACTIONS [12; 12] *May 87*
- BT1 heavy ion reactions
- BT2 nuclear reactions

MOLYBDENUM 98 TARGET [275; 275]
- BT1 targets

MOLYBDENUM 99 [916; 916]
- BT1 beta-minus decay radioisotopes
- BT2 beta decay radioisotopes
- BT3 radioisotopes
- BT4 isotopes
- BT1 days living radioisotopes
- BT2 radioisotopes
- BT3 isotopes
- BT1 even-odd nuclei
- BT2 nuclei
- BT1 intermediate mass nuclei
- BT2 nuclei
- BT1 molybdenum isotopes
- RT radioisotope generators

MOLYBDOPHOSPHATES [37; 37] *Sep 85*
(Specific compounds should be indexed by coordination of a descriptor of the form (CATION) COMPOUNDS and the above anion descriptor.)
- BT1 molybdenum compounds
- BT2 transition element compounds
- BT1 oxygen compounds
- BT1 phosphorus compounds

MOLYBDOPHOSPHORIC ACID [62; 62] *May 80*
- UF *phosphomolybdic acid*
- BT1 inorganic acids
- BT2 hydrogen compounds
- BT2 inorganic compounds
- BT1 molybdenum compounds
- BT2 transition element compounds
- BT1 oxygen compounds
- BT1 phosphorus compounds
- RT heteropolyanions
- RT molybdenum oxides
- RT phosphoric acid

MOMENT OF INERTIA [2,011; 2,011]
- UF *inertia*
- RT backbending
- RT kinetic energy
- RT mass
- RT mechanics
- RT rotation
- RT vmi model
- RT yrast states

MOMENTS METHOD [562; 562]
  RT   plasma fluid equations
  RT   transport theory

momentum (angular)
  USE   angular momentum

momentum (linear)
  USE   linear momentum

momentum (longitudinal)
  USE   longitudinal momentum

momentum (transverse)
  USE   transverse momentum

MOMENTUM COOLING [36; 36]
  Apr 82
  (Gradual reduction of emittance of coasting charged-particle beams by feedback sensing and correcting statistical fluctuations of beam momentum.)
  UF   *stochastic momentum cooling*
  BT1   stochastic cooling
  BT2   beam cooling

MOMENTUM TRANSFER [3,016; 4,683]
  Feb 78
  UF   *transfer (momentum)*
  NT1   angular momentum transfer
  NT1   four momentum transfer
  NT1   linear momentum transfer

MONACO [9; 9]
  BT1   developed countries
  BT1   europe

MONAZITES [477; 477]
  BT1   phosphate minerals
  BT2   minerals
  BT1   thorium minerals
  BT2   radioactive minerals
  BT3   minerals
  BT3   radioactive materials
  BT4   materials
  RT   thorium phosphates

MONEL [73; 95]
  BT1   nickel base alloys
  BT2   nickel alloys
  BT3   alloys
  NT1   alloy-ni66cu32

monel r-405
  USE   alloy-ni66cu32

monel 400
  USE   alloy-ni66cu32

MONEX PROCESS [0; 0]
  BT1   reprocessing
  BT2   separation processes
  RT   solvent extraction

MONGOLIAN PEOPLES REPUBLIC
  [4; 4] Oct 88
  BT1   asia
  RT   centrally planned economies

mongolism
  USE   downs syndrome

monilia
  USE   candida

MONIQUE EVENT [1; 1]
  BT1   contained explosions
  BT2   underground explosions
  BT3   explosions
  BT1   nuclear explosions
  BT2   explosions
  RT   granites

monitor codes
  USE   executive codes

§ **MONITORING** [6,822; 26,957]
  (Use of a more specific term is recommended.)
  UF   *monitoring network*
  NT1   acoustic monitoring
  NT1   aerosol monitoring
  NT1   air pollution monitoring
  NT1   beam monitoring
  NT1   loose parts monitoring
  NT1   radiation monitoring
  NT2   aerial monitoring
  NT2   personnel monitoring
  NT1   temperature monitoring
  RT   control
  RT   detection
  RT   reactor monitoring systems

monitoring network
  USE   monitoring

MONITORS [337; 2,931] Dec 84
  (Use of a more specific term is recommended.)
  BT1   measuring instruments
  NT1   air pollution monitors
  NT1   beam monitors
  NT2   beam scanners
  NT2   faraday cups
  NT2   magnetoinduction sensors
  NT1   failed element monitors
  NT1   radiation monitors
  NT2   exposure ratemeters
  NT2   liquid contamination monitors
  NT2   neutron monitors
  NT2   surface contamination monitors
  NT2   survey monitors
  RT   reactor monitoring systems

→ *monitors (air pollution)*
  USE   air pollution monitors

monitors (reactor)
  SEE   reactor control systems
  OR   reactor monitoring systems

MONJU REACTOR [341; 341]
  (Tsuruga, Fukui, Japan)
  UF   *fast prototype reactor japan*
  UF   *japan prototype fast reactor*
  UF   *jpfr reactor*
  UF   *prototype fast reactor japan*
  BT1   lmfbr type reactors
  BT2   fbr type reactors
  DT3   breeder reactors
  BT4   reactors
  BT3   fast reactors
  BT4   epithermal reactors
  BT5   reactors
  BT2   liquid metal cooled reactors
  BT3   reactors
  BT1   power reactors
  BT2   reactors
  BT1   sodium cooled reactors
  BT2   liquid metal cooled reactors
  BT3   reactors

MONKEYS [795; 1,148]
  BT1   primates
  BT2   mammals
  BT3   vertebrates
  BT4   animals
  NT1   baboons
  NT1   macacus

monobutyl phosphate
  USE   mbp

MONOCARBOXYLIC ACIDS
  [681; 4,680]
  BT1   carboxylic acids
  BT2   organic acids
  BT3   organic compounds
  NT1   acetic acid
  NT1   acrylic acid
  NT1   arachidonic acid
  NT1   benzoic acid
  NT2   ioglycamic acid
  NT1   butyric acid
  NT1   cinnamic acid
  NT1   crotonic acid
  NT1   decanoic acid
  NT1   dodecanoic acid
  NT1   eicosanoic acid
  NT1   formic acid
  NT1   glycolic acid
  NT1   heptanoic acid
  NT1   hexadecanoic acid
  NT1   hexanoic acid
  NT1   isobutyric acid
  NT1   isovaleric acid
  NT1   linoleic acid
  NT1   linolenic acid
  NT1   methacrylic acid
  NT1   nicotinic acid
  NT1   nonanoic acid
  NT1   octadecanoic acid
  NT1   octanoic acid
  NT1   oleic acid
  NT1   pethidine
  NT1   pivalic acid
  NT1   propionic acid
  NT1   sorbic acid
  NT1   tetradecanoic acid
  NT1   valeric acid

MONOCHROMATIC RADIATION
  [428; 428] Feb 78
  BT1   electromagnetic radiation
  BT2   radiations
  RT   laser radiation
  RT   visible radiation

MONOCHROMATORS [1,422; 1,422]
  RT   beam analyzers
  RT   beam optics
  RT   spectrometers

MONOCLINIC LATTICES [1,640; 1,640]
  BT1   crystal lattices
  BT2   crystal structure

MONOCLONAL ANTIBODIES
  [2,824; 2,824] Sep 82
  BT1   antibodies
  RT   clone cells
  RT   hybridomas

MONOCRYSTALS [22,822; 23,055]
  UF   *single crystals*
  BT1   crystals
  NT1   whiskers

MONOCYTES [296; 296]
  BT1   leukocytes
  BT2   blood cells
  BT3   blood
  BT4   body fluids
  BT5   biological materials
  BT6   materials

monododecylphosphoric acid
  USE   mdpa

MONOMERS [768; 1,324]
  NT1   vinyl monomers
  RT   dimers
  RT   polymerization
  RT   polymers

MONOPOLES [1,061; 3,106]
NT1 magnetic monopoles
RT multipoles

MONOSACCHARIDES [92; 3,925]
BT1 saccharides
BT2 carbohydrates
BT3 organic compounds
NT1 erythritol
NT1 hexoses
NT2 fructose
NT2 galactose
NT2 glucose
NT2 hexosamines
NT3 glucosamine
NT2 mannose
NT2 sorbose
NT1 inositols
NT2 inositol
NT1 pentoses
NT2 arabinose
NT2 deoxyribose
NT2 ribose
NT2 ribulose
NT2 xylose
NT1 sedoheptulose
NT1 sorbitol
RT gluconic acid

MONOTECTICS [14; 14]
RT eutectics
RT phase diagrams

MONOTECTOIDS [9; 9]
RT eutectoids
RT phase diagrams

MONTAGUE-1 REACTOR [5; 5]
BT1 bwr type reactors
BT2 enriched uranium reactors
BT3 reactors
BT2 power reactors
BT3 reactors
BT2 thermal reactors
BT3 reactors
BT2 water cooled reactors
BT3 reactors
BT2 water moderated reactors
BT3 reactors

MONTAGUE-2 REACTOR [5; 5]
BT1 bwr type reactors
BT2 enriched uranium reactors
BT3 reactors
BT2 power reactors
BT3 reactors
BT2 thermal reactors
BT3 reactors
BT2 water cooled reactors
BT3 reactors
BT2 water moderated reactors
BT3 reactors

MONTALTO DI CASTRO-1 REACTOR
[17; 17] *Mar 85*
(Latium, Italy.)
UF *alto lazio-1 reactor*
UF *enel-6 reactor*
BT1 bwr type reactors
BT2 enriched uranium reactors
BT3 reactors
BT2 power reactors
BT3 reactors
BT2 thermal reactors
BT3 reactors
BT2 water cooled reactors
BT3 reactors
BT2 water moderated reactors
BT3 reactors

MONTALTO DI CASTRO-2 REACTOR
[13; 13] *Mar 85*
(Latium, Italy.)
UF *alto lazio-2 reactor*
UF *enel-8 reactor*
BT1 bwr type reactors
BT2 enriched uranium reactors

BT3 reactors
BT2 power reactors
BT3 reactors
BT2 thermal reactors
BT3 reactors
BT2 water cooled reactors
BT3 reactors
BT2 water moderated reactors
BT3 reactors

MONTANA [201; 201]
BT1 usa
BT2 developed countries
BT2 north america

MONTE CARLO METHOD
[14,861; 14,861]
RT fault tree analysis
RT neutron transport theory
RT probability
RT randomness
RT stochastic processes
RT transport theory

montecuccolino rb-1 reactor
USE rb-1 reactor

montecuccolino rb-2 reactor
USE rb-2 reactor

montecuccolino rb-3 reactor
USE rb-3 reactor

§§ **MONTHLY VARIATIONS** [223; 223]
Sep 79
BT1 variations

MONTICELLO REACTOR [172; 172]
(Monticello, Minnesota, USA)
UF *northern states monticello rea*
BT1 bwr type reactors
BT2 enriched uranium reactors
BT3 reactors
BT2 power reactors
BT3 reactors
BT2 thermal reactors
BT3 reactors
BT2 water cooled reactors
BT3 reactors
BT2 water moderated reactors
BT3 reactors

MONTMORILLONITE [226; 226]
UF *hectorite*
BT1 clays
BT2 silicate minerals
BT3 minerals
BT1 inorganic ion exchangers
BT2 ion exchange materials
BT3 materials
RT bentonite

montreal univ. slowpoke react.
USE slowpoke-montreal reactor

MOON [936; 936]
BT1 satellites
RT apollo project
RT lunar atmosphere
RT lunar materials

MORAINES [14; 14]
BT1 geologic deposits

MORIN [44; 44]
BT1 dyes
BT1 flavones
BT2 flavenoids
BT3 organic oxygen compounds
BT4 organic compounds
BT1 polyphenols
BT2 phenols

BT3 aromatics
BT4 organic compounds
BT3 hydroxy compounds
BT4 organic compounds
BT1 reagents

MOROCCO [35; 35]
BT1 africa
BT1 developing countries

MORPHINE [174; 174]
BT1 alkaloids
BT2 organic compounds
BT1 analgesics
BT2 central nervous system depress
BT3 central nervous system agents
BT4 drugs
BT1 narcotics
BT2 central nervous system depress
BT3 central nervous system agents
BT4 drugs
RT codeine
RT heroin
RT papaver somniferum
RT thebaine

MORPHOLINES [83; 83]
BT1 amines
BT2 organic compounds
BT1 ethers
BT2 organic oxygen compounds
BT3 organic compounds
BT1 heterocyclic compounds
BT2 organic compounds
BT1 organic nitrogen compounds
BT2 organic compounds

MORPHOLOGICAL CHANGES
[6,580; 7,502]
SF *morphology*
NT1 ultrastructural changes
RT ogical effects
RT microscopy
RT plant breeding
RT tissues

morphology
(Branch of biology dealing with structure and form of organisms.)
SEE anatomy
OR crystal structure
OR morphological changes
OR structural models

MORRISON RULE [20; 20]
(An empirical rule for pomeron exchange.)
RT exchange interactions
RT parity
RT particle interactions
RT pomeranchuk particles
RT spin

MORSE POTENTIAL [335; 335]
BT1 potentials
RT interatomic forces

MORTALITY [2,859; 2,859]
RT death
RT lethal irradiation
RT life span
RT supralethal irradiation
RT survival curves
RT time dependence

MORTARS [117; 117]
RT building materials
RT cements
RT concretes
RT grouting

MOS TRANSISTORS [787; 1,120]
(Metal Oxide Silicon transistors)
BT1 transistors
BT2 semiconductor devices
NT1 mosfet

MOSAICISM [36; 570]
- NT1 chimeras
- NT2 radiation chimeras
- NT1 parabiosis
- RT genetic effects
- RT mutations

moscow irt-2000 reactor
- USE irt-2000 moscow reactor

moscow wwr-s reactor
- USE wwr-s-moscow reactor

MOSFET [344; 344]
(Metal Oxide Silicon Field Effect Transistors)
- BT1 field effect transistors
- BT2 transistors
- BT3 semiconductor devices
- BT1 mos transistors
- BT2 transistors
- BT3 semiconductor devices

MOSQUITOES [76; 76]
- UF *aedes*
- UF *anopheles*
- BT1 insects
- BT2 arthropods
- BT3 invertebrates
- BT4 animals
- RT malaria

MOSSES [28; 28]
- BT1 plants

MOTHS [163; 238]
- BT1 lepidoptera
- BT2 insects
- BT3 arthropods
- BT4 invertebrates
- BT5 animals
- NT1 bollworm
- NT1 codling moth
- NT1 lymantria dispar
- NT1 rice stem borers
- NT1 silkworm

§ ## MOTION [3,311; 4,858]
- NT1 ground motion
- NT1 proper motion
- RT angular momentum
- RT guiding-center approximation
- RT kinetic energy
- RT linear momentum
- RT trajectories

MOTION DETECTION SYSTEMS [82; 82] *Feb 80*
- RT detection
- RT nuclear materials diversion
- RT physical protection devices
- RT safeguards
- RT security

MOTOR VEHICLE ACCIDENTS [68; 68]
- BT1 accidents
- RT road transport
- RT vehicles

motor vehicles
- USE vehicles

MOTORS [580; 1,503]
- UF *engines*
- NT1 diesel engines
- NT1 electric motors
- NT2 superconducting motors
- NT1 ramjet engines
- NT1 stirling engines

MOTT SCATTERING [126; 126]
- BT1 elastic scattering
- BT2 scattering

mottelson-nilson model
- USE nilsson-mottelson model

moulting
- USE molting

MOUND LABORATORY [129; 129]
- BT1 us aec
- BT2 us organizations
- BT3 national organizations
- BT1 us doe
- BT2 us organizations
- BT3 national organizations
- BT1 us erda
- BT2 us organizations
- BT3 national organizations
- RT ohio

MOUNTAINS [204; 1,589]
- NT1 alps
- NT1 andes
- NT1 appalachian mountains
- NT1 appennines
- NT1 carrizo mountains
- NT1 colorado plateau
- NT1 himalayas
- NT1 rocky mountains
- NT1 san bernardino mountains
- NT1 sierra nevada colorado
- NT1 urals
- NT1 witwatersrand
- NT1 yucca mountain
- RT orogenesis

mouth
- USE oral cavity

MOVING COIL MAGNETOMETERS [22; 22]
- BT1 magnetometers
- BT2 measuring instruments

MOVING-BOUNDARY CONDITIONS [50; 50]
- BT1 boundary conditions

MOZAMBIQUE [9; 9]
- BT1 africa
- BT1 developing countries

mp tandem accelerator
- USE crnl mp tandem accelerator

mpa
- USE maximum permissible activity

mpbb
- USE maximum permissible body burde

mpc
- USE maximum permissible concentrat

mpd
- USE maximum permissible dose

mpe
- USE maximum permissible exposure

MPG [55; 55] *Dec 81*
- UF *2-mercaptopropionylglycine*
- BT1 amino acids
- BT2 carboxylic acids
- BT3 organic acids
- BT4 organic compounds
- BT1 radioprotective substances
- BT2 drugs
- BT2 response modifying factors
- BT1 thiols
- BT2 organic sulfur compounds
- BT3 organic compounds

mpi
- USE maximum permissible intake

mpl
- USE maximum permissible level

mr-2 moscow reactor
- USE rpt reactor

MRR REACTOR [19; 19]
(Association of Universities Inc., Upton, New York, USA)
- UF *brookhaven medical res. reacto*
- UF *medical res. reactor, bnl*
- UF *us aec mrr*
- BT1 enriched uranium reactors
- BT2 reactors
- BT1 isotope production reactors
- BT2 irradiation reactors
- BT3 reactors
- BT1 research reactors
- BT2 research and test reactors
- BT3 reactors
- BT1 tank type reactors
- BT2 reactors
- BT1 thermal reactors
- BT2 reactors
- BT1 water cooled reactors
- BT2 reactors
- BT1 water moderated reactors
- BT2 reactors

msmr reactor
(Missouri School of Mines, Rolla.)
- USE umrr reactor

MSRE REACTOR [56; 56]
- UF *molten salt reactor experiment*
- BT1 enriched uranium reactors
- BT2 reactors
- BT1 experimental reactors
- BT2 research and test reactors
- BT3 reactors
- BT1 graphite moderated reactors
- BT2 reactors
- BT1 molten salt cooled reactors
- BT2 molten salt reactors
- BT3 reactors
- BT1 power reactors
- BT2 reactors
- BT1 thermal reactors
- BT2 reactors

MSU CYCLOTRONS [133; 133]
(Includes 56 MeV proton cyclotron and heavy ion K500 and K800 superconducting cyclotrons.)
- UF *michigan state univ cyclotrons*
- BT1 isochronous cyclotrons
- BT2 cyclotrons
- BT3 cyclic accelerators
- BT4 accelerators

MT-1 TOKAMAK [4; 4] *Nov 89*
(Hungarian Academy of Sciences, Budapest, Hungary.)
- BT1 tokamak devices
- BT2 closed plasma devices
- BT3 thermonuclear devices

mta atommagkutato intezete
USE   atomki

mthf
(Methyltetrahydrofuran)
USE   furans

MTR REACTOR [67; 67]
UF   *idaho materials testing reacto*
UF   *materials testing react. idaho*
UF   *us aec-mat. test. react.-idaho*
BT1   enriched uranium reactors
BT2   reactors
BT1   materials testing reactors
BT2   irradiation reactors
BT3   reactors
BT1   tank type reactors
BT2   reactors
BT1   thermal reactors
BT2   reactors
BT1   water cooled reactors
BT2   reactors
BT1   water moderated reactors
BT2   reactors

mu sr
USE   muon spin relaxation

MUCOPOLYSACCHARIDES [135; 538]
BT1   amines
BT2   organic compounds
BT1   polysaccharides
BT2   saccharides
BT3   carbohydrates
BT4   organic compounds
NT1   chitin
NT1   chondroitin
NT1   heparin
NT1   hyaluronic acid

MUCOPROTEINS [18; 405]
BT1   polysaccharides
BT2   saccharides
BT3   carbohydrates
BT4   organic compounds
BT1   proteins
BT2   organic compounds
NT1   haptoglobins
NT1   intrinsic factor
NT1   phytohemagglutinin
RT   chondroitin
RT   lysozyme

mucosa
USE   mucous membranes

MUCOUS MEMBRANES [1,125; 1,167]
UF   *mucosa*
NT1   conjunctiva
RT   epithelium

MUEHLEBERG REACTOR [189; 189]
(Muehleberg, Bern, Switzerland)
UF   *akm muehleberg reactor*
UF   *akm reactor*
UF   *atomkraftwerk muehleberg*
BT1   bwr type reactors
BT2   enriched uranium reactors
BT3   reactors
BT2   power reactors
BT3   reactors
BT2   thermal reactors
BT3   reactors
BT2   water cooled reactors
BT3   reactors
BT2   water moderated reactors
BT3   reactors

MUELHEIM-KAERLICH REACTOR
[197; 197]
(Muehlheimkaerlich, Rheinlandpfalz, Federal Republic of Germany)

BT1   pwr type reactors
BT2   enriched uranium reactors
BT3   reactors
BT2   power reactors
BT3   reactors
BT2   thermal reactors
BT3   reactors
BT2   water cooled reactors
BT3   reactors
BT2   water moderated reactors
BT3   reactors

muf
USE   material unaccounted for

MUFFIN-TIN POTENTIAL [436; 436]
BT1   potentials
RT   electronic structure
RT   wave functions

mulberry alloy
USE   alloy-u90nb7zr3

mule deer
USE   deer

MULLITE [105; 105]
BT1   inorganic ion exchangers
BT2   ion exchange materials
BT3   materials
BT1   oxide minerals
BT2   minerals

MULTI-CENTER SHELL MODEL
[33; 33] *Nov 81*
UF   *multicenter shell model*
BT1   shell models
BT2   nuclear models
BT3   mathematical models

MULTI-CHANNEL ANALYZERS
[1,640; 1,640]
UF   *multichannel analyzers*
BT1   pulse analyzers
BT2   electronic equipment
BT3   equipment

multi-charged ions
USE   multicharged ions

MULTI-ELEMENT ANALYSIS
[2,979; 2,979]
(For analysis of 2 or more elements or isotopes of different elements.)
UF   *multielement analysis*
BT1   chemical analysis

MULTI-ELEMENT SEPARATION
[418; 418]
(For mutual separation of 2 or more elements or isotopes of different elements.)
UF   *multielement separation*
BT1   separation processes

multi-level analysis
USE   multilevel analysis

MULTI-NUCLEON TRANSFER
REACTIO [430; 4,942]
(More than one nucleon transfered.)
UF   *multinucleon transfer reaction*
BT1   transfer reactions
BT2   direct reactions
BT3   nuclear reactions
NT1   four-nucleon transfer reaction
NT2   alpha-transfer reactions
NT1   many-nucleon transfer reaction
NT1   three-nucleon transfer reactio
NT1   two-nucleon transfer reactions

MULTI-PARAMETER ANALYSIS
[2,314; 2,314]
UF   *multiparameter analysis*
UF   *parametric analysis*
RT   data processing

multi-particle spectrometers
USE   multiparticle spectrometers

MULTI-PHOTON PROCESSES
[1,227; 1,227] *Mar 83*
UF   *multiphoton processes*
RT   energy-level transitions
RT   lasers
RT   photon emission

multi-wire ionization chambers
USE   multiwire ionization chambers

multi-wire proportional chambe
USE   multiwire proportional chamber

multicenter shell model
USE   multi-center shell model

multichannel analyzers
USE   multi-channel analyzers

MULTICHARGED IONS [4,374; 4,381]
(With charge 3 and above.)
UF   *multi-charged ions*
BT1   ions
BT2   charged particles
RT   heavy ions
RT   light ions

multielement analysis
USE   multi-element analysis

multielement separation
USE   multi-element separation

MULTIGROUP THEORY [2,275; 2,275]
BT1   transport theory
RT   group constants
RT   neutron transport theory

multilat consult mechan, oecd
(Multilateral Consultation and surveillance Mechanism for Sea Dumping of Radioactive Waste.)
USE   oecd mcmsdrw

MULTILATERAL AGREEMENTS
[89; 89]
BT1   international agreements
BT2   agreements

MULTILEVEL ANALYSIS [295; 295]
UF   *multi-level analysis*
RT   breit-wigner formula
RT   cross sections
RT   r matrix
RT   resonance

multinucleon transfer reaction
USE   multi-nucleon transfer reactio

multiparameter analysis
USE   multi-parameter analysis

MULTIPARTICLE SPECTROMETERS
[198; 198]
- UF *multi-particle spectrometers*
- BT1 spectrometers
- BT2 measuring instruments

MULTIPERIPHERAL MODEL
[908; 1,421]
- UF+ *diffractive dissociation*
- BT1 peripheral models
- BT2 particle models
-   BT3 mathematical models
- NT1 cluster emission model
- NT2 space-time model
- RT abfst equation

MULTIPHASE FLOW [142; 142] *Aug 81*
(Simultaneous flow of more than two fluid phases in the same flow channel or pipe.)
- BT1 fluid flow

multiphoton processes
- USE multi-photon processes

MULTIPLE COLLISION METHOD
[110; 110]
- RT multiple scattering

MULTIPLE PRODUCTION
[6,589; 7,212]
- BT1 particle production
- NT1 pionization
- RT charge distribution
- RT coherent tube model
- RT correlated-particle models
- RT limiting fragmentation
- RT multiplicity
- RT particle decay
- RT particle interactions

MULTIPLE SCATTERING [3,915; 3,915]
- BT1 scattering
- RT faddeev equations
- RT glauber theory
- RT many-body problem
- RT moliere theory
- RT multiple collision method

MULTIPLETS [1,349; 4,640]
- NT1 particle multiplets
- NT2 baryon decuplets
- NT2 baryon octets
- NT2 meson nonets
- NT2 meson octets
- NT1 supermultiplets
- NT1 triplets

MULTIPLEXERS [379; 379]
- BT1 electronic equipment
- BT2 equipment
- RT data transmission

MULTIPLICATION FACTORS
[1,597; 1,597]
- RT criticality
- RT disadvantage factor
- RT fast fission factor
- RT fission neutrons
- RT resonance escape probability
- RT thermal fission factor
- RT thermal utilization

MULTIPLICITY [9,365; 9,365]
- RT eigenvalues
- RT multiple production
- RT quantum numbers

multiplier tubes
- USE electron multipliers

MULTIPOLAR CONFIGURATIONS
[183; 680]
- BT1 closed configurations
- BT2 magnetic field configurations
- NT1 hexapolar configurations
- NT1 octupolar configurations
- NT1 quadrupolar configurations
- RT fm devices
- RT internal ring devices
- RT lm devices

MULTIPOLARITY [2,427; 2,427]
- RT mixing ratio
- RT multipole radiation
- RT multipoles

MULTIPOLE RADIATION [293; 293]
- UF *octupole radiation*
- BT1 electromagnetic radiation
- BT2 radiations
- RT multipolarity
- RT multipoles

MULTIPOLE TRANSITIONS
[1,045; 9,068] *Feb 78*
- BT1 energy-level transitions
- NT1 e0-transitions
- NT1 e1-transitions
- NT1 e2-transitions
- NT1 e3-transitions
- NT1 e4-transitions
- NT1 m1-transitions
- NT1 m2-transitions
- NT1 m3-transitions
- NT1 m4-transitions

MULTIPOLES [1,308; 8,218]
- NT1 dipoles
- NT2 electric dipoles
- NT2 magnetic dipoles
- NT1 hexadecapoles
- NT1 hexapoles
- NT1 octupoles
- NT1 quadrupoles
- RT mixing ratio
- RT monopoles
- RT multipolarity
- RT multipole radiation
- RT sternheimer formula

multipurpose appl phys latt r.
- USE maple reactor

multipurpose vhtr reactor
- USE vhtr reactor

multisphere neutron detectors
- USE bonner sphere detectors

MULTIVIBRATORS [78; 186]
- UF *schmitt trigger circuits*
- BT1 pulse circuits
- BT2 electronic circuits
- NT1 flip-flop circuits
- RT pulse generators

multiwire drift chambers
- USE drift chambers

MULTIWIRE IONIZATION CHAMBERS [95; 95]
- UF *multi-wire ionization chambers*
- BT1 ionization chambers
- BT2 radiation detectors
-   BT3 measuring instruments

MULTIWIRE PROPORTIONAL CHAMBER [2,431; 4,714]
- UF *charpak chambers*
- UF *multi-wire proportional chambe*
- UF *mwpc*
- BT1 proportional counters
- BT2 radiation detectors
-   BT3 measuring instruments
- NT1 drift chambers
- NT2 time projection chambers
- RT ionization chambers
- RT wire spark chambers

MUNGBEANS [56; 56] *Aug 81*
- BT1 leguminosae
- BT2 plants
- BT1 seeds
- BT1 vegetables
- BT2 food
- RT phaseolus

MUNICH COMPACT CYCLOTRON
[7; 7] *Jun 83*
- BT1 isochronous cyclotrons
- BT2 cyclotrons
-   BT3 cyclic accelerators
-    BT4 accelerators

munich research reactor
- USE frm reactor

munich supercon. sector cyclot
- USE munich suse cyclotron

MUNICH SUSE CYCLOTRON [10; 10]
Jul 84
- UF *munich supercon. sector cyclot*
- UF *suse cyclotron (munich)*
- BT1 heavy ion accelerators
- BT2 accelerators
- BT1 isochronous cyclotrons
- BT2 cyclotrons
-   BT3 cyclic accelerators
-    BT4 accelerators

municipal law
(Prior to December 1990, this was a valid descriptor.)
- USE laws

municipal sludge
- USE sewage sludge

MUNICIPAL WASTES [80; 80] *Nov 75*
(Wastes generated in households, commercial and business establishments, schools, hospitals, etc. It excludes industrial and biological wastes, abandoned automobiles, ashes, street sweepings, construction and demolition debris, and sewage sludge. Prior to August 1985 DOMESTIC WASTES was a valid descriptor. See also INDUSTRIAL WASTES, BIOLOGICAL WASTES, ASHES, and SEWAGE SLUDGE.)
- UF *domestic wastes*
- BT1 wastes
- RT chemical wastes
- RT pollutants
- RT scrap
- RT solid wastes

municipal wastes (biological)
- USE biological wastes

municipal wastes (industrial)
- USE industrial wastes

MUON ANTINEUTRINOS [361; 361]
- BT1 antineutrinos
- BT2 antileptons
-   BT3 antiparticles
-    BT4 antimatter
-     BT5 matter
-    BT4 elementary particles
-   BT3 leptons
-    BT4 elementary particles

        BT4   fermions
        BT2   neutrinos
          BT3   leptons
            BT4   elementary particles
            BT4   fermions
          BT3   massless particles
            BT4   elementary particles
  BT1   muon neutrinos
        BT2   neutrinos
          BT3   leptons
            BT4   elementary particles
            BT4   fermions
          BT3   massless particles
            BT4   elementary particles

MUON BEAMS [646; 646]
  BT1   lepton beams
        BT2   particle beams
          BT3   beams
  RT   muon probes

MUON DETECTION [898; 898]
  BT1   charged particle detection
        BT2   radiation detection
          BT3   detection
  RT   cosmic ray detection
  RT   dumand project

MUON NEUTRINOS [1,376; 1,645]
  UF   *neutrettos*
  BT1   neutrinos
        BT2   leptons
          BT3   elementary particles
          BT3   fermions
        BT2   massless particles
          BT3   elementary particles
  NT1   muon antineutrinos

MUON NUMBER [171; 171] *Feb 78*
  BT1   lepton number
  RT   muons

MUON PAIRS [1,070; 1,070] *Sep 75*
  RT   muons minus
  RT   muons plus
  RT   pair production

MUON PROBES [813; 813] *Aug 75*
(Polarized positive muon beams used to investigate properties of condensed matter.)
  BT1   probes
  RT   muon beams
  RT   muon spin relaxation
  RT   muonium
  RT   muons plus

MUON REACTIONS [1,269; 1,269]
  UF+   *muon-deuteron interactions*
  BT1   lepton reactions
        BT2   nuclear reactions

MUON SPIN RELAXATION [185; 185]
Feb 88
  UF   *mu sr*
  UF   *muon spin resonance*
  UF   *muon spin rotation*
  BT1   relaxation
  RT   crystal lattices
  RT   magnetic properties
  RT   magnetic resonance
  RT   muon probes
  RT   spin orientation

muon spin resonance
  USE   muon spin relaxation

muon spin rotation
  USE   muon spin relaxation

MUON-ATOM COLLISIONS [31; 31]
Jan 86
  BT1   atom collisions
        BT2   collisions

MUON-CATALYZED FUSION
[488; 488] *Apr 85*
  BT1   thermonuclear reactions
        BT2   nuclear reactions
        BT2   nucleosynthesis
          BT3   synthesis
  RT   deuterium tritide
  RT   muonic molecules
  RT   muons minus

muon-deuteron interactions
  USE   deuterium target
  AND   muon reactions

MUON-MESON INTERACTIONS [5; 5]
  BT1   lepton-meson interactions
        BT2   lepton-hadron interactions
          BT3   particle interactions
            BT4   interactions

MUON-MUON INTERACTIONS [25; 25]
  BT1   lepton-lepton interactions
        BT2   particle interactions
          BT3   interactions

MUON-NEUTRON INTERACTIONS
[34; 34]
  BT1   muon-nucleon interactions
        BT2   lepton-nucleon interactions
          BT3   lepton-baryon interactions
            BT4   lepton-hadron interactions
              BT5   particle interactions
                BT6   interactions

MUON-NUCLEON INTERACTIONS
[483; 891]
  BT1   lepton-nucleon interactions
        BT2   lepton-baryon interactions
          BT3   lepton-hadron interactions
            BT4   particle interactions
              BT5   interactions
  NT1   muon-neutron interactions
  NT1   muon-proton interactions

MUON-PROTON INTERACTIONS
[421; 421]
  BT1   muon-nucleon interactions
        BT2   lepton-nucleon interactions
          BT3   lepton-baryon interactions
            BT4   lepton-hadron interactions
              BT5   particle interactions
                BT6   interactions

MUONIC ATOMS [1,414; 1,414]
  BT1   mesic atoms
        BT2   hadronic atoms
          BT3   atoms
  RT   muonic ions
  RT   muonic molecules
  RT   muons minus
  RT   pi-mu atoms

MUONIC IONS [90; 90] *Jan 78*
  BT1   ions
        BT2   charged particles
  RT   muonic atoms
  RT   muonic molecules

MUONIC MOLECULES [585; 585]
  BT1   mesic molecules
        BT2   molecules
  RT   muon-catalyzed fusion
  RT   muonic atoms
  RT   muonic ions
  RT   muons minus
  RT   muons plus

MUONIUM [818; 818]
  RT   atoms
  RT   charmonium
  RT   electrons
  RT   kaonium
  RT   muon probes
  RT   muons plus
  RT   pionium

  RT   positronium
  RT   protonium

MUONS [4,515; 9,419]
  BT1   leptons
        BT2   elementary particles
        BT2   fermions
  NT1   cosmic muons
  NT1   muons minus
  NT1   muons plus
  RT   electron-muon universality
  RT   electron-muon-tau universality
  RT   muon number
  RT   pi-mu atoms

MUONS MINUS [3,156; 3,156]
  BT1   muons
        BT2   leptons
          BT3   elementary particles
          BT3   fermions
  RT   muon pairs
  RT   muon-catalyzed fusion
  RT   muonic atoms
  RT   muonic molecules

MUONS PLUS [3,116; 3,116]
  UF   *antimuons*
  BT1   antileptons
        BT2   antiparticles
          BT3   antimatter
            BT4   matter
          BT3   elementary particles
        BT2   leptons
          BT3   elementary particles
          BT3   fermions
  BT1   muons
        BT2   leptons
          BT3   elementary particles
          BT3   fermions
  RT   muon pairs
  RT   muon probes
  RT   muonic molecules
  RT   muonium

MURA SYNCHROTRON [7; 7]
  UF   *mark v synchrotron*
  BT1   synchrotrons
        BT2   cyclic accelerators
          BT3   accelerators

MUREXIDE [4; 4]
  UF   *purpuric acid*
  BT1   dyes
  BT1   organic oxygen compounds
        BT2   organic compounds
  BT1   pyrimidines
        BT2   azines
          BT3   heterocyclic compounds
            BT4   organic compounds
          BT3   organic nitrogen compounds
            BT4   organic compounds
  BT1   reagents

MURR REACTOR [80; 80]
(University of Missouri, Research Park, Columbia, Missouri, USA)
  UF   *columbia (missouri) res. reac*
  UF   *missouri univ./columbia res. r*
  UF   *univ. of missouri/colu. res. r*
  BT1   enriched uranium reactors
        BT2   reactors
  BT1   research reactors
        BT2   research and test reactors
          BT3   reactors
  BT1   tank type reactors
        BT2   reactors
  BT1   training reactors
        BT2   research and test reactors
          BT3   reactors
  BT1   water cooled reactors
        BT2   reactors
  BT1   water moderated reactors
        BT2   reactors

musashi inst. of tech. triga r
  USE   triga-2-musashi reactor

MUSCLES [3,050; 7,792]
  UF   *tendons*
  UF+ *muscular tissue*
  NT1 diaphragm
  NT1 myoblasts
  NT1 myocardium
  RT   actin
  RT   exercise
  RT   limbs
  RT   myoglobin
  RT   myosarcomas
  RT   radiation syndrome
  RT   tongue
  RT   trichinosis

MUSCOVITE [241; 241]
  BT1 mica
  BT2 silicate minerals
  BT3 minerals

musculamine
  USE spermine

muscular tissue
  USE muscles
  AND tissues

museum objects
  USE cultural objects

museums
  USE educational facilities

MUSHROOMS [145; 145]
  BT1 fungi
  BT2 plants

mussels
  USE molluscs

mustard
  USE brassica

mustard (nitrogen)
  USE nitrogen mustard

MUTAGENESIS [2,294; 2,294]
  RT   dna adducts
  RT   doxorubicin
  RT   genetic control
  RT   genotype
  RT   mutagens
  RT   mutants
  RT   mutations

mutagenic pathways
  USE biological pathways

MUTAGENS [1,071; 1,625]
(For both chemical and physical agents.)
  UF   *chemical mutagens*
  NT1 ems
  NT1 methyl methanesulfonate
  NT1 proflavine
  RT   antibiotics
  RT   antimitotic drugs
  RT   carcinogens
  RT   dna adducts
  RT   drugs
  RT   ionizing radiations
  RT   mutagenesis
  RT   neocarcinostatin
  RT   nitrogen mustard
  RT   pesticides
  RT   plant breeding
  RT   radiomimetic drugs
  RT   teratogens
  RT   tumor promoters
  RT   viruses

MUTANTS [2,438; 3,648]
  NT1 radiation induced mutants
  NT1 revertants
  RT   adventitious bud technique
  RT   disease resistance
  RT   hereditary diseases
  RT   mutagenesis
  RT   mutations
  RT   plant breeding

MUTATION FREQUENCY [1,596; 1,596]
  UF   *aberration yield*
  RT   mutations

mutation induction pathways
  USE biological pathways

MUTATIONS [2,360; 7,933]
  NT1 chromosomal aberrations
    NT2 chromosome breakage
  NT1 dominant mutations
  NT1 gene mutations
  NT1 genome mutations
  NT1 lethal mutations
  NT1 recessive mutations
  NT1 sister chromatid exchanges
  NT1 somatic mutations
  NT1 spontaneous mutations
  RT   adventitious bud technique
  RT   congenital malformations
  RT   genetic control
  RT   genetic effects
  RT   hereditary diseases
  RT   meiosis
  RT   mosaicism
  RT   mutagenesis
  RT   mutants
  RT   mutation frequency
  RT   plant breeding
  RT   pyrimidine dimers
  RT   reproduction
  RT   revertants

mutsu (nuclear ship)
  USE ns mutsu

MUTSU REACTOR [82; 82]
  UF   *japan oceanog. ship rea. mutsu*
  UF   *nucl. ship mutsu reactor*
  BT1 pwr type reactors
    BT2 enriched uranium reactors
      BT3 reactors
    BT2 power reactors
      BT3 reactors
    BT2 thermal reactors
      BT3 reactors
    BT2 water cooled reactors
      BT3 reactors
    BT2 water moderated reactors
      BT3 reactors
  BT1 ship propulsion reactors
    BT2 propulsion reactors
      BT3 power reactors
        BT4 reactors
  RT   ns mutsu

mutualism
  USE symbiosis

mwpc
  USE multiwire proportional chamber

MYCELIUM [96; 96]
  BT1 plant tissues
  RT   fungi

MYCOBACTERIUM [80; 140]
  BT1 bacteria
    BT2 microorganisms
  NT1 mycobacterium tuberculosis
  RT   leprosy

MYCOBACTERIUM TUBERCULOSIS [63; 63]
  BT1 mycobacterium
    BT2 bacteria
      BT3 microorganisms
  RT   tuberculosis

MYCOPLASMA [46; 54]
  BT1 microorganisms
  NT1 acholeplasma laidlawii b
  RT   bacteria

MYCOSES [91; 91]
  BT1 fungal diseases
    BT2 infectious diseases
      BT3 diseases
  RT   fungi

MYELIN [167; 167]
  BT1 lipoproteins
    BT2 lipids
      BT3 organic compounds
    BT2 proteins
      BT3 organic compounds
  RT   cholesterol

MYELITIS [142; 142]
  BT1 nervous system diseases
    BT2 diseases
  RT   spinal cord

MYELOID LEUKEMIA [257; 257]
  BT1 leukemia
    BT2 immune system diseases
      BT3 diseases
    BT2 neoplasms
      BT3 diseases
  RT   philadelphia chromosome
  RT   polycythemia

MYLAR [279; 279]
  BT1 polyesters
    BT2 esters
      BT3 organic compounds
    BT2 organic polymers
      BT3 organic compounds
      BT3 polymers
  RT   glycols

MYLERAN [30; 30]
  UF   *busulfan*
  BT1 alkylating agents
    BT2 antimitotic drugs
      BT3 drugs

MYOBLASTS [31; 31]
  BT1 muscles
  RT   myocardium

MYOCARDIAL INFARCTION [2,316; 2,316]
  BT1 cardiovascular diseases
    BT2 diseases
  RT   blood circulation
  RT   coronaries
  RT   ischemia
  RT   myocardium

MYOCARDIUM [4,653; 4,653]
  BT1 heart
    BT2 cardiovascular system
    BT2 organs
      BT3 body
  BT1 muscles
  RT   coronaries
  RT   myoblasts
  RT   myocardial infarction

MYOGLOBIN [219; 219]
  BT1 globins
    BT2 proteins
      BT3 organic compounds
  BT1 pigments
  BT1 porphyrins
    BT2 heterocyclic acids
      BT3 carboxylic acids

BT4 organic acids
BT5 organic compounds
BT3 heterocyclic compounds
BT4 organic compounds
BT2 organic nitrogen compounds
BT3 organic compounds
RT muscles

myometrium
USE uterus

MYOSARCOMAS [48; 236]
BT1 sarcomas
BT2 neoplasms
BT3 diseases
NT1 rhabdomyosarcomas
RT muscles

MYOSIN [192; 192]
BT1 globulins
BT2 proteins
BT3 organic compounds

myristic acid
USE tetradecanoic acid

myxedema
USE hypothyroidism

MYXOMYCETES [64; 64]
UF *slime fungi*
BT1 fungi
BT2 plants

MZFR REACTOR [88; 88]
(Leopoldshafen, Karlsruhe, Federal Republic of Germany)
UF *mehrzweck-forschungsreaktor*
BT1 natural uranium reactors
BT2 reactors
BT1 phwr type reactors
BT2 heavy water cooled reactors
BT3 reactors
BT2 heavy water moderated reactors
BT3 reactors
BT1 power reactors
BT2 reactors
BT1 test reactors
BT2 research and test reactors
BT3 reactors
BT2 test facilities
BT1 thermal reactors
BT2 reactors

M1-TRANSITIONS [3,045; 3,045] *Feb 78*
(Magnetic dipole transitions.)
UF *magnetic dipole transitions*
BT1 multipole transitions
BT2 energy-level transitions

M2-TRANSITIONS [425; 425] *Feb 78*
(Magnetic quadrupole transitions.)
UF *magnetic quadrupole transition*
BT1 multipole transitions
BT2 energy-level transitions

M3-TRANSITIONS [141; 141] *Feb 78*
(Magnetic octupole transitions.)
UF *magnetic octupole transitions*
BT1 multipole transitions
BT2 energy-level transitions

M4-TRANSITIONS [157; 157] *Feb 78*
(Magnetic hexadecapole transitions.)
UF *magnetic hexadecapole transiti*
BT1 multipole transitions
BT2 energy-level transitions

N BARYONS [20; 99] *Dec 87*
UF *n-1150 resonances*
UF *n-1780 resonances*
UF *n-1860 resonances*
UF *n-2040 resonances*
BT1 n*baryons
BT2 baryons
BT3 fermions
BT3 hadrons
BT4 elementary particles
NT1 n-1440 baryons
NT1 n-1520 baryons
NT1 n-1535 baryons
NT1 n-1540 baryons
NT1 n-1650 baryons
NT1 n-1675 baryons
NT1 n-1680 baryons
NT1 n-1700 baryons
NT1 n-1710 baryons
NT1 n-1720 baryons
NT1 n-1960 baryons
NT1 n-1990 baryons
NT1 n-2000 baryons
NT1 n-2080 baryons
NT1 n-2090 baryons
NT1 n-2100 baryons
NT1 n-2190 baryons
NT1 n-2200 baryons
NT1 n-2220 baryons
NT1 n-2250 baryons
NT1 n-2600 baryons
NT1 n-2700 baryons
NT1 n-3000 baryons

N CODES [1,023; 1,023]
BT1 computer codes

N SHELL [46; 46] *Nov 79*
(Atomic electron shells.)
UF *atomic shells (n)*
BT1 electronic structure

N*BARYONS [1,095; 4,203]
(Prior to December 1987 this concept was indexed by N*RESONANCES.)
UF *delta resonances (baryon)*
UF *isobars (nucleon)*
UF *n*resonances*
UF *nucleon isobars*
BT1 baryons
BT2 fermions
BT2 hadrons
BT3 elementary particles
NT1 delta baryons
NT2 delta-1232 baryons
NT2 delta-1550 baryons
NT2 delta-1600 baryons
NT2 delta-1620 baryons
NT2 delta-1700 baryons
NT2 delta-1900 baryons
NT2 delta-1905 baryons
NT2 delta-1910 baryons
NT2 delta-1920 baryons
NT2 delta-1930 baryons
NT2 delta-1940 baryons
NT2 delta-1950 baryons
NT2 delta-2000 baryons
NT2 delta-2150 baryons
NT2 delta-2200 baryons
NT2 delta-2300 baryons
NT2 delta-2350 baryons
NT2 delta-2390 baryons
NT2 delta-2400 baryons
NT2 delta-2420 baryons
NT2 delta-2750 baryons
NT2 delta-2950 baryons
NT2 delta-3000 baryons
NT1 n baryons
NT2 n-1440 baryons
NT2 n-1520 baryons
NT2 n-1535 baryons
NT2 n-1540 baryons
NT2 n-1650 baryons
NT2 n-1675 baryons
NT2 n-1680 baryons
NT2 n-1700 baryons
NT2 n-1710 baryons
NT2 n-1720 baryons
NT2 n-1960 baryons
NT2 n-1990 baryons
NT2 n-2000 baryons
NT2 n-2080 baryons
NT2 n-2090 baryons
NT2 n-2100 baryons
NT2 n-2190 baryons
NT2 n-2200 baryons
NT2 n-2220 baryons
NT2 n-2250 baryons
NT2 n-2600 baryons
NT2 n-2700 baryons
NT2 n-3000 baryons
RT fractional-parentage coefficie

*n*resonances*
(Prior to December 1987 this was a valid descriptor.)
USE n*baryons

N-D METHOD [177; 177]
RT dispersion relations
RT partial waves

n-ethyl maleimide
USE nem

n-o-iodobenzoylaminoacetate
USE hippuran

N-REACTOR [340; 340]
UF *npr reactor*
UF *pow.-plut. prod. react. richla*
UF *richland npr reactor*
UF *richland pow.-plut. prod. reac*
BT1 enriched uranium reactors
BT2 reactors
BT1 lwgr type reactors
BT2 graphite moderated reactors
BT3 reactors
BT2 water cooled reactors
BT3 reactors
BT1 plutonium production reactors
BT2 production reactors
BT3 reactors
BT1 power reactors
BT2 reactors

N-TYPE CONDUCTORS [2,944; 2,944]
BT1 semiconductor materials
BT2 materials
RT p-n junctions

n-1150 resonances
(Prior to December 1987 this was a vali descriptor.)
USE n baryons

N-1440 BARYONS [185; 185]
(Prior to December 1987 this concept wa indexed by N-1470 RESONANCES.)
UF *n-1470 resonances*
UF *roper resonance*
BT1 n baryons
BT2 n*baryons
BT3 baryons
BT4 fermions
BT4 hadrons
BT5 elementary particles

n-1470 resonances
(Prior to December 1987 this was a vali descriptor.)
USE n-1440 baryons

N-1520 BARYONS [143; 143]
(Prior to December 1987 this concept wa indexed by N-1520 RESONANCES.)
UF *n-1520 resonances*
BT1 n baryons
BT2 n*baryons
BT3 baryons
BT4 fermions

n-1520 resonances
(Prior to December 1987 this was a valid descriptor.)
USE   n-1520 baryons

N-1535 BARYONS [76; 76]
(Prior to December 1987 this concept was indexed by N-1535 RESONANCES.)
UF   n-1535 resonances
BT1   n baryons
BT2   n*baryons
BT3   baryons
BT4   fermions
BT4   hadrons
BT5   elementary particles

n-1535 resonances
(Prior to December 1987 this was a valid descriptor.)
USE   n-1535 baryons

N-1540 BARYONS [2; 2] Dec 87
BT1   n baryons
BT2   n*baryons
BT3   baryons
BT4   fermions
BT4   hadrons
BT5   elementary particles

N-1650 BARYONS [6; 6] Dec 87
BT1   n baryons
BT2   n*baryons
BT3   baryons
BT4   fermions
BT4   hadrons
BT5   elementary particles

N-1675 BARYONS [5; 5] Dec 87
BT1   n baryons
BT2   n*baryons
BT3   baryons
BT4   fermions
BT4   hadrons
BT5   elementary particles

N-1680 BARYONS [35; 35]
(Prior to December 1987 this concept was indexed by N-1680 RESONANCES.)
UF   n-1680 resonances
UF   n-1688 resonances
BT1   n baryons
BT2   n*baryons
BT3   baryons
BT4   fermions
BT4   hadrons
BT5   elementary particles

n-1680 resonances
(Prior to December 1987 this was a valid descriptor.)
USE   n-1680 baryons

n-1688 resonances
(Prior to December 1987 this was a valid descriptor.)
USE   n-1680 baryons

N-1700 BARYONS [42; 42]
(Prior to December 1987 this concept was indexed by N-1700 RESONANCES.)
UF   n-1700 resonances
BT1   n baryons
BT2   n*baryons
BT3   baryons
BT4   fermions
BT4   hadrons
BT5   elementary particles

n-1700 resonances
(Prior to December 1987 this was a valid descriptor.)
USE   n-1700 baryons

N-1710 BARYONS [4; 4] Dec 87
BT1   n baryons
BT2   n*baryons
BT3   baryons
BT4   fermions
BT4   hadrons
BT5   elementary particles

N-1720 BARYONS [4; 4] Dec 87
BT1   n baryons
BT2   n*baryons
BT3   baryons
BT4   fermions
BT4   hadrons
BT5   elementary particles

n-1780 resonances
(Prior to December 1987 this was a valid descriptor.)
USE   n baryons

n-1860 resonances
(Prior to December 1987 this was a valid descriptor.)
USE   n baryons

N-1960 BARYONS [3; 3] Dec 87
BT1   n baryons
BT2   n*baryons
BT3   baryons
BT4   fermions
BT4   hadrons
BT5   elementary particles

N-1990 BARYONS [6; 6]
(Prior to December 1987 this concept was indexed by N-1990 RESONANCES.)
UF   n-1990 resonances
BT1   n baryons
BT2   n*baryons
BT3   baryons
BT4   fermions
BT4   hadrons
BT5   elementary particles

n-1990 resonances
(Prior to December 1987 this was a valid descriptor.)
USE   n-1990 baryons

N-2000 BARYONS [0; 0] Dec 87
BT1   n baryons
BT2   n*baryons
BT3   baryons
BT4   fermions
BT4   hadrons
BT5   elementary particles

n-2040 resonances
(Prior to December 1987 this was a valid descriptor.)
USE   n baryons

N-2080 BARYONS [2; 2] Dec 87
BT1   n baryons
BT2   n*baryons
BT3   baryons
BT4   fermions
BT4   hadrons
BT5   elementary particles

N-2090 BARYONS [0; 0] Dec 87
BT1   n baryons
BT2   n*baryons
BT3   baryons
BT4   fermions
BT4   hadrons
BT5   elementary particles

N-2100 BARYONS [3; 3] Dec 87
BT1   n baryons
BT2   n*baryons
BT3   baryons
BT4   fermions
BT4   hadrons
BT5   elementary particles

N-2190 BARYONS [11; 11]
(Prior to December 1987 this concept was indexed by N-2190 RESONANCES.)
UF   n-2190 resonances
BT1   n baryons
BT2   n*baryons
BT3   baryons
BT4   fermions
BT4   hadrons
BT5   elementary particles

n-2190 resonances
(Prior to December 1987 this was a valid descriptor.)
USE   n-2190 baryons

N-2200 BARYONS [0; 0] Dec 87
BT1   n baryons
BT2   n*baryons
BT3   baryons
BT4   fermions
BT4   hadrons
BT5   elementary particles

N-2220 BARYONS [0; 0] Dec 87
BT1   n baryons
BT2   n*baryons
BT3   baryons
BT4   fermions
BT4   hadrons
BT5   elementary particles

N-2250 BARYONS [0; 0] Dec 87
BT1   n baryons
BT2   n*baryons
BT3   baryons
BT4   fermions
BT4   hadrons
BT5   elementary particles

N-2600 BARYONS [1; 1]
(Prior to December 1987 this concept was indexed by N-2650 RESONANCES.)
UF   n-2650 resonances
BT1   n baryons
BT2   n*baryons
BT3   baryons
BT4   fermions
BT4   hadrons
BT5   elementary particles

n-2650 resonances
(Prior to December 1987 this was a valid descriptor.)
USE   n-2600 baryons

N-2700 BARYONS [0; 0] Dec 87
BT1   n baryons
BT2   n*baryons
BT3   baryons
BT4   fermions
BT4   hadrons
BT5   elementary particles

N-3000 BARYONS [0; 0]
(Prior to December 1987 this concept was indexed by N-3030 RESONANCES.)
UF   n-3030 resonances
BT1   n baryons
BT2   n*baryons
BT3   baryons
BT4   fermions
BT4   hadrons
BT5   elementary particles

n-3030 resonances
(Prior to December 1987 this was a valid descriptor.)
USE   n-3000 baryons

NABARLEK DEPOSIT [78; 78] *Jul 78*
BT1   uranium deposits
BT2   geologic deposits
RT   northern territory
RT   uranium ores

NAC CYCLOTRON [286; 286] *Jun 83*
(Separated-sector cyclotron of the National Accelerator Centre, Faure, Republic of South Africa.)
UF   *faure cyclotron*
UF   *nacssc*
UF   *nat. accel. cent. (sa) cyclotr*
UF   *south africa nac cyclotron*
BT1   heavy ion accelerators
BT2   accelerators
BT1   isochronous cyclotrons
BT2   cyclotrons
BT3   cyclic accelerators
BT4   accelerators

nacssc
(Separated-sector cyclotron of the National Accelerator Centre, Faure, Republic of South Africa.)
USE   nac cyclotron

NAD [231; 231]
(Nicotinamide-Adenine Dinucleotide)
UF   *coenzyme i*
UF   *nicotinamide-adenine dinucleot*
BT1   coenzymes
BT1   nucleotides
BT2   organic compounds
RT   nicotinamide
RT   pyridines

NADH2 [68; 68]
UF   *diphosphodihydropyridine nucle*
UF   *reduced nad*
BT1   coenzymes
BT1   nucleotides
BT2   organic compounds
RT   nicotinamide

NADP [141; 141]
(Nicotinamide-Adenine Dinucleotide Phosphate)
UF   *coenzyme ii*
UF   *nicotinamide-aden dinucle phos*
BT1   coenzymes
BT1   nucleotides
BT2   organic compounds
RT   nicotinamide

NAGASAKI [714; 714]
BT1   japan
BT2   asia
BT2   developed countries
RT   a-bomb survivors
RT   nuclear explosions
RT   nuclear weapons

NAI DETECTORS [1,753; 1,753] *Sep 79*
UF   *sodium iodide detectors*
BT1   solid scintillation detectors
BT2   scintillation counters
BT3   radiation detectors
BT4   measuring instruments

NAILS [69; 69]
BT1   skin
BT2   organs
BT3   body
RT   fingers

nak
(Use the descriptors below or their appropriate narrower terms.)
USE   potassium alloys
AND   sodium alloys

NAK COOLED REACTORS [4; 18]
(Prior to March 1986 this concept was indexed by coordination of POTASSIUM COOLED REACTORS and SODIUM COOLED REACTORS.)
BT1   liquid metal cooled reactors
BT2   reactors
NT1   ebr-1 reactor
NT1   ser reactor
NT1   snaptran reactors
NT1   s10fs-1 reactor
NT1   s10fs-3 reactor
NT1   s10fs-4 reactor
NT1   s2ds reactor
NT1   s8dr reactor
NT1   s8er reactor
RT   potassium cooled reactors
RT   sodium cooled reactors

nal synchrotron
(Prior to December 1990, this was a valid descriptor.)
USE   fermilab accelerator

NANO AMP BEAM CURRENTS [194; 194] *Feb 76*
(From 10 exp -9 to 10 exp -6 amp.)
BT1   beam currents
BT2   currents

* NANOSEC LIVING RADIOISOTOPES [3; 1,227] *Nov 80*
(From 10 exp -9 to 10 exp -6 sec. For specific terms, consult the Appendix.)
BT1   radioisotopes
BT2   isotopes
RT   half-life

NAP-M STORAGE RING [25; 25] *Aug 75*
BT1   storage rings

NAPHTHALENE [454; 454]
BT1   condensed aromatics
BT2   aromatics
BT3   organic compounds
BT1   hydrocarbons
BT2   organic compounds
RT   acenaphthene
RT   decalin
RT   tetralin

naphthalic acid
USE   phthalic acid

NAPHTHOLS [156; 344]
UF   *hydroxynaphthalenes*
UF   *naphthols-alpha*
UF   *naphthols-beta*
BT1   phenols
BT2   aromatics
BT3   organic compounds
BT2   hydroxy compounds
BT3   organic compounds
NT1   acid chrome dyes
NT1   beryllon
NT1   nitroso-r salt
NT1   pan
NT1   thorin
NT1   trypan blue
NT1   1-nitroso-2-naphthol

naphthols-alpha
USE   naphthols

naphthols-beta
USE   naphthols

NAPHTHYL RADICALS [11; 11]
BT1   aryl radicals
BT2   radicals

NARCOTICS [119; 300]
BT1   central nervous system depress
BT2   central nervous system agents
BT3   drugs
NT1   heroin
NT1   methadone hydrochloride
NT1   morphine
NT1   pethidine
NT1   thebaine
RT   analgesics
RT   anesthetics
RT   enkephalins
RT   hypnotics and sedatives

NARORA-1 REACTOR [64; 64]
(Narora, Uttar Pradesh, India)
BT1   natural uranium reactors
BT2   reactors
BT1   phwr type reactors
BT2   heavy water cooled reactors
BT3   reactors
BT2   heavy water moderated reactors
BT3   reactors
BT1   power reactors
BT2   reactors

NARORA-2 REACTOR [61; 61]
(Narora, Uttar Pradesh, India)
BT1   natural uranium reactors
BT2   reactors
BT1   phwr type reactors
BT2   heavy water cooled reactors
BT3   reactors
BT2   heavy water moderated reactor
BT3   reactors
BT1   power reactors
BT2   reactors

NASA [225; 225]
UF   *nat. aeronautics and space adm*
BT1   us organizations
BT2   national organizations

nasa-test reactor
(Plum Brook Reactor Facility)
USE   pbr reactor

nasa-tr reactor
(Plum Brook Reactor Facility)
USE   pbr reactor

nasopharynx
USE   pharynx

nat. accel. cent. (sa) cyclotr
USE   nac cyclotron

nat. aeronautics and space adm
USE   nasa

nat. bur. of standards reactor
USE   nbsr reactor

nat. cent. systems reliability
(National Centre of Systems Reliability)
USE   ncsr

nat. inst. kern. hoge-energief
USE   nikhef

nat. inst. radiol. sci. cyclo.
USE   nirs cyclotron

nat. radiological prot. board
　　USE　　nrpb

national bureau of standards
　　USE　　us nbs

NATIONAL CONTROL [180; 180]
　　BT1　　atomic energy control
　　RT　　reactor commissioning
　　RT　　reactor decommissioning
　　RT　　reactor dismantling

national council radiation pro
　　USE　　us ncrp

NATIONAL DEFENSE [252; 459]
　　UF　　*national security*
　　NT1　　civil defense
　　RT　　nuclear weapons

NATIONAL GOVERNMENT [490; 490] *Nov 80*
　　UF　　*federal government*
　　RT　　centrally planned economies
　　RT　　government policies
　　RT　　legislation
　　RT　　local government
　　RT　　national organizations
　　RT　　public officials
　　RT　　regulations
　　RT　　state government

NATIONAL ORGANIZATIONS [454; 34,227]
　　NT1　　argentine organizations
　　NT1　　australian organizations
　　　NT2　　ansto
　　　　NT3　　aaec
　　NT1　　austrian organizations
　　　NT2　　seibersdorf research centre
　　NT1　　bangladesh organizations
　　NT1　　belgian organizations
　　NT1　　brazilian organizations
　　　NT2　　brazilian cnen
　　　NT2　　brazilian lnls
　　　NT2　　nuclebras
　　NT1　　canadian organizations
　　　NT2　　atomic energy of canada ltd
　　　　NT3　　chalk river nuclear labs
　　　　NT3　　wnre
　　　NT2　　canadian aecb
　　NT1　　chinese organizations
　　NT1　　colombian organizations
　　　NT2　　ian
　　NT1　　czechoslovak organizations
　　　NT2　　ujv
　　　NT2　　uvvvr
　　NT1　　danish organizations
　　　NT2　　danish atomic energy commissio
　　　NT2　　risoe national laboratory
　　　　NT3　　risoe research establishment
　　NT1　　finnish organizations
　　NT1　　french organizations
　　　NT2　　cea
　　　　NT3　　cea bruyeres le chatel
　　　　NT3　　cea cadarache
　　　　NT3　　cea fontenay-aux-roses
　　　　NT3　　cea grenoble
　　　　NT3　　cea la hague
　　　　NT3　　cea marcoule
　　　　NT3　　cea pierrelatte
　　　　NT3　　cea saclay
　　　NT2　　cogema
　　　　NT3　　cogema la hague
　　　　NT3　　cogema marcoule
　　　　NT3　　cogema pierrelatte
　　NT1　　german fr organizations
　　　NT2　　bundesamt fuer strahlenschutz
　　　NT2　　ges fuer reaktorsicherheit
　　　NT2　　ipp garching
　　　NT2　　kernforschungsanlage juelich
　　　NT2　　kernforschungszentrum karlsruh
　　　NT2　　reaktorsicherheitskommission
　　　NT2　　strahlenschutzkommission
　　　NT2　　wak
　　　NT2　　zfi leipzig
　　　NT2　　zfk rossendorf
　　NT1　　greek organizations
　　NT1　　hungarian organizations
　　　NT2　　atomki
　　NT1　　indian organizations
　　　NT2　　barc
　　　NT2　　igcar
　　NT1　　iranian organizations
　　　NT2　　iranian atomic energy organiza
　　　NT2　　tehran nuclear research centre
　　NT1　　iraqi organizations
　　　NT2　　iraqi atomic energy commission
　　　　NT3　　iraqi nuclear research centre
　　NT1　　israeli organizations
　　　NT2　　israel atomic energy commissio
　　　　NT3　　negev nuclear research center
　　　　NT3　　soreq nuclear research center
　　NT1　　italian organizations
　　　NT2　　agip nucleare
　　　NT2　　cise
　　　NT2　　italian enea
　　　　NT3　　cnen
　　NT1　　japanese organizations
　　　NT2　　jaeri
　　　NT2　　jnsda
　　　NT2　　pnc
　　NT1　　korean organizations
　　　NT2　　kaeri
　　NT1　　malaysian organizations
　　　NT2　　puspati
　　NT1　　mexican organizations
　　NT1　　netherlands organizations
　　　NT2　　ecn
　　　　NT3　　rcn
　　　NT2　　iko
　　　NT2　　iri
　　　NT2　　kvi
　　　NT2　　nikhef
　　NT1　　new zealand organizations
　　NT1　　norwegian organizations
　　NT1　　philippine organizations
　　　NT2　　philippine nuclear research in
　　　　NT3　　philippine atomic energy commi
　　　　NT3　　philippine atomic research cen
　　NT1　　polish organizations
　　NT1　　south african organizations
　　NT1　　spanish organizations
　　NT1　　swedish organizations
　　NT1　　swiss organizations
　　NT1　　united kingdom organizations
　　　NT2　　bnfl
　　　NT2　　ncsr
　　　NT2　　nrpb
　　　NT2　　uk national physical lab
　　　NT2　　uk nii
　　　NT2　　ukaea
　　　　NT3　　aere
　　　　NT3　　culham laboratory
　　NT1　　us organizations
　　　NT2　　federal radiation council
　　　NT2　　nasa
　　　NT2　　national science foundation
　　　NT2　　naval research laboratory
　　　NT2　　orau
　　　NT2　　tennessee valley authority
　　　NT2　　ucla
　　*NT2　　us aec
　　　NT2　　us bureau of mines
　　　NT2　　us doe
　　　　NT3　　ames laboratory
　　　　NT3　　anl
　　　　NT3　　atomics international canoga p
　　　　NT3　　battelle pacific northwest lab
　　　　NT3　　bettis
　　　　NT3　　bnl
　　　　NT3　　bonneville power administratio
　　　　NT3　　feed materials production cent
　　　　NT3　　hanford engineering developmen
　　　　NT3　　hanford reservation
　　　　NT3　　hapo
　　　　NT3　　idaho chemical processing plan
　　　　NT3　　idaho national engineering lab
　　　　　NT4　　nrts
　　　　NT3　　kansas city plant
　　　　NT3　　kapl
　　　　NT3　　lanl
　　　　　NT4　　lasl
　　　　NT3　　lawrence berkeley laboratory
　　　　NT3　　lawrence livermore national la
　　　　　NT4　　lawrence livermore laboratory
　　　　NT3　　mound laboratory
　　　　NT3　　oak ridge reservation
　　　　NT3　　orgdp
　　　　NT3　　ornl
　　　　NT3　　paducah plant
　　　　NT3　　pantex plant
　　　　NT3　　pinellas plant
　　　　NT3　　portsmouth centrifuge enrichme
　　　　NT3　　portsmouth gaseous diffusion p
　　　　NT3　　rocky flats plant
　　　　NT3　　sandia national laboratories
　　　　　NT4　　sandia laboratories
　　　　NT3　　savannah river plant
　　　　NT3　　sequoyah uf6 production plant
　　　　NT3　　stanford linear accelerator ce
　　　　NT3　　wipp
　　　　NT3　　y-12 plant
　　　NT2　　us dot
　　　NT2　　us epa
　　*NT2　　us erda
　　　NT2　　us fda
　　　NT2　　us fea
　　　NT2　　us hud
　　　NT2　　us jcae
　　　NT2　　us national academy of science
　　　NT2　　us nbs
　　　NT2　　us ncrp
　　　NT2　　us nrc
　　　NT2　　us osha
　　NT1　　ussr organizations
　　　NT2　　gosatomnadzor
　　　NT2　　ihep
　　　NT2　　leningrad institute of nuclear
　　RT　　international organizations
　　RT　　national government
　　RT　　nuclear operators

national r. test st. burst f.
　　USE　　pbf reactor

national reactor testing stati
　　USE　　nrts

NATIONAL SCIENCE FOUNDATION [15; 15]
　　BT1　　us organizations
　　BT2　　national organizations

national security
　　USE　　national defense

national synchrotron light sou
　　USE　　nsls

NATIONALIZATION [4; 4] *Mar 86*
(Takeover by government, with or without compensation, of a public or private activity.)
　　RT　　centrally planned economies
　　RT　　economic policy
　　RT　　government policies

NATO [11; 11] *Jun 87*
　　UF　　*north atlantic treaty organiza*
　　BT1　　international organizations

natural activity
   USE   natural radioactivity

natural circulation
   USE   natural convection

NATURAL CONVECTION [2,135; 2,135]
(Heat transfer by natural convection.)
- UF   *free convection*
- UF   *natural circulation*
- BT1   convection
-   BT2   heat transfer
-     BT3   energy transfer
- RT   thermosyphons

natural disaster (exceptional)
   USE   exceptional natural disaster

NATURAL GAS [1,451; 1,451]
- UF   *liquefied natural gas*
- BT1   fossil fuels
-   BT2   energy sources
-   BT2   fuels
- BT1   fuel gas
-   BT2   energy sources
-   BT2   fuels
-   BT2   gases
-     BT3   fluids
- RT   explosive stimulation
- RT   gasbuggy event
- RT   petrochemistry
- RT   rio blanco event
- RT   rulison event
- RT   wagon wheel event
- RT   wasatch formation

→ **NATURAL GAS DEPOSITS** [0; 0]
Aug 91
- BT1   geologic deposits
- BT1   mineral resources
-   BT2   resources

natural mutations
   USE   spontaneous mutations

NATURAL NUCLEAR REACTORS
[24; 165] *Jan 79*
- NT1   oklo phenomenon
- RT   chain reactions
- RT   criticality
- RT   reactors
- RT   uranium ores

§ **NATURAL OCCURRENCE** [118; 118]
Jul 85
- RT   earth crust
- RT   geochemistry
- RT   isotope ratio
- RT   ore composition
- RT   radioisotopes

NATURAL RADIOACTIVITY
[3,641; 3,641]
(For unspecified naturally occurring radioisotopes only.)
- UF   *natural activity*
- BT1   radioactivity
- RT   background radiation
- RT   daughter products
- RT   gamma logging
- RT   polonium
- RT   potassium 40
- RT   radium
- RT   radon
- RT   thermal springs
- RT   thorium
- RT   uranium

natural reactor oklo
   USE   oklo phenomenon

NATURAL RUBBER [104; 104]
- UF   *rubber (natural)*
- BT1   rubbers
-   BT2   elastomers
-     BT3   polymers
-   BT2   organic polymers
-     BT3   organic compounds
-     BT3   polymers
- RT   dielectric materials
- RT   latex

NATURAL UNITS [15; 20]
(Based on fundamental constants.)
- BT1   units
- NT1   uniton
- RT   fundamental constants

NATURAL URANIUM [893; 893]
- BT1   uranium
-   BT2   actinides
-     BT3   metals
-       BT4   elements

NATURAL URANIUM REACTORS
[90; 4,229]
(Reactors primarily fueled with natural uranium.)
- BT1   reactors
- NT1   agesta reactor
- NT1   aquilon reactor
- NT1   atucha reactor
- NT1   atucha-2 reactor
- NT1   bepo reactor
- NT1   bohunice a-1 reactor
- NT1   bohunice a-2 reactor
- NT1   br-1 reactor
- NT1   bruce-1 reactor
- NT1   bruce-2 reactor
- NT1   bruce-3 reactor
- NT1   bruce-4 reactor
- NT1   bruce-5 reactor
- NT1   bruce-6 reactor
- NT1   bruce-7 reactor
- NT1   bruce-8 reactor
- NT1   cernavoda-1 reactor
- NT1   cesar reactor
- NT1   cirus reactor
- NT1   cordoba reactor
- NT1   cp-2 reactor
- NT1   cp-3 reactor
- NT1   darlington-1 reactor
- NT1   darlington-2 reactor
- NT1   darlington-3 reactor
- NT1   darlington-4 reactor
- NT1   dhruva reactor
- NT1   diorit reactor
- NT1   douglas point ontario reactor
- NT1   eco reactor
- NT1   el-1 reactor
- NT1   el-2 reactor
- NT1   essor reactor
- NT1   f-1 reactor
- NT1   fr-2 reactor
- NT1   gentilly reactor
- NT1   gentilly-2 reactor
- NT1   gleep reactor
- NT1   jatr reactor
- NT1   jrr-3 reactor
- NT1   kanupp reactor
- NT1   magnox type reactors
-   NT2   berkeley reactor
-   NT2   bradwell reactor
-   NT2   calder hall a-1 reactor
-   NT2   calder hall a-2 reactor
-   NT2   calder hall b-3 reactor
-   NT2   calder hall b-4 reactor
-   NT2   chapelcross-1 reactor
-   NT2   chapelcross-2 reactor
-   NT2   chapelcross-3 reactor
-   NT2   chapelcross-4 reactor
-   NT2   dungeness-a reactor
-   NT2   hinkley point-a reactor
-   NT2   hunterston-a reactor
-   NT2   latina reactor
-   NT2   oldbury-a reactor
-   NT2   sizewell-a reactor
-   NT2   tokai-mura reactor
-   NT2   trawsfynydd reactor
-   NT2   wylfa reactor
- NT1   marius reactor
- NT1   mzfr reactor
- NT1   narora-1 reactor
- NT1   narora-2 reactor
- NT1   npd reactor
- NT1   nru reactor
- NT1   nrx reactor
- NT1   pickering-1 reactor
- NT1   pickering-2 reactor
- NT1   pickering-3 reactor
- NT1   pickering-4 reactor
- NT1   pickering-5 reactor
- NT1   pickering-6 reactor
- NT1   pickering-7 reactor
- NT1   pickering-8 reactor
- NT1   point lepreau-1 reactor
- NT1   point lepreau-2 reactor
- NT1   pse reactor
- NT1   r-b reactor
- NT1   r-1 reactor
- NT1   rajasthan-1 reactor
- NT1   rajasthan-2 reactor
- NT1   taiwan research reactor
- NT1   windscale production reactors
- NT1   wolsung-1 reactor
- NT1   x-10 reactor
- NT1   zed-2 reactor
- NT1   zeep reactor
- NT1   zephyr reactor
- RT   ebr-1 reactor
- RT   eole reactor
- RT   nora reactor
- RT   pdp reactor

natural uranium target
   USE   uranium 238 target

NAURU [2; 2] *Mar 87*
- BT1   micronesia
-   BT2   australasia
-   BT2   islands
- RT   pacific ocean

NAUSEA [135; 135]
- BT1   symptoms
- RT   digestive system diseases

naval res lab cyclotron
   USE   nrl cyclotron

naval res lab linac
   USE   nrl linac

NAVAL RESEARCH LABORATORY
[31; 31]
- BT1   us organizations
-   BT2   national organizations

NAVIER-STOKES EQUATIONS
[782; 782]
(Prior to January 1983 the form NAVIER-STOKES EQUATION was used)
- BT1   partial differential equations
-   BT2   differential equations
-     BT3   equations
- RT   incompressible flow
- RT   viscous flow

NAVIGATIONAL INSTRUMENTS
[36; 36]
- RT   aircraft
- RT   electronic guidance
- RT   rockets
- RT   ships
- RT   space vehicles

NBI CYCLOTRON [3; 3] *Jun 85*
- UF   *niels bohr institute cyclotron*
- BT1   cyclotrons
-   BT2   cyclic accelerators
-     BT3   accelerators

nbs (us)
   USE   us nbs

nbs synchrotron uv rad. fac.
   USE   surf ii storage ring

NBSR REACTOR [63; 63]
(National Bureau of Standards, Washington, D.C., USA)
   UF   *nat. bur. of standards reactor*
   UF   *us nbs reactor*
   BT1   heavy water cooled reactors
     BT2   reactors
   BT1   heavy water moderated reactors
     BT2   reactors
   BT1   materials testing reactors
     BT2   irradiation reactors
       BT3   reactors
   BT1   research reactors
     BT2   research and test reactors
       BT3   reactors
   BT1   tank type reactors
     BT2   reactors
   BT1   thermal reactors
     BT2   reactors

ncrp (us)
(National Council for Radiation Protection)
   USE   us ncrp

NCSCR-1 REACTOR [3; 3]
   UF   *north carol. st. col. res. r-1*
   UF   *raleigh-ncsc research react.-1*
   BT1   aqueous homogeneous reactors
     BT2   liquid homogeneous reactors
       BT3   fluid fueled reactors
         BT4   reactors
       BT3   homogeneous reactors
         BT4   reactors
     BT2   water cooled reactors
       BT3   reactors
     BT2   water moderated reactors
       BT3   reactors
   BT1   enriched uranium reactors
     BT2   reactors
   BT1   research reactors
     BT2   research and test reactors
       BT3   reactors
   BT1   thermal reactors
     BT2   reactors
   BT1   training reactors
     BT2   research and test reactors
       BT3   reactors

NCSR [6; 6] *Nov 75*
(National Centre of Systems Reliability)
   UF   *nat. cent. systems reliability*
   BT1   united kingdom organizations
     BT2   national organizations
   RT   systems analysis

ncuspr reactor
   USE   pulstar-raleigh reactor

nda remote experiment station
   USE   prr reactor

ndpp
(p-nitro-3-dimethylaminopropiophenone-HCl)
   USE   amines
   AND   aromatics
   AND   ketones
   AND   nitro compounds

NEA [383; 421]
(Nuclear Energy Agency of the OECD; prior to April 1972 known as European Nuclear Energy Agency, and documents written before that date should be indexed to ENEA.)
   UF   *nuclear energy agency (oecd)*
   BT1   oecd
     BT2   international organizations
   NT1   enea

NEAR INFRARED RADIATION [1,501; 1,501]
(Wavelength range 0.8-2.5 microns)
   BT1   infrared radiation
     BT2   electromagnetic radiation
       BT3   radiations

NEAR ULTRAVIOLET RADIATION [1,980; 1,980]
(Wavelength range 4000-2000 A.)
   BT1   ultraviolet radiation
     BT2   electromagnetic radiation
       BT3   radiations

NEBRASKA [97; 97]
   BT1   usa
     BT2   developed countries
     BT2   north america

NEBULAE [3,004; 5,193]
   NT1   crab nebula
   NT1   planetary nebulae
   NT1   solar nebula
   RT   cosmic dust
   RT   cosmic gases
   RT   galaxies
   RT   h2 regions

NECK [2,207; 2,207]
   BT1   body areas
     BT2   body
   RT   carotid arteries
   RT   larynx
   RT   parathyroid glands
   RT   pharynx
   RT   thyroid

NECKAR REACTOR [133; 133]
   UF   *gemeinschaftskernkraftwerk nec*
   UF   *gkn-1 reactor (neckar)*
   BT1   pwr type reactors
     BT2   enriched uranium reactors
       BT3   reactors
     BT2   power reactors
       BT3   reactors
     BT2   thermal reactors
       BT3   reactors
     BT2   water cooled reactors
       BT3   reactors
     BT2   water moderated reactors
       BT3   reactors

NECKAR-2 REACTOR [64; 64] *Nov 79*
   UF   *gkn-2 reaktor (neckar)*
   BT1   pwr type reactors
     BT2   enriched uranium reactors
       BT3   reactors
     BT2   power reactors
       BT3   reactors
     BT2   thermal reactors
       BT3   reactors
     BT2   water cooled reactors
       BT3   reactors
     BT2   water moderated reactors
       BT3   reactors

NECROSIS [1,599; 1,905]
   BT1   pathological changes
     BT2   diseases
   NT1   gangrene
   NT1   osteoradionecrosis
   RT   fistulae
   RT   ischemia
   RT   ulcers
   RT   wounds

NEEDLE CHAMBERS [32; 32]
   BT1   proportional counters
     BT2   radiation detectors
       BT3   measuring instruments

neel point
   USE   neel temperature

NEEL TEMPERATURE [1,203; 1,203]
   UF   *neel point*
   BT1   transition temperature
     BT2   thermodynamic properties
       BT3   physical properties
   RT   antiferromagnetism
   RT   magnetic susceptibility

NEGATIVE ENERGY STATES [106; 106]
   BT1   energy levels

negative ions
   USE   anions

NEGATIVE MASS [37; 37]
   BT1   hypothesis
   BT1   mass
   RT   relativity theory

NEGATIVE MASS EFFECT [24; 24]
   RT   beam dynamics
   RT   negative mass instability
   RT   plasma instability

NEGATIVE MASS INSTABILITY [45; 45]
   BT1   plasma microinstabilities
     BT2   plasma instability
       BT3   instability
   RT   negative mass effect

negatons
   USE   electrons

negatrons
   USE   electrons

NEGEV NUCLEAR RESEARCH CENTER [3; 3] *Nov 79*
   BT1   israel atomic energy commissio
     BT2   israeli organizations
       BT3   national organizations

NELKIN THEORY [19; 19]
   BT1   transport theory

NEM [37; 37] *May 76*
(N-ethyl maleimide)
   UF   *n-ethyl maleimide*
   BT1   antimitotic drugs
     BT2   drugs
   BT1   imides
     BT2   organic nitrogen compounds
       BT3   organic compounds
   BT1   radiosensitizers
     BT2   drugs
     BT2   response modifying factors

NEMATODES [143; 232]
   UF   *worms (round)*
   BT1   invertebrates
     BT2   animals
   NT1   ascaridae
     NT2   ascaris
   NT1   dictyocaulus
   NT1   hookworm
   NT1   nippostrongylus
   NT1   syngamus
   NT1   trichinella
   RT   filariasis
   RT   helminths
   RT   parasites

NEMBUTAL [41; 41]
   UF   *pentobarbital*
   BT1   barbiturates
     BT2   anesthetics
       BT3   central nervous system depress

	BT4	central nervous system agents
	BT5	drugs
BT2	hypnotics and sedatives	
BT3	central nervous system depress	
BT4	central nervous system agents	
BT5	drugs	
BT2	organic oxygen compounds	
BT3	organic compounds	
BT2	pyrimidines	
BT3	azines	
BT4	heterocyclic compounds	
BT5	organic compounds	
BT4	organic nitrogen compounds	
BT5	organic compounds	

NEOCARCINOSTATIN [21; 21] *Dec 79*
- BT1 antibiotics
- BT2 drugs
- BT2 organic compounds
- BT1 antineoplastic drugs
- BT2 drugs
- BT1 radiomimetic drugs
- BT2 drugs
- RT antimitotic drugs
- RT chemotherapy
- RT mutagens
- RT neoplasms

NEOCLASSICAL TRANSPORT THEORY [388; 388] *Nov 82*
- BT1 transport theory
- RT banana regime
- RT bootstrap current
- RT pfirsch-schlueter regime
- RT plasma
- RT plateau regime

NEODYMIUM [1,246; 1,246]
- BT1 rare earths
- BT2 metals
- BT3 elements

NEODYMIUM ADDITIONS [174; 174]
(Alloys containing not more than 1% Nd are listed here.)
- BT1 rare earth additions
- RT neodymium alloys
- RT neodymium compounds

NEODYMIUM ALLOYS [788; 817]
(Alloys containing more than 1% Nd.)
- BT1 rare earth alloys
- BT2 alloys
- NT1 neodymium base alloys
- RT neodymium additions

NEODYMIUM BASE ALLOYS [22; 22]
- BT1 neodymium alloys
- BT2 rare earth alloys
- BT3 alloys

NEODYMIUM BORIDES [157; 157]
- BT1 borides
- BT2 boron compounds
- BT1 neodymium compounds
- BT2 rare earth compounds

NEODYMIUM BROMIDES [24; 24]
- BT1 bromides
- BT2 bromine compounds
- BT3 halogen compounds
- BT2 halides
- BT3 halogen compounds
- BT1 neodymium compounds
- BT2 rare earth compounds

NEODYMIUM CARBIDES [25; 25]
- BT1 carbides
- BT2 carbon compounds
- BT1 neodymium compounds
- BT2 rare earth compounds

NEODYMIUM CARBONATES [15; 15]
- BT1 carbonates
- BT2 carbon compounds
- BT2 oxygen compounds
- BT1 neodymium compounds
- BT2 rare earth compounds

NEODYMIUM CHLORIDES [182; 182]
- BT1 chlorides
- BT2 chlorine compounds
- BT3 halogen compounds
- BT2 halides
- BT3 halogen compounds
- BT1 neodymium compounds
- BT2 rare earth compounds

NEODYMIUM COMPLEXES [914; 914]
- BT1 rare earth complexes
- BT2 complexes

NEODYMIUM COMPOUNDS [909; 2,557]
- BT1 rare earth compounds
- NT1 neodymium borides
- NT1 neodymium bromides
- NT1 neodymium carbides
- NT1 neodymium carbonates
- NT1 neodymium chlorides
- NT1 neodymium fluorides
- NT1 neodymium hydrides
- NT1 neodymium hydroxides
- NT1 neodymium iodides
- NT1 neodymium nitrates
- NT1 neodymium nitrides
- NT1 neodymium oxides
- NT1 neodymium perchlorates
- NT1 neodymium phosphates
- NT1 neodymium silicates
- NT1 neodymium silicides
- NT1 neodymium sulfates
- NT1 neodymium sulfides
- NT1 neodymium tellurides
- NT1 neodymium tungstates
- RT neodymium additions

NEODYMIUM FLUORIDES [91; 91]
- BT1 fluorides
- BT2 fluorine compounds
- BT3 halogen compounds
- BT2 halides
- BT3 halogen compounds
- BT1 neodymium compounds
- BT2 rare earth compounds

NEODYMIUM HYDRIDES [24; 24]
- BT1 hydrides
- BT2 hydrogen compounds
- BT1 neodymium compounds
- BT2 rare earth compounds

NEODYMIUM HYDROXIDES [27; 27]
- BT1 hydroxides
- BT2 hydrogen compounds
- BT2 oxygen compounds
- BT1 neodymium compounds
- BT2 rare earth compounds

NEODYMIUM IODIDES [18; 18]
- BT1 iodides
- BT2 halides
- BT3 halogen compounds
- BT2 iodine compounds
- BT3 halogen compounds
- BT1 neodymium compounds
- BT2 rare earth compounds

NEODYMIUM IONS [408; 408]
- BT1 ions
- BT2 charged particles

NEODYMIUM ISOTOPES [439; 1,908]
- NT1 neodymium 127
- NT1 neodymium 128
- NT1 neodymium 129
- NT1 neodymium 130
- NT1 neodymium 131
- NT1 neodymium 132
- NT1 neodymium 133
- NT1 neodymium 134
- NT1 neodymium 135
- NT1 neodymium 136
- NT1 neodymium 137
- NT1 neodymium 138
- NT1 neodymium 139
- NT1 neodymium 140
- NT1 neodymium 141
- NT1 neodymium 142
- NT1 neodymium 143
- NT1 neodymium 144
- NT1 neodymium 145
- NT1 neodymium 146
- NT1 neodymium 147
- NT1 neodymium 148
- NT1 neodymium 149
- NT1 neodymium 150
- NT1 neodymium 151
- NT1 neodymium 152
- NT1 neodymium 153
- NT1 neodymium 154
- NT1 neodymium 155
- NT1 neodymium 156

NEODYMIUM LASERS [1,594; 1,594]
- BT1 solid state lasers
- BT2 lasers
- BT3 amplifiers
- BT4 equipment
- RT gdl facility
- RT gekko facility
- RT nova facility
- RT novette facility
- RT octal 82 facility
- RT omega facility
- RT shiva facility

NEODYMIUM NITRATES [96; 96]
- BT1 neodymium compounds
- BT2 rare earth compounds
- BT1 nitrates
- BT2 nitrogen compounds
- BT2 oxygen compounds

NEODYMIUM NITRIDES [11; 11]
- BT1 neodymium compounds
- BT2 rare earth compounds
- BT1 nitrides
- BT2 nitrogen compounds
- BT2 pnictides

NEODYMIUM OXIDES [755; 755]
- BT1 neodymium compounds
- BT2 rare earth compounds
- BT1 oxides
- BT2 chalcogenides
- BT2 oxygen compounds

NEODYMIUM PERCHLORATES [15; 15]
- BT1 neodymium compounds
- BT2 rare earth compounds
- BT1 perchlorates
- BT2 chlorine compounds
- BT3 halogen compounds
- BT2 oxygen compounds

NEODYMIUM PHOSPHATES [99; 99]
- BT1 neodymium compounds
- BT2 rare earth compounds
- BT1 phosphates
- BT2 oxygen compounds
- BT2 phosphorus compounds

NEODYMIUM SILICATES [35; 35]
- BT1 neodymium compounds
- BT2 rare earth compounds
- BT1 silicates
- BT2 oxygen compounds
- BT2 silicon compounds

NEODYMIUM SILICIDES [22; 22]
BT1 neodymium compounds
BT2 rare earth compounds
BT1 silicides
BT2 silicon compounds

NEODYMIUM SULFATES [40; 40]
BT1 neodymium compounds
BT2 rare earth compounds
BT1 sulfates
BT2 oxygen compounds
BT2 sulfur compounds

NEODYMIUM SULFIDES [77; 77]
BT1 neodymium compounds
BT2 rare earth compounds
BT1 sulfides
BT2 chalcogenides
BT2 sulfur compounds

NEODYMIUM TELLURIDES [7; 7] Mar 76
BT1 neodymium compounds
BT2 rare earth compounds
BT1 tellurides
BT2 chalcogenides
BT2 tellurium compounds

NEODYMIUM TUNGSTATES [14; 14] Feb 80
BT1 neodymium compounds
BT2 rare earth compounds
BT1 tungstates
BT2 oxygen compounds
BT2 tungsten compounds
BT3 transition element compounds

NEODYMIUM 127 [3; 3] Oct 84
BT1 beta-plus decay radioisotopes
BT2 beta decay radioisotopes
BT3 radioisotopes
BT4 isotopes
BT1 even-odd nuclei
BT2 nuclei
BT1 neodymium isotopes
BT1 rare earth nuclei
BT2 intermediate mass nuclei
BT3 nuclei
BT1 seconds living radioisotopes
BT2 radioisotopes
BT3 isotopes

NEODYMIUM 128 [5; 5] Oct 84
BT1 beta-plus decay radioisotopes
BT2 beta decay radioisotopes
BT3 radioisotopes
BT4 isotopes
BT1 even-even nuclei
BT2 nuclei
BT1 neodymium isotopes
BT1 rare earth nuclei
BT2 intermediate mass nuclei
BT3 nuclei

NEODYMIUM 129 [5; 5] Jun 77
BT1 beta-plus decay radioisotopes
BT2 beta decay radioisotopes
BT3 radioisotopes
BT4 isotopes
BT1 electron capture radioisotopes
BT2 beta decay radioisotopes
BT3 radioisotopes
BT4 isotopes
BT1 even-odd nuclei
BT2 nuclei
BT1 neodymium isotopes
BT1 rare earth nuclei
BT2 intermediate mass nuclei
BT3 nuclei
BT1 seconds living radioisotopes
BT2 radioisotopes
BT3 isotopes

NEODYMIUM 130 [10; 10]
BT1 beta-plus decay radioisotopes
BT2 beta decay radioisotopes
BT3 radioisotopes
BT4 isotopes
BT1 electron capture radioisotopes
BT2 beta decay radioisotopes
BT3 radioisotopes
BT4 isotopes
BT1 even-even nuclei
BT2 nuclei
BT1 neodymium isotopes
BT1 rare earth nuclei
BT2 intermediate mass nuclei
BT3 nuclei
BT1 seconds living radioisotopes
BT2 radioisotopes
BT3 isotopes

NEODYMIUM 131 [4; 4] Jun 77
BT1 beta-plus decay radioisotopes
BT2 beta decay radioisotopes
BT3 radioisotopes
BT4 isotopes
BT1 even-odd nuclei
BT2 nuclei
BT1 neodymium isotopes
BT1 rare earth nuclei
BT2 intermediate mass nuclei
BT3 nuclei
BT1 seconds living radioisotopes
BT2 radioisotopes
BT3 isotopes

NEODYMIUM 132 [20; 20] Jun 77
BT1 beta-plus decay radioisotopes
BT2 beta decay radioisotopes
BT3 radioisotopes
BT4 isotopes
BT1 electron capture radioisotopes
BT2 beta decay radioisotopes
BT3 radioisotopes
BT4 isotopes
BT1 even-even nuclei
BT2 nuclei
BT1 minutes living radioisotopes
BT2 radioisotopes
BT3 isotopes
BT1 neodymium isotopes
BT1 rare earth nuclei
BT2 intermediate mass nuclei
BT3 nuclei

NEODYMIUM 133 [16; 16] Jun 77
BT1 beta-plus decay radioisotopes
BT2 beta decay radioisotopes
BT3 radioisotopes
BT4 isotopes
BT1 electron capture radioisotopes
BT2 beta decay radioisotopes
BT3 radioisotopes
BT4 isotopes
BT1 even-odd nuclei
BT2 nuclei
BT1 minutes living radioisotopes
BT2 radioisotopes
BT3 isotopes
BT1 neodymium isotopes
BT1 rare earth nuclei
BT2 intermediate mass nuclei
BT3 nuclei

NEODYMIUM 134 [30; 30] Jan 76
BT1 beta-plus decay radioisotopes
BT2 beta decay radioisotopes
BT3 radioisotopes
BT4 isotopes
BT1 electron capture radioisotopes
BT2 beta decay radioisotopes
BT3 radioisotopes
BT4 isotopes
BT1 even-even nuclei
BT2 nuclei
BT1 minutes living radioisotopes
BT2 radioisotopes
BT3 isotopes
BT1 neodymium isotopes
BT1 rare earth nuclei
BT2 intermediate mass nuclei
BT3 nuclei

NEODYMIUM 135 [33; 33]
BT1 beta-plus decay radioisotopes
BT2 beta decay radioisotopes
BT3 radioisotopes
BT4 isotopes
BT1 electron capture radioisotopes
BT2 beta decay radioisotopes
BT3 radioisotopes
BT4 isotopes
BT1 even-odd nuclei
BT2 nuclei
BT1 minutes living radioisotopes
BT2 radioisotopes
BT3 isotopes
BT1 neodymium isotopes
BT1 rare earth nuclei
BT2 intermediate mass nuclei
BT3 nuclei

NEODYMIUM 136 [33; 33]
BT1 beta-plus decay radioisotopes
BT2 beta decay radioisotopes
BT3 radioisotopes
BT4 isotopes
BT1 electron capture radioisotopes
BT2 beta decay radioisotopes
BT3 radioisotopes
BT4 isotopes
BT1 even-even nuclei
BT2 nuclei
BT1 minutes living radioisotopes
BT2 radioisotopes
BT3 isotopes
BT1 neodymium isotopes
BT1 rare earth nuclei
BT2 intermediate mass nuclei
BT3 nuclei

NEODYMIUM 137 [22; 22]
BT1 beta-plus decay radioisotopes
BT2 beta decay radioisotopes
BT3 radioisotopes
BT4 isotopes
BT1 electron capture radioisotopes
BT2 beta decay radioisotopes
BT3 radioisotopes
BT4 isotopes
BT1 even-odd nuclei
BT2 nuclei
BT1 isomeric transition isotopes
BT2 radioisotopes
BT3 isotopes
BT1 minutes living radioisotopes
BT2 radioisotopes
BT3 isotopes
BT1 neodymium isotopes
BT1 rare earth nuclei
BT2 intermediate mass nuclei
BT3 nuclei
BT1 seconds living radioisotopes
BT2 radioisotopes
BT3 isotopes

NEODYMIUM 138 [28; 28]
BT1 electron capture radioisotopes
BT2 beta decay radioisotopes
BT3 radioisotopes
BT4 isotopes
BT1 even-even nuclei
BT2 nuclei
BT1 hours living radioisotopes
BT2 radioisotopes
BT3 isotopes
BT1 neodymium isotopes
BT1 rare earth nuclei
BT2 intermediate mass nuclei
BT3 nuclei

NEODYMIUM 139 [23; 23]
BT1 beta-plus decay radioisotopes
BT2 beta decay radioisotopes
BT3 radioisotopes
BT4 isotopes
BT1 electron capture radioisotopes
BT2 beta decay radioisotopes
BT3 radioisotopes

```
        BT4      isotopes
   BT1   even-odd nuclei
     BT2    nuclei
   BT1   hours living radioisotopes
     BT2    radioisotopes
       BT3     isotopes
   BT1   isomeric transition isotopes
     BT2    radioisotopes
       BT3     isotopes
   BT1   minutes living radioisotopes
     BT2    radioisotopes
       BT3     isotopes
   BT1   neodymium isotopes
   BT1   rare earth nuclei
     BT2    intermediate mass nuclei
       BT3     nuclei

NEODYMIUM 140 [31; 31]
   BT1   days living radioisotopes
     BT2    radioisotopes
       BT3     isotopes
   BT1   electron capture radioisotopes
     BT2    beta decay radioisotopes
       BT3     radioisotopes
         BT4      isotopes
   BT1   even-even nuclei
     BT2    nuclei
   BT1   neodymium isotopes
   BT1   rare earth nuclei
     BT2    intermediate mass nuclei
       BT3     nuclei

NEODYMIUM 141 [53; 53]
   BT1   beta-plus decay radioisotopes
     BT2    beta decay radioisotopes
       BT3     radioisotopes
         BT4      isotopes
   BT1   electron capture radioisotopes
     BT2    beta decay radioisotopes
       BT3     radioisotopes
         BT4      isotopes
   BT1   even-odd nuclei
     BT2    nuclei
   BT1   hours living radioisotopes
     BT2    radioisotopes
       BT3     isotopes
   BT1   isomeric transition isotopes
     BT2    radioisotopes
       BT3     isotopes
   BT1   minutes living radioisotopes
     BT2    radioisotopes
       BT3     isotopes
   BT1   neodymium isotopes
   BT1   rare earth nuclei
     BT2    intermediate mass nuclei
       BT3     nuclei

NEODYMIUM 142 [186; 186]
   BT1   even-even nuclei
     BT2    nuclei
   BT1   neodymium isotopes
   BT1   rare earth nuclei
     BT2    intermediate mass nuclei
       BT3     nuclei
   BT1   stable isotopes
     BT2    isotopes

NEODYMIUM 142 REACTIONS [6; 6]
Feb 84
   BT1   heavy ion reactions
     BT2    nuclear reactions

NEODYMIUM 142 TARGET [223; 223]
   BT1   targets

NEODYMIUM 143 [366; 366]
   BT1   even-odd nuclei
     BT2    nuclei
   BT1   neodymium isotopes
   BT1   rare earth nuclei
     BT2    intermediate mass nuclei
       BT3     nuclei
   BT1   stable isotopes
     BT2    isotopes

NEODYMIUM 143 TARGET [111; 111]
   BT1   targets

NEODYMIUM 144 [495; 495]
   BT1   alpha decay radioisotopes
     BT2    radioisotopes
       BT3     isotopes
   BT1   even-even nuclei
     BT2    nuclei
   BT1   neodymium isotopes
   BT1   rare earth nuclei
     BT2    intermediate mass nuclei
       BT3     nuclei
   BT1   years living radioisotopes
     BT2    radioisotopes
       BT3     isotopes

NEODYMIUM 144 TARGET [140; 140]
   BT1   targets

NEODYMIUM 145 [91; 91]
   BT1   even-odd nuclei
     BT2    nuclei
   BT1   neodymium isotopes
   BT1   rare earth nuclei
     BT2    intermediate mass nuclei
       BT3     nuclei
   BT1   stable isotopes
     BT2    isotopes

NEODYMIUM 145 TARGET [52; 52]
   BT1   targets

NEODYMIUM 146 [161; 161]
   BT1   even-even nuclei
     BT2    nuclei
   BT1   neodymium isotopes
   BT1   rare earth nuclei
     BT2    intermediate mass nuclei
       BT3     nuclei
   BT1   stable isotopes
     BT2    isotopes

NEODYMIUM 146 TARGET [141; 141]
   BT1   targets

NEODYMIUM 147 [136; 136]
   BT1   beta-minus decay radioisotopes
     BT2    beta decay radioisotopes
       BT3     radioisotopes
         BT4      isotopes
   BT1   days living radioisotopes
     BT2    radioisotopes
       BT3     isotopes
   BT1   even-odd nuclei
     BT2    nuclei
   BT1   internal conversion radioisoto
     BT2    radioisotopes
       BT3     isotopes
   BT1   neodymium isotopes
   BT1   rare earth nuclei
     BT2    intermediate mass nuclei
       BT3     nuclei

NEODYMIUM 147 TARGET [3; 3]
Jul 80
   BT1   targets

NEODYMIUM 148 [168; 168]
   BT1   even-even nuclei
     BT2    nuclei
   BT1   neodymium isotopes
   BT1   rare earth nuclei
     BT2    intermediate mass nuclei
       BT3     nuclei
   BT1   stable isotopes
     BT2    isotopes

NEODYMIUM 148 TARGET [97; 97]
   BT1   targets

NEODYMIUM 149 [33; 33]
   BT1   beta-minus decay radioisotopes
     BT2    beta decay radioisotopes
       BT3     radioisotopes
         BT4      isotopes
   BT1   even-odd nuclei
     BT2    nuclei
   BT1   hours living radioisotopes
     BT2    radioisotopes
       BT3     isotopes
   BT1   neodymium isotopes
   BT1   rare earth nuclei
     BT2    intermediate mass nuclei
       BT3     nuclei

NEODYMIUM 149 TARGET [2; 2]
Jul 80
   BT1   targets

NEODYMIUM 150 [150; 150]
   BT1   even-even nuclei
     BT2    nuclei
   BT1   neodymium isotopes
   BT1   rare earth nuclei
     BT2    intermediate mass nuclei
       BT3     nuclei
   BT1   stable isotopes
     BT2    isotopes

NEODYMIUM 150 REACTIONS [4; 4]
   BT1   heavy ion reactions
     BT2    nuclear reactions

NEODYMIUM 150 TARGET [199; 199]
   BT1   targets

NEODYMIUM 151 [19; 19]
   BT1   beta-minus decay radioisotopes
     BT2    beta decay radioisotopes
       BT3     radioisotopes
         BT4      isotopes
   BT1   even-odd nuclei
     BT2    nuclei
   BT1   minutes living radioisotopes
     BT2    radioisotopes
       BT3     isotopes
   BT1   neodymium isotopes
   BT1   rare earth nuclei
     BT2    intermediate mass nuclei
       BT3     nuclei

NEODYMIUM 152 [16; 16]
   BT1   beta-minus decay radioisotopes
     BT2    beta decay radioisotopes
       BT3     radioisotopes
         BT4      isotopes
   BT1   even-even nuclei
     BT2    nuclei
   BT1   minutes living radioisotopes
     BT2    radioisotopes
       BT3     isotopes
   BT1   neodymium isotopes
   BT1   rare earth nuclei
     BT2    intermediate mass nuclei
       BT3     nuclei

NEODYMIUM 153 [0; 0] Aug 87
   BT1   beta-minus decay radioisotopes
     BT2    beta decay radioisotopes
       BT3     radioisotopes
         BT4      isotopes
   BT1   even-odd nuclei
     BT2    nuclei
   BT1   neodymium isotopes
   BT1   rare earth nuclei
     BT2    intermediate mass nuclei
       BT3     nuclei
   BT1   seconds living radioisotopes
     BT2    radioisotopes
       BT3     isotopes

NEODYMIUM 154 [10; 10]
   BT1   beta-minus decay radioisotopes
     BT2    beta decay radioisotopes
       BT3     radioisotopes
         BT4      isotopes
   BT1   even-even nuclei
```

BT2 nuclei
BT1 neodymium isotopes
BT1 rare earth nuclei
BT2 intermediate mass nuclei
BT3 nuclei
BT1 seconds living radioisotopes
BT2 radioisotopes
BT3 isotopes

NEODYMIUM 155 [3; 3] *Aug 87*
BT1 beta-minus decay radioisotopes
BT2 beta decay radioisotopes
BT3 radioisotopes
BT4 isotopes
BT1 even-odd nuclei
BT2 nuclei
BT1 neodymium isotopes
BT1 rare earth nuclei
BT2 intermediate mass nuclei
BT3 nuclei
BT1 seconds living radioisotopes
BT2 radioisotopes
BT3 isotopes

NEODYMIUM 156 [2; 2] *Aug 87*
BT1 beta-minus decay radioisotopes
BT2 beta decay radioisotopes
BT3 radioisotopes
BT4 isotopes
BT1 even-even nuclei
BT2 nuclei
BT1 neodymium isotopes
BT1 rare earth nuclei
BT2 intermediate mass nuclei
BT3 nuclei
BT1 seconds living radioisotopes
BT2 radioisotopes
BT3 isotopes

NEOHYDRIN [72; 72]
UF *chlormerodrin*
BT1 diuretics
BT2 drugs

neomycin
USE antibiotics

NEON [4,569; 4,610]
BT1 rare gases
BT2 nonmetals
BT3 elements

NEON CHLORIDES [1; 1]
BT1 chlorides
BT2 chlorine compounds
BT3 halogen compounds
BT2 halides
BT3 halogen compounds
BT1 neon compounds
BT2 rare gas compounds

NEON COMPLEXES [5; 5]
BT1 complexes

NEON COMPOUNDS [18; 40]
BT1 rare gas compounds
NT1 neon chlorides
NT1 neon fluorides
NT1 neon hydrides
NT1 neon iodides
NT1 neon oxides

NEON FLUORIDES [5; 5]
BT1 fluorides
BT2 fluorine compounds
BT3 halogen compounds
BT2 halides
BT3 halogen compounds
BT1 neon compounds
BT2 rare gas compounds

NEON HYDRIDES [14; 14]
BT1 hydrides
BT2 hydrogen compounds
BT1 neon compounds
BT2 rare gas compounds

NEON IODIDES [2; 2]
BT1 iodides
BT2 halides
BT3 halogen compounds
BT2 iodine compounds
BT3 halogen compounds
BT1 neon compounds
BT2 rare gas compounds

NEON IONS [2,139; 2,139]
BT1 ions
BT2 charged particles

NEON ISOTOPES [277; 2,999]
NT1 neon 16
NT1 neon 17
NT1 neon 18
NT1 neon 19
NT1 neon 20
NT1 neon 21
NT1 neon 22
NT1 neon 23
NT1 neon 24
NT1 neon 25
NT1 neon 26
NT1 neon 27
NT1 neon 28
NT1 neon 29
NT1 neon 30
NT1 neon 32

NEON OXIDES [1; 1]
BT1 neon compounds
BT2 rare gas compounds
BT1 oxides
BT2 chalcogenides
BT2 oxygen compounds

NEON 16 [32; 32]
BT1 even-even nuclei
BT2 nuclei
BT1 light nuclei
BT2 nuclei
BT1 neon isotopes

NEON 17 [12; 12]
BT1 beta-plus decay radioisotopes
BT2 beta decay radioisotopes
BT3 radioisotopes
BT4 isotopes
BT1 even-odd nuclei
BT2 nuclei
BT1 light nuclei
BT2 nuclei
BT1 millisec living radioisotopes
BT2 radioisotopes
BT3 isotopes
BT1 neon isotopes

NEON 18 [122; 122]
BT1 beta-plus decay radioisotopes
BT2 beta decay radioisotopes
BT3 radioisotopes
BT4 isotopes
BT1 even-even nuclei
BT2 nuclei
BT1 light nuclei
BT2 nuclei
BT1 neon isotopes
BT1 seconds living radioisotopes
BT2 radioisotopes
BT3 isotopes

NEON 19 [141; 141]
BT1 beta-plus decay radioisotopes
BT2 beta decay radioisotopes
BT3 radioisotopes
BT4 isotopes
BT1 even-odd nuclei
BT2 nuclei
BT1 light nuclei
BT2 nuclei
BT1 neon isotopes
BT1 seconds living radioisotopes
BT2 radioisotopes
BT3 isotopes

NEON 19 BEAMS [4; 4] *Nov 88*
BT1 ion beams
BT2 beams

NEON 20 [1,727; 1,727]
BT1 even-even nuclei
BT2 nuclei
BT1 light nuclei
BT2 nuclei
BT1 neon isotopes
BT1 stable isotopes
BT2 isotopes
RT neon 20 beams

NEON 20 BEAMS [347; 347]
BT1 ion beams
BT2 beams
RT neon 20

NEON 20 REACTIONS [1,237; 1,237]
BT1 heavy ion reactions
BT2 nuclear reactions

NEON 20 TARGET [646; 646]
BT1 targets

NEON 21 [395; 395]
BT1 even-odd nuclei
BT2 nuclei
BT1 light nuclei
BT2 nuclei
BT1 neon isotopes
BT1 stable isotopes
BT2 isotopes

NEON 21 TARGET [58; 58]
BT1 targets

NEON 22 [532; 532]
BT1 even-even nuclei
BT2 nuclei
BT1 light nuclei
BT2 nuclei
BT1 neon isotopes
BT1 stable isotopes
BT2 isotopes
RT neon 22 beams

NEON 22 BEAMS [68; 68]
BT1 ion beams
BT2 beams
RT neon 22

NEON 22 REACTIONS [363; 363]
BT1 heavy ion reactions
BT2 nuclear reactions

NEON 22 TARGET [142; 142]
BT1 targets

NEON 23 [52; 52]
BT1 beta-minus decay radioisotopes
BT2 beta decay radioisotopes
BT3 radioisotopes
BT4 isotopes
BT1 even-odd nuclei
BT2 nuclei
BT1 light nuclei
BT2 nuclei
BT1 neon isotopes
BT1 seconds living radioisotopes
BT2 radioisotopes
BT3 isotopes

NEON 24 [68; 68]
 BT1 beta-minus decay radioisotopes
 BT2 beta decay radioisotopes
 BT3 radioisotopes
 BT4 isotopes
 BT1 even-even nuclei
 BT2 nuclei
 BT1 light nuclei
 BT2 nuclei
 BT1 minutes living radioisotopes
 BT2 radioisotopes
 BT3 isotopes
 BT1 neon isotopes

NEON 24 DECAY RADIOISOTOPES
 [0; 798] *Mar 86*
 BT1 heavy ion decay radioisotopes
 BT2 radioisotopes
 BT3 isotopes
 NT1 protactinium 231
 NT1 thorium 230
 NT1 uranium 232
 NT1 uranium 233
 NT1 uranium 234
 RT neon 24 emission decay

NEON 24 EMISSION DECAY [31; 31]
 Mar 86
 BT1 heavy ion emission decay
 BT2 nuclear decay
 BT3 decay
 RT neon 24 decay radioisotopes

NEON 25 [25; 25]
 BT1 beta-minus decay radioisotopes
 BT2 beta decay radioisotopes
 BT3 radioisotopes
 BT4 isotopes
 BT1 even-odd nuclei
 BT2 nuclei
 BT1 light nuclei
 BT2 nuclei
 BT1 millisec living radioisotopes
 BT2 radioisotopes
 BT3 isotopes
 BT1 neon isotopes

NEON 26 [21; 21]
 BT1 beta-minus decay radioisotopes
 BT2 beta decay radioisotopes
 BT3 radioisotopes
 BT4 isotopes
 BT1 even-even nuclei
 BT2 nuclei
 BT1 light nuclei
 BT2 nuclei
 BT1 millisec living radioisotopes
 BT2 radioisotopes
 BT3 isotopes
 BT1 neon isotopes

NEON 27 [7; 7]
 BT1 even-odd nuclei
 BT2 nuclei
 BT1 light nuclei
 BT2 nuclei
 BT1 neon isotopes

NEON 28 [8; 8] *Sep 79*
 BT1 even-even nuclei
 BT2 nuclei
 BT1 light nuclei
 BT2 nuclei
 BT1 neon isotopes

NEON 29 [5; 5] *Oct 85*
 BT1 beta-minus decay radioisotopes
 BT2 beta decay radioisotopes
 BT3 radioisotopes
 BT4 isotopes
 BT1 even-odd nuclei
 BT2 nuclei
 BT1 light nuclei
 BT2 nuclei
 BT1 neon isotopes

NEON 30 [6; 6] *Oct 85*
 BT1 beta-minus decay radioisotopes
 BT2 beta decay radioisotopes
 BT3 radioisotopes
 BT4 isotopes
 BT1 even-even nuclei
 BT2 nuclei
 BT1 light nuclei
 BT2 nuclei
 BT1 neon isotopes

NEON 32 [0; 0] *Jul 90*
 BT1 even-even nuclei
 BT2 nuclei
 BT1 light nuclei
 BT2 nuclei
 BT1 neon isotopes

NEONATES [809; 809] *Jul 76*
 (Newborn animals)
 UF *newborns*
 BT1 animals
 RT age groups
 RT infants
 RT teratogens

neopentane
 USE 2-2-dimethylpropane

NEOPLASMS [21,384; 46,628]
 UF *astrocytomas*
 UF *cancer*
 UF *tumors*
 BT1 diseases
 NT1 adenomas
 NT1 angiomas
 NT1 carcinomas
 NT1 epitheliomas
 NT1 experimental neoplasms
 NT2 ehrlich ascites tumor
 NT1 gliomas
 NT1 hepatomas
 NT1 leukemia
 NT2 myeloid leukemia
 NT1 lymphomas
 NT2 hodgkins disease
 NT2 lymphosarcomas
 NT1 melanomas
 NT1 sarcomas
 NT2 fibrosarcomas
 NT2 lymphosarcomas
 NT2 myosarcomas
 NT3 rhabdomyosarcomas
 NT2 osteosarcomas
 RT antimitotic drugs
 RT ascites tumor cells
 RT bleomycin
 RT carcinoembryonic antigen
 RT carcinogenesis
 RT carcinogens
 RT delayed radiation effects
 RT dimethylbenzanthracene
 RT granulomas
 RT in vivo
 RT metastases
 RT neocarcinostatin
 RT radioimmunodetection
 RT tumor cells
 RT tumor promoters

NEOPRENE [78; 78]
 UF *chlorobutadiene*
 UF *chloroprene*
 UF *2-chloro-1,3-butadiene*
 BT1 elastomers
 BT2 polymers
 BT1 organic chlorine compounds
 BT2 organic halogen compounds
 BT3 organic compounds
 BT1 organic polymers
 BT2 organic compounds
 BT2 polymers
 RT butadiene

NEP-1 REACTOR [4; 4] *Jun 77*
 UF *new england power co.-1 reacto*
 UF *new england power-1 reactor*
 BT1 pwr type reactors
 BT2 enriched uranium reactors
 BT3 reactors
 BT2 power reactors
 BT3 reactors
 BT2 thermal reactors
 BT3 reactors
 BT2 water cooled reactors
 BT3 reactors
 BT2 water moderated reactors
 BT3 reactors

NEP-2 REACTOR [4; 4] *Jun 77*
 UF *new england power co.-2 reacto*
 UF *new england power-2 reactor*
 BT1 pwr type reactors
 BT2 enriched uranium reactors
 BT3 reactors
 BT2 power reactors
 BT3 reactors
 BT2 thermal reactors
 BT3 reactors
 BT2 water cooled reactors
 BT3 reactors
 BT2 water moderated reactors
 BT3 reactors

nepa
 USE us natl environment policy act

NEPAL [14; 14]
 BT1 asia
 BT1 developing countries

NEPHRECTOMY [140; 140]
 BT1 surgery
 BT2 medicine
 RT kidneys

NEPHRITIS [245; 245]
 BT1 urogenital system diseases
 BT2 diseases
 RT kidneys

NEPHROSCLEROSIS [38; 38]
 BT1 cardiovascular diseases
 BT2 diseases
 BT1 urogenital system diseases
 BT2 diseases
 RT kidneys

NEPTEX PROCESS [1; 1]
 BT1 reprocessing
 BT2 separation processes
 RT solvent extraction

NEPTUNE PLANET [253; 253]
 BT1 planets

NEPTUNE REACTOR [5; 5]
 UF *derby zpr neptune*
 BT1 zero power reactors
 BT2 experimental reactors
 BT3 research and test reactors
 BT4 reactors

NEPTUNIUM [1,067; 1,084]
 BT1 actinides
 BT2 metals
 BT3 elements
 BT1 transuranium elements
 BT2 elements
 NT1 neptunium-alpha
 NT1 neptunium-beta
 NT1 neptunium-gamma

NEPTUNIUM ADDITIONS [7; 7]
 (Alloys containing not more than 1% Np are listed here.)
 RT neptunium alloys
 RT neptunium compounds

NEPTUNIUM ALLOYS [162; 169]
(Alloys containing more than 1% Np.)
- BT1 actinide alloys
- BT2 alloys
- NT1 neptunium base alloys
- RT neptunium additions

NEPTUNIUM ARSENIDES [31; 31]
- BT1 arsenides
- BT2 arsenic compounds
- BT2 pnictides
- BT1 neptunium compounds
- BT2 actinide compounds
- BT2 transuranium compounds

NEPTUNIUM BASE ALLOYS [7; 7]
- BT1 neptunium alloys
- BT2 actinide alloys
- BT3 alloys

NEPTUNIUM BORIDES [6; 6]
- BT1 borides
- BT2 boron compounds
- BT1 neptunium compounds
- BT2 actinide compounds
- BT2 transuranium compounds

NEPTUNIUM BROMIDES [13; 13]
- BT1 bromides
- BT2 bromine compounds
- BT3 halogen compounds
- BT2 halides
- BT3 halogen compounds
- BT1 neptunium compounds
- BT2 actinide compounds
- BT2 transuranium compounds

NEPTUNIUM CARBIDES [11; 11]
- BT1 carbides
- BT2 carbon compounds
- BT1 neptunium compounds
- BT2 actinide compounds
- BT2 transuranium compounds

NEPTUNIUM CARBONATES [18; 18]
- BT1 carbonates
- BT2 carbon compounds
- BT2 oxygen compounds
- BT1 neptunium compounds
- BT2 actinide compounds
- BT2 transuranium compounds

NEPTUNIUM CHLORIDES [32; 32]
- BT1 chlorides
- BT2 chlorine compounds
- BT3 halogen compounds
- BT2 halides
- BT3 halogen compounds
- BT1 neptunium compounds
- BT2 actinide compounds
- BT2 transuranium compounds

NEPTUNIUM COMPLEXES [394; 445]
- BT1 actinide complexes
- BT2 complexes
- BT1 transuranium complexes
- NT1 neptunyl complexes

NEPTUNIUM COMPOUNDS [670; 1,236]
- BT1 actinide compounds
- BT1 transuranium compounds
- NT1 neptunium arsenides
- NT1 neptunium borides
- NT1 neptunium bromides
- NT1 neptunium carbides
- NT1 neptunium carbonates
- NT1 neptunium chlorides
- NT1 neptunium fluorides
- NT1 neptunium hydrides
- NT1 neptunium hydroxides
- NT1 neptunium iodides
- NT1 neptunium nitrates
- NT1 neptunium nitrides
- NT1 neptunium oxides
- NT1 neptunium perchlorates
- NT1 neptunium phosphates
- NT1 neptunium phosphides
- NT1 neptunium selenides
- NT1 neptunium sulfates
- NT1 neptunium sulfides
- NT1 neptunium tellurides
- NT1 neptunyl compounds
- RT neptunium additions

NEPTUNIUM FLUORIDES [75; 75]
- BT1 fluorides
- BT2 fluorine compounds
- BT3 halogen compounds
- BT2 halides
- BT3 halogen compounds
- BT1 neptunium compounds
- BT2 actinide compounds
- BT2 transuranium compounds

NEPTUNIUM HYDRIDES [11; 11]
Nov 76
- BT1 hydrides
- BT2 hydrogen compounds
- BT1 neptunium compounds
- BT2 actinide compounds
- BT2 transuranium compounds

NEPTUNIUM HYDROXIDES [17; 17]
- BT1 hydroxides
- BT2 hydrogen compounds
- BT2 oxygen compounds
- BT1 neptunium compounds
- BT2 actinide compounds
- BT2 transuranium compounds

NEPTUNIUM IODIDES [10; 10]
- BT1 iodides
- BT2 halides
- BT3 halogen compounds
- BT2 iodine compounds
- BT3 halogen compounds
- BT1 neptunium compounds
- BT2 actinide compounds
- BT2 transuranium compounds

NEPTUNIUM IONS [62; 62]
- BT1 ions
- BT2 charged particles

NEPTUNIUM ISOTOPES [94; 1,822]
- NT1 neptunium 226
- NT1 neptunium 227
- NT1 neptunium 228
- NT1 neptunium 229
- NT1 neptunium 230
- NT1 neptunium 231
- NT1 neptunium 232
- NT1 neptunium 233
- NT1 neptunium 234
- NT1 neptunium 235
- NT1 neptunium 236
- NT1 neptunium 237
- NT1 neptunium 238
- NT1 neptunium 239
- NT1 neptunium 240
- NT1 neptunium 241
- NT1 neptunium 242
- NT1 neptunium 243
- NT1 neptunium 244

NEPTUNIUM NITRATES [46; 46]
- BT1 neptunium compounds
- BT2 actinide compounds
- BT2 transuranium compounds
- BT1 nitrates
- BT2 nitrogen compounds
- BT2 oxygen compounds

NEPTUNIUM NITRIDES [11; 11]
- BT1 neptunium compounds
- BT2 actinide compounds
- BT2 transuranium compounds
- BT1 nitrides
- BT2 nitrogen compounds
- BT2 pnictides

NEPTUNIUM OXIDES [224; 224]
- BT1 neptunium compounds
- BT2 actinide compounds
- BT2 transuranium compounds
- BT1 oxides
- BT2 chalcogenides
- BT2 oxygen compounds

NEPTUNIUM PERCHLORATES [12; 12]
Jan 77
- BT1 neptunium compounds
- BT2 actinide compounds
- BT2 transuranium compounds
- BT1 perchlorates
- BT2 chlorine compounds
- BT3 halogen compounds
- BT2 oxygen compounds

NEPTUNIUM PHOSPHATES [5; 5]
Feb 82
- BT1 neptunium compounds
- BT2 actinide compounds
- BT2 transuranium compounds
- BT1 phosphates
- BT2 oxygen compounds
- BT2 phosphorus compounds

NEPTUNIUM PHOSPHIDES [6; 6]
- BT1 neptunium compounds
- BT2 actinide compounds
- BT2 transuranium compounds
- BT1 phosphides
- BT2 phosphorus compounds
- BT2 pnictides

NEPTUNIUM SELENIDES [17; 17]
Jun 77
- BT1 neptunium compounds
- BT2 actinide compounds
- BT2 transuranium compounds
- BT1 selenides
- BT2 chalcogenides
- BT2 selenium compounds

NEPTUNIUM SULFATES [13; 13]
- BT1 neptunium compounds
- BT2 actinide compounds
- BT2 transuranium compounds
- BT1 sulfates
- BT2 oxygen compounds
- BT2 sulfur compounds

NEPTUNIUM SULFIDES [14; 14]
- BT1 neptunium compounds
- BT2 actinide compounds
- BT2 transuranium compounds
- BT1 sulfides
- BT2 chalcogenides
- BT2 sulfur compounds

NEPTUNIUM TELLURIDES [15; 15]
Feb 76
- BT1 neptunium compounds
- BT2 actinide compounds
- BT2 transuranium compounds
- BT1 tellurides
- BT2 chalcogenides
- BT2 tellurium compounds

NEPTUNIUM 226 [2; 2] *Dec 90*
- BT1 actinide nuclei
- BT2 heavy nuclei
- BT3 nuclei
- BT1 alpha decay radioisotopes
- BT2 radioisotopes
- BT3 isotopes
- BT1 millisec living radioisotopes
- BT2 radioisotopes
- BT3 isotopes
- BT1 neptunium isotopes
- BT1 odd-odd nuclei
- BT2 nuclei

NEPTUNIUM 227 [5; 5]
 BT1 actinide nuclei
 BT2 heavy nuclei
 BT3 nuclei
 BT1 alpha decay radioisotopes
 BT2 radioisotopes
 BT3 isotopes
 BT1 millisec living radioisotopes
 BT2 radioisotopes
 BT3 isotopes
 BT1 neptunium isotopes
 BT1 odd-even nuclei
 BT2 nuclei

NEPTUNIUM 228 [1; 1]
 BT1 actinide nuclei
 BT2 heavy nuclei
 BT3 nuclei
 BT1 neptunium isotopes
 BT1 odd-odd nuclei
 BT2 nuclei

NEPTUNIUM 229 [2; 2]
 BT1 actinide nuclei
 BT2 heavy nuclei
 BT3 nuclei
 BT1 alpha decay radioisotopes
 BT2 radioisotopes
 BT3 isotopes
 BT1 minutes living radioisotopes
 BT2 radioisotopes
 BT3 isotopes
 BT1 neptunium isotopes
 BT1 odd-even nuclei
 BT2 nuclei

NEPTUNIUM 230 [1; 1]
 BT1 actinide nuclei
 BT2 heavy nuclei
 BT3 nuclei
 BT1 alpha decay radioisotopes
 BT2 radioisotopes
 BT3 isotopes
 BT1 electron capture radioisotopes
 BT2 beta decay radioisotopes
 BT3 radioisotopes
 BT4 isotopes
 BT1 minutes living radioisotopes
 BT2 radioisotopes
 BT3 isotopes
 BT1 neptunium isotopes
 BT1 odd-odd nuclei
 BT2 nuclei

NEPTUNIUM 231 [1; 1]
 BT1 actinide nuclei
 BT2 heavy nuclei
 BT3 nuclei
 BT1 alpha decay radioisotopes
 BT2 radioisotopes
 BT3 isotopes
 BT1 electron capture radioisotopes
 BT2 beta decay radioisotopes
 BT3 radioisotopes
 BT4 isotopes
 BT1 minutes living radioisotopes
 BT2 radioisotopes
 BT3 isotopes
 BT1 neptunium isotopes
 BT1 odd-even nuclei
 BT2 nuclei

NEPTUNIUM 232 [2; 2]
 BT1 actinide nuclei
 BT2 heavy nuclei
 BT3 nuclei
 BT1 electron capture radioisotopes
 BT2 beta decay radioisotopes
 BT3 radioisotopes
 BT4 isotopes
 BT1 minutes living radioisotopes
 BT2 radioisotopes
 BT3 isotopes
 BT1 neptunium isotopes
 BT1 odd-odd nuclei
 BT2 nuclei

NEPTUNIUM 232 TARGET [3; 3]
Jul 76
 BT1 targets

NEPTUNIUM 233 [8; 8]
 BT1 actinide nuclei
 BT2 heavy nuclei
 BT3 nuclei
 BT1 alpha decay radioisotopes
 BT2 radioisotopes
 BT3 isotopes
 BT1 electron capture radioisotopes
 BT2 beta decay radioisotopes
 BT3 radioisotopes
 BT4 isotopes
 BT1 minutes living radioisotopes
 BT2 radioisotopes
 BT3 isotopes
 BT1 neptunium isotopes
 BT1 odd-even nuclei
 BT2 nuclei

NEPTUNIUM 234 [13; 13]
 BT1 actinide nuclei
 BT2 heavy nuclei
 BT3 nuclei
 BT1 beta-plus decay radioisotopes
 BT2 beta decay radioisotopes
 BT3 radioisotopes
 BT4 isotopes
 BT1 days living radioisotopes
 BT2 radioisotopes
 BT3 isotopes
 BT1 electron capture radioisotopes
 BT2 beta decay radioisotopes
 BT3 radioisotopes
 BT4 isotopes
 BT1 neptunium isotopes
 BT1 odd-odd nuclei
 BT2 nuclei

NEPTUNIUM 235 [74; 74]
 BT1 actinide nuclei
 BT2 heavy nuclei
 BT3 nuclei
 BT1 alpha decay radioisotopes
 BT2 radioisotopes
 BT3 isotopes
 BT1 electron capture radioisotopes
 BT2 beta decay radioisotopes
 BT3 radioisotopes
 BT4 isotopes
 BT1 neptunium isotopes
 BT1 odd-even nuclei
 BT2 nuclei
 BT1 years living radioisotopes
 BT2 radioisotopes
 BT3 isotopes

NEPTUNIUM 236 [74; 74]
 BT1 actinide nuclei
 BT2 heavy nuclei
 BT3 nuclei
 BT1 beta-minus decay radioisotopes
 BT2 beta decay radioisotopes
 BT3 radioisotopes
 BT4 isotopes
 BT1 electron capture radioisotopes
 BT2 beta decay radioisotopes
 BT3 radioisotopes
 BT4 isotopes
 BT1 hours living radioisotopes
 BT2 radioisotopes
 BT3 isotopes
 BT1 internal conversion radioisoto
 BT2 radioisotopes
 BT3 isotopes
 BT1 neptunium isotopes
 BT1 odd-odd nuclei
 BT2 nuclei
 BT1 years living radioisotopes
 BT2 radioisotopes
 BT3 isotopes

NEPTUNIUM 236 TARGET [10; 10]
Jul 81
 BT1 targets

NEPTUNIUM 237 [1,257; 1,257]
 BT1 actinide nuclei
 BT2 heavy nuclei
 BT3 nuclei
 BT1 alpha decay radioisotopes
 BT2 radioisotopes
 BT3 isotopes
 BT1 isomeric transition isotopes
 BT2 radioisotopes
 BT3 isotopes
 BT1 nanosec living radioisotopes
 BT2 radioisotopes
 BT3 isotopes
 BT1 neptunium isotopes
 BT1 odd-even nuclei
 BT2 nuclei
 BT1 spontaneous fission radioisoto
 BT2 radioisotopes
 BT3 isotopes
 BT1 years living radioisotopes
 BT2 radioisotopes
 BT3 isotopes

NEPTUNIUM 237 TARGET [320; 320]
 BT1 targets

NEPTUNIUM 238 [107; 107]
 BT1 actinide nuclei
 BT2 heavy nuclei
 BT3 nuclei
 BT1 beta-minus decay radioisotopes
 BT2 beta decay radioisotopes
 BT3 radioisotopes
 BT4 isotopes
 BT1 days living radioisotopes
 BT2 radioisotopes
 BT3 isotopes
 BT1 neptunium isotopes
 BT1 odd-odd nuclei
 BT2 nuclei

NEPTUNIUM 238 TARGET [8; 8]
Nov 77
 BT1 targets

NEPTUNIUM 239 [342; 342]
 BT1 actinide nuclei
 BT2 heavy nuclei
 BT3 nuclei
 BT1 beta-minus decay radioisotopes
 BT2 beta decay radioisotopes
 BT3 radioisotopes
 BT4 isotopes
 BT1 days living radioisotopes
 BT2 radioisotopes
 BT3 isotopes
 BT1 neptunium isotopes
 BT1 odd-even nuclei
 BT2 nuclei

NEPTUNIUM 239 TARGET [4; 4]
Feb 84
 BT1 targets

NEPTUNIUM 240 [10; 10]
 BT1 actinide nuclei
 BT2 heavy nuclei
 BT3 nuclei
 BT1 beta-minus decay radioisotopes
 BT2 beta decay radioisotopes
 BT3 radioisotopes
 BT4 isotopes
 BT1 hours living radioisotopes
 BT2 radioisotopes
 BT3 isotopes
 BT1 minutes living radioisotopes
 BT2 radioisotopes
 BT3 isotopes
 BT1 neptunium isotopes
 BT1 odd-odd nuclei
 BT2 nuclei

NEPTUNIUM 241 [6; 6]
BT1 actinide nuclei
BT2 heavy nuclei
BT3 nuclei
BT1 beta-minus decay radioisotopes
BT2 beta decay radioisotopes
BT3 radioisotopes
BT4 isotopes
BT1 minutes living radioisotopes
BT2 radioisotopes
BT3 isotopes
BT1 neptunium isotopes
BT1 odd-even nuclei
BT2 nuclei

NEPTUNIUM 242 [7; 7] *Sep 81*
BT1 actinide nuclei
BT2 heavy nuclei
BT3 nuclei
BT1 beta-minus decay radioisotopes
BT2 beta decay radioisotopes
BT3 radioisotopes
BT4 isotopes
BT1 minutes living radioisotopes
BT2 radioisotopes
BT3 isotopes
BT1 neptunium isotopes
BT1 odd-odd nuclei
BT2 nuclei

NEPTUNIUM 243 [5; 5] *Sep 79*
BT1 actinide nuclei
BT2 heavy nuclei
BT3 nuclei
BT1 beta-minus decay radioisotopes
BT2 beta decay radioisotopes
BT3 radioisotopes
BT4 isotopes
BT1 minutes living radioisotopes
BT2 radioisotopes
BT3 isotopes
BT1 neptunium isotopes
BT1 odd-even nuclei
BT2 nuclei

NEPTUNIUM 244 [4; 4] *Feb 87*
BT1 actinide nuclei
BT2 heavy nuclei
BT3 nuclei
BT1 beta-minus decay radioisotopes
BT2 beta decay radioisotopes
BT3 radioisotopes
BT4 isotopes
BT1 minutes living radioisotopes
BT2 radioisotopes
BT3 isotopes
BT1 neptunium isotopes
BT1 odd-odd nuclei
BT2 nuclei

NEPTUNIUM-ALPHA [13; 13]
BT1 neptunium
BT2 actinides
BT3 metals
BT4 elements
BT2 transuranium elements
BT3 elements

NEPTUNIUM-BETA [1; 1]
BT1 neptunium
BT2 actinides
BT3 metals
BT4 elements
BT2 transuranium elements
BT3 elements

NEPTUNIUM-GAMMA [7; 7]
BT1 neptunium
BT2 actinides
BT3 metals
BT4 elements
BT2 transuranium elements
BT3 elements

NEPTUNYL COMPLEXES [54; 54]
Sep 83
BT1 neptunium complexes
BT2 actinide complexes
BT3 complexes
BT2 transuranium complexes
RT neptunyl compounds

NEPTUNYL COMPOUNDS [111; 111]
BT1 neptunium compounds
BT2 actinide compounds
BT2 transuranium compounds
RT neptunyl complexes

NERNST EFFECT [163; 163]
UF *nernst-ettinghausen effect*
RT hall effect

NERNST HEAT THEOREM [13; 13]
RT thermodynamics

nernst-ettinghausen effect
USE nernst effect

nerva nrx-a2 reactor
USE nrx-a2 reactor

nerva nrx-a3 reactor
USE nrx-a3 reactor

nerva nrx-a4 eng. syst. test r
USE nrx-a4-est reactor

nerva nrx-a5 reactor
USE nrx-a5 reactor

nerva nrx-a6 reactor
USE nrx-a6 reactor

nerva nuclear rocket engine
USE nerva reactor

NERVA REACTOR [73; 73]
UF *nerva nuclear rocket engine*
BT1 space propulsion reactors
BT2 propulsion reactors
BT3 power reactors
BT4 reactors
BT2 space power reactors
BT3 mobile reactors
BT4 reactors
BT3 power reactors
BT4 reactors

NERVE CELLS [1,438; 1,438]
UF *axons*
UF *neurons*
BT1 somatic cells
BT2 animal cells
RT bioelectricity
RT nerve tissue
RT nervous system
RT receptors

NERVE TISSUE [235; 235]
BT1 tissues
BT2 body
RT nerve cells
RT nerves

NERVES [659; 785]
BT1 nervous system
NT1 sciatic nerve
NT1 vagus
RT herpes zoster
RT nerve tissue
RT reflexes

NERVOUS SYSTEM [318; 18,211]
NT1 autonomic nervous system
NT2 vagus
NT1 central nervous system
NT2 brain
NT3 cerebellum
NT3 cerebrum
NT4 cerebral cortex
NT3 hippocampus
NT3 hypothalamus
NT3 olfactory bulbs
NT3 thalamus
NT2 spinal cord
NT1 ganglions
NT1 nerves
NT2 sciatic nerve
NT2 vagus
RT nerve cells
RT nervous system diseases
RT organs
RT pain
RT poliomyelitis
RT reflexes
RT retina
RT sense organs

NERVOUS SYSTEM DISEASES
[3,275; 4,741]
BT1 diseases
NT1 encephalitis
NT1 epilepsy
NT1 gliomas
NT1 mental disorders
NT1 myelitis
NT1 poliomyelitis
NT1 rabies
RT meningococcus
RT nervous system
RT neurology

NESTOR REACTOR [12; 12]
(UKAEA, Winfrith, United Kingdom)
UF *neutron source thermal reactor*
UF *ukaea-nestor reactor*
BT1 argonaut type reactors
BT2 enriched uranium reactors
BT3 reactors
BT2 research and test reactors
BT3 reactors
BT2 water cooled reactors
BT3 reactors
BT2 water moderated reactors
BT3 reactors
BT1 research reactors
BT2 research and test reactors
BT3 reactors
BT1 thermal reactors
BT2 reactors

→ **NESTS** [0; 0] *Aug 91*
(The place where the eggs of animals are laid and hatched and the young are reared.)
RT animal breeding
RT habitat
RT reproduction

NET TOKAMAK [626; 626] *Feb 86*
UF *next european torus*
BT1 tokamak devices
BT2 closed plasma devices
BT3 thermonuclear devices

NETHERLANDS [1,137; 1,137]
BT1 developed countries
BT1 europe

NETHERLANDS ORGANIZATIONS
[87; 303]
BT1 national organizations
NT1 ecn
NT2 rcn
NT1 iko
NT1 iri
NT1 kvi
NT1 nikhef

NETWORK ANALYSIS [74; 74] *Jun 83*
(Derivation of the electrical properties of a network from its configuration, element values and driving forces.)
  RT   circuit theory
  RT   electronic circuits

networks (computers)
  USE   computer networks

neuherberg research reactor
  USE   frn reactor

neumann functions
  USE   bessel functions

NEUMANN SERIES [31; 31] *Feb 84*
  BT1   series expansion
  RT   bessel functions

NEUPOTZ-1 REACTOR [10; 10] *Jul 78*
(Neupotz, Rheinlandpfalz, Federal Republic of Germany)
  BT1   pwr type reactors
    BT2   enriched uranium reactors
      BT3   reactors
    BT2   power reactors
      BT3   reactors
    BT2   thermal reactors
      BT3   reactors
    BT2   water cooled reactors
      BT3   reactors
    BT2   water moderated reactors
      BT3   reactors

NEUPOTZ-2 REACTOR [4; 4] *Jul 78*
(Neupotz, Rheinlandpfalz, Federal Republic of Germany)
  BT1   pwr type reactors
    BT2   enriched uranium reactors
      BT3   reactors
    BT2   power reactors
      BT3   reactors
    BT2   thermal reactors
      BT3   reactors
    BT2   water cooled reactors
      BT3   reactors
    BT2   water moderated reactors
      BT3   reactors

NEURAL NETWORKS [62; 62] *Sep 89*
(Computer programs built of linear arrays of processing elements grouped together to simulate the interconnections between the neurons and the learning rules of the brain.)
  RT   artificial intelligence
  RT   computer architecture
  RT   expert systems

neuridine
  USE   spermine

NEUROLOGY [453; 453]
  BT1   medicine
  RT   nervous system diseases

neurons
  USE   nerve cells

NEUROREGULATORS [152; 2,213] *May 84*
  BT1   autonomic nervous system agent
  BT2   drugs
  NT1   acetylcholine
  NT1   adrenaline
  NT1   aminobutyric acid
  NT1   dopa
  NT1   dopamine
  NT1   endorphins
    NT2   enkephalins
  NT1   noradrenaline
  NT1   serotonin

NEUROSPORA [120; 120]
  BT1   fungi
    BT2   plants

neutr int stand uranium source
  USE   nisus facility

NEUTRAL ATOM BEAM INJECTION [3,468; 3,468]
  BT1   beam injection
  RT   atomic beam sources
  RT   neutral beam sources

NEUTRAL BEAM SOURCES [689; 922] *Nov 82*
(Not for subatomic species.)
  NT1   atomic beam sources
  RT   ion sources
  RT   neutral atom beam injection

NEUTRAL CURRENTS [1,117; 2,645]
  BT1   algebraic currents
    BT2   currents
  NT1   weak neutral currents
  RT   charged currents
  RT   electromagnetic interactions
  RT   neutral-current interactions
  RT   weak interactions

NEUTRAL PARTICLES [1,378; 1,380]
  RT   missing mass
  RT   missing-mass spectrometers
  RT   neutral-particle transport
  RT   particles

NEUTRAL RED [9; 9]
  UF   *toluylene red*
  BT1   amines
    BT2   organic compounds
  BT1   indicators
  BT1   pyrazines
    BT2   azines
      BT3   heterocyclic compounds
        BT4   organic compounds
      BT3   organic nitrogen compounds
        BT4   organic compounds

NEUTRAL-CURRENT INTERACTIONS [1,945; 1,945]
  BT1   particle interactions
    BT2   interactions
  RT   basic interactions
  RT   neutral currents
  RT   weinberg lepton model

NEUTRAL-PARTICLE TRANSPORT [253; 4,331] *Sep 75*
  UF   *transport (neutral-particle)*
  BT1   radiation transport
  NT1   atom transport
  NT1   neutron transport
  NT1   photon transport
  RT   neutral particles

neutralization (beam)
  USE   beam neutralization

neutralization (chemical)
  USE   ph value

neutralization (physical)
(Of electrons, holes, or radicals; not for the concept covered by BEAM NEUTRALIZATION.)
  USE   recombination

neutrettos
  USE   muon neutrinos

NEUTRINO BEAMS [682; 682]
  BT1   lepton beams
    BT2   particle beams
      BT3   beams

NEUTRINO DETECTION [1,185; 1,185]
  BT1   radiation detection
    BT2   detection
  RT   dumand project

NEUTRINO OSCILLATION [941; 941] *Oct 83*
(Periodic transformation of two or more kinds of neutrinos into each other; interference of mass and charge eigenstates.)
  RT   mixing ratio
  RT   neutrinos
  RT   weak interactions

NEUTRINO REACTIONS [1,327; 1,327]
  UF+ *neutrino-deuteron interactions*
  BT1   lepton reactions
    BT2   nuclear reactions

neutrino-deuteron interactions
  USE   deuterium target
  AND   neutrino reactions

NEUTRINO-ELECTRON INTERACTIONS [712; 846]
  BT1   lepton-lepton interactions
    BT2   particle interactions
      BT3   interactions
  NT1   antineutrino-electron interact

NEUTRINO-MESON INTERACTIONS [15; 15]
  BT1   lepton-meson interactions
    BT2   lepton-hadron interactions
      BT3   particle interactions
        BT4   interactions

NEUTRINO-MUON INTERACTIONS [21; 21]
  BT1   lepton-lepton interactions
    BT2   particle interactions
      BT3   interactions

NEUTRINO-NEUTRINO INTERACTIONS [109; 109]
  BT1   lepton-lepton interactions
    BT2   particle interactions
      BT3   interactions

NEUTRINO-NEUTRON INTERACTIONS [206; 270]
  BT1   neutrino-nucleon interactions
    BT2   lepton-nucleon interactions
      BT3   lepton-baryon interactions
        BT4   lepton-hadron interactions
          BT5   particle interactions
            BT6   interactions
  NT1   antineutrino-neutron interacti

NEUTRINO-NUCLEON INTERACTIONS [1,711; 2,909]
  BT1   lepton-nucleon interactions
    BT2   lepton-baryon interactions
      BT3   lepton-hadron interactions
        BT4   particle interactions
          BT5   interactions
  NT1   antineutrino-nucleon interacti
    NT2   antineutrino-neutron interacti
    NT2   antineutrino-proton interactio
  NT1   neutrino-neutron interactions
    NT2   antineutrino-neutron interacti
  NT1   neutrino-proton interactions
    NT2   antineutrino-proton interactio

NEUTRINO-PROTON INTERACTIONS [551; 829]
  BT1   neutrino-nucleon interactions
    BT2   lepton-nucleon interactions
      BT3   lepton-baryon interactions
        BT4   lepton-hadron interactions

    BT5   particle interactions
    BT6   interactions
NT1   antineutrino-proton interactio

NEUTRINOS [6,049; 10,624]
- BT1 leptons
  - BT2 elementary particles
  - BT2 fermions
- BT1 massless particles
  - BT2 elementary particles
- NT1 antineutrinos
  - NT2 electron antineutrinos
  - NT2 muon antineutrinos
- NT1 cosmic neutrinos
- NT1 electron neutrinos
  - NT2 electron antineutrinos
- NT1 muon neutrinos
  - NT2 muon antineutrinos
- NT1 solar neutrinos
- NT1 tau neutrinos
- RT feynman-gell-mann theory
- RT neutrino oscillation
- RT two-component neutrino theory

NEUTRON ABSORBERS [1,448; 2,284]
- NT1 burnable poisons
- RT control elements
- RT reactor control systems
- RT reactor materials
- RT regulating rods
- RT scram rods
- RT shim rods

NEUTRON ACTIVATION ANALYSIS [5,449; 5,449]
- UF analysis (neutron activation)
- BT1 activation analysis
  - BT2 nondestructive analysis
    - BT3 chemical analysis
- RT neutron activation analyzers

NEUTRON ACTIVATION ANALYZERS [294; 294]
- BT1 measuring instruments
- RT neutron activation analysis

NEUTRON AGE [45; 45]
- UF+ fermi age
- RT fermi age theory
- RT neutron flux
- RT slowing-down

NEUTRON BEAMS [9,952; 9,952]
- BT1 nucleon beams
  - BT2 particle beams
    - BT3 beams
- RT neutron guides
- RT neutrons
- RT pulsed neutron techniques

NEUTRON CAMERAS [62; 62] Jul 78
- BT1 cameras
- RT neutron diffractometers
- RT neutron radiography

neutron capture
    USE   capture
    AND   neutron reactions

NEUTRON CAPTURE THERAPY [575; 575]
- BT1 neutron therapy
  - BT2 radiotherapy
    - BT3 therapy
      - BT4 medicine
- RT radioactivation

neutron capture-to-fissi ratio
    USE   capture-to-fission ratio

NEUTRON CHOPPERS [232; 232]
- UF choppers (neutron)
- BT1 beam pulsers
- RT neutron spectrometers
- RT shutters

NEUTRON CONVERTERS [119; 119]
- RT neutron sources
- RT slowing-down
- RT ultracold neutrons

NEUTRON DENSITY [1,005; 1,005]
- UF density (neutron)
- RT neutrons
- RT power density

NEUTRON DETECTION [2,821; 2,821]
- BT1 radiation detection
  - BT2 detection
- RT neutron detectors
- RT neutron dosimetry
- RT neutron monitors
- RT neutron spectrometers
- RT neutron spectroscopy
- RT neutron-photon converters
- RT radiation detectors

NEUTRON DETECTORS [2,463; 6,057]
- BT1 radiation detectors
  - BT2 measuring instruments
- NT1 activation detectors
- NT1 bf3 counters
- NT1 boron coated ion chambers
- NT1 boron lined counters
- NT1 fission chambers
- NT1 fission foil detectors
- NT1 he-3 counters
- NT1 moderating detectors
  - NT2 bonner sphere detectors
  - NT2 long counters
- NT1 proton recoil detectors
- NT1 self-powered neutron detectors
- NT1 threshold detectors
- RT neutron detection
- RT neutron dosimetry
- RT neutron monitors
- RT neutron thermopiles
- RT reactor control systems

NEUTRON DIFFRACTION [7,565; 7,565]
- UF rocking curve
- BT1 diffraction
  - BT2 coherent scattering
    - BT3 scattering
- RT crystallography
- RT neutron diffractometers
- RT neutron-photon converters
- RT structural chemical analysis

NEUTRON DIFFRACTOMETERS [490; 490]
- BT1 diffractometers
  - BT2 measuring instruments
- RT crystallography
- RT neutron cameras
- RT neutron diffraction

NEUTRON DIFFUSION EQUATION [1,944; 1,944]
- RT fick laws
- RT flux synthesis
- RT homogenization methods
- RT neutron transport theory

NEUTRON DOSIMETRY [4,219; 4,219]
- BT1 dosimetry
- RT albedo-neutron dosemeters
- RT neutron detection
- RT neutron detectors
- RT neutron monitors

neutron economy
    USE   neutron flux

NEUTRON EMISSION [1,686; 1,686]
- UF neutron evaporation
- BT1 emission
- RT liquid drop model

neutron evaporation
    USE   neutron emission

NEUTRON FLUENCE [3,583; 4,368]
- UF fluence (neutron)
- NT1 damaging neutron fluence
- NT2 equivalent fission fluence
- RT neutron flux

NEUTRON FLUX [10,779; 10,929]
- UF flux (neutron)
- UF neutron economy
- UF+ neutron flux density
- BT1 radiation flux
- NT1 adjoint flux
- RT damaging neutron fluence
- RT disadvantage factor
- RT flux synthesis
- RT heterogeneous effects
- RT homogenization methods
- RT neutron age
- RT neutron fluence
- RT neutron flux flattening
- RT neutron flux tilting
- RT neutron importance function
- RT neutrons

neutron flux density
    USE   flux density
    AND   neutron flux

NEUTRON FLUX FLATTENING [203; 203]
- UF flattening (neutron flux)
- RT neutron flux

NEUTRON FLUX TILTING [55; 55]
- UF tilting (neutron flux)
- RT neutron flux

NEUTRON GENERATORS [485; 485]
Dec 82
(Usually low-energy accelerators used to produce neutrons by nuclear reactions, e.g. T(d,n).)
- BT1 neutron sources
  - BT2 particle sources
    - BT3 radiation sources

NEUTRON GUIDES [105; 105] Nov 85
- RT neutron beams
- RT neutron reflectors
- RT neutron sources
- RT neutron transport
- RT pulsed neutron techniques
- RT reactor channels
- RT ultracold neutrons

NEUTRON IMPORTANCE FUNCTION [172; 172]
- UF importance function (neutron)
- RT adjoint flux
- RT neutron flux
- RT perturbation theory

NEUTRON LEAKAGE [696; 696]
- UF leakage (neutron)
- RT neutron transport theory

NEUTRON LOGGING [413; 942] Jan 77
(Well logging using neutron source.)
- BT1 radioactivity logging
  - BT2 well logging
- NT1 neutron-gamma logging
- NT1 neutron-neutron logging
- RT neutron probes

neutron matter
  USE   nuclear matter

neutron moisture meters
  USE   moisture gages

NEUTRON MONITORS [869; 869]
  BT1   radiation monitors
    BT2   monitors
      BT3   measuring instruments
  RT   neutron detection
  RT   neutron detectors
  RT   neutron dosimetry
  RT   reactor control systems

neutron multiplier facility
  USE   subcritical assemblies

NEUTRON OSCILLATION [59; 59]
Nov 85
(Process of a reversible neutron-antineutron transformation.)
  RT   antineutrons
  RT   baryon number
  RT   neutrons

NEUTRON PROBES [50; 50] *Mar 86*
  BT1   probes
  RT   moisture gages
  RT   neutron logging
  RT   neutron reactions
  RT   neutron sources

NEUTRON RADIOGRAPHY
[1,360; 1,360]
  RT   industrial radiography
  RT   neutron cameras
  RT   neutron-photon converters
  RT   nondestructive testing

NEUTRON REACTIONS [20,489; 21,661]
  UF+   neutron capture
  UF+   neutron-deuteron interactions
  BT1   nucleon reactions
    BT2   baryon reactions
      BT3   hadron reactions
        BT4   nuclear reactions
  NT1   fast fission
  NT1   thermal fission
  RT   neutron probes

NEUTRON REFLECTORS [986; 986]
  UF   reflectors (neutron)
  RT   configuration control
  RT   neutron guides
  RT   reflector savings

NEUTRON SEPARATION ENERGY
[325; 325]
  BT1   binding energy
    BT2   energy
  RT   neutrons

NEUTRON SLOWING-DOWN THEORY
[325; 356]
  UF   slowing-down theory (neutron)
  NT1   fermi age theory
  RT   moderators
  RT   neutron spectra
  RT   neutron transport theory
  RT   placzec function
  RT   reactor physics
  RT   selengut-goertzel equation
  RT   slowing-down
  RT   slowing-down kernels
  RT   spencer-fano theory
  RT   wick method

neutron source facilities
  SEE   neutron sources

neutron source thermal reactor
  USE   nestor reactor

NEUTRON SOURCES [6,331; 6,616]
(Excludes reactors even when used as neutron sources.)
  SF   neutron source facilities
  BT1   particle sources
    BT2   radiation sources
  NT1   neutron generators
  NT1   nisus facility
  RT   neutron converters
  RT   neutron guides
  RT   neutron probes
  RT   neutrons
  RT   radioactivation
  RT   sigma piles
  RT   sora reactor
  RT   thermal columns

NEUTRON SPECTRA [8,309; 8,329]
  BT1   spectra
  NT1   watt fission spectrum
  RT   neutron slowing-down theory
  RT   neutrons
  RT   spectra unfolding
  RT   spectral hardening

NEUTRON SPECTROMETERS
[1,565; 1,652]
  BT1   spectrometers
    BT2   measuring instruments
  NT1   bonner sphere spectrometers
  RT   neutron choppers
  RT   neutron detection

neutron spectrometry
  USE   neutron spectroscopy

NEUTRON SPECTROSCOPY
[1,207; 1,207]
  UF   neutron spectrometry
  BT1   spectroscopy
  RT   neutron detection

NEUTRON STARS [3,777; 3,777]
  BT1   stars
  RT   accretion disks
  RT   gravitational collapse
  RT   neutrons
  RT   nuclear matter
  RT   pulsars

NEUTRON TEMPERATURE [134; 134]
  UF   temperature (neutron)
  RT   energy
  RT   neutrons
  RT   thermal neutrons

NEUTRON THERAPY [1,109; 1,643]
Feb 76
  BT1   radiotherapy
    BT2   therapy
      BT3   medicine
  NT1   neutron capture therapy

NEUTRON THERMOPILES [2; 2]
  RT   neutron detectors

NEUTRON TRANSFER [965; 965]
  RT   neutrons
  RT   transfer reactions

NEUTRON TRANSPORT [2,989; 2,989]
  UF   transport (neutron)
  BT1   neutral-particle transport
    BT2   radiation transport
  RT   neutron guides
  RT   neutron transport theory

NEUTRON TRANSPORT THEORY
[3,039; 3,528]
  BT1   transport theory
  RT   adjoint difference method
  RT   albedo
  RT   amouyal-benoist-horowitz method
  RT   extrapolation length
  RT   feynman method
  RT   fick laws
  RT   homogenization methods
  RT   milne problem
  RT   monte carlo method
  RT   multigroup theory
  RT   neutron diffusion equation
  RT   neutron leakage
  RT   neutron slowing-down theory
  RT   neutron transport
  RT   one-group theory
  RT   perturbation theory
  RT   reactor physics
  RT   serber-wilson method
  RT   slowing-down
  RT   spherical harmonics method
  RT   transfer matrix method
  RT   variational methods
  RT   yvon method

NEUTRON-ANTINEUTRON INTERACTIO [47; 47]
  BT1   nucleon-antinucleon interactio
    BT2   baryon-baryon interactions
      BT3   hadron-hadron interactions
        BT4   particle interactions
          BT5   interactions

NEUTRON-DEFICIENT ISOTOPES
[908; 908]
  BT1   radioisotopes
    BT2   isotopes
  RT   delayed protons

neutron-deuteron interactions
  USE   deuterium target
  AND   neutron reactions

NEUTRON-GAMMA LOGGING
[360; 360] *Oct 76*
(Neutron source and gamma detector.)
  BT1   neutron logging
    BT2   radioactivity logging
      BT3   well logging

NEUTRON-NEUTRON INTERACTIONS
[259; 259]
  BT1   nucleon-nucleon interactions
    BT2   baryon-baryon interactions
      BT3   hadron-hadron interactions
        BT4   particle interactions
          BT5   interactions

NEUTRON-NEUTRON LOGGING
[231; 231] *Oct 76*
(Neutron source and neutron detector.)
  BT1   neutron logging
    BT2   radioactivity logging
      BT3   well logging

NEUTRON-PHOTON CONVERTERS
[22; 22]
  RT   neutron detection
  RT   neutron diffraction
  RT   neutron radiography
  RT   photographic film detectors

NEUTRON-RICH ISOTOPES [892; 892]
Jul 76
  BT1   beta-minus decay radioisotopes
    BT2   beta decay radioisotopes
      BT3   radioisotopes
        BT4   isotopes
  RT   beta-delayed neutrons

NEUTRONIC DAMAGE FUNCTIONS
[193; 193] *May 76*
- RT   damaging neutron fluence
- RT   equivalent fission fluence
- RT   irradiation
- RT   physical radiation effects

NEUTRONS [29,918; 54,744]
- BT1   nucleons
  - BT2   baryons
    - BT3   fermions
    - BT3   hadrons
      - BT4   elementary particles
- NT1   antineutrons
- NT1   beta-delayed neutrons
- NT1   cold neutrons
  - NT2   ultracold neutrons
- NT1   cosmic neutrons
- NT1   epithermal neutrons
- NT1   fast neutrons
- NT1   fission neutrons
  - NT2   delayed neutrons
  - NT2   prompt neutrons
- NT1   intermediate neutrons
- NT1   photoneutrons
- NT1   pile neutrons
- NT1   polyneutrons
  - NT2   dineutrons
  - NT2   tetraneutrons
  - NT2   trineutrons
- NT1   resonance neutrons
- NT1   slow neutrons
- NT1   solar neutrons
- NT1   thermal neutrons
- RT   cinda
- RT   haywood model
- RT   neutron beams
- RT   neutron density
- RT   neutron flux
- RT   neutron oscillation
- RT   neutron separation energy
- RT   neutron sources
- RT   neutron spectra
- RT   neutron stars
- RT   neutron temperature
- RT   neutron transfer
- RT   rosenbluth-nelkin model

NEUTROPHILS [446; 446]
- BT1   leukocytes
  - BT2   blood cells
    - BT3   blood
      - BT4   body fluids
        - BT5   biological materials
          - BT6   materials

NEVADA [756; 784]
- BT1   usa
  - BT2   developed countries
  - BT2   north america
- NT1   tonopah test range
- RT   nevada test site

NEVADA TEST SITE [1,419; 1,419]
- RT   arbor project
- RT   nevada
- RT   nuclear explosions
- RT   nuclear weapons
- RT   tonopah test range
- RT   yucca mountain

NEW BRUNSWICK [46; 46]
- BT1   canada
  - BT2   developed countries
  - BT2   north america

new england power co.-1 reacto
- USE   nep-1 reactor

new england power co.-2 reacto
- USE   nep-2 reactor

new england power-1 reactor
- USE   nep-1 reactor

new england power-2 reactor
- USE   nep-2 reactor

NEW GUINEA [23; 23]
- BT1   australasia
- BT1   islands
- RT   australia
- RT   new zealand
- RT   pacific ocean

NEW HAMPSHIRE [112; 112]
- BT1   usa
  - BT2   developed countries
  - BT2   north america

NEW JERSEY [335; 335]
- BT1   usa
  - BT2   developed countries
  - BT2   north america

NEW MEXICO [1,255; 1,255]
- BT1   usa
  - BT2   developed countries
  - BT2   north america
- RT   lanl
- RT   lasl
- RT   sandia laboratories
- RT   sandia national laboratories
- RT   wipp

NEW SOUTH WALES [87; 87]
- BT1   australia
  - BT2   australasia
  - BT2   developed countries

NEW YORK [543; 590]
- BT1   usa
  - BT2   developed countries
  - BT2   north america
- NT1   new york city
- RT   bnl
- RT   kapl

NEW YORK CITY [49; 49]
- BT1   new york
  - BT2   usa
    - BT3   developed countries
    - BT3   north america

NEW ZEALAND [222; 222]
- BT1   australasia
- BT1   developed countries
- BT1   islands
- RT   new guinea
- RT   pacific ocean

NEW ZEALAND ORGANIZATIONS
[3; 3] *Apr 86*
- BT1   national organizations

NEWBOLD ISLAND-1 REACTOR
[15; 15]
(Name changed to HOPE CREEK-1 REACTOR in November 1973 because of change in construction site, and more recent material should be so indexed.)
- UF   *bordentown nj newbold island-1*
- UF   *public service newbold isl.-1*
- BT1   hope creek-1 reactor
  - BT2   bwr type reactors
    - BT3   enriched uranium reactors
      - BT4   reactors
    - BT3   power reactors
      - BT4   reactors
    - BT3   thermal reactors
      - BT4   reactors
    - BT3   water cooled reactors
      - BT4   reactors
    - BT3   water moderated reactors
      - BT4   reactors

NEWBOLD ISLAND-2 REACTOR
[15; 15]
(Name changed to HOPE CREEK-2 REACTOR in November 1973 because of change in construction site, and more recent material should be so indexed.)
- UF   *bordentown nj newbold island-2*
- UF   *public service newbold isl.-2*
- BT1   hope creek-2 reactor
  - BT2   bwr type reactors
    - BT3   enriched uranium reactors
      - BT4   reactors
    - BT3   power reactors
      - BT4   reactors
    - BT3   thermal reactors
      - BT4   reactors
    - BT3   water cooled reactors
      - BT4   reactors
    - BT3   water moderated reactors
      - BT4   reactors

newborns
- USE   neonates

NEWCASTLE DISEASE [14; 14]
- BT1   viral diseases
  - BT2   infectious diseases
    - BT3   diseases
- RT   birds
- RT   viruses

NEWFOUNDLAND [34; 34]
- BT1   canada
  - BT2   developed countries
  - BT2   north america
- RT   atlantic ocean
- RT   islands

newton mechanics
- USE   classical mechanics

NEWTON METHOD [198; 198] *Aug 78*
- BT1   iterative methods
- RT   mathematics
- RT   numerical solution
- RT   polynomials

newts
- USE   salamanders

next european torus
- USE   net tokamak

niacin
- USE   nicotinic acid

NICARAGUA [6; 6]
- BT1   central america
  - BT2   latin america
- BT1   developing countries

nichrome
- USE   alloy-ni60fe24cr16

nichrome v
- USE   alloy-ni80cr20

NICKEL [7,992; 7,992]
- BT1   transition elements
  - BT2   metals
    - BT3   elements
- RT   td-nickel

NICKEL ADDITIONS [546; 2,255]
(Alloys containing not more than 1% Ni are listed here.)
- NT1   alloy-zr98sn-2
- NT1   steel-cralnimo
- NT1   steel-crmo

NT1	steel-crmov
NT1	steel-crni
NT1	steel-cr12moniv
NT1	steel-cr17mn15nni
NT1	steel-cr2moninb
NT1	steel-cr2mov
NT1	steel-mncumo
NT1	steel-mnnimo
NT1	steel-nimocr
RT	nickel alloys
RT	nickel compounds

NICKEL ALLOYS [6,224; 25,095]
(Alloys containing more than 1% Ni.)

UF	*nickel steels*
BT1	alloys
NT1	alloy-co36cr22ni22w15fe3
NT1	alloy-co43cr20fe18ni13w3
NT1	alloy-co54cr20w15ni10
NT1	alloy-co60cr30w4
NT1	alloy-co62cr28mo6ni3
NT1	alloy-cu52ni47
NT1	alloy-fe31cr21co20ni20mo3w2
NT1	alloy-fe36ni33cr26
NT1	alloy-fe40ni35cr22
NT1	alloy-fe44ni33cr21
NT1	alloy-fe46ni33cr21
NT1	alloy-fe48cr24ni24
NT1	alloy-fe53ni29co18
NT1	alnico alloys
*NT1	chromium-nickel steels
NT1	german silver
NT1	invar
*NT1	nickel base alloys
NT1	refractaloy
NT1	steel-cr16ni
NT1	steel-cr17cu4ni4nb-l
NT1	steel-cr17ni4mo3
NT1	steel-cr2nimov
NT1	steel-cr21mn9ni6
NT1	steel-cr21ni5ti
NT1	steel-cr22ni5ti
NT1	steel-cr26ni5mo-l
NT1	steel-mnnimov
NT1	steel-nicr
NT1	steel-nicrmo
NT1	steel-ni3cr
NT1	steel-ni3crmo
NT1	steel-ni3crmov
NT1	steel-ni3mov
NT1	steel-ni4
NT1	steel-ni4crw
NT1	tikonal
RT	nickel additions

→ **NICKEL ARSENIDES** [0; 0] *Sep 91*

BT1	arsenides
BT2	arsenic compounds
BT2	pnictides
BT1	nickel compounds
BT2	transition element compounds

NICKEL BASE ALLOYS [3,283; 6,337]

BT1	nickel alloys
BT2	alloys
NT1	alloy-ni42fe36cr12mo6ti3
NT1	alloy-ni43fe30cr22mo3
NT1	alloy-ni45cr23fe19co3mo3w3
NT1	alloy-ni45fe34cr20
NT1	alloy-ni50mo32cr15si3
NT1	alloy-ni55co17cr15mo5al4ti4
NT1	alloy-ni55cr19co11mo10ti3
NT1	alloy-ni56cr21w10mo5fe4al2
NT1	alloy-ni58cr14co8al4mo4nb4w4
NT1	alloy-ni58cr20co14mo4ti3
NT1	alloy-ni60cr14co10ti5mo4w4al3
NT1	alloy-ni60cr25w15
NT1	alloy-ni60mo13co9cr8nb4al3
NT1	alloy-ni65mo16cr15w4
NT1	alloy-ni67cr19mo5w5ti3
NT1	alloy-ni68cr15w6al3mo3fe2
NT1	alloy-ni77cr17al5
NT1	alloy-ni77cr20ti2
NT1	alloy-ni78cr21
NT1	alloy-ni79fe16mo4
NT1	alloy-ni80fe16mo4
NT1	alloy-ni94mn3al2

NT1	chromel
NT2	alloy-ni60fe24cr16
NT2	alloy-ni80cr20
NT2	alloy-ni85cr15
NT1	colmonoy
NT1	hastelloys
NT2	alloy-ni49cr22fe18mo9
NT2	alloy-ni50cr22fe18mo9
NT2	alloy-ni54mo17cr17fe6w4
NT2	alloy-ni62cr16mo15fe3
NT2	alloy-ni65mo28fe5
NT2	alloy-ni70mo17cr7fe5
NT1	inconel alloys
NT2	alloy-ni41fe40cr16nb3
NT2	alloy-ni46cr23co19ti5al4
NT2	alloy-ni47cr25co12w9fe3
NT2	alloy-ni48co28cr15al3mo3ti2
NT2	alloy-ni51cr48
NT2	alloy-ni53cr19fe19nb5mo3
NT2	alloy-ni54cr22co13mo9
NT2	alloy-ni59cr30fe9
NT2	alloy-ni60co15cr10al6ti5mo3
NT2	alloy-ni61cr16co9al3ti3w3
NT2	alloy-ni61cr22mo9nb4fe3
NT2	alloy-ni61cr23fe14
NT2	alloy-ni73cr15fe7ti3
NT2	alloy-ni73cr20mn3nb3
NT2	alloy-ni74cr13al6mo4
NT2	alloy-ni75cr12al6mo5
NT2	alloy-ni76cr15fe8
NT2	alloy-ni78cr16al4
NT1	monel
NT2	alloy-ni66cu32
NT1	nimonic
NT2	alloy-ni43fe33cr16mo3
NT2	alloy-ni48cr22fe18mo9
NT2	alloy-ni50co20cr15al5mo5
NT2	alloy-ni59cr20co17ti2
NT2	alloy-ni65cr25mo10
NT2	alloy-ni76cr15fe8
NT2	alloy-ni76cr20ti2
NT1	td-nickel chromium
NT1	udimet alloys
NT2	alloy-ni53co19cr15mo5al4ti3

NICKEL BORIDES [167; 167]

BT1	borides
BT2	boron compounds
BT1	nickel compounds
BT2	transition element compounds

NICKEL BROMIDES [13; 13]

BT1	bromides
BT2	bromine compounds
BT3	halogen compounds
BT2	halides
BT3	halogen compounds
BT1	nickel compounds
BT2	transition element compounds

NICKEL CARBIDES [51; 51]

BT1	carbides
BT2	carbon compounds
BT1	nickel compounds
BT2	transition element compounds

NICKEL CARBONATES [9; 9]

BT1	carbonates
BT2	carbon compounds
BT2	oxygen compounds
BT1	nickel compounds
BT2	transition element compounds

NICKEL CHLORIDES [111; 111]

BT1	chlorides
BT2	chlorine compounds
BT3	halogen compounds
BT2	halides
BT3	halogen compounds
BT1	nickel compounds
BT2	transition element compounds

nickel chromium-td
USE   td-nickel chromium

NICKEL COMPLEXES [396; 396]

BT1	transition element complexes
BT2	complexes

NICKEL COMPOUNDS [887; 2,572]

BT1	transition element compounds
NT1	nickel arsenides
NT1	nickel borides
NT1	nickel bromides
NT1	nickel carbides
NT1	nickel carbonates
NT1	nickel chlorides
NT1	nickel fluorides
NT1	nickel hydrides
NT1	nickel hydroxides
NT1	nickel iodides
NT1	nickel nitrates
NT1	nickel nitrides
NT1	nickel oxides
NT1	nickel phosphates
NT1	nickel phosphides
NT1	nickel selenides
NT1	nickel silicates
NT1	nickel silicides
NT1	nickel sulfates
NT1	nickel sulfides
NT1	nickel tellurides
NT1	nickel tungstates
NT1	nickelates
RT	nickel additions

NICKEL FLUORIDES [110; 110]

BT1	fluorides
BT2	fluorine compounds
BT3	halogen compounds
BT2	halides
BT3	halogen compounds
BT1	nickel compounds
BT2	transition element compounds

NICKEL HYDRIDES [139; 139]

BT1	hydrides
BT2	hydrogen compounds
BT1	nickel compounds
BT2	transition element compounds

NICKEL HYDROXIDES [29; 29]

BT1	hydroxides
BT2	hydrogen compounds
BT2	oxygen compounds
BT1	nickel compounds
BT2	transition element compounds

NICKEL IODIDES [20; 20]

BT1	iodides
BT2	halides
BT3	halogen compounds
BT2	iodine compounds
BT3	halogen compounds
BT1	nickel compounds
BT2	transition element compounds

NICKEL IONS [1,021; 1,021]

BT1	ions
BT2	charged particles

NICKEL ISOTOPES [405; 3,403]

NT1	nickel 53
NT1	nickel 54
NT1	nickel 55
NT1	nickel 56
NT1	nickel 57
NT1	nickel 58
NT1	nickel 59
NT1	nickel 60
NT1	nickel 61
NT1	nickel 62
NT1	nickel 63
NT1	nickel 64
NT1	nickel 65
NT1	nickel 66
NT1	nickel 67
NT1	nickel 68
NT1	nickel 69
NT1	nickel 71
NT1	nickel 72
NT1	nickel 73

NT1 nickel 78

NICKEL NITRATES [24; 24]
BT1 nickel compounds
BT2 transition element compounds
BT1 nitrates
BT2 nitrogen compounds
BT2 oxygen compounds

NICKEL NITRIDES [6; 6]
BT1 nickel compounds
BT2 transition element compounds
BT1 nitrides
BT2 nitrogen compounds
BT2 pnictides

NICKEL ORES [65; 65]
BT1 ores

NICKEL OXIDES [675; 675]
BT1 nickel compounds
BT2 transition element compounds
BT1 oxides
BT2 chalcogenides
BT2 oxygen compounds
RT nickelates

NICKEL PHOSPHATES [9; 9]
BT1 nickel compounds
BT2 transition element compounds
BT1 phosphates
BT2 oxygen compounds
BT2 phosphorus compounds

NICKEL PHOSPHIDES [63; 63] *Jan 76*
BT1 nickel compounds
BT2 transition element compounds
BT1 phosphides
BT2 phosphorus compounds
BT2 pnictides

→ **NICKEL SELENIDES** [0; 0] *Sep 91*
BT1 nickel compounds
BT2 transition element compounds
BT1 selenides
BT2 chalcogenides
BT2 selenium compounds

NICKEL SILICATES [4; 4]
BT1 nickel compounds
BT2 transition element compounds
BT1 silicates
BT2 oxygen compounds
BT2 silicon compounds

NICKEL SILICIDES [147; 147] *Jan 76*
BT1 nickel compounds
BT2 transition element compounds
BT1 silicides
BT2 silicon compounds

nickel silver
USE german silver

nickel steels
(Steels containing Ni as main alloying element. Prior to November 1983 this was a valid descriptor, and older material is so indexed. Coordinate descriptor below with most specific appropriate term from STEELS hierarchy.)
USE nickel alloys

NICKEL SULFATES [71; 71]
BT1 nickel compounds
BT2 transition element compounds
BT1 sulfates
BT2 oxygen compounds
BT2 sulfur compounds

NICKEL SULFIDES [108; 108]
BT1 nickel compounds
BT2 transition element compounds
BT1 sulfides
BT2 chalcogenides
BT2 sulfur compounds

NICKEL TELLURIDES [13; 13] *Jul 84*
BT1 nickel compounds
BT2 transition element compounds
BT1 tellurides
BT2 chalcogenides
BT2 tellurium compounds

→ **NICKEL TUNGSTATES** [0; 0] *Sep 91*
BT1 nickel compounds
BT2 transition element compounds
BT1 tungstates
BT2 oxygen compounds
BT2 tungsten compounds
BT3 transition element compounds

NICKEL 53 [8; 8] *May 76*
BT1 beta-plus decay radioisotopes
BT2 beta decay radioisotopes
BT3 radioisotopes
BT4 isotopes
BT1 even-odd nuclei
BT2 nuclei
BT1 intermediate mass nuclei
BT2 nuclei
BT1 millisec living radioisotopes
BT2 radioisotopes
BT3 isotopes
BT1 nickel isotopes

NICKEL 54 [10; 10] *Feb 78*
BT1 even-even nuclei
BT2 nuclei
BT1 intermediate mass nuclei
BT2 nuclei
BT1 nickel isotopes

NICKEL 55 [19; 19]
BT1 beta-plus decay radioisotopes
BT2 beta decay radioisotopes
BT3 radioisotopes
BT4 isotopes
BT1 even-odd nuclei
BT2 nuclei
BT1 intermediate mass nuclei
BT2 nuclei
BT1 millisec living radioisotopes
BT2 radioisotopes
BT3 isotopes
BT1 nickel isotopes

NICKEL 56 [287; 287]
BT1 days living radioisotopes
BT2 radioisotopes
BT3 isotopes
BT1 electron capture radioisotopes
BT2 beta decay radioisotopes
BT3 radioisotopes
BT4 isotopes
BT1 even-even nuclei
BT2 nuclei
BT1 intermediate mass nuclei
BT2 nuclei
BT1 nickel isotopes

NICKEL 57 [182; 182]
BT1 beta-plus decay radioisotopes
BT2 beta decay radioisotopes
BT3 radioisotopes
BT4 isotopes
BT1 days living radioisotopes
BT2 radioisotopes
BT3 isotopes
BT1 electron capture radioisotopes
BT2 beta decay radioisotopes
BT3 radioisotopes
BT4 isotopes
BT1 even-odd nuclei

BT2 nuclei
BT1 intermediate mass nuclei
BT2 nuclei
BT1 nickel isotopes

NICKEL 57 TARGET [3; 3] *Dec 85*
BT1 targets

NICKEL 58 [1,071; 1,071]
BT1 even-even nuclei
BT2 nuclei
BT1 intermediate mass nuclei
BT2 nuclei
BT1 nickel isotopes
BT1 stable isotopes
BT2 isotopes

NICKEL 58 BEAMS [120; 120] *Oct 76*
BT1 ion beams
BT2 beams

NICKEL 58 REACTIONS [436; 436]
BT1 heavy ion reactions
BT2 nuclear reactions

NICKEL 58 TARGET [2,210; 2,210]
BT1 targets

NICKEL 59 [283; 283]
BT1 electron capture radioisotopes
BT2 beta decay radioisotopes
BT3 radioisotopes
BT4 isotopes
BT1 even-odd nuclei
BT2 nuclei
BT1 intermediate mass nuclei
BT2 nuclei
BT1 nickel isotopes
BT1 years living radioisotopes
BT2 radioisotopes
BT3 isotopes

NICKEL 59 REACTIONS [3; 3] *Jun 84*
BT1 heavy ion reactions
BT2 nuclear reactions

NICKEL 59 TARGET [32; 32]
BT1 targets

NICKEL 60 [628; 628]
BT1 even-even nuclei
BT2 nuclei
BT1 intermediate mass nuclei
BT2 nuclei
BT1 nickel isotopes
BT1 stable isotopes
BT2 isotopes

NICKEL 60 BEAMS [20; 20] *Jan 79*
BT1 ion beams
BT2 beams

NICKEL 60 REACTIONS [52; 52] *Oct 76*
BT1 heavy ion reactions
BT2 nuclear reactions

NICKEL 60 TARGET [778; 778]
BT1 targets

NICKEL 61 [186; 186]
BT1 even-odd nuclei
BT2 nuclei
BT1 intermediate mass nuclei
BT2 nuclei
BT1 nickel isotopes
BT1 stable isotopes
BT2 isotopes

NICKEL 61 REACTIONS [3; 3] *Dec 86*
BT1 heavy ion reactions
BT2 nuclear reactions

NICKEL 61 TARGET [101; 101]
BT1 targets

NICKEL 62 [339; 339]
BT1 even-even nuclei
BT2 nuclei
BT1 intermediate mass nuclei
BT2 nuclei
BT1 nickel isotopes
BT1 stable isotopes
BT2 isotopes

NICKEL 62 TARGET [462; 462]
BT1 targets

NICKEL 63 [427; 427]
BT1 beta-minus decay radioisotopes
BT2 beta decay radioisotopes
BT3 radioisotopes
BT4 isotopes
BT1 even-odd nuclei
BT2 nuclei
BT1 intermediate mass nuclei
BT2 nuclei
BT1 nickel isotopes
BT1 years living radioisotopes
BT2 radioisotopes
BT3 isotopes

NICKEL 64 [231; 231]
BT1 even-even nuclei
BT2 nuclei
BT1 intermediate mass nuclei
BT2 nuclei
BT1 nickel isotopes
BT1 stable isotopes
BT2 isotopes

NICKEL 64 REACTIONS [119; 119]
Feb 78
BT1 heavy ion reactions
BT2 nuclear reactions

NICKEL 64 TARGET [602; 602]
BT1 targets

NICKEL 65 [97; 97]
BT1 beta-minus decay radioisotopes
BT2 beta decay radioisotopes
BT3 radioisotopes
BT4 isotopes
BT1 even-odd nuclei
BT2 nuclei
BT1 hours living radioisotopes
BT2 radioisotopes
BT3 isotopes
BT1 intermediate mass nuclei
BT2 nuclei
BT1 nickel isotopes

NICKEL 66 [32; 32]
BT1 beta-minus decay radioisotopes
BT2 beta decay radioisotopes
BT3 radioisotopes
BT4 isotopes
BT1 days living radioisotopes
BT2 radioisotopes
BT3 isotopes
BT1 even-even nuclei
BT2 nuclei
BT1 intermediate mass nuclei
BT2 nuclei
BT1 nickel isotopes

NICKEL 67 [20; 20]
BT1 beta-minus decay radioisotopes
BT2 beta decay radioisotopes
BT3 radioisotopes
BT4 isotopes
BT1 even-odd nuclei
BT2 nuclei
BT1 intermediate mass nuclei
BT2 nuclei
BT1 nickel isotopes
BT1 seconds living radioisotopes
BT2 radioisotopes
BT3 isotopes

NICKEL 68 [26; 26]
BT1 even-even nuclei
BT2 nuclei
BT1 intermediate mass nuclei
BT2 nuclei
BT1 nickel isotopes

NICKEL 69 [19; 19]
BT1 beta-minus decay radioisotopes
BT2 beta decay radioisotopes
BT3 radioisotopes
BT4 isotopes
BT1 even-odd nuclei
BT2 nuclei
BT1 intermediate mass nuclei
BT2 nuclei
BT1 nickel isotopes
BT1 seconds living radioisotopes
BT2 radioisotopes
BT3 isotopes

NICKEL 71 [2; 2] *May 90*
BT1 beta-minus decay radioisotopes
BT2 beta decay radioisotopes
BT3 radioisotopes
BT4 isotopes
BT1 even-odd nuclei
BT2 nuclei
BT1 intermediate mass nuclei
BT2 nuclei
BT1 nickel isotopes
BT1 seconds living radioisotopes
BT2 radioisotopes
BT3 isotopes

NICKEL 72 [2; 2] *May 90*
BT1 beta-minus decay radioisotopes
BT2 beta decay radioisotopes
BT3 radioisotopes
BT4 isotopes
BT1 even-even nuclei
BT2 nuclei
BT1 intermediate mass nuclei
BT2 nuclei
BT1 nickel isotopes
BT1 seconds living radioisotopes
BT2 radioisotopes
BT3 isotopes

NICKEL 73 [2; 2] *May 90*
BT1 beta-minus decay radioisotopes
BT2 beta decay radioisotopes
BT3 radioisotopes
BT4 isotopes
BT1 even-odd nuclei
BT2 nuclei
BT1 intermediate mass nuclei
BT2 nuclei
BT1 millisec living radioisotopes
BT2 radioisotopes
BT3 isotopes
BT1 nickel isotopes

NICKEL 74 [0; 0] *Aug 90*
BT1 beta-minus decay radioisotopes
BT2 beta decay radioisotopes
BT3 radioisotopes
BT4 isotopes
BT1 even-even nuclei
BT2 nuclei
BT1 intermediate mass nuclei
BT2 nuclei
BT1 seconds living radioisotopes
BT2 radioisotopes
BT3 isotopes

NICKEL 78 [11; 11] *Nov 80*
BT1 even-even nuclei
BT2 nuclei
BT1 intermediate mass nuclei
BT2 nuclei
BT1 nickel isotopes

nickel-chromium steels
(Steels containing Ni and Cr as main alloying elements; Ni content is higher than Cr content. Prior to November 1983 this was a valid descriptor, and older material is so indexed.)
USE chromium-nickel steels

NICKELATES [18; 18]
(Specific compounds should be indexed by coordination of a descriptor of the form (CATION) COMPOUNDS and the above anion descriptor.)
BT1 nickel compounds
BT2 transition element compounds
BT1 oxygen compounds
RT nickel oxides

NICOTIANA [209; 209]
UF *tobacco plant*
BT1 plants
RT tobacco

NICOTINAMIDE [117; 117]
UF *pp-factor*
UF *vitamin pp*
BT1 amides
BT2 organic nitrogen compounds
BT3 organic compounds
BT1 pyridines
BT2 azines
BT3 heterocyclic compounds
BT4 organic compounds
BT3 organic nitrogen compounds
BT4 organic compounds
BT1 vitamin b group
BT2 vitamins
RT heterocyclic acids
RT nad
RT nadh2
RT nadp
RT nicotinic acid

nicotinamide-aden dinucle phos
(Nicotinamide-Adenine Dinucleotide Phosphate)
USE nadp

nicotinamide-adenine dinucleot
(Nicotinamide-Adenine Dinucleotide)
USE nad

NICOTINE [116; 116]
BT1 alkaloids
BT2 organic compounds
BT1 pyridines
BT2 azines
BT3 heterocyclic compounds
BT4 organic compounds
BT3 organic nitrogen compounds
BT4 organic compounds
BT1 pyrrolidines
BT2 amines
BT3 organic compounds
BT2 pyrroles
BT3 azoles
BT4 heterocyclic compounds
BT5 organic compounds
BT4 organic nitrogen compounds
BT5 organic compounds

NICOTINIC ACID [63; 63] *Feb 76*
UF *niacin*
BT1 monocarboxylic acids
BT2 carboxylic acids
BT3 organic acids
BT4 organic compounds
BT1 pyridines
BT2 azines
BT3 heterocyclic compounds
BT4 organic compounds
BT3 organic nitrogen compounds
BT4 organic compounds
BT1 vitamin b group
BT2 vitamins
RT nicotinamide

NIEDERAICHBACH REACTOR [75; 75]
UF   *kernkraftwerk niederaichbach*
UF   *kkn reactor*
BT1   enriched uranium reactors
BT2   reactors
BT1   hwgcr type reactors
BT2   gas cooled reactors
BT3   reactors
BT2   heavy water moderated reactors
BT3   reactors
BT1   pressure tube reactors
BT2   power reactors
BT3   reactors
BT1   thermal reactors
BT2   reactors

niels bohr institute cyclotron
USE   nbi cyclotron

NIFLEX PROCESS [0; 0]
BT1   reprocessing
BT2   separation processes
RT   solvent extraction

nigella
USE   ranunculaceae

NIGER [55; 55]
BT1   africa
BT1   developing countries

NIGER RIVER [3; 3] *Jul 76*
BT1   rivers
BT2   surface waters

NIGERIA [93; 93]
BT1   africa
BT1   developing countries

NIGHT SKY [183; 183] *Apr 84*
(Prior to December 1990, this concept was indexed by NIGHTTIME plus other descriptors from the wordblock EARTH ATMOSPHERE.)
UF   *nighttime (sky)*
RT   aurorae
RT   daily variations

nightglow
USE   airglow

nighttime (sky)
USE   night sky

nii (uk)
(Nuclear Installations Inspectorate.)
USE   uk nii

NIKHEF [81; 81] *Jul 77*
(National Instituut voor Kernfysica en Hoge-energiefysica.)
UF   *nat. inst. kern. hoge-energief*
BT1   netherlands organizations
BT2   national organizations

NILE RIVER [15; 15]
BT1   rivers
BT2   surface waters

nilsson model
USE   nilsson-mottelson model

nilsson potential
USE   nilsson-mottelson model

nilsson scheme
USE   nilsson-mottelson model

NILSSON-MOTTELSON MODEL [1,363; 1,363]
UF   *approximation (bohr)*
UF   *bohr approximation*
UF   *bohr-mottelson model*
UF   *mottelson-nilsson model*
UF   *nilsson model*
UF   *nilsson potential*
UF   *nilsson scheme*
BT1   nuclear models
BT2   mathematical models

nim
USE   nuclear instrument modules

NIMBUS SATELLITES [14; 14] *Sep 83*
BT1   satellites

NIMONIC [119; 745]
(For unspecified Nimonic alloys.)
BT1   nickel base alloys
BT2   nickel alloys
BT3   alloys
NT1   alloy-ni43fe33cr16mo3
NT1   alloy-ni48cr22fe18mo9
NT1   alloy-ni50co20cr15al5mo5
NT1   alloy-ni59cr20co17ti2
NT1   alloy-ni65cr25mo10
NT1   alloy-ni76cr15fe8
NT1   alloy-ni76cr20ti2
RT   inconel alloys

nimonic pe13
USE   alloy-ni48cr22fe18mo9

nimonic pe16
USE   alloy-ni43fe33cr16mo3

nimonic 105
USE   alloy-ni50co20cr15al5mo5

nimonic 80a
USE   alloy-ni76cr20ti2

nimonic 86
USE   alloy-ni65cr25mo10

nimonic 90
USE   alloy-ni59cr20co17ti2

NIMROD [117; 117]
UF   *harwell synchrotron*
BT1   synchrotrons
BT2   cyclic accelerators
BT3   accelerators

NINA [82; 82]
UF   *daresbury synchrotron*
BT1   synchrotrons
BT2   cyclic accelerators
BT3   accelerators

NINE MILE POINT-1 REACTOR [114; 114]
(Scriba, New York, USA)
UF   *scriba nuclear power plant*
BT1   bwr type reactors
BT2   enriched uranium reactors
BT3   reactors
BT2   power reactors
BT3   reactors
BT2   thermal reactors
BT3   reactors
BT2   water cooled reactors
BT3   reactors
BT2   water moderated reactors
BT3   reactors

NINE MILE POINT-2 REACTOR [67; 67]
(Scriba, New York, USA)
UF   *osweso nuclear power plant*
BT1   bwr type reactors
BT2   enriched uranium reactors
BT3   reactors
BT2   power reactors
BT3   reactors
BT2   thermal reactors
BT3   reactors
BT2   water cooled reactors
BT3   reactors
BT2   water moderated reactors
BT3   reactors

NINGYOITE [13; 13]
BT1   phosphate minerals
BT2   minerals
BT1   uranium minerals
BT2   radioactive minerals
BT3   minerals
BT3   radioactive materials
BT4   materials
RT   uranium phosphates

NINHYDRIN [11; 11]
UF   *triketohydrindane*
BT1   ketones
BT2   organic compounds
BT1   reagents
RT   aromatics

NIOBATES [1,321; 1,321]
(Specific compounds should be indexed by coordination of a descriptor of the form (CATION) COMPOUNDS and the above anion descriptor.)
BT1   niobium compounds
BT2   transition element compounds
BT1   oxygen compounds

NIOBIUM [6,908; 6,921]
UF   *columbium*
BT1   transition elements
BT2   metals
BT3   elements
NT1   niobium-alpha
NT1   niobium-beta

NIOBIUM ADDITIONS [826; 1,380]
(Alloys containing not more than 1% Nb are listed here.)
NT1   alloy-fe31cr21co20ni20mo3w2
NT1   alloy-fe36ni33cr26
NT1   alloy-ni45fe34cr20
NT1   alloy-ni46cr23co19ti5al4
NT1   alloy-ni61cr16co9al3ti3w3
NT1   alloy-ni73cr15fe7ti3
NT1   steel-cr16ni13monbv
NT1   steel-cr16ni15mo3nb
NT1   steel-cr16ni16monb
NT1   steel-cr17cu4ni4nb-l
NT1   steel-cr17ni12monb
NT1   steel-cr18ni11nb
NT1   steel-cr18ni11nbco
NT1   steel-cr2moninb
NT1   steel-cr9monbv
RT   niobium alloys
RT   niobium compounds

NIOBIUM ALLOYS [5,120; 8,459]
(Alloys containing more than 1% Nb.)
BT1   alloys
NT1   alloy-fe48cr24ni24
NT1   alloy-ni41fe40cr16nb3
NT1   alloy-ni47cr25co12w9fe3
NT1   alloy-ni53cr19fe19nb5mo3
NT1   alloy-ni58cr14co8al4mo4nb4w4
NT1   alloy-ni60mo13co9cr8nb4al3
NT1   alloy-ni61cr22mo9nb4fe3
NT1   alloy-ni73cr20mn3nb3
NT1   alloy-ni74cr13al6mo4
NT1   alloy-ni75cr12al6mo5
NT1   alloy-u90nb7zr3
NT1   alloy-zr97nb3
NT1   niobium base alloys
NT2   alloy-nb94mo4

RT   niobium additions

NIOBIUM ARSENIDES [4; 4] *Aug 82*
  BT1   arsenides
   BT2   arsenic compounds
   BT2   pnictides
  BT1   niobium compounds
   BT2   transition element compounds

NIOBIUM BASE ALLOYS [2,204; 2,225]
  BT1   niobium alloys
   BT2   alloys
  NT1   alloy-nb94mo4

NIOBIUM BORIDES [65; 65]
  BT1   borides
   BT2   boron compounds
  BT1   niobium compounds
   BT2   transition element compounds

NIOBIUM BROMIDES [40; 40]
  BT1   bromides
   BT2   bromine compounds
    BT3   halogen compounds
   BT2   halides
    BT3   halogen compounds
  BT1   niobium compounds
   BT2   transition element compounds

NIOBIUM CARBIDES [780; 780]
  BT1   carbides
   BT2   carbon compounds
  BT1   niobium compounds
   BT2   transition element compounds

NIOBIUM CHLORIDES [210; 210]
  BT1   chlorides
   BT2   chlorine compounds
    BT3   halogen compounds
   BT2   halides
    BT3   halogen compounds
  BT1   niobium compounds
   BT2   transition element compounds

NIOBIUM COMPLEXES [485; 485]
  BT1   transition element complexes
   BT2   complexes

NIOBIUM COMPOUNDS [1,005; 6,168]
  BT1   transition element compounds
  NT1   niobates
  NT1   niobium arsenides
  NT1   niobium borides
  NT1   niobium bromides
  NT1   niobium carbides
  NT1   niobium chlorides
  NT1   niobium fluorides
  NT1   niobium hydrides
  NT1   niobium hydroxides
  NT1   niobium iodides
  NT1   niobium nitrates
  NT1   niobium nitrides
  NT1   niobium oxides
  NT1   niobium phosphates
  NT1   niobium phosphides
  NT1   niobium selenides
  NT1   niobium silicates
  NT1   niobium silicides
  NT1   niobium sulfates
  NT1   niobium sulfides
  NT1   niobium tellurides
  RT   niobium additions

NIOBIUM FLUORIDES [97; 97]
  BT1   fluorides
   BT2   fluorine compounds
    BT3   halogen compounds
   BT2   halides
    BT3   halogen compounds
  BT1   niobium compounds
   BT2   transition element compounds

NIOBIUM HYDRIDES [317; 317]
  BT1   hydrides
   BT2   hydrogen compounds
  BT1   niobium compounds
   BT2   transition element compounds

NIOBIUM HYDROXIDES [50; 50]
  BT1   hydroxides
   BT2   hydrogen compounds
   BT2   oxygen compounds
  BT1   niobium compounds
   BT2   transition element compounds

NIOBIUM IODIDES [32; 32]
  BT1   iodides
   BT2   halides
    BT3   halogen compounds
   BT2   iodine compounds
    BT3   halogen compounds
  BT1   niobium compounds
   BT2   transition element compounds

NIOBIUM IONS [177; 177]
  BT1   ions
   BT2   charged particles

NIOBIUM ISOTOPES [98; 1,877]
  NT1   niobium 100
  NT1   niobium 101
  NT1   niobium 102
  NT1   niobium 103
  NT1   niobium 104
  NT1   niobium 105
  NT1   niobium 106
  NT1   niobium 83
  NT1   niobium 84
  NT1   niobium 85
  NT1   niobium 86
  NT1   niobium 87
  NT1   niobium 88
  NT1   niobium 89
  NT1   niobium 90
  NT1   niobium 91
  NT1   niobium 92
  NT1   niobium 93
  NT1   niobium 94
  NT1   niobium 95
  NT1   niobium 96
  NT1   niobium 97
  NT1   niobium 98
  NT1   niobium 99

NIOBIUM NITRATES [4; 4]
  BT1   niobium compounds
   BT2   transition element compounds
  BT1   nitrates
   BT2   nitrogen compounds
   BT2   oxygen compounds

NIOBIUM NITRIDES [568; 568]
  BT1   niobium compounds
   BT2   transition element compounds
  BT1   nitrides
   BT2   nitrogen compounds
   BT2   pnictides

NIOBIUM ORES [37; 37]
  BT1   ores

NIOBIUM OXIDES [1,532; 1,534]
  BT1   niobium compounds
   BT2   transition element compounds
  BT1   oxides
   BT2   chalcogenides
   BT2   oxygen compounds
  RT   aeschynite
  RT   hatchettolite
  RT   oxide minerals

NIOBIUM PHOSPHATES [26; 26]
  BT1   niobium compounds
   BT2   transition element compounds
  BT1   phosphates
   BT2   oxygen compounds
   BT2   phosphorus compounds

→ **NIOBIUM PHOSPHIDES** [0; 0] *Sep 91*
  BT1   niobium compounds
   BT2   transition element compounds
  BT1   phosphides
   BT2   phosphorus compounds
   BT2   pnictides

NIOBIUM SELENIDES [280; 280]
  BT1   niobium compounds
   BT2   transition element compounds
  BT1   selenides
   BT2   chalcogenides
   BT2   selenium compounds

NIOBIUM SILICATES [6; 6]
  BT1   niobium compounds
   BT2   transition element compounds
  BT1   silicates
   BT2   oxygen compounds
   BT2   silicon compounds
  RT   silicate minerals

NIOBIUM SILICIDES [82; 82] *Jan 76*
  BT1   niobium compounds
   BT2   transition element compounds
  BT1   silicides
   BT2   silicon compounds

NIOBIUM SULFATES [13; 13]
  BT1   niobium compounds
   BT2   transition element compounds
  BT1   sulfates
   BT2   oxygen compounds
   BT2   sulfur compounds

NIOBIUM SULFIDES [107; 107]
  BT1   niobium compounds
   BT2   transition element compounds
  BT1   sulfides
   BT2   chalcogenides
   BT2   sulfur compounds

NIOBIUM TELLURIDES [19; 19] *May 79*
  BT1   niobium compounds
   BT2   transition element compounds
  BT1   tellurides
   BT2   chalcogenides
   BT2   tellurium compounds

NIOBIUM 100 [17; 17]
  BT1   beta-minus decay radioisotopes
   BT2   beta decay radioisotopes
    BT3   radioisotopes
     BT4   isotopes
  BT1   intermediate mass nuclei
   BT2   nuclei
  BT1   niobium isotopes
  BT1   odd-odd nuclei
   BT2   nuclei
  BT1   seconds living radioisotopes
   BT2   radioisotopes
    BT3   isotopes

NIOBIUM 101 [21; 21]
  BT1   beta-minus decay radioisotopes
   BT2   beta decay radioisotopes
    BT3   radioisotopes
     BT4   isotopes
  BT1   intermediate mass nuclei
   BT2   nuclei
  BT1   niobium isotopes
  BT1   odd-even nuclei
   BT2   nuclei
  BT1   seconds living radioisotopes
   BT2   radioisotopes
    BT3   isotopes

NIOBIUM 102 [17; 17]
  BT1   beta-minus decay radioisotopes
   BT2   beta decay radioisotopes
    BT3   radioisotopes
     BT4   isotopes
  BT1   intermediate mass nuclei
   BT2   nuclei
  BT1   niobium isotopes
  BT1   odd-odd nuclei

BT2   nuclei
BT1   seconds living radioisotopes
BT2   radioisotopes
BT3   isotopes

NIOBIUM 103 [20; 20]
BT1   beta-minus decay radioisotopes
BT2   beta decay radioisotopes
BT3   radioisotopes
BT4   isotopes
BT1   intermediate mass nuclei
BT2   nuclei
BT1   niobium isotopes
BT1   odd-even nuclei
BT2   nuclei
BT1   seconds living radioisotopes
BT2   radioisotopes
BT3   isotopes

NIOBIUM 104 [13; 13] *Nov 76*
BT1   beta-minus decay radioisotopes
BT2   beta decay radioisotopes
BT3   radioisotopes
BT4   isotopes
BT1   intermediate mass nuclei
BT2   nuclei
BT1   niobium isotopes
BT1   odd-odd nuclei
BT2   nuclei
BT1   seconds living radioisotopes
BT2   radioisotopes
BT3   isotopes

NIOBIUM 105 [8; 8]
BT1   beta-minus decay radioisotopes
BT2   beta decay radioisotopes
BT3   radioisotopes
BT4   isotopes
BT1   intermediate mass nuclei
BT2   nuclei
BT1   niobium isotopes
BT1   odd-even nuclei
BT2   nuclei
BT1   seconds living radioisotopes
BT2   radioisotopes
BT3   isotopes

NIOBIUM 106 [3; 3] *Jul 81*
BT1   beta-minus decay radioisotopes
BT2   beta decay radioisotopes
BT3   radioisotopes
BT4   isotopes
BT1   intermediate mass nuclei
BT2   nuclei
BT1   niobium isotopes
BT1   odd-odd nuclei
BT2   nuclei
BT1   seconds living radioisotopes
BT2   radioisotopes
BT3   isotopes

NIOBIUM 83 [3; 3] *Oct 88*
BT1   beta-plus decay radioisotopes
BT2   beta decay radioisotopes
BT3   radioisotopes
BT4   isotopes
BT1   intermediate mass nuclei
BT2   nuclei
BT1   niobium isotopes
BT1   odd-even nuclei
BT2   nuclei
BT1   seconds living radioisotopes
BT2   radioisotopes
BT3   isotopes

NIOBIUM 84 [7; 7] *Nov 77*
BT1   beta-plus decay radioisotopes
BT2   beta decay radioisotopes
BT3   radioisotopes
BT4   isotopes
BT1   electron capture radioisotopes
BT2   beta decay radioisotopes
BT3   radioisotopes
BT4   isotopes
BT1   intermediate mass nuclei
BT2   nuclei

BT1   niobium isotopes
BT1   odd-odd nuclei
BT2   nuclei
BT1   seconds living radioisotopes
BT2   radioisotopes
BT3   isotopes

NIOBIUM 85 [5; 5] *Apr 80*
BT1   beta decay radioisotopes
BT2   radioisotopes
BT3   isotopes
BT1   intermediate mass nuclei
BT2   nuclei
BT1   minutes living radioisotopes
BT2   radioisotopes
BT3   isotopes
BT1   niobium isotopes
BT1   odd-even nuclei
BT2   nuclei
BT1   seconds living radioisotopes
BT2   radioisotopes
BT3   isotopes

NIOBIUM 86 [9; 9]
BT1   electron capture radioisotopes
BT2   beta decay radioisotopes
BT3   radioisotopes
BT4   isotopes
BT1   intermediate mass nuclei
BT2   nuclei
BT1   minutes living radioisotopes
BT2   radioisotopes
BT3   isotopes
BT1   niobium isotopes
BT1   odd-odd nuclei
BT2   nuclei

NIOBIUM 87 [11; 11]
BT1   beta-plus decay radioisotopes
BT2   beta decay radioisotopes
BT3   radioisotopes
BT4   isotopes
BT1   electron capture radioisotopes
BT2   beta decay radioisotopes
BT3   radioisotopes
BT4   isotopes
BT1   intermediate mass nuclei
BT2   nuclei
BT1   minutes living radioisotopes
BT2   radioisotopes
BT3   isotopes
BT1   niobium isotopes
BT1   odd-even nuclei
BT2   nuclei

NIOBIUM 88 [8; 8]
BT1   beta-plus decay radioisotopes
BT2   beta decay radioisotopes
BT3   radioisotopes
BT4   isotopes
BT1   electron capture radioisotopes
BT2   beta decay radioisotopes
BT3   radioisotopes
BT4   isotopes
BT1   intermediate mass nuclei
BT2   nuclei
BT1   minutes living radioisotopes
BT2   radioisotopes
BT3   isotopes
BT1   niobium isotopes
BT1   odd-odd nuclei
BT2   nuclei

NIOBIUM 89 [30; 30]
BT1   beta-plus decay radioisotopes
BT2   beta decay radioisotopes
BT3   radioisotopes
BT4   isotopes
BT1   hours living radioisotopes
BT2   radioisotopes
BT3   isotopes
BT1   intermediate mass nuclei
BT2   nuclei
BT1   niobium isotopes
BT1   odd-even nuclei
BT2   nuclei

NIOBIUM 90 [177; 177]
BT1   beta-plus decay radioisotopes
BT2   beta decay radioisotopes
BT3   radioisotopes
BT4   isotopes
BT1   electron capture radioisotopes
BT2   beta decay radioisotopes
BT3   radioisotopes
BT4   isotopes
BT1   hours living radioisotopes
BT2   radioisotopes
BT3   isotopes
BT1   intermediate mass nuclei
BT2   nuclei
BT1   isomeric transition isotopes
BT2   radioisotopes
BT3   isotopes
BT1   niobium isotopes
BT1   odd-odd nuclei
BT2   nuclei
BT1   seconds living radioisotopes
BT2   radioisotopes
BT3   isotopes

NIOBIUM 91 [135; 135]
BT1   days living radioisotopes
BT2   radioisotopes
BT3   isotopes
BT1   electron capture radioisotopes
BT2   beta decay radioisotopes
BT3   radioisotopes
BT4   isotopes
BT1   intermediate mass nuclei
BT2   nuclei
BT1   internal conversion radioisoto
BT2   radioisotopes
BT3   isotopes
BT1   isomeric transition isotopes
BT2   radioisotopes
BT3   isotopes
BT1   niobium isotopes
BT1   odd-even nuclei
BT2   nuclei
BT1   years living radioisotopes
BT2   radioisotopes
BT3   isotopes

NIOBIUM 92 [148; 148]
BT1   beta-plus decay radioisotopes
BT2   beta decay radioisotopes
BT3   radioisotopes
BT4   isotopes
BT1   days living radioisotopes
BT2   radioisotopes
BT3   isotopes
BT1   electron capture radioisotopes
BT2   beta decay radioisotopes
BT3   radioisotopes
BT4   isotopes
BT1   intermediate mass nuclei
BT2   nuclei
BT1   niobium isotopes
BT1   odd-odd nuclei
BT2   nuclei
BT1   years living radioisotopes
BT2   radioisotopes
BT3   isotopes

NIOBIUM 92 TARGET [4; 4] *May 88*
BT1   targets

NIOBIUM 93 [406; 406]
BT1   intermediate mass nuclei
BT2   nuclei
BT1   internal conversion radioisoto
BT2   radioisotopes
BT3   isotopes
BT1   isomeric transition isotopes
BT2   radioisotopes
BT3   isotopes
BT1   niobium isotopes
BT1   odd-even nuclei
BT2   nuclei
BT1   stable isotopes
BT2   isotopes
BT1   years living radioisotopes
BT2   radioisotopes
BT3   isotopes

NIOBIUM 93 REACTIONS [167; 167]
Jan 76
- BT1 heavy ion reactions
- BT2 nuclear reactions

NIOBIUM 93 TARGET [827; 827]
- BT1 targets

NIOBIUM 94 [119; 119]
- BT1 beta-minus decay radioisotopes
- BT2 beta decay radioisotopes
- BT3 radioisotopes
- BT4 isotopes
- BT1 intermediate mass nuclei
- BT2 nuclei
- BT1 internal conversion radioisoto
- BT2 radioisotopes
- BT3 isotopes
- BT1 isomeric transition isotopes
- BT2 radioisotopes
- BT3 isotopes
- BT1 minutes living radioisotopes
- BT2 radioisotopes
- BT3 isotopes
- BT1 niobium isotopes
- BT1 odd-odd nuclei
- BT2 nuclei
- BT1 years living radioisotopes
- BT2 radioisotopes
- BT3 isotopes

NIOBIUM 94 TARGET [7; 7] *Oct 76*
- BT1 targets

NIOBIUM 95 [686; 686]
- BT1 beta-minus decay radioisotopes
- BT2 beta decay radioisotopes
- BT3 radioisotopes
- BT4 isotopes
- BT1 days living radioisotopes
- BT2 radioisotopes
- BT3 isotopes
- BT1 intermediate mass nuclei
- BT2 nuclei
- BT1 isomeric transition isotopes
- BT2 radioisotopes
- BT3 isotopes
- BT1 niobium isotopes
- BT1 odd-even nuclei
- BT2 nuclei

NIOBIUM 95 TARGET [3; 3] *Nov 79*
- BT1 targets

NIOBIUM 96 [56; 56]
- BT1 beta-minus decay radioisotopes
- BT2 beta decay radioisotopes
- BT3 radioisotopes
- BT4 isotopes
- BT1 hours living radioisotopes
- BT2 radioisotopes
- BT3 isotopes
- BT1 intermediate mass nuclei
- BT2 nuclei
- BT1 niobium isotopes
- BT1 odd-odd nuclei
- BT2 nuclei

NIOBIUM 96 TARGET [5; 5] *Oct 76*
- BT1 targets

NIOBIUM 97 [58; 58]
- BT1 beta-minus decay radioisotopes
- BT2 beta decay radioisotopes
- BT3 radioisotopes
- BT4 isotopes
- BT1 hours living radioisotopes
- BT2 radioisotopes
- BT3 isotopes
- BT1 intermediate mass nuclei
- BT2 nuclei
- BT1 isomeric transition isotopes
- BT2 radioisotopes
- BT3 isotopes
- BT1 niobium isotopes
- BT1 odd-even nuclei

- BT2 nuclei
- BT1 seconds living radioisotopes
- BT2 radioisotopes
- BT3 isotopes

NIOBIUM 98 [19; 19]
- BT1 beta-minus decay radioisotopes
- BT2 beta decay radioisotopes
- BT3 radioisotopes
- BT4 isotopes
- BT1 intermediate mass nuclei
- BT2 nuclei
- BT1 minutes living radioisotopes
- BT2 radioisotopes
- BT3 isotopes
- BT1 niobium isotopes
- BT1 odd-odd nuclei
- BT2 nuclei
- BT1 seconds living radioisotopes
- BT2 radioisotopes
- BT3 isotopes

NIOBIUM 99 [28; 28]
- BT1 beta-minus decay radioisotopes
- BT2 beta decay radioisotopes
- BT3 radioisotopes
- BT4 isotopes
- BT1 intermediate mass nuclei
- BT2 nuclei
- BT1 minutes living radioisotopes
- BT2 radioisotopes
- BT3 isotopes
- BT1 niobium isotopes
- BT1 odd-even nuclei
- BT2 nuclei
- BT1 seconds living radioisotopes
- BT2 radioisotopes
- BT3 isotopes

NIOBIUM-ALPHA [8; 8]
- BT1 niobium
- BT2 transition elements
- BT3 metals
- BT4 elements

NIOBIUM-BETA [7; 7]
- BT1 niobium
- BT2 transition elements
- BT3 metals
- BT4 elements

NIPPOSTRONGYLUS [7; 7]
- BT1 nematodes
- BT2 invertebrates
- BT3 animals
- RT gastrointestinal tract
- RT rodents

NIRS CYCLOTRON [35; 35] *Dec 79*
(Installed at the National Institute of Radiological Science in Japan.)
- UF *nat. inst. radiol. sci. cyclo.*
- BT1 isochronous cyclotrons
- BT2 cyclotrons
- BT3 cyclic accelerators
- BT4 accelerators

NISUS FACILITY [15; 15]
- UF *neutr int stand uranium source*
- BT1 neutron sources
- BT2 particle sources
- BT3 radiation sources
- RT calibration standards
- RT fast neutrons
- RT measuring instruments

NITELLA [12; 12]
- BT1 algae
- BT2 plants

NITRATES [2,075; 6,986]
- BT1 nitrogen compounds
- BT1 oxygen compounds
- NT1 aluminium nitrates
- NT1 americium nitrates
- NT1 ammonium nitrates
- NT1 barium nitrates
- NT1 berkelium nitrates
- NT1 beryllium nitrates
- NT1 bismuth nitrates
- NT1 cadmium nitrates
- NT1 calcium nitrates
- NT1 californium nitrates
- NT1 cerium nitrates
- NT1 cesium nitrates
- NT1 chromium nitrates
- NT1 cobalt nitrates
- NT1 copper nitrates
- NT1 curium nitrates
- NT1 dysprosium nitrates
- NT1 einsteinium nitrates
- NT1 erbium nitrates
- NT1 europium nitrates
- NT1 gadolinium nitrates
- NT1 gallium nitrates
- NT1 hafnium nitrates
- NT1 holmium nitrates
- NT1 indium nitrates
- NT1 iron nitrates
- NT1 lanthanum nitrates
- NT1 lead nitrates
- NT1 lithium nitrates
- NT1 lutetium nitrates
- NT1 magnesium nitrates
- NT1 manganese nitrates
- NT1 mercury nitrates
- NT1 molybdenum nitrates
- NT1 neodymium nitrates
- NT1 neptunium nitrates
- NT1 nickel nitrates
- NT1 niobium nitrates
- NT1 palladium nitrates
- NT1 petn
- NT1 plutonium nitrates
- NT1 polonium nitrates
- NT1 potassium nitrates
- NT1 praseodymium nitrates
- NT1 promethium nitrates
- NT1 protactinium nitrates
- NT1 rubidium nitrates
- NT1 ruthenium nitrates
- NT1 samarium nitrates
- NT1 scandium nitrates
- NT1 silver nitrates
- NT1 sodium nitrates
- NT1 strontium nitrates
- NT1 tantalum nitrates
- NT1 tellurium nitrates
- NT1 terbium nitrates
- NT1 thallium nitrates
- NT1 thorium nitrates
- NT1 thulium nitrates
- NT1 titanium nitrates
- NT1 uranium nitrates
- NT1 uranyl nitrates
- NT2 unh
- NT1 vanadium nitrates
- NT1 ytterbium nitrates
- NT1 yttrium nitrates
- NT1 zinc nitrates
- NT1 zirconium nitrates
- RT nitric acid

§ **NITRATION** [40; 40] *Jul 78*
- BT1 chemical reactions
- RT nitro compounds

NITRIC ACID [4,463; 4,463]
- UF *hydrogen nitrates*
- BT1 inorganic acids
- BT2 hydrogen compounds
- BT2 inorganic compounds
- BT1 nitrogen compounds
- BT1 oxygen compounds
- RT aqua regia
- RT denitration
- RT nitrates

NITRIC ACID ESTERS [21; 350]
- BT1 esters
- BT2 organic compounds
- NT1 nitrocellulose
- NT1 petn

NITRIC OXIDE [305; 305] *Apr 84*
- BT1 nitrogen oxides
  - BT2 nitrogen compounds
  - BT2 oxides
    - BT3 chalcogenides
    - BT3 oxygen compounds

NITRIDATION [450; 450]
- BT1 chemical reactions
- RT nitrides

NITRIDES [641; 5,097]
- BT1 nitrogen compounds
- BT1 pnictides
- NT1 aluminium nitrides
- NT1 americium nitrides
- NT1 argon nitrides
- NT1 barium nitrides
- NT1 berkelium nitrides
- NT1 beryllium nitrides
- NT1 boron nitrides
- NT1 calcium nitrides
- NT1 californium nitrides
- NT1 carbon nitrides
- NT1 cerium nitrides
- NT1 cesium nitrides
- NT1 chromium nitrides
- NT1 copper nitrides
- NT1 curium nitrides
- NT1 dysprosium nitrides
- NT1 einsteinium nitrides
- NT1 erbium nitrides
- NT1 europium nitrides
- NT1 fermium nitrides
- NT1 gadolinium nitrides
- NT1 gallium nitrides
- NT1 germanium nitrides
- NT1 hafnium nitrides
- NT1 helium nitrides
- NT1 holmium nitrides
- NT1 indium nitrides
- NT1 iron nitrides
- NT1 lanthanum nitrides
- NT1 lead nitrides
- NT1 lithium nitrides
- NT1 magnesium nitrides
- NT1 manganese nitrides
- NT1 mendelevium nitrides
- NT1 molybdenum nitrides
- NT1 neodymium nitrides
- NT1 neptunium nitrides
- NT1 nickel nitrides
- NT1 niobium nitrides
- NT1 nobelium nitrides
- NT1 phosphorus nitrides
- NT1 plutonium nitrides
- NT1 potassium nitrides
- NT1 praseodymium nitrides
- NT1 rhenium nitrides
- NT1 ruthenium nitrides
- NT1 samarium nitrides
- NT1 scandium nitrides
- NT1 silicon nitrides
- NT1 silver nitrides
- NT1 sodium nitrides
- NT1 sulfur nitrides
- NT1 tantalum nitrides
- NT1 terbium nitrides
- NT1 thorium nitrides
- NT1 thulium nitrides
- NT1 tin nitrides
- NT1 titanium nitrides
- NT1 tungsten nitrides
- NT1 uranium nitrides
- NT1 vanadium nitrides
- NT1 ytterbium nitrides
- NT1 yttrium nitrides
- NT1 zirconium nitrides
- RT carbonitrides
- RT ceramics
- RT nitridation

NITRILES [652; 1,251]
- UF+ *ttf-tcnq*
- BT1 organic nitrogen compounds
  - BT2 organic compounds
- NT1 acetonitrile
- NT1 acrylonitrile
- RT carboxylic acids
- RT isonitriles

nitrilotriacetic acid
- USE nta

NITRITES [473; 473]
(Specific compounds should be indexed by coordination of a descriptor of the form (CATION) COMPOUNDS and the above anion descriptor.)
- BT1 nitrogen compounds
- BT1 oxygen compounds
- RT nitrous acid

NITRO COMPOUNDS [983; 2,401]
- UF+ *ndpp*
- UF+ *p-nitrodimethylaminopropiophen*
- BT1 organic nitrogen compounds
  - BT2 organic compounds
- NT1 dinitrophenol
- NT1 dpph
- NT1 metronidazole
- NT1 misonidazole
- NT1 nitrobenzene
- NT1 nitromethane
- NT1 nitrophenol
- NT1 picric acid
- NT1 sdpph
- NT1 tnt
- RT nitration

NITROBENZENE [333; 333]
- BT1 nitro compounds
  - BT2 organic nitrogen compounds
    - BT3 organic compounds
- RT benzene

NITROCELLULOSE [328; 328]
- UF *collodion*
- UF *gun cotton*
- UF *pyroxylin*
- BT1 nitric acid esters
  - BT2 esters
    - BT3 organic compounds
- BT1 polysaccharides
  - BT2 saccharides
    - BT3 carbohydrates
      - BT4 organic compounds
- RT celluloid
- RT explosives

NITROGEN [10,290; 10,371]
- UF *nitrogen nitrides*
- BT1 nonmetals
  - BT2 elements
- RT cryogenic fluids
- RT inert atmosphere
- RT kjeldahl method
- RT nitrogen fixation

NITROGEN ADDITIONS [619; 663]
- NT1 alloy-fe31cr21co20ni20mo3w2
- NT1 steel-cr17mn15nni
- NT1 steel-cr21mn9ni6
- NT1 steel-nicrmo

NITROGEN CARBIDES [9; 9]
- BT1 carbides
  - BT2 carbon compounds
- BT1 nitrogen compounds

NITROGEN CHLORIDES [7; 7]
- BT1 chlorides
  - BT2 chlorine compounds
    - BT3 halogen compounds
  - BT2 halides
    - BT3 halogen compounds
- BT1 nitrogen compounds

NITROGEN COMPLEXES [33; 33]
- BT1 complexes

NITROGEN COMPOUNDS [712; 21,164]
- NT1 azides
- NT1 carbonitrides
- NT1 cyanates
- *NT1 nitrates
- NT1 nitric acid
- *NT1 nitrides
- NT1 nitrites
- NT1 nitrogen carbides
- NT1 nitrogen chlorides
- NT1 nitrogen fluorides
- NT1 nitrogen hydrides
  - NT2 ammonia
- NT1 nitrogen iodides
- NT1 nitrogen oxides
  - NT2 nitric oxide
  - NT2 nitrogen dioxide
  - NT2 nitrous oxide
- NT1 nitrous acid
- RT organic nitrogen compounds

NITROGEN COOLED REACTORS [5; 26]
- UF *nitrogen-cooled reactors*
- BT1 gas cooled reactors
  - BT2 reactors
- NT1 htltr reactor

NITROGEN CYCLE [125; 125]
- RT fertilizers
- RT metabolism
- RT nitrogen fixation

NITROGEN DIOXIDE [323; 323] *Sep 77*
- BT1 nitrogen oxides
  - BT2 nitrogen compounds
  - BT2 oxides
    - BT3 chalcogenides
    - BT3 oxygen compounds

NITROGEN FIXATION [351; 351]
- UF *fixation (nitrogen)*
- RT air
- RT bacteria
- RT metabolism
- RT nitrogen
- RT nitrogen cycle
- RT nitrogenase
- RT plant growth
- RT soils

NITROGEN FLUORIDES [82; 82]
- BT1 fluorides
  - BT2 fluorine compounds
    - BT3 halogen compounds
  - BT2 halides
    - BT3 halogen compounds
- BT1 nitrogen compounds

NITROGEN HYDRIDES [110; 2,813]
- BT1 hydrides
  - BT2 hydrogen compounds
- BT1 nitrogen compounds
- NT1 ammonia

→ **NITROGEN IODIDES** [0; 0] *Sep 91*
- BT1 iodides
  - BT2 halides
    - BT3 halogen compounds
  - BT2 iodine compounds
    - BT3 halogen compounds
- BT1 nitrogen compounds

NITROGEN IONS [2,707; 2,707]
- BT1 ions
  - BT2 charged particles

NITROGEN ISOTOPES [366; 6,752]
- NT1 nitrogen 11
- NT1 nitrogen 12
- NT1 nitrogen 13
- NT1 nitrogen 14
- NT1 nitrogen 15
- NT1 nitrogen 16
- NT1 nitrogen 17
- NT1 nitrogen 18
- NT1 nitrogen 19

NT1 nitrogen 20
NT1 nitrogen 21
NT1 nitrogen 22
NT1 nitrogen 23

NITROGEN MUSTARD [85; 85]
UF *bis-chloroethylamine*
UF *dichlorodiethylamine*
UF *mustard (nitrogen)*
BT1 alkylating agents
BT2 antimitotic drugs
BT3 drugs
BT1 amines
BT2 organic compounds
BT1 organic chlorine compounds
BT2 organic halogen compounds
BT3 organic compounds
RT mutagens

nitrogen nitrides
USE nitrogen

NITROGEN OXIDES [2,682; 3,452]
BT1 nitrogen compounds
BT1 oxides
BT2 chalcogenides
BT2 oxygen compounds
NT1 nitric oxide
NT1 nitrogen dioxide
NT1 nitrous oxide

nitrogen sulfides
USE sulfur nitrides

NITROGEN TRANSFERASES [4; 83] Dec 86
BT1 transferases
BT2 enzymes
BT3 organic compounds
NT1 aminotransferases

NITROGEN 11 [7; 7]
BT1 light nuclei
BT2 nuclei
BT1 nitrogen isotopes
BT1 odd-even nuclei
BT2 nuclei

NITROGEN 12 [279; 279]
BT1 beta-plus decay radioisotopes
BT2 beta decay radioisotopes
BT3 radioisotopes
BT4 isotopes
BT1 light nuclei
BT2 nuclei
BT1 millisec living radioisotopes
BT2 radioisotopes
BT3 isotopes
BT1 nitrogen isotopes
BT1 odd-odd nuclei
BT2 nuclei

NITROGEN 12 TARGET [4; 4]
BT1 targets

NITROGEN 13 [1,365; 1,365]
BT1 beta-plus decay radioisotopes
BT2 beta decay radioisotopes
BT3 radioisotopes
BT4 isotopes
BT1 electron capture radioisotopes
BT2 beta decay radioisotopes
BT3 radioisotopes
BT4 isotopes
BT1 light nuclei
BT2 nuclei
BT1 minutes living radioisotopes
BT2 radioisotopes
BT3 isotopes
BT1 nitrogen isotopes
BT1 odd-even nuclei
BT2 nuclei

NITROGEN 13 BEAMS [6; 6] *Jan 84*
BT1 ion beams
BT2 beams

NITROGEN 13 TARGET [19; 19]
BT1 targets

NITROGEN 14 [1,489; 1,489]
BT1 light nuclei
BT2 nuclei
BT1 nitrogen isotopes
BT1 odd-odd nuclei
BT2 nuclei
BT1 stable isotopes
BT2 isotopes
RT nitrogen 14 beams

NITROGEN 14 BEAMS [342; 342]
BT1 ion beams
BT2 beams
RT nitrogen 14

NITROGEN 14 REACTIONS [1,090; 1,090]
BT1 heavy ion reactions
BT2 nuclear reactions

NITROGEN 14 TARGET [905; 905]
BT1 targets

NITROGEN 15 [3,123; 3,123]
BT1 light nuclei
BT2 nuclei
BT1 nitrogen isotopes
BT1 odd-even nuclei
BT2 nuclei
BT1 stable isotopes
BT2 isotopes

NITROGEN 15 BEAMS [41; 41] *May 80*
BT1 ion beams
BT2 beams

NITROGEN 15 REACTIONS [215; 215]
BT1 heavy ion reactions
BT2 nuclear reactions

NITROGEN 15 TARGET [387; 387]
BT1 targets

NITROGEN 16 [526; 526]
BT1 beta-minus decay radioisotopes
BT2 beta decay radioisotopes
BT3 radioisotopes
BT4 isotopes
BT1 light nuclei
BT2 nuclei
BT1 nitrogen isotopes
BT1 odd-odd nuclei
BT2 nuclei
BT1 seconds living radioisotopes
BT2 radioisotopes
BT3 isotopes

NITROGEN 16 TARGET [4; 4] *Sep 77*
BT1 targets

NITROGEN 17 [69; 69]
BT1 beta-minus decay radioisotopes
BT2 beta decay radioisotopes
BT3 radioisotopes
BT4 isotopes
BT1 light nuclei
BT2 nuclei
BT1 nitrogen isotopes
BT1 odd-even nuclei
BT2 nuclei
BT1 seconds living radioisotopes
BT2 radioisotopes
BT3 isotopes

NITROGEN 18 [24; 24]
BT1 beta-minus decay radioisotopes
BT2 beta decay radioisotopes
BT3 radioisotopes
BT4 isotopes
BT1 light nuclei
BT2 nuclei
BT1 millisec living radioisotopes
BT2 radioisotopes
BT3 isotopes
BT1 nitrogen isotopes
BT1 odd-odd nuclei
BT2 nuclei

NITROGEN 19 [40; 40]
BT1 beta-minus decay radioisotopes
BT2 beta decay radioisotopes
BT3 radioisotopes
BT4 isotopes
BT1 light nuclei
BT2 nuclei
BT1 millisec living radioisotopes
BT2 radioisotopes
BT3 isotopes
BT1 nitrogen isotopes
BT1 odd-even nuclei
BT2 nuclei

NITROGEN 20 [19; 19] *Jun 85*
BT1 beta-minus decay radioisotopes
BT2 beta decay radioisotopes
BT3 radioisotopes
BT4 isotopes
BT1 light nuclei
BT2 nuclei
BT1 nitrogen isotopes
BT1 odd-odd nuclei
BT2 nuclei

NITROGEN 21 [7; 7] *Apr 86*
BT1 light nuclei
BT2 nuclei
BT1 nitrogen isotopes
BT1 odd-even nuclei
BT2 nuclei

NITROGEN 22 [8; 8]
BT1 beta-minus decay radioisotopes
BT2 beta decay radioisotopes
BT3 radioisotopes
BT4 isotopes
BT1 light nuclei
BT2 nuclei
BT1 nitrogen isotopes
BT1 odd-odd nuclei
BT2 nuclei

NITROGEN 23 [7; 7] *Oct 85*
BT1 beta-minus decay radioisotopes
BT2 beta decay radioisotopes
BT3 radioisotopes
BT4 isotopes
BT1 light nuclei
BT2 nuclei
BT1 nitrogen isotopes
BT1 odd-even nuclei
BT2 nuclei

nitrogen-cooled reactors
USE nitrogen cooled reactors

NITROGENASE [35; 35] *Oct 83*
BT1 dehydrogenases
BT2 oxidoreductases
BT3 enzymes
BT4 organic compounds
RT nitrogen fixation

NITROMETHANE [72; 72] *Dec 80*
BT1 chemical explosives
BT2 explosives
BT1 nitro compounds
BT2 organic nitrogen compounds
BT3 organic compounds
RT methane

nitronic 40
   USE   steel-cr21mn9ni6

NITROPHENOL [59; 59]
BT1   nitro compounds
  BT2   organic nitrogen compounds
    BT3   organic compounds
BT1   phenols
  BT2   aromatics
    BT3   organic compounds
  BT2   hydroxy compounds
    BT3   organic compounds
RT   dinitrophenol

NITROSO COMPOUNDS [692; 857]
UF+   *streptozocin*
UF+   *streptozotocin*
BT1   organic nitrogen compounds
  BT2   organic compounds
NT1   nitroso-r salt
NT1   nitrosoureas
NT1   1-nitroso-2-naphthol

NITROSO-R SALT [25; 25]
BT1   naphthols
  BT2   phenols
    BT3   aromatics
      BT4   organic compounds
    BT3   hydroxy compounds
      BT4   organic compounds
BT1   nitroso compounds
  BT2   organic nitrogen compounds
    BT3   organic compounds
BT1   sulfonic acids
  BT2   organic acids
    BT3   organic compounds
  BT2   organic sulfur compounds
    BT3   organic compounds

NITROSOUREAS [130; 130] *Jan 85*
BT1   nitroso compounds
  BT2   organic nitrogen compounds
    BT3   organic compounds
RT   urea

NITROUS ACID [196; 196]
BT1   inorganic acids
  BT2   hydrogen compounds
  BT2   inorganic compounds
BT1   nitrogen compounds
BT1   oxygen compounds
RT   nitrites

NITROUS OXIDE [244; 244] *Apr 84*
BT1   nitrogen oxides
  BT2   nitrogen compounds
  BT2   oxides
    BT3   chalcogenides
    BT3   oxygen compounds

NITROXYL RADICALS [58; 58] *Aug 81*
BT1   radicals

nmr
   USE   nuclear magnetic resonance

NMR IMAGING [6,286; 6,286] *May 86*
BT1   diagnostic techniques
RT   nuclear magnetic resonance

nmr logging
   USE   nuclear magnetic logging

NMR SPECTRA [4,965; 4,965] *Apr 78*
(Nuclear Magnetic Resonance spectra.)
UF   *nuclear magnetic resonance spe*
UF+   *pmr spectra*
UF+   *proton magnetic resonance spec*
BT1   spectra
RT   nuclear magnetic resonance

NMR SPECTROMETERS [434; 434]
BT1   spectrometers
  BT2   measuring instruments

NN-2170 DIBARYONS [2; 2] *Dec 87*
BT1   dibaryons
  BT2   baryons
    BT3   fermions
    BT3   hadrons
      BT4   elementary particles

NN-2250 DIBARYONS [0; 0] *Dec 87*
BT1   dibaryons
  BT2   baryons
    BT3   fermions
    BT3   hadrons
      BT4   elementary particles

NOBELIUM [51; 51]
BT1   actinides
  BT2   metals
    BT3   elements
BT1   transplutonium elements
  BT2   transuranium elements
    BT3   elements

NOBELIUM CARBIDES [0; 0]
BT1   carbides
  BT2   carbon compounds
BT1   nobelium compounds
  BT2   actinide compounds
  BT2   transplutonium compounds
    BT3   transuranium compounds

NOBELIUM CHLORIDES [0; 0]
BT1   chlorides
  BT2   chlorine compounds
    BT3   halogen compounds
  BT2   halides
    BT3   halogen compounds
BT1   nobelium compounds
  BT2   actinide compounds
  BT2   transplutonium compounds
    BT3   transuranium compounds

NOBELIUM COMPLEXES [7; 7]
BT1   actinide complexes
  BT2   complexes
BT1   transuranium complexes

NOBELIUM COMPOUNDS [6; 8]
BT1   actinide compounds
BT1   transplutonium compounds
  BT2   transuranium compounds
NT1   nobelium carbides
NT1   nobelium chlorides
NT1   nobelium nitrides
NT1   nobelium oxides
NT1   nobelium sulfides

NOBELIUM IONS [2; 2]
BT1   ions
  BT2   charged particles

NOBELIUM ISOTOPES [48; 135]
NT1   nobelium 250
NT1   nobelium 251
NT1   nobelium 252
NT1   nobelium 253
NT1   nobelium 254
NT1   nobelium 255
NT1   nobelium 256
NT1   nobelium 257
NT1   nobelium 258
NT1   nobelium 259
NT1   nobelium 260
NT1   nobelium 261
NT1   nobelium 262

NOBELIUM NITRIDES [0; 0]
BT1   nitrides
  BT2   nitrogen compounds
  BT2   pnictides

BT1   nobelium compounds
  BT2   actinide compounds
  BT2   transplutonium compounds
    BT3   transuranium compounds

NOBELIUM OXIDES [2; 2]
BT1   nobelium compounds
  BT2   actinide compounds
  BT2   transplutonium compounds
    BT3   transuranium compounds
BT1   oxides
  BT2   chalcogenides
  BT2   oxygen compounds

NOBELIUM SULFIDES [0; 0]
BT1   nobelium compounds
  BT2   actinide compounds
  BT2   transplutonium compounds
    BT3   transuranium compounds
BT1   sulfides
  BT2   chalcogenides
  BT2   sulfur compounds

NOBELIUM 250 [6; 6] *Mar 76*
BT1   actinide nuclei
  BT2   heavy nuclei
    BT3   nuclei
BT1   even-even nuclei
  BT2   nuclei
BT1   microsec living radioisotopes
  BT2   radioisotopes
    BT3   isotopes
BT1   nobelium isotopes
BT1   spontaneous fission radioisoto
  BT2   radioisotopes
    BT3   isotopes

NOBELIUM 251 [2; 2]
BT1   actinide nuclei
  BT2   heavy nuclei
    BT3   nuclei
BT1   alpha decay radioisotopes
  BT2   radioisotopes
    BT3   isotopes
BT1   even-odd nuclei
  BT2   nuclei
BT1   millisec living radioisotopes
  BT2   radioisotopes
    BT3   isotopes
BT1   nobelium isotopes

NOBELIUM 252 [18; 18]
BT1   actinide nuclei
  BT2   heavy nuclei
    BT3   nuclei
BT1   alpha decay radioisotopes
  BT2   radioisotopes
    BT3   isotopes
BT1   even-even nuclei
  BT2   nuclei
BT1   nobelium isotopes
BT1   seconds living radioisotopes
  BT2   radioisotopes
    BT3   isotopes
BT1   spontaneous fission radioisoto
  BT2   radioisotopes
    BT3   isotopes

NOBELIUM 253 [6; 6]
BT1   actinide nuclei
  BT2   heavy nuclei
    BT3   nuclei
BT1   alpha decay radioisotopes
  BT2   radioisotopes
    BT3   isotopes
BT1   electron capture radioisotopes
  BT2   beta decay radioisotopes
    BT3   radioisotopes
      BT4   isotopes
BT1   even-odd nuclei
  BT2   nuclei
BT1   minutes living radioisotopes
  BT2   radioisotopes
    BT3   isotopes
BT1   nobelium isotopes

NOBELIUM 254 [22; 22]
BT1 actinide nuclei
BT2 heavy nuclei
BT3 nuclei
BT1 alpha decay radioisotopes
BT2 radioisotopes
BT3 isotopes
BT1 electron capture radioisotopes
BT2 beta decay radioisotopes
BT3 radioisotopes
BT4 isotopes
BT1 even-even nuclei
BT2 nuclei
BT1 isomeric transition isotopes
BT2 radioisotopes
BT3 isotopes
BT1 millisec living radioisotopes
BT2 radioisotopes
BT3 isotopes
BT1 nobelium isotopes
BT1 seconds living radioisotopes
BT2 radioisotopes
BT3 isotopes
BT1 spontaneous fission radioisoto
BT2 radioisotopes
BT3 isotopes

NOBELIUM 255 [9; 9]
BT1 actinide nuclei
BT2 heavy nuclei
BT3 nuclei
BT1 alpha decay radioisotopes
BT2 radioisotopes
BT3 isotopes
BT1 electron capture radioisotopes
BT2 beta decay radioisotopes
BT3 radioisotopes
BT4 isotopes
BT1 even-odd nuclei
BT2 nuclei
BT1 minutes living radioisotopes
BT2 radioisotopes
BT3 isotopes
BT1 nobelium isotopes

NOBELIUM 256 [10; 10]
BT1 actinide nuclei
BT2 heavy nuclei
BT3 nuclei
BT1 alpha decay radioisotopes
BT2 radioisotopes
BT3 isotopes
BT1 even-even nuclei
BT2 nuclei
BT1 nobelium isotopes
BT1 seconds living radioisotopes
BT2 radioisotopes
BT3 isotopes
BT1 spontaneous fission radioisoto
BT2 radioisotopes
BT3 isotopes

NOBELIUM 257 [3; 3]
BT1 actinide nuclei
BT2 heavy nuclei
BT3 nuclei
BT1 alpha decay radioisotopes
BT2 radioisotopes
BT3 isotopes
BT1 even-odd nuclei
BT2 nuclei
BT1 nobelium isotopes
BT1 seconds living radioisotopes
BT2 radioisotopes
BT3 isotopes

NOBELIUM 258 [20; 20]
BT1 actinide nuclei
BT2 heavy nuclei
BT3 nuclei
BT1 even-even nuclei
BT2 nuclei
BT1 millisec living radioisotopes
BT2 radioisotopes
BT3 isotopes
BT1 nobelium isotopes
BT1 spontaneous fission radioisoto
BT2 radioisotopes
BT3 isotopes

NOBELIUM 259 [15; 15]
BT1 actinide nuclei
BT2 heavy nuclei
BT3 nuclei
BT1 alpha decay radioisotopes
BT2 radioisotopes
BT3 isotopes
BT1 electron capture radioisotopes
BT2 beta decay radioisotopes
BT3 radioisotopes
BT4 isotopes
BT1 even-odd nuclei
BT2 nuclei
BT1 minutes living radioisotopes
BT2 radioisotopes
BT3 isotopes
BT1 nobelium isotopes

NOBELIUM 260 [14; 14] *Aug 78*
BT1 actinide nuclei
BT2 heavy nuclei
BT3 nuclei
BT1 alpha decay radioisotopes
BT2 radioisotopes
BT3 isotopes
BT1 even-even nuclei
BT2 nuclei
BT1 nobelium isotopes

NOBELIUM 261 [2; 2] *Feb 87*
BT1 actinide nuclei
BT2 heavy nuclei
BT3 nuclei
BT1 even-odd nuclei
BT2 nuclei
BT1 nobelium isotopes

NOBELIUM 262 [6; 6] *Feb 87*
BT1 actinide nuclei
BT2 heavy nuclei
BT3 nuclei
BT1 even-even nuclei
BT2 nuclei
BT1 nobelium isotopes

noble gases
USE rare gases

NOCARDIA [13; 13]
BT1 bacteria
BT2 microorganisms
RT actinomyces

NODAL EXPANSION METHOD [75; 75] *Sep 89*
RT finite difference method
RT finite element method
RT mathematics
RT mesh generation

NOGENT SUR SEINE-1 REACTOR [9; 9] *Jul 84*
BT1 pwr type reactors
BT2 enriched uranium reactors
BT3 reactors
BT2 power reactors
BT3 reactors
BT2 thermal reactors
BT3 reactors
BT2 water cooled reactors
BT3 reactors
BT2 water moderated reactors
BT3 reactors

NOGENT SUR SEINE-2 REACTOR [6; 6] *Jul 84*
BT1 pwr type reactors
BT2 enriched uranium reactors
BT3 reactors
BT2 power reactors
BT3 reactors
BT2 thermal reactors
BT3 reactors
BT2 water cooled reactors
BT3 reactors

BT2 water moderated reactors
BT3 reactors

NOISE [3,558; 7,138]
NT1 background noise
NT1 radio noise
NT2 atmospherics
NT2 whistlers
NT1 seismic noise
NT1 temperature noise
RT fluctuations
RT signal-to-noise ratio

noise (reactor)
USE reactor noise

NOISE THERMOMETERS [62; 62] *Nov 78*
(Operation based on the Nyquist theorem of thermal noise.)
BT1 thermometers
BT2 measuring instruments
RT in core instruments
RT temperature measurement

nok-1 reactor
(Nordost Schweizerische Kraftwerke AG-1 reactor.)
USE beznau-1 reactor

nok-2 reactor
(Nordost Schweizerische Kraftwerke AG-2 reactor.)
USE beznau-2 reactor

NOLEN-SCHIFFER ANOMALY [32; 32]
RT coulomb energy
RT isobaric analogs

NOMOGRAMS [289; 289]
BT1 diagrams
BT2 information

non lagrangian quantum field t
USE axiomatic field theory

non-aqueous solvents
USE nonaqueous solvents

non-canonical dimension
USE anomalous dimension

non-central forces
USE noncentral forces

non-destructive analysis
USE nondestructive analysis

non-destructive testing
USE nondestructive testing

NON-DISJUNCTION [39; 39]
UF *nondisjunction*
RT aneuploidy
RT cell division
RT genome mutations

non-dispersive ion waves
USE ion acoustic waves

NON-EQUILIBRIUM PLASMA [535; 535]
UF *nonequilibrium plasma*
BT1 plasma

NON-INDUCTIVE CURRENT DRIVE
[247; 365] *Jun 87*
(Generation of a plasma current by a non-inductive technique.)
- NT1   lower hybrid current drive
- RT   bootstrap current
- RT   current-drive heating
- RT   electric currents
- RT   plasma

non-lagrangian quantum field t
- USE   axiomatic field theory

non-leptonic decay
- USE   weak hadronic decay

non-linear field theory
- USE   nonlinear problems
- AND   quantum field theory

non-linear optics
- USE   nonlinear optics

non-linear plasma instabilitie
- USE   parametric instabilities

non-linear problems
- USE   nonlinear problems

non-linear programming
- USE   nonlinear programming

non-linear systems
- USE   nonlinear problems

non-local potential
- USE   nonlocal potential

non-local quantum field theory
- USE   yukawa nonlocal theory

non-measurable variables
- USE   hidden variables

non-metals
- USE   nonmetals

NON-PEPTIDE C-N HYDROLASES
[15; 57] *Dec 86*
- BT1   hydrolases
- BT2   enzymes
- BT3   organic compounds
- NT1   amidases
- NT2   urease
- NT1   amidinases
- NT2   arginase

non-proliferation
- USE   proliferation

NON-PROLIFERATION POLICY
[173; 173] *Mar 86*
- RT   government policies
- RT   non-proliferation treaty
- RT   nuclear materials diversion
- RT   nuclear weapons
- RT   proliferation

NON-PROLIFERATION TREATY
[844; 844]
- UF   nonproliferation treaty
- BT1   treaties
- RT   non-proliferation policy
- RT   nuclear materials possession
- RT   proliferation
- RT   safeguards

non-radioactive waste disposal
- USE   nonradioactive waste disposal

non-radioactive wastes
- USE   nonradioactive wastes

non-uniform irradiation
- USE   nonuniform irradiation

non-unitary representations
- USE   nonunitary representations

NONANOIC ACID [17; 17]
- UF   nonylic acid
- UF   pelargonic acid
- BT1   monocarboxylic acids
- BT2   carboxylic acids
- BT3   organic acids
- BT4   organic compounds

NONAQUEOUS SOLVENTS [257; 2,441]
(See also ORGANIC SOLVENTS.)
- UF   non-aqueous solvents
- BT1   solvents
- NT1   organic solvents
- NT2   amsco
- NT2   carbitols
- NT2   cellosolves
- NT2   solvesso
- NT2   turpentine
- RT   solvation

nonaxial nuclei
- USE   deformed nuclei

noncanonical dimension
- USE   anomalous dimension

NONCENTRAL FORCES [36; 36]
- UF   non-central forces
- RT   potentials
- RT   tensor mesons

NONDESTRUCTIVE ANALYSIS
[2,215; 15,618]
- UF   non-destructive analysis
- UF   nondestructive chemical anal
- BT1   chemical analysis
- NT1   activation analysis
- NT2   charged-particle activation an
- NT2   neutron activation analysis
- NT2   photon activation analysis
- NT1   delayed neutron analysis
- NT1   deuteron microprobe analysis
- NT1   electron microprobe analysis
- NT1   ion microprobe analysis
- NT1   ion scattering analysis
- NT1   nuclear reaction analysis
- NT1   proton microprobe analysis
- NT1   radiation absorption analysis
- NT1   radiation scattering analysis
- NT1   x-ray emission analysis
- NT2   pixe analysis
- NT2   x-ray fluorescence analysis

nondestructive chemical anal
- USE   nondestructive analysis

NONDESTRUCTIVE TESTING
[3,867; 13,816]
- UF   non-destructive testing
- BT1   materials testing
- BT2   testing
- NT1   acoustic testing
- NT2   acoustic emission testing
- NT2   ultrasonic testing
- NT1   electrical testing
- NT1   electromagnetic testing
- NT2   eddy current testing
- NT1   industrial radiography
- NT1   liquid penetrant inspection
- NT1   magnetic testing
- NT1   radiation attenuation testing
- NT1   thermal testing
- NT2   frost tests
- NT2   thermography
- RT   autoradiography
- RT   beta radiography
- RT   fuel scanning
- RT   gamma radiography
- RT   in-service inspection
- RT   inspection
- RT   neutron radiography
- RT   proton radiography
- RT   quality control
- RT   radiometric gages
- RT   x-ray radiography

nondisjunction
- USE   non-disjunction

nondispersive ion waves
- USE   ion acoustic waves

nonequilibrium plasma
- USE   non-equilibrium plasma

nonlagrangian quantum field th
- USE   axiomatic field theory

nonleptonic decay
- USE   weak hadronic decay

nonlinear field theory
- USE   nonlinear problems
- AND   quantum field theory

NONLINEAR OPTICS [489; 489]
Mar 86
(Study of the interaction of radiation with matter in which certain variables describing the response of the matter are not proportional to variables describing the radiation.)
- UF   non-linear optics
- BT1   optics
- RT   frequency mixing
- RT   harmonic generation
- RT   nonlinear problems

nonlinear plasma instabilities
- USE   parametric instabilities

NONLINEAR PROBLEMS
[13,865; 13,865]
- UF   non-linear problems
- UF   non-linear systems
- UF   nonlinear systems
- UF+   non-linear field theory
- UF+   nonlinear field theory
- RT   baecklund transformation
- RT   frequency mixing
- RT   harmonic generation
- RT   harmonics
- RT   mathematics
- RT   nonlinear optics
- RT   plasma disruption
- RT   plasma instability
- RT   quasilinear problems

RT   reactor stability

NONLINEAR PROGRAMMING [94; 94]
UF   non-linear programming
RT   dynamic programming
RT   econometrics
RT   linear programming
RT   mathematical models
RT   optimization

nonlinear systems
USE   nonlinear problems

NONLOCAL POTENTIAL [761; 761]
UF   non-local potential
BT1   potentials
RT   locality
RT   nuclear potential
RT   perey-buck model

nonlocal quantum field theory
USE   yukawa nonlocal theory

NONLUMINOUS MATTER
[1,233; 1,233] Jan 85
(Unseen mass in the Universe assumed from discrepancies in cosmological model values and observation.)
UF   dark matter
UF   unobserved matter
UF   unseen matter
BT1   matter
RT   galaxies
RT   intergalactic space
RT   universe

nonmeasurable variables
(Prior to December 1985 this was a valid descriptor.)
USE   hidden variables

NONMETALS [189; 109,888]
UF   non-metals
BT1   elements
NT1   carbon
  NT2   activated carbon
  NT2   carbon black
  NT2   carbynes
  NT2   diamonds
  NT2   graphite
  NT2   pyrolytic carbon
NT1   halogens
  NT2   astatine
  NT2   bromine
  NT2   chlorine
  NT2   fluorine
  NT2   iodine
NT1   hydrogen
NT1   nitrogen
NT1   oxygen
NT1   phosphorus
NT1   rare gases
  NT2   argon
  NT2   helium
  NT2   krypton
  NT2   neon
  NT2   radon
  NT2   xenon
NT1   sulfur
RT   semimetals

nonproliferation
USE   proliferation

nonproliferation treaty
USE   non-proliferation treaty

NONRADIOACTIVE WASTE DISPOSAL [110; 110]
UF   non-radioactive waste disposal
BT1   nonradioactive waste managemen
BT2   waste management
BT3   management
BT1   waste disposal
BT2   waste management
BT3   management
RT   chemical effluents

NONRADIOACTIVE WASTE MANAGEMEN [0; 131] Dec 90
BT1   waste management
BT2   management
NT1   nonradioactive waste disposal
NT1   nonradioactive wastes
NT2   chemical wastes
NT3   chemical effluents

NONRADIOACTIVE WASTES
[207; 1,129]
UF   non-radioactive wastes
BT1   nonradioactive waste managemen
BT2   waste management
BT3   management
BT1   wastes
NT1   chemical wastes
NT2   chemical effluents
RT   hazardous materials

NONSPECIFIC PEPTIDASES [2; 114] Dec 86
(Prior to December 1990, this concept was indexed by NONSPECIFIC PROTEINASES.)
UF   nonspecific proteinases
BT1   peptide hydrolases
BT2   hydrolases
BT3   enzymes
BT4   organic compounds
NT1   renin
NT1   urokinase

nonspecific proteinases
(Prior to December 1990, this was a valid descriptor.)
USE   nonspecific peptidases

NONUNIFORM IRRADIATION
[256; 256]
UF   non-uniform irradiation
BT1   irradiation
RT   critical organs
RT   isodose curves
RT   radionuclide kinetics
RT   spatial dose distributions

NONUNITARY REPRESENTATIONS
[91; 91]
UF   non-unitary representations
UF   representations (nonunitary)
RT   group theory
RT   irreducible representations
RT   symmetry groups
RT   unitarity

nonviscous flow
USE   ideal flow

NONYL RADICALS [1; 1]
BT1   alkyl radicals
BT2   radicals

nonylic acid
USE   nonanoic acid

NORA REACTOR [2; 2]
UF   norwegian research react. nora
BT1   heavy water cooled reactors
BT2   reactors
BT1   heavy water moderated reactors
BT2   reactors
BT1   research reactors

BT2   research and test reactors
BT3   reactors
BT1   tank type reactors
BT2   reactors
BT1   thermal reactors
BT2   reactors
RT   enriched uranium reactors
RT   natural uranium reactors

NORADRENALINE [500; 500]
BT1   adrenal hormones
BT2   hormones
BT1   cardiotonics
BT2   cardiovascular agents
BT3   drugs
BT1   neuroregulators
BT2   autonomic nervous system agent
BT3   drugs
BT1   sympathomimetics
BT2   autonomic nervous system agent
BT3   drugs

NORD COMPUTERS [17; 17] Aug 76
BT1   computers

nordheim equation
USE   inhour equation

NORDHEIM-SCALETTAR METHOD
[8; 8]
RT   control rod worths

nordost schweiz kraftw-1 react
USE   beznau-1 reactor

nordost schweiz kraftw-2 react
USE   beznau-2 reactor

norilsk res. reactor rg-1m
USE   rg-1m reactor

NORMAL-MODE ANALYSIS [274; 274]
UF   analysis (normal-mode)
RT   fourier analysis
RT   plasma waves

NORTH AMERICA [143; 19,897]
NT1   canada
  NT2   alberta
  NT2   british columbia
  NT2   manitoba
  NT2   new brunswick
  NT2   newfoundland
  NT2   northwest territories
    NT3   port radium
  NT2   nova scotia
  NT2   ontario
    NT3   chalk river
    NT3   deep river
    NT3   elliot lake
  NT2   prince edward island
  NT2   quebec
  NT2   saskatchewan
    NT3   beaverlodge
  NT2   yukon territory
NT1   mexico
NT1   usa
  NT2   alabama
  NT2   alaska
  NT2   arizona
  NT2   arkansas
  NT2   california
  NT2   colorado
  NT2   connecticut
  NT2   delaware
  NT2   florida
    NT3   cape kennedy
  NT2   georgia
  NT2   hawaii
  NT2   idaho
  NT2   illinois

NT2 indiana
NT2 iowa
NT2 kansas
NT2 kentucky
NT2 louisiana
NT2 maine
NT2 maryland
NT2 massachusetts
NT2 michigan
NT2 minnesota
NT2 mississippi
NT2 missouri
NT2 montana
NT2 nebraska
NT2 nevada
NT3 tonopah test range
NT2 new hampshire
NT2 new jersey
NT2 new mexico
NT2 new york
NT3 new york city
NT2 north carolina
NT2 north dakota
NT2 ohio
NT2 oklahoma
NT2 oregon
NT2 pennsylvania
NT2 puerto rico
NT2 rhode island
NT2 south carolina
NT2 south dakota
NT2 tennessee
NT2 texas
NT2 utah
NT2 vermont
NT2 virginia
NT2 washington
NT2 washington dc
NT2 west virginia
NT2 wisconsin
NT2 wyoming

NORTH ANNA-1 REACTOR [78; 78]
(Mineral, Virginia, USA)
UF *mineral va. north anna-1 react*
BT1 pwr type reactors
BT2 enriched uranium reactors
BT3 reactors
BT2 power reactors
BT3 reactors
BT2 thermal reactors
BT3 reactors
BT2 water cooled reactors
BT3 reactors
BT2 water moderated reactors
BT3 reactors

NORTH ANNA-2 REACTOR [65; 65]
(Mineral, Virginia, USA)
UF *mineral va. north anna-2 react*
BT1 pwr type reactors
BT2 enriched uranium reactors
BT3 reactors
BT2 power reactors
BT3 reactors
BT2 thermal reactors
BT3 reactors
BT2 water cooled reactors
BT3 reactors
BT2 water moderated reactors
BT3 reactors

NORTH ANNA-3 REACTOR [55; 55]
(Mineral, Virginia, USA)
UF *mineral va. north anna-3 react*
BT1 pwr type reactors
BT2 enriched uranium reactors
BT3 reactors
BT2 power reactors
BT3 reactors
BT2 thermal reactors
BT3 reactors
BT2 water cooled reactors
BT3 reactors
BT2 water moderated reactors
BT3 reactors

NORTH ANNA-4 REACTOR [54; 54]
(Mineral, Virginia, USA)
BT1 pwr type reactors
BT2 enriched uranium reactors
BT3 reactors
BT2 power reactors
BT3 reactors
BT2 thermal reactors
BT3 reactors
BT2 water cooled reactors
BT3 reactors
BT2 water moderated reactors
BT3 reactors

north atlantic treaty organiza
USE nato

north carol. st. col. res. r-1
USE ncscr-1 reactor

NORTH CAROLINA [241; 241]
BT1 usa
BT2 developed countries
BT2 north america
RT cape fear river

north carolina pulstar reactor
USE pulstar-raleigh reactor

NORTH COAST-1 REACTOR [4; 4]
(Formerly the Aguirre-1 Reactor, relocated and renamed.)
UF *aguirre-1 reactor*
BT1 pwr type reactors
BT2 enriched uranium reactors
BT3 reactors
BT2 power reactors
BT3 reactors
BT2 thermal reactors
BT3 reactors
BT2 water cooled reactors
BT3 reactors
BT2 water moderated reactors
BT3 reactors

NORTH DAKOTA [102; 102]
BT1 usa
BT2 developed countries
BT2 north america

NORTH KOREA [10; 10]
UF *korea (north)*
BT1 asia
BT1 developing countries
RT centrally planned economies

NORTH SEA [187; 187]
BT1 atlantic ocean
BT2 seas
BT3 surface waters

NORTH-SOUTH ASYMMETRY [117; 117]
(For cosmic radiation only.)
BT1 asymmetry
RT cosmic radiation

NORTHERN HEMISPHERE [59; 59]
Dec 86
(Both for the surface and the celestial hemisphere.)
RT earth planet

northern ireland
USE united kingdom

northern rhodesia
USE zambia

northern states monticello rea
USE monticello reactor

NORTHERN TERRITORY [444; 444]
BT1 australia
BT2 australasia
BT2 developed countries
RT jabiluka deposit
RT koongarra deposit
RT nabarlek deposit
RT ranger deposit
RT south alligator deposit

NORTHWEST TERRITORIES [57; 58]
BT1 canada
BT2 developed countries
BT2 north america
NT1 port radium

NORWAY [733; 733]
BT1 developed countries
BT1 scandinavia
BT2 europe

NORWEGIAN ORGANIZATIONS [116; 116]
BT1 national organizations

norwegian research react. nora
USE nora reactor

NOSE [474; 474]
BT1 face
BT2 head
BT3 body areas
BT4 body
BT1 respiratory system
RT sense organs

NOTCHES [639; 639]
RT cracks
RT impact tests

NOTIFICATION PROCEDURES [39; 39]
Dec 76
(Procedures to be followed by a nuclear operator in compliance with his legal obligation to notify certain actions or incidents to the authorities.)
BT1 administrative procedures
RT nuclear operators

noto-1 reactor
USE shika-1 reactor

NOVA FACILITY [337; 337] *Aug 81*
(Upgrade of SHIVA FACILITY at LLL for laser fusion experiments.)
RT lawrence livermore laboratory
RT lawrence livermore national la
RT neodymium lasers
RT novette facility
RT shiva facility

NOVA MODEL [20; 20]
BT1 particle models
BT2 mathematical models

NOVA SCOTIA [45; 45]
BT1 canada
BT2 developed countries
BT2 north america

NOVAE [1,133; 1,133]
BT1 eruptive variable stars
BT2 binary stars
BT3 stars
BT2 variable stars
BT3 stars
RT supernovae

novain
   USE   carnitine

NOVETTE FACILITY [54; 54] *Oct 85*
(Two-beam Nd glass laser at LLNL operating at fundamental or harmonic wavelengths used for target irradiation experiments.)
   RT   lawrence livermore national la
   RT   neodymium lasers
   RT   nova facility
   RT   shiva facility

novo voronezh-1 reactor
   USE   wwer-1 reactor

novo voronezh-2 reactor
   USE   wwer-2 reactor

novo voronezh-3 reactor
   USE   wwer-3 reactor

novo voronezh-4 reactor
   USE   wwer-4 reactor

novo voronezh-5 reactor
   USE   wwer-5 reactor

novocaine
   USE   procaine

NOZZLES [2,140; 2,140]
   RT   aerosol generators
   RT   flowmeters
   RT   jets
   RT   orifices
   RT   pipe fittings
   RT   separation nozzle method

NPD REACTOR [43; 43]
(Nuclear Power Demonstration reactor, Rolphton, Ontario, Canada)
   UF   *nucl. pow. demon. react. canad*
   UF   *rolphton npd-2 reactor*
   BT1   candu type reactors
     BT2   heavy water moderated reactors
       BT3   reactors
     BT2   pressure tube reactors
       BT3   power reactors
         BT4   reactors
     BT2   thermal reactors
       BT3   reactors
   BT1   natural uranium reactors
     BT2   reactors
   BT1   phwr type reactors
     BT2   heavy water cooled reactors
       BT3   reactors
     BT2   heavy water moderated reactors
       BT3   reactors

npr reactor
   USE   n-reactor

NRL CYCLOTRON [14; 14]
   UF   *naval res lab cyclotron*
   UF   *us naval res lab cyclotron*
   BT1   isochronous cyclotrons
     BT2   cyclotrons
       BT3   cyclic accelerators
         BT4   accelerators

NRL LINAC [6; 6]
   UF   *naval res lab linac*
   UF   *us naval res lab linac*
   BT1   linear accelerators
     BT2   accelerators

NRPB [271; 271] *Dec 79*
(National Radiological Protection Board.)
   UF   *nat. radiological prot. board*
   BT1   united kingdom organizations
     BT2   national organizations

NRTS [37; 37]
(Name changed in 1976 to Idaho National Engineering Laboratory and more recent material should be so indexed.)
   UF   *national reactor testing stati*
   BT1   idaho national engineering lab
     BT2   us doe
       BT3   us organizations
         BT4   national organizations
     BT2   us erda
       BT3   us organizations
         BT4   national organizations
   BT1   us aec
     BT2   us organizations
       BT3   national organizations

nrts-etr reactor
   USE   etr reactor

nrts-lptf reactor
   USE   lptf reactor

nru canada reactor
   USE   nru reactor

NRU REACTOR [74; 74]
(Atomic Energy of Canada, Ltd., Chalk River Nuclear Labs., Ontario, Canada)
   UF   *canadian nru reactor*
   UF   *nru canada reactor*
   BT1   heavy water cooled reactors
     BT2   reactors
   BT1   heavy water moderated reactors
     BT2   reactors
   BT1   isotope production reactors
     BT2   irradiation reactors
       BT3   reactors
   BT1   natural uranium reactors
     BT2   reactors
   BT1   research reactors
     BT2   research and test reactors
       BT3   reactors
   BT1   tank type reactors
     BT2   reactors
   BT1   test reactors
     BT2   research and test reactors
       BT3   reactors
     BT2   test facilities

NRX REACTOR [55; 55]
(Atomic Energy of Canada, Ltd., Chalk River Nuclear Labs., Ontario, Canada)
   UF   *canada nrx research reactor*
   BT1   heavy water cooled reactors
     BT2   reactors
   BT1   heavy water moderated reactors
     BT2   reactors
   BT1   isotope production reactors
     BT2   irradiation reactors
       BT3   reactors
   BT1   materials testing reactors
     BT2   irradiation reactors
       BT3   reactors
   BT1   natural uranium reactors
     BT2   reactors
   BT1   research reactors
     BT2   research and test reactors
       BT3   reactors
   BT1   tank type reactors
     BT2   reactors
   BT1   thermal reactors
     BT2   reactors

NRX-A2 REACTOR [6; 6]
   UF   *nerva nrx-a2 reactor*
   BT1   experimental reactors
     BT2   research and test reactors
       BT3   reactors
   BT1   hydrogen cooled reactors
     BT2   gas cooled reactors
       BT3   reactors
   BT1   space propulsion reactors
     BT2   propulsion reactors
       BT3   power reactors
         BT4   reactors
     BT2   space power reactors
       BT3   mobile reactors
         BT4   reactors
       BT3   power reactors
         BT4   reactors

NRX-A3 REACTOR [3; 3]
   UF   *nerva nrx-a3 reactor*
   BT1   experimental reactors
     BT2   research and test reactors
       BT3   reactors
   BT1   hydrogen cooled reactors
     BT2   gas cooled reactors
       BT3   reactors
   BT1   space propulsion reactors
     BT2   propulsion reactors
       BT3   power reactors
         BT4   reactors
     BT2   space power reactors
       BT3   mobile reactors
         BT4   reactors
       BT3   power reactors
         BT4   reactors

NRX-A4-EST REACTOR [2; 2]
   UF   *nerva nrx-a4 eng. syst. test r*
   BT1   experimental reactors
     BT2   research and test reactors
       BT3   reactors
   BT1   hydrogen cooled reactors
     BT2   gas cooled reactors
       BT3   reactors
   BT1   space propulsion reactors
     BT2   propulsion reactors
       BT3   power reactors
         BT4   reactors
     BT2   space power reactors
       BT3   mobile reactors
         BT4   reactors
       BT3   power reactors
         BT4   reactors

NRX-A5 REACTOR [3; 3]
   UF   *nerva nrx-a5 reactor*
   BT1   experimental reactors
     BT2   research and test reactors
       BT3   reactors
   BT1   hydrogen cooled reactors
     BT2   gas cooled reactors
       BT3   reactors
   BT1   space propulsion reactors
     BT2   propulsion reactors
       BT3   power reactors
         BT4   reactors
     BT2   space power reactors
       BT3   mobile reactors
         BT4   reactors
       BT3   power reactors
         BT4   reactors

NRX-A6 REACTOR [4; 4]
   UF   *nerva nrx-a6 reactor*
   BT1   experimental reactors
     BT2   research and test reactors
       BT3   reactors
   BT1   hydrogen cooled reactors
     BT2   gas cooled reactors
       BT3   reactors
   BT1   space propulsion reactors
     BT2   propulsion reactors
       BT3   power reactors
         BT4   reactors
     BT2   space power reactors
       BT3   mobile reactors
         BT4   reactors
       BT3   power reactors
         BT4   reactors

ns arktika

NS ARKTIKA
(Prior to the name change in November 1982 this was a valid descriptor, and older material is so indexed.)
USE   ns leonid brezhnev

NS LENIN [9; 9]
UF   *lenin (nuclear ship)*
BT1   nuclear ships
BT2   ships
RT   lenin reactor

NS LEONID BREZHNEV [8; 8] *Jul 76*
(Prior to November 1982 known as NS ARKTIKA.)
UF   *arktika (nuclear ship)*
UF   *leonid brezhnev (nuclear ship)*
UF   *ns arktika*
BT1   nuclear ships
BT2   ships
RT   leonid brezhnev reactor

NS MUTSU [89; 89]
UF   *mutsu (nuclear ship)*
BT1   nuclear merchant ships
BT2   nuclear ships
BT3   ships
RT   mutsu reactor

NS OTTO HAHN [169; 169]
UF   *otto hahn (nuclear ship)*
BT1   nuclear merchant ships
BT2   nuclear ships
BT3   ships
RT   otto hahn reactor

NS SAVANNAH [26; 26]
UF   *savannah (nuclear ship)*
BT1   nuclear merchant ships
BT2   nuclear ships
BT3   ships
RT   savannah reactor

NS SIBIR [2; 2] *Sep 85*
UF   *sibir (nuclear ship)*
BT1   nuclear ships
BT2   ships
RT   sibir reactor

NSCR REACTOR [31; 31]
(Texas A and M University, College Station, Texas, USA)
UF   *college station texas train. r*
UF   *nucl. science center re. texas*
UF   *texas college station train. r*
BT1   pool type reactors
BT2   water cooled reactors
BT3   reactors
BT2   water moderated reactors
BT3   reactors
BT1   training reactors
BT2   research and test reactors
BT3   reactors
BT1   triga type reactors
BT2   enriched uranium reactors
BT3   reactors
BT2   hydride moderated reactors
BT3   reactors
BT2   research and test reactors
BT3   reactors
BT2   solid homogeneous reactors
BT3   homogeneous reactors
BT4   reactors
BT2   water cooled reactors
BT3   reactors
BT2   water moderated reactors
BT3   reactors

NSF-RFP REACTOR [13; 13]
UF   *nucl. safety facility-rfp reac*
UF   *rocky flats pl.-nucl. saf. fac*
BT1   zero power reactors
BT2   experimental reactors
BT3   research and test reactors
BT4   reactors

NSLS [441; 441] *Sep 79*
UF   *national synchrotron light sou*
BT1   synchrotron radiation sources
BT2   radiation sources
RT   light sources
RT   synchrotron radiation
RT   synchrotrons
RT   x-ray sources

nspp
USE   nuclear safety pilot plant

NSRR REACTOR [148; 148]
(Nuclear Safety Research Reactor in Japan)
UF   *nucl. saf. res. reactor (jap.)*
BT1   enriched uranium reactors
BT2   reactors
BT1   hydride moderated reactors
BT2   reactors
BT1   mixed spectrum reactors
BT2   reactors
BT1   pulsed reactors
BT2   reactors
BT1   research reactors
BT2   research and test reactors
BT3   reactors
BT1   solid homogeneous reactors
BT2   homogeneous reactors
BT3   reactors
BT1   water cooled reactors
BT2   reactors
BT1   water moderated reactors
BT2   reactors

NTA [292; 292]
UF   *nitrilotriacetic acid*
BT1   amino acids
BT2   carboxylic acids
BT3   organic acids
BT4   organic compounds
BT1   chelating agents

NTR REACTOR [3; 3]
(General Electric Company, Vallecitos Nuclear Center, Pleasanton, California, USA)
UF   *gen. electric nuclear test rea*
UF   *nucl. test reactor gen. el. co*
UF   *pleasanton usa ntr reactor*
BT1   enriched uranium reactors
BT2   reactors
BT1   graphite moderated reactors
BT2   reactors
BT1   research reactors
BT2   research and test reactors
BT3   reactors
BT1   tank type reactors
BT2   reactors
BT1   test reactors
BT2   research and test reactors
BT3   reactors
BT2   test facilities
BT1   thermal reactors
BT2   reactors
BT1   water cooled reactors
BT2   reactors
BT1   water moderated reactors
BT2   reactors

nucl mater, conv phys protec
USE   cppnm

nucl weapons lat am prohib tre
USE   tlatelolco treaty

nucl. phys. res. in. amsterdam
USE   iko

nucl. pow. demon. react. canad
USE   npd reactor

nucl. saf. res. reactor (jap.)
USE   nsrr reactor

nucl. safety facility-rfp reac
USE   nsf-rfp reactor

nucl. science center re. texas
USE   nscr reactor

nucl. ship arktika reactor
USE   leonid brezhnev reactor

nucl. ship lenin reactor
USE   lenin reactor

nucl. ship leonid brezhnev rea
USE   leonid brezhnev reactor

nucl. ship mutsu reactor
USE   mutsu reactor

nucl. ship oper. lia. conv,bru
(Brussels Convention on Liability for Operation of Nuclear Ships)
USE   bcolons

nucl. ship otto hahn reactor
USE   otto hahn reactor

nucl. ship savannah reactor
USE   savannah reactor

nucl. ship sibir reactor
USE   sibir reactor

nucl. test reactor gen. el. co
USE   ntr reactor

nuclear accidents
USE   accidents

nuclear acoustic resonance
USE   acoustic nmr

NUCLEAR ALIGNMENT [1,228; 1,228]
RT   oriented nuclei
RT   spin orientation

nuclear attacks
USE   nuclear weapons

NUCLEAR CASCADES [1,183; 3,408]
UF   *cascades (nuclear)*
UF   *intranuclear cascades*
BT1   energy-level transitions
NT1   gamma cascades
RT   energy levels

nuclear charge
USE   atomic number

NUCLEAR CHEMISTRY [283; 283]
(Study of nuclei and nuclear reactions using chemical methods. Prior to March 1986 RADIOCHEMISTRY was used for this concept.)
RT   chemistry
RT   nuclear physics
RT   radiochemistry

nuclear contestation
   USE   public relations

nuclear controversy
(Prior to January 1983 PUBLIC RELATIONS was used for this concept.)
   USE   public opinion

NUCLEAR CORES [911; 911]
   UF   *cores (nuclear)*
   UF+ *core polarization (nuclei)*
   RT   nuclear structure

NUCLEAR DAMAGE [143; 143] *Dec 76*
(All physical or material damage caused by a nuclear incident, i.e. resulting from the radioactive or other hazardous properties of nuclear materials.)
   UF   *damage (nuclear)*
   RT   accidents
   RT   vcoclnd

nuclear damage, vienna liabil
   USE   vcoclnd

NUCLEAR DATA COLLECTIONS [2,905; 2,905]
(Use only for items about nuclear data collections, not for items which contain nuclear data.)
   RT   cinda
   RT   compiled data
   RT   data base management
   RT   data compilation
   RT   evaluated data
   RT   information systems
   RT   international nuclear data com

NUCLEAR DECAY [1,199; 15,091]
Feb 78
   BT1 decay
   NT1 alpha decay
   NT1 beta decay
     NT2 beta-minus decay
       NT3 double beta decay
     NT2 beta-plus decay
     NT2 electron capture decay
       NT3 k capture
       NT3 l capture
       NT3 m capture
   NT1 gamma decay
   NT1 heavy ion emission decay
     NT2 carbon 12 emission decay
     NT2 carbon 14 emission decay
     NT2 magnesium 28 emission decay
     NT2 magnesium 30 emission decay
     NT2 neon 24 emission decay
     NT2 oxygen 16 emission decay
     NT2 silicon 32 emission decay
     NT2 silicon 34 emission decay
   NT1 internal conversion
     NT2 internal pair production
     NT2 k conversion
     NT2 l conversion
     NT2 m conversion
   NT1 proton-emission decay
   NT1 spontaneous fission

NUCLEAR DEFORMATION [5,012; 5,012]
(For the deformation in the excited state of nuclei which are not deformed in the ground state.)
   BT1 deformation
   RT   deformed nuclei

nuclear density
(Coordinate descriptor below with NEUTRON DENSITY and/or PROTON DENSITY.)
   USE   nuclear matter

NUCLEAR DISARMAMENT [152; 152]
Dec 76
   RT   nuclear weapons
   RT   safeguards

NUCLEAR ELECTRIC MOMENTS [1,384; 1,384]
   UF   *nuclear moments (electric)*
   BT1 electric moments
   BT1 nuclear properties
   RT   electric dipole moments
   RT   nuclear quadrupole resonance
   RT   perturbed angular correlation
   RT   quadrupole moments

NUCLEAR EMULSIONS [2,661; 2,661]
   RT   autoradiography
   RT   images
   RT   latent images
   RT   photographic film detectors
   RT   photographic film dosemeters
   RT   photographic films
   RT   radiator counters

NUCLEAR ENERGY [4,417; 4,417]
(Use only in the general sense, such as for energy production or the comparison of different sources of energy.)
   UF   *atomic energy*
   BT1 energy
   RT   nuclear power plants

nuclear energy agency (oecd)
   USE   nea

NUCLEAR ENGINEERING [1,879; 1,879]
   BT1 engineering
   RT   nuclear industry
   RT   reactor technology
   RT   reactors
   RT   technology transfer

nuclear evaporation
   USE   evaporation model

NUCLEAR EXCAVATION [81; 81]
   BT1 excavation
   RT   cratering explosions
   RT   nuclear explosions
   RT   plowshare project
   RT   surface explosions
   RT   underground explosions
   RT   underwater explosions

NUCLEAR EXPLOSION DETECTION [136; 136]
   BT1 detection
   RT   atmospheric explosions
   RT   nuclear explosions
   RT   seismic detection
   RT   underground explosions

NUCLEAR EXPLOSIONS [3,020; 3,542]
(Specifically named single nuclear explosions are listed by name and the word EVENT, e.g., BOXCAR EVENT. All projects involving nuclear explosions are listed by the project name and the word PROJECT, e.g., PLOWSHARE PROJECT.)
   UF   *atomic explosions*
   UF   *events (nuclear explosions)*
   UF   *nuclear weapon tests*
   BT1 explosions
   NT1 almendro event
   NT1 annie event
   NT1 argus event
   NT1 baneberry event
   NT1 benham event
   NT1 boxcar event
   NT1 cabriolet event
   NT1 calabash event
   NT1 cannikin event
   NT1 carpetbag event
   NT1 danny boy event
   NT1 dining car event
   NT1 faultless event
   NT1 gasbuggy event
   NT1 greeley event
   NT1 halfbeak event
   NT1 handcar event
   NT1 handley event
   NT1 harry event
   NT1 holly event
   NT1 hutch event
   NT1 jorum event
   NT1 marvel event
   NT1 milrow event
   NT1 monique event
   NT1 orange event
   NT1 pokhran event
   NT1 rio blanco event
   NT1 romeo event
   NT1 rulison event
   NT1 scotch event
   NT1 smoky event
   NT1 starfish event
   NT1 swordfish event
   NT1 teak event
   NT1 tewa event
   NT1 thermonuclear explosions
     NT2 bravo event
     NT2 mike event
     NT2 schooner event
   NT1 trinity event
   NT1 wagon wheel event
   NT1 yankee event
   NT1 zuni event
   RT   aleutian islands
   RT   anvil project
   RT   arbor project
   RT   artificial radiation belts
   RT   atmospheric explosions
   RT   bedrock project
   RT   buffalo project
   RT   castle project
   RT   cavities
   RT   civil defense
   RT   contained explosions
   RT   cratering explosions
   RT   crossroads project
   RT   dominic project
   RT   electromagnetic pulses
   RT   excavation
   RT   explosive fracturing
   RT   explosive stimulation
   RT   fallout
   RT   fission
   RT   fission products
   RT   global fallout
   RT   greenhouse project
   RT   ground motion
   RT   hardtack project
   RT   hiroshima
   RT   ivy project
   RT   jangle project
   RT   marshall islands
   RT   nagasaki
   RT   nevada test site
   RT   nuclear excavation
   RT   nuclear explosion detection
   RT   nuclear fireballs
   RT   nuclear weapons
   RT   nuclear winter
   RT   plowshare project
   RT   plumbbob project
   RT   radioactive clouds
   RT   redwing project
   RT   seismic effects
   RT   shelters
   RT   shock waves
   RT   surface explosions
   RT   thunderbird project
   RT   underground explosions
   RT   underwater explosions
   RT   upshot project
   RT   vela project

NUCLEAR EXPLOSIVES [94; 94]
   BT1 explosives

NUCLEAR FACILITIES [5,619; 57,265]
- UF *installation sites*
- UF *nuclear installation sites*
- UF *sites (nuclear installations)*
- NT1 feed materials plants
  - NT2 anaconda uranium mill
  - NT2 feed materials production cent
  - NT2 highland uranium mill
  - NT2 shirley basin uranium mill
  - NT2 west valley uf6 facility
- NT1 fuel cycle centers
- NT1 fuel fabrication plants
  - NT2 cimarron plutonium plant
  - NT2 cimarron uranium plant
  - NT2 exxon fuel fabrication facilit
  - NT2 general atomic fuel fabricatio
  - NT2 mixed oxide fuel plant
  - NT2 westinghouse recycle fuels pla
- NT1 fuel reprocessing plants
  - NT2 barnwell fuel processing plant
  - NT2 cea la hague
  - NT2 cogema la hague
  - NT2 hef
  - NT2 idaho chemical processing plan
  - NT2 midwest fuel recovery plant
  - NT2 nuclear fuel recovery and recy
  - NT2 sellafield reprocessing plant
  - NT2 wackersdorf reprocessing plant
  - NT2 wak
  - NT2 west valley processing plant
  - NT2 westinghouse recycle fuels pla
- NT1 hot labs
- NT1 humeca uranium mill
- NT1 irradiation plants
  - NT2 isomed
- NT1 isotope separation plants
  - NT2 centrifuge enrichment plants
    - NT3 portsmouth centrifuge enrichme
  - NT2 gaseous diffusion plants
    - NT3 cogema pierrelatte
    - NT3 orgdp
    - NT3 paducah plant
    - NT3 portsmouth gaseous diffusion p
  - NT2 heavy water plants
  - NT2 tritium extraction plants
- NT1 nuclear power plants
  - NT2 bopssar standard plant
  - NT2 ebasco standard plant
  - NT2 gibbssar standard plant
  - NT2 offshore nuclear power plants
  - NT2 swessar standard plant
  - NT2 thermonuclear power plants
  - NT2 underground nuclear stations
- NT1 radioactive waste facilities
  - NT2 asse salt mine
  - NT2 gorleben salt dome
  - NT2 konrad ore mine
  - NT2 pamela plant
  - NT2 vaalputs radioactive waste dis
  - NT2 wipp
- RT biointrusion
- RT controlled areas
- RT external zones
- RT human intrusion
- RT laboratories
- RT site approvals
- RT storage facilities
- RT test facilities
- RT underground facilities

nuclear ferromagnetism
(Ordering of nuclear spins occurring when the temperature is lowered to the microkelvin region.)
- USE ferromagnetism
- AND nuclear magnetism

NUCLEAR FIREBALL MODEL
[200; 200] *Sep 78*
(A nuclear reaction model for the total disintegration of the two nuclei in relativistic heavy ion reactions.)
- UF *firestreak model*
- BT1 nuclear models
  - BT2 mathematical models
- RT evaporation model
- RT heavy ion reactions

- RT inclusive interactions
- RT quasi-fission
- RT spallation

NUCLEAR FIREBALLS [103; 103]
Aug 75
- UF *fireballs (nuclear)*
- RT nuclear explosions

NUCLEAR FORCES [1,576; 1,609]
- NT1 wigner force
- RT binding energy
- RT mass defect
- RT nuclear potential
- RT tensor forces

NUCLEAR FRAGMENTATION
[566; 566] *Nov 75*
- UF *fragmentation (nuclear)*
- BT1 nuclear reactions
- RT deep inelastic heavy ion react
- RT fission
- RT incomplete fusion reactions
- RT nuclear fragments
- RT spallation

NUCLEAR FRAGMENTS [2,404; 6,470]
Nov 78
- UF *fragments (nuclear)*
- NT1 anomalons
- NT1 fission fragments
- NT1 spallation fragments
- RT fission
- RT nuclear fragmentation
- RT spallation

nuclear fuel centers
- USE fuel cycle centers

NUCLEAR FUEL CONVERSION
[288; 1,330]
(Conversion of a fertile substance into a fissile substance.)
- UF *conversion (nuclear fuel)*
- NT1 breeding
- RT conversion ratio
- RT fertile materials

nuclear fuel elements
- USE fuel elements

NUCLEAR FUEL RECOVERY AND RECY [8; 8] *Apr 84*
(EXXON NUCLEAR FACILITY ROANE COUNTY, Tennessee, USA. Prior to December 1990, this concept was indexed by EXXON RECOVERY AND RECYCLE PLA.)
- UF *exxon recovery and recycle pla*
- BT1 fuel reprocessing plants
  - BT2 nuclear facilities

NUCLEAR FUELS [7,475; 16,999]
- UF *reactor fuels (fission)*
- BT1 energy sources
- BT1 fuels
- BT1 reactor materials
  - BT2 materials
- NT1 denatured fuel
- NT1 fuel slurries
- NT1 gas fuels
- NT1 solid fuels
  - NT2 alloy nuclear fuels
  - NT2 dispersion nuclear fuels
  - NT2 mixed carbide fuels
  - NT2 mixed nitride fuels
  - NT2 mixed oxide fuels
- NT1 spent fuels
- RT accelerator breeders
- RT burnup
- RT fertile materials
- RT fissile materials
- RT fissium
- RT fuel cycle
- RT fuel densification

- RT fuel elements
- RT fuel integrity
- RT fuel particles
- RT fuel pellets
- RT fuel washers
- RT fuel-cladding interactions
- RT fuel-coolant interactions
- RT nuclear materials management
- RT plutonium
- RT reactors
- RT thorium cycle
- RT uranium

NUCLEAR FURNACE REACTOR
[7; 7]
- BT1 beryllium moderated reactors
  - BT2 metal moderated reactors
    - BT3 reactors
- BT1 enriched uranium reactors
  - BT2 reactors
- BT1 research and test reactors
  - BT2 reactors
- BT1 tank type reactors
  - BT2 reactors
- BT1 water moderated reactors
  - BT2 reactors

NUCLEAR INDUSTRY [4,518; 4,518]
- BT1 industry
- RT construction
- RT fuel fabrication plants
- RT fuel reprocessing plants
- RT gaseous diffusion plants
- RT nuclear engineering
- RT nuclear parks

nuclear install. inspect. (uk)
- USE uk nii

nuclear installation sites
(If appropriate use one of the specific types of facilities.)
- USE nuclear facilities

NUCLEAR INSTRUMENT MODULES
[418; 418]
(Standard instrumentation modules designed to be interchangeable physically and electrically.)
- UF *aec-nim*
- UF *nim*
- RT electronic circuits
- RT electronic equipment
- RT fastbus system
- RT modular structures

NUCLEAR INSURANCE [398; 398]
- BT1 insurance

NUCLEAR LIABILITY [327; 327]
Dec 76
(The special liability regime, for nuclear damage, of the operators of nuclear installations.)
- BT1 liabilities
- RT liability exclusions
- RT liability limitations
- RT nuclear operators
- RT pcotpl
- RT price-anderson act
- RT time limitations
- RT vcoclnd

NUCLEAR MAGNETIC LOGGING
[38; 38] *Apr 78*
- UF *nmr logging*
- BT1 well logging

NUCLEAR MAGNETIC MOMENTS
[2,045; 2,045]
- UF *nuclear moments (magnetic)*
- BT1 magnetic moments
- BT1 nuclear properties
- RT magnetic dipole moments
- RT nuclear magnetism

NUCLEAR MAGNETIC MOMENTS

RT	perturbed angular correlation
RT	quadrupole moments
RT	schmidt lines

NUCLEAR MAGNETIC RESONANCE
[11,614; 11,712]

UF	*nmr*
UF	*nuclear spin resonance*
UF	*paramagnetic resonance (nuclea*
BT1	magnetic resonance
BT2	resonance
NT1	acoustic nmr
RT	chemical shift
RT	contrast media
RT	double resonance methods
RT	knight shift
RT	level mixing resonance
RT	nmr imaging
RT	nmr spectra
RT	nuclear magnetism
RT	overhauser effect
RT	spin echo
RT	spin-lattice relaxation
RT	spin-spin relaxation
RT	structural chemical analysis

nuclear magnetic resonance spe
USE   nmr spectra

NUCLEAR MAGNETISM [16; 16]
Mar 85
(Refers to ordering of nuclear spins at extremely low temperatures.)

UF+	*nuclear ferromagnetism*
BT1	magnetism
RT	nuclear magnetic moments
RT	nuclear magnetic resonance
RT	spin orientation

NUCLEAR MATERIALS DIVERSION
[920; 920]

RT	cppnm
RT	detection
RT	motion detection systems
RT	non-proliferation policy
RT	safeguards
RT	security personnel

NUCLEAR MATERIALS MANAGEMENT [3,574; 5,147]

UF	*fissionable materials manageme*
BT1	management
NT1	fuel management
RT	accounting
RT	cost
RT	cppnm
RT	detection
RT	fissile materials
RT	fissionable materials
RT	fuel cycle
RT	identification systems
RT	nuclear fuels
RT	nuclear materials possession
RT	radioactive wastes
RT	reprocessing
RT	safeguards

NUCLEAR MATERIALS POSSESSION
[203; 203] *Dec 76*

UF	*possession (nuclear materials)*
RT	non-proliferation treaty
RT	nuclear materials management
RT	nuclear trade
RT	proliferation
RT	safeguard regulations
RT	safeguards

NUCLEAR MATRIX [152; 152]
BT1   matrices

NUCLEAR MATTER [6,617; 6,617]

UF	*neutron matter*
UF	*nuclear density*
UF	*nuclear matter density*
BT1	matter
RT	neutron stars
RT	nuclei
RT	pion condensation
RT	quark matter
RT	walecka model

nuclear matter density
(Coordinate descriptor below with NEUTRON DENSITY and/or PROTON DENSITY.)
USE   nuclear matter

NUCLEAR MEDICINE [7,638; 12,562]

UF+	*radiodiagnosis (radionuclides)*
BT1	medicine
RT	biomedical radiography
RT	clearance
RT	diagnosis
RT	diagnostic techniques
RT	gamma cameras
RT	labelled compounds
RT	positron cameras
RT	radioisotope scanning
RT	radioisotopes
RT	radiology
RT	radiopharmaceuticals
RT	radiotherapy
RT	renography
RT	scintiscanning
RT	tracer techniques

NUCLEAR MERCHANT SHIPS
[58; 205] *Mar 76*

UF	*commercial nuclear ships*
BT1	nuclear ships
BT2	ships
NT1	ns mutsu
NT1	ns otto hahn
NT1	ns savannah

NUCLEAR MODELS [4,215; 31,630]

UF	*models (nuclear)*
BT1	mathematical models
NT1	bjorklund-fernbach model
NT1	black nucleus model
NT1	brueckner model
NT1	cloudy crystal ball model
NT1	cluster model
NT1	collective model
NT2	rotation-vibration model
NT1	cranking model
NT1	davydov-filipov model
NT1	droplet model
NT1	elliot model
NT1	evaporation model
NT2	weisskopf model
NT1	exciton model
NT1	fermi gas model
NT1	folding model
NT1	goldberger model
NT1	lane-thomas-wigner model
NT1	liquid drop model
NT1	nilsson-mottelson model
NT1	nuclear fireball model
NT1	order-disorder model
NT1	particle-core coupling model
NT1	particle-hole model
NT1	perey-buck model
NT1	quartet model
NT1	quasiparticle-phonon model
NT1	scission-point model
NT1	shell models
NT2	governor model
NT2	interacting boson model
NT2	multi-center shell model
NT1	spherical model
NT1	strong-absorption model
NT1	superfluid model
NT1	unified model
NT1	vmi model
NT1	walecka model
NT1	weak-coupling model
RT	bohr-wheeler theory
RT	brueckner method
RT	compound nuclei
RT	deformed nuclei
RT	hamada-johnston potential
RT	harmonic oscillator models
RT	hartree-fock method
RT	hartree-fock-bogolyubov theory
RT	hill-wheeler theory
RT	hurwitz effect
RT	hydrodynamic model
RT	kisslinger-sorensen theory
RT	nuclear radii
RT	nuclear structure
RT	nucleon-nucleon potential
RT	optical models
RT	single-particle model
RT	strutinsky theory
RT	thomas-fermi model

NUCLEAR MOLECULES [643; 643]

RT	interactions
RT	nuclei

nuclear moments (electric)
USE   nuclear electric moments

nuclear moments (magnetic)
USE   nuclear magnetic moments

NUCLEAR OPERATORS [151; 151]
Dec 76
(The financially responsible organizations or persons.)

UF	*operators (nuclear facilities)*
RT	national organizations
RT	notification procedures
RT	nuclear liability
RT	wano

NUCLEAR PARKS [183; 183]
(A facility containing a nuclear power plant plus on-site support industries such as fuel fabrication plants, reprocessing plants, etc.)

RT	fuel fabrication plants
RT	fuel reprocessing plants
RT	nuclear industry
RT	nuclear power plants

NUCLEAR PHYSICS [2,446; 2,446]
(Use only for indexing articles of very broad coverage, such as annual reviews, text books, etc.)

BT1	physics
RT	high energy physics
RT	nuclear chemistry
RT	nuclear theory

NUCLEAR POISONS [274; 1,344]
(Neutron absorbers in a reactor.)

UF	*poisons (nuclear)*
BT1	reactor materials
BT2	materials
NT1	burnable poisons
NT1	fission poisons
NT1	soluble poisons
RT	poisoning
RT	reactor poison removal

NUCLEAR POTENTIAL [5,988; 10,722]

BT1	potentials
NT1	hard-core potential
NT1	harmonic potential
NT1	hulthen potential
NT1	soft-core potential
NT1	square-well potential
NT1	woods-saxon potential
NT1	yukawa potential
RT	hamada-johnston potential
RT	nonlocal potential
RT	nuclear forces
RT	optical models
RT	signell-marshak potential
RT	tabakin potential
RT	wigner-eisenbud theory

NUCLEAR POWER [6,734; 6,832]
- BT1 power
- NT1 residual power
- RT electric power
- RT nuclear power phaseout
- RT power generation

NUCLEAR POWER PHASEOUT
[224; 224] Dec 82
(Policy scenario wherein plants now operating or under construction are allowed normal-life operation, but no additional plants are allowed.)
- RT energy policy
- RT government policies
- RT nuclear power

NUCLEAR POWER PLANTS
[36,124; 37,068]
- UF *nuclear power stations*
- BT1 nuclear facilities
- BT1 thermal power plants
  - BT2 power plants
- NT1 bopssar standard plant
- NT1 ebasco standard plant
- NT1 gibbssar standard plant
- NT1 offshore nuclear power plants
- NT1 swessar standard plant
- NT1 thermonuclear power plants
- NT1 underground nuclear stations
- RT nuclear energy
- RT nuclear parks
- RT power reactors

nuclear power stations
- USE nuclear power plants

NUCLEAR PROPERTIES [1,042; 6,493]
- NT1 nuclear electric moments
- NT1 nuclear magnetic moments
- NT1 nuclear radii
- RT limiting values
- RT nuclear structure

NUCLEAR PUMPING [176; 176]
(Laser-like pumping in nuclei, produced by electrons or, in general, by beams of charged particles.)
- UF *nuclear-pumped lasers*
- UF *pumping (nuclear)*
- RT electrical pumping
- RT gasers
- RT optical pumping
- RT stimulated emission

NUCLEAR QUADRUPOLE RESONANCE [876; 876]
- BT1 resonance
- RT electric fields
- RT level mixing resonance
- RT nuclear electric moments
- RT quadrupole moments

NUCLEAR RADII [2,868; 2,868]
- UF *charge radius (nuclear)*
- UF *mass radius (nuclear)*
- BT1 nuclear properties
- RT charge distribution
- RT nuclear models
- RT nuclear structure
- RT particle radii

NUCLEAR REACTION ANALYSIS
[1,687; 1,687]
(Chemical analysis based on detection and analysis of prompt nuclear reaction products, e.g., gamma rays, neutrons, or charged particles.)
- UF *analysis (nuclear reaction)*
- UF+ *pige analysis*
- BT1 nondestructive analysis
  - BT2 chemical analysis
- RT activation analysis
- RT nuclear reaction analyzers

NUCLEAR REACTION ANALYZERS
[21; 21] Jan 86
- BT1 measuring instruments
- RT nuclear reaction analysis

NUCLEAR REACTION KINETICS
[5,495; 5,495]
- BT1 reaction kinetics
  - BT2 kinetics
- RT coupled channel born approxima
- RT distorted wave theory
- RT dwba
- RT finite-range interactions
- RT nuclear reactions
- RT q-value
- RT rescattering
- RT resonating-group method
- RT spin flip
- RT zero-range approximation

NUCLEAR REACTION YIELD
[3,833; 6,419]
- UF *yield (nuclear reaction)*
- NT1 fission yield
- NT1 fusion yield
- RT nuclear reactions

NUCLEAR REACTIONS [8,558; 123,036]
- NT1 alpha reactions
- NT1 antineutrino reactions
- NT1 breakup reactions
- NT1 charge-exchange reactions
- NT1 cold fusion
- NT1 compound-nucleus reactions
- NT1 deuteron reactions
  - NT2 antideuteron reactions
- NT1 direct reactions
  - NT2 knock-on reactions
  - NT2 knock-out reactions
  - NT2 quasi-free reactions
  - NT2 transfer reactions
    - NT3 multi-nucleon transfer reactio
      - NT4 four-nucleon transfer reaction
        - NT5 alpha-transfer reactions
      - NT4 many-nucleon transfer reaction
      - NT4 three-nucleon transfer reactio
      - NT4 two-nucleon transfer reactions
    - NT3 one-nucleon transfer reactions
    - NT3 pickup reactions
    - NT3 stripping
- NT1 fission
  - NT2 binary fission
  - NT2 electrofission
  - NT2 fast fission
  - NT2 photofission
  - NT2 quaternary fission
  - NT2 spontaneous fission
  - NT2 ternary fission
  - NT2 thermal fission
- NT1 hadron reactions
  - NT2 baryon reactions
    - NT3 hyperon reactions
    - NT3 nucleon reactions
      - NT4 antinucleon reactions
        - NT5 antineutron reactions
        - NT5 antiproton reactions
      - NT4 neutron reactions
        - NT5 fast fission
        - NT5 thermal fission
      - NT4 proton reactions
  - NT2 meson reactions
    - NT3 kaon reactions
      - NT4 kaon minus reactions
      - NT4 kaon neutral reactions
      - NT4 kaon plus reactions
    - NT3 pion reactions
      - NT4 pion minus reactions
      - NT4 pion plus reactions
- NT1 heavy ion reactions
  - NT2 aluminium 27 reactions
  - NT2 argon 36 reactions
  - NT2 argon 40 reactions
  - NT2 beryllium 7 reactions
  - NT2 beryllium 8 reactions
  - NT2 beryllium 9 reactions
  - NT2 bismuth 209 reactions
  - NT2 boron 10 reactions
  - NT2 boron 11 reactions
  - NT2 bromine 79 reactions
  - NT2 bromine 81 reactions
  - NT2 calcium 40 reactions
  - NT2 calcium 42 reactions
  - NT2 calcium 44 reactions
  - NT2 calcium 48 reactions
  - NT2 carbon 12 reactions
  - NT2 carbon 13 reactions
  - NT2 carbon 14 reactions
  - NT2 chlorine 35 reactions
  - NT2 chlorine 37 reactions
  - NT2 chromium 52 reactions
  - NT2 chromium 54 reactions
  - NT2 cobalt 59 reactions
  - NT2 copper 63 reactions
  - NT2 copper 65 reactions
  - NT2 deep inelastic heavy ion react
  - NT2 dysprosium 161 reactions
  - NT2 erbium 166 reactions
  - NT2 fluorine 19 reactions
  - NT2 gadolinium 155 reactions
  - NT2 germanium 74 reactions
  - NT2 germanium 76 reactions
  - NT2 gold 197 reactions
  - NT2 heavy ion fusion reactions
  - NT2 helium 6 reactions
  - NT2 helium 8 reactions
  - NT2 holmium 165 reactions
  - NT2 incomplete fusion reactions
  - NT2 iodine 127 reactions
  - NT2 iron 54 reactions
  - NT2 iron 56 reactions
  - NT2 iron 58 reactions
  - NT2 krypton 80 reactions
  - NT2 krypton 82 reactions
  - NT2 krypton 83 reactions
  - NT2 krypton 84 reactions
  - NT2 krypton 86 reactions
  - NT2 lanthanum 139 reactions
  - NT2 lead 206 reactions
  - NT2 lead 208 reactions
  - NT2 lithium 11 reactions
  - NT2 lithium 6 reactions
  - NT2 lithium 7 reactions
  - NT2 lithium 8 reactions
  - NT2 lithium 9 reactions
  - NT2 magnesium 24 reactions
  - NT2 magnesium 25 reactions
  - NT2 magnesium 26 reactions
  - NT2 manganese 55 reactions
  - NT2 molybdenum 100 reactions
  - NT2 molybdenum 92 reactions
  - NT2 molybdenum 96 reactions
  - NT2 molybdenum 98 reactions
  - NT2 neodymium 142 reactions
  - NT2 neodymium 150 reactions
  - NT2 neon 20 reactions
  - NT2 neon 22 reactions
  - NT2 nickel 58 reactions
  - NT2 nickel 59 reactions
  - NT2 nickel 60 reactions
  - NT2 nickel 61 reactions
  - NT2 nickel 64 reactions
  - NT2 niobium 93 reactions
  - NT2 nitrogen 14 reactions
  - NT2 nitrogen 15 reactions
  - NT2 oxygen 16 reactions
  - NT2 oxygen 17 reactions
  - NT2 oxygen 18 reactions
  - NT2 palladium 118 reactions
  - NT2 phosphorus 31 reactions
  - NT2 potassium 39 reactions
  - NT2 quasi-fission
  - NT2 ruthenium 104 reactions
  - NT2 samarium 144 reactions
  - NT2 samarium 154 reactions
  - NT2 scandium 45 reactions
  - NT2 selenium 76 reactions
  - NT2 selenium 80 reactions
  - NT2 selenium 82 reactions
  - NT2 silicon 28 reactions
  - NT2 silicon 29 reactions
  - NT2 silicon 30 reactions
  - NT2 silver 109 reactions
  - NT2 sodium 23 reactions
  - NT2 sulfur 32 reactions
  - NT2 sulfur 33 reactions

NT2	sulfur 34 reactions
NT2	sulfur 36 reactions
NT2	tellurium 130 reactions
NT2	thallium 205 reactions
NT2	thorium 232 reactions
NT2	tin 112 reactions
NT2	tin 116 reactions
NT2	tin 118 reactions
NT2	tin 120 reactions
NT2	tin 122 reactions
NT2	tin 124 reactions
NT2	titanium 46 reactions
NT2	titanium 48 reactions
NT2	titanium 50 reactions
NT2	tungsten 183 reactions
NT2	tungsten 184 reactions
NT2	uranium 235 reactions
NT2	uranium 238 reactions
NT2	vanadium 51 reactions
NT2	xenon 129 reactions
NT2	xenon 132 reactions
NT2	xenon 134 reactions
NT2	xenon 136 reactions
NT2	zinc 64 reactions
NT2	zinc 68 reactions
NT2	zinc 70 reactions
NT2	zirconium 90 reactions
NT2	zirconium 92 reactions
NT2	zirconium 96 reactions
NT1	helium 3 reactions
NT1	lepton reactions
NT2	electron reactions
NT3	electrofission
NT2	muon reactions
NT2	neutrino reactions
NT2	positron reactions
NT1	nuclear fragmentation
NT1	photonuclear reactions
NT2	photofission
NT1	precompound-nucleus emission
NT1	quasi-elastic scattering
NT1	secondary reactions
NT1	spallation
NT1	strangeness-exchange reactions
NT1	thermonuclear reactions
NT2	impact fusion
NT2	muon-catalyzed fusion
NT1	triton reactions
RT	capture
RT	capture-to-fission ratio
RT	chain reactions
RT	cinda
RT	coherent tube model
RT	coupled channel born approxima
RT	coupled channel theory
RT	cross sections
RT	delayed gamma radiation
RT	detailed balance principle
RT	excitation functions
RT	feshbach-weisskopf model
RT	form factors
RT	g matrix
RT	giant resonance
RT	hauser-feshbach theory
RT	hot atom chemistry
RT	impact parameter
RT	integral cross sections
RT	intermediate resonance
RT	intermediate structure
RT	jackson model
RT	k matrix
RT	lane-robson theory
RT	lewis peak
RT	longitudinal momentum
RT	nuclear reaction kinetics
RT	nuclear reaction yield
RT	oppenheimer-phillips process
RT	polarized products
RT	prompt gamma radiation
RT	proximity scattering
RT	r matrix
RT	reaction product transport
RT	reich-moore formula
RT	rescattering
RT	scattering
RT	shadow effect
RT	skyrme potential
RT	spectroscopic factors

RT	strangeness analog resonances
RT	targets
RT	threshold energy
RT	transverse energy
RT	transverse momentum
RT	yang theorem

nuclear reactors
USE   reactors

nuclear research centre,tehran
USE   tehran nuclear research centre

nuclear safety
USE   radiation protection

NUCLEAR SAFETY PILOT PLANT
[28; 28]
UF   *nspp*
BT1   reactor safety experiments

NUCLEAR SCREENING [353; 353]
RT   coulomb field
RT   effective charge

NUCLEAR SHIP VISITS [44; 44]
Dec 76
RT	bcolons
RT	maritime laws
RT	nuclear ships
RT	territorial waters
RT	transport regulations

NUCLEAR SHIPS [463; 760]
BT1	ships
NT1	ns lenin
NT1	ns leonid brezhnev
NT1	ns sibir
NT1	nuclear merchant ships
NT2	ns mutsu
NT2	ns otto hahn
NT2	ns savannah
RT	bcolons
RT	nuclear ship visits
RT	ship propulsion reactors
RT	solas convention
RT	submarines

NUCLEAR SPECIFIC HEAT [29; 29]
Mar 76
(Contribution to specific heat by lattice vibrations)
BT1	specific heat
BT2	thermodynamic properties
BT3	physical properties
RT	electronic specific heat
RT	lattice vibrations

nuclear spin resonance
USE   nuclear magnetic resonance

NUCLEAR STRUCTURE
[14,041; 14,041]
RT	backbending
RT	belyaev theory
RT	energy levels
RT	even-even nuclei
RT	even-odd nuclei
RT	generator-coordinate method
RT	hartree-fock method
RT	hartree-fock-bogolyubov theory
RT	heavy nuclei
RT	interacting boson model
RT	intermediate mass nuclei
RT	k-harmonics method
RT	light nuclei
RT	magic nuclei
RT	nuclear cores
RT	nuclear models
RT	nuclear properties
RT	nuclear radii

RT	nuclei
RT	odd-even nuclei
RT	odd-odd nuclei
RT	particle-core coupling model
RT	quartet model
RT	yrast states

NUCLEAR SUPERHEATING [65; 65]
BT1   superheating
BT2   heating

NUCLEAR TEMPERATURE
[1,465; 1,465]
UF	*temperature (nuclear)*
RT	energy
RT	evaporation model
RT	nuclei

NUCLEAR THEORY [859; 2,160]
NT1	hauser-feshbach theory
RT	broken-pair approximation
RT	nuclear physics

NUCLEAR TRADE [925; 925] *Dec 76*
(Trade or commerce involving special nuclear material or any other radioactive materials, instruments, equipment, plants, etc., of nuclear interest.)
UF	*commerce (nuclear)*
BT1	trade
RT	economic development
RT	economic policy
RT	nuclear materials possession
RT	transport

nuclear transmutation
USE   transmutation

NUCLEAR WASTE POLICY ACTS
[653; 653] *Jul 85*
(For legislation of any country relating to the handling of nuclear radioactive wastes.)
UF	*radioactive waste policy acts*
BT1	atomic energy laws
BT2	laws
RT	radioactive waste disposal
RT	radioactive wastes
RT	spent fuel storage
RT	spent fuels

nuclear weapon tests
USE   nuclear explosions

NUCLEAR WEAPONS [2,271; 2,271]
UF	*atomic bombs*
UF	*atomic weapons*
UF	*nuclear attacks*
UF	*thermonuclear weapons*
RT	arms control
RT	castle project
RT	civil defense
RT	fallout
RT	hiroshima
RT	local fallout
RT	manhattan project
RT	nagasaki
RT	national defense
RT	nevada test site
RT	non-proliferation policy
RT	nuclear disarmament
RT	nuclear explosions
RT	nuclear winter
RT	plumbbob project
RT	projectiles
RT	redwing project
RT	shelters
RT	teapot project
RT	tlatelolco treaty
RT	tumbler project

nuclear weapons proliferation
USE   proliferation

NUCLEAR WINTER [65; 65] *Sep 86*
(The atmospheric effects resulting from nuclear war. The major effect is considered to be a hemispheric temperature drop to as low as -40 deg C lasting several months.)
RT climates
RT environmental impacts
RT nuclear explosions
RT nuclear weapons

nuclear-pumped lasers
(Coordinate descriptor below with appropriate descriptor from word block for LASERS.)
USE nuclear pumping

nuclease (deoxyribonuclease)
USE dna-ase

nuclease (ribonuclease)
USE rna-ase

NUCLEASES [419; 706]
BT1 phosphodiesterases
BT2 esterases
BT3 hydrolases
BT4 enzymes
BT5 organic compounds
NT1 dna-ase
NT1 endonucleases
NT1 rna-ase
RT micrococcus luteus
RT nucleic acids
RT nucleoproteins

NUCLEATE BOILING [645; 1,111]
BT1 boiling
BT2 phase transformations
NT1 departure nucleate boiling
RT heat transfer
RT nucleation

NUCLEATION [2,093; 2,093]
RT crystal growth
RT crystallization
RT nucleate boiling

NUCLEBRAS [108; 108] *Mar 77*
BT1 brazilian organizations
BT2 national organizations

NUCLEI [5,707; 272,607]
NT1 antinuclei
NT2 antideuterons
NT2 antiprotons
NT2 antitritons
NT1 cosmic nuclei
NT1 deformed nuclei
*NT1 even-even nuclei
*NT1 even-odd nuclei
*NT1 heavy nuclei
NT1 hypernuclei
*NT1 intermediate mass nuclei
NT1 isobaric nuclei
NT1 isomeric nuclei
NT1 isotonic nuclei
*NT1 light nuclei
NT1 magic nuclei
NT1 mirror nuclei
*NT1 odd-even nuclei
*NT1 odd-odd nuclei
NT1 oriented nuclei
RT fundamental constants
RT isotopes
RT nuclear matter
RT nuclear molecules
RT nuclear structure
RT nuclear temperature
RT overhauser effect

nuclei (cells)
USE cell nuclei

NUCLEIC ACID DENATURATION [120; 120]
(Breaking of H-bonds between strands of NA.)
UF denaturation (nucleic acid)
RT decomposition
RT dna sequencing
RT heat treatments
RT molecular structure
RT nucleic acids
RT ph value

NUCLEIC ACID REPLICATION [14; 1,435]
NT1 dna replication

NUCLEIC ACIDS [508; 13,016]
BT1 organic compounds
NT1 dna
NT2 recombinant dna
NT1 rna
NT2 messenger-rna
NT2 ribosomal rna
NT2 transfer rna
NT1 thymonucleic acid
RT biological repair
RT cell nuclei
RT genetics
RT nucleases
RT nucleic acid denaturation
RT nucleoproteins
RT nucleotides
RT photoreactivation
RT precursor
RT ribosides

nucleogenesis
USE nucleosynthesis

NUCLEOLI [73; 73]
BT1 cell nuclei
BT2 cell constituents
RT chromosomes
RT human chromosomes
RT ribosomal rna
RT rna

NUCLEON BEAMS [103; 19,177]
BT1 particle beams
BT2 beams
NT1 neutron beams
NT1 proton beams

nucleon isobars
USE n*baryons

NUCLEON REACTIONS [923; 39,582]
UF+ nucleon-deuteron interactions
BT1 baryon reactions
BT2 hadron reactions
BT3 nuclear reactions
NT1 antinucleon reactions
NT2 antineutron reactions
NT2 antiproton reactions
NT1 neutron reactions
NT2 fast fission
NT2 thermal fission
NT1 proton reactions

NUCLEON-ANTINUCLEON INTERACTIO [596; 5,963]
BT1 baryon-baryon interactions
BT2 hadron-hadron interactions
BT3 particle interactions
BT4 interactions
NT1 antiproton-neutron interaction
NT1 neutron-antineutron interactio
NT1 proton-antineutron interaction
NT1 proton-antiproton interactions

nucleon-deuteron interactions
USE deuterium target
AND nucleon reactions

NUCLEON-HYPERON INTERACTIONS [457; 457]
BT1 baryon-baryon interactions
BT2 hadron-hadron interactions
BT3 particle interactions
BT4 interactions

NUCLEON-NUCLEON INTERACTIONS [6,210; 15,067]
BT1 baryon-baryon interactions
BT2 hadron-hadron interactions
BT3 particle interactions
BT4 interactions
NT1 neutron-neutron interactions
NT1 proton-nucleon interactions
NT2 proton-neutron interactions
NT2 proton-proton interactions
RT reid potential
RT schiffer potential

NUCLEON-NUCLEON POTENTIAL [3,547; 6,254]
BT1 potentials
NT1 gauss potential
NT1 hamada-johnston potential
NT1 reid potential
NT1 schiffer potential
NT1 signell-marshak potential
NT1 skyrme potential
NT1 yamaguchi potential
RT gartenhaus potential
RT interactions
RT jastrow theory
RT levy-klein potential
RT nuclear models
RT nucleons
RT ope potential
RT resonating-group method
RT rosenfeld force
RT surface delta potential
RT tabakin potential
RT yukawa potential

NUCLEONS [6,576; 89,099]
BT1 baryons
BT2 fermions
BT2 hadrons
BT3 elementary particles
NT1 antinucleons
NT2 antineutrons
NT2 antiprotons
NT1 neutrons
NT2 antineutrons
NT2 beta-delayed neutrons
NT2 cold neutrons
NT3 ultracold neutrons
NT2 cosmic neutrons
NT2 epithermal neutrons
NT2 fast neutrons
NT2 fission neutrons
NT3 delayed neutrons
NT3 prompt neutrons
NT2 intermediate neutrons
NT2 photoneutrons
NT2 pile neutrons
NT2 polyneutrons
NT3 dineutrons
NT3 tetraneutrons
NT3 trineutrons
NT2 resonance neutrons
NT2 slow neutrons
NT2 solar neutrons
NT2 thermal neutrons
NT1 photonucleons
NT2 photoneutrons
NT2 photoprotons
NT1 protons
NT2 antiprotons
NT2 cosmic protons
NT2 delayed protons
NT2 diprotons
NT2 photoprotons
NT2 prompt protons
NT2 solar protons
NT2 trapped protons

RT	brueckner method
RT	charge independence
RT	effective range theory
RT	hard-core potential
RT	levinger-bethe theory
RT	massey-mohr equation
RT	nucleon-nucleon potential
RT	ope potential
RT	pseudovector coupling
RT	rosenfeld force
RT	signell-marshak potential
RT	stapp theory
RT	tabakin potential
RT	wolfenstein parameters
RT	yamaguchi potential
RT	yukawa potential

NUCLEOPROTEINS [261; 261]
- BT1 proteins
  - BT2 organic compounds
- RT nucleases
- RT nucleic acids

NUCLEOSIDES [388; 4,893]
- BT1 nucleotides
  - BT2 organic compounds
- BT1 ribosides
- NT1 adenosine
- NT1 budr
- NT1 cytidine
- NT1 deoxycytidine
- NT1 deoxyuridine
- NT1 fudr
- NT1 guanosine
- NT1 inosine
- NT1 iododeoxyuridine
- NT1 thymidine
- NT1 uridine
- RT biological indicators
- RT purines
- RT pyrimidines

NUCLEOSOMES [62; 62] *Aug 84*
(Chromatin subunits composed of DNA-histone complexes.)
- RT chromatin
- RT dna
- RT histones

NUCLEOSYNTHESIS [2,505; 12,048]
- UF *nucleogenesis*
- BT1 synthesis
- NT1 heavy ion fusion reactions
- NT1 thermonuclear reactions
  - NT2 impact fusion
  - NT2 muon-catalyzed fusion
- RT carbon burning
- RT cno cycle
- RT cosmochemistry
- RT helium burning
- RT hydrogen burning
- RT origin
- RT r process
- RT s process
- RT stars

NUCLEOTIDASES [63; 63]
- BT1 phosphatases
  - BT2 esterases
    - BT3 hydrolases
      - BT4 enzymes
        - BT5 organic compounds

NUCLEOTIDES [1,532; 8,778]
- UF *oligonucleotides*
- BT1 organic compounds
- NT1 adp
- NT1 amp
- NT1 atp
- NT1 cytidylic acid
- NT1 deoxycytidylic acid
- NT1 guanylic acid
- NT1 nad
- NT1 nadh2
- NT1 nadp
- NT1 nucleosides
  - NT2 adenosine
  - NT2 budr
  - NT2 cytidine
  - NT2 deoxycytidine
  - NT2 deoxyuridine
  - NT2 fudr
  - NT2 guanosine
  - NT2 inosine
  - NT2 iododeoxyuridine
  - NT2 thymidine
  - NT2 uridine
- NT1 thymidylic acid
- NT1 udpg
- NT1 ump
- NT1 uridylic acid
- NT1 utp
- RT codons
- RT dna sequencing
- RT hypoxanthine
- RT nucleic acids
- RT organic acids

NUCLEOTIDYLTRANSFERASES [11; 348] *Dec 86*
- BT1 phosphorus-group transferases
  - BT2 transferases
    - BT3 enzymes
      - BT4 organic compounds
- NT1 polymerases
  - NT2 dna polymerases
  - NT2 rna polymerases

nuclides
- USE isotopes

numak reactors
(University of Wisconsin Tokamak upgrade of UWMAK I, II, and III.)
- USE uwmak devices

NUMATRON ACCELERATOR [21; 21] *Feb 84*
- BT1 heavy ion accelerators
  - BT2 accelerators

NUMBER CODES [84; 84]
- BT1 computer codes

NUMERICAL DATA [1,505; 122,099] *Oct 78*
(For data flagging one of the more specific terms should be used.)
- BT1 data
  - BT2 information
- NT1 compiled data
- NT1 evaluated data
- NT1 experimental data
- NT1 statistical data
- NT1 theoretical data

NUMERICAL SOLUTION [18,409; 30,338]
(For the procedure only.)
- NT1 extrapolation
- NT1 finite difference method
- NT1 finite element method
- NT1 interpolation
  - NT2 runge-kutta method
- NT1 maximum-likelihood fit
  - NT2 least square fit
- RT analytical solution
- RT asymptotic solutions
- RT galerkin-petrov method
- RT iterative methods
- RT mathematics
- RT newton method

NUSSELT NUMBER [789; 789]
- RT heat transfer
- RT prandtl number

NUTRIENTS [746; 746]
- RT culture media
- RT diet
- RT eutrophication
- RT feeding
- RT fertilizers
- RT food
- RT nutrition
- RT xenobiotics

NUTRITION [645; 645]
- RT animal breeding
- RT animal feeds
- RT diet
- RT food
- RT mass rearing
- RT nutrients
- RT nutritional deficiency
- RT rearing

NUTRITIONAL DEFICIENCY [435; 435]
- UF *deficiency (nutritional)*
- UF *malnutrition*
- RT diet
- RT nutrition

NUTS [20; 75] *Jan 82*
- BT1 fruits
  - BT2 food
- NT1 chestnuts
- NT1 peanuts

nuts (mechanical)
- USE fasteners

NYLON [190; 190]
- BT1 polyamides
  - BT2 organic polymers
    - BT3 organic compounds
    - BT3 polymers

nymphs
- USE larvae

NYQUIST DIAGRAMS [80; 80]
- BT1 diagrams
  - BT2 information
- RT feedback
- RT oscillations
- RT reactor stability

O CODES [614; 614]
- BT1 computer codes

O GROUPS [2,002; 2,002]
- BT1 dynamical groups
  - BT2 symmetry groups
- BT1 lie groups
  - BT2 symmetry groups

O-GLYCOSYL HYDROLASES [27; 214] *Dec 86*
- BT1 glycosyl hydrolases
  - BT2 hydrolases
    - BT3 enzymes
      - BT4 organic compounds
- NT1 amylase
- NT1 galactosidase
- NT1 glucuronidase
- NT1 lysozyme

oak harbor ohio reactor
- USE davis besse-1 reactor

oak ridge associated univ.
- USE orau

oak ridge critical exp. facili
- USE or-cef reactor

oak ridge gaseous diffusion pl
- USE orgdp

oak ridge national laboratory
   USE   ornl

oak ridge research reactor
   USE   orr reactor

OAK RIDGE RESERVATION [73; 73]
Jul 85
   BT1   us doe
      BT2   us organizations
         BT3   national organizations
   RT   orgdp
   RT   ornl
   RT   tennessee
   RT   y-12 plant

OAKS [58; 58]
   UF   *quercus*
   BT1   trees
      BT2   plants

OATS [159; 159]
   UF   *avena*
   BT1   cereals
      BT2   gramineae
         BT3   plants

ob. inst. yadern. issled.
   USE   jinr

OBE MODEL [1,074; 2,689]
   UF   *one-boson-exchange model*
   BT1   boson-exchange models
      BT2   peripheral models
         BT3   particle models
            BT4   mathematical models
   NT1   ope model
   NT2   electric born model

obesity
   USE   metabolic diseases

OBRIGHEIM REACTOR [253; 253]
   UF   *kernkraftwerk obrigheim*
   UF   *kwo reactor*
   BT1   pwr type reactors
      BT2   enriched uranium reactors
         BT3   reactors
      BT2   power reactors
         BT3   reactors
      BT2   thermal reactors
         BT3   reactors
      BT2   water cooled reactors
         BT3   reactors
      BT2   water moderated reactors
         BT3   reactors

obsidianites
   USE   tektites

obstetrics
   USE   gynecology

occlusion complexes
   USE   clathrates

occultation
   USE   eclipse

OCCUPATION NUMBER [729; 729]
   RT   pauli principle
   RT   quantum mechanics
   RT   statistical mechanics

OCCUPATIONAL DISEASES [497; 497]
   BT1   diseases
   RT   industrial medicine
   RT   occupational exposure
   RT   occupational safety
   RT   occupations
   RT   work

OCCUPATIONAL EXPOSURE
[1,449; 1,449] *Apr 85*
   RT   icrp critical group
   RT   occupational diseases
   RT   occupational safety
   RT   occupations
   RT   radiation doses

OCCUPATIONAL SAFETY
[1,284; 1,284] *Feb 81*
   BT1   safety
   RT   drug abuse
   RT   health hazards
   RT   industrial medicine
   RT   occupational diseases
   RT   occupational exposure
   RT   occupations
   RT   personnel
   RT   working conditions

occupational safety health adm
   USE   us osha

OCCUPATIONS [934; 934]
   UF   *employment*
   UF   *professions*
   UF+   *caste (insects)*
   RT   icrp critical group
   RT   occupational diseases
   RT   occupational exposure
   RT   occupational safety
   RT   personnel
   RT   personnel dosimetry
   RT   sociology
   RT   work

OCEANIC CRUST [39; 39] *Dec 86*
   BT1   earth crust
   RT   earth planet

OCEANOGRAPHY [392; 392]
   RT   earth planet
   RT   geography
   RT   limnology
   RT   seas

oceans
   USE   seas

OCONEE-1 REACTOR [306; 306]
(Oconee, South Carolina, USA)
   BT1   pwr type reactors
      BT2   enriched uranium reactors
         BT3   reactors
      BT2   power reactors
         BT3   reactors
      BT2   thermal reactors
         BT3   reactors
      BT2   water cooled reactors
         BT3   reactors
      BT2   water moderated reactors
         BT3   reactors

OCONEE-2 REACTOR [150; 150]
(Oconee, South Carolina, USA)
   BT1   pwr type reactors
      BT2   enriched uranium reactors
         BT3   reactors
      BT2   power reactors
         BT3   reactors
      BT2   thermal reactors
         BT3   reactors
      BT2   water cooled reactors
         BT3   reactors
      BT2   water moderated reactors
         BT3   reactors

OCONEE-3 REACTOR [139; 139]
(Oconee, South Carolina, USA)
   BT1   pwr type reactors
      BT2   enriched uranium reactors
         BT3   reactors
      BT2   power reactors
         BT3   reactors
      BT2   thermal reactors
         BT3   reactors
      BT2   water cooled reactors
         BT3   reactors
      BT2   water moderated reactors
         BT3   reactors

OCTADECANOIC ACID [117; 117]
   UF   *stearic acid*
   BT1   monocarboxylic acids
      BT2   carboxylic acids
         BT3   organic acids
            BT4   organic compounds

octadecyl glyceryl ether-alpha
   USE   batyl alcohol

OCTAL 82 FACILITY [13; 13] *Sep 83*
(Neodymium glass laser facility at Limeil, France for laser fusion experiments.)
   RT   neodymium lasers

OCTANE [149; 149]
   BT1   alkanes
      BT2   hydrocarbons
         BT3   organic compounds

OCTANOIC ACID [43; 43]
   UF   *caprylic acid*
   BT1   monocarboxylic acids
      BT2   carboxylic acids
         BT3   organic acids
            BT4   organic compounds

OCTANOLS [79; 79]
   UF   *octyl alcohols*
   BT1   alcohols
      BT2   hydroxy compounds
         BT3   organic compounds

OCTET MODEL [87; 87]
   UF   *eightfold way*
   BT1   particle models
      BT2   mathematical models
   RT   baryon octets

OCTUPOLAR CONFIGURATIONS
[147; 147]
   BT1   multipolar configurations
      BT2   closed configurations
         BT3   magnetic field configurations

octupole radiation
   USE   multipole radiation

OCTUPOLES [438; 438]
   BT1   multipoles

octyl alcohols
   USE   octanols

OCTYL RADICALS [10; 10]
   BT1   alkyl radicals
      BT2   radicals

* **ODD-EVEN NUCLEI** [588; 106,300]
(Odd protons, even neutrons. For specific terms, consult the Appendix.)
   BT1   nuclei
   RT   nuclear structure

* **ODD-ODD NUCLEI** [470; 62,725]
(Odd protons, odd neutrons. For specific terms, consult the Appendix.)
  BT1 nuclei
  RT nuclear structure

odocoileus
(For specific terms, consult the Appendix.)
  USE deer

§ **ODOR** [72; 72]
  BT1 organoleptic properties
  RT chemoreceptors

OECD [224; 628]
  UF organization econ co-op and de
  BT1 international organizations
  NT1 nea
  NT2 enea

OECD MCMSDRW [16; 16] *Aug 78*
(Multilateral Consultation and surveillance Mechanism for Sea Dumping of Radioactive Waste, set up by the OECD Council on 22 July 1977.)
  UF consult mechan on sea dumping
  UF multilat consult mechan, oecd
  BT1 international regulations
  BT2 regulations
  BT3 laws
  RT contamination
  RT lcpmpdpw
  RT marine disposal

oefzs
  USE seibersdorf research centre

oer
  USE oxygen enhancement ratio

OFF-GAS SYSTEMS [1,509; 1,509]
  RT gaseous wastes
  RT pollution control equipment
  RT scrubbing

off-peak energy storage
  USE energy storage

OFFSHORE NUCLEAR POWER PLANTS [222; 229]
  UF floating nuclear power plants
  UF platform mounted nuclear plant
  BT1 nuclear power plants
  BT2 nuclear facilities
  BT2 thermal power plants
  BT3 power plants
  RT atlantic-1 reactor
  RT atlantic-2 reactor
  RT estuaries
  RT offshore sites
  RT reactor sites
  RT seas
  RT shores
  RT site selection

OFFSHORE SITES [192; 192]
  RT coastal waters
  RT estuaries
  RT offshore nuclear power plants
  RT reactor sites
  RT seas
  RT shores
  RT site selection
  RT territorial waters

offsprings
  USE progeny

OGO SATELLITES [99; 99]
  UF orbiting geophysical observato
  BT1 satellites
  RT space flight

OGRA [38; 38]
  BT1 magnetic mirrors
  BT2 open plasma devices
  BT3 thermonuclear devices

ohi-3 reactor
  USE oi-3 reactor

ohi-4 reactor
  USE oi-4 reactor

OHIO [219; 219]
  BT1 usa
  BT2 developed countries
  BT2 north america
  RT feed materials production cent
  RT mound laboratory
  RT portsmouth centrifuge enrichme
  RT portsmouth gaseous diffusion p

OHIO RIVER [8; 8]
  BT1 rivers
  BT2 surface waters

ohio state univ. reactor
  USE osur reactor

OHM LAW [229; 229]
  RT electric conductivity

ohmic plasma heating
  USE joule heating

ohmic plasma losses
  USE energy losses

ohmic resistance
  USE electric conductivity

OI-1 REACTOR [35; 35]
  UF kepco oshima oi-1 reactor
  UF oshima oi-1 reactor
  BT1 pwr type reactors
  BT2 enriched uranium reactors
  BT3 reactors
  BT2 power reactors
  BT3 reactors
  BT2 thermal reactors
  BT3 reactors
  BT2 water cooled reactors
  BT3 reactors
  BT2 water moderated reactors
  BT3 reactors

OI-2 REACTOR [30; 30]
  UF kepco oshima oi-2 reactor
  UF oshima oi-2 reactor
  BT1 pwr type reactors
  BT2 enriched uranium reactors
  BT3 reactors
  BT2 power reactors
  BT3 reactors
  BT2 thermal reactors
  BT3 reactors
  BT2 water cooled reactors
  BT3 reactors
  BT2 water moderated reactors
  BT3 reactors

OI-3 REACTOR [6; 6] *Feb 90*
(Oi, Fukui, Japan.)
  UF ohi-3 reactor
  BT1 pwr type reactors
  BT2 enriched uranium reactors
  BT3 reactors
  BT2 power reactors
  BT3 reactors
  BT2 thermal reactors
  BT3 reactors
  BT2 water cooled reactors
  BT3 reactors
  BT2 water moderated reactors
  BT3 reactors

OI-4 REACTOR [5; 5] *Feb 90*
(Oi, Fukui, Japan.)
  UF ohi-4 reactor
  BT1 pwr type reactors
  BT2 enriched uranium reactors
  BT3 reactors
  BT2 power reactors
  BT3 reactors
  BT2 thermal reactors
  BT3 reactors
  BT2 water cooled reactors
  BT3 reactors
  BT2 water moderated reactors
  BT3 reactors

OIL PALMS [13; 13] *Sep 75*
  BT1 trees
  BT2 plants
  RT oils

OIL SANDS [79; 79] *Sep 75*
  UF tar sands
  BT1 carbonaceous materials
  BT2 materials
  BT1 sand
  RT bitumens
  RT oil shales

OIL SHALES [315; 315]
  BT1 carbonaceous materials
  BT2 materials
  BT1 shales
  BT2 sedimentary rocks
  BT3 rocks
  RT bitumens
  RT explosive stimulation
  RT gasbuggy event
  RT green river formation
  RT in-situ processing
  RT oil sands
  RT retorting
  RT rulison event
  RT shale oil
  RT uinta formation
  RT wasatch formation

→ **OIL SPILLS** [0; 0] *Aug 91*
  BT1 accidents

→ **OIL WELLS** [0; 0] *Aug 91*
  BT1 wells
  RT blowouts

OILS [655; 1,026]
  BT1 other organic compounds
  BT2 organic compounds
  NT1 castor oil
  NT1 corn oil
  NT1 cottonseed oil
  NT1 croton oil
  NT1 essential oils
  NT1 fish oil
  NT1 linseed oil
  NT1 lipiodol
  NT1 olive oil
  NT1 peanut oil
  NT1 sesame oil
  NT1 soybean oil
  NT1 triolein
  RT coolants
  RT greases
  RT hydrocarbons
  RT oil palms
  RT petroleum
  RT petroleum products
  RT terpenes
  RT triglycerides

OINTMENTS [52; 52]
RT drugs
RT skin

oiyai
USE jinr

OKG-1 REACTOR [59; 59]
UF *oskarshamn-1 reactor*
BT1 bwr type reactors
  BT2 enriched uranium reactors
    BT3 reactors
  BT2 power reactors
    BT3 reactors
  BT2 thermal reactors
    BT3 reactors
  BT2 water cooled reactors
    BT3 reactors
  BT2 water moderated reactors
    BT3 reactors

OKG-2 REACTOR [55; 55]
UF *oskarshamn-2 reactor*
BT1 bwr type reactors
  BT2 enriched uranium reactors
    BT3 reactors
  BT2 power reactors
    BT3 reactors
  BT2 thermal reactors
    BT3 reactors
  BT2 water cooled reactors
    BT3 reactors
  BT2 water moderated reactors
    BT3 reactors

OKG-3 REACTOR [21; 21]
UF *oskarshamn-3 reactor*
BT1 power reactors
  BT2 reactors

OKG-4 REACTOR [2; 2]
UF *oskarshamn-4 reactor*
BT1 power reactors
  BT2 reactors

OKLAHOMA [117; 117]
BT1 usa
  BT2 developed countries
  BT2 north america
RT sequoyah uf6 production plant

OKLO PHENOMENON [219; 219]
Jan 76
UF *natural reactor oklo*
BT1 natural nuclear reactors
RT chain reactions
RT criticality
RT uranium ores

oktemberian-1 reactor
USE armenian-1 reactor

oktemberian-2 reactor
USE armenian-2 reactor

OKUBO MASS FORMULA [100; 100]
BT1 mass formulae
RT particle multiplets

OLDBURY-A REACTOR [46; 46]
(Oldbury on Severn, Gloucestershire, UK)
BT1 carbon dioxide cooled reactors
  BT2 gas cooled reactors
    BT3 reactors
BT1 magnox type reactors
  BT2 gcr type reactors
    BT3 gas cooled reactors
      BT4 reactors
    BT3 graphite moderated reactors
      BT4 reactors
  BT2 natural uranium reactors
    BT3 reactors
  BT2 power reactors
    BT3 reactors
BT1 thermal reactors
  BT2 reactors

OLDBURY-B REACTOR [23; 23]
(Oldbury on Severn, Gloucestershire, UK)
BT1 carbon dioxide cooled reactors
  BT2 gas cooled reactors
    BT3 reactors
BT1 enriched uranium reactors
  BT2 reactors
BT1 power reactors
  BT2 reactors
BT1 thermal reactors
  BT2 reactors

olefins
USE alkenes

OLEIC ACID [203; 203]
BT1 monocarboxylic acids
  BT2 carboxylic acids
    BT3 organic acids
      BT4 organic compounds
RT triolein

olein
USE triolein

OLFACTORY BULBS [53; 53]
BT1 brain
  BT2 central nervous system
    BT3 nervous system
  BT2 organs
    BT3 body
RT sense organs

oligonucleotides
USE nucleotides

OLIGOPHENYLENES [3; 3]
BT1 aromatics
  BT2 organic compounds
BT1 hydrocarbons
  BT2 organic compounds

OLIGOSACCHARIDES [167; 916]
BT1 saccharides
  BT2 carbohydrates
    BT3 organic compounds
NT1 disaccharides
  NT2 cellobiose
  NT2 lactose
  NT2 maltose
  NT2 melibiose
  NT2 saccharose
NT1 raffinose

OLIVE OIL [29; 29]
UF *florence oil*
UF *luccu oil*
BT1 oils
  BT2 other organic compounds
    BT3 organic compounds
BT1 triglycerides
  BT2 esters
    BT3 organic compounds
  BT2 lipids
    BT3 organic compounds
RT olives

OLIVE TREES [6; 6] *Dec 75*
BT1 trees
  BT2 plants

OLIVES [12; 12]
BT1 fruits
  BT2 food
RT dacus oleae
RT olive oil

OLIVINE [268; 268]
BT1 silicate minerals
  BT2 minerals
RT anorthosites
RT basalt
RT dielectric track detectors
RT iron silicates
RT kimberlites
RT magnesium silicates
RT peridotites

olkiluoto (halmholmen)-1 reac
USE tvo-1 reactor

olkiluoto (halmholmen)-2 reac
USE tvo-2 reactor

OLYMPIC DAM MINE [6; 6] *Apr 90*
BT1 uranium mines
  BT2 mines
    BT3 underground facilities
RT roxby downs deposit
RT south australia

omaha veterans triga-mk-1
USE triga-veterans reactor

OMAN [10; 10] *Sep 81*
BT1 asia
BT1 developing countries
BT1 middle east

OMEGA BARYONS [10; 134] *Dec 87*
BT1 hyperons
  BT2 baryons
    BT3 fermions
    BT3 hadrons
      BT4 elementary particles
  BT2 strange particles
    BT3 elementary particles
NT1 omega particles
NT2 antiomega particles

OMEGA C NEUTRAL BARYONS
[12; 12] *Dec 87*
BT1 charmed baryons
  BT2 baryons
    BT3 fermions
    BT3 hadrons
      BT4 elementary particles
  BT2 charm particles
    BT3 elementary particles

OMEGA FACILITY [112; 112] *May 84*
(Large Nd laser facility at University of Rochester to be used for laser fusion experiments.)
RT laser fusion reactors
RT neodymium lasers

omega minus
(Prior to December 1987 this was a valid descriptor.)
USE omega particles

OMEGA PARTICLE BEAMS [2; 2]
BT1 hyperon beams
  BT2 particle beams
    BT3 beams

OMEGA PARTICLES [247; 415]
UF *omega minus*
BT1 omega baryons
  BT2 hyperons
    BT3 baryons
      BT4 fermions
      BT4 hadrons
        BT5 elementary particles
    BT3 strange particles
      BT4 elementary particles
NT1 antiomega particles

omega west reactor
   USE   owr reactor

omega-1675 resonances
(Prior to December 1987 this was a valid descriptor.)
   USE   omega3-1670 mesons

omega-1778 resonances
(Prior to December 1987 this was a valid descriptor.)
   USE   mesons

OMEGA-783 MESONS [1,136; 1,136]
(Prior to December 1987 this concept was indexed by OMEGA-784 RESONANCES.)
   UF   *omega-784 resonances*
   BT1   vector mesons
      BT2   mesons
         BT3   bosons
         BT3   hadrons
            BT4   elementary particles

omega-784 resonances
(Prior to December 1987 this was a valid descriptor.)
   USE   omega-783 mesons

OMEGA3-1670 MESONS [30; 30] *Sep 77*
(Prior to December 1987 this concept was indexed by OMEGA-1675 RESONANCES.)
   UF   *omega-1675 resonances*
   BT1   tensor mesons
      BT2   mesons
         BT3   bosons
         BT3   hadrons
            BT4   elementary particles

omentum
   USE   mesentery

OMNES-MUSKHELISHVILI METHOD [16; 16]
   RT   partial waves

OMNITRON [1; 1]
   BT1   synchrotrons
      BT2   cyclic accelerators
         BT3   accelerators

OMR TYPE REACTORS [10; 41]
   UF   *organic cooled and moder. reac*
   BT1   organic cooled reactors
      BT2   reactors
   BT1   organic moderated reactors
      BT2   reactors
   NT1   arbus reactor
   NT1   omre reactor
   NT1   pnpf reactor
   RT   power reactors

OMRE REACTOR [10; 10]
   UF   *organic moderated r. experimen*
   BT1   enriched uranium reactors
      BT2   reactors
   BT1   experimental reactors
      BT2   research and test reactors
         BT3   reactors
   BT1   mixed spectrum reactors
      BT2   reactors
   BT1   omr type reactors
      BT2   organic cooled reactors
         BT3   reactors
      BT2   organic moderated reactors
         BT3   reactors

on-line computers
   USE   computers
   AND   on-line systems

ON-LINE CONTROL SYSTEMS [5,172; 5,172]
   BT1   control systems
   BT1   on-line systems
   NT1   computerized control systems
   RT   camac system
   RT   computer-aided manufacturing
   RT   fastbus system
   RT   process computers
   RT   reactor control systems
   RT   real time systems

ON-LINE MEASUREMENT SYSTEMS [3,715; 3,715]
   BT1   on-line systems
   RT   digitizers
   RT   fastbus system
   RT   measuring instruments
   RT   reactor monitoring systems

ON-LINE SYSTEMS [1,764; 10,311]
   UF+   *on-line computers*
   NT1   on-line control systems
      NT2   computerized control systems
   NT1   on-line measurement systems
   RT   computer networks
   RT   real time systems

ON-SITE POWER GENERATION [13; 13] *Apr 86*
(Production of power at location of use instead of purchase of power from a utility.)
   BT1   power generation
   RT   accidents
   RT   emergency plans
   RT   reactor sites

ONAGAWA-1 REACTOR [31; 31]
(Onagawa, Miyagi, Japan)
   UF   *tohoku-1 reactor*
   BT1   bwr type reactors
      BT2   enriched uranium reactors
         BT3   reactors
      BT2   power reactors
         BT3   reactors
      BT2   thermal reactors
         BT3   reactors
      BT2   water cooled reactors
         BT3   reactors
      BT2   water moderated reactors
         BT3   reactors

ONAGAWA-2 REACTOR [3; 3] *Nov 89*
(Onagawa, Miyagi, Japan.)
   BT1   bwr type reactors
      BT2   enriched uranium reactors
         BT3   reactors
      BT2   power reactors
         BT3   reactors
      BT2   thermal reactors
         BT3   reactors
      BT2   water cooled reactors
         BT3   reactors
      BT2   water moderated reactors
         BT3   reactors

ONCOGENES [321; 321] *Apr 87*
   BT1   genes
   RT   carcinogenesis
   RT   growth factors
   RT   oncogenic transformations
   RT   oncogenic viruses

ONCOGENIC TRANSFORMATIONS [577; 685] *Jul 81*
(The chemical alterations induced in a cell by exposure to carcinogens and leading ultimately to the development of a neoplastic condition.)
   UF   *transformations (oncogenic)*
   NT1   cell transformations
   RT   carcinogenesis
   RT   carcinogens
   RT   oncogenes

ONCOGENIC VIRUSES [186; 428] *Mar 76*
   UF   *epstein-barr virus*
   UF   *rous sarcoma virus*
   UF   *sv40 virus*
   UF   *tumor viruses*
   BT1   viruses
      BT2   microorganisms
      BT2   parasites
   NT1   adenovirus
   NT1   leukemia viruses
   NT1   polyoma virus
   RT   carcinogenesis
   RT   leukemia
   RT   oncogenes

ONCOVIN [88; 88] *May 76*
   UF   *vincristine sulphate*
   BT1   alkaloids
      BT2   organic compounds
   BT1   antimitotic drugs
      BT2   drugs

ONDULATOR RADIATION [310; 310]
   BT1   bremsstrahlung
      BT2   electromagnetic radiation
         BT3   radiations

one-boson-exchange model
   USE   obe model

ONE-DIMENSIONAL CALCULATIONS [6,178; 6,178]
   UF   *calculations (1-dimensional)*
   UF   *1-dimensional calculations*
   RT   adjoint difference method
   RT   mathematics

ONE-GROUP THEORY [288; 288]
   BT1   transport theory
   RT   neutron transport theory

ONE-NUCLEON TRANSFER REACTIONS [3,507; 3,507]
   BT1   transfer reactions
      BT2   direct reactions
         BT3   nuclear reactions

ONIONS [289; 289]
   BT1   vegetables
      BT2   food
   RT   allium cepa
   RT   bulbs
   RT   hylemya antiqua
   RT   sprout inhibition

onsager principle
   USE   onsager relations

ONSAGER RELATIONS [160; 160]
   UF   *onsager principle*
   UF   *onsager symmetry relations*
   RT   irreversible processes
   RT   pressure gradients
   RT   temperature gradients
   RT   thermodynamics

onsager symmetry relations
   USE   onsager relations

ONTARIO [419; 508]
   BT1   canada
      BT2   developed countries
      BT2   north america
   NT1   chalk river
   NT1   deep river
   NT1   elliot lake

ontario phwr pickering-1 r.
   USE   pickering-1 reactor

ontario phwr pickering-2 r.
  USE   pickering-2 reactor

ontario phwr pickering-3 r.
  USE   pickering-3 reactor

ontario phwr pickering-4 r.
  USE   pickering-4 reactor

ontario phwr pickering-5 r.
  USE   pickering-5 reactor

ontario phwr pickering-6 r.
  USE   pickering-6 reactor

ontario phwr pickering-7 r.
  USE   pickering-7 reactor

ontario phwr pickering-8 r.
  USE   pickering-8 reactor

ONTOGENESIS [507; 507]
  RT   cell differentiation
  RT   embryos
  RT   fetuses
  RT   genotype
  RT   metamorphosis
  RT   phenotype

OOCYTES [363; 363]
  BT1   germ cells

OOGENESIS [78; 78]
  BT1   gametogenesis
  RT   oogonia
  RT   ova
  RT   ovaries
  RT   reproduction

OOGONIA [20; 20] *Nov 75*
  BT1   germ cells
  RT   oogenesis

OPACITY [4,331; 4,331]
  UF   *absorptivity (optical)*
  UF   *optical density*
  UF   *transparency*
  BT1   optical properties
    BT2   physical properties
  RT   attenuation
  RT   schlieren method
  RT   transmission
  RT   visibility
  RT   visible radiation

OPE MODEL [1,629; 1,640]
  UF   *pion-exchange model*
  BT1   obe model
    BT2   boson-exchange models
      BT3   peripheral models
        BT4 particle models
          BT5 mathematical models
  NT1   electric born model
  RT   ope potential

OPE POTENTIAL [347; 354]
  BT1   potentials
  NT1   gammel-thaler potential
  RT   nucleon-nucleon potential
  RT   nucleons
  RT   ope model

OPEN CONFIGURATIONS [140; 1,399]
  UF   *magnetic traps (open)*
  BT1   magnetic field configurations
  NT1   baseball seam configurations
  NT1   cusped geometries
  NT1   magnetic mirror configurations
    NT2   tlm configurations
  NT1   minimum-b configurations
  RT   open plasma devices

open cycle cooling systems
  USE   open-cycle cooling systems

open cycle mhd generators
  USE   open-cycle mhd generators

open pit mining
  USE   mining

OPEN PLASMA DEVICES [178; 6,805]
  BT1   thermonuclear devices
  NT1   baseball devices
  NT1   linear pinch devices
    NT2   linear hard core pinch devices
    NT2   linear screw pinch devices
    NT2   linear theta pinch devices
      NT3   bsg devices
      NT3   chalice devices
      NT3   isar devices
      NT3   pharos devices
      NT3   scylla devices
    NT2   linear z pinch devices
    NT2   megatron
  NT1   magnetic mirrors
    NT2   alice
    NT2   aspa device
    NT2   beta ii devices
    NT2   bsg devices
    NT2   bumpy tori
      NT3   elmo bumpy torus
    NT2   burnout devices
    NT2   circe devices
      NT3   circe-25kw device
    NT2   dcx devices
    NT2   deca devices
    NT2   elmo devices
      NT3   elmo bumpy torus
    NT2   imp device
    NT2   interem device
    NT2   mftf devices
    NT2   ogra
    NT2   phoenix devices
    NT2   pleiade device
    NT2   pr devices
      NT3   pr-6 device
      NT3   pr-7 device
      NT3   pr-8 device
    NT2   reversed-field mirrors
    NT2   tandem mirrors
      NT3   gamma 10 devices
      NT3   phaedrus mirror devices
      NT3   tara devices
      NT3   tmx devices
    NT2   vgl devices
    NT2   2x devices
  NT1   plasma focus devices
  NT1   q devices
    NT2   helios devices
    NT2   qp devices
  RT   open configurations

OPEN-CYCLE COOLING SYSTEMS [55; 55] *Jul 76*
  UF   *open cycle cooling systems*
  BT1   cooling systems
  RT   cooling towers
  RT   reactor cooling systems

OPEN-CYCLE MHD GENERATORS [151; 151]
  UF   *open cycle mhd generators*
  BT1   mhd generators
    BT2   direct energy converters
  RT   closed-cycle mhd generators

OPEN-LOOP CONTROL [22; 22] *Sep 76*
(Without feedback.)
  BT1   control

OPENINGS [582; 2,855]
  NT1   apertures
  NT1   doors
  NT1   orifices
  NT1   windows
  RT   boreholes
  RT   caves
  RT   cavities
  RT   craters
  RT   ducts
  RT   shutters
  RT   vents

OPERATING COST [407; 407] *Dec 82*
  BT1   cost
  RT   economic analysis

OPERATING LICENSES [448; 448] *Dec 76*
  BT1   licenses
  RT   licensing procedures
  RT   licensing regulations

operating systems (computer)
  USE   executive codes

OPERATION [11,323; 24,590]
  NT1   reactor operation
  RT   maintenance
  RT   modifications
  RT   start-up

operation (fission reactor)
  USE   reactor operation

OPERATIONAL AMPLIFIERS [219; 219]
  BT1   amplifiers
    BT2   equipment
  BT1   electronic equipment
    BT2   equipment

operations research
  SEE   management
  OR   optimization

OPERATOR PRODUCT EXPANSION [15; 15] *Nov 88*
  BT1   series expansion
  RT   gauge invariance
  RT   quantum operators

operators (mathematical)
  USE   mathematical operators

operators (nuclear facilities)
  USE   nuclear operators

operators(quantum field theo)
  USE   quantum operators

operators(quantum mechanical)
  USE   quantum operators

OPHTHALMOLOGY [176; 176]
  BT1   medicine
  RT   eyes
  RT   sense organs diseases

opossum
  USE   marsupials

OPPENHEIMER-PHILLIPS PROCESS [2; 2]
  RT   direct reactions
  RT   nuclear reactions
  RT   stripping

OPTICAL ACTIVITY [190; 190] *Jun 77*
(The ability to rotate the plane of vibration of polarized light.)
- UF   *activity (optical)*
- BT1   optical properties
  - BT2   physical properties
- RT   crystal structure
- RT   molecular structure
- RT   polarization
- RT   stereochemistry

optical density
- USE   opacity

OPTICAL DEPTH CURVE [189; 290]
Aug 75
- BT1   diagrams
  - BT2   information
- NT1   spectroscopic curve of growth
- RT   absorption spectra
- RT   cosmic gases
- RT   element abundance
- RT   line broadening
- RT   optical properties
- RT   oscillator strengths

OPTICAL DISPERSION [522; 522]
- RT   diffraction
- RT   optics
- RT   refraction
- RT   refractive index

optical equipment
- USE   optical systems

OPTICAL FIBERS [821; 821] *Sep 82*
(Long, thin threads of transparent materials used to transmit light.)
- BT1   fibers
- RT   fiber optics
- RT   optical systems

OPTICAL FILTERS [412; 412]
- BT1   filters
- RT   optical systems

OPTICAL MICROSCOPES [135; 135]
- BT1   microscopes

OPTICAL MICROSCOPY [978; 978]
- BT1   microscopy

OPTICAL MODELS [9,058; 9,058]
- UF   *feshbach-porter-weisskopf mode*
- UF   *kisslinger model*
- UF   *models (optical)*
- BT1   mathematical models
- RT   atomic models
- RT   bjorklund-fernbach model
- RT   cloudy crystal ball model
- RT   fsc approximation
- RT   nuclear models
- RT   nuclear potential
- RT   particle models
- RT   perey-buck model
- RT   woods-saxon potential

OPTICAL MODES [355; 355]
- UF   *modes (optical)*
- BT1   oscillation modes

OPTICAL PROPERTIES [4,371; 23,667]
- UF   *reflectance (spectral)*
- UF   *spectral reflectance*
- BT1   physical properties
- NT1   brightness
- NT1   color
- NT1   emissivity
- NT1   luminosity
- NT1   opacity
- NT1   optical activity
- NT1   refractive index
- RT   antireflection coatings
- RT   dichroism
- RT   electro-optical effects
- RT   fiber optics
- RT   magneto-optical effects
- RT   mirrors
- RT   optical depth curve
- RT   optical systems
- RT   optics
- RT   reflective coatings
- RT   spectroscopic curve of growth
- RT   visibility

OPTICAL PUMPING [2,083; 2,083]
- UF   *laser pumping*
- UF   *pumping (laser)*
- RT   double resonance methods
- RT   electrical pumping
- RT   excitation
- RT   lasers
- RT   nuclear pumping
- RT   stimulated emission

OPTICAL PYROMETERS [52; 52]
- BT1   pyrometers
  - BT2   measuring instruments
- RT   temperature measurement

OPTICAL SPECTROMETERS [375; 375]
- BT1   spectrometers
  - BT2   measuring instruments

OPTICAL SYSTEMS [2,595; 2,619]
- UF   *optical equipment*
- NT1   periscopes
- RT   antireflection coatings
- RT   beam optics
- RT   diffraction gratings
- RT   fiber optics
- RT   lenses
- RT   lighting systems
- RT   mirrors
- RT   optical fibers
- RT   optical filters
- RT   optical properties
- RT   optics
- RT   remote viewing equipment
- RT   shutters
- RT   telescopes

OPTICAL THEOREM [224; 224]
- RT   small angle scattering

OPTICALLY THICK PLASMA [134; 134]
- BT1   plasma

OPTICALLY THIN PLASMA [174; 174]
- BT1   plasma

OPTICS [690; 2,104] *Jan 78*
- NT1   fiber optics
- NT1   nonlinear optics
- RT   incidence angle
- RT   optical dispersion
- RT   optical properties
- RT   optical systems
- RT   quantum electronics

OPTIMAL CONTROL [231; 231] *Sep 76*
- BT1   control
- RT   optimization

§§ ## OPTIMIZATION [13,468; 14,067]
- SF   operations research
- NT1   minimization
- RT   alara
- RT   augmentation
- RT   control
- RT   control systems
- RT   control theory
- RT   dynamic programming
- RT   econometrics
- RT   linear programming
- RT   mitigation
- RT   modifications
- RT   nonlinear programming
- RT   optimal control
- RT   planning
- RT   variational methods

optoacoustic cells
- USE   photoacoustic spectrometers

OR-CEF REACTOR [4; 4]
- UF   *cef-or reactor*
- UF   *critical exp. facility oak rid*
- UF   *oak ridge critical exp. facili*
- BT1   zero power reactors
  - BT2   experimental reactors
    - BT3   research and test reactors
      - BT4   reactors

ORAL ADMINISTRATION [1,265; 1,265]
- UF   *gastric administration*
- BT1   intake
- RT   ingestion
- RT   intestinal absorption
- RT   radionuclide administration

ORAL CAVITY [915; 1,988]
- UF   *lips*
- UF   *mouth*
- BT1   digestive system
- NT1   teeth
- NT1   tongue
- RT   head
- RT   ingestion
- RT   pharynx
- RT   salivary glands

ORANGE EVENT [3; 3] *Jan 76*
- BT1   atmospheric explosions
  - BT2   explosions
- BT1   nuclear explosions
  - BT2   explosions
- RT   hardtack project

orange-type spectrometers
- USE   flat magnetic spectrometers

ORANGES [72; 72]
- BT1   fruits
  - BT2   food
- RT   citrus

ORAU [27; 27]
- UF   *oak ridge associated univ.*
- BT1   us organizations
  - BT2   national organizations

ORBIT STABILITY [215; 215]
- BT1   stability
- RT   beam dynamics

ORBITAL ANGULAR MOMENTUM [1,451; 1,451]
- BT1   angular momentum
- RT   fractional-parentage coefficie
- RT   j-j coupling
- RT   l-s coupling
- RT   spin

ORBITAL MOMENTUM OPERATORS [52; 52]
- BT1   angular momentum operators
  - BT2   quantum operators
    - BT3   mathematical operators

orbiting geophysical observato
- USE   ogo satellites

ORBITING SOLAR OBSERVATORIES [130; 130]
- BT1   satellites
- RT   space flight
- RT   sun

ORBITS [3,752; 3,752]
(For electron orbits in atoms use ELECTRONIC STRUCTURE.)
  RT   beam dynamics
  RT   precession
  RT   trajectories

ORDER PARAMETERS [3,614; 3,614]
  RT   crystal structure
  RT   wilson loop

ORDER-DISORDER MODEL [50; 50]
  Sep 77
  BT1   nuclear models
    BT2   mathematical models
  RT   fission

ORDER-DISORDER TRANSFORMATIONS [2,560; 2,560]
  BT1   phase transformations
  RT   crystal-phase transformations
  RT   ising model
  RT   superlattices

ORE COMPOSITION [398; 398]
  UF   *abundance (mineral)*
  RT   availability
  RT   mining
  RT   natural occurrence
  RT   ores

ORE CONCENTRATES [369; 668]
  UF   *concentrates (ore)*
  UF   *enriched materials (ores)*
  NT1   uranium concentrates
  RT   ore enrichment

ORE ENRICHMENT [306; 306]
  UF   *enrichment (ores)*
  BT1   ore processing
  BT1   separation processes
  RT   flotation
  RT   leaching
  RT   ore concentrates
  RT   slurex process

ORE PROCESSING [2,505; 3,526]
  UF   *processing (ores)*
  NT1   in-situ processing
    NT2   solution mining
  NT1   ore enrichment
  NT1   retorting
  RT   anaconda uranium mill
  RT   crushing
  RT   flotation
  RT   highland uranium mill
  RT   humeca uranium mill
  RT   leaching
  RT   ores
  RT   radiometric sorting
  RT   refining
  RT   shirley basin uranium mill
  RT   slurex process
  RT   slurries
  RT   tailings
  RT   thiobacillus oxidans
  RT   uranium concentrates

ore reserves
(Index by coordination of RESERVES with ORES or with the descriptor for a specific type of ore.)
  USE   reserves

OREGON [200; 200]
  BT1   usa
    BT2   developed countries
    BT2   north america
  RT   columbia river basin

oregon state triga reactor
  USE   ostr reactor

ORELA [90; 90]
(Oak Ridge Electron Linear Accelerator)
  BT1   linear accelerators
    BT2   accelerators

ORES [1,255; 12,139]
  NT1   aluminium ores
    NT2   bauxite
  NT1   bismuth ores
  NT1   chromium ores
  NT1   cobalt ores
  NT1   copper ores
  NT1   gold ores
  NT1   iron ores
    NT2   hematite
    NT2   limonite
    NT2   magnetite
  NT1   lead ores
  NT1   manganese ores
  NT1   molybdenum ores
  NT1   nickel ores
  NT1   niobium ores
  NT1   polymetallic ores
  NT1   rhenium ores
  NT1   selenium ores
  NT1   silver ores
  NT1   tantalum ores
  NT1   tellurium ores
  NT1   thorium ores
  NT1   tin ores
  NT1   tungsten ores
  NT1   uranium ores
    NT2   uranium concentrates
  NT1   vanadium ores
  NT1   yttrium ores
  NT1   zinc ores
  NT1   zirconium ores
  RT   environmental materials
  RT   geologic deposits
  RT   minerals
  RT   ore composition
  RT   ore processing

organ cultures
  USE   tissue cultures

ORGANIC ACIDS [531; 30,885]
(Not for the concepts covered by NUCLEIC ACIDS and NUCLEOTIDES.)
  UF   *acids (organic)*
  UF+   *sulfinic acids*
  BT1   organic compounds
  NT1   arsonic acids
    NT2   arsanilic acid
    NT2   arsenazo
    NT2   beryllon
  NT1   boronic acids
  NT1   cacodylic acid
  *NT1 carboxylic acids
  NT1   fulvic acids
  NT1   humic acids
  NT1   mdpa
  NT1   organophosphinic acids
  NT1   phytic acid
  NT1   sulfonic acids
    NT2   acid chrome dyes
    NT2   arsenazo
    NT2   beryllon
    NT2   bromosulfophthalein
    NT2   chromotropic acid
    NT2   congo red
    NT2   eriochrome dyes
    NT2   erioglaucine
    NT2   evans blue
    NT2   ferron
    NT2   methyl orange
    NT2   nitroso-r salt
    NT2   sdpph
    NT2   spadns
    NT2   sulfanilic acid
    NT2   taurine
    NT2   thorin
    NT2   tiron
    NT2   trypan blue
    NT2   unithiol
  NT1   thioic acids
  RT   acidification
  RT   anhydrides
  RT   chloranilic acid
  RT   hydrazides
  RT   hydroxamic acids
  RT   nucleotides
  RT   ph value
  RT   picric acid
  RT   rhodizonic acid
  RT   sialic acid
  RT   soaps
  RT   uric acid

ORGANIC ARSENIC COMPOUNDS [107; 107] Mar 77
  UF   *arsonates*
  BT1   organic compounds
  RT   arsenic compounds

ORGANIC BORON COMPOUNDS [482; 605]
  BT1   organic compounds
  NT1   carboranes
  RT   boron compounds

ORGANIC BROMINE COMPOUNDS [1,015; 1,693]
  UF   *brominated hydrocarbons*
  UF+   *bromamines*
  BT1   organic halogen compounds
    BT2   organic compounds
  NT1   brominated aliphatic hydrocarb
  NT1   brominated aromatic hydrocarbo
  NT1   bromoform
  NT1   bromosulfophthalein
  NT1   bromouracils
    NT2   budr
  NT1   eosin
  NT1   methyl bromide
  RT   bromine compounds

organic c. hw m. chalk river
  USE   zed-2 reactor

ORGANIC CHLORINE COMPOUNDS [2,662; 6,318]
  UF   *chlorinated hydrocarbons*
  UF+   *pcb (polychlorinated biphenyl)*
  BT1   organic halogen compounds
    BT2   organic compounds
  NT1   chloral
  NT1   chloramines
  NT1   chloranil
  NT1   chlorinated aliphatic hydrocar
    NT2   carbon tetrachloride
    NT2   chloroform
    NT2   methyl chloride
    NT2   pvc
  NT1   chlorinated aromatic hydrocarb
    NT2   aldrin
  NT1   chlorouracils
  NT1   chlorpromazine
  NT1   ddt
  NT1   iodochloroquine
  NT1   kel-f
  NT1   lindane
  NT1   methylene chloride
  NT1   neoprene
  NT1   nitrogen mustard
  NT1   phosgene
  NT1   rose bengal
  RT   chlorine compounds

ORGANIC COMPOUNDS [2,659; 159,500]
  UF   *compounds (organic)*
  *NT1 aldehydes
  *NT1 alkaloids
  *NT1 amines
  *NT1 antibiotics
  *NT1 aromatics
  *NT1 carbohydrates
  *NT1 carbonic acid derivatives
  *NT1 enzymes
  *NT1 esters
  *NT1 heterocyclic compounds
  *NT1 hydrocarbons
  *NT1 hydroxy compounds
  NT1   isoenzymes

* NT1 ketones
* NT1 lipids
* NT1 nucleic acids
* NT1 nucleotides
* NT1 organic acids
  NT1 organic arsenic compounds
* NT1 organic boron compounds
* NT1 organic halogen compounds
  NT1 organic mercury compounds
* NT1 organic nitrogen compounds
* NT1 organic oxygen compounds
* NT1 organic phosphorus compounds
* NT1 organic polymers
  NT1 organic silicon compounds
* NT1 organic sulfur compounds
* NT1 organometallic compounds
* NT1 other organic compounds
* NT1 proteins
* NT1 steroids
* NT1 terpenes
  RT clathrates
  RT translocation

ORGANIC COOLANTS [111; 111]
BT1 coolants
RT aromatics
RT organic cooled reactors
RT polyphenyls
RT refrigerants

organic cooled and moder. reac
USE   omr type reactors

ORGANIC COOLED REACTORS
[82; 235]
BT1 reactors
NT1 eco reactor
NT1 eocr reactor
NT1 essor reactor
NT1 lwor type reactors
NT1 omr type reactors
  NT2 arbus reactor
  NT2 omre reactor
  NT2 pnpf reactor
NT1 wr-1 reactor
NT1 zed-2 reactor
RT organic coolants

ORGANIC CRYSTAL PHOSPHORS
[79; 79]
BT1 phosphors
RT anthracene
RT solid scintillation detectors
RT stilbene

ORGANIC FLUORINE COMPOUNDS
[2,242; 4,360]
UF   *fluorinated hydrocarbons*
BT1 organic halogen compounds
  BT2 organic compounds
NT1 carbon tetrafluoride
NT1 fluorinated aliphatic hydrocar
NT1 fluorinated aromatic hydrocarb
NT1 fluoroform
NT1 fluorouracils
  NT2 fudr
NT1 kel-f
NT1 methyl fluoride
NT1 teflon
NT1 tta
RT fluorine compounds

ORGANIC HALOGEN COMPOUNDS
[642; 16,112]
UF   *halogenated hydrocarbons*
BT1 organic compounds
NT1 freons
NT1 halogenated aliphatic hydrocar
  NT2 brominated aliphatic hydrocarb
  NT2 chlorinated aliphatic hydrocar
    NT3 carbon tetrachloride
    NT3 chloroform
    NT3 methyl chloride
    NT3 pvc
  NT2 fluorinated aliphatic hydrocar
  NT2 iodinated aliphatic hydrocarbo
NT1 halogenated aromatic hydrocarb
  NT2 brominated aromatic hydrocarbo
  NT2 chlorinated aromatic hydrocarb
    NT3 aldrin
  NT2 fluorinated aromatic hydrocarb
  NT2 iodinated aromatic hydrocarbon
NT1 organic bromine compounds
  NT2 brominated aliphatic hydrocarb
  NT2 brominated aromatic hydrocarbo
  NT2 bromoform
  NT2 bromosulfophthalein
  NT2 bromouracils
    NT3 budr
  NT2 eosin
  NT2 methyl bromide
NT1 organic chlorine compounds
  NT2 chloral
  NT2 chloramines
  NT2 chloranil
  NT2 chlorinated aliphatic hydrocar
    NT3 carbon tetrachloride
    NT3 chloroform
    NT3 methyl chloride
    NT3 pvc
  NT2 chlorinated aromatic hydrocarb
    NT3 aldrin
  NT2 chlorouracils
  NT2 chlorpromazine
  NT2 ddt
  NT2 iodochloroquine
  NT2 kel-f
  NT2 lindane
  NT2 methylene chloride
  NT2 neoprene
  NT2 nitrogen mustard
  NT2 phosgene
  NT2 rose bengal
NT1 organic fluorine compounds
  NT2 carbon tetrafluoride
  NT2 fluorinated aliphatic hydrocar
  NT2 fluorinated aromatic hydrocarb
  NT2 fluoroform
  NT2 fluorouracils
    NT3 fudr
  NT2 kel-f
  NT2 methyl fluoride
  NT2 teflon
  NT2 tta
NT1 organic iodine compounds
  NT2 diiodotyrosine
  NT2 diodrast
  NT2 erythrosine
  NT2 ferron
  NT2 hypaque
  NT2 iodinated aliphatic hydrocarbo
  NT2 iodinated aromatic hydrocarbon
  NT2 iodochloroquine
  NT2 iodoform
  NT2 iodouracils
    NT3 iododeoxyuridine
  NT2 ioglycamic acid
  NT2 lipiodol
  NT2 methyl iodide
  NT2 pbi
  NT2 rose bengal
  NT2 thyroxine
RT halogen compounds
RT refrigerants

ORGANIC INSULATORS [96; 96]
RT dielectric materials
RT electrical insulation

ORGANIC IODINE COMPOUNDS
[1,621; 4,020]
UF   *iodinated hydrocarbons*
UF+   *risa*
BT1 organic halogen compounds
  BT2 organic compounds
NT1 diiodotyrosine
NT1 diodrast
NT1 erythrosine
NT1 ferron
NT1 hypaque
NT1 iodinated aliphatic hydrocarbo
NT1 iodinated aromatic hydrocarbon
NT1 iodochloroquine
NT1 iodoform
NT1 iodouracils
  NT2 iododeoxyuridine
NT1 ioglycamic acid
NT1 lipiodol
NT1 methyl iodide
NT1 pbi
NT1 rose bengal
NT1 thyroxine
RT iodine compounds

ORGANIC ION EXCHANGERS
[1,453; 1,576]
UF   *amberlite*
UF   *dowex*
UF   *permutit (organic)*
BT1 ion exchange materials
  BT2 materials
NT1 polystyrene-dvb

ORGANIC MATTER [369; 369] *Jul 82*
(Only for unspecified materials containing chain and ring compounds of carbon; if specific organic compounds are studied, use descriptors for the compounds.)
BT1 matter
RT carbonaceous materials
RT geochemistry

ORGANIC MERCURY COMPOUNDS
[181; 181]
UF   *methylmercury*
BT1 organic compounds

organic moderated r. experimen
USE   omre reactor

organic moderated r. piqua
USE   pnpf reactor

ORGANIC MODERATED REACTORS
[7; 107]
UF   *organic-moderated reactors*
BT1 reactors
NT1 eocr reactor
NT1 omr type reactors
  NT2 arbus reactor
  NT2 omre reactor
  NT2 pnpf reactor
NT1 rospo reactor
NT1 sur-100 series reactor
NT1 viper reactor
NT1 zerlina reactor
RT organic moderators

ORGANIC MODERATORS [66; 66]
BT1 moderators
RT aromatics
RT organic moderated reactors
RT polyphenyls

ORGANIC NITROGEN COMPOUNDS
[1,698; 34,133]
(Excluding those concepts included under the descriptors: PROTEINS, AMINES, ALKALOIDS, AMINO ACIDS, NUCLEIC ACIDS, and NUCLEOTIDES.)
BT1 organic compounds
NT1 amides
* NT2 acetamide
  NT2 acrylamide
  NT2 asparagine
  NT2 formamide
  NT2 glutamine
  NT2 hypaque
* NT2 lactams
  NT2 metrizamide
  NT2 nicotinamide
  NT2 phenatine
* NT2 sulfonamides
  NT2 thionalide
NT1 amidines
  NT2 stilbamidine
NT1 azido compounds
NT1 azines
* NT2 phenothiazines

* NT2   pyrazines
* NT2   pyridazines
* NT2   pyridines
* NT2   pyrimidines
* NT2   triazines
NT1   azo compounds
NT2   arsenazo
* NT2   azo dyes
NT1   azoles
NT2   carbazoles
* NT2   imidazoles
NT2   oxadiazoles
* NT2   oxazoles
* NT2   pyrazoles
* NT2   pyrroles
* NT2   tetrazoles
NT2   thiadiazoles
* NT2   thiazoles
NT2   triazoles
NT1   carbamates
NT2   dedtc
NT2   urethane
NT1   carbazides
NT1   carbazones
NT2   diphenylcarbazones
NT2   dithizone
NT1   cyanamides
NT1   diazo compounds
NT2   pan
NT2   pyridylazoresorcinol
NT2   thorin
NT1   dpca
NT1   gangliosides
NT1   guanethidine
NT1   guanidines
NT1   hydrazides
* NT2   isoniazid
NT1   hydrazones
NT1   imides
NT2   nem
NT1   imidines
NT1   imines
NT2   creatinine
NT2   pemoline
NT2   schiff bases
NT1   imipramine
NT1   isoalloxazines
NT2   diaphorases
NT1   melanin
NT1   morpholines
NT1   nitriles
NT2   acetonitrile
NT2   acrylonitrile
NT1   nitro compounds
NT2   dinitrophenol
NT2   dpph
NT2   metronidazole
NT2   misonidazole
NT2   nitrobenzene
NT2   nitromethane
NT2   nitrophenol
NT2   picric acid
NT2   sdpph
NT2   tnt
NT1   nitroso compounds
NT2   nitroso-r salt
NT2   nitrosoureas
NT2   1-nitroso-2-naphthol
NT1   oximes
NT2   benzoinoxime
NT2   dimethylglyoxime
NT2   furildioxime
NT1   phenanthrolines
NT2   ferroin
NT2   phenanthroline-ortho
NT1   porphyrins
NT2   chlorophyll
NT2   hematoporphyrins
NT2   heme
* NT2   hemoglobin
NT2   hemosiderin
NT2   myoglobin
* NT2   peroxidases
NT2   protoporphyrins
NT1   pteridines
NT2   aminopterin
NT2   folic acid
NT1   purines
* NT2   adenines
NT2   guanine

NT2   guanosine
NT2   hypoxanthine
NT2   inosine
NT2   mercaptopurine
* NT2   xanthines
NT1   semicarbazides
NT1   semicarbazones
NT1   tamoxifen
NT1   thionine
NT1   urea
RT   diazotization
RT   nitrogen compounds

ORGANIC OXYGEN COMPOUNDS
[700; 8,147]
(Excluding those concepts included under the descriptors: HYDROXY COMPOUNDS, CARBONIC ACID DERIVATIVES, LIPIDS, ORGANIC ACIDS, ALDEHYDES, KETONES, and ESTERS.)
UF+   *heterocyclic oxygen compounds*
UF+   *parabanic acid*
BT1   organic compounds
NT1   allantoin
NT1   alloxan
NT1   barbiturates
NT2   amytal
NT2   nembutal
NT2   phenobarbital
NT2   thiopental
NT1   benzoyl peroxide
NT1   cyanurates
NT1   cytosine
NT1   dioxane
NT1   dioxin
NT1   epoxides
NT2   araldite
NT1   ethers
NT2   acetals
NT3   acetal
NT2   anisole
NT2   batyl alcohol
NT2   butyl ether
NT2   carbitols
NT2   cellosolves
NT2   curcumin
NT2   dme
NT2   ethyl ether
NT2   ioglycamic acid
NT2   isopropyl ether
NT2   methyl ether
NT2   methylal
NT2   mexamine
NT2   morpholines
NT1   flavenoids
NT2   flavones
NT3   hesperidin
NT3   morin
NT3   quercetin
NT1   furans
NT2   benzofurans
NT2   furfural
NT2   furildioxime
NT2   tetrahydrofuran
NT1   isoalloxazines
NT2   diaphorases
NT1   ketenes
NT1   malathion
NT1   murexide
NT1   oxadiazoles
NT1   oxazoles
NT2   benzoxazoles
NT2   pemoline
NT2   popop
NT1   phenatine
NT1   psoralen
NT1   pyrans
NT2   coumarin
NT2   hematoxylin
NT2   quercetin
NT2   tetrahydropyran
NT1   pyridoxal
NT1   quinones
NT2   anthraquinones
NT3   alizarin
NT3   carminic acid
NT3   quinizarin
NT2   benzoquinones
NT3   chloranil
NT3   chloranilic acid

NT3   quinhydrone
NT3   ubiquinone
NT2   rhodizonic acid
NT2   vitamin k
NT1   rhodamines
NT1   saccharin
NT1   semicarbazides
NT1   tmpn
NT1   triacetoneamine-n-oxyl
NT1   trioxanes
NT1   xanthines
NT2   caffeine
NT2   theobromine
NT2   theophylline
NT2   uric acid
RT   oxygen compounds

ORGANIC PHOSPHORUS COMPOUNDS [1,958; 9,352]
(Excluding those concepts covered by NUCLEIC ACIDS and NUCLEOTIDES.)
UF   *diphenylphosphine oxide*
UF   *dpo*
BT1   organic compounds
NT1   casein
NT1   malathion
NT1   organophosphinic acids
NT1   parathion
NT1   phosphinic acid esters
NT1   phosphocreatine
NT1   phospholipids
NT2   cardiolipin
NT2   cephalins
NT2   lecithins
NT2   sphingomyelins
NT1   phosphonates
NT1   phosphonic acid esters
NT2   dampa
NT2   dhdecmp
NT1   phosphoric acid esters
NT2   butyl phosphates
NT3   dbp
NT3   mbp
NT3   tbp
NT2   hdehp
NT2   mdpa
NT2   phytic acid
NT2   tcp
NT1   tbpo
NT1   topo
NT1   tops
NT1   tpo
NT1   udpg
RT   phosphines
RT   phosphorus compounds
RT   thiophosphoric acid esters

ORGANIC POLYMERS [2,591; 16,284]
UF   *plastics*
BT1   organic compounds
BT1   polymers
NT1   araldite
NT1   bakelite
NT1   copolymers
NT1   graft polymers
NT1   neoprene
NT1   plastic foams
NT1   polyacetals
NT2   formvar
NT2   polyoxymethylenes
NT1   polyamides
NT2   nylon
NT2   polyurethanes
NT1   polycarbonates
NT1   polyesters
NT2   dacron
NT2   homalite
NT2   laminac
NT2   mylar
NT1   polyethylene glycols
NT2   carbowax
NT2   pluronics
NT1   polyisoprene
NT1   polyolefins
NT2   polyethylenes
NT3   kel-f
NT3   marlex
NT3   teflon
NT2   polypropylene

	NT2	polystyrene
	NT2	polystyrene-dvb
	NT1	polyvinyls
	NT2	polyacrylates
	NT3	lucite
	NT3	perspex
	NT3	plexiglas
	NT3	pmma
	NT2	polystyrene
	NT2	pva
	NT2	pvc
	NT2	pvp
	NT1	resins
	NT1	rubbers
	NT2	buna
	NT2	latex
	NT2	natural rubber
	NT2	silastic
	NT2	viton
	NT1	textolite
	NT1	thermoplastics
	RT	acrylonitrile
	RT	benzofurans
	RT	butadiene
	RT	concrete-plastic composites
	RT	fiberglass
	RT	melamine
	RT	plasticizers
	RT	polyphenyls
	RT	wood-plastic composites
	RT	xenobiotics

ORGANIC SILICON COMPOUNDS
[54; 54] Jul 86
BT1 organic compounds

ORGANIC SOLVENTS [2,750; 2,789]
BT1 nonaqueous solvents
BT2 solvents
NT1 amsco
NT1 carbitols
NT1 cellosolves
NT1 solvesso
NT1 turpentine
RT   butyl ether
RT   carbon tetrachloride
RT   chloroform
RT   dhdecmp
RT   dme
RT   ethyl ether
RT   isopropyl ether
RT   methyl ether
RT   solutions
RT   trioxanes

ORGANIC SULFUR COMPOUNDS
[2,019; 13,403]
UF   *thio compounds*
UF+ *sulfinic acids*
UF+ *tetrathiafulvalene*
UF+ *ttf*
UF+ *ttf-tcnq*
BT1 organic compounds
NT1 biotin
NT1 cystamine
NT1 dedtc
NT1 disulfides
NT2 cystine
NT2 thioctic acid
NT1 dithizone
NT1 ethionine
NT1 heparin
NT1 methionine
NT1 phenothiazines
NT2 chlorpromazine
NT2 methylene blue
NT1 sulfonamides
NT2 sulfadiazine
NT1 sulfonates
NT2 indocyanine green
NT1 sulfones
NT2 spadns
NT1 sulfonic acid esters
NT2 abs
NT2 ems
NT2 methyl methanesulfonate
NT1 sulfonic acids
NT2 acid chrome dyes

	NT2	arsenazo
	NT2	beryllon
	NT2	bromosulfophthalein
	NT2	chromotropic acid
	NT2	congo red
	NT2	eriochrome dyes
	NT2	erioglaucine
	NT2	evans blue
	NT2	ferron
	NT2	methyl orange
	NT2	nitroso-r salt
	NT2	sdpph
	NT2	spadns
	NT2	sulfanilic acid
	NT2	taurine
	NT2	thorin
	NT2	tiron
	NT2	trypan blue
	NT2	unithiol
	NT1	sulfoxides
	NT2	dmso
	NT2	dpso
	NT1	sulfuric acid esters
	NT1	thiadiazoles
	NT1	thiazoles
	NT2	benzothiazoles
	NT2	saccharin
	NT2	thiamine
	NT1	thiocyanates
	NT2	ammonium thiocyanates
	NT1	thioic acids
	NT1	thiols
	NT2	cysteine
	NT2	dithiols
	NT3	bal
	NT3	unithiol
	NT2	malathion
	NT2	mea
	NT2	meg
	NT2	mercaptopurine
	NT2	mpg
	NT2	penicillamine
	NT2	thionalide
	NT2	thiouracil
	NT1	thionaphthenes
	NT1	thionine
	NT1	thiopental
	NT1	thiophene
	NT1	thiophenols
	NT1	thioureas
	NT2	aet
	NT2	thiourea
	NT1	tops
	NT1	tta
	NT1	xanthates
	NT2	viscose
	RT	sulfur compounds
	RT	thiophosphoric acid esters

organic-moderated reactors
USE organic moderated reactors

organization econ co-op and de
USE oecd

ORGANIZATIONAL MODELS
[342; 342] Nov 75
UF   *models (organizational)*
RT   management
RT   organizing
RT   planning

ORGANIZING [2,703; 2,703]
RT   organizational models
RT   planning
RT   schedules

ORGANOIDS [120; 2,166]
UF   *golgi apparatus*
BT1 cell constituents
NT1 endoplasmic reticulum
NT1 lysosomes
NT1 ribosomes
RT   subcellular distribution
RT   ultracentrifugation
RT   ultrastructural changes

ORGANOLEPTIC PROPERTIES
[304; 3,663]
NT1 color
NT1 flavor
NT1 odor
RT   food
RT   preservation
RT   sense organs

ORGANOMETALLIC COMPOUNDS
[2,610; 2,686]
(For compounds of metals and semimetals with organic compounds, but only when the metal or semimetal is directly bound to carbon.)
BT1 organic compounds
NT1 grignard reagents
NT1 lactoferrin
NT1 tel

ORGANOPHOSPHINIC ACIDS [35; 35]
BT1 organic acids
BT2 organic compounds
BT1 organic phosphorus compounds
BT2 organic compounds
RT   phosphinic acid esters

ORGANS [1,804; 106,077]
BT1 body
NT1 blood vessels
NT2 arteries
NT3 aorta
NT3 carotid arteries
NT3 coronaries
NT2 capillaries
NT2 veins
NT3 portal system
NT1 bone marrow
NT1 brain
NT2 cerebellum
NT2 cerebrum
NT3 cerebral cortex
NT2 hippocampus
NT2 hypothalamus
NT2 olfactory bulbs
NT2 thalamus
NT1 critical organs
NT1 diaphragm
NT1 esophagus
NT1 female genitals
NT2 ovaries
NT2 uterus
NT1 glands
NT2 endocrine glands
NT3 adrenal glands
NT3 pancreas
NT3 parathyroid glands
NT3 pituitary gland
NT3 thyroid
NT2 liver
NT2 mammary glands
NT2 pineal gland
NT2 prostate
NT2 salivary glands
NT1 heart
NT2 myocardium
NT2 pericardium
NT1 intestines
NT2 large intestine
NT3 rectum
NT2 small intestine
NT1 kidneys
NT2 glomeruli
NT2 tubules
NT1 lungs
NT1 male genitals
NT2 prostate
NT2 testes
NT1 perfused organs
NT1 pharynx
NT1 sense organs
NT2 auditory organs
NT2 eyes
NT3 conjunctiva
NT3 cornea
NT3 crystalline lens
NT3 lacrimal ducts
NT3 retina
NT3 uvea

NT2	taste buds
NT2	vestibular apparatus
NT1	skeleton
NT2	bone joints
NT2	exoskeleton
NT2	femur
NT2	skull
NT3	jaw
NT2	tibia
NT2	vertebrae
NT1	skin
NT2	epidermis
NT2	feathers
NT2	hair
NT2	nails
NT1	spleen
NT1	stomach
NT1	thymus
NT1	tongue
NT1	urinary tract
NT2	bladder
NT2	ureters
RT	artificial organs
RT	biological regeneration
RT	biology
RT	blood flow
RT	cardiovascular system
RT	digestive system
RT	homogenates
RT	in vivo
RT	lymphatic system
RT	nervous system
RT	respiratory system
RT	retention
RT	tissues

ORGDP [148; 148]
UF   k-25 plant
UF   oak ridge gaseous diffusion pl
BT1   gaseous diffusion plants
  BT2   isotope separation plants
    BT3   industrial plants
    BT3   nuclear facilities
BT1   us doe
  BT2   us organizations
    BT3   national organizations
BT1   us erda
  BT2   us organizations
    BT3   national organizations
RT   oak ridge reservation
RT   tennessee

orgel reactor
USE   essor reactor

ORIENTATION [4,654; 15,108]
NT1   grain orientation
NT1   spin orientation
RT   anisotropy
RT   asymmetry
RT   configuration
RT   incidence angle
RT   isotropy
RT   symmetry

ORIENTED NUCLEI [1,006; 1,006]
UF   *polarized nuclei*
BT1   nuclei
RT   nuclear alignment
RT   polarization

ORIFICES [345; 345]
BT1   openings
RT   apertures
RT   flowmeters
RT   nozzles
RT   pipe fittings

ORIGIN [3,387; 3,387]
RT   cosmology
RT   nucleosynthesis
RT   protostars
RT   star evolution
RT   white holes

ORION COMPUTERS [0; 0]
BT1   computers

ORMAK DEVICES [175; 175]
BT1   tokamak devices
  BT2   closed plasma devices
    BT3   thermonuclear devices

ORNAMENTAL PLANTS [128; 128]
BT1   plants
RT   aesthetics

ORNITHINE [78; 78]
UF   *2,5-diaminovaleric acid*
BT1   amino acids
  BT2   carboxylic acids
    BT3   organic acids
      BT4   organic compounds

ORNL [1,737; 1,737]
UF   *oak ridge national laboratory*
BT1   us aec
  BT2   us organizations
    BT3   national organizations
BT1   us doe
  BT2   us organizations
    BT3   national organizations
BT1   us erda
  BT2   us organizations
    BT3   national organizations
RT   oak ridge reservation
RT   tennessee

ORNL ISOCHRONOUS CYCLOTRON [120; 120]
BT1   isochronous cyclotrons
  BT2   cyclotrons
    BT3   cyclic accelerators
      BT4   accelerators
RT   hhirf accelerator

ornl research reactor
USE   orr reactor

ORNL SEPARATED ORBIT CYCLOTRON [0; 0]
BT1   separated orbit cyclotrons
  BT2   cyclotrons
    BT3   cyclic accelerators
      BT4   accelerators

ornl x-10 area graphite reacto
USE   x-10 reactor

ORNL-PCA REACTOR [47; 47]
UF   *pca-ornl reactor*
UF   *pool critical assembly ornl*
BT1   zero power reactors
  BT2   experimental reactors
    BT3   research and test reactors
      BT4   reactors

OROGENESIS [226; 226]
RT   mountains
RT   petrogenesis
RT   rocks

OROTIC ACID [83; 83]
UF   *uracil-6-carboxylic acid*
UF   *6-carboxyuracil*
BT1   heterocyclic acids
  BT2   carboxylic acids
    BT3   organic acids
      BT4   organic compounds
  BT2   heterocyclic compounds
    BT3   organic compounds
BT1   uracils
  BT2   hydroxy compounds
    BT3   organic compounds
  BT2   pyrimidines
    BT3   azines
      BT4   heterocyclic compounds
        BT5   organic compounds

      BT4   organic nitrogen compounds
        BT5   organic compounds

ORPHEE REACTOR [26; 26] *Nov 79*
(High flux reactor at Saclay Nuclear Research Centre, Gif-sur-Yvette, France.)
BT1   research reactors
  BT2   research and test reactors
    BT3   reactors
BT1   tank type reactors
  BT2   reactors
BT1   test reactors
  BT2   research and test reactors
    BT3   reactors
  BT2   test facilities
BT1   water cooled reactors
  BT2   reactors

ORR REACTOR [226; 226]
UF   *oak ridge research reactor*
UF   *ornl research reactor*
BT1   enriched uranium reactors
  BT2   reactors
BT1   tank type reactors
  BT2   reactors
BT1   water cooled reactors
  BT2   reactors
BT1   water moderated reactors
  BT2   reactors

ORSAT APPARATUS [0; 0]
RT   gas analysis

orsay alice cyclotron
USE   alice cyclotron

ORSAY CYCLOTRON [18; 18]
BT1   isochronous cyclotrons
  BT2   cyclotrons
    BT3   cyclic accelerators
      BT4   accelerators

ORSAY LINAC [24; 24]
BT1   linear accelerators
  BT2   accelerators

ORSAY SYNCHROCYCLOTRON [30; 30]
BT1   synchrocyclotrons
  BT2   cyclic accelerators
    BT3   accelerators

ORSAY TANDEM ACCELERATOR [34; 34] *Jan 77*
BT1   tandem electrostatic accelerat
  BT2   electrostatic accelerators
    BT3   accelerators
BT1   van de graaff accelerators
  BT2   electrostatic accelerators
    BT3   accelerators

ORTHICONS [4; 4]
BT1   camera tubes
  BT2   image tubes

ORTHITE [6; 6]
BT1   allanite
  BT2   silicate minerals
    BT3   minerals
  BT2   thorium minerals
    BT3   radioactive minerals
      BT4   minerals
      BT4   radioactive materials
        BT5   materials
RT   lanthanum silicates

orthogonal pinch devices (line
USE   linear theta pinch devices

ORTHOGONAL TRANSFORMATIONS [160; 160]
BT1   transformations

orthoiodohippurate
USE   hippuran

ORTHORHOMBIC LATTICES
[1,944; 1,944]
BT1   crystal lattices
BT2   crystal structure

oryza
USE   rice

OSCILLATION MODES [3,225; 4,243]
UF   *modes (oscillation)*
UF   *vibration modes*
NT1   bernstein mode
NT1   optical modes
NT1   single-particle modes
RT   harmonics
RT   lattice vibrations
RT   mode control
RT   mode conversion
RT   oscillations
RT   plasma waves

oscillation techniques (pile)
USE   pile oscillation techniques

OSCILLATIONS [6,088; 10,142]
NT1   betatron oscillations
NT1   harmonics
NT2   cyclotron harmonics
NT1   phase oscillations
NT1   sawtooth oscillations
NT1   synchrotron oscillations
RT   amplitudes
RT   disturbances
RT   mechanical vibrations
RT   nyquist diagrams
RT   oscillation modes
RT   pulsations
RT   variations

oscillations (plasma)
USE   plasma waves

OSCILLATOR STRENGTHS
[1,734; 1,734]
RT   einstein coefficients
RT   energy-level transitions
RT   optical depth curve
RT   spectroscopic curve of growth
RT   strength functions

OSCILLATORS [846; 901]
BT1   electronic equipment
BT2   equipment
NT1   blocking oscillators
NT1   transistor oscillators
RT   electronic circuits
RT   pulse techniques
RT   resonators
RT   semiconductor devices

oscillators (reactor)
USE   reactor oscillators

OSCILLOGRAPHS [256; 256]
BT1   electronic equipment
BT2   equipment
RT   cathode ray tubes

OSEEN METHOD [7; 7]
RT   fluid flow

oshima oi-1 reactor
USE   oi-1 reactor

oshima oi-2 reactor
USE   oi-2 reactor

OSIRIS REACTOR [96; 96]
(CEA/CEN de Saclay, Gif-sur-Yvette, France)
BT1   enriched uranium reactors
BT2   reactors
BT1   materials testing reactors
BT2   irradiation reactors
BT3   reactors
BT1   research reactors
BT2   research and test reactors
BT3   reactors
BT1   tank type reactors
BT2   reactors
BT1   thermal reactors
BT2   reactors
BT1   water cooled reactors
BT2   reactors
BT1   water moderated reactors
BT2   reactors

oskarshamn-1 reactor
USE   okg-1 reactor

oskarshamn-2 reactor
USE   okg-2 reactor

oskarshamn-3 reactor
USE   okg-3 reactor

oskarshamn-4 reactor
USE   okg-4 reactor

OSLO CYCLOTRON [23; 23] *Jul 80*
BT1   isochronous cyclotrons
BT2   cyclotrons
BT3   cyclic accelerators
BT4   accelerators

OSMIUM [300; 300]
BT1   platinum metals
BT2   transition elements
BT3   metals
BT4   elements

OSMIUM ADDITIONS [16; 16]
(Alloys containing not more than 1% Os are listed here.)
RT   osmium alloys
RT   osmium compounds

OSMIUM ALLOYS [123; 140]
(Alloys containing more than 1% Os.)
BT1   platinum metal alloys
BT2   alloys
NT1   osmium base alloys
RT   osmium additions

OSMIUM BASE ALLOYS [14; 14]
BT1   osmium alloys
BT2   platinum metal alloys
BT3   alloys

OSMIUM BORIDES [17; 17] *Feb 76*
BT1   borides
BT2   boron compounds
BT1   osmium compounds
BT2   transition element compounds

→ **OSMIUM CARBIDES** [0; 0] *Sep 91*
BT1   carbides
BT2   carbon compounds
BT1   osmium compounds
BT2   transition element compounds

OSMIUM CHLORIDES [17; 17]
BT1   chlorides
BT2   chlorine compounds
BT3   halogen compounds
BT2   halides
BT3   halogen compounds
BT1   osmium compounds
BT2   transition element compounds

OSMIUM COMPLEXES [130; 130]
BT1   transition element complexes
BT2   complexes

OSMIUM COMPOUNDS [95; 195]
BT1   transition element compounds
NT1   osmium borides
NT1   osmium carbides
NT1   osmium chlorides
NT1   osmium fluorides
NT1   osmium oxides
NT1   osmium phosphides
NT1   osmium sulfates
NT1   osmium sulfides
RT   osmium additions

OSMIUM FLUORIDES [11; 11]
BT1   fluorides
BT2   fluorine compounds
BT3   halogen compounds
BT2   halides
BT3   halogen compounds
BT1   osmium compounds
BT2   transition element compounds

OSMIUM IONS [14; 14]
BT1   ions
BT2   charged particles

OSMIUM ISOTOPES [214; 1,103]
NT1   osmium 162
NT1   osmium 163
NT1   osmium 164
NT1   osmium 165
NT1   osmium 166
NT1   osmium 167
NT1   osmium 168
NT1   osmium 169
NT1   osmium 170
NT1   osmium 171
NT1   osmium 172
NT1   osmium 173
NT1   osmium 174
NT1   osmium 175
NT1   osmium 176
NT1   osmium 177
NT1   osmium 178
NT1   osmium 179
NT1   osmium 180
NT1   osmium 181
NT1   osmium 182
NT1   osmium 183
NT1   osmium 184
NT1   osmium 185
NT1   osmium 186
NT1   osmium 187
NT1   osmium 188
NT1   osmium 189
NT1   osmium 190
NT1   osmium 191
NT1   osmium 192
NT1   osmium 193
NT1   osmium 194
NT1   osmium 195
NT1   osmium 196

OSMIUM OXIDES [59; 59]
BT1   osmium compounds
BT2   transition element compounds
BT1   oxides
BT2   chalcogenides
BT2   oxygen compounds

→ **OSMIUM PHOSPHIDES** [0; 0] *Sep 91*
BT1   osmium compounds
BT2   transition element compounds
BT1   phosphides
BT2   phosphorus compounds
BT2   pnictides

OSMIUM SULFATES [2; 2] *Mar 77*
BT1   osmium compounds
BT2   transition element compounds
BT1   sulfates
BT2   oxygen compounds
BT2   sulfur compounds

OSMIUM SULFIDES [0; 0] *Sep 91*
BT1 osmium compounds
BT2 transition element compounds
BT1 sulfides
BT2 chalcogenides
BT2 sulfur compounds

OSMIUM 162 [2; 2] *Jul 89*
BT1 alpha decay radioisotopes
BT2 radioisotopes
BT3 isotopes
BT1 even-even nuclei
BT2 nuclei
BT1 intermediate mass nuclei
BT2 nuclei
BT1 millisec living radioisotopes
BT2 radioisotopes
BT3 isotopes
BT1 osmium isotopes

OSMIUM 163 [0; 0] *May 86*
BT1 alpha decay radioisotopes
BT2 radioisotopes
BT3 isotopes
BT1 even-odd nuclei
BT2 nuclei
BT1 intermediate mass nuclei
BT2 nuclei
BT1 osmium isotopes

OSMIUM 164 [0; 0] *May 86*
BT1 alpha decay radioisotopes
BT2 radioisotopes
BT3 isotopes
BT1 even-even nuclei
BT2 nuclei
BT1 intermediate mass nuclei
BT2 nuclei
BT1 millisec living radioisotopes
BT2 radioisotopes
BT3 isotopes
BT1 osmium isotopes

OSMIUM 165 [4; 4] *Nov 78*
BT1 alpha decay radioisotopes
BT2 radioisotopes
BT3 isotopes
BT1 even-odd nuclei
BT2 nuclei
BT1 intermediate mass nuclei
BT2 nuclei
BT1 millisec living radioisotopes
BT2 radioisotopes
BT3 isotopes
BT1 osmium isotopes

OSMIUM 166 [5; 5] *Feb 78*
BT1 alpha decay radioisotopes
BT2 radioisotopes
BT3 isotopes
BT1 electron capture radioisotopes
BT2 beta decay radioisotopes
BT3 radioisotopes
BT4 isotopes
BT1 even-even nuclei
BT2 nuclei
BT1 intermediate mass nuclei
BT2 nuclei
BT1 millisec living radioisotopes
BT2 radioisotopes
BT3 isotopes
BT1 osmium isotopes

OSMIUM 167 [5; 5] *Feb 78*
BT1 alpha decay radioisotopes
BT2 radioisotopes
BT3 isotopes
BT1 electron capture radioisotopes
BT2 beta decay radioisotopes
BT3 radioisotopes
BT4 isotopes
BT1 even-odd nuclei
BT2 nuclei
BT1 intermediate mass nuclei
BT2 nuclei
BT1 millisec living radioisotopes
BT2 radioisotopes
BT3 isotopes
BT1 osmium isotopes

OSMIUM 168 [11; 11] *Feb 78*
BT1 alpha decay radioisotopes
BT2 radioisotopes
BT3 isotopes
BT1 electron capture radioisotopes
BT2 beta decay radioisotopes
BT3 radioisotopes
BT4 isotopes
BT1 even-even nuclei
BT2 nuclei
BT1 intermediate mass nuclei
BT2 nuclei
BT1 osmium isotopes
BT1 seconds living radioisotopes
BT2 radioisotopes
BT3 isotopes

OSMIUM 169 [3; 3] *Aug 82*
BT1 alpha decay radioisotopes
BT2 radioisotopes
BT3 isotopes
BT1 electron capture radioisotopes
BT2 beta decay radioisotopes
BT3 radioisotopes
BT4 isotopes
BT1 even-odd nuclei
BT2 nuclei
BT1 intermediate mass nuclei
BT2 nuclei
BT1 osmium isotopes
BT1 seconds living radioisotopes
BT2 radioisotopes
BT3 isotopes

OSMIUM 170 [14; 14]
BT1 alpha decay radioisotopes
BT2 radioisotopes
BT3 isotopes
BT1 electron capture radioisotopes
BT2 beta decay radioisotopes
BT3 radioisotopes
BT4 isotopes
BT1 even-even nuclei
BT2 nuclei
BT1 intermediate mass nuclei
BT2 nuclei
BT1 osmium isotopes
BT1 seconds living radioisotopes
BT2 radioisotopes
BT3 isotopes

OSMIUM 171 [10; 10]
BT1 alpha decay radioisotopes
BT2 radioisotopes
BT3 isotopes
BT1 electron capture radioisotopes
BT2 beta decay radioisotopes
BT3 radioisotopes
BT4 isotopes
BT1 even-odd nuclei
BT2 nuclei
BT1 intermediate mass nuclei
BT2 nuclei
BT1 osmium isotopes
BT1 seconds living radioisotopes
BT2 radioisotopes
BT3 isotopes

OSMIUM 172 [24; 24]
BT1 alpha decay radioisotopes
BT2 radioisotopes
BT3 isotopes
BT1 beta-plus decay radioisotopes
BT2 beta decay radioisotopes
BT3 radioisotopes
BT4 isotopes
BT1 electron capture radioisotopes
BT2 beta decay radioisotopes
BT3 radioisotopes
BT4 isotopes
BT1 even-even nuclei
BT2 nuclei
BT1 intermediate mass nuclei
BT2 nuclei
BT1 osmium isotopes
BT1 seconds living radioisotopes
BT2 radioisotopes
BT3 isotopes

OSMIUM 173 [11; 11]
BT1 alpha decay radioisotopes
BT2 radioisotopes
BT3 isotopes
BT1 beta-plus decay radioisotopes
BT2 beta decay radioisotopes
BT3 radioisotopes
BT4 isotopes
BT1 electron capture radioisotopes
BT2 beta decay radioisotopes
BT3 radioisotopes
BT4 isotopes
BT1 even-odd nuclei
BT2 nuclei
BT1 intermediate mass nuclei
BT2 nuclei
BT1 osmium isotopes
BT1 seconds living radioisotopes
BT2 radioisotopes
BT3 isotopes

OSMIUM 174 [23; 23]
BT1 alpha decay radioisotopes
BT2 radioisotopes
BT3 isotopes
BT1 beta-plus decay radioisotopes
BT2 beta decay radioisotopes
BT3 radioisotopes
BT4 isotopes
BT1 electron capture radioisotopes
BT2 beta decay radioisotopes
BT3 radioisotopes
BT4 isotopes
BT1 even-even nuclei
BT2 nuclei
BT1 intermediate mass nuclei
BT2 nuclei
BT1 osmium isotopes
BT1 seconds living radioisotopes
BT2 radioisotopes
BT3 isotopes

OSMIUM 175 [13; 13]
BT1 beta-plus decay radioisotopes
BT2 beta decay radioisotopes
BT3 radioisotopes
BT4 isotopes
BT1 electron capture radioisotopes
BT2 beta decay radioisotopes
BT3 radioisotopes
BT4 isotopes
BT1 even-odd nuclei
BT2 nuclei
BT1 intermediate mass nuclei
BT2 nuclei
BT1 minutes living radioisotopes
BT2 radioisotopes
BT3 isotopes
BT1 osmium isotopes

OSMIUM 176 [19; 19]
BT1 beta-plus decay radioisotopes
BT2 beta decay radioisotopes
BT3 radioisotopes
BT4 isotopes
BT1 electron capture radioisotopes
BT2 beta decay radioisotopes
BT3 radioisotopes
BT4 isotopes
BT1 even-even nuclei
BT2 nuclei
BT1 intermediate mass nuclei
BT2 nuclei
BT1 minutes living radioisotopes
BT2 radioisotopes
BT3 isotopes
BT1 osmium isotopes

OSMIUM 177 [9; 9]
BT1 beta-plus decay radioisotopes
BT2 beta decay radioisotopes
BT3 radioisotopes
BT4 isotopes
BT1 electron capture radioisotopes
BT2 beta decay radioisotopes

         BT3   radioisotopes
            BT4   isotopes
     BT1   even-odd nuclei
     BT2   nuclei
     BT1   intermediate mass nuclei
     BT2   nuclei
     BT1   minutes living radioisotopes
     BT2   radioisotopes
         BT3   isotopes
     BT1   osmium isotopes

OSMIUM 178 [28; 28]
     BT1   beta-plus decay radioisotopes
     BT2   beta decay radioisotopes
         BT3   radioisotopes
            BT4   isotopes
     BT1   electron capture radioisotopes
     BT2   beta decay radioisotopes
         BT3   radioisotopes
            BT4   isotopes
     BT1   even-even nuclei
     BT2   nuclei
     BT1   intermediate mass nuclei
     BT2   nuclei
     BT1   minutes living radioisotopes
     BT2   radioisotopes
         BT3   isotopes
     BT1   osmium isotopes

OSMIUM 179 [11; 11]
     BT1   beta-plus decay radioisotopes
     BT2   beta decay radioisotopes
         BT3   radioisotopes
            BT4   isotopes
     BT1   electron capture radioisotopes
     BT2   beta decay radioisotopes
         BT3   radioisotopes
            BT4   isotopes
     BT1   even-odd nuclei
     BT2   nuclei
     BT1   intermediate mass nuclei
     BT2   nuclei
     BT1   minutes living radioisotopes
     BT2   radioisotopes
         BT3   isotopes
     BT1   osmium isotopes

OSMIUM 180 [54; 54]
     BT1   electron capture radioisotopes
     BT2   beta decay radioisotopes
         BT3   radioisotopes
            BT4   isotopes
     BT1   even-even nuclei
     BT2   nuclei
     BT1   intermediate mass nuclei
     BT2   nuclei
     BT1   internal conversion radioisoto
     BT2   radioisotopes
         BT3   isotopes
     BT1   minutes living radioisotopes
     BT2   radioisotopes
         BT3   isotopes
     BT1   osmium isotopes

OSMIUM 181 [32; 32]
     BT1   beta-plus decay radioisotopes
     BT2   beta decay radioisotopes
         BT3   radioisotopes
            BT4   isotopes
     BT1   electron capture radioisotopes
     BT2   beta decay radioisotopes
         BT3   radioisotopes
            BT4   isotopes
     BT1   even-odd nuclei
     BT2   nuclei
     BT1   heavy nuclei
     BT2   nuclei
     BT1   hours living radioisotopes
     BT2   radioisotopes
         BT3   isotopes
     BT1   minutes living radioisotopes
     BT2   radioisotopes
         BT3   isotopes
     BT1   osmium isotopes

OSMIUM 182 [67; 67]
     BT1   electron capture radioisotopes
     BT2   beta decay radioisotopes
         BT3   radioisotopes
            BT4   isotopes
     BT1   even-even nuclei
     BT2   nuclei
     BT1   heavy nuclei
     BT2   nuclei
     BT1   hours living radioisotopes
     BT2   radioisotopes
         BT3   isotopes
     BT1   isomeric transition isotopes
     BT2   radioisotopes
         BT3   isotopes
     BT1   nanosec living radioisotopes
     BT2   radioisotopes
         BT3   isotopes
     BT1   osmium isotopes

OSMIUM 183 [36; 36]
     BT1   beta-plus decay radioisotopes
     BT2   beta decay radioisotopes
         BT3   radioisotopes
            BT4   isotopes
     BT1   electron capture radioisotopes
     BT2   beta decay radioisotopes
         BT3   radioisotopes
            BT4   isotopes
     BT1   even-odd nuclei
     BT2   nuclei
     BT1   heavy nuclei
     BT2   nuclei
     BT1   hours living radioisotopes
     BT2   radioisotopes
         BT3   isotopes
     BT1   isomeric transition isotopes
     BT2   radioisotopes
         BT3   isotopes
     BT1   osmium isotopes

OSMIUM 184 [42; 42]
     BT1   even-even nuclei
     BT2   nuclei
     BT1   heavy nuclei
     BT2   nuclei
     BT1   osmium isotopes
     BT1   stable isotopes
     BT2   isotopes

OSMIUM 184 TARGET [5; 5]
     BT1   targets

OSMIUM 185 [43; 43]
     BT1   days living radioisotopes
     BT2   radioisotopes
         BT3   isotopes
     BT1   electron capture radioisotopes
     BT2   beta decay radioisotopes
         BT3   radioisotopes
            BT4   isotopes
     BT1   even-odd nuclei
     BT2   nuclei
     BT1   heavy nuclei
     BT2   nuclei
     BT1   osmium isotopes

OSMIUM 186 [129; 129]
     BT1   alpha decay radioisotopes
     BT2   radioisotopes
         BT3   isotopes
     BT1   even-even nuclei
     BT2   nuclei
     BT1   heavy nuclei
     BT2   nuclei
     BT1   osmium isotopes
     BT1   stable isotopes
     BT2   isotopes
     BT1   years living radioisotopes
     BT2   radioisotopes
         BT3   isotopes

OSMIUM 186 TARGET [30; 30]
     BT1   targets

OSMIUM 187 [91; 91]
     BT1   even-odd nuclei
     BT2   nuclei
     BT1   heavy nuclei
     BT2   nuclei
     BT1   osmium isotopes
     BT1   stable isotopes
     BT2   isotopes

OSMIUM 187 TARGET [46; 46]
     BT1   targets

OSMIUM 188 [151; 151]
     BT1   even-even nuclei
     BT2   nuclei
     BT1   heavy nuclei
     BT2   nuclei
     BT1   osmium isotopes
     BT1   stable isotopes
     BT2   isotopes

OSMIUM 188 TARGET [48; 48]
     BT1   targets

OSMIUM 189 [63; 63]
     BT1   even-odd nuclei
     BT2   nuclei
     BT1   heavy nuclei
     BT2   nuclei
     BT1   hours living radioisotopes
     BT2   radioisotopes
         BT3   isotopes
     BT1   internal conversion radioisoto
     BT2   radioisotopes
         BT3   isotopes
     BT1   isomeric transition isotopes
     BT2   radioisotopes
         BT3   isotopes
     BT1   osmium isotopes
     BT1   stable isotopes
     BT2   isotopes

OSMIUM 189 TARGET [36; 36]
     BT1   targets

OSMIUM 190 [133; 133]
     BT1   even-even nuclei
     BT2   nuclei
     BT1   heavy nuclei
     BT2   nuclei
     BT1   internal conversion radioisoto
     BT2   radioisotopes
         BT3   isotopes
     BT1   isomeric transition isotopes
     BT2   radioisotopes
         BT3   isotopes
     BT1   minutes living radioisotopes
     BT2   radioisotopes
         BT3   isotopes
     BT1   osmium isotopes
     BT1   stable isotopes
     BT2   isotopes

OSMIUM 190 TARGET [43; 43]
     BT1   targets

OSMIUM 191 [118; 118]
     BT1   beta-minus decay radioisotopes
     BT2   beta decay radioisotopes
         BT3   radioisotopes
            BT4   isotopes
     BT1   days living radioisotopes
     BT2   radioisotopes
         BT3   isotopes
     BT1   even-odd nuclei
     BT2   nuclei
     BT1   heavy nuclei
     BT2   nuclei
     BT1   hours living radioisotopes
     BT2   radioisotopes
         BT3   isotopes
     BT1   internal conversion radioisoto
     BT2   radioisotopes
         BT3   isotopes
     BT1   isomeric transition isotopes
     BT2   radioisotopes
         BT3   isotopes

BT1 osmium isotopes

OSMIUM 191 TARGET [0; 0] *Apr 79*
BT1 targets

OSMIUM 192 [152; 152]
BT1 even-even nuclei
BT2 nuclei
BT1 heavy nuclei
BT2 nuclei
BT1 isomeric transition isotopes
BT2 radioisotopes
BT3 isotopes
BT1 osmium isotopes
BT1 seconds living radioisotopes
BT2 radioisotopes
BT3 isotopes
BT1 stable isotopes
BT2 isotopes

OSMIUM 192 TARGET [98; 98]
BT1 targets

OSMIUM 193 [32; 32]
BT1 beta-minus decay radioisotopes
BT2 beta decay radioisotopes
BT3 radioisotopes
BT4 isotopes
BT1 days living radioisotopes
BT2 radioisotopes
BT3 isotopes
BT1 even-odd nuclei
BT2 nuclei
BT1 heavy nuclei
BT2 nuclei
BT1 osmium isotopes

OSMIUM 194 [10; 10]
BT1 beta-minus decay radioisotopes
BT2 beta decay radioisotopes
BT3 radioisotopes
BT4 isotopes
BT1 even-even nuclei
BT2 nuclei
BT1 heavy nuclei
BT2 nuclei
BT1 internal conversion radioisoto
BT2 radioisotopes
BT3 isotopes
BT1 osmium isotopes
BT1 years living radioisotopes
BT2 radioisotopes
BT3 isotopes

OSMIUM 195 [2; 2]
BT1 beta-minus decay radioisotopes
BT2 beta decay radioisotopes
BT3 radioisotopes
BT4 isotopes
BT1 even-odd nuclei
BT2 nuclei
BT1 heavy nuclei
BT2 nuclei
BT1 minutes living radioisotopes
BT2 radioisotopes
BT3 isotopes
BT1 osmium isotopes

OSMIUM 196 [11; 11] *Jan 77*
BT1 beta-minus decay radioisotopes
BT2 beta decay radioisotopes
BT3 radioisotopes
BT4 isotopes
BT1 even-even nuclei
BT2 nuclei
BT1 heavy nuclei
BT2 nuclei
BT1 minutes living radioisotopes
BT2 radioisotopes
BT3 isotopes
BT1 osmium isotopes

OSMOSIS [465; 465]
UF *reverse osmosis*
RT advection
RT diffusion
RT donnan theory
RT hypertonic solutions
RT isotonic solutions
RT mass transfer
RT membrane transport
RT membranes
RT molecular weight
RT permeability

osteitis (radioinduced)
USE osteoradionecrosis

osteoblasts
USE connective tissue cells

osteocytes
USE bone cells

OSTEODENSITOMETRY [317; 317]
BT1 biomedical radiography
BT2 diagnostic techniques
BT2 medicine
RT bone tissues
RT osteoporosis
RT scintiscanning

OSTEOMYELITIS [435; 435]
BT1 skeletal diseases
BT2 diseases
RT bone tissues

OSTEOPOROSIS [489; 489]
BT1 skeletal diseases
BT2 diseases
RT bone tissues
RT osteodensitometry

OSTEORADIONECROSIS [301; 301]
UF *osteitis (radioinduced)*
BT1 local radiation effects
BT2 biological radiation effects
BT3 biological effects
BT3 radiation effects
BT1 necrosis
BT2 pathological changes
BT3 diseases
BT1 radiation injuries
BT2 biological radiation effects
BT3 biological effects
BT3 radiation effects
BT2 injuries
BT3 diseases
BT1 skeletal diseases
BT2 diseases
RT bone tissues

OSTEOSARCOMAS [915; 915]
BT1 sarcomas
BT2 neoplasms
BT3 diseases
BT1 skeletal diseases
BT2 diseases
RT bone tissues

OSTR REACTOR [12; 12]
(Oregon State University, Corvallis, Oregon, USA)
UF *oregon state triga reactor*
BT1 isotope production reactors
BT2 irradiation reactors
BT3 reactors
BT1 pulsed reactors
BT2 reactors
BT1 training reactors
BT2 research and test reactors
BT3 reactors
BT1 triga type reactors
BT2 enriched uranium reactors
BT3 reactors
BT2 hydride moderated reactors
BT3 reactors
BT2 research and test reactors
BT3 reactors
BT2 solid homogeneous reactors
BT3 homogeneous reactors
BT4 reactors
BT2 water cooled reactors
BT3 reactors
BT2 water moderated reactors
BT3 reactors

OSUR REACTOR [20; 20]
(Ohio State University, Columbus, Ohio, USA)
UF *ohio state univ. reactor*
BT1 pool type reactors
BT2 water cooled reactors
BT3 reactors
BT2 water moderated reactors
BT3 reactors
BT1 training reactors
BT2 research and test reactors
BT3 reactors

osweso nuclear power plant
USE nine mile point-2 reactor

OTHER ORGANIC COMPOUNDS [18; 2,620]
(For organic materials, usually naturally occurring, composed of undetermined or mixed organic compounds.)
BT1 organic compounds
NT1 amber
NT1 asphaltite
NT1 oils
NT2 castor oil
NT2 corn oil
NT2 cottonseed oil
NT2 croton oil
NT2 essential oils
NT2 fish oil
NT2 linseed oil
NT2 lipiodol
NT2 olive oil
NT2 peanut oil
NT2 sesame oil
NT2 soybean oil
NT2 triolein
NT1 pitches
NT1 soaps
NT1 tar
NT2 bitumens
NT3 asphalts
NT3 carburan
NT3 coal tar
NT3 thucholite
NT1 waxes
NT2 carbowax
NT2 paraffin
NT2 santowax

OTTAWA RIVER [7; 7]
BT1 rivers
BT2 surface waters

ottawa slowpoke reactor
USE slowpoke ottawa reactor

otto hahn (nuclear ship)
USE ns otto hahn

OTTO HAHN REACTOR [177; 177]
UF *nucl. ship otto hahn reactor*
BT1 pwr type reactors
BT2 enriched uranium reactors
BT3 reactors
BT2 power reactors
BT3 reactors
BT2 thermal reactors
BT3 reactors
BT2 water cooled reactors
BT3 reactors
BT2 water moderated reactors
BT3 reactors

BT1 ship propulsion reactors
BT2 propulsion reactors
BT3 power reactors
BT4 reactors
RT ns otto hahn

OUABAIN [246; 246]
BT1 cardiotonics
BT2 cardiovascular agents
BT3 drugs
BT1 glycosides
BT2 carbohydrates
BT3 organic compounds

OUTAGES [884; 884] *May 81*
(Accidental or planned shutdown of all or part of an electrical or thermal power system.)
UF *blackouts*
RT accidents
RT availability
RT capacity
RT failures
RT maintenance
RT power losses
RT power plants
RT power supplies
RT power systems
RT power transmission
RT reliability
RT shutdown

outgassing
USE degassing

OVA [116; 116]
BT1 gametes
BT2 germ cells
RT eggs
RT life cycle
RT oogenesis
RT ovulation

OVALBUMIN [28; 28]
BT1 glycoproteins
BT2 proteins
BT3 organic compounds
BT2 saccharides
BT3 carbohydrates
BT4 organic compounds

OVARIES [1,569; 1,569]
BT1 female genitals
BT2 organs
BT3 body
BT1 gonads
RT estrogens
RT oogenesis
RT ovulation
RT progesterone

OVERBURDEN [191; 191]
(The loose soil, silt, sand, gravel, or other unconsolidated material overlying bedrock, either transported or formed in place.)
UF *regolith*
RT dusts
RT rocks
RT soils

OVERCURRENT [7; 7] *Apr 86*
BT1 electric currents
BT2 currents
RT electrical transients
RT surges

OVERHAUSER EFFECT [304; 304] *Jul 80*
RT electron spin resonance
RT nuclear magnetic resonance
RT nuclei
RT polarization

OVERVOLTAGE [16; 16] *Apr 86*
BT1 electric potential
RT breakdown
RT electrical transients
RT surges

OVULATION [142; 142]
RT estrous cycle
RT fertilization
RT menstrual cycle
RT ova
RT ovaries
RT reproduction

OWNERSHIP [81; 81] *Nov 78*
RT legal aspects
RT property rights

OWR REACTOR [38; 38]
(University of California, Los Alamos Scientific Lab., Los Alamos, New Mexico, USA)
UF *los alam. omega west reactor*
UF *omega west reactor*
BT1 enriched uranium reactors
BT2 reactors
BT1 research reactors
BT2 research and test reactors
BT3 reactors
BT1 tank type reactors
BT2 reactors
BT1 test reactors
BT2 research and test reactors
BT3 reactors
BT2 test facilities
BT1 thermal reactors
BT2 reactors
BT1 water cooled reactors
BT2 reactors
BT1 water moderated reactors
BT2 reactors

OXADIAZOLES [30; 30]
(Compounds that contain a five-membered heterocyclic ring containing one oxygen and two nitrogen atoms.)
BT1 azoles
BT2 heterocyclic compounds
BT3 organic compounds
BT2 organic nitrogen compounds
BT3 organic compounds
BT1 organic oxygen compounds
BT2 organic compounds

oxalaldehyde
USE glyoxal

OXALATES [955; 955]
BT1 carboxylic acid salts
RT oxalic acid esters

OXALIC ACID [450; 450]
BT1 dicarboxylic acids
BT2 carboxylic acids
BT3 organic acids
BT4 organic compounds

OXALIC ACID ESTERS [10; 10]
BT1 carboxylic acid esters
BT2 esters
BT3 organic compounds
RT oxalates

OXAZOLES [108; 186]
(Compounds that contain a five-membered heterocyclic ring containing one nitrogen and one oxygen atom.)
BT1 azoles
BT2 heterocyclic compounds
BT3 organic compounds
BT2 organic nitrogen compounds
BT3 organic compounds
BT1 organic oxygen compounds
BT2 organic compounds
NT1 benzoxazoles
NT1 pemoline

NT1 popop

oxidants
USE oxidizers

OXIDASES [187; 308]
BT1 oxidoreductases
BT2 enzymes
BT3 organic compounds
NT1 amine oxidases
NT1 cytochrome oxidase
NT1 histaminase
NT1 luciferase
NT1 uricase

OXIDATION [12,767; 15,984]
UF+ *disproportionation*
BT1 chemical reactions
NT1 combustion
NT2 cocombustion
NT2 fluidized-bed combustion
NT1 roasting
RT anoxia
RT antioxidants
RT corrosion
RT corrosion products
RT oxidizers
RT redox potential
RT reduction
RT thiobacillus ferroxidans
RT thiobacillus oxidans

OXIDE MINERALS [58; 3,784] *Apr 84*
SF *perovskites*
BT1 minerals
NT1 aeschynite
NT1 baddeleyite
NT1 bastnaesite
NT1 becquerelite
NT1 brannerite
NT1 cerianite
NT1 clarkeite
NT1 corundum
NT2 ruby
NT2 sapphire
NT1 cristobalite
NT1 curite
NT1 davidite
NT1 demesmaekerite
NT1 ferrite garnets
NT1 francevillite
NT1 gummite
NT1 hatchettolite
NT1 hematite
NT1 hollandite
NT1 ilmenite
NT1 iriginite
NT1 ishikawaite
NT1 kaolin
NT1 limonite
NT1 magnetite
NT1 masuyite
NT1 moluranite
NT1 mullite
NT1 perovskite
NT1 quartz
NT1 rutile
NT1 schoepite
NT1 spinels
NT1 strelkinite
NT1 tantalite
NT1 thorianite
NT1 tyuyamunite
NT1 umohoite
NT1 uraninites
NT2 pitchblende
NT1 uranium black
NT1 uranothorianite
NT1 wolframite
NT1 wulfenite
NT1 zeunerite
NT1 zirconolite
RT aluminium oxides
RT arsenic oxides
RT barium oxides
RT calcium oxides
RT cerium oxides
RT cobalt oxides

```
RT      copper oxides
RT      hafnium oxides
RT      iron oxides
RT      kimberlites
RT      lead oxides
RT      magnesium oxides
RT      manganese oxides
RT      molybdenum oxides
RT      niobium oxides
RT      potassium oxides
RT      selenium oxides
RT      shales
RT      silicon oxides
RT      sodium oxides
RT      tantalum oxides
RT      tellurium oxides
RT      thorium oxides
RT      titanium oxides
RT      tungsten oxides
RT      uranium oxides
RT      vanadium oxides
RT      zirconium oxides

OXIDES [3,310; 74,480]
BT1     chalcogenides
BT1     oxygen compounds
NT1     actinium oxides
NT1     aluminium oxides
NT1     americium oxides
NT1     antimony oxides
NT1     argon oxides
NT1     arsenic oxides
NT1     barium oxides
NT1     berkelium oxides
NT1     beryllium oxides
NT1     bismuth oxides
NT1     boron oxides
NT1     bromine oxides
NT1     cadmium oxides
NT1     calcium oxides
NT1     californium oxides
NT1     carbon oxides
  NT2       carbon dioxide
  NT2       carbon monoxide
NT1     cerium oxides
NT1     cesium oxides
NT1     chlorine oxides
NT1     chromium oxides
NT1     cobalt oxides
NT1     copper oxides
NT1     curium oxides
NT1     dysprosium oxides
NT1     einsteinium oxides
NT1     erbium oxides
NT1     europium oxides
NT1     fermium oxides
NT1     fluorine oxides
NT1     francium oxides
NT1     gadolinium oxides
NT1     gallium oxides
NT1     germanium oxides
NT1     gold oxides
NT1     hafnium oxides
NT1     helium oxides
NT1     holmium oxides
NT1     indium oxides
NT1     iodine oxides
NT1     iridium oxides
NT1     iron oxides
NT1     krypton oxides
NT1     lanthanum oxides
NT1     lawrencium oxides
NT1     lead oxides
NT1     lithium oxides
NT1     lutetium oxides
NT1     magnesium oxides
NT1     manganese oxides
NT1     mendelevium oxides
NT1     mercury oxides
NT1     molybdenum oxides
  NT2       molybdenum blue
NT1     neodymium oxides
NT1     neon oxides
NT1     neptunium oxides
NT1     nickel oxides
NT1     niobium oxides
NT1     nitrogen oxides
  NT2       nitric oxide
  NT2       nitrogen dioxide
  NT2       nitrous oxide
NT1     nobelium oxides
NT1     osmium oxides
NT1     palladium oxides
NT1     phosphorus oxides
NT1     platinum oxides
NT1     plutonium oxides
  NT2       plutonium dioxide
NT1     polonium oxides
NT1     potassium oxides
NT1     praseodymium oxides
NT1     promethium oxides
NT1     protactinium oxides
NT1     radium oxides
NT1     radon oxides
NT1     rhenium oxides
NT1     rhodium oxides
NT1     rubidium oxides
NT1     ruthenium oxides
NT1     samarium oxides
NT1     scandium oxides
NT1     selenium oxides
NT1     silicon oxides
NT1     silver oxides
NT1     sodium oxides
NT1     strontium oxides
NT1     sulfur oxides
NT1     tantalum oxides
NT1     technetium oxides
NT1     tellurium oxides
NT1     terbium oxides
NT1     thallium oxides
NT1     thorium oxides
  NT2       thorotrast
NT1     thulium oxides
NT1     tin oxides
NT1     titanium oxides
NT1     tungsten oxides
NT1     uranium oxides
  NT2       uranium dioxide
  NT2       uranium oxides u3o8
  NT2       uranium trioxide
NT1     vanadium oxides
NT1     xenon oxides
NT1     ytterbium oxides
NT1     yttrium oxides
NT1     zinc oxides
NT1     zirconium oxides
RT      ceramics
RT      corrosion products
RT      oxybromides
RT      oxycarbides
RT      oxychlorides
RT      oxyfluorides
RT      oxygen additions
RT      oxyiodides
RT      oxysulfides

OXIDIZERS [228; 228] Feb 83
UF      oxidants
UF      oxidizing agents
RT      antioxidants
RT      oxidation


oxidizing agents
USE     oxidizers


OXIDOREDUCTASES [958; 2,738]
UF      reductases
BT1     enzymes
  BT2       organic compounds
NT1     dehydrogenases
  NT2       diaphorases
  NT2       lactate dehydrogenase
  NT2       nitrogenase
NT1     hydrogenases
NT1     hydroxylases
  NT2       tyrosinase
NT1     oxidases
  NT2       amine oxidases
  NT2       cytochrome oxidase
  NT2       histaminase
  NT2       luciferase
  NT2       uricase
NT1     oxygenases
  NT2       tryptophan oxygenase
NT1     peroxidases
  NT2       catalase
NT1     superoxide dismutase

RT      redox process
RT      reduction
RT      respiration


OXIMES [591; 662]
BT1     amines
  BT2       organic compounds
BT1     hydroxy compounds
  BT2       organic compounds
BT1     organic nitrogen compounds
  BT2       organic compounds
NT1     benzoinoxime
NT1     dimethylglyoxime
NT1     furildioxime
RT      aldehydes
RT      hydroxylamine
RT      ketones


OXINE [513; 513] Jul 80
UF      8-hydroxyquinoline
BT1     hydroxy compounds
  BT2       organic compounds
BT1     quinolines
  BT2       pyridines
    BT3       azines
      BT4       heterocyclic compounds
        BT5       organic compounds
      BT4       organic nitrogen compounds
        BT5       organic compounds


oxirans
USE     epoxides


oxoacetic acid
USE     glyoxylic acid


oxocarboxylic acids
USE     keto acids


OXONIUM IONS [72; 72]
BT1     molecular ions
  BT2       ions
    BT3       charged particles
RT      hydrogen ions 1 plus
RT      radiation chemistry


oxopropane
USE     acetone


OXYBROMIDES [96; 96]
(Specific compounds should be indexed
by coordination of a descriptor of the form
(CATION) COMPOUNDS and the above
anion descriptor.)
BT1     bromine compounds
  BT2       halogen compounds
BT1     oxyhalides
  BT2       halogen compounds
  BT2       oxygen compounds
RT      bromides
RT      bromine oxides
RT      oxides


OXYCARBIDES [25; 25] Aug 84
(Specific compounds should be indexed
by coordination of a descriptor of the form
(CATION) COMPOUNDS and the above
anion descriptor.)
BT1     carbon compounds
BT1     oxygen compounds
RT      carbides
RT      carbon oxides
RT      oxides


OXYCHLORIDES [572; 572]
(Specific compounds should be indexed
by coordination of a descriptor of the form
(CATION) COMPOUNDS and the above
anion descriptor.)
BT1     chlorine compounds
  BT2       halogen compounds
BT1     oxyhalides
  BT2       halogen compounds
```

BT2   oxygen compounds
RT   chlorides
RT   chlorine oxides
RT   oxides

OXYFLUORIDES [336; 336]
(Specific compounds should be indexed by coordination of a descriptor of the form (CATION) COMPOUNDS and the above anion descriptor.)
BT1   fluorine compounds
BT2   halogen compounds
BT1   oxyhalides
BT2   halogen compounds
BT2   oxygen compounds
RT   fluorides
RT   fluorine oxides
RT   oxides

OXYGEN [16,278; 16,614]
BT1   nonmetals
BT2   elements
RT   cryogenic fluids
RT   ozone

OXYGEN ADDITIONS [583; 583]
RT   oxides

OXYGEN COMPLEXES [31; 31]
BT1   complexes

OXYGEN COMPOUNDS [2,060; 148,602]
UF+   *chlorites*
UF+   *polythionates*
UF+   *polythionic acids*
UF+   *thionates*
NT1   aluminates
NT1   antimonates
NT1   arsenates
NT1   aurates
*NT1 borates
NT1   boric acid
NT1   bromates
NT1   bromic acid
*NT1 carbonates
NT1   carbonic acid
NT1   chlorates
NT1   chloric acid
NT1   chlorous acid
NT1   chromates
NT1   chromic acid
NT1   cuprates
NT1   dichromates
NT1   ferrates
NT1   fluorates
*NT1 germanates
NT1   hafnates
*NT1 hydroxides
NT1   hypochlorous acid
NT1   hypoiodous acid
NT1   hypophosphorous acid
NT1   iodates
NT1   iodic acid
NT1   manganates
NT1   molybdates
NT1   molybdophosphates
NT1   molybdophosphoric acid
NT1   nickelates
NT1   niobates
*NT1 nitrates
NT1   nitric acid
NT1   nitrites
NT1   nitrous acid
*NT1 oxides
NT1   oxycarbides
*NT1 oxyhalides
NT1   oxysulfides
NT1   perbromates
*NT1 perchlorates
NT1   perchloric acid
NT1   periodates
NT1   periodic acid
NT1   permanganates
*NT1 peroxides
NT1   perrhenates
NT1   persulfates
NT1   persulfuric acid
NT1   pertechnetates
*NT1 phosphates
NT1   phosphoric acid
NT1   phosphorous acid
NT1   plumbates
NT1   pyrophosphates
NT1   rhenates
NT1   selenates
NT1   selenites
*NT1 silicates
NT1   silicic acid
NT1   stannates
*NT1 sulfates
NT1   sulfites
NT1   sulfuric acid
NT1   sulfurous acid
NT1   tantalates
NT1   technetates
NT1   tellurates
NT1   telluric acid
*NT1 titanates
*NT1 tungstates
NT1   tungstophosphates
NT1   tungstophosphoric acid
*NT1 vanadates
*NT1 water
*NT1 zirconates
RT   cyanates
RT   hydroxyl radicals
RT   organic oxygen compounds
RT   ozone

oxygen effect (radiobiology)
USE   response modifying factors

OXYGEN ENHANCEMENT RATIO [845; 845]
UF   *oer*
RT   aerobic conditions
RT   anaerobic conditions
RT   biological radiation effects
RT   let
RT   quality factor
RT   rbe
RT   response modifying factors

oxygen fluorides
USE   fluorine oxides

oxygen hydrides
USE   water

OXYGEN IONS [3,707; 3,707]
BT1   ions
BT2   charged particles

OXYGEN ISOTOPES [583; 10,123]
NT1   oxygen 12
NT1   oxygen 13
NT1   oxygen 14
NT1   oxygen 15
NT1   oxygen 16
NT1   oxygen 17
NT1   oxygen 18
NT1   oxygen 19
NT1   oxygen 20
NT1   oxygen 21
NT1   oxygen 22
NT1   oxygen 23
NT1   oxygen 24
NT1   oxygen 28

OXYGEN METERS [136; 136]
BT1   measuring instruments
RT   chemical analysis

OXYGEN POTENTIAL [115; 115]
Apr 81
(Partial molar free enthalpy of oxygen in an oxide phase.)
BT1   free enthalpy
BT2   energy
BT2   thermodynamic properties
BT3   physical properties

OXYGEN 12 [23; 23]
BT1   even-even nuclei
BT2   nuclei
BT1   light nuclei
BT2   nuclei
BT1   oxygen isotopes

OXYGEN 13 [22; 22]
BT1   beta-plus decay radioisotopes
BT2   beta decay radioisotopes
BT3   radioisotopes
BT4   isotopes
BT1   even-odd nuclei
BT2   nuclei
BT1   light nuclei
BT2   nuclei
BT1   millisec living radioisotopes
BT2   radioisotopes
BT3   isotopes
BT1   oxygen isotopes

OXYGEN 14 [230; 230]
BT1   beta-plus decay radioisotopes
BT2   beta decay radioisotopes
BT3   radioisotopes
BT4   isotopes
BT1   even-even nuclei
BT2   nuclei
BT1   light nuclei
BT2   nuclei
BT1   minutes living radioisotopes
BT2   radioisotopes
BT3   isotopes
BT1   oxygen isotopes

OXYGEN 15 [1,153; 1,153]
BT1   beta-plus decay radioisotopes
BT2   beta decay radioisotopes
BT3   radioisotopes
BT4   isotopes
BT1   even-odd nuclei
BT2   nuclei
BT1   light nuclei
BT2   nuclei
BT1   minutes living radioisotopes
BT2   radioisotopes
BT3   isotopes
BT1   oxygen isotopes

OXYGEN 15 TARGET [8; 8] *Apr 76*
BT1   targets

OXYGEN 16 [4,778; 4,778]
BT1   even-even nuclei
BT2   nuclei
BT1   light nuclei
BT2   nuclei
BT1   oxygen isotopes
BT1   stable isotopes
BT2   isotopes
RT   oxygen 16 beams

OXYGEN 16 BEAMS [779; 779]
BT1   ion beams
BT2   beams
RT   oxygen 16

OXYGEN 16 EMISSION DECAY [2; 2] *Jul 91*
BT1   heavy ion emission decay
BT2   nuclear decay
BT3   decay

OXYGEN 16 REACTIONS [4,434; 4,434]
BT1   heavy ion reactions
BT2   nuclear reactions

OXYGEN 16 TARGET [3,172; 3,172]
BT1   targets

OXYGEN 17 [1,022; 1,022]
BT1   even-odd nuclei
BT2   nuclei
BT1   light nuclei
BT2   nuclei
BT1   oxygen isotopes

OXYGEN 17
- BT1 stable isotopes
- BT2 isotopes

OXYGEN 17 REACTIONS [172; 172]
- BT1 heavy ion reactions
- BT2 nuclear reactions

OXYGEN 17 TARGET [207; 207]
- BT1 targets

OXYGEN 18 [3,211; 3,211]
- BT1 even-even nuclei
- BT2 nuclei
- BT1 light nuclei
- BT2 nuclei
- BT1 oxygen isotopes
- BT1 stable isotopes
- BT2 isotopes
- RT oxygen 18 beams

OXYGEN 18 BEAMS [121; 121]
- BT1 ion beams
- BT2 beams
- RT oxygen 18

OXYGEN 18 REACTIONS [893; 893]
- BT1 heavy ion reactions
- BT2 nuclear reactions

OXYGEN 18 TARGET [620; 620]
- BT1 targets

OXYGEN 19 [107; 107]
- BT1 beta-minus decay radioisotopes
- BT2 beta decay radioisotopes
- BT3 radioisotopes
- BT4 isotopes
- BT1 even-odd nuclei
- BT2 nuclei
- BT1 light nuclei
- BT2 nuclei
- BT1 oxygen isotopes
- BT1 seconds living radioisotopes
- BT2 radioisotopes
- BT3 isotopes

OXYGEN 20 [73; 73]
- BT1 beta-minus decay radioisotopes
- BT2 beta decay radioisotopes
- BT3 radioisotopes
- BT4 isotopes
- BT1 even-even nuclei
- BT2 nuclei
- BT1 light nuclei
- BT2 nuclei
- BT1 oxygen isotopes
- BT1 seconds living radioisotopes
- BT2 radioisotopes
- BT3 isotopes

OXYGEN 21 [21; 21]
- BT1 beta-minus decay radioisotopes
- BT2 beta decay radioisotopes
- BT3 radioisotopes
- BT4 isotopes
- BT1 even-odd nuclei
- BT2 nuclei
- BT1 light nuclei
- BT2 nuclei
- BT1 oxygen isotopes
- BT1 seconds living radioisotopes
- BT2 radioisotopes
- BT3 isotopes

OXYGEN 22 [35; 35]
- BT1 beta-minus decay radioisotopes
- BT2 beta decay radioisotopes
- BT3 radioisotopes
- BT4 isotopes
- BT1 even-even nuclei
- BT2 nuclei
- BT1 light nuclei
- BT2 nuclei
- BT1 millisec living radioisotopes
- BT2 radioisotopes
- BT3 isotopes
- BT1 oxygen isotopes

OXYGEN 23 [11; 11]
- BT1 even-odd nuclei
- BT2 nuclei
- BT1 light nuclei
- BT2 nuclei
- BT1 oxygen isotopes

OXYGEN 24 [10; 10] *Feb 78*
- BT1 even-even nuclei
- BT2 nuclei
- BT1 light nuclei
- BT2 nuclei
- BT1 oxygen isotopes

OXYGEN 28 [3; 3] *Feb 79*
- BT1 even-even nuclei
- BT2 nuclei
- BT1 light nuclei
- BT2 nuclei
- BT1 oxygen isotopes

OXYGENASES [52; 53] *Apr 84*
- BT1 oxidoreductases
- BT2 enzymes
- BT3 organic compounds
- NT1 tryptophan oxygenase

OXYHALIDES [6; 84] *Nov 89*
- BT1 halogen compounds
- BT1 oxygen compounds
- NT1 oxybromides
- NT1 oxychlorides
- NT1 oxyfluorides
- NT1 oxyiodides

OXYIODIDES [52; 52]
(Specific compounds should be indexed by coordination of a descriptor of the form (CATION) COMPOUNDS and the above anion descriptor.)
- BT1 iodine compounds
- BT2 halogen compounds
- BT1 oxyhalides
- BT2 halogen compounds
- BT2 oxygen compounds
- RT iodides
- RT iodine oxides
- RT oxides

oxymethylene
- USE formaldehyde

OXYSULFIDES [203; 203]
(Specific compounds should be indexed by coordination of a descriptor of the form (CATION) COMPOUNDS and the above anion descriptor.)
- BT1 oxygen compounds
- BT1 sulfur compounds
- RT oxides
- RT sulfides
- RT sulfur oxides

OXYTETRACYCLINE [17; 17]
- UF *terramycin*
- BT1 tetracyclines
- BT2 antibiotics
- BT3 drugs
- BT3 organic compounds

OXYTOCIN [64; 64]
- BT1 pituitary hormones
- BT2 peptide hormones
- BT3 hormones
- RT parturition
- RT uterus

OYSTER CREEK-1 REACTOR [245; 245]
(Forked River, New Jersey, USA)
- BT1 bwr type reactors
- BT2 enriched uranium reactors
- BT3 reactors
- BT2 power reactors
- BT3 reactors
- BT2 thermal reactors
- BT3 reactors
- BT2 water cooled reactors
- BT3 reactors
- BT2 water moderated reactors
- BT3 reactors

oyster creek-2 reactor
- USE forked river-1 reactor

OYSTERS [114; 114]
- BT1 molluscs
- BT2 aquatic organisms
- BT2 invertebrates
- BT3 animals
- RT seafood

OZONE [977; 977]
- RT atmospheric chemistry
- RT oxygen
- RT oxygen compounds

OZONE LAYER [55; 55] *Feb 83*
- BT1 layers
- RT stratosphere

P CODES [2,092; 2,092]
- BT1 computer codes

P INVARIANCE [3,125; 3,125]
- UF *parity nonconservation*
- UF *space reflection*
- BT1 invariance principles
- RT lee-yang theory
- RT parity

P REACTOR [66; 66]
- UF *savannah riv. plant p reactor*
- BT1 heavy water moderated reactors
- BT2 reactors
- BT1 special production reactors
- BT2 production reactors
- BT3 reactors

P STATES [3,005; 3,005]
- BT1 energy levels

P WAVES [2,102; 2,102]
(For seismic waves use SEISMIC P WAVES.)
- BT1 partial waves
- RT angular momentum
- RT quantum mechanics

p waves (seismic)
- USE seismic p waves

p-n counters
- USE junction detectors

P-N JUNCTIONS [626; 626] *Jan 77*
- BT1 semiconductor junctions
- RT n-type conductors
- RT p-type conductors

p-nitrodimethylaminopropiophen
- USE amines
- AND aromatics
- AND ketones
- AND nitro compounds

P-TYPE CONDUCTORS [2,177; 2,177]
- BT1 semiconductor materials
- BT2 materials
- RT p-n junctions

PABA [32; 32]
  UF   *aminobenzoic acid-para*
  UF   *para-aminobenzoic acid*
  UF   *vitamin h-1*
  BT1   amino acids
    BT2   carboxylic acids
      BT3   organic acids
        BT4   organic compounds
  RT   folic acid
  RT   vitamin b group

pacemakers
  USE   cardiac pacemakers

pacific gas diablo canyon-1 r.
  USE   diablo canyon-1 reactor

pacific gas diablo canyon-2 r.
  USE   diablo canyon-2 reactor

PACIFIC OCEAN [789; 814]
  BT1   seas
    BT2   surface waters
  NT1   bering sea
  NT1   humboldt bay
  NT1   san francisco bay
  NT1   sequim bay
  RT   aleutian islands
  RT   fiji
  RT   hawaii
  RT   indonesia
  RT   kiribati
  RT   marshall islands
  RT   micronesia
  RT   nauru
  RT   new guinea
  RT   new zealand
  RT   philippines
  RT   singapore
  RT   tasmania
  RT   tuvalu

PACKAGE REACTORS [16; 16]
(Compact power reactors specially designed to simplify shipping and assembly.)
  BT1   power reactors
    BT2   reactors
  BT1   transportable reactors
    BT2   reactors

PACKAGING [2,845; 2,845]
  RT   containers
  RT   packaging rules
  RT   transport

PACKAGING RULES [322; 322] *Dec 76*
(Including labelling.)
  UF   *labelling (packages)*
  BT1   regulations
    BT2   laws
  RT   packaging
  RT   transport

packing (column)
  USE   column packing

PADE APPROXIMATION [758; 758]
  RT   series expansion

PADUCAH PLANT [77; 77]
  BT1   gaseous diffusion plants
    BT2   isotope separation plants
      BT3   industrial plants
      BT3   nuclear facilities
  BT1   us aec
    BT2   us organizations
      BT3   national organizations
  BT1   us doe
    BT2   us organizations
      BT3   national organizations
  BT1   us erda
    BT2   us organizations
      BT3   national organizations
  RT   kentucky

paec
  USE   philippine atomic energy commi

pahr
(Post-accident heat removal)
  USE   after-heat removal

PAIN [684; 684]
  BT1   symptoms
  RT   analgesics
  RT   anesthesia
  RT   nervous system

paintings
  USE   cultural objects

PAINTS [408; 505]
  BT1   coatings
  NT1   luminous paints
  RT   corrosion protection
  RT   pigments

pair conversion
  USE   internal pair production

PAIR PRODUCTION [8,786; 8,929]
(For production of particle pairs only; ion pairs should be indexed to IONIZATION and ION PAIRS.)
  BT1   particle production
  NT1   internal pair production
  RT   bethe-heitler theory
  RT   electron pairs
  RT   muon pairs

PAIR SPECTROMETERS [137; 137]
  BT1   gamma spectrometers
    BT2   spectrometers
      BT3   measuring instruments

PAIRING ENERGY [579; 579]
  BT1   binding energy
    BT2   energy

PAIRING INTERACTIONS [2,143; 2,143]
  BT1   interactions
  RT   generator-coordinate method

PAKHRA SYNCHROTRON [20; 20]
  BT1   synchrotrons
    BT2   cyclic accelerators
      BT3   accelerators

PAKISTAN [223; 223]
  BT1   asia
  BT1   developing countries

pakistan atomic research r.
  USE   parr reactor

PAKS-1 REACTOR [348; 348]
(Paks, Tolna, Hungary)
  UF   *hungarian paks-1 reactor*
  BT1   wwer type reactors
    BT2   pwr type reactors
      BT3   enriched uranium reactors
        BT4   reactors
      BT3   power reactors
        BT4   reactors
      BT3   thermal reactors
        BT4   reactors
      BT3   water cooled reactors
        BT4   reactors
      BT3   water moderated reactors
        BT4   reactors

PAKS-2 REACTOR [138; 138]
(Paks, Tolna, Hungary)
  UF   *hungarian paks-2 reactor*
  BT1   wwer type reactors
    BT2   pwr type reactors
      BT3   enriched uranium reactors
        BT4   reactors
      BT3   power reactors
        BT4   reactors
      BT3   thermal reactors
        BT4   reactors
      BT3   water cooled reactors
        BT4   reactors
      BT3   water moderated reactors
        BT4   reactors

PAKS-3 REACTOR [58; 58] *Jul 80*
(Paks, Tolna, Hungary)
  UF   *hungarian paks-3 reactor*
  BT1   wwer type reactors
    BT2   pwr type reactors
      BT3   enriched uranium reactors
        BT4   reactors
      BT3   power reactors
        BT4   reactors
      BT3   thermal reactors
        BT4   reactors
      BT3   water cooled reactors
        BT4   reactors
      BT3   water moderated reactors
        BT4   reactors

PAKS-4 REACTOR [50; 50] *Jul 80*
(Paks, Tolna, Hungary)
  UF   *hungarian paks-4 reactor*
  BT1   wwer type reactors
    BT2   pwr type reactors
      BT3   enriched uranium reactors
        BT4   reactors
      BT3   power reactors
        BT4   reactors
      BT3   thermal reactors
        BT4   reactors
      BT3   water cooled reactors
        BT4   reactors
      BT3   water moderated reactors
        BT4   reactors

PALANQUIN EVENT [1; 1]
  BT1   chemical explosions
    BT2   explosions
  BT1   cratering explosions
    BT2   explosions
  BT1   underground explosions
    BT2   explosions

PALEONTOLOGY [288; 288]
  RT   age estimation
  RT   biological evolution
  RT   fossils

PALISADES-1 REACTOR [139; 139]
  UF   *consumers michigan palisades*
  UF   *south haven michigan reactor*
  BT1   pwr type reactors
    BT2   enriched uranium reactors
      BT3   reactors
    BT2   power reactors
      BT3   reactors
    BT2   thermal reactors
      BT3   reactors
    BT2   water cooled reactors
      BT3   reactors
    BT2   water moderated reactors
      BT3   reactors

PALLADIUM [1,966; 1,966]
  BT1   platinum metals
    BT2   transition elements
      BT3   metals
        BT4   elements

PALLADIUM ADDITIONS [100; 100]
(Alloys containing not more than 1% Pd are listed here.)
  RT   palladium alloys
  RT   palladium compounds

PALLADIUM ALLOYS [912; 1,248]
(Alloys containing more than 1% Pd.)
- BT1 platinum metal alloys
- BT2 alloys
- NT1 palladium base alloys
- RT palladium additions

→ **PALLADIUM ARSENIDES** [0; 0] *Sep 91*
- BT1 arsenides
- BT2 arsenic compounds
- BT2 pnictides
- BT1 palladium compounds
- BT2 transition element compounds

PALLADIUM BASE ALLOYS [324; 324]
- BT1 palladium alloys
- BT2 platinum metal alloys
- BT3 alloys

→ **PALLADIUM BORIDES** [0; 0] *Sep 91*
- BT1 borides
- BT2 boron compounds
- BT1 palladium compounds
- BT2 transition element compounds

PALLADIUM BROMIDES [3; 3] *May 79*
- BT1 bromides
- BT2 bromine compounds
- BT3 halogen compounds
- BT2 halides
- BT3 halogen compounds
- BT1 palladium compounds
- BT2 transition element compounds

PALLADIUM CARBIDES [6; 6]
- BT1 carbides
- BT2 carbon compounds
- BT1 palladium compounds
- BT2 transition element compounds

PALLADIUM CHLORIDES [46; 46]
- BT1 chlorides
- BT2 chlorine compounds
- BT3 halogen compounds
- BT2 halides
- BT3 halogen compounds
- BT1 palladium compounds
- BT2 transition element compounds

PALLADIUM COMPLEXES [199; 199]
- BT1 transition element complexes
- BT2 complexes

PALLADIUM COMPOUNDS [221; 668]
- BT1 transition element compounds
- NT1 palladium arsenides
- NT1 palladium borides
- NT1 palladium bromides
- NT1 palladium carbides
- NT1 palladium chlorides
- NT1 palladium fluorides
- NT1 palladium hydrides
- NT1 palladium hydroxides
- NT1 palladium iodides
- NT1 palladium nitrates
- NT1 palladium oxides
- NT1 palladium phosphides
- NT1 palladium selenides
- NT1 palladium silicides
- NT1 palladium sulfides
- NT1 palladium tellurides
- RT palladium additions

PALLADIUM FLUORIDES [8; 8]
- BT1 fluorides
- BT2 fluorine compounds
- BT3 halogen compounds
- BT2 halides
- BT3 halogen compounds
- BT1 palladium compounds
- BT2 transition element compounds

PALLADIUM HYDRIDES [240; 240]
- BT1 hydrides
- BT2 hydrogen compounds
- BT1 palladium compounds
- BT2 transition element compounds

PALLADIUM HYDROXIDES [4; 4]
Apr 79
- BT1 hydroxides
- BT2 hydrogen compounds
- BT2 oxygen compounds
- BT1 palladium compounds
- BT2 transition element compounds

PALLADIUM IODIDES [13; 13]
- BT1 iodides
- BT2 halides
- BT3 halogen compounds
- BT2 iodine compounds
- BT3 halogen compounds
- BT1 palladium compounds
- BT2 transition element compounds

PALLADIUM IONS [78; 78]
- BT1 ions
- BT2 charged particles

PALLADIUM ISOTOPES [188; 1,004]
- NT1 palladium 100
- NT1 palladium 101
- NT1 palladium 102
- NT1 palladium 103
- NT1 palladium 104
- NT1 palladium 105
- NT1 palladium 106
- NT1 palladium 107
- NT1 palladium 108
- NT1 palladium 109
- NT1 palladium 110
- NT1 palladium 111
- NT1 palladium 112
- NT1 palladium 113
- NT1 palladium 114
- NT1 palladium 115
- NT1 palladium 116
- NT1 palladium 117
- NT1 palladium 118
- NT1 palladium 119
- NT1 palladium 95
- NT1 palladium 96
- NT1 palladium 97
- NT1 palladium 98
- NT1 palladium 99

PALLADIUM NITRATES [16; 16]
Jul 78
- BT1 nitrates
- BT2 nitrogen compounds
- BT2 oxygen compounds
- BT1 palladium compounds
- BT2 transition element compounds

PALLADIUM OXIDES [36; 36]
- BT1 oxides
- BT2 chalcogenides
- BT2 oxygen compounds
- BT1 palladium compounds
- BT2 transition element compounds

→ **PALLADIUM PHOSPHIDES** [0; 0]
Sep 91
- BT1 palladium compounds
- BT2 transition element compounds
- BT1 phosphides
- BT2 phosphorus compounds
- BT2 pnictides

→ **PALLADIUM SELENIDES** [0; 0] *Sep 91*
- BT1 palladium compounds
- BT2 transition element compounds
- BT1 selenides
- BT2 chalcogenides
- BT2 selenium compounds

PALLADIUM SILICIDES [86; 86]
Oct 76
- BT1 palladium compounds
- BT2 transition element compounds
- BT1 silicides
- BT2 silicon compounds

PALLADIUM SULFIDES [7; 7] *Oct 76*
- BT1 palladium compounds
- BT2 transition element compounds
- BT1 sulfides
- BT2 chalcogenides
- BT2 sulfur compounds

PALLADIUM TELLURIDES [6; 6]
Feb 78
- BT1 palladium compounds
- BT2 transition element compounds
- BT1 tellurides
- BT2 chalcogenides
- BT2 tellurium compounds

PALLADIUM 100 [50; 50]
- BT1 days living radioisotopes
- BT2 radioisotopes
- BT3 isotopes
- BT1 electron capture radioisotopes
- BT2 beta decay radioisotopes
- BT3 radioisotopes
- BT4 isotopes
- BT1 even-even nuclei
- BT2 nuclei
- BT1 intermediate mass nuclei
- BT2 nuclei
- BT1 palladium isotopes

PALLADIUM 101 [40; 40]
- BT1 beta-plus decay radioisotopes
- BT2 beta decay radioisotopes
- BT3 radioisotopes
- BT4 isotopes
- BT1 electron capture radioisotopes
- BT2 beta decay radioisotopes
- BT3 radioisotopes
- BT4 isotopes
- BT1 even-odd nuclei
- BT2 nuclei
- BT1 hours living radioisotopes
- BT2 radioisotopes
- BT3 isotopes
- BT1 intermediate mass nuclei
- BT2 nuclei
- BT1 palladium isotopes

PALLADIUM 102 [83; 83]
- BT1 even-even nuclei
- BT2 nuclei
- BT1 intermediate mass nuclei
- BT2 nuclei
- BT1 palladium isotopes
- BT1 stable isotopes
- BT2 isotopes

PALLADIUM 102 TARGET [61; 61]
- BT1 targets

PALLADIUM 103 [104; 104]
- BT1 days living radioisotopes
- BT2 radioisotopes
- BT3 isotopes
- BT1 electron capture radioisotopes
- BT2 beta decay radioisotopes
- BT3 radioisotopes
- BT4 isotopes
- BT1 even-odd nuclei
- BT2 nuclei
- BT1 intermediate mass nuclei
- BT2 nuclei
- BT1 palladium isotopes

PALLADIUM 104 [98; 98]
- BT1 even-even nuclei
- BT2 nuclei
- BT1 intermediate mass nuclei
- BT2 nuclei
- BT1 palladium isotopes
- BT1 stable isotopes

BT2   isotopes

PALLADIUM 104 TARGET [97; 97]
BT1   targets

PALLADIUM 105 [88; 88]
BT1   even-odd nuclei
BT2   nuclei
BT1   intermediate mass nuclei
BT2   nuclei
BT1   palladium isotopes
BT1   stable isotopes
BT2   isotopes

PALLADIUM 105 TARGET [61; 61]
BT1   targets

PALLADIUM 106 [153; 153]
BT1   even-even nuclei
BT2   nuclei
BT1   intermediate mass nuclei
BT2   nuclei
BT1   palladium isotopes
BT1   stable isotopes
BT2   isotopes

PALLADIUM 106 TARGET [102; 102]
BT1   targets

PALLADIUM 107 [52; 52]
BT1   beta-minus decay radioisotopes
BT2   beta decay radioisotopes
BT3   radioisotopes
BT4   isotopes
BT1   even-odd nuclei
BT2   nuclei
BT1   intermediate mass nuclei
BT2   nuclei
BT1   isomeric transition isotopes
BT2   radioisotopes
BT3   isotopes
BT1   palladium isotopes
BT1   seconds living radioisotopes
BT2   radioisotopes
BT3   isotopes
BT1   years living radioisotopes
BT2   radioisotopes
BT3   isotopes

PALLADIUM 107 TARGET [7; 7]
Jul 78
BT1   targets

PALLADIUM 108 [123; 123]
BT1   even-even nuclei
BT2   nuclei
BT1   intermediate mass nuclei
BT2   nuclei
BT1   palladium isotopes
BT1   stable isotopes
BT2   isotopes

PALLADIUM 108 TARGET [127; 127]
BT1   targets

PALLADIUM 109 [111; 111]
BT1   beta-minus decay radioisotopes
BT2   beta decay radioisotopes
BT3   radioisotopes
BT4   isotopes
BT1   even-odd nuclei
BT2   nuclei
BT1   hours living radioisotopes
BT2   radioisotopes
BT3   isotopes
BT1   intermediate mass nuclei
BT2   nuclei
BT1   isomeric transition isotopes
BT2   radioisotopes
BT3   isotopes
BT1   minutes living radioisotopes
BT2   radioisotopes
BT3   isotopes
BT1   palladium isotopes

PALLADIUM 110 [113; 113]
BT1   even-even nuclei
BT2   nuclei
BT1   intermediate mass nuclei
BT2   nuclei
BT1   palladium isotopes
BT1   stable isotopes
BT2   isotopes

PALLADIUM 110 TARGET [223; 223]
BT1   targets

PALLADIUM 111 [25; 25]
BT1   beta-minus decay radioisotopes
BT2   beta decay radioisotopes
BT3   radioisotopes
BT4   isotopes
BT1   even-odd nuclei
BT2   nuclei
BT1   hours living radioisotopes
BT2   radioisotopes
BT3   isotopes
BT1   intermediate mass nuclei
BT2   nuclei
BT1   isomeric transition isotopes
BT2   radioisotopes
BT3   isotopes
BT1   minutes living radioisotopes
BT2   radioisotopes
BT3   isotopes
BT1   palladium isotopes

PALLADIUM 112 [25; 25]
BT1   beta-minus decay radioisotopes
BT2   beta decay radioisotopes
BT3   radioisotopes
BT4   isotopes
BT1   even-even nuclei
BT2   nuclei
BT1   hours living radioisotopes
BT2   radioisotopes
BT3   isotopes
BT1   intermediate mass nuclei
BT2   nuclei
BT1   internal conversion radioisoto
BT2   radioisotopes
BT3   isotopes
BT1   palladium isotopes

PALLADIUM 113 [6; 6]
BT1   beta-minus decay radioisotopes
BT2   beta decay radioisotopes
BT3   radioisotopes
BT4   isotopes
BT1   even-odd nuclei
BT2   nuclei
BT1   intermediate mass nuclei
BT2   nuclei
BT1   minutes living radioisotopes
BT2   radioisotopes
BT3   isotopes
BT1   palladium isotopes

PALLADIUM 114 [16; 16]
BT1   beta-minus decay radioisotopes
BT2   beta decay radioisotopes
BT3   radioisotopes
BT4   isotopes
BT1   even-even nuclei
BT2   nuclei
BT1   intermediate mass nuclei
BT2   nuclei
BT1   minutes living radioisotopes
BT2   radioisotopes
BT3   isotopes
BT1   palladium isotopes

PALLADIUM 115 [10; 10]
BT1   beta-minus decay radioisotopes
BT2   beta decay radioisotopes
BT3   radioisotopes
BT4   isotopes
BT1   even-odd nuclei
BT2   nuclei
BT1   intermediate mass nuclei
BT2   nuclei
BT1   palladium isotopes
BT1   seconds living radioisotopes

BT2   radioisotopes
BT3   isotopes

PALLADIUM 116 [12; 12]
BT1   beta-minus decay radioisotopes
BT2   beta decay radioisotopes
BT3   radioisotopes
BT4   isotopes
BT1   even-even nuclei
BT2   nuclei
BT1   intermediate mass nuclei
BT2   nuclei
BT1   palladium isotopes
BT1   seconds living radioisotopes
BT2   radioisotopes
BT3   isotopes

PALLADIUM 117 [2; 2]
BT1   beta-minus decay radioisotopes
BT2   beta decay radioisotopes
BT3   radioisotopes
BT4   isotopes
BT1   even-odd nuclei
BT2   nuclei
BT1   intermediate mass nuclei
BT2   nuclei
BT1   isomeric transition isotopes
BT2   radioisotopes
BT3   isotopes
BT1   millisec living radioisotopes
BT2   radioisotopes
BT3   isotopes
BT1   palladium isotopes
BT1   seconds living radioisotopes
BT2   radioisotopes
BT3   isotopes

PALLADIUM 118 [9; 9] *Jul 76*
BT1   beta-minus decay radioisotopes
BT2   beta decay radioisotopes
BT3   radioisotopes
BT4   isotopes
BT1   even-even nuclei
BT2   nuclei
BT1   intermediate mass nuclei
BT2   nuclei
BT1   palladium isotopes
BT1   seconds living radioisotopes
BT2   radioisotopes
BT3   isotopes

PALLADIUM 118 REACTIONS [2; 2]
Dec 79
BT1   heavy ion reactions
BT2   nuclear reactions

PALLADIUM 118 TARGET [3; 3]
Dec 79
BT1   targets

→ **PALLADIUM 119** [3; 3] *Mar 91*
BT1   beta-minus decay radioisotopes
BT2   beta decay radioisotopes
BT3   radioisotopes
BT4   isotopes
BT1   even-odd nuclei
BT2   nuclei
BT1   intermediate mass nuclei
BT2   nuclei
BT1   millisec living radioisotopes
BT2   radioisotopes
BT3   isotopes
BT1   palladium isotopes

PALLADIUM 95 [9; 9] *Sep 81*
BT1   beta-plus decay radioisotopes
BT2   beta decay radioisotopes
BT3   radioisotopes
BT4   isotopes
BT1   electron capture radioisotopes
BT2   beta decay radioisotopes
BT3   radioisotopes
BT4   isotopes
BT1   even-odd nuclei
BT2   nuclei
BT1   intermediate mass nuclei
BT2   nuclei

BT1 palladium isotopes
BT1 seconds living radioisotopes
BT2 radioisotopes
BT3 isotopes

PALLADIUM 96 [33; 33]
BT1 electron capture radioisotopes
BT2 beta decay radioisotopes
BT3 radioisotopes
BT4 isotopes
BT1 even-even nuclei
BT2 nuclei
BT1 intermediate mass nuclei
BT2 nuclei
BT1 minutes living radioisotopes
BT2 radioisotopes
BT3 isotopes
BT1 palladium isotopes

PALLADIUM 97 [10; 10]
BT1 beta-plus decay radioisotopes
BT2 beta decay radioisotopes
BT3 radioisotopes
BT4 isotopes
BT1 electron capture radioisotopes
BT2 beta decay radioisotopes
BT3 radioisotopes
BT4 isotopes
BT1 even-odd nuclei
BT2 nuclei
BT1 intermediate mass nuclei
BT2 nuclei
BT1 minutes living radioisotopes
BT2 radioisotopes
BT3 isotopes
BT1 palladium isotopes

PALLADIUM 98 [18; 18]
BT1 beta-plus decay radioisotopes
BT2 beta decay radioisotopes
BT3 radioisotopes
BT4 isotopes
BT1 electron capture radioisotopes
BT2 beta decay radioisotopes
BT3 radioisotopes
BT4 isotopes
BT1 even-even nuclei
BT2 nuclei
BT1 intermediate mass nuclei
BT2 nuclei
BT1 minutes living radioisotopes
BT2 radioisotopes
BT3 isotopes
BT1 palladium isotopes

PALLADIUM 99 [15; 15]
BT1 beta-plus decay radioisotopes
BT2 beta decay radioisotopes
BT3 radioisotopes
BT4 isotopes
BT1 electron capture radioisotopes
BT2 beta decay radioisotopes
BT3 radioisotopes
BT4 isotopes
BT1 even-odd nuclei
BT2 nuclei
BT1 intermediate mass nuclei
BT2 nuclei
BT1 minutes living radioisotopes
BT2 radioisotopes
BT3 isotopes
BT1 palladium isotopes

palmitic acid
USE hexadecanoic acid

PALO VERDE-1 REACTOR [77; 77]
(Wintersburg, Arizona, USA)
BT1 pwr type reactors
BT2 enriched uranium reactors
BT3 reactors
BT2 power reactors
BT3 reactors
BT2 thermal reactors
BT3 reactors
BT2 water cooled reactors
BT3 reactors
BT2 water moderated reactors
BT3 reactors

PALO VERDE-2 REACTOR [62; 62]
(Wintersburg, Arizona, USA)
BT1 pwr type reactors
BT2 enriched uranium reactors
BT3 reactors
BT2 power reactors
BT3 reactors
BT2 thermal reactors
BT3 reactors
BT2 water cooled reactors
BT3 reactors
BT2 water moderated reactors
BT3 reactors

PALO VERDE-3 REACTOR [58; 58]
(Wintersburg, Arizona, USA)
BT1 pwr type reactors
BT2 enriched uranium reactors
BT3 reactors
BT2 power reactors
BT3 reactors
BT2 thermal reactors
BT3 reactors
BT2 water cooled reactors
BT3 reactors
BT2 water moderated reactors
BT3 reactors

PALO VERDE-4 REACTOR [24; 24] *Jul 78*
(Wintersburg, Arizona, USA)
BT1 pwr type reactors
BT2 enriched uranium reactors
BT3 reactors
BT2 power reactors
BT3 reactors
BT2 thermal reactors
BT3 reactors
BT2 water cooled reactors
BT3 reactors
BT2 water moderated reactors
BT3 reactors

PALO VERDE-5 REACTOR [21; 21] *Jul 78*
(Wintersburg, Arizona, USA)
BT1 pwr type reactors
BT2 enriched uranium reactors
BT3 reactors
BT2 power reactors
BT3 reactors
BT2 thermal reactors
BT3 reactors
BT2 water cooled reactors
BT3 reactors
BT2 water moderated reactors
BT3 reactors

PALUEL-1 REACTOR [38; 38] *May 81*
BT1 pwr type reactors
BT2 enriched uranium reactors
BT3 reactors
BT2 power reactors
BT3 reactors
BT2 thermal reactors
BT3 reactors
BT2 water cooled reactors
BT3 reactors
BT2 water moderated reactors
BT3 reactors

PALUEL-2 REACTOR [21; 21] *Jul 81*
BT1 pwr type reactors
BT2 enriched uranium reactors
BT3 reactors
BT2 power reactors
BT3 reactors
BT2 thermal reactors
BT3 reactors
BT2 water cooled reactors
BT3 reactors
BT2 water moderated reactors
BT3 reactors

PALUEL-3 REACTOR [19; 19] *Jul 81*
BT1 pwr type reactors
BT2 enriched uranium reactors
BT3 reactors
BT2 power reactors
BT3 reactors
BT2 thermal reactors
BT3 reactors
BT2 water cooled reactors
BT3 reactors
BT2 water moderated reactors
BT3 reactors

PALUEL-4 REACTOR [14; 14] *Jul 81*
BT1 pwr type reactors
BT2 enriched uranium reactors
BT3 reactors
BT2 power reactors
BT3 reactors
BT2 thermal reactors
BT3 reactors
BT2 water cooled reactors
BT3 reactors
BT2 water moderated reactors
BT3 reactors

PAMELA PLANT [8; 8] *Feb 88*
(Vitrification plant for high-level radioactive wastes in Mol, Belgium.)
BT1 radioactive waste facilities
BT2 nuclear facilities
RT high-level radioactive wastes
RT pilot plants
RT radioactive waste processing
RT vitrification

PAMPUS STORAGE RING [19; 19] *Sep 77*
(Photons for Atomic and Molecular Processes and Universal Studies storage ring facility in Amsterdam.)
BT1 storage rings

PAN [104; 104]
UF *pyridineazohydroxynaphthalene*
UF *pyridylazonaphthol*
BT1 diazo compounds
BT2 organic nitrogen compounds
BT3 organic compounds
BT1 naphthols
BT2 phenols
BT3 aromatics
BT4 organic compounds
BT3 hydroxy compounds
BT4 organic compounds
BT1 pyridines
BT2 azines
BT3 heterocyclic compounds
BT4 organic compounds
BT3 organic nitrogen compounds
BT4 organic compounds

PANAMA [13; 13]
BT1 central america
BT2 latin america
BT1 developing countries

PANAMA CANAL [3; 3]
BT1 surface waters
RT panama canal zone

PANAMA CANAL ZONE [2; 2]
BT1 central america
BT2 latin america
RT panama canal

PANCREAS [2,189; 2,189]
BT1 digestive system
BT1 endocrine glands
BT2 glands
BT3 organs
BT4 body
RT amylase
RT chymotrypsin
RT glucagon
RT insulin
RT trypsin

PANOFSKY RATIO [23; 23]
RT   photoproduction

PANTEX PLANT [24; 24] *Sep 77*
BT1   us doe
BT2   us organizations
BT3   national organizations
BT1   us erda
BT2   us organizations
BT3   national organizations
RT   texas

PANTOTHENIC ACID [26; 26]
UF   *vitamin b-5*
BT1   amino acids
BT2   carboxylic acids
BT3   organic acids
BT4   organic compounds
BT1   hydroxy acids
BT2   carboxylic acids
BT3   organic acids
BT4   organic compounds
BT1   vitamin b group
BT2   vitamins
RT   alanine-beta

PAPAIN [57; 57]
BT1   sh-proteinases
BT2   peptide hydrolases
BT3   hydrolases
BT4   enzymes
BT5   organic compounds

PAPAVER SOMNIFERUM [14; 14]
BT1   medicinal plants
BT2   plants
RT   morphine

PAPAYAS [60; 60]
BT1   fruits
BT2   food

PAPER [393; 393]
RT   dielectric materials

paper chromatography
USE   chromatography

PAPP [4; 4]
UF   *aminopropiophenone-para*
BT1   amines
BT2   organic compounds
BT1   ketones
BT2   organic compounds

paprika
USE   peppers

para-aminobenzoic acid
USE   paba

parabanic acid
USE   imidazoles
AND   organic oxygen compounds

PARABIOSIS [44; 44]
BT1   mosaicism
RT   blood circulation

PARACHARGE [3; 3] *Aug 76*
BT1   particle properties

paradox basin
USE   colorado plateau

PARAELECTRIC RESONANCE [11; 11]
(Resonant rotation of electric dipoles in ionic crystals.)
UF   *per*
BT1   electric resonance
BT2   resonance

PARAFFIN [300; 300]
BT1   alkanes
BT2   hydrocarbons
BT3   organic compounds
BT1   waxes
BT2   other organic compounds
BT3   organic compounds
RT   shielding materials

paraffins
USE   alkanes

paragenes
USE   plasmids

PARAGUAY [10; 10] *Feb 82*
BT1   developing countries
BT1   south america
BT2   latin america

PARALLEL PROCESSING [631; 631]
Nov 85
BT1   programming
RT   algorithms
RT   computers
RT   supercomputers
RT   vector processing

paramagn. res. (elec. acoust.)
USE   acoustic esr

paramagn. res. (nucl. acoust.)
USE   acoustic nmr

paramagnetic resonance (electr
USE   electron spin resonance

paramagnetic resonance (nuclea
USE   nuclear magnetic resonance

PARAMAGNETISM [2,383; 2,383]
BT1   magnetism
RT   van vleck theory

PARAMECIUM [53; 53]
BT1   protozoa
BT2   invertebrates
BT3   animals
BT2   microorganisms

PARAMETER COMPUTERS [7; 7]
BT1   digital computers
BT2   computers

PARAMETRIC AMPLIFIERS [89; 89]
BT1   amplifiers
BT2   equipment
BT1   electronic equipment
BT2   equipment
RT   frequency converters

parametric analysis
USE   multi-parameter analysis

PARAMETRIC INSTABILITIES
[1,383; 1,383]
UF   *non-linear plasma instabilitie*
UF   *nonlinear plasma instabilities*
BT1   plasma macroinstabilities

BT2   plasma instability
BT3   instability
RT   alternating current
RT   electric fields

PARASITES [373; 4,323]
NT1   ascaridae
NT2   ascaris
NT1   claviceps
NT1   fusarium
NT1   helminths
NT2   ascaris
NT2   cestodes
NT3   hymenolepis
NT2   trematodes
NT3   fasciola
NT3   schistosoma
NT2   trichinella
NT1   mildew
NT1   plasmodium
NT1   syngamus
NT1   trypanosoma
NT1   ustilago
NT1   viruses
NT2   aids virus
NT2   bacteriophages
NT2   influenza viruses
NT2   measles virus
NT2   oncogenic viruses
NT3   adenovirus
NT3   leukemia viruses
NT3   polyoma virus
NT2   polio virus
NT2   simian virus
NT2   tobacco mosaic virus
NT2   vaccinia virus
RT   babesidae
RT   disease vectors
RT   filariasis
RT   fungi
RT   hookworm
RT   hydatidosis
RT   insects
RT   microorganisms
RT   mites
RT   nematodes
RT   parasitic diseases
RT   pest control
RT   pest eradication
RT   pesticides
RT   plant diseases
RT   protozoa
RT   screwworm fly
RT   sterile male technique

PARASITIC DISEASES [147; 359]
Dec 82
BT1   infectious diseases
BT2   diseases
NT1   fascioliasis
NT1   filariasis
NT1   hydatidosis
NT1   malaria
NT1   schistosomiasis
NT1   trichinosis
NT1   trypanosomiasis
RT   dictyocaulus
RT   hookworm
RT   parasites

PARASTATISTICS [98; 98] *Jan 77*
RT   bose-einstein statistics
RT   fermi statistics
RT   field algebra
RT   statistical mechanics

parasympathetic nervous system
USE   autonomic nervous system

PARASYMPATHOLYTICS [51; 145]
BT1   autonomic nervous system agen
BT2   drugs
NT1   atropine
RT   autonomic nervous system

PARASYMPATHOMIMETICS [91; 596]
- BT1 autonomic nervous system agent
- BT2 drugs
- NT1 acetylcholine
- NT1 eserine
- NT1 pilocarpine
- RT autonomic nervous system
- RT vagus

PARATHION [39; 39] *May 76*
- BT1 insecticides
- BT2 pesticides
- BT1 organic phosphorus compounds
- BT2 organic compounds
- BT1 thiophosphoric acid esters
- BT2 esters
- BT3 organic compounds

PARATHORMONE [294; 294]
- BT1 peptide hormones
- BT2 hormones
- RT bone tissues
- RT calcium
- RT parathyroid glands

PARATHYROID GLANDS [460; 460]
- BT1 endocrine glands
- BT2 glands
- BT3 organs
- BT4 body
- RT calcitonin
- RT hyperparathyroidism
- RT neck
- RT parathormone
- RT thyroid

PARATYPHOID [3; 3]
- BT1 bacterial diseases
- BT2 infectious diseases
- BT3 diseases
- RT intestines
- RT salmonella

paris convention-third party l
- USE pcotpl

PARITY [12,262; 12,262]
- BT1 particle properties
- RT minami ambiguity
- RT morrison rule
- RT p invariance
- RT quantum numbers

parity nonconservation
- USE p invariance

PARKA REACTOR [4; 4] *Feb 79*
- UF *lasl critical assembly*
- BT1 zero power reactors
- BT2 experimental reactors
- BT3 research and test reactors
- BT4 reactors

parr carolinas cvtr reactor
- USE cvtr reactor

PARR REACTOR [33; 33]
(Pakistan Atomic Energy Commission, Islamabad, Pakistan)
- UF *islamabad reactor pakistan*
- UF *pakistan atomic research r.*
- UF *rawalpindi research reactor*
- BT1 enriched uranium reactors
- BT2 reactors
- BT1 pool type reactors
- BT2 water cooled reactors
- BT3 reactors
- BT2 water moderated reactors
- BT3 reactors
- BT1 research reactors
- BT2 research and test reactors
- BT3 reactors

PARSONSITE [2; 2]
- BT1 phosphate minerals
- BT2 minerals
- BT1 uranium minerals
- BT2 radioactive minerals
- BT3 minerals
- BT3 radioactive materials
- BT4 materials
- RT lead phosphates
- RT uranium phosphates

parthenogenesis
- USE reproduction

PARTIAL BODY IRRADIATION [1,463; 1,463]
- UF *shielded organs*
- BT1 external irradiation
- BT2 irradiation
- RT abscopal radiation effects
- RT body areas
- RT local irradiation
- RT spatial dose distributions

partial conser. axial currents
- USE pcac theory

partial conser. vector current
- USE pcvc theory

PARTIAL DIFFERENTIAL EQUATIONS [732; 20,787] *Dec 82*
- BT1 differential equations
- BT2 equations
- NT1 boltzmann equation
- NT1 boltzmann-vlasov equation
- NT2 plasma fluid equations
- NT1 continuity equations
- NT1 equations of motion
- NT1 fokker-planck equation
- NT1 fourier heat equation
- NT1 grad-shafranov equation
- NT1 hamilton-jacobi equations
- NT1 korteweg-de vries equation
- NT1 lagrange equations
- NT1 laplace equation
- NT1 maxwell equations
- NT1 navier-stokes equations
- NT1 poisson equation
- NT1 proca equations
- NT1 wave equations
- NT2 dirac equation
- NT2 klein-gordon equation
- NT2 schroedinger equation
- RT cauchy problem
- RT dirichlet problem

PARTIAL PRESSURE [406; 406] *Jul 85*
- BT1 thermodynamic properties
- BT2 physical properties

PARTIAL WAVES [3,501; 8,095]
- NT1 d waves
- NT1 f waves
- NT1 p waves
- NT1 s waves
- RT angular momentum
- RT cdd poles
- RT dispersion relations
- RT linear absorption models
- RT n-d method
- RT omnes-muskhelishvili method
- RT phase shift
- RT quantum mechanics
- RT scattering
- RT scattering amplitudes

PARTICLE BEAM FUSION ACCELERAT [431; 431] *Sep 82*
- UF *pbfa*
- BT1 accelerators
- RT energy deposition
- RT inertial confinement
- RT ion beam fusion reactors

PARTICLE BEAMS [1,315; 51,976]
- BT1 beams
- NT1 hyperon beams
- NT2 lambda particle beams
- NT2 omega particle beams
- NT2 sigma particle beams
- NT2 xi particle beams
- NT1 lepton beams
- NT2 electron beams
- NT2 muon beams
- NT2 neutrino beams
- NT2 positron beams
- NT1 meson beams
- NT2 eta meson beams
- NT2 kaon beams
- NT2 pion beams
- NT1 nucleon beams
- NT2 neutron beams
- NT2 proton beams
- RT beam neutralization
- RT ion beams
- RT photon beams
- RT pomeranchuk theorem
- RT q-shift

PARTICLE BOOSTERS [873; 873]
(First stage of a multistage accelerator.)
- UF *boosters (particle)*
- RT accelerators
- RT beam injection

PARTICLE DECAY [4,959; 19,971]
- SF *disintegration (nuclear part.)*
- BT1 decay
- NT1 electromagnetic particle decay
- NT1 hadronic particle decay
- NT1 radiative decay
- NT1 weak particle decay
- NT2 leptonic decay
- NT2 semileptonic decay
- NT2 weak hadronic decay
- RT multiple production
- RT particle production

PARTICLE DISCRIMINATION [1,043; 1,043]
(Particle or radiation discrimination in a mixed field.)
- BT1 particle identification
- RT measuring methods
- RT radiation detection
- RT resolution

PARTICLE IDENTIFICATION [2,665; 3,633]
- NT1 particle discrimination

PARTICLE INTERACTIONS [3,177; 74,875]
- BT1 interactions
- NT1 annihilation
- NT1 charged-current interactions
- NT1 coherent production
- NT1 electron-quark interactions
- NT1 electroproduction
- NT1 exclusive interactions
- NT2 semi-exclusive interactions
- NT1 gluon-gluon interactions
- NT1 hadron-hadron interactions
- NT2 baryon-baryon interactions
- NT3 hyperon-hyperon interactions
- NT3 nucleon-antinucleon interactio
- NT4 antiproton-neutron interaction
- NT4 neutron-antineutron interactio
- NT4 proton-antineutron interaction
- NT4 proton-antiproton interactions
- NT3 nucleon-hyperon interactions
- NT3 nucleon-nucleon interactions
- NT4 neutron-neutron interactions
- NT4 proton-nucleon interactions
- NT5 proton-neutron interactions
- NT5 proton-proton interactions
- NT2 meson-baryon interactions
- NT3 meson-hyperon interactions

PARTICLE INTERACTIONS 548 PARTICLE PROPERTIES

    NT4   kaon-hyperon interactions
    NT4   pion-hyperon interactions
  NT3 meson-nucleon interactions
    NT4   kaon-nucleon interactions
      NT5   kaon-neutron interactions
        NT6   kaon minus-neutron interaction
        NT6   kaon neutral-neutron interacti
        NT6   kaon plus-neutron interactions
      NT5   kaon-proton interactions
        NT6   kaon minus-proton interactions
        NT6   kaon neutral-proton interactio
        NT6   kaon plus-proton interactions
    NT4   pion-nucleon interactions
      NT5   pion-neutron interactions
        NT6   pion minus-neutron interaction
        NT6   pion plus-neutron interactions
      NT5   pion-proton interactions
        NT6   pion minus-proton interactions
        NT6   pion plus-proton interactions
  NT2 meson-meson interactions
    NT3   kaon-kaon interactions
    NT3   pion-kaon interactions
    NT3   pion-pion interactions
NT1 inclusive interactions
  NT2 semi-inclusive interactions
NT1 incoherent production
NT1 lepton-hadron interactions
  NT2 lepton-baryon interactions
    NT3   lepton-hyperon interactions
    NT3   lepton-nucleon interactions
      NT4   deep inelastic scattering
      NT4   electron-nucleon interactions
        NT5   electron-neutron interactions
        NT5   electron-proton interactions
      NT4   lepton-neutron interactions
        NT5   antilepton-neutron interaction
          NT6   antineutrino-neutron interacti
      NT4   lepton-proton interactions
        NT5   antilepton-proton interactions
          NT6   antineutrino-proton interactio
      NT4   muon-nucleon interactions
        NT5   muon-neutron interactions
        NT5   muon-proton interactions
      NT4   neutrino-nucleon interactions
        NT5   antineutrino-nucleon interacti
          NT6   antineutrino-neutron interacti
          NT6   antineutrino-proton interactio
        NT5   neutrino-neutron interactions
          NT6   antineutrino-neutron interacti
        NT5   neutrino-proton interactions
          NT6   antineutrino-proton interactio
  NT2 lepton-meson interactions
    NT3   electron-meson interactions
      NT4   electron-pion interactions
    NT3   muon-meson interactions
    NT3   neutrino-meson interactions
NT1 lepton-lepton interactions
  NT2 electron-electron interactions
  NT2 electron-muon interactions
  NT2 electron-positron interactions
  NT2 muon-muon interactions
  NT2 neutrino-electron interactions
    NT3   antineutrino-electron interact
  NT2 neutrino-muon interactions
  NT2 neutrino-neutrino interactions

  NT2 positron-positron interactions
NT1 neutral-current interactions
NT1 photon-hadron interactions
  NT2 photon-baryon interactions
    NT3   photon-hyperon interactions
    NT3   photon-nucleon interactions
      NT4   photon-neutron interactions
      NT4   photon-proton interactions
  NT2 photon-meson interactions
NT1 photon-lepton interactions
  NT2 photon-electron interactions
  NT2 photon-muon interactions
  NT2 photon-neutrino interactions
NT1 photon-photon interactions
NT1 photoproduction
  NT2 primakoff effect
NT1 quark-antiquark interactions
NT1 quark-gluon interactions
NT1 quark-hadron interactions
NT1 quark-quark interactions
RT   coherent tube model
RT   four momentum transfer
RT   longitudinal momentum
RT   morrison rule
RT   multiple production
RT   particle kinematics
RT   particle production
RT   polarized products
RT   s channel
RT   straight-line path approximati
RT   string models
RT   t channel
RT   transverse energy
RT   transverse momentum
RT   u channel

PARTICLE KINEMATICS [1,896; 1,896]
UF   kinematics (particle)
RT   angular correlation
RT   collisions
RT   conservation laws
RT   decay
RT   distribution
RT   equations of motion
RT   particle interactions
RT   particle rapidity

PARTICLE LOSSES [469; 469] Mar 83
UF   losses (particles)
RT   energy losses
RT   plasma confinement
RT   plasma disruption

PARTICLE MOBILITY [209; 1,796]
BT1 mobility
NT1 electron mobility
NT1 ion mobility

PARTICLE MODELS [2,905; 62,161]
UF   models (particle)
BT1 mathematical models
NT1 composite models
  NT2 bootstrap model
  NT2 cim model
  NT2 parton model
  NT2 quark model
    NT3   color model
    NT3   flavor model
NT1 correlated-particle models
NT1 diffraction models
NT1 dual absorption model
NT1 extended particle model
  NT2 bag model
  NT2 string models
NT1 feynman gas model
NT1 fireball model
NT1 gluon model
NT1 hard collision models
NT1 higgs model
NT1 isobar model
NT1 jet model
NT1 lee model
NT1 linear absorption models
NT1 nova model
NT1 octet model
NT1 peripheral models
  NT2 baryon-exchange models

  NT2 boson-exchange models
    NT3   obe model
      NT4   ope model
        NT5   electric born model
    NT3   sigma model
  NT2 multiperipheral model
    NT3   cluster emission model
      NT4   space-time model
NT1 strong-coupling model
NT1 tensor dominance model
NT1 thermodynamic model
  NT2 hydrodynamic model
NT1 uncorrelated-particle model
NT1 unified gauge models
  NT2 grand unified theory
    NT3   standard model
  NT2 weinberg lepton model
NT1 van hove model
NT1 vector dominance model
NT1 veneziano model
  NT2 dual resonance model
RT   harmonic oscillator models
RT   leading particles
RT   limiting fragmentation
RT   optical models
RT   particle multiplets
RT   particle structure
RT   statistical models
RT   structure functions

PARTICLE MULTIPLETS [1,718; 2,279]
BT1 multiplets
NT1 baryon decuplets
NT1 baryon octets
NT1 meson nonets
NT1 meson octets
RT   okubo mass formula
RT   particle models
RT   spectra

PARTICLE PRODUCTION
[18,193; 37,301]
UF   production mechanisms, particl
UF+ cumulative effect
UF+ diffractive dissociation
NT1 coherent production
NT1 electroproduction
NT1 incoherent production
NT1 multiple production
  NT2 pionization
NT1 pair production
  NT2 internal pair production
NT1 photoproduction
  NT2 primakoff effect
RT   blankenbecler-sugar equations
RT   hydrodynamic model
RT   leading particles
RT   mixing ratio
RT   particle decay
RT   particle interactions
RT   regeneration

PARTICLE PROPERTIES [874; 57,004]
(Use only for data compilations or paper of a similar broad nature; otherwise use the specific terms listed below.)
NT1 chirality
NT1 form factors
  NT2 dirac form factors
  NT2 electromagnetic form factors
  NT2 pauli form factors
NT1 g parity
NT1 helicity
NT1 hypercharge
NT1 isospin
NT1 mass difference
NT1 paracharge
NT1 parity
NT1 particle radii
NT1 particle rapidity
NT1 particle widths
NT1 spin
NT1 strangeness
RT   lifetime
RT   limiting values
RT   quantum numbers
RT   spin orientation

PARTICLE RADII [992; 992]
(For quantum objects only; otherwise use PARTICLE SIZE.)
  UF   charge radius (particle)
  UF   mass radius (particle)
  BT1   particle properties
  RT   nuclear radii
  RT   particle structure

PARTICLE RAPIDITY [3,237; 3,237]
(Defined as $(1/2)\ln((E+p)/(E-p))$; widely used in high energy physics.)
  UF   rapidity
  BT1   particle properties
  RT   kinetic energy
  RT   longitudinal momentum
  RT   particle kinematics
  RT   scale invariance

PARTICLE RESUSPENSION [225; 225] Sep 77
  UF   resuspension (particles)
  RT   aerodynamics
  RT   air pollution
  RT   chemical effluents
  RT   diffusion
  RT   dispersions
  RT   dusts
  RT   earth crust
  RT   erosion
  RT   fallout
  RT   radioactive aerosols
  RT   radioactive effluents
  RT   radionuclide migration
  RT   surface air
  RT   wind

PARTICLE SIZE [5,457; 5,457]
(For quantum objects see PARTICLE RADII.)
  BT1   size
  RT   aerosols
  RT   ceramography
  RT   colloids
  RT   dispersions
  RT   droplets
  RT   dusts
  RT   elutriation
  RT   microspheres
  RT   particles
  RT   powders

PARTICLE SOURCES [130; 9,854]
  BT1   radiation sources
  NT1   alpha sources
  NT1   antiproton sources
  NT1   beta sources
  NT1   deuteron sources
  NT1   electron sources
    NT2   pierce electron guns
  NT1   neutron sources
    NT2   neutron generators
    NT2   nisus facility
  NT1   positron sources
  NT1   proton sources
  RT   ion sources

PARTICLE STRUCTURE [1,516; 1,516]
  RT   bach-tamaid theory
  RT   emc effect
  RT   landau quasi particles
  RT   particle models
  RT   particle radii
  RT   string models
  RT   structure functions

PARTICLE TRACKS [5,436; 6,728]
  UF   prongs
  UF   tracks
  NT1   fission tracks
  RT   dielectric track detectors
  RT   etching
  RT   image scanners
  RT   particles
  RT   pattern recognition
  RT   trajectories

PARTICLE WIDTHS [3,913; 3,913]
  BT1   particle properties
  RT   lifetime

PARTICLE-CORE COUPLING MODEL [528; 528] Jan 77
  UF   particle-core model
  UF   particle-rotor model
  BT1   nuclear models
  BT2   mathematical models
  RT   coupling
  RT   nuclear structure
  RT   weak-coupling model

particle-core model
  USE   particle-core coupling model

PARTICLE-HOLE MODEL [2,084; 2,084]
  BT1   nuclear models
  BT2   mathematical models
  RT   aligned coupling scheme
  RT   weak-coupling model

particle-rotor model
  USE   particle-core coupling model

§ **PARTICLES** [4,848; 7,880]
(When appropriate, see the more specific descriptors listed under CHARGED PARTICLES, ELEMENTARY PARTICLES, and QUASI PARTICLES.)
  UF   fragments (particles)
  UF+   fallout particulates
  UF+   radioactive particulates
  NT1   droplets
  NT1   interstellar grains
  NT1   particulates
  RT   aerosols
  RT   colloids
  RT   condensation nuclei
  RT   dispersions
  RT   dusts
  RT   elutriation
  RT   granular materials
  RT   neutral particles
  RT   particle size
  RT   particle tracks
  RT   powders
  RT   sedimentation
  RT   virial theorem
  RT   viruses

particles (fuel)
  USE   fuel particles

→ **PARTICULATES** [5; 5] Jun 83
(Prior to August 1991, this concept was indexed to AEROSOLS and PARTICLES.)
  UF   airborne particles
  UF   airborne particulates
  UF   waterborne particles
  UF   waterborne particulates
  BT1   particles

PARTITION [654; 654]
(Not to be used in connection with ion exchange or ion exchange chromatography.)
  RT   arrhenius equation
  RT   equilibrium
  RT   gas chromatography
  RT   solvent extraction

partition chromatography
  USE   chromatography

PARTITION FUNCTIONS [2,788; 2,788]
  BT1   functions
  RT   statistical mechanics
  RT   thermodynamics

PARTON MODEL [4,015; 4,015]
  BT1   composite models
  BT2   particle models
  BT3   mathematical models
  RT   deep inelastic scattering
  RT   partons
  RT   quark model

PARTONS [938; 938] Feb 80
  BT1   postulated particles
  BT2   elementary particles
  RT   parton model
  RT   quarks

PARTURITION [126; 126]
  UF   birth
  RT   oxytocin
  RT   pregnancy
  RT   progeny

PAS [3; 3]
  UF   aminosalicylic acid-para
  BT1   amino acids
  BT2   carboxylic acids
  BT3   organic acids
  BT4   organic compounds
  BT1   antibiotics
  BT2   drugs
  BT2   organic compounds
  RT   salicylic acid
  RT   tuberculosis

paschen curve
  USE   paschen law

PASCHEN LAW [32; 32]
  UF   paschen curve
  UF   paschen minimum
  RT   breakdown
  RT   electric discharges
  RT   electric potential
  RT   gases
  RT   spark gaps

PASCHEN LINES [82; 82]
  RT   spectra

paschen minimum
  USE   paschen law

PASCHEN-BACK EFFECT [19; 19]
  RT   fine structure
  RT   zeeman effect

PASSIVATION [722; 722]
  RT   corrosion protection

PASSIVITY [160; 160]
  RT   corrosion
  RT   corrosion resistance

PASTEURIZATION [126; 616]
  BT1   food processing
  NT1   radicidation
  RT   preservation
  RT   sterilization

PASTURES [148; 148] Dec 79
  RT   cattle
  RT   forage
  RT   gramineae

PATENT LAWS [4; 4] Dec 76
(Prior to December 1990, this descriptor was spelled PATENT LAW.)
  BT1   laws

PATENTS [590; 590]
(Use only for items about patents, not for items which are patents.)
  RT   document types
  RT   legal aspects
  RT   licensing

RT specifications

PATHFINDER REACTOR [9; 9]
UF *sioux falls pathfinder reactor*
BT1 bwr type reactors
BT2 enriched uranium reactors
BT3 reactors
BT2 power reactors
BT3 reactors
BT2 thermal reactors
BT3 reactors
BT2 water cooled reactors
BT3 reactors
BT2 water moderated reactors
BT3 reactors

PATHOGENESIS [1,448; 5,309]
NT1 carcinogenesis
NT2 leukemogenesis

PATHOGENS [113; 113] *May 81*
RT diseases
RT fungi
RT microorganisms

PATHOLOGICAL CHANGES
[5,757; 19,063]
BT1 diseases
NT1 abscesses
NT1 allergy
NT1 ascites
NT1 atrophy
NT1 biological shock
NT1 caries
NT1 cysts
NT1 edema
NT1 emphysema
NT1 fibrosis
NT1 fistulae
NT1 granulomas
NT1 hemorrhage
NT1 hypertrophy
NT1 inflammation
NT1 jaundice
NT1 leukopenia
NT2 lymphopenia
NT1 malformations
NT2 congenital malformations
NT3 downs syndrome
NT1 necrosis
NT2 gangrene
NT2 osteoradionecrosis
NT1 splenomegaly
NT1 ulcers
RT hemolysis
RT pathology

PATHOLOGY [2,249; 2,249]
RT autopsy
RT diseases
RT medicine
RT pathological changes

PATIENTS [55,233; 55,233]
BT1 man
BT2 primates
BT3 mammals
BT4 vertebrates
BT5 animals
RT human populations
RT medicine
RT therapy

PATTERN RECOGNITION
[1,776; 1,776] *May 76*
(Identification of shapes and patterns without active human participation.)
RT data processing
RT diagrams
RT display devices
RT identification systems
RT image scanners
RT image tubes
RT images
RT particle tracks
RT visibility

PATTERSON METHOD [101; 101]
RT crystallography
RT diffraction methods

pauli exclusion principle
USE pauli principle

PAULI FORM FACTORS [28; 28]
BT1 form factors
BT2 particle properties

pauli matrices
USE pauli spin operators

PAULI PRINCIPLE [1,503; 1,503]
UF *exclusion principle*
UF *pauli exclusion principle*
RT occupation number
RT quantum mechanics

PAULI SPIN OPERATORS [451; 451]
UF *pauli matrices*
BT1 angular momentum operators
BT2 quantum operators
BT3 mathematical operators
RT spin

pavia triga-mk-2 reactor
USE triga-2-pavia reactor

pawling research reactor
USE prr reactor

PAYBACK PERIOD [5; 5] *Apr 86*
(Time required for the cost savings from a new installation to equal the initial capital investment.)
RT cost
RT economics
RT financial incentives
RT investment

PBF REACTOR [205; 205]
UF *national r. test st. burst f.*
UF *power-burst facility usaec*
BT1 pulsed reactors
BT2 reactors
BT1 tank type reactors
BT2 reactors

pbfa
USE particle beam fusion accelerat

PBI [101; 101]
UF *protein-bound iodine*
BT1 cpb
BT1 organic iodine compounds
BT2 organic halogen compounds
BT3 organic compounds
BT1 proteins
BT2 organic compounds
RT blood-plasma clearance
RT thyroid hormones

PBR REACTOR [9; 9]
(NASA, Lewis Research Center, Plum Brook Station, Sandusky, Ohio, USA)
UF *nasa-test reactor*
UF *nasa-tr reactor*
UF *plum brook nasa-tr*
UF *plum brook reactor facility*
BT1 enriched uranium reactors
BT2 reactors
BT1 materials testing reactors
BT2 irradiation reactors
BT3 reactors
BT1 research reactors
BT2 research and test reactors
BT3 reactors
BT1 tank type reactors
BT2 reactors

BT1 water cooled reactors
BT2 reactors
BT1 water moderated reactors
BT2 reactors

PBX DEVICES [63; 63] *Nov 88*
(A modification of the PDX device with a rearrangement of the divertor coils.)
UF *princeton beta experiment*
BT1 tokamak devices
BT2 closed plasma devices
BT3 thermonuclear devices
RT pdx devices
RT poloidal field divertors

pca
USE polar-cap absorption

pca-ornl reactor
USE ornl-pca reactor

PCAC THEORY [950; 950]
UF *partial conser. axial currents*
RT axial-vector currents
RT current algebra

→ *pcb*
USE chlorinated aromatic hydrocarb

pcb (polychlorinated biphenyl)
USE aromatics
AND organic chlorine compounds

pcm accidents
USE power-cooling-mismatch acciden

PCOTPL [206; 206]
(Paris Convention on Third Party Liability
UF *liabil conv on third party, pa*
UF *paris convention-third party l*
UF *third party liabil conv, paris*
BT1 international agreements
BT2 agreements
RT bcstpc
RT civil liability
RT liabilities
RT nuclear liability

PCTR REACTOR [4; 4]
(Pacific Northwest Lab., Battelle Memoria Institute, Richland, Washington, USA)
UF *physical constants testing r.*
UF *richland phys. const. test. r.*
BT1 enriched uranium reactors
BT2 reactors
BT1 graphite moderated reactors
BT2 reactors
BT1 research reactors
BT2 research and test reactors
BT3 reactors
BT1 thermal reactors
BT2 reactors

PCVC THEORY [26; 26]
UF *partial conser. vector current*
RT current algebra
RT vector currents

PDP COMPUTERS [809; 809]
BT1 dec computers
BT2 computers

PDP REACTOR [7; 7]
UF *process development pile*
UF *savannah river process dvl. r.*
BT1 heavy water cooled reactors
BT2 reactors
BT1 heavy water moderated reactor
BT2 reactors
BT1 zero power reactors
BT2 experimental reactors

         BT3   research and test reactors
         BT4   reactors
    RT   enriched uranium reactors
    RT   natural uranium reactors

pdus
(Process Development Units.)
    USE   pilot plants

PDX DEVICES [385; 385] *Jul 78*
    UF   *poloidal divertor experiment*
    RT   pbx devices
    RT   poloidal field divertors
    RT   tokamak devices

pe-13
    USE   alloy-ni48cr22fe18mo9

pe-16
    USE   alloy-ni43fe33cr16mo3

pea plant
    USE   pisum

PEACH BOTTOM-1 REACTOR
[214; 214]
(York county, Pennsylvania, USA)
    UF   *htgr peach bottom reactor*
    BT1   enriched uranium reactors
      BT2   reactors
    BT1   helium cooled reactors
      BT2   gas cooled reactors
        BT3   reactors
    BT1   htgr type reactors
      BT2   gas cooled reactors
        BT3   reactors
      BT2   graphite moderated reactors
        BT3   reactors
    BT1   power reactors
      BT2   reactors
    BT1   thermal reactors
      BT2   reactors

PEACH BOTTOM-2 REACTOR
[277; 277]
(York county, Pennsylvania, USA)
    BT1   bwr type reactors
      BT2   enriched uranium reactors
        BT3   reactors
      BT2   power reactors
        BT3   reactors
      BT2   thermal reactors
        BT3   reactors
      BT2   water cooled reactors
        BT3   reactors
      BT2   water moderated reactors
        BT3   reactors

PEACH BOTTOM-3 REACTOR
[156; 156]
(York county, Pennsylvania, USA)
    BT1   bwr type reactors
      BT2   enriched uranium reactors
        BT3   reactors
      BT2   power reactors
        BT3   reactors
      BT2   thermal reactors
        BT3   reactors
      BT2   water cooled reactors
        BT3   reactors
      BT2   water moderated reactors
        BT3   reactors

PEACHES [33; 33]
    BT1   fruits
    BT2   food

PEAK LOAD [99; 99] *Dec 82*
(Maximum instantaneous load or maximum average load over a designated interval of time.)

    UF+   *peak-load pricing*
    RT   electric utilities
    RT   load management
    RT   power demand

peak-load pricing
    USE   charges
    AND   peak load

PEAKS [1,885; 1,964]
    NT1   escape peaks
    RT   pulse rise time
    RT   transients

PEANUT OIL [10; 10]
    BT1   oils
      BT2   other organic compounds
        BT3   organic compounds
    BT1   triglycerides
      BT2   esters
        BT3   organic compounds
      BT2   lipids
        BT3   organic compounds

PEANUTS [114; 114]
    UF   *groundnuts*
    BT1   nuts
      BT2   fruits
        BT3   food
    RT   leguminosae
    RT   proteins

pearl pulsations
    USE   pulsations

PEARLITE [144; 144]
(An aggregate in steel of ferrite and cementite.)
    UF   *perlite (iron-carbon alloy)*
    RT   cast iron
    RT   cementite
    RT   ferrite
    RT   steels

PEARS [23; 23]
    BT1   fruits
    BT2   food

PEAS [175; 175]
    BT1   seeds
    BT1   vegetables
      BT2   food
    RT   pisum

PEAT [194; 194]
    BT1   fossil fuels
      BT2   energy sources
      BT2   fuels
    RT   coal
    RT   soils

PEBBLE BED REACTORS [1,116; 1,922]
    BT1   solid homogeneous reactors
      BT2   homogeneous reactors
        BT3   reactors
    NT1   avr reactor
    NT1   thtr-300 reactor
    NT1   vg-400 reactor
    NT1   vgr-50 reactor

PEBBLE SPRINGS-1 REACTOR [6; 6]
(Arlington, Oregon, USA)
    BT1   pwr type reactors
      BT2   enriched uranium reactors
        BT3   reactors
      BT2   power reactors
        BT3   reactors
      BT2   thermal reactors
        BT3   reactors
      BT2   water cooled reactors
        BT3   reactors
      BT2   water moderated reactors
        BT3   reactors

PEBBLE SPRINGS-2 REACTOR [6; 6]
(Arlington, Oregon, USA)
    BT1   pwr type reactors
      BT2   enriched uranium reactors
        BT3   reactors
      BT2   power reactors
        BT3   reactors
      BT2   thermal reactors
        BT3   reactors
      BT2   water cooled reactors
        BT3   reactors
      BT2   water moderated reactors
        BT3   reactors

PEC BRASIMONE REACTOR
[155; 155]
    UF   *brasimone pec reactor*
    BT1   fbr type reactors
      BT2   breeder reactors
        BT3   reactors
      BT2   fast reactors
        BT3   epithermal reactors
          BT4   reactors
    BT1   power reactors
      BT2   reactors

PECTINS [47; 47]
    BT1   polysaccharides
      BT2   saccharides
        BT3   carbohydrates
          BT4   organic compounds
    RT   galacturonic acid
    RT   glucuronic acid

peculiar a-stars
    USE   magnetic stars

PEDIATRICS [660; 660]
    BT1   medicine
    RT   children
    RT   congenital malformations

peening
    USE   shot peening

pegase critical experiments
    USE   peggy reactor

PEGASE REACTOR [11; 11]
(Cadarache Nuclear Research Center, France.)
    UF   *cadarache fuel el. testing r.*
    BT1   enriched uranium reactors
      BT2   reactors
    BT1   tank type reactors
      BT2   reactors
    BT1   test reactors
      BT2   research and test reactors
        BT3   reactors
      BT2   test facilities
    BT1   thermal reactors
      BT2   reactors
    BT1   water cooled reactors
      BT2   reactors
    BT1   water moderated reactors
      BT2   reactors

PEGGY REACTOR [1; 1]
    UF   *pegase critical experiments*
    BT1   enriched uranium reactors
      BT2   reactors
    BT1   water cooled reactors
      BT2   reactors
    BT1   water moderated reactors
      BT2   reactors
    BT1   zero power reactors
      BT2   experimental reactors
        BT3   research and test reactors
          BT4   reactors

PEGMATITES [174; 174]
- BT1 plutonic rocks
- BT2 igneous rocks
- BT3 rocks
- RT feldspars
- RT granites
- RT mica
- RT xenotime

PEIERLS METHOD [50; 50]
- UF *kapur-peierls method*
- UF *wigner method*
- RT bremsstrahlung
- RT compound nuclei
- RT cross sections
- RT photoneutrons

PEIERLS-NABARRO FORCE [52; 52]
- RT crystal structure
- RT dislocations

pelargonic acid
- USE nonanoic acid

PELINDUNA REACTOR [3; 3]
- BT1 enriched uranium reactors
- BT2 reactors
- BT1 heavy water cooled reactors
- BT2 reactors
- BT1 heavy water moderated reactors
- BT2 reactors
- BT1 tank type reactors
- BT2 reactors
- BT1 thermal reactors
- BT2 reactors
- BT1 zero power reactors
- BT2 experimental reactors
- BT3 research and test reactors
- BT4 reactors

PELLET INJECTION [848; 848] Mar 83
- UF *injection (pellets)*
- RT fuel feeding systems
- RT fuel pellets
- RT thermonuclear fuels
- RT thermonuclear reactor fueling

PELLETIZING [188; 188] Feb 81
- BT1 molding
- BT2 fabrication
- RT breeding pellets
- RT compacting
- RT fuel pellets
- RT moderator pellets
- RT waste pellets

PELLETRON ACCELERATORS [181; 183] Dec 79
- BT1 electrostatic accelerators
- BT2 accelerators
- NT1 5u pelletron accelerator

pellets (breeding)
- USE breeding pellets

pellets (fuel)
- USE fuel pellets

pellets (moderator)
- USE moderator pellets

PELVIS [1,851; 1,851]
- BT1 body areas
- BT2 body
- RT bladder
- RT female genitals
- RT gonads
- RT rectum

PEMOLINE [0; 0]
- BT1 imines
- BT2 organic nitrogen compounds
- BT3 organic compounds
- BT1 oxazoles
- BT2 azoles
- BT3 heterocyclic compounds
- BT4 organic compounds
- BT3 organic nitrogen compounds
- BT4 organic compounds
- BT2 organic oxygen compounds
- BT3 organic compounds

penetrant inspection (liquid)
- USE liquid penetrant inspection

PENETRATION DEPTH [1,111; 1,111]
Nov 78
(May be used in any field; in particular in the field of superconductivity it is the depth to which an external magnetic field penetrates a superconductor.)
- RT electric conductors
- RT ginzburg-landau theory
- RT skin effect
- RT superconductivity

PENFOLD-LEISS METHOD [25; 25]
- RT bremsstrahlung

PENICILLAMINE [115; 115]
- UF *mercaptoaminoisovaleric acid*
- UF *mercaptovaline*
- BT1 amino acids
- BT2 carboxylic acids
- BT3 organic acids
- BT4 organic compounds
- BT1 chelating agents
- BT1 radioprotective substances
- BT2 drugs
- BT2 response modifying factors
- BT1 thiols
- BT2 organic sulfur compounds
- BT3 organic compounds

PENICILLIN [97; 97]
- BT1 antibiotics
- BT2 drugs
- BT2 organic compounds

PENICILLIUM [95; 95]
- BT1 fungi
- BT2 plants

PENLY-1 REACTOR [3; 3] Jul 84
- BT1 pwr type reactors
- BT2 enriched uranium reactors
- BT3 reactors
- BT2 power reactors
- BT3 reactors
- BT2 thermal reactors
- BT3 reactors
- BT2 water cooled reactors
- BT3 reactors
- BT2 water moderated reactors
- BT3 reactors

PENNING DISCHARGES [222; 222]
- UF *pig discharges*
- BT1 electric discharges
- RT penning ion sources
- RT sputter-ion pumps

PENNING EFFECT [419; 419]
- RT ionization

penning gages
- USE philips gages

PENNING ION SOURCES [488; 488]
- UF *pig ion sources*
- BT1 ion sources
- RT penning discharges

PENNSYLVANIA [370; 370]
- BT1 usa
- BT2 developed countries
- BT2 north america
- RT bettis

pennsylvania state triga reac
- USE pstr reactor

pennsylvania state un. res. re
- USE pstr reactor

pentaerythritol tetranitrate
- USE petn

pentamethylenediamine
- USE cadaverine

pentamethyleneimines
- USE piperidines

PENTANE [228; 228]
- BT1 alkanes
- BT2 hydrocarbons
- BT3 organic compounds

pentanedione (2,3)
- USE 2-3-pentanedione

pentanoic acid
- USE valeric acid

PENTANOLS [111; 111]
- UF *amyl alcohols*
- UF *pentyl alcohols*
- BT1 alcohols
- BT2 hydroxy compounds
- BT3 organic compounds

PENTENES [66; 66]
- BT1 alkenes
- BT2 hydrocarbons
- BT3 organic compounds

pentobarbital
- USE nembutal

PENTOSES [41; 326]
- BT1 monosaccharides
- BT2 saccharides
- BT3 carbohydrates
- BT4 organic compounds
- NT1 arabinose
- NT1 deoxyribose
- NT1 ribose
- NT1 ribulose
- NT1 xylose
- RT ribosides

pentothal
- USE thiopental

pentyl alcohols
- USE pentanols

PENTYL RADICALS [14; 14]
- UF *amyl radicals*
- BT1 alkyl radicals
- BT2 radicals

peos
(Plasma Erosion Opening Switches.)
- USE plasma switches

PEP STORAGE RINGS [877; 891]
  UF   *positron-electron-proton st ri*
  BT1   storage rings

PEPPERS [91; 91]
  (Fruit of Capsicum plant.)
  UF   *paprika*
  UF   *red peppers*
  BT1   vegetables
    BT2   food
  RT   capsicum
  RT   spices

pepr devices
  USE   cathode ray tube digitizers

PEPSIN [62; 62]
  BT1   acid proteinases
    BT2   peptide hydrolases
      BT3   hydrolases
        BT4   enzymes
          BT5   organic compounds
  RT   digestion
  RT   stomach

PEPTIDE HORMONES [256; 6,167]
  UF+   *bradykinin*
  BT1   hormones
  NT1   calcitonin
  NT1   gastrin
  NT1   glucagon
  NT1   insulin
  NT1   lactogens
    NT2   hpl
  NT1   parathormone
  NT1   pituitary hormones
    NT2   acth
    NT2   gonadotropins
      NT3   fsh
      NT3   hcg
      NT3   lh
      NT3   lth
    NT2   liberins
      NT3   lh-rh
    NT2   oxytocin
    NT2   sth
    NT2   tsh
    NT2   vasopressin
  NT1   thyroid hormones
    NT2   diiodothyronine
    NT2   thyrocalcitonin
    NT2   thyroxine
    NT2   triiodothyronine
  NT1   thyronine
  NT1   trh

PEPTIDE HYDROLASES [369; 1,581]
  BT1   hydrolases
    BT2   enzymes
      BT3   organic compounds
  NT1   acid proteinases
    NT2   pepsin
  NT1   aminopeptidases
  NT1   carboxypeptidases
  NT1   nonspecific peptidases
    NT2   renin
    NT2   urokinase
  NT1   serine proteinases
    NT2   chymotrypsin
    NT2   fibrinolysin
    NT2   kallikrein
    NT2   thrombin
    NT2   trypsin
  NT1   sh-proteinases
    NT2   cathepsins
    NT2   papain
    NT2   streptococcal proteinase
  RT   proteolysis

PEPTIDES [1,554; 3,754]
  BT1   proteins
    BT2   organic compounds
  NT1   polypeptides
    NT2   calcitonin
    NT2   endorphins
  NT3   enkephalins
  NT2   gastrin
  NT2   glucagon
  NT2   glutathione
  NT2   kinins
  RT   glycylglycine
  RT   pyrogens

PEPTONE [8; 8]
  BT1   proteins
    BT2   organic compounds

per
  USE   paraelectric resonance

peratization procedure
  USE   feinberg-pais theory

PERBROMATES [27; 27]
  (Specific compounds should be indexed by coordination of a descriptor of the form (CATION) COMPOUNDS and the above anion descriptor.)
  BT1   bromine compounds
    BT2   halogen compounds
  BT1   oxygen compounds

PERCHLORATES [717; 1,169]
  BT1   chlorine compounds
    BT2   halogen compounds
  BT1   oxygen compounds
  NT1   aluminium perchlorates
  NT1   americium perchlorates
  NT1   ammonium perchlorates
  NT1   barium perchlorates
  NT1   cadmium perchlorates
  NT1   calcium perchlorates
  NT1   cerium perchlorates
  NT1   cesium perchlorates
  NT1   chromium perchlorates
  NT1   cobalt perchlorates
  NT1   copper perchlorates
  NT1   dysprosium perchlorates
  NT1   erbium perchlorates
  NT1   europium perchlorates
  NT1   gadolinium perchlorates
  NT1   hafnium perchlorates
  NT1   holmium perchlorates
  NT1   indium perchlorates
  NT1   iron perchlorates
  NT1   lanthanum perchlorates
  NT1   lithium perchlorates
  NT1   lutetium perchlorates
  NT1   magnesium perchlorates
  NT1   manganese perchlorates
  NT1   neodymium perchlorates
  NT1   neptunium perchlorates
  NT1   plutonium perchlorates
  NT1   potassium perchlorates
  NT1   praseodymium perchlorates
  NT1   rubidium perchlorates
  NT1   samarium perchlorates
  NT1   scandium perchlorates
  NT1   silver perchlorates
  NT1   sodium perchlorates
  NT1   strontium perchlorates
  NT1   terbium perchlorates
  NT1   thallium perchlorates
  NT1   thorium perchlorates
  NT1   uranium perchlorates
  NT1   uranyl perchlorates
  NT1   ytterbium perchlorates
  NT1   yttrium perchlorates
  NT1   zinc perchlorates
  NT1   zirconium perchlorates
  RT   perchloric acid

PERCHLORIC ACID [963; 963]
  BT1   chlorine compounds
    BT2   halogen compounds
  BT1   inorganic acids
    BT2   hydrogen compounds
    BT2   inorganic compounds
  BT1   oxygen compounds
  RT   perchlorates

PERCUS-YEVICK EQUATION [49; 49]
  BT1   equations
  RT   many-body problem

PEREY-BUCK MODEL [27; 27]
  UF   *perey-wilkins model*
  BT1   nuclear models
    BT2   mathematical models
  RT   nonlocal potential
  RT   optical models

perey-wilkins model
  USE   perey-buck model

PERFECT FLOW [0; 0]
  (Non-viscous fluid flow obeying the Euler equation. Use INCOMPRESSIBLE FLOW and/or STEADY FLOW.)

§§ **PERFORMANCE** [34,733; 34,733]
  UF   *figure of merit*
  RT   efficiency
  RT   errors
  RT   evaluation
  RT   feasibility studies
  RT   performance testing
  RT   productivity
  RT   reliability
  RT   resolution
  RT   uses

PERFORMANCE TESTING [16,853; 18,641]
  BT1   testing
  NT1   bioassay
  RT   certification
  RT   inspection
  RT   performance
  RT   post-irradiation examination
  RT   quality control

PERFUSED ORGANS [1,162; 1,162]
  BT1   organs
    BT2   body
  RT   perfused tissues

PERFUSED TISSUES [577; 577] *Oct 75*
  BT1   tissues
    BT2   body
  RT   perfused organs

PERICARDIUM [151; 151] *Sep 80*
  BT1   heart
    BT2   cardiovascular system
    BT2   organs
      BT3   body
  BT1   serous membranes
    BT2   membranes

PERIDOTITES [19; 56] *Sep 83*
  BT1   plutonic rocks
    BT2   igneous rocks
      BT3   rocks
  NT1   kimberlites
  RT   hornblende
  RT   olivine
  RT   silicate minerals

PERINATAL IRRADIATION [69; 69]
  (A combination of prenatal and postnatal irradiation.)
  BT1   irradiation
  RT   prenatal irradiation

period (reactor)
  USE   reactor period

PERIODATES [134; 134]
  (Specific compounds should be indexed by coordination of a descriptor of the form (CATION) COMPOUNDS and the above anion descriptor.)
  BT1   iodine compounds
    BT2   halogen compounds

BT1 oxygen compounds
RT periodic acid

PERIODIC ACID [15; 15]
BT1 inorganic acids
BT2 hydrogen compounds
BT2 inorganic compounds
BT1 iodine compounds
BT2 halogen compounds
BT1 oxygen compounds
RT periodates

PERIODIC SYSTEM [275; 275]
UF *mendeleev periodic system*
RT atomic number
RT elements

periodicity
USE variations

periosteum
USE bone tissues

PERIPHERAL COLLISIONS [204; 204]
BT1 strong interactions
BT2 basic interactions
BT2 interactions
RT heavy ion reactions
RT impact parameter

PERIPHERAL MODELS [373; 7,294]
UF *exchange models*
BT1 particle models
BT2 mathematical models
NT1 baryon-exchange models
NT1 boson-exchange models
NT2 obe model
NT3 ope model
NT4 electric born model
NT2 sigma model
NT1 multiperipheral model
NT2 cluster emission model
NT3 space-time model

PERISCOPES [27; 27]
BT1 optical systems
RT hot cells
RT hot labs
RT remote handling

PERITONEUM [403; 403]
BT1 serous membranes
BT2 membranes
RT abdomen
RT ascites
RT gastrointestinal tract
RT intraperitoneal injection
RT liver
RT mesentery
RT peritonitis
RT spleen

PERITONITIS [54; 54]
BT1 digestive system diseases
BT2 diseases
BT1 symptoms
RT peritoneum

PERKINS-1 REACTOR [8; 8]
(In Davie County, North Carolina, USA.)
BT1 pwr type reactors
BT2 enriched uranium reactors
BT3 reactors
BT2 power reactors
BT3 reactors
BT2 thermal reactors
BT3 reactors
BT2 water cooled reactors
BT3 reactors
BT2 water moderated reactors
BT3 reactors

PERKINS-2 REACTOR [7; 7]
(In Davie County, North Carolina, USA.)
BT1 pwr type reactors
BT2 enriched uranium reactors
BT3 reactors
BT2 power reactors
BT3 reactors
BT2 thermal reactors
BT3 reactors
BT2 water cooled reactors
BT3 reactors
BT2 water moderated reactors
BT3 reactors

PERKINS-3 REACTOR [7; 7]
(In Davie County, North Carolina, USA.)
BT1 pwr type reactors
BT2 enriched uranium reactors
BT3 reactors
BT2 power reactors
BT3 reactors
BT2 thermal reactors
BT3 reactors
BT2 water cooled reactors
BT3 reactors
BT2 water moderated reactors
BT3 reactors

perlite (iron-carbon alloy)
USE pearlite

PERMALLOY [127; 132]
BT1 alloys
NT1 alloy-ni80fe16mo4

permalloy c
USE alloy-ni80fe16mo4

PERMANENT MAGNETS [1,041; 1,041]
BT1 magnets
BT2 equipment
RT magnetic properties

PERMANGANATES [208; 208]
(Specific compounds should be indexed by coordination of a descriptor of the form (CATION) COMPOUNDS and the above anion descriptor.)
BT1 manganese compounds
BT2 transition element compounds
BT1 oxygen compounds
RT manganese oxides

§ **PERMEABILITY** [3,947; 3,947]
RT dialysis
RT membranes
RT osmosis
RT porosity

permeability (magnetic)
USE magnetic susceptibility

permeability coef (fluid mech)
USE hydraulic conductivity

permendur
USE alloy-co50fe50

permit applications
USE administrative procedures

permits
USE licenses

PERMITTIVITY [1,998; 1,998]
UF *dielectric constant*
BT1 dielectric properties
BT2 electrical properties
BT3 physical properties

permutit (inorganic)
USE inorganic ion exchangers

permutit (organic)
USE organic ion exchangers

pernicious anemia
USE anemias

PEROVSKITE [849; 849]
(CaTiO/sub 3/.)
BT1 oxide minerals
BT2 minerals
RT calcium oxides
RT kimberlites
RT synroc process
RT titanium oxides

perovskite crystal structure
USE cubic lattices

perovskites
SEE oxide minerals

PEROXIDASES [481; 546]
BT1 oxidoreductases
BT2 enzymes
BT3 organic compounds
BT1 porphyrins
BT2 heterocyclic acids
BT3 carboxylic acids
BT4 organic acids
BT5 organic compounds
BT3 heterocyclic compounds
BT4 organic compounds
BT2 organic nitrogen compounds
BT3 organic compounds
NT1 catalase

PEROXIDES [659; 2,094]
BT1 oxygen compounds
NT1 benzoyl peroxide
NT1 hydrogen peroxide
NT1 plutonium peroxide
NT1 uranium peroxide

PEROXY RADICALS [345; 345]
UF *superoxide radicals*
BT1 radicals

PERRHENATES [217; 217]
(Specific compounds should be indexed by coordination of a descriptor of the form (CATION) COMPOUNDS and the above anion descriptor.)
BT1 oxygen compounds
BT1 rhenium compounds
BT2 transition element compounds
RT rhenium oxides

PERRY-1 REACTOR [56; 56]
(Perry, Ohio, USA)
BT1 bwr type reactors
BT2 enriched uranium reactors
BT3 reactors
BT2 power reactors
BT3 reactors
BT2 thermal reactors
BT3 reactors
BT2 water cooled reactors
BT3 reactors
BT2 water moderated reactors
BT3 reactors

PERRY-2 REACTOR [49; 49]
(Perry, Ohio, USA)
BT1 bwr type reactors
BT2 enriched uranium reactors
BT3 reactors
BT2 power reactors
BT3 reactors
BT2 thermal reactors

```
    BT3    reactors
    BT2    water cooled reactors
    BT3    reactors
    BT2    water moderated reactors
    BT3    reactors
```

PERRYMAN-1 REACTOR [2; 2] *Jan 78*
```
    BT1    enriched uranium reactors
    BT2    reactors
    BT1    power reactors
    BT2    reactors
    BT1    thermal reactors
    BT2    reactors
    BT1    water cooled reactors
    BT2    reactors
    BT1    water moderated reactors
    BT2    reactors
```

PERRYMAN-2 REACTOR [2; 2] *Jan 78*
```
    BT1    enriched uranium reactors
    BT2    reactors
    BT1    power reactors
    BT2    reactors
    BT1    thermal reactors
    BT2    reactors
    BT1    water cooled reactors
    BT2    reactors
    BT1    water moderated reactors
    BT2    reactors
```

personal computers
```
    USE    microcomputers
```

PERSONNEL [8,773; 15,365]
(Studies of groups of persons employed in a particular field of endeavor. For studies on individuals in a group see also MAN.)
```
    UF     employees
    UF     manpower
    UF     workers
    NT1    astronauts
    NT1    aviation personnel
    NT1    dial painters
    NT1    medical personnel
    NT1    military personnel
    NT1    miners
    NT1    public officials
    NT1    radiological personnel
    NT1    reactor operators
    NT1    security personnel
    RT     human factors
    RT     human populations
    RT     labor relations
    RT     man
    RT     man-machine systems
    RT     management
    RT     medical surveillance
    RT     occupational safety
    RT     occupations
    RT     work
```

PERSONNEL DOSIMETRY [3,589; 3,589]
```
    UF     personnel film dosimetry
    BT1    dosimetry
    RT     external irradiation
    RT     occupations
    RT     personnel monitoring
    RT     thermoluminescent dosemeters
```

personnel film dosimetry
```
    USE    personnel dosimetry
```

PERSONNEL MONITORING [2,659; 2,659]
(To include medical surveillance of early and late radiation effects)
```
    UF+    excretion analysis
    BT1    radiation monitoring
    BT2    monitoring
    RT     albedo-neutron dosemeters
    RT     medical surveillance
    RT     personnel dosimetry
    RT     radiation doses
```

```
    RT     radioactivity
    RT     radionuclide kinetics
    RT     whole-body counting
```

PERSPEX [111; 111]
```
    BT1    polyacrylates
    BT2    esters
    BT3    organic compounds
    BT2    polyvinyls
    BT3    organic polymers
    BT4    organic compounds
    BT4    polymers
```

PERSULFATES [95; 95]
(Specific compounds should be indexed by coordination of a descriptor of the form (CATION) COMPOUNDS and the above anion descriptor.)
```
    BT1    oxygen compounds
    BT1    sulfur compounds
    RT     persulfuric acid
```

PERSULFURIC ACID [18; 18]
```
    BT1    oxygen compounds
    BT1    sulfur compounds
    RT     persulfates
    RT     sulfuric acid
```

PERT METHOD [42; 42]
(Program Evaluation and Review Technique.)
```
    UF     cpm
    UF     critical path method
    RT     planning
    RT     schedules
```

PERTECHNETATES [1,795; 1,795]
(Specific compounds should be indexed by coordination of a descriptor of the form (CATION) COMPOUNDS and the above anion descriptor.)
```
    BT1    oxygen compounds
    BT1    technetium compounds
    BT2    transition element compounds
    RT     technetium oxides
```

PERTURBATION THEORY [14,901; 14,911]
```
    UF     reductive perturbation method
    NT1    hsk procedure
    RT     adjoint flux
    RT     born approximation
    RT     brinkman-kramers approximation
    RT     mathematics
    RT     neutron importance function
    RT     neutron transport theory
    RT     p1-approximation
    RT     p3-approximation
    RT     quantum mechanics
    RT     quasilinear problems
    RT     rayleigh-schroedinger formula
    RT     reactor kinetics
    RT     ritchie-eldridge theory
    RT     scattering
```

perturbations
```
    USE    disturbances
```

perturbed ang. corr. (differ.)
```
    USE    differential pac
```

perturbed ang. corr. (integr.)
```
    USE    integral pac
```

PERTURBED ANGULAR CORRELATION [976; 1,973]
```
    BT1    angular correlation
    BT2    correlations
    NT1    differential pac
    NT1    integral pac
    RT     nuclear electric moments
    RT     nuclear magnetic moments
```

perturbed stationary states me
```
    USE    pss method
```

PERU [84; 84]
```
    BT1    developing countries
    BT1    south america
    BT2    latin america
    RT     amazon river
```

PERYLENE [34; 34]
```
    BT1    condensed aromatics
    BT2    aromatics
    BT3    organic compounds
```

PEST CONTROL [420; 611]
```
    NT1    genetic control
    NT1    pest eradication
    RT     insects
    RT     mites
    RT     parasites
    RT     pesticides
    RT     phosphines
    RT     quarantine
    RT     rodents
    RT     sterile insect release
    RT     sterile male technique
```

PEST ERADICATION [51; 51] *Sep 75*
```
    BT1    pest control
    RT     insects
    RT     parasites
```

PESTICIDES [544; 1,856]
```
    NT1    fumigants
    NT1    fungicides
    NT2    cycloheximide
    NT1    herbicides
    NT1    insecticides
    NT2    aldrin
    NT2    ddt
    NT2    dieldrin
    NT2    lindane
    NT2    malathion
    NT2    parathion
    RT     agriculture
    RT     disinfectants
    RT     disinfestation
    RT     ecosystems
    RT     grain disinfestation
    RT     mutagens
    RT     parasites
    RT     pest control
    RT     phosphines
    RT     pollutants
    RT     pollution
```

→ *pet scanning*
```
    USE    positron computed tomography
```

PETHIDINE [10; 10]
```
    UF     demerol
    UF     dolantal
    BT1    analgesics
    BT2    central nervous system depress
    BT3    central nervous system agents
    BT4    drugs
    BT1    aromatics
    BT2    organic compounds
    BT1    monocarboxylic acids
    BT2    carboxylic acids
    BT3    organic acids
    BT4    organic compounds
    BT1    narcotics
    BT2    central nervous system depress
    BT3    central nervous system agents
    BT4    drugs
    BT1    piperidines
    BT2    amines
    BT3    organic compounds
    BT2    pyridines
    BT3    azines
    BT4    heterocyclic compounds
    BT5    organic compounds
    BT4    organic nitrogen compounds
    BT5    organic compounds
```

PETN [22; 22]
UF *pentaerythritol tetranitrate*
BT1 chemical explosives
BT2 explosives
BT1 nitrates
BT2 nitrogen compounds
BT2 oxygen compounds
BT1 nitric acid esters
BT2 esters
BT3 organic compounds

PETRA STORAGE RING [573; 573]
Jul 76
(Positron-Elektron-Tandem-
Ringbeschleuniger Anlage)
BT1 storage rings

PETROCHEMISTRY [120; 120]
BT1 chemistry
RT cracking
RT natural gas
RT petroleum
RT petroleum products

PETROGENESIS [562; 562]
RT orogenesis
RT petrology
RT rocks
RT tectonics

petrography
USE petrology

PETROLEUM [2,099; 2,160]
UF *crude oil*
BT1 fossil fuels
BT2 energy sources
BT2 fuels
NT1 shale oil
RT distillation
RT hydrocarbons
RT oils
RT petrochemistry
RT petroleum refineries

→ *petroleum coke*
USE coke

→ **PETROLEUM DEPOSITS** [0; 0] *Aug 91*
BT1 geologic deposits
BT1 mineral resources
BT2 resources

→ **PETROLEUM INDUSTRY** [0; 0] *Aug 91*
BT1 industry

PETROLEUM PRODUCTS [268; 846]
NT1 diesel fuels
NT1 gasoline
NT1 kerosene
NT1 lubricating oils
RT oils
RT petrochemistry
RT petroleum refineries
RT refining

PETROLEUM REFINERIES [118; 118]
RT distillation
RT distillation equipment
RT industrial plants
RT petroleum
RT petroleum products

PETROLOGY [1,241; 1,241]
UF *lithology*
UF *petrography*
RT petrogenesis
RT rocks

petrov-galerkin method
USE galerkin-petrov method

petten high flux reactor
USE hfr reactor

petten low flux reactor
USE lfr reactor

petten stek reactor
USE stek reactor

PETULA TOKAMAK [116; 116] *Nov 75*
BT1 tokamak devices
BT2 closed plasma devices
BT3 thermonuclear devices

PEV RANGE [495; 495] *Jan 77*
(From 10 exp 15 to 10 exp 18 ev.)
BT1 energy range

PEWEE-1 REACTOR [2; 2]
BT1 space propulsion reactors
BT2 propulsion reactors
BT3 power reactors
BT4 reactors
BT2 space power reactors
BT3 mobile reactors
BT4 reactors
BT3 power reactors
BT4 reactors

PEWEE-2 REACTOR [1; 1]
BT1 space propulsion reactors
BT2 propulsion reactors
BT3 power reactors
BT4 reactors
BT2 space power reactors
BT3 mobile reactors
BT4 reactors
BT3 power reactors
BT4 reactors

PEWEE-3 REACTOR [1; 1]
BT1 space propulsion reactors
BT2 propulsion reactors
BT3 power reactors
BT4 reactors
BT2 space power reactors
BT3 mobile reactors
BT4 reactors
BT3 power reactors
BT4 reactors

PEWEE-4 REACTOR [0; 0]
BT1 space propulsion reactors
BT2 propulsion reactors
BT3 power reactors
BT4 reactors
BT2 space power reactors
BT3 mobile reactors
BT4 reactors
BT3 power reactors
BT4 reactors

PFIRSCH-SCHLUETER REGIME
[113; 113] *Oct 81*
RT collisional plasma
RT neoclassical transport theory
RT stellarators
RT tokamak devices

PFR REACTOR [466; 466]
UF *dounreay prototype fast r.*
UF *prototype fast r. dounreay*
BT1 lmfbr type reactors
BT2 fbr type reactors
BT3 breeder reactors
BT4 reactors
BT3 fast reactors
BT4 epithermal reactors
BT5 reactors
BT2 liquid metal cooled reactors
BT3 reactors
BT1 power reactors
BT2 reactors
BT1 sodium cooled reactors
BT2 liquid metal cooled reactors

BT3 reactors
RT enriched uranium reactors
RT plutonium reactors

PH VALUE [14,526; 14,526]
UF *acidity*
UF *neutralization (chemical)*
RT bases
RT buffers
RT inorganic acids
RT nucleic acid denaturation
RT organic acids
RT protein denaturation

ph'chromosome
USE philadelphia chromosome

PHAEDRUS MIRROR DEVICES
[12; 12] *Feb 89*
BT1 tandem mirrors
BT2 magnetic mirrors
BT3 open plasma devices
BT4 thermonuclear devices

phages
USE bacteriophages

PHAGOCYTES [74; 942]
BT1 somatic cells
BT2 animal cells
NT1 macrophages
RT leukocytes
RT phagocytosis

PHAGOCYTOSIS [404; 404]
RT amoeba
RT excretion
RT immune reactions
RT intracellular digestion
RT macrophages
RT phagocytes
RT reticuloendothelial system

PHANTOMS [6,315; 6,315]
BT1 mockup
BT2 structural models
RT biological models
RT depth dose distributions
RT functional models
RT isodose curves
RT radiotherapy
RT tissue-equivalent materials

pharmaceuticals
USE drugs

PHARMACOLOGY [768; 768]
RT antiandrogens
RT drugs
RT radiopharmaceuticals

pharmacotherapy
USE chemotherapy

PHAROS DEVICES [0; 0]
BT1 linear theta pinch devices
BT2 linear pinch devices
BT3 open plasma devices
BT4 thermonuclear devices
BT3 pinch devices
BT4 thermonuclear devices

PHARYNX [1,036; 1,036]
UF *nasopharynx*
UF *throat*
UF+ *tonsils*
BT1 digestive system
BT1 organs
BT2 body
BT1 respiratory system
RT neck
RT oral cavity

PHASE DIAGRAMS [11,722; 11,722]
- UF state diagrams
- BT1 diagrams
  - BT2 information
- RT allotropy
- RT alloy systems
- RT critical temperature
- RT eutectics
- RT eutectoids
- RT gases
- RT glass
- RT liquids
- RT melting points
- RT microstructure
- RT monotectics
- RT monotectoids
- RT phase rule
- RT phase studies
- RT phase transformations
- RT solid solutions
- RT solids
- RT thermal analysis
- RT triple point

PHASE OSCILLATIONS [291; 291]
- BT1 beam dynamics
  - BT2 dynamics
    - BT3 mechanics
- BT1 oscillations

PHASE RULE [12; 12]
- RT phase diagrams

PHASE SHIFT [6,533; 6,533]
- RT aharonov-bohm effect
- RT argand diagrams
- RT partial waves
- RT scattering

PHASE SPACE [4,709; 4,709]
- BT1 mathematical space
  - BT2 space
- RT attractors
- RT dalitz plot
- RT ergodic hypothesis
- RT liouville theorem
- RT mathematics
- RT prism plot

PHASE STABILITY [760; 760]
- BT1 stability
- RT beam dynamics

PHASE STUDIES [10,238; 10,238]
- RT phase diagrams
- RT phase transformations
- RT thermodynamic activity

PHASE TRANSFORMATIONS [14,160; 41,438]
- UF transitions (phase)
- NT1 boiling
  - NT2 film boiling
  - NT2 nucleate boiling
    - NT3 departure nucleate boiling
  - NT2 pool boiling
  - NT2 subcooled boiling
  - NT2 transition boiling
- NT1 crystal-phase transformations
- NT1 crystallization
- NT1 evaporation
  - NT2 sublimation
  - NT2 vacuum evaporation
- NT1 melting
  - NT2 electron beam melting
  - NT2 vacuum melting
  - NT2 zone melting
- NT1 order-disorder transformations
- RT allotropy
- RT critical temperature
- RT dew point
- RT eutectics
- RT eutectoids
- RT freezing
- RT glass
- RT guinier-preston zones
- RT habit planes
- RT microstructure
- RT phase diagrams
- RT phase studies
- RT physical chemistry
- RT shape memory effect
- RT solidification
- RT thermal analysis
- RT transition heat
- RT transition temperature
- RT triple point
- RT widmanstaetten structure

PHASE VELOCITY [582; 582]
- BT1 velocity
- RT wave propagation

PHASEOLUS [368; 368]
- UF bean plant
- BT1 leguminosae
  - BT2 plants
- RT beans
- RT mungbeans
- RT phytohemagglutinin

phasotrons
- USE synchrocyclotrons

PHEBUS REACTOR [13; 13] *May 90*
(Nuclear Protection and Safety Institute, CEA St. Paul lez Durance, France.)
- BT1 enriched uranium reactors
  - BT2 reactors
- BT1 pool type reactors
  - BT2 water cooled reactors
    - BT3 reactors
  - BT2 water moderated reactors
    - BT3 reactors
- BT1 research reactors
  - BT2 research and test reactors
    - BT3 reactors
- BT1 thermal reactors
  - BT2 reactors

phenacetin
- USE analgesics
- AND antipyretics

PHENANTHRENE [81; 81]
- BT1 condensed aromatics
  - BT2 aromatics
    - BT3 organic compounds
- BT1 hydrocarbons
  - BT2 organic compounds

PHENANTHROLINE-ORTHO [145; 145]
- BT1 phenanthrolines
  - BT2 heterocyclic compounds
    - BT3 organic compounds
  - BT2 organic nitrogen compounds
    - BT3 organic compounds
- BT1 reagents
- RT ferroin

PHENANTHROLINES [248; 411]
- BT1 heterocyclic compounds
  - BT2 organic compounds
- BT1 organic nitrogen compounds
  - BT2 organic compounds
- NT1 ferroin
- NT1 phenanthroline-ortho

PHENATINE [0; 0]
- BT1 amides
  - BT2 organic nitrogen compounds
    - BT3 organic compounds
- BT1 organic oxygen compounds
  - BT2 organic compounds
- BT1 pyridines
  - BT2 azines
    - BT3 heterocyclic compounds
      - BT4 organic compounds
    - BT3 organic nitrogen compounds
      - BT4 organic compounds

PHENAZINE [25; 25]
- BT1 pyrazines
  - BT2 azines
    - BT3 heterocyclic compounds
      - BT4 organic compounds
    - BT3 organic nitrogen compounds
      - BT4 organic compounds

PHENETHYL RADICALS [7; 7]
- BT1 aryl radicals
  - BT2 radicals

PHENIX REACTOR [526; 526]
(Marcoule, Gard, France)
- UF marcoule phenix reactor
- BT1 enriched uranium reactors
  - BT2 reactors
- BT1 lmfbr type reactors
  - BT2 fbr type reactors
    - BT3 breeder reactors
      - BT4 reactors
    - BT3 fast reactors
      - BT4 epithermal reactors
        - BT5 reactors
  - BT2 liquid metal cooled reactors
    - BT3 reactors
- BT1 plutonium reactors
  - BT2 reactors
- BT1 power reactors
  - BT2 reactors
- BT1 sodium cooled reactors
  - BT2 liquid metal cooled reactors
    - BT3 reactors

PHENOBARBITAL [112; 112]
- UF luminal
- BT1 anticonvulsants
  - BT2 central nervous system depress
    - BT3 central nervous system agents
      - BT4 drugs
- BT1 barbiturates
  - BT2 anesthetics
    - BT3 central nervous system depress
      - BT4 central nervous system agents
        - BT5 drugs
  - BT2 hypnotics and sedatives
    - BT3 central nervous system depress
      - BT4 central nervous system agents
        - BT5 drugs
  - BT2 organic oxygen compounds
    - BT3 organic compounds
  - BT2 pyrimidines
    - BT3 azines
      - BT4 heterocyclic compounds
        - BT5 organic compounds
      - BT4 organic nitrogen compounds
        - BT5 organic compounds

PHENOL [225; 225]
- UF hydroxybenzene
- BT1 phenols
  - BT2 aromatics
    - BT3 organic compounds
  - BT2 hydroxy compounds
    - BT3 organic compounds

phenolates
- USE alkoxides

PHENOLPHTHALEIN [15; 15]
- BT1 carboxylic acid esters
  - BT2 esters
    - BT3 organic compounds
- BT1 indicators
- BT1 phenols
  - BT2 aromatics
    - BT3 organic compounds
  - BT2 hydroxy compounds
    - BT3 organic compounds
- RT phthalic acid

PHENOLS [778; 4,254]
- BT1 aromatics
  - BT2 organic compounds
- BT1 hydroxy compounds
  - BT2 organic compounds
- NT1 amidol
- NT1 bambp
- NT1 cresols
- NT1 dinitrophenol
- NT1 eriochrome dyes
- NT1 naphthols
  - NT2 acid chrome dyes
  - NT2 beryllon
  - NT2 nitroso-r salt
  - NT2 pan
  - NT2 thorin
  - NT2 trypan blue
  - NT2 1-nitroso-2-naphthol
- NT1 nitrophenol
- NT1 phenol
- NT1 phenolphthalein
- NT1 picric acid
- NT1 polyphenols
  - NT2 arsenazo
  - NT2 aurin
  - NT2 bromosulfophthalein
  - NT2 catecholamines
  - NT2 curcumin
  - NT2 dopamine
  - NT2 fluorescein
  - NT2 hematoxylin
  - NT2 morin
  - NT2 pyridylazoresorcinol
  - NT2 pyrocatechol
  - NT2 pyrogallol
  - NT2 quercetin
  - NT2 resorcinol
  - NT2 stilbestrol
  - NT2 tannic acid
  - NT2 tiron
- NT1 pop
- NT1 thymol
- NT1 tyramine
- RT alkoxides
- RT bakelite

PHENOTHIAZINES [77; 322]
- UF+ *promethazine*
- BT1 azines
  - BT2 heterocyclic compounds
    - BT3 organic compounds
  - BT2 organic nitrogen compounds
    - BT3 organic compounds
- BT1 organic sulfur compounds
  - BT2 organic compounds
- NT1 chlorpromazine
- NT1 methylene blue
- RT thionine

PHENOTYPE [527; 527]
- RT genotype
- RT ontogenesis

PHENOXY RADICALS [54; 54]
- BT1 radicals

phenyl methyl ether
- USE anisole

PHENYL RADICALS [150; 150]
- BT1 aryl radicals
  - BT2 radicals

phenylacetylene
- USE tolan

phenylacrylic acid-beta
- USE cinnamic acid

PHENYLALANINE [438; 438]
- UF *aminophenylacetic acid-alpha*
- BT1 amino acids
  - BT2 carboxylic acids
    - BT3 organic acids
      - BT4 organic compounds
- BT1 aromatics
  - BT2 organic compounds
- RT dopa
- RT tyrosine

phenylamine
- USE aniline

phenylcarbinol
- USE benzyl alcohol

PHENYLENE RADICALS [9; 9]
- BT1 radicals

phenylethylene
- USE styrene

phenylhydroxylamine
- USE cupferron

phenylisopropylamine
- USE benzedrine

PHEROMONE [30; 30]
- BT1 secretion
- RT insects
- RT sex

PHI J-1850 MESONS [3; 3] *Dec 87*
- BT1 strangeonium
  - BT2 mesons
    - BT3 bosons
    - BT3 hadrons
      - BT4 elementary particles
  - BT2 quarkonium
- BT1 tensor mesons
  - BT2 mesons
    - BT3 bosons
    - BT3 hadrons
      - BT4 elementary particles

phi-1019 resonances
(Prior to December 1987 this was a valid descriptor.)
- USE phi-1020 mesons

PHI-1020 MESONS [881; 881]
(Prior to December 1987 this concept was indexed by PHI-1019 RESONANCES.)
- UF *phi-1019 resonances*
- BT1 strangeonium
  - BT2 mesons
    - BT3 bosons
    - BT3 hadrons
      - BT4 elementary particles
  - BT2 quarkonium
- BT1 vector mesons
  - BT2 mesons
    - BT3 bosons
    - BT3 hadrons
      - BT4 elementary particles

PHI-1680 MESONS [10; 10] *Dec 87*
- BT1 strangeonium
  - BT2 mesons
    - BT3 bosons
    - BT3 hadrons
      - BT4 elementary particles
  - BT2 quarkonium
- BT1 vector mesons
  - BT2 mesons
    - BT3 bosons
    - BT3 hadrons
      - BT4 elementary particles

philadelp. elect.-pow. reac.-1
- USE limerick-1 reactor

philadelp. elect.-pow. reac.-2
- USE limerick-2 reactor

PHILADELPHIA CHROMOSOME [19; 19]
- UF *ph'chromosome*
- BT1 human chromosomes
  - BT2 chromosomes
- RT myeloid leukemia

PHILCO COMPUTERS [0; 0]
- BT1 computers

PHILIPPINE ATOMIC ENERGY COMMI [24; 27] *Sep 77*
(Philippine Atomic Energy Commission, abolished in 1988 and replaced by the philippine Nuclear Research Institute.)
- UF *paec*
- BT1 philippine nuclear research in
  - BT2 philippine organizations
    - BT3 national organizations

PHILIPPINE ATOMIC RESEARCH CEN [3; 3] *Sep 77*
(Philippine Atomic Research Center)
- BT1 philippine nuclear research in
  - BT2 philippine organizations
    - BT3 national organizations

philippine nucl res inst
(From June to December 1990, this was a valid descriptor.)
- USE philippine nuclear research in

philippine nucl. power plant-1
- USE pnpp-1 reactor

PHILIPPINE NUCLEAR RESEARCH IN [0; 0] *Jun 90*
(Philippine Nuclear Research Institute, created in 1988 and replacing the Philippine Atomic Energy Commission.)
- UF *philippine nucl res inst*
- BT1 philippine organizations
  - BT2 national organizations
- NT1 philippine atomic energy commi
- NT1 philippine atomic research cen

PHILIPPINE ORGANIZATIONS [1; 28] *Sep 77*
- BT1 national organizations
- NT1 philippine nuclear research in
  - NT2 philippine atomic energy commi
  - NT2 philippine atomic research cen

philippine research reactor-1
- USE prr-1 reactor

PHILIPPINES [259; 259]
- BT1 asia
- BT1 developing countries
- BT1 islands
- RT pacific ocean

PHILIPPSBURG-1 REACTOR [106; 106]
- UF *kernkraftwerk philippsburg-1*
- UF *kkp-1 philippsburg reactor*
- BT1 bwr type reactors
  - BT2 enriched uranium reactors
    - BT3 reactors
  - BT2 power reactors
    - BT3 reactors
  - BT2 thermal reactors
    - BT3 reactors
  - BT2 water cooled reactors
    - BT3 reactors
  - BT2 water moderated reactors
    - BT3 reactors

PHILIPPSBURG-2 REACTOR [115; 115]
- UF *kernkraftwerk philippsburg-2*
- UF *kkp-2 philippsburg reactor*
- BT1 pwr type reactors
- BT2 enriched uranium reactors
- BT3 reactors
- BT2 power reactors
- BT3 reactors
- BT2 thermal reactors
- BT3 reactors
- BT2 water cooled reactors
- BT3 reactors
- BT2 water moderated reactors
- BT3 reactors

PHILIPS GAGES [14; 14]
- UF *penning gages*
- BT1 ionization gages
- BT2 vacuum gages
- BT3 pressure gages
- BT4 measuring instruments
- RT sputter-ion pumps

PHIPPS BEND-1 REACTOR [6; 6]
Jan 78
(Surgoinsville, Tennessee, USA)
- BT1 bwr type reactors
- BT2 enriched uranium reactors
- BT3 reactors
- BT2 power reactors
- BT3 reactors
- BT2 thermal reactors
- BT3 reactors
- BT2 water cooled reactors
- BT3 reactors
- BT2 water moderated reactors
- BT3 reactors
- RT ge standard reactor

PHIPPS BEND-2 REACTOR [6; 6]
Jan 78
(Surgoinsville, Tennessee, USA)
- BT1 bwr type reactors
- BT2 enriched uranium reactors
- BT3 reactors
- BT2 power reactors
- BT3 reactors
- BT2 thermal reactors
- BT3 reactors
- BT2 water cooled reactors
- BT3 reactors
- BT2 water moderated reactors
- BT3 reactors
- RT ge standard reactor

PHI4-FIELD THEORY [868; 868]
Feb 78
- BT1 quantum field theory
- BT2 field theories
- RT boundary conditions
- RT haag theorem
- RT heisenberg model
- RT ising model
- RT locality
- RT radiative corrections

phloredzin
- USE phlorizin

phlorhizin
- USE phlorizin

PHLORIZIN [9; 9]
- UF *phloredzin*
- UF *phlorhizin*
- BT1 glycosides
- BT2 carbohydrates
- BT3 organic compounds
- BT1 ketones
- BT2 organic compounds

PHOEBUS-1A REACTOR [2; 2]
- UF *rocket reactor exp. phoebus-1a*
- BT1 gas cooled reactors
- BT2 reactors
- BT1 space propulsion reactors
- BT2 propulsion reactors
- BT3 power reactors
- BT4 reactors
- BT2 space power reactors
- BT3 mobile reactors
- BT4 reactors
- BT3 power reactors
- BT4 reactors

PHOEBUS-1B REACTOR [3; 3]
- UF *rocket reactor exp. phoebus-1b*
- BT1 gas cooled reactors
- BT2 reactors
- BT1 space propulsion reactors
- BT2 propulsion reactors
- BT3 power reactors
- BT4 reactors
- BT2 space power reactors
- BT3 mobile reactors
- BT4 reactors
- BT3 power reactors
- BT4 reactors

PHOEBUS-2A REACTOR [7; 7]
- UF *rocket reactor exp. phoebus-2a*
- BT1 gas cooled reactors
- BT2 reactors
- BT1 space propulsion reactors
- BT2 propulsion reactors
- BT3 power reactors
- BT4 reactors
- BT2 space power reactors
- BT3 mobile reactors
- BT4 reactors
- BT3 power reactors
- BT4 reactors

PHOENIX DEVICES [5; 5]
- BT1 magnetic mirrors
- BT2 open plasma devices
- BT3 thermonuclear devices

PHONONS [6,642; 6,642]
- BT1 quasi particles
- RT acoustic esr
- RT acoustic nmr
- RT electron-phonon coupling
- RT landau liquid helium theory
- RT photoacoustic effect
- RT quasiparticle-phonon model
- RT solitons
- RT umklapp processes

PHORBOL ESTERS [456; 456] *Dec 81*
- BT1 esters
- BT2 organic compounds

PHOSGENE [45; 45]
- UF *carbon oxychloride*
- UF *carbonyl chloride*
- BT1 carbonic acid derivatives
- BT2 organic compounds
- BT1 organic chlorine compounds
- BT2 organic halogen compounds
- BT3 organic compounds

PHOSPHATASES [254; 1,369]
- BT1 esterases
- BT2 hydrolases
- BT3 enzymes
- BT4 organic compounds
- NT1 acid phosphatase
- NT1 alkaline phosphatase
- NT1 nucleotidases

PHOSPHATE GLASS [409; 439]
(Glass with phosphorus pentoxide as a major component.)
- BT1 glass
- NT1 borophosphate glass
- RT rpl dosemeters

PHOSPHATE MINERALS [38; 566]
Apr 84
- BT1 minerals
- NT1 apatites
- NT1 autunite
- NT1 dumontite
- NT1 florencite
- NT1 lermontovite
- NT1 monazites
- NT1 ningyoite
- NT1 parsonsite
- NT1 phosphuranylite
- NT1 saleeite
- NT1 steenstrupine
- NT1 torbernite
- NT1 uranocircite
- NT1 xenotime
- RT aluminium phosphates
- RT barium phosphates
- RT cerium phosphates
- RT copper phosphates
- RT lead phosphates
- RT magnesium phosphates
- RT phosphate rocks
- RT phosphorites
- RT uranium phosphates
- RT yttrium phosphates

PHOSPHATE ROCKS [166; 260]
May 80
- BT1 sedimentary rocks
- BT2 rocks
- NT1 phosphorites
- RT calcium carbonates
- RT calcium phosphates
- RT phosphate minerals

PHOSPHATES [2,442; 5,382]
(For salts only; see also PHOSPHORIC ACID ESTERS.)
- BT1 oxygen compounds
- BT1 phosphorus compounds
- NT1 aluminium phosphates
- NT1 americium phosphates
- NT1 ammonium phosphates
- NT1 barium phosphates
- NT1 berkelium phosphates
- NT1 beryllium phosphates
- NT1 bismuth phosphates
- NT1 boron phosphates
- NT1 cadmium phosphates
- NT1 calcium phosphates
- NT1 cerium phosphates
- NT1 cesium phosphates
- NT1 chromium phosphates
- NT1 cobalt phosphates
- NT1 copper phosphates
- NT1 dysprosium phosphates
- NT1 erbium phosphates
- NT1 europium phosphates
- NT1 gadolinium phosphates
- NT1 gallium phosphates
- NT1 germanium phosphates
- NT1 hafnium phosphates
- NT1 holmium phosphates
- NT1 indium phosphates
- NT1 iron phosphates
- NT1 lanthanum phosphates
- NT1 lead phosphates
- NT1 lithium phosphates
- NT1 lutetium phosphates
- NT1 magnesium phosphates
- NT1 manganese phosphates
- NT1 molybdenum phosphates
- NT1 neodymium phosphates
- NT1 neptunium phosphates
- NT1 nickel phosphates
- NT1 niobium phosphates
- NT1 plutonium phosphates
- NT1 potassium phosphates
- NT1 praseodymium phosphates
- NT1 promethium phosphates
- NT1 protactinium phosphates
- NT1 rubidium phosphates
- NT1 samarium phosphates
- NT1 scandium phosphates
- NT1 silicon phosphates
- NT1 silver phosphates
- NT1 sodium phosphates

```
NT1    strontium phosphates
NT1    superphosphates
NT1    tantalum phosphates
NT1    technetium phosphates
NT1    terbium phosphates
NT1    thallium phosphates
NT1    thorium phosphates
NT1    thulium phosphates
NT1    tin phosphates
NT1    titanium phosphates
NT1    uranium phosphates
NT1    uranyl phosphates
NT1    vanadium phosphates
NT1    xenon phosphates
NT1    ytterbium phosphates
NT1    yttrium phosphates
NT1    zinc phosphates
NT1    zirconium phosphates
RT     phosphoric acid
RT     phosphorites
```

phosphatides
USE   phospholipids

PHOSPHIDES [612; 2,892]
```
BT1    phosphorus compounds
BT1    pnictides
NT1    aluminium phosphides
NT1    berkelium phosphides
NT1    beryllium phosphides
NT1    boron phosphides
NT1    cadmium phosphides
NT1    cerium phosphides
NT1    cobalt phosphides
NT1    copper phosphides
NT1    curium phosphides
NT1    dysprosium phosphides
NT1    erbium phosphides
NT1    europium phosphides
NT1    gadolinium phosphides
NT1    gallium phosphides
NT1    germanium phosphides
NT1    hafnium phosphides
NT1    holmium phosphides
NT1    indium phosphides
NT1    iron phosphides
NT1    lanthanum phosphides
NT1    lithium phosphides
NT1    manganese phosphides
NT1    molybdenum phosphides
NT1    neptunium phosphides
NT1    nickel phosphides
NT1    niobium phosphides
NT1    osmium phosphides
NT1    palladium phosphides
NT1    platinum phosphides
NT1    plutonium phosphides
NT1    potassium phosphides
NT1    praseodymium phosphides
NT1    rhodium phosphides
NT1    ruthenium phosphides
NT1    samarium phosphides
NT1    scandium phosphides
NT1    silicon phosphides
NT1    tantalum phosphides
NT1    terbium phosphides
NT1    thorium phosphides
NT1    thulium phosphides
NT1    tin phosphides
NT1    titanium phosphides
NT1    tungsten phosphides
NT1    uranium phosphides
NT1    vanadium phosphides
NT1    yttrium phosphides
NT1    zinc phosphides
NT1    zirconium phosphides
RT     phosphorus additions
```

PHOSPHINES [486; 486]
```
BT1    phosphorus compounds
RT     organic phosphorus compounds
RT     pest control
RT     pesticides
RT     phosphorus hydrides
RT     tpo
```

PHOSPHINIC ACID ESTERS [56; 56]
```
BT1    esters
BT2      organic compounds
BT1    organic phosphorus compounds
BT2      organic compounds
RT     organophosphinic acids
```

phosphites
(Specific phosphites should be indexed by coordination of a descriptor of the form (CATION) COMPOUNDS and PHOSPHOROUS ACID.)
USE   phosphorous acid

PHOSPHOCREATINE [79; 79]
```
BT1    amino acids
BT2      carboxylic acids
BT3        organic acids
BT4          organic compounds
BT1    organic phosphorus compounds
BT2      organic compounds
RT     creatine
```

PHOSPHODIESTERASES [81; 499]
Dec 86
```
BT1    esterases
BT2      hydrolases
BT3        enzymes
BT4          organic compounds
NT1    nucleases
NT2      dna-ase
NT2      endonucleases
NT2      rna-ase
```

PHOSPHOHYDROLASES [10; 585]
Sep 85
```
BT1    acid anhydrases
BT2      hydrolases
BT3        enzymes
BT4          organic compounds
NT1    atp-ase
```

PHOSPHOLIPIDS [1,315; 1,469]
```
UF     phosphatides
BT1    esters
BT2      organic compounds
BT1    lipids
BT2      organic compounds
BT1    organic phosphorus compounds
BT2      organic compounds
NT1    cardiolipin
NT1    cephalins
NT1    lecithins
NT1    sphingomyelins
```

phosphomolybdic acid
USE   molybdophosphoric acid

PHOSPHONATES [1,000; 1,000] Feb 76
(For salts only; see also PHOSPHONIC ACID ESTERS.)
```
BT1    organic phosphorus compounds
BT2      organic compounds
```

PHOSPHONIC ACID ESTERS [500; 549]
```
SF     dehpa
BT1    esters
BT2      organic compounds
BT1    organic phosphorus compounds
BT2      organic compounds
NT1    dampa
NT1    dhdecmp
```

PHOSPHORESCENCE [327; 327]
```
BT1    luminescence
BT2      photon emission
BT3        emission
RT     afterglow
RT     phosphors
```

PHOSPHORIC ACID [1,310; 1,312]
```
UF     hydrogen phosphates
BT1    inorganic acids
BT2      hydrogen compounds
BT2      inorganic compounds
BT1    oxygen compounds
BT1    phosphorus compounds
RT     molybdophosphoric acid
RT     phosphates
RT     tungstophosphoric acid
```

PHOSPHORIC ACID ESTERS [656; 3,827]
```
BT1    esters
BT2      organic compounds
BT1    organic phosphorus compounds
BT2      organic compounds
NT1    butyl phosphates
NT2      dbp
NT2      mbp
NT2      tbp
NT1    hdehp
NT1    mdpa
NT1    phytic acid
NT1    tcp
```

PHOSPHORITES [137; 137]
```
BT1    phosphate rocks
BT2      sedimentary rocks
BT3        rocks
RT     phosphate minerals
RT     phosphates
```

PHOSPHOROUS ACID [131; 131]
```
UF     phosphites
BT1    inorganic acids
BT2      hydrogen compounds
BT2      inorganic compounds
BT1    oxygen compounds
BT1    phosphorus compounds
```

PHOSPHORS [1,145; 6,422]
```
UF     fluors
UF     scintillators
NT1    glass scintillators
NT1    inorganic phosphors
NT1    liquid scintillators
NT1    organic crystal phosphors
NT1    plastic scintillators
RT     luminescent chambers
RT     luminescent dosemeters
RT     phosphorescence
RT     scintillation counters
```

PHOSPHORUS [2,131; 2,131]
```
BT1    nonmetals
BT2      elements
```

PHOSPHORUS ADDITIONS [529; 529]
```
RT     phosphides
```

PHOSPHORUS BROMIDES [12; 12]
```
BT1    bromides
BT2      bromine compounds
BT3        halogen compounds
BT2      halides
BT3        halogen compounds
BT1    phosphorus compounds
```

PHOSPHORUS CHLORIDES [74; 74]
```
BT1    chlorides
BT2      chlorine compounds
BT3        halogen compounds
BT2      halides
BT3        halogen compounds
BT1    phosphorus compounds
```

PHOSPHORUS COMPLEXES [86; 86]
```
BT1    complexes
```

PHOSPHORUS COMPOUNDS [847; 11,877]
```
NT1    hypophosphorous acid
NT1    molybdophosphates
NT1    molybdophosphoric acid
*NT1   phosphates
```

* NT1   phosphides
  NT1   phosphines
  NT1   phosphoric acid
  NT1   phosphorous acid
  NT1   phosphorus bromides
  NT1   phosphorus chlorides
  NT1   phosphorus fluorides
  NT1   phosphorus hydrides
  NT1   phosphorus iodides
  NT1   phosphorus nitrides
  NT1   phosphorus oxides
  NT1   phosphorus sulfides
  NT1   pyrophosphates
  NT1   tungstophosphates
  NT1   tungstophosphoric acid
  RT   organic phosphorus compounds

PHOSPHORUS FLUORIDES [92; 92]
  BT1   fluorides
    BT2   fluorine compounds
      BT3   halogen compounds
    BT2   halides
      BT3   halogen compounds
  BT1   phosphorus compounds

PHOSPHORUS HYDRIDES [48; 48]
  BT1   hydrides
    BT2   hydrogen compounds
  BT1   phosphorus compounds
  RT   phosphines

PHOSPHORUS IODIDES [12; 12]
  BT1   iodides
    BT2   halides
      BT3   halogen compounds
    BT2   iodine compounds
      BT3   halogen compounds
  BT1   phosphorus compounds

PHOSPHORUS IONS [676; 676]
  BT1   ions
    BT2   charged particles

PHOSPHORUS ISOTOPES [190; 7,192]
  NT1   phosphorus 21
  NT1   phosphorus 24
  NT1   phosphorus 26
  NT1   phosphorus 27
  NT1   phosphorus 28
  NT1   phosphorus 29
  NT1   phosphorus 30
  NT1   phosphorus 31
  NT1   phosphorus 32
  NT1   phosphorus 33
  NT1   phosphorus 34
  NT1   phosphorus 35
  NT1   phosphorus 36
  NT1   phosphorus 37
  NT1   phosphorus 38
  NT1   phosphorus 39
  NT1   phosphorus 40
  NT1   phosphorus 41
  NT1   phosphorus 42
  NT1   phosphorus 43
  NT1   phosphorus 44
  NT1   phosphorus 45
  NT1   phosphorus 46

PHOSPHORUS NITRIDES [10; 10]
  BT1   nitrides
    BT2   nitrogen compounds
    BT2   pnictides
  BT1   phosphorus compounds

PHOSPHORUS OXIDES [348; 348]
  BT1   oxides
    BT2   chalcogenides
    BT2   oxygen compounds
  BT1   phosphorus compounds

PHOSPHORUS SULFIDES [26; 26]
  BT1   phosphorus compounds
  BT1   sulfides
    BT2   chalcogenides
    BT2   sulfur compounds

PHOSPHORUS 21 [2; 2]
  BT1   light nuclei
    BT2   nuclei
  BT1   odd-even nuclei
    BT2   nuclei
  BT1   phosphorus isotopes

PHOSPHORUS 24 [3; 3] *Feb 78*
  BT1   light nuclei
    BT2   nuclei
  BT1   odd-odd nuclei
    BT2   nuclei
  BT1   phosphorus isotopes

PHOSPHORUS 26 [15; 15] *Sep 83*
  BT1   beta-plus decay radioisotopes
    BT2   beta decay radioisotopes
      BT3   radioisotopes
        BT4   isotopes
  BT1   light nuclei
    BT2   nuclei
  BT1   millisec living radioisotopes
    BT2   radioisotopes
      BT3   isotopes
  BT1   odd-odd nuclei
    BT2   nuclei
  BT1   phosphorus isotopes

PHOSPHORUS 27 [3; 3] *Apr 86*
  BT1   light nuclei
    BT2   nuclei
  BT1   millisec living radioisotopes
    BT2   radioisotopes
      BT3   isotopes
  BT1   odd-even nuclei
    BT2   nuclei
  BT1   phosphorus isotopes

PHOSPHORUS 28 [53; 53]
  BT1   beta-plus decay radioisotopes
    BT2   beta decay radioisotopes
      BT3   radioisotopes
        BT4   isotopes
  BT1   light nuclei
    BT2   nuclei
  BT1   millisec living radioisotopes
    BT2   radioisotopes
      BT3   isotopes
  BT1   odd-odd nuclei
    BT2   nuclei
  BT1   phosphorus isotopes

PHOSPHORUS 29 [123; 123]
  BT1   beta-plus decay radioisotopes
    BT2   beta decay radioisotopes
      BT3   radioisotopes
        BT4   isotopes
  BT1   light nuclei
    BT2   nuclei
  BT1   odd-even nuclei
    BT2   nuclei
  BT1   phosphorus isotopes
  BT1   seconds living radioisotopes
    BT2   radioisotopes
      BT3   isotopes

PHOSPHORUS 30 [187; 187]
  BT1   beta-plus decay radioisotopes
    BT2   beta decay radioisotopes
      BT3   radioisotopes
        BT4   isotopes
  BT1   light nuclei
    BT2   nuclei
  BT1   minutes living radioisotopes
    BT2   radioisotopes
      BT3   isotopes
  BT1   odd-odd nuclei
    BT2   nuclei
  BT1   phosphorus isotopes

PHOSPHORUS 31 [1,555; 1,555]
  BT1   light nuclei
    BT2   nuclei
  BT1   odd-even nuclei
    BT2   nuclei
  BT1   phosphorus isotopes
  BT1   stable isotopes
    BT2   isotopes

PHOSPHORUS 31 BEAMS [37; 37]
Sep 83
  BT1   ion beams
    BT2   beams

PHOSPHORUS 31 REACTIONS [20; 20]
Apr 78
  BT1   heavy ion reactions
    BT2   nuclear reactions

PHOSPHORUS 31 TARGET [228; 228]
  BT1   targets

PHOSPHORUS 32 [5,020; 5,020]
  BT1   beta-minus decay radioisotopes
    BT2   beta decay radioisotopes
      BT3   radioisotopes
        BT4   isotopes
  BT1   days living radioisotopes
    BT2   radioisotopes
      BT3   isotopes
  BT1   light nuclei
    BT2   nuclei
  BT1   odd-odd nuclei
    BT2   nuclei
  BT1   phosphorus isotopes

PHOSPHORUS 32 TARGET [5; 5]
  BT1   targets

PHOSPHORUS 33 [152; 152]
  BT1   beta-minus decay radioisotopes
    BT2   beta decay radioisotopes
      BT3   radioisotopes
        BT4   isotopes
  BT1   days living radioisotopes
    BT2   radioisotopes
      BT3   isotopes
  BT1   light nuclei
    BT2   nuclei
  BT1   odd-even nuclei
    BT2   nuclei
  BT1   phosphorus isotopes

PHOSPHORUS 34 [18; 18]
  BT1   beta-minus decay radioisotopes
    BT2   beta decay radioisotopes
      BT3   radioisotopes
        BT4   isotopes
  BT1   light nuclei
    BT2   nuclei
  BT1   odd-odd nuclei
    BT2   nuclei
  BT1   phosphorus isotopes
  BT1   seconds living radioisotopes
    BT2   radioisotopes
      BT3   isotopes

PHOSPHORUS 35 [31; 31]
  BT1   beta-minus decay radioisotopes
    BT2   beta decay radioisotopes
      BT3   radioisotopes
        BT4   isotopes
  BT1   light nuclei
    BT2   nuclei
  BT1   odd-even nuclei
    BT2   nuclei
  BT1   phosphorus isotopes
  BT1   seconds living radioisotopes
    BT2   radioisotopes
      BT3   isotopes

PHOSPHORUS 36 [23; 23]
  BT1   beta-minus decay radioisotopes
    BT2   beta decay radioisotopes
      BT3   radioisotopes
        BT4   isotopes
  BT1   light nuclei
    BT2   nuclei
  BT1   odd-odd nuclei
    BT2   nuclei
  BT1   phosphorus isotopes
  BT1   seconds living radioisotopes
    BT2   radioisotopes
      BT3   isotopes

PHOSPHORUS 37 [19; 19]
- BT1 beta-minus decay radioisotopes
- BT2 beta decay radioisotopes
- BT3 radioisotopes
- BT4 isotopes
- BT1 light nuclei
- BT2 nuclei
- BT1 odd-even nuclei
- BT2 nuclei
- BT1 phosphorus isotopes
- BT1 seconds living radioisotopes
- BT2 radioisotopes
- BT3 isotopes

PHOSPHORUS 38 [9; 9]
- BT1 beta-minus decay radioisotopes
- BT2 beta decay radioisotopes
- BT3 radioisotopes
- BT4 isotopes
- BT1 light nuclei
- BT2 nuclei
- BT1 millisec living radioisotopes
- BT2 radioisotopes
- BT3 isotopes
- BT1 odd-odd nuclei
- BT2 nuclei
- BT1 phosphorus isotopes

PHOSPHORUS 39 [6; 6] *Oct 77*
- BT1 light nuclei
- BT2 nuclei
- BT1 odd-even nuclei
- BT2 nuclei
- BT1 phosphorus isotopes

PHOSPHORUS 40 [7; 7] *Sep 79*
- BT1 beta-minus decay radioisotopes
- BT2 beta decay radioisotopes
- BT3 radioisotopes
- BT4 isotopes
- BT1 light nuclei
- BT2 nuclei
- BT1 odd-odd nuclei
- BT2 nuclei
- BT1 phosphorus isotopes

PHOSPHORUS 41 [7; 7] *Jul 80*
- BT1 beta-minus decay radioisotopes
- BT2 beta decay radioisotopes
- BT3 radioisotopes
- BT4 isotopes
- BT1 intermediate mass nuclei
- BT2 nuclei
- BT1 odd-even nuclei
- BT2 nuclei
- BT1 phosphorus isotopes

PHOSPHORUS 42 [7; 7] *Jul 80*
- BT1 beta-minus decay radioisotopes
- BT2 beta decay radioisotopes
- BT3 radioisotopes
- BT4 isotopes
- BT1 intermediate mass nuclei
- BT2 nuclei
- BT1 odd-odd nuclei
- BT2 nuclei
- BT1 phosphorus isotopes

PHOSPHORUS 43 [2; 2] *Sep 89*
- BT1 intermediate mass nuclei
- BT2 nuclei
- BT1 odd-even nuclei
- BT2 nuclei
- BT1 phosphorus isotopes

PHOSPHORUS 44 [2; 2] *Sep 89*
- BT1 intermediate mass nuclei
- BT2 nuclei
- BT1 odd-odd nuclei
- BT2 nuclei
- BT1 phosphorus isotopes

PHOSPHORUS 45 [0; 0] *Apr 90*
- BT1 intermediate mass nuclei
- BT2 nuclei
- BT1 odd-even nuclei
- BT2 nuclei
- BT1 phosphorus isotopes

PHOSPHORUS 46 [0; 0] *Apr 90*
- BT1 intermediate mass nuclei
- BT2 nuclei
- BT1 odd-odd nuclei
- BT2 nuclei
- BT1 phosphorus isotopes

PHOSPHORUS-GROUP TRANSFERASES [9; 1,220] *Dec 86*
- BT1 transferases
- BT2 enzymes
- BT3 organic compounds
- NT1 nucleotidyltransferases
- NT2 polymerases
- NT3 dna polymerases
- NT3 rna polymerases
- NT1 phosphotransferases
- NT2 hexokinase

phosphorylases
- USE phosphotransferases

PHOSPHORYLATION [1,000; 1,000]
- BT1 chemical reactions

PHOSPHOTRANSFERASES [1,150; 1,654]
- UF *kinases (phosphotransferases)*
- UF *phosphorylases*
- BT1 phosphorus-group transferases
- BT2 transferases
- BT3 enzymes
- BT4 organic compounds
- NT1 hexokinase

phosphotungstic acid
- USE tungstophosphoric acid

phosphowolframic acid
- USE tungstophosphoric acid

PHOSPHURANYLITE [3; 3]
- BT1 phosphate minerals
- BT2 minerals
- BT1 uranium minerals
- BT2 radioactive minerals
- BT3 minerals
- BT3 radioactive materials
- BT4 materials
- RT uranium phosphates

PHOTOACOUSTIC EFFECT [140; 140] *Sep 80*
- RT phonons
- RT photoacoustic spectrometers
- RT photoacoustic spectroscopy
- RT radiation effects

PHOTOACOUSTIC SPECTROMETERS [65; 65] *Feb 78*
- UF *optoacoustic cells*
- UF *spectrophones*
- BT1 infrared spectrometers
- BT2 spectrometers
- BT3 measuring instruments
- RT absorption spectroscopy
- RT gas analysis
- RT photoacoustic effect
- RT photoacoustic spectroscopy

PHOTOACOUSTIC SPECTROSCOPY [126; 126] *Apr 86*
- BT1 spectroscopy
- RT photoacoustic effect
- RT photoacoustic spectrometers

PHOTOCATHODES [409; 409] *Nov 80*
- BT1 cathodes
- BT2 electrodes
- RT photocurrents
- RT photoelectric effect
- RT photoemission
- RT quantum efficiency

photocells
- USE photoelectric cells

PHOTOCHEMISTRY [2,302; 2,302]
- BT1 chemistry
- RT photolysis
- RT photosynthesis
- RT radiation chemistry
- RT reaction intermediates

PHOTOCONDUCTIVE CELLS [13; 13]
- BT1 photoelectric cells
- BT2 direct energy converters
- RT photoconductivity

PHOTOCONDUCTIVITY [1,746; 1,746]
- BT1 electric conductivity
- BT2 electrical properties
- BT3 physical properties
- RT photoconductive cells
- RT photoconductors
- RT photocurrents
- RT traps

PHOTOCONDUCTORS [124; 124]
- RT electric conductors
- RT photoconductivity
- RT photodetectors
- RT photoelectric cells
- RT semiconductor materials

PHOTOCURRENTS [168; 168] *Mar 85*
- BT1 electric currents
- BT2 currents
- RT photocathodes
- RT photoconductivity
- RT photodiodes
- RT photoelectric cells
- RT photoelectric effect

PHOTODETECTORS [483; 483]
- RT photoconductors
- RT photodiodes
- RT photoelectric cells
- RT phototransistors

PHOTODIODES [805; 805]
- BT1 semiconductor diodes
- BT2 semiconductor devices
- RT photocurrents
- RT photodetectors
- RT photoelectric cells
- RT phototransistors

photodisintegration
- USE photonuclear reactions

PHOTOELASTICITY [164; 164]
- BT1 elasticity
- BT2 mechanical properties
- RT homalite
- RT materials testing
- RT stress analysis

PHOTOELECTRIC CELLS [150; 305]
- UF *photocells*
- BT1 direct energy converters
- NT1 photoconductive cells
- NT1 photovoltaic cells
- RT image tubes
- RT photoconductors
- RT photocurrents
- RT photodetectors
- RT photodiodes
- RT photomultipliers
- RT phototransistors

PHOTOELECTRIC CELLS

 RT phototubes
 RT semiconductor devices
 RT solar cells

PHOTOELECTRIC EFFECT [728; 1,012]
 UF+ *photoelectromagnetic effect*
 UF+ *photomagnetoelectric effect*
 NT1 photoelectric emission
 NT1 photovoltaic effect
 RT fowler-nordheim theory
 RT photocathodes
 RT photocurrents

PHOTOELECTRIC EMISSION
[543; 543]
 BT1 electron emission
  BT2 emission
 BT1 photoelectric effect
 RT photoelectron counting
 RT quantum efficiency

photoelectromagnetic effect
 USE magnetic fields
 AND photoelectric effect

PHOTOELECTRON COUNTING
[162; 162] *Aug 76*
 BT1 counting techniques
 RT photoelectric emission
 RT photons

PHOTOELECTRON SPECTROSCOPY
[2,940; 2,940]
 BT1 electron spectroscopy
  BT2 spectroscopy
 RT electronic structure
 RT molecular structure

PHOTOEMISSION [1,652; 1,652]
(Photon-induced emission)
 BT1 secondary emission
  BT2 emission
 RT photocathodes

PHOTOFISSION [675; 675]
 BT1 fission
  BT2 nuclear reactions
 BT1 photonuclear reactions
  BT2 nuclear reactions

PHOTOGRAPHIC EMULSIONS
[276; 276]
 RT latent images
 RT photographic film dosemeters

PHOTOGRAPHIC FILM DETECTORS
[598; 598]
 UF *track detectors (photographic)*
 BT1 radiation detectors
  BT2 measuring instruments
 RT neutron-photon converters
 RT nuclear emulsions
 RT photographic film dosemeters
 RT photographic films

PHOTOGRAPHIC FILM DOSEMETERS [729; 729]
 UF *film badges*
 UF *film dosemeters*
 BT1 dosemeters
  BT2 measuring instruments
 RT film dosimetry
 RT nuclear emulsions
 RT photographic emulsions
 RT photographic film detectors

PHOTOGRAPHIC FILMS [1,553; 1,553]
 RT image scanners
 RT images
 RT latent images
 RT nuclear emulsions
 RT photographic film detectors

photographs
 USE images

PHOTOGRAPHY [1,300; 2,467]
 NT1 cinematography
 NT1 photomicrography
 NT1 schlieren method
 NT1 streak photography
 NT1 ultrahigh-speed photography
 RT cameras
 RT developers
 RT holography
 RT image processing
 RT xerography

PHOTOIONIZATION [3,979; 3,979]
 BT1 ionization

PHOTOLUMINESCENCE [2,017; 2,017]
 BT1 luminescence
  BT2 photon emission
   BT3 emission

PHOTOLYSIS [2,159; 2,159]
 BT1 decomposition
  BT2 chemical reactions
 RT dissociation
 RT photochemistry
 RT radiolysis
 RT traps

photomagnetic effect
 USE magnetic susceptibility
 AND visible radiation

photomagnetoelectric effect
 USE magnetic fields
 AND photoelectric effect

PHOTOMETERS [324; 882]
 BT1 measuring instruments
 NT1 densitometers
 RT photometry

PHOTOMETRY [5,961; 5,961]
 RT densitometers
 RT photometers
 RT spectrophotometry
 RT spectroscopy

PHOTOMICROGRAPHY [400; 400]
 BT1 photography
 RT ceramography
 RT fractography
 RT metallography
 RT microscopy

PHOTOMULTIPLIERS [2,335; 2,335]
 BT1 phototubes
 RT electron multipliers
 RT photoelectric cells
 RT scintillation counters

PHOTON ACTIVATION ANALYSIS
[276; 276] *Nov 78*
 UF *analysis (photon activation)*
 BT1 activation analysis
  BT2 nondestructive analysis
   BT3 chemical analysis

PHOTON BEAMS [5,397; 5,397]
 BT1 beams
 RT light sources
 RT particle beams
 RT photons
 RT visible radiation

PHOTON COLLISIONS [521; 2,057]
 BT1 collisions
 NT1 photon-atom collisions
 NT1 photon-electron collisions
 NT1 photon-ion collisions
 NT1 photon-molecule collisions

PHOTON-ELECTRON INTERACTIONS

 NT1 photon-positron collisions

PHOTON EMISSION [1,473; 8,263]
(Emission of photons)
 BT1 emission
 NT1 luminescence
  NT2 cathodoluminescence
  NT2 chemiluminescence
   NT3 bioluminescence
  NT2 electroluminescence
  NT2 fluorescence
   NT3 resonance fluorescence
  NT2 lyoluminescence
  NT2 phosphorescence
  NT2 photoluminescence
  NT2 radioluminescence
   NT3 radiothermoluminescence
  NT2 thermoluminescence
   NT3 radiothermoluminescence
 NT1 superradiance
 RT multi-photon processes
 RT secondary emission

PHOTON EMISSION SCANNING
[28; 28] *Apr 86*
 BT1 diagnostic techniques
 RT emission computed tomography
 RT photons

PHOTON TEMPERATURE [18; 18]
 UF *temperature (photon)*
 RT energy
 RT photons

PHOTON TRANSMISSION SCANNING
[202; 406]
 UF *gamma transmission scanning*
 UF *x-ray transmission scanning*
 BT1 diagnostic techniques
 RT single photon ect

PHOTON TRANSPORT [851; 851]
 UF *transport (gamma)*
 UF *transport (photon)*
 BT1 neutral-particle transport
  BT2 radiation transport
 RT gamma transport theory

PHOTON-ATOM COLLISIONS
[877; 877]
 BT1 atom collisions
  BT2 collisions
 BT1 photon collisions
  BT2 collisions

PHOTON-BARYON INTERACTIONS
[10; 1,618]
 BT1 photon-hadron interactions
  BT2 electromagnetic interactions
   BT3 basic interactions
   BT3 interactions
  BT2 particle interactions
   BT3 interactions
 NT1 photon-hyperon interactions
 NT1 photon-nucleon interactions
  NT2 photon-neutron interactions
  NT2 photon-proton interactions

photon-deuteron interactions
 USE deuterium target
 AND photonuclear reactions

PHOTON-ELECTRON COLLISIONS
[105; 105]
 BT1 electron collisions
  BT2 collisions
 BT1 photon collisions
  BT2 collisions

PHOTON-ELECTRON INTERACTIONS
[432; 432]
 BT1 photon-lepton interactions
  BT2 particle interactions
   BT3 interactions

PHOTON-HADRON INTERACTIONS
[102; 1,784]
- BT1 electromagnetic interactions
- BT2 basic interactions
- BT2 interactions
- BT1 particle interactions
- BT2 interactions
- NT1 photon-baryon interactions
- NT2 photon-hyperon interactions
- NT2 photon-nucleon interactions
- NT3 photon-neutron interactions
- NT3 photon-proton interactions
- NT1 photon-meson interactions

PHOTON-HYPERON INTERACTIONS
[5; 5]
- BT1 photon-baryon interactions
- BT2 photon-hadron interactions
- BT3 electromagnetic interactions
- BT4 basic interactions
- BT4 interactions
- BT3 particle interactions
- BT4 interactions

PHOTON-ION COLLISIONS [203; 203]
- BT1 ion collisions
- BT2 collisions
- BT1 photon collisions
- BT2 collisions

PHOTON-LEPTON INTERACTIONS
[23; 495]
- BT1 particle interactions
- BT2 interactions
- NT1 photon-electron interactions
- NT1 photon-muon interactions
- NT1 photon-neutrino interactions
- RT electromagnetic interactions
- RT weak interactions

PHOTON-MESON INTERACTIONS
[80; 80]
- BT1 photon-hadron interactions
- BT2 electromagnetic interactions
- BT3 basic interactions
- BT3 interactions
- BT2 particle interactions
- BT3 interactions

PHOTON-MOLECULE COLLISIONS
[469; 469]
- BT1 molecule collisions
- BT2 collisions
- BT1 photon collisions
- BT2 collisions

PHOTON-MUON INTERACTIONS
[4; 4]
- BT1 photon-lepton interactions
- BT2 particle interactions
- BT3 interactions

PHOTON-NEUTRINO INTERACTIONS
[38; 38]
- BT1 photon-lepton interactions
- BT2 particle interactions
- BT3 interactions

PHOTON-NEUTRON INTERACTIONS
[171; 171]
- BT1 photon-nucleon interactions
- BT2 photon-baryon interactions
- BT3 photon-hadron interactions
- BT4 electromagnetic interactions
- BT5 basic interactions
- BT5 interactions
- BT4 particle interactions
- BT5 interactions

PHOTON-NUCLEON INTERACTIONS
[516; 1,604]
- BT1 photon-baryon interactions
- BT2 photon-hadron interactions
- BT3 electromagnetic interactions
- BT4 basic interactions
- BT4 interactions
- BT3 particle interactions
- BT4 interactions
- NT1 photon-neutron interactions
- NT1 photon-proton interactions

photon-photon collisions
- USE photon-photon interactions

PHOTON-PHOTON INTERACTIONS
[1,357; 1,357]
- UF *photon-photon collisions*
- BT1 electromagnetic interactions
- BT2 basic interactions
- BT2 interactions
- BT1 particle interactions
- BT2 interactions
- RT equivalent-photon approximatio

PHOTON-POSITRON COLLISIONS
[12; 12]
- BT1 photon collisions
- BT2 collisions
- BT1 positron collisions
- BT2 collisions

PHOTON-PROTON INTERACTIONS
[996; 996]
- BT1 photon-nucleon interactions
- BT2 photon-baryon interactions
- BT3 photon-hadron interactions
- BT4 electromagnetic interactions
- BT5 basic interactions
- BT5 interactions
- BT4 particle interactions
- BT5 interactions

PHOTONEUTRONS [1,032; 1,032]
- BT1 neutrons
- BT2 nucleons
- BT3 baryons
- BT4 fermions
- BT4 hadrons
- BT5 elementary particles
- BT1 photonucleons
- BT2 nucleons
- BT3 baryons
- BT4 fermions
- BT4 hadrons
- BT5 elementary particles
- RT peierls method
- RT photonuclear reactions

PHOTONS [14,458; 15,044]
- BT1 bosons
- BT1 massless particles
- BT2 elementary particles
- NT1 cosmic photons
- RT delayed gamma radiation
- RT electromagnetic radiation
- RT gamma radiation
- RT photoelectron counting
- RT photon beams
- RT photon emission scanning
- RT photon temperature
- RT prompt gamma radiation
- RT single photon ect
- RT tagged photon method
- RT x radiation

PHOTONUCLEAR REACTIONS
[5,869; 6,482]
- UF *photodisintegration*
- UF+ *photon-deuteron interactions*
- BT1 nuclear reactions
- NT1 photofission
- RT giant resonance
- RT giant resonance model
- RT photoneutrons
- RT photonucleons
- RT photoproduction
- RT photoprotons

PHOTONUCLEONS [41; 1,066]
- BT1 nucleons
- BT2 baryons
- BT3 fermions
- BT3 hadrons
- BT4 elementary particles
- NT1 photoneutrons
- NT1 photoprotons
- RT photonuclear reactions

PHOTOPRODUCTION [4,438; 4,523]
- BT1 electromagnetic interactions
- BT2 basic interactions
- BT2 interactions
- BT1 particle interactions
- BT2 interactions
- BT1 particle production
- NT1 primakoff effect
- RT drell model
- RT electric born model
- RT kroll-ruderman theorem
- RT levinger-bethe theory
- RT panofsky ratio
- RT photonuclear reactions

PHOTOPROTONS [407; 407]
- BT1 photonucleons
- BT2 nucleons
- BT3 baryons
- BT4 fermions
- BT4 hadrons
- BT5 elementary particles
- BT1 protons
- BT2 hydrogen ions 1 plus
- BT3 cations
- BT4 ions
- BT5 charged particles
- BT3 hydrogen ions
- BT4 ions
- BT5 charged particles
- BT2 nucleons
- BT3 baryons
- BT4 fermions
- BT4 hadrons
- BT5 elementary particles
- RT photonuclear reactions

PHOTOREACTIVATION [558; 558]
- UF+ *pre*
- BT1 biological repair
- BT2 biological recovery
- RT microorganisms
- RT molecular structure
- RT nucleic acids
- RT radiation injuries
- RT ultrastructural changes
- RT ultraviolet radiation
- RT visible radiation

PHOTORESISTORS [82; 82]
- BT1 resistors
- BT2 electrical equipment
- BT3 equipment

PHOTOSENSITIVITY [1,058; 1,058]
- BT1 sensitivity

PHOTOSPHERE [1,437; 1,437]
- BT1 solar atmosphere
- BT2 stellar atmospheres
- BT3 atmospheres
- RT chromosphere
- RT faculae
- RT solar granulation
- RT sun
- RT sunspots

PHOTOSYNTHESIS [994; 994]
- BT1 chemical reactions
- BT1 synthesis
- RT biosynthesis
- RT carbon cycle
- RT carbon dioxide fixation
- RT chlorophyll
- RT chloroplasts
- RT leaves
- RT photochemistry

PHOTOTRANSISTORS [38; 38]
  BT1   transistors
    BT2   semiconductor devices
  RT   photodetectors
  RT   photodiodes
  RT   photoelectric cells

PHOTOTUBES [78; 2,401]
  NT1   photomultipliers
  RT   electron tubes
  RT   photoelectric cells

PHOTOVOLTAIC CELLS [145; 145]
  BT1   photoelectric cells
    BT2   direct energy converters
  RT   photovoltaic conversion
  RT   photovoltaic effect
  RT   semiconductor diodes
  RT   solar cells

PHOTOVOLTAIC CONVERSION
[65; 65] *Dec 82*
  BT1   direct energy conversion
    BT2   energy conversion
      BT3   conversion
  RT   photovoltaic cells

PHOTOVOLTAIC EFFECT [188; 188]
  BT1   photoelectric effect
  RT   energy conversion
  RT   photovoltaic cells

photovoltaic power plants
  USE   solar power plants

PHTHALATES [133; 133]
  BT1   carboxylic acid salts
  RT   phthalic acid esters

PHTHALAZINES [6; 6]
  BT1   pyridazines
    BT2   azines
      BT3   heterocyclic compounds
        BT4   organic compounds
      BT3   organic nitrogen compounds
        BT4   organic compounds

PHTHALIC ACID [89; 89]
  UF   *benzenedicarboxylic acid-ortho*
  UF   *naphthalic acid*
  BT1   dicarboxylic acids
    BT2   carboxylic acids
      BT3   organic acids
        BT4   organic compounds
  RT   bromosulfophthalein
  RT   eosin
  RT   fluorescein
  RT   phenolphthalein
  RT   rhodamines
  RT   rose bengal

PHTHALIC ACID ESTERS [66; 66]
  BT1   esters
    BT2   organic compounds
  RT   phthalates

PHTHALOCYANINES [238; 238]
  BT1   dyes
  BT1   heterocyclic compounds
    BT2   organic compounds
  RT   copper complexes

PHWR TYPE REACTORS [640; 2,045]
  UF   *pressur. heavy water cool./mod*
  BT1   heavy water cooled reactors
    BT2   reactors
  BT1   heavy water moderated reactors
    BT2   reactors
  NT1   agesta reactor
  NT1   atucha reactor
  NT1   atucha-2 reactor
  NT1   bruce-1 reactor
  NT1   bruce-2 reactor
  NT1   bruce-3 reactor
  NT1   bruce-4 reactor
  NT1   bruce-5 reactor
  NT1   bruce-6 reactor
  NT1   bruce-7 reactor
  NT1   bruce-8 reactor
  NT1   cernavoda-1 reactor
  NT1   cordoba reactor
  NT1   cvtr reactor
  NT1   darlington-1 reactor
  NT1   darlington-2 reactor
  NT1   darlington-3 reactor
  NT1   darlington-4 reactor
  NT1   douglas point ontario reactor
  NT1   gentilly-2 reactor
  NT1   kalpakkam-1 reactor
  NT1   kalpakkam-2 reactor
  NT1   kanupp reactor
  NT1   mzfr reactor
  NT1   narora-1 reactor
  NT1   narora-2 reactor
  NT1   npd reactor
  NT1   pickering-1 reactor
  NT1   pickering-2 reactor
  NT1   pickering-3 reactor
  NT1   pickering-4 reactor
  NT1   pickering-5 reactor
  NT1   pickering-6 reactor
  NT1   pickering-7 reactor
  NT1   pickering-8 reactor
  NT1   point lepreau-1 reactor
  NT1   point lepreau-2 reactor
  NT1   rajasthan-1 reactor
  NT1   rajasthan-2 reactor
  NT1   wolsung-1 reactor
  RT   power reactors

PHYCOCYANIN [4; 4]
  BT1   pigments

PHYCOMYCES [8; 8]
  BT1   fungi
    BT2   plants

phys protec nucl mater, conv
  USE   cppnm

phys.-tech. res. r. moscow
  USE   rpt reactor

PHYSARUM [32; 32]
  BT1   fungi
    BT2   plants

PHYSICAL CHEMISTRY [88; 88]
Apr 86
  BT1   chemistry
  RT   phase transformations

physical constants testing r.
  USE   pctr reactor

physical effort
  USE   exercise

PHYSICAL METALLURGY [160; 160]
Jul 77
  BT1   metallurgy
  RT   crystal structure
  RT   mechanical properties
  RT   mechanics
  RT   physical properties
  RT   thermodynamics

§ **PHYSICAL PROPERTIES**
[4,447; 133,022]
  NT1   density
  NT1   electrical properties
    NT2   capacitance
    NT2   dielectric properties
      NT3   kerr effect
      NT3   permittivity
    NT2   electric conductivity
      NT3   ionic conductivity
      NT3   magnetoresistance
      NT3   photoconductivity
      NT3   superconductivity
    NT2   polarizability
    NT2   thermoelectric properties
  NT1   half-thickness
  NT1   magnetic properties
    NT2   magnetic susceptibility
    NT2   magnetization
    NT2   magnetostriction
  NT1   optical properties
    NT2   brightness
    NT2   color
    NT2   emissivity
    NT2   luminosity
    NT2   opacity
    NT2   optical activity
    NT2   refractive index
  NT1   specific surface area
  NT1   thermodynamic properties
    NT2   critical pressure
    NT2   enthalpy
      NT3   absorption heat
      NT3   adsorption heat
      NT3   mixing heat
      NT3   reaction heat
        NT4   combustion heat
        NT4   dissociation heat
        NT4   formation heat
      NT3   solution heat
      NT3   transition heat
        NT4   fusion heat
        NT4   sublimation heat
        NT4   vaporization heat
    NT2   entropy
    NT2   free energy
      NT3   formation free energy
    NT2   free enthalpy
      NT3   formation free enthalpy
      NT3   oxygen potential
    NT2   partial pressure
    NT2   specific heat
      NT3   electronic specific heat
      NT3   nuclear specific heat
    NT2   stored energy
    NT2   thermal conductivity
    NT2   thermal diffusivity
    NT2   transition temperature
      NT3   boiling points
      NT3   critical temperature
      NT3   curie point
      NT3   dew point
      NT3   lambda point
      NT3   melting points
      NT3   neel temperature
    NT2   vapor pressure
  RT   physical metallurgy
  RT   surface properties
  RT   thermal degradation

PHYSICAL PROTECTION [619; 619]
Apr 76
(Concerning the need for physical protection of facilities, devices, or materials from intentional damage or theft, and proposed or existing methods for meeting those needs. See also PHYSICAL PROTECTION DEVICES.)
  RT   biointrusion
  RT   cppnm
  RT   entry control systems
  RT   human intrusion
  RT   sabotage
  RT   safeguards
  RT   secrecy protection
  RT   security
  RT   security personnel

PHYSICAL PROTECTION DEVICES
[541; 654]
  UF   *locks (security)*
  NT1   security seals
  RT   entry control systems
  RT   identification systems
  RT   motion detection systems
  RT   sabotage
  RT   safeguards
  RT   security

§ **PHYSICAL RADIATION EFFECTS**
[34,215; 36,124]
- UF *damage (radiation, physical)*
- UF *radiation damage (physical)*
- BT1 radiation effects
- NT1 atomic displacements
- NT1 interstitial helium generation
- NT1 interstitial hydrogen generati
- NT1 radiation hardening
- RT amoeba effect
- RT damaging neutron fluence
- RT equivalent fission fluence
- RT fuel densification
- RT metamict state
- RT neutronic damage functions

PHYSICS [749; 5,408] *Apr 79*
(Use only for articles of very broad coverage, such as annual reviews, text books, etc.)
- NT1 atomic physics
- NT1 high energy physics
- NT1 nuclear physics
- NT1 solid state physics

PHYSIOLOGY [2,394; 2,394]
- RT anatomy
- RT antiandrogens
- RT behavior
- RT biological functions
- RT biological stress
- RT blood circulation
- RT blood-brain barrier
- RT body temperature
- RT digestion
- RT excretion
- RT growth
- RT homeostasis
- RT hormones
- RT metabolism
- RT molecular biology
- RT reproduction
- RT respiration
- RT ripening
- RT sleep
- RT transpiration

physostigmine
USE eserine

PHYTIC ACID [95; 95]
- BT1 lipotropic factors
- BT2 drugs
- BT1 organic acids
- BT2 organic compounds
- BT1 phosphoric acid esters
- BT2 esters
- BT3 organic compounds
- BT2 organic phosphorus compounds
- BT3 organic compounds
- RT inositol

phytochrome
(Prior to August 1985 this was a valid descriptor.)
USE phytochromes

PHYTOCHROMES [31; 373]
(Prior to August 1985 the singular form was used.)
- UF *phytochrome*
- BT1 pigments
- NT1 chlorophyll

PHYTOHEMAGGLUTININ [324; 324]
- BT1 hemagglutinins
- BT2 agglutinins
- BT1 mitogens
- BT1 mucoproteins
- BT2 polysaccharides
- BT3 saccharides
- BT4 carbohydrates
- BT5 organic compounds
- BT2 proteins
- BT3 organic compounds

- RT cell proliferation
- RT lymphocytes
- RT mitosis
- RT phaseolus

phytoplankton
USE plankton

pi condensate
USE pion condensation

PI-K ATOMS [9; 9] *Nov 85*
(A charged pion and an oppositely charged kaon in a Coulomb bound state.)
- RT bound state
- RT kaons
- RT mesic atoms
- RT pions

PI-MU ATOMS [11; 11] *Feb 83*
(A charged pion and an oppositely charged muon in a Coulomb bound state.)
- RT bound state
- RT mesic atoms
- RT muonic atoms
- RT muons
- RT pions

PI-1300 MESONS [9; 9] *Dec 87*
- BT1 pseudoscalar mesons
- BT2 mesons
- BT3 bosons
- BT3 hadrons
- BT4 elementary particles

pi-1640 resonances
(Prior to December 1987 this was a valid descriptor.)
USE pi2-1680 mesons

PI-1770 MESONS [4; 4] *Dec 87*
- BT1 pseudoscalar mesons
- BT2 mesons
- BT3 bosons
- BT3 hadrons
- BT4 elementary particles

PICKERING-1 REACTOR [212; 212]
(Pickering, Ontario, Canada)
- UF *ontario phwr pickering-1 r.*
- BT1 candu type reactors
- BT2 heavy water moderated reactors
- BT3 reactors
- BT2 pressure tube reactors
- BT3 power reactors
- BT4 reactors
- BT2 thermal reactors
- BT3 reactors
- BT1 natural uranium reactors
- BT2 reactors
- BT1 phwr type reactors
- BT2 heavy water cooled reactors
- BT3 reactors
- BT2 heavy water moderated reactors
- BT3 reactors

PICKERING-2 REACTOR [174; 174]
(Pickering, Ontario, Canada)
- UF *ontario phwr pickering-2 r.*
- BT1 candu type reactors
- BT2 heavy water moderated reactors
- BT3 reactors
- BT2 pressure tube reactors
- BT3 power reactors
- BT4 reactors
- BT2 thermal reactors
- BT3 reactors
- BT1 natural uranium reactors
- BT2 reactors
- BT1 phwr type reactors
- BT2 heavy water cooled reactors
- BT3 reactors
- BT2 heavy water moderated reactors
- BT3 reactors

PICKERING-3 REACTOR [110; 110]
(Pickering, Ontario, Canada)
- UF *ontario phwr pickering-3 r.*
- BT1 candu type reactors
- BT2 heavy water moderated reactors
- BT3 reactors
- BT2 pressure tube reactors
- BT3 power reactors
- BT4 reactors
- BT2 thermal reactors
- BT3 reactors
- BT1 natural uranium reactors
- BT2 reactors
- BT1 phwr type reactors
- BT2 heavy water cooled reactors
- BT3 reactors
- BT2 heavy water moderated reactors
- BT3 reactors

PICKERING-4 REACTOR [92; 92]
(Pickering, Ontario, Canada)
- UF *ontario phwr pickering-4 r.*
- BT1 candu type reactors
- BT2 heavy water moderated reactors
- BT3 reactors
- BT2 pressure tube reactors
- BT3 power reactors
- BT4 reactors
- BT2 thermal reactors
- BT3 reactors
- BT1 natural uranium reactors
- BT2 reactors
- BT1 phwr type reactors
- BT2 heavy water cooled reactors
- BT3 reactors
- BT2 heavy water moderated reactors
- BT3 reactors

PICKERING-5 REACTOR [31; 31]
Nov 77
(Pickering, Ontario, Canada)
- UF *ontario phwr pickering-5 r.*
- BT1 candu type reactors
- BT2 heavy water moderated reactors
- BT3 reactors
- BT2 pressure tube reactors
- BT3 power reactors
- BT4 reactors
- BT2 thermal reactors
- BT3 reactors
- BT1 natural uranium reactors
- BT2 reactors
- BT1 phwr type reactors
- BT2 heavy water cooled reactors
- BT3 reactors
- BT2 heavy water moderated reactor
- BT3 reactors

PICKERING-6 REACTOR [16; 16]
Nov 77
(Pickering, Ontario, Canada)
- UF *ontario phwr pickering-6 r.*
- BT1 candu type reactors
- BT2 heavy water moderated reactor
- BT3 reactors
- BT2 pressure tube reactors
- BT3 power reactors
- BT4 reactors
- BT2 thermal reactors
- BT3 reactors
- BT1 natural uranium reactors
- BT2 reactors
- BT1 phwr type reactors
- BT2 heavy water cooled reactors
- BT3 reactors
- BT2 heavy water moderated reacto
- BT3 reactors

PICKERING-7 REACTOR [18; 18]
Nov 77
(Pickering, Ontario, Canada)
- UF *ontario phwr pickering-7 r.*
- BT1 candu type reactors
- BT2 heavy water moderated reacto
- BT3 reactors
- BT2 pressure tube reactors
- BT3 power reactors
- BT4 reactors
- BT2 thermal reactors

```
       BT3    reactors
  BT1    natural uranium reactors
       BT2    reactors
  BT1    phwr type reactors
       BT2    heavy water cooled reactors
         BT3    reactors
       BT2    heavy water moderated reactors
         BT3    reactors
```

PICKERING-8 REACTOR [19; 19]
Nov 77
(Pickering, Ontario, Canada)
```
  UF     ontario phwr pickering-8 r.
  BT1    candu type reactors
       BT2    heavy water moderated reactors
         BT3    reactors
       BT2    pressure tube reactors
         BT3    power reactors
           BT4    reactors
       BT2    thermal reactors
         BT3    reactors
  BT1    natural uranium reactors
       BT2    reactors
  BT1    phwr type reactors
       BT2    heavy water cooled reactors
         BT3    reactors
       BT2    heavy water moderated reactors
         BT3    reactors
```

picket fence
  USE   cusped geometries

PICKLING [138; 175]
  BT1   surface treatments
  NT1   corrosion pickling

PICKUP REACTIONS [3,113; 3,113]
  BT1   transfer reactions
       BT2   direct reactions
         BT3   nuclear reactions

PICO AMP BEAM CURRENTS [61; 61]
(From 10 exp -12 to 10 exp -9 amp.)
  BT1   beam currents
       BT2   currents

PICOLINES [125; 191]
  UF   *methyl pyridines*
  BT1   pyridines
       BT2   azines
         BT3   heterocyclic compounds
           BT4   organic compounds
         BT3   organic nitrogen compounds
           BT4   organic compounds
  NT1   picolinic acid
  RT   pyridoxal

PICOLINIC ACID [66; 66]
  UF   *2-pyridinecarboxylic acid*
  BT1   heterocyclic acids
       BT2   carboxylic acids
         BT3   organic acids
           BT4   organic compounds
       BT2   heterocyclic compounds
         BT3   organic compounds
  BT1   picolines
       BT2   pyridines
         BT3   azines
           BT4   heterocyclic compounds
             BT5   organic compounds
           BT4   organic nitrogen compounds
             BT5   organic compounds

PICRIC ACID [48; 48]
  UF   *picronitric acid*
  UF   *tnp*
  UF   *trinitrophenol*
  BT1   explosives
  BT1   nitro compounds
       BT2   organic nitrogen compounds
         BT3   organic compounds
  BT1   phenols
       BT2   aromatics
         BT3   organic compounds
       BT2   hydroxy compounds
         BT3   organic compounds

  RT   organic acids

picronitric acid
  USE   picric acid

PICRYL RADICALS [2; 2]
  BT1   radicals

PIERCE ELECTRON GUNS [64; 64]
  BT1   electron sources
       BT2   particle sources
         BT3   radiation sources

PIERCE INSTABILITY [30; 30] *Sep 83*
  BT1   instability
  RT   beam-plasma systems
  RT   electron beams

pierrelatte (cea)
  USE   cea pierrelatte

PIEZOELECTRICITY [698; 698]
  BT1   electricity

pig discharges
  USE   penning discharges

pig ion sources
  USE   penning ion sources

pige analysis
(Proton-Induced Gamma Emission analysis.)
  USE   nuclear reaction analysis
  AND   prompt gamma radiation
  AND   proton reactions

PIGEONS [43; 43]
  BT1   birds
       BT2   vertebrates
         BT3   animals

pigment cells
  USE   animal cells
  AND   pigments

PIGMENTS [340; 2,766]
  UF+   *pigment cells*
  SF   *chemicals*
  NT1   bilirubin
  NT1   biliverdin
  NT1   carotenoids
  NT1   cytochromes
  NT1   hematoporphyrins
  NT1   heme
  NT1   hemoglobin
    NT2   carboxyhemoglobin
    NT2   methemoglobin
  NT1   hemosiderin
  NT1   india ink
  NT1   melanin
  NT1   molybdenum blue
  NT1   myoglobin
  NT1   phycocyanin
  NT1   phytochromes
    NT2   chlorophyll
  NT1   protoporphyrins
  NT1   rhodopsin
  NT1   stercobilin
  NT1   ultramarine
  NT1   urobilinogen
  RT   paints
  RT   porphyrins

PIGMI FACILITIES [7; 7] *Sep 82*
  UF   *pion generator medical irradia*
  RT   accelerator facilities
  RT   irradiation devices
  RT   linear accelerators
  RT   meson factories

  RT   quadrupole linacs

pigs
  USE   swine

PIKAS [3; 3]
  UF   *cony*
  BT1   mammals
       BT2   vertebrates
         BT3   animals

PILE NEUTRONS [304; 304]
  BT1   neutrons
       BT2   nucleons
         BT3   baryons
           BT4   fermions
           BT4   hadrons
             BT5   elementary particles

PILE OSCILLATION TECHNIQUES
[87; 87]
  UF   *oscillation techniques (pile)*
  RT   reactivity
  RT   reactor oscillators

PILE REPLACEMENT TECHNIQUES
[30; 30]
  UF   *substitution techniques*
  RT   reactivity

pilgrim reactor
(Prior to December 1990, this was a valid descriptor.)
  USE   pilgrim-1 reactor

PILGRIM-1 REACTOR [70; 70]
(Plymouth, Massachusetts, USA)
  UF   *pilgrim reactor*
  UF   *plymouth pilgrim power reactor*
  BT1   pwr type reactors
       BT2   enriched uranium reactors
         BT3   reactors
       BT2   power reactors
         BT3   reactors
       BT2   thermal reactors
         BT3   reactors
       BT2   water cooled reactors
         BT3   reactors
       BT2   water moderated reactors
         BT3   reactors

PILGRIM-2 REACTOR [31; 31]
(Plymouth, Massachusetts, USA)
  BT1   pwr type reactors
       BT2   enriched uranium reactors
         BT3   reactors
       BT2   power reactors
         BT3   reactors
       BT2   thermal reactors
         BT3   reactors
       BT2   water cooled reactors
         BT3   reactors
       BT2   water moderated reactors
         BT3   reactors

PILGRIM-3 REACTOR [22; 22]
(Plymouth, Massachusetts, USA)
  BT1   pwr type reactors
       BT2   enriched uranium reactors
         BT3   reactors
       BT2   power reactors
         BT3   reactors
       BT2   thermal reactors
         BT3   reactors
       BT2   water cooled reactors
         BT3   reactors
       BT2   water moderated reactors
         BT3   reactors

PILOCARPINE [11; 11]
  BT1   alkaloids
       BT2   organic compounds
  BT1   parasympathomimetics
       BT2   autonomic nervous system
              agent

PILOT PLANTS [2,028; 2,667]
- UF   *demonstration plants*
- UF   *pdus*
- UF   *plants (pilot)*
- UF   *process development units*
- BT1 functional models
- NT1 wipp
- RT   industrial plants
- RT   mockup
- RT   pamela plant

PINACOL [8; 8]
- UF   *tetramethylethylene glycol*
- BT1 glycols
- BT2 alcohols
- BT3 hydroxy compounds
- BT4 organic compounds

PINCH DEVICES [421; 2,741]
- BT1 thermonuclear devices
- NT1 field-reversed theta pinch dev
- NT1 linear pinch devices
- NT2 linear hard core pinch devices
- NT2 linear screw pinch devices
- NT2 linear theta pinch devices
- NT3 bsg devices
- NT3 chalice devices
- NT3 isar devices
- NT3 pharos devices
- NT3 scylla devices
- NT2 linear z pinch devices
- NT2 megatron
- NT1 toroidal pinch devices
- NT2 hbtx devices
- NT2 tlp devices
- NT3 alpha device
- NT3 zeta devices
- NT2 toroidal screw pinch devices
- NT3 tpe-2 device
- NT2 toroidal theta pinch devices
- NT3 scyllac devices
- NT2 tpe-1rm15 device
- NT2 zt-p devices
- NT2 zt-40 devices
- RT   end effects
- RT   limiters
- RT   pinch effect

PINCH EFFECT [890; 3,921]
- NT1 hard core pinch
- NT1 longitudinal pinch
- NT2 belt pinch
- NT1 reverse-field pinch
- NT1 screw pinch
- NT1 theta pinch
- RT   limiters
- RT   magnetic compression
- RT   magnetic field configurations
- RT   pinch devices
- RT   plasma
- RT   plasma filament
- RT   plasma focus

PINEAL GLAND [119; 119]
- UF   *epiphysis (pineal gland)*
- BT1 glands
- BT2 organs
- BT3 body
- RT   brain
- RT   endocrine glands
- RT   melatonin

PINELLAS PLANT [18; 18] *Sep 77*
- BT1 us doe
- BT2 us organizations
- BT3 national organizations
- BT1 us erda
- BT2 us organizations
- BT3 national organizations
- RT   florida

PINES [281; 281]
- BT1 conifers
- BT2 plants
- BT1 trees
- BT2 plants

PINES-BOHM THEORY [10; 10]
- UF   *bohm-pines theory*
- RT   electron gas

pinning force
- USE   magnetic flux

pins (fuel)
- USE   fuel pins

PION BEAMS [2,014; 2,014]
- BT1 meson beams
- BT2 particle beams
- BT3 beams

PION CONDENSATION [547; 547] *Aug 78*
- UF   *pi condensate*
- RT   bose-einstein condensation
- RT   nuclear matter
- RT   pions

PION DETECTION [625; 625]
- BT1 radiation detection
- BT2 detection
- RT   pion dosimetry

PION DOSIMETRY [106; 106]
- BT1 dosimetry
- RT   pion detection

pion generator medical irradia
- USE   pigmi facilities

PION MINUS REACTIONS [2,542; 2,542] *Jan 77*
- BT1 pion reactions
- BT2 meson reactions
- BT3 hadron reactions
- BT4 nuclear reactions

PION MINUS-NEUTRON INTERACTION [145; 145] *Jan 77*
- BT1 pion-neutron interactions
- BT2 pion-nucleon interactions
- BT3 meson-nucleon interactions
- BT4 meson-baryon interactions
- BT5 hadron-hadron interactions
- BT6 particle interactions
- BT7 interactions

PION MINUS-PROTON INTERACTIONS [2,130; 2,130] *Jan 77*
- BT1 pion-proton interactions
- BT2 pion-nucleon interactions
- BT3 meson-nucleon interactions
- BT4 meson-baryon interactions
- BT5 hadron-hadron interactions
- BT6 particle interactions
- BT7 interactions

PION PLUS REACTIONS [1,823; 1,823] *Jan 77*
- BT1 pion reactions
- BT2 meson reactions
- BT3 hadron reactions
- BT4 nuclear reactions

PION PLUS-NEUTRON INTERACTIONS [76; 76] *Jan 77*
- BT1 pion-neutron interactions
- BT2 pion-nucleon interactions
- BT3 meson-nucleon interactions
- BT4 meson-baryon interactions
- BT5 hadron-hadron interactions
- BT6 particle interactions
- BT7 interactions

PION PLUS-PROTON INTERACTIONS [863; 863] *Jan 77*
- BT1 pion-proton interactions
- BT2 pion-nucleon interactions
- BT3 meson-nucleon interactions
- BT4 meson-baryon interactions
- BT5 hadron-hadron interactions
- BT6 particle interactions
- BT7 interactions

PION REACTIONS [3,411; 6,749]
- UF+ *pion-deuteron interactions*
- BT1 meson reactions
- BT2 hadron reactions
- BT3 nuclear reactions
- NT1 pion minus reactions
- NT1 pion plus reactions

pion-deuteron interactions
- USE   deuterium target
- AND   pion reactions

pion-exchange model
- USE   ope model

PION-HYPERON INTERACTIONS [24; 24]
- BT1 meson-hyperon interactions
- BT2 meson-baryon interactions
- BT3 hadron-hadron interactions
- BT4 particle interactions
- BT5 interactions

PION-KAON INTERACTIONS [144; 144]
- BT1 meson-meson interactions
- BT2 hadron-hadron interactions
- BT3 particle interactions
- BT4 interactions

PION-NEUTRON INTERACTIONS [101; 312]
- BT1 pion-nucleon interactions
- BT2 meson-nucleon interactions
- BT3 meson-baryon interactions
- BT4 hadron-hadron interactions
- BT5 particle interactions
- BT6 interactions
- NT1 pion minus-neutron interaction
- NT1 pion plus-neutron interactions

PION-NUCLEON INTERACTIONS [2,975; 7,462]
- BT1 meson-nucleon interactions
- BT2 meson-baryon interactions
- BT3 hadron-hadron interactions
- BT4 particle interactions
- BT5 interactions
- NT1 pion-neutron interactions
- NT2 pion minus-neutron interaction
- NT2 pion plus-neutron interactions
- NT1 pion-proton interactions
- NT2 pion minus-proton interactions
- NT2 pion plus-proton interactions

PION-PION INTERACTIONS [932; 932]
- BT1 meson-meson interactions
- BT2 hadron-hadron interactions
- BT3 particle interactions
- BT4 interactions

PION-PROTON INTERACTIONS [1,768; 4,361]
- BT1 pion-nucleon interactions
- BT2 meson-nucleon interactions
- BT3 meson-baryon interactions
- BT4 hadron-hadron interactions
- BT5 particle interactions
- BT6 interactions
- NT1 pion minus-proton interactions
- NT1 pion plus-proton interactions

PIONEER SPACE PROBES [407; 407]
  BT1   space vehicles

PIONIC ATOMS [537; 537]
  BT1   mesic atoms
    BT2   hadronic atoms
      BT3   atoms
  RT   pionium

PIONIUM [18; 18] *Nov 85*
  RT   bound state
  RT   kaonium
  RT   muonium
  RT   pionic atoms
  RT   pions minus
  RT   pions plus

PIONIZATION [682; 682]
  BT1   multiple production
    BT2   particle production

PIONS [10,386; 25,352]
  BT1   pseudoscalar mesons
    BT2   mesons
      BT3   bosons
      BT3   hadrons
        BT4   elementary particles
  NT1   cosmic pions
  NT1   pions minus
  NT1   pions neutral
  NT1   pions plus
  RT   abc effect
  RT   goldberger-treiman relation
  RT   pi-k atoms
  RT   pi-mu atoms
  RT   pion condensation

PIONS MINUS [9,502; 9,502]
  BT1   pions
    BT2   pseudoscalar mesons
      BT3   mesons
        BT4   bosons
        BT4   hadrons
          BT5   elementary particles
  RT   pionium

PIONS NEUTRAL [5,079; 5,079]
  BT1   pions
    BT2   pseudoscalar mesons
      BT3   mesons
        BT4   bosons
        BT4   hadrons
          BT5   elementary particles
  RT   primakoff effect

PIONS PLUS [8,345; 8,345]
  BT1   pions
    BT2   pseudoscalar mesons
      BT3   mesons
        BT4   bosons
        BT4   hadrons
          BT5   elementary particles
  RT   pionium

PIPE FITTINGS [553; 553]
  RT   expansion joints
  RT   nozzles
  RT   orifices
  RT   pipelines
  RT   pipes
  RT   pressure vessels
  RT   restraints
  RT   seals
  RT   valves

PIPE JOINTS [372; 372]
  BT1   joints
  RT   expansion joints

pipe restraints
  USE   pipes
  AND   restraints

PIPE WHIP [58; 58] *Jan 84*
(Large amplitude mechanical motion of a pipe due to changes in the flow of the fluid in the pipe.)
  RT   dynamic loads
  RT   pipes
  RT   steam lines

PIPELINES [2,302; 2,950]
  NT1   steam lines
  RT   hydraulic transport
  RT   pipe fittings
  RT   pipes
  RT   pneumatic transport
  RT   positioning

PIPERAZINES [93; 93]
  BT1   pyrazines
    BT2   azines
      BT3   heterocyclic compounds
        BT4   organic compounds
      BT3   organic nitrogen compounds
        BT4   organic compounds
  RT   amines

PIPERIDINES [277; 322]
  UF   *hexahydropyridines*
  UF   *pentamethyleneimines*
  BT1   amines
    BT2   organic compounds
  BT1   pyridines
    BT2   azines
      BT3   heterocyclic compounds
        BT4   organic compounds
      BT3   organic nitrogen compounds
        BT4   organic compounds
  NT1   pethidine
  NT1   tmpn
  NT1   triacetoneamine-n-oxyl

PIPES [8,436; 8,436]
  UF   *tubes (conduits)*
  UF+   *pipe restraints*
  RT   borescopes
  RT   cylinders
  RT   ducts
  RT   pipe fittings
  RT   pipe whip
  RT   pipelines
  RT   restraints
  RT   tubes

PIPPARD THEORY [22; 22]
  RT   superconductivity

piqua nuclear power facility
  USE   pnpf reactor

piqua organic moderated reacto
  USE   pnpf reactor

PIRANI GAGES [17; 17]
  BT1   hot-wire gages
    BT2   pressure gages
      BT3   measuring instruments
  BT1   vacuum gages
    BT2   pressure gages
      BT3   measuring instruments

PISUM [290; 290]
  UF   *pea plant*
  BT1   leguminosae
    BT2   plants
  RT   peas

pitch (reactor parameters)
  USE   reactor lattice parameters

pitch angle
  USE   inclination

PITCHBLENDE [202; 202]
  BT1   uraninites
    BT2   oxide minerals
      BT3   minerals
    BT2   uranium minerals
      BT3   radioactive minerals
        BT4   minerals
        BT4   radioactive materials
          BT5   materials

PITCHES [44; 44]
(The residues from the destructive distillation of tars.)
  BT1   other organic compounds
    BT2   organic compounds
  RT   tar

PITOT TUBES [54; 54]
  RT   flowmeters

PITTING CORROSION [624; 624]
  BT1   corrosion
    BT2   chemical reactions

PITUITARY GLAND [1,147; 1,147]
  UF   *hypophysis*
  BT1   endocrine glands
    BT2   glands
      BT3   organs
        BT4   body
  RT   acromegaly
  RT   cushing syndrome
  RT   homeostasis
  RT   hypophysectomy
  RT   hypothalamus
  RT   lactogens
  RT   pituitary hormones

PITUITARY HORMONES [120; 3,013]
  BT1   peptide hormones
    BT2   hormones
  NT1   acth
  NT1   gonadotropins
    NT2   fsh
    NT2   hcg
    NT2   lh
    NT2   lth
  NT1   liberins
    NT2   lh-rh
  NT1   oxytocin
  NT1   sth
  NT1   tsh
  NT1   vasopressin
  RT   hypophysectomy
  RT   pituitary gland

PIVALIC ACID [19; 19]
  UF   *dimethylpropionic acid*
  UF   *trimethylacetic acid*
  BT1   monocarboxylic acids
    BT2   carboxylic acids
      BT3   organic acids
        BT4   organic compounds

PIXE ANALYSIS [1,026; 1,026] *Sep 80*
  UF   *proton-induced x-ray emiss ana*
  BT1   x-ray emission analysis
    BT2   nondestructive analysis
      BT3   chemical analysis

PI2-1680 MESONS [55; 55]
(Prior to December 1987 this concept was indexed by PI-1640 RESONANCES.)
  UF   *pi-1640 resonances*
  BT1   tensor mesons
    BT2   mesons
      BT3   bosons
      BT3   hadrons
        BT4   elementary particles

PI2-2100 MESONS [0; 0] *Dec 87*
  BT1   tensor mesons
    BT2   mesons
      BT3   bosons
      BT3   hadrons
        BT4   elementary particles

PL-1 LANGUAGE [47; 47]
BT1 programming languages

PL-11 LANGUAGE [4; 4]
BT1 programming languages

PLACENTA [587; 587]
BT1 fetal membranes
BT2 membranes
RT hpl
RT lactogens
RT pregnancy

PLACERS [42; 42]
BT1 geologic deposits
RT alluvial deposits

PLACZEC FUNCTION [32; 32]
UF *bethe-placzec model*
UF+ *cn method*
BT1 functions
RT neutron slowing-down theory

PLAGES [204; 204]
BT1 solar activity
RT chromosphere
RT faculae

PLAICE [28; 28]
BT1 fishes
BT2 aquatic organisms
BT2 vertebrates
BT3 animals
RT seafood

plainsboro irl pool type react
USE irl reactor

PLANARIA [8; 8]
BT1 turbellaria
BT2 platyhelminths
BT3 invertebrates
BT4 animals

PLANCK LAW [190; 190]
RT quantum mechanics

PLANCK RADIATION FORMULA [95; 95]
RT blackbody radiation
RT thermodynamics

plane-wave born approximation
USE born approximation

PLANET-SYSTEM ACCRETION [288; 288]
UF *accretion (planet-system)*
RT cosmological models
RT galactic evolution
RT solar system evolution
RT star accretion

PLANETARY ATMOSPHERES [1,306; 2,150]
(Excludes the concept covered by EARTH ATMOSPHERE.)
BT1 atmospheres
NT1 planetary ionospheres
NT1 planetary magnetospheres

planetary evolution
(When appropriate, see also PLANETS or descriptors for specific planets.)
USE solar system evolution

PLANETARY IONOSPHERES [203; 203]
Sep 78
(Excludes the Earth's ionosphere for which use IONOSPHERE.)
BT1 planetary atmospheres
BT2 atmospheres

PLANETARY MAGNETOSPHERES [701; 701] *Jul 76*
(Excludes the Earth's magnetosphere.)
UF *magnetospheres (planetary)*
BT1 planetary atmospheres
BT2 atmospheres
RT earth magnetosphere

PLANETARY NEBULAE [1,203; 1,203]
BT1 nebulae
RT stars

PLANETS [674; 5,249]
NT1 earth planet
NT1 jupiter planet
NT1 mars planet
NT1 mercury planet
NT1 neptune planet
NT1 pluto planet
NT1 saturn planet
NT1 uranus planet
NT1 venus planet
RT asteroids
RT comets
RT protoplanets
RT solar system

PLANKTON [754; 754]
UF *phytoplankton*
UF *zooplankton*
UF+ *diatoms*
BT1 aquatic organisms
RT bacteria
RT biological materials
RT biomass
RT crustaceans
RT daphnia
RT protozoa
RT surface waters
RT unicellular algae

§§ **PLANNING** [24,208; 25,877]
(Projected design of plants or equipment as well as projected human efforts.)
NT1 experiment planning
RT allocations
RT cancellation
RT computer-aided design
RT construction
RT coordinated research programs
RT decision tree analysis
RT demonstration programs
RT design
RT emergency plans
RT energy policy
RT environmental policy
RT fault tree analysis
RT feasibility studies
RT forecasting
RT government policies
RT implementation
RT modifications
RT optimization
RT organizational models
RT organizing
RT pert method
RT production
RT regional cooperation
RT research programs
RT schedules
RT site selection

PLANT BREEDING [1,830; 1,830]
RT adventitious bud technique
RT disease resistance
RT irradiation
RT morphological changes
RT mutagens
RT mutants
RT mutations
RT plant growth
RT productivity
RT reproduction

PLANT CELLS [823; 823]
UF *cells (plant)*
UF *protoplasts*
UF+ *cell growth (plant)*
RT cell constituents
RT cell cultures
RT cell flow systems
RT cell wall
RT chloroplasts
RT clone cells
RT cytology
RT in vivo

plant cultivation
USE cultivation techniques

PLANT DISEASES [254; 815]
RT disease incidence
RT disease resistance
RT mildew
RT parasites
RT tobacco mosaic virus

plant fossils
USE fossils

PLANT GROWTH [1,871; 1,871]
BT1 growth
RT carbon dioxide fixation
RT kinetin
RT nitrogen fixation
RT plant breeding
RT plants
RT sprouting

PLANT GROWTH REGULATORS [117; 259]
NT1 auxins
RT kinetin

PLANT STEMS [436; 436]
UF *stem (plant)*
RT bark
RT plants

PLANT TISSUES [335; 708]
NT1 bark
NT1 endosperm
NT1 meristems
NT1 mycelium
RT tissues

PLANTS [4,068; 17,381]
UF *vegetation*
NT1 algae
NT2 acetabularia
NT2 fucus
NT2 laminaria
NT2 lichens
NT2 nitella
NT2 porphyra
NT2 ulva
NT2 unicellular algae
NT3 chlamydomonas
NT3 chlorella
NT3 euglena
NT3 scenedesmus
NT1 allium cepa
NT1 arabidopsis
NT1 banana plants
NT1 brassica
NT1 buckwheat
NT1 cacti
NT1 capsicum
NT1 carnations
NT1 cassava
NT1 citrus
NT1 coffee plants
NT1 conifers
NT2 pines
NT1 corchorus
NT1 cotton plants
NT1 crepis
NT1 ferns
NT1 flax plants

```
NT1     forage
NT1     fungi
   NT2      aspergillus
   NT2      claviceps
   NT2      fusarium
   NT2      lichens
   NT2      mildew
   NT2      mushrooms
   NT2      myxomycetes
   NT2      neurospora
   NT2      penicillium
   NT2      phycomyces
   NT2      physarum
   NT2      rhizopus
   NT2      ustilago
   NT2      yeasts
      NT3      candida
      NT3      saccharomyces
         NT4      saccharomyces cerevisiae
      NT3      torula
NT1     gramineae
   NT2      cereals
      NT3      barley
      NT3      maize
      NT3      millet
      NT3      oats
      NT3      rice
      NT3      rye
      NT3      sorghum
      NT3      wheat
   NT2      sugar cane
NT1     herbs
   NT2      coleus
NT1     jute
NT1     leguminosae
   NT2      alfalfa
   NT2      clover
   NT2      glycine hispida
   NT2      mungbeans
   NT2      phaseolus
   NT2      pisum
   NT2      vicia
NT1     lilium
NT1     medicinal plants
   NT2      aloe
   NT2      atropa belladonna
   NT2      castor
   NT2      digitalis
   NT2      papaver somniferum
NT1     mosses
NT1     nicotiana
NT1     ornamental plants
NT1     preferred species
NT1     ranunculaceae
NT1     shrubs
NT1     solanum
   NT2      solanum tuberosum
NT1     sunflowers
NT1     tea plants
NT1     tradescantia
NT1     trees
   NT2      cacao trees
   NT2      coconut palms
   NT2      eucalyptuses
   NT2      fruit trees
   NT2      hevea
   NT2      oaks
   NT2      oil palms
   NT2      olive trees
   NT2      pines
   NT2      poplars
NT1     trillium
NT1     weeds
RT      agriculture
RT      alkaloids
RT      aquatic organisms
RT      biological materials
RT      biology
RT      biomass
RT      botany
RT      buds
RT      bulbs
RT      chlorophyll
RT      endangered species
RT      essential oils
RT      fertilizers
RT      flowers
RT      ground cover
RT      leaves
RT      plant growth
```

```
RT      plant stems
RT      renewable energy sources
RT      roots
RT      seedlings
RT      seeds
RT      soils
RT      sprouting
RT      symbiosis
RT      translocation
RT      transpiration
RT      tubers
RT      vegetative propagation
```

plants (industrial)
   USE   industrial plants

plants (pilot)
   USE   pilot plants

plants (power)
   USE   power plants

PLAQUE FORMATION [71; 71] *Apr 78*
   RT   bacteriophages
   RT   bioassay
   RT   clone cells
   RT   viruses

PLASMA [24,968; 46,416]
   NT1   ambiplasma
   NT1   cold plasma
   NT1   collisional plasma
   NT1   collisionless plasma
   NT1   equilibrium plasma
   NT1   fissioning plasma
   NT1   high-beta plasma
   NT1   homogeneous plasma
   NT1   hot plasma
   NT1   inhomogeneous plasma
   NT1   laser-produced plasma
   NT1   low-beta plasma
   NT1   medium-beta plasma
   NT1   non-equilibrium plasma
   NT1   optically thick plasma
   NT1   optically thin plasma
   NT1   quantum plasma
   NT1   quiescent plasma
   NT1   relativistic plasma
   NT1   rotating plasma
   NT1   solid-state plasma
   RT   aspect ratio
   RT   beam-plasma systems
   RT   bohm criterion
   RT   boltzmann-vlasov equation
   RT   bootstrap current
   RT   breakeven
   RT   compact torus
   RT   confinement time
   RT   distribution functions
   RT   electric arcs
   RT   gas blankets
   RT   grad-shafranov equation
   RT   guiding-center approximation
   RT   holtsmark theory
   RT   impurities
   RT   ionic composition
   RT   ionized gases
   RT   kinetic equations
   RT   langmuir frequency
   RT   loss cone
   RT   magnetic field configurations
   RT   magnetic field ripples
   RT   magnetic islands
   RT   magnetohydrodynamics
   RT   mass balance
   RT   neoclassical transport theory
   RT   non-inductive current drive
   RT   pinch effect
   RT   plasma acceleration
   RT   plasma confinement
   RT   plasma density
   RT   plasma diagnostics
   RT   plasma diamagnetism
   RT   plasma drift
   RT   plasma eaters
   RT   plasma expansion

```

```
RT   plasma filament
RT   plasma focus
RT   plasma heating
RT   plasma impurities
RT   plasma instability
RT   plasma production
RT   plasma radial profiles
RT   plasma rings
RT   plasma scrape-off layer
RT   plasma simulation
RT   plasma waves
RT   plasmoids
RT   sawtooth oscillations
RT   solar wind
RT   spitzer theory
RT   voigt effect
RT   wall effects
```

*plasma (blood)*
   USE     blood plasma

**PLASMA ACCELERATION**
[1,189; 1,189]
   BT1     acceleration
   RT      plasma
   RT      plasma guns
   RT      plasma jets

*plasma accelerators*
   USE     plasma guns

**PLASMA ARC SPRAYING** [402; 402]
   BT1     spray coating
      BT2      surface coating
         BT3      deposition

**PLASMA ARC WELDING** [105; 105]
   BT1     arc welding
      BT2      welding
         BT3      joining
            BT4      fabrication

**PLASMA BEAM INJECTION** [227; 227]
   BT1     beam injection

**PLASMA BETATRONS** [25; 25]
   UF      *budker accelerators*
   BT1     collective accelerators
      BT2      accelerators
   RT      betatrons

**PLASMA CELLS** [74; 74]
   UF      *plasmocytes*
   BT1     connective tissue cells
      BT2      somatic cells
         BT3      animal cells
   RT      bone marrow
   RT      lymphocytes

**PLASMA CENTRIFUGES** [29; 29]
*Jul 85*
   UF      *vacuum arc centrifuges*
   BT1     centrifuges
   RT      isotope separation

*plasma clearance*
   USE     blood-plasma clearance

**PLASMA CONFINEMENT** [3,216; 6,357]
(Prior to January 1983 this concept was
indexed by CONFINEMENT.)
   BT1     confinement
   NT1     h-mode plasma confinement
   NT1     inertial confinement
   NT1     magnetic confinement
   RT      confinement time
   RT      gas blankets
   RT      limiters
   RT      magnetic surfaces
   RT      marfe
   RT      particle losses
   RT      plasma
   RT      plasma disruption
```

```
             RT   plateau regime
             RT   sawtooth oscillations
             RT   thermal barriers
             RT   tritium recovery

PLASMA CORE ASSEMBLY [14; 14]
  Apr 77
     UF    lasl cold critical assembly
     BT1   gas fueled reactors
       BT2   fluid fueled reactors
         BT3   reactors
       BT2   homogeneous reactors
         BT3   reactors
     BT1   zero power reactors
       BT2   experimental reactors
         BT3   research and test reactors
           BT4   reactors


plasma currents
     USE   electric currents

PLASMA DENSITY [9,149; 9,149]
     UF    density (plasma)
     RT    debye length
     RT    lawson criterion
     RT    plasma
     RT    plasma expansion
     RT    plasma focus

PLASMA DIAGNOSTICS
  [11,180; 11,180]
     RT    plasma
     RT    plasma eaters
     RT    sonic probes

PLASMA DIAMAGNETISM [208; 208]
     BT1   diamagnetism
       BT2   magnetism
     RT    plasma


plasma diodes
     USE   thermionic diodes

PLASMA DISRUPTION [820; 820]
  Sep 83
     RT    confinement time
     RT    nonlinear problems
     RT    particle losses
     RT    plasma confinement
     RT    plasma macroinstabilities
     RT    sawtooth oscillations
     RT    tearing instability
     RT    tokamak devices

PLASMA DRIFT [2,339; 2,339]
     UF    drift (plasma)
     RT    ambipolar diffusion
     RT    drift instability
     RT    plasma
     RT    plasma expansion
     RT    plasma fluid equations

PLASMA EATERS [44; 44]
     BT1   electric probes
       BT2   probes
     BT1   flowmeters
       BT2   measuring instruments
     RT    electron density
     RT    flow rate
     RT    plasma
     RT    plasma diagnostics


plasma erosion opening switche
     USE   plasma switches

PLASMA EXPANSION [957; 957]
     BT1   expansion
     RT    plasma
     RT    plasma density
     RT    plasma drift
     RT    plasma instability

PLASMA FILAMENT [890; 890]
     UF    filament (plasma)
     RT    pinch effect
     RT    plasma
     RT    plasma focus
     RT    plasma jets

PLASMA FLUID EQUATIONS [99; 99]
  Nov 88
     UF    fluid equations (plasma)
     BT1   boltzmann-vlasov equation
       BT2   partial differential equations
         BT3   differential equations
           BT4   equations
     RT    magnetohydrodynamics
     RT    moments method
     RT    plasma drift
     RT    plasma simulation

PLASMA FOCUS [747; 747]
     RT    pinch effect
     RT    plasma
     RT    plasma density
     RT    plasma filament
     RT    plasma focus devices
     RT    plasma guns

PLASMA FOCUS DEVICES [462; 462]
     BT1   open plasma devices
       BT2   thermonuclear devices
     RT    plasma focus


plasma frequency
     USE   langmuir frequency

PLASMA FURNACES [85; 85]
     BT1   furnaces
     RT    arc furnaces

PLASMA GUNS [926; 926]
     UF    guns (plasma)
     UF    plasma accelerators
     RT    impact fusion drivers
     RT    plasma acceleration
     RT    plasma focus
     RT    plasma jets
     RT    plasma rings

PLASMA HEATING [4,348; 15,205]
     BT1   heating
     NT1   adiabatic compression heating
     NT1   beam injection heating
     NT1   current-drive heating
     NT1   high-frequency heating
       NT2   ecr heating
       NT2   icr heating
       NT2   lower hybrid heating
       NT2   magnetic-pumping heating
         NT3   acoustic heating
         NT3   collisional heating
         NT3   transit-time magnetic pump-
                 ing
     NT1   laser-radiation heating
     NT1   shock heating
     NT1   turbulent heating
     RT    auxiliary heating
     RT    bernstein mode
     RT    energy deposition
     RT    joule heating
     RT    mode conversion
     RT    plasma
     RT    plasma potential
     RT    plasma production
     RT    thermonuclear devices

PLASMA IMPURITIES [178; 178]
  Apr 90
     BT1   impurities
     RT    divertors
     RT    limiters
     RT    plasma
     RT    plasma scrape-off layer
     RT    wall effects

PLASMA INSTABILITY [6,217; 16,024]
     BT1   instability
     NT1   absolute instabilities
     NT1   convective instabilities
     NT1   decay instability
     NT1   drift instability
     NT1   explosive instability
     NT1   plasma macroinstabilities
       NT2   ballooning instability
       NT2   edge localized modes
       NT2   fishbone instability
       NT2   flute instability
       NT2   helical instability
       NT2   helmholtz instability
       NT2   kink instability
       NT2   parametric instabilities
       NT2   sausage instability
       NT2   tearing instability
       NT2   tilting instability
     NT1   plasma microinstabilities
       NT2   bump-in-tail instability
       NT2   cyclotron instability
       NT2   hose instability
       NT2   ion wave instability
       NT2   loss cone instability
       NT2   negative mass instability
       NT2   two-stream instability
       NT2   whistler instability
     NT1   trapped-particle instability
     RT    dispersion relations
     RT    instability growth rates
     RT    marfe
     RT    mercier criterion
     RT    mhd equilibrium
     RT    negative mass effect
     RT    nonlinear problems
     RT    plasma
     RT    plasma expansion
     RT    suydam criterion

PLASMA JETS [905; 905]
     RT    plasma acceleration
     RT    plasma filament
     RT    plasma guns


plasma lens
     USE   electromagnetic lenses

PLASMA MACROINSTABILITIES
  [977; 6,277]
     UF    mhd instabilities (plasma)
     BT1   plasma instability
       BT2   instability
     NT1   ballooning instability
     NT1   edge localized modes
     NT1   fishbone instability
     NT1   flute instability
     NT1   helical instability
     NT1   helmholtz instability
     NT1   kink instability
     NT1   parametric instabilities
     NT1   sausage instability
     NT1   tearing instability
     NT1   tilting instability
     RT    decay instability
     RT    plasma disruption
     RT    rayleigh-taylor instability

PLASMA MICROINSTABILITIES
  [642; 3,544]
     BT1   plasma instability
       BT2   instability
     NT1   bump-in-tail instability
     NT1   cyclotron instability
     NT1   hose instability
     NT1   ion wave instability
     NT1   loss cone instability
     NT1   negative mass instability
     NT1   two-stream instability
     NT1   whistler instability
     RT    decay instability


plasma opening switches
     USE   plasma switches
```

plasma oscillations
  USE   plasma waves

PLASMA POTENTIAL [138; 138]
Nov 88
(The electrostatic potential of a plasma along a magnetic field line.)
  BT1   electric potential
  RT   charge exchange
  RT   magnetic mirror configurations
  RT   magnetic mirrors
  RT   plasma heating

PLASMA PRESSURE [1,165; 1,165]
  UF   *pressure (plasma)*
  RT   beta ratio

PLASMA PRODUCTION [2,829; 2,829]
  RT   high-frequency discharges
  RT   ionization
  RT   laser-produced plasma
  RT   plasma
  RT   plasma heating
  RT   thermonuclear devices

PLASMA RADIAL PROFILES [362; 362] *Sep 89*
  UF   *radial profiles (plasma)*
  RT   magnetic flux coordinates
  RT   magnetic surfaces
  RT   plasma
  RT   spatial distribution
  RT   stellarators
  RT   tokamak devices

PLASMA RINGS [68; 68] *Feb 84*
  RT   compact torus
  RT   plasma
  RT   plasma guns

PLASMA SCRAPE-OFF LAYER [905; 905] *Sep 83*
  BT1   boundary layers
    BT2   layers
  RT   plasma
  RT   plasma impurities

PLASMA SEEDING [118; 118] *Oct 76*
  UF   *seeding (plasma)*
  RT   ionization
  RT   ionization potential
  RT   mhd channels
  RT   mhd generators
  RT   seed-slag interactions

PLASMA SHEATH [1,230; 1,230]
  RT   boundary layers
  RT   marfe
  RT   reentry

PLASMA SHEET [880; 880]
  RT   earth magnetosphere
  RT   magnetotail

PLASMA SIMULATION [4,337; 4,337]
  UF   *models (plasma)*
  BT1   simulation
  RT   functional models
  RT   plasma
  RT   plasma fluid equations
  RT   simulators

PLASMA SWITCHES [313; 313] *Jan 86*
(Switches employing a current-conducting plasma for operation.)
  UF   *peos*
  UF   *plasma erosion opening switche*
  UF   *plasma opening switches*
  UF   *pos*
  UF   *reflex switches*
  BT1   switches
    BT2   electrical equipment
      BT3   equipment
  RT   energy storage systems
  RT   pulse generators
  RT   pulse techniques

plasma temperature
  USE   electron temperature
  AND   ion temperature

PLASMA WAVES [8,576; 12,219]
  UF   *electrostatic waves*
  UF   *langmuir oscillations*
  UF   *oscillations (plasma)*
  UF   *plasma oscillations*
  NT1   electron plasma waves
  NT1   ion waves
    NT2   ion acoustic waves
    NT2   ion plasma waves
  RT   alfven waves
  RT   beat wave accelerators
  RT   decay instability
  RT   dispersion relations
  RT   frequency mixing
  RT   harmonics
  RT   hydromagnetic waves
  RT   landau damping
  RT   normal-mode analysis
  RT   oscillation modes
  RT   plasma
  RT   plasmons
  RT   tonks-langmuir theory
  RT   wakefield accelerators
  RT   whistler instability

plasma-wall interactions
  USE   wall effects

PLASMAPAUSE [378; 378]
  BT1   boundary layers
    BT2   layers
  RT   earth magnetosphere
  RT   international magnetospheric s
  RT   loss cone
  RT   magnetotail
  RT   plasmasphere

PLASMASPHERE [573; 573]
  RT   earth magnetosphere
  RT   international magnetospheric s
  RT   magnetotail
  RT   plasmapause

PLASMATRONS [210; 665]
  BT1   electron tubes
  NT1   duoplasmatrons
  NT1   triplasmatrons

PLASMIDS [522; 522] *Jan 82*
  UF   *paragenes*
  BT1   cell constituents
  RT   cytoplasm
  RT   genes
  RT   genetics
  RT   transposons

PLASMINOGEN [98; 98] *May 84*
  BT1   blood coagulation factors
    BT2   coagulants
      BT3   hematologic agents
        BT4   drugs

plasmocytes
  USE   plasma cells

PLASMODIUM [70; 70]
  BT1   parasites
  BT1   protozoa
    BT2   invertebrates
      BT3   animals
    BT2   microorganisms
  RT   malaria

PLASMOIDS [211; 211]
  RT   plasma

PLASMONS [1,304; 1,304]
  BT1   quasi particles
  RT   plasma waves
  RT   solid-state plasma

plaster of paris
  USE   gypsum cements

PLASTIC FOAMS [56; 56]
  BT1   organic polymers
    BT2   organic compounds
    BT2   polymers

plastic properties
  USE   plasticity

plastic scintillation counters
  USE   plastic scintillation detector

PLASTIC SCINTILLATION DETECTOR [1,699; 1,699]
  UF   *plastic scintillation counters*
  BT1   solid scintillation detectors
    BT2   scintillation counters
      BT3   radiation detectors
        BT4   measuring instruments
  RT   plastic scintillators

PLASTIC SCINTILLATORS [573; 573]
  BT1   phosphors
  RT   anthracene
  RT   plastic scintillation detector
  RT   terphenyls

PLASTIC SURGERY [190; 190]
  BT1   surgery
    BT2   medicine
  RT   transplants

PLASTICITY [4,216; 4,216]
  UF   *plastic properties*
  BT1   mechanical properties
  RT   creep
  RT   deformation
  RT   ductility
  RT   flow stress

PLASTICIZERS [98; 98]
(A chemical such as castor oil or linseed oil added to rubbers, resins, or other material to impart flexibility, workability, or stretchability.)
  RT   castor oil
  RT   linseed oil
  RT   organic polymers
  RT   rubbers

plastics
  USE   organic polymers

PLATEAU REGIME [80; 80] *Nov 82*
(The collision frequency regime characterized by an effective Coulomb scattering rate equal to or greater than the poloidal transit frequency, but a mean free path less than the connection length. In this regime the transport coefficients are independent of collision frequency.)
  RT   neoclassical transport theory
  RT   plasma confinement
  RT   tokamak devices
  RT   trapping

PLATES [3,273; 3,273]
(Thicker than sheets or foils.)
  RT   foils
  RT   prismatic configuration
  RT   rectangular configuration
  RT   shape
  RT   sheets
  RT   slabs

plates (fuel)
  USE   fuel plates

platform mounted nuclear plant
  USE   offshore nuclear power plants

PLATING [311; 873]
(For the process only.)
  BT1   surface coating
    BT2   deposition
  NT1   electroplating
  NT1   vapor plating
  RT   cladding
  RT   rolling

PLATINUM [2,487; 2,487]
  BT1   platinum metals
    BT2   transition elements
      BT3   metals
        BT4   elements

PLATINUM ADDITIONS [48; 48]
(Alloys containing not more than 1% Pt are listed here.)
  RT   platinum alloys
  RT   platinum compounds

PLATINUM ALLOYS [768; 959]
(Alloys containing more than 1% Pt.)
  BT1   platinum metal alloys
    BT2   alloys
  NT1   platinum base alloys
  RT   platinum additions

→ **PLATINUM ARSENIDES** [0; 0] *Sep 91*
  BT1   arsenides
    BT2   arsenic compounds
    BT2   pnictides
  BT1   platinum compounds
    BT2   transition element compounds

PLATINUM BASE ALLOYS [188; 188]
  BT1   platinum alloys
    BT2   platinum metal alloys
      BT3   alloys

PLATINUM BROMIDES [7; 7]
  BT1   bromides
    BT2   bromine compounds
      BT3   halogen compounds
    BT2   halides
      BT3   halogen compounds
  BT1   platinum compounds
    BT2   transition element compounds

PLATINUM CARBIDES [11; 11]
  BT1   carbides
    BT2   carbon compounds
  BT1   platinum compounds
    BT2   transition element compounds

PLATINUM CHLORIDES [56; 56]
  BT1   chlorides
    BT2   chlorine compounds
      BT3   halogen compounds
    BT2   halides
      BT3   halogen compounds
  BT1   platinum compounds
    BT2   transition element compounds

PLATINUM COMPLEXES [469; 469]
  BT1   transition element complexes
    BT2   complexes

PLATINUM COMPOUNDS [309; 525]
  BT1   transition element compounds
  NT1   platinum arsenides
  NT1   platinum bromides
  NT1   platinum carbides
  NT1   platinum chlorides
  NT1   platinum fluorides
  NT1   platinum hydrides
  NT1   platinum hydroxides
  NT1   platinum iodides
  NT1   platinum oxides
  NT1   platinum phosphides
  NT1   platinum silicides
  NT1   platinum sulfides
  NT1   platinum tellurides
  RT   platinum additions

PLATINUM FLUORIDES [11; 11]
  BT1   fluorides
    BT2   fluorine compounds
      BT3   halogen compounds
    BT2   halides
      BT3   halogen compounds
  BT1   platinum compounds
    BT2   transition element compounds

PLATINUM HYDRIDES [12; 12] *Nov 79*
  BT1   hydrides
    BT2   hydrogen compounds
  BT1   platinum compounds
    BT2   transition element compounds

PLATINUM HYDROXIDES [0; 0]
Sep 91
  BT1   hydroxides
    BT2   hydrogen compounds
    BT2   oxygen compounds
  BT1   platinum compounds
    BT2   transition element compounds

PLATINUM IODIDES [10; 10]
  BT1   iodides
    BT2   halides
      BT3   halogen compounds
    BT2   iodine compounds
      BT3   halogen compounds
  BT1   platinum compounds
    BT2   transition element compounds

PLATINUM IONS [65; 65]
  BT1   ions
    BT2   charged particles

PLATINUM ISOTOPES [250; 1,201]
  NT1   platinum 168
  NT1   platinum 169
  NT1   platinum 170
  NT1   platinum 171
  NT1   platinum 172
  NT1   platinum 173
  NT1   platinum 174
  NT1   platinum 175
  NT1   platinum 176
  NT1   platinum 177
  NT1   platinum 178
  NT1   platinum 179
  NT1   platinum 180
  NT1   platinum 181
  NT1   platinum 182
  NT1   platinum 183
  NT1   platinum 184
  NT1   platinum 185
  NT1   platinum 186
  NT1   platinum 187
  NT1   platinum 188
  NT1   platinum 189
  NT1   platinum 190
  NT1   platinum 191
  NT1   platinum 192
  NT1   platinum 193
  NT1   platinum 194
  NT1   platinum 195
  NT1   platinum 196
  NT1   platinum 197
  NT1   platinum 198
  NT1   platinum 199
  NT1   platinum 200
  NT1   platinum 201
  NT1   platinum 202
  NT1   platinum 203
  NT1   platinum 204
  NT1   platinum 205
  NT1   platinum 206
  NT1   platinum 207
  NT1   platinum 208

PLATINUM METAL ALLOYS [1; 889]
Jul 86
  BT1   alloys
  NT1   iridium alloys
    NT2   iridium base alloys
  NT1   osmium alloys
    NT2   osmium base alloys
  NT1   palladium alloys
    NT2   palladium base alloys
  NT1   platinum alloys
    NT2   platinum base alloys
  NT1   rhodium alloys
    NT2   rhodium base alloys
  NT1   ruthenium alloys
    NT2   ruthenium base alloys

PLATINUM METALS [85; 5,372]
  BT1   transition elements
    BT2   metals
      BT3   elements
  NT1   iridium
  NT1   osmium
  NT1   palladium
  NT1   platinum
  NT1   rhodium
  NT1   ruthenium

PLATINUM OXIDES [56; 56]
  BT1   oxides
    BT2   chalcogenides
    BT2   oxygen compounds
  BT1   platinum compounds
    BT2   transition element compounds

→ **PLATINUM PHOSPHIDES** [0; 0] *Sep 91*
  BT1   phosphides
    BT2   phosphorus compounds
    BT2   pnictides
  BT1   platinum compounds
    BT2   transition element compounds

PLATINUM SILICIDES [57; 57] *Jul 78*
  BT1   platinum compounds
    BT2   transition element compounds
  BT1   silicides
    BT2   silicon compounds

PLATINUM SULFIDES [3; 3]
  BT1   platinum compounds
    BT2   transition element compounds
  BT1   sulfides
    BT2   chalcogenides
    BT2   sulfur compounds

PLATINUM TELLURIDES [4; 4]
Dec 85
  BT1   platinum compounds
    BT2   transition element compounds
  BT1   tellurides
    BT2   chalcogenides
    BT2   tellurium compounds

PLATINUM 168 [0; 0] *May 86*
  BT1   alpha decay radioisotopes
    BT2   radioisotopes
      BT3   isotopes
  BT1   even-even nuclei
    BT2   nuclei
  BT1   intermediate mass nuclei
    BT2   nuclei
  BT1   platinum isotopes

PLATINUM 169 [0; 0] *May 86*
  BT1   alpha decay radioisotopes
    BT2   radioisotopes
      BT3   isotopes
  BT1   even-odd nuclei
    BT2   nuclei
  BT1   intermediate mass nuclei
    BT2   nuclei
  BT1   millisec living radioisotopes
    BT2   radioisotopes
      BT3   isotopes
  BT1   platinum isotopes

PLATINUM 170 [3; 3] *May 86*
  BT1   alpha decay radioisotopes
  BT2   radioisotopes
   BT3   isotopes
  BT1   even-even nuclei
  BT2   nuclei
  BT1   intermediate mass nuclei
  BT2   nuclei
  BT1   millisec living radioisotopes
  BT2   radioisotopes
   BT3   isotopes
  BT1   platinum isotopes

PLATINUM 171 [2; 2] *May 86*
  BT1   alpha decay radioisotopes
  BT2   radioisotopes
   BT3   isotopes
  BT1   even-odd nuclei
  BT2   nuclei
  BT1   intermediate mass nuclei
  BT2   nuclei
  BT1   millisec living radioisotopes
  BT2   radioisotopes
   BT3   isotopes
  BT1   platinum isotopes

PLATINUM 172 [3; 3] *Jun 85*
  BT1   alpha decay radioisotopes
  BT2   radioisotopes
   BT3   isotopes
  BT1   even-even nuclei
  BT2   nuclei
  BT1   intermediate mass nuclei
  BT2   nuclei
  BT1   millisec living radioisotopes
  BT2   radioisotopes
   BT3   isotopes
  BT1   platinum isotopes

PLATINUM 173 [7; 7]
  BT1   alpha decay radioisotopes
  BT2   radioisotopes
   BT3   isotopes
  BT1   electron capture radioisotopes
  BT2   beta decay radioisotopes
   BT3   radioisotopes
    BT4   isotopes
  BT1   even-odd nuclei
  BT2   nuclei
  BT1   intermediate mass nuclei
  BT2   nuclei
  BT1   millisec living radioisotopes
  BT2   radioisotopes
   BT3   isotopes
  BT1   platinum isotopes

PLATINUM 174 [10; 10]
  BT1   alpha decay radioisotopes
  BT2   radioisotopes
   BT3   isotopes
  BT1   electron capture radioisotopes
  BT2   beta decay radioisotopes
   BT3   radioisotopes
    BT4   isotopes
  BT1   even-even nuclei
  BT2   nuclei
  BT1   intermediate mass nuclei
  BT2   nuclei
  BT1   millisec living radioisotopes
  BT2   radioisotopes
   BT3   isotopes
  BT1   platinum isotopes

PLATINUM 175 [12; 12]
  BT1   alpha decay radioisotopes
  BT2   radioisotopes
   BT3   isotopes
  BT1   electron capture radioisotopes
  BT2   beta decay radioisotopes
   BT3   radioisotopes
    BT4   isotopes
  BT1   even-odd nuclei
  BT2   nuclei
  BT1   intermediate mass nuclei
  BT2   nuclei
  BT1   platinum isotopes
  BT1   seconds living radioisotopes

  BT2   radioisotopes
   BT3   isotopes

PLATINUM 176 [24; 24]
  BT1   alpha decay radioisotopes
  BT2   radioisotopes
   BT3   isotopes
  BT1   electron capture radioisotopes
  BT2   beta decay radioisotopes
   BT3   radioisotopes
    BT4   isotopes
  BT1   even-even nuclei
  BT2   nuclei
  BT1   intermediate mass nuclei
  BT2   nuclei
  BT1   platinum isotopes
  BT1   seconds living radioisotopes
  BT2   radioisotopes
   BT3   isotopes

PLATINUM 177 [10; 10]
  BT1   alpha decay radioisotopes
  BT2   radioisotopes
   BT3   isotopes
  BT1   electron capture radioisotopes
  BT2   beta decay radioisotopes
   BT3   radioisotopes
    BT4   isotopes
  BT1   even-odd nuclei
  BT2   nuclei
  BT1   intermediate mass nuclei
  BT2   nuclei
  BT1   platinum isotopes
  BT1   seconds living radioisotopes
  BT2   radioisotopes
   BT3   isotopes

PLATINUM 178 [22; 22]
  BT1   alpha decay radioisotopes
  BT2   radioisotopes
   BT3   isotopes
  BT1   electron capture radioisotopes
  BT2   beta decay radioisotopes
   BT3   radioisotopes
    BT4   isotopes
  BT1   even-even nuclei
  BT2   nuclei
  BT1   intermediate mass nuclei
  BT2   nuclei
  BT1   platinum isotopes
  BT1   seconds living radioisotopes
  BT2   radioisotopes
   BT3   isotopes

PLATINUM 179 [5; 5]
  BT1   alpha decay radioisotopes
  BT2   radioisotopes
   BT3   isotopes
  BT1   electron capture radioisotopes
  BT2   beta decay radioisotopes
   BT3   radioisotopes
    BT4   isotopes
  BT1   even-odd nuclei
  BT2   nuclei
  BT1   intermediate mass nuclei
  BT2   nuclei
  BT1   platinum isotopes
  BT1   seconds living radioisotopes
  BT2   radioisotopes
   BT3   isotopes

PLATINUM 180 [14; 14]
  BT1   alpha decay radioisotopes
  BT2   radioisotopes
   BT3   isotopes
  BT1   electron capture radioisotopes
  BT2   beta decay radioisotopes
   BT3   radioisotopes
    BT4   isotopes
  BT1   even-even nuclei
  BT2   nuclei
  BT1   intermediate mass nuclei
  BT2   nuclei
  BT1   platinum isotopes
  BT1   seconds living radioisotopes
  BT2   radioisotopes
   BT3   isotopes

PLATINUM 181 [11; 11]
  BT1   alpha decay radioisotopes
  BT2   radioisotopes
   BT3   isotopes
  BT1   electron capture radioisotopes
  BT2   beta decay radioisotopes
   BT3   radioisotopes
    BT4   isotopes
  BT1   even-odd nuclei
  BT2   nuclei
  BT1   heavy nuclei
  BT2   nuclei
  BT1   platinum isotopes
  BT1   seconds living radioisotopes
  BT2   radioisotopes
   BT3   isotopes

PLATINUM 182 [17; 17]
  BT1   alpha decay radioisotopes
  BT2   radioisotopes
   BT3   isotopes
  BT1   beta-plus decay radioisotopes
  BT2   beta decay radioisotopes
   BT3   radioisotopes
    BT4   isotopes
  BT1   electron capture radioisotopes
  BT2   beta decay radioisotopes
   BT3   radioisotopes
    BT4   isotopes
  BT1   even-even nuclei
  BT2   nuclei
  BT1   heavy nuclei
  BT2   nuclei
  BT1   minutes living radioisotopes
  BT2   radioisotopes
   BT3   isotopes
  BT1   platinum isotopes

PLATINUM 183 [18; 18]
  BT1   alpha decay radioisotopes
  BT2   radioisotopes
   BT3   isotopes
  BT1   beta-plus decay radioisotopes
  BT2   beta decay radioisotopes
   BT3   radioisotopes
    BT4   isotopes
  BT1   electron capture radioisotopes
  BT2   beta decay radioisotopes
   BT3   radioisotopes
    BT4   isotopes
  BT1   even-odd nuclei
  BT2   nuclei
  BT1   heavy nuclei
  BT2   nuclei
  BT1   minutes living radioisotopes
  BT2   radioisotopes
   BT3   isotopes
  BT1   platinum isotopes
  BT1   seconds living radioisotopes
  BT2   radioisotopes
   BT3   isotopes

PLATINUM 184 [48; 48]
  BT1   alpha decay radioisotopes
  BT2   radioisotopes
   BT3   isotopes
  BT1   beta-plus decay radioisotopes
  BT2   beta decay radioisotopes
   BT3   radioisotopes
    BT4   isotopes
  BT1   electron capture radioisotopes
  BT2   beta decay radioisotopes
   BT3   radioisotopes
    BT4   isotopes
  BT1   even-even nuclei
  BT2   nuclei
  BT1   heavy nuclei
  BT2   nuclei
  BT1   minutes living radioisotopes
  BT2   radioisotopes
   BT3   isotopes
  BT1   platinum isotopes

PLATINUM 185 [34; 34]
  BT1   alpha decay radioisotopes
  BT2   radioisotopes
   BT3   isotopes
  BT1   beta-plus decay radioisotopes
  BT2   beta decay radioisotopes

PLATINUM 185

  BT3   radioisotopes
  BT4   isotopes
BT1   electron capture radioisotopes
BT2   beta decay radioisotopes
  BT3   radioisotopes
  BT4   isotopes
BT1   even-odd nuclei
BT2   nuclei
BT1   heavy nuclei
BT2   nuclei
BT1   hours living radioisotopes
BT2   radioisotopes
BT3   isotopes
BT1   minutes living radioisotopes
BT2   radioisotopes
BT3   isotopes
BT1   platinum isotopes

PLATINUM 186 [46; 46]
BT1   alpha decay radioisotopes
BT2   radioisotopes
BT3   isotopes
BT1   electron capture radioisotopes
BT2   beta decay radioisotopes
  BT3   radioisotopes
  BT4   isotopes
BT1   even-even nuclei
BT2   nuclei
BT1   heavy nuclei
BT2   nuclei
BT1   hours living radioisotopes
BT2   radioisotopes
BT3   isotopes
BT1   platinum isotopes

PLATINUM 187 [35; 35]
BT1   beta-plus decay radioisotopes
BT2   beta decay radioisotopes
  BT3   radioisotopes
  BT4   isotopes
BT1   electron capture radioisotopes
BT2   beta decay radioisotopes
  BT3   radioisotopes
  BT4   isotopes
BT1   even-odd nuclei
BT2   nuclei
BT1   heavy nuclei
BT2   nuclei
BT1   hours living radioisotopes
BT2   radioisotopes
BT3   isotopes
BT1   platinum isotopes

PLATINUM 188 [66; 66]
BT1   alpha decay radioisotopes
BT2   radioisotopes
BT3   isotopes
BT1   days living radioisotopes
BT2   radioisotopes
BT3   isotopes
BT1   electron capture radioisotopes
BT2   beta decay radioisotopes
  BT3   radioisotopes
  BT4   isotopes
BT1   even-even nuclei
BT2   nuclei
BT1   heavy nuclei
BT2   nuclei
BT1   platinum isotopes

PLATINUM 189 [35; 35]
BT1   beta-plus decay radioisotopes
BT2   beta decay radioisotopes
  BT3   radioisotopes
  BT4   isotopes
BT1   electron capture radioisotopes
BT2   beta decay radioisotopes
  BT3   radioisotopes
  BT4   isotopes
BT1   even-odd nuclei
BT2   nuclei
BT1   heavy nuclei
BT2   nuclei
BT1   hours living radioisotopes
BT2   radioisotopes
BT3   isotopes
BT1   platinum isotopes

PLATINUM 190 [78; 78]
BT1   alpha decay radioisotopes
BT2   radioisotopes
BT3   isotopes
BT1   even-even nuclei
BT2   nuclei
BT1   heavy nuclei
BT2   nuclei
BT1   platinum isotopes
BT1   years living radioisotopes
BT2   radioisotopes
BT3   isotopes

PLATINUM 190 TARGET [6; 6] *Sep 79*
BT1   targets

PLATINUM 191 [69; 69]
BT1   days living radioisotopes
BT2   radioisotopes
BT3   isotopes
BT1   electron capture radioisotopes
BT2   beta decay radioisotopes
  BT3   radioisotopes
  BT4   isotopes
BT1   even-odd nuclei
BT2   nuclei
BT1   heavy nuclei
BT2   nuclei
BT1   platinum isotopes

PLATINUM 192 [132; 132]
BT1   even-even nuclei
BT2   nuclei
BT1   heavy nuclei
BT2   nuclei
BT1   platinum isotopes
BT1   stable isotopes
BT2   isotopes

PLATINUM 192 TARGET [25; 25]
Jan 78
BT1   targets

PLATINUM 193 [61; 61]
BT1   days living radioisotopes
BT2   radioisotopes
BT3   isotopes
BT1   electron capture radioisotopes
BT2   beta decay radioisotopes
  BT3   radioisotopes
  BT4   isotopes
BT1   even-odd nuclei
BT2   nuclei
BT1   heavy nuclei
BT2   nuclei
BT1   internal conversion radioisoto
BT2   radioisotopes
BT3   isotopes
BT1   isomeric transition isotopes
BT2   radioisotopes
BT3   isotopes
BT1   platinum isotopes
BT1   years living radioisotopes
BT2   radioisotopes
BT3   isotopes

PLATINUM 194 [167; 167]
BT1   even-even nuclei
BT2   nuclei
BT1   heavy nuclei
BT2   nuclei
BT1   platinum isotopes
BT1   stable isotopes
BT2   isotopes

PLATINUM 194 TARGET [108; 108]
BT1   targets

PLATINUM 195 [221; 221]
BT1   days living radioisotopes
BT2   radioisotopes
BT3   isotopes
BT1   even-odd nuclei
BT2   nuclei
BT1   heavy nuclei
BT2   nuclei
BT1   internal conversion radioisoto
BT2   radioisotopes
BT3   isotopes
BT1   isomeric transition isotopes
BT2   radioisotopes
BT3   isotopes
BT1   platinum isotopes
BT1   stable isotopes
BT2   isotopes

PLATINUM 195 TARGET [75; 75]
BT1   targets

PLATINUM 196 [156; 156]
BT1   even-even nuclei
BT2   nuclei
BT1   heavy nuclei
BT2   nuclei
BT1   platinum isotopes
BT1   stable isotopes
BT2   isotopes

PLATINUM 196 TARGET [107; 107]
BT1   targets

PLATINUM 197 [67; 67]
BT1   beta-minus decay radioisotopes
BT2   beta decay radioisotopes
  BT3   radioisotopes
  BT4   isotopes
BT1   even-odd nuclei
BT2   nuclei
BT1   heavy nuclei
BT2   nuclei
BT1   hours living radioisotopes
BT2   radioisotopes
BT3   isotopes
BT1   internal conversion radioisoto
BT2   radioisotopes
BT3   isotopes
BT1   isomeric transition isotopes
BT2   radioisotopes
BT3   isotopes
BT1   platinum isotopes

PLATINUM 198 [63; 63]
BT1   even-even nuclei
BT2   nuclei
BT1   heavy nuclei
BT2   nuclei
BT1   platinum isotopes
BT1   stable isotopes
BT2   isotopes

PLATINUM 198 TARGET [100; 100]
BT1   targets

PLATINUM 199 [21; 21]
BT1   beta-minus decay radioisotopes
BT2   beta decay radioisotopes
  BT3   radioisotopes
  BT4   isotopes
BT1   even-odd nuclei
BT2   nuclei
BT1   heavy nuclei
BT2   nuclei
BT1   internal conversion radioisoto
BT2   radioisotopes
BT3   isotopes
BT1   isomeric transition isotopes
BT2   radioisotopes
BT3   isotopes
BT1   minutes living radioisotopes
BT2   radioisotopes
BT3   isotopes
BT1   platinum isotopes
BT1   seconds living radioisotopes
BT2   radioisotopes
BT3   isotopes

PLATINUM 200 [11; 11]
BT1   beta-minus decay radioisotopes
BT2   beta decay radioisotopes
  BT3   radioisotopes
  BT4   isotopes
BT1   even-even nuclei
BT2   nuclei
BT1   heavy nuclei

PLATINUM 200

```
    BT2    nuclei
    BT1    hours living radioisotopes
    BT2    radioisotopes
      BT3    isotopes
    BT1    platinum isotopes
```

PLATINUM 201 [1; 1]
```
    BT1    beta-minus decay radioisotopes
    BT2    beta decay radioisotopes
      BT3    radioisotopes
        BT4    isotopes
    BT1    even-odd nuclei
    BT2    nuclei
    BT1    heavy nuclei
    BT2    nuclei
    BT1    minutes living radioisotopes
    BT2    radioisotopes
      BT3    isotopes
    BT1    platinum isotopes
```

PLATINUM 202 [0; 0]
```
    BT1    even-even nuclei
    BT2    nuclei
    BT1    heavy nuclei
    BT2    nuclei
    BT1    platinum isotopes
```

PLATINUM 203 [0; 0]
```
    BT1    even-odd nuclei
    BT2    nuclei
    BT1    heavy nuclei
    BT2    nuclei
    BT1    platinum isotopes
```

PLATINUM 204 [2; 2]
```
    BT1    even-even nuclei
    BT2    nuclei
    BT1    heavy nuclei
    BT2    nuclei
    BT1    platinum isotopes
```

PLATINUM 205 [0; 0]
```
    BT1    even-odd nuclei
    BT2    nuclei
    BT1    heavy nuclei
    BT2    nuclei
    BT1    platinum isotopes
```

PLATINUM 206 [0; 0]
```
    BT1    even-even nuclei
    BT2    nuclei
    BT1    heavy nuclei
    BT2    nuclei
    BT1    platinum isotopes
```

PLATINUM 207 [0; 0]
```
    BT1    even-odd nuclei
    BT2    nuclei
    BT1    heavy nuclei
    BT2    nuclei
    BT1    platinum isotopes
```

PLATINUM 208 [1; 1]
```
    BT1    even-even nuclei
    BT2    nuclei
    BT1    heavy nuclei
    BT2    nuclei
    BT1    platinum isotopes
```

platr reactor
```
    USE    prr reactor
```

PLATYHELMINTHS [24; 290]
```
    UF     cercaria
    UF     worms (flat)
    BT1    invertebrates
    BT2    animals
    NT1    cestodes
      NT2    hymenolepis
    NT1    trematodes
      NT2    fasciola
      NT2    schistosoma
    NT1    turbellaria
      NT2    planaria
```

PLBR REACTOR [24; 24] *Jul 78*
```
    UF     prototype large breeder react
    BT1    lmfbr type reactors
    BT2    fbr type reactors
      BT3    breeder reactors
        BT4    reactors
      BT3    fast reactors
        BT4    epithermal reactors
          BT5    reactors
    BT2    liquid metal cooled reactors
      BT3    reactors
    BT1    power reactors
    BT2    reactors
```

pleasanton usa ntr reactor
```
    USE    ntr reactor
```

PLEIADE DEVICE [8; 8]
```
    BT1    magnetic mirrors
    BT2    open plasma devices
      BT3    thermonuclear devices
```

plesiotherapy
```
    USE    radiotherapy
```

PLEURA [313; 313]
```
    BT1    serous membranes
    BT2    membranes
    RT     chest
    RT     lungs
    RT     mediastinum
```

PLEXIGLAS [221; 221]
```
    BT1    polyacrylates
    BT2    esters
      BT3    organic compounds
    BT2    polyvinyls
      BT3    organic polymers
        BT4    organic compounds
        BT4    polymers
    RT     pmma
```

PLOIDY [163; 542]
```
    NT1    aneuploidy
    NT1    diploidy
    NT1    haploidy
    NT1    polyploidy
    RT     genome mutations
```

PLOTTERS [230; 230]
```
    BT1    computer-graphics devices
    BT2    computer output devices
    RT     computer graphics
    RT     display devices
```

PLOWSHARE PROJECT [113; 390]
```
    UF     project plowshare
    NT1    cabriolet event
    NT1    chariot event
    NT1    danny boy event
    NT1    gasbuggy event
    NT1    gnome event
    NT1    hardhat event
    NT1    marvel event
    NT1    pre-gondola i event
    NT1    pre-gondola ii event
    NT1    rio blanco event
    NT1    rulison event
    NT1    schooner event
    NT1    sedan event
    NT1    sloop event
    NT1    wagon wheel event
    RT     contained explosions
    RT     cratering explosions
    RT     nuclear excavation
    RT     nuclear explosions
    RT     surface explosions
    RT     underground explosions
```

PLT DEVICES [634; 634] *Oct 75*
```
    UF     princeton large torus
    BT1    tokamak devices
    BT2    closed plasma devices
      BT3    thermonuclear devices
```

plugs
```
    USE    closures
```

plum brook nasa-tr
```
    USE    pbr reactor
```

plum brook reactor facility
```
    USE    pbr reactor
```

PLUMBATES [5; 5]
(Specific compounds should be indexed by coordination of a descriptor of the form (CATION) COMPOUNDS and the above anion descriptor.)
```
    BT1    lead compounds
    BT1    oxygen compounds
    RT     lead oxides
```

PLUMBBOB PROJECT [5; 11]
```
    UF     project plumbbob
    NT1    smoky event
    RT     nuclear explosions
    RT     nuclear weapons
```

PLUMES [1,306; 1,306]
```
    RT     air pollution
    RT     gaseous wastes
    RT     liquid wastes
    RT     smokes
    RT     stack disposal
    RT     stacks
    RT     thermal pollution
    RT     waste heat
    RT     water pollution
```

PLUMS [17; 17]
```
    BT1    fruits
    BT2    food
```

plunger method
(Method for the determination of lifetimes of nuclear levels.)
```
    USE    charge plunger method
```

PLURONICS [4; 4]
```
    BT1    detergents
    BT2    emulsifiers
      BT3    additives
    BT2    wetting agents
      BT3    surfactants
    BT1    polyethylene glycols
    BT2    organic polymers
      BT3    organic compounds
      BT3    polymers
```

PLUTO PLANET [77; 77]
```
    BT1    planets
```

PLUTO REACTOR [54; 54]
```
    UF     harwell pluto reactor
    BT1    enriched uranium reactors
    BT2    reactors
    BT1    heavy water cooled reactors
    BT2    reactors
    BT1    heavy water moderated reactors
    BT2    reactors
    BT1    materials testing reactors
    BT2    irradiation reactors
      BT3    reactors
    BT1    tank type reactors
    BT2    reactors
    BT1    thermal reactors
    BT2    reactors
```

PLUTONIC ROCKS [141; 1,486] *Oct 85*
(Rocks formed at considerable depth by crystallization of magma or by chemical alteration.)
```
    UF     intrusion (rock)
    UF     intrusive rocks
    UF     rock intrusion
    UF     sedimentary intrusive rocks
    BT1    igneous rocks
```

```
      BT2       rocks
      NT1       anorthosites
      NT1       gabbros
      NT1       granites
      NT2        aplites
      NT2        granodiorites
      NT2        quartz monzonite
      NT1       pegmatites
      NT1       peridotites
      NT2        kimberlites
      NT1       syenites
      RT        mineralization

PLUTONIUM [8,576; 8,690]
      BT1       actinides
      BT2        metals
      BT3         elements
      BT1       transuranium elements
      BT2        elements
      NT1       plutonium-alpha
      NT1       plutonium-beta
      NT1       plutonium-delta
      NT1       plutonium-epsilon
      NT1       plutonium-eta
      NT1       plutonium-gamma
      RT        nuclear fuels
      RT        plutonium recycle

PLUTONIUM ADDITIONS [16; 16]
(Alloys containing not more than 1% Pu
are listed here.)
      RT        plutonium alloys
      RT        plutonium compounds

PLUTONIUM ALLOYS [329; 428]
(Alloys containing more than 1% Pu.)
      BT1       actinide alloys
      BT2        alloys
      NT1       plutonium base alloys
      RT        plutonium additions

PLUTONIUM ARSENIDES [12; 12]
      Feb 79
      BT1       arsenides
      BT2        arsenic compounds
      BT2        pnictides
      BT1       plutonium compounds
      BT2        actinide compounds
      BT2        transuranium compounds

PLUTONIUM BASE ALLOYS [95; 95]
      BT1       plutonium alloys
      BT2        actinide alloys
      BT3         alloys

PLUTONIUM BORIDES [6; 6]
      BT1       borides
      BT2        boron compounds
      BT1       plutonium compounds
      BT2        actinide compounds
      BT2        transuranium compounds

PLUTONIUM BROMIDES [9; 9]
      BT1       bromides
      BT2        bromine compounds
      BT3         halogen compounds
      BT2        halides
      BT3         halogen compounds
      BT1       plutonium compounds
      BT2        actinide compounds
      BT2        transuranium compounds

PLUTONIUM CARBIDES [669; 669]
      BT1       carbides
      BT2        carbon compounds
      BT1       plutonium compounds
      BT2        actinide compounds
      BT2        transuranium compounds

PLUTONIUM CARBONATES [23; 23]
      BT1       carbonates
      BT2        carbon compounds
      BT2        oxygen compounds
      BT1       plutonium compounds
      BT2        actinide compounds
      BT2        transuranium compounds

PLUTONIUM CHLORIDES [95; 95]
      BT1       chlorides
      BT2        chlorine compounds
      BT3         halogen compounds
      BT2        halides
      BT3         halogen compounds
      BT1       plutonium compounds
      BT2        actinide compounds
      BT2        transuranium compounds

PLUTONIUM COMPLEXES [585; 609]
      BT1       actinide complexes
      BT2        complexes
      BT1       transuranium complexes
      NT1       plutonyl complexes

PLUTONIUM COMPOUNDS
[1,023; 6,960]
      BT1       actinide compounds
      BT1       transuranium compounds
      NT1       plutonium arsenides
      NT1       plutonium borides
      NT1       plutonium bromides
      NT1       plutonium carbides
      NT1       plutonium carbonates
      NT1       plutonium chlorides
      NT1       plutonium fluorides
      NT1       plutonium hydrides
      NT1       plutonium hydroxides
      NT1       plutonium iodides
      NT1       plutonium nitrates
      NT1       plutonium nitrides
      NT1       plutonium oxides
       NT2       plutonium dioxide
      NT1       plutonium perchlorates
      NT1       plutonium peroxide
      NT1       plutonium phosphates
      NT1       plutonium phosphides
      NT1       plutonium selenides
      NT1       plutonium silicates
      NT1       plutonium sulfates
      NT1       plutonium sulfides
      NT1       plutonium tellurides
      NT1       plutonyl compounds
      RT        plutonium additions

PLUTONIUM DIOXIDE [2,175; 2,175]
      BT1       plutonium oxides
      BT2        oxides
      BT3         chalcogenides
      BT3         oxygen compounds
      BT2        plutonium compounds
      BT3         actinide compounds
      BT3         transuranium compounds

PLUTONIUM FLUORIDES [193; 193]
      BT1       fluorides
      BT2        fluorine compounds
      BT3         halogen compounds
      BT2        halides
      BT3         halogen compounds
      BT1       plutonium compounds
      BT2        actinide compounds
      BT2        transuranium compounds

PLUTONIUM HYDRIDES [37; 37]
      BT1       hydrides
      BT2        hydrogen compounds
      BT1       plutonium compounds
      BT2        actinide compounds
      BT2        transuranium compounds

PLUTONIUM HYDROXIDES [57; 57]
      BT1       hydroxides
      BT2        hydrogen compounds
      BT2        oxygen compounds
      BT1       plutonium compounds
      BT2        actinide compounds
      BT2        transuranium compounds

PLUTONIUM IODIDES [14; 14]
      BT1       iodides
      BT2        halides
      BT3         halogen compounds
      BT2        iodine compounds
      BT3         halogen compounds
      BT1       plutonium compounds
      BT2        actinide compounds
      BT2        transuranium compounds

PLUTONIUM IONS [80; 80]
      BT1       ions
      BT2        charged particles

PLUTONIUM ISOTOPES [1,023; 10,023]
      NT1       plutonium 230
      NT1       plutonium 231
      NT1       plutonium 232
      NT1       plutonium 233
      NT1       plutonium 234
      NT1       plutonium 235
      NT1       plutonium 236
      NT1       plutonium 237
      NT1       plutonium 238
      NT1       plutonium 239
      NT1       plutonium 240
      NT1       plutonium 241
      NT1       plutonium 242
      NT1       plutonium 243
      NT1       plutonium 244
      NT1       plutonium 245
      NT1       plutonium 246
      NT1       plutonium 247
      NT1       plutonium 248
      NT1       plutonium 250

PLUTONIUM NITRATES [616; 616]
      BT1       nitrates
      BT2        nitrogen compounds
      BT2        oxygen compounds
      BT1       plutonium compounds
      BT2        actinide compounds
      BT2        transuranium compounds

PLUTONIUM NITRIDES [242; 242]
      BT1       nitrides
      BT2        nitrogen compounds
      BT2        pnictides
      BT1       plutonium compounds
      BT2        actinide compounds
      BT2        transuranium compounds
      RT        mixed nitride fuels

PLUTONIUM OXIDES [2,308; 4,471]
      BT1       oxides
      BT2        chalcogenides
      BT2        oxygen compounds
      BT1       plutonium compounds
      BT2        actinide compounds
      BT2        transuranium compounds
      NT1       plutonium dioxide

PLUTONIUM PERCHLORATES [7; 7]
      Jan 77
      BT1       perchlorates
      BT2        chlorine compounds
      BT3         halogen compounds
      BT2        oxygen compounds
      BT1       plutonium compounds
      BT2        actinide compounds
      BT2        transuranium compounds

PLUTONIUM PEROXIDE [6; 6] Dec
      BT1       peroxides
      BT2        oxygen compounds
      BT1       plutonium compounds
      BT2        actinide compounds
      BT2        transuranium compounds

PLUTONIUM PHOSPHATES [14; 14]
      BT1       phosphates
      BT2        oxygen compounds
      BT2        phosphorus compounds
      BT1       plutonium compounds
      BT2        actinide compounds
      BT2        transuranium compounds

PLUTONIUM PHOSPHIDES [9; 9]
      BT1       phosphides
      BT2        phosphorus compounds
      BT2        pnictides
      BT1       plutonium compounds
      BT2        actinide compounds
      BT2        transuranium compounds
```

PLUTONIUM PRODUCTION REACTORS [49; 592]
- BT1 production reactors
- BT2 reactors
- NT1 calder hall a-1 reactor
- NT1 calder hall a-2 reactor
- NT1 calder hall b-3 reactor
- NT1 calder hall b-4 reactor
- NT1 chapelcross-1 reactor
- NT1 chapelcross-2 reactor
- NT1 chapelcross-3 reactor
- NT1 chapelcross-4 reactor
- NT1 g-1 reactor
- NT1 g-2 reactor
- NT1 g-3 reactor
- NT1 hanford production reactors
- NT1 n-reactor
- NT1 windscale production reactors

PLUTONIUM REACTORS [54; 1,936]
- BT1 reactors
- NT1 clementine reactor
- NT1 ebr-1 reactor
- NT1 hclwr type reactors
- NT1 jatr reactor
- NT1 lampre-1 reactor
- NT1 masurca reactor
- NT1 phenix reactor
- NT1 prcf reactor
- NT1 rapsodie reactor
- NT1 sbr-1 reactor
- NT1 sbr-2 reactor
- NT1 sbr-5 reactor
- NT1 sefor reactor
- NT1 super phenix reactor
- NT1 zeep reactor
- NT1 zephyr reactor
- RT beloyarsk-3 reactor
- RT bn-350 reactor
- RT clinch river breeder reactor
- RT ebr-2 reactor
- RT pfr reactor
- RT sneak reactor
- RT vera reactor
- RT zebra reactor
- RT zenith reactor

PLUTONIUM RECYCLE [912; 912]
- BT1 fuel cycle
- RT fuel cycle centers
- RT plutonium

plutonium recycle critical fac
- USE prcf reactor

plutonium recycle test reactor
- USE prtr reactor

PLUTONIUM SELENIDES [10; 10]
Feb 79
- BT1 plutonium compounds
- BT2 actinide compounds
- BT2 transuranium compounds
- BT1 selenides
- BT2 chalcogenides
- BT2 selenium compounds

PLUTONIUM SILICATES [2; 2] *Jul 84*
- BT1 plutonium compounds
- BT2 actinide compounds
- BT2 transuranium compounds
- BT1 silicates
- BT2 oxygen compounds
- BT2 silicon compounds

PLUTONIUM SULFATES [41; 41]
- BT1 plutonium compounds
- BT2 actinide compounds
- BT2 transuranium compounds
- BT1 sulfates
- BT2 oxygen compounds
- BT2 sulfur compounds

PLUTONIUM SULFIDES [9; 9]
- BT1 plutonium compounds
- BT2 actinide compounds
- BT2 transuranium compounds
- BT1 sulfides
- BT2 chalcogenides
- BT2 sulfur compounds

PLUTONIUM TELLURIDES [20; 20]
Feb 76
- BT1 plutonium compounds
- BT2 actinide compounds
- BT2 transuranium compounds
- BT1 tellurides
- BT2 chalcogenides
- BT2 tellurium compounds

PLUTONIUM 230 [2; 2] *Dec 90*
- BT1 actinide nuclei
- BT2 heavy nuclei
- BT3 nuclei
- BT1 alpha decay radioisotopes
- BT2 radioisotopes
- BT3 isotopes
- BT1 even-even nuclei
- BT2 nuclei
- BT1 millisec living radioisotopes
- BT2 radioisotopes
- BT3 isotopes
- BT1 plutonium isotopes

PLUTONIUM 231 [0; 0]
- BT1 actinide nuclei
- BT2 heavy nuclei
- BT3 nuclei
- BT1 even-odd nuclei
- BT2 nuclei
- BT1 plutonium isotopes

PLUTONIUM 232 [14; 14]
- BT1 actinide nuclei
- BT2 heavy nuclei
- BT3 nuclei
- BT1 alpha decay radioisotopes
- BT2 radioisotopes
- BT3 isotopes
- BT1 electron capture radioisotopes
- BT2 beta decay radioisotopes
- BT3 radioisotopes
- BT4 isotopes
- BT1 even-even nuclei
- BT2 nuclei
- BT1 minutes living radioisotopes
- BT2 radioisotopes
- BT3 isotopes
- BT1 plutonium isotopes

PLUTONIUM 233 [8; 8]
- BT1 actinide nuclei
- BT2 heavy nuclei
- BT3 nuclei
- BT1 alpha decay radioisotopes
- BT2 radioisotopes
- BT3 isotopes
- BT1 electron capture radioisotopes
- BT2 beta decay radioisotopes
- BT3 radioisotopes
- BT4 isotopes
- BT1 even-odd nuclei
- BT2 nuclei
- BT1 minutes living radioisotopes
- BT2 radioisotopes
- BT3 isotopes
- BT1 plutonium isotopes

PLUTONIUM 234 [19; 19]
- BT1 actinide nuclei
- BT2 heavy nuclei
- BT3 nuclei
- BT1 alpha decay radioisotopes
- BT2 radioisotopes
- BT3 isotopes
- BT1 electron capture radioisotopes
- BT2 beta decay radioisotopes
- BT3 radioisotopes
- BT4 isotopes
- BT1 even-even nuclei
- BT2 nuclei
- BT1 hours living radioisotopes
- BT2 radioisotopes
- BT3 isotopes
- BT1 plutonium isotopes

PLUTONIUM 235 [18; 18]
- BT1 actinide nuclei
- BT2 heavy nuclei
- BT3 nuclei
- BT1 alpha decay radioisotopes
- BT2 radioisotopes
- BT3 isotopes
- BT1 electron capture radioisotopes
- BT2 beta decay radioisotopes
- BT3 radioisotopes
- BT4 isotopes
- BT1 even-odd nuclei
- BT2 nuclei
- BT1 internal conversion radioisoto
- BT2 radioisotopes
- BT3 isotopes
- BT1 minutes living radioisotopes
- BT2 radioisotopes
- BT3 isotopes
- BT1 plutonium isotopes
- BT1 spontaneous fission radioisoto
- BT2 radioisotopes
- BT3 isotopes

PLUTONIUM 235 TARGET [2; 2]
- BT1 targets

PLUTONIUM 236 [156; 156]
- BT1 actinide nuclei
- BT2 heavy nuclei
- BT3 nuclei
- BT1 alpha decay radioisotopes
- BT2 radioisotopes
- BT3 isotopes
- BT1 even-even nuclei
- BT2 nuclei
- BT1 magnesium 28 decay radioisotop
- BT2 heavy ion decay radioisotopes
- BT3 radioisotopes
- BT4 isotopes
- BT1 plutonium isotopes
- BT1 spontaneous fission radioisoto
- BT2 radioisotopes
- BT3 isotopes
- BT1 years living radioisotopes
- BT2 radioisotopes
- BT3 isotopes

PLUTONIUM 236 TARGET [6; 6]
Nov 77
- BT1 targets

PLUTONIUM 237 [220; 220]
- BT1 actinide nuclei
- BT2 heavy nuclei
- BT3 nuclei
- BT1 alpha decay radioisotopes
- BT2 radioisotopes
- BT3 isotopes
- BT1 days living radioisotopes
- BT2 radioisotopes
- BT3 isotopes
- DT1 electron capture radioisotopes
- BT2 beta decay radioisotopes
- BT3 radioisotopes
- BT4 isotopes
- BT1 even-odd nuclei
- BT2 nuclei
- BT1 internal conversion radioisoto
- BT2 radioisotopes
- BT3 isotopes
- BT1 isomeric transition isotopes
- BT2 radioisotopes
- BT3 isotopes
- BT1 nanosec living radioisotopes
- BT2 radioisotopes
- BT3 isotopes
- BT1 plutonium isotopes
- BT1 spontaneous fission radioisoto
- BT2 radioisotopes
- BT3 isotopes

PLUTONIUM 237 TARGET [5; 5]
Jan 77
BT1   targets

PLUTONIUM 238 [2,920; 2,920]
BT1   actinide nuclei
 BT2   heavy nuclei
  BT3   nuclei
BT1   alpha decay radioisotopes
 BT2   radioisotopes
  BT3   isotopes
BT1   even-even nuclei
 BT2   nuclei
BT1   plutonium isotopes
BT1   silicon 32 decay radioisotopes
 BT2   heavy ion decay radioisotopes
  BT3   radioisotopes
   BT4   isotopes
BT1   spontaneous fission radioisoto
 BT2   radioisotopes
  BT3   isotopes
BT1   years living radioisotopes
 BT2   radioisotopes
  BT3   isotopes

PLUTONIUM 238 TARGET [42; 42]
BT1   targets

PLUTONIUM 239 [6,148; 6,148]
BT1   actinide nuclei
 BT2   heavy nuclei
  BT3   nuclei
BT1   alpha decay radioisotopes
 BT2   radioisotopes
  BT3   isotopes
BT1   even-odd nuclei
 BT2   nuclei
BT1   plutonium isotopes
BT1   spontaneous fission radioisoto
 BT2   radioisotopes
  BT3   isotopes
BT1   years living radioisotopes
 BT2   radioisotopes
  BT3   isotopes

PLUTONIUM 239 TARGET [677; 677]
BT1   targets

PLUTONIUM 240 [2,038; 2,038]
BT1   actinide nuclei
 BT2   heavy nuclei
  BT3   nuclei
BT1   alpha decay radioisotopes
 BT2   radioisotopes
  BT3   isotopes
BT1   even-even nuclei
 BT2   nuclei
BT1   plutonium isotopes
BT1   spontaneous fission radioisoto
 BT2   radioisotopes
  BT3   isotopes
BT1   years living radioisotopes
 BT2   radioisotopes
  BT3   isotopes

PLUTONIUM 240 TARGET [157; 157]
BT1   targets

PLUTONIUM 241 [787; 787]
BT1   actinide nuclei
 BT2   heavy nuclei
  BT3   nuclei
BT1   alpha decay radioisotopes
 BT2   radioisotopes
  BT3   isotopes
BT1   beta-minus decay radioisotopes
 BT2   beta decay radioisotopes
  BT3   radioisotopes
   BT4   isotopes
BT1   even-odd nuclei
 BT2   nuclei
BT1   plutonium isotopes
BT1   spontaneous fission radioisoto
 BT2   radioisotopes
  BT3   isotopes

BT1   years living radioisotopes
 BT2   radioisotopes
  BT3   isotopes

PLUTONIUM 241 TARGET [163; 163]
BT1   targets

PLUTONIUM 242 [506; 506]
BT1   actinide nuclei
 BT2   heavy nuclei
  BT3   nuclei
BT1   alpha decay radioisotopes
 BT2   radioisotopes
  BT3   isotopes
BT1   even-even nuclei
 BT2   nuclei
BT1   plutonium isotopes
BT1   spontaneous fission radioisoto
 BT2   radioisotopes
  BT3   isotopes
BT1   years living radioisotopes
 BT2   radioisotopes
  BT3   isotopes

PLUTONIUM 242 TARGET [147; 147]
BT1   targets

PLUTONIUM 243 [46; 46]
BT1   actinide nuclei
 BT2   heavy nuclei
  BT3   nuclei
BT1   beta-minus decay radioisotopes
 BT2   beta decay radioisotopes
  BT3   radioisotopes
   BT4   isotopes
BT1   even-odd nuclei
 BT2   nuclei
BT1   hours living radioisotopes
 BT2   radioisotopes
  BT3   isotopes
BT1   plutonium isotopes
BT1   spontaneous fission radioisoto
 BT2   radioisotopes
  BT3   isotopes

PLUTONIUM 243 TARGET [5; 5]
Nov 77
BT1   targets

PLUTONIUM 244 [198; 198]
BT1   actinide nuclei
 BT2   heavy nuclei
  BT3   nuclei
BT1   alpha decay radioisotopes
 BT2   radioisotopes
  BT3   isotopes
BT1   even-even nuclei
 BT2   nuclei
BT1   plutonium isotopes
BT1   spontaneous fission radioisoto
 BT2   radioisotopes
  BT3   isotopes
BT1   years living radioisotopes
 BT2   radioisotopes
  BT3   isotopes

PLUTONIUM 244 TARGET [49; 49]
Jul 76
BT1   targets

PLUTONIUM 245 [6; 6]
BT1   actinide nuclei
 BT2   heavy nuclei
  BT3   nuclei
BT1   beta-minus decay radioisotopes
 BT2   beta decay radioisotopes
  BT3   radioisotopes
   BT4   isotopes
BT1   even-odd nuclei
 BT2   nuclei
BT1   hours living radioisotopes
 BT2   radioisotopes
  BT3   isotopes
BT1   plutonium isotopes

PLUTONIUM 246 [10; 10]
BT1   actinide nuclei
 BT2   heavy nuclei
  BT3   nuclei
BT1   beta-minus decay radioisotopes
 BT2   beta decay radioisotopes
  BT3   radioisotopes
   BT4   isotopes
BT1   days living radioisotopes
 BT2   radioisotopes
  BT3   isotopes
BT1   even-even nuclei
 BT2   nuclei
BT1   plutonium isotopes

PLUTONIUM 247 [4; 4] *Mar 85*
BT1   actinide nuclei
 BT2   heavy nuclei
  BT3   nuclei
BT1   days living radioisotopes
 BT2   radioisotopes
  BT3   isotopes
BT1   even-odd nuclei
 BT2   nuclei
BT1   plutonium isotopes

PLUTONIUM 248 [2; 2]
BT1   actinide nuclei
 BT2   heavy nuclei
  BT3   nuclei
BT1   even-even nuclei
 BT2   nuclei
BT1   plutonium isotopes

PLUTONIUM 250 [1; 1]
BT1   actinide nuclei
 BT2   heavy nuclei
  BT3   nuclei
BT1   even-even nuclei
 BT2   nuclei
BT1   plutonium isotopes

PLUTONIUM-ALPHA [72; 72]
BT1   plutonium
 BT2   actinides
  BT3   metals
   BT4   elements
 BT2   transuranium elements
  BT3   elements

PLUTONIUM-BETA [21; 21]
BT1   plutonium
 BT2   actinides
  BT3   metals
   BT4   elements
 BT2   transuranium elements
  BT3   elements

PLUTONIUM-DELTA [55; 55]
BT1   plutonium
 BT2   actinides
  BT3   metals
   BT4   elements
 BT2   transuranium elements
  BT3   elements

PLUTONIUM-EPSILON [16; 16]
BT1   plutonium
 BT2   actinides
  BT3   metals
   BT4   elements
 BT2   transuranium elements
  BT3   elements

PLUTONIUM-ETA [0; 0]
BT1   plutonium
 BT2   actinides
  BT3   metals
   BT4   elements
 BT2   transuranium elements
  BT3   elements

PLUTONIUM-GAMMA [7; 7]
- BT1 plutonium
  - BT2 actinides
    - BT3 metals
      - BT4 elements
  - BT2 transuranium elements
    - BT3 elements

PLUTONYL COMPLEXES [26; 26]
Sep 83
- BT1 plutonium complexes
  - BT2 actinide complexes
    - BT3 complexes
  - BT2 transuranium complexes
- RT plutonyl compounds

PLUTONYL COMPOUNDS [72; 72]
- BT1 plutonium compounds
  - BT2 actinide compounds
  - BT2 transuranium compounds
- RT plutonyl complexes

plymouth pilgrim power reactor
- USE pilgrim-1 reactor

PLZT [25; 25] *Apr 84*
(Lead lanthanum zirconate titanate.)
- BT1 lanthanum compounds
  - BT2 rare earth compounds
- BT1 lead compounds
- BT1 titanates
  - BT2 oxygen compounds
  - BT2 titanium compounds
    - BT3 transition element compounds
- BT1 zirconates
  - BT2 oxygen compounds
  - BT2 zirconium compounds
    - BT3 transition element compounds

PM-2A REACTOR [1; 1]
- UF *camp century medium p. p. 2a*
- UF *portable medium power plant 2a*
- BT1 process heat reactors
  - BT2 power reactors
    - BT3 reactors
- BT1 pwr type reactors
  - BT2 enriched uranium reactors
    - BT3 reactors
  - BT2 power reactors
    - BT3 reactors
  - BT2 thermal reactors
    - BT3 reactors
  - BT2 water cooled reactors
    - BT3 reactors
  - BT2 water moderated reactors
    - BT3 reactors

PM-3A REACTOR [2; 2]
- UF *mcmurdo sound medium p. p. 3a*
- UF *portable medium power plant 3a*
- BT1 pwr type reactors
  - BT2 enriched uranium reactors
    - BT3 reactors
  - BT2 power reactors
    - BT3 reactors
  - BT2 thermal reactors
    - BT3 reactors
  - BT2 water cooled reactors
    - BT3 reactors
  - BT2 water moderated reactors
    - BT3 reactors

PMMA [328; 328] *Feb 81*
- UF *polymethylmethacrylates*
- BT1 polyacrylates
  - BT2 esters
    - BT3 organic compounds
  - BT2 polyvinyls
    - BT3 organic polymers
      - BT4 organic compounds
      - BT4 polymers
- RT lucite
- RT methacrylic acid esters
- RT plexiglas

pmr spectra
(Proton Magnetic Resonance spectra.)
- USE nmr spectra
- AND protons

PNC [390; 390]
(Power Reactor and Nuclear Fuel Development Corporation)
- UF *power react nucl fuel dev corp*
- BT1 japanese organizations
  - BT2 national organizations

PNEUMATIC CONTROLLERS [76; 76]
- BT1 control equipment
  - BT2 equipment

PNEUMATIC TRANSPORT [182; 182]
Sep 76
- BT1 transport
- RT pipelines
- RT pneumatics
- RT remote handling equipment

PNEUMATICS [160; 160]
- RT hydraulics
- RT pneumatic transport

PNEUMOCOCCUS [34; 34]
- UF *diplococcus pneumoniae*
- BT1 bacteria
  - BT2 microorganisms
- RT pneumonia

PNEUMOCONIOSES [182; 198]
- UF *silicosis*
- BT1 respiratory system diseases
  - BT2 diseases
- NT1 berylliosis
- RT dusts
- RT lungs

PNEUMONIA [335; 352]
- BT1 respiratory system diseases
  - BT2 diseases
- NT1 bronchopneumonia
- RT lungs
- RT pneumococcus

PNEUMONITIS [601; 601]
- RT inflammation
- RT lungs

PNICTIDES [5; 1,838] *Nov 89*
- NT1 antimonides
  - NT2 indium antimonides
- NT1 arsenides
  - NT2 aluminium arsenides
  - NT2 americium arsenides
  - NT2 berkelium arsenides
  - NT2 boron arsenides
  - NT2 cadmium arsenides
  - NT2 californium arsenides
  - NT2 cerium arsenides
  - NT2 cobalt arsenides
  - NT2 copper arsenides
  - NT2 curium arsenides
  - NT2 europium arsenides
  - NT2 gadolinium arsenides
  - NT2 gallium arsenides
  - NT2 germanium arsenides
  - NT2 indium arsenides
  - NT2 lithium arsenides
  - NT2 magnesium arsenides
  - NT2 manganese arsenides
  - NT2 molybdenum arsenides
  - NT2 neptunium arsenides
  - NT2 nickel arsenides
  - NT2 niobium arsenides
  - NT2 palladium arsenides
  - NT2 platinum arsenides
  - NT2 plutonium arsenides
  - NT2 praseodymium arsenides
  - NT2 ruthenium arsenides
  - NT2 samarium arsenides
  - NT2 silicon arsenides
  - NT2 silver arsenides
  - NT2 terbium arsenides
  - NT2 thorium arsenides
  - NT2 thulium arsenides
  - NT2 tin arsenides
  - NT2 uranium arsenides
  - NT2 vanadium arsenides
  - NT2 yttrium arsenides
  - NT2 zinc arsenides
  - NT2 zirconium arsenides
- NT1 nitrides
  - NT2 aluminium nitrides
  - NT2 americium nitrides
  - NT2 argon nitrides
  - NT2 barium nitrides
  - NT2 berkelium nitrides
  - NT2 beryllium nitrides
  - NT2 boron nitrides
  - NT2 calcium nitrides
  - NT2 californium nitrides
  - NT2 carbon nitrides
  - NT2 cerium nitrides
  - NT2 cesium nitrides
  - NT2 chromium nitrides
  - NT2 copper nitrides
  - NT2 curium nitrides
  - NT2 dysprosium nitrides
  - NT2 einsteinium nitrides
  - NT2 erbium nitrides
  - NT2 europium nitrides
  - NT2 fermium nitrides
  - NT2 gadolinium nitrides
  - NT2 gallium nitrides
  - NT2 germanium nitrides
  - NT2 hafnium nitrides
  - NT2 helium nitrides
  - NT2 holmium nitrides
  - NT2 indium nitrides
  - NT2 iron nitrides
  - NT2 lanthanum nitrides
  - NT2 lead nitrides
  - NT2 lithium nitrides
  - NT2 magnesium nitrides
  - NT2 manganese nitrides
  - NT2 mendelevium nitrides
  - NT2 molybdenum nitrides
  - NT2 neodymium nitrides
  - NT2 neptunium nitrides
  - NT2 nickel nitrides
  - NT2 niobium nitrides
  - NT2 nobelium nitrides
  - NT2 phosphorus nitrides
  - NT2 plutonium nitrides
  - NT2 potassium nitrides
  - NT2 praseodymium nitrides
  - NT2 rhenium nitrides
  - NT2 ruthenium nitrides
  - NT2 samarium nitrides
  - NT2 scandium nitrides
  - NT2 silicon nitrides
  - NT2 silver nitrides
  - NT2 sodium nitrides
  - NT2 sulfur nitrides
  - NT2 tantalum nitrides
  - NT2 terbium nitrides
  - NT2 thorium nitrides
  - NT2 thulium nitrides
  - NT2 tin nitrides
  - NT2 titanium nitrides
  - NT2 tungsten nitrides
  - NT2 uranium nitrides
  - NT2 vanadium nitrides
  - NT2 ytterbium nitrides
  - NT2 yttrium nitrides
  - NT2 zirconium nitrides
- NT1 phosphides
  - NT2 aluminium phosphides
  - NT2 berkelium phosphides
  - NT2 beryllium phosphides
  - NT2 boron phosphides
  - NT2 cadmium phosphides
  - NT2 cerium phosphides
  - NT2 cobalt phosphides
  - NT2 copper phosphides
  - NT2 curium phosphides
  - NT2 dysprosium phosphides
  - NT2 erbium phosphides
  - NT2 europium phosphides
  - NT2 gadolinium phosphides
  - NT2 gallium phosphides
  - NT2 germanium phosphides
  - NT2 hafnium phosphides

NT2 holmium phosphides
NT2 indium phosphides
NT2 iron phosphides
NT2 lanthanum phosphides
NT2 lithium phosphides
NT2 manganese phosphides
NT2 molybdenum phosphides
NT2 neptunium phosphides
NT2 nickel phosphides
NT2 niobium phosphides
NT2 osmium phosphides
NT2 palladium phosphides
NT2 platinum phosphides
NT2 plutonium phosphides
NT2 potassium phosphides
NT2 praseodymium phosphides
NT2 rhodium phosphides
NT2 ruthenium phosphides
NT2 samarium phosphides
NT2 scandium phosphides
NT2 silicon phosphides
NT2 tantalum phosphides
NT2 terbium phosphides
NT2 thorium phosphides
NT2 thulium phosphides
NT2 tin phosphides
NT2 titanium phosphides
NT2 tungsten phosphides
NT2 uranium phosphides
NT2 vanadium phosphides
NT2 yttrium phosphides
NT2 zinc phosphides
NT2 zirconium phosphides

pnl-cml reactor
  USE cml reactor

pnl-prcf reactor
  USE prcf reactor

PNPF REACTOR [5; 5]
  UF *organic moderated r. piqua*
  UF *piqua nuclear power facility*
  UF *piqua organic moderated reacto*
  BT1 enriched uranium reactors
    BT2 reactors
  BT1 omr type reactors
    BT2 organic cooled reactors
      BT3 reactors
    BT2 organic moderated reactors
      BT3 reactors
  BT1 power reactors
    BT2 reactors
  BT1 thermal reactors
    BT2 reactors

PNPP-1 REACTOR [28; 28] *Jun 82*
  UF *bataan philippine power plant*
  UF *philippine nucl. power plant-1*
  BT1 pwr type reactors
    BT2 enriched uranium reactors
      BT3 reactors
    BT2 power reactors
      BT3 reactors
    BT2 thermal reactors
      BT3 reactors
    BT2 water cooled reactors
      BT3 reactors
    BT2 water moderated reactors
      BT3 reactors

PO RIVER [22; 22] *Dec 75*
  BT1 rivers
    BT2 surface waters

pocket calculators
  USE calculators

pocket chambers
  USE condenser ionization chambers

PODBIELNIAK CONTACTORS [7; 7]
  BT1 extraction apparatuses
    BT2 separation equipment
      BT3 equipment
  RT centrifugation
  RT solvent extraction

PODOPHYLLIC ACID [6; 6]
  BT1 hydroxy acids
    BT2 carboxylic acids
      BT3 organic acids
        BT4 organic compounds

POINCARE GROUPS [1,447; 2,204]
  BT1 lie groups
    BT2 symmetry groups
  NT1 lorentz groups
  RT lorentz transformations

POINT BEACH-1 REACTOR [125; 125]
(Two Creeks, Wisconsin, USA)
  UF *wisconsin point beach-1 reacto*
  BT1 pwr type reactors
    BT2 enriched uranium reactors
      BT3 reactors
    BT2 power reactors
      BT3 reactors
    BT2 thermal reactors
      BT3 reactors
    BT2 water cooled reactors
      BT3 reactors
    BT2 water moderated reactors
      BT3 reactors

POINT BEACH-2 REACTOR [92; 92]
(Two Creeks, Wisconsin, USA)
  UF *wisconsin point beach-2 reacto*
  BT1 pwr type reactors
    BT2 enriched uranium reactors
      BT3 reactors
    BT2 power reactors
      BT3 reactors
    BT2 thermal reactors
      BT3 reactors
    BT2 water cooled reactors
      BT3 reactors
    BT2 water moderated reactors
      BT3 reactors

POINT CHARGE [295; 295]
  BT1 electric charges

point contacts
  USE electric contacts

POINT DEFECTS [2,536; 15,724]
  BT1 crystal defects
    BT2 crystal structure
  NT1 interstitials
    NT2 i centers
  NT1 vacancies
    NT2 color centers
      NT3 a centers
      NT3 e centers
      NT3 f centers
      NT3 h centers
      NT3 i centers
      NT3 m centers
      NT3 q centers
      NT3 r centers
      NT3 s centers
      NT3 u centers
      NT3 v centers
      NT3 z centers
    NT2 frenkel defects
    NT2 schottky defects
  RT electron transfer
  RT holes

POINT KERNELS [96; 96] *Nov 77*
  BT1 kernels
  RT absorption
  RT integral equations
  RT radiation flux
  RT shielding

POINT LEPREAU-1 REACTOR [91; 91]
Feb 77
(St. John, New Brunswick, Canada)
  BT1 candu type reactors
    BT2 heavy water moderated reactors
      BT3 reactors
    BT2 pressure tube reactors
      BT3 power reactors
        BT4 reactors
    BT2 thermal reactors
      BT3 reactors
  BT1 natural uranium reactors
    BT2 reactors
  BT1 phwr type reactors
    BT2 heavy water cooled reactors
      BT3 reactors
    BT2 heavy water moderated reactors
      BT3 reactors

POINT LEPREAU-2 REACTOR [26; 26]
Aug 86
(St. John, New Brunswick, Canada.)
  BT1 candu type reactors
    BT2 heavy water moderated reactors
      BT3 reactors
    BT2 pressure tube reactors
      BT3 power reactors
        BT4 reactors
    BT2 thermal reactors
      BT3 reactors
  BT1 natural uranium reactors
    BT2 reactors
  BT1 phwr type reactors
    BT2 heavy water cooled reactors
      BT3 reactors
    BT2 heavy water moderated reactors
      BT3 reactors

point mutations
  USE gene mutations

POINT SOURCES [683; 683]
  BT1 radiation sources

poiseuille flow
  USE laminar flow

POISONING [425; 483]
(Reduction of the reactivity by materials produced in a reactor, e.g., xenon, and samarium, or materials such as boron introduced into the reactor.)
  UF *samarium effect*
  UF *xenon effect*
  NT1 xenon oscillations
  RT burnable poisons
  RT fluid poison control
  RT nuclear poisons
  RT reactivity
  RT reactor kinetics
  RT soluble poisons

poisons (chemical)
  USE hazardous materials

poisons (nuclear)
  USE nuclear poisons

POISSON EQUATION [1,163; 1,163]
  BT1 partial differential equations
    BT2 differential equations
      BT3 equations
  RT laplace equation

POISSON RATIO [326; 326]
  BT1 mechanical properties
  RT elasticity
  RT hooke law
  RT strains

POKHRAN EVENT [15; 15] *Dec 75*
  BT1   contained explosions
    BT2   underground explosions
      BT3 explosions
  BT1   nuclear explosions
    BT2   explosions

POLAND [540; 540]
  BT1   developing countries
  BT1   europe
  RT   centrally planned economies

polar blackout
  USE   polar-cap absorption

POLAR CUSP [226; 226] *Dec 75*
  RT   auroral oval
  RT   earth magnetosphere
  RT   electron precipitation
  RT   ionosphere
  RT   proton precipitation

POLAR REGIONS [752; 1,404]
  NT1   antarctic regions
    NT2   antarctica
  NT1   arctic regions
  RT   polar-cap absorption

polar solvents
(Prior to December 1990, this was a valid descriptor.)
  USE   solvents

polar substorms
  USE   magnetic bays

POLAR-CAP ABSORPTION [109; 109]
  UF   pca
  UF   *polar blackout*
  BT1   absorption
  RT   polar regions
  RT   radiowave radiation
  RT   solar particles

POLAR-CAP AURORAE [144; 144]
  BT1   aurorae
  RT   antarctic regions
  RT   arctic regions
  RT   auroral oval
  RT   auroral zones
  RT   ionosphere

POLARIMETERS [849; 849]
  RT   polarization
  RT   radiation detectors

polaritons
  USE   polarons

POLARIZABILITY [1,164; 1,164]
(Induced dipole moment to external electric field ratio.)
  BT1   electrical properties
  BT2   physical properties
  RT   electric dipole moments
  RT   polarization

POLARIZATION [12,913; 12,913]
(For the process and condition in classical physics only; see also SPIN ORIENTATION.)
  UF+   *pyroelectricity*
  RT   depolarization
  RT   electrets
  RT   faraday effect
  RT   kerr effect
  RT   optical activity
  RT   oriented nuclei
  RT   overhauser effect
  RT   polarimeters
  RT   polarizability
  RT   stokes parameters
  RT   tagged photon method
  RT   voigt effect
  RT   wave forms
  RT   wave propagation

POLARIZATION-ASYMMETRY RATIO [5,279; 5,279]
  UF   *analyzing power*
  RT   scattering
  RT   spin orientation
  RT   targets

POLARIZED BEAMS [8,549; 8,549]
  BT1   beams
  RT   spin orientation

polarized nuclei
  USE   oriented nuclei

POLARIZED PRODUCTS [1,739; 1,739]
(Use only for indexing the products of nuclear reactions or particle interactions.)
  RT   nuclear reactions
  RT   particle interactions

POLARIZED TARGETS [2,352; 2,352]
  BT1   targets
  RT   spin orientation

POLAROGRAPHY [1,666; 1,666]
  RT   electrolysis
  RT   quantitative chemical analysis

POLARONS [604; 604]
  UF   *polaritons*
  BT1   quasi particles

POLIO VIRUS [53; 53]
  BT1   viruses
    BT2   microorganisms
    BT2   parasites
  RT   poliomyelitis

POLIOMYELITIS [7; 7]
  BT1   nervous system diseases
    BT2   diseases
  BT1   viral diseases
    BT2   infectious diseases
      BT3 diseases
  RT   nervous system
  RT   polio virus

polish government maryla reac
  USE   maryla reactor

POLISH ORGANIZATIONS [7; 7]
Nov 88
  BT1   national organizations

POLISHING [266; 797]
  BT1   surface finishing
  NT1   chemical polishing
  NT1   electropolishing
  NT1   mechanical polishing
  RT   metallography
  RT   surface cleaning

POLITICAL ASPECTS [1,396; 1,396]
Feb 82
(Features of an enterprise or undertaking affected by or affecting political establishments.)
  RT   ethical aspects
  RT   government policies
  RT   legal aspects
  RT   public officials
  RT   public opinion
  RT   socio-economic factors

POLLEN [359; 359]
  BT1   gametes
    BT2   germ cells
  RT   flowers
  RT   microspores
  RT   reproduction

POLLUCITE [20; 20] *Jun 83*
  BT1   silicate minerals
    BT2   minerals
  RT   aluminium silicates
  RT   cesium silicates
  RT   sodium silicates

POLLUTANTS [488; 488] *Feb 81*
(Not for radioactive contaminants for which use RADIOACTIVE WASTES or other related terminology.)
  RT   biological wastes
  RT   chemical effluents
  RT   industrial wastes
  RT   municipal wastes
  RT   pesticides
  RT   pollution
  RT   pollution abatement

POLLUTION [1,495; 9,121]
(For nonradioactive pollution only; for radioactive pollution use CONTAMINATION.)
  NT1   air pollution
  NT1   land pollution
  NT1   thermal pollution
  NT1   transfrontier pollution
  NT1   water pollution
  RT   aesthetics
  RT   body burden
  RT   environment
  RT   global aspects
  RT   lcpmpdpw
  RT   pesticides
  RT   pollutants
  RT   pollution abatement
  RT   pollution control equipment
  RT   pollution regulations
  RT   wastes

POLLUTION ABATEMENT [281; 281] *Jun 83*
(For the prevention of pollutants at the source.)
  UF+   *land pollution abatement*
  UF+   *water pollution abatement*
  NT1   air pollution abatement
  RT   chemical effluents
  RT   mitigation
  RT   pollutants
  RT   pollution
  RT   pollution control
  RT   pollution control equipment
  RT   pollution regulations
  RT   wastes

POLLUTION CONTROL [186; 186] *Apr 86*
(For management or removal of pollutants after they are formed by a source.)
  UF+   *land pollution control*
  BT1   control
  NT1   air pollution control
  NT1   water pollution control
  RT   pollution abatement
  RT   pollution control equipment
  RT   pollution regulations

POLLUTION CONTROL EQUIPMENT [278; 1,800] *Jun 76*
  BT1   equipment
  NT1   air filters
  NT1   baghouses
  NT1   electrostatic precipitators
  NT1   scrubbers
  RT   air cleaning
  RT   environmental engineering
  RT   inertial separators
  RT   off-gas systems
  RT   pollution
  RT   pollution abatement

RT　　pollution control
　　　RT　　scrubbing
　　　RT　　stack disposal
　　　RT　　sulfur meters

POLLUTION LAWS [255; 256]
(Prior to December 1990, this descriptor was spelled POLLUTION LAW.)
　　　BT1　　laws
　　　NT1　　us water pollution control act
　　　RT　　pollution regulations
　　　RT　　transfrontier pollution

pollution prev mar, london con
　　　USE　　lcpmpdpw

POLLUTION REGULATIONS [333; 333]
(Regulations for nonradioactive pollution only; see also CONTAMINATION REGULATIONS.)
　　　BT1　　regulations
　　　　BT2　　laws
　　　RT　　pollution
　　　RT　　pollution abatement
　　　RT　　pollution control
　　　RT　　pollution laws
　　　RT　　us natl environment policy act

poloidal divertor experiment
　　　USE　　pdx devices

POLOIDAL FIELD DIVERTORS [511; 511] *Jul 81*
(Divertors that displace the poloidal field lines to form a separatrix in the poloidal field.)
　　　BT1　　divertors
　　　RT　　pbx devices
　　　RT　　pdx devices

POLONIUM [188; 188]
　　　BT1　　metals
　　　　BT2　　elements
　　　RT　　natural radioactivity

POLONIUM ADDITIONS [4; 4]
(Alloys containing not more than 1% Po are listed here.)
　　　RT　　polonium alloys
　　　RT　　polonium compounds

POLONIUM ALLOYS [8; 8]
(Alloys containing more than 1% Po.)
　　　BT1　　alloys
　　　NT1　　polonium base alloys
　　　RT　　polonium additions

POLONIUM BASE ALLOYS [0; 0]
　　　BT1　　polonium alloys
　　　　BT2　　alloys

POLONIUM BROMIDES [1; 1]
　　　BT1　　bromides
　　　　BT2　　bromine compounds
　　　　　BT3　　halogen compounds
　　　　BT2　　halides
　　　　　BT3　　halogen compounds
　　　BT1　　polonium compounds

POLONIUM CHLORIDES [2; 2]
　　　BT1　　chlorides
　　　　BT2　　chlorine compounds
　　　　　BT3　　halogen compounds
　　　　BT2　　halides
　　　　　BT3　　halogen compounds
　　　BT1　　polonium compounds

POLONIUM COMPLEXES [13; 13]
　　　BT1　　complexes

POLONIUM COMPOUNDS [45; 84]
　　　NT1　　polonium bromides
　　　NT1　　polonium chlorides
　　　NT1　　polonium fluorides
　　　NT1　　polonium hydroxides
　　　NT1　　polonium iodides
　　　NT1　　polonium nitrates
　　　NT1　　polonium oxides
　　　NT1　　polonium sulfides
　　　RT　　polonium additions

POLONIUM FLUORIDES [1; 1]
　　　BT1　　fluorides
　　　　BT2　　fluorine compounds
　　　　　BT3　　halogen compounds
　　　　BT2　　halides
　　　　　BT3　　halogen compounds
　　　BT1　　polonium compounds

POLONIUM HYDROXIDES [0; 0]
　　　BT1　　hydroxides
　　　　BT2　　hydrogen compounds
　　　　BT2　　oxygen compounds
　　　BT1　　polonium compounds

POLONIUM IODIDES [4; 4]
　　　BT1　　iodides
　　　　BT2　　halides
　　　　　BT3　　halogen compounds
　　　　BT2　　iodine compounds
　　　　　BT3　　halogen compounds
　　　BT1　　polonium compounds

POLONIUM IONS [13; 13]
　　　BT1　　ions
　　　　BT2　　charged particles

POLONIUM ISOTOPES [134; 2,179]
　　　NT1　　polonium 192
　　　NT1　　polonium 193
　　　NT1　　polonium 194
　　　NT1　　polonium 195
　　　NT1　　polonium 196
　　　NT1　　polonium 197
　　　NT1　　polonium 198
　　　NT1　　polonium 199
　　　NT1　　polonium 200
　　　NT1　　polonium 201
　　　NT1　　polonium 202
　　　NT1　　polonium 203
　　　NT1　　polonium 204
　　　NT1　　polonium 205
　　　NT1　　polonium 206
　　　NT1　　polonium 207
　　　NT1　　polonium 208
　　　NT1　　polonium 209
　　　NT1　　polonium 210
　　　NT1　　polonium 211
　　　NT1　　polonium 212
　　　NT1　　polonium 213
　　　NT1　　polonium 214
　　　NT1　　polonium 215
　　　NT1　　polonium 216
　　　NT1　　polonium 217
　　　NT1　　polonium 218
　　　NT1　　polonium 219
　　　NT1　　polonium 220

POLONIUM NITRATES [5; 5]
　　　BT1　　nitrates
　　　　BT2　　nitrogen compounds
　　　　BT2　　oxygen compounds
　　　BT1　　polonium compounds

POLONIUM OXIDES [29; 29]
　　　BT1　　oxides
　　　　BT2　　chalcogenides
　　　　BT2　　oxygen compounds
　　　BT1　　polonium compounds

POLONIUM SULFIDES [0; 0]
　　　BT1　　polonium compounds
　　　BT1　　sulfides
　　　　BT2　　chalcogenides
　　　　BT2　　sulfur compounds

POLONIUM 192 [3; 3]
　　　BT1　　alpha decay radioisotopes
　　　　BT2　　radioisotopes
　　　　　BT3　　isotopes
　　　BT1　　even-even nuclei
　　　　BT2　　nuclei
　　　BT1　　heavy nuclei
　　　　BT2　　nuclei
　　　BT1　　millisec living radioisotopes
　　　　BT2　　radioisotopes
　　　　　BT3　　isotopes
　　　BT1　　polonium isotopes

POLONIUM 193 [4; 4]
　　　BT1　　alpha decay radioisotopes
　　　　BT2　　radioisotopes
　　　　　BT3　　isotopes
　　　BT1　　even-odd nuclei
　　　　BT2　　nuclei
　　　BT1　　heavy nuclei
　　　　BT2　　nuclei
　　　BT1　　millisec living radioisotopes
　　　　BT2　　radioisotopes
　　　　　BT3　　isotopes
　　　BT1　　polonium isotopes

POLONIUM 194 [9; 9]
　　　BT1　　alpha decay radioisotopes
　　　　BT2　　radioisotopes
　　　　　BT3　　isotopes
　　　BT1　　even-even nuclei
　　　　BT2　　nuclei
　　　BT1　　heavy nuclei
　　　　BT2　　nuclei
　　　BT1　　millisec living radioisotopes
　　　　BT2　　radioisotopes
　　　　　BT3　　isotopes
　　　BT1　　polonium isotopes

POLONIUM 195 [9; 9]
　　　BT1　　alpha decay radioisotopes
　　　　BT2　　radioisotopes
　　　　　BT3　　isotopes
　　　BT1　　even-odd nuclei
　　　　BT2　　nuclei
　　　BT1　　heavy nuclei
　　　　BT2　　nuclei
　　　BT1　　polonium isotopes
　　　BT1　　seconds living radioisotopes
　　　　BT2　　radioisotopes
　　　　　BT3　　isotopes

POLONIUM 196 [8; 8]
　　　BT1　　alpha decay radioisotopes
　　　　BT2　　radioisotopes
　　　　　BT3　　isotopes
　　　BT1　　electron capture radioisotopes
　　　　BT2　　beta decay radioisotopes
　　　　　BT3　　radioisotopes
　　　　　　BT4　　isotopes
　　　BT1　　even-even nuclei
　　　　BT2　　nuclei
　　　BT1　　heavy nuclei
　　　　BT2　　nuclei
　　　BT1　　polonium isotopes
　　　BT1　　seconds living radioisotopes
　　　　BT2　　radioisotopes
　　　　　BT3　　isotopes

POLONIUM 197 [6; 6]
　　　BT1　　alpha decay radioisotopes
　　　　BT2　　radioisotopes
　　　　　BT3　　isotopes
　　　BT1　　electron capture radioisotopes
　　　　BT2　　beta decay radioisotopes
　　　　　BT3　　radioisotopes
　　　　　　BT4　　isotopes
　　　BT1　　even-odd nuclei
　　　　BT2　　nuclei
　　　BT1　　heavy nuclei
　　　　BT2　　nuclei
　　　BT1　　polonium isotopes
　　　BT1　　seconds living radioisotopes
　　　　BT2　　radioisotopes
　　　　　BT3　　isotopes

POLONIUM 198 [18; 18]
BT1 alpha decay radioisotopes
BT2 radioisotopes
BT3 isotopes
BT1 beta-plus decay radioisotopes
BT2 beta decay radioisotopes
BT3 radioisotopes
BT4 isotopes
BT1 electron capture radioisotopes
BT2 beta decay radioisotopes
BT3 radioisotopes
BT4 isotopes
BT1 even-even nuclei
BT2 nuclei
BT1 heavy nuclei
BT2 nuclei
BT1 minutes living radioisotopes
BT2 radioisotopes
BT3 isotopes
BT1 polonium isotopes

POLONIUM 199 [21; 21]
BT1 alpha decay radioisotopes
BT2 radioisotopes
BT3 isotopes
BT1 beta-plus decay radioisotopes
BT2 beta decay radioisotopes
BT3 radioisotopes
BT4 isotopes
BT1 electron capture radioisotopes
BT2 beta decay radioisotopes
BT3 radioisotopes
BT4 isotopes
BT1 even-odd nuclei
BT2 nuclei
BT1 heavy nuclei
BT2 nuclei
BT1 internal conversion radioisoto
BT2 radioisotopes
BT3 isotopes
BT1 minutes living radioisotopes
BT2 radioisotopes
BT3 isotopes
BT1 polonium isotopes

POLONIUM 200 [20; 20]
BT1 alpha decay radioisotopes
BT2 radioisotopes
BT3 isotopes
BT1 beta-plus decay radioisotopes
BT2 beta decay radioisotopes
BT3 radioisotopes
BT4 isotopes
BT1 electron capture radioisotopes
BT2 beta decay radioisotopes
BT3 radioisotopes
BT4 isotopes
BT1 even-even nuclei
BT2 nuclei
BT1 heavy nuclei
BT2 nuclei
BT1 minutes living radioisotopes
BT2 radioisotopes
BT3 isotopes
BT1 polonium isotopes

POLONIUM 201 [19; 19]
BT1 alpha decay radioisotopes
BT2 radioisotopes
BT3 isotopes
BT1 beta-plus decay radioisotopes
BT2 beta decay radioisotopes
BT3 radioisotopes
BT4 isotopes
BT1 electron capture radioisotopes
BT2 beta decay radioisotopes
BT3 radioisotopes
BT4 isotopes
BT1 even-odd nuclei
BT2 nuclei
BT1 heavy nuclei
BT2 nuclei
BT1 internal conversion radioisoto
BT2 radioisotopes
BT3 isotopes
BT1 isomeric transition isotopes
BT2 radioisotopes
BT3 isotopes
BT1 minutes living radioisotopes

BT2 radioisotopes
BT3 isotopes
BT1 polonium isotopes

POLONIUM 202 [18; 18]
BT1 alpha decay radioisotopes
BT2 radioisotopes
BT3 isotopes
BT1 beta-plus decay radioisotopes
BT2 beta decay radioisotopes
BT3 radioisotopes
BT4 isotopes
BT1 electron capture radioisotopes
BT2 beta decay radioisotopes
BT3 radioisotopes
BT4 isotopes
BT1 even-even nuclei
BT2 nuclei
BT1 heavy nuclei
BT2 nuclei
BT1 internal conversion radioisoto
BT2 radioisotopes
BT3 isotopes
BT1 minutes living radioisotopes
BT2 radioisotopes
BT3 isotopes
BT1 polonium isotopes

POLONIUM 203 [10; 10]
BT1 alpha decay radioisotopes
BT2 radioisotopes
BT3 isotopes
BT1 beta-plus decay radioisotopes
BT2 beta decay radioisotopes
BT3 radioisotopes
BT4 isotopes
BT1 electron capture radioisotopes
BT2 beta decay radioisotopes
BT3 radioisotopes
BT4 isotopes
BT1 even-odd nuclei
BT2 nuclei
BT1 heavy nuclei
BT2 nuclei
BT1 internal conversion radioisoto
BT2 radioisotopes
BT3 isotopes
BT1 isomeric transition isotopes
BT2 radioisotopes
BT3 isotopes
BT1 minutes living radioisotopes
BT2 radioisotopes
BT3 isotopes
BT1 polonium isotopes
BT1 seconds living radioisotopes
BT2 radioisotopes
BT3 isotopes

POLONIUM 204 [26; 26]
BT1 alpha decay radioisotopes
BT2 radioisotopes
BT3 isotopes
BT1 electron capture radioisotopes
BT2 beta decay radioisotopes
BT3 radioisotopes
BT4 isotopes
BT1 even-even nuclei
BT2 nuclei
BT1 heavy nuclei
BT2 nuclei
BT1 hours living radioisotopes
BT2 radioisotopes
BT3 isotopes
BT1 polonium isotopes

POLONIUM 205 [24; 24]
BT1 alpha decay radioisotopes
BT2 radioisotopes
BT3 isotopes
BT1 beta-plus decay radioisotopes
BT2 beta decay radioisotopes
BT3 radioisotopes
BT4 isotopes
BT1 electron capture radioisotopes
BT2 beta decay radioisotopes
BT3 radioisotopes
BT4 isotopes
BT1 even-odd nuclei
BT2 nuclei

BT1 heavy nuclei
BT2 nuclei
BT1 hours living radioisotopes
BT2 radioisotopes
BT3 isotopes
BT1 internal conversion radioisoto
BT2 radioisotopes
BT3 isotopes
BT1 polonium isotopes

POLONIUM 206 [45; 45]
BT1 alpha decay radioisotopes
BT2 radioisotopes
BT3 isotopes
BT1 days living radioisotopes
BT2 radioisotopes
BT3 isotopes
BT1 electron capture radioisotopes
BT2 beta decay radioisotopes
BT3 radioisotopes
BT4 isotopes
BT1 even-even nuclei
BT2 nuclei
BT1 heavy nuclei
BT2 nuclei
BT1 internal conversion radioisoto
BT2 radioisotopes
BT3 isotopes
BT1 polonium isotopes

POLONIUM 207 [29; 29]
BT1 alpha decay radioisotopes
BT2 radioisotopes
BT3 isotopes
BT1 beta-plus decay radioisotopes
BT2 beta decay radioisotopes
BT3 radioisotopes
BT4 isotopes
BT1 electron capture radioisotopes
BT2 beta decay radioisotopes
BT3 radioisotopes
BT4 isotopes
BT1 even-odd nuclei
BT2 nuclei
BT1 heavy nuclei
BT2 nuclei
BT1 hours living radioisotopes
BT2 radioisotopes
BT3 isotopes
BT1 internal conversion radioisoto
BT2 radioisotopes
BT3 isotopes
BT1 isomeric transition isotopes
BT2 radioisotopes
BT3 isotopes
BT1 polonium isotopes
BT1 seconds living radioisotopes
BT2 radioisotopes
BT3 isotopes

POLONIUM 208 [90; 90]
BT1 alpha decay radioisotopes
BT2 radioisotopes
BT3 isotopes
BT1 electron capture radioisotopes
BT2 beta decay radioisotopes
BT3 radioisotopes
BT4 isotopes
BT1 even-even nuclei
BT2 nuclei
BT1 heavy nuclei
BT2 nuclei
BT1 polonium isotopes
BT1 years living radioisotopes
BT2 radioisotopes
BT3 isotopes

POLONIUM 208 TARGET [6; 6]
Mar 83
BT1 targets

POLONIUM 209 [74; 74]
BT1 alpha decay radioisotopes
BT2 radioisotopes
BT3 isotopes
BT1 electron capture radioisotopes
BT2 beta decay radioisotopes
BT3 radioisotopes

        BT4   isotopes
   BT1   even-odd nuclei
      BT2   nuclei
   BT1   heavy nuclei
      BT2   nuclei
   BT1   polonium isotopes
   BT1   years living radioisotopes
      BT2   radioisotopes
         BT3   isotopes

POLONIUM 210 [1,272; 1,272]
   UF   *radium f*
   BT1   alpha decay radioisotopes
      BT2   radioisotopes
         BT3   isotopes
   BT1   days living radioisotopes
      BT2   radioisotopes
         BT3   isotopes
   BT1   even-even nuclei
      BT2   nuclei
   BT1   heavy nuclei
      BT2   nuclei
   BT1   isomeric transition isotopes
      BT2   radioisotopes
         BT3   isotopes
   BT1   nanosec living radioisotopes
      BT2   radioisotopes
         BT3   isotopes
   BT1   polonium isotopes

POLONIUM 210 TARGET [13; 13]
   BT1   targets

POLONIUM 211 [56; 56]
   UF   *actinium c/*
   BT1   alpha decay radioisotopes
      BT2   radioisotopes
         BT3   isotopes
   BT1   even-odd nuclei
      BT2   nuclei
   BT1   heavy nuclei
      BT2   nuclei
   BT1   millisec living radioisotopes
      BT2   radioisotopes
         BT3   isotopes
   BT1   polonium isotopes
   BT1   seconds living radioisotopes
      BT2   radioisotopes
         BT3   isotopes

POLONIUM 212 [136; 136]
   UF   *thorium c/*
   BT1   alpha decay radioisotopes
      BT2   radioisotopes
         BT3   isotopes
   BT1   even-even nuclei
      BT2   nuclei
   BT1   heavy nuclei
      BT2   nuclei
   BT1   nanosec living radioisotopes
      BT2   radioisotopes
         BT3   isotopes
   BT1   polonium isotopes
   BT1   seconds living radioisotopes
      BT2   radioisotopes
         BT3   isotopes

POLONIUM 213 [7; 7]
   BT1   alpha decay radioisotopes
      BT2   radioisotopes
         BT3   isotopes
   BT1   even-odd nuclei
      BT2   nuclei
   BT1   heavy nuclei
      BT2   nuclei
   BT1   microsec living radioisotopes
      BT2   radioisotopes
         BT3   isotopes
   BT1   polonium isotopes

POLONIUM 214 [161; 161]
   UF   *radium c/*
   BT1   alpha decay radioisotopes
      BT2   radioisotopes
         BT3   isotopes
   BT1   even-even nuclei

      BT2   nuclei
   BT1   heavy nuclei
      BT2   nuclei
   BT1   microsec living radioisotopes
      BT2   radioisotopes
         BT3   isotopes
   BT1   polonium isotopes

POLONIUM 215 [9; 9]
   UF   *actinium a*
   BT1   alpha decay radioisotopes
      BT2   radioisotopes
         BT3   isotopes
   BT1   beta-minus decay radioisotopes
      BT2   beta decay radioisotopes
         BT3   radioisotopes
            BT4   isotopes
   BT1   even-odd nuclei
      BT2   nuclei
   BT1   heavy nuclei
      BT2   nuclei
   BT1   millisec living radioisotopes
      BT2   radioisotopes
         BT3   isotopes
   BT1   polonium isotopes

POLONIUM 216 [37; 37]
   UF   *thorium a*
   BT1   alpha decay radioisotopes
      BT2   radioisotopes
         BT3   isotopes
   BT1   even-even nuclei
      BT2   nuclei
   BT1   heavy nuclei
      BT2   nuclei
   BT1   millisec living radioisotopes
      BT2   radioisotopes
         BT3   isotopes
   BT1   polonium isotopes

POLONIUM 217 [4; 4]
   BT1   alpha decay radioisotopes
      BT2   radioisotopes
         BT3   isotopes
   BT1   even-odd nuclei
      BT2   nuclei
   BT1   heavy nuclei
      BT2   nuclei
   BT1   polonium isotopes
   BT1   seconds living radioisotopes
      BT2   radioisotopes
         BT3   isotopes

POLONIUM 218 [310; 310]
   UF   *radium a*
   BT1   alpha decay radioisotopes
      BT2   radioisotopes
         BT3   isotopes
   BT1   beta-minus decay radioisotopes
      BT2   beta decay radioisotopes
         BT3   radioisotopes
            BT4   isotopes
   BT1   even-even nuclei
      BT2   nuclei
   BT1   heavy nuclei
      BT2   nuclei
   BT1   minutes living radioisotopes
      BT2   radioisotopes
         BT3   isotopes
   BT1   polonium isotopes

POLONIUM 219 [1; 1]
   BT1   even-odd nuclei
      BT2   nuclei
   BT1   polonium isotopes

POLONIUM 220 [0; 0]
   BT1   even-even nuclei
      BT2   nuclei
   BT1   polonium isotopes

POLYACETALS [23; 105]
   BT1   organic polymers
      BT2   organic compounds
      BT2   polymers
   NT1   formvar

   NT1   polyoxymethylenes
   RT   acetals
   RT   cellulose
   RT   chitin
   RT   inulin
   RT   lignin
   RT   starch

POLYACRYLATES [480; 1,245]
   UF   *acrylic polymers*
   BT1   esters
      BT2   organic compounds
   BT1   polyvinyls
      BT2   organic polymers
         BT3   organic compounds
         BT3   polymers
   NT1   lucite
   NT1   perspex
   NT1   plexiglas
   NT1   pmma
   RT   methacrylic acid

POLYAMIDES [288; 758]
   UF   *aramids*
   BT1   organic polymers
      BT2   organic compounds
      BT2   polymers
   NT1   nylon
   NT1   polyurethanes
   RT   albumins
   RT   amides
   RT   proteins

POLYCARBONATES [692; 692]
   BT1   carbonates
      BT2   carbon compounds
      BT2   oxygen compounds
   BT1   organic polymers
      BT2   organic compounds
      BT2   polymers

→ *polychlorinated biphenyl*
   USE   chlorinated aromatic hydrocarb

POLYCRYSTALS [5,606; 5,606]
   UF   *bicrystals*
   BT1   crystals

polycyclic aromatic hydrocarbo
   USE   aromatics

POLYCYTHEMIA [88; 88]
   BT1   hemic diseases
      BT2   diseases
   RT   bone marrow
   RT   myeloid leukemia

POLYENES [185; 1,517]
   BT1   hydrocarbons
      BT2   organic compounds
   NT1   dienes
   NT2   allene
   NT2   butadiene
   NT2   cyclopentadiene
   NT2   ferrocene
   NT2   isoprene
   NT1   squalene
   RT   alkenes

POLYESTERS [616; 949]
   BT1   esters
      BT2   organic compounds
   BT1   organic polymers
      BT2   organic compounds
      BT2   polymers
   NT1   dacron
   NT1   homalite
   NT1   laminac
   NT1   mylar

polyethers
   USE   polyethylene glycols

POLYETHYLENE GLYCOLS [670; 681]
- UF *polyethers*
- BT1 organic polymers
  - BT2 organic compounds
  - BT2 polymers
- NT1 carbowax
- NT1 pluronics
- RT ethers
- RT glycols

POLYETHYLENES [3,042; 3,903]
- UF *ethylene polymers*
- UF *polythene*
- BT1 polyolefins
  - BT2 organic polymers
    - BT3 organic compounds
    - BT3 polymers
- NT1 kel-f
- NT1 marlex
- NT1 teflon

POLYHALITE [11; 11] Oct 82
- BT1 sulfate minerals
  - BT2 minerals
- RT calcium sulfates
- RT magnesium sulfates
- RT potassium sulfates

polyhydroxyaromatics
- USE polyphenols

POLYISOPRENE [40; 40]
- BT1 elastomers
  - BT2 polymers
- BT1 organic polymers
  - BT2 organic compounds
  - BT2 polymers
- RT isoprene

POLYMERASES [388; 766]
- BT1 nucleotidyltransferases
  - BT2 phosphorus-group transferases
    - BT3 transferases
      - BT4 enzymes
        - BT5 organic compounds
- NT1 dna polymerases
- NT1 rna polymerases

POLYMERIZATION [3,185; 6,314]
- UF+ *radiation hardening (chemical)*
- UF+ *radiopolymerization*
- BT1 chemical reactions
- NT1 copolymerization
- NT1 cross-linking
- NT1 dimerization
- NT1 telomerization
- RT curing
- RT depolymerization
- RT molecular weight
- RT monomers

POLYMERS [3,260; 19,614]
- NT1 elastomers
  - NT2 neoprene
  - NT2 polyisoprene
  - NT2 rubbers
    - NT3 buna
    - NT3 latex
    - NT3 natural rubber
    - NT3 silastic
    - NT3 viton
  - NT2 vulcanized elastomers
    - NT3 ebonite
- NT1 inorganic polymers
- NT1 organic polymers
  - NT2 araldite
  - NT2 bakelite
  - NT2 copolymers
  - NT2 graft polymers
  - NT2 neoprene
  - NT2 plastic foams
  - NT2 polyacetals
    - NT3 formvar
    - NT3 polyoxymethylenes
  - NT2 polyamides
    - NT3 nylon
    - NT3 polyurethanes
  - NT2 polycarbonates
  - NT2 polyesters
    - NT3 dacron
    - NT3 homalite
    - NT3 laminac
    - NT3 mylar
  - NT2 polyethylene glycols
    - NT3 carbowax
    - NT3 pluronics
  - NT2 polyisoprene
  - NT2 polyolefins
    - NT3 polyethylenes
      - NT4 kel-f
      - NT4 marlex
      - NT4 teflon
    - NT3 polypropylene
    - NT3 polystyrene
    - NT3 polystyrene-dvb
  - NT2 polyvinyls
    - NT3 polyacrylates
      - NT4 lucite
      - NT4 perspex
      - NT4 plexiglas
      - NT4 pmma
    - NT3 polystyrene
    - NT3 pva
    - NT3 pvc
    - NT3 pvp
  - NT2 resins
  - NT2 rubbers
    - NT3 buna
    - NT3 latex
    - NT3 natural rubber
    - NT3 silastic
    - NT3 viton
  - NT2 textolite
  - NT2 thermoplastics
- NT1 silicones
  - NT2 dc resins
  - NT2 silastic
- RT colorimetric dosemeters
- RT dielectric track detectors
- RT dimers
- RT monomers

POLYMETALLIC ORES [81; 81]
- BT1 ores

polymethylmethacrylates
- USE pmma

POLYNEUTRONS [32; 133] Aug 78
(Particle-stable many-body system composed of neutrons.)
- BT1 neutrons
  - BT2 nucleons
    - BT3 baryons
      - BT4 fermions
      - BT4 hadrons
        - BT5 elementary particles
- NT1 dineutrons
- NT1 tetraneutrons
- NT1 trineutrons

POLYNOMIALS [1,680; 3,130]
- UF *tschebyscheff approximation*
- BT1 functions
- NT1 hermite polynomials
- NT1 laguerre polynomials
- NT1 legendre polynomials
- RT mathematics
- RT newton method
- RT spline functions

polynuclear hydrocarbons
- USE condensed aromatics

POLYOLEFINS [211; 5,524]
- BT1 organic polymers
  - BT2 organic compounds
  - BT2 polymers
- NT1 polyethylenes
  - NT2 kel-f
  - NT2 marlex
  - NT2 teflon
- NT1 polypropylene

- NT1 polystyrene
- NT1 polystyrene-dvb

POLYOMA VIRUS [13; 13]
- BT1 oncogenic viruses
  - BT2 viruses
    - BT3 microorganisms
    - BT3 parasites

POLYOXYMETHYLENES [52; 52]
- BT1 polyacetals
  - BT2 organic polymers
    - BT3 organic compounds
    - BT3 polymers
- RT formaldehyde

POLYPEPTIDES [764; 2,275]
- BT1 peptides
  - BT2 proteins
    - BT3 organic compounds
- NT1 calcitonin
- NT1 endorphins
  - NT2 enkephalins
- NT1 gastrin
- NT1 glucagon
- NT1 glutathione
- NT1 kinins
- RT somatostatin

POLYPHENOLS [262; 2,554]
- UF *dihydroxyaromatics*
- UF *polyhydroxyaromatics*
- UF *trihydroxyaromatics*
- BT1 phenols
  - BT2 aromatics
    - BT3 organic compounds
  - BT2 hydroxy compounds
    - BT3 organic compounds
- NT1 arsenazo
- NT1 aurin
- NT1 bromosulfophthalein
- NT1 catecholamines
- NT1 curcumin
- NT1 dopamine
- NT1 fluorescein
- NT1 hematoxylin
- NT1 morin
- NT1 pyridylazoresorcinol
- NT1 pyrocatechol
- NT1 pyrogallol
- NT1 quercetin
- NT1 resorcinol
- NT1 stilbestrol
- NT1 tannic acid
- NT1 tiron

POLYPHENYLS [51; 148]
- BT1 aromatics
  - BT2 organic compounds
- BT1 hydrocarbons
  - BT2 organic compounds
- NT1 santowax
- NT1 terphenyls
  - NT2 terphenyl-meta
  - NT2 terphenyl-ortho
  - NT2 terphenyl-para
- RT organic coolants
- RT organic moderators
- RT organic polymers

POLYPLOIDY [132; 132]
- UF *tetraploidy*
- BT1 ploidy
- RT colchicine
- RT genome mutations

POLYPROPYLENE [535; 535]
- BT1 polyolefins
  - BT2 organic polymers
    - BT3 organic compounds
    - BT3 polymers
- RT propylene

polysaccharide-lyases
(Prior to December 1990, this was a valid descriptor.)

```
                USE     carbon-oxygen lyases

POLYSACCHARIDES [357; 4,196]
    BT1     saccharides
        BT2     carbohydrates
            BT3     organic compounds
    NT1     agar
    NT1     alginic acid
    NT1     cellophane
    NT1     cellulose
    NT1     dextran
    NT1     dextrin
    NT1     glycogen
    NT1     gum acacia
    NT1     inulin
    NT1     lignin
    NT1     lipopolysaccharides
    NT1     mucopolysaccharides
        NT2     chitin
        NT2     chondroitin
        NT2     heparin
        NT2     hyaluronic acid
    NT1     mucoproteins
        NT2     haptoglobins
        NT2     intrinsic factor
        NT2     phytohemagglutinin
    NT1     nitrocellulose
    NT1     pectins
    NT1     rayon
    NT1     sialic acid
    NT1     starch
    NT1     viscose
    RT      endotoxins
    RT      lysozyme
    RT      pyrogens
    RT      zymosan


POLYSTYRENE [1,087; 1,087]
    UF      styrene polymers
    BT1     polyolefins
        BT2     organic polymers
            BT3     organic compounds
            BT3     polymers
    BT1     polyvinyls
        BT2     organic polymers
            BT3     organic compounds
            BT3     polymers
    RT      styrene

POLYSTYRENE-DVB [176; 176]
    UF      styrene-divinylbenzene copolym
    BT1     organic ion exchangers
        BT2     ion exchange materials
            BT3     materials
    BT1     polyolefins
        BT2     organic polymers
            BT3     organic compounds
            BT3     polymers


polysulfides
    USE     sulfides


polytetrafluorethylene
    USE     teflon


polythene
    USE     polyethylenes


polythionates
    USE     oxygen compounds
    AND     sulfur compounds


polythionic acids
    USE     inorganic acids
    AND     oxygen compounds
    AND     sulfur compounds


POLYURETHANES [288; 288]
    BT1     polyamides
        BT2     organic polymers
```

```
        BT3     organic compounds
        BT3     polymers
    RT      urethane


polyvinyl alcohol
    USE     pva


polyvinyl chloride
    USE     pvc


polyvinylpyrrolidone
    USE     pvp


POLYVINYLS [439; 3,443]
    UF      vinoflex
    UF      vinyl acetate
    BT1     organic polymers
        BT2     organic compounds
        BT2     polymers
    NT1     polyacrylates
        NT2     lucite
        NT2     perspex
        NT2     plexiglas
        NT2     pmma
    NT1     polystyrene
    NT1     pva
    NT1     pvc
    NT1     pvp


POMERANCHUK PARTICLES
[1,684; 1,684]
    UF      pomerons
    BT1     mesons
        BT2     bosons
        BT2     hadrons
            BT3     elementary particles
    BT1     postulated particles
        BT2     elementary particles
    RT      morrison rule
    RT      regge poles


POMERANCHUK POLES [335; 335]
    RT      regge poles


POMERANCHUK THEOREM [134; 134]
    RT      antiparticle beams
    RT      interactions
    RT      particle beams
    RT      total cross sections


pomerons
    USE     pomeranchuk particles


ponderomotive effect
    USE     ponderomotive force


PONDEROMOTIVE FORCE [63; 63]
Apr 89
    UF      ponderomotive effect
    RT      charged particles
    RT      coulomb field
    RT      electromagnetic fields
    RT      lorentz force


ponds
    USE     lakes


POOL BOILING [328; 328]
    BT1     boiling
        BT2     phase transformations


pool critical assembly ornl
    USE     ornl-pca reactor


pool test react. chalk river
    USE     ptr reactor
```

```
POOL TYPE REACTORS [333; 2,515]
    UF      swimming pool reactors
    BT1     water cooled reactors
        BT2     reactors
    BT1     water moderated reactors
        BT2     reactors
    NT1     agata reactor
    NT1     apsara reactor
    NT1     armf-1 reactor
    NT1     astra reactor
    NT1     atrc reactor
    NT1     avogadro rs-1 reactor
    NT1     barn reactor
    NT1     bawtr reactor
    NT1     ber-2 reactor
    NT1     brr reactor
    NT1     bsr-1 reactor
    NT1     bsr-2 reactor
    NT1     cabri reactor
    NT1     consort-2 reactor
    NT1     crocus reactor
    NT1     democritus reactor
    NT1     dr-2 reactor
    NT1     fmrb reactor
    NT1     fnr reactor
    NT1     frg-1 reactor
    NT1     frg-2 reactor
    NT1     frj-1 reactor
    NT1     frm reactor
    NT1     frn reactor
    NT1     gtr reactor
    NT1     gulf triga-mk-3 reactor
    NT1     herald reactor
    NT1     hor reactor
    NT1     horace reactor
    NT1     htr reactor
    NT1     ian-r1 reactor
    NT1     iear-1 reactor
    NT1     irl reactor
    NT1     irr-1 reactor
    NT1     irt reactor
    NT1     irt-sofia reactor
    NT1     irt-2000 djakarta reactor
    NT1     irt-2000 moscow reactor
    NT1     isis reactor
    NT1     jen reactor
    NT1     jen-1 reactor
    NT1     jen-2 reactor
    NT1     jrr-4 reactor
    NT1     kmr reactor
    NT1     kur reactor
    NT1     la reina rech-1 reactor
    NT1     lido reactor
    NT1     lo aguirre rech-2 reactor
    NT1     lptr reactor
    NT1     ltir reactor
    NT1     maria reactor
    NT1     maryla reactor
    NT1     melusine-1 reactor
    NT1     minerve reactor
    NT1     mnr reactor
    NT1     nscr reactor
    NT1     osur reactor
    NT1     parr reactor
    NT1     phebus reactor
    NT1     prpr reactor
    NT1     prr-1 reactor
    NT1     pstr reactor
    NT1     ptr reactor
    NT1     pulstar-buffalo reactor
    NT1     pulstar-raleigh reactor
    NT1     rana reactor
    NT1     rinsc reactor
    NT1     ritmo reactor
    NT1     rp-10 reactor
    NT1     rts-1 reactor
    NT1     rv-1 reactor
    NT1     r2-0 reactor
    NT1     saphir reactor
    NT1     siloe reactor
    NT1     siloette reactor
    NT1     slowpoke type reactors
        NT2     slowpoke-alberta reactor
        NT2     slowpoke-dalhousie reactor
        NT2     slowpoke-montreal reactor
        NT2     slowpoke-ottawa reactor
        NT2     slowpoke-toronto reactor
        NT2     slowpoke-wnre reactor
    NT1     spert-4 reactor
    NT1     stek reactor
```

NT1 stir reactor
NT1 thetis reactor
NT1 thor reactor
NT1 toshiba reactor
NT1 tr-1 reactor
NT1 tr-2 reactor
NT1 triton reactor
NT1 trr-1 reactor
NT1 tz1 reactor
NT1 tz2 reactor
NT1 umne-1 reactor
NT1 umrr reactor
NT1 utrr reactor
NT1 uvar reactor
NT1 uwnr reactor
NT1 vr-1 reactor
NT1 wpir reactor
NT1 wsur reactor

pools (fuel storage)
USE fuel storage pools

POP [6; 6]
UF hydroxypropiophenone
BT1 ketones
BT2 organic compounds
BT1 phenols
BT2 aromatics
BT3 organic compounds
BT2 hydroxy compounds
BT3 organic compounds

POPAE STORAGE RING [11; 11]
Feb 76
(Protons On Protons And Electrons storage ring facility at Fermilab.)
BT1 storage rings

POPLARS [33; 33]
BT1 trees
BT2 plants

POPOP [64; 64]
UF bis-phenyloxazolylbenzene
BT1 oxazoles
BT2 azoles
BT3 heterocyclic compounds
BT4 organic compounds
BT3 organic nitrogen compounds
BT4 organic compounds
BT2 organic oxygen compounds
BT3 organic compounds

POPULATION DENSITY [443; 443]
UF density (population)
RT population dynamics
RT populations

POPULATION DYNAMICS [668; 668]
RT competition
RT ecological succession
RT ecosystems
RT equilibrium
RT growth
RT migration
RT population density
RT population relocation
RT populations
RT reproduction

POPULATION INVERSION [511; 511]
RT energy levels

POPULATION RELOCATION [104; 104]
Jul 81
RT accidents
RT civil defense
RT evacuation
RT external zones
RT human populations
RT population dynamics
RT populations
RT reactor accidents

POPULATIONS [974; 8,056]
UF colonies
UF+ caste (insects)
NT1 human populations
NT2 eskimos
NT2 lapps
NT2 rural populations
NT2 urban populations
RT age groups
RT biosphere
RT ecosystems
RT environment
RT genetically significant dose
RT population density
RT population dynamics
RT population relocation

PORCELAIN [69; 69]
RT ceramics

pork
USE meat

POROSIMETERS [47; 47]
BT1 measuring instruments

§ POROSITY [4,649; 4,649]
RT ceramography
RT defects
RT leaks
RT permeability
RT porous materials
RT sintering

POROUS MATERIALS [1,362; 1,362]
Jul 77
BT1 materials
RT porosity

PORPHYRA [16; 16]
BT1 algae
BT2 plants

PORPHYRINS [406; 2,460]
BT1 heterocyclic acids
BT2 carboxylic acids
BT3 organic acids
BT4 organic compounds
BT2 heterocyclic compounds
BT3 organic compounds
BT1 organic nitrogen compounds
BT2 organic compounds
NT1 chlorophyll
NT1 hematoporphyrins
NT1 heme
NT1 hemoglobin
NT2 carboxyhemoglobin
NT2 methemoglobin
NT1 hemosiderin
NT1 myoglobin
NT1 peroxidases
NT2 catalase
NT1 protoporphyrins
RT pigments

→ *porpoises*
USE cetaceans

PORT RADIUM [1; 1]
BT1 northwest territories
BT2 canada
BT3 developed countries
BT3 north america

PORTABLE EQUIPMENT [459; 480]
Jun 83
(To be used only if portability is unusual or is the significant aspect of the equipment.)
BT1 equipment
NT1 calculators
RT laboratory equipment
RT portable sources

portable medium power plant 2a
USE pm-2a reactor

portable medium power plant 3a
USE pm-3a reactor

PORTABLE SOURCES [69; 69]
BT1 radiation sources
RT portable equipment

PORTAL SYSTEM [411; 411]
BT1 veins
BT2 blood vessels
BT3 cardiovascular system
BT3 organs
BT4 body
RT intestinal absorption
RT intestines
RT liver

PORTER-THOMAS DISTRIBUTION [99; 99]
RT compound nuclei
RT level widths

PORTSMOUTH CENTRIFUGE ENRICHME [21; 21] *Aug 82*
UF gcep
BT1 centrifuge enrichment plants
BT2 isotope separation plants
BT3 industrial plants
BT3 nuclear facilities
BT1 us doe
BT2 us organizations
BT3 national organizations
RT ohio

PORTSMOUTH GASEOUS DIFFUSION P [108; 108] *Oct 75*
BT1 gaseous diffusion plants
BT2 isotope separation plants
BT3 industrial plants
BT3 nuclear facilities
BT1 us doe
BT2 us organizations
BT3 national organizations
BT1 us erda
BT2 us organizations
BT3 national organizations
RT ohio

PORTUGAL [128; 128]
BT1 developing countries
BT1 europe

portuguese jen research reacto
USE jen reactor

pos
(Plasma Opening Switches.)
USE plasma switches

position (optical)
USE coordinates

position (radio)
USE coordinates

position indicators
USE displacement gages

POSITION OPERATORS [187; 187]
BT1 quantum operators
BT2 mathematical operators
RT coordinates

POSITION SENSITIVE DETECTORS [2,515; 2,515]
BT1 radiation detectors
BT2 measuring instruments
RT counting techniques
RT superconducting colloid detect

POSITIONING [1,255; 1,255] *Dec 82*
(Not for SITE SELECTION.)
UF *emplacement*
RT alignment
RT fuel elements
RT in core instruments
RT pipelines
RT ships
RT targets

POSITIVE COLUMN [387; 387]
RT electric discharges

POSITIVE EXCESS [4; 4]
RT cosmic radiation
RT electric charges

positive ions
USE cations

POSITRON BEAMS [1,586; 1,586]
UF *beta beams (positrons)*
BT1 lepton beams
BT2 particle beams
BT3 beams
RT positrons

POSITRON CAMERAS [432; 432]
(Coincidence gamma cameras for positron annihilation imaging.)
BT1 gamma cameras
BT2 cameras
RT coincidence methods
RT emission computed tomography
RT nuclear medicine
RT positron computed tomography
RT positron detection
RT radioisotope scanners

POSITRON CHANNELING [380; 380]
BT1 channeling

POSITRON COLLISIONS [232; 1,572]
BT1 collisions
NT1 electron-positron collisions
NT1 photon-positron collisions
NT1 positron-atom collisions
NT1 positron-ion collisions
NT1 positron-molecule collisions
NT1 positron-positron collisions

POSITRON COMPUTED TOMOGRAPHY [3,016; 3,016] *Apr 80*
UF *pet scanning*
BT1 emission computed tomography
BT2 computerized tomography
BT3 tomography
RT positron cameras
RT radioisotope scanning

positron decay
USE beta-plus decay

POSITRON DETECTION [127; 127] *Sep 75*
(Prior to April 1986 this concept was expressed by co-ordination of ELECTRON DETECTION and POSITRONS.)
BT1 charged particle detection
BT2 radiation detection
BT3 detection
RT beta detection
RT electron detection
RT positron cameras

POSITRON REACTIONS [150; 150] *Sep 77*
BT1 lepton reactions
BT2 nuclear reactions

POSITRON SOURCES [330; 330] *Sep 75*
BT1 particle sources
BT2 radiation sources
RT positrons

POSITRON-ATOM COLLISIONS [570; 570]
BT1 atom collisions
BT2 collisions
BT1 positron collisions
BT2 collisions

positron-electron-proton st ri
USE pep storage rings

POSITRON-ION COLLISIONS [43; 43]
BT1 ion collisions
BT2 collisions
BT1 positron collisions
BT2 collisions

POSITRON-MOLECULE COLLISIONS [152; 152]
BT1 molecule collisions
BT2 collisions
BT1 positron collisions
BT2 collisions

POSITRON-POSITRON COLLISIONS [4; 4]
BT1 positron collisions
BT2 collisions

POSITRON-POSITRON INTERACTIONS [10; 10] *May 86*
BT1 lepton-lepton interactions
BT2 particle interactions
BT3 interactions

POSITRONIUM [1,785; 1,785]
RT atoms
RT charmonium
RT electrons
RT muonium
RT positronium compounds
RT positrons
RT protonium

POSITRONIUM COMPOUNDS [27; 27] *Sep 85*
(Atom-positronium systems of the type (X;Ps) or (X-;e+).)
RT positronium

POSITRONS [7,848; 7,908]
BT1 antileptons
BT2 antiparticles
BT3 antimatter
BT4 matter
BT3 elementary particles
BT2 leptons
BT3 elementary particles
BT3 fermions
NT1 cosmic positrons
RT beta particles
RT electron pairs
RT electrons
RT positron beams
RT positron sources
RT positronium

possession (nuclear materials)
USE nuclear materials possession

POST-IRRADIATION EXAMINATION [1,204; 1,204] *Apr 81*
RT ceramography
RT chemical analysis
RT destructive testing
RT electron microprobe analysis
RT fuel elements
RT inspection
RT performance testing
RT spectroscopy

POST-IRRADIATION THERAPY [660; 660]
BT1 therapy
BT2 medicine
RT biological recovery
RT blood substitutes

→ **POST-TRANSLATION MODIFICATION** [5; 5] *Jul 91*
BT1 biosynthesis
BT2 synthesis
RT acylation
RT glycoproteins
RT methylation
RT precursor
RT protein structure
RT proteins
RT proteolysis

POSTULATED PARTICLES [1,333; 33,731]
BT1 elementary particles
NT1 dyons
NT1 gluons
NT1 goldstone bosons
NT2 axions
NT1 grace particles
NT1 gravitons
NT1 higgs bosons
NT1 magnetic monopoles
NT1 partons
NT1 pomeranchuk particles
NT1 preons
NT1 quarks
NT1 sparticles
NT1 spurions
NT1 tachyons
NT1 taste particles
NT1 top particles

POTASSIUM [4,390; 4,390]
BT1 alkali metals
BT2 metals
BT3 elements

POTASSIUM ADDITIONS [59; 59]
(Alloys containing not more than 1% K are listed here.)
RT potassium alloys
RT potassium compounds

POTASSIUM ALLOYS [224; 237]
(Alloys containing more than 1% K.)
UF+ *nak*
BT1 alloys
NT1 potassium base alloys
RT potassium additions

POTASSIUM BASE ALLOYS [10; 10]
BT1 potassium alloys
BT2 alloys

POTASSIUM BORIDES [6; 6]
BT1 borides
BT2 boron compounds
BT1 potassium compounds
BT2 alkali metal compounds

POTASSIUM BROMIDES [758; 758]
BT1 bromides
BT2 bromine compounds
BT3 halogen compounds
BT2 halides
BT3 halogen compounds
BT1 potassium compounds
BT2 alkali metal compounds

POTASSIUM CARBIDES [17; 17]
- BT1 carbides
- BT2 carbon compounds
- BT1 potassium compounds
- BT2 alkali metal compounds

POTASSIUM CARBONATES [199; 199]
- BT1 carbonates
- BT2 carbon compounds
- BT2 oxygen compounds
- BT1 potassium compounds
- BT2 alkali metal compounds

POTASSIUM CHLORIDES [2,467; 2,485]
- BT1 chlorides
- BT2 chlorine compounds
- BT3 halogen compounds
- BT2 halides
- BT3 halogen compounds
- BT1 potassium compounds
- BT2 alkali metal compounds
- RT carnallite
- RT halide minerals

POTASSIUM COMPLEXES [80; 80]
- BT1 alkali metal complexes
- BT2 complexes

POTASSIUM COMPOUNDS [2,999; 9,262]
- UF+ prussian blue
- BT1 alkali metal compounds
- NT1 potassium borides
- NT1 potassium bromides
- NT1 potassium carbides
- NT1 potassium carbonates
- NT1 potassium chlorides
- NT1 potassium fluorides
- NT1 potassium hydrides
- NT1 potassium hydroxides
- NT1 potassium iodides
- NT1 potassium nitrates
- NT1 potassium nitrides
- NT1 potassium oxides
- NT1 potassium perchlorates
- NT1 potassium phosphates
- NT1 potassium phosphides
- NT1 potassium selenides
- NT1 potassium silicates
- NT1 potassium silicides
- NT1 potassium sulfates
- NT1 potassium sulfides
- NT1 potassium tellurides
- NT1 potassium tungstates
- NT1 potassium uranates
- NT1 potassium vanadates
- NT1 rochelle salt
- RT potassium additions

POTASSIUM COOLED REACTORS [25; 79]
- UF potassium-cooled reactors
- BT1 liquid metal cooled reactors
- BT2 reactors
- NT1 ebr-1 reactor
- NT1 ser reactor
- NT1 snap 10 reactor
- NT2 s10fs-1 reactor
- NT2 s10fs-3 reactor
- NT2 s10fs-4 reactor
- NT1 snaptran reactors
- RT nak cooled reactors

POTASSIUM FLUORIDES [693; 693]
- BT1 fluorides
- BT2 fluorine compounds
- BT3 halogen compounds
- BT2 halides
- BT3 halogen compounds
- BT1 potassium compounds
- BT2 alkali metal compounds

POTASSIUM HYDRIDES [45; 45]
- BT1 hydrides
- BT2 hydrogen compounds
- BT1 potassium compounds
- BT2 alkali metal compounds

POTASSIUM HYDROXIDES [498; 498]
- BT1 hydroxides
- BT2 hydrogen compounds
- BT2 oxygen compounds
- BT1 potassium compounds
- BT2 alkali metal compounds

POTASSIUM IODIDES [763; 763]
- BT1 iodides
- BT2 halides
- BT3 halogen compounds
- BT2 iodine compounds
- BT3 halogen compounds
- BT1 potassium compounds
- BT2 alkali metal compounds
- RT lugol

POTASSIUM IONS [576; 576]
- BT1 ions
- BT2 charged particles

POTASSIUM ISOTOPES [244; 2,911]
- NT1 potassium 35
- NT1 potassium 36
- NT1 potassium 37
- NT1 potassium 38
- NT1 potassium 39
- NT1 potassium 40
- NT1 potassium 41
- NT1 potassium 42
- NT1 potassium 43
- NT1 potassium 44
- NT1 potassium 45
- NT1 potassium 46
- NT1 potassium 47
- NT1 potassium 48
- NT1 potassium 49
- NT1 potassium 50
- NT1 potassium 51
- NT1 potassium 52
- NT1 potassium 53
- NT1 potassium 54

POTASSIUM NITRATES [350; 350]
- BT1 nitrates
- BT2 nitrogen compounds
- BT2 oxygen compounds
- BT1 potassium compounds
- BT2 alkali metal compounds

POTASSIUM NITRIDES [10; 10]
- BT1 nitrides
- BT2 nitrogen compounds
- BT2 pnictides
- BT1 potassium compounds
- BT2 alkali metal compounds

POTASSIUM OXIDES [441; 442]
- BT1 oxides
- BT2 chalcogenides
- BT2 oxygen compounds
- BT1 potassium compounds
- BT2 alkali metal compounds
- RT clarkeite
- RT oxide minerals

POTASSIUM PERCHLORATES [41; 41]
- BT1 perchlorates
- BT2 chlorine compounds
- BT3 halogen compounds
- BT2 oxygen compounds
- BT1 potassium compounds
- BT2 alkali metal compounds

POTASSIUM PHOSPHATES [245; 245]
- BT1 phosphates
- BT2 oxygen compounds
- BT2 phosphorus compounds
- BT1 potassium compounds
- BT2 alkali metal compounds

→ ## POTASSIUM PHOSPHIDES [0; 0] Sep 91
- BT1 phosphides
- BT2 phosphorus compounds
- BT2 pnictides
- BT1 potassium compounds
- BT2 alkali metal compounds

→ ## POTASSIUM SELENIDES [0; 0] Sep 91
- BT1 potassium compounds
- BT2 alkali metal compounds
- BT1 selenides
- BT2 chalcogenides
- BT2 selenium compounds

POTASSIUM SILICATES [45; 48]
- BT1 potassium compounds
- BT2 alkali metal compounds
- BT1 silicates
- BT2 oxygen compounds
- BT2 silicon compounds
- RT boltwoodite
- RT silicate minerals

POTASSIUM SILICIDES [2; 2] Jun 77
- BT1 potassium compounds
- BT2 alkali metal compounds
- BT1 silicides
- BT2 silicon compounds

POTASSIUM SULFATES [282; 284]
- BT1 potassium compounds
- BT2 alkali metal compounds
- BT1 sulfates
- BT2 oxygen compounds
- BT2 sulfur compounds
- RT polyhalite
- RT sulfate minerals

POTASSIUM SULFIDES [28; 28]
- BT1 potassium compounds
- BT2 alkali metal compounds
- BT1 sulfides
- BT2 chalcogenides
- BT2 sulfur compounds

POTASSIUM TELLURIDES [8; 8] Sep 79
- BT1 potassium compounds
- BT2 alkali metal compounds
- BT1 tellurides
- BT2 chalcogenides
- BT2 tellurium compounds

POTASSIUM TUNGSTATES [84; 84] May 78
- BT1 potassium compounds
- BT2 alkali metal compounds
- BT1 tungstates
- BT2 oxygen compounds
- BT2 tungsten compounds
- BT3 transition element compounds

POTASSIUM URANATES [21; 21] Nov 75
- BT1 potassium compounds
- BT2 alkali metal compounds
- BT1 uranates
- BT2 uranium compounds
- BT3 actinide compounds

→ ## POTASSIUM VANADATES [0; 0] Sep 91
- BT1 potassium compounds
- BT2 alkali metal compounds
- BT1 vanadates
- BT2 oxygen compounds
- BT2 vanadium compounds
- BT3 transition element compounds

POTASSIUM 35 [5; 5] Jul 76
- BT1 beta-plus decay radioisotopes
- BT2 beta decay radioisotopes
- BT3 radioisotopes
- BT4 isotopes
- BT1 light nuclei
- BT2 nuclei
- BT1 millisec living radioisotopes
- BT2 radioisotopes
- BT3 isotopes
- BT1 odd-even nuclei
- BT2 nuclei

BT1 potassium isotopes

POTASSIUM 36 [13; 13]
BT1 beta-plus decay radioisotopes
BT2 beta decay radioisotopes
BT3 radioisotopes
BT4 isotopes
BT1 light nuclei
BT2 nuclei
BT1 millisec living radioisotopes
BT2 radioisotopes
BT3 isotopes
BT1 odd-odd nuclei
BT2 nuclei
BT1 potassium isotopes

POTASSIUM 37 [33; 33]
BT1 beta-plus decay radioisotopes
BT2 beta decay radioisotopes
BT3 radioisotopes
BT4 isotopes
BT1 light nuclei
BT2 nuclei
BT1 odd-even nuclei
BT2 nuclei
BT1 potassium isotopes
BT1 seconds living radioisotopes
BT2 radioisotopes
BT3 isotopes

POTASSIUM 38 [169; 169]
BT1 beta-plus decay radioisotopes
BT2 beta decay radioisotopes
BT3 radioisotopes
BT4 isotopes
BT1 light nuclei
BT2 nuclei
BT1 minutes living radioisotopes
BT2 radioisotopes
BT3 isotopes
BT1 odd-odd nuclei
BT2 nuclei
BT1 potassium isotopes
BT1 seconds living radioisotopes
BT2 radioisotopes
BT3 isotopes

POTASSIUM 39 [448; 448]
BT1 light nuclei
BT2 nuclei
BT1 odd-even nuclei
BT2 nuclei
BT1 potassium isotopes
BT1 stable isotopes
BT2 isotopes
RT potassium 39 beams

POTASSIUM 39 BEAMS [6; 6] *Jul 76*
BT1 ion beams
BT2 beams
RT potassium 39

→ **POTASSIUM 39 REACTIONS** [2; 2]
Sep 91
BT1 heavy ion reactions
BT2 nuclear reactions

POTASSIUM 39 TARGET [210; 210]
BT1 targets

POTASSIUM 40 [1,405; 1,405]
BT1 beta-minus decay radioisotopes
BT2 beta decay radioisotopes
BT3 radioisotopes
BT4 isotopes
BT1 beta-plus decay radioisotopes
BT2 beta decay radioisotopes
BT3 radioisotopes
BT4 isotopes
BT1 electron capture radioisotopes
BT2 beta decay radioisotopes
BT3 radioisotopes
BT4 isotopes
BT1 isomeric transition isotopes
BT2 radioisotopes
BT3 isotopes

BT1 light nuclei
BT2 nuclei
BT1 nanosec living radioisotopes
BT2 radioisotopes
BT3 isotopes
BT1 odd-odd nuclei
BT2 nuclei
BT1 potassium isotopes
BT1 years living radioisotopes
BT2 radioisotopes
BT3 isotopes
RT natural radioactivity

POTASSIUM 40 TARGET [18; 18]
BT1 targets

POTASSIUM 41 [202; 202]
BT1 intermediate mass nuclei
BT2 nuclei
BT1 odd-even nuclei
BT2 nuclei
BT1 potassium isotopes
BT1 stable isotopes
BT2 isotopes
RT potassium 41 beams

POTASSIUM 41 BEAMS [3; 3] *Jul 76*
BT1 ion beams
BT2 beams
RT potassium 41

POTASSIUM 41 TARGET [54; 54]
BT1 targets

POTASSIUM 42 [349; 349]
BT1 beta-minus decay radioisotopes
BT2 beta decay radioisotopes
BT3 radioisotopes
BT4 isotopes
BT1 hours living radioisotopes
BT2 radioisotopes
BT3 isotopes
BT1 intermediate mass nuclei
BT2 nuclei
BT1 odd-odd nuclei
BT2 nuclei
BT1 potassium isotopes

POTASSIUM 43 [157; 157]
BT1 beta-minus decay radioisotopes
BT2 beta decay radioisotopes
BT3 radioisotopes
BT4 isotopes
BT1 hours living radioisotopes
BT2 radioisotopes
BT3 isotopes
BT1 intermediate mass nuclei
BT2 nuclei
BT1 odd-even nuclei
BT2 nuclei
BT1 potassium isotopes

POTASSIUM 44 [16; 16]
BT1 beta-minus decay radioisotopes
BT2 beta decay radioisotopes
BT3 radioisotopes
BT4 isotopes
BT1 intermediate mass nuclei
BT2 nuclei
BT1 minutes living radioisotopes
BT2 radioisotopes
BT3 isotopes
BT1 odd-odd nuclei
BT2 nuclei
BT1 potassium isotopes

POTASSIUM 45 [17; 17]
BT1 beta-minus decay radioisotopes
BT2 beta decay radioisotopes
BT3 radioisotopes
BT4 isotopes
BT1 intermediate mass nuclei
BT2 nuclei
BT1 minutes living radioisotopes
BT2 radioisotopes
BT3 isotopes

BT1 odd-even nuclei
BT2 nuclei
BT1 potassium isotopes

POTASSIUM 46 [29; 29]
BT1 beta-minus decay radioisotopes
BT2 beta decay radioisotopes
BT3 radioisotopes
BT4 isotopes
BT1 intermediate mass nuclei
BT2 nuclei
BT1 minutes living radioisotopes
BT2 radioisotopes
BT3 isotopes
BT1 odd-odd nuclei
BT2 nuclei
BT1 potassium isotopes

POTASSIUM 47 [20; 20]
BT1 beta-minus decay radioisotopes
BT2 beta decay radioisotopes
BT3 radioisotopes
BT4 isotopes
BT1 intermediate mass nuclei
BT2 nuclei
BT1 odd-even nuclei
BT2 nuclei
BT1 potassium isotopes
BT1 seconds living radioisotopes
BT2 radioisotopes
BT3 isotopes

POTASSIUM 48 [20; 20]
BT1 beta-minus decay radioisotopes
BT2 beta decay radioisotopes
BT3 radioisotopes
BT4 isotopes
BT1 intermediate mass nuclei
BT2 nuclei
BT1 odd-odd nuclei
BT2 nuclei
BT1 potassium isotopes
BT1 seconds living radioisotopes
BT2 radioisotopes
BT3 isotopes

POTASSIUM 49 [17; 17]
BT1 beta-minus decay radioisotopes
BT2 beta decay radioisotopes
BT3 radioisotopes
BT4 isotopes
BT1 intermediate mass nuclei
BT2 nuclei
BT1 odd-even nuclei
BT2 nuclei
BT1 potassium isotopes
BT1 seconds living radioisotopes
BT2 radioisotopes
BT3 isotopes

POTASSIUM 50 [15; 15]
BT1 beta-minus decay radioisotopes
BT2 beta decay radioisotopes
BT3 radioisotopes
BT4 isotopes
BT1 intermediate mass nuclei
BT2 nuclei
BT1 millisec living radioisotopes
BT2 radioisotopes
BT3 isotopes
BT1 odd-odd nuclei
BT2 nuclei
BT1 potassium isotopes

POTASSIUM 51 [3; 3] *Jun 84*
BT1 beta-minus decay radioisotopes
BT2 beta decay radioisotopes
BT3 radioisotopes
BT4 isotopes
BT1 intermediate mass nuclei
BT2 nuclei
BT1 millisec living radioisotopes
BT2 radioisotopes
BT3 isotopes
BT1 odd-even nuclei
BT2 nuclei
BT1 potassium isotopes

POTASSIUM 52 [5; 5] *Jun 84*
- BT1 beta-minus decay radioisotopes
- BT2 beta decay radioisotopes
- BT3 radioisotopes
- BT4 isotopes
- BT1 intermediate mass nuclei
- BT2 nuclei
- BT1 millisec living radioisotopes
- BT2 radioisotopes
- BT3 isotopes
- BT1 odd-odd nuclei
- BT2 nuclei
- BT1 potassium isotopes

POTASSIUM 53 [4; 4] *Jun 84*
- BT1 beta-minus decay radioisotopes
- BT2 beta decay radioisotopes
- BT3 radioisotopes
- BT4 isotopes
- BT1 intermediate mass nuclei
- BT2 nuclei
- BT1 millisec living radioisotopes
- BT2 radioisotopes
- BT3 isotopes
- BT1 odd-even nuclei
- BT2 nuclei
- BT1 potassium isotopes

POTASSIUM 54 [4; 4] *Jun 84*
- BT1 beta-minus decay radioisotopes
- BT2 beta decay radioisotopes
- BT3 radioisotopes
- BT4 isotopes
- BT1 intermediate mass nuclei
- BT2 nuclei
- BT1 millisec living radioisotopes
- BT2 radioisotopes
- BT3 isotopes
- BT1 odd-odd nuclei
- BT2 nuclei
- BT1 potassium isotopes

potassium-cooled reactors
- USE potassium cooled reactors

potato plant
- USE solanum tuberosum

potato tubers
- USE potatoes

POTATOES [582; 582]
- UF *potato tubers*
- BT1 tubers
- BT1 vegetables
- BT2 food
- RT solanum tuberosum
- RT sprout inhibition

potential (electric)
- USE electric potential

POTENTIAL ENERGY [3,612; 4,825]
- BT1 energy
- NT1 fission barrier
- RT kinetic energy
- RT lagrangian function
- RT landau-zener formula
- RT potentials

POTENTIAL FLOW [66; 66]
- BT1 fluid flow

POTENTIAL SCATTERING [2,208; 2,208]
- BT1 elastic scattering
- BT2 scattering
- RT coulomb scattering
- RT potentials

POTENTIALS [5,972; 16,489] *Oct 81*
(For the mathematical construct from which forces are derived by differentiation; not for ELECTRIC POTENTIAL.)
- NT1 buckingham potential
- NT1 central potential
- NT1 gartenhaus potential
- NT1 kihara potential
- NT1 lennard-jones potential
- NT1 levy-klein potential
- NT1 morse potential
- NT1 muffin-tin potential
- NT1 nonlocal potential
- NT1 nuclear potential
- NT2 hard-core potential
- NT2 harmonic potential
- NT2 hulthen potential
- NT2 soft-core potential
- NT2 square-well potential
- NT2 woods-saxon potential
- NT2 yukawa potential
- NT1 nucleon-nucleon potential
- NT2 gauss potential
- NT2 hamada-johnston potential
- NT2 reid potential
- NT2 schiffer potential
- NT2 signell-marshak potential
- NT2 skyrme potential
- NT2 yamaguchi potential
- NT1 ope potential
- NT2 gammel-thaler potential
- NT1 roche equipotentials
- NT1 surface potential
- NT2 surface delta potential
- NT1 tabakin potential
- RT basic interactions
- RT electromagnetic fields
- RT gravitational fields
- RT interatomic forces
- RT intermolecular forces
- RT noncentral forces
- RT potential energy
- RT potential scattering
- RT rosenfeld force
- RT tensor forces

POTENTIOMETERS [24; 24] *Feb 83*
- BT1 electric measuring instruments
- BT2 electrical equipment
- BT3 equipment
- BT2 measuring instruments
- RT electric potential
- RT resistors

potentiometers (var resistors)
- USE resistors

POTENTIOMETRY [1,911; 1,911]
- BT1 titration
- RT electromotive force
- RT quantitative chemical analysis
- RT quinhydrone
- RT redox potential

POTOMAC RIVER [3; 3] *Sep 77*
- BT1 rivers
- BT2 surface waters

potorous
- USE marsupials

POTTING [0; 0] *Apr 86*
(Encapsulation with a shock-absorbing dielectric material.)
- RT dielectric materials
- RT electrical equipment
- RT electronic equipment
- RT encapsulation
- RT impact shock
- RT potting materials

POTTING MATERIALS [6; 6] *Apr 86*
(Shock-absorbing dielectric materials used for encapsulation.)
- BT1 materials
- RT dielectric materials
- RT electrical equipment
- RT electronic equipment
- RT encapsulation
- RT epoxides
- RT potting
- RT shock absorbers

poultry
- USE fowl

pow.-plut. prod. react. richla
- USE n-reactor

POWDER METALLURGY [1,211; 1,214]
- BT1 metallurgy
- RT compacting
- RT powders
- RT sintered materials
- RT sintering

POWDERS [6,050; 6,050]
- RT compacts
- RT debye-scherrer method
- RT dusts
- RT elutriation
- RT granular materials
- RT particle size
- RT particles
- RT powder metallurgy
- RT sintered materials

POWER [1,623; 12,159]
- NT1 electric power
- NT2 hydroelectric power
- NT1 nuclear power
- NT2 residual power
- NT1 wave power
- NT1 wind power
- RT energy consumption
- RT power generation
- RT power input
- RT power range
- RT thermonuclear reactors

POWER AMPLIFIERS [228; 228]
- BT1 amplifiers
- BT2 equipment
- BT1 electronic equipment
- BT2 equipment

POWER COEFFICIENT [171; 171]
- BT1 reactivity coefficients

POWER CONDITIONING CIRCUITS [266; 266] *Sep 75*
(Prior to December 1990, this concept was indexed by POWER CONDITIONING SYSTEMS and ELECTRONIC CIRCUITS.)
- UF *power conditioning systems*
- RT control systems
- RT inverters
- RT power supplies

power conditioning systems
(Prior to December 1990, this was a valid descriptor.)
- USE power conditioning circuits

POWER DEMAND [1,736; 1,736]
- UF *loads (power demand)*
- BT1 demand
- RT demand factors
- RT electric power
- RT energy demand
- RT peak load

POWER DENSITY [2,282; 3,068]
  UF   density (power)
  NT1   wall loading
  RT   neutron density
  RT   power distribution
  RT   reactor cores
  RT   reactor lattices

POWER DISTRIBUTION [2,672; 2,672] Feb 76
(The spatial distribution of power level throughout a reactor core or fuel element. Not to be confused with the movement of power from one point to another, for which see POWER TRANSMISSION.)
  BT1   spatial distribution
  BT2   distribution
  RT   power density

power excursions
  USE   excursions

POWER GENERATION [3,823; 4,115]
  UF   power production
  UF+   brayton cycle power systems
  NT1   cogeneration
  NT1   on-site power generation
  RT   capacity
  RT   dual-purpose power plants
  RT   electric power
  RT   energy sources
  RT   nuclear power
  RT   power
  RT   power plants
  RT   power systems

POWER INPUT [78; 78] Jan 85
(Power required to operate machinery, appliance, or other device.)
  UF   wattage
  RT   power
  RT   power supplies

POWER LOSSES [364; 364] Jun 83
  UF   losses (power)
  RT   electric power
  RT   energy losses
  RT   outages
  RT   power transmission

POWER PLANTS [1,480; 40,042]
  UF   plants (power)
  NT1   dual-purpose power plants
  NT1   gas turbine power plants
  NT1   hydroelectric power plants
  NT1   solar power plants
  NT1   thermal power plants
    NT2   combined-cycle power plants
    NT2   fossil-fuel power plants
    NT2   geothermal power plants
    NT2   nuclear power plants
      NT3   bopssar standard plant
      NT3   ebasco standard plant
      NT3   gibbssar standard plant
      NT3   offshore nuclear power plants
      NT3   swessar standard plant
      NT3   thermonuclear power plants
      NT3   underground nuclear stations
  RT   combined cycles
  RT   electric power
  RT   outages
  RT   power generation
  RT   power systems

power production
  USE   power generation

POWER RANGE [8; 180] Apr 88
  NT1   gigawatt power range
    NT2   power range 01-10 gw
    NT2   power range 10-100 gw
    NT2   power range 100-1000 gw
  NT1   kilowatt power range
    NT2   power range 01-10 kw
    NT2   power range 10-100 kw
    NT2   power range 100-1000 kw
  NT1   megawatt power range
    NT2   power range 01-10 mw
    NT2   power range 10-100 mw
    NT2   power range 100-1000 mw
  NT1   milliwatt power range
  NT1   terawatt power range
  NT1   watt power range
    NT2   power range 01-10 w
    NT2   power range 10-100 w
    NT2   power range 100-1000 w
  RT   power

POWER RANGE 01-10 GW [14; 14] Apr 88
  BT1   gigawatt power range
  BT2   power range

POWER RANGE 01-10 KW [5; 5] Apr 88
  BT1   kilowatt power range
  BT2   power range

POWER RANGE 01-10 MW [33; 33] Apr 88
  BT1   megawatt power range
  BT2   power range

POWER RANGE 01-10 W [0; 0] Apr 88
  BT1   watt power range
  BT2   power range

POWER RANGE 10-100 GW [0; 0] Apr 88
  BT1   gigawatt power range
  BT2   power range

POWER RANGE 10-100 KW [13; 13] Apr 88
  BT1   kilowatt power range
  BT2   power range

POWER RANGE 10-100 MW [23; 23] Apr 88
  BT1   megawatt power range
  BT2   power range

POWER RANGE 10-100 W [2; 2] Apr 88
  BT1   watt power range
  BT2   power range

POWER RANGE 100-1000 GW [0; 0] Apr 88
  BT1   gigawatt power range
  BT2   power range

POWER RANGE 100-1000 KW [14; 14] Apr 88
  BT1   kilowatt power range
  BT2   power range

POWER RANGE 100-1000 MW [61; 61] Apr 88
  BT1   megawatt power range
  BT2   power range

POWER RANGE 100-1000 W [2; 2] Apr 88
  BT1   watt power range
  BT2   power range

power react nucl fuel dev corp
  USE   pnc

POWER REACTORS [5,273; 68,813]
  BT1   reactors
  NT1   aipfr reactor
  NT1   ao-phai-1 reactor
  NT1   aps reactor
  NT1   arbus reactor
  NT1   avr reactor
  NT1   beloyarsk-1 reactor
  NT1   beloyarsk-2 reactor
  NT1   beloyarsk-3 reactor
  NT1   beloyarsk-4 reactor
  NT1   bilibin reactor
  NT1   bn-1600 reactor
  NT1   bn-800 reactor
  NT1   bohunice a-1 reactor
  NT1   bohunice a-2 reactor
  NT1   bor-60 reactor
  NT1   borax-3 reactor
  NT1   borax-4 reactor
  NT1   bugey-1 reactor
  NT1   bwr type reactors
    NT2   allens creek-1 reactor
    NT2   allens creek-2 reactor
    NT2   bailly-1 reactor
    NT2   barsebaeck-1 reactor
    NT2   barsebaeck-2 reactor
    NT2   barton-1 reactor
    NT2   barton-2 reactor
    NT2   barton-3 reactor
    NT2   barton-4 reactor
    NT2   bell reactor
    NT2   big rock point reactor
    NT2   black fox-1 reactor
    NT2   black fox-2 reactor
    NT2   bonus reactor
    NT2   browns ferry-1 reactor
    NT2   browns ferry-2 reactor
    NT2   browns ferry-3 reactor
    NT2   brunsbuettel reactor
    NT2   brunswick-1 reactor
    NT2   brunswick-2 reactor
    NT2   chinshan-1 reactor
    NT2   chinshan-2 reactor
    NT2   clinton-1 reactor
    NT2   clinton-2 reactor
    NT2   cofrentes reactor
    NT2   cooper reactor
    NT2   dodewaard reactor
    NT2   douglas point-1 reactor
    NT2   douglas point-2 reactor
    NT2   dresden-1 reactor
    NT2   dresden-2 reactor
    NT2   dresden-3 reactor
    NT2   duane arnold-1 reactor
    NT2   ebwr reactor
    NT2   enel-4 reactor
    NT2   enrico fermi-2 reactor
    NT2   err reactor
    NT2   fitzpatrick reactor
    NT2   forsmark-1 reactor
    NT2   forsmark-2 reactor
    NT2   forsmark-3 reactor
    NT2   fukushima-ii-1 reactor
    NT2   fukushima-ii-2 reactor
    NT2   fukushima-ii-3 reactor
    NT2   fukushima-ii-4 reactor
    NT2   fukushima-1 reactor
    NT2   fukushima-2 reactor
    NT2   fukushima-3 reactor
    NT2   fukushima-4 reactor
    NT2   fukushima-5 reactor
    NT2   fukushima-6 reactor
    NT2   garigliano reactor
    NT2   garona reactor
    NT2   ge standard reactor
    NT2   graben-1 reactor
    NT2   grand gulf-1 reactor
    NT2   grand gulf-2 reactor
    NT2   gundremmingen-2 reactor
    NT2   gundremmingen-3 reactor
    NT2   hamaoka-1 reactor
    NT2   hamaoka-2 reactor
    NT2   hamaoka-3 reactor
    NT2   hartsville-1 reactor
    NT2   hartsville-2 reactor
    NT2   hartsville-3 reactor
    NT2   hartsville-4 reactor
    NT2   hatch-1 reactor
    NT2   hatch-2 reactor
    NT2   hdr reactor
    NT2   hope creek-1 reactor
      NT3   newbold island-1 reactor
    NT2   hope creek-2 reactor
      NT3   newbold island-2 reactor
    NT2   humboldt bay reactor
    NT2   isar reactor
    NT2   jpdr reactor
    NT2   jpdr-2 reactor
    NT2   kaiseraugst reactor

NT2	kashiwazaki-kariwa-1 reactor	NT1	dungeness-b reactor	NT3	darlington-1 reactor
NT2	kashiwazaki-kariwa-2 reactor	NT1	ebor reactor	NT3	darlington-2 reactor
NT2	kashiwazaki-kariwa-3 reactor	NT1	ebr-1 reactor	NT3	darlington-3 reactor
NT2	kashiwazaki-kariwa-4 reactor	NT1	ebr-2 reactor	NT3	darlington-4 reactor
NT2	kashiwazaki-kariwa-5 reactor	NT1	egcr reactor	NT3	douglas point ontario reactor
NT2	kashiwazaki-kariwa-6 reactor	NT1	enrico fermi-1 reactor	NT3	gentilly reactor
NT2	kashiwazaki-kariwa-7 reactor	NT1	epec reactor	NT3	gentilly-2 reactor
NT2	kruemmel reactor	NT1	escom reactor	NT3	kanupp reactor
NT2	kuosheng-1 reactor	NT1	fessenheim-2 reactor	NT3	npd reactor
NT2	kuosheng-2 reactor	NT1	fulton-1 reactor	NT3	pickering-1 reactor
NT2	la salle county-1 reactor	NT1	fulton-2 reactor	NT3	pickering-2 reactor
NT2	la salle county-2 reactor	NT1	ga standard reactor	NT3	pickering-3 reactor
NT2	lacbwr reactor	NT1	ginna-2 reactor	NT3	pickering-4 reactor
NT2	laguna verde-1 reactor	NT1	hartlepool reactor	NT3	pickering-5 reactor
NT2	laguna verde-2 reactor	NT1	hbwr reactor	NT3	pickering-6 reactor
NT2	leibstadt reactor	NT1	heysham-a reactor	NT3	pickering-7 reactor
NT2	limerick-1 reactor	NT1	heysham-b reactor	NT3	pickering-8 reactor
NT2	limerick-2 reactor	NT1	hinkley point-b reactor	NT3	point lepreau-1 reactor
NT2	lingen reactor	NT1	hnpf reactor	NT3	point lepreau-2 reactor
NT2	mendocino-1 reactor	NT1	hunterston-b reactor	NT3	rajasthan-1 reactor
NT2	mendocino-2 reactor	NT1	ignalinsk-1 reactor	NT3	rajasthan-2 reactor
NT2	millstone-1 reactor	NT1	ignalinsk-2 reactor	NT3	wolsung-1 reactor
NT2	montague-1 reactor	NT1	jervis bay reactor	NT2	cirene reactor
NT2	montague-2 reactor	NT1	joyo reactor	NT2	cvtr reactor
NT2	montalto di castro-1 reactor	NT1	knk reactor	NT2	el-4 reactor
NT2	montalto di castro-2 reactor	NT1	knk-2 reactor	NT2	jatr reactor
NT2	monticello reactor	NT1	koeberg-1 reactor	NT2	kalpakkam-1 reactor
NT2	muehleberg reactor	NT1	koeberg-2 reactor	NT2	kalpakkam-2 reactor
NT2	nine mile point-1 reactor	NT1	kursk-1 reactor	NT2	lucens reactor
NT2	nine mile point-2 reactor	NT1	kursk-2 reactor	NT2	niederaichbach reactor
NT2	okg-1 reactor	NT1	kursk-3 reactor	NT2	prtr reactor
NT2	okg-2 reactor	NT1	kursk-4 reactor	NT2	sghwr reactor
NT2	onagawa-1 reactor	NT1	lampre-1 reactor	NT1	process heat reactors
NT2	onagawa-2 reactor	NT1	leningrad-1 reactor	NT2	agesta reactor
NT2	oyster creek-1 reactor	NT1	leningrad-2 reactor	NT2	midland-1 reactor
NT2	pathfinder reactor	NT1	leningrad-3 reactor	NT2	midland-2 reactor
NT2	peach bottom-2 reactor	NT1	leningrad-4 reactor	NT2	pm-2a reactor
NT2	peach bottom-3 reactor	NT1	magnox type reactors	NT2	ser reactor
NT2	perry-1 reactor	NT2	berkeley reactor	NT2	sl-1 reactor
NT2	perry-2 reactor	NT2	bradwell reactor	NT2	slowpoke-wnre reactor
NT2	philippsburg-1 reactor	NT2	calder hall a-1 reactor	NT2	sm-1a reactor
NT2	phipps bend-1 reactor	NT2	calder hall a-2 reactor	NT2	snap 10 reactor
NT2	phipps bend-2 reactor	NT2	calder hall b-3 reactor	NT3	s10fs-1 reactor
NT2	quad cities-1 reactor	NT2	calder hall b-4 reactor	NT3	s10fs-3 reactor
NT2	quad cities-2 reactor	NT2	chapelcross-1 reactor	NT3	s10fs-4 reactor
NT2	ringhals-1 reactor	NT2	chapelcross-2 reactor	NT2	thermos reactor
NT2	river bend-1 reactor	NT2	chapelcross-3 reactor	NT2	thr reactor
NT2	river bend-2 reactor	NT2	chapelcross-4 reactor	NT1	propulsion reactors
NT2	rwe-bayernwerk reactor	NT2	dungeness-a reactor	NT2	aircraft propulsion reactors
NT2	shika-1 reactor	NT2	hinkley point-a reactor	NT2	ship propulsion reactors
NT2	shimane-1 reactor	NT2	hunterston-a reactor	NT3	efdr-50 reactor
NT2	shimane-2 reactor	NT2	latina reactor	NT3	lenin reactor
NT2	shoreham reactor	NT2	oldbury-a reactor	NT3	leonid brezhnev reactor
NT2	skagit-1 reactor	NT2	sizewell-a reactor	NT3	mutsu reactor
NT2	skagit-2 reactor	NT2	tokai-mura reactor	NT3	otto hahn reactor
NT2	sl-1 reactor	NT2	trawsfynydd reactor	NT3	savannah reactor
NT2	susquehanna-1 reactor	NT2	wylfa reactor	NT3	sibir reactor
NT2	susquehanna-2 reactor	NT1	marviken reactor	NT2	space propulsion reactors
NT2	tarapur-1 reactor	NT1	monju reactor	NT3	kiwi reactors
NT2	tarapur-2 reactor	NT1	msre reactor	NT3	nerva reactor
NT2	tokai-2 reactor	NT1	mzfr reactor	NT3	nrx-a2 reactor
NT2	tsuruga reactor	NT1	n-reactor	NT3	nrx-a3 reactor
NT2	tullnerfeld reactor	NT1	narora-1 reactor	NT3	nrx-a4-est reactor
NT2	tvo-1 reactor	NT1	narora-2 reactor	NT3	nrx-a5 reactor
NT2	tvo-2 reactor	NT1	okg-3 reactor	NT3	nrx-a6 reactor
NT2	vak reactor	NT1	okg-4 reactor	NT3	pewee-1 reactor
NT2	vbwr reactor	NT1	oldbury-b reactor	NT3	pewee-2 reactor
NT2	vermont yankee reactor	NT1	package reactors	NT3	pewee-3 reactor
NT2	verplanck-1 reactor	NT1	peach bottom-1 reactor	NT3	pewee-4 reactor
NT2	verplanck-2 reactor	NT1	pec brasimone reactor	NT3	phoebus-1a reactor
NT2	vk-50 reactor	NT1	perryman-1 reactor	NT3	phoebus-1b reactor
NT2	wnp-2 reactor	NT1	perryman-2 reactor	NT3	phoebus-2a reactor
NT3	hanford-2 reactor	NT1	pfr reactor	NT3	rover reactors
NT2	wuergassen reactor	NT1	phenix reactor	NT2	tory-2c reactor
NT2	zimmer-1 reactor	NT1	plbr reactor	NT1	pwr type reactors
NT2	zimmer-2 reactor	NT1	pnpf reactor	NT2	almaraz-1 reactor
NT1	cdfr reactor	NT1	pressure tube reactors	NT2	almaraz-2 reactor
NT1	chernobylsk-1 reactor	NT2	atucha reactor	NT2	angra-1 reactor
NT1	chernobylsk-2 reactor	NT2	atucha-2 reactor	NT2	angra-2 reactor
NT1	chernobylsk-3 reactor	NT2	candu type reactors	NT2	angra-3 reactor
NT1	chernobylsk-4 reactor	NT3	bruce-1 reactor	NT2	ardennes b-1 reactor
NT1	chinon-1 reactor	NT3	bruce-2 reactor	NT2	ardennes reactor
NT1	chinon-2 reactor	NT3	bruce-3 reactor	NT2	arkansas-1 reactor
NT1	chinon-3 reactor	NT3	bruce-4 reactor	NT2	arkansas-2 reactor
NT1	clinch river breeder reactor	NT3	bruce-5 reactor	NT2	asco-1 reactor
NT1	connah quay-b reactor	NT3	bruce-6 reactor	NT2	asco-2 reactor
NT1	desalination reactors	NT3	bruce-7 reactor	NT2	atlantic-1 reactor
NT2	bn-350 reactor	NT3	bruce-8 reactor	NT2	atlantic-2 reactor
NT1	dfr reactor	NT3	cernavoda-1 reactor	NT2	basf-1 reactor
NT1	dragon reactor	NT3	cordoba reactor	NT2	basf-2 reactor

NT2	beaver valley-1 reactor	NT2	harris-4 reactor	NT2	prairie island-1 reactor
NT2	beaver valley-2 reactor	NT2	haven-1 reactor	NT2	prairie island-2 reactor
NT2	bellefonte-1 reactor	NT3	koshkonong-1 reactor	NT2	qinshan reactor
NT2	bellefonte-2 reactor	NT2	haven-2 reactor	NT2	quanicassee-1 reactor
NT2	belleville sur loire-1 reactor	NT3	koshkonong-2 reactor	NT2	quanicassee-2 reactor
NT2	belleville sur loire-2 reactor	NT2	ikata reactor	NT2	rancho seco-1 reactor
NT2	beznau-1 reactor	NT2	ikata-2 reactor	NT2	remerschen reactor
NT2	beznau-2 reactor	NT2	ikata-3 reactor	NT2	rheinsberg akw1 reactor
NT2	biblis-1 reactor	NT2	indian point-1 reactor	NT2	ringhals-2 reactor
NT2	biblis-2 reactor	NT2	indian point-2 reactor	NT2	ringhals-3 reactor
NT2	biblis-3 reactor	NT2	indian point-3 reactor	NT2	ringhals-4 reactor
NT2	biblis-4 reactor	NT2	iran-1 reactor	NT2	robinson-2 reactor
NT2	blue hills-1 reactor	NT2	iran-2 reactor	NT2	rooppur reactor
NT2	blue hills-2 reactor	NT2	isar-2 reactor	NT2	rowe yankee reactor
NT2	borssele reactor	NT2	jamesport-1 reactor	NT2	saint alban-1 reactor
NT2	br-3 reactor	NT2	jamesport-2 reactor	NT2	saint alban-2 reactor
NT2	braidwood-1 reactor	NT2	kewaunee reactor	NT2	salem-1 reactor
NT2	braidwood-2 reactor	NT2	kori-1 reactor	NT2	salem-2 reactor
NT2	brokdorf reactor	NT2	kori-2 reactor	NT2	san onofre-1 reactor
NT2	bugey-2 reactor	NT2	krsko reactor	NT2	san onofre-2 reactor
NT2	bugey-3 reactor	NT2	lemoniz-1 reactor	NT2	san onofre-3 reactor
NT2	bugey-4 reactor	NT2	lemoniz-2 reactor	NT2	savannah reactor
NT2	bugey-5 reactor	NT2	lenin reactor	NT2	saxton reactor
NT2	bw standard reactor	NT2	leonid brezhnev reactor	NT2	seabrook-1 reactor
NT2	byron-1 reactor	NT2	loft reactor	NT2	seabrook-2 reactor
NT2	byron-2 reactor	NT2	lucie-1 reactor	NT2	selni reactor
NT2	calhoun-1 reactor	NT2	lucie-2 reactor	NT2	sendai-1 reactor
NT2	calhoun-2 reactor	NT2	maanshan-1 reactor	NT2	sendai-2 reactor
NT2	callaway-1 reactor	NT2	maine yankee reactor	NT2	sequoyah-1 reactor
NT2	callaway-2 reactor	NT2	marble hill-1 reactor	NT2	sequoyah-2 reactor
NT2	calvert cliffs-1 reactor	NT2	marble hill-2 reactor	NT2	shippingport reactor
NT2	calvert cliffs-2 reactor	NT2	mc guire-1 reactor	NT2	sizewell-b reactor
NT2	catawba-1 reactor	NT2	mc guire-2 reactor	NT2	sm-1 reactor
NT2	catawba-2 reactor	NT2	mh-1a reactor	NT2	sm-1a reactor
NT2	cattenom-1 reactor	NT2	midland-1 reactor	NT2	south texas project-1 reactor
NT2	cattenom-2 reactor	NT2	midland-2 reactor	NT2	south texas project-2 reactor
NT2	cattenom-3 reactor	NT2	mihama-1 reactor	NT2	stade reactor
NT2	cattenom-4 reactor	NT2	mihama-2 reactor	NT2	sterling-1 reactor
NT2	ce standard reactor	NT2	mihama-3 reactor	NT2	summer-1 reactor
NT2	cherokee-1 reactor	NT2	millstone-2 reactor	NT2	sundesert-1 reactor
NT2	cherokee-2 reactor	NT2	millstone-3 reactor	NT2	sundesert-2 reactor
NT2	cherokee-3 reactor	NT2	muelheim-kaerlich reactor	NT2	surry-1 reactor
NT2	comanche peak-1 reactor	NT2	mutsu reactor	NT2	surry-2 reactor
NT2	comanche peak-2 reactor	NT2	neckar reactor	NT2	surry-3 reactor
NT2	connecticut yankee reactor	NT2	neckar-2 reactor	NT2	surry-4 reactor
NT2	cook-1 reactor	NT2	nep-1 reactor	NT2	s1c prototype reactor
NT2	cook-2 reactor	NT2	nep-2 reactor	NT2	takahama-1 reactor
NT2	cruas-2 reactor	NT2	neupotz-1 reactor	NT2	takahama-2 reactor
NT2	cruas-3 reactor	NT2	neupotz-2 reactor	NT2	takahama-3 reactor
NT2	crystal river-3 reactor	NT2	nogent sur seine-1 reactor	NT2	takahama-4 reactor
NT2	crystal river-4 reactor	NT2	nogent sur seine-2 reactor	NT2	thr reactor
NT2	dampierre-1 reactor	NT2	north anna-1 reactor	NT2	three mile island-1 reactor
NT2	davis besse-1 reactor	NT2	north anna-2 reactor	NT2	three mile island-2 reactor
NT2	davis besse-2 reactor	NT2	north anna-3 reactor	NT2	tihange reactor
NT2	davis besse-3 reactor	NT2	north anna-4 reactor	NT2	tihange-2 reactor
NT2	daya bay reactor	NT2	north coast-1 reactor	NT2	tihange-3 reactor
NT2	diablo canyon-1 reactor	NT2	obrigheim reactor	NT2	tomari-1 reactor
NT2	diablo canyon-2 reactor	NT2	oconee-1 reactor	NT2	tomari-2 reactor
NT2	doel-1 reactor	NT2	oconee-2 reactor	NT2	tricastin-1 reactor
NT2	doel-2 reactor	NT2	oconee-3 reactor	NT2	tricastin-4 reactor
NT2	doel-3 reactor	NT2	oi-1 reactor	NT2	trillo-1 reactor
NT2	doel-4 reactor	NT2	oi-2 reactor	NT2	trojan reactor
NT2	efdr-50 reactor	NT2	oi-3 reactor	NT2	tsuruga-2 reactor
NT2	emsland reactor	NT2	oi-4 reactor	NT2	turkey point-3 reactor
NT2	erie-1 reactor	NT2	otto hahn reactor	NT2	turkey point-4 reactor
NT2	erie-2 reactor	NT2	palisades-1 reactor	NT2	tva-1 reactor
NT2	farley-1 reactor	NT2	palo verde-1 reactor	NT2	tva-2 reactor
NT2	farley-2 reactor	NT2	palo verde-2 reactor	NT2	tyrone-1 reactor
NT2	fessenheim-1 reactor	NT2	palo verde-3 reactor	NT2	tyrone-2 reactor
NT2	flamanville-1 reactor	NT2	palo verde-4 reactor	NT2	ulchin-1 reactor
NT2	flamanville-2 reactor	NT2	palo verde-5 reactor	NT2	ulchin-2 reactor
NT2	forked river-1 reactor	NT2	paluel-1 reactor	NT2	unterweser reactor
NT2	genkai-1 reactor	NT2	paluel-2 reactor	NT2	vahnum-1 reactor
NT2	genkai-2 reactor	NT2	paluel-3 reactor	NT2	vahnum-2 reactor
NT2	genkai-3 reactor	NT2	paluel-4 reactor	NT2	vogtle-1 reactor
NT2	genkai-4 reactor	NT2	pebble springs-1 reactor	NT2	vogtle-2 reactor
NT2	ginna-1 reactor	NT2	pebble springs-2 reactor	NT2	vogtle-3 reactor
NT2	goesgen reactor	NT2	penly-1 reactor	NT2	vogtle-4 reactor
NT2	golfech-1 reactor	NT2	perkins-1 reactor	NT2	waterford-3 reactor
NT2	grafenrheinfeld reactor	NT2	perkins-2 reactor	NT2	waterford-4 reactor
NT2	gravelines-b1 reactor	NT2	perkins-3 reactor	NT2	watts bar-1 reactor
NT2	gravelines-c6 reactor	NT2	philippsburg-2 reactor	NT2	watts bar-2 reactor
NT2	greene county reactor	NT2	pilgrim-1 reactor	NT2	westinghouse standard reactor
NT2	greenwood-2 reactor	NT2	pilgrim-2 reactor	NT2	wnp-1 reactor
NT2	greenwood-3 reactor	NT2	pilgrim-3 reactor	NT2	wnp-3 reactor
NT2	grohnde reactor	NT2	pm-2a reactor	NT2	wnp-4 reactor
NT2	hamm-uentrop reactor	NT2	pm-3a reactor	NT2	wnp-5 reactor
NT2	harris-1 reactor	NT2	pnpp-1 reactor	NT2	wolf creek-1 reactor
NT2	harris-2 reactor	NT2	point beach-1 reactor	NT2	wup-3 reactor
NT2	harris-3 reactor	NT2	point beach-2 reactor	NT2	wup-4 reactor

NT2	wup-5 reactor	NT3	nrx-a6 reactor		
NT2	wup-6 reactor	NT3	pewee-1 reactor		
NT2	wwer type reactors	NT3	pewee-2 reactor		
NT3	armenian-1 reactor	NT3	pewee-3 reactor		
NT3	armenian-2 reactor	NT3	pewee-4 reactor		
NT3	balakovo-1 reactor	NT3	phoebus-1a reactor		
NT3	balakovo-2 reactor	NT3	phoebus-1b reactor		
NT3	blahutovice-1 reactor	NT3	phoebus-2a reactor		
NT3	bohunice v-1 reactor	NT3	rover reactors		

POWER TRANSMISSION LINES [517; 517]
- RT current limiters
- RT electric cables
- RT electric power
- RT gas-insulated cables
- RT power systems
- RT power transmission

NT3 bohunice v-2 reactor
NT3 dukovany v-2 reactor
NT3 greifswald-1 reactor
NT3 greifswald-2 reactor
NT3 greifswald-3 reactor
NT3 greifswald-4 reactor
NT3 greifswald-5 reactor
NT3 greifswald-6 reactor
NT3 kalinin-1 reactor
NT3 kalinin-3 reactor
NT3 kecerovce-1 reactor
NT3 khmelnitskij-1 reactor
NT3 kola-1 reactor
NT3 kola-2 reactor
NT3 kola-3 reactor
NT3 kola-4 reactor
NT3 kozloduy-1 reactor
NT3 kozloduy-2 reactor
NT3 kozloduy-3 reactor
NT3 loviisa-1 reactor
NT3 loviisa-2 reactor
NT3 mochovce-1 reactor
NT3 paks-1 reactor
NT3 paks-2 reactor
NT3 paks-3 reactor
NT3 paks-4 reactor
NT3 rovno-1 reactor
NT3 rovno-2 reactor
NT3 rovno-3 reactor
NT3 rovno-4 reactor
NT3 rovno-5 reactor
NT3 south ukrainian-1 reactor
NT3 south ukrainian-2 reactor
NT3 south ukrainian-3 reactor
NT3 stendal-1 reactor
NT3 tatarian reactor
NT3 temelin-1 reactor
NT3 wwer-1 reactor
NT3 wwer-2 reactor
NT3 wwer-3 reactor
NT3 wwer-4 reactor
NT3 wwer-5 reactor
NT3 zaporozhe-1 reactor
NT3 zaporozhe-2 reactor
NT3 zaporozhe-3 reactor
NT3 zaporozhe-4 reactor
NT2 wyhl-1 reactor
NT2 wyhl-2 reactor
NT2 yellow creek-1 reactor
NT2 yellow creek-2 reactor
NT2 zion-1 reactor
NT2 zion-2 reactor
NT2 zorita-1 reactor
NT1 rancho seco-2 reactor
NT1 saint laurent-1 reactor
NT1 saint laurent-2 reactor
NT1 sefor reactor
NT1 smolensk-1 reactor
NT1 smolensk-2 reactor
NT1 snr reactor
NT1 snr-2 reactor
NT1 space power reactors
NT2 snap reactors
NT3 snap 10 reactor
NT4 s10fs-1 reactor
NT4 s10fs-3 reactor
NT4 s10fs-4 reactor
NT3 snap 2 reactor
NT4 s2ds reactor
NT3 snap 8 reactor
NT4 s8dr reactor
NT4 s8er reactor
NT2 space propulsion reactors
NT3 kiwi reactors
NT3 nerva reactor
NT3 nrx-a2 reactor
NT3 nrx-a3 reactor
NT3 nrx-a4-est reactor
NT3 nrx-a5 reactor

NT1 sre reactor
NT1 summit-1 reactor
NT1 summit-2 reactor
NT1 thermionic reactors
NT1 thtr-300 reactor
NT1 topaz reactor
NT1 torness reactor
NT1 vandellos reactor
NT1 vg-400 reactor
NT1 vgr-50 reactor
NT1 vhtr reactor
NT1 vidal-1 reactor
NT1 vidal-2 reactor
NT1 vrain reactor
NT1 wagr reactor
RT agr type reactors
RT bhwr type reactors
RT fbr type reactors
RT gcr type reactors
RT htgr type reactors
RT hwgcr type reactors
RT hwlwr type reactors
RT lwgr type reactors
RT lwor type reactors
RT nuclear power plants
RT omr type reactors
RT phwr type reactors
RT present worth method
RT sgr type reactors
RT szr type reactors
RT underground nuclear stations

POWER SERIES [1,589; 1,589]
- BT1 series expansion
- RT mathematics

power substations
- USE power systems

POWER SUPPLIES [4,931; 5,564]
- BT1 electronic equipment
- BT2 equipment
- NT1 spacecraft power supplies
- RT capacitors
- RT direct energy converters
- RT electric power
- RT gyrocons
- RT inverters
- RT klystrons
- RT lasertrons
- RT outages
- RT power conditioning circuits
- RT power input
- RT rf systems

POWER SYSTEMS [702; 702] *Dec 82*
(Includes electric power networks with associated generating and transmission facilities.)
- UF *electric power systems*
- UF *power substations*
- RT electrical transients
- RT outages
- RT power generation
- RT power plants
- RT power transmission
- RT power transmission lines

POWER TRANSMISSION [1,076; 1,076]
- UF *energy transmission*
- RT district heating
- RT electric power
- RT gears
- RT outages
- RT power losses
- RT power systems
- RT power transmission lines

power-burst facility usaec
- USE pbf reactor

POWER-COOLING-MISMATCH ACCIDEN [191; 191]
- UF *pcm accidents*
- BT1 reactor accidents
- BT2 accidents

POYNTING THEOREM [195; 195]
- UF *poynting vector*
- RT flux density
- RT maxwell equations
- RT radiation flux
- RT vectors

poynting vector
- USE poynting theorem

pp chain
- USE hydrogen burning

pp-factor
- USE nicotinamide

PR DEVICES [2; 8]
- BT1 magnetic mirrors
- BT2 open plasma devices
- BT3 thermonuclear devices
- NT1 pr-6 device
- NT1 pr-7 device
- NT1 pr-8 device
- RT trapping

pr-10 aeg pruefreaktor
- USE aeg-pr-10 reactor

PR-6 DEVICE [6; 6]
- BT1 pr devices
- BT2 magnetic mirrors
- BT3 open plasma devices
- BT4 thermonuclear devices

PR-7 DEVICE [0; 0]
- BT1 pr devices
- BT2 magnetic mirrors
- BT3 open plasma devices
- BT4 thermonuclear devices

PR-8 DEVICE [0; 0]
- BT1 pr devices
- BT2 magnetic mirrors
- BT3 open plasma devices
- BT4 thermonuclear devices

prague wwr-s reactor
- USE wwr-s-prague reactor

PRAIRIE ISLAND-1 REACTOR [151; 151]
(Red Wing, Minnesota, USA)
- UF *red wing prairie island-1 reac*
- BT1 pwr type reactors
- BT2 enriched uranium reactors
- BT3 reactors
- BT2 power reactors
- BT3 reactors
- BT2 thermal reactors
- BT3 reactors
- BT2 water cooled reactors
- BT3 reactors

BT2 water moderated reactors
BT3 reactors

PRAIRIE ISLAND-2 REACTOR
[108; 108]
(Red Wing, Minnesota, USA)
UF *red wing prairie island-2 reac*
BT1 pwr type reactors
BT2 enriched uranium reactors
BT3 reactors
BT2 power reactors
BT3 reactors
BT2 thermal reactors
BT3 reactors
BT2 water cooled reactors
BT3 reactors
BT2 water moderated reactors
BT3 reactors

PRANDTL NUMBER [497; 497]
RT nusselt number
RT thermodynamic properties
RT viscous flow

PRASEODYMIUM [675; 675]
BT1 rare earths
BT2 metals
BT3 elements

PRASEODYMIUM ADDITIONS [72; 72]
(Alloys containing not more than 1% Pr are listed here.)
BT1 rare earth additions
RT praseodymium alloys
RT praseodymium compounds

PRASEODYMIUM ALLOYS [599; 635]
(Alloys containing more than 1% Pr.)
BT1 rare earth alloys
BT2 alloys
NT1 praseodymium base alloys
RT praseodymium additions

PRASEODYMIUM ARSENIDES [13; 13]
Feb 76
BT1 arsenides
BT2 arsenic compounds
BT2 pnictides
BT1 praseodymium compounds
BT2 rare earth compounds

PRASEODYMIUM BASE ALLOYS
[31; 31]
BT1 praseodymium alloys
BT2 rare earth alloys
BT3 alloys

PRASEODYMIUM BORIDES [51; 51]
BT1 borides
BT2 boron compounds
BT1 praseodymium compounds
BT2 rare earth compounds

PRASEODYMIUM BROMIDES [14; 14]
BT1 bromides
BT2 bromine compounds
BT3 halogen compounds
BT2 halides
BT3 halogen compounds
BT1 praseodymium compounds
BT2 rare earth compounds

PRASEODYMIUM CARBIDES [20; 20]
BT1 carbides
BT2 carbon compounds
BT1 praseodymium compounds
BT2 rare earth compounds

PRASEODYMIUM CARBONATES
[11; 11]
BT1 carbonates
BT2 carbon compounds
BT2 oxygen compounds
BT1 praseodymium compounds
BT2 rare earth compounds

PRASEODYMIUM CHLORIDES
[108; 108]
BT1 chlorides
BT2 chlorine compounds
BT3 halogen compounds
BT2 halides
BT3 halogen compounds
BT1 praseodymium compounds
BT2 rare earth compounds

PRASEODYMIUM COMPLEXES
[617; 617]
BT1 rare earth complexes
BT2 complexes

PRASEODYMIUM COMPOUNDS
[503; 1,486]
BT1 rare earth compounds
NT1 praseodymium arsenides
NT1 praseodymium borides
NT1 praseodymium bromides
NT1 praseodymium carbides
NT1 praseodymium carbonates
NT1 praseodymium chlorides
NT1 praseodymium fluorides
NT1 praseodymium hydrides
NT1 praseodymium hydroxides
NT1 praseodymium iodides
NT1 praseodymium nitrates
NT1 praseodymium nitrides
NT1 praseodymium oxides
NT1 praseodymium perchlorates
NT1 praseodymium phosphates
NT1 praseodymium phosphides
NT1 praseodymium selenides
NT1 praseodymium silicates
NT1 praseodymium silicides
NT1 praseodymium sulfates
NT1 praseodymium sulfides
NT1 praseodymium tellurides
NT1 praseodymium tungstates
RT praseodymium additions

PRASEODYMIUM FLUORIDES [71; 71]
BT1 fluorides
BT2 fluorine compounds
BT3 halogen compounds
BT2 halides
BT3 halogen compounds
BT1 praseodymium compounds
BT2 rare earth compounds

PRASEODYMIUM HYDRIDES [31; 31]
BT1 hydrides
BT2 hydrogen compounds
BT1 praseodymium compounds
BT2 rare earth compounds

PRASEODYMIUM HYDROXIDES
[13; 13]
BT1 hydroxides
BT2 hydrogen compounds
BT2 oxygen compounds
BT1 praseodymium compounds
BT2 rare earth compounds

PRASEODYMIUM IODIDES [20; 20]
BT1 iodides
BT2 halides
BT3 halogen compounds
BT2 iodine compounds
BT3 halogen compounds
BT1 praseodymium compounds
BT2 rare earth compounds

PRASEODYMIUM IONS [200; 200]
BT1 ions
BT2 charged particles

PRASEODYMIUM ISOTOPES [51; 712]
NT1 praseodymium 124
NT1 praseodymium 126
NT1 praseodymium 128
NT1 praseodymium 129
NT1 praseodymium 130
NT1 praseodymium 131
NT1 praseodymium 132
NT1 praseodymium 133
NT1 praseodymium 134
NT1 praseodymium 135
NT1 praseodymium 136
NT1 praseodymium 137
NT1 praseodymium 138
NT1 praseodymium 139
NT1 praseodymium 140
NT1 praseodymium 141
NT1 praseodymium 142
NT1 praseodymium 143
NT1 praseodymium 144
NT1 praseodymium 145
NT1 praseodymium 146
NT1 praseodymium 147
NT1 praseodymium 148
NT1 praseodymium 149
NT1 praseodymium 150
NT1 praseodymium 151
NT1 praseodymium 152
NT1 praseodymium 153
NT1 praseodymium 154

PRASEODYMIUM NITRATES [57; 57]
BT1 nitrates
BT2 nitrogen compounds
BT2 oxygen compounds
BT1 praseodymium compounds
BT2 rare earth compounds

PRASEODYMIUM NITRIDES [17; 17]
BT1 nitrides
BT2 nitrogen compounds
BT2 pnictides
BT1 praseodymium compounds
BT2 rare earth compounds

PRASEODYMIUM OXIDES [451; 451]
BT1 oxides
BT2 chalcogenides
BT2 oxygen compounds
BT1 praseodymium compounds
BT2 rare earth compounds

PRASEODYMIUM PERCHLORATES
[12; 12]
BT1 perchlorates
BT2 chlorine compounds
BT3 halogen compounds
BT2 oxygen compounds
BT1 praseodymium compounds
BT2 rare earth compounds

PRASEODYMIUM PHOSPHATES
[23; 23] *Oct 75*
BT1 phosphates
BT2 oxygen compounds
BT2 phosphorus compounds
BT1 praseodymium compounds
BT2 rare earth compounds

PRASEODYMIUM PHOSPHIDES
[25; 25] *Jul 77*
BT1 phosphides
BT2 phosphorus compounds
BT2 pnictides
BT1 praseodymium compounds
BT2 rare earth compounds

PRASEODYMIUM SELENIDES [21; 2
BT1 praseodymium compounds
BT2 rare earth compounds
BT1 selenides
BT2 chalcogenides
BT2 selenium compounds

PRASEODYMIUM SILICATES [0; 0]
Oct 88
BT1 praseodymium compounds
BT2 rare earth compounds
BT1 silicates
BT2 oxygen compounds
BT2 silicon compounds

PRASEODYMIUM SILICIDES [11; 11]
Oct 75
BT1   praseodymium compounds
BT2   rare earth compounds
BT1   silicides
BT2   silicon compounds

PRASEODYMIUM SULFATES [41; 41]
BT1   praseodymium compounds
BT2   rare earth compounds
BT1   sulfates
BT2   oxygen compounds
BT2   sulfur compounds

PRASEODYMIUM SULFIDES [55; 55]
BT1   praseodymium compounds
BT2   rare earth compounds
BT1   sulfides
BT2   chalcogenides
BT2   sulfur compounds

PRASEODYMIUM TELLURIDES [16; 16]
BT1   praseodymium compounds
BT2   rare earth compounds
BT1   tellurides
BT2   chalcogenides
BT2   tellurium compounds

→ **PRASEODYMIUM TUNGSTATES** [0; 0]
Sep 91
BT1   praseodymium compounds
BT2   rare earth compounds
BT1   tungstates
BT2   oxygen compounds
BT2   tungsten compounds
BT3   transition element compounds

PRASEODYMIUM 124 [4; 4] *Feb 87*
BT1   odd-odd nuclei
BT2   nuclei
BT1   praseodymium isotopes
BT1   rare earth nuclei
BT2   intermediate mass nuclei
BT3   nuclei
BT1   seconds living radioisotopes
BT2   radioisotopes
BT3   isotopes

PRASEODYMIUM 126 [3; 3] *Oct 84*
BT1   beta-plus decay radioisotopes
BT2   beta decay radioisotopes
BT3   radioisotopes
BT4   isotopes
BT1   odd-odd nuclei
BT2   nuclei
BT1   praseodymium isotopes
BT1   rare earth nuclei
BT2   intermediate mass nuclei
BT3   nuclei
BT1   seconds living radioisotopes
BT2   radioisotopes
BT3   isotopes

PRASEODYMIUM 128 [6; 6] *Jul 85*
BT1   electron capture radioisotopes
BT2   beta decay radioisotopes
BT3   radioisotopes
BT4   isotopes
BT1   odd-odd nuclei
BT2   nuclei
BT1   praseodymium isotopes
BT1   rare earth nuclei
BT2   intermediate mass nuclei
BT3   nuclei
BT1   seconds living radioisotopes
BT2   radioisotopes
BT3   isotopes

PRASEODYMIUM 129 [4; 4] *Jun 77*
BT1   beta-plus decay radioisotopes
BT2   beta decay radioisotopes
BT3   radioisotopes
BT4   isotopes
BT1   electron capture radioisotopes
BT2   beta decay radioisotopes
BT3   radioisotopes
BT4   isotopes
BT1   odd-even nuclei
BT2   nuclei
BT1   praseodymium isotopes
BT1   rare earth nuclei
BT2   intermediate mass nuclei
BT3   nuclei
BT1   seconds living radioisotopes
BT2   radioisotopes
BT3   isotopes

PRASEODYMIUM 130 [10; 10] *Jun 77*
BT1   beta-plus decay radioisotopes
BT2   beta decay radioisotopes
BT3   radioisotopes
BT4   isotopes
BT1   electron capture radioisotopes
BT2   beta decay radioisotopes
BT3   radioisotopes
BT4   isotopes
BT1   odd-odd nuclei
BT2   nuclei
BT1   praseodymium isotopes
BT1   rare earth nuclei
BT2   intermediate mass nuclei
BT3   nuclei
BT1   seconds living radioisotopes
BT2   radioisotopes
BT3   isotopes

PRASEODYMIUM 131 [10; 10] *Jun 77*
BT1   beta-plus decay radioisotopes
BT2   beta decay radioisotopes
BT3   radioisotopes
BT4   isotopes
BT1   minutes living radioisotopes
BT2   radioisotopes
BT3   isotopes
BT1   odd-even nuclei
BT2   nuclei
BT1   praseodymium isotopes
BT1   rare earth nuclei
BT2   intermediate mass nuclei
BT3   nuclei

PRASEODYMIUM 132 [10; 10]
BT1   beta-plus decay radioisotopes
BT2   beta decay radioisotopes
BT3   radioisotopes
BT4   isotopes
BT1   electron capture radioisotopes
BT2   beta decay radioisotopes
BT3   radioisotopes
BT4   isotopes
BT1   minutes living radioisotopes
BT2   radioisotopes
BT3   isotopes
BT1   odd-odd nuclei
BT2   nuclei
BT1   praseodymium isotopes
BT1   rare earth nuclei
BT2   intermediate mass nuclei
BT3   nuclei

PRASEODYMIUM 133 [12; 12]
BT1   beta-plus decay radioisotopes
BT2   beta decay radioisotopes
BT3   radioisotopes
BT4   isotopes
BT1   electron capture radioisotopes
BT2   beta decay radioisotopes
BT3   radioisotopes
BT4   isotopes
BT1   minutes living radioisotopes
BT2   radioisotopes
BT3   isotopes
BT1   odd-even nuclei
BT2   nuclei
BT1   praseodymium isotopes
BT1   rare earth nuclei
BT2   intermediate mass nuclei
BT3   nuclei

PRASEODYMIUM 134 [14; 14]
BT1   beta-plus decay radioisotopes
BT2   beta decay radioisotopes
BT3   radioisotopes
BT4   isotopes
BT1   electron capture radioisotopes
BT2   beta decay radioisotopes
BT3   radioisotopes
BT4   isotopes
BT1   minutes living radioisotopes
BT2   radioisotopes
BT3   isotopes
BT1   odd-odd nuclei
BT2   nuclei
BT1   praseodymium isotopes
BT1   rare earth nuclei
BT2   intermediate mass nuclei
BT3   nuclei

PRASEODYMIUM 135 [21; 21]
BT1   beta-plus decay radioisotopes
BT2   beta decay radioisotopes
BT3   radioisotopes
BT4   isotopes
BT1   electron capture radioisotopes
BT2   beta decay radioisotopes
BT3   radioisotopes
BT4   isotopes
BT1   minutes living radioisotopes
BT2   radioisotopes
BT3   isotopes
BT1   odd-even nuclei
BT2   nuclei
BT1   praseodymium isotopes
BT1   rare earth nuclei
BT2   intermediate mass nuclei
BT3   nuclei

PRASEODYMIUM 136 [9; 9]
BT1   beta-plus decay radioisotopes
BT2   beta decay radioisotopes
BT3   radioisotopes
BT4   isotopes
BT1   electron capture radioisotopes
BT2   beta decay radioisotopes
BT3   radioisotopes
BT4   isotopes
BT1   minutes living radioisotopes
BT2   radioisotopes
BT3   isotopes
BT1   odd-odd nuclei
BT2   nuclei
BT1   praseodymium isotopes
BT1   rare earth nuclei
BT2   intermediate mass nuclei
BT3   nuclei

PRASEODYMIUM 137 [15; 15]
BT1   beta-plus decay radioisotopes
BT2   beta decay radioisotopes
BT3   radioisotopes
BT4   isotopes
BT1   electron capture radioisotopes
BT2   beta decay radioisotopes
BT3   radioisotopes
BT4   isotopes
BT1   hours living radioisotopes
BT2   radioisotopes
BT3   isotopes
BT1   odd-even nuclei
BT2   nuclei
BT1   praseodymium isotopes
BT1   rare earth nuclei
BT2   intermediate mass nuclei
BT3   nuclei

PRASEODYMIUM 138 [11; 11]
BT1   beta-plus decay radioisotopes
BT2   beta decay radioisotopes
BT3   radioisotopes
BT4   isotopes
BT1   electron capture radioisotopes
BT2   beta decay radioisotopes
BT3   radioisotopes
BT4   isotopes
BT1   hours living radioisotopes
BT2   radioisotopes
BT3   isotopes
BT1   minutes living radioisotopes
BT2   radioisotopes
BT3   isotopes
BT1   odd-odd nuclei
BT2   nuclei
BT1   praseodymium isotopes

PRASEODYMIUM 139 [39; 39]
- BT1   beta-plus decay radioisotopes
- BT2   beta decay radioisotopes
- BT3   radioisotopes
- BT4   isotopes
- BT1   electron capture radioisotopes
- BT2   beta decay radioisotopes
- BT3   radioisotopes
- BT4   isotopes
- BT1   hours living radioisotopes
- BT2   radioisotopes
- BT3   isotopes
- BT1   odd-even nuclei
- BT2   nuclei
- BT1   praseodymium isotopes
- BT1   rare earth nuclei
- BT2   intermediate mass nuclei
- BT3   nuclei

PRASEODYMIUM 140 [30; 30]
- BT1   beta-plus decay radioisotopes
- BT2   beta decay radioisotopes
- BT3   radioisotopes
- BT4   isotopes
- BT1   electron capture radioisotopes
- BT2   beta decay radioisotopes
- BT3   radioisotopes
- BT4   isotopes
- BT1   minutes living radioisotopes
- BT2   radioisotopes
- BT3   isotopes
- BT1   odd-odd nuclei
- BT2   nuclei
- BT1   praseodymium isotopes
- BT1   rare earth nuclei
- BT2   intermediate mass nuclei
- BT3   nuclei

PRASEODYMIUM 141 [187; 187]
- BT1   odd-even nuclei
- BT2   nuclei
- BT1   praseodymium isotopes
- BT1   rare earth nuclei
- BT2   intermediate mass nuclei
- BT3   nuclei
- BT1   stable isotopes
- BT2   isotopes

PRASEODYMIUM 141 TARGET [161; 161]
- BT1   targets

PRASEODYMIUM 142 [52; 52]
- BT1   beta-minus decay radioisotopes
- BT2   beta decay radioisotopes
- BT3   radioisotopes
- BT4   isotopes
- BT1   electron capture radioisotopes
- BT2   beta decay radioisotopes
- BT3   radioisotopes
- BT4   isotopes
- BT1   hours living radioisotopes
- BT2   radioisotopes
- BT3   isotopes
- BT1   internal conversion radioisoto
- BT2   radioisotopes
- BT3   isotopes
- BT1   isomeric transition isotopes
- BT2   radioisotopes
- BT3   isotopes
- BT1   minutes living radioisotopes
- BT2   radioisotopes
- BT3   isotopes
- BT1   odd-odd nuclei
- BT2   nuclei
- BT1   praseodymium isotopes
- BT1   rare earth nuclei
- BT2   intermediate mass nuclei
- BT3   nuclei

PRASEODYMIUM 143 [50; 50]
- BT1   beta-minus decay radioisotopes
- BT2   beta decay radioisotopes
- BT3   radioisotopes
- BT4   isotopes
- BT1   days living radioisotopes
- BT2   radioisotopes
- BT3   isotopes
- BT1   odd-even nuclei
- BT2   nuclei
- BT1   praseodymium isotopes
- BT1   rare earth nuclei
- BT2   intermediate mass nuclei
- BT3   nuclei

PRASEODYMIUM 144 [133; 133]
- BT1   beta-minus decay radioisotopes
- BT2   beta decay radioisotopes
- BT3   radioisotopes
- BT4   isotopes
- BT1   isomeric transition isotopes
- BT2   radioisotopes
- BT3   isotopes
- BT1   minutes living radioisotopes
- BT2   radioisotopes
- BT3   isotopes
- BT1   odd-odd nuclei
- BT2   nuclei
- BT1   praseodymium isotopes
- BT1   rare earth nuclei
- BT2   intermediate mass nuclei
- BT3   nuclei

PRASEODYMIUM 145 [13; 13]
- BT1   beta-minus decay radioisotopes
- BT2   beta decay radioisotopes
- BT3   radioisotopes
- BT4   isotopes
- BT1   hours living radioisotopes
- BT2   radioisotopes
- BT3   isotopes
- BT1   odd-even nuclei
- BT2   nuclei
- BT1   praseodymium isotopes
- BT1   rare earth nuclei
- BT2   intermediate mass nuclei
- BT3   nuclei

PRASEODYMIUM 146 [10; 10]
- BT1   beta-minus decay radioisotopes
- BT2   beta decay radioisotopes
- BT3   radioisotopes
- BT4   isotopes
- BT1   minutes living radioisotopes
- BT2   radioisotopes
- BT3   isotopes
- BT1   odd-odd nuclei
- BT2   nuclei
- BT1   praseodymium isotopes
- BT1   rare earth nuclei
- BT2   intermediate mass nuclei
- BT3   nuclei

PRASEODYMIUM 147 [29; 29]
- BT1   beta-minus decay radioisotopes
- BT2   beta decay radioisotopes
- BT3   radioisotopes
- BT4   isotopes
- BT1   minutes living radioisotopes
- BT2   radioisotopes
- BT3   isotopes
- BT1   odd-even nuclei
- BT2   nuclei
- BT1   praseodymium isotopes
- BT1   rare earth nuclei
- BT2   intermediate mass nuclei
- BT3   nuclei

PRASEODYMIUM 148 [28; 28]
- BT1   beta-minus decay radioisotopes
- BT2   beta decay radioisotopes
- BT3   radioisotopes
- BT4   isotopes
- BT1   minutes living radioisotopes
- BT2   radioisotopes
- BT3   isotopes
- BT1   odd-odd nuclei
- BT2   nuclei
- BT1   praseodymium isotopes
- BT1   rare earth nuclei
- BT2   intermediate mass nuclei
- BT3   nuclei

PRASEODYMIUM 149 [13; 13]
- BT1   beta-minus decay radioisotopes
- BT2   beta decay radioisotopes
- BT3   radioisotopes
- BT4   isotopes
- BT1   minutes living radioisotopes
- BT2   radioisotopes
- BT3   isotopes
- BT1   odd-even nuclei
- BT2   nuclei
- BT1   praseodymium isotopes
- BT1   rare earth nuclei
- BT2   intermediate mass nuclei
- BT3   nuclei

PRASEODYMIUM 150 [14; 14]
- BT1   beta-minus decay radioisotopes
- BT2   beta decay radioisotopes
- BT3   radioisotopes
- BT4   isotopes
- BT1   odd-odd nuclei
- BT2   nuclei
- BT1   praseodymium isotopes
- BT1   rare earth nuclei
- BT2   intermediate mass nuclei
- BT3   nuclei
- BT1   seconds living radioisotopes
- BT2   radioisotopes
- BT3   isotopes

PRASEODYMIUM 151 [4; 4] Jan 77
- BT1   beta-minus decay radioisotopes
- BT2   beta decay radioisotopes
- BT3   radioisotopes
- BT4   isotopes
- BT1   odd-even nuclei
- BT2   nuclei
- BT1   praseodymium isotopes
- BT1   rare earth nuclei
- BT2   intermediate mass nuclei
- BT3   nuclei
- BT1   seconds living radioisotopes
- BT2   radioisotopes
- BT3   isotopes

PRASEODYMIUM 152 [8; 8] Jun 84
- BT1   beta-minus decay radioisotopes
- BT2   beta decay radioisotopes
- BT3   radioisotopes
- BT4   isotopes
- BT1   odd-odd nuclei
- BT2   nuclei
- BT1   praseodymium isotopes
- BT1   rare earth nuclei
- BT2   intermediate mass nuclei
- BT3   nuclei
- BT1   seconds living radioisotopes
- BT2   radioisotopes
- BT3   isotopes

PRASEODYMIUM 153 [0; 0] Aug 87
- BT1   beta-minus decay radioisotopes
- BT2   beta decay radioisotopes
- BT3   radioisotopes
- BT4   isotopes
- BT1   odd-even nuclei
- BT2   nuclei
- BT1   praseodymium isotopes
- BT1   rare earth nuclei
- BT2   intermediate mass nuclei
- BT3   nuclei
- BT1   seconds living radioisotopes
- BT2   radioisotopes
- BT3   isotopes

PRASEODYMIUM 154 [5; 5] Oct 88
- BT1   beta-minus decay radioisotopes
- BT2   beta decay radioisotopes
- BT3   radioisotopes
- BT4   isotopes
- BT1   odd-odd nuclei
- BT2   nuclei
- BT1   praseodymium isotopes

(continued from PRASEODYMIUM 138)
- BT1   rare earth nuclei
- BT2   intermediate mass nuclei
- BT3   nuclei

```
BT1     rare earth nuclei
BT2       intermediate mass nuclei
BT3         nuclei
BT1     seconds living radioisotopes
BT2       radioisotopes
BT3         isotopes
```

PRAWNS [25; 25] *Apr 77*
```
BT1     crustaceans
BT2       aquatic organisms
BT2       arthropods
BT3         invertebrates
BT4           animals
RT      seafood
```

PRCF REACTOR [2; 2]
```
UF      plutonium recycle critical fac
UF      pnl-prcf reactor
BT1     plutonium reactors
BT2       reactors
BT1     tank type reactors
BT2       reactors
BT1     zero power reactors
BT2       experimental reactors
BT3         research and test reactors
BT4           reactors
```

pre
(Photoreactivation enzyme.)
```
USE     enzymes
AND     photoreactivation
```

PRE-GONDOLA I EVENT [2; 2]
```
BT1     chemical explosions
BT2       explosions
BT1     cratering explosions
BT2       explosions
BT1     plowshare project
BT1     underground explosions
BT2       explosions
```

PRE-GONDOLA II EVENT [2; 2]
```
BT1     chemical explosions
BT2       explosions
BT1     cratering explosions
BT2       explosions
BT1     plowshare project
BT1     underground explosions
BT2       explosions
```

PREAMPLIFIERS [837; 837]
```
BT1     amplifiers
BT2       equipment
BT1     electronic equipment
BT2       equipment
```

PRECESSION [832; 1,217]
```
NT1     larmor precession
RT      gyroscopes
RT      migma devices
RT      orbits
RT      rotation
```

PRECETRON STORAGE RING [3; 3]
```
BT1     storage rings
```

PRECIPITATION [4,889; 6,361]
(In chemical processes only; see also ATMOSPHERIC PRECIPITATIONS, ELECTRON PRECIPITATION, PROTON PRECIPITATION, and PRECIPITATION HARDENING.)
```
BT1     separation processes
NT1     coprecipitation
NT1     flocculation
RT      agglomeration
RT      crystallization
RT      deposition
RT      hydrometallurgy
RT      salting-out agents
RT      sedimentation
RT      solubility
RT      supersaturation
RT      waste processing
```

PRECIPITATION HARDENING [699; 699]
```
BT1     hardening
RT      age hardening
```

PRECIPITATION SCAVENGING [127; 127]
```
BT1     separation processes
RT      washout
```

precipitations (atmospheric)
```
USE     atmospheric precipitations
```

PRECIPITINS [17; 17]
```
BT1     antibodies
```

precision
```
USE     accuracy
```

PRECOMPOUND-NUCLEUS EMISSION [1,288; 1,288]
(Emission of a few high-energy nucleons resulting from direct processes before establishment of the statistical equilibrium of the compound nucleus.)
```
BT1     nuclear reactions
RT      deep inelastic heavy ion react
RT      incomplete fusion reactions
RT      quasi-fission
```

§§ **PRECURSOR** [824; 824]
```
RT      biosynthesis
RT      enzymes
RT      metabolism
RT      nucleic acids
RT      post-translation modification
```

precursors (delayed neutrons)
```
USE     delayed neutron precursors
```

precursors (delayed protons)
```
USE     delayed proton precursors
```

prediction
```
USE     forecasting
```

PREDICTION EQUATIONS [199; 199]
```
BT1     equations
```

PREDISSOCIATION [223; 223]
```
BT1     dissociation
```

PREDNISOLONE [97; 97]
```
BT1     glucocorticoids
BT2       corticosteroids
BT3         adrenal hormones
BT4           hormones
BT3         hydroxy compounds
BT4           organic compounds
BT3         ketones
BT4           organic compounds
BT3         pregnanes
BT4           steroids
BT5             organic compounds
BT3         steroid hormones
BT4           hormones
```

PREDNISONE [93; 93]
```
BT1     glucocorticoids
BT2       corticosteroids
BT3         adrenal hormones
BT4           hormones
BT3         hydroxy compounds
BT4           organic compounds
BT3         ketones
BT4           organic compounds
BT3         pregnanes
BT4           steroids
BT5             organic compounds
BT3         steroid hormones
BT4           hormones
```

preferred orientation
```
USE     grain orientation
```

PREFERRED SPECIES [0; 0] *Jul 86*
(Species particularly suited for revegetation of reclaimed land.)
```
BT1     plants
RT      gramineae
RT      land reclamation
RT      revegetation
RT      shrubs
RT      trees
```

PREGNANCY [1,989; 1,989]
```
RT      abortion
RT      embryos
RT      fetuses
RT      gynecology
RT      hpl
RT      life cycle
RT      parturition
RT      placenta
RT      prenatal exposure
RT      prenatal irradiation
RT      progesterone
RT      reproduction
RT      reproductive disorders
RT      uterus
```

PREGNANEDIOL [7; 7] *Nov 80*
```
BT1     hydroxy compounds
BT2       organic compounds
BT1     pregnanes
BT2       steroids
BT3         organic compounds
RT      metabolites
RT      progesterone
```

PREGNANES [28; 2,086]
```
BT1     steroids
BT2       organic compounds
NT1     corticosteroids
NT2       glucocorticoids
NT3         corticosterone
NT3         cortisone
NT3         dexamethasone
NT3         hydrocortisone
NT3         prednisolone
NT3         prednisone
NT2       mineralocorticoids
NT3         aldosterone
NT3         doca
NT1     hydroxypregnenone
NT1     pregnanediol
NT1     pregnanetriol
NT1     progesterone
```

PREGNANETRIOL [3; 3] *Nov 80*
```
BT1     hydroxy compounds
BT2       organic compounds
BT1     pregnanes
BT2       steroids
BT3         organic compounds
RT      metabolites
RT      progesterone
```

pregnenolone
```
USE     hydroxypregnenone
```

PRENATAL EXPOSURE [115; 392] *Apr 86*
(For prenatal exposure to radiation use PRENATAL IRRADIATION.)
```
NT1     prenatal irradiation
RT      biological effects
RT      biological stress
RT      fetuses
RT      pregnancy
RT      toxicity
```

PRENATAL IRRADIATION [933; 933]
```
UF      in utero irradiation
BT1     irradiation
BT1     prenatal exposure
RT      embryos
RT      fetuses
```

RT perinatal irradiation
RT pregnancy

PREONS [213; 213] *Jul 84*
(Postulated particles which are constituents of both quarks and leptons.)
BT1 postulated particles
BT2 elementary particles
RT color model
RT composite models
RT leptons
RT quarks

preparation (chemical)
USE chemical preparation

preparation (sample)
USE sample preparation

PRESENT WORTH METHOD [33; 33]
RT cost
RT fuel cycle
RT power reactors

PRESERVATION [865; 2,279]
NT1 radiopreservation
  NT2 radurization
RT bacterial spores
RT cultural objects
RT disinfestation
RT food
RT food processing
RT fumigants
RT grain disinfestation
RT inactivation
RT organoleptic properties
RT pasteurization
RT sterilization
RT wholesomeness

PRESSES [94; 94]
RT extrusion
RT forging
RT machine tools
RT pressing
RT tools

PRESSING [694; 1,969]
BT1 materials working
BT2 fabrication
NT1 cold pressing
NT1 hot pressing
RT compacting
RT dies
RT extrusion
RT forging
RT presses

pressur. heavy water cool./mod
USE phwr type reactors

pressur. subcrit. exp. savanna
USE pse reactor

pressur. water cooled/moderate
USE pwr type reactors

pressure (1-760 torr)
USE low pressure

pressure (critical)
USE critical pressure

pressure (plasma)
USE plasma pressure

pressure (radiation)
USE radiation pressure

pressure (vapor)
USE vapor pressure

pressure (0.1-10 mpa)
USE medium pressure

pressure (0001-0100 atm)
USE medium pressure

pressure (0100-1000 atm)
USE high pressure

pressure (1-10(-3) torr)
USE medium vacuum

pressure (10-100 mpa)
USE high pressure

pressure (100 mpa and above)
USE very high pressure

pressure (1000 atm and above)
USE very high pressure

pressure (133 pa-0.1 mpa)
USE low pressure

pressure (133-0.13 pa)
USE medium vacuum

PRESSURE COEFFICIENT [65; 65]
BT1 reactivity coefficients

PRESSURE CONTROL [169; 169]
Apr 86
BT1 control
RT pressure measurement
RT pressure regulators
RT pressure release
RT pressure suppression
RT pressure vessels

§§ **PRESSURE DEPENDENCE** [12,899; 12,899]
RT high pressure
RT high vacuum
RT low pressure
RT medium pressure
RT medium vacuum
RT pressure drop
RT ultrahigh vacuum
RT very high pressure

PRESSURE DROP [1,878; 1,878]
RT flow rate
RT fluid flow
RT pressure dependence
RT pressure gradients

PRESSURE GAGES [520; 827]
UF *gages (pressure)*
UF *manometers*
BT1 measuring instruments
NT1 barometers
NT1 hot-wire gages
  NT2 pirani gages
NT1 vacuum gages
  NT2 ionization gages
    NT3 bayard-alpert gages
    NT3 philips gages
    NT3 radioactive ionization gages
  NT2 knudsen gages
  NT2 mc leod gages
  NT2 pirani gages
RT bellows
RT pressure measurement

§ **PRESSURE GRADIENTS** [2,377; 2,377]
RT onsager relations
RT pressure drop
RT pressurization

pressure groups
USE interest groups

pressure maintenance
USE pressurization

PRESSURE MEASUREMENT [1,507; 1,508]
RT pressure control
RT pressure gages

PRESSURE REGULATORS [275; 275]
BT1 control equipment
  BT2 equipment
RT pressure control

PRESSURE RELEASE [468; 468]
RT hazards
RT pressure control
RT reactor safety
RT safety engineering

PRESSURE SUPPRESSION [948; 948]
(The suppression of pressure within a containment by some technique such as a water spray.)
RT condensation chambers
RT containment spray systems
RT pressure control
RT pressure vessels
RT reactor accidents
RT reactor safety

PRESSURE TUBE REACTORS [272; 4,261]
BT1 power reactors
  BT2 reactors
NT1 atucha reactor
NT1 atucha-2 reactor
NT1 candu type reactors
  NT2 bruce-1 reactor
  NT2 bruce-2 reactor
  NT2 bruce-3 reactor
  NT2 bruce-4 reactor
  NT2 bruce-5 reactor
  NT2 bruce-6 reactor
  NT2 bruce-7 reactor
  NT2 bruce-8 reactor
  NT2 cernavoda-1 reactor
  NT2 cordoba reactor
  NT2 darlington-1 reactor
  NT2 darlington-2 reactor
  NT2 darlington-3 reactor
  NT2 darlington-4 reactor
  NT2 douglas point ontario reactor
  NT2 gentilly reactor
  NT2 gentilly-2 reactor
  NT2 kanupp reactor
  NT2 npd reactor
  NT2 pickering-1 reactor
  NT2 pickering-2 reactor
  NT2 pickering-3 reactor
  NT2 pickering-4 reactor
  NT2 pickering-5 reactor
  NT2 pickering-6 reactor
  NT2 pickering-7 reactor
  NT2 pickering-8 reactor
  NT2 point lepreau-1 reactor
  NT2 point lepreau-2 reactor
  NT2 rajasthan-1 reactor
  NT2 rajasthan-2 reactor
  NT2 wolsung-1 reactor
NT1 cirene reactor
NT1 cvtr reactor
NT1 el-4 reactor
NT1 jatr reactor

NT1 kalpakkam-1 reactor
NT1 kalpakkam-2 reactor
NT1 lucens reactor
NT1 niederaichbach reactor
NT1 prtr reactor
NT1 sghwr reactor

PRESSURE TUBES [1,024; 1,024]
BT1 tubes
RT borescopes
RT calandrias
RT reactor cooling systems

PRESSURE VESSELS [10,979; 10,979]
UF *vessels (pressure)*
BT1 containers
RT autoclaves
RT depressurization
RT depressurization systems
RT pipe fittings
RT pressure control
RT pressure suppression

PRESSURIZATION [439; 439] *Dec 84*
UF *pressure maintenance*
UF *pressurizing*
UF *repressuring*
RT compression
RT depressurization
RT fluid injection
RT pressure gradients
RT pressurizers
RT transients

pressurized water reactors
USE pwr type reactors

PRESSURIZERS [652; 652]
RT compressors
RT pressurization
RT reactor cooling systems

pressurizing
USE pressurization

PRESTRESSED CONCRETE
[1,408; 1,408]
BT1 composite materials
BT2 materials
BT1 concretes
BT2 building materials
BT3 materials

preven marine poll, london con
USE lcpmpdpw

PREVENTIVE MEDICINE [831; 2,014]
UF *prophylaxis*
BT1 medicine
NT1 public health
RT accidents
RT environment
RT epidemiology
RT health hazards
RT immunity
RT inspection
RT medical examinations
RT medical surveillance
RT radiation protection

PRICE-ANDERSON ACT [94; 94]
Apr 78
BT1 laws
RT nuclear liability

prices
USE charges

PRIGOGINE THEOREM [29; 29]
UF *balescu theory*
UF *prigogine-balescu theory*
UF *van hove-prigogine theory*
RT irreversible processes

prigogine-balescu theory
USE prigogine theorem

PRIMAKOFF EFFECT [99; 99]
BT1 photoproduction
BT2 electromagnetic interactions
BT3 basic interactions
BT3 interactions
BT2 particle interactions
BT3 interactions
BT2 particle production
RT pions neutral

PRIMAKOFF THEORY [24; 24]
RT fermi interactions

PRIMARY COOLANT CIRCUITS
[8,299; 8,299]
BT1 reactor cooling systems
BT2 cooling systems
BT2 reactor components
RT coolant cleanup systems
RT electromagnetic filters

PRIMARY COSMIC RADIATION
[2,323; 3,871]
BT1 cosmic radiation
BT2 ionizing radiations
BT3 radiations
NT1 cosmic alpha particles
NT1 cosmic gamma bursts
NT1 cosmic nuclei
NT1 cosmic x-ray bursts
RT cosmic gamma sources
RT cosmic ray sources

PRIMATES [61; 23,372]
BT1 mammals
BT2 vertebrates
BT3 animals
NT1 apes
NT1 man
NT2 children
NT3 infants
NT2 elderly people
NT2 men
NT2 patients
NT2 women
NT1 monkeys
NT2 baboons
NT2 macacus

PRIMENE [15; 15]
BT1 amines
BT2 organic compounds

PRINCE EDWARD ISLAND [2; 2]
Feb 79
BT1 canada
BT2 developed countries
BT2 north america
BT1 islands
RT atlantic ocean

princeton beta experiment
USE pbx devices

PRINCETON CYCLOTRON [18; 18]
BT1 isochronous cyclotrons
BT2 cyclotrons
BT3 cyclic accelerators
BT4 accelerators

princeton large torus
USE plt devices

PRINCETON SYNCHROTRON [7; 7]
BT1 synchrotrons
BT2 cyclic accelerators
BT3 accelerators

PRINTED CIRCUITS [174; 174]
BT1 electronic circuits
RT microelectronic circuits

PRISM PLOT [15; 15] *Sep 75*
(Phase-space plot of a three-particle final state.)
BT1 scatterplots
BT2 diagrams
BT3 information
RT linear momentum
RT phase space
RT resonance particles

PRISMATIC CONFIGURATION
[128; 128]
BT1 configuration
RT plates
RT slabs

private law
(Prior to December 1990, this was a valid descriptor.)
USE laws

PRNC-L-77 REACTOR [5; 5]
(University of Puerto Rico, College Station, Mayaguez, Puerto Rico, USA)
UF *l-77 puerto rico reactor*
UF *mayaguez puerto rico l-77 r.*
UF *puerto rico nuclear c. l-77 r.*
BT1 aqueous homogeneous reactors
BT2 liquid homogeneous reactors
BT3 fluid fueled reactors
BT4 reactors
BT3 homogeneous reactors
BT4 reactors
BT2 water cooled reactors
BT3 reactors
BT2 water moderated reactors
BT3 reactors
BT1 enriched uranium reactors
BT2 reactors
BT1 research reactors
BT2 research and test reactors
BT3 reactors
BT1 training reactors
BT2 research and test reactors
BT3 reactors

PROBABILISTIC ESTIMATION
[1,396; 1,396] *Apr 86*
(Analytical technique for assessment of unknown quantities and the uncertainty associated with the estimates of those quantities.)
RT fault tree analysis
RT forecasting
RT probability
RT risk assessment
RT safety analysis
RT statistics

§§ **PROBABILITY** [13,133; 13,133]
RT ergodic hypothesis
RT expectation value
RT fuzzy logic
RT maximum-likelihood fit
RT monte carlo method
RT probabilistic estimation
RT risk assessment
RT statistics

PROBES [2,148; 6,342]
NT1 deuteron probes
NT1 electric probes
NT2 langmuir probe
NT2 plasma eaters
NT1 electron probes
NT1 electrostatic probes
NT1 ion probes

NT1	magnetic probes	
NT1	muon probes	
NT1	neutron probes	
NT1	proton probes	
NT1	sonic probes	
RT	measuring instruments	
RT	well logging equipment	

PROCA EQUATIONS [86; 86]
- BT1 partial differential equations
- BT2 differential equations
- BT3 equations
- RT quantum mechanics

PROCAINE [51; 51]
- UF *novocaine*
- BT1 anesthetics
- BT2 central nervous system depress
- BT3 central nervous system agents
- BT4 drugs

PROCEEDINGS [1,120; 1,120]
(Use only for items about proceedings, not for items which are proceedings.)
- RT document types

PROCESS COMPUTERS [852; 852]
Jul 76
(Computers - usually digital - used for the control of technical processes.)
- BT1 computers
- RT on-line control systems
- RT reactor control systems
- RT real time systems

process development pile
- USE pdp reactor

process development units
- USE pilot plants

PROCESS HEAT [637; 637] *Aug 78*
(Heat for industrial processes.)
- UF *heat (process)*
- RT district heating
- RT dual-purpose power plants
- RT process heat reactors
- RT retorting

PROCESS HEAT REACTORS [1,574; 1,717]
- BT1 power reactors
- BT2 reactors
- NT1 agesta reactor
- NT1 midland-1 reactor
- NT1 midland-2 reactor
- NT1 pm-2a reactor
- NT1 ser reactor
- NT1 sl-1 reactor
- NT1 slowpoke-wnre reactor
- NT1 sm-1a reactor
- NT1 snap 10 reactor
- NT2 s10fs-1 reactor
- NT2 s10fs-3 reactor
- NT2 s10fs-4 reactor
- NT1 thermos reactor
- NT1 thr reactor
- RT process heat

processes (adiabatic)
- USE adiabatic processes

processes (isentropic)
- USE isentropic processes

processes (isothermal)
- USE isothermal processes

processing
- SEE fabrication
- OR refining
- OR reprocessing

processing (data)
- USE data processing

processing (ores)
- USE ore processing

processing (wastes)
- USE waste processing

PROCTITIS [91; 91]
- BT1 digestive system diseases
- BT2 diseases
- RT rectum

§ **PRODUCTION** [6,325; 6,325]
(Limited to industrial production; see also PARTICLE PRODUCTION.)
- UF+ *hydrogen production*
- RT capacity
- RT computer-aided manufacturing
- RT fabrication
- RT isotope production
- RT planning
- RT productivity

production (beam)
- USE beam production

production capacity
- USE capacity

production mechanisms, particl
(Production of elementary particles; when appropriate, more specific descriptors listed under PARTICLE PRODUCTION should be used instead.)
- USE particle production

PRODUCTION REACTORS [134; 876]
(For the production of fissile materials only; see also IRRADIATION REACTORS.)
- BT1 reactors
- NT1 plutonium production reactors
- NT2 calder hall a-1 reactor
- NT2 calder hall a-2 reactor
- NT2 calder hall b-3 reactor
- NT2 calder hall b-4 reactor
- NT2 chapelcross-1 reactor
- NT2 chapelcross-2 reactor
- NT2 chapelcross-3 reactor
- NT2 chapelcross-4 reactor
- NT2 g-1 reactor
- NT2 g-2 reactor
- NT2 g-3 reactor
- NT2 hanford production reactors
- NT2 n-reactor
- NT2 windscale production reactors
- NT1 rtr reactor
- NT1 special production reactors
- NT2 c reactor
- NT2 k reactor
- NT2 l reactor
- NT2 p reactor
- NT2 r reactor
- NT1 sr-305 reactor

PRODUCTIVITY [1,556; 1,556]
- UF *yield (biological)*
- RT efficiency
- RT feasibility studies
- RT performance
- RT plant breeding
- RT production

professions
- USE occupations

PROFLAVINE [38; 38]
- BT1 flavines
- BT2 acridines
- BT3 pyridines
- BT4 azines
- BT5 heterocyclic compounds
- BT6 organic compounds
- BT5 organic nitrogen compounds
- BT6 organic compounds
- BT2 amines
- BT3 organic compounds
- BT1 mutagens
- RT acriflavine

PROGENY [581; 581]
- UF *offsprings*
- RT animal breeding
- RT children
- RT fertility
- RT litter size
- RT parturition
- RT reproduction
- RT sex ratio

PROGESTERONE [593; 593]
- BT1 ketones
- BT2 organic compounds
- BT1 pregnanes
- BT2 steroids
- BT3 organic compounds
- BT1 steroid hormones
- BT2 hormones
- RT hydroxypregnenone
- RT lth
- RT ovaries
- RT pregnancy
- RT pregnanediol
- RT pregnanetriol

PROGNOZ SATELLITES [281; 281]
- BT1 satellites

PROGRAMMING [3,513; 4,246]
(Limited to computer programming. See also PLANNING.)
- UF *computer programming*
- NT1 parallel processing
- NT1 vector processing
- RT artificial intelligence
- RT computer codes
- RT computer program documentati
- RT computers
- RT executive codes
- RT programming languages
- RT translators

PROGRAMMING LANGUAGES [660; 3,784]
- UF *computer languages*
- UF *languages (programming)*
- NT1 algol
- NT1 basic
- NT1 cobol
- NT1 fortran
- NT1 pl-1 language
- NT1 pl-11 language
- NT1 prolog
- RT computer codes
- RT computer program documenta
- RT programming
- RT translators

PROGRESS REPORT [5,743; 5,743]
Sep 87
(Use only in conjunction with the liter indicator Y for indexing progress repor

prohib nucl weapons lat am tre
- USE tlatelolco treaty

project anvil
   USE   anvil project

project apollo
   USE   apollo project

project bedrock
   USE   bedrock project

project buffalo
   USE   buffalo project

project castle
   USE   castle project

project crossroads
   USE   crossroads project

project dominic
   USE   dominic project

project greenhouse
   USE   greenhouse project

project hardtack
   USE   hardtack project

project ivy
   USE   ivy project

project jangle
   USE   jangle project

project plowshare
   USE   plowshare project

project plumbbob
   USE   plumbbob project

project redwing
   USE   redwing project

project thunderbird
   USE   thunderbird project

project upshot
   USE   upshot project

project vela
   USE   vela project

PROJECTILES [537; 537]
   RT   explosions
   RT   guns
   RT   nuclear weapons
   RT   rockets

PROJECTION OPERATORS [1,216; 1,216]
(A mathematical operator for projecting a quantity, e.g., angular momentum, on a given coordinate.)
   BT1   mathematical operators
   RT   aligned coupling scheme
   RT   quantum mechanics
   RT   wave functions

PROJECTION SPARK CHAMBERS [329; 329]
   BT1   spark chambers
   BT2   gas track detectors
   BT3   radiation detectors
   BT4   measuring instruments

PROJECTION WELDING [3; 3]
   BT1   resistance welding
   BT2   welding
   BT3   joining
   BT4   fabrication

projectors (scanning)
   USE   scanning measuring projectors

prolactin
   USE   lth

PROLIFERATION [1,283; 1,283] *Feb 78*
   UF   *non-proliferation*
   UF   *nonproliferation*
   UF   *nuclear weapons proliferation*
   RT   denatured fuel
   RT   fuel cycle
   RT   non-proliferation policy
   RT   non-proliferation treaty
   RT   nuclear materials possession
   RT   safeguards

proliferation (cell)
   USE   cell proliferation

PROLINE [371; 371]
   UF   *2-pyrrolidinecarboxylic acid*
   BT1   amino acids
   BT2   carboxylic acids
   BT3   organic acids
   BT4   organic compounds
   BT1   heterocyclic acids
   BT2   carboxylic acids
   BT3   organic acids
   BT4   organic compounds
   BT2   heterocyclic compounds
   BT3   organic compounds
   BT1   pyrrolidines
   BT2   amines
   BT3   organic compounds
   BT2   pyrroles
   BT3   azoles
   BT4   heterocyclic compounds
   BT5   organic compounds
   BT4   organic nitrogen compounds
   BT5   organic compounds
   RT   collagen
   RT   hydroxyproline

PROLOG [8; 8] *Apr 89*
   BT1   programming languages

promazine
   USE   tranquilizers

promethazine
   USE   amines
   AND   antihistaminics
   AND   hypnotics and sedatives
   AND   phenothiazines

PROMETHIUM [119; 119]
   UF   *illinium*
   BT1   rare earths
   BT2   metals
   BT3   elements

PROMETHIUM ADDITIONS [1; 1]
(Alloys containing not more than 1% Pm are listed here.)
   BT1   rare earth additions
   RT   promethium alloys
   RT   promethium compounds

PROMETHIUM ALLOYS [2; 3]
(Alloys containing more than 1% Pm.)
   BT1   rare earth alloys
   BT2   alloys
   NT1   promethium base alloys
   RT   promethium additions

PROMETHIUM BASE ALLOYS [1; 1]
   BT1   promethium alloys
   BT2   rare earth alloys
   BT3   alloys

PROMETHIUM BROMIDES [5; 5]
   BT1   bromides
   BT2   bromine compounds
   BT3   halogen compounds
   BT2   halides
   BT3   halogen compounds
   BT1   promethium compounds
   BT2   rare earth compounds

PROMETHIUM CHLORIDES [7; 7]
   BT1   chlorides
   BT2   chlorine compounds
   BT3   halogen compounds
   BT2   halides
   BT3   halogen compounds
   BT1   promethium compounds
   BT2   rare earth compounds

PROMETHIUM COMPLEXES [57; 57]
   BT1   rare earth complexes
   BT2   complexes

PROMETHIUM COMPOUNDS [57; 109]
   BT1   rare earth compounds
   NT1   promethium bromides
   NT1   promethium chlorides
   NT1   promethium fluorides
   NT1   promethium hydroxides
   NT1   promethium iodides
   NT1   promethium nitrates
   NT1   promethium oxides
   NT1   promethium phosphates
   RT   promethium additions

PROMETHIUM FLUORIDES [10; 10]
   BT1   fluorides
   BT2   fluorine compounds
   BT3   halogen compounds
   BT2   halides
   BT3   halogen compounds
   BT1   promethium compounds
   BT2   rare earth compounds

PROMETHIUM HYDROXIDES [0; 0] *Sep 91*
   BT1   hydroxides
   BT2   hydrogen compounds
   BT2   oxygen compounds
   BT1   promethium compounds
   BT2   rare earth compounds

PROMETHIUM IODIDES [5; 5]
   BT1   iodides
   BT2   halides
   BT3   halogen compounds
   BT2   iodine compounds
   BT3   halogen compounds
   BT1   promethium compounds
   BT2   rare earth compounds

PROMETHIUM IONS [18; 18]
   BT1   ions
   BT2   charged particles

PROMETHIUM ISOTOPES [53; 1,020]
   NT1   promethium 130
   NT1   promethium 132
   NT1   promethium 133
   NT1   promethium 134
   NT1   promethium 135
   NT1   promethium 136
   NT1   promethium 137
   NT1   promethium 138
   NT1   promethium 139

NT1 promethium 140
NT1 promethium 141
NT1 promethium 142
NT1 promethium 143
NT1 promethium 144
NT1 promethium 145
NT1 promethium 146
NT1 promethium 147
NT1 promethium 148
NT1 promethium 149
NT1 promethium 150
NT1 promethium 151
NT1 promethium 152
NT1 promethium 153
NT1 promethium 154
NT1 promethium 155
NT1 promethium 156
NT1 promethium 157
NT1 promethium 158

PROMETHIUM NITRATES [7; 7]
BT1 nitrates
BT2 nitrogen compounds
BT2 oxygen compounds
BT1 promethium compounds
BT2 rare earth compounds

PROMETHIUM OXIDES [31; 31]
BT1 oxides
BT2 chalcogenides
BT2 oxygen compounds
BT1 promethium compounds
BT2 rare earth compounds

PROMETHIUM PHOSPHATES [1; 1]
BT1 phosphates
BT2 oxygen compounds
BT2 phosphorus compounds
BT1 promethium compounds
BT2 rare earth compounds

PROMETHIUM 130 [3; 3] *Jul 85*
BT1 electron capture radioisotopes
BT2 beta decay radioisotopes
BT3 radioisotopes
BT4 isotopes
BT1 odd-odd nuclei
BT2 nuclei
BT1 promethium isotopes
BT1 rare earth nuclei
BT2 intermediate mass nuclei
BT3 nuclei
BT1 seconds living radioisotopes
BT2 radioisotopes
BT3 isotopes

PROMETHIUM 132 [6; 6] *Jun 77*
BT1 beta-plus decay radioisotopes
BT2 beta decay radioisotopes
BT3 radioisotopes
BT4 isotopes
BT1 electron capture radioisotopes
BT2 beta decay radioisotopes
BT3 radioisotopes
BT4 isotopes
BT1 odd-odd nuclei
BT2 nuclei
BT1 promethium isotopes
BT1 rare earth nuclei
BT2 intermediate mass nuclei
BT3 nuclei
BT1 seconds living radioisotopes
BT2 radioisotopes
BT3 isotopes

PROMETHIUM 133 [4; 4] *Jun 77*
BT1 beta-plus decay radioisotopes
BT2 beta decay radioisotopes
BT3 radioisotopes
BT4 isotopes
BT1 electron capture radioisotopes
BT2 beta decay radioisotopes
BT3 radioisotopes
BT4 isotopes
BT1 odd-even nuclei
BT2 nuclei
BT1 promethium isotopes
BT1 rare earth nuclei

BT2 intermediate mass nuclei
BT3 nuclei
BT1 seconds living radioisotopes
BT2 radioisotopes
BT3 isotopes

PROMETHIUM 134 [11; 11] *Apr 77*
BT1 beta-plus decay radioisotopes
BT2 beta decay radioisotopes
BT3 radioisotopes
BT4 isotopes
BT1 electron capture radioisotopes
BT2 beta decay radioisotopes
BT3 radioisotopes
BT4 isotopes
BT1 odd-odd nuclei
BT2 nuclei
BT1 promethium isotopes
BT1 rare earth nuclei
BT2 intermediate mass nuclei
BT3 nuclei
BT1 seconds living radioisotopes
BT2 radioisotopes
BT3 isotopes

PROMETHIUM 135 [12; 12] *Jan 76*
BT1 beta-plus decay radioisotopes
BT2 beta decay radioisotopes
BT3 radioisotopes
BT4 isotopes
BT1 electron capture radioisotopes
BT2 beta decay radioisotopes
BT3 radioisotopes
BT4 isotopes
BT1 odd-even nuclei
BT2 nuclei
BT1 promethium isotopes
BT1 rare earth nuclei
BT2 intermediate mass nuclei
BT3 nuclei
BT1 seconds living radioisotopes
BT2 radioisotopes
BT3 isotopes

PROMETHIUM 136 [13; 13]
BT1 beta-plus decay radioisotopes
BT2 beta decay radioisotopes
BT3 radioisotopes
BT4 isotopes
BT1 electron capture radioisotopes
BT2 beta decay radioisotopes
BT3 radioisotopes
BT4 isotopes
BT1 minutes living radioisotopes
BT2 radioisotopes
BT3 isotopes
BT1 odd-odd nuclei
BT2 nuclei
BT1 promethium isotopes
BT1 rare earth nuclei
BT2 intermediate mass nuclei
BT3 nuclei

PROMETHIUM 137 [12; 12]
BT1 beta-plus decay radioisotopes
BT2 beta decay radioisotopes
BT3 radioisotopes
BT4 isotopes
BT1 electron capture radioisotopes
BT2 beta decay radioisotopes
BT3 radioisotopes
BT4 isotopes
BT1 minutes living radioisotopes
BT2 radioisotopes
BT3 isotopes
BT1 odd-even nuclei
BT2 nuclei
BT1 promethium isotopes
BT1 rare earth nuclei
BT2 intermediate mass nuclei
BT3 nuclei

PROMETHIUM 138 [9; 9]
BT1 beta-plus decay radioisotopes
BT2 beta decay radioisotopes
BT3 radioisotopes
BT4 isotopes
BT1 electron capture radioisotopes

BT2 beta decay radioisotopes
BT3 radioisotopes
BT4 isotopes
BT1 minutes living radioisotopes
BT2 radioisotopes
BT3 isotopes
BT1 odd-odd nuclei
BT2 nuclei
BT1 promethium isotopes
BT1 rare earth nuclei
BT2 intermediate mass nuclei
BT3 nuclei

PROMETHIUM 139 [13; 13]
BT1 beta-plus decay radioisotopes
BT2 beta decay radioisotopes
BT3 radioisotopes
BT4 isotopes
BT1 electron capture radioisotopes
BT2 beta decay radioisotopes
BT3 radioisotopes
BT4 isotopes
BT1 minutes living radioisotopes
BT2 radioisotopes
BT3 isotopes
BT1 odd-even nuclei
BT2 nuclei
BT1 promethium isotopes
BT1 rare earth nuclei
BT2 intermediate mass nuclei
BT3 nuclei

PROMETHIUM 140 [14; 14]
BT1 beta-plus decay radioisotopes
BT2 beta decay radioisotopes
BT3 radioisotopes
BT4 isotopes
BT1 electron capture radioisotopes
BT2 beta decay radioisotopes
BT3 radioisotopes
BT4 isotopes
BT1 minutes living radioisotopes
BT2 radioisotopes
BT3 isotopes
BT1 odd-odd nuclei
BT2 nuclei
BT1 promethium isotopes
BT1 rare earth nuclei
BT2 intermediate mass nuclei
BT3 nuclei
BT1 seconds living radioisotopes
BT2 radioisotopes
BT3 isotopes

PROMETHIUM 141 [38; 38]
BT1 beta-plus decay radioisotopes
BT2 beta decay radioisotopes
BT3 radioisotopes
BT4 isotopes
BT1 electron capture radioisotopes
BT2 beta decay radioisotopes
BT3 radioisotopes
BT4 isotopes
BT1 minutes living radioisotopes
BT2 radioisotopes
BT3 isotopes
BT1 odd-even nuclei
BT2 nuclei
BT1 promethium isotopes
BT1 rare earth nuclei
BT2 intermediate mass nuclei
BT3 nuclei

PROMETHIUM 142 [21; 21]
BT1 beta-plus decay radioisotopes
BT2 beta decay radioisotopes
BT3 radioisotopes
BT4 isotopes
BT1 electron capture radioisotopes
BT2 beta decay radioisotopes
BT3 radioisotopes
BT4 isotopes
BT1 odd-odd nuclei
BT2 nuclei
BT1 promethium isotopes
BT1 rare earth nuclei
BT2 intermediate mass nuclei
BT3 nuclei
BT1 seconds living radioisotopes

PROMETHIUM 143 [77; 77]
- BT1 days living radioisotopes
- BT2 radioisotopes
- BT3 isotopes
- BT1 electron capture radioisotopes
- BT2 beta decay radioisotopes
- BT3 radioisotopes
- BT4 isotopes
- BT1 odd-even nuclei
- BT2 nuclei
- BT1 promethium isotopes
- BT1 rare earth nuclei
- BT2 intermediate mass nuclei
- BT3 nuclei

PROMETHIUM 144 [42; 42]
- BT1 electron capture radioisotopes
- BT2 beta decay radioisotopes
- BT3 radioisotopes
- BT4 isotopes
- BT1 odd-odd nuclei
- BT2 nuclei
- BT1 promethium isotopes
- BT1 rare earth nuclei
- BT2 intermediate mass nuclei
- BT3 nuclei
- BT1 years living radioisotopes
- BT2 radioisotopes
- BT3 isotopes

PROMETHIUM 145 [37; 37]
- BT1 alpha decay radioisotopes
- BT2 radioisotopes
- BT3 isotopes
- BT1 electron capture radioisotopes
- BT2 beta decay radioisotopes
- BT3 radioisotopes
- BT4 isotopes
- BT1 internal conversion radioisoto
- BT2 radioisotopes
- BT3 isotopes
- BT1 odd-even nuclei
- BT2 nuclei
- BT1 promethium isotopes
- BT1 rare earth nuclei
- BT2 intermediate mass nuclei
- BT3 nuclei
- BT1 years living radioisotopes
- BT2 radioisotopes
- BT3 isotopes

PROMETHIUM 146 [20; 20]
- BT1 beta-minus decay radioisotopes
- BT2 beta decay radioisotopes
- BT3 radioisotopes
- BT4 isotopes
- BT1 electron capture radioisotopes
- BT2 beta decay radioisotopes
- BT3 radioisotopes
- BT4 isotopes
- BT1 odd-odd nuclei
- BT2 nuclei
- BT1 promethium isotopes
- BT1 rare earth nuclei
- BT2 intermediate mass nuclei
- BT3 nuclei
- BT1 years living radioisotopes
- BT2 radioisotopes
- BT3 isotopes

PROMETHIUM 147 [552; 552]
- BT1 beta-minus decay radioisotopes
- BT2 beta decay radioisotopes
- BT3 radioisotopes
- BT4 isotopes
- BT1 odd-even nuclei
- BT2 nuclei
- BT1 promethium isotopes
- BT1 rare earth nuclei
- BT2 intermediate mass nuclei
- BT3 nuclei
- BT1 years living radioisotopes
- BT2 radioisotopes
- BT3 isotopes

PROMETHIUM 147 TARGET [3; 3]
May 84
- BT1 targets

PROMETHIUM 148 [42; 42]
- BT1 beta-minus decay radioisotopes
- BT2 beta decay radioisotopes
- BT3 radioisotopes
- BT4 isotopes
- BT1 days living radioisotopes
- BT2 radioisotopes
- BT3 isotopes
- BT1 isomeric transition isotopes
- BT2 radioisotopes
- BT3 isotopes
- BT1 odd-odd nuclei
- BT2 nuclei
- BT1 promethium isotopes
- BT1 rare earth nuclei
- BT2 intermediate mass nuclei
- BT3 nuclei

PROMETHIUM 149 [51; 51]
- BT1 beta-minus decay radioisotopes
- BT2 beta decay radioisotopes
- BT3 radioisotopes
- BT4 isotopes
- BT1 days living radioisotopes
- BT2 radioisotopes
- BT3 isotopes
- BT1 odd-even nuclei
- BT2 nuclei
- BT1 promethium isotopes
- BT1 rare earth nuclei
- BT2 intermediate mass nuclei
- BT3 nuclei

PROMETHIUM 149 TARGET [0; 0]
Mar 76
- BT1 targets

PROMETHIUM 150 [14; 14]
- BT1 beta-minus decay radioisotopes
- BT2 beta decay radioisotopes
- BT3 radioisotopes
- BT4 isotopes
- BT1 hours living radioisotopes
- BT2 radioisotopes
- BT3 isotopes
- BT1 odd-odd nuclei
- BT2 nuclei
- BT1 promethium isotopes
- BT1 rare earth nuclei
- BT2 intermediate mass nuclei
- BT3 nuclei

PROMETHIUM 151 [46; 46]
- BT1 beta-minus decay radioisotopes
- BT2 beta decay radioisotopes
- BT3 radioisotopes
- BT4 isotopes
- BT1 days living radioisotopes
- BT2 radioisotopes
- BT3 isotopes
- BT1 odd-even nuclei
- BT2 nuclei
- BT1 promethium isotopes
- BT1 rare earth nuclei
- BT2 intermediate mass nuclei
- BT3 nuclei

PROMETHIUM 152 [12; 12]
- BT1 beta-minus decay radioisotopes
- BT2 beta decay radioisotopes
- BT3 radioisotopes
- BT4 isotopes
- BT1 minutes living radioisotopes
- BT2 radioisotopes
- BT3 isotopes
- BT1 odd-odd nuclei
- BT2 nuclei
- BT1 promethium isotopes
- BT1 rare earth nuclei
- BT2 intermediate mass nuclei
- BT3 nuclei

PROMETHIUM 153 [14; 14]
- BT1 beta-minus decay radioisotopes
- BT2 beta decay radioisotopes
- BT3 radioisotopes
- BT4 isotopes
- BT1 minutes living radioisotopes
- BT2 radioisotopes
- BT3 isotopes
- BT1 odd-even nuclei
- BT2 nuclei
- BT1 promethium isotopes
- BT1 rare earth nuclei
- BT2 intermediate mass nuclei
- BT3 nuclei

PROMETHIUM 154 [9; 9]
- BT1 beta-minus decay radioisotopes
- BT2 beta decay radioisotopes
- BT3 radioisotopes
- BT4 isotopes
- BT1 minutes living radioisotopes
- BT2 radioisotopes
- BT3 isotopes
- BT1 odd-odd nuclei
- BT2 nuclei
- BT1 promethium isotopes
- BT1 rare earth nuclei
- BT2 intermediate mass nuclei
- BT3 nuclei

PROMETHIUM 155 [5; 5] *Apr 82*
- BT1 beta-minus decay radioisotopes
- BT2 beta decay radioisotopes
- BT3 radioisotopes
- BT4 isotopes
- BT1 odd-even nuclei
- BT2 nuclei
- BT1 promethium isotopes
- BT1 rare earth nuclei
- BT2 intermediate mass nuclei
- BT3 nuclei
- BT1 seconds living radioisotopes
- BT2 radioisotopes
- BT3 isotopes

PROMETHIUM 156 [7; 7] *Oct 86*
- BT1 beta-minus decay radioisotopes
- BT2 beta decay radioisotopes
- BT3 radioisotopes
- BT4 isotopes
- BT1 odd-odd nuclei
- BT2 nuclei
- BT1 promethium isotopes
- BT1 rare earth nuclei
- BT2 intermediate mass nuclei
- BT3 nuclei
- BT1 seconds living radioisotopes
- BT2 radioisotopes
- BT3 isotopes

PROMETHIUM 157 [2; 2] *Aug 87*
- BT1 beta-minus decay radioisotopes
- BT2 beta decay radioisotopes
- BT3 radioisotopes
- BT4 isotopes
- BT1 odd-even nuclei
- BT2 nuclei
- BT1 promethium isotopes
- BT1 rare earth nuclei
- BT2 intermediate mass nuclei
- BT3 nuclei
- BT1 seconds living radioisotopes
- BT2 radioisotopes
- BT3 isotopes

PROMETHIUM 158 [2; 2] *Aug 87*
- BT1 beta-minus decay radioisotopes
- BT2 beta decay radioisotopes
- BT3 radioisotopes
- BT4 isotopes
- BT1 odd-odd nuclei
- BT2 nuclei
- BT1 promethium isotopes
- BT1 rare earth nuclei
- BT2 intermediate mass nuclei
- BT3 nuclei
- BT1 seconds living radioisotopes
- BT2 radioisotopes

BT3 isotopes

prominences (solar)
USE solar prominences

promoters
SEE catalysts
OR efficiency
OR tumor promoters

PROMPT ELECTRONS [48; 48]
BT1 electrons
BT2 leptons
BT3 elementary particles
BT3 fermions

PROMPT GAMMA RADIATION [865; 865]
UF+ *pige analysis*
BT1 gamma radiation
BT2 electromagnetic radiation
BT3 radiations
BT2 ionizing radiations
BT3 radiations
RT nuclear reactions
RT photons

PROMPT NEUTRONS [1,085; 1,085]
BT1 fission neutrons
BT2 neutrons
BT3 nucleons
BT4 baryons
BT5 fermions
BT5 hadrons
BT6 elementary particles
RT fission spectra
RT watt fission spectrum

PROMPT PROTONS [83; 83]
BT1 protons
BT2 hydrogen ions 1 plus
BT3 cations
BT4 ions
BT5 charged particles
BT3 hydrogen ions
BT4 ions
BT5 charged particles
BT2 nucleons
BT3 baryons
BT4 fermions
BT4 hadrons
BT5 elementary particles

prongs
USE particle tracks

proof test facility un. nu. co
USE ptf-unc reactor

propadiene
USE allene

propagation (wave)
USE wave propagation

PROPAGATOR [4,930; 4,930]
RT feynman path integral
RT quantum field theory

PROPANE [533; 533]
BT1 alkanes
BT2 hydrocarbons
BT3 organic compounds

propanol (1-)
USE propanols

PROPANOLS [644; 644]
UF *propanol (1-)*
UF *propyl alcohols*
UF *1-propanol*
UF *2-propanol*
BT1 alcohols
BT2 hydroxy compounds
BT3 organic compounds

propanone
USE acetone

PROPARGYL RADICALS [6; 6]
BT1 alkyl radicals
BT2 radicals

propenal
USE acrolein

propene
USE propylene

PROPER MOTION [240; 240]
(Motion of a star with relation to the celestial sphere.)
BT1 motion
RT stars

PROPERDIN [1; 1]
BT1 proteins
BT2 organic compounds
RT immunity
RT zymosan

property insurance
(Prior to December 1990, this was a valid descriptor.)
USE insurance

PROPERTY RIGHTS [2; 2] Jul 86
RT legal aspects
RT licenses
RT ownership
RT regulations
RT site approvals

property tax exemption
USE financial incentives

prophase
USE mitosis

prophylaxis
USE preventive medicine

propine
USE propyne

PROPIONIC ACID [172; 172]
BT1 monocarboxylic acids
BT2 carboxylic acids
BT3 organic acids
BT4 organic compounds

PROPORTIONAL COUNTERS [3,256; 8,660]
BT1 radiation detectors
BT2 measuring instruments
NT1 bf3 counters
NT1 boron lined counters
NT1 he-3 counters
NT1 liquid proportional counters
NT1 multiwire proportional chamber
NT2 drift chambers
NT3 time projection chambers
NT1 needle chambers

RT avalanche quenching
RT corona counters
RT flow counters
RT gas scintillation detectors
RT proton recoil detectors
RT wall effects
RT wall-less counters

PROPULSION [188; 215]
NT1 ion propulsion
RT propulsion reactors
RT propulsion systems
RT transport

PROPULSION REACTORS [72; 1,122]
BT1 power reactors
BT2 reactors
NT1 aircraft propulsion reactors
NT1 ship propulsion reactors
NT2 efdr-50 reactor
NT2 lenin reactor
NT2 leonid brezhnev reactor
NT2 mutsu reactor
NT2 otto hahn reactor
NT2 savannah reactor
NT2 sibir reactor
NT1 space propulsion reactors
NT2 kiwi reactors
NT2 nerva reactor
NT2 nrx-a2 reactor
NT2 nrx-a3 reactor
NT2 nrx-a4-est reactor
NT2 nrx-a5 reactor
NT2 nrx-a6 reactor
NT2 pewee-1 reactor
NT2 pewee-2 reactor
NT2 pewee-3 reactor
NT2 pewee-4 reactor
NT2 phoebus-1a reactor
NT2 phoebus-1b reactor
NT2 phoebus-2a reactor
NT2 rover reactors
NT1 tory-2c reactor
RT propulsion
RT propulsion systems
RT zpr-9 reactor

PROPULSION SYSTEMS [93; 93] Jan 86
RT aircraft
RT ion thrusters
RT missiles
RT propulsion
RT propulsion reactors
RT rockets
RT vehicles

propyl alcohols
USE propanols

PROPYL RADICALS [35; 35]
BT1 alkyl radicals
BT2 radicals

PROPYLENE [487; 487]
UF *propene*
BT1 alkenes
BT2 hydrocarbons
BT3 organic compounds
RT polypropylene

PROPYNE [37; 37]
UF *methylacetylene*
UF *propine*
BT1 alkynes
BT2 hydrocarbons
BT3 organic compounds

PROSPECTING [1,551; 2,483]
NT1 aerial prospecting
RT electrical surveys
RT exploration
RT geochemical surveys
RT geologic surveys
RT geophysical surveys

PROSTAGLANDINS [746; 746]
  RT   hormones
  RT   prostate

PROSTATE [1,102; 1,102]
  BT1   glands
    BT2   organs
      BT3   body
  BT1   male genitals
    BT2   organs
      BT3   body
  RT   prostaglandins

PROSTHESES [539; 653]
  BT1   medical supplies
  NT1   mechanical heart
  RT   cardiac pacemakers
  RT   surgical materials

PROTACTINIUM [217; 217]
  BT1   actinides
    BT2   metals
      BT3   elements

PROTACTINIUM ADDITIONS [1; 1]
(Alloys containing not more than 1% Pa are listed here.)
  RT   protactinium alloys
  RT   protactinium compounds

PROTACTINIUM ALLOYS [7; 7]
(Alloys containing more than 1% Pa.)
  BT1   actinide alloys
    BT2   alloys
  NT1   protactinium base alloys
  RT   protactinium additions

PROTACTINIUM BASE ALLOYS
[0; 0]
  BT1   protactinium alloys
    BT2   actinide alloys
      BT3   alloys

PROTACTINIUM BROMIDES [11; 11]
  BT1   bromides
    BT2   bromine compounds
      BT3   halogen compounds
    BT2   halides
      BT3   halogen compounds
  BT1   protactinium compounds
    BT2   actinide compounds

PROTACTINIUM CARBIDES [9; 9]
  BT1   carbides
    BT2   carbon compounds
  BT1   protactinium compounds
    BT2   actinide compounds

PROTACTINIUM CHLORIDES [15; 15]
  BT1   chlorides
    BT2   chlorine compounds
      BT3   halogen compounds
    BT2   halides
      BT3   halogen compounds
  BT1   protactinium compounds
    BT2   actinide compounds

PROTACTINIUM COMPLEXES [75; 75]
  BT1   actinide complexes
    BT2   complexes

PROTACTINIUM COMPOUNDS
[82; 164]
  BT1   actinide compounds
  NT1   protactinium bromides
  NT1   protactinium carbides
  NT1   protactinium chlorides
  NT1   protactinium fluorides
  NT1   protactinium hydrides
  NT1   protactinium hydroxides
  NT1   protactinium iodides
  NT1   protactinium nitrates
  NT1   protactinium oxides
  NT1   protactinium phosphates
  NT1   protactinium sulfates
  RT   protactinium additions

PROTACTINIUM FLUORIDES [22; 22]
  BT1   fluorides
    BT2   fluorine compounds
      BT3   halogen compounds
    BT2   halides
      BT3   halogen compounds
  BT1   protactinium compounds
    BT2   actinide compounds

PROTACTINIUM HYDRIDES [8; 8]
Oct 84
  BT1   hydrides
    BT2   hydrogen compounds
  BT1   protactinium compounds
    BT2   actinide compounds

PROTACTINIUM HYDROXIDES [2; 2]
  BT1   hydroxides
    BT2   hydrogen compounds
    BT2   oxygen compounds
  BT1   protactinium compounds
    BT2   actinide compounds

PROTACTINIUM IODIDES [9; 9]
  BT1   iodides
    BT2   halides
      BT3   halogen compounds
    BT2   iodine compounds
      BT3   halogen compounds
  BT1   protactinium compounds
    BT2   actinide compounds

PROTACTINIUM IONS [10; 10]
  BT1   ions
    BT2   charged particles

PROTACTINIUM ISOTOPES [69; 708]
  NT1   protactinium 215
  NT1   protactinium 216
  NT1   protactinium 217
  NT1   protactinium 218
  NT1   protactinium 219
  NT1   protactinium 220
  NT1   protactinium 221
  NT1   protactinium 222
  NT1   protactinium 223
  NT1   protactinium 224
  NT1   protactinium 225
  NT1   protactinium 226
  NT1   protactinium 227
  NT1   protactinium 228
  NT1   protactinium 229
  NT1   protactinium 230
  NT1   protactinium 231
  NT1   protactinium 232
  NT1   protactinium 233
  NT1   protactinium 234
  NT1   protactinium 235
  NT1   protactinium 236
  NT1   protactinium 237
  NT1   protactinium 238

PROTACTINIUM NITRATES [1; 1]
  BT1   nitrates
    BT2   nitrogen compounds
    BT2   oxygen compounds
  BT1   protactinium compounds
    BT2   actinide compounds

PROTACTINIUM OXIDES [30; 30]
  BT1   oxides
    BT2   chalcogenides
    BT2   oxygen compounds
  BT1   protactinium compounds
    BT2   actinide compounds

→ **PROTACTINIUM PHOSPHATES** [0; 0]
Sep 91
  BT1   phosphates
    BT2   oxygen compounds
    BT2   phosphorus compounds
  BT1   protactinium compounds
    BT2   actinide compounds

PROTACTINIUM SULFATES [1; 1]
  BT1   protactinium compounds
    BT2   actinide compounds
  BT1   sulfates
    BT2   oxygen compounds
    BT2   sulfur compounds

PROTACTINIUM 215 [2; 2] Sep 79
  BT1   actinide nuclei
    BT2   heavy nuclei
      BT3   nuclei
  BT1   alpha decay radioisotopes
    BT2   radioisotopes
      BT3   isotopes
  BT1   millisec living radioisotopes
    BT2   radioisotopes
      BT3   isotopes
  BT1   odd-even nuclei
    BT2   nuclei
  BT1   protactinium isotopes

PROTACTINIUM 216 [5; 5]
  BT1   actinide nuclei
    BT2   heavy nuclei
      BT3   nuclei
  BT1   alpha decay radioisotopes
    BT2   radioisotopes
      BT3   isotopes
  BT1   millisec living radioisotopes
    BT2   radioisotopes
      BT3   isotopes
  BT1   odd-odd nuclei
    BT2   nuclei
  BT1   protactinium isotopes

PROTACTINIUM 217 [6; 6] Sep 77
  BT1   actinide nuclei
    BT2   heavy nuclei
      BT3   nuclei
  BT1   alpha decay radioisotopes
    BT2   radioisotopes
      BT3   isotopes
  BT1   millisec living radioisotopes
    BT2   radioisotopes
      BT3   isotopes
  BT1   odd-even nuclei
    BT2   nuclei
  BT1   protactinium isotopes

PROTACTINIUM 218 [4; 4] Sep 77
  BT1   actinide nuclei
    BT2   heavy nuclei
      BT3   nuclei
  BT1   alpha decay radioisotopes
    BT2   radioisotopes
      BT3   isotopes
  BT1   microsec living radioisotopes
    BT2   radioisotopes
      BT3   isotopes
  BT1   odd-odd nuclei
    BT2   nuclei
  BT1   protactinium isotopes

PROTACTINIUM 219 [3; 3] Dec 86
  BT1   actinide nuclei
    BT2   heavy nuclei
      BT3   nuclei
  BT1   alpha decay radioisotopes
    BT2   radioisotopes
      BT3   isotopes
  BT1   nanosec living radioisotopes
    BT2   radioisotopes
      BT3   isotopes
  BT1   odd-even nuclei
    BT2   nuclei
  BT1   protactinium isotopes

PROTACTINIUM 220 [3; 3] Nov 84
  BT1   actinide nuclei
    BT2   heavy nuclei
      BT3   nuclei
  BT1   alpha decay radioisotopes
    BT2   radioisotopes
      BT3   isotopes
  BT1   nanosec living radioisotopes
    BT2   radioisotopes
      BT3   isotopes
  BT1   odd-odd nuclei

PROTACTINIUM 220

- BT2 nuclei
- BT1 protactinium isotopes

PROTACTINIUM 221 [4; 4] Nov 84
- BT1 actinide nuclei
- BT2 heavy nuclei
- BT3 nuclei
- BT1 alpha decay radioisotopes
- BT2 radioisotopes
- BT3 isotopes
- BT1 microsec living radioisotopes
- BT2 radioisotopes
- BT3 isotopes
- BT1 odd-even nuclei
- BT2 nuclei
- BT1 protactinium isotopes

PROTACTINIUM 222 [7; 7] Mar 77
- BT1 actinide nuclei
- BT2 heavy nuclei
- BT3 nuclei
- BT1 alpha decay radioisotopes
- BT2 radioisotopes
- BT3 isotopes
- BT1 millisec living radioisotopes
- BT2 radioisotopes
- BT3 isotopes
- BT1 odd-odd nuclei
- BT2 nuclei
- BT1 protactinium isotopes

PROTACTINIUM 223 [4; 4]
- BT1 actinide nuclei
- BT2 heavy nuclei
- BT3 nuclei
- BT1 alpha decay radioisotopes
- BT2 radioisotopes
- BT3 isotopes
- BT1 millisec living radioisotopes
- BT2 radioisotopes
- BT3 isotopes
- BT1 odd-even nuclei
- BT2 nuclei
- BT1 protactinium isotopes

PROTACTINIUM 224 [3; 3]
- BT1 actinide nuclei
- BT2 heavy nuclei
- BT3 nuclei
- BT1 alpha decay radioisotopes
- BT2 radioisotopes
- BT3 isotopes
- BT1 millisec living radioisotopes
- BT2 radioisotopes
- BT3 isotopes
- BT1 odd-odd nuclei
- BT2 nuclei
- BT1 protactinium isotopes

PROTACTINIUM 225 [3; 3]
- BT1 actinide nuclei
- BT2 heavy nuclei
- BT3 nuclei
- BT1 alpha decay radioisotopes
- BT2 radioisotopes
- BT3 isotopes
- BT1 odd-even nuclei
- BT2 nuclei
- BT1 protactinium isotopes
- BT1 seconds living radioisotopes
- BT2 radioisotopes
- BT3 isotopes

PROTACTINIUM 226 [2; 2]
- BT1 actinide nuclei
- BT2 heavy nuclei
- BT3 nuclei
- BT1 alpha decay radioisotopes
- BT2 radioisotopes
- BT3 isotopes
- BT1 electron capture radioisotopes
- BT2 beta decay radioisotopes
- BT3 radioisotopes
- BT4 isotopes
- BT1 minutes living radioisotopes
- BT2 radioisotopes
- BT3 isotopes
- BT1 odd-odd nuclei
- BT2 nuclei
- BT1 protactinium isotopes

PROTACTINIUM 227 [12; 12]
- BT1 actinide nuclei
- BT2 heavy nuclei
- BT3 nuclei
- BT1 alpha decay radioisotopes
- BT2 radioisotopes
- BT3 isotopes
- BT1 electron capture radioisotopes
- BT2 beta decay radioisotopes
- BT3 radioisotopes
- BT4 isotopes
- BT1 minutes living radioisotopes
- BT2 radioisotopes
- BT3 isotopes
- BT1 odd-even nuclei
- BT2 nuclei
- BT1 protactinium isotopes

PROTACTINIUM 228 [6; 6]
- BT1 actinide nuclei
- BT2 heavy nuclei
- BT3 nuclei
- BT1 alpha decay radioisotopes
- BT2 radioisotopes
- BT3 isotopes
- BT1 electron capture radioisotopes
- BT2 beta decay radioisotopes
- BT3 radioisotopes
- BT4 isotopes
- BT1 hours living radioisotopes
- BT2 radioisotopes
- BT3 isotopes
- BT1 odd-odd nuclei
- BT2 nuclei
- BT1 protactinium isotopes

PROTACTINIUM 229 [13; 13]
- BT1 actinide nuclei
- BT2 heavy nuclei
- BT3 nuclei
- BT1 alpha decay radioisotopes
- BT2 radioisotopes
- BT3 isotopes
- BT1 days living radioisotopes
- BT2 radioisotopes
- BT3 isotopes
- BT1 electron capture radioisotopes
- BT2 beta decay radioisotopes
- BT3 radioisotopes
- BT4 isotopes
- BT1 odd-even nuclei
- BT2 nuclei
- BT1 protactinium isotopes

PROTACTINIUM 230 [11; 11]
- BT1 actinide nuclei
- BT2 heavy nuclei
- BT3 nuclei
- BT1 alpha decay radioisotopes
- BT2 radioisotopes
- BT3 isotopes
- BT1 beta-minus decay radioisotopes
- BT2 beta decay radioisotopes
- BT3 radioisotopes
- BT4 isotopes
- BT1 days living radioisotopes
- BT2 radioisotopes
- BT3 isotopes
- BT1 electron capture radioisotopes
- BT2 beta decay radioisotopes
- BT3 radioisotopes
- BT4 isotopes
- BT1 odd-odd nuclei
- BT2 nuclei
- BT1 protactinium isotopes

PROTACTINIUM 231 [280; 280]
- BT1 actinide nuclei
- BT2 heavy nuclei
- BT3 nuclei
- BT1 alpha decay radioisotopes
- BT2 radioisotopes
- BT3 isotopes
- BT1 neon 24 decay radioisotopes
- BT2 heavy ion decay radioisotopes
- BT3 radioisotopes
- BT4 isotopes
- BT1 odd-even nuclei
- BT2 nuclei
- BT1 protactinium isotopes
- BT1 years living radioisotopes
- BT2 radioisotopes
- BT3 isotopes

PROTACTINIUM 231 TARGET [51; 51]
- BT1 targets

PROTACTINIUM 232 [36; 36]
- BT1 actinide nuclei
- BT2 heavy nuclei
- BT3 nuclei
- BT1 beta-minus decay radioisotopes
- BT2 beta decay radioisotopes
- BT3 radioisotopes
- BT4 isotopes
- BT1 days living radioisotopes
- BT2 radioisotopes
- BT3 isotopes
- BT1 odd-odd nuclei
- BT2 nuclei
- BT1 protactinium isotopes

PROTACTINIUM 232 TARGET [4; 4] Nov 79
- BT1 targets

PROTACTINIUM 233 [224; 224]
- BT1 actinide nuclei
- BT2 heavy nuclei
- BT3 nuclei
- BT1 beta-minus decay radioisotopes
- BT2 beta decay radioisotopes
- BT3 radioisotopes
- BT4 isotopes
- BT1 days living radioisotopes
- BT2 radioisotopes
- BT3 isotopes
- BT1 odd-even nuclei
- BT2 nuclei
- BT1 protactinium isotopes

PROTACTINIUM 233 TARGET [8; 8] Jul 80
- BT1 targets

PROTACTINIUM 234 [61; 61]
- BT1 actinide nuclei
- BT2 heavy nuclei
- BT3 nuclei
- BT1 beta-minus decay radioisotopes
- BT2 beta decay radioisotopes
- BT3 radioisotopes
- BT4 isotopes
- BT1 hours living radioisotopes
- BT2 radioisotopes
- BT3 isotopes
- BT1 isomeric transition isotopes
- BT2 radioisotopes
- BT3 isotopes
- BT1 minutes living radioisotopes
- BT2 radioisotopes
- BT3 isotopes
- BT1 odd-odd nuclei
- BT2 nuclei
- BT1 protactinium isotopes

PROTACTINIUM 235 [9; 9]
- BT1 actinide nuclei
- BT2 heavy nuclei
- BT3 nuclei
- BT1 beta-minus decay radioisotopes
- BT2 beta decay radioisotopes
- BT3 radioisotopes
- BT4 isotopes
- BT1 minutes living radioisotopes
- BT2 radioisotopes
- BT3 isotopes
- BT1 odd-even nuclei
- BT2 nuclei
- BT1 protactinium isotopes

PROTACTINIUM 236 [9; 9]
- BT1 actinide nuclei
- BT2 heavy nuclei
- BT3 nuclei
- BT1 beta-minus decay radioisotopes
- BT2 beta decay radioisotopes
- BT3 radioisotopes
- BT4 isotopes
- BT1 minutes living radioisotopes
- BT2 radioisotopes
- BT3 isotopes
- BT1 odd-odd nuclei
- BT2 nuclei
- BT1 protactinium isotopes

PROTACTINIUM 237 [11; 11]
- BT1 actinide nuclei
- BT2 heavy nuclei
- BT3 nuclei
- BT1 beta-minus decay radioisotopes
- BT2 beta decay radioisotopes
- BT3 radioisotopes
- BT4 isotopes
- BT1 minutes living radioisotopes
- BT2 radioisotopes
- BT3 isotopes
- BT1 odd-even nuclei
- BT2 nuclei
- BT1 protactinium isotopes

PROTACTINIUM 238 [16; 16]
- BT1 actinide nuclei
- BT2 heavy nuclei
- BT3 nuclei
- BT1 beta-minus decay radioisotopes
- BT2 beta decay radioisotopes
- BT3 radioisotopes
- BT4 isotopes
- BT1 minutes living radioisotopes
- BT2 radioisotopes
- BT3 isotopes
- BT1 odd-odd nuclei
- BT2 nuclei
- BT1 protactinium isotopes

PROTAMINES [19; 20]
- BT1 blood coagulation factors
- BT2 coagulants
- BT3 hematologic agents
- BT4 drugs
- BT1 proteins
- BT2 organic compounds
- NT1 salmin

protec nucl mater, conv
- USE cppnm

protection (corrosion)
- USE corrosion protection

protection (radiation)
- USE radiation protection

protection (safety)
- USE safety

PROTECTIVE CLOTHING [367; 433]
- BT1 clothing
- NT1 gloves
- RT radiation protection
- RT respirators
- RT skin absorption

PROTECTIVE COATINGS [1,453; 1,453]
- BT1 coatings
- RT decontamination
- RT latex

PROTEIN DENATURATION [118; 118]
- UF *denaturation (protein)*
- RT enzymes
- RT heat treatments
- RT molecular structure
- RT ph value
- RT protein structure
- RT proteins

PROTEIN STRUCTURE [942; 942]
Dec 84
- UF *amino acid sequence*
- RT amino acids
- RT molecular structure
- RT post-translation modification
- RT protein denaturation
- RT proteins
- RT structure-activity relationshi

protein-bound iodine
- USE pbi

PROTEINS [7,677; 21,827]
- BT1 organic compounds
- NT1 actin
- NT1 albumins
- NT2 luciferin
- NT1 casein
- NT1 ferritin
- NT1 gelatin
- NT1 globins
- NT2 hemoglobin
- NT3 carboxyhemoglobin
- NT3 methemoglobin
- NT2 myoglobin
- NT1 globulins
- NT2 angiotensin
- NT2 fibrinogen
- NT2 globulins-alpha
- NT3 ceruloplasmin
- NT3 haptoglobins
- NT2 globulins-beta
- NT3 transferrin
- NT2 globulins-gamma
- NT2 immunoglobulins
- NT2 lactoferrin
- NT2 myosin
- NT2 thyroglobulin
- NT1 glycoproteins
- NT2 lactoferrin
- NT2 lh
- NT2 ovalbumin
- NT1 growth factors
- NT1 hemocyanin
- NT1 histones
- NT1 lipoproteins
- NT2 myelin
- NT1 metallothionein
- NT1 mucoproteins
- NT2 haptoglobins
- NT2 intrinsic factor
- NT2 phytohemagglutinin
- NT1 nucleoproteins
- NT1 pbi
- NT1 peptides
- NT2 polypeptides
- NT3 calcitonin
- NT3 endorphins
- NT4 enkephalins
- NT3 gastrin
- NT3 glucagon
- NT3 glutathione
- NT3 kinins
- NT1 peptone
- NT1 properdin
- NT1 protamines
- NT2 salmin
- NT1 rhodopsin
- NT1 scleroproteins
- NT2 collagen
- NT2 fibrin
- NT2 glutin
- NT2 keratin
- NT1 transcription factors
- RT amino acids
- RT blood plasma
- RT cpb
- RT dialysis
- RT food
- RT microtubules
- RT peanuts
- RT polyamides
- RT post-translation modification
- RT protein denaturation
- RT protein structure
- RT proteolysis

proteolipids
- USE lipoproteins

PROTEOLYSIS [225; 334]
- BT1 decomposition
- BT2 chemical reactions
- NT1 fibrinolysis
- RT catabolism
- RT clostridium
- RT peptide hydrolases
- RT post-translation modification
- RT proteins

PROTEUS [46; 46]
- BT1 bacteria
- BT2 microorganisms
- RT feces
- RT soils

PROTEUS REACTOR [81; 81]
(Eidgenoessiches Institut fuer Reaktorforschung, Wuerlingen, Argovie, Switzerland)
- UF *wuerenlingen proteus reactor*
- BT1 enriched uranium reactors
- BT2 reactors
- BT1 graphite moderated reactors
- BT2 reactors
- BT1 research reactors
- BT2 research and test reactors
- BT3 reactors
- BT1 test reactors
- BT2 research and test reactors
- BT3 reactors
- BT2 test facilities

PROTHROMBIN [20; 20]
- BT1 blood coagulation factors
- BT2 coagulants
- BT3 hematologic agents
- BT4 drugs

protium
- USE hydrogen 1

PROTO-CLEO STELLARATORS [50; 50]
- BT1 stellarators
- BT2 closed plasma devices
- BT3 thermonuclear devices
- RT cleo stellarator

PROTON BEAMS [10,725; 10,725]
- BT1 nucleon beams
- BT2 particle beams
- BT3 beams
- RT electron cooling
- RT proton channeling
- RT protons

proton blocking
- USE proton channeling

PROTON CHANNELING [425; 425]
- UF *proton blocking*
- BT1 channeling
- RT proton beams

PROTON COMPUTED TOMOGRAPHY [94; 94] *Apr 80*
- UF *proton scanners (tomography)*
- BT1 computerized tomography
- BT2 tomography
- RT biomedical radiography

RT image scanners
RT proton radiography

proton decay (nuclear decay)
(Emission of protons from ground states of nuclei.)
USE proton-emission decay

proton decay (particle decay)
(Decay of the proton. Coordinate the descriptor below with a descriptor for the decay, e.g. SEMILEPTONIC DECAY.)
USE protons

PROTON DECAY RADIOISOTOPES
[13; 46] Nov 84
BT1 radioisotopes
BT2 isotopes
NT1 cesium 113
NT1 cobalt 53
NT1 iodine 109
NT1 lutetium 151
NT1 scandium 39
NT1 thulium 147
RT proton-emission decay

PROTON DENSITY [751; 751]
UF density (proton)
RT protons

PROTON DETECTION [659; 659]
BT1 charged particle detection
BT2 radiation detection
BT3 detection
RT proton dosimetry
RT recoils

PROTON DOSIMETRY [113; 113]
BT1 dosimetry
RT proton detection

proton magnetic resonance spec
USE nmr spectra
AND protons

PROTON MICROPROBE ANALYSIS
[185; 185] Apr 79
BT1 microanalysis
BT1 nondestructive analysis
BT2 chemical analysis
RT proton probes

PROTON PRECESSION MAGNETOMETER [23; 23]
BT1 magnetometers
BT2 measuring instruments

PROTON PRECIPITATION [256; 256]
BT1 charged-particle precipitation
RT aurorae
RT auroral oval
RT midday aurorae
RT polar cusp
RT radiation belts
RT trapped protons

PROTON PROBES [91; 91] Apr 78
BT1 probes
RT ion probes
RT proton microprobe analysis
RT proton sources

PROTON RADIOGRAPHY [51; 51]
Aug 76
RT biomedical radiography
RT industrial radiography
RT nondestructive testing
RT proton computed tomography

PROTON REACTIONS [17,415; 17,415]
UF+ *pige analysis*
UF+ *proton-deuteron interactions*
BT1 nucleon reactions
BT2 baryon reactions
BT3 hadron reactions
BT4 nuclear reactions

PROTON RECOIL DETECTORS
[519; 520]
BT1 neutron detectors
BT2 radiation detectors
BT3 measuring instruments
RT proportional counters
RT radiator counters
RT recoils
RT scintillation counters

PROTON SATELLITES [11; 11]
BT1 satellites
RT interkosmos satellites
RT kosmos satellites

proton scanners (tomography)
USE proton computed tomography

PROTON SOURCES [153; 153]
BT1 particle sources
BT2 radiation sources
RT proton probes
RT protons

PROTON SPECTRA [3,017; 3,017]
BT1 spectra
RT protons

PROTON SPECTROMETERS [163; 163]
BT1 spectrometers
BT2 measuring instruments

PROTON TEMPERATURE [110; 110]
UF temperature (proton)
RT energy
RT protons

PROTON TRANSPORT [174; 174]
UF transport (proton)
BT1 charged-particle transport
BT2 radiation transport

PROTON-ANTINEUTRON INTERACTION [40; 40]
BT1 nucleon-antinucleon interactio
BT2 baryon-baryon interactions
BT3 hadron-hadron interactions
BT4 particle interactions
BT5 interactions

PROTON-ANTIPROTON INTERACTIONS [5,279; 5,279]
UF antiproton-proton interactions
BT1 nucleon-antinucleon interactio
BT2 baryon-baryon interactions
BT3 hadron-hadron interactions
BT4 particle interactions
BT5 interactions

proton-atom collisions
USE hydrogen ions 1 plus
AND ion-atom collisions

proton-deuteron interactions
USE deuterium target
AND proton reactions

PROTON-EMISSION DECAY [236; 236]
Nov 84
(Emission of protons from ground states of nuclei.)
UF proton decay (nuclear decay)
BT1 nuclear decay
BT2 decay

RT proton decay radioisotopes
RT protons

proton-induced x-ray emiss ana
USE pixe analysis

proton-molecule collisions
USE hydrogen ions 1 plus
AND ion-molecule collisions

PROTON-NEUTRON INTERACTIONS
[2,006; 2,006]
BT1 proton-nucleon interactions
BT2 nucleon-nucleon interactions
BT3 baryon-baryon interactions
BT4 hadron-hadron interactions
BT5 particle interactions
BT6 interactions

PROTON-NUCLEON INTERACTIONS
[188; 2,817]
(Prior to April 1986 the coordination of PROTON-NEUTRON INTERACTIONS and PROTON-PROTON INTERACTIONS was used for this concept.)
BT1 nucleon-nucleon interactions
BT2 baryon-baryon interactions
BT3 hadron-hadron interactions
BT4 particle interactions
BT5 interactions
NT1 proton-neutron interactions
NT1 proton-proton interactions

proton-proton cycle
USE hydrogen burning

PROTON-PROTON INTERACTIONS
[7,404; 7,404]
BT1 proton-nucleon interactions
BT2 nucleon-nucleon interactions
BT3 baryon-baryon interactions
BT4 hadron-hadron interactions
BT5 particle interactions
BT6 interactions

PROTONIUM [172; 172]
RT antiprotons
RT atoms
RT muonium
RT positronium
RT protons

PROTONS [32,969; 35,745]
UF proton decay (particle decay)
UF+ pmr spectra
UF+ proton magnetic resonance spe
BT1 hydrogen ions 1 plus
BT2 cations
BT3 ions
BT4 charged particles
BT2 hydrogen ions
BT3 ions
BT4 charged particles
BT1 nucleons
BT2 baryons
BT3 fermions
BT3 hadrons
BT4 elementary particles
NT1 antiprotons
NT1 cosmic protons
NT1 delayed protons
NT1 diprotons
NT1 photoprotons
NT1 prompt protons
NT1 solar protons
NT1 trapped protons
RT proton beams
RT proton density
RT proton sources
RT proton spectra
RT proton temperature
RT proton-emission decay
RT protonium

PROTOPLANETS [270; 270]
- RT cosmological models
- RT planets
- RT solar nebula
- RT solar system evolution

protoplasts
- USE plant cells

PROTOPORPHYRINS [46; 46]
- BT1 pigments
- BT1 porphyrins
  - BT2 heterocyclic acids
    - BT3 carboxylic acids
      - BT4 organic acids
        - BT5 organic compounds
    - BT3 heterocyclic compounds
      - BT4 organic compounds
  - BT2 organic nitrogen compounds
    - BT3 organic compounds
- RT hemoglobin

PROTOSTARS [760; 760]
- RT cosmological models
- RT origin
- RT star accretion
- RT stars

prototype fast r. dounreay
- USE pfr reactor

prototype fast reactor japan
- USE monju reactor

prototype large breeder react
- USE plbr reactor

PROTOZOA [205; 607]
- BT1 invertebrates
  - BT2 animals
- BT1 microorganisms
- NT1 amoeba
- NT1 babesidae
- NT1 dinoflagellate
- NT1 paramecium
- NT1 plasmodium
- NT1 tetrahymena
- NT1 trypanosoma
- RT parasites
- RT plankton

protracted irradiation
- USE chronic irradiation

provincial government
- USE state government

PROXIMITY EFFECT [503; 503]
- RT superconductivity

PROXIMITY SCATTERING [3; 3]
Apr 86
(Mutual scatterings of two outgoing particles from sequential nuclear reactions.)
- BT1 scattering
- RT final-state interactions
- RT nuclear reactions

PRPR REACTOR [4; 4]
- UF *mayaguez p. r. pool reactor*
- UF *puerto rico pool type reactor*
- BT1 pool type reactors
  - BT2 water cooled reactors
    - BT3 reactors
  - BT2 water moderated reactors
    - BT3 reactors
- BT1 triga type reactors
  - BT2 enriched uranium reactors
    - BT3 reactors
  - BT2 hydride moderated reactors
    - BT3 reactors
  - BT2 research and test reactors
    - BT3 reactors
  - BT2 solid homogeneous reactors
    - BT3 homogeneous reactors
      - BT4 reactors
  - BT2 water cooled reactors
    - BT3 reactors
  - BT2 water moderated reactors
    - BT3 reactors

PRR REACTOR [2; 2]
- UF *nda remote experiment station*
- UF *pawling research reactor*
- UF *platr reactor*
- BT1 enriched uranium reactors
  - BT2 reactors
- BT1 heavy water cooled reactors
  - BT2 reactors
- BT1 heavy water moderated reactors
  - BT2 reactors
- BT1 tank type reactors
  - BT2 reactors
- BT1 thermal reactors
  - BT2 reactors

PRR-1 REACTOR [21; 21]
(Quezon City, Philippines.)
- UF *philippine research reactor-1*
- UF *quezon philippine reactor*
- BT1 enriched uranium reactors
  - BT2 reactors
- BT1 pool type reactors
  - BT2 water cooled reactors
    - BT3 reactors
  - BT2 water moderated reactors
    - BT3 reactors

PRTR REACTOR [13; 13]
(Richland, Washington, USA)
- UF *plutonium recycle test reactor*
- BT1 heavy water cooled reactors
  - BT2 reactors
- BT1 heavy water moderated reactors
  - BT2 reactors
- BT1 pressure tube reactors
  - BT2 power reactors
    - BT3 reactors
- BT1 research reactors
  - BT2 research and test reactors
    - BT3 reactors

prussian blue
- USE ferrocyanides
- AND potassium compounds

PSE REACTOR [2; 2]
- UF *pressur. subcrit. exp. savanna*
- UF *savannah press. subcrit. exper*
- BT1 heavy water cooled reactors
  - BT2 reactors
- BT1 heavy water moderated reactors
  - BT2 reactors
- BT1 natural uranium reactors
  - BT2 reactors
- BT1 subcritical assemblies
  - BT2 experimental reactors
    - BT3 research and test reactors
      - BT4 reactors
- BT1 tank type reactors
  - BT2 reactors
- BT1 thermal reactors
  - BT2 reactors

PSEUDOMONAS [312; 312]
- BT1 bacteria
  - BT2 microorganisms

pseudoscalar antimesons
(Prior to December 1987 this was a valid descriptor.)
- USE antiparticles
- AND pseudoscalar mesons

PSEUDOSCALAR MESONS [1,256; 33,662]
(Mesons with spin and parity 0-.)
- UF+ *pseudoscalar antimesons*
- BT1 mesons
  - BT2 bosons
  - BT2 hadrons
    - BT3 elementary particles
- NT1 b mesons
  - NT2 b minus mesons
  - NT2 b neutral mesons
    - NT3 anti-b neutral mesons
  - NT2 b plus mesons
- NT1 d mesons
  - NT2 d minus mesons
  - NT2 d neutral mesons
    - NT3 anti-d neutral mesons
  - NT2 d plus mesons
- NT1 eta c-2980 mesons
- NT1 eta c-3590 mesons
- NT1 eta mesons
- NT1 eta prime-958 mesons
- NT1 eta-1275 mesons
- NT1 eta-1440 mesons
- NT1 k-1460 mesons
- NT1 k-1830 mesons
- NT1 kaons
  - NT2 antikaons
    - NT3 antikaons neutral
  - NT2 cosmic kaons
  - NT2 kaons minus
  - NT2 kaons neutral
    - NT3 antikaons neutral
    - NT3 kaons neutral long-lived
    - NT3 kaons neutral short-lived
  - NT2 kaons plus
- NT1 pi-1300 mesons
- NT1 pi-1770 mesons
- NT1 pions
  - NT2 cosmic pions
  - NT2 pions minus
  - NT2 pions neutral
  - NT2 pions plus
- RT sigma model

PSEUDOSCALARS [245; 245]
- RT scalars

PSEUDOVECTOR COUPLING [63; 63]
- BT1 coupling
- RT nucleons

pseudovector mesons
- USE axial vector mesons

psi resonances
(Prior to December 1987 this was a valid descriptor.)
- USE mesons

psi-3105 resonances
(Prior to December 1987 this was a valid descriptor.)
- USE j psi-3097 mesons

PSI-3685 MESONS [675; 675]
(Prior to December 1987 this concept was indexed by PSI-3695 RESONANCES.)
- UF *psi-3695 resonances*
- BT1 charmonium
  - BT2 mesons
    - BT3 bosons
    - BT3 hadrons
      - BT4 elementary particles
  - BT2 quarkonium
- BT1 vector mesons
  - BT2 mesons
    - BT3 bosons
    - BT3 hadrons
      - BT4 elementary particles

psi-3695 resonances
(Prior to December 1987 this was a valid descriptor.)

USE psi-3685 mesons

PSI-3770 MESONS [88; 88] *Jul 78*
(Prior to December 1987 this concept was indexed by PSI-3772 RESONANCES.)
UF   *psi-3772 resonances*
BT1   charmonium
  BT2   mesons
    BT3   bosons
    BT3   hadrons
      BT4   elementary particles
  BT2   quarkonium
BT1   vector mesons
  BT2   mesons
    BT3   bosons
    BT3   hadrons
      BT4   elementary particles

psi-3772 resonances
(Prior to December 1987 this was a valid descriptor.)
USE   psi-3770 mesons

psi-4028 resonances
(Prior to December 1987 this was a valid descriptor.)
USE   psi-4030 mesons

PSI-4030 MESONS [32; 32] *Apr 78*
(Prior to December 1987 this concept was indexed by PSI-4028 RESONANCES.)
UF   *psi-4028 resonances*
BT1   charmonium
  BT2   mesons
    BT3   bosons
    BT3   hadrons
      BT4   elementary particles
  BT2   quarkonium
BT1   vector mesons
  BT2   mesons
    BT3   bosons
    BT3   hadrons
      BT4   elementary particles

psi-4100 resonances
(Prior to December 1987 this was a valid descriptor.)
USE   psi-4160 mesons

PSI-4160 MESONS [63; 63] *Sep 75*
(Prior to December 1987 this concept was indexed by PSI-4100 RESONANCES.)
UF   *psi-4100 resonances*
BT1   charmonium
  BT2   mesons
    BT3   bosons
    BT3   hadrons
      BT4   elementary particles
  BT2   quarkonium
BT1   vector mesons
  BT2   mesons
    BT3   bosons
    BT3   hadrons
      BT4   elementary particles

psi-4300 resonances
(Prior to December 1987 this was a valid descriptor.)
USE   mesons

psi-4414 resonances
(Prior to December 1987 this was a valid descriptor.)
USE   psi-4415 mesons

PSI-4415 MESONS [21; 21] *Apr 78*
(Prior to December 1987 this concept was indexed by PSI-4414 RESONANCES.)
UF   *psi-4414 resonances*
BT1   charmonium
  BT2   mesons
    BT3   bosons
    BT3   hadrons
      BT4   elementary particles
  BT2   quarkonium
BT1   vector mesons
  BT2   mesons
    BT3   bosons
    BT3   hadrons
      BT4   elementary particles

PSORALEN [364; 364]
BT1   anticoagulants
  BT2   hematologic agents
    BT3   drugs
BT1   heterocyclic compounds
  BT2   organic compounds
BT1   organic oxygen compounds
  BT2   organic compounds
RT   benzofurans
RT   coumarin

PSORIASIS [120; 120]
BT1   skin diseases
  BT2   diseases
RT   skin

psr reactor
USE   pstr reactor

PSS METHOD [67; 67]
(Perturbed stationary states method.)
UF   *perturbed stationary states me*
RT   collisions

PSTR REACTOR [42; 42]
UF   *pennsylvania state triga reac*
UF   *pennsylvania state un. res. re*
UF   *psr reactor*
UF   *triga-pennsylvania reactor*
BT1   pool type reactors
  BT2   water cooled reactors
    BT3   reactors
  BT2   water moderated reactors
    BT3   reactors
BT1   research reactors
  BT2   research and test reactors
    BT3   reactors
BT1   thermal reactors
  BT2   reactors
BT1   training reactors
  BT2   research and test reactors
    BT3   reactors
BT1   triga type reactors
  BT2   enriched uranium reactors
    BT3   reactors
  BT2   hydride moderated reactors
    BT3   reactors
  BT2   research and test reactors
    BT3   reactors
  BT2   solid homogeneous reactors
    BT3   homogeneous reactors
      BT4   reactors
  BT2   water cooled reactors
    BT3   reactors
  BT2   water moderated reactors
    BT3   reactors

psychology
USE   behavior

psychoses
USE   mental disorders

PSYCHOTROPIC DRUGS [152; 741]
BT1   central nervous system agents
  BT2   drugs
NT1   antidepressants
  NT2   cocaine
  NT2   imipramine
  NT2   iproniazid
NT1   hallucinogens
  NT2   bufotenine
NT1   tranquilizers
  NT2   chlorpromazine
  NT2   reserpine
RT   mental disorders

PTERIDINES [29; 204]
UF   *pterins*
BT1   heterocyclic compounds
  BT2   organic compounds
BT1   organic nitrogen compounds
  BT2   organic compounds
NT1   aminopterin
NT1   folic acid
RT   pyrazines
RT   pyrimidines

pterins
USE   pteridines

pteroylglutamic acid
USE   folic acid

PTF-UNC REACTOR [1; 1]
UF   *proof test facility un. nu. co*
UF   *united nucl. corp. proof test*
BT1   zero power reactors
  BT2   experimental reactors
    BT3   research and test reactors
      BT4   reactors

ptfe
USE   teflon

PTR REACTOR [3; 3]
(Atomic Energy of Canada, Ltd., Chalk River, Ontario, Canada)
UF   *chalk river pool test reactor*
UF   *pool test react. chalk river*
BT1   enriched uranium reactors
  BT2   reactors
BT1   pool type reactors
  BT2   water cooled reactors
    BT3   reactors
  BT2   water moderated reactors
    BT3   reactors
BT1   research reactors
  BT2   research and test reactors
    BT3   reactors

public attitudes
USE   public opinion

PUBLIC HEALTH [1,199; 1,199]
UF   *health (public)*
BT1   preventive medicine
  BT2   medicine
RT   health hazards
RT   human populations
RT   medical establishments
RT   quarantine
RT   radiation protection

public information
USE   public relations

PUBLIC LANDS [11; 11] *Jul 86*
(Lands not owned by private persons, corporations, etc.)
RT   recreational areas

PUBLIC LAW [134; 134] *Dec 76*
(Body of rules governing State action a relationship with citizens.)
BT1   laws

PUBLIC OFFICIALS [54; 54] *Sep 85*
BT1   personnel
RT   government policies
RT   local government
RT   national government
RT   political aspects
RT   state government

PUBLIC OPINION [3,751; 3,751] *Jan 78*
- UF *nuclear controversy*
- UF *public attitudes*
- SF *public policy*
- RT aesthetics
- RT attitudes
- RT ethical aspects
- RT political aspects
- RT public relations

public policy
- SEE government policies
- OR public opinion
- OR public relations

PUBLIC RELATIONS [4,064; 4,064]
- UF *nuclear contestation*
- UF *public information*
- SF *public policy*
- RT aesthetics
- RT hazards
- RT management
- RT public opinion
- RT risk assessment
- RT safety analysis
- RT sociology

public service newbold isl.-1
- USE newbold island-1 reactor

public service newbold isl.-2
- USE newbold island-2 reactor

PUBLIC UTILITIES [277; 1,662] *Jan 76*
(A business organization performing some public service and subject to special government regulation.)
- NT1 electric utilities
- RT electric power
- RT fuel gas
- RT water supply

PUERTO RICO [87; 87]
- BT1 latin america
- BT1 usa
- BT2 developed countries
- BT2 north america
- BT1 west indies
- BT2 islands

puerto rico bonus reactor
- USE bonus reactor

puerto rico nuclear c. l-77 r.
- USE prnc-l-77 reactor

puerto rico pool type reactor
- USE prpr reactor

pullman wash. stat. uni. react
- USE wsur reactor

pulmonary cancer
(Use LUNGS and/or BRONCHI, as appropriate, in coordination with the descriptors below.)
- USE carcinomas

pulmonary lavage
- USE lavage
- AND lungs

pulps
- USE slurries

PULSARS [3,538; 3,538]
- BT1 cosmic radio sources
- RT crab nebula
- RT neutron stars
- RT supernova remnants

PULSATING VARIABLE STARS [237; 677] *Nov 78*
- BT1 variable stars
- BT2 stars
- NT1 cepheids

PULSATIONS [2,080; 2,080]
- UF *micropulsations*
- UF *pearl pulsations*
- RT disturbances
- RT oscillations
- RT pulses
- RT variations

PULSATOR STELLARATOR [33; 33]
- BT1 stellarators
- BT2 closed plasma devices
- BT3 thermonuclear devices

PULSE AMPLIFIERS [670; 670]
- BT1 amplifiers
- BT2 equipment
- BT1 electronic equipment
- BT2 equipment
- RT cathode followers
- RT pulse circuits
- RT pulse techniques

PULSE ANALYZERS [585; 2,228]
- UF *analyzers (pulse)*
- UF *kicksorters*
- BT1 electronic equipment
- BT2 equipment
- NT1 multi-channel analyzers
- RT pulse circuits
- RT pulse discriminators
- RT pulse techniques
- RT spectrometers

PULSE CIRCUITS [407; 3,568]
- BT1 electronic circuits
- NT1 multivibrators
- NT2 flip-flop circuits
- NT1 pulse discriminators
- NT1 pulse shapers
- NT1 trigger circuits
- NT2 transistor trigger circuits
- RT coincidence circuits
- RT counting circuits
- RT pulse amplifiers
- RT pulse analyzers
- RT pulse generators
- RT pulse techniques
- RT transistor oscillators

pulse columns
- USE extraction columns

PULSE CONVERTERS [212; 552]
- UF *converters (pulse)*
- BT1 electronic equipment
- BT2 equipment
- NT1 time-to-amplitude converters
- RT pulse shapers
- RT pulse techniques

PULSE DISCRIMINATORS [814; 814]
- BT1 discriminators
- BT2 electronic circuits
- BT1 pulse circuits
- BT2 electronic circuits
- RT pulse analyzers

PULSE GENERATORS [1,313; 2,211]
- UF *generators (pulse)*
- BT1 function generators
- BT2 electronic equipment
- BT3 equipment
- NT1 high-voltage pulse generators
- NT2 marx generators
- RT blocking oscillators
- RT frequency converters
- RT multivibrators
- RT plasma switches
- RT pulse circuits
- RT pulse shapers
- RT pulse techniques

PULSE INTEGRATORS [200; 200]
- UF *integrators (pulse)*
- BT1 electronic equipment
- BT2 equipment
- RT counting ratemeters
- RT pulse techniques

PULSE PILEUP [214; 214]
- RT time resolution
- RT timing properties

PULSE RISE TIME [948; 948]
- UF *rise time*
- BT1 timing properties
- RT peaks
- RT pulses
- RT time measurement

PULSE SHAPERS [956; 956]
- UF *clipping circuits*
- UF *pulse stretchers*
- BT1 pulse circuits
- BT2 electronic circuits
- RT pulse converters
- RT pulse generators
- RT signal conditioning

pulse stretchers
- USE pulse shapers

PULSE TECHNIQUES [3,271; 3,271]
- RT counting circuits
- RT counting ratemeters
- RT counting techniques
- RT counting tubes
- RT delay circuits
- RT electronic equipment
- RT oscillators
- RT plasma switches
- RT pulse amplifiers
- RT pulse analyzers
- RT pulse circuits
- RT pulse converters
- RT pulse generators
- RT pulse integrators
- RT pulses
- RT radiation detection
- RT radiation detectors
- RT resonators
- RT scalers

PULSED D-T REACTORS [111; 158]
- BT1 d-t reactors
- BT2 thermonuclear reactors
- BT1 pulsed fusion reactors
- BT2 thermonuclear reactors
- NT1 reference theta pinch reactor

PULSED FUSION REACTORS [226; 382]
- BT1 thermonuclear reactors
- NT1 pulsed d-t reactors
- NT2 reference theta pinch reactor
- RT laser implosions

PULSED IRRADIATION [2,941; 2,941]
- BT1 irradiation
- RT dose rates
- RT temporal dose distributions

PULSED MAGNET COILS [234; 234]
- BT1 magnet coils
- BT2 electric coils
- BT3 electrical equipment
- BT4 equipment

PULSED NEUTRON TECHNIQUES [1,229; 1,229]
- RT neutron beams
- RT neutron guides
- RT pulses

PULSED REACTORS [286; 1,304]
- UF *burst reactors*
- BT1 reactors
- NT1 acpr reactor
- NT1 bigr reactor
- NT1 bir reactor
- NT1 fbrf reactor
- NT1 fir-1 reactor
- NT1 hector reactor
- NT1 hprr reactor
- NT1 ibr-2 reactor
- NT1 ibr-30 reactor
- NT1 kalpakkam pfr reactor
- NT1 nsrr reactor
- NT1 ostr reactor
- NT1 pbf reactor
- NT1 sora reactor
- NT1 spr-2 reactor
- NT1 spr-3 reactor
- NT1 spr-4 reactor
- NT1 super kukla reactor
- NT1 tibr reactor
- NT1 triga-texas reactor
- NT1 triga-1-california reactor
- NT1 triga-1-michigan reactor
- NT1 triga-2-illinois reactor
- NT1 triga-2-kansas reactor
- NT1 triga-2-mainz reactor
- NT1 triga-2-pavia reactor
- NT1 ucbrr reactor
- NT1 viper reactor
- NT1 wsur reactor
- RT reactivity insertions

PULSES [8,058; 8,058]
(Not for edible seeds of leguminous crops.)
- UF *electric pulses*
- UF *impulse (pulses)*
- RT electrical transients
- RT electrocardiograms
- RT pulsations
- RT pulse rise time
- RT pulse techniques
- RT pulsed neutron techniques
- RT signals
- RT surges

PULSTAR-BUFFALO REACTOR [8; 8]
- UF *buffalo pulstar reactor*
- UF *buspr reactor*
- UF *western n. y. nucl. res. react*
- BT1 enriched uranium reactors
- BT2 reactors
- BT1 isotope production reactors
- BT2 irradiation reactors
- BT3 reactors
- BT1 pool type reactors
- BT2 water cooled reactors
- BT3 reactors
- BT2 water moderated reactors
- BT3 reactors
- BT1 research reactors
- BT2 research and test reactors
- BT3 reactors

PULSTAR-RALEIGH REACTOR [7; 7]
(North Carolina State University, Department of Nuclear Engineering, Raleigh, North Carolina, USA)
- UF *ncuspr reactor*
- UF *north carolina pulstar reactor*
- UF *raleigh pulstar reactor*
- BT1 pool type reactors
- BT2 water cooled reactors
- BT3 reactors
- BT2 water moderated reactors
- BT3 reactors
- BT1 research reactors
- BT2 research and test reactors
- BT3 reactors

pulverizing
- USE crushing

PUMPED LIMITERS [156; 156] *Jul 86*
- BT1 limiters
- RT helium ash

PUMPED STORAGE [20; 20] *Dec 82*
- BT1 energy storage
- BT2 storage
- RT hydroelectric power plants

pumping (laser)
- USE optical pumping

pumping (nuclear)
- USE nuclear pumping

PUMPS [4,352; 5,931]
- BT1 equipment
- NT1 electromagnetic pumps
- NT1 heat pumps
- NT1 vacuum pumps
- NT2 cryopumps
- NT2 sputter-ion pumps
- NT2 turbomolecular pumps
- RT bellows
- RT blowers
- RT compressors
- RT reactor components
- RT reactor cooling systems

PUNCHED CARDS [39; 39]
- RT memory devices

PUNCHED TAPES [31; 31]
- RT memory devices

PUPAE [247; 247]
- RT age groups
- RT insects
- RT life cycle
- RT metamorphosis

PUREX PROCESS [1,308; 1,309]
- BT1 reprocessing
- BT2 separation processes
- NT1 halex process
- NT1 saltex process
- RT solvent extraction

PURIFICATION [4,165; 4,165]
- RT cleaning
- RT coolant cleanup systems
- RT crystallization
- RT decontamination
- RT impurities
- RT refining
- RT scrubbing
- RT separation processes

PURINES [277; 1,939]
- BT1 heterocyclic compounds
- BT2 organic compounds
- BT1 organic nitrogen compounds
- BT2 organic compounds
- NT1 adenines
- NT2 kinetin
- NT1 guanine
- NT1 guanosine
- NT1 hypoxanthine
- NT1 inosine
- NT1 mercaptopurine
- NT1 xanthines
- NT2 caffeine
- NT2 theobromine
- NT2 theophylline
- NT2 uric acid
- RT nucleosides

purity
- USE impurities

PURNIMA REACTOR [39; 39]
- UF *purnima-1 reactor*
- BT1 fast reactors
- BT2 epithermal reactors
- BT3 reactors
- BT1 zero power reactors
- BT2 experimental reactors
- BT3 research and test reactors
- BT4 reactors

purnima-1 reactor
- USE purnima reactor

PURNIMA-2 REACTOR [6; 6] *Oct 81*
- BT1 fast reactors
- BT2 epithermal reactors
- BT3 reactors
- BT1 zero power reactors
- BT2 experimental reactors
- BT3 research and test reactors
- BT4 reactors

PUROMYCIN [48; 48]
- BT1 antibiotics
- BT2 drugs
- BT2 organic compounds
- BT1 antineoplastic drugs
- BT2 drugs

PURPURA [38; 38]
- BT1 hemic diseases
- BT2 diseases

purpuric acid
- USE murexide

pusan kori-1 reactor
- USE kori-1 reactor

pusan kori-2 reactor
- USE kori-2 reactor

PUSPATI [55; 55] *Dec 84*
- UF *tun ismail atomic research cen*
- UF *unit tenaga nuklear (malaysia)*
- BT1 malaysian organizations
- BT2 national organizations

puspati triga reactor
- USE rtp reactor

PUTRESCINE [66; 66]
- UF *tetramethylenediamine*
- UF *1,4-diaminobutane*
- BT1 amines
- BT2 organic compounds

PVA [181; 181]
- UF *polyvinyl alcohol*
- BT1 alcohols
- BT2 hydroxy compounds
- BT3 organic compounds
- BT1 polyvinyls
- BT2 organic polymers
- BT3 organic compounds
- BT3 polymers

PVC [666; 666]
- UF *polyvinyl chloride*
- BT1 chlorinated aliphatic hydrocar
- BT2 halogenated aliphatic hydroca
- BT3 organic halogen compound
- BT4 organic compounds
- BT2 organic chlorine compounds
- BT3 organic halogen compound
- BT4 organic compounds
- BT1 polyvinyls
- BT2 organic polymers
- BT3 organic compounds
- BT3 polymers

PVP [84; 84]
  UF   *polyvinylpyrrolidone*
  BT1   blood substitutes
  BT1   polyvinyls
    BT2   organic polymers
      BT3   organic compounds
      BT3   polymers
  BT1   pyrrolidones
    BT2   lactams
      BT3   amides
        BT4   organic nitrogen compounds
          BT5   organic compounds
    BT2   pyrroles
      BT3   azoles
        BT4   heterocyclic compounds
          BT5   organic compounds
        BT4   organic nitrogen compounds
          BT5   organic compounds

pwba
  USE   born approximation

PWR TYPE REACTORS [28,270; 46,474]
  UF   *pressur. water cooled/moderate*
  UF   *pressurized water reactors*
  BT1   enriched uranium reactors
    BT2   reactors
  BT1   power reactors
    BT2   reactors
  BT1   thermal reactors
    BT2   reactors
  BT1   water cooled reactors
    BT2   reactors
  BT1   water moderated reactors
    BT2   reactors
  NT1   almaraz-1 reactor
  NT1   almaraz-2 reactor
  NT1   angra-1 reactor
  NT1   angra-2 reactor
  NT1   angra-3 reactor
  NT1   ardennes b-1 reactor
  NT1   ardennes reactor
  NT1   arkansas-1 reactor
  NT1   arkansas-2 reactor
  NT1   asco-1 reactor
  NT1   asco-2 reactor
  NT1   atlantic-1 reactor
  NT1   atlantic-2 reactor
  NT1   basf-1 reactor
  NT1   basf-2 reactor
  NT1   beaver valley-1 reactor
  NT1   beaver valley-2 reactor
  NT1   bellefonte-1 reactor
  NT1   bellefonte-2 reactor
  NT1   belleville sur loire-1 reactor
  NT1   belleville sur loire-2 reactor
  NT1   beznau-1 reactor
  NT1   beznau-2 reactor
  NT1   biblis-1 reactor
  NT1   biblis-2 reactor
  NT1   biblis-3 reactor
  NT1   biblis-4 reactor
  NT1   blue hills-1 reactor
  NT1   blue hills-2 reactor
  NT1   borssele reactor
  NT1   br-3 reactor
  NT1   braidwood-1 reactor
  NT1   braidwood-2 reactor
  NT1   brokdorf reactor
  NT1   bugey-2 reactor
  NT1   bugey-3 reactor
  NT1   bugey-4 reactor
  NT1   bugey-5 reactor
  NT1   bw standard reactor
  NT1   byron-1 reactor
  NT1   byron-2 reactor
  NT1   calhoun-1 reactor
  NT1   calhoun-2 reactor
  NT1   callaway-1 reactor
  NT1   callaway-2 reactor
  NT1   calvert cliffs-1 reactor
  NT1   calvert cliffs-2 reactor
  NT1   catawba-1 reactor
  NT1   catawba-2 reactor
  NT1   cattenom-1 reactor
  NT1   cattenom-2 reactor
  NT1   cattenom-3 reactor
  NT1   cattenom-4 reactor
  NT1   ce standard reactor

  NT1   cherokee-1 reactor
  NT1   cherokee-2 reactor
  NT1   cherokee-3 reactor
  NT1   comanche peak-1 reactor
  NT1   comanche peak-2 reactor
  NT1   connecticut yankee reactor
  NT1   cook-1 reactor
  NT1   cook-2 reactor
  NT1   cruas-2 reactor
  NT1   cruas-3 reactor
  NT1   crystal river-3 reactor
  NT1   crystal river-4 reactor
  NT1   dampierre-1 reactor
  NT1   davis besse-1 reactor
  NT1   davis besse-2 reactor
  NT1   davis besse-3 reactor
  NT1   daya bay reactor
  NT1   diablo canyon-1 reactor
  NT1   diablo canyon-2 reactor
  NT1   doel-1 reactor
  NT1   doel-2 reactor
  NT1   doel-3 reactor
  NT1   doel-4 reactor
  NT1   efdr-50 reactor
  NT1   emsland reactor
  NT1   erie-1 reactor
  NT1   erie-2 reactor
  NT1   farley-1 reactor
  NT1   farley-2 reactor
  NT1   fessenheim-1 reactor
  NT1   flamanville-1 reactor
  NT1   flamanville-2 reactor
  NT1   forked river-1 reactor
  NT1   genkai-1 reactor
  NT1   genkai-2 reactor
  NT1   genkai-3 reactor
  NT1   genkai-4 reactor
  NT1   ginna-1 reactor
  NT1   goesgen reactor
  NT1   golfech-1 reactor
  NT1   grafenrheinfeld reactor
  NT1   gravelines-b1 reactor
  NT1   gravelines-c6 reactor
  NT1   greene county reactor
  NT1   greenwood-2 reactor
  NT1   greenwood-3 reactor
  NT1   grohnde reactor
  NT1   hamm-uentrop reactor
  NT1   harris-1 reactor
  NT1   harris-2 reactor
  NT1   harris-3 reactor
  NT1   harris-4 reactor
  NT1   haven-1 reactor
    NT2   koshkonong-1 reactor
  NT1   haven-2 reactor
    NT2   koshkonong-2 reactor
  NT1   ikata reactor
  NT1   ikata-2 reactor
  NT1   ikata-3 reactor
  NT1   indian point-1 reactor
  NT1   indian point-2 reactor
  NT1   indian point-3 reactor
  NT1   iran-1 reactor
  NT1   iran-2 reactor
  NT1   isar-2 reactor
  NT1   jamesport-1 reactor
  NT1   jamesport-2 reactor
  NT1   kewaunee reactor
  NT1   kori-1 reactor
  NT1   kori-2 reactor
  NT1   krsko reactor
  NT1   lemoniz-1 reactor
  NT1   lemoniz-2 reactor
  NT1   lenin reactor
  NT1   leonid brezhnev reactor
  NT1   loft reactor
  NT1   lucie-1 reactor
  NT1   lucie-2 reactor
  NT1   maanshan-1 reactor
  NT1   maine yankee reactor
  NT1   marble hill-1 reactor
  NT1   marble hill-2 reactor
  NT1   mc guire-1 reactor
  NT1   mc guire-2 reactor
  NT1   mh-1a reactor
  NT1   midland-1 reactor
  NT1   midland-2 reactor
  NT1   mihama-1 reactor
  NT1   mihama-2 reactor
  NT1   mihama-3 reactor

  NT1   millstone-2 reactor
  NT1   millstone-3 reactor
  NT1   muelheim-kaerlich reactor
  NT1   mutsu reactor
  NT1   neckar reactor
  NT1   neckar-2 reactor
  NT1   nep-1 reactor
  NT1   nep-2 reactor
  NT1   neupotz-1 reactor
  NT1   neupotz-2 reactor
  NT1   nogent sur seine-1 reactor
  NT1   nogent sur seine-2 reactor
  NT1   north anna-1 reactor
  NT1   north anna-2 reactor
  NT1   north anna-3 reactor
  NT1   north anna-4 reactor
  NT1   north coast-1 reactor
  NT1   obrigheim reactor
  NT1   oconee-1 reactor
  NT1   oconee-2 reactor
  NT1   oconee-3 reactor
  NT1   oi-1 reactor
  NT1   oi-2 reactor
  NT1   oi-3 reactor
  NT1   oi-4 reactor
  NT1   otto hahn reactor
  NT1   palisades-1 reactor
  NT1   palo verde-1 reactor
  NT1   palo verde-2 reactor
  NT1   palo verde-3 reactor
  NT1   palo verde-4 reactor
  NT1   palo verde-5 reactor
  NT1   paluel-1 reactor
  NT1   paluel-2 reactor
  NT1   paluel-3 reactor
  NT1   paluel-4 reactor
  NT1   pebble springs-1 reactor
  NT1   pebble springs-2 reactor
  NT1   penly-1 reactor
  NT1   perkins-1 reactor
  NT1   perkins-2 reactor
  NT1   perkins-3 reactor
  NT1   philippsburg-2 reactor
  NT1   pilgrim-1 reactor
  NT1   pilgrim-2 reactor
  NT1   pilgrim-3 reactor
  NT1   pm-2a reactor
  NT1   pm-3a reactor
  NT1   pnpp-1 reactor
  NT1   point beach-1 reactor
  NT1   point beach-2 reactor
  NT1   prairie island-1 reactor
  NT1   prairie island-2 reactor
  NT1   qinshan reactor
  NT1   quanicassee-1 reactor
  NT1   quanicassee-2 reactor
  NT1   rancho seco-1 reactor
  NT1   remerschen reactor
  NT1   rheinsberg akw1 reactor
  NT1   ringhals-2 reactor
  NT1   ringhals-3 reactor
  NT1   ringhals-4 reactor
  NT1   robinson-2 reactor
  NT1   rooppur reactor
  NT1   rowe yankee reactor
  NT1   saint alban-1 reactor
  NT1   saint alban-2 reactor
  NT1   salem-1 reactor
  NT1   salem-2 reactor
  NT1   san onofre-1 reactor
  NT1   san onofre-2 reactor
  NT1   san onofre-3 reactor
  NT1   savannah reactor
  NT1   saxton reactor
  NT1   seabrook-1 reactor
  NT1   seabrook-2 reactor
  NT1   selni reactor
  NT1   sendai-1 reactor
  NT1   sendai-2 reactor
  NT1   sequoyah-1 reactor
  NT1   sequoyah-2 reactor
  NT1   shippingport reactor
  NT1   sizewell-b reactor
  NT1   sm-1 reactor
  NT1   sm-1a reactor
  NT1   south texas project-1 reactor
  NT1   south texas project-2 reactor
  NT1   stade reactor
  NT1   sterling-1 reactor
  NT1   summer-1 reactor

NT1 sundesert-1 reactor
NT1 sundesert-2 reactor
NT1 surry-1 reactor
NT1 surry-2 reactor
NT1 surry-3 reactor
NT1 surry-4 reactor
NT1 s1c prototype reactor
NT1 takahama-1 reactor
NT1 takahama-2 reactor
NT1 takahama-3 reactor
NT1 takahama-4 reactor
NT1 thr reactor
NT1 three mile island-1 reactor
NT1 three mile island-2 reactor
NT1 tihange reactor
NT1 tihange-2 reactor
NT1 tihange-3 reactor
NT1 tomari-1 reactor
NT1 tomari-2 reactor
NT1 tricastin-1 reactor
NT1 tricastin-4 reactor
NT1 trillo-1 reactor
NT1 trojan reactor
NT1 tsuruga-2 reactor
NT1 turkey point-3 reactor
NT1 turkey point-4 reactor
NT1 tva-1 reactor
NT1 tva-2 reactor
NT1 tyrone-1 reactor
NT1 tyrone-2 reactor
NT1 ulchin-1 reactor
NT1 ulchin-2 reactor
NT1 unterweser reactor
NT1 vahnum-1 reactor
NT1 vahnum-2 reactor
NT1 vogtle-1 reactor
NT1 vogtle-2 reactor
NT1 vogtle-3 reactor
NT1 vogtle-4 reactor
NT1 waterford-3 reactor
NT1 waterford-4 reactor
NT1 watts bar-1 reactor
NT1 watts bar-2 reactor
NT1 westinghouse standard reactor
NT1 wnp-1 reactor
NT1 wnp-3 reactor
NT1 wnp-4 reactor
NT1 wnp-5 reactor
NT1 wolf creek-1 reactor
NT1 wup-3 reactor
NT1 wup-4 reactor
NT1 wup-5 reactor
NT1 wup-6 reactor
NT1 wwer type reactors
NT2 armenian-1 reactor
NT2 armenian-2 reactor
NT2 balakovo-1 reactor
NT2 balakovo-2 reactor
NT2 blahutovice-1 reactor
NT2 bohunice v-1 reactor
NT2 bohunice v-2 reactor
NT2 dukovany v-2 reactor
NT2 greifswald-1 reactor
NT2 greifswald-2 reactor
NT2 greifswald-3 reactor
NT2 greifswald-4 reactor
NT2 greifswald-5 reactor
NT2 greifswald-6 reactor
NT2 kalinin-1 reactor
NT2 kalinin-3 reactor
NT2 kecerovce-1 reactor
NT2 khmelnitskij-1 reactor
NT2 kola-1 reactor
NT2 kola-2 reactor
NT2 kola-3 reactor
NT2 kola-4 reactor
NT2 kozloduy-1 reactor
NT2 kozloduy-2 reactor
NT2 kozloduy-3 reactor
NT2 loviisa-1 reactor
NT2 loviisa-2 reactor
NT2 mochovce-1 reactor
NT2 paks-1 reactor
NT2 paks-2 reactor
NT2 paks-3 reactor
NT2 paks-4 reactor
NT2 rovno-1 reactor
NT2 rovno-2 reactor
NT2 rovno-3 reactor
NT2 rovno-4 reactor
NT2 rovno-5 reactor
NT2 south ukrainian-1 reactor
NT2 south ukrainian-2 reactor
NT2 south ukrainian-3 reactor
NT2 stendal-1 reactor
NT2 tatarian reactor
NT2 temelin-1 reactor
NT2 wwer-1 reactor
NT2 wwer-2 reactor
NT2 wwer-3 reactor
NT2 wwer-4 reactor
NT2 wwer-5 reactor
NT2 zaporozhe-1 reactor
NT2 zaporozhe-2 reactor
NT2 zaporozhe-3 reactor
NT2 zaporozhe-4 reactor
NT1 wyhl-1 reactor
NT1 wyhl-2 reactor
NT1 yellow creek-1 reactor
NT1 yellow creek-2 reactor
NT1 zion-1 reactor
NT1 zion-2 reactor
NT1 zorita-1 reactor

pwr/241 type reactor
USE bw standard reactor

pwr/41 type reactor
USE westinghouse standard reactor

pwr/80 type reactor
USE ce standard reactor

PYCNOMETERS [21; 21]
BT1 densimeters
BT2 measuring instruments

PYRANS [96; 256]
(Compounds that contain a six-membered heterocyclic ring containing one oxygen atom.)
BT1 heterocyclic compounds
BT2 organic compounds
BT1 organic oxygen compounds
BT2 organic compounds
NT1 coumarin
NT1 hematoxylin
NT1 quercetin
NT1 tetrahydropyran

PYRAZINES [97; 224]
(Compounds that contain a six-membered heterocyclic ring containing nitrogen atoms in the 1 and 4 positions.)
UF 1,4-diazines
BT1 azines
BT2 heterocyclic compounds
BT3 organic compounds
BT2 organic nitrogen compounds
BT3 organic compounds
NT1 neutral red
NT1 phenazine
NT1 piperazines
RT pteridines

PYRAZOLES [300; 771]
(Compounds that contain a five-membered heterocyclic ring containing nitrogen atoms in the 1 and 2 positions.)
BT1 azoles
BT2 heterocyclic compounds
BT3 organic compounds
BT2 organic nitrogen compounds
BT3 organic compounds
NT1 indazoles
NT1 pyrazolines
NT2 antipyrine

PYRAZOLINES [231; 466]
UF dam
UF diantipyrylmethane
UF+ aminopyrine
BT1 pyrazoles
BT2 azoles
BT3 heterocyclic compounds
BT4 organic compounds
BT3 organic nitrogen compounds
BT4 organic compounds
NT1 antipyrine

PYRENE [167; 167]
BT1 condensed aromatics
BT2 aromatics
BT3 organic compounds
BT1 hydrocarbons
BT2 organic compounds

PYREX [109; 109]
BT1 borosilicate glass
BT2 glass

PYRIDAZINES [26; 31]
(Compounds that contain a six-membered heterocyclic ring containing nitrogen atoms in the 1 and 2 positions.)
BT1 azines
BT2 heterocyclic compounds
BT3 organic compounds
BT2 organic nitrogen compounds
BT3 organic compounds
NT1 phthalazines

pyridineazohydroxynaphthalene
USE pan

PYRIDINES [1,376; 4,346]
(Compounds that contain a six-membered heterocyclic ring containing one nitrogen atom.)
BT1 azines
BT2 heterocyclic compounds
BT3 organic compounds
BT2 organic nitrogen compounds
BT3 organic compounds
NT1 acridines
NT2 acridine orange
NT2 flavines
NT3 acriflavine
NT3 proflavine
NT1 bipyridines
NT1 diodrast
NT1 nicotinamide
NT1 nicotine
NT1 nicotinic acid
NT1 pan
NT1 phenatine
NT1 picolines
NT2 picolinic acid
NT1 piperidines
NT2 pethidine
NT2 tmpn
NT2 triacetoneamine-n-oxyl
NT1 pyridinium compounds
NT1 pyridoxal
NT1 pyridoxine
NT1 pyridoxylideneglutamate
NT1 pyridylazoresorcinol
NT1 quinolines
NT2 ferron
NT2 kynurenic acid
NT2 oxine
NT2 quinaldine
RT isoniazid
RT nad

PYRIDINIUM COMPOUNDS [242; 242]
BT1 pyridines
BT2 azines
BT3 heterocyclic compounds
BT4 organic compounds
BT3 organic nitrogen compounds
BT4 organic compounds
BT1 quaternary compounds
BT2 amines
BT3 organic compounds

PYRIDOXAL [50; 50]
  BT1   aldehydes
    BT2   organic compounds
  BT1   organic oxygen compounds
    BT2   organic compounds
  BT1   pyridines
    BT2   azines
      BT3   heterocyclic compounds
        BT4   organic compounds
      BT3   organic nitrogen compounds
        BT4   organic compounds
  RT   coenzymes
  RT   picolines
  RT   vitamin b group

PYRIDOXINE [74; 74]
  UF   *vitamin b-6*
  BT1   hydroxy compounds
    BT2   organic compounds
  BT1   pyridines
    BT2   azines
      BT3   heterocyclic compounds
        BT4   organic compounds
      BT3   organic nitrogen compounds
        BT4   organic compounds
  BT1   vitamin b group
    BT2   vitamins

PYRIDOXYLIDENEGLUTAMATE
[41; 41] *Nov 77*
  BT1   glutamic acid
    BT2   amino acids
      BT3   carboxylic acids
        BT4   organic acids
          BT5   organic compounds
  BT1   pyridines
    BT2   azines
      BT3   heterocyclic compounds
        BT4   organic compounds
      BT3   organic nitrogen compounds
        BT4   organic compounds
  RT   radiopharmaceuticals

PYRIDYL RADICALS [13; 13]
  BT1   radicals

pyridylazonaphthol
  USE   pan

PYRIDYLAZORESORCINOL [95; 95]
  BT1   diazo compounds
    BT2   organic nitrogen compounds
      BT3   organic compounds
  BT1   polyphenols
    BT2   phenols
      BT3   aromatics
        BT4   organic compounds
      BT3   hydroxy compounds
        BT4   organic compounds
  BT1   pyridines
    BT2   azines
      BT3   heterocyclic compounds
        BT4   organic compounds
      BT3   organic nitrogen compounds
        BT4   organic compounds
  BT1   reagents

PYRIMIDINE DIMERS [213; 213]
Mar 86
  BT1   dimers
  RT   dna repair
  RT   mutations
  RT   pyrimidines
  RT   strand breaks

PYRIMIDINES [776; 6,656]
(Compounds that contain a six-membered heterocyclic ring containing nitrogen atoms in the 1 and 3 positions.)
  UF   *1,3-diazines*
  BT1   azines
    BT2   heterocyclic compounds
      BT3   organic compounds
    BT2   organic nitrogen compounds
      BT3   organic compounds
  NT1   alloxan
  NT1   barbiturates
    NT2   amytal
    NT2   nembutal
    NT2   phenobarbital
    NT2   thiopental
  NT1   cytidine
  NT1   cytosine
  NT1   deoxycytidine
  NT1   murexide
  NT1   sulfadiazine
  NT1   thiamine
  NT1   thymidine
  NT1   uracils
    NT2   bromouracils
      NT3   budr
    NT2   chlorouracils
    NT2   deoxyuridine
    NT2   fluorouracils
      NT3   fudr
    NT2   iodouracils
      NT3   iododeoxyuridine
    NT2   orotic acid
    NT2   thiouracil
    NT2   thymine
    NT2   uridine
  RT   nucleosides
  RT   pteridines
  RT   pyrimidine dimers

PYRITE [292; 292] *Jul 78*
  BT1   sulfide minerals
    BT2   minerals
  RT   iron ores
  RT   iron sulfides
  RT   marcasite

pyrocatechin
  USE   pyrocatechol

PYROCATECHOL [176; 176]
  UF   *catechol*
  UF   *dihydroxybenzene-ortho*
  UF   *pyrocatechin*
  UF   *1,2-dihydroxybenzene*
  BT1   developers
  BT1   polyphenols
    BT2   phenols
      BT3   aromatics
        BT4   organic compounds
      BT3   hydroxy compounds
        BT4   organic compounds
  RT   catecholamines
  RT   dopamine
  RT   pyrocatechol violet

PYROCATECHOL VIOLET [54; 54]
  BT1   dyes
  BT1   indicators
  RT   pyrocatechol

PYROCHEMICAL REPROCESSING
[119; 119] *Jul 80*
  UF   *melt refining process*
  UF   *salt transport process*
  UF   *zinc distillation process*
  BT1   reprocessing
  BT2   separation processes

PYROELECTRIC DETECTORS [39; 39]
Nov 78
  BT1   radiation detectors
  BT2   measuring instruments

pyroelectricity
(Property of certain crystals to produce a state of electrical polarity by a change of temperature.)
  USE   electric charges
  AND   polarization
  AND   temperature dependence

pyrogallic acid
  USE   pyrogallol

PYROGALLOL [60; 60]
  UF   *pyrogallic acid*
  UF   *1,2,3-trihydroxybenzene*
  BT1   developers
  BT1   polyphenols
    BT2   phenols
      BT3   aromatics
        BT4   organic compounds
      BT3   hydroxy compounds
        BT4   organic compounds

PYROGENS [36; 36]
  RT   fever
  RT   peptides
  RT   polysaccharides

PYROLYSIS [3,368; 5,263]
  UF   *thermal decomposition*
  BT1   decomposition
    BT2   chemical reactions
  NT1   calcination
  NT1   cracking
  RT   dissociation
  RT   pyrolysis products
  RT   slagging pyrolysis process
  RT   thermal degradation

PYROLYSIS PRODUCTS [350; 350]
Feb 83
  NT1   chars
  RT   by-products
  RT   combustion products
  RT   pyrolysis
  RT   synthetic fuels
  RT   volatile matter
  RT   volatility

PYROLYTIC CARBON [907; 907]
  BT1   carbon
    BT2   nonmetals
      BT3   elements

PYROMETALLURGY [146; 309]
  BT1   extractive metallurgy
    BT2   metallurgy
  NT1   chloride volatility process
  NT1   fluoride volatility process
  RT   calcination
  RT   reduction
  RT   roasting
  RT   smelting

PYROMETERS [92; 142]
  BT1   measuring instruments
  NT1   optical pyrometers
  RT   temperature measurement

PYROPHOSPHATES [987; 987]
  BT1   oxygen compounds
  BT1   phosphorus compounds

pyroxenes
  USE   silicate minerals

pyroxylin
  USE   nitrocellulose

pyrrhotite
(Prior to August 1981 this concept was indexed by using IRON METEORITES. From then till April 1984 MINERALS was coordinated with IRON SULFIDES.)
  USE   sulfide minerals

pyrrolase (tryptophan)
  USE   tryptophan oxygenase

PYRROLES [109; 2,608]
(Compounds that contain a five-membered heterocyclic ring containing one nitrogen atom.)
  BT1   azoles

PYRROLES

- BT2 heterocyclic compounds
- BT3 organic compounds
- BT2 organic nitrogen compounds
- BT3 organic compounds
- NT1 bilirubin
- NT1 biliverdin
- NT1 indoles
  - NT2 indocyanine green
  - NT2 lysergic acid
  - NT2 reserpine
  - NT2 strychnine
  - NT2 tryptamines
    - NT3 bufotenine
    - NT3 melatonin
    - NT3 serotonin
  - NT2 tryptophan
  - NT2 vinblastine
- NT1 pyrrolidines
  - NT2 hydroxyproline
  - NT2 nicotine
  - NT2 proline
- NT1 pyrrolidones
  - NT2 pvp
- NT1 stercobilin
- NT1 urobilinogen
- RT carbazoles

PYRROLIDINES [95; 670]
- UF *tetrahydropyrroles*
- BT1 amines
- BT2 organic compounds
- BT1 pyrroles
- BT2 azoles
- BT3 heterocyclic compounds
- BT4 organic compounds
- BT3 organic nitrogen compounds
- BT4 organic compounds
- NT1 hydroxyproline
- NT1 nicotine
- NT1 proline

PYRROLIDONES [81; 164]
- BT1 lactams
- BT2 amides
- BT3 organic nitrogen compounds
- BT4 organic compounds
- BT1 pyrroles
- BT2 azoles
- BT3 heterocyclic compounds
- BT4 organic compounds
- BT3 organic nitrogen compounds
- BT4 organic compounds
- NT1 pvp

PYRUVIC ACID [189; 189]
- UF *ketopropionic acid-alpha*
- BT1 keto acids
- BT2 carboxylic acids
- BT3 organic acids
- BT4 organic compounds

PZT [61; 61] *Sep 86*
(Lead zirconate titanate.)
- BT1 lead compounds
- BT1 titanates
- BT2 oxygen compounds
- BT2 titanium compounds
- BT3 transition element compounds
- BT1 zirconates
- BT2 oxygen compounds
- BT2 zirconium compounds
- BT3 transition element compounds

P1-APPROXIMATION [108; 108]
- UF *approximation (p1)*
- BT1 spherical harmonics method
- RT boltzmann equation
- RT perturbation theory

P2-APPROXIMATION [16; 16]
- UF *approximation (p2)*
- BT1 spherical harmonics method

P3-APPROXIMATION [49; 49]
- UF *approximation (p3)*
- BT1 spherical harmonics method
- RT boltzmann equation
- RT perturbation theory

Q CENTERS [4; 4] *Sep 77*
- BT1 color centers
- BT2 vacancies
- BT3 point defects
- BT4 crystal defects
- BT5 crystal structure

Q CODES [162; 162]
- BT1 computer codes

Q DEVICES [248; 267]
- BT1 open plasma devices
- BT2 thermonuclear devices
- NT1 helios devices
- NT1 qp devices
- RT magnetic mirrors

q resonances
(Prior to December 1987 this was a valid descriptor.)
- SEE kl-1280 mesons
- OR kl-1400 mesons

Q-SHIFT [31; 31] *Mar 76*
- RT betatron oscillations
- RT particle beams

Q-SWITCHING [269; 269]
- RT lasers
- RT switches

Q-VALUE [2,834; 2,834]
- BT1 energy
- RT nuclear reaction kinetics

QATAR [0; 0] *Nov 91*
- BT1 asia
- BT1 developing countries
- BT1 middle east

qf (radiation)
- USE quality factor

QINSHAN REACTOR [63; 63] *Aug 86*
(Near Shanghai, China.)
- BT1 pwr type reactors
- BT2 enriched uranium reactors
- BT3 reactors
- BT2 power reactors
- BT3 reactors
- BT2 thermal reactors
- BT3 reactors
- BT2 water cooled reactors
- BT3 reactors
- BT2 water moderated reactors
- BT3 reactors

QP DEVICES [9; 9]
- BT1 q devices
- BT2 open plasma devices
- BT3 thermonuclear devices

QUAD CITIES-1 REACTOR [156; 156]
(Cordova, Illinois, USA)
- UF *cordova quad cities-1 reactor*
- BT1 bwr type reactors
- BT2 enriched uranium reactors
- BT3 reactors
- BT2 power reactors
- BT3 reactors
- BT2 thermal reactors
- BT3 reactors
- BT2 water cooled reactors
- BT3 reactors
- BT2 water moderated reactors
- BT3 reactors

QUAD CITIES-2 REACTOR [165; 165]
(Cordova, Illinois, USA)
- UF *cordova quad cities-2 reactor*
- BT1 bwr type reactors
- BT2 enriched uranium reactors
- BT3 reactors
- BT2 power reactors
- BT3 reactors
- BT2 thermal reactors
- BT3 reactors
- BT2 water cooled reactors
- BT3 reactors
- BT2 water moderated reactors
- BT3 reactors

QUADRATURES [187; 187]
- UF *gauss quadratures*
- RT integrals

QUADRUPOLAR CONFIGURATIONS [350; 350]
- BT1 multipolar configurations
- BT2 closed configurations
- BT3 magnetic field configurations

QUADRUPOLE LINACS [340; 340]
Feb 83
- UF *radio frequency quadrupoles*
- UF *rfq (accelerators)*
- BT1 linear accelerators
- BT2 accelerators
- RT fmit linac
- RT pigmi facilities

QUADRUPOLE MOMENTS [4,360; 4,360]
- RT electric moments
- RT magnetic moments
- RT nuclear electric moments
- RT nuclear magnetic moments
- RT nuclear quadrupole resonance
- RT quadrupoles

QUADRUPOLES [3,530; 3,530]
- BT1 multipoles
- RT quadrupole moments

QUALITATIVE CHEMICAL ANALYSIS [1,343; 1,343]
- UF *analysis (qualitative chemical)*
- UF *assaying (qualitative)*
- UF+ *urinalysis*
- BT1 chemical analysis
- RT activation analysis
- RT chemistry
- RT emission spectroscopy
- RT microanalysis

QUALITY ASSURANCE [5,703; 5,703]
(The planned and systematic actions necessary to provide adequate confidence that a structure, system, or component will perform satisfactorily in service.)
- RT audits
- RT certification
- RT evaluation
- RT licensing
- RT quality control
- RT reliability
- RT safety
- RT standardization

QUALITY CONTROL [6,641; 6,641]
- BT1 control
- RT errors
- RT inspection
- RT materials testing
- RT nondestructive testing
- RT performance testing
- RT quality assurance
- RT reliability
- RT safety
- RT sampling
- RT specifications
- RT standardization

QUALITY FACTOR [566; 566]
- UF   qf (radiation)
- RT   dose equivalents
- RT   let
- RT   oxygen enhancement ratio
- RT   radiation quality
- RT   rbe

QUANICASSEE-1 REACTOR [2; 2]
- BT1   pwr type reactors
- BT2   enriched uranium reactors
- BT3   reactors
- BT2   power reactors
- BT3   reactors
- BT2   thermal reactors
- BT3   reactors
- BT2   water cooled reactors
- BT3   reactors
- BT2   water moderated reactors
- BT3   reactors

QUANICASSEE-2 REACTOR [2; 2]
- BT1   pwr type reactors
- BT2   enriched uranium reactors
- BT3   reactors
- BT2   power reactors
- BT3   reactors
- BT2   thermal reactors
- BT3   reactors
- BT2   water cooled reactors
- BT3   reactors
- BT2   water moderated reactors
- BT3   reactors

QUANTITATIVE CHEMICAL ANALYSIS [18,372; 24,415]
- UF   analysis (quantitative chemica
- UF   assaying (quantitative)
- BT1   chemical analysis
- NT1   gravimetric analysis
- NT2   thermal gravimetric analysis
- NT1   radio-release analysis
- NT1   radiometric analysis
- NT1   volumetric analysis
- RT   activation analysis
- RT   amperometry
- RT   body composition
- RT   chemical composition
- RT   chemistry
- RT   element abundance
- RT   emission spectroscopy
- RT   fluorescence spectroscopy
- RT   gas analysis
- RT   iodometry
- RT   isotope dilution
- RT   kjeldahl method
- RT   microanalysis
- RT   polarography
- RT   potentiometry
- RT   quantity ratio
- RT   radioenzymatic assay
- RT   raman spectroscopy
- RT   sensitivity
- RT   substoichiometry
- RT   titration
- RT   voltametry
- RT   x-ray emission analysis

§ **QUANTITY RATIO** [30,489; 33,783]
(Quantitative values of at least one entity in another; also for relative concentrating ability; see also ISOTOPE RATIO.)
- UF   concentration (analytical)
- UF   concentration dependence
- NT1   element abundance
- RT   quantitative chemical analysis
- RT   thermodynamic activity

QUANTIZATION [2,751; 3,843] Mar 83
(Transition from a description of a system of particles or fields in the classical approximation to a description in which canonically conjugate variables are treated as noncommuting operators.)
- NT1   second quantization
- RT   quantum field theory
- RT   quantum mechanics
- RT   quantum operators

QUANTUM CHROMODYNAMICS [16,031; 16,031] Feb 78
(Renormalizable quantum field theory, in which colored quark fields are coupled to gluon fields.)
- BT1   quantum field theory
- BT2   field theories
- RT   bag model
- RT   cim model
- RT   color model
- RT   flavor model
- RT   gauge invariance
- RT   gluon model
- RT   gluon-gluon interactions
- RT   gluons
- RT   grand unified theory
- RT   instantons
- RT   quantum electrodynamics
- RT   quark-gluon interactions
- RT   standard model
- RT   string models
- RT   su-3 groups
- RT   wilson loop

QUANTUM EFFICIENCY [586; 586] Jun 82
(Average number of electrons emitted per incident photon.)
- BT1   efficiency
- RT   photocathodes
- RT   photoelectric emission

QUANTUM ELECTRODYNAMICS [5,636; 5,829]
- BT1   electrodynamics
- BT1   quantum field theory
- BT2   field theories
- NT1   schwinger-tomonaga formalism
- RT   bhabha scattering
- RT   dirac equation
- RT   dirac operators
- RT   equivalent-photon approximatio
- RT   infrared divergences
- RT   joos-weinberg equation
- RT   moeller scattering
- RT   quantum chromodynamics
- RT   self-energy
- RT   standard model
- RT   ultraviolet divergences
- RT   vacuum polarization
- RT   ward identity

QUANTUM ELECTRONICS [190; 190] May 81
(Unites the classical areas of electronics with those of optics, spectroscopy and quantum mechanics and is based upon the quantum nature of waves and atomic and molecular systems.)
- UF   electronics (quantum)
- RT   lasers
- RT   masers
- RT   optics
- RT   quantum mechanics
- RT   spectroscopy

QUANTUM FIELD THEORY [9,806; 52,989]
- UF+   non-linear field theory
- UF+   nonlinear field theory
- BT1   field theories
- NT1   axiomatic field theory
- NT2   algebraic field theory
- NT2   lsz theory
- NT2   wightman field theory
- NT1   constructive field theory
- NT2   lattice field theory
- NT1   lagrangian field theory
- NT1   phi4-field theory
- NT1   quantum chromodynamics
- NT1   quantum electrodynamics
- NT2   schwinger-tomonaga formalism
- NT1   quantum flavordynamics
- NT1   quantum gravity
- NT1   unified gauge models
- NT2   grand unified theory
- NT3   standard model
- NT2   weinberg lepton model
- NT1   yukawa nonlocal theory
- RT   bethe-salpeter equation
- RT   current algebra
- RT   dispersion relations
- RT   dyson representation
- RT   feynman diagram
- RT   field algebra
- RT   field operators
- RT   fock representation
- RT   gauge invariance
- RT   goldberger-treiman relation
- RT   haag theorem
- RT   heisenberg picture
- RT   higgs model
- RT   ladder approximation
- RT   lehmann-kaellen representation
- RT   locality
- RT   mass formulae
- RT   massless particles
- RT   melosh transformation
- RT   propagator
- RT   quantization
- RT   quantum mechanics
- RT   quasipotential equation
- RT   radiative corrections
- RT   regge poles
- RT   renormalization
- RT   s matrix
- RT   scalar fields
- RT   scale dimension
- RT   schroedinger picture
- RT   schwinger functional equations
- RT   schwinger source theory
- RT   second quantization
- RT   sine-gordon equation
- RT   spinor fields
- RT   sugawara theory
- RT   supergravity
- RT   supersymmetry
- RT   thirring model
- RT   vector fields
- RT   vertex functions
- RT   wick theorem
- RT   yang-feldman formalism
- RT   yang-mills theory
- RT   zachariasen model

QUANTUM FLAVORDYNAMICS [263; 263] Jul 82
- BT1   quantum field theory
- BT2   field theories
- RT   flavor model

QUANTUM FLUIDS [251; 960] Feb 83
- BT1   fluids
- NT1   helium ii
- RT   helium 3
- RT   helium 4
- RT   quantum plasma

QUANTUM GRAVITY [1,901; 1,901] Nov 78
- BT1   quantum field theory
- BT2   field theories
- RT   general relativity theory
- RT   gravitation
- RT   gravitational fields
- RT   gravitons
- RT   supergravity
- RT   unified-field theories

QUANTUM MECHANICS [12,894; 12,894]
- BT1   mechanics
- RT   adiabatic approximation
- RT   adiabatic invariance
- RT   aharonov-bohm effect
- RT   angular momentum
- RT   bell theorem
- RT   bloch theory
- RT   born approximation
- RT   canonical transformations
- RT   causality
- RT   chirality
- RT   commutation relations
- RT   d waves
- RT   de broglie wavelength
- RT   density matrix
- RT   diabatic approximation
- RT   dirac approximation

QUANTUM MECHANICS

RT eigenfunctions
RT eigenstates
RT eigenvalues
RT energy density
RT expectation value
RT f waves
RT feynman path integral
RT fierz-pauli theory
RT generator-coordinate method
RT heisenberg picture
RT hidden variables
RT hsk procedure
RT hylleraas coordinates
RT klein-gordon equation
RT kramers theorem
RT levinson theorem
RT lippmann-schwinger equation
RT mathematical operators
RT occupation number
RT p waves
RT partial waves
RT pauli principle
RT perturbation theory
RT planck law
RT proca equations
RT projection operators
RT quantization
RT quantum electronics
RT quantum field theory
RT quantum numbers
RT racah coefficients
RT rarita-schwinger theory
RT s waves
RT schroedinger equation
RT schroedinger picture
RT schwinger variational method
RT second quantization
RT selection rules
RT semiclassical approximation
RT seniority number
RT sommerfeld-watson theory
RT sudden approximation
RT sum rules
RT superselection rules
RT tamm-dancoff method
RT twistor theory
RT uncertainty principle
RT wigner coefficients
RT wigner theory
RT zitterbewegung

QUANTUM NUMBERS [3,917; 4,160]
NT1 seniority number
RT flavor model
RT gell-mann theory
RT multiplicity
RT parity
RT particle properties
RT quantum mechanics
RT spin

QUANTUM OPERATORS [3,899; 28,163]
UF *operators(quantum field theo)*
UF *operators(quantum mechanical)*
BT1 mathematical operators
NT1 angular momentum operators
NT2 orbital momentum operators
NT2 pauli spin operators
NT1 annihilation operators
NT1 commutators
NT2 current commutators
NT3 sigma terms
NT1 creation operators
NT1 dirac operators
NT1 field operators
NT1 hamiltonians
NT1 linear momentum operators
NT1 position operators
RT boson expansion
RT gluon condensation
RT operator product expansion
RT quantization
RT quark condensation

QUANTUM PLASMA [61; 61]
BT1 plasma
RT quantum fluids

QUARANTINE [42; 42]
RT diseases
RT health hazards
RT incubation
RT latency period
RT pest control
RT public health
RT time dependence

QUARK CONDENSATION [25; 25]
Apr 89
RT quantum operators
RT quarks
RT vacuum states

quark confinement
USE bag model

QUARK MATTER [1,601; 1,601] *Jan 84*
UF *quark plasma*
UF *quark-gluon plasma*
BT1 matter
RT gluons
RT nuclear matter
RT quark model
RT quarks

QUARK MODEL [8,838; 15,479]
BT1 composite models
BT2 particle models
BT3 mathematical models
NT1 color model
NT1 flavor model
RT charm particles
RT landau quasi particles
RT merons
RT parton model
RT quark matter
RT quark-hadron interactions
RT quarkonium
RT quarks

quark plasma
USE quark matter

QUARK-ANTIQUARK INTERACTIONS [1,888; 1,888] *Jan 79*
BT1 particle interactions
BT2 interactions

QUARK-GLUON INTERACTIONS [836; 836] *Feb 83*
BT1 particle interactions
BT2 interactions
RT gluons
RT quantum chromodynamics
RT quarks
RT strong interactions

quark-gluon plasma
USE quark matter

QUARK-HADRON INTERACTIONS [326; 326] *Nov 78*
BT1 particle interactions
BT2 interactions
RT cim model
RT exchange interactions
RT quark model

QUARK-QUARK INTERACTIONS [1,031; 1,031] *Sep 79*
BT1 particle interactions
BT2 interactions

QUARKONIUM [1,399; 3,014] *May 80*
(A bound state of a quark and an antiquark.)
NT1 bottomonium
NT2 chi b0-10235 mesons
NT2 chi b0-9860 mesons
NT2 chi b1-10255 mesons
NT2 chi b1-9895 mesons
NT2 chi b2-10270 mesons
NT2 chi b2-9915 mesons
NT2 upsilon-10023 mesons
NT2 upsilon-10355 mesons
NT2 upsilon-10575 mesons
NT2 upsilon-10860 mesons
NT2 upsilon-11020 mesons
NT2 upsilon-9460 mesons
NT1 charmonium
NT2 chi0-3415 mesons
NT2 chi1-3510 mesons
NT2 chi2-3555 mesons
NT2 eta c-2980 mesons
NT2 eta c-3590 mesons
NT2 j psi-3097 mesons
NT2 psi-3685 mesons
NT2 psi-3770 mesons
NT2 psi-4030 mesons
NT2 psi-4160 mesons
NT2 psi-4415 mesons
NT1 strangeonium
NT2 f2-1525 mesons
NT2 phi j-1850 mesons
NT2 phi-1020 mesons
NT2 phi-1680 mesons
NT1 toponium
RT baryonium
RT quark model

QUARKS [17,136; 17,136]
UF *aces*
UF *triplet particles*
BT1 fermions
BT1 postulated particles
BT2 elementary particles
RT composite models
RT grace particles
RT melosh transformation
RT partons
RT preons
RT quark condensation
RT quark matter
RT quark model
RT quark-gluon interactions
RT taste particles

quarrying
USE mining

QUARTET MODEL [126; 126]
UF *four-nucleon structure*
BT1 nuclear models
BT2 mathematical models
RT cluster model
RT nuclear structure

QUARTZ [2,003; 2,003]
BT1 oxide minerals
BT2 minerals
RT aplites
RT cristobalite
RT granites
RT granodiorites
RT quartz monzonite
RT quartzites
RT shales
RT silicate minerals
RT silicon oxides

QUARTZ MONZONITE [13; 13] *Nov*
UF *adamellite*
BT1 granites
BT2 plutonic rocks
BT3 igneous rocks
BT4 rocks
RT feldspars
RT quartz

QUARTZITES [82; 82]
- UF cheralite
- BT1 metamorphic rocks
  - BT2 rocks
- RT quartz
- RT sandstones

QUASARS [3,424; 3,453]
- BT1 cosmic radio sources
- NT1 blue stellar objects
- RT radio galaxies
- RT seyfert galaxies
- RT stars

QUASI PARTICLES [2,577; 19,595]
- NT1 excitons
- NT1 focusons
- NT1 instantons
- NT1 landau quasi particles
- NT1 magnons
- NT1 merons
- NT1 phonons
- NT1 plasmons
- NT1 polarons
- NT1 rotons
- NT1 solitons
- RT holes
- RT many-body problem

quasi-elastic reactions
(Reactions between heavy ions, dominant at low energies, in which small amounts of energy and a few particles are transferred.)
- USE transfer reactions

QUASI-ELASTIC SCATTERING
[3,442; 3,442]
- BT1 nuclear reactions
- BT1 scattering
- RT elastic scattering
- RT quasi-free reactions

QUASI-FISSION [659; 659] Apr 77
- UF deep inelastic heavy ion colli
- UF fission-like reactions
- BT1 heavy ion reactions
  - BT2 nuclear reactions
- RT compound-nucleus reactions
- RT deep inelastic heavy ion react
- RT fission
- RT heavy ion fusion reactions
- RT nuclear fireball model
- RT precompound-nucleus emission

QUASI-FREE REACTIONS [810; 810]
- BT1 direct reactions
  - BT2 nuclear reactions
- RT quasi-elastic scattering

quasi-linear problems
- USE quasilinear problems

quasi-particle-phonon model
- USE quasiparticle-phonon model

quasi-potential equation
- USE quasipotential equation

QUASIBOUND STATE [12; 12] Nov 88
- RT bound state
- RT coupling
- RT energy levels

QUASILINEAR PROBLEMS [612; 612]
- UF quasi-linear problems
- UF quasilinear theory
- RT boltzmann-vlasov equation
- RT mathematics
- RT maxwell equations
- RT nonlinear problems
- RT perturbation theory

quasilinear theory
- USE quasilinear problems

QUASIPARTICLE-PHONON MODEL
[640; 640] Feb 81
- UF quasi-particle-phonon model
- BT1 nuclear models
  - BT2 mathematical models
- RT collective model
- RT phonons
- RT single-particle model

QUASIPOTENTIAL EQUATION
[336; 336]
- UF quasi-potential equation
- BT1 integral equations
  - BT2 equations
- RT lippmann-schwinger equation
- RT quantum field theory
- RT scattering amplitudes

QUATERNARY ALLOY SYSTEMS
[296; 296]
- BT1 alloy systems

QUATERNARY COMPOUNDS
[1,028; 2,156]
(For quaternary ammonium compounds.)
- BT1 amines
  - BT2 organic compounds
- NT1 acetylcholine
- NT1 betaine
- NT1 choline
- NT1 pyridinium compounds
- NT1 teab

QUATERNARY FISSION [19; 19]
(Fission with emission of two light charged particles.)
- BT1 fission
  - BT2 nuclear reactions

QUATERPHENYLS [1; 1]
- BT1 aromatics
  - BT2 organic compounds
- BT1 hydrocarbons
  - BT2 organic compounds

QUEBEC [83; 83]
- BT1 canada
  - BT2 developed countries
  - BT2 north america

QUEEN MARY COLLEGE UTR-B REACT [2; 2]
(Queen Mary College, London, United Kingdom)
- UF univ. training r. queen mary c
- UF utr-b queen mary college r.
- BT1 argonaut type reactors
  - BT2 enriched uranium reactors
    - BT3 reactors
  - BT2 research and test reactors
    - BT3 reactors
  - BT2 water cooled reactors
    - BT3 reactors
  - BT2 water moderated reactors
    - BT3 reactors
- BT1 training reactors
  - BT2 research and test reactors
    - BT3 reactors

QUEENSLAND [108; 108]
- BT1 australia
  - BT2 australasia
  - BT2 developed countries

QUENCH AGING [114; 114]
- BT1 aging
- RT quenching

QUENCH HARDENING [129; 129]
- BT1 hardening
- BT1 heat treatments
- RT jominy end-quench technique
- RT quenching
- RT splat cooling

QUENCHING [3,813; 3,813]
- BT1 heat treatments
- RT quench aging
- RT quench hardening

quenching (avalanche)
- USE avalanche quenching

quenching (fluorescence)
- USE fluorescence

quenching (scintillation)
- USE scintillation quenching

QUERCETIN [28; 28]
- BT1 flavones
  - BT2 flavenoids
    - BT3 organic oxygen compounds
      - BT4 organic compounds
- BT1 polyphenols
  - BT2 phenols
    - BT3 aromatics
      - BT4 organic compounds
    - BT3 hydroxy compounds
      - BT4 organic compounds
- BT1 pyrans
  - BT2 heterocyclic compounds
    - BT3 organic compounds
  - BT2 organic oxygen compounds
    - BT3 organic compounds
- RT glycosides

quercus
- USE oaks

quezon philippine reactor
- USE prr-1 reactor

QUIESCENT PLASMA [168; 168]
- BT1 plasma

QUINALDINE [10; 10]
- UF 2-methylquinoline
- BT1 quinolines
  - BT2 pyridines
    - BT3 azines
      - BT4 heterocyclic compounds
        - BT5 organic compounds
      - BT4 organic nitrogen compounds
        - BT5 organic compounds
- RT kynurenic acid

quinalizarin
- USE quinizarin

QUINHYDRONE [11; 11]
- BT1 benzoquinones
  - BT2 quinones
    - BT3 aromatics
      - BT4 organic compounds
    - BT3 organic oxygen compounds
      - BT4 organic compounds
- RT potentiometry

QUININE [19; 19]
- BT1 alkaloids
  - BT2 organic compounds
- BT1 antibiotics
  - BT2 drugs
  - BT2 organic compounds
- BT1 antipyretics
  - BT2 central nervous system depress
    - BT3 central nervous system agents

BT4 drugs

QUINIZARIN [22; 22]
UF quinalizarin
UF 1,4-dihydroxyanthraquinone
BT1 anthraquinones
BT2 quinones
BT3 aromatics
BT4 organic compounds
BT3 organic oxygen compounds
BT4 organic compounds
BT1 dyes
BT1 hydroxy compounds
BT2 organic compounds

QUINOLINES [729; 1,260]
BT1 pyridines
BT2 azines
BT3 heterocyclic compounds
BT4 organic compounds
BT3 organic nitrogen compounds
BT4 organic compounds
NT1 ferron
NT1 kynurenic acid
NT1 oxine
NT1 quinaldine
RT cinchonine

quinone
USE benzoquinones

QUINONES [305; 717]
BT1 aromatics
BT2 organic compounds
BT1 organic oxygen compounds
BT2 organic compounds
NT1 anthraquinones
NT2 alizarin
NT2 carminic acid
NT2 quinizarin
NT1 benzoquinones
NT2 chloranil
NT2 chloranilic acid
NT2 quinhydrone
NT2 ubiquinone
NT1 rhodizonic acid
NT1 vitamin k
RT ketones

r (exposure unit)
USE radiation dose units

R CENTERS [80; 80]
BT1 color centers
BT2 vacancies
BT3 point defects
BT4 crystal defects
BT5 crystal structure

R CODES [2,692; 2,692]
BT1 computer codes

R MATRIX [1,583; 1,583]
BT1 matrices
RT group theory
RT multilevel analysis
RT nuclear reactions

R PROCESS [351; 351]
BT1 star evolution
RT capture
RT nucleosynthesis
RT stars

R REACTOR [42; 42]
UF savannah riv. plant r reactor
BT1 heavy water moderated reactors
BT2 reactors
BT1 special production reactors
BT2 production reactors
BT3 reactors

R-A REACTOR [31; 31]
(Boris Kidric Institute of Nuclear Sciences, Nuclear Reactor RA Dept., Beograd, Yugoslavia)
UF vinca r-a reactor yugoslavia
UF yugoslavia r-a reactor vinca
BT1 enriched uranium reactors
BT2 reactors
BT1 heavy water cooled reactors
BT2 reactors
BT1 heavy water moderated reactors
BT2 reactors
BT1 isotope production reactors
BT2 irradiation reactors
BT3 reactors
BT1 research reactors
BT2 research and test reactors
BT3 reactors
BT1 tank type reactors
BT2 reactors
BT1 thermal reactors
BT2 reactors

R-B REACTOR [29; 29]
(Boris Kidric Institute of Nuclear Sciences, Beograd, Yugoslavia)
UF vinca r-b reactor yugoslavia
UF yugoslavia r-b reactor vinca
BT1 heavy water moderated reactors
BT2 reactors
BT1 natural uranium reactors
BT2 reactors
BT1 training reactors
BT2 research and test reactors
BT3 reactors
BT1 zero power reactors
BT2 experimental reactors
BT3 research and test reactors
BT4 reactors

r-f mass spectrometers
USE dynamic mass spectrometers

r-rna
USE ribosomal rna

R-1 REACTOR [7; 7]
(Stockholm, Sweden.)
UF stockholm r-1 reactor
UF swedish reactor r-1
BT1 heavy water cooled reactors
BT2 reactors
BT1 heavy water moderated reactors
BT2 reactors
BT1 isotope production reactors
BT2 irradiation reactors
BT3 reactors
BT1 natural uranium reactors
BT2 reactors
BT1 research reactors
BT2 research and test reactors
BT3 reactors
BT1 tank type reactors
BT2 reactors
BT1 thermal reactors
BT2 reactors

r-1650 resonances
(Prior to December 1987 this was a valid descriptor.)
USE mesons

R-2 REACTOR [49; 49]
(Aktiebolaget Atomenergi, Nyoking, Studsvik, Sweden)
UF studsvik r-2 reactor
UF swedish reactor r-2
BT1 enriched uranium reactors
BT2 reactors
BT1 materials testing reactors
BT2 irradiation reactors
BT3 reactors
BT1 research reactors
BT2 research and test reactors
BT3 reactors
BT1 tank type reactors
BT2 reactors
BT1 water cooled reactors
BT2 reactors
BT1 water moderated reactors
BT2 reactors

r-2510 resonances
(Prior to December 1987 this was a valid descriptor.)
USE f6-2510 mesons

r-3/adam reactor
USE agesta reactor

RA-0 REACTOR [7; 7]
(UN Cordoba/CNEA, Argentinian Atomic Energy Commission, Cordoba, Argentina)
UF argentine reactor ra-0
UF reactor argentin-0
BT1 research reactors
BT2 research and test reactors
BT3 reactors
BT1 tank type reactors
BT2 reactors
BT1 zero power reactors
BT2 experimental reactors
BT3 research and test reactors
BT4 reactors

RA-1 REACTOR [10; 10]
(CNEA, Argentinian Atomic Energy Agency, Buenos Aires, Argentina)
UF argentine reactor ra-1
UF reactor argentin-1
BT1 argonaut type reactors
BT2 enriched uranium reactors
BT3 reactors
BT2 research and test reactors
BT3 reactors
BT2 water cooled reactors
BT3 reactors
BT2 water moderated reactors
BT3 reactors
BT1 training reactors
BT2 research and test reactors
BT3 reactors

RA-2 REACTOR [15; 15]
(CNEA, Argentinian Atomic Energy Commission, Buenos Aires, Argentina)
UF argentine reactor ra-2
UF reactor argentin-2
BT1 research reactors
BT2 research and test reactors
BT3 reactors
BT1 tank type reactors
BT2 reactors
BT1 zero power reactors
BT2 experimental reactors
BT3 research and test reactors
BT4 reactors

RA-3 REACTOR [22; 22]
(CNEA, Argentinian Atomic Energy Commission, Buenos Aires, Argentina)
UF argentine reactor ra-3
UF ezeiza argentine ra-3 reactor
UF reactor argentin-3
BT1 research reactors
BT2 research and test reactors
BT3 reactors
BT1 tank type reactors
BT2 reactors
BT1 test reactors
BT2 research and test reactors
BT3 reactors
BT2 test facilities

RA-5 REACTOR [4; 4] Feb 76
UF argentine reactor ra-5
UF reactor argentin-5
BT1 enriched uranium reactors
BT2 reactors
BT1 research reactors
BT2 research and test reactors

```
BT3      reactors
BT1    tank type reactors
  BT2    reactors
BT1    test reactors
  BT2    research and test reactors
    BT3      reactors
  BT2    test facilities
BT1    thermal reactors
  BT2    reactors
BT1    water cooled reactors
  BT2    reactors
BT1    water moderated reactors
  BT2    reactors
```

RABBIT TUBES [138; 138]
UF   *shuttles*
BT1   reactor experimental facilitie
  BT2   reactor components

RABBITS [3,769; 3,769]
BT1   mammals
  BT2   vertebrates
    BT3   animals

RABIES [7; 7] *Apr 82*
BT1   nervous system diseases
  BT2   diseases
BT1   viral diseases
  BT2   infectious diseases
    BT3   diseases
RT   central nervous system
RT   viruses

RACAH COEFFICIENTS [199; 199]
UF   *6j-symbols*
RT   angular momentum
RT   clebsch-gordan coefficients
RT   group theory
RT   quantum mechanics
RT   wigner coefficients

RACEMIZATION [83; 83]
RT   stereochemistry

RACETRACK MICROTRONS [79; 79] *Jul 85*
(Microtrons with two bending magnets and linear accelerators between them.)
BT1   microtrons
  BT2   cyclotrons
    BT3   cyclic accelerators
      BT4   accelerators

rachitis
USE   rickets

racks (fuel)
USE   fuel racks

rad
USE   radiation dose units

RADAPPERTIZATION [590; 590]
(Use of irradiation to sterilize foodstuff.)
UF   *food irradiation (radiosterili*
UF   *radiosterilization (food)*
BT1   food processing
BT1   radiosterilization
  BT2   irradiation
  BT2   sterilization
RT   food
RT   ifip

RADAR [654; 654]
UF   *radiation detection and range*
BT1   range finders
  BT2   measuring instruments
RT   electrical equipment
RT   electronic equipment
RT   frequency range
RT   radio equipment
RT   radiowave radiation

radial distribution
USE   spatial distribution

radial profiles (plasma)
USE   plasma radial profiles

RADIAL VELOCITY [2,400; 2,400]
BT1   velocity

RADIANT HEAT TRANSFER [736; 736]
UF   *radiative transfer*
BT1   heat transfer
  BT2   energy transfer
RT   emissivity
RT   radiative cooling
RT   thermal radiation

RADIATION ABSORPTION ANALYSIS [287; 287]
(Analysis based on the determination of the absorption of X-ray, gamma-ray, or other ionizing radiation by the sample.)
BT1   nondestructive analysis
  BT2   chemical analysis

RADIATION ACCIDENTS [2,785; 2,785]
UF+   *accidental irradiation*
UF+   *criticality accidents*
UF+   *goiania radiological emergency*
BT1   accidents
RT   canare
RT   emergency plans

RADIATION ATTENUATION TESTING [88; 88] *Nov 75*
(Prior to April 1986 INDUSTRIAL RADIOGRAPHY was used for this concept.)
BT1   nondestructive testing
  BT2   materials testing
    BT3   testing
RT   industrial radiography

RADIATION BELTS [721; 726]
UF   *van allen belts*
NT1   artificial radiation belts
RT   charged-particle precipitation
RT   earth magnetosphere
RT   electron precipitation
RT   proton precipitation

radiation buildup
USE   buildup

radiation burden
USE   radiation doses

RADIATION BURNS [117; 117]
BT1   burns
  BT2   injuries
    BT3   diseases
BT1   local radiation effects
  BT2   biological radiation effects
    BT3   biological effects
    BT3   radiation effects
BT1   radiation injuries
  BT2   biological radiation effects
    BT3   biological effects
    BT3   radiation effects
  BT2   injuries
    BT3   diseases
RT   radiodermatitis

RADIATION CHEMISTRY [3,413; 3,413]
(The chemistry of the effects of high-energy radiation on matter. Not to be used for RADIOCHEMISTRY.)
UF   *radioinduced reactions*
BT1   chemistry
RT   chemical radiation effects
RT   g value
RT   oxonium ions
RT   photochemistry

RT   radiochemistry
RT   radiolysis
RT   reaction intermediates
RT   recombination
RT   scavenging
RT   valence

RADIATION CHIMERAS [404; 404]
BT1   chimeras
  BT2   mosaicism
RT   biological radiation effects
RT   spleen colony formation

RADIATION CURING [505; 505] *Sep 81*
(Prior to November 1982 this concept was indexed by the coordination of CHEMICAL RADIATION EFFECTS and CROSS-LINKING.)
BT1   chemical radiation effects
  BT2   radiation effects
BT1   curing
RT   cross-linking

radiation damage (biological)
USE   radiation injuries

radiation damage (chemical)
USE   radiolysis

radiation damage (physical)
USE   physical radiation effects

RADIATION DETECTION [2,429; 23,207]
BT1   detection
NT1   charged particle detection
  NT2   acoustic detection
  NT2   alpha detection
  NT2   beta detection
  NT2   electron detection
  NT2   ion detection
  NT2   muon detection
  NT2   positron detection
  NT2   proton detection
NT1   cosmic ray detection
NT1   fission fragment detection
NT1   gamma detection
NT1   kaon detection
NT1   neutrino detection
NT1   neutron detection
NT1   pion detection
NT1   x-ray detection
RT   coincidence spectrometry
RT   counting circuits
RT   dosemeters
RT   dosimetry
RT   particle discrimination
RT   pulse techniques
RT   radiation detectors
RT   radiation monitoring
RT   radiations
RT   spectrometers
RT   spectroscopy

radiation detection and range
USE   radar

RADIATION DETECTORS [6,177; 56,450]
UF   *counters (radiation)*
UF   *detectors (radiation)*
BT1   measuring instruments
NT1   chemical radiation detectors
NT1   cherenkov counters
NT1   compton diode detectors
NT1   corona counters
NT1   crystal counters
  NT2   filament crystal counters
NT1   dielectric track detectors
NT1   directional radiation detector
NT1   electron multiplier detectors
NT1   emanometers
NT1   flow counters
NT1   gas track detectors

NT2	bubble chambers		RT	charged particle detection		RT	radiation dose distributions
	NT3	cryogenic bubble chambers	RT	cosmic ray detection		RT	radiation dose units
	NT3	heavy liquid bubble chambers	RT	counting circuits		RT	radiation effects
	NT3	ultrasonic bubble chambers	RT	counting techniques		RT	radiations
NT2	cloud chambers		RT	dosemeters		RT	remedial action
	NT3	diffusion chambers	RT	fission fragment detection		RT	source terms
	NT3	expansion chambers	RT	gamma detection		RT	sublethal irradiation
NT2	spark chambers		RT	neutron detection		RT	supralethal irradiation

RADIATION DETECTORS (continued)

- NT2 bubble chambers
  - NT3 cryogenic bubble chambers
  - NT3 heavy liquid bubble chambers
  - NT3 ultrasonic bubble chambers
- NT2 cloud chambers
  - NT3 diffusion chambers
  - NT3 expansion chambers
- NT2 spark chambers
  - NT3 filmless spark chambers
    - NT4 sonic spark chambers
    - NT4 wire spark chambers
  - NT3 projection spark chambers
  - NT3 streamer spark chambers
  - NT3 wide gap spark chambers
- NT1 geiger-mueller counters
- NT1 gravitational wave detectors
- NT1 ionization chambers
  - NT2 boron coated ion chambers
  - NT2 bragg gray chambers
  - NT2 condenser ionization chambers
  - NT2 extrapolation chambers
  - NT2 fission chambers
  - NT2 liquid ionization chambers
  - NT2 multiwire ionization chambers
- NT1 low level counters
- NT1 neutron detectors
  - NT2 activation detectors
  - NT2 bf3 counters
  - NT2 boron coated ion chambers
  - NT2 boron lined counters
  - NT2 fission chambers
  - NT2 fission foil detectors
  - NT2 he-3 counters
  - NT2 moderating detectors
    - NT3 bonner sphere detectors
    - NT3 long counters
  - NT2 proton recoil detectors
  - NT2 self-powered neutron detectors
  - NT2 threshold detectors
- NT1 photographic film detectors
- NT1 position sensitive detectors
- NT1 proportional counters
  - NT2 bf3 counters
  - NT2 boron lined counters
  - NT2 he-3 counters
  - NT2 liquid proportional counters
  - NT2 multiwire proportional chamber
    - NT3 drift chambers
      - NT4 time projection chambers
  - NT2 needle chambers
- NT1 pyroelectric detectors
- NT1 radiometers
- NT1 scintillation counters
  - NT2 gas scintillation detectors
  - NT2 liquid scintillation detectors
  - NT2 scintillator-photodiode detect
  - NT2 solid scintillation detectors
    - NT3 bgo detectors
    - NT3 nai detectors
    - NT3 plastic scintillation detector
- NT1 secondary emission detectors
- NT1 self-powered detectors
  - NT2 self-powered gamma detectors
  - NT2 self-powered neutron detectors
- NT1 semiconductor detectors
  - NT2 bulk semiconductor detectors
  - NT2 cdte semiconductor detectors
  - NT2 ge semiconductor detectors
    - NT3 high-purity ge detectors
    - NT3 li-drifted ge detectors
  - NT2 hgi2 semiconductor detectors
  - NT2 insb semiconductor detectors
  - NT2 junction detectors
    - NT3 li-drifted junction detectors
  - NT2 li-drifted detectors
    - NT3 li-drifted ge detectors
    - NT3 li-drifted junction detectors
    - NT3 li-drifted si detectors
  - NT2 si semiconductor detectors
    - NT3 li-drifted si detectors
  - NT2 surface barrier detectors
- NT1 shower counters
- NT1 spark counters
- NT1 superconducting colloid detect
- NT1 tissue-equivalent detectors
- NT1 transition radiation detectors
- NT1 wall-less counters
- NT1 whole-body counters
- RT charged particle detection
- RT cosmic ray detection
- RT counting circuits
- RT counting techniques
- RT dosemeters
- RT fission fragment detection
- RT gamma detection
- RT neutron detection
- RT polarimeters
- RT pulse techniques
- RT radiation detection
- RT radiation monitors
- RT radioisotope scanners
- RT scalers
- RT spectrometers
- RT streak cameras
- RT telescope counters
- RT well logging equipment

RADIATION DOSE DISTRIBUTIONS [3,474; 8,765]
- UF *dose distributions*
- NT1 spatial dose distributions
  - NT2 depth dose distributions
- NT1 temporal dose distributions
- RT dose-response relationships
- RT irradiation
- RT isodose curves
- RT radiation doses

RADIATION DOSE UNITS [650; 672]
(For studies concerning units, concepts or definitions.)
- UF *gray*
- UF *r (exposure unit)*
- UF *rad*
- UF *roentgen (exposure unit)*
- UF+ *rem*
- UF+ *roentgen equivalent man*
- BT1 units
- NT1 sievert unit
- RT dosimetry
- RT icru
- RT radiation doses

radiation dosemeters
- USE dosemeters

RADIATION DOSES [44,437; 47,315]
- UF *absorbed doses*
- UF *doses (radiation)*
- UF *exposure (radiation doses)*
- UF *radiation burden*
- UF *radiation exposure (doses)*
- NT1 genetically significant dose
- NT1 integral doses
- NT1 lethal radiation dose
- NT1 somatically significant dose
- NT1 threshold dose
- RT alara
- RT biological indicators
- RT biological radiation effects
- RT biophysics
- RT buildup
- RT chronic irradiation
- RT critical organs
- RT cumulative radiation effects
- RT dose commitments
- RT dose equivalents
- RT dose limits
- RT dose rates
- RT dose-response relationships
- RT dosemeters
- RT dosimetry
- RT energy deposition
- RT fractionated irradiation
- RT icrp critical group
- RT irradiation
- RT kerma
- RT lethal irradiation
- RT low dose irradiation
- RT maximum permissible dose
- RT maximum permissible exposure
- RT medical surveillance
- RT occupational exposure
- RT personnel monitoring
- RT radiation dose distributions
- RT radiation dose units
- RT radiation effects
- RT radiations
- RT remedial action
- RT source terms
- RT sublethal irradiation
- RT supralethal irradiation

radiation dosimetry
- USE dosimetry

RADIATION EFFECTS [13,326; 111,633]
- UF *radioinduction*
- NT1 biological radiation effects
  - NT2 abscopal radiation effects
  - NT2 delayed radiation effects
  - NT2 early radiation effects
  - NT2 genetic radiation effects
  - NT2 local radiation effects
    - NT3 osteoradionecrosis
    - NT3 radiation burns
    - NT3 radiodermatitis
  - NT2 radiation injuries
    - NT3 osteoradionecrosis
    - NT3 radiation burns
    - NT3 radiodermatitis
- NT1 chemical radiation effects
  - NT2 lyoluminescence
  - NT2 radiation curing
  - NT2 radiolysis
    - NT3 autoradiolysis
- NT1 cumulative radiation effects
- NT1 physical radiation effects
  - NT2 atomic displacements
  - NT2 interstitial helium generation
  - NT2 interstitial hydrogen generati
  - NT2 radiation hardening
- RT biological localization
- RT biophysics
- RT blisters
- RT comparative evaluations
- RT crystal defects
- RT dose rates
- RT dose-response relationships
- RT energy losses
- RT irradiation
- RT photoacoustic effect
- RT radiation doses
- RT radiation quality
- RT radiations
- RT radiobiology
- RT radiosensitivity
- RT rbe
- RT recoils
- RT response modifying factors
- RT self-irradiation
- RT strand breaks
- RT thermal spikes
- RT varley mechanism
- RT wigner effect

radiation exposure (doses)
- USE radiation doses

RADIATION FLUX [4,251; 17,009]
- UF *flux (radiation)*
- NT1 cosmic ray flux
- NT1 neutron flux
  - NT2 adjoint flux
- RT flux density
- RT point kernels
- RT poynting theorem

RADIATION HARDENING [1,459; 1,459]
- BT1 hardening
- BT1 physical radiation effects
- BT2 radiation effects

radiation hardening (chemical)
- USE chemical radiation effects
- AND polymerization

RADIATION HAZARDS [9,215; 9,215]
- BT1 health hazards
  - BT2 hazards
- RT alara
- RT fallout
- RT fission product release
- RT fuel element failure
- RT genetically significant dose
- RT hot labs
- RT icrp critical group
- RT irradiation
- RT radiation protection
- RT radiation protection laws
- RT radioactive wastes
- RT release limits
- RT somatically significant dose
- RT unscear

RADIATION HEATING [623; 623]
- UF *gamma heating*
- BT1 heating

radiation hygiene
- USE radiation protection

RADIATION INDUCED MUTANTS [1,208; 1,208] *Feb 78*
- UF *radiation-induced mutants*
- BT1 mutants

RADIATION INJURIES [6,883; 7,459]
(For damage to molecules of biological significance use CHEMICAL RADIATION EFFECTS or STRAND BREAKS.)
- UF *damage (radiation, biological)*
- UF *radiation damage (biological)*
- UF+ *delayed radiation injuries*
- UF+ *early radiation injuries*
- BT1 biological radiation effects
  - BT2 biological effects
  - BT2 radiation effects
- BT1 injuries
  - BT2 diseases
- NT1 osteoradionecrosis
- NT1 radiation burns
- NT1 radiodermatitis
- RT biological indicators
- RT biological repair
- RT host-cell reactivation
- RT photoreactivation
- RT radiation syndrome
- RT radiobiology

RADIATION LENGTH [60; 60]
- RT bremsstrahlung
- RT charged particle detection
- RT energy losses
- RT half-thickness
- RT thickness

RADIATION MONITORING [12,289; 16,224]
- UF *control (radioactivity)*
- UF *surveillance (radioactivity)*
- UF *survey (radioactivity)*
- BT1 monitoring
- NT1 aerial monitoring
- NT1 personnel monitoring
- RT aerosol monitoring
- RT alarm systems
- RT controlled areas
- RT dosemeters
- RT dosimetry
- RT exposure ratemeters
- RT inspection
- RT radiation detection
- RT radiation protection
- RT radioactivity
- RT radioassay
- RT site surveys

RADIATION MONITORS [1,621; 3,097]
- UF *alarm dosemeters*
- BT1 monitors
  - BT2 measuring instruments
- NT1 exposure ratemeters
- NT1 liquid contamination monitors
- NT1 neutron monitors
- NT1 surface contamination monitors
- NT1 survey monitors
- RT alarm systems
- RT dosemeters
- RT radiation detectors
- RT radioactivity

RADIATION PRESSURE [681; 681]
- UF *pressure (radiation)*
- RT electromagnetic radiation
- RT solar wind

RADIATION PROTECTION [21,043; 21,043]
- UF *health physics*
- UF *nuclear safety*
- UF *protection (radiation)*
- UF *radiation hygiene*
- UF *radiation safety*
- UF *radiological protection*
- UF *safety (nuclear)*
- RT accidents
- RT afterloading
- RT alara
- RT biological shielding
- RT biophysics
- RT civil defense
- RT containment
- RT controlled areas
- RT decontamination
- RT distance
- RT dosimetry
- RT environment
- RT ethical aspects
- RT external irradiation
- RT fallout
- RT fallout shelters
- RT federal radiation council
- RT gloveboxes
- RT gloves
- RT half-thickness
- RT health hazards
- RT hot cells
- RT hot labs
- RT icrp
- RT image intensifiers
- RT industrial medicine
- RT inspection
- RT legal aspects
- RT licensing
- RT preventive medicine
- RT protective clothing
- RT public health
- RT radiation hazards
- RT radiation monitoring
- RT radiation protection laws
- RT radiation quality
- RT radiation sources
- RT radioprotective substances
- RT reactor safety
- RT recommendations
- RT reference man
- RT regulations
- RT reliability
- RT remedial action
- RT remote handling
- RT respirators
- RT safety
- RT safety standards
- RT shelters
- RT shielding
- RT shielding materials
- RT shields
- RT space flight
- RT television
- RT whole-body counting
- RT working conditions

radiation protection guides
- USE recommendations

RADIATION PROTECTION LAWS [766; 766] *Dec 76*
(Prior to December 1990, this descriptor was spelled RADIATION PROTECTION LAW.)
- BT1 laws
- RT federal radiation council
- RT radiation hazards
- RT radiation protection
- RT safety standards

RADIATION QUALITY [816; 816]
(For comparative studies on different types of radiation.)
- RT energy losses
- RT half-thickness
- RT ionization
- RT let
- RT quality factor
- RT radiation effects
- RT radiation protection
- RT radiations
- RT rbe

radiation safety
- USE radiation protection

RADIATION SCATTERING ANALYSIS [425; 425]
- BT1 nondestructive analysis
  - BT2 chemical analysis
- RT ion scattering analysis
- RT radiometric analysis
- RT scattering

RADIATION SOURCE IMPLANTS [1,463; 1,463]
- BT1 implants
- BT1 radiation sources
- RT afterloading
- RT internal irradiation
- RT irradiation capsules
- RT radiotherapy

RADIATION SOURCES [3,722; 22,632]
(For cosmic sources of radiation see also COSMIC GAMMA SOURCES, COSMIC RADIO SOURCES, and COSMIC X-RAY SOURCES.)
- UF *applicators (radiotherapy)*
- UF *radioapplicators*
- NT1 gamma sources
- NT1 light sources
- NT1 particle sources
  - NT2 alpha sources
  - NT2 antiproton sources
  - NT2 beta sources
  - NT2 deuteron sources
  - NT2 electron sources
    - NT3 pierce electron guns
  - NT2 neutron sources
    - NT3 neutron generators
    - NT3 nisus facility
  - NT2 positron sources
  - NT2 proton sources
- NT1 point sources
- NT1 portable sources
- NT1 radiation source implants
- NT1 sealed sources
- NT1 synchrotron radiation sources
  - NT2 kek photon factory
  - NT2 lnls storage ring
  - NT2 nsls
  - NT2 spring-8 storage ring
  - NT2 surf ii storage ring
- NT1 unsealed sources
- NT1 x-ray sources
- RT containers
- RT irradiation
- RT irradiation devices
- RT irradiation plants
- RT masers
- RT radiation protection
- RT radiations
- RT radioactivity
- RT radioisotopes
- RT well logging equipment

RADIATION STREAMING [729; 729]
- UF streaming (radiation)
- RT radiations

RADIATION SYNDROME [1,084; 1,084]
- RT acute irradiation
- RT autonomic nervous system
- RT behavior
- RT bone marrow
- RT central nervous system
- RT chronic irradiation
- RT delayed radiation effects
- RT gastrointestinal tract
- RT latency period
- RT lymphatic system
- RT lymphocytes
- RT muscles
- RT radiation injuries

RADIATION TRANSPORT [1,893; 9,825]
- UF transport (radiation)
- NT1 charged-particle transport
- NT2 proton transport
- NT1 neutral-particle transport
- NT2 atom transport
- NT2 neutron transport
- NT2 photon transport
- RT transport theory

radiation-induced mutants
- USE radiation induced mutants

RADIATIONLESS DECAY [285; 285]
(Emissionless transfer of excited-state energy from one quantum system to another, e.g. between atoms in gas mixtures.)
- UF radiationless transitions
- BT1 de-excitation
- BT2 energy-level transitions
- BT1 energy transfer
- RT fluorescence

radiationless transitions
- USE radiationless decay

RADIATIONS [1,509; 192,578]
- NT1 background radiation
- NT1 delta rays
- NT1 electromagnetic radiation
- NT2 auroral hiss
- NT2 blackbody radiation
- NT2 bremsstrahlung
- NT3 cyclotron radiation
- NT3 internal bremsstrahlung
- NT3 ondulator radiation
- NT3 synchrotron radiation
- NT2 cherenkov radiation
- NT2 coherent radiation
- NT2 electromagnetic pulses
- NT3 internal electromagnetic pulse
- NT2 gamma radiation
- NT3 delayed gamma radiation
- NT3 prompt gamma radiation
- NT2 helicon waves
- NT2 infrared radiation
- NT3 far infrared radiation
- NT3 intermediate infrared radiatio
- NT3 near infrared radiation
- NT2 laser radiation
- NT2 microwave radiation
- NT3 relict radiation
- NT2 monochromatic radiation
- NT2 multipole radiation
- NT2 radiowave radiation
- NT3 long wave radiation
- NT3 luxemburg effect
- NT3 medium wave radiation
- NT3 radio noise
- NT4 atmospherics
- NT4 whistlers
- NT3 radioecho
- NT3 short wave radiation
- NT3 solar radio bursts
- NT2 thermal radiation
- NT2 transition radiation
- NT2 ultralow frequency radiation
- NT2 ultraviolet radiation
- NT3 extreme ultraviolet radiation
- NT3 far ultraviolet radiation
- NT3 near ultraviolet radiation
- NT2 visible radiation
- NT2 x radiation
- NT3 hard x radiation
- NT3 soft x radiation
- NT2 zodiacal light
- NT1 gravitational radiation
- NT2 gravitons
- NT1 ionizing radiations
- NT2 alpha particles
- NT3 cosmic alpha particles
- NT3 delayed alpha particles
- NT3 solar alpha particles
- NT2 beta particles
- NT2 cosmic radiation
- NT3 cosmic neutrinos
- NT3 cosmic photons
- NT3 cosmic protons
- NT3 hard component
- NT3 primary cosmic radiation
- NT4 cosmic alpha particles
- NT4 cosmic gamma bursts
- NT4 cosmic nuclei
- NT4 cosmic x-ray bursts
- NT3 secondary cosmic radiation
- NT4 cosmic electrons
- NT4 cosmic kaons
- NT4 cosmic muons
- NT4 cosmic neutrons
- NT4 cosmic pions
- NT4 cosmic positrons
- NT4 cosmic showers
- NT5 extensive air showers
- NT3 soft component
- NT2 gamma radiation
- NT3 delayed gamma radiation
- NT3 prompt gamma radiation
- NT2 x radiation
- NT3 hard x radiation
- NT3 soft x radiation
- NT1 stellar radiation
- NT2 solar radiation
- NT3 solar particles
- NT4 solar alpha particles
- NT4 solar electrons
- NT4 solar neutrinos
- NT4 solar neutrons
- NT4 solar protons
- NT1 stray radiation
- RT absorption
- RT biophysics
- RT buildup
- RT dosimetry
- RT irradiation
- RT radiation detection
- RT radiation doses
- RT radiation effects
- RT radiation quality
- RT radiation sources
- RT radiation streaming

radiative capture
- USE capture

RADIATIVE COOLING [367; 367]
Feb 77
- BT1 cooling
- RT air conditioning
- RT radiant heat transfer

RADIATIVE CORRECTIONS
[2,637; 2,637]
- BT1 corrections
- RT electromagnetic interactions
- RT phi4-field theory
- RT quantum field theory

RADIATIVE DECAY [2,894; 2,894]
Sep 80
(Weak or electromagnetic decay involving photons.)
- BT1 particle decay
- BT2 decay
- RT electromagnetic particle decay
- RT weak particle decay

radiative transfer
(Energy transfer by radiation.)
- USE radiant heat transfer

RADIATOR COUNTERS [103; 103]
- RT activation detectors
- RT nuclear emulsions
- RT proton recoil detectors
- RT semiconductor detectors

RADIATORS [138; 138]
(Limited to heat radiators.)
- BT1 heat exchangers

RADICALS [5,894; 10,501]
(Not to be used for chemical compounds.)
- UF free radicals
- NT1 acyl radicals
- NT2 acetyl radicals
- NT2 butyryl radicals
- NT2 formyl radicals
- NT1 alkoxy radicals
- NT2 butoxy radicals
- NT2 ethoxy radicals
- NT2 methoxy radicals
- NT1 alkyl radicals
- NT2 allyl radicals
- NT2 butyl radicals
- NT2 dodecyl radicals
- NT2 ethyl radicals
- NT2 heptyl radicals
- NT2 hexyl radicals
- NT2 isobutyl radicals
- NT2 isopropyl radicals
- NT2 methyl radicals
- NT2 nonyl radicals
- NT2 octyl radicals
- NT2 pentyl radicals
- NT2 propargyl radicals
- NT2 propyl radicals
- NT2 tridecyl radicals
- NT2 vinyl radicals
- NT1 aryl radicals
- NT2 anisyl radicals
- NT2 benzyl radicals
- NT2 mesityl radicals
- NT2 naphthyl radicals
- NT2 phenethyl radicals
- NT2 phenyl radicals
- NT2 tolyl radicals
- NT1 benzoyl radicals
- NT1 carbenes
- NT1 carbonyl radicals
- NT1 dpph
- NT1 hydronium radicals
- NT1 hydroperoxy radicals
- NT1 hydroxyl radicals
- NT1 methylene radicals
- NT1 nitroxyl radicals
- NT1 peroxy radicals
- NT1 phenoxy radicals
- NT1 phenylene radicals
- NT1 picryl radicals
- NT1 pyridyl radicals
- NT1 sdpph
- NT1 sulfhydryl radicals
- NT1 thiyl radicals
- NT1 vinylidene radicals
- RT reaction intermediates
- RT scavenging

RADICIDATION [492; 492]
(Use of irradiation to destroy microorganisms in food which are detrimental to health.)
- UF food irradiation (radiopasteur
- UF radiopasteurization
- BT1 irradiation
- BT1 pasteurization
- BT2 food processing
- RT food
- RT health hazards
- RT ifip

RADIO EQUIPMENT [89; 483] *Mar 81*
- UF *radio receivers*
- UF *radio transmitters*
- BT1 electronic equipment
  - BT2 equipment
- NT1 heterodyne receivers
- NT1 ionosondes
- NT1 radio telescopes
- RT antennas
- RT communications
- RT microwave equipment
- RT radar
- RT radiowave radiation
- RT rf systems
- RT television

radio frequency quadrupoles
- USE quadrupole linacs

RADIO GALAXIES [1,430; 1,430]
- BT1 cosmic radio sources
- BT1 galaxies
- RT quasars

RADIO NOISE [230; 1,130]
- UF *cosmic noise*
- BT1 noise
- BT1 radiowave radiation
  - BT2 electromagnetic radiation
    - BT3 radiations
- NT1 atmospherics
- NT1 whistlers
- RT background noise
- RT interference

radio receivers
- USE radio equipment

RADIO TELESCOPES [461; 461]
- BT1 radio equipment
  - BT2 electronic equipment
    - BT3 equipment
- BT1 telescopes
- RT interferometers

radio transmitters
- USE radio equipment

radio-receptor assay
- USE radioreceptor assay

RADIO-RELEASE ANALYSIS [123; 123]
(Substance to be measured reacts chemically with a converter substance to release a radioactive material.)
- UF *radiorelease analysis*
- BT1 quantitative chemical analysis
  - BT2 chemical analysis
- RT gas analysis
- RT tracer techniques

RADIOACTIVATION [2,141; 2,141]
(For activation cross sections see also INTEGRAL CROSS SECTIONS.)
- UF *activation (radio)*
- RT activation analysis
- RT labelling
- RT neutron capture therapy
- RT neutron sources

RADIOACTIVE AEROSOLS [3,837; 3,837]
- UF+ *radioactive particulates*
- BT1 aerosols
  - BT2 sols
    - BT3 colloids
      - BT4 dispersions
- RT aerosol monitoring
- RT fallout
- RT particle resuspension
- RT radioactive clouds

radioactive biological wastes
- USE biological wastes
- AND radioactive wastes

RADIOACTIVE CLOUDS [449; 449]
- UF *atomic clouds*
- BT1 clouds
- RT accidents
- RT aerial monitoring
- RT aerosols
- RT air
- RT earth atmosphere
- RT external irradiation
- RT fallout
- RT nuclear explosions
- RT radioactive aerosols
- RT radioactivity
- RT stacks
- RT washout
- RT wind

radioactive decontamination
- USE decontamination

RADIOACTIVE EFFLUENTS [4,497; 4,497]
- UF *effluents (radioactive)*
- BT1 radioactive wastes
  - BT2 radioactive materials
    - BT3 materials
  - BT2 wastes
- RT gaseous wastes
- RT liquid wastes
- RT particle resuspension
- RT radioactive waste disposal
- RT stack disposal

radioactive gaseous wastes
- USE gaseous wastes
- AND radioactive wastes

RADIOACTIVE IONIZATION GAGES [30; 30]
- BT1 ionization gages
  - BT2 vacuum gages
    - BT3 pressure gages
      - BT4 measuring instruments

RADIOACTIVE MATERIALS [3,549; 66,198]
- BT1 materials
- NT1 fission products
- *NT1 radioactive minerals
- NT1 radioactive wastes
  - NT2 alpha-bearing wastes
  - NT2 calcined wastes
  - NT2 high-level radioactive wastes
  - NT2 intermediate-level radioactive
  - NT2 low-level radioactive wastes
  - NT2 radioactive effluents
- NT1 radiopharmaceuticals
- RT radioactivity
- RT radioisotopes

RADIOACTIVE MINERALS [169; 2,241]
- BT1 minerals
- BT1 radioactive materials
  - BT2 materials
- NT1 baddeleyite
- NT1 cordylite
- NT1 florencite
- NT1 rutile
- NT1 thorium minerals
  - NT2 aeschynite
  - NT2 allanite
    - NT3 orthite
  - NT2 bastnaesite
  - NT2 brannerite
  - NT2 cerianite
  - NT2 huttonite
  - NT2 monazites
  - NT2 steenstrupine
  - NT2 thorianite
  - NT2 thorite
  - NT2 thorogummite
  - NT2 thucholite
  - NT2 uranothorianite
  - NT2 uranothorite
  - NT2 yttrialite
- NT1 uranium minerals
  - NT2 andersonite
  - NT2 autunite
  - NT2 bayleyite
  - NT2 becquerelite
  - NT2 boltwoodite
  - NT2 brannerite
  - NT2 carburan
  - NT2 carnotite
  - NT2 clarkeite
  - NT2 coffinite
  - NT2 cuprosklodowskite
  - NT2 curite
  - NT2 cyrtolite
  - NT2 davidite
  - NT2 demesmaekerite
  - NT2 dumontite
  - NT2 francevillite
  - NT2 gummite
  - NT2 haiweeite
  - NT2 hatchettolite
  - NT2 iriginite
  - NT2 ishikawaite
  - NT2 johannite
  - NT2 lermontovite
  - NT2 liebigite
  - NT2 masuyite
  - NT2 moluranite
  - NT2 ningyoite
  - NT2 parsonsite
  - NT2 phosphuranylite
  - NT2 rutherfordite
  - NT2 saleeite
  - NT2 schoepite
  - NT2 schroeckingerite
  - NT2 soddyite
  - NT2 steenstrupine
  - NT2 strelkinite
  - NT2 thorianite
  - NT2 thucholite
  - NT2 torbernite
  - NT2 tyuyamunite
  - NT2 umohoite
  - NT2 uraninites
    - NT3 pitchblende
  - NT2 uranium black
  - NT2 uranocircite
  - NT2 uranophane
  - NT2 uranothorianite
  - NT2 uranothorite
  - NT2 uranotile
  - NT2 zeunerite
  - NT2 zippeite

radioactive particulates
- USE particles
- AND radioactive aerosols

RADIOACTIVE TRACER LOGGING [123; 123] *Jun 77*
(Well logging using radioactive tracers for measuring fluid movement and for obtaining source and sink information.)
- BT1 radioactivity logging
  - BT2 well logging
- BT1 tracer techniques
  - BT2 isotope applications

RADIOACTIVE WASTE DISPOSAL [20,535; 20,535]
- BT1 waste disposal
  - BT2 waste management
    - BT3 management
- RT actinide burner reactors
- RT asse salt mine
- RT backfilling
- RT biointrusion
- RT environmental exposure pathway
- RT fission product release
- RT fuel cycle centers
- RT gorleben salt dome
- RT ground release
- RT konrad ore mine
- RT marine disposal
- RT nuclear waste policy acts

RT radioactive effluents
RT radioactive waste facilities
RT radioactive waste storage
RT salt caverns
RT salt deposits
RT shaft excavations
RT stack disposal
RT underground disposal
RT waste-rock interactions
RT wipp

RADIOACTIVE WASTE FACILITIES
[7,524; 8,278]
BT1 nuclear facilities
NT1 asse salt mine
NT1 gorleben salt dome
NT1 konrad ore mine
NT1 pamela plant
NT1 vaalputs radioactive waste dis
NT1 wipp
RT biointrusion
RT fuel cycle centers
RT fuel reprocessing plants
RT radioactive waste disposal
RT radioactive waste processing
RT storage facilities
RT waste retrieval

RADIOACTIVE WASTE MANAGE-
MENT [491;, 491] Nov 90
BT1 waste management
BT2 management

radioactive waste policy acts
USE nuclear waste policy acts

RADIOACTIVE WASTE PROCESSING
[11,779; 11,779]
BT1 waste processing
BT2 waste management
BT3 management
RT calcination
RT calcined wastes
RT ceramic melters
RT encapsulation
RT fuel cycle centers
RT pamela plant
RT radioactive waste facilities
RT slagging pyrolysis process
RT synroc process
RT vitrification

RADIOACTIVE WASTE STORAGE
[5,891; 5,891]
BT1 waste storage
BT2 storage
BT2 waste management
BT3 management
RT dry storage
RT fuel cycle centers
RT radioactive waste disposal
RT us mrs project

RADIOACTIVE WASTES
[14,679; 35,000]
UF *residues (radioactive)*
UF+ *radioactive biological wastes*
UF+ *radioactive gaseous wastes*
BT1 radioactive materials
BT2 materials
BT1 wastes
NT1 alpha-bearing wastes
NT1 calcined wastes
NT1 high-level radioactive wastes
NT1 intermediate-level radioactive
NT1 low-level radioactive wastes
NT1 radioactive effluents
RT contamination
RT fission products
RT fissionable materials
RT ground disposal
RT mill tailings
RT nuclear materials management
RT nuclear waste policy acts
RT radiation hazards
RT radiocolloids
RT radioisotope heat sources

RT release limits
RT salt vault project
RT spent fuels
RT vaalputs radioactive waste dis
RT waste disposal
RT waste forms
RT waste management
RT waste pellets
RT waste processing
RT waste retrieval

RADIOACTIVITY [13,374; 16,851]
(For measured values of radioactivity and for unidentified radiation sources.)
UF *concentrations (radionuclides)*
UF *induced radioactivity*
UF *radionuclide concentration*
NT1 natural radioactivity
RT activity levels
RT annual limit of intake
RT body burden
RT contamination
RT hot labs
RT maximum inhalation quantity
RT maximum permissible activity
RT maximum permissible body burde
RT maximum permissible intake
RT maximum permissible level
RT personnel monitoring
RT radiation monitoring
RT radiation monitors
RT radiation sources
RT radioactive clouds
RT radioactive materials
RT radioassay
RT radioecological concentration
RT radioisotopes
RT radiometric analysis
RT radionuclide kinetics
RT residence half-time
RT surface contamination
RT whole-body counting

RADIOACTIVITY LOGGING
[251; 1,957] Oct 76
(Well logging using either natural or induced nuclear radiation.)
BT1 well logging
NT1 gamma logging
NT1 gamma-gamma logging
NT1 neutron logging
NT2 neutron-gamma logging
NT2 neutron-neutron logging
NT1 radioactive tracer logging
NT1 x-ray fluorescence logging

RADIOACTIVITY TRANSPORT
[995; 995] May 76
(The processes by which radioactive materials move and become deposited throughout a reactor system.)
UF *activity transport*
RT contamination

radioapplicators
USE radiation sources

RADIOASSAY [2,013; 2,561]
(The measurement of radioactive samples including the identification of unknown samples and the determination of activity or energy.)
RT counting techniques
RT radiation monitoring
RT radioactivity
RT radioenzymatic assay
RT radioimmunoassay
RT radioreceptor assay
RT spectroscopy

RADIOASTRONOMY [698; 698]
BT1 astronomy
RT cosmic radio sources
RT ghz range
RT mhz range
RT solar radio bursts

radioautography
USE autoradiography

radiobiological effects
USE biological radiation effects

RADIOBIOLOGY [2,258; 2,258]
BT1 biology
RT biological radiation effects
RT biophysics
RT molecular biology
RT radiation effects
RT radiation injuries
RT radiosensitivity
RT tracer techniques

radiocarbon dating
USE carbon 14
AND isotope dating

RADIOCARDIOGRAPHY [1,158; 1,158]
BT1 cardiography
BT2 diagnostic techniques

radiochemical activation analy
(Use one of the narrower terms of the descriptor below if appropriate.)
USE activation analysis

radiochemical analysis
USE radiometric analysis

radiochemical laboratories
USE hot labs

RADIOCHEMISTRY [2,519; 4,194]
(The chemistry of radioactive materials. Not to be used for RADIATION CHEMISTRY.)
UF *reactor chemistry*
BT1 chemistry
NT1 hot atom chemistry
NT2 szilard-chalmers reaction
RT emanation method
RT nuclear chemistry
RT radiation chemistry

RADIOCHROMATOGRAPHY [784; 78
BT1 chromatography
BT2 separation processes

RADIOCOLLOIDS [1,292; 1,642]
BT1 colloids
BT2 dispersions
NT1 thorotrast
RT gold 198
RT isotope applications
RT radioactive wastes

radiocrystallography
USE crystallography

radiodecomposition
USE radiolysis

RADIODERMATITIS [281; 281]
BT1 dermatitis
BT2 skin diseases
BT3 diseases
BT1 local radiation effects
BT2 biological radiation effects
BT3 biological effects
BT3 radiation effects
BT1 radiation injuries
BT2 biological radiation effects
BT3 biological effects
BT3 radiation effects
BT2 injuries
BT3 diseases

RT radiation burns

radiodiagnosis (radionuclides)
USE diagnosis
AND nuclear medicine

RADIODISINFESTATION [245; 245]
Dec 80
BT1 disinfestation
BT1 irradiation
RT grain disinfestation
RT insects
RT radiosterilization

RADIOECHO [30; 30]
BT1 radiowave radiation
 BT2 electromagnetic radiation
  BT3 radiations

RADIOECOLOGICAL CONCEN-TRATION [4,739; 4,739]
UF *accumulation (radioecological)*
BT1 ecological concentration
RT biological localization
RT buildup
RT contamination
RT ecosystems
RT food chains
RT radioactivity
RT radionuclide migration

RADIOECOLOGY [1,021; 1,021]
BT1 ecology
RT radionuclide migration

radioelectric cells
USE direct collection converters

RADIOENZYMATIC ASSAY [324; 324]
Sep 81
RT enzymes
RT labelled compounds
RT quantitative chemical analysis
RT radioassay

radiofrequency systems
USE rf systems

radiographs
USE images

radiography (auto)
USE autoradiography

radiography (biomedical)
USE biomedical radiography

radiography (industrial)
USE industrial radiography

radiography (micro)
USE microradiography

RADIOIMMUNOASSAY [9,036; 9,036]
UF *ria (radioimmunoassay)*
BT1 immunoassay
BT1 tracer techniques
 BT2 isotope applications
RT antibodies
RT antigen-antibody reactions
RT antigens
RT cpb
RT labelled compounds
RT radioassay
RT radioisotopes
RT somatostatin

RADIOIMMUNODETECTION [652; 652]
Feb 82
BT1 diagnostic techniques
BT1 tracer techniques
 BT2 isotope applications
RT antibodies
RT labelled compounds
RT neoplasms
RT therapy

RADIOIMMUNOLOGY [351; 351]
BT1 immunology
RT biological radiation effects
RT grafts
RT immunity
RT irradiation
RT therapy

radioimmunotherapy
USE immunotherapy
AND radiotherapy

radioinduced reactions
USE radiation chemistry

radioinduction
USE radiation effects

RADIOISOTOPE BATTERIES [530; 628]
UF *batteries (isotopic)*
BT1 direct energy converters
NT1 snap batteries
 NT2 snap 1 battery
 NT2 snap 11 battery
 NT2 snap 13 battery
 NT2 snap 15 battery
 NT2 snap 17 battery
 NT2 snap 19 battery
 NT2 snap 21 battery
 NT2 snap 23 battery
 NT2 snap 25 battery
 NT2 snap 27 battery
 NT2 snap 29 battery
 NT2 snap 3 battery
 NT2 snap 5 battery
 NT2 snap 7 battery
 NT2 snap 9 battery
RT cardiac pacemakers
RT direct collection converters
RT mechanical heart
RT radioisotope heat sources
RT radioisotopes
RT spacecraft power supplies
RT thermoelectric generators

RADIOISOTOPE GENERATORS [1,368; 1,368]
UF *cow-milkers*
UF *generators (radioisotope)*
RT cesium 137
RT daughter products
RT decay
RT diagnostic techniques
RT germanium 68
RT half-life
RT isotope production
RT isotope separation
RT magnesium 28
RT molybdenum 99
RT strontium 90
RT tellurium 132
RT tin 113
RT yttrium 87

RADIOISOTOPE HEAT SOURCES [1,056; 1,056]
UF *heat sources (radioisotope)*
BT1 energy sources
RT energy
RT radioactive wastes
RT radioisotope batteries
RT thermoelectric generators

radioisotope kinetics
USE radionuclide kinetics

radioisotope migration
USE radionuclide migration

RADIOISOTOPE SCANNERS [577; 577]
UF *scanners (radioisotope)*
RT gamma cameras
RT image processing
RT image scanners
RT images
RT positron cameras
RT radiation detectors
RT radioisotope scanning

RADIOISOTOPE SCANNING [2,590; 24,319]
UF *scanning (radioisotope)*
BT1 counting techniques
NT1 scintiscanning
RT cameras
RT emission computed tomography
RT gamma detection
RT nuclear medicine
RT positron computed tomography
RT radioisotope scanners
RT single photon ect

RADIOISOTOPES [8,236; 199,693]
UF *radionuclides*
BT1 isotopes
*NT1 alpha decay radioisotopes
NT1 beta decay radioisotopes
*NT2 beta-minus decay radioisotopes
*NT2 beta-plus decay radioisotopes
*NT2 electron capture radioisotopes
 NT2 iron 45
 NT2 niobium 85
 NT2 vanadium 42
 NT2 vanadium 45
NT1 bone seekers
*NT1 days living radioisotopes
NT1 heavy ion decay radioisotopes
 NT2 carbon 14 decay radioisotopes
  NT3 radium 222
  NT3 radium 223
  NT3 radium 224
  NT3 radium 226
 NT2 magnesium 28 decay radioisotop
  NT3 plutonium 236
  NT3 uranium 234
 NT2 neon 24 decay radioisotopes
  NT3 protactinium 231
  NT3 thorium 230
  NT3 uranium 232
  NT3 uranium 233
  NT3 uranium 234
 NT2 silicon 32 decay radioisotopes
  NT3 plutonium 238
*NT1 hours living radioisotopes
*NT1 internal conversion radioisoto
*NT1 isomeric transition isotopes
*NT1 microsec living radioisotopes
*NT1 millisec living radioisotopes
*NT1 minutes living radioisotopes
*NT1 nanosec living radioisotopes
NT1 neutron-deficient isotopes
NT1 proton decay radioisotopes
 NT2 cesium 113
 NT2 cobalt 53
 NT2 iodine 109
 NT2 lutetium 151
 NT2 scandium 39
 NT2 thulium 147
*NT1 seconds living radioisotopes
*NT1 spontaneous fission radioisoto
*NT1 years living radioisotopes
RT biological localization
RT carrier-free isotopes
RT carriers
RT hutch event
RT natural occurrence
RT nuclear medicine
RT radiation sources
RT radioactive materials
RT radioactivity

RT radioimmunoassay
RT radioisotope batteries
RT radionuclide administration
RT radionuclide kinetics
RT radionuclide migration

RADIOLOGICAL PERSONNEL
[1,682; 1,682]
BT1 personnel
RT biomedical radiography
RT industrial radiography
RT medical personnel

radiological protection
USE radiation protection

RADIOLOGY [1,981; 4,659]
(For the use of radiant energy in medicine.)
BT1 medicine
RT biomedical radiography
RT diagnosis
RT diagnostic techniques
RT nuclear medicine
RT radiotherapy

RADIOLUMINESCENCE [596; 740]
BT1 luminescence
BT2 photon emission
BT3 emission
NT1 radiothermoluminescence
RT scintillations

RADIOLYSIS [11,567; 11,679]
UF *damage (radiation, chemical)*
UF *degradation (radioinduced)*
UF *radiation damage (chemical)*
UF *radiodecomposition*
BT1 chemical radiation effects
BT2 radiation effects
BT1 decomposition
BT2 chemical reactions
NT1 autoradiolysis
RT dissociation
RT g value
RT photolysis
RT radiation chemistry

RADIOMETERS [514; 514]
BT1 radiation detectors
BT2 measuring instruments
RT heterodyne receivers

RADIOMETRIC ANALYSIS
[4,067; 4,067]
(Quantitative analysis for a radioactive component with known specific activity, based on measurement of its absolute disintegration rate.)
UF *radiochemical analysis*
BT1 quantitative chemical analysis
BT2 chemical analysis
RT radiation scattering analysis
RT radioactivity

RADIOMETRIC GAGES [2,279; 2,367]
UF *beta backscattering gages*
BT1 measuring instruments
NT1 electron-capture detectors
RT densimeters
RT level indicators
RT moisture gages
RT nondestructive testing
RT radiometric sorting
RT thickness gages

RADIOMETRIC SORTING [186; 186]
BT1 sorting
RT ore processing
RT radiometric gages

RADIOMETRIC SURVEYS
[1,356; 1,356] *Nov 78*
BT1 geologic surveys
RT aerial prospecting
RT exploration

RADIOMIMETIC DRUGS [83; 103]
BT1 drugs
NT1 neocarcinostatin
RT antimitotic drugs
RT carcinogens
RT dna adducts
RT mutagens

RADIONUCLIDE ADMINISTRATION
[1,518; 1,518]
RT blood-plasma clearance
RT inhalation
RT injection
RT intake
RT intratracheal administration
RT oral administration
RT radioisotopes
RT radionuclide kinetics

radionuclide concentration
USE radioactivity

radionuclide distributions
USE radionuclide kinetics

RADIONUCLIDE KINETICS
[12,728; 12,728]
(For radionuclides in living organisms only; see also TRANSLOCATION.)
UF *contamination (internal)*
UF *internal contamination*
UF *radioisotope kinetics*
UF *radionuclide distributions*
UF *radionuclide metabolism*
UF *radionuclide transfer (in org)*
UF *radionuclide turnover*
UF *transfer (radionuc in organis)*
UF *transport (radionuc in organi)*
UF *transport (radionucl. in biol)*
UF *turnover (radionuclides)*
BT1 kinetics
RT biological half-life
RT biological hot spots
RT biological localization
RT biophysics
RT blood-plasma clearance
RT body burden
RT bone seekers
RT carriers
RT compartments
RT critical organs
RT dose commitments
RT dynamic function studies
RT excretion
RT intake
RT internal irradiation
RT metabolism
RT nonuniform irradiation
RT personnel monitoring
RT radioactivity
RT radioisotopes
RT radionuclide administration
RT retention
RT retention functions
RT tissue distribution
RT tracer techniques
RT transmission
RT unsealed sources
RT uptake
RT whole-body counting

radionuclide metabolism
USE radionuclide kinetics

RADIONUCLIDE MIGRATION
[14,236; 14,236]
(In environment.)
UF *migration (radionuclide)*
UF *radioisotope migration*
UF *radionuclide transfer (in env)*
UF *transfer (environ. radionucl.)*
UF *transport (environ. radionuc.)*
BT1 environmental transport
BT2 mass transfer
RT backfilling
RT biological availability
RT clays
RT diffusion
RT ecosystems
RT environment
RT environmental exposure pathway
RT fallout deposits
RT food chains
RT ground water
RT irrigation
RT particle resuspension
RT radioecological concentration
RT radioecology
RT radioisotopes
RT soils
RT tracer techniques
RT translocation

radionuclide transfer (in env)
USE radionuclide migration

radionuclide transfer (in org)
USE radionuclide kinetics

radionuclide turnover
USE radionuclide kinetics

radionuclides
USE radioisotopes

radiopasteurization
USE radicidation

RADIOPHARMACEUTICALS
[15,456; 15,456]
BT1 drugs
BT1 labelled compounds
BT1 radioactive materials
BT2 materials
RT biological localization
RT bromosulfophthalein
RT diagnosis
RT dual-isotope subtraction tec
RT iodochloroquine
RT methyl tyrosine
RT microspheres
RT nuclear medicine
RT pharmacology
RT pyridoxylideneglutamate
RT scintiscanning

radiophotoluminescent dosemete
USE rpl dosemeters

radiopolymerization
USE chemical radiation effects
AND polymerization

RADIOPRESERVATION [261; 782]
(Prior to August 1985 RADURIZATION was used.)
BT1 irradiation
BT1 preservation
NT1 radurization
RT storage life

RADIOPROTECTIVE SUBSTANCES
[2,374; 6,119]
- UF+ *dose reduction factor*
- UF+ *dose relative factor*
- UF+ *drf*
- BT1 drugs
- BT1 response modifying factors
- NT1 aet
- NT1 bal
- NT1 bufotenine
- NT1 cystamine
- NT1 cystaphos
- NT1 dianabol
- NT1 dtpa
- NT1 gammaphos
- NT1 glutathione
- NT1 hydroxytryptophan
- NT1 kallikrein
- NT1 mea
- NT1 meg
- NT1 mercaptopropylamine
- NT1 mexamine
- NT1 mpg
- NT1 penicillamine
- NT1 royal jelly
- NT1 serotonin
- RT radiation protection
- RT scavenging
- RT tissue extracts

RADIORECEPTOR ASSAY [883; 883]
May 80
- UF *radio-receptor assay*
- UF *rra*
- BT1 tracer techniques
- BT2 isotope applications
- RT bioassay
- RT cell membranes
- RT radioassay

radiorelease analysis
- USE radio-release analysis

radioresistance
- USE radiosensitivity

RADIOSENSITIVITY [12,120; 12,120]
- UF *radioresistance*
- UF *radiosensitivity effects*
- RT biological radiation effects
- RT dose-response relationships
- RT radiation effects
- RT radiobiology
- RT radiosensitizers
- RT response modifying factors
- RT survival curves

radiosensitivity effects
- USE radiosensitivity

RADIOSENSITIZERS [1,683; 2,475]
- BT1 drugs
- BT1 response modifying factors
- NT1 fudr
- NT1 metronidazole
- NT1 misonidazole
- NT1 nem
- NT1 triacetoneamine-n-oxyl
- RT antimitotic drugs
- RT cmni
- RT radiosensitivity
- RT tmpn

RADIOSTERILIZATION [446; 769]
Jul 85
(Prior to August 1985 STERILIZATION was used for the radiosterilization of non-food items.)
- BT1 irradiation
- BT1 sterilization
- NT1 radappertization
- RT isomed
- RT radiodisinfestation
- RT sterile insect release
- RT sterile male technique

radiosterilization (food)
- USE radappertization

radiosurgery
- USE radiotherapy
- AND surgery

RADIOTHERAPY [27,578; 29,665]
- UF *contact radiotherapy*
- UF *high energy radiotherapy*
- UF *plesiotherapy*
- UF *supervoltage radiotherapy*
- UF *teletherapy*
- UF+ *radioimmunotherapy*
- UF+ *radiosurgery*
- BT1 therapy
- BT2 medicine
- NT1 afterloading
- NT1 neutron therapy
- NT2 neutron capture therapy
- RT collimators
- RT cumulative radiation effects
- RT depth dose distributions
- RT fractionated irradiation
- RT irradiation
- RT isodose curves
- RT nuclear medicine
- RT phantoms
- RT radiation source implants
- RT radiology
- RT shutters

RADIOTHERMOLUMINESCENCE
[148; 148] *Dec 80*
- BT1 radioluminescence
- BT2 luminescence
- BT3 photon emission
- BT4 emission
- BT1 thermoluminescence
- BT2 luminescence
- BT3 photon emission
- BT4 emission

radiothorium
- USE thorium 228

RADIOTOXINS [96; 96]
- RT abscopal radiation effects
- RT toxins

RADIOWAVE RADIATION
[7,801; 10,447]
- UF+ *decimeter wave radiat (1-3 dm)*
- UF+ *decimeter wave radiat (3-10dm)*
- UF+ *meter wave radiation*
- UF+ *shf radiation*
- UF+ *solar radiowave radiation*
- UF+ *super high freq radiation*
- UF+ *uhf radiation (lower range)*
- UF+ *uhf radiation (upper range)*
- UF+ *uhf radiation (01-100 ghz)*
- UF+ *uhf radiation (100-1000 mhz)*
- UF+ *ultrahi. fr rad (100-1000 mhz)*
- UF+ *ultrahigh fr rad (01-100 ghz)*
- UF+ *ultrahigh freq rad (lower r.)*
- UF+ *ultrahigh freq rad (upper r.)*
- UF+ *very high frequency radiation*
- UF+ *vhf radiation*
- BT1 electromagnetic radiation
- BT2 radiations
- NT1 long wave radiation
- NT1 luxemburg effect
- NT1 medium wave radiation
- NT1 radio noise
- NT2 atmospherics
- NT2 whistlers
- NT1 radioecho
- NT1 short wave radiation
- NT1 solar radio bursts
- RT cosmic radio sources
- RT critical frequency
- RT polar-cap absorption
- RT radar
- RT radio equipment
- RT rf systems

RADISHES [106; 106]
- BT1 vegetables
- BT2 food

RADIUM [1,301; 1,301]
- BT1 alkaline earth metals
- BT2 metals
- BT3 elements
- RT natural radioactivity

radium a
- USE polonium 218

radium b
- USE lead 214

RADIUM BROMIDES [2; 2]
- BT1 bromides
- BT2 bromine compounds
- BT3 halogen compounds
- BT2 halides
- BT3 halogen compounds
- BT1 radium compounds
- BT2 alkaline earth metal compounds

radium c
- USE bismuth 214

radium c/
- USE polonium 214

radium c//
- USE thallium 210

RADIUM CARBONATES [2; 2]
- BT1 carbonates
- BT2 carbon compounds
- BT2 oxygen compounds
- BT1 radium compounds
- BT2 alkaline earth metal compounds

RADIUM CHLORIDES [16; 16]
- BT1 chlorides
- BT2 chlorine compounds
- BT3 halogen compounds
- BT2 halides
- BT3 halogen compounds
- BT1 radium compounds
- BT2 alkaline earth metal compounds

RADIUM COMPLEXES [14; 14]
- BT1 alkaline earth metal complexes
- BT2 complexes

RADIUM COMPOUNDS [50; 100]
- BT1 alkaline earth metal compounds
- NT1 radium bromides
- NT1 radium carbonates
- NT1 radium chlorides
- NT1 radium fluorides
- NT1 radium oxides
- NT1 radium sulfates

radium d
- USE lead 210

radium e
- USE bismuth 210

radium e//
- USE thallium 206

radium f
- USE polonium 210

RADIUM FLUORIDES [2; 2]
- BT1 fluorides
  - BT2 fluorine compounds
    - BT3 halogen compounds
  - BT2 halides
    - BT3 halogen compounds
- BT1 radium compounds
  - BT2 alkaline earth metal compounds

radium g
USE lead 206

RADIUM IONS [11; 11]
- BT1 ions
  - BT2 charged particles

RADIUM ISOTOPES [311; 4,491]
- NT1 radium 205
- NT1 radium 206
- NT1 radium 207
- NT1 radium 208
- NT1 radium 209
- NT1 radium 210
- NT1 radium 211
- NT1 radium 212
- NT1 radium 213
- NT1 radium 214
- NT1 radium 215
- NT1 radium 216
- NT1 radium 217
- NT1 radium 218
- NT1 radium 219
- NT1 radium 220
- NT1 radium 221
- NT1 radium 222
- NT1 radium 223
- NT1 radium 224
- NT1 radium 225
- NT1 radium 226
- NT1 radium 227
- NT1 radium 228
- NT1 radium 229
- NT1 radium 230
- NT1 radium 231
- NT1 radium 232
- NT1 radium 233
- NT1 radium 234
- RT bone seekers

→ **RADIUM OXIDES** [0; 0] *Sep 91*
- BT1 oxides
  - BT2 chalcogenides
  - BT2 oxygen compounds
- BT1 radium compounds
  - BT2 alkaline earth metal compounds

RADIUM SULFATES [32; 32]
- BT1 radium compounds
  - BT2 alkaline earth metal compounds
- BT1 sulfates
  - BT2 oxygen compounds
  - BT2 sulfur compounds

RADIUM 205 [0; 0] *Apr 88*
- BT1 alpha decay radioisotopes
  - BT2 radioisotopes
    - BT3 isotopes
- BT1 even-odd nuclei
  - BT2 nuclei
- BT1 heavy nuclei
  - BT2 nuclei
- BT1 millisec living radioisotopes
  - BT2 radioisotopes
    - BT3 isotopes
- BT1 radium isotopes

RADIUM 206 [4; 4]
- BT1 alpha decay radioisotopes
  - BT2 radioisotopes
    - BT3 isotopes
- BT1 even-even nuclei
  - BT2 nuclei
- BT1 heavy nuclei
  - BT2 nuclei
- BT1 millisec living radioisotopes
  - BT2 radioisotopes
    - BT3 isotopes
- BT1 radium isotopes

RADIUM 207 [3; 3]
- BT1 alpha decay radioisotopes
  - BT2 radioisotopes
    - BT3 isotopes
- BT1 even-odd nuclei
  - BT2 nuclei
- BT1 heavy nuclei
  - BT2 nuclei
- BT1 radium isotopes
- BT1 seconds living radioisotopes
  - BT2 radioisotopes
    - BT3 isotopes

RADIUM 208 [5; 5]
- BT1 alpha decay radioisotopes
  - BT2 radioisotopes
    - BT3 isotopes
- BT1 even-even nuclei
  - BT2 nuclei
- BT1 heavy nuclei
  - BT2 nuclei
- BT1 radium isotopes
- BT1 seconds living radioisotopes
  - BT2 radioisotopes
    - BT3 isotopes

RADIUM 209 [3; 3]
- BT1 alpha decay radioisotopes
  - BT2 radioisotopes
    - BT3 isotopes
- BT1 even-odd nuclei
  - BT2 nuclei
- BT1 heavy nuclei
  - BT2 nuclei
- BT1 radium isotopes
- BT1 seconds living radioisotopes
  - BT2 radioisotopes
    - BT3 isotopes

RADIUM 210 [8; 8]
- BT1 alpha decay radioisotopes
  - BT2 radioisotopes
    - BT3 isotopes
- BT1 even-even nuclei
  - BT2 nuclei
- BT1 heavy nuclei
  - BT2 nuclei
- BT1 radium isotopes
- BT1 seconds living radioisotopes
  - BT2 radioisotopes
    - BT3 isotopes

RADIUM 211 [6; 6]
- BT1 alpha decay radioisotopes
  - BT2 radioisotopes
    - BT3 isotopes
- BT1 even-odd nuclei
  - BT2 nuclei
- BT1 heavy nuclei
  - BT2 nuclei
- BT1 radium isotopes
- BT1 seconds living radioisotopes
  - BT2 radioisotopes
    - BT3 isotopes

RADIUM 212 [8; 8]
- BT1 alpha decay radioisotopes
  - BT2 radioisotopes
    - BT3 isotopes
- BT1 even-even nuclei
  - BT2 nuclei
- BT1 heavy nuclei
  - BT2 nuclei
- BT1 radium isotopes
- BT1 seconds living radioisotopes
  - BT2 radioisotopes
    - BT3 isotopes

RADIUM 213 [20; 20]
- BT1 alpha decay radioisotopes
  - BT2 radioisotopes
    - BT3 isotopes
- BT1 electron capture radioisotopes
  - BT2 beta decay radioisotopes
    - BT3 radioisotopes
      - BT4 isotopes
- BT1 even-odd nuclei
  - BT2 nuclei
- BT1 heavy nuclei
  - BT2 nuclei
- BT1 internal conversion radioisoto
  - BT2 radioisotopes
    - BT3 isotopes
- BT1 isomeric transition isotopes
  - BT2 radioisotopes
    - BT3 isotopes
- BT1 millisec living radioisotopes
  - BT2 radioisotopes
    - BT3 isotopes
- BT1 minutes living radioisotopes
  - BT2 radioisotopes
    - BT3 isotopes
- BT1 radium isotopes

RADIUM 214 [18; 18]
- BT1 alpha decay radioisotopes
  - BT2 radioisotopes
    - BT3 isotopes
- BT1 electron capture radioisotopes
  - BT2 beta decay radioisotopes
    - BT3 radioisotopes
      - BT4 isotopes
- BT1 even-even nuclei
  - BT2 nuclei
- BT1 heavy nuclei
  - BT2 nuclei
- BT1 radium isotopes
- BT1 seconds living radioisotopes
  - BT2 radioisotopes
    - BT3 isotopes

RADIUM 215 [5; 5]
- BT1 alpha decay radioisotopes
  - BT2 radioisotopes
    - BT3 isotopes
- BT1 even-odd nuclei
  - BT2 nuclei
- BT1 heavy nuclei
  - BT2 nuclei
- BT1 millisec living radioisotopes
  - BT2 radioisotopes
    - BT3 isotopes
- BT1 radium isotopes

RADIUM 216 [22; 22]
- BT1 alpha decay radioisotopes
  - BT2 radioisotopes
    - BT3 isotopes
- BT1 even-even nuclei
  - BT2 nuclei
- BT1 heavy nuclei
  - BT2 nuclei
- BT1 nanosec living radioisotopes
  - BT2 radioisotopes
    - BT3 isotopes
- BT1 radium isotopes

RADIUM 217 [16; 16]
- BT1 alpha decay radioisotopes
  - BT2 radioisotopes
    - BT3 isotopes
- BT1 even-odd nuclei
  - BT2 nuclei
- BT1 heavy nuclei
  - BT2 nuclei
- BT1 microsec living radioisotopes
  - BT2 radioisotopes
    - BT3 isotopes
- BT1 radium isotopes

RADIUM 218 [38; 38]
- BT1 alpha decay radioisotopes
  - BT2 radioisotopes
    - BT3 isotopes
- BT1 even-even nuclei
  - BT2 nuclei
- BT1 heavy nuclei
  - BT2 nuclei
- BT1 microsec living radioisotopes
  - BT2 radioisotopes
    - BT3 isotopes
- BT1 radium isotopes

RADIUM 219 [20; 20]
 BT1 alpha decay radioisotopes
  BT2 radioisotopes
   BT3 isotopes
 BT1 even-odd nuclei
  BT2 nuclei
 BT1 heavy nuclei
  BT2 nuclei
 BT1 millisec living radioisotopes
  BT2 radioisotopes
   BT3 isotopes
 BT1 radium isotopes

RADIUM 220 [35; 35]
 BT1 alpha decay radioisotopes
  BT2 radioisotopes
   BT3 isotopes
 BT1 even-even nuclei
  BT2 nuclei
 BT1 heavy nuclei
  BT2 nuclei
 BT1 millisec living radioisotopes
  BT2 radioisotopes
   BT3 isotopes
 BT1 radium isotopes

RADIUM 221 [23; 23]
 BT1 alpha decay radioisotopes
  BT2 radioisotopes
   BT3 isotopes
 BT1 even-odd nuclei
  BT2 nuclei
 BT1 heavy nuclei
  BT2 nuclei
 BT1 radium isotopes
 BT1 seconds living radioisotopes
  BT2 radioisotopes
   BT3 isotopes

RADIUM 222 [88; 88]
 BT1 alpha decay radioisotopes
  BT2 radioisotopes
   BT3 isotopes
 BT1 carbon 14 decay radioisotopes
  BT2 heavy ion decay radioisotopes
   BT3 radioisotopes
    BT4 isotopes
 BT1 even-even nuclei
  BT2 nuclei
 BT1 heavy nuclei
  BT2 nuclei
 BT1 radium isotopes
 BT1 seconds living radioisotopes
  BT2 radioisotopes
   BT3 isotopes

RADIUM 223 [124; 124]
 UF   actinium x
 BT1 alpha decay radioisotopes
  BT2 radioisotopes
   BT3 isotopes
 BT1 carbon 14 decay radioisotopes
  BT2 heavy ion decay radioisotopes
   BT3 radioisotopes
    BT4 isotopes
 BT1 days living radioisotopes
  BT2 radioisotopes
   BT3 isotopes
 BT1 even-odd nuclei
  BT2 nuclei
 BT1 heavy nuclei
  BT2 nuclei
 BT1 radium isotopes

RADIUM 224 [449; 449]
 UF   thorium x
 BT1 alpha decay radioisotopes
  BT2 radioisotopes
   BT3 isotopes
 BT1 carbon 14 decay radioisotopes
  BT2 heavy ion decay radioisotopes
   BT3 radioisotopes
    BT4 isotopes
 BT1 days living radioisotopes
  BT2 radioisotopes
   BT3 isotopes
 BT1 even-even nuclei
  BT2 nuclei
 BT1 heavy nuclei
  BT2 nuclei
 BT1 radium isotopes

RADIUM 225 [47; 47]
 BT1 beta-minus decay radioisotopes
  BT2 beta decay radioisotopes
   BT3 radioisotopes
    BT4 isotopes
 BT1 days living radioisotopes
  BT2 radioisotopes
   BT3 isotopes
 BT1 even-odd nuclei
  BT2 nuclei
 BT1 heavy nuclei
  BT2 nuclei
 BT1 internal conversion radioisoto
  BT2 radioisotopes
   BT3 isotopes
 BT1 radium isotopes

RADIUM 226 [3,454; 3,454]
 BT1 alpha decay radioisotopes
  BT2 radioisotopes
   BT3 isotopes
 BT1 carbon 14 decay radioisotopes
  BT2 heavy ion decay radioisotopes
   BT3 radioisotopes
    BT4 isotopes
 BT1 even-even nuclei
  BT2 nuclei
 BT1 heavy nuclei
  BT2 nuclei
 BT1 radium isotopes
 BT1 years living radioisotopes
  BT2 radioisotopes
   BT3 isotopes

RADIUM 226 TARGET [56; 56]
 BT1 targets

RADIUM 227 [38; 38]
 BT1 beta-minus decay radioisotopes
  BT2 beta decay radioisotopes
   BT3 radioisotopes
    BT4 isotopes
 BT1 even-odd nuclei
  BT2 nuclei
 BT1 heavy nuclei
  BT2 nuclei
 BT1 minutes living radioisotopes
  BT2 radioisotopes
   BT3 isotopes
 BT1 radium isotopes

RADIUM 228 [574; 574]
 BT1 beta-minus decay radioisotopes
  BT2 beta decay radioisotopes
   BT3 radioisotopes
    BT4 isotopes
 BT1 even-even nuclei
  BT2 nuclei
 BT1 heavy nuclei
  BT2 nuclei
 BT1 internal conversion radioisoto
  BT2 radioisotopes
   BT3 isotopes
 BT1 radium isotopes
 BT1 years living radioisotopes
  BT2 radioisotopes
   BT3 isotopes

RADIUM 229 [9; 9]
 BT1 beta-minus decay radioisotopes
  BT2 beta decay radioisotopes
   BT3 radioisotopes
    BT4 isotopes
 BT1 even-odd nuclei
  BT2 nuclei
 BT1 heavy nuclei
  BT2 nuclei
 BT1 minutes living radioisotopes
  BT2 radioisotopes
   BT3 isotopes
 BT1 radium isotopes

RADIUM 230 [13; 13]
 BT1 beta-minus decay radioisotopes
  BT2 beta decay radioisotopes
   BT3 radioisotopes
    BT4 isotopes
 BT1 even-even nuclei
  BT2 nuclei
 BT1 heavy nuclei
  BT2 nuclei
 BT1 hours living radioisotopes
  BT2 radioisotopes
   BT3 isotopes
 BT1 internal conversion radioisoto
  BT2 radioisotopes
   BT3 isotopes
 BT1 radium isotopes

RADIUM 231 [1; 1]
 BT1 beta-minus decay radioisotopes
  BT2 beta decay radioisotopes
   BT3 radioisotopes
    BT4 isotopes
 BT1 even-odd nuclei
  BT2 nuclei
 BT1 heavy nuclei
  BT2 nuclei
 BT1 minutes living radioisotopes
  BT2 radioisotopes
   BT3 isotopes
 BT1 radium isotopes

RADIUM 232 [7; 7]
 BT1 beta-minus decay radioisotopes
  BT2 beta decay radioisotopes
   BT3 radioisotopes
    BT4 isotopes
 BT1 even-even nuclei
  BT2 nuclei
 BT1 heavy nuclei
  BT2 nuclei
 BT1 minutes living radioisotopes
  BT2 radioisotopes
   BT3 isotopes
 BT1 radium isotopes

RADIUM 233 [1; 1]
 BT1 even-odd nuclei
  BT2 nuclei
 BT1 heavy nuclei
  BT2 nuclei
 BT1 radium isotopes
 BT1 seconds living radioisotopes
  BT2 radioisotopes
   BT3 isotopes

RADIUM 234 [3; 3]
 BT1 even-even nuclei
  BT2 nuclei
 BT1 heavy nuclei
  BT2 nuclei
 BT1 radium isotopes
 BT1 seconds living radioisotopes
  BT2 radioisotopes
   BT3 isotopes

RADON [3,990; 3,990]
 BT1 rare gases
  BT2 nonmetals
   BT3 elements
 RT   natural radioactivity

RADON CHLORIDES [0; 0]
 BT1 chlorides
  BT2 chlorine compounds
   BT3 halogen compounds
  BT2 halides
   BT3 halogen compounds
 BT1 radon compounds
  BT2 rare gas compounds

RADON COMPLEXES [1; 1]
 BT1 complexes

RADON COMPOUNDS [12; 29]
  BT1　rare gas compounds
  NT1　radon chlorides
  NT1　radon fluorides
  NT1　radon oxides

RADON FLUORIDES [14; 14]
  BT1　fluorides
  　BT2　fluorine compounds
  　　BT3　halogen compounds
  　BT2　halides
  　　BT3　halogen compounds
  BT1　radon compounds
  　BT2　rare gas compounds

RADON IONS [7; 7]
  BT1　ions
  　BT2　charged particles

RADON ISOTOPES [283; 3,573]
  NT1　radon 199
  NT1　radon 200
  NT1　radon 201
  NT1　radon 202
  NT1　radon 203
  NT1　radon 204
  NT1　radon 205
  NT1　radon 206
  NT1　radon 207
  NT1　radon 208
  NT1　radon 209
  NT1　radon 210
  NT1　radon 211
  NT1　radon 212
  NT1　radon 213
  NT1　radon 214
  NT1　radon 215
  NT1　radon 216
  NT1　radon 217
  NT1　radon 218
  NT1　radon 219
  NT1　radon 220
  NT1　radon 221
  NT1　radon 222
  NT1　radon 223
  NT1　radon 224
  NT1　radon 225
  NT1　radon 226
  NT1　radon 227
  NT1　radon 228

radon monitors
  USE　emanometers

RADON OXIDES [7; 7]
  BT1　oxides
  　BT2　chalcogenides
  　BT2　oxygen compounds
  BT1　radon compounds
  　BT2　rare gas compounds

RADON 199 [6; 6] *Nov 80*
  BT1　alpha decay radioisotopes
  　BT2　radioisotopes
  　　BT3　isotopes
  BT1　even-odd nuclei
  　BT2　nuclei
  BT1　heavy nuclei
  　BT2　nuclei
  BT1　millisec living radioisotopes
  　BT2　radioisotopes
  　　BT3　isotopes
  BT1　radon isotopes

RADON 200 [3; 3]
  BT1　alpha decay radioisotopes
  　BT2　radioisotopes
  　　BT3　isotopes
  BT1　electron capture radioisotopes
  　BT2　beta decay radioisotopes
  　　BT3　radioisotopes
  　　　BT4　isotopes
  BT1　even-even nuclei
  　BT2　nuclei
  BT1　heavy nuclei
  　BT2　nuclei
  BT1　radon isotopes
  BT2　radioisotopes
  BT3　isotopes

RADON 201 [1; 1]
  BT1　alpha decay radioisotopes
  　BT2　radioisotopes
  　　BT3　isotopes
  BT1　electron capture radioisotopes
  　BT2　beta decay radioisotopes
  　　BT3　radioisotopes
  　　　BT4　isotopes
  BT1　even-odd nuclei
  　BT2　nuclei
  BT1　heavy nuclei
  　BT2　nuclei
  BT1　radon isotopes
  BT1　seconds living radioisotopes
  　BT2　radioisotopes
  　　BT3　isotopes

RADON 202 [4; 4]
  BT1　alpha decay radioisotopes
  　BT2　radioisotopes
  　　BT3　isotopes
  BT1　electron capture radioisotopes
  　BT2　beta decay radioisotopes
  　　BT3　radioisotopes
  　　　BT4　isotopes
  BT1　even-even nuclei
  　BT2　nuclei
  BT1　heavy nuclei
  　BT2　nuclei
  BT1　radon isotopes
  BT1　seconds living radioisotopes
  　BT2　radioisotopes
  　　BT3　isotopes

RADON 203 [2; 2]
  BT1　alpha decay radioisotopes
  　BT2　radioisotopes
  　　BT3　isotopes
  BT1　electron capture radioisotopes
  　BT2　beta decay radioisotopes
  　　BT3　radioisotopes
  　　　BT4　isotopes
  BT1　even-odd nuclei
  　BT2　nuclei
  BT1　heavy nuclei
  　BT2　nuclei
  BT1　radon isotopes
  BT1　seconds living radioisotopes
  　BT2　radioisotopes
  　　BT3　isotopes

RADON 204 [8; 8]
  BT1　alpha decay radioisotopes
  　BT2　radioisotopes
  　　BT3　isotopes
  BT1　electron capture radioisotopes
  　BT2　beta decay radioisotopes
  　　BT3　radioisotopes
  　　　BT4　isotopes
  BT1　even-even nuclei
  　BT2　nuclei
  BT1　heavy nuclei
  　BT2　nuclei
  BT1　minutes living radioisotopes
  　BT2　radioisotopes
  　　BT3　isotopes
  BT1　radon isotopes

RADON 205 [6; 6]
  BT1　alpha decay radioisotopes
  　BT2　radioisotopes
  　　BT3　isotopes
  BT1　electron capture radioisotopes
  　BT2　beta decay radioisotopes
  　　BT3　radioisotopes
  　　　BT4　isotopes
  BT1　even-odd nuclei
  　BT2　nuclei
  BT1　heavy nuclei
  　BT2　nuclei
  BT1　minutes living radioisotopes
  　BT2　radioisotopes
  　　BT3　isotopes
  BT1　radon isotopes

RADON 206 [18; 18]
  BT1　alpha decay radioisotopes
  　BT2　radioisotopes
  　　BT3　isotopes
  BT1　electron capture radioisotopes
  　BT2　beta decay radioisotopes
  　　BT3　radioisotopes
  　　　BT4　isotopes
  BT1　even-even nuclei
  　BT2　nuclei
  BT1　heavy nuclei
  　BT2　nuclei
  BT1　minutes living radioisotopes
  　BT2　radioisotopes
  　　BT3　isotopes
  BT1　radon isotopes

RADON 207 [11; 11]
  BT1　alpha decay radioisotopes
  　BT2　radioisotopes
  　　BT3　isotopes
  BT1　beta-plus decay radioisotopes
  　BT2　beta decay radioisotopes
  　　BT3　radioisotopes
  　　　BT4　isotopes
  BT1　electron capture radioisotopes
  　BT2　beta decay radioisotopes
  　　BT3　radioisotopes
  　　　BT4　isotopes
  BT1　even-odd nuclei
  　BT2　nuclei
  BT1　heavy nuclei
  　BT2　nuclei
  BT1　minutes living radioisotopes
  　BT2　radioisotopes
  　　BT3　isotopes
  BT1　radon isotopes

RADON 208 [28; 28]
  BT1　alpha decay radioisotopes
  　BT2　radioisotopes
  　　BT3　isotopes
  BT1　electron capture radioisotopes
  　BT2　beta decay radioisotopes
  　　BT3　radioisotopes
  　　　BT4　isotopes
  BT1　even-even nuclei
  　BT2　nuclei
  BT1　heavy nuclei
  　BT2　nuclei
  BT1　minutes living radioisotopes
  　BT2　radioisotopes
  　　BT3　isotopes
  BT1　radon isotopes

RADON 209 [15; 15]
  BT1　alpha decay radioisotopes
  　BT2　radioisotopes
  　　BT3　isotopes
  BT1　beta-plus decay radioisotopes
  　BT2　beta decay radioisotopes
  　　BT3　radioisotopes
  　　　BT4　isotopes
  BT1　electron capture radioisotopes
  　BT2　beta decay radioisotopes
  　　BT3　radioisotopes
  　　　BT4　isotopes
  BT1　even-odd nuclei
  　BT2　nuclei
  BT1　heavy nuclei
  　BT2　nuclei
  BT1　minutes living radioisotopes
  　BT2　radioisotopes
  　　BT3　isotopes
  BT1　radon isotopes

RADON 210 [30; 30]
  BT1　alpha decay radioisotopes
  　BT2　radioisotopes
  　　BT3　isotopes
  BT1　electron capture radioisotopes
  　BT2　beta decay radioisotopes
  　　BT3　radioisotopes
  　　　BT4　isotopes
  BT1　even-even nuclei
  　BT2　nuclei
  BT1　heavy nuclei
  　BT2　nuclei
  BT1　hours living radioisotopes

RADON 210

- BT2 radioisotopes
- BT3 isotopes
- BT1 internal conversion radioisoto
- BT2 radioisotopes
- BT3 isotopes
- BT1 isomeric transition isotopes
- BT2 radioisotopes
- BT3 isotopes
- BT1 nanosec living radioisotopes
- BT2 radioisotopes
- BT3 isotopes
- BT1 radon isotopes

RADON 211 [67; 67]

- BT1 alpha decay radioisotopes
- BT2 radioisotopes
- BT3 isotopes
- BT1 electron capture radioisotopes
- BT2 beta decay radioisotopes
- BT3 radioisotopes
- BT4 isotopes
- BT1 even-odd nuclei
- BT2 nuclei
- BT1 heavy nuclei
- BT2 nuclei
- BT1 hours living radioisotopes
- BT2 radioisotopes
- BT3 isotopes
- BT1 internal conversion radioisoto
- BT2 radioisotopes
- BT3 isotopes
- BT1 isomeric transition isotopes
- BT2 radioisotopes
- BT3 isotopes
- BT1 nanosec living radioisotopes
- BT2 radioisotopes
- BT3 isotopes
- BT1 radon isotopes

RADON 212 [46; 46]

- BT1 alpha decay radioisotopes
- BT2 radioisotopes
- BT3 isotopes
- BT1 even-even nuclei
- BT2 nuclei
- BT1 heavy nuclei
- BT2 nuclei
- BT1 minutes living radioisotopes
- BT2 radioisotopes
- BT3 isotopes
- BT1 radon isotopes

RADON 213 [10; 10]

- BT1 alpha decay radioisotopes
- BT2 radioisotopes
- BT3 isotopes
- BT1 even-odd nuclei
- BT2 nuclei
- BT1 heavy nuclei
- BT2 nuclei
- BT1 millisec living radioisotopes
- BT2 radioisotopes
- BT3 isotopes
- BT1 radon isotopes

RADON 214 [12; 12]

- BT1 alpha decay radioisotopes
- BT2 radioisotopes
- BT3 isotopes
- BT1 even-even nuclei
- BT2 nuclei
- BT1 heavy nuclei
- BT2 nuclei
- BT1 nanosec living radioisotopes
- BT2 radioisotopes
- BT3 isotopes
- BT1 radon isotopes

RADON 215 [6; 6]

- BT1 alpha decay radioisotopes
- BT2 radioisotopes
- BT3 isotopes
- BT1 even-odd nuclei
- BT2 nuclei
- BT1 heavy nuclei
- BT2 nuclei
- BT1 microsec living radioisotopes
- BT2 radioisotopes
- BT3 isotopes
- BT1 radon isotopes

RADON 216 [5; 5]

- BT1 alpha decay radioisotopes
- BT2 radioisotopes
- BT3 isotopes
- BT1 even-even nuclei
- BT2 nuclei
- BT1 heavy nuclei
- BT2 nuclei
- BT1 microsec living radioisotopes
- BT2 radioisotopes
- BT3 isotopes
- BT1 radon isotopes

RADON 217 [3; 3]

- BT1 alpha decay radioisotopes
- BT2 radioisotopes
- BT3 isotopes
- BT1 even-odd nuclei
- BT2 nuclei
- BT1 heavy nuclei
- BT2 nuclei
- BT1 microsec living radioisotopes
- BT2 radioisotopes
- BT3 isotopes
- BT1 radon isotopes

RADON 218 [13; 13]

- BT1 alpha decay radioisotopes
- BT2 radioisotopes
- BT3 isotopes
- BT1 even-even nuclei
- BT2 nuclei
- BT1 heavy nuclei
- BT2 nuclei
- BT1 millisec living radioisotopes
- BT2 radioisotopes
- BT3 isotopes
- BT1 radon isotopes

RADON 219 [42; 42]

- BT1 alpha decay radioisotopes
- BT2 radioisotopes
- BT3 isotopes
- BT1 even-odd nuclei
- BT2 nuclei
- BT1 heavy nuclei
- BT2 nuclei
- BT1 radon isotopes
- BT1 seconds living radioisotopes
- BT2 radioisotopes
- BT3 isotopes

RADON 220 [699; 699]

- UF thoron
- BT1 alpha decay radioisotopes
- BT2 radioisotopes
- BT3 isotopes
- BT1 even-even nuclei
- BT2 nuclei
- BT1 heavy nuclei
- BT2 nuclei
- BT1 radon isotopes
- BT1 seconds living radioisotopes
- BT2 radioisotopes
- BT3 isotopes

RADON 221 [7; 7]

- BT1 alpha decay radioisotopes
- BT2 radioisotopes
- BT3 isotopes
- BT1 beta-minus decay radioisotopes
- BT2 beta decay radioisotopes
- BT3 radioisotopes
- BT4 isotopes
- BT1 even-odd nuclei
- BT2 nuclei
- BT1 heavy nuclei
- BT2 nuclei
- BT1 minutes living radioisotopes
- BT2 radioisotopes
- BT3 isotopes
- BT1 radon isotopes

RADON 222 [2,543; 2,543]

- BT1 alpha decay radioisotopes
- BT2 radioisotopes
- BT3 isotopes
- BT1 days living radioisotopes
- BT2 radioisotopes
- BT3 isotopes
- BT1 even-even nuclei
- BT2 nuclei
- BT1 heavy nuclei
- BT2 nuclei
- BT1 radon isotopes

RADON 223 [12; 12] Sep 83

- BT1 beta-minus decay radioisotopes
- BT2 beta decay radioisotopes
- BT3 radioisotopes
- BT4 isotopes
- BT1 even-odd nuclei
- BT2 nuclei
- BT1 heavy nuclei
- BT2 nuclei
- BT1 minutes living radioisotopes
- BT2 radioisotopes
- BT3 isotopes
- BT1 radon isotopes

RADON 224 [25; 25]

- BT1 beta-minus decay radioisotopes
- BT2 beta decay radioisotopes
- BT3 radioisotopes
- BT4 isotopes
- BT1 even-even nuclei
- BT2 nuclei
- BT1 heavy nuclei
- BT2 nuclei
- BT1 hours living radioisotopes
- BT2 radioisotopes
- BT3 isotopes
- BT1 radon isotopes

RADON 225 [7; 7]

- BT1 beta-minus decay radioisotopes
- BT2 beta decay radioisotopes
- BT3 radioisotopes
- BT4 isotopes
- BT1 even-odd nuclei
- BT2 nuclei
- BT1 heavy nuclei
- BT2 nuclei
- BT1 minutes living radioisotopes
- BT2 radioisotopes
- BT3 isotopes
- BT1 radon isotopes

RADON 226 [148; 148]

- BT1 beta-minus decay radioisotopes
- BT2 beta decay radioisotopes
- BT3 radioisotopes
- BT4 isotopes
- BT1 even-even nuclei
- BT2 nuclei
- BT1 heavy nuclei
- BT2 nuclei
- BT1 minutes living radioisotopes
- BT2 radioisotopes
- BT3 isotopes
- BT1 radon isotopes

RADON 227 [4; 4] Jan 87

- BT1 beta-minus decay radioisotopes
- BT2 beta decay radioisotopes
- BT3 radioisotopes
- BT4 isotopes
- BT1 even-odd nuclei
- BT2 nuclei
- BT1 heavy nuclei
- BT2 nuclei
- BT1 radon isotopes
- BT1 seconds living radioisotopes
- BT2 radioisotopes
- BT3 isotopes

RADON 228 [4; 4] *Jul 89*
- BT1 beta-minus decay radioisotopes
- BT2 beta decay radioisotopes
- BT3 radioisotopes
- BT4 isotopes
- BT1 even-even nuclei
- BT2 nuclei
- BT1 heavy nuclei
- BT2 nuclei
- BT1 radon isotopes
- BT1 seconds living radioisotopes
- BT2 radioisotopes
- BT3 isotopes

RADURIZATION [1,281; 1,281]
(Use of irradiation to prolong shelf-life of food.)
- UF food irradiation (radiopreserv
- BT1 food processing
- BT1 radiopreservation
- BT2 irradiation
- BT2 preservation
- RT food
- RT ifip

RAFFINOSE [7; 7]
- BT1 oligosaccharides
- BT2 saccharides
- BT3 carbohydrates
- BT4 organic compounds

RAIL TRANSPORT [432; 432] *Dec 76*
- BT1 land transport
- BT2 transport
- RT railroad cars
- RT routing
- RT vehicles

RAILGUN ACCELERATORS [193; 193]
Sep 81
(Type of macroparticle accelerator to be used in inertial confinement fusion.)
- BT1 impact fusion drivers
- RT impact fusion

RAILROAD CARS [32; 32] *Mar 81*
- BT1 vehicles
- RT rail transport

RAIN [1,036; 1,036]
- BT1 atmospheric precipitations
- NT1 acid rain
- RT droplets
- RT landslides
- RT rain water
- RT snow
- RT washout

RAIN WATER [642; 642]
- BT1 water
- BT2 hydrogen compounds
- BT2 oxygen compounds
- RT rain

rainout
- USE washout

RAJASTHAN-1 REACTOR [213; 213]
(Kota, Rajasthan, India)
- UF *raps-1 reactor*
- BT1 candu type reactors
- BT2 heavy water moderated reactors
- BT3 reactors
- BT2 pressure tube reactors
- BT3 power reactors
- BT4 reactors
- BT2 thermal reactors
- BT3 reactors
- BT1 natural uranium reactors
- BT2 reactors
- BT1 phwr type reactors
- BT2 heavy water cooled reactors
- BT3 reactors
- BT2 heavy water moderated reactors
- BT3 reactors

RAJASTHAN-2 REACTOR [159; 159]
(Kota, Rajasthan, India)
- UF *raps-2 reactor*
- BT1 candu type reactors
- BT2 heavy water moderated reactors
- BT3 reactors
- BT2 pressure tube reactors
- BT3 power reactors
- BT4 reactors
- BT2 thermal reactors
- BT3 reactors
- BT1 natural uranium reactors
- BT2 reactors
- BT1 phwr type reactors
- BT2 heavy water cooled reactors
- BT3 reactors
- BT2 heavy water moderated reactors
- BT3 reactors

RAKE-2 REACTOR [19; 19]
(Central Institute for Nuclear Research Rossendorf, Dresden, Federal Republic of Germany.)
- UF *rossendorf ass. for crit. exp.*
- BT1 research reactors
- BT2 research and test reactors
- BT3 reactors
- BT1 tank type reactors
- BT2 reactors
- BT1 water moderated reactors
- BT2 reactors
- BT1 zero power reactors
- BT2 experimental reactors
- BT3 research and test reactors
- BT4 reactors

raleigh pulstar reactor
- USE pulstar-raleigh reactor

raleigh-ncsc research react.-1
- USE ncscr-1 reactor

RAMAN EFFECT [1,894; 1,894]
- RT raman spectra
- RT raman spectroscopy
- RT scattering
- RT spectra
- RT ultraviolet radiation
- RT visible radiation

RAMAN SPECTRA [2,490; 2,490]
Feb 76
- BT1 spectra
- RT laser spectroscopy
- RT raman effect
- RT raman spectroscopy

RAMAN SPECTROSCOPY [331; 331]
Apr 86
- UF *cars (spectroscopy)*
- UF *coherent anti-stokes raman spe*
- BT1 laser spectroscopy
- BT2 spectroscopy
- RT quantitative chemical analysis
- RT raman effect
- RT raman spectra

RAMJET ENGINES [11; 11]
- BT1 motors

RAMSAUER EFFECT [82; 82]
- UF *ramsauer-townsend effect*
- RT elastic scattering

ramsauer-townsend effect
- USE ramsauer effect

rana
- USE frogs

RANA REACTOR [2; 2]
(National Nuclear Energy Committee, Rome, Italy)
- UF *casaccia rana reactor*
- UF *ispra-2 rana reactor*
- BT1 enriched uranium reactors
- BT2 reactors
- BT1 pool type reactors
- BT2 water cooled reactors
- BT3 reactors
- BT2 water moderated reactors
- BT3 reactors
- BT1 research reactors
- BT2 research and test reactors
- BT3 reactors

RANCHO SECO-1 REACTOR [114; 114]
(Sacramento, California, USA)
- UF *sacramento rancho seco-1 react*
- BT1 pwr type reactors
- BT2 enriched uranium reactors
- BT3 reactors
- BT2 power reactors
- BT3 reactors
- BT2 thermal reactors
- BT3 reactors
- BT2 water cooled reactors
- BT3 reactors
- BT2 water moderated reactors
- BT3 reactors

RANCHO SECO-2 REACTOR [34; 34]
(Sacramento, California, USA)
- UF *sacramento rancho seco-2 react*
- BT1 power reactors
- BT2 reactors

RANDOM PHASE APPROXIMATION [2,647; 2,647]
- RT boson expansion
- RT ericson theory
- RT statistics

RANDOMNESS [1,809; 1,809]
- RT attractors
- RT monte carlo method

RANGE [2,012; 2,012]
(The range of particles and radiations in matter; not for the concepts covered by ENERGY RANGE or INTERACTION RANGE.)
- RT absorption
- RT depth dose distributions
- RT distance
- RT energy losses
- RT stopping power

RANGE FINDERS [30; 359] *Mar 76*
- UF *sonar*
- BT1 measuring instruments
- NT1 radar

RANGER DEPOSIT [185; 185] *Mar 77*
- BT1 uranium deposits
- BT2 geologic deposits
- RT northern territory
- RT uranium ores

RANKINE CYCLE [235; 235]
- BT1 thermodynamic cycles
- RT thermodynamics

RANKINE-HUGONIOT EQUATIONS [91; 91]
- RT shock waves

RANSTAD DEPOSIT [4; 4] *Dec 80*
- BT1 uranium deposits
- BT2 geologic deposits
- RT sweden
- RT uranium ores

RANUNCULACEAE [7; 7]
- UF *buttercups*
- UF *caraway*
- UF *crowfoot*
- UF *delphinium*
- UF *nigella*
- BT1 plants

rapidity
- USE particle rapidity

raps-1 reactor
- USE rajasthan-1 reactor

raps-2 reactor
- USE rajasthan-2 reactor

RAPSODIE REACTOR [223; 223]
(CEA/CEN Cadarache, st. Paul Lez Durance, France)
- UF *cadarache rapsodie reactor*
- BT1 enriched uranium reactors
- BT2 reactors
- BT1 lmfbr type reactors
- BT2 fbr type reactors
- BT3 breeder reactors
- BT4 reactors
- BT3 fast reactors
- BT4 epithermal reactors
- BT5 reactors
- BT2 liquid metal cooled reactors
- BT3 reactors
- BT1 plutonium reactors
- BT2 reactors
- BT1 sodium cooled reactors
- BT2 liquid metal cooled reactors
- BT3 reactors
- BT1 test reactors
- BT2 research and test reactors
- BT3 reactors
- BT2 test facilities

RARE EARTH ADDITIONS [216; 1,534]
- NT1 cerium additions
- NT2 alloy-ni60cr25w15
- NT2 alloy-ni60mo13co9cr8nb4al3
- NT2 alloy-ni67cr19mo5w5ti3
- NT1 dysprosium additions
- NT1 erbium additions
- NT1 europium additions
- NT1 gadolinium additions
- NT1 holmium additions
- NT1 lanthanum additions
- NT2 alloy-co36cr22ni22w15fe3
- NT1 lutetium additions
- NT1 neodymium additions
- NT1 praseodymium additions
- NT1 promethium additions
- NT1 samarium additions
- NT1 terbium additions
- NT1 thulium additions
- NT1 ytterbium additions
- RT rare earth alloys

RARE EARTH ALLOYS [1,009; 8,414]
- BT1 alloys
- NT1 cerium alloys
- NT2 cerium base alloys
- NT3 misch metal
- NT1 dysprosium alloys
- NT2 dysprosium base alloys
- NT1 erbium alloys
- NT2 erbium base alloys
- NT1 europium alloys
- NT2 europium base alloys
- NT1 gadolinium alloys
- NT2 gadolinium base alloys
- NT1 holmium alloys
- NT2 holmium base alloys
- NT1 lanthanum alloys
- NT2 lanthanum base alloys
- NT2 misch metal
- NT1 lutetium alloys
- NT2 lutetium base alloys
- NT1 neodymium alloys
- NT2 neodymium base alloys
- NT1 praseodymium alloys
- NT2 praseodymium base alloys
- NT1 promethium alloys
- NT2 promethium base alloys
- NT1 samarium alloys
- NT2 samarium base alloys
- NT1 terbium alloys
- NT2 terbium base alloys
- NT1 thulium alloys
- NT2 thulium base alloys
- NT1 ytterbium alloys
- NT2 ytterbium base alloys
- RT actinide alloys
- RT rare earth additions

RARE EARTH COMPLEXES [1,841; 5,054]
- BT1 complexes
- NT1 cerium complexes
- NT1 dysprosium complexes
- NT1 erbium complexes
- NT1 europium complexes
- NT1 gadolinium complexes
- NT1 holmium complexes
- NT1 lanthanum complexes
- NT1 lutetium complexes
- NT1 neodymium complexes
- NT1 praseodymium complexes
- NT1 promethium complexes
- NT1 samarium complexes
- NT1 terbium complexes
- NT1 thulium complexes
- NT1 ytterbium complexes

RARE EARTH COMPOUNDS [3,901; 23,651]
- *NT1 cerium compounds
- *NT1 dysprosium compounds
- *NT1 erbium compounds
- *NT1 europium compounds
- *NT1 gadolinium compounds
- *NT1 holmium compounds
- *NT1 lanthanum compounds
- *NT1 lutetium compounds
- *NT1 neodymium compounds
- *NT1 praseodymium compounds
- *NT1 promethium compounds
- *NT1 samarium compounds
- *NT1 terbium compounds
- *NT1 thulium compounds
- *NT1 ytterbium compounds

rare earth elements
- USE rare earths

*RARE EARTH NUCLEI [692; 13,209]
(For specific terms, consult the Appendix.)
- BT1 intermediate mass nuclei
- BT2 nuclei

RARE EARTHS [3,813; 12,812]
- UF *lanthanides*
- UF *rare earth elements*
- BT1 metals
- BT2 elements
- NT1 cerium
- NT2 cerium-alpha
- NT2 cerium-beta
- NT2 cerium-gamma
- NT1 dysprosium
- NT1 erbium
- NT1 europium
- NT1 gadolinium
- NT1 holmium
- NT1 lanthanum
- NT1 lutetium
- NT1 neodymium
- NT1 praseodymium
- NT1 promethium
- NT1 samarium
- NT1 terbium
- NT1 thulium
- NT1 ytterbium
- RT thucholite

RARE GAS COMPOUNDS [37; 1,117]
- NT1 argon compounds
- NT2 argon borides
- NT2 argon chlorides
- NT2 argon fluorides
- NT2 argon hydrides
- NT2 argon iodides
- NT2 argon nitrides
- NT2 argon oxides
- NT1 helium compounds
- NT2 helium carbides
- NT2 helium chlorides
- NT2 helium fluorides
- NT2 helium hydrides
- NT2 helium hydroxides
- NT2 helium nitrides
- NT2 helium oxides
- NT2 helium tritides
- NT1 krypton compounds
- NT2 krypton chlorides
- NT2 krypton fluorides
- NT2 krypton hydrides
- NT2 krypton oxides
- NT1 neon compounds
- NT2 neon chlorides
- NT2 neon fluorides
- NT2 neon hydrides
- NT2 neon iodides
- NT2 neon oxides
- NT1 radon compounds
- NT2 radon chlorides
- NT2 radon fluorides
- NT2 radon oxides
- NT1 xenon compounds
- NT2 xenon bromides
- NT2 xenon chlorides
- NT2 xenon fluorides
- NT2 xenon hydrides
- NT2 xenon hydroxides
- NT2 xenon iodides
- NT2 xenon oxides
- NT2 xenon phosphates

RARE GASES [2,204; 38,899]
- UF *noble gases*
- BT1 nonmetals
- BT2 elements
- NT1 argon
- NT1 helium
- NT1 krypton
- NT1 neon
- NT1 radon
- NT1 xenon
- RT clathrates
- RT emanation method
- RT emanation thermal analysis
- RT gas scintillation detectors
- RT inert atmosphere

RAREFIED GASES [149; 149]
- BT1 gases
- BT2 fluids

RARITA-SCHWINGER THEORY [223; 223]
- RT quantum mechanics
- RT wave equations

raschig rings
- USE column packing

RASPBERRIES [3; 3] *Jun 76*
- BT1 fruits
- BT2 food

RATCHETING [75; 75] *Aug 84*
(Progressive distortion resulting from or enhanced by cyclic loading.)
- BT1 deformation
- RT creep
- RT dynamic loads
- RT mechanical structures
- RT strains
- RT stresses

ratemeters (counting)
  USE   counting ratemeters

ratemeters (dose)
  USE   dose ratemeters

ratemeters (exposure)
  USE   exposure ratemeters

→ *rational surfaces*
  USE   mode rational surfaces

rationing
  USE   allocations

RATS [19,476; 19,476]
  BT1   rodents
    BT2   mammals
      BT3   vertebrates
        BT4   animals

rawalpindi research reactor
  USE   parr reactor

RAYLEIGH SCATTERING [448; 448]
  BT1   coherent scattering
  BT2   scattering

RAYLEIGH WAVES [101; 101]
  RT   earthquakes
  RT   lattice vibrations
  RT   seismic detection
  RT   seismic surface waves
  RT   underground explosions

rayleigh-ritz method
  USE   ritz method

RAYLEIGH-SCHROEDINGER FORMULA [169; 169]
  RT   perturbation theory

RAYLEIGH-TAYLOR INSTABILITY [671; 671]
  BT1   instability
  RT   fluid flow
  RT   hydrodynamics
  RT   plasma macroinstabilities

RAYON [26; 26]
  BT1   polysaccharides
    BT2   saccharides
      BT3   carbohydrates
        BT4   organic compounds
  RT   cellulose
  RT   fibers
  RT   textiles

RAZDAN COMPUTERS [11; 11]
  BT1   computers

RB-1 REACTOR [3; 3]
(Montecuccolino Nuclear Engineering Lab., Univ. of Bologna, Bologna, Italy)
  UF   *montecuccolino rb-1 reactor*
  UF   *reattore bologna-1*
  BT1   enriched uranium reactors
    BT2   reactors
  BT1   graphite moderated reactors
    BT2   reactors
  BT1   research reactors
    BT2   research and test reactors
      BT3   reactors
  BT1   thermal reactors
    BT2   reactors
  BT1   zero power reactors
    BT2   experimental reactors
      BT3   research and test reactors
        BT4   reactors

RB-2 REACTOR [7; 7]
  UF   *montecuccolino rb-2 reactor*
  UF   *reattore bologna-2*
  BT1   argonaut type reactors
    BT2   enriched uranium reactors
      BT3   reactors
    BT2   research and test reactors
      BT3   reactors
    BT2   water cooled reactors
      BT3   reactors
    BT2   water moderated reactors
      BT3   reactors
  BT1   thermal reactors
    BT2   reactors

RB-3 REACTOR [6; 6]
  UF   *montecuccolino rb-3 reactor*
  UF   *reattore bologna-3*
  BT1   heavy water moderated reactors
    BT2   reactors
  BT1   tank type reactors
    BT2   reactors
  BT1   zero power reactors
    BT2   experimental reactors
      BT3   research and test reactors
        BT4   reactors

RBE [2,957; 2,957]
  UF   *relative biological effectiven*
  RT   biological radiation effects
  RT   let
  RT   oxygen enhancement ratio
  RT   quality factor
  RT   radiation effects
  RT   radiation quality

rbmk type reactors
(High-power channel-cooled graphite-moderated reactor type.)
  USE   lwgr type reactors

rbmk-1000 reactor
  USE   leningrad-1 reactor

rbmk-1500 reactor
  USE   ignalinsk-1 reactor

rc-1 reactor
  USE   triga-2-rome reactor

rc-4 reactor casaccia
  USE   ritmo reactor

RCN [13; 13]
(Reactor Centrum Nederland; name changed on 1 August 1976 to Energieonderzoek Centrum Nederland, and documents written after that date should be indexed to ECN.)
  UF   *reactor centrum nederland (pet*
  BT1   ecn
    BT2   netherlands organizations
      BT3   national organizations

RCNP CYCLOTRON [71; 71] *Jun 83*
(Research Center for Nuclear Physics, Osaka University.)
  UF   *res. cent. nuc. phy. cyclotron*
  BT1   heavy ion accelerators
    BT2   accelerators
  BT1   isochronous cyclotrons
    BT2   cyclotrons
      BT3   cyclic accelerators
        BT4   accelerators

re-entry
  USE   reentry

REACTION HEAT [450; 2,578]
  UF   *heat of reaction*
  BT1   enthalpy
    BT2   thermodynamic properties
      BT3   physical properties
  NT1   combustion heat
  NT1   dissociation heat
  NT1   formation heat

REACTION INTERMEDIATES [648; 648] *Mar 83*
  RT   chemical reaction kinetics
  RT   chemical reactions
  RT   photochemistry
  RT   radiation chemistry
  RT   radicals
  RT   transients

REACTION KINETICS [6,273; 42,789]
  UF   *reaction mechanisms*
  UF   *reaction rate*
  BT1   kinetics
  NT1   biochemical reaction kinetics
  NT1   chemical reaction kinetics
    NT2   combustion kinetics
  NT1   nuclear reaction kinetics
  RT   activation energy
  RT   arrhenius equation
  RT   dissociation
  RT   equilibrium

reaction mechanisms
  USE   reaction kinetics

REACTION PRODUCT TRANSPORT [323; 323]
  UF   *helium jet method*
  UF   *transport (reaction product)*
  RT   nuclear reactions
  RT   sampling

reaction rate
  USE   reaction kinetics

REACTIVITY [3,944; 4,025]
  RT   inhour equation
  RT   pile oscillation techniques
  RT   pile replacement techniques
  RT   poisoning
  RT   reactivity coefficients
  RT   reactivity insertions
  RT   reactivity meters
  RT   reactivity units
  RT   reactivity worths
  RT   reactor kinetics
  RT   rod drop method

REACTIVITY COEFFICIENTS [778; 2,320]
  NT1   danger coefficient
  NT1   doppler coefficient
  NT1   power coefficient
  NT1   pressure coefficient
  NT1   temperature coefficient
  NT1   void coefficient
  RT   reactivity
  RT   reactivity insertions
  RT   reactor kinetics

REACTIVITY INSERTIONS [512; 654
  NT1   rod drop accidents
  RT   pulsed reactors
  RT   reactivity
  RT   reactivity coefficients
  RT   reactivity units
  RT   reactivity worths
  RT   reactor kinetics
  RT   rod ejection accidents

REACTIVITY METERS [172; 172]
  RT   reactivity

REACTIVITY UNITS [3; 13]
- NT1 dollars
- NT1 inhours
- RT reactivity
- RT reactivity insertions

REACTIVITY WORTHS [902; 902]
- RT reactivity
- RT reactivity insertions

reactor (fiss) control theory
- USE reactor kinetics

REACTOR ACCIDENTS [15,513; 32,446]
(Includes abnormal conditions of other than major significance sometimes referred to as incidents, events, etc.; for fission reactors only.)
- SF ria (reactor accidents)
- BT1 accidents
- NT1 design basis accidents
  - NT2 atws
  - NT2 maximum credible accident
- NT1 excursions
- NT1 fuel element failure
- NT1 loss of coolant
- NT1 loss of flow
- NT1 meltdown
- NT1 power-cooling-mismatch acciden
- NT1 reactor core disruption
- NT1 rod drop accidents
- NT1 rod ejection accidents
- NT1 transient overpower accidents
- RT burnout
- RT canare
- RT cenna
- RT emergency plans
- RT fuel-coolant interactions
- RT missile protection
- RT molten metal-water reactions
- RT population relocation
- RT pressure suppression
- RT reactor operation
- RT reactor safety
- RT source terms

reactor argentin-0
- USE ra-0 reactor

reactor argentin-1
- USE ra-1 reactor

reactor argentin-2
- USE ra-2 reactor

reactor argentin-3
- USE ra-3 reactor

reactor argentin-5
- USE ra-5 reactor

REACTOR CELLS [568; 568]
- UF cells (reactor)
- RT reactor lattices

reactor centrum nederland (pet
- USE rcn

REACTOR CHANNELS [671; 2,244]
(Passages through reactors.)
- UF channels (reactor)
- BT1 reactor components
- NT1 beam holes
- NT1 experimental channels
- NT1 fuel channels
- RT neutron guides

REACTOR CHARGING MACHINES [747; 747]
- UF *charging machines (fiss react)*
- UF *fueling machines (fiss react)*
- UF *loading machines (fiss react)*
- BT1 reactor components
- RT reactor fueling
- RT remote handling

reactor chemistry
- USE radiochemistry

REACTOR COMMISSIONING [573; 573]
(For fission reactors only.)
- UF *commissioning (reactor)*
- RT national control
- RT reactor decommissioning

REACTOR COMPONENTS [11,108; 66,146]
(For fission reactors only.)
- UF *reactor internals*
- NT1 control elements
  - NT2 regulating rods
  - NT2 scram rods
  - NT2 shim rods
- NT1 control rod drives
- NT1 core catchers
- NT1 fuel elements
  - NT2 annular fuel elements
  - NT2 fuel pins
  - NT2 fuel plates
  - NT2 fuel rods
    - NT3 hollow fuel rods
  - NT2 fuel wires
  - NT2 spent fuel elements
  - NT2 thermionic fuel elements
- NT1 reactor channels
  - NT2 beam holes
  - NT2 experimental channels
  - NT2 fuel channels
- NT1 reactor charging machines
- NT1 reactor cooling systems
  - NT2 direct cycle cooling systems
  - NT2 dual cycle cooling systems
  - NT2 integrated cooling systems
  - NT2 primary coolant circuits
  - NT2 secondary coolant circuits
  - NT2 shrouds
- NT1 reactor cores
  - NT2 coupled reactor cores
  - NT2 heterogeneous reactor cores
- NT1 reactor experimental facilitie
  - NT2 beam holes
  - NT2 experimental channels
  - NT2 in pile loops
  - NT2 rabbit tubes
  - NT2 tristan separator
- NT1 reactor safety fuses
- RT alarm systems
- RT breeding blankets
- RT condensation chambers
- RT containers
- RT containment
- RT control equipment
- RT cooling towers
- RT electrical equipment
- RT electronic equipment
- RT exhaust systems
- RT fins
- RT fluid-structure interactions
- RT heat exchangers
- RT jackets
- RT leak detectors
- RT pumps
- RT reactor materials
- RT shielding materials
- RT shields
- RT sleeves
- RT spacers
- RT vanes

reactor control rods
- USE control elements

REACTOR CONTROL SYSTEMS [6,387; 6,387]
(The processes and operations ensuring the control and safe running of a nuclear fission reactor.)
- SF *monitors (reactor)*
- BT1 control systems
- RT automation
- RT boiling detection
- RT burnable poisons
- RT configuration control
- RT control elements
- RT control rod drives
- RT control rooms
- RT fluid poison control
- RT neutron absorbers
- RT neutron detectors
- RT neutron monitors
- RT on-line control systems
- RT process computers
- RT reactor instrumentation
- RT reactor monitoring systems
- RT reactor safety fuses
- RT thermocouples

REACTOR COOLING SYSTEMS [8,119; 17,709]
(For fission reactors only.)
- UF *cooling systems (fiss reactor)*
- BT1 cooling systems
- BT1 reactor components
- NT1 direct cycle cooling systems
- NT1 dual cycle cooling systems
- NT1 integrated cooling systems
- NT1 primary coolant circuits
- NT1 secondary coolant circuits
- NT1 shrouds
- RT auxiliary water systems
- RT blowers
- RT boilers
- RT bypasses
- RT closed-cycle cooling systems
- RT compressors
- RT condensation chambers
- RT condenser cooling systems
- RT coolants
- RT cooling
- RT demineralizers
- RT dissolved gases
- RT economizers
- RT feedwater
- RT feedwater heaters
- RT fluid flow
- RT fluid-structure interactions
- RT heat exchangers
- RT heat transfer
- RT hot channel
- RT hot spots
- RT ice condensers
- RT loss of coolant
- RT open-cycle cooling systems
- RT pressure tubes
- RT pressurizers
- RT pumps
- RT recombiners
- RT restraints
- RT steam condensers
- RT steam generators
- RT steam jet ejectors
- RT steam lines
- RT steam separators
- RT steam turbines
- RT superheaters
- RT tubes
- RT valves
- RT vapor generators
- RT water chemistry
- RT water supply

reactor cooling systems (fus)
- USE thermonuclear reactor cooling

REACTOR CORE DISRUPTION [2,633; 2,633]
- BT1 reactor accidents
  - BT2 accidents
- RT reactor cores

REACTOR CORE RESTRAINTS
[294; 294]
- BT1 reactor protection systems
- BT1 restraints
- RT reactor cores
- RT reactor safety
- RT supports

REACTOR CORES [13,427; 13,776]
- UF *cores (reactor)*
- BT1 reactor components
- NT1 coupled reactor cores
- NT1 heterogeneous reactor cores
- RT control elements
- RT core catchers
- RT corium
- RT fluid-structure interactions
- RT fuel assemblies
- RT fuel elements
- RT fuel management
- RT in core instruments
- RT moderators
- RT power density
- RT reactor core disruption
- RT reactor core restraints
- RT reactor lattices

REACTOR DECOMMISSIONING
[1,696; 1,696]
(For fission reactors only.)
- BT1 decommissioning
- RT national control
- RT reactor commissioning

REACTOR DISMANTLING [979; 979]
(For fission reactors only.)
- UF *dismantling (fission reactor)*
- BT1 demolition
- RT fuel assembly dismantling
- RT national control

REACTOR EXPERIMENTAL FACILITIE [651; 2,058]
- BT1 reactor components
- NT1 beam holes
- NT1 experimental channels
- NT1 in pile loops
- NT1 rabbit tubes
- NT1 tristan separator

reactor fuel elements
- USE fuel elements

REACTOR FUELING [3,212; 3,274]
(For fission reactors only.)
- UF *charging (fission reactor)*
- UF *discharging (fission reactor)*
- UF *fuel loading (fission reactor)*
- UF *loading (fission reactor)*
- UF *unloading (fission reactor)*
- NT1 batch loading
- RT fuel management
- RT reactor charging machines
- RT reactor operation
- RT remote handling

reactor fueling (fusion reac)
- USE thermonuclear reactor fueling

reactor fuels (fission)
- USE nuclear fuels

reactor fuels (fusion)
- USE thermonuclear fuels

REACTOR INSTRUMENTATION
[3,466; 3,466]
(For fission reactors only.)
- RT acoustic monitoring
- RT control rooms
- RT in core instruments
- RT loose parts monitoring
- RT measuring instruments
- RT reactor control systems
- RT reactor monitoring systems
- RT reactor operation
- RT reactor protection systems
- RT reactor safety
- RT reactor shutdown

reactor internals
(If appropriate, use descriptors for specific components.)
- USE reactor components

REACTOR KINETICS [5,522; 5,522]
(For fission reactors only.)
- UF *control theory (fiss reactor)*
- UF *fission reactor control theory*
- UF *reactor (fiss) control theory*
- BT1 kinetics
- RT burnable poisons
- RT control elements
- RT control rod worths
- RT criticality
- RT delayed neutrons
- RT heterogeneous effects
- RT inhour equation
- RT perturbation theory
- RT poisoning
- RT reactivity
- RT reactivity coefficients
- RT reactivity insertions
- RT reactor kinetics equations
- RT reactor noise
- RT reactor period
- RT reactor physics
- RT reactor simulators
- RT reactor stability
- RT rod drop method

REACTOR KINETICS EQUATIONS
[651; 769]
(For fission reactors only.)
- UF *kinetics equations (reactor)*
- BT1 equations
- NT1 response matrix method
- RT reactor kinetics

REACTOR LATTICE PARAMETERS
[562; 562]
- UF *pitch (reactor parameters)*
- UF *reactor lattice pitch*
- RT homogenization methods
- RT reactor lattices
- RT reactor physics

reactor lattice pitch
- USE reactor lattice parameters

REACTOR LATTICES [1,497; 1,497]
- UF *lattices (reactor)*
- RT configuration
- RT configuration control
- RT fuel elements
- RT power density
- RT reactor cells
- RT reactor cores
- RT reactor lattice parameters
- RT zero power reactors

REACTOR LICENSING [6,469; 6,469]
(For fission reactors only.)
- BT1 licensing
- RT antitrust review
- RT ges fuer reaktorsicherheit
- RT reactor safety

REACTOR MAINTENANCE
[3,978; 3,978]
(For fission reactors only.)
- BT1 maintenance
- RT in-service inspection
- RT inspection
- RT reactor operation
- RT repair

REACTOR MATERIALS [5,776; 24,207]
(For fission reactors only; see also descriptors for specific materials.)
- BT1 materials
- NT1 nuclear fuels
- NT2 denatured fuel
- NT2 fuel slurries
- NT2 gas fuels
- NT2 solid fuels
- NT3 alloy nuclear fuels
- NT3 dispersion nuclear fuels
- NT3 mixed carbide fuels
- NT3 mixed nitride fuels
- NT3 mixed oxide fuels
- NT2 spent fuels
- NT1 nuclear poisons
- NT2 burnable poisons
- NT2 fission poisons
- NT2 soluble poisons
- RT coolants
- RT matrix materials
- RT moderators
- RT neutron absorbers
- RT reactor components
- RT shielding materials

reactor materials (fus react)
- USE thermonuclear reactor material

REACTOR MONITORING SYSTEMS
[1,828; 1,828] *Oct 84*
(Measuring and evaluation systems for performance monitoring of reactor or its components. Not to be confused with REACTOR CONTROL SYSTEMS.)
- SF *monitors (reactor)*
- RT acoustic monitoring
- RT failed element monitors
- RT loose parts monitoring
- RT monitoring
- RT monitors
- RT on-line measurement systems
- RT reactor control systems
- RT reactor instrumentation
- RT temperature monitoring

REACTOR NOISE [1,591; 1,591]
- UF *noise (reactor)*
- RT correlation functions
- RT reactor kinetics
- RT variations

REACTOR OPERATION
[12,950; 13,356]
(For fission reactors only.)
- UF *operation (fission reactor)*
- BT1 operation
- RT fuel element failure
- RT reactor accidents
- RT reactor fueling
- RT reactor instrumentation
- RT reactor maintenance
- RT reactor operators
- RT reactor shutdown
- RT reactor start-up
- RT repair

REACTOR OPERATORS [2,901; 2,90
Feb 81
(For fission reactors only.)
- BT1 personnel
- RT reactor operation

REACTOR OSCILLATORS [35; 35]
- UF *oscillators (reactor)*
- RT pile oscillation techniques

REACTOR PERIOD [142; 142]
- UF *period (reactor)*
- RT reactor kinetics
- RT rossi alpha method

REACTOR PHYSICS [1,468; 1,468]
Feb 78
(Use only for indexing articles of very broad coverage, such as annual reviews or textbooks, dealing with fission reactors.)
- RT neutron slowing-down theory
- RT neutron transport theory
- RT reactor kinetics
- RT reactor lattice parameters
- RT reactor safety

REACTOR POISON REMOVAL [42; 42]
- UF *removal (reactor poison)*
- BT1 removal
- RT nuclear poisons

REACTOR PROTECTION SYSTEMS [2,393; 6,274]
(For fission reactors only.)
- NT1 eccs
  - NT2 core flooding systems
  - NT2 core spray systems
  - NT2 high pressure coolant injectio
  - NT2 low pressure coolant injection
- NT1 reactor core restraints
- RT depressurization systems
- RT equipment protection devices
- RT missile protection
- RT reactor instrumentation
- RT reactor safety
- RT scram
- RT systems analysis

REACTOR SAFETY [30,386; 30,672]
(Theoretical and experimental investigations of the behavior of fission reactor types and designs under various real or hypothetical accidents.)
- BT1 safety
- RT accidents
- RT bethe-tait method
- RT boiling detection
- RT condensation chambers
- RT containment
- RT containment spray systems
- RT criticality
- RT depressurization
- RT fuel densification
- RT fuel element failure
- RT ges fuer reaktorsicherheit
- RT high pressure coolant injectio
- RT hot channel factor
- RT hot spot factor
- RT low pressure coolant injection
- RT maximum credible accident
- RT missile protection
- RT molten metal-water reactions
- RT pressure release
- RT pressure suppression
- RT radiation protection
- RT reactor accidents
- RT reactor core restraints
- RT reactor instrumentation
- RT reactor licensing
- RT reactor physics
- RT reactor protection systems
- RT reactor technology
- RT reactors
- RT reliability
- RT safety engineering
- RT safety standards
- RT site selection
- RT systems analysis

REACTOR SAFETY EXPERIMENTS [3,075; 3,499]
(For fission reactors only.)
- NT1 containment mockup facility
- NT1 containment research installat
- NT1 containment systems experiment
- NT1 nuclear safety pilot plant
- RT eccs

REACTOR SAFETY FUSES [51; 51]
- UF *fuses (reactor safety)*
- BT1 reactor components
- RT reactor control systems
- RT scram

REACTOR SHUTDOWN [2,571; 3,744]
(For fission reactors only.)
- BT1 shutdown
- NT1 scram
- RT after-heat
- RT reactor instrumentation
- RT reactor operation
- RT residual power

REACTOR SIMULATORS [1,660; 1,660]
(For fission reactors only.)
- UF *simulators (fission reactor)*
- BT1 simulators
  - BT2 analog systems
  - BT2 functional models
- RT control rooms
- RT reactor kinetics

REACTOR SITES [3,065; 3,065]
(For fission reactors only.)
- UF *sites (fission reactor)*
- RT environment
- RT external zones
- RT offshore nuclear power plants
- RT offshore sites
- RT on-site power generation
- RT site approvals
- RT site preparation
- RT site selection
- RT site surveys
- RT underground nuclear stations

reactor siting
- USE site selection

REACTOR STABILITY [638; 638]
(For fission reactors only.)
- UF *stability (fission reactor)*
- BT1 stability
- RT frequency response testing
- RT nonlinear problems
- RT nyquist diagrams
- RT reactor kinetics
- RT transfer functions

REACTOR START-UP [1,805; 1,805]
(For fission reactors only.)
- UF *start-up (fission reactor)*
- BT1 start-up
- RT reactor operation

reactor start-up (therm ignit)
- USE thermonuclear ignition

REACTOR TECHNOLOGY [822; 822]
Aug 75
(Use only for indexing articles of very broad coverage, such as annual reviews or textbooks, dealing with fission reactors.)
- RT nuclear engineering
- RT reactor safety
- RT reactors

reactor thermal columns
- USE thermal columns

reactor triga puspati
(Malaysia)
- USE rtp reactor

reactor venezolano-1
- USE rv-1 reactor

REACTOR VESSELS [2,903; 2,903]
(For nonpressurized containers of reactor cores and associated components.)
- UF *vessels (reactor)*
- BT1 containers

REACTORS [3,303; 141,265]
(Fission reactors only. For fusion reactors, use THERMONUCLEAR REACTORS, and for reactors combining both types of reactions, use HYBRID REACTORS.)
- UF *nuclear reactors*
- *NT1 breeder reactors
- NT1 dust cooled reactors
- *NT1 enriched uranium reactors
- *NT1 epithermal reactors
- *NT1 fluid fueled reactors
- NT1 fog cooled reactors
- *NT1 gas cooled reactors
- *NT1 graphite moderated reactors
- *NT1 heavy water cooled reactors
- *NT1 heavy water moderated reactors
- *NT1 homogeneous reactors
- *NT1 hydride moderated reactors
- *NT1 irradiation reactors
- *NT1 liquid metal cooled reactors
- *NT1 metal moderated reactors
- *NT1 mixed spectrum reactors
- *NT1 mobile reactors
- *NT1 molten salt reactors
- *NT1 natural uranium reactors
- *NT1 organic cooled reactors
- *NT1 organic moderated reactors
- *NT1 plutonium reactors
- *NT1 power reactors
- *NT1 production reactors
- *NT1 pulsed reactors
- *NT1 research and test reactors
- *NT1 tank type reactors
- *NT1 thermal reactors
- *NT1 thorium reactors
- *NT1 transportable reactors
- *NT1 water cooled reactors
- *NT1 water moderated reactors
- RT criticality
- RT excursions
- RT fission
- RT fission products
- RT fuel elements
- RT hybrid reactors
- RT natural nuclear reactors
- RT nuclear engineering
- RT nuclear fuels
- RT reactor safety
- RT reactor technology
- RT spent fuels

READOUT SYSTEMS [2,355; 2,355]
- RT data acquisition systems
- RT recording systems

REAGENTS [1,472; 4,176]
- NT1 acetylacetone
- NT1 alizarin
- NT1 aluminon
- NT1 amidol
- NT1 arsenazo
- NT1 bromosulfophthalein
- NT1 cupferron
- NT1 dimethylglyoxime
- NT1 dithiols
  - NT2 bal
  - NT2 unithiol
- NT1 dithizone
- NT1 evans blue
- NT1 ferroin
- NT1 ferron
- NT1 furildioxime
- NT1 morin
- NT1 murexide
- NT1 ninhydrin
- NT1 phenanthroline-ortho
- NT1 pyridylazoresorcinol
- NT1 rhodamines
- NT1 rhodizonic acid
- NT1 rose bengal
- NT1 sensitizers
- NT1 starch
- NT1 thionalide
- NT1 thorin
- NT1 tiron
- NT1 1-nitroso-2-naphthol
- RT reducing agents

REAKTORSICHERHEITSKOMMISSION
[97; 97] *Jan 78*
- BT1 german fr organizations
- BT2 national organizations

REAL TIME SYSTEMS [2,039; 2,039]
- RT analog systems
- RT computer networks
- RT computers
- RT control systems
- RT on-line control systems
- RT on-line systems
- RT process computers
- RT transfer functions

REARING [45; 45]
- RT animal growth
- RT diet
- RT domestic animals
- RT insects
- RT nutrition

reatt. org. sp. pot. zero
- USE rospo reactor

reattore bologna-1
- USE rb-1 reactor

reattore bologna-2
- USE rb-2 reactor

reattore bologna-3
- USE rb-3 reactor

reattore casaccia-1
- USE triga-2-rome reactor

reattore casaccia-4
- USE ritmo reactor

RECEPTORS [5,335; 5,335] *Apr 78*
- RT biochemistry
- RT bioelectricity
- RT central nervous system
- RT endocrine glands
- RT hippocampus
- RT immunity
- RT nerve cells
- RT sense organs
- RT tamoxifen

RECESSIVE MUTATIONS [121; 121]
- BT1 mutations

reciprocal translocations
- USE chromosomal aberrations

RECIPROCAL V LAW [18; 18]
- UF *1/v law*
- RT cross sections

recoil chemistry
- USE hot atom chemistry

recoil distance method
(Method for the determination of lifetimes of nuclear levels.)
- USE charge plunger method

RECOILS [5,165; 5,165]
- RT chemical state
- RT delta rays
- RT fission
- RT hot atom chemistry
- RT knock-on
- RT knock-out reactions
- RT moessbauer effect

- RT proton detection
- RT proton recoil detectors
- RT radiation effects

RECOMBINANT DNA [670; 670] *Jul 84*
- BT1 dna
- BT2 nucleic acids
- BT3 organic compounds
- RT crossing-over
- RT gene mutations
- RT gene recombination

RECOMBINATION [5,572; 5,572]
(Of electrons, holes, ions, radicals or atoms.)
- UF *neutralization (physical)*
- RT electron capture
- RT radiation chemistry

recombination (genetic)
- USE gene recombination

RECOMBINERS [138; 138]
- RT reactor cooling systems
- RT water

RECOMMENDATIONS [7,144; 7,144]
- UF *guidelines*
- UF *radiation protection guides*
- RT agreements
- RT iaea
- RT icrp
- RT icru
- RT implementation
- RT inspection
- RT iso
- RT licensing
- RT manuals
- RT radiation protection
- RT reference man
- RT regulations
- RT regulatory guides
- RT research programs
- RT safety standards
- RT solas convention

recorded information
- USE information

RECORDING SYSTEMS [1,420; 1,420]
- RT counting techniques
- RT data acquisition
- RT data acquisition systems
- RT data processing
- RT electrocardiograms
- RT electronic equipment
- RT measuring instruments
- RT readout systems

records retrieval
- USE information retrieval

recovery (biological)
- USE biological recovery

recovery (tritium)
- USE tritium recovery

RECREATIONAL AREAS [27; 27]
Sep 85
- RT ecosystems
- RT environment
- RT land use
- RT public lands
- RT socio-economic factors

RECRYSTALLIZATION [1,985; 1,985]
- RT annealing
- RT crystallization
- RT grain growth
- RT heat treatments

RECTAL ADMINISTRATION [42; 42]
Oct 75
- BT1 intake
- RT intestinal absorption
- RT uptake

RECTANGULAR CONFIGURATION [575; 708]
- BT1 configuration
- NT1 square configuration
- RT plates

RECTIFIER TUBES [11; 58]
- BT1 electron tubes
- BT1 rectifiers
- BT2 electrical equipment
- BT3 equipment
- NT1 capacitrons
- NT1 ignitrons
- RT thyratrons

RECTIFIERS [195; 306]
- BT1 electrical equipment
- BT2 equipment
- NT1 rectifier tubes
- NT2 capacitrons
- NT2 ignitrons
- NT1 semiconductor rectifiers
- RT dc to dc converters
- RT thyristors

RECTUM [1,373; 1,373]
- BT1 large intestine
- BT2 intestines
- BT3 gastrointestinal tract
- BT4 digestive system
- BT3 organs
- BT4 body
- RT feces
- RT pelvis
- RT proctitis

recurrence relations
- USE recursion relations

RECURSION RELATIONS [1,032; 1,03?]
- UF *recurrence relations*
- RT differential equations
- RT functions

recycle (fuel)
- USE fuel cycle

RECYCLING [926; 926] *May 81*
- RT energy conservation
- RT energy recovery
- RT materials handling
- RT resource conservation
- RT resources
- RT scrap
- RT waste processing
- RT wastes

RED DWARF STARS [185; 185]
- BT1 dwarf stars
- BT2 stars

RED GIANT STARS [810; 810]
- BT1 giant stars
- BT2 stars
- RT helium burning

red level-3 reactor
- USE crystal river-3 reactor

red level-4 reactor
- USE crystal river-4 reactor

red peppers
- USE peppers

RED SEA [29; 29]
  BT1 seas
    BT2 surface waters

RED SHIFT [2,841; 2,841]
  RT astrophysics
  RT cosmology
  RT doppler effect
  RT einstein effect
  RT hubble effect

red wing prairie island-1 reac
  USE prairie island-1 reactor

red wing prairie island-2 reac
  USE prairie island-2 reactor

REDOX POTENTIAL [1,240; 1,240]
  RT oxidation
  RT potentiometry
  RT reduction
  RT valence

REDOX PROCESS [223; 223]
  BT1 reprocessing
    BT2 separation processes
  RT ascorbic acid
  RT coenzymes
  RT cytochromes
  RT oxidoreductases
  RT solvent extraction

reduced nad
  USE nadh2

REDUCING AGENTS [273; 273] *Nov 80*
  RT reagents
  RT reduction

reductases
  USE oxidoreductases

REDUCTION [6,791; 6,880]
(For chemical reactions only; for size or volume change, see COMPRESSION, SHRINKAGE, or CONTRACTION.)
  UF *deoxidation*
  UF+ *disproportionation*
  BT1 chemical reactions
  NT1 bomb reduction
  NT1 thermite process
  RT kroll process
  RT oxidation
  RT oxidoreductases
  RT pyrometallurgy
  RT redox potential
  RT reducing agents

REDUCTIVE EXTRACTION [48; 48]
  BT1 separation processes
  RT molten salt reactors

reductive perturbation method
  USE perturbation theory

REDWING PROJECT [0; 1]
  UF *project redwing*
  NT1 tewa event
  NT1 zuni event
  RT atmospheric explosions
  RT bikini
  RT nuclear explosions
  RT nuclear weapons
  RT surface explosions

REENTRY [189; 189]
  UF *re-entry*
  RT ablation
  RT aerodynamics
  RT missiles
  RT plasma sheath
  RT rockets
  RT space flight
  RT space vehicles

REFERENCE MAN [911; 911]
  UF *standard man*
  RT adults
  RT icrp
  RT man
  RT radiation protection
  RT recommendations

reference materials (bio mark)
  USE biological markers

reference materials (standard)
  USE calibration standards

REFERENCE THETA PINCH REACTOR [48; 48]
  BT1 pulsed d-t reactors
    BT2 d-t reactors
      BT3 thermonuclear reactors
    BT2 pulsed fusion reactors
      BT3 thermonuclear reactors
  RT theta pinch
  RT toroidal theta pinch devices

refinement (grain)
  USE grain refinement

REFINING [784; 1,173]
  SF *processing*
  NT1 electrorefining
  NT1 zone refining
  RT chloride volatility process
  RT extractive metallurgy
  RT fluoride volatility process
  RT ore processing
  RT petroleum products
  RT purification
  RT separation processes
  RT sublimation

reflectance (spectral)
  USE optical properties

REFLECTION [5,068; 6,764]
  NT1 bragg reflection
  RT albedo
  RT backscattering
  RT electrostatic mirrors
  RT greenhouse effect
  RT incidence angle

REFLECTIVE COATINGS [74; 74] *Jan 85*
  BT1 coatings
  RT antireflection coatings
  RT optical properties

REFLECTOR SAVINGS [53; 53]
(A measure of the decrease in the critical size of a reactor as a consequence of the reflector.)
  RT configuration control
  RT critical mass
  RT critical size
  RT criticality
  RT neutron reflectors

reflectors (neutron)
  USE neutron reflectors

reflex switches
(Switches employing a current-conducting plasma for operation.)
  USE plasma switches

REFLEXES [65; 96]
  NT1 conditioned reflexes
  RT behavior
  RT nerves
  RT nervous system
  RT sense organs
  RT spinal cord

REFRACTALOY [10; 10]
  BT1 chromium alloys
    BT2 alloys
  BT1 corrosion resistant alloys
    BT2 alloys
  BT1 heat resisting alloys
    BT2 alloys
  BT1 iron alloys
    BT2 alloys
  BT1 molybdenum alloys
    BT2 alloys
  BT1 nickel alloys
    BT2 alloys

REFRACTION [1,218; 1,218]
  UF *birefringence*
  RT fresnel coefficient
  RT incidence angle
  RT optical dispersion
  RT refractive index
  RT schlieren method
  RT wave propagation

REFRACTIVE INDEX [1,361; 1,361] *May 76*
  UF *index of refraction*
  UF *refractivity*
  BT1 optical properties
    BT2 physical properties
  RT fresnel coefficient
  RT optical dispersion
  RT refraction
  RT wave propagation

refractivity
(Prior to January 1983 this concept was indexed by REFRACTION.)
  USE refractive index

REFRACTORIES [1,283; 1,283]
  RT ablation
  RT asbestos
  RT ceramics
  RT cermets
  RT graphite
  RT heat resisting alloys

REFRIGERANTS [127; 129] *Apr 78*
  RT ammonia
  RT coolants
  RT cryogenic fluids
  RT freons
  RT organic coolants
  RT organic halogen compounds
  RT refrigeration

REFRIGERATION [581; 932]
  BT1 cooling
  NT1 helium dilution refrigeration
  RT magnetic refrigerators
  RT refrigerants

REFRIGERATORS [269; 596] *Apr 80*
  NT1 helium dilution refrigerators
  NT1 magnetic refrigerators
  NT1 thermoelectric refrigerators
  RT cooling systems
  RT cryostats

refuse
  USE solid wastes

regenerating liver
  USE biological regeneration

REGENERATION [209; 209] *Nov 81*
- RT   particle production
- RT   waste processing

regeneration (biological)
- USE   biological regeneration

REGENERATORS [19; 19] *Apr 86*
- RT   heat exchangers
- RT   heat storage
- RT   stirling engines

REGGE CALCULUS [503; 503]
- RT   general relativity theory
- RT   mathematics

REGGE CUTS [549; 549]
- RT   regge poles

REGGE POLES [3,165; 3,165]
- RT   abfst equation
- RT   conspiracy relations
- RT   exchange degeneracy
- RT   linear absorption models
- RT   lorentz poles
- RT   pomeranchuk particles
- RT   pomeranchuk poles
- RT   quantum field theory
- RT   regge cuts
- RT   regge trajectories
- RT   scattering amplitudes
- RT   van hove model

REGGE TRAJECTORIES [1,989; 1,989]
- RT   regge poles

REGIONAL ANALYSIS [982; 982]
(Evaluation of the characteristics of a region and their economic, ecological, or social implications.)
- RT   ecology
- RT   economic analysis
- RT   economics
- RT   environment
- RT   fallout
- RT   geology
- RT   geomorphology
- RT   human populations
- RT   land use
- RT   regional cooperation
- RT   sociology
- RT   water use

REGIONAL COOPERATION [168; 168]
Mar 83
- BT1   cooperation
- RT   ecology
- RT   environment
- RT   government policies
- RT   land use
- RT   local government
- RT   management
- RT   planning
- RT   regional analysis
- RT   state government

regolith
(Prior to December 1990, this was a valid descriptor.)
- USE   overburden

REGRESSION ANALYSIS [890; 890]
Jul 81
- BT1   statistics
- BT2   mathematics
- RT   correlations
- RT   economic analysis
- RT   forecasting

REGULATING RODS [329; 329]
- UF   *fine control rods*
- BT1   control elements
- BT2   reactor components
- RT   neutron absorbers

REGULATIONS [7,501; 10,600]
- BT1   laws
- NT1   contamination regulations
- NT2   maximum acceptable contaminati
- NT1   international regulations
- NT2   oecd mcmsdrw
- NT1   licensing regulations
- NT1   packaging rules
- NT1   pollution regulations
- NT1   safeguard regulations
- NT1   transport regulations
- RT   administrative procedures
- RT   agreements
- RT   deregulation
- RT   enforcement
- RT   government policies
- RT   implementation
- RT   legislation
- RT   legislative text
- RT   licensing
- RT   local government
- RT   national government
- RT   property rights
- RT   radiation protection
- RT   recommendations
- RT   regulatory guides
- RT   reporting requirements
- RT   safety standards
- RT   state government

regulators (voltage)
- USE   voltage regulators

REGULATORY GUIDES [1,320; 1,320]
(Should be used to index all pieces of literature which are regulatory guides.)
- BT1   document types
- RT   legal aspects
- RT   recommendations
- RT   regulations
- RT   us aec

REICH-MOORE FORMULA [61; 61]
- RT   nuclear reactions
- RT   resonance

REID POTENTIAL [690; 690]
- BT1   nucleon-nucleon potential
- BT2   potentials
- RT   nucleon-nucleon interactions

reindeer
- USE   deer

REINFORCED CONCRETE [1,321; 1,321]
- BT1   composite materials
- BT2   materials
- BT1   concretes
- BT2   building materials
- BT3   materials
- BT1   reinforced materials
- BT2   materials
- RT   concrete stringers

REINFORCED MATERIALS [503; 1,938]
- BT1   materials
- NT1   reinforced concrete
- NT1   reinforced plastics
- RT   building materials
- RT   composite materials

REINFORCED PLASTICS [117; 117]
- BT1   reinforced materials
- BT2   materials

relat. heavy ion collid. (bnl)
- USE   brookhaven rhic

relative biological effectiven
- USE   rbe

RELATIVISTIC BEAM INJECTION [455; 455]
- BT1   beam injection

RELATIVISTIC PLASMA [1,362; 1,362]
- BT1   plasma

RELATIVISTIC RANGE [12,225; 12,225]
- BT1   energy range
- RT   relativity theory

RELATIVITY THEORY [3,494; 4,132]
- UF   *special relativity theory*
- BT1   field theories
- RT   cosmology
- RT   dirac equation
- RT   galilei transformations
- RT   joos-weinberg equation
- RT   light cone
- RT   lorentz transformations
- RT   massless particles
- RT   metrics
- RT   negative mass
- RT   relativistic range
- RT   rest mass
- RT   space-time

RELAXATION [5,566; 9,962]
- NT1   muon spin relaxation
- NT1   spin-lattice relaxation
- NT1   spin-spin relaxation
- RT   de-excitation
- RT   relaxation losses
- RT   relaxation time

relaxation (stress)
- USE   stress relaxation

RELAXATION LOSSES [128; 128]
- BT1   energy losses
- RT   dielectric properties
- RT   dipoles
- RT   relaxation

RELAXATION TIME [2,159; 2,159]
Aug 81
- RT   relaxation
- RT   time dependence

RELAYS [299; 299]
- BT1   electrical equipment
- BT2   equipment
- RT   equipment protection devices
- RT   switches
- RT   switching circuits

release (fission product)
- USE   fission product release

RELEASE LIMITS [272; 272]
- RT   radiation hazards
- RT   radioactive wastes
- RT   stack disposal

releasing factors
- USE   liberins

releasing hormones
- USE   liberins

§ **RELIABILITY** [11,999; 11,999]
- RT   accuracy
- RT   amoeba effect
- RT   errors
- RT   failure mode analysis
- RT   failures
- RT   fault tolerant computers
- RT   hazards
- RT   outages
- RT   performance
- RT   quality assurance
- RT   quality control

RT	radiation protection
RT	reactor safety
RT	risk assessment
RT	specifications
RT	systems analysis

relic radiation
    USE   relict radiation

RELICT RADIATION [533; 533] *Apr 84*
(Thermal microwave background radiation of the universe believed to date from the earliest moments of the universe.)
UF	*relic radiation*
BT1	microwave radiation
BT2	electromagnetic radiation
BT3	radiations
RT	background radiation
RT	cosmic radiation
RT	universe

RELIEF VALVES [136; 136] *Feb 76*
UF	*rupture disks*
BT1	valves
BT2	flow regulators
BT3	control equipment
BT4	equipment

relieving (stress)
    USE   stress relaxation

rem
USE	dose equivalents
AND	radiation dose units

REMEDIAL ACTION [1,442; 1,442] *Apr 85*
(Activities conducted to reduce potential radiation exposure to people and potential harm to the environment from radioactive contamination.)
UF	*mine site rehabilitation*
UF	*site rehabilitation*
RT	abandoned sites
RT	decontamination
RT	environmental engineering
RT	land reclamation
RT	radiation doses
RT	radiation protection
RT	tailings
RT	ventilation

REMERSCHEN REACTOR [3; 3] *Jul 76*
BT1	pwr type reactors
BT2	enriched uranium reactors
BT3	reactors
BT2	power reactors
BT3	reactors
BT2	thermal reactors
BT3	reactors
BT2	water cooled reactors
BT3	reactors
BT2	water moderated reactors
BT3	reactors

REMOTE CONTROL [1,479; 1,479]
BT1	control
RT	hydraulic control devices
RT	remote handling
RT	servomechanisms

REMOTE HANDLING [2,436; 2,436]
RT	automation
RT	clean rooms
RT	contact handling
RT	distance
RT	gloveboxes
RT	hot cells
RT	hot labs
RT	man-machine systems
RT	manipulators
RT	materials handling
RT	periscopes
RT	radiation protection

RT	reactor charging machines
RT	reactor fueling
RT	remote control
RT	remote handling equipment
RT	sample changers
RT	sample holders
RT	work

REMOTE HANDLING EQUIPMENT [2,066; 3,290]
BT1	materials handling equipment
BT2	equipment
NT1	cranes
NT1	manipulators
RT	auxiliary systems
RT	hot cells
RT	laboratory equipment
RT	pneumatic transport
RT	remote handling
RT	remote viewing equipment
RT	robots

REMOTE SENSING [865; 865] *Sep 78*
(Techniques for conducting measurements from aeroplanes or satellites such as for geologic exploration.)
RT	aerial prospecting
RT	aerial surveying
RT	exploration
RT	satellites

REMOTE VIEWING EQUIPMENT [806; 806]
BT1	equipment
RT	hot cells
RT	laboratory equipment
RT	lighting systems
RT	optical systems
RT	remote handling equipment
RT	television
RT	video tapes

REMOVAL [2; 34] *Aug 91*
NT1	after-heat removal
NT1	reactor poison removal
NT1	water removal

removal (after-heat)
    USE   after-heat removal

removal (reactor poison)
    USE   reactor poison removal

RENAL CLEARANCE [1,131; 1,131]
BT1	excretion
BT2	clearance
RT	glomeruli
RT	kidneys
RT	metabolism
RT	renography
RT	tubules

rene 41
    USE   alloy-ni55cr19co11mo10ti3

rene 80
    USE   alloy-ni60cr14co10ti5mo4w4al3

rene 95
    USE   alloy-ni58cr14co8al4mo4nb4w4

RENEWABLE ENERGY SOURCES [271; 1,159] *Feb 81*
BT1	energy sources
NT1	biomass
NT1	geothermal energy
NT1	hydroelectric power
NT1	solar energy
NT1	tidal power
NT1	wave power
NT1	wind power
RT	plants

RENIN [203; 203]
BT1	nonspecific peptidases
BT2	peptide hydrolases
BT3	hydrolases
BT4	enzymes
BT5	organic compounds
RT	blood pressure
RT	kidneys

RENOGRAPHY [487; 487] *May 80*
BT1	diagnostic techniques
RT	kidneys
RT	nuclear medicine
RT	renal clearance
RT	tracer techniques

RENORMALIZATION [10,101; 10,599]
NT1	charge renormalization
NT1	mass renormalization
RT	quantum field theory

RENSSELAER CRITICAL FACILITY [14; 14]
BT1	zero power reactors
BT2	experimental reactors
BT3	research and test reactors
BT4	reactors

REPAIR [2,373; 2,373]
RT	maintenance
RT	reactor maintenance
RT	reactor operation

repair (biological)
    USE   biological repair

repair pathways
    USE   biological pathways

REPLICA TECHNIQUES [87; 87]
RT	ceramography
RT	replicas

REPLICAS [79; 79]
RT	crystal models
RT	electron microscopy
RT	replica techniques

REPORTING REQUIREMENTS [293; 293] *Apr 86*
(Also includes the reports generated as a result of the requirements.)
UF	*reports required*
UF	*required reports*
RT	administrative procedures
RT	data acquisition
RT	documentation
RT	information needs
RT	regulations

reports required
    USE   reporting requirements

representations (irreducible)
    USE   irreducible representations

representations (nonunitary)
    USE   nonunitary representations

repressuring
    USE   pressurization

REPROCESSING [5,991; 7,740]
UF	*arco process*
UF	*fuel reprocessing*
SF	*processing*
BT1	separation processes
NT1	airox process
NT1	amex process
NT1	butex process

NT1 chloride volatility process
NT1 civex process
NT1 csrex process
NT1 dapex process
NT1 darex process
NT1 eurex process
NT1 excer process
NT1 fluoride volatility process
NT1 fluorox process
NT1 flurex process
NT1 hermex process
NT1 iodox process
NT1 monex process
NT1 neptex process
NT1 niflex process
NT1 purex process
NT2 halex process
NT2 saltex process
NT1 pyrochemical reprocessing
NT1 redox process
NT1 sulfex process
NT1 talspeak process
NT1 thermox process
NT1 thorex process
NT1 tramex process
NT1 zircex process
NT1 zirflex process
RT cfrp program
RT decladding
RT denitration
RT eurochemic
RT fuel cycle
RT fuel reprocessing plants
RT head end processes
RT nuclear materials management
RT sol-gel process
RT solvent extraction
RT spent fuel elements
RT wackersdorf reprocessing plant
RT wak
RT zone refining

REPRODUCTION [878; 878]
UF *parthenogenesis*
RT adults
RT embryos
RT female genitals
RT fertility
RT fertilization
RT flowers
RT gonads
RT life cycle
RT male genitals
RT mating
RT mutations
RT nests
RT oogenesis
RT ovulation
RT physiology
RT plant breeding
RT pollen
RT population dynamics
RT pregnancy
RT progeny
RT reproductive disorders
RT sex
RT spermatogenesis
RT spores
RT vegetative propagation
RT viability

REPRODUCTIVE DISORDERS
[195; 195]
BT1 urogenital system diseases
BT2 diseases
RT abortion
RT castration
RT fertility
RT menstruation disorders
RT pregnancy
RT reproduction
RT sterility

REPTILES [34; 193]
BT1 vertebrates
BT2 animals
NT1 lizards
NT1 snakes
NT1 turtles

REPUBLIC OF KOREA [395; 395]
UF *korea (south)*
UF *south korea*
BT1 asia
BT1 developing countries

republic of zaire
USE zaire republic

required reports
USE reporting requirements

res. cent. nuc. phy. cyclotron
(Research Center for Nuclear Physics, Osaka University.)
USE rcnp cyclotron

RESCATTERING [535; 535]
BT1 scattering
RT nuclear reaction kinetics
RT nuclear reactions
RT strong interactions

RESEARCH AND TEST REACTORS
[473; 19,169]
BT1 reactors
*NT1 argonaut type reactors
*NT1 experimental reactors
NT1 kalpakkam pfr reactor
NT1 kamini reactor
NT1 maple reactor
NT1 maria reactor
NT1 nuclear furnace reactor
*NT1 research reactors
NT1 super kukla reactor
*NT1 test reactors
*NT1 training reactors
*NT1 triga type reactors
NT1 yayoi reactor

research establishment risoe
USE risoe research establishment

research licenses
(Prior to December 1990, this was a valid descriptor.)
USE licenses

§ **RESEARCH PROGRAMS**
[27,171; 29,479]
(To be used jointly with descriptor(s) for subject field and/or organization concerned.)
NT1 coordinated research programs
NT2 cfrp program
NT2 ifip
RT demonstration programs
RT experiment planning
RT historical aspects
RT information needs
RT laboratories
RT planning
RT recommendations
RT reviews

RESEARCH REACTORS [1,322; 9,722]
BT1 research and test reactors
BT2 reactors
NT1 acpr reactor
NT1 aeg-pr-10 reactor
NT1 aerojet-general nucleonics r
NT1 afrri reactor
NT1 afsr reactor
NT1 agata reactor
NT1 ai-l-77 reactor
NT1 alrr reactor
NT1 anna reactor
NT1 aprf reactor
NT1 apsara reactor
NT1 arbi reactor
NT1 argonaut reactor
NT1 argos reactor
NT1 armf-1 reactor
NT1 astra reactor
NT1 avogadro rs-1 reactor
NT1 barn reactor
NT1 bepo reactor
NT1 ber-2 reactor
NT1 bgrr reactor
NT1 bigr reactor
NT1 bir reactor
NT1 br-02 reactor
NT1 br-1 reactor
NT1 brr reactor
NT1 bsr-1 reactor
NT1 bsr-2 reactor
NT1 cabri reactor
NT1 cesar reactor
NT1 cesnef reactor
NT1 cirus reactor
NT1 clementine reactor
NT1 consort-2 reactor
NT1 coral-1 reactor
NT1 cp-2 reactor
NT1 cp-3 reactor
NT1 cp-5 reactor
NT1 crocus reactor
NT1 democritus reactor
NT1 dhruva reactor
NT1 dido reactor
NT1 diorit reactor
NT1 dmtr reactor
NT1 dow triga-mk-1 reactor
NT1 dr-1 reactor
NT1 dr-2 reactor
NT1 dr-3 reactor
NT1 ebor reactor
NT1 ebr-1 reactor
NT1 eco reactor
NT1 el-1 reactor
NT1 el-2 reactor
NT1 el-3 reactor
NT1 eocr reactor
NT1 eole reactor
NT1 etr reactor
NT1 etrr-1 reactor
NT1 ewa reactor
NT1 f-1 reactor
NT1 fbrf reactor
NT1 fftf reactor
NT1 fir-1 reactor
NT1 fmrb reactor
NT1 fnr reactor
NT1 fr-0 reactor
NT1 fr-2 reactor
NT1 frf reactor
NT1 frg-1 reactor
NT1 frg-2 reactor
NT1 frj-1 reactor
NT1 frj-2 reactor
NT1 frm reactor
NT1 frn reactor
NT1 fursov pile
NT1 gleep reactor
NT1 grenoble reactor
NT1 gtrr reactor
NT1 gulf triga-mk-3 reactor
NT1 harmonie reactor
NT1 hector reactor
NT1 herald reactor
NT1 hero reactor
NT1 hfbr reactor
NT1 hfir reactor
NT1 hfr reactor
NT1 hifar reactor
NT1 hor reactor
NT1 horace reactor
NT1 hprr reactor
NT1 htltr reactor
NT1 htr reactor
NT1 ian-r1 reactor
NT1 ibr-2 reactor
NT1 ibr-30 reactor
NT1 iea-zpr reactor
NT1 iear-1 reactor
NT1 irl reactor
NT1 irr-1 reactor
NT1 irr-2 reactor
NT1 irt reactor
NT1 irt-baghdad reactor
NT1 irt-sofia reactor
NT1 irt-2000 djakarta reactor

NT1	irt-2000 moscow reactor	NT2	slowpoke-wnre reactor	UF	ore reserves
NT1	isis reactor	NT1	sneak reactor	UF+	*fossil fuel reserves*
NT1	ispra-1 reactor	NT1	sora reactor	BT1	resources
NT1	janus reactor	NT1	spert-1 reactor	NT1	coal reserves
NT1	jason reactor	NT1	spr-2 reactor	NT1	thorium reserves
NT1	jeep-2 reactor	NT1	spr-3 reactor	NT1	uranium reserves
NT1	jen reactor	NT1	spr-4 reactor		
NT1	jen-1 reactor	NT1	sr-oa reactor	**RESERVOIR PRESSURE** [19; 19] *Jul 86*	
NT1	jen-2 reactor	NT1	sr-1 reactor	UF	*datum pressure*
NT1	jmtr reactor	NT1	srrc-utr-100 reactor	UF	*formation pressure*
NT1	jrr-1 reactor	NT1	stf reactor	UF	*initial reservoir pressure*
NT1	jrr-2 reactor	NT1	supo reactor	UF	*sand pressure*
NT1	jrr-3 reactor	NT1	taiwan research reactor	UF	*shutin pressure*
NT1	jrr-4 reactor	NT1	tapiro reactor	UF	*static reservoir pressure*
NT1	juno reactor	NT1	tca reactor	UF	*well pressure*
NT1	king reactor	NT1	thetis reactor	RT	aquifers
NT1	kmr reactor	NT1	thor reactor	RT	geologic formations
NT1	kstr reactor	NT1	tibr reactor	RT	ground water
NT1	kuhfr reactor	NT1	toshiba reactor		
NT1	kur reactor	NT1	tr-1 reactor	*reservoirs (water)*	
NT1	la reina rech-1 reactor	NT1	tr-2 reactor	USE	water reservoirs
NT1	lfr reactor	NT1	triga-1-michigan reactor		
NT1	lido reactor	NT1	triton reactor	**RESIDENCE HALF-TIME** [91; 91]	
NT1	lo aguirre rech-2 reactor	NT1	trr-1 reactor	*Dec 82*	
NT1	lptr reactor	NT1	tsr-2 reactor	RT	earth atmosphere
NT1	ltir reactor	NT1	uftr reactor	RT	fallout
NT1	marius reactor	NT1	umne-1 reactor	RT	half-life
NT1	maryla reactor	NT1	umrr reactor	RT	radioactivity
NT1	melusine-1 reactor	NT1	utr-10-kinki reactor		
NT1	minerve reactor	NT1	utrr reactor		
NT1	mitr reactor	NT1	uvar reactor	*residential buildings (apartm)*	
NT1	mnr reactor	NT1	vera reactor	USE	apartment buildings
NT1	mns reactor	NT1	viper reactor		
NT1	moata reactor	NT1	vpi-utr-10 reactor		
NT1	mrr reactor	NT1	wrrr reactor	*residential buildings (houses)*	
NT1	murr reactor	NT1	wsur reactor	USE	houses
NT1	nbsr reactor	NT1	wtr reactor		
NT1	ncscr-1 reactor	NT1	wwr-k-alma-ata reactor	**RESIDUAL INTERACTIONS** [607; 607]	
NT1	nestor reactor	NT1	wwr-m-kiev reactor	BT1	interactions
NT1	nora reactor	NT1	wwr-m-leningrad reactor		
NT1	nru reactor	NT1	wwr-s-bucharest reactor	**RESIDUAL POWER** [99; 99]	
NT1	nrx reactor	NT1	wwr-s-cairo reactor	(Radiation power released by decaying fission products in irradiated nuclear fuel after irradiation has ceased, e.g., after reactor shutdown.)	
NT1	nsrr reactor	NT1	wwr-s-moscow reactor		
NT1	ntr reactor	NT1	wwr-s-prague reactor		
NT1	orphee reactor	NT1	wwr-s-tashkent reactor		
NT1	osiris reactor	NT1	wwr-sm rossendorf reactor	BT1	nuclear power
NT1	owr reactor	NT1	wwr-2 reactor	BT2	power
NT1	parr reactor	NT1	x-10 reactor	RT	after-heat
NT1	pbr reactor	NT1	zebra reactor	RT	reactor shutdown
NT1	pctr reactor	NT1	zeep reactor		
NT1	phebus reactor	NT1	zenith reactor	**RESIDUAL STRESSES** [1,130; 1,130]	
NT1	prnc-l-77 reactor	NT1	zerlina reactor	BT1	stresses
NT1	proteus reactor	NT1	zlfr reactor		
NT1	prtr reactor	NT1	zppr reactor	*residual-heat removal*	
NT1	pstr reactor			USE	after-heat removal
NT1	ptr reactor	**RESERPINE** [52; 52]			
NT1	pulstar-buffalo reactor	BT1	alkaloids	**RESIDUES** [781; 1,517]	
NT1	pulstar-raleigh reactor	BT2	organic compounds	NT1	gangue
NT1	r-a reactor	BT1	antihypertensive agents	NT1	smokes
NT1	r-1 reactor	BT2	cardiovascular agents	NT2	tobacco smokes
NT1	r-2 reactor	BT3	drugs	RT	ashes
NT1	ra-0 reactor	BT1	hypnotics and sedatives	RT	wastes
NT1	ra-2 reactor	BT2	central nervous system depress		
NT1	ra-3 reactor	BT3	central nervous system agents §		
NT1	ra-5 reactor	BT4	drugs	*residues (mathematical)*	
NT1	rake-2 reactor	BT1	indoles	USE	integral calculus
NT1	rana reactor	BT2	pyrroles	AND	singularity
NT1	rb-1 reactor	BT3	azoles		
NT1	rg-1m reactor	BT4	heterocyclic compounds		
NT1	rien-1 reactor	BT5	organic compounds	*residues (radioactive)*	
NT1	rinsc reactor	BT4	organic nitrogen compounds	USE	radioactive wastes
NT1	ritmo reactor	BT5	organic compounds		
NT1	romashka reactor	BT1	sympatholytics	**RESINS** [2,969; 2,969]	
NT1	rp-10 reactor	BT2	autonomic nervous system agent	BT1	organic polymers
NT1	rpt reactor	BT3	drugs	BT2	organic compounds
NT1	rts-1 reactor	BT1	tranquilizers	BT2	polymers
NT1	rv-1 reactor	BT2	psychotropic drugs	RT	araldite
NT1	r2-0 reactor	BT3	central nervous system agents	RT	bakelite
NT1	sbr-1 reactor	BT4	drugs	RT	desiccants
NT1	sbr-2 reactor			RT	ion exchange chromatography
NT1	sbr-5 reactor			RT	ion exchange materials
NT1	sca reactor	*reserve capacity*		RT	matrix materials
NT1	silene reactor	USE	capacity		
NT1	slowpoke type reactors				
NT2	slowpoke-alberta reactor	**RESERVES** [1,471; 1,729]			
NT2	slowpoke-dalhousie reactor	(Available and economically recoverable natural resources.)			
NT2	slowpoke-montreal reactor				
NT2	slowpoke-ottawa reactor				
NT2	slowpoke-toronto reactor				

RESISTANCE WELDING [54; 71]
  BT1 welding
    BT2 joining
      BT3 fabrication
  NT1 flash welding
  NT1 projection welding

resistivity (electric)
  USE electric conductivity

resistivity logging
  USE well logging

resistivity surveys
  USE electrical surveys

RESISTORS [494; 666]
  UF *potentiometers (var resistors)*
  BT1 electrical equipment
    BT2 equipment
  NT1 photoresistors
  NT1 rheostats
  NT1 semiconductor resistors
  RT conductor devices
  RT potentiometers
  RT thermistors

§ **RESOLUTION** [5,697; 20,141]
  NT1 energy resolution
  NT1 linear momentum resolution
  NT1 mass resolution
  NT1 spatial resolution
  NT1 time resolution
  RT accuracy
  RT comparative evaluations
  RT electron microscopy
  RT errors
  RT particle discrimination
  RT performance
  RT sensitivity
  RT signal-to-noise ratio

RESONANCE [12,107; 43,273]
  UF+ *analog resonances (isobaric)*
  NT1 cyclotron resonance
    NT2 azbel-kaner resonance
    NT2 electron cyclotron-resonance
    NT2 ion cyclotron-resonance
  NT1 electric resonance
    NT2 paraelectric resonance
  NT1 fermi resonance
  NT1 giant resonance
  NT1 helicon resonance
  NT1 hybrid resonance
  NT1 intermediate resonance
  NT1 level mixing resonance
  NT1 magnetic resonance
    NT2 eldor
    NT2 electron spin resonance
      NT3 acoustic esr
    NT2 endor
    NT2 ferrimagnetic resonance
    NT2 ferromagnetic resonance
    NT2 nuclear magnetic resonance
      NT3 acoustic nmr
  NT1 nuclear quadrupole resonance
  RT bump-in-tail instability
  RT giant resonance model
  RT harmonics
  RT mode conversion
  RT multilevel analysis
  RT reich-moore formula
  RT resonance fluorescence
  RT resonance integrals
  RT resonance particles
  RT resonance scattering
  RT resonators
  RT synchronization
  RT tuning

RESONANCE ABSORPTION
[1,160; 1,160]
  BT1 absorption

resonance cavities
  USE cavity resonators

RESONANCE ESCAPE PROBABILITY
[49; 49]
  RT dancoff correction
  RT multiplication factors

RESONANCE FLUORESCENCE
[275; 275] *Jul 80*
  BT1 fluorescence
    BT2 luminescence
      BT3 photon emission
        BT4 emission
  RT moessbauer effect
  RT resonance
  RT resonance scattering

RESONANCE INTEGRALS [514; 514]
  BT1 integrals
  RT resonance

RESONANCE IONIZATION MASS SPEC [171; 171] *Mar 86*
  BT1 mass spectroscopy
    BT2 spectroscopy

RESONANCE NEUTRONS [777; 777]
  BT1 neutrons
    BT2 nucleons
      BT3 baryons
        BT4 fermions
        BT4 hadrons
          BT5 elementary particles
  RT fission ratio
  RT intermediate neutrons
  RT intermediate reactors
  RT stein theory

RESONANCE PARTICLES [923; 17,744]
  BT1 hadrons
    BT2 elementary particles
  NT1 exotic resonances
  RT dalitz plot
  RT deck effect
  RT prism plot
  RT resonance

RESONANCE SCATTERING
[1,833; 1,833]
  BT1 inelastic scattering
    BT2 scattering
  RT acoustic esr
  RT acoustic nmr
  RT deep inelastic scattering
  RT resonance
  RT resonance fluorescence

resonance states
  USE energy levels

resonance test reactor savanna
  USE rtr reactor

RESONATING-GROUP METHOD
[800; 800]
  BT1 variational methods
  RT nuclear reaction kinetics
  RT nucleon-nucleon potential
  RT scattering
  RT two-body problem

RESONATORS [421; 3,276] *Sep 79*
  BT1 equipment
  NT1 cavity resonators
    NT2 superconducting cavity resonat
  RT electronic equipment
  RT microwave equipment
  RT oscillators

  RT pulse techniques
  RT resonance
  RT rf systems

resorcin
  USE resorcinol

RESORCINOL [70; 70]
  UF *dihydroxybenzene-meta*
  UF *resorcin*
  UF *1,3-dihydroxybenzene*
  BT1 developers
  BT1 polyphenols
    BT2 phenols
      BT3 aromatics
        BT4 organic compounds
      BT3 hydroxy compounds
        BT4 organic compounds

resource assessment
  USE resources

RESOURCE CONSERVATION [85; 85]
Dec 82
  UF *conservation (resources)*
  RT energy conservation
  RT recycling
  RT resources

resource development
  USE economic development
  AND resources

RESOURCES [749; 1,961] *Aug 76*
(The totality of the discovered and undiscovered quantities of a particular mineral or similar commodity.)
  UF *resource assessment*
  UF+ *geothermal resources*
  UF+ *resource development*
  UF+ *water resources*
  NT1 mineral resources
    NT2 natural gas deposits
    NT2 petroleum deposits
  NT1 reserves
    NT2 coal reserves
    NT2 thorium reserves
    NT2 uranium reserves
  RT recycling
  RT resource conservation

RESPIRATION [1,116; 1,116]
  RT air
  RT anoxia
  RT blood
  RT breath
  RT capillaries
  RT carboxyhemoglobin
  RT diaphragm
  RT hemoglobin
  RT inhalation
  RT krebs cycle
  RT lungs
  RT metabolism
  RT methemoglobin
  RT oxidoreductases
  RT physiology
  RT respirators
  RT respiratory system

RESPIRATORS [203; 203]
  UF *masks*
  UF *respiratory equipment*
  RT aerosols
  RT air
  RT breath
  RT dusts
  RT face
  RT filters
  RT inhalation
  RT protective clothing
  RT radiation protection
  RT respiration
  RT respiratory system

respiratory equipment
   USE   respirators

RESPIRATORY SYSTEM [628; 15,711]
NT1	bronchi
NT1	gills
NT1	larynx
NT1	lungs
NT1	nose
NT1	pharynx
NT1	trachea
RT	air
RT	breath
RT	chest
RT	inhalation
RT	lavage
RT	lung clearance
RT	organs
RT	respiration
RT	respirators
RT	respiratory system diseases

RESPIRATORY SYSTEM DISEASES [2,069; 2,773]
UF+	*bronchogenic carcinoma*
BT1	diseases
NT1	asthma
NT1	bronchitis
NT1	pneumoconioses
NT2	berylliosis
NT1	pneumonia
NT2	bronchopneumonia
RT	emphysema
RT	respiratory system

RESPIRATORY TRACT CELLS [168; 168] *Nov 78*
UF	*lung cells*
BT1	somatic cells
BT2	animal cells
RT	bronchi
RT	lungs

RESPONSE FUNCTIONS [6,507; 6,507]
(Describing the response of a system to external action.)
BT1	functions
RT	electronic circuits
RT	mathematical models
RT	measuring instruments
RT	mechanical structures
RT	structural models

RESPONSE MATRIX METHOD [123; 123]
BT1	reactor kinetics equations
BT2	equations
RT	criticality

RESPONSE MODIFYING FACTORS [6,340; 14,154]
(For biological effects.)
UF	*oxygen effect (radiobiology)*
NT1	radioprotective substances
NT2	aet
NT2	hal
NT2	bufotenine
NT2	cystamine
NT2	cystaphos
NT2	dianabol
NT2	dtpa
NT2	gammaphos
NT2	glutathione
NT2	hydroxytryptophan
NT2	kallikrein
NT2	mea
NT2	meg
NT2	mercaptopropylamine
NT2	mexamine
NT2	mpg
NT2	penicillamine
NT2	royal jelly
NT2	serotonin
NT1	radiosensitizers
NT2	fudr
NT2	metronidazole
NT2	misonidazole
NT2	nem
NT2	triacetoneamine-n-oxyl
RT	adrenalectomy
RT	biological effects
RT	biological recovery
RT	mitogens
RT	oxygen enhancement ratio
RT	radiation effects
RT	radiosensitivity

REST MASS [7,353; 7,353]
BT1	mass
RT	relativity theory

restoration
   USE   biological recovery

RESTRAINTS [267; 441] *Feb 81*
UF+	*pipe restraints*
NT1	reactor core restraints
RT	damping
RT	fasteners
RT	pipe fittings
RT	pipes
RT	reactor cooling systems
RT	shock absorbers
RT	supports

resuspension (particles)
   USE   particle resuspension

§§ **RETENTION** [4,856; 4,856]
(In living organisms.)
RT	biological availability
RT	biological hot spots
RT	biological localization
RT	body
RT	compartments
RT	critical organs
RT	edema
RT	excretion
RT	maximum permissible body burde
RT	organs
RT	radionuclide kinetics
RT	retention functions
RT	tissues
RT	uptake
RT	whole-body counting

RETENTION FUNCTIONS [637; 637]
UF	*excretion functions*
RT	compartments
RT	radionuclide kinetics
RT	retention
RT	time dependence

reticular cells
   USE   reticuloendothelial system

RETICULOCYTES [167; 167]
BT1	erythrocytes
BT2	blood cells
BT3	blood
BT4	body fluids
BT5	biological materials
BT6	materials

RETICULOENDOTHELIAL SYSTEM [441; 441]
UF	*kupffer cells*
UF	*reticular cells*
BT1	tissues
BT2	body
RT	bone marrow
RT	connective tissue
RT	liver
RT	lymph nodes
RT	lymphatic system
RT	macrophages
RT	phagocytosis
RT	spleen

RETINA [530; 530]
BT1	eyes
BT2	sense organs
BT3	organs
BT4	body
RT	nervous system
RT	rhodopsin

retinal pigment
   USE   rhodopsin

RETORTING [31; 31] *Jul 80*
(The process of extracting a desirable substance from a naturally occurring deposit.)
BT1	ore processing
RT	coking
RT	heating
RT	in-situ processing
RT	oil shales
RT	process heat

RETROFITTING [628; 628] *Apr 79*
(Modification during operation of the requirements binding on the operator.)
UF	*backfitting*
RT	construction
RT	licensing regulations
RT	modifications
RT	safety standards

REVEGETATION [119; 119] *Jul 76*
RT	deforestation
RT	ground cover
RT	land reclamation
RT	preferred species

reverse osmosis
   USE   osmosis

REVERSE-FIELD PINCH [1,896; 1,896]
BT1	pinch effect
RT	hbtx devices
RT	magnetic field reversal
RT	reversed-field mirrors
RT	tpe-1rm15 device
RT	zt-p devices
RT	zt-40 devices

REVERSED-FIELD MIRRORS [77; 77] *Nov 82*
UF	*field-reversed mirrors*
UF	*frm reactors (thermonuclear)*
BT1	magnetic mirrors
BT2	open plasma devices
BT3	thermonuclear devices
RT	magnetic field reversal
RT	reverse-field pinch

REVERTANTS [80; 80] *Nov 78*
BT1	mutants
RT	mutations

§§ **REVIEWS** [34,842; 34,842]
(Critical assessment of work and data usually accompanied by an extensive bibliography.)
BT1	document types
RT	research programs

REWETTING [381; 381] *Aug 75*
RT	dryout
RT	heat transfer
RT	hot spots
RT	surfaces

REYNOLDS NUMBER [1,708; 1,932]
NT1	magnetic reynolds number
RT	fluid flow
RT	friction factor
RT	grashof number
RT	turbulent flow
RT	viscous flow

rez lr-0 reactor
  USE   lr-0 reactor

rez tr-0 reactor
  USE   tr-0 reactor

RF SYSTEMS [5,721; 5,721]
  UF   *radiofrequency systems*
  RT   cavity resonators
  RT   cyclic accelerators
  RT   gyrocons
  RT   klystrons
  RT   lasertrons
  RT   magnetrons
  RT   power supplies
  RT   radio equipment
  RT   radiowave radiation
  RT   resonators
  RT   squid devices
  RT   superconducting cavity resonat
  RT   travelling wave tubes
  RT   tuning

→ **RFLPS** [5; 5] *Jul 91*
(Restriction Fragment Length Polymorphisms.)
  BT1   genetic variability
    BT2   biological variability
  RT   chromosomes
  RT   endonucleases
  RT   genes
  RT   genetic mapping
  RT   human chromosomes

→ *rfq (accelerators)*
  USE   quadrupole linacs

RG-1M REACTOR [5; 5]
  UF   *norilsk res. reactor rg-1m*
  BT1   enriched uranium reactors
    BT2   reactors
  BT1   research reactors
    BT2   research and test reactors
      BT3   reactors
  BT1   thermal reactors
    BT2   reactors
  BT1   water cooled reactors
    BT2   reactors
  BT1   water moderated reactors
    BT2   reactors

RHABDOMYOSARCOMAS [188; 188]
  BT1   myosarcomas
    BT2   sarcomas
      BT3   neoplasms
        BT4   diseases

RHAGOLETIS CERASI [5; 5] *Dec 75*
  UF   *cherry fruit fly*
  BT1   fruit flies
    BT2   flies
      BT3   insects
        BT4   arthropods
          BT5   invertebrates
            BT6   animals

RHEINSBERG AKW1 REACTOR [89; 89]
(Gransee, Rheinsberg, Federal Republic of Germany.)
  UF   *akw1 rheinsberg reactor*
  UF   *atomkraftw. rheinsberg akw1 re*
  BT1   pwr type reactors
    BT2   enriched uranium reactors
      BT3   reactors
    BT2   power reactors
      BT3   reactors
    BT2   thermal reactors
      BT3   reactors
    BT2   water cooled reactors
      BT3   reactors
    BT2   water moderated reactors
      BT3   reactors

RHENATES [64; 64]
(Specific compounds should be indexed by coordination of a descriptor of the form (CATION) COMPOUNDS and the above anion descriptor.)
  BT1   oxygen compounds
  BT1   rhenium compounds
    BT2   transition element compounds
  RT   rhenium oxides

RHENIUM [1,057; 1,057]
  BT1   transition elements
    BT2   metals
      BT3   elements

RHENIUM ADDITIONS [76; 76]
(Alloys containing not more than 1% Re are listed here.)
  RT   rhenium alloys
  RT   rhenium compounds

RHENIUM ALLOYS [835; 888]
(Alloys containing more than 1% Re.)
  BT1   alloys
  NT1   rhenium base alloys
  RT   rhenium additions

RHENIUM BASE ALLOYS [46; 46]
  BT1   rhenium alloys
    BT2   alloys

RHENIUM BORIDES [19; 19]
  BT1   borides
    BT2   boron compounds
  BT1   rhenium compounds
    BT2   transition element compounds

RHENIUM BROMIDES [24; 24]
  BT1   bromides
    BT2   bromine compounds
      BT3   halogen compounds
    BT2   halides
      BT3   halogen compounds
  BT1   rhenium halides
    BT2   halides
      BT3   halogen compounds
    BT2   rhenium compounds
      BT3   transition element compounds

RHENIUM CARBIDES [15; 15]
  BT1   carbides
    BT2   carbon compounds
  BT1   rhenium compounds
    BT2   transition element compounds

→ **RHENIUM CARBONATES** [0; 0] *Sep 91*
  BT1   carbonates
    BT2   carbon compounds
    BT2   oxygen compounds
  BT1   rhenium compounds
    BT2   transition element compounds

RHENIUM CHLORIDES [83; 83]
  BT1   chlorides
    BT2   chlorine compounds
      BT3   halogen compounds
    BT2   halides
      BT3   halogen compounds
  BT1   rhenium halides
    BT2   halides
      BT3   halogen compounds
    BT2   rhenium compounds
      BT3   transition element compounds

RHENIUM COMPLEXES [577; 577]
  BT1   transition element complexes
    BT2   complexes

RHENIUM COMPOUNDS [338; 1,044]
  BT1   transition element compounds
  NT1   perrhenates
  NT1   rhenates
  NT1   rhenium borides
  NT1   rhenium carbides
  NT1   rhenium carbonates
  NT1   rhenium halides
    NT2   rhenium bromides
    NT2   rhenium chlorides
    NT2   rhenium fluorides
    NT2   rhenium iodides
  NT1   rhenium hydrides
  NT1   rhenium hydroxides
  NT1   rhenium nitrides
  NT1   rhenium oxides
  NT1   rhenium selenides
  NT1   rhenium silicides
  NT1   rhenium sulfates
  NT1   rhenium sulfides
  NT1   rhenium tellurides
  RT   rhenium additions

RHENIUM FLUORIDES [37; 37]
  BT1   fluorides
    BT2   fluorine compounds
      BT3   halogen compounds
    BT2   halides
      BT3   halogen compounds
  BT1   rhenium halides
    BT2   halides
      BT3   halogen compounds
    BT2   rhenium compounds
      BT3   transition element compound

→ **RHENIUM HALIDES** [0; 0] *Sep 91*
  BT1   halides
    BT2   halogen compounds
  BT1   rhenium compounds
    BT2   transition element compounds
  NT1   rhenium bromides
  NT1   rhenium chlorides
  NT1   rhenium fluorides
  NT1   rhenium iodides

RHENIUM HYDRIDES [11; 11] *Nov 7*
  BT1   hydrides
    BT2   hydrogen compounds
  BT1   rhenium compounds
    BT2   transition element compounds

RHENIUM HYDROXIDES [4; 4] *Dec*
  BT1   hydroxides
    BT2   hydrogen compounds
    BT2   oxygen compounds
  BT1   rhenium compounds
    BT2   transition element compounds

RHENIUM IODIDES [8; 8] *Jan 79*
  BT1   iodides
    BT2   halides
      BT3   halogen compounds
    BT2   iodine compounds
      BT3   halogen compounds
  BT1   rhenium halides
    BT2   halides
      BT3   halogen compounds
    BT2   rhenium compounds
      BT3   transition element compoun

RHENIUM IONS [26; 26]
  BT1   ions
    BT2   charged particles

RHENIUM ISOTOPES [83; 717]
  NT1   rhenium 161
  NT1   rhenium 162
  NT1   rhenium 163
  NT1   rhenium 164
  NT1   rhenium 165
  NT1   rhenium 166
  NT1   rhenium 167
  NT1   rhenium 168
  NT1   rhenium 169
  NT1   rhenium 170
  NT1   rhenium 171
  NT1   rhenium 172
  NT1   rhenium 173
  NT1   rhenium 174
  NT1   rhenium 175
  NT1   rhenium 176
  NT1   rhenium 177
  NT1   rhenium 178
  NT1   rhenium 179
  NT1   rhenium 180

NT1 rhenium 181
 NT1 rhenium 182
 NT1 rhenium 183
 NT1 rhenium 184
 NT1 rhenium 185
 NT1 rhenium 186
 NT1 rhenium 187
 NT1 rhenium 188
 NT1 rhenium 189
 NT1 rhenium 190
 NT1 rhenium 191
 NT1 rhenium 192

RHENIUM NITRIDES [6; 6] *Jun 77*
 BT1 nitrides
 BT2 nitrogen compounds
 BT2 pnictides
 BT1 rhenium compounds
 BT2 transition element compounds

RHENIUM ORES [3; 3]
 BT1 ores

RHENIUM OXIDES [188; 188]
 BT1 oxides
 BT2 chalcogenides
 BT2 oxygen compounds
 BT1 rhenium compounds
 BT2 transition element compounds
 RT perrhenates
 RT rhenates

RHENIUM SELENIDES [0; 0] *Sep 91*
 BT1 rhenium compounds
 BT2 transition element compounds
 BT1 selenides
 BT2 chalcogenides
 BT2 selenium compounds

RHENIUM SILICIDES [21; 21] *Nov 78*
 BT1 rhenium compounds
 BT2 transition element compounds
 BT1 silicides
 BT2 silicon compounds

RHENIUM SULFATES [5; 5] *Mar 77*
 BT1 rhenium compounds
 BT2 transition element compounds
 BT1 sulfates
 BT2 oxygen compounds
 BT2 sulfur compounds

RHENIUM SULFIDES [75; 75]
 BT1 rhenium compounds
 BT2 transition element compounds
 BT1 sulfides
 BT2 chalcogenides
 BT2 sulfur compounds

RHENIUM TELLURIDES [0; 0] *Sep 91*
 BT1 rhenium compounds
 BT2 transition element compounds
 BT1 tellurides
 BT2 chalcogenides
 BT2 tellurium compounds

RHENIUM 161 [4; 4] *Sep 79*
 BT1 alpha decay radioisotopes
 BT2 radioisotopes
 BT3 isotopes
 BT1 intermediate mass nuclei
 BT2 nuclei
 BT1 millisec living radioisotopes
 BT2 radioisotopes
 BT3 isotopes
 BT1 odd-even nuclei
 BT2 nuclei
 BT1 rhenium isotopes

RHENIUM 162 [3; 3] *Sep 79*
 BT1 alpha decay radioisotopes
 BT2 radioisotopes
 BT3 isotopes
 BT1 intermediate mass nuclei
 BT2 nuclei

 BT1 millisec living radioisotopes
 BT2 radioisotopes
 BT3 isotopes
 BT1 odd-odd nuclei
 BT2 nuclei
 BT1 rhenium isotopes

RHENIUM 163 [4; 4] *Sep 79*
 BT1 alpha decay radioisotopes
 BT2 radioisotopes
 BT3 isotopes
 BT1 electron capture radioisotopes
 BT2 beta decay radioisotopes
 BT3 radioisotopes
 BT4 isotopes
 BT1 intermediate mass nuclei
 BT2 nuclei
 BT1 millisec living radioisotopes
 BT2 radioisotopes
 BT3 isotopes
 BT1 odd-even nuclei
 BT2 nuclei
 BT1 rhenium isotopes

RHENIUM 164 [3; 3] *Sep 79*
 BT1 alpha decay radioisotopes
 BT2 radioisotopes
 BT3 isotopes
 BT1 electron capture radioisotopes
 BT2 beta decay radioisotopes
 BT3 radioisotopes
 BT4 isotopes
 BT1 intermediate mass nuclei
 BT2 nuclei
 BT1 millisec living radioisotopes
 BT2 radioisotopes
 BT3 isotopes
 BT1 odd-odd nuclei
 BT2 nuclei
 BT1 rhenium isotopes

RHENIUM 165 [2; 2] *Sep 83*
 BT1 alpha decay radioisotopes
 BT2 radioisotopes
 BT3 isotopes
 BT1 beta-plus decay radioisotopes
 BT2 beta decay radioisotopes
 BT3 radioisotopes
 BT4 isotopes
 BT1 electron capture radioisotopes
 BT2 beta decay radioisotopes
 BT3 radioisotopes
 BT4 isotopes
 BT1 intermediate mass nuclei
 BT2 nuclei
 BT1 odd-even nuclei
 BT2 nuclei
 BT1 rhenium isotopes
 BT1 seconds living radioisotopes
 BT2 radioisotopes
 BT3 isotopes

RHENIUM 166 [7; 7] *Apr 79*
 BT1 alpha decay radioisotopes
 BT2 radioisotopes
 BT3 isotopes
 BT1 intermediate mass nuclei
 BT2 nuclei
 BT1 odd-odd nuclei
 BT2 nuclei
 BT1 rhenium isotopes
 BT1 seconds living radioisotopes
 BT2 radioisotopes
 BT3 isotopes

RHENIUM 167 [7; 7] *Apr 79*
 BT1 alpha decay radioisotopes
 BT2 radioisotopes
 BT3 isotopes
 BT1 intermediate mass nuclei
 BT2 nuclei
 BT1 odd-even nuclei
 BT2 nuclei
 BT1 rhenium isotopes
 BT1 seconds living radioisotopes
 BT2 radioisotopes
 BT3 isotopes

RHENIUM 168 [8; 8] *Nov 78*
 BT1 alpha decay radioisotopes
 BT2 radioisotopes
 BT3 isotopes
 BT1 electron capture radioisotopes
 BT2 beta decay radioisotopes
 BT3 radioisotopes
 BT4 isotopes
 BT1 intermediate mass nuclei
 BT2 nuclei
 BT1 odd-odd nuclei
 BT2 nuclei
 BT1 rhenium isotopes
 BT1 seconds living radioisotopes
 BT2 radioisotopes
 BT3 isotopes

RHENIUM 169 [5; 5] *Nov 78*
 BT1 alpha decay radioisotopes
 BT2 radioisotopes
 BT3 isotopes
 BT1 intermediate mass nuclei
 BT2 nuclei
 BT1 odd-even nuclei
 BT2 nuclei
 BT1 rhenium isotopes
 BT1 seconds living radioisotopes
 BT2 radioisotopes
 BT3 isotopes

RHENIUM 170 [9; 9]
 BT1 beta-plus decay radioisotopes
 BT2 beta decay radioisotopes
 BT3 radioisotopes
 BT4 isotopes
 BT1 electron capture radioisotopes
 BT2 beta decay radioisotopes
 BT3 radioisotopes
 BT4 isotopes
 BT1 intermediate mass nuclei
 BT2 nuclei
 BT1 odd-odd nuclei
 BT2 nuclei
 BT1 rhenium isotopes
 BT1 seconds living radioisotopes
 BT2 radioisotopes
 BT3 isotopes

RHENIUM 171 [9; 9] *Sep 87*
 BT1 beta-plus decay radioisotopes
 BT2 beta decay radioisotopes
 BT3 radioisotopes
 BT4 isotopes
 BT1 electron capture radioisotopes
 BT2 beta decay radioisotopes
 BT3 radioisotopes
 BT4 isotopes
 BT1 intermediate mass nuclei
 BT2 nuclei
 BT1 odd-even nuclei
 BT2 nuclei
 BT1 rhenium isotopes
 BT1 seconds living radioisotopes
 BT2 radioisotopes
 BT3 isotopes

RHENIUM 172 [9; 9]
 BT1 beta-plus decay radioisotopes
 BT2 beta decay radioisotopes
 BT3 radioisotopes
 BT4 isotopes
 BT1 electron capture radioisotopes
 BT2 beta decay radioisotopes
 BT3 radioisotopes
 BT4 isotopes
 BT1 intermediate mass nuclei
 BT2 nuclei
 BT1 odd-odd nuclei
 BT2 nuclei
 BT1 rhenium isotopes
 BT1 seconds living radioisotopes
 BT2 radioisotopes
 BT3 isotopes

RHENIUM 173 [9; 9]
  BT1   electron capture radioisotopes
    BT2   beta decay radioisotopes
      BT3   radioisotopes
        BT4   isotopes
  BT1   intermediate mass nuclei
    BT2   nuclei
  BT1   minutes living radioisotopes
    BT2   radioisotopes
      BT3   isotopes
  BT1   odd-even nuclei
    BT2   nuclei
  BT1   rhenium isotopes

RHENIUM 174 [12; 12]
  BT1   beta-plus decay radioisotopes
    BT2   beta decay radioisotopes
      BT3   radioisotopes
        BT4   isotopes
  BT1   electron capture radioisotopes
    BT2   beta decay radioisotopes
      BT3   radioisotopes
        BT4   isotopes
  BT1   intermediate mass nuclei
    BT2   nuclei
  BT1   minutes living radioisotopes
    BT2   radioisotopes
      BT3   isotopes
  BT1   odd-odd nuclei
    BT2   nuclei
  BT1   rhenium isotopes

RHENIUM 175 [9; 9]
  BT1   beta-plus decay radioisotopes
    BT2   beta decay radioisotopes
      BT3   radioisotopes
        BT4   isotopes
  BT1   electron capture radioisotopes
    BT2   beta decay radioisotopes
      BT3   radioisotopes
        BT4   isotopes
  BT1   intermediate mass nuclei
    BT2   nuclei
  BT1   minutes living radioisotopes
    BT2   radioisotopes
      BT3   isotopes
  BT1   odd-even nuclei
    BT2   nuclei
  BT1   rhenium isotopes

RHENIUM 176 [13; 13]
  BT1   beta-plus decay radioisotopes
    BT2   beta decay radioisotopes
      BT3   radioisotopes
        BT4   isotopes
  BT1   electron capture radioisotopes
    BT2   beta decay radioisotopes
      BT3   radioisotopes
        BT4   isotopes
  BT1   intermediate mass nuclei
    BT2   nuclei
  BT1   minutes living radioisotopes
    BT2   radioisotopes
      BT3   isotopes
  BT1   odd-odd nuclei
    BT2   nuclei
  BT1   rhenium isotopes

RHENIUM 177 [17; 17]
  BT1   beta-plus decay radioisotopes
    BT2   beta decay radioisotopes
      BT3   radioisotopes
        BT4   isotopes
  BT1   electron capture radioisotopes
    BT2   beta decay radioisotopes
      BT3   radioisotopes
        BT4   isotopes
  BT1   intermediate mass nuclei
    BT2   nuclei
  BT1   minutes living radioisotopes
    BT2   radioisotopes
      BT3   isotopes
  BT1   odd-even nuclei
    BT2   nuclei
  BT1   rhenium isotopes

RHENIUM 178 [13; 13]
  BT1   beta-plus decay radioisotopes
    BT2   beta decay radioisotopes
      BT3   radioisotopes
        BT4   isotopes
  BT1   electron capture radioisotopes
    BT2   beta decay radioisotopes
      BT3   radioisotopes
        BT4   isotopes
  BT1   intermediate mass nuclei
    BT2   nuclei
  BT1   minutes living radioisotopes
    BT2   radioisotopes
      BT3   isotopes
  BT1   odd-odd nuclei
    BT2   nuclei
  BT1   rhenium isotopes

RHENIUM 179 [17; 17]
  BT1   beta-plus decay radioisotopes
    BT2   beta decay radioisotopes
      BT3   radioisotopes
        BT4   isotopes
  BT1   electron capture radioisotopes
    BT2   beta decay radioisotopes
      BT3   radioisotopes
        BT4   isotopes
  BT1   intermediate mass nuclei
    BT2   nuclei
  BT1   minutes living radioisotopes
    BT2   radioisotopes
      BT3   isotopes
  BT1   odd-even nuclei
    BT2   nuclei
  BT1   rhenium isotopes

RHENIUM 180 [11; 11]
  BT1   beta-plus decay radioisotopes
    BT2   beta decay radioisotopes
      BT3   radioisotopes
        BT4   isotopes
  BT1   electron capture radioisotopes
    BT2   beta decay radioisotopes
      BT3   radioisotopes
        BT4   isotopes
  BT1   intermediate mass nuclei
    BT2   nuclei
  BT1   minutes living radioisotopes
    BT2   radioisotopes
      BT3   isotopes
  BT1   odd-odd nuclei
    BT2   nuclei
  BT1   rhenium isotopes

RHENIUM 181 [44; 44]
  BT1   electron capture radioisotopes
    BT2   beta decay radioisotopes
      BT3   radioisotopes
        BT4   isotopes
  BT1   heavy nuclei
    BT2   nuclei
  BT1   hours living radioisotopes
    BT2   radioisotopes
      BT3   isotopes
  BT1   odd-even nuclei
    BT2   nuclei
  BT1   rhenium isotopes

RHENIUM 182 [55; 55]
  BT1   beta-plus decay radioisotopes
    BT2   beta decay radioisotopes
      BT3   radioisotopes
        BT4   isotopes
  BT1   days living radioisotopes
    BT2   radioisotopes
      BT3   isotopes
  BT1   electron capture radioisotopes
    BT2   beta decay radioisotopes
      BT3   radioisotopes
        BT4   isotopes
  BT1   heavy nuclei
    BT2   nuclei
  BT1   hours living radioisotopes
    BT2   radioisotopes
      BT3   isotopes
  BT1   odd-odd nuclei
    BT2   nuclei
  BT1   rhenium isotopes

RHENIUM 183 [82; 82]
  BT1   days living radioisotopes
    BT2   radioisotopes
      BT3   isotopes
  BT1   electron capture radioisotopes
    BT2   beta decay radioisotopes
      BT3   radioisotopes
        BT4   isotopes
  BT1   heavy nuclei
    BT2   nuclei
  BT1   internal conversion radioisoto
    BT2   radioisotopes
      BT3   isotopes
  BT1   odd-even nuclei
    BT2   nuclei
  BT1   rhenium isotopes

RHENIUM 184 [75; 75]
  BT1   days living radioisotopes
    BT2   radioisotopes
      BT3   isotopes
  BT1   electron capture radioisotopes
    BT2   beta decay radioisotopes
      BT3   radioisotopes
        BT4   isotopes
  BT1   heavy nuclei
    BT2   nuclei
  BT1   internal conversion radioisoto
    BT2   radioisotopes
      BT3   isotopes
  BT1   isomeric transition isotopes
    BT2   radioisotopes
      BT3   isotopes
  BT1   odd-odd nuclei
    BT2   nuclei
  BT1   rhenium isotopes

RHENIUM 184 TARGET [3; 3] *Sep 79*
  BT1   targets

RHENIUM 185 [70; 70]
  BT1   heavy nuclei
    BT2   nuclei
  BT1   odd-even nuclei
    BT2   nuclei
  BT1   rhenium isotopes
  BT1   stable isotopes
    BT2   isotopes

RHENIUM 185 TARGET [39; 39]
  BT1   targets

RHENIUM 186 [127; 127]
  BT1   beta-minus decay radioisotopes
    BT2   beta decay radioisotopes
      BT3   radioisotopes
        BT4   isotopes
  BT1   days living radioisotopes
    BT2   radioisotopes
      BT3   isotopes
  BT1   electron capture radioisotopes
    BT2   beta decay radioisotopes
      BT3   radioisotopes
        BT4   isotopes
  BT1   heavy nuclei
    BT2   nuclei
  BT1   isomeric transition isotopes
    BT2   radioisotopes
      BT3   isotopes
  BT1   odd-odd nuclei
    BT2   nuclei
  BT1   rhenium isotopes
  BT1   years living radioisotopes
    BT2   radioisotopes
      BT3   isotopes

RHENIUM 186 TARGET [3; 3]
  BT1   targets

RHENIUM 187 [168; 168]
  BT1   beta-minus decay radioisotopes
    BT2   beta decay radioisotopes
      BT3   radioisotopes
        BT4   isotopes
  BT1   heavy nuclei
    BT2   nuclei
  BT1   odd-even nuclei

BT2 nuclei
BT1 rhenium isotopes
BT1 stable isotopes
BT2 isotopes
BT1 years living radioisotopes
BT2 radioisotopes
BT3 isotopes

RHENIUM 187 TARGET [35; 35]
BT1 targets

RHENIUM 188 [75; 75]
BT1 beta-minus decay radioisotopes
BT2 beta decay radioisotopes
BT3 radioisotopes
BT4 isotopes
BT1 heavy nuclei
BT2 nuclei
BT1 hours living radioisotopes
BT2 radioisotopes
BT3 isotopes
BT1 internal conversion radioisoto
BT2 radioisotopes
BT3 isotopes
BT1 isomeric transition isotopes
BT2 radioisotopes
BT3 isotopes
BT1 minutes living radioisotopes
BT2 radioisotopes
BT3 isotopes
BT1 odd-odd nuclei
BT2 nuclei
BT1 rhenium isotopes

RHENIUM 189 [8; 8]
BT1 beta-minus decay radioisotopes
BT2 beta decay radioisotopes
BT3 radioisotopes
BT4 isotopes
BT1 days living radioisotopes
BT2 radioisotopes
BT3 isotopes
BT1 heavy nuclei
BT2 nuclei
BT1 internal conversion radioisoto
BT2 radioisotopes
BT3 isotopes
BT1 odd-even nuclei
BT2 nuclei
BT1 rhenium isotopes

RHENIUM 190 [8; 8]
BT1 beta-minus decay radioisotopes
BT2 beta decay radioisotopes
BT3 radioisotopes
BT4 isotopes
BT1 heavy nuclei
BT2 nuclei
BT1 hours living radioisotopes
BT2 radioisotopes
BT3 isotopes
BT1 isomeric transition isotopes
BT2 radioisotopes
BT3 isotopes
BT1 minutes living radioisotopes
BT2 radioisotopes
BT3 isotopes
BT1 odd-odd nuclei
BT2 nuclei
BT1 rhenium isotopes

RHENIUM 191 [5; 5]
BT1 beta-minus decay radioisotopes
BT2 beta decay radioisotopes
BT3 radioisotopes
BT4 isotopes
BT1 heavy nuclei
BT2 nuclei
BT1 minutes living radioisotopes
BT2 radioisotopes
BT3 isotopes
BT1 odd-even nuclei
BT2 nuclei
BT1 rhenium isotopes

RHENIUM 192 [1; 1]
BT1 beta-minus decay radioisotopes
BT2 beta decay radioisotopes
BT3 radioisotopes
BT4 isotopes
BT1 heavy nuclei
BT2 nuclei
BT1 odd-odd nuclei
BT2 nuclei
BT1 rhenium isotopes
BT1 seconds living radioisotopes
BT2 radioisotopes
BT3 isotopes

RHEOLOGY [192; 192] *Oct 82*
RT deformation
RT fluid flow
RT matter
RT mechanical properties
RT viscosity

RHEOSTATS [3; 3]
BT1 resistors
BT2 electrical equipment
BT3 equipment

rhesus monkeys
USE macacus

RHEUMATIC DISEASES [781; 781]
UF *arthritis*
UF *rheumatoid diseases*
BT1 skeletal diseases
BT2 diseases
RT bone joints
RT bone tissues

rheumatoid diseases
USE rheumatic diseases

rhic (brookhaven)
USE brookhaven rhic

RHINE RIVER [124; 124]
BT1 rivers
BT2 surface waters

rhizopterin
USE folic acid

RHIZOPUS [32; 32]
BT1 fungi
BT2 plants

rho-prime resonances
USE rho-1600 mesons

RHO-1250 MESONS [75; 75] *Dec 75*
(Prior to December 1987 this concept was indexed by RHO-1250 RESONANCES.)
UF *rho-1250 resonances*
BT1 vector mesons
BT2 mesons
BT3 bosons
BT3 hadrons
BT4 elementary particles

rho-1250 resonances
(Prior to December 1987 this was a valid descriptor.)
USE rho-1250 mesons

rho-1500 resonances
(Prior to December 1987 this was a valid descriptor.)
USE mesons

RHO-1600 MESONS [172; 172]
(Prior to December 1987 this concept was indexed by RH0-1600 RESONANCES.)
UF *rho-prime resonances*
UF *rho-1600 resonances*
BT1 vector mesons
BT2 mesons
BT3 bosons
BT3 hadrons
BT4 elementary particles

rho-1600 resonances
(Prior to December 1987 this was a valid descriptor.)
USE rho-1600 mesons

rho-1670 resonances
(Prior to December 1987 this was a valid descriptor.)
USE rho3-1690 mesons

rho-1700 resonances
(Prior to December 1987 this was a valid descriptor.)
USE mesons

RHO-2150 MESONS [5; 5] *Dec 87*
BT1 vector mesons
BT2 mesons
BT3 bosons
BT3 hadrons
BT4 elementary particles

rho-765 resonances
(Prior to December 1987 this was a valid descriptor.)
USE rho-770 mesons

RHO-770 MESONS [2,190; 2,190]
(Prior to December 1987 this concept was indexed by RHO-765 RESONANCES.)
UF *rho-765 resonances*
BT1 vector mesons
BT2 mesons
BT3 bosons
BT3 hadrons
BT4 elementary particles

RHODAMINES [235; 235]
BT1 amines
BT2 organic compounds
BT1 dyes
BT1 heterocyclic acids
BT2 carboxylic acids
BT3 organic acids
BT4 organic compounds
BT2 heterocyclic compounds
BT3 organic compounds
BT1 organic oxygen compounds
BT2 organic compounds
BT1 reagents
RT phthalic acid

rhodanates
USE thiocyanates

rhodanides
USE thiocyanates

RHODE ISLAND [66; 66]
BT1 usa
BT2 developed countries
BT2 north america

rhode island nuclear science c
USE rinsc reactor

rhodesia (northern)
USE zambia

rhodesia (southern)
USE southern rhodesia

RHODIUM [681; 681]
BT1 platinum metals
 BT2 transition elements
  BT3 metals
   BT4 elements

RHODIUM ADDITIONS [32; 32]
(Alloys containing not more than 1% Rh are listed here.)
RT rhodium alloys
RT rhodium compounds

RHODIUM ALLOYS [493; 530]
(Alloys containing more than 1% Rh.)
BT1 platinum metal alloys
 BT2 alloys
NT1 rhodium base alloys
RT rhodium additions

RHODIUM BASE ALLOYS [35; 35]
BT1 rhodium alloys
 BT2 platinum metal alloys
  BT3 alloys

RHODIUM BORIDES [260; 260] *Sep 77*
BT1 borides
 BT2 boron compounds
BT1 rhodium compounds
 BT2 transition element compounds

RHODIUM BROMIDES [5; 5] *Feb 76*
BT1 bromides
 BT2 bromine compounds
  BT3 halogen compounds
 BT2 halides
  BT3 halogen compounds
BT1 rhodium compounds
 BT2 transition element compounds

RHODIUM CARBIDES [15; 15]
BT1 carbides
 BT2 carbon compounds
BT1 rhodium compounds
 BT2 transition element compounds

RHODIUM CHLORIDES [41; 41]
BT1 chlorides
 BT2 chlorine compounds
  BT3 halogen compounds
 BT2 halides
  BT3 halogen compounds
BT1 rhodium compounds
 BT2 transition element compounds

RHODIUM COMPLEXES [183; 183]
BT1 transition element complexes
 BT2 complexes

RHODIUM COMPOUNDS [158; 556]
BT1 transition element compounds
NT1 rhodium borides
NT1 rhodium bromides
NT1 rhodium carbides
NT1 rhodium chlorides
NT1 rhodium fluorides
NT1 rhodium hydrides
NT1 rhodium hydroxides
NT1 rhodium oxides
NT1 rhodium phosphides
NT1 rhodium selenides
NT1 rhodium silicides
NT1 rhodium sulfides
NT1 rhodium tellurides
RT rhodium additions

RHODIUM FLUORIDES [9; 9]
BT1 fluorides
 BT2 fluorine compounds
  BT3 halogen compounds
 BT2 halides
  BT3 halogen compounds
BT1 rhodium compounds
 BT2 transition element compounds

RHODIUM HYDRIDES [17; 17] *Nov 78*
BT1 hydrides
 BT2 hydrogen compounds
BT1 rhodium compounds
 BT2 transition element compounds

RHODIUM HYDROXIDES [3; 3] *Feb 76*
BT1 hydroxides
 BT2 hydrogen compounds
 BT2 oxygen compounds
BT1 rhodium compounds
 BT2 transition element compounds

RHODIUM IONS [30; 30]
BT1 ions
 BT2 charged particles

RHODIUM ISOTOPES [59; 838]
NT1 rhodium 100
NT1 rhodium 101
NT1 rhodium 102
NT1 rhodium 103
NT1 rhodium 104
NT1 rhodium 105
NT1 rhodium 106
NT1 rhodium 107
NT1 rhodium 108
NT1 rhodium 109
NT1 rhodium 110
NT1 rhodium 111
NT1 rhodium 112
NT1 rhodium 113
NT1 rhodium 114
NT1 rhodium 115
NT1 rhodium 116
NT1 rhodium 117
NT1 rhodium 94
NT1 rhodium 95
NT1 rhodium 96
NT1 rhodium 97
NT1 rhodium 98
NT1 rhodium 99

RHODIUM OXIDES [45; 45]
BT1 oxides
 BT2 chalcogenides
 BT2 oxygen compounds
BT1 rhodium compounds
 BT2 transition element compounds

RHODIUM PHOSPHIDES [0; 0] *Feb 90*
BT1 phosphides
 BT2 phosphorus compounds
 BT2 pnictides
BT1 rhodium compounds
 BT2 transition element compounds

→ **RHODIUM SELENIDES** [0; 0] *Sep 91*
BT1 rhodium compounds
 BT2 transition element compounds
BT1 selenides
 BT2 chalcogenides
 BT2 selenium compounds

RHODIUM SILICIDES [17; 17] *Aug 87*
BT1 rhodium compounds
 BT2 transition element compounds
BT1 silicides
 BT2 silicon compounds

→ **RHODIUM SULFIDES** [0; 0] *Sep 91*
BT1 rhodium compounds
 BT2 transition element compounds
BT1 sulfides
 BT2 chalcogenides
 BT2 sulfur compounds

→ **RHODIUM TELLURIDES** [0; 0] *Sep 91*
BT1 rhodium compounds
 BT2 transition element compounds
BT1 tellurides
 BT2 chalcogenides
 BT2 tellurium compounds

RHODIUM 100 [53; 53]
BT1 beta-plus decay radioisotopes
 BT2 beta decay radioisotopes
  BT3 radioisotopes
   BT4 isotopes
BT1 electron capture radioisotopes
 BT2 beta decay radioisotopes
  BT3 radioisotopes
   BT4 isotopes
BT1 hours living radioisotopes
 BT2 radioisotopes
  BT3 isotopes
BT1 intermediate mass nuclei
 BT2 nuclei
BT1 internal conversion radioisoto
 BT2 radioisotopes
  BT3 isotopes
BT1 isomeric transition isotopes
 BT2 radioisotopes
  BT3 isotopes
BT1 minutes living radioisotopes
 BT2 radioisotopes
  BT3 isotopes
BT1 odd-odd nuclei
 BT2 nuclei
BT1 rhodium isotopes

RHODIUM 101 [50; 50]
BT1 days living radioisotopes
 BT2 radioisotopes
  BT3 isotopes
BT1 electron capture radioisotopes
 BT2 beta decay radioisotopes
  BT3 radioisotopes
   BT4 isotopes
BT1 intermediate mass nuclei
 BT2 nuclei
BT1 internal conversion radioisoto
 BT2 radioisotopes
  BT3 isotopes
BT1 isomeric transition isotopes
 BT2 radioisotopes
  BT3 isotopes
BT1 odd-even nuclei
 BT2 nuclei
BT1 rhodium isotopes
BT1 years living radioisotopes
 BT2 radioisotopes
  BT3 isotopes

RHODIUM 102 [38; 38]
BT1 beta-minus decay radioisotopes
 BT2 beta decay radioisotopes
  BT3 radioisotopes
   BT4 isotopes
BT1 beta-plus decay radioisotopes
 BT2 beta decay radioisotopes
  BT3 radioisotopes
   BT4 isotopes
BT1 days living radioisotopes
 BT2 radioisotopes
  BT3 isotopes
BT1 electron capture radioisotopes
 BT2 beta decay radioisotopes
  BT3 radioisotopes
   BT4 isotopes
BT1 intermediate mass nuclei
 BT2 nuclei
BT1 odd-odd nuclei
 BT2 nuclei
BT1 rhodium isotopes

RHODIUM 103 [196; 196]
BT1 intermediate mass nuclei
 BT2 nuclei
BT1 internal conversion radioisoto
 BT2 radioisotopes
  BT3 isotopes
BT1 isomeric transition isotopes
 BT2 radioisotopes
  BT3 isotopes
BT1 minutes living radioisotopes

```
    BT2     radioisotopes
      BT3     isotopes
    BT1     odd-even nuclei
      BT2     nuclei
    BT1     rhodium isotopes
    BT1     stable isotopes
      BT2     isotopes

**RHODIUM 103 TARGET** [184; 184]
    BT1     targets

**RHODIUM 104** [57; 57]
    BT1     beta-minus decay radioisotopes
      BT2     beta decay radioisotopes
        BT3     radioisotopes
          BT4     isotopes
    BT1     electron capture radioisotopes
      BT2     beta decay radioisotopes
        BT3     radioisotopes
          BT4     isotopes
    BT1     intermediate mass nuclei
      BT2     nuclei
    BT1     isomeric transition isotopes
      BT2     radioisotopes
        BT3     isotopes
    BT1     minutes living radioisotopes
      BT2     radioisotopes
        BT3     isotopes
    BT1     odd-odd nuclei
      BT2     nuclei
    BT1     rhodium isotopes
    BT1     seconds living radioisotopes
      BT2     radioisotopes
        BT3     isotopes

**RHODIUM 105** [55; 55]
    BT1     beta-minus decay radioisotopes
      BT2     beta decay radioisotopes
        BT3     radioisotopes
          BT4     isotopes
    BT1     days living radioisotopes
      BT2     radioisotopes
        BT3     isotopes
    BT1     intermediate mass nuclei
      BT2     nuclei
    BT1     internal conversion radioisoto
      BT2     radioisotopes
        BT3     isotopes
    BT1     isomeric transition isotopes
      BT2     radioisotopes
        BT3     isotopes
    BT1     odd-even nuclei
      BT2     nuclei
    BT1     rhodium isotopes
    BT1     seconds living radioisotopes
      BT2     radioisotopes
        BT3     isotopes

**RHODIUM 106** [253; 253]
    BT1     beta-minus decay radioisotopes
      BT2     beta decay radioisotopes
        BT3     radioisotopes
          BT4     isotopes
    BT1     hours living radioisotopes
      BT2     radioisotopes
        BT3     isotopes
    BT1     intermediate mass nuclei
      BT2     nuclei
    BT1     odd-odd nuclei
      BT2     nuclei
    BT1     rhodium isotopes
    BT1     seconds living radioisotopes
      BT2     radioisotopes
        BT3     isotopes

**RHODIUM 107** [13; 13]
    BT1     beta-minus decay radioisotopes
      BT2     beta decay radioisotopes
        BT3     radioisotopes
          BT4     isotopes
    BT1     intermediate mass nuclei
      BT2     nuclei
    BT1     minutes living radioisotopes
      BT2     radioisotopes
        BT3     isotopes
    BT1     odd-even nuclei
      BT2     nuclei
    BT1     rhodium isotopes

**RHODIUM 108** [13; 13]
    BT1     beta-minus decay radioisotopes
      BT2     beta decay radioisotopes
        BT3     radioisotopes
          BT4     isotopes
    BT1     intermediate mass nuclei
      BT2     nuclei
    BT1     minutes living radioisotopes
      BT2     radioisotopes
        BT3     isotopes
    BT1     odd-odd nuclei
      BT2     nuclei
    BT1     rhodium isotopes
    BT1     seconds living radioisotopes
      BT2     radioisotopes
        BT3     isotopes

**RHODIUM 109** [24; 24]
    BT1     beta-minus decay radioisotopes
      BT2     beta decay radioisotopes
        BT3     radioisotopes
          BT4     isotopes
    BT1     intermediate mass nuclei
      BT2     nuclei
    BT1     minutes living radioisotopes
      BT2     radioisotopes
        BT3     isotopes
    BT1     odd-even nuclei
      BT2     nuclei
    BT1     rhodium isotopes

**RHODIUM 110** [9; 9]
    BT1     beta-minus decay radioisotopes
      BT2     beta decay radioisotopes
        BT3     radioisotopes
          BT4     isotopes
    BT1     intermediate mass nuclei
      BT2     nuclei
    BT1     odd-odd nuclei
      BT2     nuclei
    BT1     rhodium isotopes
    BT1     seconds living radioisotopes
      BT2     radioisotopes
        BT3     isotopes

**RHODIUM 111** [6; 6] *Jan 79*
    BT1     beta-minus decay radioisotopes
      BT2     beta decay radioisotopes
        BT3     radioisotopes
          BT4     isotopes
    BT1     intermediate mass nuclei
      BT2     nuclei
    BT1     odd-even nuclei
      BT2     nuclei
    BT1     rhodium isotopes
    BT1     seconds living radioisotopes
      BT2     radioisotopes
        BT3     isotopes

**RHODIUM 112** [8; 8] *Jan 85*
    BT1     beta-minus decay radioisotopes
      BT2     beta decay radioisotopes
        BT3     radioisotopes
          BT4     isotopes
    BT1     intermediate mass nuclei
      BT2     nuclei
    BT1     millisec living radioisotopes
      BT2     radioisotopes
        BT3     isotopes
    BT1     odd-odd nuclei
      BT2     nuclei
    BT1     rhodium isotopes

**RHODIUM 113** [0; 0] *Nov 88*
    BT1     beta-minus decay radioisotopes
      BT2     beta decay radioisotopes
        BT3     radioisotopes
          BT4     isotopes
    BT1     intermediate mass nuclei
      BT2     nuclei
    BT1     odd-even nuclei
      BT2     nuclei
    BT1     rhodium isotopes
    BT1     seconds living radioisotopes
      BT2     radioisotopes
        BT3     isotopes

**RHODIUM 114** [2; 2] *Jun 88*
    BT1     beta-minus decay radioisotopes
      BT2     beta decay radioisotopes
        BT3     radioisotopes
          BT4     isotopes
    BT1     intermediate mass nuclei
      BT2     nuclei
    BT1     odd-odd nuclei
      BT2     nuclei
    BT1     rhodium isotopes
    BT1     seconds living radioisotopes
      BT2     radioisotopes
        BT3     isotopes

**RHODIUM 115** [0; 0] *Nov 88*
    BT1     beta-minus decay radioisotopes
      BT2     beta decay radioisotopes
        BT3     radioisotopes
          BT4     isotopes
    BT1     intermediate mass nuclei
      BT2     nuclei
    BT1     millisec living radioisotopes
      BT2     radioisotopes
        BT3     isotopes
    BT1     odd-even nuclei
      BT2     nuclei
    BT1     rhodium isotopes

**RHODIUM 116** [6; 6]
    BT1     beta-minus decay radioisotopes
      BT2     beta decay radioisotopes
        BT3     radioisotopes
          BT4     isotopes
    BT1     intermediate mass nuclei
      BT2     nuclei
    BT1     millisec living radioisotopes
      BT2     radioisotopes
        BT3     isotopes
    BT1     odd-odd nuclei
      BT2     nuclei
    BT1     rhodium isotopes

**RHODIUM 117** [2; 2]
    BT1     beta-minus decay radioisotopes
      BT2     beta decay radioisotopes
        BT3     radioisotopes
          BT4     isotopes
    BT1     intermediate mass nuclei
      BT2     nuclei
    BT1     odd-even nuclei
      BT2     nuclei
    BT1     rhodium isotopes
    BT1     seconds living radioisotopes
      BT2     radioisotopes
        BT3     isotopes

**RHODIUM 94** [9; 9]
    BT1     beta-plus decay radioisotopes
      BT2     beta decay radioisotopes
        BT3     radioisotopes
          BT4     isotopes
    BT1     intermediate mass nuclei
      BT2     nuclei
    BT1     minutes living radioisotopes
      BT2     radioisotopes
        BT3     isotopes
    BT1     odd-odd nuclei
      BT2     nuclei
    BT1     rhodium isotopes
    BT1     seconds living radioisotopes
      BT2     radioisotopes
        BT3     isotopes

**RHODIUM 95** [19; 19]
    BT1     beta-plus decay radioisotopes
      BT2     beta decay radioisotopes
        BT3     radioisotopes
          BT4     isotopes
    BT1     electron capture radioisotopes
      BT2     beta decay radioisotopes
        BT3     radioisotopes
          BT4     isotopes
    BT1     intermediate mass nuclei
      BT2     nuclei
    BT1     isomeric transition isotopes
      BT2     radioisotopes
        BT3     isotopes
    BT1     minutes living radioisotopes
```

```
        BT2    radioisotopes
        BT3    isotopes
    BT1    odd-even nuclei
        BT2    nuclei
    BT1    rhodium isotopes

**RHODIUM 96** [16; 16]
    BT1    beta-plus decay radioisotopes
        BT2    beta decay radioisotopes
            BT3    radioisotopes
                BT4    isotopes
    BT1    electron capture radioisotopes
        BT2    beta decay radioisotopes
            BT3    radioisotopes
                BT4    isotopes
    BT1    intermediate mass nuclei
        BT2    nuclei
    BT1    internal conversion radioisoto
        BT2    radioisotopes
            BT3    isotopes
    BT1    isomeric transition isotopes
        BT2    radioisotopes
            BT3    isotopes
    BT1    minutes living radioisotopes
        BT2    radioisotopes
            BT3    isotopes
    BT1    odd-odd nuclei
        BT2    nuclei
    BT1    rhodium isotopes

**RHODIUM 96 TARGET** [2; 2] *Nov 75*
    BT1    targets

**RHODIUM 97** [23; 23]
    BT1    beta-plus decay radioisotopes
        BT2    beta decay radioisotopes
            BT3    radioisotopes
                BT4    isotopes
    BT1    electron capture radioisotopes
        BT2    beta decay radioisotopes
            BT3    radioisotopes
                BT4    isotopes
    BT1    intermediate mass nuclei
        BT2    nuclei
    BT1    isomeric transition isotopes
        BT2    radioisotopes
            BT3    isotopes
    BT1    minutes living radioisotopes
        BT2    radioisotopes
            BT3    isotopes
    BT1    odd-even nuclei
        BT2    nuclei
    BT1    rhodium isotopes

**RHODIUM 98** [13; 13]
    BT1    beta-plus decay radioisotopes
        BT2    beta decay radioisotopes
            BT3    radioisotopes
                BT4    isotopes
    BT1    electron capture radioisotopes
        BT2    beta decay radioisotopes
            BT3    radioisotopes
                BT4    isotopes
    BT1    intermediate mass nuclei
        BT2    nuclei
    BT1    minutes living radioisotopes
        BT2    radioisotopes
            BT3    isotopes
    BT1    odd-odd nuclei
        BT2    nuclei
    BT1    rhodium isotopes

**RHODIUM 99** [36; 36]
    BT1    beta-plus decay radioisotopes
        BT2    beta decay radioisotopes
            BT3    radioisotopes
                BT4    isotopes
    BT1    days living radioisotopes
        BT2    radioisotopes
            BT3    isotopes
    BT1    electron capture radioisotopes
        BT2    beta decay radioisotopes
            BT3    radioisotopes
                BT4    isotopes
    BT1    hours living radioisotopes
        BT2    radioisotopes
            BT3    isotopes
```

```
    BT1    intermediate mass nuclei
        BT2    nuclei
    BT1    odd-even nuclei
        BT2    nuclei
    BT1    rhodium isotopes

**RHODIZONIC ACID** [5; 5]
    BT1    hydroxy compounds
        BT2    organic compounds
    BT1    quinones
        BT2    aromatics
            BT3    organic compounds
        BT2    organic oxygen compounds
            BT3    organic compounds
    BT1    reagents
    RT     organic acids

**RHODOPSEUDOMONAS** [26; 26]
    BT1    bacteria
        BT2    microorganisms

**RHODOPSIN** [88; 88] *Mar 86*
    UF     *retinal pigment*
    UF     *visual purple*
    BT1    pigments
    BT1    proteins
        BT2    organic compounds
    RT     retina

**RHODOSPIRILLUM** [40; 40]
    BT1    bacteria
        BT2    microorganisms

*rhombohedral lattices*
    USE    trigonal lattices

**RHONE RIVER** [33; 33]
    BT1    rivers
        BT2    surface waters

**RHO3-1690 MESONS** [101; 101]
(Prior to December 1987 this concept was
indexed by RHO-1670 RESONANCES.)
    UF     *g resonances*
    UF     *rho-1670 resonances*
    BT1    tensor mesons
        BT2    mesons
            BT3    bosons
            BT3    hadrons
                BT4    elementary particles

**RHO3-2250 MESONS** [27; 27]
(Prior to December 1987 this concept was
indexed by T-2200 RESONANCES.)
    UF     *t-2200 resonances*
    BT1    tensor mesons
        BT2    mesons
            BT3    bosons
            BT3    hadrons
                BT4    elementary particles

**RHO5-2350 MESONS** [3; 3] *Dec 87*
    BT1    tensor mesons
        BT2    mesons
            BT3    bosons
            BT3    hadrons
                BT4    elementary particles

*rhr*
(Residual heat removal)
    USE    after-heat removal

**RHYOLITES** [79; 79] *Aug 78*
    BT1    igneous rocks
        BT2    rocks
    RT     feldspars
    RT     granites
    RT     silicon oxides

**RHYTHMICITY** [20; 20]
    RT     estrous cycle
    RT     menstrual cycle
```

```
*ria (radioimmunoassay)*
    USE    radioimmunoassay

*ria (reactor accidents)*
(Reactivity Initiated Accidents.)
    SEE    reactor accidents

**RIBOFLAVIN** [84; 84]
    UF     *vitamin b-2*
    BT1    vitamin b group
        BT2    vitamins
    RT     ribose

*ribonuclease*
    USE    rna-ase

*ribonucleic acid*
    USE    rna

**RIBOSE** [119; 119]
    BT1    aldehydes
        BT2    organic compounds
    BT1    pentoses
        BT2    monosaccharides
            BT3    saccharides
                BT4    carbohydrates
                    BT5    organic compounds
    RT     riboflavin

**RIBOSIDES** [31; 4,917]
    NT1    nucleosides
        NT2    adenosine
        NT2    budr
        NT2    cytidine
        NT2    deoxycytidine
        NT2    deoxyuridine
        NT2    fudr
        NT2    guanosine
        NT2    inosine
        NT2    iododeoxyuridine
        NT2    thymidine
        NT2    uridine
    RT     deoxyribose
    RT     nucleic acids
    RT     pentoses

**RIBOSOMAL RNA** [15; 15] *Apr 90*
    UF     *r-rna*
    BT1    rna
        BT2    nucleic acids
            BT3    organic compounds
    RT     nucleoli
    RT     ribosomes

**RIBOSOMES** [374; 374]
    BT1    organoids
        BT2    cell constituents
    RT     codons
    RT     microsomes
    RT     ribosomal rna
    RT     rna

**RIBULOSE** [18; 18]
    BT1    ketones
        BT2    organic compounds
    BT1    pentoses
        BT2    monosaccharides
            BT3    saccharides
                BT4    carbohydrates
                    BT5    organic compounds

**RICCATI EQUATION** [132; 132]
    BT1    differential equations
        BT2    equations

**RICCI TENSOR** [606; 606]
    BT1    tensors
    RT     riemann space
```

RICE [1,041; 1,041]
  UF   *oryza*
    BT1   cereals
      BT2   gramineae
        BT3   plants

RICE STEM BORERS [14; 14]
  BT1   moths
    BT2   lepidoptera
      BT3   insects
        BT4   arthropods
          BT5   invertebrates
            BT6   animals

RICHARDSON EQUATION [23; 23]
  UF   *richardson-dushman equation*
  BT1   equations
  RT   thermionics

RICHARDSON NUMBER [48; 48]
  RT   turbulent flow

richardson-dushman equation
  USE   richardson equation

richland ffft reactor
  USE   fftf reactor

richland npr reactor
  USE   n-reactor

richland phys. const. test. r.
  USE   pctr reactor

richland pow.-plut. prod. reac
  USE   n-reactor

ricinum communis
  USE   castor

RICKETS [30; 30]
  UF   *rachitis*
  BT1   skeletal diseases
    BT2   diseases
  RT   bone tissues
  RT   vitamin d

RICKETTSIAE [21; 21]
  BT1   microorganisms
  RT   insects
  RT   rickettsial diseases
  RT   typhus

RICKETTSIAL DISEASES [5; 10]
  Dec 82
  BT1   infectious diseases
    BT2   diseases
  NT1   typhus
  RT   rickettsiae

riemann curvature tensor
  USE   riemann space

RIEMANN FUNCTION [152; 152]
  BT1   functions
  RT   differential equations

riemann geometry
  USE   riemann space

riemann manifolds
  USE   riemann space

riemann metric
  USE   riemann space

RIEMANN SHEET [239; 239]
  RT   riemann space

RIEMANN SPACE [3,344; 5,682]
  UF   *riemann curvature tensor*
  UF   *riemann geometry*
  UF   *riemann manifolds*
  UF   *riemann metric*
  UF   *riemann sphere*
  BT1   mathematical space
    BT2   space
  NT1   euclidean space
  RT   curvilinear coordinates
  RT   ricci tensor
  RT   riemann sheet
  RT   smooth manifolds

riemann sphere
  USE   riemann space

riemann waves
  USE   shock waves

RIEN-1 REACTOR [10; 10]
(Instituto de Energenharia
Nuclear/Nuclebras, Rio de Janeiro, Brazil)
  UF   *argonauta rien-1 reactor*
  UF   *argonauta rio reactor*
  UF   *instituto engen. nucl. rio r.*
  BT1   argonaut type reactors
    BT2   enriched uranium reactors
      BT3   reactors
    BT2   research and test reactors
      BT3   reactors
    BT2   water cooled reactors
      BT3   reactors
    BT2   water moderated reactors
      BT3   reactors
  BT1   research reactors
    BT2   research and test reactors
      BT3   reactors
  BT1   training reactors
    BT2   research and test reactors
      BT3   reactors

rift zones
  USE   geologic faults

RIGHI-LEDUC EFFECT [18; 18]
  RT   hall effect
  RT   heat transfer
  RT   magnetic fields
  RT   thermal conductivity

riken linac
  USE   rilac

riken ssc
  USE   ipcr cyclotron

rikkyo univ. triga-mk-2 react.
  USE   triga-2-rikkyo reactor

RILAC [16; 16] *May 86*
(Frequency-tunable heavy ion linac at Institute of Physical and Chemical Research, Saitama, Japan.)
  UF   *inst phys chem res rilac*
  UF   *ipcr linac*
  UF   *riken linac*
  UF   *saitama tunable h.i. linac*
  BT1   heavy ion accelerators
    BT2   accelerators
  BT1   linear accelerators
    BT2   accelerators

→ *rinderpest*
  USE   viral diseases

RING CHROMOSOMES [45; 45]
  BT1   chromosomes

RING CURRENTS [492; 492]
  BT1   electric currents
    BT2   currents
  RT   electrojets

RINGHALS-1 REACTOR [93; 93]
(Ringhals, Vaeroebacka, Sweden)
  BT1   bwr type reactors
    BT2   enriched uranium reactors
      BT3   reactors
    BT2   power reactors
      BT3   reactors
    BT2   thermal reactors
      BT3   reactors
    BT2   water cooled reactors
      BT3   reactors
    BT2   water moderated reactors
      BT3   reactors

RINGHALS-2 REACTOR [111; 111]
(Ringhals, Vaeroebacka, Sweden)
  BT1   pwr type reactors
    BT2   enriched uranium reactors
      BT3   reactors
    BT2   power reactors
      BT3   reactors
    BT2   thermal reactors
      BT3   reactors
    BT2   water cooled reactors
      BT3   reactors
    BT2   water moderated reactors
      BT3   reactors

RINGHALS-3 REACTOR [73; 73]
(Ringhals, Vaeroebacka, Sweden)
  BT1   pwr type reactors
    BT2   enriched uranium reactors
      BT3   reactors
    BT2   power reactors
      BT3   reactors
    BT2   thermal reactors
      BT3   reactors
    BT2   water cooled reactors
      BT3   reactors
    BT2   water moderated reactors
      BT3   reactors

RINGHALS-4 REACTOR [34; 34]
Oct 82
  BT1   pwr type reactors
    BT2   enriched uranium reactors
      BT3   reactors
    BT2   power reactors
      BT3   reactors
    BT2   thermal reactors
      BT3   reactors
    BT2   water cooled reactors
      BT3   reactors
    BT2   water moderated reactors
      BT3   reactors

ringotron
  USE   electron-ring accelerators

RINGS [904; 904]
  RT   configuration
  RT   shape
  RT   tori

rings (storage)
  USE   storage rings

RINSC REACTOR [6; 6]
(Rhode Island Atomic Energy Commission, Rhode Island Nuclear Science Center, Narragansett, Rhode Island, USA)
  UF   *rhode island nuclear science c*
  BT1   pool type reactors
    BT2   water cooled reactors

```
        BT3    reactors
        BT2    water moderated reactors
        BT3    reactors
     BT1    research reactors
        BT2    research and test reactors
        BT3    reactors

RIO BLANCO EVENT [138; 138]
     BT1    contained explosions
        BT2    underground explosions
        BT3    explosions
     BT1    nuclear explosions
        BT2    explosions
     BT1    plowshare project
     RT     natural gas

RIOMETERS [59; 59]
     BT1    measuring instruments

RIPENING [123; 123]
     RT     age dependence
     RT     growth
     RT     life cycle
     RT     physiology

risa
     USE    albumins
     AND    organic iodine compounds

rise time
     USE    pulse rise time

risk analysis
(Prior to August 1985 this was a valid
descriptor.)
     USE    risk assessment

RISK ASSESSMENT [12,773; 12,773]
Dec 76
(Prior to August 1985 RISK ANALYSIS
was used.)
     UF     risk analysis
     RT     alara
     RT     hazards
     RT     licensing regulations
     RT     probabilistic estimation
     RT     probability
     RT     public relations
     RT     reliability
     RT     safety analysis
     RT     source terms

risks
     USE    hazards

RISOE NATIONAL LABORATORY
[158; 160] Apr 78
(Prior to 1978 known as RISOE RE-
SEARCH ESTABLISHMENT, and docu-
ments written before that date should be
so indexed.)
     BT1    danish organizations
        BT2    national organizations
     NT1    risoe research establishment

RISOE RESEARCH ESTABLISHMENT
[9; 9] Mar 77
(Name changed in early 1978 to RISOE
NATIONAL LABORATORY, and docu-
ments written after that date should be so
indexed.)
     UF     research establishment risoe
     BT1    risoe national laboratory
        BT2    danish organizations
        BT3    national organizations

RITAC DOSEMETERS [14; 14]
(Passive solid-state dosemeters based on
Radiation Induced Thermally Activated
Current.)
     BT1    dosemeters
        BT2    measuring instruments
```

```
     RT     ritad dosemeters

RITAD DOSEMETERS [6; 6]
(Integral solid-state dosemeters based on
Radiation Induced Thermally Activated
Depolarization.)
     BT1    dosemeters
        BT2    measuring instruments
     RT     dielectric materials
     RT     ritac dosemeters

RITCHIE-ELDRIDGE THEORY [2; 2]
     RT     perturbation theory

RITMO REACTOR [4; 4]
(National Nuclear Energy Committee,
Rome, Italy)
     UF     rc-4 reactor casaccia
     UF     reattore casaccia-4
     BT1    enriched uranium reactors
        BT2    reactors
     BT1    pool type reactors
        BT2    water cooled reactors
        BT3    reactors
        BT2    water moderated reactors
        BT3    reactors
     BT1    research reactors
        BT2    research and test reactors
        BT3    reactors
     BT1    thermal reactors
        BT2    reactors
     BT1    zero power reactors
        BT2    experimental reactors
        BT3    research and test reactors
        BT4    reactors

RITZ METHOD [193; 193]
     UF     rayleigh-ritz method
     UF     ritz variation method
     UF     ritz-rayleigh method
     RT     variational methods

ritz variation method
     USE    ritz method

ritz-rayleigh method
     USE    ritz method

RIVER BEND-1 REACTOR [56; 56]
(St. Francisville, Louisiana, USA)
     BT1    bwr type reactors
        BT2    enriched uranium reactors
        BT3    reactors
        BT2    power reactors
        BT3    reactors
        BT2    thermal reactors
        BT3    reactors
        BT2    water cooled reactors
        BT3    reactors
        BT2    water moderated reactors
        BT3    reactors

RIVER BEND-2 REACTOR [39; 39]
(St. Francisville, Louisiana, USA)
     BT1    bwr type reactors
        BT2    enriched uranium reactors
        BT3    reactors
        BT2    power reactors
        BT3    reactors
        BT2    thermal reactors
        BT3    reactors
        BT2    water cooled reactors
        BT3    reactors
        BT2    water moderated reactors
        BT3    reactors

RIVERS [2,087; 3,117]
     UF     creeks
     UF     streams
     BT1    surface waters
     NT1    allegheny river
     NT1    amazon river
     NT1    blind river
     NT1    cape fear river
```

```
     NT1    clinch river
     NT1    colorado river
     NT1    columbia river
     NT1    connecticut river
     NT1    cumberland river
     NT1    danube river
     NT1    delaware river
     NT1    ganga river
     NT1    gunnison river
     NT1    hudson river
     NT1    james river
     NT1    mississippi river
     NT1    missouri river
     NT1    mohawk river
     NT1    niger river
     NT1    nile river
     NT1    ohio river
     NT1    ottawa river
     NT1    po river
     NT1    potomac river
     NT1    rhine river
     NT1    rhone river
     NT1    savannah river
     NT1    scioto river
     NT1    st lawrence river
     NT1    susquehanna river
     NT1    tennessee river
     NT1    thames river
     NT1    tigris river
     NT1    volga river
     RT     drainage
     RT     estuaries
     RT     fresh water
     RT     hydrology
     RT     inland waterways
     RT     intake structures

riveting
     USE    fastening

rivets
     USE    fasteners

rkr method
     USE    rydberg-klein-rees method

RNA [1,745; 2,716]
     UF     ribonucleic acid
     BT1    nucleic acids
        BT2    organic compounds
     NT1    messenger-rna
     NT1    ribosomal rna
     NT1    transfer rna
     RT     gene operons
     RT     microsomes
     RT     nucleoli
     RT     ribosomes
     RT     rna polymerases
     RT     strand breaks

RNA POLYMERASES [111; 111] Jun
     BT1    polymerases
        BT2    nucleotidyltransferases
        BT3    phosphorus-group transferas
        BT4    transferases
        BT5    enzymes
        BT6    organic compounds
     RT     dna polymerases
     RT     rna
     RT     transcription
     RT     transcription factors

RNA-ASE [261; 261]
     UF     nuclease (ribonuclease)
     UF     ribonuclease
     BT1    nucleases
        BT2    phosphodiesterases
        BT3    esterases
        BT4    hydrolases
        BT5    enzymes
        BT6    organic compounds

rnpp-rooppur reactor
     USE    rooppur reactor
```

ro-07-0582
   USE   misonidazole

ROAD TRANSPORT [412; 412] *Dec 76*
   UF   *truck transport*
   BT1   land transport
     BT2   transport
   RT   motor vehicle accidents
   RT   routing
   RT   vehicles

ROASTING [130; 130]
   BT1   oxidation
     BT2   chemical reactions
   RT   pyrometallurgy

robert e. ginna-1 reactor
   USE   ginna-1 reactor

robert e. ginna-2 reactor
   USE   ginna-2 reactor

ROBINSON-2 REACTOR [238; 238]
   UF   *carol. pow. light robinson-2 r*
   UF   *hb robinson-2*
   BT1   pwr type reactors
     BT2   enriched uranium reactors
       BT3   reactors
     BT2   power reactors
       BT3   reactors
     BT2   thermal reactors
       BT3   reactors
     BT2   water cooled reactors
       BT3   reactors
     BT2   water moderated reactors
       BT3   reactors

ROBOTS [881; 881] *Apr 84*
   BT1   equipment
   RT   control equipment
   RT   control systems
   RT   remote handling equipment

ROCHE EQUIPOTENTIALS [338; 338]
   UF   *roche lobes*
   BT1   potentials
   RT   binary stars
   RT   gravitational fields

roche lobes
   USE   roche equipotentials

ROCHELLE SALT [26; 26]
   BT1   potassium compounds
     BT2   alkali metal compounds
   BT1   sodium compounds
     BT2   alkali metal compounds
   BT1   tartrates
     BT2   carboxylic acid salts
   RT   tartaric acid

ROCK DRILLING [592; 595]
   UF   *drilling (rock)*
   BT1   drilling
   BT1   materials drilling
     BT2   machining
   RT   boreholes
   RT   subterrene penetrators

rock intrusion
(Process of emplacement of fluid material into pre-existing rock. Coordinate the descriptor below with other appropriate descriptor(s), e.g. POSITIONING, PETROGENESIS.)
   USE   plutonic rocks

ROCK MECHANICS [919; 919]
(Application of principles of mechanics and geology to quantify the response of rock to environmental forces.)
   BT1   mechanics
   RT   geology
   RT   mechanical properties
   RT   rocks
   RT   soil mechanics

ROCK-FLUID INTERACTIONS [291; 291] *Apr 86*
   RT   chemical reactions
   RT   ground water
   RT   hydrology
   RT   rocks
   RT   waste-rock interactions

rocket reactor exp. phoebus-1a
   USE   phoebus-1a reactor

rocket reactor exp. phoebus-1b
   USE   phoebus-1b reactor

rocket reactor exp. phoebus-2a
   USE   phoebus-2a reactor

rocket reactor exp. rover
   USE   rover reactors

ROCKETS [822; 824]
   NT1   atlas rockets
   RT   electronic guidance
   RT   launching
   RT   missiles
   RT   navigational instruments
   RT   projectiles
   RT   propulsion systems
   RT   reentry
   RT   space flight
   RT   space vehicles

rocking curve
   USE   neutron diffraction

ROCKS [4,857; 16,086]
   NT1   caldasite
   NT1   conglomerates
   NT1   igneous rocks
     NT2   basalt
     NT2   lava
     NT2   plutonic rocks
       NT3   anorthosites
       NT3   gabbros
       NT3   granites
         NT4   aplites
         NT4   granodiorites
         NT4   quartz monzonite
       NT3   pegmatites
       NT3   peridotites
         NT4   kimberlites
       NT3   syenites
     NT2   rhyolites
     NT2   tuff
   NT1   metamorphic rocks
     NT2   gneisses
     NT2   quartzites
     NT2   schists
   NT1   sedimentary rocks
     NT2   carbonate rocks
       NT3   limestone
     NT2   phosphate rocks
       NT3   phosphorites
     NT2   sandstones
       NT3   graywacke
     NT2   shales
       NT3   oil shales
   NT1   synthetic rocks
   RT   aquifers
   RT   environmental materials
   RT   lunar materials
   RT   minerals
   RT   orogenesis
   RT   overburden
   RT   petrogenesis
   RT   petrology
   RT   rock mechanics
   RT   rock-fluid interactions
   RT   stone meteorites
   RT   tectonics
   RT   waste-rock interactions

ROCKWELL HARDNESS [61; 61]
   RT   hardness

rocky flats pl.-nucl. saf. fac
   USE   nsf-rfp reactor

ROCKY FLATS PLANT [388; 388]
   BT1   us aec
     BT2   us organizations
       BT3   national organizations
   BT1   us doe
     BT2   us organizations
       BT3   national organizations
   BT1   us erda
     BT2   us organizations
       BT3   national organizations
   RT   colorado

ROCKY MOUNTAINS [24; 24]
   BT1   mountains

rod bundles
   USE   fuel element clusters

ROD DROP ACCIDENTS [153; 153]
   BT1   reactivity insertions
   BT1   reactor accidents
     BT2   accidents
   RT   control elements

ROD DROP METHOD [133; 133]
   RT   control elements
   RT   reactivity
   RT   reactor kinetics

ROD EJECTION ACCIDENTS [120; 120]
   BT1   reactor accidents
     BT2   accidents
   RT   control elements
   RT   reactivity insertions

RODENTS [266; 37,217]
   UF   *kangaroo rat*
   BT1   mammals
     BT2   vertebrates
       BT3   animals
   NT1   chipmunks
   NT1   gerbils
   NT1   guinea pigs
   NT1   hamsters
   NT1   mice
   NT1   rats
   NT1   squirrels
   NT1   voles
   RT   disease vectors
   RT   nippostrongylus
   RT   pest control

RODS [720; 720]
   RT   cylinders
   RT   shape
   RT   wires

rods (control)
   USE   control elements

rods (fuel)
   USE   fuel rods

roentgen (exposure unit)
   USE   radiation dose units

roentgen equivalent man
   USE   dose equivalents
   AND   radiation dose units

ROGOWSKI COIL [105; 105]
BT1 electric coils
BT2 electrical equipment
BT3 equipment

roll welding
USE forge welding

rolla research reactor
USE umrr reactor

ROLLER BEARINGS [39; 39]
BT1 bearings

§ **ROLLING** [1,420; 1,420]
BT1 materials working
BT2 fabrication
RT cladding
RT cold working
RT compacting
RT hot working
RT plating

ROLLING FRICTION [34; 34]
BT1 friction
RT gears
RT wear

rolphton npd-2 reactor
USE npd reactor

ROMANIA [139; 139]
UF *rumania*
BT1 developing countries
BT1 europe
RT centrally planned economies

romanian wwr-c reactor
USE wwr-s-bucharest reactor

ROMASHKA REACTOR [5; 5]
(Kurchatov Inst., USSR)
UF *kurchatov institute romashka r*
BT1 research reactors
BT2 research and test reactors
BT3 reactors
BT1 solid homogeneous reactors
BT2 homogeneous reactors
BT3 reactors

rome triga-mk-2 reactor
USE triga-2-rome reactor

ROMEO EVENT [2; 2] *Jan 85*
BT1 atmospheric explosions
BT2 explosions
BT1 castle project
BT1 nuclear explosions
BT2 explosions

ROOFS [35; 35] *Apr 86*
BT1 mechanical structures
RT buildings

ROOPPUR REACTOR [3; 3]
UF *rnpp-rooppur reactor*
BT1 pwr type reactors
BT2 enriched uranium reactors
BT3 reactors
BT2 power reactors
BT3 reactors
BT2 thermal reactors
BT3 reactors
BT2 water cooled reactors
BT3 reactors
BT2 water moderated reactors
BT3 reactors

ROOT ABSORPTION [765; 879]
UF *absorption (root)*
BT1 uptake
RT roots

ROOTS [1,112; 1,112]
RT plants
RT root absorption
RT soils

roper resonance
USE n-1440 baryons

ROSE BENGAL [158; 158]
BT1 dyes
BT1 hydroxy acids
BT2 carboxylic acids
BT3 organic acids
BT4 organic compounds
BT1 indicators
BT1 organic chlorine compounds
BT2 organic halogen compounds
BT3 organic compounds
BT1 organic iodine compounds
BT2 organic halogen compounds
BT3 organic compounds
BT1 reagents
RT phthalic acid

rosenblum counters
USE spark counters

ROSENBLUTH FORMULA [35; 35]
RT cross sections
RT elastic scattering
RT four momentum transfer

ROSENBLUTH-NELKIN MODEL [1; 1]
RT neutrons
RT transport theory

ROSENFELD FORCE [23; 23]
UF *rosenfeld mixture*
RT nucleon-nucleon potential
RT nucleons
RT potentials

rosenfeld mixture
USE rosenfeld force

ROSPO REACTOR [1; 1]
UF *casaccia rospo reactor*
UF *reatt. org. sp. pot. zero*
BT1 enriched uranium reactors
BT2 reactors
BT1 organic moderated reactors
BT2 reactors
BT1 tank type reactors
BT2 reactors
BT1 zero power reactors
BT2 experimental reactors
BT3 research and test reactors
BT4 reactors

ROSSELAND APPROXIMATION [20; 20]
RT boundary layers
RT heat transfer
RT thermal radiation

rossendorf ass. for crit. exp.
USE rake-2 reactor

rossendorf wwr-sm reactor
USE wwr-sm rossendorf reactor

rossendorf zfk
USE zfk rossendorf

ROSSI ALPHA METHOD [50; 50]
RT reactor period

ROTAMAK DEVICES [56; 56] *Aug 86*
(A compact torus device in which a rotating magnetic field is used to maintain the toroidal plasma current.)
BT1 compact torus
BT2 tori

ROTATING CRYSTAL METHOD [90; 90]
BT1 diffraction methods
RT weissenberg method

ROTATING GENERATORS [105; 219]
UF *homopolar generators*
BT1 electric generators
BT2 electrical equipment
BT3 equipment
NT1 superconducting generators

ROTATING PLASMA [374; 374] *Aug 8*
BT1 plasma

ROTATION [8,771; 8,771]
RT backbending
RT coriolis force
RT guiding-center approximation
RT gyroscopes
RT moment of inertia
RT precession

→ **ROTATION-VIBRATION MODEL** [2; 2] *Sep 91*
BT1 collective model
BT2 nuclear models
BT3 mathematical models
RT deformed nuclei
RT rotational states
RT vibrational states

rotational band
USE rotational states

ROTATIONAL INVARIANCE [302; 30
BT1 invariance principles
RT axial symmetry

ROTATIONAL STATES [10,370; 10,37
UF *collective states (rotational)*
UF *rotational band*
BT1 excited states
BT2 energy levels
RT backbending
RT rotation-vibration model

ROTATIONAL TRANSFORM [498; 4
Sep 77
(The displacement of a magnetic line o force in a single circuit about a toroid tube so that it does not close upon itse
RT magnetic confinement
RT magnetic field configurations
RT magnetic fields
RT magnetic flux coordinates
RT magnetic surfaces
RT sawtooth oscillations
RT shear
RT thermonuclear devices
RT toroidal configuration

ROTONS [345; 345]
BT1 quasi particles
RT landau liquid helium theory

ROTORS [866; 997]
NT1 flywheels
RT armatures
RT machine parts
RT stators

rough vacuum
   USE   low pressure

ROUGHNESS [1,417; 1,417]
   UF   *smoothness*
   BT1   surface properties

rous sarcoma virus
   USE   oncogenic viruses

ROUTING [92; 92] *Jan 84*
   RT   evacuation
   RT   external zones
   RT   rail transport
   RT   road transport
   RT   waste transportation

ROVER REACTORS [36; 36]
   UF   *rocket reactor exp. rover*
   BT1   experimental reactors
     BT2   research and test reactors
       BT3   reactors
   BT1   hydrogen cooled reactors
     BT2   gas cooled reactors
       BT3   reactors
   BT1   space propulsion reactors
     BT2   propulsion reactors
       BT3   power reactors
         BT4   reactors
     BT2   space power reactors
       BT3   mobile reactors
         BT4   reactors
       BT3   power reactors
         BT4   reactors

ROVNO-1 REACTOR [20; 20] *Aug 84*
   BT1   wwer type reactors
     BT2   pwr type reactors
       BT3   enriched uranium reactors
         BT4   reactors
       BT3   power reactors
         BT4   reactors
       BT3   thermal reactors
         BT4   reactors
       BT3   water cooled reactors
         BT4   reactors
       BT3   water moderated reactors
         BT4   reactors

ROVNO-2 REACTOR [17; 17] *Aug 84*
   BT1   wwer type reactors
     BT2   pwr type reactors
       BT3   enriched uranium reactors
         BT4   reactors
       BT3   power reactors
         BT4   reactors
       BT3   thermal reactors
         BT4   reactors
       BT3   water cooled reactors
         BT4   reactors
       BT3   water moderated reactors
         BT4   reactors

ROVNO-3 REACTOR [19; 19] *Aug 84*
   BT1   wwer type reactors
     BT2   pwr type reactors
       BT3   enriched uranium reactors
         BT4   reactors
       BT3   power reactors
         BT4   reactors
       BT3   thermal reactors
         BT4   reactors
       BT3   water cooled reactors
         BT4   reactors
       BT3   water moderated reactors
         BT4   reactors

ROVNO-4 REACTOR [6; 6] *Aug 84*
   BT1   wwer type reactors
     BT2   pwr type reactors
       BT3   enriched uranium reactors
         BT4   reactors
       BT3   power reactors
         BT4   reactors
       BT3   thermal reactors
         BT4   reactors
       BT3   water cooled reactors
         BT4   reactors
       BT3   water moderated reactors
         BT4   reactors

ROVNO-5 REACTOR [3; 3] *Aug 84*
   BT1   wwer type reactors
     BT2   pwr type reactors
       BT3   enriched uranium reactors
         BT4   reactors
       BT3   power reactors
         BT4   reactors
       BT3   thermal reactors
         BT4   reactors
       BT3   water cooled reactors
         BT4   reactors
       BT3   water moderated reactors
         BT4   reactors

ROWE YANKEE REACTOR [141; 141]
   UF   *yankee rowe reactor*
   BT1   pwr type reactors
     BT2   enriched uranium reactors
       BT3   reactors
     BT2   power reactors
       BT3   reactors
     BT2   thermal reactors
       BT3   reactors
     BT2   water cooled reactors
       BT3   reactors
     BT2   water moderated reactors
       BT3   reactors

ROXBY DOWNS DEPOSIT [34; 34]
Dec 80
   BT1   uranium deposits
     BT2   geologic deposits
   RT   olympic dam mine
   RT   south australia
   RT   uranium ores

ROYAL JELLY [1; 1]
   BT1   radioprotective substances
     BT2   drugs
     BT2   response modifying factors
   RT   insects

RP-10 REACTOR [9; 9] *Aug 87*
(Peruvian Nuclear Energy Institute, lima, Peru.)
   BT1   pool type reactors
     BT2   water cooled reactors
       BT3   reactors
     BT2   water moderated reactors
       BT3   reactors
   BT1   research reactors
     BT2   research and test reactors
       BT3   reactors

RPL DOSEMETERS [290; 290]
   UF   *fluorod*
   UF   *glass dosemeters*
   UF   *radiophotoluminescent dosemete*
   BT1   luminescent dosemeters
     BT2   dosemeters
       BT3   measuring instruments
   RT   phosphate glass

RPT REACTOR [18; 18]
(Moscow, USSR)
   UF   *mr-2 moscow reactor*
   UF   *phys.-tech. res. r. moscow*
   BT1   enriched uranium reactors
     BT2   reactors
   BT1   lwgr type reactors
     BT2   graphite moderated reactors
       BT3   reactors
     BT2   water cooled reactors
       BT3   reactors
   BT1   mixed spectrum reactors
     BT2   reactors
   BT1   research reactors
     BT2   research and test reactors
       BT3   reactors
   BT1   tank type reactors
     BT2   reactors

rra
   USE   radioreceptor assay

rrc, kalpakkam
   USE   igcar

rscw reactor
   USE   wsur reactor

rsi avogadro reactor
   USE   avogadro rs-1 reactor

RTP REACTOR [31; 31] *Dec 84*
(Reaktor Triga Puspati.)
   UF   *puspati triga reactor*
   UF   *reactor triga puspati*
   UF   *triga puspati reactor*
   BT1   isotope production reactors
     BT2   irradiation reactors
       BT3   reactors
   BT1   triga type reactors
     BT2   enriched uranium reactors
       BT3   reactors
     BT2   hydride moderated reactors
       BT3   reactors
     BT2   research and test reactors
       BT3   reactors
     BT2   solid homogeneous reactors
       BT3   homogeneous reactors
         BT4   reactors
     BT2   water cooled reactors
       BT3   reactors
     BT2   water moderated reactors
       BT3   reactors

RTR REACTOR [5; 5]
   UF   *resonance test reactor savanna*
   UF   *savannah river lab rtr reactor*
   BT1   heavy water moderated reactors
     BT2   reactors
   BT1   production reactors
     BT2   reactors

RTS-1 REACTOR [1; 1]
(Centre for Military Applications of Nuclear Energy, Pisa, Italy)
   UF   *galileo galilei italy*
   UF   *san piero a grado pisa reactor*
   BT1   enriched uranium reactors
     BT2   reactors
   BT1   isotope production reactors
     BT2   irradiation reactors
       BT3   reactors
   BT1   pool type reactors
     BT2   water cooled reactors
       BT3   reactors
     BT2   water moderated reactors
       BT3   reactors
   BT1   research reactors
     BT2   research and test reactors
       BT3   reactors
   BT1   test reactors
     BT2   research and test reactors
       BT3   reactors
     BT2   test facilities
   BT1   thermal reactors
     BT2   reactors
   BT1   training reactors
     BT2   research and test reactors
       BT3   reactors

rubber (natural)
   USE   natural rubber

rubber trees
   USE   hevea

RUBBERS [527; 801]
   BT1   elastomers
     BT2   polymers
   BT1   organic polymers
     BT2   organic compounds

- BT2 polymers
- NT1 buna
- NT1 latex
- NT1 natural rubber
- NT1 silastic
- NT1 viton
- RT dielectric materials
- RT plasticizers
- RT vulcanization

rubella virus
- USE measles virus

rubeola
- USE measles

rubeola virus
- USE measles virus

RUBIDIUM [1,798; 1,798]
- BT1 alkali metals
- BT2 metals
- BT3 elements

RUBIDIUM ADDITIONS [17; 17]
(Alloys containing not more than 1% Rb are listed here.)
- RT rubidium alloys
- RT rubidium compounds

RUBIDIUM ALLOYS [72; 74]
(Alloys containing more than 1% Rb.)
- BT1 alloys
- NT1 rubidium base alloys
- RT rubidium additions

RUBIDIUM BASE ALLOYS [1; 1]
- BT1 rubidium alloys
- BT2 alloys

RUBIDIUM BROMIDES [136; 136]
- BT1 bromides
- BT2 bromine compounds
- BT3 halogen compounds
- BT2 halides
- BT3 halogen compounds
- BT1 rubidium compounds
- BT2 alkali metal compounds

RUBIDIUM CARBIDES [9; 9] *Feb 81*
- BT1 carbides
- BT2 carbon compounds
- BT1 rubidium compounds
- BT2 alkali metal compounds

RUBIDIUM CARBONATES [16; 16]
- BT1 carbonates
- BT2 carbon compounds
- BT2 oxygen compounds
- BT1 rubidium compounds
- BT2 alkali metal compounds

RUBIDIUM CHLORIDES [349; 349]
- BT1 chlorides
- BT2 chlorine compounds
- BT3 halogen compounds
- BT2 halides
- BT3 halogen compounds
- BT1 rubidium compounds
- BT2 alkali metal compounds

RUBIDIUM COMPLEXES [45; 45]
- BT1 alkali metal complexes
- BT2 complexes

RUBIDIUM COMPOUNDS [600; 1,733]
- BT1 alkali metal compounds
- NT1 rubidium bromides
- NT1 rubidium carbides
- NT1 rubidium carbonates
- NT1 rubidium chlorides
- NT1 rubidium fluorides
- NT1 rubidium hydrides
- NT1 rubidium hydroxides
- NT1 rubidium iodides
- NT1 rubidium nitrates
- NT1 rubidium oxides
- NT1 rubidium perchlorates
- NT1 rubidium phosphates
- NT1 rubidium selenides
- NT1 rubidium silicates
- NT1 rubidium silicides
- NT1 rubidium sulfates
- NT1 rubidium sulfides
- NT1 rubidium tungstates
- NT1 rubidium uranates
- RT rubidium additions

RUBIDIUM FLUORIDES [204; 204]
- BT1 fluorides
- BT2 fluorine compounds
- BT3 halogen compounds
- BT2 halides
- BT3 halogen compounds
- BT1 rubidium compounds
- BT2 alkali metal compounds

RUBIDIUM HYDRIDES [14; 14]
- BT1 hydrides
- BT2 hydrogen compounds
- BT1 rubidium compounds
- BT2 alkali metal compounds

RUBIDIUM HYDROXIDES [22; 22]
- BT1 hydroxides
- BT2 hydrogen compounds
- BT2 oxygen compounds
- BT1 rubidium compounds
- BT2 alkali metal compounds

RUBIDIUM IODIDES [203; 203]
- BT1 iodides
- BT2 halides
- BT3 halogen compounds
- BT2 iodine compounds
- BT3 halogen compounds
- BT1 rubidium compounds
- BT2 alkali metal compounds

RUBIDIUM IONS [146; 146]
- BT1 ions
- BT2 charged particles

RUBIDIUM ISOTOPES [459; 2,690]
- NT1 rubidium 100
- NT1 rubidium 101
- NT1 rubidium 102
- NT1 rubidium 103
- NT1 rubidium 74
- NT1 rubidium 75
- NT1 rubidium 76
- NT1 rubidium 77
- NT1 rubidium 78
- NT1 rubidium 79
- NT1 rubidium 80
- NT1 rubidium 81
- NT1 rubidium 82
- NT1 rubidium 83
- NT1 rubidium 84
- NT1 rubidium 85
- NT1 rubidium 86
- NT1 rubidium 87
- NT1 rubidium 88
- NT1 rubidium 89
- NT1 rubidium 90
- NT1 rubidium 91
- NT1 rubidium 92
- NT1 rubidium 93
- NT1 rubidium 94
- NT1 rubidium 95
- NT1 rubidium 96
- NT1 rubidium 97
- NT1 rubidium 98
- NT1 rubidium 99

RUBIDIUM NITRATES [65; 65]
- BT1 nitrates
- BT2 nitrogen compounds
- BT2 oxygen compounds
- BT1 rubidium compounds
- BT2 alkali metal compounds

RUBIDIUM OXIDES [64; 64]
- BT1 oxides
- BT2 chalcogenides
- BT2 oxygen compounds
- BT1 rubidium compounds
- BT2 alkali metal compounds

→ **RUBIDIUM PERCHLORATES** [0; 0] *Sep 91*
- BT1 perchlorates
- BT2 chlorine compounds
- BT3 halogen compounds
- BT2 oxygen compounds
- BT1 rubidium compounds
- BT2 alkali metal compounds

RUBIDIUM PHOSPHATES [44; 44]
- BT1 phosphates
- BT2 oxygen compounds
- BT2 phosphorus compounds
- BT1 rubidium compounds
- BT2 alkali metal compounds

→ **RUBIDIUM SELENIDES** [0; 0] *Sep 91*
- BT1 rubidium compounds
- BT2 alkali metal compounds
- BT1 selenides
- BT2 chalcogenides
- BT2 selenium compounds

RUBIDIUM SILICATES [5; 5] *Jan 77*
- BT1 rubidium compounds
- BT2 alkali metal compounds
- BT1 silicates
- BT2 oxygen compounds
- BT2 silicon compounds

→ **RUBIDIUM SILICIDES** [0; 0] *Sep 91*
- BT1 rubidium compounds
- BT2 alkali metal compounds
- BT1 silicides
- BT2 silicon compounds

RUBIDIUM SULFATES [82; 82]
- BT1 rubidium compounds
- BT2 alkali metal compounds
- BT1 sulfates
- BT2 oxygen compounds
- BT2 sulfur compounds

→ **RUBIDIUM SULFIDES** [0; 0] *Sep 91*
- BT1 rubidium compounds
- BT2 alkali metal compounds
- BT1 sulfides
- BT2 chalcogenides
- BT2 sulfur compounds

RUBIDIUM TUNGSTATES [26; 26] *May 78*
- BT1 rubidium compounds
- BT2 alkali metal compounds
- BT1 tungstates
- BT2 oxygen compounds
- BT2 tungsten compounds
- BT3 transition element compounds

RUBIDIUM URANATES [10; 10] *Nov*
- BT1 rubidium compounds
- BT2 alkali metal compounds
- BT1 uranates
- BT2 uranium compounds
- BT3 actinide compounds

RUBIDIUM 100 [18; 18] *Mar 76*
- BT1 beta-minus decay radioisotopes
- BT2 beta decay radioisotopes
- BT3 radioisotopes
- BT4 isotopes
- BT1 intermediate mass nuclei
- BT2 nuclei
- BT1 millisec living radioisotopes
- BT2 radioisotopes
- BT3 isotopes
- BT1 odd-odd nuclei

RUBIDIUM 100
- BT2 nuclei
- BT1 rubidium isotopes

RUBIDIUM 101 [8; 8]
- BT1 intermediate mass nuclei
- BT2 nuclei
- BT1 odd-even nuclei
- BT2 nuclei
- BT1 rubidium isotopes

RUBIDIUM 102 [9; 9]
- BT1 intermediate mass nuclei
- BT2 nuclei
- BT1 odd-odd nuclei
- BT2 nuclei
- BT1 rubidium isotopes

RUBIDIUM 103 [20; 20] *Jun 82*
- BT1 intermediate mass nuclei
- BT2 nuclei
- BT1 odd-even nuclei
- BT2 nuclei
- BT1 rubidium isotopes

RUBIDIUM 74 [4; 4] *Jun 77*
- BT1 beta-plus decay radioisotopes
- BT2 beta decay radioisotopes
- BT3 radioisotopes
- BT4 isotopes
- BT1 intermediate mass nuclei
- BT2 nuclei
- BT1 millisec living radioisotopes
- BT2 radioisotopes
- BT3 isotopes
- BT1 odd-odd nuclei
- BT2 nuclei
- BT1 rubidium isotopes

RUBIDIUM 75 [8; 8]
- BT1 beta-plus decay radioisotopes
- BT2 beta decay radioisotopes
- BT3 radioisotopes
- BT4 isotopes
- BT1 intermediate mass nuclei
- BT2 nuclei
- BT1 odd-even nuclei
- BT2 nuclei
- BT1 rubidium isotopes
- BT1 seconds living radioisotopes
- BT2 radioisotopes
- BT3 isotopes

RUBIDIUM 76 [22; 22]
- BT1 beta-plus decay radioisotopes
- BT2 beta decay radioisotopes
- BT3 radioisotopes
- BT4 isotopes
- BT1 electron capture radioisotopes
- BT2 beta decay radioisotopes
- BT3 radioisotopes
- BT4 isotopes
- BT1 intermediate mass nuclei
- BT2 nuclei
- BT1 isomeric transition isotopes
- BT2 radioisotopes
- BT3 isotopes
- BT1 microsec living radioisotopes
- BT2 radioisotopes
- BT3 isotopes
- BT1 odd-odd nuclei
- BT2 nuclei
- BT1 rubidium isotopes
- BT1 seconds living radioisotopes
- BT2 radioisotopes
- BT3 isotopes

RUBIDIUM 77 [36; 36]
- BT1 beta-plus decay radioisotopes
- BT2 beta decay radioisotopes
- BT3 radioisotopes
- BT4 isotopes
- BT1 electron capture radioisotopes
- BT2 beta decay radioisotopes
- BT3 radioisotopes
- BT4 isotopes
- BT1 intermediate mass nuclei
- BT2 nuclei
- BT1 minutes living radioisotopes
- BT2 radioisotopes
- BT3 isotopes
- BT1 odd-even nuclei
- BT2 nuclei
- BT1 rubidium isotopes

RUBIDIUM 78 [24; 24]
- BT1 beta-plus decay radioisotopes
- BT2 beta decay radioisotopes
- BT3 radioisotopes
- BT4 isotopes
- BT1 electron capture radioisotopes
- BT2 beta decay radioisotopes
- BT3 radioisotopes
- BT4 isotopes
- BT1 intermediate mass nuclei
- BT2 nuclei
- BT1 isomeric transition isotopes
- BT2 radioisotopes
- BT3 isotopes
- BT1 minutes living radioisotopes
- BT2 radioisotopes
- BT3 isotopes
- BT1 odd-odd nuclei
- BT2 nuclei
- BT1 rubidium isotopes

RUBIDIUM 79 [43; 43]
- BT1 beta-plus decay radioisotopes
- BT2 beta decay radioisotopes
- BT3 radioisotopes
- BT4 isotopes
- BT1 electron capture radioisotopes
- BT2 beta decay radioisotopes
- BT3 radioisotopes
- BT4 isotopes
- BT1 intermediate mass nuclei
- BT2 nuclei
- BT1 minutes living radioisotopes
- BT2 radioisotopes
- BT3 isotopes
- BT1 odd-even nuclei
- BT2 nuclei
- BT1 rubidium isotopes

RUBIDIUM 80 [14; 14]
- BT1 beta-plus decay radioisotopes
- BT2 beta decay radioisotopes
- BT3 radioisotopes
- BT4 isotopes
- BT1 intermediate mass nuclei
- BT2 nuclei
- BT1 odd-odd nuclei
- BT2 nuclei
- BT1 rubidium isotopes
- BT1 seconds living radioisotopes
- BT2 radioisotopes
- BT3 isotopes

RUBIDIUM 81 [218; 218]
- BT1 beta-plus decay radioisotopes
- BT2 beta decay radioisotopes
- BT3 radioisotopes
- BT4 isotopes
- BT1 electron capture radioisotopes
- BT2 beta decay radioisotopes
- BT3 radioisotopes
- BT4 isotopes
- BT1 hours living radioisotopes
- BT2 radioisotopes
- BT3 isotopes
- BT1 intermediate mass nuclei
- BT2 nuclei
- BT1 internal conversion radioisoto
- BT2 radioisotopes
- BT3 isotopes
- BT1 isomeric transition isotopes
- BT2 radioisotopes
- BT3 isotopes
- BT1 minutes living radioisotopes
- BT2 radioisotopes
- BT3 isotopes
- BT1 odd-even nuclei
- BT2 nuclei
- BT1 rubidium isotopes

RUBIDIUM 82 [228; 228]
- BT1 beta-plus decay radioisotopes
- BT2 beta decay radioisotopes
- BT3 radioisotopes
- BT4 isotopes
- BT1 electron capture radioisotopes
- BT2 beta decay radioisotopes
- BT3 radioisotopes
- BT4 isotopes
- BT1 hours living radioisotopes
- BT2 radioisotopes
- BT3 isotopes
- BT1 intermediate mass nuclei
- BT2 nuclei
- BT1 minutes living radioisotopes
- BT2 radioisotopes
- BT3 isotopes
- BT1 odd-odd nuclei
- BT2 nuclei
- BT1 rubidium isotopes

RUBIDIUM 83 [75; 75]
- BT1 days living radioisotopes
- BT2 radioisotopes
- BT3 isotopes
- BT1 electron capture radioisotopes
- BT2 beta decay radioisotopes
- BT3 radioisotopes
- BT4 isotopes
- BT1 intermediate mass nuclei
- BT2 nuclei
- BT1 odd-even nuclei
- BT2 nuclei
- BT1 rubidium isotopes

RUBIDIUM 84 [78; 78]
- BT1 beta-minus decay radioisotopes
- BT2 beta decay radioisotopes
- BT3 radioisotopes
- BT4 isotopes
- BT1 beta-plus decay radioisotopes
- BT2 beta decay radioisotopes
- BT3 radioisotopes
- BT4 isotopes
- BT1 days living radioisotopes
- BT2 radioisotopes
- BT3 isotopes
- BT1 electron capture radioisotopes
- BT2 beta decay radioisotopes
- BT3 radioisotopes
- BT4 isotopes
- BT1 intermediate mass nuclei
- BT2 nuclei
- BT1 isomeric transition isotopes
- BT2 radioisotopes
- BT3 isotopes
- BT1 minutes living radioisotopes
- BT2 radioisotopes
- BT3 isotopes
- BT1 odd-odd nuclei
- BT2 nuclei
- BT1 rubidium isotopes

RUBIDIUM 84 TARGET [4; 4] *Jul 76*
- BT1 targets

RUBIDIUM 85 [135; 135]
- BT1 intermediate mass nuclei
- BT2 nuclei
- BT1 isomeric transition isotopes
- BT2 radioisotopes
- BT3 isotopes
- BT1 nanosec living radioisotopes
- BT2 radioisotopes
- BT3 isotopes
- BT1 odd-even nuclei
- BT2 nuclei
- BT1 rubidium isotopes
- BT1 stable isotopes
- BT2 isotopes

RUBIDIUM 85 TARGET [74; 74]
- BT1 targets

RUBIDIUM 86 [652; 652]
  BT1   beta-minus decay radioisotopes
    BT2   beta decay radioisotopes
      BT3   radioisotopes
        BT4   isotopes
  BT1   days living radioisotopes
    BT2   radioisotopes
      BT3   isotopes
  BT1   electron capture radioisotopes
    BT2   beta decay radioisotopes
      BT3   radioisotopes
        BT4   isotopes
  BT1   intermediate mass nuclei
    BT2   nuclei
  BT1   isomeric transition isotopes
    BT2   radioisotopes
      BT3   isotopes
  BT1   minutes living radioisotopes
    BT2   radioisotopes
      BT3   isotopes
  BT1   odd-odd nuclei
    BT2   nuclei
  BT1   rubidium isotopes

RUBIDIUM 87 [602; 602]
  BT1   beta-minus decay radioisotopes
    BT2   beta decay radioisotopes
      BT3   radioisotopes
        BT4   isotopes
  BT1   intermediate mass nuclei
    BT2   nuclei
  BT1   odd-even nuclei
    BT2   nuclei
  BT1   rubidium isotopes
  BT1   years living radioisotopes
    BT2   radioisotopes
      BT3   isotopes

RUBIDIUM 87 TARGET [48; 48]
  BT1   targets

RUBIDIUM 88 [53; 53]
  BT1   beta-minus decay radioisotopes
    BT2   beta decay radioisotopes
      BT3   radioisotopes
        BT4   isotopes
  BT1   intermediate mass nuclei
    BT2   nuclei
  BT1   minutes living radioisotopes
    BT2   radioisotopes
      BT3   isotopes
  BT1   odd-odd nuclei
    BT2   nuclei
  BT1   rubidium isotopes

RUBIDIUM 88 TARGET [2; 2] *Jul 80*
  BT1   targets

RUBIDIUM 89 [32; 32]
  BT1   beta-minus decay radioisotopes
    BT2   beta decay radioisotopes
      BT3   radioisotopes
        BT4   isotopes
  BT1   intermediate mass nuclei
    BT2   nuclei
  BT1   minutes living radioisotopes
    BT2   radioisotopes
      BT3   isotopes
  BT1   odd-even nuclei
    BT2   nuclei
  BT1   rubidium isotopes

RUBIDIUM 90 [30; 30]
  BT1   beta-minus decay radioisotopes
    BT2   beta decay radioisotopes
      BT3   radioisotopes
        BT4   isotopes
  BT1   intermediate mass nuclei
    BT2   nuclei
  BT1   isomeric transition isotopes
    BT2   radioisotopes
      BT3   isotopes
  BT1   minutes living radioisotopes
    BT2   radioisotopes
      BT3   isotopes
  BT1   odd-odd nuclei
    BT2   nuclei
  BT1   rubidium isotopes

RUBIDIUM 91 [31; 31]
  BT1   beta-minus decay radioisotopes
    BT2   beta decay radioisotopes
      BT3   radioisotopes
        BT4   isotopes
  BT1   intermediate mass nuclei
    BT2   nuclei
  BT1   odd-even nuclei
    BT2   nuclei
  BT1   rubidium isotopes
  BT1   seconds living radioisotopes
    BT2   radioisotopes
      BT3   isotopes

RUBIDIUM 92 [27; 27]
  BT1   beta-minus decay radioisotopes
    BT2   beta decay radioisotopes
      BT3   radioisotopes
        BT4   isotopes
  BT1   intermediate mass nuclei
    BT2   nuclei
  BT1   odd-odd nuclei
    BT2   nuclei
  BT1   rubidium isotopes
  BT1   seconds living radioisotopes
    BT2   radioisotopes
      BT3   isotopes

RUBIDIUM 93 [60; 60]
  BT1   beta-minus decay radioisotopes
    BT2   beta decay radioisotopes
      BT3   radioisotopes
        BT4   isotopes
  BT1   intermediate mass nuclei
    BT2   nuclei
  BT1   odd-even nuclei
    BT2   nuclei
  BT1   rubidium isotopes
  BT1   seconds living radioisotopes
    BT2   radioisotopes
      BT3   isotopes

RUBIDIUM 94 [65; 65]
  BT1   beta-minus decay radioisotopes
    BT2   beta decay radioisotopes
      BT3   radioisotopes
        BT4   isotopes
  BT1   intermediate mass nuclei
    BT2   nuclei
  BT1   odd-odd nuclei
    BT2   nuclei
  BT1   rubidium isotopes
  BT1   seconds living radioisotopes
    BT2   radioisotopes
      BT3   isotopes

RUBIDIUM 95 [70; 70]
  BT1   beta-minus decay radioisotopes
    BT2   beta decay radioisotopes
      BT3   radioisotopes
        BT4   isotopes
  BT1   intermediate mass nuclei
    BT2   nuclei
  BT1   millisec living radioisotopes
    BT2   radioisotopes
      BT3   isotopes
  BT1   odd-even nuclei
    BT2   nuclei
  BT1   rubidium isotopes

RUBIDIUM 96 [51; 51]
  BT1   beta-minus decay radioisotopes
    BT2   beta decay radioisotopes
      BT3   radioisotopes
        BT4   isotopes
  BT1   intermediate mass nuclei
    BT2   nuclei
  BT1   millisec living radioisotopes
    BT2   radioisotopes
      BT3   isotopes
  BT1   odd-odd nuclei
    BT2   nuclei
  BT1   rubidium isotopes

RUBIDIUM 97 [52; 52]
  BT1   beta-minus decay radioisotopes
    BT2   beta decay radioisotopes
      BT3   radioisotopes
        BT4   isotopes
  BT1   intermediate mass nuclei
    BT2   nuclei
  BT1   millisec living radioisotopes
    BT2   radioisotopes
      BT3   isotopes
  BT1   odd-even nuclei
    BT2   nuclei
  BT1   rubidium isotopes

RUBIDIUM 98 [38; 38]
  BT1   beta-minus decay radioisotopes
    BT2   beta decay radioisotopes
      BT3   radioisotopes
        BT4   isotopes
  BT1   intermediate mass nuclei
    BT2   nuclei
  BT1   millisec living radioisotopes
    BT2   radioisotopes
      BT3   isotopes
  BT1   odd-odd nuclei
    BT2   nuclei
  BT1   rubidium isotopes

RUBIDIUM 99 [29; 29]
  BT1   beta-minus decay radioisotopes
    BT2   beta decay radioisotopes
      BT3   radioisotopes
        BT4   isotopes
  BT1   intermediate mass nuclei
    BT2   nuclei
  BT1   millisec living radioisotopes
    BT2   radioisotopes
      BT3   isotopes
  BT1   odd-even nuclei
    BT2   nuclei
  BT1   rubidium isotopes

RUBY [134; 134]
  BT1   corundum
    BT2   oxide minerals
      BT3   minerals

RUBY LASERS [414; 414]
  BT1   solid state lasers
    BT2   lasers
      BT3   amplifiers
        BT4   equipment

RUDERMAN-KITTEL COUPLING [77; 77]
  BT1   coupling

RUDSTAM FORMULA [50; 50]
  RT   spallation

RULISON EVENT [72; 72]
  BT1   contained explosions
    BT2   underground explosions
      BT3   explosions
  BT1   nuclear explosions
    BT2   explosions
  BT1   plowshare project
  RT   natural gas
  RT   oil shales

RUM JUNGLE [63; 63]
  BT1   uranium mines
    BT2   mines
      BT3   underground facilities
  RT   australia

rumania
  USE   romania

rumen
  USE   ruminants
  AND   stomach

RUMINANTS [196; 3,802]
- UF+ *rumen*
- BT1 mammals
  - BT2 vertebrates
    - BT3 animals
- NT1 antelopes
- NT1 buffalo
- NT1 cattle
  - NT2 calves
  - NT2 cows
- NT1 deer
- NT1 goats
- NT1 llamas
- NT1 sheep

runaway (reactor accident)
- USE excursions

RUNAWAY ELECTRONS [482; 482]
- BT1 electrons
  - BT2 leptons
    - BT3 elementary particles
    - BT3 fermions

RUNGE-KUTTA METHOD [148; 148]
Mar 81
(A self-optimizing interpolation method.)
- BT1 interpolation
  - BT2 numerical solution

rupture disks
- USE relief valves

RUPTURES [3,395; 3,395]
- BT1 failures
- RT fracture properties
- RT fractures

RURAL AREAS [75; 75]
- RT rural populations

RURAL POPULATIONS [77; 77]
- BT1 human populations
  - BT2 populations
- RT rural areas

russell-saunders coupling
- USE l-s coupling

russellville-1 arkansas react.
- USE arkansas-1 reactor

russellville-2 arkansas react.
- USE arkansas-2 reactor

RUTHENIUM [1,338; 1,338]
- BT1 platinum metals
  - BT2 transition elements
    - BT3 metals
      - BT4 elements

RUTHENIUM ADDITIONS [48; 48]
(Alloys containing not more than 1% Ru are listed here.)
- RT ruthenium alloys
- RT ruthenium compounds

RUTHENIUM ALLOYS [522; 596]
(Alloys containing more than 1% Ru.)
- BT1 platinum metal alloys
  - BT2 alloys
- NT1 ruthenium base alloys
- RT ruthenium additions

RUTHENIUM ARSENIDES [0; 0]
Sep 91
- BT1 arsenides
  - BT2 arsenic compounds
  - BT2 pnictides
- BT1 ruthenium compounds
  - BT2 transition element compounds

RUTHENIUM BASE ALLOYS [62; 62]
- BT1 ruthenium alloys
  - BT2 platinum metal alloys
    - BT3 alloys

RUTHENIUM BORIDES [43; 43] *Feb 76*
- BT1 borides
  - BT2 boron compounds
- BT1 ruthenium compounds
  - BT2 transition element compounds

RUTHENIUM BROMIDES [6; 6] *Jun 77*
- BT1 bromides
  - BT2 bromine compounds
    - BT3 halogen compounds
  - BT2 halides
    - BT3 halogen compounds
- BT1 ruthenium compounds
  - BT2 transition element compounds

RUTHENIUM CARBIDES [22; 22]
- BT1 carbides
  - BT2 carbon compounds
- BT1 ruthenium compounds
  - BT2 transition element compounds

RUTHENIUM CHLORIDES [109; 109]
- BT1 chlorides
  - BT2 chlorine compounds
    - BT3 halogen compounds
  - BT2 halides
    - BT3 halogen compounds
- BT1 ruthenium compounds
  - BT2 transition element compounds

RUTHENIUM COMPLEXES [1,296; 1,296]
- BT1 transition element complexes
  - BT2 complexes

RUTHENIUM COMPOUNDS [440; 1,171]
- BT1 transition element compounds
- NT1 ruthenium arsenides
- NT1 ruthenium borides
- NT1 ruthenium bromides
- NT1 ruthenium carbides
- NT1 ruthenium chlorides
- NT1 ruthenium fluorides
- NT1 ruthenium hydrides
- NT1 ruthenium hydroxides
- NT1 ruthenium nitrates
- NT1 ruthenium nitrides
- NT1 ruthenium nitrosyls
- NT1 ruthenium oxides
- NT1 ruthenium phosphides
- NT1 ruthenium selenides
- NT1 ruthenium silicides
- NT1 ruthenium sulfates
- NT1 ruthenium sulfides
- NT1 ruthenium tellurides
- RT ruthenium additions

RUTHENIUM FLUORIDES [47; 47]
- BT1 fluorides
  - BT2 fluorine compounds
    - BT3 halogen compounds
  - BT2 halides
    - BT3 halogen compounds
- BT1 ruthenium compounds
  - BT2 transition element compounds

RUTHENIUM HYDRIDES [26; 26]
Feb 76
- BT1 hydrides
  - BT2 hydrogen compounds
- BT1 ruthenium compounds
  - BT2 transition element compounds

RUTHENIUM HYDROXIDES [20; 20]
- BT1 hydroxides
  - BT2 hydrogen compounds
  - BT2 oxygen compounds
- BT1 ruthenium compounds
  - BT2 transition element compounds

RUTHENIUM IONS [57; 57]
- BT1 ions
  - BT2 charged particles

RUTHENIUM ISOTOPES [195; 2,582]
- NT1 ruthenium 100
- NT1 ruthenium 101
- NT1 ruthenium 102
- NT1 ruthenium 103
- NT1 ruthenium 104
- NT1 ruthenium 105
- NT1 ruthenium 106
- NT1 ruthenium 107
- NT1 ruthenium 108
- NT1 ruthenium 109
- NT1 ruthenium 110
- NT1 ruthenium 111
- NT1 ruthenium 112
- NT1 ruthenium 113
- NT1 ruthenium 91
- NT1 ruthenium 92
- NT1 ruthenium 93
- NT1 ruthenium 94
- NT1 ruthenium 95
- NT1 ruthenium 96
- NT1 ruthenium 97
- NT1 ruthenium 98
- NT1 ruthenium 99

RUTHENIUM NITRATES [22; 22]
- BT1 nitrates
  - BT2 nitrogen compounds
  - BT2 oxygen compounds
- BT1 ruthenium compounds
  - BT2 transition element compounds

→ **RUTHENIUM NITRIDES** [0; 0] *Sep 91*
- BT1 nitrides
  - BT2 nitrogen compounds
  - BT2 pnictides
- BT1 ruthenium compounds
  - BT2 transition element compounds

RUTHENIUM NITROSYLS [30; 30]
- BT1 ruthenium compounds
  - BT2 transition element compounds

RUTHENIUM OXIDES [395; 395]
- BT1 oxides
  - BT2 chalcogenides
  - BT2 oxygen compounds
- BT1 ruthenium compounds
  - BT2 transition element compounds

RUTHENIUM PHOSPHIDES [12; 12]
Jul 78
- BT1 phosphides
  - BT2 phosphorus compounds
  - BT2 pnictides
- BT1 ruthenium compounds
  - BT2 transition element compounds

→ **RUTHENIUM SELENIDES** [0; 0] *Sep 91*
- BT1 ruthenium compounds
  - BT2 transition element compounds
- BT1 selenides
  - BT2 chalcogenides
  - BT2 selenium compounds

RUTHENIUM SILICIDES [55; 55]
Jul 86
- BT1 ruthenium compounds
  - BT2 transition element compounds
- BT1 silicides
  - BT2 silicon compounds

RUTHENIUM SULFATES [14; 14]
- BT1 ruthenium compounds
  - BT2 transition element compounds
- BT1 sulfates
  - BT2 oxygen compounds
  - BT2 sulfur compounds

RUTHENIUM SULFIDES [9; 9] *Nov 78*
BT1 ruthenium compounds
BT2 transition element compounds
BT1 sulfides
BT2 chalcogenides
BT2 sulfur compounds

→ **RUTHENIUM TELLURIDES** [0; 0]
Sep 91
BT1 ruthenium compounds
BT2 transition element compounds
BT1 tellurides
BT2 chalcogenides
BT2 tellurium compounds

RUTHENIUM 100 [88; 88]
BT1 even-even nuclei
BT2 nuclei
BT1 intermediate mass nuclei
BT2 nuclei
BT1 ruthenium isotopes
BT1 stable isotopes
BT2 isotopes

RUTHENIUM 100 TARGET [53; 53]
BT1 targets

RUTHENIUM 101 [74; 74]
BT1 even-odd nuclei
BT2 nuclei
BT1 intermediate mass nuclei
BT2 nuclei
BT1 ruthenium isotopes
BT1 stable isotopes
BT2 isotopes

RUTHENIUM 101 TARGET [33; 33]
Oct 76
BT1 targets

RUTHENIUM 102 [98; 98]
BT1 even-even nuclei
BT2 nuclei
BT1 intermediate mass nuclei
BT2 nuclei
BT1 ruthenium isotopes
BT1 stable isotopes
BT2 isotopes

RUTHENIUM 102 TARGET [70; 70]
Oct 75
BT1 targets

RUTHENIUM 103 [814; 814]
BT1 beta-minus decay radioisotopes
BT2 beta decay radioisotopes
BT3 radioisotopes
BT4 isotopes
BT1 days living radioisotopes
BT2 radioisotopes
BT3 isotopes
BT1 even-odd nuclei
BT2 nuclei
BT1 intermediate mass nuclei
BT2 nuclei
BT1 ruthenium isotopes

RUTHENIUM 103 TARGET [3; 3]
Feb 84
BT1 targets

RUTHENIUM 104 [95; 95]
BT1 even-even nuclei
BT2 nuclei
BT1 intermediate mass nuclei
BT2 nuclei
BT1 ruthenium isotopes
BT1 stable isotopes
BT2 isotopes

RUTHENIUM 104 REACTIONS [8; 8]
Aug 84
BT1 heavy ion reactions
BT2 nuclear reactions

RUTHENIUM 104 TARGET [96; 96]
BT1 targets

RUTHENIUM 105 [59; 59]
BT1 beta-minus decay radioisotopes
BT2 beta decay radioisotopes
BT3 radioisotopes
BT4 isotopes
BT1 even-odd nuclei
BT2 nuclei
BT1 hours living radioisotopes
BT2 radioisotopes
BT3 isotopes
BT1 intermediate mass nuclei
BT2 nuclei
BT1 ruthenium isotopes

RUTHENIUM 106 [1,354; 1,354]
BT1 beta-minus decay radioisotopes
BT2 beta decay radioisotopes
BT3 radioisotopes
BT4 isotopes
BT1 even-even nuclei
BT2 nuclei
BT1 intermediate mass nuclei
BT2 nuclei
BT1 ruthenium isotopes
BT1 years living radioisotopes
BT2 radioisotopes
BT3 isotopes

RUTHENIUM 107 [19; 19]
BT1 beta-minus decay radioisotopes
BT2 beta decay radioisotopes
BT3 radioisotopes
BT4 isotopes
BT1 even-odd nuclei
BT2 nuclei
BT1 intermediate mass nuclei
BT2 nuclei
BT1 minutes living radioisotopes
BT2 radioisotopes
BT3 isotopes
BT1 ruthenium isotopes

RUTHENIUM 108 [37; 37]
BT1 beta-minus decay radioisotopes
BT2 beta decay radioisotopes
BT3 radioisotopes
BT4 isotopes
BT1 even-even nuclei
BT2 nuclei
BT1 intermediate mass nuclei
BT2 nuclei
BT1 minutes living radioisotopes
BT2 radioisotopes
BT3 isotopes
BT1 ruthenium isotopes

RUTHENIUM 109 [21; 21]
BT1 beta-minus decay radioisotopes
BT2 beta decay radioisotopes
BT3 radioisotopes
BT4 isotopes
BT1 even-odd nuclei
BT2 nuclei
BT1 intermediate mass nuclei
BT2 nuclei
BT1 ruthenium isotopes
BT1 seconds living radioisotopes
BT2 radioisotopes
BT3 isotopes

RUTHENIUM 110 [15; 15]
BT1 beta-minus decay radioisotopes
BT2 beta decay radioisotopes
BT3 radioisotopes
BT4 isotopes
BT1 even-even nuclei
BT2 nuclei
BT1 intermediate mass nuclei
BT2 nuclei
BT1 ruthenium isotopes
BT1 seconds living radioisotopes
BT2 radioisotopes
BT3 isotopes

RUTHENIUM 111 [9; 9]
BT1 beta-minus decay radioisotopes
BT2 beta decay radioisotopes
BT3 radioisotopes
BT4 isotopes
BT1 even-odd nuclei
BT2 nuclei
BT1 intermediate mass nuclei
BT2 nuclei
BT1 ruthenium isotopes
BT1 seconds living radioisotopes
BT2 radioisotopes
BT3 isotopes

RUTHENIUM 112 [12; 12] *Jan 79*
BT1 beta-minus decay radioisotopes
BT2 beta decay radioisotopes
BT3 radioisotopes
BT4 isotopes
BT1 even-even nuclei
BT2 nuclei
BT1 intermediate mass nuclei
BT2 nuclei
BT1 ruthenium isotopes
BT1 seconds living radioisotopes
BT2 radioisotopes
BT3 isotopes

RUTHENIUM 113 [3; 3] *Jan 79*
BT1 beta-minus decay radioisotopes
BT2 beta decay radioisotopes
BT3 radioisotopes
BT4 isotopes
BT1 even-odd nuclei
BT2 nuclei
BT1 intermediate mass nuclei
BT2 nuclei
BT1 ruthenium isotopes
BT1 seconds living radioisotopes
BT2 radioisotopes
BT3 isotopes

RUTHENIUM 91 [5; 5] *Sep 83*
BT1 even-odd nuclei
BT2 nuclei
BT1 intermediate mass nuclei
BT2 nuclei
BT1 ruthenium isotopes

RUTHENIUM 92 [15; 15]
BT1 beta-plus decay radioisotopes
BT2 beta decay radioisotopes
BT3 radioisotopes
BT4 isotopes
BT1 electron capture radioisotopes
BT2 beta decay radioisotopes
BT3 radioisotopes
BT4 isotopes
BT1 even-even nuclei
BT2 nuclei
BT1 intermediate mass nuclei
BT2 nuclei
BT1 minutes living radioisotopes
BT2 radioisotopes
BT3 isotopes
BT1 ruthenium isotopes

RUTHENIUM 93 [21; 21]
BT1 beta-plus decay radioisotopes
BT2 beta decay radioisotopes
BT3 radioisotopes
BT4 isotopes
BT1 electron capture radioisotopes
BT2 beta decay radioisotopes
BT3 radioisotopes
BT4 isotopes
BT1 even-odd nuclei
BT2 nuclei
BT1 intermediate mass nuclei
BT2 nuclei
BT1 isomeric transition isotopes
BT2 radioisotopes
BT3 isotopes
BT1 minutes living radioisotopes
BT2 radioisotopes
BT3 isotopes
BT1 ruthenium isotopes
BT1 seconds living radioisotopes

BT2 radioisotopes
BT3 isotopes

RUTHENIUM 94 [47; 47]
BT1 electron capture radioisotopes
BT2 beta decay radioisotopes
BT3 radioisotopes
BT4 isotopes
BT1 even-even nuclei
BT2 nuclei
BT1 intermediate mass nuclei
BT2 nuclei
BT1 minutes living radioisotopes
BT2 radioisotopes
BT3 isotopes
BT1 ruthenium isotopes

RUTHENIUM 95 [20; 20]
BT1 beta-plus decay radioisotopes
BT2 beta decay radioisotopes
BT3 radioisotopes
BT4 isotopes
BT1 electron capture radioisotopes
BT2 beta decay radioisotopes
BT3 radioisotopes
BT4 isotopes
BT1 even-odd nuclei
BT2 nuclei
BT1 hours living radioisotopes
BT2 radioisotopes
BT3 isotopes
BT1 intermediate mass nuclei
BT2 nuclei
BT1 ruthenium isotopes

RUTHENIUM 96 [42; 42]
BT1 even-even nuclei
BT2 nuclei
BT1 intermediate mass nuclei
BT2 nuclei
BT1 ruthenium isotopes
BT1 stable isotopes
BT2 isotopes

RUTHENIUM 96 TARGET [61; 61]
BT1 targets

RUTHENIUM 97 [107; 107]
BT1 days living radioisotopes
BT2 radioisotopes
BT3 isotopes
BT1 electron capture radioisotopes
BT2 beta decay radioisotopes
BT3 radioisotopes
BT4 isotopes
BT1 even-odd nuclei
BT2 nuclei
BT1 intermediate mass nuclei
BT2 nuclei
BT1 ruthenium isotopes

RUTHENIUM 98 [32; 32]
BT1 even-even nuclei
BT2 nuclei
BT1 intermediate mass nuclei
BT2 nuclei
BT1 ruthenium isotopes
BT1 stable isotopes
BT2 isotopes

RUTHENIUM 98 TARGET [9; 9]
Feb 79
BT1 targets

RUTHENIUM 99 [107; 107]
BT1 even-odd nuclei
BT2 nuclei
BT1 intermediate mass nuclei
BT2 nuclei
BT1 ruthenium isotopes
BT1 stable isotopes
BT2 isotopes

RUTHENIUM 99 TARGET [19; 19]
Nov 78
BT1 targets

RUTHERFORD SCATTERING
[1,871; 1,871]
BT1 elastic scattering
BT2 scattering

RUTHERFORDITE [4; 4]
BT1 carbonate minerals
BT2 minerals
BT1 uranium minerals
BT2 radioactive minerals
BT3 minerals
BT3 radioactive materials
BT4 materials
RT uranium carbonates

rutherfordium
USE element 104

RUTILE [170; 170]
BT1 oxide minerals
BT2 minerals
BT1 radioactive minerals
BT2 minerals
BT2 radioactive materials
BT3 materials
RT titanium oxides

RV-1 REACTOR [3; 3]
(Venezuelan Scientific Research Institute, IVIC, Caracas, Venezuela)
UF *reactor venezolano-1*
BT1 enriched uranium reactors
BT2 reactors
BT1 materials testing reactors
BT2 irradiation reactors
BT3 reactors
BT1 pool type reactors
BT2 water cooled reactors
BT3 reactors
BT2 water moderated reactors
BT3 reactors
BT1 research reactors
BT2 research and test reactors
BT3 reactors
BT1 training reactors
BT2 research and test reactors
BT3 reactors

→ **RWANDA** [0; 0] Oct 91
BT1 africa
BT1 developing countries

RWE-BAYERNWERK REACTOR
[179; 179]
UF *gundremmingen-1 reactor*
UF *kernkraftwerk rwe-bayernwerk*
UF *krb reactor*
UF *rwe-bayernwerk-a reactor*
BT1 bwr type reactors
BT2 enriched uranium reactors
BT3 reactors
BT2 power reactors
BT3 reactors
BT2 thermal reactors
BT3 reactors
BT2 water cooled reactors
BT3 reactors
BT2 water moderated reactors
BT3 reactors

rwe-bayernwerk-a reactor
USE rwe-bayernwerk reactor

rwe-bayernwerk-b reactor
USE gundremmingen-2 reactor

rwe-bayernwerk-c reactor
USE gundremmingen-3 reactor

rwsu reactor
USE wsur reactor

rydberg constant
USE rydberg correction

RYDBERG CORRECTION [394; 394]
UF *rydberg constant*
BT1 corrections
RT balmer lines
RT energy levels
RT energy spectra
RT rydberg states

RYDBERG EQUATION [24; 24]
BT1 equations

RYDBERG STATES [1,085; 1,085]
Nov 77
BT1 excited states
BT2 energy levels
RT electronic structure
RT rydberg correction

RYDBERG-KLEIN-REES METHOD
[30; 30]
UF *rkr method*
RT electronic structure
RT spectra
RT vibrational states

RYE [114; 114]
UF *secale*
BT1 cereals
BT2 gramineae
BT3 plants
RT claviceps

R2-0 REACTOR [9; 9]
(Aktiebolaget Atomenergi, Nykoping, Studsvik, Sweden)
UF *studsvik r2-0 reactor*
UF *swedish reactor r2-0*
BT1 enriched uranium reactors
BT2 reactors
BT1 isotope production reactors
BT2 irradiation reactors
BT3 reactors
BT1 pool type reactors
BT2 water cooled reactors
BT3 reactors
BT2 water moderated reactors
BT3 reactors
BT1 research reactors
BT2 research and test reactors
BT3 reactors

S CENTERS [19; 19] Apr 78
BT1 color centers
BT2 vacancies
BT3 point defects
BT4 crystal defects
BT5 crystal structure

S CHANNEL [886; 886]
RT mandelstam representation
RT particle interactions
RT t channel
RT u channel

S CODES [3,953; 3,953]
BT1 computer codes

S MATRIX [7,248; 7,248]
UF *collision matrix*
UF *t matrix*
BT1 matrices
RT analytic functions
RT detailed balance principle
RT landau curves
RT quantum field theory
RT scattering
RT scattering amplitudes
RT singularity
RT unitarity

RT unitary pole approximation
RT yang-feldman formalism

S PROCESS [371; 371]
(Slow process in stellar nucleosynthesis.)
BT1 star evolution
RT nucleosynthesis
RT stars

S STATES [3,669; 3,669]
BT1 energy levels

S WAVES [3,584; 3,584]
(For seismic waves use SEISMIC S WAVES.)
BT1 partial waves
RT angular momentum
RT quantum mechanics

s waves (seismic)
USE seismic s waves

S-N DIAGRAM [763; 763]
BT1 diagrams
BT2 information
RT fatigue
RT materials testing
RT stresses

s-1000 resonances
(Prior to December 1987 this was a valid descriptor.)
USE mesons

s-1930 resonances
(Prior to December 1987 this was a valid descriptor.)
USE x-1935 mesons

s-993 resonances
(Prior to December 1987 this was a valid descriptor.)
USE f0-975 mesons

saas
(Prior to May 1991, this was a valid descriptor.)
USE bundesamt fuer strahlenschutz

SABOTAGE [443; 443]
RT hazards
RT human intrusion
RT physical protection
RT physical protection devices
RT safety
RT secrecy protection
RT security
RT security personnel

SACCHARIDES [319; 9,999]
UF *glycides*
UF *sugars*
UF+ *amino sugars*
UF+ *aminoglycides*
UF+ *streptozocin*
UF+ *streptozotocin*
BT1 carbohydrates
BT2 organic compounds
NT1 gangliosides
NT1 glycolipids
NT2 cerebrosides
NT1 glycoproteins
NT2 lactoferrin
NT2 lh
NT2 ovalbumin
NT1 monosaccharides
NT2 erythritol
NT2 hexoses
NT3 fructose
NT3 galactose
NT3 glucose
NT3 hexosamines
NT4 glucosamine
NT3 mannose
NT3 sorbose
NT2 inositols
NT3 inositol
NT2 pentoses
NT3 arabinose
NT3 deoxyribose
NT3 ribose
NT3 ribulose
NT3 xylose
NT2 sedoheptulose
NT2 sorbitol
NT1 oligosaccharides
NT2 disaccharides
NT3 cellobiose
NT3 lactose
NT3 maltose
NT3 melibiose
NT3 saccharose
NT2 raffinose
NT1 polysaccharides
NT2 agar
NT2 alginic acid
NT2 cellophane
NT2 cellulose
NT2 dextran
NT2 dextrin
NT2 glycogen
NT2 gum acacia
NT2 inulin
NT2 lignin
NT2 lipopolysaccharides
NT2 mucopolysaccharides
NT3 chitin
NT3 chondroitin
NT3 heparin
NT3 hyaluronic acid
NT2 mucoproteins
NT3 haptoglobins
NT3 intrinsic factor
NT3 phytohemagglutinin
NT2 nitrocellulose
NT2 pectins
NT2 rayon
NT2 sialic acid
NT2 starch
NT2 viscose
RT glycolysis
RT glycosuria
RT hyperglycemia

SACCHARIN [24; 24]
BT1 organic oxygen compounds
BT2 organic compounds
BT1 thiazoles
BT2 azoles
BT3 heterocyclic compounds
BT4 organic compounds
BT3 organic nitrogen compounds
BT4 organic compounds
BT2 organic sulfur compounds
BT3 organic compounds

SACCHAROMYCES [148; 929]
BT1 yeasts
BT2 fungi
BT3 plants
BT2 microorganisms
NT1 saccharomyces cerevisiae

SACCHAROMYCES CEREVISIAE [782; 782]
BT1 saccharomyces
BT2 yeasts
BT3 fungi
BT4 plants
BT3 microorganisms

SACCHAROSE [568; 568]
UF *sucrose*
UF *sugar*
BT1 disaccharides
BT2 oligosaccharides
BT3 saccharides
BT4 carbohydrates
BT5 organic compounds

saclay (cea)
USE cea saclay

SACLAY LINAC [154; 154]
BT1 linear accelerators
BT2 accelerators

saclay synchrotron
USE saturne

sacramento rancho seco-1 react
USE rancho seco-1 reactor

sacramento rancho seco-2 react
USE rancho seco-2 reactor

SADDLE-POINT METHOD [301; 301]
RT mathematics

SAFARI-1 REACTOR [37; 37]
(South African Atomic Energy Board, Pretoria, South Africa)
BT1 enriched uranium reactors
BT2 reactors
BT1 tank type reactors
BT2 reactors
BT1 test reactors
BT2 research and test reactors
BT3 reactors
BT2 test facilities
BT1 thermal reactors
BT2 reactors
BT1 water cooled reactors
BT2 reactors
BT1 water moderated reactors
BT2 reactors

safe low power critical experi
USE slowpoke type reactors

SAFEGUARD REGULATIONS [466; 466]
BT1 regulations
BT2 laws
RT nuclear materials possession
RT safeguards

SAFEGUARDS [4,378; 5,648]
(Those measures designed to guard against the diversion of material such as source and special nuclear material from uses permitted by law or treaty, and to give timely indication of possible diversion or credible assurance that no diversion has occurred.)
NT1 domestic safeguards
NT1 iaea safeguards
RT accounting
RT atomic energy control
RT denatured fuel
RT detection
RT identification systems
RT inspection
RT inventories
RT legal aspects
RT losses
RT material balance area
RT material unaccounted for
RT motion detection systems
RT non-proliferation treaty
RT nuclear disarmament
RT nuclear materials diversion
RT nuclear materials management
RT nuclear materials possession
RT physical protection
RT physical protection devices
RT proliferation
RT safeguard regulations
RT security personnel
RT security seals
RT strategic points

SAFETY [10,587; 42,173]
(For general aspects of safety and protection of personnel.)
- UF protection (safety)
- NT1 occupational safety
- NT1 reactor safety
- RT accidents
- RT alara
- RT civil defense
- RT ethical aspects
- RT failures
- RT fire extinguishers
- RT fire prevention
- RT hazards
- RT health hazards
- RT human factors
- RT injuries
- RT quality assurance
- RT quality control
- RT radiation protection
- RT sabotage
- RT safety engineering
- RT safety showers
- RT safety standards
- RT security
- RT working conditions

safety (nuclear)
- USE radiation protection

SAFETY ANALYSIS [3,125; 3,125] Dec 76
- RT licensing regulations
- RT probabilistic estimation
- RT public relations
- RT risk assessment
- RT safety reports

SAFETY ENGINEERING [4,840; 4,840]
- RT alarm systems
- RT fires
- RT hazards
- RT human factors
- RT pressure release
- RT reactor safety
- RT safety
- RT seismic isolation
- RT smoke detectors
- RT systems analysis

safety of life at sea conv.
- USE solas convention

SAFETY REPORTS [198; 198] Dec 76
(For items about safety reports, not for items which are safety reports.)
- RT document types
- RT licensing regulations
- RT safety analysis

safety res. exper. facility re
- USE saref reactor

safety rods
- USE scram rods

SAFETY SHOWERS [9; 9]
- UF emergency showers
- RT burns
- RT decontamination
- RT first aid
- RT safety

SAFETY STANDARDS [3,475; 6,732]
- UF standards (safety)
- BT1 standards
- NT1 annual limit of intake
- NT1 dose limits
- NT1 maximum acceptable contaminati
- NT1 maximum inhalation quantity
- NT1 maximum permissible activity
- NT1 maximum permissible body burde
- NT1 maximum permissible concentrat
- NT1 maximum permissible dose
- NT1 maximum permissible exposure
- NT1 maximum permissible intake
- NT1 maximum permissible level
- RT federal radiation council
- RT ges fuer reaktorsicherheit
- RT legal aspects
- RT licensing
- RT radiation protection
- RT radiation protection laws
- RT reactor safety
- RT recommendations
- RT regulations
- RT retrofitting
- RT safety
- RT standardization
- RT standards document

safety test facility reactor
- USE stf reactor

safety valves
- USE valves

SAHA EQUATION [156; 156]
- UF saha-langmuir equation
- BT1 equations
- RT electric discharges
- RT thermodynamics

saha-langmuir equation
- USE saha equation

SAINT ALBAN-1 REACTOR [7; 7] Jul 84
- BT1 pwr type reactors
- BT2 enriched uranium reactors
- BT3 reactors
- BT2 power reactors
- BT3 reactors
- BT2 thermal reactors
- BT3 reactors
- BT2 water cooled reactors
- BT3 reactors
- BT2 water moderated reactors
- BT3 reactors

SAINT ALBAN-2 REACTOR [6; 6] Jul 84
- BT1 pwr type reactors
- BT2 enriched uranium reactors
- BT3 reactors
- BT2 power reactors
- BT3 reactors
- BT2 thermal reactors
- BT3 reactors
- BT2 water cooled reactors
- BT3 reactors
- BT2 water moderated reactors
- BT3 reactors

SAINT LAURENT-1 REACTOR [46; 46]
(St. Laurent des Eaux, Loir et Cher, France)
- UF edf-4 reactor
- BT1 gcr type reactors
- BT2 gas cooled reactors
- BT3 reactors
- BT2 graphite moderated reactors
- BT3 reactors
- BT1 power reactors
- BT2 reactors
- BT1 thermal reactors
- BT2 reactors

SAINT LAURENT-2 REACTOR [33; 33]
(St. Laurent des Eaux, Loir et Cher, France)
- BT1 gcr type reactors
- BT2 gas cooled reactors
- BT3 reactors
- BT2 graphite moderated reactors
- BT3 reactors
- BT1 power reactors
- BT2 reactors
- BT1 thermal reactors
- BT2 reactors

SAINT LUCIA [2; 2] Jun 90
- BT1 developing countries
- BT1 latin america
- BT1 west indies
- BT2 islands

saitama cyclotron
- USE ipcr cyclotron

saitama tunable h.i. linac
- USE rilac

salam hypothesis
- USE lee-yang theory

SALAM-POLKINGHORNE THEORY [0; 0]
- RT isospin

salam-weinberg gauge model
- USE weinberg lepton model

SALAMANDERS [46; 74]
- UF newts
- BT1 amphibians
- BT2 aquatic organisms
- BT2 vertebrates
- BT3 animals
- NT1 axolotl
- NT1 triturus

salazar triga-mk3 reactor
- USE triga-3-salazar reactor

SALEEITE [8; 8]
- BT1 phosphate minerals
- BT2 minerals
- BT1 uranium minerals
- BT2 radioactive minerals
- BT3 minerals
- BT3 radioactive materials
- BT4 materials
- RT magnesium phosphates
- RT uranium phosphates

salem nucl. gener. stat. un.-1
- USE salem-1 reactor

salem nucl. gener. stat. un.-2
- USE salem-2 reactor

SALEM-1 REACTOR [80; 80]
(Salem, New Jersey, USA)
- UF salem nucl. gener. stat. un.-1
- BT1 pwr type reactors
- BT2 enriched uranium reactors
- BT3 reactors
- BT2 power reactors
- BT3 reactors
- BT2 thermal reactors
- BT3 reactors
- BT2 water cooled reactors
- BT3 reactors
- BT2 water moderated reactors
- BT3 reactors

SALEM-2 REACTOR [60; 60]
(Salem, New Jersey, USA)
- UF salem nucl. gener. stat. un.-2
- BT1 pwr type reactors
- BT2 enriched uranium reactors
- BT3 reactors
- BT2 power reactors
- BT3 reactors

```
                BT2     thermal reactors
                BT3        reactors
                BT2     water cooled reactors
                BT3        reactors
                BT2     water moderated reactors
                BT3        reactors


        sales
            USE     trade

        SALICYLIC ACID [285; 285]
            UF      hydroxybenzoic acid-ortho
            BT1     hydroxy acids
                BT2     carboxylic acids
                    BT3     organic acids
                        BT4     organic compounds
            RT      pas

    §   SALINITY [602; 602]
            RT      desalination
            RT      estuaries
            RT      salts
            RT      seawater

        SALIVA [194; 194]
            BT1     body fluids
                BT2     biological materials
                    BT3     materials
            RT      amylase
            RT      salivary glands


        SALIVARY GLANDS [745; 745]
            BT1     glands
                BT2     organs
                    BT3     body
            RT      oral cavity
            RT      saliva


        SALMIN [1; 1]
            BT1     protamines
                BT2     blood coagulation factors
                    BT3     coagulants
                        BT4     hematologic agents
                            BT5     drugs
                BT2     proteins
                    BT3     organic compounds

        SALMON [96; 96]
            BT1     anadromous fishes
                BT2     fishes
                    BT3     aquatic organisms
                    BT3     vertebrates
                        BT4     animals

        SALMON EVENT [12; 12]
            BT1     vela project

        SALMONELLA [224; 465]
            BT1     bacteria
                BT2     microorganisms
            NT1     salmonella typhimurium
            RT      paratyphoid
            RT      typhoid

        SALMONELLA TYPHIMURIUM
        [244; 244]
            BT1     salmonella
                BT2     bacteria
                    BT3     microorganisms


        SALT CAVERNS [242; 242] Feb 83
            BT1     cavities
            RT      gorleben salt dome
            RT      radioactive waste disposal
            RT      salt deposits
            RT      underground disposal
            RT      underground storage
            RT      waste-rock interactions

        SALT DEPOSITS [3,085; 3,085]
            BT1     geologic deposits
            RT      asse salt mine
```

```
            RT      gorleben salt dome
            RT      radioactive waste disposal
            RT      salt caverns
            RT      salt vault project
            RT      underground disposal
            RT      wipp


    salt transport process
        USE     pyrochemical reprocessing


        SALT VAULT PROJECT [65; 65]
            RT      radioactive wastes
            RT      salt deposits
            RT      waste disposal


        SALTEX PROCESS [1; 1]
            BT1     purex process
                BT2     reprocessing
                    BT3     separation processes



        SALTING-OUT AGENTS [231; 231]
            RT      precipitation
            RT      solvent extraction


        SALTS [921; 3,570]
            (See also descriptors for specific salts.)
            NT1     molten salts
                NT2     flibe
            RT      brines
            RT      desalination
            RT      salinity


        SALYUT ORBITAL STATIONS [74; 74]
            BT1     satellites
            BT1     space vehicles


        SAMARIUM [1,409; 1,409]
            BT1     rare earths
                BT2     metals
                    BT3     elements


        SAMARIUM ADDITIONS [74; 74]
            (Alloys containing not more than 1% Sm
            are listed here.)
            BT1     rare earth additions
            RT      samarium alloys
            RT      samarium compounds


        SAMARIUM ALLOYS [909; 939]
            (Alloys containing more than 1% Sm.)
            BT1     rare earth alloys
                BT2     alloys
            NT1     samarium base alloys
            RT      samarium additions


    →   SAMARIUM ARSENIDES [0; 0] Sep 91
            BT1     arsenides
                BT2     arsenic compounds
                BT2     pnictides
            BT1     samarium compounds
                BT2     rare earth compounds


        SAMARIUM BASE ALLOYS [29; 29]
            BT1     samarium alloys
            BT2     rare earth alloys
                BT3     alloys


        SAMARIUM BORIDES [140; 140]
            BT1     borides
                BT2     boron compounds
            BT1     samarium compounds
                BT2     rare earth compounds


        SAMARIUM BROMIDES [13; 13]
            BT1     bromides
                BT2     bromine compounds
                    BT3     halogen compounds
                BT2     halides
                    BT3     halogen compounds
            BT1     samarium compounds
                BT2     rare earth compounds
```

```
        SAMARIUM CARBIDES [20; 20]
            BT1     carbides
                BT2     carbon compounds
            BT1     samarium compounds
                BT2     rare earth compounds


        SAMARIUM CARBONATES [11; 11]
            BT1     carbonates
                BT2     carbon compounds
                BT2     oxygen compounds
            BT1     samarium compounds
                BT2     rare earth compounds


        SAMARIUM CHLORIDES [116; 116]
            BT1     chlorides
                BT2     chlorine compounds
                    BT3     halogen compounds
                BT2     halides
                    BT3     halogen compounds
            BT1     samarium compounds
                BT2     rare earth compounds


        SAMARIUM COMPLEXES [507; 507]
            BT1     rare earth complexes
                BT2     complexes


        SAMARIUM COMPOUNDS [695; 1,899]
            BT1     rare earth compounds
            NT1     samarium arsenides
            NT1     samarium borides
            NT1     samarium bromides
            NT1     samarium carbides
            NT1     samarium carbonates
            NT1     samarium chlorides
            NT1     samarium fluorides
            NT1     samarium hydrides
            NT1     samarium hydroxides
            NT1     samarium iodides
            NT1     samarium nitrates
            NT1     samarium nitrides
            NT1     samarium oxides
            NT1     samarium perchlorates
            NT1     samarium phosphates
            NT1     samarium phosphides
            NT1     samarium selenides
            NT1     samarium silicates
            NT1     samarium silicides
            NT1     samarium sulfates
            NT1     samarium sulfides
            NT1     samarium tellurides
            NT1     samarium tungstates
            RT      samarium additions


    samarium effect
        USE     poisoning


        SAMARIUM FLUORIDES [53; 53]
            BT1     fluorides
                BT2     fluorine compounds
                    BT3     halogen compounds
                BT2     halides
                    BT3     halogen compounds
            BT1     samarium compounds
                BT2     rare earth compounds


        SAMARIUM HYDRIDES [22; 22]
            BT1     hydrides
                BT2     hydrogen compounds
            BT1     samarium compounds
                BT2     rare earth compounds


        SAMARIUM HYDROXIDES [10; 10]
            BT1     hydroxides
                BT2     hydrogen compounds
                BT2     oxygen compounds
            BT1     samarium compounds
                BT2     rare earth compounds


        SAMARIUM IODIDES [28; 28]
            BT1     iodides
                BT2     halides
                    BT3     halogen compounds
                BT2     iodine compounds
                    BT3     halogen compounds
            BT1     samarium compounds
                BT2     rare earth compounds
```

SAMARIUM IONS [173; 173]
  BT1   ions
    BT2   charged particles

SAMARIUM ISOTOPES [429; 2,287]
  NT1   samarium 131
  NT1   samarium 133
  NT1   samarium 134
  NT1   samarium 135
  NT1   samarium 136
  NT1   samarium 137
  NT1   samarium 138
  NT1   samarium 139
  NT1   samarium 140
  NT1   samarium 141
  NT1   samarium 142
  NT1   samarium 143
  NT1   samarium 144
  NT1   samarium 145
  NT1   samarium 146
  NT1   samarium 147
  NT1   samarium 148
  NT1   samarium 149
  NT1   samarium 150
  NT1   samarium 151
  NT1   samarium 152
  NT1   samarium 153
  NT1   samarium 154
  NT1   samarium 155
  NT1   samarium 156
  NT1   samarium 157
  NT1   samarium 158
  NT1   samarium 159
  NT1   samarium 160

SAMARIUM NITRATES [51; 51]
  BT1   nitrates
    BT2   nitrogen compounds
    BT2   oxygen compounds
  BT1   samarium compounds
    BT2   rare earth compounds

SAMARIUM NITRIDES [11; 11]
  BT1   nitrides
    BT2   nitrogen compounds
    BT2   pnictides
  BT1   samarium compounds
    BT2   rare earth compounds

SAMARIUM OXIDES [439; 439]
  BT1   oxides
    BT2   chalcogenides
    BT2   oxygen compounds
  BT1   samarium compounds
    BT2   rare earth compounds

SAMARIUM PERCHLORATES [0; 0]
Sep 91
  BT1   perchlorates
    BT2   chlorine compounds
      BT3   halogen compounds
    BT2   oxygen compounds
  BT1   samarium compounds
    BT2   rare earth compounds

SAMARIUM PHOSPHATES [17; 17]
  BT1   phosphates
    BT2   oxygen compounds
    BT2   phosphorus compounds
  BT1   samarium compounds
    BT2   rare earth compounds

SAMARIUM PHOSPHIDES [8; 8]
Apr 79
  BT1   phosphides
    BT2   phosphorus compounds
    BT2   pnictides
  BT1   samarium compounds
    BT2   rare earth compounds

SAMARIUM SELENIDES [32; 32]
Feb 80
  BT1   samarium compounds
    BT2   rare earth compounds
  BT1   selenides
    BT2   chalcogenides
    BT2   selenium compounds

SAMARIUM SILICATES [3; 3]
  BT1   samarium compounds
    BT2   rare earth compounds
  BT1   silicates
    BT2   oxygen compounds
    BT2   silicon compounds

SAMARIUM SILICIDES [9; 9] *Oct 75*
  BT1   samarium compounds
    BT2   rare earth compounds
  BT1   silicides
    BT2   silicon compounds

SAMARIUM SULFATES [15; 15]
  BT1   samarium compounds
    BT2   rare earth compounds
  BT1   sulfates
    BT2   oxygen compounds
    BT2   sulfur compounds

SAMARIUM SULFIDES [268; 268]
  BT1   samarium compounds
    BT2   rare earth compounds
  BT1   sulfides
    BT2   chalcogenides
    BT2   sulfur compounds

SAMARIUM TELLURIDES [19; 19]
Oct 77
  BT1   samarium compounds
    BT2   rare earth compounds
  BT1   tellurides
    BT2   chalcogenides
    BT2   tellurium compounds

SAMARIUM TUNGSTATES [8; 8]
Feb 80
  BT1   samarium compounds
    BT2   rare earth compounds
  BT1   tungstates
    BT2   oxygen compounds
    BT2   tungsten compounds
      BT3   transition element compounds

SAMARIUM 131 [3; 3] *Feb 87*
  BT1   even-odd nuclei
    BT2   nuclei
  BT1   rare earth nuclei
    BT2   intermediate mass nuclei
      BT3   nuclei
  BT1   samarium isotopes
  BT1   seconds living radioisotopes
    BT2   radioisotopes
      BT3   isotopes

SAMARIUM 133 [5; 5] *Jun 77*
  BT1   beta-plus decay radioisotopes
    BT2   beta decay radioisotopes
      BT3   radioisotopes
        BT4   isotopes
  BT1   electron capture radioisotopes
    BT2   beta decay radioisotopes
      BT3   radioisotopes
        BT4   isotopes
  BT1   even-odd nuclei
    BT2   nuclei
  BT1   rare earth nuclei
    BT2   intermediate mass nuclei
      BT3   nuclei
  BT1   samarium isotopes
  BT1   seconds living radioisotopes
    BT2   radioisotopes
      BT3   isotopes

SAMARIUM 134 [10; 10] *Jun 77*
  BT1   beta-plus decay radioisotopes
    BT2   beta decay radioisotopes
      BT3   radioisotopes
        BT4   isotopes
  BT1   electron capture radioisotopes
    BT2   beta decay radioisotopes
      BT3   radioisotopes
        BT4   isotopes
  BT1   even-even nuclei
    BT2   nuclei
  BT1   rare earth nuclei
    BT2   intermediate mass nuclei
      BT3   nuclei
  BT1   samarium isotopes
  BT1   seconds living radioisotopes
    BT2   radioisotopes
      BT3   isotopes

SAMARIUM 135 [8; 8] *Jun 77*
  BT1   beta-plus decay radioisotopes
    BT2   beta decay radioisotopes
      BT3   radioisotopes
        BT4   isotopes
  BT1   electron capture radioisotopes
    BT2   beta decay radioisotopes
      BT3   radioisotopes
        BT4   isotopes
  BT1   even-odd nuclei
    BT2   nuclei
  BT1   rare earth nuclei
    BT2   intermediate mass nuclei
      BT3   nuclei
  BT1   samarium isotopes
  BT1   seconds living radioisotopes
    BT2   radioisotopes
      BT3   isotopes

SAMARIUM 136 [20; 20] *Aug 82*
  BT1   beta-plus decay radioisotopes
    BT2   beta decay radioisotopes
      BT3   radioisotopes
        BT4   isotopes
  BT1   electron capture radioisotopes
    BT2   beta decay radioisotopes
      BT3   radioisotopes
        BT4   isotopes
  BT1   even-even nuclei
    BT2   nuclei
  BT1   rare earth nuclei
    BT2   intermediate mass nuclei
      BT3   nuclei
  BT1   samarium isotopes
  BT1   seconds living radioisotopes
    BT2   radioisotopes
      BT3   isotopes

SAMARIUM 137 [11; 11]
  BT1   beta-plus decay radioisotopes
    BT2   beta decay radioisotopes
      BT3   radioisotopes
        BT4   isotopes
  BT1   electron capture radioisotopes
    BT2   beta decay radioisotopes
      BT3   radioisotopes
        BT4   isotopes
  BT1   even-odd nuclei
    BT2   nuclei
  BT1   rare earth nuclei
    BT2   intermediate mass nuclei
      BT3   nuclei
  BT1   samarium isotopes
  BT1   seconds living radioisotopes
    BT2   radioisotopes
      BT3   isotopes

SAMARIUM 138 [22; 22]
  BT1   beta-plus decay radioisotopes
    BT2   beta decay radioisotopes
      BT3   radioisotopes
        BT4   isotopes
  BT1   electron capture radioisotopes
    BT2   beta decay radioisotopes
      BT3   radioisotopes
        BT4   isotopes
  BT1   even-even nuclei
    BT2   nuclei
  BT1   minutes living radioisotopes
    BT2   radioisotopes
      BT3   isotopes
  BT1   rare earth nuclei
    BT2   intermediate mass nuclei
      BT3   nuclei
  BT1   samarium isotopes

SAMARIUM 139 [15; 15]
  BT1   beta-plus decay radioisotopes
    BT2   beta decay radioisotopes
      BT3   radioisotopes
        BT4   isotopes
  BT1   electron capture radioisotopes

SAMARIUM 139

- BT2 beta decay radioisotopes
- BT3 radioisotopes
- BT4 isotopes
- BT1 even-odd nuclei
- BT2 nuclei
- BT1 isomeric transition isotopes
- BT2 radioisotopes
- BT3 isotopes
- BT1 minutes living radioisotopes
- BT2 radioisotopes
- BT3 isotopes
- BT1 rare earth nuclei
- BT2 intermediate mass nuclei
- BT3 nuclei
- BT1 samarium isotopes
- BT1 seconds living radioisotopes
- BT2 radioisotopes
- BT3 isotopes

SAMARIUM 140 [31; 31]

- BT1 beta-plus decay radioisotopes
- BT2 beta decay radioisotopes
- BT3 radioisotopes
- BT4 isotopes
- BT1 electron capture radioisotopes
- BT2 beta decay radioisotopes
- BT3 radioisotopes
- BT4 isotopes
- BT1 even-even nuclei
- BT2 nuclei
- BT1 minutes living radioisotopes
- BT2 radioisotopes
- BT3 isotopes
- BT1 rare earth nuclei
- BT2 intermediate mass nuclei
- BT3 nuclei
- BT1 samarium isotopes

SAMARIUM 141 [25; 25]

- BT1 beta-plus decay radioisotopes
- BT2 beta decay radioisotopes
- BT3 radioisotopes
- BT4 isotopes
- BT1 electron capture radioisotopes
- BT2 beta decay radioisotopes
- BT3 radioisotopes
- BT4 isotopes
- BT1 even-odd nuclei
- BT2 nuclei
- BT1 isomeric transition isotopes
- BT2 radioisotopes
- BT3 isotopes
- BT1 minutes living radioisotopes
- BT2 radioisotopes
- BT3 isotopes
- BT1 rare earth nuclei
- BT2 intermediate mass nuclei
- BT3 nuclei
- BT1 samarium isotopes

SAMARIUM 142 [42; 42]

- BT1 beta-plus decay radioisotopes
- BT2 beta decay radioisotopes
- BT3 radioisotopes
- BT4 isotopes
- BT1 electron capture radioisotopes
- BT2 beta decay radioisotopes
- BT3 radioisotopes
- BT4 isotopes
- BT1 even-even nuclei
- BT2 nuclei
- BT1 hours living radioisotopes
- BT2 radioisotopes
- BT3 isotopes
- BT1 rare earth nuclei
- BT2 intermediate mass nuclei
- BT3 nuclei
- BT1 samarium isotopes

SAMARIUM 143 [69; 69]

- BT1 beta-plus decay radioisotopes
- BT2 beta decay radioisotopes
- BT3 radioisotopes
- BT4 isotopes
- BT1 electron capture radioisotopes
- BT2 beta decay radioisotopes
- BT3 radioisotopes
- BT4 isotopes
- BT1 even-odd nuclei
- BT2 nuclei
- BT1 isomeric transition isotopes
- BT2 radioisotopes
- BT3 isotopes
- BT1 minutes living radioisotopes
- BT2 radioisotopes
- BT3 isotopes
- BT1 rare earth nuclei
- BT2 intermediate mass nuclei
- BT3 nuclei
- BT1 samarium isotopes

SAMARIUM 144 [179; 179]

- BT1 even-even nuclei
- BT2 nuclei
- BT1 rare earth nuclei
- BT2 intermediate mass nuclei
- BT3 nuclei
- BT1 samarium isotopes
- BT1 stable isotopes
- BT2 isotopes

SAMARIUM 144 REACTIONS [23; 23]
Jul 80
- BT1 heavy ion reactions
- BT2 nuclear reactions

SAMARIUM 144 TARGET [400; 400]
- BT1 targets

SAMARIUM 145 [105; 105]

- BT1 days living radioisotopes
- BT2 radioisotopes
- BT3 isotopes
- BT1 electron capture radioisotopes
- BT2 beta decay radioisotopes
- BT3 radioisotopes
- BT4 isotopes
- BT1 even-odd nuclei
- BT2 nuclei
- BT1 internal conversion radioisoto
- BT2 radioisotopes
- BT3 isotopes
- BT1 rare earth nuclei
- BT2 intermediate mass nuclei
- BT3 nuclei
- BT1 samarium isotopes

SAMARIUM 145 TARGET [7; 7] *Oct 75*
- BT1 targets

SAMARIUM 146 [109; 109]

- BT1 alpha decay radioisotopes
- BT2 radioisotopes
- BT3 isotopes
- BT1 even-even nuclei
- BT2 nuclei
- BT1 rare earth nuclei
- BT2 intermediate mass nuclei
- BT3 nuclei
- BT1 samarium isotopes
- BT1 years living radioisotopes
- BT2 radioisotopes
- BT3 isotopes

SAMARIUM 146 TARGET [76; 76]
- BT1 targets

SAMARIUM 147 [229; 229]

- BT1 alpha decay radioisotopes
- BT2 radioisotopes
- BT3 isotopes
- BT1 even-odd nuclei
- BT2 nuclei
- BT1 rare earth nuclei
- BT2 intermediate mass nuclei
- BT3 nuclei
- BT1 samarium isotopes
- BT1 years living radioisotopes
- BT2 radioisotopes
- BT3 isotopes

SAMARIUM 147 TARGET [137; 137]
- BT1 targets

SAMARIUM 148 [235; 235]

- BT1 alpha decay radioisotopes
- BT2 radioisotopes
- BT3 isotopes
- BT1 even-even nuclei
- BT2 nuclei
- BT1 rare earth nuclei
- BT2 intermediate mass nuclei
- BT3 nuclei
- BT1 samarium isotopes
- BT1 stable isotopes
- BT2 isotopes
- BT1 years living radioisotopes
- BT2 radioisotopes
- BT3 isotopes

SAMARIUM 148 TARGET [219; 219]
- BT1 targets

SAMARIUM 149 [173; 173]

- BT1 even-odd nuclei
- BT2 nuclei
- BT1 rare earth nuclei
- BT2 intermediate mass nuclei
- BT3 nuclei
- BT1 samarium isotopes
- BT1 stable isotopes
- BT2 isotopes

SAMARIUM 149 TARGET [119; 119]
- BT1 targets

SAMARIUM 150 [272; 272]

- BT1 even-even nuclei
- BT2 nuclei
- BT1 rare earth nuclei
- BT2 intermediate mass nuclei
- BT3 nuclei
- BT1 samarium isotopes
- BT1 stable isotopes
- BT2 isotopes

SAMARIUM 150 TARGET [216; 216]
- BT1 targets

SAMARIUM 151 [109; 109]

- BT1 beta-minus decay radioisotope
- BT2 beta decay radioisotopes
- BT3 radioisotopes
- BT4 isotopes
- BT1 even-odd nuclei
- BT2 nuclei
- BT1 internal conversion radioisoto
- BT2 radioisotopes
- BT3 isotopes
- BT1 rare earth nuclei
- BT2 intermediate mass nuclei
- BT3 nuclei
- BT1 samarium isotopes
- BT1 years living radioisotopes
- BT2 radioisotopes
- BT3 isotopes

SAMARIUM 151 TARGET [10; 10]
- BT1 targets

SAMARIUM 152 [454; 454]

- BT1 even-even nuclei
- BT2 nuclei
- BT1 rare earth nuclei
- BT2 intermediate mass nuclei
- BT3 nuclei
- BT1 samarium isotopes
- BT1 stable isotopes
- BT2 isotopes

SAMARIUM 152 TARGET [255; 255]
- BT1 targets

SAMARIUM 153 [163; 163]
  BT1   beta-minus decay radioisotopes
    BT2   beta decay radioisotopes
      BT3   radioisotopes
        BT4   isotopes
  BT1   days living radioisotopes
    BT2   radioisotopes
      BT3   isotopes
  BT1   even-odd nuclei
    BT2   nuclei
  BT1   rare earth nuclei
    BT2   intermediate mass nuclei
      BT3   nuclei
  BT1   samarium isotopes

SAMARIUM 154 [273; 273]
  BT1   even-even nuclei
    BT2   nuclei
  BT1   rare earth nuclei
    BT2   intermediate mass nuclei
      BT3   nuclei
  BT1   samarium isotopes
  BT1   stable isotopes
    BT2   isotopes

SAMARIUM 154 REACTIONS [21; 21] *Jul 80*
  BT1   heavy ion reactions
  BT2   nuclear reactions

SAMARIUM 154 TARGET [446; 446]
  BT1   targets

SAMARIUM 155 [32; 32]
  BT1   beta-minus decay radioisotopes
    BT2   beta decay radioisotopes
      BT3   radioisotopes
        BT4   isotopes
  BT1   even-odd nuclei
    BT2   nuclei
  BT1   minutes living radioisotopes
    BT2   radioisotopes
      BT3   isotopes
  BT1   rare earth nuclei
    BT2   intermediate mass nuclei
      BT3   nuclei
  BT1   samarium isotopes

SAMARIUM 156 [24; 24]
  BT1   beta-minus decay radioisotopes
    BT2   beta decay radioisotopes
      BT3   radioisotopes
        BT4   isotopes
  BT1   even-even nuclei
    BT2   nuclei
  BT1   hours living radioisotopes
    BT2   radioisotopes
      BT3   isotopes
  BT1   rare earth nuclei
    BT2   intermediate mass nuclei
      BT3   nuclei
  BT1   samarium isotopes

SAMARIUM 157 [8; 8]
  BT1   beta-minus decay radioisotopes
    BT2   beta decay radioisotopes
      BT3   radioisotopes
        BT4   isotopes
  BT1   even-odd nuclei
    BT2   nuclei
  BT1   minutes living radioisotopes
    BT2   radioisotopes
      BT3   isotopes
  BT1   rare earth nuclei
    BT2   intermediate mass nuclei
      BT3   nuclei
  BT1   samarium isotopes

SAMARIUM 158 [10; 10]
  BT1   beta-minus decay radioisotopes
    BT2   beta decay radioisotopes
      BT3   radioisotopes
        BT4   isotopes
  BT1   even-even nuclei
    BT2   nuclei
  BT1   minutes living radioisotopes
    BT2   radioisotopes
      BT3   isotopes
  BT1   rare earth nuclei
    BT2   intermediate mass nuclei
      BT3   nuclei
  BT1   samarium isotopes

SAMARIUM 159 [4; 4] *Oct 86*
  BT1   beta-minus decay radioisotopes
    BT2   beta decay radioisotopes
      BT3   radioisotopes
        BT4   isotopes
  BT1   even-odd nuclei
    BT2   nuclei
  BT1   rare earth nuclei
    BT2   intermediate mass nuclei
      BT3   nuclei
  BT1   samarium isotopes
  BT1   seconds living radioisotopes
    BT2   radioisotopes
      BT3   isotopes

SAMARIUM 160 [0; 0] *Oct 86*
  BT1   beta-minus decay radioisotopes
    BT2   beta decay radioisotopes
      BT3   radioisotopes
        BT4   isotopes
  BT1   even-even nuclei
    BT2   nuclei
  BT1   rare earth nuclei
    BT2   intermediate mass nuclei
      BT3   nuclei
  BT1   samarium isotopes
  BT1   seconds living radioisotopes
    BT2   radioisotopes
      BT3   isotopes

SAMPLE CHANGERS [256; 256]
  RT   laboratory equipment
  RT   materials handling
  RT   remote handling
  RT   sample holders

SAMPLE HOLDERS [434; 434] *Mar 76*
  UF   *specimen holders*
  UF   *target holders*
  RT   remote handling
  RT   sample changers

SAMPLE PREPARATION [6,575; 6,575]
  UF   *preparation (sample)*
  RT   ceramography
  RT   dry ashing
  RT   electron microscopy
  RT   surface treatments
  RT   wet ashing

SAMPLERS [445; 1,260]
  BT1   laboratory equipment
    BT2   equipment
  NT1   air samplers
  RT   filters
  RT   sampling

§ **SAMPLING** [6,314; 6,314]
  RT   elutriation
  RT   inspection
  RT   quality control
  RT   reaction product transport
  RT   samplers
  RT   testing
  RT   ultrafiltration

SAN ANTONIO BAY [0; 0]
  BT1   gulf of mexico
    BT2   caribbean sea
      BT3   atlantic ocean
        BT4   seas
          BT5   surface waters

SAN BERNARDINO MOUNTAINS [0; 0]
  BT1   mountains

SAN FRANCISCO BAY [11; 11]
  BT1   pacific ocean
    BT2   seas
      BT3   surface waters

SAN ONOFRE-1 REACTOR [172; 172]
(San Clemente, California, USA)
  BT1   pwr type reactors
    BT2   enriched uranium reactors
      BT3   reactors
    BT2   power reactors
      BT3   reactors
    BT2   thermal reactors
      BT3   reactors
    BT2   water cooled reactors
      BT3   reactors
    BT2   water moderated reactors
      BT3   reactors

SAN ONOFRE-2 REACTOR [110; 110]
(San Clemente, California, USA)
  BT1   pwr type reactors
    BT2   enriched uranium reactors
      BT3   reactors
    BT2   power reactors
      BT3   reactors
    BT2   thermal reactors
      BT3   reactors
    BT2   water cooled reactors
      BT3   reactors
    BT2   water moderated reactors
      BT3   reactors

SAN ONOFRE-3 REACTOR [84; 84]
(San Clemente, California, USA)
  BT1   pwr type reactors
    BT2   enriched uranium reactors
      BT3   reactors
    BT2   power reactors
      BT3   reactors
    BT2   thermal reactors
      BT3   reactors
    BT2   water cooled reactors
      BT3   reactors
    BT2   water moderated reactors
      BT3   reactors

san piero a grado pisa reactor
  USE   rts-1 reactor

SAND [971; 1,058]
  NT1   black sands
  NT1   oil sands
  RT   alluvial deposits
  RT   aquifers
  RT   building materials
  RT   clays
  RT   concretes
  RT   deserts
  RT   sandstones
  RT   silicon oxides
  RT   soils

sand pressure
  USE   reservoir pressure

SANDIA LABORATORIES [663; 663]
(Name changed to Sandia National Laboratories, and more recent material should be so indexed.)
  BT1   sandia national laboratories
    BT2   us doe
      BT3   us organizations
        BT4   national organizations
  BT1   us aec
    BT2   us organizations
      BT3   national organizations
  BT1   us erda
    BT2   us organizations
      BT3   national organizations
  RT   california
  RT   new mexico
  RT   tonopah test range

SANDIA NATIONAL LABORATORIES
[5; 538] *Apr 84*
(Formerly known as Sandia Laboratories, and older material is so indexed.)
 BT1 us doe
 BT2 us organizations
 BT3 national organizations
 NT1 sandia laboratories
 RT california
 RT new mexico
 RT tonopah test range

sandia pulsed reactor-ii
 USE spr-2 reactor

sandia pulsed reactor-iii
 USE spr-3 reactor

sandia pulsed reactor-iv
 USE spr-4 reactor

SANDSTONES [874; 877]
 BT1 sedimentary rocks
 BT2 rocks
 NT1 graywacke
 RT quartzites
 RT sand

sandvik-ht8x6
 USE steel-cr2moninb

sanicro 30
 USE alloy-fe46ni33cr21

sanicro 70
 USE alloy-ni76cr15fe8

SANITARY LANDFILLS [141; 141]
Sep 82
(Sites for biologically safe disposal of wastes by burial.)
 UF *land fills*
 UF *landfills*
 RT ground disposal

santa maria de garona pow. rea
 USE garona reactor

SANTOWAX [3; 3]
 BT1 polyphenyls
 BT2 aromatics
 BT3 organic compounds
 BT2 hydrocarbons
 BT3 organic compounds
 BT1 waxes
 BT2 other organic compounds
 BT3 organic compounds

sao paulo iea zero power reac.
 USE iea-zpr reactor

sao paulo iear-1 reactor
 USE iear-1 reactor

SAP [50; 50]
 UF *sintered aluminum powders*
 BT1 sintered materials
 BT2 materials
 RT aluminium

SAPHIR REACTOR [40; 40]
 BT1 enriched uranium reactors
 BT2 reactors
 BT1 pool type reactors
 BT2 water cooled reactors
 BT3 reactors
 BT2 water moderated reactors
 BT3 reactors
 BT1 thermal reactors
 BT2 reactors

SAPONIFICATION [21; 21]
 BT1 hydrolysis
 BT2 solvolysis
 BT3 decomposition
 BT4 chemical reactions

SAPONINS [28; 28]
 BT1 glycosides
 BT2 carbohydrates
 BT3 organic compounds

SAPPHIRE [405; 405] *May 76*
 BT1 corundum
 BT2 oxide minerals
 BT3 minerals

sar-2 reactor
(Schnell-Thermischen Argonaut Reaktor Karlsruhe)
 USE stark reactor

SARA CYCLOTRON [28; 28] *Jun 84*
(Systeme Accelerateur Rhone-Alpes -- consists of two cyclotrons, the injector cyclotron and the post-accelerator cyclotron.)
 UF *systeme acceler. rhone-alpes*
 BT1 isochronous cyclotrons
 BT2 cyclotrons
 BT3 cyclic accelerators
 BT4 accelerators
 RT grenoble cyclotron

SARCOMAS [1,583; 3,123]
 UF+ *chondrosarcomas*
 BT1 neoplasms
 BT2 diseases
 NT1 fibrosarcomas
 NT1 lymphosarcomas
 NT1 myosarcomas
 NT2 rhabdomyosarcomas
 NT1 osteosarcomas

SARCOSINE [15; 15]
 UF *methyl glycocoll*
 UF *methylaminoacetic acid*
 BT1 amino acids
 BT2 carboxylic acids
 BT3 organic acids
 BT4 organic compounds
 RT glycine

SAREF REACTOR [19; 19] *Jan 77*
 UF *inel safety res exper fac reac*
 UF *safety res. exper. facility re*
 BT1 fast reactors
 BT2 epithermal reactors
 BT3 reactors
 BT1 zero power reactors
 BT2 experimental reactors
 BT3 research and test reactors
 BT4 reactors

SARGASSO SEA [10; 10]
 BT1 atlantic ocean
 BT2 seas
 BT3 surface waters

SARGENT DIAGRAMS [0; 0]
 BT1 diagrams
 BT2 information
 RT beta decay
 RT energy

sarson
 USE brassica

SASKATCHEWAN [254; 256]
 BT1 canada
 BT2 developed countries
 BT2 north america
 NT1 beaverlodge
 RT beaverlodge mine
 RT cluff lake mine
 RT key lake mine

SATELLITE ATMOSPHERES [123; 126]
Nov 81
(For atmospheres of the natural satellites.)
 BT1 atmospheres
 NT1 lunar atmosphere

SATELLITES [3,544; 6,614]
 NT1 alouette satellites
 NT1 ariel satellites
 NT1 astron satellites
 NT1 ats satellites
 NT1 biosatellites
 NT1 early bird satellites
 NT1 explorer satellites
 NT1 geos satellites
 NT1 goes satellites
 NT1 imp satellites
 NT1 interkosmos satellites
 NT1 kosmos satellites
 NT1 landsat satellites
 NT1 mir orbital station
 NT1 molniya satellites
 NT1 moon
 NT1 nimbus satellites
 NT1 ogo satellites
 NT1 orbiting solar observatories
 NT1 prognoz satellites
 NT1 proton satellites
 NT1 salyut orbital stations
 NT1 skylab
 RT remote sensing
 RT space flight
 RT space vehicles

saturable core magnetometers
 USE fluxgate magnetometers

§§ **SATURATION** [1,885; 2,123]
 NT1 supersaturation
 RT solubility
 RT solutions

SATURN PLANET [726; 726]
 BT1 planets

SATURNE [170; 170]
 UF *saclay synchrotron*
 BT1 synchrotrons
 BT2 cyclic accelerators
 BT3 accelerators

SATURNE II [101; 101] *Dec 79*
 BT1 synchrotrons
 BT2 cyclic accelerators
 BT3 accelerators

SAUDI ARABIA [79; 79]
 BT1 asia
 BT1 developing countries
 BT1 middle east

SAUSAGE INSTABILITY [108; 108]
 BT1 plasma macroinstabilities
 BT2 plasma instability
 BT3 instability

savannah (nuclear ship)
 USE ns savannah

savannah press. subcrit. exper
 USE pse reactor

SAVANNAH REACTOR [19; 19]
- UF   nucl. ship savannah reactor
- BT1   pwr type reactors
  - BT2   enriched uranium reactors
    - BT3   reactors
  - BT2   power reactors
    - BT3   reactors
  - BT2   thermal reactors
    - BT3   reactors
  - BT2   water cooled reactors
    - BT3   reactors
  - BT2   water moderated reactors
    - BT3   reactors
- BT1   ship propulsion reactors
  - BT2   propulsion reactors
    - BT3   power reactors
      - BT4   reactors
- RT   ns savannah

savannah riv. plant c reactor
- USE   c reactor

savannah riv. plant k reactor
- USE   k reactor

savannah riv. plant l reactor
- USE   l reactor

savannah riv. plant p reactor
- USE   p reactor

savannah riv. plant r reactor
- USE   r reactor

SAVANNAH RIVER [96; 96]
- BT1   rivers
  - BT2   surface waters

savannah river lab rtr reactor
- USE   rtr reactor

SAVANNAH RIVER PLANT [1,748; 1,748]
- BT1   us aec
  - BT2   us organizations
    - BT3   national organizations
- BT1   us doe
  - BT2   us organizations
    - BT3   national organizations
- BT1   us erda
  - BT2   us organizations
    - BT3   national organizations
- RT   south carolina

savannah river process dvl. r.
- USE   pdp reactor

savannah river test pile-305
- USE   sr-305 reactor

sawada method
- USE   goldstone diagrams

SAWTOOTH OSCILLATIONS [377; 377] *Nov 88*
- BT1   oscillations
- RT   kink instability
- RT   magnetic reconnection
- RT   plasma
- RT   plasma confinement
- RT   plasma disruption
- RT   rotational transform
- RT   stellarators
- RT   tokamak devices

saxon-woods potential
- USE   woods-saxon potential

SAXTON REACTOR [29; 29]
- BT1   pwr type reactors
  - BT2   enriched uranium reactors
    - BT3   reactors
  - BT2   power reactors
    - BT3   reactors
  - BT2   thermal reactors
    - BT3   reactors
  - BT2   water cooled reactors
    - BT3   reactors
  - BT2   water moderated reactors
    - BT3   reactors

SBR-1 REACTOR [2; 2]
- UF   br-1 reactor (ussr)
- UF   soviet breeder reactor-1
- BT1   enriched uranium reactors
  - BT2   reactors
- BT1   fbr type reactors
  - BT2   breeder reactors
    - BT3   reactors
  - BT2   fast reactors
    - BT3   epithermal reactors
      - BT4   reactors
- BT1   plutonium reactors
  - BT2   reactors
- BT1   research reactors
  - BT2   research and test reactors
    - BT3   reactors

SBR-2 REACTOR [1; 1]
(Obninsk, USSR)
- UF   br-2 reactor (ussr)
- UF   soviet breeder reactor-2
- BT1   lmfbr type reactors
  - BT2   fbr type reactors
    - BT3   breeder reactors
      - BT4   reactors
    - BT3   fast reactors
      - BT4   epithermal reactors
        - BT5   reactors
  - BT2   liquid metal cooled reactors
    - BT3   reactors
- BT1   mercury cooled reactors
  - BT2   liquid metal cooled reactors
    - BT3   reactors
- BT1   plutonium reactors
  - BT2   reactors
- BT1   research reactors
  - BT2   research and test reactors
    - BT3   reactors

SBR-5 REACTOR [45; 45]
(Obninsk, USSR)
- UF   br-5 reactor (ussr)
- UF   soviet breeder reactor-5
- BT1   lmfbr type reactors
  - BT2   fbr type reactors
    - BT3   breeder reactors
      - BT4   reactors
    - BT3   fast reactors
      - BT4   epithermal reactors
        - BT5   reactors
  - BT2   liquid metal cooled reactors
    - BT3   reactors
- BT1   plutonium reactors
  - BT2   reactors
- BT1   research reactors
  - BT2   research and test reactors
    - BT3   reactors
- BT1   sodium cooled reactors
  - BT2   liquid metal cooled reactors
    - BT3   reactors
- BT1   test reactors
  - BT2   research and test reactors
    - BT3   reactors
  - BT2   test facilities

sca model
(SemiClassical Approximation model.)
- USE   semiclassical approximation

SCA REACTOR [1; 1]
- BT1   research reactors
  - BT2   research and test reactors
    - BT3   reactors
- BT1   tank type reactors
  - BT2   reactors
- BT1   training reactors
  - BT2   research and test reactors
    - BT3   reactors
- BT1   water cooled reactors
  - BT2   reactors
- BT1   water moderated reactors
  - BT2   reactors

SCALAR FIELDS [7,890; 7,890]
- RT   quantum field theory

SCALAR MESONS [1,005; 1,123]
(Mesons with spin and parity 0+.)
- BT1   mesons
  - BT2   bosons
  - BT2   hadrons
    - BT3   elementary particles
- NT1   a0-980 mesons
- NT1   chi0-3415 mesons
- NT1   f0-1240 mesons
- NT1   f0-1300 mesons
- NT1   f0-1590 mesons
- NT1   f0-1730 mesons
- NT1   f0-975 mesons
- NT1   k*0-1350 mesons
- RT   sigma model

SCALARS [853; 853]
- RT   mathematics
- RT   pseudoscalars
- RT   tensors

SCALE DIMENSION [428; 1,177]
(A natural number characteristic of the scale-transformation properties of a given quantum field.)
- NT1   anomalous dimension
- NT1   canonical dimension
- RT   conformal invariance
- RT   quantum field theory
- RT   scale invariance

SCALE HEIGHT [8; 8] *Apr 86*
(Measure of the relation between density and temperature of points in an atmosphere.)
- RT   height
- RT   ionosphere

SCALE INVARIANCE [2,239; 2,239]
- BT1   invariance principles
- RT   conformal invariance
- RT   particle rapidity
- RT   scale dimension

SCALE MODELS [962; 962] *Jul 80*
(A three-dimensional representation of an object or structure containing all parts in the same proportion as their true size.)
- UF   models (scale)
- BT1   structural models
- RT   functional models
- RT   scaling laws
- RT   simulators

SCALERS [256; 256]
- UF   scaling units
- BT1   electronic equipment
  - BT2   equipment
- RT   counting circuits
- RT   counting tubes
- RT   pulse techniques
- RT   radiation detectors

SCALING [672; 672]
- BT1   corrosion
  - BT2   chemical reactions
- RT   corrosion products
- RT   descaling
- RT   high temperature

SCALING LAWS [7,775; 7,775]
  RT   calibration
  RT   mathematical models
  RT   scale models
  RT   simulation

scaling units
  USE   scalers

SCANDINAVIA [150; 4,250]
  BT1   europe
  NT1   denmark
  NT1   finland
  NT1   norway
  NT1   sweden

SCANDIUM [1,448; 1,448]
  BT1   transition elements
    BT2   metals
      BT3   elements

SCANDIUM ADDITIONS [82; 82]
(Alloys containing not more than 1% Sc are listed here.)
  RT   scandium alloys
  RT   scandium compounds

SCANDIUM ALLOYS [338; 376]
(Alloys containing more than 1% Sc.)
  BT1   alloys
  NT1   scandium base alloys
  RT   scandium additions

SCANDIUM BASE ALLOYS [36; 36]
  BT1   scandium alloys
    BT2   alloys

SCANDIUM BORIDES [18; 18]
  BT1   borides
    BT2   boron compounds
  BT1   scandium compounds
    BT2   transition element compounds

SCANDIUM BROMIDES [10; 10]
Aug 76
  BT1   bromides
    BT2   bromine compounds
      BT3   halogen compounds
    BT2   halides
      BT3   halogen compounds
  BT1   scandium compounds
    BT2   transition element compounds

SCANDIUM CARBIDES [24; 24]
  BT1   carbides
    BT2   carbon compounds
  BT1   scandium compounds
    BT2   transition element compounds

SCANDIUM CARBONATES [0; 0]
Feb 89
  BT1   carbonates
    BT2   carbon compounds
    BT2   oxygen compounds
  BT1   scandium compounds
    BT2   transition element compounds

SCANDIUM CHLORIDES [82; 82]
  BT1   chlorides
    BT2   chlorine compounds
      BT3   halogen compounds
    BT2   halides
      BT3   halogen compounds
  BT1   scandium compounds
    BT2   transition element compounds

SCANDIUM COMPLEXES [379; 379]
  BT1   transition element complexes
    BT2   complexes

SCANDIUM COMPOUNDS [555; 1,426]
  BT1   transition element compounds
  NT1   scandium borides
  NT1   scandium bromides
  NT1   scandium carbides
  NT1   scandium carbonates
  NT1   scandium chlorides
  NT1   scandium fluorides
  NT1   scandium hydrides
  NT1   scandium hydroxides
  NT1   scandium iodides
  NT1   scandium nitrates
  NT1   scandium nitrides
  NT1   scandium oxides
  NT1   scandium perchlorates
  NT1   scandium phosphates
  NT1   scandium phosphides
  NT1   scandium selenides
  NT1   scandium silicates
  NT1   scandium silicides
  NT1   scandium sulfates
  NT1   scandium sulfides
  NT1   scandium tungstates
  RT   scandium additions

SCANDIUM FLUORIDES [60; 60]
  BT1   fluorides
    BT2   fluorine compounds
      BT3   halogen compounds
    BT2   halides
      BT3   halogen compounds
  BT1   scandium compounds
    BT2   transition element compounds

SCANDIUM HYDRIDES [82; 82]
  BT1   hydrides
    BT2   hydrogen compounds
  BT1   scandium compounds
    BT2   transition element compounds

SCANDIUM HYDROXIDES [24; 24]
  BT1   hydroxides
    BT2   hydrogen compounds
    BT2   oxygen compounds
  BT1   scandium compounds
    BT2   transition element compounds

SCANDIUM IODIDES [9; 9]
  BT1   iodides
    BT2   halides
      BT3   halogen compounds
    BT2   iodine compounds
      BT3   halogen compounds
  BT1   scandium compounds
    BT2   transition element compounds

SCANDIUM IONS [119; 119]
  BT1   ions
    BT2   charged particles

SCANDIUM ISOTOPES [91; 1,534]
  NT1   scandium 39
  NT1   scandium 40
  NT1   scandium 41
  NT1   scandium 42
  NT1   scandium 43
  NT1   scandium 44
  NT1   scandium 45
  NT1   scandium 46
  NT1   scandium 47
  NT1   scandium 48
  NT1   scandium 49
  NT1   scandium 50
  NT1   scandium 51
  NT1   scandium 52
  NT1   scandium 53
  NT1   scandium 54
  NT1   scandium 55

SCANDIUM NITRATES [17; 17]
  BT1   nitrates
    BT2   nitrogen compounds
    BT2   oxygen compounds
  BT1   scandium compounds
    BT2   transition element compounds

SCANDIUM NITRIDES [19; 19]
  BT1   nitrides
    BT2   nitrogen compounds
    BT2   pnictides
  BT1   scandium compounds
    BT2   transition element compounds

SCANDIUM OXIDES [434; 434]
  BT1   oxides
    BT2   chalcogenides
    BT2   oxygen compounds
  BT1   scandium compounds
    BT2   transition element compounds

→ SCANDIUM PERCHLORATES [0; 0]
Sep 91
  BT1   perchlorates
    BT2   chlorine compounds
      BT3   halogen compounds
    BT2   oxygen compounds
  BT1   scandium compounds
    BT2   transition element compounds

SCANDIUM PHOSPHATES [48; 48]
Sep 76
  BT1   phosphates
    BT2   oxygen compounds
    BT2   phosphorus compounds
  BT1   scandium compounds
    BT2   transition element compounds

SCANDIUM PHOSPHIDES [4; 4]
Feb 81
  BT1   phosphides
    BT2   phosphorus compounds
    BT2   pnictides
  BT1   scandium compounds
    BT2   transition element compounds

SCANDIUM SELENIDES [3; 3] *Feb 79*
  BT1   scandium compounds
    BT2   transition element compounds
  BT1   selenides
    BT2   chalcogenides
    BT2   selenium compounds

SCANDIUM SILICATES [13; 13]
  BT1   scandium compounds
    BT2   transition element compounds
  BT1   silicates
    BT2   oxygen compounds
    BT2   silicon compounds

SCANDIUM SILICIDES [31; 31] *May*
  BT1   scandium compounds
    BT2   transition element compounds
  BT1   silicides
    BT2   silicon compounds

SCANDIUM SULFATES [22; 22]
  BT1   scandium compounds
    BT2   transition element compounds
  BT1   sulfates
    BT2   oxygen compounds
    BT2   sulfur compounds

SCANDIUM SULFIDES [22; 22]
  BT1   scandium compounds
    BT2   transition element compounds
  BT1   sulfides
    BT2   chalcogenides
    BT2   sulfur compounds

SCANDIUM TUNGSTATES [8; 8]
Jun 82
  BT1   scandium compounds
    BT2   transition element compounds
  BT1   tungstates
    BT2   oxygen compounds
    BT2   tungsten compounds
      BT3   transition element compounds

SCANDIUM 39 [0; 0] *Jul 89*
 BT1 light nuclei
 BT2 nuclei
 BT1 odd-even nuclei
 BT2 nuclei
 BT1 proton decay radioisotopes
 BT2 radioisotopes
  BT3 isotopes
 BT1 scandium isotopes

SCANDIUM 40 [39; 39]
 BT1 beta-plus decay radioisotopes
 BT2 beta decay radioisotopes
  BT3 radioisotopes
   BT4 isotopes
 BT1 light nuclei
 BT2 nuclei
 BT1 millisec living radioisotopes
 BT2 radioisotopes
  BT3 isotopes
 BT1 odd-odd nuclei
 BT2 nuclei
 BT1 scandium isotopes

SCANDIUM 41 [116; 116]
 BT1 beta-plus decay radioisotopes
 BT2 beta decay radioisotopes
  BT3 radioisotopes
   BT4 isotopes
 BT1 intermediate mass nuclei
 BT2 nuclei
 BT1 millisec living radioisotopes
 BT2 radioisotopes
  BT3 isotopes
 BT1 odd-even nuclei
 BT2 nuclei
 BT1 scandium isotopes

SCANDIUM 42 [112; 112]
 BT1 beta-plus decay radioisotopes
 BT2 beta decay radioisotopes
  BT3 radioisotopes
   BT4 isotopes
 BT1 intermediate mass nuclei
 BT2 nuclei
 BT1 millisec living radioisotopes
 BT2 radioisotopes
  BT3 isotopes
 BT1 odd-odd nuclei
 BT2 nuclei
 BT1 scandium isotopes
 BT1 seconds living radioisotopes
 BT2 radioisotopes
  BT3 isotopes

SCANDIUM 43 [118; 118]
 BT1 beta-plus decay radioisotopes
 BT2 beta decay radioisotopes
  BT3 radioisotopes
   BT4 isotopes
 BT1 hours living radioisotopes
 BT2 radioisotopes
  BT3 isotopes
 BT1 intermediate mass nuclei
 BT2 nuclei
 BT1 odd-even nuclei
 BT2 nuclei
 BT1 scandium isotopes

SCANDIUM 44 [181; 181]
 BT1 beta-plus decay radioisotopes
 BT2 beta decay radioisotopes
  BT3 radioisotopes
   BT4 isotopes
 BT1 days living radioisotopes
 BT2 radioisotopes
  BT3 isotopes
 BT1 electron capture radioisotopes
 BT2 beta decay radioisotopes
  BT3 radioisotopes
   BT4 isotopes
 BT1 hours living radioisotopes
 BT2 radioisotopes
  BT3 isotopes
 BT1 intermediate mass nuclei
 BT2 nuclei
 BT1 isomeric transition isotopes
 BT2 radioisotopes
  BT3 isotopes
 BT1 odd-odd nuclei
 BT2 nuclei
 BT1 scandium isotopes

SCANDIUM 45 [231; 231]
 BT1 intermediate mass nuclei
 BT2 nuclei
 BT1 odd-even nuclei
 BT2 nuclei
 BT1 scandium isotopes
 BT1 stable isotopes
 BT2 isotopes

SCANDIUM 45 REACTIONS [18; 18] *Nov 80*
 BT1 heavy ion reactions
 BT2 nuclear reactions

SCANDIUM 45 TARGET [234; 234]
 BT1 targets

SCANDIUM 46 [433; 433]
 BT1 beta-minus decay radioisotopes
 BT2 beta decay radioisotopes
  BT3 radioisotopes
   BT4 isotopes
 BT1 days living radioisotopes
 BT2 radioisotopes
  BT3 isotopes
 BT1 intermediate mass nuclei
 BT2 nuclei
 BT1 internal conversion radioisoto
 BT2 radioisotopes
  BT3 isotopes
 BT1 isomeric transition isotopes
 BT2 radioisotopes
  BT3 isotopes
 BT1 odd-odd nuclei
 BT2 nuclei
 BT1 scandium isotopes
 BT1 seconds living radioisotopes
 BT2 radioisotopes
  BT3 isotopes

SCANDIUM 47 [133; 133]
 BT1 beta-minus decay radioisotopes
 BT2 beta decay radioisotopes
  BT3 radioisotopes
   BT4 isotopes
 BT1 days living radioisotopes
 BT2 radioisotopes
  BT3 isotopes
 BT1 intermediate mass nuclei
 BT2 nuclei
 BT1 odd-even nuclei
 BT2 nuclei
 BT1 scandium isotopes

SCANDIUM 48 [198; 198]
 BT1 beta-minus decay radioisotopes
 BT2 beta decay radioisotopes
  BT3 radioisotopes
   BT4 isotopes
 BT1 days living radioisotopes
 BT2 radioisotopes
  BT3 isotopes
 BT1 intermediate mass nuclei
 BT2 nuclei
 BT1 odd-odd nuclei
 BT2 nuclei
 BT1 scandium isotopes

SCANDIUM 49 [94; 94]
 BT1 beta-minus decay radioisotopes
 BT2 beta decay radioisotopes
  BT3 radioisotopes
   BT4 isotopes
 BT1 intermediate mass nuclei
 BT2 nuclei
 BT1 minutes living radioisotopes
 BT2 radioisotopes
  BT3 isotopes
 BT1 odd-even nuclei
 BT2 nuclei
 BT1 scandium isotopes

SCANDIUM 50 [18; 18]
 BT1 beta-minus decay radioisotopes
 BT2 beta decay radioisotopes
  BT3 radioisotopes
   BT4 isotopes
 BT1 intermediate mass nuclei
 BT2 nuclei
 BT1 isomeric transition isotopes
 BT2 radioisotopes
  BT3 isotopes
 BT1 millisec living radioisotopes
 BT2 radioisotopes
  BT3 isotopes
 BT1 minutes living radioisotopes
 BT2 radioisotopes
  BT3 isotopes
 BT1 odd-odd nuclei
 BT2 nuclei
 BT1 scandium isotopes

SCANDIUM 51 [8; 8]
 BT1 beta-minus decay radioisotopes
 BT2 beta decay radioisotopes
  BT3 radioisotopes
   BT4 isotopes
 BT1 intermediate mass nuclei
 BT2 nuclei
 BT1 odd-even nuclei
 BT2 nuclei
 BT1 scandium isotopes
 BT1 seconds living radioisotopes
 BT2 radioisotopes
  BT3 isotopes

SCANDIUM 52 [4; 4] *Oct 84*
 BT1 beta-minus decay radioisotopes
 BT2 beta decay radioisotopes
  BT3 radioisotopes
   BT4 isotopes
 BT1 intermediate mass nuclei
 BT2 nuclei
 BT1 odd-odd nuclei
 BT2 nuclei
 BT1 scandium isotopes
 BT1 seconds living radioisotopes
 BT2 radioisotopes
  BT3 isotopes

→ **SCANDIUM 53** [0; 0] *Feb 91*
 BT1 intermediate mass nuclei
 BT2 nuclei
 BT1 odd-even nuclei
 BT2 nuclei
 BT1 scandium isotopes

→ **SCANDIUM 54** [0; 0] *Feb 91*
 BT1 intermediate mass nuclei
 BT2 nuclei
 BT1 odd-odd nuclei
 BT2 nuclei
 BT1 scandium isotopes

→ **SCANDIUM 55** [0; 0] *Feb 91*
 BT1 intermediate mass nuclei
 BT2 nuclei
 BT1 odd-even nuclei
 BT2 nuclei
 BT1 scandium isotopes

scanners (beam)
 USE beam scanners

scanners (image)
 USE image scanners

scanners (radioisotope)
 USE radioisotope scanners

scanning (electron)
 USE electron scanning

scanning (fuel)
  USE   fuel scanning

scanning (radioisotope)
  USE   radioisotope scanning

SCANNING ELECTRON MICROSCOPY [2,382; 2,382] *Mar 81*
(Prior to January 1983 this concept was indexed by coordination of ELECTRON MICROSCOPY and ELECTRON SCANNING.)
  UF   *sem*
  BT1   electron microscopy
  BT2   microscopy

SCANNING MEASURING PROJECTORS [230; 230]
  UF   *franckenstein*
  UF   *projectors (scanning)*
  UF   *smp devices*
  BT1   digitizers

scatter-plots
  USE   scatterplots

SCATTERING [17,882; 111,490]
  NT1   backscattering
  NT1   coherent scattering
  NT2   brillouin effect
  NT2   diffraction
  NT3   atomic beam diffraction
  NT3   electron diffraction
  NT3   neutron diffraction
  NT3   x-ray diffraction
  NT2   rayleigh scattering
  NT1   elastic scattering
  NT2   bhabha scattering
  NT2   compton effect
  NT2   coulomb scattering
  NT2   moeller scattering
  NT2   mott scattering
  NT2   potential scattering
  NT2   rutherford scattering
  NT2   wigner scattering
  NT1   incoherent scattering
  NT1   inelastic scattering
  NT2   deep inelastic scattering
  NT2   delbrueck scattering
  NT2   resonance scattering
  NT2   thomson scattering
  NT1   multiple scattering
  NT1   proximity scattering
  NT1   quasi-elastic scattering
  NT1   rescattering
  NT1   small angle scattering
  RT   adiabatic approximation
  RT   binary encounter method
  RT   blankenbecler-sugar equations
  RT   born approximation
  RT   born-oppenheimer approximation
  RT   brinkman-kramers approximation
  RT   buildup
  RT   center-of-mass system
  RT   collisions
  RT   conspiracy relations
  RT   coupled channel born approxima
  RT   detailed balance principle
  RT   diabatic approximation
  RT   dispersion relations
  RT   dwba
  RT   effective range theory
  RT   four momentum transfer
  RT   fsc approximation
  RT   glauber theory
  RT   gribov-lipatov relation
  RT   haywood model
  RT   impact parameter
  RT   impulse approximation
  RT   incidence angle
  RT   interactions
  RT   inverse scattering problem
  RT   ion scattering analysis
  RT   jost function
  RT   laboratory system
  RT   landau curves
  RT   lane-robson theory
  RT   levinson theorem
  RT   nuclear reactions
  RT   partial waves
  RT   perturbation theory
  RT   phase shift
  RT   polarization-asymmetry ratio
  RT   radiation scattering analysis
  RT   raman effect
  RT   resonating-group method
  RT   s matrix
  RT   scattering amplitudes
  RT   scattering lengths
  RT   semiclassical approximation
  RT   shadow effect
  RT   shielding
  RT   spectroscopic factors
  RT   stray radiation
  RT   targets
  RT   threshold energy
  RT   transport theory
  RT   wkb approximation
  RT   zemach-glauber formalism

SCATTERING AMPLITUDES [13,412; 13,412]
  BT1   amplitudes
  RT   abfst equation
  RT   argand diagrams
  RT   crossing symmetry
  RT   dispersion relations
  RT   duality
  RT   eikonal approximation
  RT   linear absorption models
  RT   partial waves
  RT   quasipotential equation
  RT   regge poles
  RT   s matrix
  RT   scattering
  RT   singularity
  RT   veneziano model

SCATTERING LENGTHS [1,812; 1,812]
  RT   scattering

SCATTERPLOTS [328; 999]
(Two-dimensional projections of multidimensional data.)
  UF   *scatter-plots*
  BT1   diagrams
  BT2   information
  NT1   dalitz plot
  NT1   prism plot

SCAVENGING [1,389; 1,389]
  RT   hot atom chemistry
  RT   radiation chemistry
  RT   radicals
  RT   radioprotective substances

scavenging (atmospheric)
  USE   washout

SCENEDESMUS [36; 36]
  BT1   unicellular algae
  BT2   algae
  BT3   plants
  BT2   microorganisms

SCHEDULES [438; 438] *Jul 86*
  RT   forecasting
  RT   management
  RT   organizing
  RT   pert method
  RT   planning

SCHIFF BASES [386; 386]
  BT1   imines
  BT2   organic nitrogen compounds
  BT3   organic compounds

SCHIFFER POTENTIAL [11; 11] *Oct 76*
  BT1   nucleon-nucleon potential
  BT2   potentials
  RT   nucleon-nucleon interactions

SCHISTOSOMA [156; 156]
  BT1   trematodes
  BT2   helminths
  BT3   parasites
  BT2   platyhelminths
  BT3   invertebrates
  BT4   animals
  RT   schistosomiasis

SCHISTOSOMIASIS [114; 114]
  BT1   parasitic diseases
  BT2   infectious diseases
  BT3   diseases
  RT   schistosoma
  RT   snails

SCHISTS [60; 60] *Jun 77*
  BT1   metamorphic rocks
  BT2   rocks

SCHLIEREN METHOD [143; 143]
  BT1   photography
  RT   opacity
  RT   refraction
  RT   visible radiation

SCHMEHAUSEN REACTOR [17; 17]
  BT1   enriched uranium reactors
  BT2   reactors
  BT1   helium cooled reactors
  BT2   gas cooled reactors
  BT3   reactors
  BT1   htgr type reactors
  BT2   gas cooled reactors
  BT3   reactors
  BT2   graphite moderated reactors
  BT3   reactors

schmehausen thtr reactor
  USE   thtr-300 reactor

SCHMIDT LINES [15; 15]
  RT   nuclear magnetic moments
  RT   spin

SCHMIDT MODEL [17; 17]
  RT   single-particle model
  RT   spin

schmitt trigger circuits
  USE   multivibrators

schnelle null-en. anord./kar
  USE   sneak reactor

schneller natriumgekuehlter re
  USE   snr reactor

SCHOEPITE [15; 15]
  BT1   oxide minerals
  BT2   minerals
  BT1   uranium minerals
  BT2   radioactive minerals
  BT3   minerals
  BT3   radioactive materials
  BT4   materials
  RT   uranium oxides

schools
  USE   educational facilities

SCHOONER EVENT [13; 13]
  BT1   cratering explosions
  BT2   explosions
  BT1   plowshare project
  BT1   thermonuclear explosions
  BT2   nuclear explosions
  BT3   explosions
  BT1   underground explosions
  BT2   explosions
  RT   excavation

SCHOTTKY BARRIER DIODES [509; 509]
- BT1 semiconductor diodes
- BT2 semiconductor devices
- RT tunnel diodes

SCHOTTKY DEFECTS [93; 93]
- BT1 vacancies
- BT2 point defects
- BT3 crystal defects
- BT4 crystal structure

SCHOTTKY EFFECT [197; 197]
- RT thermionics

SCHROECKINGERITE [2; 2]
- BT1 carbonate minerals
- BT2 minerals
- BT1 halide minerals
- BT2 minerals
- BT1 sulfate minerals
- BT2 minerals
- BT1 uranium minerals
- BT2 radioactive minerals
- BT3 minerals
- BT3 radioactive materials
- BT4 materials
- RT calcium carbonates
- RT sodium sulfates
- RT uranium carbonates

SCHROEDINGER EQUATION [8,130; 8,130]
- BT1 wave equations
- BT2 partial differential equations
- BT3 differential equations
- BT4 equations
- RT dirac equation
- RT jost function
- RT quantum mechanics
- RT wave functions

SCHROEDINGER PICTURE [284; 284]
Mar 76
- UF *schroedinger representation*
- RT heisenberg picture
- RT quantum field theory
- RT quantum mechanics

schroedinger representation
- USE schroedinger picture

SCHULZ METHOD [10; 10]
- RT diffraction methods
- RT texture

SCHUMANN-RUNGE BANDS [13; 13]
- RT spectra

schwarzschild field
- USE schwarzschild metric

SCHWARZSCHILD METRIC [1,159; 1,159]
- UF *schwarzschild field*
- UF *schwarzschild solution*
- UF *schwarzschild space*
- BT1 metrics
- RT cosmology
- RT general relativity theory
- RT gravitation

SCHWARZSCHILD RADIUS [336; 336]
- RT black holes
- RT gravitational collapse

schwarzschild solution
- USE schwarzschild metric

schwarzschild space
- USE schwarzschild metric

SCHWINGER FUNCTIONAL EQUATIONS [454; 454]
- BT1 differential equations
- BT2 equations
- RT quantum field theory

SCHWINGER SOURCE THEORY [200; 200]
- RT causality
- RT elementary particles
- RT quantum field theory

SCHWINGER TERMS [177; 177]
- RT current commutators
- RT delta function

SCHWINGER VARIATIONAL METHOD [181; 181]
- BT1 variational methods
- RT lippmann-schwinger equation
- RT quantum mechanics

SCHWINGER-TOMONAGA FORMALISM [218; 218]
- BT1 quantum electrodynamics
- BT2 electrodynamics
- BT2 quantum field theory
- BT3 field theories

SCIATIC NERVE [87; 87]
- BT1 nerves
- BT2 nervous system
- RT legs

scintigraphy
- USE scintiscanning

scintillation cameras
- USE gamma cameras

scintillation chambers
- USE scintillation counters

SCINTILLATION COUNTERS [4,169; 12,621]
- UF *scintillation chambers*
- UF *scintillation detectors*
- BT1 radiation detectors
- BT2 measuring instruments
- NT1 gas scintillation detectors
- NT1 liquid scintillation detectors
- NT1 scintillator-photodiode detect
- NT1 solid scintillation detectors
- NT2 bgo detectors
- NT2 nai detectors
- NT2 plastic scintillation detector
- RT dosemeters
- RT light pipes
- RT luminescent chambers
- RT phosphors
- RT photomultipliers
- RT proton recoil detectors
- RT scintillation counting

SCINTILLATION COUNTING [1,820; 1,820]
- BT1 counting techniques
- RT scintillation counters
- RT scintillation quenching

scintillation detectors
- USE scintillation counters

SCINTILLATION QUENCHING [340; 340]
- UF *quenching (scintillation)*
- RT liquid scintillation detectors
- RT scintillation counting

SCINTILLATIONS [930; 930]
- RT radioluminescence

SCINTILLATOR-PHOTODIODE DETECT [261; 261]
- BT1 scintillation counters
- BT2 radiation detectors
- BT3 measuring instruments

scintillators
- USE phosphors

SCINTISCANNING [21,816; 21,816]
- UF *scintigraphy*
- BT1 diagnostic techniques
- BT1 radioisotope scanning
- BT2 counting techniques
- RT diagnosis
- RT dual-isotope subtraction tec
- RT images
- RT labelled compounds
- RT nuclear medicine
- RT osteodensitometry
- RT radiopharmaceuticals

SCIOTO RIVER [0; 0]
- BT1 rivers
- BT2 surface waters

SCISSION-POINT MODEL [57; 57]
Oct 86
- BT1 nuclear models
- BT2 mathematical models
- RT fission

sclera
- USE eyes

SCLEROPROTEINS [18; 852]
- BT1 proteins
- BT2 organic compounds
- NT1 collagen
- NT1 fibrin
- NT1 glutin
- NT1 keratin

SCORPIONS [25; 25]
- BT1 arachnids
- BT2 arthropods
- BT3 invertebrates
- BT4 animals

scot. res. re. cen. utr-100 re
- USE srrc-utr-100 reactor

SCOTCH EVENT [2; 2] *Jun 77*
- BT1 contained explosions
- BT2 underground explosions
- BT3 explosions
- BT1 nuclear explosions
- BT2 explosions

scotland
- USE united kingdom

SCRAM [1,304; 1,304]
- UF *emergency shutdown*
- BT1 reactor shutdown
- BT2 shutdown
- RT atws
- RT fluid poison control
- RT reactor protection systems
- RT reactor safety fuses
- RT scram rods
- RT soluble poisons

SCRAM RODS [282; 282]
- UF *emergency rods*
- UF *safety rods*
- BT1 control elements
- BT2 reactor components
- RT neutron absorbers

RT scram

SCRAP [93; 93] *Mar 83*
(Material, usually from production processes, which can be reprocessed or recycled to become useful.)
- BT1 solid wastes
  - BT2 wastes
- RT industrial wastes
- RT municipal wastes
- RT recycling
- RT waste processing

SCREENS [296; 296] *Sep 77*
(Permeable barriers, frequently of perforated plates or metal wire mesh, used to prevent particles or objects larger than a specified size from passing beyond a given point in a flow stream, while permitting everything of smaller size to pass. Not to be used for viewing screens on which any type of image is displayed as on a cathode ray tube.)
- UF+ *impingement*
- SF *gratings*
- RT filters
- RT fouling
- RT intake structures
- RT separation processes
- RT sorting

SCREW DISLOCATIONS [324; 324]
- UF *frank dislocations*
- UF *frank loops*
- BT1 dislocations
  - BT2 line defects
    - BT3 crystal defects
      - BT4 crystal structure

screw instability
- USE helical instability

SCREW PINCH [116; 116]
- BT1 pinch effect
- RT linear screw pinch devices
- RT toroidal screw pinch devices

screwing
- USE fastening

screws
- USE fasteners

SCREWWORM FLY [11; 11] *Sep 75*
- BT1 flies
  - BT2 insects
    - BT3 arthropods
      - BT4 invertebrates
        - BT5 animals
- RT domestic animals
- RT parasites

scriba nuclear power plant
- USE nine mile point-1 reactor

SCRUBBERS [73; 73]
- BT1 pollution control equipment
  - BT2 equipment
- RT air cleaning
- RT air filters
- RT air pollution
- RT cyclone separators
- RT dust collectors
- RT scrubbing
- RT sprays
- RT waste processing

SCRUBBING [220; 220] *Sep 83*
- RT chemisorption
- RT cleaning
- RT decontamination
- RT descaling

- RT filters
- RT filtration
- RT flue gas
- RT off-gas systems
- RT pollution control equipment
- RT purification
- RT scrubbers
- RT separation processes
- RT solutions
- RT sprays

SCYLLA DEVICES [64; 64]
- BT1 linear theta pinch devices
  - BT2 linear pinch devices
    - BT3 open plasma devices
      - BT4 thermonuclear devices
    - BT3 pinch devices
      - BT4 thermonuclear devices

SCYLLAC DEVICES [114; 114]
- BT1 toroidal theta pinch devices
  - BT2 toroidal pinch devices
    - BT3 closed plasma devices
      - BT4 thermonuclear devices
    - BT3 pinch devices
      - BT4 thermonuclear devices

SDPPH [1; 1]
- UF *disulfodiphenylpicrylhydrazyl*
- BT1 nitro compounds
  - BT2 organic nitrogen compounds
    - BT3 organic compounds
- BT1 radicals
- BT1 sulfonic acids
  - BT2 organic acids
    - BT3 organic compounds
  - BT2 organic sulfur compounds
    - BT3 organic compounds
- RT hydrazine

SDS COMPUTERS [12; 12]
- BT1 computers

SEA BED [1,034; 1,034]
- RT earth crust
- RT geomorphology
- RT seas
- RT sediment-water interfaces

sea disposal
- USE marine disposal

SEA LEVEL [394; 394]
- BT1 levels

SEA URCHINS [62; 62]
- BT1 echinoderms
  - BT2 aquatic organisms
  - BT2 invertebrates
    - BT3 animals

sea, safety of life at, conv.
- USE solas convention

SEABROOK-1 REACTOR [95; 95]
(Seabrook, New Hampshire, USA)
- BT1 pwr type reactors
  - BT2 enriched uranium reactors
    - BT3 reactors
  - BT2 power reactors
    - BT3 reactors
  - BT2 thermal reactors
    - BT3 reactors
  - BT2 water cooled reactors
    - BT3 reactors
  - BT2 water moderated reactors
    - BT3 reactors

SEABROOK-2 REACTOR [81; 81]
(Seabrook, New Hampshire, USA)
- BT1 pwr type reactors
  - BT2 enriched uranium reactors
    - BT3 reactors
  - BT2 power reactors

  - BT3 reactors
  - BT2 thermal reactors
    - BT3 reactors
  - BT2 water cooled reactors
    - BT3 reactors
  - BT2 water moderated reactors
    - BT3 reactors

seacoast
- USE shores

SEAFOOD [488; 488]
- BT1 fish products
- BT1 food
- RT fishes
- RT lobsters
- RT oysters
- RT plaice
- RT prawns

SEALED SOURCES [596; 596]
- BT1 radiation sources
- RT containment
- RT leak testing
- RT leaks

SEALING MATERIALS [482; 482]
- BT1 materials
- RT grouting
- RT seals

SEALS [2,262; 2,433]
- NT1 gaskets
- NT1 inflatable seals
- RT closures
- RT grouting
- RT liners
- RT pipe fittings
- RT sealing materials

seals (security)
- USE security seals

seam welding
- USE welding

seam welds
- USE welded joints

SEAS [1,202; 3,600]
(For use only in its geographic connotation; for the legal connotation se HIGH SEAS and TERRITORIAL WATERS.)
- UF *oceans*
- BT1 surface waters
- NT1 arctic ocean
  - NT2 beaufort sea
  - NT2 chukchi sea
- NT1 atlantic ocean
  - NT2 bay of biscay
  - NT2 bay of fundy
  - NT2 biscayne bay
  - NT2 caribbean sea
    - NT3 gulf of mexico
      - NT4 san antonio bay
  - NT2 chesapeake bay
  - NT2 gulf of maine
  - NT2 irish sea
  - NT2 north sea
  - NT2 sargasso sea
- NT1 baltic sea
- NT1 black sea
- NT1 caspian sea
- NT1 indian ocean
  - NT2 arabian sea
- NT1 marmara sea
- NT1 mediterranean sea
- NT1 pacific ocean
  - NT2 bering sea
  - NT2 humboldt bay
  - NT2 san francisco bay
  - NT2 sequim bay

NT1   red sea
RT   coastal waters
RT   estuaries
RT   harbors
RT   high seas
RT   islands
RT   oceanography
RT   offshore nuclear power plants
RT   offshore sites
RT   sea bed
RT   seawater
RT   shores
RT   territorial waters
RT   tide
RT   tsunamis

SEASONAL VARIATIONS [1,756; 1,756]
BT1   variations
RT   seasons

SEASONS [171; 171]
RT   atmospheric precipitations
RT   climates
RT   meteorology
RT   seasonal variations
RT   vernalization
RT   weather

SEAWATER [3,851; 3,851]
BT1   water
BT2   hydrogen compounds
BT2   oxygen compounds
RT   desalination
RT   desalination plants
RT   estuaries
RT   salinity
RT   seas
RT   sediment-water interfaces

SEAWEEDS [201; 289]
NT1   fucus
NT1   laminaria

sebaceous glands
USE   glands
AND   skin

SEBACIC ACID [10; 10]
BT1   dicarboxylic acids
BT2   carboxylic acids
BT3   organic acids
BT4   organic compounds

secale
USE   rye

second class currents
USE   second-class currents

SECOND QUANTIZATION [1,378; 1,378]
BT1   quantization
RT   annihilation operators
RT   creation operators
RT   quantum field theory
RT   quantum mechanics

SECOND SOUND [363; 363]
RT   superfluidity

SECOND-CLASS CURRENTS [265; 265]
(Classification of currents according to their properties under G- parity transformations.)
UF   *second class currents*
BT1   algebraic currents
BT2   currents
RT   weak interactions

SECONDARY BEAMS [423; 424]
BT1   beams
RT   ion probes

SECONDARY COOLANT CIRCUITS [1,474; 1,474]
BT1   reactor cooling systems
BT2   cooling systems
BT2   reactor components

SECONDARY COSMIC RADIATION [822; 4,041]
BT1   cosmic radiation
BT2   ionizing radiations
BT3   radiations
NT1   cosmic electrons
NT1   cosmic kaons
NT1   cosmic muons
NT1   cosmic neutrons
NT1   cosmic pions
NT1   cosmic positrons
NT1   cosmic showers
NT2   extensive air showers

SECONDARY EMISSION [2,441; 4,085]
BT1   emission
NT1   photoemission
RT   ion probes
RT   photon emission

SECONDARY EMISSION DETECTORS [186; 186]
BT1   radiation detectors
BT2   measuring instruments

SECONDARY REACTIONS [91; 91]
BT1   nuclear reactions

secondary recovery
USE   enhanced recovery

secondary standard dosimet lab
USE   ssdl

* **SECONDS LIVING RADIOISOTOPES** [227; 20,523]
(For specific terms, consult the Appendix.)
BT1   radioisotopes
BT2   isotopes
RT   half-life

SECRECY PROTECTION [34; 34]
Mar 77
(Measures, regulations or orders established to protect the secrecy of certain places, installations or offices.)
RT   atomic energy laws
RT   identification systems
RT   physical protection
RT   sabotage
RT   security
RT   security personnel

SECRETIN [61; 61]
BT1   hormones
RT   secretion
RT   small intestine

SECRETION [1,141; 1,167]
NT1   pheromone
RT   body fluids
RT   excretion
RT   gastric acid
RT   gastrin
RT   glands
RT   secretin

SECULAR EQUATION [170; 170]
BT1   equations
RT   eigenvalues
RT   matrices

SECURITY [1,390; 1,390]
UF   *security control*
RT   biointrusion
RT   entry control systems
RT   human intrusion
RT   identification systems
RT   motion detection systems
RT   physical protection
RT   physical protection devices
RT   sabotage
RT   safety
RT   secrecy protection
RT   security personnel

security (financial)
USE   financial security

security control
(Prior to December 1990, this was a valid descriptor.)
USE   security

SECURITY PERSONNEL [83; 83]
Jun 83
UF   *guards*
BT1   personnel
RT   nuclear materials diversion
RT   physical protection
RT   sabotage
RT   safeguards
RT   secrecy protection
RT   security

SECURITY SEALS [123; 123] *Sep 76*
UF   *seals (security)*
BT1   physical protection devices
RT   safeguards

SEDAN EVENT [8; 8]
BT1   cratering explosions
BT2   explosions
BT1   plowshare project

sedatives
USE   hypnotics and sedatives

SEDIMENT-WATER INTERFACES [113; 113] *Apr 85*
(Boundary between sediment surface and overlying water.)
BT1   interfaces
RT   limnology
RT   sea bed
RT   seawater
RT   sediments
RT   surface waters

sedimentary basins
USE   geologic structures

sedimentary intrusive rocks
USE   plutonic rocks

SEDIMENTARY ROCKS [705; 2,752]
UF   *evaporites*
BT1   rocks
NT1   carbonate rocks
NT2   limestone
NT1   phosphate rocks
NT2   phosphorites
NT1   sandstones
NT2   graywacke
NT1   shales
NT2   oil shales

SEDIMENTATION [1,210; 1,210]
UF   *deposition (gravitational)*
RT   aerosols
RT   centrifugation
RT   decantation
RT   dusts
RT   fallout

```
       RT     fallout deposits
       RT     particles
       RT     precipitation
       RT     sediments
       RT     settling ponds

SEDIMENTS [5,593; 5,593]
       RT     alluvial deposits
       RT     diagenesis
       RT     dredge spoil
       RT     environmental materials
       RT     geologic deposits
       RT     sediment-water interfaces
       RT     sedimentation
       RT     silt

SEDOHEPTULOSE [0; 0]
       BT1    ketones
       BT2      organic compounds
       BT1    monosaccharides
       BT2      saccharides
       BT3        carbohydrates
       BT4          organic compounds

SEEBECK EFFECT [248; 248]
       RT     thermoelectricity

SEED-SLAG INTERACTIONS [3; 3]
Jul 85
       RT     chemical reactions
       RT     mhd generators
       RT     plasma seeding
       RT     slags

seeding (plasma)
       USE    plasma seeding

SEEDLINGS [816; 816]
       RT     coleoptile
       RT     germination
       RT     plants

SEEDS [2,371; 2,736]
       UF     fruit (seeds)
       UF+    grains (cereal)
       NT1    coffee beans
       NT1    mungbeans
       NT1    peas
       NT1    soybeans
       RT     beans
       RT     endosperm
       RT     food
       RT     germination
       RT     plants
       RT     vernalization

SEFOR REACTOR [82; 82]
       UF     southwest exper. fast oxide r.
       BT1    experimental reactors
       BT2      research and test reactors
       BT3        reactors
       BT1    fast reactors
       BT2      epithermal reactors
       BT3        reactors
       BT1    plutonium reactors
       BT2      reactors
       BT1    power reactors
       BT2      reactors
       BT1    sodium cooled reactors
       BT2      liquid metal cooled reactors
       BT3        reactors

SEGREGATION [1,388; 1,388]
       RT     guinier-preston zones
       RT     impurities
       RT     solidification

SEIBERSDORF IAEA LABORATORY
[17; 17] Apr 88
       UF     iaea seibersdorf laboratory
       BT1    iaea
       BT2      international organizations

SEIBERSDORF RESEARCH CENTRE
[8; 8] Jun 88
       UF     austrian res cent seibersdorf
       UF     oefzs
       BT1    austrian organizations
       BT2      national organizations
       RT     astra reactor

SEISMIC DETECTION [509; 509]
       BT1    detection
       RT     benham event
       RT     boxcar event
       RT     nuclear explosion detection
       RT     rayleigh waves
       RT     seismic noise
       RT     seismic p waves
       RT     seismic s waves
       RT     seismic waves
       RT     seismographs
       RT     underground explosions
       RT     vela project

SEISMIC EFFECTS [4,904; 5,606]
       NT1    ground motion
       RT     blast effects
       RT     earthquakes
       RT     landslides
       RT     nuclear explosions
       RT     seismic isolation
       RT     seismic noise
       RT     seismic waves
       RT     shock absorbers
       RT     shock waves
       RT     soil-structure interactions
       RT     underground explosions

SEISMIC ISOLATION [11; 11] Sep 90
       RT     earthquakes
       RT     safety engineering
       RT     seismic effects
       RT     shock absorbers
       RT     soil-structure interactions

SEISMIC NOISE [22; 22] Oct 76
(A more or less continuous motion in the
earth unrelated to an earthquake with a
period of 1 to 9 seconds.)
       BT1    noise
       RT     seismic detection
       RT     seismic effects
       RT     seismic waves

SEISMIC P WAVES [141; 141]
       UF     body waves p (seismic)
       UF     p waves (seismic)
       BT1    seismic waves
       RT     earthquakes
       RT     seismic detection
       RT     underground explosions

SEISMIC S WAVES [42; 42] May 80
       UF     body waves s (seismic)
       UF     s waves (seismic)
       UF     shear waves (seismic)
       BT1    seismic waves
       RT     earthquakes
       RT     seismic detection
       RT     underground explosions

SEISMIC SURFACE WAVES [12; 33]
Mar 83
       UF     surface waves (seismic)
       BT1    seismic waves
       RT     rayleigh waves

SEISMIC SURVEYS [375; 375] Nov 75
       BT1    geologic surveys
       RT     acoustic measurements
       RT     geologic structures
       RT     seismic waves
       RT     seismology

SEISMIC WAVES [788; 1,012]
       NT1    seismic p waves
       NT1    seismic s waves
       NT1    seismic surface waves
       RT     earthquakes
       RT     epicenters
       RT     ground motion
       RT     milrow event
       RT     seismic detection
       RT     seismic effects
       RT     seismic noise
       RT     seismic surveys
       RT     seismographs
       RT     seismology
       RT     tsunamis
       RT     underground explosions

seismicity
(The relative frequency or distribution of
earthquakes.)
       USE    earthquakes

SEISMOGRAPHS [140; 140]
       BT1    measuring instruments
       RT     acoustic measurements
       RT     earthquakes
       RT     ground motion
       RT     seismic detection
       RT     seismic waves
       RT     underground explosions

SEISMOLOGY [788; 788]
       RT     earthquakes
       RT     faultless event
       RT     geologic faults
       RT     geologic structures
       RT     ground motion
       RT     seismic surveys
       RT     seismic waves
       RT     shock waves
       RT     underground explosions
       RT     vela project

SELECTION RULES [1,368; 1,526]
       NT1    superselection rules
       RT     decay
       RT     energy-level transitions
       RT     forbidden transitions
       RT     interactions
       RT     quantum mechanics
       RT     spurions

SELENATES [215; 215]
(Specific compounds should be indexed
by coordination of a descriptor of the for
(CATION) COMPOUNDS and the above
anion descriptor.)
       BT1    oxygen compounds
       BT1    selenium compounds
       RT     selenium oxides

selengut approximation
       USE    selengut-goertzel equation

SELENGUT-GOERTZEL EQUATION
[4; 4]
       UF     selengut approximation
       BT1    equations
       RT     neutron slowing-down theory
       RT     slowing-down
       RT     transport theory

SELENIDES [969; 3,908]
       BT1    chalcogenides
       BT1    selenium compounds
       NT1    aluminium selenides
       NT1    americium selenides
       NT1    antimony selenides
       NT1    arsenic selenides
       NT1    berkelium selenides
       NT1    beryllium selenides
       NT1    bismuth selenides
       NT1    cadmium selenides
       NT1    californium selenides
       NT1    cerium selenides
```

NT1 cesium selenides
NT1 chromium selenides
NT1 cobalt selenides
NT1 copper selenides
NT1 curium selenides
NT1 dysprosium selenides
NT1 erbium selenides
NT1 europium selenides
NT1 gadolinium selenides
NT1 gallium selenides
NT1 germanium selenides
NT1 hafnium selenides
NT1 holmium selenides
NT1 indium selenides
NT1 iron selenides
NT1 lanthanum selenides
NT1 lead selenides
NT1 lithium selenides
NT1 lutetium selenides
NT1 manganese selenides
NT1 mercury selenides
NT1 molybdenum selenides
NT1 neptunium selenides
NT1 nickel selenides
NT1 niobium selenides
NT1 palladium selenides
NT1 plutonium selenides
NT1 potassium selenides
NT1 praseodymium selenides
NT1 rhenium selenides
NT1 rhodium selenides
NT1 rubidium selenides
NT1 ruthenium selenides
NT1 samarium selenides
NT1 scandium selenides
NT1 silver selenides
NT1 sodium selenides
NT1 tantalum selenides
NT1 terbium selenides
NT1 thallium selenides
NT1 thorium selenides
NT1 thulium selenides
NT1 tin selenides
NT1 titanium selenides
NT1 tungsten selenides
NT1 uranium selenides
NT1 vanadium selenides
NT1 ytterbium selenides
NT1 yttrium selenides
NT1 zinc selenides
NT1 zirconium selenides
RT intermetallic compounds
RT selenium alloys

SELENITES [162; 162]
(Specific compounds should be indexed by coordination of a descriptor of the form (CATION) COMPOUNDS and the above anion descriptor.)
BT1 oxygen compounds
BT1 selenium compounds

SELENIUM [1,766; 1,766]
BT1 semimetals
BT2 elements

SELENIUM ADDITIONS [81; 81]
RT selenium alloys
RT selenium compounds

SELENIUM ALLOYS [230; 230]
(Alloys containing more than 1% Se.)
BT1 alloys
RT selenides
RT selenium additions

SELENIUM BROMIDES [11; 11]
BT1 bromides
BT2 bromine compounds
BT3 halogen compounds
BT2 halides
BT3 halogen compounds
BT1 selenium compounds

SELENIUM CARBIDES [2; 2]
BT1 carbides
BT2 carbon compounds
BT1 selenium compounds

SELENIUM CHLORIDES [13; 13]
BT1 chlorides
BT2 chlorine compounds
BT3 halogen compounds
BT2 halides
BT3 halogen compounds
BT1 selenium compounds

SELENIUM COMPLEXES [59; 59]
BT1 complexes

SELENIUM COMPOUNDS [553; 4,857]
NT1 selenates
NT1 selenides
NT2 aluminium selenides
NT2 americium selenides
NT2 antimony selenides
NT2 arsenic selenides
NT2 berkelium selenides
NT2 beryllium selenides
NT2 bismuth selenides
NT2 cadmium selenides
NT2 californium selenides
NT2 cerium selenides
NT2 cesium selenides
NT2 chromium selenides
NT2 cobalt selenides
NT2 copper selenides
NT2 curium selenides
NT2 dysprosium selenides
NT2 erbium selenides
NT2 europium selenides
NT2 gadolinium selenides
NT2 gallium selenides
NT2 germanium selenides
NT2 hafnium selenides
NT2 holmium selenides
NT2 indium selenides
NT2 iron selenides
NT2 lanthanum selenides
NT2 lead selenides
NT2 lithium selenides
NT2 lutetium selenides
NT2 manganese selenides
NT2 mercury selenides
NT2 molybdenum selenides
NT2 neptunium selenides
NT2 nickel selenides
NT2 niobium selenides
NT2 palladium selenides
NT2 plutonium selenides
NT2 potassium selenides
NT2 praseodymium selenides
NT2 rhenium selenides
NT2 rhodium selenides
NT2 rubidium selenides
NT2 ruthenium selenides
NT2 samarium selenides
NT2 scandium selenides
NT2 silver selenides
NT2 sodium selenides
NT2 tantalum selenides
NT2 terbium selenides
NT2 thallium selenides
NT2 thorium selenides
NT2 thulium selenides
NT2 tin selenides
NT2 titanium selenides
NT2 tungsten selenides
NT2 uranium selenides
NT2 vanadium selenides
NT2 ytterbium selenides
NT2 yttrium selenides
NT2 zinc selenides
NT2 zirconium selenides
NT1 selenites
NT1 selenium bromides
NT1 selenium carbides
NT1 selenium chlorides
NT1 selenium fluorides
NT1 selenium hydrides
NT1 selenium hydroxides
NT1 selenium iodides
NT1 selenium oxides
NT1 selenium sulfides
NT1 selenium tellurides
NT1 tmtsf
RT selenium additions

SELENIUM FLUORIDES [29; 29]
BT1 fluorides
BT2 fluorine compounds
BT3 halogen compounds
BT2 halides
BT3 halogen compounds
BT1 selenium compounds

SELENIUM HYDRIDES [31; 31]
BT1 hydrides
BT2 hydrogen compounds
BT1 selenium compounds

SELENIUM HYDROXIDES [0; 0]
BT1 hydroxides
BT2 hydrogen compounds
BT2 oxygen compounds
BT1 selenium compounds

SELENIUM IODIDES [14; 14]
BT1 iodides
BT2 halides
BT3 halogen compounds
BT2 iodine compounds
BT3 halogen compounds
BT1 selenium compounds

SELENIUM IONS [214; 214]
BT1 ions
BT2 charged particles

SELENIUM ISOTOPES [163; 2,314]
NT1 selenium 68
NT1 selenium 69
NT1 selenium 70
NT1 selenium 71
NT1 selenium 72
NT1 selenium 73
NT1 selenium 74
NT1 selenium 75
NT1 selenium 76
NT1 selenium 77
NT1 selenium 78
NT1 selenium 79
NT1 selenium 80
NT1 selenium 81
NT1 selenium 82
NT1 selenium 83
NT1 selenium 84
NT1 selenium 85
NT1 selenium 86
NT1 selenium 87
NT1 selenium 88
NT1 selenium 89
NT1 selenium 91

SELENIUM ORES [4; 4]
BT1 ores

SELENIUM OXIDES [67; 67]
BT1 oxides
BT2 chalcogenides
BT2 oxygen compounds
BT1 selenium compounds
RT oxide minerals
RT selenates

SELENIUM SULFIDES [8; 8]
BT1 selenium compounds
BT1 sulfides
BT2 chalcogenides
BT2 sulfur compounds

→ **SELENIUM TELLURIDES** [0; 0] *Sep 91*
BT1 selenium compounds
BT1 tellurides
BT2 chalcogenides
BT2 tellurium compounds

SELENIUM 68 [11; 11]
- BT1 beta-plus decay radioisotopes
  - BT2 beta decay radioisotopes
    - BT3 radioisotopes
      - BT4 isotopes
- BT1 even-even nuclei
  - BT2 nuclei
- BT1 intermediate mass nuclei
  - BT2 nuclei
- BT1 minutes living radioisotopes
  - BT2 radioisotopes
    - BT3 isotopes
- BT1 selenium isotopes

SELENIUM 69 [25; 25]
- BT1 beta-plus decay radioisotopes
  - BT2 beta decay radioisotopes
    - BT3 radioisotopes
      - BT4 isotopes
- BT1 electron capture radioisotopes
  - BT2 beta decay radioisotopes
    - BT3 radioisotopes
      - BT4 isotopes
- BT1 even-odd nuclei
  - BT2 nuclei
- BT1 intermediate mass nuclei
  - BT2 nuclei
- BT1 seconds living radioisotopes
  - BT2 radioisotopes
    - BT3 isotopes
- BT1 selenium isotopes

SELENIUM 70 [37; 37]
- BT1 beta-plus decay radioisotopes
  - BT2 beta decay radioisotopes
    - BT3 radioisotopes
      - BT4 isotopes
- BT1 electron capture radioisotopes
  - BT2 beta decay radioisotopes
    - BT3 radioisotopes
      - BT4 isotopes
- BT1 even-even nuclei
  - BT2 nuclei
- BT1 intermediate mass nuclei
  - BT2 nuclei
- BT1 minutes living radioisotopes
  - BT2 radioisotopes
    - BT3 isotopes
- BT1 selenium isotopes

SELENIUM 71 [17; 17]
- BT1 beta-plus decay radioisotopes
  - BT2 beta decay radioisotopes
    - BT3 radioisotopes
      - BT4 isotopes
- BT1 electron capture radioisotopes
  - BT2 beta decay radioisotopes
    - BT3 radioisotopes
      - BT4 isotopes
- BT1 even-odd nuclei
  - BT2 nuclei
- BT1 intermediate mass nuclei
  - BT2 nuclei
- BT1 minutes living radioisotopes
  - BT2 radioisotopes
    - BT3 isotopes
- BT1 selenium isotopes

SELENIUM 72 [102; 102]
- BT1 days living radioisotopes
  - BT2 radioisotopes
    - BT3 isotopes
- BT1 electron capture radioisotopes
  - BT2 beta decay radioisotopes
    - BT3 radioisotopes
      - BT4 isotopes
- BT1 even-even nuclei
  - BT2 nuclei
- BT1 intermediate mass nuclei
  - BT2 nuclei
- BT1 selenium isotopes

SELENIUM 72 TARGET [3; 3] *Feb 76*
- BT1 targets

SELENIUM 73 [90; 90]
- BT1 beta-plus decay radioisotopes
  - BT2 beta decay radioisotopes
    - BT3 radioisotopes
      - BT4 isotopes
- BT1 electron capture radioisotopes
  - BT2 beta decay radioisotopes
    - BT3 radioisotopes
      - BT4 isotopes
- BT1 even-odd nuclei
  - BT2 nuclei
- BT1 hours living radioisotopes
  - BT2 radioisotopes
    - BT3 isotopes
- BT1 intermediate mass nuclei
  - BT2 nuclei
- BT1 isomeric transition isotopes
  - BT2 radioisotopes
    - BT3 isotopes
- BT1 minutes living radioisotopes
  - BT2 radioisotopes
    - BT3 isotopes
- BT1 selenium isotopes

SELENIUM 74 [116; 116]
- BT1 even-even nuclei
  - BT2 nuclei
- BT1 intermediate mass nuclei
  - BT2 nuclei
- BT1 selenium isotopes
- BT1 stable isotopes
  - BT2 isotopes

SELENIUM 74 TARGET [51; 51]
- BT1 targets

SELENIUM 75 [1,200; 1,200]
- BT1 days living radioisotopes
  - BT2 radioisotopes
    - BT3 isotopes
- BT1 electron capture radioisotopes
  - BT2 beta decay radioisotopes
    - BT3 radioisotopes
      - BT4 isotopes
- BT1 even-odd nuclei
  - BT2 nuclei
- BT1 intermediate mass nuclei
  - BT2 nuclei
- BT1 selenium isotopes

SELENIUM 75 TARGET [2; 2] *Jun 84*
- BT1 targets

SELENIUM 76 [184; 184]
- BT1 even-even nuclei
  - BT2 nuclei
- BT1 intermediate mass nuclei
  - BT2 nuclei
- BT1 selenium isotopes
- BT1 stable isotopes
  - BT2 isotopes

SELENIUM 76 REACTIONS [2; 2] *Jun 88*
- BT1 heavy ion reactions
- BT2 nuclear reactions

SELENIUM 76 TARGET [124; 124]
- BT1 targets

SELENIUM 77 [176; 176]
- BT1 even-odd nuclei
  - BT2 nuclei
- BT1 intermediate mass nuclei
  - BT2 nuclei
- BT1 isomeric transition isotopes
  - BT2 radioisotopes
    - BT3 isotopes
- BT1 seconds living radioisotopes
  - BT2 radioisotopes
    - BT3 isotopes
- BT1 selenium isotopes
- BT1 stable isotopes
  - BT2 isotopes

SELENIUM 77 TARGET [60; 60]
- BT1 targets

SELENIUM 78 [125; 125]
- BT1 even-even nuclei
  - BT2 nuclei
- BT1 intermediate mass nuclei
  - BT2 nuclei
- BT1 selenium isotopes
- BT1 stable isotopes
  - BT2 isotopes

SELENIUM 78 TARGET [129; 129]
- BT1 targets

SELENIUM 79 [69; 69]
- BT1 beta-minus decay radioisotopes
  - BT2 beta decay radioisotopes
    - BT3 radioisotopes
      - BT4 isotopes
- BT1 even-odd nuclei
  - BT2 nuclei
- BT1 intermediate mass nuclei
  - BT2 nuclei
- BT1 internal conversion radioisoto
  - BT2 radioisotopes
    - BT3 isotopes
- BT1 isomeric transition isotopes
  - BT2 radioisotopes
    - BT3 isotopes
- BT1 minutes living radioisotopes
  - BT2 radioisotopes
    - BT3 isotopes
- BT1 selenium isotopes
- BT1 years living radioisotopes
  - BT2 radioisotopes
    - BT3 isotopes

SELENIUM 80 [83; 83]
- BT1 even-even nuclei
  - BT2 nuclei
- BT1 intermediate mass nuclei
  - BT2 nuclei
- BT1 selenium isotopes
- BT1 stable isotopes
  - BT2 isotopes

SELENIUM 80 REACTIONS [24; 24] *Jan 86*
- BT1 heavy ion reactions
- BT2 nuclear reactions

SELENIUM 80 TARGET [158; 158]
- BT1 targets

SELENIUM 81 [52; 52]
- BT1 beta-minus decay radioisotopes
  - BT2 beta decay radioisotopes
    - BT3 radioisotopes
      - BT4 isotopes
- BT1 even-odd nuclei
  - BT2 nuclei
- BT1 intermediate mass nuclei
  - BT2 nuclei
- BT1 internal conversion radioisoto
  - BT2 radioisotopes
    - BT3 isotopes
- BT1 isomeric transition isotopes
  - BT2 radioisotopes
    - BT3 isotopes
- BT1 minutes living radioisotopes
  - BT2 radioisotopes
    - BT3 isotopes
- BT1 selenium isotopes

SELENIUM 82 [175; 175]
- BT1 even-even nuclei
  - BT2 nuclei
- BT1 intermediate mass nuclei
  - BT2 nuclei
- BT1 selenium isotopes
- BT1 stable isotopes
  - BT2 isotopes

SELENIUM 82 REACTIONS [12; 12]
Dec 80
BT1 heavy ion reactions
BT2 nuclear reactions

SELENIUM 82 TARGET [139; 139]
BT1 targets

SELENIUM 83 [21; 21]
BT1 beta-minus decay radioisotopes
BT2 beta decay radioisotopes
BT3 radioisotopes
BT4 isotopes
BT1 even-odd nuclei
BT2 nuclei
BT1 intermediate mass nuclei
BT2 nuclei
BT1 minutes living radioisotopes
BT2 radioisotopes
BT3 isotopes
BT1 selenium isotopes

SELENIUM 84 [25; 25]
BT1 beta-minus decay radioisotopes
BT2 beta decay radioisotopes
BT3 radioisotopes
BT4 isotopes
BT1 even-even nuclei
BT2 nuclei
BT1 intermediate mass nuclei
BT2 nuclei
BT1 minutes living radioisotopes
BT2 radioisotopes
BT3 isotopes
BT1 selenium isotopes

SELENIUM 85 [20; 20]
BT1 beta-minus decay radioisotopes
BT2 beta decay radioisotopes
BT3 radioisotopes
BT4 isotopes
BT1 even-odd nuclei
BT2 nuclei
BT1 intermediate mass nuclei
BT2 nuclei
BT1 seconds living radioisotopes
BT2 radioisotopes
BT3 isotopes
BT1 selenium isotopes

SELENIUM 86 [13; 13]
BT1 beta-minus decay radioisotopes
BT2 beta decay radioisotopes
BT3 radioisotopes
BT4 isotopes
BT1 even-even nuclei
BT2 nuclei
BT1 intermediate mass nuclei
BT2 nuclei
BT1 seconds living radioisotopes
BT2 radioisotopes
BT3 isotopes
BT1 selenium isotopes

SELENIUM 87 [11; 11]
BT1 beta-minus decay radioisotopes
BT2 beta decay radioisotopes
BT3 radioisotopes
BT4 isotopes
BT1 even-odd nuclei
BT2 nuclei
BT1 intermediate mass nuclei
BT2 nuclei
BT1 seconds living radioisotopes
BT2 radioisotopes
BT3 isotopes
BT1 selenium isotopes

SELENIUM 88 [9; 9]
BT1 beta-minus decay radioisotopes
BT2 beta decay radioisotopes
BT3 radioisotopes
BT4 isotopes
BT1 even-even nuclei
BT2 nuclei
BT1 intermediate mass nuclei

BT2 nuclei
BT1 seconds living radioisotopes
BT2 radioisotopes
BT3 isotopes
BT1 selenium isotopes

SELENIUM 89 [4; 4] *Jul 76*
BT1 beta-minus decay radioisotopes
BT2 beta decay radioisotopes
BT3 radioisotopes
BT4 isotopes
BT1 even-odd nuclei
BT2 nuclei
BT1 intermediate mass nuclei
BT2 nuclei
BT1 millisec living radioisotopes
BT2 radioisotopes
BT3 isotopes
BT1 selenium isotopes

SELENIUM 91 [3; 3] *Mar 76*
BT1 beta-minus decay radioisotopes
BT2 beta decay radioisotopes
BT3 radioisotopes
BT4 isotopes
BT1 even-odd nuclei
BT2 nuclei
BT1 intermediate mass nuclei
BT2 nuclei
BT1 millisec living radioisotopes
BT2 radioisotopes
BT3 isotopes
BT1 selenium isotopes

SELF-ABSORPTION [465; 465]
BT1 absorption

SELF-CONSISTENT FIELD
[3,065; 3,065]
RT atomic models
RT hartree-fock method
RT hartree-fock-bogolyubov theory
RT lcao method
RT mean-field theory

SELF-DIFFUSION [1,235; 1,235]
BT1 diffusion

SELF-ENERGY [1,765; 1,765]
BT1 energy
RT quantum electrodynamics

SELF-IRRADIATION [166; 166]
BT1 irradiation
RT autoradiolysis
RT radiation effects

self-potential logging
USE well logging

SELF-POWERED DETECTORS
[67; 461]
BT1 radiation detectors
BT2 measuring instruments
NT1 self-powered gamma detectors
NT1 self-powered neutron detectors
RT compton diode detectors

SELF-POWERED GAMMA DETECTORS [56; 56]
BT1 self-powered detectors
BT2 radiation detectors
BT3 measuring instruments

SELF-POWERED NEUTRON DETECTORS [366; 366]
UF *collectrons*
BT1 neutron detectors
BT2 radiation detectors
BT3 measuring instruments
BT1 self-powered detectors
BT2 radiation detectors
BT3 measuring instruments

SELF-SHIELDING [573; 573]
RT absorption
RT shielding

SELLAFIELD REPROCESSING PLANT
[565; 565] *Jun 84*
UF *windscale reprocessing plant*
BT1 fuel reprocessing plants
BT2 nuclear facilities

SELNI REACTOR [48; 48]
UF *trino vercellese reactor*
BT1 pwr type reactors
BT2 enriched uranium reactors
BT3 reactors
BT2 power reactors
BT3 reactors
BT2 thermal reactors
BT3 reactors
BT2 water cooled reactors
BT3 reactors
BT2 water moderated reactors
BT3 reactors

sem
USE scanning electron microscopy

SEMI-EXCLUSIVE INTERACTIONS
[15; 15] *Nov 87*
BT1 exclusive interactions
BT2 particle interactions
BT3 interactions
RT semi-inclusive interactions

semi-homog. critical assembly
USE shca reactor

SEMI-INCLUSIVE INTERACTIONS
[112; 112] *Oct 81*
BT1 inclusive interactions
BT2 particle interactions
BT3 interactions
RT semi-exclusive interactions

SEMICARBAZIDES [68; 68]
BT1 carbonic acid derivatives
BT2 organic compounds
BT1 organic nitrogen compounds
BT2 organic compounds
BT1 organic oxygen compounds
BT2 organic compounds

SEMICARBAZONES [75; 75]
BT1 carbonic acid derivatives
BT2 organic compounds
BT1 organic nitrogen compounds
BT2 organic compounds
RT aldehydes
RT ketones

semicircular spectrometers
USE flat magnetic spectrometers

SEMICLASSICAL APPROXIMATION
[3,740; 3,740]
UF *approximation (semiclassical)*
UF *sca model*
RT quantum mechanics
RT scattering

semiconductor counters
USE semiconductor detectors

SEMICONDUCTOR DETECTORS
[1,552; 9,625]
UF *semiconductor counters*
BT1 radiation detectors
BT2 measuring instruments
NT1 bulk semiconductor detectors
NT1 cdte semiconductor detectors
NT1 ge semiconductor detectors
NT2 high-purity ge detectors

	NT2	li-drifted ge detectors
	NT1	hgi2 semiconductor detectors
	NT1	insb semiconductor detectors
	NT1	junction detectors
	NT2	li-drifted junction detectors
	NT1	li-drifted detectors
	NT2	li-drifted ge detectors
	NT2	li-drifted junction detectors
	NT2	li-drifted si detectors
	NT1	si semiconductor detectors
	NT2	li-drifted si detectors
	NT1	surface barrier detectors
	RT	dosemeters
	RT	radiator counters
	RT	semiconductor devices

SEMICONDUCTOR DEVICES
[1,054; 8,188]
	NT1	charge-coupled devices
	NT1	semiconductor diodes
	NT2	germanium diodes
•	NT2	junction diodes
	NT2	light emitting diodes
	NT2	photodiodes
	NT2	schottky barrier diodes
	NT2	silicon diodes
	NT2	switching diodes
	NT2	tunnel diodes
	NT2	variable capacitance diodes
	NT1	semiconductor lasers
	NT1	semiconductor rectifiers
	NT1	semiconductor resistors
	NT1	semiconductor storage devices
	NT1	semiconductor switches
	NT1	thermistors
	NT1	thyristors
	NT1	transistors
	NT2	field effect transistors
	NT3	mosfet
	NT2	junction transistors
	NT2	mis transistors
	NT2	mos transistors
	NT3	mosfet
	NT2	phototransistors
	NT2	surface barrier transistors
	RT	display devices
	RT	electrical equipment
	RT	electronic equipment
	RT	miniaturization
	RT	oscillators
	RT	photoelectric cells
	RT	semiconductor detectors
	RT	solid state physics

SEMICONDUCTOR DIODES
[669; 2,955]
	UF	*diodes (semiconductor)*
	BT1	semiconductor devices
	NT1	germanium diodes
	NT1	junction diodes
	NT1	light emitting diodes
	NT1	photodiodes
	NT1	schottky barrier diodes
	NT1	silicon diodes
	NT1	switching diodes
	NT1	tunnel diodes
	NT1	variable capacitance diodes
	RT	betavoltaic cells
	RT	photovoltaic cells
	RT	semiconductor junctions
	RT	semiconductor rectifiers
	RT	thermionic diodes

SEMICONDUCTOR JUNCTIONS
[640; 3,984]
	UF	*junctions (semiconductor)*
	NT1	heterojunctions
	NT1	josephson junctions
	NT1	mim junctions
	NT1	p-n junctions
	RT	junction detectors
	RT	junction transistors
	RT	semiconductor diodes
	RT	semiconductor materials

SEMICONDUCTOR LASERS [578; 578]
	BT1	semiconductor devices
	BT1	solid state lasers
	BT2	lasers
	BT3	amplifiers
	BT4	equipment

SEMICONDUCTOR MATERIALS
[6,470; 10,854]
(If known, coordinate with descriptors for the specific materials.)
	BT1	materials
	NT1	magnetic semiconductors
	NT1	n-type conductors
	NT1	p-type conductors
	RT	electric conductors
	RT	electron mobility
	RT	fano factor
	RT	photoconductors
	RT	semiconductor junctions
	RT	semimetals
	RT	solid state physics
	RT	traps

SEMICONDUCTOR RECTIFIERS
[56; 56]
	BT1	rectifiers
	BT2	electrical equipment
	BT3	equipment
	BT1	semiconductor devices
	RT	semiconductor diodes

SEMICONDUCTOR RESISTORS
[90; 90]
	UF	*varistors*
	BT1	resistors
	BT2	electrical equipment
	BT3	equipment
	BT1	semiconductor devices

SEMICONDUCTOR STORAGE DEVICES [182; 182]
	BT1	memory devices
	BT1	semiconductor devices

SEMICONDUCTOR SWITCHES
[105; 105]
	BT1	semiconductor devices
	BT1	switches
	BT2	electrical equipment
	BT3	equipment

semidiurnal variation
  USE daily variations

semihomog. critical assembly
  USE shca reactor

SEMILEPTONIC DECAY [2,533; 2,533]
Feb 78
(For neutron and nuclear beta decay see BETA DECAY.)
	BT1	weak particle decay
	BT2	particle decay
	BT3	decay

SEMIMETALS [135; 21,716]
	UF	*metalloids*
	BT1	elements
	NT1	arsenic
	NT1	boron
	NT1	selenium
	NT1	silicon
	NT1	tellurium
	RT	alloys
	RT	intermetallic compounds
	RT	metals
	RT	nonmetals
	RT	semiconductor materials

seminal vesicles
  USE male genitals

sena reactor
(Societe d'Energie Nucleaire des Ardennes reactor, Chooz.)
  USE ardennes reactor

sendai cyclotron
  USE tohoku cyclotron

SENDAI-1 REACTOR [18; 18] *Sep 79*
(Sendai, Kagoshima, Japan)
	UF+	*kyushu-3 reactor*
	BT1	pwr type reactors
	BT2	enriched uranium reactors
	BT3	reactors
	BT2	power reactors
	BT3	reactors
	BT2	thermal reactors
	BT3	reactors
	BT2	water cooled reactors
	BT3	reactors
	BT2	water moderated reactors
	BT3	reactors

SENDAI-2 REACTOR [11; 11] *Jun 82*
	BT1	pwr type reactors
	BT2	enriched uranium reactors
	BT3	reactors
	BT2	power reactors
	BT3	reactors
	BT2	thermal reactors
	BT3	reactors
	BT2	water cooled reactors
	BT3	reactors
	BT2	water moderated reactors
	BT3	reactors

SENEGAL [26; 26]
	BT1	africa
	BT1	developing countries

SENIORITY NUMBER [245; 245]
	BT1	quantum numbers
	RT	quantum mechanics

senn reactor
  USE garigliano reactor

SENSE ORGANS [30; 3,224]
	BT1	organs
	BT2	body
	NT1	auditory organs
	NT1	eyes
	NT2	conjunctiva
	NT2	cornea
	NT2	crystalline lens
	NT2	lacrimal ducts
	NT2	retina
	NT2	uvea
	NT1	taste buds
	NT1	vestibular apparatus
	RT	chemoreceptors
	RT	head
	RT	nervous system
	RT	nose
	RT	olfactory bulbs
	RT	organoleptic properties
	RT	receptors
	RT	reflexes
	RT	sense organs diseases

SENSE ORGANS DISEASES [350; 676]
	BT1	diseases
	NT1	cataracts
	NT1	conjunctivitis
	RT	ophthalmology
	RT	sense organs

§§ **SENSITIVITY** [21,293; 22,337]
(The quantitative aspect concerned with the threshold for detecting a given material, property, etc.)
	UF	*detection limits*
	UF+	*heat stability*
	NT1	photosensitivity
	RT	accuracy

RT	dead time		NT2	gaseous diffusion process			*seq. nucl. pow. plant un.-1*
RT	quantitative chemical analysis		NT2	laser isotope separation			USE sequoyah-1 reactor
RT	resolution		NT2	separation nozzle method			
RT	specificity		NT1	leaching			
RT	spectroscopy		NT1	metal transfer process			*seq. nucl. pow. plant un.-2*

SENSITIVITY ANALYSIS [1,625; 1,625]
Feb 81
(Response of a mathematical model to variations of the input parameters.)
RT   computer calculations
RT   errors
RT   mathematical models

SENSITIZERS [277; 277]
BT1   reagents

seoul triga-mk-2 reactor
USE   triga-2-seoul reactor

seoul triga-mk-3 reactor
USE   triga-3-seoul reactor

SEPARATED ORBIT CYCLOTRONS
[36; 36]
BT1   cyclotrons
  BT2   cyclic accelerators
    BT3   accelerators
NT1   ornl separated orbit cyclotron

separation energy
USE   binding energy

SEPARATION EQUIPMENT [124; 745]
Jul 86
BT1   equipment
NT1   extraction apparatuses
  NT2   extraction columns
  NT2   mixer-settlers
  NT2   podbielniak contactors
NT1   inertial separators
  NT2   cyclone separators
NT1   vapor separators
  NT2   steam separators
RT   separation processes

SEPARATION NOZZLE METHOD
[302; 302]
BT1   isotope separation
  BT2   separation processes
RT   nozzles

SEPARATION PROCESSES
[6,892; 59,001]
NT1   centrifugation
  NT2   gas centrifugation
  NT2   ultracentrifugation
NT1   chemisorption
NT1   chromatography
  NT2   extraction chromatography
  NT2   gas chromatography
  NT2   gel permeation chromatography
  NT2   ion exchange chromatography
  NT2   liquid column chromatography
  NT2   radiochromatography
  NT2   thermochromatography
  NT2   thin-layer chromatography
NT1   decantation
NT1   demineralization
  NT2   desalination
NT1   dialysis
NT1   distillation
NT1   elutriation
NT1   filtration
  NT2   ultrafiltration
NT1   flotation
NT1   foam separation
NT1   fractionation
NT1   freezing out
NT1   isotope separation
  NT2   dual temperature process
  NT2   electromagnetic isotope separa
  NT2   gaseous diffusion process
  NT2   laser isotope separation
  NT2   separation nozzle method
NT1   leaching
NT1   metal transfer process
NT1   multi-element separation
NT1   ore enrichment
NT1   precipitation
  NT2   coprecipitation
  NT2   flocculation
NT1   precipitation scavenging
NT1   reductive extraction
NT1   reprocessing
  NT2   airox process
  NT2   amex process
  NT2   butex process
  NT2   chloride volatility process
  NT2   civex process
  NT2   csrex process
  NT2   dapex process
  NT2   darex process
  NT2   eurex process
  NT2   excer process
  NT2   fluoride volatility process
  NT2   fluorox process
  NT2   flurex process
  NT2   hermex process
  NT2   iodox process
  NT2   monex process
  NT2   neptex process
  NT2   niflex process
  NT2   purex process
    NT3   halex process
    NT3   saltex process
  NT2   pyrochemical reprocessing
  NT2   redox process
  NT2   sulfex process
  NT2   talspeak process
  NT2   thermox process
  NT2   thorex process
  NT2   tramex process
  NT2   zircex process
  NT2   zirflex process
NT1   slurex process
NT1   solvent extraction
NT1   truex process
NT1   zone refining
RT   adsorption
RT   crystallization
RT   cyclone separators
RT   dust collectors
RT   electrostatic precipitators
RT   in-situ processing
RT   ion exchange
RT   purification
RT   refining
RT   screens
RT   scrubbing
RT   separation equipment
RT   sorting
RT   sublimation
RT   tailings

separators (inertial)
USE   inertial separators

separators (steam)
USE   steam separators

separators (vapor)
USE   vapor separators

SEPTICEMIA [93; 93]
RT   blood
RT   infectious diseases

SEPTUM MAGNETS [200; 200]
BT1   magnets
  BT2   equipment
RT   beam extraction
RT   beam optics
RT   electrostatic septa
RT   magnet coils
RT   magnetic analyzers

seq. nucl. pow. plant un.-2
USE   sequoyah-2 reactor

sequence analysis
(Analysis of nucleotide and protein chains by means of radioisotope labelling.)
USE   structural chemical analysis

SEQUENTIAL CIRCUITS [39; 39]
BT1   electronic circuits
RT   digital circuits

SEQUENTIAL SCANNING [629; 629]
Jun 83
BT1   counting techniques
RT   biomedical radiography
RT   computerized tomography
RT   dynamic function studies
RT   image scanners

sequestrene
USE   edta

SEQUIM BAY [5; 5]
BT1   pacific ocean
  BT2   seas
    BT3   surface waters
RT   hapo
RT   washington

SEQUOYAH UF6 PRODUCTION PLANT [17; 17]
BT1   industrial plants
BT1   us aec
  BT2   us organizations
    BT3   national organizations
BT1   us doe
  BT2   us organizations
    BT3   national organizations
BT1   us erda
  BT2   us organizations
    BT3   national organizations
RT   oklahoma
RT   uranium hexafluoride

SEQUOYAH-1 REACTOR [166; 166]
(Daisy, Tennessee, USA)
UF   *seq. nucl. pow. plant un.-1*
BT1   pwr type reactors
  BT2   enriched uranium reactors
    BT3   reactors
  BT2   power reactors
    BT3   reactors
  BT2   thermal reactors
    BT3   reactors
  BT2   water cooled reactors
    BT3   reactors
  BT2   water moderated reactors
    BT3   reactors

SEQUOYAH-2 REACTOR [116; 116]
(Daisy, Tennessee, USA)
UF   *seq. nucl. pow. plant un.-2*
BT1   pwr type reactors
  BT2   enriched uranium reactors
    BT3   reactors
  BT2   power reactors
    BT3   reactors
  BT2   thermal reactors
    BT3   reactors
  BT2   water cooled reactors
    BT3   reactors
  BT2   water moderated reactors
    BT3   reactors

SER REACTOR [2; 2]
UF   *snap-2 experimental reactor*
BT1   enriched uranium reactors
  BT2   reactors
BT1   nak cooled reactors
  BT2   liquid metal cooled reactors

```
          BT3    reactors
     BT1    potassium cooled reactors
          BT2    liquid metal cooled reactors
               BT3    reactors
     BT1    process heat reactors
          BT2    power reactors
               BT3    reactors
     BT1    sodium cooled reactors
          BT2    liquid metal cooled reactors
               BT3    reactors

SERAC COMPUTERS [0; 0]
     BT1    computers

SERBER THEORY [23; 23]
     RT     stripping


*serber-goldberger model*
     USE    goldberger model

SERBER-WILSON METHOD [0; 0]
     RT     neutron transport theory
     RT     transport theory

SERIES EXPANSION [4,820; 6,392]
     NT1    neumann series
     NT1    operator product expansion
     NT1    power series
     RT     boson expansion
     RT     continued fractions
     RT     convergence
     RT     equations
     RT     functions
     RT     mathematics
     RT     pade approximation
     RT     spline functions
     RT     superconvergence relations

SERINE [288; 288]
     UF     *hydroxy-alpha-alanine-beta*
     BT1    amino acids
          BT2    carboxylic acids
               BT3    organic acids
                    BT4    organic compounds
     BT1    hydroxy acids
          BT2    carboxylic acids
               BT3    organic acids
                    BT4    organic compounds

SERINE PROTEINASES [69; 374]
     *Dec 86*
     BT1    peptide hydrolases
          BT2    hydrolases
               BT3    enzymes
                    BT4    organic compounds
     NT1    chymotrypsin
     NT1    fibrinolysin
     NT1    kallikrein
     NT1    thrombin
     NT1    trypsin

SEROTONIN [653; 745]
     BT1    hydroxy compounds
          BT2    organic compounds
     BT1    neuroregulators
          BT2    autonomic nervous system
                 agent
               BT3    drugs
     BT1    radioprotective substances
          BT2    drugs
          BT2    response modifying factors
     BT1    sympathomimetics
          BT2    autonomic nervous system
                 agent
               BT3    drugs
     BT1    tryptamines
          BT2    amines
               BT3    organic compounds
          BT2    indoles
               BT3    pyrroles
                    BT4    azoles
                         BT5    heterocyclic compounds
                              BT6    organic compounds
                         BT5    organic nitrogen com-
                                pounds
                              BT6    organic compounds
     RT     mexamine

SEROUS MEMBRANES [19; 966]
     BT1    membranes
     NT1    mesentery
     NT1    pericardium
     NT1    peritoneum
     NT1    pleura

SERPUKHOV SYNCHROTRON
[585; 585]
     BT1    synchrotrons
          BT2    cyclic accelerators
               BT3    accelerators
     RT     ihep
     RT     serpukhov tevatron

SERPUKHOV TEVATRON [85; 85]
     *Nov 85*
     (3-TeV accelerating-storage complex based
     on the Serpukhov synchrotron.)
     BT1    storage rings
     BT1    synchrotrons
          BT2    cyclic accelerators
               BT3    accelerators
     RT     serpukhov synchrotron

SERRATIA [48; 48]
     BT1    bacteria
          BT2    microorganisms


*serum (blood)*
     USE    blood serum


*serum (immune)*
     USE    immune serums


*service life*
     USE    lifetime


*service water systems*
     USE    auxiliary water systems

SERVOMECHANISMS [285; 285]
     BT1    control equipment
          BT2    equipment
     RT     actuators
     RT     feedback
     RT     remote control

SESAME OIL [9; 9]
     UF     *beni oil*
     UF     *benne oil*
     UF     *gigily oil*
     UF     *gingelly oil*
     UF     *gingily oil*
     UF     *teal oil*
     UF     *teel oil*
     UF     *til oil*
     BT1    oils
          BT2    other organic compounds
               BT3    organic compounds

SET THEORY [52; 52] *Jul 89*
     BT1    mathematics
     RT     fuzzy logic


*settlements (disputes)*
     USE    dispute settlements

SETTLING PONDS [7; 7] *Apr 90*
     BT1    surface waters
     RT     drainage
     RT     sedimentation
     RT     waste processing


*sewage*
     USE    liquid wastes

*sewage disposal*
     USE    liquid wastes
     AND    waste disposal

SEWAGE SLUDGE [501; 501] *Jul 76*
(Precipitated solid matter from sewage
treatment processes)
     UF     *municipal sludge*
     UF     *sludges (sewage)*
     BT1    biological wastes
          BT2    biological materials
               BT3    materials
          BT2    wastes
     RT     anaerobic digestion
     RT     ground disposal


*sewage treatment*
     USE    liquid wastes
     AND    waste processing

SEX [201; 201]
     RT     female genitals
     RT     females
     RT     gonads
     RT     heterochromosomes
     RT     male genitals
     RT     males
     RT     mating
     RT     pheromone
     RT     reproduction
     RT     sex chromatin
     RT     sex dependence
     RT     sex ratio

SEX CHROMATIN [7; 7]
     BT1    chromatin
     RT     sex


*sex chromosomes*
     USE    heterochromosomes

SEX DEPENDENCE [950; 950] *Oct 76*
     RT     females
     RT     males
     RT     sex

SEX RATIO [117; 117]
     RT     progeny
     RT     sex

SEYFERT GALAXIES [1,485; 1,485]
     BT1    galaxies
     RT     bl lacertae objects
     RT     quasars


*sferics*
     USE    atmospherics

SGHWR REACTOR [320; 320]
     UF     *steam generating heavy wat. r*
     BT1    enriched uranium reactors
          BT2    reactors
     BT1    heavy water moderated reactor
          BT2    reactors
     BT1    pressure tube reactors
          BT2    power reactors
               BT3    reactors
     BT1    thermal reactors
          BT2    reactors
     BT1    water cooled reactors
          BT2    reactors

SGR TYPE REACTORS [0; 23]
     UF     *sodium cooled graphite mod.*
     BT1    graphite moderated reactors
          BT2    reactors
     BT1    sodium cooled reactors
          BT2    liquid metal cooled reactors
               BT3    reactors
     NT1    sre reactor
     RT     power reactors
```

SH-PROTEINASES [3; 46] *Dec 86*
  BT1   peptide hydrolases
    BT2   hydrolases
      BT3   enzymes
        BT4   organic compounds
  NT1   cathepsins
  NT1   papain
  NT1   streptococcal proteinase

SHADOW EFFECT [489; 489]
  RT   cross sections
  RT   nuclear reactions
  RT   scattering

SHAFT EXCAVATIONS [460; 460]
  Mar 81
(Vertical or inclined openings of uniform and limited cross section, as made for mining ore.)
  UF   *mine shafts*
  UF   *shafts (mines)*
  RT   earthmoving equipment
  RT   excavation
  RT   konrad ore mine
  RT   mines
  RT   radioactive waste disposal
  RT   tunnels
  RT   underground disposal

shafts (mechanical)
  USE   mechanical shafts

shafts (mines)
  USE   shaft excavations

SHALE OIL [79; 79]
  BT1   petroleum
    BT2   fossil fuels
      BT3   energy sources
      BT3   fuels
  RT   oil shales

SHALES [546; 859]
  UF   *argillite*
  BT1   sedimentary rocks
    BT2   rocks
  NT1   oil shales
  RT   carbonate minerals
  RT   clays
  RT   feldspars
  RT   iron oxides
  RT   oxide minerals
  RT   quartz
  RT   silt

shanghai inr cyclotron
  USE   inr cyclotron

SHAPE [2,997; 2,997]
  RT   cones
  RT   configuration
  RT   cylinders
  RT   dimensions
  RT   mass distribution
  RT   plates
  RT   rings
  RT   rods
  RT   slabs
  RT   spheres
  RT   spheroids
  RT   tubes

SHAPE MEMORY EFFECT [55; 55]
  Aug 86
(A shape recovery effect in metal specimens. It is associated with the martensite parent transformation.)
  UF   *marmen effect*
  RT   iron alloys
  RT   phase transformations

shaped charges
  USE   chemical explosives

shattering
  USE   mechanical fragmentation

SHCA REACTOR [8; 8]
  UF   *semi-homog. critical assembly*
  UF   *semihomog. critical assembly*
  BT1   enriched uranium reactors
    BT2   reactors
  BT1   graphite moderated reactors
    BT2   reactors
  BT1   solid homogeneous reactors
    BT2   homogeneous reactors
      BT3   reactors
  BT1   thermal reactors
    BT2   reactors
  BT1   zero power reactors
    BT2   experimental reactors
      BT3   research and test reactors
        BT4   reactors

SHEAR [2,561; 2,561]
  RT   fluid flow
  RT   magnetic fields
  RT   rotational transform
  RT   stresses
  RT   tensile properties

SHEAR PROPERTIES [968; 968]
  UF   *shear strength*
  UF   *strength (shear)*
  BT1   mechanical properties

shear strength
  USE   shear properties

shear waves (seismic)
  USE   seismic s waves

shearon harris-1 reactor
  USE   harris-1 reactor

shearon harris-2 reactor
  USE   harris-2 reactor

shearon harris-3 reactor
  USE   harris-3 reactor

shearon harris-4 reactor
  USE   harris-4 reactor

sheathing
  USE   canning

sheaths (fuel)
  USE   fuel cans

SHEEP [920; 920]
  UF   *lambs*
  BT1   domestic animals
    BT2   animals
  BT1   ruminants
    BT2   mammals
      BT3   vertebrates
        BT4   animals
  RT   dictyocaulus
  RT   meat

SHEETS [1,325; 1,325]
(Thinner than plates but thicker than foils.)
  RT   foils
  RT   plates

SHEILA HELIAC [26; 26] *Jun 87*
  BT1   heliac stellarators
    BT2   stellarators
      BT3   closed plasma devices
        BT4   thermonuclear devices
  RT   h-1 heliac

SHELL MODELS [9,328; 11,215]
(Nuclear shell models only; for electron shell models use ELECTRONIC STRUCTURE.)
  UF   *continuum shell model*
  UF   *models (shell)*
  BT1   nuclear models
    BT2   mathematical models
  NT1   governor model
  NT1   interacting boson model
  NT1   multi-center shell model
  RT   aligned coupling scheme
  RT   broken-pair approximation
  RT   elliot model
  RT   talmi integrals
  RT   weak-coupling model
  RT   wilkinson theory

SHELLS [2,086; 2,086]
(Structural forms; for electron shells in atoms use ELECTRONIC STRUCTURE.)
  RT   liners
  RT   mechanical structures

shells (containment)
  USE   containment shells

SHELTERS [122; 181]
  NT1   fallout shelters
  RT   buildings
  RT   civil defense
  RT   local fallout
  RT   nuclear explosions
  RT   nuclear weapons
  RT   radiation protection
  RT   shielding
  RT   subsurface structures

sherardizing
  USE   diffusion coating

SHERMAN TABLES [7; 7]
  RT   anisotropy
  RT   spin

SHERWOOD PROJECT [1; 1]
  RT   thermonuclear reactions

shf radiation
  USE   ghz range 01-100
  AND   radiowave radiation

shield test reactor
  USE   stir reactor

SHIELDED METAL-ARC WELDING [73; 73]
  BT1   arc welding
    BT2   welding
      BT3   joining
        BT4   fabrication

shielded organs
  USE   partial body irradiation

SHIELDING [6,919; 7,663]
  UF+   *magnetic shielding*
  NT1   biological shielding
  RT   absorption
  RT   alara
  RT   buildup
  RT   collimators
  RT   containers
  RT   distance

SHIELDING

RT external irradiation
RT gloveboxes
RT gloves
RT half-thickness
RT heterogeneous effects
RT hot cells
RT manipulators
RT point kernels
RT radiation protection
RT scattering
RT self-shielding
RT shelters
RT shielding materials
RT shields
RT shutters
RT stray radiation
RT thermal insulation
RT thickness

SHIELDING MATERIALS [1,590; 1,590]
BT1 materials
RT building materials
RT concretes
RT lead
RT paraffin
RT radiation protection
RT reactor components
RT reactor materials
RT shielding
RT shields

SHIELDS [2,180; 3,284]
NT1 biological shields
NT1 thermal shields
RT radiation protection
RT reactor components
RT shielding
RT shielding materials

SHIGELLA [22; 22]
BT1 bacteria
BT2 microorganisms

SHIKA-1 REACTOR [4; 4] Sep 89
(Shika, Ishikawa, Japan.)
UF noto-1 reactor
BT1 bwr type reactors
BT2 enriched uranium reactors
BT3 reactors
BT2 power reactors
BT3 reactors
BT2 thermal reactors
BT3 reactors
BT2 water cooled reactors
BT3 reactors
BT2 water moderated reactors
BT3 reactors

SHIKIMIC ACID [16; 16]
BT1 hydroxy acids
BT2 carboxylic acids
BT3 organic acids
BT4 organic compounds

SHIM RODS [92; 92]
UF coarse control rods
BT1 control elements
BT2 reactor components
RT neutron absorbers

SHIMANE-1 REACTOR [63; 63]
(Kashima, Shimane, Japan)
UF chugoku el. power co. reactor
UF chugoku-1 reactor
UF kashima-1 reactor
BT1 bwr type reactors
BT2 enriched uranium reactors
BT3 reactors
BT2 power reactors
BT3 reactors
BT2 thermal reactors
BT3 reactors
BT2 water cooled reactors
BT3 reactors
BT2 water moderated reactors
BT3 reactors

SHIMANE-2 REACTOR [11; 11] Nov 85
(Kashima, Shimane, Japan)
UF chugoku-2 reactor
UF kashima-2 reactor
BT1 bwr type reactors
BT2 enriched uranium reactors
BT3 reactors
BT2 power reactors
BT3 reactors
BT2 thermal reactors
BT3 reactors
BT2 water cooled reactors
BT3 reactors
BT2 water moderated reactors
BT3 reactors

SHIP PROPULSION REACTORS
[294; 579]
BT1 propulsion reactors
BT2 power reactors
BT3 reactors
NT1 efdr-50 reactor
NT1 lenin reactor
NT1 leonid brezhnev reactor
NT1 mutsu reactor
NT1 otto hahn reactor
NT1 savannah reactor
NT1 sibir reactor
RT nuclear ships

shipment
USE transport

SHIPPER-RECEIVER DIFFERENCES
[29; 29] Sep 76
RT material balance
RT material unaccounted for

shippingport pressur. wat. re.
USE shippingport reactor

SHIPPINGPORT REACTOR [333; 333]
UF shippingport pressur. wat. re.
BT1 pwr type reactors
BT2 enriched uranium reactors
BT3 reactors
BT2 power reactors
BT3 reactors
BT2 thermal reactors
BT3 reactors
BT2 water cooled reactors
BT3 reactors
BT2 water moderated reactors
BT3 reactors

SHIPS [265; 1,060]
NT1 nuclear ships
NT2 ns lenin
NT2 ns leonid brezhnev
NT2 ns sibir
NT2 nuclear merchant ships
NT3 ns mutsu
NT3 ns otto hahn
NT3 ns savannah
NT1 submarines
RT navigational instruments
RT positioning

SHIRLEY BASIN URANIUM MILL
[3; 3]
BT1 feed materials plants
BT2 industrial plants
BT2 nuclear facilities
RT ore processing
RT uranium ores

SHIVA FACILITY [168; 168] Apr 78
(Large Nd laser facility at LLL to be used for laser fusion.)
RT lawrence livermore laboratory
RT lawrence livermore national la
RT neodymium lasers
RT nova facility
RT novette facility

SHOAL EVENT [2; 2]
BT1 vela project

shock (biological)
USE biological shock

shock (impact)
USE impact shock

shock (medical)
USE biological shock

shock (thermal)
USE thermal shock

SHOCK ABSORBERS [499; 499]
RT damping
RT energy losses
RT impact shock
RT potting materials
RT restraints
RT seismic effects
RT seismic isolation
RT shock waves

SHOCK HEATING [323; 323]
BT1 plasma heating
BT2 heating

SHOCK TUBES [296; 296]
RT shock waves

shock wave hardening
USE strain hardening

SHOCK WAVES [7,197; 7,244]
UF riemann waves
UF waves (shock)
NT1 detonation waves
RT blast effects
RT earthquakes
RT explosions
RT ground motion
RT hydromagnetic waves
RT impact shock
RT implosions
RT lax theorem
RT mach number
RT nuclear explosions
RT rankine-hugoniot equations
RT seismic effects
RT seismology
RT shock absorbers
RT shock tubes
RT soil-structure interactions
RT solitons
RT supersonic flow
RT transonic flow
RT water hammer

shock-wave hardening
USE strain hardening

shoes
USE clothing

SHOREHAM REACTOR [69; 69]
(Shoreham, New York, USA)
BT1 bwr type reactors
BT2 enriched uranium reactors
BT3 reactors
BT2 power reactors
BT3 reactors
BT2 thermal reactors
BT3 reactors
BT2 water cooled reactors
BT3 reactors
BT2 water moderated reactors
BT3 reactors

SHORES [476; 476]
(For both lake- and sea-land boundaries.)
UF *coast*
UF *seacoast*
BT1 coastal regions
RT coastal waters
RT lakes
RT offshore nuclear power plants
RT offshore sites
RT seas

short circuits
USE electrical faults

short range interactions
USE interaction range

SHORT WAVE RADIATION [367; 367]
UF *hf radiation*
UF *high frequency radiation*
UF *high-frequency radiation*
UF *short-wave radiation*
BT1 radiowave radiation
BT2 electromagnetic radiation
BT3 radiations

short-lens spectrometers
USE magnetic lens spectrometers

short-range interactions
USE interaction range

short-wave radiation
USE short wave radiation

shorts (electrical)
USE electrical faults

SHOT PEENING [72; 72]
UF *peening*
BT1 cold working
BT2 materials working
BT3 fabrication
BT1 surface treatments
RT descaling
RT surface cleaning
RT surface hardening

SHOWER COUNTERS [2,237; 2,237]
(Detects high energy gamma radiation or high energy particles on basis of cascade showers in layered absorbers.)
UF *calorimeter detectors*
BT1 radiation detectors
BT2 measuring instruments
RT cosmic ray detection
RT gev range

SHOWERS [210; 3,951]
(For rain showers use RAIN; for safety showers use SAFETY SHOWERS.)
NT1 cascade showers
NT1 cosmic showers
NT2 extensive air showers

SHREDDERS [17; 17] *May 87*
BT1 materials handling equipment
BT2 equipment
RT cutting tools
RT waste processing

SHREWS [18; 18]
BT1 mammals
BT2 vertebrates
BT3 animals

SHRIMP [97; 97]
BT1 crustaceans
BT2 aquatic organisms
BT2 arthropods
BT3 invertebrates
BT4 animals

SHRINKAGE [632; 632]
RT augmentation
RT contraction
RT dilatometry

SHROUDS [373; 373]
(Cover enveloping the active length of a fuel assembly, to stabilize the coolant flow through the assembly.)
BT1 reactor cooling systems
BT2 cooling systems
BT2 reactor components
RT fuel assemblies
RT fuel channels
RT jackets

SHRUBS [114; 114]
BT1 plants
RT conifers
RT preferred species

SHUBNIKOV-DE HAAS EFFECT [154; 154]
RT hall effect
RT magnetic fields
RT magnetoresistance

shunt (biomedical)
USE bypasses

shunts
USE bypasses

SHUTDOWN [186; 2,229] *Mar 83*
(For temporary cessation of operation of a facility later to be reactivated.)
NT1 reactor shutdown
NT2 scram
RT cancellation
RT decommissioning
RT modifications
RT outages

shutin pressure
USE reservoir pressure

SHUTTERS [72; 72] *Oct 82*
RT collimators
RT neutron choppers
RT openings
RT optical systems
RT radiotherapy
RT shielding
RT thermal insulation
RT windows

shuttles
USE rabbit tubes

SI SEMICONDUCTOR DETECTORS [1,862; 2,918]
BT1 semiconductor detectors
BT2 radiation detectors
BT3 measuring instruments
NT1 li-drifted si detectors

SI UNITS [57; 80] *May 81*
BT1 units
NT1 sievert unit

si(li) detectors
USE li-drifted si detectors

SIALIC ACID [84; 84]
BT1 polysaccharides
BT2 saccharides
BT3 carbohydrates
BT4 organic compounds
RT amines
RT organic acids

sialon
USE aluminium oxides
AND silicon nitrides

sibir (nuclear ship)
USE ns sibir

SIBIR REACTOR [0; 0] *Sep 85*
UF *icebreaker sibir reactor*
UF *nucl. ship sibir reactor*
BT1 ship propulsion reactors
BT2 propulsion reactors
BT3 power reactors
BT4 reactors
RT ns sibir

SICKLE CELL ANEMIA [68; 68] *Dec 82*
BT1 anemias
BT2 hemic diseases
BT3 diseases
BT2 symptoms
RT erythrocytes

sid
USE sudden ionospheric disturbance

SIDE EFFECTS [7,377; 7,377]
RT therapy

siegbahn spectrometers
USE flat magnetic spectrometers

SIEMENS COMPUTERS [32; 32] *Oct 77*
BT1 computers

siemens unterrichtsreaktor
USE sur-100 series reactor

SIERRA LEONE [5; 5]
BT1 africa
BT1 developing countries

SIERRA NEVADA COLORADO [1; 1]
BT1 mountains

SIEVERT UNIT [26; 26] *May 81*
BT1 radiation dose units
BT2 units
BT1 si units
BT2 units

SIGMA BARYONS [15; 417] *Dec 87*
BT1 hyperons
BT2 baryons
BT3 fermions
BT3 hadrons
BT4 elementary particles
BT2 strange particles
BT3 elementary particles
NT1 sigma particles
NT2 antisigma particles
NT2 sigma minus particles
NT2 sigma neutral particles
NT2 sigma plus particles
NT1 sigma-1385 baryons
NT1 sigma-1480 baryons
NT1 sigma-1560 baryons
NT1 sigma-1580 baryons
NT1 sigma-1620 baryons
NT1 sigma-1660 baryons
NT1 sigma-1670 baryons
NT1 sigma-1690 baryons

NT1 sigma-1750 baryons
NT1 sigma-1770 baryons
NT1 sigma-1775 baryons
NT1 sigma-1840 baryons
NT1 sigma-1880 baryons
NT1 sigma-1915 baryons
NT1 sigma-1940 baryons
NT1 sigma-2000 baryons
NT1 sigma-2030 baryons
NT1 sigma-2070 baryons
NT1 sigma-2080 baryons
NT1 sigma-2100 baryons
NT1 sigma-2250 baryons
NT1 sigma-2455 baryons
NT1 sigma-2620 baryons
NT1 sigma-3000 baryons
NT1 sigma-3170 baryons

SIGMA C-2450 BARYONS [53; 53]
Apr 80
(Prior to December 1987 this concept was indexed by SIGMA-2430 RESONANCES.)
UF   *sigma-2430 resonances*
BT1   charmed baryons
  BT2   baryons
    BT3   fermions
    BT3   hadrons
      BT4   elementary particles
  BT2   charm particles
    BT3   elementary particles

sigma minus
(Prior to December 1987 this was a valid descriptor.)
USE   sigma minus particles

SIGMA MINUS PARTICLES [563; 563]
(Prior to December 1987 this concept was indexed by SIGMA MINUS.)
UF   *sigma minus*
SF   *sigma-1193 resonances*
BT1   sigma particles
  BT2   sigma baryons
    BT3   hyperons
      BT4   baryons
        BT5   fermions
        BT5   hadrons
          BT6   elementary particles
      BT4   strange particles
        BT5   elementary particles

SIGMA MODEL [2,141; 2,141]
UF   *sigma-410 resonances*
BT1   boson-exchange models
  BT2   peripheral models
    BT3   particle models
      BT4   mathematical models
RT   pseudoscalar mesons
RT   scalar mesons

sigma neutral
(Prior to December 1987 this was a valid descriptor.)
USE   sigma neutral particles

SIGMA NEUTRAL PARTICLES [416; 416]
(Prior to December 1987 this concept was indexed by SIGMA NEUTRAL.)
UF   *sigma neutral*
SF   *sigma-1193 resonances*
BT1   sigma particles
  BT2   sigma baryons
    BT3   hyperons
      BT4   baryons
        BT5   fermions
        BT5   hadrons
          BT6   elementary particles
      BT4   strange particles
        BT5   elementary particles

SIGMA PARTICLE BEAMS [25; 25]
BT1   hyperon beams
  BT2   particle beams
    BT3   beams

SIGMA PARTICLES [638; 1,739]
BT1   sigma baryons
  BT2   hyperons
    BT3   baryons
      BT4   fermions
      BT4   hadrons
        BT5   elementary particles
    BT3   strange particles
      BT4   elementary particles
NT1   antisigma particles
NT1   sigma minus particles
NT1   sigma neutral particles
NT1   sigma plus particles

SIGMA PILES [7; 7]
RT   moderators
RT   neutron sources

sigma plus
(Prior to December 1987 this was a valid descriptor.)
USE   sigma plus particles

SIGMA PLUS PARTICLES [501; 501]
(Prior to December 1987 this concept was indexed by SIGMA PLUS.)
UF   *sigma plus*
SF   *sigma-1193 resonances*
BT1   sigma particles
  BT2   sigma baryons
    BT3   hyperons
      BT4   baryons
        BT5   fermions
        BT5   hadrons
          BT6   elementary particles
      BT4   strange particles
        BT5   elementary particles

SIGMA TERMS [193; 193]
BT1   current commutators
  BT2   commutators
    BT3   quantum operators
      BT4   mathematical operators

sigma-minus atoms
USE   hadronic atoms

sigma-1193 resonances
SEE   sigma minus particles
OR   sigma neutral particles
OR   sigma plus particles

SIGMA-1385 BARYONS [370; 370]
(Prior to December 1987 this concept was indexed by SIGMA-1385 RESONANCES.)
UF   *sigma-1385 resonances*
BT1   sigma baryons
  BT2   hyperons
    BT3   baryons
      BT4   fermions
      BT4   hadrons
        BT5   elementary particles
    BT3   strange particles
      BT4   elementary particles

sigma-1385 resonances
(Prior to December 1987 this was a valid descriptor.)
USE   sigma-1385 baryons

SIGMA-1480 BARYONS [0; 0] *Dec 87*
BT1   sigma baryons
  BT2   hyperons
    BT3   baryons
      BT4   fermions
      BT4   hadrons
        BT5   elementary particles
    BT3   strange particles
      BT4   elementary particles

SIGMA-1560 BARYONS [0; 0] *Dec 87*
BT1   sigma baryons
  BT2   hyperons
    BT3   baryons
      BT4   fermions
      BT4   hadrons
        BT5   elementary particles
    BT3   strange particles
      BT4   elementary particles

SIGMA-1580 BARYONS [11; 11]
(Prior to December 1987 this concept was indexed by SIGMA-1580 RESONANCES.)
UF   *sigma-1580 resonances*
BT1   sigma baryons
  BT2   hyperons
    BT3   baryons
      BT4   fermions
      BT4   hadrons
        BT5   elementary particles
    BT3   strange particles
      BT4   elementary particles

sigma-1580 resonances
(Prior to December 1987 this was a valid descriptor.)
USE   sigma-1580 baryons

SIGMA-1620 BARYONS [5; 5]
(Prior to December 1987 this concept was indexed by SIGMA-1620 RESONANCES.)
UF   *sigma-1620 resonances*
BT1   sigma baryons
  BT2   hyperons
    BT3   baryons
      BT4   fermions
      BT4   hadrons
        BT5   elementary particles
    BT3   strange particles
      BT4   elementary particles

sigma-1620 resonances
(Prior to December 1987 this was a valid descriptor.)
USE   sigma-1620 baryons

SIGMA-1660 BARYONS [8; 8] *Mar 77*
(Prior to December 1987 this concept was indexed by SIGMA-1660 RESONANCES.)
UF   *sigma-1660 resonances*
BT1   sigma baryons
  BT2   hyperons
    BT3   baryons
      BT4   fermions
      BT4   hadrons
        BT5   elementary particles
    BT3   strange particles
      BT4   elementary particles

sigma-1660 resonances
(Prior to December 1987 this was a valid descriptor.)
USE   sigma-1660 baryons

SIGMA-1670 BARYONS [32; 32]
(Prior to December 1987 this concept was indexed by SIGMA-1670 RESONANCES.)
UF   *sigma-1670 resonances*
BT1   sigma baryons
  BT2   hyperons
    BT3   baryons
      BT4   fermions
      BT4   hadrons
        BT5   elementary particles
    BT3   strange particles
      BT4   elementary particles

sigma-1670 resonances
(Prior to December 1987 this was a valid descriptor.)
USE   sigma-1670 baryons

SIGMA-1690 BARYONS [0; 0] *Dec 87*
  BT1   sigma baryons
    BT2   hyperons
      BT3   baryons
        BT4   fermions
        BT4   hadrons
          BT5   elementary particles
      BT3   strange particles
        BT4   elementary particles

SIGMA-1750 BARYONS [8; 8]
(Prior to December 1987 this concept was indexed by SIGMA-1750 RESONANCES.)
  UF   *sigma-1750 resonances*
  BT1   sigma baryons
    BT2   hyperons
      BT3   baryons
        BT4   fermions
        BT4   hadrons
          BT5   elementary particles
      BT3   strange particles
        BT4   elementary particles

sigma-1750 resonances
(Prior to December 1987 this was a valid descriptor.)
  USE   sigma-1750 baryons

sigma-1765 resonances
(Prior to December 1987 this was a valid descriptor.)
  USE   sigma-1775 baryons

SIGMA-1770 BARYONS [2; 2] *Dec 87*
  BT1   sigma baryons
    BT2   hyperons
      BT3   baryons
        BT4   fermions
        BT4   hadrons
          BT5   elementary particles
      BT3   strange particles
        BT4   elementary particles

SIGMA-1775 BARYONS [12; 12]
(Prior to December 1987 this concept was indexed by SIGMA-1765 RESONANCES.)
  UF   *sigma-1765 resonances*
  BT1   sigma baryons
    BT2   hyperons
      BT3   baryons
        BT4   fermions
        BT4   hadrons
          BT5   elementary particles
      BT3   strange particles
        BT4   elementary particles

SIGMA-1840 BARYONS [0; 0] *Dec 87*
  BT1   sigma baryons
    BT2   hyperons
      BT3   baryons
        BT4   fermions
        BT4   hadrons
          BT5   elementary particles
      BT3   strange particles
        BT4   elementary particles

SIGMA-1880 BARYONS [0; 0] *Dec 87*
  BT1   sigma baryons
    BT2   hyperons
      BT3   baryons
        BT4   fermions
        BT4   hadrons
          BT5   elementary particles
      BT3   strange particles
        BT4   elementary particles

sigma-1910 resonances
(Prior to December 1987 this was a valid descriptor.)
  USE   sigma-1915 baryons

SIGMA-1915 BARYONS [7; 7]
(Prior to December 1987 this concept was indexed by SIGMA-1910 RESONANCES.)
  UF   *sigma-1910 resonances*
  BT1   sigma baryons
    BT2   hyperons
      BT3   baryons
        BT4   fermions
        BT4   hadrons
          BT5   elementary particles
      BT3   strange particles
        BT4   elementary particles

SIGMA-1940 BARYONS [8; 8]
(Prior to December 1987 this concept was indexed by SIGMA-1940 RESONANCES.)
  UF   *sigma-1940 resonances*
  BT1   sigma baryons
    BT2   hyperons
      BT3   baryons
        BT4   fermions
        BT4   hadrons
          BT5   elementary particles
      BT3   strange particles
        BT4   elementary particles

sigma-1940 resonances
(Prior to December 1987 this was a valid descriptor.)
  USE   sigma-1940 baryons

SIGMA-2000 BARYONS [0; 0] *Dec 87*
  BT1   sigma baryons
    BT2   hyperons
      BT3   baryons
        BT4   fermions
        BT4   hadrons
          BT5   elementary particles
      BT3   strange particles
        BT4   elementary particles

SIGMA-2030 BARYONS [16; 16]
(Prior to December 1987 this concept was indexed by SIGMA-2030 RESONANCES.)
  UF   *sigma-2030 resonances*
  BT1   sigma baryons
    BT2   hyperons
      BT3   baryons
        BT4   fermions
        BT4   hadrons
          BT5   elementary particles
      BT3   strange particles
        BT4   elementary particles

sigma-2030 resonances
(Prior to December 1987 this was a valid descriptor.)
  USE   sigma-2030 baryons

SIGMA-2070 BARYONS [0; 0] *Dec 87*
  BT1   sigma baryons
    BT2   hyperons
      BT3   baryons
        BT4   fermions
        BT4   hadrons
          BT5   elementary particles
      BT3   strange particles
        BT4   elementary particles

SIGMA-2080 BARYONS [0; 0] *Dec 87*
  BT1   sigma baryons
    BT2   hyperons
      BT3   baryons
        BT4   fermions
        BT4   hadrons
          BT5   elementary particles
      BT3   strange particles
        BT4   elementary particles

SIGMA-2100 BARYONS [0; 0] *Dec 87*
  BT1   sigma baryons
    BT2   hyperons
      BT3   baryons
        BT4   fermions
        BT4   hadrons
          BT5   elementary particles
      BT3   strange particles
        BT4   elementary particles

SIGMA-2250 BARYONS [1; 1]
(Prior to December 1987 this concept was indexed by SIGMA-2250 RESONANCES.)
  UF   *sigma-2250 resonances*
  BT1   sigma baryons
    BT2   hyperons
      BT3   baryons
        BT4   fermions
        BT4   hadrons
          BT5   elementary particles
      BT3   strange particles
        BT4   elementary particles

sigma-2250 resonances
(Prior to December 1987 this was a valid descriptor.)
  USE   sigma-2250 baryons

sigma-2430 resonances
(Prior to December 1987 this was a valid descriptor.)
  USE   sigma c-2450 baryons

SIGMA-2455 BARYONS [4; 4]
(Prior to December 1987 this concept was indexed by SIGMA-2455 RESONANCES.)
  UF   *sigma-2455 resonances*
  BT1   sigma baryons
    BT2   hyperons
      BT3   baryons
        BT4   fermions
        BT4   hadrons
          BT5   elementary particles
      BT3   strange particles
        BT4   elementary particles

sigma-2455 resonances
(Prior to December 1987 this was a valid descriptor.)
  USE   sigma-2455 baryons

sigma-2595 resonances
(Prior to December 1987 this was a valid descriptor.)
  USE   sigma-2620 baryons

SIGMA-2620 BARYONS [0; 0]
(Prior to December 1987 this concept was indexed by SIGMA-2595 RESONANCES.)
  UF   *sigma-2595 resonances*
  BT1   sigma baryons
    BT2   hyperons
      BT3   baryons
        BT4   fermions
        BT4   hadrons
          BT5   elementary particles
      BT3   strange particles
        BT4   elementary particles

SIGMA-3000 BARYONS [0; 0] *Dec 87*
  BT1   sigma baryons
    BT2   hyperons
      BT3   baryons
        BT4   fermions
        BT4   hadrons
          BT5   elementary particles
      BT3   strange particles
        BT4   elementary particles

SIGMA-3170 BARYONS [0; 0] *Dec 87*
  BT1   sigma baryons
    BT2   hyperons
      BT3   baryons
        BT4   fermions
        BT4   hadrons
          BT5   elementary particles
      BT3   strange particles
        BT4   elementary particles

sigma-410 resonances
(Prior to December 1987 this was a valid descriptor.)
    USE   sigma model

SIGNAL CONDITIONING [151; 151]
Apr 86
(Processing of the form or mode of a signal to make it compatible with a given device.)
    RT   data transmission
    RT   digitizers
    RT   pulse shapers
    RT   signals

SIGNAL DISTORTION [110; 110]
Mar 76
    RT   data transmission
    RT   electromagnetic radiation
    RT   signals
    RT   sound waves

SIGNAL-TO-NOISE RATIO [1,031; 1,031] *Apr 86*
(Prior to April 1986 NOISE was used for this concept.)
    RT   accuracy
    RT   noise
    RT   resolution
    RT   signals

SIGNALS [2,700; 2,700]
    RT   communications
    RT   data transmission
    RT   pulses
    RT   signal conditioning
    RT   signal distortion
    RT   signal-to-noise ratio

SIGNELL-MARSHAK POTENTIAL [1; 1]
    BT1   nucleon-nucleon potential
      BT2   potentials
    RT   nuclear potential
    RT   nucleons

SILANES [802; 802]
    UF   *silicon hydrides*
    BT1   hydrides
      BT2   hydrogen compounds
    BT1   silicon compounds

SILASTIC [35; 35]
    BT1   rubbers
      BT2   elastomers
        BT3   polymers
      BT2   organic polymers
        BT3   organic compounds
        BT3   polymers
    BT1   silicones
      BT2   polymers
      BT2   siloxanes

SILENE REACTOR [15; 15] *Jun 82*
    BT1   enriched uranium reactors
      BT2   reactors
    BT1   research reactors
      BT2   research and test reactors
        BT3   reactors
    BT1   zero power reactors
      BT2   experimental reactors
        BT3   research and test reactors
          BT4   reactors

SILICA GEL [820; 820]
    BT1   adsorbents
    RT   adsorption
    RT   ion exchange materials
    RT   silicon oxides

SILICATE MINERALS [129; 3,800]
Apr 84
    UF   *pyroxenes*
    BT1   minerals
    NT1   allanite
      NT2   orthite
    NT1   alvite
    NT1   amphibole
      NT2   hornblende
    NT1   beryl
    NT1   boltwoodite
    NT1   catapleite
    NT1   cerite
    NT1   chlorite minerals
    NT1   clays
      NT2   attapulgite
      NT2   bentonite
      NT2   clinoptilolite
      NT2   fullers earth
      NT2   illite
      NT2   kaolin
      NT2   montmorillonite
      NT2   smectite
    NT1   coffinite
    NT1   cuprosklodowskite
    NT1   cyrtolite
    NT1   elpidite
    NT1   eudialyte
    NT1   feldspars
    NT1   garnets
      NT2   andradite
    NT1   haiweeite
    NT1   huttonite
    NT1   ilvaite
    NT1   mica
      NT2   biotite
      NT2   muscovite
    NT1   olivine
    NT1   pollucite
    NT1   soddyite
    NT1   steenstrupine
    NT1   talc
    NT1   thorite
    NT1   thorogummite
    NT1   titanite
    NT1   tourmaline
    NT1   uranophane
    NT1   uranothorite
    NT1   vermiculite
    NT1   yttrialite
    NT1   zeolites
    NT1   zircon
    RT   aluminium silicates
    RT   beryllium silicates
    RT   boron silicates
    RT   calcium silicates
    RT   cerium silicates
    RT   cristobalite
    RT   gabbros
    RT   iron silicates
    RT   kimberlites
    RT   lava
    RT   magnesium silicates
    RT   manganese silicates
    RT   niobium silicates
    RT   peridotites
    RT   potassium silicates
    RT   quartz
    RT   silicon oxides
    RT   sodium silicates
    RT   thorium silicates
    RT   titanium silicates
    RT   uranium silicates
    RT   yttrium silicates
    RT   zirconium silicates

SILICATES [1,388; 3,928]
    BT1   oxygen compounds
    BT1   silicon compounds
    NT1   aluminium silicates
    NT1   americium silicates
    NT1   barium silicates
    NT1   berkelium silicates
    NT1   beryllium silicates
    NT1   boron silicates
    NT1   cadmium silicates
    NT1   calcium silicates
      NT2   andradite
      NT2   uranotile
    NT1   cerium silicates
    NT1   cesium silicates
    NT1   chromium silicates
    NT1   cobalt silicates
    NT1   copper silicates
    NT1   curium silicates
    NT1   dysprosium silicates
    NT1   europium silicates
    NT1   germanium silicates
    NT1   hafnium silicates
    NT1   holmium silicates
    NT1   indium silicates
    NT1   iron silicates
      NT2   andradite
    NT1   lanthanum silicates
    NT1   lead silicates
    NT1   lithium silicates
    NT1   lutetium silicates
    NT1   magnesium silicates
    NT1   manganese silicates
    NT1   molybdenum silicates
    NT1   neodymium silicates
    NT1   nickel silicates
    NT1   niobium silicates
    NT1   plutonium silicates
    NT1   potassium silicates
    NT1   praseodymium silicates
    NT1   rubidium silicates
    NT1   samarium silicates
    NT1   scandium silicates
    NT1   sodium silicates
    NT1   strontium silicates
    NT1   tantalum silicates
    NT1   thorium silicates
    NT1   titanium silicates
    NT1   uranium silicates
      NT2   uranotile
    NT1   uranyl silicates
    NT1   vanadium silicates
    NT1   ytterbium silicates
    NT1   yttrium silicates
    NT1   zinc silicates
    NT1   zirconium silicates
    RT   silicic acid
    RT   silicon oxides

SILICIC ACID [72; 72]
    UF   *hydrogen silicates*
    BT1   inorganic acids
      BT2   hydrogen compounds
      BT2   inorganic compounds
    BT1   oxygen compounds
    BT1   silicon compounds
    RT   silicates

SILICIDES [785; 2,574]
    BT1   silicon compounds
    NT1   aluminium silicides
    NT1   americium silicides
    NT1   boron silicides
    NT1   calcium silicides
    NT1   cerium silicides
    NT1   cesium silicides
    NT1   chromium silicides
    NT1   cobalt silicides
    NT1   copper silicides
    NT1   curium silicides
    NT1   dysprosium silicides
    NT1   erbium silicides
    NT1   europium silicides
    NT1   gadolinium silicides
    NT1   germanium silicides
    NT1   gold silicides
    NT1   hafnium silicides
    NT1   holmium silicides
    NT1   iridium silicides
    NT1   iron silicides
    NT1   lanthanum silicides
    NT1   lithium silicides
    NT1   lutetium silicides
    NT1   magnesium silicides
    NT1   manganese silicides
    NT1   molybdenum silicides
    NT1   neodymium silicides
    NT1   nickel silicides
    NT1   niobium silicides
    NT1   palladium silicides
    NT1   platinum silicides
    NT1   potassium silicides
    NT1   praseodymium silicides
    NT1   rhenium silicides
    NT1   rhodium silicides
    NT1   rubidium silicides
    NT1   ruthenium silicides
    NT1   samarium silicides
    NT1   scandium silicides

NT1 sodium silicides
NT1 tantalum silicides
NT1 terbium silicides
NT1 thorium silicides
NT1 thulium silicides
NT1 titanium silicides
NT1 tungsten silicides
NT1 uranium silicides
NT1 vanadium silicides
NT1 ytterbium silicides
NT1 yttrium silicides
NT1 zinc silicides
NT1 zirconium silicides
RT intermetallic compounds
RT silicon additions
RT silicon alloys

SILICON [14,398; 14,398]
BT1 semimetals
BT2 elements

SILICON ADDITIONS [661; 1,734]
(Alloys containing not more than 1% Si are listed here.)
NT1 alloy-al95cu4
NT1 alloy-fe40ni35cr22
NT1 alloy-ni56cr21w10mo5fe4al2
NT1 alloy-ni60cr25w15
NT1 alloy-ni67cr19mo5w5ti3
NT1 alloy-ni68cr15w6al3mo3fe2
NT1 alloy-ni78cr21
NT1 alloy-ni80cr20
NT1 alloy-ni94mn3al2
RT silicides
RT silicon alloys

SILICON ALLOYS [1,997; 2,552]
(Alloys containing more than 1% Si.)
BT1 alloys
NT1 alloy-co52cr17fe15mo3si3
NT1 alloy-fe36ni33cr26
NT1 alloy-ni45cr23fe19co3mo3w3
NT1 alloy-ni50mo32cr15si3
NT1 cast iron
NT1 colmonoy
RT silicides
RT silicon additions

SILICON ARSENIDES [11; 11] *Sep 79*
BT1 arsenides
BT2 arsenic compounds
BT2 pnictides
BT1 silicon compounds

SILICON BORIDES [31; 31]
BT1 borides
BT2 boron compounds
RT1 silicon halides
BT2 halides
BT3 halogen compounds
BT2 silicon compounds

SILICON BROMIDES [4; 4]
BT1 bromides
BT2 bromine compounds
BT3 halogen compounds
BT2 halides
BT3 halogen compounds
BT1 silicon compounds

SILICON CARBIDES [1,891; 1,891]
BT1 carbides
BT2 carbon compounds
BT1 silicon compounds

SILICON CHLORIDES [84; 84]
BT1 chlorides
BT2 chlorine compounds
BT3 halogen compounds
BT2 halides
BT3 halogen compounds
BT1 silicon halides
BT2 halides
BT3 halogen compounds
BT2 silicon compounds

SILICON COMPLEXES [81; 81]
BT1 complexes

SILICON COMPOUNDS [745; 15,999]
(See also SILANES, SILOXANES and SILICONES.)
NT1 silanes
*NT1 silicates
NT1 silicic acid
*NT1 silicides
NT1 silicon arsenides
NT1 silicon bromides
NT1 silicon carbides
NT1 silicon halides
NT2 silicon borides
NT2 silicon chlorides
NT2 silicon fluorides
NT2 silicon iodides
NT1 silicon hydroxides
NT1 silicon nitrides
NT1 silicon oxides
NT1 silicon phosphates
NT1 silicon phosphides
NT1 silicon sulfides

SILICON DIODES [497; 497]
BT1 semiconductor diodes
BT2 semiconductor devices

SILICON FLUORIDES [150; 150]
BT1 fluorides
BT2 fluorine compounds
BT3 halogen compounds
BT2 halides
BT3 halogen compounds
BT1 silicon halides
BT2 halides
BT3 halogen compounds
BT2 silicon compounds

→ **SILICON HALIDES** [0; 3] *Sep 91*
BT1 halides
BT2 halogen compounds
BT1 silicon compounds
NT1 silicon borides
NT1 silicon chlorides
NT1 silicon fluorides
NT1 silicon iodides

silicon hydrides
USE silanes

SILICON HYDROXIDES [21; 21]
BT1 hydroxides
BT2 hydrogen compounds
BT2 oxygen compounds
BT1 silicon compounds

SILICON IODIDES [23; 23]
BT1 iodides
BT2 halides
BT3 halogen compounds
BT2 iodine compounds
BT3 halogen compounds
BT1 silicon halides
BT2 halides
BT3 halogen compounds
BT2 silicon compounds

SILICON IONS [1,026; 1,026]
BT1 ions
BT2 charged particles

SILICON ISOTOPES [204; 3,061]
NT1 silicon 22
NT1 silicon 23
NT1 silicon 24
NT1 silicon 25
NT1 silicon 26
NT1 silicon 27
NT1 silicon 28
NT1 silicon 29
NT1 silicon 30
NT1 silicon 31
NT1 silicon 32
NT1 silicon 33
NT1 silicon 34
NT1 silicon 35
NT1 silicon 36
NT1 silicon 37
NT1 silicon 38
NT1 silicon 39
NT1 silicon 40
NT1 silicon 41
NT1 silicon 42

SILICON NITRIDES [784; 784]
UF+ *sialon*
BT1 nitrides
BT2 nitrogen compounds
BT2 pnictides
BT1 silicon compounds

SILICON OXIDES [4,685; 5,739]
BT1 oxides
BT2 chalcogenides
BT2 oxygen compounds
BT1 silicon compounds
RT cristobalite
RT glass
RT oxide minerals
RT quartz
RT rhyolites
RT sand
RT silica gel
RT silicate minerals
RT silicates
RT siloxanes

SILICON PHOSPHATES [9; 9]
BT1 phosphates
BT2 oxygen compounds
BT2 phosphorus compounds
BT1 silicon compounds

SILICON PHOSPHIDES [24; 24] *Apr 78*
BT1 phosphides
BT2 phosphorus compounds
BT2 pnictides
BT1 silicon compounds

SILICON SOLAR CELLS [250; 250] *Oct 75*
BT1 solar cells
BT2 direct energy converters
BT2 electronic equipment
BT3 equipment

SILICON SULFIDES [21; 21]
BT1 silicon compounds
BT1 sulfides
BT2 chalcogenides
BT2 sulfur compounds

SILICON 22 [7; 7] *Nov 87*
BT1 even-even nuclei
BT2 nuclei
BT1 light nuclei
BT2 nuclei
BT1 silicon isotopes

SILICON 23 [4, 4] *Aug 86*
BT1 even-odd nuclei
BT2 nuclei
BT1 light nuclei
BT2 nuclei
BT1 silicon isotopes

SILICON 24 [24; 24]
BT1 beta-plus decay radioisotopes
BT2 beta decay radioisotopes
BT3 radioisotopes
BT4 isotopes
BT1 even-even nuclei
BT2 nuclei
BT1 light nuclei
BT2 nuclei
BT1 millisec living radioisotopes
BT2 radioisotopes
BT3 isotopes
BT1 silicon isotopes

SILICON 25 [19; 19]
  BT1   beta-plus decay radioisotopes
    BT2   beta decay radioisotopes
      BT3   radioisotopes
        BT4   isotopes
  BT1   even-odd nuclei
    BT2   nuclei
  BT1   light nuclei
    BT2   nuclei
  BT1   millisec living radioisotopes
    BT2   radioisotopes
      BT3   isotopes
  BT1   silicon isotopes

SILICON 26 [51; 51]
  BT1   beta-plus decay radioisotopes
    BT2   beta decay radioisotopes
      BT3   radioisotopes
        BT4   isotopes
  BT1   even-even nuclei
    BT2   nuclei
  BT1   light nuclei
    BT2   nuclei
  BT1   seconds living radioisotopes
    BT2   radioisotopes
      BT3   isotopes
  BT1   silicon isotopes

SILICON 27 [163; 163]
  BT1   beta-plus decay radioisotopes
    BT2   beta decay radioisotopes
      BT3   radioisotopes
        BT4   isotopes
  BT1   even-odd nuclei
    BT2   nuclei
  BT1   light nuclei
    BT2   nuclei
  BT1   seconds living radioisotopes
    BT2   radioisotopes
      BT3   isotopes
  BT1   silicon isotopes

SILICON 28 [1,714; 1,714]
  BT1   even-even nuclei
    BT2   nuclei
  BT1   light nuclei
    BT2   nuclei
  BT1   silicon isotopes
  BT1   stable isotopes
    BT2   isotopes
  RT   silicon 28 beams

SILICON 28 BEAMS [151; 151]
  BT1   ion beams
    BT2   beams
  RT   silicon 28

SILICON 28 REACTIONS [589; 589]
  BT1   heavy ion reactions
    BT2   nuclear reactions

SILICON 28 TARGET [1,785; 1,785]
  BT1   targets

SILICON 29 [542; 542]
  BT1   even-odd nuclei
    BT2   nuclei
  BT1   light nuclei
    BT2   nuclei
  BT1   silicon isotopes
  BT1   stable isotopes
    BT2   isotopes
  RT   silicon 29 beams

→ SILICON 29 BEAMS [2; 2] *Mar 91*
  BT1   ion beams
    BT2   beams
  RT   silicon 29

SILICON 29 REACTIONS [28; 28]
Apr 78
  BT1   heavy ion reactions
    BT2   nuclear reactions

SILICON 29 TARGET [190; 190]
  BT1   targets

SILICON 30 [332; 332]
  BT1   even-even nuclei
    BT2   nuclei
  BT1   light nuclei
    BT2   nuclei
  BT1   silicon isotopes
  BT1   stable isotopes
    BT2   isotopes

SILICON 30 REACTIONS [87; 87]
Feb 80
  BT1   heavy ion reactions
    BT2   nuclear reactions

SILICON 30 TARGET [292; 292]
  BT1   targets

SILICON 31 [162; 162]
  BT1   beta-minus decay radioisotopes
    BT2   beta decay radioisotopes
      BT3   radioisotopes
        BT4   isotopes
  BT1   even-odd nuclei
    BT2   nuclei
  BT1   hours living radioisotopes
    BT2   radioisotopes
      BT3   isotopes
  BT1   light nuclei
    BT2   nuclei
  BT1   silicon isotopes

SILICON 32 [104; 104]
  BT1   beta-minus decay radioisotopes
    BT2   beta decay radioisotopes
      BT3   radioisotopes
        BT4   isotopes
  BT1   even-even nuclei
    BT2   nuclei
  BT1   light nuclei
    BT2   nuclei
  BT1   silicon isotopes
  BT1   years living radioisotopes
    BT2   radioisotopes
      BT3   isotopes

SILICON 32 DECAY RADIOISOTOPES
[0; 167] *Jan 90*
  BT1   heavy ion decay radioisotopes
    BT2   radioisotopes
      BT3   isotopes
  NT1   plutonium 238
  RT   silicon 32 emission decay

SILICON 32 EMISSION DECAY [0; 0]
Jan 90
  BT1   heavy ion emission decay
    BT2   nuclear decay
      BT3   decay
  RT   silicon 32 decay radioisotopes

SILICON 32 TARGET [6; 6] *Jul 81*
  BT1   targets

SILICON 33 [23; 23]
  BT1   beta-minus decay radioisotopes
    BT2   beta decay radioisotopes
      BT3   radioisotopes
        BT4   isotopes
  BT1   even-odd nuclei
    BT2   nuclei
  BT1   light nuclei
    BT2   nuclei
  BT1   seconds living radioisotopes
    BT2   radioisotopes
      BT3   isotopes
  BT1   silicon isotopes

SILICON 34 [28; 28]
  BT1   beta-minus decay radioisotopes
    BT2   beta decay radioisotopes
      BT3   radioisotopes
        BT4   isotopes
  BT1   even-even nuclei
    BT2   nuclei
  BT1   light nuclei
    BT2   nuclei
  BT1   seconds living radioisotopes
    BT2   radioisotopes
      BT3   isotopes
  BT1   silicon isotopes

SILICON 34 EMISSION DECAY [0; 0]
Oct 89
  BT1   heavy ion emission decay
    BT2   nuclear decay
      BT3   decay

SILICON 35 [17; 17]
  BT1   beta-minus decay radioisotopes
    BT2   beta decay radioisotopes
      BT3   radioisotopes
        BT4   isotopes
  BT1   even-odd nuclei
    BT2   nuclei
  BT1   light nuclei
    BT2   nuclei
  BT1   millisec living radioisotopes
    BT2   radioisotopes
      BT3   isotopes
  BT1   silicon isotopes

SILICON 36 [13; 13]
  BT1   beta-minus decay radioisotopes
    BT2   beta decay radioisotopes
      BT3   radioisotopes
        BT4   isotopes
  BT1   even-even nuclei
    BT2   nuclei
  BT1   light nuclei
    BT2   nuclei
  BT1   millisec living radioisotopes
    BT2   radioisotopes
      BT3   isotopes
  BT1   silicon isotopes

SILICON 37 [3; 3] *Sep 79*
  BT1   beta-minus decay radioisotopes
    BT2   beta decay radioisotopes
      BT3   radioisotopes
        BT4   isotopes
  BT1   even-odd nuclei
    BT2   nuclei
  BT1   light nuclei
    BT2   nuclei
  BT1   silicon isotopes

SILICON 38 [3; 3] *Jul 80*
  BT1   beta-minus decay radioisotopes
    BT2   beta decay radioisotopes
      BT3   radioisotopes
        BT4   isotopes
  BT1   even-even nuclei
    BT2   nuclei
  BT1   light nuclei
    BT2   nuclei
  BT1   silicon isotopes

SILICON 39 [3; 3] *Jul 80*
  BT1   beta-minus decay radioisotopes
    BT2   beta decay radioisotopes
      BT3   radioisotopes
        BT4   isotopes
  BT1   even-odd nuclei
    BT2   nuclei
  BT1   light nuclei
    BT2   nuclei
  BT1   silicon isotopes

SILICON 40 [2; 2] *Sep 89*
  BT1   even-even nuclei
    BT2   nuclei
  BT1   light nuclei
    BT2   nuclei
  BT1   silicon isotopes

SILICON 41 [2; 2] *Sep 89*
  BT1   even-odd nuclei
    BT2   nuclei
  BT1   intermediate mass nuclei
    BT2   nuclei
  BT1   silicon isotopes

SILICON 42 [4; 4] *Feb 79*
  BT1   even-even nuclei
    BT2   nuclei
  BT1   intermediate mass nuclei
    BT2   nuclei
  BT1   silicon isotopes

SILICONES [219; 255]
  BT1   polymers
  BT1   siloxanes
  NT1   dc resins
  NT1   silastic

siliconizing
  USE   diffusion coating

silicosis
  USE   pneumoconioses

SILKWORM [81; 81]
  UF   *bombyx*
  BT1   moths
    BT2   lepidoptera
      BT3   insects
        BT4   arthropods
          BT5   invertebrates
            BT6   animals

SILLIAC COMPUTERS [0; 0]
  BT1   computers

SILOE REACTOR [70; 70]
(CEA/CEN Grenoble, Grenoble, France)
  BT1   enriched uranium reactors
    BT2   reactors
  BT1   isotope production reactors
    BT2   irradiation reactors
      BT3   reactors
  BT1   pool type reactors
    BT2   water cooled reactors
      BT3   reactors
    BT2   water moderated reactors
      BT3   reactors
  BT1   thermal reactors
    BT2   reactors

SILOETTE REACTOR [17; 17]
  UF   *grenoble reactor melusine-2*
  UF   *melusine-2 reactor*
  BT1   enriched uranium reactors
    BT2   reactors
  BT1   pool type reactors
    BT2   water cooled reactors
      BT3   reactors
    BT2   water moderated reactors
      BT3   reactors
  BT1   thermal reactors
    BT2   reactors
  BT1   zero power reactors
    BT2   experimental reactors
      BT3   research and test reactors
        BT4   reactors

SILOXANES [200; 449]
  NT1   silicones
    NT2   dc resins
    NT2   silastic
  RT   silicon oxides

SILT [250; 250]
  RT   sediments
  RT   shales

SILVER [4,685; 4,685]
  BT1   transition elements
    BT2   metals
      BT3   elements

SILVER ADDITIONS [332; 332]
(Alloys containing not more than 1% Ag are listed here.)
  RT   silver alloys
  RT   silver compounds

SILVER ALLOYS [772; 984]
(Alloys containing more than 1% Ag.)
  BT1   alloys
  NT1   silver base alloys
  RT   silver additions

→ SILVER ARSENIDES [0; 0] *Sep 91*
  BT1   arsenides
    BT2   arsenic compounds
    BT2   pnictides
  BT1   silver compounds
    BT2   transition element compounds

SILVER BASE ALLOYS [195; 195]
  BT1   silver alloys
    BT2   alloys

SILVER BROMIDES [136; 136]
  BT1   bromides
    BT2   bromine compounds
      BT3   halogen compounds
    BT2   halides
      BT3   halogen compounds
  BT1   silver compounds
    BT2   transition element compounds

SILVER CARBONATES [4; 4]
  BT1   carbonates
    BT2   carbon compounds
    BT2   oxygen compounds
  BT1   silver compounds
    BT2   transition element compounds

SILVER CHLORIDES [238; 238]
  BT1   chlorides
    BT2   chlorine compounds
      BT3   halogen compounds
    BT2   halides
      BT3   halogen compounds
  BT1   silver compounds
    BT2   transition element compounds

SILVER COMPLEXES [82; 82]
  BT1   transition element complexes
    BT2   complexes

SILVER COMPOUNDS [494; 1,661]
  BT1   transition element compounds
  NT1   silver arsenides
  NT1   silver bromides
  NT1   silver carbonates
  NT1   silver chlorides
  NT1   silver fluorides
  NT1   silver hydrides
  NT1   silver iodides
  NT1   silver nitrates
  NT1   silver nitrides
  NT1   silver oxides
  NT1   silver perchlorates
  NT1   silver phosphates
  NT1   silver selenides
  NT1   silver sulfates
  NT1   silver sulfides
  NT1   silver tellurides
  NT1   silver tungstates
  RT   silver additions

SILVER FLUORIDES [34; 34]
  BT1   fluorides
    BT2   fluorine compounds
      BT3   halogen compounds
    BT2   halides
      BT3   halogen compounds
  BT1   silver compounds
    BT2   transition element compounds

SILVER HYDRIDES [13; 13] *Sep 79*
  BT1   hydrides
    BT2   hydrogen compounds
  BT1   silver compounds
    BT2   transition element compounds

SILVER IODIDES [277; 277]
  BT1   iodides
    BT2   halides
      BT3   halogen compounds
    BT2   iodine compounds
      BT3   halogen compounds
  BT1   silver compounds
    BT2   transition element compounds

SILVER IONS [303; 303]
  BT1   ions
    BT2   charged particles

SILVER ISOTOPES [149; 1,559]
  NT1   silver 100
  NT1   silver 101
  NT1   silver 102
  NT1   silver 103
  NT1   silver 104
  NT1   silver 105
  NT1   silver 106
  NT1   silver 107
  NT1   silver 108
  NT1   silver 109
  NT1   silver 110
  NT1   silver 111
  NT1   silver 112
  NT1   silver 113
  NT1   silver 114
  NT1   silver 115
  NT1   silver 116
  NT1   silver 117
  NT1   silver 118
  NT1   silver 119
  NT1   silver 120
  NT1   silver 121
  NT1   silver 122
  NT1   silver 123
  NT1   silver 95
  NT1   silver 96
  NT1   silver 97
  NT1   silver 98
  NT1   silver 99

SILVER NITRATES [158; 158]
  BT1   nitrates
    BT2   nitrogen compounds
    BT2   oxygen compounds
  BT1   silver compounds
    BT2   transition element compounds

SILVER NITRIDES [8; 8]
  BT1   nitrides
    BT2   nitrogen compounds
    BT2   pnictides
  BT1   silver compounds
    BT2   transition element compounds

SILVER ORES [40; 40]
  BT1   ores

SILVER OXIDES [122; 122]
  BT1   oxides
    BT2   chalcogenides
    BT2   oxygen compounds
  BT1   silver compounds
    BT2   transition element compounds

SILVER PERCHLORATES [20; 20]
  BT1   perchlorates
    BT2   chlorine compounds
      BT3   halogen compounds
    BT2   oxygen compounds
  BT1   silver compounds
    BT2   transition element compounds

SILVER PHOSPHATES [25; 25]
- BT1 phosphates
- BT2 oxygen compounds
- BT2 phosphorus compounds
- BT1 silver compounds
- BT2 transition element compounds

SILVER SELENIDES [60; 60] *Jul 78*
- BT1 selenides
- BT2 chalcogenides
- BT2 selenium compounds
- BT1 silver compounds
- BT2 transition element compounds

SILVER SULFATES [10; 10]
- BT1 silver compounds
- BT2 transition element compounds
- BT1 sulfates
- BT2 oxygen compounds
- BT2 sulfur compounds

SILVER SULFIDES [107; 107]
- BT1 silver compounds
- BT2 transition element compounds
- BT1 sulfides
- BT2 chalcogenides
- BT2 sulfur compounds

SILVER TELLURIDES [104; 104] *Sep 78*
- BT1 silver compounds
- BT2 transition element compounds
- BT1 tellurides
- BT2 chalcogenides
- BT2 tellurium compounds

SILVER TUNGSTATES [12; 12] *May 78*
- BT1 silver compounds
- BT2 transition element compounds
- BT1 tungstates
- BT2 oxygen compounds
- BT2 tungsten compounds
- BT3 transition element compounds

SILVER 100 [16; 16]
- BT1 beta-plus decay radioisotopes
- BT2 beta decay radioisotopes
- BT3 radioisotopes
- BT4 isotopes
- BT1 electron capture radioisotopes
- BT2 beta decay radioisotopes
- BT3 radioisotopes
- BT4 isotopes
- BT1 intermediate mass nuclei
- BT2 nuclei
- BT1 minutes living radioisotopes
- BT2 radioisotopes
- BT3 isotopes
- BT1 odd-odd nuclei
- BT2 nuclei
- BT1 silver isotopes

SILVER 101 [23; 23]
- BT1 beta-plus decay radioisotopes
- BT2 beta decay radioisotopes
- BT3 radioisotopes
- BT4 isotopes
- BT1 electron capture radioisotopes
- BT2 beta decay radioisotopes
- BT3 radioisotopes
- BT4 isotopes
- BT1 intermediate mass nuclei
- BT2 nuclei
- BT1 isomeric transition isotopes
- BT2 radioisotopes
- BT3 isotopes
- BT1 minutes living radioisotopes
- BT2 radioisotopes
- BT3 isotopes
- BT1 odd-even nuclei
- BT2 nuclei
- BT1 seconds living radioisotopes
- BT2 radioisotopes
- BT3 isotopes
- BT1 silver isotopes

SILVER 102 [30; 30]
- BT1 beta-plus decay radioisotopes
- BT2 beta decay radioisotopes
- BT3 radioisotopes
- BT4 isotopes
- BT1 electron capture radioisotopes
- BT2 beta decay radioisotopes
- BT3 radioisotopes
- BT4 isotopes
- BT1 intermediate mass nuclei
- BT2 nuclei
- BT1 isomeric transition isotopes
- BT2 radioisotopes
- BT3 isotopes
- BT1 minutes living radioisotopes
- BT2 radioisotopes
- BT3 isotopes
- BT1 odd-odd nuclei
- BT2 nuclei
- BT1 silver isotopes

SILVER 103 [32; 32]
- BT1 beta-plus decay radioisotopes
- BT2 beta decay radioisotopes
- BT3 radioisotopes
- BT4 isotopes
- BT1 electron capture radioisotopes
- BT2 beta decay radioisotopes
- BT3 radioisotopes
- BT4 isotopes
- BT1 hours living radioisotopes
- BT2 radioisotopes
- BT3 isotopes
- BT1 intermediate mass nuclei
- BT2 nuclei
- BT1 internal conversion radioisoto
- BT2 radioisotopes
- BT3 isotopes
- BT1 isomeric transition isotopes
- BT2 radioisotopes
- BT3 isotopes
- BT1 odd-even nuclei
- BT2 nuclei
- BT1 seconds living radioisotopes
- BT2 radioisotopes
- BT3 isotopes
- BT1 silver isotopes

SILVER 104 [51; 51]
- BT1 beta-plus decay radioisotopes
- BT2 beta decay radioisotopes
- BT3 radioisotopes
- BT4 isotopes
- BT1 electron capture radioisotopes
- BT2 beta decay radioisotopes
- BT3 radioisotopes
- BT4 isotopes
- BT1 hours living radioisotopes
- BT2 radioisotopes
- BT3 isotopes
- BT1 intermediate mass nuclei
- BT2 nuclei
- BT1 minutes living radioisotopes
- BT2 radioisotopes
- BT3 isotopes
- BT1 odd-odd nuclei
- BT2 nuclei
- BT1 silver isotopes

SILVER 105 [112; 112]
- BT1 beta-plus decay radioisotopes
- BT2 beta decay radioisotopes
- BT3 radioisotopes
- BT4 isotopes
- BT1 days living radioisotopes
- BT2 radioisotopes
- BT3 isotopes
- BT1 electron capture radioisotopes
- BT2 beta decay radioisotopes
- BT3 radioisotopes
- BT4 isotopes
- BT1 intermediate mass nuclei
- BT2 nuclei
- BT1 internal conversion radioisoto
- BT2 radioisotopes
- BT3 isotopes
- BT1 isomeric transition isotopes
- BT2 radioisotopes
- BT3 isotopes
- BT1 minutes living radioisotopes
- BT2 radioisotopes
- BT3 isotopes
- BT1 odd-even nuclei
- BT2 nuclei
- BT1 silver isotopes

SILVER 106 [91; 91]
- BT1 beta-plus decay radioisotopes
- BT2 beta decay radioisotopes
- BT3 radioisotopes
- BT4 isotopes
- BT1 days living radioisotopes
- BT2 radioisotopes
- BT3 isotopes
- BT1 electron capture radioisotopes
- BT2 beta decay radioisotopes
- BT3 radioisotopes
- BT4 isotopes
- BT1 intermediate mass nuclei
- BT2 nuclei
- BT1 minutes living radioisotopes
- BT2 radioisotopes
- BT3 isotopes
- BT1 odd-odd nuclei
- BT2 nuclei
- BT1 silver isotopes

SILVER 106 TARGET [2; 2] *Jan 86*
- BT1 targets

SILVER 107 [180; 180]
- BT1 intermediate mass nuclei
- BT2 nuclei
- BT1 internal conversion radioisoto
- BT2 radioisotopes
- BT3 isotopes
- BT1 isomeric transition isotopes
- BT2 radioisotopes
- BT3 isotopes
- BT1 odd-even nuclei
- BT2 nuclei
- BT1 seconds living radioisotopes
- BT2 radioisotopes
- BT3 isotopes
- BT1 silver isotopes
- BT1 stable isotopes
- BT2 isotopes

SILVER 107 BEAMS [19; 19]
- BT1 ion beams
- BT2 beams

SILVER 107 TARGET [498; 498]
- BT1 targets

SILVER 108 [134; 134]
- BT1 beta-minus decay radioisotopes
- BT2 beta decay radioisotopes
- BT3 radioisotopes
- BT4 isotopes
- BT1 beta-plus decay radioisotopes
- BT2 beta decay radioisotopes
- BT3 radioisotopes
- BT4 isotopes
- BT1 electron capture radioisotopes
- BT2 beta decay radioisotopes
- BT3 radioisotopes
- BT4 isotopes
- BT1 intermediate mass nuclei
- BT2 nuclei
- BT1 isomeric transition isotopes
- BT2 radioisotopes
- BT3 isotopes
- BT1 minutes living radioisotopes
- BT2 radioisotopes
- BT3 isotopes
- BT1 odd-odd nuclei
- BT2 nuclei
- BT1 silver isotopes
- BT1 years living radioisotopes
- BT2 radioisotopes
- BT3 isotopes

SILVER 108 TARGET [127; 127]
Feb 77
  BT1   targets

SILVER 109 [254; 254]
  BT1   intermediate mass nuclei
    BT2   nuclei
  BT1   internal conversion radioisoto
    BT2   radioisotopes
      BT3   isotopes
  BT1   isomeric transition isotopes
    BT2   radioisotopes
      BT3   isotopes
  BT1   odd-even nuclei
    BT2   nuclei
  BT1   seconds living radioisotopes
    BT2   radioisotopes
      BT3   isotopes
  BT1   silver isotopes
  BT1   stable isotopes
    BT2   isotopes

SILVER 109 REACTIONS [5; 5]
May 86
  BT1   heavy ion reactions
    BT2   nuclear reactions

SILVER 109 TARGET [497; 497]
  BT1   targets

SILVER 110 [590; 590]
  BT1   beta-minus decay radioisotopes
    BT2   beta decay radioisotopes
      BT3   radioisotopes
        BT4   isotopes
  BT1   days living radioisotopes
    BT2   radioisotopes
      BT3   isotopes
  BT1   electron capture radioisotopes
    BT2   beta decay radioisotopes
      BT3   radioisotopes
        BT4   isotopes
  BT1   intermediate mass nuclei
    BT2   nuclei
  BT1   isomeric transition isotopes
    BT2   radioisotopes
      BT3   isotopes
  BT1   odd-odd nuclei
    BT2   nuclei
  BT1   seconds living radioisotopes
    BT2   radioisotopes
      BT3   isotopes
  BT1   silver isotopes

SILVER 111 [101; 101]
  BT1   beta-minus decay radioisotopes
    BT2   beta decay radioisotopes
      BT3   radioisotopes
        BT4   isotopes
  BT1   days living radioisotopes
    BT2   radioisotopes
      BT3   isotopes
  BT1   intermediate mass nuclei
    BT2   nuclei
  BT1   internal conversion radioisoto
    BT2   radioisotopes
      BT3   isotopes
  BT1   isomeric transition isotopes
    BT2   radioisotopes
      BT3   isotopes
  BT1   minutes living radioisotopes
    BT2   radioisotopes
      BT3   isotopes
  BT1   odd-even nuclei
    BT2   nuclei
  BT1   silver isotopes

SILVER 112 [15; 15]
  BT1   beta-minus decay radioisotopes
    BT2   beta decay radioisotopes
      BT3   radioisotopes
        BT4   isotopes
  BT1   hours living radioisotopes
    BT2   radioisotopes
      BT3   isotopes
  BT1   intermediate mass nuclei
    BT2   nuclei
  BT1   odd-odd nuclei
    BT2   nuclei
  BT1   silver isotopes

SILVER 113 [21; 21]
  BT1   beta-minus decay radioisotopes
    BT2   beta decay radioisotopes
      BT3   radioisotopes
        BT4   isotopes
  BT1   hours living radioisotopes
    BT2   radioisotopes
      BT3   isotopes
  BT1   intermediate mass nuclei
    BT2   nuclei
  BT1   isomeric transition isotopes
    BT2   radioisotopes
      BT3   isotopes
  BT1   minutes living radioisotopes
    BT2   radioisotopes
      BT3   isotopes
  BT1   odd-even nuclei
    BT2   nuclei
  BT1   silver isotopes

SILVER 114 [10; 10]
  BT1   beta-minus decay radioisotopes
    BT2   beta decay radioisotopes
      BT3   radioisotopes
        BT4   isotopes
  BT1   intermediate mass nuclei
    BT2   nuclei
  BT1   odd-odd nuclei
    BT2   nuclei
  BT1   seconds living radioisotopes
    BT2   radioisotopes
      BT3   isotopes
  BT1   silver isotopes

SILVER 115 [17; 17]
  BT1   beta-minus decay radioisotopes
    BT2   beta decay radioisotopes
      BT3   radioisotopes
        BT4   isotopes
  BT1   intermediate mass nuclei
    BT2   nuclei
  BT1   minutes living radioisotopes
    BT2   radioisotopes
      BT3   isotopes
  BT1   odd-even nuclei
    BT2   nuclei
  BT1   seconds living radioisotopes
    BT2   radioisotopes
      BT3   isotopes
  BT1   silver isotopes

SILVER 116 [15; 15]
  BT1   beta-minus decay radioisotopes
    BT2   beta decay radioisotopes
      BT3   radioisotopes
        BT4   isotopes
  BT1   intermediate mass nuclei
    BT2   nuclei
  BT1   isomeric transition isotopes
    BT2   radioisotopes
      BT3   isotopes
  BT1   minutes living radioisotopes
    BT2   radioisotopes
      BT3   isotopes
  BT1   odd-odd nuclei
    BT2   nuclei
  BT1   seconds living radioisotopes
    BT2   radioisotopes
      BT3   isotopes
  BT1   silver isotopes

SILVER 117 [9; 9]
  BT1   beta-minus decay radioisotopes
    BT2   beta decay radioisotopes
      BT3   radioisotopes
        BT4   isotopes
  BT1   intermediate mass nuclei
    BT2   nuclei
  BT1   minutes living radioisotopes
    BT2   radioisotopes
      BT3   isotopes
  BT1   odd-even nuclei
    BT2   nuclei
  BT1   seconds living radioisotopes
    BT2   radioisotopes
      BT3   isotopes
  BT1   silver isotopes

SILVER 118 [10; 10]
  BT1   beta-minus decay radioisotopes
    BT2   beta decay radioisotopes
      BT3   radioisotopes
        BT4   isotopes
  BT1   intermediate mass nuclei
    BT2   nuclei
  BT1   isomeric transition isotopes
    BT2   radioisotopes
      BT3   isotopes
  BT1   odd-odd nuclei
    BT2   nuclei
  BT1   seconds living radioisotopes
    BT2   radioisotopes
      BT3   isotopes
  BT1   silver isotopes

SILVER 119 [5; 5]
  BT1   beta-minus decay radioisotopes
    BT2   beta decay radioisotopes
      BT3   radioisotopes
        BT4   isotopes
  BT1   intermediate mass nuclei
    BT2   nuclei
  BT1   odd-even nuclei
    BT2   nuclei
  BT1   seconds living radioisotopes
    BT2   radioisotopes
      BT3   isotopes
  BT1   silver isotopes

SILVER 120 [4; 4]
  BT1   beta-minus decay radioisotopes
    BT2   beta decay radioisotopes
      BT3   radioisotopes
        BT4   isotopes
  BT1   intermediate mass nuclei
    BT2   nuclei
  BT1   isomeric transition isotopes
    BT2   radioisotopes
      BT3   isotopes
  BT1   millisec living radioisotopes
    BT2   radioisotopes
      BT3   isotopes
  BT1   odd-odd nuclei
    BT2   nuclei
  BT1   seconds living radioisotopes
    BT2   radioisotopes
      BT3   isotopes
  BT1   silver isotopes

SILVER 121 [9; 9]
  BT1   beta-minus decay radioisotopes
    BT2   beta decay radioisotopes
      BT3   radioisotopes
        BT4   isotopes
  BT1   intermediate mass nuclei
    BT2   nuclei
  BT1   millisec living radioisotopes
    BT2   radioisotopes
      BT3   isotopes
  BT1   odd-even nuclei
    BT2   nuclei
  BT1   silver isotopes

SILVER 122 [13; 13]
  BT1   beta-minus decay radioisotopes
    BT2   beta decay radioisotopes
      BT3   radioisotopes
        BT4   isotopes
  BT1   intermediate mass nuclei
    BT2   nuclei
  BT1   odd-odd nuclei
    BT2   nuclei
  BT1   seconds living radioisotopes
    BT2   radioisotopes
      BT3   isotopes
  BT1   silver isotopes

SILVER 123 [8; 8] *Jul 76*
  BT1   beta-minus decay radioisotopes
    BT2   beta decay radioisotopes
      BT3   radioisotopes
        BT4   isotopes
  BT1   intermediate mass nuclei

BT2   nuclei
BT1   millisec living radioisotopes
  BT2   radioisotopes
    BT3   isotopes
BT1   odd-even nuclei
  BT2   nuclei
BT1   silver isotopes

SILVER 95 [2; 2] *Jun 84*
BT1   electron capture radioisotopes
  BT2   beta decay radioisotopes
    BT3   radioisotopes
      BT4   isotopes
BT1   intermediate mass nuclei
  BT2   nuclei
BT1   millisec living radioisotopes
  BT2   radioisotopes
    BT3   isotopes
BT1   odd-even nuclei
  BT2   nuclei
BT1   silver isotopes

SILVER 96 [5; 5] *Jun 82*
BT1   beta-plus decay radioisotopes
  BT2   beta decay radioisotopes
    BT3   radioisotopes
      BT4   isotopes
BT1   electron capture radioisotopes
  BT2   beta decay radioisotopes
    BT3   radioisotopes
      BT4   isotopes
BT1   intermediate mass nuclei
  BT2   nuclei
BT1   odd-odd nuclei
  BT2   nuclei
BT1   seconds living radioisotopes
  BT2   radioisotopes
    BT3   isotopes
BT1   silver isotopes

SILVER 97 [8; 8] *Feb 79*
BT1   electron capture radioisotopes
  BT2   beta decay radioisotopes
    BT3   radioisotopes
      BT4   isotopes
BT1   intermediate mass nuclei
  BT2   nuclei
BT1   odd-even nuclei
  BT2   nuclei
BT1   seconds living radioisotopes
  BT2   radioisotopes
    BT3   isotopes
BT1   silver isotopes

SILVER 98 [5; 5] *Feb 79*
BT1   beta-plus decay radioisotopes
  BT2   beta decay radioisotopes
    BT3   radioisotopes
      BT4   isotopes
BT1   electron capture radioisotopes
  BT2   beta decay radioisotopes
    BT3   radioisotopes
      BT4   isotopes
BT1   intermediate mass nuclei
  BT2   nuclei
BT1   odd-odd nuclei
  BT2   nuclei
BT1   seconds living radioisotopes
  BT2   radioisotopes
    BT3   isotopes
BT1   silver isotopes

SILVER 99 [10; 10]
BT1   beta-plus decay radioisotopes
  BT2   beta decay radioisotopes
    BT3   radioisotopes
      BT4   isotopes
BT1   electron capture radioisotopes
  BT2   beta decay radioisotopes
    BT3   radioisotopes
      BT4   isotopes
BT1   intermediate mass nuclei
  BT2   nuclei
BT1   internal conversion radioisoto
  BT2   radioisotopes
    BT3   isotopes
BT1   isomeric transition isotopes

  BT2   radioisotopes
    BT3   isotopes
BT1   minutes living radioisotopes
  BT2   radioisotopes
    BT3   isotopes
BT1   odd-even nuclei
  BT2   nuclei
BT1   seconds living radioisotopes
  BT2   radioisotopes
    BT3   isotopes
BT1   silver isotopes

SIMIAN VIRUS [133; 133]
UF   *sv 40 virus*
BT1   viruses
  BT2   microorganisms
  BT2   parasites

§§ **SIMULATION** [15,191; 35,785]
UF   *modeling*
NT1   computerized simulation
NT1   plasma simulation
RT   essex i project
RT   functional models
RT   scaling laws
RT   simulators

SIMULATORS [677; 2,329]
BT1   analog systems
BT1   functional models
NT1   reactor simulators
RT   mockup
RT   plasma simulation
RT   scale models
RT   simulation

simulators (fission reactor)
USE   reactor simulators

SIN CYCLOTRON [209; 209]
UF   *swiss inst nucl res cyclotron*
UF   *villigen cyclotron*
BT1   isochronous cyclotrons
  BT2   cyclotrons
    BT3   cyclic accelerators
      BT4   accelerators

sine generators
USE   function generators

SINE-GORDON EQUATION [736; 736]
Jun 77
BT1   field equations
  BT2   equations
RT   quantum field theory
RT   space-time

SINGAPORE [12; 12]
BT1   asia
BT1   developing countries
BT1   islands
RT   pacific ocean

single administration
USE   single intake

single crystals
USE   monocrystals

SINGLE INTAKE [247; 247]
UF   *single administration*
UF+   *accidental intake*
BT1   intake
RT   accidents
RT   first aid
RT   injuries

SINGLE PHOTON ECT [3,089; 3,089]
Apr 80
UF   *single-photon ect*
BT1   emission computed tomography

  BT2   computerized tomography
    BT3   tomography
RT   gamma cameras
RT   photon transmission scanning
RT   photons
RT   radioisotope scanning

single-level resonance formula
USE   breit-wigner formula

SINGLE-PARTICLE MODEL
[1,905; 1,905]
UF   *independent-particle model*
RT   atomic models
RT   nuclear models
RT   quasiparticle-phonon model
RT   schmidt model

SINGLE-PARTICLE MODES [228; 228]
UF   *modes (single-particle)*
BT1   oscillation modes

single-photon ect
USE   single photon ect

SINGULARITY [4,367; 4,367]
UF+   *residues (mathematical)*
RT   functions
RT   landau curves
RT   s matrix
RT   scattering amplitudes

sintered aluminum powders
USE   sap

SINTERED MATERIALS [2,191; 2,239]
BT1   materials
NT1   sap
RT   powder metallurgy
RT   powders
RT   sintering

SINTERING [3,638; 3,638]
UF   *liquid-phase sintering*
BT1   fabrication
RT   agglomeration
RT   furnaces
RT   porosity
RT   powder metallurgy
RT   sintered materials

SINUSES [385; 385] *May 81*
(In anatomical nomenclature to designate a cavity or hollow space.)
BT1   cavities
RT   face

sioux falls pathfinder reactor
USE   pathfinder reactor

siredon
USE   axolotl

SIRIUS DEVICE [23; 23]
BT1   stellarators
  BT2   closed plasma devices
    BT3   thermonuclear devices

sirius synchrotron
USE   tomsk synchrotron

→ **SIS SYNCHROTRON** [7; 7] *Feb 91*
UF   *darmstadt synchrotron*
BT1   heavy ion accelerators
  BT2   accelerators
BT1   synchrotrons
  BT2   cyclic accelerators
    BT3   accelerators

SISTER CHROMATID EXCHANGES
[305; 305] *Oct 77*
- BT1 mutations
- RT genetic effects
- RT genetic radiation effects
- RT hereditary diseases

SITE APPROVALS [158; 158] *Dec 76*
- RT licenses
- RT nuclear facilities
- RT property rights
- RT reactor sites
- RT site preparation
- RT site selection

site characterization
- USE site surveys

SITE PREPARATION [80; 80] *Dec 82*
- RT reactor sites
- RT site approvals
- RT site selection

site rehabilitation
- USE remedial action

SITE SELECTION [6,651; 6,651]
(See also descriptors for concepts involved in site selection, such as ENVIRONMENT, SEISMOLOGY and SOILS plus LIQUEFACTION.)
- UF *reactor siting*
- RT accidents
- RT environment
- RT external zones
- RT land use
- RT licensing
- RT meteorology
- RT offshore nuclear power plants
- RT offshore sites
- RT planning
- RT reactor safety
- RT reactor sites
- RT site approvals
- RT site preparation
- RT site surveys
- RT water use

SITE SURVEYS [537; 537] *Jul 86*
(Surveys of particular sites to establish their characteristics, e.g. hydrology, geological and topographical features, etc.)
- UF *site characterization*
- RT baseline ecology
- RT environmental impacts
- RT geologic surveys
- RT hydrology
- RT meteorology
- RT radiation monitoring
- RT reactor sites
- RT site selection

sites (fission reactor)
- USE reactor sites

sites (nuclear installations)
(If appropriate use one of the specific types of facilities.)
- USE nuclear facilities

SITOSTEROL [14; 14]
- BT1 sterols
- BT2 hydroxy compounds
- BT3 organic compounds
- BT2 steroids
- BT3 organic compounds

SIZE [5,550; 15,077]
- NT1 critical size
- NT1 grain size
- NT1 particle size
- RT dimensions

- RT thickness
- RT volume

sizew. nucl. pow. stat. a
- USE sizewell-a reactor

sizew. nucl. pow. stat. b
- USE sizewell-b reactor

SIZEWELL-A REACTOR [39; 39]
(Sizewell, Suffolk, UK)
- UF *sizew. nucl. pow. stat. a*
- BT1 carbon dioxide cooled reactors
- BT2 gas cooled reactors
- BT3 reactors
- BT1 magnox type reactors
- BT2 gcr type reactors
- BT3 gas cooled reactors
- BT4 reactors
- BT3 graphite moderated reactors
- BT4 reactors
- BT2 natural uranium reactors
- BT3 reactors
- BT2 power reactors
- BT3 reactors
- BT1 thermal reactors
- BT2 reactors

SIZEWELL-B REACTOR [555; 555]
(Sizewell, Suffolk, UK)
- UF *sizew. nucl. pow. stat. b*
- BT1 pwr type reactors
- BT2 enriched uranium reactors
- BT3 reactors
- BT2 power reactors
- BT3 reactors
- BT2 thermal reactors
- BT3 reactors
- BT2 water cooled reactors
- BT3 reactors
- BT2 water moderated reactors
- BT3 reactors

SKAGIT-1 REACTOR [12; 12]
(Hanford, Washington, USA)
- BT1 bwr type reactors
- BT2 enriched uranium reactors
- BT3 reactors
- BT2 power reactors
- BT3 reactors
- BT2 thermal reactors
- BT3 reactors
- BT2 water cooled reactors
- BT3 reactors
- BT2 water moderated reactors
- BT3 reactors

SKAGIT-2 REACTOR [12; 12]
(Hanford, Washington, USA)
- BT1 bwr type reactors
- BT2 enriched uranium reactors
- BT3 reactors
- BT2 power reactors
- BT3 reactors
- BT2 thermal reactors
- BT3 reactors
- BT2 water cooled reactors
- BT3 reactors
- BT2 water moderated reactors
- BT3 reactors

SKELETAL DISEASES [2,794; 6,602]
- UF *bone diseases*
- UF+ *chondrosarcomas*
- BT1 diseases
- NT1 bone fractures
- NT1 osteomyelitis
- NT1 osteoporosis
- NT1 osteoradionecrosis
- NT1 osteosarcomas
- NT1 rheumatic diseases
- NT1 rickets
- NT1 spondylitis
- RT skeleton

skeletal fossils
- USE fossils

SKELETON [7,309; 14,190]
- UF *bones*
- BT1 organs
- BT2 body
- NT1 bone joints
- NT1 exoskeleton
- NT1 femur
- NT1 skull
- NT2 jaw
- NT1 tibia
- NT1 vertebrae
- RT bone tissues
- RT limbs
- RT skeletal diseases

SKIN [4,126; 5,189]
- UF+ *sebaceous glands*
- UF+ *sweat glands*
- BT1 organs
- BT2 body
- NT1 epidermis
- NT1 feathers
- NT1 hair
- NT1 nails
- RT epilation
- RT erythema
- RT gloves
- RT hair follicles
- RT leather
- RT lupus
- RT melanin
- RT ointments
- RT psoriasis
- RT skin absorption
- RT skin diseases
- RT sweat
- RT tissues
- RT wounds

SKIN ABSORPTION [283; 283]
- UF *absorption (skin)*
- BT1 uptake
- RT gloves
- RT protective clothing
- RT skin

SKIN DISEASES [437; 1,275]
- BT1 diseases
- NT1 dermatitis
- NT2 radiodermatitis
- NT1 eczema
- NT1 herpes simplex
- NT1 psoriasis
- RT burns
- RT erythema
- RT skin

SKIN EFFECT [403; 403]
- RT electric conductors
- RT electric currents
- RT magnetic flux
- RT penetration depth

skoda (plzen) reactor
- USE sr-oa reactor

SKULL [1,502; 2,296]
- BT1 skeleton
- BT2 organs
- BT3 body
- NT1 jaw
- RT brain
- RT head

SKYLAB [184; 184]
- BT1 satellites

SKYRME POTENTIAL [1,475; 1,475]
- BT1 nucleon-nucleon potential
- BT2 potentials
- RT elastic scattering
- RT inelastic scattering
- RT nuclear reactions

SL GROUPS [619; 619]
BT1 lie groups
BT2 symmetry groups

SL-1 REACTOR [22; 22]
UF *stationary low power plant-1*
BT1 bwr type reactors
BT2 enriched uranium reactors
BT3 reactors
BT2 power reactors
BT3 reactors
BT2 thermal reactors
BT3 reactors
BT2 water cooled reactors
BT3 reactors
BT2 water moderated reactors
BT3 reactors
BT1 process heat reactors
BT2 power reactors
BT3 reactors

SLABS [1,105; 1,105]
(Thicker than plates; primarily for use in shielding studies.)
RT plates
RT prismatic configuration
RT shape

slac
USE stanford linear accelerator ce

slac 2-mile linac
USE stanford 20-gev linac

SLAGGIE MODEL [3; 3]
RT transport theory

SLAGGING PYROLYSIS PROCESS
[15; 15] *Oct 83*
UF *andco-torrax slagging pyrolysi*
RT alpha-bearing wastes
RT pyrolysis
RT radioactive waste processing

SLAGS [506; 506]
RT gangue
RT seed-slag interactions

slater determinant
USE slater method

slater integrals
USE slater method

SLATER METHOD [955; 955]
UF *slater determinant*
UF *slater integrals*
UF *slater orbitals*
RT aligned coupling scheme
RT electronic structure
RT wave functions

slater orbitals
USE slater method

slatis-siegbahn spectrometers
USE magnetic lens spectrometers

slc
USE stanford linear collider

SLEEP [65; 65]
RT hibernation
RT hypnotics and sedatives
RT physiology

SLEEVES [368; 368]
RT jackets
RT reactor components

SLIDING FRICTION [211; 211]
SF *tribology*
BT1 friction

SLIGHTLY ENRICHED URANIUM
[580; 580]
(0 - 5 per cent.)
BT1 enriched uranium
BT2 isotope enriched materials
BT3 materials
BT2 uranium
BT3 actinides
BT4 metals
BT5 elements

slime fungi
USE myxomycetes

SLIP [1,001; 1,001]
RT deformation
RT dislocations
RT slip ratio
RT slip velocity
RT twinning

SLIP CASTING [35; 35]
(A procedure in ceramics not metallurgy.)
BT1 casting
BT2 fabrication
RT ceramics

SLIP FLOW [47; 47]
(Rarefied gas flow in the region between Knudsen numbers 0.01 and 0.1 only.)
BT1 gas flow
BT2 fluid flow

SLIP RATIO [37; 37]
RT slip

SLIP VELOCITY [40; 40]
RT slip

SLOOP EVENT [0; 0]
BT1 plowshare project
RT mining

SLOPE STABILITY [32; 32] *Apr 86*
(Resistance of an inclined surface to failure by sliding or collapsing.)
BT1 stability
RT earthmoving equipment
RT excavation
RT ground motion
RT landslides
RT soil-structure interactions
RT surface mining

SLOW NEUTRONS [675; 675]
BT1 neutrons
BT2 nucleons
BT3 baryons
BT4 fermions
BT4 hadrons
BT5 elementary particles

slowdown
USE slowing-down

SLOWING-DOWN [1,255; 1,757]
UF *slowdown*
NT1 thermalization
RT absorption
RT energy losses
RT fermi age theory
RT neutron age
RT neutron converters
RT neutron slowing-down theory
RT neutron transport theory
RT selengut-goertzel equation
RT slowing-down kernels
RT slowing-down length
RT van hove theory
RT wick method
RT wigner-wilkins model
RT wilkins equation

slowing-down area
USE slowing-down length

SLOWING-DOWN KERNELS [73; 73]
UF *kernels (slowing-down)*
RT neutron slowing-down theory
RT slowing-down

SLOWING-DOWN LENGTH [76; 76]
UF *slowing-down area*
RT migration length
RT slowing-down

slowing-down theory (neutron)
USE neutron slowing-down theory

SLOWPOKE TYPE REACTORS
[80; 111] *Dec 79*
UF *safe low power critical experi*
BT1 enriched uranium reactors
BT2 reactors
BT1 isotope production reactors
BT2 irradiation reactors
BT3 reactors
BT1 pool type reactors
BT2 water cooled reactors
BT3 reactors
BT2 water moderated reactors
BT3 reactors
BT1 research reactors
BT2 research and test reactors
BT3 reactors
NT1 slowpoke-alberta reactor
NT1 slowpoke-dalhousie reactor
NT1 slowpoke-montreal reactor
NT1 slowpoke-ottawa reactor
NT1 slowpoke-toronto reactor
NT1 slowpoke-wnre reactor

SLOWPOKE-ALBERTA REACTOR
[2; 2] *Dec 79*
(University of Alberta, Faculty of Pharmacy, Edmonton, Alberta, Canada)
UF *alberta univ. slowpoke reactor*
UF *univ. of alta. slowpoke reacto*
BT1 slowpoke type reactors
BT2 enriched uranium reactors
BT3 reactors
BT2 isotope production reactors
BT3 irradiation reactors
BT4 reactors
BT2 pool type reactors
BT3 water cooled reactors
BT4 reactors
BT3 water moderated reactors
BT4 reactors
BT2 research reactors
BT3 research and test reactors
BT4 reactors

SLOWPOKE-DALHOUSIE REACTOR
[8; 8] *Dec 79*
(Dalhousie University Trace Analysis Research Centre, Halifax, Nova Scotia, Canada)
UF *dalhousie univ. slowpoke reac*
BT1 slowpoke type reactors
BT2 enriched uranium reactors
BT3 reactors
BT2 isotope production reactors
BT3 irradiation reactors
BT4 reactors
BT2 pool type reactors
BT3 water cooled reactors
BT4 reactors
BT3 water moderated reactors
BT4 reactors
BT2 research reactors

          BT3   research and test reactors
          BT4   reactors

SLOWPOKE-MONTREAL REACTOR
[8; 8] *Dec 79*
(University of Montreal, Polytechnical School, Montreal, Quebec, Canada)
   UF   *montreal univ. slowpoke react.*
   UF   *univ. de montreal slowpoke rea*
   BT1   slowpoke type reactors
     BT2   enriched uranium reactors
       BT3   reactors
     BT2   isotope production reactors
       BT3   irradiation reactors
         BT4   reactors
     BT2   pool type reactors
       BT3   water cooled reactors
         BT4   reactors
       BT3   water moderated reactors
         BT4   reactors
     BT2   research reactors
       BT3   research and test reactors
         BT4   reactors

SLOWPOKE-OTTAWA REACTOR
[12; 12]
(Atomic Energy of Canada Ltd, Commercial Products, Ottawa, Ontario, Canada)
   UF   *aecl radiochemical slowpoke re*
   UF   *ottawa slowpoke reactor*
   BT1   slowpoke type reactors
     BT2   enriched uranium reactors
       BT3   reactors
     BT2   isotope production reactors
       BT3   irradiation reactors
         BT4   reactors
     BT2   pool type reactors
       BT3   water cooled reactors
         BT4   reactors
       BT3   water moderated reactors
         BT4   reactors
     BT2   research reactors
       BT3   research and test reactors
         BT4   reactors

SLOWPOKE-TORONTO REACTOR
[20; 20]
(University of Toronto, Dept. of Chemical Engineering, Toronto, Ontario, Canada)
   UF   *toronto univ. slowpoke reactor*
   UF   *univ. of toronto slowpoke reac*
   BT1   slowpoke type reactors
     BT2   enriched uranium reactors
       BT3   reactors
     BT2   isotope production reactors
       BT3   irradiation reactors
         BT4   reactors
     BT2   pool type reactors
       BT3   water cooled reactors
         BT4   reactors
       BT3   water moderated reactors
         BT4   reactors
     BT2   research reactors
       BT3   research and test reactors
         BT4   reactors

SLOWPOKE-WNRE REACTOR [9; 9]
Oct 86
(Whiteshell Nuclear Research Establishment, Pinawa, Manitoba, Canada.)
   BT1   process heat reactors
     BT2   power reactors
       BT3   reactors
   BT1   slowpoke type reactors
     BT2   enriched uranium reactors
       BT3   reactors
     BT2   isotope production reactors
       BT3   irradiation reactors
         BT4   reactors
     BT2   pool type reactors
       BT3   water cooled reactors
         BT4   reactors
       BT3   water moderated reactors
         BT4   reactors
     BT2   research reactors
       BT3   research and test reactors
         BT4   reactors
   RT   district heating

sludges
   USE   slurries

sludges (sewage)
   USE   sewage sludge

slugs (fuel)
   USE   fuel rods

SLUREX PROCESS [3; 3]
   BT1   separation processes
   RT   leaching
   RT   ore enrichment
   RT   ore processing
   RT   slurries
   RT   solvent extraction
   RT   uranium concentrates

SLURRIES [1,595; 1,595]
   UF   *pulps*
   UF   *sludges*
   BT1   mixtures
     BT2   dispersions
   BT1   suspensions
     BT2   dispersions
   RT   hydraulic transport
   RT   ore processing
   RT   slurex process

slurries (fuel)
   USE   fuel slurries

SLURRY REACTORS [4; 4]
   BT1   fuel dispersion reactors
     BT2   homogeneous reactors
       BT3   reactors
   RT   fuel slurries

SM-1 REACTOR [3; 3]
   UF   *stationary med. pow. plant-1*
   BT1   pwr type reactors
     BT2   enriched uranium reactors
       BT3   reactors
     BT2   power reactors
       BT3   reactors
     BT2   thermal reactors
       BT3   reactors
     BT2   water cooled reactors
       BT3   reactors
     BT2   water moderated reactors
       BT3   reactors

SM-1A REACTOR [2; 2]
   UF   *stationary med. pow. plant-1a*
   BT1   process heat reactors
     BT2   power reactors
       BT3   reactors
   BT1   pwr type reactors
     BT2   enriched uranium reactors
       BT3   reactors
     BT2   power reactors
       BT3   reactors
     BT2   thermal reactors
       BT3   reactors
     BT2   water cooled reactors
       BT3   reactors
     BT2   water moderated reactors
       BT3   reactors

SM-2 REACTOR [82; 82]
   UF   *melekess-sm-2 reactor*
   BT1   materials testing reactors
     BT2   irradiation reactors
       BT3   reactors
   BT1   tank type reactors
     BT2   reactors
   BT1   thermal reactors
     BT2   reactors
   BT1   water cooled reactors
     BT2   reactors
   BT1   water moderated reactors
     BT2   reactors

SMALL ANGLE SCATTERING
[2,102; 2,102]
   UF   *small-angle scattering*
   BT1   scattering
   RT   angular distribution
   RT   optical theorem

SMALL INTESTINE [1,928; 1,928]
   UF   *duodenum*
   UF   *ileum*
   UF   *jejunum*
   BT1   intestines
     BT2   gastrointestinal tract
       BT3   digestive system
     BT2   organs
       BT3   body
   RT   ascaris
   RT   intestinal absorption
   RT   mesentery
   RT   secretin

small-angle scattering
   USE   small angle scattering

SMECTITE [110; 110] *Feb 81*
   BT1   clays
     BT2   silicate minerals
       BT3   minerals
   RT   aluminium silicates

SMELTING [210; 210]
   RT   melting
   RT   pyrometallurgy

smes
(Superconducting Magnetic Energy Storage.)
   USE   superconductive energy storage

smog
   USE   air pollution

smokatron
   USE   electron-ring accelerators

SMOKE DETECTORS [58; 58] *Feb 81*
   UF   *icsd*
   UF   *ionization chamber smoke detec*
   BT1   measuring instruments
   RT   aerosol monitoring
   RT   aerosols
   RT   alarm systems
   RT   fires
   RT   safety engineering
   RT   smokes

SMOKES [262; 712]
   BT1   aerosols
     BT2   sols
       BT3   colloids
         BT4   dispersions
   BT1   residues
   NT1   tobacco smokes
   RT   plumes
   RT   smoke detectors
   RT   stacks
   RT   visibility

SMOKY EVENT [8; 8] *Feb 82*
   BT1   atmospheric explosions
     BT2   explosions
   BT1   nuclear explosions
     BT2   explosions
   BT1   plumbbob project

SMOLENSK-1 REACTOR [16; 16]
Aug 84
   BT1   enriched uranium reactors
     BT2   reactors
   BT1   lwgr type reactors
     BT2   graphite moderated reactors
       BT3   reactors

    BT2   water cooled reactors
      BT3   reactors
    BT1   power reactors
      BT2   reactors
    BT1   thermal reactors
      BT2   reactors

SMOLENSK-2 REACTOR [13; 13]
Aug 84
    BT1   enriched uranium reactors
      BT2   reactors
    BT1   lwgr type reactors
      BT2   graphite moderated reactors
        BT3   reactors
      BT2   water cooled reactors
        BT3   reactors
    BT1   power reactors
      BT2   reactors
    BT1   thermal reactors
      BT2   reactors

SMOOTH MANIFOLDS [1,124; 1,124]
    BT1   mathematical manifolds
    RT   conformal mapping
    RT   differential topology
    RT   riemann space
    RT   topological foliation

smoothness
    USE   roughness

smp devices
    USE   scanning measuring projectors

sn method
    USE   discrete ordinate method

SNAILS [155; 155]
    BT1   molluscs
      BT2   aquatic organisms
      BT2   invertebrates
        BT3   animals
    RT   disease vectors
    RT   schistosomiasis

SNAKES [76; 76]
    BT1   reptiles
      BT2   vertebrates
        BT3   animals

SNAP BATTERIES [45; 104]
(Battery Systems for Nuclear Auxiliary Power.)
    BT1   radioisotope batteries
      BT2   direct energy converters
    NT1   snap 1 battery
    NT1   snap 11 battery
    NT1   snap 13 battery
    NT1   snap 15 battery
    NT1   snap 17 battery
    NT1   snap 19 battery
    NT1   snap 21 battery
    NT1   snap 23 battery
    NT1   snap 25 battery
    NT1   snap 27 battery
    NT1   snap 29 battery
    NT1   snap 3 battery
    NT1   snap 5 battery
    NT1   snap 7 battery
    NT1   snap 9 battery

SNAP REACTORS [222; 237]
(Reactor Systems for Nuclear Auxiliary Power.)
    BT1   space power reactors
      BT2   mobile reactors
        BT3   reactors
      BT2   power reactors
        BT3   reactors
    NT1   snap 10 reactor
      NT2   s10fs-1 reactor
      NT2   s10fs-3 reactor
      NT2   s10fs-4 reactor

    NT1   snap 2 reactor
      NT2   s2ds reactor
    NT1   snap 8 reactor
      NT2   s8dr reactor
      NT2   s8er reactor
    RT   thermionic reactors

SNAP 1 BATTERY [0; 0]
    BT1   snap batteries
      BT2   radioisotope batteries
        BT3   direct energy converters

SNAP 10 REACTOR [4; 6]
    BT1   enriched uranium reactors
      BT2   reactors
    BT1   potassium cooled reactors
      BT2   liquid metal cooled reactors
        BT3   reactors
    BT1   process heat reactors
      BT2   power reactors
        BT3   reactors
    BT1   snap reactors
      BT2   space power reactors
        BT3   mobile reactors
          BT4   reactors
        BT3   power reactors
          BT4   reactors
    BT1   sodium cooled reactors
      BT2   liquid metal cooled reactors
        BT3   reactors
    NT1   s10fs-1 reactor
    NT1   s10fs-3 reactor
    NT1   s10fs-4 reactor

SNAP 11 BATTERY [3; 3]
    BT1   snap batteries
      BT2   radioisotope batteries
        BT3   direct energy converters

SNAP 13 BATTERY [1; 1]
    BT1   snap batteries
      BT2   radioisotope batteries
        BT3   direct energy converters

SNAP 15 BATTERY [0; 0]
    BT1   snap batteries
      BT2   radioisotope batteries
        BT3   direct energy converters

SNAP 17 BATTERY [0; 0]
    BT1   snap batteries
      BT2   radioisotope batteries
        BT3   direct energy converters

SNAP 19 BATTERY [37; 37]
    BT1   snap batteries
      BT2   radioisotope batteries
        BT3   direct energy converters

SNAP 2 REACTOR [2; 2]
    BT1   enriched uranium reactors
      BT2   reactors
    BT1   snap reactors
      BT2   space power reactors
        BT3   mobile reactors
          BT4   reactors
        BT3   power reactors
          BT4   reactors
    NT1   s2ds reactor

SNAP 21 BATTERY [3; 3]
    BT1   snap batteries
      BT2   radioisotope batteries
        BT3   direct energy converters

SNAP 23 BATTERY [4; 4]
    BT1   snap batteries
      BT2   radioisotope batteries
        BT3   direct energy converters

SNAP 25 BATTERY [0; 0]
    BT1   snap batteries
      BT2   radioisotope batteries
        BT3   direct energy converters

SNAP 27 BATTERY [10; 10]
    BT1   snap batteries
      BT2   radioisotope batteries
        BT3   direct energy converters

SNAP 29 BATTERY [1; 1]
    BT1   snap batteries
      BT2   radioisotope batteries
        BT3   direct energy converters

SNAP 3 BATTERY [4; 4]
    BT1   snap batteries
      BT2   radioisotope batteries
        BT3   direct energy converters

SNAP 5 BATTERY [0; 0]
    BT1   snap batteries
      BT2   radioisotope batteries
        BT3   direct energy converters

SNAP 7 BATTERY [0; 0]
    BT1   snap batteries
      BT2   radioisotope batteries
        BT3   direct energy converters

SNAP 8 REACTOR [8; 16]
    BT1   enriched uranium reactors
      BT2   reactors
    BT1   snap reactors
      BT2   space power reactors
        BT3   mobile reactors
          BT4   reactors
        BT3   power reactors
          BT4   reactors
    NT1   s8dr reactor
    NT1   s8er reactor

SNAP 9 BATTERY [6; 6]
    BT1   snap batteries
      BT2   radioisotope batteries
        BT3   direct energy converters

snap-10a flight syst. test-1
    USE   s10fs-1 reactor

snap-10a flight syst. test-3
    USE   s10fs-3 reactor

snap-10a flight syst. test-4
    USE   s10fs-4 reactor

snap-10a transient test react.
    USE   snaptran reactors

snap-2 developmental system
    USE   s2ds reactor

snap-2 experimental reactor
    USE   ser reactor

snap-8 developmental reactor
    USE   s8dr reactor

snap-8 experimental reactor
    USE   s8er reactor

SNAPTRAN REACTORS [8; 8]
    UF   *snap-10a transient test react.*
    UF   *snaptran-1 reactor*
    UF   *snaptran-2 reactor*
    UF   *snaptran-3 reactor*
    BT1   enriched uranium reactors
      BT2   reactors
    BT1   nak cooled reactors
      BT2   liquid metal cooled reactor
        BT3   reactors
    BT1   potassium cooled reactors
      BT2   liquid metal cooled reactor

BT3 reactors
BT1 sodium cooled reactors
BT2 liquid metal cooled reactors
BT3 reactors
BT1 test reactors
BT2 research and test reactors
BT3 reactors
BT2 test facilities

snaptran-1 reactor
   USE   snaptran reactors

snaptran-2 reactor
   USE   snaptran reactors

snaptran-3 reactor
   USE   snaptran reactors

SNEAK REACTOR [84; 84]
(Gesellschaft fuer Kernforschung mbH, Karlsruhe, Baden-Wuerttemberg, Federal Republic of Germany)
   UF   *schnelle null-en. anord./kar*
BT1 air cooled reactors
BT2 gas cooled reactors
BT3 reactors
BT1 fast reactors
BT2 epithermal reactors
BT3 reactors
BT1 research reactors
BT2 research and test reactors
BT3 reactors
BT1 zero power reactors
BT2 experimental reactors
BT3 research and test reactors
BT4 reactors
RT enriched uranium reactors
RT plutonium reactors

SNELL EXPERIMENT [0; 0]
RT fission

SNOW [328; 328]
BT1 atmospheric precipitations
RT antarctic regions
RT arctic regions
RT glaciers
RT ice
RT rain

SNR REACTOR [1,170; 1,170]
(Kalkar, North Rhine Westfalia, Federal Republic of Germany)
   UF   *schneller natriumgekuehlter re*
   UF   *snr-1 reactor*
   UF   *snr-300 reactor*
BT1 lmfbr type reactors
BT2 fbr type reactors
BT3 breeder reactors
BT4 reactors
BT3 fast reactors
BT4 epithermal reactors
BT5 reactors
BT2 liquid metal cooled reactors
BT3 reactors
BT1 power reactors
BT2 reactors
BT1 sodium cooled reactors
BT2 liquid metal cooled reactors
BT3 reactors

snr-1 reactor
   USE   snr reactor

SNR-2 REACTOR [108; 108] *Oct 76*
(Kalkar, North Rhine Westfalia, Federal Republic of Germany)
BT1 lmfbr type reactors
BT2 fbr type reactors
BT3 breeder reactors
BT4 reactors
BT3 fast reactors
BT4 epithermal reactors
BT5 reactors
BT2 liquid metal cooled reactors
BT3 reactors
BT1 power reactors
BT2 reactors
BT1 sodium cooled reactors
BT2 liquid metal cooled reactors
BT3 reactors

snr-300 reactor
   USE   snr reactor

SO GROUPS [1,361; 2,790]
BT1 lie groups
BT2 symmetry groups
NT1 so-10 groups
NT1 so-12 groups
NT1 so-2 groups
NT1 so-3 groups
NT1 so-4 groups
NT1 so-6 groups
NT1 so-8 groups

SO-10 GROUPS [512; 512] *Mar 81*
BT1 so groups
BT2 lie groups
BT3 symmetry groups

SO-12 GROUPS [19; 19] *Jan 86*
BT1 so groups
BT2 lie groups
BT3 symmetry groups

SO-2 GROUPS [224; 224] *Feb 78*
BT1 so groups
BT2 lie groups
BT3 symmetry groups

SO-3 GROUPS [574; 574]
BT1 so groups
BT2 lie groups
BT3 symmetry groups

SO-4 GROUPS [238; 238] *Oct 77*
BT1 so groups
BT2 lie groups
BT3 symmetry groups

SO-6 GROUPS [114; 114] *Sep 81*
BT1 so groups
BT2 lie groups
BT3 symmetry groups

SO-8 GROUPS [70; 70] *Apr 87*
BT1 so groups
BT2 lie groups
BT3 symmetry groups

SOAPS [82; 82]
BT1 other organic compounds
BT2 organic compounds
RT detergents
RT emulsifiers
RT organic acids

socio-economic aspects
(Prior to December 1985 this was a valid descriptor.)
   USE   socio-economic factors

SOCIO-ECONOMIC FACTORS [1,433; 1,433] *Dec 82*
(Prior to December 1985 SOCIO-ECONOMIC ASPECTS was used for this concept.)
UF *socio-economic aspects*
RT aesthetics
RT economic impact
RT economics
RT financial incentives
RT political aspects
RT recreational areas
RT sociology
RT technology impacts

SOCIOLOGY [1,985; 1,985]
RT aesthetics
RT ethical aspects
RT historical aspects
RT human factors
RT human populations
RT man
RT occupations
RT public relations
RT regional analysis
RT socio-economic factors
RT urban populations

sod
   USE   superoxide dismutase

sod (soil)
   USE   soils

SODDYITE [3; 3]
BT1 silicate minerals
BT2 minerals
BT1 uranium minerals
BT2 radioactive minerals
BT3 minerals
BT3 radioactive materials
BT4 materials
RT uranium silicates

SODIUM [11,638; 11,638]
BT1 alkali metals
BT2 metals
BT3 elements

SODIUM ADDITIONS [115; 115]
(Alloys containing not more than 1% Na are listed here.)
RT sodium alloys
RT sodium compounds

SODIUM ALLOYS [316; 338]
(Alloys containing more than 1% Na.)
UF+ *nak*
BT1 alloys
NT1 sodium base alloys
RT sodium additions

sodium aminoethylthiophosphate
   USE   cystaphos

SODIUM BASE ALLOYS [20; 20]
BT1 sodium alloys
BT2 alloys

SODIUM BORIDES [16; 16]
BT1 borides
BT2 boron compounds
BT1 sodium compounds
BT2 alkali metal compounds

SODIUM BROMIDES [215; 215]
BT1 bromides
BT2 bromine compounds
BT3 halogen compounds
BT2 halides
BT3 halogen compounds
BT1 sodium compounds
BT2 alkali metal compounds

SODIUM CARBIDES [10; 10]
BT1 carbides
BT2 carbon compounds
BT1 sodium compounds
BT2 alkali metal compounds

SODIUM CARBONATES [619; 619]
BT1 carbonates
BT2 carbon compounds
BT2 oxygen compounds
BT1 sodium compounds
BT2 alkali metal compounds
RT carbonate minerals

SODIUM CHLORIDES [3,341; 3,341]
BT1 chlorides
BT2 chlorine compounds
BT3 halogen compounds
BT2 halides
BT3 halogen compounds
BT1 sodium compounds
BT2 alkali metal compounds

SODIUM COMPLEXES [98; 98]
BT1 alkali metal complexes
BT2 complexes

SODIUM COMPOUNDS [3,565; 13,706]
BT1 alkali metal compounds
NT1 borax
NT1 hypaque
NT1 rochelle salt
NT1 sodium borides
NT1 sodium bromides
NT1 sodium carbides
NT1 sodium carbonates
NT1 sodium chlorides
NT1 sodium fluorides
NT1 sodium hydrides
NT1 sodium hydroxides
NT1 sodium iodides
NT1 sodium nitrates
NT1 sodium nitrides
NT1 sodium oxides
NT1 sodium perchlorates
NT1 sodium phosphates
NT1 sodium selenides
NT1 sodium silicates
NT1 sodium silicides
NT1 sodium sulfates
NT1 sodium sulfides
NT1 sodium tellurides
NT1 sodium tungstates
NT1 sodium uranates
NT1 tiron
RT sodium additions

sodium cooled graphite mod. re
USE sgr type reactors

SODIUM COOLED REACTORS [1,885; 9,704]
UF *sodium-cooled reactors*
BT1 liquid metal cooled reactors
BT2 reactors
NT1 beloyarsk-3 reactor
NT1 beloyarsk-4 reactor
NT1 bn-1600 reactor
NT1 bn-350 reactor
NT1 bn-800 reactor
NT1 bor-60 reactor
NT1 cdfr reactor
NT1 clinch river breeder reactor
NT1 ebr-1 reactor
NT1 ebr-2 reactor
NT1 enrico fermi-1 reactor
NT1 fftf reactor
NT1 hnpf reactor
NT1 knk reactor
NT1 knk-2 reactor
NT1 lampre-1 reactor
NT1 monju reactor
NT1 pfr reactor
NT1 phenix reactor
NT1 rapsodie reactor
NT1 sbr-5 reactor
NT1 sefor reactor
NT1 ser reactor
NT1 sgr type reactors
NT2 sre reactor
NT1 snap 10 reactor
NT2 s10fs-1 reactor
NT2 s10fs-3 reactor
NT2 s10fs-4 reactor
NT1 snaptran reactors
NT1 snr reactor
NT1 snr-2 reactor
NT1 super phenix reactor
NT1 zrr reactor
RT nak cooled reactors

sodium cooled zirc. hydr. mode
USE szr type reactors

SODIUM FLUORIDES [896; 896]
BT1 fluorides
BT2 fluorine compounds
BT3 halogen compounds
BT2 halides
BT3 halogen compounds
BT1 sodium compounds
BT2 alkali metal compounds

SODIUM HYDRIDES [122; 122]
BT1 hydrides
BT2 hydrogen compounds
BT1 sodium compounds
BT2 alkali metal compounds

SODIUM HYDROXIDES [1,313; 1,313]
BT1 hydroxides
BT2 hydrogen compounds
BT2 oxygen compounds
BT1 sodium compounds
BT2 alkali metal compounds

sodium iodide detectors
USE nai detectors

SODIUM IODIDES [1,406; 1,406]
BT1 iodides
BT2 halides
BT3 halogen compounds
BT2 iodine compounds
BT3 halogen compounds
BT1 sodium compounds
BT2 alkali metal compounds

sodium iodohippurate
USE hippuran

SODIUM IONS [797; 797]
BT1 ions
BT2 charged particles

SODIUM ISOTOPES [159; 3,186]
NT1 sodium 19
NT1 sodium 20
NT1 sodium 21
NT1 sodium 22
NT1 sodium 23
NT1 sodium 24
NT1 sodium 25
NT1 sodium 26
NT1 sodium 27
NT1 sodium 28
NT1 sodium 29
NT1 sodium 30
NT1 sodium 31
NT1 sodium 32
NT1 sodium 33
NT1 sodium 34
NT1 sodium 35

sodium n-o-iodobenzoylaminoace
USE hippuran

SODIUM NITRATES [598; 598]
BT1 nitrates
BT2 nitrogen compounds
BT2 oxygen compounds
BT1 sodium compounds
BT2 alkali metal compounds

SODIUM NITRIDES [16; 16] *Feb 80*
BT1 nitrides
BT2 nitrogen compounds
BT2 pnictides
BT1 sodium compounds
BT2 alkali metal compounds

sodium orthoiodohippurate
USE hippuran

SODIUM OXIDES [802; 803]
BT1 oxides
BT2 chalcogenides
BT2 oxygen compounds
BT1 sodium compounds
BT2 alkali metal compounds
RT clarkeite
RT oxide minerals

SODIUM PERCHLORATES [202; 202]
BT1 perchlorates
BT2 chlorine compounds
BT3 halogen compounds
BT2 oxygen compounds
BT1 sodium compounds
BT2 alkali metal compounds

SODIUM PHOSPHATES [351; 351]
BT1 phosphates
BT2 oxygen compounds
BT2 phosphorus compounds
BT1 sodium compounds
BT2 alkali metal compounds

sodium reactor experiment
USE sre reactor

→ **SODIUM SELENIDES** [0; 0] *Sep 91*
BT1 selenides
BT2 chalcogenides
BT2 selenium compounds
BT1 sodium compounds
BT2 alkali metal compounds

SODIUM SILICATES [250; 252]
BT1 silicates
BT2 oxygen compounds
BT2 silicon compounds
BT1 sodium compounds
BT2 alkali metal compounds
RT catapleite
RT elpidite
RT pollucite
RT silicate minerals

SODIUM SILICIDES [5; 5] *Jun 77*
BT1 silicides
BT2 silicon compounds
BT1 sodium compounds
BT2 alkali metal compounds

SODIUM SULFATES [634; 635]
BT1 sodium compounds
BT2 alkali metal compounds
BT1 sulfates
BT2 oxygen compounds
BT2 sulfur compounds
RT schroeckingerite
RT sulfate minerals

SODIUM SULFIDES [101; 101]
BT1 sodium compounds
BT2 alkali metal compounds
BT1 sulfides
BT2 chalcogenides
BT2 sulfur compounds

SODIUM TELLURIDES [18; 18] *Feb*
BT1 sodium compounds
BT2 alkali metal compounds
BT1 tellurides
BT2 chalcogenides
BT2 tellurium compounds

SODIUM TUNGSTATES [162; 162] *Oct 76*
BT1 sodium compounds
BT2 alkali metal compounds
BT1 tungstates
BT2 oxygen compounds
BT2 tungsten compounds
BT3 transition element compou

SODIUM URANATES [49; 49]
  BT1 sodium compounds
    BT2 alkali metal compounds
  BT1 uranates
    BT2 uranium compounds
      BT3 actinide compounds

SODIUM 19 [5; 5]
  BT1 beta-plus decay radioisotopes
    BT2 beta decay radioisotopes
      BT3 radioisotopes
        BT4 isotopes
  BT1 light nuclei
    BT2 nuclei
  BT1 millisec living radioisotopes
    BT2 radioisotopes
      BT3 isotopes
  BT1 odd-even nuclei
    BT2 nuclei
  BT1 sodium isotopes

SODIUM 20 [68; 68]
  BT1 beta-plus decay radioisotopes
    BT2 beta decay radioisotopes
      BT3 radioisotopes
        BT4 isotopes
  BT1 light nuclei
    BT2 nuclei
  BT1 odd-odd nuclei
    BT2 nuclei
  BT1 seconds living radioisotopes
    BT2 radioisotopes
      BT3 isotopes
  BT1 sodium isotopes

SODIUM 21 [100; 100]
  BT1 beta-plus decay radioisotopes
    BT2 beta decay radioisotopes
      BT3 radioisotopes
        BT4 isotopes
  BT1 light nuclei
    BT2 nuclei
  BT1 odd-even nuclei
    BT2 nuclei
  BT1 seconds living radioisotopes
    BT2 radioisotopes
      BT3 isotopes
  BT1 sodium isotopes

SODIUM 21 TARGET [2; 2] *Dec 86*
  BT1 targets

SODIUM 22 [1,215; 1,215]
  BT1 beta-plus decay radioisotopes
    BT2 beta decay radioisotopes
      BT3 radioisotopes
        BT4 isotopes
  BT1 isomeric transition isotopes
    BT2 radioisotopes
      BT3 isotopes
  BT1 light nuclei
    BT2 nuclei
  BT1 nanosec living radioisotopes
    BT2 radioisotopes
      BT3 isotopes
  BT1 odd-odd nuclei
    BT2 nuclei
  BT1 sodium isotopes
  BT1 years living radioisotopes
    BT2 radioisotopes
      BT3 isotopes

SODIUM 22 TARGET [32; 32] *Oct 76*
  BT1 targets

SODIUM 23 [732; 732]
  BT1 light nuclei
    BT2 nuclei
  BT1 odd-even nuclei
    BT2 nuclei
  BT1 sodium isotopes
  BT1 stable isotopes
    BT2 isotopes
  RT   sodium 23 beams

SODIUM 23 BEAMS [63; 63] *Jul 76*
  BT1 ion beams
    BT2 beams
  RT   sodium 23

SODIUM 23 REACTIONS [57; 57]
Sep 78
  BT1 heavy ion reactions
    BT2 nuclear reactions

SODIUM 23 TARGET [351; 351]
  BT1 targets

SODIUM 24 [1,011; 1,011]
  BT1 beta-minus decay radioisotopes
    BT2 beta decay radioisotopes
      BT3 radioisotopes
        BT4 isotopes
  BT1 hours living radioisotopes
    BT2 radioisotopes
      BT3 isotopes
  BT1 isomeric transition isotopes
    BT2 radioisotopes
      BT3 isotopes
  BT1 light nuclei
    BT2 nuclei
  BT1 millisec living radioisotopes
    BT2 radioisotopes
      BT3 isotopes
  BT1 odd-odd nuclei
    BT2 nuclei
  BT1 sodium isotopes

SODIUM 25 [59; 59]
  BT1 beta-minus decay radioisotopes
    BT2 beta decay radioisotopes
      BT3 radioisotopes
        BT4 isotopes
  BT1 light nuclei
    BT2 nuclei
  BT1 odd-even nuclei
    BT2 nuclei
  BT1 seconds living radioisotopes
    BT2 radioisotopes
      BT3 isotopes
  BT1 sodium isotopes

SODIUM 26 [21; 21]
  BT1 beta-minus decay radioisotopes
    BT2 beta decay radioisotopes
      BT3 radioisotopes
        BT4 isotopes
  BT1 light nuclei
    BT2 nuclei
  BT1 odd-odd nuclei
    BT2 nuclei
  BT1 seconds living radioisotopes
    BT2 radioisotopes
      BT3 isotopes
  BT1 sodium isotopes

SODIUM 27 [25; 25]
  BT1 beta-minus decay radioisotopes
    BT2 beta decay radioisotopes
      BT3 radioisotopes
        BT4 isotopes
  BT1 light nuclei
    BT2 nuclei
  BT1 millisec living radioisotopes
    BT2 radioisotopes
      BT3 isotopes
  BT1 odd-even nuclei
    BT2 nuclei
  BT1 sodium isotopes

SODIUM 28 [22; 22]
  BT1 beta-minus decay radioisotopes
    BT2 beta decay radioisotopes
      BT3 radioisotopes
        BT4 isotopes
  BT1 light nuclei
    BT2 nuclei
  BT1 millisec living radioisotopes
    BT2 radioisotopes
      BT3 isotopes
  BT1 odd-odd nuclei
    BT2 nuclei
  BT1 sodium isotopes

SODIUM 29 [31; 31]
  BT1 beta-minus decay radioisotopes
    BT2 beta decay radioisotopes
      BT3 radioisotopes
        BT4 isotopes
  BT1 light nuclei
    BT2 nuclei
  BT1 millisec living radioisotopes
    BT2 radioisotopes
      BT3 isotopes
  BT1 odd-even nuclei
    BT2 nuclei
  BT1 sodium isotopes

SODIUM 30 [34; 34]
  BT1 beta-minus decay radioisotopes
    BT2 beta decay radioisotopes
      BT3 radioisotopes
        BT4 isotopes
  BT1 light nuclei
    BT2 nuclei
  BT1 millisec living radioisotopes
    BT2 radioisotopes
      BT3 isotopes
  BT1 odd-odd nuclei
    BT2 nuclei
  BT1 sodium isotopes

SODIUM 31 [31; 31]
  BT1 beta-minus decay radioisotopes
    BT2 beta decay radioisotopes
      BT3 radioisotopes
        BT4 isotopes
  BT1 light nuclei
    BT2 nuclei
  BT1 millisec living radioisotopes
    BT2 radioisotopes
      BT3 isotopes
  BT1 odd-even nuclei
    BT2 nuclei
  BT1 sodium isotopes

SODIUM 32 [28; 28]
  BT1 beta-minus decay radioisotopes
    BT2 beta decay radioisotopes
      BT3 radioisotopes
        BT4 isotopes
  BT1 light nuclei
    BT2 nuclei
  BT1 millisec living radioisotopes
    BT2 radioisotopes
      BT3 isotopes
  BT1 odd-odd nuclei
    BT2 nuclei
  BT1 sodium isotopes

SODIUM 33 [10; 10]
  BT1 beta-minus decay radioisotopes
    BT2 beta decay radioisotopes
      BT3 radioisotopes
        BT4 isotopes
  BT1 light nuclei
    BT2 nuclei
  BT1 millisec living radioisotopes
    BT2 radioisotopes
      BT3 isotopes
  BT1 odd-even nuclei
    BT2 nuclei
  BT1 sodium isotopes

SODIUM 34 [5; 5] *Jun 84*
  BT1 beta-minus decay radioisotopes
    BT2 beta decay radioisotopes
      BT3 radioisotopes
        BT4 isotopes
  BT1 light nuclei
    BT2 nuclei
  BT1 millisec living radioisotopes
    BT2 radioisotopes
      BT3 isotopes
  BT1 odd-odd nuclei
    BT2 nuclei
  BT1 sodium isotopes

SODIUM 35 [5; 5] *Feb 84*
- BT1 beta-minus decay radioisotopes
- BT2 beta decay radioisotopes
- BT3 radioisotopes
- BT4 isotopes
- BT1 light nuclei
- BT2 nuclei
- BT1 millisec living radioisotopes
- BT2 radioisotopes
- BT3 isotopes
- BT1 odd-even nuclei
- BT2 nuclei
- BT1 sodium isotopes

sodium(liquid)-water reactions
- USE molten metal-water reactions

sodium-cooled reactors
- USE sodium cooled reactors

sofia irt-2000 reactor
- USE irt-sofia reactor

SOFT COMPONENT [104; 104]
- BT1 cosmic radiation
- BT2 ionizing radiations
- BT3 radiations

soft soldering
- USE soldering

SOFT X RADIATION [3,075; 3,075]
- BT1 x radiation
- BT2 electromagnetic radiation
- BT3 radiations
- BT2 ionizing radiations
- BT3 radiations

SOFT-CORE POTENTIAL [446; 446]
- BT1 nuclear potential
- BT2 potentials

SOIL MECHANICS [225; 225] *Mar 77*
(Application of principles of mechanics and geology to quantify the response of soils to environmental forces.)
- BT1 mechanics
- RT earth crust
- RT ground water
- RT rock mechanics
- RT soils

SOIL-STRUCTURE INTERACTIONS [551; 551] *Oct 84*
- RT buildings
- RT dynamic loads
- RT earthquakes
- RT foundations
- RT ground motion
- RT mechanical structures
- RT seismic effects
- RT seismic isolation
- RT shock waves
- RT slope stability

SOILS [10,694; 10,770]
- UF sod (soil)
- NT1 loam
- RT aerobacter
- RT agriculture
- RT alluvial deposits
- RT clays
- RT ecosystems
- RT environmental materials
- RT fallout deposits
- RT fulvic acids
- RT ground water
- RT humic acids
- RT humus
- RT irrigation
- RT nitrogen fixation
- RT overburden
- RT peat
- RT plants
- RT proteus
- RT radionuclide migration
- RT roots
- RT sand
- RT soil mechanics
- RT terrestrial ecosystems

soja bean oil
- USE soybean oil

SOL-GEL PROCESS [440; 440]
- RT colloids
- RT fuel cycle
- RT gelation
- RT reprocessing

SOLANUM [26; 66] *Jan 79*
- BT1 plants
- NT1 solanum tuberosum

SOLANUM TUBEROSUM [62; 62]
- UF potato plant
- BT1 solanum
- BT2 plants
- RT potatoes

SOLAR ACTIVITY [2,317; 13,399]
- NT1 faculae
- NT1 plages
- NT1 solar flares
- NT1 solar granulation
- NT1 solar prominences
- NT1 solar radio bursts
- NT1 solar wind
- NT1 solar x-ray bursts
- NT1 sunspots
- RT activity levels
- RT solar cycle
- RT sun

SOLAR ALPHA PARTICLES [41; 41] *Nov 75*
(Prior to August 1985 this concept was expressed by coordination of ALPHA PARTICLES and ENERGETIC SOLAR PARTICLES.)
- BT1 alpha particles
- BT2 helium ions
- BT3 ions
- BT4 charged particles
- BT2 ionizing radiations
- BT3 radiations
- BT1 solar particles
- BT2 solar radiation
- BT3 stellar radiation
- BT4 radiations

SOLAR ATMOSPHERE [1,450; 3,709]
- BT1 stellar atmospheres
- BT2 atmospheres
- NT1 chromosphere
- NT1 heliosphere
- NT1 photosphere
- NT1 solar corona
- RT sun

SOLAR CELLS [633; 854]
- BT1 direct energy converters
- BT1 electronic equipment
- BT2 equipment
- NT1 silicon solar cells
- RT photoelectric cells
- RT photovoltaic cells
- RT solar collectors

SOLAR COLLECTORS [0; 0] *Dec 90*
- BT1 equipment
- RT solar cells
- RT solar furnaces

SOLAR CONSTANT [52; 52] *Jan 79*
(Solar energy flux just outside the earth's atmosphere at the earth's mean distance from the sun.)
- RT solar radiation

SOLAR CORONA [3,036; 3,036]
- UF corona (solar)
- BT1 solar atmosphere
- BT2 stellar atmospheres
- BT3 atmospheres
- BT1 stellar coronae
- BT2 stellar atmospheres
- BT3 atmospheres
- RT solar prominences
- RT solar wind
- RT sun

SOLAR CYCLE [1,476; 1,476]
- RT international solar maximum ye
- RT solar activity
- RT sun
- RT sunspots

solar distillation
- USE distillation
- AND solar energy

solar drying
- USE drying

solar electron events
(Prior to August 1985 this concept was expressed by coordination of ELECTRON and ENERGETIC SOLAR PARTICLES.)
- USE solar electrons

SOLAR ELECTRONS [209; 209] *Jan 7*
(Prior to August 1985 this concept was expressed by coordination of ELECTRON and ENERGETIC SOLAR PARTICLES.
- UF solar electron events
- BT1 electrons
- BT2 leptons
- BT3 elementary particles
- BT3 fermions
- BT1 solar particles
- BT2 solar radiation
- BT3 stellar radiation
- BT4 radiations

SOLAR ENERGY [598; 598]
- UF+ solar distillation
- UF+ solar heating
- BT1 energy
- BT1 renewable energy sources
- BT2 energy sources
- RT solar radiation
- RT sun

SOLAR FLARES [4,756; 4,756]
- BT1 solar activity
- BT1 stellar flares
- BT2 stellar activity
- RT chromosphere
- RT forbush decrease
- RT solar particles
- RT solar radiation
- RT solar radio bursts
- RT solar wind
- RT solar x-ray bursts
- RT space flight
- RT sun
- RT sunspots
- RT supersonic transport

SOLAR FURNACES [44; 44]
- BT1 equipment
- BT1 furnaces
- RT solar collectors

SOLAR GRANULATION [370; 370]
  UF   *granulation (solar)*
  UF   *supergranulation*
  BT1   solar activity
  RT   photosphere
  RT   sun

solar heating
  USE   heating
  AND   solar energy

solar models
  USE   star models

SOLAR NEBULA [353; 353]
  BT1   nebulae
  RT   cosmological models
  RT   protoplanets
  RT   solar system evolution

SOLAR NEUTRINOS [879; 879] *Nov 75*
(Prior to August 1985 this concept was expressed by coordination of ENERGETIC SOLAR PARTICLES and NEUTRINOS.)
  BT1   neutrinos
    BT2   leptons
      BT3   elementary particles
      BT3   fermions
    BT2   massless particles
      BT3   elementary particles
  BT1   solar particles
    BT2   solar radiation
      BT3   stellar radiation
        BT4   radiations

SOLAR NEUTRONS [70; 70] *Jul 76*
(Prior to August 1985 this concept was expressed by coordination of ENERGETIC SOLAR PARTICLES and NEUTRONS.)
  BT1   neutrons
    BT2   nucleons
      BT3   baryons
        BT4   fermions
        BT4   hadrons
          BT5   elementary particles
  BT1   solar particles
    BT2   solar radiation
      BT3   stellar radiation
        BT4   radiations

solar occultation
  USE   eclipse

SOLAR PARTICLES [1,406; 2,730]
(Prior to December 1985 SOLAR RADIATION was used for this concept except where ENERGETIC SOLAR PARTICLES was appropriate.)
  UF   *energetic solar particles*
  BT1   solar radiation
    BT2   stellar radiation
      BT3   radiations
  NT1   solar alpha particles
  NT1   solar electrons
  NT1   solar neutrinos
  NT1   solar neutrons
  NT1   solar protons
  RT   polar-cap absorption
  RT   solar flares

SOLAR POWER PLANTS [150; 150]
Jul 76
  UF   *photovoltaic power plants*
  BT1   power plants

SOLAR PROMINENCES [779; 779]
  UF   *prominences (solar)*
  UF   *spicules*
  BT1   solar activity
  RT   solar corona
  RT   sun

solar proton events
(Prior to August 1985 this concept was expressed by coordination of ENERGETIC SOLAR PARTICLES and PROTONS.)
  USE   solar protons

SOLAR PROTONS [290; 290] *Nov 75*
(Prior to August 1985 this concept was expressed by coordination of ENERGETIC SOLAR PARTICLES and PROTONS.)
  UF   *solar proton events*
  UF   *spe*
  BT1   protons
    BT2   hydrogen ions 1 plus
      BT3   cations
        BT4   ions
          BT5   charged particles
      BT3   hydrogen ions
        BT4   ions
          BT5   charged particles
    BT2   nucleons
      BT3   baryons
        BT4   fermions
        BT4   hadrons
          BT5   elementary particles
  BT1   solar particles
    BT2   solar radiation
      BT3   stellar radiation
        BT4   radiations

SOLAR RADIATION [3,601; 6,112]
  UF   *insolation*
  UF+   *solar radiowave radiation*
  BT1   stellar radiation
    BT2   radiations
  NT1   solar particles
    NT2   solar alpha particles
    NT2   solar electrons
    NT2   solar neutrinos
    NT2   solar neutrons
    NT2   solar protons
  RT   cosmic radiation
  RT   solar constant
  RT   solar energy
  RT   solar flares
  RT   solar radio bursts
  RT   solar wind
  RT   solar x-ray bursts
  RT   sun
  RT   zodiacal light

SOLAR RADIO BURSTS [1,250; 1,250]
  BT1   radiowave radiation
    BT2   electromagnetic radiation
      BT3   radiations
  BT1   solar activity
  RT   radioastronomy
  RT   solar flares
  RT   solar radiation
  RT   sun

solar radiowave radiation
  USE   radiowave radiation
  AND   solar radiation

SOLAR SYSTEM [1,358; 1,358]
  RT   asteroids
  RT   comets
  RT   halley comet
  RT   interplanetary space
  RT   meteoroids
  RT   planets
  RT   solar system evolution
  RT   sun

SOLAR SYSTEM EVOLUTION [1,382; 1,382]
  UF   *planetary evolution*
  RT   planet-system accretion
  RT   protoplanets
  RT   solar nebula
  RT   solar system
  RT   star evolution

SOLAR WIND [5,004; 5,004]
  BT1   solar activity
  BT1   stellar winds
    BT2   stellar activity
  RT   chapman-ferraro problem
  RT   expansion
  RT   forbush decrease
  RT   geocorona
  RT   loss cone
  RT   magnetosheath
  RT   plasma
  RT   radiation pressure
  RT   solar corona
  RT   solar flares
  RT   solar radiation
  RT   sun

SOLAR X-RAY BURSTS [679; 679]
  BT1   solar activity
  RT   solar flares
  RT   solar radiation
  RT   sun
  RT   x radiation

SOLAS CONVENTION [20; 20]
(London Convention on Safety of Life at Sea)
  UF   *london safety of life at sea c*
  UF   *safety of life at sea conv.*
  UF   *sea, safety of life at, conv.*
  BT1   international agreements
    BT2   agreements
  RT   civil liability
  RT   nuclear ships
  RT   recommendations

SOLDERED JOINTS [133; 133]
  BT1   joints
  RT   soldering

SOLDERING [141; 141]
  UF   *soft soldering*
  BT1   welding
    BT2   joining
      BT3   fabrication
  RT   brazing
  RT   soldered joints

soldering fluxes
  USE   metallurgical flux

SOLENOIDS [1,669; 1,669]
  UF   *inductors*
  UF+   *superconducting solenoids*
  BT1   electric coils
    BT2   electrical equipment
      BT3   equipment
  RT   actuators
  RT   magnet coils

SOLID CLUSTERS [1,110; 1,110]
  UF   *clusters (solid)*
  RT   solids

SOLID ELECTROLYTES [350; 350]
Oct 81
  BT1   electrolytes

SOLID FUELS [548; 2,608]
(Limited to nuclear fuels.)
  BT1   nuclear fuels
    BT2   energy sources
    BT2   fuels
    BT2   reactor materials
      BT3   materials
  NT1   alloy nuclear fuels
  NT1   dispersion nuclear fuels
  NT1   mixed carbide fuels
  NT1   mixed nitride fuels
  NT1   mixed oxide fuels

SOLID HOMOGENEOUS REACTORS [8; 3,456]
- BT1 homogeneous reactors
- BT2 reactors
- NT1 acpr reactor
- NT1 aerojet-general nucleonics r
- NT1 anex reactor
- NT1 ebor reactor
- NT1 nsrr reactor
- NT1 pebble bed reactors
  - NT2 avr reactor
  - NT2 thtr-300 reactor
  - NT2 vg-400 reactor
  - NT2 vgr-50 reactor
- NT1 romashka reactor
- NT1 shca reactor
- NT1 sur-100 series reactor
- NT1 treat reactor
- NT1 triga type reactors
  - NT2 afrri reactor
  - NT2 cornell triga-mk-2 reactor
  - NT2 dow triga-mk-1 reactor
  - NT2 fir-1 reactor
  - NT2 frf-2 reactor
  - NT2 frn reactor
  - NT2 gulf triga-mk-3 reactor
  - NT2 lopra reactor
  - NT2 nscr reactor
  - NT2 ostr reactor
  - NT2 prpr reactor
  - NT2 pstr reactor
  - NT2 rtp reactor
  - NT2 trico reactor
  - NT2 triga-brazil reactor
  - NT2 triga-texas reactor
  - NT2 triga-veterans reactor
  - NT2 triga-1-arizona reactor
  - NT2 triga-1-california reactor
  - NT2 triga-1-hanford reactor
  - NT2 triga-1-hanover reactor
  - NT2 triga-1-heidelberg reactor
  - NT2 triga-1-michigan reactor
  - NT2 triga-2 reactor
  - NT2 triga-2-dalat reactor
  - NT2 triga-2-illinois reactor
  - NT2 triga-2-kansas reactor
  - NT2 triga-2-ljubljana reactor
  - NT2 triga-2-mainz reactor
  - NT2 triga-2-musashi reactor
  - NT2 triga-2-pavia reactor
  - NT2 triga-2-rikkyo reactor
  - NT2 triga-2-rome reactor
  - NT2 triga-2-seoul reactor
  - NT2 triga-2-vienna reactor
  - NT2 triga-3-la jolla reactor
  - NT2 triga-3-salazar reactor
  - NT2 triga-3-seoul reactor
  - NT2 ucbrr reactor
  - NT2 wsur reactor

SOLID LUBRICANTS [76; 76]
- BT1 lubricants
- RT graphite

SOLID SCINTILLATION DETECTORS [2,302; 5,863]
- BT1 scintillation counters
  - BT2 radiation detectors
    - BT3 measuring instruments
- NT1 bgo detectors
- NT1 nai detectors
- NT1 plastic scintillation detector
- RT glass scintillators
- RT inorganic phosphors
- RT organic crystal phosphors

SOLID SOLUTIONS [10,016; 10,016]
- BT1 solutions
  - BT2 homogeneous mixtures
    - BT3 mixtures
      - BT4 dispersions
- RT alloys
- RT austenite
- RT ferrite
- RT phase diagrams
- RT solids
- RT superlattices

SOLID STATE LASERS [447; 2,921]
- UF *solid-state lasers*
- BT1 lasers
  - BT2 amplifiers
    - BT3 equipment
- NT1 neodymium lasers
- NT1 ruby lasers
- NT1 semiconductor lasers

SOLID STATE PHYSICS [663; 663]
Aug 76
(Use only for articles of a very broad nature such as an annual research program, etc.)
- UF *solid-state physics*
- BT1 physics
- RT crystal structure
- RT semiconductor devices
- RT semiconductor materials

solid state plasma
- USE solid-state plasma

SOLID WASTES [3,719; 6,051]
- UF *refuse*
- BT1 wastes
- NT1 ashes
  - NT2 fly ash
- NT1 scrap
- NT1 tailings
  - NT2 mill tailings
- NT1 waste pellets
- RT biological wastes
- RT calcined wastes
- RT combustion products
- RT dredge spoil
- RT ground disposal
- RT municipal wastes
- RT waste disposal

solid-state lasers
- USE solid state lasers

solid-state physics
- USE solid state physics

SOLID-STATE PLASMA [1,064; 1,064]
- UF *electron-hole plasma*
- UF *solid state plasma*
- BT1 plasma
- RT electron gas
- RT electron-hole droplets
- RT plasmons

SOLIDIFICATION [5,364; 5,364]
- UF *fixation (waste treatment)*
- SF *immobilization (wastes)*
- RT castings
- RT crystallization
- RT freezing
- RT melting
- RT phase transformations
- RT segregation
- RT solids
- RT vitrification
- RT waste processing

SOLIDS [6,836; 6,836]
- RT crystals
- RT dispersions
- RT glass
- RT microstructure
- RT phase diagrams
- RT solid clusters
- RT solid solutions
- RT solidification
- RT structure factors

SOLITONS [4,755; 4,755]
- BT1 quasi particles
- RT baecklund transformation
- RT phonons
- RT shock waves

SOLS [202; 8,803]
- BT1 colloids
  - BT2 dispersions
- NT1 aerosols
  - NT2 radioactive aerosols
  - NT2 smokes
    - NT3 tobacco smokes
- RT solutions

SOLUBILITY [8,408; 8,408]
- RT crystallization
- RT dissolution
- RT leaching
- RT mixing
- RT precipitation
- RT saturation
- RT solutes
- RT solutions
- RT solvents
- RT supersaturation

SOLUBLE POISONS [115; 115]
- BT1 nuclear poisons
  - BT2 reactor materials
    - BT3 materials
- RT fluid poison control
- RT poisoning
- RT scram

SOLUTES [214; 317] *May 86*
- UF *dissolved liquids*
- UF *dissolved solids*
- NT1 dissolved gases
- RT additives
- RT dissolution
- RT solubility
- RT solutions
- RT solvents

SOLUTION HEAT [708; 708]
- UF *heat of solution*
- BT1 enthalpy
  - BT2 thermodynamic properties
    - BT3 physical properties
- RT mixing heat

SOLUTION MINING [374; 374] *Jul 76*
- BT1 in-situ processing
  - BT2 ore processing
- BT1 mining
- RT leaching
- RT solvent extraction

SOLUTIONS [6,359; 33,711]
(For mathematical solutions see ANALYTICAL SOLUTION or NUMERICAL SOLUTION.)
- BT1 homogeneous mixtures
  - BT2 mixtures
    - BT3 dispersions
- NT1 aqueous solutions
- NT1 hypertonic solutions
- NT1 isotonic solutions
- NT1 leachates
- NT1 solid solutions
- RT brines
- RT buffers
- RT dilution
- RT dissolution
- RT organic solvents
- RT saturation
- RT scrubbing
- RT sols
- RT solubility
- RT solutes
- RT solvents
- RT supersaturation

solvatation
- USE solvation

SOLVATED ELECTRONS [1,377; 1,37
- UF+ *hydrated electrons*
- BT1 electrons
  - BT2 leptons
    - BT3 elementary particles

```
            BT3   fermions
            RT    solvation

SOLVATION [970; 2,409]
     UF     solvatation
     NT1    hydration
     RT     nonaqueous solvents
     RT     solvated electrons

SOLVENT EXTRACTION
[11,090; 11,095]
     UF     extraction (solvent)
     UF     liquid-liquid extraction
     BT1    separation processes
     RT     amex process
     RT     butex process
     RT     civex process
     RT     counter current
     RT     csrex process
     RT     dapex process
     RT     darex process
     RT     dissolution
     RT     distribution functions
     RT     entrainment
     RT     eurex process
     RT     excer process
     RT     extraction apparatuses
     RT     fluorox process
     RT     flurex process
     RT     hermex process
     RT     hydrometallurgy
     RT     leachates
     RT     leaching
     RT     monex process
     RT     neptex process
     RT     niflex process
     RT     partition
     RT     podbielniak contactors
     RT     purex process
     RT     redox process
     RT     reprocessing
     RT     salting-out agents
     RT     slurex process
     RT     solution mining
     RT     sulfex process
     RT     talspeak process
     RT     thermox process
     RT     thorex process
     RT     tramex process
     RT     truex process
     RT     zircex process
     RT     zirflex process

SOLVENTS [1,342; 17,588]
     UF     diluents
     UF     polar solvents
     NT1    mixed solvents
     NT1    nonaqueous solvents
        NT2    organic solvents
           NT3    amsco
           NT3    carbitols
           NT3    cellosolves
           NT3    solvesso
           NT3    turpentine
     RT     dissolution
     RT     solubility
     RT     solutes
     RT     solutions

SOLVESSO [9; 9]
     BT1    organic solvents
        BT2    nonaqueous solvents
           BT3    solvents
     RT     aromatics

SOLVOLYSIS [151; 2,732]
     BT1    decomposition
        BT2    chemical reactions
     NT1    acetolysis
     NT1    ammonolysis
     NT1    hydrolysis
        NT2    saponification
```

```
SOMALIA [5; 5]
     BT1    africa
     BT1    developing countries

SOMATIC CELLS [346; 15,551]
     BT1    animal cells
     NT1    cho cells
     NT1    connective tissue cells
        NT2    bone cells
        NT2    bone marrow cells
        NT2    fat cells
        NT2    fibroblasts
        NT2    lymphocytes
        NT2    macrophages
        NT2    mast cells
        NT2    plasma cells
     NT1    crypt cells
     NT1    liver cells
     NT1    nerve cells
     NT1    phagocytes
        NT2    macrophages
     NT1    respiratory tract cells
     NT1    spleen cells
     NT1    stem cells
     NT1    thymocytes
     NT1    thymus cells
     NT1    thyroid cells

SOMATIC MUTATIONS [228; 228]
     BT1    mutations

SOMATICALLY SIGNIFICANT DOSE
[106; 106] Jan 76
     BT1    radiation doses
     RT     radiation hazards

SOMATOSTATIN [139; 139] May 80
     UF     somatotropin release inhib fac
     RT     hormones
     RT     polypeptides
     RT     radioimmunoassay
     RT     sth

somatotropic hormone
     USE    sth


somatotropin release inhib fac
     USE    somatostatin

SOMMERFELD CONSTANT [94; 94]
     UF     sommerfeld fine structure cons
     RT     fine structure

sommerfeld fine structure cons
     USE    sommerfeld constant

SOMMERFELD-WATSON THEORY
[91; 91]
     UF     watson method
     RT     quantum mechanics

sonar
     USE    range finders

sonic logging
     USE    well logging

→ sonic measurements
     USE    acoustic measurements

SONIC PROBES [110; 110] Aug 75
(Probes using sonics for plasma diagnostics.)
     BT1    probes
     RT     acoustic measurements
     RT     ion acoustic waves
     RT     plasma diagnostics
```

```
SONIC SPARK CHAMBERS [29; 29]
     UF     acoustic spark chambers
     BT1    filmless spark chambers
        BT2    spark chambers
           BT3    gas track detectors
              BT4    radiation detectors
                 BT5    measuring instruments

soot
     USE    combustion products

SORA REACTOR [17; 17]
     BT1    fast reactors
        BT2    epithermal reactors
           BT3    reactors
     BT1    pulsed reactors
        BT2    reactors
     BT1    research reactors
        BT2    research and test reactors
           BT3    reactors
     RT     neutron sources

SORBIC ACID [12; 12]
     BT1    monocarboxylic acids
        BT2    carboxylic acids
           BT3    organic acids
              BT4    organic compounds

SORBITOL [47; 47]
     BT1    monosaccharides
        BT2    saccharides
           BT3    carbohydrates
              BT4    organic compounds
     RT     sorbose

SORBOSE [7; 7]
     BT1    hexoses
        BT2    monosaccharides
           BT3    saccharides
              BT4    carbohydrates
                 BT5    organic compounds
     BT1    ketones
        BT2    organic compounds
     RT     sorbitol

SOREQ NUCLEAR RESEARCH CENTER [8; 8] Nov 79
     BT1    israel atomic energy commissio
        BT2    israeli organizations
           BT3    national organizations

SORGHUM [87; 87]
     BT1    cereals
        BT2    gramineae
           BT3    plants

sorption
     SEE    adsorption
     OR     chemisorption
     OR     ion exchange

SORTING [39; 90] Apr 84
     NT1    radiometric sorting
     RT     filters
     RT     screens
     RT     separation processes

sound
     USE    sound waves

SOUND WAVES [2,319; 6,048]
(See also FOURTH SOUND, SECOND SOUND, and THIRD SOUND.)
     UF     sound
     NT1    ultrasonic waves
     RT     acoustic detection
     RT     acoustic esr
     RT     acoustic measurements
     RT     acoustic monitoring
     RT     acoustic nmr
     RT     frequency mixing
     RT     harmonic generation
     RT     magnetoacoustics
```

    RT   signal distortion
    RT   zero sound

SOURCE TERMS [909; 909] *Nov 85*
(Activities and amounts of the different radionuclides per unit time leaving a nuclear installation or facility and entering the environment, as during a severe reactor accident.)
    RT   containment
    RT   environment
    RT   fission product release
    RT   fission products
    RT   meltdown
    RT   radiation doses
    RT   reactor accidents
    RT   risk assessment

SOUTH AFRICA [1,323; 1,408]
    BT1   africa
    BT1   developed countries
    NT1   transvaal
    RT   south west africa
    RT   vaalputs radioactive waste dis

south africa nac cyclotron
    USE   nac cyclotron

SOUTH AFRICAN ORGANIZATIONS [81; 81] *May 87*
    BT1   national organizations

SOUTH ALLIGATOR DEPOSIT [13; 13] *Jul 78*
    BT1   uranium deposits
      BT2   geologic deposits
    RT   northern territory
    RT   uranium ores

SOUTH AMERICA [211; 2,400]
    BT1   latin america
    NT1   argentina
      NT2   mendoza
    NT1   bolivia
      NT2   chacaltaya
    NT1   brazil
    NT1   chile
    NT1   colombia
    NT1   ecuador
    NT1   french guiana
    NT1   guyana
      NT2   british guiana
    NT1   paraguay
    NT1   peru
    NT1   surinam
    NT1   uruguay
    NT1   venezuela

SOUTH AUSTRALIA [168; 168]
    BT1   australia
      BT2   australasia
      BT2   developed countries
    RT   olympic dam mine
    RT   roxby downs deposit

SOUTH CAROLINA [293; 293]
    BT1   usa
      BT2   developed countries
      BT2   north america
    RT   savannah river plant

SOUTH DAKOTA [144; 144]
    BT1   usa
      BT2   developed countries
      BT2   north america

south haven michigan reactor
    USE   palisades-1 reactor

south korea
    USE   republic of korea

SOUTH TEXAS PROJECT-1 REACTOR [38; 38]
(Bay City, Texas, USA)
    BT1   pwr type reactors
      BT2   enriched uranium reactors
        BT3 reactors
      BT2   power reactors
        BT3 reactors
      BT2   thermal reactors
        BT3 reactors
      BT2   water cooled reactors
        BT3 reactors
      BT2   water moderated reactors
        BT3 reactors

SOUTH TEXAS PROJECT-2 REACTOR [35; 35]
(Bay City, Texas, USA)
    BT1   pwr type reactors
      BT2   enriched uranium reactors
        BT3 reactors
      BT2   power reactors
        BT3 reactors
      BT2   thermal reactors
        BT3 reactors
      BT2   water cooled reactors
        BT3 reactors
      BT2   water moderated reactors
        BT3 reactors

SOUTH UKRAINIAN-1 REACTOR [34; 34] *Aug 84*
    BT1   wwer type reactors
      BT2   pwr type reactors
        BT3 enriched uranium reactors
          BT4 reactors
        BT3 power reactors
          BT4 reactors
        BT3 thermal reactors
          BT4 reactors
        BT3 water cooled reactors
          BT4 reactors
        BT3 water moderated reactors
          BT4 reactors

SOUTH UKRAINIAN-2 REACTOR [5; 5] *Feb 89*
    BT1   wwer type reactors
      BT2   pwr type reactors
        BT3 enriched uranium reactors
          BT4 reactors
        BT3 power reactors
          BT4 reactors
        BT3 thermal reactors
          BT4 reactors
        BT3 water cooled reactors
          BT4 reactors
        BT3 water moderated reactors
          BT4 reactors

SOUTH UKRAINIAN-3 REACTOR [2; 2] *Jan 90*
(Ukrainian SSR, USSR.)
    BT1   wwer type reactors
      BT2   pwr type reactors
        BT3 enriched uranium reactors
          BT4 reactors
        BT3 power reactors
          BT4 reactors
        BT3 thermal reactors
          BT4 reactors
        BT3 water cooled reactors
          BT4 reactors
        BT3 water moderated reactors
          BT4 reactors

SOUTH WEST AFRICA [117; 117]
    UF   *southwest africa*
    BT1   africa
    RT   south africa

SOUTHERN HEMISPHERE [93; 93] *Dec 86*
(Both for the surface and the celestial hemisphere.)
    RT   earth planet

SOUTHERN RHODESIA [13; 13]
    UF   *rhodesia (southern)*
    BT1   zimbabwe
      BT2   africa
      BT2   developing countries

southwest africa
    USE   south west africa

southwest exper. fast oxide r.
    USE   sefor reactor

soviet breeder reactor-1
    USE   sbr-1 reactor

soviet breeder reactor-2
    USE   sbr-2 reactor

soviet breeder reactor-5
    USE   sbr-5 reactor

soviet research reactor irt
    USE   irt reactor

soviet union
    USE   ussr

soy oil
    USE   soybean oil

SOYBEAN OIL [30; 30]
    UF   *chinese bean oil*
    UF   *soja bean oil*
    UF   *soy oil*
    BT1   oils
      BT2   other organic compounds
        BT3 organic compounds
    BT1   triglycerides
      BT2   esters
        BT3 organic compounds
      BT2   lipids
        BT3 organic compounds

soybean plant
    USE   glycine hispida

SOYBEANS [328; 328]
    BT1   seeds
    BT1   vegetables
      BT2   food
    RT   glycine hispida

SP GROUPS [821; 821]
    UF   *symplectic groups*
    BT1   lie groups
      BT2   symmetry groups

sp logging
    USE   well logging

SPACE [549; 26,261]
    NT1   intergalactic space
    NT1   interplanetary space
    NT1   interstellar space
    NT1   mathematical space
      NT2   banach space
        NT3 hilbert space
      NT2   hausdorff space
      NT2   minkowski space
      NT2   phase space
      NT2   riemann space
        NT3 euclidean space
    RT   space flight
    RT   space vehicles

SPACE CHARGE [2,901; 2,901]
  RT   charge distribution
  RT   electric charges
  RT   electron tubes

SPACE DEPENDENCE [2,051; 2,051]
(The dependence of any quantity or variable on space coordinates.)
  RT   mathematical space

SPACE FLIGHT [880; 880]
  RT   apollo project
  RT   cosmic radiation
  RT   ogo satellites
  RT   orbiting solar observatories
  RT   radiation protection
  RT   reentry
  RT   rockets
  RT   satellites
  RT   solar flares
  RT   space
  RT   space shuttles
  RT   space vehicles
  RT   venera space probes

SPACE GROUPS [3,189; 3,189]
  UF   *groups (space)*
  BT1 symmetry groups
  RT   crystal lattices
  RT   group theory

SPACE HEATING [135; 135] *Feb 76*
  BT1 heating
  RT   district heating

space lattices
  USE crystal lattices

SPACE POWER REACTORS
[973; 1,418]
  BT1   mobile reactors
   BT2   reactors
  BT1   power reactors
   BT2   reactors
  NT1   snap reactors
   NT2   snap 10 reactor
    NT3   s10fs-1 reactor
    NT3   s10fs-3 reactor
    NT3   s10fs-4 reactor
   NT2   snap 2 reactor
    NT3   s2ds reactor
   NT2   snap 8 reactor
    NT3   s8dr reactor
    NT3   s8er reactor
  NT1   space propulsion reactors
   NT2   kiwi reactors
   NT2   nerva reactor
   NT2   nrx-a2 reactor
   NT2   nrx a3 reactor
   NT2   nrx-a4-est reactor
   NT2   nrx-a5 reactor
   NT2   nrx-a6 reactor
   NT2   pewee-1 reactor
   NT2   pewee-2 reactor
   NT2   pewee-3 reactor
   NT2   pewee-4 reactor
   NT2   phoebus-1a reactor
   NT2   phoebus-1b reactor
   NT2   phoebus-2a reactor
   NT2   rover reactors

SPACE PROPULSION REACTORS
[346; 466]
  BT1   propulsion reactors
   BT2   power reactors
    BT3   reactors
  BT1   space power reactors
   BT2   mobile reactors
    BT3   reactors
   BT2   power reactors
    BT3   reactors
  NT1   kiwi reactors
  NT1   nerva reactor
  NT1   nrx-a2 reactor
  NT1   nrx-a3 reactor
  NT1   nrx-a4-est reactor
  NT1   nrx-a5 reactor
  NT1   nrx-a6 reactor
  NT1   pewee-1 reactor
  NT1   pewee-2 reactor
  NT1   pewee-3 reactor
  NT1   pewee-4 reactor
  NT1   phoebus-1a reactor
  NT1   phoebus-1b reactor
  NT1   phoebus-2a reactor
  NT1   rover reactors
  RT   fissioning plasma

space reflection
  USE p invariance

SPACE SHUTTLES [161; 161] *Feb 83*
  BT1 space vehicles
  RT   aircraft
  RT   space flight

SPACE VEHICLES [1,494; 3,092]
  NT1 luna space probes
  NT1 mariner space probes
  NT1 mars space probes
  NT1 mir orbital station
  NT1 pioneer space probes
  NT1 salyut orbital stations
  NT1 space shuttles
  NT1 vega space probes
  NT1 venera space probes
  NT1 viking space probes
  NT1 voyager space probes
  RT   electronic guidance
  RT   ionosondes
  RT   launching
  RT   navigational instruments
  RT   reentry
  RT   rockets
  RT   satellites
  RT   space
  RT   space flight
  RT   spacecraft power supplies

SPACE-TIME [11,807; 13,383]
  UF   *spacetime*
  NT1 light cone
  RT   compactification
  RT   cosmological constant
  RT   cosmology
  RT   energy-momentum tensor
  RT   galilei transformations
  RT   lorentz transformations
  RT   mach principle
  RT   mathematical space
  RT   metrics
  RT   relativity theory
  RT   sine-gordon equation
  RT   twistor theory

SPACE-TIME MODEL [89; 89] *Dec 82*
(Particle-interaction model in which particles at the instant of creation are immature or bare and their maturity rate is enhanced in the presence of other hadronic matter, as in a nucleus.)
  BT1   cluster emission model
   BT2   multiperipheral model
    BT3   peripheral models
     BT4   particle models
      BT5   mathematical models
  RT   hadron reactions

SPACECRAFT POWER SUPPLIES
[657; 657]
  BT1   power supplies
   BT2   electronic equipment
    BT3   equipment
  RT   electric batteries
  RT   energy sources
  RT   radioisotope batteries
  RT   space vehicles

SPACERS [1,487; 1,487]
  RT   fins
  RT   fuel element clusters
  RT   reactor components

spacetime
  USE space-time

SPADNS [9; 9]
(Sulfophenyl-naphthalene-sulfonic acid)
  UF   *sulfophenyl-naphthalene-sulfon*
  BT1 sulfones
   BT2   organic sulfur compounds
    BT3   organic compounds
  BT1 sulfonic acids
   BT2   organic acids
    BT3   organic compounds
   BT2   organic sulfur compounds
    BT3   organic compounds

SPAIN [597; 597]
  BT1 developing countries
  BT1 europe
  RT   bay of biscay

SPALLATION [2,633; 2,633]
(High-energy nuclear reaction resulting in the release of numerous nucleons, alpha particles or heavier nuclei as reaction products; not to be used for fission.)
  BT1 nuclear reactions
  RT   fission
  RT   nuclear fireball model
  RT   nuclear fragmentation
  RT   nuclear fragments
  RT   rudstam formula
  RT   spallation fragments

SPALLATION FRAGMENTS [578; 578]
Nov 78
  UF   *fragments (spallation)*
  UF   *spallation products*
  BT1 nuclear fragments
  RT   spallation

spallation products
  USE spallation fragments

spanish jen-1 research reactor
  USE jen-1 reactor

spanish jen-2 research reactor
  USE jen-2 reactor

SPANISH ORGANIZATIONS [41; 41]
Apr 77
  BT1 national organizations

SPARK CHAMBERS [781; 2,424]
  BT1   gas track detectors
   BT2   radiation detectors
    BT3   measuring instruments
  NT1   filmless spark chambers
   NT2   sonic spark chambers
   NT2   wire spark chambers
  NT1   projection spark chambers
  NT1   streamer spark chambers
  NT1   wide gap spark chambers
  RT   digitizers
  RT   spark counters

SPARK COUNTERS [237; 237]
  UF   *rosenblum counters*
  BT1 radiation detectors
   BT2   measuring instruments
  RT   corona counters
  RT   spark chambers

SPARK GAPS [577; 577]
  RT   breakdown
  RT   electric discharges
  RT   electric sparks
  RT   paschen law

SPARK MACHINING [71; 71]
BT1 machining

SPARK MASS SPECTROMETERS
[141; 141]
BT1 mass spectrometers
BT2 spectrometers
BT3 measuring instruments

sparks (electric)
USE electric sparks

SPARTICLES [422; 422] *Dec 87*
UF *supersymmetric particles*
BT1 postulated particles
BT2 elementary particles

§§ **SPATIAL DISTRIBUTION**
[23,907; 29,125]
(Use for the distribution of any property or quantity in space, e.g. density or particle velocity.)
UF *radial distribution*
UF+ *depth distribution*
BT1 distribution
NT1 mass distribution
NT1 power distribution
NT1 spatial dose distributions
NT2 depth dose distributions
RT angular distribution
RT charge distribution
RT plasma radial profiles
RT temperature distribution

SPATIAL DOSE DISTRIBUTIONS
[1,875; 4,962]
UF *distribution factor (rad doses*
UF+ *absorbed fraction (internal ir*
UF+ *effective energy (internal irr*
BT1 radiation dose distributions
BT1 spatial distribution
BT2 distribution
NT1 depth dose distributions
RT buildup
RT integral doses
RT irradiation procedures
RT isodose curves
RT local irradiation
RT microdosimetry
RT nonuniform irradiation
RT partial body irradiation

SPATIAL RESOLUTION [6,063; 6,063]
BT1 resolution

spe
USE solar protons

SPEAR [425; 425]
(Stanford Positron-Electron Asymmetric Ring)
BT1 storage rings

special power excursion re.-1
USE spert-1 reactor

special power excursion re.-2
USE spert-2 reactor

special power excursion re.-3
USE spert-3 reactor

special power excursion re.-4
USE spert-4 reactor

SPECIAL PRODUCTION REACTORS
[50; 166]
(For producing fissile materials such as uranium 233, californium 252, thorium 232, etc. See also PLUTONIUM PRODUCTION REACTORS.)
BT1 production reactors
BT2 reactors
NT1 c reactor
NT1 k reactor
NT1 l reactor
NT1 p reactor
NT1 r reactor

special relativity theory
USE relativity theory

speciation (biological)
USE biological evolution

speciation (chemical)
USE chemical state

specific gravity
USE density

SPECIFIC HEAT [5,217; 5,656]
UF *heat capacity*
BT1 thermodynamic properties
BT2 physical properties
NT1 electronic specific heat
NT1 nuclear specific heat
RT born-von karman theory
RT debye temperature
RT grueneisen constant

SPECIFIC SURFACE AREA [107; 107]
Sep 82
(Surface area per unit weight or volume of a particulate solid.)
UF *surface area (specific)*
BT1 physical properties

specific volume
USE density

specific weight
USE density

§§ **SPECIFICATIONS** [61,871; 61,871]
UF *design (technical specificat.)*
UF *technical specifications*
RT camac system
RT design
RT inspection
RT modifications
RT patents
RT quality control
RT reliability
RT standardization
RT standards

SPECIFICITY [2,461; 2,461]
(The qualitative attribute of accurately distinguishing among different materials, properties, radiations, etc. as compared with the quantitative aspect of the threshold for detecting a given material, property, etc.; for which see SENSITIVITY.)
RT accuracy
RT sensitivity

specimen holders
USE sample holders

SPECTRA [15,991; 137,197]
NT1 absorption spectra
NT1 alpha spectra
NT1 beta spectra
NT1 deuteron spectra
NT1 electron spectra
NT1 emission spectra
NT1 energy spectra
NT1 extreme ultraviolet spectra
NT1 fission spectra
NT1 gamma spectra
NT1 infrared spectra
NT1 mass spectra
NT1 microwave spectra
NT1 missing-mass spectra
NT1 neutron spectra
NT2 watt fission spectrum
NT1 nmr spectra
NT1 proton spectra
NT1 raman spectra
NT1 ultraviolet spectra
NT1 visible spectra
NT1 x-ray spectra
RT balmer lines
RT eddington theory
RT fine structure
RT fraunhofer lines
RT hyperfine structure
RT line broadening
RT line narrowing
RT line widths
RT lyman lines
RT particle multiplets
RT paschen lines
RT raman effect
RT rydberg-klein-rees method
RT schumann-runge bands
RT spectral shift

SPECTRA UNFOLDING [1,579; 1,579]
BT1 data processing
RT neutron spectra

spectral broadening
USE line broadening

SPECTRAL DENSITY [1,577; 1,577]
UF *density (spectral)*
BT1 spectral functions
BT2 functions
RT energy spectra

SPECTRAL FUNCTIONS [1,444; 3,001
BT1 functions
NT1 spectral density
RT dispersion relations

SPECTRAL HARDENING [54; 54]
UF *hardening (spectral)*
RT neutron spectra

spectral narrowing
USE line narrowing

spectral reflectance
USE optical properties

SPECTRAL SHIFT [3,957; 4,589]
UF *isotope shift*
UF *isotopic shift*
NT1 lamb shift
RT chemical shift
RT doppler effect
RT knight effect
RT knight shift
RT spectra
RT stark effect
RT zeeman effect

SPECTRAL SHIFT CONTROL [97;
(Type of moderator control in which t neutron spectrum is intentionally chang
BT1 configuration control

spectrochemistry
    SEE   absorption spectroscopy
    OR   emission spectroscopy

SPECTROMETERS [2,735; 19,481]
    BT1   measuring instruments
    NT1   alpha spectrometers
    NT1   beta spectrometers
    NT1   cosmic ray spectrometers
    NT1   electron spectrometers
    NT1   electrostatic spectrometers
    NT1   epr spectrometers
    NT1   fission fragment spectrometers
    NT1   fourier transform spectrometer
    NT1   gamma spectrometers
      NT2   compton spectrometers
      NT2   moessbauer spectrometers
      NT2   pair spectrometers
    NT1   heavy ion spectrometers
    NT1   infrared spectrometers
      NT2   photoacoustic spectrometers
    NT1   magnetic spectrometers
      NT2   flat magnetic spectrometers
      NT2   magnetic lens spectrometers
    NT1   mass spectrometers
      NT2   dynamic mass spectrometers
        NT3   energy balance mass spectromet
        NT3   time-of-flight mass spectromet
      NT2   spark mass spectrometers
      NT2   static mass spectrometers
    NT1   missing-mass spectrometers
    NT1   multiparticle spectrometers
    NT1   neutron spectrometers
      NT2   bonner sphere spectrometers
    NT1   nmr spectrometers
    NT1   optical spectrometers
    NT1   proton spectrometers
    NT1   time-of-flight spectrometers
      NT2   time-of-flight mass spectromet
    NT1   ultraviolet spectrometers
    NT1   x-ray spectrometers
    RT   coincidence spectrometry
    RT   diffraction gratings
    RT   interferometers
    RT   monochromators
    RT   pulse analyzers
    RT   radiation detection
    RT   radiation detectors
    RT   spectrophotometers
    RT   spectroscopy

spectrometry
    USE   spectroscopy

spectrophones
    USE   photoacoustic spectrometers

SPECTROPHOTOMETERS [273; 273]
    BT1   measuring instruments
    RT   spectrometers
    RT   spectrophotometry

SPECTROPHOTOMETRY [5,933; 5,933]
    RT   photometry
    RT   spectrophotometers
    RT   spectroscopy

SPECTROSCOPIC CURVE OF GROWTH [102; 102] *Aug 75*
    UF   *curve of growth (spectroscopic*
    UF   *curve of growth(spectroscopic)*
    BT1   optical depth curve
      BT2   diagrams
        BT3   information
    RT   absorption spectra
    RT   cosmic gases
    RT   element abundance
    RT   line broadening
    RT   optical properties
    RT   oscillator strengths

SPECTROSCOPIC FACTORS [3,548; 3,548]
    RT   nuclear reactions
    RT   scattering

SPECTROSCOPY [7,087; 45,310]
    UF   *spectrometry*
    NT1   absorption spectroscopy
    NT1   alpha spectroscopy
    NT1   baryon spectroscopy
    NT1   beta spectroscopy
    NT1   electron spectroscopy
      NT2   auger electron spectroscopy
      NT2   photoelectron spectroscopy
    NT1   emission spectroscopy
      NT2   fluorescence spectroscopy
    NT1   energy-loss spectroscopy
    NT1   gamma spectroscopy
    NT1   in-beam spectroscopy
    NT1   ion spectroscopy
    NT1   laser spectroscopy
      NT2   raman spectroscopy
    NT1   mass spectroscopy
      NT2   resonance ionization mass spec
    NT1   meson spectroscopy
    NT1   neutron spectroscopy
    NT1   photoacoustic spectroscopy
    NT1   x-ray spectroscopy
    RT   matrix isolation
    RT   photometry
    RT   post-irradiation examination
    RT   quantum electronics
    RT   radiation detection
    RT   radioassay
    RT   sensitivity
    RT   spectrometers
    RT   spectrophotometry

speed
    USE   velocity

speed indicators
    USE   velocimeters

SPEED REGULATORS [87; 87]
    BT1   control equipment
      BT2   equipment

SPENCER-FANO THEORY [14; 14]
    RT   neutron slowing-down theory

spent fuel casks
    USE   casks

SPENT FUEL ELEMENTS [3,105; 3,105]
    UF   *irradiated fuel elements*
    BT1   fuel elements
      BT2   reactor components
    RT   burnup
    RT   reprocessing
    RT   spent fuels
    RT   wackersdorf reprocessing plant
    RT   wak

SPENT FUEL STORAGE [3,488; 3,761]
    UF   *fuel cooling installations*
    BT1   storage
    NT1   away-from-reactor storage
    RT   after-heat
    RT   dry storage
    RT   fuel cooling time
    RT   fuel cycle centers
    RT   fuel racks
    RT   fuel storage pools
    RT   nuclear waste policy acts
    RT   us mrs project

SPENT FUELS [6,832; 6,943]
    UF   *irradiated fuels*
    BT1   nuclear fuels
      BT2   energy sources
      BT2   fuels
      BT2   reactor materials
        BT3   materials
    RT   fission products
    RT   fuel cooling time
    RT   fuel reprocessing plants
    RT   nuclear waste policy acts
    RT   radioactive wastes
    RT   reactors
    RT   spent fuel elements
    RT   storage facilities
    RT   us mrs project
    RT   wackersdorf reprocessing plant
    RT   wak

sperm
    USE   spermatozoa

spermatids
    USE   spermatozoa

SPERMATOCYTES [182; 182]
    BT1   germ cells

SPERMATOGENESIS [291; 291]
    BT1   gametogenesis
    RT   reproduction
    RT   spermatogonia
    RT   spermatozoa
    RT   stem cells
    RT   testes

SPERMATOGONIA [417; 417]
    BT1   germ cells
    RT   spermatogenesis

SPERMATOZOA [670; 670]
    UF   *sperm*
    UF   *spermatids*
    BT1   gametes
      BT2   germ cells
    RT   spermatogenesis

SPERMIDINE [62; 62]
    BT1   amines
      BT2   organic compounds

SPERMINE [42; 42]
    UF   *gerontine*
    UF   *musculamine*
    UF   *neuridine*
    BT1   amines
      BT2   organic compounds

SPERT-1 REACTOR [21; 21]
(Phillips Petroleum Company, USA)
    UF   *special power excursion re.-1*
    BT1   enriched uranium reactors
      BT2   reactors
    BT1   experimental reactors
      BT2   research and test reactors
        BT3   reactors
    BT1   research reactors
      BT2   research and test reactors
        BT3   reactors
    BT1   tank type reactors
      BT2   reactors
    BT1   thermal reactors
      BT2   reactors
    BT1   water moderated reactors
      BT2   reactors

SPERT-2 REACTOR [10; 10]
    UF   *special power excursion re.-2*
    BT1   enriched uranium reactors
      BT2   reactors
    BT1   experimental reactors
      BT2   research and test reactors
        BT3   reactors
    BT1   heavy water cooled reactors
      BT2   reactors
    BT1   heavy water moderated reactors
      BT2   reactors
    BT1   tank type reactors
      BT2   reactors
    BT1   thermal reactors
      BT2   reactors
    BT1   water cooled reactors

         BT2   reactors
         BT1   water moderated reactors
         BT2   reactors

SPERT-3 REACTOR [9; 9]
    UF   *special power excursion re.-3*
    BT1   enriched uranium reactors
    BT2   reactors
    BT1   experimental reactors
    BT2   research and test reactors
         BT3   reactors
    BT1   tank type reactors
    BT2   reactors
    BT1   thermal reactors
    BT2   reactors
    BT1   water cooled reactors
    BT2   reactors
    BT1   water moderated reactors
    BT2   reactors

SPERT-4 REACTOR [6; 6]
    UF   *special power excursion re.-4*
    BT1   enriched uranium reactors
    BT2   reactors
    BT1   experimental reactors
    BT2   research and test reactors
         BT3   reactors
    BT1   pool type reactors
    BT2   water cooled reactors
         BT3   reactors
    BT2   water moderated reactors
         BT3   reactors
    BT1   thermal reactors
    BT2   reactors

sphene
    USE   titanite

SPHERATOR [70; 70]
    BT1   internal ring devices
         BT2   closed plasma devices
            BT3   thermonuclear devices

SPHERES [1,750; 1,750]
    RT   geometry
    RT   shape

§ **SPHERICAL CONFIGURATION**
    [2,476; 2,476]
    BT1   configuration

SPHERICAL HARMONICS [544; 544]
    UF+   *cn method*
    BT1   functions
    RT   laplace equation
    RT   mathematics
    RT   yvon method

SPHERICAL HARMONICS METHOD
    [236; 400]
    NT1   p1-approximation
    NT1   p2-approximation
    NT1   p3-approximation
    RT   legendre polynomials
    RT   marshak boundary conditions
    RT   neutron transport theory

SPHERICAL MODEL [674; 674]
    BT1   nuclear models
         BT2   mathematical models

SPHEROIDS [261; 261] *Feb 76*
    RT   geometry
    RT   shape

SPHEROMAK DEVICES [552; 600]
    Jul 81
    (Tokamak with aspect ratio approximately equal to one.)
    BT1   tokamak devices
         BT2   closed plasma devices
            BT3   thermonuclear devices
    NT1   ctx spheromak

SPHINGOMYELINS [26; 26]
    BT1   phospholipids
    BT2   esters
         BT3   organic compounds
    BT2   lipids
         BT3   organic compounds
    BT2   organic phosphorus compounds
         BT3   organic compounds

SPICES [209; 209]
    RT   flavor
    RT   food
    RT   peppers

spicules
    USE   solar prominences

SPIDERS [10; 10]
    BT1   arachnids
    BT2   arthropods
         BT3   invertebrates
            BT4   animals

spikes (thermal)
    USE   thermal spikes

SPIN [26,546; 26,546]
    BT1   angular momentum
    BT1   particle properties
    RT   chirality
    RT   heisenberg model
    RT   helicity
    RT   high spin states
    RT   joos-weinberg equation
    RT   morrison rule
    RT   orbital angular momentum
    RT   pauli spin operators
    RT   quantum numbers
    RT   schmidt lines
    RT   schmidt model
    RT   sherman tables
    RT   spin exchange
    RT   spin flip
    RT   spin orientation
    RT   spin-lattice relaxation
    RT   spin-spin relaxation
    RT   spinors
    RT   two-component neutrino theory
    RT   weil equation

SPIN ECHO [1,587; 1,587]
    RT   nuclear magnetic resonance

SPIN EXCHANGE [496; 496]
    (Not for chemical reactions.)
    RT   exchange interactions
    RT   spin

SPIN FLIP [1,779; 1,779]
    RT   inelastic scattering
    RT   nuclear reaction kinetics
    RT   spin

SPIN GLASS STATE [831; 831] *Jul 78*
    (A magnetic state in alloys of ferromagnetic material and nonmagnetic material in which the magnetic atoms are frozen into random orientation.)
    UF   *spin-glass state*
    RT   ferromagnetic materials
    RT   magnetism

SPIN ORIENTATION [9,426; 9,426]
    (For the process and condition in quantum physics only; see also POLARIZATION.)
    BT1   orientation
    RT   muon spin relaxation
    RT   nuclear alignment
    RT   nuclear magnetism
    RT   particle properties
    RT   polarization-asymmetry ratio
    RT   polarized beams
    RT   polarized targets
    RT   spin
    RT   stern-gerlach experiment

SPIN WAVES [1,298; 1,298]
    RT   magnons

spin-glass state
    USE   spin glass state

SPIN-LATTICE RELAXATION
    [3,521; 3,521]
    BT1   relaxation
    RT   nuclear magnetic resonance
    RT   spin

spin-orbit interaction
    USE   l-s coupling

spin-spin interaction
    USE   j-j coupling

SPIN-SPIN RELAXATION [1,806; 1,806]
    BT1   relaxation
    RT   nuclear magnetic resonance
    RT   spin

SPINACH [208; 208]
    BT1   vegetables
    BT2   food

SPINAL CORD [1,835; 1,835]
    BT1   central nervous system
    BT2   nervous system
    RT   ganglions
    RT   myelitis
    RT   reflexes
    RT   vertebrae

spine
    USE   vertebrae

SPINELS [495; 495]
    BT1   oxide minerals
    BT2   minerals
    RT   aluminium oxides
    RT   magnesium oxides
    RT   magnetite

SPINOR FIELDS [2,262; 2,262] *Feb 78*
    RT   quantum field theory

spinor symmetry
    USE   boson-fermion symmetry

SPINORS [2,612; 2,612]
    RT   spin
    RT   vectors

§ **SPIRAL CONFIGURATION**
    [1,447; 1,447]
    BT1   configuration

spiral orbit spectrometers
    USE   flat magnetic spectrometers

SPIRAL READER DIGITIZERS [42; 4
    BT1   digitizers

SPIROCHAETES [13; 13]
    BT1   bacteria
    BT2   microorganisms
    RT   syphilis

spitzer self-collision time
    USE   spitzer theory

SPITZER THEORY [98; 98]
UF   *spitzer self-collision time*
UF   *spitzer value*
RT   plasma
RT   transport theory

spitzer value
USE   spitzer theory

SPLAT COOLING [94; 94]
BT1   cooling
RT   quench hardening

SPLEEN [3,574; 3,574]
BT1   organs
BT2   body
RT   abdomen
RT   blood circulation
RT   blood formation
RT   lymphatic system
RT   macrophages
RT   peritoneum
RT   reticuloendothelial system
RT   spleen cells
RT   spleen colony formation
RT   splenectomy
RT   splenomegaly

SPLEEN CELLS [787; 787]
BT1   somatic cells
BT2   animal cells
RT   spleen

SPLEEN COLONY FORMATION [285; 285]
BT1   colony formation
RT   blood formation
RT   cfu
RT   chimeras
RT   radiation chimeras
RT   spleen

SPLENECTOMY [172; 172]
BT1   surgery
BT2   medicine
RT   lymphatic system
RT   spleen

SPLENOMEGALY [106; 106]
BT1   pathological changes
BT2   diseases
BT1   symptoms
RT   hemic diseases
RT   leukemia
RT   spleen

SPLINE FUNCTIONS [220; 220] *Sep 78*
BT1   functions
RT   interpolation
RT   mathematics
RT   polynomials
RT   series expansion

split dose irradiation
USE   fractionated irradiation

SPLIT TABLE REACTOR [4; 4]
UF   *str reactor (split table)*
BT1   zero power reactors
BT2   experimental reactors
BT3   research and test reactors
BT4   reactors

SPONDYLITIS [207; 207]
UF   *ankylosing spondylitis*
BT1   skeletal diseases
BT2   diseases
RT   vertebrae

spontaneous combustion
USE   combustion

spontaneous emission (cooperat
USE   superradiance

SPONTANEOUS FISSION [2,438; 2,438]
BT1   fission
BT2   nuclear reactions
BT1   nuclear decay
BT2   decay
RT   fission isomers
RT   spontaneous fission radioisoto

* **SPONTANEOUS FISSION RADIOISOTO** [15; 7,014] *Jun 86*
(For specific terms, consult the Appendix.)
BT1   radioisotopes
BT2   isotopes
RT   spontaneous fission

SPONTANEOUS MUTATIONS [75; 75] *Feb 78*
UF   *natural mutations*
BT1   mutations

spontaneous potential logging
USE   well logging

SPORADIC E [117; 117]
BT1   e region
BT2   ionosphere
BT3   earth atmosphere

SPORES [269; 648]
NT1   bacterial spores
NT1   conidia
NT1   microspores
RT   fungi
RT   reproduction

spot welding
USE   welding

spot welds
USE   welded joints

spr-ii reactor
USE   spr-2 reactor

spr-iii reactor
USE   spr-3 reactor

spr-iv reactor
USE   spr-4 reactor

SPR-2 REACTOR [41; 41]
(Sandia Laboratories, Albuquerque, New Mexico, USA)
UF   *sandia pulsed reactor-ii*
UF   *spr-ii reactor*
BT1   pulsed reactors
BT2   reactors
BT1   research reactors
BT2   research and test reactors
BT3   reactors
BT1   thermal reactors
BT2   reactors

SPR-3 REACTOR [54; 54]
(Sandia Laboratories, Albuquerque, New Mexico, USA)
UF   *sandia pulsed reactor-iii*
UF   *spr-iii reactor*
BT1   pulsed reactors
BT2   reactors
BT1   research reactors
BT2   research and test reactors
BT3   reactors

SPR-4 REACTOR [0; 0] *Jun 84*
UF   *sandia pulsed reactor-iv*
UF   *spr-iv reactor*
BT1   pulsed reactors
BT2   reactors
BT1   research reactors
BT2   research and test reactors
BT3   reactors

SPRAY COATING [222; 636]
UF   *metal spraying*
BT1   surface coating
BT2   deposition
NT1   flame spraying
NT1   plasma arc spraying
RT   sprayed coatings

SPRAY COOLING [139; 139] *Jul 76*
BT1   cooling
RT   droplets
RT   fog cooling
RT   sprays

SPRAY DRYING [52; 52]
BT1   drying
RT   evaporation

spray systems (containment)
USE   containment spray systems

SPRAYED COATINGS [466; 466]
BT1   coatings
RT   spray coating

SPRAYS [448; 448]
UF   *fog (sprays)*
RT   atomization
RT   dispersions
RT   droplets
RT   scrubbers
RT   scrubbing
RT   spray cooling
RT   washout

SPREAD F [144; 144]
BT1   f region
BT2   ionosphere
BT3   earth atmosphere

SPRING-8 STORAGE RING [35; 35] *Sep 90*
BT1   storage rings
BT1   synchrotron radiation sources
BT2   radiation sources

SPRINGS [523; 523]
(Mechanical springs only; for springs of water see GROUND WATER.)
BT1   machine parts
RT   mechanical vibrations
RT   torsion

SPROUT INHIBITION [259; 259]
RT   onions
RT   potatoes
RT   storage life

SPROUTING [98; 98]
RT   plant growth
RT   plants
RT   vernalization

SPURIONS [50; 50]
BT1   postulated particles
BT2   elementary particles
BT1   strange particles
BT2   elementary particles
RT   selection rules

SPUTTER-ION PUMPS [125; 125]
BT1   vacuum pumps
BT2   pumps
BT3   equipment
RT   getters

RT penning discharges
RT philips gages
RT sputtering
RT ultrahigh vacuum

SPUTTERING [7,302; 7,595]
NT1 cathode sputtering
RT arc welding
RT deposition
RT ion beams
RT sputter-ion pumps
RT vacuum coating

SQUALANE [17; 17]
BT1 alkanes
BT2 hydrocarbons
BT3 organic compounds

SQUALENE [25; 25]
BT1 polyenes
BT2 hydrocarbons
BT3 organic compounds
BT1 terpenes
BT2 organic compounds

SQUARE CONFIGURATION [153; 153]
BT1 rectangular configuration
BT2 configuration

square-wave generators
USE function generators

SQUARE-WELL POTENTIAL [428; 428]
BT1 nuclear potential
BT2 potentials

SQUID DEVICES [972; 972]
(Superconducting Quantum Interference Devices)
UF *supercond. quantum interf. dev*
BT1 fluxmeters
BT2 measuring instruments
BT1 microwave equipment
BT2 electronic equipment
BT3 equipment
BT1 superconducting devices
RT interferometers
RT rf systems
RT superconductors

SQUIRRELS [27; 27]
BT1 rodents
BT2 mammals
BT3 vertebrates
BT4 animals
RT chipmunks

SR-OA REACTOR [23; 23]
(Skoda National Corporations, Plzen, Czechoslovakia)
UF *skoda (plzen) reactor*
BT1 enriched uranium reactors
BT2 reactors
BT1 research reactors
BT2 research and test reactors
BT3 reactors
BT1 tank type reactors
BT2 reactors
BT1 water cooled reactors
BT2 reactors
BT1 water moderated reactors
BT2 reactors
BT1 zero power reactors
BT2 experimental reactors
BT3 research and test reactors
BT4 reactors

sr-ob reactor
USE subcritical assemblies

SR-1 REACTOR [2; 2]
BT1 enriched uranium reactors
BT2 reactors
BT1 research reactors
BT2 research and test reactors
BT3 reactors
BT1 tank type reactors
BT2 reactors
BT1 thermal reactors
BT2 reactors
BT1 water cooled reactors
BT2 reactors
BT1 water moderated reactors
BT2 reactors

SR-3P REACTOR [2; 2]
BT1 thermal reactors
BT2 reactors
BT1 training reactors
BT2 research and test reactors
BT3 reactors
BT1 water cooled reactors
BT2 reactors

SR-305 REACTOR [3; 3]
UF *savannah river test pile-305*
BT1 graphite moderated reactors
BT2 reactors
BT1 production reactors
BT2 reactors
BT1 thermal reactors
BT2 reactors

SRE REACTOR [23; 23]
UF *sodium reactor experiment*
BT1 enriched uranium reactors
BT2 reactors
BT1 experimental reactors
BT2 research and test reactors
BT3 reactors
BT1 power reactors
BT2 reactors
BT1 sgr type reactors
BT2 graphite moderated reactors
BT3 reactors
BT2 sodium cooled reactors
BT3 liquid metal cooled reactors
BT4 reactors
BT1 thermal reactors
BT2 reactors
BT1 thorium reactors
BT2 reactors

SRI LANKA [30; 30]
UF *ceylon*
BT1 asia
BT1 developing countries
BT1 islands
RT indian ocean

sriracha reactor
USE ao-phai-1 reactor

srm
(Standard Reference Materials)
USE calibration standards

SRRC-UTR-100 REACTOR [13; 13]
(Scottish Universities Research and Reactor Centre, East Kilbride by Glasgow, UK)
UF *glasgow utr-100 reactor*
UF *scot. res. re. cen. utr-100 re*
BT1 argonaut type reactors
BT2 enriched uranium reactors
BT3 reactors
BT2 research and test reactors
BT3 reactors
BT2 water cooled reactors
BT3 reactors
BT2 water moderated reactors
BT3 reactors
BT1 research reactors
BT2 research and test reactors
BT3 reactors
BT1 thermal reactors
BT2 reactors

BT1 training reactors
BT2 research and test reactors
BT3 reactors

ssc
(Superconducting Super Collider.)
USE superconducting super collider

SSDL [64; 64] *Jul 80*
(Secondary Standard Dosimetry Laboratories.)
UF *secondary standard dosimet lab*
RT calibration standards
RT dosimetry

ST LAWRENCE RIVER [12; 12] *Jul 7*
BT1 rivers
BT2 surface waters

st lucie-1 reactor
USE lucie-1 reactor

st lucie-2 reactor
USE lucie-2 reactor

ST TOKAMAK [65; 65]
UF *tokamak model st*
BT1 tokamak devices
BT2 closed plasma devices
BT3 thermonuclear devices

sta maria garona nuc. pow. pla
USE garona reactor

staat amt atomsich strahlensch
USE bundesamt fuer strahlenschutz

§ **STABILITY** [20,255; 21,728]
UF *stabilization*
NT1 orbit stability
NT1 phase stability
NT1 reactor stability
NT1 slope stability
RT equilibrium
RT instability
RT lyapunov method

stability (fission reactor)
USE reactor stability

stabilization
USE stability

STABILIZED SUPERCONDUCTORS [213; 213]
BT1 superconductors

* **STABLE ISOTOPES** [658; 91,521]
(For specific terms, consult the Append
BT1 isotopes
RT carriers
RT magic nuclei
RT translocation

STACK DISPOSAL [1,044; 1,044]
BT1 waste disposal
BT2 waste management
BT3 management
RT chemical effluents
RT electrostatic precipitators
RT gaseous wastes
RT ground release
RT plumes
RT pollution control equipment
RT radioactive effluents
RT radioactive waste disposal
RT release limits
RT stacks

STACKING FAULTS [769; 769]
- BT1 crystal defects
- BT2 crystal structure
- *RT* dislocations

STACKS [235; 235]
- *RT* buildings
- *RT* gaseous wastes
- *RT* plumes
- *RT* radioactive clouds
- *RT* smokes
- *RT* stack disposal
- *RT* ventilation

STADE REACTOR [153; 153]
- UF *kernkraftwerk stade*
- UF *kks reactor*
- BT1 pwr type reactors
- BT2 enriched uranium reactors
- BT3 reactors
- BT2 power reactors
- BT3 reactors
- BT2 thermal reactors
- BT3 reactors
- BT2 water cooled reactors
- BT3 reactors
- BT2 water moderated reactors
- BT3 reactors

STAGNATION [122; 122]
- *RT* fluid flow

stainless steel-am-350
USE steel-cr17ni4mo3

stainless steel-fv548
USE steel-cr17ni12monb

stainless steel-zcnd17-13
USE steel-cr17ni12mo3-l

stainless steel-z2cnd17-12
USE steel-cr17ni12mo3-l

stainless steel-z2cn18-10
USE steel-cr18ni10-l

stainless steel-z3cnd17-12
USE steel-cr17ni12mo3-l

stainless steel-z6cnd17-12
USE steel-cr17ni12mo3

stainless steel-z6cnt18-10
USE steel-cr18ni10ti

stainless steel-z6cn18-10
USE steel-cr18ni10

stainless steel-z8cnt18-10
USE steel-cr18ni10ti

stainless steel-16-8-2
USE steel-cr16ni8mo2

stainless steel-17-4ph
USE steel-cr17cu4ni4nb-l

stainless steel-18-10
USE steel-cr18ni10

stainless steel-18-8
USE steel-cr18ni8

stainless steel-20-25
USE steel-ni25cr20

stainless steel-21-6-9
USE steel-cr21mn9ni6

stainless steel-301
USE steel-cr17ni7

stainless steel-302
USE steel-cr18ni9

stainless steel-304
USE steel-cr19ni10

stainless steel-304l
USE steel-cr19ni10-l

stainless steel-305
USE steel-cr18ni12

stainless steel-308
USE steel-cr20ni11

stainless steel-308l
USE steel-cr20ni11-l

stainless steel-309
USE steel-cr23ni14

stainless steel-309s
USE steel-cr23ni14

stainless steel-310
USE steel-cr25ni20

stainless steel-316
USE steel-cr17ni12mo3

stainless steel-316l
USE steel-cr17ni12mo3-l

stainless steel-321
USE steel-cr18ni10ti

stainless steel-330
USE steel-ni36cr18

stainless steel-347
USE steel-cr18ni11nb

stainless steel-348
USE steel-cr18ni11nbco

stainless steel-403
USE steel-cr12

stainless steel-405
USE steel-cr13al

stainless steel-410
USE steel-cr13

stainless steel-430
USE steel-cr16

stainless steel-431
USE steel-cr16ni

stainless steel-44ln
USE steel-cr26ni5mo-l

stainless steel-440
USE steel-cr17mo

stainless steel-446
USE steel-cr25

STAINLESS STEELS [6,531; 16,936]
- BT1 high alloy steels
- BT2 steels
- BT3 carbon additions
- BT3 iron base alloys
- BT4 iron alloys
- BT5 alloys
- NT1 chromium steels
- NT2 steel-cr10mo2
- NT2 steel-cr12
- NT2 steel-cr12moniv
- NT2 steel-cr12mov
- NT2 steel-cr13
- NT2 steel-cr13al
- NT2 steel-cr16
- NT2 steel-cr16ni
- NT2 steel-cr17cu4ni4nb-l
- NT2 steel-cr17mo
- NT2 steel-cr17ni4mo3
- NT2 steel-cr18
- NT2 steel-cr21ni5ti
- NT2 steel-cr22ni5ti
- NT2 steel-cr25
- NT2 steel-cr26ni5mo-l
- NT2 steel-cr9mo
- NT2 steel-cr9monbv
- NT1 chromium-nickel steels
- NT2 chromium-nickel-molybdenum ste
- NT3 steel-cr11ni10mo2ti-l
- NT3 steel-cr13ni6mo-l
- NT3 steel-cr15ni15motib
- NT3 steel-cr16ni13monbv
- NT3 steel-cr16ni15mo3nb
- NT3 steel-cr16ni16monb
- NT3 steel-cr16ni8mo2
- NT3 steel-cr17ni12monb
- NT3 steel-cr17ni12mo3
- NT3 steel-cr17ni12mo3-l
- NT3 steel-cr17ni13mo2ti
- NT3 steel-cr17ni13mo3ti
- NT3 steel-ni17cr14moti-l
- NT3 steel-ni26cr15ti2movalb
- NT3 steel-ni35cr18mo4ti2al
- NT2 steel-cr13mn8ni8
- NT2 steel-cr17ni13
- NT2 steel-cr17ni7
- NT2 steel-cr18ni10
- NT2 steel-cr18ni10-l
- NT2 steel-cr18ni10ti
- NT2 steel-cr18ni11
- NT2 steel-cr18ni11nb
- NT2 steel-cr18ni11nbco
- NT2 steel-cr18ni12
- NT2 steel-cr18ni12ti
- NT2 steel-cr18ni8
- NT2 steel-cr18ni9
- NT2 steel-cr18ni9ti
- NT2 steel-cr19ni10
- NT2 steel-cr19ni10-l
- NT2 steel-cr20ni11
- NT2 steel-cr20ni11-l
- NT2 steel-cr23ni14
- NT2 steel-cr23ni18
- NT2 steel-cr25ni20
- NT2 steel-ni25cr20

STAINLESS STEELS

- NT2 steel-ni36cr12ti3al-l
- NT2 steel-ni36cr18
- NT1 low carbon-high alloy steels
  - NT2 steel-cr11ni10mo2ti-l
  - NT2 steel-cr13ni6mo-l
  - NT2 steel-cr17cu4ni4nb-l
  - NT2 steel-cr17ni12mo3-l
  - NT2 steel-cr18ni10-l
  - NT2 steel-cr19ni10-l
  - NT2 steel-cr20ni11-l
  - NT2 steel-cr26ni5mo-l
  - NT2 steel-ni17cr14moti-l
  - NT2 steel-ni36cr12ti3al-l
- NT1 steel-cr17mn15nni
- NT1 steel-cr21mn9ni6
- RT corrosion resistant alloys
- RT heat resisting alloys

STAINS [176; 176]
- RT banding techniques
- RT cleaning
- RT dyes
- RT histological techniques

STAMEN [62; 62]
- UF *anthers*
- UF *stamen hairs*
- BT1 flowers

stamen hairs
  USE stamen

standard man
  USE reference man

STANDARD MODEL [2,774; 2,774]
Sep 86
(For the local gauge theory based on a SU(3)xSU(2)xU(1) symmetry that describes strong, weak and electromagnetic interactions among elementary particles.)
- BT1 grand unified theory
  - BT2 unified gauge models
    - BT3 particle models
      - BT4 mathematical models
    - BT3 quantum field theory
      - BT4 field theories
- RT electromagnetic interactions
- RT kobayashi-maskawa matrix
- RT quantum chromodynamics
- RT quantum electrodynamics
- RT strong interactions
- RT unified-field theories
- RT weak interactions
- RT weinberg angle
- RT weinberg lepton model

standard reference materials
  USE calibration standards

STANDARDIZATION [2,522; 2,522]
Feb 77
- RT benchmarks
- RT calibration standards
- RT quality assurance
- RT quality control
- RT safety standards
- RT specifications
- RT standards document

STANDARDIZED TERMINOLOGY [518; 518]
- UF *controlled terminology*
- UF *thesauri*
- UF *vocabulary (controlled)*
- RT information retrieval
- RT information systems
- RT iso

→ § STANDARDS [0; 174] *Aug 91*
- NT1 calibration standards
- NT1 energy efficiency standards
- NT1 safety standards
  - NT2 annual limit of intake
  - NT2 dose limits
  - NT2 maximum acceptable contaminati
  - NT2 maximum inhalation quantity
  - NT2 maximum permissible activity
  - NT2 maximum permissible body burde
  - NT2 maximum permissible concentrat
  - NT2 maximum permissible dose
  - NT2 maximum permissible exposure
  - NT2 maximum permissible intake
  - NT2 maximum permissible level
- RT benchmarks
- RT certification
- RT specifications

standards (calibration)
  USE calibration standards

standards (safety)
  USE safety standards

STANDARDS DOCUMENT [344; 344]
Sep 87
(Use only in conjunction with literary indicator W for indexing the text of national or international standards.)
- RT calibration standards
- RT iso
- RT safety standards
- RT standardization

STANDING WAVES [666; 666]
- UF *waves (standing)*
- RT electromagnetic radiation
- RT mechanical vibrations
- RT steady-state conditions
- RT travelling waves
- RT wave propagation
- RT waveguides
- RT wavelengths

STANFORD LINEAR ACCELERATOR CE [389; 389] *Sep 77*
- UF *slac*
- BT1 us doe
  - BT2 us organizations
    - BT3 national organizations
- BT1 us erda
  - BT2 us organizations
    - BT3 national organizations
- RT california
- RT stanford linear collider
- RT stanford 1200-mev linac
- RT stanford 20-gev linac

STANFORD LINEAR COLLIDER [907; 907] *Feb 84*
- UF *slc*
- BT1 linear accelerators
  - BT2 accelerators
- RT stanford linear accelerator ce
- RT stanford 20-gev linac

STANFORD 1.2-GEV LINAC [0; 0]
Nov 75
  USE stanford 1200-mev linac

STANFORD 1200-MEV LINAC [11; 11]
- UF *stanford 1.2-gev linac*
- BT1 linear accelerators
  - BT2 accelerators
- RT stanford linear accelerator ce

STANFORD 20-GEV LINAC [191; 191]
- UF *slac 2-mile linac*
- BT1 linear accelerators
  - BT2 accelerators
- RT stanford linear accelerator ce
- RT stanford linear collider

STANLEIGH MINE [5; 5] *Oct 82*
- BT1 uranium mines
  - BT2 mines
    - BT3 underground facilities
- RT elliot lake

STANNATES [67; 67]
(Specific compounds should be indexed by coordination of a descriptor of the f (CATION) COMPOUNDS and the abo anion descriptor.)
- BT1 oxygen compounds
- BT1 tin compounds
- RT tin oxides

STAPHYLOCOCCUS [356; 356]
- BT1 bacteria
  - BT2 microorganisms

STAPP THEORY [3; 3]
- UF *stapp-ypsilantis-metropolis th*
- RT nucleons
- RT wave propagation

stapp-ypsilantis-metropolis th
  USE stapp theory

STAR ACCRETION [2,576; 2,576]
- UF *accretion (stars)*
- BT1 star evolution
- RT accretion disks
- RT cosmic dust
- RT cosmological models
- RT eruptive variable stars
- RT interstellar grains
- RT interstellar space
- RT planet-system accretion
- RT protostars
- RT stars

STAR BURNING [294; 932] *Aug 78*
(Astrophysical processes only.)
- UF *stellar burning*
- NT1 carbon burning
- NT1 cno cycle
- NT1 helium burning
- NT1 hydrogen burning

STAR CLUSTERS [2,928; 2,928]
- UF *clusters (star)*
- RT stars

STAR EVOLUTION [7,344; 10,104]
- NT1 r process
- NT1 s process
- NT1 star accretion
- RT carbon burning
- RT cno cycle
- RT cosmology
- RT galactic evolution
- RT gravitational collapse
- RT helium burning
- RT hertzsprung-russell diagram
- RT hydrogen burning
- RT origin
- RT solar system evolution
- RT star models
- RT stars

STAR MODELS [5,678; 5,678] *Oct 7*
(Mathematical models of stars)
- UF *models (star)*
- UF *solar models*
- BT1 mathematical models
- RT carbon burning
- RT cno cycle
- RT hydrogen burning
- RT star evolution
- RT stars

STARCH [319; 319]
- UF *amylum*
- BT1 polysaccharides
  - BT2 saccharides
    - BT3 carbohydrates

```
           BT4    organic compounds
    BT1    reagents
    RT     polyacetals

starch gum
    USE    dextrin

STARFIRE TOKAMAK [156; 156]
  Jul 81
    BT1    tokamak devices
      BT2    closed plasma devices
        BT3    thermonuclear devices

STARFISH EVENT [10; 10]
    BT1    atmospheric explosions
      BT2    explosions
    BT1    dominic project
    BT1    nuclear explosions
      BT2    explosions

STARK EFFECT [1,717; 1,717]
    RT     electric fields
    RT     line broadening
    RT     magneto-optical effects
    RT     spectral shift

STARK REACTOR [7; 7]
  (Schnell-Thermischen Argonaut Reaktor
  Karlsruhe)
    UF     sar-2 reactor
    BT1    argonaut type reactors
      BT2    enriched uranium reactors
        BT3    reactors
      BT2    research and test reactors
        BT3    reactors
      BT2    water cooled reactors
        BT3    reactors
      BT2    water moderated reactors
        BT3    reactors
    BT1    thermal reactors
      BT2    reactors
    BT1    training reactors
      BT2    research and test reactors
        BT3    reactors

STARS [5,773; 28,918]
    NT1    binary stars
    NT2    eruptive variable stars
      NT3    novae
      NT3    supernovae
      NT3    t tauri stars
    NT1    dwarf stars
      NT2    black dwarf stars
      NT2    red dwarf stars
      NT2    white dwarf stars
    NT1    giant stars
      NT2    red giant stars
      NT2    supergiant stars
    NT1    magnetic stars
    NT1    main sequence stars
      NT2    carbon stars
      NT2    sun
      NT2    wolf-rayet stars
    NT1    neutron stars
    NT1    supermassive stars
    NT1    symbiotic stars
    NT1    variable stars
      NT2    eruptive variable stars
        NT3    novae
        NT3    supernovae
        NT3    t tauri stars
      NT2    pulsating variable stars
        NT3    cepheids
    RT     astronomy
    RT     black holes
    RT     carbon burning
    RT     chandrasekhar theory
    RT     nucleosynthesis
    RT     planetary nebulae
    RT     proper motion
    RT     protostars
    RT     quasars
    RT     r process
    RT     s process
    RT     star accretion
```

```
    RT     star clusters
    RT     star evolution
    RT     star models
    RT     stellar activity
    RT     stellar atmospheres
    RT     stellar flares
    RT     stellar winds
    RT     white holes

STARSPOTS [78; 778] Feb 84
  (Small regions of stellar surfaces that have
  a luminosity different from that of their
  surroundings. For the Sun use
  SUNSPOTS.)
    UF     stellar spots
    BT1    stellar activity
    NT1    sunspots
    RT     stellar atmospheres
    RT     stellar flares
    RT     variable stars

START-UP [209; 765] Feb 81
    NT1    reactor start-up
    RT     operation

start-up (fission reactor)
    USE    reactor start-up

starvation
    USE    fasting

state diagrams
    USE    phase diagrams

STATE GOVERNMENT [746; 746]
  Nov 80
  (For the government of a major subdivi-
  sion of a nation, e.g., the governments of
  the individual States of the United States
  of America. For the government of a na-
  tion state use NATIONAL GOVERN-
  MENT.)
    UF     provincial government
    RT     government policies
    RT     legislation
    RT     local government
    RT     national government
    RT     public officials
    RT     regional cooperation
    RT     regulations

state liability
  (Prior to December 1990, this was a valid
  descriptor.)
    USE    liabilities

states (energy)
    USE    energy levels

static electricity eliminators
    USE    electrostatic charge eliminato

STATIC LOADS [712; 712] Feb 81
    UF     loads (static)
    RT     deformation
    RT     dynamic loads
    RT     mechanical tests
    RT     strain rate
    RT     stresses

STATIC MASS SPECTROMETERS
  [55; 55]
    BT1    mass spectrometers
      BT2    spectrometers
        BT3    measuring instruments

static reservoir pressure
    USE    reservoir pressure
```

```
stationary low power plant-1
    USE    sl-1 reactor

stationary med. pow. plant-1
    USE    sm-1 reactor

stationary med. pow. plant-1a
    USE    sm-1a reactor

STATISTICAL DATA [1,782; 1,782]
  Sep 80
  (Use only in conjunction with literary in-
  dicator N for data flagging.)
    BT1    numerical data
      BT2    data
        BT3    information

STATISTICAL MECHANICS
  [3,198; 3,198]
    BT1    mechanics
    RT     bbgky equation
    RT     boltzmann equation
    RT     boltzmann statistics
    RT     bose-einstein statistics
    RT     ergodic hypothesis
    RT     fermi statistics
    RT     kinetic equations
    RT     kinetics
    RT     kubo formula
    RT     liouville theorem
    RT     mean-field theory
    RT     occupation number
    RT     parastatistics
    RT     partition functions

STATISTICAL MODELS [4,708; 6,496]
    UF     models (statistical)
    BT1    mathematical models
    NT1    feynman gas model
    NT1    thermodynamic model
    NT2    hydrodynamic model
    RT     particle models

STATISTICS [6,941; 7,996]
  (Limited to the indexing of information
  on the mathematical discipline of statistics
  or its application in nuclear science; for
  indexing numerical values of a statistical
  nature use STATISTICAL DATA.)
    UF+    demography
    BT1    mathematics
    NT1    regression analysis
    NT1    time-series analysis
    RT     data covariances
    RT     degrees of freedom
    RT     expectation value
    RT     fault tree analysis
    RT     gauss function
    RT     maximum-likelihood fit
    RT     probabilistic estimation
    RT     probability
    RT     random phase approximation
    RT     stochastic processes
    RT     virial theorem
    RT     weighting functions

STATOR-B DEVICE [2; 2]
    BT1    internal ring devices
      BT2    closed plasma devices
        BT3    thermonuclear devices

STATORS [82; 82] Jan 77
    RT     armatures
    RT     machine parts
    RT     rotors

STEADY FLOW [403; 502]
    BT1    fluid flow
    NT1    ideal flow
    RT     steady-state conditions
```

STEADY-STATE CONDITIONS
[3,044; 3,044]
(Reached when all transients fade out.)
- RT equilibrium
- RT standing waves
- RT steady flow
- RT steady-state fusion reactors
- RT transients

STEADY-STATE D-T REACTORS
[76; 76]
- BT1 d-t reactors
- BT2 thermonuclear reactors
- BT1 steady-state fusion reactors
- BT2 thermonuclear reactors

STEADY-STATE FUSION REACTORS
[164; 234]
- BT1 thermonuclear reactors
- NT1 steady-state d-t reactors
- RT steady-state conditions

STEAM [4,346; 4,346]
- UF *steam coolant*
- RT coolants
- RT district heating
- RT flash heating
- RT mollier diagrams
- RT steam generation
- RT steam generators
- RT steam quality
- RT superheating
- RT water
- RT water vapor

STEAM CONDENSERS [791; 900]
- UF *condensers (steam)*
- BT1 vapor condensers
- NT1 ice condensers
- RT film condensation
- RT heat exchangers
- RT heat transfer
- RT reactor cooling systems
- RT steam separators

steam coolant
- USE steam

STEAM COOLED REACTORS [26; 26]
- UF *steam-cooled reactors*
- BT1 gas cooled reactors
- BT2 reactors
- RT water cooled reactors

steam generating heavy wat. r.
- USE sghwr reactor

STEAM GENERATION [72; 238] *Jul 86*
- NT1 cogeneration
- RT steam
- RT steam generators

STEAM GENERATORS [8,422; 8,422]
- UF *generators (steam)*
- BT1 vapor generators
- BT2 boilers
- RT boiling
- RT economizers
- RT feedwater
- RT heat exchangers
- RT heat transfer
- RT reactor cooling systems
- RT steam
- RT steam generation
- RT superheaters

STEAM JET EJECTORS [13; 13]
- BT1 vapor jet ejectors
- RT reactor cooling systems

STEAM LINES [696; 696] *Nov 75*
- BT1 pipelines
- RT pipe whip
- RT reactor cooling systems

STEAM QUALITY [224; 224]
- RT steam
- RT thermodynamics

STEAM SEPARATORS [398; 398]
- UF *separators (steam)*
- BT1 vapor separators
- BT2 separation equipment
- BT3 equipment
- RT reactor cooling systems
- RT steam condensers

steam superheaters
- USE superheaters

STEAM TURBINES [1,616; 1,616]
- BT1 turbines
- RT reactor cooling systems

steam-cooled reactors
- USE steam cooled reactors

stearic acid
- USE octadecanoic acid

steel-astm-a105
- USE carbon steels

steel-astm-a106
- USE carbon steels

steel-astm-a212
(Prior to November 1983 this was a valid descriptor, and older material is so indexed.)
- USE carbon steels

steel-astm-a285
(Prior to November 1983 this was a valid descriptor, and older material is so indexed.)
- USE carbon steels

steel-astm-a302
- USE steel-mnmo

steel-astm-a350 (gr 1)
- USE carbon steels

steel-astm-a350 (gr 2)
- USE carbon steels

steel-astm-a350 (gr 3)
- USE steel-ni4

steel-astm-a350 (gr 4)
- USE steel-crni

steel-astm-a387 (gr 11)
- USE steel-crmo

steel-astm-a387 (gr 12)
- USE steel-crmo

steel-astm-a387 (gr 2)
- USE steel-crmo

steel-astm-a387 (gr 21)
- USE steel-cr2mo

steel-astm-a387 (gr 22)
- USE steel-cr2mo

steel-astm-a387 (gr 5)
- USE steel-cr5mo

steel-astm-a416
(Prior to November 1983 this was a valid descriptor, and older material is so indexed.)
- USE carbon steels

steel-astm-a508 (gr 2)
- USE steel-nimocr

steel-astm-a508 (gr 3)
- USE steel-mnnimo

steel-astm-a508 (gr 4)
- USE steel-ni3crmo

steel-astm-a508 (gr 5)
- USE steel-ni3crmov

steel-astm-a516
(Prior to November 1983 this was a valid descriptor, and older material is so indexed.)
- USE carbon steels

steel-astm-a533 (gr a)
- USE steel-mnnimo

steel-astm-a533 (gr b)
- USE steel-mnnimo

steel-astm-a533 (gr c)
- USE steel-mnmo

steel-astm-a533 (gr d)
- USE steel-mnmo

steel-astm-a537
- USE steel-mncumo

steel-astm-a542
- USE steel-cr2mo

steel-astm-a543
- USE steel-ni3crmo

STEEL-CRALNIMO [17; 17]
- UF *steel-38khmyua*
- BT1 aluminium additions
- BT1 chromium alloys
- BT2 alloys
- BT1 low alloy steels
- BT2 steels
- BT3 carbon additions
- BT3 iron base alloys
- BT4 iron alloys
- BT5 alloys
- BT1 molybdenum additions
- BT1 nickel additions

STEEL-CRMO [115; 115]
- UF *steel-astm-a387 (gr 11)*
- UF *steel-astm-a387 (gr 12)*
- UF *steel-astm-a387 (gr 2)*
- UF *steel-12khm*
- BT1 chromium additions
- BT1 low alloy steels
  - BT2 steels
    - BT3 carbon additions
    - BT3 iron base alloys
      - BT4 iron alloys
        - BT5 alloys
- BT1 molybdenum additions
- BT1 nickel additions

STEEL-CRMOV [332; 332]
- UF *steel-12kh1mf*
- UF *steel-15kh1m1f*
- UF *steel-15kh1m1fl*
- UF *steel-28cdv508*
- UF *steel-5kh2mf*
- BT1 chromium alloys
  - BT2 alloys
- BT1 copper additions
- BT1 low alloy steels
  - BT2 steels
    - BT3 carbon additions
    - BT3 iron base alloys
      - BT4 iron alloys
        - BT5 alloys
- BT1 molybdenum additions
- BT1 nickel additions
- BT1 vanadium additions

STEEL-CRNI [168; 168]
- UF *steel-astm-a350 (gr 4)*
- UF *steel-20kh*
- UF *steel-40kh*
- BT1 chromium additions
- BT1 copper additions
- BT1 low alloy steels
  - BT2 steels
    - BT3 carbon additions
    - BT3 iron base alloys
      - BT4 iron alloys
        - BT5 alloys
- BT1 nickel additions

STEEL-CR10MO2 [9; 9] *Mar 88*
- UF *steel-jfms*
- UF *steel-9cr*
- BT1 chromium steels
  - BT2 chromium alloys
    - BT3 alloys
  - BT2 stainless steels
    - BT3 high alloy steels
      - BT4 steels
        - BT5 carbon additions
        - BT5 iron base alloys
          - BT6 iron alloys
            - BT7 alloys
- BT1 martensitic steels
  - BT2 steels
    - BT3 carbon additions
    - BT3 iron base alloys
      - BT4 iron alloys
        - BT5 alloys
- BT1 molybdenum alloys
  - BT2 alloys
- RT first wall

STEEL-CR11NI10MO2TI-L [26; 26]
- UF *steel-ehp 678*
- UF *steel-ehp 679*
- UF *steel-03kh11n10m2t*
- BT1 chromium-nickel-molybdenum ste
  - BT2 chromium-nickel steels
    - BT3 chromium alloys
      - BT4 alloys
    - BT3 nickel alloys
      - BT4 alloys
    - BT3 stainless steels
      - BT4 high alloy steels
        - BT5 steels
          - BT6 carbon additions
          - BT6 iron base alloys
            - BT7 iron alloys
  - BT2 molybdenum alloys
    - BT3 alloys

- BT1 corrosion resistant alloys
  - BT2 alloys
- BT1 low carbon-high alloy steels
  - BT2 stainless steels
    - BT3 high alloy steels
      - BT4 steels
        - BT5 carbon additions
        - BT5 iron base alloys
          - BT6 iron alloys
            - BT7 alloys
- BT1 titanium alloys
  - BT2 alloys

STEEL-CR12 [31; 31]
- UF *stainless steel-403*
- UF *steel-kh12*
- BT1 chromium steels
  - BT2 chromium alloys
    - BT3 alloys
  - BT2 stainless steels
    - BT3 high alloy steels
      - BT4 steels
        - BT5 carbon additions
        - BT5 iron base alloys
          - BT6 iron alloys
            - BT7 alloys
- BT1 corrosion resistant alloys
  - BT2 alloys
- BT1 heat resisting alloys
  - BT2 alloys
- BT1 martensitic steels
  - BT2 steels
    - BT3 carbon additions
    - BT3 iron base alloys
      - BT4 iron alloys
        - BT5 alloys

STEEL-CR12MONIV [8; 8] *Feb 84*
- UF *steel-x20crmov 121*
- BT1 chromium steels
  - BT2 chromium alloys
    - BT3 alloys
  - BT2 stainless steels
    - BT3 high alloy steels
      - BT4 steels
        - BT5 carbon additions
        - BT5 iron base alloys
          - BT6 iron alloys
            - BT7 alloys
- BT1 corrosion resistant alloys
  - BT2 alloys
- BT1 ferritic steels
  - BT2 steels
    - BT3 carbon additions
    - BT3 iron base alloys
      - BT4 iron alloys
        - BT5 alloys
- BT1 heat resisting alloys
  - BT2 alloys
- BT1 molybdenum additions
- BT1 nickel additions
- BT1 vanadium additions

STEEL-CR12MOV [324; 324] *Sep 79*
- UF *alloy-ht-9*
- UF *steel-ht-9*
- UF *steel-kh12m*
- BT1 chromium steels
  - BT2 chromium alloys
    - BT3 alloys
  - BT2 stainless steels
    - BT3 high alloy steels
      - BT4 steels
        - BT5 carbon additions
        - BT5 iron base alloys
          - BT6 iron alloys
            - BT7 alloys
- BT1 corrosion resistant alloys
  - BT2 alloys
- BT1 heat resisting alloys
  - BT2 alloys
- BT1 martensitic steels
  - BT2 steels
    - BT3 carbon additions
    - BT3 iron base alloys
      - BT4 iron alloys
        - BT5 alloys
- BT1 molybdenum additions
- BT1 vanadium additions

STEEL-CR13 [76; 76]
- UF *croloy 12*
- UF *stainless steel-410*
- UF *steel-kh13*
- UF *steel-2kh13*
- BT1 chromium steels
  - BT2 chromium alloys
    - BT3 alloys
  - BT2 stainless steels
    - BT3 high alloy steels
      - BT4 steels
        - BT5 carbon additions
        - BT5 iron base alloys
          - BT6 iron alloys
            - BT7 alloys
- BT1 corrosion resistant alloys
  - BT2 alloys
- BT1 croloy
  - BT2 steels
    - BT3 carbon additions
    - BT3 iron base alloys
      - BT4 iron alloys
        - BT5 alloys
- BT1 heat resisting alloys
  - BT2 alloys
- BT1 martensitic steels
  - BT2 steels
    - BT3 carbon additions
    - BT3 iron base alloys
      - BT4 iron alloys
        - BT5 alloys

STEEL-CR13AL [23; 23]
- UF *stainless steel-405*
- BT1 aluminium additions
- BT1 chromium steels
  - BT2 chromium alloys
    - BT3 alloys
  - BT2 stainless steels
    - BT3 high alloy steels
      - BT4 steels
        - BT5 carbon additions
        - BT5 iron base alloys
          - BT6 iron alloys
            - BT7 alloys
- BT1 corrosion resistant alloys
  - BT2 alloys
- BT1 ferritic steels
  - BT2 steels
    - BT3 carbon additions
    - BT3 iron base alloys
      - BT4 iron alloys
        - BT5 alloys
- BT1 heat resisting alloys
  - BT2 alloys

STEEL-CR13MN8NI8 [8; 8]
- UF *steel-40kh13n8g8*
- BT1 austenitic steels
  - BT2 steels
    - BT3 carbon additions
    - BT3 iron base alloys
      - BT4 iron alloys
        - BT5 alloys
- BT1 chromium-nickel steels
  - BT2 chromium alloys
    - BT3 alloys
  - BT2 nickel alloys
    - BT3 alloys
  - BT2 stainless steels
    - BT3 high alloy steels
      - BT4 steels
        - BT5 carbon additions
        - BT5 iron base alloys
          - BT6 iron alloys
            - BT7 alloys
- BT1 corrosion resistant alloys
  - BT2 alloys
- BT1 manganese alloys
  - BT2 alloys

STEEL-CR13NI6MO-L [4; 4] *Feb 84*
- UF *steel-13cr6nimo*
- BT1 austenitic steels
  - BT2 steels
    - BT3 carbon additions
    - BT3 iron base alloys
      - BT4 iron alloys
        - BT5 alloys

STEEL-CR13NI6MO-L (continued)

- BT1 chromium-nickel-molybdenum ste
- BT2 chromium-nickel steels
  - BT3 chromium alloys
    - BT4 alloys
  - BT3 nickel alloys
    - BT4 alloys
  - BT3 stainless steels
    - BT4 high alloy steels
      - BT5 steels
        - BT6 carbon additions
        - BT6 iron base alloys
          - BT7 iron alloys
- BT2 molybdenum alloys
  - BT3 alloys
- BT1 corrosion resistant alloys
  - BT2 alloys
- BT1 heat resisting alloys
  - BT2 alloys
- BT1 low carbon-high alloy steels
  - BT2 stainless steels
    - BT3 high alloy steels
      - BT4 steels
        - BT5 carbon additions
        - BT5 iron base alloys
          - BT6 iron alloys
            - BT7 alloys

STEEL-CR15NI15MOTIB [113; 113]

- UF steel-din-1-4970
- BT1 austenitic steels
  - BT2 steels
    - BT3 carbon additions
    - BT3 iron base alloys
      - BT4 iron alloys
        - BT5 alloys
- BT1 boron additions
- BT1 chromium-nickel-molybdenum ste
- BT2 chromium-nickel steels
  - BT3 chromium alloys
    - BT4 alloys
  - BT3 nickel alloys
    - BT4 alloys
  - BT3 stainless steels
    - BT4 high alloy steels
      - BT5 steels
        - BT6 carbon additions
        - BT6 iron base alloys
          - BT7 iron alloys
- BT2 molybdenum alloys
  - BT3 alloys
- BT1 corrosion resistant alloys
  - BT2 alloys
- BT1 heat resisting alloys
  - BT2 alloys
- BT1 titanium additions

STEEL-CR16 [27; 27]

- UF croloy 18
- UF stainless steel-430
- BT1 chromium steels
  - BT2 chromium alloys
    - BT3 alloys
  - BT2 stainless steels
    - BT3 high alloy steels
      - BT4 steels
        - BT5 carbon additions
        - BT5 iron base alloys
          - BT6 iron alloys
            - BT7 alloys
- BT1 corrosion resistant alloys
  - BT2 alloys
- BT1 croloy
  - BT2 steels
    - BT3 carbon additions
    - BT3 iron base alloys
      - BT4 iron alloys
        - BT5 alloys
- BT1 ferritic steels
  - BT2 steels
    - BT3 carbon additions
    - BT3 iron base alloys
      - BT4 iron alloys
        - BT5 alloys
- BT1 heat resisting alloys
  - BT2 alloys

STEEL-CR16NI [5; 5] Mar 77

- UF stainless steel-431
- BT1 chromium steels
  - BT2 chromium alloys
    - BT3 alloys
  - BT2 stainless steels
    - BT3 high alloy steels
      - BT4 steels
        - BT5 carbon additions
        - BT5 iron base alloys
          - BT6 iron alloys
            - BT7 alloys
- BT1 corrosion resistant alloys
  - BT2 alloys
- BT1 heat resisting alloys
  - BT2 alloys
- BT1 martensitic steels
  - BT2 steels
    - BT3 carbon additions
    - BT3 iron base alloys
      - BT4 iron alloys
        - BT5 alloys
- BT1 nickel alloys
  - BT2 alloys

STEEL-CR16NI13MONBV [41; 41]

- UF steel-din-1-4988
- BT1 austenitic steels
  - BT2 steels
    - BT3 carbon additions
    - BT3 iron base alloys
      - BT4 iron alloys
        - BT5 alloys
- BT1 chromium-nickel-molybdenum ste
- BT2 chromium-nickel steels
  - BT3 chromium alloys
    - BT4 alloys
  - BT3 nickel alloys
    - BT4 alloys
  - BT3 stainless steels
    - BT4 high alloy steels
      - BT5 steels
        - BT6 carbon additions
        - BT6 iron base alloys
          - BT7 iron alloys
- BT2 molybdenum alloys
  - BT3 alloys
- BT1 corrosion resistant alloys
  - BT2 alloys
- BT1 heat resisting alloys
  - BT2 alloys
- BT1 niobium additions
- BT1 vanadium additions

STEEL-CR16NI15MO3NB [177; 177] Nov 75

- UF steel-kh16n15m3b
- UF steel-0kh16n15m3b
- UF steel-1kh16n15m3b
- BT1 austenitic steels
  - BT2 steels
    - BT3 carbon additions
    - BT3 iron base alloys
      - BT4 iron alloys
        - BT5 alloys
- BT1 chromium-nickel-molybdenum ste
- BT2 chromium-nickel steels
  - BT3 chromium alloys
    - BT4 alloys
  - BT3 nickel alloys
    - BT4 alloys
  - BT3 stainless steels
    - BT4 high alloy steels
      - BT5 steels
        - BT6 carbon additions
        - BT6 iron base alloys
          - BT7 iron alloys
- BT2 molybdenum alloys
  - BT3 alloys
- BT1 corrosion resistant alloys
  - BT2 alloys
- BT1 heat resisting alloys
  - BT2 alloys
- BT1 niobium additions

STEEL-CR16NI16MONB [55; 55]

- UF steel-din-1-4981
- BT1 austenitic steels
  - BT2 steels
    - BT3 carbon additions
    - BT3 iron base alloys
      - BT4 iron alloys
        - BT5 alloys
- BT1 chromium-nickel-molybdenum ste
- BT2 chromium-nickel steels
  - BT3 chromium alloys
    - BT4 alloys
  - BT3 nickel alloys
    - BT4 alloys
  - BT3 stainless steels
    - BT4 high alloy steels
      - BT5 steels
        - BT6 carbon additions
        - BT6 iron base alloys
          - BT7 iron alloys
- BT2 molybdenum alloys
  - BT3 alloys
- BT1 corrosion resistant alloys
  - BT2 alloys
- BT1 heat resisting alloys
  - BT2 alloys
- BT1 niobium additions

STEEL-CR16NI8MO2 [9; 9] Sep 79

- UF stainless steel-16-8-2
- BT1 austenitic steels
  - BT2 steels
    - BT3 carbon additions
    - BT3 iron base alloys
      - BT4 iron alloys
        - BT5 alloys
- BT1 chromium-nickel-molybdenum s
- BT2 chromium-nickel steels
  - BT3 chromium alloys
    - BT4 alloys
  - BT3 nickel alloys
    - BT4 alloys
  - BT3 stainless steels
    - BT4 high alloy steels
      - BT5 steels
        - BT6 carbon additions
        - BT6 iron base alloys
          - BT7 iron alloys
- BT2 molybdenum alloys
  - BT3 alloys
- BT1 corrosion resistant alloys
  - BT2 alloys
- BT1 heat resisting alloys
  - BT2 alloys

STEEL-CR17CU4NI4NB-L [11; 11]

- UF stainless steel-17-4ph
- BT1 chromium steels
  - BT2 chromium alloys
    - BT3 alloys
  - BT2 stainless steels
    - BT3 high alloy steels
      - BT4 steels
        - BT5 carbon additions
        - BT5 iron base alloys
          - BT6 iron alloys
            - BT7 alloys
- BT1 copper alloys
  - BT2 alloys
- BT1 corrosion resistant alloys
  - BT2 alloys
- BT1 heat resisting alloys
  - BT2 alloys
- BT1 low carbon-high alloy steels
  - BT2 stainless steels
    - BT3 high alloy steels
      - BT4 steels
        - BT5 carbon additions
        - BT5 iron base alloys
          - BT6 iron alloys
            - BT7 alloys
- BT1 martensitic steels
  - BT2 steels
    - BT3 carbon additions
    - BT3 iron base alloys
      - BT4 iron alloys
        - BT5 alloys
- BT1 nickel alloys
  - BT2 alloys

```
                BT1     niobium additions


STEEL-CR17MN15NNI [4; 4] Sep 79
    UF      croloy 299
    UF      tenelon
    BT1     austenitic steels
      BT2     steels
        BT3     carbon additions
        BT3     iron base alloys
          BT4     iron alloys
            BT5     alloys
    BT1     chromium alloys
      BT2     alloys
    BT1     corrosion resistant alloys
      BT2     alloys
    BT1     croloy
      BT2     steels
        BT3     carbon additions
        BT3     iron base alloys
          BT4     iron alloys
            BT5     alloys
    BT1     manganese alloys
      BT2     alloys
    BT1     nickel additions
    BT1     nitrogen additions
    BT1     stainless steels
      BT2     high alloy steels
        BT3     steels
          BT4     carbon additions
          BT4     iron base alloys
            BT5     iron alloys
              BT6     alloys


STEEL-CR17MO [19; 19]
    UF      stainless steel-440
    BT1     chromium steels
      BT2     chromium alloys
        BT3     alloys
      BT2     stainless steels
        BT3     high alloy steels
          BT4     steels
            BT5     carbon additions
            BT5     iron base alloys
              BT6     iron alloys
                BT7     alloys
    BT1     corrosion resistant alloys
      BT2     alloys
    BT1     heat resisting alloys
      BT2     alloys
    BT1     martensitic steels
      BT2     steels
        BT3     carbon additions
        BT3     iron base alloys
          BT4     iron alloys
            BT5     alloys
    BT1     molybdenum additions


STEEL-CR17NI12MONB [26; 26]
    UF      stainless steel-fv548
    BT1     austenitic steels
      BT2     steels
        BT3     carbon additions
        BT3     iron base alloys
          BT4     iron alloys
            BT5     alloys
    BT1     chromium-nickel-molybdenum ste
      BT2     chromium-nickel steels
        BT3     chromium alloys
          BT4     alloys
        BT3     nickel alloys
          BT4     alloys
        BT3     stainless steels
          BT4     high alloy steels
            BT5     steels
              BT6     carbon additions
              BT6     iron base alloys
                BT7     iron alloys
      BT2     molybdenum alloys
        BT3     alloys
    BT1     corrosion resistant alloys
      BT2     alloys
    BT1     heat resisting alloys
      BT2     alloys
    BT1     niobium additions


STEEL-CR17NI12MO3 [3,500; 3,500]
    UF      stainless steel-z6cnd17-12
    UF      stainless steel-316
    UF      steel-din-1-4919
    BT1     austenitic steels
      BT2     steels
        BT3     carbon additions
        BT3     iron base alloys
          BT4     iron alloys
            BT5     alloys
    BT1     chromium-nickel-molybdenum ste
      BT2     chromium-nickel steels
        BT3     chromium alloys
          BT4     alloys
        BT3     nickel alloys
          BT4     alloys
        BT3     stainless steels
          BT4     high alloy steels
            BT5     steels
              BT6     carbon additions
              BT6     iron base alloys
                BT7     iron alloys
      BT2     molybdenum alloys
        BT3     alloys
    BT1     corrosion resistant alloys
      BT2     alloys
    BT1     heat resisting alloys
      BT2     alloys


STEEL-CR17NI12MO3-L [479; 479]
    UF      stainless steel-zcnd17-13
    UF      stainless steel-z2cnd17-12
    UF      stainless steel-z3cnd17-12
    UF      stainless steel-316l
    BT1     austenitic steels
      BT2     steels
        BT3     carbon additions
        BT3     iron base alloys
          BT4     iron alloys
            BT5     alloys
    BT1     chromium-nickel-molybdenum ste
      BT2     chromium-nickel steels
        BT3     chromium alloys
          BT4     alloys
        BT3     nickel alloys
          BT4     alloys
        BT3     stainless steels
          BT4     high alloy steels
            BT5     steels
              BT6     carbon additions
              BT6     iron base alloys
                BT7     iron alloys
      BT2     molybdenum alloys
        BT3     alloys
    BT1     corrosion resistant alloys
      BT2     alloys
    BT1     heat resisting alloys
      BT2     alloys
    BT1     low carbon-high alloy steels
      BT2     stainless steels
        BT3     high alloy steels
          BT4     steels
            BT5     carbon additions
            BT5     iron base alloys
              BT6     iron alloys
                BT7     alloys


STEEL-CR17NI13 [2; 2] Sep 85
    BT1     austenitic steels
      BT2     steels
        BT3     carbon additions
        BT3     iron base alloys
          BT4     iron alloys
            BT5     alloys
    BT1     chromium-nickel steels
      BT2     chromium alloys
        BT3     alloys
      BT2     nickel alloys
        BT3     alloys
      BT2     stainless steels
        BT3     high alloy steels
          BT4     steels
            BT5     carbon additions
            BT5     iron base alloys
              BT6     iron alloys
                BT7     alloys
    BT1     corrosion resistant alloys
      BT2     alloys
    BT1     heat resisting alloys

                BT2     alloys

STEEL-CR17NI13MO2TI [10; 10]
    UF      steel-kh17n13m2t
    BT1     austenitic steels
      BT2     steels
        BT3     carbon additions
        BT3     iron base alloys
          BT4     iron alloys
            BT5     alloys
    BT1     chromium-nickel-molybdenum ste
      BT2     chromium-nickel steels
        BT3     chromium alloys
          BT4     alloys
        BT3     nickel alloys
          BT4     alloys
        BT3     stainless steels
          BT4     high alloy steels
            BT5     steels
              BT6     carbon additions
              BT6     iron base alloys
                BT7     iron alloys
      BT2     molybdenum alloys
        BT3     alloys
    BT1     corrosion resistant alloys
      BT2     alloys
    BT1     heat resisting alloys
      BT2     alloys
    BT1     titanium additions


STEEL-CR17NI13MO3TI [11; 11]
    UF      alloy-ehi 183
    UF      alloy-ehi 397
    UF      alloy-ehi 432
    UF      steel-kh17n13m3t
    BT1     austenitic steels
      BT2     steels
        BT3     carbon additions
        BT3     iron base alloys
          BT4     iron alloys
            BT5     alloys
    BT1     chromium-nickel-molybdenum ste
      BT2     chromium-nickel steels
        BT3     chromium alloys
          BT4     alloys
        BT3     nickel alloys
          BT4     alloys
        BT3     stainless steels
          BT4     high alloy steels
            BT5     steels
              BT6     carbon additions
              BT6     iron base alloys
                BT7     iron alloys
      BT2     molybdenum alloys
        BT3     alloys
    BT1     corrosion resistant alloys
      BT2     alloys
    BT1     heat resisting alloys
      BT2     alloys
    BT1     titanium additions


STEEL-CR17NI4MO3 [13; 13]
    UF      stainless steel-am-350
    BT1     chromium steels
      BT2     chromium alloys
        BT3     alloys
      BT2     stainless steels
        BT3     high alloy steels
          BT4     steels
            BT5     carbon additions
            BT5     iron base alloys
              BT6     iron alloys
                BT7     alloys
    BT1     corrosion resistant alloys
      BT2     alloys
    BT1     heat resisting alloys
      BT2     alloys
    BT1     molybdenum alloys
      BT2     alloys
    BT1     nickel alloys
      BT2     alloys


STEEL-CR17NI7 [21; 21]
    UF      stainless steel-301
    BT1     austenitic steels
      BT2     steels
        BT3     carbon additions
        BT3     iron base alloys
          BT4     iron alloys
```

                BT5   alloys
        BT1   chromium-nickel steels
        BT2   chromium alloys
            BT3   alloys
        BT2   nickel alloys
            BT3   alloys
        BT2   stainless steels
            BT3   high alloy steels
              BT4   steels
                BT5   carbon additions
                BT5   iron base alloys
                  BT6   iron alloys
                    BT7   alloys
    BT1   corrosion resistant alloys
        BT2   alloys
    BT1   heat resisting alloys
        BT2   alloys

STEEL-CR18 [11; 11]
    UF   *steel-kh18*
    UF   *steel-9kh18*
    BT1   chromium steels
        BT2   chromium alloys
            BT3   alloys
        BT2   stainless steels
            BT3   high alloy steels
              BT4   steels
                BT5   carbon additions
                BT5   iron base alloys
                  BT6   iron alloys
                    BT7   alloys
    BT1   corrosion resistant alloys
        BT2   alloys
    BT1   martensitic steels
        BT2   steels
            BT3   carbon additions
            BT3   iron base alloys
              BT4   iron alloys
                BT5   alloys

STEEL-CR18NI10 [73; 73] *Nov 75*
    UF   *croloy 3035*
    UF   *stainless steel-z6cn18-10*
    UF   *stainless steel-18-10*
    UF   *steel-kh18n10*
    BT1   austenitic steels
        BT2   steels
            BT3   carbon additions
            BT3   iron base alloys
              BT4   iron alloys
                BT5   alloys
    BT1   chromium-nickel steels
        BT2   chromium alloys
            BT3   alloys
        BT2   nickel alloys
            BT3   alloys
        BT2   stainless steels
            BT3   high alloy steels
              BT4   steels
                BT5   carbon additions
                BT5   iron base alloys
                  BT6   iron alloys
                    BT7   alloys
    BT1   corrosion resistant alloys
        BT2   alloys
    BT1   croloy
        BT2   steels
            BT3   carbon additions
            BT3   iron base alloys
              BT4   iron alloys
                BT5   alloys
    BT1   heat resisting alloys
        BT2   alloys

STEEL-CR18NI10-L [25; 25]
    UF   *stainless steel-z2cn18-10*
    BT1   austenitic steels
        BT2   steels
            BT3   carbon additions
            BT3   iron base alloys
              BT4   iron alloys
                BT5   alloys
    BT1   chromium-nickel steels
        BT2   chromium alloys
            BT3   alloys
        BT2   nickel alloys
            BT3   alloys
        BT2   stainless steels
            BT3   high alloy steels
              BT4   steels
                BT5   carbon additions
                BT5   iron base alloys
                  BT6   iron alloys
                    BT7   alloys
    BT1   corrosion resistant alloys
        BT2   alloys
    BT1   heat resisting alloys
        BT2   alloys
    BT1   low carbon-high alloy steels
        BT2   stainless steels
            BT3   high alloy steels
              BT4   steels
                BT5   carbon additions
                BT5   iron base alloys
                  BT6   iron alloys
                    BT7   alloys

STEEL-CR18NI10TI [937; 937]
    UF   *stainless steel-z6cnt18-10*
    UF   *stainless steel-z8cnt18-10*
    UF   *stainless steel-321*
    UF   *steel-kh18n10t*
    UF   *steel-0kh18n10t*
    UF   *steel-08kh18n10t*
    UF   *steel-1kh18n10t*
    BT1   austenitic steels
        BT2   steels
            BT3   carbon additions
            BT3   iron base alloys
              BT4   iron alloys
                BT5   alloys
    BT1   chromium-nickel steels
        BT2   chromium alloys
            BT3   alloys
        BT2   nickel alloys
            BT3   alloys
        BT2   stainless steels
            BT3   high alloy steels
              BT4   steels
                BT5   carbon additions
                BT5   iron base alloys
                  BT6   iron alloys
                    BT7   alloys
    BT1   corrosion resistant alloys
        BT2   alloys
    BT1   heat resisting alloys
        BT2   alloys
    BT1   titanium additions

STEEL-CR18NI11 [125; 125]
    UF   *steel-din-1-4948*
    UF   *steel-x6crni1811*
    BT1   austenitic steels
        BT2   steels
            BT3   carbon additions
            BT3   iron base alloys
              BT4   iron alloys
                BT5   alloys
    BT1   chromium-nickel steels
        BT2   chromium alloys
            BT3   alloys
        BT2   nickel alloys
            BT3   alloys
        BT2   stainless steels
            BT3   high alloy steels
              BT4   steels
                BT5   carbon additions
                BT5   iron base alloys
                  BT6   iron alloys
                    BT7   alloys
    BT1   corrosion resistant alloys
        BT2   alloys
    BT1   heat resisting alloys
        BT2   alloys

STEEL-CR18NI11NB [163; 163]
    UF   *stainless steel-347*
    BT1   austenitic steels
        BT2   steels
            BT3   carbon additions
            BT3   iron base alloys
              BT4   iron alloys
                BT5   alloys
    BT1   chromium-nickel steels
        BT2   chromium alloys
            BT3   alloys
        BT2   nickel alloys
            BT3   alloys
        BT2   stainless steels
            BT3   high alloy steels
              BT4   steels
                BT5   carbon additions
                BT5   iron base alloys
                  BT6   iron alloys
                    BT7   alloys
    BT1   corrosion resistant alloys
        BT2   alloys
    BT1   heat resisting alloys
        BT2   alloys
    BT1   niobium additions

STEEL-CR18NI11NBCO [23; 23]
    UF   *stainless steel-348*
    BT1   austenitic steels
        BT2   steels
            BT3   carbon additions
            BT3   iron base alloys
              BT4   iron alloys
                BT5   alloys
    BT1   chromium-nickel steels
        BT2   chromium alloys
            BT3   alloys
        BT2   nickel alloys
            BT3   alloys
        BT2   stainless steels
            BT3   high alloy steels
              BT4   steels
                BT5   carbon additions
                BT5   iron base alloys
                  BT6   iron alloys
                    BT7   alloys
    BT1   cobalt additions
    BT1   corrosion resistant alloys
        BT2   alloys
    BT1   heat resisting alloys
        BT2   alloys
    BT1   niobium additions

STEEL-CR18NI12 [10; 10] *Jul 76*
    UF   *stainless steel-305*
    BT1   austenitic steels
        BT2   steels
            BT3   carbon additions
            BT3   iron base alloys
              BT4   iron alloys
                BT5   alloys
    BT1   chromium-nickel steels
        BT2   chromium alloys
            BT3   alloys
        BT2   nickel alloys
            BT3   alloys
        BT2   stainless steels
            BT3   high alloy steels
              BT4   steels
                BT5   carbon additions
                BT5   iron base alloys
                  BT6   iron alloys
                    BT7   alloys
    BT1   corrosion resistant alloys
        BT2   alloys
    BT1   heat resisting alloys
        BT2   alloys

STEEL-CR18NI12TI [32; 32]
    UF   *steel-kh18n12t*
    BT1   austenitic steels
        BT2   steels
            BT3   carbon additions
            BT3   iron base alloys
              BT4   iron alloys
                BT5   alloys
    BT1   chromium-nickel steels
        BT2   chromium alloys
            BT3   alloys
        BT2   nickel alloys
            BT3   alloys
        BT2   stainless steels
            BT3   high alloy steels
              BT4   steels
                BT5   carbon additions
                BT5   iron base alloys
                  BT6   iron alloys
                    BT7   alloys
    BT1   corrosion resistant alloys
        BT2   alloys
    BT1   heat resisting alloys
        BT2   alloys

BT1 titanium additions

STEEL-CR18NI8 [73; 73]
UF *stainless steel-18-8*
BT1 austenitic steels
  BT2 steels
    BT3 carbon additions
    BT3 iron base alloys
      BT4 iron alloys
        BT5 alloys
BT1 chromium-nickel steels
  BT2 chromium alloys
    BT3 alloys
  BT2 nickel alloys
    BT3 alloys
  BT2 stainless steels
    BT3 high alloy steels
      BT4 steels
        BT5 carbon additions
        BT5 iron base alloys
          BT6 iron alloys
            BT7 alloys
BT1 corrosion resistant alloys
  BT2 alloys
BT1 heat resisting alloys
  BT2 alloys

STEEL-CR18NI9 [76; 76]
UF *stainless steel-302*
UF *steel-din-1-4301*
UF *steel-kh18n9*
UF *steel-1kh18n9*
UF *steel-7kh18n9*
BT1 austenitic steels
  BT2 steels
    BT3 carbon additions
    BT3 iron base alloys
      BT4 iron alloys
        BT5 alloys
BT1 chromium-nickel steels
  BT2 chromium alloys
    BT3 alloys
  BT2 nickel alloys
    BT3 alloys
  BT2 stainless steels
    BT3 high alloy steels
      BT4 steels
        BT5 carbon additions
        BT5 iron base alloys
          BT6 iron alloys
            BT7 alloys
BT1 corrosion resistant alloys
  BT2 alloys
BT1 heat resisting alloys
  BT2 alloys

STEEL-CR18NI9TI [137; 137]
UF *steel-kh18n9t*
UF *steel-0kh18n9t*
UF *steel-1kh18n9t*
BT1 austenitic steels
  BT2 steels
    BT3 carbon additions
    BT3 iron base alloys
      BT4 iron alloys
        BT5 alloys
BT1 chromium-nickel steels
  BT2 chromium alloys
    BT3 alloys
  BT2 nickel alloys
    BT3 alloys
  BT2 stainless steels
    BT3 high alloy steels
      BT4 steels
        BT5 carbon additions
        BT5 iron base alloys
          BT6 iron alloys
            BT7 alloys
BT1 corrosion resistant alloys
  BT2 alloys
BT1 heat resisting alloys
  BT2 alloys
BT1 titanium additions

STEEL-CR19NI10 [2,676; 2,676]
UF *stainless steel-304*
BT1 austenitic steels
  BT2 steels
    BT3 carbon additions
    BT3 iron base alloys
      BT4 iron alloys
        BT5 alloys
BT1 chromium-nickel steels
  BT2 chromium alloys
    BT3 alloys
  BT2 nickel alloys
    BT3 alloys
  BT2 stainless steels
    BT3 high alloy steels
      BT4 steels
        BT5 carbon additions
        BT5 iron base alloys
          BT6 iron alloys
            BT7 alloys
BT1 corrosion resistant alloys
  BT2 alloys
BT1 heat resisting alloys
  BT2 alloys

STEEL-CR19NI10-L [486; 486]
UF *stainless steel-304l*
BT1 austenitic steels
  BT2 steels
    BT3 carbon additions
    BT3 iron base alloys
      BT4 iron alloys
        BT5 alloys
BT1 chromium-nickel steels
  BT2 chromium alloys
    BT3 alloys
  BT2 nickel alloys
    BT3 alloys
  BT2 stainless steels
    BT3 high alloy steels
      BT4 steels
        BT5 carbon additions
        BT5 iron base alloys
          BT6 iron alloys
            BT7 alloys
BT1 corrosion resistant alloys
  BT2 alloys
BT1 heat resisting alloys
  BT2 alloys
BT1 low carbon-high alloy steels
  BT2 stainless steels
    BT3 high alloy steels
      BT4 steels
        BT5 carbon additions
        BT5 iron base alloys
          BT6 iron alloys
            BT7 alloys

STEEL-CR2MO [151; 151]
UF *croloy 2*
UF *steel-astm-a387 (gr 21)*
UF *steel-astm-a387 (gr 22)*
UF *steel-astm-a542*
UF *steel-10cd9-10*
UF *steel-15cd9-10*
BT1 chromium alloys
  BT2 alloys
BT1 croloy
  BT2 steels
    BT3 carbon additions
    BT3 iron base alloys
      BT4 iron alloys
        BT5 alloys
BT1 low alloy steels
  BT2 steels
    BT3 carbon additions
    BT3 iron base alloys
      BT4 iron alloys
        BT5 alloys
BT1 molybdenum additions

STEEL-CR2MONINB [16; 16]
UF *sandvik-ht8x6*
UF *steel-din-1-6770*
UF *steel-10crninb910*
UF *steel-3hk5s*
BT1 chromium alloys
  BT2 alloys
BT1 heat resisting alloys
  BT2 alloys
BT1 low alloy steels
  BT2 steels
    BT3 carbon additions
    BT3 iron base alloys
      BT4 iron alloys
        BT5 alloys
BT1 molybdenum additions
BT1 nickel additions
BT1 niobium additions
RT ferrite

STEEL-CR2MOV [155; 155] *Nov 81*
UF *steel-15kh2mfa*
BT1 chromium alloys
  BT2 alloys
BT1 copper additions
BT1 low alloy steels
  BT2 steels
    BT3 carbon additions
    BT3 iron base alloys
      BT4 iron alloys
        BT5 alloys
BT1 molybdenum additions
BT1 nickel additions
BT1 vanadium additions

STEEL-CR2NIMOV [45; 45] *May 86*
BT1 chromium alloys
  BT2 alloys
BT1 copper additions
BT1 low alloy steels
  BT2 steels
    BT3 carbon additions
    BT3 iron base alloys
      BT4 iron alloys
        BT5 alloys
BT1 molybdenum additions
BT1 nickel alloys
  BT2 alloys
BT1 vanadium additions

STEEL-CR20NI11 [111; 111]
UF *stainless steel-308*
BT1 austenitic steels
  BT2 steels
    BT3 carbon additions
    BT3 iron base alloys
      BT4 iron alloys
        BT5 alloys
BT1 chromium-nickel steels
  BT2 chromium alloys
    BT3 alloys
  BT2 nickel alloys
    BT3 alloys
  BT2 stainless steels
    BT3 high alloy steels
      BT4 steels
        BT5 carbon additions
        BT5 iron base alloys
          BT6 iron alloys
            BT7 alloys
BT1 corrosion resistant alloys
  BT2 alloys
BT1 heat resisting alloys
  BT2 alloys

STEEL-CR20NI11-L [23; 23] *May 80*
UF *stainless steel-308l*
BT1 austenitic steels
  BT2 steels
    BT3 carbon additions
    BT3 iron base alloys
      BT4 iron alloys
        BT5 alloys
BT1 chromium-nickel steels
  BT2 chromium alloys
    BT3 alloys
  BT2 nickel alloys
    BT3 alloys
  BT2 stainless steels
    BT3 high alloy steels
      BT4 steels
        BT5 carbon additions
        BT5 iron base alloys
          BT6 iron alloys
            BT7 alloys
BT1 corrosion resistant alloys
  BT2 alloys

STEEL-CR21MN9NI6 [17; 17] *Sep 80*
- UF   *nitronic 40*
- UF   *stainless steel-21-6-9*
- BT1   austenitic steels
  - BT2   steels
    - BT3   carbon additions
    - BT3   iron base alloys
      - BT4   iron alloys
        - BT5   alloys
- BT1   chromium alloys
  - BT2   alloys
- BT1   corrosion resistant alloys
  - BT2   alloys
- BT1   heat resisting alloys
  - BT2   alloys
- BT1   manganese alloys
  - BT2   alloys
- BT1   nickel alloys
  - BT2   alloys
- BT1   nitrogen additions
- BT1   stainless steels
  - BT2   high alloy steels
    - BT3   steels
      - BT4   carbon additions
      - BT4   iron base alloys
        - BT5   iron alloys
          - BT6   alloys

STEEL-CR21NI5TI [7; 7]
- UF   *steel-0kh21n5t*
- BT1   chromium steels
  - BT2   chromium alloys
    - BT3   alloys
  - BT2   stainless steels
    - BT3   high alloy steels
      - BT4   steels
        - BT5   carbon additions
        - BT5   iron base alloys
          - BT6   iron alloys
            - BT7   alloys
- BT1   corrosion resistant alloys
  - BT2   alloys
- BT1   nickel alloys
  - BT2   alloys
- BT1   titanium additions

STEEL-CR22NI5TI [7; 7]
- UF   *steel-0kh22n5t*
- BT1   chromium steels
  - BT2   chromium alloys
    - BT3   alloys
  - BT2   stainless steels
    - BT3   high alloy steels
      - BT4   steels
        - BT5   carbon additions
        - BT5   iron base alloys
          - BT6   iron alloys
            - BT7   alloys
- BT1   corrosion resistant alloys
  - BT2   alloys
- BT1   nickel alloys
  - BT2   alloys
- BT1   titanium additions

STEEL-CR23NI14 [43; 43]
- UF   *stainless steel-309*
- UF   *stainless steel-309s*
- BT1   austenitic steels
  - BT2   steels
    - BT3   carbon additions
    - BT3   iron base alloys
      - BT4   iron alloys
        - BT5   alloys
- BT1   chromium-nickel steels
  - BT2   chromium alloys
    - BT3   alloys
  - BT2   nickel alloys
    - BT3   alloys
  - BT2   stainless steels
    - BT3   high alloy steels
      - BT4   steels
        - BT5   carbon additions
        - BT5   iron base alloys
          - BT6   iron alloys
            - BT7   alloys
- BT1   corrosion resistant alloys
  - BT2   alloys
- BT1   heat resisting alloys
  - BT2   alloys

STEEL-CR23NI18 [15; 15]
- UF   *steel-kh23n18*
- BT1   austenitic steels
  - BT2   steels
    - BT3   carbon additions
    - BT3   iron base alloys
      - BT4   iron alloys
        - BT5   alloys
- BT1   chromium-nickel steels
  - BT2   chromium alloys
    - BT3   alloys
  - BT2   nickel alloys
    - BT3   alloys
  - BT2   stainless steels
    - BT3   high alloy steels
      - BT4   steels
        - BT5   carbon additions
        - BT5   iron base alloys
          - BT6   iron alloys
            - BT7   alloys
- BT1   corrosion resistant alloys
  - BT2   alloys
- BT1   heat resisting alloys
  - BT2   alloys

STEEL-CR25 [10; 10]
- UF   *stainless steel-446*
- UF   *steel-kh25*
- BT1   chromium steels
  - BT2   chromium alloys
    - BT3   alloys
  - BT2   stainless steels
    - BT3   high alloy steels
      - BT4   steels
        - BT5   carbon additions
        - BT5   iron base alloys
          - BT6   iron alloys
            - BT7   alloys
- BT1   corrosion resistant alloys
  - BT2   alloys
- BT1   ferritic steels
  - BT2   steels
    - BT3   carbon additions
    - BT3   iron base alloys
      - BT4   iron alloys
        - BT5   alloys
- BT1   heat resisting alloys
  - BT2   alloys

STEEL-CR25NI20 [108; 108]
- UF   *alloy-ck-20*
- UF   *alloy-hk-40*
- UF   *stainless steel-310*
- BT1   austenitic steels
  - BT2   steels
    - BT3   carbon additions
    - BT3   iron base alloys
      - BT4   iron alloys
        - BT5   alloys
- BT1   chromium-nickel steels
  - BT2   chromium alloys
    - BT3   alloys
  - BT2   nickel alloys
    - BT3   alloys
  - BT2   stainless steels
    - BT3   high alloy steels
      - BT4   steels
        - BT5   carbon additions
        - BT5   iron base alloys
          - BT6   iron alloys
            - BT7   alloys
- BT1   corrosion resistant alloys
  - BT2   alloys
- BT1   heat resisting alloys
  - BT2   alloys

(continued from STEEL-CR20NI11-L)
- BT1   heat resisting alloys
  - BT2   alloys
- BT1   low carbon-high alloy steels
  - BT2   stainless steels
    - BT3   high alloy steels
      - BT4   steels
        - BT5   carbon additions
        - BT5   iron base alloys
          - BT6   iron alloys
            - BT7   alloys

STEEL-CR26NI5MO-L [2; 2] *Feb 81*
- UF   *stainless steel-44ln*
- BT1   chromium steels
  - BT2   chromium alloys
    - BT3   alloys
  - BT2   stainless steels
    - BT3   high alloy steels
      - BT4   steels
        - BT5   carbon additions
        - BT5   iron base alloys
          - BT6   iron alloys
            - BT7   alloys
- BT1   corrosion resistant alloys
  - BT2   alloys
- BT1   heat resisting alloys
  - BT2   alloys
- BT1   low carbon-high alloy steels
  - BT2   stainless steels
    - BT3   high alloy steels
      - BT4   steels
        - BT5   carbon additions
        - BT5   iron base alloys
          - BT6   iron alloys
            - BT7   alloys
- BT1   molybdenum alloys
  - BT2   alloys
- BT1   nickel alloys
  - BT2   alloys

STEEL-CR5MO [5; 5] *Nov 83*
- UF   *croloy 5*
- UF   *steel-astm-a387 (gr 5)*
- UF   *steel-kh5m*
- BT1   chromium alloys
  - BT2   alloys
- BT1   croloy
  - BT2   steels
    - BT3   carbon additions
    - BT3   iron base alloys
      - BT4   iron alloys
        - BT5   alloys
- BT1   low alloy steels
  - BT2   steels
    - BT3   carbon additions
    - BT3   iron base alloys
      - BT4   iron alloys
        - BT5   alloys
- BT1   molybdenum additions

STEEL-CR9MO [79; 79] *Feb 84*
- BT1   chromium steels
  - BT2   chromium alloys
    - BT3   alloys
  - BT2   stainless steels
    - BT3   high alloy steels
      - BT4   steels
        - BT5   carbon additions
        - BT5   iron base alloys
          - BT6   iron alloys
            - BT7   alloys
- BT1   ferritic steels
  - BT2   steels
    - BT3   carbon additions
    - BT3   iron base alloys
      - BT4   iron alloys
        - BT5   alloys
- BT1   molybdenum additions

STEEL-CR9MONBV [45; 45]
- UF   *steel-z10cdnbv9*
- BT1   chromium steels
  - BT2   chromium alloys
    - BT3   alloys
  - BT2   stainless steels
    - BT3   high alloy steels
      - BT4   steels
        - BT5   carbon additions
        - BT5   iron base alloys
          - BT6   iron alloys
            - BT7   alloys
- BT1   ferritic steels
  - BT2   steels
    - BT3   carbon additions
    - BT3   iron base alloys
      - BT4   iron alloys
        - BT5   alloys
- BT1   molybdenum alloys
  - BT2   alloys
- BT1   niobium additions

BT1   vanadium additions

steel-din-1-4301
  USE   steel-cr18ni9

steel-din-1-4919
  USE   steel-cr17ni12mo3

steel-din-1-4948
  USE   steel-cr18ni11

steel-din-1-4970
  USE   steel-cr15ni15motib

steel-din-1-4981
  USE   steel-cr16ni16monb

steel-din-1-4988
  USE   steel-cr16ni13monbv

steel-din-1-6310
  USE   steel-mnnimo

steel-din-1-6342
  USE   steel-mnnimov

steel-din-1-6343
  USE   steel-mnnimo

steel-din-1-6348
  USE   steel-ni3mov

steel-din-1-6742
  USE   steel-ni3crmo

steel-din-1-6751
  USE   steel-nimocr

steel-din-1-6770
  USE   steel-cr2moninb

steel-din-1-6950
  USE   steel-ni3crmov

steel-ehp 678
  USE   steel-cr11ni10mo2ti-l

steel-ehp 679
  USE   steel-cr11ni10mo2ti-l

steel-ht-9
  USE   steel-cr12mov

steel-ifms
  USE   steel-cr10mo2

steel-kh12
  USE   steel-cr12

steel-kh12m
  USE   steel-cr12mov

steel-kh13
  USE   steel-cr13

steel-kh16n15m3b
  USE   steel-cr16ni15mo3nb

steel-kh17n13m2t
  USE   steel-cr17ni13mo2ti

steel-kh17n13m3t
  USE   steel-cr17ni13mo3ti

steel-kh18
  USE   steel-cr18

steel-kh18n10
  USE   steel-cr18ni10

steel-kh18n10t
  USE   steel-cr18ni10ti

steel-kh18n12t
  USE   steel-cr18ni12ti

steel-kh18n9
  USE   steel-cr18ni9

steel-kh18n9t
  USE   steel-cr18ni9ti

steel-kh20n45b
  USE   alloy-ni45fe34cr20

steel-kh23n18
  USE   steel-cr23ni18

steel-kh25
  USE   steel-cr25

steel-kh5m
  USE   steel-cr5mo

STEEL-MNCUMO [11; 11] *Mar 81*
  UF   *steel-astm-a537*
  BT1   chromium additions
  BT1   copper additions
  BT1   low alloy steels
    BT2   steels
      BT3   carbon additions
      BT3   iron base alloys
        BT4   iron alloys
          BT5   alloys
  BT1   manganese alloys
    BT2   alloys
  BT1   molybdenum additions
  BT1   nickel additions

STEEL-MNMO [133; 133]
  UF   *steel-astm-a302*
  UF   *steel-astm-a533 (gr c)*
  UF   *steel-astm-a533 (gr d)*
  BT1   low alloy steels
    BT2   steels
      BT3   carbon additions
      BT3   iron base alloys
        BT4   iron alloys
          BT5   alloys
  BT1   manganese alloys
    BT2   alloys
  BT1   molybdenum additions

STEEL-MNNIMO [833; 833]
  UF   *steel-astm-a508 (gr 3)*
  UF   *steel-astm-a533 (gr a)*
  UF   *steel-astm-a533 (gr b)*
  UF   *steel-din-1-6310*
  UF   *steel-din-1-6343*
  BT1   low alloy steels
    BT2   steels
      BT3   carbon additions
      BT3   iron base alloys
        BT4   iron alloys
          BT5   alloys
  BT1   manganese alloys
    BT2   alloys
  BT1   molybdenum additions
  BT1   nickel additions

STEEL-MNNIMOV [14; 14] *Jul 80*
  UF   *steel-din-1-6342*
  BT1   low alloy steels
    BT2   steels
      BT3   carbon additions
      BT3   iron base alloys
        BT4   iron alloys
          BT5   alloys
  BT1   manganese alloys
    BT2   alloys
  BT1   molybdenum additions
  BT1   nickel alloys
    BT2   alloys
  BT1   vanadium additions

STEEL-NICR [21; 21]
  UF   *steel-40khn*
  BT1   chromium additions
  BT1   copper additions
  BT1   low alloy steels
    BT2   steels
      BT3   carbon additions
      BT3   iron base alloys
        BT4   iron alloys
          BT5   alloys
  BT1   nickel alloys
    BT2   alloys

STEEL-NICRMO [33; 33]
  UF   *steel-40khnma*
  BT1   chromium additions
  BT1   copper additions
  BT1   low alloy steels
    BT2   steels
      BT3   carbon additions
      BT3   iron base alloys
        BT4   iron alloys
          BT5   alloys
  BT1   molybdenum additions
  BT1   nickel alloys
    BT2   alloys
  BT1   nitrogen additions

STEEL-NIMOCR [192; 192]
  UF   *steel-astm-a508 (gr 2)*
  UF   *steel-din-1-6751*
  UF   *steel-22nimocr37*
  BT1   chromium additions
  BT1   heat resisting alloys
    BT2   alloys
  BT1   low alloy steels
    BT2   steels
      BT3   carbon additions
      BT3   iron base alloys
        BT4   iron alloys
          BT5   alloys
  BT1   molybdenum additions
  BT1   nickel additions

STEEL-NI17CR14MOTI-L [0; 0] *Nov 84*
  BT1   austenitic steels
    BT2   steels
      BT3   carbon additions
      BT3   iron base alloys
        BT4   iron alloys
          BT5   alloys
  BT1   chromium-nickel-molybdenum ste
    BT2   chromium-nickel steels
      BT3   chromium alloys
        BT4   alloys
      BT3   nickel alloys

                BT4   alloys
            BT3   stainless steels
                BT4   high alloy steels
                    BT5   steels
                        BT6   carbon additions
                        BT6   iron base alloys
                            BT7   iron alloys
        BT2   molybdenum alloys
            BT3   alloys
    BT1   corrosion resistant alloys
        BT2   alloys
    BT1   heat resisting alloys
        BT2   alloys
    BT1   low carbon-high alloy steels
        BT2   stainless steels
            BT3   high alloy steels
                BT4   steels
                    BT5   carbon additions
                    BT5   iron base alloys
                        BT6   iron alloys
                            BT7   alloys
    BT1   titanium additions

STEEL-NI25CR20 [108; 108]
    UF   *stainless steel-20-25*
    BT1   austenitic steels
        BT2   steels
            BT3   carbon additions
            BT3   iron base alloys
                BT4   iron alloys
                    BT5   alloys
    BT1   chromium-nickel steels
        BT2   chromium alloys
            BT3   alloys
        BT2   nickel alloys
            BT3   alloys
        BT2   stainless steels
            BT3   high alloy steels
                BT4   steels
                    BT5   carbon additions
                    BT5   iron base alloys
                        BT6   iron alloys
                            BT7   alloys
    BT1   corrosion resistant alloys
        BT2   alloys
    BT1   heat resisting alloys
        BT2   alloys

STEEL-NI26CR15TI2MOVALB [74; 74]
    UF   *alloy-a-286*
    BT1   aluminium additions
    BT1   austenitic steels
        BT2   steels
            BT3   carbon additions
            BT3   iron base alloys
                BT4   iron alloys
                    BT5   alloys
    BT1   boron additions
    BT1   chromium-nickel-molybdenum ste
        BT2   chromium-nickel steels
            BT3   chromium alloys
                BT4   alloys
            BT3   nickel alloys
                BT4   alloys
            BT3   stainless steels
                BT4   high alloy steels
                    BT5   steels
                        BT6   carbon additions
                        BT6   iron base alloys
                            BT7   iron alloys
        BT2   molybdenum alloys
            BT3   alloys
    BT1   corrosion resistant alloys
        BT2   alloys
    BT1   heat resisting alloys
        BT2   alloys
    BT1   titanium alloys
        BT2   alloys
    BT1   vanadium additions

STEEL-NI3CR [14; 14]
    UF   *steel-12khn3*
    UF   *steel-12khn3a*
    UF   *steel-12kh2nch*
    BT1   chromium additions
    BT1   copper additions
    BT1   low alloy steels
        BT2   steels
            BT3   carbon additions
            BT3   iron base alloys
                BT4   iron alloys
                    BT5   alloys
    BT1   nickel alloys
        BT2   alloys

STEEL-NI3CRMO [38; 38]
    UF   *steel-astm-a508 (gr 4)*
    UF   *steel-astm-a543*
    UF   *steel-din-1-6742*
    BT1   chromium alloys
        BT2   alloys
    BT1   low alloy steels
        BT2   steels
            BT3   carbon additions
            BT3   iron base alloys
                BT4   iron alloys
                    BT5   alloys
    BT1   molybdenum additions
    BT1   nickel alloys
        BT2   alloys
    BT1   vanadium additions

STEEL-NI3CRMOV [9; 9] *Jul 80*
    UF   *steel-astm-a508 (gr 5)*
    UF   *steel-din-1-6950*
    BT1   chromium alloys
        BT2   alloys
    BT1   low alloy steels
        BT2   steels
            BT3   carbon additions
            BT3   iron base alloys
                BT4   iron alloys
                    BT5   alloys
    BT1   molybdenum additions
    BT1   nickel alloys
        BT2   alloys
    BT1   vanadium additions

STEEL-NI3MOV [2; 2] *Jul 80*
    UF   *steel-din-1-6348*
    BT1   low alloy steels
        BT2   steels
            BT3   carbon additions
            BT3   iron base alloys
                BT4   iron alloys
                    BT5   alloys
    BT1   molybdenum additions
    BT1   nickel alloys
        BT2   alloys
    BT1   vanadium additions

STEEL-NI35CR18MO4TI2AL [3; 3] *Dec 80*
    UF   *alloy-m-813*
    BT1   aluminium alloys
        BT2   alloys
    BT1   chromium-nickel-molybdenum ste
        BT2   chromium-nickel steels
            BT3   chromium alloys
                BT4   alloys
            BT3   nickel alloys
                BT4   alloys
            BT3   stainless steels
                BT4   high alloy steels
                    BT5   steels
                        BT6   carbon additions
                        BT6   iron base alloys
                            BT7   iron alloys
        BT2   molybdenum alloys
            BT3   alloys
    BT1   corrosion resistant alloys
        BT2   alloys
    BT1   titanium alloys
        BT2   alloys

STEEL-NI36CR12TI3AL-L [15; 15]
    UF   *alloy-ehi 702*
    UF   *steel-n36khtyu*
    BT1   aluminium additions
    BT1   chromium-nickel steels
        BT2   chromium alloys
            BT3   alloys
        BT2   nickel alloys
            BT3   alloys
        BT2   stainless steels
            BT3   high alloy steels
                BT4   steels
                    BT5   carbon additions
                    BT5   iron base alloys
                        BT6   iron alloys
                            BT7   alloys
    BT1   corrosion resistant alloys
        BT2   alloys
    BT1   low carbon-high alloy steels
        BT2   stainless steels
            BT3   high alloy steels
                BT4   steels
                    BT5   carbon additions
                    BT5   iron base alloys
                        BT6   iron alloys
                            BT7   alloys
    BT1   titanium alloys
        BT2   alloys

STEEL-NI36CR18 [3; 3] *Dec 80*
    UF   *stainless steel-330*
    BT1   austenitic steels
        BT2   steels
            BT3   carbon additions
            BT3   iron base alloys
                BT4   iron alloys
                    BT5   alloys
    BT1   chromium-nickel steels
        BT2   chromium alloys
            BT3   alloys
        BT2   nickel alloys
            BT3   alloys
        BT2   stainless steels
            BT3   high alloy steels
                BT4   steels
                    BT5   carbon additions
                    BT5   iron base alloys
                        BT6   iron alloys
                            BT7   alloys
    BT1   corrosion resistant alloys
        BT2   alloys
    BT1   heat resisting alloys
        BT2   alloys

STEEL-NI4 [0; 0] *Nov 83*
    UF   *steel-astm-a350 (gr 3)*
    UF   *steel-20n14*
    BT1   low alloy steels
        BT2   steels
            BT3   carbon additions
            BT3   iron base alloys
                BT4   iron alloys
                    BT5   alloys
    BT1   nickel alloys
        BT2   alloys

STEEL-NI4CRW [15; 15]
    UF   *steel-18kh2n4va*
    BT1   chromium alloys
        BT2   alloys
    BT1   copper additions
    BT1   low alloy steels
        BT2   steels
            BT3   carbon additions
            BT3   iron base alloys
                BT4   iron alloys
                    BT5   alloys
    BT1   nickel alloys
        BT2   alloys
    BT1   tungsten additions

steel-n36khtyu
    USE   steel-ni36cr12ti3al-l

steel-sae-1006
    USE   carbon steels

steel-sae-1045
    USE   carbon steels

steel-x20crmov 121
    USE   steel-cr12moniv

steel-x6crni1811
   USE   steel-cr18ni11

steel-z10cdnbv9
   USE   steel-cr9monbv

steel-0kh16n15m3b
   USE   steel-cr16ni15mo3nb

steel-0kh18n10t
   USE   steel-cr18ni10ti

steel-0kh18n9t
   USE   steel-cr18ni9ti

steel-0kh21n5t
   USE   steel-cr21ni5ti

steel-0kh22n5t
   USE   steel-cr22ni5ti

steel-03kh11n10m2t
   USE   steel-cr11ni10mo2ti-l

steel-08kh18n10t
   USE   steel-cr18ni10ti

steel-1kh16n15m3b
   USE   steel-cr16ni15mo3nb

steel-1kh18n10t
   USE   steel-cr18ni10ti

steel-1kh18n9
   USE   steel-cr18ni9

steel-1kh18n9t
   USE   steel-cr18ni9ti

steel-10cd9-10
   USE   steel-cr2mo

steel-10crninb910
   USE   steel-cr2moninb

steel-12khm
   USE   steel-crmo

steel-12khn3
   USE   steel-ni3cr

steel-12khn3a
   USE   steel-ni3cr

steel-12kh1mf
   USE   steel-crmov

steel-12kh2nch
   USE   steel-ni3cr

steel-13cr6nimo
   USE   steel-cr13ni6mo-l

steel-15cd9-10
   USE   steel-cr2mo

steel-15kh1m1f
   USE   steel-crmov

steel-15kh1m1fl
   USE   steel-crmov

steel-15kh2mfa
   USE   steel-cr2mov

steel-18kh2n4va
   USE   steel-ni4crw

steel-2kh13
   USE   steel-cr13

steel-20kh
   USE   steel-crni

steel-20n14
   USE   steel-ni4

steel-22nimocr37
   USE   steel-nimocr

steel-28cdv508
   USE   steel-crmov

steel-3hk5s
   USE   steel-cr2moninb

steel-38khmyua
   USE   steel-cralnimo

steel-40kh
   USE   steel-crni

steel-40khn
   USE   steel-nicr

steel-40khnma
   USE   steel-nicrmo

steel-40kh13n8g8
   USE   steel-cr13mn8ni8

steel-5kh2mf
   USE   steel-crmov

steel-7kh18n9
   USE   steel-cr18ni9

steel-9cr
   USE   steel-cr10mo2

steel-9kh18
   USE   steel-cr18

STEELS [8,086; 34,105]
   BT1   carbon additions
   BT1   iron base alloys
      BT2   iron alloys
         BT3   alloys
  *NT1   austenitic steels
   NT1   carbon steels
   NT1   croloy
    NT2   steel-cr13
    NT2   steel-cr16
    NT2   steel-cr17mn15nni
    NT2   steel-cr18ni10
    NT2   steel-cr2mo
    NT2   steel-cr5mo
  *NT1   ferritic steels
   NT1   high alloy steels
    NT2   stainless steels
     *NT3   chromium steels
      NT3   chromium-nickel steels
       *NT4   chromium-nickel-molybdenum ste
        NT4   steel-cr13mn8ni8
        NT4   steel-cr17ni13
        NT4   steel-cr17ni7
        NT4   steel-cr18ni10
        NT4   steel-cr18ni10-l
        NT4   steel-cr18ni10ti
        NT4   steel-cr18ni11
        NT4   steel-cr18ni11nb
        NT4   steel-cr18ni11nbco
        NT4   steel-cr18ni12
        NT4   steel-cr18ni12ti
        NT4   steel-cr18ni8
        NT4   steel-cr18ni9
        NT4   steel-cr18ni9ti
        NT4   steel-cr19ni10
        NT4   steel-cr19ni10-l
        NT4   steel-cr20ni11
        NT4   steel-cr20ni11-l
        NT4   steel-cr23ni14
        NT4   steel-cr23ni18
        NT4   steel-cr25ni20
        NT4   steel-ni25cr20
        NT4   steel-ni36cr12ti3al-l
        NT4   steel-ni36cr18
     *NT3   low carbon-high alloy steels
      NT3   steel-cr17mn15nni
      NT3   steel-cr21mn9ni6
  *NT1   low alloy steels
   NT1   martensitic steels
    NT2   maraging steels
    NT2   steel-cr10mo2
    NT2   steel-cr12
    NT2   steel-cr12mov
    NT2   steel-cr13
    NT2   steel-cr16ni
    NT2   steel-cr17cu4ni4nb-l
    NT2   steel-cr17mo
    NT2   steel-cr18
   RT   bainite
   RT   cementite
   RT   decarburization
   RT   ferrite
   RT   martensite
   RT   pearlite

STEENSTRUPINE [6; 6] *Dec 82*
   BT1   phosphate minerals
    BT2   minerals
   BT1   silicate minerals
    BT2   minerals
   BT1   thorium minerals
    BT2   radioactive minerals
     BT3   minerals
     BT3   radioactive materials
      BT4   materials
   BT1   uranium minerals
    BT2   radioactive minerals
     BT3   minerals
     BT3   radioactive materials
      BT4   materials

STEIN THEORY [0; 0]
   RT   capture
   RT   resonance neutrons

STEK REACTOR [60; 60]
   UF   *krito critical assembly*
   UF   *petten stek reactor*
   BT1   enriched uranium reactors
    BT2   reactors
   BT1   pool type reactors
    BT2   water cooled reactors
     BT3   reactors
    BT2   water moderated reactors

```
        BT3     reactors
  BT1   thermal reactors
  BT2   reactors

STELLAR ACTIVITY [217; 5,450]
  Dec 84
  NT1   starspots
   NT2    sunspots
  NT1   stellar flares
   NT2    solar flares
  NT1   stellar winds
   NT2    solar wind
  RT    cosmic radiation
  RT    stars
  RT    stellar radiation

STELLAR ATMOSPHERES
  [3,001; 5,819]
  (For the Sun use SOLAR ATMOSPHERE
  or one of its NTs.)
  BT1   atmospheres
  NT1   solar atmosphere
   NT2    chromosphere
   NT2    heliosphere
   NT2    photosphere
   NT2    solar corona
  NT1   stellar chromospheres
  NT1   stellar coronae
   NT2    solar corona
  NT1   stellar magnetospheres
  RT    stars
  RT    starspots

*stellar burning*
  USE   star burning

STELLAR CHROMOSPHERES
  [121; 121] *Nov 84*
  BT1   stellar atmospheres
  BT2   atmospheres

STELLAR CORONAE [171; 1,270]
  *Feb 84*
  (For the Sun use SOLAR CORONA.)
  UF    *coronae (stellar)*
  BT1   stellar atmospheres
  BT2   atmospheres
  NT1   solar corona

STELLAR FLARES [706; 2,660]
  (For the Sun use SOLAR FLARES.)
  BT1   stellar activity
  NT1   solar flares
  RT    stars
  RT    starspots
  RT    stellar winds

STELLAR MAGNETOSPHERES
  [527; 527]
  UF    *magnetospheres (stellar)*
  BT1   stellar atmospheres
  BT2   atmospheres
  RT    magnetic stars

STELLAR RADIATION [1,076; 6,057]
  *Nov 75*
  BT1   radiations
  NT1   solar radiation
   NT2    solar particles
    NT3     solar alpha particles
    NT3     solar electrons
    NT3     solar neutrinos
    NT3     solar neutrons
    NT3     solar protons
  RT    cosmic radiation
  RT    stellar activity

*stellar spots*
  USE   starspots

STELLAR WINDS [1,828; 3,828]
  (For the Sun use SOLAR WIND.)
  SF    *mass loss*
  BT1   stellar activity
  NT1   solar wind
  RT    stars
  RT    stellar flares

STELLARATOR MODEL C [11; 11]
  BT1   stellarators
  BT2   closed plasma devices
  BT3   thermonuclear devices

STELLARATORS [1,546; 3,243]
  BT1   closed plasma devices
  BT2   thermonuclear devices
  NT1   clasp device
  NT1   cleo stellarator
  NT1   h-1 heliac
  NT1   harmonica-2 device
  NT1   heliac stellarators
   NT2    sheila heliac
  NT1   ims stellarator
  NT1   jipp stellarator
  NT1   jippt-2 device
  NT1   l-2 stellarator
  NT1   proto-cleo stellarators
  NT1   pulsator stellarator
  NT1   sirius device
  NT1   stellarator model c
  NT1   torsatron stellarators
   NT2    atf torsatron
   NT2    chs torsatron
   NT2    vint torsatron
  NT1   uragan stellarator
  NT1   wega stellarator
  NT1   wendelstein-2b stellarator
  NT1   wendelstein-7 stellarator
  RT    banana regime
  RT    divertors
  RT    kruskal limit
  RT    magnetic surfaces
  RT    marfe
  RT    mode rational surfaces
  RT    pfirsch-schlueter regime
  RT    plasma radial profiles
  RT    sawtooth oscillations

STELLITE [88; 129]
  BT1   cobalt base alloys
  BT2   cobalt alloys
  BT3   alloys
  NT1   alloy-co54cr20w15ni10
  NT1   alloy-co60cr30w4
  NT1   alloy-co62cr28mo6ni3
  NT1   alloy-co64cr29w4
  NT1   alloy-co66cr26w6

*stellite 156*
  USE   alloy-co64cr29w4

*stellite 6*
  USE   alloy-co60cr30w4

*stellite 6 (deloro)*
  USE   alloy-co66cr26w6

*stem (plant)*
  USE   plant stems

STEM CELLS [1,154; 1,154]
  BT1   somatic cells
  BT2   animal cells
  RT    blood formation
  RT    bone marrow
  RT    cfu
  RT    spermatogenesis

STENDAL-1 REACTOR [5; 5] *Aug 86*
  (Stendal, Federal Republic of Germany.)
  BT1   wwer type reactors
  BT2   pwr type reactors

  BT3   enriched uranium reactors
   BT4    reactors
  BT3   power reactors
   BT4    reactors
  BT3   thermal reactors
   BT4    reactors
  BT3   water cooled reactors
   BT4    reactors
  BT3   water moderated reactors
   BT4    reactors

STERCOBILIN [0; 0]
  BT1   heterocyclic acids
   BT2    carboxylic acids
    BT3     organic acids
     BT4      organic compounds
   BT2    heterocyclic compounds
    BT3     organic compounds
  BT1   pigments
  BT1   pyrroles
   BT2    azoles
    BT3     heterocyclic compounds
     BT4      organic compounds
    BT3     organic nitrogen compounds
     BT4      organic compounds
  RT    bile

STEREOCHEMISTRY [1,225; 1,225]
  RT    isomers
  RT    ligands
  RT    molecular structure
  RT    optical activity
  RT    racemization

STERILE INSECT RELEASE [149; 149]
  RT    insect dispersal
  RT    pest control
  RT    radiosterilization
  RT    sterile male technique
  RT    sterility

STERILE MALE TECHNIQUE
  [294; 294]
  RT    agriculture
  RT    insect dispersal
  RT    insects
  RT    mass rearing
  RT    parasites
  RT    pest control
  RT    radiosterilization
  RT    sterile insect release

STERILITY [491; 491]
  RT    fertility
  RT    genetic control
  RT    reproductive disorders
  RT    sterile insect release

STERILIZATION [1,797; 2,781]
  UF    *disinfection*
  NT1   radiosterilization
   NT2    radappertization
  RT    bacterial spores
  RT    chemosterilants
  RT    disinfestation
  RT    food
  RT    grain disinfestation
  RT    inactivation
  RT    pasteurization
  RT    preservation

STERLING EVENT [6; 6]
  BT1   vela project

STERLING-1 REACTOR [6; 6]
  BT1   pwr type reactors
  BT2   enriched uranium reactors
   BT3    reactors
  BT2   power reactors
   BT3    reactors
  BT2   thermal reactors
   BT3    reactors
  BT2   water cooled reactors
   BT3    reactors
  BT2   water moderated reactors
   BT3    reactors
```

STERN-GERLACH EXPERIMENT [83; 83]
- RT beams
- RT measuring methods
- RT spin orientation

STERNHEIMER FORMULA [43; 43]
- RT multipoles

STEROID HORMONES [131; 3,942]
- BT1 hormones
- NT1 androgens
  - NT2 androstenedione
  - NT2 androsterone
  - NT2 dianabol
  - NT2 hydroxyandrostenone
  - NT2 testosterone
- NT1 corticosteroids
  - NT2 glucocorticoids
    - NT3 corticosterone
    - NT3 cortisone
    - NT3 dexamethasone
    - NT3 hydrocortisone
    - NT3 prednisolone
    - NT3 prednisone
  - NT2 mineralocorticoids
    - NT3 aldosterone
    - NT3 doca
- NT1 estrogens
  - NT2 estradiol
  - NT2 estriol
  - NT2 estrone
- NT1 progesterone

STEROIDS [393; 5,924]
- BT1 organic compounds
- NT1 androstanes
  - NT2 androgens
    - NT3 androstenedione
    - NT3 androsterone
    - NT3 dianabol
    - NT3 hydroxyandrostenone
    - NT3 testosterone
- NT1 estranes
  - NT2 estradiol
  - NT2 estriol
  - NT2 estrone
- NT1 pregnanes
  - NT2 corticosteroids
    - NT3 glucocorticoids
      - NT4 corticosterone
      - NT4 cortisone
      - NT4 dexamethasone
      - NT4 hydrocortisone
      - NT4 prednisolone
      - NT4 prednisone
    - NT3 mineralocorticoids
      - NT4 aldosterone
      - NT4 doca
  - NT2 hydroxypregnenone
  - NT2 pregnanediol
  - NT2 pregnanetriol
  - NT2 progesterone
- NT1 sterols
  - NT2 bile acids
    - NT3 cholic acid
  - NT2 cholesterol
  - NT2 ergosterol
  - NT2 lanolin
  - NT2 sitosterol
- RT cardiotonics
- RT hormones
- RT urinary ketosteroids

STEROLS [125; 1,239]
- BT1 hydroxy compounds
  - BT2 organic compounds
- BT1 steroids
  - BT2 organic compounds
- NT1 bile acids
  - NT2 cholic acid
- NT1 cholesterol
- NT1 ergosterol
- NT1 lanolin
- NT1 sitosterol

STF REACTOR [20; 20] Jun 77
- UF *safety test facility reactor*
- BT1 air cooled reactors
  - BT2 gas cooled reactors
    - BT3 reactors
- BT1 fast reactors
  - BT2 epithermal reactors
    - BT3 reactors
- BT1 research reactors
  - BT2 research and test reactors
    - BT3 reactors
- BT1 test reactors
  - BT2 research and test reactors
    - BT3 reactors
  - BT2 test facilities

STH [450; 450]
- UF *growth hormone*
- UF *somatotropic hormone*
- BT1 pituitary hormones
  - BT2 peptide hormones
    - BT3 hormones
- RT acromegaly
- RT anabolism
- RT growth
- RT hpl
- RT somatostatin

stiffness
- USE flexibility

STILBAMIDINE [1; 1]
- BT1 amidines
  - BT2 organic nitrogen compounds
    - BT3 organic compounds

STILBENE [206; 206]
- UF *1,2-diphenylethylene*
- BT1 aromatics
  - BT2 organic compounds
- BT1 hydrocarbons
  - BT2 organic compounds
- RT organic crystal phosphors
- RT stilbestrol

STILBESTROL [38; 38]
- BT1 polyphenols
  - BT2 phenols
    - BT3 aromatics
      - BT4 organic compounds
    - BT3 hydroxy compounds
      - BT4 organic compounds
- RT estrogens
- RT stilbene

stimulants (central nerv syst)
- USE analeptics

STIMULATED EMISSION [1,230; 1,230]
- BT1 emission
- BT1 energy-level transitions
- RT einstein coefficients
- RT electrical pumping
- RT gasers
- RT lasers
- RT masers
- RT nuclear pumping
- RT optical pumping

STIMULATION [1,102; 1,102]
- UF+ *growth stimulation*
- RT hormones
- RT mitogens
- RT stimuli

stimulation (explosive)
- USE explosive stimulation

STIMULI [49; 49]
- RT bioelectricity
- RT stimulation

STIR REACTOR [1; 1]
- UF *shield test reactor*
- UF *str reactor (shield test)*
- BT1 enriched uranium reactors
  - BT2 reactors
- BT1 hydride moderated reactors
  - BT2 reactors
- BT1 pool type reactors
  - BT2 water cooled reactors
    - BT3 reactors
  - BT2 water moderated reactors
    - BT3 reactors
- BT1 thermal reactors
  - BT2 reactors

STIRLING CYCLE [89; 89]
- BT1 thermodynamic cycles
- RT stirling engines
- RT thermodynamics

STIRLING ENGINES [69; 69]
- BT1 motors
- RT regenerators
- RT stirling cycle

STIRRING [183; 183]
- RT mixing
- RT turbulence

STOCHASTIC COOLING [198; 232]
Aug 81
(Gradual reduction of emittance of coasting charged-particle beams by feedback sensing and correcting statistical fluctuations of beam position or momentum.)
- BT1 beam cooling
- NT1 momentum cooling

stochastic momentum cooling
- USE momentum cooling

STOCHASTIC PROCESSES
[3,823; 4,472]
- NT1 markov process
- RT chapman-kolmogorov equation
- RT gaussian processes
- RT monte carlo method
- RT statistics

STOCKBARGER METHOD [29; 29]
- RT crystal growth

stockholm r-1 reactor
- USE r-1 reactor

stockpiles
- USE inventories

STOERMER THEORY [14; 14]
- RT charged particles
- RT magnetic fields

STOICHIOMETRY [1,321; 1,321]
(Prior to June 1986 CHEMICAL COMPOSITION was used for this concept.)
- RT chemical composition
- RT chemical reactions
- RT chemistry

STOKES LAW [89; 89]
- RT viscous flow

STOKES PARAMETERS [464; 464]
- RT polarization

STOMACH [2,103; 2,103]
- UF+ *rumen*
- BT1 gastrointestinal tract
  - BT2 digestive system
- BT1 organs
  - BT2 body
- RT gastrectomy

STOMACH

- RT gastric acid
- RT gastrin
- RT intrinsic factor
- RT pepsin
- RT vomiting

STONE METEORITES [75; 990]
- BT1 meteorites
- NT1 achondrites
- NT1 chondrites
- RT rocks

stone-webster reference pwr
- USE swessar standard plant

stopping
- USE absorption

STOPPING POWER [2,904; 2,904]
- UF *stopping power (total atomic)*
- UF *stopping power (total linear)*
- UF *stopping power (total mass)*
- RT absorption
- RT atomic number
- RT density
- RT energy losses
- RT range

stopping power (total atomic)
- USE stopping power

stopping power (total linear)
- USE stopping power

stopping power (total mass)
- USE stopping power

§§ STORAGE [2,457; 13,716]
- NT1 dry storage
- NT1 energy storage
  - NT2 heat storage
  - NT2 pumped storage
  - NT2 superconductive energy storage
- NT1 spent fuel storage
  - NT2 away-from-reactor storage
- NT1 underground storage
- NT1 waste storage
  - NT2 radioactive waste storage
- RT inventories
- RT storage facilities
- RT transport
- RT water reservoirs

storage devices (data)
- USE memory devices

STORAGE FACILITIES [841; 841] *Jan 84*
- RT inventories
- RT nuclear facilities
- RT radioactive waste facilities
- RT spent fuels
- RT storage
- RT wastes

STORAGE LIFE [756; 756]
- UF *market life*
- RT radiopreservation
- RT sprout inhibition

storage pools (fuel)
- USE fuel storage pools

STORAGE RINGS [4,666; 12,711]
- UF *rings (storage)*
- NT1 aco
- NT1 adone
- NT1 bessy storage ring
- NT1 brookhaven rhic
- NT1 celsius storage ring
- NT1 cern cesar
- NT1 cern isr
- NT1 cesr storage ring
- NT1 dci orsay storage ring
- NT1 doris storage ring
- NT1 epic storage ring
- NT1 escar storage ring
- NT1 hera storage ring
- NT1 isabelle storage rings
- NT1 lep storage rings
- NT1 lnls storage ring
- NT1 nap-m storage ring
- NT1 pampus storage ring
- NT1 pep storage rings
- NT1 petra storage ring
- NT1 popae storage ring
- NT1 precetron storage ring
- NT1 serpukhov tevatron
- NT1 spear
- NT1 spring-8 storage ring
- NT1 superconducting super collider
- NT1 surf ii storage ring
- NT1 tristan storage rings
- NT1 vep-1
- NT1 vepp-2
- NT1 vepp-3
- NT1 vepp-4
- RT accelerators
- RT kek photon factory

storage tubes
- USE electron tubes
- AND image storage tubes

STORED ENERGY [369; 369]
- BT1 energy
- BT1 thermodynamic properties
  - BT2 physical properties
- RT tank circuits

str reactor (shield test)
- USE stir reactor

str reactor (split table)
- USE split table reactor

STRAHLENSCHUTZKOMMISSION [62; 62] *Nov 78*
- BT1 german fr organizations
  - BT2 national organizations

STRAIGHT-LINE PATH APPROXIMATI [18; 18] *Sep 75*
(Assumes that transverse-momentum transfer is small in high-energy particle interactions.)
- UF *approximation (straight-line)*
- RT eikonal approximation
- RT linear momentum transfer
- RT particle interactions
- RT transverse momentum

STRAIN AGING [260; 260]
- BT1 aging
- RT cold working

STRAIN GAGES [522; 522]
- UF *gages (strain)*
- BT1 measuring instruments
- RT extensometers
- RT mechanical tests
- RT strains

STRAIN HARDENING [1,113; 1,113]
- UF *shock wave hardening*
- UF *shock-wave hardening*
- UF *work hardening*
- BT1 hardening
- RT cold working
- RT strains

STRAIN RATE [257; 257] *May 86*
- RT static loads
- RT strains
- RT tensile properties

STRAIN SOFTENING [55; 55] *Jul 77*
- UF *work softening*
- RT strains

STRAINS [7,460; 7,460]
- RT deformation
- RT elasticity
- RT poisson ratio
- RT ratcheting
- RT strain gages
- RT strain hardening
- RT strain rate
- RT strain softening
- RT stresses
- RT tensile properties

STRAND BREAKS [2,748; 2,748]
- RT biological radiation effects
- RT chemical radiation effects
- RT decomposition
- RT dna
- RT dna repair
- RT dna sequencing
- RT molecular biology
- RT pyrimidine dimers
- RT radiation effects
- RT rna

strange baryons
- USE hyperons

STRANGE MESONS [76; 2,359] *Dec 8*
- UF *k*resonances*
- UF *k-1240 resonances*
- UF *k-1871 resonances*
- BT1 mesons
  - BT2 bosons
  - BT2 hadrons
    - BT3 elementary particles
- BT1 strange particles
  - BT2 elementary particles
- NT1 k*-1410 mesons
- NT1 k*-1790 mesons
- NT1 k*-892 mesons
- NT1 k*0-1350 mesons
- NT1 k*2-1430 mesons
- NT1 k*3-1780 mesons
- NT1 k*4-2060 mesons
- NT1 k-1460 mesons
- NT1 k-1830 mesons
- NT1 kaons
  - NT2 antikaons
    - NT3 antikaons neutral
  - NT2 cosmic kaons
  - NT2 kaons minus
  - NT2 kaons neutral
    - NT3 antikaons neutral
    - NT3 kaons neutral long-lived
    - NT3 kaons neutral short-lived
  - NT2 kaons plus
- NT1 k1-1280 mesons
- NT1 k1-1400 mesons
- NT1 k2-1580 mesons
- NT1 k2-1770 mesons
- NT1 k2-2250 mesons
- NT1 k3-2320 mesons
- NT1 k4-2500 mesons

STRANGE PARTICLES [874; 14,314]
- BT1 elementary particles
- NT1 d*s-2110 mesons
- NT1 hyperons
  - NT2 antihyperons
    - NT3 antilambda particles
    - NT3 antiomega particles
    - NT3 antisigma particles
    - NT3 antixi particles
  - NT2 lambda baryons
    - NT3 lambda particles
      - NT4 antilambda particles
    - NT3 lambda-1405 baryons
    - NT3 lambda-1520 baryons

NT3 lambda-1600 baryons
NT3 lambda-1670 baryons
NT3 lambda-1690 baryons
NT3 lambda-1800 baryons
NT3 lambda-1820 baryons
NT3 lambda-1830 baryons
NT3 lambda-1890 baryons
NT3 lambda-2000 baryons
NT3 lambda-2020 baryons
NT3 lambda-2100 baryons
NT3 lambda-2110 baryons
NT3 lambda-2325 baryons
NT3 lambda-2350 baryons
NT3 lambda-2585 baryons
NT2 lambda-n-2130 dibaryons
NT2 omega baryons
NT3 omega particles
NT4 antiomega particles
NT2 sigma baryons
NT3 sigma particles
NT4 antisigma particles
NT4 sigma minus particles
NT4 sigma neutral particles
NT4 sigma plus particles
NT3 sigma-1385 baryons
NT3 sigma-1480 baryons
NT3 sigma-1560 baryons
NT3 sigma-1580 baryons
NT3 sigma-1620 baryons
NT3 sigma-1660 baryons
NT3 sigma-1670 baryons
NT3 sigma-1690 baryons
NT3 sigma-1750 baryons
NT3 sigma-1770 baryons
NT3 sigma-1775 baryons
NT3 sigma-1840 baryons
NT3 sigma-1880 baryons
NT3 sigma-1915 baryons
NT3 sigma-1940 baryons
NT3 sigma-2000 baryons
NT3 sigma-2030 baryons
NT3 sigma-2070 baryons
NT3 sigma-2080 baryons
NT3 sigma-2100 baryons
NT3 sigma-2250 baryons
NT3 sigma-2455 baryons
NT3 sigma-2620 baryons
NT3 sigma-3000 baryons
NT3 sigma-3170 baryons
NT2 xi baryons
NT3 xi particles
NT4 antixi particles
NT4 xi minus particles
NT4 xi neutral particles
NT3 xi-1530 baryons
NT3 xi-1630 baryons
NT3 xi-1680 baryons
NT3 xi-1820 baryons
NT3 xi-1940 baryons
NT3 xi-2030 baryons
NT3 xi-2120 baryons
NT3 xi-2250 baryons
NT3 xi-2370 baryons
NT3 xi-2500 baryons
NT2 z*baryons
NT3 z0-1780 baryons
NT3 z0-1865 baryons
NT3 z1-1725 baryons
NT3 z1-1900 baryons
NT3 z1-2150 baryons
NT3 z1-2500 baryons
NT1 spurions
NT1 strange mesons
NT2 k*-1410 mesons
NT2 k*-1790 mesons
NT2 k*-892 mesons
NT2 k*0-1350 mesons
NT2 k*2-1430 mesons
NT2 k*3-1780 mesons
NT2 k*4-2060 mesons
NT2 k-1460 mesons
NT2 k-1830 mesons
NT2 kaons
NT3 antikaons
NT4 antikaons neutral
NT3 cosmic kaons
NT3 kaons minus
NT3 kaons neutral
NT4 antikaons neutral

NT4 kaons neutral long-lived
NT4 kaons neutral short-lived
NT3 kaons plus
NT2 k1-1280 mesons
NT2 k1-1400 mesons
NT2 k2-1580 mesons
NT2 k2-1770 mesons
NT2 k2-2250 mesons
NT2 k3-2320 mesons
NT2 k4-2500 mesons
RT   strangeness

STRANGENESS [996; 996]
BT1 particle properties
RT   gauge invariance
RT   gell-mann theory
RT   strange particles
RT   strangeness analog resonances

STRANGENESS ANALOG RESONANCES [24; 24]
UF   analog resonances (strangeness
RT   energy levels
RT   nuclear reactions
RT   strangeness

STRANGENESS-EXCHANGE REACTIONS [213; 213] Nov 81
BT1 nuclear reactions

STRANGEONIUM [26; 276] Dec 87
(A bound state of strange and antistrange quarks.)
BT1 mesons
BT2 bosons
BT2 hadrons
BT3 elementary particles
BT1 quarkonium
NT1 f2-1525 mesons
NT1 phi j-1850 mesons
NT1 phi-1020 mesons
NT1 phi-1680 mesons

STRASBOURG-CRONENBOURG REACTOR [6; 6]
(University of Strasbourg Reactor Dept., Strasbourg, France)
BT1 argonaut type reactors
BT2 enriched uranium reactors
BT3 reactors
BT2 research and test reactors
BT3 reactors
BT2 water cooled reactors
BT3 reactors
BT2 water moderated reactors
BT3 reactors
BT1 training reactors
BT2 research and test reactors
BT3 reactors

STRATEGIC POINTS [60; 60]
(Points in the fuel cycle at which measurement of the flow of nuclear material would be useful for safeguards purposes.)
RT   material balance area
RT   safeguards

STRATIFICATION [583; 583]
RT   geologic strata
RT   layers

STRATIGRAPHY [1,132; 1,132]
RT   geologic strata
RT   geology
RT   geomorphology
RT   layers

STRATOSPHERE [756; 756]
UF   high altitude (stratosphere)
BT1 earth atmosphere
RT   global fallout
RT   magnetic rigidity
RT   ozone layer
RT   supersonic transport
RT   tropopause

STRAWBERRIES [108; 108]
BT1 fruits
BT2 food

STRAY RADIATION [314; 314]
BT1 radiations
RT   scattering
RT   shielding

STREAK CAMERAS [172; 172] Oct 86
(Cameras which produce two-dimensional images where time is one coordinate.)
BT1 cameras
RT   radiation detectors
RT   streak photography

STREAK PHOTOGRAPHY [412; 412]
BT1 photography
RT   streak cameras

STREAMER SPARK CHAMBERS [858; 858]
BT1 spark chambers
BT2 gas track detectors
BT3 radiation detectors
BT4 measuring instruments

streaming (radiation)
USE radiation streaming

streams
USE rivers

STRELKINITE [2; 2] Oct 75
BT1 oxide minerals
BT2 minerals
BT1 uranium minerals
BT2 radioactive minerals
BT3 minerals
BT3 radioactive materials
BT4 materials

strength (compression)
USE compression strength

strength (flexural)
USE flexural strength

strength (fracture)
USE fracture properties

strength (impact)
USE impact strength

strength (shear)
USE shear properties

strength (tensile)
USE tensile properties

strength (ultimate)
USE ultimate strength

strength (yield)
USE yield strength

STRENGTH FUNCTIONS [4,050; 4,050]
BT1 functions
RT   energy levels
RT   oscillator strengths

STREPTOCOCCAL PROTEINASE
[75; 75]
UF streptokinase
BT1 sh-proteinases
BT2 peptide hydrolases
BT3 hydrolases
BT4 enzymes
BT5 organic compounds
RT fibrinolysis
RT streptococcus
RT thrombosis

STREPTOCOCCUS [191; 191]
BT1 bacteria
BT2 microorganisms
RT streptococcal proteinase

streptokinase
(Prior to January 1984 this was a valid descriptor, and older material is so indexed.)
USE streptococcal proteinase

STREPTOMYCES [103; 103]
BT1 bacteria
BT2 microorganisms
RT streptomycin

STREPTOMYCIN [59; 59]
BT1 antibiotics
BT2 drugs
BT2 organic compounds
RT streptomyces
RT tuberculosis

streptozocin
(Coordinate the descriptors below with a descriptor for the application, e.g. ANTIBIOTICS, ANTINEOPLASTIC DRUGS.)
USE nitroso compounds
AND saccharides

streptozotocin
(Coordinate the descriptors below with a descriptor for the application, e.g. ANTIBIOTICS, ANTINEOPLASTIC DRUGS.)
USE nitroso compounds
AND saccharides

stress (biological)
USE biological stress

STRESS ANALYSIS [6,147; 6,147]
RT homalite
RT photoelasticity
RT stress intensity factors
RT stresses

stress concentration factors
USE stress intensity factors

§ **STRESS CORROSION** [3,334; 3,334]
BT1 corrosion
BT2 chemical reactions

STRESS INTENSITY FACTORS
[1,469; 1,469] *Aug 78*
UF *stress concentration factors*
RT crack propagation
RT cracks
RT defects
RT fracture mechanics
RT fracture properties
RT fractures
RT mechanical tests
RT stress analysis

STRESS RELAXATION [1,306; 1,306]
UF *relaxation (stress)*
UF *relieving (stress)*
UF *stress relieving*
RT annealing
RT creep
RT heat treatments
RT stresses

stress relieving
USE stress relaxation

STRESSES [10,979; 16,122]
(For mechanical stress only; see also BIOLOGICAL STRESS.)
UF *loads (stresses)*
NT1 flow stress
NT1 residual stresses
NT1 thermal stresses
RT dynamic loads
RT materials testing
RT mechanical properties
RT mechanical tests
RT ratcheting
RT s-n diagram
RT shear
RT static loads
RT strains
RT stress analysis
RT stress relaxation
RT tensile properties

stretch model
USE aligned coupling scheme

STRIATIONS [184; 184]
RT electric discharges

STRING MODELS [7,912; 7,912]
(Treating the interactions of extended particles through breaking and connection of strings.)
BT1 extended particle model
BT2 particle models
BT3 mathematical models
RT particle interactions
RT particle structure
RT quantum chromodynamics

strip mining
USE mining

stripper foils
USE beam strippers

strippers
USE beam strippers

STRIPPING [3,814; 3,814]
(For nuclear reactions only; for electron stripping use ELECTRON LOSS.)
BT1 transfer reactions
BT2 direct reactions
BT3 nuclear reactions
RT butler theory
RT oppenheimer-phillips process
RT serber theory

STRONG INTERACTIONS [5,239; 6,739]
BT1 basic interactions
BT1 interactions
NT1 charge-exchange interactions
NT1 peripheral collisions
RT annihilation
RT charge independence
RT chew-low method
RT cim model
RT grand unified theory
RT hadron-hadron interactions
RT quark-gluon interactions

RT rescattering
RT standard model
RT strong-coupling model

STRONG-ABSORPTION MODEL
[71; 71]
BT1 nuclear models
BT2 mathematical models

STRONG-COUPLING MODEL
[921; 921]
BT1 particle models
BT2 mathematical models
RT coupling
RT strong interactions
RT weak-coupling model

strongly damped heavy ion reac
USE deep inelastic heavy ion react

STRONGLY IONIZED GASES [41; 41]
(Ionization factor above 10(-4).)
BT1 ionized gases
BT2 gases
BT3 fluids

STRONTIUM [2,776; 2,776]
BT1 alkaline earth metals
BT2 metals
BT3 elements

STRONTIUM ADDITIONS [86; 86]
(Alloys containing not more than 1% Sr are listed here.)
RT strontium alloys
RT strontium compounds

STRONTIUM ALLOYS [119; 125]
(Alloys containing more than 1% Sr.)
BT1 alloys
NT1 strontium base alloys
RT strontium additions

STRONTIUM BASE ALLOYS [5; 5]
BT1 strontium alloys
BT2 alloys

STRONTIUM BORIDES [4; 4]
BT1 borides
BT2 boron compounds
BT1 strontium compounds
BT2 alkaline earth metal compou

STRONTIUM BROMIDES [37; 37]
BT1 bromides
BT2 bromine compounds
BT3 halogen compounds
BT2 halides
BT3 halogen compounds
BT1 strontium compounds
BT2 alkaline earth metal compou

STRONTIUM CARBIDES [5; 5]
BT1 carbides
BT2 carbon compounds
BT1 strontium compounds
BT2 alkaline earth metal compou

STRONTIUM CARBONATES [100; 10
BT1 carbonates
BT2 carbon compounds
BT2 oxygen compounds
BT1 strontium compounds
BT2 alkaline earth metal compou

STRONTIUM CHLORIDES [382; 382
BT1 chlorides
BT2 chlorine compounds
BT3 halogen compounds
BT2 halides
BT3 halogen compounds
BT1 strontium compounds
BT2 alkaline earth metal compou

STRONTIUM COMPLEXES [216; 216]
- BT1　alkaline earth metal complexes
- BT2　complexes

STRONTIUM COMPOUNDS [1,765; 6,100]
- BT1　alkaline earth metal compounds
- NT1　strontium borides
- NT1　strontium bromides
- NT1　strontium carbides
- NT1　strontium carbonates
- NT1　strontium chlorides
- NT1　strontium fluorides
- NT1　strontium hydrides
- NT1　strontium hydroxides
- NT1　strontium iodides
- NT1　strontium nitrates
- NT1　strontium oxides
- NT1　strontium perchlorates
- NT1　strontium phosphates
- NT1　strontium silicates
- NT1　strontium sulfates
- NT1　strontium sulfides
- NT1　strontium titanates
- NT1　strontium tungstates
- NT1　strontium uranates
- RT　strontium additions

STRONTIUM FLUORIDES [449; 449]
- BT1　fluorides
  - BT2　fluorine compounds
    - BT3　halogen compounds
  - BT2　halides
    - BT3　halogen compounds
- BT1　strontium compounds
  - BT2　alkaline earth metal compounds

STRONTIUM HYDRIDES [18; 18]
- BT1　hydrides
  - BT2　hydrogen compounds
- BT1　strontium compounds
  - BT2　alkaline earth metal compounds

STRONTIUM HYDROXIDES [39; 39]
- BT1　hydroxides
  - BT2　hydrogen compounds
  - BT2　oxygen compounds
- BT1　strontium compounds
  - BT2　alkaline earth metal compounds

STRONTIUM IODIDES [32; 32]
- BT1　iodides
  - BT2　halides
    - BT3　halogen compounds
  - BT2　iodine compounds
    - BT3　halogen compounds
- BT1　strontium compounds
  - BT2　alkaline earth metal compounds

STRONTIUM IONS [195; 195]
- BT1　ions
  - BT2　charged particles

STRONTIUM ISOTOPES [656; 9,626]
- NT1　strontium 100
- NT1　strontium 101
- NT1　strontium 102
- NT1　strontium 77
- NT1　strontium 78
- NT1　strontium 79
- NT1　strontium 80
- NT1　strontium 81
- NT1　strontium 82
- NT1　strontium 83
- NT1　strontium 84
- NT1　strontium 85
- NT1　strontium 86
- NT1　strontium 87
- NT1　strontium 88
- NT1　strontium 89
- NT1　strontium 90
- NT1　strontium 91
- NT1　strontium 92
- NT1　strontium 93
- NT1　strontium 94
- NT1　strontium 95
- NT1　strontium 96
- NT1　strontium 97
- NT1　strontium 98
- NT1　strontium 99
- RT　bone seekers

STRONTIUM NITRATES [158; 158]
- BT1　nitrates
  - BT2　nitrogen compounds
  - BT2　oxygen compounds
- BT1　strontium compounds
  - BT2　alkaline earth metal compounds

STRONTIUM OXIDES [2,892; 2,892]
- BT1　oxides
  - BT2　chalcogenides
  - BT2　oxygen compounds
- BT1　strontium compounds
  - BT2　alkaline earth metal compounds

STRONTIUM PERCHLORATES [3; 3] *Feb 88*
- BT1　perchlorates
  - BT2　chlorine compounds
    - BT3　halogen compounds
  - BT2　oxygen compounds
- BT1　strontium compounds
  - BT2　alkaline earth metal compounds

STRONTIUM PHOSPHATES [50; 50]
- BT1　phosphates
  - BT2　oxygen compounds
  - BT2　phosphorus compounds
- BT1　strontium compounds
  - BT2　alkaline earth metal compounds

STRONTIUM SILICATES [53; 53]
- BT1　silicates
  - BT2　oxygen compounds
  - BT2　silicon compounds
- BT1　strontium compounds
  - BT2　alkaline earth metal compounds

STRONTIUM SULFATES [128; 128]
- BT1　strontium compounds
  - BT2　alkaline earth metal compounds
- BT1　sulfates
  - BT2　oxygen compounds
  - BT2　sulfur compounds

STRONTIUM SULFIDES [105; 105]
- BT1　strontium compounds
  - BT2　alkaline earth metal compounds
- BT1　sulfides
  - BT2　chalcogenides
  - BT2　sulfur compounds

STRONTIUM TITANATES [24; 24] *May 90*
- BT1　strontium compounds
  - BT2　alkaline earth metal compounds
- BT1　titanates
  - BT2　oxygen compounds
  - BT2　titanium compounds
    - BT3　transition element compounds

STRONTIUM TUNGSTATES [34; 34] *Apr 79*
- BT1　strontium compounds
  - BT2　alkaline earth metal compounds
- BT1　tungstates
  - BT2　oxygen compounds
  - BT2　tungsten compounds
    - BT3　transition element compounds

→ **STRONTIUM URANATES** [0; 0] *Sep 91*
- BT1　strontium compounds
  - BT2　alkaline earth metal compounds
- BT1　uranates
  - BT2　uranium compounds
    - BT3　actinide compounds

STRONTIUM 100 [25; 25] *Apr 79*
- BT1　beta-minus decay radioisotopes
  - BT2　beta decay radioisotopes
    - BT3　radioisotopes
      - BT4　isotopes
- BT1　even-even nuclei
  - BT2　nuclei
- BT1　intermediate mass nuclei
  - BT2　nuclei
- BT1　millisec living radioisotopes
  - BT2　radioisotopes
    - BT3　isotopes
- BT1　strontium isotopes

STRONTIUM 101 [8; 8] *Jun 84*
- BT1　beta-minus decay radioisotopes
  - BT2　beta decay radioisotopes
    - BT3　radioisotopes
      - BT4　isotopes
- BT1　even-odd nuclei
  - BT2　nuclei
- BT1　intermediate mass nuclei
  - BT2　nuclei
- BT1　millisec living radioisotopes
  - BT2　radioisotopes
    - BT3　isotopes
- BT1　strontium isotopes

STRONTIUM 102 [7; 7] *Jan 86*
- BT1　beta-minus decay radioisotopes
  - BT2　beta decay radioisotopes
    - BT3　radioisotopes
      - BT4　isotopes
- BT1　even-even nuclei
  - BT2　nuclei
- BT1　intermediate mass nuclei
  - BT2　nuclei
- BT1　millisec living radioisotopes
  - BT2　radioisotopes
    - BT3　isotopes
- BT1　strontium isotopes

STRONTIUM 77 [11; 11] *Oct 76*
- BT1　beta-plus decay radioisotopes
  - BT2　beta decay radioisotopes
    - BT3　radioisotopes
      - BT4　isotopes
- BT1　even-odd nuclei
  - BT2　nuclei
- BT1　intermediate mass nuclei
  - BT2　nuclei
- BT1　seconds living radioisotopes
  - BT2　radioisotopes
    - BT3　isotopes
- BT1　strontium isotopes

STRONTIUM 78 [18; 18] *Jan 76*
- BT1　beta-plus decay radioisotopes
  - BT2　beta decay radioisotopes
    - BT3　radioisotopes
      - BT4　isotopes
- BT1　electron capture radioisotopes
  - BT2　beta decay radioisotopes
    - BT3　radioisotopes
      - BT4　isotopes
- BT1　even-even nuclei
  - BT2　nuclei
- BT1　intermediate mass nuclei
  - BT2　nuclei
- BT1　minutes living radioisotopes
  - BT2　radioisotopes
    - BT3　isotopes
- BT1　strontium isotopes

STRONTIUM 79 [31; 31]
- BT1　beta-plus decay radioisotopes
  - BT2　beta decay radioisotopes
    - BT3　radioisotopes
      - BT4　isotopes
- BT1　electron capture radioisotopes
  - BT2　beta decay radioisotopes
    - BT3　radioisotopes
      - BT4　isotopes
- BT1　even-odd nuclei
  - BT2　nuclei
- BT1　intermediate mass nuclei
  - BT2　nuclei
- BT1　minutes living radioisotopes

BT2   radioisotopes
BT3   isotopes
BT1   strontium isotopes

STRONTIUM 80 [52; 52]
BT1   beta-plus decay radioisotopes
BT2   beta decay radioisotopes
BT3   radioisotopes
BT4   isotopes
BT1   electron capture radioisotopes
BT2   beta decay radioisotopes
BT3   radioisotopes
BT4   isotopes
BT1   even-even nuclei
BT2   nuclei
BT1   hours living radioisotopes
BT2   radioisotopes
BT3   isotopes
BT1   intermediate mass nuclei
BT2   nuclei
BT1   strontium isotopes

STRONTIUM 81 [28; 28]
BT1   beta-plus decay radioisotopes
BT2   beta decay radioisotopes
BT3   radioisotopes
BT4   isotopes
BT1   electron capture radioisotopes
BT2   beta decay radioisotopes
BT3   radioisotopes
BT4   isotopes
BT1   even-odd nuclei
BT2   nuclei
BT1   intermediate mass nuclei
BT2   nuclei
BT1   minutes living radioisotopes
BT2   radioisotopes
BT3   isotopes
BT1   strontium isotopes

STRONTIUM 82 [138; 138]
BT1   days living radioisotopes
BT2   radioisotopes
BT3   isotopes
BT1   electron capture radioisotopes
BT2   beta decay radioisotopes
BT3   radioisotopes
BT4   isotopes
BT1   even-even nuclei
BT2   nuclei
BT1   intermediate mass nuclei
BT2   nuclei
BT1   strontium isotopes

STRONTIUM 83 [39; 39]
BT1   beta-plus decay radioisotopes
BT2   beta decay radioisotopes
BT3   radioisotopes
BT4   isotopes
BT1   days living radioisotopes
BT2   radioisotopes
BT3   isotopes
BT1   electron capture radioisotopes
BT2   beta decay radioisotopes
BT3   radioisotopes
BT4   isotopes
BT1   even-odd nuclei
BT2   nuclei
BT1   intermediate mass nuclei
BT2   nuclei
BT1   isomeric transition isotopes
BT2   radioisotopes
BT3   isotopes
BT1   seconds living radioisotopes
BT2   radioisotopes
BT3   isotopes
BT1   strontium isotopes

STRONTIUM 84 [78; 78]
BT1   even-even nuclei
BT2   nuclei
BT1   intermediate mass nuclei
BT2   nuclei
BT1   stable isotopes
BT2   isotopes
BT1   strontium isotopes

STRONTIUM 84 TARGET [23; 23]
BT1   targets

STRONTIUM 85 [1,126; 1,126]
BT1   days living radioisotopes
BT2   radioisotopes
BT3   isotopes
BT1   electron capture radioisotopes
BT2   beta decay radioisotopes
BT3   radioisotopes
BT4   isotopes
BT1   even-odd nuclei
BT2   nuclei
BT1   hours living radioisotopes
BT2   radioisotopes
BT3   isotopes
BT1   intermediate mass nuclei
BT2   nuclei
BT1   isomeric transition isotopes
BT2   radioisotopes
BT3   isotopes
BT1   strontium isotopes

STRONTIUM 86 [986; 986]
BT1   even-even nuclei
BT2   nuclei
BT1   intermediate mass nuclei
BT2   nuclei
BT1   stable isotopes
BT2   isotopes
BT1   strontium isotopes

STRONTIUM 86 TARGET [73; 73]
BT1   targets

STRONTIUM 87 [1,111; 1,111]
BT1   electron capture radioisotopes
BT2   beta decay radioisotopes
BT3   radioisotopes
BT4   isotopes
BT1   even-odd nuclei
BT2   nuclei
BT1   hours living radioisotopes
BT2   radioisotopes
BT3   isotopes
BT1   intermediate mass nuclei
BT2   nuclei
BT1   isomeric transition isotopes
BT2   radioisotopes
BT3   isotopes
BT1   stable isotopes
BT2   isotopes
BT1   strontium isotopes

STRONTIUM 87 TARGET [70; 70] *Mar 76*
BT1   targets

STRONTIUM 88 [288; 288]
BT1   even-even nuclei
BT2   nuclei
BT1   intermediate mass nuclei
BT2   nuclei
BT1   stable isotopes
BT2   isotopes
BT1   strontium isotopes

STRONTIUM 88 TARGET [242; 242]
BT1   targets

STRONTIUM 89 [862; 862]
BT1   beta-minus decay radioisotopes
BT2   beta decay radioisotopes
BT3   radioisotopes
BT4   isotopes
BT1   days living radioisotopes
BT2   radioisotopes
BT3   isotopes
BT1   even-odd nuclei
BT2   nuclei
BT1   intermediate mass nuclei
BT2   nuclei
BT1   strontium isotopes

STRONTIUM 90 [5,656; 5,656]
BT1   beta-minus decay radioisotopes
BT2   beta decay radioisotopes
BT3   radioisotopes
BT4   isotopes
BT1   even-even nuclei
BT2   nuclei
BT1   intermediate mass nuclei
BT2   nuclei
BT1   strontium isotopes
BT1   years living radioisotopes
BT2   radioisotopes
BT3   isotopes
RT   radioisotope generators

STRONTIUM 90 TARGET [5; 5] *Sep 8.*
BT1   targets

STRONTIUM 91 [40; 40]
BT1   beta-minus decay radioisotopes
BT2   beta decay radioisotopes
BT3   radioisotopes
BT4   isotopes
BT1   even-odd nuclei
BT2   nuclei
BT1   hours living radioisotopes
BT2   radioisotopes
BT3   isotopes
BT1   intermediate mass nuclei
BT2   nuclei
BT1   strontium isotopes

STRONTIUM 92 [35; 35]
BT1   beta-minus decay radioisotopes
BT2   beta decay radioisotopes
BT3   radioisotopes
BT4   isotopes
BT1   even-even nuclei
BT2   nuclei
BT1   hours living radioisotopes
BT2   radioisotopes
BT3   isotopes
BT1   intermediate mass nuclei
BT2   nuclei
BT1   strontium isotopes

STRONTIUM 93 [37; 37]
BT1   beta-minus decay radioisotopes
BT2   beta decay radioisotopes
BT3   radioisotopes
BT4   isotopes
BT1   even-odd nuclei
BT2   nuclei
BT1   intermediate mass nuclei
BT2   nuclei
BT1   minutes living radioisotopes
BT2   radioisotopes
BT3   isotopes
BT1   strontium isotopes

STRONTIUM 94 [32; 32]
BT1   beta-minus decay radioisotopes
BT2   beta decay radioisotopes
BT3   radioisotopes
BT4   isotopes
BT1   even-even nuclei
BT2   nuclei
BT1   intermediate mass nuclei
BT2   nuclei
BT1   minutes living radioisotopes
BT2   radioisotopes
BT3   isotopes
BT1   strontium isotopes

STRONTIUM 95 [37; 37]
BT1   beta-minus decay radioisotopes
BT2   beta decay radioisotopes
BT3   radioisotopes
BT4   isotopes
BT1   even-odd nuclei
BT2   nuclei
BT1   intermediate mass nuclei
BT2   nuclei
BT1   seconds living radioisotopes
BT2   radioisotopes
BT3   isotopes
BT1   strontium isotopes

STRONTIUM 96 [27; 27]
BT1   beta-minus decay radioisotopes
  BT2   beta decay radioisotopes
    BT3   radioisotopes
      BT4   isotopes
BT1   even-even nuclei
  BT2   nuclei
BT1   intermediate mass nuclei
  BT2   nuclei
BT1   seconds living radioisotopes
  BT2   radioisotopes
    BT3   isotopes
BT1   strontium isotopes

STRONTIUM 97 [28; 28]
BT1   beta-minus decay radioisotopes
  BT2   beta decay radioisotopes
    BT3   radioisotopes
      BT4   isotopes
BT1   even-odd nuclei
  BT2   nuclei
BT1   intermediate mass nuclei
  BT2   nuclei
BT1   millisec living radioisotopes
  BT2   radioisotopes
    BT3   isotopes
BT1   strontium isotopes

STRONTIUM 98 [43; 43]
BT1   beta-minus decay radioisotopes
  BT2   beta decay radioisotopes
    BT3   radioisotopes
      BT4   isotopes
BT1   even-even nuclei
  BT2   nuclei
BT1   intermediate mass nuclei
  BT2   nuclei
BT1   millisec living radioisotopes
  BT2   radioisotopes
    BT3   isotopes
BT1   strontium isotopes

STRONTIUM 99 [29; 29] *Mar 76*
BT1   beta-minus decay radioisotopes
  BT2   beta decay radioisotopes
    BT3   radioisotopes
      BT4   isotopes
BT1   even-odd nuclei
  BT2   nuclei
BT1   intermediate mass nuclei
  BT2   nuclei
BT1   millisec living radioisotopes
  BT2   radioisotopes
    BT3   isotopes
BT1   strontium isotopes

strophanthin
(Prior to December 1990, this was a valid descriptor.)
  USE   cardiotonics

structural beams
  USE   supports

structural buckling
  USE   deformation

STRUCTURAL CHEMICAL ANALYSIS [7,404; 8,364]
UF   *analysis (structural chemical)*
UF   *sequence analysis*
NT1   dna sequencing
RT   absorption spectroscopy
RT   coordination valences
RT   debye-scherrer method
RT   electron spin resonance
RT   infrared spectra
RT   laue method
RT   moessbauer effect
RT   molecular structure
RT   neutron diffraction
RT   nuclear magnetic resonance
RT   thermal analysis
RT   ultraviolet spectra
RT   x-ray diffraction
RT   x-ray diffractometers

structural materials
  USE   building materials

STRUCTURAL MODELS [2,028; 11,919]
UF   *models (structural)*
SF   *morphology*
NT1   mockup
  NT2   phantoms
NT1   scale models
RT   comparative evaluations
RT   functional models
RT   hypothesis
RT   mathematical models
RT   response functions

structure (crystal)
  USE   crystal structure

STRUCTURE FACTORS [901; 901]
May 81
(In macroscopic particle systems, for factors related to intensity of diffracted beam used in structure determination for liquids and solids, as by X-ray diffraction.)
RT   crystal structure
RT   liquids
RT   solids

STRUCTURE FUNCTIONS [5,095; 5,095]
(Momentum distribution of constituents within an elementary particle.)
BT1   functions
RT   emc effect
RT   gribov-lipatov relation
RT   particle models
RT   particle structure

STRUCTURE-ACTIVITY RELATIONSHI [499; 499] *Dec 84*
RT   biological functions
RT   dynamic function studies
RT   enzyme activity
RT   protein structure

structures (buildings)
  USE   buildings

structures (mechanics)
  USE   mechanical structures

STRUTINSKY THEORY [406; 406]
RT   fission
RT   nuclear models

STRYCHNINE [12; 12]
BT1   alkaloids
  BT2   organic compounds
BT1   indoles
  BT2   pyrroles
    BT3   azoles
      BT4   heterocyclic compounds
        BT5   organic compounds
      BT4   organic nitrogen compounds
        BT5   organic compounds

STSF ASSEMBLY [6; 6]
(Subcritical Time-of-Flight Spectrum Facility)
UF   *subcr time-of-flight spec faci*
BT1   subcritical assemblies
  BT2   experimental reactors
    BT3   research and test reactors
      BT4   reactors

stud welding
  USE   welding

studs
  USE   fasteners

studsvik fr-0 reactor
  USE   fr-0 reactor

studsvik r-2 reactor
  USE   r-2 reactor

studsvik r2-0 reactor
  USE   r2-0 reactor

sturgis-float. nuc. pow. plant
  USE   mh-1a reactor

STURM-LIOUVILLE EQUATION [201; 201]
BT1   differential equations
  BT2   equations
RT   eigenfunctions
RT   green function

STYRENE [674; 674]
UF   *phenylethylene*
UF   *vinylbenzene*
BT1   aromatics
  BT2   organic compounds
BT1   hydrocarbons
  BT2   organic compounds
RT   polystyrene
RT   vinyl monomers

styrene polymers
  USE   polystyrene

styrene-divinylbenzene copolym
  USE   polystyrene-dvb

SU GROUPS [2,105; 17,807]
BT1   lie groups
  BT2   symmetry groups
NT1   su-2 groups
NT1   su-3 groups
NT1   su-4 groups
NT1   su-5 groups
NT1   su-6 groups
NT1   su-7 groups
NT1   su-8 groups
NT1   su-9 groups
RT   goldstone bosons
RT   instantons
RT   unitary symmetry

SU-2 GROUPS [8,023; 8,023]
BT1   su groups
  BT2   lie groups
    BT3   symmetry groups

SU-3 GROUPS [7,200; 7,200]
BT1   su groups
  BT2   lie groups
    BT3   symmetry groups
RT   charm particles
RT   grace particles
RT   higgs model
RT   quantum chromodynamics
RT   taste particles

SU-4 GROUPS [1,360; 1,360]
BT1   su groups
  BT2   lie groups
    BT3   symmetry groups

SU-5 GROUPS [1,302; 1,302]
BT1   su groups
  BT2   lie groups
    BT3   symmetry groups
RT   grand unified theory

SU-6 GROUPS [980; 980]
BT1 su groups
BT2 lie groups
BT3 symmetry groups

SU-7 GROUPS [73; 73] *Feb 81*
BT1 su groups
BT2 lie groups
BT3 symmetry groups

SU-8 GROUPS [155; 155] *Oct 76*
BT1 su groups
BT2 lie groups
BT3 symmetry groups

SU-9 GROUPS [27; 27] *Feb 81*
BT1 su groups
BT2 lie groups
BT3 symmetry groups

SUBCELLULAR DISTRIBUTION
[189; 189] *Apr 87*
BT1 distribution
RT cell membranes
RT cell nuclei
RT organoids
RT ultracentrifugation

subcontractors
USE contractors

SUBCOOLED BOILING [354; 354]
UF *local boiling*
UF *surface boiling*
BT1 boiling
BT2 phase transformations

SUBCOOLING [534; 534]
BT1 cooling
RT vapor condensation

subcr time-of-flight spec faci
USE stsf assembly

SUBCRITICAL ASSEMBLIES [367; 372]
UF *exponential piles*
UF *neutron multiplier facility*
UF *sr-ob reactor*
BT1 experimental reactors
BT2 research and test reactors
BT3 reactors
NT1 pse reactor
NT1 stsf assembly

subcritical flow
USE laminar flow

subcriticality
USE criticality

SUBCUTANEOUS INJECTION
[357; 357]
BT1 injection
BT2 intake

SUBLETHAL IRRADIATION [808; 808]
BT1 irradiation
RT dose-response relationships
RT lethal irradiation
RT lethal radiation dose
RT radiation doses

SUBLIMATION [764; 764]
BT1 evaporation
BT2 phase transformations
RT refining
RT separation processes
RT sublimation cooling
RT sublimation heat

SUBLIMATION COOLING [4; 4]
BT1 cooling
RT sublimation

SUBLIMATION HEAT [289; 289]
UF *heat of sublimation*
UF *latent heat of sublimation*
BT1 transition heat
BT2 enthalpy
BT3 thermodynamic properties
BT4 physical properties
RT ablation
RT sublimation

SUBMARINES [133; 133]
BT1 ships
RT nuclear ships

SUBMERGED ARC WELDING
[316; 316]
BT1 arc welding
BT2 welding
BT3 joining
BT4 fabrication

subsidence (ground)
USE ground subsidence

subsidies
USE financial incentives

SUBSONIC FLOW [137; 137]
BT1 fluid flow
RT aerodynamics
RT compressible flow

substitution techniques
USE pile replacement techniques

SUBSTOICHIOMETRY [455; 455]
RT activation analysis
RT impurities
RT isotope dilution
RT quantitative chemical analysis

SUBSTRATES [4,773; 4,773]
RT enzymes
RT layers
RT thin films

SUBSURFACE STRUCTURES [129; 129]
BT1 underground facilities
RT civil defense
RT fallout shelters
RT shelters
RT tunnels

SUBTERRENE PENETRATORS [39; 39]
(Rock-melting equipment for excavation, drilling, and tunneling.)
BT1 equipment
RT boreholes
RT excavation
RT heating
RT materials drilling
RT melting
RT rock drilling
RT tunnels

suburbs
USE urban areas

SUCCINIC ACID [392; 392]
BT1 dicarboxylic acids
BT2 carboxylic acids
BT3 organic acids
BT4 organic compounds
RT aspartic acid

sucrose
USE saccharose

SUDAN [32; 32]
BT1 africa
BT1 developing countries

SUDDEN APPROXIMATION [358; 358]
Aug 75
(A high energy limit which assumes that the internal motions of the target are slow compared with the duration of the collision.)
UF *approximation (sudden)*
RT hamiltonians
RT quantum mechanics
RT transients
RT wave functions

SUDDEN COMMENCEMENTS
[159; 159]
RT magnetic storms

SUDDEN IONOSPHERIC DISTURBANCE [215; 215]
UF *sid*
BT1 ionospheric storms
BT2 disturbances
RT ionosphere

sugar
USE saccharose

SUGAR CANE [127; 127]
BT1 gramineae
BT2 plants
RT crops

sugars
USE saccharides

SUGAWARA THEORY [16; 16]
RT quantum field theory

SULFADIAZINE [9; 9]
BT1 pyrimidines
BT2 azines
BT3 heterocyclic compounds
BT4 organic compounds
BT3 organic nitrogen compound
BT4 organic compounds
BT1 sulfonamides
BT2 amides
BT3 organic nitrogen compound
BT4 organic compounds
BT2 antibiotics
BT3 drugs
BT3 organic compounds
BT2 organic sulfur compounds
BT3 organic compounds

SULFANILIC ACID [15; 15]
UF *aminobenzenesulfonic acid-par*
BT1 amines
BT2 organic compounds
BT1 sulfonic acids
BT2 organic acids
BT3 organic compounds
BT2 organic sulfur compounds
BT3 organic compounds

SULFATE MINERALS [10; 226] *Apr*
BT1 minerals
NT1 anhydrite
NT1 barite
NT1 gypsum
NT1 johannite
NT1 polyhalite
NT1 schroeckingerite
NT1 zippeite
RT aluminium sulfates
RT barium sulfates
RT calcium sulfates
RT copper sulfates

RT magnesium sulfates
RT potassium sulfates
RT sodium sulfates
RT uranium sulfates

→ **SULFATE-REDUCING BACTERIA**
[0; 0] *Oct 91*
BT1 bacteria
  BT2 microorganisms
RT desulfurization
RT sulfur cycle

SULFATES [2,034; 6,751]
(For salts only; see also SULFURIC ACID ESTERS.)
BT1 oxygen compounds
BT1 sulfur compounds
NT1 actinium sulfates
NT1 aluminium sulfates
NT1 americium sulfates
NT1 ammonium sulfates
NT1 barium sulfates
NT1 berkelium sulfates
NT1 beryllium sulfates
NT1 bismuth sulfates
NT1 cadmium sulfates
NT1 calcium sulfates
NT1 californium sulfates
NT1 cerium sulfates
NT1 cesium sulfates
NT1 chromium sulfates
NT1 cobalt sulfates
NT1 copper sulfates
NT1 curium sulfates
NT1 dysprosium sulfates
NT1 erbium sulfates
NT1 europium sulfates
NT1 gadolinium sulfates
NT1 gallium sulfates
NT1 hafnium sulfates
NT1 holmium sulfates
NT1 indium sulfates
NT1 iron sulfates
NT1 lanthanum sulfates
NT1 lead sulfates
NT1 lithium sulfates
NT1 lutetium sulfates
NT1 magnesium sulfates
NT1 manganese sulfates
NT1 mercury sulfates
NT1 molybdenum sulfates
NT1 neodymium sulfates
NT1 neptunium sulfates
NT1 nickel sulfates
NT1 niobium sulfates
NT1 osmium sulfates
NT1 plutonium sulfates
NT1 potassium sulfates
NT1 praseodymium sulfates
NT1 protactinium sulfates
NT1 radium sulfates
NT1 rhenium sulfates
NT1 rubidium sulfates
NT1 ruthenium sulfates
NT1 samarium sulfates
NT1 scandium sulfates
NT1 silver sulfates
NT1 sodium sulfates
NT1 strontium sulfates
NT1 tantalum sulfates
NT1 terbium sulfates
NT1 thallium sulfates
NT1 thorium sulfates
NT1 thulium sulfates
NT1 tin sulfates
NT1 titanium sulfates
NT1 uranium sulfates
NT1 uranyl sulfates
NT1 vanadium sulfates
NT1 ytterbium sulfates
NT1 yttrium sulfates
NT1 zinc sulfates
NT1 zirconium sulfates
RT sulfuric acid
RT thiosulfates

SULFEX PROCESS [2; 2]
BT1 reprocessing
  BT2 separation processes
RT solvent extraction

sulfhydryl compounds
USE thiols

SULFHYDRYL RADICALS [133; 133]
BT1 radicals

§ **SULFIDATION** [81; 81] *Sep 82*
BT1 chemical reactions

SULFIDE MINERALS [53; 274] *Apr 84*
UF *pyrrhotite*
UF *troilite*
BT1 minerals
NT1 chalcopyrite
NT1 galena
NT1 marcasite
NT1 pyrite
RT copper sulfides
RT iron sulfides
RT lead sulfides
RT mercury sulfides

SULFIDES [1,076; 8,680]
UF *polysulfides*
UF *thioethers*
BT1 chalcogenides
BT1 sulfur compounds
NT1 aluminium sulfides
NT1 americium sulfides
NT1 antimony sulfides
NT1 arsenic sulfides
NT1 barium sulfides
NT1 berkelium sulfides
NT1 beryllium sulfides
NT1 bismuth sulfides
NT1 boron sulfides
NT1 cadmium sulfides
NT1 calcium sulfides
NT1 californium sulfides
NT1 carbon sulfides
NT1 cerium sulfides
NT1 cesium sulfides
NT1 chromium sulfides
NT1 cobalt sulfides
NT1 copper sulfides
NT1 curium sulfides
NT1 dysprosium sulfides
NT1 einsteinium sulfides
NT1 erbium sulfides
NT1 europium sulfides
NT1 fermium sulfides
NT1 gadolinium sulfides
NT1 gallium sulfides
NT1 germanium sulfides
NT1 hafnium sulfides
NT1 holmium sulfides
NT1 hydrogen sulfides
NT1 indium sulfides
NT1 iron sulfides
NT1 lanthanum sulfides
NT1 lead sulfides
NT1 lithium sulfides
NT1 lutetium sulfides
NT1 magnesium sulfides
NT1 manganese sulfides
NT1 mendelevium sulfides
NT1 mercury sulfides
NT1 molybdenum sulfides
NT1 neodymium sulfides
NT1 neptunium sulfides
NT1 nickel sulfides
NT1 niobium sulfides
NT1 nobelium sulfides
NT1 osmium sulfides
NT1 palladium sulfides
NT1 phosphorus sulfides
NT1 platinum sulfides
NT1 plutonium sulfides
NT1 polonium sulfides
NT1 potassium sulfides
NT1 praseodymium sulfides
NT1 rhenium sulfides
NT1 rhodium sulfides
NT1 rubidium sulfides
NT1 ruthenium sulfides
NT1 samarium sulfides
NT1 scandium sulfides
NT1 selenium sulfides
NT1 silicon sulfides
NT1 silver sulfides
NT1 sodium sulfides
NT1 strontium sulfides
NT1 tantalum sulfides
NT1 technetium sulfides
NT1 tellurium sulfides
NT1 terbium sulfides
NT1 thallium sulfides
NT1 thorium sulfides
NT1 thulium sulfides
NT1 tin sulfides
NT1 titanium sulfides
NT1 tungsten sulfides
NT1 uranium sulfides
NT1 vanadium sulfides
NT1 ytterbium sulfides
NT1 yttrium sulfides
NT1 zinc sulfides
NT1 zirconium sulfides
RT oxysulfides
RT sulfur additions

sulfinic acids
USE organic acids
AND organic sulfur compounds

SULFITES [231; 231]
BT1 oxygen compounds
BT1 sulfur compounds
RT sulfurous acid

SULFOCHLORINATION [17; 17]
BT1 chlorination
  BT2 halogenation
    BT3 chemical reactions
BT1 sulfonation
  BT2 chemical reactions

sulfocyanides
USE thiocyanates

SULFONAMIDES [73; 74]
BT1 amides
  BT2 organic nitrogen compounds
    BT3 organic compounds
BT1 antibiotics
  BT2 drugs
  BT2 organic compounds
BT1 organic sulfur compounds
  BT2 organic compounds
NT1 sulfadiazine
RT sulfonic acids

SULFONATES [276; 308]
(For salts of sulfonic acids; for esters see SULFONIC ACID ESTERS.)
BT1 organic sulfur compounds
  BT2 organic compounds
NT1 indocyanine green
RT sulfonic acid esters
RT sulfonic acids

SULFONATION [39; 56]
BT1 chemical reactions
NT1 sulfochlorination

SULFONES [127; 136]
BT1 organic sulfur compounds
  BT2 organic compounds
NT1 spadns

SULFONIC ACID ESTERS [117; 670]
BT1 esters
  BT2 organic compounds
BT1 organic sulfur compounds
  BT2 organic compounds
NT1 abs
NT1 ems

SULFONIC ACID ESTERS

   NT1   methyl methanesulfonate
   RT   sulfonates
   RT   sulfonic acids

SULFONIC ACIDS [517; 1,309]

   BT1   organic acids
     BT2   organic compounds
   BT1   organic sulfur compounds
     BT2   organic compounds
   NT1   acid chrome dyes
   NT1   arsenazo
   NT1   beryllon
   NT1   bromosulfophthalein
   NT1   chromotropic acid
   NT1   congo red
   NT1   eriochrome dyes
   NT1   erioglaucine
   NT1   evans blue
   NT1   ferron
   NT1   methyl orange
   NT1   nitroso-r salt
   NT1   sdpph
   NT1   spadns
   NT1   sulfanilic acid
   NT1   taurine
   NT1   thorin
   NT1   tiron
   NT1   trypan blue
   NT1   unithiol
   RT   chloramines
   RT   sulfonamides
   RT   sulfonates
   RT   sulfonic acid esters

sulfophenyl-naphthalene-sulfon
(Sulfophenyl-naphthalene-sulfonic acid)
   USE   spadns

SULFOXIDES [341; 1,139]

   BT1   organic sulfur compounds
     BT2   organic compounds
   NT1   dmso
   NT1   dpso

SULFUR [2,352; 2,352]

   UF   *sulfur sulfides*
   BT1   nonmetals
     BT2   elements

SULFUR ADDITIONS [186; 186]

   RT   sulfides

sulfur carbides
   USE   carbon sulfides

SULFUR CHLORIDES [37; 37]

   BT1   chlorides
     BT2   chlorine compounds
       BT3   halogen compounds
     BT2   halides
       BT3   halogen compounds
   BT1   sulfur compounds

SULFUR COMPLEXES [127; 127]

   BT1   complexes

SULFUR COMPOUNDS [872; 19,718]

   UF+   *polythionates*
   UF+   *polythionic acids*
   UF+   *thionates*
   NT1   oxysulfides
   NT1   persulfates
   NT1   persulfuric acid
* NT1   sulfates
* NT1   sulfides
   NT1   sulfites
   NT1   sulfur chlorides
   NT1   sulfur fluorides
   NT1   sulfur nitrides
   NT1   sulfur oxides
   NT1   sulfuric acid
   NT1   sulfurous acid
   RT   organic sulfur compounds

→ SULFUR CYCLE [0; 0] *Oct 91*
   RT   ecosystems
   RT   metabolism
   RT   sulfate-reducing bacteria
   RT   thiobacillus oxidans

sulfur dioxide
   USE   sulfur oxides

SULFUR FLUORIDES [990; 990]

   BT1   fluorides
     BT2   fluorine compounds
       BT3   halogen compounds
     BT2   halides
       BT3   halogen compounds
   BT1   sulfur compounds

sulfur hydrides
   USE   hydrogen sulfides

SULFUR IONS [756; 756]

   BT1   ions
     BT2   charged particles

SULFUR ISOTOPES [328; 4,738]

   NT1   sulfur 24
   NT1   sulfur 27
   NT1   sulfur 28
   NT1   sulfur 29
   NT1   sulfur 30
   NT1   sulfur 31
   NT1   sulfur 32
   NT1   sulfur 33
   NT1   sulfur 34
   NT1   sulfur 35
   NT1   sulfur 36
   NT1   sulfur 37
   NT1   sulfur 38
   NT1   sulfur 39
   NT1   sulfur 40
   NT1   sulfur 41
   NT1   sulfur 42
   NT1   sulfur 43
   NT1   sulfur 44
   NT1   sulfur 45
   NT1   sulfur 46
   NT1   sulfur 47
   NT1   sulfur 48

SULFUR METERS [5; 5] *Feb 83*

   BT1   measuring instruments
   RT   chemical analysis
   RT   pollution control equipment

SULFUR NITRIDES [48; 48]

   UF   *nitrogen sulfides*
   BT1   nitrides
     BT2   nitrogen compounds
     BT2   pnictides
   BT1   sulfur compounds

SULFUR OXIDES [1,391; 1,391]

   UF   *sulfur dioxide*
   BT1   oxides
     BT2   chalcogenides
     BT2   oxygen compounds
   BT1   sulfur compounds
   RT   oxysulfides

sulfur sulfides
   USE   sulfur

SULFUR 24 [2; 2] *Feb 78*

   BT1   even-even nuclei
     BT2   nuclei
   BT1   light nuclei
     BT2   nuclei
   BT1   sulfur isotopes

SULFUR 27 [7; 7] *Aug 86*

   BT1   even-odd nuclei
     BT2   nuclei
   BT1   light nuclei
     BT2   nuclei
   BT1   sulfur isotopes

SULFUR 28 [4; 4] *Sep 89*

   BT1   beta-plus decay radioisotopes
     BT2   beta decay radioisotopes
       BT3   radioisotopes
         BT4   isotopes
   BT1   even-even nuclei
     BT2   nuclei
   BT1   light nuclei
     BT2   nuclei
   BT1   millisec living radioisotopes
     BT2   radioisotopes
       BT3   isotopes
   BT1   sulfur isotopes

SULFUR 29 [10; 10]

   BT1   beta-plus decay radioisotopes
     BT2   beta decay radioisotopes
       BT3   radioisotopes
         BT4   isotopes
   BT1   even-odd nuclei
     BT2   nuclei
   BT1   light nuclei
     BT2   nuclei
   BT1   millisec living radioisotopes
     BT2   radioisotopes
       BT3   isotopes
   BT1   sulfur isotopes

SULFUR 30 [29; 29]

   BT1   beta-plus decay radioisotopes
     BT2   beta decay radioisotopes
       BT3   radioisotopes
         BT4   isotopes
   BT1   even-even nuclei
     BT2   nuclei
   BT1   light nuclei
     BT2   nuclei
   BT1   seconds living radioisotopes
     BT2   radioisotopes
       BT3   isotopes
   BT1   sulfur isotopes

SULFUR 31 [58; 58]

   BT1   beta-plus decay radioisotopes
     BT2   beta decay radioisotopes
       BT3   radioisotopes
         BT4   isotopes
   BT1   even-odd nuclei
     BT2   nuclei
   BT1   light nuclei
     BT2   nuclei
   BT1   seconds living radioisotopes
     BT2   radioisotopes
       BT3   isotopes
   BT1   sulfur isotopes

SULFUR 32 [1,041; 1,041]

   BT1   even-even nuclei
     BT2   nuclei
   BT1   light nuclei
     BT2   nuclei
   BT1   stable isotopes
     BT2   isotopes
   BT1   sulfur isotopes

SULFUR 32 BEAMS [141; 141]

   BT1   ion beams
     BT2   beams

SULFUR 32 REACTIONS [995; 995]

   BT1   heavy ion reactions
     BT2   nuclear reactions

SULFUR 32 TARGET [574; 574]

   BT1   targets

SULFUR 33 [186; 186]
  BT1   even-odd nuclei
    BT2   nuclei
  BT1   light nuclei
    BT2   nuclei
  BT1   stable isotopes
    BT2   isotopes
  BT1   sulfur isotopes

SULFUR 33 REACTIONS [11; 11]
Apr 78
  BT1   heavy ion reactions
    BT2   nuclear reactions

SULFUR 33 TARGET [41; 41]
  BT1   targets

SULFUR 34 [605; 605]
  BT1   even-even nuclei
    BT2   nuclei
  BT1   light nuclei
    BT2   nuclei
  BT1   stable isotopes
    BT2   isotopes
  BT1   sulfur isotopes

SULFUR 34 REACTIONS [93; 93]
  BT1   heavy ion reactions
    BT2   nuclear reactions

SULFUR 34 TARGET [182; 182]
  BT1   targets

SULFUR 35 [2,680; 2,680]
  BT1   beta-minus decay radioisotopes
    BT2   beta decay radioisotopes
      BT3   radioisotopes
        BT4   isotopes
  BT1   days living radioisotopes
    BT2   radioisotopes
      BT3   isotopes
  BT1   even-odd nuclei
    BT2   nuclei
  BT1   light nuclei
    BT2   nuclei
  BT1   sulfur isotopes

SULFUR 36 [84; 84]
  BT1   even-even nuclei
    BT2   nuclei
  BT1   light nuclei
    BT2   nuclei
  BT1   stable isotopes
    BT2   isotopes
  BT1   sulfur isotopes

SULFUR 36 REACTIONS [89; 89]
Jul 80
  BT1   heavy ion reactions
    BT2   nuclear reactions

SULFUR 36 TARGET [87; 87]
  BT1   targets

SULFUR 37 [42; 42]
  BT1   beta-minus decay radioisotopes
    BT2   beta decay radioisotopes
      BT3   radioisotopes
        BT4   isotopes
  BT1   even-odd nuclei
    BT2   nuclei
  BT1   light nuclei
    BT2   nuclei
  BT1   minutes living radioisotopes
    BT2   radioisotopes
      BT3   isotopes
  BT1   sulfur isotopes

SULFUR 38 [47; 47]
  BT1   beta-minus decay radioisotopes
    BT2   beta decay radioisotopes
      BT3   radioisotopes
        BT4   isotopes
  BT1   even-even nuclei
    BT2   nuclei
  BT1   hours living radioisotopes
    BT2   radioisotopes
      BT3   isotopes
  BT1   light nuclei
    BT2   nuclei
  BT1   sulfur isotopes

SULFUR 38 BEAMS [2; 2] *Dec 86*
  BT1   ion beams
    BT2   beams

SULFUR 39 [11; 11]
  BT1   beta-minus decay radioisotopes
    BT2   beta decay radioisotopes
      BT3   radioisotopes
        BT4   isotopes
  BT1   even-odd nuclei
    BT2   nuclei
  BT1   light nuclei
    BT2   nuclei
  BT1   seconds living radioisotopes
    BT2   radioisotopes
      BT3   isotopes
  BT1   sulfur isotopes

SULFUR 40 [10; 10]
  BT1   beta-minus decay radioisotopes
    BT2   beta decay radioisotopes
      BT3   radioisotopes
        BT4   isotopes
  BT1   even-even nuclei
    BT2   nuclei
  BT1   light nuclei
    BT2   nuclei
  BT1   seconds living radioisotopes
    BT2   radioisotopes
      BT3   isotopes
  BT1   sulfur isotopes

SULFUR 41 [3; 3] *Mar 76*
  BT1   even-odd nuclei
    BT2   nuclei
  BT1   intermediate mass nuclei
    BT2   nuclei
  BT1   sulfur isotopes

SULFUR 42 [3; 3] *Mar 76*
  BT1   even-even nuclei
    BT2   nuclei
  BT1   intermediate mass nuclei
    BT2   nuclei
  BT1   sulfur isotopes

SULFUR 43 [8; 8] *Jul 80*
  BT1   beta-minus decay radioisotopes
    BT2   beta decay radioisotopes
      BT3   radioisotopes
        BT4   isotopes
  BT1   even-odd nuclei
    BT2   nuclei
  BT1   intermediate mass nuclei
    BT2   nuclei
  BT1   sulfur isotopes

SULFUR 44 [7; 7] *Apr 86*
  BT1   even-even nuclei
    BT2   nuclei
  BT1   intermediate mass nuclei
    BT2   nuclei
  BT1   sulfur isotopes

SULFUR 45 [2; 2] *Sep 89*
  BT1   even-odd nuclei
    BT2   nuclei
  BT1   intermediate mass nuclei
    BT2   nuclei
  BT1   sulfur isotopes

SULFUR 46 [2; 2] *Sep 89*
  BT1   even-even nuclei
    BT2   nuclei
  BT1   intermediate mass nuclei
    BT2   nuclei
  BT1   sulfur isotopes

SULFUR 47 [2; 2] *Sep 89*
  BT1   even-odd nuclei
    BT2   nuclei
  BT1   intermediate mass nuclei
    BT2   nuclei
  BT1   sulfur isotopes

SULFUR 48 [0; 0] *Apr 90*
  BT1   even-even nuclei
    BT2   nuclei
  BT1   intermediate mass nuclei
    BT2   nuclei
  BT1   sulfur isotopes

SULFUR-OXIDIZING BACTERIA [0; 0]
Oct 91
  BT1   bacteria
    BT2   microorganisms
  NT1   thiobacillus ferroxidans
  NT1   thiobacillus oxidans

SULFURIC ACID [3,139; 3,143]
  UF   *hydrogen sulfates*
  BT1   inorganic acids
    BT2   hydrogen compounds
    BT2   inorganic compounds
  BT1   oxygen compounds
  BT1   sulfur compounds
  RT   persulfuric acid
  RT   sulfates
  RT   sulfuric acid esters

SULFURIC ACID ESTERS [68; 68]
Apr 78
  BT1   esters
    BT2   organic compounds
  BT1   organic sulfur compounds
    BT2   organic compounds
  RT   sulfuric acid

SULFUROUS ACID [24; 24]
  BT1   inorganic acids
    BT2   hydrogen compounds
    BT2   inorganic compounds
  BT1   oxygen compounds
  BT1   sulfur compounds
  RT   sulfites

SUM RULES [5,015; 5,015]
  BT1   equations
  RT   quantum mechanics

SUMMER-1 REACTOR [44; 44]
  UF   *virgil c summer-1 reactor*
  BT1   pwr type reactors
    BT2   enriched uranium reactors
      BT3   reactors
    BT2   power reactors
      BT3   reactors
    BT2   thermal reactors
      BT3   reactors
    BT2   water cooled reactors
      BT3   reactors
    BT2   water moderated reactors
      BT3   reactors

SUMMIT-1 REACTOR [20; 20]
  BT1   enriched uranium reactors
    BT2   reactors
  BT1   htgr type reactors
    BT2   gas cooled reactors
      BT3   reactors
    BT2   graphite moderated reactors
      BT3   reactors
  BT1   power reactors
    BT2   reactors

SUMMIT-2 REACTOR [19; 19]
  BT1   enriched uranium reactors
    BT2   reactors
  BT1   htgr type reactors
    BT2   gas cooled reactors
      BT3   reactors
    BT2   graphite moderated reactors
      BT3   reactors
  BT1   power reactors
    BT2   reactors

SUN [4,825; 4,825]
- BT1 main sequence stars
- BT2 stars
- RT chromosphere
- RT energy sources
- RT international geophysical year
- RT international quiet sun year
- RT international solar maximum ye
- RT orbiting solar observatories
- RT photosphere
- RT solar activity
- RT solar atmosphere
- RT solar corona
- RT solar cycle
- RT solar energy
- RT solar flares
- RT solar granulation
- RT solar prominences
- RT solar radiation
- RT solar radio bursts
- RT solar system
- RT solar wind
- RT solar x-ray bursts

SUNDESERT-1 REACTOR [10; 10]
Oct 77
(Blythe, California, USA)
- BT1 pwr type reactors
- BT2 enriched uranium reactors
- BT3 reactors
- BT2 power reactors
- BT3 reactors
- BT2 thermal reactors
- BT3 reactors
- BT2 water cooled reactors
- BT3 reactors
- BT2 water moderated reactors
- BT3 reactors

SUNDESERT-2 REACTOR [10; 10]
Oct 77
(Blythe, California, USA)
- BT1 pwr type reactors
- BT2 enriched uranium reactors
- BT3 reactors
- BT2 power reactors
- BT3 reactors
- BT2 thermal reactors
- BT3 reactors
- BT2 water cooled reactors
- BT3 reactors
- BT2 water moderated reactors
- BT3 reactors

SUNFLOWERS [79; 79]
- UF *helianthus annuus*
- BT1 plants

SUNSHINE PROJECT [1; 1]
- RT fallout

SUNSPOTS [1,821; 1,821]
- BT1 solar activity
- BT1 starspots
- BT2 stellar activity
- RT photosphere
- RT solar cycle
- RT solar flares

super high freq radiation
- USE ghz range 01-100
- AND radiowave radiation

SUPER KUKLA REACTOR [4; 4]
Nov 75
(Lawrence Livermore Laboratory prompt burst reactor)
- BT1 pulsed reactors
- BT2 reactors
- BT1 research and test reactors
- BT2 reactors

SUPER PHENIX REACTOR [667; 667]
(Creys Malville, Isere, France)
- UF *creys-malville reactor*
- BT1 enriched uranium reactors
- BT2 reactors
- BT1 lmfbr type reactors
- BT2 fbr type reactors
- BT3 breeder reactors
- BT4 reactors
- BT3 fast reactors
- BT4 epithermal reactors
- BT5 reactors
- BT2 liquid metal cooled reactors
- BT3 reactors
- BT1 plutonium reactors
- BT2 reactors
- BT1 sodium cooled reactors
- BT2 liquid metal cooled reactors
- BT3 reactors

super power water boiler
- USE supo reactor

SUPERCOMPUTERS [359; 359] *Oct 86*
(The largest, fastest, most powerful computers available at any given time.)
- BT1 digital computers
- BT2 computers
- RT hypercube computers
- RT parallel processing
- RT vector processing

supercond. quantum interf. dev
- USE squid devices

SUPERCONDUCTING CABLES
[880; 880]
- BT1 electric cables
- BT2 cables
- BT2 conductor devices
- BT3 electrical equipment
- BT4 equipment
- RT cryogenic cables
- RT gas-insulated cables
- RT superconducting devices
- RT superconductivity

SUPERCONDUCTING CAVITY RESONAT [914; 914]
- BT1 cavity resonators
- BT2 electronic equipment
- BT3 equipment
- BT2 resonators
- BT3 equipment
- BT1 superconducting devices
- RT cyclic accelerators
- RT microwave equipment
- RT rf systems

SUPERCONDUCTING COILS
[1,165; 1,165] *May 76*
(Prior to January 1983 this concept was indexed by SUPERCONDUCTING DEVICES.)
- BT1 electric coils
- BT2 electrical equipment
- BT3 equipment
- RT magnet coils
- RT superconducting magnets
- RT superconductive energy storage

SUPERCONDUCTING COLLOID DETECT [58; 58] *Oct 76*
(Operates on the principle that a charged particle passing through a superconducting colloid in the metastable, superheated state leads to a measurable change in the inductance of a surrounding pick-up coil.)
- BT1 radiation detectors
- BT2 measuring instruments
- RT charged particle detection
- RT colloids
- RT position sensitive detectors
- RT superconductors

SUPERCONDUCTING COMPOSITES
[1,151; 1,151]
- BT1 composite materials
- BT2 materials
- RT superconducting devices
- RT superconducting wires

SUPERCONDUCTING CYCLOTRONS
[0; 0] *Oct 91*
- BT1 cyclotrons
- BT2 cyclic accelerators
- BT3 accelerators
- NT1 milan superconducting cyclotro
- NT1 texas superconducting cyclotro
- RT superconducting devices

SUPERCONDUCTING DEVICES
[941; 8,991] *Feb 76*
(Restricted to general or review articles and bibliographies.)
- NT1 cryotrons
- NT1 squid devices
- NT1 superconducting cavity resonat
- NT1 superconducting generators
- NT1 superconducting magnets
- NT1 superconducting motors
- RT flux pumps
- RT superconducting cables
- RT superconducting composites
- RT superconducting cyclotrons
- RT superconducting junctions

SUPERCONDUCTING FILMS
[2,157; 2,157] *Jun 83*
- BT1 films
- RT superconducting junctions
- RT superconductors

SUPERCONDUCTING GENERATORS
[238; 238]
- BT1 rotating generators
- BT2 electric generators
- BT3 electrical equipment
- BT4 equipment
- BT1 superconducting devices

SUPERCONDUCTING JUNCTIONS
[1,244; 1,244]
- RT josephson junctions
- RT superconducting devices
- RT superconducting films
- RT superconductors
- RT tunnel effect

superconducting magnetic energ
(Superconducting magnetic energy storage)
- USE superconductive energy storage

SUPERCONDUCTING MAGNETS
[6,732; 6,732]
- UF+ *superconducting solenoids*
- BT1 electromagnets
- BT2 electrical equipment
- BT3 equipment
- BT2 magnets
- BT3 equipment
- BT1 superconducting devices
- RT magnet coils
- RT superconducting coils
- RT superconductive energy storage
- RT superconductors

SUPERCONDUCTING MOTORS
[67; 67]
- BT1 electric motors
- BT2 electrical equipment
- BT3 equipment
- BT2 motors
- BT1 superconducting devices

superconducting solenoids
- USE solenoids
- AND superconducting magnets

SUPERCONDUCTING SUPER COLLIDER [1,783; 1,783] *Jan 85*
UF   *desertron*
UF   *ssc*
BT1   storage rings
BT1   synchrotrons
  BT2   cyclic accelerators
    BT3   accelerators

SUPERCONDUCTING WIRES [897; 897] *Nov 82*
BT1   wires
RT   superconducting composites
RT   superconductors

SUPERCONDUCTIVE ENERGY STORAGE [121; 121] *Feb 84*
UF   *smes*
UF   *superconducting magnetic energ*
BT1   energy storage
  BT2   storage
RT   superconducting coils
RT   superconducting magnets

SUPERCONDUCTIVITY [15,333; 15,333]
BT1   electric conductivity
  BT2   electrical properties
    BT3   physical properties
RT   abrikosov theory
RT   ac losses
RT   bcs theory
RT   belyaev theory
RT   bogolyubov method
RT   coherence length
RT   collective excitations
RT   cooper pairs
RT   critical current
RT   critical field
RT   cryogenics
RT   electron-hole coupling
RT   electron-phonon coupling
RT   energy gap
RT   flux quantization
RT   ginzburg-landau theory
RT   gorkov-eliashberg theory
RT   helicon resonance
RT   high-tc superconductors
RT   josephson effect
RT   kisslinger-sorensen theory
RT   london equation
RT   meissner-ochsenfeld effect
RT   mendelssohn model
RT   penetration depth
RT   pippard theory
RT   proximity effect
RT   superconducting cables
RT   tunnel effect

SUPERCONDUCTORS [11,020; 15,549]
NT1   high-tc superconductors
NT1   stabilized superconductors
NT1   type-i superconductors
NT1   type-ii superconductors
RT   abrikosov theory
RT   electric conductors
RT   squid devices
RT   superconducting colloid detect
RT   superconducting films
RT   superconducting junctions
RT   superconducting magnets
RT   superconducting wires

SUPERCONVERGENCE RELATIONS [51; 51]
RT   convergence
RT   mathematics
RT   series expansion

supercritical flow
USE   turbulent flow

SUPERDISLOCATIONS [23; 23]
(Groups of dislocations with specific space configuration.)
RT   dislocations

SUPERFLUID MODEL [351; 351]
BT1   nuclear models
  BT2   mathematical models

SUPERFLUIDITY [3,368; 3,368]
RT   bose-einstein condensation
RT   cryogenics
RT   fifth sound
RT   film flow
RT   fluid flow
RT   fourth sound
RT   ginzburg-pitaevskii theory
RT   helium ii
RT   helium 3 a
RT   helium 3 a1
RT   helium 3 b
RT   khalatnikov theory
RT   lambda point
RT   landau liquid helium theory
RT   second sound
RT   third sound
RT   viscosity
RT   vortex flow
RT   zero sound

superfluorescence
USE   superradiance

SUPERGIANT STARS [1,022; 1,022]
BT1   giant stars
  BT2   stars

supergranulation
USE   solar granulation

SUPERGRAVITY [3,421; 3,421] *Sep 77*
(A theory connecting fermion-boson supersymmetry with gravitation.)
BT1   unified-field theories
  BT2   field theories
RT   compactification
RT   gauge invariance
RT   graded lie groups
RT   gravitation
RT   gravitons
RT   kaluza-klein theory
RT   quantum field theory
RT   quantum gravity
RT   supersymmetry

SUPERHEATERS [343; 343]
UF   *steam superheaters*
RT   reactor cooling systems
RT   steam generators
RT   superheating

SUPERHEATING [655; 719]
BT1   heating
NT1   nuclear superheating
RT   steam
RT   superheaters

superheavy elements
USE   trans 104 elements

superheterodyne receivers
USE   heterodyne receivers

SUPERHILAC [186; 186]
UF   *berkeley superhilac*
BT1   hilacs
  BT2   heavy ion accelerators
    BT3   accelerators
  BT2   linear accelerators
    BT3   accelerators
RT   bevalac

SUPERLATTICES [1,423; 1,423]
RT   order-disorder transformations
RT   solid solutions

SUPERMASSIVE STARS [141; 141]
(Of the order of 100000 solar masses.)
BT1   stars

SUPERMULTIPLETS [491; 491]
BT1   multiplets

SUPERNOVA REMNANTS [1,855; 2,477]
BT1   cosmic radio sources
NT1   crab nebula
RT   pulsars
RT   supernovae

SUPERNOVAE [3,296; 3,296]
BT1   eruptive variable stars
  BT2   binary stars
    BT3   stars
  BT2   variable stars
    BT3   stars
RT   novae
RT   supernova remnants

SUPEROPERATORS [55; 55]
(Acting on other mathematical operator(s).)
BT1   mathematical operators

SUPEROXIDE DISMUTASE [130; 130] *Apr 84*
UF   *sod*
BT1   oxidoreductases
  BT2   enzymes
    BT3   organic compounds

superoxide radicals
USE   peroxy radicals

SUPERPARAMAGNETISM [125; 125] *Feb 76*
(Quasiparamagnetism of small magnetically ordered particles.)
BT1   magnetism

SUPERPHOSPHATES [161; 161]
BT1   fertilizers
BT1   phosphates
  BT2   oxygen compounds
  BT2   phosphorus compounds

SUPERRADIANCE [110; 110] *Feb 84*
UF   *cooperative spontaneous emissi*
UF   *emission (cooperative spontane*
UF   *spontaneous emission (cooperat*
UF   *superfluorescence*
BT1   photon emission
  BT2   emission
RT   fluorescence
RT   laser radiation

SUPERSATURATION [240; 240]
BT1   saturation
RT   precipitation
RT   solubility
RT   solutions

SUPERSELECTION RULES [159; 159]
BT1   selection rules
RT   quantum mechanics

SUPERSONIC FLOW [877; 877]
BT1   fluid flow
RT   aerodynamics
RT   compressible flow
RT   shock waves
RT   transonic flow
RT   wind tunnels

SUPERSONIC TRANSPORT [83; 83]
BT1   air transport
  BT2   transport
RT   aircraft
RT   cosmic radiation
RT   solar flares
RT   stratosphere

supersymmetric particles
  USE   sparticles

SUPERSYMMETRY [10,478; 10,478]
    Feb 78
  BT1   symmetry
  RT   graded lie groups
  RT   group theory
  RT   quantum field theory
  RT   supergravity

supervisor codes
  USE   executive codes

supervoltage radiotherapy
  USE   radiotherapy

SUPO REACTOR [3; 3]
(Los Alamos Scientific Lab., Los Alamos, New Mexico, USA)
  UF   *super power water boiler*
  BT1   aqueous homogeneous reactors
    BT2   liquid homogeneous reactors
      BT3   fluid fueled reactors
        BT4   reactors
      BT3   homogeneous reactors
        BT4   'reactors
    BT2   water cooled reactors
      BT3   reactors
    BT2   water moderated reactors
      BT3   reactors
  BT1   enriched uranium reactors
    BT2   reactors
  BT1   research reactors
    BT2   research and test reactors
      BT3   reactors
  BT1   thermal reactors
    BT2   reactors

supply
  USE   availability

→ SUPPLY AND DEMAND [0; 0] *Oct 91*
  RT   demand
  RT   energy demand
  RT   energy supplies

SUPPORTS [3,789; 4,863]
  UF   *beams (structural)*
  UF   *columns (structural)*
  UF   *structural beams*
  BT1   mechanical structures
  NT1   foundations
  NT1   fuel racks
  RT   reactor core restraints
  RT   restraints

supralethal doses
  USE   supralethal irradiation

SUPRALETHAL IRRADIATION [141; 141]
  UF   *supralethal doses*
  BT1   irradiation
  RT   death
  RT   dose-response relationships
  RT   lethal irradiation
  RT   lethal radiation dose
  RT   mortality
  RT   radiation doses

sur-100 aachen
  USE   sur-100 series reactor

sur-100 berlin
  USE   sur-100 series reactor

sur-100 bremen
  USE   sur-100 series reactor

sur-100 darmstadt
  USE   sur-100 series reactor

sur-100 hamburg
  USE   sur-100 series reactor

sur-100 karlsruhe
  USE   sur-100 series reactor

sur-100 kiel
  USE   sur-100 series reactor

sur-100 muenchen
  USE   sur-100 series reactor

SUR-100 SERIES REACTOR [10; 10]
  UF   *siemens unterrichtsreaktor*
  UF   *sur-100 aachen*
  UF   *sur-100 berlin*
  UF   *sur-100 bremen*
  UF   *sur-100 darmstadt*
  UF   *sur-100 hamburg*
  UF   *sur-100 karlsruhe*
  UF   *sur-100 kiel*
  UF   *sur-100 muenchen*
  UF   *sur-100 stuttgart*
  UF   *sur-100 ulm*
  BT1   enriched uranium reactors
    BT2   reactors
  BT1   organic moderated reactors
    BT2   reactors
  BT1   solid homogeneous reactors
    BT2   homogeneous reactors
      BT3   reactors
  BT1   thermal reactors
    BT2   reactors
  BT1   training reactors
    BT2   research and test reactors
      BT3   reactors

sur-100 stuttgart
  USE   sur-100 series reactor

sur-100 ulm
  USE   sur-100 series reactor

SURF II STORAGE RING [7; 7] *Jul 84*
(NBS Synchrotron Ultraviolet Radiation Facility.)
  UF   *nbs synchrotron uv rad. fac.*
  UF   *synchrotron uv rad. fac. (nbs)*
  BT1   storage rings
  BT1   synchrotron radiation sources
    BT2   radiation sources

SURFACE AIR [1,261; 1,261]
  BT1   air
    BT2   gases
      BT3   fluids
  RT   earth atmosphere
  RT   particle resuspension

SURFACE AREA [161; 161] *May 86*
(Extent of the area covered by a surface. See also SPECIFIC SURFACE AREA.)
  RT   surface properties
  RT   surfaces

surface area (specific)
  USE   specific surface area

SURFACE BARRIER DETECTORS [1,131; 1,131]
  UF   *surface-barrier detectors*
  BT1   semiconductor detectors
    BT2   radiation detectors
      BT3   measuring instruments
  RT   surface barrier transistors

SURFACE BARRIER TRANSISTORS [16; 16]
  UF   *surface-barrier transistors*
  BT1   transistors
    BT2   semiconductor devices
  RT   surface barrier detectors

surface boiling
  USE   subcooled boiling

SURFACE CLEANING [1,124; 1,124]
  BT1   cleaning
  BT1   surface finishing
  RT   decontamination
  RT   descaling
  RT   polishing
  RT   shot peening

SURFACE COATING [2,233; 8,693]
  UF   *coating (surface)*
  UF   *coating processes*
  BT1   deposition
  NT1   chemical coating
    NT2   chemical vapor deposition
    NT2   electrochemical coating
      NT3   anodization
  NT1   cladding
  NT1   diffusion coating
  NT1   dip coating
    NT2   hot dipping
  NT1   electrodeposition
    NT2   electroplating
  NT1   plating
    NT2   electroplating
    NT2   vapor plating
  NT1   spray coating
    NT2   flame spraying
    NT2   plasma arc spraying
  NT1   vacuum coating
  RT   coatings
  RT   corrosion protection
  RT   liners
  RT   lining processes
  RT   surface finishing

SURFACE CONTAMINATION [1,458; 1,458]
(For radioactive contamination only; see also POLLUTION.)
  BT1   contamination
  RT   decontamination
  RT   radioactivity
  RT   surface contamination monitors

SURFACE CONTAMINATION MONITORS [191; 191]
  BT1   radiation monitors
    BT2   monitors
      BT3   measuring instruments
  RT   surface contamination

surface delta interaction
  USE   surface delta potential

SURFACE DELTA POTENTIAL [74;
  UF   *modified surface delta potenti*
  UF   *surface delta interaction*
  UF   *surface-delta potential*
  BT1   surface potential
    BT2   potentials
  RT   nucleon-nucleon potential

SURFACE ENERGY [77; 77]
(The energy per unit area of an expose surface of a liquid; generally greater th the surface tension. Prior to June 1986 SURFACE TENSION was used for thi concept.)
  RT   surface tension

SURFACE EXPLOSIONS [55; 60]
- BT1 explosions
- NT1 bravo event
- NT1 holly event
- NT1 mike event
- NT1 zuni event
- RT buffalo project
- RT castle project
- RT cratering explosions
- RT craters
- RT ivy project
- RT jangle project
- RT nuclear excavation
- RT nuclear explosions
- RT plowshare project
- RT redwing project

SURFACE FINISHING [298; 3,819]
- UF *finishing (surface)*
- NT1 descaling
- NT1 polishing
  - NT2 chemical polishing
  - NT2 electropolishing
  - NT2 mechanical polishing
- NT1 surface cleaning
- RT coatings
- RT etching
- RT machining
- RT metallography
- RT surface coating
- RT surface hardening

SURFACE HARDENING [347; 915]
- BT1 hardening
- BT1 surface treatments
- NT1 carburization
- RT cold working
- RT shot peening
- RT surface finishing

SURFACE IONIZATION [286; 289]
- BT1 ionization
- NT1 adiabatic surface ionization
- RT ion thrusters

SURFACE MINING [0; 0] Oct 75
- BT1 mining
- RT coal mining
- RT excavation
- RT fracturing
- RT mines
- RT slope stability
- RT underground mining

SURFACE POTENTIAL [120; 143]
Oct 83
- BT1 potentials
- NT1 surface delta potential
- RT surface properties
- RT work functions

SURFACE PROPERTIES [5,047; 8,285]
- SF *tribology*
- NT1 emissivity
- NT1 roughness
- NT1 surface tension
- RT adhesion
- RT adsorption
- RT ceramography
- RT corrosion
- RT physical properties
- RT surface area
- RT surface potential
- RT surface treatments
- RT wettability

SURFACE TENSION [1,341; 1,341]
(The force acting on the surface of a liquid, tending to minimize the area of the surface; it equals the free energy per unit surface.)
- UF *tension (surface)*
- BT1 surface properties
- RT surface energy
- RT surfactants

SURFACE TREATMENTS [1,076; 2,210]
- NT1 pickling
  - NT2 corrosion pickling
- NT1 shot peening
- NT1 surface hardening
  - NT2 carburization
- RT sample preparation
- RT surface properties

SURFACE WATERS [2,773; 11,463]
- NT1 coastal waters
  - NT2 estuaries
- NT1 lakes
  - NT2 ambrosia lake
  - NT2 athabasca lake
  - NT2 dead sea
  - NT2 great lakes
    - NT3 lake erie
    - NT3 lake huron
    - NT3 lake michigan
    - NT3 lake ontario
    - NT3 lake superior
  - NT2 lago maggiore
  - NT2 lake baikal
  - NT2 lake balaton
- NT1 panama canal
- NT1 rivers
  - NT2 allegheny river
  - NT2 amazon river
  - NT2 blind river
  - NT2 cape fear river
  - NT2 clinch river
  - NT2 colorado river
  - NT2 columbia river
  - NT2 connecticut river
  - NT2 cumberland river
  - NT2 danube river
  - NT2 delaware river
  - NT2 ganga river
  - NT2 gunnison river
  - NT2 hudson river
  - NT2 james river
  - NT2 mississippi river
  - NT2 missouri river
  - NT2 mohawk river
  - NT2 niger river
  - NT2 nile river
  - NT2 ohio river
  - NT2 ottawa river
  - NT2 po river
  - NT2 potomac river
  - NT2 rhine river
  - NT2 rhone river
  - NT2 savannah river
  - NT2 scioto river
  - NT2 st lawrence river
  - NT2 susquehanna river
  - NT2 tennessee river
  - NT2 thames river
  - NT2 tigris river
  - NT2 volga river
- NT1 seas
  - NT2 arctic ocean
    - NT3 beaufort sea
    - NT3 chukchi sea
  - NT2 atlantic ocean
    - NT3 bay of biscay
    - NT3 bay of fundy
    - NT3 biscayne bay
    - NT3 caribbean sea
      - NT4 gulf of mexico
        - NT5 san antonio bay
    - NT3 chesapeake bay
    - NT3 gulf of maine
    - NT3 irish sea
    - NT3 north sea
    - NT3 sargasso sea
  - NT2 baltic sea
  - NT2 black sea
  - NT2 caspian sea
  - NT2 indian ocean
    - NT3 arabian sea
  - NT2 marmara sea
  - NT2 mediterranean sea
  - NT2 pacific ocean
    - NT3 bering sea
    - NT3 humboldt bay
    - NT3 san francisco bay
    - NT3 sequim bay
  - NT2 red sea
- NT1 settling ponds
- NT1 water reservoirs
- RT air-water interactions
- RT alluvial deposits
- RT atmospheric precipitations
- RT fishes
- RT floods
- RT ground water
- RT hydrology
- RT hydrosphere
- RT irrigation
- RT liquid wastes
- RT plankton
- RT sediment-water interfaces
- RT swamps
- RT water
- RT water currents

surface waves (seismic)
- USE seismic surface waves

surface-active agents
- USE surfactants

surface-barrier detectors
- USE surface barrier detectors

surface-barrier transistors
- USE surface barrier transistors

surface-delta potential
- USE surface delta potential

SURFACES [14,266; 14,266]
- RT adsorption
- RT blisters
- RT infrared thermography
- RT interfaces
- RT rewetting
- RT surface area
- RT topological foliation
- RT two-dimensional calculations

SURFACTANTS [832; 1,225]
- UF *surface-active agents*
- NT1 wetting agents
  - NT2 detergents
    - NT3 pluronics
- RT surface tension

SURGERY [7,799; 9,178]
- UF+ *radiosurgery*
- UF+ *sympathectomy*
- UF+ *vagotomy*
- BT1 medicine
- NT1 adrenalectomy
- NT1 castration
- NT1 gastrectomy
- NT1 hepatectomy
- NT1 hypophysectomy
- NT1 laryngectomy
- NT1 nephrectomy
- NT1 plastic surgery
- NT1 splenectomy
- NT1 thymectomy
- NT1 thyroidectomy
- RT anesthesia
- RT surgical materials
- RT therapy

SURGES [99; 99]
- RT electric controllers
- RT electric currents
- RT electric potential
- RT electrical transients
- RT fluid flow
- RT hydraulics
- RT overcurrent
- RT overvoltage
- RT pulses
- RT voltage regulators

SURGICAL MATERIALS [345; 345]
- BT1 materials
- BT1 medical supplies
- RT isomed
- RT prostheses
- RT surgery

SURINAM [9; 9]
- BT1 developing countries
- BT1 south america
  - BT2 latin america

SURMAC TOKAMAK [4; 4] *Nov 82*
- BT1 tokamak devices
  - BT2 closed plasma devices
    - BT3 thermonuclear devices

surry power station unit-1
- USE surry-1 reactor

surry power station unit-2
- USE surry-2 reactor

SURRY-1 REACTOR [298; 298]
(Gravel Neck, Virginia, USA)
- UF *surry power station unit-1*
- BT1 pwr type reactors
  - BT2 enriched uranium reactors
    - BT3 reactors
  - BT2 power reactors
    - BT3 reactors
  - BT2 thermal reactors
    - BT3 reactors
  - BT2 water cooled reactors
    - BT3 reactors
  - BT2 water moderated reactors
    - BT3 reactors

SURRY-2 REACTOR [249; 249]
(Gravel Neck, Virginia, USA)
- UF *surry power station unit-2*
- BT1 pwr type reactors
  - BT2 enriched uranium reactors
    - BT3 reactors
  - BT2 power reactors
    - BT3 reactors
  - BT2 thermal reactors
    - BT3 reactors
  - BT2 water cooled reactors
    - BT3 reactors
  - BT2 water moderated reactors
    - BT3 reactors

SURRY-3 REACTOR [102; 102]
(Gravel Neck, Virginia, USA)
- BT1 pwr type reactors
  - BT2 enriched uranium reactors
    - BT3 reactors
  - BT2 power reactors
    - BT3 reactors
  - BT2 thermal reactors
    - BT3 reactors
  - BT2 water cooled reactors
    - BT3 reactors
  - BT2 water moderated reactors
    - BT3 reactors

SURRY-4 REACTOR [101; 101]
(Gravel Neck, Virginia, USA)
- BT1 pwr type reactors
  - BT2 enriched uranium reactors
    - BT3 reactors
  - BT2 power reactors
    - BT3 reactors
  - BT2 thermal reactors
    - BT3 reactors
  - BT2 water cooled reactors
    - BT3 reactors
  - BT2 water moderated reactors
    - BT3 reactors

surveillance
- USE inspection

surveillance (medical)
- USE medical surveillance

surveillance (radioactivity)
- USE radiation monitoring

survey (radioactivity)
- USE radiation monitoring

SURVEY MONITORS [257; 257]
- BT1 radiation monitors
  - BT2 monitors
    - BT3 measuring instruments

SURVIVAL CURVES [8,143; 8,143]
- UF *survival fraction*
- RT biological effects
- RT dose-response relationships
- RT lethal irradiation
- RT mortality
- RT radiosensitivity

survival fraction
- USE survival curves

SURVIVAL TIME [3,484; 3,484]
- RT lethal irradiation
- RT time dependence

susceptibility (magnetic)
- USE magnetic susceptibility

suse cyclotron (munich)
- USE munich suse cyclotron

SUSPENSIONS [966; 2,542]
- BT1 dispersions
- NT1 slurries
- RT drilling fluids
- RT filters
- RT fluidization
- RT fluidized beds
- RT turbidity

suspensions (fuel)
- USE fuel slurries

susq. steam elect. stat. un.-1
- USE susquehanna-1 reactor

susq. steam elect. stat. un.-2
- USE susquehanna-2 reactor

SUSQUEHANNA RIVER [14; 14]
- BT1 rivers
  - BT2 surface waters

SUSQUEHANNA-1 REACTOR [65; 65]
(Salem, Pennsylvania, USA)
- UF *susq. steam elect. stat. un.-1*
- BT1 bwr type reactors
  - BT2 enriched uranium reactors
    - BT3 reactors
  - BT2 power reactors
    - BT3 reactors
  - BT2 thermal reactors
    - BT3 reactors
  - BT2 water cooled reactors
    - BT3 reactors
  - BT2 water moderated reactors
    - BT3 reactors

SUSQUEHANNA-2 REACTOR [59; 59]
(Salem, Pennsylvania, USA)
- UF *susq. steam elect. stat. un.-2*
- BT1 bwr type reactors
  - BT2 enriched uranium reactors
    - BT3 reactors
  - BT2 power reactors
    - BT3 reactors
  - BT2 thermal reactors
    - BT3 reactors
  - BT2 water cooled reactors
    - BT3 reactors
  - BT2 water moderated reactors
    - BT3 reactors

SUYDAM CRITERION [59; 59]
- UF *suydam theory*
- RT mercier criterion
- RT plasma instability

suydam theory
- USE suydam criterion

sv 40 virus
- USE simian virus

sv40 virus
- USE oncogenic viruses

SW GROUPS [6; 9]
- BT1 lie groups
  - BT2 symmetry groups
- NT1 sw-3 groups

SW-3 GROUPS [3; 3]
- BT1 sw groups
  - BT2 lie groups
    - BT3 symmetry groups

SWAGING [97; 97]
- BT1 materials working
  - BT2 fabrication
- RT forging

SWAMPS [137; 137] *Oct 76*
- UF *bogs*
- UF *marshes*
- UF *wetlands*
- RT aquatic ecosystems
- RT surface waters

SWAZILAND [11; 11]
- BT1 africa
- BT1 developing countries

SWEAT [19; 19]
- UF *transpiration (animal)*
- BT1 biological wastes
  - BT2 biological materials
    - BT3 materials
  - BT2 wastes
- BT1 body fluids
  - BT2 biological materials
    - BT3 materials
- RT excretion
- RT skin

sweat glands
- USE glands
- AND skin

SWEDEN [2,436; 2,436]
- BT1 developed countries
- BT1 scandinavia
  - BT2 europe
- RT ranstad deposit

SWEDISH ORGANIZATIONS [129; 1
Sep 76
- BT1 national organizations

swedish reactor r-1
- USE r-1 reactor

swedish reactor r-2
   USE   r-2 reactor

swedish reactor r2-0
   USE   r2-0 reactor

SWEEP CIRCUITS [49; 49]
   BT1   electronic circuits
   RT   timing circuits

SWELLING [4,805; 4,805]
   BT1   deformation
   RT   blisters
   RT   expansion
   RT   thermal expansion

SWESSAR STANDARD PLANT [9; 9]
(Stone and Webster reference PWR nuclear power plant)
   UF   *stone-webster reference pwr*
   BT1   nuclear power plants
     BT2   nuclear facilities
     BT2   thermal power plants
       BT3   power plants

swierk agata reactor
   USE   agata reactor

swierk anna reactor
   USE   anna reactor

swierk ewa reactor
   USE   ewa reactor

SWIERK LINAC [8; 8]
   BT1   linear accelerators
     BT2   accelerators

swierk maria reactor
   USE   maria reactor

swierk research reactor maryla
   USE   maryla reactor

swimming
   USE   exercise

swimming pool reactors
   USE   pool type reactors

swimming pool tank r. austria
   USE   astra reactor

SWINE [1,374; 1,485]
   UF   *pigs*
   BT1   domestic animals
     BT2   animals
   BT1   mammals
     BT2   vertebrates
       BT3   animals
   NT1   miniature swine
   RT   meat

swirl flow
   USE   vortex flow

swiss inst nucl res cyclotron
   USE   sin cyclotron

SWISS ORGANIZATIONS [122; 122]
Sep 80
   BT1   national organizations

SWITCHES [1,294; 1,716]
   UF   *contactors*
   UF   *electric contactors*
   UF   *electric switches*
   BT1   electrical equipment
     BT2   equipment
   NT1   cryotrons
   NT1   plasma switches
   NT1   semiconductor switches
   RT   bimetals
   RT   circuit breakers
   RT   connectors
   RT   electric contacts
   RT   electric discharges
   RT   electric fuses
   RT   equipment protection devices
   RT   interlocks
   RT   q-switching
   RT   relays
   RT   switching circuits

SWITCHING CIRCUITS [532; 635]
   BT1   electronic circuits
   NT1   transistor switching circuits
   RT   circuit breakers
   RT   counting circuits
   RT   gating circuits
   RT   relays
   RT   switches
   RT   thyratrons
   RT   thyristors

SWITCHING DIODES [28; 28]
   BT1   semiconductor diodes
     BT2   semiconductor devices
   RT   transistor switching circuits

SWITZERLAND [1,561; 1,561]
   BT1   developed countries
   BT1   europe

SWORDFISH EVENT [0; 0]
   BT1   atmospheric explosions
     BT2   explosions
   BT1   dominic project
   BT1   nuclear explosions
     BT2   explosions
   BT1   underwater explosions
     BT2   explosions

sydsvenska kraft ab reactor 1
   USE   barsebaeck-1 reactor

sydsvenska kraft ab reactor 2
   USE   barsebaeck-2 reactor

SYENITES [26; 26] *Nov 84*
   BT1   plutonic rocks
     BT2   igneous rocks
       BT3   rocks
   RT   feldspars

SYMBIOSIS [43; 43] *Dec 84*
(Limited to biology.)
   UF   *commensalism*
   UF   *mutualism*
   RT   animals
   RT   biology
   RT   metabolism
   RT   plants

SYMBIOTIC STARS [204; 204] *Mar 83*
(Objects whose spectra have characteristics of disparate spectral classes.)
   BT1   stars
   RT   accretion disks
   RT   binary stars

symbolic logic
   USE   mathematical logic

SYMMETRY [6,954; 24,491]
   NT1   axial symmetry
   NT1   boson-fermion symmetry
   NT1   chiral symmetry
   NT1   crossing symmetry
   NT1   supersymmetry
   NT1   unitary symmetry
   RT   asymmetry
   RT   configuration
   RT   distribution
   RT   invariance principles
   RT   orientation
   RT   symmetry breaking
   RT   symmetry groups

SYMMETRY BREAKING
[13,254; 13,254]
   RT   compactification
   RT   higgs bosons
   RT   instantons
   RT   symmetry
   RT   symmetry groups

SYMMETRY GROUPS [1,298; 32,604]
   NT1   dynamical groups
     NT2   o groups
   NT1   lie groups
     NT2   conformal groups
     NT2   de sitter group
     NT2   graded lie groups
     NT2   o groups
     NT2   poincare groups
       NT3   lorentz groups
     NT2   sl groups
     NT2   so groups
       NT3   so-10 groups
       NT3   so-12 groups
       NT3   so-2 groups
       NT3   so-3 groups
       NT3   so-4 groups
       NT3   so-6 groups
       NT3   so-8 groups
     NT2   sp groups
     NT2   su groups
       NT3   su-2 groups
       NT3   su-3 groups
       NT3   su-4 groups
       NT3   su-5 groups
       NT3   su-6 groups
       NT3   su-7 groups
       NT3   su-8 groups
       NT3   su-9 groups
     NT2   sw groups
       NT3   sw-3 groups
     NT2   u groups
       NT3   u-1 groups
       NT3   u-12 groups
       NT3   u-2 groups
       NT3   u-3 groups
       NT3   u-4 groups
       NT3   u-5 groups
       NT3   u-6 groups
   NT1   space groups
   RT   casimir operators
   RT   current algebra
   RT   group theory
   RT   irreducible representations
   RT   nonunitary representations
   RT   symmetry
   RT   symmetry breaking

sympathectomy
   USE   autonomic nervous system
   AND   surgery

sympathetic nervous system
   USE   autonomic nervous system

SYMPATHOLYTICS [146; 193]
   BT1   autonomic nervous system agent
     BT2   drugs
   NT1   ergotamine
   NT1   reserpine
   RT   autonomic nervous system

SYMPATHOMIMETICS [434; 3,140]
- BT1 autonomic nervous system agent
- BT2 drugs
- NT1 adrenaline
- NT1 amphetamines
- NT2 benzedrine
- NT1 dopamine
- NT1 ephedrine
- NT1 noradrenaline
- NT1 serotonin
- NT1 tyramine
- RT autonomic nervous system
- RT vasoconstriction
- RT vasodilation

symplectic groups
- USE sp groups

symposia
- USE meetings

§§ **SYMPTOMS** [1,410; 10,064]
- NT1 anemias
- NT2 ischemia
- NT2 megaloblastic anemia
- NT2 sickle cell anemia
- NT2 thalassemia
- NT1 ascites
- NT1 constipation
- NT1 diarrhea
- NT1 edema
- NT1 erythema
- NT1 fever
- NT1 heart failure
- NT1 hemorrhage
- NT1 hypertension
- NT1 jaundice
- NT1 leukopenia
- NT2 lymphopenia
- NT1 nausea
- NT1 pain
- NT1 peritonitis
- NT1 splenomegaly
- NT1 uremia
- NT1 vomiting
- RT diagnosis
- RT diseases

SYNCHROCYCLOTRONS [197; 626]
- UF *fm cyclotrons*
- UF *frequency modulated cyclotrons*
- UF *phasotrons*
- BT1 cyclic accelerators
- BT2 accelerators
- NT1 berkeley synchrocyclotron
- NT1 cern synchrocyclotron
- NT1 chicago synchrocyclotron
- NT1 dubna synchrocyclotron
- NT1 goettingen synchrocyclotron
- NT1 harvard synchrocyclotron
- NT1 harwell synchrocyclotron
- NT1 iko synchrocyclotron
- NT1 mcgill synchrocyclotron
- NT1 orsay synchrocyclotron
- NT1 uppsala synchrocyclotron
- RT cyclotrons
- RT synchrotrons

SYNCHRONIZATION [512; 512] Oct 77
- RT antimetabolites
- RT cell cycle
- RT coincidence methods
- RT resonance
- RT synchronous cultures
- RT tuning

SYNCHRONOUS CULTURES [265; 265]
- BT1 cell cultures
- RT antimetabolites
- RT cell cycle
- RT synchronization

synchrophasotrons
- USE synchrotrons

SYNCHROTRON OSCILLATIONS [378; 378]
- BT1 beam dynamics
- BT2 dynamics
- BT3 mechanics
- BT1 oscillations

SYNCHROTRON RADIATION [5,743; 5,743]
- UF *bremsstrahlung (magnetic)*
- UF *magnetic bremsstrahlung*
- BT1 bremsstrahlung
- BT2 electromagnetic radiation
- BT3 radiations
- RT cyclotron radiation
- RT kek photon factory
- RT nsls
- RT synchrotron radiation sources
- RT wiggler magnets

SYNCHROTRON RADIATION SOURCES [1,240; 1,783] Jul 81
- BT1 radiation sources
- NT1 kek photon factory
- NT1 lnls storage ring
- NT1 nsls
- NT1 spring-8 storage ring
- NT1 surf ii storage ring
- RT synchrotron radiation

synchrotron uv rad. fac. (nbs)
- USE surf ii storage ring

SYNCHROTRONS [1,716; 10,925]
- UF *synchrophasotrons*
- BT1 cyclic accelerators
- BT2 accelerators
- NT1 bevatron
- NT1 birmingham synchrotron
- NT1 bonn synchrotron
- NT1 brookhaven ags
- NT1 caltech synchrotron
- NT1 cambridge electron accelerator
- NT1 cern ps synchrotron
- NT1 cern sps synchrotron
- NT1 cornell 10-gev synchrotron
- NT1 cornell 2-gev synchrotron
- NT1 cosmotron
- NT1 desy
- NT1 erevan synchrotron
- NT1 escar storage ring
- NT1 fermilab accelerator
- NT1 fermilab tevatron
- NT1 fian synchrotron
- NT1 frascati synchrotron
- NT1 glasgow synchrotron
- NT1 ipns-i synchrotron
- NT1 itep synchrotron
- NT1 jinr synchrotron
- NT1 kek synchrotron
- NT1 lampf ii synchrotron
- NT1 lusy
- NT1 mura synchrotron
- NT1 nimrod
- NT1 nina
- NT1 omnitron
- NT1 pakhra synchrotron
- NT1 princeton synchrotron
- NT1 saturne
- NT1 saturne ii
- NT1 serpukhov synchrotron
- NT1 serpukhov tevatron
- NT1 sis synchrotron
- NT1 superconducting super collider
- NT1 tokyo synchrotron
- NT1 tomsk synchrotron
- NT1 zgs
- RT nsls
- RT synchrocyclotrons

SYNERGISM [1,936; 1,936]
- RT biochemistry
- RT biological effects

SYNGAMUS [2; 2]
- BT1 nematodes
- BT2 invertebrates
- BT3 animals
- BT1 parasites
- RT chickens
- RT mammals

synovia
- USE bone joints

synroc
- USE synthetic rocks

SYNROC PROCESS [225; 225] Nov 81
- RT hollandite
- RT perovskite
- RT radioactive waste processing
- RT zirconolite

§ **SYNTHESIS** [4,004; 39,965]
- UF *formation*
- NT1 biosynthesis
- NT2 post-translation modification
- NT1 chemical preparation
- NT1 nucleosynthesis
- NT2 heavy ion fusion reactions
- NT2 thermonuclear reactions
- NT3 impact fusion
- NT3 muon-catalyzed fusion
- NT1 photosynthesis

synthetases
- USE ligases

SYNTHETIC FUELS [272; 272]
(No natural occurrence; produced by chemical techniques.)
- BT1 fuels
- RT coal gasification
- RT coal liquefaction
- RT pyrolysis products

SYNTHETIC ROCKS [375; 375] Feb
- UF *synroc*
- BT1 rocks

SYPHILIS [17; 17]
- BT1 bacterial diseases
- BT2 infectious diseases
- BT3 diseases
- RT spirochaetes

SYRIA [37; 37]
- BT1 asia
- BT1 developing countries
- BT1 middle east

syrian hamster
- USE hamsters

SYSTEM FAILURE ANALYSIS [975; 4,123]
(Techniques for analysing the events leading to, or following from, a potential, actual, system failure.)
- BT1 systems analysis
- NT1 failure mode analysis
- NT1 fault tree analysis
- RT mathematical logic

systeme acceler. rhone-alpes
- USE sara cyclotron

SYSTEMS ANALYSIS [2,361; 6,307] Nov 75
(Used in the fields of technology research and management for problems such as calculation of failure probabilities and reliability studies of systems and components.)

NT1 system failure analysis
NT2 failure mode analysis
NT2 fault tree analysis
RT   control systems
RT   energy accounting
RT   energy analysis
RT   failures
RT   man-machine systems
RT   ncsr
RT   reactor protection systems
RT   reactor safety
RT   reliability
RT   safety engineering

SZILARD-CHALMERS REACTION [116; 116]
BT1 hot atom chemistry
BT2 radiochemistry
BT3 chemistry

SZR TYPE REACTORS [0; 378]
UF   sodium cooled zirc. hydr. mode
BT1 hydride moderated reactors
BT2 reactors
BT1 liquid metal cooled reactors
BT2 reactors
NT1 knk reactor
NT1 knk-2 reactor
RT   hydride moderators
RT   power reactors

S1C PROTOTYPE REACTOR [3; 3]
(General Electric, Knowles Atomic Power Lab., USA)
BT1 mobile reactors
BT2 reactors
BT1 pwr type reactors
BT2 enriched uranium reactors
BT3 reactors
BT2 power reactors
BT3 reactors
BT2 thermal reactors
BT3 reactors
BT2 water cooled reactors
BT3 reactors
BT2 water moderated reactors
BT3 reactors
BT1 test reactors
BT2 research and test reactors
BT3 reactors
BT2 test facilities

S10FS-1 REACTOR [3; 3]
UF   snap-10a flight syst. test-1
BT1 nak cooled reactors
BT2 liquid metal cooled reactors
BT3 reactors
BT1 snap 10 reactor
BT2 enriched uranium reactors
BT3 reactors
BT2 potassium cooled reactors
BT3 liquid metal cooled reactors
BT4 reactors
BT2 process heat reactors
BT3 power reactors
BT4 reactors
BT2 snap reactors
BT3 space power reactors
BT4 mobile reactors
BT5 reactors
BT4 power reactors
BT5 reactors
BT2 sodium cooled reactors
BT3 liquid metal cooled reactors
BT4 reactors

S10FS-3 REACTOR [1; 1]
UF   snap-10a flight syst. test-3
BT1 nak cooled reactors
BT2 liquid metal cooled reactors
BT3 reactors
BT1 snap 10 reactor
BT2 enriched uranium reactors
BT3 reactors
BT2 potassium cooled reactors
BT3 liquid metal cooled reactors
BT4 reactors

BT2 process heat reactors
BT3 power reactors
BT4 reactors
BT2 snap reactors
BT3 space power reactors
BT4 mobile reactors
BT5 reactors
BT4 power reactors
BT5 reactors
BT2 sodium cooled reactors
BT3 liquid metal cooled reactors
BT4 reactors

S10FS-4 REACTOR [1; 1]
UF   snap-10a flight syst. test-4
BT1 nak cooled reactors
BT2 liquid metal cooled reactors
BT3 reactors
BT1 snap 10 reactor
BT2 enriched uranium reactors
BT3 reactors
BT2 potassium cooled reactors
BT3 liquid metal cooled reactors
BT4 reactors
BT2 process heat reactors
BT3 power reactors
BT4 reactors
BT2 snap reactors
BT3 space power reactors
BT4 mobile reactors
BT5 reactors
BT4 power reactors
BT5 reactors
BT2 sodium cooled reactors
BT3 liquid metal cooled reactors
BT4 reactors

S2DS REACTOR [2; 2]
UF   snap-2 developmental system
BT1 nak cooled reactors
BT2 liquid metal cooled reactors
BT3 reactors
BT1 snap 2 reactor
BT2 enriched uranium reactors
BT3 reactors
BT2 snap reactors
BT3 space power reactors
BT4 mobile reactors
BT5 reactors
BT4 power reactors
BT5 reactors

S8DR REACTOR [14; 14]
UF   snap-8 developmental reactor
BT1 nak cooled reactors
BT2 liquid metal cooled reactors
BT3 reactors
BT1 snap 8 reactor
BT2 enriched uranium reactors
BT3 reactors
BT2 snap reactors
BT3 space power reactors
BT4 mobile reactors
BT5 reactors
BT4 power reactors
BT5 reactors

S8ER REACTOR [7; 7]
UF   snap-8 experimental reactor
BT1 nak cooled reactors
BT2 liquid metal cooled reactors
BT3 reactors
BT1 snap 8 reactor
BT2 enriched uranium reactors
BT3 reactors
BT2 snap reactors
BT3 space power reactors
BT4 mobile reactors
BT5 reactors
BT4 power reactors
BT5 reactors

T CHANNEL [881; 881]
RT   mandelstam representation
RT   particle interactions
RT   s channel
RT   u channel

T CODES [2,735; 2,735]
BT1 computer codes

T INVARIANCE [1,116; 1,258]
UF   time-reversal invariance
BT1 invariance principles
NT1 detailed balance principle

t matrix
USE s matrix

T TAURI STARS [395; 395]
BT1 eruptive variable stars
BT2 binary stars
BT3 stars
BT2 variable stars
BT3 stars

T-10 TOKAMAK [172; 172] *Oct 83*
BT1 tokamak devices
BT2 closed plasma devices
BT3 thermonuclear devices

T-15 TOKAMAK [100; 100] *Jun 84*
BT1 tokamak devices
BT2 closed plasma devices
BT3 thermonuclear devices

t-2200 resonances
(Prior to December 1987 this was a valid descriptor.)
USE rho3-2250 mesons

T-7 TOKAMAK [26; 26] *Oct 83*
BT1 tokamak devices
BT2 closed plasma devices
BT3 thermonuclear devices

TABAKIN POTENTIAL [91; 91]
BT1 potentials
RT   nuclear potential
RT   nucleon-nucleon potential
RT   nucleons

TACHYONS [715; 715]
(Hypothesized particles that travel faster than the velocity of light; they have an imaginary rest mass.)
BT1 postulated particles
BT2 elementary particles

tadpoles
USE amphibians
AND larvae

TAGGED PHOTON METHOD [227; 227]
BT1 coincidence methods
BT2 counting techniques
RT   bremsstrahlung
RT   photons
RT   polarization

TAILINGS [1,134; 1,617] *Feb 81*
(Solid residue separated in the preparation of various products.)
UF   mine tailings
BT1 solid wastes
BT2 wastes
NT1 mill tailings
RT   biointrusion
RT   ore processing
RT   remedial action
RT   separation processes

TAIWAN RESEARCH REACTOR [21; 21]
BT1 heavy water cooled reactors
BT2 reactors
BT1 heavy water moderated reactors
BT2 reactors
BT1 isotope production reactors
BT2 irradiation reactors

BT3 reactors
BT1 materials testing reactors
BT2 irradiation reactors
BT3 reactors
BT1 natural uranium reactors
BT2 reactors
BT1 research reactors
BT2 research and test reactors
BT3 reactors
BT1 tank type reactors
BT2 reactors
BT1 thermal reactors
BT2 reactors

TAKAHAMA-1 REACTOR [33; 33]
(Takahama, Fukui, Japan)
UF *kansai-3 reactor*
BT1 pwr type reactors
BT2 enriched uranium reactors
BT3 reactors
BT2 power reactors
BT3 reactors
BT2 thermal reactors
BT3 reactors
BT2 water cooled reactors
BT3 reactors
BT2 water moderated reactors
BT3 reactors

TAKAHAMA-2 REACTOR [29; 29]
(Takahama, Fukui, Japan)
UF *kansai-4 reactor*
BT1 pwr type reactors
BT2 enriched uranium reactors
BT3 reactors
BT2 power reactors
BT3 reactors
BT2 thermal reactors
BT3 reactors
BT2 water cooled reactors
BT3 reactors
BT2 water moderated reactors
BT3 reactors

TAKAHAMA-3 REACTOR [21; 21]
Jul 81
BT1 pwr type reactors
BT2 enriched uranium reactors
BT3 reactors
BT2 power reactors
BT3 reactors
BT2 thermal reactors
BT3 reactors
BT2 water cooled reactors
BT3 reactors
BT2 water moderated reactors
BT3 reactors

TAKAHAMA-4 REACTOR [20; 20]
Jul 81
BT1 pwr type reactors
BT2 enriched uranium reactors
BT3 reactors
BT2 power reactors
BT3 reactors
BT2 thermal reactors
BT3 reactors
BT2 water cooled reactors
BT3 reactors
BT2 water moderated reactors
BT3 reactors

TALC [37; 37]
BT1 silicate minerals
BT2 minerals
RT magnesium silicates

TALMI INTEGRALS [38; 38]
BT1 integrals
RT shell models

TALSPEAK PROCESS [6; 6] *Jan 79*
BT1 reprocessing
BT2 separation processes
RT solvent extraction

tam
USE tamoxifen

TAMM-DANCOFF METHOD [296; 296]
RT boson expansion
RT quantum mechanics

tammuz-1 reactor
USE tz1 reactor

tammuz-2 reactor
USE tz2 reactor

TAMOXIFEN [40; 40] *May 81*
UF *tam*
BT1 organic nitrogen compounds
BT2 organic compounds
RT estrogens
RT receptors

tan
USE triacetoneamine-n-oxyl

TANDEM ELECTROSTATIC ACCELERAT [915; 1,065] *Apr 80*
BT1 electrostatic accelerators
BT2 accelerators
NT1 crnl mp tandem accelerator
NT1 jaeri tandem accelerator
NT1 learn tandem accelerator
NT1 orsay tandem accelerator
NT1 vivitron tandem accelerator

tandem mirror exp. at uclll
USE tmx devices

tandem mirror type reactors
USE tmr reactors

TANDEM MIRRORS [530; 1,039]
Sep 83
BT1 magnetic mirrors
BT2 open plasma devices
BT3 thermonuclear devices
NT1 gamma 10 devices
NT1 phaedrus mirror devices
NT1 tara devices
NT1 tmx devices
RT tlm configurations
RT tmr reactors

TANK CIRCUITS [17; 17]
BT1 electronic circuits
RT stored energy

tank type critical assembly
USE tca reactor

TANK TYPE REACTORS [142; 5,728]
BT1 reactors
NT1 alrr reactor
NT1 aquilon reactor
NT1 atr reactor
NT1 borax-1 reactor
NT1 borax-2 reactor
NT1 borax-3 reactor
NT1 borax-4 reactor
NT1 br-02 reactor
NT1 br-1 reactor
NT1 br-2 reactor
NT1 br-3-vn reactor
NT1 cirus reactor
NT1 cp-3 reactor
NT1 cp-5 reactor
NT1 dca reactor
NT1 dido reactor
NT1 diorit reactor
NT1 dmtr reactor
NT1 dr-3 reactor
NT1 eco reactor
NT1 el-1 reactor
NT1 el-2 reactor
NT1 el-3 reactor
NT1 eocr reactor
NT1 eole reactor
NT1 esada-vesr reactor
NT1 essor reactor
NT1 etr reactor
NT1 etrr-1 reactor
NT1 ewa reactor
NT1 fir-1 reactor
NT1 fr-2 reactor
NT1 frj-2 reactor
NT1 getr reactor
NT1 grenoble reactor
NT1 gtrr reactor
NT1 hbwr reactor
NT1 hfbr reactor
NT1 hfir reactor
NT1 hfr reactor
NT1 hifar reactor
NT1 hwctr reactor
NT1 irr-2 reactor
NT1 ispra-1 reactor
NT1 janus reactor
NT1 jeep-2 reactor
NT1 jmtr reactor
NT1 jrr-2 reactor
NT1 jrr-3 reactor
NT1 juno reactor
NT1 kamini reactor
NT1 litr reactor
NT1 loft reactor
NT1 lptr reactor
NT1 mir reactor
NT1 mitr reactor
NT1 mrr reactor
NT1 mtr reactor
NT1 murr reactor
NT1 nbsr reactor
NT1 nora reactor
NT1 nru reactor
NT1 nrx reactor
NT1 ntr reactor
NT1 nuclear furnace reactor
NT1 orphee reactor
NT1 orr reactor
NT1 osiris reactor
NT1 owr reactor
NT1 pbf reactor
NT1 pbr reactor
NT1 pegase reactor
NT1 pelinduna reactor
NT1 pluto reactor
NT1 prcf reactor
NT1 prr reactor
NT1 pse reactor
NT1 r-a reactor
NT1 r-1 reactor
NT1 r-2 reactor
NT1 ra-0 reactor
NT1 ra-2 reactor
NT1 ra-3 reactor
NT1 ra-5 reactor
NT1 rake-2 reactor
NT1 rb-3 reactor
NT1 rospo reactor
NT1 rpt reactor
NT1 safari-1 reactor
NT1 sca reactor
NT1 sm-2 reactor
NT1 spert-1 reactor
NT1 spert-2 reactor
NT1 spert-3 reactor
NT1 sr-oa reactor
NT1 sr-1 reactor
NT1 taiwan research reactor
NT1 tca reactor
NT1 thermos reactor
NT1 triga-1-michigan reactor
NT1 tsr-1 reactor
NT1 venus reactor
NT1 wntr reactor
NT1 wr-1 reactor
NT1 wtr reactor
NT1 wwr type reactors
NT2 budapest training reactor
NT2 irt-baghdad reactor
NT2 wwr-k-alma-ata reactor
NT2 wwr-m-kiev reactor

NT2	wwr-m-leningrad reactor	
NT2	wwr-s-bucharest reactor	
NT2	wwr-s-budapest reactor	
NT2	wwr-s-cairo reactor	
NT2	wwr-s-moscow reactor	
NT2	wwr-s-prague reactor	
NT2	wwr-s-tashkent reactor	
NT2	wwr-sm rossendorf reactor	
NT2	wwr-2 reactor	
NT1	zed-2 reactor	
NT1	zeep reactor	
NT1	zlfr reactor	
NT1	zpr reactor	
RT	mns reactor	

TANKS [1,343; 1,343]
  BT1   containers

TANNIC ACID [49; 49]
  UF   *digallic acid*
  UF   *gallotannic acid*
  UF   *tannin*
  BT1   carboxylic acids
    BT2   organic acids
      BT3   organic compounds
  BT1   polyphenols
    BT2   phenols
      BT3   aromatics
        BT4   organic compounds
      BT3   hydroxy compounds
        BT4   organic compounds

tannin
  USE   tannic acid

TANTALATES [373; 373]
(Specific compounds should be indexed by coordination of a descriptor of the form (CATION) COMPOUNDS and the above anion descriptor.)
  BT1   oxygen compounds
  BT1   tantalum compounds
    BT2   transition element compounds
  RT   tantalum oxides

TANTALITE [16; 16]
  BT1   oxide minerals
    BT2   minerals
  RT   iron oxides
  RT   manganese oxides
  RT   tantalum oxides

TANTALUM [3,885; 3,885]
  BT1   transition elements
    BT2   metals
      BT3   elements

TANTALUM ADDITIONS [148; 191]
(Alloys containing not more than 1% Ta are listed here.)
  NT1   alloy-nb94mo4
  RT   tantalum alloys
  RT   tantalum compounds

tantalum alloy-t111
  USE   alloy-ta90w8hf

TANTALUM ALLOYS [901; 1,422]
(Alloys containing more than 1% Ta.)
  BT1   alloys
  NT1   alloy-ni46cr23co19ti5al4
  NT1   alloy-ni61cr16co9al3ti3w3
  NT1   tantalum base alloys
    NT2   alloy-ta90w8hf
  RT   tantalum additions

TANTALUM BASE ALLOYS [225; 305]
  BT1   tantalum alloys
    BT2   alloys
  NT1   alloy-ta90w8hf

TANTALUM BORIDES [62; 62]
  BT1   borides
    BT2   boron compounds
  BT1   tantalum compounds
    BT2   transition element compounds

TANTALUM BROMIDES [32; 32]
  BT1   bromides
    BT2   bromine compounds
      BT3   halogen compounds
    BT2   halides
      BT3   halogen compounds
  BT1   tantalum compounds
    BT2   transition element compounds

TANTALUM CARBIDES [475; 475]
  BT1   carbides
    BT2   carbon compounds
  BT1   tantalum compounds
    BT2   transition element compounds

TANTALUM CHLORIDES [127; 127]
  BT1   chlorides
    BT2   chlorine compounds
      BT3   halogen compounds
    BT2   halides
      BT3   halogen compounds
  BT1   tantalum compounds
    BT2   transition element compounds

TANTALUM COMPLEXES [282; 282]
  BT1   transition element complexes
    BT2   complexes

TANTALUM COMPOUNDS [316; 2,815]
  BT1   transition element compounds
  NT1   tantalates
  NT1   tantalum borides
  NT1   tantalum bromides
  NT1   tantalum carbides
  NT1   tantalum chlorides
  NT1   tantalum fluorides
  NT1   tantalum hydrides
  NT1   tantalum hydroxides
  NT1   tantalum iodides
  NT1   tantalum nitrates
  NT1   tantalum nitrides
  NT1   tantalum oxides
  NT1   tantalum phosphates
  NT1   tantalum phosphides
  NT1   tantalum selenides
  NT1   tantalum silicates
  NT1   tantalum silicides
  NT1   tantalum sulfates
  NT1   tantalum sulfides
  NT1   tantalum tellurides
  NT1   tantalum tungstates
  RT   tantalum additions

TANTALUM FLUORIDES [103; 103]
  BT1   fluorides
    BT2   fluorine compounds
      BT3   halogen compounds
    BT2   halides
      BT3   halogen compounds
  BT1   tantalum compounds
    BT2   transition element compounds

TANTALUM HYDRIDES [148; 148]
  BT1   hydrides
    BT2   hydrogen compounds
  BT1   tantalum compounds
    BT2   transition element compounds

TANTALUM HYDROXIDES [19; 19]
  BT1   hydroxides
    BT2   hydrogen compounds
    BT2   oxygen compounds
  BT1   tantalum compounds
    BT2   transition element compounds

TANTALUM IODIDES [18; 18]
  BT1   iodides
    BT2   halides
      BT3   halogen compounds
    BT2   iodine compounds
      BT3   halogen compounds
  BT1   tantalum compounds
    BT2   transition element compounds

TANTALUM IONS [123; 123]
  BT1   ions
    BT2   charged particles

TANTALUM ISOTOPES [79; 1,268]
  NT1   tantalum 156
  NT1   tantalum 157
  NT1   tantalum 158
  NT1   tantalum 159
  NT1   tantalum 160
  NT1   tantalum 161
  NT1   tantalum 162
  NT1   tantalum 163
  NT1   tantalum 164
  NT1   tantalum 165
  NT1   tantalum 166
  NT1   tantalum 167
  NT1   tantalum 168
  NT1   tantalum 169
  NT1   tantalum 170
  NT1   tantalum 171
  NT1   tantalum 172
  NT1   tantalum 173
  NT1   tantalum 174
  NT1   tantalum 175
  NT1   tantalum 176
  NT1   tantalum 177
  NT1   tantalum 178
  NT1   tantalum 179
  NT1   tantalum 180
  NT1   tantalum 181
  NT1   tantalum 182
  NT1   tantalum 183
  NT1   tantalum 184
  NT1   tantalum 185
  NT1   tantalum 186

TANTALUM NITRATES [0; 0] *Feb 84*
  BT1   nitrates
    BT2   nitrogen compounds
    BT2   oxygen compounds
  BT1   tantalum compounds
    BT2   transition element compounds

TANTALUM NITRIDES [137; 137]
  BT1   nitrides
    BT2   nitrogen compounds
    BT2   pnictides
  BT1   tantalum compounds
    BT2   transition element compounds

TANTALUM ORES [26; 26]
  BT1   ores

TANTALUM OXIDES [780; 789]
  BT1   oxides
    BT2   chalcogenides
    BT2   oxygen compounds
  BT1   tantalum compounds
    BT2   transition element compounds
  RT   hatchettolite
  RT   oxide minerals
  RT   tantalates
  RT   tantalite

TANTALUM PHOSPHATES [4; 4]
Jan 84
  BT1   phosphates
    BT2   oxygen compounds
    BT2   phosphorus compounds
  BT1   tantalum compounds
    BT2   transition element compounds

→ **TANTALUM PHOSPHIDES** [0; 0]
Sep 91
  BT1   phosphides
    BT2   phosphorus compounds
    BT2   pnictides
  BT1   tantalum compounds
    BT2   transition element compounds

TANTALUM SELENIDES [107; 107]
  Feb 76
  BT1   selenides
  BT2   chalcogenides
  BT2   selenium compounds
  BT1   tantalum compounds
  BT2   transition element compounds

→ **TANTALUM SILICATES** [0; 0] *Sep 91*
  BT1   silicates
  BT2   oxygen compounds
  BT2   silicon compounds
  BT1   tantalum compounds
  BT2   transition element compounds

TANTALUM SILICIDES [48; 48] *Jan 79*
  BT1   silicides
  BT2   silicon compounds
  BT1   tantalum compounds
  BT2   transition element compounds

TANTALUM SULFATES [4; 4] *Feb 82*
  BT1   sulfates
  BT2   oxygen compounds
  BT2   sulfur compounds
  BT1   tantalum compounds
  BT2   transition element compounds

TANTALUM SULFIDES [239; 239]
  BT1   sulfides
  BT2   chalcogenides
  BT2   sulfur compounds
  BT1   tantalum compounds
  BT2   transition element compounds

TANTALUM TELLURIDES [15; 15]
  Jul 80
  BT1   tantalum compounds
  BT2   transition element compounds
  BT1   tellurides
  BT2   chalcogenides
  BT2   tellurium compounds

TANTALUM TUNGSTATES [8; 8]
  Sep 79
  BT1   tantalum compounds
  BT2   transition element compounds
  BT1   tungstates
  BT2   oxygen compounds
  BT2   tungsten compounds
  BT3   transition element compounds

TANTALUM 156 [2; 2] *Jul 89*
  BT1   intermediate mass nuclei
  BT2   nuclei
  BT1   millisec living radioisotopes
  BT2   radioisotopes
  BT3   isotopes
  BT1   odd-odd nuclei
  BT2   nuclei
  BT1   tantalum isotopes

TANTALUM 157 [3; 3] *Sep 79*
  BT1   alpha decay radioisotopes
  BT2   radioisotopes
  BT3   isotopes
  BT1   intermediate mass nuclei
  BT2   nuclei
  BT1   millisec living radioisotopes
  BT2   radioisotopes
  BT3   isotopes
  BT1   odd-even nuclei
  BT2   nuclei
  BT1   tantalum isotopes

TANTALUM 158 [3; 3] *Sep 79*
  BT1   alpha decay radioisotopes
  BT2   radioisotopes
  BT3   isotopes
  BT1   electron capture radioisotopes
  BT2   beta decay radioisotopes
  BT3   radioisotopes
  BT4   isotopes
  BT1   intermediate mass nuclei
  BT2   nuclei
  BT1   millisec living radioisotopes
  BT2   radioisotopes
  BT3   isotopes
  BT1   odd-odd nuclei
  BT2   nuclei
  BT1   tantalum isotopes

TANTALUM 159 [3; 3] *Sep 79*
  BT1   alpha decay radioisotopes
  BT2   radioisotopes
  BT3   isotopes
  BT1   electron capture radioisotopes
  BT2   beta decay radioisotopes
  BT3   radioisotopes
  BT4   isotopes
  BT1   intermediate mass nuclei
  BT2   nuclei
  BT1   millisec living radioisotopes
  BT2   radioisotopes
  BT3   isotopes
  BT1   odd-even nuclei
  BT2   nuclei
  BT1   tantalum isotopes

TANTALUM 160 [4; 4] *Sep 79*
  BT1   alpha decay radioisotopes
  BT2   radioisotopes
  BT3   isotopes
  BT1   electron capture radioisotopes
  BT2   beta decay radioisotopes
  BT3   radioisotopes
  BT4   isotopes
  BT1   intermediate mass nuclei
  BT2   nuclei
  BT1   odd-odd nuclei
  BT2   nuclei
  BT1   seconds living radioisotopes
  BT2   radioisotopes
  BT3   isotopes
  BT1   tantalum isotopes

TANTALUM 161 [7; 7] *Sep 79*
  BT1   alpha decay radioisotopes
  BT2   radioisotopes
  BT3   isotopes
  BT1   intermediate mass nuclei
  BT2   nuclei
  BT1   odd-even nuclei
  BT2   nuclei
  BT1   seconds living radioisotopes
  BT2   radioisotopes
  BT3   isotopes
  BT1   tantalum isotopes

TANTALUM 162 [5; 5] *Oct 85*
  BT1   intermediate mass nuclei
  BT2   nuclei
  BT1   odd-odd nuclei
  BT2   nuclei
  BT1   seconds living radioisotopes
  BT2   radioisotopes
  BT3   isotopes
  BT1   tantalum isotopes

TANTALUM 163 [10; 10] *Dec 80*
  BT1   alpha decay radioisotopes
  BT2   radioisotopes
  BT3   isotopes
  BT1   intermediate mass nuclei
  BT2   nuclei
  BT1   odd-even nuclei
  BT2   nuclei
  BT1   seconds living radioisotopes
  BT2   radioisotopes
  BT3   isotopes
  BT1   tantalum isotopes

TANTALUM 164 [10; 10] *Aug 82*
  BT1   alpha decay radioisotopes
  BT2   radioisotopes
  BT3   isotopes
  BT1   intermediate mass nuclei
  BT2   nuclei
  BT1   odd-odd nuclei
  BT2   nuclei
  BT1   seconds living radioisotopes
  BT2   radioisotopes
  BT3   isotopes
  BT1   tantalum isotopes

TANTALUM 165 [7; 7] *Aug 82*
  BT1   beta-plus decay radioisotopes
  BT2   beta decay radioisotopes
  BT3   radioisotopes
  BT4   isotopes
  BT1   electron capture radioisotopes
  BT2   beta decay radioisotopes
  BT3   radioisotopes
  BT4   isotopes
  BT1   intermediate mass nuclei
  BT2   nuclei
  BT1   odd-even nuclei
  BT2   nuclei
  BT1   seconds living radioisotopes
  BT2   radioisotopes
  BT3   isotopes
  BT1   tantalum isotopes

TANTALUM 166 [5; 5] *Aug 75*
  BT1   beta-plus decay radioisotopes
  BT2   beta decay radioisotopes
  BT3   radioisotopes
  BT4   isotopes
  BT1   electron capture radioisotopes
  BT2   beta decay radioisotopes
  BT3   radioisotopes
  BT4   isotopes
  BT1   intermediate mass nuclei
  BT2   nuclei
  BT1   odd-odd nuclei
  BT2   nuclei
  BT1   seconds living radioisotopes
  BT2   radioisotopes
  BT3   isotopes
  BT1   tantalum isotopes

TANTALUM 167 [8; 8] *Jul 76*
  BT1   beta-plus decay radioisotopes
  BT2   beta decay radioisotopes
  BT3   radioisotopes
  BT4   isotopes
  BT1   electron capture radioisotopes
  BT2   beta decay radioisotopes
  BT3   radioisotopes
  BT4   isotopes
  BT1   intermediate mass nuclei
  BT2   nuclei
  BT1   minutes living radioisotopes
  BT2   radioisotopes
  BT3   isotopes
  BT1   odd-even nuclei
  BT2   nuclei
  BT1   tantalum isotopes

TANTALUM 168 [10; 10]
  BT1   beta-plus decay radioisotopes
  BT2   beta decay radioisotopes
  BT3   radioisotopes
  BT4   isotopes
  BT1   electron capture radioisotopes
  BT2   beta decay radioisotopes
  BT3   radioisotopes
  BT4   isotopes
  BT1   intermediate mass nuclei
  BT2   nuclei
  BT1   minutes living radioisotopes
  BT2   radioisotopes
  BT3   isotopes
  BT1   odd-odd nuclei
  BT2   nuclei
  BT1   tantalum isotopes

TANTALUM 169 [14; 14] *Oct 75*
  BT1   beta-plus decay radioisotopes
  BT2   beta decay radioisotopes
  BT3   radioisotopes
  BT4   isotopes
  BT1   electron capture radioisotopes
  BT2   beta decay radioisotopes
  BT3   radioisotopes
  BT4   isotopes
  BT1   intermediate mass nuclei
  BT2   nuclei
  BT1   minutes living radioisotopes
  BT2   radioisotopes
  BT3   isotopes
  BT1   odd-even nuclei
  BT2   nuclei
  BT1   tantalum isotopes

TANTALUM 170 [7; 7]
- BT1 beta-plus decay radioisotopes
  - BT2 beta decay radioisotopes
    - BT3 radioisotopes
      - BT4 isotopes
- BT1 electron capture radioisotopes
  - BT2 beta decay radioisotopes
    - BT3 radioisotopes
      - BT4 isotopes
- BT1 intermediate mass nuclei
  - BT2 nuclei
- BT1 minutes living radioisotopes
  - BT2 radioisotopes
    - BT3 isotopes
- BT1 odd-odd nuclei
  - BT2 nuclei
- BT1 tantalum isotopes

TANTALUM 171 [12; 12]
- BT1 beta-plus decay radioisotopes
  - BT2 beta decay radioisotopes
    - BT3 radioisotopes
      - BT4 isotopes
- BT1 electron capture radioisotopes
  - BT2 beta decay radioisotopes
    - BT3 radioisotopes
      - BT4 isotopes
- BT1 intermediate mass nuclei
  - BT2 nuclei
- BT1 minutes living radioisotopes
  - BT2 radioisotopes
    - BT3 isotopes
- BT1 odd-even nuclei
  - BT2 nuclei
- BT1 tantalum isotopes

TANTALUM 172 [7; 7]
- BT1 beta-plus decay radioisotopes
  - BT2 beta decay radioisotopes
    - BT3 radioisotopes
      - BT4 isotopes
- BT1 electron capture radioisotopes
  - BT2 beta decay radioisotopes
    - BT3 radioisotopes
      - BT4 isotopes
- BT1 intermediate mass nuclei
  - BT2 nuclei
- BT1 minutes living radioisotopes
  - BT2 radioisotopes
    - BT3 isotopes
- BT1 odd-odd nuclei
  - BT2 nuclei
- BT1 tantalum isotopes

TANTALUM 173 [17; 17]
- BT1 beta-plus decay radioisotopes
  - BT2 beta decay radioisotopes
    - BT3 radioisotopes
      - BT4 isotopes
- BT1 electron capture radioisotopes
  - BT2 beta decay radioisotopes
    - BT3 radioisotopes
      - BT4 isotopes
- BT1 hours living radioisotopes
  - BT2 radioisotopes
    - BT3 isotopes
- BT1 intermediate mass nuclei
  - BT2 nuclei
- BT1 odd-even nuclei
  - BT2 nuclei
- BT1 tantalum isotopes

TANTALUM 174 [11; 11]
- BT1 beta-plus decay radioisotopes
  - BT2 beta decay radioisotopes
    - BT3 radioisotopes
      - BT4 isotopes
- BT1 electron capture radioisotopes
  - BT2 beta decay radioisotopes
    - BT3 radioisotopes
      - BT4 isotopes
- BT1 hours living radioisotopes
  - BT2 radioisotopes
    - BT3 isotopes
- BT1 intermediate mass nuclei
  - BT2 nuclei
- BT1 odd-odd nuclei
  - BT2 nuclei
- BT1 tantalum isotopes

TANTALUM 175 [19; 19]
- BT1 beta-plus decay radioisotopes
  - BT2 beta decay radioisotopes
    - BT3 radioisotopes
      - BT4 isotopes
- BT1 electron capture radioisotopes
  - BT2 beta decay radioisotopes
    - BT3 radioisotopes
      - BT4 isotopes
- BT1 hours living radioisotopes
  - BT2 radioisotopes
    - BT3 isotopes
- BT1 intermediate mass nuclei
  - BT2 nuclei
- BT1 odd-even nuclei
  - BT2 nuclei
- BT1 tantalum isotopes

TANTALUM 176 [6; 6]
- BT1 beta-plus decay radioisotopes
  - BT2 beta decay radioisotopes
    - BT3 radioisotopes
      - BT4 isotopes
- BT1 electron capture radioisotopes
  - BT2 beta decay radioisotopes
    - BT3 radioisotopes
      - BT4 isotopes
- BT1 hours living radioisotopes
  - BT2 radioisotopes
    - BT3 isotopes
- BT1 intermediate mass nuclei
  - BT2 nuclei
- BT1 odd-odd nuclei
  - BT2 nuclei
- BT1 tantalum isotopes

TANTALUM 177 [35; 35]
- BT1 beta-plus decay radioisotopes
  - BT2 beta decay radioisotopes
    - BT3 radioisotopes
      - BT4 isotopes
- BT1 days living radioisotopes
  - BT2 radioisotopes
    - BT3 isotopes
- BT1 electron capture radioisotopes
  - BT2 beta decay radioisotopes
    - BT3 radioisotopes
      - BT4 isotopes
- BT1 intermediate mass nuclei
  - BT2 nuclei
- BT1 odd-even nuclei
  - BT2 nuclei
- BT1 tantalum isotopes

TANTALUM 178 [53; 53]
- BT1 beta-plus decay radioisotopes
  - BT2 beta decay radioisotopes
    - BT3 radioisotopes
      - BT4 isotopes
- BT1 electron capture radioisotopes
  - BT2 beta decay radioisotopes
    - BT3 radioisotopes
      - BT4 isotopes
- BT1 hours living radioisotopes
  - BT2 radioisotopes
    - BT3 isotopes
- BT1 intermediate mass nuclei
  - BT2 nuclei
- BT1 minutes living radioisotopes
  - BT2 radioisotopes
    - BT3 isotopes
- BT1 odd-odd nuclei
  - BT2 nuclei
- BT1 tantalum isotopes

TANTALUM 179 [29; 29]
- BT1 electron capture radioisotopes
  - BT2 beta decay radioisotopes
    - BT3 radioisotopes
      - BT4 isotopes
- BT1 intermediate mass nuclei
  - BT2 nuclei
- BT1 odd-even nuclei
  - BT2 nuclei
- BT1 tantalum isotopes
- BT1 years living radioisotopes
  - BT2 radioisotopes
    - BT3 isotopes

TANTALUM 179 TARGET [2; 2]
Apr 86
- BT1 targets

TANTALUM 180 [91; 91]
- BT1 beta-minus decay radioisotopes
  - BT2 beta decay radioisotopes
    - BT3 radioisotopes
      - BT4 isotopes
- BT1 electron capture radioisotopes
  - BT2 beta decay radioisotopes
    - BT3 radioisotopes
      - BT4 isotopes
- BT1 hours living radioisotopes
  - BT2 radioisotopes
    - BT3 isotopes
- BT1 intermediate mass nuclei
  - BT2 nuclei
- BT1 odd-odd nuclei
  - BT2 nuclei
- BT1 tantalum isotopes

TANTALUM 180 TARGET [19; 19]
Feb 76
- BT1 targets

TANTALUM 181 [658; 658]
- BT1 heavy nuclei
  - BT2 nuclei
- BT1 odd-even nuclei
  - BT2 nuclei
- BT1 stable isotopes
  - BT2 isotopes
- BT1 tantalum isotopes

TANTALUM 181 TARGET [1,007; 1,007]
- BT1 targets

TANTALUM 182 [250; 250]
- BT1 beta-minus decay radioisotopes
  - BT2 beta decay radioisotopes
    - BT3 radioisotopes
      - BT4 isotopes
- BT1 days living radioisotopes
  - BT2 radioisotopes
    - BT3 isotopes
- BT1 heavy nuclei
  - BT2 nuclei
- BT1 internal conversion radioisoto
  - BT2 radioisotopes
    - BT3 isotopes
- BT1 isomeric transition isotopes
  - BT2 radioisotopes
    - BT3 isotopes
- BT1 millisec living radioisotopes
  - BT2 radioisotopes
    - BT3 isotopes
- BT1 minutes living radioisotopes
  - BT2 radioisotopes
    - BT3 isotopes
- BT1 odd-odd nuclei
  - BT2 nuclei
- BT1 tantalum isotopes

TANTALUM 182 TARGET [4; 4]
Aug 76
- BT1 targets

TANTALUM 183 [16; 16]
- BT1 beta-minus decay radioisotopes
  - BT2 beta decay radioisotopes
    - BT3 radioisotopes
      - BT4 isotopes
- BT1 days living radioisotopes
  - BT2 radioisotopes
    - BT3 isotopes
- BT1 heavy nuclei
  - BT2 nuclei
- BT1 odd-even nuclei
  - BT2 nuclei
- BT1 tantalum isotopes

TANTALUM 184 [13; 13]
- BT1 beta-minus decay radioisotopes
- BT2 beta decay radioisotopes
- BT3 radioisotopes
- BT4 isotopes
- BT1 heavy nuclei
- BT2 nuclei
- BT1 hours living radioisotopes
- BT2 radioisotopes
- BT3 isotopes
- BT1 odd-odd nuclei
- BT2 nuclei
- BT1 tantalum isotopes

TANTALUM 185 [5; 5]
- BT1 beta-minus decay radioisotopes
- BT2 beta decay radioisotopes
- BT3 radioisotopes
- BT4 isotopes
- BT1 heavy nuclei
- BT2 nuclei
- BT1 minutes living radioisotopes
- BT2 radioisotopes
- BT3 isotopes
- BT1 odd-even nuclei
- BT2 nuclei
- BT1 tantalum isotopes

TANTALUM 186 [2; 2]
- BT1 beta-minus decay radioisotopes
- BT2 beta decay radioisotopes
- BT3 radioisotopes
- BT4 isotopes
- BT1 heavy nuclei
- BT2 nuclei
- BT1 minutes living radioisotopes
- BT2 radioisotopes
- BT3 isotopes
- BT1 odd-odd nuclei
- BT2 nuclei
- BT1 tantalum isotopes

TANZANIA [32; 32]
- BT1 africa
- BT1 developing countries

tapeworms
- USE cestodes

TAPIRO REACTOR [18; 18]
(CNEN, Casaccia Center, Rome, Italy)
- BT1 fast reactors
- BT2 epithermal reactors
- BT3 reactors
- BT1 research reactors
- BT2 research and test reactors
- BT3 reactors
- BT1 test reactors
- BT2 research and test reactors
- BT3 reactors
- BT2 test facilities

TAR [23; 1,085]
- BT1 other organic compounds
- BT2 organic compounds
- NT1 bitumens
- NT2 asphalts
- NT2 carburan
- NT2 coal tar
- NT2 thucholite
- RT pitches

tar sands
- USE oil sands

TARA DEVICES [104; 104] *Jul 84*
(Tandem mirror experiment at MIT.)
- BT1 tandem mirrors
- BT2 magnetic mirrors
- BT3 open plasma devices
- BT4 thermonuclear devices

TARAPUR-1 REACTOR [230; 230]
(Boisar, Maharastra, India)
- BT1 bwr type reactors
- BT2 enriched uranium reactors
- BT3 reactors
- BT2 power reactors
- BT3 reactors
- BT2 thermal reactors
- BT3 reactors
- BT2 water cooled reactors
- BT3 reactors
- BT2 water moderated reactors
- BT3 reactors

TARAPUR-2 REACTOR [216; 216]
(Boisar, Maharastra, India)
- BT1 bwr type reactors
- BT2 enriched uranium reactors
- BT3 reactors
- BT2 power reactors
- BT3 reactors
- BT2 thermal reactors
- BT3 reactors
- BT2 water cooled reactors
- BT3 reactors
- BT2 water moderated reactors
- BT3 reactors

TARGET CHAMBERS [1,661; 1,661]
- BT1 accelerator facilities
- RT accelerators
- RT targets

target holders
- USE sample holders

TARGETS [9,725; 78,778]
- NT1 actinium 227 target
- NT1 aluminium 25 target
- NT1 aluminium 26 target
- NT1 aluminium 27 target
- NT1 aluminium 28 target
- NT1 americium 241 target
- NT1 americium 242 target
- NT1 americium 243 target
- NT1 antimony 120 target
- NT1 antimony 121 target
- NT1 antimony 123 target
- NT1 antimony 127 target
- NT1 argon 36 target
- NT1 argon 37 target
- NT1 argon 38 target
- NT1 argon 40 target
- NT1 arsenic 75 target
- NT1 barium 130 target
- NT1 barium 134 target
- NT1 barium 135 target
- NT1 barium 136 target
- NT1 barium 137 target
- NT1 barium 138 target
- NT1 barium 139 target
- NT1 berkelium 249 target
- NT1 beryllium 10 target
- NT1 beryllium 11 target
- NT1 beryllium 7 target
- NT1 beryllium 8 target
- NT1 beryllium 9 target
- NT1 bismuth 207 target
- NT1 bismuth 208 target
- NT1 bismuth 209 target
- NT1 bismuth 210 target
- NT1 boron 10 target
- NT1 boron 11 target
- NT1 boron 12 target
- NT1 boron 13 target
- NT1 bromine 71 target
- NT1 bromine 76 target
- NT1 bromine 79 target
- NT1 bromine 81 target
- NT1 cadmium 106 target
- NT1 cadmium 108 target
- NT1 cadmium 109 target
- NT1 cadmium 110 target
- NT1 cadmium 111 target
- NT1 cadmium 112 target
- NT1 cadmium 113 target
- NT1 cadmium 114 target
- NT1 cadmium 116 target
- NT1 calcium 40 target
- NT1 calcium 41 target
- NT1 calcium 42 target
- NT1 calcium 43 target
- NT1 calcium 44 target
- NT1 calcium 46 target
- NT1 calcium 48 target
- NT1 calcium 49 target
- NT1 californium 249 target
- NT1 californium 250 target
- NT1 californium 251 target
- NT1 californium 252 target
- NT1 californium 254 target
- NT1 carbon 11 target
- NT1 carbon 12 target
- NT1 carbon 13 target
- NT1 carbon 14 target
- NT1 cerium 136 target
- NT1 cerium 138 target
- NT1 cerium 140 target
- NT1 cerium 141 target
- NT1 cerium 142 target
- NT1 cesium 131 target
- NT1 cesium 132 target
- NT1 cesium 133 target
- NT1 cesium 134 target
- NT1 cesium 135 target
- NT1 cesium 137 target
- NT1 chlorine 35 target
- NT1 chlorine 36 target
- NT1 chlorine 37 target
- NT1 chromium 50 target
- NT1 chromium 52 target
- NT1 chromium 53 target
- NT1 chromium 54 target
- NT1 chromium 56 target
- NT1 cobalt 56 target
- NT1 cobalt 57 target
- NT1 cobalt 58 target
- NT1 cobalt 59 target
- NT1 cobalt 60 target
- NT1 copper 61 target
- NT1 copper 63 target
- NT1 copper 64 target
- NT1 copper 65 target
- NT1 curium 242 target
- NT1 curium 243 target
- NT1 curium 244 target
- NT1 curium 245 target
- NT1 curium 246 target
- NT1 curium 247 target
- NT1 curium 248 target
- NT1 curium 250 target
- NT1 deuterium target
- NT1 dysprosium 154 target
- NT1 dysprosium 156 target
- NT1 dysprosium 158 target
- NT1 dysprosium 160 target
- NT1 dysprosium 161 target
- NT1 dysprosium 162 target
- NT1 dysprosium 163 target
- NT1 dysprosium 164 target
- NT1 dysprosium 165 target
- NT1 einsteinium 253 target
- NT1 einsteinium 254 target
- NT1 einsteinium 255 target
- NT1 electron beam targets
- NT1 erbium 162 target
- NT1 erbium 163 target
- NT1 erbium 164 target
- NT1 erbium 165 target
- NT1 erbium 166 target
- NT1 erbium 167 target
- NT1 erbium 168 target
- NT1 erbium 170 target
- NT1 europium 151 target
- NT1 europium 152 target
- NT1 europium 153 target
- NT1 europium 154 target
- NT1 europium 155 target
- NT1 fermium 253 target
- NT1 fermium 254 target
- NT1 fermium 255 target
- NT1 fermium 256 target
- NT1 fermium 257 target
- NT1 fermium 258 target
- NT1 fermium 259 target
- NT1 fermium 260 target
- NT1 fluorine 18 target
- NT1 fluorine 19 target

NT1 gadolinium 148 target
NT1 gadolinium 152 target
NT1 gadolinium 154 target
NT1 gadolinium 155 target
NT1 gadolinium 156 target
NT1 gadolinium 157 target
NT1 gadolinium 158 target
NT1 gadolinium 159 target
NT1 gadolinium 160 target
NT1 gallium 65 target
NT1 gallium 67 target
NT1 gallium 69 target
NT1 gallium 71 target
NT1 germanium 70 target
NT1 germanium 71 target
NT1 germanium 72 target
NT1 germanium 73 target
NT1 germanium 74 target
NT1 germanium 75 target
NT1 germanium 76 target
NT1 germanium 86 target
NT1 gold 187 target
NT1 gold 193 target
NT1 gold 194 target
NT1 gold 195 target
NT1 gold 196 target
NT1 gold 197 target
NT1 gold 198 target
NT1 gold 199 target
NT1 hafnium 174 target
NT1 hafnium 176 target
NT1 hafnium 177 target
NT1 hafnium 178 target
NT1 hafnium 179 target
NT1 hafnium 180 target
NT1 helium 3 target
NT1 helium 4 target
NT1 helium 6 target
NT1 holmium 165 target
NT1 hydrogen 1 target
NT1 indium 110 target
NT1 indium 113 target
NT1 indium 115 target
NT1 indium 127 target
NT1 iodine 127 target
NT1 iodine 128 target
NT1 iodine 129 target
NT1 ion beam targets
NT1 iridium 189 target
NT1 iridium 191 target
NT1 iridium 193 target
NT1 iridium 194 target
NT1 iron 54 target
NT1 iron 55 target
NT1 iron 56 target
NT1 iron 57 target
NT1 iron 58 target
NT1 krypton 78 target
NT1 krypton 80 target
NT1 krypton 82 target
NT1 krypton 83 target
NT1 krypton 84 target
NT1 krypton 85 target
NT1 krypton 86 target
NT1 lanthanum 139 target
NT1 laser targets
NT1 lead 200 target
NT1 lead 202 target
NT1 lead 204 target
NT1 lead 205 target
NT1 lead 206 target
NT1 lead 207 target
NT1 lead 208 target
NT1 lead 209 target
NT1 lead 210 target
NT1 lithium 6 target
NT1 lithium 7 target
NT1 lithium 8 target
NT1 lithium 9 target
NT1 lutetium 174 target
NT1 lutetium 175 target
NT1 lutetium 176 target
NT1 magnesium 23 target
NT1 magnesium 24 target
NT1 magnesium 25 target
NT1 magnesium 26 target
NT1 magnesium 27 target
NT1 manganese 51 target
NT1 manganese 53 target
NT1 manganese 54 target
NT1 manganese 55 target
NT1 mercury 196 target
NT1 mercury 199 target
NT1 mercury 200 target
NT1 mercury 201 target
NT1 mercury 202 target
NT1 mercury 204 target
NT1 mercury 206 target
NT1 molybdenum 100 target
NT1 molybdenum 92 target
NT1 molybdenum 94 target
NT1 molybdenum 95 target
NT1 molybdenum 96 target
NT1 molybdenum 97 target
NT1 molybdenum 98 target
NT1 neodymium 142 target
NT1 neodymium 143 target
NT1 neodymium 144 target
NT1 neodymium 145 target
NT1 neodymium 146 target
NT1 neodymium 147 target
NT1 neodymium 148 target
NT1 neodymium 149 target
NT1 neodymium 150 target
NT1 neon 20 target
NT1 neon 21 target
NT1 neon 22 target
NT1 neptunium 232 target
NT1 neptunium 236 target
NT1 neptunium 237 target
NT1 neptunium 238 target
NT1 neptunium 239 target
NT1 nickel 57 target
NT1 nickel 58 target
NT1 nickel 59 target
NT1 nickel 60 target
NT1 nickel 61 target
NT1 nickel 62 target
NT1 nickel 64 target
NT1 niobium 92 target
NT1 niobium 93 target
NT1 niobium 94 target
NT1 niobium 95 target
NT1 niobium 96 target
NT1 nitrogen 12 target
NT1 nitrogen 13 target
NT1 nitrogen 14 target
NT1 nitrogen 15 target
NT1 nitrogen 16 target
NT1 osmium 184 target
NT1 osmium 186 target
NT1 osmium 187 target
NT1 osmium 188 target
NT1 osmium 189 target
NT1 osmium 190 target
NT1 osmium 191 target
NT1 osmium 192 target
NT1 oxygen 15 target
NT1 oxygen 16 target
NT1 oxygen 17 target
NT1 oxygen 18 target
NT1 palladium 102 target
NT1 palladium 104 target
NT1 palladium 105 target
NT1 palladium 106 target
NT1 palladium 107 target
NT1 palladium 108 target
NT1 palladium 110 target
NT1 palladium 118 target
NT1 phosphorus 31 target
NT1 phosphorus 32 target
NT1 platinum 190 target
NT1 platinum 192 target
NT1 platinum 194 target
NT1 platinum 195 target
NT1 platinum 196 target
NT1 platinum 198 target
NT1 plutonium 235 target
NT1 plutonium 236 target
NT1 plutonium 237 target
NT1 plutonium 238 target
NT1 plutonium 239 target
NT1 plutonium 240 target
NT1 plutonium 241 target
NT1 plutonium 242 target
NT1 plutonium 243 target
NT1 plutonium 244 target
NT1 polarized targets
NT1 polonium 208 target
NT1 polonium 210 target
NT1 potassium 39 target
NT1 potassium 40 target
NT1 potassium 41 target
NT1 praseodymium 141 target
NT1 promethium 147 target
NT1 promethium 149 target
NT1 protactinium 231 target
NT1 protactinium 232 target
NT1 protactinium 233 target
NT1 radium 226 target
NT1 rhenium 184 target
NT1 rhenium 185 target
NT1 rhenium 186 target
NT1 rhenium 187 target
NT1 rhodium 103 target
NT1 rhodium 96 target
NT1 rubidium 84 target
NT1 rubidium 85 target
NT1 rubidium 87 target
NT1 rubidium 88 target
NT1 ruthenium 100 target
NT1 ruthenium 101 target
NT1 ruthenium 102 target
NT1 ruthenium 103 target
NT1 ruthenium 104 target
NT1 ruthenium 96 target
NT1 ruthenium 98 target
NT1 ruthenium 99 target
NT1 samarium 144 target
NT1 samarium 145 target
NT1 samarium 146 target
NT1 samarium 147 target
NT1 samarium 148 target
NT1 samarium 149 target
NT1 samarium 150 target
NT1 samarium 151 target
NT1 samarium 152 target
NT1 samarium 154 target
NT1 scandium 45 target
NT1 selenium 72 target
NT1 selenium 74 target
NT1 selenium 75 target
NT1 selenium 76 target
NT1 selenium 77 target
NT1 selenium 78 target
NT1 selenium 80 target
NT1 selenium 82 target
NT1 silicon 28 target
NT1 silicon 29 target
NT1 silicon 30 target
NT1 silicon 32 target
NT1 silver 106 target
NT1 silver 107 target
NT1 silver 108 target
NT1 silver 109 target
NT1 sodium 21 target
NT1 sodium 22 target
NT1 sodium 23 target
NT1 strontium 84 target
NT1 strontium 86 target
NT1 strontium 87 target
NT1 strontium 88 target
NT1 strontium 90 target
NT1 sulfur 32 target
NT1 sulfur 33 target
NT1 sulfur 34 target
NT1 sulfur 36 target
NT1 tantalum 179 target
NT1 tantalum 180 target
NT1 tantalum 181 target
NT1 tantalum 182 target
NT1 technetium 99 target
NT1 tellurium 119 target
NT1 tellurium 120 target
NT1 tellurium 122 target
NT1 tellurium 123 target
NT1 tellurium 124 target
NT1 tellurium 125 target
NT1 tellurium 126 target
NT1 tellurium 128 target
NT1 tellurium 130 target
NT1 terbium 159 target
NT1 terbium 160 target
NT1 thallium 203 target
NT1 thallium 205 target
NT1 thallium 207 target
NT1 thallium 209 target
NT1 thorium 228 target
NT1 thorium 229 target

NT1 thorium 230 target
NT1 thorium 231 target
NT1 thorium 232 target
NT1 thorium 233 target
NT1 thorium 239 target
NT1 thulium 169 target
NT1 tin 110 target
NT1 tin 112 target
NT1 tin 114 target
NT1 tin 115 target
NT1 tin 116 target
NT1 tin 117 target
NT1 tin 118 target
NT1 tin 119 target
NT1 tin 120 target
NT1 tin 122 target
NT1 tin 124 target
NT1 tin 126 target
NT1 titanium 44 target
NT1 titanium 45 target
NT1 titanium 46 target
NT1 titanium 47 target
NT1 titanium 48 target
NT1 titanium 49 target
NT1 titanium 50 target
NT1 tritium target
NT1 tungsten 180 target
NT1 tungsten 182 target
NT1 tungsten 183 target
NT1 tungsten 184 target
NT1 tungsten 185 target
NT1 tungsten 186 target
NT1 uranium 232 target
NT1 uranium 233 target
NT1 uranium 234 target
NT1 uranium 235 target
NT1 uranium 236 target
NT1 uranium 237 target
NT1 uranium 238 target
NT1 uranium 239 target
NT1 uranium 240 target
NT1 vanadium 48 target
NT1 vanadium 49 target
NT1 vanadium 50 target
NT1 vanadium 51 target
NT1 xenon 123 target
NT1 xenon 124 target
NT1 xenon 125 target
NT1 xenon 126 target
NT1 xenon 127 target
NT1 xenon 128 target
NT1 xenon 129 target
NT1 xenon 130 target
NT1 xenon 131 target
NT1 xenon 132 target
NT1 xenon 134 target
NT1 xenon 136 target
NT1 ytterbium 168 target
NT1 ytterbium 170 target
NT1 ytterbium 171 target
NT1 ytterbium 172 target
NT1 ytterbium 173 target
NT1 ytterbium 174 target
NT1 ytterbium 176 target
NT1 yttrium 87 target
NT1 yttrium 88 target
NT1 yttrium 89 target
NT1 zinc 64 target
NT1 zinc 65 target
NT1 zinc 66 target
NT1 zinc 67 target
NT1 zinc 68 target
NT1 zinc 70 target
NT1 zirconium 90 target
NT1 zirconium 91 target
NT1 zirconium 92 target
NT1 zirconium 93 target
NT1 zirconium 94 target
NT1 zirconium 96 target
RT nuclear reactions
RT polarizati n-asymmetry ratio
RT positioning
RT scattering
RT target chambers

TARTARIC ACID [129; 129]
UF *dihydroxysuccinic acid*
BT1 hydroxy acids
BT2 carboxylic acids
BT3 organic acids
BT4 organic compounds
RT rochelle salt

TARTARIC ACID ESTERS [3; 3]
BT1 carboxylic acid esters
BT2 esters
BT3 organic compounds

TARTRATES [149; 175]
BT1 carboxylic acid salts
NT1 rochelle salt

tashkent wwr-s reactor
USE wwr-s-tashkent reactor

TASMANIA [32; 32]
BT1 australia
BT2 australasia
BT2 developed countries
BT1 islands
RT indian ocean
RT pacific ocean

TASTE BUDS [49; 49]
BT1 sense organs
BT2 organs
BT3 body
RT flavor

TASTE PARTICLES [15; 15] *Aug 78*
BT1 postulated particles
BT2 elementary particles
RT color model
RT hadrons
RT hypercharge
RT quarks
RT su-3 groups

TATARIAN REACTOR [2; 2] *Jan 90*
(Tatar, USSR.)
BT1 wwer type reactors
BT2 pwr type reactors
BT3 enriched uranium reactors
BT4 reactors
BT3 power reactors
BT4 reactors
BT3 thermal reactors
BT4 reactors
BT3 water cooled reactors
BT4 reactors
BT3 water moderated reactors
BT4 reactors

tau leptons
USE tau particles

TAU NEUTRINOS [495; 495] *Aug 78*
BT1 heavy leptons
BT2 leptons
BT3 elementary particles
BT3 fermions
BT1 neutrinos
BT2 leptons
BT3 elementary particles
BT3 fermions
BT2 massless particles
BT3 elementary particles

TAU PARTICLES [1,302; 1,302] *Jul 78*
UF *tau leptons*
UF *tauons*
BT1 heavy leptons
BT2 leptons
BT3 elementary particles
BT3 fermions
RT electron-muon-tau universality

tauons
USE tau particles

TAURINE [97; 97]
UF *aminoethanesulfonic acid*
BT1 amines
BT2 organic compounds
BT1 sulfonic acids
BT2 organic acids
BT3 organic compounds
BT2 organic sulfur compounds
BT3 organic compounds

tax credits
USE financial incentives

TAX LAWS [18; 18] *Dec 76*
(Prior to December 1990, this descriptor was spelled TAX LAW.)
BT1 laws

TAXES [82; 82] *Jun 76*
RT economic policy
RT financial incentives
RT trade

TAXONOMY [68; 68] *May 76*
(The study of the general principles of classification.)
RT biology

TBP [2,392; 2,392]
UF *tributyl phosphate*
BT1 butyl phosphates
BT2 phosphoric acid esters
BT3 esters
BT4 organic compounds
BT3 organic phosphorus compounds
BT4 organic compounds

TBPO [58; 58]
UF *tributylphosphine oxide*
BT1 organic phosphorus compounds
BT2 organic compounds

TBR TOKAMAK [84; 84] *Mar 83*
BT1 tokamak devices
BT2 closed plasma devices
BT3 thermonuclear devices

TCA REACTOR [21; 21]
(Tokai Research Establishment of JAERI Ibaraki Prefecture, Japan)
UF *tank type critical assembly*
BT1 enriched uranium reactors
BT2 reactors
BT1 research reactors
BT2 research and test reactors
BT3 reactors
BT1 tank type reactors
BT2 reactors
BT1 water cooled reactors
BT2 reactors
BT1 water moderated reactors
BT2 reactors
BT1 zero power reactors
BT2 experimental reactors
BT3 research and test reactors
BT4 reactors

TCA TOKAMAK [90; 90] *Apr 84*
(Experimental tokamak at Centre de Recherches en Physique des Plasmas, Lausanne.)
UF *lausanne tokamak*
UF *tokamak chaufage alfven*
BT1 tokamak devices
BT2 closed plasma devices
BT3 thermonuclear devices

TCP [7; 7]
  UF   *tricresyl phosphates*
  BT1   phosphoric acid esters
    BT2   esters
      BT3   organic compounds
    BT2   organic phosphorus compounds
      BT3   organic compounds

tct
  USE   two-component torus

TD-NICKEL [35; 35]
(Ni-ThO2 dispersion.)
  BT1   cermets
    BT2   composite materials
      BT3   materials
  BT1   dispersions
  RT   nickel
  RT   thorium oxides

TD-NICKEL CHROMIUM [47; 47]
(Ni-Cr-ThO2 dispersion.)
  UF   *nickel chromium-td*
  BT1   cermets
    BT2   composite materials
      BT3   materials
  BT1   chromium alloys
    BT2   alloys
  BT1   dispersions
  BT1   nickel base alloys
    BT2   nickel alloys
      BT3   alloys
  RT   thorium oxides

TDA [14; 14]
  UF   *decylamine-tris*
  BT1   amines
    BT2   organic compounds
  BT1   chelating agents

tea
  USE   beverages

TEA LEAVES [65; 65]
  BT1   leaves
  RT   beverages
  RT   tea plants

TEA PLANTS [17; 17] *Jul 80*
  UF   *camellia sinensis*
  BT1   plants
  RT   beverages
  RT   tea leaves

TEAB [9; 9]
  UF   *tetraethylammonium bromide*
  BT1   bromides
    BT2   bromine compounds
      BT3   halogen compounds
    BT2   halides
      BT3   halogen compounds
  BT1   quaternary compounds
    BT2   amines
      BT3   organic compounds

teaching
  USE   education

teaching facilities
  USE   educational facilities

TEAK EVENT [3; 3]
  BT1   atmospheric explosions
    BT2   explosions
  BT1   nuclear explosions
    BT2   explosions

teal oil
  USE   sesame oil

TEAPOT PROJECT [3; 3]
  RT   nuclear weapons

tear canals
  USE   lacrimal ducts

TEARING INSTABILITY [1,121; 1,121]
Nov 78
  BT1   plasma macroinstabilities
    BT2   plasma instability
      BT3   instability
  RT   plasma disruption

TECHNETATES [93; 93]
(Specific compounds should be indexed by coordination of a descriptor of the form (CATION) COMPOUNDS and the above anion descriptor.)
  BT1   oxygen compounds
  BT1   technetium compounds
    BT2   transition element compounds
  RT   technetium oxides

TECHNETIUM [932; 932]
  UF   *masurium*
  BT1   transition elements
    BT2   metals
      BT3   elements

TECHNETIUM ADDITIONS [10; 10]
(Alloys containing not more than 1% Tc are listed here.)
  RT   technetium alloys
  RT   technetium compounds

TECHNETIUM ALLOYS [46; 65]
(Alloys containing more than 1% Tc.)
  BT1   alloys
  NT1   technetium base alloys
  RT   technetium additions

TECHNETIUM BASE ALLOYS [19; 19]
  BT1   technetium alloys
    BT2   alloys

TECHNETIUM BROMIDES [15; 15]
Aug 84
  BT1   bromides
    BT2   bromine compounds
      BT3   halogen compounds
    BT2   halides
      BT3   halogen compounds
  BT1   technetium compounds
    BT2   transition element compounds

TECHNETIUM CARBIDES [6; 6]
  BT1   carbides
    BT2   carbon compounds
  BT1   technetium compounds
    BT2   transition element compounds

TECHNETIUM CHLORIDES [40; 40]
  BT1   chlorides
    BT2   chlorine compounds
      BT3   halogen compounds
    BT2   halides
      BT3   halogen compounds
  BT1   technetium compounds
    BT2   transition element compounds

TECHNETIUM COMPLEXES [1,888; 1,888]
  BT1   transition element complexes
    BT2   complexes

TECHNETIUM COMPOUNDS [975; 3,129]
  BT1   transition element compounds
  NT1   pertechnetates
  NT1   technetates
  NT1   technetium bromides
  NT1   technetium carbides
  NT1   technetium chlorides
  NT1   technetium fluorides
  NT1   technetium hydrides
  NT1   technetium iodides
  NT1   technetium oxides
  NT1   technetium phosphates
  NT1   technetium sulfides
  RT   technetium additions

TECHNETIUM FLUORIDES [15; 15]
  BT1   fluorides
    BT2   fluorine compounds
      BT3   halogen compounds
    BT2   halides
      BT3   halogen compounds
  BT1   technetium compounds
    BT2   transition element compounds

TECHNETIUM HYDRIDES [12; 12]
Mar 83
  BT1   hydrides
    BT2   hydrogen compounds
  BT1   technetium compounds
    BT2   transition element compounds

TECHNETIUM IODIDES [6; 6]
  BT1   iodides
    BT2   halides
      BT3   halogen compounds
    BT2   iodine compounds
      BT3   halogen compounds
  BT1   technetium compounds
    BT2   transition element compounds

TECHNETIUM IONS [16; 16]
  BT1   ions
    BT2   charged particles

TECHNETIUM ISOTOPES [242; 18,901]
  NT1   technetium 100
  NT1   technetium 101
  NT1   technetium 102
  NT1   technetium 103
  NT1   technetium 104
  NT1   technetium 105
  NT1   technetium 106
  NT1   technetium 107
  NT1   technetium 108
  NT1   technetium 109
  NT1   technetium 110
  NT1   technetium 111
  NT1   technetium 112
  NT1   technetium 90
  NT1   technetium 91
  NT1   technetium 92
  NT1   technetium 93
  NT1   technetium 94
  NT1   technetium 95
  NT1   technetium 96
  NT1   technetium 97
  NT1   technetium 98
  NT1   technetium 99

TECHNETIUM OXIDES [131; 131]
  BT1   oxides
    BT2   chalcogenides
    BT2   oxygen compounds
  BT1   technetium compounds
    BT2   transition element compounds
  RT   pertechnetates
  RT   technetates

TECHNETIUM PHOSPHATES [105; 105] *Mar 81*
  BT1   phosphates
    BT2   oxygen compounds
    BT2   phosphorus compounds
  BT1   technetium compounds
    BT2   transition element compounds

TECHNETIUM SULFIDES [82; 82]
  BT1   sulfides
    BT2   chalcogenides
    BT2   sulfur compounds
  BT1   technetium compounds
    BT2   transition element compounds

TECHNETIUM 100 [31; 31]
- BT1 beta-minus decay radioisotopes
  - BT2 beta decay radioisotopes
    - BT3 radioisotopes
      - BT4 isotopes
- BT1 intermediate mass nuclei
  - BT2 nuclei
- BT1 odd-odd nuclei
  - BT2 nuclei
- BT1 seconds living radioisotopes
  - BT2 radioisotopes
    - BT3 isotopes
- BT1 technetium isotopes

TECHNETIUM 101 [44; 44]
- BT1 beta-minus decay radioisotopes
  - BT2 beta decay radioisotopes
    - BT3 radioisotopes
      - BT4 isotopes
- BT1 intermediate mass nuclei
  - BT2 nuclei
- BT1 minutes living radioisotopes
  - BT2 radioisotopes
    - BT3 isotopes
- BT1 odd-even nuclei
  - BT2 nuclei
- BT1 technetium isotopes

TECHNETIUM 102 [10; 10]
- BT1 beta-minus decay radioisotopes
  - BT2 beta decay radioisotopes
    - BT3 radioisotopes
      - BT4 isotopes
- BT1 intermediate mass nuclei
  - BT2 nuclei
- BT1 isomeric transition isotopes
  - BT2 radioisotopes
    - BT3 isotopes
- BT1 minutes living radioisotopes
  - BT2 radioisotopes
    - BT3 isotopes
- BT1 odd-odd nuclei
  - BT2 nuclei
- BT1 seconds living radioisotopes
  - BT2 radioisotopes
    - BT3 isotopes
- BT1 technetium isotopes

TECHNETIUM 103 [19; 19]
- BT1 beta-minus decay radioisotopes
  - BT2 beta decay radioisotopes
    - BT3 radioisotopes
      - BT4 isotopes
- BT1 intermediate mass nuclei
  - BT2 nuclei
- BT1 odd-even nuclei
  - BT2 nuclei
- BT1 seconds living radioisotopes
  - BT2 radioisotopes
    - BT3 isotopes
- BT1 technetium isotopes

TECHNETIUM 104 [30; 30]
- BT1 beta-minus decay radioisotopes
  - BT2 beta decay radioisotopes
    - BT3 radioisotopes
      - BT4 isotopes
- BT1 intermediate mass nuclei
  - BT2 nuclei
- BT1 minutes living radioisotopes
  - BT2 radioisotopes
    - BT3 isotopes
- BT1 odd-odd nuclei
  - BT2 nuclei
- BT1 technetium isotopes

TECHNETIUM 105 [22; 22]
- BT1 beta-minus decay radioisotopes
  - BT2 beta decay radioisotopes
    - BT3 radioisotopes
      - BT4 isotopes
- BT1 intermediate mass nuclei
  - BT2 nuclei
- BT1 minutes living radioisotopes
  - BT2 radioisotopes
    - BT3 isotopes
- BT1 odd-even nuclei
  - BT2 nuclei
- BT1 technetium isotopes

TECHNETIUM 106 [20; 20]
- BT1 beta-minus decay radioisotopes
  - BT2 beta decay radioisotopes
    - BT3 radioisotopes
      - BT4 isotopes
- BT1 intermediate mass nuclei
  - BT2 nuclei
- BT1 odd-odd nuclei
  - BT2 nuclei
- BT1 seconds living radioisotopes
  - BT2 radioisotopes
    - BT3 isotopes
- BT1 technetium isotopes

TECHNETIUM 107 [14; 14]
- BT1 beta-minus decay radioisotopes
  - BT2 beta decay radioisotopes
    - BT3 radioisotopes
      - BT4 isotopes
- BT1 intermediate mass nuclei
  - BT2 nuclei
- BT1 odd-even nuclei
  - BT2 nuclei
- BT1 seconds living radioisotopes
  - BT2 radioisotopes
    - BT3 isotopes
- BT1 technetium isotopes

TECHNETIUM 108 [16; 16]
- BT1 beta-minus decay radioisotopes
  - BT2 beta decay radioisotopes
    - BT3 radioisotopes
      - BT4 isotopes
- BT1 intermediate mass nuclei
  - BT2 nuclei
- BT1 odd-odd nuclei
  - BT2 nuclei
- BT1 seconds living radioisotopes
  - BT2 radioisotopes
    - BT3 isotopes
- BT1 technetium isotopes

TECHNETIUM 109 [9; 9] *Jul 76*
- BT1 beta-minus decay radioisotopes
  - BT2 beta decay radioisotopes
    - BT3 radioisotopes
      - BT4 isotopes
- BT1 intermediate mass nuclei
  - BT2 nuclei
- BT1 odd-even nuclei
  - BT2 nuclei
- BT1 seconds living radioisotopes
  - BT2 radioisotopes
    - BT3 isotopes
- BT1 technetium isotopes

TECHNETIUM 110 [4; 4] *Jul 76*
- BT1 beta-minus decay radioisotopes
  - BT2 beta decay radioisotopes
    - BT3 radioisotopes
      - BT4 isotopes
- BT1 intermediate mass nuclei
  - BT2 nuclei
- BT1 millisec living radioisotopes
  - BT2 radioisotopes
    - BT3 isotopes
- BT1 odd-odd nuclei
  - BT2 nuclei
- BT1 technetium isotopes

TECHNETIUM 111 [0; 0] *Nov 88*
- BT1 beta-minus decay radioisotopes
  - BT2 beta decay radioisotopes
    - BT3 radioisotopes
      - BT4 isotopes
- BT1 intermediate mass nuclei
  - BT2 nuclei
- BT1 millisec living radioisotopes
  - BT2 radioisotopes
    - BT3 isotopes
- BT1 odd-even nuclei
  - BT2 nuclei
- BT1 technetium isotopes

TECHNETIUM 112 [3; 3] *Dec 90*
- BT1 beta-minus decay radioisotopes
  - BT2 beta decay radioisotopes
    - BT3 radioisotopes
      - BT4 isotopes
- BT1 intermediate mass nuclei
  - BT2 nuclei
- BT1 millisec living radioisotopes
  - BT2 radioisotopes
    - BT3 isotopes
- BT1 odd-odd nuclei
  - BT2 nuclei
- BT1 technetium isotopes

TECHNETIUM 90 [17; 17]
- BT1 beta-plus decay radioisotopes
  - BT2 beta decay radioisotopes
    - BT3 radioisotopes
      - BT4 isotopes
- BT1 intermediate mass nuclei
  - BT2 nuclei
- BT1 odd-odd nuclei
  - BT2 nuclei
- BT1 seconds living radioisotopes
  - BT2 radioisotopes
    - BT3 isotopes
- BT1 technetium isotopes

TECHNETIUM 91 [21; 21]
- BT1 beta-plus decay radioisotopes
  - BT2 beta decay radioisotopes
    - BT3 radioisotopes
      - BT4 isotopes
- BT1 electron capture radioisotopes
  - BT2 beta decay radioisotopes
    - BT3 radioisotopes
      - BT4 isotopes
- BT1 intermediate mass nuclei
  - BT2 nuclei
- BT1 minutes living radioisotopes
  - BT2 radioisotopes
    - BT3 isotopes
- BT1 odd-even nuclei
  - BT2 nuclei
- BT1 technetium isotopes

TECHNETIUM 92 [27; 27]
- BT1 beta-plus decay radioisotopes
  - BT2 beta decay radioisotopes
    - BT3 radioisotopes
      - BT4 isotopes
- BT1 electron capture radioisotopes
  - BT2 beta decay radioisotopes
    - BT3 radioisotopes
      - BT4 isotopes
- BT1 intermediate mass nuclei
  - BT2 nuclei
- BT1 minutes living radioisotopes
  - BT2 radioisotopes
    - BT3 isotopes
- BT1 odd-odd nuclei
  - BT2 nuclei
- BT1 technetium isotopes

TECHNETIUM 93 [127; 127]
- BT1 beta-plus decay radioisotopes
  - BT2 beta decay radioisotopes
    - BT3 radioisotopes
      - BT4 isotopes
- BT1 electron capture radioisotopes
  - BT2 beta decay radioisotopes
    - BT3 radioisotopes
      - BT4 isotopes
- BT1 hours living radioisotopes
  - BT2 radioisotopes
    - BT3 isotopes
- BT1 intermediate mass nuclei
  - BT2 nuclei
- BT1 isomeric transition isotopes
  - BT2 radioisotopes
    - BT3 isotopes
- BT1 minutes living radioisotopes
  - BT2 radioisotopes
    - BT3 isotopes
- BT1 odd-even nuclei
  - BT2 nuclei
- BT1 technetium isotopes

TECHNETIUM 94 [62; 62]
  BT1   beta-plus decay radioisotopes
    BT2   beta decay radioisotopes
      BT3   radioisotopes
        BT4   isotopes
  BT1   electron capture radioisotopes
    BT2   beta decay radioisotopes
      BT3   radioisotopes
        BT4   isotopes
  BT1   hours living radioisotopes
    BT2   radioisotopes
      BT3   isotopes
  BT1   intermediate mass nuclei
    BT2   nuclei
  BT1   minutes living radioisotopes
    BT2   radioisotopes
      BT3   isotopes
  BT1   odd-odd nuclei
    BT2   nuclei
  BT1   technetium isotopes

TECHNETIUM 95 [235; 235]
  BT1   beta-plus decay radioisotopes
    BT2   beta decay radioisotopes
      BT3   radioisotopes
        BT4   isotopes
  BT1   days living radioisotopes
    BT2   radioisotopes
      BT3   isotopes
  BT1   electron capture radioisotopes
    BT2   beta decay radioisotopes
      BT3   radioisotopes
        BT4   isotopes
  BT1   hours living radioisotopes
    BT2   radioisotopes
      BT3   isotopes
  BT1   intermediate mass nuclei
    BT2   nuclei
  BT1   isomeric transition isotopes
    BT2   radioisotopes
      BT3   isotopes
  BT1   odd-even nuclei
    BT2   nuclei
  BT1   technetium isotopes

TECHNETIUM 96 [64; 64]
  BT1   beta-plus decay radioisotopes
    BT2   beta decay radioisotopes
      BT3   radioisotopes
        BT4   isotopes
  BT1   days living radioisotopes
    BT2   radioisotopes
      BT3   isotopes
  BT1   electron capture radioisotopes
    BT2   beta decay radioisotopes
      BT3   radioisotopes
        BT4   isotopes
  BT1   intermediate mass nuclei
    BT2   nuclei
  BT1   internal conversion radioisoto
    BT2   radioisotopes
      BT3   isotopes
  BT1   isomeric transition isotopes
    BT2   radioisotopes
      BT3   isotopes
  BT1   minutes living radioisotopes
    BT2   radioisotopes
      BT3   isotopes
  BT1   odd-odd nuclei
    BT2   nuclei
  BT1   technetium isotopes

TECHNETIUM 97 [87; 87]
  BT1   days living radioisotopes
    BT2   radioisotopes
      BT3   isotopes
  BT1   electron capture radioisotopes
    BT2   beta decay radioisotopes
      BT3   radioisotopes
        BT4   isotopes
  BT1   intermediate mass nuclei
    BT2   nuclei
  BT1   internal conversion radioisoto
    BT2   radioisotopes
      BT3   isotopes
  BT1   isomeric transition isotopes
    BT2   radioisotopes
      BT3   isotopes
  BT1   odd-even nuclei
    BT2   nuclei
  BT1   technetium isotopes
  BT1   years living radioisotopes
    BT2   radioisotopes
      BT3   isotopes

TECHNETIUM 98 [51; 51]
  BT1   beta-minus decay radioisotopes
    BT2   beta decay radioisotopes
      BT3   radioisotopes
        BT4   isotopes
  BT1   intermediate mass nuclei
    BT2   nuclei
  BT1   odd-odd nuclei
    BT2   nuclei
  BT1   technetium isotopes
  BT1   years living radioisotopes
    BT2   radioisotopes
      BT3   isotopes

TECHNETIUM 99 [18,027; 18,027]
  BT1   beta-minus decay radioisotopes
    BT2   beta decay radioisotopes
      BT3   radioisotopes
        BT4   isotopes
  BT1   hours living radioisotopes
    BT2   radioisotopes
      BT3   isotopes
  BT1   intermediate mass nuclei
    BT2   nuclei
  BT1   internal conversion radioisoto
    BT2   radioisotopes
      BT3   isotopes
  BT1   isomeric transition isotopes
    BT2   radioisotopes
      BT3   isotopes
  BT1   odd-even nuclei
    BT2   nuclei
  BT1   technetium isotopes
  BT1   years living radioisotopes
    BT2   radioisotopes
      BT3   isotopes

TECHNETIUM 99 TARGET [39; 39]
  Oct 75
  BT1   targets

technical specifications
  USE   specifications

→ **TECHNOLOGY ASSESSMENT** [8; 8]
  Aug 91
  RT   feasibility studies
  RT   industry

technology development
  SEE   commercialization

TECHNOLOGY IMPACTS [339; 339]
  May 86
  RT   commercialization
  RT   cost benefit analysis
  RT   economic impact
  RT   economy
  RT   industry
  RT   socio-economic factors
  RT   technology transfer

TECHNOLOGY TRANSFER
  [1,499; 1,499] Nov 77
  UF   *transfer of knowledge*
  RT   commercialization
  RT   developing countries
  RT   education
  RT   industry
  RT   information
  RT   information dissemination
  RT   international cooperation
  RT   nuclear engineering
  RT   technology impacts

TECTONICS [1,171; 1,171]
  RT   metamorphism
  RT   petrogenesis
  RT   rocks

teel oil
  USE   sesame oil

TEETH [835; 835]
  BT1   oral cavity
    BT2   digestive system
  RT   bone tissues
  RT   calcium
  RT   caries
  RT   dentin
  RT   dentistry
  RT   jaw

TEFLON [928; 928]
  UF   *polytetrafluorethylene*
  UF   *ptfe*
  BT1   organic fluorine compounds
    BT2   organic halogen compounds
      BT3   organic compounds
  BT1   polyethylenes
    BT2   polyolefins
      BT3   organic polymers
        BT4   organic compounds
        BT4   polymers

teheran univ. research reactor
  USE   utrr reactor

TEHRAN NUCLEAR RESEARCH CENTRE [12; 12] Oct 76
  UF   *nuclear research centre,tehran*
  BT1   iranian organizations
    BT2   national organizations

TEKTITES [115; 115]
  UF   *australites*
  UF   *billitonites*
  UF   *moldavites*
  UF   *obsidianites*
  BT1   minerals
  RT   meteorites

TEL [11; 11]
  UF   *tetraethyl lead*
  BT1   lead compounds
  BT1   organometallic compounds
    BT2   organic compounds

TELANGIECTASIS [166; 166]
  BT1   cardiovascular diseases
    BT2   diseases
  RT   blood vessels

TELEMETRY [253; 253]
  BT1   data transmission
    BT2   communications

TELESCOPE COUNTERS [1,237; 1,237]
  RT   coincidence circuits
  RT   cosmic ray detection
  RT   counting techniques
  RT   hodoscopes
  RT   radiation detectors

TELESCOPES [1,012; 1,469]
  NT1   radio telescopes
  RT   borescopes
  RT   mirrors
  RT   optical systems

teletherapy
  USE   radiotherapy

TELEVISION [1,102; 1,102]
- RT camera tubes
- RT cameras
- RT radiation protection
- RT radio equipment
- RT remote viewing equipment
- RT video tapes
- RT x radiation

TELLURATES [121; 121]
(Specific compounds should be indexed by coordination of a descriptor of the form (CATION) COMPOUNDS and the above anion descriptor.)
- BT1 oxygen compounds
- BT1 tellurium compounds
- RT telluric acid

TELLURIC ACID [37; 37]
- BT1 inorganic acids
  - BT2 hydrogen compounds
  - BT2 inorganic compounds
- BT1 oxygen compounds
- BT1 tellurium compounds
- RT tellurates

TELLURIDES [1,615; 5,932]
- BT1 chalcogenides
- BT1 tellurium compounds
- NT1 aluminium tellurides
- NT1 americium tellurides
- NT1 antimony tellurides
- NT1 arsenic tellurides
- NT1 berkelium tellurides
- NT1 beryllium tellurides
- NT1 bismuth tellurides
- NT1 cadmium tellurides
- NT1 californium tellurides
- NT1 cerium tellurides
- NT1 cesium tellurides
- NT1 chromium tellurides
- NT1 cobalt tellurides
- NT1 copper tellurides
- NT1 curium tellurides
- NT1 dysprosium tellurides
- NT1 erbium tellurides
- NT1 europium tellurides
- NT1 gadolinium tellurides
- NT1 gallium tellurides
- NT1 germanium tellurides
- NT1 gold tellurides
- NT1 hafnium tellurides
- NT1 holmium tellurides
- NT1 indium tellurides
- NT1 iron tellurides
- NT1 lanthanum tellurides
- NT1 lead tellurides
- NT1 lithium tellurides
- NT1 magnesium tellurides
- NT1 manganese tellurides
- NT1 mercury tellurides
- NT1 molybdenum tellurides
- NT1 neodymium tellurides
- NT1 neptunium tellurides
- NT1 nickel tellurides
- NT1 niobium tellurides
- NT1 palladium tellurides
- NT1 platinum tellurides
- NT1 plutonium tellurides
- NT1 potassium tellurides
- NT1 praseodymium tellurides
- NT1 rhenium tellurides
- NT1 rhodium tellurides
- NT1 ruthenium tellurides
- NT1 samarium tellurides
- NT1 selenium tellurides
- NT1 silver tellurides
- NT1 sodium tellurides
- NT1 tantalum tellurides
- NT1 terbium tellurides
- NT1 thallium tellurides
- NT1 thorium tellurides
- NT1 thulium tellurides
- NT1 tin tellurides
- NT1 titanium tellurides
- NT1 tungsten tellurides
- NT1 uranium tellurides
- NT1 vanadium tellurides
- NT1 ytterbium tellurides
- NT1 yttrium tellurides
- NT1 zinc tellurides
- NT1 zirconium tellurides
- RT intermetallic compounds
- RT tellurium additions
- RT tellurium alloys

TELLURIUM [1,666; 1,666]
- BT1 semimetals
  - BT2 elements

TELLURIUM ADDITIONS [236; 236]
- RT tellurides
- RT tellurium alloys

TELLURIUM ALLOYS [654; 661]
(Alloys containing more than 1% Te.)
- BT1 alloys
- RT tellurides
- RT tellurium additions

TELLURIUM BROMIDES [36; 36]
Dec 75
- BT1 bromides
  - BT2 bromine compounds
    - BT3 halogen compounds
  - BT2 halides
    - BT3 halogen compounds
- BT1 tellurium halides
  - BT2 halides
    - BT3 halogen compounds
  - BT2 tellurium compounds

TELLURIUM CARBIDES [2; 2]
- BT1 carbides
  - BT2 carbon compounds
- BT1 tellurium compounds

TELLURIUM CHLORIDES [151; 151]
- BT1 chlorides
  - BT2 chlorine compounds
    - BT3 halogen compounds
  - BT2 halides
    - BT3 halogen compounds
- BT1 tellurium halides
  - BT2 halides
    - BT3 halogen compounds
  - BT2 tellurium compounds

TELLURIUM COMPLEXES [197; 197]
- BT1 complexes

TELLURIUM COMPOUNDS [709; 7,080]
- NT1 tellurates
- NT1 telluric acid
- NT1 tellurides
  - NT2 aluminium tellurides
  - NT2 americium tellurides
  - NT2 antimony tellurides
  - NT2 arsenic tellurides
  - NT2 berkelium tellurides
  - NT2 beryllium tellurides
  - NT2 bismuth tellurides
  - NT2 cadmium tellurides
  - NT2 californium tellurides
  - NT2 cerium tellurides
  - NT2 cesium tellurides
  - NT2 chromium tellurides
  - NT2 cobalt tellurides
  - NT2 copper tellurides
  - NT2 curium tellurides
  - NT2 dysprosium tellurides
  - NT2 erbium tellurides
  - NT2 europium tellurides
  - NT2 gadolinium tellurides
  - NT2 gallium tellurides
  - NT2 germanium tellurides
  - NT2 gold tellurides
  - NT2 hafnium tellurides
  - NT2 holmium tellurides
  - NT2 indium tellurides
  - NT2 iron tellurides
  - NT2 lanthanum tellurides
  - NT2 lead tellurides
  - NT2 lithium tellurides
  - NT2 magnesium tellurides
  - NT2 manganese tellurides
  - NT2 mercury tellurides
  - NT2 molybdenum tellurides
  - NT2 neodymium tellurides
  - NT2 neptunium tellurides
  - NT2 nickel tellurides
  - NT2 niobium tellurides
  - NT2 palladium tellurides
  - NT2 platinum tellurides
  - NT2 plutonium tellurides
  - NT2 potassium tellurides
  - NT2 praseodymium tellurides
  - NT2 rhenium tellurides
  - NT2 rhodium tellurides
  - NT2 ruthenium tellurides
  - NT2 samarium tellurides
  - NT2 selenium tellurides
  - NT2 silver tellurides
  - NT2 sodium tellurides
  - NT2 tantalum tellurides
  - NT2 terbium tellurides
  - NT2 thallium tellurides
  - NT2 thorium tellurides
  - NT2 thulium tellurides
  - NT2 tin tellurides
  - NT2 titanium tellurides
  - NT2 tungsten tellurides
  - NT2 uranium tellurides
  - NT2 vanadium tellurides
  - NT2 ytterbium tellurides
  - NT2 yttrium tellurides
  - NT2 zinc tellurides
  - NT2 zirconium tellurides
- NT1 tellurium carbides
- NT1 tellurium halides
  - NT2 tellurium bromides
  - NT2 tellurium chlorides
  - NT2 tellurium fluorides
  - NT2 tellurium iodides
- NT1 tellurium hydrides
- NT1 tellurium hydroxides
- NT1 tellurium nitrates
- NT1 tellurium oxides
- NT1 tellurium sulfides

TELLURIUM FLUORIDES [51; 51]
- BT1 fluorides
  - BT2 fluorine compounds
    - BT3 halogen compounds
  - BT2 halides
    - BT3 halogen compounds
- BT1 tellurium halides
  - BT2 halides
    - BT3 halogen compounds
  - BT2 tellurium compounds

→ TELLURIUM HALIDES [0; 0] *Sep 91*
- BT1 halides
  - BT2 halogen compounds
- BT1 tellurium compounds
- NT1 tellurium bromides
- NT1 tellurium chlorides
- NT1 tellurium fluorides
- NT1 tellurium iodides

TELLURIUM HYDRIDES [25; 25]
Jun 77
- BT1 hydrides
  - BT2 hydrogen compounds
- BT1 tellurium compounds

TELLURIUM HYDROXIDES [11; 11]
Feb 78
- BT1 hydroxides
  - BT2 hydrogen compounds
  - BT2 oxygen compounds
- BT1 tellurium compounds

TELLURIUM IODIDES [28; 28]
- BT1 iodides
  - BT2 halides
    - BT3 halogen compounds
  - BT2 iodine compounds
    - BT3 halogen compounds
- BT1 tellurium halides
  - BT2 halides
    - BT3 halogen compounds
  - BT2 tellurium compounds

TELLURIUM IONS [142; 142]
- BT1 ions
- BT2 charged particles

TELLURIUM ISOTOPES [244; 1,935]
- NT1 tellurium 106
- NT1 tellurium 107
- NT1 tellurium 108
- NT1 tellurium 109
- NT1 tellurium 110
- NT1 tellurium 111
- NT1 tellurium 112
- NT1 tellurium 113
- NT1 tellurium 114
- NT1 tellurium 115
- NT1 tellurium 116
- NT1 tellurium 117
- NT1 tellurium 118
- NT1 tellurium 119
- NT1 tellurium 120
- NT1 tellurium 121
- NT1 tellurium 122
- NT1 tellurium 123
- NT1 tellurium 124
- NT1 tellurium 125
- NT1 tellurium 126
- NT1 tellurium 127
- NT1 tellurium 128
- NT1 tellurium 129
- NT1 tellurium 130
- NT1 tellurium 131
- NT1 tellurium 132
- NT1 tellurium 133
- NT1 tellurium 134
- NT1 tellurium 135
- NT1 tellurium 136
- NT1 tellurium 137
- NT1 tellurium 138

TELLURIUM NITRATES [8; 8] *May 78*
- BT1 nitrates
- BT2 nitrogen compounds
- BT2 oxygen compounds
- BT1 tellurium compounds

TELLURIUM ORES [3; 3]
- BT1 ores

TELLURIUM OXIDES [362; 362]
- BT1 oxides
- BT2 chalcogenides
- BT2 oxygen compounds
- BT1 tellurium compounds
- RT oxide minerals

TELLURIUM SULFIDES [15; 15]
- BT1 sulfides
- BT2 chalcogenides
- BT2 sulfur compounds
- BT1 tellurium compounds

TELLURIUM 106 [4; 4]
- BT1 alpha decay radioisotopes
- BT2 radioisotopes
- BT3 isotopes
- BT1 even-even nuclei
- BT2 nuclei
- BT1 intermediate mass nuclei
- BT2 nuclei
- BT1 microsec living radioisotopes
- BT2 radioisotopes
- BT3 isotopes
- BT1 tellurium isotopes

TELLURIUM 107 [7; 7]
- BT1 alpha decay radioisotopes
- BT2 radioisotopes
- BT3 isotopes
- BT1 beta-plus decay radioisotopes
- BT2 beta decay radioisotopes
- BT3 radioisotopes
- BT4 isotopes
- BT1 electron capture radioisotopes
- BT2 beta decay radioisotopes
- BT3 radioisotopes
- BT4 isotopes
- BT1 even-odd nuclei
- BT2 nuclei
- BT1 intermediate mass nuclei
- BT2 nuclei
- BT1 millisec living radioisotopes
- BT2 radioisotopes
- BT3 isotopes
- BT1 tellurium isotopes

TELLURIUM 108 [16; 16]
- BT1 alpha decay radioisotopes
- BT2 radioisotopes
- BT3 isotopes
- BT1 beta-plus decay radioisotopes
- BT2 beta decay radioisotopes
- BT3 radioisotopes
- BT4 isotopes
- BT1 electron capture radioisotopes
- BT2 beta decay radioisotopes
- BT3 radioisotopes
- BT4 isotopes
- BT1 even-even nuclei
- BT2 nuclei
- BT1 intermediate mass nuclei
- BT2 nuclei
- BT1 seconds living radioisotopes
- BT2 radioisotopes
- BT3 isotopes
- BT1 tellurium isotopes

TELLURIUM 109 [20; 20]
- BT1 alpha decay radioisotopes
- BT2 radioisotopes
- BT3 isotopes
- BT1 beta-plus decay radioisotopes
- BT2 beta decay radioisotopes
- BT3 radioisotopes
- BT4 isotopes
- BT1 electron capture radioisotopes
- BT2 beta decay radioisotopes
- BT3 radioisotopes
- BT4 isotopes
- BT1 even-odd nuclei
- BT2 nuclei
- BT1 intermediate mass nuclei
- BT2 nuclei
- BT1 seconds living radioisotopes
- BT2 radioisotopes
- BT3 isotopes
- BT1 tellurium isotopes

TELLURIUM 110 [10; 10]
- BT1 alpha decay radioisotopes
- BT2 radioisotopes
- BT3 isotopes
- BT1 beta-plus decay radioisotopes
- BT2 beta decay radioisotopes
- BT3 radioisotopes
- BT4 isotopes
- BT1 electron capture radioisotopes
- BT2 beta decay radioisotopes
- BT3 radioisotopes
- BT4 isotopes
- BT1 even-even nuclei
- BT2 nuclei
- BT1 intermediate mass nuclei
- BT2 nuclei
- BT1 seconds living radioisotopes
- BT2 radioisotopes
- BT3 isotopes
- BT1 tellurium isotopes

TELLURIUM 111 [7; 7]
- BT1 beta-plus decay radioisotopes
- BT2 beta decay radioisotopes
- BT3 radioisotopes
- BT4 isotopes
- BT1 electron capture radioisotopes
- BT2 beta decay radioisotopes
- BT3 radioisotopes
- BT4 isotopes
- BT1 even-odd nuclei
- BT2 nuclei
- BT1 intermediate mass nuclei
- BT2 nuclei
- BT1 seconds living radioisotopes
- BT2 radioisotopes
- BT3 isotopes
- BT1 tellurium isotopes

TELLURIUM 112 [19; 19]
- BT1 beta-plus decay radioisotopes
- BT2 beta decay radioisotopes
- BT3 radioisotopes
- BT4 isotopes
- BT1 electron capture radioisotopes
- BT2 beta decay radioisotopes
- BT3 radioisotopes
- BT4 isotopes
- BT1 even-even nuclei
- BT2 nuclei
- BT1 intermediate mass nuclei
- BT2 nuclei
- BT1 minutes living radioisotopes
- BT2 radioisotopes
- BT3 isotopes
- BT1 tellurium isotopes

TELLURIUM 113 [17; 17]
- BT1 beta-plus decay radioisotopes
- BT2 beta decay radioisotopes
- BT3 radioisotopes
- BT4 isotopes
- BT1 electron capture radioisotopes
- BT2 beta decay radioisotopes
- BT3 radioisotopes
- BT4 isotopes
- BT1 even-odd nuclei
- BT2 nuclei
- BT1 intermediate mass nuclei
- BT2 nuclei
- BT1 minutes living radioisotopes
- BT2 radioisotopes
- BT3 isotopes
- BT1 tellurium isotopes

TELLURIUM 114 [22; 22]
- BT1 beta-plus decay radioisotopes
- BT2 beta decay radioisotopes
- BT3 radioisotopes
- BT4 isotopes
- BT1 electron capture radioisotopes
- BT2 beta decay radioisotopes
- BT3 radioisotopes
- BT4 isotopes
- BT1 even-even nuclei
- BT2 nuclei
- BT1 intermediate mass nuclei
- BT2 nuclei
- BT1 minutes living radioisotopes
- BT2 radioisotopes
- BT3 isotopes
- BT1 tellurium isotopes

TELLURIUM 115 [24; 24]
- BT1 beta-plus decay radioisotopes
- BT2 beta decay radioisotopes
- BT3 radioisotopes
- BT4 isotopes
- BT1 electron capture radioisotopes
- BT2 beta decay radioisotopes
- BT3 radioisotopes
- BT4 isotopes
- BT1 even-odd nuclei
- BT2 nuclei
- BT1 intermediate mass nuclei
- BT2 nuclei
- BT1 minutes living radioisotopes
- BT2 radioisotopes
- BT3 isotopes
- BT1 tellurium isotopes

TELLURIUM 116 [18; 18]
- BT1 beta-plus decay radioisotopes
- BT2 beta decay radioisotopes
- BT3 radioisotopes
- BT4 isotopes
- BT1 electron capture radioisotopes
- BT2 beta decay radioisotopes
- BT3 radioisotopes
- BT4 isotopes
- BT1 even-even nuclei
- BT2 nuclei
- BT1 hours living radioisotopes
- BT2 radioisotopes
- BT3 isotopes
- BT1 intermediate mass nuclei
- BT2 nuclei
- BT1 tellurium isotopes

TELLURIUM 117 [35; 35]
  BT1   beta-plus decay radioisotopes
   BT2   beta decay radioisotopes
    BT3   radioisotopes
     BT4   isotopes
  BT1   electron capture radioisotopes
   BT2   beta decay radioisotopes
    BT3   radioisotopes
     BT4   isotopes
  BT1   even-odd nuclei
   BT2   nuclei
  BT1   hours living radioisotopes
   BT2   radioisotopes
    BT3   isotopes
  BT1   intermediate mass nuclei
   BT2   nuclei
  BT1   tellurium isotopes

TELLURIUM 118 [49; 49]
  BT1   days living radioisotopes
   BT2   radioisotopes
    BT3   isotopes
  BT1   electron capture radioisotopes
   BT2   beta decay radioisotopes
    BT3   radioisotopes
     BT4   isotopes
  BT1   even-even nuclei
   BT2   nuclei
  BT1   intermediate mass nuclei
   BT2   nuclei
  BT1   tellurium isotopes

TELLURIUM 119 [58; 58]
  BT1   beta-plus decay radioisotopes
   BT2   beta decay radioisotopes
    BT3   radioisotopes
     BT4   isotopes
  BT1   days living radioisotopes
   BT2   radioisotopes
    BT3   isotopes
  BT1   electron capture radioisotopes
   BT2   beta decay radioisotopes
    BT3   radioisotopes
     BT4   isotopes
  BT1   even-odd nuclei
   BT2   nuclei
  BT1   hours living radioisotopes
   BT2   radioisotopes
    BT3   isotopes
  BT1   intermediate mass nuclei
   BT2   nuclei
  BT1   tellurium isotopes

TELLURIUM 119 TARGET [3; 3]
Sep 75
  BT1   targets

TELLURIUM 120 [44; 44]
  BT1   even-even nuclei
   BT2   nuclei
  BT1   intermediate mass nuclei
   BT2   nuclei
  BT1   stable isotopes
   BT2   isotopes
  BT1   tellurium isotopes

TELLURIUM 120 TARGET [11; 11]
  BT1   targets

TELLURIUM 121 [91; 91]
  BT1   beta-plus decay radioisotopes
   BT2   beta decay radioisotopes
    BT3   radioisotopes
     BT4   isotopes
  BT1   days living radioisotopes
   BT2   radioisotopes
    BT3   isotopes
  BT1   electron capture radioisotopes
   BT2   beta decay radioisotopes
    BT3   radioisotopes
     BT4   isotopes
  BT1   even-odd nuclei
   BT2   nuclei
  BT1   intermediate mass nuclei
   BT2   nuclei
  BT1   internal conversion radioisoto
   BT2   radioisotopes
    BT3   isotopes
  BT1   isomeric transition isotopes
   BT2   radioisotopes
    BT3   isotopes
  BT1   tellurium isotopes

TELLURIUM 122 [100; 100]
  BT1   even-even nuclei
   BT2   nuclei
  BT1   intermediate mass nuclei
   BT2   nuclei
  BT1   stable isotopes
   BT2   isotopes
  BT1   tellurium isotopes

TELLURIUM 122 TARGET [92; 92]
  BT1   targets

TELLURIUM 123 [159; 159]
  BT1   days living radioisotopes
   BT2   radioisotopes
    BT3   isotopes
  BT1   electron capture radioisotopes
   BT2   beta decay radioisotopes
    BT3   radioisotopes
     BT4   isotopes
  BT1   even-odd nuclei
   BT2   nuclei
  BT1   intermediate mass nuclei
   BT2   nuclei
  BT1   internal conversion radioisoto
   BT2   radioisotopes
    BT3   isotopes
  BT1   isomeric transition isotopes
   BT2   radioisotopes
    BT3   isotopes
  BT1   stable isotopes
   BT2   isotopes
  BT1   tellurium isotopes
  BT1   years living radioisotopes
   BT2   radioisotopes
    BT3   isotopes

TELLURIUM 123 TARGET [47; 47]
  BT1   targets

TELLURIUM 124 [129; 129]
  BT1   even-even nuclei
   BT2   nuclei
  BT1   intermediate mass nuclei
   BT2   nuclei
  BT1   stable isotopes
   BT2   isotopes
  BT1   tellurium isotopes

TELLURIUM 124 TARGET [116; 116]
  BT1   targets

TELLURIUM 125 [287; 287]
  BT1   days living radioisotopes
   BT2   radioisotopes
    BT3   isotopes
  BT1   even-odd nuclei
   BT2   nuclei
  BT1   intermediate mass nuclei
   BT2   nuclei
  BT1   internal conversion radioisoto
   BT2   radioisotopes
    BT3   isotopes
  BT1   isomeric transition isotopes
   BT2   radioisotopes
    BT3   isotopes
  BT1   stable isotopes
   BT2   isotopes
  BT1   tellurium isotopes

TELLURIUM 125 TARGET [29; 29]
  BT1   targets

TELLURIUM 126 [99; 99]
  BT1   even-even nuclei
   BT2   nuclei
  BT1   intermediate mass nuclei
   BT2   nuclei
  BT1   stable isotopes
   BT2   isotopes
  BT1   tellurium isotopes

TELLURIUM 126 TARGET [106; 106]
  BT1   targets

TELLURIUM 127 [82; 82]
  BT1   beta-minus decay radioisotopes
   BT2   beta decay radioisotopes
    BT3   radioisotopes
     BT4   isotopes
  BT1   days living radioisotopes
   BT2   radioisotopes
    BT3   isotopes
  BT1   even-odd nuclei
   BT2   nuclei
  BT1   hours living radioisotopes
   BT2   radioisotopes
    BT3   isotopes
  BT1   intermediate mass nuclei
   BT2   nuclei
  BT1   isomeric transition isotopes
   BT2   radioisotopes
    BT3   isotopes
  BT1   tellurium isotopes

TELLURIUM 128 [163; 163]
  BT1   even-even nuclei
   BT2   nuclei
  BT1   intermediate mass nuclei
   BT2   nuclei
  BT1   stable isotopes
   BT2   isotopes
  BT1   tellurium isotopes

TELLURIUM 128 TARGET [116; 116]
  BT1   targets

TELLURIUM 129 [140; 140]
  BT1   beta-minus decay radioisotopes
   BT2   beta decay radioisotopes
    BT3   radioisotopes
     BT4   isotopes
  BT1   days living radioisotopes
   BT2   radioisotopes
    BT3   isotopes
  BT1   even-odd nuclei
   BT2   nuclei
  BT1   hours living radioisotopes
   BT2   radioisotopes
    BT3   isotopes
  BT1   intermediate mass nuclei
   BT2   nuclei
  BT1   isomeric transition isotopes
   BT2   radioisotopes
    BT3   isotopes
  BT1   tellurium isotopes

TELLURIUM 130 [199; 199]
  BT1   even-even nuclei
   BT2   nuclei
  BT1   intermediate mass nuclei
   BT2   nuclei
  BT1   stable isotopes
   BT2   isotopes
  BT1   tellurium isotopes

TELLURIUM 130 REACTIONS [4; 4]
Dec 80
  BT1   heavy ion reactions
  BT2   nuclear reactions

TELLURIUM 130 TARGET [198; 198]
  BT1   targets

TELLURIUM 131 [71; 71]
  BT1   beta-minus decay radioisotopes
   BT2   beta decay radioisotopes
    BT3   radioisotopes
     BT4   isotopes
  BT1   days living radioisotopes
   BT2   radioisotopes
    BT3   isotopes
  BT1   even-odd nuclei
   BT2   nuclei
  BT1   intermediate mass nuclei
   BT2   nuclei
  BT1   isomeric transition isotopes
   BT2   radioisotopes
    BT3   isotopes

BT1 minutes living radioisotopes
   BT2 radioisotopes
      BT3 isotopes
BT1 tellurium isotopes

TELLURIUM 132 [299; 299]
BT1 beta-minus decay radioisotopes
   BT2 beta decay radioisotopes
      BT3 radioisotopes
         BT4 isotopes
BT1 days living radioisotopes
   BT2 radioisotopes
      BT3 isotopes
BT1 even-even nuclei
   BT2 nuclei
BT1 intermediate mass nuclei
   BT2 nuclei
BT1 tellurium isotopes
RT radioisotope generators

TELLURIUM 133 [39; 39]
BT1 beta-minus decay radioisotopes
   BT2 beta decay radioisotopes
      BT3 radioisotopes
         BT4 isotopes
BT1 even-odd nuclei
   BT2 nuclei
BT1 intermediate mass nuclei
   BT2 nuclei
BT1 isomeric transition isotopes
   BT2 radioisotopes
      BT3 isotopes
BT1 minutes living radioisotopes
   BT2 radioisotopes
      BT3 isotopes
BT1 tellurium isotopes

TELLURIUM 134 [71; 71]
BT1 beta-minus decay radioisotopes
   BT2 beta decay radioisotopes
      BT3 radioisotopes
         BT4 isotopes
BT1 even-even nuclei
   BT2 nuclei
BT1 intermediate mass nuclei
   BT2 nuclei
BT1 minutes living radioisotopes
   BT2 radioisotopes
      BT3 isotopes
BT1 tellurium isotopes

TELLURIUM 135 [28; 28]
BT1 beta-minus decay radioisotopes
   BT2 beta decay radioisotopes
      BT3 radioisotopes
         BT4 isotopes
BT1 even-odd nuclei
   BT2 nuclei
BT1 intermediate mass nuclei
   BT2 nuclei
BT1 seconds living radioisotopes
   BT2 radioisotopes
      BT3 isotopes
BT1 tellurium isotopes

TELLURIUM 136 [20; 20]
BT1 beta-minus decay radioisotopes
   BT2 beta decay radioisotopes
      BT3 radioisotopes
         BT4 isotopes
BT1 even-even nuclei
   BT2 nuclei
BT1 intermediate mass nuclei
   BT2 nuclei
BT1 seconds living radioisotopes
   BT2 radioisotopes
      BT3 isotopes
BT1 tellurium isotopes

TELLURIUM 137 [10; 10]
BT1 beta-minus decay radioisotopes
   BT2 beta decay radioisotopes
      BT3 radioisotopes
         BT4 isotopes
BT1 even-odd nuclei
   BT2 nuclei
BT1 intermediate mass nuclei
   BT2 nuclei
BT1 seconds living radioisotopes
   BT2 radioisotopes
      BT3 isotopes
BT1 tellurium isotopes

TELLURIUM 138 [2; 2] *Mar 76*
BT1 beta-minus decay radioisotopes
   BT2 beta decay radioisotopes
      BT3 radioisotopes
         BT4 isotopes
BT1 even-even nuclei
   BT2 nuclei
BT1 intermediate mass nuclei
   BT2 nuclei
BT1 seconds living radioisotopes
   BT2 radioisotopes
      BT3 isotopes
BT1 tellurium isotopes

TELOMERIZATION [79; 79]
BT1 polymerization
   BT2 chemical reactions

telophase
   USE mitosis

tem
   USE alkylating agents

tem (microscopy)
   USE transmission electron microsco

TEMELIN-1 REACTOR [139; 139]
Sep 86
BT1 wwer type reactors
   BT2 pwr type reactors
      BT3 enriched uranium reactors
         BT4 reactors
      BT3 power reactors
         BT4 reactors
      BT3 thermal reactors
         BT4 reactors
      BT3 water cooled reactors
         BT4 reactors
      BT3 water moderated reactors
         BT4 reactors

temperature (body)
   USE body temperature

temperature (debye)
   USE debye temperature

temperature (electron)
   USE electron temperature

temperature (ion)
   USE ion temperature

temperature (neutron)
   USE neutron temperature

temperature (nuclear)
   USE nuclear temperature

temperature (photon)
   USE photon temperature

temperature (proton)
   USE proton temperature

temperature (transition)
   USE transition temperature

temperature (0 k)
   USE absolute zero temperature

temperature (0000-0013 k)
   USE ultralow temperature

temperature (0013-0065 k)
   USE very low temperature

temperature (0065-0273 k)
   USE low temperature

temperature (0273-0400 k)
   USE medium temperature

temperature (0400-1000 k)
   USE high temperature

temperature (1000-4000 k)
   USE very high temperature

temperature (4000 k and above)
   USE ultrahigh temperature

TEMPERATURE COEFFICIENT
[664; 664]
BT1 reactivity coefficients
RT doppler coefficient
RT temperature dependence

TEMPERATURE CONTROL
[1,313; 1,313]
UF+ *thermoregulation*
BT1 control
RT air conditioning
RT cooling
RT heating
RT temperature measurement
RT temperature monitoring
RT thermal insulation
RT thermostats

§§ **TEMPERATURE DEPENDENCE**
[74,271; 74,271]
UF *temperature effects*
UF+ *pyroelectricity*
RT absolute zero temperature
RT biological adaptation
RT high temperature
RT low temperature
RT medium temperature
RT temperature coefficient
RT temperature distribution
RT thermoelasticity
RT ultrahigh temperature
RT ultralow temperature
RT vernalization
RT very high temperature
RT very low temperature

TEMPERATURE DISTRIBUTION
[3,589; 3,589]
(Coordinate with the temperature range involved, e.g. MEDIUM TEMPERATURE. Prior to January 1983 the temperature range was coordinated with SPATIAL DISTRIBUTION.)
RT spatial distribution
RT temperature dependence
RT temperature gradients

temperature effects
   USE temperature dependence

TEMPERATURE GRADIENTS
[1,120; 1,120]
(Coordinate with the temperature range involved, e.g. HIGH TEMPERATURE. Prior to June 1986 this concept was expressed with the aid of TEMPERATURE DISTRIBUTION or SPATIAL DISTRIBUTION.)
- UF *thermal gradients*
- RT onsager relations
- RT temperature distribution

TEMPERATURE INVERSIONS [65; 65]
Oct 76
(Meteorological phenomena whereby warmer air layers at higher altitudes produce a closed stable air layer at lower altitudes.)
- UF *inversions (temperature)*
- RT air pollution
- RT earth atmosphere
- RT meteorology

TEMPERATURE MEASUREMENT
[4,132; 4,132]
- RT bolometers
- RT calorimeters
- RT calorimetry
- RT isotherms
- RT measuring instruments
- RT noise thermometers
- RT optical pyrometers
- RT pyrometers
- RT temperature control
- RT temperature monitoring
- RT thermocouples
- RT thermography
- RT thermometers

TEMPERATURE MONITORING
[733; 733]
- BT1 monitoring
- RT in core instruments
- RT infrared thermography
- RT reactor monitoring systems
- RT temperature control
- RT temperature measurement

TEMPERATURE NOISE [380; 380]
- BT1 noise
- RT cooling
- RT transients
- RT variations

TEMPERING [1,032; 1,032]
- BT1 heat treatments

TEMPORAL DOSE DISTRIBUTIONS
[538; 538]
- BT1 radiation dose distributions
- RT chronic irradiation
- RT cumulative radiation effects
- RT dose rates
- RT fractionated irradiation
- RT integral doses
- RT irradiation procedures
- RT pulsed irradiation
- RT time dependence

tendons
- USE muscles

tenelon
- USE steel-cr17mn15nni

tenn. val. author. react.-1
- USE tva-1 reactor

tenn. val. author. react.-2
- USE tva-2 reactor

TENNESSEE [378; 378]
- BT1 usa
- BT2 developed countries
- BT2 north america
- RT clinch river
- RT oak ridge reservation
- RT orgdp
- RT ornl
- RT y-12 plant

TENNESSEE RIVER [22; 22]
- BT1 rivers
- BT2 surface waters

TENNESSEE VALLEY AUTHORITY
[154; 154] *Jan 77*
- UF *tva*
- BT1 us organizations
- BT2 national organizations

TENSILE PROPERTIES [7,662; 12,802]
- UF *strength (tensile)*
- UF *tensile strength*
- BT1 mechanical properties
- NT1 ductility
- NT1 flexibility
- RT compression strength
- RT shear
- RT strain rate
- RT strains
- RT stresses
- RT ultimate strength
- RT yield strength

tensile strength
- USE tensile properties

tension (surface)
- USE surface tension

TENSOR DOMINANCE MODEL
[30; 30]
- UF *tensor meson dominance*
- BT1 particle models
- BT2 mathematical models
- RT tensor mesons

TENSOR FORCES [1,042; 1,042]
- RT nuclear forces
- RT potentials
- RT tensors
- RT vectors

tensor meson dominance
- USE tensor dominance model

TENSOR MESONS [407; 653]
(Mesons with spin higher than 1.)
- BT1 mesons
- BT2 bosons
- BT2 hadrons
- BT3 elementary particles
- NT1 a2-1320 mesons
- NT1 a3-2050 mesons
- NT1 a4-2040 mesons
- NT1 a6-2450 mesons
- NT1 chi2-3555 mesons
- NT1 f2-1270 mesons
- NT1 f2-1410 mesons
- NT1 f2-1525 mesons
- NT1 f2-1720 mesons
- NT1 f2-1810 mesons
- NT1 f2-2150 mesons
- NT1 f2-2240 mesons
- NT1 f4-2030 mesons
- NT1 f4-2300 mesons
- NT1 f6-2510 mesons
- NT1 k*2-1430 mesons
- NT1 k*3-1780 mesons
- NT1 k*4-2060 mesons
- NT1 k2-1580 mesons
- NT1 k2-1770 mesons
- NT1 k2-2250 mesons
- NT1 k3-2320 mesons
- NT1 k4-2500 mesons
- NT1 omega3-1670 mesons
- NT1 phi j-1850 mesons
- NT1 pi2-1680 mesons
- NT1 pi2-2100 mesons
- NT1 rho3-1690 mesons
- NT1 rho3-2250 mesons
- NT1 rho5-2350 mesons
- RT noncentral forces
- RT tensor dominance model

TENSORS [4,064; 8,138]
- NT1 dielectric tensor
- NT1 energy-momentum tensor
- NT1 ricci tensor
- NT1 vectors
- NT2 isovectors
- RT mathematics
- RT metrics
- RT scalars
- RT tensor forces

teollisuuden voima oy-1 react.
- USE tvo-1 reactor

teollisuuden voima oy-2 react.
- USE tvo-2 reactor

TERATOGENESIS [301; 301]
- RT biological radiation effects
- RT congenital malformations
- RT growth
- RT teratogens

TERATOGENS [18; 18] *Sep 83*
- RT carcinogens
- RT congenital malformations
- RT drugs
- RT fetuses
- RT genetic effects
- RT ionizing radiations
- RT mutagens
- RT neonates
- RT teratogenesis

TERAWATT POWER RANGE [17; 17]
Apr 88
- BT1 power range

TERBIUM [906; 906]
- BT1 rare earths
- BT2 metals
- BT3 elements

TERBIUM ADDITIONS [94; 94]
(Alloys containing not more than 1% T are listed here.)
- BT1 rare earth additions
- RT terbium alloys
- RT terbium compounds

TERBIUM ALLOYS [844; 903]
(Alloys containing more than 1% Tb.)
- BT1 rare earth alloys
- BT2 alloys
- NT1 terbium base alloys
- RT terbium additions

TERBIUM ARSENIDES [2; 2] *Jan 77*
- BT1 arsenides
- BT2 arsenic compounds
- BT2 pnictides
- BT1 terbium compounds
- BT2 rare earth compounds

TERBIUM BASE ALLOYS [52; 52]
- BT1 terbium alloys
- BT2 rare earth alloys
- BT3 alloys

TERBIUM BORIDES [25; 25]
BT1 borides
BT2 boron compounds
BT1 terbium compounds
BT2 rare earth compounds

TERBIUM BROMIDES [13; 13]
BT1 bromides
BT2 bromine compounds
BT3 halogen compounds
BT2 halides
BT3 halogen compounds
BT1 terbium compounds
BT2 rare earth compounds

TERBIUM CARBIDES [13; 13]
BT1 carbides
BT2 carbon compounds
BT1 terbium compounds
BT2 rare earth compounds

TERBIUM CARBONATES [8; 8]
BT1 carbonates
BT2 carbon compounds
BT2 oxygen compounds
BT1 terbium compounds
BT2 rare earth compounds

TERBIUM CHLORIDES [63; 63]
BT1 chlorides
BT2 chlorine compounds
BT3 halogen compounds
BT2 halides
BT3 halogen compounds
BT1 terbium compounds
BT2 rare earth compounds

TERBIUM COMPLEXES [323; 323]
BT1 rare earth complexes
BT2 complexes

TERBIUM COMPOUNDS [506; 1,096]
BT1 rare earth compounds
NT1 terbium arsenides
NT1 terbium borides
NT1 terbium bromides
NT1 terbium carbides
NT1 terbium carbonates
NT1 terbium chlorides
NT1 terbium fluorides
NT1 terbium hydrides
NT1 terbium hydroxides
NT1 terbium iodides
NT1 terbium nitrates
NT1 terbium nitrides
NT1 terbium oxides
NT1 terbium perchlorates
NT1 terbium phosphates
NT1 terbium phosphides
NT1 terbium selenides
NT1 terbium silicides
NT1 terbium sulfates
NT1 terbium sulfides
NT1 terbium tellurides
RT terbium additions

TERBIUM FLUORIDES [84; 84]
BT1 fluorides
BT2 fluorine compounds
BT3 halogen compounds
BT2 halides
BT3 halogen compounds
BT1 terbium compounds
BT2 rare earth compounds

TERBIUM HYDRIDES [18; 18]
BT1 hydrides
BT2 hydrogen compounds
BT1 terbium compounds
BT2 rare earth compounds

TERBIUM HYDROXIDES [12; 12]
BT1 hydroxides
BT2 hydrogen compounds
BT2 oxygen compounds
BT1 terbium compounds
BT2 rare earth compounds

TERBIUM IODIDES [12; 12]
BT1 iodides
BT2 halides
BT3 halogen compounds
BT2 iodine compounds
BT3 halogen compounds
BT1 terbium compounds
BT2 rare earth compounds

TERBIUM IONS [167; 167]
BT1 ions
BT2 charged particles

TERBIUM ISOTOPES [76; 963]
NT1 terbium 140
NT1 terbium 141
NT1 terbium 143
NT1 terbium 144
NT1 terbium 145
NT1 terbium 146
NT1 terbium 147
NT1 terbium 148
NT1 terbium 149
NT1 terbium 150
NT1 terbium 151
NT1 terbium 152
NT1 terbium 153
NT1 terbium 154
NT1 terbium 155
NT1 terbium 156
NT1 terbium 157
NT1 terbium 158
NT1 terbium 159
NT1 terbium 160
NT1 terbium 161
NT1 terbium 162
NT1 terbium 163
NT1 terbium 164
NT1 terbium 165

TERBIUM NITRATES [20; 20]
BT1 nitrates
BT2 nitrogen compounds
BT2 oxygen compounds
BT1 terbium compounds
BT2 rare earth compounds

TERBIUM NITRIDES [3; 3]
BT1 nitrides
BT2 nitrogen compounds
BT2 pnictides
BT1 terbium compounds
BT2 rare earth compounds

TERBIUM OXIDES [236; 236]
BT1 oxides
BT2 chalcogenides
BT2 oxygen compounds
BT1 terbium compounds
BT2 rare earth compounds

TERBIUM PERCHLORATES [6; 6]
BT1 perchlorates
BT2 chlorine compounds
BT3 halogen compounds
BT2 oxygen compounds
BT1 terbium compounds
BT2 rare earth compounds

TERBIUM PHOSPHATES [39; 39]
BT1 phosphates
BT2 oxygen compounds
BT2 phosphorus compounds
BT1 terbium compounds
BT2 rare earth compounds

TERBIUM PHOSPHIDES [8; 8] *Jan 77*
BT1 phosphides
BT2 phosphorus compounds
BT2 pnictides
BT1 terbium compounds
BT2 rare earth compounds

TERBIUM SELENIDES [7; 7] *Mar 85*
BT1 selenides
BT2 chalcogenides
BT2 selenium compounds
BT1 terbium compounds
BT2 rare earth compounds

TERBIUM SILICIDES [26; 26]
BT1 silicides
BT2 silicon compounds
BT1 terbium compounds
BT2 rare earth compounds

TERBIUM SULFATES [17; 17]
BT1 sulfates
BT2 oxygen compounds
BT2 sulfur compounds
BT1 terbium compounds
BT2 rare earth compounds

TERBIUM SULFIDES [28; 28]
BT1 sulfides
BT2 chalcogenides
BT2 sulfur compounds
BT1 terbium compounds
BT2 rare earth compounds

TERBIUM TELLURIDES [11; 11]
Feb 78
BT1 tellurides
BT2 chalcogenides
BT2 tellurium compounds
BT1 terbium compounds
BT2 rare earth compounds

TERBIUM 140 [4; 4] *Feb 87*
BT1 odd-odd nuclei
BT2 nuclei
BT1 rare earth nuclei
BT2 intermediate mass nuclei
BT3 nuclei
BT1 seconds living radioisotopes
BT2 radioisotopes
BT3 isotopes
BT1 terbium isotopes

TERBIUM 141 [3; 3] *Apr 88*
BT1 beta-plus decay radioisotopes
BT2 beta decay radioisotopes
BT3 radioisotopes
BT4 isotopes
BT1 electron capture radioisotopes
BT2 beta decay radioisotopes
BT3 radioisotopes
BT4 isotopes
BT1 odd-even nuclei
BT2 nuclei
BT1 rare earth nuclei
BT2 intermediate mass nuclei
BT3 nuclei
BT1 seconds living radioisotopes
BT2 radioisotopes
BT3 isotopes
BT1 terbium isotopes

TERBIUM 143 [9; 9] *Jun 85*
BT1 beta-plus decay radioisotopes
BT2 beta decay radioisotopes
BT3 radioisotopes
BT4 isotopes
BT1 electron capture radioisotopes
BT2 beta decay radioisotopes
BT3 radioisotopes
BT4 isotopes
BT1 odd-even nuclei
BT2 nuclei
BT1 rare earth nuclei
BT2 intermediate mass nuclei
BT3 nuclei
BT1 seconds living radioisotopes
BT2 radioisotopes
BT3 isotopes
BT1 terbium isotopes

TERBIUM 144 [7; 7] *Jun 82*
- BT1 beta-plus decay radioisotopes
- BT2 beta decay radioisotopes
- BT3 radioisotopes
- BT4 isotopes
- BT1 electron capture radioisotopes
- BT2 beta decay radioisotopes
- BT3 radioisotopes
- BT4 isotopes
- BT1 isomeric transition isotopes
- BT2 radioisotopes
- BT3 isotopes
- BT1 odd-odd nuclei
- BT2 nuclei
- BT1 rare earth nuclei
- BT2 intermediate mass nuclei
- BT3 nuclei
- BT1 seconds living radioisotopes
- BT2 radioisotopes
- BT3 isotopes
- BT1 terbium isotopes

TERBIUM 145 [10; 10] *Jun 82*
- BT1 beta-plus decay radioisotopes
- BT2 beta decay radioisotopes
- BT3 radioisotopes
- BT4 isotopes
- BT1 odd-even nuclei
- BT2 nuclei
- BT1 rare earth nuclei
- BT2 intermediate mass nuclei
- BT3 nuclei
- BT1 seconds living radioisotopes
- BT2 radioisotopes
- BT3 isotopes
- BT1 terbium isotopes

TERBIUM 146 [30; 30]
- BT1 beta-plus decay radioisotopes
- BT2 beta decay radioisotopes
- BT3 radioisotopes
- BT4 isotopes
- BT1 electron capture radioisotopes
- BT2 beta decay radioisotopes
- BT3 radioisotopes
- BT4 isotopes
- BT1 isomeric transition isotopes
- BT2 radioisotopes
- BT3 isotopes
- BT1 millisec living radioisotopes
- BT2 radioisotopes
- BT3 isotopes
- BT1 odd-odd nuclei
- BT2 nuclei
- BT1 rare earth nuclei
- BT2 intermediate mass nuclei
- BT3 nuclei
- BT1 seconds living radioisotopes
- BT2 radioisotopes
- BT3 isotopes
- BT1 terbium isotopes

TERBIUM 147 [80; 80]
- BT1 beta-plus decay radioisotopes
- BT2 beta decay radioisotopes
- BT3 radioisotopes
- BT4 isotopes
- BT1 electron capture radioisotopes
- BT2 beta decay radioisotopes
- BT3 radioisotopes
- BT4 isotopes
- BT1 hours living radioisotopes
- BT2 radioisotopes
- BT3 isotopes
- BT1 minutes living radioisotopes
- BT2 radioisotopes
- BT3 isotopes
- BT1 odd-even nuclei
- BT2 nuclei
- BT1 rare earth nuclei
- BT2 intermediate mass nuclei
- BT3 nuclei
- BT1 terbium isotopes

TERBIUM 148 [63; 63]
- BT1 beta-plus decay radioisotopes
- BT2 beta decay radioisotopes
- BT3 radioisotopes
- BT4 isotopes
- BT1 electron capture radioisotopes
- BT2 beta decay radioisotopes
- BT3 radioisotopes
- BT4 isotopes
- BT1 hours living radioisotopes
- BT2 radioisotopes
- BT3 isotopes
- BT1 minutes living radioisotopes
- BT2 radioisotopes
- BT3 isotopes
- BT1 odd-odd nuclei
- BT2 nuclei
- BT1 rare earth nuclei
- BT2 intermediate mass nuclei
- BT3 nuclei
- BT1 terbium isotopes

TERBIUM 149 [86; 86]
- BT1 alpha decay radioisotopes
- BT2 radioisotopes
- BT3 isotopes
- BT1 beta-plus decay radioisotopes
- BT2 beta decay radioisotopes
- BT3 radioisotopes
- BT4 isotopes
- BT1 electron capture radioisotopes
- BT2 beta decay radioisotopes
- BT3 radioisotopes
- BT4 isotopes
- BT1 hours living radioisotopes
- BT2 radioisotopes
- BT3 isotopes
- BT1 minutes living radioisotopes
- BT2 radioisotopes
- BT3 isotopes
- BT1 odd-even nuclei
- BT2 nuclei
- BT1 rare earth nuclei
- BT2 intermediate mass nuclei
- BT3 nuclei
- BT1 terbium isotopes

TERBIUM 150 [41; 41]
- BT1 beta-plus decay radioisotopes
- BT2 beta decay radioisotopes
- BT3 radioisotopes
- BT4 isotopes
- BT1 electron capture radioisotopes
- BT2 beta decay radioisotopes
- BT3 radioisotopes
- BT4 isotopes
- BT1 hours living radioisotopes
- BT2 radioisotopes
- BT3 isotopes
- BT1 minutes living radioisotopes
- BT2 radioisotopes
- BT3 isotopes
- BT1 odd-odd nuclei
- BT2 nuclei
- BT1 rare earth nuclei
- BT2 intermediate mass nuclei
- BT3 nuclei
- BT1 terbium isotopes

TERBIUM 151 [60; 60]
- BT1 alpha decay radioisotopes
- BT2 radioisotopes
- BT3 isotopes
- BT1 beta-plus decay radioisotopes
- BT2 beta decay radioisotopes
- BT3 radioisotopes
- BT4 isotopes
- BT1 electron capture radioisotopes
- BT2 beta decay radioisotopes
- BT3 radioisotopes
- BT4 isotopes
- BT1 hours living radioisotopes
- BT2 radioisotopes
- BT3 isotopes
- BT1 internal conversion radioisoto
- BT2 radioisotopes
- BT3 isotopes
- BT1 isomeric transition isotopes
- BT2 radioisotopes
- BT3 isotopes
- BT1 odd-even nuclei
- BT2 nuclei
- BT1 rare earth nuclei
- BT2 intermediate mass nuclei
- BT3 nuclei
- BT1 seconds living radioisotopes
- BT2 radioisotopes
- BT3 isotopes
- BT1 terbium isotopes

TERBIUM 152 [28; 28]
- BT1 beta-plus decay radioisotopes
- BT2 beta decay radioisotopes
- BT3 radioisotopes
- BT4 isotopes
- BT1 electron capture radioisotopes
- BT2 beta decay radioisotopes
- BT3 radioisotopes
- BT4 isotopes
- BT1 hours living radioisotopes
- BT2 radioisotopes
- BT3 isotopes
- BT1 isomeric transition isotopes
- BT2 radioisotopes
- BT3 isotopes
- BT1 minutes living radioisotopes
- BT2 radioisotopes
- BT3 isotopes
- BT1 odd-odd nuclei
- BT2 nuclei
- BT1 rare earth nuclei
- BT2 intermediate mass nuclei
- BT3 nuclei
- BT1 terbium isotopes

TERBIUM 153 [80; 80]
- BT1 beta-plus decay radioisotopes
- BT2 beta decay radioisotopes
- BT3 radioisotopes
- BT4 isotopes
- BT1 days living radioisotopes
- BT2 radioisotopes
- BT3 isotopes
- BT1 electron capture radioisotopes
- BT2 beta decay radioisotopes
- BT3 radioisotopes
- BT4 isotopes
- BT1 odd-even nuclei
- BT2 nuclei
- BT1 rare earth nuclei
- BT2 intermediate mass nuclei
- BT3 nuclei
- BT1 terbium isotopes

TERBIUM 154 [27; 27]
- BT1 beta-plus decay radioisotopes
- BT2 beta decay radioisotopes
- BT3 radioisotopes
- BT4 isotopes
- BT1 electron capture radioisotopes
- BT2 beta decay radioisotopes
- BT3 radioisotopes
- BT4 isotopes
- BT1 hours living radioisotopes
- BT2 radioisotopes
- BT3 isotopes
- BT1 isomeric transition isotopes
- BT2 radioisotopes
- BT3 isotopes
- BT1 odd-odd nuclei
- BT2 nuclei
- BT1 rare earth nuclei
- BT2 intermediate mass nuclei
- BT3 nuclei
- BT1 terbium isotopes

TERBIUM 155 [66; 66]
- BT1 days living radioisotopes
- BT2 radioisotopes
- BT3 isotopes
- BT1 electron capture radioisotopes
- BT2 beta decay radioisotopes
- BT3 radioisotopes
- BT4 isotopes
- BT1 odd-even nuclei
- BT2 nuclei
- BT1 rare earth nuclei
- BT2 intermediate mass nuclei

BT3 nuclei
BT1 terbium isotopes

TERBIUM 156 [32; 32]
BT1 beta-minus decay radioisotopes
BT2 beta decay radioisotopes
BT3 radioisotopes
BT4 isotopes
BT1 beta-plus decay radioisotopes
BT2 beta decay radioisotopes
BT3 radioisotopes
BT4 isotopes
BT1 days living radioisotopes
BT2 radioisotopes
BT3 isotopes
BT1 electron capture radioisotopes
BT2 beta decay radioisotopes
BT3 radioisotopes
BT4 isotopes
BT1 hours living radioisotopes
BT2 radioisotopes
BT3 isotopes
BT1 isomeric transition isotopes
BT2 radioisotopes
BT3 isotopes
BT1 odd-odd nuclei
BT2 nuclei
BT1 rare earth nuclei
BT2 intermediate mass nuclei
BT3 nuclei
BT1 terbium isotopes

TERBIUM 157 [48; 48]
BT1 electron capture radioisotopes
BT2 beta decay radioisotopes
BT3 radioisotopes
BT4 isotopes
BT1 internal conversion radioisoto
BT2 radioisotopes
BT3 isotopes
BT1 odd-even nuclei
BT2 nuclei
BT1 rare earth nuclei
BT2 intermediate mass nuclei
BT3 nuclei
BT1 terbium isotopes
BT1 years living radioisotopes
BT2 radioisotopes
BT3 isotopes

TERBIUM 158 [40; 40]
BT1 beta-minus decay radioisotopes
BT2 beta decay radioisotopes
BT3 radioisotopes
BT4 isotopes
BT1 electron capture radioisotopes
BT2 beta decay radioisotopes
BT3 radioisotopes
BT4 isotopes
BT1 internal conversion radioisoto
BT2 radioisotopes
BT3 isotopes
BT1 isomeric transition isotopes
BT2 radioisotopes
BT3 isotopes
BT1 odd-odd nuclei
BT2 nuclei
BT1 rare earth nuclei
BT2 intermediate mass nuclei
BT3 nuclei
BT1 seconds living radioisotopes
BT2 radioisotopes
BT3 isotopes
BT1 terbium isotopes
BT1 years living radioisotopes
BT2 radioisotopes
BT3 isotopes

TERBIUM 159 [133; 133]
BT1 odd-even nuclei
BT2 nuclei
BT1 rare earth nuclei
BT2 intermediate mass nuclei
BT3 nuclei
BT1 stable isotopes
BT2 isotopes
BT1 terbium isotopes

TERBIUM 159 TARGET [266; 266]
BT1 targets

TERBIUM 160 [187; 187]
BT1 beta-minus decay radioisotopes
BT2 beta decay radioisotopes
BT3 radioisotopes
BT4 isotopes
BT1 days living radioisotopes
BT2 radioisotopes
BT3 isotopes
BT1 odd-odd nuclei
BT2 nuclei
BT1 rare earth nuclei
BT2 intermediate mass nuclei
BT3 nuclei
BT1 terbium isotopes

TERBIUM 160 TARGET [4; 4] *Apr 79*
BT1 targets

TERBIUM 161 [43; 43]
BT1 beta-minus decay radioisotopes
BT2 beta decay radioisotopes
BT3 radioisotopes
BT4 isotopes
BT1 days living radioisotopes
BT2 radioisotopes
BT3 isotopes
BT1 odd-even nuclei
BT2 nuclei
BT1 rare earth nuclei
BT2 intermediate mass nuclei
BT3 nuclei
BT1 terbium isotopes

TERBIUM 162 [9; 9]
BT1 beta-minus decay radioisotopes
BT2 beta decay radioisotopes
BT3 radioisotopes
BT4 isotopes
BT1 minutes living radioisotopes
BT2 radioisotopes
BT3 isotopes
BT1 odd-odd nuclei
BT2 nuclei
BT1 rare earth nuclei
BT2 intermediate mass nuclei
BT3 nuclei
BT1 terbium isotopes

TERBIUM 163 [5; 5]
BT1 beta-minus decay radioisotopes
BT2 beta decay radioisotopes
BT3 radioisotopes
BT4 isotopes
BT1 minutes living radioisotopes
BT2 radioisotopes
BT3 isotopes
BT1 odd-even nuclei
BT2 nuclei
BT1 rare earth nuclei
BT2 intermediate mass nuclei
BT3 nuclei
BT1 terbium isotopes

TERBIUM 164 [1; 1]
BT1 beta-minus decay radioisotopes
BT2 beta decay radioisotopes
BT3 radioisotopes
BT4 isotopes
BT1 minutes living radioisotopes
BT2 radioisotopes
BT3 isotopes
BT1 odd-odd nuclei
BT2 nuclei
BT1 rare earth nuclei
BT2 intermediate mass nuclei
BT3 nuclei
BT1 terbium isotopes

TERBIUM 165 [0; 0] *Apr 86*
BT1 beta-minus decay radioisotopes
BT2 beta decay radioisotopes
BT3 radioisotopes
BT4 isotopes
BT1 minutes living radioisotopes

BT2 radioisotopes
BT3 isotopes
BT1 odd-even nuclei
BT2 nuclei
BT1 rare earth nuclei
BT2 intermediate mass nuclei
BT3 nuclei
BT1 terbium isotopes

TEREPHTHALIC ACID [58; 58]
UF *benzenedicarboxylic acid-para*
BT1 dicarboxylic acids
BT2 carboxylic acids
BT3 organic acids
BT4 organic compounds
RT dacron

TERNARY ALLOY SYSTEMS
[3,287; 3,287]
BT1 alloy systems

TERNARY FISSION [316; 316]
BT1 fission
BT2 nuclear reactions

TERPENES [237; 451]
BT1 organic compounds
NT1 camphene
NT1 camphor
NT1 carotenoids
NT1 geraniol
NT1 squalene
NT1 turpentine
RT oils

TERPHENYL-META [6; 6]
BT1 terphenyls
BT2 polyphenyls
BT3 aromatics
BT4 organic compounds
BT3 hydrocarbons
BT4 organic compounds

TERPHENYL-ORTHO [7; 7]
BT1 terphenyls
BT2 polyphenyls
BT3 aromatics
BT4 organic compounds
BT3 hydrocarbons
BT4 organic compounds

TERPHENYL-PARA [50; 50]
BT1 terphenyls
BT2 polyphenyls
BT3 aromatics
BT4 organic compounds
BT3 hydrocarbons
BT4 organic compounds

TERPHENYLS [58; 113]
BT1 polyphenyls
BT2 aromatics
BT3 organic compounds
BT2 hydrocarbons
BT3 organic compounds
NT1 terphenyl-meta
NT1 terphenyl-ortho
NT1 terphenyl-para
RT liquid scintillators
RT plastic scintillators

terramycin
USE oxytetracycline

terrestrial background
USE background radiation

TERRESTRIAL ECOSYSTEMS
[1,084; 1,084]
BT1 ecosystems
RT deserts
RT forests
RT islands
RT soils

RT tundra

territorial seas
USE territorial waters

TERRITORIAL WATERS [14; 14]
(Waters under the sovereign jurisdiction of a nation or state including both marginal sea and inland waters.)
UF *territorial seas*
RT coastal waters
RT continental shelf
RT fishery laws
RT high seas
RT inland waterways
RT maritime laws
RT nuclear ship visits
RT offshore sites
RT seas

→ *tertiary recovery*
USE enhanced recovery

terylene
USE dacron

TEST FACILITIES [1,599; 3,236]
May 86
UF *facilities (test)*
NT1 test reactors
NT2 aipfr reactor
NT2 arbus reactor
NT2 astra reactor
NT2 atr reactor
NT2 barn reactor
NT2 bawtr reactor
NT2 bgrr reactor
NT2 br-02 reactor
NT2 brr reactor
NT2 cesnef reactor
NT2 cirus reactor
NT2 cp-5 reactor
NT2 dhruva reactor
NT2 dimple reactor
NT2 diorit reactor
NT2 ebor reactor
NT2 ebr-1 reactor
NT2 eco reactor
NT2 eocr reactor
NT2 esada-vesr reactor
NT2 essor reactor
NT2 etr reactor
NT2 fftf reactor
NT2 fir-1 reactor
NT2 fmrb reactor
NT2 fnr reactor
NT2 fr-2 reactor
NT2 frctf reactor
NT2 frg-1 reactor
NT2 frn reactor
NT2 getr reactor
NT2 grenoble reactor
NT2 gtr reactor
NT2 gtrr reactor
NT2 harmonie reactor
NT2 herald reactor
NT2 hero reactor
NT2 hfir reactor
NT2 hifar reactor
NT2 htltr reactor
NT2 irl reactor
NT2 irr-1 reactor
NT2 irt-baghdad reactor
NT2 irt-2000 djakarta reactor
NT2 irt-2000 moscow reactor
NT2 ispra-1 reactor
NT2 jmtr reactor
NT2 kalpakkam lmfbr reactor
NT2 kmr reactor
NT2 loft reactor
NT2 mzfr reactor
NT2 nru reactor
NT2 ntr reactor
NT2 orphee reactor
NT2 owr reactor
NT2 pegase reactor
NT2 proteus reactor
NT2 ra-3 reactor
NT2 ra-5 reactor
NT2 rapsodie reactor
NT2 rts-1 reactor
NT2 safari-1 reactor
NT2 sbr-5 reactor
NT2 snaptran reactors
NT2 stf reactor
NT2 s1c prototype reactor
NT2 tapiro reactor
NT2 tory-2c reactor
NT2 treat reactor
NT2 triga-1-michigan reactor
NT2 triga-2-pavia reactor
NT2 tsr-1 reactor
NT2 tsr-2 reactor
NT2 urr reactor
NT2 uvar reactor
NT2 viper reactor
NT2 wr-1 reactor
NT2 wtr reactor
NT1 tonopah test range
NT1 tritium systems test assembly
RT laboratories
RT laboratory equipment
RT mockup
RT nuclear facilities
RT testing

test fast breeder r. kalpakkam
USE kalpakkam lmfbr reactor

→ *test heating reactor*
USE thr reactor

TEST PARTICLES [502; 502]
RT charged particles

TEST REACTORS [231; 6,157]
(A facility to test the technical feasibility of a concept or to provide the technical basis for a similar facility in a larger size.)
BT1 research and test reactors
BT2 reactors
BT1 test facilities
NT1 aipfr reactor
NT1 arbus reactor
NT1 astra reactor
NT1 atr reactor
NT1 barn reactor
NT1 bawtr reactor
NT1 bgrr reactor
NT1 br-02 reactor
NT1 brr reactor
NT1 cesnef reactor
NT1 cirus reactor
NT1 cp-5 reactor
NT1 dhruva reactor
NT1 dimple reactor
NT1 diorit reactor
NT1 ebor reactor
NT1 ebr-1 reactor
NT1 eco reactor
NT1 eocr reactor
NT1 esada-vesr reactor
NT1 essor reactor
NT1 etr reactor
NT1 fftf reactor
NT1 fir-1 reactor
NT1 fmrb reactor
NT1 fnr reactor
NT1 fr-2 reactor
NT1 frctf reactor
NT1 frg-1 reactor
NT1 frn reactor
NT1 getr reactor
NT1 grenoble reactor
NT1 gtr reactor
NT1 gtrr reactor
NT1 harmonie reactor
NT1 herald reactor
NT1 hero reactor
NT1 hfir reactor
NT1 hifar reactor
NT1 htltr reactor
NT1 irl reactor
NT1 irr-1 reactor
NT1 irt-baghdad reactor
NT1 irt-2000 djakarta reactor
NT1 irt-2000 moscow reactor
NT1 ispra-1 reactor
NT1 jmtr reactor
NT1 kalpakkam lmfbr reactor
NT1 kmr reactor
NT1 loft reactor
NT1 mzfr reactor
NT1 nru reactor
NT1 ntr reactor
NT1 orphee reactor
NT1 owr reactor
NT1 pegase reactor
NT1 proteus reactor
NT1 ra-3 reactor
NT1 ra-5 reactor
NT1 rapsodie reactor
NT1 rts-1 reactor
NT1 safari-1 reactor
NT1 sbr-5 reactor
NT1 snaptran reactors
NT1 stf reactor
NT1 s1c prototype reactor
NT1 tapiro reactor
NT1 tory-2c reactor
NT1 treat reactor
NT1 triga-1-michigan reactor
NT1 triga-2-pavia reactor
NT1 tsr-1 reactor
NT1 tsr-2 reactor
NT1 urr reactor
NT1 uvar reactor
NT1 viper reactor
NT1 wr-1 reactor
NT1 wtr reactor

TESTES [1,525; 1,525]
BT1 gonads
BT1 male genitals
BT2 organs
BT3 body
RT androgens
RT spermatogenesis

§§ **TESTING** [9,939; 55,607]
NT1 frequency response testing
NT1 leak testing
NT1 materials testing
NT2 destructive testing
NT3 charpy test
NT2 mechanical tests
NT3 impact tests
NT4 charpy test
NT2 nondestructive testing
NT3 acoustic testing
NT4 acoustic emission testing
NT4 ultrasonic testing
NT3 electrical testing
NT3 electromagnetic testing
NT4 eddy current testing
NT3 industrial radiography
NT3 liquid penetrant inspection
NT3 magnetic testing
NT3 radiation attenuation testing
NT3 thermal testing
NT4 frost tests
NT4 thermography
NT1 performance testing
NT2 bioassay
RT bench-scale experiments
RT certification
RT evaluation
RT feasibility studies
RT field tests
RT inspection
RT sampling
RT test facilities

testing (biological)
USE bioassay

TESTOSTERONE [551; 551]
- BT1 androgens
  - BT2 androstanes
    - BT3 steroids
      - BT4 organic compounds
  - BT2 steroid hormones
    - BT3 hormones
- BT1 hydroxy compounds
  - BT2 organic compounds
- BT1 ketones
  - BT2 organic compounds

TETA [11; 11]
- UF *triethylenetetramine*
- BT1 amines
  - BT2 organic compounds

TETAHA [21; 21]
(Triethylenetetraaminehexaacetic acid)
- UF *triethylenetetraaminehexaaceti*
- BT1 amino acids
  - BT2 carboxylic acids
    - BT3 organic acids
      - BT4 organic compounds
- BT1 chelating agents

TETANUS [42; 42]
- BT1 bacterial diseases
  - BT2 infectious diseases
    - BT3 diseases

TETRACENE [28; 28]
- BT1 condensed aromatics
  - BT2 aromatics
    - BT3 organic compounds
- BT1 hydrocarbons
  - BT2 organic compounds

tetrachlorobenzoquinone
- USE chloranil

tetrachloromethane
(Prior to August 1985 this was a valid descriptor.)
- USE carbon tetrachloride

TETRACYCLINES [197; 220]
- BT1 antibiotics
  - BT2 drugs
    - BT2 organic compounds
- NT1 chlortetracycline
- NT1 oxytetracycline

TETRADECANOIC ACID [50; 50]
- UF *myristic acid*
- BT1 monocarboxylic acids
  - BT2 carboxylic acids
    - BT3 organic acids
      - BT4 organic compounds

tetraethyl lead
- USE tel

tetraethylammonium bromide
- USE teab

tetrafluoromethane
(Prior to August 1985 this was a valid descriptor.)
- USE carbon tetrafluoride

TETRAGONAL LATTICES [1,982; 1,982]
- BT1 crystal lattices
  - BT2 crystal structure

TETRAHYDROFURAN [288; 288]
Sep 80
- UF *thf*
- BT1 furans
  - BT2 heterocyclic compounds
    - BT3 organic compounds
  - BT2 organic oxygen compounds
    - BT3 organic compounds

tetrahydronaphthalene
- USE tetralin

TETRAHYDROPYRAN [16; 16]
- BT1 pyrans
  - BT2 heterocyclic compounds
    - BT3 organic compounds
  - BT2 organic oxygen compounds
    - BT3 organic compounds
- RT ethers

tetrahydropyrroles
- USE pyrrolidines

tetrahydroxybutane
- USE erythritol

TETRAHYMENA [79; 79]
- BT1 protozoa
  - BT2 invertebrates
    - BT3 animals
  - BT2 microorganisms

TETRALIN [39; 39]
- UF *tetrahydronaphthalene*
- BT1 aromatics
  - BT2 organic compounds
- BT1 hydrocarbons
  - BT2 organic compounds
- RT naphthalene

tetramethylenediamine
- USE putrescine

tetramethylethylene glycol
- USE pinacol

tetramethyltetraselenafulvalen
- USE tmtsf

TETRANEUTRONS [28; 28]
- BT1 polyneutrons
  - BT2 neutrons
    - BT3 nucleons
      - BT4 baryons
        - BT5 fermions
        - BT5 hadrons
          - BT6 elementary particles

tetraphenylethylene glycol
- USE benzopinacol

tetraploidy
- USE polyploidy

tetrathiafulvalene
- USE heterocyclic compounds
- AND organic sulfur compounds

TETRAZOLES [39; 71]
(Compounds that contain a five-membered heterocyclic ring containing four nitrogen atoms.)
- BT1 azoles
  - BT2 heterocyclic compounds
    - BT3 organic compounds
  - BT2 organic nitrogen compounds
    - BT3 organic compounds
- NT1 tetrazolium

TETRAZOLIUM [32; 32]
- BT1 chlorides
  - BT2 chlorine compounds
    - BT3 halogen compounds
  - BT2 halides
    - BT3 halogen compounds
- BT1 tetrazoles
  - BT2 azoles
    - BT3 heterocyclic compounds
      - BT4 organic compounds
    - BT3 organic nitrogen compounds
      - BT4 organic compounds

TEV RANGE [1,861; 4,410]
(From 10 exp 12 to 10 exp 15 ev.)
- BT1 energy range
- NT1 tev range 01-10
- NT1 tev range 10-100
- NT1 tev range 100-1000

TEV RANGE 01-10 [1,829; 1,829]
Oct 77
- BT1 tev range
  - BT2 energy range

TEV RANGE 10-100 [833; 833] Oct 77
- BT1 tev range
  - BT2 energy range

TEV RANGE 100-1000 [360; 360] Oct 77
- BT1 tev range
  - BT2 energy range

tevatron (fermilab)
- USE fermilab tevatron

TEWA EVENT [2; 2] Jan 85
- BT1 atmospheric explosions
  - BT2 explosions
- BT1 nuclear explosions
  - BT2 explosions
- BT1 redwing project

TEXAS [955; 955]
- BT1 usa
  - BT2 developed countries
  - BT2 north america
- RT pantex plant

TEXAS A AND M CYCLOTRON [85; 85]
- UF *texas a and m var energy cyclo*
- BT1 isochronous cyclotrons
  - BT2 cyclotrons
    - BT3 cyclic accelerators
      - BT4 accelerators

texas a and m k500 cyclotron
(Prior to December 1990, this was a valid descriptor.)
- USE texas superconducting cyclotro

texas a and m var energy cyclo
- USE texas a and m cyclotron

texas college station train. r
- USE nscr reactor

texas experimental tokamak
- USE text devices

texas supercond. cyclotron
- USE texas superconducting cyclotro

TEXAS SUPERCONDUCTING CYCLOTRO [9; 9] *Jun 83*
(Prior to December 1990, this concept was indexed by TEXAS A AND M K500 CYCLOTRON.)
UF *texas a and m k500 cyclotron*
UF *texas supercond. cyclotron*
BT1 heavy ion accelerators
BT2 accelerators
BT1 isochronous cyclotrons
BT2 cyclotrons
BT3 cyclic accelerators
BT4 accelerators
BT1 superconducting cyclotrons
BT2 cyclotrons
BT3 cyclic accelerators
BT4 accelerators

texas univ. triga reactor
USE triga-texas reactor

TEXT DEVICES [295; 295] *Jul 78*
UF *texas experimental tokamak*
BT1 tokamak devices
BT2 closed plasma devices
BT3 thermonuclear devices

TEXTILES [244; 265]
RT clothing
RT cotton
RT dacron
RT fibers
RT jute
RT rayon
RT wool

TEXTOLITE [13; 13]
BT1 organic polymers
BT2 organic compounds
BT2 polymers

TEXTOR TOKAMAK [480; 480] *Sep 77*
(Torus EXperiment for Technology Oriented Research.)
UF *torus exper techn oriented res*
BT1 tokamak devices
BT2 closed plasma devices
BT3 thermonuclear devices

§ **TEXTURE** [1,606; 1,606]
RT crystal structure
RT grain orientation
RT schulz method

TFR TOKAMAK [454; 454]
UF *tokamak fontenay-aux-roses*
BT1 tokamak devices
BT2 closed plasma devices
BT3 thermonuclear devices

tftr device
(Prior to August 1985 this was a valid descriptor.)
USE tftr tokamak

TFTR TOKAMAK [1,630; 1,630] *Nov 77*
(Prior to August 1985 TFTR DEVICE was used.)
UF *tftr device*
UF *tokamak fusion test reactor*
BT1 tokamak devices
BT2 closed plasma devices
BT3 thermonuclear devices

thai research reactor-1
USE trr-1 reactor

THAILAND [89; 89]
BT1 asia
BT1 developing countries

THALAMUS [117; 117]
BT1 brain
BT2 central nervous system
BT3 nervous system
BT2 organs
BT3 body
RT ganglions

THALASSEMIA [59; 59]
BT1 anemias
BT2 hemic diseases
BT3 diseases
BT2 symptoms

THALLIUM [922; 922]
BT1 metals
BT2 elements

THALLIUM ADDITIONS [240; 240]
(Alloys containing not more than 1% Tl are listed here.)
RT thallium alloys
RT thallium compounds

THALLIUM ALLOYS [356; 381]
(Alloys containing more than 1% Tl.)
BT1 alloys
NT1 thallium base alloys
RT thallium additions

THALLIUM BASE ALLOYS [14; 14]
BT1 thallium alloys
BT2 alloys

THALLIUM BROMIDES [56; 56]
BT1 bromides
BT2 bromine compounds
BT3 halogen compounds
BT2 halides
BT3 halogen compounds
BT1 thallium halides
BT2 halides
BT3 halogen compounds
BT2 thallium compounds

THALLIUM CARBIDES [5; 5] *Sep 77*
BT1 carbides
BT2 carbon compounds
BT1 thallium compounds

THALLIUM CARBONATES [7; 7] *Jan 77*
BT1 carbonates
BT2 carbon compounds
BT2 oxygen compounds
BT1 thallium compounds

THALLIUM CHLORIDES [217; 217]
BT1 chlorides
BT2 chlorine compounds
BT3 halogen compounds
BT2 halides
BT3 halogen compounds
BT1 thallium halides
BT2 halides
BT3 halogen compounds
BT2 thallium compounds

THALLIUM COMPLEXES [81; 81]
BT1 complexes

THALLIUM COMPOUNDS [494; 1,452]
NT1 thallium carbides
NT1 thallium carbonates
NT1 thallium halides
NT2 thallium bromides
NT2 thallium chlorides
NT2 thallium fluorides
NT2 thallium iodides
NT1 thallium hydrides
NT1 thallium hydroxides
NT1 thallium nitrates
NT1 thallium oxides
NT1 thallium perchlorates
NT1 thallium phosphates
NT1 thallium selenides
NT1 thallium sulfates
NT1 thallium sulfides
NT1 thallium tellurides
NT1 thallium tungstates
NT1 thallium uranates
RT thallium additions

THALLIUM FLUORIDES [29; 29]
BT1 fluorides
BT2 fluorine compounds
BT3 halogen compounds
BT2 halides
BT3 halogen compounds
BT1 thallium halides
BT2 halides
BT3 halogen compounds
BT2 thallium compounds

THALLIUM HALIDES [2; 139] *Jan 85*
BT1 halides
BT2 halogen compounds
BT1 thallium compounds
NT1 thallium bromides
NT1 thallium chlorides
NT1 thallium fluorides
NT1 thallium iodides

THALLIUM HYDRIDES [5; 5] *Jun 81*
BT1 hydrides
BT2 hydrogen compounds
BT1 thallium compounds

THALLIUM HYDROXIDES [4; 4]
BT1 hydroxides
BT2 hydrogen compounds
BT2 oxygen compounds
BT1 thallium compounds

THALLIUM IODIDES [65; 65]
BT1 iodides
BT2 halides
BT3 halogen compounds
BT2 iodine compounds
BT3 halogen compounds
BT1 thallium halides
BT2 halides
BT3 halogen compounds
BT2 thallium compounds

THALLIUM IONS [168; 168]
BT1 ions
BT2 charged particles

THALLIUM ISOTOPES [326; 5,006]
NT1 thallium 179
NT1 thallium 182
NT1 thallium 184
NT1 thallium 185
NT1 thallium 186
NT1 thallium 187
NT1 thallium 188
NT1 thallium 189
NT1 thallium 190
NT1 thallium 191
NT1 thallium 192
NT1 thallium 193
NT1 thallium 194
NT1 thallium 195
NT1 thallium 196
NT1 thallium 197
NT1 thallium 198
NT1 thallium 199
NT1 thallium 200
NT1 thallium 201
NT1 thallium 202
NT1 thallium 203
NT1 thallium 204
NT1 thallium 205
NT1 thallium 206
NT1 thallium 207
NT1 thallium 208
NT1 thallium 209
NT1 thallium 210

THALLIUM NITRATES [24; 24]
- BT1 nitrates
- BT2 nitrogen compounds
- BT2 oxygen compounds
- BT1 thallium compounds

THALLIUM OXIDES [386; 386]
- BT1 oxides
- BT2 chalcogenides
- BT2 oxygen compounds
- BT1 thallium compounds

THALLIUM PERCHLORATES [4; 4]
- BT1 perchlorates
- BT2 chlorine compounds
- BT3 halogen compounds
- BT2 oxygen compounds
- BT1 thallium compounds

THALLIUM PHOSPHATES [11; 11] Jan 79
- BT1 phosphates
- BT2 oxygen compounds
- BT2 phosphorus compounds
- BT1 thallium compounds

THALLIUM SELENIDES [68; 68] Sep 80
- BT1 selenides
- BT2 chalcogenides
- BT2 selenium compounds
- BT1 thallium compounds

THALLIUM SULFATES [27; 27]
- BT1 sulfates
- BT2 oxygen compounds
- BT2 sulfur compounds
- BT1 thallium compounds

THALLIUM SULFIDES [85; 85]
- BT1 sulfides
- BT2 chalcogenides
- BT2 sulfur compounds
- BT1 thallium compounds

THALLIUM TELLURIDES [86; 86] Sep 79
- BT1 tellurides
- BT2 chalcogenides
- BT2 tellurium compounds
- BT1 thallium compounds

THALLIUM TUNGSTATES [0; 0] Sep 91
- BT1 thallium compounds
- BT1 tungstates
- BT2 oxygen compounds
- BT2 tungsten compounds
- BT3 transition element compounds

THALLIUM URANATES [2; 2] Feb 79
- BT1 thallium compounds
- BT1 uranates
- BT2 uranium compounds
- BT3 actinide compounds

THALLIUM 179 [3; 3] Sep 83
- BT1 alpha decay radioisotopes
- BT2 radioisotopes
- BT3 isotopes
- BT1 intermediate mass nuclei
- BT2 nuclei
- BT1 isomeric transition isotopes
- BT2 radioisotopes
- BT3 isotopes
- BT1 millisec living radioisotopes
- BT2 radioisotopes
- BT3 isotopes
- BT1 odd-even nuclei
- BT2 nuclei
- BT1 thallium isotopes

THALLIUM 182 [4; 4] Jul 86
- BT1 alpha decay radioisotopes
- BT2 radioisotopes
- BT3 isotopes
- BT1 heavy nuclei
- BT2 nuclei
- BT1 odd-odd nuclei
- BT2 nuclei
- BT1 thallium isotopes

THALLIUM 184 [7; 7] Jan 77
- BT1 alpha decay radioisotopes
- BT2 radioisotopes
- BT3 isotopes
- BT1 beta-plus decay radioisotopes
- BT2 beta decay radioisotopes
- BT3 radioisotopes
- BT4 isotopes
- BT1 electron capture radioisotopes
- BT2 beta decay radioisotopes
- BT3 radioisotopes
- BT4 isotopes
- BT1 heavy nuclei
- BT2 nuclei
- BT1 odd-odd nuclei
- BT2 nuclei
- BT1 seconds living radioisotopes
- BT2 radioisotopes
- BT3 isotopes
- BT1 thallium isotopes

THALLIUM 185 [8; 8] Jan 77
- BT1 alpha decay radioisotopes
- BT2 radioisotopes
- BT3 isotopes
- BT1 heavy nuclei
- BT2 nuclei
- BT1 isomeric transition isotopes
- BT2 radioisotopes
- BT3 isotopes
- BT1 odd-even nuclei
- BT2 nuclei
- BT1 seconds living radioisotopes
- BT2 radioisotopes
- BT3 isotopes
- BT1 thallium isotopes

THALLIUM 186 [22; 22]
- BT1 alpha decay radioisotopes
- BT2 radioisotopes
- BT3 isotopes
- BT1 beta-plus decay radioisotopes
- BT2 beta decay radioisotopes
- BT3 radioisotopes
- BT4 isotopes
- BT1 electron capture radioisotopes
- BT2 beta decay radioisotopes
- BT3 radioisotopes
- BT4 isotopes
- BT1 heavy nuclei
- BT2 nuclei
- BT1 isomeric transition isotopes
- BT2 radioisotopes
- BT3 isotopes
- BT1 odd-odd nuclei
- BT2 nuclei
- BT1 seconds living radioisotopes
- BT2 radioisotopes
- BT3 isotopes
- BT1 thallium isotopes

THALLIUM 187 [13; 13]
- BT1 alpha decay radioisotopes
- BT2 radioisotopes
- BT3 isotopes
- BT1 electron capture radioisotopes
- BT2 beta decay radioisotopes
- BT3 radioisotopes
- BT4 isotopes
- BT1 heavy nuclei
- BT2 nuclei
- BT1 isomeric transition isotopes
- BT2 radioisotopes
- BT3 isotopes
- BT1 odd-even nuclei
- BT2 nuclei
- BT1 seconds living radioisotopes
- BT2 radioisotopes
- BT3 isotopes
- BT1 thallium isotopes

THALLIUM 188 [15; 15]
- BT1 beta-plus decay radioisotopes
- BT2 beta decay radioisotopes
- BT3 radioisotopes
- BT4 isotopes
- BT1 electron capture radioisotopes
- BT2 beta decay radioisotopes
- BT3 radioisotopes
- BT4 isotopes
- BT1 heavy nuclei
- BT2 nuclei
- BT1 minutes living radioisotopes
- BT2 radioisotopes
- BT3 isotopes
- BT1 odd-odd nuclei
- BT2 nuclei
- BT1 thallium isotopes

THALLIUM 189 [22; 22]
- BT1 beta-plus decay radioisotopes
- BT2 beta decay radioisotopes
- BT3 radioisotopes
- BT4 isotopes
- BT1 electron capture radioisotopes
- BT2 beta decay radioisotopes
- BT3 radioisotopes
- BT4 isotopes
- BT1 heavy nuclei
- BT2 nuclei
- BT1 minutes living radioisotopes
- BT2 radioisotopes
- BT3 isotopes
- BT1 odd-even nuclei
- BT2 nuclei
- BT1 thallium isotopes

THALLIUM 190 [19; 19]
- BT1 beta-plus decay radioisotopes
- BT2 beta decay radioisotopes
- BT3 radioisotopes
- BT4 isotopes
- BT1 electron capture radioisotopes
- BT2 beta decay radioisotopes
- BT3 radioisotopes
- BT4 isotopes
- BT1 heavy nuclei
- BT2 nuclei
- BT1 minutes living radioisotopes
- BT2 radioisotopes
- BT3 isotopes
- BT1 odd-odd nuclei
- BT2 nuclei
- BT1 thallium isotopes

THALLIUM 191 [26; 26]
- BT1 beta-plus decay radioisotopes
- BT2 beta decay radioisotopes
- BT3 radioisotopes
- BT4 isotopes
- BT1 electron capture radioisotopes
- BT2 beta decay radioisotopes
- BT3 radioisotopes
- BT4 isotopes
- BT1 heavy nuclei
- BT2 nuclei
- BT1 minutes living radioisotopes
- BT2 radioisotopes
- BT3 isotopes
- BT1 odd-even nuclei
- BT2 nuclei
- BT1 thallium isotopes

THALLIUM 192 [21; 21]
- BT1 beta-plus decay radioisotopes
- BT2 beta decay radioisotopes
- BT3 radioisotopes
- BT4 isotopes
- BT1 electron capture radioisotopes
- BT2 beta decay radioisotopes
- BT3 radioisotopes
- BT4 isotopes
- BT1 heavy nuclei
- BT2 nuclei
- BT1 minutes living radioisotopes
- BT2 radioisotopes
- BT3 isotopes

    DT1   odd odd nuclei
    BT2   nuclei
    BT1   thallium isotopes

THALLIUM 193 [31; 31]
    BT1   beta-plus decay radioisotopes
    BT2   beta decay radioisotopes
       BT3   radioisotopes
          BT4   isotopes
    BT1   electron capture radioisotopes
    BT2   beta decay radioisotopes
       BT3   radioisotopes
          BT4   isotopes
    BT1   heavy nuclei
    BT2   nuclei
    BT1   isomeric transition isotopes
    BT2   radioisotopes
       BT3   isotopes
    BT1   minutes living radioisotopes
    BT2   radioisotopes
       BT3   isotopes
    BT1   odd-even nuclei
    BT2   nuclei
    BT1   thallium isotopes

THALLIUM 194 [21; 21]
    BT1   beta-plus decay radioisotopes
    BT2   beta decay radioisotopes
       BT3   radioisotopes
          BT4   isotopes
    BT1   electron capture radioisotopes
    BT2   beta decay radioisotopes
       BT3   radioisotopes
          BT4   isotopes
    BT1   heavy nuclei
    BT2   nuclei
    BT1   minutes living radioisotopes
    BT2   radioisotopes
       BT3   isotopes
    BT1   odd-odd nuclei
    BT2   nuclei
    BT1   thallium isotopes

THALLIUM 195 [29; 29]
    BT1   beta-plus decay radioisotopes
    BT2   beta decay radioisotopes
       BT3   radioisotopes
          BT4   isotopes
    BT1   electron capture radioisotopes
    BT2   beta decay radioisotopes
       BT3   radioisotopes
          BT4   isotopes
    BT1   heavy nuclei
    BT2   nuclei
    BT1   hours living radioisotopes
    BT2   radioisotopes
       BT3   isotopes
    BT1   isomeric transition isotopes
    BT2   radioisotopes
       BT3   isotopes
    BT1   odd-even nuclei
    BT2   nuclei
    BT1   seconds living radioisotopes
    BT2   radioisotopes
       BT3   isotopes
    BT1   thallium isotopes

THALLIUM 196 [22; 22]
    BT1   beta-plus decay radioisotopes
    BT2   beta decay radioisotopes
       BT3   radioisotopes
          BT4   isotopes
    BT1   electron capture radioisotopes
    BT2   beta decay radioisotopes
       BT3   radioisotopes
          BT4   isotopes
    BT1   heavy nuclei
    BT2   nuclei
    BT1   hours living radioisotopes
    BT2   radioisotopes
       BT3   isotopes
    BT1   isomeric transition isotopes
    BT2   radioisotopes
       BT3   isotopes
    BT1   odd-odd nuclei
    BT2   nuclei
    BT1   thallium isotopes

THALLIUM 197 [36; 36]
    BT1   beta-plus decay radioisotopes
    BT2   beta decay radioisotopes
       BT3   radioisotopes
          BT4   isotopes
    BT1   electron capture radioisotopes
    BT2   beta decay radioisotopes
       BT3   radioisotopes
          BT4   isotopes
    BT1   heavy nuclei
    BT2   nuclei
    BT1   hours living radioisotopes
    BT2   radioisotopes
       BT3   isotopes
    BT1   isomeric transition isotopes
    BT2   radioisotopes
       BT3   isotopes
    BT1   odd-even nuclei
    BT2   nuclei
    BT1   seconds living radioisotopes
    BT2   radioisotopes
       BT3   isotopes
    BT1   thallium isotopes

THALLIUM 198 [38; 38]
    BT1   beta-plus decay radioisotopes
    BT2   beta decay radioisotopes
       BT3   radioisotopes
          BT4   isotopes
    BT1   electron capture radioisotopes
    BT2   beta decay radioisotopes
       BT3   radioisotopes
          BT4   isotopes
    BT1   heavy nuclei
    BT2   nuclei
    BT1   hours living radioisotopes
    BT2   radioisotopes
       BT3   isotopes
    BT1   internal conversion radioisoto
    BT2   radioisotopes
       BT3   isotopes
    BT1   isomeric transition isotopes
    BT2   radioisotopes
       BT3   isotopes
    BT1   odd-odd nuclei
    BT2   nuclei
    BT1   thallium isotopes

THALLIUM 199 [60; 60]
    BT1   electron capture radioisotopes
    BT2   beta decay radioisotopes
       BT3   radioisotopes
          BT4   isotopes
    BT1   heavy nuclei
    BT2   nuclei
    BT1   hours living radioisotopes
    BT2   radioisotopes
       BT3   isotopes
    BT1   odd-even nuclei
    BT2   nuclei
    BT1   thallium isotopes

THALLIUM 200 [49; 49]
    BT1   beta-plus decay radioisotopes
    BT2   beta decay radioisotopes
       BT3   radioisotopes
          BT4   isotopes
    BT1   days living radioisotopes
    BT2   radioisotopes
       BT3   isotopes
    BT1   electron capture radioisotopes
    BT2   beta decay radioisotopes
       BT3   radioisotopes
          BT4   isotopes
    BT1   heavy nuclei
    BT2   nuclei
    BT1   odd-odd nuclei
    BT2   nuclei
    BT1   thallium isotopes

THALLIUM 201 [3,554; 3,554]
    BT1   days living radioisotopes
    BT2   radioisotopes
       BT3   isotopes
    BT1   electron capture radioisotopes
    BT2   beta decay radioisotopes
       BT3   radioisotopes

    BT4   isotopes
    BT1   heavy nuclei
    BT2   nuclei
    BT1   odd-even nuclei
    BT2   nuclei
    BT1   thallium isotopes

THALLIUM 202 [68; 68]
    BT1   days living radioisotopes
    BT2   radioisotopes
       BT3   isotopes
    BT1   electron capture radioisotopes
    BT2   beta decay radioisotopes
       BT3   radioisotopes
          BT4   isotopes
    BT1   heavy nuclei
    BT2   nuclei
    BT1   odd-odd nuclei
    BT2   nuclei
    BT1   thallium isotopes

THALLIUM 203 [125; 125]
    BT1   heavy nuclei
    BT2   nuclei
    BT1   odd-even nuclei
    BT2   nuclei
    BT1   stable isotopes
    BT2   isotopes
    BT1   thallium isotopes

THALLIUM 203 TARGET [73; 73]
    BT1   targets

THALLIUM 204 [355; 355]
    BT1   beta-minus decay radioisotopes
    BT2   beta decay radioisotopes
       BT3   radioisotopes
          BT4   isotopes
    BT1   electron capture radioisotopes
    BT2   beta decay radioisotopes
       BT3   radioisotopes
          BT4   isotopes
    BT1   heavy nuclei
    BT2   nuclei
    BT1   odd-odd nuclei
    BT2   nuclei
    BT1   thallium isotopes
    BT1   years living radioisotopes
    BT2   radioisotopes
       BT3   isotopes

THALLIUM 205 [191; 191]
    BT1   heavy nuclei
    BT2   nuclei
    BT1   odd-even nuclei
    BT2   nuclei
    BT1   stable isotopes
    BT2   isotopes
    BT1   thallium isotopes

THALLIUM 205 REACTIONS [7; 7]
    Apr 78
    BT1   heavy ion reactions
    BT2   nuclear reactions

THALLIUM 205 TARGET [164; 164]
    BT1   targets

THALLIUM 206 [57; 57]
    UF   *radium e//*
    BT1   beta-minus decay radioisotope
    BT2   beta decay radioisotopes
       BT3   radioisotopes
          BT4   isotopes
    BT1   heavy nuclei
    BT2   nuclei
    BT1   isomeric transition isotopes
    BT2   radioisotopes
       BT3   isotopes
    BT1   minutes living radioisotopes
    BT2   radioisotopes
       BT3   isotopes
    BT1   odd-odd nuclei
    BT2   nuclei
    BT1   thallium isotopes

THALLIUM 207 [95; 95]
  UF   *actinium c//*
  BT1   beta-minus decay radioisotopes
    BT2   beta decay radioisotopes
      BT3   radioisotopes
        BT4   isotopes
  BT1   heavy nuclei
    BT2   nuclei
  BT1   isomeric transition isotopes
    BT2   radioisotopes
      BT3   isotopes
  BT1   minutes living radioisotopes
    BT2   radioisotopes
      BT3   isotopes
  BT1   odd-even nuclei
    BT2   nuclei
  BT1   seconds living radioisotopes
    BT2   radioisotopes
      BT3   isotopes
  BT1   thallium isotopes

THALLIUM 207 TARGET [3; 3]
  May 80
  BT1   targets

THALLIUM 208 [146; 146]
  UF   *thorium c//*
  BT1   beta-minus decay radioisotopes
    BT2   beta decay radioisotopes
      BT3   radioisotopes
        BT4   isotopes
  BT1   heavy nuclei
    BT2   nuclei
  BT1   minutes living radioisotopes
    BT2   radioisotopes
      BT3   isotopes
  BT1   odd-odd nuclei
    BT2   nuclei
  BT1   thallium isotopes

THALLIUM 209 [14; 14]
  BT1   beta-minus decay radioisotopes
    BT2   beta decay radioisotopes
      BT3   radioisotopes
        BT4   isotopes
  BT1   heavy nuclei
    BT2   nuclei
  BT1   minutes living radioisotopes
    BT2   radioisotopes
      BT3   isotopes
  BT1   odd-even nuclei
    BT2   nuclei
  BT1   thallium isotopes

THALLIUM 209 TARGET [4; 4] *Jun 84*
  BT1   targets

THALLIUM 210 [24; 24]
  UF   *radium c//*
  BT1   beta minus decay radioisotopes
    BT2   beta decay radioisotopes
      BT3   radioisotopes
        BT4   isotopes
  BT1   heavy nuclei
    BT2   nuclei
  BT1   minutes living radioisotopes
    BT2   radioisotopes
      BT3   isotopes
  BT1   odd-odd nuclei
    BT2   nuclei
  BT1   thallium isotopes

THAMES RIVER [6; 6] *Feb 76*
  BT1   rivers
    BT2   surface waters

the next step thermonuc. reac.
  USE   tns reactors

THEBAINE [3; 3]
  BT1   alkaloids
    BT2   organic compounds
  BT1   analgesics
    BT2   central nervous system depress
      BT3   central nervous system agents
        BT4   drugs
  BT1   narcotics
    BT2   central nervous system depress
      BT3   central nervous system agents
        BT4   drugs
  RT   codeine
  RT   heroin
  RT   morphine

thenoyltrifluoroacetone
  USE   tta

theobroma
  USE   cacao trees

THEOBROMINE [8; 8]
  UF   *3,7-dimethylxanthine*
  BT1   diuretics
    BT2   drugs
  BT1   vasodilators
    BT2   cardiovascular agents
      BT3   drugs
  BT1   xanthines
    BT2   organic oxygen compounds
      BT3   organic compounds
    BT2   purines
      BT3   heterocyclic compounds
        BT4   organic compounds
      BT3   organic nitrogen compounds
        BT4   organic compounds

THEOPHYLLINE [88; 88]
  UF   *1,3-dimethylxanthine*
  BT1   diuretics
    BT2   drugs
  BT1   vasodilators
    BT2   cardiovascular agents
      BT3   drugs
  BT1   xanthines
    BT2   organic oxygen compounds
      BT3   organic compounds
    BT2   purines
      BT3   heterocyclic compounds
        BT4   organic compounds
      BT3   organic nitrogen compounds
        BT4   organic compounds

THEORETICAL DATA [26,667; 26,667]
  Oct 78
  (Use only in conjunction with literary indicator N for data flagging.)
  BT1   numerical data
    BT2   data
      BT3   information

therapeutic agents
  USE   drugs

THERAPY [2,673; 34,146]
  UF   *treatment (therapy)*
  BT1   medicine
  NT1   chemotherapy
  NT1   first aid
  NT1   immunotherapy
  NT1   post-irradiation therapy
  NT1   radiotherapy
    NT2   afterloading
    NT2   neutron therapy
      NT3   neutron capture therapy
  NT1   transfusions
  RT   balneology
  RT   biological recovery
  RT   bleomycin
  RT   blood substitutes
  RT   castration
  RT   diet
  RT   drugs
  RT   injection
  RT   patients
  RT   radioimmunodetection
  RT   radioimmunology
  RT   side effects
  RT   surgery

THERMAL ANALYSIS [1,976; 6,029]
  UF   *analysis (thermal)*
  NT1   differential thermal analysis
  NT1   dilatometry
  NT1   emanation thermal analysis
  NT1   thermal gravimetric analysis
  RT   phase diagrams
  RT   phase transformations
  RT   structural chemical analysis
  RT   thermal expansion

THERMAL BARRIERS [227; 227]
  Mar 83
  (Localized depressions of field, particle density and potential which reduce thermal-energy transfer between plug and central-cell electrons in mirror devices.)
  RT   plasma confinement
  RT   tmr reactors
  RT   tmx devices

THERMAL BOUNDARY RESISTANCE [41; 186]
  (Thermal impedance at an interface at ultralow temperatures.)
  NT1   kapitza resistance
  RT   heat transfer
  RT   ultralow temperature

THERMAL COLUMNS [98; 98]
  UF   *columns (thermal)*
  UF   *reactor thermal columns*
  RT   moderators
  RT   neutron sources
  RT   thermal neutrons

THERMAL CONDUCTION [1,563; 1,563]
  (Heat transfer by conduction.)
  UF   *conduction (thermal)*
  BT1   heat transfer
    BT2   energy transfer
  RT   thermal conductivity
  RT   thermal insulation

THERMAL CONDUCTIVITY [6,013; 6,013]
  UF   *conductivity (thermal)*
  BT1   thermodynamic properties
    BT2   physical properties
  RT   heat transfer
  RT   matthiessen rule
  RT   righi-leduc effect
  RT   thermal conduction
  RT   thermal diffusivity
  RT   thermoelasticity
  RT   umklapp processes
  RT   wiedemann-franz law

THERMAL CYCLING [1,431; 1,431]
  RT   mechanical tests
  RT   thermal shock

thermal decomposition
  USE   pyrolysis

THERMAL DEGRADATION [798; 798]
  Oct 75
  UF+   *heat stability*
  RT   chemical properties
  RT   heating
  RT   mechanical properties
  RT   physical properties
  RT   pyrolysis

THERMAL DIFFUSION [1,263; 1,263]
  (Phenomenon in which a temperature gradient in a mixture of fluids gives rise to a flow of one constituent relative to the mixture as a whole.)
  UF   *thermodiffusion*
  BT1   diffusion
  RT   heat transfer
  RT   thermal diffusivity

THERMAL DIFFUSIVITY [755; 755]
(The quantity of heat passing normally through a unit area per unit time divided by the product of specific heat, density, and temperature gradient.)
- SF *heat dissipation*
- BT1 thermodynamic properties
-   BT2 physical properties
- RT thermal conductivity
- RT thermal diffusion
- RT thermal insulation

THERMAL EFFICIENCY [517; 517]
- BT1 efficiency
- RT thermodynamics

THERMAL EFFLUENTS [1,110; 1,110]
- UF *effluents (thermal)*
- UF *heated effluents*
- RT heat sinks
- RT thermal pollution
- RT waste heat

THERMAL EQUILIBRIUM
[1,317; 1,317]
- BT1 equilibrium
- RT thermodynamic properties

THERMAL EXPANSION [3,477; 3,477]
- BT1 expansion
- RT contraction
- RT dilatometry
- RT elongation
- RT expansion joints
- RT grueneisen constant
- RT swelling
- RT thermal analysis
- RT thermodynamic properties
- RT thermoelasticity

THERMAL FATIGUE [731; 731]
- BT1 fatigue
-   BT2 mechanical properties

THERMAL FISSION [1,155; 1,155]
- BT1 fission
-   BT2 nuclear reactions
- BT1 neutron reactions
-   BT2 nucleon reactions
-     BT3 baryon reactions
-       BT4 hadron reactions
-         BT5 nuclear reactions
- RT thermal neutrons
- RT watt fission spectrum

THERMAL FISSION FACTOR [12; 12]
- RT fission
- RT multiplication factors

THERMAL FRACTURES [37; 37]
May 86
- BT1 fractures
-   BT2 failures
- RT thermal stresses

thermal gradients
(Coordinate the term below with the temperature range involved, e.g. MEDIUM TEMPERATURE. Prior to June 1986 the temperature range was coordinated with TEMPERATURE DISTRIBUTION.)
- USE temperature gradients

THERMAL GRAVIMETRIC ANALYSIS
[1,813; 1,813]
- UF *thermogravimetric analysis*
- UF *thermogravimetry*
- BT1 gravimetric analysis
-   BT2 quantitative chemical analysis
-     BT3 chemical analysis
- BT1 thermal analysis
- RT decomposition

THERMAL INSULATION [1,526; 1,526]
- UF *insulation (thermal)*
- RT air conditioning
- RT energy conservation
- RT fire resistance
- RT heat transfer
- RT shielding
- RT shutters
- RT temperature control
- RT thermal conduction
- RT thermal diffusivity
- RT thermal shields

THERMAL NEUTRONS [7,431; 7,431]
(Neutrons in thermal equilibrium with the medium in which they exist.)
- BT1 neutrons
-   BT2 nucleons
-     BT3 baryons
-       BT4 fermions
-       BT4 hadrons
-         BT5 elementary particles
- RT neutron temperature
- RT thermal columns
- RT thermal fission
- RT watt fission spectrum
- RT zemach-glauber formalism

thermal photography
- USE infrared thermography

THERMAL POLLUTION [1,308; 1,308]
(Environmental temperature rise due to waste heat disposal.)
- UF+ *thermal pollution (air)*
- UF+ *thermal pollution (water)*
- BT1 pollution
- RT environmental effects
- RT plumes
- RT thermal effluents
- RT waste heat

thermal pollution (air)
- USE air pollution
- AND thermal pollution

thermal pollution (water)
- USE thermal pollution
- AND water pollution

THERMAL POWER PLANTS
[811; 36,986]
- BT1 power plants
- NT1 combined-cycle power plants
- NT1 fossil-fuel power plants
- NT1 geothermal power plants
- NT1 nuclear power plants
-   NT2 bopssar standard plant
-   NT2 ebasco standard plant
-   NT2 gibbssar standard plant
-   NT2 offshore nuclear power plants
-   NT2 swessar standard plant
-   NT2 thermonuclear power plants
-   NT2 underground nuclear stations
- RT district heating

thermal properties
- USE thermodynamic properties

THERMAL RADIATION [906; 906]
- BT1 electromagnetic radiation
-   BT2 radiations
- RT blackbody radiation
- RT heat transfer
- RT infrared radiation
- RT radiant heat transfer
- RT rosseland approximation
- RT thermodynamic properties

THERMAL REACTORS [1,002; 54,628]
- BT1 reactors
- NT1 aeg-pr-10 reactor
- NT1 aerojet-general nucleonics r
- NT1 afrri reactor
- NT1 agesta reactor
- NT1 ai-l-77 reactor
- NT1 alrr reactor
- NT1 anex reactor
- NT1 anna reactor
- NT1 aps reactor
- NT1 apsara reactor
- NT1 aquilon reactor
- NT1 arbi reactor
- NT1 arbus reactor
- NT1 argonaut reactor
- NT1 argos reactor
- NT1 armf-1 reactor
- NT1 astra reactor
- NT1 atr reactor
- NT1 atrc reactor
- NT1 atucha reactor
- NT1 atucha-2 reactor
- NT1 avogadro rs-1 reactor
- NT1 avr reactor
- NT1 bawtr reactor
- NT1 beloyarsk-1 reactor
- NT1 beloyarsk-2 reactor
- NT1 bepo reactor
- NT1 ber-2 reactor
- NT1 berkeley reactor
- NT1 bgrr reactor
- NT1 bilibin reactor
- NT1 bohunice a-1 reactor
- NT1 bohunice a-2 reactor
- NT1 borax-1 reactor
- NT1 borax-2 reactor
- NT1 borax-3 reactor
- NT1 borax-4 reactor
- NT1 br-02 reactor
- NT1 br-1 reactor
- NT1 br-2 reactor
- NT1 bradwell reactor
- NT1 brr reactor
- NT1 bsr-1 reactor
- NT1 bsr-2 reactor
- NT1 budapest training reactor
- NT1 bugey-1 reactor
- NT1 bwr type reactors
-   NT2 allens creek-1 reactor
-   NT2 allens creek-2 reactor
-   NT2 bailly-1 reactor
-   NT2 barsebaeck-1 reactor
-   NT2 barsebaeck-2 reactor
-   NT2 barton-1 reactor
-   NT2 barton-2 reactor
-   NT2 barton-3 reactor
-   NT2 barton-4 reactor
-   NT2 bell reactor
-   NT2 big rock point reactor
-   NT2 black fox-1 reactor
-   NT2 black fox-2 reactor
-   NT2 bonus reactor
-   NT2 browns ferry-1 reactor
-   NT2 browns ferry-2 reactor
-   NT2 browns ferry-3 reactor
-   NT2 brunsbuettel reactor
-   NT2 brunswick-1 reactor
-   NT2 brunswick-2 reactor
-   NT2 chinshan-1 reactor
-   NT2 chinshan-2 reactor
-   NT2 clinton-1 reactor
-   NT2 clinton-2 reactor
-   NT2 cofrentes reactor
-   NT2 cooper reactor
-   NT2 dodewaard reactor
-   NT2 douglas point-1 reactor
-   NT2 douglas point-2 reactor
-   NT2 dresden-1 reactor
-   NT2 dresden-2 reactor
-   NT2 dresden-3 reactor
-   NT2 duane arnold-1 reactor
-   NT2 ebwr reactor
-   NT2 enel-4 reactor
-   NT2 enrico fermi-2 reactor
-   NT2 err reactor
-   NT2 fitzpatrick reactor
-   NT2 forsmark-1 reactor
-   NT2 forsmark-2 reactor
-   NT2 forsmark-3 reactor

NT2	fukushima-ii-1 reactor	NT2	skagit-1 reactor	NT1	dragon reactor
NT2	fukushima-ii-2 reactor	NT2	skagit-2 reactor	NT1	dungeness-a reactor
NT2	fukushima-ii-3 reactor	NT2	sl-1 reactor	NT1	dungeness-b reactor
NT2	fukushima-ii-4 reactor	NT2	susquehanna-1 reactor	NT1	ebor reactor
NT2	fukushima-1 reactor	NT2	susquehanna-2 reactor	NT1	egcr reactor
NT2	fukushima-2 reactor	NT2	tarapur-1 reactor	NT1	el-1 reactor
NT2	fukushima-3 reactor	NT2	tarapur-2 reactor	NT1	el-2 reactor
NT2	fukushima-4 reactor	NT2	tokai-2 reactor	NT1	el-4 reactor
NT2	fukushima-5 reactor	NT2	tsuruga reactor	NT1	eocr reactor
NT2	fukushima-6 reactor	NT2	tullnerfeld reactor	NT1	esada-vesr reactor
NT2	garigliano reactor	NT2	tvo-1 reactor	NT1	essor reactor
NT2	garona reactor	NT2	tvo-2 reactor	NT1	etr reactor
NT2	ge standard reactor	NT2	vak reactor	NT1	fir-1 reactor
NT2	graben-1 reactor	NT2	vbwr reactor	NT1	fnr reactor
NT2	grand gulf-1 reactor	NT2	vermont yankee reactor	NT1	fr-2 reactor
NT2	grand gulf-2 reactor	NT2	verplanck-1 reactor	NT1	frg-1 reactor
NT2	gundremmingen-2 reactor	NT2	verplanck-2 reactor	NT1	fulton-1 reactor
NT2	gundremmingen-3 reactor	NT2	vk-50 reactor	NT1	fulton-2 reactor
NT2	hamaoka-1 reactor	NT2	wnp-2 reactor	NT1	g-1 reactor
NT2	hamaoka-2 reactor	NT3	hanford-2 reactor	NT1	g-2 reactor
NT2	hamaoka-3 reactor	NT2	wuergassen reactor	NT1	g-3 reactor
NT2	hartsville-1 reactor	NT2	zimmer-1 reactor	NT1	ga standard reactor
NT2	hartsville-2 reactor	NT2	zimmer-2 reactor	NT1	getr reactor
NT2	hartsville-3 reactor	NT1	cabri reactor	NT1	gleep reactor
NT2	hartsville-4 reactor	NT1	calder hall a-1 reactor	NT1	hartlepool reactor
NT2	hatch-1 reactor	NT1	calder hall a-2 reactor	NT1	hbwr reactor
NT2	hatch-2 reactor	NT1	calder hall b-3 reactor	NT1	hector reactor
NT2	hdr reactor	NT1	calder hall b-4 reactor	NT1	herald reactor
NT2	hope creek-1 reactor	NT1	candu type reactors	NT1	heysham-a reactor
NT3	newbold island-1 reactor	NT2	bruce-1 reactor	NT1	heysham-b reactor
NT2	hope creek-2 reactor	NT2	bruce-2 reactor	NT1	hfbr reactor
NT3	newbold island-2 reactor	NT2	bruce-3 reactor	NT1	hfetr reactor
NT2	humboldt bay reactor	NT2	bruce-4 reactor	NT1	hfir reactor
NT2	isar reactor	NT2	bruce-5 reactor	NT1	hfr reactor
NT2	jpdr reactor	NT2	bruce-6 reactor	NT1	hifar reactor
NT2	jpdr-2 reactor	NT2	bruce-7 reactor	NT1	hinkley point-a reactor
NT2	kaiseraugst reactor	NT2	bruce-8 reactor	NT1	hinkley point-b reactor
NT2	kashiwazaki-kariwa-1 reactor	NT2	cernavoda-1 reactor	NT1	hitrex-1 reactor
NT2	kashiwazaki-kariwa-2 reactor	NT2	cordoba reactor	NT1	hnpf reactor
NT2	kashiwazaki-kariwa-3 reactor	NT2	darlington-1 reactor	NT1	hor reactor
NT2	kashiwazaki-kariwa-4 reactor	NT2	darlington-2 reactor	NT1	htr reactor
NT2	kashiwazaki-kariwa-5 reactor	NT2	darlington-3 reactor	NT1	hunterston-a reactor
NT2	kashiwazaki-kariwa-6 reactor	NT2	darlington-4 reactor	NT1	hunterston-b reactor
NT2	kashiwazaki-kariwa-7 reactor	NT2	douglas point ontario reactor	NT1	hwctr reactor
NT2	kruemmel reactor	NT2	gentilly-1 reactor	NT1	ian-r1 reactor
NT2	kuosheng-1 reactor	NT2	gentilly-2 reactor	NT1	iear-1 reactor
NT2	kuosheng-2 reactor	NT2	kanupp reactor	NT1	ignalinsk-1 reactor
NT2	la salle county-1 reactor	NT2	npd reactor	NT1	ignalinsk-2 reactor
NT2	la salle county-2 reactor	NT2	pickering-1 reactor	NT1	irl reactor
NT2	lacbwr reactor	NT2	pickering-2 reactor	NT1	irr-1 reactor
NT2	laguna verde-1 reactor	NT2	pickering-3 reactor	NT1	irt reactor
NT2	laguna verde-2 reactor	NT2	pickering-4 reactor	NT1	irt-baghdad reactor
NT2	leibstadt reactor	NT2	pickering-5 reactor	NT1	irt-sofia reactor
NT2	limerick-1 reactor	NT2	pickering-6 reactor	NT1	irt-2000 djakarta reactor
NT2	limerick-2 reactor	NT2	pickering-7 reactor	NT1	irt-2000 moscow reactor
NT2	lingen reactor	NT2	pickering-8 reactor	NT1	isis reactor
NT2	mendocino-1 reactor	NT2	point lepreau-1 reactor	NT1	janus reactor
NT2	mendocino-2 reactor	NT2	point lepreau-2 reactor	NT1	jatr reactor
NT2	millstone-1 reactor	NT2	rajasthan-1 reactor	NT1	jen reactor
NT2	montague-1 reactor	NT2	rajasthan-2 reactor	NT1	jen-1 reactor
NT2	montague-2 reactor	NT2	wolsung-1 reactor	NT1	juno reactor
NT2	montalto di castro-1 reactor	NT1	cesar reactor	NT1	kamini reactor
NT2	montalto di castro-2 reactor	NT1	cesnef reactor	NT1	knk reactor
NT2	monticello reactor	NT1	chapelcross-1 reactor	NT1	kuhfr reactor
NT2	muehleberg reactor	NT1	chapelcross-2 reactor	NT1	kursk-1 reactor
NT2	nine mile point-1 reactor	NT1	chapelcross-3 reactor	NT1	kursk-2 reactor
NT2	nine mile point-2 reactor	NT1	chapelcross-4 reactor	NT1	kursk-3 reactor
NT2	okg-1 reactor	NT1	chernobylsk-1 reactor	NT1	kursk-4 reactor
NT2	okg-2 reactor	NT1	chernobylsk-2 reactor	NT1	latina reactor
NT2	onagawa-1 reactor	NT1	chernobylsk-3 reactor	NT1	leningrad-1 reactor
NT2	onagawa-2 reactor	NT1	chernobylsk-4 reactor	NT1	leningrad-2 reactor
NT2	oyster creek-1 reactor	NT1	chinon-1 reactor	NT1	leningrad-3 reactor
NT2	pathfinder reactor	NT1	chinon-2 reactor	NT1	leningrad-4 reactor
NT2	peach bottom-2 reactor	NT1	chinon-3 reactor	NT1	lfr reactor
NT2	peach bottom-3 reactor	NT1	cirene reactor	NT1	lido reactor
NT2	perry-1 reactor	NT1	cirus reactor	NT1	litr reactor
NT2	perry-2 reactor	NT1	consort-2 reactor	NT1	lptr reactor
NT2	philippsburg-1 reactor	NT1	cp-2 reactor	NT1	lucens reactor
NT2	phipps bend-1 reactor	NT1	cp-3 reactor	NT1	lwbr type reactors
NT2	phipps bend-2 reactor	NT1	cp-5 reactor	NT1	maria reactor
NT2	quad cities-1 reactor	NT1	cvtr reactor	NT1	marius reactor
NT2	quad cities-2 reactor	NT1	democritus reactor	NT1	melusine-1 reactor
NT2	ringhals-1 reactor	NT1	dhruva reactor	NT1	minerve reactor
NT2	river bend-1 reactor	NT1	dido reactor	NT1	mir reactor
NT2	river bend-2 reactor	NT1	dimple reactor	NT1	mitr reactor
NT2	rwe-bayernwerk reactor	NT1	dmtr reactor	NT1	mrr reactor
NT2	shika-1 reactor	NT1	dow triga-mk-1 reactor	NT1	msre reactor
NT2	shimane-1 reactor	NT1	dr-1 reactor	NT1	mtr reactor
NT2	shimane-2 reactor	NT1	dr-2 reactor	NT1	mzfr reactor
NT2	shoreham reactor	NT1	dr-3 reactor	NT1	nbsr reactor

NT1	ncscr-1 reactor	NT2	davis besse-1 reactor	NT2	north anna-2 reactor
NT1	nestor reactor	NT2	davis besse-2 reactor	NT2	north anna-3 reactor
NT1	niederaichbach reactor	NT2	davis besse-3 reactor	NT2	north anna-4 reactor
NT1	nora reactor	NT2	daya bay reactor	NT2	north coast-1 reactor
NT1	nrx reactor	NT2	diablo canyon-1 reactor	NT2	obrigheim reactor
NT1	ntr reactor	NT2	diablo canyon-2 reactor	NT2	oconee-1 reactor
NT1	oldbury-a reactor	NT2	doel-1 reactor	NT2	oconee-2 reactor
NT1	oldbury-b reactor	NT2	doel-2 reactor	NT2	oconee-3 reactor
NT1	osiris reactor	NT2	doel-3 reactor	NT2	oi-1 reactor
NT1	owr reactor	NT2	doel-4 reactor	NT2	oi-2 reactor
NT1	pctr reactor	NT2	efdr-50 reactor	NT2	oi-3 reactor
NT1	peach bottom-1 reactor	NT2	emsland reactor	NT2	oi-4 reactor
NT1	pegase reactor	NT2	erie-1 reactor	NT2	otto hahn reactor
NT1	pelinduna reactor	NT2	erie-2 reactor	NT2	palisades-1 reactor
NT1	perryman-1 reactor	NT2	farley-1 reactor	NT2	palo verde-1 reactor
NT1	perryman-2 reactor	NT2	farley-2 reactor	NT2	palo verde-2 reactor
NT1	phebus reactor	NT2	fessenheim-1 reactor	NT2	palo verde-3 reactor
NT1	pluto reactor	NT2	flamanville-1 reactor	NT2	palo verde-4 reactor
NT1	pnpf reactor	NT2	flamanville-2 reactor	NT2	palo verde-5 reactor
NT1	prr reactor	NT2	forked river-1 reactor	NT2	paluel-1 reactor
NT1	pse reactor	NT2	genkai-1 reactor	NT2	paluel-2 reactor
NT1	pstr reactor	NT2	genkai-2 reactor	NT2	paluel-3 reactor
NT1	pwr type reactors	NT2	genkai-3 reactor	NT2	paluel-4 reactor
NT2	almaraz-1 reactor	NT2	genkai-4 reactor	NT2	pebble springs-1 reactor
NT2	almaraz-2 reactor	NT2	ginna-1 reactor	NT2	pebble springs-2 reactor
NT2	angra-1 reactor	NT2	goesgen reactor	NT2	penly-1 reactor
NT2	angra-2 reactor	NT2	golfech-1 reactor	NT2	perkins-1 reactor
NT2	angra-3 reactor	NT2	grafenrheinfeld reactor	NT2	perkins-2 reactor
NT2	ardennes b-1 reactor	NT2	gravelines-b1 reactor	NT2	perkins-3 reactor
NT2	ardennes reactor	NT2	gravelines-c6 reactor	NT2	philippsburg-2 reactor
NT2	arkansas-1 reactor	NT2	greene county reactor	NT2	pilgrim-1 reactor
NT2	arkansas-2 reactor	NT2	greenwood-2 reactor	NT2	pilgrim-2 reactor
NT2	asco-1 reactor	NT2	greenwood-3 reactor	NT2	pilgrim-3 reactor
NT2	asco-2 reactor	NT2	grohnde reactor	NT2	pm-2a reactor
NT2	atlantic-1 reactor	NT2	hamm-uentrop reactor	NT2	pm-3a reactor
NT2	atlantic-2 reactor	NT2	harris-1 reactor	NT2	pnpp-1 reactor
NT2	basf-1 reactor	NT2	harris-2 reactor	NT2	point beach-1 reactor
NT2	basf-2 reactor	NT2	harris-3 reactor	NT2	point beach-2 reactor
NT2	beaver valley-1 reactor	NT2	harris-4 reactor	NT2	prairie island-1 reactor
NT2	beaver valley-2 reactor	NT2	haven-1 reactor	NT2	prairie island-2 reactor
NT2	bellefonte-1 reactor	NT3	koshkonong-1 reactor	NT2	qinshan reactor
NT2	bellefonte-2 reactor	NT2	haven-2 reactor	NT2	quanicassee-1 reactor
NT2	belleville sur loire-1 reactor	NT3	koshkonong-2 reactor	NT2	quanicassee-2 reactor
NT2	belleville sur loire-2 reactor	NT2	ikata reactor	NT2	rancho seco-1 reactor
NT2	beznau-1 reactor	NT2	ikata-2 reactor	NT2	remerschen reactor
NT2	beznau-2 reactor	NT2	ikata-3 reactor	NT2	rheinsberg akw1 reactor
NT2	biblis-1 reactor	NT2	indian point-1 reactor	NT2	ringhals-2 reactor
NT2	biblis-2 reactor	NT2	indian point-2 reactor	NT2	ringhals-3 reactor
NT2	biblis-3 reactor	NT2	indian point-3 reactor	NT2	ringhals-4 reactor
NT2	biblis-4 reactor	NT2	iran-1 reactor	NT2	robinson-2 reactor
NT2	blue hills-1 reactor	NT2	iran-2 reactor	NT2	rooppur reactor
NT2	blue hills-2 reactor	NT2	isar-2 reactor	NT2	rowe yankee reactor
NT2	borssele reactor	NT2	jamesport-1 reactor	NT2	saint alban-1 reactor
NT2	br-3 reactor	NT2	jamesport-2 reactor	NT2	saint alban-2 reactor
NT2	braidwood-1 reactor	NT2	kewaunee reactor	NT2	salem-1 reactor
NT2	braidwood-2 reactor	NT2	kori-1 reactor	NT2	salem-2 reactor
NT2	brokdorf reactor	NT2	kori-2 reactor	NT2	san onofre-1 reactor
NT2	bugey-2 reactor	NT2	krsko reactor	NT2	san onofre-2 reactor
NT2	bugey-3 reactor	NT2	lemoniz-1 reactor	NT2	san onofre-3 reactor
NT2	bugey-4 reactor	NT2	lemoniz-2 reactor	NT2	savannah reactor
NT2	bugey-5 reactor	NT2	lenin reactor	NT2	saxton reactor
NT2	bw standard reactor	NT2	leonid brezhnev reactor	NT2	seabrook-1 reactor
NT2	byron-1 reactor	NT2	loft reactor	NT2	seabrook-2 reactor
NT2	byron-2 reactor	NT2	lucie-1 reactor	NT2	selni reactor
NT2	calhoun-1 reactor	NT2	lucie-2 reactor	NT2	sendai-1 reactor
NT2	calhoun-2 reactor	NT2	maanshan-1 reactor	NT2	sendai-2 reactor
NT2	callaway-1 reactor	NT2	maine yankee reactor	NT2	sequoyah-1 reactor
NT2	callaway-2 reactor	NT2	marble hill-1 reactor	NT2	sequoyah-2 reactor
NT2	calvert cliffs-1 reactor	NT2	marble hill-2 reactor	NT2	shippingport reactor
NT2	calvert cliffs-2 reactor	NT2	mc guire-1 reactor	NT2	sizewell-b reactor
NT2	catawba-1 reactor	NT2	mc guire-2 reactor	NT2	sm-1 reactor
NT2	catawba-2 reactor	NT2	mh-1a reactor	NT2	sm-1a reactor
NT2	cattenom-1 reactor	NT2	midland-1 reactor	NT2	south texas project-1 reactor
NT2	cattenom-2 reactor	NT2	midland-2 reactor	NT2	south texas project-2 reactor
NT2	cattenom-3 reactor	NT2	mihama-1 reactor	NT2	stade reactor
NT2	cattenom-4 reactor	NT2	mihama-2 reactor	NT2	sterling-1 reactor
NT2	ce standard reactor	NT2	mihama-3 reactor	NT2	summer-1 reactor
NT2	cherokee-1 reactor	NT2	millstone-2 reactor	NT2	sundesert-1 reactor
NT2	cherokee-2 reactor	NT2	millstone-3 reactor	NT2	sundesert-2 reactor
NT2	cherokee-3 reactor	NT2	muelheim-kaerlich reactor	NT2	surry-1 reactor
NT2	comanche peak-1 reactor	NT2	mutsu reactor	NT2	surry-2 reactor
NT2	comanche peak-2 reactor	NT2	neckar reactor	NT2	surry-3 reactor
NT2	connecticut yankee reactor	NT2	neckar-2 reactor	NT2	surry-4 reactor
NT2	cook-1 reactor	NT2	nep-1 reactor	NT2	s1c prototype reactor
NT2	cook-2 reactor	NT2	nep-2 reactor	NT2	takahama-1 reactor
NT2	cruas-2 reactor	NT2	neupotz-1 reactor	NT2	takahama-2 reactor
NT2	cruas-3 reactor	NT2	neupotz-2 reactor	NT2	takahama-3 reactor
NT2	crystal river-3 reactor	NT2	nogent sur seine-1 reactor	NT2	takahama-4 reactor
NT2	crystal river-4 reactor	NT2	nogent sur seine-2 reactor	NT2	thr reactor
NT2	dampierre-1 reactor	NT2	north anna-1 reactor	NT2	three mile island-1 reactor

NT2	three mile island-2 reactor	NT3	zaporozhe-1 reactor	NT1	utr-10-kinki reactor
NT2	tihange reactor	NT3	zaporozhe-2 reactor	NT1	utrr reactor
NT2	tihange-2 reactor	NT3	zaporozhe-3 reactor	NT1	uvar reactor
NT2	tihange-3 reactor	NT3	zaporozhe-4 reactor	NT1	uwnr reactor
NT2	tomari-1 reactor	NT2	wyhl-1 reactor	NT1	uwtr reactor
NT2	tomari-2 reactor	NT2	wyhl-2 reactor	NT1	vandellos reactor
NT2	tricastin-1 reactor	NT2	yellow creek-1 reactor	NT1	venus reactor
NT2	tricastin-4 reactor	NT2	yellow creek-2 reactor	NT1	vg-400 reactor
NT2	trillo-1 reactor	NT2	zion-1 reactor	NT1	vgr-50 reactor
NT2	trojan reactor	NT2	zion-2 reactor	NT1	vhtr reactor
NT2	tsuruga-2 reactor	NT2	zorita-1 reactor	NT1	vidal-1 reactor
NT2	turkey point-3 reactor	NT1	r-a reactor	NT1	vidal-2 reactor
NT2	turkey point-4 reactor	NT1	r-1 reactor	NT1	voronezh ast-500 reactor
NT2	tva-1 reactor	NT1	ra-5 reactor	NT1	vpi-utr-10 reactor
NT2	tva-2 reactor	NT1	rb-1 reactor	NT1	vr-1 reactor
NT2	tyrone-1 reactor	NT1	rb-2 reactor	NT1	wagr reactor
NT2	tyrone-2 reactor	NT1	rg-1m reactor	NT1	windscale production reactors
NT2	ulchin-1 reactor	NT1	ritmo reactor	NT1	wpir reactor
NT2	ulchin-2 reactor	NT1	rts-1 reactor	NT1	wr-1 reactor
NT2	unterweser reactor	NT1	safari-1 reactor	NT1	wrrr reactor
NT2	vahnum-1 reactor	NT1	saint laurent-1 reactor	NT1	wsur reactor
NT2	vahnum-2 reactor	NT1	saint laurent-2 reactor	NT1	wtr reactor
NT2	vogtle-1 reactor	NT1	saphir reactor	NT1	wwr-k-alma-ata reactor
NT2	vogtle-2 reactor	NT1	sghwr reactor	NT1	wwr-m-kiev reactor
NT2	vogtle-3 reactor	NT1	shca reactor	NT1	wwr-m-leningrad reactor
NT2	vogtle-4 reactor	NT1	siloe reactor	NT1	wwr-s-bucharest reactor
NT2	waterford-3 reactor	NT1	siloette reactor	NT1	wwr-s-budapest reactor
NT2	waterford-4 reactor	NT1	sizewell-a reactor	NT1	wwr-s-cairo reactor
NT2	watts bar-1 reactor	NT1	sm-2 reactor	NT1	wwr-s-moscow reactor
NT2	watts bar-2 reactor	NT1	smolensk-1 reactor	NT1	wwr-s-prague reactor
NT2	westinghouse standard reactor	NT1	smolensk-2 reactor	NT1	wwr-s-tashkent reactor
NT2	wnp-1 reactor	NT1	spert-1 reactor	NT1	wwr-sm rossendorf reactor
NT2	wnp-3 reactor	NT1	spert-2 reactor	NT1	wwr-2 reactor
NT2	wnp-4 reactor	NT1	spert-3 reactor	NT1	wylfa reactor
NT2	wnp-5 reactor	NT1	spert-4 reactor	NT1	x-10 reactor
NT2	wolf creek-1 reactor	NT1	spr-2 reactor	NT1	zed-2 reactor
NT2	wup-3 reactor	NT1	sr-1 reactor	NT1	zenith reactor
NT2	wup-4 reactor	NT1	sr-3p reactor	NT1	zerlina reactor
NT2	wup-5 reactor	NT1	sr-305 reactor	NT1	zlfr reactor
NT2	wup-6 reactor	NT1	sre reactor	NT1	zpr reactor
NT2	wwer type reactors	NT1	srrc-utr-100 reactor	RT	lwgr type reactors
NT3	armenian-1 reactor	NT1	stark reactor		
NT3	armenian-2 reactor	NT1	stek reactor	**THERMAL SHIELDS** [523; 523]	
NT3	balakovo-1 reactor	NT1	stir reactor	BT1	shields
NT3	balakovo-2 reactor	NT1	supo reactor	RT	thermal insulation
NT3	blahutovice-1 reactor	NT1	sur-100 series reactor		
NT3	bohunice v-1 reactor	NT1	taiwan research reactor	**THERMAL SHOCK** [1,591; 1,591]	
NT3	bohunice v-2 reactor	NT1	thermos reactor	UF	*shock (thermal)*
NT3	dukovany v-2 reactor	NT1	thetis reactor	RT	heat treatments
NT3	greifswald-1 reactor	NT1	thtr-300 reactor	RT	thermal cycling
NT3	greifswald-2 reactor	NT1	tokai-mura reactor	RT	thermal stresses
NT3	greifswald-3 reactor	NT1	torness reactor		
NT3	greifswald-4 reactor	NT1	toshiba reactor	**THERMAL SPIKES** [174; 174]	
NT3	greifswald-5 reactor	NT1	tr-1 reactor	UF	*spikes (thermal)*
NT3	greifswald-6 reactor	NT1	trawsfynydd reactor	RT	crystal defects
NT3	kalinin-1 reactor	NT1	treat reactor	RT	radiation effects
NT3	kalinin-3 reactor	NT1	trico reactor	RT	thermal-nelson model
NT3	kecerovce-1 reactor	NT1	triga-brazil reactor		
NT3	khmelnitskij-1 reactor	NT1	triga-texas reactor	**THERMAL SPRINGS** [344; 344] *Dec 75*	
NT3	kola-1 reactor	NT1	triga-veterans reactor	UF	*geothermal springs*
NT3	kola-2 reactor	NT1	triga-1-california reactor	UF	*geysers*
NT3	kola-3 reactor	NT1	triga-1-hanover reactor	UF	*hot springs*
NT3	kola 4 reactor	NT1	triga-1-heidelberg reactor	UF	*thermal waters*
NT3	kozloduy-1 reactor	NT1	triga-1-michigan reactor	RT	geothermal energy
NT3	kozloduy-2 reactor	NT1	triga-2 reactor	RT	geothermal fields
NT3	kozloduy-3 reactor	NT1	triga-2-dalat reactor	RT	natural radioactivity
NT3	loviisa-1 reactor	NT1	triga-2-illinois reactor		
NT3	loviisa-2 reactor	NT1	triga-2-kansas reactor		
NT3	mochovce-1 reactor	NT1	triga-2-ljubljana reactor		
NT3	paks-1 reactor	NT1	triga-2-mainz reactor	*thermal storage*	
NT3	paks-2 reactor	NT1	triga-2-musashi reactor	USE	heat storage
NT3	paks-3 reactor	NT1	triga-2-pavia reactor		
NT3	paks-4 reactor	NT1	triga-2-rikkyo reactor	**THERMAL STRESSES** [3,724; 3,724]	
NT3	rovno-1 reactor	NT1	triga-2-rome reactor	BT1	stresses
NT3	rovno-2 reactor	NT1	triga-2-seoul reactor	RT	thermal fractures
NT3	rovno-3 reactor	NT1	triga-2-vienna reactor	RT	thermal shock
NT3	rovno-4 reactor	NT1	triga-3-salazar reactor	RT	thermoelasticity
NT3	rovno-5 reactor	NT1	triga-3-seoul reactor		
NT3	south ukrainian-1 reactor	NT1	triton reactor	**THERMAL TESTING** [467; 704]	
NT3	south ukrainian-2 reactor	NT1	trr-1 reactor	BT1	nondestructive testing
NT3	south ukrainian-3 reactor	NT1	tz1 reactor	BT2	materials testing
NT3	stendal-1 reactor	NT1	tz2 reactor	BT3	testing
NT3	tatarian reactor	NT1	ucbrr reactor	NT1	frost tests
NT3	temelin-1 reactor	NT1	uftr reactor	NT1	thermography
NT3	wwer-1 reactor	NT1	uhtrex reactor		
NT3	wwer-2 reactor	NT1	ulysse reactor	**THERMAL UTILIZATION** [40; 40]	
NT3	wwer-3 reactor	NT1	umne-1 reactor	RT	multiplication factors
NT3	wwer-4 reactor	NT1	umrr reactor		
NT3	wwer-5 reactor	NT1	urr reactor		

thermal waters
   USE   thermal springs

THERMAL-NELSON MODEL [2; 2]
   BT1   mathematical models
   RT   thermal spikes

THERMALIZATION [647; 1,097]
(Establishment of thermal equilibrium between neutrons and their surroundings.)
   BT1   slowing-down

thermionic cells
   USE   thermionic converters

THERMIONIC COLLECTORS [26; 26]
Aug 78
   RT   anodes
   RT   thermionic converters
   RT   thermionic diodes

THERMIONIC CONVERSION [120; 120]
   BT1   direct energy conversion
      BT2   energy conversion
         BT3   conversion
   RT   thermionic converters
   RT   thermionic diodes

THERMIONIC CONVERTERS [492; 492]
   UF   *thermionic cells*
   UF   *thermionic generators*
   BT1   direct energy converters
   RT   thermionic collectors
   RT   thermionic conversion
   RT   thermionic diodes
   RT   thermionic emitters
   RT   thermionic fuel elements
   RT   thermionic reactors
   RT   topaz reactor

THERMIONIC DIODES [358; 358]
   UF   *plasma diodes*
   BT1   diode tubes
      BT2   electron tubes
   BT1   thermionic tubes
      BT2   electron tubes
   RT   magnetic insulation
   RT   semiconductor diodes
   RT   thermionic collectors
   RT   thermionic conversion
   RT   thermionic converters
   RT   thermionic emission
   RT   thermionic emitters

THERMIONIC EMISSION [423; 423]
   BT1   emission
   RT   electron emission
   RT   electron tubes
   RT   thermionic diodes
   RT   thermionic emitters

THERMIONIC EMITTERS [132; 132]
Jul 78
   RT   cathodes
   RT   electron sources
   RT   thermionic converters
   RT   thermionic diodes
   RT   thermionic emission

THERMIONIC FUEL ELEMENTS [61; 61]
   BT1   fuel elements
      BT2   reactor components
   RT   thermionic converters
   RT   thermionic reactors

thermionic generators
   USE   thermionic converters

THERMIONIC REACTORS [156; 156]
(Limited to reactors with in-core thermionic cells.)
   BT1   power reactors
      BT2   reactors
   RT   mobile reactors
   RT   snap reactors
   RT   thermionic converters
   RT   thermionic fuel elements

THERMIONIC TUBES [17; 374]
   BT1   electron tubes
   NT1   thermionic diodes
   RT   microwave tubes

THERMIONICS [47; 47]
   RT   richardson equation
   RT   schottky effect

THERMISTORS [136; 136]
   BT1   semiconductor devices
   RT   resistors

THERMITE PROCESS [77; 77]
   BT1   reduction
      BT2   chemical reactions
   RT   welding

THERMOCHROMATOGRAPHY [202; 202] *Jan 77*
   BT1   chromatography
      BT2   separation processes

THERMOCOUPLES [1,647; 1,647]
   BT1   measuring instruments
   RT   calorimetric dosemeters
   RT   reactor control systems
   RT   temperature measurement
   RT   thermoelectric generators
   RT   thermoelectricity

thermodiffusion
   USE   thermal diffusion

THERMODYNAMIC ACTIVITY [733; 733] *Oct 76*
(Used instead of molar fractions in non-ideal solutions.)
   UF   *activity coefficient*
   UF   *chemical activity*
   RT   chemical reactions
   RT   equilibrium
   RT   phase studies
   RT   quantity ratio
   RT   thermodynamics

THERMODYNAMIC CYCLES [392; 949]
   UF   *bottoming cycles*
   UF   *cycles (thermodynamic)*
   UF   *topping cycles*
   NT1   brayton cycle
   NT1   carnot cycle
   NT1   combined cycles
   NT1   rankine cycle
   NT1   stirling cycle
   RT   closed-cycle systems
   RT   thermodynamics
   RT   working fluids

THERMODYNAMIC MODEL [631; 1,791]
   BT1   particle models
      BT2   mathematical models
   BT1   statistical models
      BT2   mathematical models
   NT1   hydrodynamic model

THERMODYNAMIC MOLECULAR MODEL [32; 32]
   BT1   molecular models
      BT2   mathematical models

THERMODYNAMIC PROPERTIES [5,780; 50,125]
   UF   *thermal properties*
   BT1   physical properties
   NT1   critical pressure
   NT1   enthalpy
   NT2   absorption heat
   NT2   adsorption heat
   NT2   mixing heat
   NT2   reaction heat
   NT3   combustion heat
   NT3   dissociation heat
   NT3   formation heat
   NT2   solution heat
   NT2   transition heat
   NT3   fusion heat
   NT3   sublimation heat
   NT3   vaporization heat
   NT1   entropy
   NT1   free energy
   NT2   formation free energy
   NT1   free enthalpy
   NT2   formation free enthalpy
   NT2   oxygen potential
   NT1   partial pressure
   NT1   specific heat
   NT2   electronic specific heat
   NT2   nuclear specific heat
   NT1   stored energy
   NT1   thermal conductivity
   NT1   thermal diffusivity
   NT1   transition temperature
   NT2   boiling points
   NT2   critical temperature
   NT2   curie point
   NT2   dew point
   NT2   lambda point
   NT2   melting points
   NT2   neel temperature
   NT1   vapor pressure
   RT   limiting values
   RT   prandtl number
   RT   thermal equilibrium
   RT   thermal expansion
   RT   thermal radiation
   RT   thermodynamics

THERMODYNAMICS [8,071; 8,071]
   RT   absolute zero temperature
   RT   adiabatic processes
   RT   brayton cycle
   RT   carnot cycle
   RT   degrees of freedom
   RT   energy
   RT   enthalpy
   RT   entropy
   RT   equations of state
   RT   exergy
   RT   heat sinks
   RT   heat transfer
   RT   irreversible processes
   RT   isentropic processes
   RT   isothermal processes
   RT   khalatnikov theory
   RT   lte
   RT   mollier diagrams
   RT   nernst heat theorem
   RT   onsager relations
   RT   partition functions
   RT   physical metallurgy
   RT   planck radiation formula
   RT   rankine cycle
   RT   saha equation
   RT   steam quality
   RT   stirling cycle
   RT   thermal efficiency
   RT   thermodynamic activity
   RT   thermodynamic cycles
   RT   thermodynamic properties
   RT   virial equation
   RT   wigner distribution

THERMOELASTICITY [195; 195] *Feb 79*
(Dependence of the stress distribution of an elastic solid on its thermal state, or of its thermal conductivity on the stress distribution.)
   BT1   elasticity

BT2	mechanical properties
RT	temperature dependence
RT	thermal conductivity
RT	thermal expansion
RT	thermal stresses

thermoelectric cells
  USE   thermoelectric generators

THERMOELECTRIC CONVERSION
[159; 159]
  BT1   direct energy conversion
    BT2   energy conversion
      BT3   conversion
  RT   thermoelectric generators
  RT   thermoelectric refrigerators

thermoelectric converters
  USE   thermoelectric generators

thermoelectric coolers
  USE   thermoelectric refrigerators

THERMOELECTRIC GENERATORS
[944; 944]
  UF   *thermoelectric cells*
  UF   *thermoelectric converters*
  BT1   direct energy converters
  RT   radioisotope batteries
  RT   radioisotope heat sources
  RT   thermocouples
  RT   thermoelectric conversion
  RT   thermoelectricity

THERMOELECTRIC PROPERTIES
[1,417; 1,417]
  BT1   electrical properties
    BT2   physical properties

THERMOELECTRIC REFRIGERATORS [16; 16] *Apr 80*
  UF   *thermoelectric coolers*
  BT1   direct energy converters
  BT1   refrigerators
  RT   thermoelectric conversion

THERMOELECTRICITY [490; 490]
  BT1   electricity
  RT   seebeck effect
  RT   thermocouples
  RT   thermoelectric generators

THERMOGRAPHY [234; 234] *Jul 78*
(Technique employing heat transfer transients.)
  BT1   thermal testing
    BT2   nondestructive testing
      BT3   materials testing
        BT4   testing
  RT   infrared radiation
  RT   temperature measurement

thermogravimetric analysis
  USE   thermal gravimetric analysis

thermogravimetry
  USE   thermal gravimetric analysis

THERMOLUMINESCENCE
[2,745; 2,888]
  BT1   luminescence
    BT2   photon emission
      BT3   emission
  NT1   radiothermoluminescence
  RT   thermoluminescent dosemeters

THERMOLUMINESCENT DOSEMETERS [3,988; 3,988]
  UF   *tld (dosemeters)*
  UF   *tld systems*
  BT1   luminescent dosemeters
    BT2   dosemeters
      BT3   measuring instruments
  RT   calcium fluorides
  RT   calcium sulfates
  RT   lithium fluorides
  RT   personnel dosimetry
  RT   thermoluminescence
  RT   thermoluminescent dosimetry

THERMOLUMINESCENT DOSIMETRY
[1,542; 1,542]
  UF   *tld (dosimetry)*
  BT1   dosimetry
  RT   thermoluminescent dosemeters

THERMOMAGNETIC CONVERSION
[14; 14]
  BT1   direct energy conversion
    BT2   energy conversion
      BT3   conversion

THERMOMAGNETISM [117; 117]
  BT1   magnetism

THERMOMETERS [560; 617]
  BT1   measuring instruments
  NT1   noise thermometers
  RT   bolometers
  RT   temperature measurement

THERMONUCLEAR DEVICES
[2,339; 40,212]
  NT1   closed plasma devices
    NT2   astron
    NT2   blascon devices
    NT2   heliotron
    NT2   internal ring devices
      NT3   fm devices
      NT3   levitron devices
      NT3   lm devices
      NT3   spherator
      NT3   stator-b device
      NT3   tokapole devices
      NT3   tornado devices
    NT2   stellarators
      NT3   clasp device
      NT3   cleo stellarator
      NT3   h-1 heliac
      NT3   harmonica-2 device
      NT3   heliac stellarators
        NT4   sheila heliac
      NT3   ims stellarator
      NT3   jipp stellarator
      NT3   jippt-2 device
      NT3   l-2 stellarator
      NT3   proto-cleo stellarators
      NT3   pulsator stellarator
      NT3   sirius device
      NT3   stellarator model c
      NT3   torsatron stellarators
        NT4   atf torsatron
        NT4   chs torsatron
        NT4   vint torsatron
      NT3   uragan stellarator
      NT3   wega stellarator
      NT3   wendelstein-2b stellarator
      NT3   wendelstein-7 stellarator
    NT2   tokamak devices
      NT3   act devices
      NT3   aditya tokamak
      NT3   alcator device
      NT3   asdex tokamak
      NT3   atc devices
      NT3   castor tokamak
      NT3   columbia high-beta tokamak
      NT3   compact ignition tokamak
      NT3   continuous current tokamak
      NT3   ct-6b tokamak
      NT3   dante tokamak
      NT3   dite tokamak
      NT3   doublet-1 device
      NT3   doublet-2 device
      NT3   doublet-3 device
      NT3   etf tokamak
      NT3   ft tokamak
      NT3   hl-1 tokamak
      NT3   ht-6b tokamak
      NT3   ht-6m tokamak
      NT3   hybtok tokamaks
      NT3   intor tokamak
      NT3   isx tokamak
      NT3   iter tokamak
      NT3   jet tokamak
      NT3   jft-2 tokamak
      NT3   jft-2a tokamak
      NT3   jft-2m tokamak
      NT3   jippt-2 device
      NT3   jt-60 tokamak
      NT3   jt-60u tokamak
      NT3   jxfr tokamak
      NT3   lt-3 tokamak
      NT3   lt-4 tokamak
      NT3   mt-1 tokamak
      NT3   net tokamak
      NT3   ormak devices
      NT3   pbx devices
      NT3   petula tokamak
      NT3   plt devices
      NT3   spheromak devices
        NT4   ctx spheromak
      NT3   st tokamak
      NT3   starfire tokamak
      NT3   surmac tokamak
      NT3   t-10 tokamak
      NT3   t-15 tokamak
      NT3   t-7 tokamak
      NT3   tbr tokamak
      NT3   tca tokamak
      NT3   text devices
      NT3   textor tokamak
      NT3   tfr tokamak
      NT3   tftr tokamak
      NT3   tiber-x tokamak
      NT3   tj-1 tokamak
      NT3   tnt-a tokamak
      NT3   tokapole devices
      NT3   tokoloshe tokamak
      NT3   tore supra tokamak
      NT3   tormac devices
      NT3   tortus tokamak
      NT3   torus-ii tokamak
      NT3   tosca tokamak
      NT3   triam-1 tokamak
      NT3   tuman devices
      NT3   two-component torus
      NT3   uwmak devices
      NT3   varennes tokamak
      NT3   versator tokamak
      NT3   wt-3 tokamak
    NT2   toroidal pinch devices
      NT3   hbtx devices
      NT3   tlp devices
        NT4   alpha device
        NT4   zeta devices
      NT3   toroidal screw pinch devices
        NT4   tpe-2 device
      NT3   toroidal theta pinch devices
        NT4   scyllac devices
      NT3   tpe-1rm15 device
      NT3   zt-p devices
      NT3   zt-40 devices
  NT1   hylife converter
  NT1   icf devices
    NT2   angara-5 device
  NT1   migma devices
  NT1   open plasma devices
    NT2   baseball devices
    NT2   linear pinch devices
      NT3   linear hard core pinch devices
      NT3   linear screw pinch devices
      NT3   linear theta pinch devices
        NT4   bsg devices
        NT4   chalice devices
        NT4   isar devices
        NT4   pharos devices
        NT4   scylla devices
      NT3   linear z pinch devices
      NT3   megatron
    NT2   magnetic mirrors
      NT3   alice
      NT3   aspa device
      NT3   beta ii devices

	NT3	bsg devices
	NT3	bumpy tori
	NT4	elmo bumpy torus
	NT3	burnout devices
	NT3	circe devices
	NT4	circe-25kw device
	NT3	dcx devices
	NT3	deca devices
	NT3	elmo devices
	NT4	elmo bumpy torus
	NT3	imp device
	NT3	interem device
	NT3	mftf devices
	NT3	ogra
	NT3	phoenix devices
	NT3	pleiade device
	NT3	pr devices
	NT4	pr-6 device
	NT4	pr-7 device
	NT4	pr-8 device
	NT3	reversed-field mirrors
	NT3	tandem mirrors
	NT4	gamma 10 devices
	NT4	phaedrus mirror devices
	NT4	tara devices
	NT4	tmx devices
	NT3	vgl devices
	NT3	2x devices
	NT2	plasma focus devices
	NT2	q devices
	NT3	helios devices
	NT3	qp devices
NT1		pinch devices
	NT2	field-reversed theta pinch dev
	NT2	linear pinch devices
	NT3	linear hard core pinch devices
	NT3	linear screw pinch devices
	NT3	linear theta pinch devices
	NT4	bsg devices
	NT4	chalice devices
	NT4	isar devices
	NT4	pharos devices
	NT4	scylla devices
	NT3	linear z pinch devices
	NT3	megatron
	NT2	toroidal pinch devices
	NT3	hbtx devices
	NT3	tlp devices
	NT4	alpha device
	NT4	zeta devices
	NT3	toroidal screw pinch devices
	NT4	tpe-2 device
	NT3	toroidal theta pinch devices
	NT4	scyllac devices
	NT3	tpe-1rm15 device
	NT3	zt-p devices
	NT3	zt-40 devices
RT		beam injection
RT		confinement time
RT		lawson criterion
RT		magnetic field configurations
RT		mass balance
RT		plasma heating
RT		plasma production
RT		rotational transform
RT		thermonuclear reactors
RT		tritium recovery

THERMONUCLEAR EXPLOSIONS
[180; 196]
- BT1 nuclear explosions
- BT2 explosions
- NT1 bravo event
- NT1 mike event
- NT1 schooner event
- RT castle project
- RT thermonuclear reactions

THERMONUCLEAR FUELS
[1,605; 1,605]
- UF *reactor fuels (fusion)*
- BT1 fuels
- RT deuterium
- RT electron beam targets
- RT fuel feeding systems
- RT fusion yield
- RT ion beam targets
- RT laser targets
- RT pellet injection
- RT thermonuclear reactor fueling
- RT tritium
- RT tritium systems test assembly

THERMONUCLEAR IGNITION
[1,283; 1,283]
- UF *ignition (thermonuclear)*
- UF *reactor start-up (therm ignit)*
- RT compact ignition tokamak
- RT thermonuclear reactors
- RT tiber-x tokamak

thermonuclear implosions(laser
- USE laser implosions

THERMONUCLEAR POWER PLANTS
[515; 515] *Apr 79*
- BT1 nuclear power plants
- BT2 nuclear facilities
- BT2 thermal power plants
- BT3 power plants
- RT thermonuclear reactors

THERMONUCLEAR REACTIONS
[4,153; 4,705]
(Exoenergetic fusion reactions between light nuclei; are always accompanied by release of the excess binding energy.)
- UF *fusion reactions (exoenergetic*
- UF *fusion reactions (thermonuclea*
- BT1 nuclear reactions
- BT1 nucleosynthesis
- BT2 synthesis
- NT1 impact fusion
- NT1 muon-catalyzed fusion
- RT chain reactions
- RT cold fusion
- RT fusion yield
- RT heavy ion fusion reactions
- RT helium ash
- RT matterhorn project
- RT sherwood project
- RT thermonuclear explosions

THERMONUCLEAR REACTOR COOLING [410; 410] *Jul 76*
(For the cooling systems, not the process.)
- UF *cooling systems (fus reactor)*
- UF *reactor cooling systems (fus)*
- BT1 cooling systems
- RT coolants
- RT cooling
- RT heat transfer

THERMONUCLEAR REACTOR FUELING [131; 131] *Nov 82*
- UF *charging (fusion reactor)*
- UF *reactor fueling (fusion reac)*
- RT fuel feeding systems
- RT gas injection
- RT pellet injection
- RT thermonuclear fuels
- RT thermonuclear reactors
- RT tritium systems test assembly

THERMONUCLEAR REACTOR MATERIAL [5,031; 5,031]
(To be assigned in conjunction with the specific descriptor for the material used.)
- UF *fusion-reactor materials*
- UF *reactor materials (fus react)*
- BT1 materials
- RT fmit linac
- RT thermonuclear reactors

THERMONUCLEAR REACTOR WALLS [897; 5,023]
- NT1 first wall
- RT flibe
- RT thermonuclear reactors

THERMONUCLEAR REACTORS
[10,443; 13,202]
(For conceptual design studies; coordinate with descriptor for existing thermonuclear device if appropriate.)
- UF *fusion reactors*
- NT1 d-d reactors
- NT1 d-t reactors
- NT2 pulsed d-t reactors
- NT3 reference theta pinch reactor
- NT2 steady-state d-t reactors
- NT1 electron beam fusion reactors
- NT1 ion beam fusion reactors
- NT1 laser fusion reactors
- NT1 linus reactors
- NT1 pulsed fusion reactors
- NT2 pulsed d-t reactors
- NT3 reference theta pinch reactor
- NT1 steady-state fusion reactors
- NT2 steady-state d-t reactors
- NT1 tmr reactors
- NT1 tns reactors
- RT breakeven
- RT breeding blankets
- RT breeding pellets
- RT confinement time
- RT fusion yield
- RT hybrid reactors
- RT mass balance
- RT power
- RT thermonuclear devices
- RT thermonuclear ignition
- RT thermonuclear power plants
- RT thermonuclear reactor fueling
- RT thermonuclear reactor material
- RT thermonuclear reactor walls
- RT tritium recovery

thermonuclear weapons
- USE nuclear weapons

THERMOPHORESIS [20; 20] *Sep 86*
- RT electrophoresis

THERMOPLASTICS [138; 138]
- BT1 organic polymers
- BT2 organic compounds
- BT2 polymers

thermoregulation
(Mechanism by which mammals and birds attempt to balance heat gain and heat loss in order to maintain a constant body temperature when exposed to variations temperature of the surroundings.)
- USE body temperature
- AND temperature control

THERMOS REACTOR [25; 25] *Feb*
- BT1 process heat reactors
- BT2 power reactors
- BT3 reactors
- BT1 tank type reactors
- BT2 reactors
- BT1 thermal reactors
- BT2 reactors

THERMOSPHERE [352; 352]
- BT1 earth atmosphere

THERMOSTATS [92; 1,734]
- BT1 control equipment
- BT2 equipment
- NT1 cryostats
- RT temperature control

THERMOSYPHONS [98; 98] *Jun 83*
(Systems of natural circulation in a flu caused by the difference between hot a cold portions.)
- RT heat transfer
- RT natural convection

THERMOX PROCESS [4; 4]
- BT1 reprocessing
- BT2 separation processes
- RT solvent extraction

thesauri
- USE standardized terminology

THETA PINCH [920; 920]
- BT1 pinch effect
- RT linear theta pinch devices
- RT reference theta pinch reactor
- RT toroidal theta pinch devices

theta-1690 resonances
(Prior to December 1987 this was a valid descriptor.)
- USE f2-1720 mesons

THETIS REACTOR [6; 6]
(University Gent, Institute for Nuclear Sciences, Pietersnieuwstraat, Belgium)
- UF *iisnr reactor*
- BT1 enriched uranium reactors
- BT2 reactors
- BT1 isotope production reactors
- BT2 irradiation reactors
- BT3 reactors
- BT1 pool type reactors
- BT2 water cooled reactors
- BT3 reactors
- BT2 water moderated reactors
- BT3 reactors
- BT1 research reactors
- BT2 research and test reactors
- BT3 reactors
- BT1 thermal reactors
- BT2 reactors
- BT1 training reactors
- BT2 research and test reactors
- BT3 reactors

thf
- USE tetrahydrofuran

THIADIAZOLES [24; 24]
(Compounds that contain a five-membered heterocyclic ring containing one sulfur and two nitrogen atoms.)
- BT1 azoles
- BT2 heterocyclic compounds
- BT3 organic compounds
- BT2 organic nitrogen compounds
- BT3 organic compounds
- BT1 organic sulfur compounds
- BT2 organic compounds

THIAMINE [103; 103]
- UF *vitamin b-1*
- BT1 amines
- BT2 organic compounds
- BT1 hydroxy compounds
- BT2 organic compounds
- BT1 pyrimidines
- BT2 azines
- BT3 heterocyclic compounds
- BT4 organic compounds
- BT3 organic nitrogen compounds
- BT4 organic compounds
- BT1 thiazoles
- BT2 azoles
- BT3 heterocyclic compounds
- BT4 organic compounds
- BT3 organic nitrogen compounds
- BT4 organic compounds
- BT2 organic sulfur compounds
- BT3 organic compounds
- BT1 vitamin b group
- BT2 vitamins

THIAZOLES [165; 351]
(Compounds that contain a five-membered heterocyclic ring containing one sulfur and one nitrogen atom.)
- UF *thiazolidines*
- BT1 azoles
- BT2 heterocyclic compounds
- BT3 organic compounds
- BT2 organic nitrogen compounds
- BT3 organic compounds
- BT1 organic sulfur compounds
- BT2 organic compounds
- NT1 benzothiazoles
- NT1 saccharin
- NT1 thiamine

thiazolidines
- USE thiazoles

§§ **THICKNESS** [9,580; 9,655]
(Index only if essential.)
- BT1 dimensions
- RT distance
- RT half-thickness
- RT radiation length
- RT shielding
- RT size

THICKNESS GAGES [712; 712]
- BT1 measuring instruments
- RT radiometric gages

THIN FILM STORAGE DEVICES [24; 24]
- BT1 memory devices

THIN FILMS [4,846; 4,846] *Dec 83*
(Films a few molecules thick deposited on a substrate.)
- BT1 films
- RT coatings
- RT deposition
- RT substrates

THIN-LAYER CHROMATOGRAPHY [1,325; 1,325]
- BT1 chromatography
- BT2 separation processes

thio compounds
- USE organic sulfur compounds

thioalcohols
- USE thiols

THIOBACILLUS FERROXIDANS [82; 82]
- BT1 bacillus
- BT2 bacteria
- BT3 microorganisms
- BT1 sulfur-oxidizing bacteria
- BT2 bacteria
- BT3 microorganisms
- RT leaching
- RT oxidation
- RT uranium ores

THIOBACILLUS OXIDANS [22; 22]
- BT1 bacillus
- BT2 bacteria
- BT3 microorganisms
- BT1 sulfur-oxidizing bacteria
- BT2 bacteria
- BT3 microorganisms
- RT desulfurization
- RT leaching
- RT ore processing
- RT oxidation
- RT sulfur cycle

thiocarbamides
- USE thioureas

THIOCTIC ACID [15; 15]
- UF *lipoic acid (alpha)*
- BT1 disulfides
- BT2 organic sulfur compounds
- BT3 organic compounds
- BT1 heterocyclic acids
- BT2 carboxylic acids
- BT3 organic acids
- BT4 organic compounds
- BT2 heterocyclic compounds
- BT3 organic compounds
- BT1 lipotropic factors
- BT2 drugs

THIOCYANATES [1,060; 1,060]
- UF *isothiocyanates*
- UF *rhodanates*
- UF *rhodanides*
- UF *sulfocyanides*
- UF *thiocyanides*
- BT1 antithyroid drugs
- BT2 drugs
- BT1 carbonic acid derivatives
- BT2 organic compounds
- BT1 organic sulfur compounds
- BT2 organic compounds
- NT1 ammonium thiocyanates
- RT thiocyanic acid

THIOCYANIC ACID [12; 12]
- RT thiocyanates

thiocyanides
- USE thiocyanates

thioethers
- USE sulfides

thioglycolicaminonaphthalide
- USE thionalide

THIOIC ACIDS [91; 91]
- BT1 organic acids
- BT2 organic compounds
- BT1 organic sulfur compounds
- BT2 organic compounds

THIOLS [1,115; 2,546]
- UF *mercaptans*
- UF *sulfhydryl compounds*
- UF *thioalcohols*
- BT1 organic sulfur compounds
- BT2 organic compounds
- NT1 cysteine
- NT1 dithiols
- NT2 bal
- NT2 unithiol
- NT1 malathion
- NT1 mea
- NT1 meg
- NT1 mercaptopurine
- NT1 mpg
- NT1 penicillamine
- NT1 thionalide
- NT1 thiouracil

THIONALIDE [15; 15]
- UF *thioglycolicaminonaphthalide*
- BT1 amides
- BT2 organic nitrogen compounds
- BT3 organic compounds
- BT1 reagents
- BT1 thiols
- BT2 organic sulfur compounds
- BT3 organic compounds
- RT glycolic acid

THIONAPHTHENES [7; 7]
- UF *benzothiophenes*
- BT1 heterocyclic compounds
- BT2 organic compounds
- BT1 organic sulfur compounds
- BT2 organic compounds

thionates
- USE oxygen compounds
- AND sulfur compounds

THIONINE [27; 27]
- BT1 amines
- BT2 organic compounds
- BT1 heterocyclic compounds
- BT2 organic compounds
- BT1 organic nitrogen compounds
- BT2 organic compounds
- BT1 organic sulfur compounds
- BT2 organic compounds
- RT phenothiazines

THIOPENTAL [9; 9]
- UF *pentothal*
- BT1 barbiturates
- BT2 anesthetics
  - BT3 central nervous system depress
    - BT4 central nervous system agents
      - BT5 drugs
- BT2 hypnotics and sedatives
  - BT3 central nervous system depress
    - BT4 central nervous system agents
      - BT5 drugs
- BT2 organic oxygen compounds
  - BT3 organic compounds
- BT2 pyrimidines
  - BT3 azines
    - BT4 heterocyclic compounds
      - BT5 organic compounds
    - BT4 organic nitrogen compounds
      - BT5 organic compounds
- BT1 organic sulfur compounds
- BT2 organic compounds

THIOPHENE [88; 88]
- BT1 heterocyclic compounds
- BT2 organic compounds
- BT1 organic sulfur compounds
- BT2 organic compounds
- RT tta

THIOPHENOLS [18; 18]
- BT1 organic sulfur compounds
- BT2 organic compounds

THIOPHOSPHORIC ACID ESTERS [61; 147]
- BT1 esters
- BT2 organic compounds
- NT1 cystaphos
- NT1 gammaphos
- NT1 parathion
- RT organic phosphorus compounds
- RT organic sulfur compounds

THIOSULFATES [128; 128]
- RT sulfates

THIOURACIL [59; 59]
- BT1 antimetabolites
- BT2 drugs
- BT1 antithyroid drugs
- BT2 drugs
- BT1 thiols
- BT2 organic sulfur compounds
- BT3 organic compounds
- BT1 uracils
- BT2 hydroxy compounds
- BT3 organic compounds
- BT2 pyrimidines
- BT3 azines
  - BT4 heterocyclic compounds
  - BT5 organic compounds
  - BT4 organic nitrogen compounds
  - BT5 organic compounds

THIOUREA [233; 233]
- BT1 antithyroid drugs
- BT2 drugs
- BT1 thioureas
- BT2 carbonic acid derivatives
- BT3 organic compounds
- BT2 organic sulfur compounds
- BT3 organic compounds

THIOUREAS [273; 810]
- UF *thiocarbamides*
- BT1 carbonic acid derivatives
- BT2 organic compounds
- BT1 organic sulfur compounds
- BT2 organic compounds
- NT1 aet
- NT1 thiourea
- RT amides

third party liabil conv, bruss
- USE bcstpc

third party liabil conv, paris
- USE pcotpl

THIRD SOUND [136; 136]
- RT superfluidity

THIRRING MODEL [465; 465]
- RT merons
- RT quantum field theory

THIYL RADICALS [36; 36]
(For RS- radicals where R is organic component.)
- BT1 radicals

THOMAS-FERMI MODEL [887; 887]
- UF *fermi-thomas model*
- UF *thomas-fermi-dirac model*
- BT1 mathematical models
- RT atomic models
- RT nuclear models

thomas-fermi-dirac model
- USE thomas-fermi model

THOMSON SCATTERING [1,206; 1,206]
- BT1 inelastic scattering
- BT2 scattering

THOR REACTOR [21; 21]
(Hsin-Chu, Taiwan)
- UF *topr reactor*
- BT1 enriched uranium reactors
- BT2 reactors
- BT1 intermediate reactors
- BT2 epithermal reactors
- BT3 reactors
- BT1 isotope production reactors
- BT2 irradiation reactors
- BT3 reactors
- BT1 pool type reactors
- BT2 water cooled reactors
- BT3 reactors
- BT2 water moderated reactors
- BT3 reactors
- BT1 research reactors
- BT2 research and test reactors
- BT3 reactors
- BT1 training reactors
- BT2 research and test reactors
- BT3 reactors

thoracic duct
- USE lymph vessels

thorax
- USE chest

THOREX PROCESS [121; 121]
- BT1 reprocessing
- BT2 separation processes
- RT solvent extraction

THORIANITE [10; 10]
- BT1 oxide minerals
- BT2 minerals
- BT1 thorium minerals
- BT2 radioactive minerals
- BT3 minerals
- BT3 radioactive materials
- BT4 materials
- BT1 uranium minerals
- BT2 radioactive minerals
- BT3 minerals
- BT3 radioactive materials
- BT4 materials
- RT black sands
- RT thorium oxides
- RT uranium oxides

THORIN [7; 7]
- BT1 arsenic compounds
- BT1 diazo compounds
- BT2 organic nitrogen compounds
- BT3 organic compounds
- BT1 naphthols
- BT2 phenols
- BT3 aromatics
- BT4 organic compounds
- BT3 hydroxy compounds
- BT4 organic compounds
- BT1 reagents
- BT1 sulfonic acids
- BT2 organic acids
- BT3 organic compounds
- BT2 organic sulfur compounds
- BT3 organic compounds

THORITE [34; 34]
- BT1 silicate minerals
- BT2 minerals
- BT1 thorium minerals
- BT2 radioactive minerals
- BT3 minerals
- BT3 radioactive materials
- BT4 materials
- RT black sands
- RT thorium silicates

THORIUM [5,142; 5,189]
- BT1 actinides
- BT2 metals
- BT3 elements
- NT1 thorium-alpha
- NT1 thorium-beta
- RT natural radioactivity

thorium a
- USE polonium 216

THORIUM ADDITIONS [45; 45]
(Alloys containing not more than 1% are listed here.)
- RT thorium alloys
- RT thorium compounds

THORIUM ALLOYS [514; 570]
(Alloys containing more than 1% Th.)
- BT1 actinide alloys
- BT2 alloys
- NT1 thorium base alloys
- RT thorium additions

THORIUM ARSENIDES [15; 15] Dec
- BT1 arsenides
- BT2 arsenic compounds
- BT2 pnictides
- BT1 thorium compounds
- BT2 actinide compounds

thorium b
USE   lead 212

THORIUM BASE ALLOYS [57; 57]
BT1   thorium alloys
BT2   actinide alloys
BT3   alloys

THORIUM BORIDES [23; 23]
BT1   borides
BT2   boron compounds
BT1   thorium compounds
BT2   actinide compounds

THORIUM BROMIDES [68; 68]
BT1   bromides
BT2   bromine compounds
BT3   halogen compounds
BT2   halides
BT3   halogen compounds
BT1   thorium compounds
BT2   actinide compounds

thorium c
USE   bismuth 212

thorium c/
USE   polonium 212

thorium c//
USE   thallium 208

THORIUM CARBIDES [256; 256]
BT1   carbides
BT2   carbon compounds
BT1   thorium compounds
BT2   actinide compounds

THORIUM CARBONATES [11; 11]
BT1   carbonates
BT2   carbon compounds
BT2   oxygen compounds
BT1   thorium compounds
BT2   actinide compounds

THORIUM CHLORIDES [180; 180]
BT1   chlorides
BT2   chlorine compounds
BT3   halogen compounds
BT2   halides
BT3   halogen compounds
BT1   thorium compounds
BT2   actinide compounds

THORIUM COMPLEXES [903; 903]
BT1   actinide complexes
BT2   complexes

THORIUM COMPOUNDS [676; 4,290]
BT1   actinide compounds
NT1   thorium arsenides
NT1   thorium borides
NT1   thorium bromides
NT1   thorium carbides
NT1   thorium carbonates
NT1   thorium chlorides
NT1   thorium fluorides
NT1   thorium hydrides
NT1   thorium hydroxides
NT1   thorium iodides
NT1   thorium nitrates
NT1   thorium nitrides
NT1   thorium oxides
NT2   thorotrast
NT1   thorium perchlorates
NT1   thorium phosphates
NT1   thorium phosphides
NT1   thorium selenides
NT1   thorium silicates
NT1   thorium silicides
NT1   thorium sulfates

NT1   thorium sulfides
NT1   thorium tellurides
NT1   thorium tungstates
RT   thorium additions

THORIUM CYCLE [514; 514] *Feb 78*
(Use of thorium as the fertile material in reactor fuels.)
BT1   fuel cycle
RT   nuclear fuels
RT   thorium 232

thorium d
USE   lead 208

THORIUM DEPOSITS [17; 17] *May 86*
BT1   geologic deposits
RT   thorium ores

THORIUM FLUORIDES [216; 216]
BT1   fluorides
BT2   fluorine compounds
BT3   halogen compounds
BT2   halides
BT3   halogen compounds
BT1   thorium compounds
BT2   actinide compounds

THORIUM HYDRIDES [74; 74]
BT1   hydrides
BT2   hydrogen compounds
BT1   thorium compounds
BT2   actinide compounds

THORIUM HYDROXIDES [44; 44]
BT1   hydroxides
BT2   hydrogen compounds
BT2   oxygen compounds
BT1   thorium compounds
BT2   actinide compounds

THORIUM IODIDES [28; 28]
BT1   iodides
BT2   halides
BT3   halogen compounds
BT2   iodine compounds
BT3   halogen compounds
BT1   thorium compounds
BT2   actinide compounds

THORIUM IONS [91; 91]
BT1   ions
BT2   charged particles

THORIUM ISOTOPES [480; 4,216]
NT1   thorium 212
NT1   thorium 213
NT1   thorium 214
NT1   thorium 215
NT1   thorium 216
NT1   thorium 217
NT1   thorium 218
NT1   thorium 219
NT1   thorium 220
NT1   thorium 221
NT1   thorium 222
NT1   thorium 223
NT1   thorium 224
NT1   thorium 225
NT1   thorium 226
NT1   thorium 227
NT1   thorium 228
NT1   thorium 229
NT1   thorium 230
NT1   thorium 231
NT1   thorium 232
NT1   thorium 233
NT1   thorium 234
NT1   thorium 235
NT1   thorium 236
NT1   thorium 238

THORIUM MINERALS [76; 713]

BT1   radioactive minerals
BT2   minerals
BT2   radioactive materials
BT3   materials
NT1   aeschynite
NT1   allanite
NT2   orthite
NT1   bastnaesite
NT1   brannerite
NT1   cerianite
NT1   huttonite
NT1   monazites
NT1   steenstrupine
NT1   thorianite
NT1   thorite
NT1   thorogummite
NT1   thucholite
NT1   uranothorianite
NT1   uranothorite
NT1   yttrialite
RT   thorium oxides
RT   thorium phosphates
RT   thorium silicates

THORIUM NITRATES [236; 236]
BT1   nitrates
BT2   nitrogen compounds
BT2   oxygen compounds
BT1   thorium compounds
BT2   actinide compounds

THORIUM NITRIDES [100; 100]
BT1   nitrides
BT2   nitrogen compounds
BT2   pnictides
BT1   thorium compounds
BT2   actinide compounds

THORIUM ORES [339; 339]
BT1   ores
RT   thorium deposits
RT   thorium reserves

THORIUM OXIDES [1,820; 2,238]
BT1   oxides
BT2   chalcogenides
BT2   oxygen compounds
BT1   thorium compounds
BT2   actinide compounds
NT1   thorotrast
RT   aeschynite
RT   bastnaesite
RT   brannerite
RT   cerianite
RT   oxide minerals
RT   td-nickel
RT   td-nickel chromium
RT   thorianite
RT   thorium minerals
RT   uranothorianite

THORIUM PERCHLORATES [3; 3]
Jun 83
BT1   perchlorates
BT2   chlorine compounds
BT3   halogen compounds
BT2   oxygen compounds
BT1   thorium compounds
BT2   actinide compounds

THORIUM PHOSPHATES [23; 285]
BT1   phosphates
BT2   oxygen compounds
BT2   phosphorus compounds
BT1   thorium compounds
BT2   actinide compounds
RT   monazites
RT   thorium minerals

THORIUM PHOSPHIDES [38; 38]
BT1   phosphides
BT2   phosphorus compounds
BT2   pnictides
BT1   thorium compounds
BT2   actinide compounds

THORIUM REACTORS [45; 1,135]
  BT1   reactors
  NT1   avr reactor
  NT1   borax-4 reactor
  NT1   dragon reactor
  NT1   err reactor
  NT1   sre reactor
  NT1   thtr-300 reactor
  RT   iea-zpr reactor
  RT   zenith reactor

THORIUM RESERVES [8; 8] *May 86*
  BT1   reserves
    BT2   resources
  RT   thorium ores

THORIUM SELENIDES [19; 19] *Oct 75*
  BT1   selenides
    BT2   chalcogenides
    BT2   selenium compounds
  BT1   thorium compounds
    BT2   actinide compounds

THORIUM SILICATES [15; 64]
  BT1   silicates
    BT2   oxygen compounds
    BT2   silicon compounds
  BT1   thorium compounds
    BT2   actinide compounds
  RT   allanite
  RT   huttonite
  RT   silicate minerals
  RT   thorite
  RT   thorium minerals
  RT   thorogummite
  RT   uranothorite
  RT   yttrialite

THORIUM SILICIDES [17; 17] *Jul 77*
  BT1   silicides
    BT2   silicon compounds
  BT1   thorium compounds
    BT2   actinide compounds

THORIUM SULFATES [27; 27]
  BT1   sulfates
    BT2   oxygen compounds
    BT2   sulfur compounds
  BT1   thorium compounds
    BT2   actinide compounds

THORIUM SULFIDES [54; 54]
  BT1   sulfides
    BT2   chalcogenides
    BT2   sulfur compounds
  BT1   thorium compounds
    BT2   actinide compounds

THORIUM TELLURIDES [12; 12]
Feb 76
  BT1   tellurides
    BT2   chalcogenides
    BT2   tellurium compounds
  BT1   thorium compounds
    BT2   actinide compounds

THORIUM TUNGSTATES [4; 4] *Jul 78*
  BT1   thorium compounds
    BT2   actinide compounds
  BT1   tungstates
    BT2   oxygen compounds
    BT2   tungsten compounds
      BT3   transition element compounds

thorium x
  USE   radium 224

THORIUM 212 [3; 3] *Sep 79*
  BT1   actinide nuclei
    BT2   heavy nuclei
      BT3   nuclei
  BT1   alpha decay radioisotopes
    BT2   radioisotopes
      BT3   isotopes

  BT1   even-even nuclei
    BT2   nuclei
  BT1   millisec living radioisotopes
    BT2   radioisotopes
      BT3   isotopes
  BT1   thorium isotopes

THORIUM 213 [5; 5]
  BT1   actinide nuclei
    BT2   heavy nuclei
      BT3   nuclei
  BT1   alpha decay radioisotopes
    BT2   radioisotopes
      BT3   isotopes
  BT1   even-odd nuclei
    BT2   nuclei
  BT1   millisec living radioisotopes
    BT2   radioisotopes
      BT3   isotopes
  BT1   thorium isotopes

THORIUM 214 [4; 4]
  BT1   actinide nuclei
    BT2   heavy nuclei
      BT3   nuclei
  BT1   alpha decay radioisotopes
    BT2   radioisotopes
      BT3   isotopes
  BT1   even-even nuclei
    BT2   nuclei
  BT1   millisec living radioisotopes
    BT2   radioisotopes
      BT3   isotopes
  BT1   thorium isotopes

THORIUM 215 [4; 4]
  BT1   actinide nuclei
    BT2   heavy nuclei
      BT3   nuclei
  BT1   alpha decay radioisotopes
    BT2   radioisotopes
      BT3   isotopes
  BT1   even-odd nuclei
    BT2   nuclei
  BT1   seconds living radioisotopes
    BT2   radioisotopes
      BT3   isotopes
  BT1   thorium isotopes

THORIUM 216 [7; 7]
  BT1   actinide nuclei
    BT2   heavy nuclei
      BT3   nuclei
  BT1   alpha decay radioisotopes
    BT2   radioisotopes
      BT3   isotopes
  BT1   even-even nuclei
    BT2   nuclei
  BT1   millisec living radioisotopes
    BT2   radioisotopes
      BT3   isotopes
  BT1   thorium isotopes

THORIUM 217 [8; 8]
  BT1   actinide nuclei
    BT2   heavy nuclei
      BT3   nuclei
  BT1   alpha decay radioisotopes
    BT2   radioisotopes
      BT3   isotopes
  BT1   even-odd nuclei
    BT2   nuclei
  BT1   microsec living radioisotopes
    BT2   radioisotopes
      BT3   isotopes
  BT1   thorium isotopes

THORIUM 218 [18; 18]
  BT1   actinide nuclei
    BT2   heavy nuclei
      BT3   nuclei
  BT1   alpha decay radioisotopes
    BT2   radioisotopes
      BT3   isotopes
  BT1   even-even nuclei
    BT2   nuclei
  BT1   nanosec living radioisotopes

    BT2   radioisotopes
      BT3   isotopes
  BT1   thorium isotopes

THORIUM 219 [4; 4]
  BT1   actinide nuclei
    BT2   heavy nuclei
      BT3   nuclei
  BT1   alpha decay radioisotopes
    BT2   radioisotopes
      BT3   isotopes
  BT1   even-odd nuclei
    BT2   nuclei
  BT1   microsec living radioisotopes
    BT2   radioisotopes
      BT3   isotopes
  BT1   thorium isotopes

THORIUM 220 [23; 23]
  BT1   actinide nuclei
    BT2   heavy nuclei
      BT3   nuclei
  BT1   alpha decay radioisotopes
    BT2   radioisotopes
      BT3   isotopes
  BT1   even-even nuclei
    BT2   nuclei
  BT1   microsec living radioisotopes
    BT2   radioisotopes
      BT3   isotopes
  BT1   thorium isotopes

THORIUM 221 [7; 7]
  BT1   actinide nuclei
    BT2   heavy nuclei
      BT3   nuclei
  BT1   alpha decay radioisotopes
    BT2   radioisotopes
      BT3   isotopes
  BT1   even-odd nuclei
    BT2   nuclei
  BT1   millisec living radioisotopes
    BT2   radioisotopes
      BT3   isotopes
  BT1   thorium isotopes

THORIUM 222 [34; 34]
  BT1   actinide nuclei
    BT2   heavy nuclei
      BT3   nuclei
  BT1   alpha decay radioisotopes
    BT2   radioisotopes
      BT3   isotopes
  BT1   even-odd nuclei
    BT2   nuclei
  BT1   millisec living radioisotopes
    BT2   radioisotopes
      BT3   isotopes
  BT1   thorium isotopes

THORIUM 223 [21; 21]
  BT1   actinide nuclei
    BT2   heavy nuclei
      BT3   nuclei
  BT1   alpha decay radioisotopes
    BT2   radioisotopes
      BT3   isotopes
  BT1   even-odd nuclei
    BT2   nuclei
  BT1   millisec living radioisotopes
    BT2   radioisotopes
      BT3   isotopes
  BT1   thorium isotopes

THORIUM 224 [35; 35]
  BT1   actinide nuclei
    BT2   heavy nuclei
      BT3   nuclei
  BT1   alpha decay radioisotopes
    BT2   radioisotopes
      BT3   isotopes
  BT1   even-even nuclei
    BT2   nuclei
  BT1   seconds living radioisotopes
    BT2   radioisotopes
      BT3   isotopes
  BT1   thorium isotopes

THORIUM 225 [10; 10]
BT1 actinide nuclei
 BT2 heavy nuclei
  BT3 nuclei
BT1 alpha decay radioisotopes
 BT2 radioisotopes
  BT3 isotopes
BT1 electron capture radioisotopes
 BT2 beta decay radioisotopes
  BT3 radioisotopes
   BT4 isotopes
BT1 even-odd nuclei
 BT2 nuclei
BT1 minutes living radioisotopes
 BT2 radioisotopes
  BT3 isotopes
BT1 thorium isotopes

THORIUM 226 [38; 38]
BT1 actinide nuclei
 BT2 heavy nuclei
  BT3 nuclei
BT1 alpha decay radioisotopes
 BT2 radioisotopes
  BT3 isotopes
BT1 even-even nuclei
 BT2 nuclei
BT1 minutes living radioisotopes
 BT2 radioisotopes
  BT3 isotopes
BT1 thorium isotopes

THORIUM 227 [79; 79]
BT1 actinide nuclei
 BT2 heavy nuclei
  BT3 nuclei
BT1 alpha decay radioisotopes
 BT2 radioisotopes
  BT3 isotopes
BT1 days living radioisotopes
 BT2 radioisotopes
  BT3 isotopes
BT1 even-odd nuclei
 BT2 nuclei
BT1 thorium isotopes

THORIUM 228 [620; 620]
UF *radiothorium*
BT1 actinide nuclei
 BT2 heavy nuclei
  BT3 nuclei
BT1 alpha decay radioisotopes
 BT2 radioisotopes
  BT3 isotopes
BT1 even-even nuclei
 BT2 nuclei
BT1 thorium isotopes
BT1 years living radioisotopes
 BT2 radioisotopes
  BT3 isotopes

THORIUM 228 TARGET [4; 4] *Oct 86*
BT1 targets

THORIUM 229 [115; 115]
BT1 actinide nuclei
 BT2 heavy nuclei
  BT3 nuclei
BT1 alpha decay radioisotopes
 BT2 radioisotopes
  BT3 isotopes
BT1 even-odd nuclei
 BT2 nuclei
BT1 thorium isotopes
BT1 years living radioisotopes
 BT2 radioisotopes
  BT3 isotopes

THORIUM 229 TARGET [37; 37]
BT1 targets

THORIUM 230 [972; 972]
BT1 actinide nuclei
 BT2 heavy nuclei
  BT3 nuclei
BT1 alpha decay radioisotopes
 BT2 radioisotopes
  BT3 isotopes
BT1 even-even nuclei
 BT2 nuclei
BT1 neon 24 decay radioisotopes
 BT2 heavy ion decay radioisotopes
  BT3 radioisotopes
   BT4 isotopes
BT1 spontaneous fission radioisoto
 BT2 radioisotopes
  BT3 isotopes
BT1 thorium isotopes
BT1 years living radioisotopes
 BT2 radioisotopes
  BT3 isotopes

THORIUM 230 TARGET [85; 85]
BT1 targets

THORIUM 231 [103; 103]
UF *uranium x 2*
BT1 actinide nuclei
 BT2 heavy nuclei
  BT3 nuclei
BT1 beta-minus decay radioisotopes
 BT2 beta decay radioisotopes
  BT3 radioisotopes
   BT4 isotopes
BT1 days living radioisotopes
 BT2 radioisotopes
  BT3 isotopes
BT1 even-odd nuclei
 BT2 nuclei
BT1 thorium isotopes

THORIUM 231 TARGET [6; 6] *Nov 77*
BT1 targets

THORIUM 232 [2,245; 2,245]
BT1 actinide nuclei
 BT2 heavy nuclei
  BT3 nuclei
BT1 alpha decay radioisotopes
 BT2 radioisotopes
  BT3 isotopes
BT1 even-even nuclei
 BT2 nuclei
BT1 spontaneous fission radioisoto
 BT2 radioisotopes
  BT3 isotopes
BT1 thorium isotopes
BT1 years living radioisotopes
 BT2 radioisotopes
  BT3 isotopes
RT thorium cycle

THORIUM 232 REACTIONS [8; 8]
Aug 87
BT1 heavy ion reactions
 BT2 nuclear reactions

THORIUM 232 TARGET [1,238; 1,238]
BT1 targets

THORIUM 233 [102; 102]
BT1 actinide nuclei
 BT2 heavy nuclei
  BT3 nuclei
BT1 beta-minus decay radioisotopes
 BT2 beta decay radioisotopes
  BT3 radioisotopes
   BT4 isotopes
BT1 even-odd nuclei
 BT2 nuclei
BT1 minutes living radioisotopes
 BT2 radioisotopes
  BT3 isotopes
BT1 thorium isotopes

THORIUM 233 TARGET [10; 10]
Nov 77
BT1 targets

THORIUM 234 [298; 298]
UF *uranium x 1*
BT1 actinide nuclei
 BT2 heavy nuclei
  BT3 nuclei
BT1 beta-minus decay radioisotopes
 BT2 beta decay radioisotopes
  BT3 radioisotopes
   BT4 isotopes
BT1 days living radioisotopes
 BT2 radioisotopes
  BT3 isotopes
BT1 even-even nuclei
 BT2 nuclei
BT1 internal conversion radioisoto
 BT2 radioisotopes
  BT3 isotopes
BT1 thorium isotopes

THORIUM 235 [8; 8]
BT1 actinide nuclei
 BT2 heavy nuclei
  BT3 nuclei
BT1 beta-minus decay radioisotopes
 BT2 beta decay radioisotopes
  BT3 radioisotopes
   BT4 isotopes
BT1 even-odd nuclei
 BT2 nuclei
BT1 minutes living radioisotopes
 BT2 radioisotopes
  BT3 isotopes
BT1 thorium isotopes

THORIUM 236 [7; 7]
BT1 actinide nuclei
 BT2 heavy nuclei
  BT3 nuclei
BT1 beta-minus decay radioisotopes
 BT2 beta decay radioisotopes
  BT3 radioisotopes
   BT4 isotopes
BT1 even-even nuclei
 BT2 nuclei
BT1 minutes living radioisotopes
 BT2 radioisotopes
  BT3 isotopes
BT1 thorium isotopes

THORIUM 238 [12; 12] *Dec 80*
BT1 actinide nuclei
 BT2 heavy nuclei
  BT3 nuclei
BT1 even-even nuclei
 BT2 nuclei
BT1 thorium isotopes

THORIUM 239 TARGET [5; 5]
BT1 targets

THORIUM-ALPHA [45; 45]
BT1 thorium
 BT2 actinides
  BT3 metals
   BT4 elements

THORIUM-BETA [32; 32]
BT1 thorium
 BT2 actinides
  BT3 metals
   BT4 elements

thorium-hochtemp. protot. rea.
USE thtr-300 reactor

THOROGUMMITE [8; 8]
BT1 silicate minerals
 BT2 minerals
BT1 thorium minerals
 BT2 radioactive minerals
  BT3 minerals
 BT3 radioactive materials
  BT4 materials
RT thorium silicates

thoron
  USE radon 220

THOROTRAST [357; 357]
  BT1 contrast media
  BT1 radiocolloids
    BT2 colloids
      BT3 dispersions
  BT1 thorium oxides
    BT2 oxides
      BT3 chalcogenides
      BT3 oxygen compounds
    BT2 thorium compounds
      BT3 actinide compounds

→ **THR REACTOR** [24; 24] *Sep 91*
  (Qinghua University, Beijing, China)
  UF *test heating reactor*
  BT1 process heat reactors
    BT2 power reactors
      BT3 reactors
  BT1 pwr type reactors
    BT2 enriched uranium reactors
      BT3 reactors
    BT2 power reactors
      BT3 reactors
    BT2 thermal reactors
      BT3 reactors
    BT2 water cooled reactors
      BT3 reactors
    BT2 water moderated reactors
      BT3 reactors

THREADED JOINTS [14; 14] *Nov 88*
  BT1 joints

THREE MILE ISLAND-1 REACTOR [229; 229]
  (Dauphin county, Pennsylvania, USA)
  BT1 pwr type reactors
    BT2 enriched uranium reactors
      BT3 reactors
    BT2 power reactors
      BT3 reactors
    BT2 thermal reactors
      BT3 reactors
    BT2 water cooled reactors
      BT3 reactors
    BT2 water moderated reactors
      BT3 reactors

THREE MILE ISLAND-2 REACTOR [2,183; 2,183]
  (Dauphin county, Pennsylvania, USA)
  BT1 pwr type reactors
    BT2 enriched uranium reactors
      BT3 reactors
    BT2 power reactors
      BT3 reactors
    BT2 thermal reactors
      BT3 reactors
    BT2 water cooled reactors
      BT3 reactors
    BT2 water moderated reactors
      BT3 reactors

THREE-BODY PROBLEM [5,057; 5,057]
  BT1 many-body problem
  RT efimov effect
  RT faddeev equations

THREE-DIMENSIONAL CALCULATIONS [8,481; 8,481]
  UF *calculations (3-dimensional)*
  UF *3-dimensional calculations*
  RT adjoint difference method
  RT general circulation models
  RT many-dimensional calculations
  RT mathematics

THREE-NUCLEON TRANSFER REACTIO [1,138; 1,138]
  BT1 multi-nucleon transfer reactio
    BT2 transfer reactions
      BT3 direct reactions
        BT4 nuclear reactions

THREONINE [110; 110]
  BT1 amino acids
    BT2 carboxylic acids
      BT3 organic acids
        BT4 organic compounds
  BT1 hydroxy acids
    BT2 carboxylic acids
      BT3 organic acids
        BT4 organic compounds

THRESHOLD DETECTORS [355; 355]
  BT1 neutron detectors
    BT2 radiation detectors
      BT3 measuring instruments
  RT activation detectors
  RT fission chambers
  RT fission foil detectors

THRESHOLD DOSE [354; 354]
  BT1 radiation doses

THRESHOLD ENERGY [3,324; 3,324]
  BT1 energy
  RT interactions
  RT nuclear reactions
  RT scattering

THRESHOLD RIGIDITY [264; 264]
  UF *geomagnetic cut-off rigidity*
  RT cosmic radiation
  RT geomagnetic field

throat
  USE pharynx

THROMBIN [167; 167]
  BT1 blood coagulation factors
    BT2 coagulants
      BT3 hematologic agents
        BT4 drugs
  BT1 serine proteinases
    BT2 peptide hydrolases
      BT3 hydrolases
        BT4 enzymes
          BT5 organic compounds
  RT thrombosis

thrombocytes
  USE blood platelets

THROMBOPLASTIN [12; 12]
  BT1 blood coagulation factors
    BT2 coagulants
      BT3 hematologic agents
        BT4 drugs

THROMBOPOIESIS [58; 58]
  BT1 blood formation
  RT blood platelets

THROMBOSIS [1,366; 1,366]
  BT1 cardiovascular diseases
    BT2 diseases
  RT blood coagulation
  RT blood vessels
  RT fibrinolysin
  RT streptococcal proteinase
  RT thrombin

THTR-300 REACTOR [568; 568]
  (Hammuentrop, North Rhein Westfalia, Federal Republic of Germany)
  UF *schmehausen thtr reactor*
  UF *thorium-hochtemp. protot. rea.*
  BT1 enriched uranium reactors
    BT2 reactors
  BT1 helium cooled reactors
    BT2 gas cooled reactors
      BT3 reactors
  BT1 htgr type reactors
    BT2 gas cooled reactors
      BT3 reactors
      BT2 graphite moderated reactors
        BT3 reactors
  BT1 pebble bed reactors
    BT2 solid homogeneous reactors
      BT3 homogeneous reactors
        BT4 reactors
  BT1 power reactors
    BT2 reactors
  BT1 thermal reactors
    BT2 reactors
  BT1 thorium reactors
    BT2 reactors

THUCHOLITE [18; 18]
  BT1 bitumens
    BT2 tar
      BT3 other organic compounds
        BT4 organic compounds
  BT1 thorium minerals
    BT2 radioactive minerals
      BT3 minerals
      BT3 radioactive materials
        BT4 materials
  BT1 uranium minerals
    BT2 radioactive minerals
      BT3 minerals
      BT3 radioactive materials
        BT4 materials
  RT carburan
  RT rare earths
  RT uraninites

THULIUM [520; 520]
  BT1 rare earths
    BT2 metals
      BT3 elements

THULIUM ADDITIONS [90; 90]
  (Alloys containing not more than 1% T are listed here.)
  BT1 rare earth additions
  RT thulium alloys
  RT thulium compounds

THULIUM ALLOYS [223; 243]
  (Alloys containing more than 1% Tm.)
  BT1 rare earth alloys
    BT2 alloys
  NT1 thulium base alloys
  RT thulium additions

THULIUM ARSENIDES [4; 4] *Feb 7*
  BT1 arsenides
    BT2 arsenic compounds
    BT2 pnictides
  BT1 thulium compounds
    BT2 rare earth compounds

THULIUM BASE ALLOYS [18; 18]
  BT1 thulium alloys
    BT2 rare earth alloys
      BT3 alloys

THULIUM BORIDES [21; 21]
  BT1 borides
    BT2 boron compounds
  BT1 thulium compounds
    BT2 rare earth compounds

THULIUM BROMIDES [8; 8]
  BT1 bromides
    BT2 bromine compounds
      BT3 halogen compounds
    BT2 halides
      BT3 halogen compounds
  BT1 thulium compounds
    BT2 rare earth compounds

THULIUM CARBIDES [12; 12]
  BT1 carbides
    BT2 carbon compounds
  BT1 thulium compounds
    BT2 rare earth compounds

THULIUM CHLORIDES [29; 29]
  BT1   chlorides
    BT2   chlorine compounds
      BT3   halogen compounds
    BT2   halides
      BT3   halogen compounds
  BT1   thulium compounds
    BT2   rare earth compounds

THULIUM COMPLEXES [126; 126]
  BT1   rare earth complexes
    BT2   complexes

THULIUM COMPOUNDS [374; 850]
  BT1   rare earth compounds
  NT1   thulium arsenides
  NT1   thulium borides
  NT1   thulium bromides
  NT1   thulium carbides
  NT1   thulium chlorides
  NT1   thulium fluorides
  NT1   thulium hydrides
  NT1   thulium hydroxides
  NT1   thulium iodides
  NT1   thulium nitrates
  NT1   thulium nitrides
  NT1   thulium oxides
  NT1   thulium phosphates
  NT1   thulium phosphides
  NT1   thulium selenides
  NT1   thulium silicides
  NT1   thulium sulfates
  NT1   thulium sulfides
  NT1   thulium tellurides
  RT   thulium additions

THULIUM FLUORIDES [43; 43]
  BT1   fluorides
    BT2   fluorine compounds
      BT3   halogen compounds
    BT2   halides
      BT3   halogen compounds
  BT1   thulium compounds
    BT2   rare earth compounds

THULIUM HYDRIDES [20; 20]
  BT1   hydrides
    BT2   hydrogen compounds
  BT1   thulium compounds
    BT2   rare earth compounds

THULIUM HYDROXIDES [0; 0] *Sep 91*
  BT1   hydroxides
    BT2   hydrogen compounds
    BT2   oxygen compounds
  BT1   thulium compounds
    BT2   rare earth compounds

THULIUM IODIDES [10; 10]
  BT1   iodides
    BT2   halides
      BT3   halogen compounds
    BT2   iodine compounds
      BT3   halogen compounds
  BT1   thulium compounds
    BT2   rare earth compounds

THULIUM IONS [128; 128]
  BT1   ions
    BT2   charged particles

THULIUM ISOTOPES [70; 1,029]
  NT1   thulium 147
  NT1   thulium 148
  NT1   thulium 149
  NT1   thulium 150
  NT1   thulium 151
  NT1   thulium 152
  NT1   thulium 153
  NT1   thulium 154
  NT1   thulium 155
  NT1   thulium 156
  NT1   thulium 157
  NT1   thulium 158
  NT1   thulium 159
  NT1   thulium 160
  NT1   thulium 161
  NT1   thulium 162
  NT1   thulium 163
  NT1   thulium 164
  NT1   thulium 165
  NT1   thulium 166
  NT1   thulium 167
  NT1   thulium 168
  NT1   thulium 169
  NT1   thulium 170
  NT1   thulium 171
  NT1   thulium 172
  NT1   thulium 173
  NT1   thulium 174
  NT1   thulium 175
  NT1   thulium 176
  NT1   thulium 177

THULIUM NITRATES [12; 12]
  BT1   nitrates
    BT2   nitrogen compounds
    BT2   oxygen compounds
  BT1   thulium compounds
    BT2   rare earth compounds

THULIUM NITRIDES [2; 2]
  BT1   nitrides
    BT2   nitrogen compounds
    BT2   pnictides
  BT1   thulium compounds
    BT2   rare earth compounds

THULIUM OXIDES [180; 180]
  BT1   oxides
    BT2   chalcogenides
    BT2   oxygen compounds
  BT1   thulium compounds
    BT2   rare earth compounds

THULIUM PHOSPHATES [22; 22] *Oct 75*
  BT1   phosphates
    BT2   oxygen compounds
    BT2   phosphorus compounds
  BT1   thulium compounds
    BT2   rare earth compounds

THULIUM PHOSPHIDES [5; 5] *Jul 77*
  BT1   phosphides
    BT2   phosphorus compounds
    BT2   pnictides
  BT1   thulium compounds
    BT2   rare earth compounds

THULIUM SELENIDES [71; 71]
  BT1   selenides
    BT2   chalcogenides
    BT2   selenium compounds
  BT1   thulium compounds
    BT2   rare earth compounds

THULIUM SILICIDES [13; 13] *Jul 78*
  BT1   silicides
    BT2   silicon compounds
  BT1   thulium compounds
    BT2   rare earth compounds

THULIUM SULFATES [11; 11]
  BT1   sulfates
    BT2   oxygen compounds
    BT2   sulfur compounds
  BT1   thulium compounds
    BT2   rare earth compounds

THULIUM SULFIDES [42; 42]
  BT1   sulfides
    BT2   chalcogenides
    BT2   sulfur compounds
  BT1   thulium compounds
    BT2   rare earth compounds

THULIUM TELLURIDES [24; 24]
  BT1   tellurides
    BT2   chalcogenides
    BT2   tellurium compounds
  BT1   thulium compounds
    BT2   rare earth compounds

THULIUM 147 [17; 17] *Jun 82*
  BT1   millisec living radioisotopes
    BT2   radioisotopes
      BT3   isotopes
  BT1   odd-even nuclei
    BT2   nuclei
  BT1   proton decay radioisotopes
    BT2   radioisotopes
      BT3   isotopes
  BT1   rare earth nuclei
    BT2   intermediate mass nuclei
      BT3   nuclei
  BT1   thulium isotopes

THULIUM 148 [2; 2] *Jun 82*
  BT1   beta-plus decay radioisotopes
    BT2   beta decay radioisotopes
      BT3   radioisotopes
        BT4   isotopes
  BT1   electron capture radioisotopes
    BT2   beta decay radioisotopes
      BT3   radioisotopes
        BT4   isotopes
  BT1   odd-odd nuclei
    BT2   nuclei
  BT1   rare earth nuclei
    BT2   intermediate mass nuclei
      BT3   nuclei
  BT1   thulium isotopes

THULIUM 149 [4; 4] *Apr 85*
  BT1   odd-even nuclei
    BT2   nuclei
  BT1   rare earth nuclei
    BT2   intermediate mass nuclei
      BT3   nuclei
  BT1   thulium isotopes

THULIUM 150 [13; 13] *Sep 81*
  BT1   isomeric transition isotopes
    BT2   radioisotopes
      BT3   isotopes
  BT1   millisec living radioisotopes
    BT2   radioisotopes
      BT3   isotopes
  BT1   odd-odd nuclei
    BT2   nuclei
  BT1   rare earth nuclei
    BT2   intermediate mass nuclei
      BT3   nuclei
  BT1   thulium isotopes

THULIUM 151 [21; 21] *Aug 82*
  BT1   odd-even nuclei
    BT2   nuclei
  BT1   rare earth nuclei
    BT2   intermediate mass nuclei
      BT3   nuclei
  BT1   seconds living radioisotopes
    BT2   radioisotopes
      BT3   isotopes
  BT1   thulium isotopes

THULIUM 152 [16; 16] *Dec 80*
  BT1   electron capture radioisotopes
    BT2   beta decay radioisotopes
      BT3   radioisotopes
        BT4   isotopes
  BT1   odd-odd nuclei
    BT2   nuclei
  BT1   rare earth nuclei
    BT2   intermediate mass nuclei
      BT3   nuclei
  BT1   seconds living radioisotopes
    BT2   radioisotopes
      BT3   isotopes
  BT1   thulium isotopes

THULIUM 153 [14; 14]
  BT1   alpha decay radioisotopes
    BT2   radioisotopes
      BT3   isotopes
  BT1   electron capture radioisotopes
    BT2   beta decay radioisotopes
      BT3   radioisotopes
        BT4   isotopes
  BT1   odd-even nuclei
    BT2   nuclei

THULIUM 153

- BT1 rare earth nuclei
  - BT2 intermediate mass nuclei
    - BT3 nuclei
- BT1 seconds living radioisotopes
  - BT2 radioisotopes
    - BT3 isotopes
- BT1 thulium isotopes

THULIUM 154 [8; 8] Feb 77

- BT1 alpha decay radioisotopes
  - BT2 radioisotopes
    - BT3 isotopes
- BT1 electron capture radioisotopes
  - BT2 beta decay radioisotopes
    - BT3 radioisotopes
      - BT4 isotopes
- BT1 odd-odd nuclei
  - BT2 nuclei
- BT1 rare earth nuclei
  - BT2 intermediate mass nuclei
    - BT3 nuclei
- BT1 seconds living radioisotopes
  - BT2 radioisotopes
    - BT3 isotopes
- BT1 thulium isotopes

THULIUM 155 [7; 7] Jan 76

- BT1 alpha decay radioisotopes
  - BT2 radioisotopes
    - BT3 isotopes
- BT1 electron capture radioisotopes
  - BT2 beta decay radioisotopes
    - BT3 radioisotopes
      - BT4 isotopes
- BT1 odd-even nuclei
  - BT2 nuclei
- BT1 rare earth nuclei
  - BT2 intermediate mass nuclei
    - BT3 nuclei
- BT1 seconds living radioisotopes
  - BT2 radioisotopes
    - BT3 isotopes
- BT1 thulium isotopes

THULIUM 156 [12; 12] Mar 76

- BT1 alpha decay radioisotopes
  - BT2 radioisotopes
    - BT3 isotopes
- BT1 beta-plus decay radioisotopes
  - BT2 beta decay radioisotopes
    - BT3 radioisotopes
      - BT4 isotopes
- BT1 electron capture radioisotopes
  - BT2 beta decay radioisotopes
    - BT3 radioisotopes
      - BT4 isotopes
- BT1 minutes living radioisotopes
  - BT2 radioisotopes
    - BT3 isotopes
- BT1 odd-odd nuclei
  - BT2 nuclei
- BT1 rare earth nuclei
  - BT2 intermediate mass nuclei
    - BT3 nuclei
- BT1 seconds living radioisotopes
  - BT2 radioisotopes
    - BT3 isotopes
- BT1 thulium isotopes

THULIUM 157 [9; 9] Jan 77

- BT1 alpha decay radioisotopes
  - BT2 radioisotopes
    - BT3 isotopes
- BT1 beta-plus decay radioisotopes
  - BT2 beta decay radioisotopes
    - BT3 radioisotopes
      - BT4 isotopes
- BT1 electron capture radioisotopes
  - BT2 beta decay radioisotopes
    - BT3 radioisotopes
      - BT4 isotopes
- BT1 minutes living radioisotopes
  - BT2 radioisotopes
    - BT3 isotopes
- BT1 odd-even nuclei
  - BT2 nuclei

- BT1 rare earth nuclei
  - BT2 intermediate mass nuclei
    - BT3 nuclei
- BT1 thulium isotopes

THULIUM 158 [19; 19]

- BT1 beta-plus decay radioisotopes
  - BT2 beta decay radioisotopes
    - BT3 radioisotopes
      - BT4 isotopes
- BT1 electron capture radioisotopes
  - BT2 beta decay radioisotopes
    - BT3 radioisotopes
      - BT4 isotopes
- BT1 minutes living radioisotopes
  - BT2 radioisotopes
    - BT3 isotopes
- BT1 odd-odd nuclei
  - BT2 nuclei
- BT1 rare earth nuclei
  - BT2 intermediate mass nuclei
    - BT3 nuclei
- BT1 thulium isotopes

THULIUM 159 [33; 33]

- BT1 beta-plus decay radioisotopes
  - BT2 beta decay radioisotopes
    - BT3 radioisotopes
      - BT4 isotopes
- BT1 electron capture radioisotopes
  - BT2 beta decay radioisotopes
    - BT3 radioisotopes
      - BT4 isotopes
- BT1 internal conversion radioisoto
  - BT2 radioisotopes
    - BT3 isotopes
- BT1 minutes living radioisotopes
  - BT2 radioisotopes
    - BT3 isotopes
- BT1 odd-even nuclei
  - BT2 nuclei
- BT1 rare earth nuclei
  - BT2 intermediate mass nuclei
    - BT3 nuclei
- BT1 thulium isotopes

THULIUM 160 [20; 20]

- BT1 beta-plus decay radioisotopes
  - BT2 beta decay radioisotopes
    - BT3 radioisotopes
      - BT4 isotopes
- BT1 electron capture radioisotopes
  - BT2 beta decay radioisotopes
    - BT3 radioisotopes
      - BT4 isotopes
- BT1 minutes living radioisotopes
  - BT2 radioisotopes
    - BT3 isotopes
- BT1 odd-odd nuclei
  - BT2 nuclei
- BT1 rare earth nuclei
  - BT2 intermediate mass nuclei
    - BT3 nuclei
- BT1 thulium isotopes

THULIUM 161 [21; 21]

- BT1 beta-plus decay radioisotopes
  - BT2 beta decay radioisotopes
    - BT3 radioisotopes
      - BT4 isotopes
- BT1 electron capture radioisotopes
  - BT2 beta decay radioisotopes
    - BT3 radioisotopes
      - BT4 isotopes
- BT1 internal conversion radioisoto
  - BT2 radioisotopes
    - BT3 isotopes
- BT1 minutes living radioisotopes
  - BT2 radioisotopes
    - BT3 isotopes
- BT1 odd-even nuclei
  - BT2 nuclei
- BT1 rare earth nuclei
  - BT2 intermediate mass nuclei
    - BT3 nuclei
- BT1 thulium isotopes

THULIUM 162 [25; 25]

- BT1 beta-plus decay radioisotopes
  - BT2 beta decay radioisotopes
    - BT3 radioisotopes
      - BT4 isotopes
- BT1 electron capture radioisotopes
  - BT2 beta decay radioisotopes
    - BT3 radioisotopes
      - BT4 isotopes
- BT1 isomeric transition isotopes
  - BT2 radioisotopes
    - BT3 isotopes
- BT1 minutes living radioisotopes
  - BT2 radioisotopes
    - BT3 isotopes
- BT1 odd-odd nuclei
  - BT2 nuclei
- BT1 rare earth nuclei
  - BT2 intermediate mass nuclei
    - BT3 nuclei
- BT1 seconds living radioisotopes
  - BT2 radioisotopes
    - BT3 isotopes
- BT1 thulium isotopes

THULIUM 163 [40; 40]

- BT1 beta-plus decay radioisotopes
  - BT2 beta decay radioisotopes
    - BT3 radioisotopes
      - BT4 isotopes
- BT1 electron capture radioisotopes
  - BT2 beta decay radioisotopes
    - BT3 radioisotopes
      - BT4 isotopes
- BT1 hours living radioisotopes
  - BT2 radioisotopes
    - BT3 isotopes
- BT1 odd-even nuclei
  - BT2 nuclei
- BT1 rare earth nuclei
  - BT2 intermediate mass nuclei
    - BT3 nuclei
- BT1 thulium isotopes

THULIUM 164 [22; 22]

- BT1 beta-plus decay radioisotopes
  - BT2 beta decay radioisotopes
    - BT3 radioisotopes
      - BT4 isotopes
- BT1 electron capture radioisotopes
  - BT2 beta decay radioisotopes
    - BT3 radioisotopes
      - BT4 isotopes
- BT1 isomeric transition isotopes
  - BT2 radioisotopes
    - BT3 isotopes
- BT1 minutes living radioisotopes
  - BT2 radioisotopes
    - BT3 isotopes
- BT1 odd-odd nuclei
  - BT2 nuclei
- BT1 rare earth nuclei
  - BT2 intermediate mass nuclei
    - BT3 nuclei
- BT1 thulium isotopes

THULIUM 165 [57; 57]

- BT1 beta-plus decay radioisotopes
  - BT2 beta decay radioisotopes
    - BT3 radioisotopes
      - BT4 isotopes
- BT1 days living radioisotopes
  - BT2 radioisotopes
    - BT3 isotopes
- BT1 electron capture radioisotopes
  - BT2 beta decay radioisotopes
    - BT3 radioisotopes
      - BT4 isotopes
- BT1 odd-even nuclei
  - BT2 nuclei
- BT1 rare earth nuclei
  - BT2 intermediate mass nuclei
    - BT3 nuclei
- BT1 thulium isotopes

THULIUM 166 [37; 37]
- BT1 beta-plus decay radioisotopes
  - BT2 beta decay radioisotopes
    - BT3 radioisotopes
      - BT4 isotopes
- BT1 electron capture radioisotopes
  - BT2 beta decay radioisotopes
    - BT3 radioisotopes
      - BT4 isotopes
- BT1 hours living radioisotopes
  - BT2 radioisotopes
    - BT3 isotopes
- BT1 odd-odd nuclei
  - BT2 nuclei
- BT1 rare earth nuclei
  - BT2 intermediate mass nuclei
    - BT3 nuclei
- BT1 thulium isotopes

THULIUM 167 [113; 113]
- BT1 days living radioisotopes
  - BT2 radioisotopes
    - BT3 isotopes
- BT1 electron capture radioisotopes
  - BT2 beta decay radioisotopes
    - BT3 radioisotopes
      - BT4 isotopes
- BT1 odd-even nuclei
  - BT2 nuclei
- BT1 rare earth nuclei
  - BT2 intermediate mass nuclei
    - BT3 nuclei
- BT1 thulium isotopes

THULIUM 168 [52; 52]
- BT1 days living radioisotopes
  - BT2 radioisotopes
    - BT3 isotopes
- BT1 electron capture radioisotopes
  - BT2 beta decay radioisotopes
    - BT3 radioisotopes
      - BT4 isotopes
- BT1 odd-odd nuclei
  - BT2 nuclei
- BT1 rare earth nuclei
  - BT2 intermediate mass nuclei
    - BT3 nuclei
- BT1 thulium isotopes

THULIUM 169 [275; 275]
- BT1 odd-even nuclei
  - BT2 nuclei
- BT1 rare earth nuclei
  - BT2 intermediate mass nuclei
    - BT3 nuclei
- BT1 stable isotopes
  - BT2 isotopes
- BT1 thulium isotopes

THULIUM 169 TARGET [140; 140]
- BT1 targets

THULIUM 170 [227; 227]
- BT1 beta-minus decay radioisotopes
  - BT2 beta decay radioisotopes
    - BT3 radioisotopes
      - BT4 isotopes
- BT1 days living radioisotopes
  - BT2 radioisotopes
    - BT3 isotopes
- BT1 electron capture radioisotopes
  - BT2 beta decay radioisotopes
    - BT3 radioisotopes
      - BT4 isotopes
- BT1 odd-odd nuclei
  - BT2 nuclei
- BT1 rare earth nuclei
  - BT2 intermediate mass nuclei
    - BT3 nuclei
- BT1 thulium isotopes

THULIUM 171 [36; 36]
- BT1 beta-minus decay radioisotopes
  - BT2 beta decay radioisotopes
    - BT3 radioisotopes
      - BT4 isotopes
- BT1 odd-even nuclei
  - BT2 nuclei
- BT1 rare earth nuclei
  - BT2 intermediate mass nuclei
    - BT3 nuclei
- BT1 thulium isotopes
- BT1 years living radioisotopes
  - BT2 radioisotopes
    - BT3 isotopes

THULIUM 172 [10; 10]
- BT1 beta-minus decay radioisotopes
  - BT2 beta decay radioisotopes
    - BT3 radioisotopes
      - BT4 isotopes
- BT1 days living radioisotopes
  - BT2 radioisotopes
    - BT3 isotopes
- BT1 odd-odd nuclei
  - BT2 nuclei
- BT1 rare earth nuclei
  - BT2 intermediate mass nuclei
    - BT3 nuclei
- BT1 thulium isotopes

THULIUM 173 [9; 9]
- BT1 beta-minus decay radioisotopes
  - BT2 beta decay radioisotopes
    - BT3 radioisotopes
      - BT4 isotopes
- BT1 hours living radioisotopes
  - BT2 radioisotopes
    - BT3 isotopes
- BT1 odd-even nuclei
  - BT2 nuclei
- BT1 rare earth nuclei
  - BT2 intermediate mass nuclei
    - BT3 nuclei
- BT1 thulium isotopes

THULIUM 174 [6; 6]
- BT1 beta-minus decay radioisotopes
  - BT2 beta decay radioisotopes
    - BT3 radioisotopes
      - BT4 isotopes
- BT1 minutes living radioisotopes
  - BT2 radioisotopes
    - BT3 isotopes
- BT1 odd-odd nuclei
  - BT2 nuclei
- BT1 rare earth nuclei
  - BT2 intermediate mass nuclei
    - BT3 nuclei
- BT1 thulium isotopes

THULIUM 175 [2; 2]
- BT1 beta-minus decay radioisotopes
  - BT2 beta decay radioisotopes
    - BT3 radioisotopes
      - BT4 isotopes
- BT1 minutes living radioisotopes
  - BT2 radioisotopes
    - BT3 isotopes
- BT1 odd-even nuclei
  - BT2 nuclei
- BT1 rare earth nuclei
  - BT2 intermediate mass nuclei
    - BT3 nuclei
- BT1 thulium isotopes

THULIUM 176 [2; 2]
- BT1 beta-minus decay radioisotopes
  - BT2 beta decay radioisotopes
    - BT3 radioisotopes
      - BT4 isotopes
- BT1 minutes living radioisotopes
  - BT2 radioisotopes
    - BT3 isotopes
- BT1 odd-odd nuclei
  - BT2 nuclei
- BT1 rare earth nuclei
  - BT2 intermediate mass nuclei
    - BT3 nuclei
- BT1 thulium isotopes

THULIUM 177 [6; 6] *Jun 84*
- BT1 beta-minus decay radioisotopes
  - BT2 beta decay radioisotopes
    - BT3 radioisotopes
      - BT4 isotopes
- BT1 minutes living radioisotopes
  - BT2 radioisotopes
    - BT3 isotopes
- BT1 odd-even nuclei
  - BT2 nuclei
- BT1 rare earth nuclei
  - BT2 intermediate mass nuclei
    - BT3 nuclei
- BT1 thulium isotopes

THUNDERBIRD PROJECT [2; 2] *Sep 83*
(In-situ gasification of coal following nuclear fragmentation of rock seams.)
- UF *project thunderbird*
- RT coal gasification
- RT contained explosions
- RT nuclear explosions
- RT underground explosions

thyme camphor
- USE thymol

THYMECTOMY [167; 167]
- BT1 surgery
  - BT2 medicine
- RT immunity
- RT thymus

thymic acid
- USE thymol

THYMIDINE [2,943; 2,943]
- BT1 nucleosides
  - BT2 nucleotides
    - BT3 organic compounds
  - BT2 ribosides
- BT1 pyrimidines
  - BT2 azines
    - BT3 heterocyclic compounds
      - BT4 organic compounds
    - BT3 organic nitrogen compounds
      - BT4 organic compounds
- RT thymine

THYMIDYLIC ACID [24; 24]
- BT1 nucleotides
  - BT2 organic compounds
- RT thymine

THYMINE [639; 639]
- UF *5-methyl uracil*
- BT1 uracils
  - BT2 hydroxy compounds
    - BT3 organic compounds
  - BT2 pyrimidines
    - BT3 azines
      - BT4 heterocyclic compounds
        - BT5 organic compounds
      - BT4 organic nitrogen compounds
        - BT5 organic compounds
- RT thymidine
- RT thymidylic acid
- RT thymonucleic acid

THYMOCYTES [607; 607]
- BT1 somatic cells
  - BT2 animal cells
- RT thymus

THYMOL [8; 8]
- UF *hydroxy-para-cymene*
- UF *isopropyl cresol*
- UF *thyme camphor*
- UF *thymic acid*
- BT1 phenols
  - BT2 aromatics
    - BT3 organic compounds
  - BT2 hydroxy compounds
    - BT3 organic compounds

RT   cymene

THYMONUCLEIC ACID [2; 2]
- BT1   nucleic acids
  - BT2   organic compounds
- RT   thymine

THYMUS [1,276; 1,276]
- BT1   lymphatic system
- BT1   organs
  - BT2   body
- RT   calcitonin
- RT   chest
- RT   lymphocytes
- RT   mediastinum
- RT   thymectomy
- RT   thymocytes
- RT   thymus cells

THYMUS CELLS [175; 175]
- BT1   somatic cells
  - BT2   animal cells
- RT   thymus

THYRATRONS [166; 166]
- BT1   gas discharge tubes
  - BT2   electron tubes
- RT   rectifier tubes
- RT   switching circuits

THYRISTORS [462; 462]
- BT1   semiconductor devices
- RT   rectifiers
- RT   switching circuits

THYROCALCITONIN [17; 17]
- BT1   thyroid hormones
  - BT2   peptide hormones
    - BT3   hormones
- RT   calcium

THYROGLOBULIN [369; 369]
- BT1   globulins
  - BT2   proteins
    - BT3   organic compounds
- RT   iodine
- RT   thyroid
- RT   thyroid hormones
- RT   thyroxine

THYROID [5,025; 5,025]
- BT1   endocrine glands
  - BT2   glands
    - BT3   organs
      - BT4   body
- RT   blood-plasma clearance
- RT   calcitonin
- RT   goiter
- RT   iodine
- RT   neck
- RT   parathyroid glands
- RT   thyroglobulin
- RT   thyroid cells
- RT   thyroid hormones
- RT   thyroidectomy
- RT   thyroiditis

thyroid antagonists
- USE   antithyroid drugs

THYROID CELLS [45; 45] *Jul 81*
- BT1   somatic cells
  - BT2   animal cells
- RT   thyroid

THYROID HORMONES [489; 1,864]
- BT1   peptide hormones
  - BT2   hormones
- NT1   diiodothyronine
- NT1   thyrocalcitonin
- NT1   thyroxine
- NT1   triiodothyronine
- RT   hyperthyroidism
- RT   hypothyroidism
- RT   iodine

RT   metabolism
RT   pbi
RT   thyroglobulin
RT   thyroid
RT   thyronine
RT   tsh

thyroid stimulating hormone
- USE   tsh

THYROIDECTOMY [287; 287]
- BT1   surgery
  - BT2   medicine
- RT   thyroid

THYROIDITIS [196; 196]
- BT1   endocrine diseases
  - BT2   diseases
- RT   thyroid

THYRONINE [78; 78]
- UF   *desiodothyroxine*
- BT1   amino acids
  - BT2   carboxylic acids
    - BT3   organic acids
      - BT4   organic compounds
- BT1   aromatics
  - BT2   organic compounds
- BT1   hydroxy acids
  - BT2   carboxylic acids
    - BT3   organic acids
      - BT4   organic compounds
- BT1   peptide hormones
  - BT2   hormones
- RT   diiodothyronine
- RT   ethers
- RT   thyroid hormones
- RT   thyroxine
- RT   triiodothyronine

thyrotoxicosis
- USE   hyperthyroidism

thyrotropin-releasing hormone
- USE   trh

THYROXINE [1,129; 1,129]
- BT1   amino acids
  - BT2   carboxylic acids
    - BT3   organic acids
      - BT4   organic compounds
- BT1   organic iodine compounds
  - BT2   organic halogen compounds
    - BT3   organic compounds
- BT1   thyroid hormones
  - BT2   peptide hormones
    - BT3   hormones
- RT   ethers
- RT   thyroglobulin
- RT   thyronine

TIBER-X TOKAMAK [102; 102] *Sep 87*
(Compact, 3-m radius, steady-state tokamak with ECH/1H current drive and profile control.)
- BT1   tokamak devices
  - BT2   closed plasma devices
    - BT3   thermonuclear devices
- RT   thermonuclear ignition

TIBIA [314; 314]
- BT1   skeleton
  - BT2   organs
    - BT3   body
- RT   legs

TIBR REACTOR [2; 2] *Dec 86*
- BT1   enriched uranium reactors
  - BT2   reactors
- BT1   fast reactors
  - BT2   epithermal reactors
    - BT3   reactors
- BT1   pulsed reactors
  - BT2   reactors

BT1   research reactors
- BT2   research and test reactors
  - BT3   reactors
- BT1   transportable reactors
  - BT2   reactors

TICKS [38; 38]
- BT1   arachnids
  - BT2   arthropods
    - BT3   invertebrates
      - BT4   animals

tid
- USE   travelling ionospheric disturb

TIDAL POWER [17; 17] *Oct 82*
- BT1   renewable energy sources
  - BT2   energy sources
- RT   water currents

tidal waves
- USE   tsunamis

TIDE [408; 408]
(Prior to August 1985 the form TIDES was used.)
- UF   *tides*
- RT   seas
- RT   water currents

tides
(Prior to August 1985 this was a valid descriptor.)
- USE   tide

tiglium oil
- USE   croton oil

TIGRIS RIVER [3; 3] *May 88*
- BT1   rivers
  - BT2   surface waters
- RT   iraq
- RT   turkey

TIHANGE REACTOR [79; 79]
(Tihange, Liege, Belgium)
- UF   *tihange-1 reactor*
- BT1   pwr type reactors
  - BT2   enriched uranium reactors
    - BT3   reactors
  - BT2   power reactors
    - BT3   reactors
  - BT2   thermal reactors
    - BT3   reactors
  - BT2   water cooled reactors
    - BT3   reactors
  - BT2   water moderated reactors
    - BT3   reactors

tihange-1 reactor
- USE   tihange reactor

TIHANGE-2 REACTOR [17; 17] *Apr*
- BT1   pwr type reactors
  - BT2   enriched uranium reactors
    - BT3   reactors
  - BT2   power reactors
    - BT3   reactors
  - BT2   thermal reactors
    - BT3   reactors
  - BT2   water cooled reactors
    - BT3   reactors
  - BT2   water moderated reactors
    - BT3   reactors

TIHANGE-3 REACTOR [12; 12] *Apr*
- BT1   pwr type reactors
  - BT2   enriched uranium reactors
    - BT3   reactors
  - BT2   power reactors
    - BT3   reactors

```
  BT2    thermal reactors
    BT3    reactors
  BT2    water cooled reactors
    BT3    reactors
  BT2    water moderated reactors
    BT3    reactors

TIKONAL [8; 8] Oct 75
  BT1    aluminium alloys
    BT2    alloys
  BT1    cobalt alloys
    BT2    alloys
  BT1    copper alloys
    BT2    alloys
  BT1    iron base alloys
    BT2    iron alloys
      BT3    alloys
  BT1    nickel alloys
    BT2    alloys
  BT1    titanium alloys
    BT2    alloys

til oil
  USE    sesame oil

tilting (neutron flux)
  USE    neutron flux tilting

TILTING INSTABILITY [85; 85] Feb 84
  BT1    plasma macroinstabilities
    BT2    plasma instability
      BT3    instability

TIME DEPENDENCE [42,355; 42,355]
  RT    blood-plasma clearance
  RT    confinement time
  RT    counting rates
  RT    delayed radiation effects
  RT    differential pac
  RT    dose rates
  RT    early radiation effects
  RT    flow rate
  RT    heating rate
  RT    incubation
  RT    instability growth rates
  RT    mortality
  RT    quarantine
  RT    relaxation time
  RT    retention functions
  RT    survival time
  RT    temporal dose distributions
  RT    velocity

TIME INTERVAL ANALYZERS
[206; 214]
  BT1    measuring instruments
  NT1    chronotrons
    NT2    vernier chronotrons
  RT    atomic clocks
  RT    time measurement

TIME LIMITATIONS [13; 13] Dec 76
(For time limitations on liability for damages.)
  RT    liabilities
  RT    liability limitations
  RT    nuclear liability

TIME MEASUREMENT [1,174; 1,174]
  RT    atomic clocks
  RT    coincidence circuits
  RT    dead time
  RT    measuring instruments
  RT    pulse rise time
  RT    time interval analyzers
  RT    timing circuits
  RT    timing properties

TIME PROJECTION CHAMBERS
[53; 53] Apr 84
(Prior to August, 1988, this concept was indexed by PROJECTION SPARK CHAMBERS.)
  UF    tpc
  BT1    drift chambers
    BT2    multiwire proportional chamber
      BT3    proportional counters
        BT4    radiation detectors
          BT5    measuring instruments

TIME RESOLUTION [3,459; 3,459]
(Minimum time interval between events to be detected.)
  BT1    resolution
  BT1    timing properties
  RT    pulse pileup

TIME-OF-FLIGHT MASS
SPECTROMET [288; 288] Jan 76
  BT1    dynamic mass spectrometers
    BT2    mass spectrometers
      BT3    spectrometers
        BT4    measuring instruments
  BT1    time-of-flight spectrometers
    BT2    spectrometers
      BT3    measuring instruments

TIME-OF-FLIGHT METHOD
[4,972; 4,972]
  RT    charge plunger method
  RT    time-of-flight spectrometers

TIME-OF-FLIGHT SPECTROMETERS
[1,415; 1,699]
  BT1    spectrometers
    BT2    measuring instruments
  NT1    time-of-flight mass spectromet
  RT    time-of-flight method

time-reversal invariance
  USE    t invariance

TIME-SERIES ANALYSIS [243; 243]
Jul 81
  BT1    statistics
    BT2    mathematics
  RT    forecasting

TIME-TO-AMPLITUDE CONVERTERS
[341; 341]
  BT1    pulse converters
    BT2    electronic equipment
      BT3    equipment

TIMING CIRCUITS [734; 734]
  BT1    electronic circuits
  RT    dead time
  RT    discriminators
  RT    sweep circuits
  RT    time measurement
  RT    timing properties

TIMING PROPERTIES [1,002, 5,894]
(Properties of a detector, circuit or other component related to time measurement, such as its pulse rise time or time resolution, etc.)
  NT1    dead time
  NT1    pulse rise time
  NT1    time resolution
  RT    pulse pileup
  RT    time measurement
  RT    timing circuits

TIN [3,029; 3,029]
  BT1    metals
    BT2    elements

TIN ADDITIONS [331; 331]
(Alloys containing not more than 1% Sn are listed here.)
  RT    tin alloys
  RT    tin compounds

TIN ALLOYS [2,979; 6,203]
(Alloys containing more than 1% Sn.)
  BT1    alloys
  NT1    alloy-bi50pb25cd12sn12
  NT1    alloy-zr98sn-2
  NT1    alloy-zr98sn-4
  NT1    bronze
  NT1    tin base alloys
  RT    tin additions

TIN ARSENIDES [0; 0] Sep 91
  BT1    arsenides
    BT2    arsenic compounds
      BT2    pnictides
  BT1    tin compounds

TIN BASE ALLOYS [119; 119]
  BT1    tin alloys
    BT2    alloys

TIN BORIDES [4; 4]
  BT1    borides
    BT2    boron compounds
  BT1    tin compounds

TIN BROMIDES [32; 32]
  BT1    bromides
    BT2    bromine compounds
      BT3    halogen compounds
    BT2    halides
      BT3    halogen compounds
  BT1    tin halides
    BT2    halides
      BT3    halogen compounds
    BT2    tin compounds

TIN CHLORIDES [333; 333]
  BT1    chlorides
    BT2    chlorine compounds
      BT3    halogen compounds
    BT2    halides
      BT3    halogen compounds
  BT1    tin halides
    BT2    halides
      BT3    halogen compounds
    BT2    tin compounds

TIN COMPLEXES [267; 267]
  BT1    complexes

TIN COMPOUNDS [936; 2,822]
  NT1    stannates
  NT1    tin arsenides
  NT1    tin borides
  NT1    tin halides
    NT2    tin bromides
    NT2    tin chlorides
    NT2    tin fluorides
    NT2    tin iodides
  NT1    tin hydrides
  NT1    tin hydroxides
  NT1    tin nitrides
  NT1    tin oxides
  NT1    tin phosphates
  NT1    tin phosphides
  NT1    tin selenides
  NT1    tin sulfates
  NT1    tin sulfides
  NT1    tin tellurides
  NT1    tin tungstates
  RT    tin additions

TIN FLUORIDES [42; 42]
  BT1    fluorides
    BT2    fluorine compounds
      BT3    halogen compounds
    BT2    halides
      BT3    halogen compounds
  BT1    tin halides
    BT2    halides
      BT3    halogen compounds
    BT2    tin compounds

TIN HALIDES [0; 3] Sep 91
  BT1    halides
    BT2    halogen compounds
  BT1    tin compounds
  NT1    tin bromides
  NT1    tin chlorides
  NT1    tin fluorides
  NT1    tin iodides
```

TIN HYDRIDES [19; 19]
  BT1 hydrides
    BT2 hydrogen compounds
  BT1 tin compounds

TIN HYDROXIDES [30; 30]
  BT1 hydroxides
    BT2 hydrogen compounds
    BT2 oxygen compounds
  BT1 tin compounds

TIN IODIDES [71; 71]
  BT1 iodides
    BT2 halides
      BT3 halogen compounds
    BT2 iodine compounds
      BT3 halogen compounds
  BT1 tin halides
    BT2 halides
      BT3 halogen compounds
    BT2 tin compounds

TIN IONS [207; 207]
  BT1 ions
    BT2 charged particles

TIN ISOTOPES [513; 3,298]
  NT1 tin 100
  NT1 tin 102
  NT1 tin 103
  NT1 tin 104
  NT1 tin 105
  NT1 tin 106
  NT1 tin 107
  NT1 tin 108
  NT1 tin 109
  NT1 tin 110
  NT1 tin 111
  NT1 tin 112
  NT1 tin 113
  NT1 tin 114
  NT1 tin 115
  NT1 tin 116
  NT1 tin 117
  NT1 tin 118
  NT1 tin 119
  NT1 tin 120
  NT1 tin 121
  NT1 tin 122
  NT1 tin 123
  NT1 tin 124
  NT1 tin 125
  NT1 tin 126
  NT1 tin 127
  NT1 tin 128
  NT1 tin 129
  NT1 tin 130
  NT1 tin 131
  NT1 tin 132
  NT1 tin 133
  NT1 tin 134

TIN NITRIDES [3; 3] *Jun 76*
  BT1 nitrides
    BT2 nitrogen compounds
    BT2 pnictides
  BT1 tin compounds

TIN ORES [72; 72] *Aug 78*
  BT1 ores

TIN OXIDES [576; 576]
  BT1 oxides
    BT2 chalcogenides
    BT2 oxygen compounds
  BT1 tin compounds
  RT   stannates

TIN PHOSPHATES [55; 55]
  BT1 phosphates
    BT2 oxygen compounds
    BT2 phosphorus compounds
  BT1 tin compounds

TIN PHOSPHIDES [25; 25] *Jan 77*
  BT1 phosphides
    BT2 phosphorus compounds
    BT2 pnictides
  BT1 tin compounds

TIN SELENIDES [84; 84] *Jul 76*
  BT1 selenides
    BT2 chalcogenides
    BT2 selenium compounds
  BT1 tin compounds

TIN SULFATES [6; 6]
  BT1 sulfates
    BT2 oxygen compounds
    BT2 sulfur compounds
  BT1 tin compounds

TIN SULFIDES [174; 174]
  BT1 sulfides
    BT2 chalcogenides
    BT2 sulfur compounds
  BT1 tin compounds

TIN TELLURIDES [502; 502]
  BT1 tellurides
    BT2 chalcogenides
    BT2 tellurium compounds
  BT1 tin compounds

→ **TIN TUNGSTATES** [0; 0] *Sep 91*
  BT1 tin compounds
  BT1 tungstates
    BT2 oxygen compounds
    BT2 tungsten compounds
      BT3 transition element compounds

TIN 100 [18; 18] *Sep 85*
  BT1 beta-plus decay radioisotopes
    BT2 beta decay radioisotopes
      BT3 radioisotopes
        BT4 isotopes
  BT1 electron capture radioisotopes
    BT2 beta decay radioisotopes
      BT3 radioisotopes
        BT4 isotopes
  BT1 even-even nuclei
    BT2 nuclei
  BT1 intermediate mass nuclei
    BT2 nuclei
  BT1 tin isotopes

TIN 102 [9; 9] *Sep 85*
  BT1 beta-plus decay radioisotopes
    BT2 beta decay radioisotopes
      BT3 radioisotopes
        BT4 isotopes
  BT1 electron capture radioisotopes
    BT2 beta decay radioisotopes
      BT3 radioisotopes
        BT4 isotopes
  BT1 even-even nuclei
    BT2 nuclei
  BT1 intermediate mass nuclei
    BT2 nuclei
  BT1 tin isotopes

TIN 103 [7; 7] *Jul 80*
  BT1 beta-plus decay radioisotopes
    BT2 beta decay radioisotopes
      BT3 radioisotopes
        BT4 isotopes
  BT1 even-odd nuclei
    BT2 nuclei
  BT1 intermediate mass nuclei
    BT2 nuclei
  BT1 seconds living radioisotopes
    BT2 radioisotopes
      BT3 isotopes
  BT1 tin isotopes

TIN 104 [32; 32] *Nov 76*
  BT1 even-even nuclei
    BT2 nuclei
  BT1 intermediate mass nuclei
    BT2 nuclei
  BT1 tin isotopes

TIN 105 [9; 9] *Jul 80*
  BT1 beta-plus decay radioisotopes
    BT2 beta decay radioisotopes
      BT3 radioisotopes
        BT4 isotopes
  BT1 even-odd nuclei
    BT2 nuclei
  BT1 intermediate mass nuclei
    BT2 nuclei
  BT1 seconds living radioisotopes
    BT2 radioisotopes
      BT3 isotopes
  BT1 tin isotopes

TIN 106 [42; 42]
  BT1 beta-plus decay radioisotopes
    BT2 beta decay radioisotopes
      BT3 radioisotopes
        BT4 isotopes
  BT1 electron capture radioisotopes
    BT2 beta decay radioisotopes
      BT3 radioisotopes
        BT4 isotopes
  BT1 even-even nuclei
    BT2 nuclei
  BT1 intermediate mass nuclei
    BT2 nuclei
  BT1 minutes living radioisotopes
    BT2 radioisotopes
      BT3 isotopes
  BT1 tin isotopes

TIN 107 [17; 17]
  BT1 beta-plus decay radioisotopes
    BT2 beta decay radioisotopes
      BT3 radioisotopes
        BT4 isotopes
  BT1 electron capture radioisotopes
    BT2 beta decay radioisotopes
      BT3 radioisotopes
        BT4 isotopes
  BT1 even-odd nuclei
    BT2 nuclei
  BT1 intermediate mass nuclei
    BT2 nuclei
  BT1 minutes living radioisotopes
    BT2 radioisotopes
      BT3 isotopes
  BT1 tin isotopes

TIN 108 [73; 73]
  BT1 beta-plus decay radioisotopes
    BT2 beta decay radioisotopes
      BT3 radioisotopes
        BT4 isotopes
  BT1 electron capture radioisotopes
    BT2 beta decay radioisotopes
      BT3 radioisotopes
        BT4 isotopes
  BT1 even-even nuclei
    BT2 nuclei
  BT1 intermediate mass nuclei
    BT2 nuclei
  BT1 minutes living radioisotopes
    BT2 radioisotopes
      BT3 isotopes
  BT1 tin isotopes

TIN 109 [31; 31]
  BT1 beta-plus decay radioisotopes
    BT2 beta decay radioisotopes
      BT3 radioisotopes
        BT4 isotopes
  BT1 electron capture radioisotopes
    BT2 beta decay radioisotopes
      BT3 radioisotopes
        BT4 isotopes
  BT1 even-odd nuclei
    BT2 nuclei
  BT1 intermediate mass nuclei
    BT2 nuclei
  BT1 minutes living radioisotopes
    BT2 radioisotopes
      BT3 isotopes
  BT1 tin isotopes

TIN 110 [67; 67]
  BT1   electron capture radioisotopes
    BT2   beta decay radioisotopes
      BT3   radioisotopes
        BT4   isotopes
  BT1   even-even nuclei
    BT2   nuclei
  BT1   hours living radioisotopes
    BT2   radioisotopes
      BT3   isotopes
  BT1   intermediate mass nuclei
    BT2   nuclei
  BT1   tin isotopes

TIN 110 TARGET [5; 5] *Jul 80*
  BT1   targets

TIN 111 [69; 69]
  BT1   beta-plus decay radioisotopes
    BT2   beta decay radioisotopes
      BT3   radioisotopes
        BT4   isotopes
  BT1   electron capture radioisotopes
    BT2   beta decay radioisotopes
      BT3   radioisotopes
        BT4   isotopes
  BT1   even-odd nuclei
    BT2   nuclei
  BT1   intermediate mass nuclei
    BT2   nuclei
  BT1   minutes living radioisotopes
    BT2   radioisotopes
      BT3   isotopes
  BT1   tin isotopes

TIN 112 [125; 125]
  BT1   even-even nuclei
    BT2   nuclei
  BT1   intermediate mass nuclei
    BT2   nuclei
  BT1   stable isotopes
    BT2   isotopes
  BT1   tin isotopes

TIN 112 REACTIONS [0; 0] *Oct 91*
  BT1   heavy ion reactions
    BT2   nuclear reactions

TIN 112 TARGET [257; 257]
  BT1   targets

TIN 113 [343; 343]
  BT1   days living radioisotopes
    BT2   radioisotopes
      BT3   isotopes
  BT1   electron capture radioisotopes
    BT2   beta decay radioisotopes
      BT3   radioisotopes
        BT4   isotopes
  BT1   even-odd nuclei
    BT2   nuclei
  BT1   intermediate mass nuclei
    BT2   nuclei
  BT1   internal conversion radioisoto
    BT2   radioisotopes
      BT3   isotopes
  BT1   isomeric transition isotopes
    BT2   radioisotopes
      BT3   isotopes
  BT1   minutes living radioisotopes
    BT2   radioisotopes
      BT3   isotopes
  BT1   tin isotopes
  RT   radioisotope generators

TIN 114 [126; 126]
  BT1   even-even nuclei
    BT2   nuclei
  BT1   intermediate mass nuclei
    BT2   nuclei
  BT1   stable isotopes
    BT2   isotopes
  BT1   tin isotopes

TIN 114 TARGET [76; 76]
  BT1   targets

TIN 115 [141; 141]
  BT1   even-odd nuclei
    BT2   nuclei
  BT1   intermediate mass nuclei
    BT2   nuclei
  BT1   stable isotopes
    BT2   isotopes
  BT1   tin isotopes

TIN 115 TARGET [28; 28] *Oct 76*
  BT1   targets

TIN 116 [275; 275]
  BT1   even-even nuclei
    BT2   nuclei
  BT1   intermediate mass nuclei
    BT2   nuclei
  BT1   stable isotopes
    BT2   isotopes
  BT1   tin isotopes

TIN 116 REACTIONS [9; 9] *Nov 87*
  BT1   heavy ion reactions
    BT2   nuclear reactions

TIN 116 TARGET [386; 386]
  BT1   targets

TIN 117 [209; 209]
  BT1   days living radioisotopes
    BT2   radioisotopes
      BT3   isotopes
  BT1   even-odd nuclei
    BT2   nuclei
  BT1   intermediate mass nuclei
    BT2   nuclei
  BT1   isomeric transition isotopes
    BT2   radioisotopes
      BT3   isotopes
  BT1   stable isotopes
    BT2   isotopes
  BT1   tin isotopes

TIN 117 TARGET [137; 137]
  BT1   targets

TIN 118 [265; 265]
  BT1   even-even nuclei
    BT2   nuclei
  BT1   intermediate mass nuclei
    BT2   nuclei
  BT1   stable isotopes
    BT2   isotopes
  BT1   tin isotopes

TIN 118 REACTIONS [4; 4] *Jun 87*
  BT1   heavy ion reactions
    BT2   nuclear reactions

TIN 118 TARGET [336; 336]
  BT1   targets

TIN 119 [933; 933]
  BT1   days living radioisotopes
    BT2   radioisotopes
      BT3   isotopes
  BT1   even-odd nuclei
    BT2   nuclei
  BT1   intermediate mass nuclei
    BT2   nuclei
  BT1   internal conversion radioisoto
    BT2   radioisotopes
      BT3   isotopes
  BT1   isomeric transition isotopes
    BT2   radioisotopes
      BT3   isotopes
  BT1   stable isotopes
    BT2   isotopes
  BT1   tin isotopes

TIN 119 TARGET [89; 89]
  BT1   targets

TIN 120 [353; 353]
  BT1   even-even nuclei
    BT2   nuclei
  BT1   intermediate mass nuclei
    BT2   nuclei
  BT1   stable isotopes
    BT2   isotopes
  BT1   tin isotopes

TIN 120 BEAMS [7; 7] *May 84*
  BT1   ion beams
    BT2   beams

TIN 120 REACTIONS [26; 26] *Jul 78*
  BT1   heavy ion reactions
    BT2   nuclear reactions

TIN 120 TARGET [614; 614]
  BT1   targets

TIN 121 [87; 87]
  BT1   beta-minus decay radioisotopes
    BT2   beta decay radioisotopes
      BT3   radioisotopes
        BT4   isotopes
  BT1   days living radioisotopes
    BT2   radioisotopes
      BT3   isotopes
  BT1   even-odd nuclei
    BT2   nuclei
  BT1   intermediate mass nuclei
    BT2   nuclei
  BT1   internal conversion radioisoto
    BT2   radioisotopes
      BT3   isotopes
  BT1   isomeric transition isotopes
    BT2   radioisotopes
      BT3   isotopes
  BT1   tin isotopes
  BT1   years living radioisotopes
    BT2   radioisotopes
      BT3   isotopes

TIN 122 [112; 112]
  BT1   even-even nuclei
    BT2   nuclei
  BT1   intermediate mass nuclei
    BT2   nuclei
  BT1   stable isotopes
    BT2   isotopes
  BT1   tin isotopes

TIN 122 REACTIONS [6; 6] *Sep 80*
  BT1   heavy ion reactions
    BT2   nuclear reactions

TIN 122 TARGET [252; 252]
  BT1   targets

TIN 123 [66; 66]
  BT1   beta-minus decay radioisotopes
    BT2   beta decay radioisotopes
      BT3   radioisotopes
        BT4   isotopes
  BT1   days living radioisotopes
    BT2   radioisotopes
      BT3   isotopes
  BT1   even-odd nuclei
    BT2   nuclei
  BT1   intermediate mass nuclei
    BT2   nuclei
  BT1   minutes living radioisotopes
    BT2   radioisotopes
      BT3   isotopes
  BT1   tin isotopes

TIN 124 [190; 190]
  BT1   even-even nuclei
    BT2   nuclei
  BT1   intermediate mass nuclei
    BT2   nuclei
  BT1   stable isotopes
    BT2   isotopes

BT1   tin isotopes

TIN 124 REACTIONS [43; 43] *Dec 80*
BT1   heavy ion reactions
BT2   nuclear reactions

TIN 124 TARGET [538; 538]
BT1   targets

TIN 125 [56; 56]
BT1   beta-minus decay radioisotopes
BT2   beta decay radioisotopes
BT3   radioisotopes
BT4   isotopes
BT1   days living radioisotopes
BT2   radioisotopes
BT3   isotopes
BT1   even-odd nuclei
BT2   nuclei
BT1   intermediate mass nuclei
BT2   nuclei
BT1   minutes living radioisotopes
BT2   radioisotopes
BT3   isotopes
BT1   tin isotopes

TIN 126 [42; 42]
BT1   beta-minus decay radioisotopes
BT2   beta decay radioisotopes
BT3   radioisotopes
BT4   isotopes
BT1   even-even nuclei
BT2   nuclei
BT1   intermediate mass nuclei
BT2   nuclei
BT1   tin isotopes
BT1   years living radioisotopes
BT2   radioisotopes
BT3   isotopes

TIN 126 TARGET [6; 6] *Apr 80*
BT1   targets

TIN 127 [11; 11]
BT1   beta-minus decay radioisotopes
BT2   beta decay radioisotopes
BT3   radioisotopes
BT4   isotopes
BT1   even-odd nuclei
BT2   nuclei
BT1   hours living radioisotopes
BT2   radioisotopes
BT3   isotopes
BT1   intermediate mass nuclei
BT2   nuclei
BT1   minutes living radioisotopes
BT2   radioisotopes
BT3   isotopes
BT1   tin isotopes

TIN 128 [30; 30]
BT1   beta-minus decay radioisotopes
BT2   beta decay radioisotopes
BT3   radioisotopes
BT4   isotopes
BT1   even-even nuclei
BT2   nuclei
BT1   intermediate mass nuclei
BT2   nuclei
BT1   minutes living radioisotopes
BT2   radioisotopes
BT3   isotopes
BT1   tin isotopes

TIN 129 [20; 20]
BT1   beta-minus decay radioisotopes
BT2   beta decay radioisotopes
BT3   radioisotopes
BT4   isotopes
BT1   even-odd nuclei
BT2   nuclei
BT1   intermediate mass nuclei
BT2   nuclei
BT1   minutes living radioisotopes
BT2   radioisotopes
BT3   isotopes
BT1   tin isotopes

TIN 130 [38; 38]
BT1   beta-minus decay radioisotopes
BT2   beta decay radioisotopes
BT3   radioisotopes
BT4   isotopes
BT1   even-even nuclei
BT2   nuclei
BT1   intermediate mass nuclei
BT2   nuclei
BT1   minutes living radioisotopes
BT2   radioisotopes
BT3   isotopes
BT1   tin isotopes

TIN 131 [24; 24]
BT1   beta-minus decay radioisotopes
BT2   beta decay radioisotopes
BT3   radioisotopes
BT4   isotopes
BT1   even-odd nuclei
BT2   nuclei
BT1   intermediate mass nuclei
BT2   nuclei
BT1   minutes living radioisotopes
BT2   radioisotopes
BT3   isotopes
BT1   seconds living radioisotopes
BT2   radioisotopes
BT3   isotopes
BT1   tin isotopes

TIN 132 [89; 89]
BT1   beta-minus decay radioisotopes
BT2   beta decay radioisotopes
BT3   radioisotopes
BT4   isotopes
BT1   even-even nuclei
BT2   nuclei
BT1   intermediate mass nuclei
BT2   nuclei
BT1   seconds living radioisotopes
BT2   radioisotopes
BT3   isotopes
BT1   tin isotopes

TIN 133 [10; 10]
BT1   beta-minus decay radioisotopes
BT2   beta decay radioisotopes
BT3   radioisotopes
BT4   isotopes
BT1   even-odd nuclei
BT2   nuclei
BT1   intermediate mass nuclei
BT2   nuclei
BT1   seconds living radioisotopes
BT2   radioisotopes
BT3   isotopes
BT1   tin isotopes

TIN 134 [8; 8]
BT1   beta-minus decay radioisotopes
BT2   beta decay radioisotopes
BT3   radioisotopes
BT4   isotopes
BT1   even-even nuclei
BT2   nuclei
BT1   intermediate mass nuclei
BT2   nuclei
BT1   seconds living radioisotopes
BT2   radioisotopes
BT3   isotopes
BT1   tin isotopes

TIRON [51; 51]
BT1   polyphenols
BT2   phenols
BT3   aromatics
BT4   organic compounds
BT3   hydroxy compounds
BT4   organic compounds
BT1   reagents
BT1   sodium compounds
BT2   alkali metal compounds
BT1   sulfonic acids
BT2   organic acids
BT3   organic compounds
BT2   organic sulfur compounds
BT3   organic compounds

TISSUE CULTURES [578; 578]
UF   *cultures (tissue)*
UF   *organ cultures*
RT   cell cultures
RT   culture media
RT   in vitro
RT   tissues

TISSUE DISTRIBUTION [2,889; 2,889]
BT1   distribution
RT   biological localization
RT   radionuclide kinetics
RT   tissues

tissue equivalent chambers
USE   bragg gray chambers

TISSUE EXTRACTS [155; 155]
BT1   biological materials
BT2   materials
RT   cell constituents
RT   mitogens
RT   radioprotective substances
RT   tissues

TISSUE-EQUIVALENT DETECTORS
[425; 425]
BT1   radiation detectors
BT2   measuring instruments
RT   dose equivalents

TISSUE-EQUIVALENT MATERIALS
[1,204; 1,204]
BT1   materials
RT   phantoms
RT   tissues

TISSUES [6,133; 17,696]
(For animal tissues only; see also PLANT
TISSUES.)
UF   *animal tissues*
UF+   *muscular tissue*
BT1   body
NT1   bone marrow
NT1   connective tissue
NT2   adipose tissue
NT2   bone tissues
NT3   antlers
NT3   trabecular bone
NT2   cartilage
NT2   fascia
NT2   ligaments
NT1   endothelium
NT1   epithelium
NT2   epidermis
NT1   nerve tissue
NT1   perfused tissues
NT1   reticuloendothelial system
RT   biological materials
RT   biological regeneration
RT   biology
RT   biopsy
RT   capillaries
RT   histological techniques
RT   histology
RT   homogenates
RT   in vivo
RT   morphological changes
RT   organs
RT   plant tissues
RT   retention
RT   skin
RT   tissue cultures
RT   tissue distribution
RT   tissue extracts
RT   tissue-equivalent materials

TITANATES [1,120; 1,220]
(Specific compounds should be indexed
by coordination of a descriptor of the form
(CATION) COMPOUNDS and the above
anion descriptor.)
BT1   oxygen compounds
BT1   titanium compounds
BT2   transition element compounds
NT1   cadmium titanates
NT1   plzt

NT1 pzt
NT1 strontium titanates
RT titanium oxides

TITANITE [80; 80]
UF *sphene*
BT1 silicate minerals
BT2 minerals
RT titanium silicates

TITANIUM [4,861; 5,036]
BT1 transition elements
BT2 metals
BT3 elements
NT1 titanium-alpha
NT1 titanium-beta
RT kroll process

TITANIUM ADDITIONS [1,065; 3,650]
(Alloys containing not more than 1% Ti are listed here.)
NT1 alloy-fe44ni33cr21
NT1 alloy-fe46ni33cr21
NT1 alloy-mo99
NT1 alloy-nb94mo4
NT1 alloy-ni43fe30cr22mo3
NT1 alloy-ni47cr25co12w9fe3
NT1 alloy-ni51cr48
NT1 alloy-ni53cr19fe19nb5mo3
NT1 alloy-ni59cr30fe9
NT1 alloy-ni60cr25w15
NT1 alloy-ni61cr22mo9nb4fe3
NT1 alloy-ni70mo17cr7fe5
NT1 alloy-ni73cr20mn3nb3
NT1 alloy-ni74cr13al6mo4
NT1 alloy-ni75cr12al6mo5
NT1 alloy-ni76cr15fe8
NT1 alloy-ni78cr16al4
NT1 alloy-ni78cr21
NT1 steel-cr15ni15motib
NT1 steel-cr17ni13mo2ti
NT1 steel-cr17ni13mo3ti
NT1 steel-cr18ni10ti
NT1 steel-cr18ni12ti
NT1 steel-cr18ni9ti
NT1 steel-cr21ni5ti
NT1 steel-cr22ni5ti
NT1 steel-ni17cr14moti-l
RT titanium alloys
RT titanium compounds

TITANIUM ALLOYS [3,738; 7,346]
(Alloys containing more than 1% Ti.)
BT1 alloys
NT1 alloy-ni41fe40cr16nb3
NT1 alloy-ni42fe36cr12mo6ti3
NT1 alloy-ni43fe33cr16mo3
NT1 alloy-ni46cr23co19ti5al4
NT1 alloy-ni48co28cr15al3mo3ti2
NT1 alloy-ni50co20cr15al5mo5
NT1 alloy-ni53co19cr15mo5al4ti3
NT1 alloy-ni55co17cr15mo5al4ti4
NT1 alloy-ni55cr19co11mo10ti3
NT1 alloy-ni56cr21w10mo5fe4al2
NT1 alloy-ni58cr14co8al4mo4nb4w4
NT1 alloy-ni58cr20co14mo4ti3
NT1 alloy-ni59cr20co17ti2
NT1 alloy-ni60co15cr10al6ti5mo3
NT1 alloy-ni60cr14co10ti5mo4w4al3
NT1 alloy-ni60mo13co9cr8nb4al3
NT1 alloy-ni61cr16co9al3ti3w3
NT1 alloy-ni67cr19mo5w5ti3
NT1 alloy-ni68cr15w6al3mo3fe2
NT1 alloy-ni73cr15fe7ti3
NT1 alloy-ni76cr20ti2
NT1 alloy-ni77cr20ti2
NT1 steel-cr11ni10mo2ti-l
NT1 steel-ni26cr15ti2movalb
NT1 steel-ni35cr18mo4ti2al
NT1 steel-ni36cr12ti3al-l
NT1 tikonal
NT1 titanium base alloys
NT2 alloy-ti78cr11mo7al3
NT2 alloy-ti88mo8al3
NT2 alloy-ti89al6mo3
NT2 alloy-ti90al6
NT2 alloy-ti90al6mo3
NT2 alloy-ti90al6v4
NT2 alloy-ti90mo7al2
NT2 alloy-ti91al4mo3
NT2 alloy-ti91al5cr2
NT2 alloy-ti99
RT titanium additions

TITANIUM BASE ALLOYS
[1,893; 2,453]
BT1 titanium alloys
BT2 alloys
NT1 alloy-ti78cr11mo7al3
NT1 alloy-ti88mo8al3
NT1 alloy-ti89al6mo3
NT1 alloy-ti90al6
NT1 alloy-ti90al6mo3
NT1 alloy-ti90al6v4
NT1 alloy-ti90mo7al2
NT1 alloy-ti91al4mo3
NT1 alloy-ti91al5cr2
NT1 alloy-ti99

TITANIUM BORIDES [338; 338]
BT1 borides
BT2 boron compounds
BT1 titanium compounds
BT2 transition element compounds

TITANIUM BROMIDES [5; 5]
BT1 bromides
BT2 bromine compounds
BT3 halogen compounds
BT2 halides
BT3 halogen compounds
BT1 titanium compounds
BT2 transition element compounds

TITANIUM CARBIDES [1,098; 1,098]
BT1 carbides
BT2 carbon compounds
BT1 titanium compounds
BT2 transition element compounds

TITANIUM CHLORIDES [124; 124]
BT1 chlorides
BT2 chlorine compounds
BT3 halogen compounds
BT2 halides
BT3 halogen compounds
BT1 titanium compounds
BT2 transition element compounds

TITANIUM COMPLEXES [161; 161]
BT1 transition element complexes
BT2 complexes

TITANIUM COMPOUNDS [618; 6,897]
BT1 transition element compounds
NT1 titanates
NT2 cadmium titanates
NT2 plzt
NT2 pzt
NT2 strontium titanates
NT1 titanium borides
NT1 titanium bromides
NT1 titanium carbides
NT1 titanium chlorides
NT1 titanium fluorides
NT1 titanium hydrides
NT1 titanium hydroxides
NT1 titanium iodides
NT1 titanium nitrates
NT1 titanium nitrides
NT1 titanium oxides
NT1 titanium phosphates
NT1 titanium phosphides
NT1 titanium selenides
NT1 titanium silicates
NT1 titanium silicides
NT1 titanium sulfates
NT1 titanium sulfides
NT1 titanium tellurides
NT1 titanium tungstates
RT titanium additions

TITANIUM FLUORIDES [29; 29]
BT1 fluorides
BT2 fluorine compounds
BT3 halogen compounds
BT2 halides
BT3 halogen compounds
BT1 titanium compounds
BT2 transition element compounds

TITANIUM HYDRIDES [321; 321]
BT1 hydrides
BT2 hydrogen compounds
BT1 titanium compounds
BT2 transition element compounds

TITANIUM HYDROXIDES [76; 76]
BT1 hydroxides
BT2 hydrogen compounds
BT2 oxygen compounds
BT1 titanium compounds
BT2 transition element compounds

TITANIUM IODIDES [20; 20]
BT1 iodides
BT2 halides
BT3 halogen compounds
BT2 iodine compounds
BT3 halogen compounds
BT1 titanium compounds
BT2 transition element compounds

TITANIUM IONS [496; 496]
BT1 ions
BT2 charged particles

TITANIUM ISOTOPES [190; 1,499]
NT1 titanium 39
NT1 titanium 40
NT1 titanium 41
NT1 titanium 42
NT1 titanium 43
NT1 titanium 44
NT1 titanium 45
NT1 titanium 46
NT1 titanium 47
NT1 titanium 48
NT1 titanium 49
NT1 titanium 50
NT1 titanium 51
NT1 titanium 52
NT1 titanium 53
NT1 titanium 54
NT1 titanium 55
NT1 titanium 56
NT1 titanium 57

TITANIUM NITRATES [6; 6]
BT1 nitrates
BT2 nitrogen compounds
BT2 oxygen compounds
BT1 titanium compounds
BT2 transition element compounds

TITANIUM NITRIDES [561; 561]
BT1 nitrides
BT2 nitrogen compounds
BT2 pnictides
BT1 titanium compounds
BT2 transition element compounds

TITANIUM OXIDES [2,304; 2,717]
BT1 oxides
BT2 chalcogenides
BT2 oxygen compounds
BT1 titanium compounds
BT2 transition element compounds
RT aeschynite
RT brannerite
RT hollandite
RT ilmenite
RT oxide minerals
RT perovskite
RT rutile
RT titanates
RT zirconolite

TITANIUM PHOSPHATES [76; 76]
  BT1   phosphates
  BT2   oxygen compounds
  BT2   phosphorus compounds
  BT1   titanium compounds
  BT2   transition element compounds

→ **TITANIUM PHOSPHIDES** [0; 0] *Sep 91*
  BT1   phosphides
  BT2   phosphorus compounds
  BT2   pnictides
  BT1   titanium compounds
  BT2   transition element compounds

TITANIUM SELENIDES [19; 19] *Jul 78*
  BT1   selenides
  BT2   chalcogenides
  BT2   selenium compounds
  BT1   titanium compounds
  BT2   transition element compounds

TITANIUM SILICATES [13; 13]
  BT1   silicates
  BT2   oxygen compounds
  BT2   silicon compounds
  BT1   titanium compounds
  BT2   transition element compounds
  RT   silicate minerals
  RT   titanite

TITANIUM SILICIDES [73; 73] *Apr 79*
  BT1   silicides
  BT2   silicon compounds
  BT1   titanium compounds
  BT2   transition element compounds

TITANIUM SULFATES [24; 24]
  BT1   sulfates
  BT2   oxygen compounds
  BT2   sulfur compounds
  BT1   titanium compounds
  BT2   transition element compounds

TITANIUM SULFIDES [58; 58]
  BT1   sulfides
  BT2   chalcogenides
  BT2   sulfur compounds
  BT1   titanium compounds
  BT2   transition element compounds

TITANIUM TELLURIDES [9; 9] *Sep 79*
  BT1   tellurides
  BT2   chalcogenides
  BT2   tellurium compounds
  BT1   titanium compounds
  BT2   transition element compounds

→ **TITANIUM TUNGSTATES** [0; 0] *Sep 91*
  BT1   titanium compounds
  BT2   transition element compounds
  BT1   tungstates
  BT2   oxygen compounds
  BT2   tungsten compounds
  BT3   transition element compounds

TITANIUM 39 [7; 7] *Nov 88*
  BT1   beta-plus decay radioisotopes
  BT2   beta decay radioisotopes
  BT3   radioisotopes
  BT4   isotopes
  BT1   even-odd nuclei
  BT2   nuclei
  BT1   light nuclei
  BT2   nuclei
  BT1   titanium isotopes

TITANIUM 40 [5; 5] *May 90*
  BT1   beta-plus decay radioisotopes
  BT2   beta decay radioisotopes
  BT3   radioisotopes
  BT4   isotopes
  BT1   even-even nuclei
  BT2   nuclei
  BT1   light nuclei

  BT2   nuclei
  BT1   millisec living radioisotopes
  BT2   radioisotopes
  BT3   isotopes
  BT1   titanium isotopes

TITANIUM 41 [10; 10]
  BT1   beta-plus decay radioisotopes
  BT2   beta decay radioisotopes
  BT3   radioisotopes
  BT4   isotopes
  BT1   even-odd nuclei
  BT2   nuclei
  BT1   intermediate mass nuclei
  BT2   nuclei
  BT1   millisec living radioisotopes
  BT2   radioisotopes
  BT3   isotopes
  BT1   titanium isotopes

TITANIUM 42 [44; 44]
  BT1   beta-plus decay radioisotopes
  BT2   beta decay radioisotopes
  BT3   radioisotopes
  BT4   isotopes
  BT1   even-even nuclei
  BT2   nuclei
  BT1   intermediate mass nuclei
  BT2   nuclei
  BT1   millisec living radioisotopes
  BT2   radioisotopes
  BT3   isotopes
  BT1   titanium isotopes

TITANIUM 43 [33; 33]
  BT1   beta-plus decay radioisotopes
  BT2   beta decay radioisotopes
  BT3   radioisotopes
  BT4   isotopes
  BT1   even-odd nuclei
  BT2   nuclei
  BT1   intermediate mass nuclei
  BT2   nuclei
  BT1   millisec living radioisotopes
  BT2   radioisotopes
  BT3   isotopes
  BT1   titanium isotopes

TITANIUM 44 [243; 243]
  BT1   electron capture radioisotopes
  BT2   beta decay radioisotopes
  BT3   radioisotopes
  BT4   isotopes
  BT1   even-even nuclei
  BT2   nuclei
  BT1   intermediate mass nuclei
  BT2   nuclei
  BT1   titanium isotopes
  BT1   years living radioisotopes
  BT2   radioisotopes
  BT3   isotopes

TITANIUM 44 TARGET [9; 9] *Nov 78*
  BT1   targets

TITANIUM 45 [79; 79]
  BT1   beta-plus decay radioisotopes
  BT2   beta decay radioisotopes
  BT3   radioisotopes
  BT4   isotopes
  BT1   electron capture radioisotopes
  BT2   beta decay radioisotopes
  BT3   radioisotopes
  BT4   isotopes
  BT1   even-odd nuclei
  BT2   nuclei
  BT1   hours living radioisotopes
  BT2   radioisotopes
  BT3   isotopes
  BT1   intermediate mass nuclei
  BT2   nuclei
  BT1   titanium isotopes

TITANIUM 45 TARGET [2; 2] *Nov 77*
  BT1   targets

TITANIUM 46 [246; 246]
  BT1   even-even nuclei
  BT2   nuclei
  BT1   intermediate mass nuclei
  BT2   nuclei
  BT1   stable isotopes
  BT2   isotopes
  BT1   titanium isotopes

TITANIUM 46 REACTIONS [19; 19] *Nov 85*
  BT1   heavy ion reactions
  BT2   nuclear reactions

TITANIUM 46 TARGET [251; 251]
  BT1   targets

TITANIUM 47 [126; 126]
  BT1   even-odd nuclei
  BT2   nuclei
  BT1   intermediate mass nuclei
  BT2   nuclei
  BT1   stable isotopes
  BT2   isotopes
  BT1   titanium isotopes

TITANIUM 47 TARGET [78; 78]
  BT1   targets

TITANIUM 48 [374; 374]
  BT1   even-even nuclei
  BT2   nuclei
  BT1   intermediate mass nuclei
  BT2   nuclei
  BT1   stable isotopes
  BT2   isotopes
  BT1   titanium isotopes

TITANIUM 48 BEAMS [2; 2] *May 89*
  BT1   ion beams
  BT2   beams

TITANIUM 48 REACTIONS [82; 82] *Sep 77*
  BT1   heavy ion reactions
  BT2   nuclear reactions

TITANIUM 48 TARGET [472; 472]
  BT1   targets

TITANIUM 49 [131; 131]
  BT1   even-odd nuclei
  BT2   nuclei
  BT1   intermediate mass nuclei
  BT2   nuclei
  BT1   stable isotopes
  BT2   isotopes
  BT1   titanium isotopes

TITANIUM 49 TARGET [61; 61]
  BT1   targets

TITANIUM 50 [284; 284]
  BT1   even-even nuclei
  BT2   nuclei
  BT1   intermediate mass nuclei
  BT2   nuclei
  BT1   stable isotopes
  BT2   isotopes
  BT1   titanium isotopes

TITANIUM 50 BEAMS [23; 23] *Sep*
  BT1   ion beams
  BT2   beams

TITANIUM 50 REACTIONS [90; 90]
  BT1   heavy ion reactions
  BT2   nuclear reactions

TITANIUM 50 TARGET [296; 296]
  BT1   targets

TITANIUM 51 [63; 63]
- BT1 beta-minus decay radioisotopes
- BT2 beta decay radioisotopes
- BT3 radioisotopes
- BT4 isotopes
- BT1 even-odd nuclei
- BT2 nuclei
- BT1 intermediate mass nuclei
- BT2 nuclei
- BT1 minutes living radioisotopes
- BT2 radioisotopes
- BT3 isotopes
- BT1 titanium isotopes

TITANIUM 52 [25; 25]
- BT1 beta-minus decay radioisotopes
- BT2 beta decay radioisotopes
- BT3 radioisotopes
- BT4 isotopes
- BT1 even-even nuclei
- BT2 nuclei
- BT1 intermediate mass nuclei
- BT2 nuclei
- BT1 minutes living radioisotopes
- BT2 radioisotopes
- BT3 isotopes
- BT1 titanium isotopes

TITANIUM 53 [7; 7] Nov 76
- BT1 beta-minus decay radioisotopes
- BT2 beta decay radioisotopes
- BT3 radioisotopes
- BT4 isotopes
- BT1 even-odd nuclei
- BT2 nuclei
- BT1 intermediate mass nuclei
- BT2 nuclei
- BT1 seconds living radioisotopes
- BT2 radioisotopes
- BT3 isotopes
- BT1 titanium isotopes

TITANIUM 54 [2; 2] Nov 80
- BT1 even-even nuclei
- BT2 nuclei
- BT1 intermediate mass nuclei
- BT2 nuclei
- BT1 titanium isotopes

TITANIUM 55 [0; 0] Feb 91
- BT1 even-odd nuclei
- BT2 nuclei
- BT1 intermediate mass nuclei
- BT2 nuclei
- BT1 titanium isotopes

TITANIUM 56 [3; 3] Aug 86
- BT1 even-even nuclei
- BT2 nuclei
- BT1 intermediate mass nuclei
- BT2 nuclei
- BT1 titanium isotopes

TITANIUM 57 [2; 2] Aug 86
- BT1 even-odd nuclei
- BT2 nuclei
- BT1 intermediate mass nuclei
- BT2 nuclei
- BT1 titanium isotopes

TITANIUM-ALPHA [110; 110]
- BT1 titanium
- BT2 transition elements
- BT3 metals
- BT4 elements

TITANIUM-BETA [101; 101]
- BT1 titanium
- BT2 transition elements
- BT3 metals
- BT4 elements

TITRATION [1,201; 3,323]
- NT1 amperometry
- NT1 iodometry
- NT1 potentiometry
- RT quantitative chemical analysis

→ ## TJ-1 TOKAMAK [2; 2] Aug 91
(CIEMAT, Madrid, Spain.)
- BT1 tokamak devices
- BT2 closed plasma devices
- BT3 thermonuclear devices

TLATELOLCO TREATY [38; 38] Dec 75
(Treaty for the Prohibition of Nuclear Weapons in Latin America)
- UF latin am nucl weap prohib trea
- UF nucl weapons lat am prohib tre
- UF prohib nucl weapons lat am tre
- UF treaty prohib nucl weap lat am
- BT1 treaties
- RT nuclear weapons

tld (dosemeters)
- USE thermoluminescent dosemeters

tld (dosimetry)
- USE thermoluminescent dosimetry

tld systems
- USE thermoluminescent dosemeters

TLM CONFIGURATIONS [10; 10] Aug 75
(Toroidally Linked Mirror configurations)
- BT1 magnetic mirror configurations
- BT2 open configurations
- BT3 magnetic field configurations
- RT magnetic fields
- RT magnetic mirrors
- RT minimum-b configurations
- RT tandem mirrors
- RT toroidal configuration

TLP DEVICES [12; 83]
- UF longitudinal pinch devices (tr
- UF toroidal longitudinal pinch de
- BT1 toroidal pinch devices
- BT2 closed plasma devices
- BT3 thermonuclear devices
- BT2 pinch devices
- BT3 thermonuclear devices
- NT1 alpha device
- NT1 zeta devices
- RT longitudinal pinch

TMPN [20; 20] Feb 76
(2,2,6,6-tetramethyl-4-piperidinol-N-oxyl)
- UF 2,2,6,6-tetramethyl-4-piperidi
- BT1 hydroxy compounds
- BT2 organic compounds
- BT1 organic oxygen compounds
- BT2 organic compounds
- BT1 piperidines
- BT2 amines
- BT3 organic compounds
- BT2 pyridines
- BT3 azines
- BT4 heterocyclic compounds
- BT5 organic compounds
- BT4 organic nitrogen compounds
- BT5 organic compounds
- RT radiosensitizers
- RT triacetoneamine-n-oxyl

TMR REACTORS [465; 465] Jul 81
- UF mars reactor
- UF tandem mirror type reactors
- BT1 thermonuclear reactors
- RT magnetic mirrors
- RT tandem mirrors
- RT thermal barriers

TMTSF [62; 62] Oct 83
- UF tetramethyltetraselenafulvalen
- BT1 heterocyclic compounds
- BT2 organic compounds
- BT1 selenium compounds

TMX DEVICES [732; 732] Apr 78
(Tandem Mirror Experiment at Lawrence Livermore Laboratory.)
- UF tandem mirror exp. at uclll
- BT1 tandem mirrors
- BT2 magnetic mirrors
- BT3 open plasma devices
- BT4 thermonuclear devices
- RT lawrence livermore laboratory
- RT thermal barriers

TNA [0; 0]
- UF trinonylamine
- BT1 amines
- BT2 organic compounds
- BT1 chelating agents

tnp
- USE picric acid

TNS REACTORS [81; 81] Sep 78
(The next tokamak confinement device beyond TFTR.)
- UF the next step thermonuc. reac.
- BT1 thermonuclear reactors
- RT tokamak devices

TNT [28; 28]
- UF trinitrotoluene
- BT1 chemical explosives
- BT2 explosives
- BT1 nitro compounds
- BT2 organic nitrogen compounds
- BT3 organic compounds
- RT toluene

TNT-A TOKAMAK [9; 9] Mar 85
- UF tokyo non-circular tokamak
- BT1 tokamak devices
- BT2 closed plasma devices
- BT3 thermonuclear devices

TOA [375; 375]
- UF trioctylamine
- BT1 amines
- BT2 organic compounds
- BT1 chelating agents

toads
- USE frogs

TOBACCO [180; 180]
- RT crops
- RT nicotiana
- RT tobacco smokes

TOBACCO MOSAIC VIRUS [37; 37]
- BT1 viruses
- BT2 microorganisms
- BT2 parasites
- RT plant diseases

tobacco plant
- USE nicotiana

TOBACCO SMOKES [453; 453]
- BT1 smokes
- BT2 aerosols
- BT3 sols
- BT4 colloids
- BT5 dispersions
- BT2 residues
- RT tobacco

tocopherols
  USE   vitamin e

TOGO [3; 3] *Feb 81*
  BT1   africa
  BT1   developing countries

tohoku avf cyclotron
  USE   tohoku cyclotron

TOHOKU CYCLOTRON [9; 9] *Jun 83*
(At Cyclotron and Radioisotope Center, Tohoku University, Sendai, Japan.)
  UF   *cyric cyclotron*
  UF   *sendai cyclotron*
  UF   *tohoku avf cyclotron*
  UF   *tohoku university cyclotron*
  BT1   heavy ion accelerators
    BT2   accelerators
  BT1   isochronous cyclotrons
    BT2   cyclotrons
      BT3   cyclic accelerators
        BT4   accelerators

tohoku university cyclotron
  USE   tohoku cyclotron

tohoku-1 reactor
  USE   onagawa-1 reactor

tokai-mura fast critical assem
  USE   fca reactor

TOKAI-MURA REACTOR [35; 35]
  UF   *japco-1 reactor*
  UF   *tokai-1 reactor*
  BT1   carbon dioxide cooled reactors
    BT2   gas cooled reactors
      BT3   reactors
  BT1   magnox type reactors
    BT2   gcr type reactors
      BT3   gas cooled reactors
        BT4   reactors
      BT3   graphite moderated reactors
        BT4   reactors
    BT2   natural uranium reactors
      BT3   reactors
    BT2   power reactors
      BT3   reactors
  BT1   thermal reactors
    BT2   reactors

tokai-1 reactor
  USE   tokai-mura reactor

TOKAI-2 REACTOR [36; 36]
(Tokaimura, Ibaraki, Japan)
  UF   *japco-3 reactor*
  BT1   bwr type reactors
    BT2   enriched uranium reactors
      BT3   reactors
    BT2   power reactors
      BT3   reactors
    BT2   thermal reactors
      BT3   reactors
    BT2   water cooled reactors
      BT3   reactors
    BT2   water moderated reactors
      BT3   reactors

tokamak chaufage alfven
  USE   tca tokamak

tokamak de varennes
  USE   varennes tokamak

TOKAMAK DEVICES [14,530; 26,907]
  BT1   closed plasma devices
    BT2   thermonuclear devices
  NT1   act devices
  NT1   aditya tokamak
  NT1   alcator device
  NT1   asdex tokamak
  NT1   atc devices
  NT1   castor tokamak
  NT1   columbia high-beta tokamak
  NT1   compact ignition tokamak
  NT1   continuous current tokamak
  NT1   ct-6b tokamak
  NT1   dante tokamak
  NT1   dite tokamak
  NT1   doublet-1 device
  NT1   doublet-2 device
  NT1   doublet-3 device
  NT1   etf tokamak
  NT1   ft tokamak
  NT1   hl-1 tokamak
  NT1   ht-6b tokamak
  NT1   ht-6m tokamak
  NT1   hybtok tokamaks
  NT1   intor tokamak
  NT1   isx tokamak
  NT1   iter tokamak
  NT1   jet tokamak
  NT1   jft-2 tokamak
  NT1   jft-2a tokamak
  NT1   jft-2m tokamak
  NT1   jippt-2 device
  NT1   jt-60 tokamak
  NT1   jt-60u tokamak
  NT1   jxfr tokamak
  NT1   lt-3 tokamak
  NT1   lt-4 tokamak
  NT1   mt-1 tokamak
  NT1   net tokamak
  NT1   ormak devices
  NT1   pbx devices
  NT1   petula tokamak
  NT1   plt devices
  NT1   spheromak devices
    NT2   ctx spheromak
  NT1   st tokamak
  NT1   starfire tokamak
  NT1   surmac tokamak
  NT1   t-10 tokamak
  NT1   t-15 tokamak
  NT1   t-7 tokamak
  NT1   tbr tokamak
  NT1   tca tokamak
  NT1   text devices
  NT1   textor tokamak
  NT1   tfr tokamak
  NT1   tftr tokamak
  NT1   tiber-x tokamak
  NT1   tj-1 tokamak
  NT1   tnt-a tokamak
  NT1   tokapole tokamak
  NT1   tokoloshe tokamak
  NT1   tore supra tokamak
  NT1   tormac devices
  NT1   tortus tokamak
  NT1   torus-ii tokamak
  NT1   tosca tokamak
  NT1   triam-1 tokamak
  NT1   tuman devices
  NT1   two-component torus
  NT1   uwmak devices
  NT1   varennes tokamak
  NT1   versator tokamak
  NT1   wt-3 tokamak
  RT   banana regime
  RT   divertors
  RT   exhaust systems
  RT   h-mode plasma confinement
  RT   magnetic surfaces
  RT   marfe
  RT   mode rational surfaces
  RT   pdx devices
  RT   pfirsch-schlueter regime
  RT   plasma disruption
  RT   plasma radial profiles
  RT   plateau regime
  RT   sawtooth oscillations
  RT   tns reactors
  RT   wega stellarator

tokamak fontenay-aux-roses
  USE   tfr tokamak

tokamak fusion test reactor
  USE   tftr tokamak

tokamak model st
  USE   st tokamak

TOKAPOLE DEVICES [69; 69] *Jul 81*
  BT1   internal ring devices
    BT2   closed plasma devices
      BT3   thermonuclear devices
  BT1   tokamak devices
    BT2   closed plasma devices
      BT3   thermonuclear devices

→ **TOKOLOSHE TOKAMAK** [4; 4] *Mar 91*
(Pelindaba, Pretoria, South Africa.)
  BT1   tokamak devices
    BT2   closed plasma devices
      BT3   thermonuclear devices

TOKYO INS CYCLOTRON [26; 26] *Jun 83*
(Sector-focused cyclotron at Institute for Nuclear Studies, University of Tokyo.)
  UF   *ins cyclotron (tokyo)*
  UF   *inst. nucl. studies cyclotron*
  BT1   heavy ion accelerators
    BT2   accelerators
  BT1   isochronous cyclotrons
    BT2   cyclotrons
      BT3   cyclic accelerators
        BT4   accelerators

tokyo non-circular tokamak
  USE   tnt-a tokamak

TOKYO SYNCHROTRON [104; 104]
(1.3-Gev electron synchrotron.)
  BT1   synchrotrons
    BT2   cyclic accelerators
      BT3   accelerators

tokyo-denrioku k-1 reactor
  USE   kashiwazaki-kariwa-1 reactor

tokyo-denryoku k-2 reactor
  USE   kashiwazaki-kariwa-2 reactor

tokyo-1 reactor
  USE   fukushima-1 reactor

tokyo-2 reactor
  USE   fukushima-2 reactor

tokyo-3 reactor
  USE   fukushima-3 reactor

tokyo-4 reactor
  USE   fukushima-4 reactor

TOLAN [27; 27]
  UF   *phenylacetylene*
  BT1   aromatics
    BT2   organic compounds
  BT1   hydrocarbons
    BT2   organic compounds

toller poles
  USE   lorentz poles

TOLUENE [932; 932]
- UF   *methylbenzene*
- BT1 aromatics
- BT2   organic compounds
- BT1 hydrocarbons
- BT2   organic compounds
- RT   tnt
- RT   toluidines

TOLUIDINE BLUE [28; 28]
- BT1 azo dyes
- BT2   azo compounds
- BT3   organic nitrogen compounds
- BT4   organic compounds
- BT2   dyes
- RT   toluidines

TOLUIDINES [38; 38]
- UF   *aminotoluenes*
- UF   *tolylamines*
- BT1 amines
- BT2   organic compounds
- RT   toluene
- RT   toluidine blue

toluylene red
- USE   neutral red

TOLYL RADICALS [6; 6]
- BT1 aryl radicals
- BT2   radicals

tolylamines
- USE   toluidines

TOMARI-1 REACTOR [4; 4] *Sep 89*
(Tomari, Hokkaido, Japan.)
- BT1 pwr type reactors
- BT2   enriched uranium reactors
- BT3   reactors
- BT2   power reactors
- BT3   reactors
- BT2   thermal reactors
- BT3   reactors
- BT2   water cooled reactors
- BT3   reactors
- BT2   water moderated reactors
- BT3   reactors

TOMARI-2 REACTOR [2; 2] *Nov 89*
(Tomari, Hokkaido, Japan.)
- BT1 pwr type reactors
- BT2   enriched uranium reactors
- BT3   reactors
- BT2   power reactors
- BT3   reactors
- BT2   thermal reactors
- BT3   reactors
- BT2   water cooled reactors
- BT3   reactors
- BT2   water moderated reactors
- BT3   reactors

TOMATOES [301; 301]
- BT1 vegetables
- BT2   food

TOMOGRAPHY [2,395; 25,819]
(A radiographic technique characterized by the movement of two of the three components - source, object, and film - so that a clear image of one plane of the object is registered, while images of all other planes are blurred.)
- UF   *laminography*
- NT1 compton scattering tomography
- NT1 computerized tomography
- NT2   cat scanning
- NT2   emission computed tomography
- NT3   positron computed tomography
- NT3   single photon ect
- NT2   proton computed tomography
- NT1 grazing incidence tomography
- RT   biomedical radiography
- RT   diagnostic techniques
- RT   industrial radiography

TOMONAGA APPROXIMATION [27; 27]
- UF   *approximation (tomonaga)*
- UF   *intermediate coupling approxim*
- RT   intermediate coupling

TOMSK SYNCHROTRON [43; 43]
- UF   *sirius synchrotron*
- BT1 synchrotrons
- BT2   cyclic accelerators
- BT3   accelerators

TONGUE [347; 347]
- BT1 oral cavity
- BT2   digestive system
- BT1 organs
- BT2   body
- RT   muscles

tonks-langmuir oscillations
- USE   tonks-langmuir theory

TONKS-LANGMUIR THEORY [15; 15]
- UF   *tonks-langmuir oscillations*
- RT   plasma waves

TONOPAH TEST RANGE [30; 30]
Feb 76
- BT1 nevada
- BT2   usa
- BT3   developed countries
- BT3   north america
- BT1 test facilities
- RT   nevada test site
- RT   sandia laboratories
- RT   sandia national laboratories

tonsils
- USE   lymphatic system
- AND   pharynx

TOOLS [284; 766]
- BT1 equipment
- NT1 cutting tools
- NT1 drill bits
- RT   machine tools
- RT   machining
- RT   presses

top accidents
- USE   transient overpower accidents

TOP PARTICLES [915; 915] *Jul 85*
(Particles with T quantum number not = 0.)
- BT1 postulated particles
- BT2   elementary particles
- RT   beauty particles
- RT   flavor model
- RT   toponium

top quark model
- USE   flavor model

TOPAZ REACTOR [20; 20]
- BT1 experimental reactors
- BT2   research and test reactors
- BT3   reactors
- BT1 hydride moderated reactors
- BT2   reactors
- BT1 power reactors
- BT2   reactors
- RT   hydride moderators
- RT   thermionic converters

tophet a
- USE   alloy-ni80cr20

tophet c
- USE   alloy-ni60fe24cr16

TOPO [433; 433]
- UF   *trioctylphosphine oxide*
- BT1 organic phosphorus compounds
- BT2   organic compounds

TOPOGRAPHY [890; 890]
- RT   earth planet
- RT   maps

TOPOLOGICAL FOLIATION [106; 106]
- RT   differential topology
- RT   smooth manifolds
- RT   surfaces

TOPOLOGICAL MAPPING
[1,438; 2,241]
- UF   *mapping (topological)*
- BT1 transformations
- NT1 conformal mapping
- RT   mapping fibration
- RT   mathematical manifolds
- RT   topology

TOPOLOGY [3,528; 3,654]
- BT1 mathematics
- NT1 differential topology
- RT   dimensions
- RT   fractals
- RT   global analysis
- RT   invariant imbedding
- RT   mathematical manifolds
- RT   topological mapping

TOPONIUM [127; 127] *May 86*
(A bound state of top and antitop quarks.)
- BT1 mesons
- BT2   bosons
- BT2   hadrons
- BT3   elementary particles
- BT1 quarkonium
- RT   flavor model
- RT   top particles

topping cycles
- USE   thermodynamic cycles

topr reactor
- USE   thor reactor

TOPS [2; 2]
- UF   *trioctylphosphine sulfide*
- BT1 organic phosphorus compounds
- BT2   organic compounds
- BT1 organic sulfur compounds
- BT2   organic compounds

TORBERNITE [17; 17]
- BT1 phosphate minerals
- BT2   minerals
- BT1 uranium minerals
- BT2   radioactive minerals
- BT3   minerals
- BT3   radioactive materials
- BT4   materials
- RT   copper phosphates
- RT   uranium phosphates

TORE SUPRA TOKAMAK [312; 312]
Jun 83
- BT1 tokamak devices
- BT2   closed plasma devices
- BT3   thermonuclear devices

TORI [716; 1,328]
- NT1 compact torus
- NT2   field-reversed theta pinch dev
- NT2   rotamak devices
- RT   annular space
- RT   aspect ratio
- RT   bumpy tori
- RT   rings

RT   toroidal configuration

TORMAC DEVICES [56; 56] *Jul 76*
- UF   *tormak devices*
- BT1   tokamak devices
- BT2   closed plasma devices
- BT3   thermonuclear devices

tormak devices
(Prior to July 1984 this was a valid descriptor.)
- USE   tormac devices

TORNADO DEVICES [15; 15]
- BT1   internal ring devices
- BT2   closed plasma devices
- BT3   thermonuclear devices

TORNADOES [225; 225]
- RT   turbulence
- RT   weather
- RT   wind

TORNESS REACTOR [136; 136] *Feb 81*
(Dunbar, East Lothian, UK)
- BT1   agr type reactors
- BT2   enriched uranium reactors
- BT3   reactors
- BT2   gas cooled reactors
- BT3   reactors
- BT2   graphite moderated reactors
- BT3   reactors
- BT1   carbon dioxide cooled reactors
- BT2   gas cooled reactors
- BT3   reactors
- BT1   power reactors
- BT2   reactors
- BT1   thermal reactors
- BT2   reactors

TOROIDAL CONFIGURATION [4,429; 4,429]
- BT1   annular space
- BT2   configuration
- BT1   closed configurations
- BT2   magnetic field configurations
- RT   compact torus
- RT   rotational transform
- RT   tlm configurations
- RT   tori

TOROIDAL FIELD DIVERTORS [36; 36] *Jul 81*
(Divertors that displace the toroidal field lines to form a separatrix in the toroidal field.)
- BT1   divertors
- RT   bundle divertors

toroidal longitudinal pinch de
- USE   tlp devices

TOROIDAL PINCH DEVICES [416; 1,020]
- BT1   closed plasma devices
- BT2   thermonuclear devices
- BT1   pinch devices
- BT2   thermonuclear devices
- NT1   hbtx devices
- NT1   tlp devices
- NT2   alpha device
- NT2   zeta devices
- NT1   toroidal screw pinch devices
- NT2   tpe-2 device
- NT1   toroidal theta pinch devices
- NT2   scyllac devices
- NT1   tpe-1rm15 device
- NT1   zt-p devices
- NT1   zt-40 devices
- RT   banana regime

TOROIDAL SCREW PINCH DEVICES [119; 119]
- BT1   toroidal pinch devices
- BT2   closed plasma devices
- BT3   thermonuclear devices
- BT2   pinch devices
- BT3   thermonuclear devices
- NT1   tpe-2 device
- RT   screw pinch

TOROIDAL THETA PINCH DEVICES [194; 295]
- BT1   toroidal pinch devices
- BT2   closed plasma devices
- BT3   thermonuclear devices
- BT2   pinch devices
- BT3   thermonuclear devices
- NT1   scyllac devices
- RT   reference theta pinch reactor
- RT   theta pinch

toronto univ. slowpoke reactor
- USE   slowpoke-toronto reactor

TORQUE [461; 461]
- RT   torsion

torrey pines triga-mk-3 react.
- USE   triga-3-la jolla reactor

TORSATRON STELLARATORS [361; 683]
(Prior to December 1990, this was spelled TORSATRON STELLARATOR.)
- UF   *uragan-3 stellarator*
- BT1   stellarators
- BT2   closed plasma devices
- BT3   thermonuclear devices
- NT1   atf torsatron
- NT1   chs torsatron
- NT1   vint torsatron

TORSION [1,045; 1,045]
- RT   deformation
- RT   springs
- RT   torque

→ **TORTUS TOKAMAK** [4; 4] *Mar 91*
(Sydney University, Sydney, Australia.)
- BT1   tokamak devices
- BT2   closed plasma devices
- BT3   thermonuclear devices

TORULA [10; 10]
- UF   *torulopsis*
- BT1   yeasts
- BT2   fungi
- BT3   plants
- BT2   microorganisms

torulopsis
- USE   torula

torus exper techn oriented res
- USE   textor tokamak

TORUS-II TOKAMAK [41; 41] *Feb 77*
(Device to be built within the EURATOM-CEA Association.)
- BT1   tokamak devices
- BT2   closed plasma devices
- BT3   thermonuclear devices

TORY-2C REACTOR [1; 1]
- UF   *exp. propulsion test reactor*
- BT1   air cooled reactors
- BT2   gas cooled reactors
- BT3   reactors
- BT1   experimental reactors
- BT2   research and test reactors
- BT3   reactors
- BT1   propulsion reactors
- BT2   power reactors
- BT3   reactors
- BT1   test reactors
- BT2   research and test reactors
- BT3   reactors
- BT2   test facilities

TOSCA TOKAMAK [8; 8] *Jun 87*
- BT1   tokamak devices
- BT2   closed plasma devices
- BT3   thermonuclear devices

TOSHIBA REACTOR [8; 8]
- UF   *toshiba training reactor*
- UF   *ttr-1 toshiba reactor*
- BT1   enriched uranium reactors
- BT2   reactors
- BT1   pool type reactors
- BT2   water cooled reactors
- BT3   reactors
- BT2   water moderated reactors
- BT3   reactors
- BT1   research reactors
- BT2   research and test reactors
- BT3   reactors
- BT1   thermal reactors
- BT2   reactors
- BT1   training reactors
- BT2   research and test reactors
- BT3   reactors

toshiba training reactor
- USE   toshiba reactor

§ **TOTAL CROSS SECTIONS** [14,862; 14,862]
(Cross sections integrated over all angles and all reaction channels.)
- BT1   cross sections
- RT   excitation functions
- RT   pomeranchuk theorem

TOTAL ENERGY SYSTEMS [38; 38] *Dec 82*
(Integral energy systems of high efficienc e.g., a system utilizing gas-fired turbines or engines that produce electrical energy and utilize exhaust heat in applications such as heating and cooling.)
- UF   *integrated utility systems*
- UF   *ius*
- RT   combined cycles
- RT   energy conservation
- RT   energy consumption

toughness (fracture)
- USE   fracture properties

TOURMALINE [55; 55]
- BT1   silicate minerals
- BT2   minerals
- RT   aluminium silicates
- RT   boron silicates
- RT   dielectric track detectors

tower shielding reactor-1
- USE   tsr-1 reactor

tower shielding reactor-2
- USE   tsr-2 reactor

towers (extraction)
- USE   extraction columns

towers (structures)
- USE   mechanical structures

townsend avalanche
- USE   townsend discharge

TOWNSEND DISCHARGE [372; 372]
- UF avalanche multiplication
- UF townsend avalanche
- UF townsend formula
- UF townsend theory
- BT1 electric discharges
- RT avalanche quenching

townsend formula
- USE townsend discharge

townsend theory
- USE townsend discharge

toxic materials
- USE hazardous materials

TOXICITY [5,099; 5,099]
- RT acute exposure
- RT aflatoxins
- RT biological effects
- RT chronic exposure
- RT detoxification
- RT dose-response relationships
- RT drugs
- RT hazardous materials
- RT lethal doses
- RT mimosine
- RT prenatal exposure
- RT toxins
- RT venoms

TOXINS [721; 1,004]
- BT1 antigens
- NT1 aflatoxins
- NT1 endotoxins
- RT antitoxins
- RT bacteria
- RT clostridium
- RT detoxification
- RT radiotoxins
- RT toxicity
- RT toxoids
- RT venoms

TOXOIDS [16; 16] *Nov 75*
- RT antibodies
- RT immune reactions
- RT immunity
- RT toxins

tpc
(Time Projection Chambers.)
- USE time projection chambers

TPE-1RM15 DEVICE [5; 5] *Dec 89*
(Electrotechnical Laboratory, Tukuba, Ibaraki, Japan.)
- BT1 toroidal pinch devices
- BT2 closed plasma devices
- BT3 thermonuclear devices
- BT2 pinch devices
- BT3 thermonuclear devices
- RT reverse-field pinch

TPE-2 DEVICE [0; 0] *Dec 89*
(Electrotechnical Laboratory, Tukuba, Ibaraki, Japan.)
- BT1 toroidal screw pinch devices
- BT2 toroidal pinch devices
- BT3 closed plasma devices
- BT4 thermonuclear devices
- BT3 pinch devices
- BT4 thermonuclear devices

TPO [116; 116]
- UF triphenylphosphine oxide
- BT1 organic phosphorus compounds
- BT2 organic compounds
- RT phosphines

TR-0 REACTOR [32; 32]
(Tezkovodni Reaktor nuloveho vykonu.)
- UF czechoslovak tr-0 reactor
- UF rez tr-0 reactor
- BT1 heavy water moderated reactors
- BT2 reactors
- BT1 zero power reactors
- BT2 experimental reactors
- BT3 research and test reactors
- BT4 reactors

TR-1 REACTOR [15; 15]
(Cekmece Nuclear Research and Training Centre, Turkish Atomic Energy Commission, Istanbul, Turkey)
- UF turkish reactor-1
- BT1 enriched uranium reactors
- BT2 reactors
- BT1 isotope production reactors
- BT2 irradiation reactors
- BT3 reactors
- BT1 pool type reactors
- BT2 water cooled reactors
- BT3 reactors
- BT2 water moderated reactors
- BT3 reactors
- BT1 research reactors
- BT2 research and test reactors
- BT3 reactors
- BT1 thermal reactors
- BT2 reactors
- BT1 training reactors
- BT2 research and test reactors
- BT3 reactors

→ ## TR-2 REACTOR [2; 2] *Jul 91*
- UF turkish reactor-2
- BT1 pool type reactors
- BT2 water cooled reactors
- BT3 reactors
- BT2 water moderated reactors
- BT3 reactors
- BT1 research reactors
- BT2 research and test reactors
- BT3 reactors

TRABECULAR BONE [87; 87]
- BT1 bone tissues
- BT2 connective tissue
- BT3 tissues
- BT4 body
- RT bone marrow

§§ ## TRACE AMOUNTS [8,459; 8,459]
- RT carrier-free isotopes
- RT crystal doping
- RT doped materials
- RT impurities
- RT inclusions
- RT ion implantation
- RT microanalysis

trace elements
(Coordinate TRACE AMOUNTS with the descriptor listed below or with descriptors for specific elements.)
- USE elements

TRACER TECHNIQUES [28,555; 40,938]
- BT1 isotope applications
- NT1 dual-isotope subtraction tec
- NT1 isotope dilution
- NT1 labelled pool techniques
- NT1 radioactive tracer logging
- NT1 radioimmunoassay
- NT1 radioimmunodetection
- NT1 radioreceptor assay
- RT autoradiography
- RT biological markers
- RT crime detection
- RT diagnosis
- RT diagnostic techniques
- RT dynamic function studies
- RT enzyme immunoassay
- RT labelled compounds
- RT nuclear medicine
- RT radio-release analysis

- RT radiobiology
- RT radionuclide kinetics
- RT radionuclide migration
- RT renography

TRACHEA [400; 400]
- BT1 respiratory system
- RT intratracheal administration
- RT mediastinum

track detectors (dielectric)
- USE dielectric track detectors

track detectors (gas)
- USE gas track detectors

track detectors (photographic)
- USE photographic film detectors

tracks
- USE particle tracks

TRADE [934; 1,840]
- UF exports
- UF imports
- UF sales
- NT1 nuclear trade
- RT commercial sector
- RT competition
- RT domestic supplies
- RT economics
- RT market
- RT taxes

TRADESCANTIA [134; 134]
- BT1 plants

training
- USE education

training facilities
- USE educational facilities

TRAINING REACTORS [61; 1,552]
- BT1 research and test reactors
- BT2 reactors
- NT1 aerojet-general nucleonics r
- NT1 afrri reactor
- NT1 ai-l-77 reactor
- NT1 apsara reactor
- NT1 arbi reactor
- NT1 argonaut reactor
- NT1 argos reactor
- NT1 bgrr reactor
- NT1 budapest training reactor
- NT1 cesnef reactor
- NT1 cirus reactor
- NT1 consort-2 reactor
- NT1 cornell triga-mk-2 reactor
- NT1 dow triga-mk-1 reactor
- NT1 dr-1 reactor
- NT1 fir-1 reactor
- NT1 fnr reactor
- NT1 fr-0 reactor
- NT1 frf reactor
- NT1 frg-1 reactor
- NT1 gleep reactor
- NT1 gtrr reactor
- NT1 gulf triga-mk-3 reactor
- NT1 hor reactor
- NT1 htr reactor
- NT1 ian-r1 reactor
- NT1 iowa utr-10 reactor
- NT1 jason reactor
- NT1 jrr-1 reactor
- NT1 kur reactor
- NT1 lfr reactor
- NT1 melusine-1 reactor
- NT1 mitr reactor
- NT1 moata reactor
- NT1 murr reactor

NT1	ncscr-1 reactor	NT1	element 111 compounds	*transfer (mass)*	
NT1	nscr reactor	NT1	element 112 compounds	USE	mass transfer
NT1	ostr reactor	NT1	element 113 compounds		
NT1	osur reactor	NT1	element 114 compounds		
NT1	prnc-l-77 reactor	NT1	element 126 compounds	*transfer (momentum)*	
NT1	pstr reactor			USE	momentum transfer
NT1	queen mary college utr-b react	**TRANS 104 ELEMENTS** [932; 1,187]			
NT1	r-b reactor	UF	superheavy elements		
NT1	ra-1 reactor	BT1	transplutonium elements	*transfer (q-squared)*	
NT1	rien-1 reactor	BT2	transuranium elements	USE	four momentum transfer
NT1	rts-1 reactor	BT3	elements		
NT1	rv-1 reactor	NT1	element 105		
NT1	sca reactor	NT1	element 106		
NT1	sr-3p reactor	NT1	element 107		
NT1	srrc-utr-100 reactor	NT1	element 108	*transfer (radionuc in organis)*	
NT1	stark reactor	NT1	element 109	USE	radionuclide kinetics
NT1	strasbourg-cronenbourg reactor	NT1	element 110		
NT1	sur-100 series reactor	NT1	element 111		
NT1	thetis reactor	NT1	element 112		
NT1	thor reactor	NT1	element 113	*transfer factors (biological)*	
NT1	toshiba reactor	NT1	element 114	USE	ecological concentration
NT1	tr-1 reactor	NT1	element 115		
NT1	trico reactor	NT1	element 116	**TRANSFER FUNCTIONS** [769; 769]	
NT1	triga-1-michigan reactor	NT1	element 117	BT1	functions
NT1	triga-2-pavia reactor	NT1	element 118	RT	reactor stability
NT1	trr-1 reactor	NT1	element 119	RT	real time systems
NT1	ucbrr reactor	NT1	element 120		
NT1	uftr reactor	NT1	element 126	**TRANSFER MATRIX METHOD**	
NT1	ulysse reactor	NT1	element 128	[358; 358]	
NT1	umne-1 reactor	NT1	element 134	RT	cross sections
NT1	umrr reactor	NT1	element 145	RT	mathematical operators
NT1	urr reactor	NT1	element 164	RT	neutron transport theory
NT1	utr-10-kinki reactor	NT1	element 173		
NT1	uvar reactor			**TRANSFER NUMBERS** [83; 83]	
NT1	uwnr reactor			RT	electrophoresis
NT1	uwtr reactor				
NT1	vpi-utr-10 reactor	*transaminases*			
NT1	vr-1 reactor	USE	aminotransferases	*transfer of knowledge*	
NT1	wntr reactor			USE	technology transfer
NT1	wpir reactor	**TRANSCRIPTION** [621; 621] *Sep 81*			
NT1	wwr-s-budapest reactor	RT	dna polymerases	**TRANSFER REACTIONS** [2,199; 12,33	
NT1	x-10 reactor	RT	dna replication	(For nuclear reactions only; see also	
NT1	zlfr reactor	RT	gene regulation	CHARGE EXCHANGE and ELECTRON	
NT1	zpr reactor	RT	genes	TRANSFER.)	
		RT	messenger-rna	UF	quasi-elastic reactions
training-research react. kyoto		RT	rna polymerases	BT1	direct reactions
USE	kur reactor	RT	transcription factors	BT2	nuclear reactions
				NT1	multi-nucleon transfer reactio
trains		→ **TRANSCRIPTION FACTORS** [0; 0]		NT2	four-nucleon transfer reaction
USE	vehicles	*Oct 91*		NT3	alpha-transfer reactions
		BT1	proteins	NT2	many-nucleon transfer reacti
TRAJECTORIES [4,920; 4,920]		BT2	organic compounds	NT2	three-nucleon transfer reactio
RT	beam dynamics	RT	gene regulation	NT2	two-nucleon transfer reaction
RT	motion	RT	rna polymerases	NT1	one-nucleon transfer reactions
RT	orbits	RT	transcription	NT1	pickup reactions
RT	particle tracks			NT1	stripping
		TRANSDUCERS [1,575; 1,575]		RT	incomplete fusion reactions
TRAMEX PROCESS [7; 7]		RT	electrical equipment	RT	neutron transfer
BT1	reprocessing	RT	measuring instruments		
BT2	separation processes			**TRANSFER RNA** [196; 196]	
RT	amines	*transfer (angular momentum)*		BT1	rna
RT	solvent extraction	USE	angular momentum transfer	BT2	nucleic acids
				BT3	organic compounds
TRANQUILIZERS [191; 377]		*transfer (electron)*			
UF	promazine	USE	electron transfer	**TRANSFERASES** [583; 2,908]	
UF	tranquillizers			BT1	enzymes
BT1	psychotropic drugs			BT2	organic compounds
BT2	central nervous system agents	*transfer (energy)*		NT1	carbon-group transferases
BT3	drugs	USE	energy transfer	NT2	methyl transferases
NT1	chlorpromazine			NT1	glycosyl transferases
NT1	reserpine			NT1	nitrogen transferases
		transfer (environ. radionucl.)		NT2	aminotransferases
tranquillizers		USE	radionuclide migration	NT1	phosphorus-group transferases
USE	tranquilizers			NT2	nucleotidyltransferases
		transfer (four momentum)		NT3	polymerases
TRANS 104 ELEMENT COMPOUNDS		USE	four momentum transfer	NT4	dna polymerases
[23; 51]				NT4	rna polymerases
BT1	transplutonium compounds			NT2	phosphotransferases
BT2	transuranium compounds	*transfer (heat)*		NT3	hexokinase
NT1	element 105 compounds	USE	heat transfer		
NT1	element 106 compounds			**TRANSFERRIN** [444; 444]	
NT1	element 107 compounds			BT1	globulins-beta
NT1	element 108 compounds	*transfer (linear momentum)*		BT2	globulins
NT1	element 109 compounds	USE	linear momentum transfer	BT3	proteins
NT1	element 110 compounds			BT4	organic compounds

TRANSFORMATIONS [1,782; 9,107]
UF   *translation (mathematics)*
NT1 baecklund transformation
NT1 canonical transformations
 NT2 bogolyubov transformation
 NT2 foldy-wouthuysen transform
NT1 integral transformations
 NT2 fourier transformation
 NT2 hankel transform
 NT2 hilbert transformation
 NT2 laplace transformation
 NT2 mellin transform
NT1 orthogonal transformations
NT1 topological mapping
 NT2 conformal mapping

transformations (oncogenic)
USE oncogenic transformations

TRANSFORMERS [838; 838]
BT1 electrical equipment
 BT2 equipment
RT   dc to dc converters
RT   electric coils

TRANSFRONTIER CONTAMINATION
[669; 669] *Dec 76*
(For radioactive contamination only; see also TRANSFRONTIER POLLUTION.)
BT1 contamination
RT   bilateral agreements
RT   contamination regulations
RT   environmental transport

TRANSFRONTIER POLLUTION
[29; 29] *Dec 76*
(For nonradioactive pollution only; for radioactive pollution use TRANSFRONTIER CONTAMINATION.)
BT1 pollution
RT   bilateral agreements
RT   environmental transport
RT   pollution laws

TRANSFUSIONS [311; 311]
BT1 therapy
 BT2 medicine
RT   blood
RT   blood groups
RT   blood substitutes
RT   transplants

TRANSIENT OVERPOWER ACCIDENTS [492; 492] *Sep 79*
UF   *top accidents*
BT1 reactor accidents
 BT2 accidents
RT   transients

transient reactor test facil.
USE treat reactor

TRANSIENTS [9,809; 9,995]
NT1 electrical transients
RT   peaks
RT   pressurization
RT   reaction intermediates
RT   steady-state conditions
RT   sudden approximation
RT   temperature noise
RT   transient overpower accidents
RT   variations

TRANSISTOR AMPLIFIERS [129; 129]
BT1 amplifiers
 BT2 equipment
BT1 electronic equipment
 BT2 equipment
RT   transistors

TRANSISTOR OSCILLATORS [44; 44]
BT1 oscillators
 BT2 electronic equipment
  BT3 equipment
RT   pulse circuits
RT   transistors

TRANSISTOR SWITCHING CIRCUITS [103; 103]
BT1 switching circuits
 BT2 electronic circuits
RT   switching diodes

TRANSISTOR TRIGGER CIRCUITS [62; 62]
BT1 trigger circuits
 BT2 pulse circuits
  BT3 electronic circuits

TRANSISTORS [524; 2,351]
UF   *diode transistors*
BT1 semiconductor devices
NT1 field effect transistors
 NT2 mosfet
NT1 junction transistors
NT1 mis transistors
NT1 mos transistors
 NT2 mosfet
NT1 phototransistors
NT1 surface barrier transistors
RT   electronic circuits
RT   transistor amplifiers
RT   transistor oscillators

transit-time heating
USE transit-time magnetic pumping

TRANSIT-TIME MAGNETIC PUMPING
[66; 66]
(Transit-time magnetic pumping heating.)
UF   *transit-time heating*
UF   *ttmp*
BT1 magnetic-pumping heating
 BT2 high-frequency heating
  BT3 plasma heating
   BT4 heating
RT   fast magnetoacoustic waves
RT   landau damping

TRANSITION AMPLITUDES
[1,850; 3,406] *Dec 75*
BT1 amplitudes
NT1 decay amplitudes

TRANSITION BOILING [155; 155]
BT1 boiling
 BT2 phase transformations

TRANSITION ELEMENT ALLOYS
[229; 35,290]
(Prior to November 1983 this was a valid descriptor. Use a descriptor for the specific alloy, or use the broader term ALLOYS.)

TRANSITION ELEMENT COMPLEXES
[393; 13,732]
BT1 complexes
NT1 chromium complexes
NT1 cobalt complexes
NT1 copper complexes
 NT2 ceruloplasmin
NT1 gold complexes
NT1 hafnium complexes
NT1 iridium complexes
NT1 iron complexes
 NT2 ferricyanides
 NT2 ferritin
 NT2 ferrocene
 NT2 ferrocyanides
NT1 manganese complexes
NT1 molybdenum complexes
NT1 nickel complexes
NT1 niobium complexes
NT1 osmium complexes
NT1 palladium complexes
NT1 platinum complexes
NT1 rhenium complexes
NT1 rhodium complexes
NT1 ruthenium complexes
NT1 scandium complexes
NT1 silver complexes
NT1 tantalum complexes
NT1 technetium complexes
NT1 titanium complexes
NT1 tungsten complexes
NT1 vanadium complexes
NT1 yttrium complexes
NT1 zirconium complexes

TRANSITION ELEMENT COMPOUNDS
[879; 72,489]
UF   *group iva metal compounds*
UF   *group va metal compounds*
UF   *group via metal compounds*
*NT1 chromium compounds
*NT1 cobalt compounds
*NT1 copper compounds
*NT1 gold compounds
*NT1 hafnium compounds
*NT1 iridium compounds
*NT1 iron compounds
*NT1 manganese compounds
*NT1 molybdenum compounds
*NT1 nickel compounds
*NT1 niobium compounds
*NT1 osmium compounds
*NT1 palladium compounds
*NT1 platinum compounds
*NT1 rhenium compounds
*NT1 rhodium compounds
*NT1 ruthenium compounds
*NT1 scandium compounds
*NT1 silver compounds
*NT1 tantalum compounds
*NT1 technetium compounds
*NT1 titanium compounds
*NT1 tungsten compounds
*NT1 vanadium compounds
*NT1 yttrium compounds
*NT1 zirconium compounds

TRANSITION ELEMENTS
[1,359; 69,608]
UF   *transition metals*
BT1 metals
 BT2 elements
NT1 chromium
NT1 cobalt
NT1 copper
NT1 gold
NT1 hafnium
 NT2 hafnium-alpha
 NT2 hafnium-beta
NT1 iron
 NT2 iron-alpha
 NT2 iron-beta
 NT2 iron-delta
 NT2 iron-gamma
NT1 manganese
 NT2 manganese-alpha
 NT2 manganese-beta
 NT2 manganese-gamma
 NT2 manganese-sigma
NT1 molybdenum
NT1 nickel
NT1 niobium
 NT2 niobium-alpha
 NT2 niobium-beta
NT1 platinum metals
 NT2 iridium
 NT2 osmium
 NT2 palladium
 NT2 platinum
 NT2 rhodium
 NT2 ruthenium
NT1 rhenium
NT1 scandium
NT1 silver
NT1 tantalum
NT1 technetium
NT1 titanium
 NT2 titanium-alpha
 NT2 titanium-beta
NT1 tungsten
 NT2 tungsten-alpha

NT1 vanadium
NT1 yttrium
NT1 zirconium
NT2 zirconium-alpha
NT2 zirconium-beta
NT2 zirconium-omega

TRANSITION FLOW [159; 159]
BT1 fluid flow

TRANSITION HEAT [252; 1,142]
UF *heat of transition*
UF *latent heat of transition*
BT1 enthalpy
BT2 thermodynamic properties
BT3 physical properties
NT1 fusion heat
NT1 sublimation heat
NT1 vaporization heat
RT differential thermal analysis
RT phase transformations

transition metals
USE transition elements

TRANSITION RADIATION [558; 558]
BT1 electromagnetic radiation
BT2 radiations

TRANSITION RADIATION DETECTORS [223; 223]
(For detection of transition radiation emitted by particles going from one medium to another.)
BT1 radiation detectors
BT2 measuring instruments

TRANSITION TEMPERATURE
[12,002; 21,848]
UF *temperature (transition)*
BT1 thermodynamic properties
BT2 physical properties
NT1 boiling points
NT1 critical temperature
NT1 curie point
NT1 dew point
NT1 lambda point
NT1 melting points
NT1 neel temperature
RT ductile-brittle transitions
RT phase transformations

transitions (ductile-brittle)
USE ductile-brittle transitions

transitions (energy level)
USE energy-level transitions

transitions (forbidden)
USE forbidden transitions

transitions (phase)
USE phase transformations

translation (computer codes)
USE translators

translation (macromolecules)
USE biosynthesis

translation (mathematics)
USE transformations

translation (mechanical)
USE mechanics

TRANSLATORS [114; 114]
(Computer codes translating programs from one programming language into another.)
UF *translation (computer codes)*
BT1 computer codes
RT programming
RT programming languages

TRANSLOCATION [1,008; 1,008]
(See also RADIOACTIVITY TRANSPORT for the movement of and deposition of radioactive materials throughout a reactor.)
RT animals
RT ions
RT kinetics
RT minerals
RT organic compounds
RT plants
RT radionuclide migration
RT stable isotopes
RT transport

TRANSMISSION [3,204; 3,204]
(Of particles and radiations through matter; see also DATA TRANSMISSION, MACHINE PARTS, or POWER TRANSMISSION.)
RT absorption
RT attenuation
RT opacity
RT radionuclide kinetics

transmission (data)
USE data transmission

transmission (heat)
USE heat transfer

TRANSMISSION ELECTRON MICROSCO [2,621; 2,621] *Feb 81*
UF *tem (microscopy)*
BT1 electron microscopy
BT2 microscopy

TRANSMUTATION [697; 697]
(Of nuclides.)
UF *nuclear transmutation*
RT breeding
RT isotope production

TRANSONIC FLOW [89; 89]
BT1 fluid flow
RT aerodynamics
RT compressible flow
RT shock waves
RT supersonic flow

transparency
USE opacity

TRANSPIRATION [120; 120]
(Plants only.)
RT evaporation
RT leaves
RT physiology
RT plants
RT water vapor

transpiration (animal)
USE sweat

TRANSPLANTS [2,518; 3,564]
NT1 grafts
RT chimeras
RT graft-host reaction
RT host
RT immunity
RT immunosuppression
RT plastic surgery
RT transfusions

transplutonides
USE transplutonium elements

TRANSPLUTONIUM COMPOUNDS
[80; 875] *May 80*
BT1 transuranium compounds
*NT1 americium compounds
*NT1 berkelium compounds
*NT1 californium compounds
*NT1 curium compounds
*NT1 einsteinium compounds
*NT1 element 104 compounds
*NT1 fermium compounds
*NT1 lawrencium compounds
*NT1 mendelevium compounds
*NT1 nobelium compounds
*NT1 trans 104 element compounds

TRANSPLUTONIUM ELEMENTS
[327; 3,454]
UF *transplutonides*
BT1 transuranium elements
BT2 elements
NT1 americium
NT1 berkelium
NT1 californium
NT1 curium
NT1 einsteinium
NT1 element 104
NT1 fermium
NT1 lawrencium
NT1 mendelevium
NT1 nobelium
NT1 trans 104 elements
NT2 element 105
NT2 element 106
NT2 element 107
NT2 element 108
NT2 element 109
NT2 element 110
NT2 element 111
NT2 element 112
NT2 element 113
NT2 element 114
NT2 element 115
NT2 element 116
NT2 element 117
NT2 element 118
NT2 element 119
NT2 element 120
NT2 element 126
NT2 element 128
NT2 element 134
NT2 element 145
NT2 element 164
NT2 element 173
RT actinides

§ **TRANSPORT** [5,951; 7,521]
(Limited to the movement of goods and persons. For other types of transport, see descriptors such as ENVIRONMENTAL TRANSPORT, RADIATION TRANSPORT, RADIONUCLIDE MIGRATION, and RADIONUCLIDE KINETICS.)
UF *shipment*
NT1 air transport
NT2 supersonic transport
NT1 hydraulic transport
NT1 land transport
NT2 rail transport
NT2 road transport
NT1 maritime transport
NT1 pneumatic transport
RT containers
RT conveyors
RT delivery
RT materials handling
RT materials handling equipment
RT nuclear trade
RT packaging
RT packaging rules
RT propulsion
RT storage
RT translocation
RT transport regulations
RT vehicles
RT waste transportation

transport (atom)
  USE   atom transport

transport (beam)
  USE   beam transport

transport (charged-particle)
  USE   charged-particle transport

transport (environ. radionuc.)
  USE   radionuclide migration

transport (gamma)
  USE   photon transport

transport (neutral-particle)
  USE   neutral-particle transport

transport (neutron)
  USE   neutron transport

transport (photon)
  USE   photon transport

transport (proton)
  USE   proton transport

transport (radiation)
  USE   radiation transport

transport (radionuc in organi)
  USE   radionuclide kinetics

transport (radionucl. in biol)
  USE   radionuclide kinetics

transport (reaction product)
  USE   reaction product transport

transport insurance
  USE   insurance

TRANSPORT REGULATIONS
[1,023; 1,023]
  BT1   regulations
    BT2 laws
  RT   maritime laws
  RT   nuclear ship visits
  RT   transport

TRANSPORT THEORY [4,785; 10,749]
  NT1   charged-particle transport the
  NT1   gamma transport theory
  NT1   multigroup theory
  NT1   nelkin theory
  NT1   neoclassical transport theory
  NT1   neutron transport theory
  NT1   one-group theory
  RT   boltzmann equation
  RT   boltzmann-vlasov equation
  RT   case method
  RT   chapman-enskog theory
  RT   chapman-ferraro problem
  RT   discrete ordinate method
  RT   feynman method
  RT   fokker-planck equation
  RT   grad-shafranov equation
  RT   haywood model
  RT   invariant imbedding
  RT   moments method
  RT   monte carlo method
  RT   radiation transport
  RT   rosenbluth-nelkin model
  RT   scattering
  RT   selengut-goertzel equation
  RT   serber-wilson method
  RT   slaggie model
  RT   spitzer theory
  RT   van hove theory
  RT   wick-chandrasekhar method
  RT   yoshimori-kitano model
  RT   young model
  RT   yvon method

TRANSPORTABLE REACTORS [16; 33]
(Capable of being moved when not critical and possibly partly dismantled.)
  BT1   reactors
  NT1   package reactors
  NT1   tibr reactor

→ **TRANSPOSONS** [3; 3] *Jul 91*
  RT   dna-cloning
  RT   genes
  RT   genetic engineering
  RT   genetic variability
  RT   plasmids

TRANSURANIUM COMPLEXES
[32; 1,444]
  NT1   americium complexes
  NT1   berkelium complexes
  NT1   californium complexes
  NT1   curium complexes
  NT1   einsteinium complexes
  NT1   fermium complexes
  NT1   lawrencium complexes
  NT1   mendelevium complexes
  NT1   neptunium complexes
    NT2 neptunyl complexes
  NT1   nobelium complexes
  NT1   plutonium complexes
    NT2 plutonyl complexes

TRANSURANIUM COMPOUNDS
[212; 9,264]
 * NT1   neptunium compounds
 * NT1   plutonium compounds
 * NT1   transplutonium compounds

TRANSURANIUM ELEMENTS
[1,370; 12,733]
  BT1   elements
  NT1   neptunium
    NT2 neptunium-alpha
    NT2 neptunium-beta
    NT2 neptunium-gamma
  NT1   plutonium
    NT2 plutonium-alpha
    NT2 plutonium-beta
    NT2 plutonium-delta
    NT2 plutonium-epsilon
    NT2 plutonium-eta
    NT2 plutonium-gamma
  NT1   transplutonium elements
    NT2 americium
    NT2 berkelium
    NT2 californium
    NT2 curium
    NT2 einsteinium
    NT2 element 104
    NT2 fermium
    NT2 lawrencium
    NT2 mendelevium
    NT2 nobelium
    NT2 trans 104 elements
      NT3 element 105
      NT3 element 106
      NT3 element 107
      NT3 element 108
      NT3 element 109
      NT3 element 110
      NT3 element 111
      NT3 element 112
      NT3 element 113
      NT3 element 114
      NT3 element 115
      NT3 element 116
      NT3 element 117
      NT3 element 118
      NT3 element 119
      NT3 element 120
      NT3 element 126
      NT3 element 128
      NT3 element 134
      NT3 element 145
      NT3 element 164
      NT3 element 173
  RT   actinides

TRANSVAAL [84; 84]
  BT1   south africa
    BT2 africa
    BT2 developed countries
  RT   witwatersrand

TRANSVERSE ENERGY [118; 118]
Apr 89
(The kinetic energy of any particle, or group of particles, detected during a particle/target or beam/target interaction at a nonzero angle measured with respect to the initial particle or beam direction.)
  BT1   kinetic energy
    BT2 energy
  RT   angular distribution
  RT   anisotropy
  RT   energy spectra
  RT   nuclear reactions
  RT   particle interactions
  RT   transverse momentum

TRANSVERSE MOMENTUM
[7,998; 7,998]
  UF   *momentum (transverse)*
  BT1   linear momentum
  RT   center-of-mass system
  RT   interactions
  RT   longitudinal momentum
  RT   nuclear reactions
  RT   particle interactions
  RT   straight-line path approximati
  RT   transverse energy

TRAPPED ELECTRONS [1,261; 1,261]
  BT1   electrons
    BT2 leptons
      BT3 elementary particles
      BT3 fermions
  RT   electron precipitation

TRAPPED PROTONS [138; 138] *Apr 77*
  BT1   protons
    BT2 hydrogen ions 1 plus
      BT3 cations
        BT4 ions
          BT5 charged particles
      BT3 hydrogen ions
        BT4 ions
          BT5 charged particles
    BT2 nucleons
      BT3 baryons
        BT4 fermions
        BT4 hadrons
          BT5 elementary particles
  RT   aurorae
  RT   proton precipitation

TRAPPED-PARTICLE INSTABILITY
[627; 627]
  BT1   plasma instability
    BT2 instability
  RT   banana regime
  RT   closed plasma devices

TRAPPING [4,949; 5,249]
(Includes trapping of electrons or holes in lattices and trapping of particles in fields.)
  NT1   banana regime
  RT   crystal lattices
  RT   greenhouse effect
  RT   holes
  RT   magnetic fields
  RT   plateau regime
  RT   pr devices

TRAPS [2,089; 2,487]
(Equipment for trapping of electrons or holes in lattices and trapping of particles in fields; see also FILTERS.)
  NT1   cold traps
  RT   electrons
  RT   holes
  RT   luminescence
  RT   photoconductivity
  RT   photolysis
  RT   semiconductor materials
  RT   vacancies

trauma
  USE   injuries

traumatic shock
  USE   biological shock
  AND   injuries

TRAVELLING IONOSPHERIC DISTURB [124; 124]
  UF   tid
  BT1   ionospheric storms
    BT2   disturbances
  RT   ionosphere

TRAVELLING WAVE TUBES [64; 64]
  BT1   microwave tubes
    BT2   electron tubes
    BT2   microwave equipment
      BT3   electronic equipment
        BT4   equipment
  RT   rf systems

TRAVELLING WAVES [702; 702]
  UF   waves (travelling)
  RT   electromagnetic radiation
  RT   mechanical vibrations
  RT   standing waves
  RT   wave propagation
  RT   waveguides
  RT   wavelengths

TRAWSFYNYDD REACTOR [29; 29]
(Merionethshire, Wales, UK)
  BT1   carbon dioxide cooled reactors
    BT2   gas cooled reactors
      BT3   reactors
  BT1   magnox type reactors
    BT2   gcr type reactors
      BT3   gas cooled reactors
        BT4   reactors
      BT3   graphite moderated reactors
        BT4   reactors
    BT2   natural uranium reactors
      BT3   reactors
    BT2   power reactors
      BT3   reactors
  BT1   thermal reactors
    BT2   reactors

TREAT REACTOR [397; 397]
(ANL, Idaho National Engineering Lab., Idaho Falls, Idaho, USA)
  UF   transient reactor test facil.
  BT1   air cooled reactors
    BT2   gas cooled reactors
      BT3   reactors
  BT1   enriched uranium reactors
    BT2   reactors
  BT1   experimental reactors
    BT2   research and test reactors
      BT3   reactors
  BT1   graphite moderated reactors
    BT2   reactors
  BT1   solid homogeneous reactors
    BT2   homogeneous reactors
      BT3   reactors
  BT1   test reactors
    BT2   research and test reactors
      BT3   reactors
    BT2   test facilities
  BT1   thermal reactors
    BT2   reactors

TREATIES [167; 991]
  NT1   non-proliferation treaty
  NT1   tlatelolco treaty
  RT   arms control
  RT   international agreements
  RT   international laws

treatment (therapy)
  USE   therapy

treaty prohib nucl weap lat am
  USE   tlatelolco treaty

TREES [647; 1,138]
  UF   *betula*
  UF   *birches*
  UF   *deciduous trees*
  UF   *mahogany trees*
  BT1   plants
  NT1   cacao trees
  NT1   coconut palms
  NT1   eucalyptuses
  NT1   fruit trees
  NT1   hevea
  NT1   oaks
  NT1   oil palms
  NT1   olive trees
  NT1   pines
  NT1   poplars
  RT   bark
  RT   biomass plantations
  RT   conifers
  RT   forests
  RT   preferred species
  RT   wood

TREMATODES [18; 199]
  UF   *flukes (trematodes)*
  BT1   helminths
    BT2   parasites
  BT1   platyhelminths
    BT2   invertebrates
      BT3   animals
  NT1   fasciola
  NT1   schistosoma

tretamine
  USE   alkylating agents

TRH [267; 267]
  UF   *thyrotropin-releasing hormone*
  BT1   peptide hormones
    BT2   hormones
  RT   hypothalamus
  RT   tsh

tri university meson facility
  USE   triumf cyclotron

TRIACETONEAMINE-N-OXYL [32; 32]
  UF   *tan*
  BT1   ketones
    BT2   organic compounds
  BT1   organic oxygen compounds
    BT2   organic compounds
  BT1   piperidines
    BT2   amines
      BT3   organic compounds
    BT2   pyridines
      BT3   azines
        BT4   heterocyclic compounds
          BT5   organic compounds
        BT4   organic nitrogen compounds
          BT5   organic compounds
  BT1   radiosensitizers
    BT2   drugs
    BT2   response modifying factors
  RT   tmpn

TRIAM-1 TOKAMAK [31; 31] *Mar 83*
  BT1   tokamak devices
    BT2   closed plasma devices
      BT3   thermonuclear devices

TRIANGULAR CONFIGURATION [220; 220]
  BT1   configuration

TRIAZINES [93; 148]
(Compounds that contain a six-membered heterocyclic ring containing three nitrogen atoms.)
  BT1   azines
    BT2   heterocyclic compounds
      BT3   organic compounds
    BT2   organic nitrogen compounds
      BT3   organic compounds
  NT1   cyanurates
  NT1   melamine

TRIAZOLES [92; 92]
(Compounds that contain a five-membered heterocyclic ring containing three nitrogen atoms.)
  BT1   azoles
    BT2   heterocyclic compounds
      BT3   organic compounds
    BT2   organic nitrogen compounds
      BT3   organic compounds

tribaloy 700
  USE   alloy-ni50mo32cr15si3

tribaloy 800
  USE   alloy-co52cr17fe15mo3si3

TRIBOLIUM [63; 63]
  BT1   beetles
    BT2   insects
      BT3   arthropods
        BT4   invertebrates
          BT5   animals

tribology
  SEE   sliding friction
  OR   surface properties
  OR   wear

tributyl phosphate
  USE   tbp

tributylphosphine oxide
  USE   tbpo

TRICARBALLYLIC ACID [8; 8]
  BT1   carboxylic acids
    BT2   organic acids
      BT3   organic compounds

TRICASTIN-1 REACTOR [11; 11] *Oct 85*
(Troischateaux, Drome, France)
  BT1   pwr type reactors
    BT2   enriched uranium reactors
      BT3   reactors
    BT2   power reactors
      BT3   reactors
    BT2   thermal reactors
      BT3   reactors
    BT2   water cooled reactors
      BT3   reactors
    BT2   water moderated reactors
      BT3   reactors

TRICASTIN-4 REACTOR [3; 3] *Apr*
(Troischateaux, Drome, France.)
  BT1   pwr type reactors
    BT2   enriched uranium reactors
      BT3   reactors
    BT2   power reactors

BT3   reactors
BT2   thermal reactors
BT3   reactors
BT2   water cooled reactors
BT3   reactors
BT2   water moderated reactors
BT3   reactors

TRICHINELLA [19; 19]
BT1   helminths
BT2   parasites
BT1   nematodes
BT2   invertebrates
BT3   animals
RT   meat
RT   trichinosis

TRICHINOSIS [16; 16]
BT1   parasitic diseases
BT2   infectious diseases
BT3   diseases
RT   gastrointestinal tract
RT   inflammation
RT   muscles
RT   trichinella

trichloroacetaldehyde
USE   chloral

trichloromethane
USE   chloroform

TRICLINIC LATTICES [364; 364]
BT1   crystal lattices
BT2   crystal structure

TRICO REACTOR [2; 2]
(Kinshasa, Zaire)
UF   *congo kinshasa triga reactor*
UF   *triga-congo reactor*
BT1   isotope production reactors
BT2   irradiation reactors
BT3   reactors
BT1   thermal reactors
BT2   reactors
BT1   training reactors
BT2   research and test reactors
BT3   reactors
BT1   triga type reactors
BT2   enriched uranium reactors
BT3   reactors
BT2   hydride moderated reactors
BT3   reactors
BT2   research and test reactors
BT3   reactors
BT2   solid homogeneous reactors
BT3   homogeneous reactors
BT4   reactors
BT2   water cooled reactors
BT3   reactors
BT2   water moderated reactors
BT3   reactors

tricresyl phosphates
USE   tcp

TRIDECYL RADICALS [0; 0]
BT1   alkyl radicals
BT2   radicals

TRIDODECYLAMINE [45; 45]
UF   *trilaurylamine*
BT1   amines
BT2   organic compounds
BT1   chelating agents

triethylenemelamine
USE   alkylating agents

triethylenetetraaminehexaaceti
(Triethylenetetraaminehexaacetic acid)
USE   tetaha

triethylenetetramine
USE   teta

triga puspati reactor
USE   rtp reactor

TRIGA TYPE REACTORS [243; 822]
BT1   enriched uranium reactors
BT2   reactors
BT1   hydride moderated reactors
BT2   reactors
BT1   research and test reactors
BT2   reactors
BT1   solid homogeneous reactors
BT2   homogeneous reactors
BT3   reactors
BT1   water cooled reactors
BT2   reactors
BT1   water moderated reactors
BT2   reactors
NT1   afrri reactor
NT1   cornell triga-mk-2 reactor
NT1   dow triga-mk-1 reactor
NT1   fir-1 reactor
NT1   frf-2 reactor
NT1   frn reactor
NT1   gulf triga-mk-3 reactor
NT1   lopra reactor
NT1   nscr reactor
NT1   ostr reactor
NT1   prpr reactor
NT1   pstr reactor
NT1   rtp reactor
NT1   trico reactor
NT1   triga-brazil reactor
NT1   triga-texas reactor
NT1   triga-veterans reactor
NT1   triga-1-arizona reactor
NT1   triga-1-california reactor
NT1   triga-1-hanford reactor
NT1   triga-1-hanover reactor
NT1   triga-1-heidelberg reactor
NT1   triga-1-michigan reactor
NT1   triga-2 reactor
NT1   triga-2-dalat reactor
NT1   triga-2-illinois reactor
NT1   triga-2-kansas reactor
NT1   triga-2-ljubljana reactor
NT1   triga-2-mainz reactor
NT1   triga-2-musashi reactor
NT1   triga-2-pavia reactor
NT1   triga-2-rikkyo reactor
NT1   triga-2-rome reactor
NT1   triga-2-seoul reactor
NT1   triga-2-vienna reactor
NT1   triga-3-la jolla reactor
NT1   triga-3-salazar reactor
NT1   triga-3-seoul reactor
NT1   ucbrr reactor
NT1   wsur reactor

TRIGA-BRAZIL REACTOR [32; 32]
(Instituto de Pesquisas Radioativas
Nuclebras, Cidade Universitaria-
Pampulma, Minas Gerais, Brazil)
UF   *brazil triga reactor*
UF   *minas gerais univ. triga react*
UF   *univ. minas gerais triga react*
BT1   isotope production reactors
BT2   irradiation reactors
BT3   reactors
BT1   thermal reactors
BT2   reactors
BT1   triga type reactors
BT2   enriched uranium reactors
BT3   reactors
BT2   hydride moderated reactors
BT3   reactors
BT2   research and test reactors
BT3   reactors
BT2   solid homogeneous reactors
BT3   homogeneous reactors
BT4   reactors
BT2   water cooled reactors
BT3   reactors
BT2   water moderated reactors
BT3   reactors

triga-congo reactor
USE   trico reactor

triga-f-dasa reactor
USE   afrri reactor

triga-mk-1-dkfz heidelberg re.
USE   triga-1-heidelberg reactor

triga-mk-2 reactor
(See also specific reactors of this type,
e.g. CORNELL TRIGA-MK-2 REACTOR.)
USE   triga-2 reactor

triga-pennsylvania reactor
USE   pstr reactor

TRIGA-TEXAS REACTOR [13; 13]
(Univ. of Texas, Balcones Research Cen-
ter, near Austin, Texas, USA)
UF   *texas univ. triga reactor*
UF   *univ. of texas triga reactor*
BT1   isotope production reactors
BT2   irradiation reactors
BT3   reactors
BT1   pulsed reactors
BT2   reactors
BT1   thermal reactors
BT2   reactors
BT1   triga type reactors
BT2   enriched uranium reactors
BT3   reactors
BT2   hydride moderated reactors
BT3   reactors
BT2   research and test reactors
BT3   reactors
BT2   solid homogeneous reactors
BT3   homogeneous reactors
BT4   reactors
BT2   water cooled reactors
BT3   reactors
BT2   water moderated reactors
BT3   reactors

TRIGA-VETERANS REACTOR [6; 6]
(Omaha V.A. Medical Center/U.S. Veter-
ans Administration, Omaha, Nebraska,
USA)
UF   *omaha veterans triga-mk-1*
UF   *veter. adm. hosp. triga react.*
BT1   isotope production reactors
BT2   irradiation reactors
BT3   reactors
BT1   thermal reactors
BT2   reactors
BT1   triga type reactors
BT2   enriched uranium reactors
BT3   reactors
BT2   hydride moderated reactors
BT3   reactors
BT2   research and test reactors
BT3   reactors
BT2   solid homogeneous reactors
BT3   homogeneous reactors
BT4   reactors
BT2   water cooled reactors
BT3   reactors
BT2   water moderated reactors
BT3   reactors

TRIGA-1-ARIZONA REACTOR [4; 4]
Nov 88
BT1   triga type reactors
BT2   enriched uranium reactors
BT3   reactors
BT2   hydride moderated reactors
BT3   reactors
BT2   research and test reactors
BT3   reactors
BT2   solid homogeneous reactors
BT3   homogeneous reactors
BT4   reactors
BT2   water cooled reactors
BT3   reactors

TRIGA-1-CALIFORNIA REACTOR
[5; 5]
- UF california irvine triga-mk-1 r
- UF irvine triga-mk-1 reactor
- UF ucirr reactor
- UF univ. of calif. irvine triga
- BT1 isotope production reactors
  - BT2 irradiation reactors
    - BT3 reactors
- BT1 pulsed reactors
  - BT2 reactors
- BT1 thermal reactors
  - BT2 reactors
- BT1 triga type reactors
  - BT2 enriched uranium reactors
    - BT3 reactors
  - BT2 hydride moderated reactors
    - BT3 reactors
  - BT2 research and test reactors
    - BT3 reactors
  - BT2 solid homogeneous reactors
    - BT3 homogeneous reactors
      - BT4 reactors
  - BT2 water cooled reactors
    - BT3 reactors
  - BT2 water moderated reactors
    - BT3 reactors

TRIGA-1-HANFORD REACTOR [5; 5]
Sep 79
- UF hanford neutron radiography fa
- BT1 materials testing reactors
  - BT2 irradiation reactors
    - BT3 reactors
- BT1 triga type reactors
  - BT2 enriched uranium reactors
    - BT3 reactors
  - BT2 hydride moderated reactors
    - BT3 reactors
  - BT2 research and test reactors
    - BT3 reactors
  - BT2 solid homogeneous reactors
    - BT3 homogeneous reactors
      - BT4 reactors
  - BT2 water cooled reactors
    - BT3 reactors
  - BT2 water moderated reactors
    - BT3 reactors

→ TRIGA-1-HANOVER REACTOR [0; 0]
Jul 91
- UF frh reactor
- UF hannover-triga-mk-1 reactor
- BT1 isotope production reactors
  - BT2 irradiation reactors
    - BT3 reactors
- BT1 thermal reactors
  - BT2 reactors
- BT1 triga type reactors
  - BT2 enriched uranium reactors
    - BT3 reactors
  - BT2 hydride moderated reactors
    - BT3 reactors
  - BT2 research and test reactors
    - BT3 reactors
  - BT2 solid homogeneous reactors
    - BT3 homogeneous reactors
      - BT4 reactors
  - BT2 water cooled reactors
    - BT3 reactors
  - BT2 water moderated reactors
    - BT3 reactors

TRIGA-1-HEIDELBERG REACTOR
[4; 4]
- UF heidelberg triga-mk-1-dkfz re.
- UF triga-mk-1-dkfz heidelberg re.
- BT1 thermal reactors
  - BT2 reactors
- BT1 triga type reactors
  - BT2 enriched uranium reactors
    - BT3 reactors
  - BT2 hydride moderated reactors
    - BT3 reactors
  - BT2 research and test reactors
    - BT3 reactors
  - BT2 solid homogeneous reactors
    - BT3 homogeneous reactors
      - BT4 reactors
  - BT2 water cooled reactors
    - BT3 reactors
  - BT2 water moderated reactors
    - BT3 reactors

TRIGA-1-MICHIGAN REACTOR [5; 5]
Feb 76
(Michigan State University, East Lansing, Michigan, USA)
- UF michigan state triga-mk-1 reac
- BT1 isotope production reactors
  - BT2 irradiation reactors
    - BT3 reactors
- BT1 pulsed reactors
  - BT2 reactors
- BT1 research reactors
  - BT2 research and test reactors
    - BT3 reactors
- BT1 tank type reactors
  - BT2 reactors
- BT1 test reactors
  - BT2 research and test reactors
    - BT3 reactors
  - BT2 test facilities
- BT1 thermal reactors
  - BT2 reactors
- BT1 training reactors
  - BT2 research and test reactors
    - BT3 reactors
- BT1 triga type reactors
  - BT2 enriched uranium reactors
    - BT3 reactors
  - BT2 hydride moderated reactors
    - BT3 reactors
  - BT2 research and test reactors
    - BT3 reactors
  - BT2 solid homogeneous reactors
    - BT3 homogeneous reactors
      - BT4 reactors
  - BT2 water cooled reactors
    - BT3 reactors
  - BT2 water moderated reactors
    - BT3 reactors

TRIGA-2 REACTOR [58; 58]
- UF triga-mk-2 reactor
- BT1 isotope production reactors
  - BT2 irradiation reactors
    - BT3 reactors
- BT1 thermal reactors
  - BT2 reactors
- BT1 triga type reactors
  - BT2 enriched uranium reactors
    - BT3 reactors
  - BT2 hydride moderated reactors
    - BT3 reactors
  - BT2 research and test reactors
    - BT3 reactors
  - BT2 solid homogeneous reactors
    - BT3 homogeneous reactors
      - BT4 reactors
  - BT2 water cooled reactors
    - BT3 reactors
  - BT2 water moderated reactors
    - BT3 reactors

triga-2-cornell reactor
- USE cornell triga-mk-2 reactor

TRIGA-2-DALAT REACTOR [10; 10]
(Dalat, Socialist Republic of Viet-Nam)
- UF dalat triga-mk-2 reactor
- UF vietnamese triga-mk-2 reactor
- BT1 isotope production reactors
  - BT2 irradiation reactors
    - BT3 reactors
- BT1 thermal reactors
  - BT2 reactors
- BT1 triga type reactors
  - BT2 enriched uranium reactors
    - BT3 reactors
  - BT2 hydride moderated reactors
    - BT3 reactors
  - BT2 research and test reactors
    - BT3 reactors
  - BT2 solid homogeneous reactors
    - BT3 homogeneous reactors
      - BT4 reactors
  - BT2 water cooled reactors
    - BT3 reactors
  - BT2 water moderated reactors
    - BT3 reactors

TRIGA-2-ILLINOIS REACTOR [12; 12]
(Univ. of Illinois, Urbana, Illinois, USA)
- UF illinois univ. triga-mk-2 reac
- UF univ. of illin. triga-mk-2 rea
- BT1 isotope production reactors
  - BT2 irradiation reactors
    - BT3 reactors
- BT1 pulsed reactors
  - BT2 reactors
- BT1 thermal reactors
  - BT2 reactors
- BT1 triga type reactors
  - BT2 enriched uranium reactors
    - BT3 reactors
  - BT2 hydride moderated reactors
    - BT3 reactors
  - BT2 research and test reactors
    - BT3 reactors
  - BT2 solid homogeneous reactors
    - BT3 homogeneous reactors
      - BT4 reactors
  - BT2 water cooled reactors
    - BT3 reactors
  - BT2 water moderated reactors
    - BT3 reactors

TRIGA-2-KANSAS REACTOR [6; 6]
(Kansas State Univ., Manhattan, Kansas, USA)
- UF kansas state univ. triga-mk-2
- BT1 isotope production reactors
  - BT2 irradiation reactors
    - BT3 reactors
- BT1 pulsed reactors
  - BT2 reactors
- BT1 thermal reactors
  - BT2 reactors
- BT1 triga type reactors
  - BT2 enriched uranium reactors
    - BT3 reactors
  - BT2 hydride moderated reactors
    - BT3 reactors
  - BT2 research and test reactors
    - BT3 reactors
  - BT2 solid homogeneous reactors
    - BT3 homogeneous reactors
      - BT4 reactors
  - BT2 water cooled reactors
    - BT3 reactors
  - BT2 water moderated reactors
    - BT3 reactors

TRIGA-2-LJUBLJANA REACTOR
[43; 43]
(J. Stefan Institute, Ljubljana, Yugoslav
- UF ljubljana triga-mk-2 reactor
- UF yugoslav triga-mk-2 reactor
- BT1 isotope production reactors
  - BT2 irradiation reactors
    - BT3 reactors
- BT1 thermal reactors
  - BT2 reactors
- BT1 triga type reactors
  - BT2 enriched uranium reactors
    - BT3 reactors
  - BT2 hydride moderated reactors
    - BT3 reactors
  - BT2 research and test reactors
    - BT3 reactors
  - BT2 solid homogeneous reactors
    - BT3 homogeneous reactors
      - BT4 reactors
  - BT2 water cooled reactors
    - BT3 reactors
  - BT2 water moderated reactors
    - BT3 reactors

TRIGA-2-MAINZ REACTOR [19; 19]
(Institut fuer Kernchemie, Univ. Mainz, Mainz, F.R. Germany)
UF   *german (mainz) triga-mk-2 reac*
UF   *mainz triga-mk-2 reactor*
BT1   isotope production reactors
  BT2   irradiation reactors
    BT3   reactors
BT1   pulsed reactors
  BT2   reactors
BT1   thermal reactors
  BT2   reactors
BT1   triga type reactors
  BT2   enriched uranium reactors
    BT3   reactors
  BT2   hydride moderated reactors
    BT3   reactors
  BT2   research and test reactors
    BT3   reactors
  BT2   solid homogeneous reactors
    BT3   homogeneous reactors
      BT4   reactors
  BT2   water cooled reactors
    BT3   reactors
  BT2   water moderated reactors
    BT3   reactors

TRIGA-2-MUSASHI REACTOR [36; 36]
(Atomic Energy Research Lab., Musashi Institute of Technology University, Kanagawa Prefecture, Japan)
UF   *musashi inst. of tech. triga r*
BT1   isotope production reactors
  BT2   irradiation reactors
    BT3   reactors
BT1   thermal reactors
  BT2   reactors
BT1   triga type reactors
  BT2   enriched uranium reactors
    BT3   reactors
  BT2   hydride moderated reactors
    BT3   reactors
  BT2   research and test reactors
    BT3   reactors
  BT2   solid homogeneous reactors
    BT3   homogeneous reactors
      BT4   reactors
  BT2   water cooled reactors
    BT3   reactors
  BT2   water moderated reactors
    BT3   reactors

TRIGA-2-PAVIA REACTOR [15; 15]
(Pavia, Italy)
UF   *lena triga-mk-2 pulsed reactor*
UF   *pavia triga-mk-2 reactor*
BT1   isotope production reactors
  BT2   irradiation reactors
    BT3   reactors
BT1   pulsed reactors
  BT2   reactors
BT1   test reactors
  BT2   research and test reactors
    BT3   reactors
  BT2   test facilities
BT1   thermal reactors
  BT2   reactors
BT1   training reactors
  BT2   research and test reactors
    BT3   reactors
BT1   triga type reactors
  BT2   enriched uranium reactors
    BT3   reactors
  BT2   hydride moderated reactors
    BT3   reactors
  BT2   research and test reactors
    BT3   reactors
  BT2   solid homogeneous reactors
    BT3   homogeneous reactors
      BT4   reactors
  BT2   water cooled reactors
    BT3   reactors
  BT2   water moderated reactors
    BT3   reactors

TRIGA-2-RIKKYO REACTOR [16; 16]
(Institute for Atomic Energy, Rikkyo University, Kanagawa Prefecture, Japan)
UF   *rikkyo univ. triga-mk-2 react.*
BT1   isotope production reactors
  BT2   irradiation reactors
    BT3   reactors
BT1   thermal reactors
  BT2   reactors
BT1   triga type reactors
  BT2   enriched uranium reactors
    BT3   reactors
  BT2   hydride moderated reactors
    BT3   reactors
  BT2   research and test reactors
    BT3   reactors
  BT2   solid homogeneous reactors
    BT3   homogeneous reactors
      BT4   reactors
  BT2   water cooled reactors
    BT3   reactors
  BT2   water moderated reactors
    BT3   reactors

TRIGA-2-ROME REACTOR [12; 12]
UF   *italian triga-mk-2 reactor*
UF   *rc-1 reactor*
UF   *reattore casaccia-1*
UF   *rome triga-mk-2 reactor*
BT1   isotope production reactors
  BT2   irradiation reactors
    BT3   reactors
BT1   thermal reactors
  BT2   reactors
BT1   triga type reactors
  BT2   enriched uranium reactors
    BT3   reactors
  BT2   hydride moderated reactors
    BT3   reactors
  BT2   research and test reactors
    BT3   reactors
  BT2   solid homogeneous reactors
    BT3   homogeneous reactors
      BT4   reactors
  BT2   water cooled reactors
    BT3   reactors
  BT2   water moderated reactors
    BT3   reactors

TRIGA-2-SEOUL REACTOR [9; 9]
(Korea Atomic Energy Research Institute, Cheong Ryang, Seoul, Korea)
UF   *korean (seoul) triga-mk-2 reac*
UF   *seoul triga-mk-2 reactor*
BT1   isotope production reactors
  BT2   irradiation reactors
    BT3   reactors
BT1   thermal reactors
  BT2   reactors
BT1   triga type reactors
  BT2   enriched uranium reactors
    BT3   reactors
  BT2   hydride moderated reactors
    BT3   reactors
  BT2   research and test reactors
    BT3   reactors
  BT2   solid homogeneous reactors
    BT3   homogeneous reactors
      BT4   reactors
  BT2   water cooled reactors
    BT3   reactors
  BT2   water moderated reactors
    BT3   reactors

TRIGA-2-VIENNA REACTOR [42; 42]
(Atominstitute of the Austrian Universities/Austrian Fed. Min. of Science and Research, Vienna, Austria)
UF   *austrian triga-mk-2 reactor*
UF   *vienna triga-mk-2 reactor*
BT1   isotope production reactors
  BT2   irradiation reactors
    BT3   reactors
BT1   thermal reactors
  BT2   reactors
BT1   triga type reactors
  BT2   enriched uranium reactors
    BT3   reactors
  BT2   hydride moderated reactors
BT3   research and test reactors
BT2   reactors
BT3   reactors
BT2   solid homogeneous reactors
BT3   homogeneous reactors
    BT4   reactors
BT2   water cooled reactors
BT3   reactors
BT2   water moderated reactors
BT3   reactors

triga-3-gulf reactor
  USE   gulf triga-mk-3 reactor

TRIGA-3-LA JOLLA REACTOR [4; 4]
UF   *la jolla triga-mk-3 reactor*
UF   *torrey pines triga-mk-3 react.*
BT1   triga type reactors
  BT2   enriched uranium reactors
    BT3   reactors
  BT2   hydride moderated reactors
    BT3   reactors
  BT2   research and test reactors
    BT3   reactors
  BT2   solid homogeneous reactors
    BT3   homogeneous reactors
      BT4   reactors
  BT2   water cooled reactors
    BT3   reactors
  BT2   water moderated reactors
    BT3   reactors

TRIGA-3-SALAZAR REACTOR [17; 17]
UF   *mexican triga-mk-3 reactor*
UF   *salazar triga-mk3 reactor*
BT1   isotope production reactors
  BT2   irradiation reactors
    BT3   reactors
BT1   thermal reactors
  BT2   reactors
BT1   triga type reactors
  BT2   enriched uranium reactors
    BT3   reactors
  BT2   hydride moderated reactors
    BT3   reactors
  BT2   research and test reactors
    BT3   reactors
  BT2   solid homogeneous reactors
    BT3   homogeneous reactors
      BT4   reactors
  BT2   water cooled reactors
    BT3   reactors
  BT2   water moderated reactors
    BT3   reactors

TRIGA-3-SEOUL REACTOR [21; 21]
May 80
(Korea Atomic Energy Research Institute, Cheong Ryang, Seoul, Korea)
UF   *korean (seoul) triga-mk-3 reac*
UF   *seoul triga-mk-3 reactor*
BT1   isotope production reactors
  BT2   irradiation reactors
    BT3   reactors
BT1   thermal reactors
  BT2   reactors
BT1   triga type reactors
  BT2   enriched uranium reactors
    BT3   reactors
  BT2   hydride moderated reactors
    BT3   reactors
  BT2   research and test reactors
    BT3   reactors
  BT2   solid homogeneous reactors
    BT3   homogeneous reactors
      BT4   reactors
  BT2   water cooled reactors
    BT3   reactors
  BT2   water moderated reactors
    BT3   reactors

TRIGGER CIRCUITS [1,421; 1,483]
BT1   pulse circuits
  BT2   electronic circuits
NT1   transistor trigger circuits

TRIGLYCERIDES [269; 422]
  BT1 esters
    BT2 organic compounds
  BT1 lipids
    BT2 organic compounds
  NT1 butter fat
  NT1 corn oil
  NT1 croton oil
  NT1 linseed oil
  NT1 olive oil
  NT1 peanut oil
  NT1 soybean oil
  NT1 triolein
  RT   glycerol
  RT   oils

TRIGONAL LATTICES [594; 594]
  UF   *rhombohedral lattices*
  BT1 crystal lattices
    BT2 crystal structure

trihydroxyaromatics
  USE polyphenols

trihydroxybenzoic acid
  USE gallic acid

TRIHYDROXYGLUTARIC ACID [13; 13]
  UF   *trioxyglutaric acid*
  BT1 hydroxy acids
    BT2 carboxylic acids
      BT3 organic acids
        BT4 organic compounds

TRIIODOTHYRONINE [839; 839]
  BT1 thyroid hormones
    BT2 peptide hormones
      BT3 hormones
  RT   diiodothyronine
  RT   thyronine

triketohydrindane
  USE ninhydrin

trilaurylamine
  USE tridodecylamine

TRILLIUM [3; 3]
  BT1 plants

TRILLO-1 REACTOR [10; 10] *May 79*
(Trillo, Guadalajara, Spain)
  BT1 pwr type reactors
    BT2 enriched uranium reactors
      BT3 reactors
    BT2 power reactors
      BT3 reactors
    BT2 thermal reactors
      BT3 reactors
    BT2 water cooled reactors
      BT3 reactors
    BT2 water moderated reactors
      BT3 reactors

trimethylacetic acid
  USE pivalic acid

trimethylbenzene-sym
  USE mesitylene

TRINEUTRONS [33; 33]
  BT1 polyneutrons
    BT2 neutrons
      BT3 nucleons
        BT4 baryons
          BT5 fermions
          BT5 hadrons
            BT6 elementary particles

trinitrophenol
  USE picric acid

trinitrotoluene
  USE tnt

TRINITY EVENT [12; 12]
  BT1 nuclear explosions
    BT2 explosions

trino vercellese reactor
  USE selni reactor

trinonylamine
  USE tna

trioctylamine
  USE toa

trioctylphosphine oxide
  USE topo

trioctylphosphine sulfide
  USE tops

TRIODE TUBES [83; 83]
  BT1 electron tubes

TRIOLEIN [71; 71]
  UF   *glyceryl trioleate*
  UF   *olein*
  BT1 oils
    BT2 other organic compounds
      BT3 organic compounds
  BT1 triglycerides
    BT2 esters
      BT3 organic compounds
    BT2 lipids
      BT3 organic compounds
  RT   oleic acid

TRIOXANES [42; 42]
  BT1 heterocyclic compounds
    BT2 organic compounds
  BT1 organic oxygen compounds
    BT2 organic compounds
  RT   organic solvents

trioxyglutaric acid
  USE trihydroxyglutaric acid

TRIPHENYLENE [15; 15]
  BT1 condensed aromatics
    BT2 aromatics
      BT3 organic compounds
  BT1 hydrocarbons
    BT2 organic compounds

TRIPHENYLMETHANE DYES [113; 164]
  BT1 dyes
  NT1 aluminon
  NT1 aurin
  NT1 methyl violet
  NT1 methylthymol blue

triphenylphosphine oxide
  USE tpo

TRIPLASMATRONS [9; 9]
  BT1 ion sources
  BT1 plasmatrons
    BT2 electron tubes

TRIPLE POINT [16; 16] *Feb 88*
(The temperature and pressure at which the solid, liquid and vapor phases of a substance coexist in equilibrium with one another.)
  RT   phase diagrams
  RT   phase transformations

triplet particles
  USE quarks

TRIPLETS [581; 581]
  BT1 multiplets

tristan project
  USE tristan storage rings

TRISTAN SEPARATOR [22; 22] *May 8*
  BT1 electromag isotope separators
  BT1 reactor experimental facilitie
    BT2 reactor components
  RT   hfbr reactor

TRISTAN STORAGE RINGS [523; 523 *Sep 81*
(Transposable Ring Intersecting STorage Accelerators in Nippon.)
  UF   *kek inters. stor. accel.*
  UF   *tristan project*
  BT1 storage rings

tritiated compounds
  USE tritium compounds

tritiated water
  USE heavy water
  AND tritium oxides

triticum
  USE wheat

TRITIDES [22; 224] *Mar 86*
  BT1 tritium compounds
    BT2 hydrogen compounds
  NT1 deuterium tritide
  NT1 helium tritides
  NT1 hydrogen tritide
  NT1 lithium tritides

TRITIUM [16,477; 16,477]
  UF   *hydrogen 3*
  BT1 beta-minus decay radioisotopes
    BT2 beta decay radioisotopes
      BT3 radioisotopes
        BT4 isotopes
  BT1 hydrogen isotopes
  BT1 light nuclei
    BT2 nuclei
  BT1 odd-even nuclei
    BT2 nuclei
  BT1 years living radioisotopes
    BT2 radioisotopes
      BT3 isotopes
  RT   thermonuclear fuels
  RT   tritium extraction plants
  RT   tritons

TRITIUM COMPOUNDS [12,173; 13,683]
  UF   *tritiated compounds*
  UF+ *dto*
  UF+ *hto*
  BT1 hydrogen compounds
  NT1 tritides
    NT2 deuterium tritide
    NT2 helium tritides
    NT2 hydrogen tritide
    NT2 lithium tritides
  NT1 tritium oxides
  RT   heavy water
  RT   labelled compounds
  RT   tritium extraction plants

TRITIUM EXTRACTION PLANTS
[122; 122] *Oct 75*
- BT1 isotope separation plants
- BT2 industrial plants
- BT2 nuclear facilities
- RT heavy water
- RT tritium
- RT tritium compounds

tritium hydride
- USE hydrogen tritide

TRITIUM IONS [142; 142]
- BT1 ions
- BT2 charged particles

TRITIUM METERS [56; 56] *Sep 81*
- BT1 measuring instruments
- RT chemical analysis

TRITIUM OXIDES [1,003; 1,003]
- UF+ *tritiated water*
- BT1 tritium compounds
- BT2 hydrogen compounds

TRITIUM PRODUCTION REACTORS
[93; 96]
- BT1 irradiation reactors
- BT2 reactors
- NT1 celestin reactor

TRITIUM RECOVERY [1,214; 1,214]
(In thermonuclear reactors and/or devices.)
- UF *recovery (tritium)*
- RT breeding blankets
- RT plasma confinement
- RT thermonuclear devices
- RT thermonuclear reactors

TRITIUM SYSTEMS TEST ASSEMBLY
[107; 107] *Jul 86*
(Facility to test and demonstrate safe handling of tritium in a manner similar to that required for a thermonuclear reactor.)
- BT1 test facilities
- RT thermonuclear fuels
- RT thermonuclear reactor fueling

TRITIUM TARGET [1,175; 1,175]
- BT1 targets

triton
- USE triturus

TRITON BEAMS [219; 219]
- BT1 ion beams
- BT2 beams
- RT tritons

TRITON REACTIONS [1,110; 1,110]
- BT1 nuclear reactions

TRITON REACTOR [26; 26]
(CEA, Paris, France)
- BT1 enriched uranium reactors
- BT2 reactors
- BT1 pool type reactors
- BT2 water cooled reactors
- BT3 reactors
- BT2 water moderated reactors
- BT3 reactors
- BT1 research reactors
- BT2 research and test reactors
- BT3 reactors
- BT1 thermal reactors
- BT2 reactors

TRITONS [3,730; 3,745]
- BT1 charged particles
- NT1 antitritons
- RT tritium
- RT triton beams

TRITURUS [19; 19]
- UF *triton*
- BT1 salamanders
- BT2 amphibians
- BT3 aquatic organisms
- BT3 vertebrates
- BT4 animals

TRIUMF CYCLOTRON [506; 506]
- UF *tri university meson facility*
- BT1 isochronous cyclotrons
- BT2 cyclotrons
- BT3 cyclic accelerators
- BT4 accelerators

trochotrons
- USE counting tubes

troilite
(Prior to August 1981 this concept was indexed by using IRON METEORITES. From then till April 1984 MINERALS was coordinated with IRON SULFIDES.)
- USE sulfide minerals

TROJAN REACTOR [99; 99]
(Prescott, Oregon, USA)
- BT1 pwr type reactors
- BT2 enriched uranium reactors
- BT3 reactors
- BT2 power reactors
- BT3 reactors
- BT2 thermal reactors
- BT3 reactors
- BT2 water cooled reactors
- BT3 reactors
- BT2 water moderated reactors
- BT3 reactors

trombay r-5 reactor
(Prior to March 1986 this was a valid descriptor, and older material is so indexed.)
- USE dhruva reactor

TROMEXAN [0; 0]
- BT1 anticoagulants
- BT2 hematologic agents
- BT3 drugs

TROPICAL MEDICINE [10; 10]
- BT1 medicine
- RT tropical regions

TROPICAL REGIONS [246; 246]
- RT climates
- RT tropical medicine

TROPONES [28; 28]
- UF *cycloheptatrienones*
- BT1 ketones
- BT2 organic compounds

TROPOPAUSE [30; 30]
- BT1 boundary layers
- BT2 layers
- RT earth atmosphere
- RT global fallout
- RT stratosphere
- RT troposphere

TROPOSPHERE [478; 478]
- BT1 earth atmosphere
- RT air
- RT air-water interactions
- RT tropopause

TROUT [172; 172]
- BT1 fishes
- BT2 aquatic organisms
- BT2 vertebrates
- BT3 animals

TRR-1 REACTOR [12; 12]
(Office of Atomic Energy for Peace (OAEP), Ministry of Industry, Bangkok, Thailand)
- UF *thai research reactor-1*
- BT1 enriched uranium reactors
- BT2 reactors
- BT1 pool type reactors
- BT2 water cooled reactors
- BT3 reactors
- BT2 water moderated reactors
- BT3 reactors
- BT1 research reactors
- BT2 research and test reactors
- BT3 reactors
- BT1 thermal reactors
- BT2 reactors
- BT1 training reactors
- BT2 research and test reactors
- BT3 reactors

truck transport
- USE road transport

trucks
- USE vehicles

TRUEX PROCESS [8; 8] *Jul 89*
- BT1 separation processes
- RT solvent extraction

truth model
- USE flavor model

trypaflavine
- USE acriflavine

TRYPAN BLUE [27; 27]
- BT1 amines
- BT2 organic compounds
- BT1 azo dyes
- BT2 azo compounds
- BT3 organic nitrogen compounds
- BT4 organic compounds
- BT2 dyes
- BT1 naphthols
- BT2 phenols
- BT3 aromatics
- BT4 organic compounds
- BT3 hydroxy compounds
- BT4 organic compounds
- BT1 sulfonic acids
- BT2 organic acids
- BT3 organic compounds
- BT2 organic sulfur compounds
- BT3 organic compounds

TRYPANOSOMA [105; 105]
- BT1 parasites
- BT1 protozoa
- BT2 invertebrates
- BT3 animals
- BT2 microorganisms
- RT glossina
- RT trypanosomiasis

TRYPANOSOMIASIS [78; 78]
- BT1 parasitic diseases
- BT2 infectious diseases
- BT3 diseases
- RT trypanosoma

TRYPSIN [352; 352]
- BT1 serine proteinases
- BT2 peptide hydrolases
- BT3 hydrolases
- BT4 enzymes
- BT5 organic compounds
- RT digestion
- RT pancreas

TRYPTAMINES [92; 882]
- BT1 amines
- BT2 organic compounds
- BT1 indoles
- BT2 pyrroles
- BT3 azoles
- BT4 heterocyclic compounds
- BT5 organic compounds
- BT4 organic nitrogen compounds
- BT5 organic compounds
- NT1 bufotenine
- NT1 melatonin
- NT1 serotonin

TRYPTOPHAN [486; 486]
- BT1 amino acids
- BT2 carboxylic acids
- BT3 organic acids
- BT4 organic compounds
- BT1 heterocyclic acids
- BT2 carboxylic acids
- BT3 organic acids
- BT4 organic compounds
- BT2 heterocyclic compounds
- BT3 organic compounds
- BT1 indoles
- BT2 pyrroles
- BT3 azoles
- BT4 heterocyclic compounds
- BT5 organic compounds
- BT4 organic nitrogen compounds
- BT5 organic compounds
- RT hydroxytryptophan

TRYPTOPHAN OXYGENASE [9; 9]
- UF *pyrrolase (tryptophan)*
- BT1 oxygenases
- BT2 oxidoreductases
- BT3 enzymes
- BT4 organic compounds

tschebyscheff approximation
- USE polynomials

tsetse fly
- USE glossina

TSH [866; 866]
- UF *thyroid stimulating hormone*
- BT1 pituitary hormones
- BT2 peptide hormones
- BT3 hormones
- RT thyroid hormones
- RT trh

TSR-1 REACTOR [14; 14]
(Oak Ridge National Lab., Oak Ridge, Tennessee, USA)
- UF *tower shielding reactor-1*
- BT1 enriched uranium reactors
- BT2 reactors
- BT1 tank type reactors
- BT2 reactors
- BT1 test reactors
- BT2 research and test reactors
- BT3 reactors
- BT2 test facilities

TSR-2 REACTOR [36; 36]
(Oak Ridge National Lab., Oak Ridge, Tennessee, USA)
- UF *tower shielding reactor-2*
- BT1 research reactors
- BT2 research and test reactors
- BT3 reactors
- BT1 test reactors
- BT2 research and test reactors
- BT3 reactors
- BT2 test facilities
- BT1 water cooled reactors
- BT2 reactors
- BT1 water moderated reactors
- BT2 reactors

tsukuba kek synchrotron
- USE kek synchrotron

TSUNAMIS [42; 42]
(A great sea wave produced by submarine earth movement or volcanic eruption.)
- UF *tidal waves*
- RT earthquakes
- RT exceptional natural disaster
- RT seas
- RT seismic waves

TSURUGA REACTOR [82; 82]
(Tsuruga, Fukui, Japan)
- UF *japco-2 reactor*
- UF *tsuruga-1 reactor*
- BT1 bwr type reactors
- BT2 enriched uranium reactors
- BT3 reactors
- BT2 power reactors
- BT3 reactors
- BT2 thermal reactors
- BT3 reactors
- BT2 water cooled reactors
- BT3 reactors
- BT2 water moderated reactors
- BT3 reactors

tsuruga-1 reactor
- USE tsuruga reactor

TSURUGA-2 REACTOR [46; 46] *Jun 83*
- UF *japco-4 reactor*
- BT1 pwr type reactors
- BT2 enriched uranium reactors
- BT3 reactors
- BT2 power reactors
- BT3 reactors
- BT2 thermal reactors
- BT3 reactors
- BT2 water cooled reactors
- BT3 reactors
- BT2 water moderated reactors
- BT3 reactors

TTA [467; 467]
- UF *thenoyltrifluoroacetone*
- BT1 heterocyclic compounds
- BT2 organic compounds
- BT1 ketones
- BT2 organic compounds
- BT1 organic fluorine compounds
- BT2 organic halogen compounds
- BT3 organic compounds
- BT1 organic sulfur compounds
- BT2 organic compounds
- RT thiophene

ttf
(Tetrathiafulvalene.)
- USE heterocyclic compounds
- AND organic sulfur compounds

ttf-tcnq
(Tetrathiafulvalene-Tetracyanoquinodimethane.)
- USE cycloalkenes
- AND heterocyclic compounds
- AND nitriles
- AND organic sulfur compounds

ttmp
- USE transit-time magnetic pumping

ttr-1 toshiba reactor
- USE toshiba reactor

TUBERCULIN [16; 16]
- BT1 antigens

TUBERCULOSIS [450; 562]
- BT1 bacterial diseases
- BT2 infectious diseases
- BT3 diseases
- NT1 lupus
- RT mycobacterium tuberculosis
- RT pas
- RT streptomycin

TUBERS [50; 619]
- NT1 potatoes
- RT plants

TUBES [8,153; 9,315]
(For objects of tubular shape; see also DRIFT TUBES, ELECTRON TUBES, or IMAGE STORAGE TUBES.)
- NT1 baffled tubes
- NT1 guide tubes
- NT1 pressure tubes
- RT borescopes
- RT corrosion denting
- RT cylinders
- RT ducts
- RT pipes
- RT reactor cooling systems
- RT shape
- RT tunnels

tubes (conduits)
- USE pipes

tubular pinch devices (linear)
- USE linear hard core pinch devices

TUBULES [205; 205]
(In kidneys.)
- BT1 kidneys
- BT2 organs
- BT3 body
- RT aldosterone
- RT renal clearance
- RT vasopressin

TUFF [1,359; 1,359]
- BT1 igneous rocks
- BT2 rocks
- RT volcanoes

TULLNERFELD REACTOR [30; 30]
- UF *zwentendorf reactor*
- BT1 bwr type reactors
- BT2 enriched uranium reactors
- BT3 reactors
- BT2 power reactors
- BT3 reactors
- BT2 thermal reactors
- BT3 reactors
- BT2 water cooled reactors
- BT3 reactors
- BT2 water moderated reactors
- BT3 reactors

TUMAN DEVICES [97; 97]
- BT1 tokamak devices
- BT2 closed plasma devices
- BT3 thermonuclear devices

TUMBLER PROJECT [1; 1]
- RT nuclear weapons

TUMOR CELLS [4,631; 5,495]
- UF *giant cells*
- BT1 animal cells
- NT1 ascites tumor cells
- NT1 hela cells
- RT cell cultures
- RT in vivo
- RT neoplasms

TUMOR PROMOTERS [149; 149]
Jul 81
(Chemical agents which are not mutagenic or carcinogenic in themselves, but which will accelerate the growth of a pre-existing tumor.)
SF   *promoters*
RT   carcinogens
RT   mutagens
RT   neoplasms

tumor viruses
USE   oncogenic viruses

tumors
USE   neoplasms

tun ismail atomic research cen
(Malaysia)
USE   puspati

TUNA [22; 22]
BT1   fishes
BT2   aquatic organisms
BT2   vertebrates
BT3   animals

TUNDRA [14; 14]
RT   arctic regions
RT   climates
RT   terrestrial ecosystems

TUNGSTATES [947; 1,593]
BT1   oxygen compounds
BT1   tungsten compounds
BT2   transition element compounds
NT1   aluminium tungstates
NT1   ammonium tungstates
NT1   barium tungstates
NT1   bismuth tungstates
NT1   cadmium tungstates
NT1   calcium tungstates
NT1   cerium tungstates
NT1   cesium tungstates
NT1   cobalt tungstates
NT1   copper tungstates
NT1   dysprosium tungstates
NT1   erbium tungstates
NT1   gadolinium tungstates
NT1   hafnium tungstates
NT1   indium tungstates
NT1   iron tungstates
NT1   lanthanum tungstates
NT1   lead tungstates
NT1   lithium tungstates
NT1   lutetium tungstates
NT1   manganese tungstates
NT1   neodymium tungstates
NT1   nickel tungstates
NT1   potassium tungstates
NT1   praseodymium tungstates
NT1   rubidium tungstates
NT1   samarium tungstates
NT1   scandium tungstates
NT1   silver tungstates
NT1   sodium tungstates
NT1   strontium tungstates
NT1   tantalum tungstates
NT1   thallium tungstates
NT1   thorium tungstates
NT1   tin tungstates
NT1   titanium tungstates
NT1   uranium tungstates
NT1   uranyl tungstates
NT1   vanadium tungstates
NT1   ytterbium tungstates
NT1   yttrium tungstates
NT1   zinc tungstates
NT1   zirconium tungstates

TUNGSTEN [7,515; 7,518]
UF   *wolfram*
BT1   transition elements
BT2   metals
BT3   elements
NT1   tungsten-alpha

TUNGSTEN ADDITIONS [230; 445]
(Alloys containing not more than 1% W are listed here.)
NT1   alloy-ni48cr22fe18mo9
NT1   alloy-ni49cr22fe18mo9
NT1   alloy-ni50cr22fe18mo9
NT1   alloy-ni62cr16mo15fe3
NT1   steel-ni4crw
RT   tungsten alloys
RT   tungsten compounds

TUNGSTEN ALLOYS [1,792; 3,027]
(Alloys containing more than 1% W.)
BT1   alloys
NT1   alloy-co36cr22ni22w15fe3
NT1   alloy-co43cr20fe18ni13w3
NT1   alloy-co54cr20w15ni10
NT1   alloy-co60cr30w4
NT1   alloy-co64cr29w4
NT1   alloy-co66cr26w6
NT1   alloy-fe31cr21co20ni20mo3w2
NT1   alloy-ni45cr23fe19co3mo3w3
NT1   alloy-ni47cr25co12w9fe3
NT1   alloy-ni54mo17cr16fe6w4
NT1   alloy-ni56cr21w10mo5fe4al2
NT1   alloy-ni58cr14co8al4mo4nb4w4
NT1   alloy-ni60cr14co10ti5mo4w4al3
NT1   alloy-ni60cr25w15
NT1   alloy-ni61cr16co9al3ti3w3
NT1   alloy-ni65mo16cr15w4
NT1   alloy-ni67cr19mo5w5ti3
NT1   alloy-ni68cr15w6al3mo3fe2
NT1   alloy-ta90w8hf
NT1   tungsten base alloys
NT1   tungsten bronze
RT   tungsten additions

TUNGSTEN BASE ALLOYS [562; 562]
BT1   tungsten alloys
BT2   alloys

TUNGSTEN BORIDES [71; 71]
BT1   borides
BT2   boron compounds
BT1   tungsten compounds
BT2   transition element compounds

TUNGSTEN BROMIDES [13; 13]
BT1   bromides
BT2   bromine compounds
BT3   halogen compounds
BT2   halides
BT3   halogen compounds
BT1   tungsten compounds
BT2   transition element compounds

TUNGSTEN BRONZE [35; 35]
BT1   copper base alloys
BT2   copper alloys
BT3   alloys
BT1   tungsten alloys
BT2   alloys

TUNGSTEN CARBIDES [818; 818]
BT1   carbides
BT2   carbon compounds
BT1   tungsten compounds
BT2   transition element compounds

TUNGSTEN CHLORIDES [162; 162]
BT1   chlorides
BT2   chlorine compounds
BT3   halogen compounds
BT2   halides
BT3   halogen compounds
BT1   tungsten compounds
BT2   transition element compounds

TUNGSTEN COMPLEXES [710; 710]
BT1   transition element complexes
BT2   complexes

TUNGSTEN COMPOUNDS [729; 4,526]
BT1   transition element compounds
NT1   tungstates
NT2   aluminium tungstates
NT2   ammonium tungstates
NT2   barium tungstates
NT2   bismuth tungstates
NT2   cadmium tungstates
NT2   calcium tungstates
NT2   cerium tungstates
NT2   cesium tungstates
NT2   cobalt tungstates
NT2   copper tungstates
NT2   dysprosium tungstates
NT2   erbium tungstates
NT2   gadolinium tungstates
NT2   hafnium tungstates
NT2   indium tungstates
NT2   iron tungstates
NT2   lanthanum tungstates
NT2   lead tungstates
NT2   lithium tungstates
NT2   lutetium tungstates
NT2   manganese tungstates
NT2   neodymium tungstates
NT2   nickel tungstates
NT2   potassium tungstates
NT2   praseodymium tungstates
NT2   rubidium tungstates
NT2   samarium tungstates
NT2   scandium tungstates
NT2   silver tungstates
NT2   sodium tungstates
NT2   strontium tungstates
NT2   tantalum tungstates
NT2   thallium tungstates
NT2   thorium tungstates
NT2   tin tungstates
NT2   titanium tungstates
NT2   uranium tungstates
NT2   uranyl tungstates
NT2   vanadium tungstates
NT2   ytterbium tungstates
NT2   yttrium tungstates
NT2   zinc tungstates
NT2   zirconium tungstates
NT1   tungsten borides
NT1   tungsten bromides
NT1   tungsten carbides
NT1   tungsten chlorides
NT1   tungsten fluorides
NT1   tungsten hydrides
NT1   tungsten hydroxides
NT1   tungsten iodides
NT1   tungsten nitrides
NT1   tungsten oxides
NT1   tungsten phosphides
NT1   tungsten selenides
NT1   tungsten silicides
NT1   tungsten sulfides
NT1   tungsten tellurides
NT1   tungstophosphates
NT1   tungstophosphoric acid
RT   tungsten additions

TUNGSTEN FLUORIDES [265; 265]
BT1   fluorides
BT2   fluorine compounds
BT3   halogen compounds
BT2   halides
BT3   halogen compounds
BT1   tungsten compounds
BT2   transition element compounds

TUNGSTEN HYDRIDES [11; 11] *Jan 77*
BT1   hydrides
BT2   hydrogen compounds
BT1   tungsten compounds
BT2   transition element compounds

TUNGSTEN HYDROXIDES [6; 6]
BT1 hydroxides
BT2 hydrogen compounds
BT2 oxygen compounds
BT1 tungsten compounds
BT2 transition element compounds

TUNGSTEN IODIDES [12; 12]
BT1 iodides
BT2 halides
BT3 halogen compounds
BT2 iodine compounds
BT3 halogen compounds
BT1 tungsten compounds
BT2 transition element compounds

TUNGSTEN IONS [195; 195]
BT1 ions
BT2 charged particles

TUNGSTEN ISOTOPES [172; 1,273]
NT1 tungsten 158
NT1 tungsten 159
NT1 tungsten 160
NT1 tungsten 161
NT1 tungsten 162
NT1 tungsten 163
NT1 tungsten 164
NT1 tungsten 165
NT1 tungsten 166
NT1 tungsten 167
NT1 tungsten 168
NT1 tungsten 169
NT1 tungsten 170
NT1 tungsten 171
NT1 tungsten 172
NT1 tungsten 173
NT1 tungsten 174
NT1 tungsten 175
NT1 tungsten 176
NT1 tungsten 177
NT1 tungsten 178
NT1 tungsten 179
NT1 tungsten 180
NT1 tungsten 181
NT1 tungsten 182
NT1 tungsten 183
NT1 tungsten 184
NT1 tungsten 185
NT1 tungsten 186
NT1 tungsten 187
NT1 tungsten 188
NT1 tungsten 189
NT1 tungsten 190
NT1 tungsten 192

TUNGSTEN NITRIDES [33; 33]
BT1 nitrides
BT2 nitrogen compounds
BT2 pnictides
BT1 tungsten compounds
BT2 transition element compounds

TUNGSTEN ORES [101; 101]
BT1 ores

TUNGSTEN OXIDES [1,072; 1,099]
BT1 oxides
BT2 chalcogenides
BT2 oxygen compounds
BT1 tungsten compounds
BT2 transition element compounds
RT oxide minerals
RT tungstophosphoric acid
RT wolframite

TUNGSTEN PHOSPHIDES [5; 5] *Sep 79*
BT1 phosphides
BT2 phosphorus compounds
BT2 pnictides
BT1 tungsten compounds
BT2 transition element compounds

TUNGSTEN SELENIDES [53; 53] *Jul 78*
BT1 selenides
BT2 chalcogenides
BT2 selenium compounds
BT1 tungsten compounds
BT2 transition element compounds

TUNGSTEN SILICIDES [107; 107]
Oct 75
BT1 silicides
BT2 silicon compounds
BT1 tungsten compounds
BT2 transition element compounds

TUNGSTEN SULFIDES [69; 69]
BT1 sulfides
BT2 chalcogenides
BT2 sulfur compounds
BT1 tungsten compounds
BT2 transition element compounds

→ **TUNGSTEN TELLURIDES** [0; 0] *Sep 91*
BT1 tellurides
BT2 chalcogenides
BT2 tellurium compounds
BT1 tungsten compounds
BT2 transition element compounds

TUNGSTEN 158 [2; 2] *May 86*
BT1 alpha decay radioisotopes
BT2 radioisotopes
BT3 isotopes
BT1 even-even nuclei
BT2 nuclei
BT1 intermediate mass nuclei
BT2 nuclei
BT1 tungsten isotopes

TUNGSTEN 159 [0; 0] *May 86*
BT1 alpha decay radioisotopes
BT2 radioisotopes
BT3 isotopes
BT1 even-odd nuclei
BT2 nuclei
BT1 intermediate mass nuclei
BT2 nuclei
BT1 millisec living radioisotopes
BT2 radioisotopes
BT3 isotopes
BT1 tungsten isotopes

TUNGSTEN 160 [3; 3] *Sep 79*
BT1 alpha decay radioisotopes
BT2 radioisotopes
BT3 isotopes
BT1 even-even nuclei
BT2 nuclei
BT1 intermediate mass nuclei
BT2 nuclei
BT1 millisec living radioisotopes
BT2 radioisotopes
BT3 isotopes
BT1 tungsten isotopes

TUNGSTEN 161 [2; 2] *May 86*
BT1 alpha decay radioisotopes
BT2 radioisotopes
BT3 isotopes
BT1 electron capture radioisotopes
BT2 beta decay radioisotopes
BT3 radioisotopes
BT4 isotopes
BT1 even-odd nuclei
BT2 nuclei
BT1 intermediate mass nuclei
BT2 nuclei
BT1 millisec living radioisotopes
BT2 radioisotopes
BT3 isotopes
BT1 tungsten isotopes

TUNGSTEN 162 [8; 8]
BT1 alpha decay radioisotopes
BT2 radioisotopes
BT3 isotopes
BT1 electron capture radioisotopes
BT2 beta decay radioisotopes

BT3 radioisotopes
BT4 isotopes
BT1 even-even nuclei
BT2 nuclei
BT1 intermediate mass nuclei
BT2 nuclei
BT1 seconds living radioisotopes
BT2 radioisotopes
BT3 isotopes
BT1 tungsten isotopes

TUNGSTEN 163 [8; 8]
BT1 alpha decay radioisotopes
BT2 radioisotopes
BT3 isotopes
BT1 electron capture radioisotopes
BT2 beta decay radioisotopes
BT3 radioisotopes
BT4 isotopes
BT1 even-odd nuclei
BT2 nuclei
BT1 intermediate mass nuclei
BT2 nuclei
BT1 seconds living radioisotopes
BT2 radioisotopes
BT3 isotopes
BT1 tungsten isotopes

TUNGSTEN 164 [14; 14]
BT1 alpha decay radioisotopes
BT2 radioisotopes
BT3 isotopes
BT1 electron capture radioisotopes
BT2 beta decay radioisotopes
BT3 radioisotopes
BT4 isotopes
BT1 even-even nuclei
BT2 nuclei
BT1 intermediate mass nuclei
BT2 nuclei
BT1 seconds living radioisotopes
BT2 radioisotopes
BT3 isotopes
BT1 tungsten isotopes

TUNGSTEN 165 [5; 5] *Feb 76*
BT1 alpha decay radioisotopes
BT2 radioisotopes
BT3 isotopes
BT1 electron capture radioisotopes
BT2 beta decay radioisotopes
BT3 radioisotopes
BT4 isotopes
BT1 even-odd nuclei
BT2 nuclei
BT1 intermediate mass nuclei
BT2 nuclei
BT1 seconds living radioisotopes
BT2 radioisotopes
BT3 isotopes
BT1 tungsten isotopes

TUNGSTEN 166 [13; 13] *Feb 76*
BT1 alpha decay radioisotopes
BT2 radioisotopes
BT3 isotopes
BT1 electron capture radioisotopes
BT2 beta decay radioisotopes
BT3 radioisotopes
BT4 isotopes
BT1 even-even nuclei
BT2 nuclei
BT1 intermediate mass nuclei
BT2 nuclei
BT1 seconds living radioisotopes
BT2 radioisotopes
BT3 isotopes
BT1 tungsten isotopes

TUNGSTEN 167 [9; 9] *Nov 85*
BT1 even-odd nuclei
BT2 nuclei
BT1 intermediate mass nuclei
BT2 nuclei
BT1 seconds living radioisotopes
BT2 radioisotopes
BT3 isotopes
BT1 tungsten isotopes

TUNGSTEN 168 [20; 20] *Feb 84*
  BT1   beta-plus decay radioisotopes
  BT2   beta decay radioisotopes
    BT3   radioisotopes
      BT4   isotopes
  BT1   electron capture radioisotopes
  BT2   beta decay radioisotopes
    BT3   radioisotopes
      BT4   isotopes
  BT1   even-even nuclei
  BT2   nuclei
  BT1   intermediate mass nuclei
  BT2   nuclei
  BT1   seconds living radioisotopes
  BT2   radioisotopes
    BT3   isotopes
  BT1   tungsten isotopes

TUNGSTEN 169 [10; 10] *Oct 85*
  BT1   beta-plus decay radioisotopes
  BT2   beta decay radioisotopes
    BT3   radioisotopes
      BT4   isotopes
  BT1   electron capture radioisotopes
  BT2   beta decay radioisotopes
    BT3   radioisotopes
      BT4   isotopes
  BT1   even-odd nuclei
  BT2   nuclei
  BT1   intermediate mass nuclei
  BT2   nuclei
  BT1   seconds living radioisotopes
  BT2   radioisotopes
    BT3   isotopes
  BT1   tungsten isotopes

TUNGSTEN 170 [32; 32]
  BT1   beta-plus decay radioisotopes
  BT2   beta decay radioisotopes
    BT3   radioisotopes
      BT4   isotopes
  BT1   electron capture radioisotopes
  BT2   beta decay radioisotopes
    BT3   radioisotopes
      BT4   isotopes
  BT1   even-even nuclei
  BT2   nuclei
  BT1   intermediate mass nuclei
  BT2   nuclei
  BT1   minutes living radioisotopes
  BT2   radioisotopes
    BT3   isotopes
  BT1   tungsten isotopes

TUNGSTEN 171 [13; 13]
  BT1   beta-plus decay radioisotopes
  BT2   beta decay radioisotopes
    BT3   radioisotopes
      BT4   isotopes
  BT1   electron capture radioisotopes
  BT2   beta decay radioisotopes
    BT3   radioisotopes
      BT4   isotopes
  BT1   even-odd nuclei
  BT2   nuclei
  BT1   intermediate mass nuclei
  BT2   nuclei
  BT1   minutes living radioisotopes
  BT2   radioisotopes
    BT3   isotopes
  BT1   tungsten isotopes

TUNGSTEN 172 [31; 31]
  BT1   beta-plus decay radioisotopes
  BT2   beta decay radioisotopes
    BT3   radioisotopes
      BT4   isotopes
  BT1   electron capture radioisotopes
  BT2   beta decay radioisotopes
    BT3   radioisotopes
      BT4   isotopes
  BT1   even-even nuclei
  BT2   nuclei
  BT1   intermediate mass nuclei
  BT2   nuclei
  BT1   minutes living radioisotopes
  BT2   radioisotopes
    BT3   isotopes
  BT1   tungsten isotopes

TUNGSTEN 173 [16; 16]
  BT1   beta-plus decay radioisotopes
  BT2   beta decay radioisotopes
    BT3   radioisotopes
      BT4   isotopes
  BT1   electron capture radioisotopes
  BT2   beta decay radioisotopes
    BT3   radioisotopes
      BT4   isotopes
  BT1   even-odd nuclei
  BT2   nuclei
  BT1   intermediate mass nuclei
  BT2   nuclei
  BT1   minutes living radioisotopes
  BT2   radioisotopes
    BT3   isotopes
  BT1   tungsten isotopes

TUNGSTEN 174 [31; 31]
  BT1   electron capture radioisotopes
  BT2   beta decay radioisotopes
    BT3   radioisotopes
      BT4   isotopes
  BT1   even-even nuclei
  BT2   nuclei
  BT1   intermediate mass nuclei
  BT2   nuclei
  BT1   minutes living radioisotopes
  BT2   radioisotopes
    BT3   isotopes
  BT1   tungsten isotopes

TUNGSTEN 175 [24; 24]
  BT1   beta-plus decay radioisotopes
  BT2   beta decay radioisotopes
    BT3   radioisotopes
      BT4   isotopes
  BT1   electron capture radioisotopes
  BT2   beta decay radioisotopes
    BT3   radioisotopes
      BT4   isotopes
  BT1   even-odd nuclei
  BT2   nuclei
  BT1   intermediate mass nuclei
  BT2   nuclei
  BT1   minutes living radioisotopes
  BT2   radioisotopes
    BT3   isotopes
  BT1   tungsten isotopes

TUNGSTEN 176 [20; 20]
  BT1   electron capture radioisotopes
  BT2   beta decay radioisotopes
    BT3   radioisotopes
      BT4   isotopes
  BT1   even-even nuclei
  BT2   nuclei
  BT1   hours living radioisotopes
  BT2   radioisotopes
    BT3   isotopes
  BT1   intermediate mass nuclei
  BT2   nuclei
  BT1   internal conversion radioisoto
  BT2   radioisotopes
    BT3   isotopes
  BT1   tungsten isotopes

TUNGSTEN 177 [10; 10]
  BT1   beta-plus decay radioisotopes
  BT2   beta decay radioisotopes
    BT3   radioisotopes
      BT4   isotopes
  BT1   electron capture radioisotopes
  BT2   beta decay radioisotopes
    BT3   radioisotopes
      BT4   isotopes
  BT1   even-odd nuclei
  BT2   nuclei
  BT1   hours living radioisotopes
  BT2   radioisotopes
    BT3   isotopes
  BT1   intermediate mass nuclei
  BT2   nuclei
  BT1   tungsten isotopes

TUNGSTEN 178 [54; 54]
  BT1   days living radioisotopes
  BT2   radioisotopes
    BT3   isotopes
  BT1   electron capture radioisotopes
  BT2   beta decay radioisotopes
    BT3   radioisotopes
      BT4   isotopes
  BT1   even-even nuclei
  BT2   nuclei
  BT1   intermediate mass nuclei
  BT2   nuclei
  BT1   tungsten isotopes

TUNGSTEN 179 [38; 38]
  BT1   electron capture radioisotopes
  BT2   beta decay radioisotopes
    BT3   radioisotopes
      BT4   isotopes
  BT1   even-odd nuclei
  BT2   nuclei
  BT1   intermediate mass nuclei
  BT2   nuclei
  BT1   isomeric transition isotopes
  BT2   radioisotopes
    BT3   isotopes
  BT1   minutes living radioisotopes
  BT2   radioisotopes
    BT3   isotopes
  BT1   tungsten isotopes

TUNGSTEN 180 [65; 65]
  BT1   even-even nuclei
  BT2   nuclei
  BT1   intermediate mass nuclei
  BT2   nuclei
  BT1   stable isotopes
  BT2   isotopes
  BT1   tungsten isotopes

TUNGSTEN 180 TARGET [28; 28]
  BT1   targets

TUNGSTEN 181 [119; 119]
  BT1   days living radioisotopes
  BT2   radioisotopes
    BT3   isotopes
  BT1   electron capture radioisotopes
  BT2   beta decay radioisotopes
    BT3   radioisotopes
      BT4   isotopes
  BT1   even-odd nuclei
  BT2   nuclei
  BT1   heavy nuclei
  BT2   nuclei
  BT1   internal conversion radioisoto
  BT2   radioisotopes
    BT3   isotopes
  BT1   tungsten isotopes

TUNGSTEN 182 [229; 229]
  BT1   even-even nuclei
  BT2   nuclei
  BT1   heavy nuclei
  BT2   nuclei
  BT1   stable isotopes
  BT2   isotopes
  BT1   tungsten isotopes

TUNGSTEN 182 TARGET [160; 160]
  BT1   targets

TUNGSTEN 183 [139; 139]
  BT1   even-odd nuclei
  BT2   nuclei
  BT1   heavy nuclei
  BT2   nuclei
  BT1   isomeric transition isotopes
  BT2   radioisotopes
    BT3   isotopes
  BT1   seconds living radioisotopes
  BT2   radioisotopes
    BT3   isotopes
  BT1   stable isotopes
  BT2   isotopes
  BT1   tungsten isotopes

TUNGSTEN 183 REACTIONS [2; 2]
Feb 84
BT1 heavy ion reactions
BT2 nuclear reactions

TUNGSTEN 183 TARGET [57; 57]
BT1 targets

TUNGSTEN 184 [222; 222]
BT1 even-even nuclei
BT2 nuclei
BT1 heavy nuclei
BT2 nuclei
BT1 stable isotopes
BT2 isotopes
BT1 tungsten isotopes

TUNGSTEN 184 BEAMS [10; 10]
Feb 77
BT1 ion beams
BT2 beams

TUNGSTEN 184 REACTIONS [6; 6]
Oct 82
BT1 heavy ion reactions
BT2 nuclear reactions

TUNGSTEN 184 TARGET [327; 327]
BT1 targets

TUNGSTEN 185 [123; 123]
BT1 beta-minus decay radioisotopes
BT2 beta decay radioisotopes
BT3 radioisotopes
BT4 isotopes
BT1 days living radioisotopes
BT2 radioisotopes
BT3 isotopes
BT1 even-odd nuclei
BT2 nuclei
BT1 heavy nuclei
BT2 nuclei
BT1 internal conversion radioisoto
BT2 radioisotopes
BT3 isotopes
BT1 isomeric transition isotopes
BT2 radioisotopes
BT3 isotopes
BT1 minutes living radioisotopes
BT2 radioisotopes
BT3 isotopes
BT1 tungsten isotopes

TUNGSTEN 185 TARGET [5; 5] *Nov 85*
BT1 targets

TUNGSTEN 186 [162; 162]
BT1 even-even nuclei
BT2 nuclei
BT1 heavy nuclei
BT2 nuclei
BT1 stable isotopes
BT2 isotopes
BT1 tungsten isotopes

TUNGSTEN 186 TARGET [164; 164]
BT1 targets

TUNGSTEN 187 [112; 112]
BT1 beta-minus decay radioisotopes
BT2 beta decay radioisotopes
BT3 radioisotopes
BT4 isotopes
BT1 days living radioisotopes
BT2 radioisotopes
BT3 isotopes
BT1 even-odd nuclei
BT2 nuclei
BT1 heavy nuclei
BT2 nuclei
BT1 tungsten isotopes

TUNGSTEN 188 [13; 13]
BT1 beta-minus decay radioisotopes
BT2 beta decay radioisotopes
BT3 radioisotopes
BT4 isotopes
BT1 days living radioisotopes
BT2 radioisotopes
BT3 isotopes
BT1 even-even nuclei
BT2 nuclei
BT1 heavy nuclei
BT2 nuclei
BT1 tungsten isotopes

TUNGSTEN 189 [1; 1]
BT1 beta-minus decay radioisotopes
BT2 beta decay radioisotopes
BT3 radioisotopes
BT4 isotopes
BT1 even-odd nuclei
BT2 nuclei
BT1 heavy nuclei
BT2 nuclei
BT1 minutes living radioisotopes
BT2 radioisotopes
BT3 isotopes
BT1 tungsten isotopes

TUNGSTEN 190 [6; 6]
BT1 beta-plus decay radioisotopes
BT2 beta decay radioisotopes
BT3 radioisotopes
BT4 isotopes
BT1 even-even nuclei
BT2 nuclei
BT1 heavy nuclei
BT2 nuclei
BT1 minutes living radioisotopes
BT2 radioisotopes
BT3 isotopes
BT1 tungsten isotopes

TUNGSTEN 192 [2; 2]
BT1 even-even nuclei
BT2 nuclei
BT1 heavy nuclei
BT2 nuclei
BT1 tungsten isotopes

TUNGSTEN-ALPHA [4; 4] *Oct 85*
BT1 tungsten
BT2 transition elements
BT3 metals
BT4 elements

TUNGSTOPHOSPHATES [54; 54]
Feb 88
BT1 oxygen compounds
BT1 phosphorus compounds
BT1 tungsten compounds
BT2 transition element compounds
RT tungstophosphoric acid

TUNGSTOPHOSPHORIC ACID [122; 122]
UF *phosphotungstic acid*
UF *phosphowolframic acid*
UF *wolframophosphoric acid*
BT1 inorganic acids
BT2 hydrogen compounds
BT2 inorganic compounds
BT1 oxygen compounds
BT1 phosphorus compounds
BT1 tungsten compounds
BT2 transition element compounds
RT heteropolyanions
RT phosphoric acid
RT tungsten oxides
RT tungstophosphates

TUNING [1,360; 1,360] *Aug 75*
UF *frequency selection*
RT cavity resonators
RT frequency control
RT resonance
RT rf systems
RT synchronization

TUNISIA [26; 26]
BT1 africa
BT1 developing countries

TUNNEL DIODES [139; 139]
BT1 semiconductor diodes
BT2 semiconductor devices
RT schottky barrier diodes

TUNNEL EFFECT [3,080; 3,080]
RT superconducting junctions
RT superconductivity

TUNNELS [349; 533]
BT1 underground facilities
NT1 wind tunnels
RT earthmoving equipment
RT excavation
RT mines
RT shaft excavations
RT subsurface structures
RT subterrene penetrators
RT tubes

TURBELLARIA [0; 8]
BT1 platyhelminths
BT2 invertebrates
BT3 animals
NT1 planaria

TURBIDITY [114; 114]
RT suspensions

TURBINE BLADES [525; 525]
UF *blades (turbines)*
UF+ *compressor blades*
RT turbines

TURBINES [820; 3,203]
NT1 gas turbines
NT1 steam turbines
NT1 wind turbines
RT hydroelectric power plants
RT turbine blades
RT working fluids

TURBOGENERATORS [520; 520]
BT1 electric generators
BT2 electrical equipment
BT3 equipment

TURBOMOLECULAR PUMPS [164; 164]
BT1 vacuum pumps
BT2 pumps
BT3 equipment
RT high vacuum
RT medium vacuum
RT ultrahigh vacuum

TURBULENCE [5,979; 5,979]
RT attractors
RT diffusion
RT fluid flow
RT hurricanes
RT mixing
RT stirring
RT tornadoes
RT turbulent flow
RT vortices
RT wind

TURBULENT FLOW [2,553; 2,553]
UF *supercritical flow*
BT1 fluid flow
RT critical flow
RT laminar flow
RT reynolds number
RT richardson number
RT turbulence
RT two-phase flow
RT viscous flow

TURBULENT HEATING [393; 393]
  BT1   plasma heating
  BT2   heating

TURKEY [209; 209]
  BT1   asia
  BT1   developing countries
  BT1   middle east
  RT   tigris river

TURKEY POINT-3 REACTOR
[164; 164]
(Turkey Point, Florida, USA)
  BT1   pwr type reactors
    BT2   enriched uranium reactors
      BT3   reactors
    BT2   power reactors
      BT3   reactors
    BT2   thermal reactors
      BT3   reactors
    BT2   water cooled reactors
      BT3   reactors
    BT2   water moderated reactors
      BT3   reactors

TURKEY POINT-4 REACTOR
[151; 151]
(Miami, Florida, USA)
  BT1   pwr type reactors
    BT2   enriched uranium reactors
      BT3   reactors
    BT2   power reactors
      BT3   reactors
    BT2   thermal reactors
      BT3   reactors
    BT2   water cooled reactors
      BT3   reactors
    BT2   water moderated reactors
      BT3   reactors

turkish reactor-1
  USE   tr-1 reactor

turkish reactor-2
  USE   tr-2 reactor

turku cyclotron
  USE   aabo cyclotron

turnips
  USE   brassica

turnover (radionuclides)
  USE   radionuclide kinetics

TURPENTINE [13; 13]
  BT1   organic solvents
    BT2   nonaqueous solvents
      BT3   solvents
  BT1   terpenes
    BT2   organic compounds
  RT   hydrocarbons

TURTLES [50; 50]
  BT1   reptiles
    BT2   vertebrates
      BT3   animals

TUVALU [2; 2] *Jul 91*
  BT1   micronesia
    BT2   australasia
    BT2   islands
  RT   pacific ocean

tva
  USE   tennessee valley authority

TVA-1 REACTOR [2; 2]
  UF   *tenn. val. author. react.-1*
  BT1   pwr type reactors
    BT2   enriched uranium reactors
      BT3   reactors
    BT2   power reactors
      BT3   reactors
    BT2   thermal reactors
      BT3   reactors
    BT2   water cooled reactors
      BT3   reactors
    BT2   water moderated reactors
      BT3   reactors

TVA-2 REACTOR [2; 2]
  UF   *tenn. val. author. react.-2*
  BT1   pwr type reactors
    BT2   enriched uranium reactors
      BT3   reactors
    BT2   power reactors
      BT3   reactors
    BT2   thermal reactors
      BT3   reactors
    BT2   water cooled reactors
      BT3   reactors
    BT2   water moderated reactors
      BT3   reactors

TVO-1 REACTOR [114; 114] *Aug 76*
(Asea-Atom BWR reactor at Olkiluoto (Halmholmen) Finland for Teollisuuden Voima OY.)
  UF   *olkiluoto (halmholmen)-1 reac*
  UF   *teollisuuden voima oy-1 react.*
  BT1   bwr type reactors
    BT2   enriched uranium reactors
      BT3   reactors
    BT2   power reactors
      BT3   reactors
    BT2   thermal reactors
      BT3   reactors
    BT2   water cooled reactors
      BT3   reactors
    BT2   water moderated reactors
      BT3   reactors

TVO-2 REACTOR [102; 102] *Aug 76*
(Asea-Atom BWR reactor at Olkiluoto (Halmholmen) Finland for Teollisuuden Voima OY.)
  UF   *olkiluoto (halmholmen)-2 reac*
  UF   *teollisuuden voima oy-2 react.*
  BT1   bwr type reactors
    BT2   enriched uranium reactors
      BT3   reactors
    BT2   power reactors
      BT3   reactors
    BT2   thermal reactors
      BT3   reactors
    BT2   water cooled reactors
      BT3   reactors
    BT2   water moderated reactors
      BT3   reactors

TWINNING [1,050; 1,050]
  RT   crystal structure
  RT   microstructure
  RT   slip

TWISTOR THEORY [460; 460] *Jul 78*
(Quantized points of space-time.)
  RT   gravitation
  RT   quantum mechanics
  RT   space-time
  RT   unified-field theories

TWO-BODY PROBLEM [3,643; 3,643]
  BT1   many-body problem
  RT   resonating-group method

TWO-COMPONENT NEUTRINO THEORY [30; 30]
  RT   beta decay
  RT   neutrinos
  RT   spin

TWO-COMPONENT TORUS [38; 38]
Mar 76
  UF   *tct*
  BT1   tokamak devices
    BT2   closed plasma devices
      BT3   thermonuclear devices

TWO-DIMENSIONAL CALCULATIONS
[11,578; 11,578]
  UF   *calculations (2-dimensional)*
  UF   *2-dimensional calculations*
  RT   adjoint difference method
  RT   ising model
  RT   many-dimensional calculations
  RT   mathematics
  RT   surfaces

two-fireball model
  USE   fireball model

two-fluid theory
  USE   landau liquid helium theory

TWO-NUCLEON TRANSFER REACTIONS [2,270; 2,270]
  BT1   multi-nucleon transfer reactio
    BT2   transfer reactions
      BT3   direct reactions
        BT4   nuclear reactions

TWO-PHASE FLOW [5,593; 5,593]
  BT1   fluid flow
  RT   boiling
  RT   gas flow
  RT   heat transfer
  RT   liquid flow
  RT   turbulent flow

TWO-STREAM INSTABILITY
[685; 685]
  BT1   plasma microinstabilities
    BT2   plasma instability
      BT3   instability
  RT   fluid flow

TYPE-I SUPERCONDUCTORS
[267; 267]
  BT1   superconductors

TYPE-II SUPERCONDUCTORS
[2,293; 2,293]
  UF   *type-iii superconductors*
  BT1   superconductors

type-iii superconductors
  USE   type-ii superconductors

TYPHOID [15; 15]
  BT1   bacterial diseases
    BT2   infectious diseases
      BT3   diseases
  RT   salmonella

TYPHUS [8; 8]
  BT1   rickettsial diseases
    BT2   infectious diseases
      BT3   diseases
  RT   rickettsiae

TYRAMINE [80; 80]
  BT1   amines
    BT2   organic compounds
  BT1   phenols
    BT2   aromatics
      BT3   organic compounds
    BT2   hydroxy compounds
      BT3   organic compounds
  BT1   sympathomimetics
    BT2   autonomic nervous system agent
      BT3   drugs

TYRONE-1 REACTOR [6; 6]
- BT1 pwr type reactors
- BT2 enriched uranium reactors
- BT3 reactors
- BT2 power reactors
- BT3 reactors
- BT2 thermal reactors
- BT3 reactors
- BT2 water cooled reactors
- BT3 reactors
- BT2 water moderated reactors
- BT3 reactors

TYRONE-2 REACTOR [3; 3]
- BT1 pwr type reactors
- BT2 enriched uranium reactors
- BT3 reactors
- BT2 power reactors
- BT3 reactors
- BT2 thermal reactors
- BT3 reactors
- BT2 water cooled reactors
- BT3 reactors
- BT2 water moderated reactors
- BT3 reactors

TYROSINASE [42; 42]
- BT1 hydroxylases
- BT2 oxidoreductases
- BT3 enzymes
- BT4 organic compounds

TYROSINE [654; 654]
- BT1 amino acids
- BT2 carboxylic acids
- BT3 organic acids
- BT4 organic compounds
- BT1 aromatics
- BT2 organic compounds
- BT1 hydroxy acids
- BT2 carboxylic acids
- BT3 organic acids
- BT4 organic compounds
- RT diiodotyrosine
- RT melanin
- RT methyl tyrosine
- RT phenylalanine

TYUYAMUNITE [12; 12]
- BT1 oxide minerals
- BT2 minerals
- BT1 uranium minerals
- BT2 radioactive minerals
- BT3 minerals
- BT3 radioactive materials
- BT4 materials
- RT calcium oxides
- RT uranium oxides
- RT vanadium oxides

TZ1 REACTOR [3; 3] *Jun 85*
- UF *tammuz-1 reactor*
- BT1 enriched uranium reactors
- BT2 reactors
- BT1 experimental reactors
- BT2 research and test reactors
- BT3 reactors
- BT1 isotope production reactors
- BT2 irradiation reactors
- BT3 reactors
- BT1 pool type reactors
- BT2 water cooled reactors
- BT3 reactors
- BT2 water moderated reactors
- BT3 reactors
- BT1 thermal reactors
- BT2 reactors

TZ2 REACTOR [3; 3] *Jun 85*
- UF *tammuz-2 reactor*
- BT1 enriched uranium reactors
- BT2 reactors
- BT1 experimental reactors
- BT2 research and test reactors
- BT3 reactors
- BT1 pool type reactors

- BT2 water cooled reactors
- BT3 reactors
- BT2 water moderated reactors
- BT3 reactors
- BT1 thermal reactors
- BT2 reactors

U CENTERS [93; 93]
- BT1 color centers
- BT2 vacancies
- BT3 point defects
- BT4 crystal defects
- BT5 crystal structure

U CHANNEL [165; 165]
- RT mandelstam representation
- RT particle interactions
- RT s channel
- RT t channel

U CODES [272; 272]
- BT1 computer codes

U GROUPS [759; 6,538]
- BT1 lie groups
- BT2 symmetry groups
- NT1 u-1 groups
- NT1 u-12 groups
- NT1 u-2 groups
- NT1 u-3 groups
- NT1 u-4 groups
- NT1 u-5 groups
- NT1 u-6 groups
- RT unitary symmetry

u processes
- USE umklapp processes

U-1 GROUPS [5,209; 5,209]
- BT1 u groups
- BT2 lie groups
- BT3 symmetry groups

U-12 GROUPS [26; 26]
- BT1 u groups
- BT2 lie groups
- BT3 symmetry groups

U-2 GROUPS [180; 180]
- BT1 u groups
- BT2 lie groups
- BT3 symmetry groups

u-2375 resonances
(Prior to December 1987 this was a valid descriptor.)
- USE f4-2300 mesons

U-3 GROUPS [215; 215]
- BT1 u groups
- BT2 lie groups
- BT3 symmetry groups

U-4 GROUPS [108; 108]
- BT1 u groups
- BT2 lie groups
- BT3 symmetry groups

U-5 GROUPS [40; 40] *Aug 86*
- BT1 u groups
- BT2 lie groups
- BT3 symmetry groups

U-6 GROUPS [163; 163]
- BT1 u groups
- BT2 lie groups
- BT3 symmetry groups

uar
- USE egyptian arab republic

UBIQUINONE [34; 34]
- BT1 benzoquinones
- BT2 quinones
- BT3 aromatics
- BT4 organic compounds
- BT3 organic oxygen compounds
- BT4 organic compounds
- BT1 coenzymes
- RT vitamin k

UCBRR REACTOR [6; 6]
(Berkeley Research Reactor, University of California, Berkeley, California, USA)
- UF *berkeley triga reactor*
- UF *california berkeley triga reac*
- UF *univ. of calif. triga reactor*
- BT1 isotope production reactors
- BT2 irradiation reactors
- BT3 reactors
- BT1 pulsed reactors
- BT2 reactors
- BT1 thermal reactors
- BT2 reactors
- BT1 training reactors
- BT2 research and test reactors
- BT3 reactors
- BT1 triga type reactors
- BT2 enriched uranium reactors
- BT3 reactors
- BT2 hydride moderated reactors
- BT3 reactors
- BT2 research and test reactors
- BT3 reactors
- BT2 solid homogeneous reactors
- BT3 homogeneous reactors
- BT4 reactors
- BT2 water cooled reactors
- BT3 reactors
- BT2 water moderated reactors
- BT3 reactors

ucirr reactor
- USE triga-1-california reactor

UCLA [35; 35]
- UF *univ. of california / los ange*
- BT1 us organizations
- BT2 national organizations
- RT california

uclbl
- USE lawrence berkeley laboratory

uclll
- USE lawrence livermore laboratory

UCLRL CYCLOTRONS [23; 34]
- BT1 isochronous cyclotrons
- BT2 cyclotrons
- BT3 cyclic accelerators
- BT4 accelerators
- NT1 lbl 88-inch cyclotron

UDIMET ALLOYS [23; 59]
- BT1 nickel base alloys
- BT2 nickel alloys
- BT3 alloys
- NT1 alloy-ni53co19cr15mo5al4ti3

udimet 700
- USE alloy-ni53co19cr15mo5al4ti3

UDPG [14; 14]
- BT1 glycosides
- BT2 carbohydrates
- BT3 organic compounds
- BT1 nucleotides
- BT2 organic compounds
- BT1 organic phosphorus compound
- BT2 organic compounds
- RT glucose
- RT uracils
- RT uridine

UFTR REACTOR [22; 22]
(University of Florida, Nuclear Sciences Center, Gainesville, Florida, USA)
  UF   *florida university reactor*
  UF   *univ. of florida reactor*
  BT1   argonaut type reactors
    BT2   enriched uranium reactors
      BT3   reactors
    BT2   research and test reactors
      BT3   reactors
    BT2   water cooled reactors
      BT3   reactors
    BT2   water moderated reactors
      BT3   reactors
  BT1   isotope production reactors
    BT2   irradiation reactors
      BT3   reactors
  BT1   research reactors
    BT2   research and test reactors
      BT3   reactors
  BT1   thermal reactors
    BT2   reactors
  BT1   training reactors
    BT2   research and test reactors
      BT3   reactors

UGANDA [11; 11]
  BT1   africa
  BT1   developing countries

uhf (lower range)
  USE   ghz range 01-100

uhf (upper range)
  USE   ghz range 100-1000

uhf radiation (lower range)
  USE   mhz range 100-1000
  AND   radiowave radiation

uhf radiation (upper range)
  USE   ghz range 01-100
  AND   radiowave radiation

uhf radiation (01-100 ghz)
  USE   ghz range 01-100
  AND   radiowave radiation

uhf radiation (100-1000 mhz)
  USE   mhz range 100-1000
  AND   radiowave radiation

UHTREX REACTOR [4; 4]
  UF   *ultrahigh temp. reactor exp.*
  BT1   enriched uranium reactors
    BT2   reactors
  BT1   experimental reactors
    BT2   research and test reactors
      BT3   reactors
  BT1   graphite moderated reactors
    BT2   reactors
  BT1   helium cooled reactors
    BT2   gas cooled reactors
      BT3   reactors
  BT1   thermal reactors
    BT2   reactors

UINTA FORMATION [0; 0] *Apr 84*
(Strata of Eocene age and continental origin occurring typically in the Uinta Basin in Utah and Colorado.)
  BT1   geologic formations
  RT   colorado
  RT   oil shales
  RT   uranium deposits
  RT   uranium ores
  RT   utah

ujm
(Uncorrelated-jet model.)
  USE   jet model

UJV [151; 151]
  UF   *ustav jadernych vyzkumu*
  BT1   czechoslovak organizations
    BT2   national organizations

uk atomic energy authority
  USE   ukaea

UK NATIONAL PHYSICAL LAB
[18; 18] *Feb 83*
  BT1   united kingdom organizations
    BT2   national organizations

UK NII [70; 70] *Jun 83*
(HM Nuclear Installations Inspectorate.)
  UF   *nii (uk)*
  UF   *nuclear install. inspect. (uk)*
  UF   *uk nuclear install. inspector.*
  BT1   united kingdom organizations
    BT2   national organizations

uk nuclear install. inspector.
  USE   uk nii

uk royal nav. coll.-jason reac
  USE   jason reactor

UKAEA [567; 806]
  UF   *uk atomic energy authority*
  BT1   united kingdom organizations
    BT2   national organizations
  NT1   aere
  NT1   culham laboratory
  RT   united kingdom

ukaea-dido reactor
  USE   dido reactor

ukaea-juno reactor
  USE   juno reactor

ukaea-lido reactor
  USE   lido reactor

ukaea-nestor reactor
  USE   nestor reactor

UKRAINIAN SSR [102; 102]
  BT1   ussr
    BT2   developed countries
    BT2   europe

ULCERS [582; 582]
  BT1   pathological changes
    BT2   diseases
  RT   fistulae
  RT   gangrene
  RT   necrosis

→ **ULCHIN-1 REACTOR** [2; 2] *Jul 91*
(Ulchin, Republic of Korea)
  UF   *knu-9 reactor*
  UF   *uljin-1 reactor*
  BT1   pwr type reactors
    BT2   enriched uranium reactors
      BT3   reactors
    BT2   power reactors
      BT3   reactors
    BT2   thermal reactors
      BT3   reactors
    BT2   water cooled reactors
      BT3   reactors
    BT2   water moderated reactors
      BT3   reactors

→ **ULCHIN-2 REACTOR** [2; 2] *Jul 91*
(Ulchin, Republic of Korea)
  UF   *knu-10 reactor*
  UF   *uljin-2 reactor*
  BT1   pwr type reactors
    BT2   enriched uranium reactors
      BT3   reactors
    BT2   power reactors
      BT3   reactors
    BT2   thermal reactors
      BT3   reactors
    BT2   water cooled reactors
      BT3   reactors
    BT2   water moderated reactors
      BT3   reactors

→ *uljin-1 reactor*
  USE   ulchin-1 reactor

→ *uljin-2 reactor*
  USE   ulchin-2 reactor

ultimate storage
  USE   waste disposal

ULTIMATE STRENGTH [428; 428]
May 80
  UF   *strength (ultimate)*
  BT1   mechanical properties
  RT   tensile properties

ULTRACENTRIFUGATION [265; 265]
  BT1   centrifugation
    BT2   separation processes
  RT   centrifuge enrichment plants
  RT   organoids
  RT   subcellular distribution

ultracentrifuge enrichment pla
  USE   centrifuge enrichment plants

ULTRACENTRIFUGES [163; 163]
  BT1   centrifuges
  RT   centrifugation
  RT   isotope separation

ULTRACOLD NEUTRONS [503; 503]
  BT1   cold neutrons
    BT2   neutrons
      BT3   nucleons
        BT4   baryons
          BT5   fermions
          BT5   hadrons
            BT6   elementary particles
  RT   neutron converters
  RT   neutron guides

ULTRAFILTRATION [349; 349]
  BT1   filtration
    BT2   separation processes
  RT   filters
  RT   glomeruli
  RT   sampling

ultrahi. fr rad (100-1000 mhz)
  USE   mhz range 100-1000
  AND   radiowave radiation

ultrahigh fr rad (01-100 ghz)
  USE   ghz range 01-100
  AND   radiowave radiation

ultrahigh freq rad (lower r.)
  USE   mhz range 100-1000
  AND   radiowave radiation

ultrahigh freq rad (upper r.)
USE ghz range 01-100
AND radiowave radiation

ultrahigh frequency (low. r.)
USE ghz range 01-100

ultrahigh frequency (upp. r.)
USE ghz range 100-1000

ultrahigh temp. reactor exp.
USE uhtrex reactor

ULTRAHIGH TEMPERATURE
[1,526; 1,526]
UF temperature (4000 k and above)
RT critical heat flux
RT temperature dependence

ULTRAHIGH VACUUM [1,629; 1,629]
UF vacuum (0.13x10(-5) pa and bel
UF vacuum (10(-8) torr and below)
RT cryopumps
RT pressure dependence
RT sputter-ion pumps
RT turbomolecular pumps
RT vacuum pumps

ULTRAHIGH-SPEED PHOTOGRAPHY
[161; 161]
BT1 photography

ULTRALOW FREQUENCY RADIATION [89; 89]
BT1 electromagnetic radiation
BT2 radiations

ULTRALOW TEMPERATURE
[17,079; 17,079]
UF milli k range
UF temperature (0000-0013 k)
RT cryogenics
RT temperature dependence
RT thermal boundary resistance

ULTRAMARINE [2; 2]
BT1 pigments

ULTRASONIC BUBBLE CHAMBERS
[10; 10]
BT1 bubble chambers
BT2 gas track detectors
BT3 radiation detectors
BT4 measuring instruments

ULTRASONIC MACHINING [43; 43]
BT1 machining

ULTRASONIC TESTING [4,157; 4,157]
BT1 acoustic testing
BT2 nondestructive testing
BT3 materials testing
BT4 testing
RT acoustic measurements
RT ultrasonic waves

ULTRASONIC WAVES [3,846; 3,846]
UF ultrasonics
UF+ echography
BT1 sound waves
RT ultrasonic testing
RT ultrasonography

ULTRASONIC WELDING [13; 13]
BT1 welding
BT2 joining
BT3 fabrication

ultrasonics
USE ultrasonic waves

ULTRASONOGRAPHY [2,238; 2,238]
May 86
BT1 diagnostic techniques
RT ultrasonic waves

ULTRASTRUCTURAL CHANGES
[959; 959]
BT1 morphological changes
RT biological repair
RT cell constituents
RT cytology
RT electron microscopy
RT organoids
RT photoreactivation

ULTRAVIOLET DIVERGENCES
[1,001; 1,001]
UF *divergences (ultraviolet)*
RT quantum electrodynamics

ULTRAVIOLET RADIATION
[11,226; 15,412]
BT1 electromagnetic radiation
BT2 radiations
NT1 extreme ultraviolet radiation
NT1 far ultraviolet radiation
NT1 near ultraviolet radiation
RT photoreactivation
RT raman effect
RT ultraviolet spectra

ULTRAVIOLET SPECTRA
[4,577; 4,577]
BT1 spectra
RT absorption spectroscopy
RT electronic structure
RT structural chemical analysis
RT ultraviolet radiation

ULTRAVIOLET SPECTROMETERS
[187; 187] *Aug 78*
BT1 spectrometers
BT2 measuring instruments

ULVA [20; 20]
BT1 algae
BT2 plants

ulyanovsk reactor vk-50
USE vk-50 reactor

ULYSSE REACTOR [6; 6]
(INSTN, CEN, Saclay, France)
BT1 argonaut type reactors
BT2 enriched uranium reactors
BT3 reactors
BT2 research and test reactors
BT3 reactors
BT2 water cooled reactors
BT3 reactors
BT2 water moderated reactors
BT3 reactors
BT1 thermal reactors
BT2 reactors
BT1 training reactors
BT2 research and test reactors
BT3 reactors

UMKLAPP PROCESSES [98; 98]
UF *u processes*
BT1 electromagnetic interactions
BT2 basic interactions
BT2 interactions
RT crystals
RT electric conductivity
RT electrons
RT phonons
RT thermal conductivity

UMNE-1 REACTOR [7; 7]
(Univ. of Maryland, College Park, Maryland, USA)
UF *maryland univ. reactor*
UF *umr reactor*

UF *univ. of maryland reactor*
BT1 enriched uranium reactors
BT2 reactors
BT1 pool type reactors
BT2 water cooled reactors
BT3 reactors
BT2 water moderated reactors
BT3 reactors
BT1 research reactors
BT2 research and test reactors
BT3 reactors
BT1 thermal reactors
BT2 reactors
BT1 training reactors
BT2 research and test reactors
BT3 reactors

UMOHOITE [3; 3]
BT1 oxide minerals
BT2 minerals
BT1 uranium minerals
BT2 radioactive minerals
BT3 minerals
BT3 radioactive materials
BT4 materials
RT molybdenum oxides
RT uranium oxides

UMP [14; 14] *Feb 82*
UF *uridine monophosphate*
BT1 nucleotides
BT2 organic compounds
RT uridine

umr reactor
USE umne-1 reactor

UMRR REACTOR [13; 13]
(University of Missouri-Rolla, Rolla, Missouri, USA)
UF *missouri school of mines reac*
UF *missouri univ./rolla res. reac*
UF *msmr reactor*
UF *rolla research reactor*
UF *univ. of missouri/rolla res. r*
BT1 enriched uranium reactors
BT2 reactors
BT1 pool type reactors
BT2 water cooled reactors
BT3 reactors
BT2 water moderated reactors
BT3 reactors
BT1 research reactors
BT2 research and test reactors
BT3 reactors
BT1 thermal reactors
BT2 reactors
BT1 training reactors
BT2 research and test reactors
BT3 reactors

un sci.comm effects atom rad
USE unscear

unbihexium
USE element 126

unbinilium
USE element 120

unbioctium
USE element 128

uncertainty in measured values
USE data covariances

UNCERTAINTY PRINCIPLE [569; 5
UF *heisenberg principle*
RT quantum mechanics

uncorrelated-jet model
   USE   jet model

UNCORRELATED-PARTICLE MODEL
[24; 24]
   BT1   particle models
     BT2   mathematical models
   RT   jet model

UNDERGROUND [977; 977]
   BT1   levels
   RT   underground storage

UNDERGROUND DISPOSAL
[9,490; 9,490]
(For disposal of wastes deep underground.)
   SF   *waste burial*
   BT1   waste disposal
     BT2   waste management
       BT3 management
   RT   asse salt mine
   RT   backfilling
   RT   fluid injection
   RT   gases
   RT   gorleben salt dome
   RT   ground cover
   RT   ground disposal
   RT   hydraulic conductivity
   RT   konrad ore mine
   RT   radioactive waste disposal
   RT   salt caverns
   RT   salt deposits
   RT   shaft excavations
   RT   underground facilities

UNDERGROUND EXPLOSIONS
[1,107; 1,497]
   BT1   explosions
   NT1   cabriolet event
   NT1   calabash event
   NT1   contained explosions
     NT2   almendro event
     NT2   baneberry event
     NT2   benham event
     NT2   boxcar event
     NT2   cannikin event
     NT2   carpetbag event
     NT2   dining car event
     NT2   gasbuggy event
     NT2   halfbeak event
     NT2   handley event
     NT2   marvel event
     NT2   monique event
     NT2   pokhran event
     NT2   rio blanco event
     NT2   rulison event
     NT2   scotch event
     NT2   wagon wheel event
   NT1   danny boy event
   NT1   faultless event
   NT1   greeley event
   NT1   handcar event
   NT1   hutch event
   NT1   jorum event
   NT1   milrow event
   NT1   palanquin event
   NT1   pre-gondola i event
   NT1   pre-gondola ii event
   NT1   schooner event
   RT   anvil project
   RT   arbor project
   RT   bedrock project
   RT   cavities
   RT   chimneys
   RT   cratering explosions
   RT   craters
   RT   explosive fracturing
   RT   explosive stimulation
   RT   ground motion
   RT   in-situ processing
   RT   jangle project
   RT   landslides
   RT   mining
   RT   nuclear excavation
   RT   nuclear explosion detection
   RT   nuclear explosions
   RT   plowshare project
   RT   rayleigh waves
   RT   seismic detection
   RT   seismic effects
   RT   seismic p waves
   RT   seismic s waves
   RT   seismic waves
   RT   seismographs
   RT   seismology
   RT   thunderbird project
   RT   underwater explosions
   RT   upshot project
   RT   vela project

UNDERGROUND FACILITIES
[479; 2,063] *Jul 86*
   UF   *facilities (underground)*
   NT1   mines
     NT2   asse salt mine
     NT2   coal mines
     NT2   konrad ore mine
     NT2   uranium mines
       NT3 beaverlodge mine
       NT3 cluff lake mine
       NT3 key lake mine
       NT3 mary kathleen mines
       NT3 mi vida mine
       NT3 olympic dam mine
       NT3 rum jungle
       NT3 stanleigh mine
   NT1   subsurface structures
   NT1   tunnels
     NT2   wind tunnels
   NT1   underground nuclear stations
   RT   nuclear facilities
   RT   underground disposal
   RT   underground storage

→ **UNDERGROUND MINING** [0; 0] *Oct 75*
   BT1   mining
   RT   coal mining
   RT   surface mining

underground nuclear power plan
   USE   underground nuclear stations

UNDERGROUND NUCLEAR STATIONS [269; 269]
   UF   *underground nuclear power plan*
   BT1   nuclear power plants
     BT2   nuclear facilities
     BT2   thermal power plants
       BT3 power plants
   BT1   underground facilities
   RT   power reactors
   RT   reactor sites

UNDERGROUND STORAGE
[1,404; 1,404] *Jun 77*
   BT1   storage
   RT   cavities
   RT   geologic deposits
   RT   salt caverns
   RT   underground
   RT   underground facilities
   RT   waste storage

UNDERWATER [516; 516]
   BT1   levels
   RT   dumand project

UNDERWATER EXPLOSIONS [32; 32]
   BT1   explosions
   NT1   swordfish event
   RT   crossroads project
   RT   dominic project
   RT   nuclear excavation
   RT   nuclear explosions
   RT   underground explosions

undulators
   USE   wiggler magnets

UNESCO [6; 6] *Nov 75*
(United Nations Educational, Scientific and Cultural Organization)
   RT   united nations

UNH [67; 67]
   UF   *uranyl nitrate hexahydrate*
   BT1   hydrates
   BT1   uranyl nitrates
     BT2   nitrates
       BT3 nitrogen compounds
       BT3 oxygen compounds
     BT2   uranyl compounds
       BT3 uranium compounds
       BT4 actinide compounds

unhexquadium
   USE   element 164

UNICELLULAR ALGAE [57; 406]
   BT1   algae
     BT2   plants
   BT1   microorganisms
   NT1   chlamydomonas
   NT1   chlorella
   NT1   euglena
   NT1   scenedesmus
   RT   plankton

UNIDO [2; 2] *Jun 88*
(United Nations Industrial Development Organization)
   BT1   international organizations
   RT   austria
   RT   united nations

UNIFIED GAUGE MODELS
[8,667; 16,958]
   BT1   particle models
     BT2   mathematical models
   BT1   quantum field theory
     BT2   field theories
   NT1   grand unified theory
   NT2   standard model
   NT1   weinberg lepton model
   RT   gauge invariance
   RT   inflationary universe
   RT   kaluza-klein theory
   RT   unified-field theories

UNIFIED MODEL [319; 319]
   BT1   nuclear models
     BT2   mathematical models

UNIFIED-FIELD THEORIES
[569; 4,770]
(Prior to April 1983 this concept was indexed by EINSTEIN-SCHROEDINGER THEORY. To be used for theories unifying gravitation with other interactions. For quantum field theory involving only electromagnetic, weak and strong interactions see GRAND UNIFIED THEORY.)
   BT1   field theories
   NT1   einstein-schroedinger theory
   NT1   kaluza-klein theory
   NT1   supergravity
   NT1   weyl unified theory
   RT   basic interactions
   RT   grand unified theory
   RT   gravitation
   RT   quantum gravity
   RT   standard model
   RT   twistor theory
   RT   unified gauge models

UNILAC [226; 226] *Oct 75*
   BT1   heavy ion accelerators
     BT2   accelerators
   BT1   linear accelerators
     BT2   accelerators

union of soviet soc reps
   USE   ussr

unipolar transistors
   USE   field effect transistors

UNISIST [3; 3]
   RT   information retrieval
   RT   information systems

unit tenaga nuklear (malaysia)
   USE   puspati

UNITARITY [3,388; 3,388]
   RT   nonunitary representations
   RT   s matrix
   RT   unitary symmetry

UNITARY POLE APPROXIMATION
[99; 99]
   RT   k matrix
   RT   many-body problem
   RT   s matrix

UNITARY SYMMETRY [450; 450]
   BT1   symmetry
   RT   su groups
   RT   u groups
   RT   unitarity

united arab rep. wwr-c reactor
   USE   wwr-s-cairo reactor

united arab republic
   USE   egyptian arab republic

UNITED KINGDOM [4,955; 4,955]
   UF   *england*
   UF   *great britain*
   UF   *northern ireland*
   UF   *scotland*
   BT1   developed countries
   BT1   europe
   RT   ukaea

UNITED KINGDOM ORGANIZATIONS
[698; 2,151]
   BT1   national organizations
   NT1   bnfl
   NT1   ncsr
   NT1   nrpb
   NT1   uk national physical lab
   NT1   uk nii
   NT1   ukaea
     NT2   aere
     NT2   culham laboratory

UNITED NATIONS [97; 183]
   BT1   international organizations
   NT1   unscear
   RT   fao
   RT   iaea
   RT   ilo
   RT   unesco
   RT   unido
   RT   who

united nucl. corp. proof test
   USE   ptf-unc reactor

united states of america
   USE   usa

UNITHIOL [22; 22]
   BT1   dithiols
     BT2   reagents
     BT2   thiols
       BT3   organic sulfur compounds
         BT4   organic compounds
   BT1   sulfonic acids
     BT2   organic acids
       BT3   organic compounds
     BT2   organic sulfur compounds
       BT3   organic compounds
   RT   bal

UNITON [6; 6]
   BT1   natural units
     BT2   units
   RT   gravitational fields
   RT   gravitons

UNITS [98; 717]
   NT1   natural units
     NT2   uniton
   NT1   radiation dose units
     NT2   sievert unit
   NT1   si units
     NT2   sievert unit

univ. catholique louvain cycl.
   USE   cyclone cyclotron

univ. de montreal slowpoke rea
   USE   slowpoke-montreal reactor

univ. minas gerais triga react
   USE   triga-brazil reactor

univ. of alta. slowpoke reacto
   USE   slowpoke-alberta reactor

univ. of calif. irvine triga
   USE   triga-1-california reactor

univ. of calif. lawr. rad. lab
   USE   lawrence berkeley laboratory

univ. of calif. triga reactor
   USE   ucbrr reactor

univ. of california / los ange
   USE   ucla

univ. of florida reactor
   USE   uftr reactor

univ. of illin. triga-mk-2 rea
   USE   triga-2-illinois reactor

univ. of maryland reactor
   USE   umne-1 reactor

univ. of missouri/colu. res. r
   USE   murr reactor

univ. of missouri/rolla res. r
   USE   umrr reactor

univ. of teheran research reac
   USE   utrr reactor

univ. of texas triga reactor
   USE   triga-texas reactor

univ. of toronto slowpoke reac
   USE   slowpoke-toronto reactor

univ. of virginia reactor
   USE   uvar reactor

univ. of washington reactor
   USE   uwtr reactor

univ. of wisconsin nucl. react
   USE   uwnr reactor

univ. of wisconsin tokamak
   USE   uwmak devices

univ. training r. queen mary c
   USE   queen mary college utr-b react

UNIVAC COMPUTERS [58; 58]
   BT1   computers

universal blackbody radiation
   USE   blackbody radiation

UNIVERSE [6,412; 6,412]
   UF   *cosmos*
   UF   *metagalaxy*
   RT   cosmological models
   RT   cosmology
   RT   galactic evolution
   RT   hubble effect
   RT   intergalactic space
   RT   nonluminous matter
   RT   relict radiation

universities
   USE   educational facilities

unloading
   USE   materials handling

unloading (fission reactor)
   USE   reactor fueling

unnilennium
   USE   element 109

unnilhexium
   USE   element 106

unniloctium
   USE   element 108

unnilpentium
   USE   element 105

unnilquadium
   USE   element 104

unnilseptium
   USE   element 107

unobserved matter
(In outer space.)
   USE   nonluminous matter

unpinch devices
   USE   linear hard core pinch devic

unquadpentium
   USE   element 145

UNSCEAR [87; 87] *Oct 75*
(United Nations Scientific Committee on Effects of Atomic Radiation)
UF   *un sci.comm effects atom rad*
BT1   united nations
BT2   international organizations
RT   dose limits
RT   radiation hazards

UNSEALED SOURCES [204; 204]
BT1   radiation sources
RT   internal irradiation
RT   radionuclide kinetics

unseen matter
(In outer space.)
USE   nonluminous matter

unsepttrium
USE   element 173

UNSTEADY FLOW [385; 385]
BT1   fluid flow

UNTERWESER REACTOR [105; 105]
UF   *kku reactor*
BT1   pwr type reactors
BT2   enriched uranium reactors
BT3   reactors
BT2   power reactors
BT3   reactors
BT2   thermal reactors
BT3   reactors
BT2   water cooled reactors
BT3   reactors
BT2   water moderated reactors
BT3   reactors

untriquadium
USE   element 134

ununbium
USE   element 112

ununennium
USE   element 119

ununhexium
USE   element 116

ununnilium
USE   element 110

ununoctium
USE   element 118

ununpentium
USE   element 115

ununquadium
USE   element 114

ununseptium
USE   element 117

ununtrium
USE   element 113

unununium
USE   element 111

UPPER VOLTA [4; 4]
BT1   africa
BT1   developing countries

UPPSALA SYNCHROCYCLOTRON [18; 18]
BT1   synchrocyclotrons
BT2   cyclic accelerators
BT3   accelerators
RT   celsius storage ring

UPSHOT PROJECT [6; 9]
UF   *project upshot*
NT1   annie event
NT1   harry event
RT   nuclear explosions
RT   underground explosions

upsilon resonances
(Prior to December 1987 this was a valid descriptor.)
SEE   bottomonium
OR   vector mesons

upsilon-10000 resonances
(Prior to December 1987 this was a valid descriptor.)
USE   upsilon-10023 mesons

UPSILON-10023 MESONS [230; 230]
Nov 78
(Prior to December 1987 this concept was indexed by UPSILON-10000 RESONANCES.)
UF   *upsilon-10000 resonances*
BT1   bottomonium
BT2   mesons
BT3   bosons
BT3   hadrons
BT4   elementary particles
BT2   quarkonium
BT1   vector mesons
BT2   mesons
BT3   bosons
BT3   hadrons
BT4   elementary particles

upsilon-10350 resonances
(Prior to December 1987 this was a valid descriptor.)
USE   upsilon-10355 mesons

UPSILON-10355 MESONS [37; 37]
May 86
(Prior to December 1987 this concept was indexed by UPSILON-10350 RESONANCES.)
UF   *upsilon-10350 resonances*
BT1   bottomonium
BT2   mesons
BT3   bosons
BT3   hadrons
BT4   elementary particles
BT2   quarkonium
BT1   vector mesons
BT2   mesons
BT3   bosons
BT3   hadrons
BT4   elementary particles

upsilon-10500 resonances
(Prior to December 1987 this was a valid descriptor.)
USE   upsilon-10575 mesons

UPSILON-10575 MESONS [142; 142]
Nov 78
(Prior to December 1987 this concept was indexed by UPSILON-10500 RESONANCES.)
UF   *upsilon-10500 resonances*
BT1   bottomonium
BT2   mesons
BT3   bosons
BT3   hadrons
BT4   elementary particles
BT2   quarkonium
BT1   vector mesons
BT2   mesons
BT3   bosons
BT3   hadrons
BT4   elementary particles

UPSILON-10860 MESONS [13; 13]
Dec 87
BT1   bottomonium
BT2   mesons
BT3   bosons
BT3   hadrons
BT4   elementary particles
BT2   quarkonium
BT1   vector mesons
BT2   mesons
BT3   bosons
BT3   hadrons
BT4   elementary particles

UPSILON-11020 MESONS [7; 7] *Dec 87*
BT1   bottomonium
BT2   mesons
BT3   bosons
BT3   hadrons
BT4   elementary particles
BT2   quarkonium
BT1   vector mesons
BT2   mesons
BT3   bosons
BT3   hadrons
BT4   elementary particles

UPSILON-9460 MESONS [385; 385]
Apr 78
(Prior to December 1987 this concept was indexed by UPSILON-9500 RESONANCES.)
UF   *upsilon-9500 resonances*
BT1   bottomonium
BT2   mesons
BT3   bosons
BT3   hadrons
BT4   elementary particles
BT2   quarkonium
BT1   vector mesons
BT2   mesons
BT3   bosons
BT3   hadrons
BT4   elementary particles

upsilon-9500 resonances
(Prior to December 1987 this was a valid descriptor.)
USE   upsilon-9460 mesons

§ **UPTAKE** [11,268; 13,578]
UF   *incorporation (biological)*
NT1   foliar uptake
NT1   intestinal absorption
NT1   root absorption
NT1   skin absorption
RT   biological availability
RT   intake
RT   radionuclide kinetics
RT   rectal administration
RT   retention

uracil-6-carboxylic acid
USE   orotic acid

URACILS [388; 2,836]
BT1   hydroxy compounds
BT2   organic compounds
BT1   pyrimidines
BT2   azines
BT3   heterocyclic compounds
BT4   organic compounds
BT3   organic nitrogen compounds
BT4   organic compounds
NT1   bromouracils
NT2   budr

URACILS

NT1 chlorouracils
NT1 deoxyuridine
NT1 fluorouracils
  NT2 fudr
NT1 iodouracils
  NT2 iododeoxyuridine
NT1 orotic acid
NT1 thiouracil
NT1 thymine
NT1 uridine
RT udpg
RT uridylic acid

URAGAN STELLARATOR [121; 121]
UF *uragan-2 stellarator*
BT1 stellarators
  BT2 closed plasma devices
    BT3 thermonuclear devices

uragan-2 stellarator
USE uragan stellarator

uragan-3 stellarator
USE torsatron stellarators

URAL COMPUTERS [3; 3]
BT1 computers

URALS [22; 22]
BT1 mountains

urals atomic power station
SEE beloyarsk-1 reactor
OR beloyarsk-2 reactor
OR beloyarsk-3 reactor

URANATES [292; 659]
BT1 uranium compounds
  BT2 actinide compounds
NT1 ammonium uranates
  NT2 adu
NT1 cesium uranates
NT1 lithium uranates
NT1 potassium uranates
NT1 rubidium uranates
NT1 sodium uranates
NT1 strontium uranates
NT1 thallium uranates

URANINITES [286; 474]
BT1 oxide minerals
  BT2 minerals
BT1 uranium minerals
  BT2 radioactive minerals
    BT3 minerals
    BT3 radioactive materials
      BT4 materials
NT1 pitchblende
RT black sands
RT thucholite

URANIUM [17,892; 21,593]
BT1 actinides
  BT2 metals
    BT3 elements
NT1 depleted uranium
NT1 enriched uranium
  NT2 highly enriched uranium
  NT2 moderately enriched uranium
  NT2 slightly enriched uranium
NT1 natural uranium
NT1 uranium-alpha
NT1 uranium-beta
NT1 uranium-gamma
RT natural radioactivity
RT nuclear fuels
RT uranium ores
RT uranium recycle
RT uranium requirements

URANIUM ADDITIONS [69; 69]
(Alloys containing not more than 1% U are listed here.)
RT uranium alloys
RT uranium compounds

URANIUM ALLOYS [1,658; 2,375]
(Alloys containing more than 1% U.)
BT1 actinide alloys
  BT2 alloys
NT1 uranium base alloys
  NT2 alloy-u90nb7zr3
RT uranium additions

URANIUM ARSENIDES [136; 136]
BT1 arsenides
  BT2 arsenic compounds
  BT2 pnictides
BT1 uranium compounds
  BT2 actinide compounds

URANIUM BASE ALLOYS [701; 717]
BT1 uranium alloys
  BT2 actinide alloys
    BT3 alloys
NT1 alloy-u90nb7zr3

URANIUM BLACK [10; 10]
BT1 oxide minerals
  BT2 minerals
BT1 uranium minerals
  BT2 radioactive minerals
    BT3 minerals
    BT3 radioactive materials
      BT4 materials
RT uranium oxides

URANIUM BORIDES [44; 44]
BT1 borides
  BT2 boron compounds
BT1 uranium compounds
  BT2 actinide compounds

URANIUM BROMIDES [97; 97]
BT1 bromides
  BT2 bromine compounds
    BT3 halogen compounds
  BT2 halides
    BT3 halogen compounds
BT1 uranium compounds
  BT2 actinide compounds

URANIUM CARBIDES [1,608; 1,608]
BT1 carbides
  BT2 carbon compounds
BT1 uranium compounds
  BT2 actinide compounds

URANIUM CARBONATES [55; 61]
BT1 carbonates
  BT2 carbon compounds
  BT2 oxygen compounds
BT1 uranium compounds
  BT2 actinide compounds
RT bayleyite
RT carbonate minerals
RT liebigite
RT rutherfordite
RT schroeckingerite
RT uranium minerals

URANIUM CHLORIDES [458; 458]
BT1 chlorides
  BT2 chlorine compounds
    BT3 halogen compounds
  BT2 halides
    BT3 halogen compounds
BT1 uranium compounds
  BT2 actinide compounds

URANIUM COMPLEXES [1,593; 3,242]
BT1 actinide complexes
  BT2 complexes
NT1 uranyl complexes

URANIUM COMPOUNDS [2,165; 21,976]
BT1 actinide compounds
NT1 uranates
  NT2 ammonium uranates
    NT3 adu
  NT2 cesium uranates
  NT2 lithium uranates
  NT2 potassium uranates
  NT2 rubidium uranates
  NT2 sodium uranates
  NT2 strontium uranates
  NT2 thallium uranates
NT1 uranium arsenides
NT1 uranium borides
NT1 uranium bromides
NT1 uranium carbides
NT1 uranium carbonates
NT1 uranium chlorides
NT1 uranium fluorides
  NT2 uranium hexafluoride
  NT2 uranium pentafluoride
  NT2 uranium tetrafluoride
NT1 uranium hydrides
NT1 uranium hydroxides
NT1 uranium iodides
NT1 uranium nitrates
NT1 uranium nitrides
NT1 uranium oxides
  NT2 uranium dioxide
  NT2 uranium oxides u3o8
  NT2 uranium trioxide
NT1 uranium perchlorates
NT1 uranium peroxide
NT1 uranium phosphates
NT1 uranium phosphides
NT1 uranium selenides
NT1 uranium silicates
  NT2 uranotile
NT1 uranium silicides
NT1 uranium sulfates
NT1 uranium sulfides
NT1 uranium tellurides
NT1 uranium tungstates
NT1 uranium vanadates
NT1 uranyl compounds
  NT2 auc
  NT2 uranyl carbonates
  NT2 uranyl chlorides
  NT2 uranyl fluorides
  NT2 uranyl nitrates
    NT3 unh
  NT2 uranyl perchlorates
  NT2 uranyl phosphates
  NT2 uranyl silicates
  NT2 uranyl sulfates
  NT2 uranyl tungstates
RT uranium additions

URANIUM CONCENTRATES [378; 3
BT1 ore concentrates
BT1 uranium ores
  BT2 ores
RT ore processing
RT slurex process

URANIUM DEPOSITS [755; 928]
BT1 geologic deposits
NT1 blizzard deposit
NT1 jabiluka deposit
NT1 koongarra deposit
NT1 nabarlek deposit
NT1 ranger deposit
NT1 ranstad deposit
NT1 roxby downs deposit
NT1 south alligator deposit
NT1 yeelirrie deposit
RT chattanooga formation
RT green river formation
RT uinta formation
RT uranium ores
RT wasatch formation

URANIUM DIOXIDE [7,654; 7,654]
BT1 uranium oxides
  BT2 oxides
    BT3 chalcogenides
    BT3 oxygen compounds
  BT2 uranium compounds
    BT3 actinide compounds

uranium enrichment
   USE   isotope separation

uranium enrichment plants
   USE   isotope separation plants

URANIUM FLUORIDES [422; 2,669]
- BT1   fluorides
  - BT2   fluorine compounds
    - BT3   halogen compounds
  - BT2   halides
    - BT3   halogen compounds
- BT1   uranium compounds
  - BT2   actinide compounds
- NT1   uranium hexafluoride
- NT1   uranium pentafluoride
- NT1   uranium tetrafluoride

URANIUM HEXAFLUORIDE [1,954; 1,954]
- BT1   uranium fluorides
  - BT2   fluorides
    - BT3   fluorine compounds
      - BT4   halogen compounds
    - BT3   halides
      - BT4   halogen compounds
  - BT2   uranium compounds
    - BT3   actinide compounds
- RT   sequoyah uf6 production plant

URANIUM HYDRIDES [147; 147]
- BT1   hydrides
  - BT2   hydrogen compounds
- BT1   uranium compounds
  - BT2   actinide compounds

URANIUM HYDROXIDES [38; 38]
- BT1   hydroxides
  - BT2   hydrogen compounds
  - BT2   oxygen compounds
- BT1   uranium compounds
  - BT2   actinide compounds

uranium i
   USE   uranium 228

uranium ii
   USE   uranium 234

URANIUM INSTITUTE [39; 39] *Dec 75*
(An international trade association)
- BT1   international organizations

URANIUM IODIDES [45; 45]
- BT1   iodides
  - BT2   halides
    - BT3   halogen compounds
  - BT2   iodine compounds
    - BT3   halogen compounds
- BT1   uranium compounds
  - BT2   actinide compounds

URANIUM IONS [882; 882]
- BT1   ions
  - BT2   charged particles

URANIUM ISOTOPES [1,651; 12,721]
- NT1   uranium 222
- NT1   uranium 223
- NT1   uranium 224
- NT1   uranium 225
- NT1   uranium 226
- NT1   uranium 227
- NT1   uranium 228
- NT1   uranium 229
- NT1   uranium 230
- NT1   uranium 231
- NT1   uranium 232
- NT1   uranium 233
- NT1   uranium 234
- NT1   uranium 235
- NT1   uranium 236
- NT1   uranium 237
- NT1   uranium 238
- NT1   uranium 239
- NT1   uranium 240
- NT1   uranium 242

URANIUM MINERALS [726; 1,407]
- BT1   radioactive minerals
  - BT2   minerals
  - BT2   radioactive materials
    - BT3   materials
- NT1   andersonite
- NT1   autunite
- NT1   bayleyite
- NT1   becquerelite
- NT1   boltwoodite
- NT1   brannerite
- NT1   carburan
- NT1   carnotite
- NT1   clarkeite
- NT1   coffinite
- NT1   cuprosklodowskite
- NT1   curite
- NT1   cyrtolite
- NT1   davidite
- NT1   demesmaekerite
- NT1   dumontite
- NT1   francevillite
- NT1   gummite
- NT1   haiweeite
- NT1   hatchettolite
- NT1   iriginite
- NT1   ishikawaite
- NT1   johannite
- NT1   lermontovite
- NT1   liebigite
- NT1   masuyite
- NT1   moluranite
- NT1   ningyoite
- NT1   parsonsite
- NT1   phosphuranylite
- NT1   rutherfordite
- NT1   saleeite
- NT1   schoepite
- NT1   schroeckingerite
- NT1   soddyite
- NT1   steenstrupine
- NT1   strelkinite
- NT1   thorianite
- NT1   thucholite
- NT1   torbernite
- NT1   tyuyamunite
- NT1   umohoite
- NT1   uraninites
  - NT2   pitchblende
- NT1   uranium black
- NT1   uranocircite
- NT1   uranophane
- NT1   uranothorianite
- NT1   uranothorite
- NT1   uranotile
- NT1   zeunerite
- NT1   zippeite
- RT   uranium carbonates
- RT   uranium oxides
- RT   uranium phosphates
- RT   uranium silicates
- RT   uranium sulfates

URANIUM MINES [2,382; 2,458] *Oct 76*
- BT1   mines
  - BT2   underground facilities
- NT1   beaverlodge mine
- NT1   cluff lake mine
- NT1   key lake mine
- NT1   mary kathleen mines
- NT1   mi vida mine
- NT1   olympic dam mine
- NT1   rum jungle
- NT1   stanleigh mine

URANIUM NITRATES [276; 276]
- BT1   nitrates
  - BT2   nitrogen compounds
  - BT2   oxygen compounds
- BT1   uranium compounds
  - BT2   actinide compounds

URANIUM NITRIDES [640; 640]
- BT1   nitrides
  - BT2   nitrogen compounds
  - BT2   pnictides
- BT1   uranium compounds
  - BT2   actinide compounds
- RT   mixed nitride fuels

uranium ore reserves
   USE   uranium reserves

URANIUM ORES [8,490; 8,799]
- BT1   ores
- NT1   uranium concentrates
- RT   anaconda uranium mill
- RT   blizzard deposit
- RT   chattanooga formation
- RT   green river formation
- RT   highland uranium mill
- RT   humeca uranium mill
- RT   jabiluka deposit
- RT   koongarra deposit
- RT   mining
- RT   nabarlek deposit
- RT   natural nuclear reactors
- RT   oklo phenomenon
- RT   ranger deposit
- RT   ranstad deposit
- RT   roxby downs deposit
- RT   shirley basin uranium mill
- RT   south alligator deposit
- RT   thiobacillus ferroxidans
- RT   uinta formation
- RT   uranium
- RT   uranium deposits
- RT   uranium reserves
- RT   wasatch formation
- RT   yeelirrie deposit

uranium oxide fuel plant
   USE   mixed oxide fuel plant

URANIUM OXIDES [2,595; 11,551]
- BT1   oxides
  - BT2   chalcogenides
  - BT2   oxygen compounds
- BT1   uranium compounds
  - BT2   actinide compounds
- NT1   uranium dioxide
- NT1   uranium oxides u3o8
- NT1   uranium trioxide
- RT   becquerelite
- RT   brannerite
- RT   clarkeite
- RT   curite
- RT   demesmaekerite
- RT   francevillite
- RT   gummite
- RT   hatchettolite
- RT   iriginite
- RT   masuyite
- RT   moluranite
- RT   oxide minerals
- RT   schoepite
- RT   thorianite
- RT   tyuyamunite
- RT   umohoite
- RT   uranium black
- RT   uranium minerals
- RT   uranothorianite
- RT   zeunerite

URANIUM OXIDES U3O8 [1,305; 1,305]
(Prior to December 1985 the form U3O8 was used.)
- UF   *u3o8*
- UF   *yellow cake*
- BT1   uranium oxides
  - BT2   oxides
    - BT3   chalcogenides
    - BT3   oxygen compounds
  - BT2   uranium compounds
    - BT3   actinide compounds

URANIUM PENTAFLUORIDE [60; 60]
Apr 77
- BT1 uranium fluorides
  - BT2 fluorides
    - BT3 fluorine compounds
      - BT4 halogen compounds
    - BT3 halides
      - BT4 halogen compounds
- BT2 uranium compounds
  - BT3 actinide compounds

URANIUM PERCHLORATES [20; 20]
Sep 75
- BT1 perchlorates
  - BT2 chlorine compounds
    - BT3 halogen compounds
  - BT2 oxygen compounds
- BT1 uranium compounds
  - BT2 actinide compounds

URANIUM PEROXIDE [31; 31] Nov 77
- BT1 peroxides
  - BT2 oxygen compounds
- BT1 uranium compounds
  - BT2 actinide compounds

URANIUM PHOSPHATES [75; 99]
- BT1 phosphates
  - BT2 oxygen compounds
  - BT2 phosphorus compounds
- BT1 uranium compounds
  - BT2 actinide compounds
- RT dumontite
- RT lermontovite
- RT ningyoite
- RT parsonsite
- RT phosphate minerals
- RT phosphuranylite
- RT saleeite
- RT torbernite
- RT uranium minerals
- RT uranocircite

URANIUM PHOSPHIDES [117; 117]
- BT1 phosphides
  - BT2 phosphorus compounds
  - BT2 pnictides
- BT1 uranium compounds
  - BT2 actinide compounds

URANIUM RECYCLE [95; 95] Mar 87
- BT1 fuel cycle
- RT fuel cycle centers
- RT uranium

URANIUM REQUIREMENTS [206; 206]
Dec 82
- BT1 demand
- RT uranium

URANIUM RESERVES [261; 261]
Oct 75
- UF uranium ore reserves
- BT1 reserves
  - BT2 resources
- RT uranium ores

URANIUM SELENIDES [103; 103]
Feb 76
- BT1 selenides
  - BT2 chalcogenides
  - BT2 selenium compounds
- BT1 uranium compounds
  - BT2 actinide compounds

URANIUM SILICATES [27; 55]
- BT1 silicates
  - BT2 oxygen compounds
  - BT2 silicon compounds
- BT1 uranium compounds
  - BT2 actinide compounds
- NT1 uranotile
- RT boltwoodite
- RT cuprosklodowskite
- RT silicate minerals
- RT soddyite
- RT uranium minerals
- RT uranophane
- RT uranothorite

URANIUM SILICIDES [312; 312]
- BT1 silicides
  - BT2 silicon compounds
- BT1 uranium compounds
  - BT2 actinide compounds

URANIUM SULFATES [71; 75]
- BT1 sulfates
  - BT2 oxygen compounds
  - BT2 sulfur compounds
- BT1 uranium compounds
  - BT2 actinide compounds
- RT johannite
- RT sulfate minerals
- RT uranium minerals
- RT zippeite

URANIUM SULFIDES [222; 222]
- BT1 sulfides
  - BT2 chalcogenides
  - BT2 sulfur compounds
- BT1 uranium compounds
  - BT2 actinide compounds

URANIUM TELLURIDES [95; 95]
Feb 76
- BT1 tellurides
  - BT2 chalcogenides
  - BT2 tellurium compounds
- BT1 uranium compounds
  - BT2 actinide compounds

URANIUM TETRAFLUORIDE [392; 392]
- BT1 uranium fluorides
  - BT2 fluorides
    - BT3 fluorine compounds
      - BT4 halogen compounds
    - BT3 halides
      - BT4 halogen compounds
- BT2 uranium compounds
  - BT3 actinide compounds

URANIUM TRIOXIDE [306; 306]
- BT1 uranium oxides
  - BT2 oxides
    - BT3 chalcogenides
    - BT3 oxygen compounds
  - BT2 uranium compounds
    - BT3 actinide compounds

URANIUM TUNGSTATES [6; 6] Nov 78
- BT1 tungstates
  - BT2 oxygen compounds
  - BT2 tungsten compounds
    - BT3 transition element compounds
- BT1 uranium compounds
  - BT2 actinide compounds

URANIUM VANADATES [3; 26]
- BT1 uranium compounds
  - BT2 actinide compounds
- BT1 vanadates
  - BT2 oxygen compounds
  - BT2 vanadium compounds
    - BT3 transition element compounds

uranium x 1
- USE thorium 234

uranium x 2
- USE thorium 231

URANIUM 222 [2; 2] Jun 86
- BT1 actinide nuclei
  - BT2 heavy nuclei
    - BT3 nuclei
- BT1 alpha decay radioisotopes
  - BT2 radioisotopes
    - BT3 isotopes
- BT1 even-even nuclei
  - BT2 nuclei
- BT1 microsec living radioisotopes
  - BT2 radioisotopes
    - BT3 isotopes
- BT1 uranium isotopes

→ ## URANIUM 223 [2; 2] Jul 91
- BT1 actinide nuclei
  - BT2 heavy nuclei
    - BT3 nuclei
- BT1 alpha decay radioisotopes
  - BT2 radioisotopes
    - BT3 isotopes
- BT1 even-odd nuclei
  - BT2 nuclei
- BT1 microsec living radioisotopes
  - BT2 radioisotopes
    - BT3 isotopes
- BT1 uranium isotopes

→ ## URANIUM 224 [3; 3] Jul 91
- BT1 actinide nuclei
  - BT2 heavy nuclei
    - BT3 nuclei
- BT1 alpha decay radioisotopes
  - BT2 radioisotopes
    - BT3 isotopes
- BT1 even-even nuclei
  - BT2 nuclei
- BT1 microsec living radioisotopes
  - BT2 radioisotopes
    - BT3 isotopes
- BT1 uranium isotopes

URANIUM 225 [6; 6] Jul 89
- BT1 actinide nuclei
  - BT2 heavy nuclei
    - BT3 nuclei
- BT1 alpha decay radioisotopes
  - BT2 radioisotopes
    - BT3 isotopes
- BT1 even-odd nuclei
  - BT2 nuclei
- BT1 millisec living radioisotopes
  - BT2 radioisotopes
    - BT3 isotopes
- BT1 uranium isotopes

URANIUM 226 [15; 15]
- BT1 actinide nuclei
  - BT2 heavy nuclei
    - BT3 nuclei
- BT1 alpha decay radioisotopes
  - BT2 radioisotopes
    - BT3 isotopes
- BT1 even-even nuclei
  - BT2 nuclei
- BT1 millisec living radioisotopes
  - BT2 radioisotopes
    - BT3 isotopes
- BT1 uranium isotopes

URANIUM 227 [3; 3]
- BT1 actinide nuclei
  - BT2 heavy nuclei
    - BT3 nuclei
- BT1 alpha decay radioisotopes
  - BT2 radioisotopes
    - BT3 isotopes
- BT1 even-odd nuclei
  - BT2 nuclei
- BT1 minutes living radioisotopes
  - BT2 radioisotopes
    - BT3 isotopes
- BT1 uranium isotopes

URANIUM 228 [9; 9]
- UF uranium i
- BT1 actinide nuclei
  - BT2 heavy nuclei
    - BT3 nuclei
- BT1 alpha decay radioisotopes
  - BT2 radioisotopes
    - BT3 isotopes
- BT1 electron capture radioisotopes
  - BT2 beta decay radioisotopes
    - BT3 radioisotopes
      - BT4 isotopes

```
         BT1     even-even nuclei
         BT2     nuclei
         BT1     minutes living radioisotopes
         BT2     radioisotopes
           BT3     isotopes
         BT1     uranium isotopes


URANIUM 229 [5; 5]
         BT1     actinide nuclei
         BT2     heavy nuclei
           BT3     nuclei
         BT1     alpha decay radioisotopes
         BT2     radioisotopes
           BT3     isotopes
         BT1     electron capture radioisotopes
         BT2     beta decay radioisotopes
           BT3     radioisotopes
             BT4     isotopes
         BT1     even-odd nuclei
         BT2     nuclei
         BT1     minutes living radioisotopes
         BT2     radioisotopes
           BT3     isotopes
         BT1     uranium isotopes


URANIUM 230 [26; 26]
         BT1     actinide nuclei
         BT2     heavy nuclei
           BT3     nuclei
         BT1     alpha decay radioisotopes
         BT2     radioisotopes
           BT3     isotopes
         BT1     days living radioisotopes
         BT2     radioisotopes
           BT3     isotopes
         BT1     even-even nuclei
         BT2     nuclei
         BT1     internal conversion radioisoto
         BT2     radioisotopes
           BT3     isotopes
         BT1     uranium isotopes


URANIUM 231 [7; 7]
         BT1     actinide nuclei
         BT2     heavy nuclei
           BT3     nuclei
         BT1     alpha decay radioisotopes
         BT2     radioisotopes
           BT3     isotopes
         BT1     days living radioisotopes
         BT2     radioisotopes
           BT3     isotopes
         BT1     electron capture radioisotopes
         BT2     beta decay radioisotopes
           BT3     radioisotopes
             BT4     isotopes
         BT1     even-odd nuclei
         BT2     nuclei
         BT1     uranium isotopes


URANIUM 232 [350; 350]
         BT1     actinide nuclei
         BT2     heavy nuclei
           BT3     nuclei
         BT1     alpha decay radioisotopes
         BT2     radioisotopes
           BT3     isotopes
         BT1     even-even nuclei
         BT2     nuclei
         BT1     neon 24 decay radioisotopes
         BT2     heavy ion decay radioisotopes
           BT3     radioisotopes
             BT4     isotopes
         BT1     spontaneous fission radioisoto
         BT2     radioisotopes
           BT3     isotopes
         BT1     uranium isotopes
         BT1     years living radioisotopes
         BT2     radioisotopes
           BT3     isotopes


URANIUM 232 TARGET [24; 24]
         BT1     targets


URANIUM 233 [1,695; 1,695]
         BT1     actinide nuclei
         BT2     heavy nuclei
           BT3     nuclei
         BT1     alpha decay radioisotopes
         BT2     radioisotopes
           BT3     isotopes
         BT1     even-odd nuclei
         BT2     nuclei
         BT1     neon 24 decay radioisotopes
         BT2     heavy ion decay radioisotopes
           BT3     radioisotopes
             BT4     isotopes
         BT1     spontaneous fission radioisoto
         BT2     radioisotopes
           BT3     isotopes
         BT1     uranium isotopes
         BT1     years living radioisotopes
         BT2     radioisotopes
           BT3     isotopes


URANIUM 233 TARGET [380; 380]
         BT1     targets


URANIUM 234 [1,166; 1,166]
         UF      uranium ii
         BT1     actinide nuclei
         BT2     heavy nuclei
           BT3     nuclei
         BT1     alpha decay radioisotopes
         BT2     radioisotopes
           BT3     isotopes
         BT1     even-even nuclei
         BT2     nuclei
         BT1     magnesium 28 decay radioisotop
         BT2     heavy ion decay radioisotopes
           BT3     radioisotopes
             BT4     isotopes
         BT1     neon 24 decay radioisotopes
         BT2     heavy ion decay radioisotopes
           BT3     radioisotopes
             BT4     isotopes
         BT1     spontaneous fission radioisoto
         BT2     radioisotopes
           BT3     isotopes
         BT1     uranium isotopes
         BT1     years living radioisotopes
         BT2     radioisotopes
           BT3     isotopes


URANIUM 234 TARGET [106; 106]
         BT1     targets


URANIUM 235 [5,743; 5,743]
         BT1     actinide nuclei
         BT2     heavy nuclei
           BT3     nuclei
         BT1     alpha decay radioisotopes
         BT2     radioisotopes
           BT3     isotopes
         BT1     even-odd nuclei
         BT2     nuclei
         BT1     internal conversion radioisoto
         BT2     radioisotopes
           BT3     isotopes
         BT1     isomeric transition isotopes
         BT2     radioisotopes
           BT3     isotopes
         BT1     minutes living radioisotopes
         BT2     radioisotopes
           BT3     isotopes
         BT1     spontaneous fission radioisoto
         BT2     radioisotopes
           BT3     isotopes
         BT1     uranium isotopes
         BT1     years living radioisotopes
         BT2     radioisotopes
           BT3     isotopes


URANIUM 235 REACTIONS [23; 23]
         Jun 77
         BT1     heavy ion reactions
         BT2     nuclear reactions


URANIUM 235 TARGET [1,553; 1,553]
         BT1     targets


URANIUM 236 [710; 710]
         BT1     actinide nuclei
         BT2     heavy nuclei
           BT3     nuclei
         BT1     alpha decay radioisotopes
         BT2     radioisotopes
           BT3     isotopes
         BT1     even-even nuclei
         BT2     nuclei
         BT1     spontaneous fission radioisoto
         BT2     radioisotopes
           BT3     isotopes
         BT1     uranium isotopes
         BT1     years living radioisotopes
         BT2     radioisotopes
           BT3     isotopes


URANIUM 236 TARGET [234; 234]
         BT1     targets


URANIUM 237 [170; 170]
         BT1     actinide nuclei
         BT2     heavy nuclei
           BT3     nuclei
         BT1     beta-minus decay radioisotopes
         BT2     beta decay radioisotopes
           BT3     radioisotopes
             BT4     isotopes
         BT1     days living radioisotopes
         BT2     radioisotopes
           BT3     isotopes
         BT1     even-odd nuclei
         BT2     nuclei
         BT1     uranium isotopes


URANIUM 237 TARGET [11; 11]
         BT1     targets


URANIUM 238 [5,127; 5,127]
         BT1     actinide nuclei
         BT2     heavy nuclei
           BT3     nuclei
         BT1     alpha decay radioisotopes
         BT2     radioisotopes
           BT3     isotopes
         BT1     even-even nuclei
         BT2     nuclei
         BT1     spontaneous fission radioisoto
         BT2     radioisotopes
           BT3     isotopes
         BT1     uranium isotopes
         BT1     years living radioisotopes
         BT2     radioisotopes
           BT3     isotopes


URANIUM 238 BEAMS [144; 144]
         Sep 77
         BT1     ion beams
         BT2     beams


URANIUM 238 REACTIONS [419; 419]
         Mar 77
         BT1     heavy ion reactions
         BT2     nuclear reactions


URANIUM 238 TARGET [2,657; 2,657]
         UF      natural uranium target
         BT1     targets


URANIUM 239 [214; 214]
         BT1     actinide nuclei
         BT2     heavy nuclei
           BT3     nuclei
         BT1     beta-minus decay radioisotopes
         BT2     beta decay radioisotopes
           BT3     radioisotopes
             BT4     isotopes
         BT1     even-odd nuclei
         BT2     nuclei
         BT1     minutes living radioisotopes
         BT2     radioisotopes
           BT3     isotopes
         BT1     uranium isotopes
```

URANIUM 239 TARGET [19; 19]
BT1 targets

URANIUM 240 [20; 20]
BT1 actinide nuclei
BT2 heavy nuclei
BT3 nuclei
BT1 beta-minus decay radioisotopes
BT2 beta decay radioisotopes
BT3 radioisotopes
BT4 isotopes
BT1 even-even nuclei
BT2 nuclei
BT1 hours living radioisotopes
BT2 radioisotopes
BT3 isotopes
BT1 internal conversion radioisoto
BT2 radioisotopes
BT3 isotopes
BT1 uranium isotopes

URANIUM 240 TARGET [6; 6] *Jul 78*
BT1 targets

URANIUM 242 [0; 0] *Jun 86*
BT1 actinide nuclei
BT2 heavy nuclei
BT3 nuclei
BT1 beta-minus decay radioisotopes
BT2 beta decay radioisotopes
BT3 radioisotopes
BT4 isotopes
BT1 even-even nuclei
BT2 nuclei
BT1 minutes living radioisotopes
BT2 radioisotopes
BT3 isotopes
BT1 uranium isotopes

URANIUM-ALPHA [170; 170]
BT1 uranium
BT2 actinides
BT3 metals
BT4 elements

URANIUM-BETA [53; 53]
BT1 uranium
BT2 actinides
BT3 metals
BT4 elements

URANIUM-GAMMA [87; 87]
BT1 uranium
BT2 actinides
BT3 metals
BT4 elements

URANOCIRCITE [5; 5]
BT1 phosphate minerals
BT2 minerals
BT1 uranium minerals
BT2 radioactive minerals
BT3 minerals
BT3 radioactive materials
BT4 materials
RT barium sulfates
RT uranium phosphates

URANOPHANE [26; 26] *Feb 76*
BT1 silicate minerals
BT2 minerals
BT1 uranium minerals
BT2 radioactive minerals
BT3 minerals
BT3 radioactive materials
BT4 materials
RT calcium silicates
RT uranium silicates

URANOTHORIANITE [9; 9]
BT1 oxide minerals
BT2 minerals
BT1 thorium minerals
BT2 radioactive minerals
BT3 minerals
BT3 radioactive materials

BT4 materials
BT1 uranium minerals
BT2 radioactive minerals
BT3 minerals
BT3 radioactive materials
BT4 materials
RT thorium oxides
RT uranium oxides

URANOTHORITE [14; 14]
BT1 silicate minerals
BT2 minerals
BT1 thorium minerals
BT2 radioactive minerals
BT3 minerals
BT3 radioactive materials
BT4 materials
BT1 uranium minerals
BT2 radioactive minerals
BT3 minerals
BT3 radioactive materials
BT4 materials
RT thorium silicates
RT uranium silicates

URANOTILE [3; 3]
BT1 calcium silicates
BT2 calcium compounds
BT3 alkaline earth metal compounds
BT2 silicates
BT3 oxygen compounds
BT3 silicon compounds
BT1 uranium minerals
BT2 radioactive minerals
BT3 minerals
BT3 radioactive materials
BT4 materials
BT1 uranium silicates
BT2 silicates
BT3 oxygen compounds
BT3 silicon compounds
BT2 uranium compounds
BT3 actinide compounds

URANUS PLANET [358; 358]
BT1 planets

URANYL CARBONATES [2; 2] *Jul 90*
BT1 carbonates
BT2 carbon compounds
BT2 oxygen compounds
BT1 uranyl compounds
BT2 uranium compounds
BT3 actinide compounds

URANYL CHLORIDES [68; 68] *Jun 82*
BT1 chlorides
BT2 chlorine compounds
BT3 halogen compounds
BT2 halides
BT3 halogen compounds
BT1 uranyl compounds
BT2 uranium compounds
BT3 actinide compounds

URANYL COMPLEXES [1,685; 1,685]
BT1 uranium complexes
BT2 actinide complexes
BT3 complexes
RT uranyl compounds

URANYL COMPOUNDS [1,723; 3,300]
BT1 uranium compounds
BT2 actinide compounds
NT1 auc
NT1 uranyl carbonates
NT1 uranyl chlorides
NT1 uranyl fluorides
NT1 uranyl nitrates
NT2 unh
NT1 uranyl perchlorates
NT1 uranyl phosphates
NT1 uranyl silicates
NT1 uranyl sulfates
NT1 uranyl tungstates
RT uranyl complexes

URANYL FLUORIDES [96; 96]
BT1 fluorides
BT2 fluorine compounds
BT3 halogen compounds
BT2 halides
BT3 halogen compounds
BT1 uranyl compounds
BT2 uranium compounds
BT3 actinide compounds

uranyl nitrate hexahydrate
USE unh

URANYL NITRATES [1,096; 1,158]
BT1 nitrates
BT2 nitrogen compounds
BT2 oxygen compounds
BT1 uranyl compounds
BT2 uranium compounds
BT3 actinide compounds
NT1 unh

URANYL PERCHLORATES [19; 19] *Sep 85*
BT1 perchlorates
BT2 chlorine compounds
BT3 halogen compounds
BT2 oxygen compounds
BT1 uranyl compounds
BT2 uranium compounds
BT3 actinide compounds

URANYL PHOSPHATES [124; 124] *Jul 78*
BT1 phosphates
BT2 oxygen compounds
BT2 phosphorus compounds
BT1 uranyl compounds
BT2 uranium compounds
BT3 actinide compounds

URANYL SILICATES [7; 7] *Feb 82*
BT1 silicates
BT2 oxygen compounds
BT2 silicon compounds
BT1 uranyl compounds
BT2 uranium compounds
BT3 actinide compounds

URANYL SULFATES [177; 177]
BT1 sulfates
BT2 oxygen compounds
BT2 sulfur compounds
BT1 uranyl compounds
BT2 uranium compounds
BT3 actinide compounds

URANYL TUNGSTATES [0; 0] *Nov 8*
BT1 tungstates
BT2 oxygen compounds
BT2 tungsten compounds
BT3 transition element compou
BT1 uranyl compounds
BT2 uranium compounds
BT3 actinide compounds

URBAN AREAS [617; 617]
UF *cities*
UF *metropolitan areas*
UF *suburbs*
RT urban populations

URBAN POPULATIONS [171; 171]
BT1 human populations
BT2 populations
RT sociology
RT urban areas

UREA [1,149; 1,149]
UF *carbamide*
BT1 carbonic acid derivatives
BT2 organic compounds
BT1 organic nitrogen compounds
BT2 organic compounds
RT allantoin

RT   amides
RT   citrulline
RT   nitrosoureas
RT   uremia

UREASE [38; 38]
BT1   amidases
BT2   non-peptide c-n hydrolases
BT3   hydrolases
BT4   enzymes
BT5   organic compounds

ureidoaminovaleric acid
USE   citrulline

UREMIA [63; 63]
BT1   symptoms
BT1   urogenital system diseases
BT2   diseases
RT   blood
RT   kidneys
RT   urea

URETERS [270; 270]
BT1   urinary tract
BT2   organs
BT3   body

URETHANE [87; 87]
BT1   carbamates
BT2   carbonic acid derivatives
BT3   organic compounds
BT2   carboxylic acid salts
BT2   organic nitrogen compounds
BT3   organic compounds
RT   polyurethanes

urethra
USE   urinary tract

URIC ACID [73; 73]
UF   *8-hydroxyxanthine*
BT1   xanthines
BT2   organic oxygen compounds
BT3   organic compounds
BT2   purines
BT3   heterocyclic compounds
BT4   organic compounds
BT3   organic nitrogen compounds
BT4   organic compounds
RT   organic acids

URICASE [0; 0]
BT1   oxidases
BT2   oxidoreductases
BT3   enzymes
BT4   organic compounds

URIDINE [596; 596]
BT1   nucleosides
BT2   nucleotides
BT3   organic compounds
BT2   ribosides
BT3   organic compounds
BT1   uracils
BT2   hydroxy compounds
BT3   organic compounds
BT2   pyrimidines
BT3   azines
BT4   heterocyclic compounds
BT5   organic compounds
BT4   organic nitrogen compounds
BT5   organic compounds
RT   udpg
RT   ump

uridine monophosphate
USE   ump

uridine triphosphate
USE   utp

URIDYLIC ACID [27; 27]
BT1   nucleotides
BT2   organic compounds
RT   uracils

urinalysis
USE   qualitative chemical analysis
AND   urine

URINARY KETOSTEROIDS [9; 9]
UF   *ketosteroids (urinary)*
RT   androgens
RT   steroids
RT   urine

URINARY TRACT [883; 2,388]
UF   *urethra*
BT1   organs
BT2   body
NT1   bladder
NT1   ureters
RT   calculi
RT   excretion
RT   kidneys
RT   urine
RT   urogenital system diseases

URINE [3,335; 3,335]
UF+   *deoxycytidinuria*
UF+   *urinalysis*
BT1   biological wastes
BT2   biological materials
BT3   materials
BT2   wastes
BT1   body fluids
BT2   biological materials
BT3   materials
RT   diuretics
RT   excretion
RT   kidneys
RT   urinary ketosteroids
RT   urinary tract

UROBILINOGEN [1; 1]
BT1   heterocyclic acids
BT2   carboxylic acids
BT3   organic acids
BT4   organic compounds
BT2   heterocyclic compounds
BT3   organic compounds
BT1   pigments
BT1   pyrroles
BT2   azoles
BT3   heterocyclic compounds
BT4   organic compounds
BT3   organic nitrogen compounds
BT4   organic compounds
RT   bile

UROCANIC ACID [9; 9]
BT1   heterocyclic acids
BT2   carboxylic acids
BT3   organic acids
BT4   organic compounds
BT2   heterocyclic compounds
BT3   organic compounds
BT1   imidazoles
BT2   azoles
BT3   heterocyclic compounds
BT4   organic compounds
BT3   organic nitrogen compounds
BT4   organic compounds

UROGENITAL SYSTEM DISEASES [3,062; 3,623]
UF+   *uterine cervix carcinoma*
BT1   diseases
NT1   menstruation disorders
NT1   nephritis
NT1   nephrosclerosis
NT1   reproductive disorders
NT1   uremia
RT   female genitals
RT   gonorrhea
RT   gynecology
RT   kidneys
RT   male genitals
RT   urinary tract

UROKINASE [84; 84]
BT1   blood coagulation factors
BT2   coagulants
BT3   hematologic agents
BT4   drugs
BT1   nonspecific peptidases
BT2   peptide hydrolases
BT3   hydrolases
BT4   enzymes
BT5   organic compounds
RT   fibrinolysis

UROTROPIN [79; 79]
UF   *cystamin*
UF   *hexamethylenetetramine*
UF   *methenamine*
BT1   amines
BT2   organic compounds

URR REACTOR [14; 14]
(Universities Research Reactor, Risley, UK)
UF   *manch. liverp. univ. res. re.*
BT1   argonaut type reactors
BT2   enriched uranium reactors
BT3   reactors
BT2   research and test reactors
BT3   reactors
BT2   water cooled reactors
BT3   reactors
BT2   water moderated reactors
BT3   reactors
BT1   test reactors
BT2   research and test reactors
BT3   reactors
BT2   test facilities
BT1   thermal reactors
BT2   reactors
BT1   training reactors
BT2   research and test reactors
BT3   reactors

URUGUAY [30; 30]
BT1   developing countries
BT1   south america
BT2   latin america

US AEC [527; 9,702]
(Includes all AEC-associated organizations.)
UF   *us atomic energy commission*
BT1   us organizations
BT2   national organizations
NT1   ames laboratory
NT1   anl
NT1   bettis
NT1   bnl
NT1   feed materials production cent
NT1   hapo
NT1   idaho chemical processing plan
NT1   kapl
NT1   lasl
NT1   lawrence berkeley laboratory
NT1   lawrence livermore laboratory
NT1   mound laboratory
NT1   nrts
NT1   ornl
NT1   paducah plant
NT1   rocky flats plant
NT1   sandia laboratories
NT1   savannah river plant
NT1   sequoyah uf6 production plant
NT1   y-12 plant
RT   regulatory guides
RT   us doe
RT   us erda
RT   us nrc
RT   usa

us aec low inten. test reactor
USE   litr reactor

us aec lptr reactor
USE   lptr reactor

us aec mrr
USE   mrr reactor

us aec-mat. test. react.-idaho
USE   mtr reactor

us atomic energy commission
USE   us aec

US BUREAU OF MINES [33; 33]
Jul 77
UF   *bureau of mines (us)*
BT1   us organizations
  BT2   national organizations

US DOE [3,443; 11,359] Feb 78
(US Department of Energy.)
BT1   us organizations
  BT2   national organizations
NT1   ames laboratory
NT1   anl
NT1   atomics international canoga p
NT1   battelle pacific northwest lab
NT1   bettis
NT1   bnl
NT1   bonneville power administratio
NT1   feed materials production cent
NT1   hanford engineering developmen
NT1   hanford reservation
NT1   hapo
NT1   idaho chemical processing plan
NT1   idaho national engineering lab
  NT2   nrts
NT1   kansas city plant
NT1   kapl
NT1   lanl
  NT2   lasl
NT1   lawrence berkeley laboratory
NT1   lawrence livermore national la
  NT2   lawrence livermore laboratory
NT1   mound laboratory
NT1   oak ridge reservation
NT1   orgdp
NT1   ornl
NT1   paducah plant
NT1   pantex plant
NT1   pinellas plant
NT1   portsmouth centrifuge enrichme
NT1   portsmouth gaseous diffusion p
NT1   rocky flats plant
NT1   sandia national laboratories
  NT2   sandia laboratories
NT1   savannah river plant
NT1   sequoyah uf6 production plant
NT1   stanford linear accelerator ce
NT1   wipp
NT1   y-12 plant
RT   us aec
RT   us erda

US DOT [104; 104] Sep 79
(US Department of Transportation.)
BT1   us organizations
  BT2   national organizations

US EPA [732; 732] Jul 78
UF   *environmental protection agenc*
UF   *epa*
BT1   us organizations
  BT2   national organizations

US ERDA [303; 10,315]
(US Energy Research and Development Administration; created in 1975 and includes part of US AEC research activities, the Office of Coal Research, and the solar and geothermal research activities from the National Science Foundation.)
BT1   us organizations
  BT2   national organizations
NT1   ames laboratory

NT1   anl
NT1   atomics international canoga p
NT1   battelle columbus laboratory
NT1   battelle pacific northwest lab
NT1   bettis
NT1   bnl
NT1   feed materials production cent
NT1   hapo
NT1   idaho chemical processing plan
NT1   idaho national engineering lab
  NT2   nrts
NT1   kansas city plant
NT1   kapl
NT1   lasl
NT1   lawrence berkeley laboratory
NT1   lawrence livermore laboratory
NT1   mound laboratory
NT1   orgdp
NT1   ornl
NT1   paducah plant
NT1   pantex plant
NT1   pinellas plant
NT1   portsmouth gaseous diffusion p
NT1   rocky flats plant
NT1   sandia laboratories
NT1   savannah river plant
NT1   sequoyah uf6 production plant
NT1   stanford linear accelerator ce
NT1   y-12 plant
RT   hanford reservation
RT   us aec
RT   us doe

US FDA [72; 72] Nov 78
UF   *food and drug administration*
BT1   us organizations
  BT2   national organizations

US FEA [11; 11] Jul 77
(US Federal Energy Administration.)
UF   *federal energy administration*
BT1   us organizations
  BT2   national organizations

US HUD [2; 2] Nov 77
(US Department of Housing and Urban Development.)
BT1   us organizations
  BT2   national organizations

US JCAE [11; 11] Nov 75
(US Joint Committee on Atomic Energy)
UF   *joint committee on atomic ener*
BT1   us organizations
  BT2   national organizations

US MRS PROJECT [331; 331] Sep 86
(Monitored Retrievable Storage project in the USA for the long-term isolation of spent fuel and radioactive wastes permitting continuous monitoring, ready retrieval and periodic maintenance as necessary to assure containment.)
RT   high-level radioactive wastes
RT   radioactive waste storage
RT   spent fuel storage
RT   spent fuels

US NATIONAL ACADEMY OF SCIENCE [22; 22]
BT1   us organizations
  BT2   national organizations

us natl counc. radiat. protec.
USE   us ncrp

US NATL ENVIRONMENT POLICY ACT [181; 181] Mar 77
(US National Environmental Policy Act.)
UF   *nepa*
BT1   laws
RT   contamination regulations
RT   environment
RT   environmental impact statement
RT   pollution regulations

us naval res lab cyclotron
USE   nrl cyclotron

us naval res lab linac
USE   nrl linac

US NBS [265; 265] Feb 79
UF   *national bureau of standards*
UF   *nbs (us)*
BT1   us organizations
  BT2   national organizations

us nbs reactor
USE   nbsr reactor

US NCRP [113; 113]
(US National Council for Radiation Protection.)
UF   *national council radiation pro*
UF   *ncrp (us)*
UF   *us natl counc. radiat. protec.*
BT1   us organizations
  BT2   national organizations

US NRC [5,724; 5,724]
(United States Nuclear Regulatory Commission; prior to 1975 was part of US AEC and earlier material is so indexed.)
BT1   us organizations
  BT2   national organizations
RT   us aec

US ORGANIZATIONS [563; 22,875]
BT1   national organizations
NT1   federal radiation council
NT1   nasa
NT1   national science foundation
NT1   naval research laboratory
NT1   orau
NT1   tennessee valley authority
NT1   ucla
*NT1   us aec
NT1   us bureau of mines
NT1   us doe
  NT2   ames laboratory
  NT2   anl
  NT2   atomics international canoga
  NT2   battelle pacific northwest lab
  NT2   bettis
  NT2   bnl
  NT2   bonneville power administra
  NT2   feed materials production ce
  NT2   hanford engineering developmen
  NT2   hanford reservation
  NT2   hapo
  NT2   idaho chemical processing p
  NT2   idaho national engineering
    NT3   nrts
  NT2   kansas city plant
  NT2   kapl
  NT2   lanl
    NT3   lasl
  NT2   lawrence berkeley laboratory
  NT2   lawrence livermore national
    NT3   lawrence livermore labora
  NT2   mound laboratory
  NT2   oak ridge reservation
  NT2   orgdp
  NT2   ornl
  NT2   paducah plant
  NT2   pantex plant
  NT2   pinellas plant
  NT2   portsmouth centrifuge enrich
  NT2   portsmouth gaseous diffusio p
  NT2   rocky flats plant
  NT2   sandia national laboratories
    NT3   sandia laboratories
  NT2   savannah river plant
  NT2   sequoyah uf6 production pl
  NT2   stanford linear accelerator
  NT2   wipp
  NT2   y-12 plant
NT1   us dot
NT1   us epa

* NT1 us erda
  NT1 us fda
  NT1 us fea
  NT1 us hud
  NT1 us jcae
  NT1 us national academy of science
  NT1 us nbs
  NT1 us ncrp
  NT1 us nrc
  NT1 us osha

US OSHA [23; 23] *Sep 80*
(US Occupational Safety and Health Administration.)
  UF *occupational safety health adm*
  BT1 us organizations
   BT2 national organizations

US WATER POLLUTION CONTROL ACT [2; 2] *Mar 77*
(US Federal Water Pollution Control Act.)
  UF *federal water pollution contro*
  UF *fwpca*
  BT1 pollution laws
   BT2 laws

USA [6,671; 16,587]
  UF *united states of america*
  BT1 developed countries
  BT1 north america
  NT1 alabama
  NT1 alaska
  NT1 arizona
  NT1 arkansas
  NT1 california
  NT1 colorado
  NT1 connecticut
  NT1 delaware
  NT1 florida
   NT2 cape kennedy
  NT1 georgia
  NT1 hawaii
  NT1 idaho
  NT1 illinois
  NT1 indiana
  NT1 iowa
  NT1 kansas
  NT1 kentucky
  NT1 louisiana
  NT1 maine
  NT1 maryland
  NT1 massachusetts
  NT1 michigan
  NT1 minnesota
  NT1 mississippi
  NT1 missouri
  NT1 montana
  NT1 nebraska
  NT1 nevada
   NT2 tonopah test range
  NT1 new hampshire
  NT1 new jersey
  NT1 new mexico
  NT1 new york
   NT2 new york city
  NT1 north carolina
  NT1 north dakota
  NT1 ohio
  NT1 oklahoma
  NT1 oregon
  NT1 pennsylvania
  NT1 puerto rico
  NT1 rhode island
  NT1 south carolina
  NT1 south dakota
  NT1 tennessee
  NT1 texas
  NT1 utah
  NT1 vermont
  NT1 virginia
  NT1 washington
  NT1 washington dc
  NT1 west virginia
  NT1 wisconsin
  NT1 wyoming
  RT us aec

USES [13,088; 13,088]
(For the evaluation of the usefulness of a procedure, material, or device.)
  UF *applications*
  RT efficiency
  RT performance

USSR [2,422; 2,597]
  UF *soviet union*
  UF *union of soviet soc reps*
  BT1 developed countries
  BT1 europe
  NT1 byelorussian ssr
  NT1 dubna
  NT1 ukrainian ssr
  RT centrally planned economies
  RT chukchi sea

USSR ORGANIZATIONS [83; 123]
Oct 75
  BT1 national organizations
  NT1 gosatomnadzor
  NT1 ihep
  NT1 leningrad institute of nuclear

ustav jadernych vyzkumu
  USE ujv

USTILAGO [18; 18]
  BT1 fungi
   BT2 plants
  BT1 parasites
  RT cereals

UTAH [554; 554]
  BT1 usa
   BT2 developed countries
   BT2 north america
  RT green river formation
  RT mi vida mine
  RT uinta formation

uterine cervix carcinoma
  USE carcinomas
  AND urogenital system diseases

UTERUS [2,066; 2,066]
  UF *endometrium*
  UF *myometrium*
  BT1 female genitals
   BT2 organs
    BT3 body
  RT embryos
  RT fetuses
  RT oxytocin
  RT pregnancy

UTP [35; 35]
  UF *uridine triphosphate*
  BT1 nucleotides
   BT2 organic compounds

utr-b queen mary college r.
  USE queen mary college utr-b react

utr-10 iowa state university r
  USE iowa utr-10 reactor

UTR-10-KINKI REACTOR [34; 34]
(Atomic Energy Research Institute, Kinki Univ., Osaka Prefecture, Japan)
  UF *kinki univ. utr-10 reactor*
  BT1 argonaut type reactors
   BT2 enriched uranium reactors
    BT3 reactors
   BT2 research and test reactors
    BT3 reactors
   BT2 water cooled reactors
    BT3 reactors
   BT2 water moderated reactors
    BT3 reactors
  BT1 research reactors
   BT2 research and test reactors
    BT3 reactors
  BT1 thermal reactors
   BT2 reactors
  BT1 training reactors
   BT2 research and test reactors

UTRR REACTOR [4; 4]
(Atomic Energy Organization of Iran, Nuclear Research Centre, Teheran, Iran)
  UF *teheran univ. research reactor*
  UF *univ. of teheran research reac*
  BT1 enriched uranium reactors
   BT2 reactors
  BT1 pool type reactors
   BT2 water cooled reactors
    BT3 reactors
   BT2 water moderated reactors
    BT3 reactors
  BT1 research reactors
   BT2 research and test reactors
    BT3 reactors
  BT1 thermal reactors
   BT2 reactors

UVAR REACTOR [23; 23]
(University of Virginia, Charlottsville, Virginia, USA)
  UF *univ. of virginia reactor*
  UF *virginia univ. reactor*
  BT1 enriched uranium reactors
   BT2 reactors
  BT1 isotope production reactors
   BT2 irradiation reactors
    BT3 reactors
  BT1 pool type reactors
   BT2 water cooled reactors
    BT3 reactors
   BT2 water moderated reactors
    BT3 reactors
  BT1 research reactors
   BT2 research and test reactors
    BT3 reactors
  BT1 test reactors
   BT2 research and test reactors
    BT3 reactors
   BT2 test facilities
  BT1 thermal reactors
   BT2 reactors
  BT1 training reactors
   BT2 research and test reactors
    BT3 reactors

UVEA [125; 125]
  UF *choroid*
  BT1 eyes
   BT2 sense organs
    BT3 organs
     BT4 body

UVVVR [66; 66] *May 79*
(Ustavu pro Vyzkum, Vyrobu a Vyuziti Radioisotopu - Institute for the Research, Production and Application of Radioisotopes, Prague.)
  BT1 czechoslovak organizations
   BT2 national organizations

UWMAK DEVICES [104; 104]
  UF *numak reactors*
  UF *univ. of wisconsin tokamak*
  UF *wisconsin university tokamak*
  BT1 tokamak devices
   BT2 closed plasma devices
    BT3 thermonuclear devices

UWNR REACTOR [19; 19]
(University of Wisconsin, Mechanical Engineering Building, Madison, Wisconsin, USA)
  UF *univ. of wisconsin nucl. react*
  UF *wisconsin univ. nucl. reactor*
  BT1 enriched uranium reactors
   BT2 reactors
  BT1 isotope production reactors
   BT2 irradiation reactors
    BT3 reactors

BT1 pool type reactors
BT2 water cooled reactors
BT3 reactors
BT2 water moderated reactors
BT3 reactors
BT1 thermal reactors
BT2 reactors
BT1 training reactors
BT2 research and test reactors
BT3 reactors

UWTR REACTOR [4; 4]
(University of Washington, Seattle, Washington, USA)
UF *univ. of washington reactor*
UF *washington univ. (seattle) rea*
BT1 enriched uranium reactors
BT2 reactors
BT1 lwgr type reactors
BT2 graphite moderated reactors
BT3 reactors
BT2 water cooled reactors
BT3 reactors
BT1 thermal reactors
BT2 reactors
BT1 training reactors
BT2 research and test reactors
BT3 reactors

uzbek wwr-s reactor
USE wwr-s-tashkent reactor

u3o8
(Prior to December 1985 this was a valid descriptor.)
USE uranium oxides u3o8

V CENTERS [444; 444]
BT1 color centers
BT2 vacancies
BT3 point defects
BT4 crystal defects
BT5 crystal structure

V CODES [515; 515]
BT1 computer codes

V-A THEORY [668; 668]
UF *vector-axial vector theory*
RT axial-vector currents
RT current algebra
RT fermi interactions
RT vector currents

v-1 reactor (bohunice)
USE bohunice v-1 reactor

v-2 reactor (bohunice)
USE bohunice v-2 reactor

v-2 reactor (dukovany)
USE dukovany v-2 reactor

va characteristic
USE electric conductivity

VAALPUTS RADIOACTIVE WASTE DIS [26; 26] *May 87*
(Vaalputs Radioactive Waste Disposal Facility in Bushmanland, South Africa .)
BT1 radioactive waste facilities
BT2 nuclear facilities
RT radioactive wastes
RT south africa
RT waste management

VACANCIES [6,572; 10,454]
(Not for HOLES.)
BT1 point defects
BT2 crystal defects
BT3 crystal structure
NT1 color centers
NT2 a centers
NT2 e centers
NT2 f centers
NT2 h centers
NT2 i centers
NT2 m centers
NT2 q centers
NT2 r centers
NT2 s centers
NT2 u centers
NT2 v centers
NT2 z centers
NT1 frenkel defects
NT1 schottky defects
RT traps

VACCINES [362; 362]
RT antigens
RT bacteria
RT fungi
RT immunity
RT inoculation
RT viruses

VACCINIA VIRUS [39; 39]
BT1 viruses
BT2 microorganisms
BT2 parasites

vacuum (rough)
USE low pressure

vacuum (0.13-0.13x10(-5) pa)
USE high vacuum

vacuum (0.13x10(-5) pa and bel
USE ultrahigh vacuum

vacuum (1-10(-3) torr)
USE medium vacuum

vacuum (1-760 torr)
USE low pressure

vacuum (10(-3)-10(-8) torr)
USE high vacuum

vacuum (10(-8) torr and below)
USE ultrahigh vacuum

vacuum (133 pa-0.1 mpa)
USE low pressure

vacuum (133-0.13 pa)
USE medium vacuum

vacuum arc centrifuges
USE plasma centrifuges

VACUUM CASTING [50; 50]
UF *continuous vacuum casting*
BT1 casting
BT2 fabrication

VACUUM COATING [380; 380] *Apr 79*
(For the process; for the product use VAPOR DEPOSITED COATINGS.)
BT1 surface coating
BT2 deposition
RT sputtering
RT vacuum evaporation
RT vapor deposited coatings

VACUUM EVAPORATION [123; 123] *May 86*
BT1 evaporation
BT2 phase transformations
RT vacuum coating
RT vapor deposited coatings
RT vapor plating

VACUUM FURNACES [123; 123]
BT1 furnaces
RT arc furnaces
RT electron beam furnaces

VACUUM GAGES [96; 287]
BT1 pressure gages
BT2 measuring instruments
NT1 ionization gages
NT2 bayard-alpert gages
NT2 philips gages
NT2 radioactive ionization gages
NT1 knudsen gages
NT1 mc leod gages
NT1 pirani gages
RT vacuum systems

VACUUM MELTING [282; 282]
BT1 melting
BT2 phase transformations

VACUUM POLARIZATION [1,215; 1,215]
RT casimir effect
RT quantum electrodynamics
RT vacuum states

VACUUM PUMPS [623; 1,458]
BT1 pumps
BT2 equipment
NT1 cryopumps
NT1 sputter-ion pumps
NT1 turbomolecular pumps
RT getters
RT high vacuum
RT laboratory equipment
RT medium vacuum
RT ultrahigh vacuum
RT vacuum systems

VACUUM STATES [5,453; 5,453]
RT annihilation operators
RT creation operators
RT field operators
RT gluon condensation
RT instantons
RT quark condensation
RT vacuum polarization

VACUUM SYSTEMS [4,508; 4,508]
RT accelerators
RT vacuum gages
RT vacuum pumps

vacuum ultraviolet radiation
USE far ultraviolet radiation

VACUUM WELDING [59; 59]
BT1 welding
BT2 joining
BT3 fabrication
RT electron beam welding

vagina
USE female genitals

vagotomy
USE surgery
AND vagus

VAGUS [43; 43]
UF+ *vagotomy*
BT1 autonomic nervous system
BT2 nervous system
BT1 nerves
BT2 nervous system
RT parasympathomimetics

VAHNUM-1 REACTOR [11; 11] *Feb 77*
(Vahnum, North Rhein Westfalia, Federal Republic of Germany)
UF *kernkraftwerk vahnum-1*
BT1 pwr type reactors
BT2 enriched uranium reactors
BT3 reactors
BT2 power reactors
BT3 reactors
BT2 thermal reactors
BT3 reactors
BT2 water cooled reactors
BT3 reactors
BT2 water moderated reactors
BT3 reactors

VAHNUM-2 REACTOR [8; 8] *Feb 77*
(Vahnum, NorthRhein Westfalia, Federal Republic of Germany)
UF *kernkraftwerk vahnum-2*
BT1 pwr type reactors
BT2 enriched uranium reactors
BT3 reactors
BT2 power reactors
BT3 reactors
BT2 thermal reactors
BT3 reactors
BT2 water cooled reactors
BT3 reactors
BT2 water moderated reactors
BT3 reactors

VAK REACTOR [88; 88]
UF *kahl-vak reactor*
UF *versuchsatomkraftwerk kahl re.*
BT1 bwr type reactors
BT2 enriched uranium reactors
BT3 reactors
BT2 power reactors
BT3 reactors
BT2 thermal reactors
BT3 reactors
BT2 water cooled reactors
BT3 reactors
BT2 water moderated reactors
BT3 reactors

VALENCE [6,902; 7,646]
UF *valency states*
UF+ *electron acceptor*
UF+ *electron donor*
UF+ *valence electrons*
NT1 coordination valences
RT electron transfer
RT hot atom chemistry
RT radiation chemistry
RT redox potential

valence electrons
USE electrons
AND valence

valency states
USE valence

VALERIC ACID [38; 38]
UF *pentanoic acid*
BT1 monocarboxylic acids
BT2 carboxylic acids
BT3 organic acids
BT4 organic compounds

validation
USE verification

VALINE [299; 299]
UF *aminoisovaleric acid-alpha*
BT1 amino acids
BT2 carboxylic acids
BT3 organic acids
BT4 organic compounds

VALINOMYCIN [26; 26] *Nov 77*
BT1 antibiotics
BT2 drugs
BT2 organic compounds
RT lipids

vallecitos vbwr reactor
USE vbwr reactor

VALVES [4,131; 4,256]
UF *safety valves*
BT1 flow regulators
BT2 control equipment
BT3 equipment
NT1 relief valves
RT bellows
RT closures
RT pipe fittings
RT reactor cooling systems

van allen belts
USE radiation belts

VAN DE GRAAFF ACCELERATORS [1,900; 2,069]
BT1 electrostatic accelerators
BT2 accelerators
NT1 crnl mp tandem accelerator
NT1 jaeri tandem accelerator
NT1 learn tandem accelerator
NT1 orsay tandem accelerator
NT1 vivitron tandem accelerator
RT vicksi accelerator

VAN DER WAALS FORCES [723; 723]
RT adsorption
RT intermolecular forces
RT molecules
RT virial equation

VAN HOVE MODEL [35; 35]
BT1 particle models
BT2 mathematical models
RT regge poles

VAN HOVE THEORY [51; 51]
RT slowing-down
RT transport theory

VAN HOVE-HUGENHOLTZ THEORY [16; 16]
UF *hugenholtz-pines theory*
RT many-body problem

van hove-prigogine theory
USE prigogine theorem

VAN VLECK THEORY [174; 174]
RT paramagnetism

VANADATES [1,144; 1,175]
(Specific compounds should be indexed by coordination of a descriptor of the form (CATION) COMPOUNDS and the above anion descriptor.)
BT1 oxygen compounds
BT1 vanadium compounds
BT2 transition element compounds
NT1 potassium vanadates
NT1 uranium vanadates
RT vanadium oxides

VANADIUM [4,358; 4,358]
BT1 transition elements
BT2 metals
BT3 elements

VANADIUM ADDITIONS [739; 1,848]
(Alloys containing not more than 1% V are listed here.)
NT1 alloy-ni54mo17cr16fe6w4
NT1 alloy-ni60co15cr10al6ti5mo3
NT1 alloy-ni62cr16mo15fe3
NT1 alloy-ni65mo28fe5
NT1 alloy-ni68cr15w6al3mo3fe2
NT1 alloy-ti90al6
NT1 steel-crmov
NT1 steel-cr12moniv
NT1 steel-cr12mov
NT1 steel-cr16ni13monbv
NT1 steel-cr2mov
NT1 steel-cr2nimov
NT1 steel-cr9monbv
NT1 steel-mnnimov
NT1 steel-ni26cr15ti2movalb
NT1 steel-ni3crmo
NT1 steel-ni3crmov
NT1 steel-ni3mov
RT vanadium alloys
RT vanadium compounds

VANADIUM ALLOYS [2,648; 3,916]
(Alloys containing more than 1% V.)
BT1 alloys
NT1 alloy-co52fe35v10
NT1 alloy-co52fe35v13
NT1 alloy-ti90al6v4
NT1 alloy-ti91al4mo3
NT1 vanadium base alloys
NT2 alloy-v87cr9fe3
RT vanadium additions

VANADIUM ARSENIDES [3; 3] *Jul 77*
BT1 arsenides
BT2 arsenic compounds
BT2 pnictides
BT1 vanadium compounds
BT2 transition element compounds

VANADIUM BASE ALLOYS [898; 907]
BT1 vanadium alloys
BT2 alloys
NT1 alloy-v87cr9fe3

VANADIUM BORIDES [43; 43]
BT1 borides
BT2 boron compounds
BT1 vanadium compounds
BT2 transition element compounds

VANADIUM BROMIDES [13; 13]
BT1 bromides
BT2 bromine compounds
BT3 halogen compounds
BT2 halides
BT3 halogen compounds
BT1 vanadium compounds
BT2 transition element compounds

VANADIUM CARBIDES [363; 363]
BT1 carbides
BT2 carbon compounds
BT1 vanadium compounds
BT2 transition element compounds

VANADIUM CHLORIDES [111; 111]
BT1 chlorides
BT2 chlorine compounds
BT3 halogen compounds
BT2 halides
BT3 halogen compounds
BT1 vanadium compounds
BT2 transition element compounds

VANADIUM COMPLEXES [1,163; 1,163]
- BT1 transition element complexes
- BT2 complexes

VANADIUM COMPOUNDS
[1,323; 5,825]
- BT1 transition element compounds
- NT1 vanadates
  - NT2 potassium vanadates
  - NT2 uranium vanadates
- NT1 vanadium arsenides
- NT1 vanadium borides
- NT1 vanadium bromides
- NT1 vanadium carbides
- NT1 vanadium chlorides
- NT1 vanadium fluorides
- NT1 vanadium hydrides
- NT1 vanadium hydroxides
- NT1 vanadium iodides
- NT1 vanadium nitrates
- NT1 vanadium nitrides
- NT1 vanadium oxides
- NT1 vanadium phosphates
- NT1 vanadium phosphides
- NT1 vanadium selenides
- NT1 vanadium silicates
- NT1 vanadium silicides
- NT1 vanadium sulfates
- NT1 vanadium sulfides
- NT1 vanadium tellurides
- NT1 vanadium tungstates
- RT vanadium additions

VANADIUM FLUORIDES [51; 51]
- BT1 fluorides
  - BT2 fluorine compounds
    - BT3 halogen compounds
  - BT2 halides
    - BT3 halogen compounds
- BT1 vanadium compounds
  - BT2 transition element compounds

VANADIUM HYDRIDES [269; 269]
- BT1 hydrides
  - BT2 hydrogen compounds
- BT1 vanadium compounds
  - BT2 transition element compounds

VANADIUM HYDROXIDES [13; 13]
- BT1 hydroxides
  - BT2 hydrogen compounds
  - BT2 oxygen compounds
- BT1 vanadium compounds
  - BT2 transition element compounds

VANADIUM IODIDES [12; 12]
- BT1 iodides
  - BT2 halides
    - BT3 halogen compounds
  - BT2 iodine compounds
    - BT3 halogen compounds
- BT1 vanadium compounds
  - BT2 transition element compounds

VANADIUM IONS [254; 254]
- BT1 ions
  - BT2 charged particles

VANADIUM ISOTOPES [97; 1,321]
- NT1 vanadium 42
- NT1 vanadium 44
- NT1 vanadium 45
- NT1 vanadium 46
- NT1 vanadium 47
- NT1 vanadium 48
- NT1 vanadium 49
- NT1 vanadium 50
- NT1 vanadium 51
- NT1 vanadium 52
- NT1 vanadium 53
- NT1 vanadium 54
- NT1 vanadium 55
- NT1 vanadium 56
- NT1 vanadium 57
- NT1 vanadium 58
- NT1 vanadium 59
- NT1 vanadium 60

VANADIUM NITRATES [6; 6] Oct 76
- BT1 nitrates
  - BT2 nitrogen compounds
  - BT2 oxygen compounds
- BT1 vanadium compounds
  - BT2 transition element compounds

VANADIUM NITRIDES [216; 216]
- BT1 nitrides
  - BT2 nitrogen compounds
  - BT2 pnictides
- BT1 vanadium compounds
  - BT2 transition element compounds

VANADIUM ORES [45; 45] Feb 76
- BT1 ores

VANADIUM OXIDES [2,050; 2,060]
- BT1 oxides
  - BT2 chalcogenides
  - BT2 oxygen compounds
- BT1 vanadium compounds
  - BT2 transition element compounds
- RT francevillite
- RT oxide minerals
- RT tyuyamunite
- RT vanadates

VANADIUM PHOSPHATES [40; 40]
- BT1 phosphates
  - BT2 oxygen compounds
  - BT2 phosphorus compounds
- BT1 vanadium compounds
  - BT2 transition element compounds

VANADIUM PHOSPHIDES [6; 6]
Nov 80
- BT1 phosphides
  - BT2 phosphorus compounds
  - BT2 pnictides
- BT1 vanadium compounds
  - BT2 transition element compounds

VANADIUM SELENIDES [24; 24]
Sep 79
- BT1 selenides
  - BT2 chalcogenides
  - BT2 selenium compounds
- BT1 vanadium compounds
  - BT2 transition element compounds

VANADIUM SILICATES [5; 5]
- BT1 silicates
  - BT2 oxygen compounds
  - BT2 silicon compounds
- BT1 vanadium compounds
  - BT2 transition element compounds

VANADIUM SILICIDES [330; 330]
- BT1 silicides
  - BT2 silicon compounds
- BT1 vanadium compounds
  - BT2 transition element compounds

VANADIUM SULFATES [36; 36]
- BT1 sulfates
  - BT2 oxygen compounds
  - BT2 sulfur compounds
- BT1 vanadium compounds
  - BT2 transition element compounds

VANADIUM SULFIDES [60; 60]
- BT1 sulfides
  - BT2 chalcogenides
  - BT2 sulfur compounds
- BT1 vanadium compounds
  - BT2 transition element compounds

→ ## VANADIUM TELLURIDES [0; 0] Jul 91
- BT1 tellurides
  - BT2 chalcogenides
  - BT2 tellurium compounds
- BT1 vanadium compounds
  - BT2 transition element compounds

VANADIUM TUNGSTATES [3; 3]
Jul 78
- BT1 tungstates
  - BT2 oxygen compounds
  - BT2 tungsten compounds
    - BT3 transition element compounds
- BT1 vanadium compounds
  - BT2 transition element compounds

VANADIUM 42 [3; 3] Sep 78
- BT1 beta decay radioisotopes
  - BT2 radioisotopes
    - BT3 isotopes
- BT1 intermediate mass nuclei
  - BT2 nuclei
- BT1 odd-odd nuclei
  - BT2 nuclei
- BT1 vanadium isotopes

VANADIUM 44 [2; 2] Apr 86
- BT1 beta-plus decay radioisotopes
  - BT2 beta decay radioisotopes
    - BT3 radioisotopes
      - BT4 isotopes
- BT1 intermediate mass nuclei
  - BT2 nuclei
- BT1 millisec living radioisotopes
  - BT2 radioisotopes
    - BT3 isotopes
- BT1 odd-odd nuclei
  - BT2 nuclei
- BT1 vanadium isotopes

VANADIUM 45 [13; 13] Nov 80
- BT1 beta decay radioisotopes
  - BT2 radioisotopes
    - BT3 isotopes
- BT1 intermediate mass nuclei
  - BT2 nuclei
- BT1 odd-even nuclei
  - BT2 nuclei
- BT1 vanadium isotopes

VANADIUM 46 [43; 43]
- BT1 beta-plus decay radioisotopes
  - BT2 beta decay radioisotopes
    - BT3 radioisotopes
      - BT4 isotopes
- BT1 intermediate mass nuclei
  - BT2 nuclei
- BT1 millisec living radioisotopes
  - BT2 radioisotopes
    - BT3 isotopes
- BT1 odd-odd nuclei
  - BT2 nuclei
- BT1 vanadium isotopes

VANADIUM 47 [82; 82]
- BT1 beta-plus decay radioisotopes
  - BT2 beta decay radioisotopes
    - BT3 radioisotopes
      - BT4 isotopes
- BT1 electron capture radioisotopes
  - BT2 beta decay radioisotopes
    - BT3 radioisotopes
      - BT4 isotopes
- BT1 intermediate mass nuclei
  - BT2 nuclei
- BT1 minutes living radioisotopes
  - BT2 radioisotopes
    - BT3 isotopes
- BT1 odd-even nuclei
  - BT2 nuclei
- BT1 vanadium isotopes

VANADIUM 48 [229; 229]
- BT1 beta-plus decay radioisotopes
  - BT2 beta decay radioisotopes
    - BT3 radioisotopes
      - BT4 isotopes
- BT1 days living radioisotopes
  - BT2 radioisotopes
    - BT3 isotopes
- BT1 electron capture radioisotopes
  - BT2 beta decay radioisotopes
    - BT3 radioisotopes
      - BT4 isotopes
- BT1 intermediate mass nuclei

BT2　　nuclei
　　BT1　　odd-odd nuclei
　　BT2　　nuclei
　　BT1　　vanadium isotopes

VANADIUM 48 TARGET [3; 3] *Oct 82*
　　BT1　　targets

VANADIUM 49 [133; 133]
　　BT1　　days living radioisotopes
　　BT2　　radioisotopes
　　　BT3　　isotopes
　　BT1　　electron capture radioisotopes
　　BT2　　beta decay radioisotopes
　　　BT3　　radioisotopes
　　　　BT4　　isotopes
　　BT1　　intermediate mass nuclei
　　BT2　　nuclei
　　BT1　　odd-even nuclei
　　BT2　　nuclei
　　BT1　　vanadium isotopes

VANADIUM 49 TARGET [7; 7]
　　BT1　　targets

VANADIUM 50 [120; 120]
　　BT1　　beta-minus decay radioisotopes
　　BT2　　beta decay radioisotopes
　　　BT3　　radioisotopes
　　　　BT4　　isotopes
　　BT1　　electron capture radioisotopes
　　BT2　　beta decay radioisotopes
　　　BT3　　radioisotopes
　　　　BT4　　isotopes
　　BT1　　intermediate mass nuclei
　　BT2　　nuclei
　　BT1　　odd-odd nuclei
　　BT2　　nuclei
　　BT1　　vanadium isotopes
　　BT1　　years living radioisotopes
　　BT2　　radioisotopes
　　　BT3　　isotopes

VANADIUM 50 TARGET [28; 28]
　　BT1　　targets

VANADIUM 51 [563; 563]
　　BT1　　intermediate mass nuclei
　　BT2　　nuclei
　　BT1　　odd-even nuclei
　　BT2　　nuclei
　　BT1　　stable isotopes
　　BT2　　isotopes
　　BT1　　vanadium isotopes

VANADIUM 51 REACTIONS [13; 13]
Nov 85
　　BT1　　heavy ion reactions
　　BT2　　nuclear reactions

VANADIUM 51 TARGET [501; 501]
　　BT1　　targets

VANADIUM 52 [126; 126]
　　BT1　　beta-minus decay radioisotopes
　　BT2　　beta decay radioisotopes
　　　BT3　　radioisotopes
　　　　BT4　　isotopes
　　BT1　　intermediate mass nuclei
　　BT2　　nuclei
　　BT1　　minutes living radioisotopes
　　BT2　　radioisotopes
　　　BT3　　isotopes
　　BT1　　odd-odd nuclei
　　BT2　　nuclei
　　BT1　　vanadium isotopes

VANADIUM 53 [15; 15]
　　BT1　　beta-minus decay radioisotopes
　　BT2　　beta decay radioisotopes
　　　BT3　　radioisotopes
　　　　BT4　　isotopes
　　BT1　　intermediate mass nuclei
　　BT2　　nuclei

　　BT1　　minutes living radioisotopes
　　BT2　　radioisotopes
　　　BT3　　isotopes
　　BT1　　odd-even nuclei
　　BT2　　nuclei
　　BT1　　vanadium isotopes

VANADIUM 54 [8; 8]
　　BT1　　beta-minus decay radioisotopes
　　BT2　　beta decay radioisotopes
　　　BT3　　radioisotopes
　　　　BT4　　isotopes
　　BT1　　intermediate mass nuclei
　　BT2　　nuclei
　　BT1　　odd-odd nuclei
　　BT2　　nuclei
　　BT1　　seconds living radioisotopes
　　BT2　　radioisotopes
　　　BT3　　isotopes
　　BT1　　vanadium isotopes

VANADIUM 55 [6; 6] *Jul 78*
　　BT1　　beta-minus decay radioisotopes
　　BT2　　beta decay radioisotopes
　　　BT3　　radioisotopes
　　　　BT4　　isotopes
　　BT1　　intermediate mass nuclei
　　BT2　　nuclei
　　BT1　　odd-even nuclei
　　BT2　　nuclei
　　BT1　　seconds living radioisotopes
　　BT2　　radioisotopes
　　　BT3　　isotopes
　　BT1　　vanadium isotopes

VANADIUM 56 [2; 2] *Nov 80*
　　BT1　　intermediate mass nuclei
　　BT2　　nuclei
　　BT1　　odd-odd nuclei
　　BT2　　nuclei
　　BT1　　vanadium isotopes

VANADIUM 57 [4; 4] *Aug 86*
　　BT1　　intermediate mass nuclei
　　BT2　　nuclei
　　BT1　　odd-even nuclei
　　BT2　　nuclei
　　BT1　　vanadium isotopes

VANADIUM 58 [3; 3] *Aug 86*
　　BT1　　intermediate mass nuclei
　　BT2　　nuclei
　　BT1　　odd-odd nuclei
　　BT2　　nuclei
　　BT1　　vanadium isotopes

VANADIUM 59 [2; 2] *Aug 86*
　　BT1　　intermediate mass nuclei
　　BT2　　nuclei
　　BT1　　odd-even nuclei
　　BT2　　nuclei
　　BT1　　vanadium isotopes

VANADIUM 60 [2; 2] *Aug 86*
　　BT1　　intermediate mass nuclei
　　BT2　　nuclei
　　BT1　　odd-odd nuclei
　　BT2　　nuclei
　　BT1　　vanadium isotopes

VANDELLOS REACTOR [21; 21]
(Vandellos, Tarragona, Spain)
　　BT1　　carbon dioxide cooled reactors
　　BT2　　gas cooled reactors
　　　BT3　　reactors
　　BT1　　gcr type reactors
　　BT2　　gas cooled reactors
　　　BT3　　reactors
　　BT2　　graphite moderated reactors
　　　BT3　　reactors
　　BT1　　power reactors
　　BT2　　reactors
　　BT1　　thermal reactors
　　BT2　　reactors

VANES [105; 105]
　　RT　　fins
　　RT　　reactor components

vanstar 7
　　USE　　alloy-v87cr9fe3

VAPOR CONDENSATION [1,428; 1,546]
　　UF　　*condensation (vapor)*
　　NT1　　dropwise condensation
　　NT1　　film condensation
　　RT　　condensates
　　RT　　condensation chambers
　　RT　　condensation nuclei
　　RT　　cooling
　　RT　　dew point
　　RT　　heat transfer
　　RT　　liquefaction
　　RT　　subcooling
　　RT　　vapor condensers

VAPOR CONDENSERS [229; 1,141]
　　UF　　*condensers (vapor)*
　　NT1　　steam condensers
　　　NT2　　ice condensers
　　RT　　cold traps
　　RT　　cooling towers
　　RT　　counterflow systems
　　RT　　crossflow systems
　　RT　　evaporators
　　RT　　heat sinks
　　RT　　vapor condensation
　　RT　　vapor separators

VAPOR DEPOSITED COATINGS
[1,421; 1,421]
　　UF　　*vapor-deposited coatings*
　　BT1　　coatings
　　RT　　chemical vapor deposition
　　RT　　vacuum coating
　　RT　　vacuum evaporation
　　RT　　vapor plating

VAPOR GENERATORS [113; 8,504]
　　UF　　*generators (vapor)*
　　BT1　　boilers
　　NT1　　steam generators
　　RT　　reactor cooling systems
　　RT　　vapors

VAPOR JET EJECTORS [10; 23]
　　NT1　　steam jet ejectors
　　RT　　mhd generators

VAPOR PLATING [217; 217]
　　BT1　　plating
　　　BT2　　surface coating
　　　　BT3　　deposition
　　RT　　cathode sputtering
　　RT　　chemical vapor deposition
　　RT　　vacuum evaporation
　　RT　　vapor deposited coatings

VAPOR PRESSURE [2,257; 2,257]
　　UF　　*pressure (vapor)*
　　BT1　　thermodynamic properties
　　　BT2　　physical properties
　　RT　　knudsen flow

VAPOR SEPARATORS [64; 453]
　　UF　　*separators (vapor)*
　　BT1　　separation equipment
　　　BT2　　equipment
　　NT1　　steam separators
　　RT　　mhd generators
　　RT　　vapor condensers

vapor-deposited coatings
　　USE　　vapor deposited coatings

vaporization
　　USE　　evaporation

VAPORIZATION HEAT [353; 353]
UF heat of vaporization
UF latent heat of vaporization
BT1 transition heat
BT2 enthalpy
BT3 thermodynamic properties
BT4 physical properties
RT evaporation
RT evaporative cooling

§ **VAPORS** [3,017; 4,965]
BT1 gases
BT2 fluids
NT1 water vapor
RT evaporation
RT liquids
RT vapor generators
RT void fraction

varactors
USE variable capacitance diodes

VARENNES TOKAMAK [51; 51] *Sep 83*
UF tokamak de varennes
BT1 tokamak devices
BT2 closed plasma devices
BT3 thermonuclear devices

variability (biological)
USE biological variability

variability (genetic)
USE genetic variability

VARIABLE CAPACITANCE DIODES [31; 31]
UF varactors
UF variable-capacitance diodes
BT1 semiconductor diodes
BT2 semiconductor devices

VARIABLE ENERGY CYCLOTRONS [167; 167]
UF variable-energy cyclotrons
BT1 cyclotrons
BT2 cyclic accelerators
BT3 accelerators

variable moment of inertia mod
USE vmi model

VARIABLE STARS [2,027; 6,772]
BT1 stars
NT1 eruptive variable stars
NT2 novae
NT2 supernovae
NT2 t tauri stars
NT1 pulsating variable stars
NT2 cepheids
RT magnetic stars
RT starspots

variable-capacitance diodes
USE variable capacitance diodes

variable-energy cyclotrons
USE variable energy cyclotrons

VARIATIONAL METHODS [4,860; 5,826]
NT1 hsk procedure
NT1 resonating-group method
NT1 schwinger variational method
RT functionals
RT mathematics
RT neutron transport theory
RT optimization
RT ritz method

§§ **VARIATIONS** [10,818; 23,688]
UF periodicity
NT1 annual variations
NT1 daily variations
NT1 fluctuations
NT1 geographical variations
NT1 hourly variations
NT1 monthly variations
NT1 seasonal variations
RT degrees of freedom
RT disturbances
RT landau fluctuations
RT modifications
RT modulation
RT oscillations
RT pulsations
RT reactor noise
RT temperature noise
RT transients

varistors
(Non-linear semiconductor resistors)
USE semiconductor resistors

VARLEY MECHANISM [0; 0]
RT crystal defects
RT crystals
RT interstitials
RT radiation effects

VARNISHES [74; 74]
BT1 coatings
RT dielectric materials

VASCULAR DISEASES [2,577; 3,688]
BT1 diseases
NT1 hypertension

VASOCONSTRICTION [228; 228]
RT blood circulation
RT blood vessels
RT capillaries
RT sympathomimetics
RT vasodilation

VASOCONSTRICTORS [68; 306] *May 84*
BT1 cardiovascular agents
BT2 drugs
NT1 angiotensin
NT1 ephedrine

vasodilatation
(Prior to December 1990, this was a valid descriptor.)
USE vasodilation

VASODILATION [275; 275] *Jun 77*
UF vasodilatation
RT blood circulation
RT blood vessels
RT capillaries
RT sympathomimetics
RT vasoconstriction

VASODILATORS [359; 405] *May 84*
BT1 cardiovascular agents
BT2 drugs
NT1 theobromine
NT1 theophylline

VASOPRESSIN [255; 255]
UF antidiuretic hormone
BT1 pituitary hormones
BT2 peptide hormones
BT3 hormones
RT tubules

vavilov-cherenkov radiation
USE cherenkov radiation

vax computers
USE dec computers

VBWR REACTOR [4; 4]
UF vallecitos vbwr reactor
BT1 bwr type reactors
BT2 enriched uranium reactors
BT3 reactors
BT2 power reactors
BT3 reactors
BT2 thermal reactors
BT3 reactors
BT2 water cooled reactors
BT3 reactors
BT2 water moderated reactors
BT3 reactors

vcocl
USE vcoclnd

VCOCLND [54; 54]
(Vienna Convention on Civil Liability fo Nuclear Damage)
UF damage, vienna conv liability
UF liabil conv nucl damage, vienn
UF nuclear damage, vienna liabil
UF vcocl
UF vienna conv. civil liability
BT1 international agreements
BT2 agreements
RT civil liability
RT nuclear damage
RT nuclear liability

VECTOR CURRENTS [1,020; 1,020]
BT1 algebraic currents
BT2 currents
RT axial-vector currents
RT cvc theory
RT pcvc theory
RT v-a theory

VECTOR DOMINANCE MODEL [1,094; 1,094]
BT1 particle models
BT2 mathematical models
RT vector mesons

VECTOR FIELDS [3,818; 3,818]
RT quantum field theory

VECTOR MESONS [2,812; 5,286]
(Mesons with spin and parity 1-.)
SF upsilon resonances
BT1 mesons
BT2 bosons
BT2 hadrons
BT3 elementary particles
NT1 d*-2010 mesons
NT1 j psi-3097 mesons
NT1 k*-1410 mesons
NT1 k*-1790 mesons
NT1 k*-892 mesons
NT1 omega-783 mesons
NT1 phi-1020 mesons
NT1 phi-1680 mesons
NT1 psi-3685 mesons
NT1 psi-3770 mesons
NT1 psi-4030 mesons
NT1 psi-4160 mesons
NT1 psi-4415 mesons
NT1 rho-1250 mesons
NT1 rho-1600 mesons
NT1 rho-2150 mesons
NT1 rho-770 mesons
NT1 upsilon-10023 mesons
NT1 upsilon-10355 mesons
NT1 upsilon-10575 mesons
NT1 upsilon-10860 mesons
NT1 upsilon-11020 mesons
NT1 upsilon-9460 mesons
RT gluon model
RT gluons
RT higgs model
RT vector dominance model

VECTOR PROCESSING [181; 181]
Sep 86
- BT1 programming
- RT algorithms
- RT computers
- RT parallel processing
- RT supercomputers

vector-axial vector theory
- USE v-a theory

VECTORS [1,784; 2,213]
- BT1 tensors
- NT1 isovectors
- RT banach space
- RT eigenvectors
- RT helmholtz theorem
- RT laplacian
- RT mathematics
- RT poynting theorem
- RT spinors
- RT tensor forces

VEGA SPACE PROBES [132; 132]
Apr 85
- BT1 space vehicles

VEGARD LAW [62; 62]
- RT alloy systems
- RT crystal lattices

VEGETABLES [630; 3,083]
(Edible parts of plants only.)
- BT1 food
- NT1 beans
- NT1 beets
- NT1 brassica
- NT1 carrots
- NT1 cucumbers
- NT1 lettuce
- NT1 mungbeans
- NT1 onions
- NT1 peas
- NT1 peppers
- NT1 potatoes
- NT1 radishes
- NT1 soybeans
- NT1 spinach
- NT1 tomatoes
- NT1 yams
- RT crops

vegetation
- USE plants

VEGETATIVE PROPAGATION [65; 65]
- RT adventitious bud technique
- RT plants
- RT reproduction

VEHICLES [683; 712]
- UF cars
- UF motor vehicles
- UF trains
- UF trucks
- NT1 automobiles
- NT1 railroad cars
- RT earthmoving equipment
- RT ignition systems
- RT motor vehicle accidents
- RT propulsion systems
- RT rail transport
- RT road transport
- RT transport

VEINS [1,613; 1,994]
- BT1 blood vessels
- BT2 cardiovascular system
- BT2 organs
- BT3 body
- NT1 portal system
- RT intravenous injection
- RT lymph vessels

VELA PROJECT [20; 68]
- UF *project vela*
- NT1 cowboy event
- NT1 gnome event
- NT1 lollipop event
- NT1 long shot event
- NT1 salmon event
- NT1 shoal event
- NT1 sterling event
- RT nuclear explosions
- RT seismic detection
- RT seismology
- RT underground explosions

VELOCIMETERS [134; 134] *Nov 78*
- UF *speed indicators*
- BT1 measuring instruments
- RT accelerometers
- RT velocity

§ **VELOCITY** [12,425; 16,914]
- UF *speed*
- NT1 angular velocity
- NT1 critical velocity
- NT1 mach number
- NT1 phase velocity
- NT1 radial velocity
- RT acceleration
- RT flow rate
- RT kinetic energy
- RT linear momentum
- RT time dependence
- RT velocimeters

VENERA SPACE PROBES [217; 217]
Sep 78
- BT1 space vehicles
- RT space flight

VENEZIANO MODEL [348; 1,131]
- BT1 particle models
- BT2 mathematical models
- NT1 dual resonance model
- RT scattering amplitudes

VENEZUELA [57; 57]
- BT1 developing countries
- BT1 south america
- BT2 latin america

VENOMS [109; 109]
- RT toxicity
- RT toxins

VENTILATION [2,278; 2,278]
- RT aerosols
- RT air
- RT air cleaning
- RT air conditioning
- RT air flow
- RT exhaust systems
- RT filters
- RT fume hoods
- RT gaseous wastes
- RT remedial action
- RT stacks

VENTS [317; 317]
- RT openings

VENTURI TUBES [69; 69]
- RT flowmeters

VENUS PLANET [778; 778]
- BT1 planets

VENUS REACTOR [32; 32]
- UF *vulcain exp. nucl. study*
- BT1 enriched uranium reactors
- BT2 reactors
- BT1 experimental reactors
- BT2 research and test reactors
- BT3 reactors
- BT1 heavy water cooled reactors
- BT2 reactors
- BT1 heavy water moderated reactors
- BT2 reactors
- BT1 tank type reactors
- BT2 reactors
- BT1 thermal reactors
- BT2 reactors
- BT1 water cooled reactors
- BT2 reactors
- BT1 water moderated reactors
- BT2 reactors

VEP-1 [8; 8]
- BT1 storage rings

VEPP-2 [98; 98]
- BT1 storage rings

VEPP-3 [92; 92]
- BT1 storage rings

VEPP-4 [118; 118]
- BT1 storage rings

VERA REACTOR [9; 9]
(UK Ministry of Defence, Berkshire, United Kingdom)
- UF *versatile exp. react. assembl.*
- BT1 fast reactors
- BT2 epithermal reactors
- BT3 reactors
- BT1 research reactors
- BT2 research and test reactors
- BT3 reactors
- BT1 zero power reactors
- BT2 experimental reactors
- BT3 research and test reactors
- BT4 reactors
- RT enriched uranium reactors
- RT plutonium reactors

VERIFICATION [2,683; 2,683] *Oct 82*
(Process or result of confirming the accuracy of reported information, data, etc.)
- UF *validation*
- UF+ *information validation*
- RT arms control
- RT audits
- RT evaluation

VERMICULITE [94; 94]
- BT1 inorganic ion exchangers
- BT2 ion exchange materials
- BT3 materials
- BT1 silicate minerals
- BT2 minerals
- RT aluminium silicates
- RT iron silicates
- RT magnesium silicates

VERMONT [72; 72]
- BT1 usa
- BT2 developed countries
- BT2 north america

VERMONT YANKEE REACTOR [194; 194]
(Vernon, Vermont, USA)
- UF *yankee vermont reactor*
- BT1 bwr type reactors
- BT2 enriched uranium reactors
- BT3 reactors
- BT2 power reactors
- BT3 reactors
- BT2 thermal reactors
- BT3 reactors
- BT2 water cooled reactors
- BT3 reactors
- BT2 water moderated reactors
- BT3 reactors

VERNALIZATION [9; 9]
- RT cereals
- RT crops
- RT seasons
- RT seeds
- RT sprouting
- RT temperature dependence

VERNIER CHRONOTRONS [1; 1]
BT1 chronotrons
BT2 time interval analyzers
BT3 measuring instruments

VERPLANCK-1 REACTOR [1; 1]
BT1 bwr type reactors
BT2 enriched uranium reactors
BT3 reactors
BT2 power reactors
BT3 reactors
BT2 thermal reactors
BT3 reactors
BT2 water cooled reactors
BT3 reactors
BT2 water moderated reactors
BT3 reactors

VERPLANCK-2 REACTOR [1; 1]
BT1 bwr type reactors
BT2 enriched uranium reactors
BT3 reactors
BT2 power reactors
BT3 reactors
BT2 thermal reactors
BT3 reactors
BT2 water cooled reactors
BT3 reactors
BT2 water moderated reactors
BT3 reactors

versat. interm. puls. exp. re.
USE viper reactor

versatile exp. react. assembl.
USE vera reactor

VERSATOR TOKAMAK [23; 23] *Mar 86*
BT1 tokamak devices
BT2 closed plasma devices
BT3 thermonuclear devices

versene
USE edta

versuchsatomkraftwerk kahl re.
USE vak reactor

VERTEBRAE [2,351; 2,351]
UF *spine*
UF+ *disks (intervertebral)*
UF+ *intervertebral disks*
BT1 skeleton
BT2 organs
BT3 body
RT spinal cord
RT spondylitis

VERTEBRATES [61; 75,680]
BT1 animals
NT1 amphibians
NT2 frogs
NT2 salamanders
NT3 axolotl
NT3 triturus
NT1 birds
NT2 fowl
NT3 chickens
NT3 ducks
NT2 pigeons
NT1 fishes
NT2 anadromous fishes
NT3 salmon
NT2 codfish
NT2 eel
NT2 goldfish
NT2 plaice
NT2 trout
NT2 tuna
NT1 mammals
NT2 burros
NT2 cats
NT2 cetaceans
NT2 dogs
NT3 beagles
NT2 horses
NT2 marsupials
NT2 pikas
NT2 primates
NT3 apes
NT3 man
NT4 children
NT5 infants
NT4 elderly people
NT4 men
NT4 patients
NT4 women
NT3 monkeys
NT4 baboons
NT4 macacus
NT2 rabbits
NT2 rodents
NT3 chipmunks
NT3 gerbils
NT3 guinea pigs
NT3 hamsters
NT3 mice
NT3 rats
NT3 squirrels
NT3 voles
NT2 ruminants
NT3 antelopes
NT3 buffalo
NT3 cattle
NT4 calves
NT4 cows
NT3 deer
NT3 goats
NT3 llamas
NT3 sheep
NT2 shrews
NT2 swine
NT3 miniature swine
NT1 reptiles
NT2 lizards
NT2 snakes
NT2 turtles

VERTEX FUNCTIONS [2,920; 2,920]
BT1 functions
RT form factors
RT quantum field theory

very high frequency
USE mhz range

very high frequency radiation
USE mhz range
AND radiowave radiation

VERY HIGH PRESSURE [2,730; 2,730]
UF *pressure (100 mpa and above)*
UF *pressure (1000 atm and above)*
RT pressure dependence

VERY HIGH TEMPERATURE
[20,791; 20,791]
UF *temperature (1000-4000 k)*
RT critical heat flux
RT temperature dependence
RT vhtr reactor

very low pressure
USE medium vacuum

VERY LOW TEMPERATURE
[9,808; 9,808]
UF *temperature (0013-0065 k)*
RT cryogenics
RT temperature dependence

vessels
USE containers

vessels (chemical reactions)
USE chemical reactors

vessels (pressure)
USE pressure vessels

vessels (reactor)
USE reactor vessels

VESTIBULAR APPARATUS [46; 46]
UF+ *labyrinth*
BT1 sense organs
BT2 organs
BT3 body
RT auditory organs

vetch
USE vicia

veter. adm. hosp. triga react.
USE triga-veterans reactor

VETERINARY MEDICINE [124; 124]
BT1 medicine
RT animals

VG-400 REACTOR [6; 6] *Apr 89*
BT1 enriched uranium reactors
BT2 reactors
BT1 helium cooled reactors
BT2 gas cooled reactors
BT3 reactors
BT1 htgr type reactors
BT2 gas cooled reactors
BT3 reactors
BT2 graphite moderated reactors
BT3 reactors
BT1 pebble bed reactors
BT2 solid homogeneous reactors
BT3 homogeneous reactors
BT4 reactors
BT1 power reactors
BT2 reactors
BT1 thermal reactors
BT2 reactors

VGL DEVICES [1; 1]
BT1 magnetic mirrors
BT2 open plasma devices
BT3 thermonuclear devices

VGR-50 REACTOR [3; 3] *Apr 89*
BT1 enriched uranium reactors
BT2 reactors
BT1 helium cooled reactors
BT2 gas cooled reactors
BT3 reactors
BT1 htgr type reactors
BT2 gas cooled reactors
BT3 reactors
BT2 graphite moderated reactors
BT3 reactors
BT1 pebble bed reactors
BT2 solid homogeneous reactors
BT3 homogeneous reactors
BT4 reactors
BT1 power reactors
BT2 reactors
BT1 thermal reactors
BT2 reactors

vhf
USE mhz range

vhf radiation
USE mhz range
AND radiowave radiation

VHTR REACTOR [349; 349] *Jan 78*
  UF   *exp multipurp high temp gas cr*
  UF   *multipurpose vhtr reactor*
  BT1   enriched uranium reactors
  BT2   reactors
  BT1   experimental reactors
  BT2   research and test reactors
  BT3   reactors
  BT1   helium cooled reactors
  BT2   gas cooled reactors
  BT3   reactors
  BT1   htgr type reactors
  BT2   gas cooled reactors
  BT3   reactors
  BT1   graphite moderated reactors
  BT3   reactors
  BT1   power reactors
  BT2   reactors
  BT1   thermal reactors
  BT2   reactors
  RT   very high temperature

VIABILITY [389; 389]
  RT   biological regeneration
  RT   growth
  RT   life cycle
  RT   reproduction

VIBRATING SAMPLE MAGNETOMETERS [45; 45]
  BT1   magnetometers
  BT2   measuring instruments

vibration modes
  USE   oscillation modes

vibrational band
  USE   vibrational states

VIBRATIONAL STATES [8,688; 8,688]
  UF   *collective states (vibrational*
  UF   *vibrational band*
  BT1   excited states
  BT2   energy levels
  RT   infrared spectra
  RT   lattice vibrations
  RT   rotation-vibration model
  RT   rydberg-klein-rees method

vibrations (lattice)
  USE   lattice vibrations

vibrations (mechanical)
  USE   mechanical vibrations

VICIA [262; 262]
  UF   *vetch*
  BT1   leguminosae
  BT2   plants

VICKERS HARDNESS [448; 448]
  RT   hardness

VICKSI ACCELERATOR [89; 89] *Feb 76*
  (Van de Graaff Isochronous Cyclotron Kombination fuer Schwere Ionen at Hahn-Meitner-Institut, Berlin.)
  UF   *hahn-meitner vicksi accelerato*
  BT1   heavy ion accelerators
  BT2   accelerators
  RT   isochronous cyclotrons
  RT   van de graaff accelerators

VICTIMS COMPENSATION [182; 182] *Dec 76*
  (For victims not covered by workmens compensation.)
  RT   accidents
  RT   exceptional natural disaster
  RT   financial security
  RT   insurance
  RT   liabilities
  RT   workmens compensation

VICTORIA [42; 42]
  BT1   australia
  BT2   australasia
  BT2   developed countries

VIDAL-1 REACTOR [2; 2] *Feb 76*
  BT1   enriched uranium reactors
  BT2   reactors
  BT1   helium cooled reactors
  BT2   gas cooled reactors
  BT3   reactors
  BT1   htgr type reactors
  BT2   gas cooled reactors
  BT3   reactors
  BT2   graphite moderated reactors
  BT3   reactors
  BT1   power reactors
  BT2   reactors
  BT1   thermal reactors
  BT2   reactors

VIDAL-2 REACTOR [2; 2] *Feb 76*
  BT1   enriched uranium reactors
  BT2   reactors
  BT1   helium cooled reactors
  BT2   gas cooled reactors
  BT3   reactors
  BT1   htgr type reactors
  BT2   gas cooled reactors
  BT3   reactors
  BT2   graphite moderated reactors
  BT3   reactors
  BT1   power reactors
  BT2   reactors
  BT1   thermal reactors
  BT2   reactors

VIDEO TAPES [143; 143] *Mar 85*
  BT1   magnetic tapes
  BT2   magnetic storage devices
  BT3   memory devices
  RT   digitizers
  RT   image processing
  RT   images
  RT   remote viewing equipment
  RT   television

VIDICONS [186; 186]
  BT1   camera tubes
  BT2   image tubes

vienna conv. civil liability
  USE   vcoclnd

vienna triga-mk-2 reactor
  USE   triga-2-vienna reactor

VIET NAM [28; 28]
  BT1   asia
  BT1   developing countries
  RT   centrally planned economies

vietnamese triga-mk-2 reactor
  USE   triga-2-dalat reactor

vikalloy 1
  USE   alloy-co52fe35v10

vikalloy 2
  USE   alloy-co52fe35v13

VIKING SPACE PROBES [94; 94] *Jun 77*
  BT1   space vehicles

villigen cyclotron
  USE   sin cyclotron

VINBLASTINE [105; 105]
  BT1   alkaloids
  BT2   organic compounds
  BT1   antimitotic drugs
  BT2   drugs
  BT1   indoles
  BT2   pyrroles
  BT3   azoles
  BT4   heterocyclic compounds
  BT5   organic compounds
  BT4   organic nitrogen compounds
  BT5   organic compounds
  RT   leukemia

vinca r-a reactor yugoslavia
  USE   r-a reactor

vinca r-b reactor yugoslavia
  USE   r-b reactor

vincristine sulphate
  USE   oncovin

vinoflex
  USE   polyvinyls

VINT TORSATRON [18; 18] *Jan 77*
  BT1   torsatron stellarators
  BT2   stellarators
  BT3   closed plasma devices
  BT4   thermonuclear devices

vinyl acetate
  USE   polyvinyls

vinyl cyanide
  USE   acrylonitrile

VINYL MONOMERS [563; 563]
  BT1   monomers
  RT   acrolein
  RT   acrylamide
  RT   acrylates
  RT   acrylic acid
  RT   acrylic acid esters
  RT   acrylonitrile
  RT   methacrylates
  RT   methacrylic acid
  RT   methacrylic acid esters
  RT   styrene

VINYL RADICALS [84; 84]
  BT1   alkyl radicals
  BT2   radicals

vinylbenzene
  USE   styrene

VINYLIDENE RADICALS [23; 23]
  BT1   radicals

VIOLANTHRONE [1; 1]
  BT1   condensed aromatics
  BT2   aromatics
  BT3   organic compounds
  BT1   hydrocarbons
  BT2   organic compounds
  BT1   ketones
  BT2   organic compounds
  RT   dyes

VIPER REACTOR [22; 22]
(UK Ministry of Defence, Berkshire, United Kingdom)
- UF   *versat. interm. puls. exp. re.*
- BT1   enriched uranium reactors
  - BT2   reactors
- BT1   fast reactors
  - BT2   epithermal reactors
    - BT3   reactors
- BT1   organic moderated reactors
  - BT2   reactors
- BT1   pulsed reactors
  - BT2   reactors
- BT1   research reactors
  - BT2   research and test reactors
    - BT3   reactors
- BT1   test reactors
  - BT2   research and test reactors
    - BT3   reactors
  - BT2   test facilities

VIRAL DISEASES [241; 625] *Dec 82*
- UF   *rinderpest*
- UF+   *hepatitis (infectious)*
- BT1   infectious diseases
  - BT2   diseases
- NT1   aids
- NT1   herpes simplex
- NT1   herpes zoster
- NT1   influenza
- NT1   measles
- NT1   newcastle disease
- NT1   poliomyelitis
- NT1   rabies
- RT   cell transformations
- RT   viruses

virgil c summer-1 reactor
- USE   summer-1 reactor

VIRGINIA [199; 199]
- BT1   usa
  - BT2   developed countries
  - BT2   north america
- RT   james river

virginia poly. inst. train. r.
- USE   vpi-utr-10 reactor

virginia univ. reactor
- USE   uvar reactor

VIRIAL EQUATION [193; 193]
(In thermodynamics only.)
- RT   equations of state
- RT   gases
- RT   thermodynamics
- RT   van der waals forces

VIRIAL THEOREM [388; 388]
(In mechanics only.)
- RT   kinetic energy
- RT   mechanics
- RT   particles
- RT   statistics

virtual mass effect
- USE   hydrodynamic mass effect

VIRTUAL PARTICLES [915; 915]
- BT1   elementary particles
- RT   deep inelastic scattering

VIRTUAL STATES [284; 284]
- BT1   energy levels

VIRULENCE [50; 50]
- RT   infectious diseases
- RT   microorganisms

VIRUSES [1,366; 3,339]
- BT1   microorganisms
- BT1   parasites
- NT1   aids virus
- NT1   bacteriophages
- NT1   influenza viruses
- NT1   measles virus
- NT1   oncogenic viruses
  - NT2   adenovirus
  - NT2   leukemia viruses
  - NT2   polyoma virus
- NT1   polio virus
- NT1   simian virus
- NT1   tobacco mosaic virus
- NT1   vaccinia virus
- RT   herpes simplex
- RT   herpes zoster
- RT   inoculation
- RT   interferon
- RT   mutagens
- RT   newcastle disease
- RT   particles
- RT   plaque formation
- RT   rabies
- RT   vaccines
- RT   viral diseases

VISCOSE [15; 15]
- BT1   polysaccharides
  - BT2   saccharides
    - BT3   carbohydrates
      - BT4   organic compounds
- BT1   xanthates
  - BT2   organic sulfur compounds
    - BT3   organic compounds

VISCOSIMETERS [60; 60]
- BT1   measuring instruments

§ **VISCOSITY** [4,051; 4,051]
- RT   fluid flow
- RT   internal friction
- RT   rheology
- RT   superfluidity
- RT   viscous flow

VISCOUS FLOW [770; 845]
- BT1   fluid flow
- NT1   couette flow
- RT   laminar flow
- RT   navier-stokes equations
- RT   prandtl number
- RT   reynolds number
- RT   stokes law
- RT   turbulent flow
- RT   viscosity

VISIBILITY [56; 56] *May 86*
- RT   images
- RT   luminosity
- RT   opacity
- RT   optical properties
- RT   pattern recognition
- RT   smokes
- RT   visible radiation

VISIBLE RADIATION [9,496; 9,496]
- UF   *light*
- UF+   *photomagnetic effect*
- BT1   electromagnetic radiation
  - BT2   radiations
- RT   fresnel coefficient
- RT   kerr effect
- RT   laser radiation
- RT   light sources
- RT   lighting systems
- RT   monochromatic radiation
- RT   opacity
- RT   photon beams
- RT   photoreactivation
- RT   raman effect
- RT   schlieren method
- RT   visibility
- RT   visible spectra
- RT   voigt effect

VISIBLE SPECTRA [3,256; 3,256] *Jul 76*
- BT1   spectra
- RT   visible radiation

VISION [248; 248]
- RT   eyes

visual purple
- USE   rhodopsin

VITAMIN A [248; 248]
- UF   *axerophtol*
- BT1   vitamins
- RT   carotenoids

VITAMIN B GROUP [36; 953]
- BT1   vitamins
- NT1   biotin
- NT1   carnitine
- NT1   folic acid
- NT1   nicotinamide
- NT1   nicotinic acid
- NT1   pantothenic acid
- NT1   pyridoxine
- NT1   riboflavin
- NT1   thiamine
- NT1   vitamin b-12
- RT   adenines
- RT   citrovorum factor
- RT   coenzymes
- RT   lipotropic factors
- RT   paba
- RT   pyridoxal

vitamin b-t
- USE   carnitine

vitamin b-1
- USE   thiamine

VITAMIN B-12 [269; 269]
- UF   *cyanocobalamin*
- BT1   blood coagulation factors
  - BT2   coagulants
    - BT3   hematologic agents
      - BT4   drugs
- BT1   vitamin b group
  - BT2   vitamins
- RT   anemias
- RT   intrinsic factor

vitamin b-2
- USE   riboflavin

vitamin b-5
- USE   pantothenic acid

vitamin b-6
- USE   pyridoxine

vitamin c
- USE   ascorbic acid

VITAMIN D [181; 302]
- BT1   vitamins
- NT1   cholecalciferol
- NT1   ergocalciferol
- RT   rickets

vitamin d-2
- USE   ergocalciferol

vitamin d-3
- USE   cholecalciferol

VITAMIN E [168; 168]
UF *tocopherols*
BT1 vitamins

vitamin h
USE biotin

vitamin h-1
USE paba

VITAMIN K [44; 44]
BT1 blood coagulation factors
BT2 coagulants
BT3 hematologic agents
BT4 drugs
BT1 quinones
BT2 aromatics
BT3 organic compounds
BT2 organic oxygen compounds
BT3 organic compounds
BT1 vitamins
RT anticoagulants
RT ubiquinone

vitamin p
USE bioflavonoids

vitamin pp
USE nicotinamide

VITAMINS [148; 2,323]
NT1 ascorbic acid
NT1 bioflavonoids
NT1 vitamin a
NT1 vitamin b group
NT2 biotin
NT2 carnitine
NT2 folic acid
NT2 nicotinamide
NT2 nicotinic acid
NT2 pantothenic acid
NT2 pyridoxine
NT2 riboflavin
NT2 thiamine
NT2 vitamin b-12
NT1 vitamin d
NT2 cholecalciferol
NT2 ergocalciferol
NT1 vitamin e
NT1 vitamin k
RT biochemistry
RT carotenoids
RT diet
RT drugs
RT food
RT metabolism

VITON [12; 12]
BT1 rubbers
BT2 elastomers
BT3 polymers
BT2 organic polymers
BT3 organic compounds
BT3 polymers

VITRIFICATION [2,617; 2,617]
SF *immobilization (wastes)*
RT ceramic melters
RT glass
RT metallic glasses
RT pamela plant
RT radioactive waste processing
RT solidification

VIVITRON TANDEM ACCELERATOR
[5; 5] *Dec 90*
(Nuclear Research Center, Strasbourg, France.)
BT1 tandem electrostatic accelerat
BT2 electrostatic accelerators

BT3 accelerators
BT1 van de graaff accelerators
BT2 electrostatic accelerators
BT3 accelerators

VK-50 REACTOR [65; 65]
(Dimitrovgrad, USSR)
UF *ulyanovsk reactor vk-50*
BT1 bwr type reactors
BT2 enriched uranium reactors
BT3 reactors
BT2 power reactors
BT3 reactors
BT2 thermal reactors
BT3 reactors
BT2 water cooled reactors
BT3 reactors
BT2 water moderated reactors
BT3 reactors

vlasov equation
USE boltzmann-vlasov equation

vlasov instability
USE boltzmann-vlasov equation

vlb systems
USE interferometers

VMI MODEL [139; 139]
UF *variable moment of inertia mod*
BT1 nuclear models
BT2 mathematical models
RT backbending
RT moment of inertia

vocabulary (controlled)
USE standardized terminology

VOGTLE-1 REACTOR [51; 51]
(Waynesboro, Georgia, USA)
BT1 pwr type reactors
BT2 enriched uranium reactors
BT3 reactors
BT2 power reactors
BT3 reactors
BT2 thermal reactors
BT3 reactors
BT2 water cooled reactors
BT3 reactors
BT2 water moderated reactors
BT3 reactors

VOGTLE-2 REACTOR [40; 40]
(Waynesboro, Georgia, USA)
BT1 pwr type reactors
BT2 enriched uranium reactors
BT3 reactors
BT2 power reactors
BT3 reactors
BT2 thermal reactors
BT3 reactors
BT2 water cooled reactors
BT3 reactors
BT2 water moderated reactors
BT3 reactors

VOGTLE-3 REACTOR [23; 23]
(Waynesboro, Georgia, USA)
BT1 pwr type reactors
BT2 enriched uranium reactors
BT3 reactors
BT2 power reactors
BT3 reactors
BT2 thermal reactors
BT3 reactors
BT2 water cooled reactors
BT3 reactors
BT2 water moderated reactors
BT3 reactors

VOGTLE-4 REACTOR [23; 23]
(Waynesboro, Georgia, USA)
BT1 pwr type reactors
BT2 enriched uranium reactors
BT3 reactors
BT2 power reactors
BT3 reactors
BT2 thermal reactors
BT3 reactors
BT2 water cooled reactors
BT3 reactors
BT2 water moderated reactors
BT3 reactors

VOID COEFFICIENT [645; 645]
BT1 reactivity coefficients

VOID FRACTION [1,556; 1,556]
RT liquids
RT vapors

VOIDS [3,507; 3,507]
RT boiling detection
RT bubbles
RT cavities
RT defects
RT water influx

VOIGT EFFECT [59; 59]
UF *cotton-mouton effect*
BT1 magneto-optical effects
RT plasma
RT polarization
RT visible radiation

VOLATILE MATTER [182; 182] *May 86*
(Materials capable of being readily evaporated.)
BT1 matter
RT pyrolysis products
RT volatility

VOLATILITY [830; 830]
RT chloride volatility process
RT distillation
RT fluoride volatility process
RT pyrolysis products
RT volatile matter

volatilization
USE evaporation

VOLCANIC REGIONS [190; 190]
RT volcanoes

volcanic rocks
USE igneous rocks

VOLCANOES [752; 752]
UF+ *calderas*
RT earth crust
RT geology
RT geothermal energy
RT lava
RT tuff
RT volcanic regions

VOLES [51; 51]
BT1 rodents
BT2 mammals
BT3 vertebrates
BT4 animals

VOLGA RIVER [5; 5]
BT1 rivers
BT2 surface waters

VOLOXIDATION PROCESS [50; 50]
(Separation process designed to remove volatile fission products from spent LMFBR fuels.)
BT1 head end processes

volt-ampere characteristic
USE electric conductivity

voltage
USE electric potential

VOLTAGE REGULATORS [259; 259]
UF *regulators (voltage)*
RT electric controllers
RT surges

voltaic cells
USE electric batteries

VOLTAMETRY [1,107; 1,107]
UF *coulometry*
RT currents
RT electrolysis
RT electrolytic cells
RT electromotive force
RT quantitative chemical analysis

volterra equations
USE volterra integral equations

VOLTERRA INTEGRAL EQUATIONS [115; 115]
UF *volterra equations*
BT1 integral equations
BT2 equations

VOLTMETERS [118; 118]
BT1 electric measuring instruments
BT2 electrical equipment
BT3 equipment
BT2 measuring instruments

§ VOLUME [3,540; 3,540]
RT dimensions
RT size

VOLUMETRIC ANALYSIS [72; 72] *Mar 83*
BT1 quantitative chemical analysis
BT2 chemical analysis

VOMITING [169; 169]
BT1 symptoms
RT digestive system diseases
RT stomach

VORONEZH AST-500 REACTOR [2; 2] *Jan 90*
(Voronezh, USSR.)
BT1 thermal reactors
BT2 reactors
BT1 water cooled reactors
BT2 reactors
BT1 water moderated reactors
BT2 reactors

VORTEX FLOW [847; 847]
UF *swirl flow*
BT1 fluid flow
RT superfluidity

VORTICES [1,685; 1,685]
RT turbulence

vortices (magnetic)
USE magnetic flux

VOYAGER SPACE PROBES [454; 454] *Apr 78*
BT1 space vehicles

vpi and su training reactor
USE vpi-utr-10 reactor

VPI-UTR-10 REACTOR [2; 2]
(Blacksburg, Virginia, USA.)
UF *virginia poly. inst. train. r.*
UF *vpi and su training reactor*
BT1 argonaut type reactors
BT2 enriched uranium reactors
BT3 reactors
BT2 research and test reactors
BT3 reactors
BT2 water cooled reactors
BT3 reactors
BT2 water moderated reactors
BT3 reactors
BT1 research reactors
BT2 research and test reactors
BT3 reactors
BT1 thermal reactors
BT2 reactors
BT1 training reactors
BT2 research and test reactors
BT3 reactors

VR-1 REACTOR [5; 5] *Aug 86*
(Czech Technical University, Faculty of Nuclear Science and Technical Engineering, Prague.)
BT1 enriched uranium reactors
BT2 reactors
BT1 pool type reactors
BT2 water cooled reactors
BT3 reactors
BT2 water moderated reactors
BT3 reactors
BT1 thermal reactors
BT2 reactors
BT1 training reactors
BT2 research and test reactors
BT3 reactors

VRAIN REACTOR [391; 391]
UF *fort st. vrain reactor*
BT1 enriched uranium reactors
BT2 reactors
BT1 htgr type reactors
BT2 gas cooled reactors
BT3 reactors
BT2 graphite moderated reactors
BT3 reactors
BT1 power reactors
BT2 reactors

vulcain exp. nucl. study
USE venus reactor

vulcain/belgian-3 reactor
USE br-3-vn reactor

VULCANIZATION [152; 152]
RT curing
RT rubbers
RT vulcanized elastomers

VULCANIZED ELASTOMERS [35; 40]
BT1 elastomers
BT2 polymers
NT1 ebonite
RT vulcanization

VYCOR [70; 70]
RT glass

w boson
USE intermediate bosons

W CODES [603; 603]
BT1 computer codes

W MINUS BOSONS [867; 867] *Mar 86*
BT1 intermediate vector bosons
BT2 intermediate bosons
BT3 bosons
BT3 elementary particles

W PLUS BOSONS [878; 878] *Mar 86*
BT1 intermediate vector bosons
BT2 intermediate bosons
BT3 bosons
BT3 elementary particles

w stellarators
SEE wendelstein-2b stellarator
OR wendelstein-7 stellarator

w. b. mc guire-1 reactor
USE mc guire-1 reactor

w. b. mc guire-2 reactor
USE mc guire-2 reactor

WACKERSDORF REPROCESSING PLANT [105; 105] *Feb 88*
(Wiederaufarbeitungsanlage Wackersdorf, Federal Republic of Germany.)
UF *waw*
UF *wiederaufarbeitungsanlage wack*
BT1 fuel reprocessing plants
BT2 nuclear facilities
RT reprocessing
RT spent fuel elements
RT spent fuels

wageningen barn reactor
USE barn reactor

WAGON WHEEL EVENT [43; 43]
BT1 contained explosions
BT2 underground explosions
BT3 explosions
BT1 nuclear explosions
BT2 explosions
BT1 plowshare project
RT natural gas

WAGR REACTOR [160; 160]
UF *agr reactor (windscale)*
UF *windscale adv. gas-cooled re.*
BT1 agr type reactors
BT2 enriched uranium reactors
BT3 reactors
BT2 gas cooled reactors
BT3 reactors
BT2 graphite moderated reactors
BT3 reactors
BT1 carbon dioxide cooled reactor
BT2 gas cooled reactors
BT3 reactors
BT1 power reactors
BT2 reactors
BT1 thermal reactors
BT2 reactors

WAK [234; 234]
(Wiederaufarbeitungsanlage Karlsruhe)
UF *karlsruhe reprocessing plant*
UF *wiederaufarbeitungsanlage ka*
BT1 fuel reprocessing plants
BT2 nuclear facilities
BT1 german fr organizations
BT2 national organizations
RT reprocessing
RT spent fuel elements
RT spent fuels

WAKEFIELD ACCELERATORS [199; 199] *Apr 87*
BT1 linear accelerators
BT2 accelerators
RT acceleration
RT plasma waves

WALECKA MODEL [94; 94] *Oct 84*
(A mean-field theory of nuclear matter with scalar and vector fields as carrier of nuclear forces.)
BT1 nuclear models
BT2 mathematical models

RT   nuclear matter

walker carcinoma
   USE   experimental neoplasms

wall effect
(Prior to January 1983 this was a valid descriptor for the contribution to ionization in an ionization chamber by electrons liberated from the chamber walls.)
   USE   wall effects

WALL EFFECTS [1,078; 1,078]
   UF   *plasma-wall interactions*
   UF   *wall effect*
   RT   end effects
   RT   ionization
   RT   ionization chambers
   RT   microdosimetry
   RT   plasma
   RT   plasma impurities
   RT   proportional counters
   RT   wall-less counters

WALL LOADING [818; 818] *Aug 75*
(Surface power density at thermonuclear reactor walls.)
   BT1   power density
   RT   first wall

WALL-LESS COUNTERS [53; 53]
   BT1   radiation detectors
   BT2   measuring instruments
   RT   ionization chambers
   RT   proportional counters
   RT   wall effects

walter reed res. reactor l-54
   USE   wrrr reactor

WANO [6; 6] *May 90*
   UF   *world assoc nuclear operators*
   BT1   international organizations
   RT   nuclear operators

WARD IDENTITY [1,496; 1,496]
   RT   gauge invariance
   RT   quantum electrodynamics

warning systems
   USE   alarm systems

WARSAW CYCLOTRON [3; 3] *Jul 82*
   BT1   heavy ion accelerators
   BT2   accelerators
   BT1   isochronous cyclotrons
   BT2   cyclotrons
   BT3   cyclic accelerators
   BT4   accelerators

WASATCH FORMATION [4; 4] *Apr 84*
   BT1   geologic formations
   RT   coal
   RT   colorado
   RT   natural gas
   RT   oil shales
   RT   uranium deposits
   RT   uranium ores
   RT   wyoming

washers (fuel)
   USE   fuel washers

WASHINGTON [599; 599]
   BT1   usa
   BT2   developed countries
   BT2   north america
   RT   columbia river
   RT   columbia river basin
   RT   hanford engineering developmen
   RT   hanford reservation

RT   sequim bay

WASHINGTON DC [26; 26]
   UF   *district of columbia*
   BT1   usa
   BT2   developed countries
   BT2   north america

washington pub power sup sys-1
   USE   wnp-1 reactor

washington pub power sup sys-2
   USE   wnp-2 reactor

washington pub power sup sys-3
   USE   wnp-3 reactor

washington pub power sup sys-4
   USE   wnp-4 reactor

washington pub power sup sys-5
   USE   wnp-5 reactor

washington state univ. reactor
   USE   wsur reactor

washington univ. (seattle) rea
   USE   uwtr reactor

WASHOUT [536; 536]
   UF   *rainout*
   UF   *scavenging (atmospheric)*
   BT1   fallout
   RT   atmospheric precipitations
   RT   decontamination
   RT   droplets
   RT   precipitation scavenging
   RT   radioactive clouds
   RT   rain
   RT   sprays
   RT   water

waspaloy
   USE   alloy-ni58cr20co14mo4ti3

WASPS [8; 15]
   BT1   insects
   BT2   arthropods
   BT3   invertebrates
   BT4   animals
   NT1   habrobracon

waste burial
   SEE   ground disposal
   OR   underground disposal

waste chemicals
   USE   chemical wastes

WASTE DISPOSAL [1,447; 26,456]
(For final disposal of wastes, with no intention of retrieval.)
   UF   *discharges (wastes)*
   UF   *disposal (wastes)*
   UF   *ultimate storage*
   UF+   *sewage disposal*
   BT1   waste management
   BT2   management
   NT1   ground disposal
   NT1   ground release
   NT1   marine disposal
   NT1   nonradioactive waste disposal
   NT1   radioactive waste disposal
   NT1   stack disposal
   NT1   underground disposal
   RT   global aspects

RT   hydraulic fracturing
RT   liquid wastes
RT   radioactive wastes
RT   salt vault project
RT   solid wastes
RT   waste processing
RT   waste storage
RT   wastes

WASTE FORMS [1,410; 1,410] *Nov 85*
(Physical and chemical forms of wastes (e.g. liquid, in concrete, in glass) without packaging.)
   BT1   wastes
   RT   radioactive wastes
   RT   waste management

WASTE HEAT [1,155; 1,155]
   BT1   energy sources
   BT1   wastes
   RT   cogeneration
   RT   district heating
   RT   energy recovery
   RT   heat recovery
   RT   heat sinks
   RT   plumes
   RT   thermal effluents
   RT   thermal pollution
   RT   waste heat utilization
   RT   waste product utilization

WASTE HEAT UTILIZATION [50; 50] *Dec 82*
   BT1   waste product utilization
   RT   heat recovery
   RT   waste heat

waste isolation pilot plant
   USE   wipp

WASTE MANAGEMENT [7,182; 44,760]
   UF   *handling (wastes)*
   BT1   management
   NT1   nonradioactive waste managemen
   NT2   nonradioactive waste disposal
   NT2   nonradioactive wastes
   NT3   chemical wastes
   NT4   chemical effluents
   NT1   radioactive waste management
   NT1   waste disposal
   NT2   ground disposal
   NT2   ground release
   NT2   marine disposal
   NT2   nonradioactive waste disposal
   NT2   radioactive waste disposal
   NT2   stack disposal
   NT2   underground disposal
   NT1   waste processing
   NT2   radioactive waste processing
   NT1   waste retrieval
   NT1   waste storage
   NT2   radioactive waste storage
   NT1   waste transportation
   RT   hazardous materials
   RT   radioactive wastes
   RT   vaalputs radioactive waste dis
   RT   waste forms
   RT   waste product utilization

WASTE PELLETS [26; 26] *Mar 81*
   BT1   solid wastes
   BT2   wastes
   RT   pelletizing
   RT   radioactive wastes

WASTE PROCESSING [1,865; 13,525]
   UF   *processing (wastes)*
   UF   *waste treatment*
   UF+   *sewage treatment*
   BT1   waste management
   BT2   management
   NT1   radioactive waste processing
   RT   anaerobic digestion
   RT   bitumens
   RT   calcination
   RT   evaporation
   RT   flotation

RT	freezing out	NT1	gaseous wastes	RT	water cooled reactors
RT	liquid wastes	NT2	exhaust gases		
RT	precipitation	NT2	flue gas	**water content**	
RT	radioactive wastes	NT1	industrial wastes	USE	humidity
RT	recycling	NT1	liquid wastes		
RT	regeneration	NT2	waste water		
RT	scrap	NT1	municipal wastes	**water coolant**	
RT	scrubbers	NT1	nonradioactive wastes	USE	water
RT	settling ponds	NT2	chemical wastes		
RT	shredders	NT3	chemical effluents		
RT	solidification	NT1	radioactive wastes	**water cooled graphite mod. rea**	
RT	waste disposal	NT2	alpha-bearing wastes	USE	lwgr type reactors
RT	wet ashing	NT2	calcined wastes		

WASTE PRODUCT UTILIZATION
[284; 332] *Dec 81*
(Use of waste products as raw material, either directly or after processing, e.g. sewage sludge for fertilizer, or radioactive waste as a source of radiation.)

		NT2	high-level radioactive wastes	**WATER COOLED REACTORS**	
		NT2	intermediate-level radioactive	[4,182; 77,157]	
		NT2	low-level radioactive wastes	UF	*water-cooled reactors*
		NT2	radioactive effluents	BT1	reactors
		NT1	solid wastes	NT1	acpr reactor
		NT2	ashes	NT1	anna reactor
		NT3	fly ash	*NT1	aqueous homogeneous reactors
		NT2	scrap	*NT1	argonaut type reactors
		NT2	tailings	NT1	atr reactor
NT1	waste heat utilization	NT3	mill tailings	NT1	borax-1 reactor
RT	cogeneration	NT2	waste pellets	NT1	borax-2 reactor
RT	energy recovery	NT1	waste forms	NT1	borax-3 reactor
RT	heat recovery	NT1	waste heat	NT1	borax-4 reactor
RT	waste heat	RT	by-products	NT1	br-02 reactor
RT	waste management	RT	hazardous materials	NT1	br-2 reactor
		RT	pollution	NT1	br-3-vn reactor
WASTE RETRIEVAL [180; 180] *Aug 81*		RT	pollution abatement	*NT1	bwr type reactors
BT1	waste management	RT	recycling	NT1	cirus reactor
BT2	management	RT	residues	NT1	esada-vesr reactor
RT	materials handling	RT	storage facilities	NT1	etr reactor
RT	radioactive waste facilities	RT	waste disposal	NT1	ewa reactor
RT	radioactive wastes			NT1	getr reactor
		WATER [20,807; 41,471]		NT1	hclwr type reactors
waste solutions		UF	*hydrogen hydroxides*	NT1	hfetr reactor
USE	liquid wastes	UF	*oxygen hydrides*	NT1	hfir reactor
		UF	*water coolant*	NT1	hfr reactor
WASTE STORAGE [519; 6,399]		UF	*water moderator*	*NT1	hwlwr type reactors
(For temporary storage of wastes.)		UF+	*water resources*	NT1	iowa utr-10 reactor
UF	*interim storage*	BT1	hydrogen compounds	NT1	janus reactor
UF	*intermediate storage*	BT1	oxygen compounds	NT1	jmtr reactor
BT1	storage	NT1	drinking water	NT1	kamini reactor
BT1	waste management	NT1	feedwater	NT1	koeberg-1 reactor
BT2	management	NT1	fresh water	NT1	koeberg-2 reactor
NT1	radioactive waste storage	NT1	ground water	NT1	kuhfr reactor
RT	underground storage	NT1	heavy water	NT1	litr reactor
RT	waste disposal	NT1	rain water	NT1	lr-0 reactor
		NT1	seawater	NT1	lwbr type reactors
WASTE TRANSPORTATION		NT1	waste water	*NT1	lwgr type reactors
[1,323; 1,323]		RT	anhydrides	NT1	maple reactor
BT1	waste management	RT	aqueous solutions	NT1	mir reactor
BT2	management	RT	atmospheric precipitations	NT1	mrr reactor
RT	away-from-reactor storage	RT	balneology	NT1	mtr reactor
RT	routing	RT	clouds	NT1	murr reactor
RT	transport	RT	coolants	NT1	nsrr reactor
		RT	cooling	NT1	ntr reactor
waste treatment		RT	demineralizers	NT1	orphee reactor
USE	waste processing	RT	electromagnetic filters	NT1	orr reactor
		RT	environmental materials	NT1	osiris reactor
WASTE WATER [732; 732] *Dec 82*		RT	glaciers	NT1	owr reactor
BT1	liquid wastes	RT	hydronium radicals	NT1	pbr reactor
BT2	wastes	RT	hydrosphere	NT1	pegase reactor
BT1	water	RT	ice	NT1	peggy reactor
BT2	hydrogen compounds	RT	intake structures	NT1	perryman-1 reactor
BT2	oxygen compounds	RT	liquid wastes	NT1	perryman-2 reactor
RT	drainage	RT	moderators	*NT1	pool type reactors
RT	water pollution	RT	recombiners	*NT1	pwr type reactors
		RT	steam	NT1	r-2 reactor
WASTE-ROCK INTERACTIONS		RT	surface waters	NT1	ra-5 reactor
[399; 399] *Oct 81*		RT	washout	NT1	rg-1m reactor
RT	backfilling	RT	water influx	NT1	safari-1 reactor
RT	chemical reactions	RT	water requirements	NT1	sca reactor
RT	radioactive waste disposal			NT1	sghwr reactor
RT	rock-fluid interactions	**WATER CHEMISTRY** [2,391; 2,391]		NT1	sm-2 reactor
RT	rocks	*Sep 75*		NT1	spert-2 reactor
RT	salt caverns	(For the chemical treatment of water. For		NT1	spert-3 reactor
		the chemical properties of water, use		NT1	sr-oa reactor
WASTES [299; 49,255]		WATER and CHEMICAL PROPERTIES.)		NT1	sr-1 reactor
NT1	aerosol wastes	UF	*cooling water chem. treatment*	NT1	sr-3p reactor
NT2	fly ash	BT1	water treatment	NT1	tca reactor
NT1	biological wastes	RT	chemical analysis	*NT1	triga type reactors
NT2	feces	RT	chemical composition	NT1	tsr-2 reactor
NT2	sewage sludge	RT	coolants	NT1	venus reactor
NT2	sweat	RT	corrosion denting	NT1	voronezh ast-500 reactor
NT2	urine	RT	demineralization	NT1	wntr reactor
		RT	feedwater	NT1	wtr reactor
		RT	reactor cooling systems		

*NT1	wwr type reactors		NT1	hfr reactor		→	**WATER QUALITY** [4; 4] *May 76*
NT1	zlfr reactor		NT1	janus reactor		BT1	environmental quality
NT1	zr-6 reactor		NT1	jmtr reactor		RT	water pollution
RT	steam cooled reactors		NT1	juno reactor			
RT	water chemistry		NT1	kamini reactor		→	**WATER REMOVAL** [0; 0] *Apr 84*

WATER CURRENTS [127; 127] *Nov 81*
(Net transport of water along a definable path.)
- BT1 currents
- RT advection
- RT surface waters
- RT tidal power
- RT tide

water demand
- USE water requirements

water distribution
- USE water supply

WATER HAMMER [256; 256]
- RT hydraulics
- RT impact shock
- RT shock waves

water infiltration
- USE water influx

WATER INFLUX [282; 282] *Oct 85*
(Entrance of water or aqueous solutions into geologic formations, underground spaces, etc.)
- UF infiltration (rock)
- UF infiltration (water)
- UF influx (water)
- UF intrusion (water)
- UF water infiltration
- UF water intrusion
- RT aqueous solutions
- RT aquifers
- RT cavities
- RT coal seams
- RT geologic structures
- RT ground water
- RT hydrology
- RT mines
- RT voids
- RT water
- RT wells

water intrusion
- USE water influx

water moderated organic cooled
- USE lwor type reactors

WATER MODERATED REACTORS [840; 69,208]
- UF water-moderated reactors
- BT1 reactors
- NT1 acpr reactor
- NT1 anna reactor
- *NT1 aqueous homogeneous reactors
- *NT1 argonaut type reactors
- NT1 atr reactor
- NT1 borax-1 reactor
- NT1 borax-2 reactor
- NT1 borax-3 reactor
- NT1 borax-4 reactor
- NT1 br-02 reactor
- NT1 br-2 reactor
- NT1 br-3-vn reactor
- *NT1 bwr type reactors
- NT1 esada-vesr reactor
- NT1 etr reactor
- NT1 ewa reactor
- NT1 getr reactor
- NT1 hclwr type reactors
- NT1 hfetr reactor
- NT1 hfir reactor

- NT1 hfr reactor
- NT1 janus reactor
- NT1 jmtr reactor
- NT1 juno reactor
- NT1 kamini reactor
- NT1 koeberg-1 reactor
- NT1 koeberg-2 reactor
- NT1 kuca reactor
- NT1 kuhfr reactor
- NT1 litr reactor
- NT1 lr-0 reactor
- NT1 lwbr type reactors
- NT1 lwor type reactors
- NT1 maple reactor
- NT1 mir reactor
- NT1 mrr reactor
- NT1 mtr reactor
- NT1 murr reactor
- NT1 nsrr reactor
- NT1 ntr reactor
- NT1 nuclear furnace reactor
- NT1 orr reactor
- NT1 osiris reactor
- NT1 owr reactor
- NT1 pbr reactor
- NT1 pegase reactor
- NT1 peggy reactor
- NT1 perryman-1 reactor
- NT1 perryman-2 reactor
- *NT1 pool type reactors
- *NT1 pwr type reactors
- NT1 r-2 reactor
- NT1 ra-5 reactor
- NT1 rake-2 reactor
- NT1 rg-1m reactor
- NT1 safari-1 reactor
- NT1 sca reactor
- NT1 sm-2 reactor
- NT1 spert-1 reactor
- NT1 spert-2 reactor
- NT1 spert-3 reactor
- NT1 sr-oa reactor
- NT1 sr-1 reactor
- NT1 tca reactor
- *NT1 triga type reactors
- NT1 tsr-2 reactor
- NT1 venus reactor
- NT1 voronezh ast-500 reactor
- NT1 wntr reactor
- NT1 wtr reactor
- *NT1 wwr type reactors
- NT1 zlfr reactor

water moderator
- USE water

WATER POLLUTION [2,843; 2,843]
(For nonradioactive pollution only; for radioactive pollution use CONTAMINATION.)
- UF+ thermal pollution (water)
- UF+ water pollution abatement
- BT1 pollution
- RT dissolved gases
- RT environmental effects
- RT eutrophication
- RT fouling
- RT plumes
- RT waste water
- RT water pollution control
- RT water quality
- RT water use

water pollution abatement
- USE pollution abatement
- AND water pollution

→ **WATER POLLUTION CONTROL** [0; 0] *Apr 86*
(The removal or management of pollutants after they are formed by a source.)
- BT1 pollution control
- BT2 control
- RT water pollution
- RT water use

→ **WATER QUALITY** [4; 4] *May 76*
- BT1 environmental quality
- RT water pollution

→ **WATER REMOVAL** [0; 0] *Apr 84*
(Prior to August 1991, this concept was indexed to DEHYDRATION.)
- BT1 removal
- RT dehydration

WATER REQUIREMENTS [32; 32] *Dec 82*
- UF water demand
- BT1 demand
- RT water
- RT water use

WATER RESERVOIRS [685; 685]
- UF cooling ponds
- UF reservoirs (water)
- BT1 surface waters
- RT dams
- RT energy storage
- RT energy storage systems
- RT fresh water
- RT lakes
- RT storage
- RT water supply
- RT water use

water resources
(Prior to January 1983 this concept was indexed by coordination of RESERVES and WATER.)
- USE resources
- AND water

water solutions
- USE aqueous solutions

water springs
- USE ground water

WATER SUPPLY [141; 141] *May 86*
(To be used in the sense of a public utility or other engineered system, e.g. an irrigation system, rather than a natural system.)
- UF water distribution
- RT public utilities
- RT reactor cooling systems
- RT water reservoirs

WATER TABLES [61; 61] *Dec 87*
- RT aquifers
- RT ground water
- RT hydrology

WATER TREATMENT [397; 2,102] *Dec 82*
- NT1 water chemistry
- RT bioreactors
- RT deaerators
- RT dissolved gases

WATER USE [31; 31] *Feb 84*
- RT environment
- RT external zones
- RT hydrology
- RT land use
- RT regional analysis
- RT site selection
- RT water pollution
- RT water pollution control
- RT water requirements
- RT water reservoirs

WATER VAPOR [1,957; 1,957]
- BT1 vapors
- BT2 gases
- BT3 fluids
- RT humidity
- RT steam

RT   transpiration

water wells
    USE   wells

water-cooled reactors
    USE   water cooled reactors

water-moderated reactors
    USE   water moderated reactors

→ *waterborne particles*
    USE   particulates

→ *waterborne particulates*
    USE   particulates

WATERFORD-3 REACTOR [66; 66]
(Taft, Louisiana, USA)
    BT1   pwr type reactors
        BT2   enriched uranium reactors
            BT3   reactors
        BT2   power reactors
            BT3   reactors
        BT2   thermal reactors
            BT3   reactors
        BT2   water cooled reactors
            BT3   reactors
        BT2   water moderated reactors
            BT3   reactors

WATERFORD-4 REACTOR [6; 6]
(Taft, Louisiana, USA)
    BT1   pwr type reactors
        BT2   enriched uranium reactors
            BT3   reactors
        BT2   power reactors
            BT3   reactors
        BT2   thermal reactors
            BT3   reactors
        BT2   water cooled reactors
            BT3   reactors
        BT2   water moderated reactors
            BT3   reactors

→ **WATERSHEDS** [0; 0] *Oct 91*
(The drainage areas or catchment basins of streams.)
    NT1   colorado river basin
    NT1   columbia river basin

watson method
    USE   sommerfeld-watson theory

watt distribution
    USE   watt fission spectrum

watt fission source
    USE   watt fission spectrum

WATT FISSION SPECTRUM [27; 27]
    UF   *watt distribution*
    UF   *watt fission source*
    BT1   neutron spectra
        BT2   spectra
    RT   fission
    RT   prompt neutrons
    RT   thermal fission
    RT   thermal neutrons

WATT POWER RANGE [1; 4] *Apr 88*
    BT1   power range
    NT1   power range 01-10 w
    NT1   power range 10-100 w
    NT1   power range 100-1000 w

wattage
    USE   power input

WATTS BAR-1 REACTOR [81; 81]
(Spring City, Tennessee, USA)
    BT1   pwr type reactors
        BT2   enriched uranium reactors
            BT3   reactors
        BT2   power reactors
            BT3   reactors
        BT2   thermal reactors
            BT3   reactors
        BT2   water cooled reactors
            BT3   reactors
        BT2   water moderated reactors
            BT3   reactors

WATTS BAR-2 REACTOR [63; 63]
(Spring City, Tennessee, USA)
    BT1   pwr type reactors
        BT2   enriched uranium reactors
            BT3   reactors
        BT2   power reactors
            BT3   reactors
        BT2   thermal reactors
            BT3   reactors
        BT2   water cooled reactors
            BT3   reactors
        BT2   water moderated reactors
            BT3   reactors

WAVE EQUATIONS [1,018; 8,107]
Oct 82
    BT1   partial differential equations
        BT2   differential equations
            BT3   equations
    NT1   dirac equation
    NT1   klein-gordon equation
    NT1   schroedinger equation
    RT   rarita-schwinger theory

WAVE FORMS [910; 910]
    RT   electromagnetic radiation
    RT   polarization
    RT   wave propagation

WAVE FUNCTIONS [23,379; 23,379]
    BT1   functions
    RT   eigenfunctions
    RT   fractional-parentage coefficie
    RT   hidden variables
    RT   hybridization
    RT   muffin-tin potential
    RT   projection operators
    RT   schroedinger equation
    RT   slater method
    RT   sudden approximation

WAVE PACKETS [1,041; 1,041]
    RT   wave propagation

WAVE POWER [27; 27] *Dec 82*
    BT1   power
    BT1   renewable energy sources
        BT2   energy sources

WAVE PROPAGATION [11,327; 11,327]
    UF   *propagation (wave)*
    RT   amplitudes
    RT   fermat principle
    RT   huygens principle
    RT   interference
    RT   mode control
    RT   mode conversion
    RT   phase velocity
    RT   polarization
    RT   refraction
    RT   refractive index
    RT   standing waves
    RT   stapp theory
    RT   travelling waves
    RT   wave forms
    RT   wave packets
    RT   wavelengths
    RT   zero sound

WAVEGUIDES [2,459; 2,497]
    NT1   helical waveguides
    RT   cyclic accelerators
    RT   electrical equipment
    RT   microwave equipment
    RT   standing waves
    RT   travelling waves

wavelength dependence
    USE   frequency dependence

WAVELENGTHS [452; 452] *Feb 76*
(Prior to July 1986 FREQUENCY RANGE was used for this concept. If the frequency of the wave is known, see the descriptor for the specific frequency range listed under FREQUENCY RANGE.)
    RT   frequency range
    RT   standing waves
    RT   travelling waves
    RT   wave propagation

waves (shock)
    USE   shock waves

waves (standing)
    USE   standing waves

waves (travelling)
    USE   travelling waves

waw
    USE   wackersdorf reprocessing plant

WAXES [82; 390]
    BT1   other organic compounds
        BT2   organic compounds
    NT1   carbowax
    NT1   paraffin
    NT1   santowax

WAY-WIGNER FORMULA [3; 3]
    RT   beta decay

weak boson
    USE   intermediate bosons

WEAK CHARGED CURRENTS
[484; 484] *Aug 76*
    BT1   charged currents
        BT2   algebraic currents
            BT3   currents
    RT   weak neutral currents

WEAK HADRONIC DECAY
[2,067; 2,067] *Feb 78*
(Decay of hadrons due to weak interactions.)
    UF   *non-leptonic decay*
    UF   *nonleptonic decay*
    BT1   weak particle decay
        BT2   particle decay
            BT3   decay

WEAK INTERACTIONS [5,860; 12,6
    BT1   basic interactions
    BT1   interactions
    NT1   fermi interactions
    NT1   leptonic decay
    RT   cabibbo angle
    RT   charged currents
    RT   electron-quark interactions
    RT   feinberg-pais theory
    RT   goldberger-treiman relation
    RT   grand unified theory
    RT   lepton-hadron interactions
    RT   lepton-lepton interactions
    RT   neutral currents
    RT   neutrino oscillation
    RT   photon-lepton interactions

    RT   second-class currents
    RT   standard model
    RT   weak neutral currents
    RT   weak particle decay
    RT   weinberg angle
    RT   weinberg lepton model

WEAK NEUTRAL CURRENTS
[1,539; 1,539]
    BT1   neutral currents
      BT2   algebraic currents
        BT3   currents
    RT   weak charged currents
    RT   weak interactions
    RT   weinberg lepton model
    RT   weyl unified theory

WEAK PARTICLE DECAY
[1,507; 7,732] *Feb 78*
    BT1   particle decay
      BT2   decay
    NT1   leptonic decay
    NT1   semileptonic decay
    NT1   weak hadronic decay
    RT   radiative decay
    RT   weak interactions

WEAK-COUPLING MODEL [888; 888]
    BT1   nuclear models
      BT2   mathematical models
    RT   coupling
    RT   particle-core coupling model
    RT   particle-hole model
    RT   shell models
    RT   strong-coupling model

WEAKLY IONIZED GASES [258; 258]
(Ionization factor under 10(-4).)
    BT1   ionized gases
      BT2   gases
        BT3   fluids

WEAR [1,356; 1,356]
    SF   *tribology*
    RT   abrasion
    RT   bearings
    RT   erosion
    RT   friction
    RT   gears
    RT   grinding
    RT   mechanical tests
    RT   rolling friction
    RT   wear resistance

WEAR RESISTANCE [827; 827]
    BT1   mechanical properties
    RT   gears
    RT   wear

WEATHER [544; 544]
    RT   atmospheric precipitations
    RT   climates
    RT   clouds
    RT   forecasting
    RT   hurricanes
    RT   meteorology
    RT   seasons
    RT   tornadoes
    RT   wind

WEATHERING [161; 161] *May 86*
(Physical disintegration and chemical decomposition (as of earthy and rocky materials) on exposure to atmospheric agents.)
    RT   corrosion
    RT   decomposition

wecs
    USE   wind turbines

WEEDS [63; 63]
    BT1   plants

weevils
    USE   beetles

wega device
    USE   wega stellarator

WEGA STELLARATOR [86; 86]
    UF   *wega device*
    UF   *wega tokamak*
    BT1   stellarators
      BT2   closed plasma devices
        BT3   thermonuclear devices
    RT   tokamak devices

wega tokamak
    USE   wega stellarator

weighing
    USE   balances

WEIGHT [1,781; 1,781]
    RT   density
    RT   mass
    RT   molecular weight
    RT   weight indicators

WEIGHT INDICATORS [76; 227]
    BT1   measuring instruments
    NT1   balances
      NT2   microbalances
    RT   densimeters
    RT   weight

WEIGHTING FUNCTIONS [769; 769]
    BT1   functions
    RT   statistics

WEIL EQUATION [30; 30]
    BT1   equations
    RT   spin

WEINBERG ANGLE [559; 559] *Jan 84*
    RT   intermediate vector bosons
    RT   mixing ratio
    RT   standard model
    RT   weak interactions
    RT   weinberg lepton model

WEINBERG LEPTON MODEL
[4,353; 4,353]
    UF   *electroweak interaction model*
    UF   *salam-weinberg gauge model*
    UF   *weinberg model*
    UF   *weinberg-salam gauge model*
    BT1   unified gauge models
      BT2   particle models
        BT3   mathematical models
      BT2   quantum field theory
        BT3   field theories
    RT   electromagnetic interactions
    RT   electron quark interactions
    RT   grand unified theory
    RT   neutral-current interactions
    RT   standard model
    RT   weak interactions
    RT   weak neutral currents
    RT   weinberg angle

weinberg model
    USE   weinberg lepton model

weinberg-salam gauge model
    USE   weinberg lepton model

WEISSENBERG METHOD [37; 37]
    RT   rotating crystal method

WEISSKOPF MODEL [108; 108]
    BT1   evaporation model
      BT2   nuclear models
        BT3   mathematical models

WEIZSAECKER FORMULA [95; 95]
    UF   *bethe-weizsaecker relation*
    UF   *weizsaecker-fermi formula*
    RT   liquid drop model
    RT   mass number

weizsaecker-fermi formula
    USE   weizsaecker formula

WELDABILITY [523; 523]
    RT   welding

WELDED JOINTS [7,055; 7,132]
    UF   *butt welds*
    UF   *lap welds*
    UF   *seam welds*
    UF   *spot welds*
    UF   *welds*
    BT1   joints
    RT   welding

WELDING [2,322; 5,499]
(All endothermic processes for material joining.)
    UF   *fusion (welding)*
    UF   *seam welding*
    UF   *spot welding*
    UF   *stud welding*
    BT1   joining
      BT2   fabrication
    NT1   arc welding
      NT2   gas metal-arc welding
        NT3   gas tungsten-arc welding
      NT2   plasma arc welding
      NT2   shielded metal-arc welding
      NT2   submerged arc welding
    NT1   brazing
    NT1   diffusion welding
    NT1   electron beam welding
    NT1   electroslag welding
    NT1   explosion welding
    NT1   forge welding
    NT1   friction welding
    NT1   gas welding
    NT1   induction welding
    NT1   laser welding
    NT1   magnetic force welding
    NT1   resistance welding
      NT2   flash welding
      NT2   projection welding
    NT1   soldering
    NT1   ultrasonic welding
    NT1   vacuum welding
    RT   filler metals
    RT   heat affected zone
    RT   melting
    RT   metallurgical flux
    RT   thermite process
    RT   weldability
    RT   welded joints
    RT   welding machines
    RT   welding rods

welding fluxes
    USE   metallurgical flux

WELDING MACHINES [248; 248]
    RT   welding

WELDING RODS [218; 218]
    RT   electrodes
    RT   welding

welds
    USE   welded joints

WELL LOGGING [1,364; 3,243]
- UF *electric logging*
- UF *gravity logging*
- UF *induction logging*
- UF *resistivity logging*
- UF *self-potential logging*
- UF *sonic logging*
- UF *sp logging*
- UF *spontaneous potential logging*
- NT1 nuclear magnetic logging
- NT1 radioactivity logging
  - NT2 gamma logging
  - NT2 gamma-gamma logging
  - NT2 neutron logging
    - NT3 neutron-gamma logging
    - NT3 neutron-neutron logging
  - NT2 radioactive tracer logging
  - NT2 x-ray fluorescence logging
- RT boreholes
- RT drill cores
- RT well logging equipment

WELL LOGGING EQUIPMENT [447; 447] *Apr 80*
(Limited to equipment based on nuclear techniques or used in exploration of materials of nuclear interest.)
- BT1 equipment
- RT probes
- RT radiation detectors
- RT radiation sources
- RT well logging

well pressure
- USE reservoir pressure

WELLS [849; 849] *May 76*
- UF *gas wells*
- UF *water wells*
- NT1 injection wells
- NT1 oil wells
- RT blowouts
- RT boreholes
- RT water influx

welton method
- USE feynman method

WENDELSTEIN-2B STELLARATOR [8; 8] *Jul 76*
- SF *w stellarators*
- BT1 stellarators
  - BT2 closed plasma devices
    - BT3 thermonuclear devices

WENDELSTEIN-7 STELLARATOR [420; 420]
- SF *w stellarators*
- BT1 stellarators
  - BT2 closed plasma devices
    - BT3 thermonuclear devices

WENDS [2; 2] *Dec 79*
(World ENergy Data System)
- UF *world energy data system*
- BT1 information systems
- RT energy policy

wentzel-kramers-brillouin appr
- USE wkb approximation

WEST INDIES [19; 197]
- BT1 islands
- NT1 bahama islands
- NT1 cuba
- NT1 dominican republic
- NT1 haiti
- NT1 jamaica
- NT1 puerto rico
- NT1 saint lucia
- RT caribbean sea
- RT latin america

WEST VALLEY PROCESSING PLANT [309; 309]
- BT1 fuel reprocessing plants
  - BT2 nuclear facilities

WEST VALLEY UF6 FACILITY [2; 2] *Jul 85*
- BT1 feed materials plants
  - BT2 industrial plants
  - BT2 nuclear facilities

WEST VIRGINIA [66; 66]
- BT1 usa
  - BT2 developed countries
  - BT2 north america

WESTERN AUSTRALIA [145; 145]
- BT1 australia
  - BT2 australasia
  - BT2 developed countries
- RT yeelirrie deposit

western n. y. nucl. res. react
- USE pulstar-buffalo reactor

westinghouse nucl. train. reac
- USE wntr reactor

WESTINGHOUSE RECYCLE FUELS PLA [21; 21]
- BT1 fuel fabrication plants
  - BT2 nuclear facilities
- BT1 fuel reprocessing plants
  - BT2 nuclear facilities
- RT fuel cycle

WESTINGHOUSE STANDARD REACTOR [192; 192] *Oct 75*
- UF *pwr/41 type reactor*
- BT1 pwr type reactors
  - BT2 enriched uranium reactors
    - BT3 reactors
  - BT2 power reactors
    - BT3 reactors
  - BT2 thermal reactors
    - BT3 reactors
  - BT2 water cooled reactors
    - BT3 reactors
  - BT2 water moderated reactors
    - BT3 reactors
- RT bopssar standard plant
- RT gibbssar standard plant

westinghouse testing reactor
- USE wtr reactor

WET ASHING [108; 108]
- UF *ashing (wet)*
- RT combustion
- RT sample preparation
- RT waste processing

wetlands
- USE swamps

WETTABILITY [444; 444]
- RT surface properties
- RT wetting agents

WETTING AGENTS [76; 439]
- BT1 surfactants
- NT1 detergents
  - NT2 pluronics
- RT wettability

weyl field
- USE weyl unified theory

WEYL UNIFIED THEORY [682; 682]
- UF *weyl field*
- BT1 unified-field theories
  - BT2 field theories
- RT electromagnetic fields
- RT gravitational fields
- RT weak neutral currents

→ *whales*
- USE cetaceans

WHEAT [1,293; 1,293]
- UF *triticum*
- BT1 cereals
  - BT2 gramineae
    - BT3 plants

WHISKERS [240; 240]
- BT1 monocrystals
  - BT2 crystals

WHISTLER INSTABILITY [30; 30] *Nov 88*
- UF *whistler mode*
- BT1 plasma microinstabilities
  - BT2 plasma instability
    - BT3 instability
- RT beam-plasma systems
- RT plasma waves

whistler mode
- USE whistler instability

WHISTLERS [857; 857]
- BT1 radio noise
  - BT2 noise
  - BT2 radiowave radiation
    - BT3 electromagnetic radiation
      - BT4 radiations
- RT atmospherics
- RT auroral hiss
- RT lightning

white copper
- USE german silver

WHITE DWARF STARS [1,844; 1,84
- BT1 dwarf stars
  - BT2 stars

WHITE HOLES [47; 47] *Oct 77*
(A time-reversed black hole, an expan source with growing intensity and pho energy.)
- RT black holes
- RT cosmology
- RT origin
- RT stars

whiteshell nuclear research es
- USE wnre

whiteshell-1 reactor
- USE wr-1 reactor

WHO [213; 213]
- UF *world health organization*
- BT1 international organizations
- RT medicine
- RT united nations

WHOLE-BODY COUNTERS [474; 4
- BT1 radiation detectors
  - BT2 measuring instruments
- RT gamma spectrometers
- RT whole-body counting

WHOLE-BODY COUNTING
[1,521; 1,521]
BT1 counting techniques
RT body
RT personnel monitoring
RT radiation protection
RT radioactivity
RT radionuclide kinetics
RT retention
RT whole-body counters

WHOLE-BODY IRRADIATION
[5,419; 5,419]
BT1 external irradiation
BT2 irradiation
RT body

WHOLESOMENESS [547; 547]
RT food
RT preservation

WICK METHOD [4; 4]
RT neutron slowing-down theory
RT slowing-down

WICK THEOREM [137; 137]
RT many-body problem
RT quantum field theory

WICK-CHANDRASEKHAR METHOD
[3; 3]
RT transport theory

WIDE GAP SPARK CHAMBERS
[86; 86]
BT1 spark chambers
BT2 gas track detectors
BT3 radiation detectors
BT4 measuring instruments

WIDMANSTAETTEN STRUCTURE
[40; 40]
BT1 microstructure
BT2 crystal structure
RT phase transformations

WIDTH [369; 369]
(For dimensions only: see also LEVEL WIDTHS, LINE WIDTHS, and PARTICLE WIDTHS.)
BT1 dimensions

WIEDEMANN-FRANZ LAW [60; 60]
RT electric conductivity
RT thermal conductivity

wiederaufarbeitungsanlage karl
USE wak

wiederaufarbeitungsanlage wack
USE wackersdorf reprocessing plant

WIGGLER MAGNETS [1,054; 1,054]
Nov 77
UF *undulators*
BT1 magnets
BT2 equipment
RT electron beams
RT synchrotron radiation

WIGHTMAN FIELD THEORY
[237; 237]
BT1 axiomatic field theory
BT2 quantum field theory
BT3 field theories

WIGNER COEFFICIENTS [134; 134]
UF *9j-symbols*
RT angular momentum
RT clebsch-gordan coefficients
RT group theory
RT quantum mechanics
RT racah coefficients

WIGNER DISTRIBUTION [267; 267]
RT thermodynamics

WIGNER EFFECT [44; 44]
RT graphite
RT radiation effects

WIGNER FORCE [35; 35]
BT1 nuclear forces

wigner method
USE peierls method

WIGNER SCATTERING [18; 18]
BT1 elastic scattering
BT2 scattering

WIGNER THEORY [281; 281]
RT quantum mechanics

WIGNER-EISENBUD THEORY [30; 30]
RT nuclear potential

WIGNER-SEITZ METHOD [124; 124]
RT band theory

WIGNER-WILKINS MODEL [8; 8]
RT slowing-down

WILD ANIMALS [276; 276]
BT1 animals

WILKINS EQUATION [1; 1]
BT1 equations
RT slowing-down

WILKINSON THEORY [0; 0]
RT shell models

william h. zimmer-1 reactor
USE zimmer-1 reactor

william h. zimmer-2 reactor
USE zimmer-2 reactor

williams-weizsaecker approxima
USE equivalent-photon approximatio

WILSON LOOP [958; 958] *Mar 83*
RT feynman path integral
RT lattice field theory
RT order parameters
RT quantum chromodynamics
RT yang-mills theory

WILZBACH METHOD [22; 22]
BT1 labelling
RT labelled compounds

WINCHES [38; 38]
BT1 equipment
RT materials handling equipment

WIND [1,948; 2,104]
RT advection
RT air
RT atmospheric circulation
RT climates
RT fallout
RT hurricanes
RT meteorology
RT particle resuspension
RT radioactive clouds
RT tornadoes
RT turbulence
RT weather

→ *wind energy conversion systems*
USE wind turbines

WIND POWER [62; 62] *Dec 82*
BT1 power
BT1 renewable energy sources
BT2 energy sources
RT wind turbines

WIND TUNNELS [184; 184]
BT1 tunnels
BT2 underground facilities
RT aerodynamics
RT supersonic flow

→ **WIND TURBINES** [0; 0] *Aug 91*
UF *wecs*
UF *wind energy conversion systems*
BT1 turbines
RT wind power

WINDOWS [658; 658]
BT1 openings
RT shutters

windscale adv. gas-cooled re.
USE wagr reactor

WINDSCALE PRODUCTION REACTORS [73; 73]
BT1 air cooled reactors
BT2 gas cooled reactors
BT3 reactors
BT1 graphite moderated reactors
BT2 reactors
BT1 natural uranium reactors
BT2 reactors
BT1 plutonium production reactors
BT2 production reactors
BT3 reactors
BT1 thermal reactors
BT2 reactors

windscale reprocessing plant
USE sellafield reprocessing plant

wine
USE beverages

WIPP [649; 649] *Apr 85*
UF *waste isolation pilot plant*
BT1 pilot plants
BT2 functional models
BT1 radioactive waste facilities
BT2 nuclear facilities
BT1 us doe
BT2 us organizations
BT3 national organizations
RT alpha-bearing wastes
RT high-level radioactive wastes
RT new mexico
RT radioactive waste disposal
RT salt deposits

WIRE SPARK CHAMBERS [367; 367]
BT1 filmless spark chambers
BT2 spark chambers
BT3 gas track detectors
BT4 radiation detectors
BT5 measuring instruments
RT multiwire proportional chamber

WIRES [2,242; 3,273]
NT1 exploding wires
NT1 superconducting wires
RT filaments
RT rods

wires (fuel)
USE fuel wires

WISCONSIN [180; 180]
- BT1 usa
- BT2 developed countries
- BT2 north america

wisconsin point beach-1 reacto
- USE point beach-1 reactor

wisconsin point beach-2 reacto
- USE point beach-2 reactor

wisconsin publ. serv. pow. rea
- USE kewaunee reactor

wisconsin univ. nucl. reactor
- USE uwnr reactor

wisconsin university tokamak
- USE uwmak devices

wisconsin utilities proj-3 rea
- USE wup-3 reactor

wisconsin utilities proj-4 rea
- USE wup-4 reactor

wisconsin utilities proj-5 rea
- USE wup-5 reactor

wisconsin utilities proj-6 rea
- USE wup-6 reactor

WITWATERSRAND [74; 74]
- BT1 mountains
- RT transvaal

WKB APPROXIMATION [1,381; 1,381]
- UF wentzel-kramers-brillouin appr
- RT scattering

WNP-1 REACTOR [37; 37]
- UF washington pub power sup sys-1
- UF wppss nuclear project no. 1
- BT1 pwr type reactors
- BT2 enriched uranium reactors
- BT3 reactors
- BT2 power reactors
- BT3 reactors
- BT2 thermal reactors
- BT3 reactors
- BT2 water cooled reactors
- BT3 reactors
- BT2 water moderated reactors
- BT3 reactors

WNP-2 REACTOR [41; 51]
(Washington Public Power Supply System Nuclear Project Number 2, previously known as Hanford-2 Reactor.)
- UF washington pub power sup sys-2
- UF wppss nuclear project no. 2
- BT1 bwr type reactors
- BT2 enriched uranium reactors
- BT3 reactors
- BT2 power reactors
- BT3 reactors
- BT2 thermal reactors
- BT3 reactors
- BT2 water cooled reactors
- BT3 reactors
- BT2 water moderated reactors
- BT3 reactors
- NT1 hanford-2 reactor

WNP-3 REACTOR [22; 22]
- UF washington pub power sup sys-3
- UF wppss nuclear project no. 3
- BT1 pwr type reactors
- BT2 enriched uranium reactors
- BT3 reactors
- BT2 power reactors
- BT3 reactors
- BT2 thermal reactors
- BT3 reactors
- BT2 water cooled reactors
- BT3 reactors
- BT2 water moderated reactors
- BT3 reactors

WNP-4 REACTOR [11; 11] Aug 75
- UF washington pub power sup sys-4
- UF wppss nuclear project no. 4
- BT1 pwr type reactors
- BT2 enriched uranium reactors
- BT3 reactors
- BT2 power reactors
- BT3 reactors
- BT2 thermal reactors
- BT3 reactors
- BT2 water cooled reactors
- BT3 reactors
- BT2 water moderated reactors
- BT3 reactors

WNP-5 REACTOR [13; 13]
- UF washington pub power sup sys-5
- UF wppss nuclear project no. 5
- BT1 pwr type reactors
- BT2 enriched uranium reactors
- BT3 reactors
- BT2 power reactors
- BT3 reactors
- BT2 thermal reactors
- BT3 reactors
- BT2 water cooled reactors
- BT3 reactors
- BT2 water moderated reactors
- BT3 reactors

WNRE [56; 56]
- UF whiteshell nuclear research es
- BT1 atomic energy of canada ltd
- BT2 canadian organizations
- BT3 national organizations

WNTR REACTOR [2; 2] Apr 85
(Zion, Illinois, USA.)
- UF westinghouse nucl. train. reac
- BT1 enriched uranium reactors
- BT2 reactors
- BT1 fast reactors
- BT2 epithermal reactors
- BT3 reactors
- BT1 tank type reactors
- BT2 reactors
- BT1 training reactors
- BT2 research and test reactors
- BT3 reactors
- BT1 water cooled reactors
- BT2 reactors
- BT1 water moderated reactors
- BT2 reactors

WOLF CREEK-1 REACTOR [33; 33]
Oct 75
(Coffey, Kansas, USA)
- BT1 pwr type reactors
- BT2 enriched uranium reactors
- BT3 reactors
- BT2 power reactors
- BT3 reactors
- BT2 thermal reactors
- BT3 reactors
- BT2 water cooled reactors
- BT3 reactors
- BT2 water moderated reactors
- BT3 reactors

WOLF-RAYET STARS [603; 603]
- BT1 main sequence stars
- BT2 stars

WOLFENSTEIN PARAMETERS [105; 105]
- RT interactions
- RT nucleons

wolfram
- USE tungsten

WOLFRAMITE [38; 38]
- BT1 oxide minerals
- BT2 minerals
- RT iron oxides
- RT tungsten oxides

wolframophosphoric acid
- USE tungstophosphoric acid

WOLSUNG-1 REACTOR [49; 49]
Feb 78
- BT1 candu type reactors
- BT2 heavy water moderated reacto
- BT3 reactors
- BT2 pressure tube reactors
- BT3 power reactors
- BT4 reactors
- BT2 thermal reactors
- BT3 reactors
- BT1 natural uranium reactors
- BT2 reactors
- BT1 phwr type reactors
- BT2 heavy water cooled reactors
- BT3 reactors
- BT2 heavy water moderated react
- BT3 reactors

WOMEN [1,872; 1,872]
- BT1 females
- BT1 man
- BT2 primates
- BT3 mammals
- BT4 vertebrates
- BT5 animals
- RT adults
- RT gynecology

WOOD [638; 638]
- RT cork
- RT creosote
- RT fuels
- RT lignin
- RT trees
- RT wood-plastic composites
- RT xylose

wood alcohol
- USE methanol

wood metal
- USE alloy-bi50pb25cd12sn12

WOOD-PLASTIC COMPOSITES [122; 122]
- BT1 composite materials
- BT2 materials
- RT organic polymers
- RT wood

WOODS-SAXON POTENTIAL [2,477; 2,477]
- UF saxon-woods potential
- BT1 nuclear potential
- BT2 potentials
- RT optical models

WOOL [76; 76]
- RT fibers
- RT textiles

wool fat
- USE lanolin

worcester polyt. inst pool re.
- USE wpir reactor

WORK [587; 587]
- UF *labor*
- RT automation
- RT ilo
- RT occupational diseases
- RT occupations
- RT personnel
- RT remote handling
- RT working conditions

WORK FUNCTIONS [1,251; 1,251]
- RT binding energy
- RT electron emission
- RT electron tubes
- RT energy
- RT metals
- RT surface potential

work hardening
- USE strain hardening

work softening
- USE strain softening

workers
- USE personnel

working (materials)
- USE materials working

WORKING CONDITIONS [1,243; 1,243]
- RT air conditioning
- RT alara
- RT icrp critical group
- RT industrial medicine
- RT labor relations
- RT occupational safety
- RT radiation protection
- RT safety
- RT work

WORKING FLUIDS [285; 285] *Jun 82*
- SF *heat transfer fluids*
- BT1 fluids
- RT energy conversion
- RT heat exchangers
- RT heat pumps
- RT heat transfer
- RT hydrodynamics
- RT thermodynamic cycles
- RT turbines

WORKMENS COMPENSATION [74; 74]
- UF *compensation (workmens)*
- RT accidents
- RT civil liability
- RT financial security
- RT hazards
- RT indemnification agreements
- RT legal aspects
- RT victims compensation

world assoc nuclear operators
- USE wano

world energy data system
- USE wends

world health organization
- USE who

world-wide fallout
- USE global fallout

worms (flat)
- USE platyhelminths

worms (round)
- USE nematodes

worms (segmented)
- USE annelids

WOUNDS [535; 535]
- BT1 injuries
- BT2 diseases
- RT healing
- RT necrosis
- RT skin

WPIR REACTOR [6; 6]
(Worcester Polytechnic Institute, Worcester, Massachusetts, USA)
- UF *worcester polyt. inst pool re.*
- BT1 enriched uranium reactors
- BT2 reactors
- BT1 pool type reactors
- BT2 water cooled reactors
- BT3 reactors
- BT2 water moderated reactors
- BT3 reactors
- BT1 thermal reactors
- BT2 reactors
- BT1 training reactors
- BT2 research and test reactors
- BT3 reactors

wppss nuclear project no. 1
- USE wnp-1 reactor

wppss nuclear project no. 2
- USE wnp-2 reactor

wppss nuclear project no. 3
- USE wnp-3 reactor

wppss nuclear project no. 4
- USE wnp-4 reactor

wppss nuclear project no. 5
- USE wnp-5 reactor

WR-1 REACTOR [34; 34]
(Atomic Energy of Canada, Ltd., Manitoba, Canada)
- UF *whiteshell-1 reactor*
- BT1 enriched uranium reactors
- BT2 reactors
- BT1 heavy water moderated reactors
- BT2 reactors
- BT1 materials testing reactors
- BT2 irradiation reactors
- BT3 reactors
- BT1 organic cooled reactors
- BT2 reactors
- BT1 tank type reactors
- BT2 reactors
- BT1 test reactors
- BT2 research and test reactors
- BT3 reactors
- BT2 test facilities
- BT1 thermal reactors
- BT2 reactors

WRRR REACTOR [1; 1]
- UF *walter reed res. reactor l-54*
- BT1 aqueous homogeneous reactors
- BT2 liquid homogeneous reactors
- BT3 fluid fueled reactors
- BT4 reactors
- BT3 homogeneous reactors
- BT4 reactors
- BT2 water cooled reactors
- BT3 reactors
- BT2 water moderated reactors
- BT3 reactors
- BT1 enriched uranium reactors
- BT2 reactors
- BT1 research reactors
- BT2 research and test reactors
- BT3 reactors
- BT1 thermal reactors
- BT2 reactors

WSUR REACTOR [10; 10]
(Washington State University, Nuclear Radiation Center, Pullman, Washington, USA)
- UF *pullman wash. stat. uni. react*
- UF *rscw reactor*
- UF *rwsu reactor*
- UF *washington state univ. reactor*
- BT1 pool type reactors
- BT2 water cooled reactors
- BT3 reactors
- BT2 water moderated reactors
- BT3 reactors
- BT1 pulsed reactors
- BT2 reactors
- BT1 research reactors
- BT2 research and test reactors
- BT3 reactors
- BT1 thermal reactors
- BT2 reactors
- BT1 triga type reactors
- BT2 enriched uranium reactors
- BT3 reactors
- BT2 hydride moderated reactors
- BT3 reactors
- BT2 research and test reactors
- BT3 reactors
- BT2 solid homogeneous reactors
- BT3 homogeneous reactors
- BT4 reactors
- BT2 water cooled reactors
- BT3 reactors
- BT2 water moderated reactors
- BT3 reactors

WT-3 TOKAMAK [12; 12] *Dec 89*
(Kyoto University, Kyoto, Japan.)
- BT1 tokamak devices
- BT2 closed plasma devices
- BT3 thermonuclear devices

WTR REACTOR [2; 2]
(Westinghouse Electric Corporation, Madison, Pennsylvania, USA)
- UF *westinghouse testing reactor*
- BT1 enriched uranium reactors
- BT2 reactors
- BT1 isotope production reactors
- BT2 irradiation reactors
- BT3 reactors
- BT1 research reactors
- BT2 research and test reactors
- BT3 reactors
- BT1 tank type reactors
- BT2 reactors
- BT1 test reactors
- BT2 research and test reactors
- BT3 reactors
- BT2 test facilities
- BT1 thermal reactors
- BT2 reactors
- BT1 water cooled reactors
- BT2 reactors
- BT1 water moderated reactors
- BT2 reactors

wuerenlingen proteus reactor
- USE proteus reactor

WUERGASSEN REACTOR [195; 195]
(Wuergassen, Niedersachsen, Federal Republic of Germany)
UF   *kernkraftwerk wuergassen*
BT1   bwr type reactors
  BT2   enriched uranium reactors
    BT3   reactors
  BT2   power reactors
    BT3   reactors
  BT2   thermal reactors
    BT3   reactors
  BT2   water cooled reactors
    BT3   reactors
  BT2   water moderated reactors
    BT3   reactors

WULFENITE [3; 3]
BT1   oxide minerals
  BT2   minerals
RT   lead oxides
RT   molybdenum oxides

wup-1 reactor
USE   haven-1 reactor

wup-2 reactor
USE   haven-2 reactor

WUP-3 REACTOR [3; 3]
UF   *wisconsin utilities proj-3 rea*
BT1   pwr type reactors
  BT2   enriched uranium reactors
    BT3   reactors
  BT2   power reactors
    BT3   reactors
  BT2   thermal reactors
    BT3   reactors
  BT2   water cooled reactors
    BT3   reactors
  BT2   water moderated reactors
    BT3   reactors

WUP-4 REACTOR [3; 3]
UF   *wisconsin utilities proj-4 rea*
BT1   pwr type reactors
  BT2   enriched uranium reactors
    BT3   reactors
  BT2   power reactors
    BT3   reactors
  BT2   thermal reactors
    BT3   reactors
  BT2   water cooled reactors
    BT3   reactors
  BT2   water moderated reactors
    BT3   reactors

WUP-5 REACTOR [3; 3]
UF   *wisconsin utilities proj-5 rea*
BT1   pwr type reactors
  BT2   enriched uranium reactors
    BT3   reactors
  BT2   power reactors
    BT3   reactors
  BT2   thermal reactors
    BT3   reactors
  BT2   water cooled reactors
    BT3   reactors
  BT2   water moderated reactors
    BT3   reactors

WUP-6 REACTOR [3; 3]
UF   *wisconsin utilities proj-6 rea*
BT1   pwr type reactors
  BT2   enriched uranium reactors
    BT3   reactors
  BT2   power reactors
    BT3   reactors
  BT2   thermal reactors
    BT3   reactors
  BT2   water cooled reactors
    BT3   reactors
  BT2   water moderated reactors
    BT3   reactors

WWER TYPE REACTORS
[3,191; 5,329]
BT1   pwr type reactors
  BT2   enriched uranium reactors
    BT3   reactors
  BT2   power reactors
    BT3   reactors
  BT2   thermal reactors
    BT3   reactors
  BT2   water cooled reactors
    BT3   reactors
  BT2   water moderated reactors
    BT3   reactors
NT1   armenian-1 reactor
NT1   armenian-2 reactor
NT1   balakovo-1 reactor
NT1   balakovo-2 reactor
NT1   blahutovice-1 reactor
NT1   bohunice v-1 reactor
NT1   bohunice v-2 reactor
NT1   dukovany v-2 reactor
NT1   greifswald-1 reactor
NT1   greifswald-2 reactor
NT1   greifswald-3 reactor
NT1   greifswald-4 reactor
NT1   greifswald-5 reactor
NT1   greifswald-6 reactor
NT1   kalinin-1 reactor
NT1   kalinin-3 reactor
NT1   kecerovce-1 reactor
NT1   khmelnitskij-1 reactor
NT1   kola-1 reactor
NT1   kola-2 reactor
NT1   kola-3 reactor
NT1   kola-4 reactor
NT1   kozloduy-1 reactor
NT1   kozloduy-2 reactor
NT1   kozloduy-3 reactor
NT1   loviisa-1 reactor
NT1   loviisa-2 reactor
NT1   mochovce-1 reactor
NT1   paks-1 reactor
NT1   paks-2 reactor
NT1   paks-3 reactor
NT1   paks-4 reactor
NT1   rovno-1 reactor
NT1   rovno-2 reactor
NT1   rovno-3 reactor
NT1   rovno-4 reactor
NT1   rovno-5 reactor
NT1   south ukrainian-1 reactor
NT1   south ukrainian-2 reactor
NT1   south ukrainian-3 reactor
NT1   stendal-1 reactor
NT1   tatarian reactor
NT1   temelin-1 reactor
NT1   wwer-1 reactor
NT1   wwer-2 reactor
NT1   wwer-3 reactor
NT1   wwer-4 reactor
NT1   wwer-5 reactor
NT1   zaporozhe-1 reactor
NT1   zaporozhe-2 reactor
NT1   zaporozhe-3 reactor
NT1   zaporozhe-4 reactor

WWER-1 REACTOR [73; 73]
UF   *novo voronezh-1 reactor*
UF   *wwer-210 reactor*
BT1   wwer type reactors
  BT2   pwr type reactors
    BT3   enriched uranium reactors
      BT4   reactors
    BT3   power reactors
      BT4   reactors
    BT3   thermal reactors
      BT4   reactors
    BT3   water cooled reactors
      BT4   reactors
    BT3   water moderated reactors
      BT4   reactors

wwer-1000 reactor
USE   wwer-5 reactor

WWER-2 REACTOR [81; 81]
UF   *novo voronezh-2 reactor*
UF   *wwer-365 reactor*
BT1   wwer type reactors
  BT2   pwr type reactors
    BT3   enriched uranium reactors
      BT4   reactors
    BT3   power reactors
      BT4   reactors
    BT3   thermal reactors
      BT4   reactors
    BT3   water cooled reactors
      BT4   reactors
    BT3   water moderated reactors
      BT4   reactors

wwer-210 reactor
USE   wwer-1 reactor

WWER-3 REACTOR [304; 304]
UF   *novo voronezh-3 reactor*
UF   *wwer-440 reactor*
BT1   wwer type reactors
  BT2   pwr type reactors
    BT3   enriched uranium reactors
      BT4   reactors
    BT3   power reactors
      BT4   reactors
    BT3   thermal reactors
      BT4   reactors
    BT3   water cooled reactors
      BT4   reactors
    BT3   water moderated reactors
      BT4   reactors

wwer-365 reactor
USE   wwer-2 reactor

WWER-4 REACTOR [86; 86]
UF   *novo voronezh-4 reactor*
BT1   wwer type reactors
  BT2   pwr type reactors
    BT3   enriched uranium reactors
      BT4   reactors
    BT3   power reactors
      BT4   reactors
    BT3   thermal reactors
      BT4   reactors
    BT3   water cooled reactors
      BT4   reactors
    BT3   water moderated reactors
      BT4   reactors

wwer-440 reactor
USE   wwer-3 reactor

WWER-5 REACTOR [257; 257]
UF   *novo voronezh-5 reactor*
UF   *wwer-1000 reactor*
UF   *wwer-500 reactor*
BT1   wwer type reactors
  BT2   pwr type reactors
    BT3   enriched uranium reactors
      BT4   reactors
    BT3   power reactors
      BT4   reactors
    BT3   thermal reactors
      BT4   reactors
    BT3   water cooled reactors
      BT4   reactors
    BT3   water moderated reactors
      BT4   reactors

wwer-500 reactor
USE   wwer-5 reactor

WWR TYPE REACTORS [135; 529]
BT1   enriched uranium reactors
  BT2   reactors
BT1   tank type reactors
  BT2   reactors
BT1   water cooled reactors
  BT2   reactors
BT1   water moderated reactors

BT2	reactors	
NT1	budapest training reactor	
NT1	irt-baghdad reactor	
NT1	wwr-k-alma-ata reactor	
NT1	wwr-m-kiev reactor	
NT1	wwr-m-leningrad reactor	
NT1	wwr-s-bucharest reactor	
NT1	wwr-s-budapest reactor	
NT1	wwr-s-cairo reactor	
NT1	wwr-s-moscow reactor	
NT1	wwr-s-prague reactor	
NT1	wwr-s-tashkent reactor	
NT1	wwr-sm rossendorf reactor	
NT1	wwr-2 reactor	

wwr-c-baghdad reactor
   USE   irt-baghdad reactor

wwr-c-bucharest reactor
   USE   wwr-s-bucharest reactor

wwr-c-budapest reactor
   USE   wwr-s-budapest reactor

wwr-c-cairo reactor
   USE   wwr-s-cairo reactor

wwr-c-moscow reactor
   USE   wwr-s-moscow reactor

wwr-c-prague reactor
   USE   wwr-s-prague reactor

wwr-c-tashkent reactor
   USE   wwr-s-tashkent reactor

WWR-K-ALMA-ATA REACTOR
[31; 31]
(Alma-Ata, Kazakhstan, USSR)
   UF   *alma-ata wwr-k reactor*
   BT1   research reactors
      BT2   research and test reactors
         BT3   reactors
   BT1   thermal reactors
      BT2   reactors
   BT1   wwr type reactors
      BT2   enriched uranium reactors
         BT3   reactors
      BT2   tank type reactors
         BT3   reactors
      BT2   water cooled reactors
         BT3   reactors
      BT2   water moderated reactors
         BT3   reactors

WWR-M-KIEV REACTOR [35; 35]
(Kiev, USSR)
   UF   *kiev wwr-m reactor*
   BT1   isotope production reactors
      BT2   irradiation reactors
         BT3   reactors
   BT1   materials testing reactors
      BT2   irradiation reactors
         BT3   reactors
   BT1   research reactors
      BT2   research and test reactors
         BT3   reactors
   BT1   thermal reactors
      BT2   reactors
   BT1   wwr type reactors
      BT2   enriched uranium reactors
         BT3   reactors
      BT2   tank type reactors
         BT3   reactors
      BT2   water cooled reactors
         BT3   reactors
      BT2   water moderated reactors
         BT3   reactors

WWR-M-LENINGRAD REACTOR
[43; 43]
(Leningrad, USSR)
   UF   *leningrad wwr-m reactor*
   BT1   isotope production reactors
      BT2   irradiation reactors
         BT3   reactors
   BT1   materials testing reactors
      BT2   irradiation reactors
         BT3   reactors
   BT1   research reactors
      BT2   research and test reactors
         BT3   reactors
   BT1   thermal reactors
      BT2   reactors
   BT1   wwr type reactors
      BT2   enriched uranium reactors
         BT3   reactors
      BT2   tank type reactors
         BT3   reactors
      BT2   water cooled reactors
         BT3   reactors
      BT2   water moderated reactors
         BT3   reactors

wwr-s-baghdad reactor
(Name changed to IRT-BAGHDAD REACTOR; prior to June 1985 this was a valid descriptor.)
   USE   irt-baghdad reactor

WWR-S-BUCHAREST REACTOR
[22; 22]
(Magurele, Romania)
   UF   *bucharest wwr-s reactor*
   UF   *romanian wwr-c reactor*
   UF   *wwr-c-bucharest reactor*
   BT1   research reactors
      BT2   research and test reactors
         BT3   reactors
   BT1   thermal reactors
      BT2   reactors
   BT1   wwr type reactors
      BT2   enriched uranium reactors
         BT3   reactors
      BT2   tank type reactors
         BT3   reactors
      BT2   water cooled reactors
         BT3   reactors
      BT2   water moderated reactors
         BT3   reactors

WWR-S-BUDAPEST REACTOR [60; 60]
(Central Research Inst. for Physics, Hungarian Academy of Sciences, Budapest, Hungary)
   UF   *budapest wwr-s reactor*
   UF   *hungarian wwr-c reactor*
   UF   *wwr-c-budapest reactor*
   BT1   isotope production reactors
      BT2   irradiation reactors
         BT3   reactors
   BT1   thermal reactors
      BT2   reactors
   BT1   training reactors
      BT2   research and test reactors
         BT3   reactors
   BT1   wwr type reactors
      BT2   enriched uranium reactors
         BT3   reactors
      BT2   tank type reactors
         BT3   reactors
      BT2   water cooled reactors
         BT3   reactors
      BT2   water moderated reactors
         BT3   reactors

WWR-S-CAIRO REACTOR [39; 39]
   UF   *cairo wwr-s reactor*
   UF   *united arab rep. wwr-c reactor*
   UF   *wwr-c-cairo reactor*
   BT1   research reactors
      BT2   research and test reactors
         BT3   reactors
   BT1   thermal reactors
      BT2   reactors
   BT1   wwr type reactors
      BT2   enriched uranium reactors
         BT3   reactors
      BT2   tank type reactors
         BT3   reactors
      BT2   water cooled reactors
         BT3   reactors
      BT2   water moderated reactors
         BT3   reactors

WWR-S-MOSCOW REACTOR [3; 3]
(Moscow, USSR)
   UF   *moscow wwr-s reactor*
   UF   *wwr-c-moscow reactor*
   BT1   isotope production reactors
      BT2   irradiation reactors
         BT3   reactors
   BT1   research reactors
      BT2   research and test reactors
         BT3   reactors
   BT1   thermal reactors
      BT2   reactors
   BT1   wwr type reactors
      BT2   enriched uranium reactors
         BT3   reactors
      BT2   tank type reactors
         BT3   reactors
      BT2   water cooled reactors
         BT3   reactors
      BT2   water moderated reactors
         BT3   reactors

WWR-S-PRAGUE REACTOR [82; 82]
(Nuclear Research Institute, Rez, Czechoslovakia)
   UF   *czech wwr-s reactor*
   UF   *prague wwr-s reactor*
   UF   *wwr-c-prague reactor*
   UF   *wwr-s-rez reactor*
   BT1   research reactors
      BT2   research and test reactors
         BT3   reactors
   BT1   thermal reactors
      BT2   reactors
   BT1   wwr type reactors
      BT2   enriched uranium reactors
         BT3   reactors
      BT2   tank type reactors
         BT3   reactors
      BT2   water cooled reactors
         BT3   reactors
      BT2   water moderated reactors
         BT3   reactors

wwr-s-rez reactor
   USE   wwr-s-prague reactor

WWR-S-TASHKENT REACTOR [5; 5]
(Tashkent, USSR)
   UF   *tashkent wwr-s reactor*
   UF   *uzbek wwr-s reactor*
   UF   *wwr-c-tashkent reactor*
   BT1   research reactors
      BT2   research and test reactors
         BT3   reactors
   BT1   thermal reactors
      BT2   reactors
   BT1   wwr type reactors
      BT2   enriched uranium reactors
         BT3   reactors
      BT2   tank type reactors
         BT3   reactors
      BT2   water cooled reactors
         BT3   reactors
      BT2   water moderated reactors
         BT3   reactors

wwr-s-zittau reactor
   USE   zlfr reactor

WWR-SM ROSSENDORF REACTOR
[58; 58]
(Zentralinstitut fuer Kernforschung, Rossendorf bei Dresden, German Democratic Republic)
   UF   *rossendorf wwr-sm reactor*
   BT1   isotope production reactors
      BT2   irradiation reactors

    BT3   reactors
  BT1   research reactors
    BT2   research and test reactors
      BT3   reactors
  BT1   thermal reactors
    BT2   reactors
  BT1   wwr type reactors
    BT2   enriched uranium reactors
      BT3   reactors
    BT2   tank type reactors
      BT3   reactors
    BT2   water cooled reactors
      BT3   reactors
    BT2   water moderated reactors
      BT3   reactors

WWR-2 REACTOR [2; 2]
(Moscow, USSR)
  BT1   isotope production reactors
    BT2   irradiation reactors
      BT3   reactors
  BT1   research reactors
    BT2   research and test reactors
      BT3   reactors
  BT1   thermal reactors
    BT2   reactors
  BT1   wwr type reactors
    BT2   enriched uranium reactors
      BT3   reactors
    BT2   tank type reactors
      BT3   reactors
    BT2   water cooled reactors
      BT3   reactors
    BT2   water moderated reactors
      BT3   reactors

WYHL-1 REACTOR [88; 88] *Oct 75*
  UF   *kws-1 wyhl reactor*
  BT1   pwr type reactors
    BT2   enriched uranium reactors
      BT3   reactors
    BT2   power reactors
      BT3   reactors
    BT2   thermal reactors
      BT3   reactors
    BT2   water cooled reactors
      BT3   reactors
    BT2   water moderated reactors
      BT3   reactors

WYHL-2 REACTOR [8; 8] *Oct 75*
  UF   *kws-2 wyhl reactor*
  BT1   pwr type reactors
    BT2   enriched uranium reactors
      BT3   reactors
    BT2   power reactors
      BT3   reactors
    BT2   thermal reactors
      BT3   reactors
    BT2   water cooled reactors
      BT3   reactors
    BT2   water moderated reactors
      BT3   reactors

wylfa nuclear power station
  USE   wylfa reactor

WYLFA REACTOR [60; 60]
(Anglesey, Wales, UK)
  UF   *wylfa nuclear power station*
  BT1   carbon dioxide cooled reactors
    BT2   gas cooled reactors
      BT3   reactors
  BT1   magnox type reactors
    BT2   gcr type reactors
      BT3   gas cooled reactors
        BT4   reactors
      BT3   graphite moderated reactors
        BT4   reactors
  BT1   natural uranium reactors
    BT2   reactors
  BT1   power reactors
    BT2   reactors
  BT1   thermal reactors
    BT2   reactors

WYOMING [492; 492]
  BT1   usa
    BT2   developed countries
    BT2   north america
  RT   green river formation
  RT   wasatch formation

X CHROMOSOME [102; 102] *Jul 78*
  BT1   heterochromosomes
    BT2   chromosomes

X CODES [125; 125]
  BT1   computer codes

X RADIATION [31,565; 35,827]
  BT1   electromagnetic radiation
    BT2   radiations
  BT1   ionizing radiations
    BT2   radiations
  NT1   hard x radiation
  NT1   soft x radiation
  RT   cosmic x-ray bursts
  RT   cosmic x-ray sources
  RT   fluoroscopy
  RT   gamma radiation
  RT   photons
  RT   solar x-ray bursts
  RT   television
  RT   x-ray fluorescence analysis
  RT   x-ray galaxies
  RT   x-ray spectroscopy

x-rasers
  USE   x-ray lasers

X-RAY DETECTION [2,780; 2,780]
  BT1   radiation detection
    BT2   detection
  RT   x-ray dosimetry
  RT   x-ray spectrometers

X-RAY DIFFRACTION [18,385; 18,385]
  BT1   diffraction
    BT2   coherent scattering
      BT3   scattering
  RT   bragg reflection
  RT   crystallography
  RT   debye-scherrer method
  RT   structural chemical analysis
  RT   x-ray diffractometers

X-RAY DIFFRACTOMETERS [558; 558]
  BT1   diffractometers
    BT2   measuring instruments
  RT   crystallography
  RT   diffraction methods
  RT   structural chemical analysis
  RT   x-ray diffraction

X-RAY DOSIMETRY [1,056; 1,056]
  BT1   dosimetry
  RT   x-ray detection

X-RAY EMISSION ANALYSIS
[1,412; 6,308]
  BT1   nondestructive analysis
    BT2   chemical analysis
  NT1   pixe analysis
  NT1   x-ray fluorescence analysis
  RT   electron probes
  RT   quantitative chemical analysis
  RT   x-ray spectroscopy

X-RAY EQUIPMENT [2,182; 3,797]
  BT1   equipment
  NT1   x-ray tubes
  RT   diagnostic techniques
  RT   diffraction gratings
  RT   electronic equipment
  RT   x-ray sources

X-RAY FLUORESCENCE ANALYSIS
[4,409; 4,409]
  UF   *xeqf spectroscopy*
  BT1   x-ray emission analysis
    BT2   nondestructive analysis
      BT3   chemical analysis
  RT   fluorescence
  RT   fluorescence spectroscopy
  RT   isotope ratio
  RT   x radiation
  RT   x-ray fluorescence analyzers
  RT   x-ray fluorescence logging

X-RAY FLUORESCENCE ANALYZER
[500; 500]
  RT   x-ray fluorescence analysis

X-RAY FLUORESCENCE LOGGING
[39; 39] *Nov 78*
  BT1   radioactivity logging
    BT2   well logging
  RT   x-ray fluorescence analysis

X-RAY GALAXIES [200; 200] *Sep 75*
(Galaxies that emit most of their radiation power in the form of x- rays.)
  BT1   cosmic x-ray sources
    BT2   cosmic ray sources
  BT1   galaxies
  RT   cosmic radiation
  RT   x radiation

X-RAY LASERS [439; 439] *Jul 78*
  UF   *x-rasers*
  BT1   lasers
    BT2   amplifiers
      BT3   equipment

X-RAY RADIOGRAPHY [7,538; 7,538]
  RT   biomedical radiography
  RT   industrial radiography
  RT   nondestructive testing

x-ray radiography (biomedical)
  USE   biomedical radiography

X-RAY SOURCES [1,987; 1,987]
(For cosmic sources of x radiation use COSMIC X-RAY SOURCES.)
  BT1   radiation sources
  RT   nsls
  RT   x-ray equipment

X-RAY SPECTRA [8,994; 8,994]
  BT1   spectra
  RT   x-ray spectroscopy

X-RAY SPECTROMETERS
[1,590; 1,590]
  BT1   spectrometers
    BT2   measuring instruments
  RT   x-ray detection

x-ray spectrometry
  USE   x-ray spectroscopy

X-RAY SPECTROSCOPY [2,952; 2,9
  UF   *x-ray spectrometry*
  BT1   spectroscopy
  RT   x radiation
  RT   x-ray emission analysis
  RT   x-ray spectra

x-ray transmission scanning
  USE   photon transmission scanning

X-RAY TUBES [1,084; 1,084]
  BT1   electron tubes
  BT1   x-ray equipment
    BT2   equipment

x-zero resonances
   USE   eta prime-958 mesons

X-10 REACTOR [1; 1]
(ORNL, Tennessee, USA)
  UF   *ornl x-10 area graphite reacto*
  BT1   air cooled reactors
    BT2 gas cooled reactors
      BT3 reactors
  BT1   graphite moderated reactors
    BT2 reactors
  BT1   isotope production reactors
    BT2 irradiation reactors
      BT3 reactors
  BT1   natural uranium reactors
    BT2 reactors
  BT1   research reactors
    BT2 research and test reactors
      BT3 reactors
  BT1   thermal reactors
    BT2 reactors
  BT1   training reactors
    BT2 research and test reactors
      BT3 reactors

X-1700 MESONS [6; 6] *Dec 87*
  BT1   mesons
    BT2 bosons
    BT2 hadrons
      BT3 elementary particles

X-1935 MESONS [67; 67]
(Pior to December 1987 this concept was indexed by S-1930 RESONANCES.)
  UF   *s-1930 resonances*
  BT1   mesons
    BT2 bosons
    BT2 hadrons
      BT3 elementary particles

X-2220 MESONS [16; 16] *Dec 87*
(Prior to December 1987 this concept was indexed by X-2220 RESONANCES.)
  UF   *x-2220 resonances*
  BT1   mesons
    BT2 bosons
    BT2 hadrons
      BT3 elementary particles

x-2220 resonances
(Prior to December 1987 this was a valid descriptor.)
  USE   x-2220 mesons

x-2830 resonances
(Prior to December 1987 this was a valid descriptor.)
  USE   mesons

X-3075 MESONS [2; 2] *May 88*
  BT1   mesons
    BT2 bosons
    BT2 hadrons
      BT3 elementary particles

XANTHATES [72; 87]
  BT1   organic sulfur compounds
    BT2 organic compounds
  NT1   viscose

XANTHINES [101; 803]
  BT1   organic oxygen compounds
    BT2 organic compounds
  BT1   purines
    BT2 heterocyclic compounds
      BT3 organic compounds
    BT2 organic nitrogen compounds
      BT3 organic compounds
  NT1   caffeine
  NT1   theobromine
  NT1   theophylline
  NT1   uric acid
  RT   hypoxanthine

XDS COMPUTERS [2; 2] *Sep 79*
  UF   *xerox data systems computers*
  BT1   computers

XENOBIOTICS [94; 94] *Feb 81*
  RT   additives
  RT   detergents
  RT   drugs
  RT   nutrients
  RT   organic polymers

XENON [4,617; 4,617]
  BT1   rare gases
    BT2 nonmetals
      BT3 elements

XENON BROMIDES [11; 11]
  BT1   bromides
    BT2 bromine compounds
      BT3 halogen compounds
    BT2 halides
      BT3 halogen compounds
  BT1   xenon compounds
    BT2 rare gas compounds

XENON CHLORIDES [72; 72]
  BT1   chlorides
    BT2 chlorine compounds
      BT3 halogen compounds
    BT2 halides
      BT3 halogen compounds
  BT1   xenon compounds
    BT2 rare gas compounds

XENON COMPLEXES [18; 18]
  BT1   complexes

XENON COMPOUNDS [72; 432]
  BT1   rare gas compounds
  NT1   xenon bromides
  NT1   xenon chlorides
  NT1   xenon fluorides
  NT1   xenon hydrides
  NT1   xenon hydroxides
  NT1   xenon iodides
  NT1   xenon oxides
  NT1   xenon phosphates

xenon effect
  USE   poisoning

XENON FLUORIDES [252; 252]
  BT1   fluorides
    BT2 fluorine compounds
      BT3 halogen compounds
    BT2 halides
      BT3 halogen compounds
  BT1   xenon compounds
    BT2 rare gas compounds

XENON HYDRIDES [1; 1]
  BT1   hydrides
    BT2 hydrogen compounds
  BT1   xenon compounds
    BT2 rare gas compounds

XENON HYDROXIDES [0; 0]
  BT1   hydroxides
    BT2 hydrogen compounds
    BT2 oxygen compounds
  BT1   xenon compounds
    BT2 rare gas compounds

XENON IODIDES [7; 7] *Nov 80*
  BT1   iodides
    BT2 halides
      BT3 halogen compounds
    BT2 iodine compounds
      BT3 halogen compounds
  BT1   xenon compounds
    BT2 rare gas compounds

XENON IONS [1,311; 1,311]
  BT1   ions
    BT2 charged particles

XENON ISOTOPES [611; 4,433]
  NT1   xenon 110
  NT1   xenon 111
  NT1   xenon 112
  NT1   xenon 113
  NT1   xenon 114
  NT1   xenon 115
  NT1   xenon 116
  NT1   xenon 117
  NT1   xenon 118
  NT1   xenon 119
  NT1   xenon 120
  NT1   xenon 121
  NT1   xenon 122
  NT1   xenon 123
  NT1   xenon 124
  NT1   xenon 125
  NT1   xenon 126
  NT1   xenon 127
  NT1   xenon 128
  NT1   xenon 129
  NT1   xenon 130
  NT1   xenon 131
  NT1   xenon 132
  NT1   xenon 133
  NT1   xenon 134
  NT1   xenon 135
  NT1   xenon 136
  NT1   xenon 137
  NT1   xenon 138
  NT1   xenon 139
  NT1   xenon 140
  NT1   xenon 141
  NT1   xenon 142
  NT1   xenon 143
  NT1   xenon 144
  NT1   xenon 145

XENON OSCILLATIONS [59; 59] *Apr 84*
(Effects of fission product xenon levels on reactor operation.)
  BT1   poisoning

XENON OXIDES [36; 36]
  BT1   oxides
    BT2 chalcogenides
    BT2 oxygen compounds
  BT1   xenon compounds
    BT2 rare gas compounds

XENON PHOSPHATES [0; 0]
  BT1   phosphates
    BT2 oxygen compounds
    BT2 phosphorus compounds
  BT1   xenon compounds
    BT2 rare gas compounds

XENON 110 [0; 0] *Apr 86*
  BT1   alpha decay radioisotopes
    BT2 radioisotopes
      BT3 isotopes
  BT1   beta-plus decay radioisotopes
    BT2 beta decay radioisotopes
      BT3 radioisotopes
        BT4 isotopes
  BT1   electron capture radioisotopes
    BT2 beta decay radioisotopes
      BT3 radioisotopes
        BT4 isotopes
  BT1   even-even nuclei
    BT2 nuclei
  BT1   intermediate mass nuclei
    BT2 nuclei
  BT1   millisec living radioisotopes
    BT2 radioisotopes
      BT3 isotopes
  BT1   xenon isotopes

XENON 111 [5; 5] *Apr 80*
  BT1   alpha decay radioisotopes
    BT2   radioisotopes
      BT3   isotopes
  BT1   beta-plus decay radioisotopes
    BT2   beta decay radioisotopes
      BT3   radioisotopes
        BT4   isotopes
  BT1   electron capture radioisotopes
    BT2   beta decay radioisotopes
      BT3   radioisotopes
        BT4   isotopes
  BT1   even-odd nuclei
    BT2   nuclei
  BT1   intermediate mass nuclei
    BT2   nuclei
  BT1   millisec living radioisotopes
    BT2   radioisotopes
      BT3   isotopes
  BT1   xenon isotopes

XENON 112 [15; 15] *Apr 79*
  BT1   alpha decay radioisotopes
    BT2   radioisotopes
      BT3   isotopes
  BT1   beta-plus decay radioisotopes
    BT2   beta decay radioisotopes
      BT3   radioisotopes
        BT4   isotopes
  BT1   electron capture radioisotopes
    BT2   beta decay radioisotopes
      BT3   radioisotopes
        BT4   isotopes
  BT1   even-even nuclei
    BT2   nuclei
  BT1   intermediate mass nuclei
    BT2   nuclei
  BT1   seconds living radioisotopes
    BT2   radioisotopes
      BT3   isotopes
  BT1   xenon isotopes

XENON 113 [22; 22]
  BT1   beta-plus decay radioisotopes
    BT2   beta decay radioisotopes
      BT3   radioisotopes
        BT4   isotopes
  BT1   electron capture radioisotopes
    BT2   beta decay radioisotopes
      BT3   radioisotopes
        BT4   isotopes
  BT1   even-odd nuclei
    BT2   nuclei
  BT1   intermediate mass nuclei
    BT2   nuclei
  BT1   seconds living radioisotopes
    BT2   radioisotopes
      BT3   isotopes
  BT1   xenon isotopes

XENON 114 [5; 5] *Feb 78*
  BT1   beta-plus decay radioisotopes
    BT2   beta decay radioisotopes
      BT3   radioisotopes
        BT4   isotopes
  BT1   electron capture radioisotopes
    BT2   beta decay radioisotopes
      BT3   radioisotopes
        BT4   isotopes
  BT1   even-even nuclei
    BT2   nuclei
  BT1   intermediate mass nuclei
    BT2   nuclei
  BT1   seconds living radioisotopes
    BT2   radioisotopes
      BT3   isotopes
  BT1   xenon isotopes

XENON 115 [6; 6]
  BT1   beta-plus decay radioisotopes
    BT2   beta decay radioisotopes
      BT3   radioisotopes
        BT4   isotopes
  BT1   electron capture radioisotopes
    BT2   beta decay radioisotopes
      BT3   radioisotopes
        BT4   isotopes
  BT1   even-odd nuclei
    BT2   nuclei
  BT1   intermediate mass nuclei
    BT2   nuclei
  BT1   seconds living radioisotopes
    BT2   radioisotopes
      BT3   isotopes
  BT1   xenon isotopes

XENON 116 [10; 10]
  BT1   beta-plus decay radioisotopes
    BT2   beta decay radioisotopes
      BT3   radioisotopes
        BT4   isotopes
  BT1   electron capture radioisotopes
    BT2   beta decay radioisotopes
      BT3   radioisotopes
        BT4   isotopes
  BT1   even-even nuclei
    BT2   nuclei
  BT1   intermediate mass nuclei
    BT2   nuclei
  BT1   seconds living radioisotopes
    BT2   radioisotopes
      BT3   isotopes
  BT1   xenon isotopes

XENON 117 [13; 13]
  BT1   beta-plus decay radioisotopes
    BT2   beta decay radioisotopes
      BT3   radioisotopes
        BT4   isotopes
  BT1   electron capture radioisotopes
    BT2   beta decay radioisotopes
      BT3   radioisotopes
        BT4   isotopes
  BT1   even-odd nuclei
    BT2   nuclei
  BT1   intermediate mass nuclei
    BT2   nuclei
  BT1   minutes living radioisotopes
    BT2   radioisotopes
      BT3   isotopes
  BT1   xenon isotopes

XENON 118 [27; 27]
  BT1   beta-plus decay radioisotopes
    BT2   beta decay radioisotopes
      BT3   radioisotopes
        BT4   isotopes
  BT1   electron capture radioisotopes
    BT2   beta decay radioisotopes
      BT3   radioisotopes
        BT4   isotopes
  BT1   even-even nuclei
    BT2   nuclei
  BT1   intermediate mass nuclei
    BT2   nuclei
  BT1   minutes living radioisotopes
    BT2   radioisotopes
      BT3   isotopes
  BT1   xenon isotopes

XENON 119 [25; 25]
  BT1   beta-plus decay radioisotopes
    BT2   beta decay radioisotopes
      BT3   radioisotopes
        BT4   isotopes
  BT1   electron capture radioisotopes
    BT2   beta decay radioisotopes
      BT3   radioisotopes
        BT4   isotopes
  BT1   even-odd nuclei
    BT2   nuclei
  BT1   intermediate mass nuclei
    BT2   nuclei
  BT1   minutes living radioisotopes
    BT2   radioisotopes
      BT3   isotopes
  BT1   xenon isotopes

XENON 120 [40; 40]
  BT1   beta-plus decay radioisotopes
    BT2   beta decay radioisotopes
      BT3   radioisotopes
        BT4   isotopes
  BT1   electron capture radioisotopes
    BT2   beta decay radioisotopes
      BT3   radioisotopes
        BT4   isotopes
  BT1   even-even nuclei
    BT2   nuclei
  BT1   intermediate mass nuclei
    BT2   nuclei
  BT1   minutes living radioisotopes
    BT2   radioisotopes
      BT3   isotopes
  BT1   xenon isotopes

XENON 121 [22; 22]
  BT1   beta-plus decay radioisotopes
    BT2   beta decay radioisotopes
      BT3   radioisotopes
        BT4   isotopes
  BT1   electron capture radioisotopes
    BT2   beta decay radioisotopes
      BT3   radioisotopes
        BT4   isotopes
  BT1   even-odd nuclei
    BT2   nuclei
  BT1   intermediate mass nuclei
    BT2   nuclei
  BT1   minutes living radioisotopes
    BT2   radioisotopes
      BT3   isotopes
  BT1   xenon isotopes

XENON 122 [60; 60]
  BT1   electron capture radioisotopes
    BT2   beta decay radioisotopes
      BT3   radioisotopes
        BT4   isotopes
  BT1   even-even nuclei
    BT2   nuclei
  BT1   hours living radioisotopes
    BT2   radioisotopes
      BT3   isotopes
  BT1   intermediate mass nuclei
    BT2   nuclei
  BT1   xenon isotopes

XENON 123 [115; 115]
  BT1   beta-plus decay radioisotopes
    BT2   beta decay radioisotopes
      BT3   radioisotopes
        BT4   isotopes
  BT1   electron capture radioisotopes
    BT2   beta decay radioisotopes
      BT3   radioisotopes
        BT4   isotopes
  BT1   even-odd nuclei
    BT2   nuclei
  BT1   hours living radioisotopes
    BT2   radioisotopes
      BT3   isotopes
  BT1   intermediate mass nuclei
    BT2   nuclei
  BT1   xenon isotopes

XENON 123 TARGET [3; 3] *Dec 75*
  BT1   targets

XENON 124 [103; 103]
  BT1   even-even nuclei
    BT2   nuclei
  BT1   intermediate mass nuclei
    BT2   nuclei
  BT1   stable isotopes
    BT2   isotopes
  BT1   xenon isotopes

XENON 124 TARGET [39; 39] *Feb*
  BT1   targets

XENON 125 [85; 85]
  BT1   beta-plus decay radioisotopes
    BT2   beta decay radioisotopes
      BT3   radioisotopes
        BT4   isotopes
  BT1   electron capture radioisotopes
    BT2   beta decay radioisotopes
      BT3   radioisotopes
        BT4   isotopes
  BT1   even-odd nuclei
    BT2   nuclei
  BT1   hours living radioisotopes
    BT2   radioisotopes

BT3   isotopes
BT1   intermediate mass nuclei
BT2   nuclei
BT1   internal conversion radioisoto
BT2   radioisotopes
BT3   isotopes
BT1   isomeric transition isotopes
BT2   radioisotopes
BT3   isotopes
BT1   seconds living radioisotopes
BT2   radioisotopes
BT3   isotopes
BT1   xenon isotopes

XENON 125 TARGET [5; 5] *Jul 78*
BT1   targets

XENON 126 [86; 86]
BT1   even-even nuclei
BT2   nuclei
BT1   intermediate mass nuclei
BT2   nuclei
BT1   stable isotopes
BT2   isotopes
BT1   xenon isotopes

XENON 126 TARGET [7; 7] *Feb 76*
BT1   targets

XENON 127 [151; 151]
BT1   days living radioisotopes
BT2   radioisotopes
BT3   isotopes
BT1   electron capture radioisotopes
BT2   beta decay radioisotopes
BT3   radioisotopes
BT4   isotopes
BT1   even-odd nuclei
BT2   nuclei
BT1   intermediate mass nuclei
BT2   nuclei
BT1   isomeric transition isotopes
BT2   radioisotopes
BT3   isotopes
BT1   minutes living radioisotopes
BT2   radioisotopes
BT3   isotopes
BT1   xenon isotopes

XENON 127 TARGET [4; 4] *Feb 79*
BT1   targets

XENON 128 [100; 100]
BT1   even-even nuclei
BT2   nuclei
BT1   intermediate mass nuclei
BT2   nuclei
BT1   stable isotopes
BT2   isotopes
BT1   xenon isotopes

XENON 128 TARGET [8; 8] *Oct 75*
BT1   targets

XENON 129 [225; 225]
BT1   days living radioisotopes
BT2   radioisotopes
BT3   isotopes
BT1   even-odd nuclei
BT2   nuclei
BT1   intermediate mass nuclei
BT2   nuclei
BT1   internal conversion radioisoto
BT2   radioisotopes
BT3   isotopes
BT1   isomeric transition isotopes
BT2   radioisotopes
BT3   isotopes
BT1   stable isotopes
BT2   isotopes
BT1   xenon isotopes

XENON 129 BEAMS [58; 58] *Jul 76*
BT1   ion beams
BT2   beams

XENON 129 REACTIONS [50; 50]
Jul 76
BT1   heavy ion reactions
BT2   nuclear reactions

XENON 129 TARGET [9; 9] *May 84*
BT1   targets

XENON 130 [102; 102]
BT1   even-even nuclei
BT2   nuclei
BT1   intermediate mass nuclei
BT2   nuclei
BT1   stable isotopes
BT2   isotopes
BT1   xenon isotopes

XENON 130 TARGET [8; 8] *Oct 75*
BT1   targets

XENON 131 [215; 215]
BT1   days living radioisotopes
BT2   radioisotopes
BT3   isotopes
BT1   even-odd nuclei
BT2   nuclei
BT1   intermediate mass nuclei
BT2   nuclei
BT1   internal conversion radioisoto
BT2   radioisotopes
BT3   isotopes
BT1   isomeric transition isotopes
BT2   radioisotopes
BT3   isotopes
BT1   stable isotopes
BT2   isotopes
BT1   xenon isotopes

XENON 131 BEAMS [11; 11] *Feb 77*
BT1   ion beams
BT2   beams

XENON 131 TARGET [44; 44] *Apr 79*
BT1   targets

XENON 132 [194; 194]
BT1   even-even nuclei
BT2   nuclei
BT1   even-odd nuclei
BT2   nuclei
BT1   intermediate mass nuclei
BT2   nuclei
BT1   stable isotopes
BT2   isotopes
BT1   xenon isotopes

XENON 132 BEAMS [89; 89] *Jan 79*
BT1   ion beams
BT2   beams

XENON 132 REACTIONS [123; 123]
Feb 77
BT1   heavy ion reactions
BT2   nuclear reactions

XENON 132 TARGET [87; 87] *Oct 75*
BT1   targets

XENON 133 [2,295; 2,295]
BT1   beta-minus decay radioisotopes
BT2   beta decay radioisotopes
BT3   radioisotopes
BT4   isotopes
BT1   days living radioisotopes
BT2   radioisotopes
BT3   isotopes
BT1   even-odd nuclei
BT2   nuclei
BT1   intermediate mass nuclei
BT2   nuclei
BT1   internal conversion radioisoto
BT2   radioisotopes
BT3   isotopes
BT1   isomeric transition isotopes
BT2   radioisotopes
BT3   isotopes
BT1   xenon isotopes

XENON 134 [94; 94]
BT1   even-even nuclei
BT2   nuclei
BT1   intermediate mass nuclei
BT2   nuclei
BT1   stable isotopes
BT2   isotopes
BT1   xenon isotopes

XENON 134 REACTIONS [6; 6] *Sep 83*
BT1   heavy ion reactions
BT2   nuclear reactions

XENON 134 TARGET [8; 8] *Oct 75*
BT1   targets

XENON 135 [331; 331]
BT1   beta-minus decay radioisotopes
BT2   beta decay radioisotopes
BT3   radioisotopes
BT4   isotopes
BT1   even-odd nuclei
BT2   nuclei
BT1   hours living radioisotopes
BT2   radioisotopes
BT3   isotopes
BT1   intermediate mass nuclei
BT2   nuclei
BT1   isomeric transition isotopes
BT2   radioisotopes
BT3   isotopes
BT1   minutes living radioisotopes
BT2   radioisotopes
BT3   isotopes
BT1   xenon isotopes

XENON 136 [224; 224]
BT1   even-even nuclei
BT2   nuclei
BT1   intermediate mass nuclei
BT2   nuclei
BT1   stable isotopes
BT2   isotopes
BT1   xenon isotopes
RT   xenon 136 beams

XENON 136 BEAMS [61; 61]
BT1   ion beams
BT2   beams
RT   xenon 136

XENON 136 REACTIONS [279; 279]
BT1   heavy ion reactions
BT2   nuclear reactions

XENON 136 TARGET [42; 42] *Oct 75*
BT1   targets

XENON 137 [69; 69]
BT1   beta-minus decay radioisotopes
BT2   beta decay radioisotopes
BT3   radioisotopes
BT4   isotopes
BT1   even-odd nuclei
BT2   nuclei
BT1   intermediate mass nuclei
BT2   nuclei
BT1   minutes living radioisotopes
BT2   radioisotopes
BT3   isotopes
BT1   xenon isotopes

XENON 138 [87; 87]
BT1   beta-minus decay radioisotopes
BT2   beta decay radioisotopes
BT3   radioisotopes
BT4   isotopes
BT1   even-even nuclei
BT2   nuclei

BT1   intermediate mass nuclei
BT2   nuclei
BT1   minutes living radioisotopes
BT2   radioisotopes
BT3   isotopes
BT1   xenon isotopes

XENON 139 [32; 32]
BT1   beta-minus decay radioisotopes
BT2   beta decay radioisotopes
BT3   radioisotopes
BT4   isotopes
BT1   even-odd nuclei
BT2   nuclei
BT1   intermediate mass nuclei
BT2   nuclei
BT1   seconds living radioisotopes
BT2   radioisotopes
BT3   isotopes
BT1   xenon isotopes

XENON 140 [21; 21]
BT1   beta-minus decay radioisotopes
BT2   beta decay radioisotopes
BT3   radioisotopes
BT4   isotopes
BT1   even-even nuclei
BT2   nuclei
BT1   intermediate mass nuclei
BT2   nuclei
BT1   seconds living radioisotopes
BT2   radioisotopes
BT3   isotopes
BT1   xenon isotopes

XENON 141 [9; 9]
BT1   beta-minus decay radioisotopes
BT2   beta decay radioisotopes
BT3   radioisotopes
BT4   isotopes
BT1   even-odd nuclei
BT2   nuclei
BT1   intermediate mass nuclei
BT2   nuclei
BT1   seconds living radioisotopes
BT2   radioisotopes
BT3   isotopes
BT1   xenon isotopes

XENON 142 [13; 13]
BT1   beta-minus decay radioisotopes
BT2   beta decay radioisotopes
BT3   radioisotopes
BT4   isotopes
BT1   even-even nuclei
BT2   nuclei
BT1   intermediate mass nuclei
BT2   nuclei
BT1   seconds living radioisotopes
BT2   radioisotopes
BT3   isotopes
BT1   xenon isotopes

XENON 143 [7; 7]
BT1   beta-minus decay radioisotopes
BT2   beta decay radioisotopes
BT3   radioisotopes
BT4   isotopes
BT1   even-odd nuclei
BT2   nuclei
BT1   intermediate mass nuclei
BT2   nuclei
BT1   millisec living radioisotopes
BT2   radioisotopes
BT3   isotopes
BT1   xenon isotopes

XENON 144 [3; 3]
BT1   beta-minus decay radioisotopes
BT2   beta decay radioisotopes
BT3   radioisotopes
BT4   isotopes
BT1   even-even nuclei
BT2   nuclei
BT1   intermediate mass nuclei
BT2   nuclei
BT1   seconds living radioisotopes
BT2   radioisotopes
BT3   isotopes
BT1   xenon isotopes

XENON 145 [4; 4]
BT1   beta-minus decay radioisotopes
BT2   beta decay radioisotopes
BT3   radioisotopes
BT4   isotopes
BT1   even-odd nuclei
BT2   nuclei
BT1   intermediate mass nuclei
BT2   nuclei
BT1   millisec living radioisotopes
BT2   radioisotopes
BT3   isotopes
BT1   xenon isotopes

XENOTIME [39; 39]
BT1   phosphate minerals
BT2   minerals
RT   granites
RT   pegmatites
RT   yttrium phosphates

xeqf spectroscopy
USE   x-ray fluorescence analysis

xeroderma pigmentosum cells
USE   xp cells

XEROGRAPHY [226; 226]
UF   *xeroradiography*
RT   electrostatics
RT   photography

xeroradiography
(Coordinate, as appropriate, with BIOMEDICAL RADIOGRAPHY or INDUSTRIAL RADIOGRAPHY.)
USE   xerography

xerox data systems computers
USE   xds computers

XI BARYONS [13; 210] *Dec 87*
BT1   hyperons
BT2   baryons
BT3   fermions
BT3   hadrons
BT4   elementary particles
BT2   strange particles
BT3   elementary particles
NT1   xi particles
NT2   antixi particles
NT2   xi minus particles
NT2   xi neutral particles
NT1   xi-1530 baryons
NT1   xi-1630 baryons
NT1   xi-1680 baryons
NT1   xi-1820 baryons
NT1   xi-1940 baryons
NT1   xi-2030 baryons
NT1   xi-2120 baryons
NT1   xi-2250 baryons
NT1   xi-2370 baryons
NT1   xi-2500 baryons

XI C PLUS BARYONS [30; 30] *Dec 87*
BT1   charmed baryons
BT2   baryons
BT3   fermions
BT3   hadrons
BT4   elementary particles
BT2   charm particles
BT3   elementary particles

xi minus
(Prior to December 1987 this was a valid descriptor.)
USE   xi minus particles

XI MINUS PARTICLES [316; 316]
(Prior to August 1985 this concept was indexed by XI-MINUS and from August 1985 to December 1987 by XI MINUS.)
UF   *xi minus*
UF   *xi-minus*
BT1   xi particles
BT2   xi baryons
BT3   hyperons
BT4   baryons
BT5   fermions
BT5   hadrons
BT6   elementary particles
BT4   strange particles
BT5   elementary particles

xi neutral
(Prior to December 1987 this was a valid descriptor.)
USE   xi neutral particles

XI NEUTRAL PARTICLES [154; 154]
(Prior to August 1985 this concept was indexed by XI-NEUTRAL and from August 1985 to December 1987 by XI NEUTRAL.)
UF   *xi neutral*
UF   *xi-neutral*
BT1   xi particles
BT2   xi baryons
BT3   hyperons
BT4   baryons
BT5   fermions
BT5   hadrons
BT6   elementary particles
BT4   strange particles
BT5   elementary particles

XI PARTICLE BEAMS [4; 4]
BT1   hyperon beams
BT2   particle beams
BT3   beams

XI PARTICLES [212; 593]
BT1   xi baryons
BT2   hyperons
BT3   baryons
BT4   fermions
BT4   hadrons
BT5   elementary particles
BT3   strange particles
BT4   elementary particles
NT1   antixi particles
NT1   xi minus particles
NT1   xi neutral particles

xi-minus
(Prior to August 1985 this was a valid descriptor.)
USE   xi minus particles

xi-neutral
(Prior to August 1985 this was a valid descriptor.)
USE   xi neutral particles

XI-1530 BARYONS [95; 95]
(Prior to December 1987 this concept was indexed by XI-1530 RESONANCES.)
UF   *xi-1530 resonances*
BT1   xi baryons
BT2   hyperons
BT3   baryons
BT4   fermions
BT4   hadrons
BT5   elementary particles
BT3   strange particles
BT4   elementary particles

xi-1530 resonances
(Prior to December 1987 this was a valid descriptor.)
USE   xi-1530 baryons

XI-1630 BARYONS [8; 8]
  UF   *xi-1630 resonances*
  BT1   xi baryons
    BT2   hyperons
      BT3   baryons
        BT4   fermions
        BT4   hadrons
          BT5   elementary particles
      BT3   strange particles
        BT4   elementary particles

xi-1630 resonances
(Prior to December 1987 this was a valid descriptor.)
  USE   xi-1630 baryons

XI-1680 BARYONS [0; 0] *Dec 87*
  BT1   xi baryons
    BT2   hyperons
      BT3   baryons
        BT4   fermions
        BT4   hadrons
          BT5   elementary particles
      BT3   strange particles
        BT4   elementary particles

XI-1820 BARYONS [24; 24]
(Prior to December 1987 this concept was indexed by XI-1820 RESONANCES.)
  UF   *xi-1820 resonances*
  BT1   xi baryons
    BT2   hyperons
      BT3   baryons
        BT4   fermions
        BT4   hadrons
          BT5   elementary particles
      BT3   strange particles
        BT4   elementary particles

xi-1820 resonances
(Prior to December 1987 this was a valid descriptor.)
  USE   xi-1820 baryons

xi-1930 resonances
(Prior to December 1987 this was a valid descriptor.)
  USE   xi-1940 baryons

XI-1940 BARYONS [14; 14]
(Prior to December 1987 this concept was indexed by XI-1930 RESONANCES.)
  UF   *xi-1930 resonances*
  BT1   xi baryons
    BT2   hyperons
      BT3   baryons
        BT4   fermions
        BT4   hadrons
          BT5   elementary particles
      BT3   strange particles
        BT4   elementary particles

XI-2030 BARYONS [13; 13]
(Prior to December 1987 this concept was indexed by XI-2030 RESONANCES.)
  UF   *xi-2030 resonances*
  BT1   xi baryons
    BT2   hyperons
      BT3   baryons
        BT4   fermions
        BT4   hadrons
          BT5   elementary particles
      BT3   strange particles
        BT4   elementary particles

xi-2030 resonances
(Prior to December 1987 this was a valid descriptor.)
  USE   xi-2030 baryons

XI-2120 BARYONS [0; 0] *Dec 87*
  BT1   xi baryons
    BT2   hyperons
      BT3   baryons
        BT4   fermions
        BT4   hadrons
          BT5   elementary particles
      BT3   strange particles
        BT4   elementary particles

XI-2250 BARYONS [7; 7] *Dec 87*
  BT1   xi baryons
    BT2   hyperons
      BT3   baryons
        BT4   fermions
        BT4   hadrons
          BT5   elementary particles
      BT3   strange particles
        BT4   elementary particles

XI-2370 BARYONS [0; 0] *Dec 87*
  BT1   xi baryons
    BT2   hyperons
      BT3   baryons
        BT4   fermions
        BT4   hadrons
          BT5   elementary particles
      BT3   strange particles
        BT4   elementary particles

XI-2500 BARYONS [2; 2] *Dec 87*
  BT1   xi baryons
    BT2   hyperons
      BT3   baryons
        BT4   fermions
        BT4   hadrons
          BT5   elementary particles
      BT3   strange particles
        BT4   elementary particles

XP CELLS [337; 337] *Jul 76*
  UF   *xeroderma pigmentosum cells*
  BT1   animal cells

xuv
  USE   extreme ultraviolet radiation

XYLENE-PARA [40; 40]
  BT1   xylenes
    BT2   aromatics
      BT3   organic compounds
    BT2   hydrocarbons
      BT3   organic compounds

XYLENES [332; 368]
  UF   *dimethylbenzenes*
  BT1   aromatics
    BT2   organic compounds
  BT1   hydrocarbons
    BT2   organic compounds
  NT1   xylene-para

XYLENOL ORANGE [169; 169]
  BT1   dyes
  BT1   indicators

XYLOSE [65; 65]
  BT1   aldehydes
    BT2   organic compounds
  BT1   pentoses
    BT2   monosaccharides
      BT3   saccharides
        BT4   carbohydrates
          BT5   organic compounds
  RT   wood

Y CHROMOSOME [17; 17]
  BT1   heterochromosomes
    BT2   chromosomes

Y CODES [31; 31]
  BT1   computer codes

*y*resonances*
(Prior to December 1987 this was a valid descriptor.)
  USE   baryons

Y-12 PLANT [153; 153]
  BT1   us aec
    BT2   us organizations
      BT3   national organizations
  BT1   us doe
    BT2   us organizations
      BT3   national organizations
  BT1   us erda
    BT2   us organizations
      BT3   national organizations
  RT   oak ridge reservation
  RT   tennessee

yamaguchi nonlocal potential
  USE   yamaguchi potential

YAMAGUCHI POTENTIAL [222; 222]
  UF   *yamaguchi nonlocal potential*
  BT1   nucleon-nucleon potential
    BT2   potentials
  RT   nucleons

YAMS [27; 27]
(Tuberous root of plants of the genus Dioscorea.)
  BT1   vegetables
    BT2   food

YANG THEOREM [17; 17]
  RT   angular distribution
  RT   nuclear reactions

YANG-FELDMAN FORMALISM [33; 33]
  RT   quantum field theory
  RT   s matrix

yang-lee distribution
  USE   lee-yang theory

YANG-MILLS THEORY [5,097; 5,097]
  RT   instantons
  RT   isospin
  RT   quantum field theory
  RT   wilson loop

yankee connecticut reactor
  USE   connecticut yankee reactor

YANKEE EVENT [2; 2] *Jan 85*
  BT1   atmospheric explosions
    BT2   explosions
  BT1   castle project
  BT1   nuclear explosions
    BT2   explosions

yankee maine reactor
  USE   maine yankee reactor

yankee rowe reactor
  USE   rowe yankee reactor

yankee vermont reactor
  USE   vermont yankee reactor

YAYOI REACTOR [142; 142]
  BT1   fast reactors
    BT2   epithermal reactors
      BT3   reactors
  BT1   research and test reactors

BT2   reactors

* YEARS LIVING RADIOISOTOPES [84; 101,714]
(For specific terms, consult the Appendix.)
BT1   radioisotopes
BT2   isotopes
RT   half-life

YEASTS [531; 1,588]
BT1   fungi
BT2   plants
BT1   microorganisms
NT1   candida
NT1   saccharomyces
NT2   saccharomyces cerevisiae
NT1   torula
RT   zymosan

YEELIRRIE DEPOSIT [16; 16] Dec 80
BT1   uranium deposits
BT2   geologic deposits
RT   uranium ores
RT   western australia

yellow cake
USE   uranium oxides u3o8

YELLOW CREEK-1 REACTOR [5; 5]
Nov 77
(Corinth, Mississippi, USA)
BT1   pwr type reactors
BT2   enriched uranium reactors
BT3   reactors
BT2   power reactors
BT3   reactors
BT2   thermal reactors
BT3   reactors
BT2   water cooled reactors
BT3   reactors
BT2   water moderated reactors
BT3   reactors

YELLOW CREEK-2 REACTOR [4; 4]
Nov 77
(Corinth, Mississippi, USA)
BT1   pwr type reactors
BT2   enriched uranium reactors
BT3   reactors
BT2   power reactors
BT3   reactors
BT2   thermal reactors
BT3   reactors
BT2   water cooled reactors
BT3   reactors
BT2   water moderated reactors
BT3   reactors

→ YEMEN [0; 0] Nov 91
BT1   developing countries
BT1   middle east

yerevan synchrotron
USE   erevan synchrotron

yield (biological)
USE   productivity

yield (chemical reaction)
USE   chemical reaction yield

yield (fission)
USE   fission yield

yield (fusion)
USE   fusion yield

yield (nuclear reaction)
USE   nuclear reaction yield

YIELD STRENGTH [2,620; 2,620]
UF   *strength (yield)*
BT1   mechanical properties
RT   tensile properties

yolk
USE   eggs

yoshida sarcoma
USE   experimental neoplasms

YOSHIMORI-KITANO MODEL [2; 2]
RT   transport theory

YOUNG DIAGRAM [118; 118]
BT1   diagrams
BT2   information
RT   group theory

YOUNG MODEL [6; 6]
RT   transport theory

YOUNG MODULUS [1,487; 1,487]
BT1   mechanical properties
RT   elasticity
RT   hooke law

YRAST STATES [2,332; 2,332]
(The lowest energy states for given angular momenta.)
BT1   energy levels
RT   angular momentum
RT   backbending
RT   moment of inertia
RT   nuclear structure

YTTERBIUM [1,081; 1,081]
BT1   rare earths
BT2   metals
BT3   elements

YTTERBIUM ADDITIONS [109; 109]
(Alloys containing not more than 1% Yb are listed here.)
BT1   rare earth additions
RT   ytterbium alloys
RT   ytterbium compounds

YTTERBIUM ALLOYS [265; 281]
(Alloys containing more than 1% Yb.)
BT1   rare earth alloys
BT2   alloys
NT1   ytterbium base alloys
RT   ytterbium additions

YTTERBIUM BASE ALLOYS [11; 11]
BT1   ytterbium alloys
BT2   rare earth alloys
BT3   alloys

YTTERBIUM BORIDES [39; 39]
BT1   borides
BT2   boron compounds
BT1   ytterbium compounds
BT2   rare earth compounds

YTTERBIUM BROMIDES [14; 14]
BT1   bromides
BT2   bromine compounds
BT3   halogen compounds
BT2   halides
BT3   halogen compounds
BT1   ytterbium compounds
BT2   rare earth compounds

YTTERBIUM CARBIDES [14; 14]
BT1   carbides
BT2   carbon compounds
BT1   ytterbium compounds
BT2   rare earth compounds

YTTERBIUM CARBONATES [4; 4]
BT1   carbonates
BT2   carbon compounds
BT2   oxygen compounds
BT1   ytterbium compounds
BT2   rare earth compounds

YTTERBIUM CHLORIDES [105; 105]
BT1   chlorides
BT2   chlorine compounds
BT3   halogen compounds
BT2   halides
BT3   halogen compounds
BT1   ytterbium compounds
BT2   rare earth compounds

YTTERBIUM COMPLEXES [320; 320]
BT1   rare earth complexes
BT2   complexes

YTTERBIUM COMPOUNDS [477; 1,257]
BT1   rare earth compounds
NT1   ytterbium borides
NT1   ytterbium bromides
NT1   ytterbium carbides
NT1   ytterbium carbonates
NT1   ytterbium chlorides
NT1   ytterbium fluorides
NT1   ytterbium hydrides
NT1   ytterbium hydroxides
NT1   ytterbium iodides
NT1   ytterbium nitrates
NT1   ytterbium nitrides
NT1   ytterbium oxides
NT1   ytterbium perchlorates
NT1   ytterbium phosphates
NT1   ytterbium selenides
NT1   ytterbium silicates
NT1   ytterbium silicides
NT1   ytterbium sulfates
NT1   ytterbium sulfides
NT1   ytterbium tellurides
NT1   ytterbium tungstates
RT   ytterbium additions

YTTERBIUM FLUORIDES [68; 68]
BT1   fluorides
BT2   fluorine compounds
BT3   halogen compounds
BT2   halides
BT3   halogen compounds
BT1   ytterbium compounds
BT2   rare earth compounds

YTTERBIUM HYDRIDES [29; 29]
BT1   hydrides
BT2   hydrogen compounds
BT1   ytterbium compounds
BT2   rare earth compounds

YTTERBIUM HYDROXIDES [6; 6]
BT1   hydroxides
BT2   hydrogen compounds
BT2   oxygen compounds
BT1   ytterbium compounds
BT2   rare earth compounds

YTTERBIUM IODIDES [30; 30]
BT1   iodides
BT2   halides
BT3   halogen compounds
BT2   iodine compounds
BT3   halogen compounds
BT1   ytterbium compounds
BT2   rare earth compounds

YTTERBIUM IONS [268; 268]
BT1 ions
BT2 charged particles

YTTERBIUM ISOTOPES [214; 2,026]
NT1 ytterbium 150
NT1 ytterbium 151
NT1 ytterbium 152
NT1 ytterbium 153
NT1 ytterbium 154
NT1 ytterbium 155
NT1 ytterbium 156
NT1 ytterbium 157
NT1 ytterbium 158
NT1 ytterbium 159
NT1 ytterbium 160
NT1 ytterbium 161
NT1 ytterbium 162
NT1 ytterbium 163
NT1 ytterbium 164
NT1 ytterbium 165
NT1 ytterbium 166
NT1 ytterbium 167
NT1 ytterbium 168
NT1 ytterbium 169
NT1 ytterbium 170
NT1 ytterbium 171
NT1 ytterbium 172
NT1 ytterbium 173
NT1 ytterbium 174
NT1 ytterbium 175
NT1 ytterbium 176
NT1 ytterbium 177
NT1 ytterbium 178
NT1 ytterbium 179
NT1 ytterbium 180

YTTERBIUM NITRATES [30; 30]
BT1 nitrates
BT2 nitrogen compounds
BT2 oxygen compounds
BT1 ytterbium compounds
BT2 rare earth compounds

YTTERBIUM NITRIDES [8; 8]
BT1 nitrides
BT2 nitrogen compounds
BT2 pnictides
BT1 ytterbium compounds
BT2 rare earth compounds

YTTERBIUM OXIDES [339; 339]
BT1 oxides
BT2 chalcogenides
BT2 oxygen compounds
BT1 ytterbium compounds
BT2 rare earth compounds

YTTERBIUM PERCHLORATES [0; 0]
Sep 91
BT1 perchlorates
BT2 chlorine compounds
BT3 halogen compounds
BT2 oxygen compounds
BT1 ytterbium compounds
BT2 rare earth compounds

YTTERBIUM PHOSPHATES [20; 20]
Oct 75
BT1 phosphates
BT2 oxygen compounds
BT2 phosphorus compounds
BT1 ytterbium compounds
BT2 rare earth compounds

YTTERBIUM SELENIDES [19; 19]
Jan 77
BT1 selenides
BT2 chalcogenides
BT2 selenium compounds
BT1 ytterbium compounds
BT2 rare earth compounds

YTTERBIUM SILICATES [6; 6]
BT1 silicates
BT2 oxygen compounds
BT2 silicon compounds
BT1 ytterbium compounds
BT2 rare earth compounds

YTTERBIUM SILICIDES [12; 12] *Jul 78*
BT1 silicides
BT2 silicon compounds
BT1 ytterbium compounds
BT2 rare earth compounds

YTTERBIUM SULFATES [20; 20]
BT1 sulfates
BT2 oxygen compounds
BT2 sulfur compounds
BT1 ytterbium compounds
BT2 rare earth compounds

YTTERBIUM SULFIDES [70; 70]
BT1 sulfides
BT2 chalcogenides
BT2 sulfur compounds
BT1 ytterbium compounds
BT2 rare earth compounds

YTTERBIUM TELLURIDES [4; 4]
Sep 87
BT1 tellurides
BT2 chalcogenides
BT2 tellurium compounds
BT1 ytterbium compounds
BT2 rare earth compounds

YTTERBIUM TUNGSTATES [5; 5]
Feb 79
BT1 tungstates
BT2 oxygen compounds
BT2 tungsten compounds
BT3 transition element compounds
BT1 ytterbium compounds
BT2 rare earth compounds

YTTERBIUM 150 [2; 2] *Apr 85*
BT1 even-even nuclei
BT2 nuclei
BT1 rare earth nuclei
BT2 intermediate mass nuclei
BT3 nuclei
BT1 ytterbium isotopes

YTTERBIUM 151 [16; 16] *Oct 85*
BT1 even-odd nuclei
BT2 nuclei
BT1 rare earth nuclei
BT2 intermediate mass nuclei
BT3 nuclei
BT1 ytterbium isotopes

YTTERBIUM 152 [24; 24] *Dec 80*
BT1 even-even nuclei
BT2 nuclei
BT1 rare earth nuclei
BT2 intermediate mass nuclei
BT3 nuclei
BT1 ytterbium isotopes

YTTERBIUM 153 [11; 11] *Jun 77*
BT1 beta-plus decay radioisotopes
BT2 beta decay radioisotopes
BT3 radioisotopes
BT4 isotopes
BT1 electron capture radioisotopes
BT2 beta decay radioisotopes
BT3 radioisotopes
BT4 isotopes
BT1 even-odd nuclei
BT2 nuclei
BT1 isomeric transition isotopes
BT2 radioisotopes
BT3 isotopes
BT1 microsec living radioisotopes
BT2 radioisotopes
BT3 isotopes
BT1 rare earth nuclei
BT2 intermediate mass nuclei
BT3 nuclei
BT1 seconds living radioisotopes
BT2 radioisotopes
BT3 isotopes
BT1 ytterbium isotopes

YTTERBIUM 154 [10; 10] *Oct 76*
BT1 alpha decay radioisotopes
BT2 radioisotopes
BT3 isotopes
BT1 even-even nuclei
BT2 nuclei
BT1 millisec living radioisotopes
BT2 radioisotopes
BT3 isotopes
BT1 rare earth nuclei
BT2 intermediate mass nuclei
BT3 nuclei
BT1 ytterbium isotopes

YTTERBIUM 155 [6; 6] *Jan 76*
BT1 alpha decay radioisotopes
BT2 radioisotopes
BT3 isotopes
BT1 electron capture radioisotopes
BT2 beta decay radioisotopes
BT3 radioisotopes
BT4 isotopes
BT1 even-odd nuclei
BT2 nuclei
BT1 rare earth nuclei
BT2 intermediate mass nuclei
BT3 nuclei
BT1 seconds living radioisotopes
BT2 radioisotopes
BT3 isotopes
BT1 ytterbium isotopes

YTTERBIUM 156 [19; 19] *Nov 76*
BT1 alpha decay radioisotopes
BT2 radioisotopes
BT3 isotopes
BT1 electron capture radioisotopes
BT2 beta decay radioisotopes
BT3 radioisotopes
BT4 isotopes
BT1 even-even nuclei
BT2 nuclei
BT1 rare earth nuclei
BT2 intermediate mass nuclei
BT3 nuclei
BT1 seconds living radioisotopes
BT2 radioisotopes
BT3 isotopes
BT1 ytterbium isotopes

YTTERBIUM 157 [12; 12] *Jul 76*
BT1 alpha decay radioisotopes
BT2 radioisotopes
BT3 isotopes
BT1 electron capture radioisotopes
BT2 beta decay radioisotopes
BT3 radioisotopes
BT4 isotopes
BT1 even-odd nuclei
BT2 nuclei
BT1 rare earth nuclei
BT2 intermediate mass nuclei
BT3 nuclei
BT1 seconds living radioisotopes
BT2 radioisotopes
BT3 isotopes
BT1 ytterbium isotopes

YTTERBIUM 158 [52; 52]
BT1 alpha decay radioisotopes
BT2 radioisotopes
BT3 isotopes
BT1 beta-plus decay radioisotopes
BT2 beta decay radioisotopes
BT3 radioisotopes
BT4 isotopes
BT1 electron capture radioisotopes
BT2 beta decay radioisotopes
BT3 radioisotopes
BT4 isotopes
BT1 even-even nuclei
BT2 nuclei

        BT1   minutes living radioisotopes
        BT2   radioisotopes
        BT3   isotopes
    BT1   rare earth nuclei
        BT2   intermediate mass nuclei
        BT3   nuclei
    BT1   ytterbium isotopes

YTTERBIUM 159 [26; 26]
    BT1   electron capture radioisotopes
        BT2   beta decay radioisotopes
        BT3   radioisotopes
            BT4   isotopes
    BT1   even-odd nuclei
        BT2   nuclei
    BT1   minutes living radioisotopes
        BT2   radioisotopes
        BT3   isotopes
    BT1   rare earth nuclei
        BT2   intermediate mass nuclei
        BT3   nuclei
    BT1   ytterbium isotopes

YTTERBIUM 160 [109; 109]
    BT1   beta-plus decay radioisotopes
        BT2   beta decay radioisotopes
        BT3   radioisotopes
            BT4   isotopes
    BT1   electron capture radioisotopes
        BT2   beta decay radioisotopes
        BT3   radioisotopes
            BT4   isotopes
    BT1   even-even nuclei
        BT2   nuclei
    BT1   minutes living radioisotopes
        BT2   radioisotopes
        BT3   isotopes
    BT1   rare earth nuclei
        BT2   intermediate mass nuclei
        BT3   nuclei
    BT1   ytterbium isotopes

YTTERBIUM 161 [72; 72]
    BT1   beta-plus decay radioisotopes
        BT2   beta decay radioisotopes
        BT3   radioisotopes
            BT4   isotopes
    BT1   electron capture radioisotopes
        BT2   beta decay radioisotopes
        BT3   radioisotopes
            BT4   isotopes
    BT1   even-odd nuclei
        BT2   nuclei
    BT1   minutes living radioisotopes
        BT2   radioisotopes
        BT3   isotopes
    BT1   rare earth nuclei
        BT2   intermediate mass nuclei
        BT3   nuclei
    BT1   ytterbium isotopes

YTTERBIUM 162 [85; 85]
    BT1   beta-plus decay radioisotopes
        BT2   beta decay radioisotopes
        BT3   radioisotopes
            BT4   isotopes
    BT1   electron capture radioisotopes
        BT2   beta decay radioisotopes
        BT3   radioisotopes
            BT4   isotopes
    BT1   even-even nuclei
        BT2   nuclei
    BT1   minutes living radioisotopes
        BT2   radioisotopes
        BT3   isotopes
    BT1   rare earth nuclei
        BT2   intermediate mass nuclei
        BT3   nuclei
    BT1   ytterbium isotopes

YTTERBIUM 163 [54; 54]
    BT1   beta-plus decay radioisotopes
        BT2   beta decay radioisotopes
        BT3   radioisotopes
            BT4   isotopes
    BT1   electron capture radioisotopes
        BT2   beta decay radioisotopes
        BT3   radioisotopes
        BT4   isotopes
    BT1   even-odd nuclei
        BT2   nuclei
    BT1   minutes living radioisotopes
        BT2   radioisotopes
        BT3   isotopes
    BT1   rare earth nuclei
        BT2   intermediate mass nuclei
        BT3   nuclei
    BT1   ytterbium isotopes

YTTERBIUM 164 [79; 79]
    BT1   electron capture radioisotopes
        BT2   beta decay radioisotopes
        BT3   radioisotopes
            BT4   isotopes
    BT1   even-even nuclei
        BT2   nuclei
    BT1   hours living radioisotopes
        BT2   radioisotopes
        BT3   isotopes
    BT1   internal conversion radioisoto
        BT2   radioisotopes
        BT3   isotopes
    BT1   rare earth nuclei
        BT2   intermediate mass nuclei
        BT3   nuclei
    BT1   ytterbium isotopes

YTTERBIUM 165 [69; 69]
    BT1   beta-plus decay radioisotopes
        BT2   beta decay radioisotopes
        BT3   radioisotopes
            BT4   isotopes
    BT1   electron capture radioisotopes
        BT2   beta decay radioisotopes
        BT3   radioisotopes
            BT4   isotopes
    BT1   even-odd nuclei
        BT2   nuclei
    BT1   internal conversion radioisoto
        BT2   radioisotopes
        BT3   isotopes
    BT1   minutes living radioisotopes
        BT2   radioisotopes
        BT3   isotopes
    BT1   rare earth nuclei
        BT2   intermediate mass nuclei
        BT3   nuclei
    BT1   ytterbium isotopes

YTTERBIUM 166 [116; 116]
    BT1   days living radioisotopes
        BT2   radioisotopes
        BT3   isotopes
    BT1   electron capture radioisotopes
        BT2   beta decay radioisotopes
        BT3   radioisotopes
            BT4   isotopes
    BT1   even-even nuclei
        BT2   nuclei
    BT1   internal conversion radioisoto
        BT2   radioisotopes
        BT3   isotopes
    BT1   rare earth nuclei
        BT2   intermediate mass nuclei
        BT3   nuclei
    BT1   ytterbium isotopes

YTTERBIUM 167 [72; 72]
    BT1   beta-plus decay radioisotopes
        BT2   beta decay radioisotopes
        BT3   radioisotopes
            BT4   isotopes
    BT1   electron capture radioisotopes
        BT2   beta decay radioisotopes
        BT3   radioisotopes
            BT4   isotopes
    BT1   even-odd nuclei
        BT2   nuclei
    BT1   minutes living radioisotopes
        BT2   radioisotopes
        BT3   isotopes
    BT1   rare earth nuclei
        BT2   intermediate mass nuclei
        BT3   nuclei
    BT1   ytterbium isotopes

YTTERBIUM 168 [169; 169]
    BT1   even-even nuclei
        BT2   nuclei
    BT1   rare earth nuclei
        BT2   intermediate mass nuclei
        BT3   nuclei
    BT1   stable isotopes
        BT2   isotopes
    BT1   ytterbium isotopes

YTTERBIUM 168 TARGET [16; 16]
    BT1   targets

YTTERBIUM 169 [497; 497]
    BT1   days living radioisotopes
        BT2   radioisotopes
        BT3   isotopes
    BT1   electron capture radioisotopes
        BT2   beta decay radioisotopes
        BT3   radioisotopes
            BT4   isotopes
    BT1   even-odd nuclei
        BT2   nuclei
    BT1   isomeric transition isotopes
        BT2   radioisotopes
        BT3   isotopes
    BT1   rare earth nuclei
        BT2   intermediate mass nuclei
        BT3   nuclei
    BT1   seconds living radioisotopes
        BT2   radioisotopes
        BT3   isotopes
    BT1   ytterbium isotopes

YTTERBIUM 170 [215; 215]
    BT1   even-even nuclei
        BT2   nuclei
    BT1   rare earth nuclei
        BT2   intermediate mass nuclei
        BT3   nuclei
    BT1   stable isotopes
        BT2   isotopes
    BT1   ytterbium isotopes

YTTERBIUM 170 TARGET [33; 33]
    BT1   targets

YTTERBIUM 171 [122; 122]
    BT1   even-odd nuclei
        BT2   nuclei
    BT1   rare earth nuclei
        BT2   intermediate mass nuclei
        BT3   nuclei
    BT1   stable isotopes
        BT2   isotopes
    BT1   ytterbium isotopes

YTTERBIUM 171 TARGET [52; 52]
    BT1   targets

YTTERBIUM 172 [166; 166]
    BT1   even-even nuclei
        BT2   nuclei
    BT1   rare earth nuclei
        BT2   intermediate mass nuclei
        BT3   nuclei
    BT1   stable isotopes
        BT2   isotopes
    BT1   ytterbium isotopes

YTTERBIUM 172 TARGET [43; 43]
    BT1   targets

YTTERBIUM 173 [90; 90]
    BT1   even-odd nuclei
        BT2   nuclei
    BT1   rare earth nuclei
        BT2   intermediate mass nuclei
        BT3   nuclei
    BT1   stable isotopes
        BT2   isotopes
    BT1   ytterbium isotopes

YTTERBIUM 173 TARGET [44; 44]
BT1   targets

YTTERBIUM 174 [185; 185]
BT1   even-even nuclei
BT2   nuclei
BT1   rare earth nuclei
BT2   intermediate mass nuclei
BT3   nuclei
BT1   stable isotopes
BT2   isotopes
BT1   ytterbium isotopes

YTTERBIUM 174 TARGET [109; 109]
BT1   targets

YTTERBIUM 175 [62; 62]
BT1   beta-minus decay radioisotopes
BT2   beta decay radioisotopes
BT3   radioisotopes
BT4   isotopes
BT1   days living radioisotopes
BT2   radioisotopes
BT3   isotopes
BT1   even-odd nuclei
BT2   nuclei
BT1   rare earth nuclei
BT2   intermediate mass nuclei
BT3   nuclei
BT1   ytterbium isotopes

YTTERBIUM 176 [65; 65]
BT1   even-even nuclei
BT2   nuclei
BT1   isomeric transition isotopes
BT2   radioisotopes
BT3   isotopes
BT1   rare earth nuclei
BT2   intermediate mass nuclei
BT3   nuclei
BT1   seconds living radioisotopes
BT2   radioisotopes
BT3   isotopes
BT1   stable isotopes
BT2   isotopes
BT1   ytterbium isotopes

YTTERBIUM 176 TARGET [137; 137]
BT1   targets

YTTERBIUM 177 [25; 25]
BT1   beta-minus decay radioisotopes
BT2   beta decay radioisotopes
BT3   radioisotopes
BT4   isotopes
BT1   even-odd nuclei
BT2   nuclei
BT1   hours living radioisotopes
BT2   radioisotopes
BT3   isotopes
BT1   internal conversion radioisoto
BT2   radioisotopes
BT3   isotopes
BT1   isomeric transition isotopes
BT2   radioisotopes
BT3   isotopes
BT1   rare earth nuclei
BT2   intermediate mass nuclei
BT3   nuclei
BT1   seconds living radioisotopes
BT2   radioisotopes
BT3   isotopes
BT1   ytterbium isotopes

YTTERBIUM 178 [5; 5]
BT1   beta-minus decay radioisotopes
BT2   beta decay radioisotopes
BT3   radioisotopes
BT4   isotopes
BT1   even-even nuclei
BT2   nuclei
BT1   hours living radioisotopes
BT2   radioisotopes
BT3   isotopes
BT1   rare earth nuclei
BT2   intermediate mass nuclei
BT3   nuclei
BT1   ytterbium isotopes

YTTERBIUM 179 [7; 7] *Jun 82*
BT1   beta-minus decay radioisotopes
BT2   beta decay radioisotopes
BT3   radioisotopes
BT4   isotopes
BT1   even-odd nuclei
BT2   nuclei
BT1   minutes living radioisotopes
BT2   radioisotopes
BT3   isotopes
BT1   rare earth nuclei
BT2   intermediate mass nuclei
BT3   nuclei
BT1   ytterbium isotopes

YTTERBIUM 180 [4; 4] *Sep 87*
BT1   beta-minus decay radioisotopes
BT2   beta decay radioisotopes
BT3   radioisotopes
BT4   isotopes
BT1   even-even nuclei
BT2   nuclei
BT1   minutes living radioisotopes
BT2   radioisotopes
BT3   isotopes
BT1   rare earth nuclei
BT2   intermediate mass nuclei
BT3   nuclei
BT1   ytterbium isotopes

YTTRIALITE [2; 2]
BT1   silicate minerals
BT2   minerals
BT1   thorium minerals
BT2   radioactive minerals
BT3   minerals
BT3   radioactive materials
BT4   materials
RT   cerium silicates
RT   thorium silicates
RT   yttrium silicates

YTTRIUM [1,759; 1,759]
BT1   transition elements
BT2   metals
BT3   elements

YTTRIUM ADDITIONS [244; 246]
(Alloys containing not more than 1% Y are listed here.)
NT1   alloy-ni77cr17al5
RT   yttrium alloys
RT   yttrium compounds

YTTRIUM ALLOYS [1,297; 1,421]
(Alloys containing more than 1% Y.)
BT1   alloys
NT1   yttrium base alloys
RT   yttrium additions

yttrium aluminium garnets
USE   aluminium oxides
AND   ferrite garnets
AND   yttrium compounds

YTTRIUM ARSENIDES [5; 5] *Jan 77*
BT1   arsenides
BT2   arsenic compounds
BT2   pnictides
BT1   yttrium compounds
BT2   transition element compounds

YTTRIUM BASE ALLOYS [99; 99]
BT1   yttrium alloys
BT2   alloys

YTTRIUM BORIDES [90; 90]
BT1   borides
BT2   boron compounds
BT1   yttrium compounds
BT2   transition element compounds

YTTRIUM BROMIDES [15; 15]
BT1   bromides
BT2   bromine compounds
BT3   halogen compounds
BT2   halides
BT3   halogen compounds
BT1   yttrium compounds
BT2   transition element compounds

YTTRIUM CARBIDES [44; 44]
BT1   carbides
BT2   carbon compounds
BT1   yttrium compounds
BT2   transition element compounds

YTTRIUM CARBONATES [21; 21]
BT1   carbonates
BT2   carbon compounds
BT2   oxygen compounds
BT1   yttrium compounds
BT2   transition element compounds

YTTRIUM CHLORIDES [143; 143]
BT1   chlorides
BT2   chlorine compounds
BT3   halogen compounds
BT2   halides
BT3   halogen compounds
BT1   yttrium compounds
BT2   transition element compounds

YTTRIUM COMPLEXES [537; 537]
BT1   transition element complexes
BT2   complexes

YTTRIUM COMPOUNDS [2,964; 11,810]
UF+   *yttrium aluminium garnets*
BT1   transition element compounds
NT1   yttrium arsenides
NT1   yttrium borides
NT1   yttrium bromides
NT1   yttrium carbides
NT1   yttrium carbonates
NT1   yttrium chlorides
NT1   yttrium fluorides
NT1   yttrium hydrides
NT1   yttrium hydroxides
NT1   yttrium iodides
NT1   yttrium nitrates
NT1   yttrium nitrides
NT1   yttrium oxides
NT1   yttrium perchlorates
NT1   yttrium phosphates
NT1   yttrium phosphides
NT1   yttrium selenides
NT1   yttrium silicates
NT1   yttrium silicides
NT1   yttrium sulfates
NT1   yttrium sulfides
NT1   yttrium tellurides
NT1   yttrium tungstates
RT   yttrium additions

YTTRIUM FLUORIDES [280; 280]
BT1   fluorides
BT2   fluorine compounds
BT3   halogen compounds
BT2   halides
BT3   halogen compounds
BT1   yttrium compounds
BT2   transition element compounds

YTTRIUM HYDRIDES [136; 136]
BT1   hydrides
BT2   hydrogen compounds
BT1   yttrium compounds
BT2   transition element compounds

YTTRIUM HYDROXIDES [45; 45]
BT1   hydroxides
BT2   hydrogen compounds
BT2   oxygen compounds
BT1   yttrium compounds
BT2   transition element compounds

YTTRIUM IODIDES [10; 10]
BT1 iodides
BT2 halides
BT3 halogen compounds
BT2 iodine compounds
BT3 halogen compounds
BT1 yttrium compounds
BT2 transition element compounds

YTTRIUM IONS [158; 158]
BT1 ions
BT2 charged particles

YTTRIUM ISOTOPES [98; 2,199]
NT1 yttrium 100
NT1 yttrium 101
NT1 yttrium 102
NT1 yttrium 77
NT1 yttrium 80
NT1 yttrium 81
NT1 yttrium 82
NT1 yttrium 83
NT1 yttrium 84
NT1 yttrium 85
NT1 yttrium 86
NT1 yttrium 87
NT1 yttrium 88
NT1 yttrium 89
NT1 yttrium 90
NT1 yttrium 91
NT1 yttrium 92
NT1 yttrium 93
NT1 yttrium 94
NT1 yttrium 95
NT1 yttrium 96
NT1 yttrium 97
NT1 yttrium 98
NT1 yttrium 99

YTTRIUM NITRATES [54; 54]
BT1 nitrates
BT2 nitrogen compounds
BT2 oxygen compounds
BT1 yttrium compounds
BT2 transition element compounds

YTTRIUM NITRIDES [25; 25]
BT1 nitrides
BT2 nitrogen compounds
BT2 pnictides
BT1 yttrium compounds
BT2 transition element compounds

YTTRIUM ORES [4; 4]
BT1 ores

YTTRIUM OXIDES [7,805; 7,806]
BT1 oxides
BT2 chalcogenides
BT2 oxygen compounds
BT1 yttrium compounds
BT2 transition element compounds

→ **YTTRIUM PERCHLORATES** [0; 0] Sep 91
BT1 perchlorates
BT2 chlorine compounds
BT3 halogen compounds
BT2 oxygen compounds
BT1 yttrium compounds
BT2 transition element compounds

YTTRIUM PHOSPHATES [81; 97]
BT1 phosphates
BT2 oxygen compounds
BT2 phosphorus compounds
BT1 yttrium compounds
BT2 transition element compounds
RT phosphate minerals
RT xenotime

YTTRIUM PHOSPHIDES [10; 10] Jan 77
BT1 phosphides
BT2 phosphorus compounds
BT2 pnictides
BT1 yttrium compounds
BT2 transition element compounds

→ **YTTRIUM SELENIDES** [0; 0] Sep 91
BT1 selenides
BT2 chalcogenides
BT2 selenium compounds
BT1 yttrium compounds
BT2 transition element compounds

YTTRIUM SILICATES [63; 65]
BT1 silicates
BT2 oxygen compounds
BT2 silicon compounds
BT1 yttrium compounds
BT2 transition element compounds
RT silicate minerals
RT yttrialite

YTTRIUM SILICIDES [39; 39] Jul 77
BT1 silicides
BT2 silicon compounds
BT1 yttrium compounds
BT2 transition element compounds

YTTRIUM SULFATES [26; 26]
BT1 sulfates
BT2 oxygen compounds
BT2 sulfur compounds
BT1 yttrium compounds
BT2 transition element compounds

YTTRIUM SULFIDES [82; 82]
BT1 sulfides
BT2 chalcogenides
BT2 sulfur compounds
BT1 yttrium compounds
BT2 transition element compounds

YTTRIUM TELLURIDES [5; 5] Nov 78
BT1 tellurides
BT2 chalcogenides
BT2 tellurium compounds
BT1 yttrium compounds
BT2 transition element compounds

YTTRIUM TUNGSTATES [25; 25] Feb 80
BT1 tungstates
BT2 oxygen compounds
BT2 tungsten compounds
BT3 transition element compounds
BT1 yttrium compounds
BT2 transition element compounds

YTTRIUM 100 [26; 26] Jun 77
BT1 beta-minus decay radioisotopes
BT2 beta decay radioisotopes
BT3 radioisotopes
BT4 isotopes
BT1 intermediate mass nuclei
BT2 nuclei
BT1 millisec living radioisotopes
BT2 radioisotopes
BT3 isotopes
BT1 odd-odd nuclei
BT2 nuclei
BT1 yttrium isotopes

YTTRIUM 101 [11; 11] Jun 84
BT1 beta-minus decay radioisotopes
BT2 beta decay radioisotopes
BT3 radioisotopes
BT4 isotopes
BT1 intermediate mass nuclei
BT2 nuclei
BT1 millisec living radioisotopes
BT2 radioisotopes
BT3 isotopes
BT1 odd-even nuclei
BT2 nuclei
BT1 yttrium isotopes

YTTRIUM 102 [15; 15] Jan 77
BT1 beta-minus decay radioisotopes
BT2 beta decay radioisotopes
BT3 radioisotopes
BT4 isotopes
BT1 intermediate mass nuclei
BT2 nuclei
BT1 millisec living radioisotopes
BT2 radioisotopes
BT3 isotopes
BT1 odd-odd nuclei
BT2 nuclei
BT1 yttrium isotopes

YTTRIUM 77 [0; 0] Dec 90
BT1 intermediate mass nuclei
BT2 nuclei
BT1 odd-even nuclei
BT2 nuclei
BT1 yttrium isotopes

YTTRIUM 80 [10; 10] May 80
BT1 beta-plus decay radioisotopes
BT2 beta decay radioisotopes
BT3 radioisotopes
BT4 isotopes
BT1 intermediate mass nuclei
BT2 nuclei
BT1 odd-odd nuclei
BT2 nuclei
BT1 seconds living radioisotopes
BT2 radioisotopes
BT3 isotopes
BT1 yttrium isotopes

YTTRIUM 81 [13; 13]
BT1 beta-plus decay radioisotopes
BT2 beta decay radioisotopes
BT3 radioisotopes
BT4 isotopes
BT1 electron capture radioisotopes
BT2 beta decay radioisotopes
BT3 radioisotopes
BT4 isotopes
BT1 intermediate mass nuclei
BT2 nuclei
BT1 minutes living radioisotopes
BT2 radioisotopes
BT3 isotopes
BT1 odd-even nuclei
BT2 nuclei
BT1 yttrium isotopes

YTTRIUM 82 [13; 13]
BT1 beta-plus decay radioisotopes
BT2 beta decay radioisotopes
BT3 radioisotopes
BT4 isotopes
BT1 intermediate mass nuclei
BT2 nuclei
BT1 odd-odd nuclei
BT2 nuclei
BT1 seconds living radioisotopes
BT2 radioisotopes
BT3 isotopes
BT1 yttrium isotopes

YTTRIUM 83 [33; 33]
BT1 beta-plus decay radioisotopes
BT2 beta decay radioisotopes
BT3 radioisotopes
BT4 isotopes
BT1 electron capture radioisotopes
BT2 beta decay radioisotopes
BT3 radioisotopes
BT4 isotopes
BT1 intermediate mass nuclei
BT2 nuclei
BT1 minutes living radioisotopes
BT2 radioisotopes
BT3 isotopes
BT1 odd-even nuclei
BT2 nuclei
BT1 yttrium isotopes

YTTRIUM 84 [8; 8]
  BT1   beta-plus decay radioisotopes
  BT2   beta decay radioisotopes
    BT3   radioisotopes
      BT4   isotopes
  BT1   electron capture radioisotopes
  BT2   beta decay radioisotopes
    BT3   radioisotopes
      BT4   isotopes
  BT1   intermediate mass nuclei
  BT2   nuclei
  BT1   minutes living radioisotopes
  BT2   radioisotopes
    BT3   isotopes
  BT1   odd-odd nuclei
  BT2   nuclei
  BT1   seconds living radioisotopes
  BT2   radioisotopes
    BT3   isotopes
  BT1   yttrium isotopes

YTTRIUM 85 [30; 30]
  BT1   beta-plus decay radioisotopes
  BT2   beta decay radioisotopes
    BT3   radioisotopes
      BT4   isotopes
  BT1   electron capture radioisotopes
  BT2   beta decay radioisotopes
    BT3   radioisotopes
      BT4   isotopes
  BT1   hours living radioisotopes
  BT2   radioisotopes
    BT3   isotopes
  BT1   intermediate mass nuclei
  BT2   nuclei
  BT1   odd-even nuclei
  BT2   nuclei
  BT1   yttrium isotopes

YTTRIUM 86 [31; 31]
  BT1   beta-plus decay radioisotopes
  BT2   beta decay radioisotopes
    BT3   radioisotopes
      BT4   isotopes
  BT1   electron capture radioisotopes
  BT2   beta decay radioisotopes
    BT3   radioisotopes
      BT4   isotopes
  BT1   hours living radioisotopes
  BT2   radioisotopes
    BT3   isotopes
  BT1   intermediate mass nuclei
  BT2   nuclei
  BT1   internal conversion radioisoto
  BT2   radioisotopes
    BT3   isotopes
  BT1   isomeric transition isotopes
  BT2   radioisotopes
    BT3   isotopes
  BT1   minutes living radioisotopes
  BT2   radioisotopes
    BT3   isotopes
  BT1   odd-odd nuclei
  BT2   nuclei
  BT1   yttrium isotopes

YTTRIUM 87 [97; 97]
  BT1   beta-plus decay radioisotopes
  BT2   beta decay radioisotopes
    BT3   radioisotopes
      BT4   isotopes
  BT1   days living radioisotopes
  BT2   radioisotopes
    BT3   isotopes
  BT1   electron capture radioisotopes
  BT2   beta decay radioisotopes
    BT3   radioisotopes
      BT4   isotopes
  BT1   hours living radioisotopes
  BT2   radioisotopes
    BT3   isotopes
  BT1   intermediate mass nuclei
  BT2   nuclei
  BT1   isomeric transition isotopes
  BT2   radioisotopes
    BT3   isotopes
  BT1   odd-even nuclei
  BT2   nuclei
  BT1   yttrium isotopes
  RT   radioisotope generators

YTTRIUM 87 TARGET [5; 5] *Jan 77*
  BT1   targets

YTTRIUM 88 [211; 211]
  BT1   beta-plus decay radioisotopes
  BT2   beta decay radioisotopes
    BT3   radioisotopes
      BT4   isotopes
  BT1   days living radioisotopes
  BT2   radioisotopes
    BT3   isotopes
  BT1   electron capture radioisotopes
  BT2   beta decay radioisotopes
    BT3   radioisotopes
      BT4   isotopes
  BT1   intermediate mass nuclei
  BT2   nuclei
  BT1   odd-odd nuclei
  BT2   nuclei
  BT1   yttrium isotopes

YTTRIUM 88 TARGET [13; 13] *Jan 77*
  BT1   targets

YTTRIUM 89 [404; 404]
  BT1   intermediate mass nuclei
  BT2   nuclei
  BT1   isomeric transition isotopes
  BT2   radioisotopes
    BT3   isotopes
  BT1   odd-even nuclei
  BT2   nuclei
  BT1   seconds living radioisotopes
  BT2   radioisotopes
    BT3   isotopes
  BT1   stable isotopes
  BT2   isotopes
  BT1   yttrium isotopes

YTTRIUM 89 TARGET [481; 481]
  BT1   targets

YTTRIUM 90 [1,028; 1,028]
  BT1   beta-minus decay radioisotopes
  BT2   beta decay radioisotopes
    BT3   radioisotopes
      BT4   isotopes
  BT1   days living radioisotopes
  BT2   radioisotopes
    BT3   isotopes
  BT1   hours living radioisotopes
  BT2   radioisotopes
    BT3   isotopes
  BT1   intermediate mass nuclei
  BT2   nuclei
  BT1   isomeric transition isotopes
  BT2   radioisotopes
    BT3   isotopes
  BT1   odd-odd nuclei
  BT2   nuclei
  BT1   yttrium isotopes

YTTRIUM 91 [212; 212]
  BT1   beta-minus decay radioisotopes
  BT2   beta decay radioisotopes
    BT3   radioisotopes
      BT4   isotopes
  BT1   days living radioisotopes
  BT2   radioisotopes
    BT3   isotopes
  BT1   intermediate mass nuclei
  BT2   nuclei
  BT1   isomeric transition isotopes
  BT2   radioisotopes
    BT3   isotopes
  BT1   minutes living radioisotopes
  BT2   radioisotopes
    BT3   isotopes
  BT1   odd-even nuclei
  BT2   nuclei
  BT1   yttrium isotopes

YTTRIUM 92 [13; 13]
  BT1   beta-minus decay radioisotopes
  BT2   beta decay radioisotopes
    BT3   radioisotopes
      BT4   isotopes
  BT1   hours living radioisotopes
  BT2   radioisotopes
    BT3   isotopes
  BT1   intermediate mass nuclei
  BT2   nuclei
  BT1   odd-odd nuclei
  BT2   nuclei
  BT1   yttrium isotopes

YTTRIUM 93 [30; 30]
  BT1   beta-minus decay radioisotopes
  BT2   beta decay radioisotopes
    BT3   radioisotopes
      BT4   isotopes
  BT1   hours living radioisotopes
  BT2   radioisotopes
    BT3   isotopes
  BT1   intermediate mass nuclei
  BT2   nuclei
  BT1   isomeric transition isotopes
  BT2   radioisotopes
    BT3   isotopes
  BT1   millisec living radioisotopes
  BT2   radioisotopes
    BT3   isotopes
  BT1   odd-even nuclei
  BT2   nuclei
  BT1   yttrium isotopes

YTTRIUM 94 [22; 22]
  BT1   beta-minus decay radioisotopes
  BT2   beta decay radioisotopes
    BT3   radioisotopes
      BT4   isotopes
  BT1   intermediate mass nuclei
  BT2   nuclei
  BT1   minutes living radioisotopes
  BT2   radioisotopes
    BT3   isotopes
  BT1   odd-odd nuclei
  BT2   nuclei
  BT1   yttrium isotopes

YTTRIUM 95 [23; 23]
  BT1   beta-minus decay radioisotopes
  BT2   beta decay radioisotopes
    BT3   radioisotopes
      BT4   isotopes
  BT1   intermediate mass nuclei
  BT2   nuclei
  BT1   minutes living radioisotopes
  BT2   radioisotopes
    BT3   isotopes
  BT1   odd-even nuclei
  BT2   nuclei
  BT1   yttrium isotopes

YTTRIUM 96 [32; 32]
  BT1   beta-minus decay radioisotopes
  BT2   beta decay radioisotopes
    BT3   radioisotopes
      BT4   isotopes
  BT1   intermediate mass nuclei
  BT2   nuclei
  BT1   odd-odd nuclei
  BT2   nuclei
  BT1   seconds living radioisotopes
  BT2   radioisotopes
    BT3   isotopes
  BT1   yttrium isotopes

YTTRIUM 97 [25; 25]
  BT1   beta-minus decay radioisotopes
  BT2   beta decay radioisotopes
    BT3   radioisotopes
      BT4   isotopes
  BT1   intermediate mass nuclei
  BT2   nuclei
  BT1   isomeric transition isotopes
  BT2   radioisotopes
    BT3   isotopes
  BT1   millisec living radioisotopes
  BT2   radioisotopes

BT3 isotopes
BT1 odd-even nuclei
BT2 nuclei
BT1 seconds living radioisotopes
BT2 radioisotopes
BT3 isotopes
BT1 yttrium isotopes

YTTRIUM 98 [27; 27]
BT1 beta-minus decay radioisotopes
BT2 beta decay radioisotopes
BT3 radioisotopes
BT4 isotopes
BT1 intermediate mass nuclei
BT2 nuclei
BT1 millisec living radioisotopes
BT2 radioisotopes
BT3 isotopes
BT1 odd-odd nuclei
BT2 nuclei
BT1 seconds living radioisotopes
BT2 radioisotopes
BT3 isotopes
BT1 yttrium isotopes

YTTRIUM 99 [38; 38]
BT1 beta-minus decay radioisotopes
BT2 beta decay radioisotopes
BT3 radioisotopes
BT4 isotopes
BT1 intermediate mass nuclei
BT2 nuclei
BT1 odd-even nuclei
BT2 nuclei
BT1 seconds living radioisotopes
BT2 radioisotopes
BT3 isotopes
BT1 yttrium isotopes

YUCCA MOUNTAIN [1,028; 1,028]
Jan 85
BT1 mountains
RT nevada test site

yugoslav triga-mk-2 reactor
USE triga-2-ljubljana reactor

YUGOSLAVIA [311; 311]
BT1 developing countries
BT1 europe

yugoslavia r-a reactor vinca
USE r-a reactor

yugoslavia r-b reactor vinca
USE r-b reactor

YUKAWA NONLOCAL THEORY [279; 279]
UF non-local quantum field theory
UF nonlocal quantum field theory
BT1 quantum field theory
BT2 field theories

YUKAWA POTENTIAL [1,005; 1,005]
BT1 nuclear potential
BT2 potentials
RT nucleon-nucleon potential
RT nucleons

YUKON TERRITORY [6; 6] Jan 79
BT1 canada
BT2 developed countries
BT2 north america

YVON METHOD [8; 8]
RT neutron transport theory
RT spherical harmonics
RT transport theory

Z CENTERS [93; 93]
BT1 color centers
BT2 vacancies
BT3 point defects
BT4 crystal defects
BT5 crystal structure

Z CODES [160; 160]
BT1 computer codes

Z NEUTRAL BOSONS [1,619; 1,619]
Mar 86
BT1 intermediate vector bosons
BT2 intermediate bosons
BT3 bosons
BT3 elementary particles

z pinch devices (linear)
USE linear z pinch devices

Z*BARYONS [73; 74]
(Prior to December 1987 this concept was indexed by Z*RESONANCES.)
UF z*resonances
BT1 hyperons
BT2 baryons
BT3 fermions
BT3 hadrons
BT4 elementary particles
BT2 strange particles
BT3 elementary particles
NT1 z0-1780 baryons
NT1 z0-1865 baryons
NT1 z1-1725 baryons
NT1 z1-1900 baryons
NT1 z1-2150 baryons
NT1 z1-2500 baryons

*z*resonances*
(Prior to December 1987 this was a valid descriptor.)
USE z*baryons

ZACHARIASEN MODEL [16; 16]
RT quantum field theory

ZAIRE REPUBLIC [41; 41]
UF congo democratic republic
UF republic of zaire
BT1 africa
BT1 developing countries

ZAMBIA [21; 21]
UF northern rhodesia
UF rhodesia (northern)
BT1 africa
BT1 developing countries

ZAPOROZHE-1 REACTOR [29; 29]
Aug 84
BT1 wwer type reactors
BT2 pwr type reactors
BT3 enriched uranium reactors
BT4 reactors
BT3 power reactors
BT4 reactors
BT3 thermal reactors
BT4 reactors
BT3 water cooled reactors
BT4 reactors
BT3 water moderated reactors
BT4 reactors

ZAPOROZHE-2 REACTOR [12; 12]
Dec 86
BT1 wwer type reactors
BT2 pwr type reactors
BT3 enriched uranium reactors
BT4 reactors
BT3 power reactors
BT4 reactors
BT3 thermal reactors
BT4 reactors
BT3 water cooled reactors
BT4 reactors
BT3 water moderated reactors
BT4 reactors

ZAPOROZHE-3 REACTOR [2; 2]
Jan 90
(Ukrainian SSR, USSR.)
BT1 wwer type reactors
BT2 pwr type reactors
BT3 enriched uranium reactors
BT4 reactors
BT3 power reactors
BT4 reactors
BT3 thermal reactors
BT4 reactors
BT3 water cooled reactors
BT4 reactors
BT3 water moderated reactors
BT4 reactors

ZAPOROZHE-4 REACTOR [3; 3]
Jan 90
(Ukrainian SSR, USSR.)
BT1 wwer type reactors
BT2 pwr type reactors
BT3 enriched uranium reactors
BT4 reactors
BT3 power reactors
BT4 reactors
BT3 thermal reactors
BT4 reactors
BT3 water cooled reactors
BT4 reactors
BT3 water moderated reactors
BT4 reactors

zea mays
USE maize

ZEBRA REACTOR [83; 83]
(UKAEA, Winfrith, United Kingdom)
UF zero energy breeder react. as.
BT1 fbr type reactors
BT2 breeder reactors
BT3 reactors
BT2 fast reactors
BT3 epithermal reactors
BT4 reactors
BT1 research reactors
BT2 research and test reactors
BT3 reactors
BT1 zero power reactors
BT2 experimental reactors
BT3 research and test reactors
BT4 reactors
RT enriched uranium reactors
RT plutonium reactors

ZED-2 REACTOR [36; 36]
UF chalk river zed-2 reactor
UF organic c. hw m. chalk river
BT1 air cooled reactors
BT2 gas cooled reactors
BT3 reactors
BT1 heavy water cooled reactors
BT2 reactors
BT1 heavy water moderated reacto
BT2 reactors
BT1 natural uranium reactors
BT2 reactors
BT1 organic cooled reactors
BT2 reactors
BT1 tank type reactors
BT2 reactors
BT1 thermal reactors
BT2 reactors

ZEEMAN EFFECT [1,333; 1,333]
UF zeeman resonance
UF zeeman spectrum
UF zeeman transition
RT double resonance methods
RT magnetic fields
RT magneto-optical effects
RT paschen-back effect
RT spectral shift

zeeman resonance
   USE   zeeman effect

zeeman spectrum
   USE   zeeman effect

zeeman transition
   USE   zeeman effect

ZEEP REACTOR [5; 5]
- UF   *zero energy experimental pile*
- BT1   heavy water moderated reactors
  - BT2   reactors
- BT1   natural uranium reactors
  - BT2   reactors
- BT1   plutonium reactors
  - BT2   reactors
- BT1   research reactors
  - BT2   research and test reactors
    - BT3   reactors
- BT1   tank type reactors
  - BT2   reactors
- BT1   zero power reactors
  - BT2   experimental reactors
    - BT3   research and test reactors
      - BT4   reactors

ZEMACH-GLAUBER FORMALISM
[2; 2]
- RT   scattering
- RT   thermal neutrons

zener diodes
   USE   junction diodes

ZENITH REACTOR [1; 1]
- UF   *zero energy nitrog. heat. ther*
- BT1   graphite moderated reactors
  - BT2   reactors
- BT1   research reactors
  - BT2   research and test reactors
    - BT3   reactors
- BT1   thermal reactors
  - BT2   reactors
- BT1   zero power reactors
  - BT2   experimental reactors
    - BT3   research and test reactors
      - BT4   reactors
- RT   enriched uranium reactors
- RT   plutonium reactors
- RT   thorium reactors

zentralinst. f kernforschung
   USE   zfk rossendorf

zentralinst. isotop. leipzig
   USE   zfi leipzig

ZEOLITES [1,363; 1,363]
- UF   *analcime*
- BT1   inorganic ion exchangers
  - BT2   ion exchange materials
    - BT3   materials
- BT1   silicate minerals
  - BT2   minerals
- RT   desiccants

ZEPHYR REACTOR [18; 18]
- UF   *zero energy fast react.-zephyr*
- BT1   fast reactors
  - BT2   epithermal reactors
    - BT3   reactors
- BT1   materials testing reactors
  - BT2   irradiation reactors
    - BT3   reactors
- BT1   natural uranium reactors
  - BT2   reactors
- BT1   plutonium reactors
  - BT2   reactors
- BT1   zero power reactors
  - BT2   experimental reactors

- BT3   research and test reactors
  - BT4   reactors

ZERAN LINAC [5; 5] *Apr 79*
- BT1   linear accelerators
  - BT2   accelerators

ZERLINA REACTOR [24; 24]
(Bhabha Atomic Research Centre,
Trombay, Maharashtra, India)
- UF   *zero energy reactor latt. inv.*
- BT1   heavy water moderated reactors
  - BT2   reactors
- BT1   organic moderated reactors
  - BT2   reactors
- BT1   research reactors
  - BT2   research and test reactors
    - BT3   reactors
- BT1   thermal reactors
  - BT2   reactors
- BT1   zero power reactors
  - BT2   experimental reactors
    - BT3   research and test reactors
      - BT4   reactors

zero energy balance
   USE   breakeven

zero energy breeder react. ass
   USE   zebra reactor

zero energy experimental pile
   USE   zeep reactor

zero energy fast react.-zephyr
   USE   zephyr reactor

zero energy nitrog. heat. ther
   USE   zenith reactor

zero energy reactor latt. inv.
   USE   zerlina reactor

zero gradient synchrotron
   USE   zgs

zero power crit. expe. minerve
   USE   minerve reactor

zero power reac (cornell univ)
   USE   zpr reactor

ZERO POWER REACTORS [876; 2,347]
- UF   *critical assemblies*
- UF   *zero-power reactors*
- BT1   experimental reactors
  - BT2   research and test reactors
    - BT3   reactors
- NT1   agata reactor
- NT1   anex reactor
- NT1   anna reactor
- NT1   apfa-3 reactor
- NT1   aquilon reactor
- NT1   big ten reactor
- NT1   cfrmf reactor
- NT1   cml reactor
- NT1   coral-1 reactor
- NT1   crocus reactor
- NT1   dca reactor
- NT1   dimple reactor
- NT1   ecel reactor
- NT1   ermine reactor
- NT1   fca reactor
- NT1   flattop reactor
- NT1   fr-0 reactor
- NT1   godiva reactor
- NT1   hero reactor

- NT1   hitrex-1 reactor
- NT1   horace reactor
- NT1   iea-zpr reactor
- NT1   ifr reactor
- NT1   ipen-mb-1 reactor
- NT1   jezebel reactor
- NT1   juno reactor
- NT1   kahter reactor
- NT1   kuca reactor
- NT1   lptf reactor
- NT1   lr-0 reactor
- NT1   marius reactor
- NT1   maryla reactor
- NT1   masurca reactor
- NT1   minerve reactor
- NT1   neptune reactor
- NT1   nsf-rfp reactor
- NT1   or-cef reactor
- NT1   ornl-pca reactor
- NT1   parka reactor
- NT1   pdp reactor
- NT1   peggy reactor
- NT1   pelinduna reactor
- NT1   plasma core assembly
- NT1   prcf reactor
- NT1   ptf-unc reactor
- NT1   purnima reactor
- NT1   purnima-2 reactor
- NT1   r-b reactor
- NT1   ra-0 reactor
- NT1   ra-2 reactor
- NT1   rake-2 reactor
- NT1   rb-1 reactor
- NT1   rb-3 reactor
- NT1   rensselaer critical facility
- NT1   ritmo reactor
- NT1   rospo reactor
- NT1   saref reactor
- NT1   shca reactor
- NT1   silene reactor
- NT1   siloette reactor
- NT1   sneak reactor
- NT1   split table reactor
- NT1   sr-oa reactor
- NT1   tca reactor
- NT1   tr-0 reactor
- NT1   vera reactor
- NT1   zebra reactor
- NT1   zeep reactor
- NT1   zenith reactor
- NT1   zephyr reactor
- NT1   zerlina reactor
- NT1   zlfr reactor
- NT1   zppr reactor
- NT1   zpr reactor
- NT1   zpr-3 reactor
- NT1   zpr-6 reactor
- NT1   zpr-9 reactor
- NT1   zr-6 reactor
- RT   reactor lattices

zero power res. react-3 (anl)
   USE   zpr-3 reactor

zero power res. react-6 (anl)
   USE   zpr-6 reactor

zero power res. react-9 (anl)
   USE   zpr-9 reactor

ZERO SOUND [216; 216]
- RT   sound waves
- RT   superfluidity
- RT   wave propagation

zero-power reactors
   USE   zero power reactors

ZERO-RANGE APPROXIMATION
[348; 348]
- RT   elastic scattering
- RT   finite-range interactions
- RT   nuclear reaction kinetics

zet pinch
    USE   longitudinal pinch

ZETA DEVICES [74; 74]
    BT1   tlp devices
      BT2   toroidal pinch devices
        BT3   closed plasma devices
          BT4   thermonuclear devices
        BT3   pinch devices
          BT4   thermonuclear devices

ZEUNERITE [2; 2]
    BT1   oxide minerals
      BT2   minerals
    BT1   uranium minerals
      BT2   radioactive minerals
        BT3   minerals
        BT3   radioactive materials
          BT4   materials
    RT   arsenic oxides
    RT   calcium oxides
    RT   uranium oxides

ZFI LEIPZIG [16; 16] *May 86*
(Zentralinstitut fuer Isotopen- und Strahlenforschung, Leipzig.)
    UF   *institut isotop. stral leipzig*
    UF   *leipzig zfi*
    UF   *zentralinst. isotop. leipzig*
    BT1   german fr organizations
      BT2   national organizations

ZFK ROSSENDORF [73; 73] *Feb 77*
(Zentralinstitut fuer Kernforschung, Rossendorf, Germany.)
    UF   *rossendorf zfk*
    UF   *zentralinst. f kernforschung*
    BT1   german fr organizations
      BT2   national organizations

ZGS [269; 269]
    UF   *argonne zgs*
    UF   *zero gradient synchrotron*
    BT1   synchrotrons
      BT2   cyclic accelerators
        BT3   accelerators

ZIEGLER CATALYST [5; 5]
    BT1   catalysts
    RT   catalysis

ZIMBABWE [14; 16] *Sep 80*
    BT1   africa
    BT1   developing countries
    NT1   southern rhodesia

ZIMMER-1 REACTOR [34; 34]
(Moscow, Ohio, USA)
    UF   *william h. zimmer-1 reactor*
    BT1   bwr type reactors
      BT2   enriched uranium reactors
        BT3   reactors
      BT2   power reactors
        BT3   reactors
      BT2   thermal reactors
        BT3   reactors
      BT2   water cooled reactors
        BT3   reactors
      BT2   water moderated reactors
        BT3   reactors

ZIMMER-2 REACTOR [13; 13] *Feb 80*
(Moscow, Ohio, USA)
    UF   *william h. zimmer-2 reactor*
    BT1   bwr type reactors
      BT2   enriched uranium reactors
        BT3   reactors
      BT2   power reactors
        BT3   reactors
      BT2   thermal reactors
        BT3   reactors
      BT2   water cooled reactors
        BT3   reactors
      BT2   water moderated reactors
        BT3   reactors

ZINC [4,230; 4,230]
    BT1   metals
      BT2   elements

ZINC ADDITIONS [265; 266]
(Alloys containing not more than 1% Zn are listed here.)
    RT   zinc alloys
    RT   zinc compounds

ZINC ALLOYS [816; 1,184]
(Alloys containing more than 1% Zn.)
    BT1   alloys
    NT1   brass
      NT2   brass-alpha
      NT2   brass-beta
    NT1   german silver
    NT1   zinc base alloys
    RT   zinc additions

ZINC ARSENIDES [25; 25] *Jul 78*
    BT1   arsenides
      BT2   arsenic compounds
      BT2   pnictides
    BT1   zinc compounds

ZINC BASE ALLOYS [72; 72]
    BT1   zinc alloys
      BT2   alloys

ZINC BORIDES [2; 2]
    BT1   borides
      BT2   boron compounds
    BT1   zinc compounds

ZINC BROMIDES [47; 47]
    BT1   bromides
      BT2   bromine compounds
        BT3   halogen compounds
      BT2   halides
        BT3   halogen compounds
    BT1   zinc halides
      BT2   halides
        BT3   halogen compounds
      BT2   zinc compounds

ZINC CARBIDES [1; 1]
    BT1   carbides
      BT2   carbon compounds
    BT1   zinc compounds

ZINC CARBONATES [12; 12]
    BT1   carbonates
      BT2   carbon compounds
      BT2   oxygen compounds
    BT1   zinc compounds

ZINC CHLORIDES [213; 213]
    BT1   chlorides
      BT2   chlorine compounds
        BT3   halogen compounds
      BT2   halides
        BT3   halogen compounds
    BT1   zinc halides
      BT2   halides
        BT3   halogen compounds
      BT2   zinc compounds

ZINC COMPLEXES [389; 389]
    BT1   complexes

ZINC COMPOUNDS [936; 3,618]
    NT1   zinc arsenides
    NT1   zinc borides
    NT1   zinc carbides
    NT1   zinc carbonates
    NT1   zinc halides
      NT2   zinc bromides
      NT2   zinc chlorides
      NT2   zinc fluorides
      NT2   zinc iodides
    NT1   zinc hydrides
    NT1   zinc hydroxides
    NT1   zinc nitrates
    NT1   zinc oxides
    NT1   zinc perchlorates
    NT1   zinc phosphates
    NT1   zinc phosphides
    NT1   zinc selenides
    NT1   zinc silicates
    NT1   zinc silicides
    NT1   zinc sulfates
    NT1   zinc sulfides
    NT1   zinc tellurides
    NT1   zinc tungstates
    RT   zinc additions

zinc distillation process
    USE   pyrochemical reprocessing

ZINC FLUORIDES [90; 90]
    BT1   fluorides
      BT2   fluorine compounds
        BT3   halogen compounds
      BT2   halides
        BT3   halogen compounds
    BT1   zinc halides
      BT2   halides
        BT3   halogen compounds
      BT2   zinc compounds

→ **ZINC HALIDES** [0; 0] *Sep 91*
    BT1   halides
      BT2   halogen compounds
    BT1   zinc compounds
    NT1   zinc bromides
    NT1   zinc chlorides
    NT1   zinc fluorides
    NT1   zinc iodides

ZINC HYDRIDES [8; 8] *Nov 76*
    BT1   hydrides
      BT2   hydrogen compounds
    BT1   zinc compounds

ZINC HYDROXIDES [17; 17]
    BT1   hydroxides
      BT2   hydrogen compounds
      BT2   oxygen compounds
    BT1   zinc compounds

ZINC IODIDES [30; 30]
    BT1   iodides
      BT2   halides
        BT3   halogen compounds
      BT2   iodine compounds
        BT3   halogen compounds
    BT1   zinc halides
      BT2   halides
        BT3   halogen compounds
      BT2   zinc compounds

ZINC IONS [328; 328]
    BT1   ions
      BT2   charged particles

ZINC ISOTOPES [190; 2,683]
    NT1   zinc 57
    NT1   zinc 58
    NT1   zinc 59
    NT1   zinc 60
    NT1   zinc 61
    NT1   zinc 62
    NT1   zinc 63
    NT1   zinc 64
    NT1   zinc 65
    NT1   zinc 66
    NT1   zinc 67
    NT1   zinc 68
    NT1   zinc 69
    NT1   zinc 70
    NT1   zinc 71
    NT1   zinc 72
    NT1   zinc 73
    NT1   zinc 74
    NT1   zinc 75
    NT1   zinc 76
    NT1   zinc 77
    NT1   zinc 78
    NT1   zinc 79
    NT1   zinc 80

ZINC NITRATES [23; 23]
  BT1   nitrates
    BT2   nitrogen compounds
    BT2   oxygen compounds
  BT1   zinc compounds

ZINC ORES [106; 106]
  BT1   ores

ZINC OXIDES [791; 791]
  BT1   oxides
    BT2   chalcogenides
    BT2   oxygen compounds
  BT1   zinc compounds

ZINC PERCHLORATES [0; 0] *Sep 91*
  BT1   perchlorates
    BT2   chlorine compounds
      BT3   halogen compounds
    BT2   oxygen compounds
  BT1   zinc compounds

ZINC PHOSPHATES [21; 21]
  BT1   phosphates
    BT2   oxygen compounds
    BT2   phosphorus compounds
  BT1   zinc compounds

ZINC PHOSPHIDES [43; 43] *Apr 78*
  BT1   phosphides
    BT2   phosphorus compounds
    BT2   pnictides
  BT1   zinc compounds

ZINC SELENIDES [327; 327]
  BT1   selenides
    BT2   chalcogenides
    BT2   selenium compounds
  BT1   zinc compounds

ZINC SILICATES [32; 32]
  BT1   silicates
    BT2   oxygen compounds
    BT2   silicon compounds
  BT1   zinc compounds

ZINC SILICIDES [0; 0] *Sep 91*
  BT1   silicides
    BT2   silicon compounds
  BT1   zinc compounds

ZINC SULFATES [117; 117]
  BT1   sulfates
    BT2   oxygen compounds
    BT2   sulfur compounds
  BT1   zinc compounds

ZINC SULFIDES [728; 728]
  BT1   sulfides
    BT2   chalcogenides
    BT2   sulfur compounds
  BT1   zinc compounds

ZINC TELLURIDES [383; 383] *Feb 76*
  BT1   tellurides
    BT2   chalcogenides
    BT2   tellurium compounds
  BT1   zinc compounds

ZINC TUNGSTATES [24; 24] *Nov 81*
  BT1   tungstates
    BT2   oxygen compounds
    BT2   tungsten compounds
      BT3   transition element compounds
  BT1   zinc compounds

ZINC 57 [7; 7] *May 76*
  BT1   beta-plus decay radioisotopes
    BT2   beta decay radioisotopes
      BT3   radioisotopes
        BT4   isotopes
  BT1   even-odd nuclei
    BT2   nuclei
  BT1   intermediate mass nuclei
    BT2   nuclei
  BT1   millisec living radioisotopes
    BT2   radioisotopes
      BT3   isotopes
  BT1   zinc isotopes

ZINC 58 [2; 2] *Sep 86*
  BT1   even-even nuclei
    BT2   nuclei
  BT1   intermediate mass nuclei
    BT2   nuclei
  BT1   zinc isotopes

ZINC 59 [9; 9] *Jun 82*
  BT1   beta-plus decay radioisotopes
    BT2   beta decay radioisotopes
      BT3   radioisotopes
        BT4   isotopes
  BT1   even-odd nuclei
    BT2   nuclei
  BT1   intermediate mass nuclei
    BT2   nuclei
  BT1   millisec living radioisotopes
    BT2   radioisotopes
      BT3   isotopes
  BT1   zinc isotopes

ZINC 60 [32; 32]
  BT1   beta-plus decay radioisotopes
    BT2   beta decay radioisotopes
      BT3   radioisotopes
        BT4   isotopes
  BT1   electron capture radioisotopes
    BT2   beta decay radioisotopes
      BT3   radioisotopes
        BT4   isotopes
  BT1   even-even nuclei
    BT2   nuclei
  BT1   intermediate mass nuclei
    BT2   nuclei
  BT1   minutes living radioisotopes
    BT2   radioisotopes
      BT3   isotopes
  BT1   zinc isotopes

ZINC 61 [17; 17]
  BT1   beta-plus decay radioisotopes
    BT2   beta decay radioisotopes
      BT3   radioisotopes
        BT4   isotopes
  BT1   electron capture radioisotopes
    BT2   beta decay radioisotopes
      BT3   radioisotopes
        BT4   isotopes
  BT1   even-odd nuclei
    BT2   nuclei
  BT1   intermediate mass nuclei
    BT2   nuclei
  BT1   minutes living radioisotopes
    BT2   radioisotopes
      BT3   isotopes
  BT1   zinc isotopes

ZINC 62 [124; 124]
  BT1   beta-plus decay radioisotopes
    BT2   beta decay radioisotopes
      BT3   radioisotopes
        BT4   isotopes
  BT1   electron capture radioisotopes
    BT2   beta decay radioisotopes
      BT3   radioisotopes
        BT4   isotopes
  BT1   even-even nuclei
    BT2   nuclei
  BT1   hours living radioisotopes
    BT2   radioisotopes
      BT3   isotopes
  BT1   intermediate mass nuclei
    BT2   nuclei
  BT1   zinc isotopes

ZINC 63 [86; 86]
  BT1   beta-plus decay radioisotopes
    BT2   beta decay radioisotopes
      BT3   radioisotopes
        BT4   isotopes
  BT1   electron capture radioisotopes
    BT2   beta decay radioisotopes
      BT3   radioisotopes
        BT4   isotopes
  BT1   even-odd nuclei
    BT2   nuclei
  BT1   intermediate mass nuclei
    BT2   nuclei
  BT1   minutes living radioisotopes
    BT2   radioisotopes
      BT3   isotopes
  BT1   zinc isotopes

ZINC 64 [305; 305]
  BT1   even-even nuclei
    BT2   nuclei
  BT1   intermediate mass nuclei
    BT2   nuclei
  BT1   stable isotopes
    BT2   isotopes
  BT1   zinc isotopes

ZINC 64 REACTIONS [29; 29] *Oct 83*
  BT1   heavy ion reactions
  BT2   nuclear reactions

ZINC 64 TARGET [266; 266]
  BT1   targets

ZINC 65 [1,519; 1,519]
  BT1   beta-plus decay radioisotopes
    BT2   beta decay radioisotopes
      BT3   radioisotopes
        BT4   isotopes
  BT1   days living radioisotopes
    BT2   radioisotopes
      BT3   isotopes
  BT1   electron capture radioisotopes
    BT2   beta decay radioisotopes
      BT3   radioisotopes
        BT4   isotopes
  BT1   even-odd nuclei
    BT2   nuclei
  BT1   intermediate mass nuclei
    BT2   nuclei
  BT1   zinc isotopes

ZINC 65 TARGET [14; 14] *May 84*
  BT1   targets

ZINC 66 [197; 197]
  BT1   even-even nuclei
    BT2   nuclei
  BT1   intermediate mass nuclei
    BT2   nuclei
  BT1   stable isotopes
    BT2   isotopes
  BT1   zinc isotopes

ZINC 66 TARGET [171; 171]
  BT1   targets

ZINC 67 [174; 174]
  BT1   even-odd nuclei
    BT2   nuclei
  BT1   intermediate mass nuclei
    BT2   nuclei
  BT1   stable isotopes
    BT2   isotopes
  BT1   zinc isotopes

ZINC 67 TARGET [72; 72]
  BT1   targets

ZINC 68 [197; 197]
  BT1   even-even nuclei
    BT2   nuclei
  BT1   intermediate mass nuclei
    BT2   nuclei
  BT1   stable isotopes
    BT2   isotopes
  BT1   zinc isotopes

ZINC 68 REACTIONS [8; 8] *Mar 76*
  BT1   heavy ion reactions
  BT2   nuclear reactions

ZINC 68 TARGET [201; 201]
BT1　targets

ZINC 69 [71; 71]
BT1　beta-minus decay radioisotopes
BT2　beta decay radioisotopes
BT3　radioisotopes
BT4　isotopes
BT1　even-odd nuclei
BT2　nuclei
BT1　hours living radioisotopes
BT2　radioisotopes
BT3　isotopes
BT1　intermediate mass nuclei
BT2　nuclei
BT1　isomeric transition isotopes
BT2　radioisotopes
BT3　isotopes
BT1　minutes living radioisotopes
BT2　radioisotopes
BT3　isotopes
BT1　zinc isotopes

ZINC 70 [81; 81]
BT1　even-even nuclei
BT2　nuclei
BT1　intermediate mass nuclei
BT2　nuclei
BT1　stable isotopes
BT2　isotopes
BT1　zinc isotopes

ZINC 70 REACTIONS [2; 2] *Feb 78*
BT1　heavy ion reactions
BT2　nuclear reactions

ZINC 70 TARGET [92; 92]
BT1　targets

ZINC 71 [13; 13]
BT1　beta-minus decay radioisotopes
BT2　beta decay radioisotopes
BT3　radioisotopes
BT4　isotopes
BT1　even-odd nuclei
BT2　nuclei
BT1　hours living radioisotopes
BT2　radioisotopes
BT3　isotopes
BT1　intermediate mass nuclei
BT2　nuclei
BT1　minutes living radioisotopes
BT2　radioisotopes
BT3　isotopes
BT1　zinc isotopes

ZINC 72 [15; 15]
BT1　beta-minus decay radioisotopes
BT2　beta decay radioisotopes
BT3　radioisotopes
BT4　isotopes
BT1　days living radioisotopes
BT2　radioisotopes
BT3　isotopes
BT1　even-even nuclei
BT2　nuclei
BT1　intermediate mass nuclei
BT2　nuclei
BT1　zinc isotopes

ZINC 73 [8; 8]
BT1　beta-minus decay radioisotopes
BT2　beta decay radioisotopes
BT3　radioisotopes
BT4　isotopes
BT1　even-odd nuclei
BT2　nuclei
BT1　intermediate mass nuclei
BT2　nuclei
BT1　seconds living radioisotopes
BT2　radioisotopes
BT3　isotopes
BT1　zinc isotopes

ZINC 74 [15; 15] *Nov 76*
BT1　beta-minus decay radioisotopes
BT2　beta decay radioisotopes
BT3　radioisotopes
BT4　isotopes
BT1　even-even nuclei
BT2　nuclei
BT1　intermediate mass nuclei
BT2　nuclei
BT1　minutes living radioisotopes
BT2　radioisotopes
BT3　isotopes
BT1　zinc isotopes

ZINC 75 [10; 10]
BT1　beta-minus decay radioisotopes
BT2　beta decay radioisotopes
BT3　radioisotopes
BT4　isotopes
BT1　even-odd nuclei
BT2　nuclei
BT1　intermediate mass nuclei
BT2　nuclei
BT1　seconds living radioisotopes
BT2　radioisotopes
BT3　isotopes
BT1　zinc isotopes

ZINC 76 [9; 9]
BT1　beta-minus decay radioisotopes
BT2　beta decay radioisotopes
BT3　radioisotopes
BT4　isotopes
BT1　even-even nuclei
BT2　nuclei
BT1　intermediate mass nuclei
BT2　nuclei
BT1　seconds living radioisotopes
BT2　radioisotopes
BT3　isotopes
BT1　zinc isotopes

ZINC 77 [8; 8]
BT1　beta-minus decay radioisotopes
BT2　beta decay radioisotopes
BT3　radioisotopes
BT4　isotopes
BT1　even-odd nuclei
BT2　nuclei
BT1　intermediate mass nuclei
BT2　nuclei
BT1　seconds living radioisotopes
BT2　radioisotopes
BT3　isotopes
BT1　zinc isotopes

ZINC 78 [7; 7]
BT1　beta-minus decay radioisotopes
BT2　beta decay radioisotopes
BT3　radioisotopes
BT4　isotopes
BT1　even-even nuclei
BT2　nuclei
BT1　intermediate mass nuclei
BT2　nuclei
BT1　seconds living radioisotopes
BT2　radioisotopes
BT3　isotopes
BT1　zinc isotopes

ZINC 79 [6; 6] *Jun 77*
BT1　even-odd nuclei
BT2　nuclei
BT1　intermediate mass nuclei
BT2　nuclei
BT1　zinc isotopes

ZINC 80 [11; 11] *Jun 85*
BT1　beta-minus decay radioisotopes
BT2　beta decay radioisotopes
BT3　radioisotopes
BT4　isotopes
BT1　even-even nuclei
BT2　nuclei
BT1　intermediate mass nuclei
BT2　nuclei
BT1　millisec living radioisotopes
BT2　radioisotopes

BT3　isotopes
BT1　zinc isotopes

zion station unit-1
USE　zion-1 reactor

zion station unit-2
USE　zion-2 reactor

ZION-1 REACTOR [356; 356]
(Zion, Illinois, USA)
UF　*zion station unit-1*
BT1　pwr type reactors
BT2　enriched uranium reactors
BT3　reactors
BT2　power reactors
BT3　reactors
BT2　thermal reactors
BT3　reactors
BT2　water cooled reactors
BT3　reactors
BT2　water moderated reactors
BT3　reactors

ZION-2 REACTOR [244; 244]
(Zion, Illinois, USA)
UF　*zion station unit-2*
BT1　pwr type reactors
BT2　enriched uranium reactors
BT3　reactors
BT2　power reactors
BT3　reactors
BT2　thermal reactors
BT3　reactors
BT2　water cooled reactors
BT3　reactors
BT2　water moderated reactors
BT3　reactors

ZIPPEITE [8; 8]
BT1　sulfate minerals
BT2　minerals
BT1　uranium minerals
BT2　radioactive minerals
BT3　minerals
BT3　radioactive materials
BT4　materials
RT　uranium sulfates

ZIRCALOY [2,167; 3,949]
(For unspecified Zircaloy alloys.)
BT1　zirconium base alloys
BT2　zirconium alloys
BT3　alloys
NT1　alloy-zr98sn-2
NT1　alloy-zr98sn-4

zircaloy 2
USE　alloy-zr98sn-2

zircaloy 4
USE　alloy-zr98sn-4

ZIRCEX PROCESS [2; 2]
BT1　reprocessing
BT2　separation processes
RT　solvent extraction

ZIRCON [796; 796]
BT1　silicate minerals
BT2　minerals
RT　caldasite
RT　zirconium silicates

ZIRCONATES [456; 538]
(Specific compounds should be indexed by coordination of a descriptor of the f (CATION) COMPOUNDS and the abc anion descriptor.)
BT1　oxygen compounds
BT1　zirconium compounds
BT2　transition element compoun

ZIRCONIUM [4,514; 4,741]
- BT1 transition elements
  - BT2 metals
    - BT3 elements
- NT1 zirconium-alpha
- NT1 zirconium-beta
- NT1 zirconium-omega

(Preceding entries on column 1:)
- NT1 plzt
- NT1 pzt
- RT zirconium oxides

ZIRCONIUM ADDITIONS [584; 895]
(Alloys containing not more than 1% Zr are listed here.)
- NT1 alloy-mo99
- NT1 alloy-mo99b
- NT1 alloy-nb94mo4
- NT1 alloy-ni43fe33cr16mo3
- NT1 alloy-ni46cr23co19ti5al4
- NT1 alloy-ni47cr25co12w9fe3
- NT1 alloy-ni55co17cr15mo5al4ti4
- NT1 alloy-ni58cr20co14mo4ti3
- NT1 alloy-ni59cr20co17ti2
- NT1 alloy-ni60co15cr10al6ti5mo3
- NT1 alloy-ni60cr14co10ti5mo4w4al3
- NT1 alloy-ni61cr16co9al3ti3w3
- NT1 alloy-ni74cr13al6mo4
- NT1 alloy-ni75cr12al6mo5
- NT1 alloy-ni76cr20ti2
- RT zirconium alloys
- RT zirconium compounds

ZIRCONIUM ALLOYS [3,450; 9,235]
(Alloys containing more than 1% Zr.)
- BT1 alloys
- NT1 alloy-ti89al6mo3
- NT1 alloy-ti90al6
- NT1 alloy-u90nb7zr3
- NT1 alloy-v87cr9fe3
- NT1 zirconium base alloys
  - NT2 alloy-zr97nb3
  - NT2 zircaloy
    - NT3 alloy-zr98sn-2
    - NT3 alloy-zr98sn-4
- RT zirconium additions

ZIRCONIUM ARSENIDES [2; 2] *Nov 76*
- BT1 arsenides
  - BT2 arsenic compounds
  - BT2 pnictides
- BT1 zirconium compounds
  - BT2 transition element compounds

ZIRCONIUM BASE ALLOYS [1,550; 5,435]
- BT1 zirconium alloys
  - BT2 alloys
- NT1 alloy-zr97nb3
- NT1 zircaloy
  - NT2 alloy-zr98sn-2
  - NT2 alloy-zr98sn-4

ZIRCONIUM BORIDES [201; 201]
- BT1 borides
  - BT2 boron compounds
- BT1 zirconium compounds
  - BT2 transition element compounds

ZIRCONIUM BROMIDES [44; 44]
- BT1 bromides
  - BT2 bromine compounds
    - BT3 halogen compounds
  - BT2 halides
    - BT3 halogen compounds
- BT1 zirconium compounds
  - BT2 transition element compounds

ZIRCONIUM CARBIDES [818; 818]
- BT1 carbides
  - BT2 carbon compounds
- BT1 zirconium compounds
  - BT2 transition element compounds

ZIRCONIUM CARBONATES [15; 15]
- BT1 carbonates
  - BT2 carbon compounds
  - BT2 oxygen compounds
- BT1 zirconium compounds
  - BT2 transition element compounds

ZIRCONIUM CHLORIDES [302; 302]
- BT1 chlorides
  - BT2 chlorine compounds
    - BT3 halogen compounds
  - BT2 halides
    - BT3 halogen compounds
- BT1 zirconium compounds
  - BT2 transition element compounds

ZIRCONIUM COMPLEXES [1,002; 1,002]
- BT1 transition element complexes
  - BT2 complexes

ZIRCONIUM COMPOUNDS [1,028; 9,234]
- BT1 transition element compounds
- NT1 zirconates
  - NT2 plzt
  - NT2 pzt
- NT1 zirconium arsenides
- NT1 zirconium borides
- NT1 zirconium bromides
- NT1 zirconium carbides
- NT1 zirconium carbonates
- NT1 zirconium chlorides
- NT1 zirconium fluorides
- NT1 zirconium hydrides
- NT1 zirconium hydroxides
- NT1 zirconium iodides
- NT1 zirconium nitrates
- NT1 zirconium nitrides
- NT1 zirconium oxides
- NT1 zirconium perchlorates
- NT1 zirconium phosphates
- NT1 zirconium phosphides
- NT1 zirconium selenides
- NT1 zirconium silicates
- NT1 zirconium silicides
- NT1 zirconium sulfates
- NT1 zirconium sulfides
- NT1 zirconium tellurides
- NT1 zirconium tungstates
- RT zirconium additions

ZIRCONIUM FLUORIDES [275; 275]
- BT1 fluorides
  - BT2 fluorine compounds
    - BT3 halogen compounds
  - BT2 halides
    - BT3 halogen compounds
- BT1 zirconium compounds
  - BT2 transition element compounds

ZIRCONIUM HYDRIDES [648; 648]
- BT1 hydrides
  - BT2 hydrogen compounds
- BT1 zirconium compounds
  - BT2 transition element compounds
- RT hydride moderators

ZIRCONIUM HYDROXIDES [154; 154]
- BT1 hydroxides
  - BT2 hydrogen compounds
  - BT2 oxygen compounds
- BT1 zirconium compounds
  - BT2 transition element compounds

ZIRCONIUM IODIDES [65; 65]
- BT1 iodides
  - BT2 halides
    - BT3 halogen compounds
  - BT2 iodine compounds
    - BT3 halogen compounds
- BT1 zirconium compounds
  - BT2 transition element compounds

ZIRCONIUM IONS [142; 142]
- BT1 ions
  - BT2 charged particles

ZIRCONIUM ISOTOPES [269; 3,168]
- NT1 zirconium 100
- NT1 zirconium 101
- NT1 zirconium 102
- NT1 zirconium 103
- NT1 zirconium 104
- NT1 zirconium 80
- NT1 zirconium 81
- NT1 zirconium 82
- NT1 zirconium 83
- NT1 zirconium 84
- NT1 zirconium 85
- NT1 zirconium 86
- NT1 zirconium 87
- NT1 zirconium 88
- NT1 zirconium 89
- NT1 zirconium 90
- NT1 zirconium 91
- NT1 zirconium 92
- NT1 zirconium 93
- NT1 zirconium 94
- NT1 zirconium 95
- NT1 zirconium 96
- NT1 zirconium 97
- NT1 zirconium 98
- NT1 zirconium 99

ZIRCONIUM NITRATES [71; 71]
- BT1 nitrates
  - BT2 nitrogen compounds
  - BT2 oxygen compounds
- BT1 zirconium compounds
  - BT2 transition element compounds

ZIRCONIUM NITRIDES [324; 324]
- BT1 nitrides
  - BT2 nitrogen compounds
  - BT2 pnictides
- BT1 zirconium compounds
  - BT2 transition element compounds

ZIRCONIUM ORES [9; 9] *Mar 86*
- BT1 ores

ZIRCONIUM OXIDES [4,189; 4,250]
- BT1 oxides
  - BT2 chalcogenides
  - BT2 oxygen compounds
- BT1 zirconium compounds
  - BT2 transition element compounds
- RT baddeleyite
- RT oxide minerals
- RT zirconates
- RT zirconolite

ZIRCONIUM PERCHLORATES [5; 5] *Feb 81*
- BT1 perchlorates
  - BT2 chlorine compounds
    - BT3 halogen compounds
  - BT2 oxygen compounds
- BT1 zirconium compounds
  - BT2 transition element compounds

ZIRCONIUM PHOSPHATES [381; 381]
- BT1 phosphates
  - BT2 oxygen compounds
  - BT2 phosphorus compounds
- BT1 zirconium compounds
  - BT2 transition element compounds

ZIRCONIUM PHOSPHIDES [25; 25]
- BT1 phosphides
  - BT2 phosphorus compounds
  - BT2 pnictides
- BT1 zirconium compounds
  - BT2 transition element compounds

ZIRCONIUM SELENIDES [27; 27]
- BT1 selenides
- BT2 chalcogenides
- BT2 selenium compounds
- BT1 zirconium compounds
- BT2 transition element compounds

ZIRCONIUM SILICATES [108; 476]
- BT1 silicates
- BT2 oxygen compounds
- BT2 silicon compounds
- BT1 zirconium compounds
- BT2 transition element compounds
- RT alvite
- RT catapleite
- RT cyrtolite
- RT elpidite
- RT eudialyte
- RT silicate minerals
- RT zircon

ZIRCONIUM SILICIDES [40; 40]
Nov 76
- BT1 silicides
- BT2 silicon compounds
- BT1 zirconium compounds
- BT2 transition element compounds

ZIRCONIUM SULFATES [110; 110]
- BT1 sulfates
- BT2 oxygen compounds
- BT2 sulfur compounds
- BT1 zirconium compounds
- BT2 transition element compounds

ZIRCONIUM SULFIDES [69; 69]
- BT1 sulfides
- BT2 chalcogenides
- BT2 sulfur compounds
- BT1 zirconium compounds
- BT2 transition element compounds

ZIRCONIUM TELLURIDES [19; 19]
Nov 76
- BT1 tellurides
- BT2 chalcogenides
- BT2 tellurium compounds
- BT1 zirconium compounds
- BT2 transition element compounds

ZIRCONIUM TUNGSTATES [17; 17]
Sep 78
- BT1 tungstates
- BT2 oxygen compounds
- BT2 tungsten compounds
- BT3 transition element compounds
- BT1 zirconium compounds
- BT2 transition element compounds

ZIRCONIUM 100 [61; 61]
- BT1 beta-minus decay radioisotopes
- BT2 beta decay radioisotopes
- BT3 radioisotopes
- BT4 isotopes
- BT1 even-even nuclei
- BT2 nuclei
- BT1 intermediate mass nuclei
- BT2 nuclei
- BT1 seconds living radioisotopes
- BT2 radioisotopes
- BT3 isotopes
- BT1 zirconium isotopes

ZIRCONIUM 101 [20; 20]
- BT1 beta-minus decay radioisotopes
- BT2 beta decay radioisotopes
- BT3 radioisotopes
- BT4 isotopes
- BT1 even-odd nuclei
- BT2 nuclei
- BT1 intermediate mass nuclei
- BT2 nuclei
- BT1 seconds living radioisotopes
- BT2 radioisotopes
- BT3 isotopes
- BT1 zirconium isotopes

ZIRCONIUM 102 [28; 28]
- BT1 beta-minus decay radioisotopes
- BT2 beta decay radioisotopes
- BT3 radioisotopes
- BT4 isotopes
- BT1 even-even nuclei
- BT2 nuclei
- BT1 intermediate mass nuclei
- BT2 nuclei
- BT1 seconds living radioisotopes
- BT2 radioisotopes
- BT3 isotopes
- BT1 zirconium isotopes

ZIRCONIUM 103 [14; 14]
- BT1 even-odd nuclei
- BT2 nuclei
- BT1 intermediate mass nuclei
- BT2 nuclei
- BT1 seconds living radioisotopes
- BT2 radioisotopes
- BT3 isotopes
- BT1 zirconium isotopes

ZIRCONIUM 104 [9; 9]
- BT1 even-even nuclei
- BT2 nuclei
- BT1 intermediate mass nuclei
- BT2 nuclei
- BT1 zirconium isotopes

ZIRCONIUM 80 [35; 35]
- BT1 even-even nuclei
- BT2 nuclei
- BT1 intermediate mass nuclei
- BT2 nuclei
- BT1 zirconium isotopes

ZIRCONIUM 81 [7; 7]
- BT1 beta-plus decay radioisotopes
- BT2 beta decay radioisotopes
- BT3 radioisotopes
- BT4 isotopes
- BT1 even-odd nuclei
- BT2 nuclei
- BT1 intermediate mass nuclei
- BT2 nuclei
- BT1 minutes living radioisotopes
- BT2 radioisotopes
- BT3 isotopes
- BT1 zirconium isotopes

ZIRCONIUM 82 [9; 9]
- BT1 beta-plus decay radioisotopes
- BT2 beta decay radioisotopes
- BT3 radioisotopes
- BT4 isotopes
- BT1 even-even nuclei
- BT2 nuclei
- BT1 intermediate mass nuclei
- BT2 nuclei
- BT1 minutes living radioisotopes
- BT2 radioisotopes
- BT3 isotopes
- BT1 zirconium isotopes

ZIRCONIUM 83 [17; 17]
- BT1 beta-plus decay radioisotopes
- BT2 beta decay radioisotopes
- BT3 radioisotopes
- BT4 isotopes
- BT1 even-odd nuclei
- BT2 nuclei
- BT1 intermediate mass nuclei
- BT2 nuclei
- BT1 seconds living radioisotopes
- BT2 radioisotopes
- BT3 isotopes
- BT1 zirconium isotopes

ZIRCONIUM 84 [24; 24]
- BT1 beta-plus decay radioisotopes
- BT2 beta decay radioisotopes
- BT3 radioisotopes
- BT4 isotopes
- BT1 electron capture radioisotopes
- BT2 beta decay radioisotopes
- BT3 radioisotopes
- BT4 isotopes
- BT1 even-even nuclei
- BT2 nuclei
- BT1 intermediate mass nuclei
- BT2 nuclei
- BT1 minutes living radioisotopes
- BT2 radioisotopes
- BT3 isotopes
- BT1 zirconium isotopes

ZIRCONIUM 85 [12; 12]
- BT1 beta-plus decay radioisotopes
- BT2 beta decay radioisotopes
- BT3 radioisotopes
- BT4 isotopes
- BT1 electron capture radioisotopes
- BT2 beta decay radioisotopes
- BT3 radioisotopes
- BT4 isotopes
- BT1 even-odd nuclei
- BT2 nuclei
- BT1 intermediate mass nuclei
- BT2 nuclei
- BT1 isomeric transition isotopes
- BT2 radioisotopes
- BT3 isotopes
- BT1 minutes living radioisotopes
- BT2 radioisotopes
- BT3 isotopes
- BT1 seconds living radioisotopes
- BT2 radioisotopes
- BT3 isotopes
- BT1 zirconium isotopes

ZIRCONIUM 86 [24; 24]
- BT1 electron capture radioisotopes
- BT2 beta decay radioisotopes
- BT3 radioisotopes
- BT4 isotopes
- BT1 even-even nuclei
- BT2 nuclei
- BT1 hours living radioisotopes
- BT2 radioisotopes
- BT3 isotopes
- BT1 intermediate mass nuclei
- BT2 nuclei
- BT1 zirconium isotopes

ZIRCONIUM 87 [16; 16]
- BT1 beta-plus decay radioisotopes
- BT2 beta decay radioisotopes
- BT3 radioisotopes
- BT4 isotopes
- BT1 electron capture radioisotopes
- BT2 beta decay radioisotopes
- BT3 radioisotopes
- BT4 isotopes
- BT1 even-odd nuclei
- BT2 nuclei
- BT1 hours living radioisotopes
- BT2 radioisotopes
- BT3 isotopes
- BT1 intermediate mass nuclei
- BT2 nuclei
- BT1 isomeric transition isotopes
- BT2 radioisotopes
- BT3 isotopes
- BT1 seconds living radioisotopes
- BT2 radioisotopes
- BT3 isotopes
- BT1 zirconium isotopes

ZIRCONIUM 88 [60; 60]
- BT1 days living radioisotopes
- BT2 radioisotopes
- BT3 isotopes
- BT1 electron capture radioisotopes
- BT2 beta decay radioisotopes
- BT3 radioisotopes
- BT4 isotopes
- BT1 even-even nuclei
- BT2 nuclei
- BT1 intermediate mass nuclei
- BT2 nuclei
- BT1 zirconium isotopes

ZIRCONIUM 89 [177; 177]
BT1   beta-plus decay radioisotopes
  BT2   beta decay radioisotopes
    BT3   radioisotopes
      BT4   isotopes
BT1   days living radioisotopes
  BT2   radioisotopes
    BT3   isotopes
BT1   electron capture radioisotopes
  BT2   beta decay radioisotopes
    BT3   radioisotopes
      BT4   isotopes
BT1   even-odd nuclei
  BT2   nuclei
BT1   intermediate mass nuclei
  BT2   nuclei
BT1   isomeric transition isotopes
  BT2   radioisotopes
    BT3   isotopes
BT1   minutes living radioisotopes
  BT2   radioisotopes
    BT3   isotopes
BT1   zirconium isotopes

ZIRCONIUM 90 [1,117; 1,117]
BT1   even-even nuclei
  BT2   nuclei
BT1   intermediate mass nuclei
  BT2   nuclei
BT1   isomeric transition isotopes
  BT2   radioisotopes
    BT3   isotopes
BT1   millisec living radioisotopes
  BT2   radioisotopes
    BT3   isotopes
BT1   stable isotopes
  BT2   isotopes
BT1   zirconium isotopes

ZIRCONIUM 90 REACTIONS [69; 69] *Jun 84*
BT1   heavy ion reactions
  BT2   nuclear reactions

ZIRCONIUM 90 TARGET [1,365; 1,365]
BT1   targets

ZIRCONIUM 91 [184; 184]
BT1   even-odd nuclei
  BT2   nuclei
BT1   intermediate mass nuclei
  BT2   nuclei
BT1   stable isotopes
  BT2   isotopes
BT1   zirconium isotopes

ZIRCONIUM 91 TARGET [143; 143]
BT1   targets

ZIRCONIUM 92 [182; 182]
BT1   even-even nuclei
  BT2   nuclei
BT1   intermediate mass nuclei
  BT2   nuclei
BT1   stable isotopes
  BT2   isotopes
BT1   zirconium isotopes

ZIRCONIUM 92 REACTIONS [11; 11] *Jan 85*
BT1   heavy ion reactions
  BT2   nuclear reactions

ZIRCONIUM 92 TARGET [284; 284]
BT1   targets

ZIRCONIUM 93 [55; 55]
BT1   beta-minus decay radioisotopes
  BT2   beta decay radioisotopes
    BT3   radioisotopes
      BT4   isotopes
BT1   even-odd nuclei
  BT2   nuclei
BT1   intermediate mass nuclei
  BT2   nuclei
BT1   years living radioisotopes
  BT2   radioisotopes
    BT3   isotopes
BT1   zirconium isotopes

ZIRCONIUM 93 TARGET [2; 2] *Jan 86*
BT1   targets

ZIRCONIUM 94 [107; 107]
BT1   even-even nuclei
  BT2   nuclei
BT1   intermediate mass nuclei
  BT2   nuclei
BT1   stable isotopes
  BT2   isotopes
BT1   zirconium isotopes

ZIRCONIUM 94 TARGET [222; 222]
BT1   targets

ZIRCONIUM 95 [955; 955]
BT1   beta-minus decay radioisotopes
  BT2   beta decay radioisotopes
    BT3   radioisotopes
      BT4   isotopes
BT1   days living radioisotopes
  BT2   radioisotopes
    BT3   isotopes
BT1   even-odd nuclei
  BT2   nuclei
BT1   intermediate mass nuclei
  BT2   nuclei
BT1   zirconium isotopes

ZIRCONIUM 96 [128; 128]
BT1   even-even nuclei
  BT2   nuclei
BT1   intermediate mass nuclei
  BT2   nuclei
BT1   stable isotopes
  BT2   isotopes
BT1   zirconium isotopes

ZIRCONIUM 96 REACTIONS [20; 20] *Jan 85*
BT1   heavy ion reactions
  BT2   nuclear reactions

ZIRCONIUM 96 TARGET [169; 169]
BT1   targets

ZIRCONIUM 97 [64; 64]
BT1   beta-minus decay radioisotopes
  BT2   beta decay radioisotopes
    BT3   radioisotopes
      BT4   isotopes
BT1   even-odd nuclei
  BT2   nuclei
BT1   hours living radioisotopes
  BT2   radioisotopes
    BT3   isotopes
BT1   intermediate mass nuclei
  BT2   nuclei
BT1   zirconium isotopes

ZIRCONIUM 98 [39; 39]
BT1   beta-minus decay radioisotopes
  BT2   beta decay radioisotopes
    BT3   radioisotopes
      BT4   isotopes
BT1   even-even nuclei
  BT2   nuclei
BT1   intermediate mass nuclei
  BT2   nuclei
BT1   seconds living radioisotopes
  BT2   radioisotopes
    BT3   isotopes
BT1   zirconium isotopes

ZIRCONIUM 99 [23; 23]
BT1   beta-minus decay radioisotopes
  BT2   beta decay radioisotopes
    BT3   radioisotopes
      BT4   isotopes
BT1   even-odd nuclei
  BT2   nuclei
BT1   intermediate mass nuclei
  BT2   nuclei
BT1   seconds living radioisotopes
  BT2   radioisotopes
    BT3   isotopes
BT1   zirconium isotopes

ZIRCONIUM-ALPHA [204; 204]
BT1   zirconium
  BT2   transition elements
    BT3   metals
      BT4   elements

ZIRCONIUM-BETA [69; 69]
BT1   zirconium
  BT2   transition elements
    BT3   metals
      BT4   elements

ZIRCONIUM-OMEGA [14; 14]
BT1   zirconium
  BT2   transition elements
    BT3   metals
      BT4   elements

ZIRCONOLITE [81; 81] *Sep 81*
BT1   oxide minerals
  BT2   minerals
RT   calcium oxides
RT   synroc process
RT   titanium oxides
RT   zirconium oxides

ZIRFLEX PROCESS [5; 5]
BT1   reprocessing
  BT2   separation processes
RT   solvent extraction

zittauer lehr- und forschungsr
USE   zlfr reactor

ZITTERBEWEGUNG [57; 57]
RT   quantum mechanics

ZLFR REACTOR [14; 14] *Nov 80*
(Ingenieurhochschule, Zittau, Federal Republic of Germany.)
UF   *wwr-s-zittau reactor*
UF   *zittauer lehr- und forschungsr*
BT1   enriched uranium reactors
  BT2   reactors
BT1   research reactors
  BT2   research and test reactors
    BT3   reactors
BT1   tank type reactors
  BT2   reactors
BT1   thermal reactors
  BT2   reactors
BT1   training reactors
  BT2   research and test reactors
    BT3   reactors
BT1   water cooled reactors
  BT2   reactors
BT1   water moderated reactors
  BT2   reactors
BT1   zero power reactors
  BT2   experimental reactors
    BT3   research and test reactors
      BT4   reactors

ZODIACAL LIGHT [97; 97]
UF   *gegenschein*
UF   *light (zodiacal)*
BT1   electromagnetic radiation
  BT2   radiations
RT   interplanetary space
RT   solar radiation

zoe reactor
USE   el-1 reactor

ZONE MELTING [452; 452]
UF   *floating zone techniques*
BT1   melting
  BT2   phase transformations
RT   crystal growth

ZONE REFINING [170; 170]
- BT1 refining
- BT1 separation processes
- RT crystallization
- RT metallurgy
- RT reprocessing

ZONES [710; 1,651]
- NT1 brillouin zones
- NT1 guinier-preston zones

zones (auroral)
- USE auroral zones

ZOOLOGY [11; 11]
- BT1 biology

zooplankton
- USE plankton

ZORITA-1 REACTOR [16; 16]
- UF *central nuclear de zorita-1*
- UF *jose cabrera reactor*
- BT1 pwr type reactors
- BT2 enriched uranium reactors
- BT3 reactors
- BT2 power reactors
- BT3 reactors
- BT2 thermal reactors
- BT3 reactors
- BT2 water cooled reactors
- BT3 reactors
- BT2 water moderated reactors
- BT3 reactors

ZPPR REACTOR [209; 209]
(Zero power reactor at Idaho Falls.)
- BT1 fast reactors
- BT2 epithermal reactors
- BT3 reactors
- BT1 research reactors
- BT2 research and test reactors
- BT3 reactors
- BT1 zero power reactors
- BT2 experimental reactors
- BT3 research and test reactors
- BT4 reactors

ZPR REACTOR [16; 16]
(Cornell University, Ward Laboratory of Nuclear Engineering, Ithaca, New York, USA)
- UF *cornell univ. zero pow. react.*
- UF *zero power reac (cornell univ)*
- BT1 enriched uranium reactors
- BT2 reactors
- BT1 tank type reactors
- BT2 reactors
- BT1 thermal reactors
- BT2 reactors
- BT1 training reactors
- BT2 research and test reactors
- BT3 reactors
- BT1 zero power reactors
- BT2 experimental reactors
- BT3 research and test reactors
- BT4 reactors

ZPR-3 REACTOR [37; 37]
(Variously fuelled, unmoderated, uncooled.)
- UF *anl zero power res. reactor-3*
- UF *zero power res. react-3 (anl)*
- BT1 fast reactors
- BT2 epithermal reactors
- BT3 reactors
- BT1 zero power reactors
- BT2 experimental reactors
- BT3 research and test reactors
- BT4 reactors

ZPR-6 REACTOR [65; 65]
(Variously fuelled, unmoderated, uncooled.)
- UF *anl zero power res. reactor-6*
- UF *zero power res. react-6 (anl)*
- BT1 fast reactors
- BT2 epithermal reactors
- BT3 reactors
- BT1 zero power reactors
- BT2 experimental reactors
- BT3 research and test reactors
- BT4 reactors

ZPR-9 REACTOR [85; 85]
(Uncooled.)
- UF *anl zero power res. reactor-9*
- UF *zero power res. react-9 (anl)*
- BT1 fast reactors
- BT2 epithermal reactors
- BT3 reactors
- BT1 zero power reactors
- BT2 experimental reactors
- BT3 research and test reactors
- BT4 reactors
- RT breeder reactors
- RT propulsion reactors

ZR-6 REACTOR [8; 8] *Oct 81*
(At Central Research Institute for Physics, Budapest.)
- BT1 water cooled reactors
- BT2 reactors
- BT1 zero power reactors
- BT2 experimental reactors
- BT3 research and test reactors
- BT4 reactors

ZRR REACTOR [9; 9]
- BT1 experimental reactors
- BT2 research and test reactors
- BT3 reactors
- BT1 fast reactors
- BT2 epithermal reactors
- BT3 reactors
- BT1 sodium cooled reactors
- BT2 liquid metal cooled reactors
- BT3 reactors

ZT-P DEVICES [17; 17] *Sep 86*
- BT1 toroidal pinch devices
- BT2 closed plasma devices
- BT3 thermonuclear devices
- BT2 pinch devices
- BT3 thermonuclear devices
- RT reverse-field pinch

ZT-40 DEVICES [190; 190] *Apr 78*
(Los Alamos Experiment on reverse-field pinch.)
- BT1 toroidal pinch devices
- BT2 closed plasma devices
- BT3 thermonuclear devices
- BT2 pinch devices
- BT3 thermonuclear devices
- RT reverse-field pinch

ZUNI EVENT [2; 2] *Jan 85*
- BT1 nuclear explosions
- BT2 explosions
- BT1 redwing project
- BT1 surface explosions
- BT2 explosions

zwentendorf reactor
- USE tullnerfeld reactor

zygotes
- USE embryos

ZYMOSAN [27; 27]
- RT polysaccharides
- RT properdin
- RT yeasts

Z0-1780 BARYONS [2; 2] *Dec 87*
- BT1 z*baryons
- BT2 hyperons
- BT3 baryons
- BT4 fermions
- BT4 hadrons
- BT5 elementary particles
- BT3 strange particles
- BT4 elementary particles

Z0-1865 BARYONS [0; 0] *Dec 87*
- BT1 z*baryons
- BT2 hyperons
- BT3 baryons
- BT4 fermions
- BT4 hadrons
- BT5 elementary particles
- BT3 strange particles
- BT4 elementary particles

Z1-1725 BARYONS [0; 0] *Dec 87*
- BT1 z*baryons
- BT2 hyperons
- BT3 baryons
- BT4 fermions
- BT4 hadrons
- BT5 elementary particles
- BT3 strange particles
- BT4 elementary particles

Z1-1900 BARYONS [0; 0] *Dec 87*
- BT1 z*baryons
- BT2 hyperons
- BT3 baryons
- BT4 fermions
- BT4 hadrons
- BT5 elementary particles
- BT3 strange particles
- BT4 elementary particles

Z1-2150 BARYONS [0; 0] *Dec 87*
- BT1 z*baryons
- BT2 hyperons
- BT3 baryons
- BT4 fermions
- BT4 hadrons
- BT5 elementary particles
- BT3 strange particles
- BT4 elementary particles

Z1-2500 BARYONS [0; 0] *Dec 87*
- BT1 z*baryons
- BT2 hyperons
- BT3 baryons
- BT4 fermions
- BT4 hadrons
- BT5 elementary particles
- BT3 strange particles
- BT4 elementary particles

1-dimensional calculations
- USE one-dimensional calculations

1-NITROSO-2-NAPHTHOL [19; 19]
- UF *alpha-nitroso-beta-naphthol*
- UF *anbn*
- BT1 naphthols
- BT2 phenols
- BT3 aromatics
- BT4 organic compounds
- BT3 hydroxy compounds
- BT4 organic compounds
- BT1 nitroso compounds
- BT2 organic nitrogen compounds
- BT3 organic compounds
- BT1 reagents

1-propanol
- USE propanols

1/v law
- USE reciprocal v law

1,1-diethoxyethane
USE   acetal

1,2-dihydroxyanthraquinone
USE   alizarin

1,2-dihydroxybenzene
USE   pyrocatechol

1,2-dimethoxyethane
USE   dme

1,2-dimethoxymethane
USE   methylal

1,2-diphenylethane
USE   bibenzyl

1,2-diphenylethylene
USE   stilbene

1,2-ethanedial
USE   glyoxal

1,2-ethanediol
USE   glycols

1,2-ethanedithiol
USE   dithiols

1,2,3-propanetriol
USE   glycerol

1,2,3-trihydroxybenzene
USE   pyrogallol

1,2,4,5-tetramethylbenzene
USE   durene

1,3-diazines
USE   pyrimidines

1,3-dihydroxybenzene
USE   resorcinol

1,3-dimethylxanthine
USE   theophylline

1,3,5-trimethylbenzene
USE   mesitylene

1,3,7-trimethylxanthine
USE   caffeine

1,4-diaminobutane
USE   putrescine

1,4-diazines
USE   pyrazines

1,4-dihydroxyanthraquinone
USE   quinizarin

1,4-dioxane
USE   dioxane

1,5-diaminopentane
USE   cadaverine

2-chloro-1,3-butadiene
USE   neoprene

2-dimensional calculations
USE   two-dimensional calculations

2-furalaldehyde
USE   furfural

2-mercaptopropionylglycine
USE   mpg

2-methylbutadiene
USE   isoprene

2-METHYLBUTANE [12; 12] *Sep 83*
    UF   *isopentane*
    UF   *methylbutane (2-)*
    BT1   alkanes
      BT2   hydrocarbons
        BT3   organic compounds

2-METHYLPROPANE [279; 279]
    UF   *isobutane*
    UF   *methylpropane (2-)*
    BT1   alkanes
      BT2   hydrocarbons
        BT3   organic compounds

2-METHYLPROPANOL [25; 25]
    UF   *isobutyl alcohol*
    UF   *methylpropanol (2-)*
    BT1   alcohols
      BT2   hydroxy compounds
        BT3   organic compounds

2-METHYLPROPENE [62; 62]
    UF   *isobutylene*
    UF   *methylpropene (2-)*
    BT1   alkenes
      BT2   hydrocarbons
        BT3   organic compounds

2-methylquinoline
USE   quinaldine

2-propanol
USE   propanols

2-pyridinecarboxylic acid
USE   picolinic acid

2-pyrrolidinecarboxylic acid
USE   proline

2-2-DIMETHYLPROPANE [117; 117]
    UF   *dimethylpropane (2,2-)*
    UF   *neopentane*
    UF   *2,2-dimethylpropane*
    BT1   alkanes
      BT2   hydrocarbons
        BT3   organic compounds

2-3-PENTANEDIONE [8; 8]
    UF   *acetyl propionyl*
    UF   *methyl ethyl diketone*
    UF   *pentanedione (2,3)*
    BT1   ketones
      BT2   organic compounds

2,2-dimethylpropane
USE   2-2-dimethylpropane

2,2-dithiobisethylamine
USE   cystamine

2,2,6,6-tetramethyl-4-piperidi
USE   tmpn

2,4-pentanedione
USE   acetylacetone

2,5-diaminovaleric acid
USE   ornithine

2X DEVICES [174; 174]
    BT1   magnetic mirrors
      BT2   open plasma devices
        BT3   thermonuclear devices

3-dimensional calculations
USE   three-dimensional calculations

3-METHYLCHOLANTHRENE [41; 41]
Feb 82
    BT1   condensed aromatics
      BT2   aromatics
        BT3   organic compounds

3,4-dihydroxyphenylalanine
USE   dopa

3,7-dimethylxanthine
USE   theobromine

3j-symbols
USE   clebsch-gordan coefficients

4-dimensional calculations
USE   four-dimensional calculations

5-methyl uracil
USE   thymine

5U PELLETRON ACCELERATOR
[7; 7] *Feb 80*
    BT1   pelletron accelerators
      BT2   electrostatic accelerators
        BT3   accelerators

6-aminopurine
USE   adenines

6-carboxyuracil
USE   orotic acid

6-furfurylaminopurine
USE   kinetin

6j-symbols
USE   racah coefficients

8-hydroxyquinoline
USE   oxine

8-hydroxyxanthine
USE   uric acid

9j-symbols USE wigner coefficients

APPENDIX

ACTINIDE NUCLEI
- NT1 actinium 209
- NT1 actinium 210
- NT1 actinium 211
- NT1 actinium 212
- NT1 actinium 213
- NT1 actinium 214
- NT1 actinium 215
- NT1 actinium 216
- NT1 actinium 217
- NT1 actinium 218
- NT1 actinium 219
- NT1 actinium 220
- NT1 actinium 221
- NT1 actinium 222
- NT1 actinium 223
- NT1 actinium 224
- NT1 actinium 225
- NT1 actinium 226
- NT1 actinium 227
- NT1 actinium 228
- NT1 actinium 229
- NT1 actinium 230
- NT1 actinium 231
- NT1 actinium 232
- NT1 actinium 233
- NT1 actinium 234
- NT1 americium 232
- NT1 americium 234
- NT1 americium 237
- NT1 americium 238
- NT1 americium 239
- NT1 americium 240
- NT1 americium 241
- NT1 americium 242
- NT1 americium 243
- NT1 americium 244
- NT1 americium 245
- NT1 americium 246
- NT1 americium 247
- NT1 berkelium 240
- NT1 berkelium 241
- NT1 berkelium 242
- NT1 berkelium 243
- NT1 berkelium 244
- NT1 berkelium 245
- NT1 berkelium 246
- NT1 berkelium 247
- NT1 berkelium 248
- NT1 berkelium 249
- NT1 berkelium 250
- NT1 berkelium 251
- NT1 californium 239
- NT1 californium 240
- NT1 californium 241
- NT1 californium 242
- NT1 californium 243
- NT1 californium 244
- NT1 californium 245
- NT1 californium 246
- NT1 californium 247
- NT1 californium 248
- NT1 californium 249
- NT1 californium 250
- NT1 californium 251
- NT1 californium 252
- NT1 californium 253
- NT1 californium 254
- NT1 californium 255
- NT1 californium 256
- NT1 curium 236
- NT1 curium 238
- NT1 curium 239
- NT1 curium 240
- NT1 curium 241
- NT1 curium 242
- NT1 curium 243
- NT1 curium 244
- NT1 curium 245
- NT1 curium 246
- NT1 curium 247
- NT1 curium 248
- NT1 curium 249
- NT1 curium 250
- NT1 curium 251
- NT1 curium 252
- NT1 einsteinium 243
- NT1 einsteinium 244
- NT1 einsteinium 245
- NT1 einsteinium 246
- NT1 einsteinium 247
- NT1 einsteinium 248
- NT1 einsteinium 249
- NT1 einsteinium 250
- NT1 einsteinium 251
- NT1 einsteinium 252
- NT1 einsteinium 253
- NT1 einsteinium 254
- NT1 einsteinium 255
- NT1 einsteinium 256
- NT1 fermium 242
- NT1 fermium 243
- NT1 fermium 244
- NT1 fermium 245
- NT1 fermium 246
- NT1 fermium 247
- NT1 fermium 248
- NT1 fermium 249
- NT1 fermium 250
- NT1 fermium 251
- NT1 fermium 252
- NT1 fermium 253
- NT1 fermium 254
- NT1 fermium 255
- NT1 fermium 256
- NT1 fermium 257
- NT1 fermium 258
- NT1 fermium 259
- NT1 lawrencium 253
- NT1 lawrencium 254
- NT1 lawrencium 255
- NT1 lawrencium 256
- NT1 lawrencium 257
- NT1 lawrencium 258
- NT1 lawrencium 259
- NT1 lawrencium 260
- NT1 lawrencium 261
- NT1 lawrencium 262
- NT1 lawrencium 263
- NT1 mendelevium 247
- NT1 mendelevium 248
- NT1 mendelevium 249
- NT1 mendelevium 250
- NT1 mendelevium 251
- NT1 mendelevium 252
- NT1 mendelevium 253
- NT1 mendelevium 254
- NT1 mendelevium 255
- NT1 mendelevium 256
- NT1 mendelevium 257
- NT1 mendelevium 258
- NT1 mendelevium 259
- NT1 mendelevium 260
- NT1 mendelevium 261
- NT1 neptunium 226
- NT1 neptunium 227
- NT1 neptunium 228
- NT1 neptunium 229
- NT1 neptunium 230
- NT1 neptunium 231
- NT1 neptunium 232
- NT1 neptunium 233
- NT1 neptunium 234
- NT1 neptunium 235
- NT1 neptunium 236
- NT1 neptunium 237
- NT1 neptunium 238
- NT1 neptunium 239
- NT1 neptunium 240
- NT1 neptunium 241
- NT1 neptunium 242
- NT1 neptunium 243
- NT1 neptunium 244
- NT1 nobelium 250
- NT1 nobelium 251
- NT1 nobelium 252
- NT1 nobelium 253
- NT1 nobelium 254
- NT1 nobelium 255
- NT1 nobelium 256
- NT1 nobelium 257
- NT1 nobelium 258
- NT1 nobelium 259
- NT1 nobelium 260
- NT1 nobelium 261
- NT1 nobelium 262
- NT1 plutonium 230
- NT1 plutonium 231
- NT1 plutonium 232
- NT1 plutonium 233
- NT1 plutonium 234
- NT1 plutonium 235
- NT1 plutonium 236
- NT1 plutonium 237
- NT1 plutonium 238
- NT1 plutonium 239
- NT1 plutonium 240
- NT1 plutonium 241
- NT1 plutonium 242
- NT1 plutonium 243
- NT1 plutonium 244
- NT1 plutonium 245
- NT1 plutonium 246
- NT1 plutonium 247
- NT1 plutonium 248
- NT1 plutonium 250
- NT1 protactinium 215
- NT1 protactinium 216
- NT1 protactinium 217
- NT1 protactinium 218
- NT1 protactinium 219
- NT1 protactinium 220
- NT1 protactinium 221
- NT1 protactinium 222
- NT1 protactinium 223
- NT1 protactinium 224
- NT1 protactinium 225
- NT1 protactinium 226
- NT1 protactinium 227
- NT1 protactinium 228
- NT1 protactinium 229
- NT1 protactinium 230
- NT1 protactinium 231
- NT1 protactinium 232
- NT1 protactinium 233
- NT1 protactinium 234
- NT1 protactinium 235
- NT1 protactinium 236
- NT1 protactinium 237
- NT1 protactinium 238
- NT1 thorium 212
- NT1 thorium 213
- NT1 thorium 214
- NT1 thorium 215
- NT1 thorium 216
- NT1 thorium 217
- NT1 thorium 218
- NT1 thorium 219
- NT1 thorium 220
- NT1 thorium 221
- NT1 thorium 222
- NT1 thorium 223
- NT1 thorium 224
- NT1 thorium 225
- NT1 thorium 226
- NT1 thorium 227
- NT1 thorium 228
- NT1 thorium 229
- NT1 thorium 230
- NT1 thorium 231
- NT1 thorium 232
- NT1 thorium 233
- NT1 thorium 234
- NT1 thorium 235
- NT1 thorium 236
- NT1 thorium 238
- NT1 uranium 222
- NT1 uranium 223
- NT1 uranium 224
- NT1 uranium 225
- NT1 uranium 226
- NT1 uranium 227
- NT1 uranium 228
- NT1 uranium 229
- NT1 uranium 230
- NT1 uranium 231
- NT1 uranium 232
- NT1 uranium 233
- NT1 uranium 234
- NT1 uranium 235
- NT1 uranium 236
- NT1 uranium 237
- NT1 uranium 238
- NT1 uranium 239
- NT1 uranium 240
- NT1 uranium 242

ALPHA DECAY RADIOISOTOPES
- NT1 actinium 209
- NT1 actinium 210
- NT1 actinium 211
- NT1 actinium 212
- NT1 actinium 213
- NT1 actinium 214
- NT1 actinium 215
- NT1 actinium 216
- NT1 actinium 217
- NT1 actinium 218
- NT1 actinium 219
- NT1 actinium 220
- NT1 actinium 221
- NT1 actinium 222
- NT1 actinium 223
- NT1 actinium 224
- NT1 actinium 225
- NT1 actinium 226
- NT1 actinium 227
- NT1 americium 232
- NT1 americium 237
- NT1 americium 238
- NT1 americium 239
- NT1 americium 240
- NT1 americium 241
- NT1 americium 242
- NT1 americium 243
- NT1 astatine 194
- NT1 astatine 196
- NT1 astatine 197
- NT1 astatine 198
- NT1 astatine 199
- NT1 astatine 200
- NT1 astatine 201
- NT1 astatine 202
- NT1 astatine 203
- NT1 astatine 204
- NT1 astatine 205
- NT1 astatine 206
- NT1 astatine 207
- NT1 astatine 208
- NT1 astatine 209
- NT1 astatine 210
- NT1 astatine 211
- NT1 astatine 212
- NT1 astatine 213
- NT1 astatine 214

- A-1 -

NT1	astatine 215	NT1	element 108 265	NT1	lawrencium 255	NT1	platinum 178
NT1	astatine 216	NT1	element 109 266	NT1	lawrencium 256	NT1	platinum 179
NT1	astatine 217	NT1	erbium 152	NT1	lawrencium 257	NT1	platinum 180
NT1	astatine 218	NT1	erbium 153	NT1	lawrencium 258	NT1	platinum 181
NT1	astatine 219	NT1	erbium 154	NT1	lawrencium 259	NT1	platinum 182
NT1	astatine 220	NT1	erbium 155	NT1	lawrencium 260	NT1	platinum 183
NT1	berkelium 243	NT1	europium 147	NT1	lead 182	NT1	platinum 184
NT1	berkelium 244	NT1	europium 148	NT1	lead 183	NT1	platinum 185
NT1	berkelium 245	NT1	fermium 243	NT1	lead 184	NT1	platinum 186
NT1	berkelium 247	NT1	fermium 245	NT1	lead 185	NT1	platinum 188
NT1	berkelium 249	NT1	fermium 246	NT1	lead 186	NT1	platinum 190
NT1	beryllium 8	NT1	fermium 247	NT1	lead 187	NT1	plutonium 230
NT1	bismuth 188	NT1	fermium 248	NT1	lead 188	NT1	plutonium 232
NT1	bismuth 189	NT1	fermium 249	NT1	lead 189	NT1	plutonium 233
NT1	bismuth 190	NT1	fermium 250	NT1	lead 190	NT1	plutonium 234
NT1	bismuth 191	NT1	fermium 251	NT1	lead 191	NT1	plutonium 235
NT1	bismuth 192	NT1	fermium 252	NT1	lead 192	NT1	plutonium 236
NT1	bismuth 193	NT1	fermium 253	NT1	lead 210	NT1	plutonium 237
NT1	bismuth 194	NT1	fermium 254	NT1	lithium 5	NT1	plutonium 238
NT1	bismuth 195	NT1	fermium 255	NT1	lutetium 155	NT1	plutonium 239
NT1	bismuth 197	NT1	fermium 256	NT1	lutetium 156	NT1	plutonium 240
NT1	bismuth 199	NT1	fermium 257	NT1	lutetium 157	NT1	plutonium 241
NT1	bismuth 201	NT1	francium 201	NT1	lutetium 158	NT1	plutonium 242
NT1	bismuth 203	NT1	francium 202	NT1	lutetium 159	NT1	plutonium 244
NT1	bismuth 210	NT1	francium 203	NT1	mendelevium 247	NT1	polonium 192
NT1	bismuth 211	NT1	francium 204	NT1	mendelevium 248	NT1	polonium 193
NT1	bismuth 212	NT1	francium 205	NT1	mendelevium 249	NT1	polonium 194
NT1	bismuth 213	NT1	francium 206	NT1	mendelevium 250	NT1	polonium 195
NT1	bismuth 214	NT1	francium 207	NT1	mendelevium 251	NT1	polonium 196
NT1	boron 9	NT1	francium 208	NT1	mendelevium 255	NT1	polonium 197
NT1	californium 239	NT1	francium 209	NT1	mendelevium 256	NT1	polonium 198
NT1	californium 240	NT1	francium 210	NT1	mendelevium 257	NT1	polonium 199
NT1	californium 241	NT1	francium 211	NT1	mendelevium 258	NT1	polonium 200
NT1	californium 242	NT1	francium 212	NT1	mendelevium 259	NT1	polonium 201
NT1	californium 243	NT1	francium 213	NT1	mercury 175	NT1	polonium 202
NT1	californium 244	NT1	francium 214	NT1	mercury 176	NT1	polonium 203
NT1	californium 245	NT1	francium 215	NT1	mercury 177	NT1	polonium 204
NT1	californium 246	NT1	francium 216	NT1	mercury 178	NT1	polonium 205
NT1	californium 247	NT1	francium 217	NT1	mercury 179	NT1	polonium 206
NT1	californium 248	NT1	francium 218	NT1	mercury 180	NT1	polonium 207
NT1	californium 249	NT1	francium 219	NT1	mercury 181	NT1	polonium 208
NT1	californium 250	NT1	francium 220	NT1	mercury 182	NT1	polonium 209
NT1	californium 251	NT1	francium 221	NT1	mercury 183	NT1	polonium 210
NT1	californium 252	NT1	francium 222	NT1	mercury 184	NT1	polonium 211
NT1	californium 253	NT1	francium 223	NT1	mercury 185	NT1	polonium 212
NT1	californium 254	NT1	gadolinium 148	NT1	mercury 186	NT1	polonium 213
NT1	curium 236	NT1	gadolinium 149	NT1	mercury 187	NT1	polonium 214
NT1	curium 238	NT1	gadolinium 150	NT1	mercury 188	NT1	polonium 215
NT1	curium 240	NT1	gadolinium 151	NT1	neodymium 144	NT1	polonium 216
NT1	curium 241	NT1	gadolinium 152	NT1	neptunium 226	NT1	polonium 217
NT1	curium 242	NT1	gold 173	NT1	neptunium 227	NT1	polonium 218
NT1	curium 243	NT1	gold 174	NT1	neptunium 229	NT1	promethium 145
NT1	curium 244	NT1	gold 175	NT1	neptunium 230	NT1	protactinium 215
NT1	curium 245	NT1	gold 176	NT1	neptunium 231	NT1	protactinium 216
NT1	curium 246	NT1	gold 177	NT1	neptunium 233	NT1	protactinium 217
NT1	curium 247	NT1	gold 178	NT1	neptunium 235	NT1	protactinium 218
NT1	curium 248	NT1	gold 179	NT1	neptunium 237	NT1	protactinium 219
NT1	curium 250	NT1	gold 181	NT1	nobelium 251	NT1	protactinium 220
NT1	dysprosium 150	NT1	gold 183	NT1	nobelium 252	NT1	protactinium 221
NT1	dysprosium 151	NT1	gold 184	NT1	nobelium 253	NT1	protactinium 222
NT1	dysprosium 152	NT1	gold 185	NT1	nobelium 254	NT1	protactinium 223
NT1	dysprosium 153	NT1	hafnium 156	NT1	nobelium 255	NT1	protactinium 224
NT1	dysprosium 154	NT1	hafnium 157	NT1	nobelium 256	NT1	protactinium 225
NT1	einsteinium 243	NT1	hafnium 158	NT1	nobelium 257	NT1	protactinium 226
NT1	einsteinium 244	NT1	hafnium 159	NT1	nobelium 259	NT1	protactinium 227
NT1	einsteinium 245	NT1	hafnium 160	NT1	nobelium 260	NT1	protactinium 228
NT1	einsteinium 246	NT1	hafnium 161	NT1	osmium 162	NT1	protactinium 229
NT1	einsteinium 247	NT1	hafnium 162	NT1	osmium 163	NT1	protactinium 230
NT1	einsteinium 248	NT1	hafnium 174	NT1	osmium 164	NT1	protactinium 231
NT1	einsteinium 249	NT1	helium 5	NT1	osmium 165	NT1	radium 205
NT1	einsteinium 251	NT1	holmium 151	NT1	osmium 166	NT1	radium 206
NT1	einsteinium 252	NT1	holmium 152	NT1	osmium 167	NT1	radium 207
NT1	einsteinium 253	NT1	holmium 153	NT1	osmium 168	NT1	radium 208
NT1	einsteinium 254	NT1	holmium 154	NT1	osmium 169	NT1	radium 209
NT1	einsteinium 255	NT1	holmium 155	NT1	osmium 170	NT1	radium 210
NT1	element 104 255	NT1	iodine 111	NT1	osmium 171	NT1	radium 211
NT1	element 104 257	NT1	iridium 166	NT1	osmium 172	NT1	radium 212
NT1	element 104 259	NT1	iridium 167	NT1	osmium 173	NT1	radium 213
NT1	element 104 261	NT1	iridium 168	NT1	osmium 174	NT1	radium 214
NT1	element 105 257	NT1	iridium 169	NT1	osmium 186	NT1	radium 215
NT1	element 105 258	NT1	iridium 170	NT1	platinum 168	NT1	radium 216
NT1	element 105 260	NT1	iridium 171	NT1	platinum 169	NT1	radium 217
NT1	element 105 261	NT1	iridium 172	NT1	platinum 170	NT1	radium 218
NT1	element 105 262	NT1	iridium 173	NT1	platinum 171	NT1	radium 219
NT1	element 106 260	NT1	iridium 174	NT1	platinum 172	NT1	radium 220
NT1	element 106 261	NT1	iridium 175	NT1	platinum 173	NT1	radium 221
NT1	element 106 263	NT1	iridium 176	NT1	platinum 174	NT1	radium 222
NT1	element 107 261	NT1	iridium 177	NT1	platinum 175	NT1	radium 223
NT1	element 107 262	NT1	lawrencium 253	NT1	platinum 176	NT1	radium 224
NT1	element 108 264	NT1	lawrencium 254	NT1	platinum 177	NT1	radium 226

ALPHA DECAY RADIOISOTOPES

- NT1 radon 199
- NT1 radon 200
- NT1 radon 201
- NT1 radon 202
- NT1 radon 203
- NT1 radon 204
- NT1 radon 205
- NT1 radon 206
- NT1 radon 207
- NT1 radon 208
- NT1 radon 209
- NT1 radon 210
- NT1 radon 211
- NT1 radon 212
- NT1 radon 213
- NT1 radon 214
- NT1 radon 215
- NT1 radon 216
- NT1 radon 217
- NT1 radon 218
- NT1 radon 219
- NT1 radon 220
- NT1 radon 221
- NT1 radon 222
- NT1 rhenium 161
- NT1 rhenium 162
- NT1 rhenium 163
- NT1 rhenium 164
- NT1 rhenium 165
- NT1 rhenium 166
- NT1 rhenium 167
- NT1 rhenium 168
- NT1 rhenium 169
- NT1 samarium 146
- NT1 samarium 147
- NT1 samarium 148
- NT1 tantalum 157
- NT1 tantalum 158
- NT1 tantalum 159
- NT1 tantalum 160
- NT1 tantalum 161
- NT1 tantalum 163
- NT1 tantalum 164
- NT1 tellurium 106
- NT1 tellurium 107
- NT1 tellurium 108
- NT1 tellurium 109
- NT1 tellurium 110
- NT1 terbium 149
- NT1 terbium 151
- NT1 thallium 179
- NT1 thallium 182
- NT1 thallium 184
- NT1 thallium 185
- NT1 thallium 186
- NT1 thallium 187
- NT1 thorium 212
- NT1 thorium 213
- NT1 thorium 214
- NT1 thorium 215
- NT1 thorium 216
- NT1 thorium 217
- NT1 thorium 218
- NT1 thorium 219
- NT1 thorium 220
- NT1 thorium 221
- NT1 thorium 222
- NT1 thorium 223
- NT1 thorium 224
- NT1 thorium 225
- NT1 thorium 226
- NT1 thorium 227
- NT1 thorium 228
- NT1 thorium 229
- NT1 thorium 230
- NT1 thorium 232
- NT1 thulium 153
- NT1 thulium 154
- NT1 thulium 155
- NT1 thulium 156
- NT1 thulium 157
- NT1 tungsten 158
- NT1 tungsten 159
- NT1 tungsten 160
- NT1 tungsten 161
- NT1 tungsten 162
- NT1 tungsten 163
- NT1 tungsten 164
- NT1 tungsten 165
- NT1 tungsten 166
- NT1 uranium 222
- NT1 uranium 223
- NT1 uranium 224
- NT1 uranium 225
- NT1 uranium 226
- NT1 uranium 227
- NT1 uranium 228
- NT1 uranium 229
- NT1 uranium 230
- NT1 uranium 231
- NT1 uranium 232
- NT1 uranium 233
- NT1 uranium 234
- NT1 uranium 235
- NT1 uranium 236
- NT1 uranium 238
- NT1 xenon 110
- NT1 xenon 111
- NT1 xenon 112
- NT1 ytterbium 154
- NT1 ytterbium 155
- NT1 ytterbium 156
- NT1 ytterbium 157
- NT1 ytterbium 158

BETA-MINUS DECAY RADIOISOTOPES

- NT1 actinium 226
- NT1 actinium 227
- NT1 actinium 228
- NT1 actinium 229
- NT1 actinium 230
- NT1 actinium 231
- NT1 actinium 232
- NT1 actinium 233
- NT1 actinium 234
- NT1 aluminium 28
- NT1 aluminium 29
- NT1 aluminium 30
- NT1 aluminium 31
- NT1 aluminium 32
- NT1 aluminium 34
- NT1 aluminium 36
- NT1 aluminium 37
- NT1 americium 242
- NT1 americium 244
- NT1 americium 245
- NT1 americium 246
- NT1 americium 247
- NT1 antimony 122
- NT1 antimony 124
- NT1 antimony 125
- NT1 antimony 126
- NT1 antimony 127
- NT1 antimony 128
- NT1 antimony 129
- NT1 antimony 130
- NT1 antimony 131
- NT1 antimony 132
- NT1 antimony 133
- NT1 antimony 134
- NT1 antimony 135
- NT1 antimony 136
- NT1 argon 39
- NT1 argon 41
- NT1 argon 42
- NT1 argon 43
- NT1 argon 44
- NT1 argon 45
- NT1 argon 46
- NT1 arsenic 74
- NT1 arsenic 76
- NT1 arsenic 77
- NT1 arsenic 78
- NT1 arsenic 79
- NT1 arsenic 80
- NT1 arsenic 81
- NT1 arsenic 82
- NT1 arsenic 83
- NT1 arsenic 84
- NT1 arsenic 85
- NT1 arsenic 86
- NT1 arsenic 87
- NT1 astatine 217
- NT1 astatine 218
- NT1 astatine 219
- NT1 astatine 220
- NT1 astatine 221
- NT1 astatine 222
- NT1 astatine 223
- NT1 barium 139
- NT1 barium 140
- NT1 barium 141
- NT1 barium 142
- NT1 barium 143
- NT1 barium 144
- NT1 barium 145
- NT1 barium 146
- NT1 barium 147
- NT1 barium 148
- NT1 barium 149
- NT1 berkelium 248
- NT1 berkelium 249
- NT1 berkelium 250
- NT1 berkelium 251
- NT1 beryllium 10
- NT1 beryllium 11
- NT1 beryllium 12
- NT1 beryllium 14
- NT1 bismuth 210
- NT1 bismuth 211
- NT1 bismuth 212
- NT1 bismuth 213
- NT1 bismuth 214
- NT1 bismuth 215
- NT1 bismuth 216
- NT1 boron 12
- NT1 boron 13
- NT1 boron 14
- NT1 boron 15
- NT1 boron 17
- NT1 boron 19
- NT1 bromine 80
- NT1 bromine 82
- NT1 bromine 83
- NT1 bromine 84
- NT1 bromine 85
- NT1 bromine 86
- NT1 bromine 87
- NT1 bromine 88
- NT1 bromine 89
- NT1 bromine 90
- NT1 bromine 91
- NT1 bromine 92
- NT1 bromine 93
- NT1 cadmium 113
- NT1 cadmium 115
- NT1 cadmium 117
- NT1 cadmium 118
- NT1 cadmium 119
- NT1 cadmium 120
- NT1 cadmium 121
- NT1 cadmium 122
- NT1 cadmium 123
- NT1 cadmium 124
- NT1 cadmium 125
- NT1 cadmium 126
- NT1 cadmium 130
- NT1 calcium 45
- NT1 calcium 47
- NT1 calcium 49
- NT1 calcium 50
- NT1 calcium 51
- NT1 calcium 52
- NT1 calcium 53
- NT1 californium 253
- NT1 californium 255
- NT1 carbon 14
- NT1 carbon 15
- NT1 carbon 16
- NT1 carbon 17
- NT1 carbon 18
- NT1 cerium 141
- NT1 cerium 143
- NT1 cerium 144
- NT1 cerium 145
- NT1 cerium 146
- NT1 cerium 147
- NT1 cerium 148
- NT1 cerium 149
- NT1 cerium 150
- NT1 cerium 151
- NT1 cerium 152
- NT1 cesium 130
- NT1 cesium 132
- NT1 cesium 134
- NT1 cesium 135
- NT1 cesium 136
- NT1 cesium 137
- NT1 cesium 138
- NT1 cesium 139
- NT1 cesium 140
- NT1 cesium 141
- NT1 cesium 142
- NT1 cesium 143
- NT1 cesium 144
- NT1 cesium 145
- NT1 cesium 146
- NT1 cesium 147
- NT1 cesium 148
- NT1 chlorine 36
- NT1 chlorine 38
- NT1 chlorine 39
- NT1 chlorine 40
- NT1 chlorine 41
- NT1 chromium 55
- NT1 chromium 56
- NT1 chromium 57
- NT1 chromium 58
- NT1 chromium 59
- NT1 cobalt 60
- NT1 cobalt 61
- NT1 cobalt 62
- NT1 cobalt 63
- NT1 cobalt 64
- NT1 cobalt 65
- NT1 cobalt 66
- NT1 cobalt 67
- NT1 copper 64
- NT1 copper 66
- NT1 copper 67
- NT1 copper 68
- NT1 copper 69
- NT1 copper 70
- NT1 copper 71
- NT1 copper 72
- NT1 copper 73
- NT1 copper 74
- NT1 copper 75
- NT1 curium 249
- NT1 curium 250
- NT1 curium 251
- NT1 dysprosium 165
- NT1 dysprosium 166
- NT1 dysprosium 167
- NT1 dysprosium 168
- NT1 dysprosium 169
- NT1 einsteinium 254
- NT1 einsteinium 255
- NT1 einsteinium 256
- NT1 erbium 169
- NT1 erbium 171
- NT1 erbium 172
- NT1 erbium 173
- NT1 erbium 174
- NT1 europium 150
- NT1 europium 152
- NT1 europium 154
- NT1 europium 155
- NT1 europium 156
- NT1 europium 157
- NT1 europium 158
- NT1 europium 159
- NT1 europium 160
- NT1 europium 161
- NT1 europium 162
- NT1 fluorine 20
- NT1 fluorine 21
- NT1 fluorine 22
- NT1 fluorine 23
- NT1 fluorine 24
- NT1 fluorine 26
- NT1 francium 220
- NT1 francium 222
- NT1 francium 223
- NT1 francium 224
- NT1 francium 225
- NT1 francium 226
- NT1 francium 227
- NT1 francium 228
- NT1 francium 229
- NT1 francium 230
- NT1 francium 231
- NT1 gadolinium 159
- NT1 gadolinium 161
- NT1 gadolinium 162
- NT1 gadolinium 163
- NT1 gadolinium 164
- NT1 gallium 70
- NT1 gallium 72

NT1 gallium 73
NT1 gallium 74
NT1 gallium 75
NT1 gallium 76
NT1 gallium 77
NT1 gallium 78
NT1 gallium 79
NT1 gallium 80
NT1 gallium 81
NT1 gallium 82
NT1 gallium 83
NT1 germanium 75
NT1 germanium 77
NT1 germanium 78
NT1 germanium 79
NT1 germanium 80
NT1 germanium 81
NT1 germanium 82
NT1 germanium 83
NT1 germanium 84
NT1 germanium 85
NT1 gold 196
NT1 gold 198
NT1 gold 199
NT1 gold 200
NT1 gold 201
NT1 gold 202
NT1 gold 203
NT1 gold 204
NT1 hafnium 181
NT1 hafnium 182
NT1 hafnium 183
NT1 hafnium 184
NT1 helium 6
NT1 helium 7
NT1 helium 8
NT1 holmium 164
NT1 holmium 166
NT1 holmium 167
NT1 holmium 168
NT1 holmium 169
NT1 holmium 170
NT1 holmium 171
NT1 holmium 172
NT1 indium 112
NT1 indium 114
NT1 indium 115
NT1 indium 116
NT1 indium 117
NT1 indium 118
NT1 indium 119
NT1 indium 120
NT1 indium 121
NT1 indium 122
NT1 indium 123
NT1 indium 124
NT1 indium 125
NT1 indium 126
NT1 indium 127
NT1 indium 128
NT1 indium 129
NT1 indium 130
NT1 indium 131
NT1 indium 132
NT1 iodine 126
NT1 iodine 128
NT1 iodine 129
NT1 iodine 130
NT1 iodine 131
NT1 iodine 132
NT1 iodine 133
NT1 iodine 134
NT1 iodine 135
NT1 iodine 136
NT1 iodine 137
NT1 iodine 138
NT1 iodine 139
NT1 iodine 140
NT1 iodine 141
NT1 iodine 142
NT1 iridium 192
NT1 iridium 194
NT1 iridium 195
NT1 iridium 196
NT1 iridium 197
NT1 iridium 198
NT1 iron 59
NT1 iron 60
NT1 iron 61
NT1 iron 62

NT1 iron 63
NT1 iron 64
NT1 krypton 85
NT1 krypton 87
NT1 krypton 88
NT1 krypton 89
NT1 krypton 90
NT1 krypton 91
NT1 krypton 92
NT1 krypton 93
NT1 krypton 94
NT1 krypton 95
NT1 krypton 97
NT1 lanthanum 138
NT1 lanthanum 140
NT1 lanthanum 141
NT1 lanthanum 142
NT1 lanthanum 143
NT1 lanthanum 144
NT1 lanthanum 145
NT1 lanthanum 146
NT1 lanthanum 147
NT1 lanthanum 148
NT1 lanthanum 149
NT1 lead 209
NT1 lead 210
NT1 lead 211
NT1 lead 212
NT1 lead 213
NT1 lead 214
NT1 lithium 11
NT1 lithium 13
NT1 lithium 8
NT1 lithium 9
NT1 lutetium 176
NT1 lutetium 177
NT1 lutetium 178
NT1 lutetium 179
NT1 lutetium 180
NT1 lutetium 181
NT1 lutetium 182
NT1 lutetium 183
NT1 lutetium 184
NT1 magnesium 27
NT1 magnesium 28
NT1 magnesium 29
NT1 magnesium 30
NT1 magnesium 31
NT1 magnesium 32
NT1 magnesium 33
NT1 magnesium 34
NT1 manganese 56
NT1 manganese 57
NT1 manganese 58
NT1 manganese 59
NT1 manganese 60
NT1 manganese 61
NT1 manganese 62
NT1 manganese 63
NT1 mercury 203
NT1 mercury 205
NT1 mercury 206
NT1 molybdenum 101
NT1 molybdenum 102
NT1 molybdenum 103
NT1 molybdenum 104
NT1 molybdenum 105
NT1 molybdenum 106
NT1 molybdenum 107
NT1 molybdenum 108
NT1 molybdenum 99
NT1 neodymium 147
NT1 neodymium 149
NT1 neodymium 151
NT1 neodymium 152
NT1 neodymium 153
NT1 neodymium 154
NT1 neodymium 155
NT1 neodymium 156
NT1 neon 23
NT1 neon 24
NT1 neon 25
NT1 neon 26
NT1 neon 29
NT1 neon 30
NT1 neptunium 236
NT1 neptunium 238
NT1 neptunium 239
NT1 neptunium 240
NT1 neptunium 241

NT1 neptunium 242
NT1 neptunium 243
NT1 neptunium 244
NT1 neutron-rich isotopes
NT1 nickel 63
NT1 nickel 65
NT1 nickel 66
NT1 nickel 67
NT1 nickel 69
NT1 nickel 71
NT1 nickel 72
NT1 nickel 73
NT1 nickel 74
NT1 niobium 100
NT1 niobium 101
NT1 niobium 102
NT1 niobium 103
NT1 niobium 104
NT1 niobium 105
NT1 niobium 106
NT1 niobium 94
NT1 niobium 95
NT1 niobium 96
NT1 niobium 97
NT1 niobium 98
NT1 niobium 99
NT1 nitrogen 16
NT1 nitrogen 17
NT1 nitrogen 18
NT1 nitrogen 19
NT1 nitrogen 20
NT1 nitrogen 22
NT1 nitrogen 23
NT1 osmium 191
NT1 osmium 193
NT1 osmium 194
NT1 osmium 195
NT1 osmium 196
NT1 oxygen 19
NT1 oxygen 20
NT1 oxygen 21
NT1 oxygen 22
NT1 palladium 107
NT1 palladium 109
NT1 palladium 111
NT1 palladium 112
NT1 palladium 113
NT1 palladium 114
NT1 palladium 115
NT1 palladium 116
NT1 palladium 117
NT1 palladium 118
NT1 palladium 119
NT1 phosphorus 32
NT1 phosphorus 33
NT1 phosphorus 34
NT1 phosphorus 35
NT1 phosphorus 36
NT1 phosphorus 37
NT1 phosphorus 38
NT1 phosphorus 40
NT1 phosphorus 41
NT1 phosphorus 42
NT1 platinum 197
NT1 platinum 199
NT1 platinum 200
NT1 platinum 201
NT1 plutonium 241
NT1 plutonium 243
NT1 plutonium 245
NT1 plutonium 246
NT1 polonium 215
NT1 polonium 218
NT1 potassium 40
NT1 potassium 42
NT1 potassium 43
NT1 potassium 44
NT1 potassium 45
NT1 potassium 46
NT1 potassium 47
NT1 potassium 48
NT1 potassium 49
NT1 potassium 50
NT1 potassium 51
NT1 potassium 52
NT1 potassium 53
NT1 potassium 54
NT1 praseodymium 142
NT1 praseodymium 143

NT1 praseodymium 144
NT1 praseodymium 145
NT1 praseodymium 146
NT1 praseodymium 147
NT1 praseodymium 148
NT1 praseodymium 149
NT1 praseodymium 150
NT1 praseodymium 151
NT1 praseodymium 152
NT1 praseodymium 153
NT1 praseodymium 154
NT1 promethium 146
NT1 promethium 147
NT1 promethium 148
NT1 promethium 149
NT1 promethium 150
NT1 promethium 151
NT1 promethium 152
NT1 promethium 153
NT1 promethium 154
NT1 promethium 155
NT1 promethium 156
NT1 promethium 157
NT1 promethium 158
NT1 protactinium 230
NT1 protactinium 232
NT1 protactinium 233
NT1 protactinium 234
NT1 protactinium 235
NT1 protactinium 236
NT1 protactinium 237
NT1 protactinium 238
NT1 radium 225
NT1 radium 227
NT1 radium 228
NT1 radium 229
NT1 radium 230
NT1 radium 231
NT1 radium 232
NT1 radon 221
NT1 radon 223
NT1 radon 224
NT1 radon 225
NT1 radon 226
NT1 radon 227
NT1 radon 228
NT1 rhenium 186
NT1 rhenium 187
NT1 rhenium 188
NT1 rhenium 189
NT1 rhenium 190
NT1 rhenium 191
NT1 rhenium 192
NT1 rhodium 102
NT1 rhodium 104
NT1 rhodium 105
NT1 rhodium 106
NT1 rhodium 107
NT1 rhodium 108
NT1 rhodium 109
NT1 rhodium 110
NT1 rhodium 111
NT1 rhodium 112
NT1 rhodium 113
NT1 rhodium 114
NT1 rhodium 115
NT1 rhodium 116
NT1 rhodium 117
NT1 rubidium 100
NT1 rubidium 84
NT1 rubidium 86
NT1 rubidium 87
NT1 rubidium 88
NT1 rubidium 89
NT1 rubidium 90
NT1 rubidium 91
NT1 rubidium 92
NT1 rubidium 93
NT1 rubidium 94
NT1 rubidium 95
NT1 rubidium 96
NT1 rubidium 97
NT1 rubidium 98
NT1 rubidium 99
NT1 ruthenium 103
NT1 ruthenium 105
NT1 ruthenium 106
NT1 ruthenium 107
NT1 ruthenium 108
NT1 ruthenium 109

BETA-MINUS DECAY RADIOISOTOPES

NT1 ruthenium 110
NT1 ruthenium 111
NT1 ruthenium 112
NT1 ruthenium 113
NT1 samarium 151
NT1 samarium 153
NT1 samarium 155
NT1 samarium 156
NT1 samarium 157
NT1 samarium 158
NT1 samarium 159
NT1 samarium 160
NT1 scandium 46
NT1 scandium 47
NT1 scandium 48
NT1 scandium 49
NT1 scandium 50
NT1 scandium 51
NT1 scandium 52
NT1 selenium 79
NT1 selenium 81
NT1 selenium 83
NT1 selenium 84
NT1 selenium 85
NT1 selenium 86
NT1 selenium 87
NT1 selenium 88
NT1 selenium 89
NT1 selenium 91
NT1 silicon 31
NT1 silicon 32
NT1 silicon 33
NT1 silicon 34
NT1 silicon 35
NT1 silicon 36
NT1 silicon 37
NT1 silicon 38
NT1 silicon 39
NT1 silver 108
NT1 silver 110
NT1 silver 111
NT1 silver 112
NT1 silver 113
NT1 silver 114
NT1 silver 115
NT1 silver 116
NT1 silver 117
NT1 silver 118
NT1 silver 119
NT1 silver 120
NT1 silver 121
NT1 silver 122
NT1 silver 123
NT1 sodium 24
NT1 sodium 25
NT1 sodium 26
NT1 sodium 27
NT1 sodium 28
NT1 sodium 29
NT1 sodium 30
NT1 sodium 31
NT1 sodium 32
NT1 sodium 33
NT1 sodium 34
NT1 sodium 35
NT1 strontium 100
NT1 strontium 101
NT1 strontium 102
NT1 strontium 89
NT1 strontium 90
NT1 strontium 91
NT1 strontium 92
NT1 strontium 93
NT1 strontium 94
NT1 strontium 95
NT1 strontium 96
NT1 strontium 97
NT1 strontium 98
NT1 strontium 99
NT1 sulfur 35
NT1 sulfur 37
NT1 sulfur 38
NT1 sulfur 39
NT1 sulfur 40
NT1 sulfur 43
NT1 tantalum 180
NT1 tantalum 182
NT1 tantalum 183
NT1 tantalum 184
NT1 tantalum 185
NT1 tantalum 186
NT1 technetium 100
NT1 technetium 101
NT1 technetium 102
NT1 technetium 103
NT1 technetium 104
NT1 technetium 105
NT1 technetium 106
NT1 technetium 107
NT1 technetium 108
NT1 technetium 109
NT1 technetium 110
NT1 technetium 111
NT1 technetium 112
NT1 technetium 98
NT1 technetium 99
NT1 tellurium 127
NT1 tellurium 129
NT1 tellurium 131
NT1 tellurium 132
NT1 tellurium 133
NT1 tellurium 134
NT1 tellurium 135
NT1 tellurium 136
NT1 tellurium 137
NT1 tellurium 138
NT1 terbium 156
NT1 terbium 158
NT1 terbium 160
NT1 terbium 161
NT1 terbium 162
NT1 terbium 163
NT1 terbium 164
NT1 terbium 165
NT1 thallium 204
NT1 thallium 206
NT1 thallium 207
NT1 thallium 208
NT1 thallium 209
NT1 thallium 210
NT1 thorium 231
NT1 thorium 233
NT1 thorium 234
NT1 thorium 235
NT1 thorium 236
NT1 thulium 170
NT1 thulium 171
NT1 thulium 172
NT1 thulium 173
NT1 thulium 174
NT1 thulium 175
NT1 thulium 176
NT1 thulium 177
NT1 tin 121
NT1 tin 123
NT1 tin 125
NT1 tin 126
NT1 tin 127
NT1 tin 128
NT1 tin 129
NT1 tin 130
NT1 tin 131
NT1 tin 132
NT1 tin 133
NT1 tin 134
NT1 titanium 51
NT1 titanium 52
NT1 titanium 53
NT1 tritium
NT1 tungsten 185
NT1 tungsten 187
NT1 tungsten 188
NT1 tungsten 189
NT1 uranium 237
NT1 uranium 239
NT1 uranium 240
NT1 uranium 242
NT1 vanadium 50
NT1 vanadium 52
NT1 vanadium 53
NT1 vanadium 54
NT1 vanadium 55
NT1 xenon 133
NT1 xenon 135
NT1 xenon 137
NT1 xenon 138
NT1 xenon 139
NT1 xenon 140
NT1 xenon 141
NT1 xenon 142
NT1 xenon 143
NT1 xenon 144
NT1 xenon 145
NT1 ytterbium 175
NT1 ytterbium 177
NT1 ytterbium 178
NT1 ytterbium 179
NT1 ytterbium 180
NT1 yttrium 100
NT1 yttrium 101
NT1 yttrium 102
NT1 yttrium 90
NT1 yttrium 91
NT1 yttrium 92
NT1 yttrium 93
NT1 yttrium 94
NT1 yttrium 95
NT1 yttrium 96
NT1 yttrium 97
NT1 yttrium 98
NT1 yttrium 99
NT1 zinc 69
NT1 zinc 71
NT1 zinc 72
NT1 zinc 73
NT1 zinc 74
NT1 zinc 75
NT1 zinc 76
NT1 zinc 77
NT1 zinc 78
NT1 zinc 80
NT1 zirconium 100
NT1 zirconium 101
NT1 zirconium 102
NT1 zirconium 93
NT1 zirconium 95
NT1 zirconium 97
NT1 zirconium 98
NT1 zirconium 99

BETA-PLUS DECAY RADIOISOTOPES

NT1 aluminium 22
NT1 aluminium 23
NT1 aluminium 24
NT1 aluminium 25
NT1 aluminium 26
NT1 antimony 108
NT1 antimony 110
NT1 antimony 111
NT1 antimony 112
NT1 antimony 113
NT1 antimony 114
NT1 antimony 115
NT1 antimony 116
NT1 antimony 117
NT1 antimony 118
NT1 antimony 120
NT1 antimony 122
NT1 argon 31
NT1 argon 32
NT1 argon 33
NT1 argon 34
NT1 argon 35
NT1 arsenic 66
NT1 arsenic 67
NT1 arsenic 68
NT1 arsenic 69
NT1 arsenic 70
NT1 arsenic 71
NT1 arsenic 72
NT1 arsenic 74
NT1 astatine 205
NT1 astatine 206
NT1 barium 117
NT1 barium 119
NT1 barium 120
NT1 barium 121
NT1 barium 122
NT1 barium 123
NT1 barium 124
NT1 barium 125
NT1 barium 126
NT1 barium 127
NT1 barium 129
NT1 bismuth 194
NT1 bismuth 197
NT1 bismuth 200
NT1 bismuth 202
NT1 bismuth 203
NT1 bismuth 205
NT1 bismuth 206
NT1 bismuth 207
NT1 boron 8
NT1 bromine 69
NT1 bromine 70
NT1 bromine 71
NT1 bromine 72
NT1 bromine 73
NT1 bromine 74
NT1 bromine 75
NT1 bromine 76
NT1 bromine 77
NT1 bromine 78
NT1 bromine 80
NT1 cadmium 100
NT1 cadmium 101
NT1 cadmium 102
NT1 cadmium 103
NT1 cadmium 104
NT1 cadmium 105
NT1 cadmium 107
NT1 cadmium 97
NT1 cadmium 98
NT1 cadmium 99
NT1 calcium 36
NT1 calcium 37
NT1 calcium 38
NT1 calcium 39
NT1 carbon 10
NT1 carbon 11
NT1 carbon 9
NT1 cerium 125
NT1 cerium 127
NT1 cerium 128
NT1 cerium 129
NT1 cerium 130
NT1 cerium 131
NT1 cerium 133
NT1 cerium 135
NT1 cerium 137
NT1 cesium 114
NT1 cesium 115
NT1 cesium 116
NT1 cesium 117
NT1 cesium 118
NT1 cesium 119
NT1 cesium 120
NT1 cesium 121
NT1 cesium 122
NT1 cesium 123
NT1 cesium 124
NT1 cesium 125
NT1 cesium 126
NT1 cesium 127
NT1 cesium 128
NT1 cesium 129
NT1 cesium 130
NT1 cesium 132
NT1 chlorine 31
NT1 chlorine 32
NT1 chlorine 33
NT1 chlorine 34
NT1 chlorine 36
NT1 chromium 42
NT1 chromium 45
NT1 chromium 46
NT1 chromium 47
NT1 chromium 49
NT1 cobalt 53
NT1 cobalt 54
NT1 cobalt 55
NT1 cobalt 56
NT1 cobalt 58
NT1 copper 57
NT1 copper 58
NT1 copper 59
NT1 copper 60
NT1 copper 61
NT1 copper 62
NT1 copper 64
NT1 dysprosium 145
NT1 dysprosium 146
NT1 dysprosium 147
NT1 dysprosium 148
NT1 dysprosium 149
NT1 dysprosium 150
NT1 dysprosium 151
NT1 dysprosium 153
NT1 dysprosium 155

NT1 erbium 145	NT1 indium 103	NT1 manganese 51	NT1 praseodymium 130
NT1 erbium 147	NT1 indium 104	NT1 manganese 52	NT1 praseodymium 131
NT1 erbium 148	NT1 indium 105	NT1 mercury 179	NT1 praseodymium 132
NT1 erbium 149	NT1 indium 106	NT1 mercury 181	NT1 praseodymium 133
NT1 erbium 150	NT1 indium 107	NT1 mercury 182	NT1 praseodymium 134
NT1 erbium 151	NT1 indium 108	NT1 mercury 183	NT1 praseodymium 135
NT1 erbium 152	NT1 indium 109	NT1 mercury 184	NT1 praseodymium 136
NT1 erbium 153	NT1 indium 110	NT1 mercury 185	NT1 praseodymium 137
NT1 erbium 154	NT1 indium 112	NT1 mercury 186	NT1 praseodymium 138
NT1 erbium 155	NT1 indium 114	NT1 mercury 187	NT1 praseodymium 139
NT1 erbium 156	NT1 iodine 110	NT1 mercury 188	NT1 praseodymium 140
NT1 erbium 157	NT1 iodine 111	NT1 mercury 191	NT1 promethium 132
NT1 erbium 158	NT1 iodine 112	NT1 mercury 193	NT1 promethium 133
NT1 erbium 159	NT1 iodine 113	NT1 molybdenum 87	NT1 promethium 134
NT1 erbium 161	NT1 iodine 114	NT1 molybdenum 88	NT1 promethium 135
NT1 erbium 163	NT1 iodine 115	NT1 molybdenum 89	NT1 promethium 136
NT1 europium 134	NT1 iodine 116	NT1 molybdenum 90	NT1 promethium 137
NT1 europium 135	NT1 iodine 117	NT1 molybdenum 91	NT1 promethium 138
NT1 europium 136	NT1 iodine 118	NT1 neodymium 127	NT1 promethium 139
NT1 europium 138	NT1 iodine 119	NT1 neodymium 128	NT1 promethium 140
NT1 europium 139	NT1 iodine 120	NT1 neodymium 129	NT1 promethium 141
NT1 europium 140	NT1 iodine 121	NT1 neodymium 130	NT1 promethium 142
NT1 europium 141	NT1 iodine 122	NT1 neodymium 131	NT1 radon 207
NT1 europium 142	NT1 iodine 124	NT1 neodymium 132	NT1 radon 209
NT1 europium 143	NT1 iodine 126	NT1 neodymium 133	NT1 rhenium 165
NT1 europium 144	NT1 iodine 128	NT1 neodymium 134	NT1 rhenium 170
NT1 europium 145	NT1 iridium 178	NT1 neodymium 135	NT1 rhenium 171
NT1 europium 146	NT1 iridium 179	NT1 neodymium 136	NT1 rhenium 172
NT1 europium 147	NT1 iridium 180	NT1 neodymium 137	NT1 rhenium 174
NT1 europium 148	NT1 iridium 181	NT1 neodymium 139	NT1 rhenium 175
NT1 europium 150	NT1 iridium 182	NT1 neodymium 141	NT1 rhenium 176
NT1 europium 152	NT1 iridium 183	NT1 neon 17	NT1 rhenium 177
NT1 fluorine 17	NT1 iridium 184	NT1 neon 18	NT1 rhenium 178
NT1 fluorine 18	NT1 iridium 185	NT1 neon 19	NT1 rhenium 179
NT1 gadolinium 137	NT1 iridium 186	NT1 neptunium 234	NT1 rhenium 180
NT1 gadolinium 139	NT1 iridium 188	NT1 nickel 53	NT1 rhenium 182
NT1 gadolinium 142	NT1 iridium 190	NT1 nickel 55	NT1 rhodium 100
NT1 gadolinium 143	NT1 iron 49	NT1 nickel 57	NT1 rhodium 102
NT1 gadolinium 144	NT1 iron 51	NT1 niobium 83	NT1 rhodium 94
NT1 gadolinium 145	NT1 iron 52	NT1 niobium 84	NT1 rhodium 95
NT1 gadolinium 146	NT1 iron 53	NT1 niobium 87	NT1 rhodium 96
NT1 gadolinium 147	NT1 krypton 71	NT1 niobium 88	NT1 rhodium 97
NT1 gallium 62	NT1 krypton 72	NT1 niobium 89	NT1 rhodium 98
NT1 gallium 63	NT1 krypton 73	NT1 niobium 90	NT1 rhodium 99
NT1 gallium 64	NT1 krypton 74	NT1 niobium 92	NT1 rubidium 74
NT1 gallium 65	NT1 krypton 75	NT1 nitrogen 12	NT1 rubidium 75
NT1 gallium 66	NT1 krypton 77	NT1 nitrogen 13	NT1 rubidium 76
NT1 gallium 68	NT1 krypton 79	NT1 osmium 172	NT1 rubidium 77
NT1 germanium 61	NT1 lanthanum 121	NT1 osmium 173	NT1 rubidium 78
NT1 germanium 64	NT1 lanthanum 125	NT1 osmium 174	NT1 rubidium 79
NT1 germanium 65	NT1 lanthanum 126	NT1 osmium 175	NT1 rubidium 80
NT1 germanium 66	NT1 lanthanum 127	NT1 osmium 176	NT1 rubidium 81
NT1 germanium 67	NT1 lanthanum 128	NT1 osmium 177	NT1 rubidium 82
NT1 germanium 69	NT1 lanthanum 129	NT1 osmium 178	NT1 rubidium 84
NT1 gold 182	NT1 lanthanum 130	NT1 osmium 179	NT1 ruthenium 92
NT1 gold 184	NT1 lanthanum 131	NT1 osmium 181	NT1 ruthenium 93
NT1 gold 185	NT1 lanthanum 132	NT1 osmium 183	NT1 ruthenium 95
NT1 gold 186	NT1 lanthanum 133	NT1 oxygen 13	NT1 samarium 133
NT1 gold 187	NT1 lanthanum 134	NT1 oxygen 14	NT1 samarium 134
NT1 gold 188	NT1 lanthanum 135	NT1 oxygen 15	NT1 samarium 135
NT1 gold 189	NT1 lanthanum 136	NT1 palladium 101	NT1 samarium 136
NT1 gold 190	NT1 lead 187	NT1 palladium 95	NT1 samarium 137
NT1 gold 192	NT1 lead 188	NT1 palladium 97	NT1 samarium 138
NT1 gold 194	NT1 lead 189	NT1 palladium 98	NT1 samarium 139
NT1 gold 196	NT1 lead 190	NT1 palladium 99	NT1 samarium 140
NT1 hafnium 154	NT1 lead 191	NT1 phosphorus 26	NT1 samarium 141
NT1 hafnium 155	NT1 lead 192	NT1 phosphorus 28	NT1 samarium 142
NT1 hafnium 162	NT1 lead 193	NT1 phosphorus 29	NT1 samarium 143
NT1 hafnium 163	NT1 lead 194	NT1 phosphorus 30	NT1 scandium 40
NT1 hafnium 166	NT1 lead 195	NT1 platinum 182	NT1 scandium 41
NT1 hafnium 167	NT1 lead 199	NT1 platinum 183	NT1 scandium 42
NT1 hafnium 168	NT1 lead 201	NT1 platinum 184	NT1 scandium 43
NT1 hafnium 169	NT1 lutetium 153	NT1 platinum 185	NT1 scandium 44
NT1 holmium 145	NT1 lutetium 162	NT1 platinum 187	NT1 selenium 68
NT1 holmium 146	NT1 lutetium 163	NT1 platinum 189	NT1 selenium 69
NT1 holmium 147	NT1 lutetium 164	NT1 polonium 198	NT1 selenium 70
NT1 holmium 148	NT1 lutetium 165	NT1 polonium 199	NT1 selenium 71
NT1 holmium 149	NT1 lutetium 166	NT1 polonium 200	NT1 selenium 73
NT1 holmium 150	NT1 lutetium 167	NT1 polonium 201	NT1 silicon 24
NT1 holmium 151	NT1 lutetium 168	NT1 polonium 202	NT1 silicon 25
NT1 holmium 152	NT1 lutetium 169	NT1 polonium 203	NT1 silicon 26
NT1 holmium 153	NT1 lutetium 170	NT1 polonium 205	NT1 silicon 27
NT1 holmium 154	NT1 lutetium 171	NT1 polonium 207	NT1 silver 100
NT1 holmium 155	NT1 lutetium 174	NT1 potassium 35	NT1 silver 101
NT1 holmium 156	NT1 magnesium 20	NT1 potassium 36	NT1 silver 102
NT1 holmium 157	NT1 magnesium 21	NT1 potassium 37	NT1 silver 103
NT1 holmium 158	NT1 magnesium 22	NT1 potassium 38	NT1 silver 104
NT1 holmium 160	NT1 magnesium 23	NT1 potassium 40	NT1 silver 105
NT1 holmium 162	NT1 manganese 49	NT1 praseodymium 126	NT1 silver 106
NT1 indium 100	NT1 manganese 50	NT1 praseodymium 129	NT1 silver 108

BETA-PLUS DECAY RADIOISOTOPES

- NT1 silver 96
- NT1 silver 98
- NT1 silver 99
- NT1 sodium 19
- NT1 sodium 20
- NT1 sodium 21
- NT1 sodium 22
- NT1 strontium 77
- NT1 strontium 78
- NT1 strontium 79
- NT1 strontium 80
- NT1 strontium 81
- NT1 strontium 83
- NT1 sulfur 28
- NT1 sulfur 29
- NT1 sulfur 30
- NT1 sulfur 31
- NT1 tantalum 165
- NT1 tantalum 166
- NT1 tantalum 167
- NT1 tantalum 168
- NT1 tantalum 169
- NT1 tantalum 170
- NT1 tantalum 171
- NT1 tantalum 172
- NT1 tantalum 173
- NT1 tantalum 174
- NT1 tantalum 175
- NT1 tantalum 176
- NT1 tantalum 177
- NT1 tantalum 178
- NT1 technetium 90
- NT1 technetium 91
- NT1 technetium 92
- NT1 technetium 93
- NT1 technetium 94
- NT1 technetium 95
- NT1 technetium 96
- NT1 tellurium 107
- NT1 tellurium 108
- NT1 tellurium 109
- NT1 tellurium 110
- NT1 tellurium 111
- NT1 tellurium 112
- NT1 tellurium 113
- NT1 tellurium 114
- NT1 tellurium 115
- NT1 tellurium 116
- NT1 tellurium 117
- NT1 tellurium 119
- NT1 tellurium 121
- NT1 terbium 141
- NT1 terbium 143
- NT1 terbium 144
- NT1 terbium 145
- NT1 terbium 146
- NT1 terbium 147
- NT1 terbium 148
- NT1 terbium 149
- NT1 terbium 150
- NT1 terbium 151
- NT1 terbium 152
- NT1 terbium 153
- NT1 terbium 154
- NT1 terbium 156
- NT1 thallium 184
- NT1 thallium 186
- NT1 thallium 188
- NT1 thallium 189
- NT1 thallium 190
- NT1 thallium 191
- NT1 thallium 192
- NT1 thallium 193
- NT1 thallium 194
- NT1 thallium 195
- NT1 thallium 196
- NT1 thallium 197
- NT1 thallium 198
- NT1 thallium 200
- NT1 thulium 148
- NT1 thulium 156
- NT1 thulium 157
- NT1 thulium 158
- NT1 thulium 159
- NT1 thulium 160
- NT1 thulium 161
- NT1 thulium 162
- NT1 thulium 163
- NT1 thulium 164
- NT1 thulium 165
- NT1 thulium 166
- NT1 tin 100
- NT1 tin 102
- NT1 tin 103
- NT1 tin 105
- NT1 tin 106
- NT1 tin 107
- NT1 tin 108
- NT1 tin 109
- NT1 tin 111
- NT1 titanium 39
- NT1 titanium 40
- NT1 titanium 41
- NT1 titanium 42
- NT1 titanium 43
- NT1 titanium 45
- NT1 tungsten 168
- NT1 tungsten 169
- NT1 tungsten 170
- NT1 tungsten 171
- NT1 tungsten 172
- NT1 tungsten 173
- NT1 tungsten 175
- NT1 tungsten 177
- NT1 tungsten 190
- NT1 vanadium 44
- NT1 vanadium 46
- NT1 vanadium 47
- NT1 vanadium 48
- NT1 xenon 110
- NT1 xenon 111
- NT1 xenon 112
- NT1 xenon 113
- NT1 xenon 114
- NT1 xenon 115
- NT1 xenon 116
- NT1 xenon 117
- NT1 xenon 118
- NT1 xenon 119
- NT1 xenon 120
- NT1 xenon 121
- NT1 xenon 123
- NT1 xenon 125
- NT1 ytterbium 153
- NT1 ytterbium 158
- NT1 ytterbium 160
- NT1 ytterbium 161
- NT1 ytterbium 162
- NT1 ytterbium 163
- NT1 ytterbium 165
- NT1 ytterbium 167
- NT1 yttrium 80
- NT1 yttrium 81
- NT1 yttrium 82
- NT1 yttrium 83
- NT1 yttrium 84
- NT1 yttrium 85
- NT1 yttrium 86
- NT1 yttrium 87
- NT1 yttrium 88
- NT1 zinc 57
- NT1 zinc 59
- NT1 zinc 60
- NT1 zinc 61
- NT1 zinc 62
- NT1 zinc 63
- NT1 zinc 65
- NT1 zirconium 81
- NT1 zirconium 82
- NT1 zirconium 83
- NT1 zirconium 84
- NT1 zirconium 85
- NT1 zirconium 87
- NT1 zirconium 89

DAYS LIVING RADIOISOTOPES

- NT1 actinium 225
- NT1 actinium 226
- NT1 americium 240
- NT1 antimony 119
- NT1 antimony 120
- NT1 antimony 122
- NT1 antimony 124
- NT1 antimony 126
- NT1 antimony 127
- NT1 argon 37
- NT1 arsenic 71
- NT1 arsenic 72
- NT1 arsenic 73
- NT1 arsenic 74
- NT1 arsenic 76
- NT1 arsenic 77
- NT1 barium 128
- NT1 barium 131
- NT1 barium 133
- NT1 barium 135
- NT1 barium 140
- NT1 berkelium 245
- NT1 berkelium 246
- NT1 berkelium 249
- NT1 beryllium 7
- NT1 bismuth 205
- NT1 bismuth 206
- NT1 bismuth 210
- NT1 bromine 77
- NT1 bromine 82
- NT1 cadmium 115
- NT1 calcium 45
- NT1 calcium 47
- NT1 californium 246
- NT1 californium 248
- NT1 californium 253
- NT1 californium 254
- NT1 cerium 134
- NT1 cerium 137
- NT1 cerium 139
- NT1 cerium 141
- NT1 cerium 143
- NT1 cerium 144
- NT1 cesium 129
- NT1 cesium 131
- NT1 cesium 132
- NT1 cesium 136
- NT1 chromium 51
- NT1 cobalt 56
- NT1 cobalt 57
- NT1 cobalt 58
- NT1 copper 67
- NT1 curium 240
- NT1 curium 241
- NT1 curium 242
- NT1 dysprosium 159
- NT1 dysprosium 166
- NT1 einsteinium 251
- NT1 einsteinium 253
- NT1 einsteinium 254
- NT1 einsteinium 255
- NT1 erbium 160
- NT1 erbium 169
- NT1 erbium 172
- NT1 europium 145
- NT1 europium 146
- NT1 europium 147
- NT1 europium 148
- NT1 europium 149
- NT1 europium 156
- NT1 fermium 252
- NT1 fermium 253
- NT1 fermium 257
- NT1 gadolinium 146
- NT1 gadolinium 147
- NT1 gadolinium 149
- NT1 gadolinium 151
- NT1 gadolinium 153
- NT1 gallium 67
- NT1 germanium 68
- NT1 germanium 69
- NT1 germanium 71
- NT1 gold 194
- NT1 gold 195
- NT1 gold 196
- NT1 gold 198
- NT1 gold 199
- NT1 hafnium 175
- NT1 hafnium 179
- NT1 hafnium 181
- NT1 holmium 166
- NT1 indium 111
- NT1 indium 114
- NT1 iodine 124
- NT1 iodine 125
- NT1 iodine 126
- NT1 iodine 131
- NT1 iridium 188
- NT1 iridium 189
- NT1 iridium 190
- NT1 iridium 192
- NT1 iridium 193
- NT1 iridium 194
- NT1 iron 59
- NT1 krypton 79
- NT1 lanthanum 140
- NT1 lead 203
- NT1 lutetium 169
- NT1 lutetium 170
- NT1 lutetium 171
- NT1 lutetium 172
- NT1 lutetium 174
- NT1 lutetium 177
- NT1 manganese 52
- NT1 manganese 54
- NT1 mendelevium 258
- NT1 mercury 195
- NT1 mercury 197
- NT1 mercury 203
- NT1 molybdenum 99
- NT1 neodymium 140
- NT1 neodymium 147
- NT1 neptunium 234
- NT1 neptunium 238
- NT1 neptunium 239
- NT1 nickel 56
- NT1 nickel 57
- NT1 nickel 66
- NT1 niobium 91
- NT1 niobium 92
- NT1 niobium 95
- NT1 osmium 185
- NT1 osmium 191
- NT1 osmium 193
- NT1 palladium 100
- NT1 palladium 103
- NT1 phosphorus 32
- NT1 phosphorus 33
- NT1 platinum 188
- NT1 platinum 191
- NT1 platinum 193
- NT1 platinum 195
- NT1 plutonium 237
- NT1 plutonium 246
- NT1 plutonium 247
- NT1 polonium 206
- NT1 polonium 210
- NT1 praseodymium 143
- NT1 promethium 143
- NT1 promethium 148
- NT1 promethium 149
- NT1 promethium 151
- NT1 protactinium 229
- NT1 protactinium 230
- NT1 protactinium 232
- NT1 protactinium 233
- NT1 radium 223
- NT1 radium 224
- NT1 radium 225
- NT1 radon 222
- NT1 rhenium 182
- NT1 rhenium 183
- NT1 rhenium 184
- NT1 rhenium 186
- NT1 rhenium 189
- NT1 rhodium 101
- NT1 rhodium 102
- NT1 rhodium 105
- NT1 rhodium 99
- NT1 rubidium 83
- NT1 rubidium 84
- NT1 rubidium 86
- NT1 ruthenium 103
- NT1 ruthenium 97
- NT1 samarium 145
- NT1 samarium 153
- NT1 scandium 44
- NT1 scandium 46
- NT1 scandium 47
- NT1 scandium 48
- NT1 selenium 72
- NT1 selenium 75
- NT1 silver 105
- NT1 silver 106
- NT1 silver 110
- NT1 silver 111
- NT1 strontium 82
- NT1 strontium 83
- NT1 strontium 85
- NT1 strontium 89
- NT1 sulfur 35
- NT1 tantalum 177
- NT1 tantalum 182

NT1 tantalum 183
NT1 technetium 95
NT1 technetium 96
NT1 technetium 97
NT1 tellurium 118
NT1 tellurium 119
NT1 tellurium 121
NT1 tellurium 123
NT1 tellurium 125
NT1 tellurium 127
NT1 tellurium 129
NT1 tellurium 131
NT1 tellurium 132
NT1 terbium 153
NT1 terbium 155
NT1 terbium 156
NT1 terbium 160
NT1 terbium 161
NT1 thallium 200
NT1 thallium 201
NT1 thallium 202
NT1 thorium 227
NT1 thorium 231
NT1 thorium 234
NT1 thulium 165
NT1 thulium 167
NT1 thulium 168
NT1 thulium 170
NT1 thulium 172
NT1 tin 113
NT1 tin 117
NT1 tin 119
NT1 tin 121
NT1 tin 123
NT1 tin 125
NT1 tungsten 178
NT1 tungsten 181
NT1 tungsten 185
NT1 tungsten 187
NT1 tungsten 188
NT1 uranium 230
NT1 uranium 231
NT1 uranium 237
NT1 vanadium 48
NT1 vanadium 49
NT1 xenon 127
NT1 xenon 129
NT1 xenon 131
NT1 xenon 133
NT1 ytterbium 166
NT1 ytterbium 169
NT1 ytterbium 175
NT1 yttrium 87
NT1 yttrium 88
NT1 yttrium 90
NT1 yttrium 91
NT1 zinc 65
NT1 zinc 72
NT1 zirconium 88
NT1 zirconium 89
NT1 zirconium 95

ELECTRON CAPTURE RADIOISOTOPES
NT1 actinium 214
NT1 actinium 215
NT1 actinium 222
NT1 actinium 223
NT1 actinium 224
NT1 actinium 226
NT1 americium 232
NT1 americium 234
NT1 americium 237
NT1 americium 238
NT1 americium 239
NT1 americium 240
NT1 americium 242
NT1 americium 244
NT1 antimony 109
NT1 antimony 110
NT1 antimony 111
NT1 antimony 112
NT1 antimony 113
NT1 antimony 114
NT1 antimony 115
NT1 antimony 116
NT1 antimony 117
NT1 antimony 118
NT1 antimony 119
NT1 antimony 120

NT1 antimony 122
NT1 argon 37
NT1 arsenic 67
NT1 arsenic 70
NT1 arsenic 71
NT1 arsenic 72
NT1 arsenic 73
NT1 arsenic 74
NT1 astatine 195
NT1 astatine 197
NT1 astatine 199
NT1 astatine 200
NT1 astatine 201
NT1 astatine 202
NT1 astatine 203
NT1 astatine 204
NT1 astatine 205
NT1 astatine 206
NT1 astatine 207
NT1 astatine 208
NT1 astatine 209
NT1 astatine 210
NT1 astatine 211
NT1 barium 117
NT1 barium 119
NT1 barium 120
NT1 barium 121
NT1 barium 122
NT1 barium 123
NT1 barium 124
NT1 barium 125
NT1 barium 126
NT1 barium 127
NT1 barium 128
NT1 barium 129
NT1 barium 131
NT1 barium 133
NT1 berkelium 240
NT1 berkelium 242
NT1 berkelium 243
NT1 berkelium 244
NT1 berkelium 245
NT1 berkelium 246
NT1 berkelium 248
NT1 beryllium 7
NT1 bismuth 190
NT1 bismuth 191
NT1 bismuth 192
NT1 bismuth 193
NT1 bismuth 194
NT1 bismuth 195
NT1 bismuth 196
NT1 bismuth 197
NT1 bismuth 198
NT1 bismuth 199
NT1 bismuth 200
NT1 bismuth 201
NT1 bismuth 202
NT1 bismuth 203
NT1 bismuth 204
NT1 bismuth 205
NT1 bismuth 206
NT1 bismuth 207
NT1 bismuth 208
NT1 bromine 71
NT1 bromine 73
NT1 bromine 74
NT1 bromine 75
NT1 bromine 76
NT1 bromine 77
NT1 bromine 78
NT1 bromine 80
NT1 cadmium 100
NT1 cadmium 101
NT1 cadmium 102
NT1 cadmium 103
NT1 cadmium 104
NT1 cadmium 105
NT1 cadmium 107
NT1 cadmium 109
NT1 cadmium 96
NT1 cadmium 97
NT1 calcium 41
NT1 californium 241
NT1 californium 243
NT1 californium 245
NT1 californium 247
NT1 cerium 123
NT1 cerium 126
NT1 cerium 127

NT1 cerium 128
NT1 cerium 129
NT1 cerium 130
NT1 cerium 131
NT1 cerium 132
NT1 cerium 133
NT1 cerium 134
NT1 cerium 135
NT1 cerium 137
NT1 cerium 139
NT1 cesium 114
NT1 cesium 115
NT1 cesium 116
NT1 cesium 117
NT1 cesium 118
NT1 cesium 119
NT1 cesium 120
NT1 cesium 121
NT1 cesium 122
NT1 cesium 123
NT1 cesium 124
NT1 cesium 125
NT1 cesium 126
NT1 cesium 127
NT1 cesium 128
NT1 cesium 129
NT1 cesium 130
NT1 cesium 131
NT1 cesium 132
NT1 cesium 134
NT1 chlorine 36
NT1 chromium 48
NT1 chromium 49
NT1 chromium 51
NT1 cobalt 55
NT1 cobalt 56
NT1 cobalt 57
NT1 cobalt 58
NT1 copper 58
NT1 copper 60
NT1 copper 61
NT1 copper 62
NT1 copper 64
NT1 curium 238
NT1 curium 239
NT1 curium 241
NT1 dysprosium 141
NT1 dysprosium 143
NT1 dysprosium 144
NT1 dysprosium 145
NT1 dysprosium 147
NT1 dysprosium 148
NT1 dysprosium 149
NT1 dysprosium 150
NT1 dysprosium 151
NT1 dysprosium 152
NT1 dysprosium 153
NT1 dysprosium 155
NT1 dysprosium 157
NT1 dysprosium 159
NT1 einsteinium 244
NT1 einsteinium 245
NT1 einsteinium 246
NT1 einsteinium 247
NT1 einsteinium 248
NT1 einsteinium 249
NT1 einsteinium 250
NT1 einsteinium 251
NT1 einsteinium 252
NT1 einsteinium 254
NT1 element 105 258
NT1 erbium 147
NT1 erbium 149
NT1 erbium 150
NT1 erbium 151
NT1 erbium 152
NT1 erbium 153
NT1 erbium 154
NT1 erbium 155
NT1 erbium 156
NT1 erbium 157
NT1 erbium 158
NT1 erbium 159
NT1 erbium 160
NT1 erbium 161
NT1 erbium 163
NT1 erbium 165
NT1 europium 139
NT1 europium 140
NT1 europium 141

NT1 europium 142
NT1 europium 143
NT1 europium 144
NT1 europium 145
NT1 europium 146
NT1 europium 147
NT1 europium 148
NT1 europium 149
NT1 europium 150
NT1 europium 152
NT1 europium 154
NT1 fermium 247
NT1 fermium 249
NT1 fermium 251
NT1 fermium 253
NT1 francium 204
NT1 francium 206
NT1 francium 207
NT1 francium 208
NT1 francium 209
NT1 francium 210
NT1 francium 211
NT1 francium 212
NT1 francium 213
NT1 gadolinium 141
NT1 gadolinium 143
NT1 gadolinium 144
NT1 gadolinium 145
NT1 gadolinium 146
NT1 gadolinium 147
NT1 gadolinium 149
NT1 gadolinium 151
NT1 gadolinium 153
NT1 gallium 62
NT1 gallium 63
NT1 gallium 64
NT1 gallium 65
NT1 gallium 66
NT1 gallium 67
NT1 gallium 68
NT1 gallium 70
NT1 germanium 64
NT1 germanium 65
NT1 germanium 66
NT1 germanium 67
NT1 germanium 68
NT1 germanium 69
NT1 germanium 71
NT1 gold 180
NT1 gold 181
NT1 gold 182
NT1 gold 183
NT1 gold 184
NT1 gold 185
NT1 gold 186
NT1 gold 187
NT1 gold 188
NT1 gold 189
NT1 gold 190
NT1 gold 191
NT1 gold 192
NT1 gold 193
NT1 gold 194
NT1 gold 195
NT1 gold 196
NT1 hafnium 154
NT1 hafnium 155
NT1 hafnium 157
NT1 hafnium 158
NT1 hafnium 159
NT1 hafnium 160
NT1 hafnium 162
NT1 hafnium 163
NT1 hafnium 166
NT1 hafnium 167
NT1 hafnium 168
NT1 hafnium 169
NT1 hafnium 170
NT1 hafnium 171
NT1 hafnium 172
NT1 hafnium 173
NT1 hafnium 175
NT1 holmium 145
NT1 holmium 147
NT1 holmium 149
NT1 holmium 150
NT1 holmium 151
NT1 holmium 152
NT1 holmium 153
NT1 holmium 154

NT1	holmium 155	NT1	lead 188	NT1	neodymium 141	NT1	praseodymium 129
NT1	holmium 156	NT1	lead 189	NT1	neptunium 230	NT1	praseodymium 130
NT1	holmium 157	NT1	lead 190	NT1	neptunium 231	NT1	praseodymium 132
NT1	holmium 158	NT1	lead 191	NT1	neptunium 232	NT1	praseodymium 133
NT1	holmium 159	NT1	lead 192	NT1	neptunium 233	NT1	praseodymium 134
NT1	holmium 160	NT1	lead 193	NT1	neptunium 234	NT1	praseodymium 135
NT1	holmium 161	NT1	lead 194	NT1	neptunium 235	NT1	praseodymium 136
NT1	holmium 162	NT1	lead 195	NT1	neptunium 236	NT1	praseodymium 137
NT1	holmium 163	NT1	lead 196	NT1	nickel 56	NT1	praseodymium 138
NT1	holmium 164	NT1	lead 197	NT1	nickel 57	NT1	praseodymium 139
NT1	indium 102	NT1	lead 198	NT1	nickel 59	NT1	praseodymium 140
NT1	indium 103	NT1	lead 199	NT1	niobium 84	NT1	praseodymium 142
NT1	indium 104	NT1	lead 200	NT1	niobium 86	NT1	promethium 130
NT1	indium 105	NT1	lead 201	NT1	niobium 87	NT1	promethium 132
NT1	indium 106	NT1	lead 202	NT1	niobium 88	NT1	promethium 133
NT1	indium 107	NT1	lead 203	NT1	niobium 90	NT1	promethium 134
NT1	indium 108	NT1	lead 205	NT1	niobium 91	NT1	promethium 135
NT1	indium 109	NT1	lutetium 153	NT1	niobium 92	NT1	promethium 136
NT1	indium 110	NT1	lutetium 154	NT1	nitrogen 13	NT1	promethium 137
NT1	indium 111	NT1	lutetium 155	NT1	nobelium 253	NT1	promethium 138
NT1	indium 112	NT1	lutetium 156	NT1	nobelium 254	NT1	promethium 139
NT1	indium 114	NT1	lutetium 157	NT1	nobelium 255	NT1	promethium 140
NT1	iodine 110	NT1	lutetium 158	NT1	nobelium 259	NT1	promethium 141
NT1	iodine 111	NT1	lutetium 159	NT1	osmium 166	NT1	promethium 142
NT1	iodine 112	NT1	lutetium 160	NT1	osmium 167	NT1	promethium 143
NT1	iodine 113	NT1	lutetium 161	NT1	osmium 168	NT1	promethium 144
NT1	iodine 114	NT1	lutetium 162	NT1	osmium 169	NT1	promethium 145
NT1	iodine 115	NT1	lutetium 163	NT1	osmium 170	NT1	promethium 146
NT1	iodine 116	NT1	lutetium 164	NT1	osmium 171	NT1	protactinium 226
NT1	iodine 117	NT1	lutetium 165	NT1	osmium 172	NT1	protactinium 227
NT1	iodine 118	NT1	lutetium 166	NT1	osmium 173	NT1	protactinium 228
NT1	iodine 119	NT1	lutetium 167	NT1	osmium 174	NT1	protactinium 229
NT1	iodine 120	NT1	lutetium 168	NT1	osmium 175	NT1	protactinium 230
NT1	iodine 121	NT1	lutetium 169	NT1	osmium 176	NT1	radium 213
NT1	iodine 122	NT1	lutetium 170	NT1	osmium 177	NT1	radium 214
NT1	iodine 123	NT1	lutetium 171	NT1	osmium 178	NT1	radon 200
NT1	iodine 124	NT1	lutetium 172	NT1	osmium 179	NT1	radon 201
NT1	iodine 125	NT1	lutetium 173	NT1	osmium 180	NT1	radon 202
NT1	iodine 126	NT1	lutetium 174	NT1	osmium 181	NT1	radon 203
NT1	iodine 128	NT1	manganese 51	NT1	osmium 182	NT1	radon 204
NT1	iridium 178	NT1	manganese 52	NT1	osmium 183	NT1	radon 205
NT1	iridium 179	NT1	manganese 53	NT1	osmium 185	NT1	radon 206
NT1	iridium 180	NT1	manganese 54	NT1	palladium 100	NT1	radon 207
NT1	iridium 181	NT1	mendelevium 248	NT1	palladium 101	NT1	radon 208
NT1	iridium 182	NT1	mendelevium 249	NT1	palladium 103	NT1	radon 209
NT1	iridium 183	NT1	mendelevium 250	NT1	palladium 95	NT1	radon 210
NT1	iridium 184	NT1	mendelevium 251	NT1	palladium 96	NT1	radon 211
NT1	iridium 185	NT1	mendelevium 252	NT1	palladium 97	NT1	rhenium 163
NT1	iridium 186	NT1	mendelevium 254	NT1	palladium 98	NT1	rhenium 164
NT1	iridium 187	NT1	mendelevium 255	NT1	palladium 99	NT1	rhenium 165
NT1	iridium 188	NT1	mendelevium 256	NT1	platinum 173	NT1	rhenium 168
NT1	iridium 189	NT1	mendelevium 257	NT1	platinum 174	NT1	rhenium 170
NT1	iridium 190	NT1	mendelevium 258	NT1	platinum 175	NT1	rhenium 171
NT1	iridium 192	NT1	mercury 177	NT1	platinum 176	NT1	rhenium 172
NT1	iron 52	NT1	mercury 178	NT1	platinum 177	NT1	rhenium 173
NT1	iron 53	NT1	mercury 179	NT1	platinum 178	NT1	rhenium 174
NT1	iron 55	NT1	mercury 180	NT1	platinum 179	NT1	rhenium 175
NT1	krypton 71	NT1	mercury 181	NT1	platinum 180	NT1	rhenium 176
NT1	krypton 72	NT1	mercury 182	NT1	platinum 181	NT1	rhenium 177
NT1	krypton 73	NT1	mercury 183	NT1	platinum 182	NT1	rhenium 178
NT1	krypton 74	NT1	mercury 184	NT1	platinum 183	NT1	rhenium 179
NT1	krypton 75	NT1	mercury 185	NT1	platinum 184	NT1	rhenium 180
NT1	krypton 76	NT1	mercury 186	NT1	platinum 185	NT1	rhenium 181
NT1	krypton 77	NT1	mercury 187	NT1	platinum 186	NT1	rhenium 182
NT1	krypton 79	NT1	mercury 188	NT1	platinum 187	NT1	rhenium 183
NT1	krypton 81	NT1	mercury 189	NT1	platinum 188	NT1	rhenium 184
NT1	lanthanum 120	NT1	mercury 190	NT1	platinum 189	NT1	rhenium 186
NT1	lanthanum 121	NT1	mercury 191	NT1	platinum 191	NT1	rhodium 100
NT1	lanthanum 122	NT1	mercury 192	NT1	platinum 193	NT1	rhodium 101
NT1	lanthanum 123	NT1	mercury 193	NT1	plutonium 232	NT1	rhodium 102
NT1	lanthanum 124	NT1	mercury 194	NT1	plutonium 233	NT1	rhodium 104
NT1	lanthanum 125	NT1	mercury 195	NT1	plutonium 234	NT1	rhodium 95
NT1	lanthanum 126	NT1	mercury 197	NT1	plutonium 235	NT1	rhodium 96
NT1	lanthanum 127	NT1	molybdenum 87	NT1	plutonium 237	NT1	rhodium 98
NT1	lanthanum 128	NT1	molybdenum 88	NT1	polonium 196	NT1	rhodium 99
NT1	lanthanum 129	NT1	molybdenum 89	NT1	polonium 197	NT1	rubidium 76
NT1	lanthanum 130	NT1	molybdenum 90	NT1	polonium 198	NT1	rubidium 77
NT1	lanthanum 131	NT1	molybdenum 91	NT1	polonium 199	NT1	rubidium 78
NT1	lanthanum 132	NT1	molybdenum 93	NT1	polonium 200	NT1	rubidium 79
NT1	lanthanum 133	NT1	neodymium 129	NT1	polonium 201	NT1	rubidium 81
NT1	lanthanum 134	NT1	neodymium 130	NT1	polonium 202	NT1	rubidium 82
NT1	lanthanum 135	NT1	neodymium 132	NT1	polonium 203	NT1	rubidium 83
NT1	lanthanum 136	NT1	neodymium 133	NT1	polonium 204	NT1	rubidium 84
NT1	lanthanum 137	NT1	neodymium 134	NT1	polonium 205	NT1	rubidium 86
NT1	lanthanum 138	NT1	neodymium 135	NT1	polonium 206	NT1	ruthenium 92
NT1	lawrencium 254	NT1	neodymium 136	NT1	polonium 207	NT1	ruthenium 93
NT1	lawrencium 255	NT1	neodymium 137	NT1	polonium 208	NT1	ruthenium 94
NT1	lawrencium 256	NT1	neodymium 138	NT1	polonium 209	NT1	ruthenium 95
NT1	lead 186	NT1	neodymium 139	NT1	potassium 40	NT1	ruthenium 97
NT1	lead 187	NT1	neodymium 140	NT1	praseodymium 128		

NT1 samarium 133
NT1 samarium 134
NT1 samarium 135
NT1 samarium 136
NT1 samarium 137
NT1 samarium 138
NT1 samarium 139
NT1 samarium 140
NT1 samarium 141
NT1 samarium 142
NT1 samarium 143
NT1 samarium 145
NT1 scandium 44
NT1 selenium 69
NT1 selenium 70
NT1 selenium 71
NT1 selenium 72
NT1 selenium 73
NT1 selenium 75
NT1 silver 100
NT1 silver 101
NT1 silver 102
NT1 silver 103
NT1 silver 104
NT1 silver 105
NT1 silver 106
NT1 silver 108
NT1 silver 110
NT1 silver 95
NT1 silver 96
NT1 silver 97
NT1 silver 98
NT1 silver 99
NT1 strontium 78
NT1 strontium 79
NT1 strontium 80
NT1 strontium 81
NT1 strontium 82
NT1 strontium 83
NT1 strontium 85
NT1 strontium 87
NT1 tantalum 158
NT1 tantalum 159
NT1 tantalum 160
NT1 tantalum 165
NT1 tantalum 166
NT1 tantalum 167
NT1 tantalum 168
NT1 tantalum 169
NT1 tantalum 170
NT1 tantalum 171
NT1 tantalum 172
NT1 tantalum 173
NT1 tantalum 174
NT1 tantalum 175
NT1 tantalum 176
NT1 tantalum 177
NT1 tantalum 178
NT1 tantalum 179
NT1 tantalum 180
NT1 technetium 91
NT1 technetium 92
NT1 technetium 93
NT1 technetium 94
NT1 technetium 95
NT1 technetium 96
NT1 technetium 97
NT1 tellurium 107
NT1 tellurium 108
NT1 tellurium 109
NT1 tellurium 110
NT1 tellurium 111
NT1 tellurium 112
NT1 tellurium 113
NT1 tellurium 114
NT1 tellurium 115
NT1 tellurium 116
NT1 tellurium 117
NT1 tellurium 118
NT1 tellurium 119
NT1 tellurium 121
NT1 tellurium 123
NT1 terbium 141
NT1 terbium 143
NT1 terbium 144
NT1 terbium 146
NT1 terbium 147
NT1 terbium 148
NT1 terbium 149
NT1 terbium 150
NT1 terbium 151
NT1 terbium 152
NT1 terbium 153
NT1 terbium 154
NT1 terbium 155
NT1 terbium 156
NT1 terbium 157
NT1 terbium 158
NT1 thallium 184
NT1 thallium 186
NT1 thallium 187
NT1 thallium 188
NT1 thallium 189
NT1 thallium 190
NT1 thallium 191
NT1 thallium 192
NT1 thallium 193
NT1 thallium 194
NT1 thallium 195
NT1 thallium 196
NT1 thallium 197
NT1 thallium 198
NT1 thallium 199
NT1 thallium 200
NT1 thallium 201
NT1 thallium 202
NT1 thallium 204
NT1 thorium 225
NT1 thulium 148
NT1 thulium 152
NT1 thulium 153
NT1 thulium 154
NT1 thulium 155
NT1 thulium 156
NT1 thulium 157
NT1 thulium 158
NT1 thulium 159
NT1 thulium 160
NT1 thulium 161
NT1 thulium 162
NT1 thulium 163
NT1 thulium 164
NT1 thulium 165
NT1 thulium 166
NT1 thulium 167
NT1 thulium 168
NT1 thulium 170
NT1 tin 100
NT1 tin 102
NT1 tin 106
NT1 tin 107
NT1 tin 108
NT1 tin 109
NT1 tin 110
NT1 tin 111
NT1 tin 113
NT1 titanium 44
NT1 titanium 45
NT1 tungsten 161
NT1 tungsten 162
NT1 tungsten 163
NT1 tungsten 164
NT1 tungsten 165
NT1 tungsten 166
NT1 tungsten 168
NT1 tungsten 169
NT1 tungsten 170
NT1 tungsten 171
NT1 tungsten 172
NT1 tungsten 173
NT1 tungsten 174
NT1 tungsten 175
NT1 tungsten 176
NT1 tungsten 177
NT1 tungsten 178
NT1 tungsten 179
NT1 tungsten 181
NT1 uranium 228
NT1 uranium 229
NT1 uranium 231
NT1 vanadium 47
NT1 vanadium 48
NT1 vanadium 49
NT1 vanadium 50
NT1 xenon 110
NT1 xenon 111
NT1 xenon 112
NT1 xenon 113
NT1 xenon 114
NT1 xenon 115
NT1 xenon 116
NT1 xenon 117
NT1 xenon 118
NT1 xenon 119
NT1 xenon 120
NT1 xenon 121
NT1 xenon 122
NT1 xenon 123
NT1 xenon 125
NT1 xenon 127
NT1 ytterbium 153
NT1 ytterbium 155
NT1 ytterbium 156
NT1 ytterbium 157
NT1 ytterbium 158
NT1 ytterbium 159
NT1 ytterbium 160
NT1 ytterbium 161
NT1 ytterbium 162
NT1 ytterbium 163
NT1 ytterbium 164
NT1 ytterbium 165
NT1 ytterbium 166
NT1 ytterbium 167
NT1 ytterbium 169
NT1 yttrium 81
NT1 yttrium 83
NT1 yttrium 84
NT1 yttrium 85
NT1 yttrium 86
NT1 yttrium 87
NT1 yttrium 88
NT1 zinc 60
NT1 zinc 61
NT1 zinc 62
NT1 zinc 63
NT1 zinc 65
NT1 zirconium 84
NT1 zirconium 85
NT1 zirconium 86
NT1 zirconium 87
NT1 zirconium 88
NT1 zirconium 89

EVEN-EVEN NUCLEI

NT1 argon 32
NT1 argon 34
NT1 argon 36
NT1 argon 38
NT1 argon 40
NT1 argon 42
NT1 argon 44
NT1 argon 46
NT1 argon 50
NT1 barium 120
NT1 barium 122
NT1 barium 124
NT1 barium 126
NT1 barium 128
NT1 barium 130
NT1 barium 132
NT1 barium 134
NT1 barium 136
NT1 barium 138
NT1 barium 140
NT1 barium 142
NT1 barium 144
NT1 barium 146
NT1 barium 148
NT1 beryllium 10
NT1 beryllium 12
NT1 beryllium 14
NT1 beryllium 6
NT1 beryllium 8
NT1 cadmium 100
NT1 cadmium 102
NT1 cadmium 104
NT1 cadmium 106
NT1 cadmium 108
NT1 cadmium 110
NT1 cadmium 112
NT1 cadmium 114
NT1 cadmium 116
NT1 cadmium 118
NT1 cadmium 120
NT1 cadmium 122
NT1 cadmium 124
NT1 cadmium 126
NT1 cadmium 128
NT1 cadmium 130
NT1 cadmium 96
NT1 cadmium 98
NT1 calcium 36
NT1 calcium 38
NT1 calcium 40
NT1 calcium 42
NT1 calcium 44
NT1 calcium 46
NT1 calcium 48
NT1 calcium 50
NT1 calcium 52
NT1 californium 240
NT1 californium 242
NT1 californium 244
NT1 californium 246
NT1 californium 248
NT1 californium 250
NT1 californium 252
NT1 californium 254
NT1 californium 256
NT1 carbon 10
NT1 carbon 12
NT1 carbon 14
NT1 carbon 16
NT1 carbon 18
NT1 carbon 20
NT1 carbon 22
NT1 carbon 8
NT1 cerium 124
NT1 cerium 126
NT1 cerium 128
NT1 cerium 130
NT1 cerium 132
NT1 cerium 134
NT1 cerium 136
NT1 cerium 138
NT1 cerium 140
NT1 cerium 142
NT1 cerium 144
NT1 cerium 146
NT1 cerium 148
NT1 cerium 150
NT1 cerium 152
NT1 chromium 42
NT1 chromium 44
NT1 chromium 46
NT1 chromium 48
NT1 chromium 50
NT1 chromium 52
NT1 chromium 54
NT1 chromium 56
NT1 chromium 58
NT1 chromium 60
NT1 chromium 62
NT1 curium 236
NT1 curium 238
NT1 curium 240
NT1 curium 242
NT1 curium 244
NT1 curium 246
NT1 curium 248
NT1 curium 250
NT1 curium 252
NT1 dysprosium 142
NT1 dysprosium 144
NT1 dysprosium 146
NT1 dysprosium 148
NT1 dysprosium 150
NT1 dysprosium 152
NT1 dysprosium 154
NT1 dysprosium 156
NT1 dysprosium 158
NT1 dysprosium 160
NT1 dysprosium 162
NT1 dysprosium 164
NT1 dysprosium 166
NT1 dysprosium 168
NT1 element 104 25
NT1 element 104 25
NT1 element 104 25
NT1 element 104 26
NT1 element 104 26
NT1 element 106 26
NT1 element 108 26
NT1 element 108 26
NT1 erbium 148
NT1 erbium 150
NT1 erbium 152
NT1 erbium 154
NT1 erbium 156

NT1	erbium 158	NT1	krypton 96	NT1	nickel 66	NT1	polonium 208
NT1	erbium 160	NT1	krypton 98	NT1	nickel 68	NT1	polonium 210
NT1	erbium 162	NT1	lead 182	NT1	nickel 72	NT1	polonium 212
NT1	erbium 164	NT1	lead 184	NT1	nickel 74	NT1	polonium 214
NT1	erbium 166	NT1	lead 186	NT1	nickel 78	NT1	polonium 216
NT1	erbium 168	NT1	lead 188	NT1	nobelium 250	NT1	polonium 218
NT1	erbium 170	NT1	lead 190	NT1	nobelium 252	NT1	polonium 220
NT1	erbium 172	NT1	lead 192	NT1	nobelium 254	NT1	radium 206
NT1	erbium 174	NT1	lead 194	NT1	nobelium 256	NT1	radium 208
NT1	fermium 242	NT1	lead 196	NT1	nobelium 258	NT1	radium 210
NT1	fermium 244	NT1	lead 198	NT1	nobelium 260	NT1	radium 212
NT1	fermium 246	NT1	lead 200	NT1	nobelium 262	NT1	radium 214
NT1	fermium 248	NT1	lead 202	NT1	osmium 162	NT1	radium 216
NT1	fermium 250	NT1	lead 204	NT1	osmium 164	NT1	radium 218
NT1	fermium 252	NT1	lead 206	NT1	osmium 166	NT1	radium 220
NT1	fermium 254	NT1	lead 208	NT1	osmium 168	NT1	radium 222
NT1	fermium 256	NT1	lead 210	NT1	osmium 170	NT1	radium 224
NT1	fermium 258	NT1	lead 212	NT1	osmium 172	NT1	radium 226
NT1	gadolinium 138	NT1	lead 214	NT1	osmium 174	NT1	radium 228
NT1	gadolinium 140	NT1	lead 216	NT1	osmium 176	NT1	radium 230
NT1	gadolinium 142	NT1	magnesium 20	NT1	osmium 178	NT1	radium 232
NT1	gadolinium 144	NT1	magnesium 22	NT1	osmium 180	NT1	radium 234
NT1	gadolinium 146	NT1	magnesium 24	NT1	osmium 182	NT1	radon 200
NT1	gadolinium 148	NT1	magnesium 26	NT1	osmium 184	NT1	radon 202
NT1	gadolinium 150	NT1	magnesium 28	NT1	osmium 186	NT1	radon 204
NT1	gadolinium 152	NT1	magnesium 30	NT1	osmium 188	NT1	radon 206
NT1	gadolinium 154	NT1	magnesium 32	NT1	osmium 190	NT1	radon 208
NT1	gadolinium 156	NT1	magnesium 34	NT1	osmium 192	NT1	radon 210
NT1	gadolinium 158	NT1	magnesium 36	NT1	osmium 194	NT1	radon 212
NT1	gadolinium 160	NT1	mercury 176	NT1	osmium 196	NT1	radon 214
NT1	gadolinium 162	NT1	mercury 178	NT1	oxygen 12	NT1	radon 216
NT1	gadolinium 164	NT1	mercury 180	NT1	oxygen 14	NT1	radon 218
NT1	germanium 64	NT1	mercury 182	NT1	oxygen 16	NT1	radon 220
NT1	germanium 66	NT1	mercury 184	NT1	oxygen 18	NT1	radon 222
NT1	germanium 68	NT1	mercury 186	NT1	oxygen 20	NT1	radon 224
NT1	germanium 70	NT1	mercury 188	NT1	oxygen 22	NT1	radon 226
NT1	germanium 72	NT1	mercury 190	NT1	oxygen 24	NT1	radon 228
NT1	germanium 74	NT1	mercury 192	NT1	oxygen 28	NT1	ruthenium 100
NT1	germanium 76	NT1	mercury 194	NT1	palladium 100	NT1	ruthenium 102
NT1	germanium 78	NT1	mercury 196	NT1	palladium 102	NT1	ruthenium 104
NT1	germanium 80	NT1	mercury 198	NT1	palladium 104	NT1	ruthenium 106
NT1	germanium 82	NT1	mercury 200	NT1	palladium 106	NT1	ruthenium 108
NT1	germanium 84	NT1	mercury 202	NT1	palladium 108	NT1	ruthenium 110
NT1	hafnium 154	NT1	mercury 204	NT1	palladium 110	NT1	ruthenium 112
NT1	hafnium 156	NT1	mercury 206	NT1	palladium 112	NT1	ruthenium 92
NT1	hafnium 158	NT1	mercury 208	NT1	palladium 114	NT1	ruthenium 94
NT1	hafnium 160	NT1	mercury 210	NT1	palladium 116	NT1	ruthenium 96
NT1	hafnium 162	NT1	mercury 212	NT1	palladium 118	NT1	ruthenium 98
NT1	hafnium 164	NT1	molybdenum 100	NT1	palladium 96	NT1	samarium 134
NT1	hafnium 166	NT1	molybdenum 102	NT1	palladium 98	NT1	samarium 136
NT1	hafnium 168	NT1	molybdenum 104	NT1	platinum 168	NT1	samarium 138
NT1	hafnium 170	NT1	molybdenum 106	NT1	platinum 170	NT1	samarium 140
NT1	hafnium 172	NT1	molybdenum 108	NT1	platinum 172	NT1	samarium 142
NT1	hafnium 174	NT1	molybdenum 84	NT1	platinum 174	NT1	samarium 144
NT1	hafnium 176	NT1	molybdenum 88	NT1	platinum 176	NT1	samarium 146
NT1	hafnium 178	NT1	molybdenum 90	NT1	platinum 178	NT1	samarium 148
NT1	hafnium 180	NT1	molybdenum 92	NT1	platinum 180	NT1	samarium 150
NT1	hafnium 182	NT1	molybdenum 94	NT1	platinum 182	NT1	samarium 152
NT1	hafnium 184	NT1	molybdenum 96	NT1	platinum 184	NT1	samarium 154
NT1	hafnium 186	NT1	molybdenum 98	NT1	platinum 186	NT1	samarium 156
NT1	helium 10	NT1	neodymium 128	NT1	platinum 188	NT1	samarium 158
NT1	helium 4	NT1	neodymium 130	NT1	platinum 190	NT1	samarium 160
NT2	helium i	NT1	neodymium 132	NT1	platinum 192	NT1	selenium 68
NT2	helium ii	NT1	neodymium 134	NT1	platinum 194	NT1	selenium 70
NT1	helium 6	NT1	neodymium 136	NT1	platinum 196	NT1	selenium 72
NT1	helium 8	NT1	neodymium 138	NT1	platinum 198	NT1	selenium 74
NT1	iron 48	NT1	neodymium 140	NT1	platinum 200	NT1	selenium 76
NT1	iron 50	NT1	neodymium 142	NT1	platinum 202	NT1	selenium 78
NT1	iron 52	NT1	neodymium 144	NT1	platinum 204	NT1	selenium 80
NT1	iron 54	NT1	neodymium 146	NT1	platinum 206	NT1	selenium 82
NT1	iron 56	NT1	neodymium 148	NT1	platinum 208	NT1	selenium 84
NT1	iron 58	NT1	neodymium 150	NT1	plutonium 230	NT1	selenium 86
NT1	iron 60	NT1	neodymium 152	NT1	plutonium 232	NT1	selenium 88
NT1	iron 62	NT1	neodymium 154	NT1	plutonium 234	NT1	silicon 22
NT1	iron 64	NT1	neodymium 156	NT1	plutonium 236	NT1	silicon 24
NT1	iron 66	NT1	neon 16	NT1	plutonium 238	NT1	silicon 26
NT1	iron 68	NT1	neon 18	NT1	plutonium 240	NT1	silicon 28
NT1	krypton 70	NT1	neon 20	NT1	plutonium 242	NT1	silicon 30
NT1	krypton 72	NT1	neon 22	NT1	plutonium 244	NT1	silicon 32
NT1	krypton 74	NT1	neon 24	NT1	plutonium 246	NT1	silicon 34
NT1	krypton 76	NT1	neon 26	NT1	plutonium 248	NT1	silicon 36
NT1	krypton 78	NT1	neon 28	NT1	plutonium 250	NT1	silicon 38
NT1	krypton 80	NT1	neon 30	NT1	polonium 192	NT1	silicon 40
NT1	krypton 82	NT1	neon 32	NT1	polonium 194	NT1	silicon 42
NT1	krypton 84	NT1	nickel 54	NT1	polonium 196	NT1	strontium 100
NT1	krypton 86	NT1	nickel 56	NT1	polonium 198	NT1	strontium 102
NT1	krypton 88	NT1	nickel 58	NT1	polonium 200	NT1	strontium 78
NT1	krypton 90	NT1	nickel 60	NT1	polonium 202	NT1	strontium 80
NT1	krypton 92	NT1	nickel 62	NT1	polonium 204	NT1	strontium 82
NT1	krypton 94	NT1	nickel 64	NT1	polonium 206	NT1	strontium 84

EVEN-EVEN NUCLEI

NT1	strontium 86	NT1	tungsten 186	NT1	barium 123	NT1	curium 249
NT1	strontium 88	NT1	tungsten 188	NT1	barium 125	NT1	curium 251
NT1	strontium 90	NT1	tungsten 190	NT1	barium 127	NT1	dysprosium 141
NT1	strontium 92	NT1	tungsten 192	NT1	barium 129	NT1	dysprosium 143
NT1	strontium 94	NT1	uranium 222	NT1	barium 131	NT1	dysprosium 145
NT1	strontium 96	NT1	uranium 224	NT1	barium 133	NT1	dysprosium 147
NT1	strontium 98	NT1	uranium 226	NT1	barium 135	NT1	dysprosium 149
NT1	sulfur 24	NT1	uranium 228	NT1	barium 137	NT1	dysprosium 151
NT1	sulfur 28	NT1	uranium 230	NT1	barium 139	NT1	dysprosium 153
NT1	sulfur 30	NT1	uranium 232	NT1	barium 141	NT1	dysprosium 155
NT1	sulfur 32	NT1	uranium 234	NT1	barium 143	NT1	dysprosium 157
NT1	sulfur 34	NT1	uranium 236	NT1	barium 145	NT1	dysprosium 159
NT1	sulfur 36	NT1	uranium 238	NT1	barium 147	NT1	dysprosium 161
NT1	sulfur 38	NT1	uranium 240	NT1	barium 149	NT1	dysprosium 163
NT1	sulfur 40	NT1	uranium 242	NT1	beryllium 11	NT1	dysprosium 165
NT1	sulfur 42	NT1	xenon 110	NT1	beryllium 13	NT1	dysprosium 167
NT1	sulfur 44	NT1	xenon 112	NT1	beryllium 5	NT1	dysprosium 169
NT1	sulfur 46	NT1	xenon 114	NT1	beryllium 7	NT1	element 104 253
NT1	sulfur 48	NT1	xenon 116	NT1	beryllium 9	NT1	element 104 255
NT1	tellurium 106	NT1	xenon 118	NT1	cadmium 101	NT1	element 104 257
NT1	tellurium 108	NT1	xenon 120	NT1	cadmium 103	NT1	element 104 259
NT1	tellurium 110	NT1	xenon 122	NT1	cadmium 105	NT1	element 104 261
NT1	tellurium 112	NT1	xenon 124	NT1	cadmium 107	NT1	element 106 259
NT1	tellurium 114	NT1	xenon 126	NT1	cadmium 109	NT1	element 106 261
NT1	tellurium 116	NT1	xenon 128	NT1	cadmium 111	NT1	element 106 263
NT1	tellurium 118	NT1	xenon 130	NT1	cadmium 113	NT1	erbium 145
NT1	tellurium 120	NT1	xenon 132	NT1	cadmium 115	NT1	erbium 147
NT1	tellurium 122	NT1	xenon 134	NT1	cadmium 117	NT1	erbium 149
NT1	tellurium 124	NT1	xenon 136	NT1	cadmium 119	NT1	erbium 151
NT1	tellurium 126	NT1	xenon 138	NT1	cadmium 121	NT1	erbium 153
NT1	tellurium 128	NT1	xenon 140	NT1	cadmium 123	NT1	erbium 155
NT1	tellurium 130	NT1	xenon 142	NT1	cadmium 125	NT1	erbium 157
NT1	tellurium 132	NT1	xenon 144	NT1	cadmium 127	NT1	erbium 159
NT1	tellurium 134	NT1	ytterbium 150	NT1	cadmium 97	NT1	erbium 161
NT1	tellurium 136	NT1	ytterbium 152	NT1	cadmium 99	NT1	erbium 163
NT1	tellurium 138	NT1	ytterbium 154	NT1	calcium 35	NT1	erbium 165
NT1	thorium 212	NT1	ytterbium 156	NT1	calcium 37	NT1	erbium 167
NT1	thorium 214	NT1	ytterbium 158	NT1	calcium 39	NT1	erbium 169
NT1	thorium 216	NT1	ytterbium 160	NT1	calcium 41	NT1	erbium 171
NT1	thorium 218	NT1	ytterbium 162	NT1	calcium 43	NT1	erbium 173
NT1	thorium 220	NT1	ytterbium 164	NT1	calcium 45	NT1	fermium 243
NT1	thorium 224	NT1	ytterbium 166	NT1	calcium 47	NT1	fermium 245
NT1	thorium 226	NT1	ytterbium 168	NT1	calcium 49	NT1	fermium 247
NT1	thorium 228	NT1	ytterbium 170	NT1	calcium 51	NT1	fermium 249
NT1	thorium 230	NT1	ytterbium 172	NT1	calcium 53	NT1	fermium 251
NT1	thorium 232	NT1	ytterbium 174	NT1	californium 239	NT1	fermium 253
NT1	thorium 234	NT1	ytterbium 176	NT1	californium 241	NT1	fermium 255
NT1	thorium 236	NT1	ytterbium 178	NT1	californium 243	NT1	fermium 257
NT1	thorium 238	NT1	ytterbium 180	NT1	californium 245	NT1	fermium 259
NT1	tin 100	NT1	zinc 58	NT1	californium 247	NT1	gadolinium 137
NT1	tin 102	NT1	zinc 60	NT1	californium 249	NT1	gadolinium 139
NT1	tin 104	NT1	zinc 62	NT1	californium 251	NT1	gadolinium 141
NT1	tin 106	NT1	zinc 64	NT1	californium 253	NT1	gadolinium 143
NT1	tin 108	NT1	zinc 66	NT1	californium 255	NT1	gadolinium 145
NT1	tin 110	NT1	zinc 68	NT1	carbon 11	NT1	gadolinium 147
NT1	tin 112	NT1	zinc 70	NT1	carbon 13	NT1	gadolinium 149
NT1	tin 114	NT1	zinc 72	NT1	carbon 15	NT1	gadolinium 151
NT1	tin 116	NT1	zinc 74	NT1	carbon 17	NT1	gadolinium 153
NT1	tin 118	NT1	zinc 76	NT1	carbon 19	NT1	gadolinium 155
NT1	tin 120	NT1	zinc 78	NT1	carbon 9	NT1	gadolinium 157
NT1	tin 122	NT1	zinc 80	NT1	cerium 123	NT1	gadolinium 159
NT1	tin 124	NT1	zirconium 100	NT1	cerium 125	NT1	gadolinium 161
NT1	tin 126	NT1	zirconium 102	NT1	cerium 127	NT1	gadolinium 163
NT1	tin 128	NT1	zirconium 104	NT1	cerium 129	NT1	germanium 61
NT1	tin 130	NT1	zirconium 80	NT1	cerium 131	NT1	germanium 65
NT1	tin 132	NT1	zirconium 82	NT1	cerium 133	NT1	germanium 67
NT1	tin 134	NT1	zirconium 84	NT1	cerium 135	NT1	germanium 69
NT1	titanium 40	NT1	zirconium 86	NT1	cerium 137	NT1	germanium 71
NT1	titanium 42	NT1	zirconium 88	NT1	cerium 139	NT1	germanium 73
NT1	titanium 44	NT1	zirconium 90	NT1	cerium 141	NT1	germanium 75
NT1	titanium 46	NT1	zirconium 92	NT1	cerium 143	NT1	germanium 77
NT1	titanium 48	NT1	zirconium 94	NT1	cerium 145	NT1	germanium 79
NT1	titanium 50	NT1	zirconium 96	NT1	cerium 147	NT1	germanium 81
NT1	titanium 52	NT1	zirconium 98	NT1	cerium 149	NT1	germanium 83
NT1	titanium 54			NT1	cerium 151	NT1	germanium 85
NT1	titanium 56	**EVEN-ODD NUCLEI**		NT1	chromium 43	NT1	hafnium 155
NT1	tungsten 158	NT1	argon 31	NT1	chromium 45	NT1	hafnium 157
NT1	tungsten 160	NT1	argon 33	NT1	chromium 47	NT1	hafnium 159
NT1	tungsten 162	NT1	argon 35	NT1	chromium 49	NT1	hafnium 161
NT1	tungsten 164	NT1	argon 37	NT1	chromium 51	NT1	hafnium 163
NT1	tungsten 166	NT1	argon 39	NT1	chromium 53	NT1	hafnium 165
NT1	tungsten 168	NT1	argon 41	NT1	chromium 55	NT1	hafnium 167
NT1	tungsten 170	NT1	argon 43	NT1	chromium 57	NT1	hafnium 169
NT1	tungsten 172	NT1	argon 45	NT1	chromium 59	NT1	hafnium 171
NT1	tungsten 174	NT1	argon 47	NT1	chromium 61	NT1	hafnium 173
NT1	tungsten 176	NT1	argon 49	NT1	curium 239	NT1	hafnium 175
NT1	tungsten 178	NT1	argon 51	NT1	curium 241	NT1	hafnium 177
NT1	tungsten 180	NT1	barium 117	NT1	curium 243	NT1	hafnium 179
NT1	tungsten 182	NT1	barium 119	NT1	curium 245	NT1	hafnium 181
NT1	tungsten 184	NT1	barium 121	NT1	curium 247	NT1	hafnium 183

EVEN-ODD NUCLEI

NT1	hafnium 185	NT1	neodymium 127	NT1	platinum 199	NT1	selenium 79
NT1	helium 3	NT1	neodymium 129	NT1	platinum 201	NT1	selenium 81
NT2	helium 3 a	NT1	neodymium 131	NT1	platinum 203	NT1	selenium 83
NT2	helium 3 a1	NT1	neodymium 133	NT1	platinum 205	NT1	selenium 85
NT2	helium 3 b	NT1	neodymium 135	NT1	platinum 207	NT1	selenium 87
NT1	helium 5	NT1	neodymium 137	NT1	plutonium 231	NT1	selenium 89
NT1	helium 7	NT1	neodymium 139	NT1	plutonium 233	NT1	selenium 91
NT1	helium 9	NT1	neodymium 141	NT1	plutonium 235	NT1	silicon 23
NT1	iron 45	NT1	neodymium 143	NT1	plutonium 237	NT1	silicon 25
NT1	iron 47	NT1	neodymium 145	NT1	plutonium 239	NT1	silicon 27
NT1	iron 49	NT1	neodymium 147	NT1	plutonium 241	NT1	silicon 29
NT1	iron 51	NT1	neodymium 149	NT1	plutonium 243	NT1	silicon 31
NT1	iron 53	NT1	neodymium 151	NT1	plutonium 245	NT1	silicon 33
NT1	iron 55	NT1	neodymium 153	NT1	plutonium 247	NT1	silicon 35
NT1	iron 57	NT1	neodymium 155	NT1	polonium 193	NT1	silicon 37
NT1	iron 59	NT1	neon 17	NT1	polonium 195	NT1	silicon 39
NT1	iron 61	NT1	neon 19	NT1	polonium 197	NT1	silicon 41
NT1	iron 63	NT1	neon 21	NT1	polonium 199	NT1	strontium 101
NT1	iron 65	NT1	neon 23	NT1	polonium 201	NT1	strontium 77
NT1	iron 67	NT1	neon 25	NT1	polonium 203	NT1	strontium 79
NT1	krypton 71	NT1	neon 27	NT1	polonium 205	NT1	strontium 81
NT1	krypton 73	NT1	neon 29	NT1	polonium 207	NT1	strontium 83
NT1	krypton 75	NT1	nickel 53	NT1	polonium 209	NT1	strontium 85
NT1	krypton 77	NT1	nickel 55	NT1	polonium 211	NT1	strontium 87
NT1	krypton 79	NT1	nickel 57	NT1	polonium 213	NT1	strontium 89
NT1	krypton 81	NT1	nickel 59	NT1	polonium 215	NT1	strontium 91
NT1	krypton 83	NT1	nickel 61	NT1	polonium 217	NT1	strontium 93
NT1	krypton 85	NT1	nickel 63	NT1	polonium 219	NT1	strontium 95
NT1	krypton 87	NT1	nickel 65	NT1	radium 205	NT1	strontium 97
NT1	krypton 89	NT1	nickel 67	NT1	radium 207	NT1	strontium 99
NT1	krypton 91	NT1	nickel 69	NT1	radium 209	NT1	sulfur 27
NT1	krypton 93	NT1	nickel 71	NT1	radium 211	NT1	sulfur 29
NT1	krypton 95	NT1	nickel 73	NT1	radium 213	NT1	sulfur 31
NT1	krypton 97	NT1	nobelium 251	NT1	radium 215	NT1	sulfur 33
NT1	lead 183	NT1	nobelium 253	NT1	radium 217	NT1	sulfur 35
NT1	lead 185	NT1	nobelium 255	NT1	radium 219	NT1	sulfur 37
NT1	lead 187	NT1	nobelium 257	NT1	radium 221	NT1	sulfur 39
NT1	lead 189	NT1	nobelium 259	NT1	radium 223	NT1	sulfur 41
NT1	lead 191	NT1	nobelium 261	NT1	radium 225	NT1	sulfur 43
NT1	lead 193	NT1	osmium 163	NT1	radium 227	NT1	sulfur 45
NT1	lead 195	NT1	osmium 165	NT1	radium 229	NT1	sulfur 47
NT1	lead 197	NT1	osmium 167	NT1	radium 231	NT1	tellurium 107
NT1	lead 199	NT1	osmium 169	NT1	radium 233	NT1	tellurium 109
NT1	lead 201	NT1	osmium 171	NT1	radon 199	NT1	tellurium 111
NT1	lead 203	NT1	osmium 173	NT1	radon 201	NT1	tellurium 113
NT1	lead 205	NT1	osmium 175	NT1	radon 203	NT1	tellurium 115
NT1	lead 207	NT1	osmium 177	NT1	radon 205	NT1	tellurium 117
NT1	lead 209	NT1	osmium 179	NT1	radon 207	NT1	tellurium 119
NT1	lead 211	NT1	osmium 181	NT1	radon 209	NT1	tellurium 121
NT1	lead 213	NT1	osmium 183	NT1	radon 211	NT1	tellurium 123
NT1	lead 215	NT1	osmium 185	NT1	radon 213	NT1	tellurium 125
NT1	magnesium 21	NT1	osmium 187	NT1	radon 215	NT1	tellurium 127
NT1	magnesium 23	NT1	osmium 189	NT1	radon 217	NT1	tellurium 129
NT1	magnesium 25	NT1	osmium 191	NT1	radon 219	NT1	tellurium 131
NT1	magnesium 27	NT1	osmium 193	NT1	radon 221	NT1	tellurium 133
NT1	magnesium 29	NT1	osmium 195	NT1	radon 223	NT1	tellurium 135
NT1	magnesium 31	NT1	oxygen 13	NT1	radon 225	NT1	tellurium 137
NT1	magnesium 33	NT1	oxygen 15	NT1	radon 227	NT1	thorium 213
NT1	magnesium 35	NT1	oxygen 17	NT1	ruthenium 101	NT1	thorium 215
NT1	mercury 175	NT1	oxygen 19	NT1	ruthenium 103	NT1	thorium 217
NT1	mercury 177	NT1	oxygen 21	NT1	ruthenium 105	NT1	thorium 219
NT1	mercury 179	NT1	oxygen 23	NT1	ruthenium 107	NT1	thorium 221
NT1	mercury 181	NT1	palladium 101	NT1	ruthenium 109	NT1	thorium 222
NT1	mercury 183	NT1	palladium 103	NT1	ruthenium 111	NT1	thorium 223
NT1	mercury 185	NT1	palladium 105	NT1	ruthenium 113	NT1	thorium 225
NT1	mercury 187	NT1	palladium 107	NT1	ruthenium 91	NT1	thorium 227
NT1	mercury 189	NT1	palladium 109	NT1	ruthenium 93	NT1	thorium 229
NT1	mercury 191	NT1	palladium 111	NT1	ruthenium 95	NT1	thorium 231
NT1	mercury 193	NT1	palladium 113	NT1	ruthenium 97	NT1	thorium 233
NT1	mercury 195	NT1	palladium 115	NT1	ruthenium 99	NT1	thorium 235
NT1	mercury 197	NT1	palladium 117	NT1	samarium 131	NT1	tin 103
NT1	mercury 199	NT1	palladium 119	NT1	samarium 133	NT1	tin 105
NT1	mercury 201	NT1	palladium 95	NT1	samarium 135	NT1	tin 107
NT1	mercury 203	NT1	palladium 97	NT1	samarium 137	NT1	tin 109
NT1	mercury 205	NT1	palladium 99	NT1	samarium 139	NT1	tin 111
NT1	mercury 207	NT1	platinum 169	NT1	samarium 141	NT1	tin 113
NT1	mercury 209	NT1	platinum 171	NT1	samarium 143	NT1	tin 115
NT1	mercury 211	NT1	platinum 173	NT1	samarium 145	NT1	tin 117
NT1	molybdenum 101	NT1	platinum 175	NT1	samarium 147	NT1	tin 119
NT1	molybdenum 103	NT1	platinum 177	NT1	samarium 149	NT1	tin 121
NT1	molybdenum 105	NT1	platinum 179	NT1	samarium 151	NT1	tin 123
NT1	molybdenum 107	NT1	platinum 181	NT1	samarium 153	NT1	tin 125
NT1	molybdenum 85	NT1	platinum 183	NT1	samarium 155	NT1	tin 127
NT1	molybdenum 87	NT1	platinum 185	NT1	samarium 157	NT1	tin 129
NT1	molybdenum 89	NT1	platinum 187	NT1	samarium 159	NT1	tin 131
NT1	molybdenum 91	NT1	platinum 189	NT1	selenium 69	NT1	tin 133
NT1	molybdenum 93	NT1	platinum 191	NT1	selenium 71	NT1	titanium 39
NT1	molybdenum 95	NT1	platinum 193	NT1	selenium 73	NT1	titanium 41
NT1	molybdenum 97	NT1	platinum 195	NT1	selenium 75	NT1	titanium 43
NT1	molybdenum 99	NT1	platinum 197	NT1	selenium 77	NT1	titanium 45

NT1	titanium 47	**HEAVY NUCLEI**		NT2	einsteinium 246	NT2	plutonium 233
NT1	titanium 49	NT1	actinide nuclei	NT2	einsteinium 247	NT2	plutonium 234
NT1	titanium 51	NT2	actinium 209	NT2	einsteinium 248	NT2	plutonium 235
NT1	titanium 53	NT2	actinium 210	NT2	einsteinium 249	NT2	plutonium 236
NT1	titanium 55	NT2	actinium 211	NT2	einsteinium 250	NT2	plutonium 237
NT1	titanium 57	NT2	actinium 212	NT2	einsteinium 251	NT2	plutonium 238
NT1	tungsten 159	NT2	actinium 213	NT2	einsteinium 252	NT2	plutonium 239
NT1	tungsten 161	NT2	actinium 214	NT2	einsteinium 253	NT2	plutonium 240
NT1	tungsten 163	NT2	actinium 215	NT2	einsteinium 254	NT2	plutonium 241
NT1	tungsten 165	NT2	actinium 216	NT2	einsteinium 255	NT2	plutonium 242
NT1	tungsten 167	NT2	actinium 217	NT2	einsteinium 256	NT2	plutonium 243
NT1	tungsten 169	NT2	actinium 218	NT2	fermium 242	NT2	plutonium 244
NT1	tungsten 171	NT2	actinium 219	NT2	fermium 243	NT2	plutonium 245
NT1	tungsten 173	NT2	actinium 220	NT2	fermium 244	NT2	plutonium 246
NT1	tungsten 175	NT2	actinium 221	NT2	fermium 245	NT2	plutonium 247
NT1	tungsten 177	NT2	actinium 222	NT2	fermium 246	NT2	plutonium 248
NT1	tungsten 179	NT2	actinium 223	NT2	fermium 247	NT2	plutonium 250
NT1	tungsten 181	NT2	actinium 224	NT2	fermium 248	NT2	protactinium 215
NT1	tungsten 183	NT2	actinium 225	NT2	fermium 249	NT2	protactinium 216
NT1	tungsten 185	NT2	actinium 226	NT2	fermium 250	NT2	protactinium 217
NT1	tungsten 187	NT2	actinium 227	NT2	fermium 251	NT2	protactinium 218
NT1	tungsten 189	NT2	actinium 228	NT2	fermium 252	NT2	protactinium 219
NT1	uranium 223	NT2	actinium 229	NT2	fermium 253	NT2	protactinium 220
NT1	uranium 225	NT2	actinium 230	NT2	fermium 254	NT2	protactinium 221
NT1	uranium 227	NT2	actinium 231	NT2	fermium 255	NT2	protactinium 222
NT1	uranium 229	NT2	actinium 232	NT2	fermium 256	NT2	protactinium 223
NT1	uranium 231	NT2	actinium 233	NT2	fermium 257	NT2	protactinium 224
NT1	uranium 233	NT2	actinium 234	NT2	fermium 258	NT2	protactinium 225
NT1	uranium 235	NT2	americium 232	NT2	fermium 259	NT2	protactinium 226
NT1	uranium 237	NT2	americium 234	NT2	lawrencium 253	NT2	protactinium 227
NT1	uranium 239	NT2	americium 237	NT2	lawrencium 254	NT2	protactinium 228
NT1	xenon 111	NT2	americium 238	NT2	lawrencium 255	NT2	protactinium 229
NT1	xenon 113	NT2	americium 239	NT2	lawrencium 256	NT2	protactinium 230
NT1	xenon 115	NT2	americium 240	NT2	lawrencium 257	NT2	protactinium 231
NT1	xenon 117	NT2	americium 241	NT2	lawrencium 258	NT2	protactinium 232
NT1	xenon 119	NT2	americium 242	NT2	lawrencium 259	NT2	protactinium 233
NT1	xenon 121	NT2	americium 243	NT2	lawrencium 260	NT2	protactinium 234
NT1	xenon 123	NT2	americium 244	NT2	lawrencium 261	NT2	protactinium 235
NT1	xenon 125	NT2	americium 245	NT2	lawrencium 262	NT2	protactinium 236
NT1	xenon 127	NT2	americium 246	NT2	lawrencium 263	NT2	protactinium 237
NT1	xenon 129	NT2	americium 247	NT2	mendelevium 247	NT2	protactinium 238
NT1	xenon 131	NT2	berkelium 240	NT2	mendelevium 248	NT2	thorium 212
NT1	xenon 132	NT2	berkelium 241	NT2	mendelevium 249	NT2	thorium 213
NT1	xenon 133	NT2	berkelium 242	NT2	mendelevium 250	NT2	thorium 214
NT1	xenon 135	NT2	berkelium 243	NT2	mendelevium 251	NT2	thorium 215
NT1	xenon 137	NT2	berkelium 244	NT2	mendelevium 252	NT2	thorium 216
NT1	xenon 139	NT2	berkelium 245	NT2	mendelevium 253	NT2	thorium 217
NT1	xenon 141	NT2	berkelium 246	NT2	mendelevium 254	NT2	thorium 218
NT1	xenon 143	NT2	berkelium 247	NT2	mendelevium 255	NT2	thorium 219
NT1	xenon 145	NT2	berkelium 248	NT2	mendelevium 256	NT2	thorium 220
NT1	ytterbium 151	NT2	berkelium 249	NT2	mendelevium 257	NT2	thorium 221
NT1	ytterbium 153	NT2	berkelium 250	NT2	mendelevium 258	NT2	thorium 222
NT1	ytterbium 155	NT2	berkelium 251	NT2	mendelevium 259	NT2	thorium 223
NT1	ytterbium 157	NT2	californium 239	NT2	mendelevium 260	NT2	thorium 224
NT1	ytterbium 159	NT2	californium 240	NT2	mendelevium 261	NT2	thorium 225
NT1	ytterbium 161	NT2	californium 241	NT2	neptunium 226	NT2	thorium 226
NT1	ytterbium 163	NT2	californium 242	NT2	neptunium 227	NT2	thorium 227
NT1	ytterbium 165	NT2	californium 243	NT2	neptunium 228	NT2	thorium 228
NT1	ytterbium 167	NT2	californium 244	NT2	neptunium 229	NT2	thorium 229
NT1	ytterbium 169	NT2	californium 245	NT2	neptunium 230	NT2	thorium 230
NT1	ytterbium 171	NT2	californium 246	NT2	neptunium 231	NT2	thorium 231
NT1	ytterbium 173	NT2	californium 247	NT2	neptunium 232	NT2	thorium 232
NT1	ytterbium 175	NT2	californium 248	NT2	neptunium 233	NT2	thorium 233
NT1	ytterbium 177	NT2	californium 249	NT2	neptunium 234	NT2	thorium 234
NT1	ytterbium 179	NT2	californium 250	NT2	neptunium 235	NT2	thorium 235
NT1	zinc 57	NT2	californium 251	NT2	neptunium 236	NT2	thorium 236
NT1	zinc 59	NT2	californium 252	NT2	neptunium 237	NT2	thorium 238
NT1	zinc 61	NT2	californium 253	NT2	neptunium 238	NT2	uranium 222
NT1	zinc 63	NT2	californium 254	NT2	neptunium 239	NT2	uranium 223
NT1	zinc 65	NT2	californium 255	NT2	neptunium 240	NT2	uranium 224
NT1	zinc 67	NT2	californium 256	NT2	neptunium 241	NT2	uranium 225
NT1	zinc 69	NT2	curium 236	NT2	neptunium 242	NT2	uranium 226
NT1	zinc 71	NT2	curium 238	NT2	neptunium 243	NT2	uranium 227
NT1	zinc 73	NT2	curium 239	NT2	neptunium 244	NT2	uranium 228
NT1	zinc 75	NT2	curium 240	NT2	nobelium 250	NT2	uranium 229
NT1	zinc 77	NT2	curium 241	NT2	nobelium 251	NT2	uranium 230
NT1	zinc 79	NT2	curium 242	NT2	nobelium 252	NT2	uranium 231
NT1	zirconium 101	NT2	curium 243	NT2	nobelium 253	NT2	uranium 232
NT1	zirconium 103	NT2	curium 244	NT2	nobelium 254	NT2	uranium 233
NT1	zirconium 81	NT2	curium 245	NT2	nobelium 255	NT2	uranium 234
NT1	zirconium 83	NT2	curium 246	NT2	nobelium 256	NT2	uranium 235
NT1	zirconium 85	NT2	curium 247	NT2	nobelium 257	NT2	uranium 236
NT1	zirconium 87	NT2	curium 248	NT2	nobelium 258	NT2	uranium 237
NT1	zirconium 89	NT2	curium 249	NT2	nobelium 259	NT2	uranium 238
NT1	zirconium 91	NT2	curium 250	NT2	nobelium 260	NT2	uranium 239
NT1	zirconium 93	NT2	curium 251	NT2	nobelium 261	NT2	uranium 240
NT1	zirconium 95	NT2	curium 252	NT2	nobelium 262	NT2	uranium 242
NT1	zirconium 97	NT2	einsteinium 243	NT2	plutonium 230	NT1	astatine 194
NT1	zirconium 99	NT2	einsteinium 244	NT2	plutonium 231	NT1	astatine 195
		NT2	einsteinium 245	NT2	plutonium 232	NT1	astatine 196

NT1	astatine 197	NT1	gold 183	NT1	mercury 186
NT1	astatine 198	NT1	gold 184	NT1	mercury 187
NT1	astatine 199	NT1	gold 185	NT1	mercury 188
NT1	astatine 200	NT1	gold 186	NT1	mercury 189
NT1	astatine 201	NT1	gold 187	NT1	mercury 190
NT1	astatine 202	NT1	gold 188	NT1	mercury 191
NT1	astatine 203	NT1	gold 189	NT1	mercury 192
NT1	astatine 204	NT1	gold 190	NT1	mercury 193
NT1	astatine 205	NT1	gold 191	NT1	mercury 194
NT1	astatine 206	NT1	gold 192	NT1	mercury 195
NT1	astatine 207	NT1	gold 193	NT1	mercury 196
NT1	astatine 208	NT1	gold 194	NT1	mercury 197
NT1	astatine 209	NT1	gold 195	NT1	mercury 198
NT1	astatine 210	NT1	gold 196	NT1	mercury 199
NT1	astatine 211	NT1	gold 197	NT1	mercury 200
NT1	astatine 212	NT1	gold 198	NT1	mercury 201
NT1	astatine 213	NT1	gold 199	NT1	mercury 202
NT1	astatine 214	NT1	gold 200	NT1	mercury 203
NT1	astatine 215	NT1	gold 201	NT1	mercury 204
NT1	astatine 216	NT1	gold 202	NT1	mercury 205
NT1	astatine 217	NT1	gold 203	NT1	mercury 206
NT1	astatine 218	NT1	gold 204	NT1	mercury 207
NT1	astatine 219	NT1	hafnium 181	NT1	mercury 208
NT1	astatine 220	NT1	hafnium 182	NT1	mercury 209
NT1	astatine 221	NT1	hafnium 183	NT1	mercury 210
NT1	astatine 222	NT1	hafnium 184	NT1	mercury 211
NT1	astatine 223	NT1	hafnium 185	NT1	mercury 212
NT1	bismuth 188	NT1	hafnium 186	NT1	osmium 181
NT1	bismuth 189	NT1	iridium 181	NT1	osmium 182
NT1	bismuth 190	NT1	iridium 182	NT1	osmium 183
NT1	bismuth 191	NT1	iridium 183	NT1	osmium 184
NT1	bismuth 192	NT1	iridium 184	NT1	osmium 185
NT1	bismuth 193	NT1	iridium 185	NT1	osmium 186
NT1	bismuth 194	NT1	iridium 186	NT1	osmium 187
NT1	bismuth 195	NT1	iridium 187	NT1	osmium 188
NT1	bismuth 196	NT1	iridium 188	NT1	osmium 189
NT1	bismuth 197	NT1	iridium 189	NT1	osmium 190
NT1	bismuth 198	NT1	iridium 190	NT1	osmium 191
NT1	bismuth 199	NT1	iridium 191	NT1	osmium 192
NT1	bismuth 200	NT1	iridium 192	NT1	osmium 193
NT1	bismuth 201	NT1	iridium 193	NT1	osmium 194
NT1	bismuth 202	NT1	iridium 194	NT1	osmium 195
NT1	bismuth 203	NT1	iridium 195	NT1	osmium 196
NT1	bismuth 204	NT1	iridium 196	NT1	platinum 181
NT1	bismuth 205	NT1	iridium 197	NT1	platinum 182
NT1	bismuth 206	NT1	iridium 198	NT1	platinum 183
NT1	bismuth 207	NT1	lead 182	NT1	platinum 184
NT1	bismuth 208	NT1	lead 183	NT1	platinum 185
NT1	bismuth 209	NT1	lead 184	NT1	platinum 186
NT1	bismuth 210	NT1	lead 185	NT1	platinum 187
NT1	bismuth 211	NT1	lead 186	NT1	platinum 188
NT1	bismuth 212	NT1	lead 187	NT1	platinum 189
NT1	bismuth 213	NT1	lead 188	NT1	platinum 190
NT1	bismuth 214	NT1	lead 189	NT1	platinum 191
NT1	bismuth 215	NT1	lead 190	NT1	platinum 192
NT1	bismuth 216	NT1	lead 191	NT1	platinum 193
NT1	francium 201	NT1	lead 192	NT1	platinum 194
NT1	francium 202	NT1	lead 193	NT1	platinum 195
NT1	francium 203	NT1	lead 194	NT1	platinum 196
NT1	francium 204	NT1	lead 195	NT1	platinum 197
NT1	francium 205	NT1	lead 196	NT1	platinum 198
NT1	francium 206	NT1	lead 197	NT1	platinum 199
NT1	francium 207	NT1	lead 198	NT1	platinum 200
NT1	francium 208	NT1	lead 199	NT1	platinum 201
NT1	francium 209	NT1	lead 200	NT1	platinum 202
NT1	francium 210	NT1	lead 201	NT1	platinum 203
NT1	francium 211	NT1	lead 202	NT1	platinum 204
NT1	francium 212	NT1	lead 203	NT1	platinum 205
NT1	francium 213	NT1	lead 204	NT1	platinum 206
NT1	francium 214	NT1	lead 205	NT1	platinum 207
NT1	francium 215	NT1	lead 206	NT1	platinum 208
NT1	francium 216	NT1	lead 207	NT1	polonium 192
NT1	francium 217	NT1	lead 208	NT1	polonium 193
NT1	francium 218	NT1	lead 209	NT1	polonium 194
NT1	francium 219	NT1	lead 210	NT1	polonium 195
NT1	francium 220	NT1	lead 211	NT1	polonium 196
NT1	francium 221	NT1	lead 212	NT1	polonium 197
NT1	francium 222	NT1	lead 213	NT1	polonium 198
NT1	francium 223	NT1	lead 214	NT1	polonium 199
NT1	francium 224	NT1	lead 215	NT1	polonium 200
NT1	francium 225	NT1	lead 216	NT1	polonium 201
NT1	francium 226	NT1	lutetium 181	NT1	polonium 202
NT1	francium 227	NT1	lutetium 182	NT1	polonium 203
NT1	francium 228	NT1	lutetium 183	NT1	polonium 204
NT1	francium 229	NT1	lutetium 184	NT1	polonium 205
NT1	francium 230	NT1	mercury 181	NT1	polonium 206
NT1	francium 231	NT1	mercury 182	NT1	polonium 207
NT1	francium 232	NT1	mercury 183	NT1	polonium 208
NT1	gold 181	NT1	mercury 184	NT1	polonium 209
NT1	gold 182	NT1	mercury 185	NT1	polonium 210

NT1	polonium 211
NT1	polonium 212
NT1	polonium 213
NT1	polonium 214
NT1	polonium 215
NT1	polonium 216
NT1	polonium 217
NT1	polonium 218
NT1	radium 205
NT1	radium 206
NT1	radium 207
NT1	radium 208
NT1	radium 209
NT1	radium 210
NT1	radium 211
NT1	radium 212
NT1	radium 213
NT1	radium 214
NT1	radium 215
NT1	radium 216
NT1	radium 217
NT1	radium 218
NT1	radium 219
NT1	radium 220
NT1	radium 221
NT1	radium 222
NT1	radium 223
NT1	radium 224
NT1	radium 225
NT1	radium 226
NT1	radium 227
NT1	radium 228
NT1	radium 229
NT1	radium 230
NT1	radium 231
NT1	radium 232
NT1	radium 233
NT1	radium 234
NT1	radon 199
NT1	radon 200
NT1	radon 201
NT1	radon 202
NT1	radon 203
NT1	radon 204
NT1	radon 205
NT1	radon 206
NT1	radon 207
NT1	radon 208
NT1	radon 209
NT1	radon 210
NT1	radon 211
NT1	radon 212
NT1	radon 213
NT1	radon 214
NT1	radon 215
NT1	radon 216
NT1	radon 217
NT1	radon 218
NT1	radon 219
NT1	radon 220
NT1	radon 221
NT1	radon 222
NT1	radon 223
NT1	radon 224
NT1	radon 225
NT1	radon 226
NT1	radon 227
NT1	radon 228
NT1	rhenium 181
NT1	rhenium 182
NT1	rhenium 183
NT1	rhenium 184
NT1	rhenium 185
NT1	rhenium 186
NT1	rhenium 187
NT1	rhenium 188
NT1	rhenium 189
NT1	rhenium 190
NT1	rhenium 191
NT1	rhenium 192
NT1	tantalum 181
NT1	tantalum 182
NT1	tantalum 183
NT1	tantalum 184
NT1	tantalum 185
NT1	tantalum 186
NT1	thallium 182
NT1	thallium 184
NT1	thallium 185
NT1	thallium 186

NT1 thallium 187
NT1 thallium 188
NT1 thallium 189
NT1 thallium 190
NT1 thallium 191
NT1 thallium 192
NT1 thallium 193
NT1 thallium 194
NT1 thallium 195
NT1 thallium 196
NT1 thallium 197
NT1 thallium 198
NT1 thallium 199
NT1 thallium 200
NT1 thallium 201
NT1 thallium 202
NT1 thallium 203
NT1 thallium 204
NT1 thallium 205
NT1 thallium 206
NT1 thallium 207
NT1 thallium 208
NT1 thallium 209
NT1 thallium 210
NT1 tungsten 181
NT1 tungsten 182
NT1 tungsten 183
NT1 tungsten 184
NT1 tungsten 185
NT1 tungsten 186
NT1 tungsten 187
NT1 tungsten 188
NT1 tungsten 189
NT1 tungsten 190
NT1 tungsten 192

HOURS LIVING RADIOISOTOPES
NT1 actinium 224
NT1 actinium 228
NT1 actinium 229
NT1 americium 237
NT1 americium 238
NT1 americium 239
NT1 americium 242
NT1 americium 244
NT1 americium 245
NT1 antimony 116
NT1 antimony 117
NT1 antimony 118
NT1 antimony 128
NT1 antimony 129
NT1 argon 41
NT1 arsenic 78
NT1 astatine 207
NT1 astatine 208
NT1 astatine 209
NT1 astatine 210
NT1 astatine 211
NT1 barium 126
NT1 barium 129
NT1 barium 139
NT1 berkelium 243
NT1 berkelium 244
NT1 berkelium 248
NT1 berkelium 250
NT1 bismuth 201
NT1 bismuth 202
NT1 bismuth 203
NT1 bismuth 204
NT1 bismuth 212
NT1 bromine 75
NT1 bromine 76
NT1 bromine 80
NT1 bromine 83
NT1 cadmium 107
NT1 cadmium 117
NT1 californium 247
NT1 californium 255
NT1 cerium 132
NT1 cerium 133
NT1 cerium 135
NT1 cerium 137
NT1 cesium 127
NT1 cesium 134
NT1 chromium 48
NT1 cobalt 55
NT1 cobalt 58
NT1 cobalt 61
NT1 copper 61
NT1 copper 64
NT1 curium 238
NT1 curium 239
NT1 curium 249
NT1 dysprosium 152
NT1 dysprosium 153
NT1 dysprosium 155
NT1 dysprosium 157
NT1 dysprosium 165
NT1 einsteinium 249
NT1 einsteinium 250
NT1 einsteinium 256
NT1 erbium 158
NT1 erbium 161
NT1 erbium 163
NT1 erbium 165
NT1 erbium 171
NT1 europium 150
NT1 europium 152
NT1 europium 157
NT1 fermium 251
NT1 fermium 254
NT1 fermium 255
NT1 fermium 256
NT1 fluorine 18
NT1 gadolinium 159
NT1 gallium 66
NT1 gallium 68
NT1 gallium 72
NT1 gallium 73
NT1 germanium 66
NT1 germanium 75
NT1 germanium 77
NT1 germanium 78
NT1 gold 191
NT1 gold 192
NT1 gold 193
NT1 gold 196
NT1 gold 200
NT1 hafnium 170
NT1 hafnium 171
NT1 hafnium 173
NT1 hafnium 180
NT1 hafnium 182
NT1 hafnium 183
NT1 hafnium 184
NT1 holmium 160
NT1 holmium 161
NT1 holmium 162
NT1 holmium 167
NT1 indium 109
NT1 indium 110
NT1 indium 113
NT1 indium 115
NT1 indium 117
NT1 iodine 120
NT1 iodine 121
NT1 iodine 123
NT1 iodine 130
NT1 iodine 132
NT1 iodine 133
NT1 iodine 135
NT1 iridium 184
NT1 iridium 185
NT1 iridium 186
NT1 iridium 187
NT1 iridium 190
NT1 iridium 194
NT1 iridium 195
NT1 iridium 196
NT1 iron 52
NT1 krypton 76
NT1 krypton 77
NT1 krypton 83
NT1 krypton 85
NT1 krypton 87
NT1 krypton 88
NT1 lanthanum 132
NT1 lanthanum 133
NT1 lanthanum 135
NT1 lanthanum 141
NT1 lanthanum 142
NT1 lead 198
NT1 lead 199
NT1 lead 200
NT1 lead 201
NT1 lead 202
NT1 lead 204
NT1 lead 209
NT1 lead 212
NT1 lutetium 176
NT1 lutetium 179
NT1 magnesium 28
NT1 manganese 56
NT1 mendelevium 256
NT1 mendelevium 257
NT1 mendelevium 259
NT1 mercury 192
NT1 mercury 193
NT1 mercury 195
NT1 mercury 197
NT1 molybdenum 90
NT1 molybdenum 93
NT1 neodymium 138
NT1 neodymium 139
NT1 neodymium 141
NT1 neodymium 149
NT1 neptunium 236
NT1 neptunium 240
NT1 nickel 65
NT1 niobium 89
NT1 niobium 90
NT1 niobium 96
NT1 niobium 97
NT1 osmium 181
NT1 osmium 182
NT1 osmium 183
NT1 osmium 189
NT1 osmium 191
NT1 palladium 101
NT1 palladium 109
NT1 palladium 111
NT1 palladium 112
NT1 platinum 185
NT1 platinum 186
NT1 platinum 187
NT1 platinum 189
NT1 platinum 197
NT1 platinum 200
NT1 plutonium 234
NT1 plutonium 243
NT1 plutonium 245
NT1 polonium 204
NT1 polonium 205
NT1 polonium 207
NT1 potassium 42
NT1 potassium 43
NT1 praseodymium 137
NT1 praseodymium 138
NT1 praseodymium 139
NT1 praseodymium 142
NT1 praseodymium 145
NT1 promethium 150
NT1 protactinium 228
NT1 protactinium 234
NT1 radium 230
NT1 radon 210
NT1 radon 211
NT1 radon 224
NT1 rhenium 181
NT1 rhenium 182
NT1 rhenium 188
NT1 rhenium 190
NT1 rhodium 100
NT1 rhodium 106
NT1 rhodium 99
NT1 rubidium 81
NT1 rubidium 82
NT1 ruthenium 105
NT1 ruthenium 95
NT1 samarium 142
NT1 samarium 156
NT1 scandium 43
NT1 scandium 44
NT1 selenium 73
NT1 silicon 31
NT1 silver 103
NT1 silver 104
NT1 silver 112
NT1 silver 113
NT1 sodium 24
NT1 strontium 80
NT1 strontium 85
NT1 strontium 87
NT1 strontium 91
NT1 strontium 92
NT1 sulfur 38
NT1 tantalum 173
NT1 tantalum 174
NT1 tantalum 175
NT1 tantalum 176
NT1 tantalum 178
NT1 tantalum 180
NT1 tantalum 184
NT1 technetium 93
NT1 technetium 94
NT1 technetium 95
NT1 technetium 99
NT1 tellurium 116
NT1 tellurium 117
NT1 tellurium 119
NT1 tellurium 127
NT1 tellurium 129
NT1 terbium 147
NT1 terbium 148
NT1 terbium 149
NT1 terbium 150
NT1 terbium 151
NT1 terbium 152
NT1 terbium 154
NT1 terbium 156
NT1 thallium 195
NT1 thallium 196
NT1 thallium 197
NT1 thallium 198
NT1 thallium 199
NT1 thulium 163
NT1 thulium 166
NT1 thulium 173
NT1 tin 110
NT1 tin 127
NT1 titanium 45
NT1 tungsten 176
NT1 tungsten 177
NT1 uranium 240
NT1 xenon 122
NT1 xenon 123
NT1 xenon 125
NT1 xenon 135
NT1 ytterbium 164
NT1 ytterbium 177
NT1 ytterbium 178
NT1 yttrium 85
NT1 yttrium 86
NT1 yttrium 87
NT1 yttrium 90
NT1 yttrium 92
NT1 yttrium 93
NT1 zinc 62
NT1 zinc 69
NT1 zinc 71
NT1 zirconium 86
NT1 zirconium 87
NT1 zirconium 97

INTERMEDIATE MASS NUCLEI
NT1 antimony 106
NT1 antimony 108
NT1 antimony 109
NT1 antimony 110
NT1 antimony 111
NT1 antimony 112
NT1 antimony 113
NT1 antimony 114
NT1 antimony 115
NT1 antimony 116
NT1 antimony 117
NT1 antimony 118
NT1 antimony 119
NT1 antimony 120
NT1 antimony 121
NT1 antimony 122
NT1 antimony 123
NT1 antimony 124
NT1 antimony 125
NT1 antimony 126
NT1 antimony 127
NT1 antimony 128
NT1 antimony 129
NT1 antimony 130
NT1 antimony 131
NT1 antimony 132
NT1 antimony 133
NT1 antimony 134
NT1 antimony 135
NT1 antimony 136
NT1 argon 41
NT1 argon 42
NT1 argon 43

NT1	argon 44	NT1	cadmium 103	NT1	chromium 42	NT1	germanium 72
NT1	argon 45	NT1	cadmium 104	NT1	chromium 43	NT1	germanium 73
NT1	argon 46	NT1	cadmium 105	NT1	chromium 44	NT1	germanium 74
NT1	argon 47	NT1	cadmium 106	NT1	chromium 45	NT1	germanium 75
NT1	argon 49	NT1	cadmium 107	NT1	chromium 46	NT1	germanium 76
NT1	argon 50	NT1	cadmium 108	NT1	chromium 47	NT1	germanium 77
NT1	argon 51	NT1	cadmium 109	NT1	chromium 48	NT1	germanium 78
NT1	arsenic 65	NT1	cadmium 110	NT1	chromium 49	NT1	germanium 79
NT1	arsenic 66	NT1	cadmium 111	NT1	chromium 50	NT1	germanium 80
NT1	arsenic 67	NT1	cadmium 112	NT1	chromium 51	NT1	germanium 81
NT1	arsenic 68	NT1	cadmium 113	NT1	chromium 52	NT1	germanium 82
NT1	arsenic 69	NT1	cadmium 114	NT1	chromium 53	NT1	germanium 83
NT1	arsenic 70	NT1	cadmium 115	NT1	chromium 54	NT1	germanium 84
NT1	arsenic 71	NT1	cadmium 116	NT1	chromium 55	NT1	germanium 85
NT1	arsenic 72	NT1	cadmium 117	NT1	chromium 56	NT1	gold 173
NT1	arsenic 73	NT1	cadmium 118	NT1	chromium 57	NT1	gold 174
NT1	arsenic 74	NT1	cadmium 119	NT1	chromium 58	NT1	gold 175
NT1	arsenic 75	NT1	cadmium 120	NT1	chromium 59	NT1	gold 176
NT1	arsenic 76	NT1	cadmium 121	NT1	chromium 60	NT1	gold 177
NT1	arsenic 77	NT1	cadmium 122	NT1	chromium 61	NT1	gold 178
NT1	arsenic 78	NT1	cadmium 123	NT1	chromium 62	NT1	gold 179
NT1	arsenic 79	NT1	cadmium 124	NT1	cobalt 53	NT1	gold 180
NT1	arsenic 80	NT1	cadmium 125	NT1	cobalt 54	NT1	hafnium 154
NT1	arsenic 81	NT1	cadmium 126	NT1	cobalt 55	NT1	hafnium 155
NT1	arsenic 82	NT1	cadmium 127	NT1	cobalt 56	NT1	hafnium 156
NT1	arsenic 83	NT1	cadmium 128	NT1	cobalt 57	NT1	hafnium 157
NT1	arsenic 84	NT1	cadmium 130	NT1	cobalt 58	NT1	hafnium 158
NT1	arsenic 85	NT1	cadmium 96	NT1	cobalt 59	NT1	hafnium 159
NT1	arsenic 86	NT1	cadmium 97	NT1	cobalt 60	NT1	hafnium 160
NT1	arsenic 87	NT1	cadmium 98	NT1	cobalt 61	NT1	hafnium 161
NT1	barium 117	NT1	cadmium 99	NT1	cobalt 62	NT1	hafnium 162
NT1	barium 119	NT1	calcium 41	NT1	cobalt 63	NT1	hafnium 163
NT1	barium 120	NT1	calcium 42	NT1	cobalt 64	NT1	hafnium 164
NT1	barium 121	NT1	calcium 43	NT1	cobalt 65	NT1	hafnium 165
NT1	barium 122	NT1	calcium 44	NT1	cobalt 66	NT1	hafnium 166
NT1	barium 123	NT1	calcium 45	NT1	cobalt 67	NT1	hafnium 167
NT1	barium 124	NT1	calcium 46	NT1	cobalt 68	NT1	hafnium 168
NT1	barium 125	NT1	calcium 47	NT1	cobalt 69	NT1	hafnium 169
NT1	barium 126	NT1	calcium 48	NT1	cobalt 70	NT1	hafnium 170
NT1	barium 127	NT1	calcium 49	NT1	copper 57	NT1	hafnium 171
NT1	barium 128	NT1	calcium 50	NT1	copper 58	NT1	hafnium 172
NT1	barium 129	NT1	calcium 51	NT1	copper 59	NT1	hafnium 173
NT1	barium 130	NT1	calcium 52	NT1	copper 60	NT1	hafnium 174
NT1	barium 131	NT1	calcium 53	NT1	copper 61	NT1	hafnium 175
NT1	barium 132	NT1	cesium 113	NT1	copper 62	NT1	hafnium 176
NT1	barium 133	NT1	cesium 114	NT1	copper 63	NT1	hafnium 177
NT1	barium 134	NT1	cesium 115	NT1	copper 64	NT1	hafnium 178
NT1	barium 135	NT1	cesium 116	NT1	copper 65	NT1	hafnium 179
NT1	barium 136	NT1	cesium 117	NT1	copper 66	NT1	hafnium 180
NT1	barium 137	NT1	cesium 118	NT1	copper 67	NT1	indium 100
NT1	barium 138	NT1	cesium 119	NT1	copper 68	NT1	indium 101
NT1	barium 139	NT1	cesium 120	NT1	copper 69	NT1	indium 102
NT1	barium 140	NT1	cesium 121	NT1	copper 70	NT1	indium 103
NT1	barium 141	NT1	cesium 122	NT1	copper 71	NT1	indium 104
NT1	barium 142	NT1	cesium 123	NT1	copper 72	NT1	indium 105
NT1	barium 143	NT1	cesium 124	NT1	copper 73	NT1	indium 106
NT1	barium 144	NT1	cesium 125	NT1	copper 74	NT1	indium 107
NT1	barium 145	NT1	cesium 126	NT1	copper 75	NT1	indium 108
NT1	barium 146	NT1	cesium 127	NT1	gallium 61	NT1	indium 109
NT1	barium 147	NT1	cesium 128	NT1	gallium 62	NT1	indium 110
NT1	barium 148	NT1	cesium 129	NT1	gallium 63	NT1	indium 111
NT1	barium 149	NT1	cesium 130	NT1	gallium 64	NT1	indium 112
NT1	bromine 69	NT1	cesium 131	NT1	gallium 65	NT1	indium 113
NT1	bromine 70	NT1	cesium 132	NT1	gallium 66	NT1	indium 114
NT1	bromine 71	NT1	cesium 133	NT1	gallium 67	NT1	indium 115
NT1	bromine 72	NT1	cesium 134	NT1	gallium 68	NT1	indium 116
NT1	bromine 73	NT1	cesium 135	NT1	gallium 69	NT1	indium 117
NT1	bromine 74	NT1	cesium 136	NT1	gallium 70	NT1	indium 118
NT1	bromine 75	NT1	cesium 137	NT1	gallium 71	NT1	indium 119
NT1	bromine 76	NT1	cesium 138	NT1	gallium 72	NT1	indium 120
NT1	bromine 77	NT1	cesium 139	NT1	gallium 73	NT1	indium 121
NT1	bromine 78	NT1	cesium 140	NT1	gallium 74	NT1	indium 122
NT1	bromine 79	NT1	cesium 141	NT1	gallium 75	NT1	indium 123
NT1	bromine 80	NT1	cesium 142	NT1	gallium 76	NT1	indium 124
NT1	bromine 81	NT1	cesium 143	NT1	gallium 77	NT1	indium 125
NT1	bromine 82	NT1	cesium 144	NT1	gallium 78	NT1	indium 126
NT1	bromine 83	NT1	cesium 145	NT1	gallium 79	NT1	indium 127
NT1	bromine 84	NT1	cesium 146	NT1	gallium 80	NT1	indium 128
NT1	bromine 85	NT1	cesium 147	NT1	gallium 81	NT1	indium 129
NT1	bromine 86	NT1	cesium 148	NT1	gallium 82	NT1	indium 130
NT1	bromine 87	NT1	chlorine 41	NT1	gallium 83	NT1	indium 131
NT1	bromine 88	NT1	chlorine 42	NT1	germanium 61	NT1	indium 132
NT1	bromine 89	NT1	chlorine 43	NT1	germanium 64	NT1	iodine 108
NT1	bromine 90	NT1	chlorine 44	NT1	germanium 65	NT1	iodine 109
NT1	bromine 91	NT1	chlorine 45	NT1	germanium 66	NT1	iodine 110
NT1	bromine 92	NT1	chlorine 46	NT1	germanium 67	NT1	iodine 111
NT1	bromine 93	NT1	chlorine 47	NT1	germanium 68	NT1	iodine 112
NT1	cadmium 100	NT1	chlorine 48	NT1	germanium 69	NT1	iodine 113
NT1	cadmium 101	NT1	chlorine 49	NT1	germanium 70	NT1	iodine 114
NT1	cadmium 102	NT1	chlorine 51	NT1	germanium 71	NT1	iodine 115

NT1	iodine 116	NT1	krypton 95	NT1	niobium 89	NT2	cerium 124
NT1	iodine 117	NT1	krypton 96	NT1	niobium 90	NT2	cerium 125
NT1	iodine 118	NT1	krypton 97	NT1	niobium 91	NT2	cerium 126
NT1	iodine 119	NT1	krypton 98	NT1	niobium 92	NT2	cerium 127
NT1	iodine 120	NT1	manganese 44	NT1	niobium 93	NT2	cerium 128
NT1	iodine 121	NT1	manganese 46	NT1	niobium 94	NT2	cerium 129
NT1	iodine 122	NT1	manganese 47	NT1	niobium 95	NT2	cerium 130
NT1	iodine 123	NT1	manganese 48	NT1	niobium 96	NT2	cerium 131
NT1	iodine 124	NT1	manganese 49	NT1	niobium 97	NT2	cerium 132
NT1	iodine 125	NT1	manganese 50	NT1	niobium 98	NT2	cerium 133
NT1	iodine 126	NT1	manganese 51	NT1	niobium 99	NT2	cerium 134
NT1	iodine 127	NT1	manganese 52	NT1	osmium 162	NT2	cerium 135
NT1	iodine 128	NT1	manganese 53	NT1	osmium 163	NT2	cerium 136
NT1	iodine 129	NT1	manganese 54	NT1	osmium 164	NT2	cerium 137
NT1	iodine 130	NT1	manganese 55	NT1	osmium 165	NT2	cerium 138
NT1	iodine 131	NT1	manganese 56	NT1	osmium 166	NT2	cerium 139
NT1	iodine 132	NT1	manganese 57	NT1	osmium 167	NT2	cerium 140
NT1	iodine 133	NT1	manganese 58	NT1	osmium 168	NT2	cerium 141
NT1	iodine 134	NT1	manganese 59	NT1	osmium 169	NT2	cerium 142
NT1	iodine 135	NT1	manganese 60	NT1	osmium 170	NT2	cerium 143
NT1	iodine 136	NT1	manganese 61	NT1	osmium 171	NT2	cerium 144
NT1	iodine 137	NT1	manganese 62	NT1	osmium 172	NT2	cerium 145
NT1	iodine 138	NT1	manganese 63	NT1	osmium 173	NT2	cerium 146
NT1	iodine 139	NT1	manganese 64	NT1	osmium 174	NT2	cerium 147
NT1	iodine 140	NT1	manganese 65	NT1	osmium 175	NT2	cerium 148
NT1	iodine 141	NT1	mercury 175	NT1	osmium 176	NT2	cerium 149
NT1	iodine 142	NT1	mercury 176	NT1	osmium 177	NT2	cerium 150
NT1	iridium 166	NT1	mercury 177	NT1	osmium 178	NT2	cerium 151
NT1	iridium 167	NT1	mercury 178	NT1	osmium 179	NT2	cerium 152
NT1	iridium 168	NT1	mercury 179	NT1	osmium 180	NT2	dysprosium 141
NT1	iridium 169	NT1	mercury 180	NT1	palladium 100	NT2	dysprosium 142
NT1	iridium 170	NT1	molybdenum 100	NT1	palladium 101	NT2	dysprosium 143
NT1	iridium 171	NT1	molybdenum 101	NT1	palladium 102	NT2	dysprosium 144
NT1	iridium 172	NT1	molybdenum 102	NT1	palladium 103	NT2	dysprosium 145
NT1	iridium 173	NT1	molybdenum 103	NT1	palladium 104	NT2	dysprosium 146
NT1	iridium 174	NT1	molybdenum 104	NT1	palladium 105	NT2	dysprosium 147
NT1	iridium 175	NT1	molybdenum 105	NT1	palladium 106	NT2	dysprosium 148
NT1	iridium 176	NT1	molybdenum 106	NT1	palladium 107	NT2	dysprosium 149
NT1	iridium 177	NT1	molybdenum 107	NT1	palladium 108	NT2	dysprosium 150
NT1	iridium 178	NT1	molybdenum 108	NT1	palladium 109	NT2	dysprosium 151
NT1	iridium 179	NT1	molybdenum 84	NT1	palladium 110	NT2	dysprosium 152
NT1	iridium 180	NT1	molybdenum 85	NT1	palladium 111	NT2	dysprosium 153
NT1	iron 45	NT1	molybdenum 87	NT1	palladium 112	NT2	dysprosium 154
NT1	iron 47	NT1	molybdenum 88	NT1	palladium 113	NT2	dysprosium 155
NT1	iron 48	NT1	molybdenum 89	NT1	palladium 114	NT2	dysprosium 156
NT1	iron 49	NT1	molybdenum 90	NT1	palladium 115	NT2	dysprosium 157
NT1	iron 50	NT1	molybdenum 91	NT1	palladium 116	NT2	dysprosium 158
NT1	iron 51	NT1	molybdenum 92	NT1	palladium 117	NT2	dysprosium 159
NT1	iron 52	NT1	molybdenum 93	NT1	palladium 118	NT2	dysprosium 160
NT1	iron 53	NT1	molybdenum 94	NT1	palladium 119	NT2	dysprosium 161
NT1	iron 54	NT1	molybdenum 95	NT1	palladium 95	NT2	dysprosium 162
NT1	iron 55	NT1	molybdenum 96	NT1	palladium 96	NT2	dysprosium 163
NT1	iron 56	NT1	molybdenum 97	NT1	palladium 97	NT2	dysprosium 164
NT1	iron 57	NT1	molybdenum 98	NT1	palladium 98	NT2	dysprosium 165
NT1	iron 58	NT1	molybdenum 99	NT1	palladium 99	NT2	dysprosium 166
NT1	iron 59	NT1	nickel 53	NT1	phosphorus 41	NT2	dysprosium 167
NT1	iron 60	NT1	nickel 54	NT1	phosphorus 42	NT2	dysprosium 168
NT1	iron 61	NT1	nickel 55	NT1	phosphorus 43	NT2	dysprosium 169
NT1	iron 62	NT1	nickel 56	NT1	phosphorus 44	NT2	erbium 145
NT1	iron 63	NT1	nickel 57	NT1	phosphorus 45	NT2	erbium 147
NT1	iron 64	NT1	nickel 58	NT1	phosphorus 46	NT2	erbium 148
NT1	iron 65	NT1	nickel 59	NT1	platinum 168	NT2	erbium 149
NT1	iron 66	NT1	nickel 60	NT1	platinum 169	NT2	erbium 150
NT1	iron 67	NT1	nickel 61	NT1	platinum 170	NT2	erbium 151
NT1	iron 68	NT1	nickel 62	NT1	platinum 171	NT2	erbium 152
NT1	krypton 70	NT1	nickel 63	NT1	platinum 172	NT2	erbium 153
NT1	krypton 71	NT1	nickel 64	NT1	platinum 173	NT2	erbium 154
NT1	krypton 72	NT1	nickel 65	NT1	platinum 174	NT2	erbium 155
NT1	krypton 73	NT1	nickel 66	NT1	platinum 175	NT2	erbium 156
NT1	krypton 74	NT1	nickel 67	NT1	platinum 176	NT2	erbium 157
NT1	krypton 75	NT1	nickel 68	NT1	platinum 177	NT2	erbium 158
NT1	krypton 76	NT1	nickel 69	NT1	platinum 178	NT2	erbium 159
NT1	krypton 77	NT1	nickel 71	NT1	platinum 179	NT2	erbium 160
NT1	krypton 78	NT1	nickel 72	NT1	platinum 180	NT2	erbium 161
NT1	krypton 79	NT1	nickel 73	NT1	potassium 41	NT2	erbium 162
NT1	krypton 80	NT1	nickel 74	NT1	potassium 42	NT2	erbium 163
NT1	krypton 81	NT1	nickel 78	NT1	potassium 43	NT2	erbium 164
NT1	krypton 82	NT1	niobium 100	NT1	potassium 44	NT2	erbium 165
NT1	krypton 83	NT1	niobium 101	NT1	potassium 45	NT2	erbium 166
NT1	krypton 84	NT1	niobium 102	NT1	potassium 46	NT2	erbium 167
NT1	krypton 85	NT1	niobium 103	NT1	potassium 47	NT2	erbium 168
NT1	krypton 86	NT1	niobium 104	NT1	potassium 48	NT2	erbium 169
NT1	krypton 87	NT1	niobium 105	NT1	potassium 49	NT2	erbium 170
NT1	krypton 88	NT1	niobium 106	NT1	potassium 50	NT2	erbium 171
NT1	krypton 89	NT1	niobium 83	NT1	potassium 51	NT2	erbium 172
NT1	krypton 90	NT1	niobium 84	NT1	potassium 52	NT2	erbium 173
NT1	krypton 91	NT1	niobium 85	NT1	potassium 53	NT2	erbium 174
NT1	krypton 92	NT1	niobium 86	NT1	potassium 54	NT2	europium 134
NT1	krypton 93	NT1	niobium 87	NT1	rare earth nuclei	NT2	europium 135
NT1	krypton 94	NT1	niobium 88	NT2	cerium 123	NT2	europium 136

NT2 europium 137
NT2 europium 138
NT2 europium 139
NT2 europium 140
NT2 europium 141
NT2 europium 142
NT2 europium 143
NT2 europium 144
NT2 europium 145
NT2 europium 146
NT2 europium 147
NT2 europium 148
NT2 europium 149
NT2 europium 150
NT2 europium 151
NT2 europium 152
NT2 europium 153
NT2 europium 154
NT2 europium 155
NT2 europium 156
NT2 europium 157
NT2 europium 158
NT2 europium 159
NT2 europium 160
NT2 europium 161
NT2 europium 162
NT2 gadolinium 137
NT2 gadolinium 138
NT2 gadolinium 139
NT2 gadolinium 140
NT2 gadolinium 141
NT2 gadolinium 142
NT2 gadolinium 143
NT2 gadolinium 144
NT2 gadolinium 145
NT2 gadolinium 146
NT2 gadolinium 147
NT2 gadolinium 148
NT2 gadolinium 149
NT2 gadolinium 150
NT2 gadolinium 151
NT2 gadolinium 152
NT2 gadolinium 153
NT2 gadolinium 154
NT2 gadolinium 155
NT2 gadolinium 156
NT2 gadolinium 157
NT2 gadolinium 158
NT2 gadolinium 159
NT2 gadolinium 160
NT2 gadolinium 161
NT2 gadolinium 162
NT2 gadolinium 163
NT2 gadolinium 164
NT2 holmium 144
NT2 holmium 145
NT2 holmium 146
NT2 holmium 147
NT2 holmium 148
NT2 holmium 149
NT2 holmium 150
NT2 holmium 151
NT2 holmium 152
NT2 holmium 153
NT2 holmium 154
NT2 holmium 155
NT2 holmium 156
NT2 holmium 157
NT2 holmium 158
NT2 holmium 159
NT2 holmium 160
NT2 holmium 161
NT2 holmium 162
NT2 holmium 163
NT2 holmium 164
NT2 holmium 165
NT2 holmium 166
NT2 holmium 167
NT2 holmium 168
NT2 holmium 169
NT2 holmium 170
NT2 holmium 171
NT2 holmium 172
NT2 lanthanum 120
NT2 lanthanum 121
NT2 lanthanum 122
NT2 lanthanum 123
NT2 lanthanum 124
NT2 lanthanum 125
NT2 lanthanum 126
NT2 lanthanum 127
NT2 lanthanum 128
NT2 lanthanum 129
NT2 lanthanum 130
NT2 lanthanum 131
NT2 lanthanum 132
NT2 lanthanum 133
NT2 lanthanum 134
NT2 lanthanum 135
NT2 lanthanum 136
NT2 lanthanum 137
NT2 lanthanum 138
NT2 lanthanum 139
NT2 lanthanum 140
NT2 lanthanum 141
NT2 lanthanum 142
NT2 lanthanum 143
NT2 lanthanum 144
NT2 lanthanum 145
NT2 lanthanum 146
NT2 lanthanum 147
NT2 lanthanum 148
NT2 lanthanum 149
NT2 lutetium 151
NT2 lutetium 152
NT2 lutetium 153
NT2 lutetium 154
NT2 lutetium 155
NT2 lutetium 156
NT2 lutetium 157
NT2 lutetium 158
NT2 lutetium 159
NT2 lutetium 160
NT2 lutetium 161
NT2 lutetium 162
NT2 lutetium 163
NT2 lutetium 164
NT2 lutetium 165
NT2 lutetium 166
NT2 lutetium 167
NT2 lutetium 168
NT2 lutetium 169
NT2 lutetium 170
NT2 lutetium 171
NT2 lutetium 172
NT2 lutetium 173
NT2 lutetium 174
NT2 lutetium 175
NT2 lutetium 176
NT2 lutetium 177
NT2 lutetium 178
NT2 lutetium 179
NT2 lutetium 180
NT2 lutetium 181
NT2 lutetium 182
NT2 lutetium 183
NT2 lutetium 184
NT2 neodymium 127
NT2 neodymium 128
NT2 neodymium 129
NT2 neodymium 130
NT2 neodymium 131
NT2 neodymium 132
NT2 neodymium 133
NT2 neodymium 134
NT2 neodymium 135
NT2 neodymium 136
NT2 neodymium 137
NT2 neodymium 138
NT2 neodymium 139
NT2 neodymium 140
NT2 neodymium 141
NT2 neodymium 142
NT2 neodymium 143
NT2 neodymium 144
NT2 neodymium 145
NT2 neodymium 146
NT2 neodymium 147
NT2 neodymium 148
NT2 neodymium 149
NT2 neodymium 150
NT2 neodymium 151
NT2 neodymium 152
NT2 neodymium 153
NT2 neodymium 154
NT2 neodymium 155
NT2 neodymium 156
NT2 praseodymium 124
NT2 praseodymium 126
NT2 praseodymium 128
NT2 praseodymium 129
NT2 praseodymium 130
NT2 praseodymium 131
NT2 praseodymium 132
NT2 praseodymium 133
NT2 praseodymium 134
NT2 praseodymium 135
NT2 praseodymium 136
NT2 praseodymium 137
NT2 praseodymium 138
NT2 praseodymium 139
NT2 praseodymium 140
NT2 praseodymium 141
NT2 praseodymium 142
NT2 praseodymium 143
NT2 praseodymium 144
NT2 praseodymium 145
NT2 praseodymium 146
NT2 praseodymium 147
NT2 praseodymium 148
NT2 praseodymium 149
NT2 praseodymium 150
NT2 praseodymium 151
NT2 praseodymium 152
NT2 praseodymium 153
NT2 praseodymium 154
NT2 promethium 130
NT2 promethium 132
NT2 promethium 133
NT2 promethium 134
NT2 promethium 135
NT2 promethium 136
NT2 promethium 137
NT2 promethium 138
NT2 promethium 139
NT2 promethium 140
NT2 promethium 141
NT2 promethium 142
NT2 promethium 143
NT2 promethium 144
NT2 promethium 145
NT2 promethium 146
NT2 promethium 147
NT2 promethium 148
NT2 promethium 149
NT2 promethium 150
NT2 promethium 151
NT2 promethium 152
NT2 promethium 153
NT2 promethium 154
NT2 promethium 155
NT2 promethium 156
NT2 promethium 157
NT2 promethium 158
NT2 samarium 131
NT2 samarium 133
NT2 samarium 134
NT2 samarium 135
NT2 samarium 136
NT2 samarium 137
NT2 samarium 138
NT2 samarium 139
NT2 samarium 140
NT2 samarium 141
NT2 samarium 142
NT2 samarium 143
NT2 samarium 144
NT2 samarium 145
NT2 samarium 146
NT2 samarium 147
NT2 samarium 148
NT2 samarium 149
NT2 samarium 150
NT2 samarium 151
NT2 samarium 152
NT2 samarium 153
NT2 samarium 154
NT2 samarium 155
NT2 samarium 156
NT2 samarium 157
NT2 samarium 158
NT2 samarium 159
NT2 samarium 160
NT2 terbium 140
NT2 terbium 141
NT2 terbium 143
NT2 terbium 144
NT2 terbium 145
NT2 terbium 146
NT2 terbium 147
NT2 terbium 148
NT2 terbium 149
NT2 terbium 150
NT2 terbium 151
NT2 terbium 152
NT2 terbium 153
NT2 terbium 154
NT2 terbium 155
NT2 terbium 156
NT2 terbium 157
NT2 terbium 158
NT2 terbium 159
NT2 terbium 160
NT2 terbium 161
NT2 terbium 162
NT2 terbium 163
NT2 terbium 164
NT2 terbium 165
NT2 thulium 147
NT2 thulium 148
NT2 thulium 149
NT2 thulium 150
NT2 thulium 151
NT2 thulium 152
NT2 thulium 153
NT2 thulium 154
NT2 thulium 155
NT2 thulium 156
NT2 thulium 157
NT2 thulium 158
NT2 thulium 159
NT2 thulium 160
NT2 thulium 161
NT2 thulium 162
NT2 thulium 163
NT2 thulium 164
NT2 thulium 165
NT2 thulium 166
NT2 thulium 167
NT2 thulium 168
NT2 thulium 169
NT2 thulium 170
NT2 thulium 171
NT2 thulium 172
NT2 thulium 173
NT2 thulium 174
NT2 thulium 175
NT2 thulium 176
NT2 thulium 177
NT2 ytterbium 150
NT2 ytterbium 151
NT2 ytterbium 152
NT2 ytterbium 153
NT2 ytterbium 154
NT2 ytterbium 155
NT2 ytterbium 156
NT2 ytterbium 157
NT2 ytterbium 158
NT2 ytterbium 159
NT2 ytterbium 160

NT2	ytterbium 161	NT1	rubidium 96	NT1	silver 123	NT1	tellurium 108
NT2	ytterbium 162	NT1	rubidium 97	NT1	silver 95	NT1	tellurium 109
NT2	ytterbium 163	NT1	rubidium 98	NT1	silver 96	NT1	tellurium 110
NT2	ytterbium 164	NT1	rubidium 99	NT1	silver 97	NT1	tellurium 111
NT2	ytterbium 165	NT1	ruthenium 100	NT1	silver 98	NT1	tellurium 112
NT2	ytterbium 166	NT1	ruthenium 101	NT1	silver 99	NT1	tellurium 113
NT2	ytterbium 167	NT1	ruthenium 102	NT1	strontium 100	NT1	tellurium 114
NT2	ytterbium 168	NT1	ruthenium 103	NT1	strontium 101	NT1	tellurium 115
NT2	ytterbium 169	NT1	ruthenium 104	NT1	strontium 102	NT1	tellurium 116
NT2	ytterbium 170	NT1	ruthenium 105	NT1	strontium 77	NT1	tellurium 117
NT2	ytterbium 171	NT1	ruthenium 106	NT1	strontium 78	NT1	tellurium 118
NT2	ytterbium 172	NT1	ruthenium 107	NT1	strontium 79	NT1	tellurium 119
NT2	ytterbium 173	NT1	ruthenium 108	NT1	strontium 80	NT1	tellurium 120
NT2	ytterbium 174	NT1	ruthenium 109	NT1	strontium 81	NT1	tellurium 121
NT2	ytterbium 175	NT1	ruthenium 110	NT1	strontium 82	NT1	tellurium 122
NT2	ytterbium 176	NT1	ruthenium 111	NT1	strontium 83	NT1	tellurium 123
NT2	ytterbium 177	NT1	ruthenium 112	NT1	strontium 84	NT1	tellurium 124
NT2	ytterbium 178	NT1	ruthenium 113	NT1	strontium 85	NT1	tellurium 125
NT2	ytterbium 179	NT1	ruthenium 91	NT1	strontium 86	NT1	tellurium 126
NT2	ytterbium 180	NT1	ruthenium 92	NT1	strontium 87	NT1	tellurium 127
NT1	rhenium 161	NT1	ruthenium 93	NT1	strontium 88	NT1	tellurium 128
NT1	rhenium 162	NT1	ruthenium 94	NT1	strontium 89	NT1	tellurium 129
NT1	rhenium 163	NT1	ruthenium 95	NT1	strontium 90	NT1	tellurium 130
NT1	rhenium 164	NT1	ruthenium 96	NT1	strontium 91	NT1	tellurium 131
NT1	rhenium 165	NT1	ruthenium 97	NT1	strontium 92	NT1	tellurium 132
NT1	rhenium 166	NT1	ruthenium 98	NT1	strontium 93	NT1	tellurium 133
NT1	rhenium 167	NT1	ruthenium 99	NT1	strontium 94	NT1	tellurium 134
NT1	rhenium 168	NT1	scandium 41	NT1	strontium 95	NT1	tellurium 135
NT1	rhenium 169	NT1	scandium 42	NT1	strontium 96	NT1	tellurium 136
NT1	rhenium 170	NT1	scandium 43	NT1	strontium 97	NT1	tellurium 137
NT1	rhenium 171	NT1	scandium 44	NT1	strontium 98	NT1	tellurium 138
NT1	rhenium 172	NT1	scandium 45	NT1	strontium 99	NT1	thallium 179
NT1	rhenium 173	NT1	scandium 46	NT1	sulfur 41	NT1	tin 100
NT1	rhenium 174	NT1	scandium 47	NT1	sulfur 42	NT1	tin 102
NT1	rhenium 175	NT1	scandium 48	NT1	sulfur 43	NT1	tin 103
NT1	rhenium 176	NT1	scandium 49	NT1	sulfur 44	NT1	tin 104
NT1	rhenium 177	NT1	scandium 50	NT1	sulfur 45	NT1	tin 105
NT1	rhenium 178	NT1	scandium 51	NT1	sulfur 46	NT1	tin 106
NT1	rhenium 179	NT1	scandium 52	NT1	sulfur 47	NT1	tin 107
NT1	rhenium 180	NT1	scandium 53	NT1	sulfur 48	NT1	tin 108
NT1	rhodium 100	NT1	scandium 54	NT1	tantalum 156	NT1	tin 109
NT1	rhodium 101	NT1	scandium 55	NT1	tantalum 157	NT1	tin 110
NT1	rhodium 102	NT1	selenium 68	NT1	tantalum 158	NT1	tin 111
NT1	rhodium 103	NT1	selenium 69	NT1	tantalum 159	NT1	tin 112
NT1	rhodium 104	NT1	selenium 70	NT1	tantalum 160	NT1	tin 113
NT1	rhodium 105	NT1	selenium 71	NT1	tantalum 161	NT1	tin 114
NT1	rhodium 106	NT1	selenium 72	NT1	tantalum 162	NT1	tin 115
NT1	rhodium 107	NT1	selenium 73	NT1	tantalum 163	NT1	tin 116
NT1	rhodium 108	NT1	selenium 74	NT1	tantalum 164	NT1	tin 117
NT1	rhodium 109	NT1	selenium 75	NT1	tantalum 165	NT1	tin 118
NT1	rhodium 110	NT1	selenium 76	NT1	tantalum 166	NT1	tin 119
NT1	rhodium 111	NT1	selenium 77	NT1	tantalum 167	NT1	tin 120
NT1	rhodium 112	NT1	selenium 78	NT1	tantalum 168	NT1	tin 121
NT1	rhodium 113	NT1	selenium 79	NT1	tantalum 169	NT1	tin 122
NT1	rhodium 114	NT1	selenium 80	NT1	tantalum 170	NT1	tin 123
NT1	rhodium 115	NT1	selenium 81	NT1	tantalum 171	NT1	tin 124
NT1	rhodium 116	NT1	selenium 82	NT1	tantalum 172	NT1	tin 125
NT1	rhodium 117	NT1	selenium 83	NT1	tantalum 173	NT1	tin 126
NT1	rhodium 94	NT1	selenium 84	NT1	tantalum 174	NT1	tin 127
NT1	rhodium 95	NT1	selenium 85	NT1	tantalum 175	NT1	tin 128
NT1	rhodium 96	NT1	selenium 86	NT1	tantalum 176	NT1	tin 129
NT1	rhodium 97	NT1	selenium 87	NT1	tantalum 177	NT1	tin 130
NT1	rhodium 98	NT1	selenium 88	NT1	tantalum 178	NT1	tin 131
NT1	rhodium 99	NT1	selenium 89	NT1	tantalum 179	NT1	tin 132
NT1	rubidium 100	NT1	selenium 91	NT1	tantalum 180	NT1	tin 133
NT1	rubidium 101	NT1	silicon 41	NT1	technetium 100	NT1	tin 134
NT1	rubidium 102	NT1	silicon 42	NT1	technetium 101	NT1	titanium 41
NT1	rubidium 103	NT1	silver 100	NT1	technetium 102	NT1	titanium 42
NT1	rubidium 74	NT1	silver 101	NT1	technetium 103	NT1	titanium 43
NT1	rubidium 75	NT1	silver 102	NT1	technetium 104	NT1	titanium 44
NT1	rubidium 76	NT1	silver 103	NT1	technetium 105	NT1	titanium 45
NT1	rubidium 77	NT1	silver 104	NT1	technetium 106	NT1	titanium 46
NT1	rubidium 78	NT1	silver 105	NT1	technetium 107	NT1	titanium 47
NT1	rubidium 79	NT1	silver 106	NT1	technetium 108	NT1	titanium 48
NT1	rubidium 80	NT1	silver 107	NT1	technetium 109	NT1	titanium 49
NT1	rubidium 81	NT1	silver 108	NT1	technetium 110	NT1	titanium 50
NT1	rubidium 82	NT1	silver 109	NT1	technetium 111	NT1	titanium 51
NT1	rubidium 83	NT1	silver 110	NT1	technetium 112	NT1	titanium 52
NT1	rubidium 84	NT1	silver 111	NT1	technetium 90	NT1	titanium 53
NT1	rubidium 85	NT1	silver 112	NT1	technetium 91	NT1	titanium 54
NT1	rubidium 86	NT1	silver 113	NT1	technetium 92	NT1	titanium 55
NT1	rubidium 87	NT1	silver 114	NT1	technetium 93	NT1	titanium 56
NT1	rubidium 88	NT1	silver 115	NT1	technetium 94	NT1	titanium 57
NT1	rubidium 89	NT1	silver 116	NT1	technetium 95	NT1	tungsten 158
NT1	rubidium 90	NT1	silver 117	NT1	technetium 96	NT1	tungsten 159
NT1	rubidium 91	NT1	silver 118	NT1	technetium 97	NT1	tungsten 160
NT1	rubidium 92	NT1	silver 119	NT1	technetium 98	NT1	tungsten 161
NT1	rubidium 93	NT1	silver 120	NT1	technetium 99	NT1	tungsten 162
NT1	rubidium 94	NT1	silver 121	NT1	tellurium 106	NT1	tungsten 163
NT1	rubidium 95	NT1	silver 122	NT1	tellurium 107	NT1	tungsten 164

NT1	tungsten 165	NT1	yttrium 96	NT1	gold 197	NT1	technetium 97
NT1	tungsten 166	NT1	yttrium 97	NT1	hafnium 178	NT1	technetium 99
NT1	tungsten 167	NT1	yttrium 98	NT1	hafnium 179	NT1	tellurium 121
NT1	tungsten 168	NT1	yttrium 99	NT1	hafnium 180	NT1	tellurium 123
NT1	tungsten 169	NT1	zinc 57	NT1	holmium 158	NT1	tellurium 125
NT1	tungsten 170	NT1	zinc 58	NT1	holmium 160	NT1	terbium 151
NT1	tungsten 171	NT1	zinc 59	NT1	holmium 164	NT1	terbium 157
NT1	tungsten 172	NT1	zinc 60	NT1	indium 112	NT1	terbium 158
NT1	tungsten 173	NT1	zinc 61	NT1	indium 114	NT1	thallium 198
NT1	tungsten 174	NT1	zinc 62	NT1	indium 115	NT1	thorium 234
NT1	tungsten 175	NT1	zinc 63	NT1	indium 116	NT1	thulium 159
NT1	tungsten 176	NT1	zinc 64	NT1	indium 121	NT1	thulium 161
NT1	tungsten 177	NT1	zinc 65	NT1	iodine 125	NT1	tin 113
NT1	tungsten 178	NT1	zinc 66	NT1	iodine 129	NT1	tin 119
NT1	tungsten 179	NT1	zinc 67	NT1	iodine 130	NT1	tin 121
NT1	tungsten 180	NT1	zinc 68	NT1	iodine 132	NT1	tungsten 176
NT1	vanadium 42	NT1	zinc 69	NT1	iodine 133	NT1	tungsten 181
NT1	vanadium 44	NT1	zinc 70	NT1	iridium 190	NT1	tungsten 185
NT1	vanadium 45	NT1	zinc 71	NT1	iridium 191	NT1	uranium 230
NT1	vanadium 46	NT1	zinc 72	NT1	iridium 192	NT1	uranium 235
NT1	vanadium 47	NT1	zinc 73	NT1	iridium 193	NT1	uranium 240
NT1	vanadium 48	NT1	zinc 74	NT1	krypton 79	NT1	xenon 125
NT1	vanadium 49	NT1	zinc 75	NT1	krypton 83	NT1	xenon 129
NT1	vanadium 50	NT1	zinc 76	NT1	lead 199	NT1	xenon 131
NT1	vanadium 51	NT1	zinc 77	NT1	lead 202	NT1	xenon 133
NT1	vanadium 52	NT1	zinc 78	NT1	lutetium 169	NT1	ytterbium 164
NT1	vanadium 53	NT1	zinc 79	NT1	lutetium 170	NT1	ytterbium 165
NT1	vanadium 54	NT1	zinc 80	NT1	lutetium 171	NT1	ytterbium 166
NT1	vanadium 55	NT1	zirconium 100	NT1	lutetium 172	NT1	ytterbium 177
NT1	vanadium 56	NT1	zirconium 101	NT1	lutetium 176	NT1	yttrium 86
NT1	vanadium 57	NT1	zirconium 102	NT1	mercury 193		
NT1	vanadium 58	NT1	zirconium 103	NT1	mercury 195	**ISOMERIC TRANSITION**	
NT1	vanadium 59	NT1	zirconium 104	NT1	mercury 197	**ISOTOPES**	
NT1	vanadium 60	NT1	zirconium 80	NT1	mercury 199	NT1	actinium 222
NT1	xenon 110	NT1	zirconium 81	NT1	molybdenum 93	NT1	aluminium 24
NT1	xenon 111	NT1	zirconium 82	NT1	neodymium 147	NT1	americium 242
NT1	xenon 112	NT1	zirconium 83	NT1	neptunium 236	NT1	antimony 113
NT1	xenon 113	NT1	zirconium 84	NT1	niobium 91	NT1	antimony 117
NT1	xenon 114	NT1	zirconium 85	NT1	niobium 93	NT1	antimony 122
NT1	xenon 115	NT1	zirconium 86	NT1	niobium 94	NT1	antimony 124
NT1	xenon 116	NT1	zirconium 87	NT1	osmium 180	NT1	antimony 126
NT1	xenon 117	NT1	zirconium 88	NT1	osmium 189	NT1	antimony 131
NT1	xenon 118	NT1	zirconium 89	NT1	osmium 190	NT1	astatine 202
NT1	xenon 119	NT1	zirconium 90	NT1	osmium 191	NT1	barium 131
NT1	xenon 120	NT1	zirconium 91	NT1	osmium 194	NT1	barium 133
NT1	xenon 121	NT1	zirconium 92	NT1	palladium 112	NT1	barium 135
NT1	xenon 122	NT1	zirconium 93	NT1	platinum 193	NT1	barium 136
NT1	xenon 123	NT1	zirconium 94	NT1	platinum 195	NT1	barium 137
NT1	xenon 124	NT1	zirconium 95	NT1	platinum 197	NT1	barium 138
NT1	xenon 125	NT1	zirconium 96	NT1	platinum 199	NT1	bismuth 198
NT1	xenon 126	NT1	zirconium 97	NT1	plutonium 235	NT1	bismuth 201
NT1	xenon 127	NT1	zirconium 98	NT1	plutonium 237	NT1	bismuth 211
NT1	xenon 128	NT1	zirconium 99	NT1	polonium 199	NT1	bromine 76
NT1	xenon 129			NT1	polonium 201	NT1	bromine 77
NT1	xenon 130	**INTERNAL CONVERSION**		NT1	polonium 202	NT1	bromine 79
NT1	xenon 131	**RADIOISOTO**		NT1	polonium 203	NT1	bromine 80
NT1	xenon 132	NT1	actinium 227	NT1	polonium 205	NT1	bromine 82
NT1	xenon 133	NT1	antimony 119	NT1	polonium 206	NT1	bromine 83
NT1	xenon 134	NT1	antimony 122	NT1	polonium 207	NT1	cadmium 100
NT1	xenon 135	NT1	antimony 124	NT1	praseodymium 142	NT1	cadmium 111
NT1	xenon 136	NT1	antimony 126	NT1	promethium 145	NT1	cadmium 113
NT1	xenon 137	NT1	astatine 212	NT1	radium 213	NT1	cerium 135
NT1	xenon 138	NT1	barium 131	NT1	radium 225	NT1	cerium 137
NT1	xenon 139	NT1	barium 133	NT1	radium 228	NT1	cerium 139
NT1	xenon 140	NT1	barium 135	NT1	radium 230	NT1	cesium 121
NT1	xenon 141	NT1	berkelium 243	NT1	radon 210	NT1	cesium 123
NT1	xenon 142	NT1	bromine 77	NT1	radon 211	NT1	cesium 134
NT1	xenon 143	NT1	bromine 80	NT1	rhenium 183	NT1	cesium 135
NT1	xenon 144	NT1	bromine 82	NT1	rhenium 184	NT1	cesium 136
NT1	xenon 145	NT1	cadmium 111	NT1	rhenium 188	NT1	cesium 138
NT1	yttrium 100	NT1	cadmium 113	NT1	rhenium 189	NT1	chlorine 34
NT1	yttrium 101	NT1	californium 247	NT1	rhodium 100	NT1	chlorine 38
NT1	yttrium 102	NT1	californium 250	NT1	rhodium 101	NT1	cobalt 58
NT1	yttrium 77	NT1	cerium 133	NT1	rhodium 103	NT1	cobalt 60
NT1	yttrium 80	NT1	cerium 137	NT1	rhodium 105	NT1	copper 68
NT1	yttrium 81	NT1	cesium 123	NT1	rhodium 96	NT1	dysprosium 147
NT1	yttrium 82	NT1	cesium 134	NT1	rubidium 81	NT1	dysprosium 149
NT1	yttrium 83	NT1	cesium 138	NT1	samarium 145	NT1	dysprosium 165
NT1	yttrium 84	NT1	cobalt 58	NT1	samarium 151	NT1	erbium 151
NT1	yttrium 85	NT1	cobalt 60	NT1	scandium 46	NT1	erbium 167
NT1	yttrium 86	NT1	dysprosium 159	NT1	selenium 79	NT1	europium 141
NT1	yttrium 87	NT1	einsteinium 254	NT1	selenium 81	NT1	europium 152
NT1	yttrium 88	NT1	erbium 156	NT1	silver 103	NT1	europium 154
NT1	yttrium 89	NT1	erbium 169	NT1	silver 105	NT1	fermium 250
NT1	yttrium 90	NT1	germanium 73	NT1	silver 107	NT1	fermium 256
NT1	yttrium 91	NT1	germanium 75	NT1	silver 109	NT1	fluorine 18
NT1	yttrium 92	NT1	gold 191	NT1	silver 111	NT1	francium 206
NT1	yttrium 93	NT1	gold 193	NT1	silver 99	NT1	francium 211
NT1	yttrium 94	NT1	gold 195	NT1	tantalum 182	NT1	francium 212
NT1	yttrium 95	NT1	gold 196	NT1	technetium 96	NT1	francium 213

ISOMERIC TRANSITION ISOTOPES

- NT1 gadolinium 141
- NT1 gadolinium 145
- NT1 gadolinium 147
- NT1 gadolinium 148
- NT1 gallium 74
- NT1 germanium 73
- NT1 germanium 75
- NT1 germanium 77
- NT1 gold 191
- NT1 gold 193
- NT1 gold 195
- NT1 gold 196
- NT1 gold 197
- NT1 gold 198
- NT1 gold 200
- NT1 hafnium 177
- NT1 hafnium 178
- NT1 hafnium 179
- NT1 hafnium 180
- NT1 hafnium 182
- NT1 holmium 148
- NT1 holmium 156
- NT1 holmium 158
- NT1 holmium 159
- NT1 holmium 160
- NT1 holmium 161
- NT1 holmium 162
- NT1 holmium 163
- NT1 holmium 164
- NT1 holmium 168
- NT1 indium 104
- NT1 indium 107
- NT1 indium 109
- NT1 indium 111
- NT1 indium 112
- NT1 indium 113
- NT1 indium 114
- NT1 indium 115
- NT1 indium 116
- NT1 indium 117
- NT1 indium 118
- NT1 indium 119
- NT1 indium 121
- NT1 iodine 116
- NT1 iodine 121
- NT1 iodine 122
- NT1 iodine 130
- NT1 iodine 132
- NT1 iodine 133
- NT1 iodine 134
- NT1 iridium 190
- NT1 iridium 191
- NT1 iridium 192
- NT1 iridium 193
- NT1 iron 53
- NT1 krypton 79
- NT1 krypton 81
- NT1 krypton 83
- NT1 krypton 84
- NT1 krypton 85
- NT1 krypton 86
- NT1 lanthanum 132
- NT1 lead 194
- NT1 lead 197
- NT1 lead 199
- NT1 lead 200
- NT1 lead 201
- NT1 lead 202
- NT1 lead 203
- NT1 lead 204
- NT1 lead 207
- NT1 lutetium 153
- NT1 lutetium 154
- NT1 lutetium 169
- NT1 lutetium 170
- NT1 lutetium 171
- NT1 lutetium 172
- NT1 lutetium 174
- NT1 lutetium 177
- NT1 mercury 193
- NT1 mercury 195
- NT1 mercury 197
- NT1 mercury 199
- NT1 mercury 201
- NT1 molybdenum 89
- NT1 molybdenum 91
- NT1 molybdenum 92
- NT1 molybdenum 93
- NT1 molybdenum 94
- NT1 neodymium 137
- NT1 neodymium 139
- NT1 neodymium 141
- NT1 neptunium 237
- NT1 niobium 90
- NT1 niobium 91
- NT1 niobium 93
- NT1 niobium 94
- NT1 niobium 95
- NT1 niobium 97
- NT1 nobelium 254
- NT1 osmium 182
- NT1 osmium 183
- NT1 osmium 189
- NT1 osmium 190
- NT1 osmium 191
- NT1 osmium 192
- NT1 palladium 107
- NT1 palladium 109
- NT1 palladium 111
- NT1 palladium 117
- NT1 platinum 193
- NT1 platinum 195
- NT1 platinum 197
- NT1 platinum 199
- NT1 plutonium 237
- NT1 polonium 201
- NT1 polonium 203
- NT1 polonium 207
- NT1 polonium 210
- NT1 potassium 40
- NT1 praseodymium 142
- NT1 praseodymium 144
- NT1 promethium 148
- NT1 protactinium 234
- NT1 radium 213
- NT1 radon 210
- NT1 radon 211
- NT1 rhenium 184
- NT1 rhenium 186
- NT1 rhenium 188
- NT1 rhenium 190
- NT1 rhodium 100
- NT1 rhodium 101
- NT1 rhodium 103
- NT1 rhodium 104
- NT1 rhodium 105
- NT1 rhodium 95
- NT1 rhodium 96
- NT1 rhodium 97
- NT1 rubidium 76
- NT1 rubidium 78
- NT1 rubidium 81
- NT1 rubidium 84
- NT1 rubidium 85
- NT1 rubidium 86
- NT1 rubidium 90
- NT1 ruthenium 93
- NT1 samarium 139
- NT1 samarium 141
- NT1 samarium 143
- NT1 scandium 44
- NT1 scandium 46
- NT1 scandium 50
- NT1 selenium 73
- NT1 selenium 77
- NT1 selenium 79
- NT1 selenium 81
- NT1 silver 101
- NT1 silver 102
- NT1 silver 103
- NT1 silver 105
- NT1 silver 107
- NT1 silver 108
- NT1 silver 109
- NT1 silver 110
- NT1 silver 111
- NT1 silver 113
- NT1 silver 116
- NT1 silver 118
- NT1 silver 120
- NT1 silver 99
- NT1 sodium 22
- NT1 sodium 24
- NT1 strontium 83
- NT1 strontium 85
- NT1 strontium 87
- NT1 tantalum 182
- NT1 technetium 102
- NT1 technetium 93
- NT1 technetium 95
- NT1 technetium 96
- NT1 technetium 97
- NT1 technetium 99
- NT1 tellurium 121
- NT1 tellurium 123
- NT1 tellurium 125
- NT1 tellurium 127
- NT1 tellurium 129
- NT1 tellurium 131
- NT1 tellurium 133
- NT1 terbium 144
- NT1 terbium 146
- NT1 terbium 151
- NT1 terbium 152
- NT1 terbium 154
- NT1 terbium 156
- NT1 terbium 158
- NT1 thallium 179
- NT1 thallium 185
- NT1 thallium 186
- NT1 thallium 187
- NT1 thallium 193
- NT1 thallium 195
- NT1 thallium 196
- NT1 thallium 197
- NT1 thallium 198
- NT1 thallium 206
- NT1 thallium 207
- NT1 thulium 150
- NT1 thulium 162
- NT1 thulium 164
- NT1 tin 113
- NT1 tin 117
- NT1 tin 119
- NT1 tin 121
- NT1 tungsten 179
- NT1 tungsten 183
- NT1 tungsten 185
- NT1 uranium 235
- NT1 xenon 125
- NT1 xenon 127
- NT1 xenon 129
- NT1 xenon 131
- NT1 xenon 133
- NT1 xenon 135
- NT1 ytterbium 153
- NT1 ytterbium 169
- NT1 ytterbium 176
- NT1 ytterbium 177
- NT1 yttrium 86
- NT1 yttrium 87
- NT1 yttrium 89
- NT1 yttrium 90
- NT1 yttrium 91
- NT1 yttrium 93
- NT1 yttrium 97
- NT1 zinc 69
- NT1 zirconium 85
- NT1 zirconium 87
- NT1 zirconium 89
- NT1 zirconium 90

LIGHT NUCLEI

- NT1 aluminium 22
- NT1 aluminium 23
- NT1 aluminium 24
- NT1 aluminium 25
- NT1 aluminium 26
- NT1 aluminium 27
- NT1 aluminium 28
- NT1 aluminium 29
- NT1 aluminium 30
- NT1 aluminium 31
- NT1 aluminium 32
- NT1 aluminium 33
- NT1 aluminium 34
- NT1 aluminium 35
- NT1 aluminium 36
- NT1 aluminium 37
- NT1 aluminium 38
- NT1 aluminium 39
- NT1 argon 31
- NT1 argon 32
- NT1 argon 33
- NT1 argon 34
- NT1 argon 35
- NT1 argon 36
- NT1 argon 37
- NT1 argon 38
- NT1 argon 39
- NT1 argon 40
- NT1 beryllium 10
- NT1 beryllium 11
- NT1 beryllium 12
- NT1 beryllium 13
- NT1 beryllium 14
- NT1 beryllium 5
- NT1 beryllium 6
- NT1 beryllium 7
- NT1 beryllium 8
- NT1 beryllium 9
- NT1 boron 10
- NT1 boron 11
- NT1 boron 12
- NT1 boron 13
- NT1 boron 14
- NT1 boron 15
- NT1 boron 17
- NT1 boron 18
- NT1 boron 19
- NT1 boron 7
- NT1 boron 8
- NT1 boron 9
- NT1 calcium 35
- NT1 calcium 36
- NT1 calcium 37
- NT1 calcium 38
- NT1 calcium 39
- NT1 calcium 40
- NT1 carbon 10
- NT1 carbon 11
- NT1 carbon 12
- NT1 carbon 13
- NT1 carbon 14
- NT1 carbon 15
- NT1 carbon 16
- NT1 carbon 17
- NT1 carbon 18
- NT1 carbon 19
- NT1 carbon 20
- NT1 carbon 22
- NT1 carbon 8
- NT1 carbon 9
- NT1 chlorine 31
- NT1 chlorine 32
- NT1 chlorine 33
- NT1 chlorine 34
- NT1 chlorine 35
- NT1 chlorine 36
- NT1 chlorine 37
- NT1 chlorine 38
- NT1 chlorine 39
- NT1 chlorine 40
- NT1 deuterium
- NT1 fluorine 14
- NT1 fluorine 15
- NT1 fluorine 16
- NT1 fluorine 17
- NT1 fluorine 18
- NT1 fluorine 19
- NT1 fluorine 20
- NT1 fluorine 21
- NT1 fluorine 22
- NT1 fluorine 23
- NT1 fluorine 24
- NT1 fluorine 25
- NT1 fluorine 26
- NT1 fluorine 27
- NT1 fluorine 29
- NT1 helium 10
- NT1 helium 2
- NT1 helium 3
- NT2 helium 3 a
- NT2 helium 3 a1
- NT2 helium 3 b
- NT1 helium 4
- NT2 helium i
- NT2 helium ii
- NT1 helium 5
- NT1 helium 6
- NT1 helium 7
- NT1 helium 8
- NT1 helium 9
- NT1 hydrogen 1
- NT1 hydrogen 4
- NT1 hydrogen 5
- NT1 hydrogen 6
- NT1 hydrogen 7
- NT1 lithium 10
- NT1 lithium 11

LIGHT NUCLEI / A-23 / MILLISEC LIVING RADIOISOTOPES

NT1	lithium 13	NT1	potassium 40	NT1	radon 217	NT1	cobalt 67
NT1	lithium 3	NT1	scandium 39	NT1	rubidium 76	NT1	copper 57
NT1	lithium 4	NT1	scandium 40	NT1	tellurium 106	NT1	dysprosium 149
NT1	lithium 5	NT1	silicon 22	NT1	thorium 217	NT1	element 104 256
NT1	lithium 6	NT1	silicon 23	NT1	thorium 219	NT1	element 104 258
NT1	lithium 7	NT1	silicon 24	NT1	thorium 220	NT1	element 104 260
NT1	lithium 8	NT1	silicon 25	NT1	uranium 222	NT1	element 104 262
NT1	lithium 9	NT1	silicon 26	NT1	uranium 223	NT1	element 106 259
NT1	magnesium 20	NT1	silicon 27	NT1	uranium 224	NT1	element 106 260
NT1	magnesium 21	NT1	silicon 28	NT1	ytterbium 153	NT1	element 106 261
NT1	magnesium 22	NT1	silicon 29			NT1	element 106 263
NT1	magnesium 23	NT1	silicon 30	**MILLISEC LIVING**		NT1	element 107 261
NT1	magnesium 24	NT1	silicon 31	**RADIOISOTOPES**		NT1	element 107 262
NT1	magnesium 25	NT1	silicon 32	NT1	actinium 209	NT1	element 108 265
NT1	magnesium 26	NT1	silicon 33	NT1	actinium 210	NT1	erbium 151
NT1	magnesium 27	NT1	silicon 34	NT1	actinium 211	NT1	europium 134
NT1	magnesium 28	NT1	silicon 35	NT1	actinium 212	NT1	fermium 243
NT1	magnesium 29	NT1	silicon 36	NT1	actinium 213	NT1	fermium 244
NT1	magnesium 30	NT1	silicon 37	NT1	actinium 215	NT1	fluorine 24
NT1	magnesium 31	NT1	silicon 38	NT1	actinium 220	NT1	francium 201
NT1	magnesium 32	NT1	silicon 39	NT1	actinium 221	NT1	francium 202
NT1	magnesium 33	NT1	silicon 40	NT1	aluminium 22	NT1	francium 203
NT1	magnesium 34	NT1	sodium 19	NT1	aluminium 23	NT1	francium 206
NT1	magnesium 35	NT1	sodium 20	NT1	aluminium 24	NT1	francium 214
NT1	magnesium 36	NT1	sodium 21	NT1	aluminium 31	NT1	francium 219
NT1	neon 16	NT1	sodium 22	NT1	aluminium 32	NT1	gallium 62
NT1	neon 17	NT1	sodium 23	NT1	aluminium 34	NT1	gallium 82
NT1	neon 18	NT1	sodium 24	NT1	antimony 134	NT1	gallium 83
NT1	neon 19	NT1	sodium 25	NT1	antimony 136	NT1	germanium 61
NT1	neon 20	NT1	sodium 26	NT1	argon 31	NT1	germanium 73
NT1	neon 21	NT1	sodium 27	NT1	argon 32	NT1	germanium 85
NT1	neon 22	NT1	sodium 28	NT1	argon 33	NT1	gold 173
NT1	neon 23	NT1	sodium 29	NT1	argon 34	NT1	gold 174
NT1	neon 24	NT1	sodium 30	NT1	arsenic 66	NT1	gold 175
NT1	neon 25	NT1	sodium 31	NT1	arsenic 84	NT1	gold 191
NT1	neon 26	NT1	sodium 32	NT1	arsenic 86	NT1	hafnium 155
NT1	neon 27	NT1	sodium 33	NT1	arsenic 87	NT1	hafnium 156
NT1	neon 28	NT1	sodium 34	NT1	astatine 194	NT1	hafnium 157
NT1	neon 29	NT1	sodium 35	NT1	astatine 195	NT1	helium 6
NT1	neon 30	NT1	sulfur 24	NT1	astatine 196	NT1	helium 8
NT1	neon 32	NT1	sulfur 27	NT1	astatine 197	NT1	holmium 144
NT1	nitrogen 11	NT1	sulfur 28	NT1	astatine 212	NT1	holmium 148
NT1	nitrogen 12	NT1	sulfur 29	NT1	astatine 217	NT1	indium 114
NT1	nitrogen 13	NT1	sulfur 30	NT1	barium 136	NT1	indium 128
NT1	nitrogen 14	NT1	sulfur 31	NT1	barium 147	NT1	indium 129
NT1	nitrogen 15	NT1	sulfur 32	NT1	barium 148	NT1	indium 130
NT1	nitrogen 16	NT1	sulfur 33	NT1	barium 149	NT1	indium 131
NT1	nitrogen 17	NT1	sulfur 34	NT1	beryllium 12	NT1	indium 132
NT1	nitrogen 18	NT1	sulfur 35	NT1	beryllium 14	NT1	iodine 110
NT1	nitrogen 19	NT1	sulfur 36	NT1	boron 12	NT1	iodine 140
NT1	nitrogen 20	NT1	sulfur 37	NT1	boron 13	NT1	iodine 141
NT1	nitrogen 21	NT1	sulfur 38	NT1	boron 14	NT1	iodine 142
NT1	nitrogen 22	NT1	sulfur 39	NT1	boron 15	NT1	iridium 166
NT1	nitrogen 23	NT1	sulfur 40	NT1	boron 17	NT1	iridium 167
NT1	oxygen 12	NT1	titanium 39	NT1	boron 8	NT1	iridium 169
NT1	oxygen 13	NT1	titanium 40	NT1	bromine 70	NT1	iron 49
NT1	oxygen 14	NT1	tritium	NT1	bromine 91	NT1	iron 51
NT1	oxygen 15			NT1	bromine 92	NT1	krypton 71
NT1	oxygen 16	**MICROSEC LIVING**		NT1	bromine 93	NT1	krypton 94
NT1	oxygen 17	**RADIOISOTOPES**		NT1	cadmium 124	NT1	krypton 95
NT1	oxygen 18	NT1	actinium 216	NT1	cadmium 125	NT1	krypton 97
NT1	oxygen 19	NT1	actinium 218	NT1	cadmium 126	NT1	lawrencium 257
NT1	oxygen 20	NT1	actinium 219	NT1	cadmium 127	NT1	lead 182
NT1	oxygen 21	NT1	astatine 214	NT1	cadmium 128	NT1	lead 184
NT1	oxygen 22	NT1	astatine 215	NT1	cadmium 130	NT1	lead 207
NT1	oxygen 23	NT1	astatine 216	NT1	cadmium 96	NT1	lithium 10
NT1	oxygen 24	NT1	element 104 254	NT1	calcium 36	NT1	lithium 11
NT1	oxygen 28	NT1	element 108 264	NT1	calcium 37	NT1	lithium 8
NT1	phosphorus 21	NT1	fermium 242	NT1	calcium 38	NT1	lithium 9
NT1	phosphorus 24	NT1	fermium 258	NT1	calcium 39	NT1	lutetium 151
NT1	phosphorus 26	NT1	francium 212	NT1	calcium 53	NT1	lutetium 152
NT1	phosphorus 27	NT1	francium 213	NT1	carbon 16	NT1	lutetium 153
NT1	phosphorus 28	NT1	francium 217	NT1	carbon 17	NT1	lutetium 155
NT1	phosphorus 29	NT1	francium 218	NT1	carbon 18	NT1	lutetium 156
NT1	phosphorus 30	NT1	iodine 116	NT1	carbon 9	NT1	lutetium 170
NT1	phosphorus 31	NT1	iodine 121	NT1	cesium 114	NT1	magnesium 20
NT1	phosphorus 32	NT1	iodine 122	NT1	cesium 116	NT1	magnesium 21
NT1	phosphorus 33	NT1	krypton 84	NT1	cesium 145	NT1	magnesium 30
NT1	phosphorus 34	NT1	krypton 85	NT1	cesium 146	NT1	magnesium 31
NT1	phosphorus 35	NT1	lutetium 154	NT1	cesium 147	NT1	manganese 49
NT1	phosphorus 36	NT1	mercury 201	NT1	cesium 148	NT1	manganese 50
NT1	phosphorus 37	NT1	nobelium 250	NT1	chlorine 31	NT1	manganese 61
NT1	phosphorus 38	NT1	polonium 213	NT1	chlorine 32	NT1	manganese 62
NT1	phosphorus 39	NT1	polonium 214	NT1	chromium 45	NT1	manganese 63
NT1	phosphorus 40	NT1	protactinium 218	NT1	chromium 46	NT1	mercury 175
NT1	potassium 35	NT1	protactinium 221	NT1	chromium 47	NT1	mercury 176
NT1	potassium 36	NT1	radium 217	NT1	cobalt 53	NT1	mercury 177
NT1	potassium 37	NT1	radium 218	NT1	cobalt 54	NT1	mercury 178
NT1	potassium 38	NT1	radon 215	NT1	cobalt 64	NT1	molybdenum 89
NT1	potassium 39	NT1	radon 216	NT1	cobalt 66	NT1	neon 17

MILLISEC LIVING RADIOISOTOPES

- NT1 neon 25
- NT1 neon 26
- NT1 neptunium 226
- NT1 neptunium 227
- NT1 nickel 53
- NT1 nickel 55
- NT1 nickel 73
- NT1 nitrogen 12
- NT1 nitrogen 18
- NT1 nitrogen 19
- NT1 nobelium 251
- NT1 nobelium 254
- NT1 nobelium 258
- NT1 osmium 162
- NT1 osmium 164
- NT1 osmium 165
- NT1 osmium 166
- NT1 osmium 167
- NT1 oxygen 13
- NT1 oxygen 22
- NT1 palladium 117
- NT1 palladium 119
- NT1 phosphorus 26
- NT1 phosphorus 27
- NT1 phosphorus 28
- NT1 phosphorus 38
- NT1 platinum 169
- NT1 platinum 170
- NT1 platinum 171
- NT1 platinum 172
- NT1 platinum 173
- NT1 platinum 174
- NT1 plutonium 230
- NT1 polonium 192
- NT1 polonium 193
- NT1 polonium 194
- NT1 polonium 211
- NT1 polonium 215
- NT1 polonium 216
- NT1 potassium 35
- NT1 potassium 36
- NT1 potassium 50
- NT1 potassium 51
- NT1 potassium 52
- NT1 potassium 53
- NT1 potassium 54
- NT1 protactinium 215
- NT1 protactinium 216
- NT1 protactinium 217
- NT1 protactinium 222
- NT1 protactinium 223
- NT1 protactinium 224
- NT1 radium 205
- NT1 radium 206
- NT1 radium 213
- NT1 radium 215
- NT1 radium 219
- NT1 radium 220
- NT1 radon 199
- NT1 radon 213
- NT1 radon 218
- NT1 rhenium 161
- NT1 rhenium 162
- NT1 rhenium 163
- NT1 rhenium 164
- NT1 rhodium 112
- NT1 rhodium 115
- NT1 rhodium 116
- NT1 rubidium 100
- NT1 rubidium 74
- NT1 rubidium 95
- NT1 rubidium 96
- NT1 rubidium 97
- NT1 rubidium 98
- NT1 rubidium 99
- NT1 scandium 40
- NT1 scandium 41
- NT1 scandium 42
- NT1 scandium 50
- NT1 selenium 89
- NT1 selenium 91
- NT1 silicon 24
- NT1 silicon 25
- NT1 silicon 35
- NT1 silicon 36
- NT1 silver 120
- NT1 silver 121
- NT1 silver 123
- NT1 silver 95
- NT1 sodium 19
- NT1 sodium 24
- NT1 sodium 27
- NT1 sodium 28
- NT1 sodium 29
- NT1 sodium 30
- NT1 sodium 31
- NT1 sodium 32
- NT1 sodium 33
- NT1 sodium 34
- NT1 sodium 35
- NT1 strontium 100
- NT1 strontium 101
- NT1 strontium 102
- NT1 strontium 97
- NT1 strontium 98
- NT1 strontium 99
- NT1 sulfur 28
- NT1 sulfur 29
- NT1 tantalum 156
- NT1 tantalum 157
- NT1 tantalum 158
- NT1 tantalum 159
- NT1 tantalum 182
- NT1 technetium 110
- NT1 technetium 111
- NT1 technetium 112
- NT1 tellurium 107
- NT1 terbium 146
- NT1 thallium 179
- NT1 thorium 212
- NT1 thorium 213
- NT1 thorium 214
- NT1 thorium 216
- NT1 thorium 221
- NT1 thorium 222
- NT1 thorium 223
- NT1 thulium 147
- NT1 thulium 150
- NT1 titanium 40
- NT1 titanium 41
- NT1 titanium 42
- NT1 titanium 43
- NT1 tungsten 159
- NT1 tungsten 160
- NT1 tungsten 161
- NT1 uranium 225
- NT1 uranium 226
- NT1 vanadium 44
- NT1 vanadium 46
- NT1 xenon 110
- NT1 xenon 111
- NT1 xenon 143
- NT1 xenon 145
- NT1 ytterbium 154
- NT1 yttrium 100
- NT1 yttrium 101
- NT1 yttrium 102
- NT1 yttrium 93
- NT1 yttrium 97
- NT1 yttrium 98
- NT1 zinc 57
- NT1 zinc 59
- NT1 zinc 80
- NT1 zirconium 90

MINUTES LIVING RADIOISOTOPES

- NT1 actinium 222
- NT1 actinium 223
- NT1 actinium 230
- NT1 actinium 231
- NT1 actinium 232
- NT1 actinium 233
- NT1 aluminium 28
- NT1 aluminium 29
- NT1 americium 234
- NT1 americium 244
- NT1 americium 246
- NT1 americium 247
- NT1 antimony 111
- NT1 antimony 113
- NT1 antimony 114
- NT1 antimony 115
- NT1 antimony 116
- NT1 antimony 118
- NT1 antimony 120
- NT1 antimony 122
- NT1 antimony 124
- NT1 antimony 126
- NT1 antimony 128
- NT1 antimony 129
- NT1 antimony 130
- NT1 antimony 131
- NT1 antimony 132
- NT1 antimony 133
- NT1 argon 43
- NT1 argon 44
- NT1 arsenic 68
- NT1 arsenic 69
- NT1 arsenic 70
- NT1 arsenic 79
- NT1 astatine 201
- NT1 astatine 202
- NT1 astatine 203
- NT1 astatine 204
- NT1 astatine 205
- NT1 astatine 206
- NT1 astatine 220
- NT1 astatine 221
- NT1 barium 122
- NT1 barium 123
- NT1 barium 124
- NT1 barium 125
- NT1 barium 127
- NT1 barium 131
- NT1 barium 137
- NT1 barium 141
- NT1 barium 142
- NT1 berkelium 240
- NT1 berkelium 242
- NT1 berkelium 251
- NT1 bismuth 193
- NT1 bismuth 194
- NT1 bismuth 195
- NT1 bismuth 196
- NT1 bismuth 197
- NT1 bismuth 198
- NT1 bismuth 199
- NT1 bismuth 200
- NT1 bismuth 201
- NT1 bismuth 211
- NT1 bismuth 212
- NT1 bismuth 213
- NT1 bismuth 214
- NT1 bismuth 215
- NT1 bismuth 216
- NT1 bromine 72
- NT1 bromine 73
- NT1 bromine 74
- NT1 bromine 77
- NT1 bromine 78
- NT1 bromine 80
- NT1 bromine 82
- NT1 bromine 84
- NT1 bromine 85
- NT1 cadmium 100
- NT1 cadmium 101
- NT1 cadmium 102
- NT1 cadmium 103
- NT1 cadmium 104
- NT1 cadmium 105
- NT1 cadmium 111
- NT1 cadmium 118
- NT1 cadmium 119
- NT1 calcium 49
- NT1 californium 240
- NT1 californium 241
- NT1 californium 242
- NT1 californium 243
- NT1 californium 244
- NT1 californium 245
- NT1 californium 256
- NT1 carbon 11
- NT1 cerium 128
- NT1 cerium 129
- NT1 cerium 130
- NT1 cerium 131
- NT1 cerium 145
- NT1 cerium 146
- NT1 cesium 120
- NT1 cesium 121
- NT1 cesium 122
- NT1 cesium 123
- NT1 cesium 125
- NT1 cesium 126
- NT1 cesium 128
- NT1 cesium 130
- NT1 cesium 135
- NT1 cesium 138
- NT1 cesium 139
- NT1 cesium 140
- NT1 chlorine 34
- NT1 chlorine 38
- NT1 chlorine 39
- NT1 chlorine 40
- NT1 chromium 49
- NT1 chromium 55
- NT1 chromium 56
- NT1 cobalt 54
- NT1 cobalt 60
- NT1 cobalt 62
- NT1 copper 59
- NT1 copper 60
- NT1 copper 62
- NT1 copper 66
- NT1 copper 68
- NT1 copper 69
- NT1 curium 236
- NT1 curium 251
- NT1 dysprosium 147
- NT1 dysprosium 148
- NT1 dysprosium 149
- NT1 dysprosium 150
- NT1 dysprosium 151
- NT1 dysprosium 165
- NT1 dysprosium 167
- NT1 dysprosium 168
- NT1 einsteinium 245
- NT1 einsteinium 246
- NT1 einsteinium 247
- NT1 einsteinium 248
- NT1 einsteinium 256
- NT1 element 104 261
- NT1 erbium 154
- NT1 erbium 155
- NT1 erbium 156
- NT1 erbium 157
- NT1 erbium 159
- NT1 erbium 173
- NT1 erbium 174
- NT1 europium 142
- NT1 europium 143
- NT1 europium 154
- NT1 europium 158
- NT1 europium 159
- NT1 fermium 249
- NT1 fermium 250
- NT1 fluorine 17
- NT1 francium 210
- NT1 francium 211
- NT1 francium 212
- NT1 francium 221
- NT1 francium 222
- NT1 francium 223
- NT1 francium 224
- NT1 francium 225
- NT1 francium 227
- NT1 gadolinium 142
- NT1 gadolinium 143
- NT1 gadolinium 144
- NT1 gadolinium 145
- NT1 gadolinium 161
- NT1 gadolinium 162
- NT1 gadolinium 163
- NT1 gallium 64
- NT1 gallium 65
- NT1 gallium 70
- NT1 gallium 74
- NT1 gallium 75
- NT1 germanium 64
- NT1 germanium 67
- NT1 gold 185
- NT1 gold 186
- NT1 gold 187
- NT1 gold 188
- NT1 gold 189
- NT1 gold 190
- NT1 gold 200
- NT1 gold 201
- NT1 hafnium 164
- NT1 hafnium 165
- NT1 hafnium 166
- NT1 hafnium 167
- NT1 hafnium 168
- NT1 hafnium 169
- NT1 hafnium 177
- NT1 holmium 150
- NT1 holmium 152
- NT1 holmium 153
- NT1 holmium 154

NT1 holmium 155	NT1 manganese 50	NT1 polonium 200	NT1 ruthenium 93
NT1 holmium 156	NT1 manganese 51	NT1 polonium 201	NT1 ruthenium 94
NT1 holmium 157	NT1 manganese 52	NT1 polonium 202	NT1 samarium 138
NT1 holmium 158	NT1 manganese 57	NT1 polonium 203	NT1 samarium 139
NT1 holmium 159	NT1 manganese 58	NT1 polonium 218	NT1 samarium 140
NT1 holmium 160	NT1 mendelevium 251	NT1 potassium 38	NT1 samarium 141
NT1 holmium 162	NT1 mendelevium 252	NT1 potassium 44	NT1 samarium 143
NT1 holmium 164	NT1 mendelevium 254	NT1 potassium 45	NT1 samarium 155
NT1 holmium 168	NT1 mendelevium 255	NT1 potassium 46	NT1 samarium 157
NT1 holmium 169	NT1 mendelevium 258	NT1 praseodymium 131	NT1 samarium 158
NT1 holmium 170	NT1 mercury 186	NT1 praseodymium 132	NT1 scandium 49
NT1 indium 103	NT1 mercury 187	NT1 praseodymium 133	NT1 scandium 50
NT1 indium 104	NT1 mercury 188	NT1 praseodymium 134	NT1 selenium 68
NT1 indium 105	NT1 mercury 189	NT1 praseodymium 135	NT1 selenium 70
NT1 indium 106	NT1 mercury 190	NT1 praseodymium 136	NT1 selenium 71
NT1 indium 107	NT1 mercury 191	NT1 praseodymium 138	NT1 selenium 73
NT1 indium 108	NT1 mercury 199	NT1 praseodymium 140	NT1 selenium 79
NT1 indium 109	NT1 mercury 205	NT1 praseodymium 142	NT1 selenium 81
NT1 indium 111	NT1 mercury 206	NT1 praseodymium 144	NT1 selenium 83
NT1 indium 112	NT1 molybdenum 101	NT1 praseodymium 146	NT1 selenium 84
NT1 indium 114	NT1 molybdenum 102	NT1 praseodymium 147	NT1 silver 100
NT1 indium 116	NT1 molybdenum 103	NT1 praseodymium 148	NT1 silver 101
NT1 indium 117	NT1 molybdenum 104	NT1 praseodymium 149	NT1 silver 102
NT1 indium 118	NT1 molybdenum 88	NT1 promethium 136	NT1 silver 104
NT1 indium 119	NT1 molybdenum 89	NT1 promethium 137	NT1 silver 105
NT1 indium 121	NT1 molybdenum 91	NT1 promethium 138	NT1 silver 106
NT1 iodine 115	NT1 neodymium 132	NT1 promethium 139	NT1 silver 108
NT1 iodine 117	NT1 neodymium 133	NT1 promethium 140	NT1 silver 111
NT1 iodine 118	NT1 neodymium 134	NT1 promethium 141	NT1 silver 113
NT1 iodine 119	NT1 neodymium 135	NT1 promethium 152	NT1 silver 115
NT1 iodine 120	NT1 neodymium 136	NT1 promethium 153	NT1 silver 116
NT1 iodine 122	NT1 neodymium 137	NT1 promethium 154	NT1 silver 117
NT1 iodine 128	NT1 neodymium 139	NT1 protactinium 226	NT1 silver 99
NT1 iodine 130	NT1 neodymium 141	NT1 protactinium 227	NT1 strontium 78
NT1 iodine 134	NT1 neodymium 151	NT1 protactinium 234	NT1 strontium 79
NT1 iodine 136	NT1 neodymium 152	NT1 protactinium 235	NT1 strontium 81
NT1 iridium 179	NT1 neon 24	NT1 protactinium 236	NT1 strontium 93
NT1 iridium 180	NT1 neptunium 229	NT1 protactinium 237	NT1 strontium 94
NT1 iridium 181	NT1 neptunium 230	NT1 protactinium 238	NT1 sulfur 37
NT1 iridium 182	NT1 neptunium 231	NT1 radium 213	NT1 tantalum 167
NT1 iridium 183	NT1 neptunium 232	NT1 radium 227	NT1 tantalum 168
NT1 iridium 192	NT1 neptunium 233	NT1 radium 229	NT1 tantalum 169
NT1 iridium 197	NT1 neptunium 240	NT1 radium 231	NT1 tantalum 170
NT1 iron 53	NT1 neptunium 241	NT1 radium 232	NT1 tantalum 171
NT1 iron 61	NT1 neptunium 242	NT1 radon 204	NT1 tantalum 172
NT1 iron 62	NT1 neptunium 243	NT1 radon 205	NT1 tantalum 178
NT1 krypton 74	NT1 neptunium 244	NT1 radon 206	NT1 tantalum 182
NT1 krypton 75	NT1 niobium 85	NT1 radon 207	NT1 tantalum 185
NT1 krypton 89	NT1 niobium 86	NT1 radon 208	NT1 tantalum 186
NT1 lanthanum 125	NT1 niobium 87	NT1 radon 209	NT1 technetium 101
NT1 lanthanum 126	NT1 niobium 88	NT1 radon 212	NT1 technetium 102
NT1 lanthanum 127	NT1 niobium 94	NT1 radon 221	NT1 technetium 104
NT1 lanthanum 128	NT1 niobium 98	NT1 radon 223	NT1 technetium 105
NT1 lanthanum 129	NT1 niobium 99	NT1 radon 225	NT1 technetium 91
NT1 lanthanum 130	NT1 nitrogen 13	NT1 radon 226	NT1 technetium 92
NT1 lanthanum 131	NT1 nobelium 253	NT1 rhenium 173	NT1 technetium 93
NT1 lanthanum 132	NT1 nobelium 255	NT1 rhenium 174	NT1 technetium 94
NT1 lanthanum 134	NT1 nobelium 259	NT1 rhenium 175	NT1 technetium 96
NT1 lanthanum 136	NT1 osmium 175	NT1 rhenium 176	NT1 tellurium 112
NT1 lanthanum 143	NT1 osmium 176	NT1 rhenium 177	NT1 tellurium 113
NT1 lawrencium 260	NT1 osmium 177	NT1 rhenium 178	NT1 tellurium 114
NT1 lead 190	NT1 osmium 178	NT1 rhenium 179	NT1 tellurium 115
NT1 lead 191	NT1 osmium 179	NT1 rhenium 180	NT1 tellurium 131
NT1 lead 192	NT1 osmium 180	NT1 rhenium 188	NT1 tellurium 133
NT1 lead 193	NT1 osmium 181	NT1 rhenium 190	NT1 tellurium 134
NT1 lead 194	NT1 osmium 190	NT1 rhenium 191	NT1 terbium 147
NT1 lead 195	NT1 osmium 195	NT1 rhodium 100	NT1 terbium 148
NT1 lead 196	NT1 osmium 196	NT1 rhodium 103	NT1 terbium 149
NT1 lead 197	NT1 oxygen 14	NT1 rhodium 104	NT1 terbium 150
NT1 lead 199	NT1 oxygen 15	NT1 rhodium 107	NT1 terbium 152
NT1 lead 201	NT1 palladium 109	NT1 rhodium 108	NT1 terbium 162
NT1 lead 211	NT1 palladium 111	NT1 rhodium 109	NT1 terbium 163
NT1 lead 213	NT1 palladium 113	NT1 rhodium 94	NT1 terbium 164
NT1 lead 214	NT1 palladium 114	NT1 rhodium 95	NT1 terbium 165
NT1 lutetium 161	NT1 palladium 96	NT1 rhodium 96	NT1 thallium 188
NT1 lutetium 162	NT1 palladium 97	NT1 rhodium 97	NT1 thallium 189
NT1 lutetium 163	NT1 palladium 98	NT1 rhodium 98	NT1 thallium 190
NT1 lutetium 164	NT1 palladium 99	NT1 rubidium 77	NT1 thallium 191
NT1 lutetium 165	NT1 phosphorus 30	NT1 rubidium 78	NT1 thallium 192
NT1 lutetium 166	NT1 platinum 182	NT1 rubidium 79	NT1 thallium 193
NT1 lutetium 167	NT1 platinum 183	NT1 rubidium 81	NT1 thallium 194
NT1 lutetium 168	NT1 platinum 184	NT1 rubidium 82	NT1 thallium 206
NT1 lutetium 169	NT1 platinum 185	NT1 rubidium 84	NT1 thallium 207
NT1 lutetium 171	NT1 platinum 199	NT1 rubidium 86	NT1 thallium 208
NT1 lutetium 172	NT1 platinum 201	NT1 rubidium 88	NT1 thallium 209
NT1 lutetium 178	NT1 plutonium 232	NT1 rubidium 89	NT1 thallium 210
NT1 lutetium 180	NT1 plutonium 233	NT1 rubidium 90	NT1 thorium 225
NT1 lutetium 181	NT1 plutonium 235	NT1 ruthenium 107	NT1 thorium 226
NT1 lutetium 182	NT1 polonium 198	NT1 ruthenium 108	NT1 thorium 233
NT1 magnesium 27	NT1 polonium 199	NT1 ruthenium 92	NT1 thorium 235

MINUTES LIVING RADIOISOTOPES

NT1 thorium 236
NT1 thulium 156
NT1 thulium 157
NT1 thulium 158
NT1 thulium 159
NT1 thulium 160
NT1 thulium 161
NT1 thulium 162
NT1 thulium 164
NT1 thulium 174
NT1 thulium 175
NT1 thulium 176
NT1 thulium 177
NT1 tin 106
NT1 tin 107
NT1 tin 108
NT1 tin 109
NT1 tin 111
NT1 tin 113
NT1 tin 123
NT1 tin 125
NT1 tin 127
NT1 tin 128
NT1 tin 129
NT1 tin 130
NT1 tin 131
NT1 titanium 51
NT1 titanium 52
NT1 tungsten 170
NT1 tungsten 171
NT1 tungsten 172
NT1 tungsten 173
NT1 tungsten 174
NT1 tungsten 175
NT1 tungsten 179
NT1 tungsten 185
NT1 tungsten 189
NT1 tungsten 190
NT1 uranium 227
NT1 uranium 228
NT1 uranium 229
NT1 uranium 235
NT1 uranium 239
NT1 uranium 242
NT1 vanadium 47
NT1 vanadium 52
NT1 vanadium 53
NT1 xenon 117
NT1 xenon 118
NT1 xenon 119
NT1 xenon 120
NT1 xenon 121
NT1 xenon 127
NT1 xenon 135
NT1 xenon 137
NT1 xenon 138
NT1 ytterbium 158
NT1 ytterbium 159
NT1 ytterbium 160
NT1 ytterbium 161
NT1 ytterbium 162
NT1 ytterbium 163
NT1 ytterbium 165
NT1 ytterbium 167
NT1 ytterbium 179
NT1 ytterbium 180
NT1 yttrium 81
NT1 yttrium 83
NT1 yttrium 84
NT1 yttrium 86
NT1 yttrium 91
NT1 yttrium 94
NT1 yttrium 95
NT1 zinc 60
NT1 zinc 61
NT1 zinc 63
NT1 zinc 69
NT1 zinc 71
NT1 zinc 74
NT1 zirconium 81
NT1 zirconium 82
NT1 zirconium 84
NT1 zirconium 85
NT1 zirconium 89

NANOSEC LIVING RADIOISOTOPES

NT1 actinium 217
NT1 antimony 113
NT1 antimony 117
NT1 astatine 213
NT1 barium 138
NT1 bismuth 211
NT1 bromine 83
NT1 cesium 113
NT1 fermium 256
NT1 fluorine 18
NT1 francium 211
NT1 francium 212
NT1 francium 213
NT1 francium 215
NT1 francium 216
NT1 gadolinium 147
NT1 gadolinium 148
NT1 krypton 86
NT1 lead 194
NT1 lead 200
NT1 molybdenum 92
NT1 molybdenum 94
NT1 neptunium 237
NT1 osmium 182
NT1 plutonium 237
NT1 polonium 210
NT1 polonium 212
NT1 potassium 40
NT1 protactinium 219
NT1 protactinium 220
NT1 radium 216
NT1 radon 210
NT1 radon 211
NT1 radon 214
NT1 rubidium 85
NT1 sodium 22
NT1 thorium 218

ODD-EVEN NUCLEI

NT1 actinium 209
NT1 actinium 211
NT1 actinium 213
NT1 actinium 215
NT1 actinium 217
NT1 actinium 219
NT1 actinium 221
NT1 actinium 223
NT1 actinium 225
NT1 actinium 227
NT1 actinium 229
NT1 actinium 231
NT1 actinium 233
NT1 aluminium 23
NT1 aluminium 25
NT1 aluminium 27
NT1 aluminium 29
NT1 aluminium 31
NT1 aluminium 33
NT1 aluminium 35
NT1 aluminium 37
NT1 aluminium 39
NT1 americium 237
NT1 americium 239
NT1 americium 241
NT1 americium 243
NT1 americium 245
NT1 americium 247
NT1 antimony 109
NT1 antimony 111
NT1 antimony 113
NT1 antimony 115
NT1 antimony 117
NT1 antimony 119
NT1 antimony 121
NT1 antimony 123
NT1 antimony 125
NT1 antimony 127
NT1 antimony 129
NT1 antimony 131
NT1 antimony 133
NT1 antimony 135
NT1 arsenic 65
NT1 arsenic 67
NT1 arsenic 69
NT1 arsenic 71
NT1 arsenic 73
NT1 arsenic 75
NT1 arsenic 77
NT1 arsenic 79
NT1 arsenic 81
NT1 arsenic 83
NT1 arsenic 85
NT1 arsenic 87
NT1 astatine 195
NT1 astatine 197
NT1 astatine 199
NT1 astatine 201
NT1 astatine 203
NT1 astatine 205
NT1 astatine 207
NT1 astatine 209
NT1 astatine 211
NT1 astatine 213
NT1 astatine 215
NT1 astatine 217
NT1 astatine 219
NT1 astatine 221
NT1 astatine 223
NT1 berkelium 241
NT1 berkelium 243
NT1 berkelium 245
NT1 berkelium 247
NT1 berkelium 249
NT1 berkelium 251
NT1 bismuth 189
NT1 bismuth 191
NT1 bismuth 193
NT1 bismuth 195
NT1 bismuth 197
NT1 bismuth 199
NT1 bismuth 201
NT1 bismuth 203
NT1 bismuth 205
NT1 bismuth 207
NT1 bismuth 209
NT1 bismuth 211
NT1 bismuth 213
NT1 bismuth 215
NT1 boron 11
NT1 boron 13
NT1 boron 15
NT1 boron 17
NT1 boron 19
NT1 boron 7
NT1 boron 9
NT1 bromine 69
NT1 bromine 71
NT1 bromine 73
NT1 bromine 75
NT1 bromine 77
NT1 bromine 79
NT1 bromine 81
NT1 bromine 83
NT1 bromine 85
NT1 bromine 87
NT1 bromine 89
NT1 bromine 91
NT1 bromine 93
NT1 cesium 113
NT1 cesium 115
NT1 cesium 117
NT1 cesium 119
NT1 cesium 121
NT1 cesium 123
NT1 cesium 125
NT1 cesium 127
NT1 cesium 129
NT1 cesium 131
NT1 cesium 133
NT1 cesium 135
NT1 cesium 137
NT1 cesium 139
NT1 cesium 141
NT1 cesium 143
NT1 cesium 145
NT1 cesium 147
NT1 chlorine 31
NT1 chlorine 33
NT1 chlorine 35
NT1 chlorine 37
NT1 chlorine 39
NT1 chlorine 41
NT1 chlorine 43
NT1 chlorine 45
NT1 chlorine 47
NT1 chlorine 49
NT1 chlorine 51
NT1 cobalt 53
NT1 cobalt 55
NT1 cobalt 57
NT1 cobalt 59
NT1 cobalt 61
NT1 cobalt 63
NT1 cobalt 65
NT1 cobalt 67
NT1 cobalt 69
NT1 copper 57
NT1 copper 59
NT1 copper 61
NT1 copper 63
NT1 copper 65
NT1 copper 67
NT1 copper 69
NT1 copper 71
NT1 copper 73
NT1 copper 75
NT1 einsteinium 243
NT1 einsteinium 245
NT1 einsteinium 247
NT1 einsteinium 249
NT1 einsteinium 251
NT1 einsteinium 253
NT1 einsteinium 255
NT1 element 105 255
NT1 element 105 257
NT1 element 105 259
NT1 element 105 261
NT1 element 107 261
NT1 europium 135
NT1 europium 137
NT1 europium 139
NT1 europium 141
NT1 europium 143
NT1 europium 145
NT1 europium 147
NT1 europium 149
NT1 europium 151
NT1 europium 153
NT1 europium 155
NT1 europium 157
NT1 europium 159
NT1 europium 161
NT1 fluorine 15
NT1 fluorine 17
NT1 fluorine 19
NT1 fluorine 21
NT1 fluorine 23
NT1 fluorine 25
NT1 fluorine 27
NT1 fluorine 29
NT1 francium 201
NT1 francium 203
NT1 francium 205
NT1 francium 207
NT1 francium 209
NT1 francium 211
NT1 francium 213
NT1 francium 215
NT1 francium 217
NT1 francium 219
NT1 francium 221
NT1 francium 223
NT1 francium 225
NT1 francium 227
NT1 francium 229
NT1 francium 231
NT1 gallium 61
NT1 gallium 63
NT1 gallium 65
NT1 gallium 67
NT1 gallium 69
NT1 gallium 71
NT1 gallium 73
NT1 gallium 75
NT1 gallium 77
NT1 gallium 79
NT1 gallium 81
NT1 gallium 83
NT1 gold 173
NT1 gold 175
NT1 gold 177
NT1 gold 179
NT1 gold 181
NT1 gold 183
NT1 gold 185
NT1 gold 187
NT1 gold 189
NT1 gold 191

NT1 gold 193	NT1 lawrencium 259	NT1 potassium 49	NT1 scandium 51
NT1 gold 195	NT1 lawrencium 261	NT1 potassium 51	NT1 scandium 53
NT1 gold 197	NT1 lawrencium 263	NT1 potassium 53	NT1 scandium 55
NT1 gold 199	NT1 lithium 11	NT1 praseodymium 129	NT1 silver 101
NT1 gold 201	NT1 lithium 13	NT1 praseodymium 131	NT1 silver 103
NT1 gold 203	NT1 lithium 3	NT1 praseodymium 133	NT1 silver 105
NT1 holmium 145	NT1 lithium 5	NT1 praseodymium 135	NT1 silver 107
NT1 holmium 147	NT1 lithium 7	NT1 praseodymium 137	NT1 silver 109
NT1 holmium 149	NT1 lithium 9	NT1 praseodymium 139	NT1 silver 111
NT1 holmium 151	NT1 lutetium 151	NT1 praseodymium 141	NT1 silver 113
NT1 holmium 153	NT1 lutetium 153	NT1 praseodymium 143	NT1 silver 115
NT1 holmium 155	NT1 lutetium 155	NT1 praseodymium 145	NT1 silver 117
NT1 holmium 157	NT1 lutetium 157	NT1 praseodymium 147	NT1 silver 119
NT1 holmium 159	NT1 lutetium 159	NT1 praseodymium 149	NT1 silver 121
NT1 holmium 161	NT1 lutetium 161	NT1 praseodymium 151	NT1 silver 123
NT1 holmium 163	NT1 lutetium 163	NT1 praseodymium 153	NT1 silver 95
NT1 holmium 165	NT1 lutetium 165	NT1 promethium 133	NT1 silver 97
NT1 holmium 167	NT1 lutetium 167	NT1 promethium 135	NT1 silver 99
NT1 holmium 169	NT1 lutetium 169	NT1 promethium 137	NT1 sodium 19
NT1 holmium 171	NT1 lutetium 171	NT1 promethium 139	NT1 sodium 21
NT1 hydrogen 1	NT1 lutetium 173	NT1 promethium 141	NT1 sodium 23
NT1 hydrogen 5	NT1 lutetium 175	NT1 promethium 143	NT1 sodium 25
NT1 hydrogen 7	NT1 lutetium 177	NT1 promethium 145	NT1 sodium 27
NT1 indium 101	NT1 lutetium 179	NT1 promethium 147	NT1 sodium 29
NT1 indium 103	NT1 lutetium 181	NT1 promethium 149	NT1 sodium 31
NT1 indium 105	NT1 lutetium 183	NT1 promethium 151	NT1 sodium 33
NT1 indium 107	NT1 manganese 47	NT1 promethium 153	NT1 sodium 35
NT1 indium 109	NT1 manganese 49	NT1 promethium 155	NT1 tantalum 157
NT1 indium 111	NT1 manganese 51	NT1 promethium 157	NT1 tantalum 159
NT1 indium 113	NT1 manganese 53	NT1 protactinium 215	NT1 tantalum 161
NT1 indium 115	NT1 manganese 55	NT1 protactinium 217	NT1 tantalum 163
NT1 indium 117	NT1 manganese 57	NT1 protactinium 219	NT1 tantalum 165
NT1 indium 119	NT1 manganese 59	NT1 protactinium 221	NT1 tantalum 167
NT1 indium 121	NT1 manganese 61	NT1 protactinium 223	NT1 tantalum 169
NT1 indium 123	NT1 manganese 63	NT1 protactinium 225	NT1 tantalum 171
NT1 indium 125	NT1 manganese 65	NT1 protactinium 227	NT1 tantalum 173
NT1 indium 127	NT1 mendelevium 247	NT1 protactinium 229	NT1 tantalum 175
NT1 indium 129	NT1 mendelevium 249	NT1 protactinium 231	NT1 tantalum 177
NT1 indium 131	NT1 mendelevium 251	NT1 protactinium 233	NT1 tantalum 179
NT1 iodine 109	NT1 mendelevium 253	NT1 protactinium 235	NT1 tantalum 181
NT1 iodine 111	NT1 mendelevium 255	NT1 protactinium 237	NT1 tantalum 183
NT1 iodine 113	NT1 mendelevium 257	NT1 rhenium 161	NT1 tantalum 185
NT1 iodine 115	NT1 mendelevium 259	NT1 rhenium 163	NT1 technetium 101
NT1 iodine 117	NT1 mendelevium 261	NT1 rhenium 165	NT1 technetium 103
NT1 iodine 119	NT1 neptunium 227	NT1 rhenium 167	NT1 technetium 105
NT1 iodine 121	NT1 neptunium 229	NT1 rhenium 169	NT1 technetium 107
NT1 iodine 123	NT1 neptunium 231	NT1 rhenium 171	NT1 technetium 109
NT1 iodine 125	NT1 neptunium 233	NT1 rhenium 173	NT1 technetium 91
NT1 iodine 127	NT1 neptunium 235	NT1 rhenium 175	NT1 technetium 93
NT1 iodine 129	NT1 neptunium 237	NT1 rhenium 177	NT1 technetium 95
NT1 iodine 131	NT1 neptunium 239	NT1 rhenium 179	NT1 technetium 97
NT1 iodine 133	NT1 neptunium 241	NT1 rhenium 181	NT1 technetium 99
NT1 iodine 135	NT1 neptunium 243	NT1 rhenium 183	NT1 terbium 141
NT1 iodine 137	NT1 niobium 101	NT1 rhenium 185	NT1 terbium 143
NT1 iodine 139	NT1 niobium 103	NT1 rhenium 187	NT1 terbium 145
NT1 iodine 141	NT1 niobium 105	NT1 rhenium 189	NT1 terbium 147
NT1 iridium 167	NT1 niobium 83	NT1 rhenium 191	NT1 terbium 149
NT1 iridium 169	NT1 niobium 85	NT1 rhodium 101	NT1 terbium 151
NT1 iridium 171	NT1 niobium 87	NT1 rhodium 103	NT1 terbium 153
NT1 iridium 173	NT1 niobium 89	NT1 rhodium 105	NT1 terbium 155
NT1 iridium 175	NT1 niobium 91	NT1 rhodium 107	NT1 terbium 157
NT1 iridium 177	NT1 niobium 93	NT1 rhodium 109	NT1 terbium 159
NT1 iridium 179	NT1 niobium 95	NT1 rhodium 111	NT1 terbium 161
NT1 iridium 181	NT1 niobium 97	NT1 rhodium 113	NT1 terbium 163
NT1 iridium 183	NT1 niobium 99	NT1 rhodium 115	NT1 terbium 165
NT1 iridium 185	NT1 nitrogen 11	NT1 rhodium 117	NT1 thallium 179
NT1 iridium 187	NT1 nitrogen 13	NT1 rhodium 95	NT1 thallium 185
NT1 iridium 189	NT1 nitrogen 15	NT1 rhodium 97	NT1 thallium 187
NT1 iridium 191	NT1 nitrogen 17	NT1 rhodium 99	NT1 thallium 189
NT1 iridium 193	NT1 nitrogen 19	NT1 rubidium 101	NT1 thallium 191
NT1 iridium 195	NT1 nitrogen 21	NT1 rubidium 103	NT1 thallium 193
NT1 iridium 197	NT1 nitrogen 23	NT1 rubidium 75	NT1 thallium 195
NT1 lanthanum 121	NT1 phosphorus 21	NT1 rubidium 77	NT1 thallium 197
NT1 lanthanum 123	NT1 phosphorus 27	NT1 rubidium 79	NT1 thallium 199
NT1 lanthanum 125	NT1 phosphorus 29	NT1 rubidium 81	NT1 thallium 201
NT1 lanthanum 127	NT1 phosphorus 31	NT1 rubidium 83	NT1 thallium 203
NT1 lanthanum 129	NT1 phosphorus 33	NT1 rubidium 85	NT1 thallium 205
NT1 lanthanum 131	NT1 phosphorus 35	NT1 rubidium 87	NT1 thallium 207
NT1 lanthanum 133	NT1 phosphorus 37	NT1 rubidium 89	NT1 thallium 209
NT1 lanthanum 135	NT1 phosphorus 39	NT1 rubidium 91	NT1 thulium 147
NT1 lanthanum 137	NT1 phosphorus 41	NT1 rubidium 93	NT1 thulium 149
NT1 lanthanum 139	NT1 phosphorus 43	NT1 rubidium 95	NT1 thulium 151
NT1 lanthanum 141	NT1 phosphorus 45	NT1 rubidium 97	NT1 thulium 153
NT1 lanthanum 143	NT1 potassium 35	NT1 rubidium 99	NT1 thulium 155
NT1 lanthanum 145	NT1 potassium 37	NT1 scandium 39	NT1 thulium 157
NT1 lanthanum 147	NT1 potassium 39	NT1 scandium 41	NT1 thulium 159
NT1 lanthanum 149	NT1 potassium 41	NT1 scandium 43	NT1 thulium 161
NT1 lawrencium 253	NT1 potassium 43	NT1 scandium 45	NT1 thulium 163
NT1 lawrencium 255	NT1 potassium 45	NT1 scandium 47	NT1 thulium 165
NT1 lawrencium 257	NT1 potassium 47	NT1 scandium 49	NT1 thulium 167

ODD-EVEN NUCLEI

NT1	thulium 169
NT1	thulium 171
NT1	thulium 173
NT1	thulium 175
NT1	thulium 177
NT1	tritium
NT1	vanadium 45
NT1	vanadium 47
NT1	vanadium 49
NT1	vanadium 51
NT1	vanadium 53
NT1	vanadium 55
NT1	vanadium 57
NT1	vanadium 59
NT1	yttrium 101
NT1	yttrium 77
NT1	yttrium 81
NT1	yttrium 83
NT1	yttrium 85
NT1	yttrium 87
NT1	yttrium 89
NT1	yttrium 91
NT1	yttrium 93
NT1	yttrium 95
NT1	yttrium 97
NT1	yttrium 99

ODD-ODD NUCLEI

NT1	actinium 210
NT1	actinium 212
NT1	actinium 214
NT1	actinium 216
NT1	actinium 218
NT1	actinium 220
NT1	actinium 222
NT1	actinium 224
NT1	actinium 226
NT1	actinium 228
NT1	actinium 230
NT1	actinium 232
NT1	actinium 234
NT1	aluminium 22
NT1	aluminium 24
NT1	aluminium 26
NT1	aluminium 28
NT1	aluminium 30
NT1	aluminium 32
NT1	aluminium 34
NT1	aluminium 36
NT1	aluminium 38
NT1	americium 232
NT1	americium 234
NT1	americium 238
NT1	americium 240
NT1	americium 242
NT1	americium 244
NT1	americium 246
NT1	antimony 106
NT1	antimony 108
NT1	antimony 110
NT1	antimony 112
NT1	antimony 114
NT1	antimony 116
NT1	antimony 118
NT1	antimony 120
NT1	antimony 122
NT1	antimony 124
NT1	antimony 126
NT1	antimony 128
NT1	antimony 130
NT1	antimony 132
NT1	antimony 134
NT1	antimony 136
NT1	arsenic 66
NT1	arsenic 68
NT1	arsenic 70
NT1	arsenic 72
NT1	arsenic 74
NT1	arsenic 76
NT1	arsenic 78
NT1	arsenic 80
NT1	arsenic 82
NT1	arsenic 84
NT1	arsenic 86
NT1	astatine 194
NT1	astatine 196
NT1	astatine 198
NT1	astatine 200
NT1	astatine 202
NT1	astatine 204
NT1	astatine 206
NT1	astatine 208
NT1	astatine 210
NT1	astatine 212
NT1	astatine 214
NT1	astatine 216
NT1	astatine 218
NT1	astatine 220
NT1	astatine 222
NT1	berkelium 240
NT1	berkelium 242
NT1	berkelium 244
NT1	berkelium 246
NT1	berkelium 248
NT1	berkelium 250
NT1	bismuth 188
NT1	bismuth 190
NT1	bismuth 192
NT1	bismuth 194
NT1	bismuth 196
NT1	bismuth 198
NT1	bismuth 200
NT1	bismuth 202
NT1	bismuth 204
NT1	bismuth 206
NT1	bismuth 208
NT1	bismuth 210
NT1	bismuth 212
NT1	bismuth 214
NT1	bismuth 216
NT1	boron 10
NT1	boron 12
NT1	boron 14
NT1	boron 18
NT1	boron 8
NT1	bromine 70
NT1	bromine 72
NT1	bromine 74
NT1	bromine 76
NT1	bromine 78
NT1	bromine 80
NT1	bromine 82
NT1	bromine 84
NT1	bromine 86
NT1	bromine 88
NT1	bromine 90
NT1	bromine 92
NT1	cesium 114
NT1	cesium 116
NT1	cesium 118
NT1	cesium 120
NT1	cesium 122
NT1	cesium 124
NT1	cesium 126
NT1	cesium 128
NT1	cesium 130
NT1	cesium 132
NT1	cesium 134
NT1	cesium 136
NT1	cesium 138
NT1	cesium 140
NT1	cesium 142
NT1	cesium 144
NT1	cesium 146
NT1	cesium 148
NT1	chlorine 32
NT1	chlorine 34
NT1	chlorine 36
NT1	chlorine 38
NT1	chlorine 40
NT1	chlorine 42
NT1	chlorine 44
NT1	chlorine 46
NT1	chlorine 48
NT1	cobalt 54
NT1	cobalt 56
NT1	cobalt 58
NT1	cobalt 60
NT1	cobalt 62
NT1	cobalt 64
NT1	cobalt 66
NT1	cobalt 68
NT1	cobalt 70
NT1	copper 58
NT1	copper 60
NT1	copper 62
NT1	copper 64
NT1	copper 66
NT1	copper 68
NT1	copper 70
NT1	copper 72
NT1	copper 74
NT1	deuterium
NT1	einsteinium 244
NT1	einsteinium 246
NT1	einsteinium 248
NT1	einsteinium 250
NT1	einsteinium 252
NT1	einsteinium 254
NT1	einsteinium 256
NT1	element 105 258
NT1	element 105 260
NT1	element 105 262
NT1	element 107 262
NT1	element 109 266
NT1	europium 134
NT1	europium 136
NT1	europium 138
NT1	europium 140
NT1	europium 142
NT1	europium 144
NT1	europium 146
NT1	europium 148
NT1	europium 150
NT1	europium 152
NT1	europium 154
NT1	europium 156
NT1	europium 158
NT1	europium 160
NT1	europium 162
NT1	fluorine 14
NT1	fluorine 16
NT1	fluorine 18
NT1	fluorine 20
NT1	fluorine 22
NT1	fluorine 24
NT1	fluorine 26
NT1	francium 202
NT1	francium 204
NT1	francium 206
NT1	francium 208
NT1	francium 210
NT1	francium 212
NT1	francium 214
NT1	francium 216
NT1	francium 218
NT1	francium 220
NT1	francium 222
NT1	francium 224
NT1	francium 226
NT1	francium 228
NT1	francium 230
NT1	francium 232
NT1	gallium 62
NT1	gallium 64
NT1	gallium 66
NT1	gallium 68
NT1	gallium 70
NT1	gallium 72
NT1	gallium 74
NT1	gallium 76
NT1	gallium 78
NT1	gallium 80
NT1	gallium 82
NT1	gold 174
NT1	gold 176
NT1	gold 178
NT1	gold 180
NT1	gold 182
NT1	gold 184
NT1	gold 186
NT1	gold 188
NT1	gold 190
NT1	gold 192
NT1	gold 194
NT1	gold 196
NT1	gold 198
NT1	gold 200
NT1	gold 202
NT1	gold 204
NT1	holmium 144
NT1	holmium 146
NT1	holmium 148
NT1	holmium 150
NT1	holmium 152
NT1	holmium 154
NT1	holmium 156
NT1	holmium 158
NT1	holmium 160
NT1	holmium 162

ODD-ODD NUCLEI

NT1	holmium 164
NT1	holmium 166
NT1	holmium 168
NT1	holmium 170
NT1	holmium 172
NT1	hydrogen 4
NT1	hydrogen 6
NT1	indium 100
NT1	indium 102
NT1	indium 104
NT1	indium 106
NT1	indium 108
NT1	indium 110
NT1	indium 112
NT1	indium 114
NT1	indium 116
NT1	indium 118
NT1	indium 120
NT1	indium 122
NT1	indium 124
NT1	indium 126
NT1	indium 128
NT1	indium 130
NT1	indium 132
NT1	iodine 108
NT1	iodine 110
NT1	iodine 112
NT1	iodine 114
NT1	iodine 116
NT1	iodine 118
NT1	iodine 120
NT1	iodine 122
NT1	iodine 124
NT1	iodine 126
NT1	iodine 128
NT1	iodine 130
NT1	iodine 132
NT1	iodine 134
NT1	iodine 136
NT1	iodine 138
NT1	iodine 140
NT1	iodine 142
NT1	iridium 166
NT1	iridium 168
NT1	iridium 170
NT1	iridium 172
NT1	iridium 174
NT1	iridium 176
NT1	iridium 178
NT1	iridium 180
NT1	iridium 182
NT1	iridium 184
NT1	iridium 186
NT1	iridium 188
NT1	iridium 190
NT1	iridium 192
NT1	iridium 194
NT1	iridium 196
NT1	iridium 198
NT1	lanthanum 120
NT1	lanthanum 122
NT1	lanthanum 124
NT1	lanthanum 126
NT1	lanthanum 128
NT1	lanthanum 130
NT1	lanthanum 132
NT1	lanthanum 134
NT1	lanthanum 136
NT1	lanthanum 138
NT1	lanthanum 140
NT1	lanthanum 142
NT1	lanthanum 144
NT1	lanthanum 146
NT1	lanthanum 148
NT1	lawrencium 254
NT1	lawrencium 256
NT1	lawrencium 258
NT1	lawrencium 260
NT1	lawrencium 262
NT1	lithium 10
NT1	lithium 4
NT1	lithium 6
NT1	lithium 8
NT1	lutetium 152
NT1	lutetium 154
NT1	lutetium 156
NT1	lutetium 158
NT1	lutetium 160
NT1	lutetium 162
NT1	lutetium 164

ODD-ODD NUCLEI

NT1	lutetium 166	NT1	praseodymium 148	NT1	silver 116	NT1	vanadium 54
NT1	lutetium 168	NT1	praseodymium 150	NT1	silver 118	NT1	vanadium 56
NT1	lutetium 170	NT1	praseodymium 152	NT1	silver 120	NT1	vanadium 58
NT1	lutetium 172	NT1	praseodymium 154	NT1	silver 122	NT1	vanadium 60
NT1	lutetium 174	NT1	promethium 130	NT1	silver 96	NT1	yttrium 100
NT1	lutetium 176	NT1	promethium 132	NT1	silver 98	NT1	yttrium 102
NT1	lutetium 178	NT1	promethium 134	NT1	sodium 20	NT1	yttrium 80
NT1	lutetium 180	NT1	promethium 136	NT1	sodium 22	NT1	yttrium 82
NT1	lutetium 182	NT1	promethium 138	NT1	sodium 24	NT1	yttrium 84
NT1	lutetium 184	NT1	promethium 140	NT1	sodium 26	NT1	yttrium 86
NT1	manganese 44	NT1	promethium 142	NT1	sodium 28	NT1	yttrium 88
NT1	manganese 46	NT1	promethium 144	NT1	sodium 30	NT1	yttrium 90
NT1	manganese 48	NT1	promethium 146	NT1	sodium 32	NT1	yttrium 92
NT1	manganese 50	NT1	promethium 148	NT1	sodium 34	NT1	yttrium 94
NT1	manganese 52	NT1	promethium 150	NT1	tantalum 156	NT1	yttrium 96
NT1	manganese 54	NT1	promethium 152	NT1	tantalum 158	NT1	yttrium 98
NT1	manganese 56	NT1	promethium 154	NT1	tantalum 160		
NT1	manganese 58	NT1	promethium 156	NT1	tantalum 162	**RARE EARTH NUCLEI**	
NT1	manganese 60	NT1	promethium 158	NT1	tantalum 164	NT1	cerium 123
NT1	manganese 62	NT1	protactinium 216	NT1	tantalum 166	NT1	cerium 124
NT1	manganese 64	NT1	protactinium 218	NT1	tantalum 168	NT1	cerium 125
NT1	mendelevium 248	NT1	protactinium 220	NT1	tantalum 170	NT1	cerium 126
NT1	mendelevium 250	NT1	protactinium 222	NT1	tantalum 172	NT1	cerium 127
NT1	mendelevium 252	NT1	protactinium 224	NT1	tantalum 174	NT1	cerium 128
NT1	mendelevium 254	NT1	protactinium 226	NT1	tantalum 176	NT1	cerium 129
NT1	mendelevium 256	NT1	protactinium 228	NT1	tantalum 178	NT1	cerium 130
NT1	mendelevium 258	NT1	protactinium 230	NT1	tantalum 180	NT1	cerium 131
NT1	mendelevium 260	NT1	protactinium 232	NT1	tantalum 182	NT1	cerium 132
NT1	neptunium 226	NT1	protactinium 234	NT1	tantalum 184	NT1	cerium 133
NT1	neptunium 228	NT1	protactinium 236	NT1	tantalum 186	NT1	cerium 134
NT1	neptunium 230	NT1	protactinium 238	NT1	technetium 100	NT1	cerium 135
NT1	neptunium 232	NT1	rhenium 162	NT1	technetium 102	NT1	cerium 136
NT1	neptunium 234	NT1	rhenium 164	NT1	technetium 104	NT1	cerium 137
NT1	neptunium 236	NT1	rhenium 166	NT1	technetium 106	NT1	cerium 138
NT1	neptunium 238	NT1	rhenium 168	NT1	technetium 108	NT1	cerium 139
NT1	neptunium 240	NT1	rhenium 170	NT1	technetium 110	NT1	cerium 140
NT1	neptunium 242	NT1	rhenium 172	NT1	technetium 112	NT1	cerium 141
NT1	neptunium 244	NT1	rhenium 174	NT1	technetium 90	NT1	cerium 142
NT1	niobium 100	NT1	rhenium 176	NT1	technetium 92	NT1	cerium 143
NT1	niobium 102	NT1	rhenium 178	NT1	technetium 94	NT1	cerium 144
NT1	niobium 104	NT1	rhenium 180	NT1	technetium 96	NT1	cerium 145
NT1	niobium 106	NT1	rhenium 182	NT1	technetium 98	NT1	cerium 146
NT1	niobium 84	NT1	rhenium 184	NT1	terbium 140	NT1	cerium 147
NT1	niobium 86	NT1	rhenium 186	NT1	terbium 144	NT1	cerium 148
NT1	niobium 88	NT1	rhenium 188	NT1	terbium 146	NT1	cerium 149
NT1	niobium 90	NT1	rhenium 190	NT1	terbium 148	NT1	cerium 150
NT1	niobium 92	NT1	rhenium 192	NT1	terbium 150	NT1	cerium 151
NT1	niobium 94	NT1	rhodium 100	NT1	terbium 152	NT1	cerium 152
NT1	niobium 96	NT1	rhodium 102	NT1	terbium 154	NT1	dysprosium 141
NT1	niobium 98	NT1	rhodium 104	NT1	terbium 156	NT1	dysprosium 142
NT1	nitrogen 12	NT1	rhodium 106	NT1	terbium 158	NT1	dysprosium 143
NT1	nitrogen 14	NT1	rhodium 108	NT1	terbium 160	NT1	dysprosium 144
NT1	nitrogen 16	NT1	rhodium 110	NT1	terbium 162	NT1	dysprosium 145
NT1	nitrogen 18	NT1	rhodium 112	NT1	terbium 164	NT1	dysprosium 146
NT1	nitrogen 20	NT1	rhodium 114	NT1	thallium 182	NT1	dysprosium 147
NT1	nitrogen 22	NT1	rhodium 116	NT1	thallium 184	NT1	dysprosium 148
NT1	phosphorus 24	NT1	rhodium 94	NT1	thallium 186	NT1	dysprosium 149
NT1	phosphorus 26	NT1	rhodium 96	NT1	thallium 188	NT1	dysprosium 150
NT1	phosphorus 28	NT1	rhodium 98	NT1	thallium 190	NT1	dysprosium 151
NT1	phosphorus 30	NT1	rubidium 100	NT1	thallium 192	NT1	dysprosium 152
NT1	phosphorus 32	NT1	rubidium 102	NT1	thallium 194	NT1	dysprosium 153
NT1	phosphorus 34	NT1	rubidium 74	NT1	thallium 196	NT1	dysprosium 154
NT1	phosphorus 36	NT1	rubidium 76	NT1	thallium 198	NT1	dysprosium 155
NT1	phosphorus 38	NT1	rubidium 78	NT1	thallium 200	NT1	dysprosium 156
NT1	phosphorus 40	NT1	rubidium 80	NT1	thallium 202	NT1	dysprosium 157
NT1	phosphorus 42	NT1	rubidium 82	NT1	thallium 204	NT1	dysprosium 158
NT1	phosphorus 44	NT1	rubidium 84	NT1	thallium 206	NT1	dysprosium 159
NT1	phosphorus 46	NT1	rubidium 86	NT1	thallium 208	NT1	dysprosium 160
NT1	potassium 36	NT1	rubidium 88	NT1	thallium 210	NT1	dysprosium 161
NT1	potassium 38	NT1	rubidium 90	NT1	thulium 148	NT1	dysprosium 162
NT1	potassium 40	NT1	rubidium 92	NT1	thulium 150	NT1	dysprosium 163
NT1	potassium 42	NT1	rubidium 94	NT1	thulium 152	NT1	dysprosium 164
NT1	potassium 44	NT1	rubidium 96	NT1	thulium 154	NT1	dysprosium 165
NT1	potassium 46	NT1	rubidium 98	NT1	thulium 156	NT1	dysprosium 166
NT1	potassium 48	NT1	scandium 40	NT1	thulium 158	NT1	dysprosium 167
NT1	potassium 50	NT1	scandium 42	NT1	thulium 160	NT1	dysprosium 168
NT1	potassium 52	NT1	scandium 44	NT1	thulium 162	NT1	dysprosium 169
NT1	potassium 54	NT1	scandium 46	NT1	thulium 164	NT1	erbium 145
NT1	praseodymium 124	NT1	scandium 48	NT1	thulium 166	NT1	erbium 147
NT1	praseodymium 126	NT1	scandium 50	NT1	thulium 168	NT1	erbium 148
NT1	praseodymium 128	NT1	scandium 52	NT1	thulium 170	NT1	erbium 149
NT1	praseodymium 130	NT1	scandium 54	NT1	thulium 172	NT1	erbium 150
NT1	praseodymium 132	NT1	silver 100	NT1	thulium 174	NT1	erbium 151
NT1	praseodymium 134	NT1	silver 102	NT1	thulium 176	NT1	erbium 152
NT1	praseodymium 136	NT1	silver 104	NT1	vanadium 42	NT1	erbium 153
NT1	praseodymium 138	NT1	silver 106	NT1	vanadium 44	NT1	erbium 154
NT1	praseodymium 140	NT1	silver 108	NT1	vanadium 46	NT1	erbium 155
NT1	praseodymium 142	NT1	silver 110	NT1	vanadium 48	NT1	erbium 156
NT1	praseodymium 144	NT1	silver 112	NT1	vanadium 50	NT1	erbium 157
NT1	praseodymium 146	NT1	silver 114	NT1	vanadium 52	NT1	erbium 158

NT1 erbium 159	NT1 holmium 161	NT1 neodymium 141	NT1 samarium 149
NT1 erbium 160	NT1 holmium 162	NT1 neodymium 142	NT1 samarium 150
NT1 erbium 161	NT1 holmium 163	NT1 neodymium 143	NT1 samarium 151
NT1 erbium 162	NT1 holmium 164	NT1 neodymium 144	NT1 samarium 152
NT1 erbium 163	NT1 holmium 165	NT1 neodymium 145	NT1 samarium 153
NT1 erbium 164	NT1 holmium 166	NT1 neodymium 146	NT1 samarium 154
NT1 erbium 165	NT1 holmium 167	NT1 neodymium 147	NT1 samarium 155
NT1 erbium 166	NT1 holmium 168	NT1 neodymium 148	NT1 samarium 156
NT1 erbium 167	NT1 holmium 169	NT1 neodymium 149	NT1 samarium 157
NT1 erbium 168	NT1 holmium 170	NT1 neodymium 150	NT1 samarium 158
NT1 erbium 169	NT1 holmium 171	NT1 neodymium 151	NT1 samarium 159
NT1 erbium 170	NT1 holmium 172	NT1 neodymium 152	NT1 samarium 160
NT1 erbium 171	NT1 lanthanum 120	NT1 neodymium 153	NT1 terbium 140
NT1 erbium 172	NT1 lanthanum 121	NT1 neodymium 154	NT1 terbium 141
NT1 erbium 173	NT1 lanthanum 122	NT1 neodymium 155	NT1 terbium 143
NT1 erbium 174	NT1 lanthanum 123	NT1 neodymium 156	NT1 terbium 144
NT1 europium 134	NT1 lanthanum 124	NT1 praseodymium 124	NT1 terbium 145
NT1 europium 135	NT1 lanthanum 125	NT1 praseodymium 126	NT1 terbium 146
NT1 europium 136	NT1 lanthanum 126	NT1 praseodymium 128	NT1 terbium 147
NT1 europium 137	NT1 lanthanum 127	NT1 praseodymium 129	NT1 terbium 148
NT1 europium 138	NT1 lanthanum 128	NT1 praseodymium 130	NT1 terbium 149
NT1 europium 139	NT1 lanthanum 129	NT1 praseodymium 131	NT1 terbium 150
NT1 europium 140	NT1 lanthanum 130	NT1 praseodymium 132	NT1 terbium 151
NT1 europium 141	NT1 lanthanum 131	NT1 praseodymium 133	NT1 terbium 152
NT1 europium 142	NT1 lanthanum 132	NT1 praseodymium 134	NT1 terbium 153
NT1 europium 143	NT1 lanthanum 133	NT1 praseodymium 135	NT1 terbium 154
NT1 europium 144	NT1 lanthanum 134	NT1 praseodymium 136	NT1 terbium 155
NT1 europium 145	NT1 lanthanum 135	NT1 praseodymium 137	NT1 terbium 156
NT1 europium 146	NT1 lanthanum 136	NT1 praseodymium 138	NT1 terbium 157
NT1 europium 147	NT1 lanthanum 137	NT1 praseodymium 139	NT1 terbium 158
NT1 europium 148	NT1 lanthanum 138	NT1 praseodymium 140	NT1 terbium 159
NT1 europium 149	NT1 lanthanum 139	NT1 praseodymium 141	NT1 terbium 160
NT1 europium 150	NT1 lanthanum 140	NT1 praseodymium 142	NT1 terbium 161
NT1 europium 151	NT1 lanthanum 141	NT1 praseodymium 143	NT1 terbium 162
NT1 europium 152	NT1 lanthanum 142	NT1 praseodymium 144	NT1 terbium 163
NT1 europium 153	NT1 lanthanum 143	NT1 praseodymium 145	NT1 terbium 164
NT1 europium 154	NT1 lanthanum 144	NT1 praseodymium 146	NT1 terbium 165
NT1 europium 155	NT1 lanthanum 145	NT1 praseodymium 147	NT1 thulium 147
NT1 europium 156	NT1 lanthanum 146	NT1 praseodymium 148	NT1 thulium 148
NT1 europium 157	NT1 lanthanum 147	NT1 praseodymium 149	NT1 thulium 149
NT1 europium 158	NT1 lanthanum 148	NT1 praseodymium 150	NT1 thulium 150
NT1 europium 159	NT1 lanthanum 149	NT1 praseodymium 151	NT1 thulium 151
NT1 europium 160	NT1 lutetium 151	NT1 praseodymium 152	NT1 thulium 152
NT1 europium 161	NT1 lutetium 152	NT1 praseodymium 153	NT1 thulium 153
NT1 europium 162	NT1 lutetium 153	NT1 praseodymium 154	NT1 thulium 154
NT1 gadolinium 137	NT1 lutetium 154	NT1 promethium 130	NT1 thulium 155
NT1 gadolinium 138	NT1 lutetium 155	NT1 promethium 132	NT1 thulium 156
NT1 gadolinium 139	NT1 lutetium 156	NT1 promethium 133	NT1 thulium 157
NT1 gadolinium 140	NT1 lutetium 157	NT1 promethium 134	NT1 thulium 158
NT1 gadolinium 141	NT1 lutetium 158	NT1 promethium 135	NT1 thulium 159
NT1 gadolinium 142	NT1 lutetium 159	NT1 promethium 136	NT1 thulium 160
NT1 gadolinium 143	NT1 lutetium 160	NT1 promethium 137	NT1 thulium 161
NT1 gadolinium 144	NT1 lutetium 161	NT1 promethium 138	NT1 thulium 162
NT1 gadolinium 145	NT1 lutetium 162	NT1 promethium 139	NT1 thulium 163
NT1 gadolinium 146	NT1 lutetium 163	NT1 promethium 140	NT1 thulium 164
NT1 gadolinium 147	NT1 lutetium 164	NT1 promethium 141	NT1 thulium 165
NT1 gadolinium 148	NT1 lutetium 165	NT1 promethium 142	NT1 thulium 166
NT1 gadolinium 149	NT1 lutetium 166	NT1 promethium 143	NT1 thulium 167
NT1 gadolinium 150	NT1 lutetium 167	NT1 promethium 144	NT1 thulium 168
NT1 gadolinium 151	NT1 lutetium 168	NT1 promethium 145	NT1 thulium 169
NT1 gadolinium 152	NT1 lutetium 169	NT1 promethium 146	NT1 thulium 170
NT1 gadolinium 153	NT1 lutetium 170	NT1 promethium 147	NT1 thulium 171
NT1 gadolinium 154	NT1 lutetium 171	NT1 promethium 148	NT1 thulium 172
NT1 gadolinium 155	NT1 lutetium 172	NT1 promethium 149	NT1 thulium 173
NT1 gadolinium 156	NT1 lutetium 173	NT1 promethium 150	NT1 thulium 174
NT1 gadolinium 157	NT1 lutetium 174	NT1 promethium 151	NT1 thulium 175
NT1 gadolinium 158	NT1 lutetium 175	NT1 promethium 152	NT1 thulium 176
NT1 gadolinium 159	NT1 lutetium 176	NT1 promethium 153	NT1 thulium 177
NT1 gadolinium 160	NT1 lutetium 177	NT1 promethium 154	NT1 ytterbium 150
NT1 gadolinium 161	NT1 lutetium 178	NT1 promethium 155	NT1 ytterbium 151
NT1 gadolinium 162	NT1 lutetium 179	NT1 promethium 156	NT1 ytterbium 152
NT1 gadolinium 163	NT1 lutetium 180	NT1 promethium 157	NT1 ytterbium 153
NT1 gadolinium 164	NT1 lutetium 181	NT1 promethium 158	NT1 ytterbium 154
NT1 holmium 144	NT1 lutetium 182	NT1 samarium 131	NT1 ytterbium 155
NT1 holmium 145	NT1 lutetium 183	NT1 samarium 133	NT1 ytterbium 156
NT1 holmium 146	NT1 lutetium 184	NT1 samarium 134	NT1 ytterbium 157
NT1 holmium 147	NT1 neodymium 127	NT1 samarium 135	NT1 ytterbium 158
NT1 holmium 148	NT1 neodymium 128	NT1 samarium 136	NT1 ytterbium 159
NT1 holmium 149	NT1 neodymium 129	NT1 samarium 137	NT1 ytterbium 160
NT1 holmium 150	NT1 neodymium 130	NT1 samarium 138	NT1 ytterbium 161
NT1 holmium 151	NT1 neodymium 131	NT1 samarium 139	NT1 ytterbium 162
NT1 holmium 152	NT1 neodymium 132	NT1 samarium 140	NT1 ytterbium 163
NT1 holmium 153	NT1 neodymium 133	NT1 samarium 141	NT1 ytterbium 164
NT1 holmium 154	NT1 neodymium 134	NT1 samarium 142	NT1 ytterbium 165
NT1 holmium 155	NT1 neodymium 135	NT1 samarium 143	NT1 ytterbium 166
NT1 holmium 156	NT1 neodymium 136	NT1 samarium 144	NT1 ytterbium 167
NT1 holmium 157	NT1 neodymium 137	NT1 samarium 145	NT1 ytterbium 168
NT1 holmium 158	NT1 neodymium 138	NT1 samarium 146	NT1 ytterbium 169
NT1 holmium 159	NT1 neodymium 139	NT1 samarium 147	NT1 ytterbium 170
NT1 holmium 160	NT1 neodymium 140	NT1 samarium 148	NT1 ytterbium 171

RARE EARTH NUCLEI

- NT1 ytterbium 172
- NT1 ytterbium 173
- NT1 ytterbium 174
- NT1 ytterbium 175
- NT1 ytterbium 176
- NT1 ytterbium 177
- NT1 ytterbium 178
- NT1 ytterbium 179
- NT1 ytterbium 180

SECONDS LIVING RADIOISOTOPES

- NT1 actinium 214
- NT1 actinium 222
- NT1 actinium 234
- NT1 aluminium 24
- NT1 aluminium 25
- NT1 aluminium 26
- NT1 aluminium 30
- NT1 americium 232
- NT1 antimony 106
- NT1 antimony 108
- NT1 antimony 109
- NT1 antimony 110
- NT1 antimony 112
- NT1 antimony 126
- NT1 antimony 134
- NT1 antimony 135
- NT1 argon 35
- NT1 argon 45
- NT1 argon 46
- NT1 arsenic 67
- NT1 arsenic 80
- NT1 arsenic 81
- NT1 arsenic 82
- NT1 arsenic 83
- NT1 arsenic 84
- NT1 arsenic 85
- NT1 astatine 198
- NT1 astatine 199
- NT1 astatine 200
- NT1 astatine 202
- NT1 astatine 218
- NT1 astatine 219
- NT1 astatine 222
- NT1 astatine 223
- NT1 barium 117
- NT1 barium 119
- NT1 barium 120
- NT1 barium 121
- NT1 barium 143
- NT1 barium 144
- NT1 barium 145
- NT1 barium 146
- NT1 beryllium 11
- NT1 bismuth 189
- NT1 bismuth 190
- NT1 bismuth 191
- NT1 bismuth 192
- NT1 bismuth 193
- NT1 bismuth 198
- NT1 bromine 71
- NT1 bromine 76
- NT1 bromine 79
- NT1 bromine 86
- NT1 bromine 87
- NT1 bromine 88
- NT1 bromine 89
- NT1 bromine 90
- NT1 cadmium 120
- NT1 cadmium 121
- NT1 cadmium 122
- NT1 cadmium 123
- NT1 cadmium 97
- NT1 cadmium 98
- NT1 cadmium 99
- NT1 calcium 50
- NT1 calcium 51
- NT1 calcium 52
- NT1 californium 239
- NT1 carbon 10
- NT1 carbon 15
- NT1 cerium 123
- NT1 cerium 124
- NT1 cerium 125
- NT1 cerium 126
- NT1 cerium 127
- NT1 cerium 135
- NT1 cerium 139
- NT1 cerium 147
- NT1 cerium 148
- NT1 cerium 149
- NT1 cerium 150
- NT1 cerium 151
- NT1 cerium 152
- NT1 cesium 115
- NT1 cesium 116
- NT1 cesium 117
- NT1 cesium 118
- NT1 cesium 119
- NT1 cesium 122
- NT1 cesium 123
- NT1 cesium 124
- NT1 cesium 136
- NT1 cesium 141
- NT1 cesium 142
- NT1 cesium 143
- NT1 cesium 144
- NT1 chlorine 33
- NT1 chlorine 34
- NT1 chlorine 38
- NT1 chlorine 41
- NT1 chromium 57
- NT1 chromium 58
- NT1 chromium 59
- NT1 cobalt 63
- NT1 cobalt 65
- NT1 copper 58
- NT1 copper 68
- NT1 copper 70
- NT1 copper 71
- NT1 copper 72
- NT1 copper 73
- NT1 copper 74
- NT1 copper 75
- NT1 dysprosium 141
- NT1 dysprosium 142
- NT1 dysprosium 143
- NT1 dysprosium 144
- NT1 dysprosium 145
- NT1 dysprosium 146
- NT1 dysprosium 147
- NT1 dysprosium 169
- NT1 einsteinium 243
- NT1 einsteinium 244
- NT1 element 104 253
- NT1 element 104 255
- NT1 element 104 257
- NT1 element 104 259
- NT1 element 105 255
- NT1 element 105 257
- NT1 element 105 258
- NT1 element 105 259
- NT1 element 105 260
- NT1 element 105 261
- NT1 element 105 262
- NT1 element 109 266
- NT1 erbium 147
- NT1 erbium 148
- NT1 erbium 149
- NT1 erbium 150
- NT1 erbium 151
- NT1 erbium 152
- NT1 erbium 153
- NT1 erbium 167
- NT1 europium 135
- NT1 europium 136
- NT1 europium 138
- NT1 europium 139
- NT1 europium 140
- NT1 europium 141
- NT1 europium 142
- NT1 europium 144
- NT1 europium 160
- NT1 europium 161
- NT1 europium 162
- NT1 fermium 245
- NT1 fermium 246
- NT1 fermium 247
- NT1 fermium 248
- NT1 fermium 250
- NT1 fermium 259
- NT1 fluorine 20
- NT1 fluorine 21
- NT1 fluorine 22
- NT1 fluorine 23
- NT1 francium 204
- NT1 francium 205
- NT1 francium 206
- NT1 francium 207
- NT1 francium 208
- NT1 francium 209
- NT1 francium 213
- NT1 francium 220
- NT1 francium 226
- NT1 francium 228
- NT1 francium 229
- NT1 francium 230
- NT1 francium 231
- NT1 francium 232
- NT1 gadolinium 140
- NT1 gadolinium 141
- NT1 gadolinium 143
- NT1 gadolinium 164
- NT1 gallium 63
- NT1 gallium 74
- NT1 gallium 76
- NT1 gallium 77
- NT1 gallium 78
- NT1 gallium 79
- NT1 gallium 80
- NT1 gallium 81
- NT1 germanium 65
- NT1 germanium 75
- NT1 germanium 77
- NT1 germanium 79
- NT1 germanium 80
- NT1 germanium 81
- NT1 germanium 82
- NT1 germanium 83
- NT1 germanium 84
- NT1 gold 176
- NT1 gold 177
- NT1 gold 178
- NT1 gold 179
- NT1 gold 180
- NT1 gold 181
- NT1 gold 182
- NT1 gold 183
- NT1 gold 184
- NT1 gold 193
- NT1 gold 195
- NT1 gold 196
- NT1 gold 197
- NT1 gold 202
- NT1 gold 203
- NT1 gold 204
- NT1 hafnium 154
- NT1 hafnium 158
- NT1 hafnium 159
- NT1 hafnium 160
- NT1 hafnium 161
- NT1 hafnium 162
- NT1 hafnium 163
- NT1 hafnium 177
- NT1 hafnium 178
- NT1 hafnium 179
- NT1 holmium 145
- NT1 holmium 146
- NT1 holmium 148
- NT1 holmium 149
- NT1 holmium 150
- NT1 holmium 151
- NT1 holmium 152
- NT1 holmium 159
- NT1 holmium 161
- NT1 holmium 163
- NT1 holmium 170
- NT1 holmium 171
- NT1 holmium 172
- NT1 indium 101
- NT1 indium 102
- NT1 indium 104
- NT1 indium 105
- NT1 indium 107
- NT1 indium 116
- NT1 indium 118
- NT1 indium 120
- NT1 indium 121
- NT1 indium 122
- NT1 indium 123
- NT1 indium 124
- NT1 indium 125
- NT1 indium 126
- NT1 indium 127
- NT1 indium 129
- NT1 iodine 111
- NT1 iodine 112
- NT1 iodine 113
- NT1 iodine 114

SECONDS LIVING RADIOISOTOPES

- NT1 iodine 116
- NT1 iodine 133
- NT1 iodine 136
- NT1 iodine 137
- NT1 iodine 138
- NT1 iodine 139
- NT1 iridium 170
- NT1 iridium 171
- NT1 iridium 172
- NT1 iridium 173
- NT1 iridium 174
- NT1 iridium 175
- NT1 iridium 176
- NT1 iridium 177
- NT1 iridium 178
- NT1 iridium 191
- NT1 iridium 196
- NT1 iridium 198
- NT1 iron 52
- NT1 iron 63
- NT1 iron 64
- NT1 krypton 72
- NT1 krypton 73
- NT1 krypton 79
- NT1 krypton 81
- NT1 krypton 90
- NT1 krypton 91
- NT1 krypton 92
- NT1 krypton 93
- NT1 lanthanum 120
- NT1 lanthanum 121
- NT1 lanthanum 122
- NT1 lanthanum 123
- NT1 lanthanum 124
- NT1 lanthanum 144
- NT1 lanthanum 145
- NT1 lanthanum 146
- NT1 lanthanum 147
- NT1 lanthanum 148
- NT1 lanthanum 149
- NT1 lawrencium 253
- NT1 lawrencium 254
- NT1 lawrencium 255
- NT1 lawrencium 256
- NT1 lawrencium 258
- NT1 lawrencium 259
- NT1 lead 185
- NT1 lead 186
- NT1 lead 187
- NT1 lead 188
- NT1 lead 189
- NT1 lead 203
- NT1 lutetium 154
- NT1 lutetium 157
- NT1 lutetium 158
- NT1 lutetium 159
- NT1 lutetium 160
- NT1 lutetium 183
- NT1 lutetium 184
- NT1 magnesium 22
- NT1 magnesium 23
- NT1 magnesium 29
- NT1 manganese 58
- NT1 manganese 59
- NT1 manganese 60
- NT1 mendelevium 247
- NT1 mendelevium 248
- NT1 mendelevium 249
- NT1 mendelevium 250
- NT1 mercury 179
- NT1 mercury 180
- NT1 mercury 181
- NT1 mercury 182
- NT1 mercury 183
- NT1 mercury 184
- NT1 mercury 185
- NT1 molybdenum 105
- NT1 molybdenum 106
- NT1 molybdenum 107
- NT1 molybdenum 108
- NT1 molybdenum 87
- NT1 neodymium 127
- NT1 neodymium 129
- NT1 neodymium 130
- NT1 neodymium 131
- NT1 neodymium 137
- NT1 neodymium 153
- NT1 neodymium 154
- NT1 neodymium 155
- NT1 neodymium 156

SECONDS LIVING RADIOISOTOPES

- NT1 neon 18
- NT1 neon 19
- NT1 neon 23
- NT1 nickel 67
- NT1 nickel 69
- NT1 nickel 71
- NT1 nickel 72
- NT1 nickel 74
- NT1 niobium 100
- NT1 niobium 101
- NT1 niobium 102
- NT1 niobium 103
- NT1 niobium 104
- NT1 niobium 105
- NT1 niobium 106
- NT1 niobium 83
- NT1 niobium 84
- NT1 niobium 85
- NT1 niobium 90
- NT1 niobium 97
- NT1 niobium 98
- NT1 niobium 99
- NT1 nitrogen 16
- NT1 nitrogen 17
- NT1 nobelium 252
- NT1 nobelium 254
- NT1 nobelium 256
- NT1 nobelium 257
- NT1 osmium 168
- NT1 osmium 169
- NT1 osmium 170
- NT1 osmium 171
- NT1 osmium 172
- NT1 osmium 173
- NT1 osmium 174
- NT1 osmium 192
- NT1 oxygen 19
- NT1 oxygen 20
- NT1 oxygen 21
- NT1 palladium 107
- NT1 palladium 115
- NT1 palladium 116
- NT1 palladium 117
- NT1 palladium 118
- NT1 palladium 95
- NT1 phosphorus 29
- NT1 phosphorus 34
- NT1 phosphorus 35
- NT1 phosphorus 36
- NT1 phosphorus 37
- NT1 platinum 175
- NT1 platinum 176
- NT1 platinum 177
- NT1 platinum 178
- NT1 platinum 179
- NT1 platinum 180
- NT1 platinum 181
- NT1 platinum 183
- NT1 platinum 199
- NT1 polonium 195
- NT1 polonium 196
- NT1 polonium 197
- NT1 polonium 203
- NT1 polonium 207
- NT1 polonium 211
- NT1 polonium 212
- NT1 polonium 217
- NT1 potassium 37
- NT1 potassium 38
- NT1 potassium 47
- NT1 potassium 48
- NT1 potassium 49
- NT1 praseodymium 124
- NT1 praseodymium 126
- NT1 praseodymium 128
- NT1 praseodymium 129
- NT1 praseodymium 130
- NT1 praseodymium 150
- NT1 praseodymium 151
- NT1 praseodymium 152
- NT1 praseodymium 153
- NT1 praseodymium 154
- NT1 promethium 130
- NT1 promethium 132
- NT1 promethium 133
- NT1 promethium 134
- NT1 promethium 135
- NT1 promethium 140
- NT1 promethium 142
- NT1 promethium 155
- NT1 promethium 156
- NT1 promethium 157
- NT1 promethium 158
- NT1 protactinium 225
- NT1 radium 207
- NT1 radium 208
- NT1 radium 209
- NT1 radium 210
- NT1 radium 211
- NT1 radium 212
- NT1 radium 214
- NT1 radium 221
- NT1 radium 222
- NT1 radium 233
- NT1 radium 234
- NT1 radon 200
- NT1 radon 201
- NT1 radon 202
- NT1 radon 203
- NT1 radon 219
- NT1 radon 220
- NT1 radon 227
- NT1 radon 228
- NT1 rhenium 165
- NT1 rhenium 166
- NT1 rhenium 167
- NT1 rhenium 168
- NT1 rhenium 169
- NT1 rhenium 170
- NT1 rhenium 171
- NT1 rhenium 172
- NT1 rhenium 192
- NT1 rhodium 104
- NT1 rhodium 105
- NT1 rhodium 106
- NT1 rhodium 108
- NT1 rhodium 110
- NT1 rhodium 111
- NT1 rhodium 113
- NT1 rhodium 114
- NT1 rhodium 117
- NT1 rhodium 94
- NT1 rubidium 75
- NT1 rubidium 76
- NT1 rubidium 80
- NT1 rubidium 91
- NT1 rubidium 92
- NT1 rubidium 93
- NT1 rubidium 94
- NT1 ruthenium 109
- NT1 ruthenium 110
- NT1 ruthenium 111
- NT1 ruthenium 112
- NT1 ruthenium 113
- NT1 ruthenium 93
- NT1 samarium 131
- NT1 samarium 133
- NT1 samarium 134
- NT1 samarium 135
- NT1 samarium 136
- NT1 samarium 137
- NT1 samarium 139
- NT1 samarium 159
- NT1 samarium 160
- NT1 scandium 42
- NT1 scandium 46
- NT1 scandium 51
- NT1 scandium 52
- NT1 selenium 69
- NT1 selenium 77
- NT1 selenium 85
- NT1 selenium 86
- NT1 selenium 87
- NT1 selenium 88
- NT1 silicon 26
- NT1 silicon 27
- NT1 silicon 33
- NT1 silicon 34
- NT1 silver 101
- NT1 silver 103
- NT1 silver 107
- NT1 silver 109
- NT1 silver 110
- NT1 silver 114
- NT1 silver 115
- NT1 silver 116
- NT1 silver 117
- NT1 silver 118
- NT1 silver 119
- NT1 silver 120
- NT1 silver 122
- NT1 silver 96
- NT1 silver 97
- NT1 silver 98
- NT1 silver 99
- NT1 sodium 20
- NT1 sodium 21
- NT1 sodium 25
- NT1 sodium 26
- NT1 strontium 77
- NT1 strontium 83
- NT1 strontium 95
- NT1 strontium 96
- NT1 sulfur 30
- NT1 sulfur 31
- NT1 sulfur 39
- NT1 sulfur 40
- NT1 tantalum 160
- NT1 tantalum 161
- NT1 tantalum 162
- NT1 tantalum 163
- NT1 tantalum 164
- NT1 tantalum 165
- NT1 tantalum 166
- NT1 technetium 100
- NT1 technetium 102
- NT1 technetium 103
- NT1 technetium 106
- NT1 technetium 107
- NT1 technetium 108
- NT1 technetium 109
- NT1 technetium 90
- NT1 tellurium 108
- NT1 tellurium 109
- NT1 tellurium 110
- NT1 tellurium 111
- NT1 tellurium 135
- NT1 tellurium 136
- NT1 tellurium 137
- NT1 tellurium 138
- NT1 terbium 140
- NT1 terbium 141
- NT1 terbium 143
- NT1 terbium 144
- NT1 terbium 145
- NT1 terbium 146
- NT1 terbium 151
- NT1 terbium 158
- NT1 thallium 184
- NT1 thallium 185
- NT1 thallium 186
- NT1 thallium 187
- NT1 thallium 195
- NT1 thallium 197
- NT1 thallium 207
- NT1 thorium 215
- NT1 thorium 224
- NT1 thulium 151
- NT1 thulium 152
- NT1 thulium 153
- NT1 thulium 154
- NT1 thulium 155
- NT1 thulium 156
- NT1 thulium 162
- NT1 tin 103
- NT1 tin 105
- NT1 tin 131
- NT1 tin 132
- NT1 tin 133
- NT1 tin 134
- NT1 titanium 53
- NT1 tungsten 162
- NT1 tungsten 163
- NT1 tungsten 164
- NT1 tungsten 165
- NT1 tungsten 166
- NT1 tungsten 167
- NT1 tungsten 168
- NT1 tungsten 169
- NT1 tungsten 183
- NT1 vanadium 54
- NT1 vanadium 55
- NT1 xenon 112
- NT1 xenon 113
- NT1 xenon 114
- NT1 xenon 115
- NT1 xenon 116
- NT1 xenon 125
- NT1 xenon 139
- NT1 xenon 140
- NT1 xenon 141
- NT1 xenon 142
- NT1 xenon 144
- NT1 ytterbium 153
- NT1 ytterbium 155
- NT1 ytterbium 156
- NT1 ytterbium 157
- NT1 ytterbium 169
- NT1 ytterbium 176
- NT1 ytterbium 177
- NT1 yttrium 80
- NT1 yttrium 82
- NT1 yttrium 84
- NT1 yttrium 89
- NT1 yttrium 96
- NT1 yttrium 97
- NT1 yttrium 98
- NT1 yttrium 99
- NT1 zinc 73
- NT1 zinc 75
- NT1 zinc 76
- NT1 zinc 77
- NT1 zinc 78
- NT1 zirconium 100
- NT1 zirconium 101
- NT1 zirconium 102
- NT1 zirconium 103
- NT1 zirconium 83
- NT1 zirconium 85
- NT1 zirconium 87
- NT1 zirconium 98
- NT1 zirconium 99

SPONTANEOUS FISSION RADIOISOTO

- NT1 americium 237
- NT1 americium 238
- NT1 americium 239
- NT1 americium 240
- NT1 americium 241
- NT1 americium 242
- NT1 americium 243
- NT1 americium 244
- NT1 americium 245
- NT1 americium 246
- NT1 berkelium 242
- NT1 berkelium 243
- NT1 berkelium 244
- NT1 berkelium 245
- NT1 berkelium 249
- NT1 californium 246
- NT1 californium 248
- NT1 californium 249
- NT1 californium 250
- NT1 californium 252
- NT1 californium 254
- NT1 californium 256
- NT1 curium 240
- NT1 curium 241
- NT1 curium 242
- NT1 curium 243
- NT1 curium 244
- NT1 curium 245
- NT1 curium 246
- NT1 curium 248
- NT1 curium 250
- NT1 einsteinium 253
- NT1 einsteinium 254
- NT1 einsteinium 255
- NT1 element 104 25
- NT1 element 104 25
- NT1 element 104 25
- NT1 element 104 25
- NT1 element 104 25
- NT1 element 104 26
- NT1 element 104 26
- NT1 element 104 26
- NT1 element 105 25
- NT1 element 105 25
- NT1 element 105 25
- NT1 element 105 26
- NT1 element 105 26
- NT1 element 106 25
- NT1 element 106 26
- NT1 element 106 26
- NT1 element 107 26
- NT1 fermium 242
- NT1 fermium 244

NT1 fermium 246	NT1 dysprosium 160	NT1 neon 22	NT1 tin 118
NT1 fermium 248	NT1 dysprosium 161	NT1 nickel 58	NT1 tin 119
NT1 fermium 250	NT1 dysprosium 162	NT1 nickel 60	NT1 tin 120
NT1 fermium 252	NT1 dysprosium 163	NT1 nickel 61	NT1 tin 122
NT1 fermium 254	NT1 dysprosium 164	NT1 nickel 62	NT1 tin 124
NT1 fermium 255	NT1 erbium 162	NT1 nickel 64	NT1 titanium 46
NT1 fermium 256	NT1 erbium 164	NT1 niobium 93	NT1 titanium 47
NT1 fermium 257	NT1 erbium 166	NT1 nitrogen 14	NT1 titanium 48
NT1 fermium 258	NT1 erbium 167	NT1 nitrogen 15	NT1 titanium 49
NT1 fermium 259	NT1 erbium 168	NT1 osmium 184	NT1 titanium 50
NT1 mendelevium 259	NT1 erbium 170	NT1 osmium 186	NT1 tungsten 180
NT1 neptunium 237	NT1 europium 151	NT1 osmium 187	NT1 tungsten 182
NT1 nobelium 250	NT1 europium 153	NT1 osmium 188	NT1 tungsten 183
NT1 nobelium 252	NT1 fluorine 19	NT1 osmium 189	NT1 tungsten 184
NT1 nobelium 254	NT1 gadolinium 154	NT1 osmium 190	NT1 tungsten 186
NT1 nobelium 256	NT1 gadolinium 155	NT1 osmium 192	NT1 vanadium 51
NT1 nobelium 258	NT1 gadolinium 156	NT1 oxygen 16	NT1 xenon 124
NT1 plutonium 235	NT1 gadolinium 157	NT1 oxygen 17	NT1 xenon 126
NT1 plutonium 236	NT1 gadolinium 158	NT1 oxygen 18	NT1 xenon 128
NT1 plutonium 237	NT1 gadolinium 160	NT1 palladium 102	NT1 xenon 129
NT1 plutonium 238	NT1 gallium 69	NT1 palladium 104	NT1 xenon 130
NT1 plutonium 239	NT1 gallium 71	NT1 palladium 105	NT1 xenon 131
NT1 plutonium 240	NT1 germanium 70	NT1 palladium 106	NT1 xenon 132
NT1 plutonium 241	NT1 germanium 72	NT1 palladium 108	NT1 xenon 134
NT1 plutonium 242	NT1 germanium 73	NT1 palladium 110	NT1 xenon 136
NT1 plutonium 243	NT1 germanium 74	NT1 phosphorus 31	NT1 ytterbium 168
NT1 plutonium 244	NT1 germanium 76	NT1 platinum 192	NT1 ytterbium 170
NT1 thorium 230	NT1 gold 197	NT1 platinum 194	NT1 ytterbium 171
NT1 thorium 232	NT1 hafnium 176	NT1 platinum 195	NT1 ytterbium 172
NT1 uranium 232	NT1 hafnium 177	NT1 platinum 196	NT1 ytterbium 173
NT1 uranium 233	NT1 hafnium 178	NT1 platinum 198	NT1 ytterbium 174
NT1 uranium 234	NT1 hafnium 179	NT1 potassium 39	NT1 ytterbium 176
NT1 uranium 235	NT1 hafnium 180	NT1 potassium 41	NT1 yttrium 89
NT1 uranium 236	NT1 helium 3	NT1 praseodymium 141	NT1 zinc 64
NT1 uranium 238	NT2 helium 3 a	NT1 rhenium 185	NT1 zinc 66
	NT2 helium 3 a1	NT1 rhenium 187	NT1 zinc 67
STABLE ISOTOPES	NT2 helium 3 b	NT1 rhodium 103	NT1 zinc 68
NT1 aluminium 27	NT1 helium 4	NT1 rubidium 85	NT1 zinc 70
NT1 antimony 121	NT2 helium i	NT1 ruthenium 100	NT1 zirconium 90
NT1 antimony 123	NT2 helium ii	NT1 ruthenium 101	NT1 zirconium 91
NT1 argon 36	NT1 holmium 165	NT1 ruthenium 102	NT1 zirconium 92
NT1 argon 38	NT1 hydrogen 1	NT1 ruthenium 104	NT1 zirconium 94
NT1 argon 40	NT1 indium 113	NT1 ruthenium 96	NT1 zirconium 96
NT1 arsenic 75	NT1 iodine 127	NT1 ruthenium 98	
NT1 barium 130	NT1 iridium 191	NT1 ruthenium 99	**YEARS LIVING**
NT1 barium 132	NT1 iridium 193	NT1 samarium 144	**RADIOISOTOPES**
NT1 barium 134	NT1 iron 54	NT1 samarium 148	NT1 actinium 227
NT1 barium 135	NT1 iron 56	NT1 samarium 149	NT1 aluminium 26
NT1 barium 136	NT1 iron 57	NT1 samarium 150	NT1 americium 241
NT1 barium 137	NT1 iron 58	NT1 samarium 152	NT1 americium 242
NT1 barium 138	NT1 krypton 78	NT1 samarium 154	NT1 americium 243
NT1 beryllium 9	NT1 krypton 80	NT1 scandium 45	NT1 antimony 125
NT1 bismuth 209	NT1 krypton 82	NT1 selenium 74	NT1 argon 39
NT1 boron 10	NT1 krypton 83	NT1 selenium 76	NT1 argon 42
NT1 boron 11	NT1 krypton 84	NT1 selenium 77	NT1 barium 133
NT1 bromine 79	NT1 krypton 86	NT1 selenium 78	NT1 berkelium 247
NT1 bromine 81	NT1 lanthanum 139	NT1 selenium 80	NT1 beryllium 10
NT1 cadmium 106	NT1 lead 204	NT1 selenium 82	NT1 bismuth 207
NT1 cadmium 108	NT1 lead 206	NT1 silicon 28	NT1 bismuth 208
NT1 cadmium 110	NT1 lead 207	NT1 silicon 29	NT1 bismuth 210
NT1 cadmium 111	NT1 lead 208	NT1 silicon 30	NT1 cadmium 109
NT1 cadmium 112	NT1 lithium 6	NT1 silver 107	NT1 cadmium 113
NT1 cadmium 113	NT1 lithium 7	NT1 silver 109	NT1 calcium 41
NT1 cadmium 114	NT1 lutetium 175	NT1 sodium 23	NT1 californium 249
NT1 cadmium 116	NT1 magnesium 24	NT1 strontium 84	NT1 californium 250
NT1 calcium 40	NT1 magnesium 25	NT1 strontium 86	NT1 californium 251
NT1 calcium 42	NT1 magnesium 26	NT1 strontium 87	NT1 californium 252
NT1 calcium 43	NT1 manganese 55	NT1 strontium 88	NT1 carbon 14
NT1 calcium 44	NT1 mercury 196	NT1 sulfur 32	NT1 cesium 134
NT1 calcium 46	NT1 mercury 198	NT1 sulfur 33	NT1 cesium 135
NT1 calcium 48	NT1 mercury 199	NT1 sulfur 34	NT1 cesium 137
NT1 carbon 12	NT1 mercury 200	NT1 sulfur 36	NT1 chlorine 36
NT1 carbon 13	NT1 mercury 201	NT1 tantalum 181	NT1 cobalt 60
NT1 cerium 136	NT1 mercury 202	NT1 tellurium 120	NT1 curium 243
NT1 cerium 138	NT1 mercury 204	NT1 tellurium 122	NT1 curium 244
NT1 cerium 140	NT1 molybdenum 100	NT1 tellurium 123	NT1 curium 245
NT1 cerium 142	NT1 molybdenum 92	NT1 tellurium 124	NT1 curium 246
NT1 cesium 133	NT1 molybdenum 94	NT1 tellurium 125	NT1 curium 247
NT1 chlorine 35	NT1 molybdenum 95	NT1 tellurium 126	NT1 curium 248
NT1 chlorine 37	NT1 molybdenum 96	NT1 tellurium 128	NT1 curium 250
NT1 chromium 50	NT1 molybdenum 97	NT1 tellurium 130	NT1 dysprosium 154
NT1 chromium 52	NT1 molybdenum 98	NT1 terbium 159	NT1 einsteinium 252
NT1 chromium 53	NT1 neodymium 142	NT1 thallium 203	NT1 europium 150
NT1 chromium 54	NT1 neodymium 143	NT1 thallium 205	NT1 europium 152
NT1 cobalt 59	NT1 neodymium 145	NT1 thulium 169	NT1 europium 154
NT1 copper 63	NT1 neodymium 146	NT1 tin 112	NT1 europium 155
NT1 copper 65	NT1 neodymium 148	NT1 tin 114	NT1 gadolinium 148
NT1 deuterium	NT1 neodymium 150	NT1 tin 115	NT1 gadolinium 150
NT1 dysprosium 156	NT1 neon 20	NT1 tin 116	NT1 gadolinium 152
NT1 dysprosium 158	NT1 neon 21	NT1 tin 117	NT1 hafnium 172

NT1	hafnium 174	NT1	neptunium 235	NT1	potassium 40	NT1	technetium 97
NT1	hafnium 178	NT1	neptunium 236	NT1	promethium 144	NT1	technetium 98
NT1	hafnium 182	NT1	neptunium 237	NT1	promethium 145	NT1	technetium 99
NT1	holmium 163	NT1	nickel 59	NT1	promethium 146	NT1	tellurium 123
NT1	holmium 166	NT1	nickel 63	NT1	promethium 147	NT1	terbium 157
NT1	indium 115	NT1	niobium 91	NT1	protactinium 231	NT1	terbium 158
NT1	iodine 129	NT1	niobium 92	NT1	radium 226	NT1	thallium 204
NT1	iridium 192	NT1	niobium 93	NT1	radium 228	NT1	thorium 228
NT1	iron 55	NT1	niobium 94	NT1	rhenium 186	NT1	thorium 229
NT1	iron 60	NT1	osmium 186	NT1	rhenium 187	NT1	thorium 230
NT1	krypton 81	NT1	osmium 194	NT1	rhodium 101	NT1	thorium 232
NT1	krypton 85	NT1	palladium 107	NT1	rubidium 87	NT1	thulium 171
NT1	lanthanum 137	NT1	platinum 190	NT1	ruthenium 106	NT1	tin 121
NT1	lanthanum 138	NT1	platinum 193	NT1	samarium 146	NT1	tin 126
NT1	lead 202	NT1	plutonium 236	NT1	samarium 147	NT1	titanium 44
NT1	lead 205	NT1	plutonium 238	NT1	samarium 148	NT1	tritium
NT1	lead 210	NT1	plutonium 239	NT1	samarium 151	NT1	uranium 232
NT1	lutetium 173	NT1	plutonium 240	NT1	selenium 79	NT1	uranium 233
NT1	lutetium 174	NT1	plutonium 241	NT1	silicon 32	NT1	uranium 234
NT1	lutetium 176	NT1	plutonium 242	NT1	silver 108	NT1	uranium 235
NT1	manganese 53	NT1	plutonium 244	NT1	sodium 22	NT1	uranium 236
NT1	mercury 194	NT1	polonium 208	NT1	strontium 90	NT1	uranium 238
NT1	molybdenum 93	NT1	polonium 209	NT1	tantalum 179	NT1	vanadium 50
NT1	neodymium 144					NT1	zirconium 93

HOW TO ORDER IAEA PUBLICATIONS

 An exclusive sales agent for IAEA publications, to whom all orders and inquiries should be addressed, has been appointed for the following countries:

CANADA UNITED STATES OF AMERICA	UNIPUB, 4611-F Assembly Drive, Lanham, MD 20706-4391, USA

 In the following countries IAEA publications may be purchased from the sales agents or booksellers listed or through major local booksellers. Payment can be made in local currency or with UNESCO coupons.

ARGENTINA	Comisión Nacional de Energía Atómica, Avenida del Libertador 8250, RA-1429 Buenos Aires
AUSTRALIA	Hunter Publications, 58 A Gipps Street, Collingwood, Victoria 3066
BELGIUM	Service Courrier UNESCO, 202, Avenue du Roi, B-1060 Brussels
CHILE	Comisión Chilena de Energía Nuclear, Venta de Publicaciones, Amunategui 95, Casilla 188-D, Santiago
CHINA	IAEA Publications in Chinese: China Nuclear Energy Industry Corporation, Translation Section, P.O. Box 2103, Beijing IAEA Publications other than in Chinese: China National Publications Import & Export Corporation, Deutsche Abteilung, P.O. Box 88, Beijing
CZECHOSLOVAKIA	S.N.T.L., Mikulandska 4, CS-116 86 Prague 1 Alfa, Publishers, Hurbanovo námestie 3, CS-815 89 Bratislava
FRANCE	Office International de Documentation et Librairie, 48, rue Gay-Lussac, F-75240 Paris Cedex 05
HUNGARY	Kultura, Hungarian Foreign Trading Company, P.O. Box 149, H-1389 Budapest 62
INDIA	Oxford Book and Stationery Co., 17, Park Street, Calcutta-700 016 Oxford Book and Stationery Co., Scindia House, New Delhi-110 001
ISRAEL	YOZMOT (1989) Ltd, P.O. Box 56055, Tel Aviv 61560
ITALY	Libreria Scientifica, Dott. Lucio de Biasio "aeiou", Via Meravigli 16, I-20123 Milan
JAPAN	Maruzen Company, Ltd, P.O. Box 5050, 100-31 Tokyo International
PAKISTAN	Mirza Book Agency, 65, Shahrah Quaid-e-Azam, P.O. Box 729, Lahore 3
POLAND	Ars Polona-Ruch, Centrala Handlu Zagranicznego, Krakowskie Przedmiescie 7, PL-00-068 Warsaw
ROMANIA	Ilexim, P.O. Box 136-137, Bucharest
SOUTH AFRICA	Van Schaik Bookstore (Pty) Ltd, P.O. Box 724, Pretoria 0001
SPAIN	Díaz de Santos, Lagasca 95, E-28006 Madrid Díaz de Santos, Balmes 417, E-08022 Barcelona
SWEDEN	AB Fritzes Kungl. Hovbokhandel, Fredsgatan 2, P.O. Box 16356, S-103 27 Stockholm
UNITED KINGDOM	HMSO, Publications Centre, Agency Section, 51 Nine Elms Lane, London SW8 5DR
USSR	Mezhdunarodnaya Kniga, Smolenskaya-Sennaya 32-34, Moscow G-200
YUGOSLAVIA	Jugoslavenska Knjiga, Terazije 27, P.O. Box 36, YU-11001 Belgrade

 Orders from countries where sales agents have not yet been appointed and requests for information should be addressed directly to:

**Division of Publications
International Atomic Energy Agency
Wagramerstrasse 5, P.O. Box 100, A-1400 Vienna, Austria**